CW01112789

Encyclopedia of Private International Law

Encyclopedia of Private International Law

Volume 2

Edited by

Jürgen Basedow
Director, Max Planck Institute for Comparative and International Private Law, Germany, and Membre associé, Institut de droit international

Giesela Rühl
Professor, Friedrich Schiller University Jena, Germany

Franco Ferrari
Professor, New York University School of Law, USA

Pedro de Miguel Asensio
Professor, Complutense University of Madrid, Spain

Edward Elgar PUBLISHING

Cheltenham, UK • Northampton, MA, USA

© Jürgen Basedow, Giesela Rühl, Franco Ferrari and Pedro de Miguel Asensio 2017

All rights reserved. No part of this publication may be reproduced, stored in a retrieval system or transmitted in any form or by any means, electronic, mechanical or photocopying, recording, or otherwise without the prior permission of the publisher.

Published by
Edward Elgar Publishing Limited
The Lypiatts
15 Lansdown Road
Cheltenham
Glos GL50 2JA
UK

Edward Elgar Publishing, Inc.
William Pratt House
9 Dewey Court
Northampton
Massachusetts 01060
USA

A catalogue record for this book
is available from the British Library

Library of Congress Control Number: 2016949947

This book is available electronically on Elgaronline
DOI 10.4337/9781782547235

ISBN 978 1 78254 722 8 (4 volume set)
ISBN 978 1 78254 723 5 (eBook)

Printed by CPI Group (UK) Ltd, Croydon CR0 4YY

Contents

VOLUME 1

Preface	vi
List of authors	viii
List of entries (Volumes 1 and 2)	xx
List of national reports (Volume 3)	xxvi
List of legal instruments (Volume 4)	xxviii
List of abbreviations	xxxii
Entries A–H	1

VOLUME 2

List of abbreviations	vi
Entries I–Z	887

VOLUME 3

List of abbreviations	vi
List of national reports	xxvi
National Reports A–Z	1855
Table of legislation	2668
Index	2731

VOLUME 4

Explanatory note	vi
List of legal instruments	vii
Legal Instruments A–Z	2907

List of Abbreviations

A.2d Atlantic Reporter 2nd Series
AAA American Arbitration Association
ABA American Bar Association
ABGBl. Bundesgesetzblatt für die Republik Österreich (Official Journal of Austria)
AC Law Reports, Appeal Cases, 3rd Series
AcP Archiv für die civilistische Praxis
ACTA Anti-Counterfeiting Trade Agreement
AD Anno Domini
AD South African Law Reports, Appellate Division
ADR Alternative Dispute Resolution
ADSp. Allgemeine Deutsche Spediteursbedingungen
AEDIPr Anuario Español de Derecho Internacional Privado
A.F.D.I. Annuaire Français de Droit International
AFNOR Association française de normalisation
Afr J Int'l Comp L African Journal of International and Comparative Law
AG Advocate General
AG Amtsgericht (Local Court, Germany)
AIPDIP Interamerican Association of Private International Law Professors
AIPPI Association Internationale pour la Protection de la Propriété Intellectuelle
AIPPI Journal Journal of the Japanese Group of AIPPI
AIR All India Reporter
AJP Aktuelle Juristische Praxis
Al-Adl Al-Adl Journal (Journal of the Beirut Bar)
Alb. L.J. Sci. & Tech. Albany Law Journal of Science and Technology
ALER American Law and Economics Review
ALI American Law Institute
All ER All England Law Reports
All ER (Comm) All England Law Reports (Commercial Cases)
All NLR All-Nigeria Law Reports
ALQ Arab Law Quarterly
ALR Australian Law Reports
ALR Allgemeines Preußisches Landrecht (General Prussian Law of the Land)
Air & Space Law Air and Space Law
Am.Bus.L.J. American Business Law Journal
AMC American Maritime Cases
Am.Econ.Rev. American Economic Review
AMEDIP Mexican Academy of Private International and Comparative Law
AMEX American Stock Exchange
Am.J.Comp.L. American Journal of Comparative Law
Am.J.Comp.L. Sup. American Journal of Comparative Law (Supplement)
Am.J.Int'l L. American Journal of International Law
Am. J. Legal Hist. American Journal of Legal History
Am. Jurist & L. Mag. American Jurist and Law Magazine
Am.Pol.Sc.Rev American Political Science Review
Am.Rev.Int'l Arb. American Review of International Arbitration
Am.U.Int'l L.Rev. American University International Law Review
Am.U.J.Int'l L. & Pol'y American University Journal of International Law and Policy
Am.U.L.Rev. American University Law Review
An.Der.Mar. Anuario de Derecho maritimo
Anglo-Am.L.R. Anglo-American Law Review
Annals Am.Acad.Pol.& Soc.Sci. Annals of the American Academy of Political and Social Science
Ann.Surv.Int'l & Comp.L. Annual Survey of International and Comparative Law
A.P.D. Archives de Philosophie du Droit
APLR Asia Pacific Law Review
App Court of Appeals
App Ct Appeal Court
App. Div. Appellate Division

LIST OF ABBREVIATIONS

App no   application no
approx.   approximately
Arb.   Arbitration
Arb.Int'l   Arbitration International
ARGBl   Reichsgesetzblatt für die im Reichsrath vertretenen Königreiche und Länder (former Official Journal of Austria)
Ariz.L.Rev.   Arizona Law Review
Ariz.St.L.J.   Arizona State Law Journal
Ark   Arkansas
art/arts   article/articles
Artif.Intell.Rev.   Artificial Intelligence Review
AS   Amtliche Sammlung des Bundesrechts (Switzerland)
ASADIP   American Association of Private International Law
ASDA SVLR Bulletin   Association Suisse de Droit Aérien et Spatial/Schweizerische Vereinigung für Luft- und Raumrecht Bulletin
ASEAN   Association of Southeast Asian Nations
Asian Y. B. Int'l L.   Asian Yearbook of International Law
ASIL PROC   American Society of International Law Proceedings
ATA   Asia Trustmark Alliance
ATF   Arrêts du Tribunal fédéral (Decisions of the Swiss Federal Supreme Court)
ATS   Australian Treaty Series
Aust Bar Rev   Australian Bar Review
Aust ILJ   Australian International Law Journal
Austr.Bus.L.Rev.   Australian Business Law Review
AustralianJ.Leg.Phil   Australian Journal of Legal Philosophy
AVR   Archiv des Völkerrechts
Az.J.Int'l & Comp.L.   Arizona Journal of International and Comparative Law
b2b   business to business
b2c   business to consumer
BAG   Bundesarbeitsgericht (German Federal Labour Court)
BAnz   Bundesanzeiger
b-Arbitra   Belgian Review of Arbitration

BauR   Zeitschrift für das gesamte öffentliche und zivile Baurecht
Baz   Baz Review (Review of the decisions of the Lebanese Court of Cassation)
BBl   Bundesblatt (Official Journal of Switzerland)
BC   Before Christ
BE   Buddhist Era
BeckOK-ZPO   Beck'scher Onlinekommentar zur Zivilprozessordnung
BeckRS   Beck-Rechtsprechung
BerDtGesVR   Berichte der Deutschen Gesellschaft für Völkerrecht
Berkeley J.Int'l L.   Berkeley Journal of International Law
BFH   Bundesfinanzhof (German Federal Fiscal Court)
BFHE   Entscheidungen des BFH (Decisions of the German Federal Fiscal Court)
BFLR   Banking & Finance Law Review
BGBl.   Bundesgesetzblatt (Official Journal of Germany)
BGE   Entscheidungen des Schweizerischen Bundesgerichts (Decisions of the Swiss Federal Supreme Court)
BGH   Bundesgerichtshof (German Federal Supreme Court)
BGHZ   Entscheidungen des Bundesgerichtshofs in Zivilsachen (Decisions of the German Federal Supreme Court)
BH   Publication of Judgments of the Kúria (Supreme Court of Hungary) and of the High Courts
BIICL   British Institute of International and Comparative Law
BIMCO   Baltic and International Maritime Council
BIRPI   United International Bureaux for the Protection of Intellectual Property
BIT   Bilateral Investment Treaty
BJM   Basler Juristische Mitteilungen
BKR   Zeitschrift für Bank- und Kapitalmarktrecht
B/L   Bill of lading
B.L.I.   Business Law International
BPatG   Bundespatentgericht (German Federal Patent Court)

BO   Boletín Oficial (Official Journal of Argentina)
BOE   Boletín Oficial del Estado (Official Journal of Spain)
BOLERO   Bill of Lading Electronic Registry Organization
Bom LR   Bombay Law Reporter
BPR   Butterworths Property Reports
Brooklyn J.Int'l L.   Brooklyn Journal of International Law
BS   Bereinigte Sammlung der Bundesgesetze und Verordnungen 1848–1947 (former Official Journal of Switzerland)
BSozG   Bundessozialgericht (German Federal Court on Social Law)
Buff.L.Rev.   Buffalo Law Review
Bull.civ.   Bulletin des arrêts des chambres civiles de la Cour de Cassation
Bulletin   Bulletin des arrêts des chambre civiles
Bull.Lég.Comp.   Bulletin de la Société de Législation comparée
B.U.Int'l L.J.   Boston University International Law Journal
B.U.L.Rev.   Boston University Law Review
BVerfG   Bundesverfassungsgericht (German Federal Constitutional Court)
BVerfGE   Entscheidungen des Bundesverfassungsgerichts (Decisions of the German Federal Constitutional Court)
BYIL   British Yearbook of International Law
BYU L. Rev.   BYU Law Review
C: Case number
c2c   consumer to consumer
c2b   consumer to business
CA   Court of Appeals
CA   Civil Appeal (Israel)
Cal   Calcutta
Cal.   Supreme Court of California
Cal.2d   California Reporter, 2nd Series
Cal.App.   California Court of Appeals
Cal.App.3d   California Appellate Reports, 3rd Series
Cal.L.Rev.   California Law Review
Cal.Rptr.   California Reporter
Cal.Rptr.2d   California Reporter, 2nd Series
Cal.W.Int'l L.J.   California Western International Law Journal
Camp.   Campbell's Nisi Prius Cases
Can.Bar Rev.   Canadian Bar Review
Canadian Lab. & Emp. L.J.   Canadian Labour & Employment Law Journal
Car   Charles
Cardozo J. Confl. Res.   Cardozo Journal of Conflict Resolution
Cardozo J.Int'l & Comp.L.   Cardozo Journal of International and Comparative Law
Cardozo L.Rev.   Cardozo Law Review
Cas.t.H   Cases temp. Hardwicke
Cass   Corte Suprema di Cassazione (Italian Supreme Court)
Cass.   Cour de cassation (French Supreme Court)
Cassandre   Répertoire Cassandre
Cass. civ.   Chambre civil de la Cour de cassation (Civil Chamber of the French Supreme Court)
Cass. civ. 1ère   Première chambre civile de la Cour de cassation (First Civil Chamber of the French Supreme Court)
Cass. com.   Chambre commerciale de la Cour de cassation (Commercial Chamber of the French Supreme Court)
Cass. soc.   Chambre sociale de la Cour de cassation (Social Chamber of the French Supreme Court)
Cass.fr.   Cour de cassation (French Supreme Court)
Cass.it.   Corte Suprema di cassazione (Italian Supreme Court)
C.B.L.J.   Canadian Business Law Journal
Cass civ (1)   see Cass. civ. 1ère
CC   Civil Case
C.Cass.   Cour de Cassation (Belgium Supreme Court)
C.Cass.Soc.   see Cass. soc.
C.D.E.   Cahiers de Droit Européen
CDT   Cuadernos de Derecho Transnacional
CEDEP   Centro de Estudios de Derecho, Economía y Política
CEFL   Commission on European Family Law
CEFTA   Central European Free Trade Agreement

LIST OF ABBREVIATIONS

CEN European Committee for Standardization
CEO Chief Executive Officer
CESL Common European Sales Law
CESL-D Proposal for a Common European Sales Law
CETS Council of Europe Treaty Series
cf confer (compare)
CFA Court of Final Appeal
CFI Court of First Instance
CFLQ Child and Family Law Quarterly
CFR Common Frame of Reference
CFSP Common Foreign and Security Policy
ch/chs chapter/chapters
Ch Chancery
Ch Chancery Division (New Zealand)
Ch Law Reports, Chancery Division, 3rd Series
ChFR Charta of Fundamental Rights of the European Union
Chi.J.Int'l L. Chicago Journal of International Law
Chi-Kent L.Rev. Chicago-Kent Law Review
Chin.Yb.Priv. Int'l & Comp.L. Chinese Yearbook of Private International Law and Comparative Law
CI Consumer International
CI Constitutional Instrument (Ghana)
cic culpa in contrahendo
CIDIP Conferencia especializada interamericana de Derecho internacional privado (Inter-American Specialized Conference on Private International Law)
CIEC Commission International de l'État Civil (International Commission on Civil Status)
CILSA Comparative and International Law Journal of Southern Africa
Cir Circuit (USA)
CIS Community of Independent States
CISG United Nations Convention on Contracts for the International Sale of Goods
CITEJA Comité International Technique d'Experts Juridiques Aeriens (International Technical Committee of Aerial Legal Experts)

CivCh Hukuk Dairesi (Civil Chamber)
CJEU Court of Justice of the European Union
CJQ Civil Justice Quarterly
cl clause
Cl.& F. Clark & Finnelly's House of Lords Cases
CLB Commonwealth Law Bulletin
CLBR Coleção das leis do Império do Brasil (Collection of Laws of the Empire of Brazil)
CLC International Convention on Civil Liability for Oil Pollution Damage
C.L.C. Commercial Law Cases
CLH Comparative Legal History
CLR Commonwealth Law Reports
CLIP European Max Planck Group on Conflict of Laws in Intellectual Property
CLJ Cambridge Law Journal
CLP Current Legal Problems
Clunet see Journal du Droit International
CMI Comité Maritime International (International Maritime Committee)
CMI Yearbook Yearbook of the Comité Maritime International
CMLR Common Market Law Review
CMR Convention on the contract for the international carriage of goods by road
cmt comment[ary]
Coll Slovak Legal Collection (Zbierka Zakonov Slovenskej Republiky)
Coll. Jud. Conv. Collection of Judicial Conventions concluded between Tunisia and other countries
coord/cords Coordinator/Coordinators
Cox Crim. Cases Cox's Criminal Cases
Cogn.Psychol. Cognitive Psychology
col/cols column/columns
Colum.Bus.L.Rev. Columbia Business Law Review
Colum.Hum.Rts.L.Rev. Columbia Human Rights Review
Colum.J.Eur.L. Columbia Journal of European Law
Colum.J.Transnat'l L. Columbia Journal of Transnational Law
Colum.L.Rev. Columbia Law Review

COM   European Commission documents
COMI   Center of main interest
Comp   Compiler
Cornell Int'l L.J.   Cornell International Law Journal
Cornell L.Rev.   Cornell Law Review
Corte cost.   Corte costituzionale (Italian Constitutional Court)
Court of the EurAzEC   Court of the Eurasian Economic Community
CP Rep   Civil Procedure Reports
CQLR   Compilation of Québec Laws and Regulations
Cranch   Cranch's Supreme Court Reports
Creighton L.Rev.   Creighton Law Review
Ct.   Court
Ct App   Court of Appeals (US, State Courts)
Cth   Commonwealth of Australia
CTL   see CDT
C.T.L.R.   Computer and Telecommunications Law Review
CTS   Consolidated Treaty Series
Cuadernos de DIPr   Cuadernos de derecho internacional privado
CUP   Cambridge University Press
Customs Union   Customs Union founded by Belarus, Kazakhstan and the Russian Federation within the Eurasian Economic Community
CYELS   Cambridge Yearbook of European Legal Studies
Cyprus HR Law Rev   Cyprus Human Rights Law Review
Czech Yrbk Intl L   Czech Yearbook of International Law
Darras   Revue de droit international privé (Darras)
D   United States District Court (federal)
DB   Der Betrieb
DC Cir   United States Court of Appeals for the District of Columbia Circuit
DCFR   Draft Common Frame of Reference
DDC   United States District Court, District of Columbia
Dec: Decision number
DeCITA   Derecho del Comercio International – Temas y Actualidades
DG   Directorate General of the European Commission
DGRN   General Directorate of Registries and Public Notaries
DLR   Dominion Law Reports
Dick.L.Rev.   Dickinson Law Review
DIF   Sistema Nacional para el Desarrollo Integral de la Familia
Dir   Directive (European Union)
Dir. comm. Int   Diritto del commercio internazionale
Dir.internaz.   Diritto internazionale, Rivista trimestrale di dottrina e documentazione
Dir Marit   Il Diritto Marittimo
dir/dirs   Director/Directors
Dir. Trasp.   Diritto dei trasporti
diss   dissenting
DJT   Deutscher Juristentag
DMF   Droit maritime français
DNJ   United States District Court, District of New Jersey
Doc.   Document
DOF   Diario Oficial de la Federación (Official Journal of Mexico)
DOU   Diário Oficial da União (Official Journal of Brazil)
DP   Drejtësia Popullore
D.R.   Diário da República (Official Journal of Portugal)
Dr Marit Fr   Le Droit maritime Française
Ds   Departementsserien (Sweden)
DStJG   Deutsche Steuerjuristische Gesellschaft
DtZ   Deutsch-Deutsche Rechts-Zeitschrift
Duke Int'l & Comp.L.J.   Duke International and Comparative Law Journal
Duke L.J.   Duke Law Journal
D.U.L.J.   Dublin University Law Journal
DV   Darzhaven vestnik
DVBl   Deutsches Verwaltungsblatt
DZWIR   Deutsche Zeitschrift für Wirtschafts- und Insolvenzrecht
E&W   England and Wales
EAEC   European Atomic Energy Community
EBH   Publication of Principal Judgments of the Kúria (Supreme Court of Hungary)

LIST OF ABBREVIATIONS

E.B.L.R.   European Business Law Review
EBOR   European Business Organization Review
EC   European Community
ECB   European Central Bank
ECFI   European Court of First Instance
ECFR   European Company and Financial Law Review
ECJ   European Court of Justice
ECHR   Reports of Judgments and Decision of the European Court of Human Rights
ECLI   European Case Law Identifier
ECLR   European Competition Law Review
ECODIR   Electronic Consumer Dispute Resolution
ECOFIN   Economics and Financial Council of the European Union
Econ.Lett.   Economic Letters
ECR   European Court Reports
ECR-I   European Court Reports, Volume one
ECR-II   European Court Reports, Volume two
ECtHR   European Court of Human Rights
ECTIL   European Centre of Tort and Insurance Law
ed/eds   editor/editors
Edin.L.R.   Edinburgh Law Review
EDJ   El Derecho Jurisprudencia
edn   Edition
EDNC   Eastern District of North Carolina
EDNY   Eastern District of New York
EEA   European Economic Area
EEA   European Economic Association
EEC   European Economic Community
EEJ-Net   European Extra Judicial-Network
EEU   Eurasian Economic Union
EEZ   Exclusive Economic Zone
EFTA   European Free Trade Association
eg   exempli gratia/for example
EGC   European General Court
EHRR   European Human Rights Reports
eif   entry into force
EIPR   European Intellectual Property Review
EJCL   Electronic Journal of Comparative Law

EJHL   European Journal of Health Law
EJIL   European Journal of International Law
EJLE   European Journal of Law & Economics
E.J.L.R.   European Journal of Law Reform
eLB   electronic Bill of Lading
Elder L.J.   The Elder Law Journal
ELI   European Law Institute
ELIA   Association for a European Law Institute
ELR   Erasmus Law Review
E.L.Rev.   European Law Review
Emory Int'l L.Rev.   Emory International Law Review
Env L Rev   Environmental Law Review
EPO   European Patent Office
ER   English Reports
ERCL   European Review of Contract Law
ERPL   European Review of Private Law
et al   et alii (and others)
etc   et cetera (and so forth)
ETL   European Transport Law
et seq   et sequens (and the following)
EU   European Union
EuCML   Journal of European Consumer and Market Law
EuGRZ   Europäische Grundrechte-Zeitschrift
EuLF-I   The European Legal Forum, Section I
EuLF-II   The European Legal Forum, Section II
EuLR   European Law Reporter
EUR   Euro (currency)
E.R.P.L.   European Review of Private Law
EurAzEC   Eurasian Economic Community
Eur.J.Consum.L./R.E.D.C.   European Journal of Consumer Law/Revue Européenne de Droit de la Consommation
Eur.J.L. & Econ.   European Journal of Law & Economics
Eur.J.L.Ref.   European Journal of Law Reform
Eur.J.Leg.Stud.   European Journal of Legal Studies
Eur.L.J.   European Law Journal

Europ. Bus. Org. L. Rev.   European Business Organization Law Review

Eur.T.L.   European Transport Law

EurUP   Zeitschrift für Europäisches Umwelt- und Planungsrecht

EuZ   Zeitschrift für Europarecht

EuZA   Europäische Zeitschrift für Arbeitsrecht

EuZW   Europäische Zeitschrift für Wirtschaftsrecht

EvBl   Evidenzblatt der Rechtsmittelentscheidungen

EWCA Civ   Court of Appeal (Civil Division) (UK)

EWHC   England & Wales High Court (Administrative Court) (revision) 2000–2001

EWHC ... (Admin)   England & Wales High Court (Administrative Court) 2001- ...

EWHC ... (Comm)   High Court, Commercial Court (UK)

EWHC (TCC)   High Court, Technology & Construction Court (UK)

EWiR   Entscheidungen zum Wirtschaftsrecht

EWS   Europäisches Wirtschafts- und Steuerrecht

F.2d/3d   Federal Reporter, 2nd/3rd Series

F Cas   Federal Cases

Fam   Law Reports, Family Division

Fam Law   Family Law

Fam.L.Quart.   Family Law Quarterly

FamRZ   Zeitschrift für das gesamte Familienrecht

Fasc   fascicule

FC   Federal Court of Canada

FCA   Federal Court of Australia

FCN-Treaty   Treaty on Friendship, Commerce and Navigation

FCR   Butterworths Familiy Court Reports

F.C.R.   Australian Federal Court Reports

Fed Cir   United States Court of Appeals for the Federal Circuit

Fed. Reg.   Federal Register

FEK   Fyllo Efemeridas tes Kyverniseos (Official Journal of the Hellenic Republic)

FET   fair and equitable treatment

f/ff   following

FF   Feuille fédérale

FIATA   Fédération Internationale des Associations de Transitaires et Assimilés

FIDIC   Fédération Internationale des Ingénieurs-Conseils

Fin.Man.   Financial Management

FIOST   free in, out, stowed and trimmed

FLR   Family Law Reports

FL Rev   Australian Federal Law Review

fn/fns   footnote/footnotes

FNRJ   Federal Popular Republic of Yugoslavia

FONASBA   Federation of National Associations of Ship Brokers and Agents

Fordham Int'l L.J.   Fordham International Law Journal

Fordham L.Rev.   Fordham Law Review

Foro it.   Il foro italiano

FPRY   Federal People's Republic of Yugoslavia

FPS   full protection and security

FR   Finanzrundschau

F.R.D.   Federal Rules Decisions

FRY   Federal Republic of Yugoslavia

FSR   Fleet Street Reports

F.Supp./F.Supp.2d   Federal Supplement/Federal Supplement, 2nd Series

FTA   Free Trade Agreement

Ga.J.Int'l.& Comp.L.   Georgia Journal of International and Comparative law

Gall.   Gallison's Reports

Ga.L.Rev.   Georgia Law Review

Ga.St.U.L.Rev.   Georgia State University Law Review

GATT   General Agreement on Tariffs and Trade

Gaz. Pal.   La Gazette du Palais

Gaz. trib. lib. syr.   Gazette des tribunaux libanais et syriens

Gazz.Uff.   Gazzetta Ufficiale della Repubblica Italiana (Official Journal of Italy)

GBDe   Global Business Dialogue on E-Commerce

GC   General Court at the Court of Justice of the European Union (formerly Court of First Instance)

GCC Gulf Cooperation Council
GDR German Democratic Republic
GEDIP Group européen de droit international privé (European Group for Private International Law)
GENCON The Baltic and International Maritime Council Uniform General Charter
Geo. J. Int'l L. Georgetown Journal of International Law
Geo.L.J. Georgetown Law Journal
Geo.Mason L.Rev. George Mason Law Review
Geo.Wash.L.Rev. George Washington Law Review
German Y.B.Int'l L. German Yearbook of International Law
Giur. it. Giurisprudenza italiana
Giust. civ Mass. Giustizia civile Massimario
GLJ German Law Journal
GmbH Gesellschaft mit beschränkter Haftung
GPR Zeitschrift für Gemeinschaftsprivatrecht
GRUR Gewerblicher Rechtsschutz und Urheberrecht
GRURAusl Gewerblicher Rechtsschutz und Urheberrecht, Internationaler Teil (up until 1966)
GRURInt. Gewerblicher Rechtsschutz und Urheberrecht, Internationaler Teil (since 1967)
GRUR-RR Gewerblicher Rechtsschutz und Urheberrecht Rechtsprechungs-Report
Guernsey L.R. Guernsey Law Report
GURI see Gazz.Uff.
Hague Yrbk Intl L Hague Yearbook of International Law
Harv.Int'l L.J. Harvard International Law Journal
Harv.J.L.& Pub.Pol'y Harvard Journal of Law and Public Policy
Harv.L.Rev. Harvard Law Review
Harv.Negot.L.Rev. Harvard Negotiation Law Review
Hastings Int'l & Comp.L.Rev. Hastings International and Comparative Law
Hastings L.J. Hastings Law Journal

Hatem Recueil Hatem
HCA High Court of Australia
HCJ High Court of Justice of Israel
HD Højesteretsdom (Judgment by the Danish Supreme Court)
HKCFA Hong Kong Court of Final Appeal
HKCFAR Hong Kong Court of Final Appeal Reports
HKEC Hong Kong Electronic Cases
HKLJ Hong Kong Law Journal
HKLR Hong Kong Law Reports
HKLRD Hong Kong Law Reports & Digest
HL House of Lords (UK)
Hofstra L.Rev. Hofstra Law Review
How.L.J. Howard Law Journal
Hous.J.Int'l L. Houston Journal of International Law
Hous. L. Rev. Houston Law Review
HR Hoge Raad (Dutch Supreme Court)
HUP Harvard University Press
IAC Inter-American Convention
IAD Internal Affairs Doctrine
IAEA International Atomic Energy Agency
IAJC Inter-American Juridical Committee
IATA International Air Transport Association
IBA International Bar Association
ibid ibidem (in the same place)
ICA International Court of Arbitration of the International Chamber of Commerce
ICANN Internet Corporation for Assigned Names and Numbers
ICAO International Civil Aviation Organization
ICC International Chamber of Commerce
ICCA International Council for Commercial Arbitration
ICCLR International Company & Commercial Law Review
ICCS International Commission on Civil Status
ICDR International Center for Dispute Resolution of the American Arbitration Association
ICE Institution of Civil Engineers

ICJ   International Court of Justice
IJCP   International Journal of Cultural Property
I.C.J. Rep.   International Court of Justice Reports of Judgments
ICJ Statute   Statute of the International Court of Justice
ICLQ   International & Comparative Law Quarterly
ICLR   The International Construction Law Review
ICN   International Competition Network
ICR   Industrial Cases Reports
ICSID   International Centre for Settlement of Investment Disputes
ICT   Information and Communication Technology
id   idem (the same)
ie   id est (that is)
IECL   International Encyclopedia of Comparative Law
IFL   International Family Law
İHFM   İstanbul Üniversitesi Hukuk Fakültesi Mecmuası
IHLADI   Instituto Hispano Luso Americano de Derecho Internacional (Spanish-Portuguese-American Institute of International Law)
IHR   Internationales Handelsrecht
IIC   International Review of Intellectual Property and Competition Law
IIT   International Investment Treaty
I.J.   Irish Jurist
I.J.F.L.   Irish Journal of Family Law
IJLPF   International Journal of Law, Policy and the Family
IJODR   International Journal of Online Dispute Resolution
ILA   International Law Association
ILA Committee   Committee of the International Law Association Committee on 'Intellectual Property and Private International Law'
ILC   International Law Commission
ILI   International Law Institute
ILJ   Industrial Law Journal
Ill.   Supreme Court of Illinois
ILO   International Labor Organization
ILO CEARC   International Labor Organization Committee on the Application of Conventions and Recommendations
ILM   International Legal Materials
ILPr   International Litigation Procedure
ILQ   International Law Quarterly
ILR   International Law Reports
ILRM   Irish Law Reports Monthly
IMCO   Inter-Governmental Maritime Consultative Organization
IMF   International Monetary Fund
Imm AR   Immigration Appeal Reports
IMO   International Maritime Organization
IMSO   International Mobile Satellite Organization
INCOTERMS   International Commercial Terms
Ind.   Indiana
Ind.J.Global L.Stud.   Indiana Journal for Global Legal Studies
Indian J.Int'l L.   Indian Journal of International Law
Indiana L.J.   Indiana Law Journal
InDret   Revista para el Análisis del Derecho
infra   below
IntALR   International Arbitration Law Review
Int. Bus.& Econ. R.J.   International Business & Economics Research Journal
Int'l J.Legal Info.   International Journal of Legal Information
Int J Proc Law   International Journal of Procedural Law
Int'l Law.   International Lawyer
Int'l L.Forum   International Law Forum du droit international
Int'l Lis   Rivista di diritto processuale internazionale e arbitrato internazionale
Int'l Litg.   International Litigation
Int'l Org.   International Organization
IOPC Funds   International Oil Pollution Compensation Funds
IOSCO   International Organization of Securities Commissions
Iowa L.Rev.   Iowa Law Review

LIST OF ABBREVIATIONS XV

IP   Internet Protocol
IP   Intellectual property
IPG   Gutachten zum internationalen und ausländischen Privatrecht
IPRax   Praxis des Internationalen Privat- und Verfahrensrechts
IPRE   Österreichische Entscheidungen zum Internationalen Privatrecht
IPRspr.   Die deutsche Rechtsprechung auf dem Gebiete des Internationalen Privatrechts
IR   Irish Report
IRRC   International Review of the Red Cross
IRuD   Internationales Recht und Diplomatie
ISDS   Investor-State Dispute Settlement
Islam L & Soc   Islamic Law and Society
ISO   International Organization for Standardization
ISR   Internationale Steuer-Rundschau
IStR   Internationales Steuerrecht
ITF   International Transport Workers' Federation
ITLOS   International Tribunal for the Law of the Sea
ITR   Income Tax Reports
ITU   International Telecommunications Union
IVRA   Rivista Internazionale di Diritto Romano e Antico
IYIL   The Italian Yearbook of International Law
Iž   Izvršna žalba (appeal in enforcement procedure) (Serbia)
J Afr L   Journal of African Law
JAL(C)   Journal of Air Law (and Commerce)
Jap.Ann.Int'l L.   Japanese Annual of International Law
JBL   Journal of Business Law
JBl.   Juristische Blätter
J.Bus.   Journal of Business
JCL   Journal of Contract Law
J.-Cl. dr. int.   Juris-classeur de droit international
JCMS   Journal of Common Market Studies
J.Com.Mar.Stud.   see JCMS

J.Comp.Leg.   Journal of Comparative Legislation and International Law
J.Consum.Aff.   Journal of Consumer Affairs
J.Consum.Res.   Journal of Consumer Research
J.Corp.L.   Journal of Corporation Law
JCP   Juris-Classeur Périodique
J.C.P.   Journal of Consumer Policy
J.Dr.Int'l   Journal du Droit International
J.Dr.Int.Priv.   Journal du Droit International Privé
J.D.E.   Journal de droit européen
J East Euro L   Journal of East European Law
J.Econ.Beh. & Org.   Journal of Economic Behavior and Organization
J.Econ.Lit.   Journal of Economic Literature
J.Econ.Persp.   Journal of Economic Perspectives
J.Exp.Psychol.Hum.Percept.Perform.   Journal of Experimental Psychology: Human Perception and Performance
J.Fin.Econ.   Journal of Financial Economics
J.Fin.Quant.A.   Journal of Financial Quantitative Analysis
JGS   Justizgesetzsammlung (Collection of Laws of Austria)
JherJb   Jherings Jahrbücher für die Dogmatik des heutigen römischen und deutschen Privatrechts
J.I.B.L.R.   Journal of International Banking Law & Regulation
JIDS   Journal of International Dispute Settlement
JIML   Journal of International Maritime Law
J. Int'l & Comp. L.   Journal of International and Comparative Law
J.Int'l Arb.   Journal of International Arbitration
J.Int'l Econ.L.   Journal of International Economic Law
JIPITEC   Journal of Intellectual Property, Information Technology, and Electronic Commerce Law
JITE   Journal of Institutional and Theoretical Economics
J.L.& Com.   Journal of Law and Commerce

JLE Journal of Law and Economics
J.L.Econ.& Org. Journal of Law, Economics and Organizations
J.Leg.Pluralism Journal of Legal Pluralism and Unofficial Law
JLS Journal of Legal Studies
J. Market Res. Journal of Market Research
J.Mar.L.& Com. Journal of Maritime Law & Commerce
J.O. Journal Officiel de la République Française (Official Journal of France)
JORF see J.O.
JPA Jurisprudence du Port d'Anvers
J.Pers.Soc.Psychol. Journal of Personality and Social Psychology
J.P.I.L. Journal of Personal Injury Litigation
J.Pol.Econ. Journal of Political Economy
J Priv Int L Journal of Private International Law
JR Juristische Rundschau
JRC Jersey Reports
J.Soc.Comp. Legislation Journal of the Society of Comparative Legislation
JTL Journal des tribunaux Luxembourg
Jur.Rev. Juridical Review
J.W.T. Journal of World Trade
JZ JuristenZeitung
KB Law Reports, King's Bench
KG Kammergericht (Higher Regional Court Berlin, Germany)
KHK Kanun Hükmünde Kararname (Turkish decree law)
KunstRSp Kunstrechtsspiegel
Labeo Rassegna di Diritto Romano
La.L.Rev. Louisiana Law Review
Law & Prac. Int'l Cts. & Tribunals Law and Practice of International Courts and Tribunals
LCIA London Court of International Arbitration
LCP Law & Contemporary Problems
L.Ed. United States Supreme Court Reports, Lawyers' Edition
Legf. B. Kúria (Supreme Court of Hungary)
Legf. B. Pf. Judgment of the Kúria (Supreme Court of Hungary) in Revision

Leon. Leonard's Reports
LFMR Law & Financial Markets Review
LFN Laws of the Federation of Nigeria
LG Landgericht (Regional Court, Germany)
LHR Law & History Review
Lib liber (book)
lit littera (letter)
LJN Landelijk Jurisprudentie Nummer
Ll L Rep Lloyd's List Law Reports
Lloyd's Rep Lloyd's Law Reports
Lloyd's Rep IR Lloyd's Law Reports Insurance & Reinsurance
LLMC Convention on Limitation of Liability for Maritime Claims
LMAA London Maritime Arbitrators Association
LMCLQ Lloyd's Maritime and Commercial Law Quarterly
LMK Lindenmaier-Möhring – Kommentierte Rechtsprechung
LMR Law Magazine & Review
LNRI Lembaran Negara Republik Indonesia (Official Journal of Indonesia)
LNTS League of Nations Treaty Series
loc. cit. loco citato (in the place cited)
LOF Lloyd's Open Form
Louisiana R.S. Louisiana Laws Revised Statutes
Loy.L.A.L.Rev. Loloya of Los Angeles Law Review
Loy.U.Chi.Int'l.L.Rev. Loyola University Chicago International Law Review
L.Q. Lois du Québec
LQR Law Quarterly Review
LR Liechtensteinische Rechtssammlung (Collection of Laws of Liechtenstein)
L.R. Law Reports
LR QB Law Reports, Queen's Bench, 1st Series
LRA locus regit actum (the place governs the act)
LR (Ir) Law Reports (Ireland)
LRQ Lois refondues du Québec
LR (NSW) New South Wales Law Reports (old abbreviation)
LS Legal Studies

LSG   Landessozialgericht (Regional Court on Social Law, Germany)
ltd   limited company
Malaya L.Rev.   Malaya Law Review
MANU   Manupatra
MARPOL   International Convention for the Prevention of Pollution from Ships
Mar.Pol'y   Marine Policy
Marq.L.Rev.   Marquette Law Review
Mason   Mason's United States Circuit Court Reports
Mass.   Massachusetts
MB   Moniteur belge/Belgisch Staatsblad (Official Journal of Belgium)
MC   Model Convention
McGill L.J.   McGill Law Journal
Md.L.Rev.   Maryland Law Review
MDR   Monatsschrift für Deutsches Recht
MECLR   Middle East Commercial Law Review
Me.L.Rev.   Maine Law Review
Mémorial   Mémorial – Journal Officiel du Grand-Duché de Luxembourg (Official Journal of Luxembourg)
Mem.St.U.L.Rev.   Memphis State University Law Review
Mercer L.Rev.   Mercer Law Review
Mercosur   Mercado Común del Sur (South American Common Market)
MFN   most favoured nation
MHB   Milletlerarası Hukuk ve Milletlerarası Özel Hukuk Bülteni
Mich.J.Int'l L.   Michigan Journal of International Law
Mich.L.Rev.   Michigan Law Review
Minn   Minnesota
Minn.J.Int'l L.   Minnesota Journal of International Law
Minn.L.Rev.   Minnesota Law Review
Misc 3d.   Miscellaneous Reports, 3rd Series
Miss   Mississippi
MJ   Maastricht Journal of European and Comparative Law
MLC   Maritime Labour Convention
MLR   Modern Law Review

Mo   Missouri
Mo.L.Rev.   Missouri Law Review
MRAs   Mutual Recognition Agreements
MTO   Multimodal Transport Operator
MU   International Treaties (in the Official Journal of Montenegro)
MULR   Melbourne University Law Review
NAFTA   North American Free Trade Agreement
NASDAQ   National Association of Securities Dealers Automated Quotation
NCCUSL   National Conference of Commissioners on Uniform State Laws
N.C. J. Int'L L. & Com. Reg.   North Carolina Journal of International Law and Commercial Regulation
N.C.L.Rev.   North Carolina Law Review
N.E.2d   Northeastern Reporter 2nd Series
Neb.L.Rev.   Nebraska Law Review
Nev. L. J.   Nevada Law Journal
NGO   Non-Governmental Organization
NI   Northern Ireland
NiemZ   Zeitschrift für internationales Privat- und Strafrecht (later: Zeitschrift für Internationales Privat- und Öffentliches Recht)
NiemeyersZ   Niemeyers Zeitschrift für Internationales Recht
Nigerian LJ   Nigerian Law Journal
NILR   Netherlands International Law Review
NIPR   Nederlands Internationaal Privaatrecht
NJ   Nederlandse Jurisprudentie
N.J.   Supreme Court of New Jersey
N.J.   New Jersey Reports
NJA   Nytt Juridiskt Arkiv (Decisions of the Swedish Supreme Court)
N.J.L.   The New Law Journal
NJW   Neue Juristische Wochenschrift
NJW-RR   Neue Juristische Wochenschrift, Rechtsprechungsreport
NLCC   Le Nuove Leggi Civili Commentate
NLJ   New Law Journal
NLR   National Law Review

no/nos   number/numbers
Northwest.J.Int'l L. & Bus.   Northwestern Journal of International Law & Business
Northwest.U.L.Rev.   Northwestern University Law Review
Nordisk Tidsskrift Int'l Ret   Nordisk Tidskrift for International Ret
NOU   Norges offentlige utredninger (Official reports of Norway)
NRCD   National Redemption Council Decree
NSFNET   National Science Foundation NET
NStZ-RR   Neue Zeitschrift für Strafrecht, Rechtsprechungs- Report
NSWLR   New South Wales Law Reports (modern abbreviation)
N.W.   North Western Reporter
N.W. 2d   Northwestern Reporter 2nd Series
NWLR   Nigerian Weekly Law Reports
NY   New York
N.Y.   New York Court of Appeals
N.Y.   New York Reports
N.Y.2d   New York Reports, 2nd Series
N.Y. GOB. LAW   New York General Obligations Law
N.Y.Int'l L.Rev.   New York International Law Review
N.Y.L.Forum   New York Law Forum
NYLJ   New York Law Journal
nyp   not yet published
nyr   not yet released/reported
N.Y.S. 2d   New York Supplement, 2nd Series
N.Y.Sch.J.Int'l.& Comp.L.   New York Law School Journal of International and Comparative Law
NYSE   New York Stock Exchange
N.Y.U.Envtl.L.J.   New York University Environmental Law Journal
N.Y.U.J.Int'l Law & Pol.   New York University Journal of International Law & Politics
N.Y.U.J. Law & Lib.   New York University Journal of Law & Liberty
N.Y.U. L.Q. Rev.   New York University Law Quarterly Review
N.Y.U.L.Rev.   New York University Law Review

NZCA   New Zealand Court of Appeal
NZFam   Neue Zeitschrift für Familienrecht
NZG   Neue Zeitschrift für Gesellschaftsrecht
NZHC   New Zealand High Court
NZI   Neue Zeitschrift für das Recht der Insolvenz und Sanierung
NZJPIL   New Zealand Journal of Public and International Law
NZLR   New Zealand Law Reports
O.   Ordinance
OAPI   African Organization for Intellectual Property
OAS   Organization of American States
ODR   Online Dispute Resolution
OECD   Organisation for Economic Co-operation and Development
OEEC   Organisation for European Economic Co-operation
ÖZföR   Österreichische Zeitschrift für Öffentliches Recht
OGH   Oberster Gerichtshof (Austrian Supreme Court)
OHADA   Organisation pour l'Harmonisation en Afrique du Droit des Affaires (Organization for the Harmonization of Business Law in Africa)
OHIM   Office of Harmonization for the Internal Market
Ohio St.J.on Disp.Resol.   Ohio State Journal on Dispute Resolution
Ohio St.L.J.   Ohio State Law Journal
O.J.   Official Journal of the European Communities (since 2003: Official Journal of the European Union)
OLG   Oberlandesgericht (Higher Regional Court, Germany)
Okla.L.Rev.   Oklahoma Law Review
ONSC   Ontario Superior Court of Justice Reports
op. cit.   opera citato (in the work cited)
Or.L.Rev.   Oregon Law Review
Or.Rev.Stat.   Oregon Revised Statutes
OTIF   Organisation intergouvernementale pour les transportes internationaux ferroviaires (Intergovermental Organisation for International Carriage by Rail)
Ottawa L.Rev.   Ottawa Law Review

OUCLJ Oxford University Commonwealth Law Journal
OUP Oxford University Press
Oxford J.Leg.Stud. Oxford Journal of Legal Studies
p/pp page/pages
P Probate, Divorce and Admiralty Division (New Zealand)
P. Law Reports, Probate
P.2d Pacific Reporter, 2nd Series
P&I Protection and Indemnity
Pa Pennsylvania
Pa. Supreme Court of Pennsylvania
Pa. Pennsylvania State Reports
p.a. per annum (per year)
Pace Int'l L.Rev. Pace International Law Review
PACS Pacte civil de solidarité
para/paras paragraph/paragraphs
Paris J. Int'l Arb. Paris Journal of International Arbitration
Pas.Belge Pasicrisie belge
Pas.lux. Pasicrisie luxembourgeoise
PC Judicial Committee of the Privy Council
PC Spanish Provincial Court (Audiencia Provincial)
PCIJ Permanent Court of International Justice
PD Law Reports, Probate, Divorce & Admiralty Division
P.D. Piskei Din (Israel)
PECL Principles of European Contract Law
PEICL Principles of European Insurance Contract Law
Penn St. Int'l L. Rev. Penn State International Law Review
Peters Peters' Supreme Court Reports
PICAO Provisional International Civil Aviation Organization
P.L. Public Law
plc public limited company
POEJ Proche Orient Etudes Juridiques (Journal of the Faculty of Law and Political Science, Saint-Joseph University of Beirut)
POG Taiwanese Presidential Office Gazette (Zong-tong-fu Gong-bao)
PRC People's Republic of China
Prel. Doc. No. Preliminary Document Number
Proc.Am.Soc.Int'l L. Proceedings of the Annual Meeting of the American Society of International Law
PSLR Penn State Law Review
Psychol.Bull. Psychological Bulletin
Psychol.Rev. Psychological Review
pt/pts part/parts
pub publication
Pž Parnična žalba (appeal in litigious procedure) (Serbia)
QB Law Reports, Queen's Bench, 3rd Series
QBD Law Reports, Queen's Bench Division
Qd R Queensland Reports
QJE Quarterly Journal of Economics
R/r Rule
R. The Reports in all the Courts
RabelsZ Rabels Zeitschrift für ausländisches und internationales Privatrecht
Raj Rajasthan High Court
Rand J.Econ. The RAND Journal of Economics
RBD Revista Boliviana de Derecho
R.B.D.I. Revue Belge de Droit International
RdA Revue de l'arbitrage
RdC Revue des contrats
RDC/TBH Revue de Droit Commercial Belge//Tijdschrift voor Belgisch Handelsrecht
R.D.I.D.C. Revue de Droit international et de Droit comparé
R.D.M. Revista de Derecho mercantile
R.D.T. Revue de droit des transports
R.D.U.E. Revue du droit de l'Union Européenne
RdW Österreichisches Recht der Wirtschaft
R.E.C.D. Revue européenne de droit de la consommation/European Journal of Consumer Law
Rec. des Cours Recueil des Cours de l'Academie de Droit International de la Haye
REDI Revista Española de Derecho Internacional

REEI   Revista Electrónica de Estudios Internacionales

Reg   Regulation (European Union)

reg/regs   regulation/regulations

REIO   Regional Economic Integration Organization

REITS   Real Estate Investment Trusts

Rép. Defrénois   Defrénois – la revue du notariat

Reports Int.Arb.Awards   Reports of International Arbitral Awards

repr   reprinted

RES   Resolution

rev edn   revised edition

Rev.crit.DIP   Revue critique de droit international privé

Rev.Droit Aff.Int'les   Revue de Droit des Affaires Internationales

Rev.Dr.Unif.   Revue de Droit Uniforme

Rev.Econ. & Stat.   The Review of Economics and Statistics

Rev.Econ.Stud.   Review of Economic Studies

Rev.L. & Econ.   Review of Law and Economics

Rev. trim. dr. fam.   Revue trimestrielle de droit de la famille

Revue Scapel   Revue de Droit Commercial, Maritime, Aérien et des Transports (Scapel)

RG   Reichsgericht (German Imperial Court of Justice)

RGBl.   Reichsgesetzblatt (former Official Journal of Germany)

RGZ   Entscheidungen des Reichsgerichts in Zivilsachen (Decisions of the German Imperial Court of Justice in civil matters)

RH   Rättsfall från hovrätterna (Sweden)

RHC   Rules of the Hong Kong High Court

R.H.D.I.   Revue Héllenique de Droit International

RIDA   Revue internationale du droit d'auteur

R.I.D.C.   Revue international de droit comparé

Riv.Dir.Int.   Rivista di diritto internazionale

Riv.Dir.Int'le Priv. & Proc.   Rivista di diritto internazionale privato e processuale

Riv Dir Proc   Rivista di diritto processuale

Riv.it.dir.lav.   Rivista italiana di diritto del lavoro

RIW   Recht der internationalen Wirtschaft

R.J.   Reporting judge

RJL   Revue judiciaire libanaise (Al-Nashra al-Qadaiyya)

RMCUE   Revue du Marché Commun et de l'Union Européenne

RO   Recueil officiel des lois fédérales (Official Journal of Switzerland)

ROC   Republic of China on Taiwan

Roger Williams U.L.Rev.   Roger Williams University Law Review

Roman.J.Priv. Int'l & Comp.L.   Romanian Journal of Private International and Comparative Law

RPC   Reports of Patent Cases

Rpfleger   Der Deutsche Rechtspfleger

RS   Republic of Serbia

RSC   Bermuda Rules of the Supreme Court 1985

R.S.C.   Revised Statutes of Canada

RSDIE   Revue suisse de droit international et européen

RStBl.   Reichssteuerblatt (Official Fiscal Journal of Germany)

Rt   Norsk Retstidende (Collection of Decisions of the Norwegian Supreme Court)

RTDCiv   Revue trimestrielle de droit civil

RTDEur   Revue trimestrielle de droit européen

R.T.D.C.   Revue trimestrielle de droit commercial et de droit économique

RTDF   Revue trimestrielle de droit familial

RW   Rechtskundig Weekblad

s/ss   section/sections

SA   South African Law Reports

SA … (A)   Appellate Division

SA … (C)   Cape Provincial Division

SA … (ECG)   Eastern Cape High Court, Grahamstown

SA … (W)   Witwatersrand Local Division

SA Merc.L.J.   South African Mercantile Law Journal

San Diego Int'l L.J.   San Diego International Law Journal

SASR   South Australian State Reports
Sb   Sbírka zákonů (Collection of Laws of the Czech Republic)
SBC   Statutes of British Columbia
Sbm.s.   Sbírka mezinárodních smluv
Sc   scilicet (that is to say)
SCA   South African Supreme Court of Appeal
S.Cal.L.Rev.   Southern California Law Review
Scand. Inst. Mar. L.   Scandinavian Institute of Maritime Law
SCC   Supreme Court of Canada
SCC   Sala de Casación Civil (Civil chamber of the Venezuelan Supreme Court of Justice)
SCC   Indian Supreme Court Cases
S.C.C.   Stockholm Chamber of Commerce
SCG   Serbia and Montenegro
Sch   Schedule
SchiedsVZ   Zeitschrift für Schiedsverfahren
SchwJbIntR   Schweizerisches Jahrbuch für internationales Recht (Annuaire Suisse de Droit International)
SCJ   Supreme Court Judgment (Thailand)
SCJILB   South Carolina Journal of International Law & Business
Scot   Scotland
SCR   Supreme Court Reports
S.Ct.   Supreme Court Reporter
SD   District Court for the Southern District
SDFla   District Court for the Southern District of Florida
SDNY   District Court for the Southern District of New York
SDR   Special Drawing Rights
SE   Societas Europaea (European Company)
SEKO   Sjöfolk Facket för Service och Kommunikation (Swedish Trade Union)
SES   Single Economic Space of the Eurasian Economic Community
SFRJ/SFRY   Socialist Federal Republic of Yugoslavia
SFT   Swiss Federal Tribunal
SI   Statutory Instrument
S.Ill.U.L.J.   Southern Illinois University Law Journal

Sl. list CG br.   Official Journal of Montenegro No (new)
Sl. list RCG br.   Official Journal of Montenegro No (old)
SJ   State Journal (Lithuania)
SJIR   Schweizerisches Jahrbuch für internationales Recht
SLR   Singapore Law Reports
SLT   The Scots Law Times
SME   Small and Medium Enterprises
SMU L.Rev.   Southern Methodist University Law Review
SNS   Statutes of Nova Scotia
So.2d   Southern Reporter, 2nd Series
SOLAS   International Convention for the Safety of Life at Sea
SOU   Statens Offentliga Utredningar (Sweden)
SPA   Sala Político Administrativa (Administrative Chamber)
Span Yrbk Intl L   Spanish Yearbook of International Law
SPV   Special Purpose Vehicle
SQ   Statutes of Quebec
SR   Systematische Rechtssammlung (Collection of Laws of Switzerland)
SR   Statutory regulation
Stan. J. Civ. Rts. & Civ. Liberties   Stanford Journal of Civil Rights & Civil Liberties
Stan.J.Int'l L.   Stanford Journal of International Law
Stan.J.L.Bus.Fin   Stanford Journal of Law, Business & Finance
Stan.L.Rev.   Stanford Law Review
Stat.   Statutes at Large
StAZ   Das Standesamt
Stb   Staatsblad (Official Journal of The Netherlands)
STC   Judgment of the Spanish Constitutional Court
S.T.C.   Simons Tax Cases
S.T.C. (SDC)   Simon's Tax Cases (Special Commissioners' Decisions)
Stetson L.Rev.   Stetson Law Review
S.Tex.L.Rev.   Southern Texas Law Review

STJ   Superior Tribunal de Justiça (Brazilian Superior Court of Justice)

St. John's L.Rev.   St. John's Law Review

STS   Judgment of the Spanish Supreme Court

StuW   Steuer und Wirtschaft

subpara/subparas   subparagraph/subparagraphs

supp/supps   supplement/supplements

supra   above

SvJT   Svensk Juristtidning

SVR   Straßenverkehrsrecht

S.W.2d   Southwestern Reporter, 2nd Series

SWI   Steuer und Wirtschaft International

SYBIL   Singapore Yearbook of International Law

Syd.L.Rev.   Sydney Law Review

Syracuse J.Int'l L.& Com.   Syracuse Journal of International Law and Commerce

Syracuse L.Rev.   Syracuse Law Review

SZ   Entscheidungen des österreichischen Obersten Gerichtshofes in Zivil- und Justizverwaltungssachen (Decisions of the Austrian Supreme Court in civil and judicial administrative matters)

SZIER   Schweizerische Zeitschrift für internationales und europäisches Recht

SZW   Schweizerische Zeitschrift für Wirtschaftsrecht

T.   tomo

TA   Tesis Aislada

TASE   Tel-Aviv Stock Exchange

Tasm.U.L.Rev.   Tasmanian University Law Review

TDM   Transnational Dispute Management

TEC   Treaty establishing the European Community

Tel Aviv U.Stud.L.   Tel Aviv University Studies in Law

Temp.L.Rev.   Temple Law Review

Tenn.L.Rev.   Tennessee Law Review

TEU   Treaty on European Union

Tex.Int'l L.J.   Texas International Law Journal

Tex.L.Rev.   Texas Law Review

TFEU   Treaty on the Functioning of the European Union

TGI   Tribunal de Grande Instance

TIAS   Treaties and other International Acts Series

Tit   Titulus (title)

TLA   Treaty on Legal Assistance

TLNRI   Tambahan Lembaran Negara Republik Indonesia (Supplement to the Official Journal of Indonesia)

Torts L.J.   Torts Law Journal

tr/trs   translator/translators

Trav Com fr DIP   Travaux du Comité français de droit international privé

TranspR   Transportrecht

TRIPS   Treaty on Trade-Related Aspects of Intellectual Property Rights

Trib   Tribunal (Court of First Instance)

TSJ   Tribunal Supremo de Justicia de Venezuela (Venezuelan Supreme Court of Justice)

Tul.J.Int'l & Comp.L.   Tulane Journal of International and Comparative Law

Tul.L.Rev.   Tulane Law Review

Tul.Mar.L.J.   Tulane Maritime Law Journal

UAE   United Arab Emirates

UCC   Uniform Commercial Code

UCC L.J.   Uniform Commercial Code Law Journal

U.C. Davis L.Rev.   University of California at Davis Law Review

U.Chi.L.Rev.   University of Chicago Law Review

UCLA L.Rev.   University of California at Los Angeles Law Review

U.Colo.L.Rev.   University of Colorado Law Review

UCP   Uniform Customs and Practice for Documentary Credits of the International Chamber of Commerce

UDRP   Uniform Domain Name Dispute Resolution Policy

UfR   Ugeskrift for Retsvæsen (Danish Weekly Law Journal)

U Ghana LJ   University of Ghana Law Journal

U.Ill.L.Rev.   University of Illinois Law Review

UINL   Union Internationale du Notariat Latin

List of Abbreviations

UK United Kingdom
U.Kan.L.Rev. University of Kansas Law Review
UKEAT United Kindom Employment Appeal Tribunal
UKHL United Kingdom House of Lords
UKPC United Kingdom Privy Council
Ukr Yrbk Intl L Ukrainian Yearbook of International Law
UKSC United Kingdom Supreme Court
ULF Hague Uniform Law on the Formation of Contracts for the International Sale of Goods
ULIS Hague Uniform Law on the International Sale of Goods
U.Miami Inter-Am.L.Rev. University of Miami Inter-American Law Review
U.Miami L.Rev. University of Miami Law Review
UMKC L.Rev. UMKC Law Review
UN United Nations
UNCITRAL United Nations Commission on International Trade Law
UNCTAD United Nations Conference on Trade and Development
UNECE United Nations Economic Commission for Europe
UNESCAP United Nations Economic and Social Commission for Asia and the Pacific
UN GAOR Supp United Nations, General Assembly Official Records, Supplement
UNICEF United Nations Children's Fund
UNIDROIT International Institute for the Unification of Private Law/Institut international pour l'unification du droit privé
UNIDROIT Principles UNIDROIT Principles of International Commercial Contracts
Unif.L.Rev. Uniform Law Review
UNPROFOR United Nations Protection Force
UNTS United Nations Treaty Series
U.Pa.J.Int'l Bus.L. University of Pennsylvania Journal of International Business Law
U.Pa.J.Int'l Econ.L. University of Pennsylvania Journal for International Economic Law

U.Pa.J.Int'l L. University of Pennsylvania Journal of International Law
U.Pa.L.Rev. University of Pennsylvania Law Review
US/USA United States of America
U.S. United States Reports
USD US-Dollar (currency)
U.S.F.Mar.L.J. University of San Francisco Maritime Law Journal
USSR Union of Soviet Socialist Republics
U.Tas.L.Rev. University of Tasmania Law Review
U.T.L.J. University of Toronto Law Journal
UWLA L.Rev. University of West Los Angeles Law Review
v versus
Va.J.Int'l L. Virginia Journal of International Law
Va.L.Rev. Virginia Law Review
Val.Univ.L.Rev. Valparaiso University Law Review
Vand.J. Transnat'l L. Vanderbilt Journal of Transnational Law
Vand.L.Rev. Vanderbilt Law Review
VAT Value Added Tax
VersR Versicherungsrecht
Ves.Sen. Vesey Senior's Chancery Reports
Vict.U.Well.L.Rev. Victoria University of Wellington Law Review
Virginia J Intl L Virginia Journal of International
VLD Vestre Landsretsdom (Judgment by the Danish Western Court of Appeal)
VOB Vergabe- und Vertragsordnung für Bauleistungen
vol/vols volume/volumes
VuR Verbraucher und Recht
VwGH Verwaltungsgerichtshof (Austrian Supreme Administrative Court)
War Western Australian Reports
Wash.2d Washington Reports, 2nd Series
Washburn L.J. Washburn Law Journal
Wash. & Lee L.Rev. Washington and Lee Law Review
Wash. U. Global St. L. Rev. Washington University Global Studies Law Review

Wash.U.L.Q.   Washington University Law Quarterly
Wash.U.L.Rev.   Washington University Law Review
Wayne L.Rev.   Wayne Law Review
WCO   World Customs Organization
WFC   Work in Fishing Convention
WGO-MfOR   WGO-Monatshefte für Osteuropäisches Recht
Wheaton   Wheaton's Supreme Court Reports
Willamette J. Int'l L. & Disp. Resol.   Willamette Journal of International Law and Dispute Resolution
Willamette L.Rev.   Willamette Law Review
WIPO   World Intellectual Property Organization
Wis   Wisconsin
Wis.   Wisconsin Supreme Court
Wis.2d   Wisconsin Reports, 2nd Series
Wis.Int'l L.J.   Wisconsin International Law Journal
Wis.L.Rev.   Wisconsin Law Review
WJLGS   Wisconsin Journal of Law, Gender & Society
WL   Westlaw
WLR   Weekly Law Reports
WM   Wertpapier-Mitteilungen
WM IV   WM Zeitschrift für Wirtschafts- und Bankrecht
Wm. & Mary L.Rev.   William and Mary Law Review
WMU J Mar affairs   WMU Journal of Maritime Affairs
WPNR   Weekblad voor Privaatrecht Notariaat en Registratie
WRP   Wettbewerb in Recht und Praxis
WTO   World Trade Organization
WuW   Wirtschaft und Wettbewerb
W. Va.L.Rev.   West Virginia Law Review
Yale J.Int'l L.   Yale Journal of International Law
Yale J.on Reg.   Yale Journal on Regulation
Yale J.Reg.   Yale Journal on Regulation
Yale J. World Pub.Ord.   Yale Journal of World Public Order
Yale L. & Pol'y Rev.   Yale Law & Policy Review

Yale L.J.   Yale Law Journal
YEL   Yearbook of European Law
YIMEL   Yearbook of Islamic and Middle Eastern Law
YKD   Yargıtay Kararları Dergisi
YbPIL   Yearbook of Private International Law
ZAK   Zivilrecht aktuell
ZaöRV   Zeitschrift für ausländisches öffentliches Recht und Völkerrecht
ZASCA   see SCA
ZBGR   Schweizerische Zeitschrift für Beurkundungs- und Grundbuchrecht
ZChinR   Zeitschrift für Chinesisches Recht
Zeitschr Int Priv & StrafR   Zeitschrift für Internationales Privat- und Strafrecht
ZEuP   Zeitschrift für Europäisches Privatrecht
ZEuS   Zeitschrift für europarechtliche Studien
ZfRV   Zeitschrift für Europarecht, Internationales Privatrecht und Rechtsvergleichung
ZGR   Zeitschrift für Unternehmens- und Gesellschaftsrecht
ZgS   Zeitschrift für Vertragsgestaltung, Schuld- und Haftungsrecht (formerly Zeitschrift für das Gesamte Schuldrecht)
ZHR   Zeitschrift für das gesamte Handelsrecht und Wirtschaftsrecht
ZIEV   Zeitschrift für die internationale Eisenbahnförderung
ZIP   Zeitschrift für Wirtschaftsrecht
ZLW   Zeitschrift für Luft- und Weltraumrecht
ZSR   Zeitschrift für Schweizerisches Recht
ZVersWiss   Zeitschrift für die gesamte Versicherungswissenschaft
ZVglRWiss   Zeitschrift für Vergleichende Rechtswissenschaft
ZVR   Zeitschrift für Verkehrsrecht
ZWS   Zeitschrift für Wirtschafts- und Sozialwissenschaften
ZZP   Zeitschrift für Zivilprozess
ZZPInt   Zeitschrift für Zivilprozess International
ZZW   Zeitschrift für Zivilstandswesen

ENTRIES I–Z

ICAO[1]

I. History of ICAO

Due to the need for regulation of international air transport after the Second World War, the US government invited all states involved in the war, as well as the neutral states (except for → Argentina) to an international conference in Chicago. The founding of the International Civil Aviation Organization (ICAO) was decided on 7 December 1944 with the signing of the Chicago Convention (Convention of 7 December 1944 on International Civil Aviation, 15 UNTS 295). Of the 52 participating nations, 37 signed the agreement, whereupon the organization, with its seat in Montreal, provisionally began its work under the name Provisional International Civil Aviation Organization (PICAO). After achieving the required 26 ratifications, the Convention entered into force on 4 April 1947 and PICAO was replaced by ICAO. The seat of the organization remained in Montreal. One month later, on 13 May 1947, ICAO was accorded the status of specialized agency of the United Nations according to art 57 UN Charter (Charter of the United Nations of 26 June 1945, 1 UNTS XVI). To this day, 191 nations have joined ICAO. Seven local offices responsible for nine air service areas in Bangkok, Cairo, Dakar, Lima, Mexico City, Nairobi and Paris have been established. ICAO cooperates closely with other UN agencies, such as the World Meteorological Organization, the International Telecommunication Union, the Universal Postal Union, the World Health Organization and the International Maritime Organization. Many NGOs are involved in the work of ICAO, for example the International Air Transport Association or the International Federation of Air Line Pilots' Associations.

II. The Chicago Convention on International Civil Aviation

The convention adopted at the Chicago Convention on International Civil Aviation (also referred to as the Chicago Convention or ICAO Convention) and the simultaneously concluded supplementary agreements (International Air Services Transit Agreement of 7 December 1944 (84 UNTS 389), International Air Transport Agreement of 7 December 1944 (171 UNTS 387)) established principles that provide the basis for today's civil air traffic.

The Convention states in art 1 that each state maintains sovereignty over its airspace. It distinguishes between civil and state aircraft, whereby the Convention applies only to civil aircraft and not to state aircraft (such as aircraft used in police or military services) (art 3(a)). Furthermore, the Convention differentiates between scheduled air service and non-scheduled international air service. The latter is treated as privileged, as it permits flights into or across the territory of a contracting state without obtaining prior permission (art 5). On the other hand, according to art 6, scheduled air service may be operated only in accordance with the permission of that state. Thereafter, based on the Chicago Convention, several so-called 'freedoms of the air' have been developed that are generally accepted in the community of nations.

Bilateral aviation conventions, which govern the essential questions of air traffic between the particular parties involved, have been established based on freedoms of the air. The following freedoms of the air exist:

- the right or privilege in respect of scheduled international air services, granted by one state to another state or states, to fly across its territory without landing (1st Freedom Right);
- the right or privilege in respect of scheduled international air services, granted by one state to another state or states, to land in a state's territory for non-traffic purposes (2nd Freedom Right);
- the right or privilege in respect of scheduled international air services, granted by one state to another state, to put down, in the territory of the first state, traffic coming from the home state of the carrier (3rd Freedom Right);
- the right or privilege in respect of scheduled international air services, granted by one state to another state, to take on, in the territory of the first state, traffic destined for the home state of the carrier (4th Freedom Right);

---

[1] This entry is a revised and updated version of 'International Civil Aviation Organization (ICAO)' by Alexander von Ziegler, published in Jürgen Basedow and others (eds), *The Max Planck Encyclopedia of European Private Law*, vol 1 (OUP 2012) 962 *et seq*.

- the right or privilege in respect of scheduled international air services, granted by one state to another state, to put down and to take on, in the territory of the first state, traffic coming from or destined to a third state (5th Freedom Right);
- the right or privilege in respect of scheduled international air services, of transporting, via the home state of the carrier, traffic moving between two other states (6th Freedom Right).
- the right or privilege in respect of scheduled international air services, granted by one state to another state, of transporting traffic between the territory of the granting state and any third state with no requirement to include on such operation any point in the territory of the recipient state (7th Freedom Right);
- the right or privilege in respect of scheduled international air services of transporting cabotage traffic between two points in the territory of the granting state on a service which originates or terminates in the home country of the foreign carrier or outside the territory of the granting state (8th Freedom Right);
- the right or privilege of transporting cabotage traffic of the granting state on a service performed entirely within the territory of the granting state (9th Freedom Right).

Only the first five freedom rights have been officially recognized as such by international treaty. For this reason, ICAO characterizes the 6th to 9th Freedom Rights as 'so-called' freedom rights.

III. Tasks and targets

The main aim of ICAO is the promotion of international air traffic. Furthermore, uniform and universal regulation aims to ensure a safe and orderly development of civil aviation and to provide a uniform basis for operating international air services. According to art 44 of the Chicago Convention, ICAO develops principles and technical methods for the economical and safe development of international air traffic. More specifically, this encompasses ensuring the safe and orderly growth of international civil aviation throughout the world, promoting the construction and operation of aircraft for peaceful purposes, encouraging the development of airways, airports and air navigation facilities and preventing economic waste caused by unreasonable competition. In addition, the rights of the contracting states and their ability to operate international airlines are to be fully respected, any discrimination between the contracting states is to be avoided, and the safety of flights is to be promoted. These targets are mainly realized by directives and recommendations. There is a wide uniformity in certain domains because of the adoption of the 19 annexes in numerous jurisdictions: personal licensing, rules of the air, meteorological service, aeronautical charts, units of measurement to be used in air and ground operations, operation of aircraft, aircraft → nationality and registration marks, airworthiness of aircraft, facilitation, aeronautical telecommunications, air traffic services, search and rescue, aircraft accident and incident investigation, aerodromes, aeronautical information services, environmental protection, security, the safe transport of dangerous goods and safety management. These annexes are supplemented by numerous ICAO technical publications that foster further standardization and contribute to the integration of worldwide flight supervision, communication and search and rescue services. In other respects, ICAO grants international development aid by delegating experts to developing countries and by providing financial resources for training purposes and training institutions in many countries.

IV. Structure

ICAO comprises three main bodies: the Council, the General Assembly and the General Secretariat.

The Council, as the permanent executive body, is elected by the General Assembly for a period of three years and consists of representatives of 36 contracting states. These are first, the states of chief importance in air traffic, second, the states which make the largest contributions to the ICAO budget and third, the states which represent the major geographic areas of the world. The head of the Council is the Council President. The Council is the body with the broadest job description and in practice it plays the most important role. It carries out not only the instructions of the Assembly and attends to various administrative and management tasks within the organization and financing of ICAO, but it is also responsible for the adoption of international standards and recommended practices, which it can designate as annexes to the Convention. These annexes require the vote of two-thirds of the Council. Otherwise, decisions of the Council are made by a majority vote of its members without the possibility of veto. The Council is assisted in its work by four expert committees: the Air

Navigation Commission (on technical issues and safety regulations), the Air Transport Committee (on economic questions such as economic planning, forecasting and collecting statistics), the Committee on Joint Support of Air Navigation Services (on the construction, maintenance and improvement of internationally used air navigation service appliances in areas without sovereignty over the airspace and on the financing of air navigation services facilities in states which lack sufficient financial resources), as well as the Finance Committee (on the management, control and monitoring of the budget). Furthermore, additional committees may be formed, partly on a continuing basis, but at times as mere *ad hoc* committees.

ICAO has seven regional offices, which are responsible for nine separate air navigation regions (Bangkok for Asia and the Pacific, Cairo for the Middle East, Dakar for West and Central Africa, Lima for South America, Mexico City for North and Central America and the Caribbean, Nairobi for East and South Africa, and Paris for Europe and the North Atlantic). At the regular air navigation meetings, the particular problems of these air navigation regions are discussed and allocated to the respective Air Navigation Commission, which will then prepare recommendations for the specific region.

Furthermore, the Council performs arbitral functions in the → mediation of differences of opinion regarding the interpretation and application of the Chicago Convention and its annexes. The procedural rules are based on those of the ICJ (International Court of Justice). If the Council sees the possibility of negotiating a dispute bilaterally or multilaterally during an ongoing dispute settlement proceeding, it can encourage the parties to do so. The Council may call in individuals or groups to assist the mediation, provided the involved parties consent. If these efforts fail to result in resolution, the suspended dispute settlement proceedings may be continued. The members of the Council decide on the case at issue by a majority vote, although members of the Council are prohibited from voting in the consideration of any dispute to which they are party (art 84 Chicago Convention). The decision can be appealed to the ICJ. An arbitral tribunal may only review the decision if one of the parties is not a member of the ICJ Statute (Statute of the International Court of Justice of 26 June 1945, 15 UNTS 355). Failing agreement on the choice of the arbitral tribunal and failing to name arbitrators, arbitrators will be appointed by the Council President (art 85 Chicago Convention). The decisions made by the ICJ or an arbitral tribunal are binding on the parties. It is noteworthy that members of the Council are not to be regarded as independent judges, but rather as representatives elected by their states and who make their decisions from a political perspective.

The sovereign body of ICAO is the General Assembly, which is composed of representatives from all contracting states. The Assembly, in which every state is entitled to one vote, meets every three years. It is responsible on the one hand for determining the tasks of the other bodies, and on the other hand for supervising their operations concerning law, economics and technology. Furthermore, the Assembly determines the dues of the contracting states and outlines the budget of the organization.

The third ICAO body is the Secretariat, which is located at the seat of the organization in Montreal. It is headed by the Secretary General, who is elected for a three-year period of office. The Secretary General assumes the role of the CEO of the organization, and manages the Secretariat as well as the seven regional offices. The tasks carried out in these offices are summarized and coordinated by the Secretariat. In addition, the Secretary General is responsible for the management and appointment of personnel. The Secretariat is divided into five main divisions: the Air Navigation Bureau, the Air Transport Bureau, the Technical Cooperation Bureau, the Legal Affairs and External Relations Bureau and the Bureau of Administration and Services. Instructions by the Council are binding on the Secretariat.

V. Financing

ICAO is primarily financed by dues of the contracting states. The amount of these dues is based on the financial capability of the particular state. Seventy-five per cent of the dues are in accordance with the UN scale, by which the amount of dues payable is reduced proportional to decreasing per-capita income. The remaining 25 per cent is determined according to the specific share of the respective contracting state in global air traffic. The Assembly determines the budget and the proportional dues of each state for a three-year period.

VI. Implementation of ICAO instruments into national law

ICAO cannot directly set binding laws for its contracting states. Accordingly, the states have to convert the elaborated guidelines and recommendations, which appear in the form of annexes to the Chicago Convention, into their respective national law in order for them to take effect. After adoption of an annex by the Council by a two-thirds majority vote, according to art 90 Chicago Convention, the Council submits the annex to each contracting state. The states are given a three-month period to voice any objections, a period which can be extended by the Council. Thereafter, the annex will become effective, unless a majority of contracting states express their opposition, in which case the annex in question does not take effect. However, even if there is no opposition by a majority of contracting states, there is no automatic obligation upon the contracting states to implement the annex into their national laws. Rather, according to art 38 Chicago Convention, the states can report differences between the national rules and the ICAO rules, and are not obliged to implement the new rules into national law even where the annex is accepted. Rather, adoption is a matter for the state to decide. This so-called contracting out exists for all annexes with the exception of annex 2, which governs the so-called rules of the air.

VII. Future developments

In the time since its foundation, ICAO has provided proof of its competence, particularly concerning the unification of national rules for air traffic. The 19 annexes to the Chicago Convention are a particularly substantial contribution to the increase of flight safety. Today's civil aviation law is inconceivable without ICAO. Particularly worth mentioning is the Convention for the Unification of Certain Rules for International Carriage by Air (the Montreal Convention, [2001] OJ L 194/38), concluded at the initiative of ICAO in Montreal on 28 May 1999, which harmonizes and modernizes numerous rules on air carriage liability (→ Air law (uniform law)). Similarly, ICAO has been able to meet the needs arising from technical advances and their resulting judicial requirements. Because of the technical nature of the rules, ICAO has remained broadly unaffected by global political conflicts. The scope of ICAO has expanded over the course of time while current developments, such as the use of satellites for communication and navigation, present new challenges to the organization.

ALEXANDER VON ZIEGLER AND
JUDITH BAUMANN

Literature

Isabella Henrietta Philepina Diederiks-Verschoor, Pablo Mendes de Leon and Michael Butler, *An Introduction to Air Law* (9th edn, Kluwer Law International 2012); Stephan Hobe and Otto Kimminich, *Einführung in das Völkerrecht* (9th edn, UTB 2004); Jiefang Huang, *Aviation Safety through the Rule of Law, ICAO's Mechanisms and Practices* (Wolters Kluwer 2009); Knut Ipsen, *Völkerrecht* (6th edn, CH Beck 2004); Heinrich Mensen, *Moderne Flugsicherung* (3rd edn, Springer 2004); Michael Milde, *International Air Law and ICAO* (2nd edn, Eleven 2012); Heiko F Schäffer, 'Von Kitty Hawk nach Montreal – Der Weg zur International Civil Aviation Organisation (ICAO)' (2003) 10 TranspR 377; Walter Schwenk and Elmar Giemulla, *Handbuch des Luftverkehrsrechts* (4th edn, Heymann 2013); Günther Unser, *Die UNO: Aufgaben, Strukturen, Politik* (7th edn, Beck Rechtsberater im dtv 2004); Ludwig Weber, *International Civil Aviation Organization* (Kluwer Law International 2007).

Immovable property

I. Lex rei sitae

1. Principle

Real rights in immovable property (→ Property and proprietary rights) are governed by the *lex rei sitae*, ie the law of the state where the immovable is situated. This rule is recognized in all EU Member States and beyond. In some jurisdictions, rights in immovables are specifically subjected to the *lex situs*, see art 3(2) French Civil Code (Code Civil of 21 March 1804), art 10(1) Spanish Civil Code (Código Civil of 24 July 1998, Geceta de Madrid No 206, 25 July 1889), art 81 Bulgarian Private international law Code (Law No 42 of 17 May 2005, as amended), rule 132 in Great Britain (Lord Collins of Mapesbury and others (eds), *Dicey, Morris and Collins on the Conflict of Laws*, vol 2 (15th edn, Sweet & Maxwell 2012) henceforth *Dicey, Morris and Collins on the Conflict of Laws*), art 99(1) Swiss Private international law Act (*Bundesgesetz über das Internationale Privatrecht* of 18 December 1987, 1988 BBl I 5, as amended). In other jurisdictions, there is only a single rule relating to immovables and movables alike, see art 87 § 1 Belgian Private international law Act (*Wet Houdende het Wetboek von international privaatrecht/Code de droit international privé* of 16 July 204, BS 27 July 2004, p 57344, 57366), art 43 German Introductory Act to the German Civil Code (*Einführungsgesetz zum Bürgerlichen Gesetzbuch* of 21 September 1994, BGBl. I 2494, as amended, henceforth EGBGB), art 10:127 para 1 Dutch Civil Code (*Nieuw Burgerlijk Wetboek* of 1 January 1992), art 51 Italian Private international law Act (*Riforma del Sistema italiano di diritto internazionale private*, Act No 218 of 31 May 1995, henceforth Italian PILA), art 1.48 Lithuanian Civil Code (*Lietuvos Respublikos civilinis kodeksas*, of 6 September 2000), art 69(1) Czech Private international law Act (Act No 91/2012 Sb, on private international law), art 41 Polish Private international law Act (Official Journal 2011 No 80, pos 432, henceforth Polish PILA), art 2613 Romanian Civil Code (Law 287/2009, published in the Official Gazette No 511 of 24 July 2009, and subsequently amended and supplemented by Law 71/2011, published in the Official Gazette No 409 of 10 June 2011). Because of this unanimity, a theoretically possible *renvoi* is excluded in practice. Presumably for the same reason, there is until now no European regulation with respect to the law applicable to proprietary rights in immovables (→ Property and proprietary rights). Only Recital (18) of the preamble to the EU Succession Regulation (Regulation (EU) No 650/2012 of the European Parliament and of the Council of 4 July 2012 on jurisdiction, applicable law, recognition and enforcement of decisions and acceptance and enforcement of authentic instruments in matters of succession and on the creation of a European Certificate of Succession, [2012] OJ L 201/107; → Rome IV Regulation (succession)) mentions the *lex rei sitae* principle as a matter of course. However, if the EU should envisage a private international law regulation on proprietary rights in general (as to the necessity with respect to movables see Ulrich Drobnig, 'A Plea for European Conflict Rules on Proprietary Security' in Michael Joachim Bonell, Marie-Louise Holle and Peter Arnt Nielsen (eds), *Liber Amicorum Ole Lando* (DJØF Publishing 2012) 85 *et seq*) or a European private international law codification, then in the interests of comprehensiveness and practicability it should also include a rule on immovables.

2. *No freedom of choice of law*

The law applicable to proprietary rights in immovables is not open to a → choice of law by the parties (Heinz-Peter Mansel in Julius von Staudinger (ed), Internationales Sachenrecht (Neubearbeitung 2015, CH Beck) para 20). In contrast to many other areas of private international law, where the realm of → party autonomy has gradually been expanded, and notwithstanding academic proposals in favour of an introduction of party autonomy with respect to movables (see Louis d'Avout, *Sur les solutions du conflit de lois en droit des biens* (Economica 2006) 612 *et seq*; Jeroen van der Weide, *Mobiliteit van goederen in het IPR* (Kluwer 2006); Axel Flessner, 'Rechtswahl im internationalen Sachenrecht – neue Anstöße aus Europa' in Peter Apathy and Raimund Bollenberger (eds), *Festschrift für Helmut Koziol* (Jan Sramek 2010) 125 *et seq*, see also 10:128 (2) and (3) and art 10:133 (1) Dutch Civil Code, which under special circumstances allows a limited choice of law for movables), there is no move for a more liberal attitude with respect to immovables.

3. *Foundation of the* lex situs

Applicability of the *lex situs* is founded on practicability, the stability of the connecting factor, the necessity of registration of real rights in the state where the immovable is situated, and is in harmony with the expectations of the parties. It is also in line with the exclusive jurisdiction of the courts in the Member State where the property is situated for disputes relating to proprietary rights in immovables, see art 24 no 1 Brussels I Regulation (recast) (Regulation (EU) No 1215/2012 of the European Parliament and of the Council of 12 December 2012 on jurisdiction and the recognition and enforcement of judgments in civil and commercial matters (recast), [2012] OJ L 351/1) (→ Brussels I (Convention and Regulation)), see also VI.) and with the private international law rules relating to the underlying contractual relations such as eg a contract for the sale of an immovable, see art 4(1)(c) Rome I Regulation (Regulation (EC) No 593/2008 of the European Parliament and of the Council of 17 June 2008 on the law applicable to contractual obligations, [2008] OJ L 177/6; → Rome Convention and Rome I Regulation (contractual obligations)), and its formal requirements, see art 11 (5) Rome I Regulation. According to the latter provision, the parties, who may choose the applicable law for the obligatory contract, are nevertheless bound by formal requirements such as a notarial deed if those requirements are mandatory according to the *lex situs*, irrespective of an agreement by the parties to the contrary and irrespective of the chosen law.

4. The lex situs and the different systems of transfer of ownership

The fact that for movables in particular a number of European jurisdictions follow the so-called consent principle, where ownership passes through the conclusion of the underlying contract (see Franco Ferrari, 'Transfer of Title – Movable Goods' in Jürgen Basedow and others (eds), *The Max Planck Encyclopedia of European Private Law*, vol 2 (2012) 1678 *et seq*), a sales contract, for example, does not lead to an amalgamation of the contractual and the proprietary aspects of the transaction for matters of conflict of laws (see for English law James Fawcett, Janeen Carruthers and Peter North, *Cheshire, North & Fawcett – Private international law* (14th edn, OUP 2008) 1204 *et seq*). Even the Italian PILA, which in art 51(2) seems to provide that the law applicable to the contract should also govern its proprietary effects, is not interpreted as giving way to choice of law for the proprietary effects of the transaction (see Valentina Maglio and Karsten Thorn, 'Neues Internationales Privatrecht in Italien' (1997) 96 ZVglRWiss 347, 369 *et seq*). In systems where the effectiveness of the proprietary transfer rests upon the existence of a valid obligation to transfer (see Franco Ferrari, 'Transfer of Title: Movable Goods' in Jürgen Basedow and others (eds), *The Max Planck Encyclopedia of European Private Law*, vol 2 (2012) 1678), the validity of the contract is an incidental question and therefore subject to the law designated by the private international law of the forum, in EU Member States by the Rome I Regulation.

II. Scope of application

1. General

The applicable *lex rei sitae* determines all questions of property law, such as acquisition and loss of rights *in rem* including their causal or abstract character (see expressly art 10:127 (4) Dutch Civil Code), formalities of the conveyance (see James Fawcett, Janeen Carruthers and Peter North, *Cheshire, North & Fawcett – Private international law* (14th edn, OUP 2008) 1203) and the necessity of registration (explicitly mentioned eg in art 55 Italian PILA), possession of the immovable (expressly mentioned in art 31(1) Austrian PILA (Bundesgesetz über das international Privatrecht of 15 June 1978, BGBl. No 304/1978), art 51(1) Italian PILA, art 18 Latvian Civil Code (*Civillikums, Valdības Vēstnesis* of 1937), art 45 Polish PILA, art 2.613 Romanian Civil Code), the possible content of proprietary rights, the right to vindicate including accessory rights such as the right to → damages under §§ 989, 990 German Civil Code (*Bürgerliches Gesetzbuch* of 2 January 2002, BGBl. I 42, as amended; see German Federal Court of Justice (BGH), 25 September 1997 [1998] NJW 1321) as well as rules of substantive law connected to the registration of the immovable such as, for example, the presumption of ownership resulting from registration as owner in the land registry (see eg § 891 German Civil Code).

2. Capacity

Limitations as to the capacity (→ Capacity and emancipation) to acquire land, eg restrictions for foreigners to buy domestic immovables, are to the extent they may still exist also governed by the *lex situs*, with a *renvoi* remaining possible (see *Dicey, Morris and Collins on the Conflict of Laws*, para 23–068).

With respect to the general capacity to conclude proprietary transactions, the EU approach varies between Member States. According to German and French private international law, this question falls under the general rules on capacity, so that the law of the person's → nationality will be applicable (see for → Germany: Heinz-Peter Mansel in Julius von Staudinger (ed), Internationales Sachenrecht (Neubearbeitung 2015, CH Beck) para 1075, for → France: Vincent Bonnet 'Biens', *Juris Classeur Droit International* 6, fascicule 550 (2016) para 84). Contrastingly, English private international law (and that of other common law jurisdictions) submits capacity to deal in land to the *lex situs* but allows for a *renvoi* where foreign law is involved, so that there seems to be no practical difference if the land is situated abroad. However, if the land is situated in England, English courts will apply their own law to questions of capacity (eg age of maturity) even if the party in question is of foreign nationality (*Dicey, Morris and Collins on the Conflict of Laws*, para 23–063 *et seq*; James Fawcett, Janeen Carruthers and Peter North, *Cheshire, North & Fawcett – Private international law* (14th edn, OUP 2008) 1202 *et seq*).

III. Characterization

Whether a piece of property is movable or immovable is also for the *lex situs* of the property in question to decide (for a comparative treatise on the notion of *Grundstücke* see Christian von Bar, 'Wozu braucht man und was sind Grundstücke?' in Peter Mankowski and Wolfgang Wurmnest (ed) *Festschrift für Ulrich Magnus* (Sellier 2014) 585). The question whether something is movable or immovable is particularly relevant in the case of buildings or other equipment which are fixed to the immovable, albeit perhaps only temporarily as with so-called fixtures, or commercially related to it. In some European jurisdictions, the rule that the *lex situs* decides the character of the object in question is expressly spelled out, see for example art 1.48 Lithuanian Civil Code and art 10:127 (4(a) and (b)) Dutch Civil Code. In other jurisdictions the same result is reached by interpreting the general *lex situs* rule (see Christiane Wendehorst, 'art 43 EGBGB' in Franz Jürgen Säcker (ed), *Münchener Kommentar BGB* (6th edn, CH Beck 2015) para 78; Gerhard Kegel and Klaus Schurig, *Internationales Privatrecht* (9th edn, CH Beck 2004) § 19 II; *Dicey, Morris and Collins on the Conflict of Laws*, rule 128, para 22R-001; Yvon Loussouarn and Pierre Bourel, *Droit international privé* (10th edn, Dalloz 2013) para. 660; cf also Steffen Kirchner, *Grundpfandrechte in Europa* (Duncker & Humblot 2004) 37 *et seq*). In some cases proprietary and contractual relationships may be closely intertwined (see in general Steven E Bartels and John Michael Milo (eds), *The Contents of Real Rights* (Wolf Legal Publishers 2004), for example where timeshare contracts provide for co-ownership but subject the contractual relation between the co-owners to a law which differs from the *lex situs*. In one instance, the German Federal Court of Justice (BGH) has held that the question whether the legal relationship between the co-owners is open for a choice of law is to be decided by the private international law of the *lex rei sitae* (German Federal Court of Justice (BGH), 25 September 1997 [1998] NJW 1321).

IV. *Conflit mobile*

In international property law (→ Property and proprietary rights), difficulties may arise if property in which a real right has been created under the law of state A is subsequently moved to state B, so-called *conflit mobile* or *Statutenwechsel*. Generally, the applicable *lex situs* is determined by the place where the property is situated at the time at which the relevant act (acquisition or loss of ownership or of a limited real right, seizure etc) occurs. For immovables, the question of the material time is largely irrelevant since the *lex situs* is a stable connecting factor. A change of the applicable law can only occur if the legal regime changes because the state disappears and/or a new political and legal system is implemented. This has recently happened on several occasions in Middle and Eastern Europe and in the former German Democratic Republic. This is, however, a topic relating to inter-temporal private law and not to be dealt with here.

V. Relationship with succession and matrimonial property law

Proprietary rights in immovables (→ Property and proprietary rights) can change not only through voluntary transfer but also by operation of law, primarily through succession and marriage and/or divorce. Under the traditional English and French private international law approach, conflicts between the law governing succession and the *lex situs* cannot arise with respect to immovables because, following the 'principle of scission', these jurisdictions distinguish between movables and immovables and subject rights in immovables to the *lex rei sitae* (Dieter Martiny, 'Lex rei sitae as a Connecting Factor in EU Private international law' [2012] IPRax 119, 125 *et seq*). However, other Member States (eg Germany) used to have a unitary rule (art 25 EGBGB) subjecting both movables and immovables to the nationality of the deceased. The unitary approach is now also followed by the EU Succession Regulation and by the EU on matrimonial property (Council Regulation (EU) 2016/1103 of 24 June 2016) (see below V.2.). Accordingly, the question arises whether and to what extent the proprietary effects of succession, marriage or divorce on immovables should nevertheless be governed by the *lex situs*, or whether they should rather be covered by the private international law rules relating to succession or → matrimonial property. Generally, the statutory provisions on international property law do not expressly deal with this conflict. An exception is art 51(2) Italian PILA, which excludes transfers by way of succession or family relationships from the scope of application of the *situs* rule.

1. Succession

Under autonomous German private international law, the BGH used to distinguish between (i) the entitlement as such (who will acquire title?), which is for the law of succession to decide, and (ii) the mode of implementation, which is subject to the *lex situs*. Thus in the case of a *Vindikationslegat* creating an immediate and direct right *in rem* in favour of the legatee upon the death of the testator, the BGH has held that if the immovable is situated in Germany, the right of the legatee will not be acquired *per se*, because German law as the *lex situs* gives the legatee only an obligatory right against the estate (German Federal Court of Justice (BGH), 28 September 1994 [1995] NJW 58; Jan Peter Schmidt, Die kollisionsrechtliche Behandlung dinglich wirkender Vermächtnisse, RabelsZ 77 (2013) 1). Consequently, the parties will have to observe the necessary steps for a transfer of ownership (or other real right) in the land under German law.

Since the EU Succession Regulation has become applicable (17 August 2015) the extent to which the *lex situs* can still be applied to immovables has to be determined by autonomous interpretation (→ Interpretation, autonomous) of the Regulation. Article 1(2)(k) and (l) exempts from its scope 'the nature of rights *in rem*', and 'any recording in a register of rights in immovable or movable property, including the legal requirements for such recording, and the effects of recording or failing to record such rights in a register'. The first exemption is understood as relating to the *numerus clausus* principle (Kurt Lechner, 'Die EuErbVO im Spannungsfeld zwischen Erbstatut und Sachstatut' [2013] IPRax 497; *Kurt Lechner* was the rapporteur for the European Parliament in the negotiations of the Regulation). Thus, it will still be for the *lex situs* of each Member State to decide which kinds of proprietary rights its jurisdiction is prepared to accept in immovables being part of its territory. The second exemption relates not only to procedural questions but includes the substantive effects which the registration (or failure to register) has upon the proprietary right. This is emphasized by Recital (19) which holds that the declaratory or constitutive nature of registration for the acquisition of a real right is to be decided by the *lex situs*. Article 23(2)(e), which states that the law governing the succession extends in particular to 'the transfer to the heirs and, as the case may be, to the legatees of the assets, rights and obligations forming part of the estate', and which might be interpreted as leaving no room for the *lex situs* regarding the modes of transfer of real rights from the deceased to the heirs or legatees, is subordinated to art 1(2)(l), while art 23 cannot apply to matters standing outside the regulation. As a result, the *lex situs* will continue to decide through which mechanism, including registration, a proprietary right is transferred to an heir or legatee (see Kurt Lechner, 'Die EuErbVO im Spannungsfeld zwischen Erbstatut und Sachstatut' [2013] IPRax 497; Christoph Döbereiner, 'Vindikationslegate unter Geltung der EU-Erbrechtsverordnung' [2014] GPR 42; for a slightly different solution see Patrick Wautelet, 'art 23' in Andrea Bonomi and others (eds), *Le droit européen des successions, Commentaire du Réglement n° 650/ 2012 du 4 juillet 2012* (Bruylant 2013) para 51). According to this opinion, only registration as a means of rendering the proprietary right 'opposable' as against third parties continues to be governed by the *lex rei sitae*, whereas other aspects of the transfer are to be submitted to the *lex successionis*. In a case where the proprietary right conferred to a person by the law applicable to the succession is unknown under the *lex situs*, art 31 obliges Member States to adapt 'that right to the closest equivalent right in rem [under the *lex situs*], taking into account the aims and the interests pursued by the specific right in rem'. Accordingly, and despite art 1(2)(k), a Member State cannot deny the effectiveness of an acquisition by way of succession for the simple reason that the specific type of real right is unknown at the *situs*. For example, the usufruct of the estate as a whole under French succession law, which is unknown in Germany (see § 1085 German Civil Code), is to be interpreted as resting upon each individual piece of property forming part of the estate (Paul Lagarde, 'Les principes de base du nouveau règlement européen sur les successions' (2012) 110 Rev.crit.DIP 691, 715 *et seq*).

2. Matrimonial property

In its Regulation implementing enhanced cooperation in the area of jurisdiction, applicable law and the recognition and enforcement of decisions in matters of à matrimonial property regimes (Regulation (EU) 2016/1103), the EU Commission also follows a unitary approach. This is emphasized by art 21, which states that the law applicable to a matrimonial property regime under arts 22 or 26 shall apply to the couple's entire property. There is no possibility for the spouses to limit the effects of a choice of law to the immovable situated in the state of the chosen law. With respect to the delimitation regarding the *lex situs* the EU adopts the same solution as in the Succession Regulation, see Recitals (24), (27) and (28). Consequently, art 1(2)(g), (h) of the Regulation exclude from its scope of application 'the nature of rights *in rem* relating to a property' as well as the registration of property rights and its effects. The same problems as with the Succession Regulation may hence arise, with questions of registration and third party protection as the main concerns (see Dieter Martiny, 'Lex rei sitae as a Connecting Factor in EU Private international law' [2012] IPRax 119, 130; Caroline Rupp, 'Die Verordnung zum europäischen internationalen Ehegüterrecht aus sachenrechtlicher Perspektive' [2016] GPR 295).

VI. Jurisdiction

For 'proceedings which have as their object rights *in rem* in immovable property or tenancies of immovable property', art 24 no 1 Brussels I Regulation (recast) gives exclusive jurisdiction to the courts in the Member State where the immovable is located. Applicability of this rule does not depend on the defendant being domiciled in a Member State but rests solely on the *situs* of the immovable in one of the Member States. In conformity with ECJ jurisprudence on art 24 Brussels I Regulation in general, the Court has interpreted no 1 narrowly. Exclusive jurisdiction by no means extends to all kinds of claim associated with proprietary rights in immovables such as, for example, the claim of a buyer of a piece of land against the seller for specific performance or termination of the contract of sale or for damages under such a contract. Instead, exclusive jurisdiction requires that the claim itself rests on a right *in rem* such as ownership or a limited real right (eg a mortgage), or, in the ECJ's own words, art 24 no 1 Brussels I Regulation covers only 'actions which seek to determine the extent, content, ownership or possession of immovable property or the existence of other rights in rem therein and to provide the holders of those rights with protection for the powers which attach to their interest' (ECJ judgment of 3 April 2014, Case C-438/12 *Irmengard Weber v Mechthilde Weber* [2014] OJ C 159/6, para 42, with further references). Thus, in *Weber*, the Court affirmed that German courts had exclusive jurisdiction for the determination of party rights under a real right of pre-emption (pursuant to §§ 1094 *et seq* German Civil Code) over an immovable situated in Munich. By way of contrast, in a judgment of 5 April 2001 (Case C-518/99 *Richard Gaillard v Alaya Chekili* [2001] ECR I-2771), the Luxembourg court held that a claim for rescission of a contract of sale of an immovable and consequential damages did not fall under art 24 no 1, because the seller's rights were based on the contractual relationship between the parties, as opposed to rights *in rem* relating to the land. Since art 24 no 1 Brussels I Regulation is to be interpreted autonomously, it was irrelevant whether rescission of the contract had automatic effects on the proprietary rights of the parties under the applicable substantive law. The same result has been reached by the German BGH concerning a claim for extinction of an usufruct in a piece of land, where the claim rested on a breach of contract (see German Federal Court of Justice (BGH), 4 August 2004 [2007] IPRax 210; note Matthias Lehmann and Sánchez Lorenzo [2007] IPRax 190). But even in a case where the claim was based on ownership of the land, the ECJ declined exclusive jurisdiction according to art 24 no 1 Brussels I Regulation because in that instance, the predominant purpose was to stop a nuisance emanating from a nuclear power station located in a neighbouring state (see judgment of 18 May 2006, Case C-343/04 *Land Oberösterreich v ČEZ* [2006] ECR I-4557). The court rightly held that the main subject of such proceedings was not the right in the land possibly affected by ionizing radiation, but the question whether the way in which the nuclear power station was run complied with national and international safety standards. This issue was better to be decided by the courts in the state in which the power station was located than by the courts in a neighbouring state.

Following a general ECJ tendency in interpreting art 24 Brussels I Regulation (see ECJ judgment of 12 May 2011, Case C-144/10 *Berliner Verkehrsbetriebe (BVG) v JPMorgan Chase Bank NA* [2011] OJ C 194/6) the German BGH has held that proceedings in which the issue of ownership of or other real right in the land is only incidental to eg a claim for damages are also exempted from exclusive jurisdiction under art 24 no 1 (see German Federal Court of Justice (BGH), 18 July 2008 [2008] NJW 3502).

With regard to 'tenancies', the ECJ has continued its strict and narrow interpretation.

Claims based on the termination of a timeshare contract which took the form of a club membership were held to fall outside the ambit of art 24 no 1 Brussels I Regulation since such membership not only gave rise to the right to use a fixed apartment in a specific holiday complex, but also included various services and gave members the possibility to exchange their 'holiday rights' with other members of the club (see ECJ judgment of 13 October 2005, Case C-73/04 *Markus Klein v Rhodos Management Ltd* [2005] ECR I-8667). Finally subsection 2 of art 24 no 1 Brussels I Regulation opens the possibility for parties to bring a suit at their common domicile if the proceedings 'have as their object tenancies of immovable property concluded for temporary private use for a maximum period of six consecutive months, . . . provided that the tenant is a natural person and that the landlord and the tenant are domiciled in the same Member State'.

EVA-MARIA KIENINGER

Literature

Louis d'Avout, *Sur les solutions du conflit de lois en droit des biens* (Economica 2006); Steven E Bartels and John Michael Milo (eds), *The Contents of Real Rights* (Wolf Legal Publishers 2004); Vincent Bonnet, 'Biens', *Juris Classeur Droit International* 6, fascicule 550 (2016); Andrea Bonomi and others (eds), *Le droit européen des successions, Commentaire du Réglement n° 650/2012 du 4 juillet 2012* (Bruylant 2013); Christoph Döbereiner, 'Vindikationslegate unter Geltung der EU-Erbrechtsverordnung' [2014] GPR 42; Ulrich Drobnig, 'A Plea for European Conflict Rules on Proprietary Security' in Michael Joachim Bonell, Marie-Louise Holle and Peter Arnt Nielsen (eds), *Liber Amicorum Ole Lando* (DJØF Publishing 2012) 85; James Fawcett, Janeen Carruthers and Peter North, *Cheshire, North & Fawcett – Private international law* (14th edn, OUP 2008); Franco Ferrari, 'Transfer of Title: Movable Goods' in Jürgen Basedow and others (eds), *The Max Planck Encyclopedia of European Private Law*, vol 2 (2012) 1678; Axel Flessner, 'Rechtswahl im internationalen Sachenrecht – neue Anstöße aus Europa' in Peter Apathy and Raimund Bollenberger (eds), *Festschrift für Helmut Koziol* (Jan Sramek 2010) 125; Gerhard Kegel and Klaus Schurig, *Internationales Privatrecht* (9th edn, CH Beck 2004); Steffen Kirchner, *Grundpfandrechte in Europa* (Duncker & Humblot 2004); Paul Lagarde, 'Les principes de base du nouveau règlement européen sur les successions' (2012) 110 Rev.crit.DIP 691; Kurt Lechner, 'Die EuErbVO im Spannungsfeld zwischen Erbstatut und Sachstatut' [2013] IPRax 497; Yvon Loussouarn and Pierre Bourel, *Droit international privé* ((10th edn, Dalloz 2013) para. 660); Valentina Maglio and Karsten Thorn, 'Neues Internationales Privatrecht in Italien' (1997) 96 ZVglRWiss 347; Dieter Martiny, 'Lex rei sitae as a connecting factor in EU Private international law' [2012] IPRax 119; Lord Collins of Mapesbury and others (eds), *Dicey, Morris and Collins on the Conflict of Laws*, vol 2 (15th edn, Sweet & Maxwell 2012); Caroline Rupp, 'Die Verordnung zum europäischen internationalen Ehegüterrecht aus sachenrechtlicher Perspektive' [2016] GPR 295); Jan Peter Schmidt, Die kollisionsrechtliche Behandlung dinglich wirkender Vermächtnisse, RabelsZ 77 (2013); Heinz-Peter Mansel in Julius von Staudinger (ed), Internationales Sachenrecht (Neubearbeitung 2015, CH Beck); Jeroen van der Weide, *Mobiliteit van goederen in het IPR* (Kluwer 2006); Christian von Bar, 'Wozu braucht man und was sind Grundstücke?' in Peter Mankowski and Wolfgang Wurmnest (eds), *Festschrift für Ulrich Magnus* (Sellier 2014) 585; Christiane Wendehorst, 'art 43 EGBGB' in Franz Jürgen Säcker and others (eds), *Münchener Kommentar BGB* (6th edn, CH Beck 2015).

Immunity

I. State immunity from jurisdiction

According to international law, states (and all their organs) enjoy immunity both from jurisdiction and from execution. The principle of immunity is founded not on any technical rule of law, but rather on broad considerations of public policy, international law and → comity (House of Lords, *Rahimtoola v Nizam of Hyderabad* [1958] AC 379, 404). Judging another state, or seizing its property, was believed to be inappropriate and against the traditional principle of '*par in parem non habet iudicium*', a principle which describes the essence of the international community itself, where all states are equal. Any other solution would have resulted in a violation of another fundamental principle of international law, the principle of non-interference (GA A/RES/36/103, 91st plenary meeting, 9 December 1981).

With certain notable exceptions (Calcutta High Court, *Maharaja Bikram Kishore of Kishore v Province of Assam* (1949) 17 ITR 220 Cal), such a prerogative is accorded to those entities that qualify as 'states' according to theories of public international law, ie to entities that enjoy both internal and external juridical sovereignty.

On the other hand, international law has witnessed a significant evolution with regard to the material scope of application of the principles of state immunity. Initially, immunity was granted regardless of court proceedings being brought (Court of Appeal, *Le Parlement Belge* (1880) 5 P.D. 197, 214). Accordingly, contracts concluded by foreign states were not judicially enforceable in courts other than those of the breaching state (Court of Appeal, *Twycross v Dreyfus* (1877) 5 Law Reports, Chancery Division 605).

However, in view of the effects of recognition of foreign state immunity on cross-border contracts, and in light of the strong state intervention in international trade, a number of jurisdictions developed a new approach to the matter. Judges began to analyse how states generally exercised their competences and prerogatives, pointing out that, in practice, states either acted as political bodies utilizing their *imperium* or, as any other private entity by means of private contracts (Corte d'Appello Lucca, 1887, *Hamspohn v Bey di Tunisi*, [1887] Foro it. I, 474). States acting as a private individual were regarded as having submitted themselves to all the civil consequences of the contract, including its judicial enforcement (Tribunal Civil of Brussels, *Societe pour la fabrication de cartouches v Colonel Mutkuroff, Ministre de la guerre de la principaute de Bulgarie* (1888), in *Pandectes periodiques* 1889, 350). Thus, foreign state immunity was recognized and granted only when the conduct of the defendant constituted an expression of its *iure imperii* prerogatives. This had the consequence that, when no nexus of such conduct with the exercise of public powers of the foreign state was identified, the seized court had to declare its jurisdiction.

The theory of restricted state immunity found broad consensus, even though some states still continue to make reference to an absolute theory of state immunity, such as → China and Hong Kong (after the resumption of the Chinese sovereignty in 1997; see Hong Kong Court of Final Appeal 8 June 2011 and 8 September 2011, *Democratic Republic of the Congo and others v FG Hemisphere Associates LLC*, in (2011) 147 ILR 376, and (2011) 150 ILR 684, respectively). Nonetheless, many states nowadays espouse the idea that no immunity should be granted for private transactions. With specific reference to the European area, while some states traditionally followed the absolute theory, it must be noted that such conceptualization has to be evaluated in light of art 6 ECHR (Convention for the Protection of Human Rights and Fundamental Freedoms (ECHR) of 4 November 1950, 213 UNTS 221) as interpreted by the European Court of Human Rights (ECtHR). In proceedings before the ECtHR, where Russia purported to uphold the immunity of the Trade Counsellor of the Democratic People's Republic of Korea in connection with a loan from a Russian national, the Court held unanimously that there had been a violation of art 6 ECHR (*Oleynikov v Russia*, App no 36703/04 (ECtHR, 14 March 2013)).

The coexistence of conflicting theories of state immunity induced states and international organizations to draft instruments in an attempt to define more clearly the material scope of its application. Among these instruments, the European Convention on State Immunity (of 15 May 1972, Basel, CETS No 74, 1972), the UN Convention on Jurisdictional Immunities of States and their Property adopted by the General Assembly on 2 December 2004 (44 ILM 803, UN doc. A/RES/59/38, Annex) and the draft Inter-American Convention on Jurisdictional Immunity of States (22 ILM 292) drawn up by the Inter-American Juridical Committee of the Organization of American States (1983) can be recalled.

At the same time, even those states that still adhere to traditional theories of immunity do not recognize an immunity that is truly absolute. There are common exceptions to state immunity in proceedings related to (i) immovable property (→ Property and proprietary rights), (ii) interests of foreign states in property assets by way of succession or insolvency and (iii) infringement of copyrights, patent and trade marks registered in the state of the forum. Such exceptions are deeply connected with the location of the property and the regulatory authority to which these categories of property are subject.

On the other hand, it must also be noted that states that apply a restrictive theory differ in the methods they adopt to determine in which cases immunity is to be granted. In other terms, international law prescribes that immunity must be granted only for *acta iure imperii*, leaving it to states to decide whether to set statutory provisions setting out the immunity exceptions, or whether to allow national judges discretion to investigate the public or private nature of the foreign state conduct on a case-by-case basis.

Among those states that adopted statutory provisions setting out the immunity exceptions, the common law systems of the → USA, the → UK, → Canada, → New Zealand and → Australia may be mentioned. A principal aim of such legislation is to limit judicial

ILARIA QUEIROLO

interpretation. In these systems, judges are bound to apply statutory provisions that are quite clear and leave little room for judicial interpretation. According to such provisions, foreign states enjoy immunity except in cases where their activity is carried out by means of civil law (*acta iure privatorum*) rather than public law (*acta iure imperii*) (see the US 1976 Foreign Sovereign Immunity Act (15 ILM 1388), arts 1605 and ff).

Continental states follow a different approach, but still seem to have developed consistent case-law, generally arriving at the same results as common law systems, this despite national judges classifying sovereign acts according to national law (Federal Constitutional Court of Germany (BVerfG), *Empire of Iran case* (1963) 45 ILR 57). The reasoning followed by domestic courts is that if the action of the foreign state is carried out by private law means and the foreign state has no legitimate power to impose a decision on individuals, then said foreign state will not enjoy immunity (on the issue of treasure bonds, see for example the Austrian Oberster Gerichtshof, 20 May 2014, 4 Ob 227/13f, [2014] *The European Legal Forum*, 123).

Nevertheless, this case-by-case approach still raises the possibility of conflicting domestic and intra-state case-law (→ Interregional/Interstate law). From a domestic perspective, the default of the Republic of → Argentina offers an apt case study. Various Italian courts arrived at conflicting solutions on the issue of foreign state immunity from jurisdiction (in favour of immunity see *ex multis* Trib. Milano 11 March 2003, *Gallo v Rep. Argentina* [2004] Foro it. I, 293; against immunity, Trib. Roma 22 July 2002, *Mauri et al. v Rep. Argentina* [2003] Riv.Dir.Int'le Priv. & Proc. 174). This made it necessary for the *Corte di Cassazione* to settle the conflict, and while composing the internal case-law (Cass. Civ. GC., 27 May 2005, n 11225, *Borri v Repubblica Argentina* [2005] Riv.Dir.Int. 856), by following the pro-immunity interpretation recognizing that the state budget law of Argentina suspending payments was an *acta iure imperii*, the Court departed from the principles applied by other civil law courts that on a number of occasions had ruled in favour of the plaintiffs (see Regional Court (LG) of Frankfurt am Main, 14 March 2003, n 294/02, [2003] WM IV 783; Higher Regional Court (OLG) of Frankfurt, 13 June 2006 – 8 U 107/03, [2007] WM IV 929).

Another question that can be considered settled by case-law in both civil and common law countries is whether the distinction between *acta iure imperii* and *acta iure privatorum* should rest solely upon the nature of the state's conduct, or whether the distinction should be influenced by the general public interest pursued through the state's conduct. While some national decisions have tended to weigh public interests in granting immunity (see U.S. District Court, District of Columbia, *Turkmani v Republic of Bolivia*, 193 F. Supp. 2d 165 (D.D.C. 2002) and Cass. Civ. GC, 27 May 2005, n 11225, *Borri, cit*), the general idea is that the decision on immunity is determined solely by the public or private nature of the state's act, regardless of any public policy consideration driving that act (see *ex multis* U.S. Supreme Court, *Republic of Argentina v Weltover Inc*, 504 U.S. 607 and Cass. Civ. GC, 5 December 1966, n 2830, *Consorzio agrario della Tripolitana v Federazione italiana consorzi agrari e altri* [1967] Riv.Dir.Int'le Priv. & Proc. 602).

When the above-mentioned conditions are met, it is apparent that immunity competes not only with central organs of the state, such as the legislative, judiciary and administrative powers, but also with all bodies delegated to exercise sovereign functions. This is also confirmed in the 2004 UN Convention on Jurisdictional Immunities, by art 2.1(b)(iii). Thus, for example, classification societies acting as recognized organizations in the issuance of statutory certificates are to enjoy state immunity (see Trib. Genova 8 March 2012, *Abdel Naby Hussein Mabrouk Aly et al v RINA Spa* [2012] Il diritto marittimo 145, stating that recognized organizations enjoy functional immunity, though applying the criterion of state immunity).

Moreover, the gravity of the foreign state conduct is not an element which can jeopardize the recognition of immunity. In this regard, Italian Courts dealing with tort actions for damages suffered by individuals during the Second World War sought to argue that immunity cannot be granted for gross violation of fundamental rights (Cass. Civ. GC, 11 March 2004, n 5044, *Luigi Ferrini v Rep fed di Germania* [2004] Riv. Dir.Int. 540, para 9.2). However, the ICJ stated that customary law has not yet evolved in a way similar to the Italian Courts' interpretation of international law (ICJ, Jurisdictional Immunities of the State (*Germany v Italy*), Judgment 3 February 2012, para 83 ff). More recently, the Italian Constitutional Court (Corte Cost. 22 October 2014, n 238, in Gazzetta Ufficiale, 29

October 2014, 1) addressed the issue under a constitutional law point of view, arguing that the lack of an exception to the operability of the rules on state immunity in those circumstances where no alternative remedy is granted is against the Italian Constitution (Gazzetta Ufficiale No 298 on 27 December 1947).

The fact that immunity has to be upheld in favour of foreign states in proceedings concerning civil cases is also confirmed by ECtHR case-law. The Court recently confirmed its jurisprudence in cases of torture committed by foreign state officials (*Jones and others v United Kingdom*, App no 34356/06 & 40528/06 (ECtHR 14 January 2014)).

Such conclusions are to be read in light of the fact that the principles on state immunity are usually understood as procedural in nature, and unable completely to impair the substantial right to access a court, even in cases of an alleged violation of *jus cogens* principles.

However it is also true that this scenario could change in the future: art 12 of the 2004 UN Convention on Jurisdictional Immunities expressly states that, unless otherwise agreed between states concerned, no immunity can be invoked in a court of law in compensatory proceedings for death or personal injury. This provision will eventually be applicable, depending on the entry into force of the Convention, only between parties that ratify the Convention. On the other hand, of course, there is nothing to prevent this rule from becoming part of customary law, thereby binding all members of the international community.

Regardless of the entry into force of the Convention, art 11 must also be kept in mind, this already constituting customary law (see *Guadagnino v Italy and France* App no 2555/03 (ECtHR 18 January 2011) para 70). Accordingly, no immunity is to be granted in employment contracts if the performance was carried out in the forum state, unless (i) the activity is strictly connected with the exercise of public functions and authority, (ii) the court is asked to rule on the reintegration of the former employee and (iii) if the employee has the citizenship of the foreign state (but in the case said employee has his/her habitual residence in the forum state).

II. State immunity from execution

Apart from immunity from being summonsed in foreign state courts when exercising sovereign powers, states also have a right to immunity from execution, meaning that their assets and properties cannot be attached without their prior consent. While intrinsically linked to immunity from jurisdiction, immunity from execution has traditionally been considered an autonomous rule, with the consequence that the actual enforcement of a decision against a foreign state is not automatic and may on occasions prove difficult.

However, in determining the scope of application of immunity of foreign state's assets it must be noted that there are no uniform solutions at the international level. It is true that states developed the common idea that a restrictive approach should also be followed in this field, but state practice seems here more hesitant. When the theory of restricted immunity from jurisdiction was already developed and began to gain acceptance, a number of states continued to conceive immunity from execution as (an autonomous) absolute right of the foreign state (Cour d'Appel Paris 7 June 1969, *Clerget v Banque Commerciale pour l'Europe de Nord and Banque de Commerce Ectérieure du Vietnam* 52 ILR 310), while others, denying the existence of a clear customary rule, began to interpret such immunity narrowly, reflecting the conceptual evolution of immunity from jurisdiction (Corte Cost. 13 July 1963, n 135 [1963] I Foro it. 1597).

Even with broad acceptance of the restricted scope of application of immunity from execution, states still have different frameworks, making it at times possible to invoke such immunity even when no immunity from jurisdiction can be invoked. This happens in countries that deny execution on foreign state's assets if the assets are intended to carry out a public activity *latu sensu* (so without regard to the effective commercial use) whose attachment would compromise the exercise of the foreign state's powers (Cass. Civ. GC, 19 March 1992, n 3468, *Stati Uniti d'America v D'avola et al* [1993] Riv. Dir.Int'le Priv. & Proc. 392 and Corte Cost. 15 July 1992, n 329 [1993] Foro it. I, 2785). If the property is employed for commercial purposes though, it may be attached regardless of any connection with the enforced judgment.

On the other hand, a different approach may be followed: some countries grant execution on property only if it was used for the commercial activity upon which the claim is based (Foreign Sovereign Immunities Act (FSIA, 28 U.S.C. § 1610, litt. (a), n 2)) or on any commercial property if the judgment is based on an order confirming an arbitral award rendered against the foreign state (Foreign Sovereign Immunities Act (FSIA, 28 U.S.C. § 1610, litt. (a), n 6)).

Other countries, such as → Switzerland, not only require the presence on the territory of foreign state assets to be attached, but also require a nexus of the state with the case (eg Switzerland is the state where the legal relationship to be enforced has its origins or is at least the state of performance (Tribunal fédéral suisse 6 June 1956, *Royaume de Grèce v Banque Julius Bär & Cie* (18 ILR 195))), being some connecting factors (→ connecting factor), such as the seat of the arbitration tribunal, insufficient to establish the required connection (Tribunal fédéral Suisse 19 June 1980, *Lybie v LIAMCO* (62 ILR 228)).

Thus, the admissibility of attachment and identification of foreign state assets to be attached will broadly depend upon national provisions.

III. Functional immunity

International law also knows functional immunity, or immunity *ratione materiae*. Such immunity covers official acts of people-organs of the state, and its aim is to avoid that (i) the individual is held responsible for performing state's orders and that (ii) state immunity is 'circumvented' by the possibility of calling the individual into court (Court of Appeal, *Zoernsch v Waldock* [1964] 1 WLR 675 and Cass. Civ. GC., 11 March 2004, n 5044, Luigi Ferrini, *cit* and Court of Appeal, *Propend Finance Pty Ltd v Sing* [1997], 111 ILR 611).

In order for this immunity to be recognized, the expression of public powers must be investigated (a matter that was debated in House of Lords, *Regina v Bartle and the Commissioner of Police for the Metropolis and Others Ex Parte Pinochet* (38 ILM 581)): giving relevance to the aims driving the conduct of the agent could easily make it possible for any tribunal to prosecute the defendant on the ground that his/her public action was (only or also) driven by personal reasons (see Riccardo Luzzatto and Ilaria Queirolo, 'Sovranità territoriale, "Jurisdiction" e regole di immunità' in Sergio M Carbone, Riccardo Luzzatto and Alberto Santa Maria (eds), *Istituzioni di diritto internazionale* (4th edn, Giappichelli 2011) 256).

In addition, any individual performing orders can invoke such immunity regardless of his/her ranking position: any other solution would undermine state immunity (see Hazel Fox, 'Functions of State Officials and the Restrictive Rule of State Immunity' in Marcelo Kohen, Robert Kolb and Djacoba Tehindrazanarivelo (eds), *Perspectives of International Law in the 21st Century: Liber Amicorum Professor Christian Dominicé in Honour of his 80th Birthday* (Martinus Nijhoff 2011) 129 f). Furthermore, states have an obligation to notify the forum state regarding the agent's immunity (ICJ, Case concerning certain questions of mutual assistance in criminal matters, *Djibouti v France*, Judgment of 4 June 2008, [2008] I.C.J. Rep. 177, at para 196).

Again, the material scope of application of functional immunity is not without limits. First, it is undisputed that international treaties can provide for jurisdiction over individuals acting as agents of the state. Second, some also argue that in light of a customary rule developed by the case-law of the Nuremberg Military Tribunals, state officials cannot invoke functional immunity when committing the so-called 'core crimes' (Michaela Frulli, 'Immunities of Persons from Jurisdiction' in Antonio Cassese (ed), *The Oxford Companion to International Criminal Justice* (OUP 2009) 368; art 27 ICC Statute (2187 UNTS 90); though the ICJ stated that heads of states – according to customary law – enjoy temporal immunity even if they committed crimes against humanity: ICJ, Case Concerning the Arrest Warrant of 11 April 2000 (*Democratic Republic of Congo v Belgium*, Judgment of 14 February 2002, [2002] I.C.J. Rep. 3, para 61). Third, some also argue that no immunity can be invoked by the agent acting without authorization or without the prior consent of the host state (for the case of extraordinary renditions: Cass. Pen., 29 November 2012, n 46340 [2013] Riv.Dir.Int. 272 *et seq*; *contra* recognizing immunity in the *Lonzano* case, Cass. Pen., 24 July 2008, n 31171 [2008] Riv.Dir.Int.1223).

Ratione temporis, it is undisputed that functional immunity can be invoked at any time for an action or omission committed during the office.

Disputed are the origins and relationships of functional immunity to state immunity: some argue that the former is a corollary of the non-intervention principle and others that it is a corollary to the immunity of foreign states.

Moreover, with regard to the possibility of a waiver of immunity, only the foreign state can waive functional immunity because this privilege is not conceived as a personal right, but rather as a right of the state itself.

IV. The Act of State Doctrine

Next to state and functional immunity, common law countries can also rely on the Act of State Doctrine to avoid judging foreign state actions. According to this theory, states are sovereign within their border, with full control over their legislation; simply put, it is not for national judges to decide the validity of foreign laws and conducts that take place in the foreign state territory (U.S. Supreme Court, *Underhill v Hernandez*, 168 U.S. 250 (1897)).

Even if there are similarities between state immunity and the common law Act of State Doctrine, the differences are quite significant. In the first case the national court has no jurisdiction to hear the case, while in the second case the judge will adjudicate the case, still being unable to question the validity of the foreign state conduct (Mauro Megliani, *Debitori sovrani e obbligazionisti esteri* (Giuffrè 2009) 189). Again, the founding principle of the Doctrine is the respect of the foreign sovereignty, even though this conclusion finds no support in rules of international law, but rather in principles of separation of powers in national constitutions (U.S. Supreme Court, *Banco Nacional de Cuba v Sabbatino*, 376 U.S. 398 (1964)). Conceived this way, the Doctrine is not to be understood as a right of the foreign state, but rather as a policy of the judicial power. This means that no waiver of the foreign state is possible in this case, even though the Doctrine is not applied by domestic courts if the government, who is in the best position to assess diplomatic issues, has no objection to the adjudication of the case (so-called Bernstein Exception).

There is at least one more exception to the applicability of the Doctrine, ie the commercial activity exception, though, here, unlike in the field of state immunity, the affirmation of the exception struggled, given that the focus is not on the nature of the foreign state act, but rather on its aims (US courts affirmed that some commercial activities can have a significant sovereign component, thus being opportune for the courts not to interfere with foreign sovereignty in these cases; United States Court of Appeals, Ninth Circuit, 649 F.2d 1354 (1981)).

V. Personal immunity

Immunity *ratione personae* is also known under international law, under which certain individuals of the foreign state are entitled to immunity from civil, criminal and administrative jurisdiction for private acts. Thus, these individuals enjoy complete immunity from foreign jurisdiction since for official acts they can invoke functional immunity, while for private acts they can invoke personal immunity.

Nevertheless, only certain officials of the foreign state are entitled to such protection, while officials of non-state international actors are not accorded such immunity (Cass. Pen., 17 September 2004, n 49666 [2005] Riv.Dir.Int'le Priv. & Proc. 783). It is commonly understood that – other than diplomats (on which see below) – only heads of state, heads of government and ministers of foreign affairs enjoy such immunity from jurisdiction (ICJ, *Case Concerning the Arrest Warrant of 11 April 2000, cit*, para 51).

Personal immunity not only presents some restrictions under the personal scope of application, but also under both the temporal and the material scope of application of the rule. With regard to the temporal scope, it is settled that personal immunity can be invoked in a foreign court of law only during the term of office. As the object of immunity is to protect the head of state in the performance of his/her duty during the term of office, it follows that at the end of this term, foreign courts can adjudicate personal suits.

As to the waiver of immunity, being personal immunity a protection of the state and not of the individual, it is not for the latter to waive immunity.

With regard to the material scope of application, personal immunity knows no exception in criminal matters for acts committed during private and official visits (ICJ, *Case Concerning the Arrest Warrant of 11 April 2000, cit*, para 58, criticized, but now confirmed by the text of the ILC Draft arts 1, 3 and 4 provisionally adopted by the Drafting Committee at the sixty-fifth session of the International Law Commission, 2013). There is a debate on civil matters: some believe that no such immunity exists (U.S. Supreme Court, *The Schooner Exchange v M'Faddon*, 11 U.S. 116 (1812), 145); others think that such immunity is limited to private actions committed during official visits, while others still uphold the existence of a limited civil immunity *ratione personae* (on this topic see Rosanne van Alebeek, *The Immunity of States and their Officials in International Criminal Law and International Human Rights Law* (OUP 2008) 169). State practice seems to point towards this last solution, highlighting that there are (very few) exceptions to personal immunity with regard to (i) immovable property, (ii) succession proceedings, (iii) non-official commercial activities of the high-ranking officials and (iv) for foreign defendant counterclaims through which the jurisdiction of the state is accepted.

It must also be noted that high-ranking officials not only enjoy immunity under customary international law, but also enjoy personal inviolability, ie immunity from arrest, detention, searches and seizures.

VI. Diplomatic immunity: a self-contained system and problems following execution of judicial decisions

Historically speaking, diplomatic immunity preceded and through its evolution influenced state immunity. While state immunity now rests upon the notion of immunity *ratione materiae*, diplomatic immunity remains an immunity *ratione personae*, developed to ensure that representatives in foreign states are able to work unhindered.

The relevant principles and rules governing this immunity are now to be found in the 1961 Vienna Convention on Diplomatic Relations (500 UNTS 95). This Convention provides that mission premises are inviolable and free from seizure or search (art 22), are tax free (art 23), with inviolability extending to archives and documents (art 24). Under the Convention, mission members are free to move within the borders of the receiving state, except for areas restricted on national security grounds (art 26), the diplomat is inviolable, as are his personal dwelling and mail (art 29 and art 30), and the diplomat also enjoys absolute immunity from criminal proceedings, as well as from civil proceedings subject to the exceptions already seen for high-ranking officials (art 31).

Again, diplomatic immunity (for consular immunity see the 1963 Vienna Convention on Consular Relations (596 UNTS 261)) is conceived as a protection of the foreign state, so that only the sending state can waive immunity in proceedings (art 32).

In comparison to other immunities, immunity from jurisdiction and from execution are again independent, so that the sending state has to make an express double waiver. It must also be remembered that diplomatic immunity constitutes a self-contained system, with its own rules and principles (ICJ, Case Concerning United States Diplomatic and Consular Staff in Tehran (*United States of America v Iran*), Judgment of 24 March 1980, in [1980] I.C.J. Rep. 3, para 86; see also Federal Constitutional Court of Germany (BVerfG), 2 BvM 9/03, 6 December 2006, [2007] NJW 2605). It follows that even if the state waives all its immunity, diplomatic premises cannot be attached without a specific waiver.

The issue becomes important in light of the economic crisis and the default of some states. When the state fails to repay the bonds (→ Bonds and loans) issued on the international market, bond holders might only attach diplomatic premises and/or bank accounts when no other property of the foreign state is to be found within the borders of the seized jurisdiction (the limited possibility to attach foreign states' assets was recently highlighted by the seizure of the Argentinian Ara Libertad on 2 October 2012 in Ghana: see *Republic of Argentina v High Court (Comm Div) Accra Ex Parte*, Attorney General, No J5/10/2013 (Ghana S.C., June 20, 2013), available on the web page of the Permanent Court of Arbitration at <www.pca-cpa.org/showpage. asp?pag_id=1526>; International Tribunal for the Law of the Sea, 15 December 2012, *The 'Ara Libertad' Case (Argentina v Ghana)*, List of Cases: No. 20, available at <www.itlos.org/cases/list-of-cases/case-no-20/> ordering the release of the military ship and the crew pending international arbitration; on the relationships between immunity and the sovereign debt see Ilaria Queirolo, 'Immunità degli Stati e crisi del debito sovrano' in Giovanna Adinolfi and Michele Vellano (eds), *La crisi del debito sovrano degli Stati dell'area euro. Profili giuridici* (Giappichelli 2012) 151).

As a general rule, absent a specific waiver, diplomatic properties may not be attached; even so, only properties devolved to the public function are covered by such immunity, while other commodities not used to perform diplomatic activities are not covered. Case-law has also addressed the issue of promiscuous commodities used for both public and private activities: in Italy, in such cases, an *in dubio pro immunitate* principle grants protection also to such properties that show no actual connection to public activity (Cass. Civ. GC., 4 May 1989, n 2085, *Benamar Capizzi v Ambasciata della Repubblica Democratica Popolare di Algeria* [1989] Foro it. I, 2804 and Cass. Civ. GC., 4 April 1986, n 2316, *Paradiso v Istituto Agronomico Mediterraneo* [1986] I Foro it. 2507). More recently, the Italian Parliament has passed Law 10 November 2014, n. 162, according to which it is for the foreign state (and not for Italian courts) to declare if diplomatic bank accounts in Italy serve a public function (and are thus immune) or not.

VII. Limiting immunities of non-state-like international actors

Apart from states, other actors of the international community enjoy immunity under international law. For example the Sovereign Military Hospitaller Order of Saint John of Jerusalem of Rhodes and of Malta, the Holy See and international organizations are accorded certain immunities.

The Order of Malta is an independent Knightly Order with humanitarian goals, and even if it no longer has a territory, it is considered a subject of international law; thus, Italian courts continued to grant immunity to the Order (Cass. Civ., 13 March 1935, *Nanni v Pace and Military Order of Malta* [1935] Foro it. 1485). The Order is also one of the few non-state entities with observer status at the UN, where 64 members of the UN have recognized the full sovereignty of the Order (A/48/957 & Add 1).

Nevertheless, recent case-law has shown a tendency to reduce the immunities of non-state-like actors. In view of the lack of territory and of an 'organized systems of justice' comparable to those of the states, courts have developed the idea that international sovereignty of non-state-like entities does not automatically mean traditional immunity. Such immunity has to be recognized only within the limits of the treaties concluded by the forum state hosting the non-territorial entity: if the treaty contains no express immunity provision, no immunity will be granted (Cass. Civ. GC, 9 August 2010, n 18481, *Acismom v Di Alesio* [2010] Giustizia Civile Massimario, 7–8, 1099).

From the Italian point of view, some conclusions can be drawn with regard to the Holy See: according to art 11 of the Lateran Treaty (available at <www.aloha.net/~mikesch/treaty.htm>, last access 8 April 2015), only central organs of the Church enjoy the priviledge of non-interference. Thus, autonomous entities such as the Vatican Radio, whose aim is simply to spread the Church message, are not accorded immunity from jurisdiction (Cass. Pen., 9 April 2003, n 22516, [2003] Riv.Dir.Int. 821). Immunity of the Holy See was also questioned in the United States (*O'Bryan v Holy See*, 556 F.3d 361, 369–70 (6th Cir. 2009) and *Doe v Holy See*, 557 F.3d 1066, 1069 (9th Cir. 2009)).

VIII. Immunity and human rights: the peculiar position of the United Nations

While at first sight immunity would seem ontologically inconsistent with the right of action enshrined in art 6 ECHR, immunity does not mean impunity. The individual is only forced to seek justice in a different court of law, even if such action might prove to be more costly or difficult. The right to access a court is not absolute and can be limited as long as such limitation serves a legitimate aim, such as the respect for international customary law and the rules on immunity, and provided that the core right is not jeopardized (*Waite and Kennedy v Federal Republic of Germany*, App no 26083/94 (ECtHR 18 February 1999); *Fogarty v United Kingdom*, App no 37112/79 (ECtHR 21 November 2001); *McElhinney v Ireland*, App no 31253/96 (ECtHR 21 November 2001); *Al-Adsani v United Kingdom*, App no 35763/97 (ECtHR 21 November 2001); and *Roland Klausecker v Germany*, App no 415/07 (ECtHR 6 January 2015)).

From the ECtHR case-law it follows that immunity can be granted without violation of the Convention only if there is an equivalent protection of human rights in the state or in the system that enjoys immunity (cf the Italian system with reference to the question of Germany's immunity for civil claim actions related to the Second World War, Corte Cost. 22 October 2014, n 238, *cit*); the UN, in the framework of its UNPROFOR mission did not create an equivalent system to assess the claims of the victims of the Srebrenica massacre. Nonetheless the Court stated that it 'does not follow, however, that in the absence of an alternative remedy the recognition of immunity is *ipso facto* constitutive of a violation of the right of access to a court'

(*Stichting Mothers of Srebrenica and Others v The Netherlands*, App no 65542/12 (ECtHR 27 June 2013), para 161 ff).

The conclusion of the Court seems driven by a desire not to oblige states to interfere with the Security Council, charged as it is with the mission of securing international peace and security (*Stichting Mothers of Srebrenica and Others v The Netherlands*, App no 65542/12 (ECtHR 27 June 2013), para 154). A similar position has been recently expressed in the USA in relation to the events of Haiti (U.S. District Court, Southern District of New York, *Delama Georges et al v United Nations et al*, 13-CV-7146 (JPO) that has been confirmed on appeal).

IX. Waiver of immunity: some remarks

The founding principle of immunity is not to assure impunity, but rather to avoid interference in sovereign functions (Cass. Civ. GC., 12 November 1997, n 11150, *Cassa naz. previd. assist. avv e procuratori v Tesauro* [1997] Giust. civ Mass. 2141); immunity is also a right of the foreign state, thus it follows it can be waived.

Waiver of immunity must be (i) certain and non-ambiguous, (ii) made eventually with a waiver from execution, and either (iii) express or (iv) implied. With regard to an implied waiver, certain jurisdictions accept that a declaration of the contractual nature of the claim made by the state is sufficient to imply a waiver (*Morgan Guaranty Trust Co. of New York v Republic of Palau*, 702 F.Supp. 60 (SDNY 1988)). This conclusion can also be drawn when the foreign state, as a defendant, enters the case without contesting the jurisdiction (Cass. Civ. GC, 28 March 2006, n 7035, *Alcan Packaging Singen Gmbh v Soc Danieli Officine Meccaniche e altro* [2006] Giust civ Mass 3) or when the state submits a counterclaim (U.S. Supreme Court, *The National City Bank of New York v Republic of China*, 348 U.S. 365 (1955)), or, again, when the foreign state is the plaintiff.

No waiver of immunity can be inferred from the absence of the defendant: in *in absentia* proceedings the judge will therefore grant immunity and dismiss the case.

ILARIA QUEIROLO

Literature

Dapo Akande and Sangeeta Shah, 'Immunities of State Officials, International Crimes, and Domestic Courts' (2011) 21 EJIL 815; Rosanne van Alebeek, *The Immunity of States and their Officials in International Criminal Law and International Human Rights Law* (OUP 2008); Francesco Berlingieri, 'La Convenzione delle Nazioni Unite sull'immunità giurisdizionale degli Stati e delle loro proprietà' (2006) Dir Marit 1351; Beatrice I Bonafè, 'State Immunity and the Protection of Private Investors: The Argentine Bonds Case before Italian Courts' (2006) 17 IYIL 165; Benedetto Conforti, 'Sui privilegi e le immunità dell'Ordine di Malta' (1990) I Foro it. 2597; Andrew Dickinson, Rae Lindsay and James P Loonam, *State Immunity: Selected Materials and Commentary* (OUP 2004); Hazel Fox, 'Functions of State Officials and the Restrictive Rule of State Immunity' in Marcelo Kohen, Robert Kolb and Djacoba Tehindrazanarivelo (eds), *Perspectives of International Law in the 21st Century: Liber Amicorum Professor Christian Dominicé in Honour of his 80th Birthday* (Martinus Nijhoff 2011) 127; Hazel Fox and Philippa Webb, *The Law of State Immunity* (3rd edn, OUP 2013); Michaela Frulli, 'Immunities of Persons from Jurisdiction' in Antonio Cassese (ed), *The Oxford Companion to International Criminal Justice* (OUP 2009) 368; Riccardo Luzzatto and Ilaria Queirolo, 'Sovranità territoriale, "Jurisdiction" e regole di immunità' in Sergio Carbone, Riccardo Luzzatto and Alberto Santa Maria (eds), *Istituzioni di diritto internazionale* (4th edn, Giappichelli 2011) 235; Mauro Megliani, *Debitori sovrani e obbligazionisti esteri* (Giuffrè 2009); Ilaria Queirolo, 'Immunità degli Stati e crisi del debito sovrano' in Giovanna Adinolfi and Michele Vellano (eds), *La crisi del debito sovrano degli Stati dell'area euro. Profili giuridici* (Giappichelli 2012) 151; August Reinisch, 'European Court Practice Concerning State Immunity from Enforcement Measures' (2006) 17 EJIL 803; Luigi Sbolci, *Controversie di lavoro con gli Stati stranieri e diritto internazionale* (Giuffrè 1987); Pasquale De Sena, *Diritto internazionale e immunità funzionale degli organi statali* (Giuffrè 1996).

IMO

I. Foundation and legal nature

The International Maritime Organization, originally the Inter-Governmental Maritime Consultative Organization (IMCO), was established on 6 March 1948 under the auspices of the United Nations, building upon former attempts to address legal problems on the international level arising out of trade and the *mare liberum*.

The principle of freedom of access and trade as envisaged by Grotius clashes with the superimposing of legal systems on any particular vessel: from ownership to management, persons involved in a ship's trading may all be of different nationalities, none of which coincide with the ship's country of registration. More specifically, ships are mobile assets which are permanently moving between different jurisdictions and thus subject to different regulations. A ship may therefore fulfil a given country's requirements regarding design, construction, equipment, manning and operation, but still be in breach of another country's regulations on vessels berthing at its ports. Thus the need arises for universal standards that can be applied and recognized by all countries, and this becomes acute in view of maritime disaster. For countries to open their coastlines to foreign ships on the understanding that this poses no disproportionate risk to their safety, security and environment, and for ships to ply their trade without unreasonable obstacles, a common approach to shipping is greatly needed (see Efthimios E Mytropoulos, 'IMO: 60 Years in the Service of Shipping' in Norman A Martínez Gutiérrez (ed), *Serving the Rule of International Maritime Law: Essays in Honour of Professor David Joseph Attard* (Routledge 2010) 7–21).

Multinational cooperation in shipping dates back to the mid-19th century, a turning point being when the British Board of Trade in consultation with the French government drafted articles to prevent collisions at sea; these articles entered into force in 1863 and were adopted by more than 30 countries. The establishment of the Comité Maritime International in 1897 is also noteworthy, assisting *inter alia* with convening the Third International Conference on Maritime Law held in Brussels in 1910, at which the 1910 Salvage Convention (International Convention of 23 September 1910 for the Unification of certain Rules of Law related to Assistance and Salvage at Sea, in K Zweigert and J Kropholler, *Sources of International Uniform Law*, vol 2 (AW Sijthoff 1972) 7; 206 LNTS 220) and the Collision Convention (International Convention of 23 September 1910 for the Unification of certain Rules of Law related to Collision between Vessels, in K Zweigert and J Kropholler, *Sources of International Uniform Law*, vol 2 (AW Sijthoff 1972) 3) were adopted, and with convening the London conference held in the aftermath of the *Titanic* disaster, which concluded in 1914 with the adoption of the SOLAS (International Convention of 1 November 1974 for the safety of life at sea, 1184 UNTS 278). Between the two world wars further global developments in cooperation were pursued within the League of Nations Organization for Communication and Transit. The outcomes included the 1921 Barcelona Declaration (Declaration of 20 April 1921 recognizing the right to a → flag of states having no sea-coast, 7 LNTS 73) on the right of states with no seacoast to possess a merchant fleet, as well as the 1923 Geneva Declaration (Convention and Statute of 9 December 1923 on the International Régime of Maritime Ports, 58 LNTS 285) which established the principle of equality of treatment of vessels in maritime ports. In addition the first rules and uniform methods concerning the tonnage measurement of ships were drafted (see further Eula MacDonald, 'Towards a World Maritime Organization', Department of State Bulletin, 25.1 to 1.2 of 1948, document E/CONF.4/13, 23.2.1948; Douglas NH Johnson, 'IMCO: The First Four Years' (1963) 12 ICLQ 31–55).

Following the efforts to coordinate shipping during the Second World War, the need to pursue such aims in peace time became apparent. To this end the United Maritime Consultative Council was set up on a temporary basis; operative only until October 1946, it completed its mission by recommending the establishment of a permanent maritime organization. The newly created United Nations took on the task, and IMCO finally came into existence at a Maritime Conference in Geneva 1948 (Convention of 6 March 1948 on the Intergovernmental Maritime Consultative Organization, 289 UNTS 3), although the constitutive Convention entered into force only in 1959 with its ratification by Japan as the twenty-first Member State.

II. Function and competences

Pursuant to art 1(a) of the constitutive Convention, the main purposes of this specialized UN agency are

> to provide machinery for co-operation among Governments in the field of governmental regulation and practices relating to technical matters of all kinds affecting shipping engaged in international trade; to encourage and facilitate the general adoption of the highest practical standards in matters concerning maritime safety, efficiency of navigation and prevention and control of marine pollution from ships.

With this in mind, the Organization focuses its work on the development of international standards by adopting conventions, regulations, recommendations and guidelines. The outcome is a highly complex system which, as many developing states have complained, is difficult to implement. In view of these difficulties, IMO began to undertake the tasks of assistance and technical cooperation, a shift which was mirrored by changes in its structure.

Hence, in addition to rule-making, IMO plays a key role in helping states both to implement and comply with its own standards. At the outset IMO consisted of a handful of states, mostly traditional maritime countries; however, this composition has changed markedly over the years, thanks to open registries characterized by their lack of requirement of a close link between vessels and the countries operating them. While the financial incentives accompanying the new registries persuaded shipowners of the benefits of changing ships' country of registration, and with this a crucial problem for marine safety appeared, in that these countries lacked the human and technical resources to ensure that ships complied with the relevant domestic and international standards. In an attempt to resolve this problem, which was clearly diminishing the fleets of traditional maritime nations and jeopardizing marine safety, the idea was pursued at the diplomatic level of establishing a genuine link between a ship and its state of registration, for example by requiring beneficial ownership to be located in the state of registration. However, the constituting of IMO's Maritime Safety Committee in 1959 forced states to seek alternatives to this approach. Against the backdrop of the flags of convenience issue, Liberia and Panama were excluded from the first Maritime Safety Committee, despite their claims to rank among the largest ship-owning nations of which the Committee was comprised. The International Court of Justice was eventually asked to provide an advisory opinion on this matter of interpretation, which was duly rendered on 8 June 1960, and indicated that the largest ship-owning nations were to be determined according to tonnage figures rather than whether beneficial ownership was located in the country in question (see further Kenneth R Simmonds, 'The Constitution of the Maritime Safety Committee of IMCO' (1963) 12 ICLQ 56–87).

The underlying discussion highlighted the division between states over policy and opinion concerning the genuine link theory, which has still not been overcome. It also revealed the inability of many countries effectively to enforce domestic and international maritime safety regulations. IMO accordingly developed a more pro-active approach, first by providing flag states with guidance on standards implementation, and second by acknowledging port state control along with flag state jurisdiction; which is to say, the main IMO conventions lay down provisions placing responsibility on port and coastal states for inspecting foreign vessels arriving at their shores in order to ensure that they meet international standards. In the event of non-compliance, ships may be detained in port until repairs have been carried out (see further Z Oya Özçayir, Port State Control (2nd edn, LLP 2004)). This is likely to give rise to competition issues among ports, for which reason the IMO has encouraged cooperation in the form of regional port state control organizations, of which the Paris Memorandum of Understanding (Paris Memorandum of Understanding on Port State Control of 26 January 1982, 21 ILM 1, available at <www.parismou.org>) is a noteworthy example.

III. Organization and methods

The original structure of IMO as conceived by the constitutive Convention was restricted to an Assembly, a Council, a Secretariat and a Maritime Safety Committee, to which further committees could be added, as occurred with the establishment of the Marine Environment Protection, the Legal, the Technical Cooperation and the Facilitation Committees, whose work in turn is supported by several sub-committees. In addition to extraordinary sessions, the Assembly gathers together all Member States every two years, mainly to approve the budget and technical resolutions as well as recommendations presented by the committees. In the interim the Council performs the function of a governing body, while the technical work is carried out by the Secretariat and aforementioned committees.

According to art 28(a) IMO Convention, the Maritime Safety Committee is entrusted with rule-making on

> any matter within the scope of the Organization concerned with aids to navigation, construction and equipment of vessels, manning from a safety standpoint, rules for the prevention of collisions, handling of dangerous cargoes, maritime safety

procedures and requirements, hydrographic information, log-books and navigational records, marine casualty investigations, salvage [→ Salvage] and rescue and any other matters directly affecting maritime safety.

Preventing maritime pollution has unfortunately become more significant over the years, so that a specific committee was set up to draft standards aimed at avoiding or reducing damage to marine environments. The *Torrey Canyon* disaster drew attention to this regrettable facet of shipping and it became clear that technical regulations alone were insufficient to deal with the many legal problems arising from the disaster, such as damage caused to third parties. A Legal Committee was thus instituted in 1967, which nowadays deals with any legal matters within the scope of IMO, and has undertaken the task of drafting international conventions, among which those on private law issues are noteworthy.

Hence, all three committees focus on rule-making, seeking to keep pace with the constant technological and communications innovations in shipping. In this regard, IMO soon realized that its conventions, regulations and other instruments needed to be regularly updated in order to fulfil their functions, or risk being rendered useless. This problem arose with the updating of SOLAS, in that the Convention's traditional amendment procedure could not secure the entry into force of the relevant amendments in reasonable time. With this in mind, a tacit amendment procedure was endorsed in the 1974 version of SOLAS whereby an amendment enters into force not once a given number of contracting states have accepted it, but rather on a specific date, unless an agreed number of states have presented objections before the said date. This procedure greatly facilitates the updating of conventions and thereby enables IMO to keep abreast of technical innovations and findings as well as new challenges. Indeed, it has been contended that IMO has acquired a quasi-prescriptive jurisdiction as a result.

Over the years IMO's main objective has shifted from finalizing international conventions to implementing and enforcing international standards. Ship inspection and control are only a part of this policy, which is aimed at improving ship management and flag states' responsibilities for its oversight. In this context, the work of the entire agency is imbued by the priorities of assistance and technical cooperation. Thus the Secretariat provides for immediate assistance, the Technical Cooperation Committee carries out specific projects related to these matters, while the main purpose of the Maritime Safety and the Marine Environment Protection Committees is rule-making, by ensuring that conventions contain technical cooperation provisions, as well as developing guidelines to assist countries in implementing conventions. More specific guidance is provided by the Facilitation Committee, which is devoted to implementing the Convention of 9 April 1965 on Facilitation of International Maritime Traffic, 591 UNTS 265, with a view to eliminating bureaucracy and further unnecessary regulatory constraints on international shipping. Furthermore, with the increasing need for maritime security, the Assembly has empowered the Committee to ensure that actions undertaken for security purposes do not unnecessarily burden international maritime trade.

In addition, in the first decade of the century IMO developed an audit scheme to pursue standard implementation. Member States are assessed on how effectively they implement and enforce IMO standards, receiving feedback and recommendations based on their current performance aimed at promoting maritime safety and environmental protection. The IMO Assembly has already decided to make the scheme mandatory.

IV. Contribution to private international law

1. Uniform law: overview of the main conventions

a) Maritime safety

With the sinking of the *Titanic*, the first SOLAS came into being, directly addressing issues such as ship construction, listening watch for distress alerts and the number of lifeboats and lifejackets available on board. New versions of the Convention were adopted in 1929 and 1948, with IMO assuming responsibility over it from then on. An international conference was held in 1960, which laid down the IMO waybill for the coming years, given the many issues to be addressed and the assumed tasks to be pursued. In particular, a new version of SOLAS was adopted. This included a wide range of measures designed to improve marine safety and instructions on the carriage of dangerous goods, regarding which the 1960 conference recommended adopting a uniform international code for transportation by sea, ultimately issued by IMO in 1965. Similar concerns have led this

UN agency to intervene in the limitations on the draught to which a ship may be loaded by updating the Load Lines Convention in 1966 (International Convention on Load Lines of 5 April 1966, 640 UNTS 133), and in particular by pursuing a uniform system of ships tonnage measurement, which finally came to fruition in a convention issued in 1969 (Tonnage Convention (International Convention of 23 June 1969 on Tonnage Measurement of Ships, 1291 UNTS 3)).

SOLAS also contains detailed provisions on ship construction, including nuclear ships and bulk carriers, accompanied by further codes dealing with ship design, construction and operation standards. Navigational safety is also covered, and SOLAS requires navigational systems to be carried on board, as well as adoption of specific governmental measures such as the maintenance of meteorological services for ships or search-and-rescue services. Along similar lines, IMO also set up the International Mobile Satellite Organization (IMSO) as a way of overcoming conventional radio spectrum shortcomings (Convention of 3 September 1976 on the International Maritime Satellite Organization, 1203 UNTS 131). Commercial and other aspects of ship operating, in particular marine safety, were thus improved, as distress alerts are transmitted far more effectively by satellite than by terrestrial means. The adopting of the SAR Convention (International Convention of 27 April 1979 on maritime search and rescue, 1405 UNTS 97) was a continuation of these efforts to improve such operations following accidents at sea.

IMO is fully aware of the fact that marine safety, security and environmental protection are highly dependent on the human factor, and in 1978 issued the STCW Convention (International Convention of 7 July 1978 on Standards of Training, Certification and Watchkeeping for Seafarers, 1361 UNTS 2), which came into force in 1984 and has been modified to stress the relevance of demonstrating competence over training. The Convention was thoroughly revised in 1995 and 2010 and some responsibility fell on IMO for ensuring that its requirements are met through gathering information on its implementation by Member States and publishing a 'white list' of countries that perform well. Following in the footsteps of the Convention, in 1995, IMO issued a twin convention for fishing vessels, a sector to which the 1977 SFV Convention (Torremolinos International Convention of 2 April 1977 for the Safety of Fishing Vessels, superseded by the 1993 Torremolinos Protocol, IMO Publ IMO-793 E; Cape Town Agreement of 2012 on the Implementation of the Provisions of the 1993 Protocol relating to the Torremolinos International Convention for the Safety of Fishing Vessels) is specifically devoted.

b) Maritime security

Maritime security issues were first included on IMO's agenda in 1986, following the hijacking of the Italian cruiseship *Achille Lauro*. The first guidelines on practical measures to prevent unlawful acts against passengers and crew on board ships resulted, followed in 1988 by the SUA Convention (Convention of 10 March 1988 for the Suppression of Unlawful Acts against the Safety of Maritime Navigation, 1678 UNTS 201), itself supplemented by a protocol extending its provisions to unlawful acts against fixed platforms located on the continental shelf. The redrafted provisions allow *inter alia* the prosecution or extradition of alleged offenders wherever they happen to be. In view of terrorist attacks against transport infrastructures, new measures have been issued, and the International Ship and Port Facility Code (available at <www.imo.org/ourwork/security/instruments/pages/ispscode.aspx>) focusing on the establishment of security plans both on board ship and in ports is of particular interest. IMO has so far issued several guidelines which include combatting acts of piracy and armed robbery against ships and the prevention and suppression of the smuggling of drugs, psychotropic substances and precursor chemicals on ships engaged in international maritime traffic.

c) Protection of the marine environment and atmosphere

With the increase in the international oil trade and consequent spectacular oil spills, IMO's awareness of the need to protect the marine environment increased significantly. Nevertheless, environmental risks not only stem from maritime accidents but are also a result of routine shipping operations such as cargo tank cleaning and garbage dumping; indeed, operational pollution is acknowledged to be a greater threat than accidental pollution. IMO began its activities in this field by taking on the administration of the 1954 International Convention for the Prevention of Pollution of the Sea by Oil (of 12 May 1954, 327 UNTS 3), specifically targeting the discharge or escape of oil into the sea by intentional or negligent acts of those operating the ship. Seeking a more comprehensive approach, in 1973 IMO adopted the MARPOL (International Convention on the prevention of pollution from ships, adopted 2 November 1973, 1340 UNTS 184), revised by a Protocol in 1978 (Protocol of 1978 relating thereto, adopted 17 February 1978, 1340 UNTS 61), both addressing almost all vessel-source pollution in accordance with a Protocol to SOLAS issued the same year. Both conventions have since been further amended, in part as a consequence of major oil spills such as those caused by the sinking of the *Exxon Valdez*, the *Erika* and the *Prestige*, after which single-hull oil tankers were phased out.

IMO has targeted oil pollution more specifically by issuing the OPRC Convention (International Convention of 30 November 1990 on Oil Pollution Preparedness, Response and Cooperation, 1891 UNTS 91), aimed at achieving international cooperation and mutual assistance in preparing for and responding to major oil pollution incidents, along the same lines as the 2000 Protocol specifically addressing pollution incidents by hazardous and noxious substances other than oil. The spread of invasive species is another major ecological threat to oceans which both the BWM Convention (International Convention of 13 February 2004 for the Control and Management of Ships' Ballast Water and Sediments, IMO Doc BWM/CONF/36) and the AFS Convention (International Convention of 5 October 2001 on the Control of Harmful Anti-Fouling Systems on Ships, IMO Doc AFS/CONF/26) have addressed. In a similar vein, IMO adopted measures on ship-recycling in both the 2003 Guidelines and the 2009 Ship-Recycling Convention (Hong Kong International Convention of 15 May 2009 for the Safe and Environmentally Sound Recycling of Ships, IMO Doc SR/CONF/45), as well as on shipwrecks, with guidelines laid down in a convention adopted in 2007 (Removal of Wrecks Convention (Nairobi International Convention of 18 May 2007 on the Removal of Wrecks, IMO Doc LEG/CONF 16/17, 46 ILM 697)). Although the shipping industry is not a major contributor to atmospheric pollution it certainly produces gas emissions, but in fact is well on its way to reducing them, partly thanks to IMO's ongoing work which includes devising ship energy efficiency plans.

The role of IMO in this field is backed up by UNCLOS (United Nations Convention of 10 December 1982 on the Law of the Sea, 1833 UNTS 396). This Convention expressly refers to IMO in Annex VIII, art 2(2), acknowledging it to be responsible for the establishment and maintenance of a list of experts for special arbitration concerning the application of UNCLOS rules relating to 'navigation, including pollution from vessels and dumping'. Indeed, further UNCLOS provisions mention 'the competent international organization', which is universally interpreted as a reference to IMO. Accordingly, IMO pursues its activities within the framework provided for UNCLOS, which has resulted *inter alia* in the assumption of new functions such as those regarding the adoption of traffic separation schemes.

d) Liability and compensation
Ratification by states of the IMO constitutive Convention has been accompanied by reservations making it clear that they expected the Organization to focus on technical rather than financial and commercial matters (see Nicolai Lagoni, 'International Maritime Organization (IMO)' in Jürgen Basedow and others (eds), *The Max Planck Encyclopedia of European Private Law* (OUP 2012) 970–71). The *Torrey Canyon* disaster triggered a change in this approach on the basis that many legal issues arising from it concerned precisely financial and commercial matters. From then on, and with the institution of the Legal Committee, IMO has released numerous legal instruments classified as private law conventions.

The first was the 1969 Intervention Convention (International Convention of 29 November 1969 Relating to Intervention on the High Seas in Cases of Oil Pollution Casualties, 970 UNTS 211). This was immediately followed by the 1969 CLC (International Convention on Civil Liability for Oil Pollution Damage of 29 November 1969, 973 UNTS 3), which replaced a fault-based system with strict liability of shipowners in exchange for liability limitation and the establishment of a compulsory insurance mechanism. The underlying objective is to grant adequate compensation to the victims of oil spills at sea, for which the Fund Convention (International Convention on the Establishment of an International Fund for Compensation for Oil Pollution Damage of 18 December 1971, ceased to be in force 24 May 2002, 1110 UNTS 57) increased the amount insured by a second tier of liability. In accordance with this, liability falls on the recipients of the oil, so that should the compensation due exceed the amount available according to the 1969 CLC, victims may resort to the compensation fund provided by the Fund Convention. By this means the burden of compensation is more evenly discharged between shipowners and cargo interests. The limits of liability laid down in both conventions were increased through amendments adopted in 1992 (1992 CLC (International Convention of 27 November 1992 on civil liability for oil pollution damage, 1956 UNTS 255) and 1992 Fund Convention (Protocol to the International Fund for Compensation for Oil Pollution Damage of 27 November 1992, 1956 UNTS 255)), 2000 (of 27 September 2000) and 2003, while IMO also established a supplementary fund for oil pollution damage in a 2003 Protocol (Protocol of 16 May 2003, [2004] OJ L 78/24). Although the Compensation Funds are instituted as separate legal entities, their working activity is closely linked to the IMO in that the IMO is the depositary of the conventions giving rise to the funds and the Legal Committee is entitled to adopt revisions of the limits to compensation to be provided by the funds.

In the same vein, the Organization enshrined similar liability and compensatory schemes in the 1971 Brussels Civil Liability Convention (Convention Relating to Civil Liability in the Field of Maritime Carriage of Nuclear Material of 17 December 1971, 974 UNTS 255), the HNS Convention (International Convention of 3 May 1996 on liability and compensation for damage in connection with the carriage of hazardous and noxious substances by sea, 35 ILM 1406; as amended by the Protocol of 20 April 2010 to the International Convention on liability and compensation for damage in connection with the carriage of hazardous and noxious substances by sea, IMO Doc LEG/CONF.17/DC/1 (29 April 2010)), the Bunker Convention 2001 (International Convention of 23 March 2001 on civil liability for bunker oil pollution damage, IMO Doc LEG/CONF 12/19, 40 ILM 1406), providing for similar limits of liability as those contained in the 1976 LLMC (Convention of 19 November 1976 on limitation of liability for maritime claims, 1456 UNTS 221, as amended by the 1996 Protocol, 35 ILM 1433, and in 2012 by the amendment adopted by the Legal Committee of IMO at its ninety-ninth session (April 2012) by resolution LEG.5(99)), the Athens Convention 2002 (Athens Convention of 1 November 2002 relating to the carriage of passengers and their luggage by sea, IMO Doc LEG/CONF.13/20 (19 November 2002) which is a protocol to the Athens Convention 1974 (Athens Convention of 13 December 1974 relating to the carriage of passengers and their luggage by sea, 1463 UNTS 20)), and the Removal of Wrecks Convention.

2. The role of private international law

a) Relation between uniform substantive rules and private international law systems

While the idea of a general maritime law independent of the legislative authority of a single state dates from the 12th century, IMO uniform private law conventions respond specifically to the needs of shipping. To this end, uniform substantive rules displace domestic law within their scope of application, including the relevant private international law system. In this regard, questions have been raised as to whether conflict rules always precede the application of substantive provisions, even when laid down in international conventions. The general approach is that national courts will directly resort to uniform substantive rules rather than to private international law rules. This is on the grounds that, whereas the substantive rules are more specific in accordance with their sphere of application, they also offer a substantive solution, while private international law operates on the basis of a two-step approach which requires the applicable law to be first determined and then applied. The point is that private international law depends on the existence of a conflict of laws, as indicated by arts 1 Rome I (Regulation (EC) No 593/2008 of the European Parliament and of the Council of 17 June 2008 on the law applicable to contractual obligations (Rome I), [2008] OJ L 177/6) and Rome II (Regulation (EC) No 864/2007 of the European Parliament and of the Council of 11 July 2007 on the law applicable to non-contractual obligations (Rome II), [2007] OJ L 199/40) Regulations, which come into operation 'in situations involving a conflict of laws'. To the extent that uniform substantive law prevents such situations, resorting to conflict rules before applying IMO conventions is not necessary.

Anyway, there is still room for private international law to the extent uniform law conventions may not be exhaustive, in that they fail to cover all situations; this is the case with the Collisions Convention, which is silent regarding situations involving a vessel colliding with an oil rig (see Jürgen Basedow, 'Rome II at Sea: General

Aspects of Maritime Torts' (2010) 74 RabelsZ 118–38). In these cases, it may be necessary to determine the applicable law, as required where internal gaps arise when applying a uniform law convention such as the type of → damages or the existence of a causal link between damage and incident. Legal divergence becomes apparent while applying such conventions and their concepts, and the unification efforts are lost by an interpretation according to the relevant domestic law. In this regard, the divergence between national courts over the interpretation of conventions may be reduced by interpretative bodies, with a noteworthy role being played by the International Oil Pollution Compensation Funds in charge of administering the Oil Pollution and Funds Conventions; their Resolution No 8 of May 2003 reminds states that in the light of art 31 Vienna Convention on the Law of Treaties (of 23 May 1969, 1155 UNTS 331), national courts will give due consideration to decisions taken by the governing bodies of the IOPC Funds with a view to ensuring equal treatment of all those who claim compensation for oil pollution damage in party states. Nevertheless, national case-law has already indicated that such decisions are not conventional law and are therefore not binding. At any rate, an independent or autonomous interpretation rather than one based on the applicable law – either the *lex causae* or the → *lex fori* – is preferable as serving an international harmonized understanding of the relevant provisions, although it may also pose problems to the extent that a common understanding based on reliable criteria must be found. The general principles underlying the Convention are useful for these purposes, and only in the event they are unavailable should recourse be taken to the domestic law designated by private international law (Jürgen Basedow, 'Uniform Law Conventions and UNIDROIT Principles of International Commercial Contracts' (2000) V Unif.L.Rev. 129–39).

b) Uniform private international law rules
IMO conventions contain private international law rules which are also uniform law. In this regard, and within the scope of the relevant convention, they in principle take priority over similar laws regarding their application on the grounds that they are *lex specialis*. Where international instruments overlap, the ranking of treaties may be resolved by compatibility clauses, such as that laid down in art 71 Brussels I (Regulation (EC) No 44/2001 of 22 December 2000 on jurisdiction and the recognition and enforcement of judgments in civil and commercial matters, [2001] OJ L 12/1) and Brussels I (recast) (Regulation (EU) No 1215/2012 of the European Parliament and of the Council of 12 December 2012 on jurisdiction and the recognition and enforcement of judgments in civil and commercial matters (recast), [2012] OJ L 351/1) Regulations, by which their prevalence is acknowledged. Nevertheless, one of the remarkable features of IMO is that it closely collaborates with other specialized agencies and United Nations bodies, such as the International Labour Organization, and other intergovernmental organizations with a view to ensuring coordination on matters of common interest. By these means conflicts between treaties are likely to be avoided.

Given that IMO conventions mainly lay down uniform substantive rules, conflict rules are rare but existent, as shown by art 14 1976 Limitation Convention submitting the constitution and distribution of the limitation fund, including all relevant rules of procedure, to the law of the state in which it is instituted. Provisions dealing with international jurisdiction and recognition and enforcement of foreign judgments are more common, bearing in mind that the ultimate goals of these conventions are compensation of victims and reparation of damage without unnecessary procedural delays. Accordingly, art IX 1969 CLC submits all claims related to the Convention to the exclusive jurisdiction of the state on whose coast the maritime accident occurred. The corresponding decision is enforced in another contracting state in accordance with art X, which establishes the grounds for refusal of recognition. These are that the judgment was obtained fraudulently and the defendant was not given reasonable notice and a fair opportunity to present his or her case. Through these provisions the Convention aims to avoid concurrent jurisdictions and seeks a quick enforcement of decisions, although both objectives are undermined by the fact that these rules are not binding on non-contracting states. For this reason *lis pendens* (→ *Lis alibi pendens*) issues not addressed by the IMO conventions to the extent that they laid down an exclusive head of jurisdiction are likely to arise. In this regard and as stated in its judgment of 6 December 1994, Case C-406/92, *Tatry v Maciej Rataj* ([1994] ECR I-5439), the ECJ applies the provisions on *lis pendens* contained in the EU legal instruments to resolve the case of related actions brought before different Member States, one of them a non-contracting state to the relevant IMO convention. For this reason it is important to note that, unlike Brussels I Regulation, Brussels I Regulation (recast) contains rules on related actions brought before a court located in an EU Member State and a court of a non-Member State.

Similar rules to those provided for the 1969 CLC are enshrined in arts 38–40 HNS Convention and arts 9–10 Bunker Convention. In contrast, art 17 Athens Carriage of Passengers Convention provides for alternative heads of jurisdiction, including choice of forum (→ Choice of forum and submission to jurisdiction) after the occurrence of an incident or submission to arbitration, so that passengers involved in a maritime incident can find a forum close to them. Nevertheless, the Convention also fails to address *lis pendens* issues, for which other instruments such as those of the EU might also be of use.

LAURA CARBALLO PIÑEIRO

Literature

Jürgen Basedow, 'Uniform Law Conventions and UNIDROIT Principles of International Commercial Contracts' [2000] Unif.L.Rev, 129; Jürgen Basedow, 'Rome II at Sea: General Aspects of Maritime Torts' (2010) 74 RabelsZ 118; Jürgen Basedow and Ulrich Magnus (eds), *Pollution of the Sea: Prevention and Compensation* (Springer 2007); Douglas NH Johnson, 'IMCO: The First Four Years' (1963) 12 ICLQ 31; Nicolai Lagoni, 'International Maritime Organization (IMO)' in Jürgen Basedow and others (eds), *The Max Planck Encyclopedia of European Private Law* (OUP 2012) 970; Eula MacDonald, 'Towards a World Maritime Organization', Department of State Bulletin, 25.1 to 1.2 of 1948, document E/CONF.4/13, 23.2.1948; Javier Maseda Rodríguez, 'Responsabilidad civil por vertido de hidrocarburos en el mar: competencia judicial internacional y actividad procesal del naviero y víctimas' in José Manuel Sobrino Heredia (ed), *Mares y océanos en un mundo en cambio: Tendencias jurídicas, actores y factores* (Tirant lo Blanch 2007) 525; Thomas A Mensah, 'International Maritime Organization (IMO)' in *Max Planck Encyclopedia of Public International Law* (OUP 2011) 1001; Efthimios E Mytropoulos, 'IMO: 60 Years in the Service of Shipping' in Norman A Martínez Gutiérrez (ed), *Serving the Rule of International Maritime Law: Essays in Honour of Professor David Joseph Attard* (Routledge 2010) 7; Z Oya Özçayir, *Port State Control* (2nd edn, LLP 2004); Kenneth R Simmonds, 'The Constitution of the Maritime Safety Committee of IMCO' (1963) 12 ICLQ 56; Rüdiger Wolfrum, 'IMO Interface with the Law of the Sea Convention' in Myron H Nordquist, John Norton Moore (eds), *Current Maritime Issues and the International Maritime Organization* (Martinus Nijhoff 1999) 223.

LAURA CARBALLO PIÑEIRO / ANDREA BONOMI

Incidental (preliminary) question

I. General remarks

Lawyers commonly find that a rule of law can attach specific effects to an existing legal status or relationship. When a court or an administrative authority is required to take a decision on a legal question involving the application of such a rule, it may be required to take first a decision on the presupposed status or relationship, if its existence or validity is disputed. In such circumstances, it is common to say that the decision on the 'main' question (ie the main object of the decision) depends on the decision of a 'preliminary' or 'incidental question' (*question préalable* in French, *Vorfrage* in German).

Take, for example, a contentious → succession case in which a court is required to take a decision on the division of the estate among the heirs. If the applicable rules on intestate succession confer to the surviving spouse the right to a part of the estate, it may be that the existence or validity of the deceased's → marriage is disputed: this is the case if some other potential heirs allege that the marriage was null and void or that it had been terminated by a divorce (→ Divorce and personal separation). In such a case, the question of the existence and validity of the marriage is not the main object of the proceedings; nevertheless the court will have to decide this issue incidentally in order to determine whether the surviving spouse can inherit part of the estate.

In some cases, the decision on the main question may depend on an incidental question, which hinges in turn on another incidental question (*Vor-Vorfrage*). This is for instance the case if the rules on intestate succession grant some heirship rights to the deceased's children, but distinguish between children born during the marriage and outside the marriage. If the legitimacy of a child is in dispute, this is an incidental question. However, it may be that the decision on this incidental question depends on another (logically preliminary) incidental question: that of the existence of a valid marriage between the child's parents.

When the situation is purely domestic, incidental questions do not raise any private international law issue. The decision on the incidental question – like the decision on the main question – depends solely on the domestic rules of the → *lex fori*. Normally, the rules applicable to the main question simply refer, for the decision on the incidental question, to the rules, which would govern this question if it had been the main object of separate proceedings. Thus, the validity of a marriage for the purpose of a succession is normally decided based on the same rules which would govern proceedings for the annulment of the marriage. However, it may also be that special rules govern the disputed issue when it arises as an incidental question. Thus, the rules on so-called 'putative marriage' (as provided for in several jurisdictions) are nothing other than special rules extending some specific effects or benefits of marriage to persons who entered, in good faith, into an invalid marriage. In any case, in the absence of foreign elements, the choice between these different ways of deciding on the incidental question depends solely on domestic law and no issue of private international law arises.

If the situation is international, the law applicable to the main question is determined by the choice-of-law rules of the forum. These may designate the *lex fori* or a foreign law (the foreign *lex causae*). In the first case, it is undisputed that the solution of the incidental question will also depend on the rules of the forum, including, where appropriate, its private international law rules. Thus, if the incidental question – unlike the main question – does not involve any international element, it seems obvious that it should be decided pursuant the domestic rules of the → *lex fori*. If the incidental question has an international dimension, its solution will depend on the private international law rules of the forum; these may be choice-of-law rules or recognition rules, depending on the circumstances of the case. Thus, if the incidental question has been decided with *res judicata* effect by a foreign court, and this decision is recognized in the forum, the recognition rules of the forum will dictate the solution, thus prevailing over its choice of rules. By contrast, if the incidental question was not decided with *res judicata* effect, or if the foreign decision is not recognized in the forum, this question will have to be decided in conformity with the law designated by the choice-of-law rules of the forum.

When the main question is purely domestic, but the incidental question is not, the solution also depends on the choice-of-law and recognition rules of the *lex fori*.

From a private international law perspective, the controversial problem involving the incidental question only arises when, under the choice-of-law rules of the forum, the main question is governed by a foreign law. In such a case, the issue arises as to whether the incidental question should be decided in accordance with the law of the forum (including where appropriate its choice-of-law and recognition rules) or by reference to the *lex causae* (including where appropriate its choice-of-law or recognition rules). In the German legal literature, which first tackled the problem (George Melchior, *Die Grundlagen des deutschen internationalen Privatrechts* (De Gruyter 1932) 245 ff; Wilhelm Wengler, 'Die Vorfrage im Kollisionsrecht' (1934) 8 RabelsZ 148), the '*lex fori* approach' was traditionally described as an 'independent connection' ('*selbständige Anknüpfung*') and the '*lex causae* approach' as a 'dependent connection' ('*unselbständige Anknüpfung*'). This is the 'problem of the incidental question' in private international law. There is a clear divide among scholars on this issue, but intermediate or 'agnostic' solutions have also been proposed.

National courts only rarely take a clear stand on this issue. From a comparative perspective, the '*lex fori* approach' seems to be preponderant, at least in certain countries (in → France, see the decision of the Cour de Cassation of 22 April 1986, *Djenangi*), but important decisions have been taken based on the opposite approach (see the well-known decision of the Ontario Court of Appeal of 4 November 1963, *Schwebel v Ungar*, 42 DLR (2d) 622).

Contrary to one author's view (Wilhelm Wengler, 'Die Vorfrage im Kollisionsrecht' (1934) 8 RabelsZ 149), the incidental question is not simply a question of construction of the legal concept used by a rule of law. In the examples above, there might well be a problem of construction of the rules of the foreign *lex causae*. For instance, the effects of the annulment of the marriage on the inheritance rights of the deceased's spouse could be disputed. This is simply a question of construction of the legal notion of 'spouse' as used by the rules on intestate succession of the foreign succession law. Once it is clear that a 'spouse' loses his/her inheritance rights when the marriage is void, the question may arise as to whether the marriage is valid or not. This is the incidental question. As mentioned above, it concerns the validity of the legal status or relationship, on which the effects of the rules on intestate succession depend (Torben Svenné Schmidt, 'The Incidental Question in Private international law' (1992) 233 *Collected Courses of the Hague Academy of International Law* 305, 324).

ANDREA BONOMI

According to a traditional understanding of the problem, the alternative is between the 'application' of the choice-of-law rules of the forum and the 'application' of the choice-of-law rules of the *lex causae*. However, as rightly emphasized (Paolo Picone, 'La méthode de la reference à lordre juridique competent en droit international privé' (1986) 197 *Collected Courses of the Hague Academy of International Law* 229, 307 *et seq*), if the 'independent' approach consists indeed of the application of the private international rules of the forum, the 'dependent' approach should be more aptly described as based on a 'reference' to the solution of the incidental question under the legal system of the *lex causae* as a whole (in Italian *riferimento all'ordinamento competente*). As a matter of fact, the solution of the incidental question under the *lex causae* does not necessarily depend on its choice-of-law rules but can result from other rules of that legal system, in particular from its rules on the recognition of foreign decisions or from other principles on the recognition of foreign legal status and relationships in that country. In such a case, it would be improper to consider 'under a *lex causae* approach' that the foreign recognition rules or principles should be 'applied' in the forum state: it is self-evident that foreign recognition rules are never 'applied' by foreign courts. More exactly, if a dependent approach is adopted, the *lex causae* is taken into account as a whole with the consequence that the solution given under that law to the incidental question is accepted ('imported') as such in the legal system of the forum.

II. Conditions of the incidental question problem

As mentioned above, the logical conditions of the private international law problem of the incidental question are that (i) the main question is governed by a foreign *lex causae* and (ii) the application of a substantive law rule of this law requires a decision on an incidental legal question.

From a practical point of view, other conditions must also be fulfilled. In particular, for the alternative between the → *lex fori* approach and the *lex causae* approach to become relevant *in concreto*, it is also necessary (iii) that the two approaches lead to diverging decisions on the incidental question. This is the case when the choice-of-law rules of the *lex fori* designate, as applicable to the incidental question, a law that is different from the one that would be applicable under the *lex causae*, provided that the substantive rules of the designated laws also lead to different results. A conflict can also arise when the incidental question had already been decided by a judgment having *res judicata* effects in the forum but not recognized in the *lex causae* state, or vice versa. By contrast, a 'false conflict' arises when the choice-of-law rules of both the *lex fori* and the *lex causae* designate the same law as governing the incidental question, or when the substantive rules of the designated laws lead to the same result, or when a previous decision on the incidental question is recognized with similar effects in both states concerned.

It has been rightly argued (Paolo Picone, 'La méthode de la reference à l'ordre juridique competent en droit international privé' (1986) 197 *Collected Courses of the Hague Academy of International Law* 229, 304) that a further condition for the problem to arise is (iv) that the *lex causae* designated by the choice-of-law rules of the forum as applicable to the main question is also applicable to this question under the choice-of-law rules of the *lex causae*. *In abstracto*, this condition is not required because, from the perspective of the forum state, the alternative between the 'independent' and the 'dependent' connection of the incidental question can arise irrespective of the law that is applicable to the main question under the *lex causae*. However, the most weighty arguments for the *lex causae* approach – which are, as we will see, the uniformity of decisions between the → *lex fori* and the *lex causae* and the consistent application of the foreign *lex causae* as a whole – are devoid of their substance if the main question itself is not governed by the same law in the two states concerned. Therefore, the alternative between the two approaches mentioned will only become relevant when the choice-of-law rules of both the *lex fori* and the *lex causae* provide for the application of the substantive rules of the *lex causae* to the main question. In the examples above, it is necessary, for instance, that the succession (main question) is governed, both in state A (forum) and in state B, by the law of state B (*lex causae*).

Of course, this does not necessarily imply that both states apply the same → connecting factor, since the application of one and the same law to the main question can also result from different choice-of-law rules, as well as from the adoption, in at least one of the states concerned, of the → *renvoi* doctrine.

In the following section, we will review some of the arguments that are most often put forward in favour of the *lex fori* approach and the *lex causae* approach. Many of these considerations play an important role, but we believe that none of them can justify, in general terms, an *a priori* choice in favour of one or the other of the two proposed solutions. Nevertheless, in some circumstances, some of these arguments clearly plead in favour of one solution or the other. In other cases, they just give useful indications for a decision to be taken on a case-by-case basis.

III. The main arguments for a *lex fori* approach (independent connection)

The → *lex fori* approach is the solution that courts of most countries tend to adopt spontaneously, in the absence of particular grounds. As mentioned above, the problem of the incidental question arises when the decision of the main question depends on the existence or validity of a certain legal status or relationship involving some foreign elements. If this issue were to be decided as the main object of the proceedings, it would be decided in accordance with the choice-of-law rules of the forum. The first reflex of the courts is normally to resort to these same choice-of-law rules, even when that question arises incidentally.

Indeed, this instinctive reaction seeks to safeguard consistency within the domestic legal order. The strong interest of each country in the consistency of all decisions, which are taken (or could be taken) in those countries with regard to the existence or validity of a particular legal status or relationship, cannot be denied. Now, if a 'dependent' connection were preferred, the decision on the incidental question – based on the choice-of-law or recognition rules of the *lex causae* – could differ from the decision that a court of the forum state would take based on the conflict rules of the forum if the same question arose as the main object of separate proceedings. Moreover, the decision on the incidental question based on the *lex causae* approach could also differ from the decision, which the forum courts would take if the same question arose incidentally in proceedings relating to a different main question, governed by a distinct *lex causae* (eg the question of a marriage validity could be answered differently depending on whether the main question turns on the spouses' capacity to remarry or their inheritance rights) (Pierre Mayer, 'Le phénomène de la coordination des ordres juridiques étatiques en droit privé' (2007) 327 *Collected Courses of the Hague Academy of International Law* 9, 335 *et seq*). This leads to uncertainty. By contrast, if the courts always apply the law designated by the forum choice-of-law rules, the decision on the disputed question should always be the same, irrespective of whether it arises as the main question or as an incidental question.

The consistency argument is reinforced by the following consideration. Each legal status and relationship consists of a body of rights and effects of which that status or relationship cannot be completely devoid. If the choice-of-law rules of the forum recognize the existence and validity of such a status or relationship by referring to a certain law, it would be contradictory to deny this status or relationship all of its consequences by systematically referring to a different law when its effects are at stake. It does not make sense to consider that a marriage is valid if it produces no effects with regard to the relationships between the spouses and vis-à-vis the children and the → succession. As it has been rightly pointed out, such a paradoxical conclusion would also be problematic from a human rights perspective: thus, under art 8 of the European Convention on Human Rights (European Convention of 4 November 1950 for the Protection of Human Rights and Fundamental Freedoms, 213 UNTS 221), respect for the family life implies that a family status or relationship is recognized with its concrete effects (Andreas Bucher, 'La dimension sociale du droit international privé' (2009) 341 *Collected Courses of the Hague Academy of International Law* 9, 246).

These arguments are certainly very strong, but they are not always decisive. Inconsistent decisions on the same issue can also be rendered in purely domestic cases. This possibility is tolerated in all legal systems within the limits of *res judicata*. Now, *res judicata* is a relative principle, which only covers decisions rendered on the same question between the same parties. Moreover, decisions rendered on incidental questions are normally not covered by *res judicata*, which means that they can co-exist within the same legal system with contradictory decisions on the same question. Nevertheless, this is in practice a relatively rare occurrence. It is certainly true that some inconsistencies can be more broadly accepted in international situations, but they should be avoided unless justified by very serious reasons.

Internal consistency is very important, but its weight varies depending on the circumstances of the case. First, one should distinguish the instances, where the *res judicata* principle controls. This is generally the case when the incidental question was already decided as the main question in previous proceedings between the same parties. For example, if we assume that the deceased's marriage has been declared null and void by a final judgment in the forum state, the court seized with the same question as an incidental question is bound by *res judicata* and should therefore not be allowed to render an inconsistent decision based on the *lex causae*.

The same is also true when the same question, raised incidentally in previous proceedings concerning a different question, was decided with *res judicata* effect in conformity with the applicable procedural rules. Thus, in certain legal orders, one of the parties can require an incidental question to be decided with *res judicata* effect (eg '*Zwischenfeststellungsklage*' in → Germany, '*accertamento costitutivo*' in → Italy). In some systems, all questions relating to the existence of a → personal status must always be decided with *res judicata* effect, irrespective of whether they constitute the main object of the proceedings or an incidental question (Italy).

Of course, the preclusive effect of *res judicata* not only attaches to previous judgments rendered in the forum, but also to foreign judgments duly recognized in the forum. Thus, if the nullity of the deceased's marriage has been declared by a foreign judgment recognized in the forum, the forum courts will be bound by that judgment when they have to decide on the spouse's inheritance rights.

Even if the now incidentally disputed question was not yet decided in previous proceedings, the need for internal consistency is controlling when, in the pending proceedings, the incidental question must be decided with *res judicata* effect according to the rules of civil procedure of the forum. Since, in this case, the court's decision on the incidental question will also be binding with respect to future proceedings, it seems that it should not be based on the law governing the main question in the pending proceedings, but on the law designated by the choice-of-law rules of the forum (Carmen Christina Bernitt, *Die Anknüpfung von Vorfragen im europäischen Kollisionsrecht* (Mohr Siebeck 2010) 72 *et seq*).

Besides the cases where the decision on the incidental question is (or will be) covered by *res judicata*, the need for internal consistency is particularly stringent when the legal status or relationship, which is the object of the incidental question, was validly created or constituted in the forum (Paul Lagarde, 'La règle de conflit applicable aux questions préalables' [1960] Rev. crit.DIP 459, 481). This is for instance the case when a marriage was celebrated in the forum or an adoption constituted through a local decree. In such a case, it is very unlikely that the local courts will give priority to the foreign *lex causae*, when this leads to an invalidity decision.

The same is probably true when the legal status or relationship was created abroad, but its recognition in the forum is imposed by some higher principles of European or international law. Based on well-known case-law of the European Court of Justice regarding the effects of freedom of movement on the recognition of a person's name attributed abroad (Case C-148/02 *Carlos Garcia Avello v Belgian State* [2003] ECR I-11613; Case C-353/06 *Stefan Grunkin and Dorothee Regina Paul* [2008] ECR I-7639), it is now widely accepted that other kinds of legal status or relationships legally constituted under the law of a Member State (such as marriage or filiation) also benefit from recognition in the other Member States, under certain (although not yet entirely settled) conditions (Andreas Bucher, 'La dimension sociale du droit international privé' (2009) 341 *Collected Courses of the Hague Academy of International Law* 9, 359 *et seq*). The same is also true with respect to certain principles of the European Human Rights Convention, such as the protection of family life (art 8 ECHR). When such principles are applicable in the forum, the local authorities will not be allowed to deny recognition to the relevant foreign legal status or relationship, even if this is not valid under the *lex causae* governing the main question.

Apart from these cases, internal consistency does not always seem to be conclusive for the decision on the incidental question. Nevertheless, it still is a significant consideration, which should be balanced against the factors militating for a *lex causae* approach.

To this effect, the need for internal consistency will carry more weight when the choice-of-law rules of the forum submit the incidental question to the substantive law of the forum, and in particular when this is the result of specific policy considerations.

Another relevant factor is the more or less close connection existing between the main question and the incidental question. As it was frequently pointed out, a legal status or relationship frequently produces some 'natural' effects, which are part of its core, but also other 'side-effects' which are perceived as not belonging to the essence (Andreas Bucher, 'La dimension sociale du droit international privé' (2009) 341 *Collected Courses of the Hague Academy of International Law* 9, 246). Thus, the incapacity to remarry is regarded as a core effect of marriage in all legal systems which do not allow polygamy; by contrast, the spouses' rights to → matrimonial property and inheritance, although very frequently granted, are not always perceived as essential consequences of marriage. It follows that internal consistency is more directly threatened when opposite decisions on the existence or validity of legal status relate to its core effects rather than when 'ancillary' effects are at stake. Thus, when a marriage is void under the law designated by choice-of-law rules of the forum but valid under a *lex causae* approach, it would be nevertheless problematic to allow one of the spouses to remarry. By contrast, under the same circumstances it would be more acceptable that the same marriage confers some inheritance rights to the surviving spouse.

IV. The main arguments for the *lex causae* approach (dependent connection)

Notwithstanding the strengths of the *lex fori* approach, very important arguments can also be put forward for the *lex causae* approach (for a detailed analysis, see Carmen Christina Bernitt, *Die Anknüpfung von Vorfragen im europäischen Kollisionsrecht* (Mohr Siebeck 2010) 36 *et seq*; Torben Svenné Schmidt, 'The Incidental Question in Private international law' (1992) 233 *Collected Courses of the Hague Academy of International Law*, 305, 368 *et seq*). In the absence of compelling reasons for an independent connection, these arguments should be put in the balance with the need for internal consistency and can justify, in some instances, the choice for a dependent connection.

1. International harmony of decisions

One of the main arguments for the *lex causae* is undoubtedly the quest for international harmony of decisions (or international uniformity). It is clear that the application of a foreign law to the main question under the choice-of-law rules of the forum, is meant to promote uniformity, a goal that is attained, in particular, when the *lex causae* is also applicable to that question under its own choice-of-law rules. However, uniformity is jeopardized if the forum courts take, on the incidental question, a diverging decision that would be rendered under the foreign *lex causae*. The dependant connection avoids this, thus promoting a harmonious result.

Criticism is sometimes levied against this reasoning. Several scholars note that international decisional harmony is an ideal objective, which is often practically unattainable (Paul Lagarde, 'La règle de conflit applicable aux questions préalables' [1960] Rev.crit.DIP 459, 467 *et seq*). In situations that give rise to incidental questions, it happens that the laws of more than two states are involved, and that these provide for different solutions; then, complete uniformity cannot be achieved. Moreover, harmony of decisions does not only depend on the determination of the applicable law, but on several other factors, including the possibly diverging assessment of the disputed facts. Therefore, the importance of international uniformity of the applicable law should not be overestimated. These considerations are not unfounded, and they explain why the quest for international uniformity should not always prevail over the need for internal consistency. Therefore, a general preference for the *lex causae* approach cannot be based on the quest for uniformity.

Nevertheless, it cannot be denied that uniformity is one of the important goals of private international law. In particular it constitutes one of the main reasons why states accept, in international situations, to apply foreign laws or to recognize foreign decisions. As it has been frequently noted, international harmony promotes legal certainty, avoids limping relationships and limits forum shopping (→ Forum (and law) shopping). Therefore, the search for uniformity is an important factor when determining the way to deal with an incidental question. Its weight depends on various factors.

On one hand, uniformity is clearly more important in some private international systems and in some areas of law than in others.

Thus, the fact that the private international law system of the forum follows the *renvoi* doctrine in general or in the specific area of law covered by the dispute reflects a clear propensity to search for international harmony. This is certainly not conclusive *per se*, but constitutes a significant indication in favour of the *lex causae* approach. This indication is even stronger when all kinds of *renvoi* are accepted (not only '*Rückverweisung*', but also '*Weiterverweisung*'), and in particular when situations of 'cross-references' ('*chassé-croisé*') are solved by resorting to the so-called 'foreign court doctrine'. By contrast, the fact that *renvoi* is rejected (in general terms or in the specific area), is a very strong indication against the *lex causae* approach: why should the courts of the forum state strive for a uniform solution of the incidental question, if the *lex fori* shows no real interest in a uniform solution of the main question? (Carmen Christina Bernitt, *Die Anknüpfung von Vorfragen im europäischen Kollisionsrecht* (Mohr Siebeck 2010) 75).

On the other hand, uniformity is more important when it can be concretely achieved in the case at hand. First as mentioned, there are good reasons to consider that the problem of the incidental question does not even arise when the *lex causae* is not applicable to the main question under the choice-of-law rules of that law: in such a case it is clear that uniformity will not be achieved such that a dependent connection of the incidental question does not make much sense. Second, international uniformity can more easily be achieved when only two legal orders are concerned, ie the *lex fori* and the *lex causae*, than in the presence of several interested states. Thus, if under the choice-of-law rules of the law applicable to the main question, the incidental question is governed by the substantive rules of the *lex causae*, international uniformity can easily be attained if the courts in the forum state are ready to follow that solution, renouncing the application of the domestic substantive rules, which would apply under a → *lex fori* approach. By contrast, if a third state also comes into play (because its law is designated to govern the incidental question by the choice-of-law rules of either the *lex fori* or of the *lex causae*, or because its courts have decided on the incidental question by a judgment, which is recognized in only one of the other two states concerned) a complete uniformity cannot be achieved, and the weight of this argument is clearly reduced (Paul Lagarde, 'La règle de conflit applicable aux questions préalables' [1960] Rev.crit.DIP 459, 467 *et seq*).

International uniformity is also particularly important when the choice of rules governing the main question have been unified by virtue of an international convention or a European regulation. In such cases, several commentators plead for the adoption of the *lex causae* approach (Torger W Wienke, *Zur Anknüpfung der Vorfrage bei internationalprivatrechtlichen Staatsverträgen* (Verlag für Standesamtswesen 1977) 195; Christian Heinze, 'Bausteine eines Allgemeinen Teils des europäischen Internationalen Privatrechts' in Dietmar Baetge, Jan von Hein and Michael von Hinden (eds), *Die richtige Ordnung – Festschrift für Jan Kropholler* (Mohr Siebeck 2008) 112; Hans Jürgen Sonnenberger, 'Randbemerkungen zum Allgemeinen Teil eines europäisierten IPR' in Dietmar Baetge, Jan von Hein and Michael von Hinden (eds), *Die richtige Ordnung – Festschrift für Jan Kropholler* (Mohr Siebeck 2008) 241). However, it has been correctly pointed out that – at least when *renvoi* is excluded – uniform private international law instruments only promote international harmony among the contracting states (or the EU Member States), but not necessarily with respect to third states (Carmen Christina Bernitt, *Die Anknüpfung von Vorfragen im europäischen Kollisionsrecht* (Mohr Siebeck 2010) 467 *et seq*). Unification of the choice-of-law rules is therefore not conclusive for the adoption of a *lex causae* approach.

2. Deference for the foreign lex causae

A further argument sometimes invoked in favour of a dependent connection is the need to respect the foreign *lex causae* and to apply it consistently. If the choice-of-law rules of the forum refer to the law of a foreign country for the decision on the main question, all conditions set up by the foreign substantive rules should be construed and applied as they would be in the courts of the foreign country. Following this reasoning, the incidental question raised by those rules should also be decided in conformity with the choice-of-law rules and the recognition rules of the *lex causae* (Paul Lagarde, 'La règle de conflit applicable aux questions préalables' [1960] Rev.crit.DIP 459, 470 *et seq*; Torben Svenné Schmidt, 'The Incidental Question in Private international law' (1992) 233 *Collected Courses of the Hague Academy of International Law*, 305, 369 *et seq*).

It is certainly desirable that the foreign *lex causae* be applied exactly as it would in the courts of the relevant foreign state. However, this goal is not sufficient to impose a *lex causae* approach, in particular if this leads to inconsistencies within the legal system of the forum. As a matter of fact, there are other instances where the foreign law designated by the choice-of-law rule of the forum is not applied exactly as it should be: this is the case when the courts of the forum 'adapt' the foreign rules in order to avoid inconsistencies, or when they refuse to apply a specific rule of the foreign law because it would result in a violation of the forum's public policy. It goes even further when the → *renvoi* doctrine is not accepted by the forum state, since the foreign *lex causae* is then applied notwithstanding the fact that it would not be applicable under its own criteria. These examples show that the deference for a foreign applicable law is not without limits. It should also be noted that in private international law, separate aspects of one single relationship are commonly 'split' among different laws (eg the specific effects of a marriage such as the spouses' name, their personal relationships and the matrimonial property, are often regulated by different laws). Therefore, the fact that the main question is governed by a law does not necessarily imply that the same law should also govern the incidental question.

One could also contend that the consistency of the *lex causae* is not really threatened by the independent connection. It can happen that the *lex causae* itself refers to a foreign law for the decision on the incidental question. If this is the case, it impliedly accepts that the effects of its own substantive law rules attach to a legal status or relationship, which is not validly constituted under its domestic law rules. In this case, there is no particular need to preserve the consistency between the substantive rules applicable, respectively, to the incidental question and to the main question. Thus, it is acceptable that the effects of the substantive rules of the *lex causae* attach to a legal status or relationship, which is valid under the law of the forum.

The argument based on respect for the *lex causae* is certainly stronger when, under that law, the incidental question would be governed – as the main question – by the substantive rules of the *lex causae*. In this case, there is an intrinsic connection between the rules governing the main question and the incidental question, and this should be taken into account. The need to respect the *lex causae* is probably even stronger when the *lex fori* approach would lead to recognition of the validity of a legal status or relationship that is contrary to the public policy of the *lex causae*. In such a case, the decision on the incidental question would be in open contradiction with the rationale of the substantive rules of the *lex causae*.

3. Absence of a forum interest

As a further justification for a *lex causae* approach, it has been argued that the forum state does not have a real interest in applying its own choice-of-law rules to the incidental question (Paul Lagarde, 'La règle de conflit applicable aux questions préalables' [1960] Rev.crit.DIP 459, 468 *et seq*). According to this opinion, the fact that the main question is subject to a foreign law indicates that the forum state is not directly concerned with the decision to be taken on that question; *a fortiori* there is no interest of the forum state in imposing the application of its own choice-of-law rules to a question, which only arises incidentally and for the sole purpose of answering the main question.

It is certainly true that under certain circumstances the incidental question does not present any substantial connection with the forum state and can only arise before the courts of that state because they are seized with the main question. In such circumstances, the interest of the forum in the decision of the incidental question may appear very limited and the application of the law designated by its choice-of-law rules improper. This is so, in particular, when the disputed question could not even be the main object of proceedings in the forum because the local courts would lack jurisdiction. In that case, the application of the law designated by the choice-of-law rules of the forum is not really justified (see Georges AL Droz, 'Regards sur le droit international privé comparé' (1991) 229 *Collected Courses of the Hague Academy of International Law* 9, 361 *et seq*).

However, this is not always true. In particular, the fact that a foreign law is applicable to the main question does not always imply a lack of interest of the forum state.

On one hand, contrary to some American theories, state interests are not always paramount for the determination of the applicable law. It is widely recognized that other considerations also play an important role, in particular the desire to apply a law that is close and familiar to the parties. Therefore, the reference to a foreign law does not imply a lack of interest of the forum state.

On the other hand, even if one accepts that – at least under certain circumstances – the forum state is not directly interested in the outcome of the dispute over the main question, this does not exclude that it might well be interested in the decision on the incidental question. This may be so because the incidental question is much more closely connected to the forum state (eg when the inheritance rights in a foreign estate depend on the validity of a local marriage) and/or because it raises policy considerations which are more sensitive in the perspective of that state (eg the inheritance rights depend on the recognition of → same-sex marriages).

V. The main arguments for a 'result-oriented' solution

In light of the difficulty to opt for a general solution, some scholars have suggested to adopt a result-oriented approach to the incidental question (Kurt Siehr, 'Die rechtliche Stellung von Kindern aus hinkenden Ehen – Zur alternativen Anknüpfung der Vorfrage in favorem legitimitatis' (1971) StAZ 205, 212; Rhona Schuz, *A Modern Approach to the Incidental Question* (Springer Netherland 1997) 68 *et seq*).

In many choice-of-law systems, the traditional 'jurisdiction-selecting' rules have been replaced in certain areas of law by 'result-oriented' rules, which have as their purpose to favour the achievement of a certain substantive result in accordance with a specific policy of the forum. Thus, in the area of parent–child relationships, the choice-of-law rules often provide for alternative connections. This means that among several potentially applicable laws, the court may select the one which is more consistent with the purpose of establishing a parent–child relationship or, when relevant, the child's legitimacy. It has been suggested that a similar approach should also be adopted for incidental questions, with the consequence that the *lex fori* approach and a *lex causae* approach could be applied on an alternative basis in order to promote a certain desired substantive result.

Much can be said in favour of a result-oriented approach. In the absence of generally accepted solutions to the problem of the incidental question, it is reasonable to prefer an approach that is consistent with the existing choice-of-law rules of the forum. Therefore, when the choice-of-law rules of the forum state are based on a clear policy option, a result-oriented approach should be undoubtedly preferred.

On one hand, this is the case when the forum choice-of-law rules applicable to the incidental question are result oriented. Let us assume that the court is seized with the question of determining a child's inheritance rights and that the forum choice-of-law rules regarding filiation are based on the '*favor filiationis*' principle. This means that, where the establishment of the parent–child link constitutes the main question, it can potentially be regulated by one of several laws applicable on an alternative basis. Such a method should be extended to the solution of the incidental question with the consequence that the court should be allowed to select, between the *lex fori* approach and the *lex causae* approach, the one which fosters the creation of a parent–child relationship. The fact that the choice-of-law rules regarding the main question (ie succession) are not result oriented should not rule out this result.

In practice, this approach results in adding, to the alternative connections provided for by the choice-of-law rules of the forum, the possible solution (or solutions) based on the choice-of-law or the recognition rules of the *lex causae*. Assuming that the question of the parent–child link is governed, under the *lex fori*, either by the national law or by the law of the habitual residence of the child, and that under the law of a parent's last domicile (applicable to the succession), the same question is governed by the national law or the law of the habitual residence of the parents, the proposed 'oriented' solution would be to take into account all of these alternative connections. In the end, the existence of the parent–child relationship would be accepted if it is validly constituted under (at least) one of the mentioned laws.

On the other hand, a similar approach could also be adopted when the forum choice-of-law rules applicable to the main question (as opposed those applicable to the incidental question) are result oriented. If this is the case, several laws are potentially applicable to the main question under the choice-of-law rules of the forum. In this framework, it makes sense to favour the intended result by allowing the court to decide the dilemma of the incidental question in a way that is consistent with the goal of those rules. Thus, if the incidental question of the validity of a marriage must be decided for the purpose of establishing a child's legitimacy, the court should be able to select, between the law applicable under the *lex fori* approach and the law applicable under the *lex causae* approach, the one that upholds the validity of the marriage. The fact that the forum choice-of-law rules for the incidental question (ie the marriage validity) are not themselves result oriented should not exclude this solution.

In both cases, the relevant forum policy ('*favor filiationis*' or '*favor legitimitatis*') should prevail over the other considerations mentioned above (under points III. and IV.), because this reflects the rationale of the choice-of-law rules of the forum.

By contrast, a result-oriented approach to the incidental question would be ill founded when the choice-of-law rules of the forum (both those for the main question and those for the incidental question) are not result oriented. For instance, if the question of the validity of the marriage arises as an incidental question in a succession case, it would not be appropriate to select the solution which favours the validity of the marriage if the choice-of-law rules regarding both the succession and the validity of marriage are not result oriented. In such a case an *a priori* choice in favour of the validity or invalidity of the disputed legal status or relationship cannot be founded on a specific policy of forum law.

One should consider that a result-oriented approach affects the interests of the parties involved. This can only be justified if it reflects a specific forum policy. In our last example, a rule oriented towards upholding the validity of the deceased's marriage would affect the interests of other competing heirs (children, parents, other relatives). If such a policy is not reflected in the choice of law of the forum, then there is no sufficient reason for basing the solution of the incidental questions on such a policy.

In particular, and contrary to one author's suggestion (Rhona Schuz, *A Modern Approach to the Incidental Question* (Springer Netherland 1997) 68 *et seq*), we consider that it would be too much of a stretch to infer the principles for a result-oriented solution of the incidental question directly from the substantive rules and policies of the forum.

VI. Some suggestions for an empirical approach

As it appears from the previous remarks, no abstract preference for a general solution to the problem of the incidental question can be directly inferred from the arguments invoked by the proponents of one or the other approach. This does not mean that the decision should always be taken on a case-by-case basis. Under certain circumstances, certain solutions should be clearly preferred. When these do not apply, the decision will ultimately be in the judge's discretion; nevertheless some guidance can be inferred from the arguments mentioned above.

1. A priori *solutions*

First of all, it is important to recall that in some instances the problem of the incidental question does not even arise. Besides purely domestic instances and those in which the main question is governed by the *lex fori*, we will also mention the cases in which the law designated by the forum to govern the main question is not applicable to that question under its own choice-of-law rules. In all of these situations, it is clear that the law applicable to the incidental question should be determined under the choice-of-law rules of the forum.

The problem can be easily solved when the courts in the forum state are bound by a previous decision with *res judicata* effect between the parties. This is obviously the case when the now-incidental question was previously decided as the main question in a judgment rendered in the forum state: the *res judicata* principle takes priority over the choice-of-law rules of the forum. The same is also true when the previous judgment has exceptionally decided an incidental question with *res judicata* effect. In our opinion, the *res judicata* effect should also prevail when the previous judgment was rendered abroad, provided that it is recognized in the forum state (*ex lege* or following a registration procedure). In this case, the recognition rules of the *lex fori* prevail over its choice-of-law rules; *a fortiori*, they will take precedence over the diverging solutions possibly inferred from the *lex causae*.

Of course, the extension of *res judicata* will depend on the civil procedure rules of the state where the decision has been rendered (forum state or foreign state of origin). Normally, the *res judicata* effect is restricted to the parties of the previous proceedings. Therefore, the existence of a previous decision does not always bind the court, which is presently seized with the incidental question. However, one should consider that the notion of 'parties' normally also includes the heirs and other successors of the parties.

Failing a decision with *res judicata* effect between the parties, a result-oriented approach should be followed whenever the forum choice-of-law rules applicable either to the incidental question or to the main question are themselves result oriented. As argued above, when a clear preference for a specific result can be inferred from the choice of rules of the forum, this principle of preference should also be followed when deciding on the incidental question. The substantive goal reflected by the choice-of-law rules should prevail over the arguments invoked for a *lex fori* approach or a *lex causae* approach.

In the absence of a clear result-oriented solution based on the forum choice-of-law rules, the *lex fori* approach should in principle be preferred when the legal status or relationship, which forms the object of the incidental question, was validly created or constituted in the forum state. In such a case, a diverging decision on the incidental question will openly contradict a previous act of the forum authorities. Although the court seized with the incidental question can, in theory, opt for a *lex causae* approach, it seems very unlikely that – in the absence of a clear policy goal to that effect – the court will sacrifice the internal consistency of the domestic legal order in order to pursue the uncertain objective of international harmony of decisions.

The court will have to reach a similar result even if the disputed legal status or relationship was created or constituted abroad, provided that higher principles of European or international law – such as the freedom of movement inside the EU or the respect for family life under the ECHR – require its recognition, or the recognition of some of its specific effects, in the forum.

2. Case-by-case approach

The criteria mentioned above will help to solve a significant number of cases. In the residual situations, we think that no clear preference between a *lex fori* approach and a *lex causae* approach can be formulated *in abstracto*. As the doctrinal debate clearly shows, strong arguments can be raised in favour of both prevailing approaches and their respective weight changes with the circumstances of the case. Courts are also reluctant to adopt clear-cut solutions and prefer to benefit from a measure of discretion in order to reach a just result in each individual case.

Although a case-by-case approach is normally not in line with the goal of legal certainty, we do not believe that the risk of unpredictable results should be overestimated (*contra*: Carmen Christina Bernitt, *Die Anknüpfung von Vorfragen im europäischen Kollisionsrecht* (Mohr Siebeck 2010) 89 *et seq*). First of all, the problem of the incidental question only arises in a very limited number of cases, and the principles mentioned above further reduce the number of uncertain situations. Moreover, predictability is, in any case, extremely difficult to ensure in circumstances where incidental questions arise: in fact, even if a specific and uniform approach to incidental questions is adopted, the decision will, in any case, depend on which court is seized with the main proceedings and on which law is applicable to the main question under the forum choice-of-law rules. Since these circumstances are generally difficult to foresee, the predictability of the final decision is, in any case, not completely granted. Finally, based on the arguments discussed above, guidance can be given to the court in order to increase predictability. In particular, we think that the following criteria should be taken into account:

First, the choice between a *lex fori* approach or a *lex causae* approach will depend on the emphasis placed, by the private international law system of the forum state, on international uniformity of decisions, in particular in the dispute's specific area of law. The assessment of this should be based on the content of the choice-of-law rules of the forum. In particular, the attitude towards *renvoi* is very significant in this respect. The fact that the *renvoi* doctrine is accepted reveals a clear propensity for the search of uniform solutions, in particular when all kinds of *renvoi* are taken into account in the *forum*. The adherence to the so-called 'foreign court theory' is an even stronger indication that uniformity with the foreign *lex causae* is an important goal for the forum state. This is not sufficient in itself to impose a *lex causae* approach to the incidental question, but it certainly favours it. By contrast, the fact that the *renvoi* doctrine is excluded clearly indicates that international uniformity is not a priority for the forum; therefore, there is no particular reason to follow a *lex causae* approach.

A second factor is the probability that the incidental question will be raised – as a main question or again incidentally – in separate proceedings before the courts in the forum state. As explained above, the main reason to favour the *lex fori* approach is to avoid inconsistent decisions on the same question in the forum state. The weight of this argument is clearly reduced when, in the light of the circumstances, the risk of such inconsistent decisions is low or nonexistent.

This can result from the fact that the disputed legal status or relationship does not present significant contacts to the forum. Several scholars stress that this aspect can sometimes justify the choice in favour of a *lex causae* approach. In the absence of sufficient connections to the forum, it may even be that the courts in that country would not have jurisdiction to decide on the disputed question as the main question. Under such circumstances there seems to be no compelling reason for deciding the incidental question under the choice-of-law rules of the forum.

The risk of inconsistent decisions can also be influenced by other circumstances which *de facto* exclude or reduce the possibility of further proceedings on the same question in the forum. Thus, once the alleged parent is dead, there is no real risk that the question of the existence of a parent–child relationship will arise otherwise than in proceedings concerning the → succession.

A third aspect to consider is the more or less close relationship existing between the main question and the incidental question. As explained above, the main question can sometimes be seen as belonging to the 'core' effects of the legal status or relationship which constitutes the incidental question (eg the inability to remarry is clearly a core effect of a marriage). In such a case, it is more difficult for the courts to deviate from the application of the forum choice-of-law rules and follow the *lex causae* approach. If a legal status or relationship is valid under the choice-of-law rules of the forum it cannot be devoid of its core effects by simply referring to the *lex causae*. On the same lines, it is difficult to recognize such core effects to a relationship that does not validly exist under choice-of-law rules of the forum. By contrast, the *lex causae* approach can more easily be followed when the main question does not belong to the core effects of the disputed status or relationship. This is, for instance, the case when the main question turns on a person's surname: since the link between the name and the existence of a certain family status (→ marriage, divorce (→ Divorce and personal separation), filiation), albeit important, is not so close, we can more easily accept that the person's name will conform to the foreign *lex causae* even if this does not correspond to the person's status under the choice-of-law rules of the forum (Andreas Bucher, 'La dimension sociale du droit international privé' (2009) 341 *Collected Courses of the Hague Academy of International Law* 9 (246 *et seq*); see also the decision of the German Federal Court of Justice (BGH), 15 February 1984 [1986] IPRax 35).

ANDREA BONOMI

Literature

Carmen Christina Bernitt, *Die Anknüpfung von Vorfragen im europäischen Kollisionsrecht* (Mohr Siebeck 2010); Michael Bogdan, 'Private international law as a Component of the Law of the Forum' (2010) 34 *Collected Courses of the Hague Academy of International Law* 9; Andreas Bucher, 'La dimension sociale du droit international privé' (2009) 341 *Collected Courses of the Hague Academy of International Law* 9; Georges A L Droz, 'Regards sur le droit international privé comparé' (1991) 229 *Collected Courses of the Hague Academy of International Law* 9; Verena Fülleman-Kuhn, *Die Vorfrage im Internationalen Privatrecht unter besonderer Berücksichtigung der bundesgerechtlichen Rechtsprechung* (Zürich 1977); Allan Ezra Gotlieb, 'The Incidental Question Revisited: Theory and Practice in the Conflict of Laws' in Kenneth R Simmonds (ed), *Contemporary Problems in the Conflict of Laws: Essays in Honour of J H C Morris* (Brill 1978) 34; Christian Heinze, 'Bausteine eines Allgemeinen Teils des europäischen Internationalen Privatrechts' in Dietmar Baetge, Jan von Hein and Michael von Hinden (eds), *Die richtige Ordnung – Festschrift für Jan Kropholler* (Mohr Siebeck 2008) 112; Jan Kropholler, *Internationales Privatrecht* (5th edn, Mohr Siebeck 2004) 219; Paul Lagarde, 'La règle de conflit applicable aux questions préalables' [1960] Rev.crit.DIP 459; Pierre Mayer, 'Le phénomène de la coordination des ordres juridiques étatiques en droit privé' (2007) 327 *Collected Courses of the Hague Academy of International Law* 9; Georg Melchior, *Die Grundlagen des deutschen internationalen Privatrechts* (De Gruyter 1932); Karl H Neumayer, 'Zur Vorfrage im internationalen Privatrecht' in Friedrich-Wilhelm Baer-Kaupert (ed), *Liber amicorum B C H Aubin* (Engel 1979) 93; Paolo Picone, 'La méthode de la reference à l'ordre juridique competent en droit international privé' (1986) 197 *Collected Courses of the Hague Academy of International Law* 229; Paolo Picone, 'Die "Anwendung" einer ausländischen "Rechtsordnung" im Forumstaat: . . . perseverare est diabolicum!' in Jürgen Basedow, Isaak Meier, Anton K Schnyder, Talia Einhorn and Daniel Girsberger (eds), *Private Law in the International Arena: From National Conflict Rules towards Harmonization and Unification – Liber amicorum Kurt Siehr* (TMC Asser Press 2000) 569; Torben Svenné Schmidt, 'The Incidental Question in Private international law' (1992) 233 *Collected Courses of the Hague Academy of International Law* 305; Klaus Schurig, 'Die Struktur des kollisionsrechtlichen Vorfragenproblems' in Hans Joachim Musielak, Klaus Schurig and Gerhard Kegel (eds), *Festschrift für Gerhard Kegel zum 75. Geburtstag* (Kohlhammer 1987) 549; Rhona Schuz, *A Modern Approach to the Incidental Question* (Springer Netherland 1997); Kurt Siehr, 'Die rechtliche Stellung von Kindern aus hinkenden Ehen – Zur alternativen Anknüpfung der Vorfrage in favorem legitimitatis' (1971) StAZ 205;

Hans Jürgen Sonnenberger, 'Randbemerkungen zum Allgemeinen Teil eines europäisierten IPR' in Dietmar Baetge, Jan von Hein and Michael von Hinden (eds), *Die richtige Ordnung – Festschrift für Jan Kropholler* (Mohr Siebeck 2008) 241; Peter Winkler von Mohrenfels, 'Kollisionsrechtliche Vorfrage und materielles Recht' [1987] RabelsZ 20; Wilhelm Wengler, 'Die Vorfrage im Kollisionsrecht' (1934) 8 RabelsZ 148; Wilhelm Wengler, 'Nouvelles réflexions sur les "questions préalables"' [1966] Rev. crit.DIP 165; Wilhelm Wengler, 'The Law Applicable to Preliminary (Incidental) Questions' (1988) IECL III-7; Torger W Wienke, *Zur Anknüpfung der Vorfrage bei internationalprivatrechtlichen Staatsverträgen* (Verlag für Standesamtswesen 1977).

Injunction

I. Introduction

Pre-trial injunctions are both commonplace and significant in cross-border litigation. Two particular types of pre-trial injunction are especially important in international proceedings: the → anti-suit injunction, restraining proceedings in a foreign jurisdiction, and the freezing injunction, preserving a defendant's assets pending final judgment. Such injunctions have a decisive role in establishing the balance of advantage between litigants, and prompting settlement. To obtain a freezing injunction, preserving a defendant's assets pending judgment may rob the defendant of any possibility of escaping enforcement, while the effect of such a remedy on a defendant's business, and not least its ability to raise finance, may force a defendant into negotiation, and settlement. Again, to obtain an anti-suit injunction may prevent a party from claiming, or counter-claiming, in its preferred forum, and may thwart that party's own attempt to force a settlement favourable to itself by initiating proceedings in a forum disadvantageous to the other party. The effect may be to persuade such a party to settle on less beneficial terms, or withdraw its claim. So significant are these practical consequences that the distortion caused to the relationship of debtor and creditor was seen as one reason for the rejection of pre-trial attachment orders in the USA (*Grupo Mexicano de Desarrollo SA v Alliance Bond Fund Inc*, 527 U.S. 308, 312 (1999)).

Worldwide freezing and → anti-suit injunctions are especially associated with international commercial litigation before the English courts. They are very commonly sought in such proceedings, and often determine the final outcome of a dispute. This reflects the broad scope of such relief, born of the width of the English court's *in personam* jurisdiction in such cases (Horatia Muir Watt, 'Of Transcultural Borrowing, Hybrids, and the Complexity of Legal Knowledge' in Guy Canivet, Mads Andenas and Duncan Fairgrieve (eds), *Comparative Law Before the Courts* (BIICL 2004)), and the court's flexible, case-by-case approach, which encourages resort to such → remedies, combined with the considerable volume of cross-border litigation in the English courts (Richard Fentiman, 'The Scope of Transnational Injunctions' (2013) 11 NZJPIL 323). Both remedies are common, and take similar form, in other common law jurisdictions, though their design, scope and rationale may be different. Anti-suit injunctions may be sought in → Canada (*Amchem Products Inc v Workers Compensation Board* (1993) 102 DLR (4th) 96)) and → Australia (*CSR Ltd v Cigna Insurance Australia Ltd* (1997) 189 CLR 345) and in the → USA (*China Trade & Development Corp v MV Choong Yong*, 837 F.2d 33 (2d Cir 1987)). In the USA, however, the scope of pre-trial freezing orders is restricted. In *Grupo Mexicano de Desarrollo SA v Alliance Bond Fund Inc* (527 U.S. 308 (1999)), the US Supreme Court held that federal courts do not possess the inherent equitable jurisdiction to grant such injunctive relief which underlies the development of such relief in other common law jurisdictions, a conclusion followed in state courts (*Credit Agricole Indosuez v Rossiyskiy Kredit Bank*, 729 NE 2d 683 NY CA (2000); *US Bank Natl Assn v Angeion Corp*, 615 N.W.2d 425 Minnesota CA (2000)). Although courts may grant pre-trial attachment orders, the decision forecloses the possibility of granting worldwide asset-freezing orders, a jurisdiction dependent in common law jurisdictions on the existence of a distinctively equitable *in personam* jurisdiction, which facilitates the freezing of foreign assets (*Alliance Bond Fund v Grupo Mexicano de Desarrollo SA*, 143 F.3d 688, 693 (2d Cir 1998); Lawrence Collins, 'United States Supreme Court Rejects Mareva Jurisdiction' (1999) 115 LQR 601). Regular use is made in → France of domestic pre-trial attachment orders, but the attachment of foreign assets is impermissible (*Banque Worms SA v Ep X Brachot*, Cass civ 1ère, 19 November 2002), although disclosure may be ordered of assets located abroad

(Cour de cassation, Cass civ 1ère, 14 February 2008). In some civil law jurisdictions, although an attachment of foreign assets is unavailable, foreign assets may be indirectly affected by personal orders preventing a defendant in pending litigation from dealing in its assets (*D'Hoker v Tritan Enterprises* [2009] EWHC 949).

→ Anti-suit injunctions in the strict sense are confined to common law jurisdictions, reflecting historical and procedural differences between the common law and civil law. The courts of some civil law systems will, however, enforce anti-suit injunctions obtained in common law courts (as in France: Civ 1ère, 14 October 2009, pourvoi No 08-16.369, *In Zone Brands*). Again, mechanisms functionally equivalent to the anti-suit injunction exist in civil law jurisdictions, as in France, where a court may order a party to French proceedings to discontinue proceedings abroad, enforced by an order of *astreinte* imposing a financial penalty for each day of that party's default (*Banque Worms SA v Ep X Brachot*, Cour de Cassation, 1ère civ, 19 November 2002; Horatia Muir Watt, 'Injunctive Relief in the French Courts: A Case of Legal Borrowing' (2003) 62 CLJ 573). Similarly, in → Germany the victim of abusive foreign proceedings may sue the claimant in delict, entitling the victim to an injunction to prevent the wrongful litigation in support of its substantive right (Higher Regional Court (OLG) of Düsseldorf, 18 July 1997; § 1004 German Civil Code (*Bürgerliches Gesetzbuch* of 2 January 2002, BGBl. I 42, as amended).

Where an injunction operates intra-territoriality, as where a court freezes a defendant's assets located within its jurisdiction, no problems of practice or of private international law arise, provided that the defendant is properly subject to the court's jurisdiction in proceedings to which the injunction is ancillary. In such cases enforcement against the defendant, and the affected assets, would be straightforward, and the court's jurisdiction is uncontroversially established. Significant problems of practice and principle arise, however, where such relief is directed at a party's conduct in a foreign country, as where an anti-suit injunction purports to restrain a party from litigating in a foreign court, or a freezing injunction restrains a defendant from concealing, moving or dissipating its assets abroad. How can such an injunction be enforced? What is the legitimate scope of such an apparently extraterritorial remedy?

II. Enforcement

Direct enforcement of cross-border injunctions is possible in certain situations, but is often problematic. Direct enforcement of an anti-suit injunction is sometimes possible in the court where the enjoined party has sued, as perhaps where the injunction enforces an exclusive jurisdiction agreement (as in France; Civ 1ère, 14 October 2009, pourvoi No 08-16.369, *In Zone Brands*). At first sight surprising, this may be justified if the injunction is characterized in the enforcing court as a judgment concerning the parties' substantive rights, which does not represent any infringement of the enforcing court's sovereignty. Such recognition may not extend, however, to injunctions granted to enforce an applicant's procedural right to protection from abusive proceedings.

Again, an injunction freezing a defendant's foreign assets might be enforced where they are located, although this gives rise to a conceptual dilemma. The court granting the order may itself place limitations on the circumstances in which enforcement is possible, as in English law where permission must first be obtained (*Dadourian Group Inc v Simms* (2006) 1 WLR 2499). Many legal systems are also unable to enforce any judgments for injunctive relief, although this is possible for example if the injunction is subject to the EU enforcement regime (Case C-125/79 *Denilauler v Couchet Frères* [1980] ECR 1553). Again, if the injunction is characterized as operating *in rem*, it may be regarded as extraterritorial, and contrary to public policy, but if it is characterized as operating *in personam*, this is likely to prevent enforcement unless the defendant is present within the enforcing court's jurisdiction. Effect may be given to such an injunction, however, not by direct execution, but because it is perceived as creating a right, recognized in the enforcing court, which founds an appropriate local remedy attaching the assets. In such cases, a freezing injunction is likely to be enforced where, for example, the enforcing court is satisfied that the granting court has a sufficient connection with the remedy, and subject to general defences such as want or notice or public policy (Swiss Federal Tribunal ATF 129 III 626; Yves Donzallaz, *La Convention de Lugano* (Stämpfli 1997) No 2450; *Comet Group Plc v Unika Computer SA* [2004] ILPr 1). A worldwide freezing injunction, granted *in personam* by an English court, may be recognized in France (*Stolzenberg v Société Daimler Chrysler Canada*, Cour de Cassation, 1ère civ, 30 Jun 2004).

RICHARD FENTIMAN

Particular conceptual and practical difficulties arise concerning the indirect enforcement of freezing injunctions against a third party, typically a bank holding a defendant's assets. In practice, freezing injunctions are policed and made effective by a third-party bank, for which reason the scope of any penalty for non-compliance by such a third party is of considerable importance. In many jurisdictions a third party having notice of a court order is bound to ensure compliance with that order or face penalties for contempt of court, although it has been held that a bank owes no duty of care in tort to a claimant, and is not liable in damages for the consequences of non-compliance (*Customs and Excise Commissioners v Barclays Bank plc* [2007] 1 AC 181). This is unproblematic where non-compliance, in the form of permitting the transfer, disbursement or concealment of assets, occurs within the jurisdiction of the granting court, but it is doubtful that a court's contempt jurisdiction extends to conduct abroad (Lawrence Collins, 'The Territorial Reach of Mareva Injunctions' (1989) 105 LQR 262, 281–7). In English law, the standard worldwide freezing injunction provides that a third-party bank, even if subject to the court's jurisdiction, is not liable for contempt to the extent that its conduct complies with the local law where it has acted, or the law governing the contract with its customer (*Baltic Shipping v Translink* (1995) 1 Lloyd's Rep 673).

The difficulties associated with enforcing injunctive relief abroad suggest that such relief is more usually made effective indirectly, as where the respondent is subject to personal penalties for non-compliance, such as the award of → damages for contempt of court, reinforced by the threat of seizure of the respondent's assets in the event of non-payment, or of imprisonment (*Trafigura Pte Ltd v Emirates General Petroleum Corp* [2010] EWHC 3007). More significantly, non-compliance may preclude the respondent from participating in substantive proceedings before the granting court, exposing it to the risk of a default judgment, and from enforcing a foreign judgment obtained in breach of the injunction (*The Hari Bhum* (2004) 1 Lloyd's Rep 206). Again, the difficulty of enforcement means that claimants wishing to freeze a defendant's assets may prefer to seek in the court seized of the substantive dispute an order for disclosure of the defendant's worldwide assets, and use that order to obtain local remedies wherever they are located.

III. The legitimacy of transnational injunctions

1. The constraints of comity

Particularly difficult issues surround the compliance of cross-border injunctions with the principle of → comity. In principle, comity requires both that the granting court should have a sufficient connection with the relief sought, and that the exercise of that jurisdiction should respect a foreign court's position. Two distinct but interconnected questions therefore arise: the question of connection; the question of deference. The question of connection concerns the legitimate basis for granting relief when one party, or both, or the effects of the remedy, are foreign. When does a court have the necessary 'interest in, or connection with, the matter in question' to justify asserting jurisdiction (*Airbus Industrie GIE v Patel* [1999] 1 AC 119, 138)? The question of deference concerns the circumstances in which the principle of international comity requires a court, having jurisdiction, to abstain from exercising jurisdiction. When does the assertion of jurisdiction trespass on the exclusive preserve of a foreign court?

2. The problem of connection

What jurisdictional basis justifies the grant of worldwide injunctions? Jurisdictional connection has both a positive and negative aspect. Principle suggests both that a court must have a connection with the relief sought, and that no other court should have a greater connection. At its simplest, no controversy need arise where such relief is ancillary to substantive proceedings in the granting court. Jurisdiction in the substantive disputes supplies a jurisdictional basis for granting ancillary relief (*Masri v Consolidated Contractors International SAL* [2008] EWCA Civ 303). However, there may be circumstances, in which even ancillary injunctions may be illegitimate because another court has a greater connection with the relief sought. Principle suggests that it would be illegitimate to purport by means of an injunction to determine any issue concerning proprietary interests in foreign property (*Masri v Consolidated Contractors International SAL* [2008] EWCA Civ 303). For that reason it is generally accepted that the attachment of foreign debts is impermissible in so far as it involves an attempt to regulate property extraterritorially (*Société Eram Shipping Co Ltd v Cie Internationale de*

Navigation [2004] 1 AC 260). Such constraints do not, however, apply where an order affecting foreign property is made *in personam* against a person subject to the granting court's jurisdiction. For that reason, such orders are not in principle extraterritorial, although they have consequences in a foreign country. By the same token, → anti-suit injunctions, in so far as they have the same conceptual basis, are not extraterritorial.

Arguably, however, to restrain foreign proceedings is inherently inconsistent with comity, just as the grant of extraterritorial proprietary orders is inconsistent, because it trespasses on the exclusive province of the foreign court. For that reason, the power to grant such relief is limited in some jurisdictions to cases where a justification exists for overriding the foreign court's competence. Arguably, any remedy which prevents a foreign court from exercising its powers is illegitimate, save where the foreign court has exercised an exorbitant jurisdiction, a position adopted in Canada (*Amchem Products Inc v Workers Compensation Board* (1993) 102 DLR (4th) 96). Alternatively, relief may be confined to preventing interference in the granting court's jurisdiction, and the protection of strong public policies (*China Trade & Development Corp v MV Choong Yong*, 837 F.2d 33 (2d Cir 1987)). By contrast, in other systems, as in English law, comity is not understood as a jurisdictional concept limiting the court's power absolutely, but as an element to be considered in particular cases in the exercise of a court's discretion to grant relief (*Star Reefers Pool Inc v JFC Group Co Ltd* [2012] EWCA Civ 14).

In the absence of such absolute constraints on the court's jurisdiction, difficulty arises in particular cases, such as where relief is sought ancillary to foreign proceedings. Principle suggests that anti-suit injunctions cannot be sought ancillary to foreign proceedings, because such relief is predicated on the existence of past or present proceedings in the granting court. The very act of granting such relief collateral to foreign proceedings infringes comity, because the necessary 'interest in or connection with' the dispute is lacking (*Airbus Industrie GIE v Patel* (1999) 1 AC 119). It is commonplace, however, for courts to grant freezing injunctions collateral to foreign proceedings. In some legal systems no such jurisdiction exists in the absence of substantive proceedings (as in many common law jurisdictions, and formerly in English law (*Siskina v Distos Compania Naviera SA* [1979] AC 210)). In others, statute expressly permits such collateral relief (UK Civil Jurisdiction and Judgments Act 1982, s 25; art 35 Brussels I Regulation (recast) (Regulation (EU) No 1215/2012 of the European Parliament and of the Council of 12 December 2012 on jurisdiction and the recognition and enforcement of judgments in civil and commercial matters (recast), [2012] OJ L 351/1; → Brussels I (Convention and Regulation)). In such cases, it may be uncertain what jurisdictional connection is required, given that the most natural connecting factor, the existence of substantive proceedings, is absent. Principle suggests, and the law of many systems confirms, that the overriding consideration is that there must be a real connecting link between the subject matter of the relief sought and the territorial jurisdiction of the granting court, established in the EU context in *Van Uden Maritime BV v Firma Deco-Line* (Case C-391/95, [1999] QB 1225; cf in English law, *Mobil Cerro Negro Ltd v Petroleos De Venezuela SA* [2008] EWHC 532).

It is possible that the necessary interest in, or connection with, the grant of relief only exists if the defendant has assets in the territory of the granting court, and only in connection with such assets. In that event, jurisdiction to grant ancillary relief may be exercised only in connection with local assets. This position reflects the assumption that the necessary connecting factor is the enforceability in the granting court of any final judgment obtained in the court seized of the substantive proceedings. It is a conclusion compelled in legal systems in which injunctive relief does not operate *in personam* against local defendants, and cannot be enforced by penalties for contempt of court (Horatia Muir Watt, 'Of Transcultural Borrowing, Hybrids, and the Complexity of Legal Knowledge' in Guy Canivet, Mads Andenas and Duncan Fairgrieve (eds), *Comparative Law Before the Courts* (BIICL 2004) 43).

Other legal systems, however, where such relief operates *in personam*, and may be locally enforced by contempt proceedings, recognize the possibility of freezing foreign assets in support of foreign proceedings, as in English law (*Mobil Cerro Negro Ltd v Petroleos De Venezuela SA* [2008] EWHC 532). In that event, much uncertainty surrounds when such jurisdiction may be exercised. One possibility is that enforceability of the injunction in the territory of the granting court is the touchstone. Where, for example, non-compliance with the order is penalized by remedies for contempt of court the penalty may be personal, which requires that either the defendant or its agent is present in England, or they may be directed at a disobedient defendant's assets, which would require alternatively the presence of such assets in England. Another possibility is that the subject matter of the injunction is the localizing factor. In those legal systems in which freezing injunctions operate *in rem* by way of attachment the remedy is targeted at the defendant's assets, which represent the subject matter of the remedy. In those where relief operates *in personam*, however, as in English law, the remedy is targeted at controlling the defendant's conduct. The subject matter of the relief is therefore the restraint of the defendant, with the effect that jurisdiction is founded if the defendant is present in the territory of the granting court (*Credit Suisse Fides Trust v Cuoghi* [1998] QB 818, 827 (CA)).

Principle suggests, however, that a legitimate jurisdictional connection may exist although the subject matter of the relief is not connected with the granting court's territory (*Mobil Cerro Negro Ltd v Petroleos de Venezuela SA* [2008] EWHC 532 [28], [155] (Comm)). Such factors might include necessity, as where any final foreign judgment would be unenforceable but for the injunction (*Credit Suisse Fides Trust v Cuoghi* [1998] QB 818, 828–9); or express submission, as where a defendant has submitted to the granting court's jurisdiction over the substance of any dispute (*Royal Bank of Scotland Plc v FAL Oil Co Ltd* [2012] EWHC 3628 (Comm)); or cases where the defendant's fraud is manifest (*Republic of Haiti v Duvalier* (1990) 1 QB 202, 215 (CA); *Motorola Credit Corporation v Uzan (No 2)* [2003] EWCA Civ 752 [114]).

Difficulty arises even in legal systems in which injunctive relief operates *in personam*. Does jurisdiction exist to freeze foreign assets merely because the defendant has assets in England? The question has become prominent in English law because of a conflict of authority between two differently constituted Courts of Appeal, in *Motorola Credit Corporation v Uzan* ([2003] EWCA Civ 752), and *Banco Nacional de Comercio Exterior SNC v Empresa de Telecommunicaciones de Cuba SA* ([2007] EWCA Civ 662). In *Empresa* the Court of Appeal held that it was an insufficient basis of jurisdiction for the grant of a worldwide injunction that the defendant has assets in England. Only a domestic order was permissible in connection with local assets. There was no connecting link between the subject matter of the measure sought and the territorial jurisdiction of this court. The subject matter of such relief is control of the defendant's conduct, so no such link exists unless the defendant (or perhaps its agent) is present in England. By contrast, in *Motorola* a differently constituted Court of Appeal confirmed the grant of a worldwide injunction against a defendant who was present outside the jurisdiction but had assets in England. The justification was that the presence of the defendant's assets offered the court a means to enforce any order for contempt in the event of the defendant's disobedience to the injunction. Principle suggests that the decision in *Empresa* is correct, in so far as the subject matter of equitable *in personam* relief consists in the control of the defendant's conduct (Adam Johnson, 'Interim Injunctions and International Jurisdiction' (2008) 27 CJQ 433).

3. The problem of deference

Even if a sufficient jurisdictional connection is established, the grant of relief may infringe the principle of comity. It is possible to argue that to restrain foreign proceedings, or to freeze foreign assets is invariably an infringement of comity. But the utility of such remedies, and their role in preserving effective access to justice, suggests that a more nuanced approach is required, which seeks to isolate those particular circumstances in which the grant of relief would infringe comity (*Star Reefers Pool Inc v JFC Group Co Ltd* [2012] EWCA Civ 14).

If such a relative rather than absolute approach to comity is adopted, the enquiry is directed at identifying particular infringements of the principle. Where a court freezes foreign assets by an injunction ancillary to its own substantive proceedings, comity is unlikely to be an issue provided that the injunction operates *in personam*, because in that event the target of the relief is a party subject to the court's jurisdiction (*Masri v Consolidated Contractors International SAL* [2008] EWCA Civ 303), provided that such an order does not purport to have proprietary effect in another country (*Société Eram Shipping Co Ltd v Cie Internationale de Navigation* [2004] 1 AC 260). Where such relief is granted ancillary to foreign proceedings, and sufficient jurisdictional connection exists, difficulty surrounds when the grant of such collateral relief complies with the principle of comity. Principle suggests that comity is only infringed if relief is granted in circumstances in which the foreign court had the power to grant equivalent relief, but declined to do so (*Refco Inc v Eastern Trading Co* (1999) 1 Lloyd's Rep 159).

Again, in systems adopting a relativist approach to comity in relation to anti-suit injunctions, it may be sufficient that a court polices the requirement of comity when exercising its discretion to grant relief, a discretion predicated on the assumption that the foreign court has primacy in deciding whether a case should be heard in foreign proceedings (*Harms Offshore AHT Taurus GmbH & Co KG v Bloom* [2009] EWCA Civ 632). In English law, for example, comity is not perceived as creating a general bar to granting relief, but a court is required to establish that comity would not be infringed on the facts of particular cases (*Star Reefers Pool Inc v JFC Group Co Ltd* [2012] EWCA Civ 14). Comity is regarded as being of reduced significance, for example, in cases where an injunction is sought to enforce an exclusive jurisdiction or arbitration agreement. This was once said to be because in such cases the court has jurisdiction to enforce the applicant's substantive rights, and is merely granting a substantive remedy as it would in any case where a breach of contract is alleged (*The Angelic Grace* (1995) 1 Lloyd's Rep 87), an analysis accepted in French law (Civ 1ère, 14 October 2009, pourvoi No 08-16.369, *In Zone Brands*). It has more recently been suggested that in such cases the foreign court's right to determine the agreement's effect will be respected, but relief will be granted nonetheless where the foreign court regards the agreement as invalid for reasons unknown to English law, in which case it is assumed that the principle of comity does not engage (*Ust-Kamenogorsk Hydropower Plant JSC v AES Ust-Kamenogorsk Hydropower Plant LLP* [2013] UKSC 35). Conversely, a court may be reluctant to restrain foreign proceedings if the foreign court has asserted jurisdiction by employing rules for exercising jurisdiction similar to those of English law (*Akai Ltd v People's Insurance Co Ltd* (1998) 1 Lloyd's Rep 90). Again, relief will be granted only when essential, as when English proceedings would be concluded before the alternative proceedings, making an injunction unnecessary (*Star Reefers Pool Inc v JFC Group Co Ltd* [2012] EWCA Civ 14), and not where it would be appropriate for the applicant to exhaust any remedies available in the foreign court (*Seismic Shipping Inc v Total E&P UK plc* [2005] EWCA Civ 985).

IV. Transnational injunctions in EU law

1. Anti-suit injunctions

One EU state may not restrain by injunction proceedings in another such state (Case C-159/02 *Turner v Grovit* [2004] ECR I-3565). Such relief infringes the distinctive EU law principle requiring mutual respect between Member States, and would subvert the *effet utile* of the EU jurisdiction regime by preventing an EU national court from asserting jurisdiction pursuant to that regime. It has been held, however, that this prohibition does not extend to injunctions restraining proceedings in non-EU states (*Ust-Kamenogorsk Hydropower Plant JSC v AES Ust-Kamenogorsk Hydropower Plant LLP* [2013] UKSC 35), or those restraining proceedings in EU national courts the jurisdiction of which is beyond the scope of that regime (*Claxton Engineering Ltd v TXM KTF* [2011] EWHC 345).

Controversially, this prohibition was extended by the CJEU to injunctions sought to enforce arbitration agreements (Case C-185/07 *Allianz v West Tankers Inc* [2009] AC 1138). Although arbitration is a matter excluded from the scope of the Brussels I Regulation, the *effet utile* of the EU jurisdiction rules would be impaired if a court were prevented from addressing an issue subject to that Regulation. Arguably, however, injunctions ancillary to arbitration may be permitted under the Regulation's successor, Brussels I Regulation (recast) (Regulation (EU) No 1215/2012 of the European Parliament and of the Council of 12 December 2012 on jurisdiction and the recognition and enforcement of judgments in civil and commercial matters (recast), [2012] OJ L 351/1; → Brussels I (Convention and Regulation)). It has been suggested (for example, by Fentiman, *International Commercial Litigation* (2nd edn, OUP 2015) [16–142]–[16–149] and by AG Wathelet in Case C-536/13 *Gazprom* (Opinion) (13 May 2015), paras [125]–[133]) that the Brussels I Regulation (recast) expressly removes the conceptual assumption on which the *West Tankers* decision rests, namely that the issue of whether civil proceedings should be stayed in the light of an arbitration agreement is a matter within the Regulation, so that an injunction to prevent a court from addressing that issue is an interference in a matter subject of the Regulation (Recital (12) Brussels I Regulation (recast)). Under the Brussels I Regulation (recast) no such interference may occur.

In so far as anti-suit injunctions may be granted to enforce arbitration agreements in cases subject to the Brussels I Regulation (recast), difficulty arises concerning the effect of such relief in the court in which the restrained proceedings were initiated. Such injunctions are not in practice sought with the expectation that they should be enforced in that court, but rather with the intention that the applicant may rely upon enforcement by contempt proceedings in the English court. Nonetheless, direct enforcement may be possible in principle, in so far as such an injunction represents a substantive contractual remedy enforcing a contractual right (cf Civ 1ère, 14 October 2009, pourvoi No 08-16.369, *In Zone Brands*). The CJEU appears to have concluded, without giving reasons, that such injunctions are not enforceable pursuant to the EU enforcement regime (Case C-159/02 *Turner v Grovit* [2004] ECR I-3565, para 30). The explanation may be that such relief is procedural in character when directed at policing abusive conduct, but principle suggests that an injunction enforcing a contractual arbitration agreement, a remedy for breach of contract, should be enforceable under the EU regime.

2. Freezing injunctions

Article 35 Brussels I Regulation (recast) governs the grant of pre-trial injunctive relief collateral to proceedings in another EU state. Article 35 provides that application may be made to the courts of a Member State may order such interim injunctive relief as may be available in that court, even if the courts of another Member State have jurisdiction as to the substance of the matter. Article 35 therefore operates where primary proceedings are commenced in state A, and collateral relief is sought in state B under art 35, and where primary proceedings are commenced in state A, where collateral relief is obtained, and a claimant seeks to give effect to such a collateral award by seeking local relief in state B under art 35. Article 35 therefore regulates such relief in two principal ways: by defining which orders may be classified as → provisional measures; and, by prescribing the degree of connection that must exist between the subject matter of relief and the awarding court. A pre-trial freezing order falls unobjectionably within the scope of permitted relief, but difficulty surrounds the jurisdictional limits to such relief.

The jurisdictional scope of art 35 was clarified by the decision of the Court of Justice, concerning art 24 of the 1968 Brussels Convention (Brussels Convention of 27 September 1968 on jurisdiction and the enforcement of judgments in civil and commercial matters, [1972] OJ L 299/32, consolidated version, [1998] OJ C 27/1), in *Van Uden Maritime BV v Firma Deco-Line* (Case C-391/95, [1998] ECR I-7091). As *Van Uden* establishes, the courts of a Member State may exercise jurisdiction only if there is 'a real connecting link between the subject matter of the measures sought and the territorial jurisdiction of the contracting state of the court before which those measures are sought' (at para 20). This clearly permits a court to grant relief in respect of local assets in support of foreign proceedings, and accommodates those legal systems where such relief operates by way of an attachment of the defendant's assets. It is controversial whether collateral relief may be granted in respect of foreign assets where such relief operates *in personam*.

Controversially, the Brussels I Regulation (recast) redefines the concept of a judgment for the purposes of recognition within the EU so that only injunctive relief ancillary to substantive proceedings in the granting court may be enforced (art 2 Brussels I Regulation (recast)). It was previously required that the enforcing court should satisfy itself that the *Van Uden* test was satisfied in the granting court (Case C-99/96 *Hans-Hermann Mietz v Intership Yachting Sneek BV* [1999] ECR I-2277). This limitation does not, however, affect the court's jurisdiction to grant collateral relief, which may in any event be made effective without direct enforcement in another EU state even if granted in respect of a defendant's foreign assets. The matter remains unresolved, but principle suggests that a court may grant an injunction freezing assets in another Member State, in support of primary proceedings in another state where such relief operates *in personam*. In that event, the subject matter of the relief is the conduct of the defendant in the territory of the granting court, in compliance with the *Van Uden* test. Moreover, enforcement of the order in the granting court's territory is also possible in such cases, pursuant to the court's powers to penalize non-compliance by an order for contempt. In English law, where the issue is of particular importance, it is assumed that the *Van Uden* requirement of a 'real connecting link' is satisfied provided that the defendant whose conduct is restrained is domiciled in England (*Banco Nacional de Comercio Exterior SNC v Empresa de Telecomunicationes de Cuba SA* (2007) 2 Lloyd's Rep 484; Louise Merrett, 'Worldwide Freezing Orders in Europe' [2008] LMCLQ 71).

Uncertainty surrounds the effect of a contractual jurisdiction agreement on the operation of the *Van Uden* test. It has been held that the existence of a jurisdiction agreement in favour of the court granting relief may supply, or may reinforce, the necessary connection between that court and the relief sought (*Royal Bank of Scotland plc v FAL Oil Company Ltd* [2012] EWHC 3628 (Comm)). Conversely, it may be suggested that the necessary connection is removed if the parties have agreed to the exclusive jurisdiction of another court. It may be argued, however, that the relevant connection relates to the link between the subject matter of the remedy sought and the granting court. Where a freezing injunction operates *in personam* to restrain the conduct of the respondent the necessary connection exists, therefore, only where the defendant (or its agent) is present within the territory of that court, and is unaffected by any contractual agreement.

RICHARD FENTIMAN

Literature

George A Bermann, 'The Use of Antisuit Injunctions in International Litigation' (1990) 28 Colum.J.Transnat'l L. 589; Adrian Briggs and Peter Rees, *Civil Jurisdiction and Judgments* (5th edn, Informa 2009); Lawrence Collins, 'The Territorial Reach of Mareva Injunctions' (1989) 105 LQR 262; Lawrence Collins, 'United States Supreme Court Rejects Mareva Jurisdiction' (1999) 115 LQR 601; Lord Collins of Mapesbury and others (eds), *Dicey, Morris & Collins on the Conflict of Laws* (15th edn, Sweet & Maxwell 2012); Richard Fentiman, 'The Scope of Transnational Injunctions' (2013) NZJPIL 323; Richard Fentiman, *International Commercial Litigation* (2nd edn, OUP 2015); Steven Gee, *Gee on Commercial Injunctions* (5th edn, Sweet and Maxwell 2006); Trevor Hartley, 'Comity and the Use of Antisuit Injunctions' [1987] Am.J.Comp.L. 487; Adam Johnson, 'Interim Injunctions and International Jurisdiction' (2008) 27 CJQ 433; Louise Merrett, 'Worldwide Freezing Orders in Europe' [2008] LMCLQ 71; Horatia Muir Watt, 'Of Transcultural Borrowing, Hybrids, and the Complexity of Legal Knowledge' in Guy Canivet, Mads Andenas and Duncan Fairgrieve (eds), *Comparative Law Before the Courts* (BIICL 2004); Thomas Raphael, *Anti-Suit Injunctions* (OUP 2008).

Insolvency, applicable law

I. The close connection between jurisdiction and applicable law

Under most national laws, cross-border insolvency proceedings and their effects are governed by the → *lex fori* (*lex concursus*), which covers both procedural and substantive aspects of the insolvency. In other words, national laws generally endorse a private international law rule whereby determination of jurisdiction entails determination of the applicable law.

This approach has been justified by legal scholars on various grounds. Some scholars have stressed that insolvency proceedings involve procedural issues, which as such fall under the *lex fori*, following a well-established unilateral choice-of-law rule whereby proceedings should be governed by the law of the state in which they take place. Others have emphasized the functional relationship between law and proceedings, which implies that, if insolvency proceedings have been commenced in a state to reach certain goals, then the court should apply the *lex fori*. This is because such goals are defined by the *lex fori* and may be better achieved through the interplay between the respective roles ascribed to national authorities (court and liquidator or other insolvency practitioners) and to national substantive rules. Other scholars have classified the domestic provisions governing insolvency as overriding mandatory rules which restrain the application of foreign law. Such a view rests mainly on the role played by public interests in insolvency proceedings, that deeply affect a country's economy and welfare.

Finally, in the context of the Insolvency Regulation (Council Regulation (EC) No 1346/2000 of 29 May 2000 on insolvency proceedings, [2000] OJ L 160/1) and with certain adaptations, the so-called 'jurisdictional approach' as a private international law method has been evoked, intended to coordinate national laws by moving away from traditional criteria based on → territoriality. In particular, this method highlights that the rights and interests to be created, modified or terminated within the proceedings are 'territorially' confined to the state in which proceedings have been commenced.

However, each of these theories posits that, whenever acts, rights and obligations to be assessed in the course of insolvency proceedings neither arise within the proceedings nor stem from insolvency law, notwithstanding that their impact on the debtor's assets has to be appraised under such law, then the court should instead apply the ordinary bilateral conflict-of-laws rules applicable to such acts, rights or obligations.

II. Insolvency Regulation regime

1. General overview

The Insolvency Regulation has followed the same approach also shared by the Member States, and in arts 4 and 28 has established a rule according to which the law of the Member State where the insolvency proceedings are opened governs the proceedings, both main and secondary, and their effects. This also means that 'determination of the court with jurisdiction entails determination of the law which is to apply' (see Case C-341/04 *Eurofood IFSC Ltd* [2006] ECR I-3813, para 33; Case C-444/07 *MG Probud* [2010] ECR I-0417, para 25; Case C-191/10 *Rastelli Davide e C. Snc v Jean-Charles Hidoux, in his capacity as liquidator appointed by the court for the company Médiasucre international* [2012] OJ C 39/3, para 16; Case C-527/10 *ERSTE Bank Hungary Nyrt v Magyar Állam, BCL Trading GmbH, ERSTE Befektetési Zrt* [2012] OJ C 287/4, para 38).

However, since the Insolvency Regulation aims at protecting third party/creditor legitimate expectations and the legal certainty of transactions entered into in a Member State (or under the law of a Member State) other than that in which the proceedings are opened, the application of the *lex concursus* is subject to certain exceptions which are mainly set out in arts 5–15 (Case C-527/10 *ERSTE Bank Hungary Nyrt v Magyar Állam, BCL Trading GmbH, ERSTE Befektetési Zrt* [2012] OJ C 287/4, para 39; Case C-557/13 *Hermann Lutz v Elke Bäuerle* (16 April 2015), paras 34–5, which stress that the exceptions must be interpreted strictly, ie without going beyond what is necessary to protect legitimate expectations and the certainty of transactions; Case C-195/15 SCI Senior Home, in administration, v Gemeinde Wedemark, Hannoversche Volksbank eG (26 October 2016), para 28). In this regard, the Insolvency Regulation makes use of different techniques to determine the applicable law. It sets up a conflict-of-laws rule (for instance, as to the effects on contracts relating to immoveable property), or impliedly makes use of the relevant national, international or European conflict-of-laws rules the court has to comply with (for instance, as to the effects on transactions concluded in payments systems), or finally provides for uniform substantive rules (for instance, as to the determination of whether debtor's assets must be regarded as situated within the territory of a Member State at the time of the proceedings' opening – see Case C-649/13 *Comité d'entreprise de Nortel Networks SA and others v Cosme Rogeau* (11 June 2015), paras 50–1 – and to the obligations honoured after the opening).

All these techniques and their rationales deserve the utmost attention in order to appraise whether they bar the application of the *lex concursus* altogether or render it subject to certain conditions.

2. The effects of insolvency proceedings on the debtor, the creditors and third parties

According to art 4, the *lex concursus* governs the condition for commencing the proceedings, their conduct and their closure (see Case C-594/14 *Simona Kornhaas v Thomas Dithmar, acting as liquidator of the assets of Kornhaas Montage und Dienstleistung Ltd* (10 December 2015), para 19: '[i]n order to ensure the effectiveness of that provision, it must be interpreted as meaning that, first, the preconditions for the opening of insolvency proceedings, second, the rules which designate the persons who are obliged to request the opening of those proceedings and, third, the consequences of an infringement of that obligation fall within its scope'). Besides, it determines the effects of the proceedings on persons and assets involved in the insolvency.

Given that multiple proceedings may be opened against the same debtor, the effects could vary between proceedings according to the *lex concursus* governing them. Nevertheless, since main and secondary/territorial proceedings differ from each other in terms of extraterritoriality, only the effects determined by the centre of main interests' (COMIs') *lex concursus* are in principle recognized abroad (see extensively → Insolvency, cooperation and recognition).

The effects on the debtor concern primarily the extent of its divestment and residual powers. Accordingly, the *lex concursus* sets forth the liquidator's powers, essentially with the view to handling the debtor's assets to the creditors' satisfaction.

As regards the effects of the insolvency proceedings on creditors and third parties, according to art 4 the *lex concursus* determines the conditions under which set-offs (→ set-off) may be invoked (sub-paragraph d); the effects of the proceedings on creditors' individual actions (sub-paragraph f); the claims to be lodged and the treatment of those arising after the proceedings opening (sub-paragraph g); the rules governing the lodging verification and admission of claims (sub-paragraph h); distribution of the proceeds from the realization of assets, the ranking of claims and the right of creditors who have obtained partial satisfaction after the opening of the proceedings by means of secured rights or set-off (sub-paragraph i); creditor rights after the closure of the proceedings (sub-paragraph k).

However, as indicated above, the Insolvency Regulation aims to safeguard the legitimate expectations and certainty of commercial transactions. In particular, the Insolvency Regulation protects the interest of creditors and third parties to rely on the law which governed the transactions before the opening of insolvency proceedings, provided that this law is different from the *lex concursus*. Moreover, it may be that persons who rely on the applicability of this different law, even in the case of insolvency proceedings, are assessed as more inclined to grant credit (Recitals (11) and (25); Case C-527/10 *ERSTE Bank Hungary Nyrt v Magyar Állam, BCL Trading GmbH, ERSTE Befektetési Zrt* [2012] OJ C 287/4, para 41, as for secured creditors with rights *in rem*; see also Case C-195/15 *SCI Senior Home, in administration, v Gemeinde Wedemark, Hannoversche Volksbank eG* (26 October 2016), para 29).

3. Set-off within insolvency proceedings

Set-off consists of a means to extinguish reciprocally two or more claims, albeit at times only in part. Within insolvency proceedings, one creditor may seek to set-off its claim against a reciprocal credit of the insolvent debtor. In doing so, set-off deprives the estate and alters the *pari passu* principle, which at least covers the unsecured or same-ranking creditors' position in the proceedings. It may be that the law applicable to the debtor's claim, the law of the creditor's claim and the *lex concursus* differently govern the right to set-off and even its admissibility.

With the view to safeguarding claims arising prior to the opening of insolvency proceedings, the Insolvency Regulation establishes in arts 4(2)(d) and 6 a comparison between the *lex concursus* and the law applicable to the debtor's claim, according to which creditors may demand set-off under the latter law even though the *lex concursus* prohibits it or imposes more restrictive conditions. In other words, arts 4(2)(d) and 6 shape a set-off-friendly regime under which the creditor may rely on the law applicable to the claims of the insolvent debtor even when the *lex concursus* does not allow for set-off. The law applicable to the insolvent debtor's claim will be determined under the Rome I Regulation (Regulation (EC) No 593/2008 of the European Parliament and of the Council of 17 June 2008 on the law applicable to contractual obligations (Rome I), [2008] OJ L 177/6; → Rome Convention and Rome I Regulation (contractual obligations)) or the → Rome II Regulation (non-contractual obligations) (Regulation (EC) No 864/2007 of the European Parliament and of the Council of 11 July 2007 on the law applicable to non-contractual obligations (Rome II), [2007] OJ L 199/40), depending respectively on whether the claim is contractual or non-contractual. It is worth noting that, as regards set-off invoked out of insolvency proceedings, the Rome I Regulation draws inspiration from the Insolvency Regulation when stating the application of the law governing the claim against which the right to set-off is asserted whenever the right itself is not agreed by the parties (art 17).

Finally, although foreign laws may determine the right to set-off, the *lex concursus* should nevertheless continue to govern the procedural issues related to the set-off, such as the formalities and procedural time-limits to demand it.

4. The effects of insolvency proceedings on individual actions and lawsuits pending

It is well known that insolvency proceedings impinge on the creditor's right to bring individual actions against the debtor. As already noted, the issue falls within the scope of the *lex concursus* according to art 4.

Given that an individual action may jeopardize the purposes of insolvency proceedings and above all unity of the estate and collective satisfaction, the law of the Member State where such proceedings are commenced determines whether and to what extent a creditor retains such right. However, art 4 provides for an exception to this rule in the case of lawsuits pending at the time when insolvency proceedings are opened. The extent of this exception is stated at art 15, according to which the effects of insolvency proceedings on a pending lawsuit concerning debtor's assets or rights subject to the divestment must be governed by the law of the Member State where the lawsuit is pending (→ *lex fori*).

ANTONIO LEANDRO

In other words, the *lex concursus* governs the effects of the insolvency proceedings on enforcement actions, irrespective of where brought and whether commenced prior to or after the opening of insolvency proceedings, while the *lex fori* governs those effects as regards the lawsuits pending (see Case C-212/15 ENEFI Energiahatékonysági Nyrt v Direcţia Generală Regională a Finanţelor Publice Braşov (DGRFP) (9 November 2016), paras 31–6). In this case the *lex fori* and *lex concursus* will 'coincide' if lawsuits are pending in the Member State of the insolvency proceedings.

5. The ranking of claims: conflict and coordination between leges concursus

Priorities and other secured rights adversely affect the *par condicio creditorum*. As a general rule, the ranking of claims is determined by the *lex concursus*.

Given that the Insolvency Regulation allows for the opening of main and secondary proceedings against the same debtor in different Member States, it may happen that the ranking determined by the law of the Member State of the COMI differs from that determined by the law of the Member State of the establishment. Since creditors may lodge their claims in all the proceedings, the same claim could have different ranking positions depending on the law governing each proceedings.

Should the claims have the same ranking and multiple lodging occur, the 'hotchpot rule' of art 20(2) provides that the creditor who obtains a dividend on his claim will share in distributions made in other proceedings only where creditors of the same ranking and category have obtained an equivalent dividend thereby. Moreover, local creditors, that is those with domicile or habitual residence (→ Domicile, habitual residence and establishment) in the Member State of the establishment or whose claims arise from activities the debtor carried out from the establishment, may rely on the ranking established by the local *lex concursus* to the extent that they apply for the opening of secondary proceedings rather than lodging their claims in the main proceedings. This is particularly when the debtor has assets or exercises its activity solely in the state of the establishment.

Such tactics and situations may harm the objectives of the main proceedings which the liquidator (or other insolvency practitioner) determines and seeks (see → Insolvency, cooperation and recognition also for remarks on the practice of the 'synthetic/virtual secondary proceedings' endorsed by the Insolvency Regulation (recast)).

6. Safeguarding rights in rem *and reservation of title*

Creditor and third party rights *in rem* on assets belonging to a debtor which are located in a Member State other than that of the insolvency proceedings at the time of opening are subject to a rule aiming to protect legitimate expectations and legal certainty. Article 5 states that the opening of insolvency proceedings does not affect those rights.

The concept of 'right *in rem*' is as wide as the nature of assets involved (see Case C-195/15 *SCI Senior Home, in administration, v Gemeinde Wedemark, Hannoversche Volksbank eG* (26 October 2016), para 21). For instance, art 5 refers (i) to the right to dispose of assets or have them disposed of and to obtain satisfaction from the proceeds of or income from those assets, in particular by virtue of a lien or a mortgage, (ii) to the exclusive right to have a claim met, in particular a right guaranteed by a lien or by assignment by way of a guarantee, or (iii) to the right to demand the assets from anyone with possession or use of them.

As for the *res* at stake, art 5 encompasses tangible or intangible, moveable or immoveable assets, both specific assets and collections of indefinite assets as a whole which change from time to time. Article 5 must be applied in conjunction with art 2(g), which includes the definition of 'Member State in which assets are situated'. For instance, in case of claims, that is 'the Member State within the territory of which the third party required to meet them has the centre of his main interests, as determined in art 3(1)' (art 2(g)).

So conceived, the rule enshrined in art 5 derogates from the rule on applicability of the *lex concursus*. In particular, it safeguards the rights *in rem* following the principle affirmed in Recital (25) that 'the basis, validity and extent of [such rights] should . . . normally be determined according to the *lex situs* and not be affected by the opening of insolvency proceedings'. Therefore, the rights deserve protection insofar as they have been regularly created as rights *in rem* under the *lex rei sitae*, ie the law of the Member State on whose territory the asset concerned is situated, irrespective of whether they may be claimed according to the *lex concursus* (see Case C-527/10 *ERSTE Bank Hungary Nyrt v Magyar Állam, BCL Trading GmbH, ERSTE Befektetési Zrt* [2012] OJ C 287/4, paras 40–2; Case C-557/13 *Hermann Lutz v Elke*

Bäuerle (16 April 2015) concerning the right resulting from the attachment of a bank account; Case C-195/15 *SCI Senior Home, in administration, v Gemeinde Wedemark, Hannoversche Volksbank eG* (26 October 2016), para 18).

However, in this case the Insolvency Regulation adopts a technique that does not provide for a conflict-of-laws rule requiring application of the *lex rei sitae* to the effects of insolvency proceedings. This contrasts with the approach in other cases that derogate art 4, for example with regard to contracts relating to immoveable property (see below). In fact, art 5 provides a substantive safeguard clause which preserves the rights validly created under the *lex rei sitae* against the effects of the insolvency on such rights as determined by the *lex concursus*.

That being said, if it is true that a right *in rem* deserves protection insofar as the *res* is placed outside the state of the opening of the proceedings and that the *lex rei sitae* grants such right notwithstanding the opening of insolvency proceedings, it is also true that, if the *res* lies in the Member State of the proceedings, art 5 does not apply, and the right will be preserved only if the *lex concursus* so provides.

It should finally be noted that the transfer of assets from the state where insolvency proceedings have been requested may veil abuse where it is aimed at later invoking art 5 in order to hinder the application of the *lex concursus*.

Against these and similar tactics, the Insolvency Regulation first provides that the safeguard clause may not preclude avoidance actions as referred to in art 4(2)(m), ie the application of the suspect period rules of *lex concursus* on detrimental acts (art 5(4)). Second, it should be borne in mind that art 5 is inapplicable whenever insolvency proceeding are opened in the state where the *res* is located.

A similar provision applies to rights based on reservation of title, where the relevant goods are situated in a Member State other than that of the proceedings at the opening time. Article 7, which applies to both the seller's and the purchaser's insolvency, protects the reservation of title, while at the same time preserving application of the *lex concursus* as to avoidance actions concerning the acts causing the reservation.

7. The effects of insolvency proceedings on ongoing contracts

The *lex concursus* determines the effects of insolvency proceedings on the contracts entered into by the debtor (art 4(2)(e)). As that law governs the extent to which the debtor is divested or alternatively remains in possession, it also determines whether the contracts may be terminated or continued, and if continued, whether the derived → contractual obligations are to be performed by the debtor or liquidator.

Even in this regard, the Insolvency Regulation allows for exceptions to the direct applicability of the *lex concursus*, which provide that the effects of the opening of the insolvency on certain contracts are governed by the law applicable to them to be determined by other conflict-of-laws rules. These exceptions consist of (i) contracts relating to immoveable property, to be governed by the *lex rei sitae* under art 8, (ii) rights and obligations arising out of a payment system or a financial market, to be governed by the law applicable to the system or the market under art 9 and (iii) contracts of employment, to be governed by the *lex contractus* under art 10.

The techniques are quite different from one another. In the case of immoveable property, the Insolvency Regulation establishes a specific conflict-of-laws rule adopting the *situs rei* as connecting factor, while in the other cases the Insolvency Regulation refers to the conflict-of-laws rules provided in the private international law system of the court conducting the insolvency proceedings.

Be that as it may, the law of the state of the proceedings will eventually govern the effects in question as law designated by these conflict-of-laws rules rather than as law applicable as *lex concursus*.

Apart from the dissimilar techniques, such provisions aim to ensure legal certainty to contracts *in rem*, which are secured by their own law against the opening of the proceedings, or contracts entered into in self-governed systems, such as the payment systems and financial markets. As for employment contracts, protection of the employees, that inspires the ordinary conflict-of-laws rules, underlies the legislative choice not to provide for a different regime in case of insolvency of the employer. However, it is worth noting that the *lex contractus* will govern only the effects of the opening of the insolvency on such contracts, while other profiles such as the ranking of the employee claims pertain to the *lex concursus*.

8. The treatment of the detrimental acts

As noted above, the validity and efficacy of contracts and other acts which may diminish the debtor's assets are subject to the *lex concursus*, irrespective of whether they give rise to rights which are not affected *per se* by the opening of the insolvency proceedings, such as rights *in rem* (art 5), the right to set-off (art 6) and the rights based on a reservation of title (art 7). The competence of the *lex concursus* clearly stems from art 4(2)(m), which refers to the 'rules relating to the voidness, voidability and unenforceability of legal acts detrimental to all the creditors'.

Generally speaking, 'avoidance rules' (and related proceedings) amount to both substantive and procedural devices serving the insolvency proceedings' objectives, particularly creditor satisfaction, by means of measures preserving the debtor's assets. Many legal systems provide for rules on the so-called suspect period that may affect certain claims, and on set aside actions aimed at returning assets to the estate.

However, the scope of the *lex concursus* is restrained by two provisions. The first, set out in art 9(2), subjects 'avoidance actions' concerning payments and financial markets transactions to the law governing the system or the market concerned. The second, set out in art 13, excludes the application of art 4(2)(m) whenever the person who benefited from an act detrimental to all the creditors provides evidence both that the act is governed by the law of a Member State other than the law of the proceedings and that such law 'does not allow any means of challenging that act in the relevant case'.

While the specific rule in matters of payment and financial markets transaction is self-evident regarding the specificity of the system under which the detrimental act arises, art 13 attracts major attention as it amounts to a general exception to the applicability of the *lex concursus*. Article 13 aims to preserve the legitimate expectations of third parties who had dealings with the debtor in Member States (and under laws) other than those in which the proceedings have subsequently been opened, to rely on the validity and efficacy of the act according to its applicable law. The Insolvency Regulation does not determine such law, since its scope is confined to insolvency issues. Instead it provides third parties with a means to demonstrate that the act detrimental to collective creditors was, and still is valid and effective according to its applicable law, even though their counterparty has been declared insolvent.

This scheme certainly entails that third parties will take advantage of the *lex concursus* where more favourable than the *lex causae*.

Accordingly, art 13 should not be conceived as a special choice-of-law rule in matters of detrimental acts, which substitutes the general rule of art 4, but rather as a rule providing an exception to the application of the *lex concursus* where this would affect acts protected by the *lex causae* (see Case C-557/13 *Hermann Lutz v Elke Bäuerle* (16 April 2015), para 31). Third parties bear the burden of establishing the content of the *lex causae* 'in the relevant case' (see Case C-557/13 *Hermann Lutz v Elke Bäuerle* (16 April 2015), paras 44–56, in which the Court, aiming to safeguard the uniform application of the Insolvency Regulation, held that art 13 also covers limitation periods or other time-bars as well as both substantive and procedural requirements for the exercise of an action to set a transaction aside). It is disputed among scholars whether third parties may invoke only the provisions on insolvency of the *lex causae* to prevent the liquidator from challenging the act or may provide evidence that the act is unchallengeable according to the law governing it. However, the ECJ upheld the latter view, stating that 'a person benefiting from a detrimental act must prove that the act at issue cannot be challenged either on the basis of the insolvency provisions of the lex causae or on the basis of the lex causae, taken as a whole' (Case C-310/14 *Nike European Operations Netherlands BV v Sportland Oy* (15 October 2015), para 34).

9. Uniform rules on the protection of specific legal situations arising after the opening of insolvency proceedings

In the interests of third party expectations concerning the validity of certain acts disposed after the opening of proceedings, the Insolvency Regulation provides for other rules derogating the direct application of the *lex concursus*.

The validity of the debtor's disposal of immoveable assets, registered ships and aircraft, as well as registered securities is governed respectively by the *lex rei sitae* and by the law of the authority under which the register is kept (art 14).

Article 24 in turn sets forth a substantive rule concerning obligations honoured for the benefit of the insolvent debtor (Case C-251/12 *Christian Van Buggenhout and Ilse Van de Mierop, acting as liquidators in the insolvency of Grontimmo SA v Banque Internationale à Luxembourg SA* [2013] OJ C 344/29, para 30 ff), stating that honouring such obligations discharges only persons who were unaware of the opening of the insolvency proceedings in another Member State. In this regard, art 24(2) establishes a *iuris tantum* presumption whereby being unaware or aware of the insolvency proceedings depends on having honoured the obligation before or after the judgment opening the proceedings has been published according to art 21.

The different techniques, whereby art 14 provides for a choice-of-law rule while art 24 for a substantive rule, nevertheless share the aim of protecting third parties who enter in contact with an insolvent debtor and who, as frequently happens in cross-border situations, in good faith may be unaware of the opening of insolvency proceedings.

While art 14 protects the legitimate expectations of third parties to see the validity of their purchase governed by the proper and known law, art 24 directly derives the debt-discharging effect from the excusable ignorance as to both the opening of insolvency proceedings and the subsequent divestment of the debtor.

10. Remarks on certain issues not solved by the Insolvency Regulation

The Insolvency Regulation expressly addresses neither the issue of *renvoi* nor whether the application of a law other than the *lex concursus* should be confined to insolvency provisions.

As far as *renvoi* is concerned, given that the Insolvency Regulation provides for a uniform conflict-of-laws regime in matters of cross-border insolvency, there should be no place for national conflict-of-laws rules in order to preserve uniformity in designating the applicable law. However, it should be remembered that, for certain categories of acts and effects, the Insolvency Regulation refers to conflict-of-laws rules as provided by a Member State or EU Regulations. At least in this regard, the issue of admitting or excluding the *renvoi* will depend on the relevant choice such rules make.

In order to answer the question of whether the law to be applied should be confined to insolvency provisions, it is necessary to examine the scope of the relevant Insolvency Regulation provisions. In particular, rules devoted expressly to govern the 'effect of the insolvency' on certain acts, rights or obligations (arts 8, 9, 10 and 11) seem to seek the application of the provisions of insolvency law, as the law intended to govern such effects.

For other cases, applying the sole insolvency law proves to fit all the situations in which the Insolvency Regulation allows putting aside the insolvency provisions of the *lex concursus*.

Thus, for instance, appraising the right to demand the set-off according to art 6 seems to require an assessment on the provisions of the law applicable to the debtor's claim in the case of set-off demanded within an insolvency proceeding, so that only the insolvency provisions of the law applicable to the debtor's claim should thereby come into consideration. On the contrary, in matters of debtor's disposal of immoveable assets, registered ships and aircraft, as well as registered securities, since art 14 generically refers to the 'validity of the act', the law applicable should primarily determine the validity under civil and commercial provisions.

As for the detrimental acts regime, third parties may rely on insolvency or civil/commercial provisions of the law governing the act depending on the legal basis under which the liquidator 'in the relevant case' brings an action against them (but see the aforementioned views of the ECJ in Case C-310/14 *Nike European Operations Netherlands BV v Sportland Oy* (15 October 2015), para 34).

Finally, since arts 6 and 14 do not explicitly refer to Member State law, the question of whether they also allow for applying non-Member States law arises.

An affirmative answer finds logical reasons for both of them. As far as set-off is concerned, the relevant law should be frequently determined according to the Rome I Regulation, whose universal scope may lead to the application of non-Member States law. As for art 14, it also addresses the protection of persons unaware of the insolvency opening, ie a condition more likely to be realistic when the asset disposed of is located outside the EU, also taking into account that the publication regime concerning the notice of the judgments opening the proceedings is limited to Member States.

11. Should public policy and overriding mandatory provisions be disregarded?

Unlike the recognition and enforcement of judgments (see → Insolvency, cooperation and recognition), the → public policy (*ordre public*) exception does not work within the Insolvency Regulation in relation to the applicable law.

However, the → *lex fori* (as *lex concursus*) is so widely entitled to govern substantive and procedural issues of the proceedings that one may wonder how a foreign law infringing its fundamental principles should anyway be applied by the court.

Having regard to the wide role awarded to the *lex fori*, it seems the Insolvency Regulation impliedly remits to that law all the insolvency profiles not covered by itself, including the treatment of the public policy exception and its consequences.

Moreover, as already noted the Insolvency Regulation employs choice-of-law rules stemming from other EU private international acts or from national law, with whose provisions the court of the insolvency proceedings has to comply in matters of public policy.

Given that the public policy exception may arise at the recognition and enforcement stage, and that several principles amounting to public policy are shared among the Member States, as they may derive from international and EU law, the court is to conduct the proceedings, and in particular in view of their universal effects the main proceedings, paying attention that its judgments and the proceedings do not offend the public policy of other Member States. This should lead the courts not to apply foreign laws if the final result conflicts with the fundamental principles shared by the home and the requested state.

As noted elsewhere (see → Insolvency, cooperation and recognition), even though not expressly governed by the Insolvency Regulation, the public policy exception would nonetheless operate within the framework of EU private international law. This means in turn that it should operate and be interpreted restrictively, especially where the foreign law in question belongs to a Member State or deals with matters subject to EU harmonization measures.

Finally, as far as → overriding mandatory provisions are concerned, lacking express rules but again having regard to the wide role awarded to the → *lex fori*, they may come into consideration to prevent the functioning of bilateral choice-of-law rules with a view to protecting national public interests. This may happen, for instance, when mandatory rules govern certain substantive effects of the insolvency on employment contracts.

How and to what extent such exception should operate depends again both on the national private international law system and on the specific rules of other EU Regulations (such as the Rome I Regulation) which may interact with the Insolvency Regulation.

12. Applicable law in the Insolvency Regulation (recast)

The Insolvency Regulation (recast) (Regulation (EU) 2015/848 of the European Parliament and of the Council of 20 May 2015 on insolvency proceedings (recast) [2015] OJ L 141/19)), which will almost entirely apply from 26 June 2017, slightly addresses the applicable law.

However, arts 11(2) and 13(2) are noteworthy because they manage, in matters of contracts relating to immoveable property and contracts of employment, respectively, the effects of the insolvency laid down by the (local) *lex contractus* when the insolvency is being handled abroad in the main proceedings. In particular, pursuant to art 13(2), the courts of the Member State where the debtor has an establishment – ie the place where presumptively the employee habitually carries out his work or has been engaged – retain jurisdiction to approve the termination or modification of employment contracts even if no secondary proceedings occur in that state, in case such termination or modification requires approval by a court (see also Recital (72)).

Article 18 extends to pending arbitration proceedings, the afore-mentioned rule whereby the effects of insolvency proceedings on a pending lawsuit concerning assets or rights included in the debtor's insolvency estate must be governed by the law of the Member State where the lawsuit is pending. In other words, the law of the state where arbitration has its seat will apply (see also Recital (73), which stresses that art 18 'should not affect national rules on recognition and enforcement of arbitral awards').

Finally, in order to reduce uncertainty concerning the localization of the debtor's assets (see, again, Case C-649/13 *Comité d'entreprise de Nortel Networks SA and others v Cosme Rogeau* (11 June 2015)), the Insolvency Regulation (recast) provides for a broader and more detailed definition, including among others registered shares in companies, financial instruments, cash held in credit institutions accounts and copyrights (art 2(9)). As a result, all the rules whose functioning depends on the concept 'Member State in which assets are situated' should benefit from such a broader and more detailed definition.

ANTONIO LEANDRO

Literature

Stefania Bariatti, 'Le garanzie finanziarie nell'insolvenza transnazionale: l'attuazione della direttiva 2002/47/CE' (2004) 40 Riv.Dir.Int'le Priv. & Proc. 841; Stefania Bariatti, 'Recent Case-Law Concerning Jurisdiction and the Recognition of Judgment under the EC European Insolvency Regulation' (2009) 73 RabelsZ 629; Stefania Bariatti and Paul Omar (eds), *The Grand Project: Reform of the European Insolvency Regulation* (INSOL Europe 2014); Massimo V Benedettelli, '"Centro degli interessi principali" del debitore e forum shopping nella disciplina comunitaria delle procedure di insolvenza' (2004) 40 Riv.Dir.Int'le Priv. & Proc. 499; Reinhard Bork, Principles of Cross-Border Insolvency Law (Intersentia 2017); Reinhard Bork and Renato Mangano, European Cross-Border Insolvency Law (OUP 2016); Titia M Bos, 'The European Insolvency Regulation and the Harmonization of Private international law in Europe' (2003) 50 NILR 31; Luigi Daniele, 'Legge applicabile e diritto uniforme nel regolamento comunitario relativo alle procedure di insolvenza' (2002) 38 Riv.Dir.Int'le Priv. & Proc. 33; Ian Fletcher, *Insolvency in Private international law* (2nd edn, OUP 2005); Giulio Cesare Giorgini, *Méthodes conflictuelles et règles matérielles dans l'application des 'nouveaux instruments' de règlement de la faillite internationale* (Dalloz 2006); Burkhard Hess, Paul Oberhammer and Thomas Pfeiffer (eds), *European Insolvency Regulation: Heidelberg–Luxembourg–Vienna Report* (Beck-Hart-Nomos 2013); Antonio Leandro, *Il ruolo della lex concursus nel regolamento comunitario sulle procedure di insolvenza* (Cacucci 2008); Antonio Leandro, 'La legge applicabile alla revocatoria fallimentare nel regolamento (CE) n° 1346/2000' (2009) 1 CDT 102; Antonio Leandro, 'A First Critical Appraisal of The New European Insolvency Regulation' (2016) Il Diritto dell'Unione Europea 215; Peter Mankowski, Michael F. Müller and Jessica Schmidt, EuInsVO 2015. Europäische Insolvenzverordnung 2015. Kommentar (Beck 2016); François Mélin, 'La loi applicable à la compensation dans les procédures communautaires d'insolvabilité' (2007) 134 J.Dr.Int'l 515; Gabriel Moss, Ian Fletcher and Stuart Isaacs (eds), Moss, Fletcher and Isaacs on the EU Regulation on Insolvency Proceedings (3rd edn, OUP 2016); Klaus Pannen, *European Insolvency Regulation* (De Gruyter Recht 2007); Michaël Raimon, *Le règlement communautaire 1346/2000 du 29 mai 2000 relatif aux procédures d'insolvabilité* (LGDJ 2007); Miguel Virgós Soriano and Francisco Garcimartín Alférez, *The European Insolvency Regulation: Law and Practice* (Kluwer 2004); Bob Wessels, 'The Secured Creditor in Cross-border Finance Transactions under the EC Insolvency Regulation' (2003) 18 J.I.B.L.R. 135; Bob Wessels, *Cross-border Insolvency Law: International Instruments Commentary* (Kluwer 2007); Bob Wessels, *International Insolvency Law Part I. Global Perspectives on Cross-border Insolvency Law* (4th edn, Wolters Kluwer 2015).

Insolvency, cooperation and recognition

I. Overview of national and international approaches

When aiming to solve cross-border crises, insolvency proceedings are often designed in national legal systems with a view to realizing liquidation and distribution, or implementing a rescue plan including assets located abroad.

The so-called principle of universality serves these purposes, by virtue of its rationale to conceive the insolvency proceedings as producing effects wherever the debtor's assets are located. On the contrary, according to the principle of → territoriality the insolvency proceedings confine their effects within the state of the opening.

When the national law takes inspiration from universality *stricto sensu*, the state of the proceedings will not recognize foreign bankruptcy judgments and the effects of the proceedings over the debtor and third parties. Nor will the foreign representative's, eg the liquidator's, powers be recognized, due to the assumption that only national proceedings may produce effects. On the contrary, territoriality *stricto sensu* implies that the effects of both national and foreign proceedings are confined to the country where they have been opened.

It seems clear that, unless coordinated, these approaches run counter to the reciprocal recognition of proceedings as well as to cooperation between the authorities involved in individual proceedings, thereby adversely affecting the unity and efficiency of the insolvency administration whenever several proceedings are opened in different states against the same debtor. As a matter of principle, it makes no difference in this regard whether those proceedings aim at winding-up or rescue purposes, even though the major problems arise as to the liquidation of disseminated assets and to the distribution of proceeds.

To date, indeed, also against the background of the UNCITRAL work on cross-border insolvency (namely the Model Law on Cross-Border Insolvency (UNCITRAL (ed), Model Law (1997) on Cross-Border Insolvency with Guide to Enactment (2013): Model Law on Cross-Border Insolvency of the United Commission on International Trade Law, Resolution 52/158 adopted by the General Assembly, 30

January 1998, No E.99.V.3., General Assembly Resolution 52/158 of 15 December 1997) and the Practical Guide on Cross-border Insolvency Cooperation (UNCITRAL (ed), UNCITRAL Practice Guide on Cross-Border Insolvency Cooperation (1 July 2009)), numerous states have endorsed a combination of universality and territoriality so as to allow foreign opening judgments and proceedings to be recognized in their territory, without preventing their own courts from opening insolvency proceedings against the same debtor.

The UNCITRAL Model Law on Cross-Border Insolvency with Guide to Enactment and the Insolvency Regulation (Council Regulation (EC) No 1346/2000 of 29 May 2000 on insolvency proceedings, [2000] OJ L 160/1), as well as earlier the 1990 European Convention on Certain International Aspects of Bankruptcy (Council of Europe, Istanbul 5 June 1990, ETS No 136; 30 ILM 165) and the 1995 Brussels Convention on Insolvency Proceedings ((1996) 35 ILM 1236), all classify proceedings commenced where the debtor has its centre of main interests (COMI) as universal proceedings, and those taking place where the debtor has an establishment as territorial proceedings. Accordingly, if universality admits that other proceedings can be opened abroad, it ultimately conceives of itself as limited. On the other hand, states oriented to territoriality ultimately deem national proceedings as a device that the foreign authorities, and in the first place liquidators (or other insolvency practitioners), may employ to achieve the aims of the proceedings in which they have been appointed.

The openness towards foreign insolvency proceedings that run parallel to national proceedings leads courts and liquidators to shape practical methods to seek effective and efficient cooperation. Article 27 UNCITRAL Model Law on Cross-Border Insolvency with Guide to Enactment sets out forms of cooperation such as entering into insolvency agreements subject to court approval, or communicating information among the liquidators appointed in each proceedings.

Naturally, the more states enact the UNCITRAL Model Law on Cross-Border Insolvency with Guide to Enactment, or generically share a similar approach, the more effortless recognition and coordination become. This also occurs between states which enter into multilateral or bilateral treaties providing them with a common recognition and cooperation framework. This happens in particular among EU Member States as a result of the recognition and cooperation system enshrined in the Insolvency Regulation, which operates as follows.

II. Preliminary remarks on the Insolvency Regulation cooperation and recognition regime

As noted elsewhere (→ Insolvency, jurisdiction and *vis attractiva*), the Insolvency Regulation allows for the opening of insolvency proceedings whose features and effects differ. Main proceedings are to be opened in the Member State where the debtor has its COMI, while secondary proceedings are to be opened in the Member State where the debtor, whose COMI is in another Member State, has an establishment. Secondary proceedings may even be opened prior to main ones in compliance with art 3(4), although in this case they are properly referred to as 'territorial proceedings'.

Main proceedings produce effects across the EU (excluding → Denmark) according to the principle of universality, while secondary proceedings have local/territorial effects, restricted to assets situated in the Member State where they have been opened. As a consequence, the principle of universality *stricto sensu* characterizes the main proceedings, as long as no secondary proceedings have been opened (Case C-444/07 *MG Probud Gdynia sp. z o.o.* [2010] ECR I-0417, para 24).

Since a debtor may have only one COMI and an indefinite number of establishments, the Insolvency Regulation admits that a single main proceeding and several secondary proceedings may coexist against the same debtor. The coordination between such proceedings amounts to a crucial objective of the Insolvency Regulation, given that opening more than one proceeding entails that the debtor's crisis covers more than one state, and that accordingly the EU interest in a smooth, efficient and time-costs-oriented insolvency administration intensifies.

In this regard, Recital (20) stresses that 'main insolvency proceedings and secondary proceedings can ... contribute to the effective realization of the total assets only if all the concurrent proceedings pending are coordinated'.

However, since cooperation implies that the proceedings have been opened and have effects abroad, it is necessary to evaluate the

Insolvency Regulation regime of recognition of judgments and proceedings.

III. Recognition and enforcement framework

1. Recognition and enforcement of judgments/recognition of proceedings

The Insolvency Regulation provides for a recognition regime concerning both the judgments handed down within the proceedings and the proceedings themselves.

Judgments opening the proceedings, whether main or secondary/territorial, rendered by courts competent according to art 3, are recognized in other Member States as soon as they become effective in the state of the opening. In this regard arts 16 and 17 endorse the principle of automatic recognition, which matches that of mutual trust, and that governs the relationships between the courts of Member States from the EU private international law perspective (Case C-341/04 *Eurofood IFSC Ltd* [2006] ECR I-3813, para 39; Case C-444/07 *MG Probud* [2010] ECR I-0417, paras 27–9).

Such principles also encompass judgments concerning the course and closing of the proceedings, as well as any composition approved by courts (art 25; Case C-444/07 *MG Probud* [2010] ECR I-0417, para 26). The same treatment applies to 'ancillary' judgments, ie those deriving directly from the insolvency proceedings and which are closely linked to them.

As regards enforcement, the Insolvency Regulation provides for the application of the Brussels Convention (Brussels Convention of 27 September 1968 on jurisdiction and the enforcement of judgments in civil and commercial matters, [1972] OJ L 299/32, consolidated version, [1998] OJ C 27/1), with the exception of the provision establishing the grounds for refusal that are established directly by the Insolvency Regulation. The reference to the Convention has to be interpreted as reference to the Brussels I Regulation (Regulation (EC) No 44/2001 of 22 December 2000 on jurisdiction and the recognition and enforcement of judgments in civil and commercial matters, [2001] OJ L 12/1) and, as of 10 January 2015, to the Brussels I Regulation (recast) (Regulation (EU) No 1215/2012 of the European Parliament and of the Council of 12 December 2012 on jurisdiction and the recognition and enforcement of judgments in civil and commercial matters (recast), [2012] OJ L 351/1; → Brussels I (Convention and Regulation)), whereby the enforcement will become even easier due to the removal of the *exequatur*.

While mutual recognition applies to both main and secondary proceedings, the effects of the judgments are to be determined separately from the effects of the proceedings. In this regard the distinction between main and secondary proceedings is again of the utmost importance. Indeed, while the judgment opening the insolvency proceedings benefits from the mutual recognition irrespective of whether it opens main or secondary proceedings, the effects of the secondary proceedings judgment are limited to the Member State of the court. The Insolvency Regulation only preserves territoriality whenever third parties intend to challenge the effects of secondary proceedings. To this end, art 17(2) prevents third parties from challenging the decision opening secondary proceedings in any other Member State.

In compliance with the limited universality approach, the judgment opening main proceedings has effects in other Member States as long as no secondary proceedings are opened there. Once secondary proceedings have been opened, the courts which provide the opening has jurisdiction, concurrently with the courts of the main proceedings, to determine which debtor's assets fall within the secondary proceedings (Case C-649/13 *Comité d'entreprise de Nortel Networks SA and others v Cosme Rogeau* (11 June 2015), paras 39–46).

2. The concepts of 'opening judgment' and 'opening time'

The effects of the judgments abroad are mainly determined by the *lex concursus* of the state where insolvency proceedings have been opened (art 17(1)). Such effects depend logically on the nature and features of the proceedings opened.

Articles 1 and 2 supported by Annexes A and B provide directives on how to assess when courts pronounce a judgment aimed at opening insolvency proceedings falling within the Insolvency Regulation (Case C-341/04 *Eurofood IFSC Ltd* [2006] ECR I-3813, paras 53 ff; Case C-247/12 *Meliha Veli Mustafa v Direktor na fond 'Garantirani vzemania na rabotnitsite i sluzhitelite' kam Natsionalnia osiguritelen institut* [2013] OJ C 164/7, para 36; Case C-461/11 *Ulf Kazimierz Radziejewski v Kronofogdemyndigheten i Stockholm* (8 November 2012), paras 23–4). For the sake of brevity, it should be borne in mind that, following art 1, the Insolvency Regulation applies to collective insolvency proceedings which entail the partial or total divestment of a debtor and the appointment of a liquidator. Annex A lists which proceedings have such material scope, while Annex B lists those of a winding-up nature (which in several cases match those listed in Annex A).

While non-listed proceedings should be governed by the Insolvency Regulation insofar as they meet the requirements defined in art 1, the ECJ seems inclined to exclude proceedings not listed in the aforementioned Annexes (Case C-461/11 *Ulf Kazimierz Radziejewski v Kronofogdemyndigheten i Stockholm* (8 November 2012), para 24). The Insolvency Regulation (recast) (Regulation (EU) 2015/848 of the European Parliament and of the Council of 20 May 2015 on insolvency proceedings (recast) [2015] OJ L 141/19) upholds this approach: new Annex A 'exhaustively' lists national insolvency procedures falling within the Regulation (see Recital (9)).

In any case, according to the ECJ, the concept of 'opening judgment' 'must be regarded as including not only a decision which is formally described as an opening decision by the legislation of the Member State of the court that handed it down, but also a decision handed down following an application, based on the debtor's insolvency, seeking the opening of proceedings referred to in' the aforementioned Annexes (Case C-341/04 *Eurofood IFSC Ltd* [2006] ECR I-3813, para 54).

Appraising the 'opening time' is also of the utmost importance especially with respect to main proceedings, since the Insolvency Regulation allows for only one main proceedings: the issue of which judgment in the case of multiple openings in different states prevails must be, in fact, resolved in favour of the judgment first rendered (see Case C-341/04 *Eurofood IFSC Ltd* [2006] ECR I-3813, para 49; Case C-116/11 *Bank Handlowy w Warszawie SA and PPHU «ADAX»/Ryszard Adamiak v Christianapol sp. z o.o.* (22 November 2012), para 51).

The 'opening time' consists in the time 'at which the judgment opening the proceedings becomes effective, whether it is a final judgment or not' (art 2(f)). Elements such as effectiveness and finality depend heavily on the *lex concursus*, so that the 'opening time' concept is to be appraised on the basis of national law. This time appraisal applies to the opening of both main and secondary proceedings since, according to arts 4 and 28, the substantive scope of the *lex concursus* does not vary in this regard by reason of the nature of the proceedings.

3. Public policy as ground for refusing recognition and enforcement

The Insolvency Regulation provides for only two grounds for refusing recognition and enforcement.

First, judgments directly deriving from the proceedings or closely linked to them as well as judgments concerning the course or closure of proceedings and preservation measures granted pending the request of opening which result in a limitation of personal freedom or postal secrecy may not be recognized (art 25(3)).

Second, Member States may refuse to recognize insolvency proceedings opened in another Member State, or to enforce a judgment rendered in the context of such proceedings, where the effects of such recognition or enforcement would be manifestly contrary to their public policy, 'in particular [their] fundamental principles or the constitutional rights and liberties of the individual' (art 26).

With regard to the → public policy (*ordre public*) exception, art 26 is concerned with the substantive differences among national laws in matters of the effects of proceedings, in order to prevent them infringing the requested state's fundamental principles. Many of the principles thus invoked derive from EU law and international law, such as the procedural rights and freedoms stemming from the Charter of Fundamental Rights of the European Union (of 18 December 2000, [2000] OJ C 364/1) and the European Convention on Human Rights (European Convention of 4 November 1950 for the Protection of Human Rights and Fundamental Freedoms, 213 UNTS 221) (Case C-341/04 *Eurofood IFSC Ltd* [2006] ECR I-3813, para 65).

However, since recognition and enforcement are informed by the principle of mutual trust between Member States, public policy, as a potential obstacle to such trust, should be interpreted restrictively. This is demonstrated by the adverb 'manifestly' appearing in art 26 (Case C-341/04 *Eurofood IFSC Ltd* [2006] ECR I-3813, paras 62–3; Case C-444/07 *MG Probud* [2010] ECR I-0417, para 34).

Nor should it be overlooked that public policy may work differently between states. Accordingly, given that judgments and proceedings banned in one state may be recognized in other states, the entire treatment of an insolvency could lack harmony and coherence within the European judicial space.

As a result, even wide divergences among national insolvency laws should not in principle lead to the refusal of recognition and enforcement of judgments rendered in the other Member States.

In this regard, it must be borne in mind that, even though the Insolvency Regulation was not adopted with the view to harmonizing national laws in insolvency matters, diversity among national laws cannot undermine its *effet utile* as regards the recognition of the effects of insolvency proceedings. It is sufficient to point out that the Insolvency Regulation obliges Member States to recognize foreign opening judgments also 'where, on account of its capacity, insolvency proceedings cannot be brought against the debtor' in their territory (art 16(1)), ie also when a long-established ground for refusing recognition in terms of public policy arises, due to the divergence among national laws concerning the substantive conditions for opening insolvency proceedings.

IV. Cooperation framework

1. The liquidators' tasks, powers and duties between lex concursus *and uniform rules*

Among extraterritorial effects, those concerning the liquidator's powers deserve close attention.

It is preferable to consider separately liquidators appointed in main proceedings as opposed to those appointed in secondary proceedings (referred to below as 'main liquidator' and 'secondary liquidator', respectively), in view of the differing tasks they carry out according to the distinctions between main and secondary proceedings.

Starting with the main liquidator, he may 'exercise all the powers conferred on him by the law of the State of the opening' (art 18(1); Case C-444/07 *MG Probud* [2010] ECR I-0417, para 23). In other words, the liquidator acts by virtue of this rule as an organ entitled to exercise its powers in any other Member State in the interest of the proceedings. In particular, he may attach and recover all the debtor's assets located in Member States other than that of the proceedings, as well as employ juridical devices offered by laws different from the *lex concursus* so as to achieve the best insolvency administration and creditors' satisfaction. For instance, he may (i) bring actions *in rem* out of the Member State of the opening, (ii) realize the debtor's assets or (iii) request provisional measures to prevent removal of assets from the territory of the proceedings. Similar powers also pertain to the temporary liquidator, which should prevent removal of assets between the application for opening and the actual judgment opening the proceedings (art 38).

Apart from the powers determined by the *lex concursus*, the main liquidator may employ powers directly stemming from the Insolvency Regulation's uniform rules. The liquidator may exercise powers abroad, provided that no secondary proceedings have been opened in the relevant Member State (Case C-444/07 *MG Probud* [2010] ECR I-0417, para 23), and that no contrary preservation measures have been taken there following an application to open insolvency proceedings (art 18(1)). In particular, the main liquidator may remove the debtor's assets from the territory of a state. However, he will be barred from doing so if third parties with a right *in rem* request a preservation measure on the same assets, this under a 'safeguard clause' which allows that assets are excluded from the proceedings. This provision shares the purpose of art 5 of protecting those rights *in rem* that third parties intend to exercise within the insolvency proceedings in relation to tangible, intangible, moveable and immoveable assets situated at the time of opening in another Member State (→ Insolvency, applicable law).

Other limitations to the main liquidator's powers arise whenever the debtor's assets are located abroad and the liquidator aims to recover and realize them. In such circumstances, he must comply with the *lex loci* as regards the procedure to be followed (art 18(3)).

Finally, the main liquidator may request to open secondary proceedings in another Member State (art 29(a)).

The powers of the secondary liquidator are as follows. On the one hand the Insolvency Regulation enables him to claim in any other Member State, whether by judicial or extrajudicial means, that moveable property has been removed after the opening of secondary proceedings from the territory of the state of the opening to the territory of that other Member State. On the other hand, he may bring any action to set aside which is in the interests of the creditors (art 18(2)). In other words, secondary liquidators may recover assets pertaining to the proceedings (i) by way of judicial claims brought before the courts of the Member State where the assets are located, (ii) by seeking enforcement of judgments obtained in the proceedings or (iii) by extrajudicial means such as contracts or other transactions.

The secondary liquidator is also entitled, within the territory of the proceedings, to carry out all the tasks provided for him by the *lex concursus* (art 28). Therefore, arts 28 and 18(2) aim to strike a balance, in the event of a transfer of assets subsequent to the opening of secondary proceedings, between the creditors' interest to rely on the integrity of the debtor's assets located in the Member State of the establishment and the principle whereby the effects of the secondary proceedings as well as the secondary liquidator's powers are territorial. In other words, art 18 provides the secondary liquidator with extraterritorial powers exclusively to protect local creditors.

2. Cooperation between liquidators

Main and secondary liquidators must act in compliance with the duty of cooperation to attain an efficient cross-border insolvency administration. Cooperation requirement involves communicating information to each other.

Many aspects of these duties are governed by the Insolvency Regulation irrespective of the liquidators' roles, tasks and powers stemming from the *lex concursus*. Indeed, the liquidators again hold a distinct position with respect to the cooperation requirement as a result of scope and purposes of the proceedings, as well as of the general aim to 'ensure the dominant role of the main proceedings' (Recital (20)). As a matter of principle, the main burden of cooperation rests on the primacy of the main liquidator.

As just noted, the main liquidator may decide as a useful strategy to apply for the opening of secondary proceedings, which may for instance be suitable to liquidate the local debtor's assets or when handling the insolvency appears so complex to call for specific local proceedings. According to the ECJ, '[a]lthough secondary proceedings are intended, inter alia, to protect local interests, they may also . . . serve other purposes, which is why they may be opened at the request of the liquidator in the main proceedings, when the efficient administration of the estate so requires' (Case C-116/11 *Bank Handlowy* (22 November 2012), para 72).

Accordingly, although conceived of initially as a protection for local creditors, secondary proceedings may prove to be useful tools for achieving the optimum insolvency management of the main proceedings, thereby acting as 'auxiliary proceedings to the main proceedings'.

Once secondary proceedings have been opened, the Insolvency Regulation binds the secondary liquidator to give precedence to the main liquidator in submitting proposals on the liquidation or use of the local assets (art 31(3)). The main liquidator may request the court opening secondary proceedings to stay the process of liquidation, entirely or in part, if this is in the interest of creditors (art 33). He may suggest closing secondary proceedings without liquidation through alternative measures, such as rescue plans or composition, as provided in the local *lex concursus* (art 34).

After winding-up and distribution of the local assets to satisfy the claims lodged in the local proceedings, the secondary liquidator must immediately transfer any remaining assets to the main liquidator (art 35).

The duty of cooperation also applies in cases of 'territorial proceedings', although art 36, once the main proceedings have been opened, makes the application of the provisions safeguarding the primacy of the main liquidator conditional upon the progress of the 'former territorial' proceedings.

The primacy of the main liquidator clearly arises out of art 37, which entitles him to request the conversion of territorial proceedings into winding-up proceedings if this proves to be in the interest of creditors lodging claims in the main proceedings. This particularly occurs with respect to claims whose rank would be best satisfied by transferring the residual liquidated assets from secondary to main proceedings (art 35).

3. Cooperation between courts

The Insolvency Regulation lacks an analogous scheme of cooperation as regards the courts, which nevertheless have to comply with the effects of the proceedings.

This gap reveals its drawbacks whenever an application to open secondary proceedings is brought by local creditors after main proceedings have been opened. In particular, nothing in the Insolvency Regulation clearly binds the courts of the Member State of the establishment to rule on the application taking account of the features and purposes of the main proceedings. Moreover, it follows from ECJ case-law that the issue of whether such features and purposes may debar the opening of secondary proceedings for 'criteria as to appropriateness' depends on the law of the establishment (Case C-327/13 *Burgo Group SpA v Illochroma SA, in liquidation, Jérôme Theetten, acting in his capacity as liquidator of Illochroma SA* (4 September 2014), paras 52–67, with respect to winding-up insolvency proceedings).

However, the ECJ has emphasized that (i) 'the Regulation provides for a certain number of mandatory rules of coordination intended to ensure ... the need for unity in the Community', that (ii) 'main proceedings have a dominant role in relation to the secondary proceedings', and that (iii) the principle of sincere cooperation laid down in art 4(3) of the EU Treaty requires the court having jurisdiction to open secondary proceedings 'to have regard to the objectives of the main proceedings and to take account of the scheme of the Regulation, which ... aims to ensure efficient and effective cross-border insolvency proceedings through mandatory coordination of the main and secondary proceedings guaranteeing the priority of the main proceedings' (Case C-116/11 *Bank Handlowy* (22 November 2012), paras 60 ff; see also Case C-327/13 *Burgo Group SpA v Illochroma SA, in liquidation, Jérôme Theetten, acting in his capacity as liquidator of Illochroma SA* (4 September 2014), para 60; Case C-212/15 *ENEFI Energiahatékonysági Nyrt v Direcția Generală Regională a Finanțelor Publice Brașov (DGRFP)* (9 November 2016), para 26).

Thus the lack of coordination and sensitivity as to features and purposes of the main proceedings arises when local creditors seek the opening of secondary proceedings. This threatens the efficient insolvency administration, particularly when the main liquidator aims at restructuring without using the secondary proceedings that the local creditors conversely seek to open. The threat to the efficient insolvency administration intensifies when several secondary proceedings are opened in different Member States where the national laws governing the liquidation process diverge or lack provision for measures alternative to the liquidation.

V. The revision of the Insolvency Regulation

The Insolvency Regulation (recast), which will almost entirely apply from 26 June 2017, aims among others to improve both the coordination between several insolvency proceedings opened against the same debtor and the balancing between efficient insolvency administration and protection of local creditors.

In this regard, the Insolvency Regulation (recast) stresses, on the one hand, that the opening of secondary proceedings serves the protection of local creditors and in certain complex cases the main proceedings' purposes (Recital (40)), but, on the other hand, that secondary proceedings may 'hamper the efficient administration of the insolvency estate' (Recital (41)).

As a consequence, the Insolvency Regulation (recast), will in the first place render the opening of secondary proceedings conditional upon both the interests of local creditors and the objectives of the main proceedings, and accordingly, strengthen the main liquidator's (referred to as 'insolvency practitioner') role in this regard.

Unlike the current regime, the Insolvency Regulation (recast) will enable the court of the establishment, on request of the insolvency practitioner, to refuse or to postpone the opening of secondary proceedings whenever this is not necessary to protect the interest of local creditors. This may be the case of an investor making an offer to buy an insolvent company on a 'going-concern' basis and the offer appears more advantageous for the creditors than liquidation of the company assets.

When ruling on the request for opening brought by local creditors, the court of the establishment should give the main insolvency practitioner both notice and the opportunity to be heard before deciding (art 38). As a consequence, as the main insolvency practitioner could apply for refusal or postponement of the opening of secondary proceedings, the court of the establishment would be wholly 'aware of any rescue or reorganization options explored by the liquidator', and it would be able 'to properly assess the consequences of the opening' prior to handing down its judgment (see Proposal for a Regulation of the European Parliament and of the Council amending Council Regulation (EC) No 1346/2000 on insolvency proceedings, COM(2012) 744 final, para 3.1.3).

Such awareness may lead the court either to refuse the opening or to select proceedings different from winding-up. This contrasts with the current regime, which allows for the alternative proceedings option only for territorial proceedings, whereas the Insolvency Regulation (recast) will do so even for secondary proceedings, ie after the opening of main proceedings.

Antonio Leandro

In line with this new broadened role in evaluating whether and to what extent secondary proceedings might affect the centralized rescue or the estate administration, the main insolvency practitioner will be entitled to challenge the decision opening secondary proceedings.

More in detail, in order to avoid the opening of secondary proceedings without hampering local creditors, the main insolvency practitioner will be empowered to undertake within the main proceedings 'that he will comply with the distribution and priority rights under national law which [the local creditors] would have if secondary proceedings were opened' (art 36(1) and Recital (42)). That undertaking has to be approved by a qualified majority of known local creditors (the local rules concerning the adoption of restructuring plans will apply: art 36 (5)) and it should remove the local creditors' concern over seeing themselves deprived of interests and preferential rights based on the local *lex concursus* by the opening of the sole main proceedings and by the applicability of the COMI's *lex concursus*. At the same time, the undertaking should avoid the opening of secondary proceedings which may adversely affect the outcome of the main insolvency proceedings, in particular where the latter are aimed at rescue and restructuring. In stating so, the Insolvency Regulation (recast) draws inspiration from the 'synthetic secondary proceedings', a practice followed in certain English administrations of groups of companies (see, among others, High Court, Chancery Division, *Re Collins & Aikman III* [2006] EWHC 1343 (Ch) (9 June 2006)).

All the advantages of the undertaking depend mainly on the fact that local creditors and courts know both that main proceedings have been opened and that the main insolvency practitioner has given the undertaking. The Insolvency Regulation (recast) seems to cope with these requirements by generically improving the system of information to foreign creditors and courts (see arts 24–30, ch IV and the strictly related data protection rules of ch VI).

As a further means to balance main proceedings' purposes and interests of local creditors, the Insolvency Regulation (recast) allows the court of establishment temporarily to stay the opening of secondary proceedings. The stay, requested by the main insolvency practitioner or the debtor in possession, should follow the stay of individual enforcement proceedings which the courts of the main proceedings granted to facilitate negotiations in process between debtor and creditors, as long as 'suitable means are in place to protect the interests of local creditors' (art 38 (3) and Recital (45)).

Should secondary proceedings be opened or the request of opening be still pending, the Insolvency Regulation (recast) extends the duty to cooperate both to the courts involved and between courts and insolvency practitioners (arts 41–4). Courts and insolvency practitioners are also required to take account of principles and guidelines adopted by European and international organizations active in the area of insolvency law (Recital (48)). For instance, the courts may coordinate with each other to appoint the insolvency practitioners, while courts and insolvency practitioners may enter into generic or detailed protocols and agreements both to facilitate cross-border cooperation and to coordinate the administration of the debtor's assets and affairs.

The revision also addresses the management of multiple insolvency proceedings relating to groups of companies, introducing new rules which 'strive to ensure the efficiency of the coordination, whilst at the same time respecting each group member's separate legal personality' (Recital (54); see also → Insolvency, jurisdiction and *vis attractiva*).

In this regard, the Insolvency Regulation (recast) fills in the gap of the current regime, drawing inspiration from the UNCITRAL Model Law on Cross-Border Insolvency with Guide to Enactment and related Legislative and Practice Guides.

In particular, when more proceedings are opened in different Member States, the Insolvency Regulation (recast) requires all the actors involved (insolvency practitioners and courts) to comply with the duties of cooperation and communication applicable in case main and secondary insolvency proceedings are opened against the same debtor (ch V, s 1).

Besides, an insolvency practitioner may request – before any court having jurisdiction over the insolvency proceedings of a member – the opening of a 'group coordination proceeding', which should further facilitate the restructuring of the entire group (ch V, s 2). Such a court may also be selected by means of a choice-of-court agreement (art 66).

The request should include the proposal of the person to be appointed as the 'coordinator', an outline of the coordination plan, the list of all insolvency practitioners appointed in the proceedings concerning the members and an outline of the estimated costs (art 61). The participation of other insolvency practitioners (and, hence, other proceedings) rests on a voluntary basis (see the regime of the 'objections' enshrined in arts 64, 65, 67 – even applicable as regards the proposed coordinator – and that of subsequent 'opt-in' (art 69(a)).

The main tasks of the coordinator consist in proposing a group coordination plan and recommending the suitable conducts of all the insolvency proceedings involved, even by acting therein (arts 71–2). The coordinator may be removed from its tasks under certain circumstances (art 75).

The advantages of the 'coordination proceedings' should be worth the costs. That means that costs of the coordination should be sustainable and adequate having regard to the purpose of each proceeding involved (Recital (58)).

As noted elsewhere (see → Insolvency, jurisdiction and *vis attractiva*), the group-of-companies-oriented rules will not prevent a court from opening insolvency proceedings for several companies in a single state whenever it finds a common COMI therein (Recital (53)).

ANTONIO LEANDRO

Literature

Edward S Adams and Jason K Fincke, 'Coordinating Cross-border Bankruptcy: How Territorialism Saves Universalism' (2008) 15 Colum.J.Eur.L. 43; Stefania Bariatti, 'Recent Case-Law Concerning Jurisdiction and the Recognition of Judgment under the EC European Insolvency Regulation' (2009) 73 RabelsZ 629; Stefania Bariatti and Paul Omar (eds), *The Grand Project: Reform of the European Insolvency Regulation* (INSOL Europe 2014); Reinhard Bork, Principles of Cross-Border Insolvency Law (Intersentia 2017); Reinhard Bork and Renato Mangano, European Cross-Border Insolvency Law (OUP 2016); Horst Eidenmüller, 'A New Framework for Business Restructuring in Europe: The EU Commission's Proposals for a Reform of the European Insolvency Regulation and Beyond' (2013) 20 MJ 133; Ian Fletcher, *Insolvency in Private international law* (2nd edn, OUP 2005); Luigi Fumagalli, 'Il regolamento comunitario sulle procedure di insolvenza' (2001) 56 Riv Dir Proc 677; Giulio Cesare Giorgini, *Méthodes conflictuelles et règles matérielles dans l'application des 'nouveaux instruments' de règlement de la faillite internationale* (Dalloz 2006); Burkhard Hess, Paul Oberhammer and Thomas Pfeiffer (eds), *European Insolvency Regulation: Heidelberg–Luxembourg–Vienna Report* (Beck-Hart-Nomos 2013); Antonio Leandro, *Il ruolo della lex concursus nel regolamento comunitario sulle procedure di insolvenza* (Cacucci 2008); Antonio Leandro, 'Amending the European Insolvency Regulation to Strengthen Main Proceedings' (2014) 50 Riv. Dir.Int'le Priv. & Proc. 317; Antonio Leandro, 'A First Critical Appraisal of The New European Insolvency Regulation' (2016) Il Diritto dell'Unione Europea 215; Peter Mankowski, Michael F. Müller and Jessica Schmidt, EuInsVO 2015. Europäische Insolvenzverordnung 2015. Kommentar (Beck 2016); Gerard McCormack, 'Universalism in Insolvency Proceedings and Common Law' (2012) 32 Oxford J.Leg.Stud. 325; Gerard McCormack, 'Reforming the European Insolvency Regulation: A Legal and Policy Perspective' (2014) 10 J Priv Int L 41; Gabriel Moss, 'Group Insolvency – Choice of Forum and Law: The European Experience under the Influence of English Pragmatism' (2007) 32 Brooklyn J.Int'l L. 1005; Gabriel Moss, Ian Fletcher and Stuart Isaacs (eds), Moss, Fletcher and Isaacs on the EU Regulation on Insolvency Proceedings (3rd edn, OUP 2016); Paul Omar, *International Insolvency Law: Themes and Perspectives* (Ashgate 2010); Klaus Pannen, *European Insolvency Regulation* (De Gruyter Recht 2007); Ilaria Queirolo, *Le procedure di insolvenza nella disciplina comunitaria. Modelli di riferimento e diritto interno* (Giappichelli 2007); Michaël Raimon, *Le règlement communautaire 1346/2000 du 29 mai 2000 relatif aux procédures d'insolvabilité* (LGDJ 2007); Christoph Thole, 'Die Reform der Europäischen Insolvenzordnung: Zentrale Aspekte des Kommissionsvorschlags und offene Fragen' (2014) 22 ZEuP 39; Miguel Virgós Soriano and Francisco Garcimartín Alférez, *The European Insolvency Regulation: Law and Practice* (Kluwer 2004); Bob Wessels, *International Insolvency Law* (3rd edn, Kluwer 2012); Bob Wessels, Bruce A Markell and Jason J Kilborn, *International Cooperation in Bankruptcy and Insolvency Matters* (OUP 2009), Bob Wessels, *International Insolvency Law Part I. Global Perspectives on Cross-border Insolvency Law* (4th edn, Wolters Kluwer 2015).

Insolvency, jurisdiction and *vis attractiva*

I. Jurisdiction over insolvency proceedings in national laws

Cross-border insolvency consists in a debtor's crisis involving assets and activities in a plurality of states.

In principle, each state is free to determine the scope of its jurisdiction in matters of insolvency with regard to both the opening of insolvency proceedings and the so-called 'ancillary' actions, ie the actions which directly derive from, or are closely linked to, insolvency proceedings.

As regards the opening of insolvency proceedings, national laws provide for grounds of jurisdiction that vary between states, even though the most common ground consists of the place where the debtor has its registered or real seat. In fact, the UNCITRAL Model Law on Cross-Border Insolvency with Guide to Enactment (UNCITRAL (ed), Model Law on Cross-Border Insolvency (1997) with Guide to Enactment (2013): Model Law on Cross-Border Insolvency of the United Commission on International Trade Law, Resolution 52/158 adopted by the General Assembly, 30 January 1998, No E.99.V.3, General Assembly Resolution 52/158 of 15 December 1997) endorses the centre of main interests (COMI) and the establishment of the debtor as jurisdictional criteria to open main and secondary insolvency proceedings, respectively. The effects of these proceedings over the debtor's assets differ (see, more extensively, → Insolvency, cooperation and recognition). In doing so, the UNCITRAL Model Law on Cross-Border Insolvency with Guide to Enactment took inspiration from both the 1990 European Convention on Certain International Aspects of Bankruptcy (Council of Europe, Istanbul 5 June 1990, ETS No 136; (1991) 30 ILM 165) and from the 1995 Brussels Convention on Insolvency Proceedings ((1996) 35 ILM 1236). The latter has been almost entirely incorporated into the Insolvency Regulation (Council Regulation (EC) No 1346/2000 of 29 May 2000 on insolvency proceedings, [2000] OJ L 160/1), which in turn has been revised by the Insolvency Regulation (recast) (Regulation (EU) 2015/848 of the European Parliament and of the Council of 20 May 2015 on insolvency proceedings (recast) [2015] OJ L 141/19), whose bulk of provisions will apply from 26 June 2017 (art 92) to proceedings opened after that date (art 84).

With regard to the scope of the jurisdiction of the court opening insolvency proceedings, some national laws provide that it covers (i) the procedural phases of the proceedings, such as lodging, verification and admission of claims, which may require settling a dispute or granting reliefs or other measures, as well as (ii) ancillary actions, according to the so-called *vis attractiva* principle. This principle aims at preserving unity and coherence in the insolvency administration, taking particularly into account that several substantive issues to which such actions give rise are governed by the *lex fori* as *lex concursus* (see → Insolvency, applicable law).

Other national laws do not follow the same approach, so that jurisdiction over ancillary actions depends upon the jurisdiction criterion that applies to each action.

II. Jurisdiction to open insolvency proceedings under the Insolvency Regulation

1. General overview

The Insolvency Regulation provides for the opening of two types of insolvency proceedings with different features and effects: main proceedings, to be opened in the Member State where the debtor has its COMI, and secondary proceedings, to be opened in the Member State where the debtor has an establishment. Secondary proceedings may even be opened prior to main proceedings in compliance with art 3(4), in which case they are properly referred to as 'territorial proceedings'. Since a debtor may have one COMI and an indefinite number of establishments, the Insolvency Regulation admits the coexistence of one main proceeding and several secondary proceedings with respect to it (see → Insolvency, cooperation and recognition).

2. The centre of main interests (COMI)

a) The notion of COMI

As far as jurisdiction to open main insolvency proceedings of companies or legal persons is concerned, art 3 Insolvency Regulation provides for a rebuttable presumption, according to which the COMI is located at the registered office. At the same time according to Recital (13), the COMI corresponds to the 'place where the debtor conducts the administration of [its] interests on a regular basis and is therefore ascertainable by third parties'. As the ECJ stated, 'objectivity and the possibility of ascertainment by third parties are necessary in order to ensure legal certainty and foreseeability concerning the determination of the court with jurisdiction to open main insolvency proceedings' (Case C-341/04 *Eurofood IFSC Ltd* [2006] ECR I-3813, para 33; more recently, Case C-353/15 *Leonmobili Srl, Gennaro Leone v Homag Holzbearbeitungssysteme GmbH et alii* (24 May 2016), para 33).

b) The location of the COMI

Determining the location of the debtor's COMI is a complicated task largely because the definition set out in Recital (13), as upheld to a great extent by the ECJ from the *Eurofood* case onwards, while stressing the autonomous meaning of the concept nevertheless highlights its factual nature, which in turn implies case-by-case fact finding and consequent potential divergences among courts. The major problems that have arisen in case-law concern the insolvency of companies belonging to a group and the transfer of the COMI.

In particular, given that the presumption on the coincidence between the COMI and the registered office is rebuttable, the courts are often required to assess the factual situation and to weight the factors and elements that may overcome the presumption. In this regard, account has been taken of the place where the company exercises its activities, which vary depending upon the type of the company's business, or where it holds assets such as immoveable property, or where it carries out its administration, including financial and personnel administration.

However, the requirement that the COMI be ascertainable by third parties, mainly the creditors, implies that all relevant factors have to be assessed and weighed in a comprehensive manner. This enables the inference that the company's COMI does not correspond to the company's registered office whenever, from the view of third parties, the company on a regular basis manages its own administration in another place. The ECJ has upheld this approach in several judgments from *Eurofood* (paras 32 ff) onwards, eventually stating that the COMI is 'the company's actual centre of management and supervision and of the management of its interests' (Case C-396/09 *Interedil Srl, in liquidation v Fallimento Interedil Srl and Intesa Gestione Crediti SpA* [2011] ECR I-9915, para 53; Case C-191/10 *Rastelli Davide e C. Snc v Jean-Charles Hidoux, in his capacity as liquidator appointed by the court for the company Médiasucre international* [2012] OJ C 39/3, para 35; Case C-353/15 *Leonmobili Srl, Gennaro Leone v Homag Holzbearbeitungssysteme GmbH et alii* (24 May 2016), paras 34 ff).

On the other hand, the Insolvency Regulation provides no specific jurisdiction criterion for the opening of insolvency proceedings of → companies belonging to a group (see Miguel Virgós and Etienne Schmit, *Report on the Convention on Insolvency Proceedings*, European Council, Doc No 6500/96, 3 May 1996, para 76). Following the *Eurofood* judgment, according to which 'the mere fact that company's economic choices are or can be controlled by a parent company in another Member State is not enough to rebut the presumption laid down by the Regulation' (para 36), the jurisdiction to open insolvency proceedings of such companies has to follow the 'separate-legal-entity' approach. That is to say that the Member State of the COMI of each company retains jurisdiction to open main proceedings for each company. Nevertheless, main insolvency proceedings of a controlled company may be opened in the state where the parent company has its own COMI if the controlled company's 'centre of management and supervision and of the management of its interests' is located in this country.

This gap has been widely criticized among scholars and practitioners due to the drawbacks it engenders in terms of inefficient administration of insolvency proceedings whenever the insolvency affects the whole group or members belonging to a closely integrated group. The Insolvency Regulation (recast) aims at filling this gap by providing a system of cooperation between the proceedings opened against each member of the group similar to that established between main and secondary proceedings opened against the same debtor (arts 56–60). Moreover, the Insolvency Regulation (recast) indicates that a court may find in its country a COMI common to all the members and then appoint one liquidator, referred to as 'insolvency practitioner', for all proceedings concerned (Recital (53)).

Besides, where the proceedings are opened in different Member States, an appointed 'insolvency practitioner' may request the opening of a 'group coordination proceeding' before any court having jurisdiction over the insolvency proceedings of a member (art 61). Such a court may also be selected by means of a choice-of-court agreement (art 66). The request should include the proposal of the person to be appointed as the 'coordinator', an outline of the coordination plan, the list of all insolvency practitioners appointed in the proceedings concerning the members and an outline of the estimated costs (art 61). Participation within the group coordination proceedings is voluntary (see also → Insolvency, cooperation and recognition).

c) The transfer of COMI

The COMI may be transferred from one Member State to another according to the EU provisions on freedom of establishment (→ Freedom of establishment/persons (European Union) and private international law), which grant a company and its shareholders the right to choose the place to conduct their activities. Thus, in the case of a COMI transfer it is important to assess which date is relevant for the purpose of determining the jurisdiction.

The Insolvency Regulation provides no provisions in this regard, but the ECJ's case-law helps solve the issue.

When the COMI is moved after the application for insolvency has been filed but before insolvency proceedings have been opened, the courts of the Member State where the COMI was situated at the time of the application retain jurisdiction (Case C-1/04 *Susanne Staubitz-Schreiber* [2006] ECR I-701, para 29). Conversely, if the COMI is transferred before a request to open insolvency proceedings is lodged, the courts of the Member State where the new COMI is located are competent (Case C-396/09 *Interedil v Fallimento Interedil* [2011] ECR I-9915, para 59). As a result, the debtor's freedom of establishment is balanced against the interest of creditors to rely on certain and predictable criteria of jurisdiction when applying to open the proceedings. Forum shopping (→ Forum (and law) shopping) practices which prove to be detrimental to creditors are accordingly reduced.

It is indisputable that the main practical problems in applying this regime arise in connection with companies. Since only the transfer of the 'centre of management and supervision and of the management of their interests' before a request to open insolvency proceedings is lodged has direct bearing on jurisdiction, it may occur that the registered office remains in a Member State, while the COMI relocates to another state, the courts of which will have no jurisdiction. However, from the presumptive coincidence between COMI and registered office, it follows that the transfer of the registered office in compliance with the laws governing the company before a request to open insolvency proceedings is lodged may imply that the COMI is also transferred under the Insolvency Regulation.

In *Interedil*, concerning transfer of the registered office of an Italian company to England, the ECJ nevertheless stated that since the presumption envisaged by art 3 is rebuttable, the applicant/creditor may prove that the COMI has not followed the registered office in the new Member State, so that the courts of the Member State in which the COMI is still located should retain jurisdiction (see Case C-396/09 *Interedil v Fallimento Interedil* [2011] ECR I-9915, para 56; Case C-353/15 *Leonmobili Srl, Gennaro Leone v Homag Holzbearbeitungssysteme GmbH et alii* (24 May 2016), para 40).

It may also occur that, while either having or transferring the COMI outside the Member State of the registered office, the company leaves an establishment in that state, so that the opening of secondary proceedings may be requested there (see Case C-327/13 *Burgo Group SpA v Illochroma SA, in liquidation, Jérôme Theetten, acting in his capacity as liquidator of Illochroma SA* (4 September 2014), paras 20–39; on the other hand, the ECJ in Case C-353/15 *Leonmobili Srl, Gennaro Leone v Homag Holzbearbeitungssysteme GmbH et alii* (24 May 2016), para 38, makes it clear that the absence of an establishment in a Member State different from that of the registered office does not necessarily entail that the COMI is not located in that State).

d) *The notion of 'establishment' and the opening of secondary/territorial insolvency proceedings*

As mentioned above, the Insolvency Regulation provides that secondary insolvency proceedings may be opened in the state where the debtor has an 'establishment', as defined in art 2(h) as the 'place of operations where the debtor carries out a non-transitory economic activity with human means and goods'. Like COMI, this notion has a factual and autonomous nature.

The reference to both 'non-transitory activity' and 'human means and goods' shows that a minimum level of organization as well as a degree of stability are required to determine whether an establishment is located in the state of the court seized. In the ECJ's words, 'the presence alone of goods in isolation or bank accounts does not, in principle, meet that definition' (Case C-396/09 *Interedil v Fallimento Interedil* [2011] ECR I-9915, para 64). Indeed, as far as companies are concerned, even the presence of the registered office with COMI located abroad is insufficient if the requirements of art 2(h) are not met (Case C-327/13 *Burgo Group SpA v Illochroma SA (in liquidation) and another* (4 September 2014), para 32). Moreover, since the establishment amounts to a jurisdiction criterion, it should be assessed like the COMI on the basis of objective factors which are ascertainable by third parties, in order to ensure legal certainty and foreseeability.

Proceedings properly referred to as 'secondary' are opened after main proceedings (art 29) without debtors' insolvency being again examined (art 27; Case C-116/11 *Bank Handlowy w*

Warszawie SA and PPHU «ADAX»/Ryszard Adamiak v Christianapol sp. z o.o. (22 November 2012), paras 64 ff).

'Territorial proceedings' may be opened before main proceedings provided that (i) the debtor's COMI is located in a Member State and (ii) main proceedings cannot be opened in this country or the opening of territorial proceedings is requested by the so-called 'local creditors', namely the creditors with domicile, habitual residence or registered office in the state where the establishment is located or whose claims stem from activities that the debtor conducted through the establishment. It is worth noting that, in the ECJ's view, such limitations (which it moreover interpreted restrictively in Case C-112/10 *Procureur-generaal bij het hof van beroep te Antwerpen v Zaza Retail BV* (17 November 2011), paras 27 *et seq*) do not apply to the opening of secondary proceedings (Case C-327/13 *Burgo Group SpA v Illochroma SA (in liquidation) and another* (4 September 2014), para 48).

Main proceedings produce effects across the EU (excluding Denmark) according to the principle of universality, while secondary/territorial proceedings have local effects, ie they are restricted to assets situated in the Member State where they have been opened (see extensively → Insolvency, cooperation and recognition).

III. A European *vis attractiva* over 'ancillary' actions

As mentioned above, national laws differ with regard to the extent of the jurisdiction of the court opening main insolvency proceedings. This applies in particular to ancillary actions, and the Insolvency Regulation contains no express provision in this respect. Nor is this type of action within the scope of application of the Brussels I Regulation (Regulation (EC) No 44/2001 of 22 December 2000 on jurisdiction and the recognition and enforcement of judgments in civil and commercial matters, [2001] OJ L 12/1) (and of the Brussels I Regulation (recast) (Regulation (EU) No 1215/2012 of the European Parliament and of the Council of 12 December 2012 on jurisdiction and the recognition and enforcement of judgments in civil and commercial matters (recast), [2012] OJ L 351/1)), which does not apply to 'bankruptcy, proceedings relating to the winding-up of insolvent companies or other legal persons, judicial arrangements, compositions and analogous proceedings' (art 1(2)(b)). According to

the *Gourdain* judgment (Case C-133/78 *Henri Gourdain v Franz Nadler* [1979] ECR I-733) (and later to *Deko Marty* (Case C-339/07 *Christopher Seagon v Deko Marty Belgium NV* [2009] ECR I-767), *SCT Industri* (Case C-111/08 *SCT Industri AB (in liquidation) v AlpenblumeAB* [2009] ECR I-5655), *German Graphics* (Case C-292/08 *German Graphics Graphische Maschinen GmbH v Alice van der Schee* [2009] ECR I-8421), *F-Tex SIA* (Case C-213/10 *F-Tex SIA v Lietuvos-Anglijos UAB 'Jadecloud-Vilma'* [2012] OJ C 165/3), *Nickel & Goeldner Spedition* (Case C-157/13 *Nickel & Goeldner Spedition GmbH v «Kintra» UAB* (4 September 2014)) and *Comité d'entreprise de Nortel Networks SA and others* (Case C-649/13 *Comité d'entreprise de Nortel Networks SA and others v Cosme Rogeau* (11 June 2015))), this exception covers only actions and decisions which derive directly from the bankruptcy or winding-up and are closely connected with the proceedings aimed at realizing the assets or establishing judicial supervision.

The ECJ filled this gap when it was called upon to decide on the jurisdiction over an action to set aside, based on insolvency, brought by a liquidator against a third party with seat in a Member State other than that where main insolvency proceedings had been opened. Indeed, actions to set aside by virtue of insolvency and related judgments are subject to certain Insolvency Regulation provisions addressing the applicable law and the recognition/enforcement of judgments. Actions to set aside belong to the category of measures devoted 'to the voidness, voidability or unenforceability of legal acts detrimental to all the creditors', that are governed by the *lex concursus* according to art 4(2)(m). Judgments stemming from actions to set aside pertain to the category of decisions 'deriving directly from the insolvency proceedings and which are closely linked to them', which under art 25(1) enjoy the same regime of recognition and enforcement that applies to judgments opening the proceedings (see → Insolvency, cooperation and recognition).

Such a legal framework concerns actions brought by the liquidator of both the main and secondary proceedings. However, the liquidator of secondary proceedings may claim in any Member State other than that of the opening 'through the courts or out of court that moveable property was removed from the territory of the state of the opening of proceedings to the territory of that other Member State after the opening of the insolvency proceedings', and he may further bring any action 'to set aside which is in the interests of the creditors' (art 18(2)). This provision exceptionally entitles the liquidator of secondary proceedings to recover assets 'of the proceedings' abroad (see → Insolvency, cooperation and recognition), either by a claim lodged directly in the Member State where the assets are located, or by the enforcement of decisions rendered by the court of the Member State where the proceedings have been opened (which stated, as an example, the inefficacy of the act under which the asset has been transferred) or lastly, out of court.

In *Deko Marty* the ECJ stated that even though the Insolvency Regulation provides no jurisdiction criteria for actions directly stemming from and closely linked to the insolvency proceedings, it should nevertheless cover cases excluded from the Brussels I Regulation (and the Brussels I Regulation (recast)) whenever a jurisdictional issue arises in matters of insolvency. To this end, the Court acknowledged a *vis attractiva* in favour of the courts of the Member State where insolvency proceedings have been opened, thereby allowing them to rule on the ancillary actions as well. Indeed, *vis attractiva* strengthens the *effet utile* of the Regulation, as it centralizes all ancillary actions in the court of the insolvency proceedings, thereby enhancing the proceedings' effectiveness and efficiency.

Moreover, *vis attractiva* appears to be consistent with the scheme of interconnection between jurisdiction, recognition and enforcement framed by arts 3 and 25 Insolvency Regulation. Article 3 determines the Member State where insolvency proceedings may be opened, while art 25 sets forth the principle of mutual recognition of the judgments concerning the course and closure of proceedings rendered by the court with jurisdiction under art 3. Since as noted, art 25(1) extends the principle of mutual recognition to 'judgments deriving directly from the insolvency proceedings and which are closely linked with them', only the court identified by art 3 is empowered to issue such decisions. According to the ECJ, the sentence 'even if [the judgments at stake] were handed down by another court' in art 25(1) means that the Member States may 'determine the court with territorial and substantive jurisdiction, which does not necessarily have to be the court which opened the insolvency proceedings' (Case C-339/07 *Seagon v Deko Marty Belgium NV* [2009] ECR I-767, para 27).

Thus, actions that qualify as ancillary to insolvency proceedings are excluded from the Brussels I Regulation (and the Brussels I Regulation (recast)) and fall within the Insolvency Regulation (see recently Case C-295/13 *H v HK* (4 December 2014), para 31 *et seq*, also for references to the 2007 → Lugano Convention (Lugano Convention of 30 October 2007 on jurisdiction and the recognition and enforcement of judgments in civil and commercial matters, [2007] OJ L 339/3); see also Case C-594/14 *Simona Kornhaas v Thomas Dithmar, acting as liquidator of the assets of Kornhaas Montage und Dienstleistung Ltd* (10 December 2015), paras 15 ff). This means that actions lacking such characterization are covered by the first Regulation as it 'is intended to apply to all civil and commercial matters apart from certain well-defined matters' (Case C-213/10 *F-Tex SIA v Lietuvos-Anglijos UAB Jadecloud-Vilma* (19 April 2012), para 29). Moreover, having regard to the scope of the Brussels I Regulation, that of the Insolvency Regulation 'must not be interpreted broadly' (Case C-157/13 *Nickel & Goeldner Spedition GmbH v «Kintra» UAB* (4 September 2014), paras 22–3 and Case C-649/13 *Comité d'entreprise de Nortel Networks SA and others v Cosme Rogeau* (11 June 2015), para 27).

In this regard, the ECJ pays attention to the legal basis of the claim rather than to the procedural context of which the action is part. In other words, *vis attractiva* depends more on the action's basis in insolvency law than on its connection with insolvency proceedings (see extensively Case C-213/10 *F-Tex SIA v Lietuvos-Anglijos UAB Jadecloud-Vilma* (19 April 2012); Case C-157/13 *Nickel & Goeldner Spedition GmbH v «Kintra» UAB* (4 September 2014); Case C-295/13 *H v HK* (4 December 2014); Case C-649/13 *Comité d'entreprise de Nortel Networks SA and others v Cosme Rogeau* (11 June 2015)). On the other hand, in case C-295/13 *H v HK*, the ECJ seems to clarify that actions based on insolvency which, according to national law, 'could theoretically be brought even if there were no insolvency proceedings', may fall within the Brussels I Regulation (and the Brussels I Regulation (recast)) when brought outside – and in the absence of – insolvency proceedings: paras 20–5 while see Case C-594/14 *Simona Kornhaas v Thomas Dithmar, acting as liquidator of the assets of Kornhaas Montage und Dienstleistung Ltd* (10 December 2015), paras 16 ff, should such an action – namely the action against the managing director by virtue of § 64(2) GmbHG – be brought within an insolvency proceeding).

The rules of jurisdiction, especially the *vis attractiva*'s one, apply to both main and secondary proceedings (Case C-649/13 *Comité d'entreprise de Nortel Networks SA and others v Cosme Rogeau* (11 June 2015), para 32) and irrespective of whether the defendant's seat (or habitual residence) lies inside or outside the EU. When dealing with an action to set aside brought in the COMI's court against a person whose place of residence was located outside the EU (Case C-328/12 *Ralph Schmid (liquidator of the assets of Aletta Zimmermann) v Lilly Hertel* [2014] OJ C 85/5; Case C-295/13 *H v HK* (4 December 2014)), the ECJ decided that the universal effect of main proceedings and the need to ensure certainty and uniformity to the jurisdiction criteria imply that the *vis attractiva* principle is not limited to ancillary disputes involving defendants domiciled or resident in a Member State. The ECJ emphasized that the Insolvency Regulation does not only address cross-border situations within the EU, and that the determination of jurisdiction cannot be postponed until the time when the location of various aspects of the proceedings in addition to the COMI, such as the residence of a potential defendant to an ancillary action, are known. The ECJ stated that 'to wait for knowledge of these matters would frustrate the objectives of improving the efficiency and effectiveness' of cross-border insolvency proceedings (Case C-328/12 *Ralph Schmid v Lilly Hertel* (16 January 2014), para 28).

IV. The innovation regarding jurisdiction in the Insolvency Regulation (recast)

The Insolvency Regulation (recast) aims to strengthen the current jurisdictional framework in terms of certainty and clarity.

Apart from the aforementioned novelties concerning the groups of companies, some recitals inspired to *Eurofood* and *Interedil* have been inserted as regards the COMI of companies (see Recital (30)) and art 3 enshrines as a rule, with certain adaptations, the contents of Recital (13) of the Insolvency Regulation, thereby defining the COMI as the 'place where the debtor conducts the administration of its interests on a regular basis and which is ascertainable by third parties'.

The COMI of individuals will presumptively correspond to the 'principal place of business' in the case of independent businessmen or professional providers, and to the habitual residence in any other case.

Besides, with the aim to prevent fraudulent or abusive forum shopping (Recitals (29) and (31)), all presumptions concerning the COMI will only apply if the registered office/principal place of business/habitual residence has not been moved to another Member State within a given period prior to the request for the opening of the proceedings (art 3(1)).

The court requested to open the proceedings will rule of its own motion, and then specify in the judgment on which ground it retains jurisdiction (art 4); debtor and creditors will be entitled to challenge such decision (art 5).

Vis attractiva over 'ancillary' proceedings has been codified (art 6). Moreover, should the 'ancillary' action be related with another action based on civil and commercial law, then the liquidator (insolvency practitioner) will be empowered to bring both claims in the court of the defendant's domicile or, in the case of several defendants, in the court of the Member State where any of them is domiciled, provided that such court has jurisdiction under the Brussels I Regulation (recast) (see also Recital (35)).

Antonio Leandro

Literature

Stefania Bariatti, 'Filling in the Gaps of EC Conflicts of Laws Instruments: The Case of Jurisdiction over Actions Related to Insolvency Proceedings' in Gabriella Venturini and Stefania Bariatti (eds), *New Instruments on Private international law: Liber Fausto Pocar* (Giuffrè 2009) 23; Stefania Bariatti, 'Recent Case-Law Concerning Jurisdiction and the Recognition of Judgment under the EC European Insolvency Regulation' (2009) 73 RabelsZ 629; Stefania Bariatti and Paul Omar (eds), *The Grand Project: Reform of the European Insolvency Regulation* (INSOL Europe 2014); Reinhard Bork, *Principles of Cross-Border Insolvency Law* (Intersentia 2017); Reinhard Bork and Renato Mangano, *European Cross-Border Insolvency Law* (OUP 2016); Anatol Dutta, 'Jurisdiction for Insolvency-related Proceedings Caught between European Legislation' (2008) *LMCLQ* 88; Horst Eidenmüller, 'A New Framework for Business Restructuring in Europe: The EU Commission's Proposals for a Reform of the European Insolvency Regulation and Beyond' (2013) 20 *MJ* 133; Ian Fletcher, *Insolvency in Private international law* (2nd edn, OUP 2005); Burkhard Hess, Paul Oberhammer and Thomas Pfeiffer (eds), *European Insolvency Regulation: Heidelberg–Luxembourg–Vienna Report* (Beck-Hart-Nomos 2013); Antonio Leandro, *Il ruolo della lex concursus nel regolamento comunitario sulle procedure di insolvenza* (Cacucci 2008); Antonio Leandro, 'Effet utile of the Regulation No 1346 and Vis Attractiva

Concursus: Some Remarks on the Deko Marty Judgment' (2009) 11 YbPIL 469; Antonio Leandro, 'A First Critical Appraisal of The New European Insolvency Regulation' (2016) Il Diritto dell'Unione Europea 215; Peter Mankowski, Michael F. Müller and Jessica Schmidt, EuInsVO 2015. Europäische Insolvenzverordnung 2015. Kommentar (Beck 2016); Gabriel Moss, 'Group Insolvency – Choice of Forum and Law: The European Experience under the Influence of English Pragmatism' (2007) 32 *Brooklyn J.Int'l L.* 1005; Gabriel Moss, Ian Fletcher and Stuart Isaacs (eds), Moss, Fletcher and Isaacs on the EU Regulation on Insolvency Proceedings (3rd edn, OUP 2016); Paul Omar (ed), *International Insolvency Law: Themes and Perspectives* (Ashgate 2010); Klaus Pannen (ed), *European Insolvency Regulation* (De Gruyter Recht 2007); Michaël Raimon, *Le règlement communautaire 1346/2000 du 29 mai 2000 relatif aux procèdures d'insolvabilité* (LGDJ 2007); Vincenzo Starace, 'La disciplina comunitaria delle procedure di insolvenza: giurisdizione ed efficacia delle sentenze straniere' (2002) 85 *Riv.Dir.Int.* 295; Miguel Virgós and Etienne Schmit, *Report on the Convention on Insolvency Proceedings* (European Council, Doc No 6500/96, 3 May 1996); Miguel Virgós Soriano and Francisco Garcimartín Alférez, *The European Insolvency Regulation: Law and Practice* (Kluwer 2004); Bob Wessels (ed), *Cross-border Insolvency Law: International Instruments Commentary* (Kluwer 2007); Bob Wessels, *International Insolvency Law* (3rd edn, Kluwer 2012), Bob Wessels, *International Insolvency Law Part I. Global Perspectives on Cross-border Insolvency Law* (4th edn, Wolters Kluwer 2015).

Insurance contracts

I. Concept and notion

Dealing with questions of private international law in matters relating to insurance requires attention to several peculiarities applying in this field. First of all, the practical relevance of private international law will depend on the degree to which the cross-border provision of insurance services is actually taking place. This will depend on various circumstances, not least on the way insurance is regulated by national legislatures. Most importantly, provision of insurance services is commonly permitted only if the company obtains a licence (for the EU see art 14(1) of the Solvency II Directive (Directive 2009/138/EC of the European Parliament and of the Council of 25 November 2009 on the taking-up and pursuit of the business of Insurance and Reinsurance (Solvency II), [2009] OJ L 335/1)) and operates in compliance with the relevant supervisory requirements. As long as a licence is dependent on the insurer being established in the country in which it provides services and such licence grants access to the national market at the place of establishment only (see, eg, with a view to insurers seated in a third country, art 162, in particular section (2)(b) of the Solvency II Directive), it will not allow for cross-border trade in insurance and, thus, the relevance of private international law will remain limited. In contrast, private international law becomes more important when supervisory law no longer presents a barrier to market entry. This applies where the cross-border provision of services does not require authorization by the supervisory board (ie where under the applicable national rules of supervision non-admitted business is lawful) or where a national licence is fully recognized abroad. The latter is the case within the EU due to the imposition of a single licence system (see art 15(1) of the Solvency II Directive) and in the USA due mainly to the → Full faith and credit clause of the US Constitution (art IV, section 1 of the US Constitution). Opening national insurance markets at the regulatory level may, however, not be sufficient for an integration of markets. While it seems that there is a considerable amount of cross-border business being conducted in the USA, cross-border business in the EU remains restricted mainly to large risk insurance, where parties have the option to choose freely the applicable law. In contrast, in mass risk insurance, where party autonomy is restricted considerably, little cross-border business activity of insurers can be observed, in spite of the introduction of the single licence system. It seems that insurers shy away from the application of a foreign law to their insurance products.

The second peculiarity concerning insurance is the fact that insurance is provided for nearly all aspects of human life. It is provided to consumers, small and medium-sized enterprises (SME), large companies, groups of companies and even to insurers themselves which take out reinsurance. There is an obvious imbalance in power between insurers and consumers as well as small and medium-sized enterprises, whereas such an imbalance becomes less obvious in relation to large companies and usually disappears in relation to insurance companies taking out reinsurance. This fact strongly impacts private international law in matters relating to insurance because mass risk insurance contracts (consumer and SME contracts) are subject to protective rules, whereas large policyholders and insurers taking out reinsurance usually enjoy party autonomy. Moreover, large risk insurance and reinsurance are often governed by arbitration agreements giving parties the utmost freedom.

The third peculiarity is the fact that insurance contracts very often concern third parties which may be resident in a foreign country and, thus, provide a foreign element even to an otherwise purely domestic contract. There are many examples particularly concerning liability insurance. International groups of companies frequently contract for liability insurance through their head company but to the benefit of all members of the group, nationals as well as foreign ones. At the same time, such risks are usually very large and not borne by one insurer only. Instead, several insurers from various countries commonly share the overall risk through co-insurance, excess-insurance or similar arrangements. Thus, international insurance programmes conducted by international groups of companies raise complex questions of private international law. This is also the case when claims are brought by a foreign victim directly against the insurer.

Life insurance poses a fourth peculiarity. It is often structured as an investment product commonly used for old age provision. Thus, it is frequently subject to special legislation outside the scope of contract law. For instance, a life insurance contract will have to be structured in a particular way in order to qualify for a privileged tax treatment or for public subsidies. Equally, it may be used for structuring occupational pension schemes, requiring the life insurance contract also to be subjected to the relevant national legislation on such schemes. Tax rules as well as rules on occupational pension schemes will apply irrespective of the applicable contract law. Moreover, such life policies are commonly taken out by the employer as a group organizer on behalf of its employees. Such employees will include those working in the head offices of the employer, but also employees working abroad (expatriates). These and other group insurance policies may raise complex questions of private international law.

Much of what has been said about life insurance also applies to compulsory insurance, yet in a modified manner. For instance, when private health insurance is taken out as an alternative to social health insurance, mandatory rules of the law of the state which provides for such → substitution must be complied with (see art 206 of the Solvency II Directive). Similarly, rules setting up a regime of compulsory (liability) insurance will override the law otherwise applicable to the insurance contract (see in detail art 7(4) of the Rome I Regulation (Regulation (EC) No 593/2008 of the European Parliament and of the Council of 17 June 2008 on the law applicable to contractual obligations (Rome I), [2008] OJ L 177/6; → Rome Convention and Rome I Regulation (contractual obligations))).

II. Legal sources

1. Uniform law

Insurance contract law has thus far not been subjected to international unification. Equally, EU legislation on insurance hardly covers aspects of contract law. The Solvency II Directive only lays down very few contract law provisions, such as the right of cancellation in individual life insurance (art 186 of the Solvency II Directive) or the free choice of a lawyer in legal expenses insurance (art 201 of the Solvency II Directive). Other directives, such as the Directive 2009/103/EC (Directive 2009/103/EC of the European Parliament and of the Council of 16 September 2009 relating to insurance against civil liability in respect of the use of motor vehicles, and the enforcement of the obligation to insure against such liability, [2009] OJ L 263/11) covering motor vehicle liability insurance and the Directive on distance marketing of consumer financial services (Directive 2002/65/EC of the European Parliament and of the Council of 23 September 2002 concerning the distance marketing of consumer financial services and amending Council Directive 90/619/EEC and Directives 97/7/EC and 98/27/EC, [2002] OJ L 271/16) covering the distance selling of (among other things) insurance contracts to consumers add to this list.

Attempts have been made to prepare uniform insurance contract law. In 2016, the second edition of the Principles of European Insurance Contract Law (PEICL, Jürgen Basedow and others (eds), *Principles of European Insurance Contract Law* (2nd edn, Sellier 2016)) was published. These principles, which cover general rules as well as rules on liability, life and group insurance, represent a model optional instrument of European insurance contract law. According to art 1:102, a choice in favour of the PEICL will be freed from any restrictions of private international law. Based on the model of the PEICL, a new research group was set up in 2015, aiming at drafting international 'Principles of Reinsurance Contract Law' (PRICL). Such principles could be chosen by the parties to a reinsurance contract as the governing law at least when the contract is subject to arbitration (see the first sentence of art 28(1) of the UNCITRAL Arbitration Model Law (United Nations Commission on International Trade Law, UNCITRAL Model Law on International Commercial Arbitration as adopted on 21 June 1985, and as amended on 7 July 2006, UN doc A/40/17 and A/61/17); → Arbitration, (UNCITRAL) Model Law).

2. *Private international law of insurance*

There has hardly been any international harmonization of the private international law of insurance. The subject is barely touched upon by the Hague Convention of 4 May 1971 on the Law Applicable to Traffic Accidents (Hague Convention of 4 May 1971 on the law applicable to traffic accidents, 965 UNTS 415) which determines the law applicable to direct claims in art 9.

In contrast, private international law of insurance has been largely unified at EU level. Special rules apply to insurance for determining jurisdiction (see arts 10–16 of the Brussels I Regulation (recast) (Regulation (EU) No 1215/2012 of the European Parliament and of the Council of 12 December 2012 on jurisdiction and the recognition and enforcement of judgments in civil and commercial matters (recast), [2012] OJ L 351/1; → Brussels I (Convention and Regulation))) whenever the defendant is domiciled in a Member State within the meaning of the Regulation (ie all of the EU Member States except → Denmark). An insurer which is not domiciled in a Member State will nevertheless be subject to arts 10 ff of the Brussels I Regulation (recast) if it 'has a branch, agency or other establishment in one of the Member States' (art 11(2) of the Brussels I Regulation (recast)). If those criteria are not met, national rules on jurisdiction will apply.

Rules on the law applicable have also been unified in the EU (see in particular art 7 of the Rome I Regulation; see also art 18 (→ Direct action) and art 19 (Subrogation) of the → Rome II Regulation (non-contractual obligations) (Regulation (EC) No 864/2007 of the European Parliament and of the Council of 11 July 2007 on the law applicable to non-contractual obligations (Rome II), [2007] OJ L 199/40)). The Rome I and II Regulations do not directly apply to Denmark and the contracting states of the European Economic Area which are not EU Member States (Iceland, Liechtenstein and Norway). However, art 178 of the Solvency II Directive provides that those states must apply the Rome I Regulation, but not the Rome II Regulation, to insurance contracts falling within the scope of art 7 of the Rome I Regulation.

In the → USA, choice-of-law rules are neither unified nor do states provide for a specific and comprehensive regulation of insurance contracts. Rather, insurance contracts largely follow the common law rules governing contracts in each state. There are, however, special rules on insurance to be found. Long-arm statutes often expressly govern jurisdiction over non-resident insurance companies. Moreover, when determining the applicable law, some states provide for special statutory rules, whereas other states adhere to general principles of choice-of-law.

III. Current regulation

1. *Jurisdiction in general*

a) EU

EU rules on jurisdiction (arts 10–16 of the Brussels I Regulation (recast)) aim at protecting the weaker party (in particular the policyholder, insured and beneficiary). For that purpose, the policyholder, insured or beneficiary, as the case may be, is given an extended choice of forum (→ Choice of forum and submission to jurisdiction). Plaintiff policyholders, insured persons or beneficiaries may sue an insurer in the court of the Member State in which the insurer is domiciled or in the court where the plaintiff is domiciled (art 11(1)(a) and (b) of the Brussels I Regulation (recast)). Further options are provided to the plaintiff for specific situations. In cases of co-insurance, all participating insurers may be sued in the court of a Member State where the leading insurer is sued (art 11(1)(c) of the Brussels I Regulation (recast)). In cases where the insurance contract is concluded through a 'branch, agency or other establishment', another forum is provided at the place of such establishment (art 10 in connection with point 5 of art 7 of the Brussels I Regulation (recast)). In cases of liability insurance and insurance of immovable property, the place where the harmful event occurred provides another forum (art 12 of the Brussels I Regulation (recast)). Finally, a liability insurer may be joined in the proceedings brought by the victim against the insured (art 13(1) of the Brussels I Regulation (recast)).

In contrast, insurers 'may bring proceedings only in the courts of the Member State in which the defendant is domiciled' (art 14(1) of the Brussels I Regulation (recast); for limited exceptions, see art 14(2) and art 10 of the Brussels I Regulation (recast)).

In principle, choice-of-forum agreements may not be used to derogate from the rules on jurisdiction to the detriment of the policyholder, insured or beneficiary (see in detail the limits set out in art 15 of the Brussels I Regulation (recast)). This does, however, not apply to insurance contracts covering special and large risks as set out in art 16 of the Brussels I Regulation (recast). While such special and large risk insurances are subject to arts 10 ff of the Brussels I Regulation (recast), those rules are not mandatory in such cases and, thus, may be derogated from even to the detriment of the policyholder. Moreover, arts 10 ff of the Brussels I Regulation (recast) have been held not to be applicable to cases where an action is brought by an insurance company against another insurance company. Typically, this is the case in matters relating to reinsurance (ECJ in Case C-412/98 *Group Josi Reinsurance Company SA v Universal General Insurance Company (UGIC)* [2000] ECR I-5925) and in relation to recourse actions (ECJ in Case C-347/08 *Vorarlberger Gebietskrankenkasse v WGV-Schwäbische Allgemeine Versicherungs AG* [2009] ECR I-8866)). Thus, when bringing actions against each other, insurance companies have to follow the general rules set out in arts 4 ff of the Brussels I Regulation (recast) and cannot rely on the protective rules contained in arts 10 ff of the Brussels I Regulation (recast).

b) USA
US law on jurisdiction in matters relating to insurance is less peculiar but to a similar effect. States have enacted long-arm statutes, some of which specifically govern jurisdiction over non-resident insurers. Accordingly, jurisdiction is granted to the courts of a particular state when an insurance company is 'contracting to insure any person, property, or risk located within the state at the time the contract was made'. While other long-arm statutes do not provide for such

explicit regulation of actions brought against an insurer, they usually establish a general rule which will be applied very much in line with those statutes governing actions against insurers expressly. As a result, plaintiff policyholders are usually provided with a forum in their home state.

2. Jurisdiction for direct actions

a) EU
→ Direct action claims brought by victims are subject to art 13(2) of the Brussels I Regulation (recast). This provision refers to arts 10, 11 and 12 of the Brussels I Regulation (recast) and, thus, all choices of forum by the policyholder are also made available to the victim. This includes jurisdiction of the courts in the Member State in which the victim is domiciled (ECJ in Case C-463/06 *FBTO Schadeverzekeringen NV v Jack Odenbreit* [2007] ECR I-11321).

b) USA
In the USA, direct actions are often granted by special direct-action statutes. Such statutes may also govern questions of jurisdiction (Ronald A. Anderson and others (eds), *Couch on Insurance* (3rd edn, Sweet & Maxwell (November) 2014) § 104:17). For example, the Louisiana Direct Action Statute (Alston Johnson, 'The Louisiana Direct Action Statute' (1983) 43 La.L.Rev. 6) provides that a direct action claim may be brought 'in the parish in which the accident or injury occurred or in the parish in which an action could be brought against either the insured or the insurer under the general rules of venue prescribed by Code of Civil Procedure art 42 only' (§ 1269(B)(1) Louisiana R.S. 22:1269).

3. Law applicable in general (mass risk and large risk insurance)

a) EU
While the law applicable to insurance contracts has been unified in the EU (as to the special situation of Denmark, see *supra* section II.2.), the uniform rules themselves are quite complex and diverse. This can easily be demonstrated by setting out the substantive scope of application of the pertinent rules. Certain insurance contracts, 'the object of which is to provide benefits for employed or self-employed persons belonging to an undertaking or group of undertakings, or to a trade or group of trades, in the event of death

or survival or of discontinuance or curtailment of activity, or of sickness related to work or accidents at work', when offered by organizations other than life insurers are exempt from the Rome I Regulation under art 1(2)(i). Article 7 of the Rome I Regulation, which provides for a specific rule on insurance contracts, will not apply to reinsurance (second sentence of art 7(1) of the Rome I Regulation; as to reinsurance, see *infra* III.7.) or to mass risk insurance covering risks which are not located within the territory of a Member State (first sentence of art 7(1) of the Rome I Regulation). In contrast, insurance contracts covering large risks are fully covered by art 7 of the Rome I Regulation, irrespective of the location of the risks insured. Large risks are defined in art 7(2) of the Rome I Regulation by reference to the rather technical definition provided in the Directive 73/239 (Directive 73/239 of 24 July 1973 on the coordination of laws, regulations and administrative provisions relating to the taking-up and pursuit of the business of direct insurance other than life assurance, [1973] OJ L 228/3, as amended by the Directive 88/357 of 22 June 1988 on the coordination of laws, regulations and administrative provisions relating to the taking-up and pursuit of the business of direct insurance other than life assurance and laying down provisions to facilitate the effective exercise of freedom to provide services and amending Directive 73/239/EEC, [1988] OJ L 172/1) which has recently been replaced by the definition provided in point 27 of art 13 of the Solvency II Directive.

Large risk insurance will be subject to the law chosen by the parties. Parties may choose any law, irrespective of whether the insurance contract has any contact with such law. In the absence of a choice, the law of the country where the insurer has his habitual residence will apply. However, this conflict rule is flexible and, thus, 'where it is clear from all the circumstances of the case that the contract is manifestly more closely connected with another country, the law of that other country shall apply' (art 7(2) of the Rome I Regulation).

Mass risk insurance covering risks located within the territory of a Member State is governed by art 7(3) of the Rome I Regulation. Thus, the location of the insured risk not only determines the substantive law to be applied, but also the relevant conflict rules. The location of the risk is to be determined in accordance with points 13 and 14 of art 13 of the Solvency II Directive. In most cases, the policyholder's place of habitual residence will be decisive. However, insurance of vehicles covers risks located in the country of registration; insurance of immovable property (→ Property and proprietary rights) covers risks located in the country where the property is situated; finally, insurance 'of a duration of four months or less covering travel or holiday risks' covers risks located in the country where the policyholder took out such insurance.

Article 7(3) of the Rome I Regulation limits party autonomy by providing parties with specific options only. Member States may, however, broaden the scope of party autonomy and, ultimately, even grant a free → choice of law. Thus, uniformity of conflict rules is not achieved entirely. In the absence of a choice by the parties, the law of the Member State in which the risk is located will apply. Again, the location of the risk is to be determined in accordance with points 13 and 14 of Article 13 of the Solvency II Directive. Where an insurance contract covers risks located in more than one Member State, the contract will be split and treated as several contracts covering risks located in different Member States.

Other mass risk insurance covering risks located outside the territory of a Member State is governed by the general conflict rules, arts 3, 4 and 6, where applicable, of the Rome I Regulation. In principle, art 3 of the Rome I Regulation grants parties free choice of law. In the absence of such choice, the law of the country in which the insurer has its habitual residence will apply, unless the contract is manifestly more closely connected with another country. Consumer insurance contracts are, however, subject to art 6 of the Rome I Regulation which requires the application of the consumer's law and only permits a choice of law if such choice is not to the detriment of the consumer.

b) USA
Choce-of-law rules in matters relating to insurance in the USA are increasingly governed by special statutory provisions (Ronald A Anderson and others (eds), *Couch on Insurance* (3rd edn, Sweet & Maxwell (November) 2014) § 24:1). Such specific statutory rules usually prevail even if they conflict with the intentions of the parties. Often, statutes determine the → place of performance to be the decisive → connecting factor and, if such place is not specified in the policy, refer to the place of contract formation. Other statutes intend to protect the

insured and, thus, refer to the law of the insured (as to statutory regimes including examples, see Ronald A Anderson and others (eds), *Couch on Insurance* (3rd edn, Sweet & Maxwell (November) 2014) § 24:3).

Courts in states without a statutory conflict rule rely on general principles. Often courts tend to follow the rules set out in the Restatement (Second) of Conflict of Laws §§ 187, 188 (general provisions), § 192 (life insurance) and § 193 (casualty insurance) when determining the law applicable (American Law Institute, Restatement of the Law, Second: Conflict of Laws 2d, St Paul 1971; for courts in New York, see Raymond Cox, 'Choice of Law: New York and English Approaches to Insurance and Reinsurance Contracts' in Julian Burling and Kevin Lazarus (eds), *Research Handbook on International Insurance Law and Regulation* (Edward Elgar 2011) 195, 196 f).

Under § 187(1) Restatement (Second) of Conflict of Laws a choice of law is permitted which is free as far as non-mandatory rules are concerned. A choice of law will, however, also derogate mandatory rules if the law chosen by the parties has a substantial relationship to the case or some other reasonable basis and does not violate fundamental policies of the law otherwise applicable (in detail § 187(2) Restatement (Second) of Conflict of Laws). In any event, choice-of-law clauses contained in contracts of adhesion will be scrutinized by the court (see Comment (b) on § 188 Restatement (Second) of Conflict of Laws mentioning insurance policies as a specific example).

In the absence of a choice of law by the parties, § 188(1) Restatement (Second) of Conflict of Laws requires the application of the law of the state which has the most significant relationship to the contract in the light of the principles set out in § 6 Restatement (Second) of Conflict of Laws (Choice-of-Law Principles). § 188(2) Restatement (Second) of Conflict of Laws lists the contacts which have to be taken into account: (a) the place of contracting, (b) the place of negotiation of the contract, (c) the → place of performance, (d) the location of the subject matter of the contract and (e) the domicile (→ Domicile, habitual residence and establishment), residence, → nationality, place of incorporation and place of business of the parties. If the place of negotiation of the contract and performance coincide, this place will prevail over other contacts in accordance with § 188(3) Restatement (Second) of Conflict of Laws.

Life and casualty insurance are governed specifically in § 192 and § 193 Restatement (Second) of Conflict of Laws. Life insurance is subject to the law of the state in which the insured is domiciled at the time the contract is concluded. This connection is due to the fact that there is a particular need to protect the insured in cases of life insurance and that life insurance is subject to particularly intense statutory regulation in most states (Comment (c) on § 192 Restatement (Second) of Conflict of Laws). Exceptionally, another law with a more significant relationship to the life insurance contract may be applied. One of the examples mentioned in Comment (c) on § 192 Restatement (Second) of Conflict of Laws is the case where a policyholder changes his domicile following an application for the policy. Moreover, the law of a new domicile may govern certain aspects of the contract which are not relevant for the obligations of the insurer, such as the question of whether the appointment of the spouse as a beneficiary will automatically be revoked by a divorce (→ Divorce and personal separation). Parties may not derogate from such law to the detriment of the insured by a contract of adhesion. Detrimental choices of law will only be upheld if there was a real choice for the insured (see Comment (e) on § 192 Restatement (Second) of Conflict of Laws).

4. Law applicable to compulsory insurance

a) EU

EU → choice of law provides for a two-step regulation of compulsory insurance. First, art 7(4) of the Rome I Regulation provides that a contract for compulsory insurance will only

> satisfy the obligation to take out insurance unless it complies with the specific provisions relating to that insurance laid down by the Member State that imposes the obligation. Where the law of the Member State in which the risk is situated and the law of the Member State imposing the obligation to take out insurance contradict each other, the latter shall prevail.

Moreover, Member States are given the option to provide that the insurance contract shall be governed by the law of the Member State that imposes the duty to take out insurance.

b) USA

While any state establishing an obligation to take out liability insurance will enforce it at least by administrative means, the compulsory nature of liability insurance will have little impact on the law of contract to be applied. Courts, in principle, follow the general conflict rules applicable to insurance contracts. In doing so, they discuss the extent to which rules on the mandatory character of liability insurance form part of the public policy of a state. However, this seems to be only exceptionally the case (*State Farm Mut Auto Ins Co v Simmons's Estate*, 417 A.2d 488, 492 f (1980); *Colonial Penn Ins Co v Gibson*, 552 A.2d 644 (1989); *Rutgers Casualty Ins Co v Mcadams*, App. Div. (*per curiam*) (2007) unpublished).

5. Law applicable to direct actions

a) Hague Convention of 4 May 1971 on the law applicable to traffic accidents

Article 9 of the Hague Traffic Accident Convention (Hague Convention of 4 May 1971 on the law applicable to traffic accidents, 965 UNTS 415) provides a special conflict rule on direct claims. According to this provision, a direct action shall be granted if the law governing the tort provides for it. If this is not the case, a direct action claim may be granted by subsidiary connections, among them the law which governs the insurance contract. Thus, the Convention favours the existence of a direct claim for the victim.

b) EU

EU choice of law provides for a special rule governing direct claims. Under art 18 of the Rome II Regulation, a victim will enjoy a direct claim against the insurer of the person liable if either the law governing liability or the law governing the insurance contract provide for such direct claim (alternative connection). Thus, EU choice of law favours the existence of a direct claim for the victim.

c) USA

Direct-action statutes may determine their own scope of application, often requiring that the place where the harmful event has occurred or sometimes the place where the policy was issued or delivered to be in the state granting direct action (Ronald A Anderson and others (eds), *Couch on Insurance* (3rd edn, Sweet & Maxwell (November) 2014) § 104:46). But even direct-action statutes intending to apply independently of where the harmful event occurred have been declared as constitutional. Some courts have, however, held that a direct action claim may violate a state's public policy (see Ronald A Anderson and others (eds), *Couch on Insurance* (3rd edn, Sweet & Maxwell (November) 2014) § 104:49).

Apart from such unilateral limitations of the geographical application of direct-action statutes, Comment (b) on § 162 Restatement (Second) of Conflict of Laws refers to the law governing claims in tort in accordance with § 145 Restatement (Second) of Conflict of Laws to decide the question of whether an action may be brought directly against the insurer. This view has been followed by some courts (Ronald A Anderson and others (eds), *Couch on Insurance* (3rd edn, Sweet & Maxwell (November) 2014) § 104:57). Others have considered the direct claim to be a substantive right under the insurance contract and, thus, applied the law governing the insurance contract, ie the law where the contract was made (Ronald A Anderson and others (eds), *Couch on Insurance* (3rd edn, Sweet & Maxwell (November) 2014) § 104:56). Yet others have classified rights of direct action as procedural and, thus, as being governed by the → *lex fori* (Ronald A Anderson and others (eds), *Couch on Insurance* (3rd edn, Sweet & Maxwell (November) 2014) § 104:53).

6. Group insurance

a) EU

EU choice of law does not provide for special rules governing group insurance. From a formal point of view, the group organizer ('central entity') is the policyholder and the law of his habitual residence will apply. A critical view may regard the organizer more as an intermediary than as a policyholder and the insured more like an individual policyholder, at least where the insured ultimately pays the premium. However, such considerations are not reflected in the current text of art 7 of the Rome I Regulation.

b) USA

Under the Restatement (Second) of Conflict of Laws, § 192 Comment (h), a group life insurance contract will be governed by the law of the domicile of the group organizer ('central entity'). Thus, each and every individual insured will enjoy the same legal situation (Comment

(h) on § 192 Restatement (Second) of Conflict of Laws). At the same time, a choice of law by the parties will more readily be accepted by the parties because the central entity arranging the group insurance scheme will have a stronger bargaining position than an individual policyholder. Most courts seem to follow this approach (Ronald A Anderson and others (eds), *Couch on Insurance* (3rd edn, Sweet & Maxwell (November) 2014) § 8:7 where only a few courts are cited applying the law of the domicile of the individual insured).

7. Law applicable to reinsurance

Reinsurance is primarily governed by unfettered → party autonomy. In most cases, parties will agree on an arbitration or jurisdiction clause and determine the law applicable to their reinsurance contract by choice-of-law clauses.

If a choice-of-law clause, whether explicit or implicit, is not included in the contract, mainly two views are put forward. Under the first view, the reinsurance contract should be subject to the law of the *situs* of the direct insurer ceding a risk to a reinsurer. This approach is based on the view that the reinsurance contract has its most significant relationship to that law. There are a number of arguments why this should be the case. It is held that the reinsured has a much more pressing interest to have its law applied. Usually, it will deal with not only one, but several reinsurers each covering a share of the reinsured risk. Applying the law of the reinsured has the advantage of subjecting all of the → reinsurance contracts concerning the same risk to the same law. Moreover, the structuring of reinsurance risks, the selection of risks to be reinsured as well as the regulation of insurance claims is in the hands of the reinsured who provides these services for the reinsurer. Finally, reinsurers typically provide their services internationally, whereas many direct insurers only operate locally. Thus, submission to foreign law is more acceptable to a reinsurer than to a direct insurer (as to all these and further arguments, see Wulf-Henning Roth, *Internationales Versicherungsvertragsrecht* (Mohr Siebeck 1985) 584 ff).

Other authors have suggested that the law of the reinsurer should be applied. It is argued that the Rome I Regulation provides for a general rule covering all contracts including reinsurance contracts. According to this general rule (art 4 of the Rome I Regulation), the *situs* of the reinsurer, as the provider of the reinsurance service which at the same time is the performance giving the characteristics to a reinsurance contract, will be decisive for the law to be applied. Under such a view, the contacts of the reinsurance contract with the law at the *situs* of the reinsured would not be strong enough to justify a different solution in accordance with the flexibility rule contained in art 4(3) of the Rome I Regulation.

HELMUT HEISS

Literature

Ronald A Anderson and others (eds), *Couch on Insurance* (3rd edn, Sweet & Maxwell (November) 2014) Chapter 8 (Group Insurance: Rights and Obligations), Chapter 24 (Law Governing the Insurance Contract), Chapter 104 (Right of Direct Action Against Insurer: Generally); Jürgen Basedow and Till Fock (eds), *Europäisches Versicherungsvertragsrecht*, vols I and II (Mohr Siebeck 2002), vol III (Mohr Siebeck 2003); Jürgen Basedow and others (eds), *Principles of European Insurance Contract Law* (2nd edn, Sellier 2016); Julian Burling and Kevin Lazarus (eds), *Research Handbook on International Insurance Law and Regulation* (Edward Elgar 2011); Raymond Cox, 'Choice of Law: New York and English Approaches to Insurance and Reinsurance Contracts' in Julian Burling and Kevin Lazarus (eds), *Research Handbook on International Insurance Law and Regulation* (Edward Elgar 2011) 195; Urs Peter Gruber, 'art 7 Rome I (insurance contracts)' and 'art 18 Rome II (direct action against the insurer)' in Gralf-Peter Callies (ed), *The Rome Regulations (Rome I and II): Commentary on the European Rules for Conflicts of Law* (2nd edn Wolters Kluwer 2015); Helmut Heiss, 'Art. 7 Rome I' in Ulrich Magnus and Peter Mankowski (eds), *European Commentaries on Privat International Law, Rome I Regulation Commentary* (Otto Schmidt 2017); Helmut Heiss, 'arts 10–16' in Ulrich Magnus and Peter Mankowski (eds), *Brussels Ibis Regulation* (3rd revised edn, Sellier 2015); Wulf-Henning Roth, *Internationales Versicherungsvertragsrecht* (Mohr Siebeck 1985).

Intellectual property, applicable law

I. Concept and notion

The concept of intellectual property comprises all subjective rights over intangible or incorporeal goods, ie creations of the human mind, that may be invoked *erga omnes*. The concept therefore includes not only copyright and neighbouring rights, but also industrial property, and particularly rights over distinctive signs such as trademarks, commercial names and designations of origin, as well as intellectual creations concerning industrial products or their appearance such as inventions and design. It further covers *sui generis* rights over certain incorporeal objects, such as topographies of integrated circuits, databases, domain names, plant varieties and traditional knowledge. In contrast, trade secrets, to the extent they are protected only by the rules on unfair competition and not by exclusive rights granted to their holders, do not qualify as objects of intellectual property.

II. Purpose and function

Intangible goods, which are devoid of physical existence, are incapable of being appropriated by anyone, although the tangible things in which they materialize (their *corpus mechanicum*), such as the copies of a novel or the machines produced under a patent, can be so. Unlike tangible goods, intangibles are ubiquitous. They may be used simultaneously by an unlimited number of persons without losing their properties. On the other hand, they cannot be possessed by a single person, which is why they are sometimes termed 'public goods'. While the physical appropriation of a tangible good ensures its exclusive use and exploitation, in the case of intangible goods exclusivity requires that the law prohibits all other persons from using them, except for private purposes, and from exploiting them. This is the main function of intellectual property rules.

Exclusive rights over the use of intangible goods inevitably involve imposing restrictions upon competition and the free access of the members of the public to such goods. For this reason each legal system only usually grants those rights insofar as this is deemed to be socially useful, eg because that is the most effective way to stimulate intellectual creation or innovation. The prevailing notions as to the object, scope and content of those rights, as well as to the limitations and exceptions to which they are subject and the definition of who their original holders are, often differ from country to country. Each state therefore typically reserves for itself the prerogative of defining in what terms such rights are constituted, exercised and extinguished in its own territory. In cross-border situations, this raises the question of the extent to which intellectual property rights granted by one state may be enforced by the jurisdictions of another state. International intellectual property law addresses this problem.

III. Legal sources

1. National

Neither Roman law nor medieval law recognized exclusive rights on intangible goods. In the 15th century, after the invention of the printing press, European sovereigns began granting privileges to printers, and exceptionally also to authors of books and other intellectual works. Privileges concerning the exploitation of useful inventions were also granted in several European countries. However, the aims of these privileges were very different from those of contemporary copyrights and patents. Primarily, they were meant to compensate an investment, by protecting their beneficiaries from competition. They were also frequently a form of controlling the circulation of works and certain economic activities. This explains why they were ordinarily not granted to authors and inventors, but rather to those who reproduced or otherwise exploited their works or inventions. Moreover, those privileges were awarded discretionarily. One may therefore say that at the time intellectual creations were not the object of subjective rights.

It was only in the 18th century, when the pressure to protect authors and inventors mounted in Europe, that the idea was advanced that property should vest in the creators of intangible goods as naturally as it does in the owners of tangible goods. Thus, in 1790 *Stanislas de Boufflers* proclaimed, in his report to the French National Assembly on the draft new law on inventions, that 'If a true property exists for a man, it is his thinking'. Further in the well-known words of *Isaac Le Chapelier*, drafter of the first French law on copyright: 'The most sacred, the most legitimate, the most unassailable and, if I may say so, the most personal of all properties, is the work that is the outcome of a writer's thinking'. The notion of intellectual property was thus born.

This notion blossomed in French law, which expressly adopted it in the law of 1791 concerning discoveries and inventions, as well as in the laws of 1791 and 1793 concerning, respectively, the right of public performance of literary works in theatres and the right of reproduction of literary and artistic works. It still prevails in modern French law. This is why the *Code la propriété intellectuelle* (French Intellectual Property Code, Act No 92–597 of 1 July 1992, as amended) states in art L-111-1: 'L'auteur d'une œuvre de l'esprit jouit sur cette œuvre, du seul fait de sa création, d'un droit de propriété incorporelle exclusif et opposable à tous'.

According to this line of reasoning, authors' rights stem from a fact, the creation of a work, and not from the law, which merely recognizes them as an emanation of the nature of things. Thus they vest in principle in the creator of that work. Due to French influence, this personalist notion of intellectual property was subsequently adopted by other countries of continental Europe and the rest of the world.

A different school of thought prevailed in common law countries. The recognition of intellectual property rights first took place in England by virtue of the Statute of Anne of 1710 ('An Act for the Encouragement of Learning, by Vesting the Copies of Printed Books in the Authors or Purchasers of such Copies, during the Times therein mentioned', available at <www.copyrighthistory.com/anne.html>), which gave authors or their assignees, for a period of 14 years counting from the moment of the first publication, an exclusive right of reproduction (a 'copyright') over their literary works. This statute placed the emphasis on the commercial exploitation of works; and it made their protection dependent upon a registration prior to their publication. According to the statute's preamble, its purpose consisted of 'the encouragement of learned men to compose and write useful books'. The right enshrined in this statute was thus conceived as an incentive to create literary works, which the public could enjoy. It thus had a clearly utilitarian purpose. This concept of copyright was subsequently adopted by the United States Constitution, which proclaims in article 1(8) that 'The Congress shall have power ... to promote the progress of science and useful arts by securing for limited times to authors and inventors the exclusive rights to their respective writings and discoveries'. In England and in the USA copyright is thus not a natural right, but rather a monopoly granted by the law, which may only be exercised in the terms set out in legal rules. This is why in *Donaldson v Beckett* ([1774] 1 ER 837) the House of Lords was able to reject the existence of a perpetual common law copyright and to hold instead that copyright was a creation of statute that could be limited in its duration. A utilitarian notion of intellectual property thus emerged.

2. *International*

Intellectual property law is currently one of the most internationalized branches of private law. Many of the most significant developments in this field during the past 100 years were the fruit of international treaties, including the Paris Industrial Property Convention (Paris Convention for the Protection of Industrial Property, 20 March 1883, with later amendments, 828 UNTS 305) and the Berne Convention (Berne Convention for the Protection of Literary and Artistic Works of 9 September 1886, completed at Paris on 4 May 1896, revised at Berlin on 13 November 1908, completed at Berne on 20 March 1914, revised at Rome on 2 June 1928, revised at Brussels on 26 June 1948, revised at Stockholm on 14 July 1967 and revised at Paris on 24 July 1971, 1161 UNTS 3 and amended in 1979 Treaty Doc no 99-27, and 1985, 828 UNTS 221) of 1883 and 1886 respectively, the → TRIPS Agreement of 1994 (Agreement of 15 April 1994 on Trade-Related Aspects of Intellectual Property Rights, 1869 UNTS 299), the WIPO Internet Treaties of 1996 (WIPO Performances and Phonograms Treaty (WPPT) of 20 December 1996, WIPO Publication No 227 and WIPO Copyright Treaty (WCT) of 20 December 1996, WIPO Publication No 226) and, more recently, the Anti-Counterfeiting Trade Agreement (Anti-Counterfeiting Trade Agreement (ACTA) of 15 November 2010 (see text in Proposal for a Council Decision on the conclusion of the Agreement of 24 June 2011, COM(2011) 380 final)) concluded in 2010.

As a result of these developments, certain minimum standards concerning the protection of intellectual property rights have emerged, and are now adopted by most countries. Nevertheless, many significant differences remain between the common law and the civil law traditions. They concern among others (i) ownership of copyright in the case of works made for hire or in the course of employment, (ii) the extent to which originality may be required for the protection of intellectual creations, (iii) the scope of fair use and fair dealing, as well as of exceptions to copyright, (iv) the possibility of acquiring rights in trademarks without registration, (v) the patentability of computer programs, business methods and biotechnological inventions, (vi) the standards for determining the equivalence between a claimed invention and an allegedly infringing device and (vii) the possibility of awarding punitive or exemplary → damages in the case of an intellectual property infringement.

These differences do not merely reflect technical divergences between national legal systems. For the most part, they are the expression of divergent policies regarding the extent to which monopolies on intangible goods may be allowed, as well as the scope of the public domain (and hence of free competition) with regard to the use and exploitation of such goods. In some cases, national interests have also clashed in this field and prevented the adoption of uniform rules. In this regard it is sufficient to mention the 35-year long quest for a Unitary European Patent, which has only very recently borne its fruits. The ideal of a uniform, worldwide protection of intellectual property rights, which inspired the Universal Copyright Convention made in Geneva in 1952 (Geneva Universal Copyright Convention of 6 September 1952, as amended in Paris on 24 July 1971, 943 UNTS 194), thus remains largely unachieved.

3. *European*

In the EU, a geographically more restricted, but deeper, process of legal integration has occurred, thanks to the legal acts that have harmonized (and in some cases unified) Member States laws. This is notably the case of the 2001 Directive on copyright in the information society (Directive 2001/29/EC of 22 May 2001 on the harmonization of certain aspects of copyright and related rights in the information society [2001] OJ L 167/10), the 2004 Directive on the enforcement of intellectual property rights (Directive 2004/48/EC of 29 April 2004 on the enforcement of intellectual property rights [2004] OJ L 157/45) and the 2008 Directive on trade marks (Directive 2008/95/EC of the European Parliament and of the Council of 22 October 2008 to approximate the laws of the Member States relating to trade marks [2008] OJ L 299/25). In some cases, unitary, EU-wide exclusive rights were created by European legal acts, as was the case of the Community Design Regulation (Council Regulation (EC) No 6/2002 of 12 December 2001 on Community designs, [2002] OJ L 3/1), the Community Trade mark Regulation (Council Regulation (EC) No 207/2009 of 26 February on the Community trade mark, [2009] OJ L 78/1) and, more recently, the Regulation on a Unitary Patent Protection (Regulation (EU) No 1257/2012 of the European Parliament and of the Council of 17 December 2012 implementing enhanced cooperation in the area of the creation of unitary patent protection [2012] OJ L361/1).

European legal enactments in this field are largely based upon the idea that the establishment of an internal market in the EU requires common intellectual property rules that will ensure competitors a level playing field, although this goal has only partially been achieved. Important differences subsist between Member States' legal systems, eg regarding free uses of copyrighted works, moral rights, collective management and unregistered trademarks. This is one of the reasons why the 'Wittem Group' undertook the task of drafting a European Copyright Code (available at <www.copyrightcode.eu>), which was published in 2010. However, this code focuses on only five topics: the definition of protected works, authorship and ownership, moral rights, economic rights and limitations. Thus it contains no rules concerning for example rental rights, resale rights, technological protection measures, the enforcement of rights and neighbouring rights. The problem of the law applicable to intellectual property rights and their infringement therefore subsists within the European space.

IV. The determination of the applicable law: current regulation

1. *National*

One of the longest-standing principles in this branch of the law is that of → territoriality, according to which intellectual property rights are governed by the law of the country for the territory of which their protection is claimed, the so-called *lex loci protectionis*. This principle is currently adopted among others in art 110(1) Swiss Private international law Act (*Bundesgesetz über das Internationale Privatrecht* of 18 December 1987, 1988 BBl I 5, as amended; according to which: 'Les droits de la propriété intellectuelle sont régis par le droit de l'Etat pour lequel la protection de propriété intellectuelle est revendiquée'); art 54(1) of the Italian Private international law Act (*Riforma del Sistema italiano di diritto internazionale private*, Act No 218 of 31 May 1995 in Gazz. Uff, Supplemento Ordinario No 128 of 3 June 1995, as amended; which states that: 'I diritti su beni immateriali sono regulate dalla legge dello Stato di utilizzazione'); and art 93(1) Belgian Private international law Act (*Wet houdende het*

Wetboek von international privaatrecht/Code de droit international privé of 16 July 2004, BS 27 July 2004, p 57344, 57366; pursuant to which: 'Les droits de propriété intellectuelle sont régis par le droit de l'État pour le territoire duquel la protection de la propriété est demandée').

Despite this the scope of the → territoriality principle remains controversial. It can only be correctly defined bearing in mind the reasons that account for the adoption of that principle. In fact, applicability of the *lex protectionis* is fully justified with regard to the existence, content and scope of the protection granted to intellectual property rights. Given the public interests involved in these issues, each state should be able to regulate the exclusive rights for which protection is claimed in its own territory. Regarding initial ownership, however, it is subject to argument that such interests are at stake. If, for example, a work made for hire in the USA is deemed worthy of protection in Portugal as an intellectual creation that cannot be freely used, then this does not necessarily entail that Portuguese rules concerning the ownership of copyright over such a work should apply. This is because, from the point of view of the public interests at stake, it is irrelevant whether the copyright on that work vests in the person who has actually created the work or his employer. Other laws may thus be applied.

A possible option is the *lex originis*; another one is the *lex contractus*, ie the law that applies to the employment relationship between the author and the person for whom the work was created. Applying the *lex originis* may facilitate cross-border licensing and promote certainty as to the ownership of the right when this is exercised abroad. Application of the *lex contractus* will enhance legal harmony because the contract and the work created in performance of it will be subject to the same law. The law of the country of origin has long been applied by the Supreme Courts of France and Portugal, although French rules concerning authors' moral rights, which are deemed to be *règles d'application immédiate*, considerably restrict that law's scope of application. A *lex originis* rule may be found among others in private international law provisions of Portugal (art 48(1) Portuguese Civil Code (*Código Civil* approved by Decreto-Lei No 47.344, of 25 November 1966, [1966] Diário do Governo I série 274/1883, with subsequent amendments)), Romania (art 60 Romanian Act on Private international law (Law No 105 of 22 September 1992, effective 26 October 1993, on the Settlement of Private international law Relations, Official Gazette of Romania No 245 of 1 October 1992)) and Greece (art 67(1) Law on Copyright (Law No 2121/1993 on Copyright, Related Rights and Cultural Matters (as last amended by Law No 3057/2002 (art 81) and by Law No 3207/2003 (art 10 par 33)))).

It is equally doubtful that the applicability of the *lex loci protectionis* should systematically extend to the remedies for the infringement of intellectual property rights. In French and Portuguese private international law this issue was traditionally governed by the *lex loci delicti*, or in some cases by the parties' *lex communis*. A → *dépeçage* was therefore introduced in this regard. This seemed justified by the fact that the reasons militating in favour of the applicability of the former of these two laws do not require that remedies for the infringement of those rights also be governed by that law. The exclusive right that has been infringed and the right to → damages for its infringement are, in fact, distinct rights. Thus while the former implicates public interests, the latter basically protects a private interest. Accordingly, the right to compensation may be waived, while some intellectual property rights, such as authors' moral rights, may not.

2. International

The territoriality principle is enshrined in the Berne Convention, which states in art 5(2) that 'the extent of protection, as well as the means of redress afforded to the author to protect his rights, shall be governed exclusively by the laws of the country where protection is claimed'. The Convention thereby acknowledges the diversity of national legal systems with regard to copyright protection and the right of each country to set out the boundaries of the protection afforded to intellectual creations in its territory. However, this right is limited in two ways. On the one hand, through the national treatment principle enshrined in art 5(1) of the Convention, thanks to which foreign authors may not be discriminated against within Berne's scope of application, and on the other hand, by the minimum rights granted by the Convention itself, which are reserved in art 5(2). Notwithstanding that, copyright was essentially conceived by the drafters of the Berne Convention as a territorial right, governed by the law of the country for which protection is claimed.

The same may be said about rights in patents and trademarks. Under the Paris Convention, each Member State applies its law to nationals and foreigners without distinction (art 2(a)). Furthermore, patents and trademarks obtained in the Member States of the Paris Union for the same inventions or distinctive signs are mutually independent (see arts 4bis(1) and 6(3)). As in the Berne Convention, this entails that the protection accorded in the territory of each Member State to such intangible goods is governed by local law.

More modern formulations of the same principle were adopted in the ALI Intellectual Property Law Principles, prepared under the auspices of the American Law Institute (published in 2008) (American Law Institute, Intellectual property: principles governing jurisdiction, choice of law and judgments in transnational disputes, St Paul 2008), the Principles of Private international law on Intellectual Property Rights drafted by members of the Private international law Associations of Korea and Japan in a project coordinated by the Waseda University (published in 2010) (Joint Proposal Drafted by Members of the Private international law Association of Korea and Japan on Private international law on Intellectual Property Rights, printed in 2011 *The Quarterly Review of Corporation Law and Society* (Waseda, Japan) 112–63) and the Principles on Conflict of Laws in Intellectual Property (or → CLIP Principles) promoted by the European Max Planck Group on Conflict of Laws in Intellectual Property (published in 2011) (European Max Planck Group on Conflict of Laws in Intellectual Property, Conflict of laws in intellectual property: the → CLIP Principles and Commentary, Oxford 2013). Indeed, according to § 301 of the ALI Principles,

> Except as otherwise provided in §§ 302 and 321–323, the law applicable to determine the existence, validity, duration, attributes, and infringement of intellectual property rights and the remedies for their infringement is: (a) for registered rights, the law of each state of registration; (b) for other intellectual property rights, the law of each state for which protection is sought.

Article 301 of the Waseda Principles in turn states that

(1) All matters concerning an intellectual property right as such, including its existence, validity, content, revocation and the like, shall be governed by *lex protectionis* unless otherwise provided by these Principles.

(2) Subject to the preceding paragraph, *lex protectionis* is the law of the state for which protection is sought. In the case of a registered intellectual property right, this state is presumed to be the state in which that right is or will be registered, or which is deemed to be a state of registration under the convention to which that state belongs or the local law of that state.

Further pursuant to art 3:102 CLIP Principles, 'The law applicable to the existence, validity, registration, scope and duration of an intellectual property right and all other matters concerning the right as such is the law of the state for which protection is sought'. An absolute territoriality of intellectual property rights, in the sense that the courts of each country should only apply the *lex fori* to their enforcement, was thus rejected by these soft law instruments.

Regarding initial ownership, the ALI Principles provide in § 313 for the application of a variant of the *lex originis*, the law of the creator's residence, with regard to intellectual property rights that do not arise out of registration. The *lex contractus* applies if the subject matter was created pursuant to an employment relationship. The Waseda and the CLIP Principles have chosen a somewhat different path, by stating respectively in art 308(1) and in art 3:201(1) that initial ownership is in principle governed by the *lex loci protectionis*. Nevertheless, art 308(2) Waseda Principles provides that 'Initial ownership of a copyrighted work is governed by the law of the state in which the copyrighted work is initially created'. Under art 3:201(2) CLIP Principles, if the situation has a close connection with another state that has a work made for hire provision, effect may be given to it. Pursuant to art 3:201(3), the law applicable in the case of a registered right claimed in the framework of an employment relationship is to be determined in accordance with the conflict rules concerning employment contracts. In many cases the practical result of the three proposals will be identical. However, the ALI and Waseda rules have some advantages over the CLIP solution with regard to predictability of the outcome of the dispute.

Regarding remedies for the infringement of intellectual property rights, a limited choice of the applicable law by the parties has been proposed in these international instruments. The ALI Principles state in § 302 that 'Subject to the other provisions of this Section, the parties may agree at any time, including after a dispute arises, to designate a law that will govern all or part of their dispute'. The Waseda Principles provide in art 304(1) that 'The law applicable to an alleged infringement and remedies is the law of each state for which protection is sought, provided that this shall not apply if the parties have chosen another law under the provisions of Article 302'. The CLIP Principles adopt a more restrictive rule in this respect. According to art 3:606(1), the parties may agree to submit the remedies claimed for the infringement to the law of their choice by an agreement entered into before or after the dispute has arisen. Furthermore, pursuant to art 3:606(2), if the infringement is closely connected with a pre-existing relationship between the parties, such as a contract, then the law governing the pre-existing relationship will also govern the remedies for the infringement. This is unless the parties have expressly excluded the application of the law governing the pre-existing relationship with regard to the remedies for infringement, or it is clear from all the circumstances of the case that the claim is more closely connected with another state. These rules are in line with the disposable nature of tort claims in most jurisdictions.

A final issue concerning the scope of the *lex protectionis* relates to whether it should also apply to security rights in intellectual property. Again, this problem should be solved in the light of the reasons that justify the applicability of that law. From this point of view, the *lex protectionis* should apply in order to determine whether an intellectual property right may be given as a security, since this is an issue that pertains to the content of that right. However, the rights and obligations of each party in a contract that provides for the creation or the transfer of a security in an intellectual property right, as well as the security rights themselves, should not be governed by that law, since the public interests that account for the applicability of the *lex protectionis* are not at stake here. This distinction is clearly made in arts 3:801 and 3:802 of the CLIP Principles.

3. European

In the EU, the principle of territoriality has prevailed in the → Rome II Regulation (non-contractual obligations) (Regulation (EC) No 864/2007 of the European Parliament and of the Council of 11 July 2007 on the law applicable to non-contractual obligations (Rome II), [2007] OJ L 199/40), art 8(1) of which states: 'The law applicable to a non-contractual obligation arising from an infringement of an intellectual property right shall be the law of the country for which protection is claimed'. The Regulation has thus subjected remedies for the infringement of intellectual property rights to the law of the country for the territory of which protection is claimed. Those remedies and the preliminary question of the existence and the validity of the allegedly infringed right will accordingly be governed by the same law. Under art 8(3), the applicable law may not be derogated from by an agreement pursuant to art 14 of the Regulation. The applicability of the law governing a pre-existing relationship between the parties, such as a contract, is also not allowed. The *lex protectionis* therefore has a more extended scope of application in this Regulation than in the above-mentioned instruments.

V. Modern trends

In an era of globalization, in which the use and exploitation of intellectual creations increasingly occur on an international scale, a strictly territorial understanding of intellectual property law can hardly correspond to the needs of the economy. This is why an important deviation from this principle was enshrined in the 1968 Brussels Convention (Brussels Convention of 27 September 1968 on jurisdiction and the enforcement of judgments in civil and commercial matters, [1972] OJ L 299/32, consolidated version, [1998] OJ C 27/1; and subsequently also in the Brussels I Regulation (Regulation (EC) No 44/2001 of 22 December 2000 on jurisdiction and the recognition and enforcement of judgments in civil and commercial matters, [2001] OJ L 12/1) and Brussels I Regulation (recast) (Regulation (EU) No 1215/2012 of the European Parliament and of the Council of 12 December 2012 on jurisdiction and the recognition and enforcement of judgments in civil and commercial matters (recast), [2012] OJ L 351/1; → Brussels I (Convention and Regulation))), which allowed the enforcement of intellectual property rights by the courts of the defendant's country of domicile, even if this is not the country of protection of such rights. In the EU, the extraterritorial enforcement of intellectual property rights was thus allowed.

The AIPPI endorsed this view in its 2003 Resolution on Jurisdiction and Applicable Law in the Case of Cross-Border Infringement of Intellectual Property Rights ([2003] AIPPI Yearbook 827–9), which states in art 1(1): 'The courts of a given country should be allowed to make a ruling over infringing acts regarding certain intellectual property rights which have taken place in any other country . . .'. Article 2(1) of the same Resolution further provides that a clear distinction should be drawn between the conflict of jurisdictions and the conflict of laws.

The ALI, the Waseda and the CLIP Principles have also made this distinction since, notwithstanding the above-mentioned conflict rules, they adopt as a primary rule of jurisdiction concerning the infringement of intellectual property rights that a person may be sued in the courts of his or her state of habitual residence. In this sense, intellectual property rights are not strictly territorial in these sets of Principles.

Lucasfilm Ltd & Ors v Ainsworth & Anor [2011] UKSC 39 illustrates this problem. That case concerned an alleged infringement of US copyright committed by the defendant in that country, where he had sold a number of copies of certain artefacts (notably helmets) originally produced by himself for the first Star Wars film. In a judgment rendered on 27 July 2011, the UK Supreme Court stated that, provided there is a basis for *in personam* jurisdiction over the defendant (as was the case), an English court has jurisdiction to try a claim for an infringement of this kind. This judgment thus constitutes an endorsement of the kind of extraterritoriality that the AIPPI Resolution and the said Principles allow.

This form of extraterritoriality was not provided for in the first intellectual property Conventions, which did not clearly distinguish the *lex protectionis* from the *lex fori*. The Berne Convention, for example, refers to the 'laws of the country where protection is claimed', instead of those of the 'country for which protection is claimed'. This, of course, is due to the fact that its drafters did not contemplate the possibility of a court outside that country being competent for the enforcement of an intellectual property right.

The ECJ has also significantly contributed to this trend through its case-law on the community exhaustion of copyright, according to which distribution rights granted by the EU Member States may no longer be invoked in respect of copies of copyrighted works which have been lawfully marketed in other Member States. The degree of control that each EU Member State exercises over the monopolies that it grants on intellectual creations has thereby been considerably restricted.

Another important development in this regard concerns internet uses of protected works. The ubiquity of the internet has greatly enhanced the number of cases in which the use of a protected work may be deemed to have occurred simultaneously in several countries where it is made available online. In such cases, multiple laws may apply, exposing the user of the work to potentially contradictory requirements, that is a lawful user in one country may be held an infringer elsewhere. This in turn considerably inhibits the dissemination of intellectual creations through the internet. The ALI Principles, the Waseda Principles and the CLIP Principles attempt to solve this problem by providing that, in the case of a 'ubiquitous infringement', courts may apply the law of the state presenting the closest connection with the dispute (§ 321 ALI Principles; art 306(1) Waseda Principles; art 3:603(1) CLIP Principles). That connection may be evidenced among others by the parties' residence or place of business, the country where their activities were carried out or the market to which they were directed. By virtue of this → 'escape clause' (as it has been characterized) the cumulative applicability of different national copyright laws, which may ensue from the territoriality principle in the case of internet uses of protected works, can be avoided, and a single law may be applied. A further restriction to that principle has thus found its way into the three sets of Principles.

Still another deviation from territoriality may be found in art 3:604(2) CLIP Principles (→ CLIP), which concerns secondary infringement. According to that provision, the law applicable to the liability of persons, such as Internet Service Providers, that offer facilities or services 'capable of being used for infringing and non-infringing purposes by a multitude of users without intervention of the person offering or rendering the facilities or services in relation to the individual acts resulting in infringement', is the law of the state where the 'centre of gravity' of the person's activities relating to those facilities or services is located. That law only applies, according to art 3:604(3), if it provides at least for liability for failure to react in case of actual knowledge of a primary infringement or in case of a manifest infringement and liability for active inducement. The Principles have thus endeavoured to ensure that Internet Service Providers benefit from the rules providing for the exclusion of their liability (such as those contained in arts 12 to 15 of the e-Commerce Directive (Directive 2000/31/EC of the European Parliament and of the Council of 8 June 2000 on certain legal aspects of information society services, in particular electronic commerce, in the Internal Market (Directive on electronic commerce) [2000] OJ L178/1)) which are in force in the country where they are established. According to the Principles, under these conditions, such rules prevail, over those of the *lex protectionis*.

A trend towards a mitigated form of territoriality has thus emerged, according to which the courts of each country may enforce foreign intellectual property rights, although they are with some exceptions bound to apply the law of the country for the territory of which their protection is sought.

Yet the need for restrictions to territoriality should not be overstated. Copyright and other intellectual property rights are basically exceptions to a principle of freedom that governs the use of intellectual creations. All uses of such creations that are not legally reserved to a given category of persons should be deemed free. Furthermore, like any other exclusive rights, intellectual property rights deeply affect social interests, notably in that they restrict public access to knowledge and information, as was stressed in the Washington Declaration on Intellectual Property and the Public Interest (available at <http://infojustice.org/wp-content/uploads/2011/09/Washington-Declaration.pdf>) adopted at the Global Congress on Intellectual Property and the Public Interest on 27 August 2011.

This is why the regulation of intellectual property rights still essentially belongs to states, which reserve for themselves the prerogative of defining, in conformity with their own assessment of the interests at stake, the conditions of acquisition, exercise and extinction of such rights in their territory, as well as the limits and exceptions to which they are subject. This is also why the exclusionary powers of intellectual property rights holders can only be exercised with regard to acts performed in the territory of the state that has granted those powers. To be sure, the enforcement of intellectual property rights may be requested of the jurisdictions of a different state, but in that case those jurisdictions shall apply the law of the state for the territory of which the protection of such rights is requested.

Dário Moura Vicente

Literature

American Law Institute, *Intellectual Property: Principles Governing Jurisdiction, Choice of Law, and Judgments in Transnational Disputes* (American Law Institute Publishers 2008); Jürgen Basedow and others (eds), *Intellectual Property in the Conflict of Laws* (Siebeck 2005); Javier Carrascosa González, *La propiedad intelectual en Derecho internacional privado español* (Comares 1994); Josef Drexl and Annette Kur (eds), *Intellectual Property and Private international law. Heading for the Future* (Hart Publishing 2005); Mireille van Eechoud, *Choice of Law in Copyright and Related Rights: Alternatives to the Lex Protectionis* (Kluwer 2003); European Max Planck Group on Conflict of Laws in Intellectual Property (ed), *The Conflict of Law in Intellectual Property: The CLIP Principles and Commentary* (OUP 2013); James Fawcett and Paul Torremans, *Intellectual Property and Private international law* (2nd edn, OUP 2011); Jane Ginsburg, 'The Private international law of Copyright in an Era of Technological Change' (1998) 273 Rec. des Cours 239; Toshiyuki Kono (ed), *Intellectual Property and Private international law: Comparative Perspectives* (Hart 2012); Peter Mankowski, 'Das Internet im Internationalen Vertrags- und Deliktsrecht' (1998) 62 RabelsZ 203; Rita Matulionyte, 'IP and Applicable Law in Recent International Proposals: Report for the International Law Association' [2012] JIPITEC 3; Pedro de Miguel Asensio, *Contratos internacionales sobre propiedad industrial* (2nd edn, Civitas 2000); Pedro de Miguel Asensio, *Derecho Privado de Internet* (4th edn, Civitas 2011); Marta Pertegás Sender, *Cross-Border Enforcement of Patent Rights: An Analysis of the Interface Between Intellectual Property and Private international law* (OUP 2002); Stig Strömholm, 'Copyright: National and International Development' *IECL*, vol 14, Copyright (Mohr Siebeck & Martinus Nijhoff 2007); Stig Strömholm, 'Copyright: Comparison of Laws' *IECL*, vol 14, Copyright (Mohr Siebeck & Martinus Nijhoff 2007); Alain Strowel, *Droit d'auteur et copyright: Divergences et convergences. Etude de droit comparé* (Bruylant & LGDJ 1993); Eugen Ulmer, *Die Immaterialgüterrechte im internationalen Privatrecht. Rechtsvergleichende Untersuchung mit Vorschlägen für die Vereinheitlichung in der Europäischen Wirtschaftsgemeinschaft* (Carl Heymanns 1975); Dário Moura Vicente, *La propriété intellectuelle en droit international privé* (Martinus Nijhoff 2009).

Intellectual property, jurisdiction

I. Harmonizing international jurisdiction rules

Whereas substantive international private law is far advanced in terms of international harmonization, issues of international jurisdiction still remain national. In fact, even though states constituted international governmental organizations that centralize all or part of the administrative procedures necessary for the granting of certain intellectual property rights, those procedures typically give rise to a portfolio of national or EU intellectual property rights enforceable only as territorial rights. Yet, these procedures do not contain significant rules addressing either the international jurisdiction of the courts of the Member States to adjudicate intellectual property related claims, or the recognition and enforcement of foreign judgments in the area of intellectual property rights (see however the Protocol on Jurisdiction and Recognition of the European Patent Convention of 5 October 1973 <www.epo.org/law-practice/legal-texts/html/epc/2013/e/ma4.html>). Additionally, even though existing universal international instruments on Intellectual Property, especially the ones concluded in the past two decades (including → TRIPS (Agreement on Trade Related Aspects of Intellectual Property Rights (annex 1C of the Marrakesh Agreement Establishing the World Trade Organization, signed in Marrakesh, Morocco on 15 April 1994) 1869 UNTS 299) and ACTA (Anti-Counterfeiting Trade Agreement (ACTA) of 15 November 2010 (see text in Proposal for a Council Decision on the conclusion of the Agreement of 24 June 2011, COM(2011) 380 final)), strongly emphasize the need effectively to enforce intellectual property rights, and though enforcement of intellectual property rights across national borders is crucial for their protection, those international instruments focus on purely domestic issues, ignoring transnational disputes. So, while the first steps in the direction of harmonizing international jurisdiction on intellectual property rights were undertaken by the Hague Conference in 1999 when it launched its preliminary draft proposal for an international Convention on Jurisdiction and Enforcement in Civil and Commercial Matters which also included rules on cross-border intellectual property rights issues, this text and its intellectual property rights rules were very contentious and determined the failure of the entire Draft Convention (Preliminary Draft Convention on Jurisdiction and the Effects of Judgments in Civil and Commercial Matters, 18 June 1999, with an explanatory report by Peter Nygh and Fausto Pocar, (HC) Prel. Doc. No 11, hereinafter the Draft Convention), followed by a new draft in 2001 (Permanent Bureau, Preliminary Document No 13, Report of the experts meeting in the intellectual property aspects of the future Convention on jurisdiction and foreign judgments in civil and commercial matters ((HC) Prel. Doc. No 13, 1 February 2001)).

Reasons for this current frame are at least two. First, since the failure of the Draft Convention was mainly due to the lack of consensus on intellectual property rights rules, states are discouraged from negotiating any intellectual property cross-border litigation instrument. Second, as with other issues that do not have adequate attention at the international level, there is a lack of pressure by interested groups to place the matters on the agenda. The current system, in fact, obliges enforcement of intellectual property rights on a national basis, country by country according to the so-called mosaic approach. This causes economic inequalities, where the big multinational companies are generally able to finance litigation in every relevant jurisdiction, whereas the medium–small size enterprises typically do not have the same financial strength to defend each national proceeding. Indeed, empirical studies have shown in recent years that cross-border cases are growing in number and increasing in proportion to the total percentage of intellectual property rights transnational litigation. Additionally, this increase is seen in cases affecting intellectual property rights that are particularly relevant to the national economy of the countries involved. Therefore, given the frequent exploitation of intellectual property rights beyond national borders and the need for their cross-border enforcement, an international agreement should remain the ultimate goal to be achieved.

Thus, recent negotiations at different international *fora* of mainly an academic nature proposed four sets of principles that can serve as models for future states' negotiations of an international agreement on intellectual property and private international law. These sets of principles are the ALI Principles Governing Jurisdiction, Choice of Law, and Judgments in Transnational Disputes, adopted on 14 May 2007 (American Law Institute, Intellectual property: principles governing jurisdiction, choice of law and judgments in transnational disputes, St Paul 2008); the CLIP Principles for Conflict of Laws in Intellectual Property, prepared by the European Max Planck Group on Conflict of Laws in Intellectual Property, published on 31 August 2011 (European Max Planck Group on Conflict of Laws in Intellectual Property, Conflict of laws in intellectual property: the CLIP principles and commentary, Oxford 2013) (→ CLIP); the Transparency Proposal on Jurisdiction, Choice of Law, Recognition and Enforcement of Foreign Judgments in Intellectual Property, finalised in 2009 (available in Jürgen Basedow, Toshiyuki Kono and Axel Metzger (eds), *Intellectual Property in the Global Arena* (Mohr Siebeck 2010)); and the Principles of Private international law on Intellectual Property Rights drafted by members of the Private international law Association of → Korea and → Japan in 2011 (Commentary on Principles of Private international law on Intellectual Property Rights (Joint Proposal Drafted by Members of the Private international law Association of Korea and Japan)' (2011) 2(6) *Kigyō to Hōsōzō*: hereinafter: Joint Japanese-Korean Proposal) (hereinafter: the four sets of principles).

Furthermore, in November 2010 the ILA instituted a Committee on 'Intellectual Property and Private international law'. Building upon the four sets of principles, this Committee is currently working towards the adoption of an ILA Resolution on intellectual property and private international law, which could serve as a model for future international agreements promoting a more efficient adjudication of transnational intellectual property disputes (see [2012] *Journal of Intellectual Property, Information Technology and E-Commerce Law*, available at <www.jipitec.eu/issues/jipitec-3-3-2012>).

II. Territoriality principle and international jurisdiction

Despite the absence of harmonized rules, with regard to international jurisdiction related to cross-border intellectual property cases states reach similar solutions. The rationale for these similarities is to be found in the territoriality principle.

The territoriality principle has a substantive nature and indicates a spatial delimitation of each intellectual property right, which exists only on the territory of the state that grants it (for registered intellectual property rights) or that recognizes it (for unregistered intellectual property rights) (hereinafter: for simplicity reasons the terminology states granting or conferring intellectual property rights will be adopted to designate states recognizing unregistered intellectual property rights also). Thus, to a same intellectual creation, invention, or sign correspond as many intellectual property rights as are their granting countries. This occurs in cases of EU intellectual property rights, that are spatially delimited to the territory of the entire EU, and of European patents, that, despite being conferred after a unitary examination process, to the same holder, on the same invention, by a single body – the European Patent Office (EPO) – originate a bundle of parallel rights, which are referred to as national portions of the European patents. Intellectual property rights are then separate and independent rights, and the territoriality principle is grounded on the principle of independence, which is at the basis of all international treaties on the substantive harmonization of intellectual property, among which the Paris Industrial Property Convention (Paris Convention for the Protection of Industrial Property (adopted in 1883, recently revised on 14 July 1967) 828 UNTS 305), Berne Convention (Berne Convention for the Protection of Literary and Artistic Works of 9 September 1886, adopted in 1896, as amended and recently revised on 24 July 1971, 1161 UNTS 3 and amended in 1979 Treaty Doc No 99-27, and 1985, 828 UNTS 221) and → TRIPS.

This territorial substantive nature of intellectual property rights builds upon various rationales. First of all, it derives from the peculiar character of registered intellectual property rights, which come to existence through administrative acts of registration: then intellectual property rights, as their respective registration acts, would be born as spatially limited to the territory of their conferring countries. Second, territoriality derives from the nature of registered and unregistered intellectual property rights, which are monopolies of the states that grant the intellectual property rights owners not only the right to exploit the intellectual creation, but also the right to exclude any other person from this exploitation: then, this right of exclusion would be granted by states just as limited to their respective territories. Third, territoriality derives from the character of registered and unregistered intellectual property rights which aim at reaching interests of a public nature, like the development of culture and science, and therefore express public policies of their granting states: then these interests, like all the ones with a public character, would be intrinsically linked just to the territory of their respective countries.

More complex is the understanding of whether the territoriality principle affects the determination of the courts with international jurisdiction and the scope of their authorities.

A traditional opinion maintains that it does. In fact, since protection of an intellectual property right is limited to the territory of its granting state, intellectual property rights do not exist, cannot be infringed and do not require any protection in foreign countries. Then, intellectual property rights shall be adjudicated solely by the courts of their granting states, which shall exercise their authorities just on circumstances occurring in their respective national territories and with effects thereby limited. In addition, since changes in the administrative acts of registration might be necessary to protect intellectual property rights, and since according to the so-called act of state doctrine administrative acts can be modified just by the national competent authorities, only the courts of the intellectual property rights granting countries can order variation in their respective national acts of registration.

This traditional opinion, however, in cases of parallel intellectual property rights obliges the interested parties, intellectual property right owners or alleged infringers, to defend as many proceedings as are the intellectual property rights implied in the litigation, according to a mosaic approach. Yet, economic globalization and rapid development of information and communication technologies potentially accessible in the entire world at the same time increase the necessity of registering intellectual property rights in more countries and the consequent risks of infringing these rights in many states. Then, jurisdiction criteria grounded on territorial reasons become more and more problematic and the limits of the mosaic approach become apparent, leading to a multiplication of parallel proceedings, which raises the risk of conflicting judgments and the costs of litigation, and originates inequalities between big multinational companies and medium-small size enterprises.

III. The Brussels system

Starting from the 1960s attempts to overcome the traditional understanding of the territoriality principle, particularly with regard to its influence on international jurisdiction, initiated in Europe. These attempts aimed at internationalizing cross-border intellectual property rights litigation, concentrating adjudication of disputes before a single judicial authority even in cases of multistate infringement and reducing the risks of conflicting judgments and the inequalities between the different players. The attempts were favoured by the entry into force of the Brussels Convention of 1968 (Brussels Convention of 27 September 1968 on jurisdiction and the enforcement of judgments in civil and commercial matters, [1972] OJ L 299/32, consolidated version, [1998] OJ C 27/1), then Brussels I Regulation (Regulation (EC) No 44/2001 of December 2000 on jurisdiction and the recognition and enforcement of judgments in civil and commercial matters [2000] OJ L 12/1) and now Brussels I Regulation (recast) (Regulation (EU) No 1215/2012 of the European Parliament and of the Council of 12 December 2012 on jurisdiction and the recognition and enforcement of judgments in civil and commercial matters (recast), [2012] OJ 351/1) (→ Brussels I (Convention and Regulation)), as well as by the → Lugano Convention (Lugano Convention of 30 October 2007 on jurisdiction and the recognition and enforcement of judgments in civil and commercial matters, [2007] OJ L 339/3) (hereinafter: Brussels system).

This system, in fact, limits the traditional authority of the courts of the intellectual property rights granting states and grounds this authority on the administrative nature of the intellectual property rights acts of registration, rather than on the territoriality principle. Consequently, the Brussels system limits the scope of the (exclusive) jurisdiction of the courts of the intellectual property rights granting state to disputes that imply changes in the administrative acts of registration (ie validity of registered intellectual property rights claims); allows courts other than the ones of the intellectual property rights granting countries to adjudicate other multistate parallel intellectual property rights disputes (registered intellectual property rights pure infringement claims or non-registered intellectual property rights claims of any nature); does not pose any territorial limitation to the authorities of these courts;

and favours consolidation of cross-border intellectual property litigation.

Hereinafter the following examples of that consolidation related to exclusive, general and infringement jurisdiction will be provided.

1. Exclusive jurisdiction

Article 16(4) of the Brussels Convention (corresponding to art 24(4) of the Brussels I Regulation (recast)) establishes the exclusive jurisdiction of the court at the place of registration in proceedings relating to registration and validity of registered intellectual property rights. This norm was interpreted by the ECJ in two cases. In the first case, *Duijnstee* (Case C-288/82 *Duijnstee v Goderbauer* [1983] ECR 3663), a liquidator in the dissolution of a company requested the former manager of the company to transfer to him all patents in 22 countries for an invention made by an employee of the company. The Supreme Court of the Netherlands referred the preliminary question to the ECJ of whether the concept of proceedings concerned with the registration or validity of patents under art 16(4) of the Brussels Convention may cover a dispute having as its subject matter a transfer of intellectual property rights. The ECJ answered that art 16(4) does not cover such disputes.

In the second case, *GAT* (Case C-4/03 *Gesellschaft für Antriebstechnik mbH & Co KA (GAT) v Lamellen und Kupplungsbau Beteilgungs KG (LuK)* [2006] ECR I-6509), a German company (*LuK*) alleged out of court that *GAT* – another German company – was in breach of, *inter alia*, certain French patents of which *LuK* was the registered proprietor. In response *GAT* filed a declaratory action for non-infringement before the Regional Court in Düsseldorf (LG), asking the court to establish that *GAT* was not in breach of *LuK*'s patents, as such patents were invalid. The Higher Regional Court in Düsseldorf (OLG) stayed the proceeding and asked the ECJ if the exclusive jurisdiction of art 16(4) of the Brussels Convention only applies if proceedings with *erga omnes* effect are brought to declare the patent invalid or rather extends also to proceedings concerned with the validity of patents where the defendant in a patent infringement action or the claimant in a declaratory action to establish that a patent is not infringed pleads that the patent is invalid and that there is also no patent infringement for that reason. The ECJ answered that the rule of exclusive jurisdiction under art 16(4) of the Brussels Convention concerns all proceedings relating to the registration or validity of a patent, irrespective of whether that issue is raised by way of an action or a plea in objection. This ECJ's statement was then codified by art 24(4) of the Brussels I Regulation (recast), according to which

> in proceedings concerned with the registration or validity of patents, trade marks, designs, or other similar rights required to be deposited or registered, irrespective of whether the issue is raised by way of an action or as a defence, [shall have exclusive jurisdiction, regardless of the domicile of the parties] the courts of the Member State in which the deposit or registration has been applied for, has taken place or is under the terms of an instrument of the Union or an international convention deemed to have taken place.

In both the *Duijnstee* and the *GAT* cases, the ECJ reached its conclusions on the basis of the following main arguments. First, according to the ECJ, exclusive jurisdiction is justified by the fact that the issue of patents necessitates the involvement of the national administrative authorities. Here, the ECJ references the *Jenard* Report (<http://aei.pitt.edu/1465/1/commercial_report_jenard_C59_79.pdf>), according to which the granting of a patent is an exercise of national sovereignty. From this statement, it may be concluded that the *Jenard* Report is grounded in the Act of State doctrine. Accordingly, the ECJ decisions citing it are also based on that doctrine. Second, the Act of State doctrine is adopted to ground the scope of the exclusive jurisdiction rule. In fact, the exclusive jurisdiction rule covers only registered intellectual property rights and does not apply to unregistered intellectual property rights. The reason for this distinction is that registered intellectual property rights are granted through a public act of concession, which implies the intervention of the national administration and therefore the exercise of national sovereignty, whereas unregistered intellectual property rights come into being without these formalities. Third, exclusive jurisdiction rules cover the proceedings related to the validity of intellectual property rights, but do not encompass transfer and infringement claims. In fact proceedings concerning intellectual property rights validity challenge the validity of its granting acts, whereas proceedings related to transfer and infringement claims concern only the activity of private subjects. Since the granting act is an act of the national administration of the conferring state, this act is an expression of the state's sovereignty and validity proceedings imply an examination of the sovereign activity of foreign states.

Yet, the ECJ did not ground the exclusive jurisdiction rules on the territoriality principle. This might be explained in light of the *Tod's* case (Case C-28/04 *Tod's v Heyraud* [2005] ECR I-5781), where the ECJ stated that the Berne Convention does not relate to private international law and therefore does not determine any applicable laws, but instead establishes a national treatment and a territoriality principle of a substantive nature. This statement may be applied to the Paris Industrial Property Convention and → TRIPS agreements and also to international procedural law. Interpreted in this way, the ECJ's *Tod*'s decision determines that the territoriality principle of the Paris Industrial Property Convention, Berne Convention and TRIPS agreements neither refers to applicable law nor posits any (implicit) exclusive jurisdiction rule.

Even though the exclusive jurisdiction rule of the Brussels system is not based on the territoriality principle, it obliges litigating transnational intellectual property rights disputes country by country and expresses a strict territorial conception of intellectual property rights. To overcome that strict territoriality, favouring consolidation of cross-border intellectual property litigation, several EU and EFTA Member States have shown resistances to the *GAT*'s holding and have mitigated its scope in four different ways. A first way relates to cases where the foreign registered intellectual property right validity issue is raised in an infringement proceeding for which the forum state court has international jurisdiction. In those cases, the question arises whether the court competent to address the foreign intellectual property right infringement claim should dismiss the case and decline jurisdiction when the validity of the foreign intellectual property right is raised. Alternatively, the seized court could stay the infringement proceedings, give the party raising the validity issue a short period of time to institute validity proceedings in a court with exclusive jurisdiction to hear the claim and then continue the infringement proceedings once a decision on validity has been reached. All of this subject to the condition that if the relevant party fails to bring invalidity proceedings, this should be treated as recognition of the validity of the intellectual property right, allowing for the infringement proceeding to continue. The first option – to dismiss the case in its entirety – is adopted for instance in the → United Kingdom and in → Italy. In contrast, the second option – simply to stay the proceeding with regard to the infringement claim – is followed in the → Netherlands and in → Switzerland.

The first option is an incorrect application of the Brussels system since this system does not extend exclusive jurisdiction rules to infringement issues, but covers only validity claims. Thus, it may be argued that the second way should be favoured. This conclusion is based on a literal interpretation of the *GAT* judgment, according to which there is nothing in *GAT* to stop a plaintiff from exercising his right under the Brussels I Regulation to bring an action for infringement at the defendant's domicile or in the place of the harmful effect according to art 2 of the Brussels I Regulation and respectively to art 5(3) of the same Regulation (corresponding to art 4 and respectively art 7(2) of the Brussels I Regulation (recast)). Further support for this conclusion can be found in the ECJ *Roche* decision (Case C-539/03 *Roche Nederland BV v Primus* [2006] ECR I-6535) that was interpreted as highlighting that the issue of validity and the claim for infringement will be split between the courts of different Member States.

A second way to mitigate the scope of the exclusive jurisdiction rules of the Brussels system concerns cases where the validity claim is incidentally raised in the frame of a preliminary proceeding to award → provisional measures under art 31 Brussels I Regulation, corresponding to art 35 of the Brussels I Regulation (recast). In such cases, certain states invoked the non-application of the exclusive jurisdiction rules of the Brussels system. This approach was confirmed by the ECJ in the *Solvay* case (Case C-616/10 *Solvay SA v Honeywell Fluorine Products Europe BV, et al* [2012] ECR-I (Jul 2012)), by stating that art 22(4) of the Brussels I Regulation must be interpreted as not precluding, in cases where the validity claim is incidentally raised in the frame of a preliminary proceeding, the application of art 31 of that Regulation.

A third way to mitigate the scope of the exclusive jurisdiction rules of the Brussels system concerns cases where non-EU registered intellectual property rights are at stake. Those cases deal with the issue of whether the exclusive jurisdiction rules of the Brussels system have a so-called 'reflexive effect', and therefore are extendable also to validity issues incidentally raised with respect to intellectual property rights registered in non-Member States. Specifically, the question arises whether art 22(4) of the Brussels I Regulation, now art 24(4) of the Brussels I Regulation (recast), creates extra EU jurisdiction thereby potentially extending its scope to cases where the intellectual property right is registered in a non-EU member country and preventing courts in EU Member States from exercising jurisdiction over validity claims incidentally raised involving foreign non-EU intellectual property rights. This question has not been solved by the ECJ. Meanwhile EU Member States have dealt with this question autonomously. So, *inter alia* in → France the answer to this question is negative and therefore French courts might make a decision upon validity issues incidentally raised for foreign non-EU intellectual property rights, but this decision would have effects limited to the parties of the dispute. In the UK the same opinion was followed in *obiter dicta* by the UK Court of Appeal's *Lucasfilm* ruling (*Lucasfilm Entertainment Co v Ainsworth* [2009] EWCA (Civ) 1328), according to which art 22(4) of the Regulation provides for exclusive jurisdiction, regardless of domicile, in respect of a variety of identified matters, including validity of patent rights, but none of that would apply to non-EU matters of the type excluded by art 22(4) Brussels I Regulation: if proceedings for infringement of a US patent were brought against a person domiciled in a Member State, art 22(4) does not exclude jurisdiction over validity. Thus, the defendant could challenge the validity of the patent.

A fourth way to mitigate the scope of the exclusive jurisdiction rule regarding registered intellectual property rights validity issues incidentally raised concerns cases where the courts ascertain that the declining of jurisdiction by virtue of exclusive jurisdiction rules could lead to a denial of justice. In those cases, courts would rule that the exclusive jurisdiction rules of the Brussels system are contrary to the human right of access to a court. This conclusion was reached *inter alia* by a Dutch decision rendered by the District Court of The Hague in the 2007 *Single Buoy Moorings v Bluewater* case (11 April 2007).

To sum up, the Brussels system establishes exclusive jurisdiction rules with regard to registered intellectual property rights validity issues principally and incidentally raised. Yet, the scope of those rules may be mitigated at least in the four different ways just highlighted. Each of these mitigations reflects a tendency that overcomes a strict territorial approach with respect to intellectual property rights and favours consolidation of cross-border intellectual property litigation.

2. General jurisdiction

Further attempts to overcome the traditional understanding of the → territoriality principle, favouring consolidation of cross-border intellectual property litigation, relate to norms that vest jurisdiction in the courts of the defendant's domicile or residence (→ Domicile, habitual residence and establishment). Among these norms stands art 2 of the Brussels I Regulation, now art 4 of the Brussels I Regulation (recast), according to which jurisdiction in registered or unregistered intellectual property rights infringement claims, or registered or unregistered intellectual property rights transfer claims, or unregistered intellectual property rights validity claims principally or incidentally raised, is grounded on the courts of the state where the defendant is domiciled.

This norm does not establish any additional territorial requirement. So, it does not impose the consideration of whether the intellectual property right in question exists or was infringed in the forum state. Thus, this rule reflects a tendency that overcomes a strict territorial approach with respect to intellectual property rights and that favours a consolidation of claims in cross-border intellectual property disputes.

3. Infringement jurisdiction

Further attempts to overcome the traditional understanding of the territoriality principle, favouring consolidation of cross-border intellectual property litigation, relate to norms that vest jurisdiction in intellectual property rights infringement cases. Among these norms stands art 5(3) of the Brussels I Regulation, now art 7(2) of the Brussels I Regulation (recast), according to which 'a person domiciled in a Member State may, in another Member State, be sued: / . . . 3. in matters relating to tort, delict or quasi-delict, in the courts for the place where the harmful event occurred or may occur'.

The ECJ interpreted art 5(3) in several cases related to → torts other than intellectual property rights infringements. In *Mines de potasse* (Case C-21/76 *Handelskwekerij G J Bier BV v Mines de potasse d'Alsace SA* [1976] ECR

1735) the ECJ posed the ubiquity theory by maintaining that where the place of the happening of the event and the place where that event results in damage are not identical the expression 'place where the harmful event occurred' in art 5(3) of the Brussels Convention, must be interpreted as covering both the place where the damage occurred (*locus damni*) or that of the event giving rise to it (*locus actus*). Thus, the plaintiff may sue the defendant in both places.

With regard to the place where the damage occurred, in *Marinari* (Case C-364/93 *Antonio Marinari v Lloyd's Bank plc and Zubaidi Trading Co* [1995] ECR I-2719), *Dumez France* (Case C-220/88 *Dumez France SA and Tracoba SARL v Hessische Landesbank* [1990] I-49) and *Kronhofer* (Case C-168/02 *Rudolf Kronhofer v Marianne Meier et al* [2004] ECR I-6009) the ECJ clarified that the direct damage is the only relevant one to ground international jurisdiction, and that indirect consequences or pecuniary losses following a direct damage shall play no role in that respect. With regard to the place of the event giving rise to the damage, in *Melzer* (Case C-228/11 *Melzer v MF Global UK Ltd* (May 2013)) the ECJ emphasized that in a case where there are several supposed perpetrators of a tort, art 5(3) of the Brussels I Regulation does not allow jurisdiction to be established on the basis of the place of the event giving rise to the damage in favour of a court within whose jurisdiction the supposed perpetrator who is being sued did not act.

In *Melzer* and *Folien Fischer* (Case C-133/1 *Folien Fischer AG v Ritrama SpA* (October 2012)), the ECJ maintained that art 5(3) of the Brussels Regulation is based on the existence of a particularly close connection between the dispute and the courts of the place where the damage occurred or of the place of the event giving rise to it. In fact, these courts are objectively best placed to determine whether the elements establishing the liability of the person sued are present, since within their jurisdiction the relevant connecting factor is to be found. So, reasons relating to the sound administration of justice and the efficacious conduct of proceedings justify the attribution of jurisdiction to those courts.

In *Folien Fischer*, then, the ECJ emphasized that art 5(3) applies not only to actions for a positive declaration seeking to establish the occurrence of an infringement, but also to actions for a negative declaration seeking to establish the absence of liability in tort.

The ECJ then restricted the jurisdiction of the seized court in cases of multistate infringements. In fact, in the *Shevill* (Case C 68/93 *Shevill v Presse Alliance SA* [1993] ECR I-415) decision the ECJ allowed the consolidation of infringement proceedings interpreting the expression of art 5(3) of the Brussels I Regulation 'place where the harmful event occurred' in the sense that the victim of a libel by a newspaper article distributed in several Member States may bring an action for damages against the publisher either before the courts of the state of the place where the publisher of the defamatory publication is established or before the courts of each contracting state in which the publication was distributed and where the victim claims to have suffered injury to his reputation. In the first case, the seized court has jurisdiction to award damages for all the harm caused by the defamation. In the second case, the seized court has jurisdiction to rule solely in respect of the harm caused in the state of the court seized.

The ECJ went even further in the *eDate* case (Joined Cases C-509/09 and C-161/10 *eDate Advertising GmbH v X and Olivier Martinez, Robert Martinez v MGN Limited* [2011] OJ C 370/9) concerning an alleged infringement of → personality rights by means of content placed online on an internet website (→ Internet, liability). According to the ECJ art 5(3) of the Brussels I Regulation must be interpreted as meaning that the person who considers that his rights have been infringed has the option of bringing an action for liability either before the courts of the Member State in which the publisher of that content is established or before the courts of the Member State in which the centre of the plaintiff's interests is based (*forum actoris*). Instead of an action for liability in respect of all the damage caused, the plaintiff may also bring his action before the courts of each Member State in the territory of which content placed online is or has been effectively accessible, irrespective of the fact that the publisher targeted the forum state. Yet, when the forum state is that of accessibility, its courts have jurisdiction only with regard to the damage caused in their respective territories.

In this framework, on several occasions the ECJ clarified how to apply its case-law related to general torts to intellectual property rights infringements also. So, in *Wintersteiger* (Case C-523/10 *Wintersteiger AG v Products 4U Sondermaschinenbau GmbH* [2012] OJ C 165/5) the ECJ highlighted that the understanding of art 5(3) of the Brussels system may vary according to the nature of the right allegedly infringed. Thus, the ECJ emphasized that the *eDate* case-law does not extend to intellectual property rights in its part related to the *forum actoris*, since this forum would protect too much owners of intellectual property rights that are strong players, unlike owners of personality rights.

Yet, the ubiquity theory was extended to intellectual property rights by the ECJ with the *Wintersteiger* judgment. In fact, the ECJ clarified that art 5(3) of the Brussels I Regulation shall be interpreted as meaning that an action relating to infringement of a trade mark registered in a Member State because of the use by an advertiser of a keyword identical to that trade mark on a search engine website operating under a country-specific top-level domain of another Member State may be brought either before the courts of the Member State in which the trade mark is registered (in their quality of courts at the place of the damage), or before the courts of the Member State of the place of establishment of the advertiser (in their quality of courts at the place of the event giving rise to the damage). The courts at the place of registration are always the best placed to ascertain whether the intellectual property right at issue has been infringed, since the protection granted by registration is limited to the territory of their respective forum state. Yet, these courts always have jurisdiction to hear the action restricted to the territory of the forum state. On the contrary, the courts at the place of establishment of the advertiser have territorially unrestricted jurisdiction to adjudicate on the entire damages wherever located.

The ubiquity theory was then extended to intellectual property rights by the ECJ with the *Pinckney* judgment (Case C-170/12 *Peter Pinckney v KDG Mediatech AG* (October 2013)). In that case the author of a work brought before a French court an action to establish liability for an alleged infringement of his copyrights protected in France. The action was brought against a company established in → Austria that had reproduced in that state the relevant work on a material support which was subsequently sold by companies established in the UK through an internet site in many countries among which was France. The ECJ was requested to establish if the French court seized had jurisdiction over that action according to art 5(3) of the Brussels I Regulation. The ECJ concluded that the French court had jurisdiction it being the court at the place of the damage. In fact, within the jurisdiction of the court seized it was possible to obtain a reproduction of the work to which the rights relied on by the defendant pertained from an internet site accessible in France. Yet, since the jurisdiction of the French court was based on the criterion of accessibility, it was limited to determine the damage caused in France.

The ubiquity theory was then extended to intellectual property rights by the ECJ with the *Coty* judgment (Case C-360/12 *Coty Germany GmbH v First Note Perfumes NV* (June 2014)). First, in *Coty* the ECJ was asked to determine if the ubiquity theory applies to an infringement of a Community trademark under the Community Trade Mark Regulation (Council Regulation No 40/94 of 20 December 1993 on the Community trade mark ([1994] OJ L 11/1), now Council Regulation (EC) No 207/2009 of 26 February 2009 on the Community trade mark (codified version) ([2009] OJ L 78/1)). The ECJ excluded that the duality of linking factors, namely the place of the event giving rise to the damage and that where the damage occurred, applies to the notion of 'Member State in which the act of infringement has been committed' in art 93(5) of the Community Trade Mark Regulation. Yet, the ECJ grounded this exclusion on the wording of art 93(5), which differs from that of art 5(3) of the Brussels I Regulation. In fact, the linking factor provided for by the former refers to the Member State where the act giving rise to the alleged infringement occurred, while that provided for by the latter concerns the Member State where that infringement produces its effects. So, according to the ECJ, jurisdiction under art 93(5) of the Community Trade Mark Regulation may be established solely in favour of the courts in the Member State in which the defendant committed the alleged unlawful act. It follows that unlike under art 93(5) of the Community Trade Mark Regulation, jurisdiction under art 5(3) of the Brussels I Regulation shall be established according to the ubiquity theory.

Second, in *Coty* the ECJ was asked to interpret art 5(3) of the Brussels I Regulation in a case where there were several supposed perpetrators of an infringement of an intellectual property right protected in the forum state, so called contributory infringement. In that case, the ECJ applied the conclusions reached in *Melzer* and emphasized that art 5(3) of the Brussels

I Regulation does not allow jurisdiction to be established on the basis of the place of the event giving rise to the damage in favour of a court within whose jurisdiction the supposed perpetrator who is being sued did not act. On the contrary, the ECJ understood art 5(3) as allowing the jurisdiction of that court to be established on the basis of the place where the alleged damage occurs, provided that the damage may occur within the jurisdiction of the court seized. Then, the court has jurisdiction only to rule on the damage caused in the territory of the Member State to which it belongs. So, even though the ECJ in *Coty* excluded consolidation of claims against the contributory infringer that did not act within the jurisdiction of the court seized, it confirmed that art 5(3) of the Brussels I Regulation shall be interpreted as establishing the jurisdiction of the court at the place where the damage occurred or at that of the event giving rise to it, according to the ubiquity theory. With regard to copyright and neighbouring rights similar conclusions were reached by the ECJ in the *Hi Hotel* case (Case C-387/12 *Hi Hotel HCF SARL v Uwe Spoering* (April 2014)).

The ubiquity theory was then extended to intellectual property rights by the ECJ in *Gautzsch* (Case C-479/12 *H Gautzsch Großhandel GmbH & Co KG v Münchener Boulevard Möbel Joseph Duna GmbH* (February 2014)), where it was requested to interpret art 89(1)(d) of the Community designs Regulation (Council Regulation (EC) No 6/2002 of 12 December 2001 on Community designs ([2002] OJ L 3/1)), under which 'the law of the Member State in which the acts of infringement or threatened infringement are committed'. So, the *Gautzsch* case concerned applicable law rather than international jurisdiction. Yet, its outcome is relevant for international jurisdiction also, since the notion of commission of an intellectual property right infringement corresponds to that of the place where the harmful event occurred under art 5(3) of the Brussels I Regulation. The ECJ distinguished (the law of) the place/state of registration of an intellectual property right from (that of) the place/state in which the acts of infringements have been committed. Thus, the ECJ confirmed that art 5(3) shall be interpreted as distinguishing these places/states, according to the ubiquity theory.

To sum up, art 5(3) of the Brussels system interpreted according to the ubiquity theory by the ECJ reflects a tendency that overcomes a strict territorial approach with respect to intellectual property rights and that favours a consolidation of claims in cross-border intellectual property disputes.

IV. New trends resulting from transnational sets of principles and academic projects

Further attempts to overcome the traditional understanding of the territoriality principle, favouring consolidation of cross-border intellectual property litigation, result from the four sets of principles referred to in section I and the current work of the ILA Committee in this field. In fact, all four sets of principles allow for consolidation of claims based on their general jurisdiction norms. In addition, all four sets of principles overcome exclusive jurisdiction in cases related to validity issues incidentally raised, by establishing that those issues can be brought before a court of a state other than that of registration, provided that the judgment on validity would have *inter partes* effect. Furthermore, all four sets of principles allow for the adjudication of an intellectual property right multistate infringement in its entirety by a single court under certain conditions.

Concerning exclusive jurisdiction the four sets of principles differ with regard to the question of whether the validity issue raised as a principal claim could be adjudicated by a court of a state other than that of registration. In fact, the CLIP Principles and the Joint Japanese-Korean Proposal explicitly establish that claims principally related to validity should be brought only before the courts of the state of registration. In contrast, the ALI Principles and the Transparency Proposal enable courts of a state other than that of registration to decide upon validity issues concerning foreign intellectual property rights principally raised, provided that the effects of the judgment on validity are limited to the parties of the proceedings. The ALI Principles pose the stricter conditions that the dispute should have a multistate nature and that the claim on validity principally raised should be brought before the court at the defendant's residence. The Transparency Proposal requires only that the Japanese court seized with the validity claim principally raised related to a foreign registered intellectual property right has jurisdiction.

Concerning infringement jurisdiction the four sets of principles differ with regard to the conditions that have to be met in order to allow the seized court to adjudicate a multistate infringement in its entirety. More particularly, there are two main differences among these sets of principles. The first relates to the question of whether the centralized jurisdiction should be limited to infringements perpetrated through ubiquitous media, such as the internet, or should also cover multistate infringements perpetrated by other means. The CLIP Principles refer to 'ubiquitous infringements'. On the contrary, the other sets of principles concern infringement perpetrated by means other than the internet also, namely the ALI Principles refer to injuries 'wherever' they could occur, while the Transparency Proposal and the Joint Japanese-Korean Proposal refer to 'multiple states' infringement.

The second difference concerns the question of which court shall have jurisdiction to adjudicate multistate infringement disputes in their entirety and under which conditions. The Transparency Proposal provides that if a Japanese court is the court of the place of the action giving rise to the damage or of the damage, it could have jurisdiction to hear multistate infringement disputes in their entirety subject to two additional requirements: the infringement must occur in several states; and its results should be maximized in Japan. The Joint Japanese-Korean Proposal grounds jurisdiction to hear multistate infringement disputes in their entirety on the court at the place of injury (but not at the place of the action) if the three following conditions are met: the injuries should occur in multiple states; the major part of the initial infringing activities should be located in the forum state; and the alleged infringement shall not be directed against a particular state. The ALI Principles allow a court of the state where the substantial infringing activities were committed to assert jurisdiction over multistate infringement disputes in their entirety, unless it can be reasonably foreseen that those activities are directed to one particular state. The CLIP Principles provide that the court of the state where the alleged infringement occurs or may occur shall have jurisdiction over the ubiquitous infringement if it is reasonably foreseen that the infringer directed the activities to the forum state. Also, with regard to the extent of jurisdiction, the CLIP Principles allow the court to assert jurisdiction to hear ubiquitous infringement disputes in their entirety where four cumulative requirements are met: the infringement shall be carried out through ubiquitous media; the court shall have jurisdiction pursuant to the infringement jurisdiction rule; the activities shall have no substantial effect in the state where the infringer is habitually resident; and the substantial activities shall be located within the forum state or the harm caused by the infringement in the forum state shall be substantial in relation to the infringement in its entirety.

BENEDETTA UBERTAZZI

Literature

Stefania Bariatti (ed), *Litigating Intellectual Property Rights Disputes Cross-Border: EU Regulations, ALI Principles, CLIP Project* (CEDAM 2010); Jürgen Basedow and others (eds), *Intellectual Property in the Conflict of Laws* (Mohr Siebeck 2005); Pedro De Miguel Asensio, 'Cross-border Adjudication of Intellectual Property Rights and Competition between Jurisdictions' [2007] *Annali italiani del diritto d'autore, della cultura e dello spettacolo* 117 ff; François Dessemontet, 'The ALI Principles: Intellectual Property in Transborder Litigation' in Jürgen Basedow, Toshiyuki Kono and Axel Metzger (eds), *Intellectual Property in the Global Arena* (Mohr Siebeck 2010); Graeme Dinwoodie, 'Trademarks and Territory: Detaching Trademark Law from the Nation-state' [2004] Hous. L. Rev. 885 ff; Josef Drexl, 'Lex americana ante portas – Zur extraterritorialen Anwendung nationalen Urheberrechts' in Ulrigh Loewenheim (ed), *Urheberrecht im Informationszeitalter, Festschrift für Wilhelm Nordemann* (CH Beck 2004) 429 ff; Rochelle Dreyfuss, 'Resolution Through Conflict of Laws: The ALI Principles on Transnational Intellectual Property Disputes: Why Invite Conflicts?' [2005] Brooklyn J.Int'l L. 819 ff; European Max Planck Group on Conflict of Laws in Intellectual Property, *Conflict of Laws in Intellectual Property, The CLIP Principles and Commentary* (OUP 2013); Jane Ginsburg, 'The Private international law of Copyrights in an Era of Technological Change' [1998] Rec. des Cours 257 ff; Annette Kur, 'Durchsetzung gemeinschaftsweiter Schutzrechte: Internationale Zuständigkeit und andwendbares Recht' [2014] GRURInt 749 ff; Annette Kur and Benedetta Ubertazzi, 'The ALI Principles and the CLIP Project: A Comparison' in Stefania Bariatti (ed), *Litigating Intellectual Property Rights Disputes Cross-Border: EU Regulations, ALI Principles, CLIP Project* (CEDAM 2010); Paul Torremans and James Fawcett, *Intellectual Property and Private international law* (2nd edn, OUP 2011); Marketa Trimble Landova, *Global Patents: Limits of Transnational Enforcement* (OUP 2012); Benedetta Ubertazzi, *Exclusive Jurisdiction in Intellectual Property* (Mohr Siebeck 2012); Dario Moura Vicente, 'La propriété intellectuelle en droit international privé' [2008] Rec. des Cours 424 ff; Dai Yokomizo, 'Intellectual Property Infringement on the Internet and Conflict of Laws' [May 2011] *AIPPI Journal* 105 ff.

Interest and policy analysis in private international law

I. Introduction

All private international law in general, and → choice of law in particular, is ultimately based on underlying interests (eg of the parties in predictable outcomes) and policies (eg of states in preventing excessive forum shopping). A few approaches, however, have put the analysis of interests and policies at the very core of the choice-of-law process. In doing so, they have looked not so much at the (private and individual) interests of the litigants but rather at the (public and collective) interests and policies of the involved states. As a result, these approaches seek to select the law that best effectuates the state interests and policies behind the conflicting rules.

Interest and policy analysis experienced its rise and heyday in the → USA during the 'conflicts revolution' in the second half of the 20th century (*infra* II.; → (American) Conflict of laws revolution). While the approach has its appeal, it is troubled by several theoretical issues all of which entail practical problems (III.). The US-American discussion spilled over into Europe as well where it generated both excitement and resistance (IV.). In conclusion one finds that the American ideas enriched conflicts theory but had a very limited impact on the modification of conflicts practice (V.).

II. Rise and heyday: interest and policy analysis in the USA

1. Origins: the realist assault on territorialism and vested rights

In order to appreciate US-American policy and interest analysis, one must understand its origins. They lie in the realist assault on the strict territorialism and rigid formalism prevailing in the first half of the 20th century in the USA.

In the early 19th century, United States Supreme Court Justice *Joseph Story* (1779–1845) (→ Story, Joseph) imported strictly territorial notions of sovereignty from continental Europe and put American conflicts law on internationalist foundations (Joseph Story, *Commentaries on the Conflict of Laws, Foreign and Domestic* (Hillard Gray 1834). A century later, Harvard law professor *Joseph Beale* (1861–1943) grafted the → vested rights theory onto *Story's* paradigms. From these principles, *Beale* logically deduced a fairly closed system of general and blackletter rules, almost in the formalist style of 19th-century German conceptual jurisprudence (Joseph Beale, *A Treatise on the Conflict of Laws* (HUP 1916)). *Beale's* choice-of-law rules were exclusively jurisdiction selecting and designed to leave little judicial discretion in the individual case. He ultimately enshrined them in the (First) Restatement of Conflict of Laws (American Law Institute, Restatement of the Law, First: Conflict of Laws, St Paul 1934; → Restatement (First and Second) of Conflict of Laws).

While still at the drafting stage, *Beale's* Restatement ran into two serious problems. One was that its strict territorialism relied on state boundaries which were increasingly ignored by an ever more mobile society and national economy. This opened a gap between official rules and social needs.

The other problem was that *Beale's* approach was badly out of date in terms of legal theory. In the 1920s and 1930s, American legal thought largely abandoned a logical and systematic approach to law which came to be disparaged as 'mechanical jurisprudence' (*Roscoe Pound*). In its stead, legal realism and a sociological understanding of law were steeply on the rise. Prominent scholars affiliated with these new trends looked at *Beale's* Restatement as a symbol of the old-fashioned formalism which they regarded as intellectually bankrupt and practically pernicious. In a series of publications, especially *David Cavers* (1902–88), *Walter Wheeler Cook* (1873–1943) and *Hessel Yntema* (1891–1966) devastatingly critiqued the prevailing doctrine and called for a turn towards a realist and sociological conflicts jurisprudence. Their work was largely deconstructive, and while they suggested choice-of-law methods built on state interests and social policies, they did so merely in broadly programmatic terms.

2. The orthodox version: Currie's governmental interests analysis

The construction of a new choice-of-law method followed a generation later and was the work of *Brainerd Currie* (1912–65). In a veritable outburst of scholarly productivity, *Currie* developed this method in a series of essays published in the late 1950s and early 1960s (collected in Brainerd Currie, *Selected Essays on the Conflict of Laws* (Duke University Press 1963)). In essence, *Currie* joined the teachings of *Beale's* critics with the state interest concepts drawn from several Supreme Court decisions (especially *Pacific Employers Insurance Co v Industrial Commission*, 306 U.S. 493 (1939)). The result was his 'governmental interests analysis'. It put choice-of-law reasoning on a new foundation.

Currie's fundamental claim was that choice of law should turn on an analysis of the governmental (ie state) policies and interests underlying the substantive laws involved in the individual case. This entailed a jurisprudential revolution: *Currie* rejected reliance on choice-of-law rules ('We would be better off without choice-of-law rules' (Brainerd Currie, *Selected Essays on the Conflict of Laws* (Duke University Press 1963) 177, 183). Instead, he proposed to solve conflicts cases through an analytic process (first summarized in 1959, Brainerd Currie, *Selected Essays on the Conflict of Laws* (Duke University Press 1963) 183–4). Drafting a mock restatement of conflicts, he later presented this method as follows.

(i) When a court is asked to apply the law of a foreign state different from the law of the forum, it should inquire into the policies expressed in the respective laws, and into the circumstances in which it is reasonable for the respective states to assert an interest in the application of those policies. . . .

(ii) If the court finds that one state has an interest in the application of its policy in the circumstances of the case and the other has none, it should apply the law of the only interested state. . . .

(iv) If, upon reconsideration, the court finds that a conflict between the legitimate interests of the two states is unavoidable, it should apply the law of the forum. . . . (Brainerd Currie, 'Comments on Babcock v Jackson' [1963] Colum.L.Rev. 1233, 1242–3).

Currie was convinced that this thought process was pretty much all that was needed to decide most conflicts cases. His method looked seductively attractive. In contrast to the formalistic nature of the traditional choice-of-law regime, *Currie's* approach promised to give effect to substantive (governmental) policies. Perhaps even more importantly, it was of admirable simplicity – it did away with most of the traditional apparatus and its complex doctrines, such as characterization, → *renvoi* or → public policy.

3. *Into the courts: interest analysis in New York, California and beyond*

Beginning in the 1960s, various state supreme courts began to adopt interest analysis more or less along *Currie's* lines, primarily in interstate tort cases. The signal event was a decision by the New York Court of Appeals (the highest court in the state of New York) in 1963. In *Babcock v Jackson* (191 N.E.2d 279 (NY 1963)), two parties from New York had a single-car accident in Ontario, → Canada. Ontario's 'guest statute' barred non-paying guests from suing host-drivers; New York's law did not. The New York court openly defied the venerable *lex loci delicti* rule and applied the law of the parties' common domicile (→ Domicile, habitual residence and establishment). The court explained that Ontario had no interest in protecting the New York driver from liability while New York had an interest in seeing the New York victim compensated. Thus all the interests lay in New York. In 1967, the Supreme Court of California also adopted interest analysis for tort cases (*Reich v Purcell*, 432 P.2d 727 (Cal 1967)). In subsequent years, a growing number of other state supreme courts abandoned the *lex loci* rule as well in favour of various policy-based choice-of-law analyses, and the American 'conflicts revolution' was underway (→ (American) Conflict of laws revolution).

Today, the consideration of governmental policies and interests is a staple in the USA. It is impossible to understand American conflicts theory and practice without it. Yet, assessing its true impact requires some differentiation. On the one hand, interest analysis has affected a real revolution only in interstate tort cases; contract conflicts have largely been resolved through a contacts approach, and other areas, such as property (→ Property and proprietary rights), domestic relations or corporate law, have by and large remained on more traditional ground. On the other hand, interest analysis has had a considerable spillover effect into these other areas. In particular, courts and scholars have often reassessed the traditional rules in light of their underlying policies, though usually without causing major changes.

It is also true that even in tort cases, only very few jurisdictions openly subscribe to interest analysis as their main approach (California, the District of Columbia and New York). Yet, the courts of many other states consider policies and interest as well, albeit only as one element in a larger mix of factors (see Symeon Symeonides, 'Choice of Law in the American Courts in 2013' [2014] Am.J.Comp.L. 223, 252–280). This is also true in the very large number of jurisdictions subscribing to the Restatement of Conflicts 2d (American Law Institute, Restatement of the Law, Second: Conflict of Laws 2d, St Paul 1971) and for good reason: while the Restatement generally endorses a 'most-significant-relationship' approach (eg for torts, see § 145), it also encourages the consideration of the 'relevant policies' of the forum and other interested states (§ 6(b) and (c)).

4. The basic pattern: three permutations – and some complications

In the 1960s and 1970s, it gradually became clear that interest analysis generated three basic permutations. *Currie* had indicated two but missed the third.

In some cases, analysing the underlying policies showed that all interests lay in one state, as in *Babcock v Jackson* (191 N.E.2d 279 (NY 1963)). Since there was no clash of state interests, these cases came to be known as 'false conflicts'. Their solution seemed easy: as *Currie* had suggested (Brainerd Currie, *Selected Essays on the Conflict of Laws* (Duke University Press 1963)), courts favouring policy analysis overwhelmingly applied the law of the only interested state, typically the place of the parties' common domicile.

In other cases, however, both states could have an interest. Where the parties had their respective domiciles in different jurisdictions (split domicile cases) each of which favoured its own party, both states would prefer to have their law applied. Since state interests now truly clashed, these cases came to be known as 'true conflicts' (a well-known example is *Cipolla v Shaposka*, 267 A.2d 854 (Pa 1970)). They were much harder to resolve. *Currie's* forum law preference led him to suggest that the → *lex fori* break the tie (*supra* II.2.). Yet, that solution was widely regarded as problematic and largely replaced with other options (*infra* III.2.).

Finally, in split domicile cases, the respective states' laws could actually each disfavour its own party (eg if an accident victim was from a state barring suit while the wrongdoer was from a jurisdiction allowing it, see *Neumeier v Kuehner*, 286 N.E.2d 454 (NY 1972)). Since in that case, arguably neither state had an interest, these scenarios came to be known as 'zero-interest cases', or, since *Currie* had not directly addressed them, as 'unprovided-for cases'. *Currie's* forum law preference implied, however, simply to revert to the *lex fori* here as well.

Ever since, American courts and commentators embracing modern choice-of-law approaches have been conscious of this tripartite pattern. It is indeed useful as a basic sorting mechanism. Yet, the pattern works well only for some conflicts, but not for others. Most importantly, it applies mainly to conflicts between so-called 'loss allocating' rules, ie norms deciding whether (or to what extent) a party is entitled to recover, such as → immunity rules or damage caps. Since losses and liabilities tend to be felt primarily at the respective domiciles, the parties' home states can be said to have an interest in the application of such rules. The pattern does not work nearly so well with regard to so-called 'conduct regulating' rules, ie norms determining when an action is wrongful to begin with, such as standards of care or rules of the road. Since such norms are tied to the place of conduct, the state where the underlying act is committed will usually have the (at least primary) interest in this regard. The courts quickly grasped this distinction. As a result, interest analysis will often lead to a combination of rules from different jurisdictions, such as the law of the parties' common domicile to issues of loss allocation and the law of place of the wrongful act to conduct regulation.

III. Six pervasive issues

Whether choice-of-law decisions should turn on an analysis of governmental policies and state interests was the dominant topic of American conflicts discourse during the closing decades of the 20th century. Scholars debated the question in a veritable deluge of articles (abundant references in Peter Hay, Patrick Borchers and Symeon Symeonides, *Conflict of Laws* (5th edn, West Academic Publishing 2010) 37–41, fns 36–59), law reviews published numerous symposia (Peter Hay, Patrick Borchers and Symeon Symeonides, *Conflict of Laws* (5th edn, West Academic Publishing 2010) fn 43), and courts struggled with the practicalities in thousands of cases. Initial enthusiasm soon gave way to disillusion. In the academy, the supporters were eventually outnumbered by the critics while the majority of courts ultimately rallied under the banner of the Second Restatement, considering policies and interests on an *ad hoc* basis and often in an eclectic fashion. Over time, the discussion brought to light a cluster of theoretical concerns all of which caused practical problems. This cluster can be broken down into six major issues.

1. Unilateralism and lex fori *bias*

Interest analysis, at least *Currie*-style, is a form of conflicts → unilateralism: it begins with a (domestic) rule and seeks to determine its (spatial) reach. In other words, it is committed to an 'internal perspective' (Lea Brilmayer, *Conflict of Laws 1–5* (Little Brown 1991) (emphasis in the original)). This commitment is questionable as a theoretical matter and leads to a major problem in practice. In terms of conflicts theory, *Currie* essentially sent the discipline back to the times before the rise of multilateralism, ie before the 'Copernican Revolution' in choice of law usually credited to *Savigny*. As many commentators have noted, in a sense, *Currie's* approach is almost a modern (policy-based) version of the statutist method developed in the late Middle Ages. This makes its very premise unacceptable to those committed to multilateralism.

The more serious problem, however, is practical: due to its internal perspective, interest analysis begins by construing the reach of forum law which it vests, so to speak, with a right of first refusal. The result is a pervasive → *lex fori* bias. To be sure, *Currie* was perfectly open about that, and he shared his preference for forum law with others of his generation (see especially Albert Ehrenzweig, 'The Lex Fori: Basic Rule in the Conflict of Laws' [1960] Mich.L.Rev. 637). Still, it took some time before the true extent of the *lex fori* bias inherent in orthodox interest analysis sank in: forum law applies (i) whenever the forum is the only interested state, (ii) as a tie-breaker in all true conflicts and (iii) as a default rule in all zero-interest cases. Thus, it is displaced only if all interests lie in another state (reverse *Babcock* situation). In a sense, then, *Currie's* whole system can be condensed into one rule with one exception: apply the law of the forum unless the parties' common domicile is elsewhere (see Lea Brilmayer, *Conflict of Laws* (Little Brown 1991) 58–9). Note that the exception will rarely apply: it presumes that the plaintiff sues in a forum that is neither his nor the defendant's home – a pretty unlikely scenario. As a result, forum law will govern the vast majority of cases. Of course, this makes the approach attractive to judges who (like most) prefer to apply their own law but who (like many) hesitate to admit that and thus look for cover. Yet the approach openly encourages forum shopping (→ Forum (and law) shopping), is at odds with the maxim that like cases should be treated alike (no matter where filed) and in its parochialism it is especially unfit for international disputes.

2. Domestic interpretation and the dilemma of true conflicts

Interest analysis' unilateralism was exacerbated by *Currie's* method of interpretation. Even when defining a rule's spatial reach, *Currie* wanted to construe it just like in a domestic context.

> The process is essentially the familiar one of construction or interpretation. Just as we determine by that process how a statute applies in time, and how it applies to marginal domestic situations, so we may determine how it should be applied to cases involving foreign elements in order to effectuate the legislative purpose. (Brainerd Currie, *Selected Essays on the Conflict of Laws* (Duke University Press 1963) 183–4)

As a result, there was no need for special tools to solve conflicts problems – nor, indeed, for actual choice-of-law rules. Conflict of laws as a special discipline was essentially explained away. While *Currie* thus promised deliverance from the complexities and intricacies of that discipline, side-stepping the traditional apparatus came at a price: since *Currie's* method was not really one of conflicts law, it could not really solve conflicts.

Orthodox interest analysis provided an attractive solution for false conflicts cases, because from its perspective they were not conflicts at all. It implied an acceptable solution for zero-interest cases because they presented no real conflict either so that the forum might as well apply its own law. But it did not, and could not, proffer a real solution for true conflicts: with a *lex fori* tie-breaker, even true conflicts were decided just like domestic disputes.

Currie's forum law tie-breaker for true conflicts was widely regarded as unsatisfactory – crude, chauvinistic, difficult to reconcile with the sovereign equality of states and, again, rewarding forum shopping. For decades, courts and scholars struggled to find better solutions in constant back-and-forth between theory and practice. This produced many ideas but ultimately no consensus.

For starters, *Currie* himself eventually amended his original approach in the mock-restatement quoted above by suggesting avoidance of true conflicts whenever possible.

> (iii) If a court finds an apparent conflict between the interests of the two states it should reconsider. A more moderate and restrained interpretation of the policy or interest of one state or the other may avoid the conflict. (Brainerd Currie, 'Comments on Babcock v Jackson' [1963] Colum.L.Rev. 1233, 1242)

As the California Supreme Court had demonstrated in an earlier decision, this could work in some cases (*Bernkrant v Fowler*, 260 P.2d 906 (Cal 1961)) – but of course not in all. And it was obviously not a real solution for (unavoidable) true conflicts.

Taking their lead from these ideas, other American scholars in the 1960s and 1970s developed several variations on *Currie*. The main goal of these 'functional approaches' was to resolve true conflicts by a more searching 'process' (David F Cavers, *The Choice-of-Law Process* (University of Michigan Press 1965)). This could lead to the discovery of shared underlying policies to break the tie or at least allow a principled weighing of interests (Arthur von Mehren and Donald Trautman, *The Law of Multistate Problems* (Little Brown 1965), Russell Weintraub, *Commentary on the Conflict of Laws* (6th edn, Foundation Press 2010, 1st edn 1971) 394–405; for an excellent overview see Peter Hay, Patrick Borchers and Symeon Symeonides, *Conflict of Laws* (5th edn, West Academic Publishing 2010) 45–51).

In a seminal article published in the year of the *Babcock* decision, *William Baxter* developed a 'comparative impairment' solution for true conflicts (William Baxter, 'Choice of Law in the Federal System' (1963) 16 Stan.L.Rev. 1): apply the law of the state whose policies would be more impaired if it lost. The underlying rationale is one of overall efficiency: all states are better off if they always sacrifice the less impaired interest (Erin O'Hara and Larry Ribstein, 'From Politics to Efficiency in Choice of Law' (2000) 67 U.Chi.L.Rev. 1151, 1173). The idea was eventually adopted by the California Supreme Court (*Bernhard v Harrah's Club*, 546 P.2d 719 (Cal 1976)).

On the other side of the Continent, the New York Court of Appeals settled for a simpler tie-breaker: it eventually decided to revert to the *lex loci delicti* with an escape option. This produced a fairly predictable pattern: in false conflicts cases, apply the law of the common domicile; otherwise, apply the law of the place of the wrong; if there are good reasons to deviate from the latter, pick the law that best effectuates the underlying policies (*Neumeier v Kuehner*, 286 N.E.2d 454 (NY 1972); *Schultz v Boy Scouts of America*, 480 N.E.2d 679 (NY 1985); *Cooney v Osgood Machinery*, 612 N.E.2d 293 (1997)). Of course, reverting to territorialism is no great trick, but as the Court emphasized, at least it does not reward forum shopping.

In the meantime, other courts decided true conflicts by looking to further contacts (*Cipolla v Shaposka*, supra III.4) or by applying the 'better law' (*Conklin v Horner*, 157 N.W.2d 279 (Wis 1968); → Better law approach). Some tribunals even stuck to the *lex fori* for reasons of simplicity and efficiency (eg *Goldberg Co v Remsen Partners Ltd*, 170 F.3d 191 (DC Cir 1999)).

As a result of all these valiant efforts, today there is a panoply of true conflicts solutions. To be sure, none of them is a *panacea*. Still, scholars and courts have rendered a policy and interest approach much more sophisticated and viable than *Currie's* original model.

3. Public interests and private justice

As the label indicates, governmental interest analysis makes choice-of-law decisions turn on the policies and interests not of private parties but of states. This reflects the underlying credo of early and mid-20th-century American legal realism and sociological jurisprudence that even private law is largely an instrument of social regulation. Interest analysis thus essentially turns private international (or interlocal) law into a method of optimizing the effect of public policies.

As a result, distinctly private interests – as well as the enforcement of private rights as such – tend to disappear from view, or are at least marginalized (Lea Brilmayer, 'Rights, Fairness, and Choice of Law' (1989) 98 Yale L.J. 1277). This is surprising in a political system allegedly committed to private market activity and personal liberty in organizing one's own affairs. Especially in its American environment, governmental interest analysis appears strangely state centred.

Of course, at least in practice, basic considerations of private distributive justice cannot be entirely eliminated. The problem is that they may be at odds with governmental interests. Assume that at the time of an accident, the plaintiff is domiciled in a state barring recovery; later, he moves to another state allowing it. Does the latter state now have an interest in applying its law? The answer seems to be yes because a pro-recovery state wants its domiciliaries to be compensated. Allowing recovery, however, would put the defendant at the mercy of the plaintiff's move. Thus state interests and basic fairness point in opposite directions. Even courts committed to interest analysis have thus mostly refused to take such after-acquired domiciles into account (*Reich v Purcell*).

On the whole, in gauging state interests, courts have frequently considered aspects of basic justice between the parties, such as justified expectations (*McCann v Foster Wheeler LLC*, 225 P.3d 516 (Cal 2010)), underlying equities (*Schultz v Boy Scouts*, 480 N.E. 2d 679 (NY 1985)) and consistency of results regardless of the forum (*ditto*). But since strictly speaking, interest analysis has no place for such considerations, accommodating them within its framework has often required considerable modification and sometimes tortured reasoning.

4. Home party preference and the reality of state interests

→ Choice of law according to governmental policies needs to determine exactly which states are interested in seeing their law applied. In doing so, it faces a dilemma: orthodox assumptions create a clear pattern but are unrealistic while realistic assessments create a messy picture that is difficult to sort out.

Orthodox interest analysis was based on three (more or less implicit) assumptions: first, even in transboundary cases, states are interested (only) in promoting their domestic policies; second, states have an interest only in their own domiciliaries; and third, such interest exists only if a state's law helps the local party. Thus, in an interstate tort case in which state A's law provides for recovery while state B's law bars it, it is fairly simple to figure out which state is interested: state A is interested (only) if it is the home of the plaintiff, state B (only) if it is the home of the defendant. This leads straight to the tripartite pattern explained above (II.4.).

Yet, none of these assumptions hold up well under scrutiny. As a preliminary matter, it is far from clear exactly who or what the 'state' is nor that public actors have any real interest at all in the outcome of routine transboundary disputes between private parties. But even if they do, it is, first, unrealistic to assume that they are interested only in their domestic policies and pay no regard to any interstate concerns. In reality, few states would be so parochial as to ignore the need for mutual cooperation, decisional harmony and the prevention of forum shopping (→ Forum (and law) shopping). Second, it is equally unrealistic to assume that states are interested only in their own domiciliaries but do not care what happens to anyone else. For example, a state may very well want to ensure compensation for all traffic victims on its roads. Third, there is little reason to believe that states have an interest only in helping their own parties but never in denying them recovery. The policy underlying a charitable immunity rule, for example, may be not only to protect a (local) defendant rendering gratuitous services against liability but also to prevent a (local) plaintiff from biting the hand that feeds him.

A more realistic assessment of state interests should thus take interstate concerns, the well-being of outsiders and the policy to impose limits on a state's own citizens' rights into account. Accordingly, several of *Currie's* successors developed variations of interest analysis based on a much broader view of policies (*David Cavers*, *Robert Leflar*, *Arthur von Mehren* and *Donald Trautman*; see also Second Restatement of Conflicts (§ 6 sec 2)). Yet, this entails a rapid multiplication of interests which begin to point in all sorts of directions. In most cases, they clash in one way or another. As a result, there are few 'false conflicts' (which are easy to handle) but lots of 'true conflicts' (which are notoriously hard to resolve, *supra* III.2.).

This is no mere theory. At least since the 1970s, many courts began to transcend the orthodox view of interests and to take a broader, more realistic, perspective with the result that potentially easy cases became hard. Taking such a broader perspective was facilitated by the fact that the approach's foundational concepts – policy and interest – were not only unrealistically narrow but also inherently unclear.

5. Unclear concepts and badly indeterminate outcomes

Due to a lack of clear definition, the meaning of 'policy' and 'interest' is highly malleable. Operating with them has provided courts with enormous interpretative freedom. This has often rendered outcomes badly indeterminate.

MATHIAS W REIMANN

To begin with, it is not always obvious what exactly the policy underlying a private law rule is. One could, and perhaps should, search for actual legislative intent; yet, such a search can be labour intensive, fruitless and thus inefficient (Giesela Rühl, *Statut und Effizienz* (Mohr Siebeck 2011) 294–7). More importantly, interest analysts have usually shown little desire, and even less effort, to look for legislative intent in any serious fashion. Instead, they have simply assumed that the policy can be deduced from the rule (Lea Brilmayer, 'Interest Analysis and the Myth of Legislative Intent' (1980) 78 Mich.L.Rev. 293). As a result, even courts trying to discern policies in good faith have often wavered and disagreed. Since policies define interests, uncertainty about the former has entailed uncertainty about the latter. More confusion was added when courts claimed interests not only as the state of domicile or place of conduct but simply by virtue of being the forum (see, eg, *Griggs v Riley*, 489 S.W. 2d 469 (Mo 1972), such as a vague and general interest as a 'justice administering state' (*Milkovich v Saari*, 203 N.W.2d 408, 417 (Minn 1973) quoting *Leflar*). Worse, judges have sometimes shamelessly fabricated utterly implausible considerations (eg, avoiding hospital shopping by accident victims (*Milkovich v Saari*, 203 N.W.2d 408, 417 (Minn 1973)).

Disagreement about, and especially fast-and-loose invention of, policies scatters interests all over the place. That explodes the basic tripartite pattern of basic scenarios (*supra* III.4.) and ultimately leaves courts with almost unbridled discretion to prefer whatever interest they want. For example, by invoking an interest simply by being the forum, a court can easily turn a common domicile case pointing to another state's law into a true conflict and then break the tie in favour of the → *lex fori* (as in *Conklin v Horner*, 157 N.W.2d 279 (Wis 1968)).

For the first few decades, ie from the early 1960s through the 1980s, it seemed that new patterns were emerging at least in terms of actual outcomes: most courts decided torts conflicts in favour of (i) forum law, (ii) the local party and (iii) plaintiffs (see Patrick Borchers, 'The Choice-of-Law Revolution: An Empirical Study' (1992) 49 Wash. & Lee L.Rev. 357). If all three preferences could be combined (ie if a plaintiff sued in his own court whose law allowed recovery), the outcome would be virtually certain. Yet, as American tort law and practice began to take a more conservative turn since the 1980s, even that pattern became unreliable. Today, plaintiffs can easily lose in their own court under the pro-defendant law of another state (for example in *McCann v Foster Wheeler LLC*, 225 P.3d 516 (Cal 2010)). As a result, decisions based on the consideration of state policies and interests are notoriously unpredictable. While that problem may be just as serious with regard to the other modern American approaches, such unpredictability creates troublesome inefficiencies because it makes cases hard to settle and costly to litigate.

6. *Home bias and discrimination*

Choice-of-law decisions turning on domicile (→ Domicile, habitual residence and establishment) discriminate on the basis of the parties' home. In some areas, such as family law, that is both commonplace and justifiable because the parties' homes obviously matter. In other subjects, such as torts, it is more difficult to accept because it is not obvious why someone's recovery should depend purely on where he or she happens to live. It becomes especially questionable when states systematically prefer their own domiciliaries. Take a single-car accident with a driver from a recovery state who is being sued by two passengers – one also from a recovery state, the other from a guest statute jurisdiction. Can a court justly apply its pro-recovery rule to the first passenger while denying a remedy to the second? (see *Tooker v Lopez*, 249 N.E.2d 394 (NY 1969)).

Such discrimination raises particularly serious concerns under a constitution guaranteeing 'equal protection of the laws' (US Const., amend. XIV sec. I), declaring that '[t]he citizens of each state shall be entitled to all Privileges and Immunities of Citizens in the several states' (art IV sec 2), and ordering each state to give 'Full Faith and Credit . . . to the public Acts, Records, and judicial Proceedings in every other State' (art IV sec 1) (see Douglas Laycock, 'Equal Citizens of Equal and Territorial States: The Constitutional Foundations of Choice of Law' (1992) 92 Colum.L.Rev. 249). Yet, when the US Supreme Court tested the constitutionality of the modern choice-of-law approaches, it set the bar so low that the states remained largely free to discriminate in that fashion and to exercise self-preference (*Allstate Insurance Co v Hague*, 449 U.S. 302 (1981)).

IV. The European reaction: excitement and resistance

The American policy-based approaches received much attention among European conflicts scholars in the 1960s to the 1980s. The discussion focused not only on *Currie* and his governmental interest analysis but also on *Cavers*' 'principles of preference', *Leflar's* 'choice-influencing considerations', and *Ehrenzweig's lex fori* approach. It generated a large literature which can be cited here only selectively.

The debate was particularly lively in → Germany where Gerhard Kegel (1912–2006) (→ Kegel, Gerhard) reacted to the American approaches as early as 1961 and first spoke of a 'crisis' of the discipline (Gerhard Kegel, 'The Crisis of Conflict of Laws' (1961-II) 112 Rec. des Cours 89, 97–207), and where several other scholars took up the American challenge as well (for an overview, see Paul Heinrich Neuhaus, 'Neue Wege im europäischen internationalen Privatrecht?' (1971) 35 RabelsZ 401 (with English summary). → Switzerland was not far behind (Anton Heini, 'Neuere Strömungen im amerikanischen internationalen Privatrecht' (1962) 19 SchwJbIntR 31, 47–61; Peter Max Gutzwiller, 'Von Ziel und Methode des IPR' (1968) 25 SchwJbIntR 161; Frank Vischer, *Das Problem der Kodifikation des schweizerischen internationalen Privatrechts* (Helbing und Lichtenhahn 1971) 16–19). Scholars engaged with the American theories in other European countries as well, eg in → Austria (Fritz Schwind, 'Aspects et Sens du Droit Internationale Privé'(1984-VI) 187 Rec. des Cours 9, 54–6), → France (Bernard Audit, 'Le Caractére Functionnel de la Règle de Conflit' (1984-II) 186 Rec. des Cours 221, 242–8), → Italy (Rodolfo de Nova, *Concezioni Statiunitensi dei Conflitti di Leggi* (Universidad de Valladolid 1964) 42–8), the → Netherlands (Ted de Boer, *Beyond Lex Loci Delicti* (Kluwer 1987)) and the → United Kingdom (Otto Kahn-Freund, *Delictual Liability and the Conflict of Laws* (Sijthoff 1968)).

Views often clashed. Influenced by the American theories, several scholars, especially in Germany and Switzerland, pushed for a fundamental reorientation of conflicts law. They advocated a turn away from the purely jurisdiction-selecting approach (seeking 'conflicts justice') and the private law-oriented model based on *Savigny* which they considered outdated in the modern social and regulatory state. Thus, they envisaged a sociological approach with law-selecting elements (pursuing 'material justice') and oriented towards public policies and interests (Christian Joerges, *Zum Funktionswandel des Kollisionsrechts* (Mohr Siebeck 1971); Peter Max Gutzwiller, 'Von Ziel und Methode des IPR' (1968) 25 SchwJbIntR 161; see also Konrad Zweigert, 'Some Reflections on the Sociological Dimensions of Private international law' (1972–73) 44 U.Colo.L.Rev. 283). This 'political school' (Giesela Rühl, *Statut und Effizienz* (Mohr Siebeck 2011) 184–8) encountered resistance from the defenders of the traditional approach, ranging from massive counterattacks (Gerhard Kegel, 'Paternal Home and Dream Home' [1979] Am.J.Comp.L. 615) to calls for moderation and acceptance of adjustment (Paul Heinrich Neuhaus, 'Neue Wege im europäischen internationalen Privatrecht?' (1971) 35 RabelsZ 401, 425–6; Frank Vischer, 'General Course on Private international law' (1992-I) 232 Rec. des Cours 9, 72–3). The defenders emphasized the virtues of the traditional, content-blind and multilateral, conflicts rules. They also argued that the American approaches could not be easily transferred from a federal system to an international context and from a tradition of judge-made law to an environment of primarily legislative rulemaking. And they pointed out that the American 'conflicts revolution' had in large part been a reaction against the excessive territorialism and rigid formalism of *Beale's* (First) Restatement, ie to problems that European conflicts law did not face on the same scale.

In the end, the defenders of the traditional order by and large prevailed. The vast majority of European conflicts scholars, not to mention courts, were not ready to switch from a private to a public law perspective, from choice-of-law rules to a choice-of-law 'process', and from general (legislative) norms to *ad hoc* (judicial) results. Well conscious of the trade-offs, they ultimately prized uniformity and predictability of results more highly than the enforcement of local policies and justice in the individual case.

V. Conclusion: enrichment of theory and modification of practice

In the long run, the impact of policy and interest analysis on conflicts theory has been more important than its effect on practice.

Before the American iconoclasts entered the scene, conflicts theory had largely become stagnant. The *Savignian* paradigms – especially jurisdiction selection, multilateralism and strict private law orientation – had long gone unquestioned, and conflicts scholarship had largely busied itself with doctrinal issues on the detail level. *Currie* and his successors stirred up the field. Their radicalism challenged the time-worn assumptions and necessitated a re-evaluation of the discipline from the perspective of sociological jurisprudence and under conditions of the modern regulatory state.

This re-thinking was most fundamental and far-reaching in the USA where revolutions in legal thought are more easily embraced. Here, the way jurists approach choice-of-law problems was permanently broadened as well as deepened.

Even in Europe, where adherence to jurisprudential tradition is usually stronger, policy and interest analysis helped to refertilize conflicts theory. The nearly mechanical application of the traditional bilateral conflicts rules came under scrutiny, substantive considerations were no longer taboo, public policies were taken more seriously and unilateralism experienced a limited revival. To be sure, the American theories were not the only, and perhaps not even the leading, cause of the European reflection upon traditional assumptions; by the 1970s and 1980s, change was in the air for other reasons as well, among them a growing interest in protecting weaker parties even in conflicts law, and more generally, the integration of Europe. But the American policy and interest-based approaches were important catalysts in this process because they asked radical questions and suggested new directions. In that sense, they contributed to a 'quiet revolution' in Europe (Symeon Symeonides, *Private international law at the End of the 20th Century: Progress or Regress* (Kluwer 2000) 26–35).

The policy approaches' effect on practice has been more limited. That is true even in the USA. Even in tort (and contract) cases, the majority of jurisdictions today subscribe either to the Restatement Second with its 'most-significant-relationship' paradigm or to similar 'mixed modern' approaches. As mentioned (*supra* II.3.), in these (and other) jurisdictions, state policies and governmental interests frequently play a role but they are only one aspect in a choice-of-law process marked by eclecticism, multifactor tests, great flexibility of methods – and thus low predictability of outcomes.

In Europe, interest analysis has ultimately left no direct traces in either legislation or court opinions. It is true that European conflicts practice has been considerably modified in recent decades; in particular, it has developed in the direction of more flexibility and greater attention to substantive outcomes. But this development can be traced to American policy approaches only in the sense that these approaches have helped the Europeans understand why mechanical and content-blind conflicts rules can be problematic. It is also true that there are some parallels between *Currie's* postulates and modern European conflicts practice, such as the provisions on mandatory rules reflecting important public policies (see, eg, art 16 Regulation (EC) No 864/2007 of the European Parliament and of the Council of 11 July 2007 on the law applicable to non-contractual obligations (Rome II), [2007] OJ L 199/40). Perhaps the most striking example is the common domicile rule in tort cases (art 4 sec II Rome II Regulation) which has been adopted in the majority of recent conflicts codifications in the world (Symeon Symeonides, *Codifying Choice of Law around the World* (OUP 2014) 72–80). While its prevalence is, in a sense, *Currie's* belated triumph, his ideas – and their adoption by New York Court of Appeals in *Babcock v Jackson* (191 N.E.2d 279 (NY 1963)) – are merely one of the rule's modern origins among others.

MATHIAS W REIMANN

Literature

Patrick Borchers, 'The Choice-of-Law Revolution: An Empirical Study' (1992) Wash. & Lee L.Rev. 357; Lea Brilmayer, *Conflict of Laws* (Little Brown 1991); David F Cavers, *The Choice-of-Law Process* (University of Michigan Press 1965); Brainerd Currie, *Selected Essays on the Conflict of Laws* (Duke University Press 1963); Brainerd Currie, 'Comments on Babcock v Jackson' (1963) 63 Colum.L.Rev. 1233; Peter Hay, Patrick Borchers and Symeon Symeonides, *Conflict of Laws* (5th edn, West Academic Publishing 2010); Christian Joerges, *Zum Funktionswandel des Kollisionsrechts* (Mohr Siebeck 1971); Gerhard Kegel, 'The Crisis of the Conflict of Laws' (1961-II) 112 Rec. des Cours 89; Gerhard Kegel, 'Paternal Home and Dream Home' (1979) 27 Am.J.Comp.L. 615; Arthur von Mehren and Donald Trautman, *The Law of Multistate Problems* (Little Brown 1965); Konrad Zweigert, 'Some Reflections on the Sociological Dimensions of Private international law' (1972–73) 44 U.Colo.L.Rev. 283.

Internet, jurisdiction

I. Jurisdictional complexity of the internet

The expansion of digital networks and the ubiquitous nature of internet activities have led to a dramatic rise not only in the number of international transactions and situations, but also in their complexity and in the challenges they pose when regulating international jurisdiction (→ Jurisdiction, foundations; → Jurisdiction, limits under international law). The increase of cross-border interaction through digital networks facilitates transactions and relationships between parties who may not always know the physical location of all actors involved. The instantaneous and borderless transmission of information via the internet has increased the provision of services and the exploitation of intangible rights on a global scale. Online services have made it common for consumers to engage in international contracts from their home country (→ Consumer contracts). Activities carried out through the internet may have significant effects simultaneously within a great number of jurisdictions, regardless of national borders. This is of particular significance in areas such as the infringement of intellectual property rights and the violation of → personality rights.

Traditional jurisdictional rules have been developed for cases involving contacts with several territorial entities based on geographical considerations (→ Jurisdiction, foundations). The territorial connecting factors (→ Connecting factor) traditionally used in jurisdiction rules may result in significant uncertainties when applied to internet activities. Doubts arise as to the location of the activities and the determination and extent of the jurisdiction to adjudicate claims concerning them. Usually in internet tort disputes, the place of action and injury will not be the same and many cases deal with so-called scattered harms, where the place of action and the places of injury may become particularly difficult to locate. Furthermore, the disconnection between the effects of internet activities and geographical boundaries favours the possibility that multiple states assert jurisdiction to hear disputes arising from a particular activity. Acting on the internet may potentially establish contacts with every jurisdiction, posing the threat of universal jurisdiction over internet actors, and creating the risk for website operators of being sued in a multiplicity of jurisdictions. Furthermore, new concerns arise when applying the connecting factors. Given the virtual nature of the internet, in the application of geographical contacts, such as the domicile (→ Domicile, habitual residence and establishment), the place where services are provided or where certain activities are carried out, it may be appropriate to consider if a party has made statements which do not correspond to the facts, aimed at conferring jurisdiction on the courts of a particular state.

Concerning injunctive relief, it is noteworthy that the scope of injunctions may deserve particular attention in the internet context, since injunctions with an unrestricted or excessive territorial scope of application may unfairly prejudice the position of private parties in countries other than the forum (→ Injunction). Some of the most notorious cases – such as the High Court of Australia's decision in *Dow Jones & Co Inc v Gutnick* ((2002) 210 CLR 575 (Australia)) and the French decision and US reaction concerning *Yahoo! Inc v La Ligue Contre le Racisime et L'Antisemitisme* (433 F.3d 1199 (9th Cir 2006)) – have raised concerns about the implications of a broad assertion of jurisdiction or the adoption of territorially unrestricted injunctive measures that may affect conducts globally, but face significant obstacles regarding their recognition and enforcement in foreign countries. Furthermore, the risks of international forum shopping (→ Forum (and law) shopping) may be especially significant in areas with important differences in substantive law. Concerning internet activities such problems have arisen in several areas, including defamation, where the so-called 'libel tourism' has expanded into a field where the protection of human rights (→ Human rights and private international law), including freedom of speech, becomes a relevant factor influencing jurisdiction and the enforcement of foreign judgments (→ Recognition and enforcement of judgments (civil law); → Recognition and enforcement of judgments (common law)).

II. Regulatory models and internet evolution

At the initial stages of the commercial expansion of the internet, some authors stressed the view that global computer networks erode the power and legitimacy of national jurisdictions to regulate global phenomena and adjudicate claims regarding online activities having global or multinational effects (David R Johnson and David Post, 'Law and Borders: The Rise of Law in Cyberspace' (1995–96) 48 Stan.L.Rev. 1367). According to this approach, internet transactions and activities should not be bound to a particular territorial sovereign and 'Cyberspace' should be conceived as a separate place and regarded as an autonomous jurisdiction. Under this view, the internet could develop its own effective institutions to establish rules and enforce them. Global self-regulation was presented as an alternative to territorial jurisdictions to govern internet activities and to adjudicate claims arising out of such activities.

However, nation states remain the primary jurisdictional entities to regulate internet activities that are basically governed by territorially based legislation (Jack L Goldsmith and Wu Tim, *Who Controls the Internet? Illusions of a Borderless World* (OUP 2006) 65; Pedro A De Miguel Asensio, *Derecho privado de Internet* (5th edn, Civitas Thomson Reuters 2015)). The legitimacy of the assertion of jurisdiction by nation states with respect to internet activities that produce significant effects in their respective territories seems widely accepted. Notwithstanding this, it is clear that → online dispute resolution mechanisms may provide an alternative by which a party can obtain an effective remedy (→ Remedies).

Internet self-regulation remains dominant only with respect to technical specifications, protocol and standards that are essential in the functioning of the technical infrastructure of the internet and its global interconnectedness, such as those developed under the auspices of ISOC (Internet Society), IETF (Internet Engineering Task Force), IRTF (Internet Research Task Force) or W3C (World Wide Web Consortium), but they do not establish regulations directly concerning private rights and their use in the internet. A more prominent role is played by ICANN (Internet Corporation for Assigned Names and Numbers) that coordinates functions concerning internet addresses and numbering resources, and the domain name system.

Initial internet technologies were conceived for global access, but filtering technology based on the significance of IP addresses as reliable indications of physical location has later been developed. In particular, geolocation technologies have become very accurate to establish the location of persons accessing websites (Dan Jerker B Svantesson, *Private international law and the Internet* (3rd edn, Kluwer 2016) ch 10). This development greatly influences the ability of internet site operators to control the location of those who access the contents they provide and to arrange their online activities limiting their territorial reach. Although certain uses of geolocation technologies may undermine the openness of the internet, their availability is a valuable instrument for internet actors not only for marketing purposes, but also to control legal risks arising out of the ubiquitous reach of internet activities. The availability of geolocation technologies may also be relevant when applying jurisdictional rules to internet activities, in particular where it is necessary to establish if contents are directed to a territory or produce significant effects within it.

III. Legal sources

1. International

There are no uniform rules on jurisdiction over internet activities adopted in the framework of international organizations. Although the lack of uniformity between states' approaches undermines legal certainty, the experience at the → Hague Conference on Private International Law is illustrative of the difficulties that an international treaty on jurisdiction over internet activities faces. The impact of the internet on the Draft Convention on Jurisdiction and Foreign Judgments in Civil and Commercial Matters (Hague Conference on Private International Law (ed), Preliminary Draft Convention on Jurisdiction and Foreign Judgments in Civil and Commercial Matters adopted by the Special Commission, Preliminary Document No 11 of August 2000) has been singled out as one of the areas where progress in the Hague Judgments Project became more difficult at the beginning of the 21st century. The uncertain legal implications of the use of the internet and the development of → electronic commerce on the traditional approach based on the territorial localization of connecting factors (→ Connecting factor) was one of the main reasons behind the failure of those negotiations at The Hague. Such disagreement was the result of the conflicting policy views between business and consumers, but also of the states' → public policy (*ordre public*) concerns related to information and the protection of certain human rights, in particular with regard to the balance between freedom of expression and protection of → personality rights. Concerns were raised about the negative consequences of the envisaged Convention over the electronic commerce industry in the framework of the debate between a 'country of origin' or a 'country of destination' approach. Under the first approach, jurisdiction is granted to the courts of the country in which the source of the transmission is located. By contrast, the second approach favours granting jurisdiction to the country where the contents are received.

The 2005 Hague Choice of Court Convention (Hague Convention of 30 June 2005 on choice of court agreements, 44 ILM 1294) is of very limited significance for internet activities beyond contracts. Moreover, it is remarkable that → consumer contracts are excluded from that Convention. Other international organizations that have been active in establishing uniform rules in certain areas related to internet activities, such as → UNCITRAL, → WIPO and private international law, ITU or → UNIDROIT, have not focused their attention on jurisdiction issues in this field. This also applies to non-governmental organizations active in the field of internet governance. ICANN has been successful in establishing → alternative dispute resolution mechanisms concerning conflicts between trademark owners and domain name registrants. However, these mechanisms are not binding on national courts and does not prevent the parties from submitting the dispute to a national court.

2. National: tests for personal jurisdiction in US case-law

The adoption of special legislation on jurisdiction for internet disputes is not common. From a comparative perspective, the evolution of two systems based on different approaches when regulating international jurisdiction are particularly influential: the → USA and the European Union. This section focuses on the situation in the USA.

After the concerns raised by certain initial cases that supported the view that the mere accessibility of the contents within a state might be sufficient to justify jurisdiction (*Inset Systems, Inc v Instruction Set, Inc*, 937 F.Supp. 161 (DConn 1996)), an internet specific test was developed on the basis of the distinction between interactive and passive websites in the landmark case *Zippo Mfg Co v Zippo Dot Coin, Inc* (952 F. Supp. 1119, 1124–5 (WDPa 1997)). It established the so-called 'sliding scale' test to internet contacts: mere passive websites without additional contacts with the forum would not be subject to jurisdiction while the characterization of a website as active was regarded as sufficient to grant jurisdiction anywhere the site is accessed. In between, jurisdiction is to be determined by considering the level of interactivity of the webpage. But the sliding scale test proved unpredictable and difficult to apply.

More recently, the adaptation of the traditional due process standards or minimum contacts test for determining personal jurisdiction has led to the acceptance that also under the traditional framework, having an active web page cannot always be regarded as a purposeful availment of the benefits of doing business in every forum for the purposes of granting jurisdiction (see *ALS Scan, Inc v Digital Serv Consultants, Inc*, 293 F.3d 707 (4th Cir 2002)). A standard based on the effect of the internet activity within a jurisdiction, in line with the US Supreme Court decision in *Calder v Jones*, 465 U.S. 783 (1984) – articulating the 'effects test' for establishing personal jurisdiction – has received significant acceptance, as well as the view that judicial application of the traditional jurisdiction rules allows the standards to evolve gradually and to adapt to the challenges posed by internet technology. These developments confirm the view that the lack of interactivity of a website is not determinative to exclude that the conduct may be purposefully directed to a state in terms that justify the assertion of jurisdiction by its courts under traditional principles. However, the US due process analysis is particularly flexible and may yield unpredictable results (→ Full faith and credit clause and due process).

Some concerns about an excessive reach of US jurisdiction based on special legislation have been raised, in connection with the trend by US authorities to seize domain names under the control of US registrars and registry operators – including the entire dot-com registry system – that relate to activities that may violate US law, even if the domain name is owned by foreigners, has been registered using the services of a foreign domain name registrar and is active basically in foreign markets. Furthermore, as regards disputes between trademark and domain name owners, the ACPA (Anticybersquatting Consumer Protection Act (ACPA), 15 U.S.C. § 1125(d)) grants broad *in rem* jurisdiction to the US courts where the domain name registrar, domain name registry, or other domain name authority that registered or assigned the domain name is located.

3. European Union

Internet-related disputes typically fall within the scope of application of the Brussels I Regulation (recast) (Regulation (EU) No 1215/2012 of the European Parliament and of the Council of 12 December 2012 on jurisdiction and the recognition and enforcement of judgments in civil and commercial matters (recast), [2012] OJ L 351/1; → Brussels I (Convention and Regulation)). Therefore, the jurisdiction rules applicable in the EU are basically the uniform provisions established in the Regulation. A parallel regime is contained in the → Lugano Convention (Lugano Convention of 30 October 2007 on jurisdiction and the recognition and enforcement of judgments in civil and commercial matters, [2007] OJ L 339/3). However, other than certain provisions (such as those on exclusive jurisdiction, choice of forum and → consumer contracts), if the defendant is not domiciled in a Member State, national jurisdiction rules remain applicable, as established in art 6(1) of the Brussels I Regulation (recast).

What is peculiar to the internet is that identifying the domicile (→ Domicile, habitual residence and establishment) of the defendant becomes more difficult. According to the case-law of the ECJ, the expression 'is not domiciled in a Member State', used in art 6(1) of the Brussels I Regulation (recast), means that application of the national rules rather than the uniform rules of jurisdiction is possible only if the court seized of the case holds firm evidence that the defendant is in fact domiciled outside the EU (Case C-327/10 *Hypoteční banka, as v Udo Mike Lindner* [2011] OJ C 25/12, para 42). Furthermore, in the context of a dispute arising from the operation of an internet site, the ECJ has held that where the domicile of a defendant who is a Member State national is unknown, the uniform rules of jurisdiction established by the Brussels I Regulation (Regulation (EC) No 44/2001 of 22 December 2000 on jurisdiction and the recognition and enforcement of judgments in civil and commercial matters, [2001] OJ L 12/1) (→ Brussels I (Convention and Regulation)) apply instead of those in force in the different Member States (Case C-292/10 *G v Cornelius de Visser* [2012] OJ C 133/5, para 42).

IV. Current regulation in the EU

1. General structure

In the Brussels I Regulation (recast) system, provided that no exclusive jurisdiction is granted under art 24, general jurisdiction may be based on a prorogation agreement by the parties or, lacking such an agreement, on the defendant's domicile. In practice, the choice of the parties is particularly significant in disputes related to contracts. The main rule on jurisdiction of the Regulation is found in art 4 that establishes the competence of the court of the defendant's domicile. Based on the general nature of the jurisdiction allocated in art 4, it has an unrestricted scope. In the context of the broader reach of communications over the internet, it is therefore very significant that the courts of the defendant's domicile are competent to rule on all the injury suffered by the alleged victim anywhere in the world.

The Brussels I Regulation (recast) has some alternative jurisdiction rules. Among those, of special relevance with regard to internet activities is art 7(2) dealing with matters relating to → tort. In these cases the claimant has the choice to bring the action where the defendant is domiciled or in the Member State whose courts are competent under art 7. However, special grounds of jurisdiction are considered exceptions to the general forum of the defendant's domicile and hence have to be interpreted restrictively. Furthermore, it can be noted that it is generally agreed that an internet site by itself cannot constitute a branch office or establishment, in particular for the purposes of the jurisdiction rule in art 7(5) of the Brussels I Regulation (recast) granting jurisdiction to the place where a branch or other establishment is situated as regards disputes arising out of the operations of a branch or establishment.

According to art 7(2) of the Brussels I Regulation (recast), in matters relating to tort a person domiciled in a Member State may be sued 'in the courts of the place where the harmful event occurred or may occur'. That rule is intended to comprise all the actions which seek to establish the liability of the defendant and which are not related to a contract in the sense of art 7(1); therefore, it covers some of the main fields of litigation arising out of internet activities, such as intellectual property disputes (→ Intellectual property, jurisdiction) and violation of → personality rights. Before addressing these two fields, it is important to note that it is settled case-law that, in the case where the place in which the event which may give rise to liability in tort occurs and the place where that event results in damage are not identical, art 7(2) grants jurisdiction to the courts of both places

(→ Jurisdiction, contracts and torts). Therefore, the defendant may be sued, at the option of the claimant, in the courts for either of those places (see, eg Case C-170/12 *Peter Pinckney v KDG Mediatech AG* [2013] OJ C 344/27). By contrast with the general forum of the defendant's domicile and the jurisdiction granted to the court of the place where the harmful event occurred, the jurisdiction of the courts of the place where the damage occurs is in principle limited to damage suffered in their territory. Identification and application of those connecting factors pose special difficulties in internet-related intellectual property and defamation claims – see sections IV.2.c) and d) below.

Provisional measures to obtain injunctive relief are of particular importance in the internet context (→ Provisional measures, → Injunction). For instance, under EU law, even in situations in which intermediaries may not be held liable either as direct or as secondary infringers, they may be required by a court or authority to terminate or prevent an infringement (see arts 12(3), 13(2) and 14(3) e-Commerce Directive (Directive 2000/31/EC of the European Parliament and of the Council of 8 June 2000 on certain legal aspects of information society services, in particular electronic commerce, in the Internal Market (Directive on electronic commerce) [2000] OJ L178/1); art 8(3) Directive 2001/29/EC of 22 May 2001 on the harmonization of certain aspects of copyright and related rights in the information society [2001] OJ L 167/10; art 11 Directive 2004/48/EC of 29 April 2004 on the enforcement of intellectual property rights [2004] OJ L 157/45). Concerning injunctive relief, it should be recalled that pursuant to art 35 of the Brussels I Regulation (recast), the courts of a Member State may adopt → provisional measures even if the courts of another Member State have jurisdiction as to the substance of the matter. Article 35 does not contain uniform jurisdiction rules for the adoption of provisional measures and hence it refers to the national rules on jurisdiction of the Member States. According to the case-law of the ECJ, the granting of provisional measures on the basis of that provision is conditional on, *inter alia*, the existence of a real connecting link between the subject matter of the measures sought and the territorial jurisdiction of the court before which those measures are sought. In particular, the required link is present if the measure is to be enforced within the territory of the state to which application is made and the measure relates to goods located in that state or to intellectual property rights granted by that state.

2. *Specific subject matter areas*

a) Contracts

Choice-of-forum clauses are of great practical importance in internet contracts, since they are valuable instruments to reduce litigation risks (→ Choice of forum and submission to jurisdiction). Article 25 of the Brussels I Regulation (recast) establishes the general forum based on the autonomy of the parties. The use of electronic technologies poses challenges to the traditional form requirements (→ Formal requirements and validity). In order to accommodate prorogation agreements concluded by electronic means of communication, art 25(2) establishes that any communication by electronic means which provides a durable record of the agreement shall be equivalent to 'writing'. In its *El Majdoub* judgment (Case C-322/14, *Jaouad El Majdoub v CarsOnTheWeb.Deutschland GmbH* [2015] OJ C 236/26) the ECJ ruled on the validity of an agreement conferring jurisdiction that was accepted on a website by 'click-wrapping'. In those situations the purchaser expressly accepts the general terms containing the jurisdiction agreement by clicking the relevant box on the seller's website but that operation does not automatically lead to the opening of the general terms, as an extra click on a specific hyperlink is necessary. Since printing the text of the general terms was possible before the conclusion of the contract, the Court held that such method of accepting general terms containing an agreement conferring jurisdiction, constitutes a communication by electronic means capable of providing a durable record of that agreement for the purposes of Article 25(2). A similar provision may be found in art 3 of the Hague Choice of Court Convention. Its underlying approach is in line with art 6 of the UNCITRAL Model Law on Electronic Commerce 1996 (UNCITRAL (ed), Model Law on Electronic Commerce with Guide to Enactment 1996, New York 1997) and art 9(2) of the 2005 UNCITRAL Electronic Communications Convention (United Nations Convention of 23 November 2005 on the Use of Electronic Communications in International Contracts, adopted on 23 November 2005 during the 53rd plenary meeting of the General Assembly by resolution A/60/21, text available in UN doc A/60/515) (→ UNCITRAL).

Among the special grounds of jurisdiction laid down in art 7, the first paragraph refers to matters relating to a contract. Contracts performed online pose particular challenges as to the determination of the place of performance as connecting factor for these purposes. Classification of certain contracts on digital contents and information as sale of goods or provision of services for the purposes of that provision may be controversial (→ Classification (characterization)). Contracts on the supply of standard software that can be delivered as a physical device or online are typically regarded as sale of goods (→ Sale contracts and sale of goods). By contrast, contracts concerning the access and online use of information (services) provided by the other party tend to be considered contracts for the provision of services. Determining the place where, under the contract, the services were provided or should have been provided may raise doubts, where such contracts are performed online and connected to several countries. In principle, connections that merely result from the location of the technical means – such as a server – instrumental in the provision of the service shall not qualify as places which have a direct link to the service (in the meaning of the Case C-204/08 *Peter Rehder v Air Baltic Corporation* [2009] OJ C 205/8, para 41). In the typical situations only the place from where the service is provided (in principle, the place where the provider is established) and the place of destination (in principle, where the addressee of the service is located) have such a direct link to the service. Although further clarification by the ECJ could be appropriate, the better view seems to be that typically and unless otherwise agreed, the place of establishment of the service provider – if clearly identifiable by the other party – should prevail when determining the place of provision of online services for the purposes of art 7(1) of the Brussels I Regulation (recast).

b) Consumer contracts
The specific jurisdictional rules protecting consumers established in the Brussels Convention were subject to some amendments in the Brussels I Regulation in order to adapt them to → electronic commerce (→ Consumer contracts). Furthermore, the Brussels I Regulation (recast) has expanded the scope of these rules so that they now also apply to contractual disputes involving third state defendants (art 6). The special rules for the protection of consumers are established in arts 17–19 Brussels I Regulation (recast). Under this special regime, prorogation of jurisdiction is greatly restricted (art 19), a consumer may only be sued in the courts of his domicile (→ Domicile, habitual residence and establishment), and a consumer may bring proceedings in the courts of his own domicile or of the defendant's domicile (art 18). To determine when consumers benefit from protection, art 17(1)(c) of the Brussels I Regulation (recast) imposes certain conditions that relate to the trader. These conditions determine who is to be regarded as a passive consumer and hence beneficiary of special protection. Application of the rules that protect consumers is limited to situations where the trader pursues its commercial activities in the country of the consumer's domicile or, by any means, directs such activities to that country or to several countries including that country, and the contract must fall within the scope of such activities. The requirement that the professional directs his activities to the country where the consumer has his habitual residence deserves particular attention. This condition was developed to adapt the previous regime to the context of internet activities, where international contracts involving passive consumers have greatly expanded. There is no definition of the concept of activity 'directed to' the country of the consumer's domicile in the Regulation. According to a Joint Declaration by the Council and the Commission on art 15 Brussels I Regulation, the mere fact that an internet site is accessible is not sufficient for the protection to be applicable (Recital (24) Rome I Regulation).

In the absence of a definition, the ECJ has been requested to clarify under which circumstances activities are regarded as being directed to the country of the consumer's domicile (→ Domicile, habitual residence and establishment). Determinative in this regard is whether, before the contract was concluded, there was evidence demonstrating that the trader was envisaging doing business with consumers domiciled in the country of that consumer's domicile. Therefore, in the context of the internet, in order to establish whether a trader directs the activities to a country, attention has to be paid to the content and settings of the trader's internet presence and its overall activity. Significant guidance has been provided by the ECJ in its *Pammer* judgment (Joined Cases C-585/08 and C-144/09, *Peter Pammer v Reederei Karl Schlüter GmbH & Co KG and Hotel Alpenhof GesmbH v Oliver Heller* [2010] OJ C 55/4, paras 76 ff). The distinction between active websites, in the sense of sites enabling the conclusion of electronic contracts, and passive websites is not deemed decisive in this regard, since also websites that are not interactive may be intended to do business and promote the conclusion of contracts with consumers by other means (→ Consumer contracts). In fact, the application of the special protection rules does not require the contract between the consumer and the trader to be concluded at a distance (Case C-190/11 *Daniela Mühlleitner v Ahmad Yusufi and Wadat Yusufi* [2012] OJ C 204/14, para 45). Furthermore, the ECJ has clarified that the application of the special provisions protecting consumers does not require the existence of a causal link between the means employed to direct the commercial or professional activity to the Member State of the consumer's domicile – such as the trader's website – and the conclusion of the contract with that consumer. However, the existence of such a causal link constitutes evidence of the connection between the contract and such activity (Case C- 218/12 *Lokman Emrek v Vlado Sabranovic* [2013] OJ C 367/14).

In its *Pammer* judgment, the ECJ held that among the evidence establishing whether an activity is 'directed to' the country of the consumer's domicile are all clear expressions of the intention to solicit the custom of that country's consumers. Such clear expressions include mention by the trader that it is offering its services or its goods in one or more countries designated by name, and recourse by the trader to advertising and marketing mechanisms that promote access to its site by consumers domiciled in the country concerned. The ECJ even provided a non-exhaustive list of items of evidence that possibly, in combination with one another, are capable of demonstrating the existence of an activity 'directed to' the country of the consumer's domicile. The relevant factors may include: the international nature of the activity at issue; mention of telephone numbers with the international code; use of a top-level domain name other than that of the country in which the trader is established, or use of a non-national top-level domain name; the description of itineraries from foreign countries corresponding to the place where the service is provided; mention of an international clientele; use of a language or a currency (→ Money and currency) other than the language or currency generally used in the country in which the trader is established. The progressive development and availability of geolocation tools are very significant when assessing the trader's internet presence and its overall activity for these purposes.

c) Personality rights

The interpretation of the → connecting factor used in art 7(2) of the Brussels I Regulation (recast) with respect to an alleged infringement of → personality rights by means of content placed online on a website was the central issue addressed by the ECJ in its Joined Cases C-509/09 and C-161/10 *eDate Advertising GmbH v X, Olivier Martinez, Robert Martinez v MGN Limited* [2011] OJ C 370/9. In line with its previous case-law, the ECJ acknowledged that the expression 'place where the harmful event occurred' covers both the place where the damage occurred and the place of the event giving rise to it (→ Jurisdiction, contracts and torts). In relation to the application of those two connecting criteria to actions seeking reparation for damage caused by a defamatory publication, the Court had held that, in the case of defamation by means of a newspaper article distributed in several states, the victim may bring an action for → damages against the publisher either before the courts of the place where the publisher of the defamatory publication is established, which have jurisdiction to award damages for all of the harm caused by the defamation, or before the courts of each state in which the publication was distributed and where the victim claims to have suffered injury to his reputation, which have jurisdiction to rule solely in respect of the harm caused in the state of the court seized (Case C-68/93 *Shevill v Presse Alliance SA* [1995] ECR I-417, para 33).

The ECJ decided to adjust that standard with respect to alleged infringements committed on the internet, after considering that the placing online of content on a website is to be distinguished from the distribution of media such as printed matter in that it is intended, in principle, to ensure the ubiquity of the content, since it may be consulted instantly by an unlimited number of persons throughout the world (Joined Cases C-509/09 and C-161/10 *eDate Advertising GmbH v X, Olivier Martinez, Robert Martinez v MGN Limited* [2011] OJ C 370/9, para 45). Because the scope of the distribution of content placed online is in principle universal, the Court considered that the usefulness of the criterion relating to distribution is limited in the internet context and the connecting criteria have to be adapted to the new media. The ECJ concluded that the courts that are in the best position to assess the impact of internet content on an individual's personality rights are the courts of the place where the alleged victim has his centre of interests. Therefore, under the *eDate Advertising* standard, the alleged victim is granted the option of bringing an action for liability, in respect of all the damage caused, either before the courts of the Member State in which the publisher of that content is established or before the courts of the Member State in which the centre of his interests is based. Furthermore, that person may bring his action before the courts of each Member State in the territory of which content placed online is or has been accessible. Those courts have jurisdiction only in respect of the damage caused in the territory of the Member State of the court seized. The ECJ clarified that the place where a person has the centre of his interests corresponds in general to his habitual residence, but a person may also have his centre of interests where he does not habitually reside, in so far as other factors, such as the pursuit of a professional activity, may establish the existence of a particularly close link with that state (paras 48–52). As to the granting of unrestricted jurisdiction to the courts of the centre of the interests of the victim, the view that it would be appropriate to require that the information at issue is objectively and particularly relevant in that territory was expressed by AG Cruz Villalón in his opinion on this case delivered on 29 March 2011 (Joined Cases C-509/09 and C-161/10 *eDate Advertising GmbH v X, Olivier Martinez, Robert Martinez v MGN Limited* [2011] OJ C 370/9, Opinion of AG Cruz Villalón). However, this additional requirement is not present in the Court's ruling.

In situations where the defendant is domiciled in a third state, national jurisdiction rules remain applicable and national standards may differ. In Germany, the relevant national provision concerning jurisdiction in non-contractual claims to be applied to third state defendants is very similar to art 7(2) of the Brussels I Regulation (recast). § 32 German Code of Civil Procedure (*Zivilprozessordnung* of 5 December 2005, BGBl. I 3202, as amended) grants jurisdiction to German courts if either the place of action or the place of injury is in → Germany. Concerning its application to personality rights infringements on the internet, reference is to be made to the 2010 *The New York Times* judgment of the German Federal Court of Justice ((BGH), 2 March 2010, VI ZR 23/09). According to this judgment, what is determinative to grant jurisdiction to German courts is whether the alleged infringing content has an objective domestic connection such that a clash of the conflicting interests of plaintiff and defendant have occurred or might occur in Germany.

d) Intellectual property

In the application of art 7(2) of the Brussels I Regulation (recast), determining the place where the damage occurs has become particularly complex in situations in which intellectual property rights are used in ubiquitous media (→ Intellectual property, jurisdiction). The assessment made by the ECJ concerning the criterion of the centre of interests of the person whose rights have been infringed in the particular context of infringements of personality rights, does not apply to the determination of jurisdiction in respect of infringements of industrial property rights (Case C-523/10 *Wintersteiger AG v Products 4U Sondermaschinenbau GmbH* [2012] OJ C 30/19, para 25) or actions seeking compensation for damage sustained on account of copyright infringement (Case C-170/12 *Peter Pinckney v KDG Mediatech AG* [2013] OJ C 344/27, para 47). Therefore, the place where the alleged damage occurred within the meaning of that provision may vary according to the nature of the right allegedly infringed. The protection afforded by national intellectual property rights is, in principle, limited to the territory of one country, and hence the place where the damage occurred in a claim of infringement of such a right is located in the state that grants the right or for which protection is claimed (Case C-523/10 *Wintersteiger AG v Products 4U Sondermaschinenbau GmbH* [2012] OJ C 30/19, para 27). The court of the place where the alleged damage occurred has jurisdiction on the basis of art 7(2) of the Brussels I Regulation (recast) only to determine the damage caused in the Member State within which it is situated (Case C-441/13, *Pez Hejduk v EnergieAgentur NRW GmbH* [2015] OJ C 107/7, para 36). Therefore, the territorial scope of an injunction in those situations should be limited to the territory of the forum. Coexistence on the internet between exclusive rights granted in different jurisdictions can only be achieved if injunctions are limited to what is necessary to exclude significant commercial effects on the territories covered by the infringed intellectual property rights.

Determining the place of infringement in connection with internet activities may be complex. The digital transmission of contents protected by intellectual property rights, involve, in typical situations, a certain number of activities that may be infringements on their own (digitalization, copying, uploading, downloading . . .). It is widely accepted that the place of the server where the information is stored is not especially significant when interpreting the connecting factors used in private international law provisions. In this connection, the place of infringement as regards uploading activities tends to be located at the country of the establishment of the person uploading the contents. The downloading of contents protected by intellectual property rights typically affects the market in the countries where the contents are received and hence the place of infringement tends to be located at the country or countries where the users were situated at the time of downloading. Therefore, to the extent that making available the contents on the internet for downloading may lead to the infringement of intellectual property rights in several jurisdictions where the contents are downloaded, the alleged infringer risks being subject to the several jurisdictions where the contents are downloaded since their courts are competent to adjudicate claims regarding the infringements within the territory of the respective state. Concerning the alleged infringement acts resulting from the acts of reutilization of a database by a person sending by means of a server data previously uploaded from a protected database to the computer of another person, the ECJ has held that the infringing act takes place, at least, in the state where the person that received the protected information is located, where there is evidence from which it may be concluded that the act discloses an intention on the part of the person performing the act to target members of the public in that country (Case C-173/11 *Football Dataco Ltd, Scottish Premier League Ltd, Scottish Football League, PA Sport UK Ltd v Sportradar GmbH, Sportradar AG* [2012] OJ C 194/10, para 47).

In its more recent *Pinckney* (Case C-170/12 *Peter Pinckney v KDG Mediatech AG* [2013] OJ C 344/27, paras 40–45) and *Hejduk* judgments (C-441/13, *Pez Hejduk v EnergieAgentur NRW GmbH* [2015] OJ C 107/7, paras 32–5), the ECJ established that unlike the special provisions on consumer contracts, the rule concerning → torts does not require that the activity concerned be 'directed to' the Member State in which the court seized is situated. It also stressed that the issue as to whether a right has been infringed by the defendant belongs to the substance of the action and cannot be determinative to establish jurisdiction (→ Substance and Procedure). Furthermore, the sole condition laid down in the Brussels I Regulation (→ Brussels I (Convention and Regulation)) in this regard is that a harmful event has occurred or may occur in its territory. Regarding the alleged copyright infringement, the Court held that jurisdiction to hear an action in tort is already established in favour of the court seized if the Member State in which that court is situated protects the rights relied on by the plaintiff and the harmful event alleged may occur within the jurisdiction of the court seized. The Court considered that such likelihood may arise, in particular, from the possibility of obtaining a reproduction of the alleged infringing work from an internet site accessible within the jurisdiction of the court seized. This judgment has raised concerns as to the risks of an excessive scope of jurisdiction resulting from the acceptance of the mere accessibility of a website in the forum state where the rights have allegedly been infringed as an element to establish it as a place where the damage occurs for the purposes of art 7(2) of the Brussels I Regulation (recast) (see, concerning the dispute in the main proceedings in *Pinckney*, Arrêt No 33 du 22 janvier 2014 (10–15.890) – Cour de cassation – Première chambre civile). At any rate, in the internet context it may be doubted whether, under the particular circumstances of a case, an additional analysis may not be necessary to conclude that mere accessibility of a website in a territory is sufficient to establish that the harmful event allegedly may occur there. In the previous practice of national courts, it was significant the judgment of the Cour de cassation, chambre commerciale, of 29 March 2011, No 10-12272, *eBay Europe et al v Maceo*, which established that in a trademark dispute French courts did not have jurisdiction when the litigious website can merely be accessed in France.

The case-law of the ECJ has also provided guidance as to the determination of the place where the event giving rise to the damage occurred for the purposes of art 7(2) of the Brussels I Regulation (recast) with respect to alleged infringements of intellectual property rights (Case C-523/10 *Wintersteiger AG v Products 4U Sondermaschinenbau GmbH* [2012] OJ C 30/19, paras 34–9; Case C-441/13, *Pez Hejduk v EnergieAgentur NRW GmbH* [2015] OJ C 107/7, paras 24–5). In particular, it can be considered that as regards infringements arising out of the posting of content on the internet, the event giving rise to the damage lies in principle in the actions of the provider of the infringing content and the place where that event occurred may in principle be located at the place of establishment of the content provider, as the place where the decision to place the content online was taken and carried out. The location of the server involved in the technical process is in principle not determinative in this respect.

PEDRO DE MIGUEL ASENSIO

Literature

Paul Schiff Berman, 'The Globalization of Jurisdiction' (2002) 151 U.Pa.L.Rev. 312; Katharina Boele-Woelki and Catherine Kessedjian (eds), *Internet. Which Court Decides? Which Law Applies? Quel tribunal décide? Quel droit s'applique?* (Kluwer 1998); Pedro A De Miguel Asensio, *Derecho privado de Internet* (5th edn, Civitas Thomson Reuters 2015); Jack L Goldsmith and Wu Tim, *Who Controls the Internet? Illusions of a Borderless World* (OUP 2006); Julia Hörnle, 'The Jurisdictional Challenge of the Internet' in Lilian Edwards and Charlotte Waelde (eds), *Law and the Internet* (3rd edn, Hart 2008) 121; David R Johnson and David Post, 'Law and Borders: The Rise of Law in Cyberspace' (1995–96) 48 Stan.L.Rev. 1367; Uta Kohl, *Jurisdiction and the Internet* (Cambridge University Press, 2007); Stefan Leible (ed), *Die Bedeutung des Internationalen Privatrechts im Zeitalter der neuen Medien* (Richard Boorberg 2003); Dário Moura Vicente, *Problemática internacional da sociedade da informaçao* (Almedina 2005); Rufus Pichler, *Internationale Zuständigkeit im Zeitalter globaler Vernetzung* (CH Beck 2008); A Benjamin Spencer, 'Jurisdiction and the Internet: Returning to Traditional Principles to Analyze Network-Mediated Contacts' (2006) U.Ill.L.Rev. 71; Dan Jerker B Svantesson, *Private international law and the Internet* (3rd edn, Kluwer 2016); Faye Fangfei Wang, *Internet Jurisdiction and Choice of Law* (Cambridge University Press, 2010).

Internet, liability

I. Delimitation and scope

Activities carried out through the internet may give rise to non-contractual liability in a variety of fields. In particular, non-contractual liability issues in the internet context have arisen with regard to the protection of privacy and → personality rights and in the area of intellectual property rights. The law applicable to internet activities has become one of the central issues concerning choice-of-law analysis in both fields.

As a result of the inability to reach a balance between the conflicting interests involved in the digital context, art 1(2)(g) of the → Rome II Regulation (non-contractual obligations) (Regulation (EC) No 864/2007 of the European Parliament and of the Council of 11 July 2007 on the law applicable to non-contractual obligations (Rome II), [2007] OJ L 199/40)) excluded 'non-contractual obligations arising out of violations of privacy and rights relating to personality, including defamation' from the scope of application of the Regulation (→ Personality Rights). In the absence of common rules, national regimes are applicable, which diverge to a significant extent. Contents distributed via internet services pose special difficulties because the place of the event giving rise to the damage and the place where the damage materializes may not be the same and additionally the damage can materialize in a multitude of places. Moreover, the outcome of litigation in this field is influenced by the level of protection granted to certain fundamental rights, in particular private life and freedom of expression. Although the debate has been intense, no uniform approach has yet emerged in the EU (→ European Union and private international law). There is a wide range of proposed solutions including approaches based on the victim's habitual residence (in combination with a foreseeability rule) (→ Domicile, habitual residence and establishment), the country of the publisher's establishment, recourse to the → *lex fori*, the extension to this subject of the general rules provided for in the Rome II Regulation and even the refusal to establish uniform conflict-of-laws rules in this field.

By contrast, non-contractual obligations arising out of an infringement of an intellectual property right are the object of a special provision in art 8 of the Rome II Regulation. The expansion of the internet takes place in a context in which significant uncertainties exist as to the scope of protection of intellectual property rights and the characterization of certain activities as infringements. Concerning → choice of law, the basic standard, widely accepted from a comparative perspective, is that the applicable law to the protection and infringement of intellectual property rights is that of each country for which protection is sought (→ Intellectual property, applicable law). A formulation of the *lex loci protectionis* principle may be found in art 8 Rome II Regulation, which refers to the law of the country for which protection is claimed. A situation of multiple infringements (of parallel national rights) occurring in different states is to be governed by the laws of each of the countries for which protection is claimed. → Territoriality of intellectual property rights and the *lex loci protectionis* rule basically lead to the distributive application of the laws of all those countries in which the relevant conduct or activity – the alleged infringement of intellectual property rights – has a direct and substantial impact.

While the determination of the applicable law to liability arising out of internet activities in those two and other fields is to be addressed as part of the discussion on the respective subject matter, a specific analysis on liability issues raised by the internet is particularly justified in connection with an area where special substantive law rules have been adopted to regulate liability arising out of internet activities that may affect → torts in many different fields and that directly influence the functioning of the internet, namely, the liability of service providers acting as internet intermediaries. Determining when online service providers may be characterized as intermediary providers of information society services, and under which circumstances they may be held liable in connection with the activities of the users of their services has become of great practical importance. Due to the significant differences between legal systems as to the liability limitations and exceptions of intermediaries, applicable law issues are particularly relevant in this respect. Internet intermediaries may have to adapt their business models to reduce the exposure to liability in the light of the applicable law, for instance when assessing to what extent they have a duty to act with a view to preventing or stopping illegal activities by the users of their services and if they are required to implement prior filtering with respect to certain unlawful contents in addition to notice and takedown procedures.

II. Claims against internet intermediaries: purpose and function

Although subject to variation among jurisdictions, the concept of internet intermediaries relevant when addressing liability issues is broad, comprising providers of many different activities, facilities and services that enable others to take full advantage of the internet and information society services. Intermediaries provide access to communication networks, services related to the transmission of information in such networks, hosting services (including cloud-based services, social networking sites, auction sites, blogging sites and other platforms that enable users to post contents), hyperlinks and search engines, and more.

To the extent that the activities, facilities and services provided by intermediaries may result in infringements of third party rights and may especially support or facilitate infringements by others, the liability of internet intermediaries, the determination of the circumstances under which they may be held liable in connection with the activities of the users of their services and the possibility to bring claims against the intermediaries themselves, has become a crucial issue for the protection of rights on the internet, such as intellectual property and personality rights. In this context the relevant activities enabling intellectual property infringements may also include the distribution of tools such as software that may be used to carry out allegedly infringing activities in particular with regard to peer-to-peer file sharing or the circumvention of technical protection measures.

Recent litigation on internet-related → torts illustrate the importance of claims against intermediaries, particularly in the field of intellectual property. Reference can be made in the EU to Joined Cases C-236/08 to C-238/08 *Google France, Google, Inc v Louis Vuitton Malletier, Viaticum SA, Luteciel SARL, Centre national de recherche en relations humaines (CNRRH) SARL, Pierre-Alexis Thonet, Bruno Raboin, Tiger SARLECJ* [2010] OJ C 134/2, and Case C-324/09 *L'Oréal SA and Others v eBay International AG and Others* [2011] OJ C 269/3; and in the US to *Tiffany (NJ) Inc v eBay Inc* 600 F.3d 93 (2nd Cir 2010) and *Viacom Int'l Inc v YouTube, Inc*, 2013 WL 1689071 (SDNY

2013). In practice, the victims of internet torts may have a particular interest in bringing claims against internet intermediaries. Among the reasons for such an interest are that intermediaries are in a position to block access to the damaging content (see eg *Twentieth Century Fox Film Corp v British Telecommunications Plc* [2011] EWHC 1981 (Ch) (28 July 2011) and *Twentieth Century Fox Film Corp v British Telecommunications Plc* [2011] EWHC 2714 (Ch) (26 October 2011)), remove it from their services (see eg in France Arrêt No 827 of 12 July 2012 (11–15.165; 11–15.188) of the Cour de cassation – Première chambre civile), and prevent the infringement in the future (see in Germany German Federal Court of Justice (BGH), 29 April 2010, I ZR 69/08 *Vorschaubilder*). Additionally, intermediaries have relevant information to locate direct infringers, in particular when such infringers are users of their services. If → damages are sought by the alleged victim, the fact that intermediaries are easier to locate and usually have more financial means than individual users becomes very relevant, as well as the fact that it is much more cost efficient to sue an intermediary than a multiplicity of alleged individual infringers who may be scattered around the world.

III. Comparative perspectives

1. General remarks

From a substantive law perspective it is remarkable that significant differences exist concerning to what extent internet intermediaries are to be held liable for the activities of third parties. Only some jurisdictions establish secondary liability and even among those jurisdictions different approaches prevail as to the conditions to impose such liability. Indeed, significant uncertainty remains over international standards for secondary liability and the delimitation between direct and indirect infringement. Moreover, through the expansion of the internet, many jurisdictions have witnessed the adoption of specific provisions regarding the → immunity or limited liability of internet intermediaries. However, other jurisdictions lack specific provisions on the liability of intermediaries and uncertainty is high as to the legal position of such internet actors.

The two basic models of regulation are the US Digital Millennium Copyright Act, 17 U.S.C. § 512 (2000) (DMCA) and the EU e-Commerce Directive. In the EU, arts 12 to 15 of the e-Commerce Directive (Directive 2000/31/EC of the European Parliament and of the Council of 8 June 2000 on certain legal aspects of information society services, in particular electronic commerce, in the Internal Market (Directive on electronic commerce) [2000] OJ L178/1) basically establish that certain situations cannot give rise to intermediaries' liability since the main purpose of those provisions is to restrict the situations in which intermediaries may be held liable pursuant to the applicable national law. However, both models show important similarities since the e-Commerce Directive uses the DMCA as a reference on this issue.

These two systems have influenced the adoption of similar provisions in a number of jurisdictions. However, differences remain regarding the complex issue of secondary liability and safe harbour immunities even between jurisdictions having rules partly based on common foundations. Both the EU e-Commerce Directive and the US DMCA are intended to exclude liability for intermediaries unless they have actual knowledge of facts or circumstances indicating illegal activity and failed to react. Although both models present significant similarities, substantive differences remain. In the USA, 'safe harbour' provisions on intermediary liability do not have a horizontal nature, contrary to the situation in the EU, where the rules cover both civil and criminal liability regardless of the subject matter concerned. In the two main areas of interest, namely intellectual property rights and rights relating to personality, substantive differences remain. In particular, in the field of copyright due to the more detailed content of the provisions of the DMCA, such as those regarding the system of notice-and-takedown, that result in some practical differences, and in the area of personality rights because according to its prevailing interpretation s 230 Communications Decency Act, 47 U.S.C. § 230 (1996) (CDA) gives intermediaries immunity against claims concerning infringements of personality rights and other torts that go well beyond the liability limitations of the e-Commerce Directive.

Additionally, this is an evolving subject in which a significant level of uncertainty remains in the interpretation of substantive law even in legal systems having special provisions on the issue. For instance, technological evolution and transformation of business models have influenced a shift in some jurisdictions, favouring a more active-preventive approach. The areas most affected by such uncertainties include the application of the liability exemptions to linking sites and search engines, the level of knowledge to establish liability, whether certain services based on the distribution of user-generated content may require a certain level of prior monitoring or the interaction between the immunities (→ Immunity) and the obligations imposed on intermediaries under the various models for graduated response.

2. USA

Two separate regimes of immunities for internet intermediaries can be found in US legislation (→ USA). First, s 230(c) CDA grants interactive online services broad immunity from certain types of liability arising out of content provided by others. Section 230(c)(1) CDA establishes immunity from legal liability for 'providers or users' of an 'interactive computer service' who publish information provided by others. These provisions were adopted to protect intermediary service providers who host content provided by others and to address the difficulties in determining liability for unlawful content online, where the traditional standard regarding print media was deemed difficult to apply. This section has been interpreted broadly and its immunity covers defamation and privacy claims – eg *Zeran v AOL Inc*, 129 F.3d 327 (4th Cir 1997), *certiorari* denied, 524 U.S. 937 (1998), as well as other tort claims related to publication (*Stoner v Ebay Inc*, 2000 WL 1705637, Civ No 305666 (SupCt Cal 2000)), but it does not apply to intellectual property claims. These provisions do not include detailed rules on notice and takedown of unlawful content and some uncertainties remain as to the precise reach of the broad immunity provided.

In 1998 the US Congress passed the Online Copyright Infringement Liability Limitation Act (OCILLA), codified as s 512 of the Digital Millennium Copyright Act (DMCA). It gives web hosts and internet service providers, → immunity from copyright infringement claims. The main categories of service providers that may benefit from the protection granted by the safe harbour provisions are: conduit communications, system caching, storage systems and information location tools. To benefit from immunity, internet service providers have to implement certain notice and takedown procedures when copyright owners complain and a mechanism for removing repeat infringers from the system. The notice and takedown procedures are to be followed before having an allegedly infringing site removed from an intermediary service or disabling access to an allegedly infringing website content. Section 512 details the precise information the copyright owner must provide to the service provider in the framework of such procedure. The interpretation of this section and the scope of the safe harbours it provides has been determinative to establish the limits to the legality of certain innovative internet business models and services, as in the notorious cases *MGM Studios, Inc v Grokster, Ltd*, 545 U.S. 913 (2005) concerning peer-to-peer file sharing, and *Viacom Int'l Inc v YouTube, Inc*, 2013 WL 1689071 (SDNY 2013).

3. European Union

The general EU legal framework (→ European Union and private international law) concerning → electronic commerce and the provision of information society services is established in the e-Commerce Directive. The e-Commerce Directive lays down harmonized rules on the liability of information society services providers acting as intermediaries. The concept of information society services includes 'any service normally provided for remuneration, at a distance, by means of electronic equipment for the processing ... and storage of data, and at the individual request of a recipient of a service ...', and extends 'to services which are not remunerated by those who receive them, such as those offering on-line information or commercial communications, or those providing tools allowing for search, access and retrieval of data ...'. Difficulties may arise in some circumstances with regard to the delimitation of the different categories of intermediary services provided for under arts 12 to 15 of the Directive, such as mere conduit, caching and hosting.

The harmonizing provisions show certain limitations that result in uncertainty concerning the position of internet intermediaries under the e-Commerce Directive. In particular, further clarification seems to be required as to the activities and providers covered and the material conditions necessary to benefit from the exemptions set out in the e-Commerce Directive's arts 12 to 14; the implementation of notice and takedown procedures; and implications of art 15 that prevents Member States from imposing a monitoring obligation of a general nature. This is also an area in which the scope of enforcement of the rights of the alleged victims, such as intellectual property or → personality rights, have to be balanced against the protection of other fundamental rights, hence basic values and policies that are part of national (or European) → public policy (*ordre public*) may become determinative. The case-law of the ECJ illustrates to what extent injunctions imposed on intermediaries – such as those resulting in preventive monitoring, content filtering or website blocking and those implementing models for graduated response that may restrict users access to the internet – may infringe the fundamental freedom to conduct a business enjoyed by intermediaries and may also violate some fundamental rights of the users, namely their freedom to receive or convey information and their right to protection of their personal data (see Case C-70/10 *Scarlet Extended SA v Société belge des auteurs, compositeurs et éditeurs SCRL (SABAM)* [2012] OJ C 25/6 with regard to the position of internet access providers, Case C-360/10 *Belgische Vereniging van Auteurs, Componisten en Uitgevers CVBA (Sabam) v Netlog NV* [2012] OJ C 98/6 in connection to providers of hosting services (in particular, an online social networking platform) and Case C-461/10 *Bonnier Audio AB, Earbooks AB, Norstedts Förlagsgrupp AB, Piratförlaget Aktiebolag, Storyside AB v Perfect Communication Sweden AB* [2012] OJ C 317/24). In the UK see judgment of 6 March 2012 England and Wales Court of Appeal (Civil Division) *R. (on the application of British Telecommunications Plc) v Secretary of State for Business, Innovation and Skills* [2012] EWCA Civ 232, finding that the graduated response system to fight copyright infringements in the internet that the Digital Economy Act 2010 inserted into the Communications Act 2003 does not breach EU data protection law.

The e-Commerce Directive is aimed at ensuring the proper functioning of the Internal Market within the EU by removing the legal obstacles to the freedom of establishment (→ Freedom of establishment/persons (European Union) and private international law) and the freedom to provide services in the field of e-commerce and information society services. The obstacles which the Directive is intended to remove are those arising from legal divergences in Member States and from uncertainty as to the applicable rules. In this connection, the Directive is based on the criteria that control of information society services within the EU is basically to take place in the Member State of origin and that Member States are not allowed to restrict the freedom to provide information society services from another Member State for reasons falling within the coordinated field (art 3). Mutual recognition in tune with the requirements of the EU freedom to provide services allows information society services providers to operate within the Union if they comply with the national provisions of the Member State in which the service provider is established. Only providers established in a Member State benefit from art 3. This provision does not apply to a situation where the place of establishment of the information society services provider is unknown (Case C-292/10 *G v Cornelius de Visser* [2012] OJ C 133/5, para 72).

The e-Commerce Directive does not establish additional rules on private international law relating to → choice of law nor does it deal with the jurisdiction of courts (art 1(4)). In its judgment of 25 October 2010 in Joined Cases C-509/09 and C-161/10 *eDate Advertising GmbH v X, Olivier Martinez, Robert Martinez v MGN Limited* [2011] OJ C 370/9, concerning the alleged infringement of personality rights, the ECJ held that art 3 of the e-Commerce Directive 'must be interpreted as not requiring transposition in the form of a specific conflict-of-laws rule', but that in relation to the coordinated field, Member States must ensure that, subject to the derogations authorized in accordance with art 3(4) of the Directive 'the provider of an electronic commerce service is not made subject to stricter requirements than those provided for by the substantive law applicable in the Member State in which that service provider is established'. Therefore, mutual recognition within the Internal Market facilitates the provision of internet services at EU level by providers established in a Member State. Mutual recognition prevents service providers that comply with the requirements to initiate and pursue their activities in the Member State of origin from having to fulfil the requirements established in all other Member States where they provide their services. Such providers can extend their activities to the rest of the Member States in circumstances in which these states are not allowed to impose within the coordinated field additional requirements to the provision of services (without prejudice of the possibility to adopt restrictive measures in exceptional situations under art 3(4) e-Commerce Directive). The coordinated field includes 'requirements concerning the liability of the service provider' (art 2(h)). However, in accordance with art 3(3) and the Annex to the Directive, the Internal Market clause of art 3 does not apply to some areas, particularly intellectual property rights.

4. International legal sources

Considering that most intermediaries operate in an international or even global market place, a harmonized international legal framework concerning the liability of intermediary service providers would be of great benefit to provide predictability and foster the development of global services for digital content. The increasing reliance by governments on intermediaries to ensure law enforcement online is an additional factor when advocating further international coordination to overcome the difficulties posed to intermediaries under multiple conflicting laws. The development of balanced, model substantive law provisions could have a significant harmonizing effect at an international level in light of the absence of specific regulations in many countries and the need for further clarification in others.

Efforts to develop international substantive standards by private organizations involving stakeholders started long ago, mainly in the context of business-led projects, such as the so-called Global Business Dialogue on Electronic Commerce. However, the interest and potential benefits of developing common substantive standards for secondary liability contrast sharply with the almost complete lack of progress in this field by the international organizations active in creating uniform provisions regarding intellectual property (such as WIPO (→ WIPO and private international law) and WTO (→ WTO and private international law)) or → electronic commerce (→ UNCITRAL). Substantive harmonization concerning the liability of internet intermediaries was the focus of particular attention in the negotiations leading to the conclusion of the Anti-Counterfeiting Trade Agreement (ACTA) (the Agreement initialled on 25 November 2010 has not entered into force and its text may be found in the Proposal for a Council Decision on the conclusion of the Agreement of 24 June 2011, COM(2011) 380 final). The draft of the ACTA made public in April 2010 contained two alternative texts on liability limitations benefiting online service providers in art 2(18) para 3, that were inspired by the basic features of the DMCA and the e-Commerce Directive, although not without some changes.

Nevertheless, the final text of the Agreement, even if remaining very much focused on fighting infringement in the digital environment, did not include liability exemption provisions for internet intermediaries. More recently, the issue has also been considered in the framework of the Trans-Pacific Partnership Agreement. The Chapter on Intellectual Property of the finalized text signed on 4 February 2016 includes Section J on Internet Service Providers. It contains provisions on the legal remedies available for right holders and the obligation to establish or maintain safe harbours in respect of providers of online services. The Agreement has not entered into force.

Given the particular difficulties posed by the existence of different substantive international standards on secondary liability and the absence of international consensus as far as regulatory details are concerned, choice-of-law provisions remain of paramount importance to provide predictability and legal certainty. Moreover, due to the complexity of this subject, international harmonization of basic principles would not mean full unification of legal systems, so that applicable law issues will continue to play a significant role.

IV. Applicable law

1. General rule on indirect or secondary liability

In sharp contrast with the evolution of internet law in most major industrialized countries that have adopted specific provisions regarding the (non-)liability of internet intermediaries, the position of intermediaries has not been the subject of a similar attention from the perspective of choice of law. However, the activities and services of those intermediaries having a potentially global reach or impact pose particular challenges from a cross-border perspective.

It has become widely accepted that the law applicable to indirect or secondary liability is the law that governs the main infringement. Potential liability of intermediaries linked to the activities of the users of their services, for instance with respect to the information stored in their servers and services, can be considered an issue concerning the determination of persons who may be held liable for acts performed by another person. In the EU (→ European Union and private international law), under the → Rome II Regulation (non-contractual obligations), the law applicable to a non-contractual obligation arising from an infringement of an intellectual property right in accordance with art 8(1) also governs the determination of persons who may be held liable for acts performed by them – art 15(a) – and liability for the acts of another person – art 15(d). Concerning liability in connection with → personality rights, a similar approach based on the application of the law that governs the infringement also to determine the liability of internet intermediaries involved seems to prevail under national laws. In this area, attention is to be paid to the implications of mutual recognition provided for under art 3 of the e-Commerce Directive regarding intermediaries established in an EU Member State, as discussed above, since personality rights and defamation are not excluded from mutual recognition in contrast with intellectual property rights (art 3 and Annex to the Directive).

Article 15 of the Rome II Regulation reflects a trend to favour the application of the same law to all issues related to a non-contractual obligation in order to promote legal certainty and uniformity, which are basic goals of EU instruments in the field of private international law. Therefore, with regard to a non-contractual obligation arising from an infringement of an intellectual property right the law of the country for which protection is claimed is determinative to establish both direct and indirect or secondary liability under the Rome II regime. The same standard prevails in cases in which national courts have recourse to art 5(2) of the Berne Convention (Paris Act of 24 July 1971 relating to the Berne Convention for the Protection of Literary and Artistic Works of 9 September 1886, completed at Paris on 4 May 1896, revised at Berlin on 13 November 1908, completed at Berne on 20 March 1914, revised at Rome on 2 June 1928, revised at Brussels on 26 June 1948, revised at Stockholm on 14 July 1967 and revised at Paris on 24 July 1971, 1161 UNTS 3 and amended in 1979 Treaty Doc no 99-27, and 1985, 828 UNTS 221) as the relevant conflict rule establishing the *lex loci protectionis* principle. In this connection, see in → France Arrêt No 827 of 12 July 2012 (11–15.165; 11–15.188) of the Cour de cassation – Première chambre civile – on the application of the law of the country of protection to both the direct infringement and the liability of a search engine provider in connection with the alleged infringement of certain rights in photographs.

In the absence of specific provisions, the law of the country for which protection is claimed applies to determine the liability of internet service providers arising from an infringement of an intellectual property right including the limitations or exemptions from liability for internet intermediaries. Furthermore, according to art 15(d) of the Rome II Regulation the law applicable to the infringement governs 'the measures which a court may take to prevent or terminate injury or damage' although 'within the limits of powers conferred on the court by its procedural law'. Delimitation between the scope of application of the law applicable to the infringement and the procedural law of the → *lex fori* may raise particular difficulties with regard to the measures that can be adopted against intermediaries.

A similar trend may be identified in the USA with regard to the law applicable to secondary liability as illustrated by the approach of the ALI Intellectual Property Principles of 2008 (American Law Institute, Intellectual property: principles governing jurisdiction, choice of law and judgments in transnational disputes, St Paul 2008). Under s 301, the law that governs the determination of infringement not only establishes direct infringement but also determines to what extent activities facilitating infringement may be regarded as infringement (s 301 ALI Intellectual Property Principles, comment h). Therefore, a court should apply the laws of each jurisdiction in which infringements are alleged – in conjunction with s 321, which applies to so-called ubiquitous infringements – regardless of the fact that in some countries the relevant activities may be considered direct infringement, while in others they are considered secondary infringement.

2. *Modern trends*

Recourse to the *lex loci protectionis* to determine what law applies to the liability of internet intermediaries may pose special difficulties, particularly in those situations in which intermediaries offer their online services globally. The coordination between the system of territorially limited intellectual property rights and the ubiquitous reach of the internet favours a reassessment of principles that may lead to the application of a multiplicity of national laws to internet activities. The *lex loci protectionis* rule usually leads to the distributive application of a plurality of laws with respect to activities performed through the internet even if applied in light of the so-called principle of proportionality to achieve a reasonable balance between the → territoriality of IP rights and the internet's global reach. The law of each protecting country applies insofar as the activity allegedly infringes intellectual property rights in its territory.

As a result of the internet's global reach, to the extent that the design and functioning of a website does not result in its addressees being limited to certain markets, the finding may prevail in many situations that the site produces substantial effects in a significant number of countries. Due to the contrast between the territorial fragmentation resulting from the *lex loci protectionis* approach and the global offering by many intermediaries of services provided to users in numerous countries around the world, a special risk has been identified that intermediaries may have to bear excessive legal uncertainties regarding their liability. Subjecting the liability of intermediaries to the laws of each country of protection has been criticized as a potential source of unfair and unpredictable results. In this context, it has been proposed to establish an exception to the *lex loci protectionis* with regard to the provision of services that enable service recipients to carry out infringing activities but which are clearly detached from the service. The exception would be particularly relevant in cases in which a third party uses the services of internet intermediaries to infringe intellectual property rights.

Article 3:604(1) CLIP Principles on Conflict of Laws in Intellectual Property (European Max Planck Group on Conflict of Laws in Intellectual Property, Conflict of laws in intellectual property: the CLIP principles and commentary, Oxford 2013; → CLIP) contains an innovative provision to favour the application of a single law to the activities of internet intermediaries. However, the distinction between secondary or indirect liability and direct infringement may be uncertain in many situations since characterization of certain conducts – such as preparatory acts – as direct or contributory infringements may vary significantly among states. Furthermore, under substantive law, secondary liability is in many jurisdictions inextricably linked to direct infringement. In these circumstances recourse to a specific choice-of-law provision restricted to the liability of intermediaries may result in the introduction of additional uncertainty and complexity when compared to the general criterion leading to the application of the *lex loci protectionis* both to direct and secondary liability. Such risk becomes particularly clear with regard to situations in which a defendant is sued both under direct and secondary liability. A specific choice-of-law rule for intermediaries could also pose very complex characterization issues with regard to the determination of its beneficiaries.

Alternatively, it is remarkable that under the ALI Intellectual Property Principles, which do not contain a specific provision on the law applicable to secondary liability, recourse to a single law with regard to internet intermediaries in cases of multistate or ubiquitous exploitation of intellectual property rights can also be the result of the application of the specific provisions on ubiquitous infringement – s 321 ALI Intellectual Property Principles – without abandoning the traditional view that the law applicable to the infringement also governs secondary liability. Under this model, the same exceptional provisions envisaging the application of a single law to ubiquitous infringements are applicable to direct and indirect or secondary liability.

Although some intermediaries provide their services and facilities on a global scale it is not rare that even in those situations the possible liability of the intermediary or the possibility to require the intermediary to terminate or prevent an infringement appear closely connected to the conducts of their users that only have an impact on a geographically limited area. For instance, individual users tend to make use of global hosting services – such as social networks – to post and make available contents that in practice may have substantial repercussions in a limited number of jurisdictions (probably, in just one) and in those circumstances non-application of the *lex loci protectionis* with regard to intermediary liability, even if the service used is provided at a global level, may raise special concerns.

To the extent that global intermediaries may also adapt their services to comply with the different legal standards of the different territories (as illustrated, for instance, by the policies implemented by global microblogging sites that allow them to remove or block content only for specific jurisdictions), the idea that in connection with intellectual property infringements *lex loci protectionis* should be abandoned with respect to the provision of intermediary services seems controversial, in particular in light of the fact that such services are used frequently to post and make available contents that in practice may have substantial repercussion in a limited number of jurisdictions (or even just one). It seems that in those circumstances the burden of complying with local laws as a consequence of providing services offered to all those jurisdictions should not be overemphasized with regard to intermediaries to the extent that they have the means to implement technologies that enable territorial restrictions, and if needed they can design and provide a service to have substantial effects only in certain countries.

PEDRO DE MIGUEL ASENSIO

Literature

Roberto Bocchini, *La responsabilità civile degli intermediari del commercio elettronico* (Edizioni scientifiche italiane 2003); Pedro A de Miguel Asensio, *Derecho privado de Internet* (5th edn, Civitas Thomson Reuters 2015); Pedro A de Miguel Asensio, 'Internet Intermediaries and the Law Applicable to Intellectual Property Infringements' (2012) 3 JIPITEC 350; Graeme Dinwoodie, Rochelle Dreyfuss and Annette Kur, 'The Law Applicable to Secondary Liability in Intellectual Property Cases' (2009) 42 *Journal of International Law and Politics* 201; Lilian Edwards, 'The Fall and Rise of Intermediary Liability Online' in Lilian Edwards and Charlotte Waelde (eds), *Law and the Internet* (3rd edn, Hart 2008), 47; Susanne L. Gössl, *Internetspezifisches Kollisionsrect?* (Nomos, 2014); Martin Husovec, 'Injunctions against Innocent Third Parties: Case of Website Blocking' (2013) 4 JIPITEC 116; Sophie Neumann, 'Intellectual Property Rights Infringements in European Private international law: Meeting the Requirements of Territoriality and Private international law' (2011) 7 J Priv Int L 583; Yuko Nishitani, 'Copyright Infringement on the Internet and Service Provider's Liability: A Japanese Approach from a Comparative Perspective' in Andrea Schulz (ed), *Legal Aspects of an E-Commerce Transaction* (Sellier 2006) 41; Lynda J Oswald, 'International Issues in Secondary Liability for Intellectual Property Rights Infringement' (2008) 45 Am.Bus.L.J. 247; Pekka Savola, 'The Ultimate Copyright Shopping Opportunity: Jurisdiction and Choice of Law in Website Blocking Injunctions' (2014) 45 IIC, 287; Gerald Spindler and Fabian Schuster (eds), *Recht der elektronischen Medien (Kommentar)* (2nd edn, CH Beck 2011); Alain Strowel (ed), *Peer-to-Peer File Sharing and Secondary Liability in Copyright Law* (Edward Elgar 2009).

Interpretation, autonomous

I. Introduction

Methods of interpretation can vary depending on the jurisdiction in question and this can contribute to the divergent application of conventions and EU laws. Autonomous interpretation in international and EU law counterbalances this often rather unnoticed reliance on the particular methods, meanings and concepts of domestic law. Since private international law is increasingly composed of norms derived from such supranational sources, the avoidance of divergent understandings of legal concepts and provisions arising out of autonomous interpretation is of profound importance. In this context, it is worth noting the major differences even among the EU Member States (Stefan Vogenauer, *Die Auslegung von Gesetzen in England und auf dem Kontinent – Eine vergleichende Untersuchung der Rechtsprechung und ihrer historischen Grundlagen* (Mohr Siebeck 2001)). Some jurisdictions tend to interpret more according to the actual wording of pieces of legislation. This is frequently the case in Eastern European states with formerly socialist legal systems that follow a more positivistic approach. In contrast, other Member States tend to go beyond the wording and deploy a purposive interpretation, such as → Germany. Some legal orders, for example → France, do not expressly distinguish between interpretation and the further development of written law by judges. Other systems distinguish between the two. Germany does so whereby the latter is called *richterliche Rechtsfortbildung*, and requires more elaborate reasoning on the part of the judge.

II. Techniques of restricting the homeward domestic trends in interpretation

To counterbalance the danger that international law is interpreted differently depending on the individual forum state with its own procedural understandings, conflict of law stance, substantive solutions and generally preferred methods, many conventions expressly require that they are to be interpreted in the light of their international character and specific aims (eg art 18 Rome Convention (Rome Convention on the law applicable to contractual obligations (consolidated version), [1998] OJ C 27/34), art 7(1) → CISG (United Nations Convention of 11 April 1980 on Contracts for the International Sale of

Goods, 1489 UNTS 3), art 4 Ottawa Factoring Convention (UNIDROIT Convention on International Factoring of 28 May 1988, 2323 UNTS 373, 27 ILM 943; → Factoring (uniform law)), art 6 UNIDROIT Financial Leasing Convention (UNIDROIT Convention of 28 May 1988 on International Financial Leasing, 2312 UNTS 195, 27 ILM 931; → Financial leasing (uniform law)); see furthermore, arts 26, 31 ff Vienna Convention on the Law of Treaties (of 23 May 1969, 1155 UNTS 331)). The same is true for international principles (art 1.6 of the UNIDROIT Principles (International Institute for the Unification of Private Law/ Institut international pour l'unification du droit privé, *UNIDROIT Principles of International Commercial Contracts 2010* (3rd edn, UNIDROIT 2010)); see also art 1:104 Principles of European Insurance Contract Law (Jürgen Basedow and others (eds), *Principles of European Insurance Contract Law* (2nd edn, Sellier 2015))) and the withdrawn proposal for a Common European Sales Law (Proposal of 11 October 2011 for a Regulation of the European Parliament and of the European Council on a Common European Sales Law COM(2011) 635 final) (Annex I art 4 CESL-D; → CESL).

However, neither EU primary law nor for example the Brussels I Regulation (Regulation (EC) No 44/2001 of 22 December 2000 on jurisdiction and the recognition and enforcement of judgments in civil and commercial matters, [2001] OJ L 12/1) (→ Brussels I (Convention and Regulation)) and the Rome I Regulation (Regulation (EC) No 593/2008 of the European Parliament and of the Council of 17 June 2008 on the law applicable to contractual obligations (Rome I), [2008] OJ L 177/6; → Rome Convention and Rome I Regulation), contain such a guideline or define a similar general goal of uniform application. (Although Recital (11) of the → Rome II Regulation (Regulation (EC) No 864/2007 of the European Parliament and of the Council of 11 July 2007 on the law applicable to non-contractual obligations (Rome II), [2007] OJ L 199/40) states that 'non-contractual obligation' has to be understood as an autonomous concept.) This might surprise, considering that EU law has 24 equally official language versions with ample scope for ambiguity. In addition, the situation has become far more complex compared to the starting point in 1957, when originally the European Economic Community (EEC), the EU predecessor, had only four official languages. Looking beyond EU law, despite its many contracting parties worldwide, the → CISG has only six official language versions.

The reason for this omission of an express autonomous interpretation requirement lies in the institutional design: the establishment of the European Court of Justice (CJEU; → Court of Justice of the European Union), which lends EU law one of its most distinctive features compared to other international communities. The CJEU has an exclusive jurisdiction to provide the definitive interpretation of EU primary law, but also regarding issues of EU secondary law as referred to the ECJ by Member State courts (art 19 TEU (Consolidated Version of the Treaty on European Union [2012] OJ C 326/13), art 267 TFEU (The Treaty on the Functioning of the European Union TFEU (consolidated version), [2012] OJ C 326/47)). Thereby, the ECJ (which forms the major part of the CJEU and which is responsible for responding to such references) is the guardian of the rule of law and of equality under the law. As is commonly known, the ECJ has played a fundamental role in developing the constitutional dimension of EU law (especially, direct effect and supremacy of EU law as well as the establishment of a human rights jurisprudence).

On a smaller scale, the ECJ develops, defines and defends the concept of autonomous interpretation. The effect on the national level is self-evident. Since the Member States courts, as a matter of EU law, are under a duty to follow the meta-principle of autonomous interpretation, they also have to adhere to specific ECJ definitions of particular terms. For example, the Member States courts have to follow the ECJ's autonomous concept of 'civil and commercial matter' (as defined since Case 29/76 *LTU Lufttransportunternehmen GmbH & Co KG v Eurocontrol* [1976] ECR 1541) that determines the scope of application of both the Brussels I and the Rome I Regulation (→ Civil and commercial matters). After all, the effect of the ECJ's decisions based on the reference procedure according to art 267 TFEU is not only *inter partes*. The purpose goes beyond the resolution of a pending case. The procedure aims at achieving a uniform interpretation and application of EU law as a whole (see Hannes Rösler, *Europäische Gerichtsbarkeit auf dem Gebiet des Zivilrechts – Strukturen, Entwicklungen und Reformperspektiven des Justiz- und Verfahrensrechts der Europäischen Union* (Mohr Siebeck 2012) 447 f). Since the

EU, under the guidance of the ECJ, pursues the most developed autonomous interpretation, EU private international law and international civil procedure will be the focal point of the following considerations.

In the area of interest autonomous interpretation commenced with the Brussels Convention (Brussels Convention of 27 September 1968 on jurisdiction and the enforcement of judgments in civil and commercial matters, [1972] OJ L 299/32, consolidated version, [1998] OJ C 27/1) (→ Brussels I (Convention and Regulation)). In *Tessili* (Case 12/76 *Industrie Tessili Italiana Como v Dunlop AG* [1976] ECR 1473) the Court stated the general rule that 'words and concepts used in the Convention must be regarded as having their own independent meaning and as being thus common to all the Member States or as referring to substantive rules of the law applicable in each case under the rules of conflict of laws of the court before which the matter is first brought, the appropriate choice can only be made in respect of each of the provisions of the convention to ensure that it is fully effective having regard to the objectives of' the preliminary reference procedure (Case 12/76 *Industrie Tessili Italiana Como v Dunlop AG* [1976] ECR 1473, summary no 2).

In the *Tessili* decision, the ECJ had explained that nonetheless the 'place of performance of the obligation in question' in the Brussels Convention had to be defined according to the rules of conflict of laws of the court before which the matter is brought (→ Place of performance; → Jurisdiction, contracts and torts). Thus, under the Convention an autonomous definition of 'place of performance' was not feasible. When the EU legislator 'communitized' the Convention by transforming it into the Brussels I Regulation, it took this one further step. Also the follow-up provision in art 7(1)(b) Brussels I Regulation (recast) (Regulation (EU) No 1215/2012 of the European Parliament and of the Council of 12 December 2012 on jurisdiction and the recognition and enforcement of judgments in civil and commercial matters (recast), [2012] OJ L 351/1; → Brussels I (Convention and Regulation)) contains an autonomous definition in the case of the sale of goods and the provision of services and only where the place of performance is in an EU Member State. In all the other instances is recourse to the national substantive law, ie the *lex causae*, still required (art 7(1)(b) Brussels I Regulation (recast)).

III. Interests in autonomous interpretation

1. Normative perspective: rule of law in an integrated legal regime

The requirement of a uniform and thus autonomous interpretation is embodied in the logic of the rule of EU law. It is a natural consequence of the legislative unification effort itself. The EU intends to maintain and develop an area of freedom, security and justice (see in general arts 67 ff TFEU and eg the relevant reference in Recital (3) of the Brussels I Regulation (recast)). Without a harmonious, coherent and thus autonomous interpretation, the regulated areas now stretching from international contract and tort law to family and international succession matters would be re-nationalized through the backdoor of the Member State courts. This effect would be disastrous for EU legal unity since the Member State courts bear by far the main burden of interpreting and applying EU international procedural and private law.

These findings in favour of autonomous interpretation are backed up by the primacy of EU law. Since EU law is an independent source of law, it requires uniform interpretation. It is true that in its starting point, EU law resembled classical international law. However, EU law goes beyond international law in that it has (almost) absolute primacy over national law. Thus, autonomous interpretation is a natural consequence of the duty of loyalty towards the EU according to art 4(3) TEU, of the way the EU Treaty has created 'a new quality in the international legal order' (see, regarding the predecessor, ie the EEC Treaty (Treaty of 25 March 1957 establishing the European Economic Community, 294–8 UNTS), Case 26/62 *Van Gend en Loos v Nederlandse Administratie der Belastingen* [1963] ECR 1, 12). The primacy becomes clearer if one contrasts this with the ECHR (European Convention of 4 November 1950 for the Protection of Human Rights and Fundamental Freedoms, 213 UNTS 221), which is of interest to civil proceedings due to its art 6 on a right to fair trial (→ Human rights and private international law). On the one hand, in → Germany, the Convention only enjoys the effect of a normal statute, as art 25 of the Basic Law for the Federal Republic of Germany (Grundgesetz of 23 May 1949, BGBl. 1, as amended) prescribes. On the other hand, in → Austria the Convention has the same status as the Austrian Constitution, based on art 49(2) of the Austrian Federal Constitutional Law

(Österreichische Bundesverfassungsgesetze, of 10 November 1920, Stammfassung BGBl. 1/1930, latest version BGBl. I 194/1999, as amended).

2. *Party perspective: foreseeability of possible jurisdiction and the applicable law*

Besides the mentioned normative arguments, the parties' interests also need to be taken into account. Regarding the Brussels Convention 1968 and later the Brussels I Regulation (→ Brussels I (Convention and Regulation)), the ECJ identified legal certainty as one of its major principles. The ECJ ruled that the jurisdictional rules which in particular

> derogate from the basic principle [of ... actor sequitur forum rei to be found today in art 4(1) Brussels I Regulation (recast)] should be interpreted in such a way as to enable a normally well-informed defendant reasonably to foresee before which courts, other than those of the State in which he is domiciled, he may be sued. (Case C-26/91 *Jakob Handte & Co GmbH v Traitements Mécano-chimiques des Surfaces SA* [1992] ECR I-3967, para 18)

The principle of legal certainty is of similar value in conflict of laws. The Rome I Regulation stresses that it intends to 'contribute to the general objective of ... legal certainty in the European judicial area, [so that] the conflict-of-law rules [on international contract law] should be highly foreseeable' (Recital (16)). This objective is of relevance beyond commercial transactions. In international divorce cases the → Rome III Regulation (Council Regulation (EU) No 1259/2010 of 20 December 2010 implementing enhanced cooperation in the area of the law applicable to divorce and legal separation, [2010] OJ L 343/10) intends to 'create a clear, comprehensive legal framework in the area of the law applicable to divorce and legal separation in the participating Member States, provide citizens with appropriate outcomes in terms of legal certainty, predictability and flexibility' (Recital (9)). In addition, the Rome III Regulation expressly intends to restrict the practice of → forum (and law) shopping (Recital (9) Rome III Regulation).

These statements account for the European legislature's intent to create rather fixed conflict norms – a different approach compared to the common law countries in particular outside the EU (such as → USA, → Canada, → Australia) that prefer a flexible handling of the individual case at the inevitable expense of certainty and foreseeability. If legal certainty is one of the major objectives of EU private international law, then the foreseeability of possible venues and the applicable law must also be guaranteed in practice and this implies a uniform interpretation and application of the laws in question (for a view questioning whether the ECJ contributes to legal certainty though the Court regularly employs this concept see Johannes Schmidt, *Rechtssicherheit im europäischen Zivilverfahrensrecht – Eine Analyse der Entscheidungen des EuGH zum EuGVÜ und der EuGVVO* (Mohr Siebeck 2015)).

IV. Autonomous interpretation guiding the interpretation methods

The CJEU (→ Court of Justice of the European Union) shares the core values and tools of legal interpretation with the Member States. After all, the EU is based on the common legal traditions of its Members. This is particularly evident with the general principles of EU law identified by the Court. Among them are the mentioned principles of legal certainty and equality before the law, but also proportionality and fundamental rights, which since the Treaty of Lisbon (Treaty of Lisbon amending the Treaty on European Union and the Treaty establishing the European Community, signed at Lisbon, 13 December 2007, [2007] OJ C 306/1, consolidated version, [2012] OJ C 326/1) are also enshrined in the EU Charter of Fundamental Rights (Charter of Fundamental Rights of the European Union of 18 December 2000, [2000] OJ C 364/1 (consolidated version 2012/C 326/02, [2012] OJ C 326/391)) (→ Human rights and private international law). Thus, unlike conventions and international soft law, EU secondary laws are embedded in much more elaborate uniform legal context that can require taking other regulations (horizontal) and the larger constitutional framework (vertical) into account.

Besides the scope of a specific measure, the degree of uniformity achieved by the several regulations in the area of private international law and international civil procedure is higher than in private law where the preferred legislative instrument are directives, which in contrast to regulations require implementing legislation by the Member States. Nevertheless, also in private international law and international civil procedure the concept of a multi-level system is apt. The EU has no courts of its own in the Member States. Therefore, the national courts function also as EU courts, which, however, can interpret and apply laws differently.

That a text is potentially open to different readings is in no way a new phenomenon. After all, legal reasoning has been subject to different tensions, policies and philosophies since the earliest times. As a President of the Supreme Court and Chief Justice of → Ireland concluded:

> Plato urged that laws be interpreted according to their spirit rather than literally. Voltaire expressed the view that to interpret the law is to corrupt it. Montesquieu viewed the judge as simply the mechanical spokesman of the law. The role of the Judge has been transformed since Montesquieu's day but the historic tension still exists between the search for the 'true intent' of a legal norm and the desire for certainty and transparency in the application of the law. (John L Murray, 'Methods of Interpretation: Comparative Law Method' in European Court of Justice (ed), *Actes du colloque pour le cinquantième anniversaire des Traités de Rome. L'influence du droit national et de la jurisprudence des juridictions des États membres sur l'interprétation du droit communautaire* (Luxemburg 2007) 39)

Despite these different tendencies, the basic interpretation methods, ie the literal, historical, systematic and teleological, are shared in the European legal systems. Based on the roots of the EU in the common Member State traditions, the ECJ deploys these traditional rules that were identified by *Friedrich Carl von → Savigny* (see Hannes Rösler, 'Interpretation of EU Law' in Jürgen Basedow and others (eds), *Max Planck Encyclopedia of European Private Law*, vol 2 (OUP 2012) 979).

1. Verbal interpretation

As for all interpretation and due to the paramount principle of legal certainty, the starting point for the ECJ is the wording. However, the literal interpretation can be difficult in a Union with all its languages and the (ideal of) equal value of all the language versions (see for primary law art 55(1) TEU). After all, the ECJ ruled in *CILFIT*:

> different language versions are all equally authentic. An interpretation of a provision of Community law thus involves a comparison of the different language versions. It must also be borne in mind, even where the different language versions are entirely in accord with one another, that Community law uses terminology which is peculiar to it. Furthermore, it must be emphasized that legal concepts do not necessarily have the same meaning in Community law as under the law of the various Member States. (Case 283/81 *Srl CILFIT and Lanificio di Gavardo SpA v Ministry of Health* [1982] ECR 3415, paras 18 f)

Similarly, art 33 of the Vienna Convention on the Law of Treaties provides that to resolve discrepancies in official texts the common intention of the diplomatic conference is decisive ('the meaning which best reconciles the texts, having regard to the object and purpose of the treaty, shall be adopted').

A good illustration of this technique is *The Tatry* decision regarding (today) art 29 Brussels I Regulation (recast) (→ Brussels I (Convention and Regulation)) on the issue of another EU court first seized:

> It should be noted at the outset that the English version of art 21 [Brussels Convention, now art 29 Brussels I Regulation (recast): 'Klagen wegen desselben Anspruchs zwischen denselben Parteien'] does not expressly distinguish between the concepts of 'object' and 'cause' of action. That language version must however be construed in the same manner as the majority of the other language versions in which that distinction is made [eg: 'demandes ayant le même objet et la même cause sont formées entre les mêmes parties']. For the purposes of [. . . now art 29 Brussels I Regulation (recast)], the 'cause of action' comprises the facts and the rule of law relied on as the basis of the action. The 'object of the action' . . . means the end the action has in view. (Case C-406/92, *The owners of the cargo lately laden on board the ship 'Tatry' v The owners of the ship 'Maciej Rataj'* [1994] ECR I-5439, para 37)

2. Systematic, teleological and historical interpretation

Nonetheless, there are many instances where the plain meaning is insufficient even if one enriches it with a comparison of various language versions. The ECJ usually stresses the *telos* more than the Member States courts, in particular based on the aims of a regulation or directive as laid down in its recitals. In addition, the ECJ deploys the systematic approach. The ECJ continues in *CILFIT*:

> [f]inally, every provision of Community law must be placed in its context and interpreted in the light of the provisions of Community law as a whole,

regard being had to the objectives thereof and to its state of evolution at the date on which the provision in question is to be applied. (Case 283/81 *Srl CILFIT and Lanificio di Gavardo SpA v Ministry of Health* [1982] ECR 3415, para 19)

Compared for example to German legal methodology or the CISG (where *travaux préparatoires* are used quite actively), the historical (or originalist) method is of less importance. After all, the development of legal texts of the Union is quite political and multi-voiced due to the different nations involved. However, regarding 'Brussels I' and 'Rome I', the Official Reports to the prior Brussels and Rome Conventions are still referred to quite often (Schlosser Report (Peter Schlosser, 'Report on the Convention on the Association of the Kingdom of Denmark, Ireland and the United Kingdom of Great Britain and Northern Ireland to the Convention on jurisdiction and the enforcement of judgments in civil and commercial matters and to the Protocol on its interpretation by the Court of Justice, signed at Luxembourg, 9 October 1978' [1979] OJ C 59/71); Giuliano-Lagarde Report (Report on the Convention on the law applicable to contractual obligations by Mario Giuliano, Professor, University of Milan, and Paul Lagarde, Professor, University of Paris I, [1980] OJ C 282/1)).

3. Comparative interpretation

A fifth method, which *von Savingy* did not mention, is the comparative approach. In order to stress the autonomy of EU law, ECJ decisions seldom openly engage in comparative interpretation (see for exceptions Ulrich Magnus, 'Introduction' in Ulrich Magnus and Peter Mankowski (eds), *Brussels I Regulation* (2nd edn, Sellier 2012) para 108). More comparative references and explanations can be found in the Options of the Advocate General, which in contrast to the actual decisions quite often quote decisions by other courts and academic writing. One also has to remember that the comparative perspective is inherent in all EU law. The ECJ with a judge from each Member State is itself a constant laboratory of comparative thinking. The 28 ECJ judges are 'unity in diversity', which was the motto for the EU in the failed Treaty establishing a Constitution for Europe ([2004] OJ C 310/1) (art I-8).

4. Autonomous interpretation as a meta principle

To sum up, autonomous interpretation is a meta principle that guides the interpretation and application of a given term. Autonomous interpretation can be 'qualified as a rule of preference *in favor* of certain arguments' (Martin Gebauer, 'Uniform Law, General Principles and Autonomous Interpretation' (2000) 5 Unif.L.Rev. 683) and one has to add: a preference in favour of certain methods such as the literal, comparative and purposive. Member State courts are obliged to make use of EU law as far as the wording allows in order to give EU law full effectiveness in the dispute in question. This means that a *contra legem* interpretation is also clearly impermissible under EU law since this would violate the fundamental principles of democratic consent and legal certainty. The ECJ highlighted that in regard to the interpretation of the Unfair Terms Directive (Council Directive 93/13/EEC of 5 April 1993 on unfair terms in consumer contracts, [1993] OJ L 95/29): 'the national court is bound to interpret national law [as a whole], [only] so far as possible, in the light of the wording and the purpose of the directive concerned in order to achieve the result sought by the directive' (Joined Cases C-397/01 to C-403/01 *Bernhard Pfeiffer and others v Deutsches Rotes Kreuz, Kreisverband Waldshut eV* [2004] ECR I-8835, para 113).

V. Scope of autonomous interpretation

The ECJ strengthens unity through the definition and development of autonomous concepts. The ECJ often decides *in dubio pro communitate*. (However, exceptions to a general rule have to be interpreted narrowly; see regarding the question of jurisdiction in case of a dual use of a product bought by a consumer, Case C-464/01 *Johann Gruber v Bay Wa AG* [2005] ECR I-439, para 27.) This also implies favouring autonomous interpretation. However, the ECJ quite often defines only the more general terms and leaves the details and of course the application more or less to the Member States courts. In European private law where, as mentioned, the preferred legislative instrument is the directive, the ECJ follows this strategy also to avoid to be overburdened by cases. In contrast, EU private international law and international civil procedure is usually embodied in regulations that have in tendency a higher regulatory density and require more detailed answers by the ECJ.

There are also instances where the EU legislature deliberately leaves it to the ECJ to define complex terms. This is the case regarding the criterion of 'directed at' the consumer's state in art 17(1)(c) Brussels I Regulation (recast) and art 6(1) Rome I Regulation (→ Consumer contracts). A further example is the 'habitual residence' that art 19 Rome I Regulation largely leaves undefined for natural persons (→ Domicile, habitual residence and establishment). In these cases, autonomous interpretation provides opportunities for judicial gap filling.

At a later stage, this jurisprudence can be the basis for legislative reforms. In the case of the recast of the → Brussels I Regulation (Convention and Regulation), the EU legislature drew from ECJ case law and its *obiter dicta*. For example, the legislature inspired from an *obiter dictum* to lay down in art 26(2) Brussels I Regulation (recast) that if the defendant is an insured person, a consumer or employee, that the court will, before assuming jurisdiction by appearance under art 26(1) Brussels I Regulation (recast), ensure that the defendant is informed of his right to contest the jurisdiction of the court and of the consequences of entering or not entering an appearance (the case is Case C-111/09 *Česká podnikatelská pojišťovna as, Vienna Insurance Group v Michal Bilas* [2010] ECR I-4545, para 31; see on this Koen Lenaerts and Thilo Stapper, 'Die Entwicklung der Brüssel I-Verordnung im Dialog des Europäischen Gerichtshof mit dem Gesetzgeber' (2014) 78 RabelsZ 252, 288). In sum, the reform pursued a piecemeal approach instead of the ambitious plans of the European Commission (Proposal for a Regulation of the European Parliament and of the Council on jurisdiction and the recognition and enforcement of judgments in civil and commercial matters (recast), COM(2010) 748 final) to abolish the *exequatur* procedure also in substantive regard (see arts 39 and 46 ff Brussels I Regulation (recast)) and to extend the scope of the jurisdictional provisions to defendants domiciled in third states (Koen Lenaerts and Thilo Stapper, 'Die Entwicklung der Brüssel I-Verordnung im Dialog des Europäischen Gerichtshof mit dem Gesetzgeber' (2014) 78 RabelsZ 252; Rea-Constantina Economides-Apostolidis, 'Brussels I in the European Practice – How Autonomous European Concepts Are Developed by the ECJ – Comparative Legal Research at ECJ Level – A View from the Inside of the Research and Documentation Directorate of the ECJ' [2010] EuLF 256).

VI. Interdependent interpretation

In general, the interpretation of norms is subject to the relativity of legal terms. This means that the terms used in various instruments have to be interpreted independently from each other. It is obvious that definitions in substantive law cannot readily be transferred without further consideration. For example, a definition of 'consumer' in a substantive EU Regulation cannot be transferred to art 6(1) Rome I Regulation (see Case C-464/01 *Johann Gruber v BayWa AG* [2005] ECR I-439) (→ Consumer contracts). If a legal system rejects the concept of → same-sex marriages this need not be the case in the area of private international law.

A recent example concerns the form of choice-of-court agreements regarding contracts concluded electronically (art 23(2) of the Brussels I Regulation, now art 25(2) Brussels I Regulation (recast)) (→ Choice of forum and submission to jurisdiction). The ECJ ruled that it is sufficient if the purchaser has the possibility to click on a box stating 'click here to open the general conditions of sale in a new window' that contains a choice-of-court agreement. The ECJ argued that an interpretation regarding requirements set out by art 5(1) of the Distance Selling Directive (Directive 97/7/EC of the European Parliament and of the Council of 20 May 1997 on the protection of consumers in respect of distance selling, [1997] OJ L144/19) cannot be transferred 'since both the wording of Article 5(1) of Directive 97/7 . . . and the objective of that provision, which is specifically consumer protection, differ from those of Article 23(2)' (Case C-322/14 *Jaouad El Majdoub v CarsOnTheWeb*, ECLI:EU:C:2015:334, para 38). Thus, the ECJ gave more grounds (wording and purpose) than the fact that one of the norms stems from EU substantive law and that the other norm derives from EU international procedural law.

Further discussion is required on how far private international law and international civil procedure have to be separated due to their different functions. On the one hand, European international civil procedure ultimately favours the defendant. It offers the place of general jurisdiction following the idea *actor sequitur forum rei*, ie that the claimant must follow the forum of the defendant's residence (art 4(1) Brussels I (recast)) (→ Brussels I (Convention and Regulation)). In addition, the closeness of the forum to facts that need to be proven is usually of more relevance than under private international law. On the other hand, private international law seeks to lead to an application of the law that has the closest connection to the subject matter in question. To serve the overall objective of legal certainty, the applicable law should be 'highly foreseeable', as Recital (16) of the Rome I Regulation states. Therefore, arts 4 ff of the Rome I Regulation contain objective standard → connecting factors. Nonetheless, several → escape clauses allow the judge a degree of discretion to determine a law that is more closely connected to the situation than that foreseen by the standard connections (eg art 4(3) Rome I Regulation).

However, despite the principle of separation between private international law and international civil procedure, an interdependent interpretation can be a useful method to systematize EU law in this area that has otherwise grown unsystematically over recent years. There are instances where a regulation states that an interdependent interpretation is intended by the legislature. For example, the substantive scope and the provisions of the Rome I Regulation (as its Recital (7) states) should be 'consistent with' the Rome II Regulation and the Brussels I Regulation (recast) (similarly Recital (7) Rome II Regulation). This allows for a coherent development of the concept of 'civil and commercial matters' within the meanings of arts 1 Brussels Regulation (recast), Rome I and Rome II Regulations.

In addition, Recital (24) of the Rome I Regulation, expressly clarifies that the concept of 'directed activity' as a condition for applying the consumer protection rule of art 6(1) Rome I Regulation has to be 'interpreted harmoniously' according to (today) art 17(1)(c) Brussels I Regulation (recast) (→ Consumer contracts). The ECJ has highlighted this interpretive requirement in several decisions (see in particular Joined Cases C-585/08 and C-144/09 *Peter Pammer v Reederei Karl Schlüter GmbH & Co KG* (C-585/08) and *Hotel Alpenhof GesmbH v Oliver Heller* (C-144/09) [2010] ECR I-12527, para 39). Further legislative statements in favour of a harmonious interpretation can be found in Recital (17) of the Rome I Regulation.

In addition, the provisions of the → Rome III Regulation should conform with those of the → Brussels IIa Regulation (Council Regulation (EC) No 2201/2003 of 27 November 2003 concerning jurisdiction and the recognition and enforcement of judgments in matrimonial matters and the matters of parental responsibility, repealing Regulation (EC) No 1347/2000, [2003] OJ L 338/1) (Recital (10) of Rome III Regulation).

If such clear statements in EU legislation are absent, a transferral of definitions and concepts between enactments from the same area, but also across the two areas is possible, but with the following caveat. A certain synchronization is also conceivable, in particular where the legislative motives of enactments coincide. Such common purposes are often explained in more detail in the recitals of enactments, such as that of party autonomy (see arts 25 ff Brussels I (recast); arts 3(1) and (2) Rome I Regulation, art 14(1) Rome II Regulation), the prohibition on circumventing the law (see arts 3(3) and (4) Rome I Regulation, art 14(2), (3) Rome II Regulation), as well as in certain instances protection of the weaker party (see arts 17 ff, 20 ff Brussels I (recast), arts 6 and 8(1) Rome I Regulation, art 14 Rome II Regulation). A further common principle is the respect of predictability and legal certainty as the relevant 'principles which underlie judicial cooperation in civil and commercial matters in the European Union' (Case C-533/08 *TNT Express Nederland BV v AXA Versicherung AG* [2010] ECR I-4107, para 49), meaning that jurisdiction and applicable law should always be predictable for the parties (see in detail Jan D Lüttringhaus, 'Übergreifende Begrifflichkeiten im europäischen Zivilverfahrens- und Kollisionsrecht – Grund und Grenzen der rechtsaktsübergreifenden Auslegung dargestellt am Beispiel vertraglicher und außervertraglicher Schuldverhältnisse' (2013) 77 RabelsZ 31, 125, who rightfully stresses that a general presumption in favour of uniform interpretation is overly simplistic; cf, Markus Würdinger, 'Das Prinzip der Einheit der Schuldrechtsverordnungen im Europäischen Internationalen Privat- und Verfahrensrecht – Eine methodologische Untersuchung über die praktische Konkordanz zwischen Brüssel I-VO, Rom I-VO und Rom II-VO' (2011) 75 RabelsZ 102, according to whom the Brussels I, Rome I and Rome II Regulations 'must be seen and interpreted as a single mutually connected entity').

HANNES RÖSLER

VII. Conclusions

Autonomous interpretation avoids the re-nationalization of the considerably Europeanized fields of private international law and international civil procedure. Autonomous interpretation guides the interpretation tools common to all Member States. However, EU law requires a preference for comparing various language versions of EU legislation. In addition, the interpretation has to be in conformity with general European laws (eg the principle of non-discrimination in art 18 TFEU). The same is true for international conventions such as the ECHR (see Louwrens Rienk Kiestra, *The Impact of the European Convention on Human Rights on Private international law* (Springer/Asser Press 2014)) and the Hague conventions (see the reference of art 15 Maintenance Regulation (Council Regulation (EC) No 4/2009 of 18 December 2008 on jurisdiction, applicable law, recognition and enforcement of decisions and cooperation in matters relating to maintenance obligations, [2009] OJ L 7/1) to the Hague Maintenance Protocol 2007 (Hague Protocol of 23 November 2007 on the law applicable to maintenance obligations, [2009] OJ L 331/19)).

An interesting question is whether the ECJ has developed a specific methodology for EU private international law and international civil procedure. In → Germany such a distinct methodology was recently claimed to exist in the field of the company law jurisprudence of the Federal Court of Justice (by Peter O Mülbert, 'Einheit der Methodenlehre? – Allgemeines Zivilrecht und Gesellschaftsrecht im Vergleich' (2014) 214 AcP 188). However, in contrast to the German Federal Court of Justice, the ECJ is not composed of specialized panels that focus on specific fields such as company law. Rather the ECJ is a universal court, being at once a supreme court for all the various areas of EU law and at the same time a constitutional court. In addition, the ECJ is a multinational court that needs to stress coherence more than traditional courts. In its approach, reasoning and interpretation methods, the ECJ has proved to be quite stable over the decades, though its decisions have grown more elaborate in the recent years.

It cannot be said that the Court approaches EU private international law and international civil procedure differently than other areas of EU law. Rather, the interpretation in this field (with the systematic and conceptual incoherencies quite often common to EU law) follows the well-established jurisprudence and the pattern of stressing the uniqueness and thus autonomy of EU law. For a community based on the rule of law (as opposed to the idea of a nation state), the homogeneous application of its laws is even more decisive than for other legal systems. For the deciding ECJ judges, the danger of divergent understanding is quite apparent since their own national background might initially guide their reading of new and controversial issues. To avoid the trend towards interpreting text in the light of a judge's own domestic law, autonomous interpretation of all EU law in the sense of neutrality abstracted from national laws is required for all EU law. Thus, EU private international law and international civil procedure is part of the general endeavour to read EU law without resort to a (specific) national legal order.

Though the ECJ added the principle of autonomous interpretation to EU law, the Member State courts bear by far the largest caseload of relevance to the European judicial area. Thus, autonomous interpretation of norms gains significance on three levels. First, the CJEU interprets these norms by adopting a supranational perspective. Second, the ECJ's guidelines provide in a vertical dimension for the second level, ie how the Member State courts have to interpret EU law. On the third level, Member State courts in practice can (ideally) orientate themselve towards the cases and can be assured that in order to safeguard uniformity, the true meaning and gap-filling solutions will be found within the four corners of the legal instrument in question or related enactments or the superior EU law in general. All these three levels, each with their own backgrounds and perspectives, contribute to the creation of common civil procedural standards. While the first and the last level are already quite international, the Member State courts remain rather state-centred. The Member State court should be encouraged to take more regard of courts from other Member States in order to strengthen Europe's horizontal transjurisdictional relationships.

HANNES RÖSLER

Literature

Rea-Constantina Economides-Apostolidis, 'Brussels I in the European Practice – How Autonomous European Concepts Are Developed by the

ECJ – Comparative Legal Research at ECJ Level – A View from the Inside of the Research and Documentation Directorate of the ECJ' [2010] EuLF 256; Martin Gebauer, 'Uniform Law, General Principles and Autonomous Interpretation' (2000) 5 Unif.L.Rev. 683; Louwrens Rienk Kiestra, *The Impact of the European Convention on Human Rights on Private international law* (Springer/Asser Press 2014); Koen Lenaerts and Thilo Stapper, 'Die Entwicklung der Brüssel I-Verordnung im Dialog des Europäischen Gerichtshof mit dem Gesetzgeber' (2014) 78 RabelsZ 252; Jan D Lüttringhaus, 'Übergreifende Begrifflichkeiten im europäischen Zivilverfahrens- und Kollisionsrecht – Grund und Grenzen der rechtsaktsübergreifenden Auslegung dargestellt am Beispiel vertraglicher und außervertraglicher Schuldverhältnisse' (2013) 77 RabelsZ 31; Ulrich Magnus and Peter Mankowski (eds), *Brussels I Regulation* (Sellier 2016); Peter O Mülbert, 'Einheit der Methodenlehre? – Allgemeines Zivilrecht und Gesellschaftsrecht im Vergleich' (2014) 214 AcP 188; John L Murray, 'Methods of Interpretation: Comparative Law Method' in European Court of Justice (ed), *Actes du colloque pour le cinquantième anniversaire des Traités de Rome. L'influence du droit national et de la jurisprudence des juridictions des États membres sur l'interprétation du droit communautaire* (Luxemburg 2007) 39; Hannes Rösler, *Europäische Gerichtsbarkeit auf dem Gebiet des Zivilrechts – Strukturen, Entwicklungen und Reformperspektiven des Justiz- und Verfahrensrechts der Europäischen Union* (Mohr Siebeck 2012); Hannes Rösler, 'Interpretation of EU Law' in Jürgen Basedow and others (eds), *Max Planck Encyclopedia of European Private Law*, vol 2 (OUP 2012) 979; Johannes Schmidt, *Rechtssicherheit im europäischen Zivilverfahrensrecht – Eine Analyse der Entscheidungen des EuGH zum EuGVÜ und der EuGVVO* (Mohr Siebeck 2015); Stefan Vogenauer, *Die Auslegung von Gesetzen in England und auf dem Kontinent – Eine vergleichende Untersuchung der Rechtsprechung und ihrer historischen Grundlagen* (Mohr Siebeck 2001); Markus Würdinger, 'Das Prinzip der Einheit der Schuldrechtsverordnungen im Europäischen Internationalen Privat- und Verfahrensrecht – Eine methodologische Untersuchung über die praktische Konkordanz zwischen Brüssel I-VO, Rom I-VO und Rom II-VO' (2011) 75 RabelsZ 102.

Interregional / Interstate law

I. Concept and notion

Interregional law is intended to resolve the issues that arise in connection with states in which differing legal regimes apply in different territorial units within such states. Multi-unit states can either be federal states such as the USA, or unitary states with composite private law systems such as the UK.

The interregional law concept has two meanings. On the one hand 'interregional law' may refer to distinct choice-of-law provisions that govern internal or domestic conflicts. Most multi-unit states have no common rules to resolve such conflicts and each unit applies its own conflict rules (eg → Australia, → Canada, the → United Kingdom and the → USA). Common special provisions for domestic conflicts, however, exist in a few jurisdictions such as the Kingdom of Spain. Conflicts between Spanish laws are governed by a set of uniform choice-of-law provisions contained in the Preliminary Title of the Spanish Civil Code (Código Civil of 24 July 1889, Gaceta de Madrid No 206, 25 July 1889, henceforth Spanish CC; arts 13–16). These rules are known as interregional law. As a further example, conflicts between Mainland → China and the administrative regions of Hong Kong (→ Hong Kong, S.A.R. of China) and Macau (→ Macau, S.A.R. of China) are also dealt with by rules that are different from private international law rules and known as interregional law.

On the other hand, 'interregional law' refers to provisions contained in national private international law systems, in international private international law conventions and in EU private international law regulations in order to address the issues arising in connection to multi-unit states. Whenever the choice-of-law rules contained in these statutes, conventions or regulations refer to the law of a multi-unit state, it becomes necessary to determine which system of law or sets of rules of a territorial unit composing such a state applies. This is dealt with by provisions belonging to the general part of national private international law codifications. Private international law conventions or EU regulations on private international law usually contain similar tailor-made provisions for matters covered by the convention or regulation. Interregional law has also been called inter-local or interterritorial law.

II. Purpose and function

Interregional law aims at resolving conflicts in multi-unit states in which differing legal rules apply to different territorial units within such states, as opposed to interpersonal law, which resolves conflicts arising due to the fact that differing rules apply to different categories of people belonging to diverse ethnic or religious communities. While resolving domestic conflicts concerns only the multi-unit state itself and is best analysed within a given legal system, more general issues arise in international cases when the applicable law is the law of such a composite state. All private international law systems are in need of determining which legal system or set of rules ultimately governs and are therefore likely to develop interregional law rules for such purpose.

There are various techniques or models in order to determine the applicable law when this is the law of a composite state. The classic solution, termed 'indirect-reference model', is to understand that private international law rules refer to the rules of a national sovereign state. Reference is therefore made to the national rules of this state to further determine which of the laws within the state governs the dispute. In practice, however, the indirect-reference model often proves unworkable, particularly as most multi-unit states have no common rules on domestic conflicts. The indirect-reference model therefore requires a subsidiary rule in order to deal with such situations. The most classical solution is to apply the law of the territorial unit that has the closest connection with the dispute.

A second model is the direct-reference model that traditionally prevails in common law systems, where domestic and international conflicts are generally treated alike. Choice-of-law rules are understood as referring both to the law of a sovereign state and to the law of a territorial unit within that state. However, the direct-reference model requires suitable connecting factors of a territorial character and cannot work in connection with rules that either use personal connecting factors such as nationality, or a combination of both personal and territorial factors. The direct-reference model therefore often requires additional special rules substituting the unsuitable → connecting factor.

A compromise solution is to combine both methods, usually by starting with the indirect-reference model and using direct reference as a subsidiary rule. Further rules might be necessary for cases in which the subsidiary direct-reference model is unworkable because the connecting factor used by the choice-of-law provision is unsuitable.

III. Legal sources

1. National

Not all private international law systems have special rules addressing the situation in which the law applicable is the law of a state that has two or more systems of law or sets of rules applying in different territorial units. Common law systems traditionally make no distinction between domestic and international conflicts and are therefore in no need of developing special rules, either in order to solve domestic conflicts or to determine the applicable law when this is the law of a multi-unit state.

The situation differs in civil law systems. The Swiss Private international law Act (Bundesgesetz über das Internationale Privatrecht of 18 December 1987, 1988 BBl I 5, as amended) is silent on the matter, but most other modern private international law statutes or codes contain provisions dealing with states with more than one legal system. The Belgian Private international law Act (Wet houdende het Wetboek von international privaatrecht/Code de droit international privé of 16 July 2004, BS 27 July 2004, pp 57344, 57366) establishes in art 17 (which is part of ch I on General Provisions) that when the statute refers to the law of a state with two or more legal systems, each system is considered to be the law of a state for the purposes of the designation of the applicable law. The preferred method is the direct-reference method. Article 17 § 2 further clarifies that a reference to the law of the state of a natural person's nationality refers to the legal system designated by the rules in force in that state, or absent such rules, to the legal system with which the natural person has the closest connection. This means that, when the direct-reference model is unworkable because the choice-of-law provision uses nationality as a connecting factor, the applicable law is to be determined either according to the indirect-reference model (ie by applying the rules existing under the applicable law), or absent such rules, by determining the law most closely connected to the dispute.

Other European private international law systems prefer to start with the indirect-reference model. Such is the case of → Spain. Article 12.5 Spanish CC provides that, whenever a choice-of-law provision designates the law of a multi-unit state, then the law of the territorial unit governing the dispute is to be determined by applying the interregional law provisions of that state. The Spanish provision does not offer a solution for those cases in which the multi-unit state has no common choice-of-law provisions dealing with domestic conflicts. Article 4(3) Introductory Act to the German Civil Code (Einführungsgesetz zum Bürgerlichen Gesetzbuche of 21 September 1994, BGBl. I 2494, as amended; → Germany), art 18 Italian Private international law Act (Riforma del Sistema italiano di diritto internazionale private, Act No 218 of 31 May 1995 in Gazz.Uff., Supplemento Ordinario No 128 of 3 June 1995, as amended; → Italy), and art 9 Polish Private international law Act (Official Journal 2011 No 80, pos 432; → Poland) are also based on the indirect-reference model. They further establish a subsidiary rule according to which, absent common choice-of-law provisions on domestic conflicts, the applicable law is that of the territorial unit with the closest connection.

The indirect-reference model seems to prevail in Latin America. It is used in art 3 Venezuelan Act on Private international law (Act of 6 August 1998 on Private international law, Official Gazette No 36.511; → Venezuela), and in art 2595(b) of the new and unified Argentine Civil and Commercial Code (Argentine Civil and Commercial Code enacted by Law of Congress No 29.994 of 1 October 2014, signed into law on 7 October 2014, Official Gazette No 32.985; → Argentina). The Panamanian Private international law Act (Código de Derecho Internacional Privado, Official Gazette of 8 May 2014) is, however, silent on the matter.

The Chinese Statute of Application of Law to Foreign Civil Relations (adopted at the 17th session of the Standing Committee of the 11th National People's Congress on 28 October 2010, effective 1 April 2011) neither uses direct reference nor indirect reference. Article 6 provides that, where a foreign law is applicable to a foreign-related civil relation and different laws are implemented in the different regions of that country, then the law of the region that is most closely connected with the foreign-related civil relation will be applied. The Japanese Act on General Rules for Application of Laws (Hōno Tekiyō ni Kansuru Tsūsokuhō, Law No 10 of 1898, as newly titled and amended by Act No 78 of 21 June 2006) does not deal with the matter in general terms but includes a provision in art 38.3 establishing that where a person has the nationality of a state where the law differs by region, then that person's national law will be the law indicated according to the rules of that state (or absent such rules, the law of the region with which that person is most closely connected).

2. *International*

The first Hague Conventions containing provisions on multi-unit states were the Hague Infant Protection Convention (Hague Convention of 5 October 1961 concerning the powers of authorities and the law applicable in respect of the protection of infants, 658 UNTS 143), and the Hague Testamentary Dispositions Convention (Hague Convention of 5 October 1961 on the conflicts of laws relating to the form of testamentary dispositions, 510 UNTS 175). These provisions appeared to be necessary because both Hague Conventions use nationality as a connecting factor, and the choice-of-law rules are thus only apt to select the law of a sovereign state and not a legal system within a multi-unit state. Article 14 Hague Infant Protection Convention establishes that, for the purpose of the Convention if the domestic law of the infant's nationality consists of a non-unified system, then 'the domestic law of the state of the infant's nationality' and 'authorities of the state of the infant's nationality', will mean respectively the law and authorities determined by the rules in force in that system and, failing such rules, that law and those authorities within the system with which the infant has the closest connection. The indirect-reference model is also used in the Hague Testamentary Dispositions Convention. According to art 1, if a national law consists of a non-unified system, the law to be applied will be determined by the rules in force in that system and, failing such rules, by the most real connection which the testator had with any one of the various laws within that system.

Later Conventions of the → Hague Conference on Private International Law have continued to include special provisions dealing with multi-unit states. Some of them use indirect reference. The Convention of 15 November 1965 on Jurisdiction, Applicable Law and Recognition of Decrees Relating to Adoptions (1107 UNTS 38) addresses the matter in art 11, and refers to the rules in force in the non-unified legal system and failing those to the law most closely connected. This model is also followed in art 16 of the Hague Maintenance Recognition and Enforcement Convention 1973 (Hague

Convention of 2 October 1973 on the recognition and enforcement of decisions relating to maintenance obligations, 1021 UNTS 209).

In more recent Conventions, which use habitual residence as a → connecting factor, the indirect-reference model has largely been abandoned. In some cases the direct-reference model is established by equating territorial units within multi-unit states with states for the purposes of the Convention. The Hague Traffic Accident Convention (Hague Convention of 4 May 1971 on the law applicable to traffic accidents, 965 UNTS 415) thus establishes in art 12 that every territorial entity forming part of a state with a non-unified legal system will be considered as a state when it has its own legal system, in respect of civil non-contractual liability arising from → traffic accidents. Article 12 Hague Products Liability Convention (Hague Convention of 2 October 1973 on the law applicable to products liability, 1056 UNTS 191) similarly provides that each territorial unit will be considered as a state for the purposes of selecting the applicable law under the Convention. A provision in both the Hague Traffic Accident Convention and the Hague Products Liability Convention clarifies that a state having a non-unified legal system is not bound to apply the Convention to domestic cases. Such provisions appeared to be necessary in order to exclude that the direct-reference model is interpreted to mean that the Conventions also cover domestic conflicts.

If, however, the Convention uses both personal and territorial connecting factors, it usually combines direct reference and indirect reference. The Hague Matrimonial Property Convention (Hague Convention of 14 March 1978 on the law applicable to matrimonial property regimes, 16 ILM 14) establishes that, where a state has two or more territorial units in which different systems of law apply to matrimonial property regimes, then any reference to the national law of such a state will be construed as referring to the system determined by the rules in force in that state. It further provides subsidiary rules that apply in the absence of such rules. With regard to habitual residence, direct reference is preferred, while any reference to habitual residence in that state will be construed as referring to habitual residence in a territorial unit of that state.

Over the years, provisions on states with more than one legal system have become increasingly sophisticated. They are highly diverse and combine direct and indirect reference with tailor-made subsidiary rules in view of the subject matter of the instrument. These provisions are usually drafted either by the Permanent Bureau of the Hague Conference as was the case for the Hague Maintenance Protocol 2007 (Hague Protocol of 23 November 2007 on the law applicable to maintenance obligations, [2009] OJ L 331/19), or more commonly by a special Commission composed of a limited number of delegates and then reviewed in the diplomatic sessions by the plenary of the negotiating states. Some of the provisions on states with more than one legal system do not deal only with matters of the applicable law. Both the Hague Child Protection Convention (Hague Convention of 19 October 1996 on jurisdiction, applicable law, recognition, enforcement and co-operation in respect of parental responsibility and measures for the protection of children, 35 ILM 1391) and the Hague Maintenance Convention 2007 (Hague Convention of 23 November 2007 on the international recovery of child support and other forms of family maintenance, [2011] OJ L 192/51; 47 ILM 257) contain a comprehensive regulation addressing all the difficulties that may result from the fact that some states are composed of two or more territorial units, each with its own judicial or legal systems.

Some Inter-American Conventions also contain rules on states with more than one legal system. Article 28 Inter-American Support Obligations Convention (Inter-American Convention on Support Obligations of 15 July 1989, 29 ILM 73), signed in Montevideo, Uruguay on 15 July 1989, opts for the direct-reference model. Any reference to the domicile or habitual residence in that state refers to domicile or habitual residence in a territorial unit of that state, and any reference to the law of the state of domicile or habitual residence refers to the law of the territorial unit in which the child has its domicile or habitual residence. Article 22 Inter-American Contracts Convention (Inter-American Convention of 17 March 1994 on the Law Applicable to International Contracts, OAS, Treaty Series, No 78, 33 ILM 732), signed at Mexico DF, Mexico on 17 March 1994, provides that in the case of a state which has two or more systems of law applicable in different territorial units with respect to matters covered by the Convention: (i) any reference to the laws of the state is to be construed as a reference to the laws in the territorial unit in question and (ii) any reference to habitual residence or place of business in that state is to be construed as a reference to habitual residence or place of business in a territorial unit of that state.

3. European

Since all EU Member States are Member States of the Hague Conference on Private International Law, it is not surprising that EU private international law regulations have followed the tradition of expressly dealing with the problems posed by multi-unit states.

The Rome I Regulation (Regulation (EC) No 593/2008 of the European Parliament and of the Council of 17 June 2008 on the law applicable to contractual obligations (Rome I), [2008] OJ L 177/6; → Rome Convention and Rome I Regulation) and the → Rome II Regulation (Regulation (EC) No 864/2007 of the European Parliament and of the Council of 11 July 2007 on the law applicable to non-contractual obligations (Rome II), [2007] OJ L 199/40) use direct reference and provide that, where a state comprises several territorial units each of which has its own rules of law, then each territorial unit is to be considered as a country for the purposes of identifying the law applicable. Member States are, however, not bound to apply the Regulations to conflicts solely between the laws of such units.

The provisions in the → Rome III Regulation (Council Regulation (EU) No 1259/2010 of 20 December 2010 implementing enhanced cooperation in the area of the law applicable to divorce and legal separation, [2010] OJ L 343/10) are slightly more complex since the Regulation combines territorial → connecting factors such as habitual residence with personal connecting factors such as nationality. References to habitual residence in a state have to be construed as references to habitual residence in a territorial unit, whereas any reference to nationality is to be construed as a reference to the territorial unit designated by the law of that state, or absent relevant rules, to the territorial unit chosen by the parties, or absent such choice, to the territorial unit with which the spouse or spouses has or have the closest connection. The provision combines the direct- and indirect-reference models with tailor-made subsidiary rules for those cases in which the multi-unit state lacks rules for solving internal conflicts.

The Succession Regulation (Regulation (EU) No 650/2012 of the European Parliament and of the Council of 4 July 2012 on jurisdiction, applicable law, recognition and enforcement of decisions and acceptance and enforcement of authentic instruments in matters of succession and on the creation of a European Certificate of Succession, [2012] OJ L 201/107; → Rome IV Regulation) establishes that where the law specified by the Regulation is that of a state which comprises several territorial units each of which has its own rules of law in respect of → succession, then the internal choice-of-laws rules of that state determine the relevant territorial unit whose rules are to apply. It contains tailor-made subsidiary rules that apply absent such rules. Provisions referring to the habitual residence of the deceased have to be construed as referring to the law of the territorial unit in which the deceased had his habitual residence; provisions referring to the nationality of the deceased have to be construed as referring to the law of the territorial unit with which the deceased had the closest connection. Additionally, any other provisions referring to other elements as connecting factors have to be construed as referring to the law of the territorial unit in which the relevant element is located.

CRISTINA GONZÁLEZ BEILFUSS

Literature

Alegría Borrás, 'Les ordres plurilegislatifs dans le droit international privé actuel' (1994) 249 Rec. des Cours 145; Gregor Christandl, 'Multi-unit States in European Private international law' (2013) 9 J Priv Int L 219; Pilar Dominguez Lozano, 'Internal Conflicts and "Interregional Law" in the Spanish Legal System' [1997] Span Yrbk Intl L 43; Sixto Sánchez Lorenzo, 'La aplicación de los Convenios de la Conferencia de La Haya a los conflictos de leyes internos: perspectiva española' [1993] REDI 131; Edoardo Vitta, 'Interlocal Conflict of Laws' in Kurt Lipstein (ed), *International Encyclopedia of Comparative Law III/1* (Mohr Siebeck 1986, reprint 2011) ch 9 s 1; Guobin Zhu, 'Inter-regional Conflict of Laws under "One Country, Two Systems": Revisiting Chinese Legal Theories and Chinese and Hong Kong Law, with Special Reference to Judicial Assistance' (2002) 32 HKLJ 615.

Interreligious law

I. Definition of the phenomenon

In the legal literature, interreligious law has two connotations. First, it describes the legal system of countries where the law is not uniform for all the citizens but depends on their religious affiliation. Second, and more specifically, interreligious law designates a set of 'special choice-of-law rules' to solve the internal and interreligious conflict of laws emanating from such a system.

For the sake of clarity, I will use the term religion-based legal pluralism (henceforth RBLP) to designate the first connotation of the term and reserve the term 'interreligious law' for the second connotation.

There is undoubtedly a similarity between interreligious law and international private law since both share the same target of determining the applicable law on a matter with parties or legal acts submitted to different normative orderings. Scholars have not agreed upon the question as to whether interreligious law should be considered as part of private international law. In any case, international private law requires the application of interreligious law in order to find the law that should govern the factual matter at stake. This happens, when the choice-of-law rule designates a foreign law of a state with religion-based legal pluralism. To determine which of the religious laws relevant in that country are applicable, the judge should apply the interreligious law prevailing in the latter (eg art 4(3) Introductory Act to the German Civil Code (Einführungsgesetz zum Bürgerlichen Gesetzbuche of 21 September 1994, BGBl. I 2494, as amended), art 12(5) Spanish Civil Code (Código Civil of 24 July 1889, Gaceta de Madrid No 206, 25 July 1889), art 20 Portuguese Civil Code (Código Civil of 25 November 1966, Decreto Lei No 47–344)).

Religions are sets of beliefs based on transcendental elements. They mostly entail certain norms of conduct for their believers towards their fellow men and towards a given deity or other supernatural powers. Religions do not share the same degree of normativity. Islam and Judaism are, for instance, endowed with a huge scope of regulations that encompass all the aspects of the believers' lives of moral and of legal nature, such as food, contracts, crimes, → marriages, divorce (→ Divorce and personal separation) and → succession. Other religions, such as Christianity, have acquired a less dense scope of normativity. At present they adopt the approach as framed by the Biblical verse 'Render unto Caesar'.

Religion-based legal pluralism is at odds with the Western model of nation states having a territorial law system, where the citizens are subjected to uniform law which is enacted by a centralized state authority and which is applicable to all of them regardless of their religious affiliation. Although dominant, this model cannot claim universality either in a historical perspective or in current times. In our present era, the phenomenon of religious juridical pluralism is far from disappearing when considered from a global perspective. However, it is generally limited to family and inheritance law issues since family relationships most strongly reflect the values and the ethics of a given culture. The family is also still perceived as the best tool for the survival of the collective identity. In addition, inside the state, the family represents a private and a relatively autonomous space. The coexistence of different religion-based family laws does not hinder the functioning of the state, the economy and the society. This would not be the case, if the religious laws were to establish different rules in fields such as the legal capacity (→ Capacity and emancipation). It is indispensable for societies and for trading activities to dispose of certain common norms regardless of the religious affiliations of the parties involved.

Throughout the world, one can notice different arrangements of RBLP. Some states incorporate religious laws in their laws so that they formally become state laws. Others just recognize their binding force. There are others that combine the two methods. The religious laws in some countries must be applied by state tribunals. In other countries, those laws are applied by religious tribunals. If provided, religious tribunals coexist with state tribunals. As far as interreligious → choice of law is concerned, states have made use of two methods. Some states have enacted substantive laws to be specifically applied to religiously mixed relationships; others have preferred the elaboration of internal choice-of-law rules; and still others combine both methods.

II. Historical context

The historical evolution of RBLP is dependent on self-perception and the interactions of three factors: the state, communities and the individual. It goes without saying that the evolution of those factors has varied geographically. This entry does not aspire to cover the historical evolution of interreligious law worldwide. It will limit itself to the history of the phenomenon in certain regions of the world which were decisive for the current situation of interreligious law. These are Europe, the Islamic world, the Ottoman Empire and the former Western colonies.

1. Europe

The legal history of Europe was determined by struggles of the central state authorities with competing local authorities and with the Church. The uniformity of law slowly followed the birth of sovereign states in the wake of the Westphalian Peace of 1648. Nevertheless, family law resisted the hegemonic aspirations of the state for a longer period. The Church had succeeded in imposing its monopoly on family law issues (mainly → marriage and divorce (→ Divorce and personal separation)) since the period between the 10th and the 12th centuries. Christians remained submitted to their religious laws in these matters. Canon law regulated marriage matters for Catholics. Protestants were also submitted to canon regulations, though in a modified form. Jews were under the jurisdiction of Mosaic Law. The breakthrough was prepared by the Enlightenment and the period following the French Revolution in 1789. After the secularization of the state, the Napoleonic Civil Code (1804) established the obligatory civil marriage, whose regulations are applied to all French citizens regardless of their religious affiliations. The obligatory civil marriage was not universally introduced in Germany until as late as 1875. Some parts of southern Europe only recently abandoned their religious marriage laws. In Spain, for instance, until the passage of Law 30/1981 7 July 1981 (Boletín Oficial del Estado 20 July 1981), Spanish Catholics could marry in- and outside Spain only according to Canon Law (*Codex Iuris Canonici*). Civil marriage was provided only for Catholics who officially left the Church and for adherents of other religions. The validity of the marriage of two Spanish citizens, one of them being Catholic and the other Jewish, required first the application of the Spanish interreligious law as provided for in the Concordat of 1953.

2. Islamic world

In other parts of the world, especially in Muslim countries, RBLP is still prevailing. This is due to the history of Islam where the ruler (beginning with the Prophet *Mohamed* in the 7th century) combined his lay authority with the considerable spiritual function as commander of the believers.

Under Islamic law, non-Muslims are allowed to live in territories under Islamic authority if they pay a poll tax. In matters of marriage, divorce and succession they are submitted to their own religious laws adjudicated by their religious tribunals, since these matters are considered to be inextricably linked to faith. It should be added that this practice was carried over from the former rulers of the conquered territories, the Sassanide and the Byzantine rulers.

While allowing adherents of other religions to be submitted to their own religious law, Islamic law has enjoyed an overriding authority. In matters opposing Muslims and non-Muslims, Islamic law is applicable and Islamic tribunals have exclusive jurisdiction. Even if non-Muslims are also allowed to present their cases (without any Muslims being involved) to Islamic courts, Islamic law will be applied to them. The general and overriding nature of Islamic law in interreligious law is based on the maxim that 'Islam supersedes and cannot be superseded'. Interfaith relationships between non-Muslims fall under the exclusive jurisdiction of the Islamic tribunals which apply Islamic law to them. As far as succession is concerned, schools of Islamic law do not agree as to whether non-Muslim individuals following different faiths would be allowed to inherit from each other. There is, however, a consensus that non-Muslims cannot inherit from their Muslim relatives. Sunni Muslims consider this impediment as being bilateral while the Shiites apply it only against non-Muslim heirs. They thus allow Muslims to inherit the estate of the non-Muslim deceased.

3. Ottoman Empire

Under Ottoman rule this state of affairs was maintained and took on the name the '*millet* system' ('*millet*' means nation). The *millet* system was an organizational form based on belonging to a given faith. With the conquest

IMEN GALLALA-ARNDT

of huge new territories in the 15th century, the Ottomans dramatically increased the ethnic and religious diversity of their Empire. The Ottoman caliphs gave the leaders of the different religious communities more power in order to guarantee their allegiance to the new Ottoman Empire. They considered them the mediators between their communities and the central Ottoman government. That is why they assigned to them legislative and judicial autonomy. Accordingly, the Ottoman subjects were born inside a '*millet*' and were submitted spiritually, financially and administratively to a *millet*-linked status regulating their lives and defining their obligations. They were not allowed to leave their *millet* unless they converted to Islam. These conversions were in any event few, probably because of the lack of interaction between members of different *millets*. Most of the conversions happened inside the Christian community, with individuals changing from one denomination to another. In fact, under the Ottoman rules non-Muslim *millets* were assigned to live in different neighbourhoods and they had little contact with Muslims.

During Ottoman times, Christians and Jews appeared before the Muslim tribunals for inter-communal matters, capital crimes or matters of public order. But they also sometimes appeared before these courts on a voluntary basis. They did so to secure some benefits from the application of Islamic law. Christians and Jews were not allowed to marry each other. This practice was also confirmed by a 19th-century registration regulation (2 September 1881) obliging the persons who intended to marry to get the permission of the leaders of their religious communities. Accordingly, non-Muslims could not avoid the impediment to marriage as provided for in their religious laws. It should nevertheless be added that ever since the classical times of the Ottoman rule, the Islamic-based interreligious law had acknowledged one exception extending beyond the religious paradigm. Specifically, women who were Ottoman subjects were prohibited from marrying non-Ottoman men even if these men were Muslims. Marriages of Muslim Ottoman women with Muslim Iranian men were accordingly annulled.

Under the pressure of the European powers which considered themselves the protectors of the non-Muslim Ottoman subjects, the Ottoman regulation titled *Hatti Humayoun* was enacted on 18 February 1856. It confirmed the privileges of the non-Muslim communities concerning the free exercise of their faith. However, it abrogated their jurisdiction in civil and penal matters and limited it to matters of → personal status. The question of interreligious law was not addressed in the regulation since religiously mixed relationships were still not common.

The Ottoman Law on family Rights of 1917 (A Bergmann, M Ferid and D Henrich, *Internationales Ehe- und Kindschaftsrecht* (Israel, Lief. 205) 143) was the first personal status law in the Islamic world addressing both Muslims and non-Muslims. It entailed, however, special regulations for the Jewish and Christian Ottoman subjects. It was also opposed by the spiritual leaders who considered it an infringement upon their legislative autonomy. The 19th century saw many attempts in the Ottoman Empire to enact comprehensive legislation for all Ottomans, but they failed to be brought about.

4. Former Western colonies

The colonial rulers, however, showed less interest than the last Ottoman rulers in submitting all the peoples in their colonies to a uniform law regardless of their religious affiliations in the field of personal status law. The general trend was leaving personal status to be regulated by the religious and customary laws prevailing at the arrival of the colonizers. The colonial rulers wanted to avoid any useless conflict with the indigenous populations and the local leaders. Behind such an attitude there was also the intention to prevent the assimilation and mixture between Europeans and others, as was the case in Indonesia under Dutch colonization. In India, British colonizers similarly did not want to interfere with the existing religion-based legal diversity. But they attempted to rationalize the system by abolishing the religious tribunals and submitting all → personal status matters to Indian-British courts.

Given the increasing number of interfaith relationships, the colonial authorities could not ignore the necessity of finding solutions to the conflict of laws arising from them. While the French colonial authorities gave their own law an overriding binding force in case of conflict with indigenous law, the British and Dutch authorities sought to resolve these conflicts on the basis of abstract and objective standards. In British India, the courts developed on the basis of statutes some principles to resolve the internal conflict of laws. For instance, the courts applied the law of the defendant. They also adjudicated some cases on the basis of 'justice, equity and good conscience'. The Dutch '*intergentieel recht*' was mainly jurisprudential. The judges applied, for instance, the law of the defendant on interreligious matters. The judges generally adopted solutions provided for in the choice-of-law rules of private international law. For interreligious marriages, however, the Dutch legislator laid down some conflict-of-law rules in the 1898 Decree on Mixed Marriages (Staatsblad 1898 No 158). According to that decree the applicable law was the law of the groom. Accordingly, the marriage between a Muslim Javanese man and a Chinese woman of Christian faith was submitted to Islamic Law.

After decolonization, the new national governing elites of the new states took a different approach to the colonial legacies of interreligious law and RBLP.

III. Contemporary significance

In current times, interreligious law still prevails in different parts of the world, mainly in Asia, Africa and to a lesser extent in the Americas (Surinam). It is, however, limited to the fields of family law and → succession law. In Europe, one of the last strongholds of interreligious law is Western Thrace in → Greece. The application of Islamic Law on Muslim Greeks is limited to the residents of that region and is based on international conventions with Turkey in place since 1881 and on Greek domestic laws, mainly Law 147/1914 (Government Gazette No 25 A Series of 1 February 1914). Nevertheless, the Muslims of that region have the possibility of opting out of Islamic law by performing a civil marriage. In Muslim-majority countries this possibility is not provided.

At the beginning of the post-colonial era, most of the new states were determined to foster national unity and to build a modern legal system that would break with the colonial legacy. Nevertheless, the real impact of this intention on interreligious law depended considerably on the status of religion in the new legal order. In some countries a specific religion has a privileged status and in others all recognized religions are equally treated.

Interreligious law has clear shortcomings in terms of the respect for human rights and the preservation of legal certainty. As a consequence, members of religious communities and the legal systems themselves have developed alternative mechanisms to minimize the impact of those disadvantages. It is interesting though to notice that interreligious law systems seem to have gained in importance in the last two decades.

1. Typology

a) Countries with a religion having a privileged status

Muslim-majoritarian countries (henceforth Muslim countries) and Israel are the main representatives of this type of country.

Muslim countries, with the exception of → Turkey, assign to Islam a particular status by considering it the state religion or/and by stipulating in their constitutions or elsewhere that Islamic law is a source of legislation. These countries have retained the main features of the Ottoman *millet* system as they submit their non-Muslim citizens to their own religious laws and even in some cases to their religious tribunals in matters of → personal status. Personal status, as commonly used in Muslim countries, covers a wide range of issues such as: capacity (→ Capacity and emancipation), legal absence (→ Absence (disappearance, presumed death)), → marriage, divorce, custody, guardianship (→ Guardianship, custody and parental responsibility) and → succession. Nevertheless, the scope of RBLP is not uniform in all the Muslim countries. Some aspects of personal status have been regulated through uniform laws. In → Egypt, for instance, only marriage and divorce are regulated along interreligious lines (Law 462 of 1955 on Abolition of the Sharia and Milli Tribunals: An-nashra at-tashrīʿīya 1955, July–September, 2348). Succession issues are regulated by a uniform law applicable to all Egyptians (Law No 77/1943 on Inheritance of 6 August 1943 Official Gazette No 92 12 August 1943, 18). Such is the case for the duty of care of minor's property (Decree-Law No 119/1952 on Duty of care of minor's property: Qawānīn al-aḥwāl ashakhṣīya [Statutes on the Personal Status] (Dar al Ḥaqqānīya 2006), 131). In Morocco, however, Jewish citizens are submitted to their own religious law in extended matters of personal status: legal capacity (→ Capacity and emancipation), interdiction, guardianship (→ Guardianship, custody and parental responsibility), → marriage, divorce

(→ Divorce and personal separation) and → succession.

Despite this difference, the distinctive feature in this type of country is the overriding authority of Islamic law. In cases of interreligious relationships, where a Muslim is involved, Islamic law is automatically applied. The Moroccan personal status law (*Mudawwana*) of 2004 (Official Gazette No 5184 of 5 February 2004, 421) is to a large extent inspired by the *Maliki* School of Islamic law. It is not applicable to all Moroccans. Article 2 specifies that Jewish Moroccans are submitted to Moroccan Jewish personal status law applied by the rabbinical tribunals. Nevertheless, the same provision stipulates that the *Mudawwana* is applied to relationships between two Moroccans, one of them being Muslim. In Egypt, as well, Islamic law enjoys an overriding authority. Article 6 of the Law on the Abolishment of Religious Tribunals of 1955 stipulates that Islamic law, as embedded in Egyptian state law, is applied to non-Muslims who do not share the same rite, sect and religion. Moreover, the non-Muslims' religious laws are applied within the limits of public policy, which is mainly based on the absolute principles of Islamic law.

In many Muslim countries, such as → Egypt and Morocco, there is also a tendency to apply the internal interreligious law to private international proceedings. As soon as a Muslim is involved in a relationship, Islamic law is applied regardless of his → nationality. For example, an Egyptian tribunal considered the bigamous marriage of a British Muslim man with a Greek-Orthodox Greek woman as valid. As a matter of public policy, the tribunal applied the Egyptian Islamic law-based personal status law and held that, as a Muslim, the British citizen was allowed to be bigamous and to marry a non-Muslim monotheist woman. Interestingly, the tribunal ignored the then pertaining prohibition of such unions in Greek civil law (Cairo tribunal of 1st instance, 5 January 1954: Majallat al-qaẓā' wat-tashrī° Year 6, No 19, 357).

In the context of Muslim countries, → Tunisia represents a paradox. In fact, Islam is the state religion, but Islamic law is not considered a source of law. Moreover, the personal status code has since 1957 been applied to all Tunisians regardless of their religious affiliations. The code does not entail any explicit prohibition of marriage between a Muslim woman and a non-Muslim man – as prohibited under Islamic law – nor does it include an explicit impediment to inheritance between Muslims and non-Muslims. Nevertheless, administrative practice and case-law principally recognize these Islamic law-based proscriptions.

→ Israel defines itself as a Jewish state and Judaism has a particular status there. Israel kept the *millet* system that it inherited from the period of rule under the Ottoman Empire and the British mandate. Each recognized religious community has its own → personal status law and its own religious tribunals (rabbinical, Islamic, tribunals of different Christian denominations and Druze tribunals). Religious law is, however, in some constellations submitted to secular state law limitations. For instance, it is forbidden for a Muslim Imam to conclude the marriage of a Muslim man with a Jewish woman, although this is allowed in Islamic law. Imams are also prevented from concluding a bigamous marriage by Israeli penal law.

There is no civil marriage in Israel. Cases involving parties from different religious communities are to be submitted to the President of the Supreme Court who designates the competent jurisdiction (Section 55 of the Palestine Order-in-Council 1922/1939: in RH Drayton (ed), *The Laws of Palestine*, vol III (1934) 2569; *The Palestine Gazette* 1939, Supplement 2, 459).

Religious tribunals have exclusive jurisdiction on marriage and divorce matters among their members and a concurrent jurisdiction with the state family courts on matters of alimony, maintenance and succession.

Although Jewish law does not apply as a general law to Palestinian Arabs, it does have this function to a certain extent in relation with non-Jewish Israeli citizens who do not follow one of the recognized faiths in Israel.

b) Countries with no religion having a privileged status

In → Lebanon, there are around 18 recognized religious authorities. The constitution of 1926 guarantees the autonomy of each recognized religious community to regulate and adjudicate the personal status issues of its members (art 9). While 'committing itself to the Most High', the Lebanese constitution treats the recognized religions equally. The religious tribunals coexist with state tribunals, but they do not have any concurrent jurisdiction. In addition, the jurisdiction determines the applicable law. The legislator laid down several interreligious regulations to be applied to interreligious relationships, mainly marriages. For instance, the validity of the marriage is to be assessed by the religious authority having celebrated the marriage, which is the authority of the husband unless the spouses-to-be had chosen to marry before the religious authority of the wife-to-be (arts 14 and 15 of the Law on the Regulation of Christian Sects and the Israelite Sect: A Bergmann, M Ferid and D Henrich, *Internationales Ehe- und Kindschaftsrecht* (Libanon, Lief. 125) 44).Thus, Lebanese law does not confer to any religious law *per se* an overriding jurisdiction. The interreligious conflict of laws is to be solved according to abstract criteria, such as the religious authority having performed the marriage. This is, however, problematic in Lebanon in case of the conversion of one of the spouses to Islam. In fact, the Sharia tribunals would in that case immediately apply Islamic law. The Lebanese law does not provide any systematic solution to the inconsistencies arising from the application of different religious laws and state law. The case-law, however, intended to find new solutions pragmatically on a case-to-case basis.

Many voices have been raised in society and in the political arena in support of enacting a secular Lebanese marriage law. The advocates of an optional secular marriage law focus on the shortcomings of the interreligious → personal status system in Lebanon, which are mainly the infringement of human rights and freedoms and the reduction of legal certainty. → India could to a certain extent achieve that goal through the enactment of the Special Marriage Act of 9 October 1954 (<http://keralaregistration.gov.in/pearlpublic/downloads/The%20Special%20Marriage%20Act.pdf?tok=49sddh3ss34ff4>). This Act enables those Indians who are normally subjected to their respective religious laws (Christian, Hindu, Muslim and Parsi laws) to perform a civil marriage. It is also possible to register the marriage under this Act after it was celebrated according to religious law. Marriages concluded or registered under this Act are subjected to particular secular post-divorce remedies. Inheritance issues are regulated for these marriages according to the civil Indian Succession Act of 1925 (Indian Gazette Part IV of 10 October 1925, 69). The core aspect of this innovation is that it allows interreligious and inter-caste marriages. In opposition to other countries with a personal law system like Israel and Lebanon, India provides its citizens with the opportunity to marry outside the limits of their respective religious communities, without being obliged to renounce their faith and without being obliged to leave the country to marry abroad. These achievements stand as a goal that Indonesia, unlike India, was not able to realize. Indonesia, with the largest Muslim population in the world, is formally grounded upon 'the belief in the One and Only God'. Interreligious law was purposely kept vague and incomplete. There are no regulations governing interreligious marriage, although this phenomenon is common in the Indonesian society. The civil state tribunals have tried to find some pragmatic solutions for this problem as well as linked questions. For instance, the Indonesian Supreme court stated in the *Jazilah* case (*Jazilah v Subandiyah Ammar Asof, etc, Varia Peradilan* [1999] Supreme Court of Indonesia, case No 51 K/AG, Year XVI No 192, September 2001, 85–93 (in Indonesian)) that Christian parties could inherit from their Muslim relatives and justified this solution with a new interpretation of Islamic law.

2. Alternatives avoiding the application of state-sponsored religious laws

It seems that the interpersonal system of law can lead, in certain aspects, to the infringement upon individual rights and freedoms as enshrined in the constitutions of the examined countries. The Lebanese constitution, for instance, guarantees the freedom of religion and conscience. Nevertheless, subjecting the members of a religious community to their religious laws without giving them any possibility of opting out is considered by secular human rights activists a violation of their freedom of religion. As already mentioned, religious laws tend to assure the cohesion of the community, and this aim thus takes priority over individual rights such as the right to choose one's spouse freely. Very often, the religious laws also contain regulations which violate the equality of the citizens on the basis of religious or gender considerations. Because of these shortcomings, members of the religious communities attempt to avoid the coercive nature of interreligious law. They are often backed in this regard by the judiciary. For instance, Israeli courts recognize the institution of reputed spouses. These are couples who live together as husband and wife without being formally married and who enjoy similar rights to those derived from the status of marriage.

Couples marry abroad to avoid the religious barriers imposed on their marriage in their own country. The status of these marriages is, however, not always clear when they go back home. Others might undertake a conversion of convenience in order to be subjected to the most favourable status.

3. Revival of interreligious law

Despite the numerous shortcomings of interreligious law, in nearly all parts of the world we can observe a revival of interreligious law or at least of claims of establishing or of extending it.

In Africa, for instance, issues of religious legal pluralism have dominated the debates on constitutional reforms which have been undertaken in the last decade. This may be explained by the increase of sectarian violence in Sub-Saharan Africa. In Kenya, the new constitution adopted by referendum on 4 August 2010 recognizes the right of Islamic tribunals, so-called Khadi courts, to deal with disputes among Muslims about issues of → marriage, divorce (→ Divorce and personal separation) and → succession on the basis of Islamic law. With this reform the jurisdiction of the Khadi courts was extended to the whole territory of Kenya, whereas it was previously limited to the territory of the former Protectorate. The new Kenyan constitution seems to foster religious legal pluralism as it specifies that the provisions on equality and freedom from discrimination in the enjoyment of fundamental rights should be 'qualified to the extent strictly necessary for the application of Muslim law before the Khadi courts to persons who confess the Muslim religion, in matters relating to personal status, marriage, divorce or inheritance'. In addition, it seems that the state even intends to extend the scope of religious legal pluralism in the future. In fact, § 45(4) of the constitution enshrines the right of the parliament to recognize 'marriages concluded under any tradition, or system of religious, personal or family law'.

In South Africa, customary law has been fully recognized in the post-apartheid era as having the same status as Roman-Dutch common law. The Muslim community there has been advocating for the recognition of Islamic marriages and Islamic personal law.

The process of drafting the Muslim Marriages Bill has been very long and difficult. The bill is presently laid before the parliament for discussion. Nevertheless, Islamic marriages have been recognized since the end of April 2014.

IMEN GALLALA-ARNDT

Literature

Najwa Al-Qattan, 'Dhimmis in the Muslim Court: Legal Autonomy and Religious Discrimination' (1999) 31 *International Journal of Middle Eastern Studies* 429; Geoffrey Wilson Bartholomew, 'Private Interpersonal Law' (1952) 1 ICLQ 325; Maurits Berger, 'Secularizing Interreligious Law in Egypt' (2005) 12/3 *Islamic Law and Society* 394; Talia Einhorn, *Private international law in Israel* (2nd edn, Wolters Kluwer 2012); A Kessmat Elgeddawy, *Relations entre systèmes confessionnel et laique en droit international privé* (Dalloz 1971); Winifred Kamau, 'Law, Pluralism and the Family in Kenya: Beyond Bifurcation of Formal Law and Custom' (2009) 23 *IJLPF* 133; Kemal Karpat, 'The Ottoman Ethnic and Confessional Legacy in the Middle East' in Milton Esman and Itamar Rabinovich (eds), *Ethnicity, Pluralism and the State in the Middle East* (Cornell University Press 1988) 35; Kurt Lipstein and Istvàn Szàszy, 'Interpersonal Conflict of Laws' in Kurt Lipstein and Istvàn Szàszy (eds), *International Encyclopedia of Comparative Law*, vol 3 (Mohr Siebeck 2011) I ch 10; Ratno Lukito, *Legal Pluralism in Indonesia* (Routledge 2013); Ilber Ortayli, *Ottoman Studies* (2nd edn, Istanbul Bilgi University Press 2007); Yüksel Sezgin, *Human Rights under State-enforced Religious Family Laws in Israel, Egypt and India* (CUP 2013); Klaus Wähler, *Interreligiöses Kollisionsrecht im Bereich privatrechtlicher Rechtsbeziehungen* (Heymann 1978).

Ius gentium

I. The notion of *ius gentium* in the ancient sources

Ius gentium is a term of Roman law with several connotations. The oldest source for it is Cicero, *De officiis* 3, 17, 69:

> Hoc quamquam video propter depravationem consuetudinis neque more turpe haberi neque aut lege sanciri aut iure civili, tamen naturae lege sanctum est. Societas est enim (quod etsi saepe dictum est, dicendum est tamen saepius), latissimi quidem quae pateat, omnium inter omnes, interior eorum, qui eiusdem gentis sint, propior eorum, qui eiusdem civitatis. Itaque maiores aliud ius gentium, aliud ius civile esse voluerunt.

Owing to the low ebb of public sentiment, such a method of procedure, I find, is neither by custom accounted morally wrong nor forbidden either by statute or by civil law; nevertheless it is forbidden by the law of nature. For there is a bond of fellowship – although I have often made this statement, I must still repeat it again and again – which has the very widest application, uniting all men together and each to each. This bond of union is closer between those who belong to the same nation, and more intimate still between those who are citizens of the same city state. It is for this reason that our forefathers chose to understand one thing by the universal law (*ius gentium*) and another by the civil law. (Translation: *Walter Miller* with minor changes)

Here *ius gentium* is used on the one hand in opposition to *lex naturae* and on the other hand in opposition to *ius civile*. The latter distinction between *ius gentium* and *ius civile* is apparently already older than *Cicero* himself, because he invokes his *maiores* to underpin the importance of this distinction, although given the scarcity of Latin sources before *Cicero* we cannot trace this distinction back with certainty. For *Cicero* the *ius gentium* means the part of the law which is applicable to all people, while the *ius civile* is a special extra set of rules for the citizens of the city state. It is interesting that *Cicero* immediately links *ius gentium* with the notion of *bona fides* in the following § 70. Dieter Nörr has interpreted this link with the help of the history of international law in antiquity. *Nörr* supposes that the *fides publica* in international law, the basis of treaties in antiquity for the Roman republic, has in the long run found its counterpart in relations of private law based on *bona fides*, both inside a city state between the citizens, but also between foreigners and citizens (Dieter Nörr, *Die Fides im römischen Völkerrecht* (CF Müller 1991) 42 ff). *Nörr* wisely pointed out that the scarcity of sources only allows us to assume this hypothesis, while a conclusive proof is impossible.

We meet the term *ius gentium* again in the *Corpus Iuris Civilis* (about AD 530) with two different definitions, one by *Gaius* (± AD 160) and the other by *Ulpian* (± AD 210). *Ius gentium* in the *Gaius* definition refers to natural law, certainly under the spell of cosmopolitic stoic philosophy, in the very beginning of the *Institutes* of *Gaius* (1, 1). This text, which is lacking in the Veronese manuscript of the *Institutes* of *Gaius*, has been taken by the compilers of the *Digest* of *Justinian* as a fragment in the *Digest* (AD 533) 1, 1, 9.

Omnes populi qui legibus et moribus reguntur, partim suo proprio, partim communi omnium hominum iure utuntur; nam quod quisque populus ipse sibi ius constituit, id ipsius proprium est vocaturque ius civile, quasi ius proprium civitatis; quod vero naturalis ratio inter omnes homines constituit, id apud omnes populos peraeque custoditur vocaturque ius gentium, quasi quo iure omnes gentes utuntur. Populus itaque Romanus partim suo proprio, partim communi omnium hominum iure utitur. Quae singula qualia sint, suis locis proponemus.

All peoples which are ruled by laws and customs use partly their own, partly a law common to all mankind. Because what every people has determined to be their law is proper to that people and it is called their own [private] law, as if it is proper to their state. But what natural reason has determined is always respected by all peoples and it is called *ius gentium*, as if it is the law used by all peoples. Therefore, the Roman people uses partly their own, partly the common law. What the content of this law is, we shall explain at the proper place.

According to *Gaius*, Roman citizens apply general legal norms stemming from *ius gentium* and a supplementary set of rules from *ius civile*. *Ius gentium* is somewhat differently structured by *Ulpian* (*Digest of Justinian* (AD 533) 1, 1, 1, 3–4).

Ius naturale est quod natura omnia animalia docuit: nam ius istud non humani generis proprium sed omnium animalium quae in terra quae in mari nascuntur avium quoque commune est. Hinc descendit maris atque feminae coniunctio, quam nos matrimonium appellamus, hinc liberorum procreatio, hinc educatio: videmus etenim cetera quoque animalia, feras etiam istius iuris peritia censeri. 4. Ius gentium est, quo gentes humanae utuntur. Quod a naturali recedere facile intellegere licet, quia illud omnibus animalibus, hoc solis hominibus inter se commune sit.

Natural law is what nature teaches to all animals, for this law is not proper to mankind, but also proper to all animals which are born on the earth and in the sea and to birds. From this law the union between men and women is derived which we call → marriage, from this law stems the procreation of children, from this law stems the education. For we do see that all remaining animals, wild animals included, are supposed to have knowledge of this law. 4. *Ius gentium* is the law used by human beings. That this law differs from natural law is easily understandable, because the latter is common to all animals, the former is common to mankind only.

Possibly *Ulpian* also had the divisions of *Cicero* in mind, because he distinguishes between *ius naturale*, *ius gentium* and *ius civile*. For *Ulpian ius gentium* refers to legal principles that are common between the different peoples, whereas *ius naturale* is spread over human beings and animals alike. Slavery, according to *Ulpian* (*Digest of Justinian* (AD 533) 1, 1, 4), belongs to *ius gentium*, not to *ius naturale*. It might be that *Ulpian* sought to reconcile Aristotelian and Stoic notions of natural law with his threefold distinction (Laurens C Winkel, 'Einige Bemerkungen über ius naturale und ius gentium' in Martin Josef Schermaier and Végh Zoltán (eds), *Ius est ars boni et aequi. Festschrift für Wolfgang Waldstein zum 65. Geburtstag* (Franz Steiner Verlag 1993) 443–9). From this complicated story it is now more understandable that *ius gentium* can occasionally also refer to international law as is the case in *Digest of Justinian* (AD 533) 50, 7, 18.

II. *Ius gentium* and the relation with early forms of private international law

The most important meaning of *ius gentium* from now on refers to common commercial practice in the Mediterranean area in antiquity. This last meaning could also be relevant for the history of private international law in antiquity (→ private international law, history of). While the very existence of private international law in that period is contested, there are decisive arguments in its favour. However, strong voices were heard to deny its very existence in antiquity, one of which was *Hans Julius Wolff*, an expert in ancient Greek law, although the opposite opinion once advocated by *Hans Lewald* is now more or less prevailing (Hans Lewald, 'Conflits des lois dans le monde grec et romain' (1959) 5 Labeo 334–69; abbreviated German version in Erich Berneker (ed), *Zur griechischen Rechtsgeschichte* (Wissenschaftliche Buchgesellschaft 1968) 666–90). Another defendant of the existence of private international law was *Fritz Sturm* (see also Philippe Gauthier, *Symbola. Les étrangers et la justice dans les cités grecques* (Université de Nancy II 1972)). According to *Sturm* several passages in *Gaius' Institutes* can be read as referring to conflict of laws and to the awareness of differences between several legal systems.

This applies to the Greek and Roman world alike. One argument in favour of private international law can be found in the many treaties in antiquity in which foreigners are allowed to have access to local judges in another city state in the Mediterranean area. This practice is well documented for the Greek Eastern Mediterranean area, but there are arguments that in the Western part such treaties have also existed (Laurens C Winkel, 'Rechtshilfeverträge – Parallele Entwicklungen in Griechenland und Rom?' in Holger Altmeppen and others (eds), *Festschrift für Rolf Knütel zum 70. Geburtstag* (CF Müller 2009) 1449 ff). It is plausible to state that through the conclusion of such treaties (in German: *Rechtshilfeverträge* or *Rechtsgewährungsverträge*) commercial relations between parties of different city states can be governed not by local legislation, but by common commercial rules, in Roman terminology *ius gentium*. A counter-argument could be that the applicable law is rarely indicated in these treaties. This led *Hans Julius Wolff* (Hans Julius Wolff, *Das Problem der Konkurrenz von Rechtsordnungen in der Antike* (CH Beck 1979)) to his opinion that there was no articulated systematic approach to private international law in antiquity. For him an indication of the applicable law is essential for a notion of private international law. However, this argument has been challenged by *Nörr* in his review (Dieter Nörr, 'Review of Hans Julius Wolff: Das Problem der Konkurrenz von Rechtsordnungen' (1981) 98 *Zeitschrift der Savigny Stiftung für Rechtsgeschichte, romanistische Abteilung* 406–11; Dieter Nörr, *Historiae iuris Antiqui II* (Keip 2003) 1411*–16*). *Nörr* stresses the importance of the → *lex fori*, also in antiquity. Indeed, in the surviving treaties of mutual legal assistance there are no direct references to common commercial practice, but this could be explained by the fact that in the surviving treaties most references are made to delictual rather than contractual liability, although given the still primitive systematization of obligations in early Roman and Greek law this cannot be a decisive argument against the existence of a common commercial practice in Greece and in Rome.

A major change in the Roman world was the introduction of the role of *praetor peregrinus* in 242 BC. It is debated what his jurisdiction entailed precisely: was he only competent for litigation between *peregrini*, foreigners in Rome entitled to legal protection, or was he also competent for litigation in a dispute between a Roman citizen and a *peregrinus*? We do not know the definite answer (Max Kaser, *Ius gentium* (Böhlau 1993) 129; Laurens C Winkel, 'Some Thoughts on the *formulae ficticiae* of Citizenship in Gaius, 4, 37: A Form of Reception?' in Andrew Barrows, David Johnston and Reinhard Zimmermann (eds), *Judge and Jurist: Studies in Memory of Lord Alan Rodger* (OUP 2013) 299–308). We do know anyhow that many contractual relations are considered by Roman jurists of the time of classical Roman law as belonging to *ius gentium*. Among them the four consensual contracts, the unilateral formal oral agreement (*stipulatio*), loan of money (*mutuum*) and the contract of safe keeping (*depositum*) and loan (*commodatum*). Kaser (Max Kaser, *Ius gentium* (Böhlau 1993) 118) supposes that we only have an imprecise list of contractual relations based on *ius gentium* in our sources and mentions some more possible examples. According to him, *ius gentium* remains Roman law being the applicable law promulgated in the edict of the *praetor peregrinus*, a Roman magistrate. Wieacker (Franz Wieacker, *Römische Rechtsgeschichte*, vol 1 (Beck 1988) 443 ff) has a more differentiated opinion. Only on a formal level is *ius gentium* Roman, substantially it is not exclusively Roman.

After the promulgation of the *Constitutio Antoniniana* (AD 212) in which citizenship for nearly all free inhabitants was granted, the practical importance of *ius gentium* is certainly diminishing, although the postclassical jurist Hermogenian (± AD 290) still uses this notion. The 'rainbow' structure of the different ideas behind *ius gentium* is clearly visible in his text:

> *Digest of Justinian* (AD 533) 1, 1, 5: *Ex hoc iure gentium introducta bella, discretae gentes, regna condita, dominia distincta, agris termini positi, aedificia collocata, commercium, emptiones venditiones, locationes conductiones, obligationes introductae sunt.*
>
> As a consequence of this *ius gentium*, wars were introduced, nations differentiated, kingdoms founded, properties individuated, estate boundaries settled, buildings put up, and commerce established, including contracts of buying and selling and letting and hiring, except for certain contractual elements established through *ius civile*.

Max Kaser (Max Kaser, *Ius gentium* (Böhlau 1993) 49) considers this text as a proof that postclassical legal scholarship no longer has the quality of the classical period. In this text, however, there are references to institutions of what we in modern times call international law. Ambivalent are the parts *regna condita* and *dominia distincta*, which can be interpreted according to a perspective of international law and a perspective of private law. The text goes on to invoke instances of exclusively private law, where we see references to two consensual contracts – *emptio venditio* and *locatio/conductio* – considered by earlier Roman jurists as belonging to *ius gentium* (see for *emptio venditio*: Julius Paulus (a Roman jurist active in the first half of the 3rd century AD) *Digest of Justinian* (AD 533) 18, 11, 2; for *locatio/conductio*: Julius Paulus, *Digest of Justinian* (AD 533) 19, 2, 1). Most interesting is the word *commercium*, as this is the word used for the right of inhabitants of those foreign city states that had acquired the right to establish legally protected commercial relations with Rome since the middle of the 3rd century BC (see for the early history Luigi Capogrossi Colognesi, '"Ius commercii", "conubium", "civitas sine suffragio". Le origini del diritto internazionale privato e la romanizzazione delle comunità latino-campane' in Alessandro Corbino (ed), *Le Strade del Potere, Maiestas populi romani, Imperium, coercitio, commercium* (Libreria Editrice Torre 1994) 3–64). One could say that Hermogenian even has historical insights in this respect, an uncommon feature among Roman jurists apart from *Gaius* and *Pomponius*. Parts of the text of Hermogenian have been adopted by medieval writers, eg *Isidorus of Sevilla* (560–636):

> Etym 5, 7: *Ius gentium est sedium occupatio, edificatio, munitio, bella, captivitates, servitutes, postliminia, federa pacis, induciae, legatorum non violandorum religio, conubia inter alienigenas prohibita. Hoc inde ius gentium appellatur, quia eo iure omnes fere gentes utuntur.*
>
> The law of nations concerns the occupation of territory, building, fortification, wars, captivities, enslavements, the right of return, treaties of peace, truces, the pledge not to molest embassies, the prohibition of marriages between different races. And it is called the 'law of nations' (*ius gentium*) because nearly all nations (*gentes*) use it.

This text was incorporated in the *Decretum Gratiani* (Distinctio I canon 9) composed around 1140 and in the *Summa Theologiae* of *Thomas Aquinas* (Theo Mayer-Maly, 'Isidor

– Gratian – Thomas: Stationen einer allgemeinen Rechtslehre' (1994) 80 Zeitschrift der Savigny Stiftung für Rechtsgeschichte, kanonistische Abteilung 490–500). This wide notion of *ius gentium* continued to play a role also after the further development of commercial relations in the Mediterranean area and in other parts of Europe. Slowly *ius gentium* can be considered as referring to basic rules of commercial practice. It is significant in this respect, as Wieacker has pointed out (Franz Wieacker, 'Historische Bedingungen und Paradigmen supranationaler Privatrechtsordnungen' in Herbert Bernstein, Ulrich Drobnig and Hein Kötz (eds), *Festschrift für Konrad Zweigert zum 70. Geburtstag* (Mohr 1981) 575–93; Franz Wieacker, *Ausgewählte Schriften, vol 2 – Theorie des Rechts und der Rechtsgewinnung* (Metzner 1983) 242–58, especially 247), that the *lex Rhodia* on maritime law was transmitted to the West in a treatise of Byzantine law. This was considered a general rule for commercial practice in Europe. Moreover, *Penna* (Dafni Penna, *The Byzantine Imperial Acts to Venice, Pisa and Genova, 10th–12th Centuries: A Comparative Legal Study* (Eleven International Publishing 2012)) has given an overview of the legal basis of the commercial relations between Venice, Genova and Pisa on one hand and the Byzantine Empire on the other hand. Although *Penna* has not investigated concrete individual cases and disputes, her research is a first step in searching for common legal rules for commercial transactions in the Middle Ages. It might very well be that the notion of *ius gentium* as referring to legal practice is reviving in the Middle Ages, but the *Glossa Ordinaria* by *Accursius* (13th century) does not devote special attention to *ius gentium* in the gloss on *Digest of Justinian* (AD 533) 1, 1, 1, 4. Following this train of thought, some scholars maintain that *ius gentium* is kind of a predecessor of the → *lex mercatoria*, the latter a term with no basis in historical sources in the Middle Ages, so that then *ius gentium* would refer mainly to common commercial practice. The proof of this hypothesis is not easy. We only have fragmentary knowledge of medieval commercial practice, mainly in the form of medieval legislation (*Consolato del Mar* (possibly in part written already in the 11th century, but restated in the first half of the 14th century), *Rôles d'Oléron* (1160), *Siete Partidas* (± 1260), see *Wieacker* (Franz Wieacker, 'Historische Bedingungen und Paradigmen supranationaler Privatrechtsordnungen' in Herbert Bernstein, Ulrich Drobnig and Hein Kötz (eds), *Festschrift für Konrad Zweigert zum 70. Geburtstag* (Mohr 1981) 575–93; Franz Wieacker, *Ausgewählte Schriften, vol 2 – Theorie des Rechts und der Rechtsgewinnung* (Metzner 1983) 242–58, especially 251)). Therefore, the hypothesis of the roots of *lex mercatoria* in *ius gentium* cannot be more than likely and acceptable.

III. *Ius gentium* between private international law and public international law

In quite another way, however, *ius gentium* again became important for the legal basis of the establishment of commercial relations in the 16th century. Francesco de Vitoria (± 1480–1546), Professor of Theology at the University of Salamanca, lectured on the problem of the 'just war' waged by the Conquistadores. He developed the theory of just war on both sides, but according to him the Spanish conquerors even had an objectively just cause for war. He considered the freedom of establishing commercial relations in the Americas a part of universal *ius gentium* which even could be imposed to people with a different culture. This appears from the following text:

> *Relectio de Indis*, III, 4: *Et quidem multa hic videntur procedere ex iure gentium, quod, quia derivatur sufficienter ex iure naturali, manifestam vim habet ad dandum ius et obligandum. Et, dato quod non semper derivetur ex iure naturali, satis videtur esse consensus maioris partis totius orbis, maxime pro bono communi omnium. Si enim, post prima tempora creati orbis aut reparati post diluvium, maior pars hominum constituerit, ut legati ubique essent inviolabiles, ut mare esset commune, ut bello capti essent servi, et hoc ita expediret, ut hospites non exigerentur, certe hoc haberet vim, etiam aliis repugnantibus.*

And, indeed, there are many things in this connection which issue from the law of nations, which, because it has a sufficient derivation from natural law, is clearly capable of conferring rights and creating obligations. And even if we grant that it is not always derived from natural law, yet there exists clearly enough a consensus of the greater part of the world, especially in behalf of the common good of all. For if after the early days of the creation of the world or its recovery from the flood the majority of mankind decided that ambassadors should everywhere be reckoned inviolable and that the sea should be common and that prisoners of war should be made slaves, and, if this, namely, that strangers should not be driven out, were deemed to be a desirable principle, it would certainly have the force of law, even though the rest of mankind objected thereto. (Translation John P Pawley Bate, *The Classics of International Law* (Carnegie Institute 1916))

The opinion of *Vitoria* has its basis in Roman law, especially in the quoted text of *Hermogenian*, where the word *commercium* is important. Elsewhere we have sought to show a link with the modern doctrine of the sources of international law as was eventually laid down in art 38 of the Statute of the International Court of Justice (of 26 June 1945, 15 UNTS 355), where legal principles recognized by civilized nations are – alongside treaty law and customary law – a source of international law (Laurens C Winkel, 'The Peace Treaties of Westphalia as an Instance of the Reception of Roman Law' in Randall Lesaffer (ed), *Peace Treaties and International Law in European History* (CUP 2004) 222 ff). Following this idea, some scholars (eg Franz Wieacker, 'Historische Bedingungen und Paradigmen supranationaler Privatrechtsordnungen' in Herbert Bernstein, Ulrich Drobnig and Hein Kötz (eds), *Festschrift für Konrad Zweigert zum 70. Geburtstag* (Mohr 1981) 575–93; Franz Wieacker, *Ausgewählte Schriften, vol 2 – Theorie des Rechts und der Rechtsgewinnung* (Metzner 1983) 242–58, especially 251 ff) maintain, albeit with great caution, that *ius gentium* is a predecessor of the *lex mercatoria*, the latter a term with no basis in historical sources in the Middle Ages, whereby the continuity with *ius gentium* would be established with reference to common commercial practice. This is only possible when *ius gentium* in antiquity is not conceived purely as Roman law!

In conclusion we can say that *ius gentium* in its various connotations in the history of legal ideas can explain certain features of the history of private international law and its link with the history of public international law (→ Private international law, history of), whereby *ius gentium* since at least the 17th century has become the technical term for international law. The English 'law of nations' is merely the literary translation of *ius gentium*.

LAURENS WINKEL

Literature

Max Kaser, *Ius gentium* (older literature is quoted there; Böhlau 1993); Hans Lewald, 'Conflits des lois dans le monde grec et romain' (1959) 5 Labeo 334; Filip De Ly, *De Lex Mercatoria – Inleiding op de studie van het transnationaal handelsrecht* (Maklu 1989) especially 106 ff; Theo Mayer-Maly, 'Das ius gentium bei den späteren Klassikern' (1983) 34 IVRA 91; Theo Mayer-Maly, 'Isidor – Gratian – Thomas: Stationen einer allgemeinen Rechtslehre' (1994) 80 Zeitschrift der Savigny Stiftung für Rechtsgeschichte, kanonische Abteilung 490; Dieter Nörr, 'Review of Hans Julius Wolff: Das Problem der Konkurrenz von Rechtsordnungen' (1981) 98 *Zeitschrift der Savigny Stiftung für Rechtsgeschichte, romanistische Abteilung* 406; Dieter Nörr, *Historiae iuris Antiqui II* (Keip 2003) 1411*–16*; Dafni Penna, *The Byzantine Imperial Acts to Venice, Pisa and Genova, 10th–12th Centuries: A Comparative Legal Study* (Eleven International Publishing 2012); Fritz Sturm, 'Kollisionsrecht in Gaius 3.129?' (1978) 29 IVRA 151; Fritz Sturm, 'Unerkannte Zeugnisse römischen Kollisionsrechts' in Rudolf Strasser (ed), *Festschrift Fritz Schwind zum 65. Geburtstag. Rechtsgeschichte, Rechtsvergleichung, Rechtspolitik* (Manz 1978) 323; P Clementius a Vlissingen, *De evolutione definitionis iuris gentium* (Romae 1940); Herbert Wagner, *Studien zur allgemeinen Rechtslehre des Gaius* (Terra 1978); Franz Wieacker, 'Historische Bedingungen und Paradigmen supranationaler Privatrechtsordnungen' in Herbert Bernstein, Ulrich Drobnig and Hein Kötz (eds), *Festschrift für Konrad Zweigert zum 70. Geburtstag* (Mohr 1981) 575; Franz Wieacker, *Ausgewählte Schriften, vol 2 – Theorie des Rechts und der Rechtsgewinnung* (Metzner 1983) 242; Franz Wieacker, *Römische Rechtsgeschichte*, vol 1 (Beck 1988); Laurens C Winkel, 'Einige Bemerkungen über ius naturale und ius gentium' in Martin Josef Schermaier and Végh Zoltán (eds), *Ius est ars boni et aequi. Festschrift für Wolfgang Waldstein zum 65. Geburtstag* (Franz Steiner Verlag 1993) 443; Laurens C Winkel, 'Quelques remarques sur les traités d'assistance juridique et sur l'existence du droit international privé dans l'Antiquité' in Jean-François Gerkens (ed), *Mélanges Fritz Sturm* (Editions Juridiques de l'Université de Liège 1999) 431; Laurens C Winkel, 'The Peace Treaties of Westphalia as an Instance of the Reception of Roman Law' in Randall Lesaffer (ed), *Peace Treaties and International Law in European History* (CUP 2004) 222; Laurens C Winkel, 'Rechtshilfeverträge – Parallele Entwicklungen in Griechenland und Rom?' in Holger Altmeppen and others (eds), *Festschrift für Rolf Knütel zum 70. Geburtstag* (CF Müller 2009) 1449; Laurens C Winkel, 'Some Thoughts on the *formulae ficticiae* of Citizenship in Gaius, 4,37: A Form of Reception?' in Andrew Barrows, David Johnston and Reinhard Zimmermann (eds), *Judge and Jurist: Studies in Memory of Lord Alan Rodger* (OUP 2013) 299; Hans Julius Wolff, *Das Problem der Konkurrenz von Rechtsordnungen in der Antike* (CH Beck 1979).

Jurisdiction, contracts and torts

In civil law countries and in uniform texts elaborated under the influence of civilian concepts, jurisdiction in contracts and → torts is frequently dealt with by way of specific provisions. Rules of this kind are harder to find in common law systems, where proceedings are often classified for jurisdictional purposes according to different criteria (actions *in rem* as opposed to actions *in personam* etc), and jurisdiction is mostly asserted on the ground of factors, or tests ('minimum contacts' etc), that are not intended to apply exclusively, or specifically, to contracts or torts.

In this entry, reference will be made primarily to the Brussels I Regulation (recast) (Regulation (EU) No 1215/2012 of the European Parliament and of the Council of 12 December 2012 on jurisdiction and the recognition and enforcement of judgments in civil and commercial matters (recast), [2012] OJ L 351/1; → Brussels I (Convention and Regulation)) on jurisdiction and the recognition and enforcement of judgments in → civil and commercial matters, which recast the Brussels I Regulation (Regulation (EC) No 44/2001 of 22 December 2000 on jurisdiction and the recognition and enforcement of judgments in civil and commercial matters, [2001] OJ L 12/1). The Brussels I Regulation for its part replaced the Brussels Convention of 1968 (Brussels Convention of 27 September 1968 on jurisdiction and the enforcement of judgments in civil and commercial matters, [1972] OJ L 299/32, consolidated version, [1998] OJ C 27/1). The focus will be on two rules, almost left unchanged by the recast, that each establish a special head of jurisdiction 'in matters relating to a contract' (art 7(1) Brussels I Regulation (recast), corresponding to art 5(1) of the former text (Brussels I Regulation) and to art 5(1) of the parallel → Lugano Convention of 2007) and 'in matters relating to tort, delict or quasi-delict' (art 7(2) Brussels I Regulation (recast), formerly art 5(3) Brussels I Regulation, identical to art 5(3) of the Lugano Convention). National provisions, from European and non-European countries, will only be briefly considered.

I. The rationale of special rules of jurisdiction in contracts and torts

Contractual matters and matters relating to torts are traditionally regarded as matters the jurisdictional treatment of which may be conveniently provided by special rules, designed to reflect the peculiar features of the subject matter of the litigation.

1. The premise: the localization of the matter as a key to determining jurisdiction

In the civilian tradition, issues of jurisdiction are normally decided through *ex ante* connecting factors aimed at localizing the relationship at stake. Contractual and non-contractual obligations (→ Contractual obligations) may in fact be situated in one place or in a reasonably limited number of places. Although obligations are incorporeal and should thus be considered to have no locality, some visible phenomena exist to which the essence of obligations can be attached (Friedrich Carl von Savigny, *System des heutigen römischen Rechts*, vol 8 (Veit und Comp 1849) 206 f). Since obligations arise out of, and are also fulfilled by, visible facts, it is generally accepted that these facts may be referred to for the purpose of localizing a particular obligation with a view to determining either the applicable law or the court with jurisdiction.

This approach seems likely to lead to a rational and fair allocation of jurisdiction. The court designated on the grounds mentioned above is, in principle, a court with which the obligation features a significant connection and one whose jurisdiction is normally consistent with the reasonable expectations of the parties: as a matter of fact, the parties, based on the legal ties existing between them, should not be surprised to be sued in one of the places where the legal ties in question have left, or are due to leave, a tangible and recordable trace (Giuseppe Pisanelli, 'Sulla competenza' in Pascale Stanislao Mancini, Giuseppe Pisanelli and Antonio Scialoja (eds), *Commentario al codice di procedura civile per gli Stati Sardi* (Unione Tipografico-Editrice Torinese 1855) 501 f). Further reasons justify the conferral of jurisdiction on a court specified in accordance with the said standards. Procedural proximity and efficiency are of special importance in this connection. Making jurisdiction contingent on the localization of a significant element of the relationship in dispute is a way to ensure that litigation takes place where evidence is most likely to be found, and – more generally – where proceedings are likely to be efficiently administered.

2. Jurisdiction at the locus solutionis, at the locus contractus and at the locus delicti

Building on these assumptions, present-day rules on international jurisdiction in contracts usually refer to the place where the obligation is expected to be fulfilled (*locus destinatae solutionis*) or the place where the contract has been concluded (*locus contractus*), whereas torts are usually situated at the place where the tort was committed (*locus delicti*).

In contracts, the → place of performance represents the preferred reference. Pursuant to art 7(1)(a) of the Brussels I Regulation (recast), a person domiciled in a Member State may be sued in another Member State 'in the courts for the place of performance of the obligation in question'. The *locus solutionis* is similarly relevant to jurisdiction under the national provisions of various countries, including → Switzerland (art 113 of the Federal Act on Private international law (Bundesgesetz über das Internationale Privatrecht of 18 December 1987, 1988 BBl I 5, as amended)), → Brazil (art 21(II) of the New Code of Civil Procedure (Código de Processo Civil, Lei No 13.105 of 16 March 2015)) and → Japan (art 3-3(i) of the Code of Civil Procedure (Act No 109 of 26 June 1996, as amended)).

The place of contracting is an admissible basis of jurisdiction in relatively few countries. It is often envisaged alongside the *locus solutionis*. For example, under art 96 of the Belgian Private international law Act (Wet houdende het Wetboek von international privaatrecht/Code de droit international privé of 16 July 2004, BS 27 July 2004, pp 57344, 57366), Belgian courts are entitled to hear a claim in contract both when the obligation in dispute has been undertaken in → Belgium and, regardless of the place of contracting, when its performance is to take place in the country. The place of contracting and the place of (non-)performance of a contract are also relevant, albeit in peculiar terms, to the jurisdiction of English courts. Pursuant to Rule 6.36 of the Rules of Civil Procedure (1998 No 3132 (L.17)), taken in conjunction with the corresponding Practice Directions, the claimant may be authorized to sue a foreign resident before an English court, *inter alia*, where the contract in question was made in England or where the complained breach was committed there (Pippa Rogerson, *Collier's Conflict of Laws* (4th edn, CUP 2013) 152 ff).

As regards torts, art 7(2) of the Brussels I Regulation (recast) provides that claims against a person domiciled in a Member State may be brought in a different Member State before 'the courts for the place where the harmful event occurred or may occur'. The *locus delicti* represents in the majority of civil law countries the key → connecting factor in this area (either alone or coupled with other elements).

The expression 'place of the tort' may be understood in different ways, depending on whether reference is made to the facts that gave rise to the damage, to the ensuing damage or both. The prevailing view, today, is that reference may in fact conveniently be made to the two places. 'Ubiquity', as the doctrine is called, has found explicit support in some texts (see, eg art 129(2) of the Swiss Federal Act on Private international law). Under other legal instruments, it has rather been introduced by way of judicial interpretation. This is what happened with the rule now enshrined in art 7(2) of the Brussels I Regulation (recast), following the judgment of the European Court of Justice in *Mines de potasse d'Alsace* (Case 21/76 *Handelskwekerij GJ Bier BV v Mines de potasse d'Alsace SA* [1976] ECR 1735).

3. The further specialization of rules on jurisdiction in contracts and torts

Contracts and torts display a variety of features. Along the lines of a well-known trend experienced with conflict-of-law provisions (Julio Diego González Campos, 'Diversification, spécialisation, flexibilisation et matérialisation des règles de droit international privé' (2000) 297 Rec. des Cours 156 ff), rules on jurisdiction, too, are undergoing a process of specialization, with particular solutions being elaborated for particular types of contracts and torts.

Under the Brussels I Regulation (recast), the rule in art 7(1) is inapplicable to disputes over contracts concluded by consumers (within the meaning of art 17) and individual contracts of employment (art 20). These matters, as well as matters relating to insurance, are the object of self-standing regimes, intended to afford special protection to the weaker party. Some national legislations similarly include special provisions on consumer and labour matters (see, eg art 3–4 of the Japanese Code of Civil Procedure and arts 114 and 115 of the Swiss Federal Act on Private international law).

In the area of → torts, special rules may be found in the Brussels I Regulation (recast) (see art 7(7), relating to disputes concerning the payment of remuneration claimed in respect of the → salvage of a cargo or freight), as well as in national legislation (see, eg art 130 of the Swiss Federal Act on Private international law on jurisdiction over matters relating to damage caused by the operation of a nuclear installation or the transportation of nuclear substances). Texts adopted to regulate special classes of torts (substantively) also include, in some cases, rules of jurisdiction applicable to claims relating to such torts (see, eg art 79 Regulation (EU) 2016/679 of the European Parliament and of the Council of 27 April 2016 on the protection of natural persons with regard to the processing of personal data and on the free movement of such data, and repealing Directive 95/46/EC (General Data Protection Regulation) [2016] OJ L 119/1).

II. The place of special rules on contracts and torts within the jurisdictional system to which they belong

Special rules dealing with jurisdiction in contracts and torts are generally but one element of a wider body of provisions governing jurisdiction in → civil and commercial matters. The overall layout of the concerned jurisdictional regime is relevant to the interpretation and operation of special rules in a number of ways.

1. Special rules on contracts and torts vis-à-vis rules of general jurisdiction

The place of performance (or the place of contracting, where relevant) and the place of a tort are normally meant to serve as concurrent heads of jurisdiction, supplementing a general rule almost invariably based on the domicile (→ Domicile, habitual residence and establishment), or the residence, of the defendant.

Under national rules, the special fora for contractual and tortious matters are usually placed on the same footing as the general forum. By contrast, in the Brussels I Regulation (recast), the rule pursuant to which 'persons domiciled in a Member State shall . . . be sued in the courts of that Member State' (art 4(1), corresponding to art 2(1) of the previous text), embodies the cornerstone of the jurisdictional regime. According to a frequent statement of the ECJ, it is only by way of derogation from that principle that the Regulation provides for special rules of jurisdiction for cases in which the defendant may be sued elsewhere (see, eg Case C-98/06 *Freeport plc v Olle Arnoldsson* [2007] ECR I-8319). Special heads of jurisdiction must thus be interpreted restrictively (see, among other judgments, Case C-147/12 *ÖFAB, Östergötlands Fastigheter AB v Frank Koot and Evergreen Investments BV* [2013] OJ C 260/14; see however Case C-27/02 *Petra Engler v Janus Versand GmbH* [2005] ECR I-481, at para 48, acknowledging, in light of previous cases, that the concept of 'matters relating to contract' does not systematically require a narrow interpretation).

2. Special rules on contracts and torts vis-à-vis exclusive fora

In claims coming within the scope of rules of exclusive jurisdiction, special rules in contracts and torts have no role to play. By definition, the former are meant to designate the courts entitled to hear certain claims to the exclusion of all other courts. As such, they are particularly significant within uniform regimes, where they can effectively perform both the task of conferring jurisdiction upon the courts of a given country and that of preventing the courts of other countries from hearing the matter.

Under the Brussels I Regulation (recast), rules of special jurisdiction may be displaced in two scenarios: when the subject matter of the dispute is one falling in the scope of application of art 24 (art 22 of the Brussels I Regulation) and, when the parties have performed an explicit prorogation of jurisdiction by agreeing, under art 25, that exclusive jurisdiction should lie with a given court (or the courts) of a Member State.

Various exclusive heads of jurisdiction are likely to interfere with the rules on contracts and torts. For example, disputes arising out of tenancies of → immovable property, as understood by art 24(1) Brussels I Regulation (recast), are not governed by art 7(1), although they involve relationships of a contractual nature. Article 24(1) similarly applies to claims regarding the validity of the exercise of a right of pre-emption over immovable property which produces *erga omnes* effects, no matter whether the right in question is based on a contract (Case C-438/12 *Irmengard Weber v Mechthilde Weber* [2014] OJ C 159/6).

In some instances, the articulation of special and exclusive heads of jurisdiction follows a more complex pattern. Under art 24(4) of the Brussels I Regulation (recast), jurisdiction over matters concerning the validity of patents and trademarks belongs to the courts of the Member State in which the deposit or registration of the patent or trademark has been applied for or has taken place. Based on the views expressed by the ECJ (Case C-4/03 *Gesellschaft für Antriebstechnik mbH & Co KG v Lamellen und Kupplungsbau Beteiligungs KG* [2006] ECR I-6509), the provision, as it is now drafted, explicitly clarifies that the said court possesses exclusive jurisdiction to assess the validity of the patent or trademark 'irrespective of whether the issue is raised by way of an action or as a defence'. Thus, in proceedings relating to a licence agreement concluded in respect of a patent or a trademark, or in proceedings in respect of the infringement of such patent or trademark, the court designated through art 7(1) or (2) will be unable to decide the case whenever the issue of the validity of the patent or trademark is raised merely by way of defence.

This solution only applies to proceedings within the scope of the rule on intellectual property rights. The ECJ denied that, in a basically similar situation, the rule currently embodied in art 24(2) Brussels I Regulation (recast), which contemplates an exclusive head of jurisdiction for proceedings which have as their object the validity of the decisions of organs of corporations, may prevent, in a contractual matter, the court designated under the special provision on contracts from deciding the incidental issue of the validity of the decision of a company's organ concerning the conclusion of the contract at stake (Case C-144/10 *Berliner Verkehrsbetriebe (BVG), Anstalt des öffentlichen Rechts v JPMorgan Chase Bank NA, Frankfurt Branch* [2011] OJ C 194/6).

Forum selection agreements, whenever they designate one or more courts as possessing exclusive jurisdiction, similarly prevent the application of special rules on jurisdiction. By contrast, where the agreed conferral is intended to be non-exclusive, the designated court will be entitled to hear the case along with the courts specified by the general rule and the relevant rules of special jurisdiction.

III. The material scope of the rules on jurisdiction in contracts and torts

1. Characterization – autonomous and lege fori

It is in the nature of a special provision to include a reference, more or less precisely worded, delimiting the substantive scope of application of the provision itself. When the reference in question consists of a legal notion, such as contract or tort, the issue arises, absent an explicit definition, of the legal order that should be referred to for the purpose of defining the expression in question.

Where domestic rules are involved, the point is consistently made that technical expressions used in rules on jurisdiction should be given the meaning they possess in the legal order of the forum. This is in line with the → *lex fori* approach predominantly followed with regard to characterization in the conflict of laws. The solution applies with stronger reason to cases where international jurisdiction is governed, at the national level, by rules originally intended to regulate venue in domestic cases, as in Germany and Portugal (see, eg on the notion of contractual relationship under art 29 of the German Code of Civil Procedure (Zivilprozessordnung of 5 December 2005, BGBl. I 3202, as amended), Reinhard Patzina, '§ 29 ZPO' in Wolfgang Krüger and Thomas Rauscher (eds), *Münchener Kommentar zur Zivilprozessordnung* (4th edn, CH Beck 2013) paras 19 f).

Where jurisdiction is regulated by uniform provisions, autonomous interpretation becomes the rule (→ Interpretation, autonomous). As the ECJ repeatedly asserted with respect to the Brussels Regime, uniform rules must be construed independently from national legal systems. Rather, regard is to be had to the goals of the provisions in question and their context. The latter indication must be understood to refer, in particular, to the relevant pieces of secondary legislation enacted in the field of judicial cooperation in civil matters. Thus, when determining not only the scope, but more generally the operation of the rules now included in art 7(1) and (2) of the Brussels I Regulation (recast), reference should be made to EU provisions identifying the law applicable to contractual and non-contractual obligations, ie to the Rome I (Regulation (EC) No 593/2008 of the European Parliament and of the Council of 17 June 2008 on the law applicable to contractual obligations (Rome I), [2008] OJ L 177/6;→ Rome Convention and Rome I Regulation) and → Rome II Regulations (Regulation (EC) No 864/2007 of the European Parliament and of the Council of 11 July 2007 on the law applicable to non-contractual obligations (Rome II), [2007] OJ L 199/40).

Pietro Franzina

2. The scope of the rule on contracts under the Brussels I Regime

In *Handte*, the ECJ held that the phrase 'matters relating to a contract' cannot be understood 'as covering a situation in which there is no obligation freely assumed by one party towards another' (Case C-26/91 *Jakob Handte & Co GmbH v Traitements Mécano-chimiques des Surfaces SA* [1992] ECR I-3967). The Court was concerned then with proceedings regarding the defective quality of certain goods, brought by the sub-buyer of the goods against the manufacturer. The Court found that, in the absence of a direct relationship between the parties, bringing the defendant before a court designated by reason of its proximity to the contract concluded by the claimant would run counter to the principles underlying special jurisdiction. As a means of strengthening the legal protection of persons established in Europe, the jurisdictional provisions which derogate from the rule based on the domicile of the defendant should in fact be interpreted 'in such a way as to enable a normally well-informed defendant reasonably to predict before which courts . . . he may be sued'. In substance, for an obligation to display a contractual nature, it must be an obligation that the parties have voluntarily accepted and one intended to be in force in the relationship between them, specifically.

Relying on the first prong of the test, the Court later held that actions in pre-contractual liability, in particular where the defendant is alleged to have abruptly broken off negotiations, do not constitute contractual matters and should instead be characterized as tortious. Absent an agreement of the parties, the obligation to make good the damage allegedly caused by a *mala fide* conduct could in fact derive 'only from the breach of rules of law' (Case C-334/00 *Fonderie Officine Meccaniche Tacconi SpA v Heinrich Wagner Sinto Maschinenfabrik GmbH* [2002] ECR I-7357). The judgment has led the European legislator to address the issue of the law governing → *culpa in contrahendo* in the framework of a legal instrument – the Rome II Regulation – that relates specifically to torts and other non-contractual obligations (it is worth noting, however, as a reminder of the difficulties surrounding the demarcation of contracts from torts, that the Rome II Regulation only deals with 'non-contractual obligation[s] arising out of dealings prior to the conclusion of a contract', and that, pursuant to art 12(1) Rome II Regulation, pre-contractual liability is governed, in principle, by the law 'that applies to the contract . . . had it been entered into'; see further on this topic Paul Lagarde, 'La culpa in contrahendo à la croisée des règlements communautaires' in Gabriella Venturini and Stefania Bariatti (eds), *Liber Fausto Pocar*, vol 2 (Giuffrè 2009) 583 ff).

Article 7(1) of the Brussels I Regulation (recast) applies, in principle, to all legal relationships meeting the requirements of voluntariness and privity. The rule has thus been found to be applicable to money obligations having their basis in the relationship between an association and its members, irrespective of whether the obligation in question arose simply from the act of becoming a member or from that act in conjunction with a decision of the organs (Case 34/82 *Martin Peters Bauunternehmung GmbH v Zuid Nederlandse Aannemers Vereniging* [1983] ECR 987). The applicability of the rule has likewise been upheld in the case of → contractual obligations embodied in a negotiable instrument (Case C-419/11 *Česká spořitelna, as v Gerald Feichter* [2013] OJ C 311/21), but the ECJ has clarified that in an action brought against the issuer of a bearer bond and based on the bond conditions, breach of the information and control obligations and prospectus liability, an applicant who has acquired that bond from a third party cannot invoke jurisdiction under the rule on matters relating to a contract unless it is shown that an obligation has been freely assumed by the defendant towards the plaintiff (Case C-375/13 *Harald Kolassa v Barclays Bank plc* [2015] OJ C 107/4). Obligations arising out of unilateral declarations of will are similarly deemed to be contractual, provided that they have been 'freely undertaken' towards a given person.

In principle, all proceedings relating to a legal relationship featuring the characteristics indicated above qualify as contractual matters. Thus, the court designated under art 7(1) Brussels I Regulation (recast) may hear claims relating to the performance of a contractual obligation and the relevant remedies of the creditor (see, eg Case 14/76 *A De Bloos, SPRL v Société en commandite par actions Bouyer* [1976] ECR 1497, on proceedings for the dissolution of a contract by the court on account of the breach of the obligations undertaken thereunder by the defendant), as well as claims relating to obligations arising as a consequence of the unilateral termination of a contract (Case

9/87 *SPRL Arcado v SA Haviland* [1988] ECR 1539), and claims seeking a declaration that the contract is null and void *ab initio*, or that an agreement has never been entered into by the parties. The conclusion on claims relating to nullity, annulment and non-existence of a contract rests on a combined reading of art 7(1) of the Brussels I Regulation (recast) and the Rome I Regulation (which explicitly governs conflicts of laws in connection with the existence and the validity of the contract, both formal and substantial, as well as issues relating to the legal consequences of nullity: see arts 10, 11 and 12(1)(e) Rome I Regulation). It also finds support in the judgment of the ECJ in *Effer*, according to which a national court's jurisdiction to determine questions relating to a contract 'includes the power to consider the existence of the constituent parts of the contract itself' (Case 38/81 *Effer SpA v Hans-Joachim Kantner* [1982] ECR 825).

3. The scope of the rule on torts under the Brussels I Regime

The meaning of the words that define the material scope of art 7(2) of the Brussels I Regulation (recast) may not be immediately evident. In addition to torts, reference is made to 'delicts' and 'quasi-delicts'. The former is a concession to divergent linguistic denominations of tort; the latter reflects the particularities of French law concerning the distinction between strict and fault-based liability and indicates that the rule is meant to cover all torts, regardless of the kind of liability to which they may give rise (Peter Mankowski, 'Article 7' in Ulrich Magnus and Peter Mankowski (eds), *Brussels Ibis Regulation* (2nd edn, Sellier 2012) 271).

For its part, the ECJ has outlined the scope of the rule on torts by way of reference to the contiguous rule on contracts. In *Kalfelis*, the Court held that the term 'matters relating to tort, delict or quasi-delict' refers to 'all actions which seek to establish the liability of a defendant and which are not related to a contract' within the meaning of what is now art 7(1) Brussels I Regulation (recast) (Case 189/87 *Athanasios Kalfelis v Bankhaus Schröder, Münchmeyer, Hengst and Co and others* [1988] ECR 5565). Where → damages are sought on the ground of an act committed by the defendant in connection with a contract, the Court stated in *Brogsitter* that, for a claim to be characterized as contractual, it is necessary that the conduct complained of may be considered a breach of contract. For this, the purpose of the contract will normally need to be taken into account. If the interpretation of the contract is indispensable in establishing the lawful or unlawful nature of the conduct, then the claim will *a priori* come with the scope of the rule on contracts; otherwise, the rule on torts will apply (Case C-548/12 *Marc Brogsitter v Fabrication de Montres Normandes EURL and Karsten Fräßdorf* [2014] OJ C 135/10, regarding an action brought by the alleged victim of acts of unfair competition (→ Competition, unfair) performed by the defendant in connection with a contract concluded with the former).

Further doubts as to the applicability of the rule on torts have surfaced in three scenarios. First, the issue has been raised of whether the rule may be resorted to in proceedings for the protection of collective rights. In *Henkel*, the Court answered in the affirmative, referring to an action brought by a consumer protection organization with a view to preventing a trader from using terms considered to be unfair in contracts with private individuals (Case C-167/00 *Verein für Konsumenteninformation v Karl Heinz Henkel* [2002] ECR I-8111).

Second, the possibility has been investigated of applying the rule on torts to an action with the characteristics of the *action paulienne*, as it is known in French law, ie an action whereby a creditor seeks to have a court revoke a fraudulent contract, which led to the transfer of the creditor's rights *in rem* in immovable property (→ Property and proprietary rights) by the debtor to a third party. The ECJ denied that a claim of this kind could be regarded as tortious. Its purpose is not to have the debtor ordered to make good the damage caused by his fraudulent conduct, but rather to render ineffective, as against his creditor, the disposition made by the debtor, regardless of whether the third party in question has committed any wrongful act (Case C-261/90 *Mario Reichert, Hans-Heinz Reichert and Ingeborg Kockler v Dresdner Bank AG* [1992] ECR I-2149).

Third, the question has been raised of whether the special rule of jurisdiction in torts may be applied to actions for a negative declaration of liability (ie actions seeking to establish that the pre-conditions for liability in tort, as a result of which the defendant would have a right of redress, are not satisfied). In *Folien Fischer* the Court gave an affirmative answer. It observed that actions for a negative declaration entail a reversal of the roles normally played by litigants in tortious matters, but found that this does not prejudice the applicability of the *locus delicti* rule since the objectives of this rule (identifying a predictable court situated close to the subject matter of the dispute) 'are not connected either to the allocation of the respective roles of claimant and defendant or to the protection of either' (Case C-133/11 *Folien Fischer AG and Fofitec AG v Ritrama SpA* (October 2012)).

IV. The design and operation of the relevant connecting factor

It has been observed that special jurisdiction in contracts and torts depends on the localization of a particular element of the relationship in dispute: the performance of one of the obligations arising from the contract, the conduct from which the damage has arisen etc. Here, too, the solutions of the Brussels I Regime are particularly significant.

1. The place of performance of the obligation in question

The rule in art 7(1) Brussels I Regulation (recast) is made up of three propositions. Article 7(1)(a) provides a general provision according to which, in matters relating to a contract, jurisdiction is granted to 'the courts for the place of performance of the obligation in question'. Pursuant to art 7(1)(b), the said place, 'unless otherwise agreed', will be, 'in the case of the sale of goods', the place in a Member State where, under the contract, the goods were delivered or should have been delivered, while, 'in the case of the provision of services', it will be the place in a Member State where the services were provided or should have been provided. Article 7(1)(c) makes clear that 'if point (b) does not apply then point (a) applies'.

The general provision in art 7(1)(a) substantially corresponds to the rule originally laid down in art 5(1) of the Brussels Convention. The ECJ provided two basic clarifications in that respect. In *De Bloos*, shedding light on certain discrepancies among the linguistic versions of the rule (as it was then worded), the Court stated that jurisdiction over contractual matters must be determined by reference to the specific obligation on which the claim is based (Case 14/76 *A De Bloos, SPRL v Société en commandite par actions Bouyer* [1976] ECR 1497). In *Tessili*, the Court asserted that, in the absence of uniform provisions determining where obligations are to be performed, the court seized of the matter, in order to assess its jurisdiction under the rule in question, should start by determining, through the conflict-of-laws provisions of the forum, the substantive law applicable to the contract. The court should then go on to localize the → place of performance of the relevant obligation in conformity with the standards provided for by that law (Case 12/76 *Industrie Tessili Italiana Como v Dunlop AG* [1976] ECR 1473).

The 'traditional' interpretation of the rule on *locus solutionis* has attracted strong criticism. The 'analytical' approach proposed in *De Bloos* has been accused of being likely to result in litigation over the same contract being brought before multiple courts, depending on the place of performance of the individual obligation relied upon by the claimant in the case at hand. For its part, the 'conflictual' approach suggested in *Tessili*, apart from requiring the parties and the seized court to pass through the subtleties of contract conflicts as a preliminary step to determine jurisdiction, was criticized by some commentators on the basis that it weakened the uniformity of the jurisdictional regime and the predictability of its practical results. As a matter of fact, the *lex causae* approach, in addition to making the issue of jurisdiction contingent upon non-unified rules, leaves the task of determining the competent court to rules elaborated for purposes unrelated to jurisdiction. In particular, as far as money obligations are concerned, the reasons why substantive rules might require the debtor to pay at the domicile of the creditor rather than at his own domicile, or vice versa, may have little to do with the goals of procedural fairness and sound administration of justice, which should instead represent the key concern when it comes to regulating adjudicatory jurisdiction (→ Place of performance).

The limits of the traditional reading have been partly mitigated by the ECJ. As a means of countering the risk of fragmentation, the Court held in *Shenavai* that, where several obligations are in dispute, and each of them is to be fulfilled in a different country, the claimant may rely on the rule on special jurisdiction to bring proceedings in respect of all obligations before one court: the court for the place of performance of the principal obligation (Case 266/85 *Hassan Shenavai v Klaus Kreischer* [1987] ECR 239). As to the lack of uniformity, the Court stressed the role that may be played by internationally uniform substantive rules aimed at identifying the *locus solutionis*. In *Custom Made*, it stated that uniform rules of contract law, where applicable in the forum to the relationship concerned, must in fact be resorted to for the purpose of determining the place of performance of the obligation in question for jurisdictional purposes, instead of national provisions (Case C-288/92 *Custom Made Commercial Ltd v Stawa Metallbau GmbH* [1994] ECR I-2913). Furthermore, in *Zelger*, the Court underlined the fact that the place of performance of the obligation in question may well be agreed upon by the parties, and thereby increase the degree of legal certainty as to the determination of the *forum solutionis*. However, the Court added that the agreement in question, in order to be relevant to jurisdiction, must be made in conformity with the applicable substantive law (Case 56/79 *Siegfried Zelger v Sebastiano Salinitri* [1980] ECR 89).

Meanwhile, the unification of rules on conflicts of laws in contracts, brought about by the Rome Convention (the predecessor of the Rome I Regulation), helped to reduce the inconvenience of *Tessili*. Under a unified regime, the same contract will in fact be governed by the same law, regardless of the national viewpoint considered. It is worth recalling, however, that the unification of conflict-of-laws rules, as realized in Europe, is not absolute and complete, due in particular to the priority granted to pre-existing international conventions concluded by Member States (art 25 of the Rome I Regulation, largely corresponding to art 21 of the Rome Convention).

These (partial) improvements did not ultimately prevent the European legislator from amending the rule of special jurisdiction in contracts with a view to overcoming the difficulties mentioned above. When the Brussels Convention was 'transformed' into the Brussels I Regulation, the old rule was coupled with the innovative provisions that may now be read in art 7(1)(b) of the Brussels I Regulation (recast): sales of goods must be localized at the place of delivery and contracts for the provision of services at the place where the services are to be supplied. While the old rule in (a) remains, based on *De Bloos* and *Tessili* (Case C-533/07 *Falco Privatstiftung and Thomas Rabitsch v Gisela Weller-Lindhorst* [2009] ECR I-3327), the 'specifications' in (b) have inaugurated a new approach. In claims relating to one of the particular contracts enumerated in (b), jurisdiction is no longer determined separately for each obligation (Case C-386/05 *Color Drack GmbH v Lexx International Vertriebs GmbH* [2007] ECR I-3699), and the localization of the only relevant obligation is no longer left to the non-unified rules of the applicable law, but must rather be effected through 'pragmatic' criteria (Case C-381/08 *Car Trim GmbH v KeySafety Systems Srl* [2010] OJ C 100/4, stating that the place of delivery, under (b), is 'the place where the physical transfer of the goods took place, as a result of which the purchaser obtained, or should have obtained, actual power of disposal over those goods at the final destination of the sales transaction').

That said, an entirely positive evaluation of this development would probably be misplaced. On the one hand, the functioning of the new *forum solutionis* has proved problematic in various respects. With the introduction of special rules on sales of goods and provisions of services, the need has arisen to determine at the outset whether or not the contract in dispute belongs to one of the enumerated categories. Failing an explicit definition of the notions in question, the characterization may in fact be uneasy: the ECJ, for its part, has addressed only some of the issues of classification raised by the new text (see, eg Case C-9/12 *Corman-Collins SA v La Maison du Whisky SA* [2014] OJ C 52/6, on agreements for the distribution of goods). In addition, the actual operation of the pragmatic standards advocated by the Court has required the latter to elaborate a rather sophisticated set of guidelines, to be used outside plain cases (see, eg Case C-19/09 *Wood Floor Solutions Andreas Domberger GmbH v Silva Trade SA* [2010] OJ C 113/14, on the identification of the place of the provision of services under an independent agency agreement to be performed in more than one country).

On the other hand, the rule now enshrined in art 7(1) Brussels I Regulation (recast) has grown outstandingly complex. In applying this rule, the seized court may sometimes need to engage in a difficult sequence of assessments. For example, a court seized of a claim brought in respect of the non-payment of goods will begin by determining, pursuant to the rule in (b), whether the place of delivery of those goods (as determined 'pragmatically' and 'empirically') is situated in its jurisdiction. If this is not the case, and the place of delivery appears to be situated outside the territory of the European Union, then the rule in (b) will be displaced altogether, and – pursuant to (c) – the 'traditional' rule based on *Tessili* and *De Bloos* will need to be resorted to as a fall-back solution. In practice, the seized court will need to reconsider the contract, this time against the backdrop of art 7(1)(a), and ascertain whether or not the 'obligation in question', ie the obligation to pay the price, as determined in accordance with the *lex causae*, was to be performed in its jurisdiction.

2. The place where the harmful event occurred or may occur

As observed earlier, the reference made in the rule now laid down in art 7(2) of the Brussels I Regulation (recast) to the place of the harmful event has been interpreted by the ECJ as covering 'both the place where the damage occurred and the place of the event giving rise to it': liability in tort, the Court observed, can only arise when a causal connexion can be established between the damage and the event from which that damage originates, and accordingly it would be inappropriate to opt for one of the two connecting factors to the exclusion of the other, since each of them can lead to the designation of a court featuring a significant link with the subject matter of the dispute (Case 21/76 *Handelskwekerij GJ Bier BV v Mines de potasse d'Alsace SA* [1976] ECR 1735).

In its subsequent case-law, the Court insisted on the idea that, in determining the *locus delicti*, proximity and predictability must represent a permanent concern. It held in *Dumez* that the special rule on torts cannot be interpreted as permitting a plaintiff pleading damage that is claimed to be the consequence of the harm suffered by other persons who were direct victims of the harmful act to bring proceedings against the perpetrator of that act in the courts of the place in which he himself ascertained the damage to his assets (Case C-220/88 *Dumez France SA and Tracoba SARL v Hessische Landesbank and others* [1990] ECR I-49; in a similar vein, the Court ruled more recently in a case involving the interpretation of the → Rome II Regulation that the damage sustained by the close relatives of the victim of a car accident in connection with the death of the latter must be classified as 'indirect consequences' of that accident and have no bearing, as such, on the localization of the harmful event: Case C-350/14 *Florin Lazar v Allianz SpA* ECLI:EU:C:2015:802). In *Marinari*, the Court held that the notion of 'place where the harmful event has occurred' may not be construed so extensively as to encompass any place where the adverse consequences can be felt of an event which has already caused damage actually arising elsewhere (Case C-364/93 *Antonio Marinari v Lloyds Bank plc and Zubaidi Trading Company* [1995] ECR I-2719). Rather, regard must be had to the place where the allegedly tortious acts were committed and where those acts were, foreseeably, likely to bring about their effects. In this connection, in a case of prospectus liability, the ECJ observed that the issuer of a certificate who does not comply with his legal obligations in respect of the prospectus must, when he decides to notify the prospectus in states other than the state where it is established, anticipate that inadequately informed operators, domiciled in those states, might invest in that certificate and suffer loss there (Case C-375/13 *Harald Kolassa v Barclays Bank plc* [2015] OJ C 107/4). On a different but related note, in *Hi Hotel*, the ECJ stressed that where there are several supposed perpetrators, the rule on torts cannot be interpreted as conferring jurisdiction, on the basis of the causal event of the damage, to a court within whose jurisdiction the supposed perpetrator who is being sued did not act (Case C-387/12 *Hi Hotel HCF SARL v Uwe Spoering* [2014] OJ C 159/4).

The application of these principles has given rise to particular difficulties in three areas of the law of torts: product liability, infringement of → personality rights and infringement of intellectual property rights.

In *Zuid-Chemie*, a case concerning the damage caused to an undertaking by the delivery of a contaminated chemical product which rendered unusable the fertilizer that the undertaking produced from a number of raw materials and by the processing of the contaminated chemical, the Court stated that the words 'place where the harmful event occurred' designate 'the place where the initial damage occurred as a result of the normal use of the product for the purpose for which it was intended'. The rule on torts covers not only the place of the event giving rise to the damage but also the place where the damage occurred, such as the factory of an undertaking in which that undertaking processed a defective product causing material damage to the processed product suffered by the undertaking, going beyond the damage inherent in the product itself. (Case C-189/08 *Zuid-Chemie BV v Philippo's Mineralenfabriek NV/SA* [2009] ECR I-6917)

As far as personality rights are concerned, the Court clarified in *Fiona Shevill* how the expression 'place where the harmful event occurred' should be interpreted in proceedings brought by the victim of a libel by a newspaper article distributed in several states. It stated that an action for damages against the publisher may be initiated either before the courts of the place where the publisher is established or before the courts of each state in which the publication was distributed and where the victim claims to have suffered injury to her reputation. However, the ECJ added that while the former courts are entitled to award damages for all the harm caused by the defamation, the latter may 'rule solely in respect of the harm caused in the State of the court seised' (Case C-68/93 *Fiona Shevill, Ixora Trading Inc, Chequepoint SARL and Chequepoint International Ltd v Presse Alliance SA* [1995] ECR I-415). By espousing the so-called mosaic theory, the Court attempted to accommodate two divergent policies. On the one hand, it stressed that the rules on jurisdiction should not jeopardize the effectiveness of the protection of the victim of defamation, and should actually allow the latter to bring proceedings wherever her reputation is affected by a publication. On the other hand, it underlined the need to safeguard the predictability of subject matter jurisdiction, and to allow publishers to forecast – based on the geographic distribution of their products – the courts before which they could face liability and the economic implications of judicial orders for compensation regarding damages suffered in the various places where the publications are distributed.

The appropriateness of these solutions has later been challenged in respect of on-line defamation. In *eDate*, the Court acknowledged that torts consisting in the diffusion of information placed on a website featured peculiar characteristics, and called for an adaption of the existing interpretive rules. For the Court, since the scope of the diffusion of content placed on-line is universal, the victim of an infringement of personality rights should be given the opportunity of bringing an action for all of the damage caused in one forum. In this connection, since 'the impact which material placed on-line is liable to have on an individual's personality rights may best be assessed by the court of the place where the alleged victim has his centre of interests', the Court held that the attribution of jurisdiction to that court, to be identified in most cases with the habitual residence of the victim, 'corresponds to the objective of the sound administration of justice' and is 'in accordance with the aim of predictability of the rules governing jurisdiction also with regard to the defendant, given that the publisher of harmful content is . . . in a position to know the centres of interests of the persons who are the subject of that content' (Joined Cases C-509/09 and C-161/10 *eDate Advertising GmbH v X, Olivier Martinez, Robert Martinez v MGN Limited* [2011] ECR I-10269).

The localization of torts also proved problematic in the case of infringement of intellectual property rights, especially if committed through the web. The Court first dealt with the matter in *Wintersteiger*, where it held that, pursuant to the rule on special jurisdiction in torts, an action relating to the infringement of a trademark registered in a Member State because of the use, by an advertiser, of a keyword identical to that trademark on a search engine website operating under a country-specific top-level domain of another Member State may be brought before either the courts of the Member State in which the trademark is registered or the courts of the Member State of the place of establishment of the advertiser (Case C-523/10 *Wintersteiger AG v Products 4U Sondermaschinenbau GmbH* (April 2012)). In *Pinckney*, the Court added that in the event of an alleged infringement of copyrights protected by the Member State of the court seized, the latter has jurisdiction to hear an action to establish liability brought by the author of a work against a company established in another Member State and which has, in the latter State, reproduced that work on a material support, when the support is subsequently sold in a third Member State through an Internet site also accessible in the jurisdiction of the court seized. The court in question, however, 'has jurisdiction only to determine the damage caused in the Member State within which it is situated' (Case C-170/12 *Peter Pinckney v KDG Mediatech AG* [2013] OJ C 344/27).

PIETRO FRANZINA

Literature

Marie-Elodie Ancel, *La prestation caractéristique du contrat* (Economica 2002); Martin Dubiel, *Der Erfüllungsortbegriff des Vertragsgerichtsstands im deutschen, europäischen und internationalen Zivilprozessrecht* (Lang 2010); Pietro Franzina, *La giurisdizione in materia contrattuale* (Cedam 2006); Pietro Franzina, 'Jurisdiction Regarding Claims for the Infringement of Privacy Rights under the General Data Protection Regulation' in Alberto De Franceschi (ed) *European Contract Law and the Digital Single Market - The Implications of the Digital Revolution* (Intersentia 2016) 81; Francisco Javier Garcimartín Alférez, 'El fuero especial en materia de obligaciones contractuales en el Reglamento Bruselas I: el "status quaestionis interpretativo"' (2013) 3 Int J Proc Law 22; Keltilbjørn Hertz, *Jurisdiction in Contract and Tort under the Brussels Convention* (Jurist- og Økonomforbundets Forlag 1998); Ruja Ignatova, *Art. 5 Nr. 1 EuGVO – Chancen und Perspektiven der Reform des Gerichtsstands am Erfüllungsort* (Lang 2005); Thomas Kadner Graziano, 'Jurisdiction Under Article 7 No. 1 of the Recast Brussels I Regulation: Disconnecting the Procedural Place of Performance From Its Counterpart in Substantive Law – An Analysis of the Case Law of the ECJ and Proposals De Lege Lata and De Lege Ferenda' (2014–2015) 16 YbPIL 167; Jan-Jaap Kuipers, 'Towards a European Approach in the Cross-Border Infringement of Personality Rights' (2011) 12 GLJ 1681; Stefan Leible, 'Der Erfüllungsort iSv Art. 5 Nr. 1 lit. b Brüssel I-VO: ein Mysterium?' in Jörn Bernreuther and others (eds), *Festschrift für Ulrich Spellenberg zum 70. Geburtstag* (Sellier 2010) 451; Thomas Lynker, *Der besondere Gerichtsstand am Erfüllungsort in der Brüssel I-Verordnung (Art. 5 Nr. 1 EuGVVO)* (Lang 2006); Peter Mankowski, 'Article 7' in Ulrich Magnus and Peter Mankowski (eds), *Brussels Ibis Regulation* (3rd edn, Otto Schmidt 2016) 88; Fabrizio Marongiu Buonaiuti, *Le obbligazioni non contrattuali nel diritto internazionale privato* (Giuffrè 2013).

Jurisdiction, foundations

I. Introduction

1. Terminology and concepts

Jurisdiction, literally (the power of) saying what the law is, is at the same time the most important and the most complex area of private international law. The complexities begin with terminology. Jurisdiction, in common law parlour, encompasses two meanings that are at least partly distinct in principle, even if they sometimes overlap in practice. These terminological and conceptual differences mar many comparative law analyses (→ Comparative law and private international law); they also make it difficult to develop a general theory.

In one way, jurisdiction describes the outer limits of a body's reach. In this sense, the concept is not confined to adjudication but applies to the activities of all three branches of government and beyond. Besides jurisdiction to adjudicate there are also jurisdiction to prescribe and jurisdiction to enforce, which limit, respectively, the spaces in which a country can legislate and enforce its own laws and decisions. The meaning of jurisdiction as the scope of a court's power is encompassed within the term jurisdiction also in some other languages, thus in Italian (*giurisdizione*) and Austrian German (*Jurisdiktion*); in Germany, the term, insofar as courts are concerned, is *Gerichtsbarkeit* or *Gerichtshoheit*.

In another sense, jurisdiction describes the allocation of adjudicatory competences vis-à-vis the (potentially) competing competence of other states' courts. Insofar, Germany and Austria use the term *internationale Zuständigkeit*, the French speak of *compétence internationale*. In English, one could speak of international venue. Jurisdiction in this latter sense is frequently narrower than in the former sense.

The terminological differences show that, for purposes of theory and comparison, a functional definition is necessary. Functionally, for purposes of private international law, the law of jurisdiction can be defined as those rules and principles that determine the circumstances under which a court is entitled to adjudicate and render a substantive judgment in view of the international and/or interstate connections involved.

2. International jurisdiction and subject matter jurisdiction

Where the jurisdiction of courts is at stake, we must distinguish what can be called international jurisdiction on the one hand from subject matter jurisdiction on the other hand. What I call here international jurisdiction encompasses personal jurisdiction and jurisdiction *in rem*. Personal jurisdiction is jurisdiction over a person, most importantly over a defendant. Jurisdiction *in rem* was once understood to be jurisdiction over a thing based on its presence in the court's territory. Today, *in rem* jurisdiction is also understood ultimately to be jurisdiction over a person; the presence of the thing merely provides the basis for the jurisdiction.

Subject matter jurisdiction on the other hand is, in principle, not about international jurisdiction. Instead, it determines the subject matters about which a court is entitled to adjudicate. Nonetheless, subject matter jurisdiction can determine international limits of jurisdiction as well (→ Jurisdiction, limits under international law). This is the case, for example, when US federal courts derive their subject matter jurisdiction from the applicability of a federal statute (so-called federal question jurisdiction). In this case, courts have sometimes translated the territorial limits of the applicable federal statute into subject matter jurisdiction limits of the court. The US Supreme Court has recently suggested, however, that this should be treated as a question of merits (*Morrison v National Australia Bank*, 561 U.S. 247, 254 (2010)).

3. Direct and indirect jurisdiction

The issue whether a court has adjudicatory jurisdiction can become relevant at two very different stages in an international litigation. The first stage concerns the proceedings before the court that renders the decision, hereinafter called the rendering court. The rendering court will not hear a case, much less render a decision, unless it determines that it has jurisdiction to do so. If it renders a decision despite the lack of jurisdiction, an appellate court may declare the decision void. The second stage concerns the proceedings before the court, often in a different state, requested to recognize and/or enforce the rendering court's decision, hereinafter the requested court (→ Recognition and enforcement of judgments). The requested court will not recognize or enforce the decision of the rendering court unless it determines that the rendering court had jurisdiction.

Although they are sometimes treated as though they were similar, the issue of jurisdiction as a requirement for adjudication is analytically different from the issue of jurisdiction as a requirement for recognition. The first is governed by the law of the rendering state, the second by the law of the requested court. Neither the rendering court, nor the recognizing court, is necessarily bound to the standards of the other. In French law, the first is called direct jurisdiction, the second indirect jurisdiction. This terminology is more exact than the German terminology (*Entscheidungszuständigkeit* and *Anerkennungszuständigkeit*) and certainly preferable to the English and American tendency to draw no terminological distinction at all.

Direct and indirect jurisdiction are also different in policy terms. It may well be the case that the rendering court is justified to assert jurisdiction under its own standards, and the recognizing court is similarly justified to deny recognition to the ensuing judgment for lack of jurisdiction under its own standards.

II. Levels of regulation

With the functional concept of jurisdiction developed earlier, it is possible to distinguish three levels of jurisdictional regulation. A first level, found primarily in higher law like international or constitutional law (→ Constitutional law and private international law), lays down outer limits of jurisdiction. This higher law only constrains jurisdiction, it does not constitute a basis for jurisdiction. Such a basis can be found on a second level that provides the rules on which jurisdiction can actually be based. A third level, finally, concerns judicial discretion for the individual case, either in the application of the rules from the second level, or in special discretionary doctrines. Here, the question is whether jurisdiction that exists should be exercised.

These levels facilitate a structural comparison between different jurisdictional regimes; they reveal that the levels do not play the same role in different legal systems, and they help to understand and classify different styles of jurisdiction regulation. Importantly, in particular, civil law systems rely almost entirely on the second level of rules, while all but ignoring the first and third level. US law, by contrast, uses almost only the first and third level; actual rules of jurisdiction often just mirror on findings from the first level.

1. First level: higher law constraints

a) Public international law

At the highest level of analysis lie higher law constraints that determine the outer boundaries of jurisdiction. Such constraints could in theory come from public international law in two ways (→ Public international law and private international law). First, public international law limits the exercise of sovereign power vis-à-vis the sovereign interests of other states; to the extent that adjudicatory jurisdiction is viewed as an exercise of sovereign power, it could therefore be limited (eg German Federal Court of Justice (BGH), 2 July 1991, 115 BGHZ 90). Second, human rights law lays down certain rights that could be viewed as limiting the exercise of jurisdiction, in particular due process and fair trial rights (art 6(1) ECHR (European Convention of 4 November 1950 for the Protection of

Human Rights and Fundamental Freedoms, 213 UNTS 221)) (→ Human rights and private international law). In reality, however, public international law has played a fairly limited role in limiting jurisdiction (→ Jurisdiction, limits under international law). Where it does, it can play a role both for direct and for indirect jurisdiction.

Public international law (→ Public international law and private international law) can play a role in relation to jurisdiction also in the form of → treaties in private international law, especially if such treaties are viewed merely as constraints and not as actual codifications of jurisdictional rules. Where such treaties exist, they are regularly coupled with rules on the recognition and enforcement of judgments; a harmonization of rules on jurisdiction is viewed mainly as a prerequisite for obligations to enforce foreign judgments. While a number of bilateral treaties exist, multilateral treaties are rare. The most successful examples of such treaties (which are more codifications than constraints) were the Brussels Convention (Brussels Convention of 27 September 1968 on jurisdiction and the enforcement of judgments in civil and commercial matters, [1972] OJ L 299/32, consolidated version, [1998] OJ C 27/1) and the Brussels II Convention (Council Act of 28 May 1998 drawing up, on the basis of Article K.3 of the Treaty on European Union, the Convention on Jurisdiction and the Recognition and Enforcement of Judgments in Matrimonial Matters, [1998] OJ C 221/01) that were later turned into EU Regulations (Brussels I Regulation (Regulation (EC) No 44/2001 of 22 December 2000 on jurisdiction and the recognition and enforcement of judgments in civil and commercial matters, [2001] OJ L 12/1) (→ Brussels I (Convention and Regulation)), → Brussels IIa Regulation (Council Regulation (EC) No 2201/2003 of 27 November 2003 concerning jurisdiction and the recognition and enforcement of judgments in matrimonial matters and the matters of parental responsibility, repealing Regulation (EC) No 1347/2000, [2003] OJ L 338/1)), and the → Lugano Convention (Lugano Convention of 30 October 2007 on jurisdiction and the recognition and enforcement of judgments in civil and commercial matters, [2007] OJ L 339/3).

By contrast, negotiations towards a comprehensive worldwide Hague Recognition and Enforcement Convention were so far unsuccessful; a new project is currently underway. One among several problems was that Americans and Europeans viewed the character of such a Convention differently: while Americans thought of it as a mere constraint on possible rules of jurisdiction, Europeans thought of it as a comprehensive codification of rules on jurisdiction. The [Hague] Convention of 30 June on Choice of Court Agreements aims to unify the law of jurisdiction based on agreement.

b) Constitutional law

A practically more important higher law that limits jurisdiction is the Constitution. In US law in particular, the law of jurisdiction has been developed almost entirely on the basis of the Constitution, especially the due process clauses of the 5th and 14th Constitutional Amendments (1 Stat. 97 (1789); 14 Stat. 358 (1866)). Courts, including the US Supreme Court, have distilled a whole array of specific rules and principles from these rather abstract clauses. The fact that so much of the law of jurisdiction has been constitutionalized has made the development of the law unpredictable. The Supreme Court of Canada has also begun to constitutionalize the Canadian law of jurisdiction, suggesting that principles of federalism require, for jurisdiction to be constitutional, a real and substantive connection (*Club Resorts v Van Breda* [2012] SCC 17).

Some civil law constitutional norms also provide jurisdictional rules, such as did § 59 of the old Swiss Federal Constitution of 1874 (AS 1 1, abolished in 1998, AS 1999 2556, 2609). Mostly, however, the Constitution becomes relevant only occasionally, for example for jurisdictional rules that prioritize husbands over wives (Federal Constitutional Court of Germany (BVerfG), 3 December 1985, 71 BVerfGE 224).

2. Second level: specific rules

Higher law, on the first level, lays down only the outer limits of jurisdiction, but does not lay down its bases. This is done instead on a second level of rules on jurisdiction.

In civil law countries, this second level is by far the most important level. The European legislator has laid down mostly strict rules on jurisdiction in the so-called 'Brussels' regime of a number of regulations on jurisdiction and the recognition and enforcement of judgments. Member States retain residual rules that apply outside the scope of the Brussels Regulations. In many civil law countries, jurisdiction is based entirely on domestic rules. For some time, countries that had no special rules for jurisdiction applied their rules on venue, either by analogy or as implicit rules on international jurisdiction (eg German Federal Court of Justice (BGH), 14 June 1965, 44 BGHZ 62; Cass Civ 1re, *Scheffel*, 30 October 1962; [1963] Recueil Dalloz 109) or developed principles on the basis of abstract considerations like fairness, efficiency, etc. (Japanese Supreme Court, 16 October 1981, Minshû 35-7-1224). Now, more and more countries have moved to codify their law on jurisdiction and thereby put it on firmer ground.

Many common law countries also rest jurisdiction on detailed rules, at least beyond traditionally accepted bases of jurisdiction such as jurisdiction based on service of process within the territory. Due to the different nature and role of service of process, some of these rules are phrased as rules granting leave to serve outside the territory. Statutory rules exist also in the USA as so-called Long Arm Statutes, but their practical relevance pales in comparison to that of the constitutional constraints: many such rules largely codify existing case-law on constitutional constraints, or even merely grant jurisdiction up to the limits of the US Constitution.

3. Third level: discretion on a case-by-case level

Even where jurisdiction is not constrained by higher law and is based on a specific rule that authorizes it, the judge may nonetheless, because of characteristics of the individual case, decline to exercise it. Such judicial discretion is more common in the common law, but it exists also in civil law systems.

a) Common law, especially forum non conveniens

Whether or not jurisdiction exists, is, in common law systems, frequently a matter of case-by-case analysis, which helps administer justice in the individual case but reduces predictability and certainty. Some such elements are built into jurisdictional tests. Thus, in US law, the court has to determine, as part of the jurisdictional test, whether the exercise of jurisdiction is reasonable. In US and English law, the court may decline jurisdiction to ensure the application of mandatory forum laws.

However, the most important discretionary basis for declining jurisdiction is the doctrine of → *forum non conveniens*. First developed in Scottish law, this doctrine has now been adopted in many common law systems. Under this doctrine, a judge will decline to exercise jurisdiction when the forum is inappropriate, and an available alternative forum in another legal system is clearly better suited than the forum. Doctrinally, *forum non conveniens* is not a jurisdictional provision, because its application leaves the existence of jurisdiction in the case intact and goes merely to the exercise of such jurisdiction. Functionally, however, existence and exercise of jurisdiction are closely related. This proximity is the reason why the ECJ refused the applicability of the doctrine in the realm of the Brussels I Regulation (Case C-281/02 *Owusu v NB Jackson and others* [2005] ECR I-1445), and the French Cour de Cassation has argued similarly for the Montreal Convention (Convention of 28 May 1999 for the unification of certain rules relating to international carriage by air, 2242 UNTS 309; Cass Civ 1re, 7 December 2011, [2012] *Recueil Dalloz* 254).

b) Discretion in civil law systems

In contrast to the common law, which traditionally leaves a high degree of discretion to courts in matters of jurisdiction, the traditional civilian approach rejects such discretion and requires strict application of formal rules. *Forum non conveniens* is, as a consequence, rejected. However, discretion in the application of individual bases is sometimes accepted. This holds true in view of parallel litigation (arts 33 and 34 Brussels I Regulation (recast) (Regulation (EU) No 1215/2012 of the European Parliament and of the Council of 12 December 2012 on jurisdiction and the recognition and enforcement of judgments in civil and commercial matters (recast), [2012] OJ L 351/1)), but also in the application of open-ended terms, such as 'closely connected' in arts 8(1) and 30(3) Brussels I Regulation (recast).

III. Interests, theories and paradigms

Scholars from different legal traditions have paid very different degrees of attention to the development of theories for the law of jurisdiction. German scholarship has focused not so much on theories as on uncovering the policy interests underlying the law of jurisdiction. While US scholars have long worked on theories, in part fuelled by the need to rationalize an erratic Supreme Court case-law, other common law jurisdictions have largely preferred pragmatism over the development of general theories. In other civil law countries, theories have been developed but have played a lesser role.

1. Interests

Following *Gerhard Kegel's* (→ Kegel, Gerhard) focus on interests in choice of law, German scholars developed a list of such interests for the law of jurisdiction. Common law doctrine does something comparable when developing relevant factors for *forum non conveniens* dismissal. The individual interests and factors carry different weight in different legal regimes.

a) Party interests/private factors

A first set of interests underlying the law of jurisdiction are party interests. To some extent, these interests are antagonistic: everything else being equal, defendants and plaintiffs are typically each interested in litigating at home. Plaintiffs have an interest in access to court; defendants have an interest in not being required to defend themselves far from home. Civil law validates especially the defendant's position: plaintiffs can only exceptionally sue at a place other than the defendant's home ('*actor sequitur forum rei*'); at the same time, the defendant cannot unilaterally avoid the jurisdiction of its home court. The common law allows such avoidance through the *forum non conveniens* doctrine; on the other hand, especially US law often starts from the assumption that plaintiffs have a legitimate interest in suing at their own home and asks to what extent this can be allowed.

Plaintiffs have an interest in litigating at a place where the defendant has assets, because this facilitates enforcement. This interest can be used to justify not only *in rem* jurisdiction, but especially *quasi in rem* jurisdiction. It does not, by itself, justify the assertion of unlimited jurisdiction at a place where the defendant has some assets but not enough to fulfil the plaintiff's claim, such as in § 23 German Code of Civil Procedure (Zivilprozessordnung of 5 December 2005, BGBl. I 3202, as amended, henceforth German CCP) or § 99 Austrian Court Jurisdiction Act (Jurisdiktionsnorm of 1 August 1895, Reichsgesetzblatt No 111/1895, last amended by Bundesgesetzblatt No I 78/2014, henceforth Austrian JN). These provisions are therefore considered exorbitant.

Certain types of parties are deemed worthy of particular protection: this is the case, at least in civil law systems, for employees and consumers, for whom it would be more burdensome to litigate away from their home than for a corporate party. As a consequence, some laws of jurisdiction protect these parties by allowing them to sue and be sued exclusively at their home place or, in the case of employees, in the place where they habitually carry out their work (eg arts 18, 21 Brussels I Regulation (recast)).

Parties also have common interests in the predictability of the venue for litigation. The law acknowledges this interest by enforcing choice of court agreements, with regard to both prorogation and derogation. Exceptions exist for the protection of either specific types of parties (like, again, consumers and employees, arts 19, 23 Brussels I Regulation (recast)) or exclusive bases of jurisdiction.

In addition, parties have an interest in availability of witnesses and other evidence and records. This can suggest establishing jurisdiction at a place in proximity to the subject matter of the litigation, for example the place of the injury for tort litigation (eg art 7(3) Brussels I Regulation (recast)).

b) Court interests/public factors

Another set of interests is held by the court, both as an institution and as a representative of its state. A first interest is in maintaining a manageable court load. This interest mandates against jurisdiction over cases that have only scant connections to the court. On the other hand, courts may have an interest in attracting litigation that brings money to the local bar and enhances the court's reputation and standing; such interests are pursued particularly in courts trying to attract commercial litigation, for example New York, London and Singapore.

Another interest that is specific to the court is ease of application of law. Everything else being equal, it is easier for a court to adjudicate if it can apply its own law than if foreign law is applicable (→ *lex fori*). Some have suggested this interest to be so overwhelming that applicable law and jurisdiction should always coincide ('*lex fori in foro proprio*'). In some situations, such coincidence does occur because the connecting factors for jurisdiction and for → choice of law are the same. Applicability of foreign law is a powerful factor in favour of *forum non conveniens* dismissal. By contrast, applicability of domestic law can be the basis for jurisdiction, as is the case for federal question jurisdiction in the USA (*supra*).

Finally, a state's regulatory interests can serve as a basis for jurisdiction. A state that wants to make sure that certain of its mandatory rules are applied will frequently ensure this by giving its own courts jurisdiction, and by providing that parties cannot opt out of this jurisdiction through a choice of court agreement. As a legislative mechanism this has become common. It is more doubtful, especially under the Brussels I Regulation, whether courts are entitled to disregard a choice of court agreement in order to protect mandatory rules without an explicit jurisdictional basis.

c) Structural interests/interests of the international system
A third set of interests concerns the international system – whether a real system (as in the European Union with its widely unified law of jurisdiction) or an imagined one (as on a global level). There is, arguably, a global interest in jurisdictional certainty and harmony, suggesting that litigation should be channelled to the most appropriate forum (the *forum conveniens*). Within the European Union, this is guaranteed, to some degree, through unified jurisdictional rules on a European level, which reduce opportunities for forum shopping, without eliminating them altogether. On a global level, a similar harmonization could be brought about through a treaty, but ambitious attempts to draft and ratify a worldwide Convention have so far been unsuccessful.

A global interest in harmony is further evident through rules on → *lis alibi pendens*: a court will, under this approach, deny jurisdiction in view of litigation that is pending elsewhere, or in view of a (recognizable) judgment from the courts of another state. Civil law systems used to have rather strict rules in this regard, which enabled strategic forum shopping. Common law systems take a more flexible approach and allow courts to decline to exercise their own jurisdiction in view of the foreign proceedings (*forum non conveniens*), and sometimes attempt to discourage a party from proceeding with litigation started elsewhere by granting → anti-suit injunctions. Although anti-suit injunctions are directed against a party and not a foreign court, they are part of the law of jurisdiction in a functional sense.

2. Theories

Different theories of jurisdiction have been developed. Here, a focus lies on theories developed especially in the US context.

a) Power theories
The power theory is famously encapsulated in *Justice Holmes'* assertion that '[t]he foundation of jurisdiction is physical power'. The basis of the theory is the relationship of domination and submission between the court and the defendant. In ancient England, this meant actual power. Jurisdiction was asserted over the defendant by physical arrest, to ensure his presence at the trial. Since then, the assertion of power has changed from actual to symbolic; the public and actual assertion of power is now privatized and symbolized in service of process by the plaintiff or its attorneys, at least in common law systems. When service of process is considered sufficient for the existence of jurisdiction, unconstrained by fairness considerations or the need of other connections (eg *Maharanee of Baroda v Wildenstein* (1972) 2 QB 283 (CA); *Burnham v Superior Court of California*, 495 U.S. 604 (1990)), this is best justified on the basis of a power theory.

b) Relational theories
Closely related are relational theories of jurisdiction. A relational theory gives jurisdiction to a sovereign's courts if and because the defendant owes the sovereign allegiance. The clearest example can be found in feudal relations, where the lord's jurisdiction over his fee-holders was based on the feudal relation between the two. Although feudalism no longer exists, there are remnants of such theories: for example, arts 14 and 15 French Civil Code (Code Civil of 21 March 1804, henceforth French CC), which base jurisdiction by French courts on the parties' French nationality, can be explained by reference to relational theory.

c) Fairness theories
Today, the main focus of a fairness theory is not the power of the court over the defendant, but rather whether it would be unfair to require the defendant to defend itself in a forum it did not choose. The US Supreme Court formulated a two-prong test in *International Shoe v Washington* (326 U.S. 310 (1945)), relying on minimum contacts and substantial fairness to the defendant; a third requirement of

reasonableness was added later (*Asahi Metal Industry Co v Superior Court of California*, 480 U.S. 102 (1987)). Fairness theories focus on the relationship between the litigants and the forum, as well as that between the underlying controversy and the forum, but unlike relational theories, the question is one of fairness regardless of sovereignty considerations.

Although much has been made of the difference between power and fairness theories, the difference is smaller than is sometimes assumed. Both theories see power as necessary for jurisdiction. They differ merely on whether power is also sufficient, or whether additional factors of fairness and reasonableness must be present.

3. Paradigms

A different way of arranging for different approaches to jurisdiction is to order them by paradigms. With some simplification, two paradigms can be contrasted. Continental European law stands for the first, US law stands for the second. Traditional English law stands, in many regards, somewhere between both paradigms, which helps explain some of its clashes with the European system.

a) 'Us or them' – the European paradigm

The European paradigm can be called 'us or them'. First, this paradigm is horizontal: European jurisdictional thinking focuses on the horizontal relations between countries rather than on the vertical relation between the court and the parties. The real question of jurisdiction in Europe is neither whether there are sufficient vertical contacts between the defendant and the country whose courts are seized, nor whether such contacts exist between that country and the controversy. The real question is which of several states' courts are the most appropriate to deal with a type of litigation. Jurisdiction is justified vis-à-vis other states with a plausible claim to jurisdiction, not vis-à-vis the defendant and its interest in protection from the court.

Second, as a consequence, jurisdictional thinking in the European tradition is multilateral and international. This is so not just for the Brussels Regulations: even in national laws, jurisdiction is allocated according to principles that are at least potentially universal. The main criteria for jurisdiction are consent and the closest connection.

Third, the paradigm is apolitical: matters of private litigation are considered apolitical; the state's only task is to provide a forum. The reason is that although the focus of jurisdiction is international, its goal is the correct adjudication of relations between the parties, where state interests are thought to be largely absent.

b) 'In or out' – the US paradigm

By contrast, the US jurisdictional paradigm can be called 'in or out'. First, this paradigm is vertical: regardless of whether jurisdiction is based on the power of the court over the defendant, the relations between the court and the defendant, or the fairness of asserting jurisdiction over the defendant, nearly all attention goes to the vertical relation between the court and the defendant.

Second, the paradigm is unilateral and domestic. This means that jurisdiction is viewed as a local issue, determined by the limits that national (or state) law sets for its own courts, not the appropriateness of the jurisdiction of other states' courts. The question is whether the dispute brought to the court lies within, or outside, the state's boundaries, inside or outside the state's legal order. Unlike in an international paradigm, in a domestic paradigm it is largely irrelevant whether the courts of other states would more appropriately exercise jurisdiction. Matters of jurisdiction are domestic matters; foreign national interests are relevant only insofar as they can be translated into such domestic matters. (Note that this is true only for the law of jurisdiction proper. The appropriateness of jurisdiction elsewhere is considered in the *forum non conveniens* test, to some extent also in the reasonableness requirement.)

Third, the paradigm is political. Since the exercise of jurisdiction is viewed along a vertical dimension as a public intrusion into the defendant's freedom, the individual has a negative right to be free from state intervention unless this intervention is justified. This is why justification for jurisdiction often occurs with reference to political philosophers dealing with the justification for governmental authority, be they *Hobbes* and *Locke* or *Rawls*, *Hart* and *Nozick*.

IV. Bases

Although jurisdictional rules display a plethora of criteria, these criteria can be grouped into three different categories of bases: consent, proximity and extraordinary bases.

1. Consent

A first basis of jurisdiction is consent (→ Choice of forum and submission to jurisdiction). Such consent is least problematical when the defendant submits to the court's jurisdiction during litigation. A defendant can consent to jurisdiction either explicitly or implicitly, by pleading on the merits. Mere pleading on jurisdiction is not usually viewed as submission to the jurisdiction on the merits.

Prior consent, through a choice-of-court agreement, is in principle no different. A defendant who consents to the jurisdiction of a court cannot complain that the exercise of that jurisdiction violates its rights and interests, whether vis-à-vis the court or vis-à-vis the plaintiff. For some time, consent jurisdiction was suspicious because it seemed to oust another court of its jurisdiction; today, jurisdiction based on consent is widely accepted. Limitations emerge from general contract law, from the desire to protect weaker parties (like consumers and employees) and from the need to maintain exclusive jurisdiction for certain areas (for example litigation over land).

2. Proximity

The large majority of bases of jurisdiction are based on proximity, some connection that exists between the court and either the transaction or the parties. Both civil and common law distinguish between general and specific jurisdiction (though with slight variations in definition). General jurisdiction is party-related and is comprehensive – it exists, untechnically spoken, at the defendant's home. Specific jurisdiction, by contrast, is based on a → connecting factor and limited to issues related to this factor, for example jurisdiction in tort at the place of the tort etc.

Existing bases of jurisdiction can be grouped, parallel to the three traditional elements of the state, as those pertaining to territory, citizenship (personality) and government (state interests).

a) Territoriality

→ Territoriality is an important – for many, the dominant – basis of jurisdiction. The most important territorial connection in the law of jurisdiction is a party's domicile (eg arts 4, 5 Brussels I Regulation (recast)) or its habitual residence (eg arts 3, 8 Brussels IIa Regulation) (→ Domicile, habitual residence and establishment). In the common law, mere presence in the jurisdiction is sufficient as a ground for jurisdiction. For natural persons, this is physical presence; for corporations, it was long, in the USA, 'doing business' in the jurisdiction, until the Supreme Court significantly curtailed this basis (*Daimler AG v Bauman*, 134 S.Ct. 746 (2014)). Many bases of specific jurisdiction are also based on a certain place – the place of conduct or of injury for torts, the place of entering into a contract or of performance for contracts, and so on.

Territorial factors can be justified under power considerations, because the state has power over its territory and everything that goes on in it. Similarly, they can be justified under fairness considerations: an individual who avails himself of the benefits of a state can be required to submit to its jurisdiction. Problems of fairness arise where someone enters a territory involuntarily, or where effects on a territory were unforeseeable, as can be the case for product liability when a product creates an injury outside the market in which it was first sold (*Asahi Metal Ind Co v Sup Ct*, 480 U.S. 102 (1987), different insofar the plurality in *McIntyre Machinery Ltd v Nicastro*, 131 S.Ct. 2780 (2011)), and for Internet defamation occurring at a faraway place (see German Federal Court of Justice (BGH), 2 March 2010, 184 BGHZ 313) (→ Internet, liability).

Under conditions of globalization (→ Globalization and private international law), territoriality changes its meaning. Some authors think that territoriality should lose its importance for the law of jurisdiction. Others argue the opposite: precisely because borders become more permeable, the law has to use territorial borders to delineate jurisdictional competences (thus eg the US Supreme Court in *F Hoffmann-La Roche Ltd v Empagran*, 542 U.S. 155 (2004)). Even if the latter view prevails, territoriality still shifts its meaning: it is concerned less with considerations of power and fairness, and more with the need for formal and easily administrable criteria of jurisdictional allocation.

b) Personality

Not all jurisdictional criteria are territorial. Some systems are explicitly based on criteria of citizenship, thus for example French law in arts 14 and 15 French CC. These provisions are considered exorbitant. But for many other regimes of jurisdiction and → *forum non conveniens*, the parties' nationality plays a role. This is so especially in family law; the Brussels IIa Regulation provides for divorce jurisdiction on the basis of either habitual residence or nationality (art 3(1)). Jurisdiction based on nationality can be justified by a state's interest in regulation and protection of its own citizens. In common law countries, domicile (→ Domicile, habitual residence and establishment) plays a somewhat similar role of affiliation. Altogether, the existence of such bases of jurisdiction demonstrates that territoriality is not exclusive.

c) State interests
Finally, the third element of the state, namely a functional government, translates into governmental or state interests as the basis of jurisdiction. This can have a positive and a negative aspect. Positively, as was discussed earlier, a state may base its jurisdiction on the desire to make sure that particularly important regulatory interests are enforced. But state interests can also have a negative impact: another state's strong regulatory interests may be a reason for a court to decline exercising its jurisdiction. In reality, it appears that courts are more willing to assert jurisdiction on the basis of their own state's regulatory interests than to decline its exercise in view of such regulatory interests elsewhere. Indeed, such foreign regulatory interests can frequently be accommodated through application of the foreign state's laws.

3. *Extraordinary bases*

a) Exorbitant jurisdiction
Several bases of jurisdiction in domestic systems are viewed as exorbitant and therefore considered unjustified. Other states do not accept the exercise of jurisdiction on these bases as justified for purposes of enforcement; scholars hope for their abolition also for domestic purposes. The Brussels I Regulation abolishes these exorbitant bases in Member States' systems with regard to defendants from within the EU, but does not interfere with them with regard to defendants outside the EU (see arts 5(2), 6(2) Brussels I Regulation).

Among the bases of jurisdiction considered exorbitant are: jurisdiction based on the plaintiff's nationality (art 14 French CC), unlimited jurisdiction based on the presence of assets belonging to the defendant (§ 23 German CCP, § 99 Austrian JN); general jurisdiction based on a corporation's doing business. Jurisdiction based on service of process is sometimes considered exorbitant by civilians, although it is the main traditional basis of jurisdiction in the common law. This demonstrates that what is considered exorbitant is often a matter of perspective.

b) Jurisdiction of necessity
Such exorbitant bases appear less shocking once one recognizes their broader function. Especially at a time when travelling to a foreign court would have been cumbersome, and the recognizability and enforceability of foreign judgments was uncertain, these bases provided a local basis of jurisdiction which, although based on a rather tangential connection, was vital in order to provide plaintiffs with access to court.

Viewed as such, exorbitant jurisdiction is closely related to so-called jurisdiction of necessity. Under this doctrine, a court may, exceptionally, assume jurisdiction even absent the normal connecting factors if this is necessary to provide the plaintiff with access to court (eg art 3 Swiss Private international law Act (Bundesgesetz über das Internationale Privatrecht of 18 December 1987, 1988 BBl I 5, as amended); § 28(1) Austrian JN; art 3136 Code civil (Quebec) (SQ 1991, c 64)). Such necessity is thought to exist especially if no other competent court is available, either because other courts do not have or will not exercise jurisdiction, or because these other courts are incapable for other reasons of providing justice. Jurisdiction of necessity has always been contested, as to both its existence and its limits. Nowadays, it has arguably become less important: existing jurisdictional bases provide plaintiffs with a broader set of options, litigating abroad has become easier (though not always easy), and increased mutual recognition of judgments makes foreign judgments more valuable. Nonetheless, the doctrine still plays a practical role.

c) Universal jurisdiction
Universal jurisdiction is arguably a specific type of such jurisdiction of necessity. Under this doctrine, every court in the world has jurisdiction at least potentially, even without the need of either the parties' consent or proximity. It is granted (if at all) for claims of violation of certain rules of international law. Originally developed in international criminal law, the doctrine has been

expanded into the area of private international law. In the USA, such civil universal jurisdiction could be claimed, for some time, under the US Alien Tort Statute (28 U.S.C. § 1350). In recent years, the US Supreme Court has severely restricted applicability of the statute for private litigation (*Sosa v Alvarez-Machain* 542 U.S. 692 (2004); *Kiobel v Royal Dutch Petroleum*, 133 S.Ct. 1659 (2013)). Whether such civil universal jurisdiction exists in other legal systems is doubtful. In many cases, existing bases of jurisdiction suffice to achieve the goals of universal civil litigation, namely to provide victims of human rights abuses with a forum.

RALF MICHAELS

Literature

Paul Schiff Berman, 'The Globalization of Jurisdiction' (2002) 151 U.Pa.L.Rev. 311; Jacco Bomhoff, *Judicial Discretion in European Law of Jurisdiction* (Sdu Uitgevers 2005); Donald Francis Donovan and Anthea Roberts, 'The Emerging Recognition of Universal Civil Jurisdiction' (2006) 100 Am.J.Int'l L. 142; Andreas Heldrich, *Internationale Zuständigkeit und anwendbares Recht* (Gruyter and Mohr 1969); Mary Keyes, *Jurisdiction in International Litigation* (Federation Press 2005); Jan Kropholler, 'Internationale Zuständigkeit' in Max-Planck-Institut für Ausländisches und Internationales Privatrecht (ed), *Handbuch des internationalen Zivilverfahrensrechts*, vol 1 (Mohr Siebeck 1982) ch 3, 183–533; Ralf Michaels, 'Two Paradigms of Jurisdiction' (2006) 27 Mich.J.Int'l L. 1003; Ralf Michaels, 'Some Jurisdictional Conceptions as Applied in Judgment Conventions' in Eckart Gottschalk and others (eds), *Conflict of Laws in a Globalizing World* (CUP 2007) 29; Arnaud Nuyts, 'Due Process and Fair Trial: Jurisdiction in the United States and in Europe Compared' in Ronald A Brand (ed), *Private Law, Private international law and Judicial Cooperation in the EU-US Relationship* (2005) 2 CILE Studies 27; Etienne Pataut, *Principe de souveraineté et conflits de juridictions* (LGDJ 1999); Thomas Pfeiffer, *Internationale Zuständigkeit und prozessuale Gerechtigkeit. Die internationale Zuständigkeit im Zivilprozess zwischen effektivem Rechtsschutz und prozessualer Gerechtigkeit* (Klostermann 1995); Jochen Schröder, *Internationale Zuständigkeit. Entwurf eines Systems von Zuständigkeitsinteressen im zwischenstaatlichen Privatverfahrensrecht aufgrund rechtshistorischer, rechtsvergleichender und rechtspolitischer Betrachtungen* (Westdeutscher Verlag 1973); Piet Jan Slot and Mielle Bulterman (eds), *Globalisation and Jurisdiction* (Kluwer International 2004); Laurence Usunier, *La régulation de la compétence juridictionnelle en droit international privé* (Economica 2008); Pascal de Vareilles Sommières,

La compétence internationale de l'Etat en matière du droit privé. Droit international public et droit international privé (LGDJ 1997); Arthur T von Mehren, *Adjudicatory Authority in Private international law: A Comparative Study* (Martinus Nijhoff 2007); Arthur T von Mehren and Donald T Trautman, 'Jurisdiction to Adjudicate: A Suggested Analysis' (1966) 79 Harv.L.Rev. 1121.

Jurisdiction, limits under international law

I. Jurisdiction in international law

The term 'jurisdiction' is commonly used to refer to an actor's authority 'to create or affect legal interests' (Willis LM Reese, 'Legislative Jurisdiction' (1978) 78 Colum.L.Rev. 1587). Put another way, it is the power to 'speak ... the law', specifically as to the persons, activities or legal interests occurring within the sovereign authority of a nation (Costas Douzinas, 'The Metaphysics of Jurisdiction' in Shaun McVeigh (ed), *Jurisprudence of Jurisdiction* (Routledge-Cavendish 2007) 21). For example, does a nation have the authority to prescribe certain conduct or does a national court have the authority to hear a dispute between the parties before it? This definition of jurisdiction relates to international law to the extent that a nation seeks to regulate persons or matters outside of its territory. International law, therefore, may potentially regulate the assertion of a nation's legal power beyond its authority.

The international law of jurisdiction can be divided usefully into three categories. *First*, jurisdiction to prescribe or legislate (sometimes called prescriptive jurisdiction) refers to a nation's ability (generally through its legislature) to make its laws applicable to persons or things (Restatement (Third) of Foreign Relations Law § 401(a) (American Law Institute, Restatement of the Law, Third: The Foreign Relations Law of the United States, St. Paul 1987)). *Second*, jurisdiction to adjudicate (traditionally termed judicial jurisdiction in Europe and personal or *in personam* jurisdiction in the USA) refers to a nation's ability 'to subject persons or things to the process of its courts or administrative tribunals, whether in civil or in criminal proceedings, whether or not the state is a party to the proceedings' (Restatement (Third) of Foreign Relations Law § 401(b)). It is, in other words, a national court's power to bring a person or thing into its adjudicative process. *Third*, jurisdiction to enforce (enforcement jurisdiction) refers to the ability of a nation to implement its law through 'induc[ing] or compel[ing] compliance or to punish noncompliance with its laws or regulations' (Restatement (Third) of Foreign Relations Law § 401(c)). These categories are not hermetically sealed. For instance, courts may both make and apply law in suits at common law before them. Yet, these categories are roughly agreed upon as indicative of the landscape of jurisdiction in international law.

In this entry, we explore jurisdiction to adjudicate (judicial jurisdiction) and the limits, if any, that international law imposes on the adjudicatory authority of nations and their courts.

1. International law limits to judicial jurisdiction

Various grounds of jurisdiction are used by nations throughout the world when asserting judicial jurisdiction. In Europe, judicial jurisdiction is governed by the Brussels I Regulation (recast) (Regulation (EU) No 1215/2012 of the European Parliament and of the Council of 12 December 2012 on jurisdiction and the recognition and enforcement of judgments in civil and commercial matters (recast), [2012] OJ L 351/1) as to jurisdictional assertions against parties domiciled in Member States and governed by the forum's national law for non-Member State domiciliaries (cf arts 4, 6 Brussels I Regulation (recast)) (→ Brussels I (Convention and Regulation)). The general rule is that Member State defendants should normally be sued in their place of domicile unless special rules relating to a particular subject matter, such as contract, tort etc, permit a plaintiff to bring suit in another European forum (cf arts 4(1), 7 Brussels I Regulation (recast)). Little mention is given of international law in case-law. As such, international law does not appear to constrain directly assertions of judicial jurisdiction in Europe, as the question presented is typically one of construing the Brussels I Regulation (recast). European courts do not forthrightly engage in an international law analysis when determining their jurisdiction.

In the USA, judicial jurisdiction is largely a subject of constitutional law (→ USA; → Jurisdiction, foundations; → Constitutional law and private international law). Except for some academic commentary linking the framework of personal jurisdiction to international law principles, very few modern US judicial decisions consider international law's relevance to judicial jurisdiction. Instead, perhaps unartfully, it is said in the USA that a defendant must have such 'minimum contacts' with the forum state that the assertion of jurisdiction does not offend 'traditional notions of fair play and substantial justice' (*International Shoe Co v Washington*, 326 U.S. 310, 316 (1945)). As a result, the law of judicial jurisdiction in the USA is primarily concerned with domestic constitutional doctrine, especially the due process rights of the defendant, and is not concerned with international law.

In most other nations, judicial jurisdiction is governed by codes of civil procedure or rules of practice before courts. The judicial jurisdiction question before a court in these countries is one of domestic statutory interpretation and not one of international law – namely, do the forum's rules of civil procedure permit the assertion of judicial jurisdiction?

In light of this, the international law standards applicable to assertions of judicial jurisdiction are best described as amorphous. According to one commentator,

> when one examines the practice of states . . . one finds that states claim jurisdiction over all sorts of cases and parties having no real connection with them and that this practice has seldom if ever given rise to diplomatic protests . . . In practice the assumption of jurisdiction by a state does not seem to be subject to any requirement that the defendant or the facts of the case need to have any connection with that state; and this practice seems to have met with acquiescence by other states . . . It is hard to resist the conclusion that . . . customary international law imposes no limits on the jurisdiction of municipal courts in civil trials. (Michael Akehurst, 'Jurisdiction in International Law' (1972–73) 46 BYIL 145, 176 ff)

Because of this, Professor *Andreas Lowenfeld* explained that it is '[a] fair question . . . whether there is a unifying principle' of judicial jurisdiction under 'international law, or only separate national laws addressing similar issues' (Andreas F Lowenfeld, 'International Litigation and the Quest for Reasonableness' [1994-I] Rec. des Cours 82). In his and the Restatement (Third) of Foreign Relations Law of the United States' view, international law imposes a 'reasonableness' requirement on assertions of judicial jurisdiction. 'States exercise jurisdiction to adjudicate on the basis of various links, including

... the defendant's nationality ... reliance on other bases, such as the nationality of the plaintiff or the presence of property unrelated to the claim, is generally considered as "exorbitant"' (Restatement (Third) of Foreign Relations Law, pt 4, ch 2, intro note).

The view that international law imposes restraints on judicial jurisdiction is, however, not universally accepted. Indeed, it may be the case that such a view of international law's limits on judicial jurisdiction permits too much discretion on the part of nations and their courts. The international law limits, if any, on jurisdiction are hard to delineate because assertions of judicial jurisdiction are largely an exercise of self-restraint in light of domestic policies. Yet, even if international law does not directly constrain a national court's exercise of judicial jurisdiction, it provides perhaps a useful conceptual framework for understanding acceptable and exorbitant bases of jurisdiction, even though international law does not dictate the rules for judicial jurisdiction.

2. Acceptable bases of judicial jurisdiction

Some bases of judicial jurisdiction are clearly acceptable in most (if not all) nations, and thus might be evidence of general principles of law that provide some evidence for international law limits on judicial jurisdiction. For instance, the principle that a defendant should always be amenable to suit in its place of domicile (*actor forum rei sequitur*) is clearly established in Europe as well as in the USA. An individual's domicile is usually defined as the nation where one last was present with an intent to remain indefinitely. Legal persons, such as corporations, are domiciled in the nation in which they are organized/incorporated and, in some cases, where they maintain their principal place of business. The idea behind such jurisdiction is that on account of the privilege of being affiliated with a state, the defendant is always subject to the authority of that nation's courts.

There is general agreement that the forum chosen by the parties to resolve a dispute should be respected. The idea is that parties may consent to establish judicial jurisdiction in a particular forum and also to oust all other fora of jurisdiction by explicitly consenting to jurisdiction through a forum selection clause or implicitly consenting to jurisdiction by not challenging the jurisdiction of a court. This general agreement is based on the idea that the parties have the autonomy to agree on which court will decide their dispute.

There is also general agreement that a state may assert judicial jurisdiction where a defendant has done a particular act or caused certain effects in a nation. The idea here is that a state has an interest in regulating and adjudicating all acts that occur or have an effect in its territory.

It is arguably best to view the question not as one of what limits international law places on judicial jurisdiction, but rather as what has been permitted generally by states in matters of judicial jurisdiction.

The Brussels I Regulation (recast) provides a useful example. Under the Regulation, the starting principle is that a defendant domiciled in a contracting state should generally be sued in the courts of that state (art 4(1) Brussels I Regulation (recast)). Domiciliaries of contracting states may be sued in the courts of other contracting states only if one of the Regulation rules permits (art 5 Brussels I Regulation (recast)). For example, the permissible bases of jurisdiction are such that in matters of contract the suit may be brought in the → place of performance (art 7(1) Brussels I Regulation (recast)). In matters of tort, suit may be brought where the harmful act occurred (art 7(2) Brussels I Regulation (recast)). This is understood as covering both the place where the damage occurred and the place of the event giving rise to it. In respect to disputes arising out of the operation or a branch office or agency (→ Agency and authority of agents), suit may proceed in the place where the branch or agent is located (art 7(5) Brussels I Regulation (recast)). And in actions *in rem*, the state where the property is located has exclusive jurisdiction (art 24(1) Brussels I Regulation (recast)). Under these rules, contracting states are prohibited from exercising judicial jurisdiction against domiciliaries of other contracting states on exorbitant bases.

Based on these provisions, it can be said that the acceptable bases for judicial jurisdiction are domicile, consent, acts or effects occurring in the nation, and the location of property (→ Property and proprietary rights).

It is important to note that these jurisdictional rules only apply to defendants domiciled in EU Member States. For suits against non-Member State party domiciliaries, jurisdiction is determined by the law of the state where suit is brought (art 5 Brussels I Regulation (recast)). To the extent national laws permit exorbitant jurisdiction, then such rules would be applicable to non-Member State party domiciliaries regardless of the domicile of the Member State party plaintiff. This approach casts doubt on the Brussels I Regulation (recast) as creating international law rules. For, under international law, the same rule of judicial jurisdiction should arguably be applicable to a defending party regardless of domicile. This is so because under international law an alien should be treated in rough parity with a domiciliary to prevent a denial of justice, which is itself an actionable claim under international law.

Nonetheless, it may be argued that it is a general principle of law that a substantial connection must exist between the forum and the parties or the matters involved before a court exercises its jurisdiction. For instance, the UNIDROIT Principles of Transnational Civil Procedure (ALI/UNIDROIT Rules of Transnational Civil Procedure (text of the Principles and the accompanying commentary were adopted by the American Law Institute (ALI) in May 2004 and by the International Institute for the Unification of Private Law (→ UNIDROIT) in April 2004 (2004) 4 Unif.L.Rev. 758)) require 'substantial connection between the forum state and the party or the transaction or occurrence in dispute' (UNIDROIT Principles at cmt P2-B). Scholars have stated the 'substantial connection' standard differently, for example by requiring a 'clear connecting factor', or a factual 'linking point . . . between the legislating state and the conduct that it seeks to regulate [abroad]' (Vaughan Lowe, 'Jurisdiction' in Malcom D Evans (ed), *International Law* (2nd edn, OUP 2006) 342; see also Ian Brownlie, *Principles of Public International Law* (6th edn, OUP 2003) 309, requiring a 'substantial and bona fide connection between subject matter and the source of the jurisdiction'; Francesco Francioni, 'Extraterritorial Application of Environmental Law' in Karl Matthias Meessen (ed), *Extraterritorial Jurisdiction in Theory and Practice* (Kluwer 1996) 126, noting that an assertion of extraterritorial jurisdiction over subjects who have no significant relation to the forum, except transitory presence or an indirect effect, may well constitute a breach of an international due process standard; Dieter Lange and Gary Born (eds), *The Extraterritorial Application of National Laws* (ICC Pub 1987)

46–7: '[I]ncreasing support has developed for a jurisdictional rule of reason that would limit unreasonable exercises of national jurisdiction' and thereby 'limit . . . applications of national laws that unduly interfere with foreign interests and international trade'). By way of example, a 'substantial connection exists' when (i) 'a significant part of the transaction or occurrence occurred in the forum state', (ii) 'an individual defendant is a habitual resident of the forum state or a jural entity has received its charter of organization or has its principal place of business therein' or (iii) 'property to which the dispute relates is located in the forum state' (UNIDROIT Principles 2.1.2).

II. Exorbitant jurisdiction

Exorbitant jurisdiction refers to those assertions of jurisdiction that, though valid under national law, nonetheless appear to be unfair due to the limited contact between the forum and the parties or the dispute. The Brussels Convention (Brussels Convention of 27 September 1968 on jurisdiction and the enforcement of judgments in civil and commercial matters, [1972] OJ L 299/32, consolidated version, [1998] OJ C 27/1) outlawed certain bases of adjudicatory jurisdiction partially in response to demands made by American and British delegations to the Hague Conference of 1966 that certain grounds of jurisdiction should be declared exorbitant, and, as such, that judgments based on those grounds should not be recognized (Joseph Halpern, '"Exorbitant Jurisdiction" and the Brussels Convention: Towards a Theory of Restraint' (1983) 9 Yale J. World Pub.Ord. 369, 481). The Brussels I Regulation (recast) continues this approach (art 5(2)). It is often assumed that US courts assert jurisdiction in expansive and exorbitant ways when compared to Europe. However, in many instances European courts permit the exercise of jurisdiction on bases that can also be viewed as exorbitant.

For instance, art 14 of the French Civil Code (Code Civil of 21 March 1804) has been read to provide that a French national may sue a foreigner in French courts without regard to any connection between the cause of action and the French forum, except for the plaintiff's nationality (→ France). Similarly, Netherlands courts may assert jurisdiction based on the plaintiff's domicile (art 126(3) of the Dutch Code of Civil Procedure (Wetboek van Burgerlijke

Rechtsvordering, available at <http://wetten.overheid.nl>, last accessed on 25 November 2014)) (→ Netherlands).

Under art 23 of the German Civil Code (Bürgerliches Gesetzbuch of 2 January 2002, BGBl. I 42, as amended), German courts may assert jurisdiction over any defendant with assets in → Germany. Traditionally, the cause of action did not have to relate to the assets, but the German Federal Court of Justice has recently imposed the requirement that the plaintiff be domiciled in Germany or the cause of action have some connection to Germany. In reaching this conclusion, it is not clear that the German Federal Court of Justice was applying international law.

In the USA and the → United Kingdom, a person served with process in the forum state (transient or tag jurisdiction) is subject to judicial jurisdiction. This is viewed as exorbitant by many nations. Furthermore, the so-called 'doing business' theory of judicial jurisdiction in the USA, whereby a corporation that transacts a certain quantum of business with the forum state may be subject to all-purpose jurisdiction, is also viewed as exorbitant by many countries (→ USA).

A number of nations are willing to assert exorbitant jurisdiction, but only over the national of a country that would assert such a basis of jurisdiction over the forum's nationals. The countries employing such jurisdiction include → Belgium, → Italy and → Portugal.

The Brussels I Regulation (recast) approach that a person domiciled in a Member State may also be sued, if one of a number of defendants, in the courts of the place where any one defendant is domiciled, 'provided the claims are so closely connected that it is expedient to hear and determine them together to avoid the risk of irreconcilable judgements resulting from separate proceedings', might also be viewed as exorbitant in other systems (art 8 Brussels I Regulation (recast)).

The many bases of exorbitant jurisdiction further cast doubt on any clear principle of international law that limits judicial jurisdiction. It may be concluded, therefore, that since many nations claim judicial jurisdiction in matters where there is not a significant connection with the forum and since such assertions of jurisdiction do not often lead to protests by other nations that international law offers limited restrictions on assertions of judicial jurisdiction.

III. Appraisal

The limits, if any, that international law places on judicial jurisdiction are open to debate. At the least, it seems clear that state practice and *opinio juris* do not limit many assertions of judicial jurisdiction. It also appears that general principles of law, outside of judicial jurisdiction being appropriate in a defendant's place of domicile, are still not fully developed. It is also questionable whether the idea of reasonableness has reached the level state practice and *opinio juris* under international law to limit assertions of judicial jurisdiction.

For these reasons, it is far too soon to conclude that international law places meaningful limits on judicial jurisdiction and assertions of exorbitant jurisdiction. Such a conclusion does not take sides on the normative question of whether international law should limit assertions of adjudicatory jurisdiction. Rather, it is a conclusion based on the practice of nations and their courts at present. The current American Law Institute project on the Restatement (Fourth) of the Foreign Relations Law of the United States will, no doubt, have much to say on these matters. Yet, no matter what conclusion the new Restatement comes to, its approach will have to be proven by the general acceptance of states.

DONALD EARL CHILDRESS III

Literature

Michael Akehurst, 'Jurisdiction in International Law' (1972–73) 46 BYIL 145; Patrick J Borchers, 'Comparing Personal Jurisdiction in the United States and the European Community: Lessons for American Reform' (1992) 40 Am.J.Comp.L. 121; Ian Brownlie, *Principles of Public International Law* (6th edn, OUP 2003) 309; Costas Douzinas, 'The Metaphysics of Jurisdiction' in Shaun McVeigh (ed), *Jurisprudence of Jurisdiction* (Routledge-Cavendish 2007) 21; Francesco Francioni, 'Extraterritorial Application of Environmental Law' in Karl Matthias Meessen (ed), *Extraterritorial Jurisdiction in Theory and Practice* (Kluwer 1996) 126; Dieter Lange and Gary Born (eds), *The Extraterritorial Application of National Laws* (ICC Pub 1987) 46–7; Vaughan Lowe, 'Jurisdiction' in Malcom D Evans (ed), *International Law* (2nd edn, OUP 2006) 342; Frederick A Mann, 'The Doctrine of Jurisdiction in International Law' (1964-I) 111 Rec. des Cours 1; Frederick A Mann, 'The Doctrine of Jurisdiction in International Law Revisited after Twenty Years' (1984-III) 186 Rec. des Cours 9;

Alex Mills, *The Confluence of Public and Private international law* (CUP 2009); Willis LM Reese, 'Legislative Jurisdiction' (1978) 78 Colum.L.Rev. 1587; William Michael Reisman (ed), *Jurisdiction in International Law* (Ashgate 1999); Cedric Ryngaert, *Jurisdiction in International Law* (OUP 2008).

Kahn, Franz

Franz Kahn (1861–1904) was one of the first authors who refused to construe an international theory or system of private international law. He was convinced that private international law is national law but has to be treated by internationally orientated methods.

I. Life and work

Franz Kahn was born on 2 August 1861 in Mannheim/Baden as the oldest son of *Bernhard Kahn* (1827–1905) and his wife *Emma*, née *Eberstadt* (1840–1906). His parents were Jews who came from villages in southern Germany and settled in Mannheim which, at this time, had a comparatively large liberal Jewish community, the biggest (about 7 per cent of the citizens) of any city of the German state Großherzogtum Baden (Karl Otto Watzinger, *Geschichte der Juden in Mannheim 1650–1945* (2nd edn, Kohlhammer 1987) 24). His father was a merchant, banker and member of the city parliament (Helmut Weber, *Die Theorie der Qualifikation* (Mohr Siebeck 1986) 14). He left Baden after the revolution of 1848, immigrated to the → USA, became a naturalized American citizen and returned in 1857 (Franz Kahn dealt with the nationality of the Kahn family of 'K.B.' (abbreviated form of: Kahn, Bernhard) in his article 'Staatsangehörigkeit, Erwerb und Verlust, Heimatlosigkeit (1898) 8 NiemZ 320–27 = Franz Kahn, *Abhandlungen zum internationalen Privatrecht*, vol 1 (Otto Lenel and Hans Lewald (eds), Duncker & Humblot 1928) 480). Two of *Franz Kahn's* younger brothers were the composer *Robert Kahn* (1865–1951) and the New York banker *Otto Hermann Kahn* (1867–1934), partner of the New York bank *Kuhn, Loeb & Co.* One of his sisters was *Elisabeth (Lili) Kahn* (1869–1940), wife of *Felix Deutsch* (1858–1928, the co-founder of the big industrial plant *AEG* and successor of his colleague *Emil Rathenau*, 1838–1915), a friend of *Walther Rathenau* (1867–1922; Shulamit Volkov, *Walther Rathenau. Ein jüdisches Leben in Deutschland 1867–1922* (CH Beck 2012) 109), the murdered German Minister of Foreign Affairs. *Lili* became known as the '*grande dame*' of the upper class society of Berlin (Helmut Weber, *Die Theorie der Qualifikation* (Mohr Siebeck 1986) 15).

After having passed the final school examination (Abitur) of the Karl-Friedrich-Gymnasium in Mannheim in 1879, *Franz Kahn* enrolled as a student at Berlin University for the winter term 1880/81 and after having spent two semesters as a law student in Heidelberg and Munich, he studied three semesters at the University of Leipzig (Gisbert Lamberg, *Die kollisionsrechtliche Lehre von Franz Kahn (1861–1904)* (Dissertation, Göttingen 1975) XXIII). He finished his law studies in Heidelberg (1883/84) and Freiburg im Breisgau in 1884/85. At the University of Leipzig (having the 'best' law faculty: Max Hachenburg, *Lebenserinnerungen eines Rechtsanwalts und Briefe aus der Emigration* (Kohlhammer 1978) 35) *Franz Kahn* also participated in the Pandekten-exercises of *Otto Lenel* (1849–1935), the famous classical historian of Roman law, also a Jew from Mannheim and a close friend of *Franz Kahn* (Otto Lenel, 'Vorwort' in Franz Kahn (ed), *Abhandlungen zum internationalen Privatrecht*, vol 1 (Duncker & Humblot 1928) XV). They may have even been related by marriage (Theodor Niemeyer (*Erinnerungen und Betrachtungen aus drei Menschenaltern* (Mühlau 1963) 138) records that *Lenel* called *Franz Kahn* his 'Schwager', ie his brother-in-law) because the mother of *Franz Kahn* was *Emma Eberstadt* (daughter of *Ferdinand Eberstadt*, 1808–88) and the wife of *Otto Lenel* was *Luise Eberstadt*, daughter of *Abraham Eberstadt* (1810–92). The *Eberstadts* were a famous Jewish family of Worms, later Mannheim. *Franz Kahn* passed the two state examinations in 1885 and 1888, respectively, and became for a short time judge at the court of first instance in Karlsruhe and in Bretten, a small town east of Karlsruhe. During 1888 and 1889 *Kahn* travelled to → France and England (→ United Kingdom) in order to study French and English law. His friend *Otto Lenel* had suggested this effort of studying foreign law in the state of origin (Otto Lenel, 'Vorwort' in Franz Kahn (ed), *Abhandlungen zum internationalen Privatrecht*, vol 1 (Duncker & Humblot 1928) XIII note 2). Because of his weak health he finally quit his job and decided to devote his time to writing mainly on problems of private international law.

Franz Kahn started his career as legal author with his thesis *Zur Geschichte des Römischen Frauen-Erbrechts* (On the History of Roman Law of Succession of Women), submitted to and accepted by the University of Leipzig in 1884 (Gisbert Lamberg, *Die kollisionsrechtliche Lehre von Franz Kahn (1861–1904)* (Dissertation Göttingen 1975) XXV). Two years later *Franz Kahn* published his first paper, 'Die Natur der Interventionsklage nach der C.P.O., und deren Anwendung auf die Mobiliar-Exekution im Gebiete des französischen Rechts' ((1886) 70 AcP 409). This paper deals with the claim of a third person under § 690 German Code of Civil Procedure of 1877 (Civilprozessordnung, RGBl. vol 1877, No 6 pp 83–243, henceforth CPO), now § 771 German Code of Civil Procedure (Zivilprozessordnung of 5 December 2005, BGBl. I 3202, as amended, henceforth ZPO), alleging that the movable seized in execution belongs to him according to art 2279 of the French Civil Code (Code Civil of 21 March 1804). This problem is still open and *Kahn's* paper is cited even today (Friedrich Stein and Martin Jonas, '§ 771 ZPO' in Friedrich Stein and Martin Jonas (eds), *Kommentar zur Zivilprozessordnung* (22nd edn, Mohr Siebeck 2012) para 4, fn 18). This paper can only be explained by the legal situation in which the German Empire found itself after 1871. The uniform CPO had entered into force in Germany on 1 January 1879, but private law was still regional law. In Baden, of which Mannheim and Heidelberg were part, the Badische Landrecht was still in force, a law which was based on the French Code civil. *Franz Kahn* was therefore interested in comparative law (→ Comparative law and private international law) and in private international law which, until 1900, was also important in Germany as interregional private law. Another article of *Franz Kahn* dealt with the territorial applicability of the Maintenance Act of Baden of 1851 ((1886) 52 *Annalen der Großherzoglich Badischen Gerichte* 170). Here his interest in conflicts law had already become evident.

Very soon after the unification of Germany in 1871, commissions were appointed to prepare drafts of a German civil code (Bürgerliches Gesetzbuch of 18 August 1896, RGBl. S. 195, as amended) and of an introductory statute of the civil code, the EGBGB (Einführungsgesetz zum Bürgerlichen Gesetzbuche of 18 August 1896, RGBl. S. 604, as amended), comprising the international, interlocal and temporary dimensions of the BGB. In six extensive articles, *Franz Kahn* published on problems of private international law in the prestigious *Jahrbücher für die Dogmatik des heutigen römischen und deutschen Privatrechts* founded by *Rudolf von Jhering* (1818–92) and, after *Jhering's* death and after the entry into force of the BGB, called *Jherings Jahrbücher für die Dogmatik des bürgerlichen Rechts*. The first article 'Gesetzeskollisionen: Ein Beitrag zur Lehre des internationalen Privatrechts' ((1891) 30 JherJb 1 = Franz Kahn, *Abhandlungen zum internationalen Privatrecht*, vol 1 (Otto Lenel and Hans Lewald (eds), Duncker & Humblot 1928) 1) deals, in a realistic, bold and astute manner, with three main problems of private international law: the nature of sources are national law unless unified by conventions; → *renvoi* has to be declined because it leads to a 'logisches Spiegelkabinett'; and the 'invention' of 'latente Gesetzeskollisionen', ie the different qualification or characterization of legal institutions as *Étienne Bartin* (→ Bartin, Étienne) (1860–1948) called it a few years later in (1897) 24 J.Dr.Int.Priv. 225, 466, 720 = Bartin, *Études* 1–82. The second article ((1896) 36 JherJb 366–408 = Franz Kahn, *Abhandlungen zum internationalen Privatrecht*, vol 1 (Otto Lenel and Hans Lewald (eds), Duncker & Humblot 1928) 124) is devoted again to the problem of *renvoi*, and this paper discusses the *renvoi* provisions as they were accepted in art 27 of the German EGBGB (original old version) and in art 1 of the Hague Marriage Convention of 1902 (in preparation since 1893). He vigorously opposes *renvoi* and relies heavily on his own judgment and on mainly French authors. The third article of *Franz Kahn* 'Die Lehre vom ordre public (Prohibitivgesetze)' ((1898) 39 JherJb 1 = Franz Kahn, *Abhandlungen zum internationalen Privatrecht*, vol 1 (Otto Lenel and Hans Lewald (eds), Duncker & Humblot 1928) 161) compares the Romanistic theory of mandatory rules with the German theory of *ordre public*. Rejecting the Romanistic theory (based mainly on *Pasquale Stanislao Mancini*, 1817–88) *Kahn* stresses two important points. The first one is the experience that not all mandatory rules apply in every case. They may only concern nationals of the forum state and not have regard for foreigners. The other point is that mandatory rules of the forum state only apply in cases which have a close relation to the forum state. His conclusion is that the problem of *ordre public* is a kind of 'Sicherheitsventil' (safety valve) which is qualified as 'the yet unknown and yet unfinished part of private international law' (Franz Kahn, *Abhandlungen zum internationalen Privatrecht*, vol 1 (Otto Lenel and Hans Lewald (eds), Duncker & Humblot 1928) 251). The fourth article of *Franz Kahn* summarizes to some extent what he already had written before. In 'Über Inhalt, Natur und Methode des internationalen Privatrechts' (Meaning, Nature and Method of PIL), published in (1899) 40 JherJb 1–87 = Franz Kahn, *Abhandlungen zum internationalen Privatrecht*, vol 1 (Otto Lenel and Hans Lewald (eds), Duncker & Humblot 1928) 255, *Kahn* stresses, once more, that private international law is, with very few exceptions, national law and cannot be derived from principles of public international law as it is taught by many of his well-established German colleagues such as *Carl Ludwig von Bar* (1836–1913) and *Ernst Zitelmann* (1852–1923). The last two papers published in JherJb deal with special German problems of intertemporal law which became important and practical after the EGBGB, including the new German rules on private international law, had entered into force on 1 January 1900 (see Franz Kahn, *Abhandlungen zum internationalen Privatrecht*, vol 1 (Otto Lenel and Hans Lewald (eds), Duncker & Humblot 1928) 327, 363). Finally, *Franz Kahn* stressed the importance of comparative law for private international law in his contribution to the International Conference on Comparative Law in Paris in 1900 ('Bedeutung der Rechtsvergleichung mit Bezug auf das internationale Privatrecht' (1900) 10 NiemZ 97 = Franz Kahn, *Abhandlungen zum internationalen Privatrecht*, vol 1 (Otto Lenel and Hans Lewald (eds), Duncker & Humblot 1928) 491 = 'Rôle, fonction et méthode du droit comparé dans le domaine du droit international privé' (1900) 29 Bull.Lég.Comp. 406). He called the use of comparative law 'eine dritte Richtung' (a third direction) which may overcome the opposing theories of international law and national law as bases of private international law.

During his last years *Franz Kahn* commented on the first Hague conventions and draft conventions: the Hague Marriage Convention, the Draft Convention on Succession and the Hague Divorce Convention 1902. These critical comments on the Third Hague Conference were published in NiemZ in the years 1903–05 (Franz Kahn, *Abhandlungen zum internationalen Privatrecht*, vol 2 (Otto Lenel and Hans Lewald (eds), Duncker & Humblot 1928) 37). In 1903 *Kahn* gave a lecture in Berlin on 'The Uniform Codification of Private international law by Treaties' (Franz Kahn, *Abhandlungen zum internationalen Privatrecht*, vol 2 (Otto Lenel and Hans Lewald (eds), Duncker & Humblot 1928) 1). He welcomed the → Hague Conference on Private International Law, which started in 1893, and expected that the Conference might finally lead to a worldwide uniform private international law.

Franz Kahn died of tuberculosis on 6 December 1904. He left his library as a legacy to the University of Kiel and its Institute of International Law as the 'Franz Kahn Library' which, since the Second World War, has no longer existed (Theodor Niemeyer, *Erinnerungen und Betrachtungen aus drei Menschenaltern* (Mühlau 1963) 138; Helmut Weber, *Die Theorie der Qualifikation* (Mohr Siebeck 1986) 16). More than 20 years after the death of *Franz Kahn* his papers were collected and published as 'Abhandlungen zum internationalen Privatrecht'. The publication of the two volumes was made possible by grants made by *Franz Kahn's* sister *Elisabeth Deutsch* of Berlin and his brother *Otto Kahn* of New York (Otto Lenel, 'Vorwort' in Franz Kahn (ed), *Abhandlungen zum internationalen Privatrecht*, vol 1 (Duncker & Humblot 1928) XVI). These volumes were edited by *Otto Lenel* and *Hans Lewald* (1883–1963), the latter being himself a specialist of private international law as well as Roman and Byzantine law and an admirer of *Otto Lenel*.

II. Kahn's contribution to private international law

Franz Kahn contributed to private international law especially in five different fields: national law as a basis of private international law, qualification or characterization, *renvoi*, *ordre public* and comparative method.

1. Basis of private international law

In the 19th century many scholars of private international law based this field of law on public international law (→ Public international law and private international law). They had the idea that international law draws the limits of national jurisdictions and obliges the states to recognize foreign judgments rendered by courts of the internationally competent foreign state. *Ernst Zitelmann* (1852–1923), in the first volume of his treatise on private international law (published 1897), called this internationally based conflicts law 'Reines internationales Privatrecht' (pure private international law) and distinguished it from the 'Angewandtes internationales Privatrecht' (applied private international law) treated in the second volume. Also *Carl Ludwig von Bar* (1836–1913) emphasized in the second edition of his treatise on 'The Theory and Practice of Private international law' (published in 1889, translated in 1892) that it is not up to the sovereign states to decide whether they are competent or not. This has to be decided by the 'Natur der Sache' (nature of the subject) and by some supranational sources giving authority to the states (Carl Ludwig von Bar, *The Theory and Practice of Private international law* (2nd edn, Green 1892) I § 32). Therefore, *Carl Ludwig von Bar* does not accept *Friedrich Carl von Savigny's* theory of the 'seat of a legal relationship' (*Sitz eines Rechtsverhältnisses*) because, first, the competent jurisdiction has to be fixed (Carl Ludwig von Bar, *The Theory and Practice of Private international law* (2nd edn, Green 1892) I § 107). There is not yet unanimity with respect to such international rules of limitation of national jurisdictions. Therefore sovereign states may define themselves their jurisdiction (eg on '*nazionalità*' as *Mancini* (→ Mancini, Pasquale Stanislao) proposed as an internationally desirable principle of personal law) but have to pay respect to any internationally fixed limitation of their jurisdiction. If they do not give respect to such internationally accepted rules, the states may be held liable for violation of such rules. This internationally based concept of private international law also affected the newly enacted German private international law of the EGBGB (Oskar Hartwieg and Friedrich Korkisch, *Die geheimen Materialien zur Kodifikation des deutschen internationalen Privatrechts 1881–1896* (Mohr Siebeck 1973) 17). Many unilateral conflicts rules on the application of German law were formulated in order to avoid international disputes about foreign law to be applied in German courts.

Franz Kahn was not convinced of this approach. From the outset he wrote that private international law is basically national law and that foreign law is not to be applied because it wants to govern but because the forum state decides by its conflicts rules that it shall govern the specific case. *Carl Ludwig von Bar* reacted to this attitude of *Franz Kahn* (Franz Kahn, *Abhandlungen zum internationalen Privatrecht*, vol 1 (Otto Lenel and Hans Lewald (eds), Duncker & Humblot 1928) 153) very angrily ((1898) 8 NiemZ 187 note 14) and accused *Franz Kahn* of charging *von Bar* with 'sehr gemeinschädliche Thätigkeit' (very noxious activity). *Franz Kahn* reacted to these reproaches and expressed his concern and lack of understanding of *von Bar's* protestations (Franz Kahn, *Abhandlungen zum internationalen Privatrecht*, vol 1 (Otto Lenel and Hans Lewald (eds), Duncker & Humblot 1928) 269 note 27). More than 30 years later *George Melchior* in his *Grundlagen des deutschen internationalen Privatrechts* wrote, with reference to *Franz Kahn*, in 1932: 'In Germany of the year 1890, you still had to be very courageous to stress the national character of private international law resulting from the differences of connecting factors, an opinion which was qualified by *von Bar*, an eminent scholar, as an act of impertinence' (George Melchior, *Grundlagen des deutschen internationalen Pivatrechts* (de Gruyter 1932) 17). *Franz Kahn* had this courage.

2. Qualification or characterization in private international law

In his 1891 research on conflict of laws (Franz Kahn, *Gesetzeskollisionen: Ein Beitrag zur Lehre des internationalen Privatrechts* (Jena 1891) 92), *Franz Kahn* asked himself about the origins of such conflicts, ie differences in choosing the law applicable in the respective forum state. *Kahn* distinguished two types of conflicts: the open ones using different connecting factors like nationality (in most of the continental countries) and domicile (mainly in Anglo-American countries) and the hidden ones, called latent conflicts ('latente Gesetzeskollisionen'). These hidden or latent conflicts originate in classifying the same problem of substantive law as belonging to different rules of private international law. This happens, for example, with statutes of limitation, which are classified in continental law as a matter governed by the law applicable to the respective claim whereas in common law countries at *Kahn's* time they were classified as procedural law and therefore governed by the respective *lex fori proceduralis*. *Kahn* was the first to discover this basic problem of private international law (Hans

Dölle, 'Juristische Entdeckungen' in Ständige Deputation des Deutschen Juristentages (ed), *Verhandlungen des 42. Deutschen Juristentages II* (Mohr Siebeck 1958) B 1, B 19) and was soon followed by *Étienne Bartin*, who observed the same phenomenon and frankly admitted in 1899 that he did not know of *Kahn's* article when he wrote his contribution to this problem in 1897 (Étienne Bartin, *Études de droit international privé* (Chevalier-Marescq 1899) 2 note 2).

3. Renvoi *in private international law*

Franz Kahn criticized *renvoi* very early. Different jurisdictions may apply different laws to the same case because they use different → connecting factors in their conflicts law. If courts have to apply foreign law, they should not pay regard to foreign conflicts law but to foreign substantive law which is applicable because it should govern the case according to the conflicts rule of the forum and not because it wants to be applied. *Renvoi*, as *Kahn* correctly and astutely realized, will lead to what *John Westlake* called '*circulus inextricabilis*' (John Westlake, *A Treatise on Private international law* (5th edn, Sweet & Maxwell 1912) 31), a 'logisches Spiegelkabinett' (Franz Kahn, *Abhandlungen zum internationalen Privatrecht*, vol 1 (Otto Lenel and Hans Lewald (eds), Duncker & Humblot 1928) 20). If every state applied *renvoi* the same way, these states would not come to a final solution because each of these states will politely invite the other by saying 'after you'! What *Franz Kahn*, however, did not realize is the fact that not every state applies *renvoi* the same way and that also in other instances (especially with respect to preliminary questions which were later 'discovered') foreign conflicts law has to be observed and may have to be applied.

4. Ordre public *and mandatory rules*

What has been said about the English forms of action (Frederic William Maitland, *The Forms of Action at Common Law* (CUP 1909, reprint 1968) 1) could also be said of the theories of statutes in private international law around 1900: 'they still rule from their graves'. This became apparent, especially in French, Italian and Spanish literature, with respect to the problem of clauses and provisions of the → *lex fori* protecting the *ordre public* (→ Public policy (*ordre public*)). Anxious to apply foreign law which deviates from normal standards, the authors developed extensive theories how such foreign law may be avoided and/or its application reduced to normal standards. In his third paper on *ordre public Franz Kahn* deals with this problem diligently, correctly pointing out that the Romanist theories on *ordre public* are remnants of the old and outgrown theory of statutes delimiting their own applicability and that these theories were hardly accepted in German-speaking countries (Franz Kahn, *Abhandlungen zum internationalen Privatrecht*, vol 1 (Otto Lenel and Hans Lewald (eds), Duncker & Humblot 1928) 161). *Kahn* in his very learned and comparative study points out that *ordre public* is hardly applied in German-speaking countries and may be thought of as 'the still unknown and yet unfinished part of private international law' (Franz Kahn, *Abhandlungen zum internationalen Privatrecht*, vol 1 (Otto Lenel and Hans Lewald (eds), Duncker & Humblot 1928) 251).

5. *Comparative law and private international law*

Franz Kahn has been called a 'nationalist' and a 'positivist'. This is incorrect. He was a realist without grand visions of deriving private international law from some kind of international law or from the 'nature of the subject'. He agreed that two sentences or rules may be drawn from 'supranational' private international law: no state may prohibit the application of foreign law (→ Foreign law, application and ascertainment) by local courts, and every state must have principles of private international law (Franz Kahn, *Abhandlungen zum internationalen Privatrecht*, vol 1 (Otto Lenel and Hans Lewald (eds), Duncker & Humblot 1928) 286). But these two rules do not solve any problem. Rules have to be more specific. And *Kahn* finds such rules in national legislation, court decisions and scholarly writings. If this realistic and pragmatic attitude is called 'positivism', you may call him 'positivist'. For him public international law is the law governing the relation between states (law *inter nationes*) and has almost nothing to do with private international law, a name which *Kahn* accepts as normally used but correctly criticizes as misleading (Franz Kahn, *Abhandlungen zum internationalen Privatrecht*, vol 1 (Otto Lenel and Hans Lewald (eds), Duncker & Humblot 1928) 255). In 1931 *Max Gutzwiller* wrote: 'Whoever wants to enjoy an amusing hour, may read the literature on the question of naming [of private international law]' (Max Gutzwiller, *Internationalprivatrecht* (Stilke 1931) 1549) and agreed with *Franz Kahn's* criticism completely.

Thus, *Franz Kahn* is not a 'nationalist' but a scholar devoted to comparative legal research. All his papers on private international law are based on material which was drawn from foreign and German sources. He quoted statutes of all important countries, analysed cases from major jurisdictions and referred to authors of all states and languages. He was perhaps the most learned comparative conflicts scholar of his time, and he provides an excellent example of the comparative law method he demanded for the study of private international law (Franz Kahn, *Abhandlungen zum internationalen Privatrecht*, vol 1 (Otto Lenel and Hans Lewald (eds), Duncker & Humblot 1928) 322, 491). This attitude is accepted today almost everywhere. *Konrad Zweigert* characterized *Franz Kahn* as 'one of the most brilliant German scholars of private international law', and located in *Kahn's* papers the origin of the so-called 'third school' of private international law, ie the school which – besides the 'internationalists' and the 'positivists' – introduced comparative law as the bases of serious studies in private international law (Konrad Zweigert, 'Die dritte Schule im internationalen Privatrecht. Zur neueren Wissenschaftsgeschichte des Kollisionsrechts' in Hans Peter Ipsen (ed), *Festschrift für Leo Raape* (Rechts- und Staatswissenschaftlicher Verlag 1948) 35, 37).

III. Kahn's influence on private international law

Franz Kahn's ideas and proposals for private international law have been accepted in modern times in such a way that no one any longer realizes that his papers were fundamental for modern developments and scholarship. This is not only true with respect to the general problems of private international law but also with respect to the more specific problems of → *renvoi* and *ordre public* (→ Public policy (*ordre public*)).

1. General problems of private international law

Private international law is national law unless unified by international conventions or EU regulations. Today this is the prevailing opinion with courts and scholars of private international law. The law-of-nations doctrine of private international law is almost a relic of history (Arthur Nussbaum, 'Rise and Fall of the Law-of-Nations Doctrine in the Conflict of Laws' (1942) 42 Colum.L.Rev. 189) and can hardly be understood by contemporary students of conflicts law. What *Franz Kahn* wrote about this subject matter and for what he was emotionally reprimanded by *Carl Ludwig von Bar* (Arthur Nussbaum, 'Rise and Fall of the Law-of-Nations Doctrine in the Conflict of Laws' (1942) 42 Colum.L.Rev. 189, 203 note 69) is so normal today that you have to dig carefully into the history of private international law (→ Private international law, history of) in order to explain to your students the ancient and once prevailing law-of-nations doctrine of conflicts law. Now no one associates *Franz Kahn* with this fight between two different theories nor observes that it was *Franz Kahn* who prevailed and laid the foundation stone of modern private international law.

Today it appears that European private international law will be uniform in some years, and the European Court of Justice as a common judicial body will contribute with its preliminary rulings to the uniformity of interpretation and application of European private international law – a goal that *Franz Kahn* envisaged for an effectively working body of supranational private international law (Franz Kahn, *Abhandlungen zum internationalen Privatrecht*, vol 1 (Otto Lenel and Hans Lewald (eds), Duncker & Humblot 1928) 2 and vol 2, 1).

Comparative law is today a natural method of private international law (→ Comparative law and private international law). EU regulations are conceived and drafted after the Commission has inquired into the laws of 28 Member States of the EU. The regulations are therefore based on comparative studies prepared in memoranda for Green Papers and on drafts for such instruments. *Franz Kahn's* ideas about the important role which comparative law has to serve in conflict-of-law studies is commonly accepted in Europe.

2. Specific problems of private international law

Franz Kahn also shaped modern conflicts law as concerns some problems which today are seen as being general problems of private international law, with respect to the question of *renvoi* and the problem of *ordre public*. Also in this regard *Franz Kahn* was ahead of his time. *Renvoi* has almost vanished and *ordre public* reduced to an exceptional application.

Renvoi, as *Franz Kahn* correctly observed, cannot be regarded as an institution which must be accepted by every jurisdiction. It does not work because all these jurisdictions would defer to the others with a polite 'after you'. However, he could not anticipate that Germany would for 100 years apply *renvoi* successfully with respect to states which did not have the same system of *renvoi* as Germany. Especially Anglo-American countries limit their jurisdiction with respect to immovables located in foreign countries and with respect to family matters of persons domiciled abroad. In these cases Germany qualified this disinterest of Anglo-American states as *renvoi* and applied German law to immovables located in Germany and to Anglo-American citizens domiciled in Germany. EU regulations have almost eliminated *renvoi* (eg art 20 Rome I Regulation (Regulation (EC) No 593/2008 of the European Parliament and of the Council of 17 June 2008 on the law applicable to contractual obligations (Rome I), [2008] OJ L 177/6; → Rome Convention and Rome I Regulation); art 24 → Rome II Regulation (Regulation (EC) No 864/2007 of the European Parliament and of the Council of 11 July 2007 on the law applicable to non-contractual obligations (Rome II), [2007] OJ L 199/40)) and kept it merely with respect to third states not applying the EU regulation in question (eg art 34 Succession Regulation (Regulation (EU) No 650/2012 of the European Parliament and of the Council of 4 July 2012 on jurisdiction, applicable law, recognition and enforcement of decisions and acceptance and enforcement of authentic instruments in matters of succession and on the creation of a European Certificate of Succession, [2012] OJ L 201/107; → Rome IV Regulation)).

The exception clause for *ordre public* has been reduced considerably. The clause applies only if the application of foreign law 'is manifestly incompatible with the public policy (*ordre public*) of the forum' (art 26 Rome II Regulation).

KURT SIEHR

Literature

Étienne Bartin, 'De l'impossibilité d'arriver à la supression définitive des conflits de lois' (1897) 24 J.Dr.Int.Priv. 225–55, 466–95, 720–38 = Étienne Bartin, 'La théorie des qualifications en droit international privé' in Étienne Bartin, *Études de droit international privé* (Chevalier-Marescq 1899) 1; Dimitrios J Evrigenis, 'Les classiques du droit international privé: Franz Kahn. A propos du Cinquantenaire de sa Mort (1904–1954)' [1957] IRuD 301; Franz Gamillscheg, 'Zur Erinnerung an Franz Kahn (2.8.1861 – 6.12.1904)' (1961) 26 RabelsZ 601; Max Hachenburg, *Lebenserinnerungen eines Rechtsanwalts und Briefe aus der Emigration* (Kohlhammer 1978); Gisbert Lamberg, *Die kollisionsrechtliche Lehre von Franz Kahn (1861–1904)* (Dissertation Göttingen 1975); Otto Lenel, 'Vorwort' in Franz Kahn (ed), *Abhandlungen zum internationalen Privatrecht*, vol 1 (Duncker & Humblot 1928) XIII; Theodor Niemeyer, *Erinnerungen und Betrachtungen aus drei Menschenaltern* (Mühlau 1963); Karl Otto Watzinger, *Geschichte der Juden in Mannheim 1650–1945* (2nd edn, Kohlhammer 1987); Helmut Weber, *Die Theorie der Qualifikation* (Mohr Siebeck 1986) 14; Ernst Zitelmann, 'Franz Kahn' (1905) 15 NiemZ 1; Konrad Zweigert, 'Die dritte Schule im internationalen Privatrecht. Zur neueren Wissenschaftsgeschichte des Kollisionsrechts' in Hans Peter Ipsen (ed), *Festschrift für Leo Raape* (Rechts- und Staatswissenschaftlicher Verlag 1948) 35.

Kegel, Gerhard

Gerhard Kegel was the most influential German academic of the second half of the 20th century in the domain of conflict of laws. His theory on the interests promoted by conflict of laws (*internationalprivatrechtliche Interessen*) had a decisive impact on the methods of private international law (→ Private international law, methods of). He had great influence over the codifications of the private international law of his time.

I. Life and work

Gerhard Kegel lived from 1912 to 2006. He came from an old family of protestant pastors and jurists. He was born on 26 June 1912 in Magdeburg and raised in the Uckermark, the landscape which *Theodor Fontane* described in his famous work *Wanderungen durch die Mark Brandenburg* ('Ramblings through Brandenburg') and which is considered the Tuscany of the north. Around 70 kilometres north of Berlin lies Templin, where his father was a pastor and teacher at the old and renowned Joachimsthalsche Gymnasium, which *Kegel* attended as well. This humanistic-protestant influence on his youth might be the origin of *Kegel's* great self-discipline and his sober work ethic. He learned not only Latin, Greek and Hebrew at school, but also English and French; in addition, he also later took up Italian, Dutch and Spanish (Zoltán Csehi, 'Gerhard Kegel [1912–2006] und sein Werk' in Verein zur Förderung der Rechtswissenschaft (ed), *Akademische Gedächtnisfeier für Gerhard Kegel* (Universität zu Köln 2007) 35, 38). During his school days he learned Syriac on his own. He gave up his plan of becoming an orientalist in favour of jurisprudence. He took great interest in philosophy, which he pursued in lifelong private studies.

From 1930 to 1933 *Kegel* studied law at the universities of Erlangen (summer semester 1930) and Göttingen (winter semester 1930/31), as well as at Friedrich Wilhelms University in Berlin (Humboldt University as of 1949). In his entertaining memoirs full of wit and irony he describes his studies and his lecturers (Gerhard Kegel, *Humor und Rumor – Erinnerungen* (CH Beck 1997)). He attended the private international law lectures of *Hans Lewald* and *Martin Wolff*, as well as two seminars taught by *Ernst Rabel* (→ Rabel, Ernst). After his first presentation during one of those seminars, *Kegel* was offered an assistantship by *Rabel*. His second presentation on 'Court decisions on the right to a compulsory portion in the transitional law of Alsace-Lorraine' was published in the Zeitschrift für ausländisches und internationales Privatrecht ('RabelsZ'; (1933) 7 RabelsZ 467) edited by *Rabel*. Ernst Rabel was the sole academic mentor recognized and appreciated by *Gerhard Kegel*. *Rabel* in return supposedly called *Kegel* his only academic student in the field of private international law (Gerhard Kegel, *Humor und Rumor – Erinnerungen* (CH Beck 1997) 55).

In Berlin, he passed both state examinations in law in the years 1934 and 1938. Following the first state examination in law, *Kegel* was appointed by *Rabel* as his research assistant at the Institute for Foreign Private Law and Private international law, affiliated to the Kaiser Wilhelm Society for the Advancement of Science (Kaiser-Wilhelm Institut für ausländisches und internationales Privatrecht) in Berlin (the Max Planck Institute for Comparative and International Private Law as of 1948). The position included collaborating on expert opinions for actual court cases regarding foreign law. In 1936 *Rabel* conferred a doctorate on *Kegel* based on his dissertation 'Issues on the Concept of Set-off: Reciprocity and Liquidity from a Perspective of Comparative Law' (Gerhard Kegel, *Probleme mit der Aufrechnung: Gegenseitigkeit und Liquidität rechtsvergleichend dargestellt* (De Gruyter 1938, reprint in 1996)). This is where *Kegel* laid the foundations for his future works on comparative law. In this work, *Kegel's* typical writing style already becomes apparent: short sentences; lack of dependent clauses; restricted use of nouns; clear ideas and distinct views. As is often the case with *Kegel*, the subject matter both directly relates to legal practice and is demanding from an academic point of view. Comparative law is placed at the service of the → *lex fori*. It serves as a source of ideas and also as a measure of evaluation. In 1941, on behalf of the Kaiser Wilhelm Institute, he carried out a study on 'The Influence of the War on Treaties in the Jurisdiction of Germany, France, England and the United States of America' (Gerhard Kegel, Hans Rupp and Konrad Zweigert, *Die Einwirkung des Krieges auf Verträge in der Rechtsprechung Deutschlands, Frankreichs, Englands und der Vereinigten Staaten von Amerika* (De Gruyter 1941)) alongside *Konrad Zweigert* and *Hans Rupp*. *Kegel* worked on the extensive segment regarding German law. The study evaluates from a comparative point of view how the breach of an obligation due to war is to be treated in law. Furthermore, the doctrine of *clausula rebus sic stantibus* (the so-called 'Wegfall der Geschäftsgrundlage', frustration of contracts) is thoroughly covered. Then, in 1953, *Kegel* presented his doctrine in a speech he delivered to the Association of German Jurists (Deutscher Juristentag, Ständige Deputation des Deutschen Juristentags (DJT) (ed), *Verhandlungen des 40. DJT*, vol 1 (CH Beck 1953) 139–236). However, his opinion did not prevail and he could not achieve a codification of this legal concept. At the turn of the year 1939/40 *Kegel* got married (Gerhard Kegel, *Humor und Rumor – Erinnerungen* (CH Beck 1997) 104). He and his wife had five children who today are doctors, theologians and jurists. In 1941 he was called up by the German military. *Kegel* utterly opposed National Socialism; this can be seen in all of his publications from this time and was also witnessed.

HEINZ-PETER MANSEL

At the end of the Second World War *Kegel* went as far westwards as possible in Germany. Thus he came to Cologne and became Faculty Assistant in 1945. In 1946 he was awarded the *Habilitation* (post-doctoral lecture qualification) for his segment in the 1941 book on 'The Influence of the War on Treaties' (Gerhard Kegel, Hans Rupp and Konrad Zweigert, *Die Einwirkung des Krieges auf Verträge in der Rechtsprechung Deutschlands, Frankreichs, Englands und der Vereinigten Staaten von Amerika* (De Gruyter 1941)). The university teaching credentials (*venia legendi*) encompassed civil, commercial, private international and comparative law. In 1947 he was appointed Lecturer (*Diätendozentur*). Later, he declined offers of professorship at the universities of Darmstadt and Hamburg, but was appointed to a full professorship for international law at the University of Cologne (1 May 1950). There, he founded the Institute of Private International and Foreign Private Law of the University of Cologne, which houses a vast library of German and foreign literature regarding conflict of laws. The new institute's comparative law focus was Anglo-American law. *Kegel* followed the tradition of *Rabel* and the Berlin Kaiser Wilhelm Institute and placed his Institute at the service of court practice as a centre for legal opinions regarding foreign law. As director of the Institute, he, with the help of his research assistants, delivered a total of about 5,000 expert opinions on foreign law for German courts. In 1970 he succeeded in obtaining large private funding – an extreme rarity at the time – for the building that would house the International Legal Institutes of Cologne. But *Kegel* also made his Institute a place where foreign scholars could pursue their scientific interests in a vast library on conflicts of law. From 1961 until 1987 he was the president of the German Council of Private international law. This is a scientific council consisting only of a few professors, which advises the German Federal Ministry of Justice regarding legislation at both national and European levels, as well as legislation resulting from treaties in the conflict-of-laws field. The 1986 large-scale reform and partial codification of the German Private international law carries *Kegel's* signature.

Kegel's principal scientific work was in private international law. Nonetheless, he had a strong interest in comparative private law (see the bibliography in Heinz-Peter Mansel, *Internationales Privatrecht im 20. Jahrhundert* (Mohr Siebeck 2014) 57 ff). In private law, which *Kegel* usually approached from a comparative point of view, he focused mainly on property law (→ Property and proprietary rights) and, in particular, the law of obligations. There, he also aspired to create a new system. In the field of substantive law, *Kegel* was more revolutionary than conservative. For instance, based on studies of comparative law, he rejected the so-called '*Abstraktionsprinzip*', the German concept of distinguishing contractual obligation from the legal act of transfer of ownership (Gerhard Kegel, 'Obligation and Disposition' in Gesellschaft zur Förderung der wissenschaftlichen Zusammenarbeit mit der Universität Tel-Aviv, Universität zu Köln (ed), *Beiträge zum deutschen und israelischen Privatrecht* (P Hanstein 1977) 103–30). In doing so, he condemned one of the cornerstones and defining accomplishments of German civil law. His book 'Contract and Tort' (Gerhard Kegel, *Vertrag und Delikt* (Carl Heymanns 2001)) aimed to eradicate the boundaries between contracts and torts and to sort out all of the interdependencies in the protection of assets. The root of this reorientation, which was approved by *Kegel*, also lay in his comparative legal studies. The book found its direct sequel in *Kegel's* final article, 'Patrimony in the flow of time, *causa* and obligation' (Gerhard Kegel, 'Vermögen im Zeitfluss, causa und Obligation' in Hans-Erich Rasmussen-Bonne (ed), *Balancing of Interests: Liber amicorum Peter Hay* (Verlag Recht und Wirtschaft 2005), 219. A subsequent work titled 'Patrimony base, patrimony control, patrimony protection' (Gerhard Kegel, *Vermögensbestand, Vermögensherrschaft, Vermögensschutz* (Schöningh 2008) was published posthumously.

Kegel was a master of intellectual conciseness. Short sentences and condensed statements were his trademarks. His language was often figurative. In personal contact he was very kind, but he could also phrase scientific discourse sarcastically. His review of *Wilhelm Wengler's* voluminous Private international law book (Gerhard Kegel, 'Handwerkliche Notizen zu Wenglers neuem Werk' [1981] IPRax 185) finishes with a warning: 'Send me your books, otherwise I will review you!'

Kegel has received many honours. Almost since its establishment, he was a member of the North Rhine-Westphalian Academy of Sciences, Humanities and the Arts, where he later assumed a leadership role. Starting in

1965, he was one of three External Scientific Members of the Max Planck Institute of Foreign Private and Private international law in Hamburg. He received an honorary doctorate from the University of Mannheim (1983) and from the Colegio Mayor de Nuestra Señora del Rosario in Bogotá (1983). He was also honoured with the Berkeley Citation (1981), which was particularly important to him. Two *Festschriften* (1977 and 1987) and one *Liber amicorum* (2002) were dedicated to him; there was also a considerable number of appreciations in both German and foreign legal reviews on the occasions of his centenary birthday and his death (see the bibliography in Heinz-Peter Mansel, *Internationales Privatrecht im 20. Jahrhundert* (Mohr Siebeck 2014) 57, 65 ff). Upon his request, *Kegel* was granted *emeritus* status in 1977 and retired early in order to devote more time to research. He was an active academic researcher until his death. He held his last lecture on 2 December 2005 in Berlin on his revered teacher *Ernst Rabel* (Gerhard Kegel, 'Ernst Rabel' [2007] IPRax 1). *Gerhard Kegel* died on 16 February 2006.

II. *Kegel's* contribution to private international law

1. *Practice and science of conflict of laws: communicating vessels*

In Cologne, *Kegel* wrote his article-by-article commentary on the Introductory Act to the German Civil Code (Einführungsgesetz zum Bürgerlichen Gesetzbuche of 21 September 1994, BGBl. I 2494, as amended, henceforth EGBGB), which contains the partially codified German private international law. This commentary was part of the 8th edition (1955) of Soergel's commentary on the German Civil Code (Hans Theodor Soergel and Wolfgang Siebert (eds), *Bürgerliches Gesetzbuch: mit Einführungsgesetz und Nebengesetzen* (8th edn, Kohlhammer 1955). *Kegel's* great and comprehensive work depicted the complete German private international law. This commentary included the jurisprudence of the German courts on conflict of laws. The relevant bibliography was fully documented and discussed. It is unlikely that any other study on conflict of laws could compare to *Kegel's* commentary in the thoroughness of its evaluation of all possible sources. In his commentary, he also considered perceptions of foreign jurisdictions and authors. Every single treaty that applied to Germany and contained conflict-of-law rules was analysed. In the 12th edition (1996), *Kegel* still contributed half of the new commentary.

In 1960 he published his first edition of a private international law textbook (Gerhard Kegel, *Internationales Privatrecht. Ein Studienbuch* (CH Beck 1960)). It is a masterpiece of scholarship regarding choice of law because it combines an abundance of sources with an extraordinary clarity of analysis and a particular conciseness of proposition. This work had a worldwide effect and set standards for legal doctrine in international private law. It was translated into Spanish in its 4th edition (1977). The planned translation of its 9th edition (2004) into Chinese is not yet complete.

It was *Kegel's* objective to grasp the reality of German private international law in action. He therefore aimed to intensely analyse and depict judicial practice in legal commentaries and textbooks.

A similar motive led him to collect expert opinions on foreign legal systems that were issued by university institutes of private international law for the use in court proceedings. On behalf of the German Council of Private international law (Deutscher Rat für internationales Privatrecht), he published a selection of these opinions in annual volumes (*IPG – Gutachten zum Internationalen und Ausländischen Privatrecht*). This series was founded by *Kegel* in collaboration with *Konrad Zweigert* (Hamburg) and *Murad Ferid* (Munich) with the publication of the 1965/66 annual volume (1968). *Kegel's* series of expert opinions published in IPG complements the collection of German jurisprudence on choice of law (IPRspr) founded by → *Rabel*. By this intensive exchange with the legal practice, *Kegel* followed in the footsteps of his teacher *Rabel*. Like *Rabel*, he considered it a *nobile officium* to support the courts in applying foreign law (→ Foreign law, application and ascertainment).

2. *Legal certainty instead of doing justice in individual cases*

For *Kegel*, court practice was the source from where he gathered material for the distillation of choice-of-law rules. Until the reform of private international law in 1986, German choice-of-law rules were only partly codified. The rules on → personal status, including family law and the law of → succession, were to a great extent codified in unilateral conflict rules in the EGBGB. Most of them were declared unconstitutional after the so-called '*Spanier*' decision of the German Federal Constitutional Court (BVerfG) (4 May 1971, [1971] NJW 1509) because they one-sidedly preferred the law of the husband or father to the law of the wife or mother. In the discussion on how to fill the resulting loophole *de lege lata* and *de lege ferenda*, *Kegel* declared himself in favour of clear and easy-to-use rules. To *Kegel*, legal certainty was of paramount importance when determining the applicable law. This is why he fought choice-of-law rules that, after having weighed and taken into account all circumstances of the individual case, would call for the application of the law of the state which has 'the most significant relationship' or 'close and most real connection'. The 'closest connection', he stated, was a popular formula, but without any content. He said that it resembled 'a wind vane as direction sign' (Gerhard Kegel, 'Besprechung von Fritz Schwind: Handbuch des Österreichischen Internationalen Privatrechts' (1978) 178 AcP 118, 120). Therefore, he tried to standardize the closest connection through ranked objective points of contact. The applicable law is supposed to be determined in a standardized, abstract way and not through an individual and specific approach. This led to the creation of the now well-known '*Kegel's* Ladder' ('Kegel'sche Leiter'). Various → connecting factors are arranged in accordance with the principle of subsidiarity. Subsidiary connecting factors would only be used if the conditions of the higher-ranking connecting factor were not met. *Kegel* developed this cascade of connecting factors while working at the German Council of Private international law, when he formulated the conflict of law rule regarding the general effects of marriage (Gerhard Kegel, 'Zur Reform des deutschen internationalen Rechts der persönlichen Ehewirkungen' in Wolfgang Lauterbach (ed), *Vorschläge und Gutachten zur Reform des deutschen internationalen Eherechts* (first published 1962, reprint by DeGruyter 2014) 75; Gerhard Kegel, 'Zur Reform des internationalen Rechts der persönlichen Ehewirkungen und des internationalen Scheidungsrechts' in Günther Beitzke (ed), *Vorschläge und Gutachten zur Reform des deutschen internationalen Personen-, Familien- und Erbrechts* (Mohr Siebeck 1981) 112, 114). *Kegel* had already proposed the objective cascade of connecting factors in 1962; over 25 years later, it was codified to a great extent in art 14 EGBGB. The general effects of marriage should be governed by the law of the country of the spouses' shared → nationality or last shared nationality during the marriage if one of them is still the national of that country; otherwise, the law of the country in which both spouses have their habitual residence or last had it during marriage, if one of them still has his or her habitual residence there; otherwise, the law of the country in which both spouses have their residence or last had it during the marriage is applicable. *Kegel* was opposed to → party autonomy. The majority of members of the German Council of Private international law and the legislator agreed with *Kegel*, with the exception of the third-ranking → connecting factor. This is where art 14 EGBGB appoints the law of the state with which both spouses are jointly most closely connected. *Kegel* wanted to apply an unrelated right of residence rather than weighing and taking into account all factual circumstances of the individual case. The legislator also allowed a limited form of choice of law which *Kegel* had rejected, fearing the possibility of manipulation by the spouses.

3. The autonomy of choice of law and legislative evolution

Kegel considered → choice of law to be an autonomous field of law subject to its own principles. He considered the impact of the constitution or of European primary law as solely indirect. Early on, he emphatically advocated *de lege ferenda* the equal treatment of men and women when determining the applicable law. He therefore rejected the use of the husband's or father's personal status as the only connecting factor. However, he cited the interests promoted by choice of law as the reason for this reorientation of the choice-of-law rules rather than the constitutional imperative of equal treatment (see Alexander Lüderitz, 'Gerhard Kegel und das deutsche internationale Privatrecht' (1982) 46 RabelsZ 475, 478 f). He considered the choice-of-law rules as laws without any content relating to substantial justice (*Ordnungsnormen*), wherefore they should not be measured by the constitutional standard of gender equality (see Klaus Schurig, 'Gerhard Kegel' in Stefan Grundmann and Karl Riesenhuber (eds), *Deutschsprachige Zivilrechtslehrer des*

20. *Jahrhunderts in Berichten ihrer Schüler*, vol 2 (De Gruyter 2010) 3, 7 f). He later realized that fundamental rights are also binding for the choice-of-law legislator. This was another reason why he became a driving force in the reform of the German Private international law and worked towards it as President of the German Council of Private international law. Only after the so-called '*Spanier*'-decision of the German Federal Constitutional Court it was conceded that the constitution had a direct impact on choice-of-law rules (Gerhard Kegel, 'Chapter 1: Introduction' in Konrad Zweigert and Ulrich Drobnig (eds), *International Encyclopedia of Comparative Law III/1* (Mohr Siebeck 1986) paras 1–12). In order to ensure the functionality of the national choice-of-law rules, he also rejected direct encroachments of the primary European law on the *lex lata* choice-of-law rules of the Member States. For *Kegel*, rules for private international law could barely be found in the primary law aimed to make substantive law rather than choice of law (see in this respect Gerhard Kegel and Klaus Schurig, *Internationales Privatrecht* (9th edn, CH Beck 2004) § 4 II). Therefore, referring to the so-called '*Centros*' judgment of the ECJ (Case C-212/97 *Centros Ltd v Erhvervs- og Selskabsstyrelsen* [1999] ECR I-1484), *Kegel* (Gerhard Kegel, (1999) 8 EWS editorial) quoted *Marcellus*' words (Shakespeare, *Hamlet* act 1 scene 4): 'Something is rotten in the state of Denmark.' He was very critical of the indirect freedom of choice of law in the field of international corporate law, which allowed the applicable company law to be a function of the company's place of establishment. Taking the interests of the legal order and the creditors of the company into consideration, he was suspicious of overreaching party autonomy. Even after the *Centros* decision, he granted the company's law of establishment only a limited scope of application and otherwise adhered to the effective administrative headquarters as the connecting factor (Gerhard Kegel and Klaus Schurig, *Internationales Privatrecht* (9th edn, CH Beck 2004) § 17 II 1). *Kegel* therefore assumed that choice of law was largely autonomous. He wanted to satisfy the indirect requirements of the constitution as well as those of European primary law through a legislative evolution of the national choice-of-law rules via legal reforms rather than through a revolutionary direct impact of both metasystems to the national choice-of-law rules of the *lex lata*.

4. Conflicts justice and interests as the foundation of choice-of-law rules

Kegel ensures the autonomy of → choice of law by distinguishing justice in substantive private law (substantive justice) and justice in private international law (conflicts justice) (Gerhard Kegel, 'Begriffs- und Interessenjurisprudenz im internationalen Privatrecht' in Max Gerwig and others (eds), *Festschrift Hans Lewald* (Helbing & Lichtenhahn 1953) 259–88). The interests promoted by the conflict-of-laws rules are abstract. They are detached from the individual subject and rather refer to idealized cases. They are also isolated from the result of the applicable substantive law. Instead, they are supposed to determine the law of the state that has the closest connection to the case. *Kegel* writes: 'Justice in private international law must balance the interests in the application of this or that system of private law' (Gerhard Kegel, 'Chapter 3: Fundamental Approach' in Konrad Zweigert and Ulrich Drobnig (eds), *International Encyclopedia of Comparative Law III/1* (Mohr Siebeck 1986) paras 3–13). 'Substantive law aims at the materially best solution, private international law aims at the spatially best solution' (Gerhard Kegel, 'Paternal Home and Dream Home: Traditional Conflict Laws and the American Reformers' (1979) 27 Am.J.Comp.L. 615, 616). It was important to *Kegel* that 'substantive laws of different states [were] treated equally... Better [substantive] law is not preferred except in cases of *ordre public*' (Gerhard Kegel, 'Paternal Home and Dream Home: Traditional Conflict Laws and the American Reformers' (1979) 27 Am.J.Comp.L. 615, 618; → Better law approach). *Kegel* names several types of interests (Gerhard Kegel, 'Chapter 3: Fundamental Approach' in Konrad Zweigert and Ulrich Drobnig (eds), *International Encyclopedia of Comparative Law III/1* (Mohr Siebeck 1986) paras 3–13; Gerhard Kegel, 'The Crisis of Conflict of Laws' (1964) 112 Rec. des Cours 91, 186 ff) that must be considered while formulating choice-of-law rules: (i) Party interests. These are the normal interests of the affected persons. In the case of a contract, the interests are those of the contracting parties. *Kegel* focuses on the presumed interests of an ordinary party and not on specific-individual interests. (ii) Community interests (German: *Verkehrsinteressen*; *Kegel* first translated it in 'The Crisis of Conflict of Laws' (1964) 112 Rec. des Cours 91, 186 as 'interests of commerce'). These are the interests of undetermined persons related socially or by business to the relevant issue of private international law. (iii) Order interests are the interests of the legal order, especially the interests in a 'workable law'. A choice-of-law rule, according to *Kegel*, has to be formed in a way to bring each typically relevant interest into adequate balance when postulated as a general rule (promoting a partially critical view on this: Jan Kropholler, *Internationales Privatrecht* (6th edn, Mohr Siebeck 2006) § 5; very sceptical and disbelieving of its relevance for the practice of the choice-of-law rules: Axel Flessner, *Interessenjurisprudenz im internationalen Privatrecht* (Mohr Siebeck 1990) 44 ff. However, *Flessner* builds his own doctrine of interests on this; by contrast Klaus Schurig, 'Das Fundament trägt noch' in Heinz-Peter Mansel (ed), *Internationales Privatrecht im 20. Jahrhundert* (Mohr Siebeck 2014) 5–25, 11 f). According to *Kegel*, the interests that are served by a certain choice-of-law rule determine the rule's field of application and its delimitation to other choice-of-law rules (Gerhard Kegel, 'The Conflict-of-Laws Machine' [1996] IPRax 309, 310).

Kegel strongly defended this understanding of choice of law against the so-called 'American conflict of laws revolution' (→ (American) Conflict of laws revolution) (an earlier work about this is Heinrich Kronstein, 'Crisis of Conflict of Laws' (1949) 37 Geo.L.J. 483–513). American authors like *Brainerd Currie* (→ Currie, Brainerd), *Albert A Ehrenzweig* (→ Ehrenzweig, Albert A), *David F Cavers*, *Robert A Leflar*, *Arthur von Mehren*, *Donald T Trautmann* and *Russel J Weintraub* wanted to overcome the abstract and general choice-of-law rules. The applicable law should be determined by means of individual case-related and, more importantly, substantive rule-oriented methods of weighing interests. The → *lex fori* should be of greater importance (priority of the *lex fori*). In part, unilateral choice-of-law rules were preferred over multilateral ones. An understanding of choice of law developed that was strongly oriented towards legal policy. The American doctrine was a fundamental assault on the so-called 'traditional conflict of laws', with its multilateral reference rules without the need to weigh all of the interests in a specific case and without orientation towards the result of an application of the substantive law. *Kegel's* 1964 lecture at the Hague Academy of International Law on the Crisis of the Conflict of Laws and the US Conflict of Laws Revolution (Gerhard Kegel, 'The Crisis of Conflict of Laws' (1964) 112 Rec. des Cours 91 ff; → (American) Conflict of laws revolution), which he used to oppose the politicization of choice of law, is of outstanding significance in this context. The lecture has been translated into Chinese (by K Xiao and G Zou, *Chongtufa de Weiji*, 2008). *Kegel* fought against these doctrines with his extensive critique and justified his interest-oriented choice-of-law doctrine and, by this, the traditional understanding of the choice-of-law rules. He invested a lot of effort in combating American changes throughout his lifetime (Gerhard Kegel, 'Paternal Home and Dream Home: Traditional Conflict Laws and the American Reformers' (1979) 27 Am.J.Comp.L. 615, 616; Gerhard Kegel, 'Chapter 3: Fundamental Approach' in Konrad Zweigert and Ulrich Drobnig (eds), *International Encyclopedia of Comparative Law III/1* (Mohr Siebeck 1986) paras 3–17 to 3–53; in this respect see Zoltán Csehi, 'Gerhard Kegel [1912–2006] und sein Werk' in Verein zur Förderung der Rechtswissenschaft (ed), *Akademische Gedächtnisfeier für Gerhard Kegel* (Universität zu Köln 2007) 35, 45).

III. Kegel's influence on private international law

Kegel was considered a 'traditionalist' and a 'representative of the conservative-classic private international law' to whom 'the perception of private law and private international law as an instrument of public policy and the thereby linked weakening of individual legal positions seemed to be the wrong way' (according to Michael Martinek, 'Wissenschaftsgeschichte der Rechtsvergleichung und des Internationalen Privatrechts in der Bundesrepublik Deutschland' in Dieter Simon (ed), *Rechtswissenschaft in der Bonner Republik* (Suhrkamp 1994) 529, 593 f). One can glean the reason for that impression from the fact that *Kegel* classified private international law as private law that aims primarily to achieve justice between individuals (Gerhard Kegel, 'Chapter 1: Introduction' in Konrad Zweigert and Ulrich Drobnig (eds), *International Encyclopedia of Comparative Law III/1* (Mohr Siebeck 1986) paras 1–6). He considered the choice-of-law rules to be mostly neutral in regard to governmental or public policy considerations unless these considerations exceeded the interest in easy-to-use choice-of-law rules. He mostly took → public policy considerations into account only within the field of application of the national *ordre public* when substantive justice imperatively required it. This explains his reluctance towards special → connecting factors for → overriding mandatory provisions. He also saw choice-of-law rules as generally neutral in regard to the result of the substantive law. To that effect *Kegel* was a conservative. Through his doctrine of interests and his adherence to seemingly politically neutral, multilateral 'abstract-general' choice-of-law rules he substantially consolidated the traditional choice-of-law system (taking a critical stance on this issue: former academic disciple Rudolf Wiethölter, 'Begriffs- und Interessenjurisprudenz – falsche Fronten im IPR und Wirtschaftsverfassungsrecht' in Alexander Lüderitz (ed), *Internationales Privatrecht und Rechtsvergleichung im Ausgang des 20. Jahrhunderts – Bewahrung od der Wende? Festschrift für Gerhard Kegel* (Metzner 1977) 213 ff; in addition Christian Joerges, *Zum Funktionswandel des Kollisionsrechts: die 'Governmental Interest Analysis' und die 'Krise des Internationalen Privatrechts'* (Mohr Siebeck 1971); Christian Joerges, 'Vorüberlegungen zu einer Theorie des Internationalen Wirtschaftsrechts' (1979) 43 RabelsZ 6–79). *Kegel's* influence on the reform legislation of the German private international law of 1986 cannot be underestimated (see in this respect Alexander Lüderitz, 'Gerhard Kegel und das deutsche internationale Privatrecht' (1982) 46 RabelsZ 475 ff; by contrast Axel Flessner, *Interessenjurisprudenz im internationalen Privatrecht* (Mohr Siebeck 1990) 36 ff). Through his doctrine of interests he created a new explanatory model for the formation of choice-of-law rules and ensured the embeddedness of the choice-of-law rule in private law. This explanatory model fundamentally affected choice-of-law thinking in the second half of the 20th century and it continues to do so today. It has echoed in scholarship far outside of Germany (see Henry Batiffol, 'Actualité des intérêts en droit international privé' in Herbert Bernstein, Ulrich Drobnig and Hein Kötz (eds), *Festschrift für Konrad Zweigert: Zum 70. Geburtstag* (Mohr Siebeck 1981) 23), and also influenced the basic structures of the European regulations on international private law – even if *Kegel's* doctrines were certainly not the only ones to influence the formation of choice-of-law rules in European regulations (in respect to a stronger appreciation of political considerations and for a critique on the seemingly empty formalism of traditional conflict of laws see Horatia Muir Watt, 'Private international law Beyond the Schism' [2011] Transnational Legal Theory 347–427). The current choice-of-law rules also include a lot of characteristics that *Kegel* rejected in academic discussion because they do not correspond to his ideal of multilateral, unequivocal, clear and objective choice-of-law rules. For example, the Rome I Regulation (Regulation (EC) No 593/2008 of the European Parliament and of the Council of 17 June 2008 on the law applicable to contractual obligations (Rome I), [2008] OJ L 177/6; → Rome Convention and Rome I Regulation) and → Rome II Regulation (Regulation (EC) No 864/2007 of the European Parliament and of the Council of 11 July 2007 on the law applicable to non-contractual obligations (Rome II), [2007] OJ L 199/40) encompass different → escape clauses based on the 'closest connection' principle. They allow a variation from the primary connecting factor in particular cases (see for example arts 4(3), 5(3), 7(3) and 8(4) Rome I Regulation, arts 4(3), 5(2), 10(4), 11(4), 12(2)(c) Rome II Regulation). Article 9 Rome I Regulation, art 16 Rome II Regulation permit the application of overriding mandatory provisions, irrespective of the law otherwise applicable under the Regulations. Party autonomy is granted a wider field of application; in many areas of conflict of laws, party autonomy is the first connecting factor. This also conflicts with *Kegel's* ideal of private international law. For *Kegel*, the legal certainty and foreseeability of the applicable law were of significantly higher value than the flexibility of private international law, due to the fact that it has not been verified that flexible rules will always produce better results in individual cases.

Kegel also demonstrated that the traditional choice-of-law system is far from being non-political. Rather, it is the result of a variety of public policy decisions that are made on the basis of conflicts in justice (Rudolf Wiethölter, 'Begriffs- und Interessenjurisprudenz – falsche Fronten im IPR und Wirtschaftsverfassungsrecht' in Alexander Lüderitz (ed), *Internationales Privatrecht und Rechtsvergleichung im Ausgang des 20. Jahrhunderts – Bewahrung od der Wende? Festschrift für Gerhard Kegel* (Metzner 1977) 213, 245). Also, the delimitation between the fields of application of the various choice-of-law rules is effected in accordance with the interests promoted by private international law and is based on public policy interest evaluation. However, current choice of law is characterized by the fact that specific choice-of-law rules protect foundational principles to a far greater degree than *Kegel* had wanted (see in this respect Jürgen Basedow, 'The Law of Open Societies: Private Ordering and Public Regulation of International Relations: General Course on Private international law' (2013) 360 Rec. des Cours 416 ff). In many cases, this protection is predetermined by an imperative of the constitution or European primary law. Both have an effect on private international law to an extent that is much more far-reaching than what *Kegel* had considered to be constitutionally prescribed.

Kegel also had an influence on numerous private international law issues. For instance, his renowned technique, the '*Kegel's* Ladder' (cascade of connecting factors), was codified in art 14 EGBGB and was also adopted in art 8 → Rome III Regulation (Council Regulation (EU) No 1259/2010 of 20 December 2010 implementing enhanced cooperation in the area of the law applicable to divorce and legal separation, [2010] OJ L 343/10). He made the judicial practice accessible to scholarship and developed his theory in a way that the judicial practice could use it. The combination of both fields set new standards in legal literature. This also contributed to a large extent to *Kegel's* success as an academic (Rudolf Wiethölter, 'Begriffs- und Interessenjurisprudenz – falsche Fronten im IPR und Wirtschaftsverfassungsrecht' in Alexander Lüderitz (ed), *Internationales Privatrecht und Rechtsvergleichung im Ausgang des 20. Jahrhunderts – Bewahrung od der Wende? Festschrift für Gerhard Kegel* (Metzner 1977) 213, 247 f).

HEINZ-PETER MANSEL

Literature

Jürgen Basedow, 'The Law of Open Societies: Private Ordering and Public Regulation of International Relations: General Course on Private international law' (2013) 360 Rec. des Cours 416; Zoltán Csehi, 'Gerhard Kegel [1912–2006] und sein Werk' in Verein zur Förderung der Rechtswissenschaft (ed), *Akademische Gedächtnisfeier für Gerhard Kegel* (Universität zu Köln 2007) 35; Axel Flessner, *Interessenjurisprudenz im internationalen Privatrecht* (Mohr Siebeck 1990); Gerhard Kegel, 'The Crisis of Conflict of Laws' (1964) 112 Rec. des Cours 91; Gerhard Kegel, 'Paternal Home and Dream Home: Traditional Conflict Laws and the American Reformers' (1979) 27 Am.J.Comp.L. 615; Gerhard Kegel, 'Chapter 1: Introduction',

'Chapter 3: Fundamental Approach' in Konrad Zweigert and Ulrich Drobnig (eds), *International Encyclopedia of Comparative Law III/1* (Mohr Siebeck 1986); Gerhard Kegel, *Humor und Rumor – Erinnerungen* (CH Beck 1997); Gerhard Kegel, *Vertrag und Delikt* (Carl Heymanns 2001); Gerhard Kegel and Klaus Schurig, *Internationales Privatrecht* (9th edn, CH Beck 2004); Alexander Lüderitz, 'Gerhard Kegel und das deutsche internationale Privatrecht' (1982) 46 RabelsZ 475; Heinz-Peter Mansel, *Internationales Privatrecht im 20. Jahrhundert* (Mohr Siebeck 2014); Michael Martinek, 'Wissenschaftsgeschichte der Rechtsvergleichung und des Internationalen Privatrechts in der Bundesrepublik Deutschland' in Dieter Simon (ed), *Rechtswissenschaft in der Bonner Republik* (Suhrkamp 1994) 529; Klaus Schurig, 'Gerhard Kegel' in Stefan Grundmann and Karl Riesenhuber (eds), *Deutschsprachige Zivilrechtslehrer des 20. Jahrhunderts in Berichten ihrer Schüler*, vol 2 (De Gruyter 2010) 3; Rudolf Wiethölter, 'Begriffs- und Interessenjurisprudenz – falsche Fronten im IPR und Wirtschaftsverfassungsrecht' in Alexander Lüderitz (ed), *Internationales Privatrecht und Rechtsvergleichung im Ausgang des 20. Jahrhunderts – Bewahrung od der Wende? Festschrift für Gerhard Kegel* (Metzner 1977) 213.

Kinship and legitimation

I. Concept and notion

'Kinship' means legal parentage that attributes the child to a man as the legal father or a woman as the legal mother. Kinship is founded on biological reproduction including medically assisted procreation. However, kinship does not necessarily presuppose genetic lineage between the parent and the child. Kinship is distinguished from adoption that is legally constituted by a formal juristic act or judicial decision, independently of the original parentage (see → Adoption). In various jurisdictions, the term 'filiation', 'parentage' is used as an overarching concept to include both kinship and adoption. Legitimation is a legal institution that provides a child born out of wedlock with the status of legitimate child.

Substantive law rules on kinship and legitimation differ widely between jurisdictions. In → Germany and → Austria, for example, the legal mother is the one who gives birth to the child (§ 1591 German Civil Code (Bürgerliches Gesetzbuch of 2 January 2002, BGBl. I 42, as amended, henceforth German CC); § 143 Austrian Civil Code (Allgemeines Bürgerliches

Gesetzbuch of 1 June 1811, JGS No 946/1811, as amended, henceforth Austrian CC)). In → France and other Roman legal systems, maternity used to depend on acknowledgement, which has principally been substituted by the registration of the mother's name into the birth certificate (eg arts 311–25 and 316 *et seq* French Civil Code (Code Civil of 21 March 1804, henceforth French CC)). While surrogate motherhood is prohibited or ignored in many jurisdictions, it is now authorized in quite a few jurisdictions (eg → United Kingdom, → Greece, → India, → Ukraine, → Russian Federation and several US states), to the effect that the intending mother who provides the egg qualifies as the legal mother by registration or court decision, or through *ex post* transfer of maternity from the surrogate mother (Hague Conference on Private International Law (ed), 'A Study of Legal Parentage and the Issues Arising from International Surrogacy Arrangements' (2014) 16–24 (available at <www.hcch.net>); Katarina Trimmings and Paul Beaumont (eds), *International Surrogacy Arrangements: Legal Regulation at the International Level* (Hart Publishing 2013) 443–64; Michael Wells-Greco, *The Status of Children arising from Inter-Country Surrogacy Arrangements* (Eleven International Publishing 2015) 85–287). To ascertain the legal father, presumptions are often provided for the mother's husband, and in some jurisdictions also for the mother's registered partner. Paternity may also be based on acknowledgement, paternity registration, 'possession of status' or judicial decision (eg § 1592 ff German CC, § 144 ff Austrian CC, art 312 *et seq* French CC). The conditions to rebut paternity presumption vary between countries, depending on whether and how far → marriage or social parenthood ought to be protected over biology (Dieter Henrich, 'Streit um die Abstammung: Europäische Perspektiven' in Andreas Spickhoff, Dieter Schwab, Dieter Henrich and Peter Gottwald (eds), *Streit um die Abstammung: ein europäischer Vergleich* (Gieseking 2007) 396–404; Ingeborg Schwenzer (ed), *Tensions between Legal, Biological, and Social Conceptions of Parentage* (Intersentia 2007) 1–11). Various states also take a different position as to whether and how far a natural child can be legitimated, for example by declaration of legitimacy, the parents' subsequent marriage or putative marriage.

In light of these diverse substantive law rules on kinship and legitimation, it is necessary to ascertain in cross-border cases which law governs the question of whether and on what conditions maternity or paternity is established, surrogate motherhood is permissible, or the child can be acknowledged or legitimated. This entry does not deal with the parent–child relationship as the legal effect of kinship and legitimation, which concerns, in particular, parental responsibilities, custody, access and child abduction. For these issues, see → Child abduction and → Brussels IIa Regulation.

II. Historical developments

The status of children born out of wedlock has gradually been improved in Europe since the 1970s. National constitutions and arts 8 and 14 ECHR (European Convention of 4 November 1950 for the Protection of Human Rights and Fundamental Freedoms, 213 UNTS 221) (see also art 7 and 21 ChFR (Charter of fundamental rights of the European Union (consolidated version 2012/C 326/02), [2012] OJ C 326/391)), particularly the ECtHR case law since the 1979 *Marckx* decision (*Marckx v Belgium*, App no 6833/74 (13 June 1979)), served as the legal basis. Most European countries abolished the distinction between legitimate and illegitimate (and adulterine) children, as well as the legal institution of legitimation. The marital status of the parents no longer affects the child's status, even though the establishment of paternity may still be founded on the parents' marriage. Comparable developments can also be observed in the → USA, → Canada and most Latin American countries. However, some European countries (eg → Greece) still adhere to the distinctive status of children, as do most Asian and African countries. England exceptionally upholds this distinction and grants legitimation in relation to parental responsibilities and nationality (see Christine Budzikiewicz, *Materielle Statuseinheit und kollisionsrechtliche Statusverbesserung* (Mohr Siebeck 2007) 213–344).

These trends in substantive law largely affect conflicts rules on kinship and legitimation. Countries like Greece that continue to distinguish between legitimate and illegitimate children in substantive law uphold separate conflicts rules on marital and non-marital kinship and legitimation (arts 17–22 Greek Civil Code (Astikos Kodikas of 23 February 1946, A.N. 2250/1040; FEK A 91/1940, 597, henceforth Greek CC)). Other countries that abolished the distinctive status of children born in and out of wedlock in substantive law generally introduced uniform conflicts rules for kinship, with certain exceptions (arts 21–5 Austrian Federal Code on Private international law (Bundesgesetz über das internationale Privatrecht of 15 June 1978, BGBl. No 304/1978, as amended, henceforth Austrian PILA); arts 92–7 Book 10 of the Dutch New Civil Code (Nieuw Burgerlijk Wetboek of 1 January 1992, henceforth Dutch CC)). France has principally designated the national law of the mother for kinship since 1972 (art 311–14 French CC). The 2011 Polish choice-of-law rules designate the national law of the child (art 55 Polish Private international law Act (Official Journal 2011 No 80, pos. 432, henceforth Polish PILA), and also in principle art 33(1) Italian Private international law Act (Riforma del Sistema italiano di diritto internazionale private, Act No 218 of 31 May 1995 in Gazz.Uff., Supplemento Ordinario No 128 of 3 June l995, as amended, henceforth Italian PILA)) The 2004 Belgian choice-of-law rules designate the national law of the respective parent (art 62(1) Belgian Code of Private international law (Code de Droit International Privé, Loi du 16 juillet 2004 portant le Code de droit international privé, MB 27 July 2004, 57344, as amended, henceforth Belgian PILA)). Germany (1997), Switzerland (1987) and Spain (2015) primarily point to the child's habitual residence, supplemented by some other alternative → connecting factors (art 19(1) Introductory Act to the German Civil Code (Einführungsgesetz zum Bürgerlichen Gesetzbuche of 21 September 1994, BGBl. I 2494, as amended, henceforth German EGBGB); arts 68, 72–3 Swiss Private international law Act (Bundesgesetz über das Internationale Privatrecht of 18 December 1987, 1988 BBl I 5, as amended, henceforth Swiss PILA); art 9(4) Spanish Civil Code (Código Civil of 24 July 1889, BOE no 206, 25 July 1889, as amended, henceforth Spanish CC)). Most of these countries no longer have specific choice-of-law rules on legitimation either (see the latest abolishment of art 34 Italian PILA in 2013). Nevertheless, considering that quite a few foreign legal systems still allow the improvement of the child's status through legitimation, some countries maintained proper choice-of-law rules on legitimation in general (art 23 Austrian PILA; art 98(1)–(3) Book 10 of the Dutch CC) or rules on the recognition of legitimation effected abroad (art 74 Swiss PILA; ss 2 & 3 England and Wales Legitimacy Act 1976 (ch 31), henceforth Legitimacy Act).

III. Legal sources

1. International instruments

As for choice-of-law rules on kinship and legitimation, relevant international instruments are to date limited in number. The CIEC (→ CIEC/ICCS (International Commission on Civil Status)) on the extension of the competence of authorities qualified to receive acknowledgements of children born out of wedlock (signed at Rome on 14 September 1961, ICCS Convention No 5, 932 UNTS 63) allows nationals of a contracting state to invoke acknowledgement without kinship under their national law in a contracting state which provides for acknowledgement with kinship, or vice versa (arts 2–3). The Convention, however, *de facto* lost its meaning once all contracting states abolished former laws providing for natural paternity as an exclusively patrimonial relation between the parent and the child.

The CIEC Convention on legitimation by marriage (signed at Rome on 10 September 1970, ICCS Convention No 12, 1081 UNTS 247) provides for an alternative application of the national law of the father or the mother (art 1(1)). This does not prevent contracting states from adopting more favourable conflicts rules for legitimation (art 5), which could ultimately dispense a reference to art 1. Further, contracting states reserve the right to deny the validity of legitimation when the kinship does not exist, when the marriage is not valid under the *lex fori* or the national law of one parent, or when the child is adulterine under the *lex fori* and one of the parents is a national of the forum state (art 2(a)–(d)).

The CIEC Convention concerning the establishment of maternal filiation of children born out of wedlock (signed at Brussels on 12 September 1962, ICCS Convention No 6, 932 UNTS 76) contains no choice-of-law rules in the proper sense. It solely refers to the law of a non-contracting state by allowing a mother, whose name is already registered in the birth certificate, to make a declaration of acknowledgement pursuant to that law (art 3).

2. EU instruments

Unlike some other areas of private international law (→ maintenance obligations, divorce, → succession, matrimonial property regimes and the property consequences of registered partnerships), choice-of-law rules on kinship and legitimation have not to date been stipulated by regulations or other instruments of the EU (see V. below). Thus, to determine the law governing kinship or legitimation, reference ought to be made to national legal sources and, in limited circumstances, to the above-mentioned CIEC Conventions (→ CIEC/ICCS (International Commission on Civil Status)).

IV. Current regulation

1. The law governing kinship

Choice-of-law rules to decide the law governing kinship differ widely between jurisdictions. Traditionally, common law jurisdictions apply the *lex fori* by definition. A number of civil law countries introduced uniform conflicts rules for the entire kinship when they abolished the distinctive status of legitimate and illegitimate children in substantive law (see II. above). Polish choice-of-law rules designate the national law of the child (art 55 Polish PILA), and Belgian choice-of-law rules the national law of the respective parent (art 62(1) Belgian PILA). Italy refers to the national law of the child and, if more favourable, to the national law of the parent (arts 33(1), (2) and 35 Italian PILA). France principally designates the national law of the mother (art 311–14 French CC), while favouring the application of French law for the 'possession of status' (art 311–15 French CC) and referring alternatively to the national law of the parent or the child for acknowledgement by voluntary act (art 311–17 French CC). Article 311–14 French CC is grounded on the principle of *'mater semper certa est'*, which is justified from a legal and sociological viewpoint when it concerns the establishment of maternity. However, the exclusive reference to the mother's nationality in disregard of the father's nationality may well discriminate against the father when marital paternity presumption or non-marital paternity is at stake. An earlier rule in Germany (former art 20(1) German EGBGB) that primarily designated the national law of the mother for non-marital parentage in principle avoided this problem by alternatively pointing to the national law of the father or the law of the child's habitual residence for non-marital paternity. Also Dutch choice-of-law rules solely subject non-marital maternity to the national law of the mother (art 94(1) of the Book 10 of Dutch CC).

When Germany introduced uniform choice-of-law rules for all children in 1997, the primary connecting factor was switched to the habitual residence of the child, supplemented by other alternative connecting factors, ie nationality of the father and the mother and the law governing the effects of marriage (art 19(1) German EGBGB). The consent to establish kinship is additionally subject to the national law of the child or, when more favourable, to German law (art 23 German EGBGB). Also Swiss conflicts rules primarily point to the child's habitual residence, complemented by the alternative reference to nationality of the child or domicile (→ Domicile, habitual residence and establishment) or nationality of the parent for acknowledgement (arts 68, 72–3 Swiss PILA).

Other civil law countries uphold different conflicts rules for marital and non-marital kinship. This is in some jurisdictions a consequence of the distinctive status of legitimate and illegitimate children in substantive law. In Greece, marital kinship is governed by the law governing the effects of marriage since 1983 (art 17 Greek CC). Non-marital kinship is subject to cascading → connecting factors, ie common nationality of the child and the parent, or failing that, common habitual residence of the child and the parent, and failing that, nationality of the respective parent (arts 19–20 Greek CC). As more recent legislations influenced by new conflict of laws methods, → Japan and → Korea employ alternative connecting factors, which refer to nationality of the father or the mother for legitimate kinship, and to nationality of the respective parent at birth or acknowledgement in addition to the child's nationality (Japan) or habitual residence (Korea) for illegitimate kinship (arts 28–9 Japanese Act on General Rules for Application of Laws (Hōno Tekiyō ni Kansuru Tsūsokuhō, Law No 10 of 1898, as newly titled and amended by Act No 78 of 21 June 2006, henceforth Japanese PILA), art 40–41 Law 6465 of 7 April 2001, Amending the Conflict of Laws Act of the Republic of Korea (henceforth PILA of the Republic of Korea)).

Some other civil law countries abolished status differences of children but still focus on the parents' marriage in establishing kinship in substantive law, which is reflected in choice-of-law rules. In Austria, the establishment or revocation of marital kinship is governed by the common national law of the parents, or failing that, by the national law of the child (art 21 Austrian PILA), whereas non-marital paternity is subject to the child's national law (art 25(1) Austrian PILA). In the Netherlands, marital kinship is governed by the law of common nationality of the spouses or partners, or failing that, by the law of their common habitual residence, and failing that, by the law of the child's habitual residence (arts 92 and 93 of the Book 10 of Dutch CC). Non-marital maternity is subject to the national law of the mother (art 94 Dutch CC), while acknowledgement is subject to four cascading connecting factors to enable acknowledgement, ie nationality of the parent, habitual residence and nationality of the child, and habitual residence of the parent (arts 95(1) and 96 Dutch CC). Judicial establishment of kinship follows choice-of-law rules comparable to art 92 Dutch CC, seeking common elements between the parents (art 97 Dutch CC).

2. Implementation of choice-of-law rules on kinship

a) Nationality and habitual residence

As indicated above, jurisdictions that traditionally follow the principle of nationality mostly continue to point to the national law of the father, the mother or the child. However, the reference to the child's nationality may well result in a vicious circle when the acquisition of nationality depends on the establishment of kinship itself as an incidental question ('*jus sanguinis*'). Thus the previous Spanish conflicts rule, which pointed to the child's law of nationality in principle, had a default rule to refer to the child's habitual residence when the child's nationality could not ascertained (ex-art 9(4) Spanish CC). The principal reference to the law of the child's habitual residence under the current Spanish rule (art 9(4) Spanish CC), as well as in Germany (art 19(1) German EGBGB) and Switzerland (arts 68 and 72 Swiss PILA), avoids this problem and serves as a uniform connecting factor for all children, which reflects their centre of life. Moreover, this legislative policy accords with the tendency in Europe to turn from the principle of nationality to the principle of habitual residence.

b) Alternative connecting factors

The majority of choice-of-law rules examined above employ alternative → connecting factors to favour the legal parentage ('*favor filiationis*'). This substantive law policy incorporated in private international law is geared toward the best interests of the child. Depending on the case, however, the best interests of the child may well consist in annulling or revoking kinship rather than upholding the kinship. Thus German choice-of-law rules accept the '*favour principle*' both for the establishment and contestation of kinship (arts 19–20 German EGBGB; similarly art 33(3) Italian PILA). This policy is arguably preferable to other choice-of-law rules that solely support the establishment of kinship (eg art 96 Book 10 of the Dutch CC; arts 28–9 Japanese PILA; arts 40–41 PILA of the Republic of Korea).

In various jurisdictions that provide for → *renvoi* in general (eg France, Germany and Japan), it is questioned whether *renvoi* should be admissible also with regard to alternative connecting factors as to kinship, particularly in cases where the relevant foreign choice-of-law rules restrict the range of alternatively applicable laws or lead to an unfavourable result. While some authors support *renvoi* following the general principle, others contend to exclude *renvoi* in such cases as a corollary of the '*favour principle*', opposing to substitute alternative connecting factors of the forum state by less favourable foreign connecting factors (see Pierre Mayer and Vincent Heuzé, *Droit international privé* (11th edn, LGDJ 2014) para 643; for art 4(1) German EGBGB, Christian von Bar and Peter Mankowski, *Internationales Privatrecht*, vol 1 (2nd edn, CH Beck 2003) § 7 para 228). Article 13(3) Italian PILA explicitly provides that *renvoi* is only admissible when it leads to the establishment of parentage ('*rinvio in favorem*').

c) Timeframe and concurring paternity

Aiming to rely on a connecting factor that actually has the closest connection, the law applicable to kinship may alter in → Germany when the child's habitual residence or the parent's nationality changes (art 19 German EGBGB). It is, however, generally accepted that the status of legal father or legal mother once acquired cannot be lost by a subsequent change of the applicable law ('vested rights', see also art 25(1) Austrian PILA). Other jurisdictions generally provide for a fixed time frame to determine the applicable law to avoid difficulties in locating the relevant connecting factor (eg art 62(1) Belgian PILA; art 311–14 French CC; arts 69 and 72 Swiss PILA).

Nevertheless, alternative connecting factors that exist at the same time (eg art 19 German EGBGB) may lead to 'concurring paternity', when for example one law presumes marital paternity for the husband and another law validates the acknowledgement of the biological father. To solve this problem, some German authors advocate allowing the child to choose the legal father, which could though *de facto* result in an arbitrary decision of the mother. The majority of German authors advocate giving priority to the 'likely father' so as to realize the best interests of the child. Thus in the above example, the acknowledging father is given priority over the newly divorced husband (Dieter Henrich, 'Art 19 EGBGB' in Julius von Staudinger and others (eds), *J. von Staudingers Kommentar zum Bürgerlichen Gesetzbuch* (Sellier/de Gruyter 2014) para 36–46). In this respect, the Dutch choice-of-law rules on acknowledgement (art 95 Book 10 of Dutch CC) prevent concurring non-marital paternity by fixing the hierarchy of cascading connecting factors.

d) Particular problems of surrogate motherhood
Complex legal problems occur when intending parents from a country prohibiting or restricting → surrogacy go to a foreign country allowing surrogacy (among others → Greece, → Ukraine, Russia (→ Russian Federation) or some US states) to make a surrogacy arrangement and take home the child to whom the surrogate mother gives birth. In general, surrogacy-friendly jurisdictions establish the legal parentage of the intending parents, but surrogacy-hostile jurisdictions do not (see I. above). How should then the legal parentage be treated in the latter jurisdictions?

Choice-of-law rules which refer to nationality or domicile of the 'mother' (eg art 311–14 French CC) seem to be generally construed as pointing to the intending mother whose legal parentage is at stake. The so-called 'split maternity' caused by alternative connecting factors under art 19 German EGBGB is generally solved by selecting the most favourable law for the child (Dieter Henrich, 'Art 19 EGBGB' in Julius von Staudinger and others (eds), *J. von Staudingers Kommentar zum Bürgerlichen Gesetzbuch* (Sellier/de Gruyter 2014) para 77a). However, surrogacy-hostile countries have until recently (see below) generally refused, on grounds of → public policy (*ordre public*), the application of foreign law as well as the recognition of paternity or maternity of the intending parents established by a foreign court decision or birth certificate (French Supreme Court (Cour de Cassation), 6 April 2011, No 09-17130; 13 September 2013, No 12-18315; 12-30138; 19 March 2014, No 13-50005; Supreme Court Japan, 23 March 2007, Minshu 61–2, 619; Administrative Court (VG) Berlin, 5 September 2012 [2014] IPRax 80). Notably, however, some of these countries at least allowed the establishment of non-marital paternity of the biological father in the forum state or the recognition of his paternity confirmed in a foreign court decision or birth certificate (Local Court (AG) Nürnberg, 14 December 2009 [2010] FamRZ 1579; see Hague Conference on Private International Law (ed), 'A Study of Legal Parentage and the Issues Arising from International Surrogacy Arrangements' (2014) 36–52 (available at <www.hcch.net>); Katarina Trimmings and Paul Beaumont (eds), *International Surrogacy Arrangements. Legal Regulation at the International Level* (Hart Publishing 2013) 510–28).

Apparently, denying legal parentage of the intending parents conforms to the fundamental principles of the forum state to prohibit surrogacy or deter reproduction tourism in view of inviolability of human dignity or inalienability of the body (Christoph Benicke, 'Kollisionsrechtliche Fragen der Leihmutterschaft' [2013] StAZ 101, 110–11). However, the child born as a result of surrogacy would then be deprived of legal parents and the possibility of obtaining custody, family name, nationality, maintenance or inheritance. Thus authors increasingly argued in view of art 8 ECHR that a foreign court decree or birth certificate granting legal parentage for the intending parents should be recognized, especially when the child is already born, the surrogate mother voluntarily gave up the child, the intending parents are married and willing to foster the child and at least one of them is a genetic parent. The best interests of the child were held to prevail over ethical concern of *de facto* a authorizing surrogacy ((Konrad Duden, *Leihmutterschaft im Internationalen Privat-und Verfahrensrecht. Abstammung und ordre public im Spiegel des Verfassungs-, Völker-und Europarechts* (Mohr Siebeck 2015) 329–332; Brigitta Lurger, 'Das österreichische IPR bei Leihmutterschaft im Ausland: das Kindeswohl zwischen Anerkennung europäischer Grundrechte und inländischem Leimutterschaftsverbot' [2013] IPRax 282, 283, 287–9; Claudia Mayer, 'Ordre public und Anerkennung der rechtlichen Elternschaft in internationalen Leihmutterschaftsfällen' (2014) 78 RabelsZ 551, 570–78; Dieter Henrich, 'Art 19 EGBGB' in Julius von Staudinger and others (eds), *J. von Staudingers Kommentar zum Bürgerlichen Gesetzbuch* (Sellier/de Gruyter 2014) para 100a, 123 ; Michael Wells-Greco, *The*

Status of Children arising from Inter-Country Surrogacy Arrangements (Eleven International Publishing 2015) 602–652). Along these lines, the Constitutional Court of Austria recognized a decision of the US state of Georgia and Ukraine affirming the legal parentage of both the intending parents respectively (Austrian Constitutional Court, 14 December 2011, No B13/11-10; 11 October 2012, No B99/12). Furthermore, the ECtHR condemned on 26 June 2014 (*Mennesson v France*, App no 65192/11 and *Labassee v France*, App no 65941/11) the above-mentioned French Supreme Court decision (Cour de Cassation, 6 April 2011, No 09-17130) for violating the children right to respect for their private life under art 8 ECHR (but not that of the intending parents by refusing to establish paternity by all means. The French Supreme Court eventually altered its position to allow registration of paternity of the intended father established in a birth certificate issued in Russia (Cour de cassation, 3 July 2015, No 14-21.323 and No 15-50.002)). The German Federal Court of Justice was even more generous (German Federal Court of Justice (BGH), 10 December 2014 [2015] NJW 479) in recognizing a decision of the US state of California asserting the legal parentage of two German male registered partners, relying on *ordre public atténué*. Arguably, in light of the best interests of the child and the stability and continuity of the status, the original kinship of the intending parents is preferable to the *ex post* establishment of legal parentage by adoption ((contra: Chris Thomale, *Mietmutterschaft* (Mohr Siebeck 2015) 101-105; see → Surrogacy). It is left to further developments of case law whether to extend the scope of recognition to maternity of the intending mother, whether to require a genetic link between the child and (at least) one of the intending parents (see ECtHR, 27 January 2015, *Paradiso and Campanelli v Italy*, App no 25358/12; ECtHR, 21 July 2016, *Foulon v France*, App no 9063/14 and *Bouvet v France*, no 10410/14; Swiss Federal Supreme Court, 21 May 2015 (BGer 5A_748/2014) and 14 September 2015 (BGer 5A_443/2014)), and whether to refuse recognition when the surrogate mother turns down to give up the child.

3. Legitimation

Countries that still uphold the legal institution of legitimation in their substantive law maintain specific choice-of-law rules on legitimation as well. Pursuant to Greek choice-of-law rules, legitimation by the parents' subsequent marriage is subject to the law governing the effects of marriage, and legitimation by state act to the national law of the father (art 22 Greek CC). As more recent legislations, Japan and the Republic of Korea rely on alternative connecting factors, pointing for all types of legitimation to nationality of the father or the mother, in addition to the child's nationality (art 30 Japanese PILA) or habitual residence (art 42 PILA of the Republic of Korea). Comparable to kinship, alternative connecting factors are often employed for legitimation pursuant to the 'favour principle' to abide by the best interests of the child ('*favor legitimationis*').

On the other hand, a number of countries set aside specific conflicts rules on legitimation when they abolished legitimation in substantive law. Even so, the question of legitimation under foreign law may still arise as an incidental question of registration, family name, parental responsibilities, maintenance or inheritance. Hence, the doctrine and case-law seek to fill the gap *de lege lata* in various countries. In France and Germany, some academics characterize legitimation as a matter of constituting kinship and suggest that general choice-of-law rule on kinship, ie art 311–14 French CC or art 19 German EGBGB, be analogously applied (Pierre Mayer and Vincent Heuzé, *Droit international privé* (11th edn, LGDJ 2014) para 638; Christian von Bar and Peter Mankowski, *Internationales Privatrecht*, vol 1 (2nd edn, CH Beck 2003) para 213). However, other German authors characterize legitimation as a legal effect of the established kinship, so they either assert an analogous application of choice-of-law rules on the parent–child relationship that refer to the child's habitual residence (art 21 German EGBGB) (Peter Huber, 'Die ausländische Legitimation zwischen Aufenthaltsrecht, Heimatrecht und deutschem Geburtenbuch' [2000] IPRax 116, 118–19) or an analogous application of choice-of-law rules on adoption to designate the law governing the effects of marriage or the national law of one parent alternatively (arts 22(1) and 23 German EGBGB, see Christine Budzikiewicz, *Materielle Statuseinheit und kollisionsrechtliche Statusverbesserung* (Mohr Siebeck 2007) 364–93). The last solution arguably deserves support, given that legitimation means a subsequent improvement of the child's status in light of the child's best interests, after the legal parentage has been established.

To deal with foreign legal systems that uphold legitimation, some countries, unlike in their substantive law, retain specific choice-of-law rules on legitimation. Austria explicitly subjects legitimation to the national law of the father (art 23 Austrian PILA). The Netherlands not only incorporated art 1 of the 1970 CIEC Convention on legitimation by marriage that refers to the nationality of either parent (art 98 Book 10 of Dutch CC), but also took advantage of the possibility to introduce the child's habitual residence as an additional alternative connecting factor to facilitate legitimation (see art 5 of the 1970 CIEC Convention on legitimation by marriage). On the other hand, Switzerland adopted a special rule limited to the recognition of legitimation effected abroad, referring alternatively to habitual residence or nationality of the child, or to domicile or nationality of one parent (art 74 Swiss PILA). Similarly, England and Wales recognize foreign legitimation by marriage when it is valid under the law of the father's domicile at birth or marriage (ss 2 & 3 Legitimacy Act; Lord Collins of Mapesbury and others (eds), *Dicey, Morris & Collins on the Conflict of Laws* (15th edn, Sweet & Maxwell 2012) para 20R-048).

V. Further developments

In light of the large diversity of conflicts rules on kinship and legitimation throughout various jurisdictions, international or regional unification of choice-of-law rules may well be desirable. The Hague Conference on Private International Law is currently examining the feasibility of drawing up a multilateral instrument on legal parentage and other issues surrounding cross-border surrogacy (see Hague Conference on Private International Law (ed), 'A Study of Legal Parentage and the Issues Arising from International Surrogacy Arrangements' (2014) (available at <www.hcch.net>)). As of 2017, the main focus of this project is placed on the recognition of parentage established by foreign birth certificates or court decisions, which include surrogacy cases (see 'Report of the Experts' Group on the Parentage/Surrogacy Project (Meeting of 31 January-3 February 2017)'(2017)(available at <www.hcch.net>)).

In the EU, there are no specific instruments that regulate choice-of-law rules on kinship or legitimation to date. Pursuant to the 'Regulation on (EU) 2016/1191 of the European Parliament and of the Council of 6 July 2016 promoting the free movement of citizens by simplifying the requirements for presenting certain public documents in the EU and amending Regulation (EU) No 1024/2012', public documents on the legal parentage issued by a Member State will unfold their evidentiary effects in other Member States without legalization or similar formality. Yet, this regulation only deals with the authenticity and not with the recognition of the contents and effects of public documents. If instead the 'principle of recognition' developed by ECJ case-law for family names (among others Case C-148/02 *M Carlos Garcia Avello v Belgium* [2003] ECR I-11635; Case C-353/06 *Stefan Grunkin & Dorothee Regina Paul* [2008] OJ C 313/3) were extended to legal parentage, it could enhance the stability of the status of a person within the EU (Kees Jan Saarloos, *European Private international law on Legal Parentage? Thoughts on a European Instrument Implementing the Principle of Mutual Recognition in Legal Parentage* (Océ Business Services 2010) 289–331). However, the appropriacy of such policy, its foundation in EU primary law and its compatibility with the fundamental principles of private international law still need to be carefully examined (Heinz-Peter Mansel, 'Anerkennung als Grundprinzip des Europäischen Rechtsraums. Zur Herausbildung eines europäischen Anerkennungs-Kollisionsrechts: Anerkennung statt Verweisung als neues Strukturprinzip des Europäischen internationalen Privatrechts?' (2006) 70 RabelsZ 651, 705–31; see → Recognition of legal situations evidenced by documents).

YUKO NISHITANI

Literature

Christoph Benicke, 'Kollisionsrechtliche Fragen der Leihmutterschaft' [2013] StAZ 101; Christine Budzikiewicz, *Materielle Statuseinheit und kollisionsrechtliche Statusverbesserung* (Mohr Siebeck 2007); Lord Collins of Mapesbury and others (eds), *Dicey, Morris & Collins on the Conflict of Laws* (15th edn, Sweet & Maxwell 2012); Konrad Duden, *Leihmutterschaft im Internationalen Privat- und Verfahrensrecht. Abstammung und ordre public im Spiegel des Verfassungs-, Völker- und Europarechts* (Mohr Siebeck 2015); Hague Conference on Private International Law (ed), 'A Study of Legal Parentage and the Issues Arising from International Surrogacy Arrangements' (2014, available at <www.hcch.net>); Hague Conference on Private International Law (ed), 'The Desirability and Feasibility of Further Work on the Parentage / Surrogacy Project' (2014, available at <www.hcch.net>); Dieter Henrich, 'Art 19 EGBGB' in Julius von Staudinger and others (eds), *J. von*

Staudingers Kommentar zum Bürgerlichen Gesetzbuch (Sellier/de Gruyter 2014); Peter Huber, 'Die ausländische Legitimation zwischen Aufenthaltsrecht, Heimatrecht und deutschem Geburtenbuch' [2000] IPRax 116; Brigitta Lurger, 'Das österreichische IPR bei Leihmutterschaft im Ausland: das Kindeswohl zwischen Anerkennung europäischer Grundrechte und inländischem Leimutterschaftsverbot' [2013] IPRax 282; Heinz-Peter Mansel, 'Anerkennung als Grundprinzip des Europäischen Rechtsraums. Zur Herausbildung eines europäischen Anerkennungs-Kollisionsrechts: Anerkennung statt Verweisung als neues Strukturprinzip des Europäischen internationalen Privatrechts?' (2006) 70 RabelsZ 651; Claudia Mayer, 'Ordre public und Anerkennung der rechtlichen Elternschaft in internationalen Leihmutterschaftsfällen' (2014) 78 RabelsZ 551; Pierre Mayer and Vincent Heuzé, *Droit international privé* (11th edn, LGDJ 2014); Kees Jan Saarloos, *European Private international law on Legal Parentage? Thoughts on a European Instrument Implementing the Principle of Mutual Recognition in Legal Parentage* (Océ Business Services 2010); Ingeborg Schwenzer (ed), *Tensions between Legal, Biological, and Social Conceptions of Parentage* (Intersentia 2007); Andreas Spickhoff and others (eds), *Streit um die Abstammung: ein europäischer Vergleich* (Gieseking 2007); Chris Thomale, *Mietmutterschaft* (Mohr Siebeck 2015); Katarina Trimmings and Paul Beaumont (eds), *International Surrogacy Arrangements: Legal Regulation at the International Level* (Hart Publishing 2013); Christian von Bar and Peter Mankowski, *Internationales Privatrecht*, vol 1 (2nd edn, CH Beck 2003); Michael Wells-Greco, *The Status of Children arising from Inter-Country Surrogacy Arrangements* (Eleven International Publishing 2015).

Lease contracts and tenancies

I. General context

Lease, tenancy and related contracts can be defined as legal relationships in which the owner or rightful possessor grants another person the temporary right to occupy and use movable or → immovable property or other legal entitlements in exchange for consideration. Under Roman law, these contracts were covered by the *locatio conductio*, which, however, extended also to services, including labour as well as works contracts. Only the medieval *ius commune* introduced the distinction between *locatio conductio rei* (tenancy and lease contracts), *locatio conductio operis* (works contract) and *locatio conductio operarum* (service contract). All of these contracts had in principle only an obligatory character, which meant that due to privity of contract, lessees and tenants were not protected in case of sale of the used thing to a third party (*emptio tollit locatum*). However, the influence of natural and customary law from the 17th century onwards led to the recognition of a partially real character of leases, to the extent that the lessee was to be protected in case of sale (*emptio non tollit locatum*). The oscillation of leases and tenancies between contract and property, which induces different connections in private international law, may still be observed today. In common law, leases (also called leaseholds) and tenancies are generally considered real rights. On the Continent, however, they are generally considered contractual rights only, often complemented by real right features such as *emptio non tollit locatum*.

Lease contracts or leaseholds (*Miete, loyer, locazione, arrendamiento*) constitute the general concept for the grant of a right of use over foreign property. The English concept lease or leasehold, the French *bail* and the Italian *affitto* cover not only the German concept of *Miete* but also that of *Pacht*, which, similar to the land law category of usufruct (*Nießbrauch*), gives its holder not only a right of use but also a right to enjoy the fruits and other proceeds of a thing or a right. A related land law concept is *emphyteusis*, or ground lease (*bail emphytéotique, Erbbaurecht, enfiteusi*), which gives its holder the right to build and own a house on the ground of another person, thus constituting an exception to the principle according to which the ownership of a plot of land extends to all buildings erected on it (*superficies solo cedit*). Another relevant land law concept is easements, also called servitudes (*Grunddienstbarkeiten, servitudes*), which may include a right of residence (*Wohnrecht, droit d'habitation*). On account of its real status and registration, this right is independent of the existence of contractual relationships and, therefore, stronger than an obligatory right of residence based on a lease or tenancy agreement.

Leases may have as their object movables, immovables and intangible property (→ Property and proprietary rights). Examples for the latter category are computer programs, radio frequencies, the *clientèle* or customer base of a company or, most importantly, immaterial rights referring to the use of such intangible property – eg patents, brands and other immaterial property rights. In this context, it is worth mentioning that the delimitation of movables and immovables is not identical in different legal orders; for example, rights referring to immovables such as mortgages (*Hypotheken*) may in some systems be classified as immovables. Finally, the related term leasing prescribes a modern special contractual regime, typically employed for the use of valuable movables such as cars, which is composed of lease and sales elements. Nowadays, it is often treated as a type of contract *sui generis*.

Within contractual leases, manifold variations may be found in different legal orders. Whereas in Germanic systems leases may be, and often are, open-ended contracts without time limit, in the French legal family going back to the Code Napoléon, there is a general prohibition of open-ended contracts, which are viewed as excessively restraining. In common law systems, there is an even greater variety of concepts. For example, in the USA, art 2A of the UCC (Uniform Commercial Code, American Law Institute, Uniform Commercial Code, Official Text with Comments, St. Paul 2012) regulates commercial leases of movable property while explicitly excluding leases of immovable property from its scope. However, in England, the term lease is generally limited to immovable property, whereas the use of movables is often termed hire. A lease requires the exclusive possession of a defined area of land for a fixed period (or series of periods) of time with the intention to create an estate in land, ie an interest in the land itself which can be assigned or sold. Conversely, a licence is simply a permission to use land which allows someone access to the land of another for an agreed purpose but does not confer any interest in land. Another related common law feature is the so-called bailment, which is a general type of contract encompassing, similar to the Roman *locatio conductio*, several contracts which have as their object the temporal use of movables including deposit, works and service contracts. Moreover, in all legal systems, the instrument of a sublease exists, yet almost exclusively in relation to dwellings. A sublease (or, less formally, sublet) is the name given to a contract under which the lessee in a lease assigns the lease to a third party, thereby making the old lessee the sublessor, and the new lessee the sublessee.

Even more important than these variations of lease is the concept of tenancy, which is typically reserved to the lease of residential or commercial buildings. In all Western countries, residential tenancy law is characterized by socially motivated interventions into freedom of contract to protect the tenant beyond *emptio non tollit locatum*, such as limitations of notice by the landlord, minimum duration of contracts, minimum quality standards, rent control and succession rights. On account of their social flavour, residential tenancies are very close to labour and consumer law, though they are not normally treated as a branch of the latter area. Likewise, in several countries special regulation of commercial and agricultural tenancies (*bail commercial* and *bail rural*) exists, even though such regulation is normally based on lease law. The same is true for special regulation on the lease of water vehicles such as bareboats (termed 'charter contract') and commercial ships as well as airplanes.

Lease law is not harmonized at European level with its core branch, residential tenancy law, being politically highly sensitive and dependant on the interaction with national or subnational housing policies. Nevertheless, with the increase in mobility of European citizens, the growth of Europe-wide job markets and the boom in tourism, tenancy regulation is increasingly important to the Single European Market. Even though equal access to national housing markets is generally available to foreign citizens, national systems in the host country may place tenants in unexpectedly unfavourable conditions. The same may be true for relatively long periods of notice required of tenants in their country of origin, which may force a worker who moves to pay rent on two different properties over an extended period. Beyond the free circulation of workers, the freedom of capital is affected by tenancy law. As a consequence of globalization and the establishment of new asset classes such as Real Estate Investment Trusts (REITS), real estate and capital markets have integrated dramatically in Europe and beyond. These investments predominantly concern commercial property, but in some countries they also extend to large municipal housing stocks put on the market by cities which are under heavy financial constraints. Therefore, the tenancy laws of a country are important economic parameters for investors.

However, the European impact on tenancy law derives also from the manifold, though mostly indirect, effects on tenancy law exerted by EU regulation and policy in other fields. For example, EU social policy against poverty and social exclusion extends to selected issues of housing, such as the amelioration of housing conditions and the provision of housing to vulnerable groups. Tenancy law and housing policy have also been affected by European competition and state aid rules, particularly with regard to state-subsidised social housing for the poor. In this context, the Commission allowed → Ireland, for example, to provide bank → guarantees for borrowings by the public Housing Finance Agency, which were qualified as a service of general interest (State Aid N 209/2001 – Ireland). Likewise, the Commission has repeatedly allowed public subsidies for housing developers aimed at promoting home-ownership among socially disadvantaged groups in deprived urban areas. In tax law, the Council decided in 1992 that the supply, construction, renovation and alteration of housing provided as part of social policy may be subject to reduced VAT rates (VAT Directive (Council Directive 92/77/EEC of 19 October 1992 supplementing the common system of value added tax and amending Directive 77/388/EEC (approximation of VAT rates), [1992] OJ L 316/1)), while the letting of accommodation is completely exempted from VAT in all Member States (Sixth Council Directive 77/388/EEC of 17 May 1977 on the harmonization of the laws of the Member States relating to turnover taxes – Common system of value added tax: uniform basis of assessment, [1977] OJ L 145/1). Further aspects of tenancy law are dealt with under European consumer law. Whereas the Doorstep Sales Directive (Council Directive 85/577/EEC of 20 December 1985 to protect the consumer in respect of contracts negotiated away from business premises, [1985] OJ L 372/31) excludes lease contracts from the scope of its application (art 3(2)(a)), the Unfair Terms Directive (Council Directive 93/13/EEC of 5 April 1993 on unfair terms in consumer contracts, [1993] OJ L 95/29) extends to clauses contained in lease contracts, provided that the tenant is a consumer and the landlord is a commercial entity (which generally requires that the landlord lets several apartments). The tenant is also protected against misleading advertising and similar practices by the Unfair Commercial Practices Directive (Directive (EC) No 2005/29 of the European Parliament and of the Council of 11 May 2005 concerning unfair business-to-consumer commercial practices in the internal market and amending Council Directive 84/450/EEC, Directives 97/7/EC, 98/27/EC and 2002/65/EC of the European Parliament and of the Council and Regulation (EC) No 2006/2004 of the European Parliament and of the Council concerning unfair business-to-consumer commercial practices in the internal market, [2005] OJ L 149/22), which provides in art 2(c) that the expression 'products' includes immovable property. The Injunctions Directive further enhances these safeguards, encompassing tenants' actions for enforcing their rights (Directive 2009/22/EC of the European Parliament and of the Council of 23 April 2009 on injunctions for the protection of consumers' interests, [2009] OJ L 110/30, codifying Directive 98/27/EC on injunctions for the protection of consumers' interests ([1998] OJ L 166/51)). Tenancy law is also affected by European provisions on energy saving according to which, *inter alia*, the landlord is bound to inform the tenant about the building's energy consumption when they enter into the agreement. In several EU Member States including → Germany, these provisions have prompted the legislator to allow rent increases after modernization measures aimed at energy savings have been completed. Furthermore, the provision of housing has been incorporated in European → antidiscrimination legislation. Based on art 19 TFEU (The Treaty on the Functioning of the European Union (consolidated version), [2012] OJ C 326/47), the Council adopted Dir 2000/43/EC implementing the principle of equal treatment (Council Directive 2000/43/EC of 29 June 2000 implementing the principle of equal treatment between persons irrespective of racial or ethnic origin, [2000] OJ L 180/22) against discrimination based on race and ethnic origin. This Directive includes in art 3(1)(h) access to and the supply of goods and services available to the public, including housing, which is particularly relevant to members of ethnic minorities. Finally, European constitutional law has deployed only limited relevance in this area so far. Although a human right to housing ('*droit au logement*') is recognized in several Member States, including → France and → Italy, it is not recognized generally across the EU, and the drafters of the EU Charter of Fundamental Rights (Charter of Fundamental Rights of the European Union of 18 December 2000, [2000] OJ C 364/1) could only agree on including a right to 'housing assistance' (without defining this term) in the Solidarity chapter of the Charter (art 34(3)), which has had little legal or political impact so far.

In contrast, the European Convention on Human Rights (European Convention of 4 November 1950 for the Protection of Human Rights and Fundamental Freedoms, 213 UNTS

221) has played an increasingly important role in tenancy law in recent years. The European Court of Human Rights has recognized several social rights such as the right of foreign tenants to install a satellite TV set to receive radio and TV channels from their home country (derived from the freedom of opinion enshrined in art 10 ECHR; *Mustafa et al v Sweden* App no 23883/06 (ECtHR, 16 March 2009)) and the right of a homosexual partner to succeed in a tenancy contract after the death of his partner who had concluded the contract (derived from the non-discrimination right, art 14, and the protection of the private sphere and family life, art 8; *Kozak v Poland* App no 13102/02 (ECtHR, 2 June 2010)). Interestingly, it has also been discussed in the English House of Lords whether the protection of the private sphere laid down in art 8 ECHR extends to a protection of the tenant against eviction (*London Borough of Harrow v Qazi* [2003] UKHL 43). Moreover, the ECtHR has repeatedly found a violation of the landlord's right of property in cases concerning extremely long waiting periods for eviction in Italy – even in cases in which the landlord intended to use a house or apartment for herself or close family members (see *Immobiliare Saffi v Italy* App no 22774/93 (ECtHR, 28 July 1999); *AO v Italy* App no 22534/93 (ECtHR, 30 May 2000); *Ghidotti v Italy* App no 28272/95 (ECtHR, 21 February 2002)). Most importantly for a private law context, the ECtHR has started to balance the property rights (→ Property and proprietary rights) of the owner against national regulation protecting the tenant. As has become apparent in cases from → Malta (*Edwards v Malta* App no 17647/04 (ECtHR, 24 October 2006)), → Poland (*Hutten-Czapska v Poland* App no 35014/97 (ECtHR, 19 June 2006)) and → Norway (*Lindheim and others v Norway* App no 13221/08, 2139/10 (ECtHR, 12 June 2012)), which seem to have overruled previous jurisprudence (*Mellacher and others v Austria* App no 10522/83, 11011/84, 11070/84 (ECtHR, 19 December 1989)), the Court is prepared to intervene when the economic balance of the contractual exchange is manifestly disturbed, in particular when the rent to be gained by the landlord is so low that it does not even cover costs and/or when the landlord is prevented from repossessing the house for an excessive, or even unlimited, period of time.

As regards comparative law, lease law in general and residential tenancy law in particular remain an underrepresented area in which only selected fields have been examined. However, during the last ten years, the European Commission has funded two major comparative projects ('Tenancy Law and Procedure in the EU' and 'Tenancy Law and Housing Policy in Europe'), the results of which are available on the Internet. In addition, in the framework of the European contract law harmonization, the Study Group on a European Civil Code, a transnational academic initiative, has analysed the lease of movables in depth. This field has subsequently also been integrated into the so-called Common Frame of Reference (Study Group on a European Civil Code/Research Group on EC Private Law (Acquis Group) (ed), *Principles, Definitions and Model Rules of European Private Law, Draft Common Frame of Reference (DCFR)* (Outline Edition 2009)), which is an academic compilation of rules and principles of a European contract law similar to a draft codification in the continental European style; yet the lease of immovables, especially residential tenancies, has again been left out due to its politically sensitive character. The Common Frame of Reference has so far led only to a draft of a Common European Sales Law (Commission, 'Proposal of 11 October 2011 for a Regulation of the European Parliament and of the European Council on a Common European Sales Law' COM(2011) 635 final), which does not incorporate the rules on leases. However, in the absence of an explicit exclusion, lease and tenancy contracts might be partially covered by the general rules of a possible future European contract law.

II. European private international law

In Europe, the private international law regulation of leases and tenancy contracts is ensured by the Rome I Regulation (Regulation (EC) No 593/2008 of the European Parliament and of the Council of 17 June 2008 on the law applicable to contractual obligations (Rome I), [2008] OJ L 177/6; → Rome Convention and Rome I Regulation (contractual obligations)). In art 4(1)(c), it covers contracts 'relating to a right *in rem* in immovable property or to a tenancy of immovable property' and subjects them to the *lex rei sitae* (see II.2. below). As opposed to real property law matters (→ Property and proprietary rights), which are under most national private international laws also subjected to the *lex rei sitae*, an overriding *ex ante* choice of law remains possible (see II.1. below). Different rules apply to certain short-term tenancies (see II.3. below) and timeshare agreements (see II.4. below). The remaining constellations, in particular leases of movables and rights, are mostly governed by the general connection with the law of the characteristic performance (see II.5. below).

1. Choice of law and its limits

In line with the contractual characterization of contracts relating to a right *in rem* or to a tenancy of → immovable property, a choice of the applicable law remains possible pursuant to the general provision of art 3 Rome I Regulation. The → choice of law is subject to general requirements: first, the existence and validity of the consent of the parties as to the choice of the applicable law needs to be determined in accordance with the requirements foreseen by the chosen law itself (arts 3(5), 10, 11 and 13 Rome I Regulation). Moreover, the choice of law may be explicit or implicit, provided that it is clearly demonstrated by the terms of the contract or the circumstances of the case (art 3(1) Rome I Regulation). However, in tenancy cases such an implicit choice should not simply be assumed in favour of the law of the common citizenship of the contractual parties if the immovable property in question is located in another EU state. Importantly, when all other elements relevant to the situation at the time of the choice are located in a country other than the country whose law has been chosen, the choice of the parties shall not prejudice the application of non-dispositive provisions of the law of that other country (art 3(3) Rome I Regulation). The ensuing juxtaposition of two national laws is in principle the same as the one foreseen in contracts with passive consumers (art 6(2) Rome I Regulation) and workers (art 8(1) Rome I Regulation). For example, if both the landlord and the tenant have German nationality and are domiciled in Germany, the choice of English law as *lex contractus* in a tenancy contract which has as its object a flat located in Germany is not capable of overriding the non-dispositive provisions of German law, especially the provisions protecting the tenant. Furthermore, the sole foreign citizenship of a landlord should not be a sufficient element to enable a choice of law which allows evading the non-dispositive provisions of the law where the flat is located. Thus, a landlord of Turkish nationality domiciled in Germany for ten years should not be allowed to rent out a flat in Germany with a choice-of-law clause opting for Turkish law, thus evading all German provisions protecting the tenant.

Significantly, the restrictions on → choice of law to the disadvantage of consumers do not apply to tenants, with the exception of timeshare contracts within the meaning of the Timesharing Directive (Directive 94/47/EC of the European Parliament and the Council of 26 October 1994 on the protection of purchasers in respect of certain aspects of contracts relating to the purchase of the right to use immovable properties on a timeshare basis, [1994] OJ L 280/83), art 6(4)(c) Rome I Regulation. This exclusion is not justified, as residential tenancies providing a tenant with a home are typically of existential importance, usually higher than of most other consumer contracts. As a consequence, only mandatory provisions in the sense of art 9 Rome I Regulation may be invoked against the law chosen by the parties (often imposed on the tenant on a take-it-or-leave-it basis). However, it is accepted in the literature that one may consider mandatory provisions all important legislative devices protecting the tenant contained in the law of location of the dwelling, in particular, limitations of notice by the landlord, minimum duration of contracts, minimum quality standards, rent control and succession rights. This interpretation counteracts the shortcomings of art 6(4)(c) Rome I Regulation.

2. The objective connection of contracts relating to a right in rem in immovable property or to a tenancy of immovable property

According to art 4(1)(c) Rome I Regulation, contracts 'relating to a right *in rem* in immovable property or to a tenancy of immovable property shall be governed by the law of the country where the property is situated'. The wording of this provision is different from that of its predecessor, art 4(3) of the Rome Convention (Rome Convention on the law applicable to contractual obligations (consolidated version), [1998] OJ C 27/34), which covered contracts whose 'subject matter is a right in immovable property or a right to use immovable property'. The reason for the changed wording, which does not seem to amount to any change of substance, is to conform to the Brussels I Regulation (Regulation (EC) No 44/2001 of 22 December 2000 on jurisdiction and the recognition and enforcement of judgments in civil and commercial matters, [2001] OJ L 12/1; → Brussels I (Convention and Regulation)), an objective expressly referred to in Recital (7) of the Rome I Regulation. According to art 22 (no 1) Brussels I Regulation, the exclusive jurisdiction for 'proceedings which have as their object rights *in rem* in immovable property or tenancies of immovable property' lies 'with the courts of the Member State in which the property is situated'. Article 4(1)(c) Rome I Regulation should therefore be interpreted in line with that provision in order to achieve conformity between jurisdiction and the applicable law.

Manifold reasons militate in favour of the application of the *lex rei sitae* to lease and tenancy contracts: the permanent localization of immovable property which determines the place of delivery of the performance and thus also the closest link; public law connections, in particular to real estate tax and the land register; the respect for mandatory rules on the protection of residential tenants; the familiarity of courts with the rules and practices of their own state; conformity between jurisdiction and applicable law.

As regards its substantive scope, art 4(1)(c) Rome I Regulation includes all kinds of contracts for the use of immovable property, which means primarily plots of land and buildings, including condominiums. Relevant contracts therefore extend to residential and commercial tenancies; subleases and short-term leases or licences; agricultural tenancies and leases; leases of holiday homes, parking lots or camping spaces exceeding the period of six months (see *infra* III.3.); gratuitous loans; as well as to all contracts which have the transfer or securitization of immovable property as their subject, like contracts to sell, to donate, to exchange, to pledge or to levy charges on the immovable property (not mere brokerage or management contracts).

In accordance with the scope of the Regulation, only contractual agreements under the law of obligations are included, which, as with all provisions of the Regulation, have to be characterized autonomously, not according to the *lex rei sitae*. It is certain that real property law contracts, such as the real transfer under §§ 929 or 925 German Civil Code (Bürgerliches Gesetzbuch of 2 January 2002, BGBl. I 42, as amended, henceforth German CC), are excluded. However, it seems wrong to limit the provision on the basis of the German principle of abstraction (*Abstraktionsprinzip*) to contracts which only engender obligations and do not entail real property effects. Instead, it should be borne in mind that under most legal systems, which follow the principle of consensus, including for example → Italy, valid sales contracts entail the automatic transfer of property. Such contracts should also be covered by art 4(1)(c) Rome I Regulation. Nevertheless, their real property law effects should be governed under private international law by the property law connection. In almost all legal systems, this is also the *lex rei sitae* (eg art 43(1) Introductory Act to the German Civil Code (Einführungsgesetz zum Bürgerlichen Gesetzbuche of 21 September 1994, BGBl. I 2494, as amended)), albeit with the notable difference that a choice of the applicable law, at least on an *ex ante* basis, is generally not permitted. Thus, effects *in rem* of lease and tenancy contracts – eg the landlord's lien (§ 562 German CC), consequences related to land registration and the principle *emptio non tollit locatum* – are covered by the real property law connection.

Based on this distinction, contracts establishing usufruct agreements and easements, such as a right of residence, should be dealt with under art 4(1)(c) Rome I Regulation, while the exercise of these rights is subject to the real property law connection.

In the case of mixed contracts, ie contracts composed of multiple elements dealt with under art 4(1) Rome I Regulation, the application of art 4(1)(c) Rome I Regulation requires that the prevailing purpose of the contract concerns a right *in rem* or a tenancy of immovable property (unless, of course, art 4(1) Rome I Regulation itself identifies the applicable private international law rule, as is the case when art 4(1)(d) Rome I Regulation states that the private international law rule contained therein applies notwithstanding art 4(1)(c) Rome I Regulation). This may be held for a tenancy contract with the option for the tenant to purchase the rented dwelling at the end of the contract, as this option constitutes a minor element when compared to the prevailing lease element. The same might generally be held for the lease of an entire company (*Unternehmenspacht*), extending to a plot of land, the buildings erected on it and all other assets of the company, which normally constitute minor elements of the overall contractual obligation. Otherwise, if the contract is constituted of elements of equal or similar rank, it is governed by the general rule contained in art 4(2) Rome I Regulation, according to which the law of the country applies where the party who effects the characteristic performance has her habitual residence. Only if a characteristic performance cannot be determined is the most closely connected law applicable according to art 4(4) Rome I Regulation.

Moreover, art 4(3) of the Rome I Regulation contains a special rule based on a manifestly closer connection of the facts of the case to the law of another country than that applicable under art 4(1) and (2) Rome I Regulation. Thus, if it is clear that a lease or tenancy contract is manifestly more closely connected to a country other than that of the *lex rei sitae*, the law of the other country shall apply pursuant to art 4(3) Rome I Regulation. For this rule to apply, it is not enough, though, that the landlord and the tenant have their common domicile (→ Domicile, habitual residence and establishment) in another country, as such a rule would circumvent the narrower requirements contained in art 4(1)(d) Rome I Regulation.

Finally, under art 11(5) Rome I Regulation, the *lex rei sitae* is also the applicable law with regard to formal requirements of the transactions in the sense of art 4(1)(c) Rome I Regulation, 'if by that law those requirements are imposed irrespective of the country where the contract is concluded and irrespective of the law governing the contract and those requirements cannot be derogated from by agreement'.

3. Short-term leases and tenancies

According to art 4(1)(d) Rome I Regulation, tenancies of immovable property concluded for temporary private use for a period of no more than six consecutive months shall be governed by the law of the country where the landlord has her habitual residence. This provision applies only insofar as the tenant is a natural person and has his habitual residence in the same country as the landlord. While the provision includes all possible uses of an immovable, it is directed in particular to the lease of holiday accommodation other than package holiday contracts.

A pertinent case decided by the ECJ is at the origin of the provision (Case 241/83 *Erich Rösler v Horst Rottwinkel* [1985] ECR 109). In this case, a German landlord had let a flat in his Italian holiday villa to a German tenant for a period of three weeks; afterwards, the landlord sued the tenant *inter alia* for → damages before the Regional Court (LG) of Berlin. The ECJ, to which the case was referred under the preliminary reference procedure, denied the international jurisdiction of the German court based on art 16(1) of the Brussels Convention (Brussels Convention of 27 September 1968 on jurisdiction and the enforcement of judgments in civil and commercial matters, [1972] OJ L 299/32, consolidated version, [1998] OJ C 27/1), which provided for the exclusive jurisdiction of the courts of the country of location of the property. Therefore, the two Germans were required to bring the dispute before an Italian court. This situation was regarded as unsatisfactory and led to the introduction of art 22 (no 1, 2nd sentence) of the Brussels I Regulation as well as art 4(1)(d) Rome I Regulation.

If, however, the tenant and the landlord have their domicile in different countries, or also in the case of commercial tenancies, the *lex rei sitae* according to art 4(1)(c) Rome I Regulation remains applicable. Thus, when an Englishman rents his Italian holiday home to a German, Italian law applies. Regarding the maximum period of six consecutive months, the contractually agreed period is crucial; as far as an agreement is lacking, the actual duration of the contract is decisive.

4. Timeshare agreements

Unlike lease contracts and tenancies, timeshare agreements are not governed by the *lex rei sitae*. According to art 6(4)(c) of the Rome I Regulation, these contracts are subject to 'the law of the country where the consumer has his habitual residence provided that the professional pursues his commercial or professional activities also in this country or, by any means, directs such activities to that country and the timeshare agreement falls within the scope of such activities'.

5. Lease of movables and rights

The lease or (gratuitous) loan of movables as well as the 'lease of rights', in particular → licence contracts and similar agreements in the field of immaterial property, are not specifically regulated in art 4(1) Rome I Regulation. Therefore, they need to be dealt with under the 'catch-all rule' contained in art 4(2), according to which the law at the seat of the party who effects the characteristic performance applies. It is generally agreed that, in lease, loan, tenancy and licence contracts, the lessor, the landlord and the licensor regularly render the characteristic performance. Only if a characteristic performance cannot be determined, as for example in the case of barter contracts, is the most closely connected law applicable according to art 4(4) Rome I Regulation.

III. Private international law of other countries

1. Switzerland

Private international law in → Switzerland is contained in the Swiss Private international law Act (Bundesgesetz über das Internationale Privatrecht of 18 December 1987, 1988 BBl I 5, as amended, henceforth Swiss PILA). Article 116 Swiss PILA lays out the general principle that parties to a contract may choose the law that will govern contractual issues, and the form required for a valid choice of law is governed also by the law chosen by the parties. In addition, the Swiss act sets a minimum standard that the choice of law must be made expressly or clearly demonstrated by the terms of the contract or the attendant circumstances. Furthermore, the parties may at any time agree to or modify a choice of law. A choice of law agreed to or modified after conclusion of the contract will have effect from the time of conclusion of the contract, but such choice or modification shall not adversely affect the rights of third parties.

In the absence of a → choice of law by the parties, art 117 Swiss PILA provides that the law governing the contract is the law of the country with the closest connection to the contract. The article also provides that the country with the closest connection is assumed to be the country in which the party who is obligated to deliver the characteristic performance has his habitual residence or, in the event that the contract is concluded based on a professional or commercial activity, the country in which the party has an office or branch. Particularly, in the case of a contract to convey a right to use moveable property, the performance of the party granting the right of use is to be considered as the characteristic performance, with the result that the law of the country where the owner has his habitual residence will govern such contracts.

However, this is not the same for contracts related to → immovable property. Although art 119 Swiss PILA similarly allows parties to choose the applicable law, the article provides that, in the absence of a valid choice of law by the parties, contracts regarding immovable property or the use of immovable property shall be governed by the law of the country in which the property is situated (*lex rei sitae*). Issues regarding the form required for such contracts to be valid will also be governed by the law of the country in which the immovable property is situated, unless the law of that country allows the application of the law of another country. Furthermore, Swiss law shall always apply to the form required for contracts related to immovable property situated in Switzerland.

The Swiss PILA deals with property rights specifically in ch 7, which lays out the application of *lex rei sitae* as the general principle. Article 99 Swiss PILA provides that rights *in rem* in immovable property are governed by the law of the country in which the property is situated, and art 100 Swiss PILA extends the principle of *lex rei sitae* to movable property. Thus, the acquisition and alienation of interests in movable property shall be governed by the law of the country where the property is situated at the time of the event from which the acquisition or alienation arises, and the substance and enjoyment of interests in movable property shall also be governed by the law of the country in which the property is situated.

2. USA

In the USA, choice-of-law analysis is part of the common law of the several states, and each state has developed its own jurisprudence in this area. Consistent with the rule that there is no general US Federal common law, US Federal courts must apply the choice-of-law rules of the state in which they are located when deciding cases under diversity jurisdiction (see *Klaxon Company v Stentor Electric Manufacturing Company*, 313 U.S. 487 (1941)). Although there is no uniform set of rules, the most comprehensive overview of the choice-of-law jurisprudence of the several states is found in the Restatement (Second) of Conflict of Laws (American Law Institute, Restatement of the Law, Second: Conflict of Laws 2d, St. Paul 1971; → Restatement (First and Second) of Conflict of Laws) which does not constitute binding authority, but is among the most widely-cited sources of secondary authority on the state of and trends in the common law.

Restatement (Second) § 186 lays down the principle that contracting parties are free to choose the law to govern issues of contract law. Regarding contracts for the conveyance of interests in → immovable property, §§ 189 and 190 of the Restatement permit party choice of the law applicable to issues regarding the validity of and the contractual duties arising from such contracts. In the absence of a valid choice of law by the parties, contracts for the conveyance of interests in immovable property are governed by the law of the state where the property is situated (*lex rei sitae*; referred to in the USA more commonly as 'law of the *situs*'), subject to the limitation that the law of another state will be applied to determine a particular issue if the other state has a more significant relationship regarding that issue (§§ 189, 190 Restatement (Second) of Conflict of Laws). Additionally, issues regarding the formal requirements (→ Formal requirements and validity) for such contracts are governed by the law of the *situs*, unless the parties have designated that the law of a different state will be applied for this purpose (§ 224 Restatement (Second) of Conflict of Laws).

When determining issues concerning rights *in rem* in immovable property (→ Property and proprietary rights), particularly the validity and effect of transfers of interests in immovables, the law of the *situs* will apply without regard to a choice of law agreed by the parties in an underlying contract (§ 223 Restatement (Second) of Conflict of Laws). This rule is based on criteria enumerated in § 6 Restatement (Second) of Conflict of Laws regarding the needs of the interstate and international systems, as well as the principles of certainty, predictability and uniformity (see comment a. to § 223 Restatement (Second) of Conflict of Laws). In contrast, interests in movable property will be determined by the law of the state that has the most significant relationship to the thing and to the parties, in consideration of the criteria enumerated in § 6 Restatement (Second) of Conflict of Laws.

While no explicit provision has been promulgated to protect consumers from a disadvantageous → choice of law in contracts regarding immovable property, an analogous protection has developed in case-law. In all types of contracts, the law chosen by the parties will be applied to all issues that the parties themselves could have resolved by including an explicit provision in their agreement (§ 187(1) Restatement (Second) of Conflict of Laws), but the law of a state chosen by the parties shall not apply to issues that the parties could not have otherwise resolved by an explicit provision in their agreement unless the chosen state has a substantial relationship to the parties or to the transaction or if there is another reasonable basis for the parties' choice (§ 187(2)(a) Restatement (Second) of Conflict of Laws). In addition, the law of the state chosen by the parties will not be applied to a particular issue if such application would be contrary to a fundamental policy of a state that has a materially greater interest in the particular issue than the state chosen by the parties (§ 187(2)(b) Restatement (Second) of Conflict of Laws). This rule excludes the possibility that the chosen law could be applied in contravention of non-dispositive provisions, such as those found in consumer protection law. Comment g. to § 187 of the Restatement clarifies that a fundamental public policy may be embodied in a statute intended to protect against the 'oppressive use of superior bargaining power'. Furthermore, no rule in the Restatement excludes contracts for the transfer of interests in immovable property from the protections provided under § 187 of the Restatement.

Finally, the choice-of-law provisions of the UCC must also be considered when dealing with contracts for lease of moveable property. While lease of goods is regulated in UCC Article 2A, choice-of-law provisions are contained in the general part of the code, UCC Article 1. In its main variant, UCC § 1–301(a) allows parties to a transaction to agree a state or nation whose law shall apply to the transaction, but the choice is effective only if the 'transaction bears a reasonable relation' to the agreed state or nation. Otherwise, if an effective agreement on applicable law is lacking, UCC § 1–301(b) dictates that the law of the forum shall apply to transactions bearing an appropriate relation to the forum. Subsections (a) and (b) of the section are subject to the limitation in UCC § 1–301(c) that the specification of applicable law in eight enumerated UCC sections – including UCC § 2A-106 pertaining to lease of goods – shall govern and contrary agreement by the parties shall be effective only if permitted by the particular law specified. Specifically in the context of lease of goods, UCC § 2A-106 limits the autonomy of parties to a consumer lease to agree an applicable law and the forum for adjudication. For the agreed law to be enforceable, UCC § 2A-106(1) requires that the chosen law must be that of the jurisdiction in which the lessee resides at the time the lease agreement becomes enforceable or will reside within 30 days thereafter or the jurisdiction where the goods are to be used. Regarding personal jurisdiction, UCC § 2A-106(2) allows parties to agree a judicial forum only to the extent that the forum chosen by the parties would otherwise have personal jurisdiction over the lessee.

Notably, the commercial code of the US Virgin Islands contains a substantively different choice-of-law provision in its § 1–301 (United States Virgin Islands Code, Title 11A, Article 1 § 1–301), adopted as the result of a short-lived revision introduced from 2001 to 2008. This variant provides more party autonomy in business-to-business transactions by removing the general requirement that the chosen law bear a reasonable relation to the transaction, while the requirement is retained only for transactions involving a consumer party. However, this revised version was not enacted by any jurisdiction other than the US Virgin Islands, and the choice-of-law provisions found in all other commercial codes enacted by the states are substantively identical to one another.

3. Japan

In Japan the main statute of private international law is the Act on General Rules for Application of Laws (Hōno Tekiyō ni Kansuru Tsūsokuhō, Act No 78 of 21 June 2006, henceforth Japanese PILA). This Act is a complete revision of the former Act (Act No 10 of 1898), which was based on German law. Choice-of-law rules are stipulated by art 7 and art 8 of the Japanese PILA, and both provisions govern issues regarding the law of obligations, exemplified by contract.

If the parties agree on a choice of applicable law in a juridical act, such as a contract, that law shall apply to issues of formation and effect of the juridical act (art 7 Japanese PILA). Furthermore, art 9 Japanese PILA permits the parties to change the law applicable to contractual issues, but any change shall not be applied to prejudice the rights of third parties.

However, there is a limitation on the choice of law from the perspective of consumer protection. If a contract is concluded between a consumer and a business operator (excluding a labour contract, art 12 Japanese PILA) and the consumer has manifested to the business operator an intent that a specific mandatory provision from the law of the consumer's habitual residence should be applied, the mandatory provision shall also apply to matters stipulated by the provision regarding the formation and effect of the consumer contract, even though the applicable law (as a result of a choice or a change of law under art 7 or art 9 Japanese PILA) is a law other than the law of the consumer's habitual residence (art 11(1) Japanese PILA). Article 11(1) also covers tenancy contracts in which the tenant is a consumer residing in Japan and the landlord is a foreign business operator. In that case, tenant-protective provisions in the Act on Land and Building Leases (Act No 90 of 1991) are regarded as mandatory provisions, and they apply in addition to the law chosen by the parties if the tenant has manifested an intention that those provisions shall apply.

If there is no agreement between the parties, the law of the place with which the contract is most closely connected at the time the contract is concluded shall govern issues of formation and effect of the contract (art 8(1) Japanese PILA). If only one of the parties is to provide the characteristic performance involved in the contract, the law of the habitual residence of the party providing said performance shall be presumed to be the law of the place with which the contract is most closely connected (art 8(2) Japanese PILA). This provision is based on the principle of characteristic performance, which was similarly adopted in art 4(2) of the Rome I Regulation.

Particularly, if the subject matter of the contract is real property – eg a contract for the sale of real property or a tenancy contract – the law of the place where the real property is situated (*lex rei sitae*) shall be presumed to be the law of the place with which the contract is most closely connected (art 8(3) Japanese PILA). Regarding issues concerning real rights and other rights requiring registration in the registry, art 13(1) Japanese PILA states that they shall be governed by the law of the place where the property associated with the right is situated. Other rights requiring registration include rights which, through registration, gain countervailing power against third parties similar to that of real rights. Typical examples are a tenancy right when it is registered and a special agreement for redemption attached to a sales contract of real property. However, acquisition or loss of a right shall be governed by the law of the place where the property associated with the right was situated at the time when the facts constituting the cause of the acquisition or loss occurred (art 13(2) Japanese PILA).

CHRISTOPH U SCHMID, JASON R DINSE
AND TSUBASA WAKABAYASHI

Literature

Peter Bassenge and others, *Palandt, Bürgerliches Gesetzbuch* (73rd edn, CH Beck 2014); Gralf-Peter Calliess (ed), *Rome Regulations* (Kluwer Law International 2011); Lord Collins of Mapesbury and others (eds), *Dicey, Morris & Collins on the Conflict of Laws*, vol 2 (15th edn, Sweet & Maxwell 2012); Tony Fahey and Michelle Norris, 'Housing' in Francis G Castles and others (eds), *The Oxford Handbook of the Welfare State* (OUP 2010) 479; James Fawcett, Janeen Carruthers and Peter North, *Cheshire, North & Fawcett: Private international law* (14th edn, OUP 2008); Franco Ferrari and others (eds), *Internationales Vertragsrecht* (2nd edn, CH Beck 2012); Andreas Furrer, Daniel Girsberger and Markus Müller-Chen, *Handkommentar zum Schweizer Privatrecht – Internationales Privatrecht* (2nd edn, Schulthess Juristische Medien AG 2012); Wolfgang Hau, 'Harmonisierung des Immobiliarmietrechts in Europa – Bestandsaufnahme und Perspektiven' (2011) 65 JZ 553; Heinrich Honsell and others, *Basler Kommentar. Internationales Privatrecht* (3rd edn, Helbing Lichtenhahn Verlag 2013); Kåre Lilleholt and others, *Principles of European Law: Lease of Goods, Study Group on a European Civil Code* (Sellier European Law Publishers 2007); Ulrich Magnus, 'Article 4 Rome I Regulation: The Applicable Law in the Absence of Choice' in Franco Ferrari and Stefan Leible (eds), *Rome I Regulation: The Law Applicable to Contractual Obligations in Europe* (Sellier European Law Publishers 2009) 27; Ulrich Magnus and Peter Mankowski (eds), *Brussels I Regulation* (2nd edn, Sellier European Law Publishers 2012); Peter Mankowski, 'Verträge über unbewegliche Sachen' in Christoph Reithmann and Dieter Martiny (eds), *Internationales Vertragsrecht* (7th edn, Otto Schmidt 2010); Thomas Rüfner, 'Miete und Pacht' in Jürgen Basedow, Klaus J Hopt and Reinhard Zimmermann (eds), *Handwörterbuch des Europäischen Privatrechts*, vol 2 (Mohr Siebeck 2009) 1061; Yoshiaki Sakurada and Masato Dōgauchi (eds), *Chūshaku Kokusaishihō (Private international law Annotated)*, vol 1 (Yūhikaku 2011) §§ 1–23; Christoph U Schmid (coordinator), 'Tenancy Law and Procedure in the EU, 2002–2004' <www.eui.eu>; Christoph U Schmid (coordinator), 'Tenancy Law and Housing Policy in Europe (ongoing research project), 2012–2015' <www.tenlaw.uni-bremen.de>; Christoph U Schmid and Jason R Dinse, 'European Dimensions of Residential Tenancy Law' [2013] ERCL 201; Christoph U Schmid and Jason R Dinse, 'Towards a Common Core of Residential Tenancy Law in Europe?' in Luca Nogler and Udo Reifner (eds), *Life Time Contracts* (Eleven International Publishing 2014) 401; Eugene F Scoles and others, *Conflict of Laws* (5th edn, West 2010); Hans-Jürgen Sonnenberger (ed), *Münchener Kommentar zum Bürgerlichen Gesetzbuch – Internationales Privatrecht*, vol 10 (5th edn, CH Beck 2010); Peter Sparkes, *European Land Law* (Hart Publishing 2007); Julius von Staudinger, *Internationales Vertragsrecht 2* (14th edn, Sellier/de Gruyter 2011); Russell J Weintraub, *Commentary on the Conflict of Laws* (6th edn, Foundation Press 2010).

Legal aid

I. Legal aid and access to justice

1. Definition and development of legal aid

Legal aid generally refers to litigation funding by a government to persons who cannot afford the costs inherent in legal proceedings. Virtually all countries in the world have a legal aid scheme, but there are many variants, in that eligibility criteria vary and some countries are noticeably more generous than others. Common forms of aid are the provision of counsel (free legal advice or a lawyer paid by the state) and the waiver or reduction of court fees, or a combination of these. In some countries where the 'loser pays' principle applies, the state aided litigation scheme may also to a certain extent cover the costs of the opposing party. Legal aid is organized differently in every country. In some countries, the court decides on an application for legal aid, while in others a (state) organization is responsible for legal aid provision. Eligibility criteria generally include a 'means and merits' test. The need for legal aid also depends upon whether a lawyer is compulsory in court proceedings in a particular country, and upon the existence of other means to fund litigation. Other types of litigation funding are of increasing importance, including personal insurance, and, in countries where this is permitted, funding by lawyers (contingency fees), third party funding and crowd-funding (Christopher Hodges, Stefan Vogenauer and Magdalena Tulibacka, *The Costs and Funding of Civil Litigation* (Hart Publishing 2010) 20–27). The term 'legal aid' itself is usually reserved for government subsidized litigation.

Legal aid has historically developed as 'law for the poor' and is generally associated with the welfare state. In their famous 'three waves of access to justice', *Cappelletti* and *Garth* designated the provision of legal aid as the first wave, emerging in most countries in the 1970s (Mauro Cappelletti and Bryant Garth, 'Access to Justice. The Worldwide Movement to Make Rights Effective: General Report' in Mauro Cappelletti and Bryant Garth (eds), *Access to Justice: A World Survey* (Sijthoff and Noordhoff 1978) 21 ff). Indigent persons or generally people (or small companies) having an income or assets below a certain threshold should be able to receive legal counsel and to bring their case to court if necessary. Hence, legal aid is generally regarded as one of the crucial preconditions for the right of access to justice, securing equality of parties and the right to legal counsel, and ultimately a fair trial (Berrnard Hubeau and Ashley Terlouw (eds), *Legal Aid in the Low Countries* (Intersentia 2014) 5–6).

2. Legal aid as a fundamental right: ECHR and EU Charter of Fundamental Rights

Legal aid is also enshrined as a fundamental right in art 6 ECHR (European Convention of 4 November 1950 for the Protection of Human Rights and Fundamental Freedoms, 213 UNTS 221) regarding the right to a fair trial and art 47 EU Charter of Fundamental Rights (Charter of Fundamental Rights of the European Union of 18 December 2000, [2000] OJ C 364/1 (consolidated version 2012/C 326/02, [2012] OJ C 326/391)) on the right to an effective remedy. However, particularly as regards civil matters legal aid is not an absolute right.

Article 6(3) ECHR concerns persons charged in criminal matters. Subsection (c) provides as a minimum right that if a person charged in a criminal matter lacks sufficient means to pay for legal assistance, this will be provided for free when the interests of justice so require. No equivalent right is specifically guaranteed as regards civil matters in art 6 ECHR. However, the ECtHR first ruled in *Airy v Ireland* ((1979) 2 EHRR 305), that states may under certain circumstances be compelled to provide for the assistance of a lawyer (para 26). It is required that legal representation is indispensable for an effective access to court, either because such representation is required or by virtue of the complexity of the matter.

In a number of other cases the ECtHR further refined this right and its limits. As to the complexity of the case, it is important in how far parties applying for legal aid have the capacity to represent themselves effectively (*McVicar v the United Kingdom* (2002) 35 EHRR 22). In *Steel and Morris v the United Kingdom* (App no 68416/01 (ECtHR, 15 February 2005)) the ECtHR added that other relevant factors are what is at stake for the party in question, their financial situation, and the prospects of success in the proceedings. Indeed, many national legal aid statutes include a 'means and merits' review. Courts have to give reasons for refusing legal aid and process requests diligently (*Tabor v Poland* App no 12825/02 (ECtHR, 27 June 2006)). For the present purposes, it is interesting to note that refusing legal aid to foreign legal persons is not contrary to art 6 ECHR, as is clear from *Granos Organicos Nacionales SA v Germany* (App no 19508/07 (ECtHR, 22 March 2012)). See Council of Europe, Guide on Article 6 – Right to a fair trial (civil limb) (available at <www.echr.coe.int/Documents/Guide_Art_6_ENG.pdf>), nos 61–70.

Contrary to art 6 ECHR, the text of art 47 of the EU Charter of Fundamental Rights does not distinguish civil matters from criminal charges. Article 47(3) EU Charter of Fundamental Rights provides that legal aid shall be made available to those who lack sufficient resources to the extent such aid is necessary to ensure effective access to justice. In the Explanations relating to the EU Charter of Fundamental Rights, explanation on art 47, express reference is made to the ECtHR case-law on legal aid and securing effective access to justice. In academic literature it has been pointed out that, while in the ECHR the social and economic nature of legal aid has been emphasized, the legal aid provision of the Charter seems to be a procedural principle (Liisa Holopainen, 'Art. 47: Right to an Effective Remedy' in Steve Peers and others (eds), *The EU Charter of Fundamental Rights: A Commentary* (Hart Publishing 2014) IX Article 47(3), pp 1269, 1272). According to art 52(3) EU Charter of Fundamental Rights, regarding the meaning and scope of the rights that are also protected under the ECHR, those rights are to be the same as those laid down by the ECHR. However, as this provision specifies, this does not preclude EU law from providing more extensive protection.

In a number of cases the CJEU (→ Court of Justice of the European Union) has given further guidance to the right to legal aid in civil matters, in particular in relation to legal persons. The ECtHR, in its judgment in *VP Diffusion Sarl v France* (App no 14565/04 (ECtHR, 26 August 2008)), stated that French legislation distinguishing between legal aid for companies and natural persons was based on an objective and reasonable justification which relates to the tax arrangements governing legal aid. Referring to this case law, the CJEU in Case C-279/09 DEB *Deutsche Energiehandels- und Beratungsgesellschaft mbH v Bundesrepublik Deutschland* ([2010] ECR I-13849), ruled that 'the grant of legal aid to legal persons is not in principle impossible, but must be assessed in the light of the applicable rules and the situation of the company concerned'. The form of the company (profit or non-profit) and the financial capacity play a role. National courts must among others ascertain whether the conditions for granting legal aid are a limitation of the right of access to justice considering the subject matter of the litigation; whether the applicant has a reasonable prospect of success; the importance of what is at stake for the applicant in the proceedings; the complexity of the relevant law and procedure; and the applicant's capacity (→ Capacity and emancipation) to represent himself effectively. This case-law was confirmed in Case C-156/12 *GREP GmbH v Freistaat Bayern* (ECLI:EU:C:2012:342), concerning a case of appeal against an *exequatur* on the basis of the Brussels I Regulation (Regulation (EC) No 44/2001 of 22 December 2000 on jurisdiction and the recognition and enforcement of judgments in civil and commercial matters, [2001] OJ L 12/1; → Brussels I (Convention and Regulation)).

II. Regulation in international and European instruments

Rules on legal aid are included in a series of conventions of the Hague Conference on Private International Law. The first convention was the Hague Convention on Civil Procedure of 17 July 1905 (Convention du 17 juillet 1905 relative à la procédure civile; RGBl. 1909, 409, available at <www.hcch.net>) (art 20–23), which was replaced by the widely ratified Hague Civil Procedure Convention (Hague Convention of 1 March 1954 on civil procedure, 286 UNTS 265) containing similar rules (art 20–24). The key element of these rules is to guarantee that nationals of other contracting states will be granted free legal aid under the same conditions as nationals of the state where legal aid is sought, upon compliance with the laws of that state. The Hague Civil Procedure Convention was in turn replaced by more specific conventions. The legal aid provisions were replaced by the Hague Access to Justice Convention (Hague Convention of 25 October 1980 on international access to justice, 1510 UNTS 375) in the relation between contracting states. This Convention is currently applicable to 28 states including 21 EU Member States. It incorporates the non-discrimination principle of the earlier Conventions and extends the scope to legal advice for persons present in the state where legal aid is requested. In addition, it provides for free → service of documents, Letters of Request and social enquiry reports, as well as for legal aid in relation to the recognition and enforcement of a decision, while including rules for an expeditious transmission of requests for legal aid, as well as rules on security for costs and enforceability of orders for costs.

Another important international instrument is the European Agreement of 27 January 1977 on the Transmission of Applications for Legal Aid (ETS No 92, 1137 UNTS 81), established by the Council of Europe. The rules to a great extent coincide with those of the 1980 Hague Access to Justice Convention. The European Agreement includes the non-discrimination principle for foreign nationals and provides for a transmission system between contracting parties through central authorities. Except for Germany all EU Member States are party to the European Agreement on the Transmission of Applications for Legal Aid.

Most important for present purposes is the European Legal Aid Directive (Council Directive 2002/8/EC of 17 January 2003 to improve access to justice in cross-border disputes by establishing minimum common rules relating to legal aid for such disputes, [2003] OJ L 26/41). It was established in 2003 and had to be transposed into the national law of the Member States by 30 November 2004, with the exception of rules relating to pre-litigation advice which had to be transposed by 30 May 2006 at the latest. This Directive provides minimum rules for the provision of legal aid in cross-border disputes brought in a Member State. As is clear from art 20, this Directive takes precedence as between the Member States over the above-mentioned European Agreement on the Transmission of Applications for Legal Aid and the Hague Access to Justice Convention. The European Legal Aid Directive will be discussed in greater detail in section III.

Apart from art 47(3) EU Charter of Fundamental Rights and the case-law (see I.2. above), the right to legal aid is guaranteed and further delineated in a number of sector-specific EU Regulations. These include several Directives in the area of asylum law (Directive 2005/85/EC (Council Directive 2005/85/EC of 1 December 2005 on minimum standards on procedures in Member States for granting and withdrawing refugee status, [2005] OJ L 326/13) and the Return Directive (Directive 2008/115/EC of the European Parliament and of the Council of 16 December 2008 on common standards and procedures in Member States for returning illegally staying third-country nationals, [2008] OJ L 348/98)) and notably the Maintenance Regulation (Council Regulation (EC) No 4/2009 of 18 December 2008 on jurisdiction, applicable law, recognition and enforcement of decisions and cooperation in matters relating to maintenance obligations, [2009] OJ L 7/1). Article 44 of the Maintenance Regulation generally provides that Member States must provide legal aid to secure access to justice. Article 45 gives details on the content of legal aid to be provided, including pre-litigation legal advice on bringing a case to court, exemption from or assistance with costs, the provision of interpretation and translation services as well as travel costs. Pursuant to art 46 of the Maintenance Regulation, Member States must provide free legal aid for persons under the age of 21 concerning child–parent maintenance obligations.

III. The European Legal Aid Directive

1. Background and aim

The Presidency Conclusions of the Tampere European Council of 1999 called for an instrument to establish minimum standards to ensure an adequate level of legal aid in cross-border cases (Tampere Conclusions, No 30 (available at <http://aei.pitt.edu/43337/>)). Shortly after the Commission put forward its Green Paper (of 9 February 2000 on Legal aid in civil matters: The problems confronting the cross-border litigant, COM(2000) 51 final), pointing out the problems that cross-border litigants face. In 2002, the Commission adopted a proposal for a Directive on legal aid (Proposal for a Council Directive of 18 January 2001 to improve access to justice in cross-border disputes by establishing minimum common rules relating to legal aid and other financial aspects of civil proceedings, COM(2002) 13 final), which was adopted with several amendments early in January 2003. The Legal Aid Directive is based on art 65(c) TEC (Consolidated version of the Treaty establishing the European Community (2002) [2002] OJ C 325/33) concerning the elimination of obstacles to the good functioning of civil proceedings. The Treaty of Lisbon (Treaty of Lisbon amending the Treaty on European Union and the Treaty establishing the European Community, signed at Lisbon, 13 December 2007, [2007] OJ C 306/1, consolidated version, [2012] OJ C 326/1) introduced a more specific basis for measures to ensure access to justice in art 81(2)(e) TFEU (The Treaty on the Functioning of the European Union (consolidated version), [2012] OJ C 326/47), and was to serve as the basis for future amendments to this Directive. The European Legal Aid Directive applies in all Member States with the exception of → Denmark. Between Denmark and the other Member States the European Agreement on the Transmission of Applications for Legal Aid (see section II.) applies as far as the other Member States are party to that Agreement.

The European Legal Aid Directive promotes the application of legal aid in cross-border disputes for persons who lack sufficient resources, and supports the right of access to justice as recognized in art 47 of the EU Charter of Fundamental Rights (Recital (5)). Neither the lack of resources of a claimant or defendant, nor the difficulties resulting from the cross-border nature of the case should hamper access to justice (Recital (6)). As is specified in art 1 this instrument aims to improve access to justice in cross-border disputes by establishing minimum common rules for legal aid. These common rules concern the right to legal aid, the conditions and extent of legal aid and a procedure for applications and the transmission between the competent authorities in the Member States.

The European Legal Aid Directive is complemented by two standard forms that are available online on the e-Justice Portal and the Judicial Atlas. One form is for the application for legal aid in another Member State. The other form is for the purpose of the transmission of an application for legal aid from the transmitting authority to the receiving authority in the

Member State where legal aid is sought. These aim to simplify and harmonize the application of the European Legal Aid Directive.

2. Scope of the Directive

The European Legal Aid Directive applies in → civil and commercial matters pursuant to art 1(2). In line with other instruments in the area of cooperation in civil matters, including for instance the Brussels I Regulation (recast) (Regulation (EU) No 1215/2012 of the European Parliament and of the Council of 12 December 2012 on jurisdiction and the recognition and enforcement of judgments in civil and commercial matters (recast), [2012] OJ L 351/1; → Brussels I (Convention and Regulation)), it is added that it applies in the cases irrespective of the nature of the court and tribunal. It does not extend to revenue, customs or administrative matters. The concept of civil and commercial matters should be interpreted in conformity with other instruments, in particular the Brussels I Regulation (currently the Brussels I Regulation (recast)), as the Commission specified in its proposal.

The European Legal Aid Directive applies only in cross-border disputes. However, this express limitation to cross-border cases was not included in the Commission proposal, and in fact the Commission envisaged this instrument as being applicable in both cross-border and domestic disputes. To this end it argued that drawing a distinction between cross-border and domestic disputes would be inconsistent and discriminatory (Etienne Leroy, 'L'aide juridique et judiciaire en droit européen' in Georges de Leval and Marcel Storme (eds), *Het Europees gerechtelijk recht en procesrecht* (Die Keure 2003) 295, 317; Eva Storskrubb, *Civil Procedure and EU Law: A Policy Area Uncovered* (OUP 2008) 169, 173). In view of the prerequisite in art 65 Treaty of Amsterdam and its successor in art 81 TFEU that instruments should regard matters with 'cross-border implications', the Directive was restricted to cross-border disputes. Article 2(1) of the European Legal Aid Directive defines these as disputes where the party applying for legal aid is domiciled or habitually resident in a Member State other than that where the court is sitting or where the decision is to be enforced. The concept of domicile is to be interpreted in accordance with art 63 of the Brussels I Regulation (recast).

The European Legal Aid Directive, as evident from its art 3, is only applicable to situations where a natural person applies for legal aid. Consequently, applications by small businesses lacking sufficient financial resources or of non-profit organizations are not covered by this instrument. This corresponds to the situation in many Member States that only provide for legal aid for natural persons and not for legal persons. In section I.2. it was discussed that the ECJ in the *DEB v Germany* case (Case C-279/09, [2010] ECR I-13849) did not rule out that the right to legal aid as guaranteed by art 47 of the EU Charter of Fundamental Rights also extends to legal persons. In the circumstances listed by the Court, the right to legal aid should thus be equally ensured in relation to legal persons.

3. Substance: minimum standards for legal aid and procedure

The European Legal Aid Directive provides minimum standards regarding the scope of the right to legal aid (ch II, arts 3 and 4), the conditions for and the extent of legal aid (ch III, arts 5–11). These provisions are indeed minimum standards and they leave the Member States discretion to set specific criteria for eligibility. In addition, the Directive provides for a procedure for obtaining legal aid (ch IV, arts 12–16). The final provisions concern the information to be provided, a rule on more favourable provisions for legal aid, the relation with other instruments and the transposal into domestic Member State law (ch V, arts 17–23).

According to art 3 natural persons involved in a dispute to which the Directive applies will be entitled to appropriate legal aid to ensure effective access to justice in accordance with the conditions provided in the Directive. What is to be covered by legal aid according to the Directive is clear from art 3(2). It should cover pre-litigation advice with a view to the reaching of a settlement prior to bringing the case to court, as well as legal assistance and representation in court proceedings, including exemption from, or assistance with the cost of proceedings of the recipient, and fees to persons mandated by the court to perform acts during the proceedings. The costs relating to cross-border procedures include those of interpretation, the requisite translation of documents, as well as travel costs in cases where the physical presence of the persons concerned is required (art 7 Directive). The Directive does not generally oblige Member States to cover the costs of the winning party for which the person obtaining legal aid (the recipient) is liable. However, if the losing recipient is liable for the costs of the opposing party and domestic legal aid would have covered these costs had the recipient been domiciled or habitually resident in the Member State where the court is sitting, then legal aid obtained on the basis of the Directive should extend to these costs.

The non-discrimination principle is laid down in art 4 of the Directive. It provides that Member States are to grant legal aid without discrimination against EU citizens and third-country nationals residing lawfully in a Member State. The nationality of the applicant is thus immaterial. All natural persons having domicile or lawful residence in a Member State may apply for legal aid in accordance with the Directive.

Member States are to grant legal aid to persons who are partly or entirely unable to meet the costs of proceedings as a result of their economic situation (art 5). This situation will be assessed by the competent authority of the Member State where the court is sitting. Relevant criteria include income, capital and family situation. Member States may define thresholds above which persons are deemed partly or entirely able to bear the costs of proceedings. If other effective dispute mechanisms are available that cover the costs of proceedings, legal aid need not be granted. These would include → alternative dispute resolution mechanisms such as consumer complaint boards. Member States may also set conditions relating to the substance of the dispute, and deny legal aid for claims that appear manifestly unfounded (art 6), a merits test which in fact is common in the Member States. Member States must consider the importance of the case to the individual applicant. The Directive includes not only rules directed at the Member State where litigation is to take place, but also a provision for the Member State where the legal aid applicant is domiciled or habitually resident. The home state must provide legal aid to cover costs relating to the assistance of a local lawyer or other legal advisor until legal aid has been received in the Member State where the court is sitting, as well as the translation costs of documents required in applying for legal aid (art 8). Legal aid must also cover the costs of enforcement of the judgment (art 9) and must extend to compulsory extrajudicial procedures (art 10) and the enforcement of authentic instruments (art 11).

For the procedure to apply for legal aid in the Member State where the court is sitting, Member States have designated transmitting and receiving authorities. Applications may be submitted to either the transmitting authority in the Member State where the applicant is domiciled or has habitual residence, or to the receiving authority (art 13). The application is made using the standard form available on the e-Justice Portal and the Judicial Atlas (art 17). Information on the competent authorities, communication means and the language(s) allowed for the application has been provided by the Member States and is available on the websites mentioned.

4. Evaluation and outlook

The Commission presented its report on the application of the Legal Aid Directive in February 2012 (Report from the Commission to the European Parliament, the Council and the European Economic and Social Committee on the application of Directive 2003/8/EC to improve access to justice in cross border disputes by establishing minimum common rules relating to legal aid for such disputes, COM(2012) 71 final). It concluded that there has been hardly any litigation or complaints in relation to the implementation of this Directive. The only real issue that has so far arisen in the ECJ case-law is the eligibility of legal persons (see I.2. above). The report notes that the transposition of the factor 'importance of the individual case to the applicant' into the possibility to deny an application in relation to an action that is manifestly unfounded (see art 6 Directive) has led to conflicting interpretations in the Member States. The uniform application is also challenged by the differences in the Member States as regards the concept of 'extrajudicial procedures' (art 10) and that of 'authentic instruments' (art 11). It should be noted that the latter term has in the meantime been defined in the Brussels I Regulation (recast) (art 2(c)). The report concludes that a number of Member States have not fully implemented the provision regarding the reimbursement of travel costs (art 7), and that the obligation to provide legal aid in relation to a local lawyer before the application for legal aid in the Member State where the court is sitting poses challenges (art 8).

The overall conclusion of this Commission report regarding the application of the European Legal Aid Directive is that during the review period (2004–09) the number of persons benefitting from cross-border legal aid increased only to a limited extent. Public awareness of this Directive is relatively low. Points for reflection identified in the report are: (i) further clarification of the economic criteria to benefit for legal aid, (ii) the situation that travelling costs are to be incurred for the hearing before the judge ruling on the granting of legal aid, (iii) the facilitation of relationships between professionals and beneficiaries in another Member State, (iv) clarification of the location of the competent transmitting authority and (v) scrutiny of the situation that an application is made to both the transmitting authority and the receiving authority. The report contains little information on the actual problems that have been reported in relation to these points for attention. Neither does it give guidance on how these points may be addressed.

Since publication of this report no concrete steps for the revision of the European Legal Aid Directive have been taken. This may be for various reasons. One reason may be that especially in view of the recent financial crisis in Europe a number of Member States have reduced the availability of legal aid and have been faced with an increase in applications for legal aid, so that it seems unlikely at present that Member States are willing to further harmonize rules on legal aid. Another reason may be that the attention has shifted to legal aid in criminal proceedings and in relation to European arrest warrant proceedings. A proposal was put forward in 2013 and in 2016, Directive (EU) 2016/1919 on legal aid for suspects and accused persons in criminal proceedings and for requested persons in European arrest warrant proceedings [2016] OJ L 297/1 was adopted.

It may be concluded that the European Legal Aid Directive has only achieved minimum harmonization. Eligibility criteria, precisely which costs are covered and to what extent, as well as the domestic procedures to obtain legal aid still vary. Judging from the Commission Report of 2012 (Report from the Commission to the European Parliament, the Council and the European Economic and Social Committee on the application of Directive 2003/8/EC to improve access to justice in cross border disputes by establishing minimum common rules relating to legal aid for such disputes, COM(2012) 71 final), the Directive seems not as yet to have had a significant impact on access to justice in cross-border cases. It remains to be seen whether the revision of the Directive is prioritized in the near future and how far possible amendments will increase the harmonization of legal aid and significantly benefit the cross-border litigant.

XANDRA KRAMER

Literature

Mauro Cappelletti and Bryant Garth, 'Access to Justice. The Worldwide Movement to Make Rights Effective: General Report' in Mauro Cappelletti and Bryant Garth (eds), *Access to Justice: A World Survey* (Sijthoff and Noordhoff 1978); Mirjam Freudenthal, *Schets van het Europees civiel procesrecht* (Kluwer 2013) 183; Burkhard Hess, *Europäisches Zivilprozessrecht* (CF Müller 2010) 476; Christopher Hodges, Stefan Vogenauer and Magdalena Tulibacka, *The Costs and Funding of Civil Litigation* (Hart Publishing 2010); Liisa Holopainen, 'Art. 47: Right to an Effective Remedy' in Steve Peers and others (eds), *The EU Charter of Fundamental Rights: A Commentary* (Hart Publishing 2014) IX Article 47(3), p 1269; Berrnard Hubeau and Ashley Terlouw (eds), *Legal Aid in the Low Countries* (Intersentia 2014); Etienne Leroy, 'L'aide juridique et judiciaire en droit européen' in Georges de Leval and Marcel Storme (eds), *Het Europees gerechtelijk recht en procesrecht* (Die Keure 2003) 295; Eva Storskrubb, *Civil Procedure and EU Law: A Policy Area Uncovered* (OUP 2008) 169.

Legalization of public documents

I. Concept and definition

In civil law systems, public documents or authentic instruments enjoy probative value and may be directly enforceable. Also certain legal acts may require an authentic instrument for validity. All these legal effects depend, among others, on whether the authentic instrument is genuine or authentic. For national authentic instruments, authenticity is a given and need not be proven: the traditional rule *acta probant sese ipsa* applies in one or the other form in all civil law jurisdictions for national authentic instruments. However, the rule does not apply to foreign public documents, so that they are required to be checked for genuineness. For practical reasons, this is done by the embassy or consulate of the receiving state in the state of origin. This is what is termed 'legalization'.

Legalization is the formal procedure by which 'public documents' (or 'authentic instruments') issued in one state ('issuing state' or 'state of origin') are certified to be genuine or 'authentic' by the diplomatic or consular authorities of another state ('receiving state' or 'state of destination'), in which the documents have to be used ('produced' or 'presented'). Legalization in a narrow sense is restricted to the certification of the genuineness of the signature and the capacity of the public official who signed it, as well as the genuineness of the official seal or affixed stamp. Legalization in a broader sense also certifies that the issuing authority had the necessary competence and that it complied with the issuing procedure required under its national law. International instruments mostly use the term legalization in its narrow sense (eg art 2 Hague Legalisation Convention (Hague Convention of 5 October 1961 abolishing the requirement of legalisation for foreign public documents, 527 UNTS 189), art 1 ICCS Waiver of Authentication Convention (Convention of 15 September 1977 waiving authentication of certain certificates and documents, 1224 UNTS 127) or art 3(3) of the Public Documents Regulation (EU 2016/1191 Regulation of the European Parliament and of the Council on promoting the free movement of citizens and businesses by simplifying the acceptance of certain public documents in the European Union and amending Regulation (EU) No 1024/2012 of 6 July 2016 OJ L 200/1)).

II. Public documents – authentic instruments

Legalization applies only to certain documents, called 'public documents' or 'authentic instruments'. So which documents are we talking about?

1. Examples

Even before giving a definition, it might be helpful to list the main types of public documents. Article 1 Hague Legalisation Convention of 5 October 1961 lists the following (with examples added by the author):

(i) court documents (eg court decisions or protocols of court proceedings),
(ii) administrative documents (eg administrative decisions, including grants of patents or licences, but also civil status documents such as birth, death or marriage certificates, furthermore educational documents, criminal and police records, whereas excerpts of official registers, eg land register, company register, might be either court or administrative documents),
(iii) notarial acts (eg testament, sales contract for immovables),
(iv) official certifications of signatures under a private act (the Convention erroneously uses the term 'authentications of signatures' instead of 'certification of signatures').

2. Authentic instruments in the civil law systems

For a lawyer trained in a civil law system, it is entirely clear what a 'public document' or an 'authentic instrument' is. The French call this type of instrument an *acte authentique*, the Germans *öffentliche Urkunde*, the Italians *atto pubblico*, the Polish *dokument urzędowy*, the Portuguese *documento autêntico*, the Romanians *act autentic* and the Spanish *documento público*. All understand each other perfectly, as they share the same legal concept.

The national laws of the various civil law countries define authentic instruments by the same four characteristics (Council of the Notariats of the European Union (CNUE), 'Comparative Study on Authentic Instruments – National Provisions of Private Law, Circulation, Mutual Recognition and Enforcement, Possible Legislative Initiative by the European Union, Study for the European Parliament No IP/C/JURI/IC/2008–019' <www.europarl.europa.eu/document/activities/cont/200811/20081127ATT43123/20081127ATT43123EN.pdf>, pp 5 *et seq*): (i) only public authorities or officials may issue public documents, (ii) the issuing authority has to act within its competence – both as to the subject matter of the document in question and geographically, (iii) the document must be in a specific authentication procedure and meet the formalities required for this type of public document.

If these three requirements are met, (iv) the authentic instrument provides conclusive proof of the content of the instrument (which is the fourth part of the definition as well as the legal consequence of an authentic instrument). This proof can be rebutted, but in some countries the rebuttal requires a special court procedure for forgery (eg → Belgium, → France, → Italy and → Romania), while in others it requires full proof to the contrary (eg → Germany and → Poland). Also, the genuineness of the public document need not be proven, but rather if the genuineness is challenged, the falsification has to be proven.

A classical definition can be found in art 1317 French Civil Code (Code Civil of 21 March 1804 – Code civil des français, promulgé le 21 mars 1804 (30 ventôse an XII), édition originale et seule officielle, A paris, Imprimerie de la République and XII -1804, as amended, available at <http://gallica.bnf.fr>, as amended): '[a]n authentic instrument is one which has been received by public officers empowered to draw up such instruments at the place where the instrument was received and with the requisite formalities'. Article 1319(1) then regulates the specific evidentiary value: '[a]n authentic instrument is conclusive evidence of the agreement it contains between the contracting parties and their heirs or assigns' (English translation from Legifrance – available at <http://195.83.177.9/code/liste.phtml?lang=uk&c=22>). Many other civil law countries have basically copied these rules with certain variations in the wording, eg in Europe Belgium (arts 1317, 1319(1) Civil Code), Italy (art 2699 Civil Code (Codice Civile, Gazz. Uff. 4 April 1942, No 79 and 79bis; edizione straordinaria)), Portugal (arts 369, 370 Civil Code ((Código Civil approved by Decreto-Lei No 47.344, of 25 November 1966, [1966] DG I série 274/1883, with subsequent amendments)), Romania (arts 1171, 1173 Civil Code (Law 287/2009, published in the Official Gazette No 511 of 24 July 2009, and subsequently amended and supplemented by Law 71/2011, published in the Official Gazette No 409 of 10 June 2011)) and Spain (arts 1216, 1218 Civil Code (Código Civil of 24 July 1889, Geceta de Madrid No 206, 25 July 1889)), or in the Americas Argentina (arts 979, 980 Civil Code (Código Civil de la República Argentina of 25 September 1869, by the passage of Law 340, entry into force 1 January 1871)), Mexico (arts 129, 130 Federal Code of Civil Procedure (Código Federal de Procedimientos Civiles, DOF 24-02-1943)) and Quebec (art 2813 Civil Code (L.Q. 1991, ch 64)). Other civil law systems give the same definition, but merge the definition and the legal effect (probative force) in one article (eg art 364 Brazilian Code of Civil Procedure (Código de Processo Civil, Lei n° 5.869 de 11 de janeiro de 1973), arts 415–18 German Code of Civil Procedure (Zivilprozessordnung of 5 December 2005, BGBl. I 3202, as amended), art 244 Polish Code of Civil Procedure (Official Journal 1964 No 43, pos. 296)).

3. Public documents in the common law

This concept of authentic acts is not known in the common law (or in the Nordic countries). Of course, in the common law and the Nordic jurisdictions, the public authorities also issue documents. However, these documents are not granted probative force as such. In England, such 'public documents' may be admitted without further proof, as sec 9(1) Civil Evidence Act 1995 (c 38) provides: '[a] document which is shown to form part of the records of a business or public authority may be received in evidence in civil proceedings without further proof'. The same applies now to notarial acts, as stated by rule 32.20, inserted in the Civil Procedure Rules 1998 by the Civil Procedure (Amendment No3) Rules 2005 (2005 No 2292 L 21): '[a] notarial act or instrument may be received in evidence without further proof as duly authenticated in accordance with the requirements of law unless the contrary is proved'. However, 'public documents' (or notarial instruments) do not necessarily provide conclusive proof as is the case in civil law countries.

4. 'Public documents' under the Hague Legalisation Convention

Given these widely differing concepts, the Hague Legalisation Convention avoided giving a comprehensive definition of 'public documents'. Instead the question whether a document is public for the purposes of the Convention is determined by the national law of the issuing state (C&R No 72 of the 2009 SC; C&R No 14 of the 2012 SC – as quoted in the Apostille Handbook No 113 – available at <www.hcch.net/upload/apostille_hbe.pdf>).

Nevertheless, the Convention gave a partial definition in that documents emanating from public officials are 'deemed to be public documents' for the purposes of the Convention.

Thus, the Convention managed to bridge the gap between the differing concepts of public documents, in that all civil law authentic instruments fall under the Convention, because one necessary (though not sufficient) part of the definition is their issuance by a public official. Also the partial definition is acceptable to the common law or the Nordic countries, which do not share the civil law concept of authentic instruments (and its specific probative value).

5. Definition of 'authentic instruments' in international instruments

a) Brussels Convention and Unibank decision

Other international sources, particularly European instruments, use the term 'authentic instrument' in a more narrow sense. Under the Brussels Convention (Brussels Convention of 27 September 1968 on jurisdiction and the enforcement of judgments in civil and commercial matters, [1972] OJ L 299/32, consolidated version, [1998] OJ C 27/1), there are specific rules for the recognition and enforcement of judgments on the one hand (art 25 *et seq*) and for authentic instruments and court settlements on the other hand (art 50 *et seq*). Thus, authentic instruments under the Brussels Convention are only those public documents containing an agreement between the parties recorded by a public official. Article 50 Brussels Convention defines the authentic instrument as 'a document which has been formally drawn up or registered as an authentic instrument and is enforceable in one Contracting State shall, in another Contracting State, be declared enforceable there, on application made .... The instrument produced must satisfy the conditions necessary to establish its authenticity in the State of origin.' Therefore art 50 Brussels Convention requires not only an authentic instrument, but also an enforceable one.

The ECJ had to consider this definition in the *Unibank* case (Case C-260/97 of 17 June 1999, *Unibank A/S v Flemming G Christensen* [1999] ECR I-3715). The case concerned a Danish enforceable acknowledgement of indebtedness that had been drawn up without intervention of a public official. Referring to the *Jenard-Möller* Report (P Jenard and G Möller, 'Report on the Convention on jurisdiction and the enforcement of judgments in civil and commercial matters done at Lugano on 16 September 1988' [1990] OJ C 189/57), the ECJ decided that the term 'authentic instrument' under the Brussels Convention required (i) that the instrument had been issued by a public authority in the form demanded by the state of origin, (ii) that the authenticity relates also to the content of the instrument and not only to the signature and (iii) that the instrument is also enforceable in the issuing state.

b) European sources

Article 57 Brussels I Regulation (Regulation (EC) No 44/2001 of 22 December 2000 on jurisdiction and the recognition and enforcement of judgments in civil and commercial matters, [2001] OJ L 12/1) and now art 58 Brussels I Regulation (recast) (Regulation (EU) No 1215/2012 of the European Parliament and of the Council of 12 December 2012 on jurisdiction and the recognition and enforcement of judgments in civil and commercial matters (recast), [2012] OJ L 351/1) (→ Brussels I (Convention and Regulation)) on the enforcement of foreign authentic instruments follow almost word for word art 50 Brussels Convention, so that the same definition applies.

Article 4(3)(a) European Enforcement Order Regulation (Regulation (EC) No 805/2004 of the European Parliament and of the Council of 21 April 2004 creating a European Enforcement Order for uncontested claims, [2004] OJ L 143/15) codified this definition generally for the authentic instrument. It defines 'authentic instrument' as 'a document which has been formally drawn up or registered as an authentic instrument, and the authenticity of which: (i) relates to the signature and the content of the instrument; and (ii) has been established by a public authority or other authority empowered for that purpose by the Member State in which it originates'. Enforceability is not expressly part of the definition. However, the European Enforcement Order Regulation deals only with enforceable authentic instruments.

Article 3(1)(i) Succession Regulation (Regulation (EU) No 650/2012 of the European Parliament and of the Council of 4 July 2012 on jurisdiction, applicable law, recognition and enforcement of decisions and acceptance and enforcement of authentic instruments in matters of succession and on the creation of a European Certificate of Succession, [2012] OJ L 201/107; → Rome IV Regulation) uses the same definition as art 4(3)(a) European Enforcement Order Regulation. The Succession Regulation, however, includes non-enforceable authentic instruments as well as enforceable ones.

CHRISTIAN HERTEL

6. Terminology and types of public documents

Comparing the terminology of these instruments, they generally use the term 'public documents' when referring to all documents emanating from a public official (eg the Hague Legalisation Convention or the proposed Public Documents Regulation), whereas the term 'authentic instruments' generally signifies a recording of declarations made to a public authority by that authority (eg Brussels I Convention, Brussels I Regulation (recast), Succession Regulation). Of course, the term may be construed differently for each instrument. This is also the terminology which is applied in this entry.

More precisely, we can distinguish three main types of public documents (each with sub-types):

(i) public documents containing (court or administrative) decisions of the public authority (judgments and administrative decisions),
(ii) public documents recording statements of private persons to a public official and recorded by the official, in particular notarial instruments containing declarations of a legal act, court settlements and court records of statements made by the parties or by witnesses during the court proceedings, and
(iii) public documents recording facts, in particular civil status documents (on birth, → marriage, death etc) and extracts of the entries in public registries (register of companies, land register, criminal records etc) or the certification of a signature or a copy etc. (In the latter subgroup, only the certification is a public document, not the underlying private act under which the signatures are certified.)

The difference between civil law systems and other systems is most obvious in the second group, in the recording of legal acts or the authentic instrument in the narrow definition. Here, the function of authentic instruments to secure legal certainty within the system of preventive justice is most clear.

III. Legalization, apostille or abolishing legalization

1. Legalization of foreign public documents

a) Procedure of legalization

The procedure of legalization is not regulated by international conventions, but rather is subject to national law. Traditionally, legalization is required in most civil law states, but not in the common law states (neither eg in Japan). Since civil law states grant higher probative and other effects to authentic acts, they seek to ensure that public documents coming from abroad are genuine before they may be used.

In the various civil law countries, similar procedures have evolved. Legalization in the proper sense is the certification undertaken by the diplomatic or consular authorities of the receiving state located in the state of origin (sometimes, but seldom also by the foreign ministry of the receiving state, then usually after a preliminary certification by the embassy). The embassy is better suited to know the relevant authorities of the issuing state, their respective competences and procedures, than are the authorities in the receiving state.

Normally, however, legalization proper is proceeded by one or two additional certifications in the state of origin. First, a higher authority in the state of origin (generally the authority charged with control of the emanating authority) confirms the authenticity of the public document (at least of the authenticity of the signature and the seal or stamp and of the official capacity of the person signing it). Certain receiving states (today only a minority) might require a second confirmation by a central authority. (In some cases, the apostille is also being used as a preliminary step for legalization for non-contracting states of the Hague Legalisation Convention.) Only after these preliminary steps, does the embassy of the receiving state legalize the document. The preliminary steps facilitate the control by the embassy. However, the chain of authentications renders legalization a slow and costly procedure.

b) Refusal of legalization

The receiving state is not obliged to legalize foreign public documents. The standard procedure for legalization of comparing the signature and the seal is insufficient if many forgeries circulate in the state of origin. Thus, the receiving state may decide to deny legalization for all public documents or at least for some types of public document. Then, the authenticity of foreign public documents has to be proven individually for each case (eg by a statement of a lawyer of the country of origin describing which steps were undertaken in order to prove the authenticity) – which of course is much more costly and time consuming than legalization. Eg German embassies have presently (March 2017) suspended legalization for 52 states (India being the largest).

2. Hague Legalisation Convention (or Apostille Convention)

Several international conventions have exempted certain documents from the legalization requirement or have replaced legalization by a more simplified procedure. The most widely used is the Hague Legalisation Convention of 5 October 1961 abolishing the requirement of legalization for foreign public documents (generally and hereafter named 'Hague Legalisation Convention', although 'Hague Apostille Convention' would better characterize the main content).

a) Contracting states
The Convention currently applies to 113 contracting states (as of 14 March 2017), making it the Hague Convention with the largest number of contracting states. Thus in practice the apostille rather than the legalization is the rule in Europe and the Americas.

However, some large countries have yet to accede to the Convention (eg → Canada and the People's Republic of → China where it applies only to Hong Kong and Macao), neither have many states in Africa and Asia. Furthermore, if a state accedes to the Convention, any other contracting state may object to the accession within six months; then the Convention takes effect between the acceding and the other states, but not between it and the objecting state (art 12 (2)). At present, objections have been raised against the accession of 15 states (by one or more other contracting states).

b) Scope of application
As we have seen (II.4. above), the Hague Convention applies to all 'public documents' emanating from a public official (art 1(1)), except only 'documents executed by diplomatic or consular agents' or 'administrative documents dealing directly with commercial or customs operations' (art 1(2)). Diplomatic or consular documents will usually be presented for authentication to the Foreign Ministry in the receiving state.

c) Replacing legalization by the apostille
The Hague Legalisation Convention exempts all public documents covered by it for the use in another contracting state from the requirement of legalization (art 2). Instead the receiving state may only require an apostille (art 3). The apostille is issued by an authority of the state of origin. Thus a two- or three-step procedure involving authorities of both the issuing and the receiving state is replaced by a one-step procedure involving only authorities of the state of origin.

The state of origin designates which authority is competent to issue the apostille. It may designate a central authority or decentralized authorities. Each contracting state notifies the Ministry of Foreign Affairs of the Netherlands of its competent authorities (art 6). The list is published on the website of the Hague Conference and therefore is easily accessible for control by the authorities or by other interested parties in the state of destination.

In its annex, the Convention includes a model for the apostille (art 4). The apostille has to bear the title in French '*Apostille (Convention de La Haye du 5 octobre 1961)*' and has to contain the ten numbered standard informational items (eg who signed the document in which capacity, who issued the apostille etc). Otherwise, it should conform as closely as possible to the model apostille certificate. However, variations (eg in size or shape) are permitted as long as the document remains clearly identifiable as an apostille in all other contracting states (C&R No 13 of the 2003 SC – available at <www.hcch.net/upload/wop/lse_concl_e.pdf>). Additional text (eg explanatory remarks) is also admissible if it is clearly outside the ten numbered informational items.

Except for the title, the apostille may be issued in the official language of the authority which issues it. However, it is recommended to use a bilingual or trilingual form including the French and/or English text. (Such forms have also been developed by the Permanent Bureau of the Hague Convention.)

The issuing authority must keep a register of all its apostilles. If there is any doubt as to the authenticity of the apostille, any interested party may consult the authority which issued it (art 7(2)). Nowadays, some of these registers may be checked electronically (e-register).

d) Effects of the apostille
The apostille certifies only the authenticity of the signature and the capacity of the person who has signed the underlying public document, as well as, where appropriate, the identity of the seal or stamp which the public document bears

(art 5(2)). However, the apostille does not certify that the issuing authority was competent to issue the document or that the requirements of domestic law for the proper execution of the underlying public document have been met. Neither does it certify the content of the document for which it was issued. Also the Hague Legalisation Convention does not affect the right of the receiving state to determine the acceptance, admissibility and the probative value of the apostillized foreign public document.

e) e-Apostille

Since 2006, special fora of the Hague Apostille Convention have developed electronic forms of apostille (e-Apostille) and the operation of electronic registers of apostilles that can be accessed online by recipients to verify the origin of an apostille they have received (e-registers). Even without changes in the text of the Hague Legalisation Convention, international fora on the e-Apostille consider an e-Apostille as admitted by the Convention (Sixth (Madrid) Forum, C&R No 6, Seventh (Izmir) Forum, C&R No 9 – as quoted in the Apostille Handbook No 308 – available at <www.hcch.net/upload/apostille_hbe.pdf>) By the end of 2016, competent authorities from 29 contracting states had implemented one or both components of the e-App.

3. Other international sources

a) Sectoral Hague conventions

Several Hague conventions on legal cooperation exempt specific public documents within their scope (in particular the requests under the respective convention) not only from legalization but also from other 'similar formalities' (such as apostillization). These are (ordered by date of signature):

(i) Hague Service Convention (Hague Convention of 15 November 1965 on the service abroad of judicial and extrajudicial documents in civil or commercial matters, 658 UNTS 163),
(ii) Hague Evidence Convention (Hague Convention of 18 March 1970 on the taking of evidence abroad in civil or commercial matters, 847 UNTS 241),
(iii) Hague Child Abduction Convention (Hague Convention of 25 October 1980 on the civil aspects of international child abduction, 1343 UNTS 89),
(iv) Hague Choice of Court Convention (Hague Convention of 30 June 2005 on choice of court agreements, 44 ILM 1294).

b) ICCS conventions on extracts from civil status records

Also several conventions drafted under the auspices of the International Commission on Civil Status (ICCS or CIEC – Commission Internationale de l'État Civil; → CIEC/ICCS (International Commission on Civil Status)) and signed by various European states exempt extracts from civil status records from the requirement of both legalization and apostille. In order of date of signature, these are:

- art 5 ICCS Paris Convention of 27 September 1956 concerning the issue of certain extracts from civil status records to be sent abroad, 299 UNTS 211 (16 ratifications as of 17 October 2015),
- art 4 ICCS Luxembourg Convention of 26 September 1957 concerning the issuance free of charge of copies of civil registration documents and the waiver of authentication requirements relating thereto, 932 UNTS 35 (ten ratifications),
- art 5 ICCS Rome Convention of 14 September 1961 on the extension of the competence of authorities qualified to receive acknowledgements of children born out of wedlock, 932 UNTS 63 (ten ratifications),
- art 7(2) ICCS Rome Convention of 10 September 1970 on legitimation by marriage, 1081 UNTS 247 (seven ratifications),
- art 8 ICCS Vienna Convention of 8 September 1976 concerning the issue of plurilingual extracts from civil status records, 1327 UNTS 3 (23 ratifications) and
- art 2 ICCS Waiver of Authentication Convention (nine ratifications).

Among these conventions, the Convention on the issue of plurilingual extracts from civil status records has the most important practical impact, because it has been ratified by most continental European civil law states (25 states – see <http://ciec1.org/ListeConventions.htm>). It provides harmonized models for extracts of the birth, death and marriage registers which are exempt from legalization and apostille.

In theory, the ICCS Waiver of Authentication Convention covers the broadest scope, including all 'records and documents relating to the civil status, capacity or family situation' or 'all other records or documents if they are produced with a view to the celebration of a marriage'. However, it has been ratified by only nine states. Some states are hesitant to ratify the ICCS conventions because they are open to accession for all states – without the possibility to object to an accession (as provided by art 12 Hague Legalisation Convention).

c) European Convention on Diplomatic and Consular Instruments

The Hague Legalisation Convention expressly exempts public documents issued by diplomatic and consular authorities from its scope of application (art 1(2)(a)). Such diplomatic and consular instruments are covered by the European Legalisation Convention (European Convention of 7 June 1968 on the abolition of legalisation of documents executed by diplomatic agents or consular officers, 788 UNTS 169), which has been ratified by 23 European states (as of 26 March2017) → Russia being the latest) see <http://conventions.coe.int/Treaty/Commun/ChercheSig.asp?NT=063&CM=8&DF=02/03/2014&CL=ENG>). Among the contracting states, diplomatic and consular instruments are exempt from legalization – and impliedly also from all other certification such as apostillization (art 3). As a fallback provision, each contracting state has to establish a system for the verification, where necessary, of the authenticity of documents to which this Convention applies (art 4(2)).

d) Brussels Legalisation Convention

In 1987, the European Communities made a first attempt to abolish altogether legalization and apostille among the EC Member States by the Brussels Convention of 25 May 1987 abolishing the Legalisation of Documents in the Member States of the European Communities (hereafter the Brussels Legalisation Convention – French text, Décret No 92–383 of 1 April 1992, available at JORF No 0084 of 8 April 1992 p 5191). However, not all EC Member States ratified the Convention. Thus the Convention entered into force only between those Member States which had not only ratified the Convention, but had also expressly declared that it should apply bilaterally even without universal ratification (art 6(3)). It now applies provisionally to seven EU Member States (Belgium, Denmark, Estonia, France, Ireland, Italy and Latvia).

The Brussels Legalisation Convention closely follows the model of the Hague Legalisation Convention, in particular in its definition of the public documents within its scope (art 1(2)), but without the exceptions of the Hague Legalisation Convention, and in its definition of the term legalization (art 3). If, in exceptional cases, the authority of the state of destination has 'serious doubts, with good reason, as to the authenticity of the signature, the capacity in which the person signing the document has acted, or the identity or seal of the stamp', it may address the central authority of the state of origin (art 4).

e) MERCOSUR

Within the Member States of MERCOSUR (Southern Common Market, that is Argentina, Brazil, Paraguay and Uruguay), under the Protocol of Las Leñas (Las Leñas Protocol of 27 June 1992 on Judicial Cooperation and Assistance in Civil, Commercial, Labour and Administrative Matters, 2145 UNTS 421), public documents are exempt from legalization or other formality, but only if they are transmitted by the central authority. Article 26 reads:

> [d]ocuments emanating from judicial authorities or other authorities of one of the Contracting States, as well as notarial instruments (escrituras públicas) and documents certifying the validity, the date or the authenticity of a signature or of the conformity with the original, which are transmitted by way of the Central Authority, shall be exempted from all legalisation, apostille or other similar formality when they have to be produced in the territory of another Contracting State.

One might say that the transfer by the central authority replaces the apostille.

Article 25 goes even further, granting public documents from another Member State the same probative value as instruments of the receiving state: 'Public instruments emanating from one Contracting State have in another (Contracting State) the same probative force as its (= the receiving state's) own public instruments' (<www.mercosur.int/t_ligaenmarco.jsp?contentid=4823&site=1&channel=secretaria>).

4. European sources

a) ECJ decision Dafeki

Under the Treaty establishing the European Community (TEC) (Consolidated versions of the Treaty on European Union and of the Treaty establishing the European Community

(2002), [2002] OJ C 325/1), now the TFEU (The Treaty on the Functioning of the European Union (consolidated version), [2012] OJ C 326/47), Member States may not completely disregard public documents on → personal status issued in another Member State. Thus, the ECJ held in the *Dafeki* case:

> [i]n proceedings for determining the entitlements to social security benefits of a migrant worker who is a Community national, the competent social security institutions and the courts of a Member State must accept certificates and analogous documents relative to personal status issued by the competent authorities of the other Member States, unless their accuracy is seriously undermined by concrete evidence relating to the individual case in question. (ECJ, Case C-336/94 of 2 December 1997, *Eftalia Dafeki v Landesversicherungsanstalt Württemberg* [1997] ECR I-6761)

The ECJ concluded this from the EC Treaty provisions on the prohibition of discrimination in the freedom of movement of workers (art 45 TFEU, then art 48 TEC) and the social security system (art 48 TFEU, *ex* art 51). However, that does not oblige the Member States to accept the documents on personal status without legalization or without any weighing of the evidence.

b) Sectoral regulations

Sectoral European regulations had already abolished the requirement of legalization (or other 'similar formality' such as apostillization) for documents within their respective scope of application (art 56 Brussels I Regulation and art 61 Brussels I Regulation (recast), art 52 → Brussels IIa Regulation (Council Regulation (EC) No 2201/2003 of 27 November 2003 concerning jurisdiction and the recognition and enforcement of judgments in matrimonial matters and the matters of parental responsibility, repealing Regulation (EC) No 1347/2000, [2003] OJ L 338/1), art 4(2) Evidence Regulation (Council Regulation (EC) No 1206/2001 of 28 May 2001 on cooperation between the courts of the Member States in the taking of evidence in civil or commercial matters, [2001] OJ L 174/1), art 4(4) European Service Regulation (Regulation (EC) No 1393/2007 of the European Parliament and of the Council of 13 November 2007 on the service in the Member States of judicial and extrajudicial documents in civil or commercial matters (service of documents), and repealing Council Regulation (EC) No 1348/2000, [2007] OJ L 324/79), art 65 Maintenance Regulation (Council Regulation (EC) No 4/2009 of 18 December 2008 on jurisdiction, applicable law, recognition and enforcement of decisions and cooperation in matters relating to maintenance obligations, [2009] OJ L 7/1), art 74 Successions Regulation (Regulation (EU) No 650/2012 of the European Parliament and of the Council of 4 July 2012 on jurisdiction, applicable law, recognition and enforcement of decisions and acceptance and enforcement of authentic instruments in matters of succession and on the creation of a European Certificate of Succession, [2012] OJ L 201/107)) art 61 Matrimonial Property Regulation (Council Regulation (EU) 2016/1103 of 24 June 2016 implementing enhanced cooperation in the area of jurisdiction, applicable law and the recognition and enforcement of decisions in matters of matrimonial property regimes [2016] OJ L 183/1), art 61 Registered Partnerships Matrimonial Property Regulation (Council Regulation (EU) 2016/1104 OJ L 183/30). The older regulations normally expressly list the documents exempted whereas the more recent regulations exempt all 'documents issued in a Member State in the context of this Regulation'.

c) Public Documents Regulation

From 16 February 2019 the new Public Documents Regulation will apply (Regulation (EU) of the European Parliament and of the Council of 6 July 2017 on promoting the free movement of citizens and businesses by simplifying the acceptance of certain public documents in the European Union and amending Regulation (EU) No 1024/2012' of 24 April 2013 [2016] OJ L 200/1. The Regulation covers documents from public registers in a broad sense, such as civil status documents (concerning birth, death, → marriage, registered partnership, parenthood, → adoption), documents on residence, citizenship and → nationality, absence of a criminal record, but also on the legal status and representation of a company or other undertaking, on real estate and intellectual property rights (art 3(1)).

These extracts from registers and certificates are exempted from all forms of legalization and similar formality (art 4). The same applies for the Union multilingual standard forms (art 15(3)). Also certified copies issued in other Member States will be accepted (art 5). Authorities are to accept non-certified translations of public documents issued by the authorities of other Member States (art 6). If the authorities of the receiving Member State have reasonable doubt as to the authenticity of the public documents, they may submit a request for information to the authorities of the Member State of origin (art 7).

The regulation also establishes EU multilingual standard forms concerning birth, death, marriage, registered partnership and legal status and representation of a company or other undertaking (arts 11 *et seq*).

5. Bilateral agreements

Certain bilateral agreements abolish legalization and apostille altogether. Such agreements exist in particular between neighbouring states or states which otherwise share common links. Such more favourable bilateral (or multilateral) agreements are not affected by the Hague Legalisation Convention (art 8).

IV. Effects of legalization or apostille

1. Effect

Legalization in the narrow sense or the procedures replacing legalization prove only the authenticity of the signature, the capacity of the official signing it and, where appropriate, the seal or stamp affixed to it (art 5(2) Hague Legalisation Convention). Under national law, legalization in a broad sense might further establish the authenticity of the public document.

In civil law systems, there are many other functions of public documents or authentic instruments for which the authenticity of a foreign public document is required but generally not sufficient.

2. Evidentiary or probative value

As we have seen, the full evidentiary value is part of the definition of a public document or authentic instrument in civil law systems. Legalization or the formalities substituting legalization do not grant particular probative value to the foreign public document. However, once authenticity has been proven by the legalization, then under the respective national rules of evidence the foreign public document is often accorded the same evidentiary value as national public documents of the same type.

So far, only some European sources regulate the evidentiary value. Article 59(1) Succession Regulation (as well as art 58 of the Matrimonial Regulation and the Registered Partnerships Regulation) on the 'Acceptance of authentic instruments' rule that 'an authentic instrument established in a Member State shall have the same evidentiary effects in another Member State as it has in the Member State of origin, or the most comparable effects, provided that this is not manifestly contrary to public policy (*ordre public*) in the Member State concerned'. According to the wording, the evidentiary standard is that of the state of origin, not that of the state of destination. However, the authorities of the state of destination will invariably apply their own procedural → *lex fori*, thereby limiting the evidentiary value to that generally accepted in the state of destination. In practice, this might limit the probative value of authentic acts when used in a common law or Nordic state.

3. Enforceability

In civil law countries, authentic instruments on obligations of the parties are typically either enforceable by matter of law or can be made enforceable by a specific declaration of the obliged party (submission to direct enforcement). In some international or European sources, enforceability even forms part of the definition of an authentic instrument (eg art 50 Brussels Convention, art 4(3)(a) European Enforcement Order Regulation).

Legalization does not render the foreign authentic instrument enforceable in the state of destination. Generally, enforceability is granted in a specific procedure in the state of destination, called the '*exequatur*'.

Enforceability is regulated by many international or European sources. In the European sectoral regulations on judicial cooperation, enforcement is one of three basic parts (besides jurisdiction and recognition). In the older sources, the *exequatur* was granted by the state of destination (eg arts 50, 31 *et seq* Brussels Convention, arts 57, 38 *et seq* Brussels I Regulation, arts 46, 28 *et seq* Brussels IIa Regulation). Today within the EU, in the more recent regulations, enforceability is granted by the Member State of origin for all other Member States. This model was first introduced by art 25 European Enforcement Order Regulation, and has since been extended by a revision to art 58, 39 *et seq* Brussels I Regulation (recast). This transfer of competences from the state of destination to the state of origin parallels the change made from legalization to apostillization.

4. Formal requirements

In civil law jurisdictions, certain types of contract or other legal acts require the form of an authentic instrument (such as the sale and transfer of → immovable property, contracts on → matrimonial property, certain types of wills or the foundation of a company), and thus to guarantee legal certainty as a pillar of the system of preventive justice (in French *justice préventive* or in German *vorsorgende Rechtspflege*). Whether a foreign authentic instrument suffices to fulfil such a formal requirement is a question of private international law, not of legalization.

First, for some legal acts, the state might require an authentication by its own authenticating officials, in particular where public registers come into play, such as for the transfer of immovables or for the foundation of companies or the transfer of company shares. Such concerns for the legal security and the integrity of the public registers have been acknowledged by the European legislature in the reservation for national law of the registry and the *lex rei sitae* in Recital (18) of the Succession Regulation.

If there is no exclusive competence, the respective international private law often admits as sufficient either the form of the law applicable to the substance of the contract or the form of the place where the contract was concluded.

If the form of the place of the act does not suffice, one ultimately has to check whether an authentication by a foreign official under his national procedure might replace an authentication under the law of the receiving state as equivalent (→ Formal requirements and validity).

CHRISTIAN HERTEL

Literature

Reinhart Bindseil, 'Internationaler Urkundenverkehr' [1992] DNotZ 275; British Institute for International and Comparative Law, 'The Use of Public Documents in the EU, Study for the European Commission JLS/C4/2005/04' <http://ec.europa.eu/civiljustice/news/docs/study_public_docs_synthesis_report.pdf>; Council of the Notariats of the European Union (CNUE), 'Comparative Study on Authentic Instruments – National Provisions of Private Law, Circulation, Mutual Recognition and Enforcement, Possible Legislative Initiative by the European Union, Study for the European Parliament No IP/C/JURI/IC/2008–019' <www.europarl.europa.eu/document/activities/cont/200811/20081127ATT43123/20081127ATT43123EN.pdf>; Georges AL Droz, 'La légalisation des actes officiels étrangers, HCCH Prel Doc No 1 of March 1959' <www.hcch.net/index_en.php?act=publications.details&pid=4393&dtid=3>; Robert Freitag, 'Der Beweiswert ausländischer Urkunden vor dem deutschen Standesbeamten' [2012] StAZ 161; Reinhold Geimer and Rolf Schütze, *Internationaler Rechtsverkehr in Zivil- und Handelssachen* (CH Beck, leaflet edition); Hague Conference on Private International Law, *The ABCs of Apostilles* (HCCH (Hague Conference on Private International Law) 2010, <www.hcch.net/upload/abc12e.pdf>); Hague Conference on Private International Law, *Apostille Handbook* (HCCH (Hague Conference on Private International Law) 2013, <www.hcch.net/upload/apostille_hbe.pdf>); Claus Kierdorf, *Die Legalisation von Urkunden* (Carl Heymanns 1973); Yvon Loussouarn, 'Explanatory Report on the 1961 Hague Apostille Convention' 1961 <www.hcch.net/index_en.php?act=publications.details&pid=52&dtid=3>; see also the bibliography on the website of the Hague Conference at <www.hcch.net/index_en.php?act=conventions.publications&dtid=1&cid=41>.

Lex fori

I. Introduction

The term '*lex fori*' refers to the law of the jurisdiction or authority seized with a case, in its application either to the procedural aspects as *ordinatoria litis* or to the merits as substantive law under various entitlements.

The unquestioned domain of the *lex fori* is procedural matters, as opposed to substantive matters pertaining to the merits: *lex fori regit processum*. The applicability of local law to procedural issues regardless of the law applied to the merits is generally accepted and appears to be a legal common place, even if not always expressly incorporated into statutory law. The history and rationale of the rule, as well as its scope, are dealt with elsewhere (→ Proceedings, law governing; → Substance and procedure).

The decision on what substantive law applies to the merits of a cross-border dispute (or, absent litigation: the decision on what substantive law shall rule on the legal aspects of a cross-border situation) involves a choice between a number of methodological alternatives, beginning with the unilateralism–bilateralism binomial (→ Unilateralism). A crucial issue in this regard is whether and the extent to which the law of the forum should apply to the substance of a dispute. An extreme possibility is to accord priority to the forum legal system over foreign law as a matter of principle, the so-called *lex fori in foro proprio*.

The *lex fori* as *decisoria litis* in the adage '*lex fori in foro proprio*' designates a methodology based on a policy of correlation (a parallelism, *Gleichlauf*) between international jurisdiction and the law applicable to the merits in a cross-border setting. It would be impossible to indicate one single explanation for this methodological choice covering the rationale for all of its separate aspects (for examples see III. below). However, it is generally accepted that at a first level the rationale of a *lex fori* approach lies in the protection of specific interests of the forum in respect of persons or things, whereas at a second level the *lex fori in foro proprio* approach appears as a reaction to the difficulties encountered in the application of foreign law (→ Foreign law, application and ascertainment), which is frequently a cumbersome, expensive and time consuming process.

The advantages of the *lex fori in foro proprio* approach are readily apparent in greater predictability, speed and fluidity in the development of the proceedings. These benefits are particularly important for subject matters such as insolvency or → succession law, where substantive and procedural issues are closely intertwined. Nonetheless, the shortcomings of the approach are also easily identified. One of the most commonly alleged weaknesses is parochialism: whilst unilateralism does not necessarily lead to inward-looking rules, this is always the outcome of the *lex fori in foro proprio* solution as by definition bilateralization of the rule is not an option. However, parochialism is no longer a persuasive argument any longer: the *lex fori* approach is usually combined with multilateral rules, as well as tempered by exceptions (see III. below).

From an economic perspective, when compared to a methodology open to the application of foreign law, the *lex fori* approach has been criticized as encouraging forum shopping (→ Forum (and law) shopping), on the one hand, and for jeopardizing → regulatory competition and the comparative regulatory advantages of foreign jurisdictions on the other (Giesela Rühl, *Statut und Effizienz: ökonomische Grundlagen des Internationalen Privatrechts* (Mohr Siebeck 2011) 807, 808–15). The relative strength of these arguments is linked to the opinion on whether forum shopping, regulatory competition etc are to be promoted.

Parallelism forum/*ius* can be achieved in various ways. Strictly speaking, the *lex fori in foro proprio* methodology in its purest form is associated with common law jurisdictions. Here parallelism implies a from-the-outset general preference for the direct application of the *lex fori* rather than foreign law, thereby entirely displacing the traditional bilateral conflict-of-laws methodology. Thus a jurisdictional approach is adopted, which may lead as a consequence to the conflict-of-laws interests being subsumed under the problems and solutions relating to jurisdictional issues. A corollary of this approach is the applicability of the *lex fori* through the authorization to stay proceedings by means of the *forum non conveniens* doctrine, when the designated legal system is a foreign one.

Other more limited forms of the parallelism between forum and *ius* are also imaginable and actually identifiable in continental Europe. The association of jurisdiction and applicable law may result from subordinating the exercise of jurisdiction to the declaration of forum law as applicable (*forum legis*: Julio Diego González Campos, 'Les liens entre la compétence judiciaire et la compétence législative en droit international privé' (1977) 156 Rec. des Cours 229, 338). Another possibility is the use of identical, and identically interpreted, connecting factors for jurisdiction and choice of law. In this regard, one option is to grant the parties the liberty to choose the *lex fori* as applicable law: the correlation may occur through a double-tier agreement of the parties on the jurisdiction and the applicable law, to which the lawgiver accords full effect. Besides, parties may be allowed to choose the law of the competent jurisdiction determined in accordance with objective criteria, as happens, for instance, in art 5(1)(d) → Rome III Regulation (Council Regulation (EU) No 1259/2010 of 20 December 2010 implementing enhanced cooperation in the area of the law applicable to divorce and legal separation, [2010] OJ L 343/10). They may as well be authorized to do so pending litigation, as stated in art 5(3) of the same instrument. Along the same lines, other possibilities under the common label of → 'Optional choice of law', refer to the option given either to the parties or to the judge to retreat to the law of the forum, in order to avoid the application of the foreign law designated by the applicable choice-of-law rule (→ Optional (facultative) choice of law).

The law of the forum intervenes sometimes for eminent practical reasons rather than as a consequence of methodological considerations for resolving conflict-of-laws situations: for instance, in order to fill a gap left by the impossibility to apply the foreign law appointed by the choice-of-law rule, due to the absence of proof of such legal system, or by its contrariety (rather, of the result of applying it) with the → public policy (*ordre public*) of the forum. Here, no priority is accorded to the *lex fori*: it acts as a residual connection to be applied subsidiary. Still, the final outcome remains the parallelism forum/*ius*. Other tools, such as → renvoi of the first degree, also lead to the *lex fori*; but again, the rationale underlying resourcing to this expedient can hardly be said to correspond to a consciously sought policy of parallelism forum/*ius*.

Finally, parallelism may simply happen as a result of a (more or less questionable) move on the part of the courts: for instance when, following an instinctive dislike towards foreign law, they make appeal to escape devices in order to remain or to come back to national law ('homeward trend'). Characterization of problems as 'procedural' for choice-of-law purposes, as well as generosity in the shaping of the category of public policy, are roads leading to this goal.

II. *Lex fori* as *lex decisoria*: history up to the 20th century

1. Initial findings

The applicability of the *lex fori* to disputes involving aliens (→ Aliens law (*Condition des étrangers, Fremdenrecht*)) has been said to go back to as early as the 4th century BC in the Greek city states (→ Private international law, history of). Among the statutists it is to be found in the writings of the 16th-century French scholar *D'Argentré*. His theories gave priority to the → territoriality principle, while considering the personal law principle as an exception. *D'Argentré* classified only a limited number of laws as personal, the rest being either real ones or 'mixed' statutes to be treated as the latter. This approach naturally promoted the application of the law of the forum: in the 16th century the main element of wealth was realty, most disputes revolved around marital property and succession rights in immovables, and were lodged before the courts at the *situs* of the property. As a consequence the application of the *lex fori* was the rule.

The exclusive application of the *lex fori* was bound to be the logical outcome of the idea of territorial sovereignty underlying the elaborations of the Dutch authors of the 17th century, such as *Paul* and *John Voet* (→ Voet, Paulus and Johannes) or *Huber* (→ Huber, Ulrik). However, such a conclusion was qualified and place was made for the application of foreign law (→ Foreign law, application and ascertainment), mainly through the notion of → comity.

Up to the middle of the 18th century England also adhered to the *lex fori* approach. This was related to the fact that unless commercial or admiralty courts assumed jurisdiction, disputes arising out of foreign transactions were not triable in England. Therefore, jurisdiction in England automatically led to the application of English law. Jurisdiction was later accepted over cross-border cases, but on the basis of a legal fiction according to which the facts leading to litigation had taken place in England. Thus, *lex fori* remained the basic rule. Exceptions were found as regards foreign contract law, applied as the law presumably intended by the parties, while other exceptions derived from comity.

In the 19th century the law of the forum was strongly supported in Germany by *Carl Georg von Wächter* (→ Wächter, Carl Georg von). He nevertheless recognized some situations in which the → *lex fori* had to yield to foreign laws and limit its own scope in order to avoid hardship. This covered the express or implied → choice of law by the parties, some items related to personal capacity (→ Capacity and emancipation), domestic relations, → successions and form of legal transactions, provided the *lex fori* did not require mandatory application also for these cases. Besides, *von Wächter* proposed three 'guiding principles' to be followed by courts. According to the first, courts must abide by any express directive of the *lex fori* concerning the law to be applied to a given question. Second, absent such a directive, the judge must decide whether forum law claims to be applied in spite of the foreign elements of the case, interpreting the rule at issue in the light of its spirit. Finally, if the examination so described leads to no clear conclusion, the *lex fori* applies.

Wächter's proposals had little impact when put forward, but they were taken up later by the so-called 'modern unilateralists', namely

Brainerd Currie (→ Currie, Brainerd) and *Albert Armin Ehrenzweig* (→ Ehrenzweig, Albert A) in the framework of the → (American) Conflict of laws revolution.

2. The 20th century: the American revolution

American conflict-of-law methodologies developed since *Caver's* critique of the choice-of-law problem in 1933 share as common feature the central role assigned to the forum in the process of choice of law. Within this framework, a *lex fori in foro proprio* approach was particularly supported by two American authors, *Brainerd Currie* and *Albert A Ehrenzweig*, whose academic proposals, although fundamentally different in conception, were similar enough in presentation to be classified together as forum-oriented approaches.

Brainerd Currie's well known theory of governmental interest analysis was developed for the resolution of litigation involving apparently conflicting laws of two or more states (→ Currie, Brainerd; → Interest and policy analysis in private international law). *Currie's* approach differentiates true and false conflicts, true conflicts only arising when conflicting policies underlie the apparently conflicting rules of different jurisdictions and each jurisdiction has an interest in the application of its policy to the particular case. Otherwise the conflict is a 'false conflict'. *Currie's* method proposal follows several steps: normally, even in cases involving foreign elements, the court should be expected to apply the rule of decision found in the law of the forum as a matter of course. When it is suggested that the law of a foreign state should furnish the rule of decision, the court should first determine the governmental policy expressed in the law of the forum, and inquire whether the relation of the forum to the case is such as to provide a legitimate basis for the assertion of an interest in the application of that policy. If necessary, the court should similarly determine the policy expressed by the foreign law and whether the foreign state has an interest in the application of its policy. If the court finds that the forum state has no interest in the application of its policy, but that the foreign state has, it should apply the foreign law. Conversely, if the court finds that the forum state has an interest in the application of its policy, it should apply the law of the forum, even though the foreign state also has an interest in the application of its contrary policy. *A fortiori*, it should apply the law of the forum if the foreign state has no such interest (Brainerd Currie, 'Notes on Methods and Objectives in the Conflict of Laws' [1959] Duke L.J. 171, 178).

Currie's approach was endorsed essentially in California by Chief Justice *Traynor* of the California Supreme Court. New York courts have also embraced the approach to choice of law to some extent, particularly when a centre of gravity approach would lead to unintended results. Also, while largely rejecting *Currie's lex fori* preference and proscription of interest weighting, several modern American choice-of-law approaches have adopted two points of his proposals: first, that states have an interest in the outcome of multistate private law disputes, and second, that these interests are to be taken into account, among others, when resolving such disputes.

According to *Ehrenzweig's* doctrinal construction jurisdiction and → choice of law are closely linked. Treatment of the *lex fori* as an exception is only the result of 'academic aberrations in the history of conflicts law' (Albert Armin Ehrenzweig, 'The Lex Fori-Basic Rule in the Conflict of Law' (1960) 58 Mich.L.Rev. 637, 645; in 646–69 *Ehrenzweig* provides for a rereading of history of conflict of laws restoring *lex fori* to its due place). Observation of American practice reveals that American courts have nearly always given preference to their own laws, and that foreign law was resorted to only in situations where such preference was contrary to the intentions of the parties, or would have caused hardship on other grounds. *Ehrenzweig* submits that only certain exceptions to the basic rule, the *lex fori*, should be retained. The first, based on the parties' intention, because 'it is so firmly established that it may be regarded as the second basic rule', while other propositions such as the *lex loci delicti* or the *lex situs*, and particularly rules serving the unity of status and estates, should be retained where, and to the extent they have sufficiently crystallized in certain specific situations.

For *Ehrenzweig* the primary objective of the law of choice of law was the ascertainment of a convenient forum. A 'nascent doctrine of *forum non conveniens*' (Albert Armin Ehrenzweig, *A Treatise on the Conflict of Laws* (West Publishing 1962) 352), would allow the courts to refuse to exercise jurisdiction in the absence of sufficient contacts with the forum. This point of departure paved the way to concluding that the proper forum should apply *lex fori* as primary solution. *Ehrenzweig* acknowledged that the local law would seldom provide for its own application: therefore the court should analyse the policy underlying the local substantive rule in order to determine whether it should be displaced by the foreign rule. In practice, however, foreign law would seldom be applicable under *Ehrenzweig's* theory.

Although critics refute the desirability of determining the law applicable to the merits on the basis of the considerations that lead to determine the proper forum, *Ehrenzweig's* legacy still inspires choice-of-law solutions in topics such as → torts in some states, such as Kentucky, Michigan and Nevada. It also underlies current doctrinal developments.

III. Current examples of the *lex fori in foro proprio* approach

The common current trend for the regulation of cross-border situations is coexistence of methods, one of them being the *lex fori* approach. Thus, it is possible to find examples of the *lex fori* approach most generally by way of specific rules of limited scope, for which in addition exceptions or alternatives are provided. Examples in this direction are developed in the following subsections.

1. The extreme (albeit attenuated) case: the lex fori *as* loi de police

In certain domains regulatory policies command the enforcement of local law. The resort to *lex fori* is immediate: it applies as *'loi de police'*, in the best interests of the forum and internal harmony in the case at hand (→ Overriding mandatory provisions). Article 8 Spanish Civil Code (Código Civil of 24 July 1889, Geceta de Madrid no 206, 25 July 1889, henceforth Spanish CC); art 10:7(2) Dutch Civil Code (Dutch New Civil Code (Nieuw Burgerlijk Wetboek of 1 January 1992, henceforth Dutch CC)); art 20 Belgian Code of Private international law (Code de Droit International Privé, Loi du 16 juillet 2004 portant le Code de droit international privé, MB 27 July 2004, 57344, as amended, henceforth Belgian PILA), illustrate the *loi de police* role of the *lex fori*. In the framework of European law, examples are provided by art 9 Rome I Regulation (Regulation (EC) No 593/2008 of the European Parliament and of the Council of 17 June 2008 on the law applicable to contractual obligations (Rome I), [2008] OJ L 177/6; → Rome Convention and Rome I Regulation), art 16 → Rome II Regulation (Regulation (EC) No 864/2007 of the European Parliament and of the Council of 11 July 2007 on the law applicable to non-contractual obligations (Rome II), [2007] OJ L 199/40) or art 30 Succession Regulation (Regulation (EU) No 650/2012 of the European Parliament and of the Council of 4 July 2012 on jurisdiction, applicable law, recognition and enforcement of decisions and acceptance and enforcement of authentic instruments in matters of succession and on the creation of a European Certificate of Succession, [2012] OJ L 201/107; → Rome IV Regulation).

Theory and practice of the *lois de police* have been considered as one of the major developments of conflict of laws in the second half of the last century. From a comparative point of view, the *lois de police* doctrine has the added value of representing a meeting point between continental private international law and the American doctrine of governmental interest analysis. Divergences remain, though, in as far as for the American supporters of the doctrine it is to be generally applied, while *lois de police* are only exceptional (Bernard Audit, 'Le droit international privé à la fin du XXe siècle: progrès ou recul' (1998) 2 R.I.D.C. 421–48, 440–42).

The *règles d'application immédiate* are an extreme expression of the *lex fori in foro proprio* approach. However, two caveats apply to this assertion. On the one hand, they represent an attenuated form of the method, in that the law of the forum applies directly but exceptionally, ie only in cases where its application is of overriding importance for the local community. On the other hand, a recent phenomenon or willingness to yield (completely or, more likely, to a certain extent, by way of 'giving effect' to the foreign rules) to foreign mandatory rules in appropriate circumstances cannot be overlooked. An example is provided by art 9(3) Rome I Regulation.

2. Other constellations

a) Marriage and matrimonial crisis: the Swiss Private international law Act

The Swiss Private international law Act (Bundesgesetz über das Internationale Privatrecht of 18 December 1987, 1988 BBl I 5, as amended, henceforth Swiss PILA), is the best representative of the *lex fori* approach and the linkage between forum and *ius* in continental

Europe. Article 44 Swiss PILA, providing for the application of Swiss law to the substantive requirements for marriage, is a typical example. Parallelism here serves the task of the authorities, which is the reason why other proposals, such as distributive connecting points or choice of the parties, were rejected.

As a logical consequence of art 44 Swiss PILA, Swiss law will also be applied to claims for marriage annulment before the Swiss courts, according to art 45a(2) Swiss PILA.

Still within the scope of family law, mention has to be made of art 61(1) Swiss PILA, according to which both divorce and separation (→ Divorce and personal separation) are ruled by Swiss law. The provision has been interpreted in the sense that the common domicile (→ Domicile, habitual residence and establishment) is not the connection factor (as it would be derived from an *a contrario* reading of art 61(2) Swiss PILA), but the fact that a Swiss court has jurisdiction. Divorce or legal separation are governed by Swiss law only because and when the Swiss courts have jurisdiction. It is therefore the connection to the *lex fori* which necessarily underlies art 61(1) Swiss PILA. Scholars agree with this understanding of the provision, which helps to avoid the additional costs linked to the application of foreign law, and also stress the intrinsic relation between procedural and material aspects of the particular subject matter (Lukas Bopp, 'Article 61' in Heinrich Honsell and others (eds), *Basler Kommentar – Internationales Privatrecht* (3rd edn, Helbig Lichtenhahn 2013) para 9). The rule is certainly tempered, albeit only to an extent, by para 2 of the same provision – which is itself nuanced by para 3.

b) Urgent and provisional measures to protect a child: the Hague Child Protection Convention

The core issue of the international regime for the protection of children is the allocation of jurisdiction to adopt measures relating to parental responsibility – especially in the case of breakdown of the family unit – as well as to education and welfare protection. In a context in which the jurisprudential component is therefore essential, a trend towards a system of parallelism between jurisdiction and applicable law is easily recognizable. One example is provided by art 15(1) of the Hague Child Protection Convention (Hague Convention of 19 October 1996 on jurisdiction, applicable law, recognition, enforcement and co-operation in respect of parental responsibility and measures for the protection of children, 35 ILM 1391). It maintains the principle posed by the Hague Infant Protection Convention (Hague Convention of 5 October 1961 concerning the powers of authorities and the law applicable in respect of the protection of infants, 658 UNTS 143) according to which 'in exercising their jurisdiction under the provisions of Chapter II, the authorities of the Contracting States shall apply their internal law'. Comparable provisions can be found in other conventional instruments as well as in national law (in force unless superseded by the international regimes). It has also been extended to the protection of adults (→ Adults, protection of) who, by reason of an impairment or insufficiency of their personal faculties, are not in a position to protect their interests: see art 43 Italian Private international law Act (Riforma del Sistema italiano di diritto internazionale private, Act No 218 of 31 May 1995 in Gazz.Uff., Supplemento Ordinario No 128 of 3 June 1995, as amended, henceforth Italian PILA). Several reasons have been said to underlie the forum/*ius* parallelism in this framework such as the *ordre public* nature of the measures, urgency, although not as pressing as to allow the jurisdiction of other authorities (see art 11 Hague Child Protection Convention), advising to apply one's own law in order to avoid the difficulties linked to proof of foreign law, and more generally – and predictable also to the adoption of non-urgent measures – that it facilitates the task of the competent authority, who will apply the law it knows best. The fact that the effects of the measures, their enforcement, are to take place mainly or exclusively within the territory of the forum has also been argued (Paolo Picone, 'Les méthodes de coordination entre ordres juridiques en droit international privé: Cours général de droit international privé' (1999) 276 Rec. des Cours 9, 166).

It is worth noting that Article 15(1) of the Hague Child Protection Convention is not an absolute provision. According to art 15(3) Hague Child Protection Convention, in so far as the protection of the person or the property of the child requires it, the authorities of the contracting states may exceptionally apply or take into consideration the law of another state with which the situation has a substantial connection. The rationale of the exception lies with the best interest of the child. The typical example – mentioned also by the Explanatory Report accompanying the convention (Paul

Lagarde, 'Explanatory Report on the 1996 Hague Child Protection Convention' (1998), available at <www.hcch.net>, para 89) – is that of the authorization requested from the authorities of the habitual residence to sell the minor's property located abroad. It is certainly preferable that the authority exercising jurisdiction may in this case apply the law of the *situs* of the property and grant the authorization provided under this law, which is applicable *in rem*.

c) Examples from the EU: cross-border insolvency and successions

The correlation forum/*ius* is neither a major concern nor a general policy of EU private international law regulations. The Insolvency Regulation (Regulation (EU) 2015/848 of the European Parliament and of the Council, of 20 May 2015 [2015] OJ L 145/19) and the Succession Regulation (Regulation (EU) No 650/2012 of the European Parliament and of the Council of 4 July 2012 on jurisdiction, applicable law, recognition and enforcement of decisions and acceptance and enforcement of authentic instruments in matters of succession and on the creation of a European Certificate of Succession, [2012] OJ L 201/107; → Rome IV Regulation) nevertheless represent an exception in this respect.

The *lex fori concursus* solution – ie the law of the state of the opening of the proceedings – is the common rule in international insolvency law (→ Insolvency, applicable law). It is enshrined in art 7 Insolvency Regulation. The following arguments are usually invoked to justify this preference. First it ensures uniformity of outcomes in a context in which different states may favour different legislative policy objectives. Second, it enables all stakeholders to clearly ascertain what their rights and obligations will be – in other words, their position within the framework of the debtor's insolvency. Third, it facilitates the management of the proceedings by matching forum and *ius*, as it ensures the *par conditio creditorum* as regards choice-of-law rules, as all the creditors will be subject to the same legal system.

A number of exceptions have nonetheless been introduced to the general rule in arts 8 *et seq* Insolvency Regulation. The rationale is twofold. First, the intention is to protect legitimate expectations as well as the certainty of transactions in specific subject matter domains particularly susceptible to the interference of a law other than the one originally governing the situation. Second, there are procedural reasons, in that the administration of insolvency proceedings is usually a complex and costly endeavour. A limitation of costs by way of an exception to the *lex fori concursus* operates in the first place in favour of only some creditors. However, it is bound to benefit all of them to the extent that it leads to a reduction of the total costs linked to the procedural management. Article 8 Insolvency Regulation, ruling on rights *in rem*, provides for an example of an exemption established in order to simplify the application of the rule (Miguel Virgós Soriano and Francisco J Garcimartín Alférez, *Derecho procesal civil internacional: litigación internacional* (2th edn, Thomson Civitas 2007) para 136 on art. 5 of Council Regulation (EC) No 1346/2000, now art. 8).

The rules of the Succession Regulation are devised so as to ensure that the authority dealing with the → succession will usually apply its own domestic law. This is the normal situation as a result of the interplay between arts 4 and 21(1) Succession Regulation. International jurisdiction is accorded to the courts of the Member State in which the deceased had his habitual residence at the time of death to rule on the succession as a whole, and, unless otherwise provided for in the Regulation, the law applicable to the succession as a whole is the law of the state in which the deceased had his habitual residence at the time of death. This outcome has been praised by academia (Andrea Bonomi, in Andrea Bonomi and Patrick Wautelet, *Le droit européen des successions* (Bruylant, 2013) 286) as it allows avoiding the difficulties linked to the access and proof of foreign law. Besides, the parallelism between jurisdiction and applicable law is of particular interest in an area such as succession law, where application of a foreign regime may be especially difficult due to the intricate relation between → substance and procedure. Direct resource to *lex fori* also permits bypassing from the outset succession rules running against the philosophy of the domestic law of the forum – a phenomenon likely to happen increasingly often due to immigration waves from individuals of countries of a markedly different cultural and legal tradition.

Under particular circumstances, the Regulation nonetheless admits the dissociation between forum and *ius*. *A priori*, this is the case when the *de cuius* has used the faculty art 22 Succession Regulation accords to choose the law of a Member State of which he was a national to govern his succession. However, the lawmaker has still sought to ensure parallelism also in this setting, and to this aim he has provided for a series of mechanisms which would come into play, such as the agreement of the parties concerned that a court or the courts of the Member State of the chosen law are to have exclusive jurisdiction to rule on any succession matter (art 5(1) Succession Regulation); correspondingly, any other court seized must decline jurisdiction (art 6(b) Succession Regulation). Declining jurisdiction is mandatory under these circumstances. It is moreover conceived as a possibility, depending on the request of one of the parties to the proceedings, under art 6(a) Succession Regulation, which provides that where the law chosen by the deceased to govern his succession is the law of a Member State, the court seized may decline jurisdiction if it considers that the courts of the Member State of the chosen law are better placed to rule on the succession, taking into account the practical circumstances of the succession such as the habitual residence of the parties and the location of the assets. A mechanism akin to the doctrine of → *forum non conveniens* is thus created, which depends on the choice by the *de cuius* of his/her national law, and which aims in the first place to preserve the coincidence between jurisdiction and applicable law, and only secondarily to sidestep practical inconveniences for the parties, or to ensure the efficacy of the procedures (Andrea Bonomi, in Andrea Bonomi and Patrick Wautelet, *Le droit européen des successions* (Bruylant 2013) 197). This is the reason why the accessibility and contents of the chosen law should play a role in the decision of the authority to decline its competence: in case the application of the foreign law turns out to be easy, the seized authority should refrain from declining jurisdiction.

d) Examples from the common law:
forum non conveniens *and* lex fori
A policy of parallelism between forum and *ius* may be identified behind the English doctrine of → *forum non conveniens*, to the extent that in deciding on the motion a factor to be considered is whether the case may be better tried in the courts of the country whose laws are applicable to the subject matter (Ole Lando, 'Lex Fori in Foro Proprio' (1995) 2 MJ 359, 360).

The connection between jurisdiction and → choice of law has recently been analysed in the framework of the American → *forum non conveniens* doctrine, in the light of practice showing that one of the most frequent rationales for dismissal of a case is that it requires complex exercises in comparative law. Both *Gulf Oil Corp v Gilbert* (330 U.S. 501 (1947)) and *Piper Aircraft Co v Reyno* (454 U.S. 235 (1981)), leading cases of the US Supreme Court regarding *forum non conveniens*, include references in this regard whereby the doctrine 'is designed in part to help courts avoid conducting complex exercises in comparative law. . . . [T]he public interest factors point towards dismissal where the court would be required to "untangle problems in conflict of laws, and in law foreign to itself"' (*Piper Aircraft Co v Reyno*, 454 U.S. 235, 251 (1981), quoting *Gulf Oil Corp v Gilbert*, 330 U.S. 501, 509 (1947)). Even if the factor cannot be deemed conclusive, the fact remains that many lower courts have given it a decisive weight in the *forum non conveniens* analyses. From 2007 to 2013, 82 per cent of reported cases dismissed on grounds of *forum non conveniens* argued the application of foreign law as the grounds for dismissal; within unreported cases 75 per cent explicitly recognized the application of foreign law as a reason for dismissal (→ Foreign law, application and ascertainment; → Foreign law, judicial review). From this data scholars conclude that *forum non conveniens* motions may serve as a proxy for determination of choice of law; that historical notions of litigation convenience are being subsumed as questions of choice of law; and that the doctrine is being used to avoid adjudicating cases of foreign law (Donald E Childress III, 'Rethinking Legal Globalization: The Case of Transnational Personal Jurisdiction' (2013) 54 Wm. & Mary L.Rev. 1489, 1528, 1538). This seems to be particularly true when normativity of foreign law is at stake (Donald E Childress III, 'Rethinking Legal Globalization: The Case of Transnational Personal Jurisdiction' (2013) 54 Wm. & Mary L.Rev. 1489, 1539, 1558).

IV. Residual *lex fori*

As seen in the preceding sections, recourse to the *lex fori* may be the outcome of a conscious legislative choice in favour of a *lex fori in foro proprio* approach. However, the law of the forum also comes into play due to a practical need to fill a gap. In this scenario *lex fori* has a subsidiary role, ensuing from the impossibility of applying the foreign law appointed by the choice-of-law rule.

When, in spite of the efforts of the parties and/or the judge (depending on the → burden of proof), foreign law has not been proven, several alternatives are opened: (i) dismissal of the action, (ii) deciding the case according to what the judge deems is the probable contents of foreign law, (iii) the application of subsequent connecting factors if provided by the choice-of-law rule for the same subject matter or (iv) resorting to another law, which in almost all legal systems will be the *lex fori*. The law of the forum governs only by default, due to the inability to determine foreign law or its content at all, or to an extent considered sufficient by the judge (see art 14(2) Italian PILA, art 15(3) Belgian PILA). Despite the absence of any specific provision in this regard, this is as well the solution advocated in Greece in the Greek Code of Civil Procedure (Presidential Decree 503/1985, Government Gazette A' 182/1985); it is also common practice in Germany (German Federal Court of Justice (BGH), 69 BGHZ 387) and in France (Cour de Cassation France, 1re civ., 21 November 2006, No de pourvoi: 05-22002 (source: Legifrance)).

The law of the forum is also likely to come into play when the result of applying the designated foreign law conflicts with local → public policy, contradicting basic values of the forum. Under these circumstances one possible solution is to reject this law and replace it by a rule of the forum. Such an alternative is usually accepted, although seldom expressly stated: see art 10:6 Dutch CC; art 6 Introductory Act to the German Civil Code (Einführungsgesetz zum Bürgerlichen Gesetzbuche of 21 September 1994, BGBl. I 2494, as amended, henceforth German EGBGB); art 21 Belgian PILA; art 12(3) Spanish CC; art 21 Rome I Regulation; art 26 Rome II Regulation; art 35 Succession Regulation.

The law of the forum that comes to the forefront on grounds of public policy is applied as last resort, ie the primary aim of its application is not to assert or to protect a specific concern of the forum (actually, such task has already been performed by the putting aside of the foreign provision by means of the *ordre public* tool). This is clear, for example, in art 16 Italian PILA, which requires the exhaustion of all other available possibilities prior to resorting to the *lex fori*. However, under some conditions, the residual application itself may be inspired by a policy requiring immediate replacement of the *lex causae* by the law of the forum: see art 10 Rome III Regulation. Where the law applicable pursuant to art 5 or art 8 makes no provision for divorce or does not grant one of the spouses equal access to divorce or legal separation on grounds of their sex, the law of the forum will apply. In the same vein, art 107.2 para 2 of the Spanish CC (no longer in force) stated that the Spanish law applies 'In any case, when one of the spouses is habitually resident in Spain: c) If the laws referred to in the first paragraph of this provision do not recognize separation or divorce, or do so in a discriminatory manner or contrary to public order.'

V. *Lex fori* by way of *renvoi*

The idea of → *renvoi* originates from the perception that the traditional model of choice-of-law rules accords the forum an over-significant role, whose legitimacy may be contested to determine by means of its own choice-of-law rules that the substantive law of another system should apply, regardless of the views this system might have on the limits of its own law. Indeed, designation of foreign law under the choice-of-law rule is usually meant to cover only its substantive rules, and the choice-of-law rules of the *lex cause* are not included (expressly art 32 Greek Civil Code (Astikos Kodikas of 23 February 1946, A.N. 2250/1040; FEK A 91/1940, 597); art 10(5) Dutch CC; art 16 Belgian PILA; art 24 Rome II Regulation; art 11 Rome III Regulation; art 12 of the Hague Maintenance Protocol 2007 (Hague Protocol of 23 November 2007 on the law applicable to maintenance obligations, [2009] OJ L 331/19); with nuances, art 18 Rome I Regulation). Only sometimes does the choice-of-law rule of the forum refer to foreign law in its entirety, and as a result either accepts a return to the law of the forum, or a further referral to the legal system of another state. Examples of the former case, known as '*renvoi de premier degré*', are provided for by German law (art 4 German EGBGB), Spanish law (art 12(2) Spanish CC), as well as by the Italian PILA (art 13(1)(b)).

The application of the law of the forum by way of *renvoi* is not related to the willingness to simplify the management of the proceedings. Neither is it due to an alleged primacy over foreign law. Rather, in its original conception it results from inverse reasoning. In current practice, even in the absence of any indication in the legal provision in this respect, the use of *renvoi* is limited to particular subject matters, such as succession, where it is shaped to achieve particularly desirable outcomes, for instance supporting the principle of unity of successions, as well as the international consistency of solutions.

MARTA REQUEJO ISIDRO

Literature

David F Cavers, 'A Critique of the Choice-of-Law Problem' (1933) 47 Harv.L.Rev. 173; Brainerd Currie, 'Notes on Methods and Objectives in the Conflict of Laws' [1959] Duke L.J. 171; Brainerd Currie, *Selected Essays on the Conflict of Laws* (Duke University Press 1963); Albert Armin Ehrenzweig, 'The Lex Fori-Basic Rule in the Conflict of Law' (1960) 58 Mich.L.Rev. 637; Albert Armin Ehrenzweig, *A Treatise on the Conflict of Laws* (West Publishing 1962); Phocion Franceskakis, 'Quelques précisions sur les lois d'application immédiate et leurs rapports avec les règles de conflit de lois' (1966) 55 Rev.crit.DIP 1; Richard Garnett, *Substance and Procedure in Private international law* (OUP 2012); Julio Diego González Campos, 'Les liens entre la compétence judiciaire et la compétence législative en droit international privé' (1977) 156 Rec. des Cours 229; Friedrich K Juenger, 'A Page of History' (1983–84) 35 Mercer L.Rev. 419; Ole Lando, 'Lex Fori in Foro Proprio' (1995) 2 MJ 359; Franco Mosconi, 'Exceptions to the Operation of Choice of Law Rules' (1989) 217 Rec. des Cours 9; Paolo Picone, 'Il metodo dell'applicazione generalizzata della lex fori' in Paolo Picone (ed), *La riforma italiana del diritto internazionale privato* (CEDAM 1998) 371; Paolo Picone, 'Les méthodes de coordination entre ordres juridiques en droit international privé: Cours général de droit international privé' (1999) 276 Rec. des Cours 9; Symeon C Symeonides, 'The American Choice-of-Law Revolution: Past, Present, and Future' (2002) 298 Rec. des Cours 9; Carl Georg von Wächter, 'Über die Collision der Privatrechtsgesetze verschiedener Staaten' (1841) 24 AcP 230, (1842) 25 AcP 161, (1842) 25 AcP 361; Celia Wasserstein Fassberg, 'The Forum: Its Role and Significance in Choice of Law' (1985) 84 ZVglRWiss 1; Hessel E Yntema, 'The Historic Bases of Private international law' (1953) 2 Am.J.Comp.L. 297.

Lex maritima

I. Definition

The term '*Lex maritima*' is often translated as 'the general maritime law' in the sense of a *ius commune* that is common to most of the world's shipping nations. It is used to describe the ancient and medieval maritime law which was based on customs as well as on written documents and codes. Today the term *lex maritima* is also used to capture the emergence of a transnational maritime law that exists in privately created rules and standard contracts as well as in maritime arbitration (→ Arbitration, maritime).

II. Historical foundations of the *lex maritima*

The law of shipping and maritime trade is old. Some historical records suggest that early unwritten rules, the Rhodian Sea Law, date back to the 8th and 9th centuries BC. Actual sources, however, are vague and the only historical evidence for the existence of the Rhodian Sea Law is a reference in the Digests of the *Corpus Iuris Civilis* (Theodor Mommsen and Paul Krueger, *Corpus Iuris Civilis*, vol 1, Digesta 14.2 (Berlin 1899)). Whereas ancient sources of maritime law are rare, early medieval tradesmen in fact produced a number of historically verifiable maritime codifications, which contained rules that in part persist until today. Among the most important and best known are the *Rôles d'Oléron* and the *Consolat de Mar*. But even more important than single codifications was the emergence of local places of trade and of universal trade customs and practices. This process of local aggregation of trade in specific locations and the emergence of uniform customs and practices can be characterized as co-evolutionary. In medieval Europe, trade flourished particularly in places where tradesmen established their own tribunals, thereby institutionalizing separation of the jurisdiction over the market from local public authorities. Specialized trade courts were installed in cities with markets, trade fairs or ports. The benches of those courts were formed not by public officials but by a jury of fellow tradespeople, composed half of people from the respective trading place and half of people from other, sometimes even foreign places. They were familiar with the problems of merchants and knew about their customs. The solution of conflicts was based on the needs of merchants, particularly the case in England, where equity as a combination of justice and good faith was the basis for the resolution of mercantile conflicts. The concept of equity combined economic reasonableness with legal certainty, both of which were crucial for merchants as well as their customers. In addition, merchant courts provided for quick and speedy decisions which with reference to the allegedly dusty feet of medieval tradesmen were called 'the courts of piepowder' (Charles Gross, 'The Court of Piepowder' (1906) 20 QJE 2, 231–49). Quick decisions were crucial for tradespeople that usually were not residents of the place where the market was held.

The establishment of local markets and important trade fairs fostered not only the exchange of goods and services between those places but also the exchange of rules, customs and practices, which thus have spread widely beyond the places of their creation and have gained validity in many other locations. Examples for such universal rules are the aforementioned *Rôles d'Oléron*, which were the codification of customs and trade practices of the island of Ôleron in the 12th century, the *Consolat de Mar*, a code originating in 14th-century Barcelona, or the Visby Rules, highly influential in the 16th-century Baltic area. Those codes reflected and codified mercantile customs. They were necessary because the medieval mercantile community was not a homogenous group. Different languages, cultural backgrounds, or difficulties in communication over large distances caused significant problems for transactions, which could be mitigated or even solved through uniform rules and practices. Those rules and practices were rooted in the maritime trade but later became known as the → *lex mercatoria*. The *lex maritima* can therefore be seen as a predecessor and important part of the medieval *lex mercatoria*.

III. Contemporary debates: the *lex maritima* as transnational law

A second connotation with the notion *lex maritima* is closely linked to recent debates over the existence and the form of transnational law. Legal scholars and social scientists participating in these debates seek to conceptualize law in the 'postnational constellation' (Jürgen Habermas, *The Postnational Constellation: Political Essays* (translated, edited and with an introduction by Max Pensky, MIT Press 2001). National legal orders seem to be incapable of regulating social phenomena that are triggered by mega trends, such as the increased importance of information technology, the massive growth of cross-border trade and many other recent developments that are usually summarized as a process of 'globalization'. Neither national nor international nor private international law can explain phenomena such as corporate social responsibility, global processes of standardization and the turn to private regulation in many fields of society which were formerly regulated exclusively by law. Many of these developments are discussed under the concept of transnational law.

1. Transnational law as internationalization and privatization of law

Debates over transnational law are manifold and hard to overlook. One narrative conceives transnational law as the result of a process of internationalization and privatization. It looks for certain social realms in which economic transactions are not, or only to a minor extent regulated by state law. The main regulatory bodies in such fields tend to be privately constituted. These fields and their respective regulation are often described by the Latin word '*Lex*' combined with a second word describing the respective field. We thus see debates over a '*lex mercatoria*', a '*lex sportiva*', the '*lex informatica*' or the '*lex constructionis*'. In the respective fields (trade law, sports law, the law of the Internet or construction law), legal scholars and social scientists have found empirical evidence for an ever increasing privatization of regulation and/or conflict resolution. This also holds true for maritime law, for which reason such phenomena of privatization in maritime law are described as the '*lex maritima*'.

2. The ineffectiveness of international law

The intrinsic internationality of maritime law is one of its major and most salient characteristics. Apart from inland navigation, most transport operations by vessel are international. The shipping industry has always sought to cope with the problems caused by its internationality. Particularly the need for predictable resolution of legal conflicts was and remains a pervasive issue of maritime transport. The law on bills of lading, for instance, has a vivid history dating right back to the late 19th century. At that time, a number of attempts were made to internationally unify certain legal aspects of bills of lading, notably by private actors. Contrary to the argument to be advanced in the following, initiatives of private actors have not been successful and international law paved the way for the unification of maritime law (Rolf Stoedter, *Geschichte der Konnossementsklauseln* (Schiffahrtsverlag Hansa 1954) 20 *et seq*, 60–61). In 1924, the International Convention of 25 August 1924 for the unification of certain rules relating to bills of lading (Hague Rules, 120 LNTS 155) was eventually enacted, and established the framework for a considerable degree of unification in international maritime law (→ Maritime law (uniform law)). However, the challenge with international law is that it is difficult to change due to conflicting national interests as well as for procedural reasons. Thus the Hague Rules were never reformed but amended by the 1968 Visby Protocol (Protocol of 23 February 1968 to amend the International Convention for the unification of certain rules of law relating to bills of lading signed at Brussels on 25 August 1924 (Hague Rules), 1412 UNTS 128) and the 1979 Brussels Protocol (Protocol of 21 December 1979 to amend the International Convention for the unification of certain rules to bills of lading (Hague Rules) as modified by the Amending Protocol of 23 February 1968 (Visby Protocol), 1412 UNTS 146; the Hague Rules together with the two Protocols are called 'Hague-Visby Rules'). This protocol, however, was not adopted by all states that had joined the Hague Rules. In addition, in 1978 the Hamburg Rules (United Nations Convention of 31 March 1978 on the carriage of goods by sea, 1695 UNTS 3), and in 2009, the Rotterdam Rules (United Nations Convention of 11 December 2008 on contracts for the international carriage of goods wholly or partly by sea, UN Doc A/RES/63/122, 63 UNTS 122) were enacted in order to further unify maritime law on an international level. However, the result was clearly the opposite to what was intended. The increasing number of international conventions on the → carriage of goods by sea led to fragmentation rather than the desired unification, since these four conventions overlap each other in substantial fields of regulation. Also private international law is incapable of mitigating this degree of fragmentation. The response of the shipping industry has been a return to an all-encompassing privatization, particularly in the fields of lawmaking and dispute resolution.

3. Private lawmaking in the international shipping industry

It is highly controversial whether private actors are capable of making law and whether it is legitimate for them to do so. This certainly applies if one takes a traditional concept of state law as a basis of consideration. However, transnational law has always challenged the traditional concept of law and tried to identify and describe forms and manifestations of law beyond the nation state. In this endeavour, standard contracts and clauses have come to the attention of transnational legal scholars. Nevertheless, standard form contracts are often criticized as one-sided and unfair, or as failing to reflect public policy and the nature of public goods. This may hold true for many standard contracts. On the one hand they are usually unproblematic from an organizational point of view, since they standardize business transactions and thereby reduce transaction costs. On the other hand, though, standard contract terms become a legal problem when one, often dominant party uses them to redistribute contractual risk in its own favour. In such cases, standard form contracts may even become unconscionable.

In response, international trade, and especially the maritime industry, has established processes in which standard form contracts are developed through discursive and participatory procedures. Accordingly, they are less one-sided and coercive than effectively negotiated among many, if not all stakeholders. The opportunity for participation renders these maritime contracts interesting material for transnational law case studies.

Within the shipping industry, the Baltic and International Maritime Council (BIMCO) plays a major role in drafting and distributing standard charter parties and other standard contracts. The objective is to produce standard forms and other shipping documents that strike a fair and equitable balance between the parties, that are legally sound, and that can be understood by all concerned. The drafting process of standard contracts at BIMCO always follows a similar pattern. The 'BIMCO Documentary Committee' coordinates all BIMCO activities in the field of standard contracts. The Documentary Committee has members with various backgrounds in the shipping industry, who serve as agents and representatives for their respective organizations. Among the members of the Documentary Committee are representatives of several states, protection and indemnity insurance providers (P&I clubs), freight associations, shipping companies as well as international shipping associations such as the 'International Chamber of Shipping', or the 'Federation of National Associations of Ship Brokers and Agents' (FONASBA), and finally members of the BIMCO secretariat. In addition, prior to a modification of existing standard forms or on commencing of the drafting process of a new form, all BIMCO members are consulted for their opinion, while their experience with existing standard forms is evaluated. This form of participation also enhances acceptance of standard contracts in the industry. After preparatory evaluations, a subcommittee starts the specific drafting process in a smaller group. Again, the subcommittee is composed of members representing shipowning/shipbroking and ship-operating interests. On completion of the drafting process, the finished document is submitted to the Documentary Committee for formal approval. That means that every stakeholder in the shipping industry, together with their specific interests, is represented in the drafting process of a standard contract form, which will subsequently be widely distributed and frequently used in international shipping.

Another example for the creation of private rules in the shipping industry is the Comité Maritime International (CMI). The CMI is a private organization, founded in 1897, that along with numerous other rules and regulations drafts, publishes and administers the so-called 'York-Antwerp Rules' (YAR). The YAR are regulations on the maritime legal instrument of 'general average', that is essential in the shipping industry. The rules on general average derive from the aforementioned 8th-century BC Rhodian Sea Law, and reflect the fact that shipping has always been a risky venture for several parties. Not only does the ship-owner bear the risk of losing the ship in heavy weather or rough seas, but the cargo-owners are similarly subject to the risk of losing their property. The rules on general average accommodate this fact in that if a ship and its cargo are at risk of being lost, the master might order the crew to abandon part of the cargo and jettison it, or in the earlier days of sail they would cut the mast to save the entire ship or the rest of the cargo. In such cases, general average rules render everyone involved in the voyage liable for any loss incurred by an individual cargo-owner or by the shipowner. That means that if one cargo-owner loses his cargo, which was abandoned in order to save the ship and the rest of the cargo, he can claim proportionate compensation from the other parties involved in the voyage. These rules still apply today but periodic revisions are necessary to adapt the procedures, responding to uncertainties in their application, or adjusting them to novel forms of transport or information technology. The revisions are effected by the CMI, and as in the case of BIMCO, representatives of various stakeholders of the maritime industry such as insuring companies, shipowners, carriers and freight-forwarders, lawyers, and many other interest groups take part in the negotiations. The revision process is a discursive process in which many divergent and partly concurring interests have to be accommodated. Here, once again, the drafting and revision process is not one-sided but rather balanced in order to accommodate the needs of all involved.

This means of creating maritime standard contracts is extremely interesting for transnational legal scholars. The perennial question is how law beyond the state can be legitimate. The concept of participation might be one step towards a concept of legitimate transnational law.

4. The role and importance of maritime arbitration

The maritime industry not only creates its own rules, but also provides highly elaborate and successful forms of dispute resolution body, which are ultimately even more important to the industry than national courts. Empirical evidence will help substantiate this thesis.

Relevant data can be retrieved from legal databases such as the Juris database, which collates German court decisions. The sample from that database was based on the following parameters: court decisions of (i) all German courts, (ii) in the period 1950 until 2013 in which (iii) the decisive legal standard was based on German maritime law (until 2013 §§ 476–900 German Commercial Code (Handelsgesetzbuch of 10 May 1897, RGBl. 219, as amended). This survey yielded 626 decisions over 64 years, so that on average fewer than ten cases were decided annually in German courts in the field of maritime law. However, the situation seems to be different before English courts. In England, the Commercial Court and the Admiralty Court have jurisdiction over maritime cases. The numbers of cases observed here are considerably higher than those before German courts, although they are decreasing. Whereas in the years 1995–97 approximately 2,000 cases were decided before state courts, this declined in the following years to only 800–1,000 cases. Even though the caseload of maritime cases in English courts is much higher than in German courts, one can see a considerable decrease between the years 1995 and 2013, with an average number of cases before national courts in England of approximately 600–800 per year over recent years. The significance of these statistics becomes clear if the numbers are contrasted with the caseload of maritime arbitrators. Particularly in London, maritime arbitration (→ Arbitration, maritime) is strongly based in the London Maritime Arbitrator's Association (henceforth LMAA). In recent years, the LMAA caseload has been approximately 3,000–4,000 cases per year. Another important arbitration association in London is Lloyd's Salvage Arbitration Branch, which offers arbitration on claims resulting from the open form salvage agreement. This arbitral process is used to decide on the amount of → salvage money that a maritime salvor can claim. Summarizing, it can be concluded that maritime arbitration is significantly more important for maritime dispute resolution than the state courts. The ratio between private arbitration and litigation before state courts becomes even more pronounced if the numbers of cases before state courts and the caseload attributable to arbitration associations are combined. We then see that approximately 500–1,000 cases per year are litigated in England, whereas far more than 3,500 cases are resolved within alternative dispute resolution bodies. Naturally these numbers are valid for only England, but maritime arbitration also exists in other places. In New York, for instance, the Society of Maritime Arbitrators (henceforth SMA) is the second largest maritime arbitration institute in the world after the LMAA. The SMA has a caseload of approximately 500 cases per year. Thus, the LMAA and the SMA handle 90 per cent of the worldwide caseload in maritime arbitration. All these numbers, however, come with a caveat. The Juris-database, for instance, is reliant on courts supplying decisions, and unless decisions are submitted to Juris, they will not be published there. Further, the numbers of English courts are limited to the two largest courts in maritime affairs in London. On the other hand, numbers of LMAA cases may be even higher, because the LMAA statistics count only cases that have been decided by LMAA arbitrators. Even so, considerably more cases are administered by the LMAA but not decided by LMAA arbitrators. Against this background, the numbers may be questionable or even meaningless from the perspective of quantitative social science methodology. But despite this caveat, the numbers indicate a marked tendency, also supported by maritime lawyers, that the maritime industry is no longer necessarily reliant on litigation and state courts. Maritime arbitration has a far greater importance for dispute resolution in this field. In addition apart from other reasons, the attractiveness of arbitration as opposed to litigation in the maritime industry is based on applicability of the New York Convention of 10 June 1958 on the Recognition and Enforcement of Foreign Arbitral Awards (330 UNTS 3), allowing for enforcement of arbitral awards in almost every country in the world. It is striking that most standard contracts provided by BIMCO contain exclusively arbitration clauses. For instance the GENCON charter party, one of the most important voyage charter parties for dry cargoes, exclusively contains an arbitration clause. Litigation is not stipulated and can only be agreed by changing and amending the standard form. Against this background, arbitration seems to be the standard method of dispute resolution in the maritime industry.

5. Implications for private international law

The foregoing observations show that the maritime industry relies heavily on privately created legal rules and private arbitration. National lawmakers and national courts remain important but are far from being the only source of regulation in the field of maritime transport. The question for the private international legal scholar then becomes what that means for private international law.

The answer to this question is as simple as it is provocative. Private international law will have to identify ways of conceptualizing and integrating privately created legal rules into its concept of law and into conflicts of law theory. In the transnational sphere, traditional concepts of law and new forms of privately created norms intersect and continually collide. Notwithstanding, private international law has always only accepted national legal orders as equipollent. Attempts to overcome this paradigm have been made during the formation process of the Rome I Regulation on the European Rules for the conflict of laws (Rome I Regulation: Regulation (EC) No 593/2008 of the European Parliament and of the Council of 17 June 2008 on the law applicable to contractual obligations (Rome I), [2008] OJ L 177/6). It was proposed to allow that parties 'may also choose as the applicable law the principles and rules of the substantive law of contract recognized internationally or in the Community' (Commission Proposal for a Regulation of the European Parliament and the Council on the law applicable to contractual obligations (Rome I) COM(2005) 650 final – final, art 3 para 2). Yet this proposal was rejected so that in the enacted version of the Rome I Regulation, only state law can be subject to a → choice of law. However, against the background of the emergence and existence of transnational law in several industries, private international law will have to embrace also privately created norms. A theoretical solution to this problem could be a generalization: private international law follows the concept of deciding not cases but only which law should decide the case. This idea can be extended to a general principle of law which also encompasses privately created norms as well as societal normative claims, and reconciles them with national legal orders. Whereas traditional private international law is only applicable to different state laws, a concept of conflict of laws as a general legal paradigm broadens the horizon. If we apply the idea of private international law not only to national laws but also to private norms, the conflict lines are shifted. The basic approach ultimately remains the same in that private international law decides not the case but rather which law is applicable to it. The consequence of a modification of a transnational conflicts law is that it is no longer limited to state law but also takes privately created norms into account. Questions then arise of which privately created norms have to be considered, and whether every social norm conflicts with state law. Naturally, not every contract and every social norm has the normative power to conflict with state law, but some privately created norms do. One characteristic feature of an equipollent privately created norm could be the participative element in the creation of maritime standard contracts as described above (see also Christiana Ochoa, 'The Relationship of Participatory Democracy to Participatory Law Formation' [2008] Ind.J.Global L.Stud. 5–18; Johannes Köndgen, 'Privatisierung des Rechts' [2006] AcP 477–525). Other elements might be the fact that the body which creates the norms is independent and impartial and that rights and duties are regulated in a fair and equitable manner (Max Planck Institute for Foreign Private and Private international law, 'Comments on the European Commission's Green Paper on the conversion of the Rome Convention of 1980 on the law applicable to contractual obligations into a Community instrument and its modernization' (2004) 68 RabelsZ 1, 33). Against this background, state law loses its claim to be the sole valid source of law but also gains a new task. It has to decide whether certain private norms have sufficient normativity to conflict with national laws and thus has to mitigate the 'clash of rationalities' that arises from new forms of regulation in the transnational sphere, such as the *Lex Maritima*. In the future, international private legal scholarship will face unprecedented challenges to conceptualize the relationship between state law and privately created norms in a transnational realm. The main task will then be to develop preconditions under which privately created rules are accepted as law, and to develop strategies for national legal orders to cope with that acceptance.

ANDREAS MAURER

Literature

Gralf-Peter Calliess, 'Law, Transnational' in Mark Juergensmeyer and Helmut Anheier (eds), *Encyclopedia of Global Studies* (Sage 2012) Vol. 3, pp 1035–1039; Claire Cutler, *Global Power and Private Authority* (CUP 2003); Grant Hunter, 'Standard Forms: The BIMCO Experience' in D Rhidian Thomas (ed), *Legal Issues Relating to Time Charterparties* (Informa Law 2008) pp 1–15; Philip C Jessup, *Transnational Law* (Yale University Press 1956); Andreas Maurer, *Lex Maritima* (Mohr Siebeck 2012); Andreas Maurer, 'The Concept of Participation in the Making of Transnational Law: Legitimization and Normativity in the Transnational Sphere' in Poul Kjaer, Paulius Jurčys and Ren Yatsunami, *Regulatory Hybridization in the Transnational Sphere* (Leiden 2013) pp 203–222; Andreas Maurer, 'Transnational Maritime Law' in Jürgen Basedow, Ulrich Magnus and Rüdiger Wolfrum (eds), *The Hamburg Lectures on Maritime Affairs 2011–2013* (Springer 2015) pp 129–146; William Mitchell, *Essay on the Early*

History of the Law Merchant (Burt Franklin 1903); James Reddie, *A Historical View of the Law of Maritime Commerce* (William Blackwood and Sons 1841 (Reprint 2005)); Thomas J Stipanowich, 'Arbitration: The "New Litigation"' (2010) U. Ill.L.Rev. 1; William Tetley, 'The General Maritime Law: The Lex Maritima' (1994) 20 Syracuse J.Int'l L.& Com. 105; William Tetley, 'International Maritime Law' (2000) 24 Tul.Mar.L.J. 775; Leon E Trakman, 'The Evolution of the Law Merchant: Our Commercial Heritage – Part I and II' (1980) 12 J.Mar.L.& Com. 1, Part II 153; Dewey R Villareal, Thomas E Fotopulos and Steven D Overly, 'International Maritime Arbitration' (1983) 12 Stetson L.Rev. 342; Rudolf Wiethölter, 'Materialization and Proceduralization in Modern Law' in Gunther Teubner (ed), *Dilemmas of Law in the Welfare State* (de Gruyter 1986) pp 221–249; Peer Zumbansen, 'Transnational Law' in Jan Smits (ed), *Encyclopedia of Comparative Law* (Edward Elgar 2006) pp 738–754.

Lex mercatoria

I. Definition and concept of *lex mercatoria*

Lex mercatoria or, in England, Law Merchant is a transnational contract governance regime with socio-economic as well as legal features. Its function is to safeguard reliable contract enforcement and to create legal certainty for international commerce. Its foundations are broader ideas of self-regulation or self-help and the principle of → party autonomy. Its construction components are institutions of private (norms, arbitration and social sanctions) and public (laws, courts and enforcement) origin, where the latter are disembedded from their domestic context to a considerable extent.

This concept of *lex mercatoria* rests on three premises: first, any economic transaction more complex than the immediate exchange of goods of easily assessable quality depends on the involved parties being convinced that in case of doubt they will be able to enforce their mutual promises for performance. In other words, commerce will seldom flourish where effective and low-cost institutions to support contractual commitments are unavailable. Second, although modern lawyers tend to think predominantly of state-created commercial law, including courts and enforcement mechanisms, as the institutions fulfilling these functions, the neighbouring disciplines of legal history, legal sociology and more recently new institutional economics provide ample evidence of instances, where reliable contract enforcement institutions are created and maintained as well by social forces and private entities. Third, while most lawyers will generously admit that private ordering works in the shadow of state commercial law and may supplement it, in fact private contract enforcement institutions may also work as a substitute for state commercial law, specifically where the latter is 'very costly, slow, unreliable, biased, corrupt, weak, or simply absent' (Avinash K Dixit, *Lawlessness and Economics: Alternative Modes of Governance* (Princeton University Press 2004) 3).

If we assume that public and private contract enforcement institutions work as functional equivalents and that their relative importance depends on their competitiveness with regard to the legal needs of contract parties, the precise institutional mix prevailing on a given market is factually, geographically and historically contingent. Factually, some markets, such as the cotton trade (Lisa Bernstein, 'Private Commercial Law in the Cotton Industry' (2001) 99 Mich.L.Rev. 1724–88), or the shipping industry (→ *Lex maritima*), are governed by industry-specific private legal systems while others are not. Geographically, in some markets, mainly in the Western countries, merchants can and do rely predominantly on state commercial law, while in less-developed or transformation countries they cannot, and in other regions, like Asia, for cultural reasons they do not (John McMillan and Christopher Woodruff, 'Private Order under Dysfunctional Public Order' (2000) 98 Mich.L.Rev. 2421–58). Historically, even in the Western world the extent to which merchants were able to rely on contract enforcement institutions provided by the state was subject to change. Thus, the history of commercial law is commonly divided into different phases, where the commercial revolution in late medieval Europe was accompanied by the evolution of 'ancient' (or medieval) *lex mercatoria*, which during the 18th and 19th centuries was integrated into and absorbed by the domestic commercial laws of the rising sovereign nation states (below II.). After the Second World War, however, European commercial law scholars resurrected the idea of a transnational commercial law, which purportedly develops in international commercial arbitration (→ Arbitration, international commercial) and, today, is referred to as 'new' *lex mercatoria* (below III.).

ANDREAS MAURER / GRALF-PETER CALLIESS

II. Historical context: ancient *lex mercatoria*

The evolution of commercial law seems to have taken place in recurrent cycles: an expansion of trade leads to changed legal needs unmet by the established legal systems. Therefore, merchants have to rely on self-help and self-regulation, where best practices over time turn into trade usage and custom, which apply and develop further in commercial dispute resolution. Specialized merchant courts operate at city markets, trade fairs or harbours, often as a privilege granted by authorities interested in levying customs duties. Due to endeavours to modernize the legal system, the thus created legal innovations finally are absorbed by and reintegrated into the general legal system (see A Claire Cutler, *Private Power and Global Authority: Transnational Merchant Law in the Global Political Economy* (CUP 2003) 108 ff).

One may see the Roman *ius gentium* as an early instance of such innovation cycle. When the Romans expanded their trade throughout Italy and across the Mediterranean, their *ius civile* was ill suited to meet the needs of foreign trade, as it did not apply to foreigners and was overly formalistic. Thus, in 241 BC a special praetor was empowered to deal with litigation concerning noncitizens. This *praetor peregrinus* developed a considerably more flexible and functional body of rules, which came to be known as *ius gentium*, a transnational law representing the general principles common to all civilized nations (→ *Ius gentium*). After all inhabitants of the Roman Empire became citizens in 212 BC, the need for a separate legal order became less pressing. However, the principles developed by the peregrine praetors were not discarded, but rather absorbed into the *ius civile*, contributing to its later much appraised universalist quality (Friedrich K Juenger, 'A Page of History' (1983) 35 Mercer L.Rev. 419, 422–3).

1. Ideology: the battle of historians

The historical blueprint for new *lex mercatoria* is the ancient *lex mercatoria*, which accompanied the commercial revolution in late medieval Europe (ca 1050–1300). Scholarship on the issue of whether an ancient *lex mercatoria* ever existed or qualified as a separate and autonomous legal system is abundant (see the affirmative overview at Leon E Trakman, 'The Twenty-First-Century Law Merchant' (2011) 48 Am.Bus.L.J. 775–834; critical Emily Kadens, 'The Myth of the Customary Law Merchant' (2012) 90 Tex.L.Rev. 1153–206, both with excessive references). The case for the existence of a medieval *lex mercatoria* seemed to be more or less settled (Levin Goldschmidt, *Handbuch des Handelsrechts, vol 1: Universalgeschichte des Handelsrechts* (3rd edn, Scentia-Verlag 1891 (reprint 1973)); Francis M Burdick, 'What is the Law Merchant?' (1902) 2 Colum.L.Rev. 470–85), as indicated by its inclusion in a very influential book on the formation of the Western legal tradition (Harold J Berman, *Law and Revolution* (Harvard University Press 1983) ch 11).

However, some scholars used the ancient *lex mercatoria* as an example for the broader assumption that private legal systems can operate autonomously from the state and, indeed, produce superior results where left free from any kind of public intervention (see Leon E Trakman, *The Law Merchant: The Evolution of Commercial Law* (Rothman 1983); Bruce Benson, *The Enterprise of Law: Justice without the State* (Pacific Research Institute for Public Policy 1990); Paul R Milgrom, Douglass C North and Barry R Weingast, 'The Role of Institutions in the Revival of Trade: The Law Merchant, Private Judges, and the Champagne Fairs' (1990) 2 *Economics and Politics* 1–23; Avner Greif, *Institutions and the Path to the Modern Economy: Lessons from Medieval Trade* (CUP 2006)).

These somewhat bold claims produced a series of historical studies contending the following. First, medieval trade fairs were institutionally organized by public authorities rather than by private ordering (Stephen E Sachs, 'From St. Ives to Cyberspace: The Modern Distortion of the Medieval "Law Merchant"' (2006) 21 Am.U.Int'l L.Rev. 685–812; Jeremy Edwards and Sheilagh Ogilvie, 'What Lessons for Economic Development Can We Draw from the Champagne Fairs?' (2012) 49 *Explorations in Economic History* 131–48). Second, merchant guilds did not facilitate the expansion of trade, but were monopolies whose continued existence must be attributed to distributional rather than efficiency effects (Sheilagh Ogilvie, *Institutions and European Trade: Merchant Guilds 1000–1800* (CUP 2011)). Third, late medieval references to *lex mercatoria* were based on privileges, statutory law and contractual practice rather than hinting to the existence of a uniform (transnational) body of substantive customary law (Albrecht Cordes, 'Die Erwartungen mittelalterlicher Kaufleute an Gerichtsverfahren: Hansische Privilegien als Indikator' in Albrecht Cordes and Serge Dauchy (eds), Emily Kadens, 'The Myth of the Customary Law Merchant' (2012) 90 Tex.L.Rev. 1153, 1170); *Eine Grenze in Bewegung: Öffentliche und private Justiz im Handels- und Seerecht* (Oldenbourg 2013) 39, 56.

This led one scholar to the conclusion that ancient *lex mercatoria* was simply dreamed up by proponents of new *lex mercatoria* who are not interested in what actually happened (Ralf Michaels, 'Legal Medievalism in *Lex mercatoria* Scholarship' (2014) 90 Tex.L.Rev. 259–68). In fact, the problem seems to be that there cannot be any positive or negative empirical proof of *ius non scriptum*, where only documentary evidence – instead of expert interviews, which are used to research new *lex mercatoria*, for example – is available. Since only highest noblemen and ecclesiastics had literate clerks and monks around them, it is no wonder that the only documentary evidence available on ancient *lex mercatoria* is contained in privileges and statutes of kings or the court rolls of an abbot, while the proceedings of most merchant courts fell into oblivion. Moreover, as the customs of merchants were treated as facts to be proven in each individual case by a merchant jury, the court rolls of St Ives, for example, rarely report on the findings of merchant juries, since they did not carry any precedential value. This explains why the available documents on ancient *lex mercatoria* contain mostly procedural rules, while there is little evidence of any substantive principles (Thomas E Scrutton, 'The Work of the Commercial Courts' (1921) 1 CLJ 6, 10 ff).

To sum up, what we can observe on both sides are ideologically more or less biased interpretations of indirect historical proof (see Jeremy Edwards and Sheilagh Ogilvie, 'Contract Enforcement, Institutions, and Social Capital: The Maghribi Traders Reappraised' (2012) 65 *Economic History Review* 421–44; Avner Greif, 'The Maghribi Traders: A Reappraisal?' (2012) 65 *Economic History Review* 445–69). However, the good thing about this 'battle of historians' is that it leaves us with more accurate evidence on ancient *lex mercatoria* than ever before. In the following, I shall try to flesh out what seems to be quite uncontroversial.

2. Origin: the rise of self-governed market towns

First, when the commercial revolution took place, there was no regulator or governance system in place, which resembled by far, what we understand by modern statehood, ie externally clearly demarcated territorial jurisdictions, which internally operate on a public–private divide as well as a separation of the powers to legislate, to adjudicate and to enforce. Instead, there was a multitude of economically and politically struggling, territorially overlapping jurisdictions of local, imperial and ecclesiastical origin, each of which in the absence of functional differentiation identified the exercise of administrative power with the task of adjudication (Hendrik Spruyt, *The Sovereign State and Its Competitors* (Princeton University Press 1994)).

Second, agricultural advances resulting in a significant growth in population triggered the commercial revolution. Many people fled the feudal system to become free burgers of towns, where craft and commerce flourished. Merchants and their guilds dominated in the self-governance of cities like Cologne, Florence or London. The right of the citizens of London to elect their own sheriff and judges and to be exempt from any other jurisdiction, for example, was granted in a charter sold by *King Henry I* around 1133. Confirmed by several royal charters, including the Magna Carta of 1215, the liberties of London later extended to the right to elect the mayor, who also performed a variety of judicial tasks at Guildhall (Graham S McBain, 'Liberties and Customs of the City of London: Are There Any Left?' (2013) 2 *International Law Research* 32–95). Many cities followed suit, often based on a charter of rights issued by kings in their endeavour to dwarf local authorities (Harold J Berman, *Law and Revolution* (Harvard University Press 1983) ch 12). Other towns were founded with the support of local authorities, interested in commerce as a source of revenue. Thus, in 1122 *Konrad of Zähringen* issued the founding charter of the city of Freiburg im Breisgau, granting the merchants, which he had called to settle on his ground based on leasehold, certain rights. Among these were, next to the protection of property and freedom from customs duties, the following:

Never will I impose a bailiff (*advocatus*) or priest

on my burgess, but whomever they choose, I shall confirm. If any dispute or difference arises among my citizens, it shall be resolved neither by my judgment (or discretion) nor that of their rector (= bailiff, sheriff, mayor), but according to the customarily acquired rights of all merchants (*pro consuetudinario et legitimo iure omnium mercatorum*), especially those of Cologne, a judgment shall be found. (My translation from the latin original, in Heinrich Schreiber (ed), Die älteste Verfassungsurkunde der Stadt Freiburg im Breisgau (Groos 1833) 31; a German translation is available at Felicitas Schmieder, Die mittelalterliche Stadt (WBG 2005) 84 f)

The rector, who was elected by the burgess each year from the 24 market jurors (*conjuratores fori*, later consuls, in London also 'aldermen'), which represented the most influential merchant families (*mercatoribus*), was in charge of the administration of the market town, including the market court. The rector, thus, originally was identical with the bailiff (*judex*) and in commercial cases sat together with two market jurors, who decided the case according to *iure omnium mercatorum*. If there was uncertainty about the content of that law, the case could be referred to Cologne for advice (Heinrich Schreiber, *Geschichte der Stadt und Universität Freiburg im Breisgau* (Wangler 1857) 41 ff (on the foundation), 62 ff (on the bailiff, the court and appeals to Cologne), 69 ff (on the 24 market jurors)).

Although most cities acquired their liberties by charters sold by kings in need of money, it seems fair to state that *lex mercatoria* developed in specialized market courts, headed by elected town officials. In England, these courts where called *pepoudrous* (or piepowder) courts, or at harbours admiralty courts, and later in staple towns, which in the Statute of the Staple of 1353 were granted the right to elect their mayor who would decide disputes *secundum legem mercatoriam*, staple courts (EE Rich, 'The Mayors of the Staples' (1933) 4 *Cambridge Historical Journal* 120–42). Salient features of these courts were that they decided disputes rather quickly from day to day or from tide to tide (Francis M Burdick, 'What is the Law Merchant?' (1902) 2 Colum.L.Rev. 470–85), and that the substantive rules applicable under customary *lex mercatoria* were established by juries composed of merchants (Henry Gerald Richardson, 'Law Merchant in London in 1292' (1922) 37 *The English Historical Review* 242–9). Moreover, merchants seemed to be quite keen to be exempt from trial by battle and other forms of proof, which *Max Weber* once called 'formal-irrational'. Finally, a general feature of *lex mercatoria* seemed to be that informal contracts (*pacta*) tended to be enforced and certain rules regarding debt collection and the attachment of goods were established.

Beyond that, it is quite difficult to establish what the term *lex mercatoria* entailed, since the court rolls – even where available, as for the fair court at St Ives – rarely report on the findings of the juries (Stephen E Sachs, 'From St. Ives to Cyberspace: The Modern Distortion of the Medieval "Law Merchant"' (2006) 21 Am.U.Int'l L.Rev. 685–812). As the modern distinction between procedural and substantive law was not yet established, it seems incorrect to state that the content of ancient *lex mercatoria* was merely procedural. Also, the concrete customs even with regard to procedural issues varied from market to market (Emily Kadens, 'Order within Law, Variety within Custom: The Character of the Medieval Merchant Law' (2004–5) 5 Chi.J.Int'l L.39–65).

3. Diffusion: privileges of merchants and equal treatment of aliens

However, it was not the variety in local customary *lex mercatoria per se*, but the issue of fair and equal treatment of aliens (→ Aliens law (Condition des étrangers, Fremdenrecht)), which seemed to be crucial in the further development of *lex mercatoria*. As the rights and liberties of cities applied to their burgess only and cities were reluctant to turn aliens into burgess, for long-distance traders there always was the risk of being treated less favourably when trading abroad. So how could similar commercial rules and institutions, which tended to treat all merchants alike, emerge throughout Europe? Due to heavy competition between various commercial cities, urban governments had strong incentives for continuous institutional reform in order to attract the presence of foreign merchants (Oscar Gelderblom, *Cities of Commerce: The Institutional Foundations of International Trade in the Low Countries, 1250–1650* (Princeton University Press 2013)).

Thus, merchant guilds and coalitions of merchants like the Hanseatic League were able to negotiate privileges for their members with cities or kings. From such privileges we know that Hanseatic merchants were concerned with the following: exclusion of trial by battle and collective liability, speedy trial according to *lex mercatoria* and even composition of juries from aliens and natives (Albrecht Cordes, 'Die Erwartungen mittelalterlicher Kaufleute an Gerichtsverfahren: Hansische Privilegien als Indikator' in Albrecht Cordes and Serge Dauchy (eds), *Eine Grenze in Bewegung: Öffentliche und private Justiz im Handels- und Seerecht* (Oldenbourg 2013) 39–64). In similar terms, the English Ordinances of the Staple were much concerned with comforting alien merchants with regard to their fair and equal treatment (Stephen Brodhurst, 'The Merchants of the Staple' (1901) 17 LQR 56–76).

Moreover, local authorities like the count of Champagne or the abbot of Ramsey were keen on attracting international merchants to their fairs. As neither Champagne nor St Ives were commercial centres in their own right, the success of these fairs seems to have been grounded on the fact that they provided a level playing field for merchants from all over Europe. The count and abbot were very much engaged in ensuring effective contract enforcement and impartial dispute resolution, including merchant juries deciding cases according to *lex mercatoria*, although the meaning of that term again remained quite opaque (Stephen E Sachs, 'From St. Ives to Cyberspace: The Modern Distortion of the Medieval "Law Merchant"' (2006) 21 Am.U.Int'l L.Rev. 685–812; Jeremy Edwards and Sheilagh Ogilvie, 'What Lessons for Economic Development Can We Draw from the Champagne Fairs?' (2012) 49 *Explorations in Economic History* 131–48).

However, letters obligatory or sealed contracts provide ample evidence that the practice of registering debts for later settlement developed at the Champagne fairs as early instances of monetary instruments, which later evolved into bills of exchange (→ Bill of exchange). Along with practices regarding → agency, partnership and insurance, such monetary instruments form the main legal innovations, which emerged from commercial practice and – although subject to considerable local variations – came to be recognized throughout Europe (Emily Kadens, 'Order within Law, Variety within Custom: The Character of the Medieval Merchant Law' (2004–5) 5 Chi.J.Int'l L. 39, 58).

Interestingly, the banking and credit business at the Champagne fairs was dominated by Italian merchants. As cities like Genoa and Venice maintained commerce with the Middle East, it is likely that Italian merchants learned most of the institutional arrangements that facilitated long-distance trade from their Eastern counterparts, which in turn maintained trade with the Mongols, India and China (Janet Lippman Abu-Lughod, *Before European Hegemony: The World System A.D. 1250–1350* (OUP 1989) 67 ff; cf Peter Frankopan, The Silk Roads. A New History of the World (Bloomsbury Publishing 2015)). The fact that trading techniques and commercial customs were imported from the, at that time, economically much more sophisticated Middle East may explain references to the 'acquired rights and customs of all merchants' as early as 1120, when the commercial revolution in the West merely started.

4. Integration: turning merchant customs from facts to (codified) norms

During the 18th and 19th centuries, finally, the rising sovereign nation states modernized their judicial systems with the result that general state courts increasingly acquired jurisdiction over commercial cases and the mentioned substantive legal innovations of *lex mercatoria* were absorbed into national private and commercial laws. In England, the integration of Law Merchant into the common law is predominantly ascribed to *Lord Mansfield*. As Chief Justice of the King's Bench between 1756 and 1788, in commercial cases he was informed on merchant customs by a special jury, which he repeatedly called in from Guildhall. In contrast to earlier practice, he turned those customs from facts into general legal principles to be applied in later cases as well, thus for the first time creating a body of commercial law as part of English common law (Charles A Bane, 'From Holt and Mansfield to Story to Llewellyn and Mentschikoff: The Progressive Development of Commercial Law' (1982–83) 37 U.Miami L.Rev. 351–77; James Oldham, *English Common Law in the Age of Mansfield* (University of North Carolina Press 2004).

In continental Europe, the integration of *lex mercatoria* took place during the 19th-century codification process (Johannes W Flume, 'Law and Commerce: The Evolution of Codified Business Law in Europe' (2014) 2 CLH 45–83). In Germany, for example, the first instance at the federal level was the imperial law on bills of exchange of 1849 (Ulrich Huber, 'Das Reichsgesetz über die Einführung einer allgemeinen Wechselordnung für Deutschland vom 26. November 1848' (1978) 33 JZ 785–91), followed by the more comprehensive codification of commercial law in the *Allgemeines Deutsches Handelsgesetzbuch* (ADHGB) of 31 May 1861 (Jens Mertens, *Privatrechtsschutz und vertikale Integration im internationalen Handel* (Mohr Siebeck 2011) 46 ff). Even today, section 346 of the German Commercial Code (Handelsgesetzbuch of 10 May 1897, RGBl. 219, as amended) contains a reference to trade usage, which somehow reflects medieval references to customary *lex mercatoria*. Moreover, some procedural relics of the ancient *lex mercatoria* survived in the German codification of procedural laws, such as the participation of merchants as commercial lay judges in German chambers of commerce provided in sections 93–114 of the German Courts Constitution Act (Gerichtsverfassungsgesetz of 27 January 1877, RGBl. 41, as amended)

III. Contemporary significance: new *lex mercatoria*

The rise of state-created and -enforced commercial law is explainable by economies of scale, realized in the process of economic modernization. While state commercial law entails high fixed costs for the set-up and maintenance of institutions like courts, laws and enforcement procedures, including the education of a legal class, the marginal costs of extending that governance system to additional transactions are negligible. The opposite is true for traditional private ordering institutions. Based on reputation and ostracism, they best operate in the context of specific types of transactions, often repeated among close-knit social groups, while their transfer to new transactional contexts over time and space is costly if not impossible. Thus, the emergence of modern complex exchange on competitive markets was enabled and facilitated by state commercial law (Thomas Dietz, *Global Order Beyond Law: How Information and Communication Technologies Facilitate Relational Contracting in International Trade* (Hart Publishing 2014) 23–38).

1. Transnational commercial law: overcoming domestic fragmentation

However, from the very beginning of this process one important caveat applied: the territorial scope of the nation state's jurisdiction to prescribe, to adjudicate and to enforce was limited (→ Territoriality). While formalizing and rationalizing commercial law for the domestic market through the production of legal unity in the substantive dimension and through the provision of reliable legal services in the procedural dimension, at the same time commercial law became territorially fragmented. Although this did not result in a complete denial of justice for international commerce, in a cross-border situation additional uncertainties arose with regard to the questions of which court has jurisdiction, which national commercial law this court shall apply, and whether a resulting judgment will be recognized and enforced as well in another nation state. These issues are addressed by the conflict rules of private international law and the laws on international civil procedure, but contrary to the *prima facie* meaning of the word there are no uniform rules on the international level, each nation state has its own conflict rules (but see for the more recent unification within the EU entries → Brussels I (Convention and Regulation), → Rome Convention and Rome I Regulation (contractual obligations), and → European Union and private international law).

In order to prevent cross-border trade from suffering, the idea to create a 'world private law' by means of international treaty harmonization arose as early as the late 19th century, ie in the so-called first phase of economic globalization (Ernst Zitelmann, *Die Möglichkeit eines Weltrechts* (Manz 1888, reprint 1916)). This endeavour, however, turned out to be more difficult than expected (→ Treaties in Private international law). More than 100 years of work within different public international organizations like the → Hague Conference on Private International Law, the International Institute for the Unification of Private Law (→ UNIDROIT), and the United Nations Commission on International Trade Law (→ UNCITRAL) have resulted in little but fragments, for example the → CISG (United Nations Convention of 11 April 1980 on Contracts for the International Sale of Goods, 1489 UNTS 3). The post-Second World War ideological division into the West, the East and the South was, of course, not a particularly favourable context, but even after the fall of the Iron Curtain matters did not improve. After all, the hopes for a world private law based on multilateral treaties have been somewhat deflated (Herbert Kronke, 'International Uniform Commercial Law Conventions: Advantages, Disadvantages, Criteria for Choice' (2000) 5 Uniform Law Review 13–21).

It was against this background that in the 1960s the Anglo-German scholar *Clive Schmitthoff* (Clive Schmitthoff, 'International Business Law: A New Law Merchant' (1961) 2 *Current Law and Social Problems* 129–53) analysed the practice of international commercial law and pointed out that its sources were not only domestic laws or international law, but especially contractual practice and commercial custom. Thus, with reference to ancient *lex mercatoria*, he claimed that a new *lex mercatoria* was emerging beyond the nation state, as was proposed in similar terms by his French colleague *Berthold Goldman* (Berthold Goldman, 'Frontières du droit et *"lex mercatoria"*' (1964) 9 A.P.D. 177–92). While *Schmitthoff* pointed to the indisputable fact that private actors play an important role in the three dimensions of norm-making, dispute resolution and enforcement, indicating that transnational commercial law is a hybrid public–private regime, *Goldman* insisted on the autonomous character of new *lex mercatoria*. This claim to the existence of a transnational legal order operating independently from the nation states triggered an international debate far beyond the immediate circle of commercial law and arbitration practitioners. It increasingly involved the interest of scholars from legal theory, new institutional economics and political science (see Gralf-Peter Calliess and Peer Zumbansen, *Rough Consensus and Running Code: A Theory of Transnational Private Law (Hart Publishing 2010); Jan Dalhuisen, Dalhuisen on Transnational Comparative, Commercial, Financial and Trade Law: Volume 1: Introduction – The New* Lex mercatoria *and its Sources* (5th edn, Hart Publishing 2013)).

According to the proponents of an autonomous new *lex mercatoria*, transnational commercial law denotes a third category of legal system beyond the traditional dichotomy of domestic laws and (public) international law. (i) Its foundations are (a) general principles of law, derived from a functional comparative analysis of the common core of domestic legal systems, and (b) the usages and customs of the international business community as expressed in standard form contracts and model clauses. (ii) Its administration and further development lies in the hands of private judges involved in international commercial arbitration, and (iii) its enforcement rests predominantly on social sanctions such as reputation and exclusion. Finally (iv) its rules are codified – if at all – in the form of lists of principles, rules and standards, codes of conduct, or best practices promulgated by private norm entrepreneurs (Klaus-Peter Berger, *The Creeping Codification of the New* Lex mercatoria (2nd edn, Kluwer Law International 2010)).

In order to address the accuracy of these claims, in the following the transnationalization of commercial law, which entails the combined internationalization and privatization of the governance of cross-border commercial contracts in the three dimensions of norm-making, dispute resolution and enforcement, shall be analysed based on available empirical evidence.

2. Dispute resolution: international commercial arbitration

International commercial arbitration (→ Arbitration, international commercial) assumes a central role in theories of new *lex mercatoria*. A recent survey confirmed earlier findings that – where available – arbitration is the preferred method of dispute resolution in international commerce, with neutrality, confidentiality and enforceability as the most important reasons (2013 Queen Mary International Arbitration Survey, available at <www.pwc.com/arbitrationstudy>). Indeed, while commercial courts in many countries experience the phenomenon of a vanishing trial, the caseloads of leading arbitration houses are skyrocketing. From 1998 to 2012, the caseload of the German commercial courts decreased by 38 per cent, while the caseload of the International Court of Arbitration (ICA) of the International Chamber of Commerce (ICC) went up by 162 per cent and that of the International Centre for Dispute Resolution (ICDR) of the American Arbitration Association (AAA) even by 257 per cent. However, the absolute numbers of these leading international commercial arbitration houses, with 759 cases at the ICA and 996 cases at the ICDR in 2012, remained relatively low, when compared to the 36,324 cases litigated in that year in German commercial courts, even when we take into account that only about 10 per cent of these cases were international. Strikingly, the average amount at dispute is many times higher in arbitration than in litigation, so we may conclude that international commercial arbitration is dominating over litigation at least where high values are at stake (Gralf-Peter Calliess, 'Der Richter im Zivilprozess' in Ständige Deputation des Deutschen Juristentages (ed), *Verhandlungen des*

70. *DJT* (CH Beck 2014) A 27 ff). A special case seems to be industry-specific arbitration, where the London Maritime Arbitrators Association (LMAA) (→ Arbitration, maritime) in 2012 with 3,849 cases handled about four times as many maritime disputes as the English courts (→ *Lex maritima*).

3. *Norm-making: private codifications of general principles and trade usage*

With regard to the privatization of lawmaking, non-legislative codifications of general principles of law as well as private codifications of trade usage and commercial custom promulgated by non-state actors are essential. The most important example for the former are the UNIDROIT Principles (International Institute for the Unification of Private Law/Institut international pour l'unification du droit privé, *UNIDROIT Principles of International Commercial Contracts 2010* (3rd edn, UNIDROIT 2010)) (→ UNIDROIT). Prominent examples for the latter are the INCOTERMS (International Commercial Terms (INCOTERMS) 2010, ICC) and the UCP 600 (Uniform customs and practice for documentary credits (ICC, publication No 600, 2007)), both drafted and continuously revised under the auspices of the ICC. As these instruments aspire to express uniform rules for international commerce not attached to any specific state legal system, they form part of transnational commercial law.

In the context of new *lex mercatoria*, the question arises whether such rules are applicable as law superseding domestic laws and regulations. State courts are traditionally required to apply the law of a specific state as governing a contract (but see art 3 of the Hague Principles on Choice of Law in International Commercial Contracts (approved on 19 March 2015, available at <www.hcch.net>)). Under art 28(1) of the UNCITRAL Arbitration Model Law (United Nations Commission on International Trade Law, UNCITRAL Model Law on International Commercial Arbitration as adopted on 21 June 1985, and as amended on 7 July 2006, UN Doc A/40/17 and A/61/17), which has been adopted in 67 states (→ Arbitration, (UNCITRAL) Model Law), the arbitral tribunal shall decide a dispute in accordance with such 'rules of law' as are chosen by the parties. It is generally agreed that in the context of international commercial arbitration the term 'rules of law', as used also in art 21(1) of the ICC Arbitration Rules (2012, available at <www.iccwbo.org>), includes internationally recognized non-state rules such as the UNIDROIT Principles.

Empirical evidence indicates that, in general, the law of a specific state is governing the contract in international commercial arbitration. Although the majority of parties has at least sometimes made use of transnational codifications such as the UNIDROIT Principles, UCP, or INCOTERMS, mostly they refer to them as a supplement to the governing national law (2010 Queen Mary International Arbitration Survey, available at <www.arbitration.qmul.ac.uk/docs/123290.pdf>). However, based on published arbitral awards and judgments, a series of studies has shown that the UNIDROIT Principles are increasingly used and accepted in practice (Maud Piers and Johan Erauw, 'Application of the Unidroit Principles of International Commercial Contracts in Arbitration' (2012) 8 J Priv Int L 441; Aldo Mascareno and Elina Mereminskaya, 'The Making of World Society through Private Commercial Law: The Case of the UNIDROIT Principles' (2013) 18 Unif.L.Rev. 447). In 2011, the database UNILEX contained 55 arbitral awards, which applied the UNIDROIT Principles as the law governing the substance of the dispute. Interestingly, only 15 of these awards did so based on party choice, whereas the other 40 awards applied them *ex officio* (Enrico Finazzi Agro, 'The Impact of the UNIDROIT Principles in International Dispute Resolution in Figures' (2011) 16 Unif.L.Rev. 719). One may conclude that 20 years after their first release in 1994 the UNIDROIT Principles are well on their way from soft law to hard code (Gralf-Peter Calliess and Moritz Renner, 'Between Law and Social Norms: The Evolution of Global Governance' (2009) 22 *Ratio Juris* 260; Nils Jansen, *The Making of Legal Authority: Non-Legislative Codifications in Historical and Comparative Perspective* (OUP 2010)).

Another important source of new *lex mercatoria* are model contracts drafted by trade associations in an effort to achieve legal certainty for their international membership. Since the 1980s such standard forms, which often establish an industry standard, increasingly include dispute resolution clauses. To give an example, the BIMCO Recommended Uniform General Charter GENCON 94, being the most popular and widely used general-purpose voyage charter party in the maritime industry, provides for English law and arbitration in London as the default option. The obvious reason for this choice is that English maritime law is well developed and that the LMAA is the market-dominant dispute resolution provider of the industry. However, the English courts are also famous for their favourable attitude towards party autonomy and, therefore, in contrast to German courts, for example, are not susceptible to interfere with transnational model contracts based on mandatory provisions or a general duty of good faith. Thus, standard dispute resolution clauses are also an endeavour to fence-off the legal unity achieved by industry self-regulation from potential disintegration through domestic courts. Instead of subjecting the transnational rules of new *lex mercatoria* under the authority of a sovereign, such clauses rather pay lip service to domestic regimes that guarantee party autonomy unbound.

Finally, even where commercial contracts contain a choice-of-law clause subjecting them to the law of a specific state, in international commercial arbitration such law is disembedded from its domestic context to a considerable extent. This is because neither the arbitrators necessarily come from that jurisdiction nor is the award subject to *de novo* review as to substance (see art 34 UNCITRAL Arbitration Model Law). Lacking in-depth knowledge of the intricacies of the governing law, international arbitrators tend to construe (and misinterpret) it in the light of general legal principles, such as the UNIDROIT Principles, or what they understand as international commercial custom. The scrutiny of awards, exercised for instance by the ICA under art 33 of the ICC Arbitration Rules (2012), is limited to the form of the award and to internationally mandatory norms like the ban on cartels in art 101 TFEU (The Treaty on the Functioning of the European Union (consolidated version), [2012] OJ C 326/47), which as part of the → public policy might inhibit recognition and enforcement of the award in certain jurisdictions. Otherwise, with regard to the interpretation of the law applicable each arbitral tribunal is its own court of ultimate appeal.

Thus, arbitral tribunals may or may not take into account judicial precedent. In fact, many arbitral tribunals take into account other published arbitral awards as persuasive precedent, a practice that contributes to still another form of transnational lawmaking. Based on the analysis of published awards, some scholars argue that a juridification and constitutionalization of arbitration takes place, with transnational public policy as the most visible result (Moritz Renner, *Zwingendes Transnationales Recht* (Nomos 2011); Alec Stone Sweet and Florian Grisel, 'The Evolution of International Arbitration: Delegation, Judicialization, Governance' in Walter Mattli and Thomas Dietz (eds), *International Arbitration and Global Governance: Contending Theories and Evidence* (OUP 2014) 22; Thomas Schultz, *Transnational Legality: Stateless Law and International Arbitration* (OUP 2014)).

4. Enforcement: between legal and social sanctions

The arbitration laws of the state, where the place of arbitration is situated, govern arbitral proceedings (art 1(2) UNCITRAL Arbitration Model Law), while the parties are free to agree on the place of arbitration (art 20(1) UNCITRAL Arbitration Model Law). An arbitral award may be set aside by a court of that state for very limited reasons only (art 34 UNCITRAL Arbitration Model Law). Otherwise, it will be recognized and enforced in that state as if it was a judgment of a court of that state. However, in international commerce it is of paramount importance, if a decision will be recognized and enforced as well in other jurisdictions. The Brussels I Regulation (recast) (Regulation (EU) No 1215/2012 of the European Parliament and of the Council of 12 December 2012 on jurisdiction and the recognition and enforcement of judgments in civil and commercial matters (recast), [2012] OJ L 351/1; → Brussels I (Convention and Regulation)) regulates the mutual recognition and enforcement of judgments in civil and commercial matters in the EU. Beyond Europe, the Hague Choice of Court Convention (Hague Convention of 30 June 2005 on choice of court agreements, 44 ILM 1294) entered into force after its ratification by → Mexico and the EU, but its effects remain limited, as only Singapore has joined yet.

The New York Convention (New York Convention of 10 June 1958 on the recognition and enforcement of foreign arbitral awards, 330 UNTS 3) currently has 156 parties and, thus, is the most successful international instrument in the field of international commercial law harmonization (→ Arbitration, recognition of awards). Under art III New York Convention, each contracting state shall recognize and enforce foreign arbitral awards as if they were domestic awards. Under art V New York

Convention, recognition and enforcement may be refused on very limited grounds only, especially where that would be contrary to the public policy of the country. Thus, EU Member State courts will refuse to recognize awards that enforce contracts which are contrary to the European competition rules (arts 101 and 102 TFEU), for example, but they will not refuse to enforce an award which applies transnational norms instead of state contract law.

It follows that the almost universal recognition and enforceability of arbitral awards granted by the New York Convention is one of the most important competitive advantages of arbitration over litigation when it comes to international commercial dispute resolution. To the extent that arbitral awards in practice do apply transnational norms, new *lex mercatoria* participates in this advantage and is transnationally enforceable. However, it is precisely the fact that the sovereign nation state lends its monopoly in the legitimate use of force to awards applying transnational norms, which is used by opponents of new *lex mercatoria* in order to argue that an autonomous transnational legal order does not exist. Ultimately, new *lex mercatoria* in this perspective rests on a delegation of state powers.

Proponents of new *lex mercatoria* as a transnational legal order raise two objections to this argument. First, as mentioned above, state created contract enforcement institutions are often unreliable, mostly outside the OECD countries. This is not only a reason why parties to international commercial contracts prefer arbitration to litigation in the first place, but it equally applies to the recognition and enforcement procedures under the New York Convention in many of its contracting states. Empirical findings show that – while in 90 per cent of the cases parties voluntarily comply – a considerable number of the parties who actually were involved in local enforcement proceedings experienced complications, which they attributed to various degrees of hostility from a country to the enforcement of foreign arbitral awards. Many countries have a bad reputation in this respect. This may be one reason why parties often negotiate a settlement after an award is rendered, entailing a discount in return for prompt payment (2008 Queen Mary International Arbitration Study, available at <www.arbitration.qmul.ac.uk/docs/123294.pdf>). After all, state-backed enforcement of arbitral awards may be less reliable and, thus, less important than expected.

Second, proponents of new *lex mercatoria* argue that the high rate of 'voluntary compliance' with arbitral awards rests on social sanctions as a private enforcement mechanism. Indisputably, reputation is of paramount importance in business, domestic or international. Merchants are likely reluctant to contract with transaction partners that have a reputation for non-compliance with arbitral awards. Although the advent of the Internet has substantially facilitated the dissemination of information on past conduct of businesses across borders, we cannot refer to reputation as a reliable private enforcement mechanism, as long as the administration of social sanctions is not formally organized. Indeed, several trade associations maintain blacklists in order to provide their membership with reliable information on parties that are in default to comply with arbitral awards. In addition, certain industries, which are organized in the form of a trade club or exchange, subject their members to disciplinary procedures, which may result in a fine or expulsion, if they are caught trading with a blacklisted merchant (Thomas Dietz, *Global Order beyond Law: How Information and Communication Technologies Facilitate Relational Contracting in International Trade* (Hart Publishing 2014) 198 ff).

From these examples of industry-specific private legal systems we can conclude that transnational law is most successful in practice where private governance mechanisms in the three dimensions of norm-making, dispute resolution and enforcement are bundled into effective transnational legal regimes (Gralf-Peter Calliess and Moritz Renner, 'Between Law and Social Norms: The Evolution of Global Governance' (2009) 22 *Ratio Juris* 260). However, beyond these special cases there is no evidence that new *lex mercatoria* rests on a formally organized system of social sanctioning. The leading international commercial arbitration institutions such as the ICA of the ICC or the ICDR of the AAA do not engage in the administration of social sanctions. The majority of commercial arbitration institutions are not even monitoring their awards systematically with a view to the questions of how many awards are set aside in court at the place of arbitration, how many are complied with voluntarily, or how many of them experience problems when enforced under the New York Convention (see 2008 Queen Mary International Arbitration Study).

IV. Conclusion

The debate on *lex mercatoria*, ancient and new, is prone to ideology, as the claim to the existence of a transnational legal order operating autonomously from the state provokes confessions from both the libertarian and the etatist camps. The originally legal discourse has increasingly attracted interdisciplinary interest from sociology of law (Yves Dezalay and Bryant G Garth, *Dealing in Virtue: International Commercial Arbitration and the Construction of a Transnational Legal Order* (Chicago University Press 1996); Gunther Teubner (ed), *Global Law without a State* (Dartmouth 1997); Volkmar Gessner (ed) *Contractual Certainty in International Trade: Empirical Studies and Theoretical Debates on Institutional Support for Global Economic Exchanges* (Hart Publishing 2009)), new institutional economics (Avner Greif, *Institutions and the Path to the Modern Economy: Lessons from Medieval Trade* (CUP 2006); Sheilagh Ogilvie, *Institutions and European Trade: Merchant Guilds 1000–1800* (CUP 2011)) and political science (Walter Mattli, 'Private Justice in a Global Economy: From Litigation to Arbitration' (2001) 55 Int'l Org. 919; A Claire Cutler, *Private Power and Global Authority: Transnational Merchant Law in the Global Political Economy* (CUP 2003); Alec Stone Sweet, 'The New *Lex mercatoria* and Transnational Governance' (2006) 13 Journal of European Public Policy 627). The past decade has brought about an empirical turn, which enables a less normatively laden take on *lex mercatoria*. Based on a wealth of evidence provided by studies on both ancient and new *lex mercatoria* we can conclude that there in fact are instances of private legal systems which operate largely outside the state. However, as transnational legal regimes depend on the formally organized administration of socio-economic sanctions, they constitute rather sector-specific exceptions than a universal transnational legal order. Beyond that, transnational commercial law in general is marked by a hybrid mode of governance, where private governance mechanisms for their inherent competitive advantages on the global law market especially in the dimension of dispute resolution and less so in the dimensions of norm-making and enforcement prevail over traditional state-created commercial law.

GRALF-PETER CALLIESS

Literature

Klaus-Peter Berger, *The Creeping Codification of the New Lex mercatoria* (2nd edn, Kluwer Law International 2010); Gralf-Peter Calliess and Peer Zumbansen, *Rough Consensus and Running Code: A Theory of Transnational Private Law* (Hart Publishing 2010); Albrecht Cordes and Serge Dauchy (eds), *Eine Grenze in Bewegung: Öffentliche und private Justiz im Handels- und Seerecht* (Oldenbourg 2013); A Claire Cutler, *Private Power and Global Authority: Transnational Merchant Law in the Global Political Economy* (CUP 2003); Jan Dalhuisen, *Dalhuisen on Transnational Comparative, Commercial, Financial and Trade Law: Volume 1: Introduction – The New Lex mercatoria and its Sources* (5th edn, Hart Publishing 2013); Yves Dezalay and Bryant G Garth, *Dealing in Virtue: International Commercial Arbitration and the Construction of a Transnational Legal Order* (Chicago University Press 1996); Thomas Dietz, *Global Order beyond Law, How Information and Communication Technologies Facilitate Relational Contracting in International Trade* (Hart Publishing 2014); Horst Eidenmüller (ed), *Regulatory Competition in Contract Law and Dispute Resolution* (CH Beck/Hart/Nomos 2013); Oscar Gelderblom, *Cities of Commerce: The Institutional Foundations of International Trade in the Low Countries, 1250–1650* (Princeton University Press 2013); Volkmar Gessner (ed), *Contractual Certainty in International Trade: Empirical Studies and Theoretical Debates on Institutional Support for Global Economic Exchanges* (Hart Publishing 2009); Avner Greif, *Institutions and the Path to the Modern Economy: Lessons from Medieval Trade* (CUP 2006); Nils Jansen, *The Making of Legal Authority: Non-Legislative Codifications in Historical and Comparative Perspective* (OUP 2010); Walter Mattli and Thomas Dietz (eds), *International Arbitration and Global Governance: Contending Theories and Evidence* (OUP 2014); Sheilagh Ogilvie, *Institutions and European Trade: Merchant Guilds 1000–1800* (CUP 2011); Thomas Schultz, *Transnational Legality: Stateless Law and International Arbitration* (OUP 2014); Gunther Teubner (ed), *Global Law without a State* (Dartmouth 1997).

Liability, capital market[1]

I. Introduction: scope, concepts, terminology

The scope of this entry is extraordinarily wide for a number of reasons. First, the source of liability may be substantive private law (contract, commercial law, tort) or regulatory law (market organization and supervision). Second, liability may flow both from 'defective' products (→ financial instruments) and human activities

[1] The entry is current as of 2014.

(financial services). Third, the contracting parties are of an uncommonly varied nature, including on the one hand, institutions, such as companies or public entities seeking financing and, on the other hand, investors, both professional and retail investors, ie consumers.

Another challenge lies in different national traditions conceptualizing the area of law concerned. On the one hand, in a number of European countries as well as other jurisdictions outside North America 'capital market law' traditionally designates an area which, in the USA, is characterized as 'securities regulation', ie legislation and case-law addressing specificities of the exchange-listed and publicly traded corporations. On the other hand theory and legal practice in other countries see the 'law of finance' as the entirety of rules governing financial services including the law of regulated and other markets (stock exchanges, multilateral trading platforms, over-the-counter transactions), post-trading activities, as well as the products traded on those markets and financial techniques employed by business organizations and others.

The following text will attempt to address a cross-section of core issues identified as such across legal systems where courts and writers have been confronted with relevant conflict-of-laws and uniform-law questions relating to the aforementioned areas.

II. Trading in securities: liability pursuant to transactional law

1. Contract

a) Primary market: issue of financial instruments

In the vast majority of cases, issuers retain the services of intermediaries, in particular investment banks, for an initial (public) offering or when additional shares, bonds (→ Bonds and loans) etc are placed on the market for the purposes of raising capital. Failure to provide the services as agreed will render the investment bank (but also accountants, legal counsel etc) liable for breach of contract or non-performance. Where the contracting parties have not chosen the law governing their agreement (see eg art 3 of the Rome I Regulation (Regulation (EC) No 593/2008 of the European Parliament and of the Council of 17 June 2008 on the law applicable to contractual obligations (Rome I), [2008] OJ L 177/6; → Rome Convention and Rome I Regulation (contractual obligations))), a default rule will determine the applicable law. Although a subsequent sale of the financial instrument to investors is frequently an element, the services of the sponsoring investment bank as underwriter are predominant, leaving it to art 4(1)(b), (2)–(4) Rome I Regulation to determine the law governing the scope and content of the obligations as well as the → remedies in case of non-performance (art 12), ie liability.

The relationship between issuer and intermediary (eg the investment bank) may have to be characterized as → agency, an area of law where harmonization efforts continue to encounter formidable difficulties due to conceptual divides, in particular between the common law and certain civil law systems (Roy Goode, Herbert Kronke and Ewan McKendrick, *Transnational Commercial Law: Text, Cases, and Materials* (OUP 2007) nos 8.17–8.28). Thus the law of agency may contain specific rules on liability, both as regards the third party and the principal, eg against the unauthorized agent. Key issues are excluded from the scope of the Rome I Regulation, art 1(2)(g). The Hague Agency Convention (Hague Convention of 14 March 1978 on the law applicable to agency, Hague Conference of Private international law (ed), *Collection of Conventions (1951–2009)* (Intersentia 2009) 268) is in force only in very few states. The autonomous conflict rules proposed or adopted by the courts vary greatly and cannot be discussed here.

b) Secondary market: trading in financial instruments

As liability arises in consequence of breach of contract, in some systems called non-performance, it is a matter for the law governing the contract to determine whether there is liability and which remedies may be available (see, for example, art 12 Rome I Regulation). The Regulation's approach to contracts of interest in this context is influenced by the Community's financial markets legislation, in particular MiFID (Markets in Financial Instruments Directive) (Directive 2004/39/EC of the European Parliament and of the Council of 21 April 2004 on markets in financial instruments amending Council Directives 85/611/EEC and 93/6/EEC and Directive 2000/12/EC of the European Parliament and of the Council and repealing Council Directive 93/22/EEC, [2004] OJ L 145/1), and it is exceedingly complex (Francisco J Garcimartín Alférez, 'New

Issues in the Rome I Regulation: The Special Provisions on Financial Market Contracts' (2008) 10 YbPIL 245; Matthias Lehmann, 'Financial Instruments' in Franco Ferrari and Stefan Leible (eds), *Rome I Regulation: The Law Applicable to Contractual Obligations in Europe* (Sellier 2009) 85; Peter Mankowski, 'Finanzmarktverträge' in Christoph Reithmann and Dieter Martiny (eds), *Internationales Vertragsrecht* (7th edn, Verlag Dr Otto Schmidt 2010), nos 2341–551). However, the system does not differ from codifications or judge-made conflict-of-laws rules in other jurisdictions: (i) primarily freedom of choice (eg art 3 Rome I Regulation, art 116 Swiss Private international law Act (Bundesgesetz über das Internationale Privatrecht of 18 December 1987, 1988 BBl I 5, as amended, henceforth Swiss PILA)), (ii) absent party choice, a form of closest connection rule (art 4 Rome I Regulation, art 117 Swiss PILA), (iii) special regime for → consumer contracts (art 6 Rome I Regulation, art 114 Swiss PILA).

The types of contract whose breach is capable of triggering the non-performing party's liability range from the sale of shares and bonds (→ Bonds and loans) to futures and options, to services provided by financial institutions, advisers etc in relation to capital market transactions. The broad scope of the consumer protection provision of art 6(1) and (2) Rome I Regulation is limited by the exceptions pursuant to art 6(4) and, as far as trade on exchanges or other multilateral trade facilities is concerned, the carve-out provided for in art 4(1)(h). Sub-paragraphs (d) and (e) of art 6(1) are explained by Recitals (27) to (30). Since a sale of shares and other → financial instruments is now within the general scope, an exception was called for with a view to ensuring the functioning of financial markets which, as is obvious in case of transactions based on public offers, require that one uniform legal regime governs, rather than a multitude of domestic consumer laws (Francisco J Garcimartín Alférez, 'New Issues in the Rome I Regulation: The Special Provisions on Financial Market Contracts' (2008) 10 YbPIL 245, 251 ff).

2. Custody, clearing and settlement

Important types of service provided by banks, brokers and other financial institutions, now commonly referred to as 'intermediaries', on the basis of their contracts with investors, are the so-called post-trade activities. These actually encompass pre-trade elements, such as custody of financial instruments, which historically and before the 'paper crunch' of certificates and in recent decades are increasingly in dematerialized form and/or immobilized as (electronic) book entries in accounts maintained by investors with intermediaries (see Roy Goode, 'The Nature and Transfer of Rights in Dematerialised and Immobilised Securities' in Fidelis Oditah (ed), *The Future for the Global Securities Market: Legal and Regulatory Aspects* (Clarendon Press 1996) 107; Antoine Maffei, 'De la nature juridique des titres dématérialisés intermédiés en droit francais' [2005] Unif.L.Rev. 237; Hubert de Vauplane (ed), *20 ans de dématérialisation des titres en France – Bilan et perspectives nationales et internationales* (Revue Banque 2005); Madeleine Yates and Gerald Montagu, *The Law of Global Custody* (4th edn, Bloomsbury 2013)). The shockwave which the English case *Macmillan Inc v Bishopsgate Investment Trust plc and others (No 3)* ([1995] 1 WLR 978) sent through the private international law world concerned aspects of property law, in particular the issue as to how the connecting factor of the *situs* was to be replaced now that securities were largely dematerialized. Article 2 Hague Securities Convention (Hague Convention of 5 July 2006 on the law applicable to certain rights in respect of securities held with an intermediary, 46 ILM 649) carefully circumscribes the Convention's scope.

In relation to contractual liability, the primary source of private international law rules in EU Member States is Rome I Regulation (see in more detail Herbert Kronke, 'The Law Applicable to Intermediated Securities and to Issues of Liability in the Intermediated Securities Holding System' in Sergio Maria Carbone (ed), *L'Unione Europea a vent'anni da Maastricht – Verso nuove regole* (Editoriale Scientifica 2013) 253). Banks and the various Central Securities Depositories will generally make use of party autonomy (art 3) and provide in their general conditions of contract for the applicability of their own law. Absent party choice, the intermediary's law (art 4(1)(b)) or the law of the stock exchange (or other Multilateral Trading Facility) where the transaction is carried out governs (art 4(1) (h) and Recital (18)). The most recent piece of national legislation on matters of interest here is art 108c Swiss PILA, which incorporates the Hague Securities Convention into Swiss law. The most modern and comprehensive body of substantive law which a European legislature enacted in response to the passage to intermediated holding patterns for financial instruments is the Swiss Federal Intermediated Securities Act of 3 October 2008 (Bundesgesetz über Bucheffekten, 2008 BBl 832; henceforth FISA) (on both see Hans Kuhn, Barbara Graham-Siegenthaler and Luc Thévenoz (eds), *The Federal Intermediated Securities Act (FISA) and the Hague Securities Convention (HSC)* (Stämpfli Publishers 2010)). According to art 33(1) FISA, a custodian is liable for the loss caused to an account holder, ie an investor holding securities credited to an account with the custodian-intermediary, in relation to the custody or transfer of intermediated securities pursuant to the Swiss Code of Obligations (220 Federal Act of 30 March 1911 on the Amendment of the Swiss Civil Code (Part Five: The Code of Obligations); henceforth CO) unless otherwise provided in art 33. That reference entails characterization of the contractual relationship as mandate (arts 398 ff CO) and the applicability of the general rules on non-performance (arts 97 ff CO). Other civil law jurisdictions will largely share the underlying analysis. Of utmost importance are subparagraphs (2) to (5) of art 33 FISA focusing on the relevant substantive law on the typical structures of transborder securities holdings. In this respect, the provisions of the UNIDROIT Convention on Substantive Rules for Intermediated Securities of 9 October 2009 (available at <www.unidroit.org>) are of benchmark character (see on that instrument Hideki Kanda and others, *Official Commentary on the UNIDROIT Convention on Intermediated Securities* (OUP 2012). See also on the broader context, Thomas Keijser (ed), *Transnational Securities Law* (OUP 2014)). Relevant provisions can be found in chapter IV ('Integrity of the intermediated holding system'), addressing investor rights and interests in the insolvency of the intermediary. The provisions prohibit upper-tier attachment and impose specific duties on intermediaries, such as the duty to act only upon instructions from the account holder, to hold securities of an aggregate number of securities of the same description credited to accounts the intermediary maintains etc. Non-performance triggers duties to remedy the situation, but also naturally entails claims for → damages or other relief available under otherwise applicable non-Convention law. The cornerstone is art 28 UNIDROIT Convention on Substantive Rules for Intermediated Securities ('Obligations and liability of intermediaries'), which sets minimum standards and opens the door for more specific provisions in account agreements and by the relevant non-Convention law.

3. Extra-contractual liability

Both grossly misleading information or advice provided by intermediaries, in particular brokers, to potential investors as well as business models aimed at inducing an investor to invest in transactions without a chance of profit, whether or not criminally fraudulent, are characterized in most legal systems as some form of tort. The German Federal Court of Justice (BGH) has applied the rule now enshrined in art 4(1) of the → Rome II Regulation (Regulation (EC) No 864/2007 of the European Parliament and of the Council of 11 July 2007 on the law applicable to non-contractual obligations (Rome II), [2007] OJ L 199/40), indicating the *lex loci damni* as the governing law in a way that identifies the market on which the tortfeasor has sought out the victim as the place where the damage occurred. Significantly, the Court rejected the argument that the brokers' regulatory home regime could impact content and limitations of the tort claim under German law (German Federal Court of Justice (BGH), 15 November 2011 [2012] BKR 78; reported and commented on by Anton K Schnyder, 'Haftung ausländischer Broker für Schäden deutscher Anleger' [2013] ZEuP 659; earlier rulings discussed by Andreas Engert and Gunnar Groh, 'Internationaler Kapitalanlegerschutz vor dem Bundesgerichtshof' [2011] IPRax 458).

III. Liability for non-compliance with regulatory framework

1. Disclosure (publicity)

Among the numerous groundbreaking and politically influential writings of US Supreme Court Judge *Louis D Brandeis* (1856–1941) there is *Other People's Money and How the Bankers Use It* (Stokes 1914, reissued 1933) with the famous opening of chapter V: 'Publicity is justly commended as a remedy for social and industrial diseases. Sunlight is said to be the best of disinfectants, electric light the most efficient policeman.' The disclosure approach became the pillar, first of US securities legislation, and by now of capital market law throughout developed legal systems. Issuers of → financial instruments and intermediaries offering such instruments to the public or individual investors are typically required to disclose information relevant for evaluating the issuer's financial status and business or the instrument's characteristics. This with a view to enabling investors to make an informed assessment of the potential benefits and risks of the investment. Disclosure may be required on the issuer first seeking admission to a market or approval of a financial instrument and thereafter, for instance periodically or on an *ad hoc* basis, if and when internal matters that are relevant for investors occur.

a) Primary market: obligation to publish a prospectus

The type and form of disclosure that has given rise to the most intense and detailed discussion of conflict-of-laws issues is the prospectus as the principal means of providing information to investors. This kind of document makes information prescribed by law or regulations on securities and on their issuer available to the public. It contains representations on which investors will rely when making a decision whether to acquire those financial instruments. While there seems to be a universal consensus that the regulatory authority tasked with approving the issue and the prospectus does not make a judgment on the quality of the investment product but only on the completeness of the information as prescribed, opinions diverge as to whether and the extent to which the objective of a disclosure regime is investor protection as opposed only to market efficiency. Legislators and courts of any given jurisdiction are clearly free to take a stance in this regard, and this stance will be as important for the formulation of the relevant choice-of-laws rule as for the relationship between the disclosure obligation as such and liability for non-compliance with regulatory requirements or inaccuracy of information contained in a prospectus.

The substantive law governing prospectuses of the Member States of the European Community, now the EU, was harmonized by a series of Directives which were consolidated in the Prospectus Directive (Directive 2003/71/EC of the European Parliament and of the Council of 4 November 2003 on the prospectus to be published when securities are offered to the public or admitted to trading [2003] OJ L 345/64). As indicated in its Recitals (10), (16), (18), (20), (21), (27) and (41), the Prospectus Directive clearly pursues investor protection as one of its principal objectives, the others being market efficiency (see Recitals (10), (18), (33) and (41)) and the achievement of an integrated, or internal, financial market (Recitals (4) and (5)). The Prospectus Directive sets forth (minimum) rules regarding the content, matters of presentation, arrangements for approval and publication of the prospectus, cross-border offers, the European 'passport' for an approved prospectus, third-country issuers as well as competent authorities and co-operation between them. As to sanctions, the Directive addresses only the Member State commitment to provide appropriate administrative measures, but expressly refrains from providing any guidance in relation to criminal sanctions and, importantly, the civil liability regime.

→ Switzerland and → Belgium appear to be the only European countries whose legislators provided an express conflicts rule on liability in this area. According to art 156 Swiss PILA and art 114 of the Belgian Private international law Act (Wet houdende het Wetboek von international privaatrecht/Code de droit international privé of 16 July 2004, BS 27 July 2004, p 57344, 57366), claims based on misrepresentations and omissions in a prospectus or similar document are governed by the *lex societatis*, ie the law governing the issuer, or the law of the country where the issue took place. As has been pointed out, this rule is also imperfect, in that it omits to identify the law governing the question as to whether disclosure through publication of a prospectus is required, or the law setting forth the content of such a document (Anton K Schnyder and Lukas Bopp, 'Kollisionsrechtliche Anknüpfung von Prospektpflicht und Prospekthaftung als Fragestellung des Internationalen Kapitalmarktrechts' in Hans-Caspar von der Crone and others (eds), *Festschrift für Dieter Zobl* (Schulthess 2004) 391, 397). Admittedly, the substantive law governing a company may comprise rules addressing both issues, as indeed does Swiss law (see arts 652a, 1156(1) CO). Apart from that, there is reason to believe that many legislators simply take it as a given that both would be governed by the law of the market where the issuer is seeking to have the securities admitted for trading. Indeed, court decisions dating back to the 19th century, as well as modern statutes and regulations, do take it for granted (see Herbert Kronke, 'Capital Markets and Conflict of Laws' (2000) 286 Rec. des Cours 245, 293 ff, with references in notes 83–90).

Where no such express conflicts rule is available, courts and scholars have developed lines of reasoning leading to four basic approaches to determining the relevant → connecting factor and, thereby, the law governing liability. The starting point is clearly characterization. For example, courts and commentators in the →

United Kingdom, → France, → Spain and → Germany traditionally characterized the issue of liability for incorrect information in a prospectus as either contractual or delictual. At least implicitly some may continue to do so, in civil law jurisdictions under the principle of → *culpa in contrahendo* (perceived as breach of a pre-contractual duty to act in accordance with the trust the other party places in one's truthfulness), or in a common law context conceptualized as a misrepresentation in an offer aimed at the conclusion of a contract (see Alastair Hudson, *The Law of Finance* (2nd edn, Sweet & Maxwell 2013) nos 36–13, 63–15). Characterizing omissions and inaccuracies in a prospectus giving rise to a claim in contract would lead in any EU Member State to the applicability of arts 3, 4, 6 and 9 to 18 of the Rome I Regulation), in Switzerland to arts 112 to 126 Swiss PILA, in the USA of the conflicts rules applied in the state of the court seized (see also §§ 187, 188 Restatement (Second) of Conflict of Laws (American Law Institute, Restatement of the Law, Second: Conflict of Laws 2d, St. Paul 1971; → Restatement (First and Second) of Conflict of Laws), and Peter Hay, Russel Jay Weintraub and Patrick J Borchers, *Conflict of Laws: Cases and Materials* (14th edn, West Group 2013) 470 ff, 504 ff, 522 ff) etc.

Starting in the 1980s and 1990s and across a number of jurisdictions, the view garnered support that causing an erroneous understanding of a prospectus by omitting relevant information or by including inaccurate data, for private international law purposes is to be characterized as tort, or delict. This, along with construing the classic rule of the *lex loci delicti commissi* so as to encompass the principle of ubiquity (ie the relevant *locus* is both the place of the wrongdoing and the place where the harm occurred) and the principle to apply the law more favourable to the injured party, led to serious flaws and inconsistencies which the present writer has criticized in detail (Herbert Kronke, 'Capital Markets and Conflict of Laws' (2000) 286 Rec. des Cours 245, 308 ff). Assume a Canadian corporation hires New York- and London-based accountants and lawyers to prepare a prospectus for an offering on the stock exchanges of Toronto, Montreal, New York, London, Frankfurt and Amsterdam. Due to a negligent misrepresentation of a material fact by the London lawyers a Dutch investor (and its Japanese or Hong Kong parent company) is harmed. Should one really have to choose between the laws of Ontario, Quebec, New York, England and the Netherlands – let alone Japan and Hong Kong? Or should the court's or the plaintiff's choice be determined following the principle of the law most favourable to the injured party? Bearing in mind that under art 5 no 3 Brussels I Regulation (Regulation (EC) No 44/2001 of 22 December 2000 on jurisdiction and the recognition and enforcement of judgments in civil and commercial matters, [2001] OJ L 12/1; → Brussels I (Convention and Regulation)) as well as other rules on jurisdiction the courts of more than one country might have jurisdiction over a claim brought by the Dutch investor, it is clear that what was a perfect solution when a court had to identify the law applicable to the harm done on the Scottish side of the border by a shot fired on the English side is inadequate for the context of activities on today's capital markets. Capital markets law involves more than investor protection; issuer reputation, market efficiency, predictability and macro-economic objectives, such as the development of emerging markets, are equally at stake.

Against the backdrop of a number of court decisions that had moved away from the traditional US approach of unilateralism and simply defined territoriality of US securities laws (eg *Leasco Data Processing Equipment Corp v Maxwell* 468 F.2d 1326 (2nd Cir 1972); *Itoba Ltd v Lep Group PLC* 54 F.3d 118 (2nd Cir 1995), cert denied 516 U.S. 1044 (1996); *Europe and Overseas Commodity Traders SA v Banque Paribas London* 147 F.3d 118 (2nd Cir 1998), cert denied 525 U.S. 1139 (1999). See also the so-called Lloyd's of London cases in various Circuits), academic writers emphasized the appropriateness of developing proper choice-of-law rules (Robert W Hillman, 'Cross-Border Investment, Conflict of Laws, and the Privatization of Securities Law' (1992) 55 LCP 331). However, the immediately plausible identification of the market where the securities had been offered as the functionally adequate connecting factor met with criticism. The critics pointed to the difficulties of localizing 'a' market in global offerings and transactions as well as to the fact that each national regulator knows its own issuers best and others very little. Some commentators concluded that the disclosure regime of an issuer's home jurisdiction should apply, even where that issuer offered securities on foreign, and even the US, markets. Others went so far as to allow issuers to choose the applicable disclosure and, in case of non-compliance, liability regime, ie party autonomy (Merritt Baker Fox, 'Securities Disclosure in a Globalizing Market: Who Should Regulate Whom?' (1997) 95 Mich.L.Rev. 2498; Stephen J Choi and Andrew T Guzman, 'Portable Reciprocity: Rethinking the International Reach of Securities Regulation' (1998) 71 S.Cal.L.Rev. 903; Roberta Romano, 'Empowering Investors: A Market Approach to Securities Regulation' in Klaus J Hopt and others (eds), *Comparative Corporate Governance* (Clarendon Press 1998) 143, 212–16). The reason guiding this school of thought was the belief that competition of legal regimes and amongst regulators would have a positive effect in the search for the best solution.

In Europe, in particular in → Germany and → Switzerland, at that time the predominant opinion had settled for a straightforward rule pursuant to which the market where the securities were offered was the preferable connecting factor (Stefan Grundmann, 'Deutsches Anlegerschutzrecht in internationalen Sachverhalten' (1990) 54 RabelsZ 283, 300; Heinz-Dieter Assmann, 'Einl A-D' in Klaus J Hopt and Herbert Wiedemann (eds), *Aktiengesetz Grosskommentar*, vol 1 (4th edn, de Gruyter 1992) nos 606, 698–704; Daniel Zimmer, Internationales Gesellschaftsrecht (Verlag Recht und Wirtschaft 1996) 56; Herbert Kronke, 'Capital Markets and Conflict of Laws' (2000) 286 Rec. des Cours 245, 297, 310 ff). While certain legislative provisions to that effect were formulated unilaterally so as to protect only the legislator's home market, the arguments supporting the approach were seen as to justify its multilateralization. The three most obvious (apart from the rule's potential of becoming a universally acceptable multilateral conflict-of-laws rule) are the following. First, effects of concurrent regimes (*lex societatis* and law of the market; either one and *lex loci delicti*) and inevitable contradictions between them are avoided. Second, all investors buying on the same market are treated equally. Third, issuers entering the same market and offering their securities are treated equally. Conversely, it is difficult to make a convincing case for the need to treat investors on different markets equally by granting alternatively remedies under the *lex societatis* and the law of the relevant market (ie the Swiss and Belgian rule and in Germany and the US advocated by authoritative authors (Ernst Rabel, *The Conflict of Laws: A Comparative Study*, vol 3 (2nd edn, University of Michigan Press 1964) 13; Bernd von Hoffmann, 'Anhang IV, Art 34' in Gerhard Kegel (ed), *Soergel. Bürgerliches Gesetzbuch mit Einführungsgesetz und Nebengesetzen*, vol 10 (12th edn, Kohlhammer 1996) para 73). Why should an Argentine issuer who wishes to have a security of a certain type traded only in London comply with Argentine disclosure requirements? If the *lex societatis* requires equal treatment of shareholders the company will, obviously, comply once the investor has acquired that status. In a similar vein, where the law governing bonds – arguably again the law of the market where they have been issued (Norbert Horn, *Das Recht der internationalen Anleihen* (Athenäum 1972); Herbert Kronke and Jens Haubold, 'Börsen- und Kapitalmarktrecht' in Herbert Kronke, Werner Melis and Anton K Schnyder (eds), *Handbuch Internationales Wirtschaftsrecht* (Verlag Dr Otto Schmidt 2005) nos 334, 335 as well as Swiss case law reported there) – requires that all, or a certain group of, bondholders are treated equally, the company will comply. Apparently one must not narrow the perspective to merely one type of financial instrument, namely shares. Moreover, it is unhelpful to suggest that the only, or primary, objective of a disclosure regime such as ours is its contribution to corporate governance (for this proposition, see Wolf-Georg Ringe and Alexander Hellgardt, 'The International Dimension of Issuer Liability: Liability and Choice of Law from a Transatlantic Perspective' (2011) 31 Oxford J.Leg.Stud. 23, 25). To do so would be as misguided as it was when investor protection alone was taken into consideration. Disclosure and liability in case of failure to disclose are multi-faceted yet primarily instruments designed to constitute and support proper functioning of markets for finance.

The entry into force of the Prospectus Directive made the above-mentioned lively US discussion blossom on the European side of the Atlantic Ocean as well. Interestingly, the Directive's system of an issuer's limited freedom to choose the competent national regulator and, thereby, the applicable disclosure regime met with criticism because, the critics maintained, it tended to privilege organizational considerations flowing from the governing company law (corporate governance standards) rather than true qualitative criteria capable of identifying the optimum disclosure level for each issuer. At the same time, leading proponents of a thorough modernization conceived in terms of liberalization suggested that liability for inaccuracies be best governed by the law governing the duty to disclose as well as by the detailed disclosure requirements (in continental European parlance '*akzessorische Anknüpfung*' or '*rattachement accessoire*'; in English called by some the 'secondary connection mechanism'). The arguments supporting this solution seem plausible. First, the required content of a prospectus and the law's reaction to misrepresentations and omissions in any legal system have been developed in tandem, in that the latter is a function of the former. Second, the interests of all stakeholders are properly taken care of, as the law governing the content is known so as to make it predictable for issuers, intermediaries and investors alike. Third, all investors are treated equally, no matter where they may have acquired the security. Fourth, issuer and intermediaries need to take into account only one standard for compliance and liability in case of non-compliance, while fifth, there are lower costs. Indeed, adopting this rule neither placement of the security on more than one market nor relevance of more than one place in case of delictual characterization would entail a plurality of potentially applicable laws (Christoph Benicke, 'Prospektpflicht und Prospekthaftung bei grenzüberschreitenden Emissionen' in Heinz-Peter Mansel and others (eds), *Festschrift für Erik Jayme*, vol 1 (Sellier 2004) 25, 36 ff; concurring Herbert Kronke and Jens Haubold, 'Börsen- und Kapitalmarktrecht' in Herbert Kronke, Werner Melis and Anton K Schnyder (eds), *Handbuch Internationales Wirtschaftsrecht* (Verlag Dr Otto Schmidt 2005) no 360; Francisco J Garcimartín Alférez, 'Cross-Border Listed Companies' (2000) 328 Rec. des Cours 97; Jan von Hein, 'Die internationale Prospekthaftung im Lichte der Rom II-Verordnung' in Harald Baum and others (eds), *Perspektiven des Wirtschaftsrechts – Beiträge für Klaus J Hopt aus Anlass seiner Emeritierung* (de Gruyter 2008) 371, 392; limited to a recommendation *de lege ferenda* Anton K Schnyder, 'Internationales Kapitalmarktrecht' in Roland Rixecker and Franz Jürgen Säcker (eds), *Münchener Kommentar zum Bürgerlichen Gesetzbuch*, vol 11 (5th edn, CH Beck 2010) no 121).

In the wake of the last financial crisis, the blossoms of sympathy for economic arguments and liberalization in the sense of 'privatization' of capital-markets-related conflict-of-laws rules have withered. Indeed, the US Supreme Court dealt them a blow when it overruled the above-mentioned court rulings returning to classic unilateral principles of territoriality and applying relevant provisions of the US Securities Exchange Act 1934 (48 Stat. 881) only to transactions in securities listed on domestic exchanges (*Morrison v National Australia Bank Ltd* 561 U.S. 247, 130 S.Ct. 2869 (2010)).

Reverting to the issue as to how inaccurate information of the public and potential investors is properly characterized, the typical absence of a pre- or quasi-contractual relationship between issuers and as yet unidentified members of the public in most legal systems leads to its characterization as tortuous or delictual. Courts in an EU Member State would therefore turn to the Rome II Regulation. Only if the duty to be truthful from the point of view of relevant substantive law were conceived as owed not to the general public but to identifiable individuals, might characterization of a breach be characterized as contractual. The applicability of the Rome II Regulation is excluded neither pursuant to art 1(2)(c) nor pursuant to art 1(2)(d) Rome II Regulation. An extension of the exclusions to claims based on the admission and distribution of financial instruments generally, as proposed at some stage (a better solution would have been to add a *lex specialis* to arts 5–9 Rome II Regulation), was not adopted. There can be no doubt that the Rome II Regulation is now *sedes materiae* (Andrew Dickinson, *The Rome II Regulation: The Law Applicable to Non-Contractual Obligations* (OUP 2008) nos 3.171 ff). However, the situation has significantly improved, as neither the principle of ubiquity nor the previously widely held view of the applicability of the law most favourable for the claimant are enshrined in the Rome II Regulation. Rather, the general rule provides for applicability of the law of the country in which the damage occurs (*lex loci damni*) irrespective of the country in which the event giving rise to the damage occurred and irrespective of any other places where indirect consequences of that event occur, art 4(1) Rome II Regulation. Nevertheless, there now seems to be consensus that for a number of reasons (notably the potential plurality of places where investors are affected and the need to maintain, to the extent possible, predictability for issuers and intermediaries employed by them and, importantly, the double function of liability, ie investor protection and market integrity) the → connecting factor provided for in the general rule is ill-suited for our purposes and requires adequate modification or adaptation (Thomas MC Arons, 'All Roads Lead to Rome: Beware of the Consequences! The Law Applicable to Prospectus Liability Claims under the Rome II Regulation' [2008] NIPR 481; Christoph Weber, 'Internationale Prospekthaftung nach der Rom II-Verordnung' [2008] WM IV 1581; Dorothee Einsele, 'Internationales Prospekthaftungsrecht – Kollisionsrechtlicher Anlegerschutz nach der Rom II-Verordnung –' [2012] ZEuP 23).

One conceivable way could be the 'secondary connection mechanism' (see III.1.a) above) connecting liability to the applicable disclosure regime, as proposed before the Rome II Regulation entered into force, and which is now argued to be covered by the country-of-origin principle purportedly enshrined at least implicitly in the exception clause of art 4(3) Rome II Regulation (Jan von Hein, 'Die internationale Prospekthaftung im Lichte der Rom II-Verordnung' in Harald Baum and others (eds), *Perspektiven des Wirtschaftsrechts – Beiträge für Klaus J Hopt aus Anlass seiner Emeritierung* (de Gruyter 2008) 371, 394). As has been pointed out, however, the country-of-origin principle has its legitimate role in the area of regulatory requirements of products and services but not in the – non-harmonized – sphere of tort or delict. Here, the protection of the wronged rather than the interests of the wrongdoer (here: the issuer or its advisers) is the primary objective, as evidenced by art 4(1) Rome II Regulation (Dorothee Einsele, 'Internationales Prospekthaftungsrecht – Kollisionsrechtlicher Anlegerschutz nach der Rom II-Verordnung –' [2012] ZEuP 23, 33). Moreover, it is difficult to argue that the *lex societatis* (law of incorporation or principal place of business) or any one of a number of laws of markets where the securities have been offered is 'manifestly more closely connected' not only with the issuer but also the victim of misrepresentations set forth in a prospectus who has relied on the information only in one place, namely where he was misinformed when contemplating acquisition of the security concerned. Lastly, it would appear paradoxical, to put it mildly, if (only) an issuer from a non-Member State who can choose the applicable disclosure regime (art 2(1)(m)(iii)) were also free to choose thereby the applicable liability regime from a menu of non-harmonized laws.

In view of the foregoing, the present writer revokes his support for the generalization and multi-lateralization of the secondary-connection mechanism for purposes of determining, under the Rome II Regulation, the law governing tortuous consequences of inaccurate prospectuses. On the whole, the market and, more precisely, the 'relevant market' as employed in other areas of regulated economic law, such as antitrust and unfair-competition law (see art 6 with Recital (21) Rome II Regulation), is the preferable connecting factor. Relevant is the market where the relevant issue takes place and where issuer and (potential) investor meet, typically the place where the stock exchange is located. To the extent that liability for inaccuracies serves the function of protecting potential investors or the general public, the country where they were targeted by the offer constitutes the relevant market. For example, German law governs liability of issuers offering securities in Germany, and this is an example where the law governing disclosure requirements and liability do coincide, albeit not by operation of a conflicts rule (§§ 3(1), 21–5 Securities Prospectus Act (Wertpapierprospektgesetz, Act on the Drawing up, Approval and Publication of the Prospectus to be Published when Securities are Offered to the Public or Admitted to Trading on an Organised Market of 22 June 2005 (2005) BGBl. I 1698), the statute implementing the Prospectus Directive) (Anton K Schnyder, 'Internationales Kapitalmarktrecht' in Roland Rixecker and Franz Jürgen Säcker (eds), *Münchener Kommentar zum Bürgerlichen Gesetzbuch*, vol 11 (5th edn, CH Beck 2010) nos 97–102). The fact that securities may be offered and acquired through channels other than multilateral trading platforms, such as stock exchanges (for example, on the telephone), or that certain types of financial instrument are not listed for trade on any such localized institution, is not an argument capable of undermining the viability of this approach. Conflict-of-laws theory has developed adequate tools to cope with multi-location situations, such as identifying 'centres of gravity', 'most significant relationships', allowing for → *dépeçage*, etc.

Finally, where the relevant investors are consumers within the meaning of art 6 of Rome I Regulation, that provision's policy calls to be implemented, giving preference to the law of the consumer's habitual residence (Dorothee Einsele, 'Internationales Prospekthaftungsrecht – Kollisionsrechtlicher Anlegerschutz nach der Rom II-Verordnung –' [2012] ZEuP 23, 41).

b) Secondary market: types of disclosure obligations and sanctions
In relation to other types of disclosure, and potential sanctions where duties to disclose are

not complied with, a distinction between two functions of such disclosure regimes needs to be drawn. On the one hand, reporting and disclosure requirements are part of (internal) corporate governance arrangements designed to enhance the flow of information and, frequently, in particular (minority-) shareholder protection. Both rules establishing any such requirements and rules sanctioning instances of non-compliance are governed by the *lex societatis*, ie the law of incorporation or the law of the 'seat', ie the place where the company's decision-making process is located. On the other hand, information, and perhaps even the same type of information such as periodic accounting, may be directed at the investing public generally. Here, the law of the (relevant, cf *supra* III.1.a)) market will unilaterally impose itself (Herbert Kronke, 'The Law Applicable to Intermediated Securities and to Issues of Liability in the Intermediated Securities Holding System' in Sergio Maria Carbone (ed), *L'Unione*; *Europea a vent'anni da Maastricht – Verso nuove regole* (Editoriale Scientifica 2013) 253; Herbert Kronke and Jens Haubold, 'Börsen- und Kapitalmarktrecht' in Herbert Kronke, Werner Melis and Anton K Schnyder (eds), *Handbuch Internationales Wirtschaftsrecht* (Verlag Dr Otto Schmidt 2005) nos 362–76 with ample references to and examples from German, Austrian and Swiss law).

2. *Non-compliance with duties in takeover context*

In many respects, the development of substantive law on public takeovers is converging internationally. For example, adequate information, equal treatment of all shareholders of the target company, adequate time for assessing the offer, mechanisms for establishing a fair price, are all features of domestic and supranational rules, such as the Takeover Directive (Directive 2004/25/EC of the European Parliament and of the Council of 21 April 2004 on takeover bids, [2004] OJ L 142/12). As has been correctly pointed out, however, so far no legislative consensus on civil liability in case of violation of relevant information duties has emerged (W Wolf-Georg Ringe and Alexander Hellgardt, 'The International Dimension of Issuer Liability: Liability and Choice of Law from a Transatlantic Perspective' (2011) 31 Oxford J.Leg.Stud. 23, 29 ff). The Takeover Directive does not provide a harmonized liability regime (see art 17). By contrast in the USA, liability for incorrect information is governed by the general provision of Rule 10b-5 (prohibition of market manipulation) and a substantial body of case-law. As regards conflict-of-laws rules, the general tendency seems to be in favour of some combination of the target company's *lex societatis* and the law of the market where the target's shares are traded (see Herbert Kronke, 'Capital Markets and Conflict of Laws' (2000) 286 Rec. des Cours 245, 329 ff; Jan von Hein, 'Zur Kodifikation des europäischen Übernahmekollisionsrechts' (2005) 34 ZGR 528; Francisco J Garcimartín Alférez, 'Cross-Border Listed Companies' (2000) 328 Rec. des Cours 97, 139 ff). Within its scope (art 1), the Directive provides for matters of company law to be governed by the law of the company's registered office, whereas matters concerning the bid procedure are governed by the law of the competent supervisory authority, ie the law of the market where the target's securities are traded (art 4(1), (2)(e)). Since the content of the offer document is governed by the latter, the same must be true for the liability in case of inaccuracies. Under autonomous conflicts rules, both the characterization of incorrect information, as well as non-compliance with other duties imposed on the bidder and/or the board of the target company, are important issues. If the violation is characterized as a tort (for examples, see Herbert Kronke and Jens Haubold, 'Börsen- und Kapitalmarktrecht' in Herbert Kronke, Werner Melis and Anton K Schnyder (eds), *Handbuch Internationales Wirtschaftsrecht* (Verlag Dr Otto Schmidt 2005) no 425), then a forum's autonomous conflicts rule for torts will determine the applicable law. Unlike in the area of liability for inaccurate disclosure in prospectuses, the state of the law is far from settled. Due to their regulatory nature, autonomous conflicts rules are mostly unilateral, resulting potentially in both under-regulation, ie situations where no national takeover law purports to govern, and situations where more than one regime pretends to be applied. A situation of under-regulation arose in connection with *LVMH's* bid for *TAG Heuer*, a Luxembourg corporation whose shares were not traded there but, *inter alia*, in Zurich. The Swiss regulator rightly determined that the law of the market demanded to be applied (Order of 30 September 1999, reported by Urs Brügger and Dieter Dubs, 'Zum internationalen Anwendungsbereich der börsenrechtlichen Übernahmeanordnung bei freiwilligen Übernameangeboten' [2000] SZW 69).

3. Non-compliance with insider law and other law relating to market manipulation

Markets for financial instruments require protection against insider trading and other forms of market manipulation. The means employed vary significantly. Even Directive 2003/6/EC (Directive 2003/6/EC of the European Parliament and of the Council of 28 January 2003 on insider dealing and market manipulation (market abuse), [2003] OJ L 96/16) does not provide for civil liability. However, art 10 reflects the analysis that market integrity is the primary objective. Accordingly, unilateral choice-of-law rules based on the market as connecting factor are internationally typical, and appropriate. To the extent that potentially applicable rules are to be characterized as delictual, supranational (such as Rome II Regulation) or autonomous choice-of-law rules, will respectively guide the competent forum's determination of the governing liability regime (Herbert Kronke, 'Capital Markets and Conflict of Laws' (2000) 286 Rec des Cours 245, 334 ff; Christian Hausmaninger, 'Insiderhandel und Informationspflichten' in Herbert Kronke, Werner Melis and Anton K Schnyder (eds), *Handbuch Internationales Wirtschaftsrecht* (Verlag Dr Otto Schmidt 2005) nos 440 ff, 463–8).

HERBERT KRONKE

Literature

Thomas MC Arons, 'All Roads Lead to Rome: Beware of the Consequences! The Law Applicable to Prospectus Liability Claims under the Rome II Regulation' [2008] NIPR 481; Heinz-Dieter Assmann, 'Einl A-D' in Klaus J Hopt and Herbert Wiedemann (eds), *Aktiengesetz Grosskommentar*, vol 1 (4th edn, de Gruyter 1992); Christoph Benicke, 'Prospektpflicht und Prospekthaftung bei grenzüberschreitenden Emissionen' in Heinz-Peter Mansel and others (eds), *Festschrift für Erik Jayme*, vol 1 (Sellier 2004) 25; Louis Dembitz Brandeis, *Other People's Money and How the Bankers Use It* (Stokes 1914, reissued 1933); Urs Brügger and Dieter Dubs, 'Zum internationalen Anwendungsbereich der börsenrechtlichen Übernahmeanordnung bei freiwilligen Übernameangeboten' [2000] SZW 69; Stephen J Choi and Andrew T Guzman, 'Portable Reciprocity: Rethinking the International Reach of Securities Regulation' (1998) 71 S.Cal.L.Rev. 903; Andrew Dickinson, *The Rome II Regulation: The Law Applicable to Non-Contractual Obligations* (OUP 2008); Dorothee Einsele, 'Internationales Prospekthaftungsrecht – Kollisionsrechtlicher Anlegerschutz nach der Rom II-Verordnung –' [2012] ZEuP 23; Andreas Engert and Gunnar Groh, 'Internationaler Kapitalanlegerschutz vor dem Bundesgerichtshof' [2011] IPRax 458; Merritt Baker Fox, 'Securities Disclosure in a Globalizing Market: Who Should Regulate Whom?' (1997) 95 Mich.L.Rev. 2498; Francisco J Garcimartín Alférez, 'Cross-Border Listed Companies' (2000) 328 Rec. des Cours 97; Francisco J Garcimartín Alférez, 'New Issues in the Rome I Regulation: The Special Provisions on Financial Market Contracts' (2008) 10 YbPIL 245; Roy Goode, 'The Nature and Transfer of Rights in Dematerialised and Immobilised Securities' in Fidelis Oditah (ed), *The Future for the Global Securities Market: Legal and Regulatory Aspects* (Clarendon Press 1996) 107; Roy Goode, Herbert Kronke and Ewan McKendrick, *Transnational Commercial Law: Text, Cases, and Materials* (OUP 2007); Stefan Grundmann, 'Deutsches Anlegerschutzrecht in internationalen Sachverhalten' (1990) 54 RabelsZ 283; Christian Hausmaninger, 'Insiderhandel und Informationspflichten' in Herbert Kronke, Werner Melis and Anton K Schnyder (eds), *Handbuch Internationales Wirtschaftsrecht* (Verlag Dr Otto Schmidt 2005) no 1555; Peter Hay, Russel Jay Weintraub and Patrick J Borchers, *Conflict of Laws: Cases and Materials* (14th edn, West Group 2013); Jan von Hein, 'Zur Kodifikation des europäischen Übernahmekollisionsrechts' (2005) 34 ZGR 528; Jan von Hein, 'Die internationale Prospekthaftung im Lichte der Rom II-Verordnung' in Harald Baum and others (eds), *Perspektiven des Wirtschaftsrechts – Beiträge für Klaus J Hopt aus Anlass seiner Emeritierung* (de Gruyter 2008) 371; Robert W Hillman, 'Cross-Border Investment, Conflict of Laws, and the Privatization of Securities Law' (1992) 55 LCP 331; Bernd von Hoffmann, 'Anhang IV, Art. 34' in Gerhard Kegel (ed), *Soergel. Bürgerliches Gesetzbuch mit Einführungsgesetz und Nebengesetzen*, vol 10 (12th edn, Kohlhammer 1996); Norbert Horn, *Das Recht der internationalen Anleihen* (Athenäum 1972); Alastair Hudson, *The Law of Finance* (2nd edn, Sweet & Maxwell 2013); Hideki Kanda and others, *Official Commentary on the UNIDROIT Convention on Intermediated Securities* (OUP 2012); Thomas Keijser (ed), *Transnational Securities Law* (OUP 2014); Herbert Kronke, 'Capital Markets and Conflict of Laws' (2000) 286 Rec. des Cours 245; Herbert Kronke, 'The Law Applicable to Intermediated Securities and to Issues of Liability in the Intermediated Securities Holding System' in Sergio Maria Carbone (ed), *L'Unione Europea a vent'anni da Maastricht – Verso nuove regole* (Editoriale Scientifica 2013) 253; Herbert Kronke and Jens Haubold, 'Börsen- und Kapitalmarktrecht' in Herbert Kronke, Werner Melis and Anton K Schnyder (eds), *Handbuch Internationales Wirtschaftsrecht* (Verlag Dr Otto Schmidt 2005) no 1405; Hans Kuhn, Barbara Graham-Siegenthaler and Luc Thévenoz (eds), *The Federal Intermediated Securities Act (FISA) and the Hague Securities Convention (HSC)* (Stämpfli Publishers 2010); Matthias Lehmann, 'Financial Instruments' in Franco Ferrari and Stefan Leible (eds), *Rome I Regulation: The Law Applicable to Contractual Obligations in Europe* (Sellier 2009) 85; Antoine

Maffei, 'De la nature juridique des titres dématérialisés intermédiés en droit francais' [2005] Unif.L.Rev. 237; Peter Mankowski, 'Finanzmarktverträge' in Christoph Reithmann and Dieter Martiny (eds), *Internationales Vertragsrecht* (7th edn, Verlag Dr Otto Schmidt 2010) no 1037; Ernst Rabel, *The Conflict of Laws: A Comparative Study*, vol 3 (2nd edn, University of Michigan Press 1964); Wolf-Georg Ringe and Alexander Hellgardt, 'The International Dimension of Issuer Liability: Liability and Choice of Law from a Transatlantic Perspective' (2011) 31 Oxford J.Leg.Stud. 23; Roberta Romano, 'Empowering Investors: A Market Approach to Securities Regulation' in Klaus J Hopt and others (eds), *Comparative Corporate Governance* (Clarendon Press 1998) 143; Anton K Schnyder, 'Internationales Kapitalmarktrecht' in Roland Rixecker and Franz Jürgen Säcker (eds), *Münchener Kommentar zum Bürgerlichen Gesetzbuch*, vol 11 (5th edn, CH Beck 2010); Anton K Schnyder, 'Haftung ausländischer Broker für Schäden deutscher Anleger' [2013] ZEuP 659; Anton K Schnyder and Lukas Bopp, 'Kollisionsrechtliche Anknüpfung von Prospektpflicht und Prospekthaftung als Fragestellung des Internationalen Kapitalmarktrechts' in Hans-Caspar von der Crone and others (eds), *Festschrift für Dieter Zobl* (Schulthess 2004) 391; Hubert de Vauplane (ed), *20 ans de dématérialisation des titres en France – Bilan et perspectives nationales et internationales* (Revue Banque 2005); Christoph Weber, 'Internationale Prospekthaftung nach der Rom II-Verordnung' [2008] WM IV 1581; Philip R Wood, *Conflict of Laws and International Finance* (2nd edn, Sweet & Maxwell 2007); Madeleine Yates and Gerald Montagu, *The Law of Global Custody* (4th edn, Bloomsbury 2013); Daniel Zimmer, *Internationales Gesellschaftsrecht* (Verlag Recht und Wirtschaft 1996).

Liability, limitation of maritime

I. Limitation of liability in the maritime context

In the maritime law context there is a long-established practice of implementing rules that enable certain parties (primarily shipowners) to limit their liability in respect of defined categories of claims. Limitation of liability regimes first arose within various countries' domestic laws, but have since been made the subject of a number of conventions that have provided some degree of international uniformity (→ maritime law (uniform law)). These conventions have established regimes on both 'global' limitation of liability, covering a wide range of third-party maritime claims, as well as on more specific subjects such as the carriage of goods and passengers, and pollution-related damage from various sources. This entry focuses on these international law sources (the domestic legislation of a number of jurisdictions is surveyed in Patrick Griggs, Richard Williams and Jeremy Farr (eds), *Limitation of Liability for Maritime Claims* (4th edn, Informa Law 2005)).

Rules on limitation of liability represent a policy decision whereby the interests of shipowners (and often related parties, such as charterers) are given favourable treatment vis-à-vis parties who have suffered loss in connection with the shipowner's operations. For every shipowner relying on a limitation regime's maximum cap on liability there is another party that is going without full compensation for the loss sustained. In some situations the bargain has been made more favourable for the latter party by including provisions on strict liability, compulsory insurance and rights of → direct action against insurers. Despite this, limitation of liability, particularly in its global form, remains a controversial topic within maritime law.

1. Historical origins

Rules permitting shipowners to limit their liability appear to have developed in the maritime codes of various Italian city states at some point between the 5th and 11th centuries AD, and feature in early maritime codes such as the 14th-century Consolat del Mar of Barcelona. By the 16th century such rules had spread throughout much of continental Europe. They are found in Dutch, Hanseatic, Swedish and French ordinances of the 17th century, made their way into English law by the 18th century, and were included in the influential Code de Commerce of 1807. Following some earlier efforts at the state level, the USA adopted an Act on limitation of liability at the federal level in 1851 (Limitation of Liability Act 1851 (46 U.S.C. §§ 30501–12); James J Donovan, 'The Origins and Development of Limitation of Shipowners' Liability' (1979) 53 Tul.L.Rev. 999, 1001 ff).

Throughout this long stretch of history the primary reason for developing such laws remained the promotion of trade by creating favourable conditions for shipowners. Shipowners did not always travel with their vessels and could be out of contact with them for extended periods of time, entrusting their safety and that of any cargo to persons who may or may not prove to be skilled and trustworthy mariners. In a world of wooden ships and basic navigational technology maritime trade was particularly risky, and these factors were seen as justifying a means of limiting the personal liability of the shipowner to encourage investment and trade. In practice this meant shipowners could, instead of facing claims for large sums, simply abandon their vessel and cargo to creditors (James J Donovan, 'The Origins and Development of Limitation of Shipowners' Liability' (1979) 53 Tul.L.Rev. 999, 1002; Barnabas W B Reynolds and Michael N Tsimplis, *Shipowners' Limitation of Liability* (Kluwer Law International 2012) 3 f).

A good illustration of how these factors could conspire against shipowners comes from the 18th-century English case of *Boucher v Lawson* ((1815) Cas.t.H194 = 95 ER 125), in which the master of the *Little Job* undertook to carry a cargo of gold coins from Portugal to England. He did so without the authorization of the shipowner, who was then sued and found liable for a large sum when the master had disappeared with the coins. This caused enough concern amongst local shipowners for them to successfully petition Parliament. The Responsibility of Shipowners Act 1733 (7 Geo II, ch 15) was duly passed, limiting a shipowner's liability in the case of theft by the master or crew to the value of the ship plus any freight due for the voyage. *Lord Mustill* has argued that at this early period there was a sense that the shipowner and cargo-owner were part of a 'joint venture', each taking a risk for the benefit of both, so that this position represented an acceptable compromise (see Lord Mustill, 'Ships Are Different – Or Are They?' [1993] LMCLQ 490, 492, 496 f). Other national limitation systems were developed to achieve similar outcomes. One approach, originating in → France, permitted a shipowner to 'abandon' the vessel (and in some cases any freight earned on the voyage in question) to his creditors, thus divesting himself of personal liability. Northern European states enacted a similar system based on liability *in rem*, with creditors' claims against the abandoned property secured by maritime liens (Alex Rein, 'International Variations on Concepts of Limitation of Liability' (1979) 53 Tul.L.Rev. 1259, 1261 ff).

2. 20th-century developments

In response to these divergent national approaches, the 20th century saw a series of attempts to promote uniformity at an international level. Perhaps the most significant issue for reform was the use of the post-incident value of the ship as the limit of the shipowner's liability. This approach could lead to significant injustices given that as vessels aged they would be exposed to an increasing number of incidents where losses might arise, while at the same time steadily losing value. Moreover that value could of course be negligible if the ship was reduced to a wreck.

This approach continued to represent the international position following the first convention on the limitation of shipowners' liability (1924 Limitation Convention (International Convention of 25 August 1924 for the unification of certain rules relating to the limitation of the liability of owners of seagoing vessels, 120 LNTS 123)). Adopted in 1924, this used the value of the vessel and freight, subject in respect of certain claims to a maximum amount calculated by a tonnage-based formula, to establish a shipowner's maximum amount of liability (art 1). An additional tonnage-based limitation amount was available to compensate claims for death or personal injury (art 7). Promoted by the Comité Maritime International (→ Maritime law (uniform law)) at the same time as the cargo-specific Hague Rules (see below), this agreement had 24 States Parties by the 1950s. Although the USA continues to use the post-incident value of the ship to cap liability by virtue of its 1851 legislation (Limitation of Liability Act 1851 (46 U.S.C. §§ 30501–12)), this approach was rejected at an international level when the 1924 Convention was superseded by a further convention of 1957 (1957 Limitation Convention (International Convention of 10 October 1957 relating to the limitation of the liability of owners of seagoing ships, 1412 UNTS 73)), which went on to achieve 54 States Parties in total. This was in turn superseded by the 1976 convention (1976 LLMC (Convention of 19 November 1976 on limitation of liability for maritime claims, 1456 UNTS 221, as amended by the 1996 Protocol, 35 ILM 1433, and in 2012 by the amendment adopted by the Legal Committee of IMO at its ninety-ninth session (April 2012) by resolution LEG.5(99))), which is discussed in more detail below, but all three instruments share common elements.

Each sets out the types of claim in relation to which shipowners can limit their liability (claims arising from wreck removal are covered by all three, for example), and a mechanism for determining the applicable monetary limit (linked to the ship's tonnage in the 1957 and 1976 Limitation Conventions, and a combination of tonnage and value in the 1924 Convention). Each contains a rule outlining situations in which these limits may be 'broken', for example in cases where the damage 'resulted from the actual fault or privity of the owner' (art 1(1) 1924 Limitation Convention), and each establishes that the level of limitation applies to the aggregate of all claims arising from any distinct occasion.

The scope of application differs significantly between the earlier agreement and the two later ones, as the 1924 Limitation Convention applied only where the ship concerned operated under the → flag of a contracting party (art 12). The 1957 and 1976 Limitation Conventions do not contain this restriction: they are the → *lex fori* applicable to all vessels provided the shipowner applies for limitation in a contracting state (art 7 1957 Limitation Convention; art 15 1976 LLMC). However, in all three cases contracting states are permitted to introduce national law excluding the benefits of limitation for parties from non-contracting states if they choose.

The so-called 'global' limitation of liability regime represented by these conventions has evolved gradually, with each new instrument introducing refinements to the regime that went before it, as opposed to introducing radical changes. The 1976 LLMC notably represented a bargain whereby the limits were substantially increased from those of 1957, but the standard required to 'break' those limits became much higher (*The 'Herceg Novi' v 'Ming Galaxy'* [1998] 2 Lloyd's Rep 454 = [1998] EWCA 457). Limitation is an area that benefits from a level of uniformity at the international level, as without an international approach claims arising from a single event can be made against a shipowner in numerous jurisdictions, and courts in one jurisdiction will not necessarily view a foreign award as falling within the scope of any domestic limitation regime (Barnabas WB Reynolds and Michael N Tsimplis, *Shipowners' Limitation of Liability* (Kluwer Law International 2012) 5). The concept of a single limitation fund against which all claims can be made is therefore highly desirable for shipowners, but despite this the existence of three separate conventions (all of which remain in force to some extent) has meant that 'in this area there is, despite outward appearances, relatively little uniformity despite years of worthy endeavour' (Patrick Griggs, 'Limitation of Liability for Maritime Claims: The Search for International Uniformity' [1997] LMCLQ 369, 376).

Alongside the development of these global regimes, a series of more subject-specific liability regimes came into existence throughout the 20th century and beyond. These stem primarily from the desire for regimes addressing day-to-day events such as damage to/loss of cargo, which will not usually reach the upper limits of the global liability conventions, and from a growing awareness of the potentially extensive → environmental liability shipowners may face following maritime disasters in the post-coal age of shipping.

II. The 1976 LLMC global liability regime

Although the 1924 and the 1957 Limitation Conventions remain in force in some countries, they have largely been superseded by the 1976 LLMC. Accordingly, for the purposes of illustrating the contemporary operation of global limitation of liability, the latter is outlined below.

The 1976 LLMC currently has 53 States Parties and its 1996 Protocol 49. It permits a broadly-defined class of shipowners, defined as 'the owner, charterer and manager of a seagoing ship', as well as salvors (those who provide → salvage services to a vessel in distress) and insurers to limit liability for a wide range of maritime claims (art 1). These claims, listed in art 2, include those for personal injury, loss of life, damage to property, delay to cargo/passengers, wreck removal and other tortious claims arising in direct connection with the operation of the ship. This broad scope of application gives the regime its 'global' character, as it operates by describing the sorts of claims for which a shipowner can limit liability, as opposed to the kinds of events for which a shipowner is liable to pay compensation, which is the case in the subject-specific regimes discussed below. The Convention permits States Parties to enter a reservation in respect of some claims (art 18), and many have taken this opportunity to exclude limitation for wreck removal claims in particular.

One of the most significant provisions of the Convention is that the limits of liability can only be 'broken' where loss resulted from the shipowner's 'personal act or omission, committed with the intent to cause such loss, or recklessly and with knowledge that such loss would probably result' (art 4). Proving this level of involvement in the particular type of loss that occurred is a very difficult threshold for claimants to meet, meaning that the right to limit liability will be lost only in exceptional cases (Barnabas W B Reynolds and Michael N Tsimplis, *Shipowners' Limitation of Liability* (Kluwer Law International 2012) 88; for further discussion see Duygu Damar, *Wilful Misconduct in International Transport Law* (Springer 2011)).

To calculate the shipowner's maximum liability the Convention takes the vessel's tonnage and multiplies it by a number of Special Drawing Rights (SDR, a unit of account maintained by the International Monetary Fund with reference to a collection of major world currencies. One SDR is currently worth around EUR 1.18). The larger the vessel, the higher the shipowner's maximum limit of liability. For example, a vessel of up to 500 tons equates to 333,000 SDR, with a set number of additional SDR added for each additional ton (art 6). A higher limit applies to passenger claims for personal injury/loss of life (art 7), and limits can also be raised if a sufficient number of States Parties agree that there has been 'a significant change in their real value' (art 21, and a recently adopted Australian proposal to this effect will enter into force in 2015, see International Maritime Organization 'Proposal to add a new work programme item and planned output to consider amendments to LLMC 96 to increase limits of liability under the Bunker Convention Submitted by Australia' LEG/12/1, 31 July 2009). Once a total figure is calculated, this is the full amount that a shipowner (or group of parties within this definition) will need to pay for all art 2 claims arising from a particular event (art 9). In addition the shipowner has the option of establishing a fund for this amount, for example by depositing the total amount of potential liability with the court, and having claimants claim against the fund. This has the advantage of removing the need to have the shipowner's vessel sitting idle as security for the claim(s). If the total amount of all claims exceeds the limitation cap, claimants will receive their share of the total fund on a *pro rata* basis (arts 11–12).

III. Subject-specific liability regimes

1. Cargo and passenger regimes

Liability regimes relating to the carriage of cargo in particular have common origins with global liability regimes, given that it was liability for loss of or damage to cargo that was a shipowner's main potential risk in the days before shipping casualties were inextricably linked with environmental concerns (→ Carriage of goods by sea). Having limited liability in this area obviously benefits carriers, but given complete contractual freedom they tend to exclude all liability where possible. Mandatory rules establishing a minimum level of liability therefore provide cargo-owners with at least some degree of compensation, but the question is where to strike the balance. Who should bear what risks?

This difficult question has led to the development of a series of liability regimes agreed to at the international level, namely the Hague Rules (International Convention of 25 August 1924 for the unification of certain rules relating to bills of lading, 120 LNTS 155), Hague-Visby Rules (the Hague Rules signed at Brussels, 25 August 1924, as amended by the 1968 Visby Protocol (1412 UNTS 128) and the 1979 Brussels Protocol (1412 UNTS 146)), Hamburg Rules (United Nations Convention of 31 March 1978 on the carriage of goods by sea, 1695 UNTS 3) and Rotterdam Rules (United Nations Convention of 11 December 2008 on contracts for the international carriage of goods wholly or partly by sea, UN Doc A/RES/63/122, 63 UNTS 122). All four contain provisions on the extent to which a carrier will be liable to the cargo-owner if goods are lost or damaged during the shipment. For example, under the Hague-Visby Rules a carrier that negligently manages a shipment of cargo, causing it to spoil, will pay the higher of either 666.67 SDR per package, or per kilo. The Hague Rules (and their amended Hague-Visby form) are relatively carrier-friendly, and provide a number of defences enabling the carrier to avoid paying even the limited amount of compensation. The Hamburg Rules were intended to address this by being more cargo-friendly, but have not been particularly successful with only 34 States Parties as opposed to around 90 that base their law on the Hague Rules in one form or another.

The Athens Convention 1974 (Athens Convention of 13 December 1974 relating to the carriage of passengers and their luggage by sea, 1463 UNTS 20) provides a liability regime for passenger claims, including personal injury, death and loss of damage to luggage (→ Carriage of passengers). A Protocol of 2002 (Athens Convention 2002 (Athens Convention of 1 November 2002 relating to the carriage of passengers and their luggage by sea, IMO Doc LEG/CONF.13/20 (19 November 2002))) introduced compulsory insurance arrangements to this regime, and this has recently entered into force. Furthermore the European Union has taken steps to implement the amended Convention for its Member States by way of a 2009 Regulation (Regulation (EC) No 392/2009 of the European Parliament and of the Council of 23 April 2009 on the liability of carriers of passengers by sea in the event of accidents, [2009] OJ L 131/24 (Athens Regulation)).

2. Environmental regimes

Since the late 1960s, damage arising from pollution events has become a key concern for shipowners, coastal states, and those in the tourism, fisheries and aquaculture sectors who rely on a healthy sea for their livelihoods. The first international regime adopted to address such issues was the 1969 CLC (International Convention on Civil Liability for Oil Pollution Damage of 29 November 1969, 973 UNTS 3), which has since been replaced by a Protocol of 1992 (1992 CLC (International Convention of 27 November 1992 on civil liability for oil pollution damage, 1956 UNTS 255)) and deals specifically with claims for pollution damage resulting from the cargo of oil tankers. The 1992 CLC provides for much higher limits of liability for the owners of such tankers than the 1976 LLMC, for example. This recognizes the amount of pollution damage an oil tanker accident can potentially cause, the *Exxon Valdez*, *Erika* and *Prestige* disasters of 1989, 1999 and 2002 respectively being prime examples. Compensation payable by shipowners, currently capped at just under 90 million SDR (art V 1992 CLC), is supplemented by separate funds administered by the International Oil Pollution Compensation Funds (first established by the Fund Convention (International Convention on the Establishment of an International Fund for Compensation for Oil Pollution Damage of 18 December 1971, ceased to be in force 24 May 2002, 1110 UNTS 57; as replaced by the Protocol to the International Fund for Compensation for Oil Pollution Damage of 27 November 1992, 1956 UNTS 255; the Protocol of 27 September 2000; and the Protocol of 16 May 2003, [2004] OJ L 78/24)). These can, in the event of a large-scale pollution event, provide additional compensation up to a limit of 203 million SDR. These funds are maintained through contributions paid by oil importers. In exchange for the right to limit their liability under the CLC shipowners are held strictly liable for any pollution events emanating from their tankers (art III 1992 CLC), and must meet a compulsory insurance requirement (art VII 1992 CLC). A 2003 Protocol to the Fund Convention (adopted 16 May 2003, [2004] OJ L 78/24) has increased the limit of compensation available under the funds to 750 million SDR. This Protocol now has 30 States Parties, most of which are coastal European Union Member States along with other significant coastal states such as → Australia, → Canada and → Norway.

While the 1976 LLMC does not apply to claims covered by the 1969 CLC (art 3), other regimes dealing with pollution liability have been developed that are linked to the former Convention. This is the case in respect of the Bunker Convention 2001 (pollution damage from ships' fuel; International Convention of 23 March 2001 on civil liability for bunker oil pollution damage, IMO Doc LEG/CONF 12/19, 40 ILM 1406), the HNS Convention (International Convention of 3 May 1996 on liability and compensation for damage in connection with the carriage of hazardous and noxious substances by sea, 35 ILM 1406; as amended by the Protocol of 20 April 2010 to the International Convention on liability and compensation for damage in connection with the carriage of hazardous and noxious substances by sea, IMO Doc LEG/CONF.17/DC/1 (29 April 2010), although neither this Convention nor its Protocol of 2010 have entered into force). These conventions rely on the limit set out in the 1976 LLMC, if applicable, without creating separate 'funds' of liability. Their advantages from the perspective of claimants stem from compulsory insurance requirements and a right of direct action against insurers. Like the 1969 CLC they provide for strict liability, so that the mere fact a pollution event has happened involving that shipowner's vessel is generally enough to establish liability. A more recent agreement organized along similar lines, although without its own limitation of liability system, is the 2007 Removal of Wrecks Convention (Nairobi International Convention of 18 May 2007 on the Removal of Wrecks, IMO Doc LEG/CONF 16/17, 46 ILM 697).

3. Interaction with global liability regime

The interaction between the various international regimes is potentially complex, with each having evolved at different times in response to different issues. For example, both the Athens Carriage of Passengers Convention and the 1976 LLMC can apply to claims by passengers for personal injury, despite having been adopted only two years apart from one another. A specialist cargo regime such as the Hague-Visby Rules will apply between the carrier and an individual cargo-owner if something goes wrong in relation to that cargo-owner's shipment, but a global liability convention could come into play if all shipments have been affected and the shipowner is facing a large number of claims. The first regime would provide the 'per package' limitation, and the latter would determine how many times that limited amount would have to be paid out in total, and then reduce the payments on a pro rata basis between claimants if necessary (on interface issues of this nature see Norman A Martínez Gutiérrez, *Limitation of Liability in International Maritime Conventions* (Routledge 2011) ch 7; Barnabas W B Reynolds and Michael N Tsimplis, *Shipowners' Limitation of Liability* (Kluwer Law International 2012) chs 12 and 13).

IV. Controversy and debate

Although there is no disputing that the 'concept of limitation of liability is now deep-rooted in the field of international maritime law' (Norman A Martínez Gutiérrez, *Limitation of Liability in International Maritime Conventions* (Routledge 2011) 201), it remains a controversial topic. There has been an ongoing academic debate as to whether it should exist at all, particularly in its 'global' incarnation. A key issue has been the impact of global limitation regimes on third parties without significant connections to the maritime industry that happen to suffer loss as the result of a shipping disaster. For example, while a cargo-owner exporting tons of cargo every year may be able to calculate the risks involved in shipping and obtain insurance to cover them, a family on a waterfront stroll who are injured by a ship hitting and damaging a dock may have no such connection to the maritime industry and no reason not to expect full compensation for their losses. If limits are raised on a regular basis this may never become a problem in practice, but in principle it is worth asking why the family should effectively subsidize the shipping operator.

Part of the argument against the need for global limitation stems from changes in the shipping industry that have removed some of the earlier justifications for limitation noted above. With modern communication, navigation and ship-construction technology shipowners can remain in contact with their vessels wherever they travel, and the operation of those vessels no longer represents such a risky undertaking. *Lord Mustill* has argued that the considerations that originally led to the establishment of global limitation regimes 'have dropped away, leaving only the comparatively modern proposition that it is in the general interests of society at large that shipowners should be permitted and indeed encouraged to remain in their traditional business; performing it in a traditional way' (Lord Mustill, 'Ships Are Different – Or Are They?' [1993] LMCLQ 490, 499 f).

Indeed many of the arguments in favour of limitation tend to be those suggesting that shipping is an important and worthwhile industry that should enjoy favourable rules in order to ensure ongoing investment and a correspondingly high level of service. But apart from the shipowners themselves, the parties that benefit most from the liability regimes discussed above are insurers, who argue that the existence of caps on liability enables them to set premiums with more accuracy, and keep those premiums lower than would otherwise be the case. On this basis limitation of liability helps to keep costs down for everyone involved in the shipping business, and thus consumers throughout the world.

Members of the shipping and insurance industries have further argued that the insurance market as a whole has insufficient capacity to cover large-scale shipping losses, such as those amounting to USD 2 billion or more. The occurrence of such major casualties, but not the amount of the accompanying losses, depends on safety measures to be taken by shipowners. Accordingly, liability that exceeds the upper limits of available insurance cover would be inefficient, since it would only drive shipowners into bankruptcy without providing incentives for increased loss prevention. Finally, unlimited liability might lead to an increase in uninsured vessels, and perhaps a large number of 'undisciplined claims' (see David Steel, 'Ships Are Different: The Case for Limitation of Liability' [1995] LMCLQ 77, 79 ff). Other authors have responded that the insurance industry exists without such rules in many other areas, that there is insufficient uniformity in the international regime to give them much certainty, and that the existence of limitation removes from shipowners an economic incentive to improve their safety standards (see especially Gotthard Gauci, 'Limitation of Liability in Maritime Law: An Anachronism?'

(1995) 19 *Marine Policy* 65; Muhammad Masum Billah, 'Economic Analysis of Limitation of Shipowners' Liability' (2006) 19 U.S.F.Mar.L.J. 297).

Although this debate has occurred at an academic level, limitation of liability is unlikely to disappear from international maritime law in the near future, given the ongoing support the concept has received from the international community in both its global and its more specific forms. The 1969 CLC in particular has been a very successful convention with 132 States Parties representing 97 per cent of world tanker tonnage, and while the more controversial 1976 LLMC has only about 50 States Parties it has nonetheless been referred to in subsequent conventions (see for example art 6, Bunkers Convention). It has also formed the basis of the European Union's compulsory liability insurance regime for shipowners, requiring all vessels visiting European Union ports to carry liability insurance for the claims covered, and at the limits set, by the 1996 version of the Convention (Directive 2009/20/EC of the European Parliament and of the Council of 23 April 2009 on the Insurance of Shipowners for Maritime Claims, [2009] OJ L 131/128). This ongoing use of limitation suggests a significant level of comfort with the idea of shipowners being given special treatment in terms of their liability. Conversely, where states have not adopted a particular liability regime, it is difficult to determine whether this is because their governments remain actively against that form of limitation, or whether they are simply not sufficiently interested in addressing the topic. Given these factors it would arguably take a series of significant and well-publicized injustices for the international community to consider any significant move away from limitation of liability for shipowners.

BEVAN MARTEN

Literature

Muhammad Masum Billah, 'Economic Analysis of Limitation of Shipowners' Liability' (2006) 19 U.S.F.Mar.L.J. 297; Pierre Bonassies, 'Problèmes et Avenir de la Limitation de Responsabilité' (1993) 451 Dr Marit Fr 95; Pierre Bonassies and Christian Scapel, *Droit Maritime* (2nd edn, LGDG 2010); Duygu Damar, *Wilful Misconduct in International Transport Law* (Springer 2011); James J Donovan, 'The Origins and Development of Limitation of Shipowners' Liability' (1979) 53 Tul.L.Rev. 999; Gotthard Gauci, 'Limitation of Liability in Maritime Law: An Anachronism?' (1995) 19 Mar.Pol'y 65; Patrick Griggs, 'Limitation of Liability for Maritime Claims: The Search for International Uniformity' [1997] LMCLQ 369; Patrick Griggs, Richard Williams and Jeremy Farr (eds), *Limitation of Liability for Maritime Claims* (4th edn, Informa Law 2005); Rolf Herber, *Seehandelsrecht. Systematische Darstellung* (2nd edn, De Gruyter 2013); Norman A Martínez Gutiérrez, *Limitation of Liability in International Maritime Conventions* (Routledge 2011); Lord Mustill, 'Ships Are Different – Or Are They?' [1993] LMCLQ 490; Alex Rein, 'International Variations on Concepts of Limitation of Liability' (1979) 53 Tul.L.Rev. 1259; Barnabas WB Reynolds and Michael N Tsimplis, *Shipowners' Limitation of Liability* (Kluwer Law International 2012); David Steel, 'Ships Are Different: The Case for Limitation of Liability' [1995] LMCLQ 77; Antoine Vialard, 'La Limitation de Responsabilité, Clé de Doute pour le Droit Maritime du 21ème Siècle' (2009) 699 Dr Marit Fr 21.

Licence contracts

I. Licence contracts in general

A licence contract is a contract under which the holder of an intellectual property right such as a patent, trademark, or copyright or another exclusive right such as a personality right, trade secret or sports rights, allows another party to make use of their exclusive right. In contrast to a full transfer of right, a licensor remains holder of the licensed right whereas the licensee acquires a limited permission to make use of the protected subject matter. Licence contracts may provide exclusive or non-exclusive permission. They may be territorially restricted or on a world-wide basis, for a specific contract period or for an indefinite period. Typical licence contracts entail mutual rights and duties, including the licence grant, the licence fee to be paid by the licensee, arrangements about the licensee's duty to publish, produce, distribute or otherwise exploit the protected subject matter, provisions on warranties and liabilities with regard to third-party rights or other defects in title, choice-of-law and choice-of-court clauses etc. However, licences may also be granted as unilateral covenants or waivers without any imposition of duties on the licensee. Due to the ever-growing international trade of goods and services, many licence contracts are concluded between parties from different jurisdictions. This raises the issue of which law should govern their relationship.

Licence contracts are highly diverse. The rights and duties of the right holder and the other party to the contract differ from case to case. Even in the most typical contracts, eg publishing contracts, duties of the contracting parties may vary significantly, eg whether the already written work is simply to be delivered or whether it is still to be written, whether the editor has the right and/or duty to publish the work in one or more countries etc. Thus, simple hard-and-fast rules referring courts either to the law of the habitual residence of licensor or licensee may not reflect the law with the closest connection for all possible licence contracts. Instead, a more cautious approach with a range of solutions for varying specific cases may be appropriate.

Contracts may include a licence grant of intellectual property rights as an ancillary duty of one of the contracting parties. Distribution or franchise agreements are typical examples for such contracts. While the agreements often include trademark or patent licences for the distributor or franchisee, the licence clause is of minor importance compared with the main duties of the parties, eg the distribution of goods or the franchisee's duty to establish the franchised business. Accordingly, these contracts follow distinct principles with regard to private international law and are outside the focus of the following analysis.

II. Jurisdiction in contractual matters

Jurisdiction in disputes arising from licence contracts has to be determined before the courts of EU Member States in accordance with the Brussels I Regulation (recast) (Regulation (EU) No 1215/2012 of the European Parliament and of the Council of 12 December 2012 on jurisdiction and the recognition and enforcement of judgments in civil and commercial matters (recast), [2012] OJ L 351/1; → Brussels I (Convention and Regulation)). For EFTA Member States the → Lugano Convention (Lugano Convention of 30 October 2007 on jurisdiction and the recognition and enforcement of judgments in civil and commercial matters, [2007] OJ L 339/3) applies. Subject to the rule of exclusive jurisdiction in art 24(4) Brussels I Regulation (recast) and art 22(2) Lugano Convention, a person domiciled in a EU or Lugano Convention Member State may be sued in their domicile regarding all claims based on a licence contract (see art 4 Brussels I Regulation (recast) and art 2 Lugano Convention). As an alternative forum, a person domiciled in a Member State may also be sued in matters relating to a contract, in the courts for the → place of performance of the obligation in question (see art 7(1) Brussels I Regulation (recast) and art 5(1) Lugano Convention). For sales and service contracts, art 7(1)(b) Brussels I Regulation (recast) – art 5(1)(b) Lugano Convention – provides an autonomous definition of the place of performance. For all other contracts the place of performance under art 7(1)(a) Brussels I Regulation (recast) has to be determined pursuant to the substantive law applicable to the obligation in question (Case 12/76 *Industrie Tessili Italiana Como v Dunlop AG* [1976] ECR 1473). In the case *Falco Privatstiftung* (Case C-533/07 *Falco Privatstiftung v Weller-Lindhorst* [2009] OJ C 141/15), the ECJ was asked whether a licence contract may be qualified as a service contract under art 5(1)(b) Brussels I Regulation (Regulation (EC) No 44/2001 of 22 December 2000 on jurisdiction and the recognition and enforcement of judgments in civil and commercial matters, [2001] OJ L 12/1). The Court rejected this approach, and as a result the doctrine developed by the ECJ in *Tessili* applies to licence contracts under the Brussels I Regulation (recast). The CLIP Principles (European Max Planck Group on Conflict of Laws in Intellectual Property, *Conflict of Laws in Intellectual Property: The CLIP Principles and Commentary* (Oxford 2013)) contain a special definition of the place of performance for licence contracts. Under art 2:201(2) CLIP Principles, unless otherwise agreed, the state where the obligation in question is to be performed will be, the state for which the licence is granted or the right is transferred. This uniform and single place of performance applies to all obligations arising from the contract, particularly the obligation to license the exclusive right and the duty to pay licence fees.

III. Applicable law

1. Party autonomy

→ Party autonomy is the guiding principle for contractual relationships in all modern private law instruments. Today, the freedom to choose the law applicable to licence contracts is undisputed.

In the EU, such freedom is based on art 3 Rome I Regulation (Regulation (EC) No 593/2008 of the European Parliament and of the Council of 17 June 2008 on the law applicable to contractual obligations (Rome I), [2008] OJ L 177/6; → Rome Convention and Rome I Regulation (contractual obligations)). Party autonomy is regularly accepted by European courts with regard to intellectual property contracts and is also widely accepted in legal literature. The principle is expressly enshrined in art 122(2) Swiss Private international law Act (Bundesgesetz über das Internationale Privatrecht of 18 December 1987, 1988 BBl. I 5, as amended, henceforth Swiss PILA); art 28(1) Turkish Private international law Code (Code on Private International and International Civil Procedure Law of 27 November 2007 (Act No 5718) (Milletlerarası Özel Hukuk ve Usul Hukuku Hakkında Kanun), Resmî Gazete No 26728 of 12 December 2007); arts 35, 43 Austrian Federal Code on Private international law before the enactment of the Rome I Regulation (Bundesgesetz über das internationale Privatrecht of 15 June 1978, BGBl. No 304/1978, as amended, henceforth Austrian PILA), and in art 49 Chinese Statute of Application of Law to Foreign Civil Relations (adopted at the 17th session of the Standing Committee of the 11th National People's Congress on 28 October 2010, effective 1 April 2011). § 315(1) ALI Principles (American Law Institute, Intellectual property: principles governing jurisdiction, choice of law and judgments in transnational disputes, St. Paul 2008) expressly affirms the freedom to choose the law applicable to 'transfer of interest in, or grant or license of, intellectual property rights'. § 305(2) contains special rules on choice-of-law clauses in standard form contracts. Party autonomy is also provided for in art 306 of the Transparency Proposal (Transparency Proposal on Jurisdiction, Choice of Law, Recognition and Enforcement of Foreign Judgments in Intellectual Property, finalised in 2009, in Jürgen Basedow, Toshiyuki Kono and Axel Metzger (eds), *Intellectual Property in the Global Arena: Jurisdiction, Applicable Law, and the Recognition of Judgments in Europe, Japan and the US* (Mohr Siebeck, 2010) 394–402) and in art 302 of the Joint Japanese and Korean Principles (Principles of Private international law on Intellectual Property Rights, Joint Proposal Drafted by Members of the Private international law Association of Korea and Japan, The Quarterly Review of Corporation Law and Society (Waseda Institute 2011) 112–63).

2. *Applicable law in the absence of choice*

a) No special rule in art 4 Rome I Regulation
The determination of the law applicable to licence contracts in the absence of choice raises difficult questions. In principle, art 4 Rome I Regulation governs the issue of which law applies to a licence contract if the parties have not chosen the applicable law. However, art 4(1) Rome I Regulation provides specific rules for a variety of contracts but not for contracts concerning intellectual property rights. For contracts not covered by art 4(1) Rome I Regulation, art 4(2) Rome I Regulation refers to the characteristic performance test, ie 'the contract shall be governed by the law of the country where the party required to effect the characteristic performance of the contract has his habitual residence'. Courts may deviate from art 4(1) and art 4(2) Rome I Regulation if the contract is 'manifestly more closely connected' with another country (see art 4(3) Rome I Regulation). A court may also apply the closest connection test if the applicable law cannot be determined under art 4(1) and art 4(2) Rome I Regulation (see art 4(4) Rome I Regulation). The ECJ has yet to decide on the applicable law to licence contracts. There is also no reported national case-law of EU Member States supreme courts, since the Regulation applies only to contracts concluded after 17 December 2009. Lacking clear guidance by the Rome I Regulation or the ECJ, various solutions could be applied by European courts.

b) Application of the law of the licensor
Following the 'pre-Rome I' rules of certain EU jurisdictions and current Swiss law, the law of the licensor's habitual residence would govern a licence contract. This solution was applied in a patent case by the German Federal Court of Justice in a 2009 decision (German Federal Court of Justice (BGH), 15 September 2009 [2010] GRURInt. 334). It was also supported in a 2009 copyright case by the Austrian Supreme Court (Oberster Gerichtshof, 8 September 2009, 4 Ob 90/09b – '*F.-Privatstiftung*', [2010] JBl. 253), and in a 1975 trademark decision by the Swiss Federal Court (Swiss Bundesgericht, 22 April 1975 – *Toga/Togal*, 110 II BGE 293). The Swiss legislature adopted the same approach as a general rule in art 122 Swiss PILA. According to art 122, all intellectual property contracts are governed by the law of the state of the right holder's habitual

residence. However, art 122 Swiss PILA contains certain exceptions. If the contract has a closer connection to another state, in particular to the state of residence of transferee or licensee, then the law of that state will apply. Application of the licensor's law is also suggested as a basic presumption or fall-back provision by the currently discussed international collections of soft law principles and reform proposals on the subject (see § 315(2) ALI Principles, art 3:502(3) CLIP Principles and art 306(2) Transparency Proposal).

c) Application of the law of the licensee
Another solution would be to apply the law of the licensee's habitual residence. The Austrian PILA, before enactment of the Rome I Regulation, pointed in art 43 to the law of the habitual residence of the licensee for all multistate licence contracts, irrespective of the rights and duties of the parties. A similar rule was provided for in s 25(c) of the former Hungarian Act on Private international law (Law-decree No 13 of 1979 on Private international law). German and French courts also applied the law of the licensee to publishing contracts (German Federal Court of Justice (BGH), 29 March 2001 [2001] GRUR 1134 and Cour d'Appel de Paris, 2 June 1999 [1/2000] RIDA 302). Application of the licensee's law has also been suggested as an underlying presumption by art 307(2) of the recent joint Japanese–Korean proposal for law reform.

d) Application of the lex loci protectionis
A third solution would be to apply the law of the protecting country as *lex contractus*. This solution was applied by the Higher Regional Court of Düsseldorf in 1961 in the case of an exclusive patent licence granted by a French right holder to a German licensee as part of a cross-licence agreement (Higher Regional Court (OLG) of Düsseldorf, 4 August 1961 [1962] GRUR Ausl 256). Applying the *lex loci protections* was also supported by art 43 of the former Austrian PILA for single-state licences. Article 306 of the Transparency Proposal follows the same approach. The law of the protecting country is used as the primary fall-back provision in art 3:502(3) CLIP Principles for single-state licences. It also has some support in scholarly writing. This approach would foster legal certainty for users because they could rely on their national law when making use of the software or contents. Further, this approach would prevent → *dépeçage* between the contractual issues of the licence contracts and the intellectual property aspects. However, the protecting country approach suffers from the disadvantage inherent to all 'mosaic' theories in private international law, in that applying multiple territorial laws to ubiquitous legal relationships significantly raises the degree of complexity for the right holder. Applying a territorial approach to internationally used licence contracts may also have the effect of a race to the top with regard to the legal restrictions on freedom of contract: if, for example, a licensor wishes to exclude its liability for mistakes in a computer program, the licensor will have the choice of either using the most restrictive contract law regime or taking the risk that the waiver will be unenforceable in certain jurisdictions.

3. Characterization
a) Contractual issues
All legal issues qualified as intrinsically contractual may be concentrated under one applicable law chosen by the parties. This raises the question of which aspects of licence contracts may be characterized as issues of contract law. Article 12 Rome I Regulation provides certain indications for the most crucial aspects of licence contracts. Under art 12, the following issues must be characterized as contract law: (i) formation and validity of contracts, (ii) interpretation of contracts, including the exact determination of the rights and duties of the parties, irrespective of whether the rules of interpretation are enshrined in the general legislation on contracts or whether they are to be found in special legislation on intellectual property (see eg § 31(5) German Copyright Act (Gesetz über Urheberrecht und verwandte Schutzrechte of 9 September 1965, BGBl. I 1273, as amended) or art 122-7 French Intellectual Property Code (Code de la propriété intellectuelle, Act No 92–597 of 1 July 1992, as amended)), (iii) the consequences of a total or partial breach of obligations, including avoidance of the contract, the assessment of → damages, warranties and liabilities and indemnification clauses, (iv) the various ways of extinguishing obligations, including termination clauses, and → prescription and limitation of actions, and (v) the consequences of nullity of the contract. For these named issues, the parties are free to choose the applicable law in accordance with art 3 Rome I Regulation.

b) Law applicable to the transfer of an intellectual property right

A controversial issue of characterization is whether transfer of an intellectual property right as such is governed by the law applicable to the 'proprietary' aspects of the intellectual property right, that is in most jurisdictions the *lex loci protectionis*, or alternatively by the *lex contractus* (for the application of the *lex loci protectionis*, see eg *Corcovado Music Corp v Hollis Music, Inc*, 981 F.2d 679 (2d Cir 1993); for the application of the *lex contractus*, see eg *Campbell Connelly & Co v Noble* [1963] 1 WLR 252; Cour de Cassation France, 28 May 1963 [1963] JCP II 13347). A *dépeçage* between the contract, including the rightholder's obligation to transfer the intellectual property right and the contract effecting the transfer, would contradict legal practice in the field of intellectual property contracts. Such contracts typically contain both the obligation to transfer and the transfer as such at the same time. A European court would also be inclined by art 14(1) Rome I Regulation to apply the *lex contractus*. Article 14(1) determines the law applicable to the contract between assignor and assignee as the law applicable to the relationship between assignor and assignee, including any proprietary aspects of the assignment. Hence, one may argue that law applicable to the transfer or licence contract should also apply to the 'proprietary' aspects of the transfer or licence.

c) Intellectual property issues

Several issues of intellectual property law are of interest with regard to licence contracts (→ Intellectual property, applicable law). With regard to the proprietary aspects of licence contracts, one should bear in mind that the application of the *lex loci protectionis* is mandatory internationally. Thus a careful characterization of the various legal aspects of licence contracts is of essential importance. For all contractual aspects, the parties may choose the applicable law, whereas for all proprietary aspects, they have to accept the application of the law or laws of the states for which protection is sought. The typical issues of intellectual property law in connection with licence contracts are (i) requirements of protection of intellectual property rights, (ii) the existence, validity and registration, (iii) the scope of protection, especially the precise activities covered by the exclusive right, (iv) limitations and exceptions, including the term of protection, (v) initial ownership, ie who is considered to be the author or inventor and who has the right to register a patent etc, especially in employment relationships, (vi) transferability of the intellectual property right or of specific statutory rights of the author or inventor, (vii) infringement, (viii) liability for the acts of another person and (ix) → remedies, especially the requirements for → injunctions and the calculation of damages. For the listed issues party autonomy is either excluded or limited.

4. Formal validity

The formal validity of contracts is subject to special rules of private international law. This issue may be of relevance for licence contracts because of the numerous writing requirements in national intellectual property acts (see eg arts 131–2, 131–3(3), 132–7 French Intellectual Property Code; s 90(3) British Copyright, Designs and Patents Act 1988 (ch 48); s 30(6) UK Patents Act 1977 (ch 37); 35 U.S.C. § 261(2); § 40 German Copyright Act). Many modern jurisdictions apply conflict rules to formalities which favour the validity of the contract (*favor negotii*). The reason for this liberal approach is that formal requirements (→ Formal requirements and validity) are often invoked to invalidate contracts which have been concluded in good faith. In international transactions, formal requirements are even more because the parties often ignore formalities required by foreign law. The *favor negotii* approach has therefore gained ground in modern private international law. It is also followed by art 11 Rome I Regulation, according to which contracts are formally valid if they satisfy the formal requirements of the law which governs them in substance, eg the law chosen by the parties, or of the law of the state in which either of the parties or its agent is present at the time of contract conclusion, or of the law of the state in which either of the parties is habitually resident at that time. This alternative approach is also applicable to the formal requirements for licence contracts.

AXEL METZGER

Literature

Pedro de Miguel Asensio, 'The Law Governing International Intellectual Property Licensing Agreements (a Conflict of Laws Analysis)' in Jacques de Werra (ed), *Research Handbook on*

Intellectual Property Licensing (Edward Elgar 2013) 312; Nerina Boschiero, 'Spunti critici sulla nuova disciplina comunitaria della legge applicabile ai contratti relativi alla proprietà intellettuale in mancanza de scelta ad opera delle parti' in Gabriela Venturini and Stefania Bariatti (eds), *Liber Fausto Pocar* (Giuffrè 2009) 141; James Fawcett and Paul Torremans, *Intellectual Property and Private international law* (2nd edn, OUP 2011); Muriel Josselin-Gall, *Les contrats d'exploitation du droit de propriété littéraire et artistique* (Edition Joly 1995); Paul Katzenberger, 'Vor §§ 120 ff' in Gerhard Schricker and Ulrich Loewenheim (eds), *Urheberrecht. Kommentar* (4th edn, CH Beck 2010) para 153 ff; Dário Moura Vicente, 'La propriété intellectuelle en droit international privé' (2008) 335 Rec. des cours 105; Yuko Nishitani, 'Contracts Concerning Intellectual Property Rights' in Franco Ferrari and Stefan Leible (eds), *Rome I Regulation: The Law Applicable to Contractual Obligations in Europe* (Sellier 2009) 51; Marta Pertegás Sender, 'Artikel 93 (Recht toepasselijk op intellectuele eigendom)' in Johan Erauw and others (eds), *Het Wetboek Internationaal Privaatrecht becommentarieerd* (Intersentia 2006) 477; Paul Torremans, 'Licenses and Assignments of Intellectual Property Rights under the Rome I Regulation' [2008] J Priv Int L 397; Mireille van Eechoud, *Choice of Law in Copyright and Related Rights* (Kluwer 2003).

Life insurance contracts

I. Development of the private international law of life insurance

1. From the Middle Ages to the 20th century

The roots of life insurance as well as of private international law (see → Aldricus) both lie in medieval Northern Italy: it was in the Mediterranean marine commerce dominated by the sea-power of Upper Italian cities that the predecessors of premium-based life insurance policies developed. Although some of these contracts involved cross-border scenarios (cf Enrico Bensa, *Il Contratto di Assicurazione nel Medio Evo* (Tipografia Maritima Editrice 1884) 128 ff), private international law issues did not arise until actuarial science laid the ground for the triumphant course of modern-life insurance business. Frequently, the need to purchase life insurance abroad stemmed from the prevalent prohibition of these contracts in many European countries due to religious or moral reservations (cf *Ordonnance de la Marine, Du mois d'Août* 1681, vol 3 (Paris) ch VI art 10: 'Défendons de faire aucune assurance sur la vie des personnes'). The situation was different in England, where life insurance business had been thriving early on. In light of this, continental Europeans willing to take out life insurance policies had to contract across borders. However, given the lack of choice-of-law rules, transnational life insurance policies often proved hard to enforce. This eventually spurred the development of life insurance companies on the Continent: in Germany, for example, the *Gothaer* was founded in 1827 in part as a reaction to the inadequacies of cross-border life insurance (cf Peter Koch, *Geschichte der Versicherungswirtschaft in Deutschland* (VVW 2012) 68). Although especially English insurers continued their international business (cf eg German Imperial Court of Justice (RG), 8 February 1889 [1889] 22 RGZ 215), cross-border life insurance contracts did not reach a considerable scale until these products were included in the European Single Market.

2. European Common Market for life insurance

The Common Market for life insurance was created by aligning the regulatory environment for insurers as well as by harmonizing European private international law rules: the Third Life Assurance Directive (Council Directive 92/96/EEC of 10 November 1992 on the coordination of laws, regulations and administrative provisions relating to direct life assurance and amending Directives 79/267/EEC and 90/619/EEC, [1992] OJ L 360/1) introduced the single licence principle allowing life insurers from Member States of the EU or the EEA to serve the entire Common Market without approval by any other supervisory authority except from their home country regulator (see eg Jürgen Basedow, 'Internal Market (Insurance)' in Jürgen Basedow and others (eds), *The Max Planck Encyclopedia of European Private Law*, vol 1 (OUP 2012) 955 ff). While this allowed insurers to enjoy the freedom to provide services and freedom of establishment, the transnational life insurance business also needed reliable private international law rules. Special European provisions on jurisdiction were introduced with the Brussels Convention (Brussels Convention of 27 September 1968 on jurisdiction and the enforcement of judgments in civil and commercial matters, [1972] OJ L 299/32, consolidated version, [1998] OJ C 27/1), the predecessor of the Brussels I Regulation (recast) (Regulation (EU) No 1215/2012 of the European Parliament and of the Council of 12 December 2012 on jurisdiction and the recognition and enforcement of judgments in civil and commercial matters (recast), [2012] OJ L 351/1) (→ Brussels I (Convention and Regulation)). The first European provisions on → choice of law relevant for → insurance contracts were contained in the Rome Convention (Rome Convention on the law applicable to contractual obligations (consolidated version), [1998] OJ C 27/34). The scope of application of these provisions was, however, limited to insurance contracts covering risks situated outside the EU/EEA. Intra-EU/EEA risks were subject to the choice-of-law rules of the Second Life Assurance Directive (Council Directive 90/619/EEC of 8 November 1990 on the coordination of laws, regulations and administrative provisions relating to direct life assurance, laying down provisions to facilitate the effective exercise of freedom to provide services and amending Directive 79/267/EEC, [1990] OJ L 330/50). This Directive was replaced by the Fourth Life Assurance Directive (Directive 2002/83/EC of the European Parliament and of the Council of 5 November 2002 concerning life assurance, [2002] OJ L 345/1), which in turn will merge into the Solvency II Directive in 2016 (Directive 2009/138/EC of the European Parliament and of the Council of 25 November 2009 on the taking-up and pursuit of the business of Insurance and Reinsurance (Solvency II), [2009] OJ L 335/1, as amended).

From the beginning, these choice-of-law rules were criticized as both too complicated and too incoherent. In 2008, the European legislator introduced the Rome I Regulation (Regulation (EC) No 593/2008 of the European Parliament and of the Council of 17 June 2008 on the law applicable to contractual obligations (Rome I), [2008] OJ L 177/6; → Rome Convention and Rome I Regulation (contractual obligations)) which contains a provision on insurance contracts in art 7 and which supersedes the choice-of-law rules of the aforementioned European Directives and the Rome Convention. However, the Rome I Regulation has inherited many of the flaws already identified in the preceding choice-of-law regime. And it is also due to this unsatisfactory *status quo* of EU private international law in the field of insurance that cross-border life insurance business prospers only in certain niches: for example, most variable annuity contracts are currently being marketed from → Ireland and → Luxembourg given the favourable regulatory environment in these countries. However, the same may not be said with regard to standard life insurance policies.

II. Life insurance contracts under the Rome I Regulation

1. General outline

While European choice-of-law rules for insurance contracts have been consolidated in the Rome I Regulation, it still maintains a cumbersome fragmentation of the applicable rules (→ Insurance contracts). Whereas 'large risks' are subject to the choice-of-law regime in art 7(2) regardless of their location, the rules applicable to 'mass risks' under the Rome I Regulation vary: art 7(3) only concerns policies covering risks situated inside the EU. Insurance contracts relating to risks located outside the EU are subject to the general choice-of-law provisions, ie arts 3, 4, 6 and the rules applicable by virtue of art 23 Rome I Regulation.

It is hence of fundamental importance that art 7(1), (2) Rome I Regulation effectively determines that life insurance may never be deemed as covering a 'large risk' since this term is defined by reference to art 5(d) Dir 73/239 (First Council Directive 73/239/EEC of 24 July 1973 on the coordination of laws, regulations and administrative provisions relating to the taking-up and pursuit of the business of direct insurance other than life assurance, [1973] OJ L 228/3) and that instrument in accord with its language applies only to 'direct insurance other than life assurance'. By consequence, even experienced economic players such as multinational corporations contracting group life insurance for their employees may never benefit from the more liberal art 7(2) Rome I Regulation. Since life insurance contracts are invariably treated as 'mass risks', art 7(3)(1) Rome I Regulation imposes severe restrictions on → party autonomy in respect to these policies. At the same time, however, art 7(3)(2) Rome I Regulation allows for an expansion of choice-of-law options by virtue of national private international law and therefore openly compromises the Regulation's intention of providing a uniform set of choice-of-law rules in the EU. Finally, where a (group) life insurance contract covers risks situated in more than one Member State or risks inside as well as outside the EU, the contract shall be considered as constituting several contracts each relating to only one state (cf art 7(5) Rome I Regulation). This may lead to a fragmentation of a single contract, whereby different laws apply to the risks depending on their location (see eg Louise Merrett, 'Choice of Law in Insurance Contracts under the Rome I Regulation' (2009) 5 J Priv Int L 49, 54 ff).

2. Limitations of the scope of application in the context of life insurance

Among other exemptions, eg relating to pre-contractual obligations (see art 1(2)(i)), art 1(2)(j) Rome I Regulation also contains a carve-out provision covering certain life insurance contracts in the context of occupational pensions and similar benefits. This exception is narrowly tailored since it affects solely insurance contracts arising out of operations carried out by insurers other than those mentioned in art 2 Fourth Life Assurance Directive. The carve-out in art 1(2)(j) therefore only excludes life insurance policies that satisfy two requirements: first, these contracts must be entered into with an insurance company not established in the EU, and, second, the object of the life insurance contract at hand must be to provide benefits for employed or self-employed persons in the event of death or survival or of discontinuance or curtailment of activity, or of sickness related to work or accidents at work. Given that European insurance regulations oblige insurers from third countries to underwrite their EU/EEA life insurance business through a European branch, art 1(2)(j) Rome I Regulation applies to life insurance contracts covering risks situated outside the EU/EEA (see eg Jan D Lüttringhaus, 'Art. 1' in Franco Ferrari (ed), *Rome I Regulation* (Sellier 2014) paras 90 ff; Christian Heinze, 'Insurance Contracts under the Rome I Regulation' [2009] NIPR 445, 446; Stefan Perner, 'Das Internationale Versicherungsvertragsrecht nach Rom I' [2009] IPRax 218, 219). It is moreover important to note that art 7 Rome I Regulation applies only to direct insurance. Reinsurance contracts relating to life insurance policies are subject to the general choice-of-law regime in art 3 and art 4 (→ Reinsurance contracts).

3. Location of risk as key concept

The location of risk is a key concept under the Rome I Regulation since it defines which choice-of-law regime is applicable. With regard to life insurance contracts, art 7(6) Rome I Regulation draws upon art 1(1)(g) Fourth Life Assurance Directive (art 13(14)(a) Solvency II Directive), which locates the risk in the Member State where the policyholder has his/her habitual residence. This rule is modified by art 19(1) Rome I Regulation in view of a natural person acting in the course of his/her business activity: the habitual residence and hence the risk is located at his/her principal place of business provided that the life insurance contract is linked to the business activity.

If the policyholder is a legal person, art 1(1) (g) Fourth Life Assurance Directive (art 13(14) (a) Solvency II Directive) points to the Member State where the entity's establishment, to which the contract relates, is situated (cf Case C-191/ 99 *Kvaerner plc v Staatssecretaris van Financien* [2001] ECR I-4447, para 47). The term 'legal person' also includes entities that do not dispose of a legal personality (see Jürgen Basedow and Wolfgang Drasch, 'Das neue Internationale Versicherungsvertragsrecht' [1991] NJW 785, 788). Pursuant to art 7(5) Rome I Regulation, life insurance contracts covering risks relating to branches of a legal person in different Member States shall be considered as constituting several contracts each relating to only one Member State. By consequence, different laws will apply to the respective risks covered by the life insurance policy. The term 'place of establishment' referred to in art 1(1)(g) Fourth Life Assurance Directive (art 13(14)(a) Solvency II Directive) is defined in art 1(1)(c) Fourth Life Assurance Directive as the head office, an agency or a branch of an undertaking. The latter terms should be interpreted consistently with ECJ case-law on jurisdiction: here the terms imply a place of business which has the appearance of permanency, such as the extension of a parent body, has a management and is materially equipped to negotiate business with third parties (cf with regard to art 5(5) Brussels I Regulation (Regulation (EC) No 44/2001 of 22 December 2000 on jurisdiction and the recognition and enforcement of judgments in civil and commercial matters, [2001] OJ L 12/1; → Brussels I (Convention and Regulation)) eg Case 14/76 *De Bloos v Bouyer* [1976] ECR 1497, paras 19 ff and Case 218/86 *SAR Schotte GmbH v Parfums Rothschild SARL* [1987] ECR 4905, para 10). Insurance subsidiaries will usually satisfy these requirements (cf Case C-191/99 *Kvaerner* [2001] ECR I-4447, paras 43 ff). For the purpose of art 7 Rome I Regulation, risks which may not be attributed to a specific subsidiary or which affect the company in its entirety should be located at the head office of the legal person. Since EU private international law only focuses on the policyholder, whereas the situation of the insured as well as of the beneficiary of the life insurance policy is immaterial, group life insurance which is, for instance, taken out by a company for its employees may therefore usually be subjected to a single law.

Finally, art 7(1) and art 1(4) Rome I Regulation refer only to risks situated inside the EU without addressing risks located in EEA Member States. This raises the question whether or not a different treatment of life insurance coverage of risks in EEA States was indeed intended. If so, this would eventually lead to an unjustifiable discrimination of policyholders from EEA Member States on grounds of their nationality, although such different treatment is expressly prohibited by art 4 EEA Agreement (Helmut Heiss, 'Versicherungsverträge in "Rom I": Neuerliches Versagen des europäischen Gesetzgebers' in Dietmar Baetge, Jan von Hein and Michael von Hinden (eds), *Festschrift für Jan Kropholler zum 70. Geburtstag* (Mohr Siebeck 2008) 459, 462 ff). Therefore, art 7 Rome I Regulation should be applied at least by analogy to risks located in EEA Member States. This extensive reading of the provision is also supported by EU law: art 178 Solvency II Directive obliges all EEA Member States to apply the choice-of-law rules contained in art 7 Rome I Regulation. This underlines that the European legislator intends to establish a uniform choice-of-law regime that does not distinguish between risks located in EU or EEA Member States (Jan D Lüttringhaus, 'Art. 7 Rom I-VO Versicherungsverträge' in *beck-online.GROSSKOMMENTAR* (CH Beck 2016) para 51).

III. Law applicable to risks situated inside the EU/EEA: art 7 Rome I Regulation

Given that the European legislator decided to exclude life insurance contracts from the category of 'large risks' and hence the more liberal choice-of-law regime in art 7(2) Rome I Regulation, these policies are subject to art 7(3) Rome I Regulation which constrains party autonomy considerably.

1. Limited party autonomy under art 7(3) Rome I Regulation

Article 7(3) limits the laws that the parties to a life insurance contract may choose in accordance with art 3 Rome I Regulation to: (i) the law of the Member State where the risk is situated at the time of conclusion of the contract, (ii) the law of the country where the policyholder has his habitual residence and (iii) the law of the Member State of which the policyholder is a national (Jan D Lüttringhaus, 'Art. 7 Rom I-VO Versicherungsverträge' in *beck-online. GROSSKOMMENTAR* (CH Beck 2016) paras 106 et seq). As regards life insurance, art 7(3)(a) and (b) will always lead to the application of the same law, given that art 7(6) Rome I Regulation locates the risk at the habitual residence of the policyholder anyway. Yet, it is noteworthy that art 7(3)(b) Rome I Regulation expressly refers to the 'country' and not the 'Member State' of residence. Whereas this wording may therefore generally include third countries, the case is different with regard to life insurance: since the risk would automatically be located at the habitual residence outside the EU/EEA, the special rules for insurance contracts in art 7 are inapplicable according to art 7(1) and art 7(6) Rome I Regulation. Instead, the choice-of-law provisions in arts 3, 4, 6, 23 Rome I Regulation apply. Under art 7(3), the parties' choice is therefore *de facto* limited to the law of the Member State where the risk is situated (art 7(3)(a), (b)) or of which the policyholder is a national (art 7(3)(c) Rome I Regulation).

Article 7(3)(d) and (e) offer further choices which are, however, confined to special scenarios: art 7(3)(d) Rome I Regulation applies only if an insurance contract covers risks which are exclusively limited to events occurring in a Member State other than the Member State where the risk is situated. With regard to life insurance, this provision may become relevant in the context of travel insurance, ie life insurance coverage that relates only to the travel destination but not to the Member State where the policyholder has his habitual residence. Finally, where the policyholder pursues a commercial activity or a liberal profession and the insurance contract covers two or more risks which relate to those activities and which are situated in different Member States, art 7(3)(e) Rome I Regulation allows the parties to subject the contract in its entirety to the law of any of the Member States concerned or to the law of the country of habitual residence of the policyholder.

2. National rules expanding party autonomy: art 7(3)(2) Rome I Regulation

The limited choice-of-law options provided for in art 7(3) may, however, be expanded. Whenever in the alternatives set out in art 7(3)(a), (b) and (e) the national private international law rules of the Member States grant greater freedom of choice, the parties may take advantage of that freedom pursuant to art 7(3)(2) Rome I Regulation. Among the Member States having made use of this rule figure, for example, the → United Kingdom (cf Regulation 4 Financial Services and Markets Act 2000 (Law Applicable to Contracts of Insurance) Regulations 2009, SI 2009/3075), Italy (cf art 181 Codice delle assicurazioni, as amended by Gaz. Uff. 13 October 2005, No 239, Suppl. Ordinario No 163) and Austria (cf s 35a Austrian Federal Code on Private international law (Bundesgesetz über das internationale Privatrecht of 15 June 1978, BGBl. No 304/1978)). By contrast, other Member States such as Germany did not exercise the option to grant greater party autonomy under their national choice-of-law rules. Overall, art 7(3)(2) Rome I Regulation reflects but a compromise since the Member States were unable to find common ground with regard to the extent of party autonomy appropriate for insurance contracts covering mass risks. It is important to note that the possibility to apply national provisions instead of the uniform rules of the Rome I Regulation counteracts the very aim of European private international law and adds further complexity to the already thorny choice-of-law regime for insurance contracts.

3. Law applicable in the absence of choice: art 7(3)(3) Rome I Regulation

In the absence of a choice of law by the parties to a life insurance contract, art 7(3)(3) Rome I Regulation points to the law of the Member State in which the risk is situated at the time of conclusion of the contract. Since the risk covered by an insurance policy is usually located at the habitual residence of the policyholder (see art 7(6) Rome I, art 1(1)(g) Fourth Life Assurance Directive and art 13(14) Solvency II Directive; see as to the relevance of art 19(1) Rome I *supra* II.3.), the contract will be governed by this law. As regards insurance policies taken out by legal persons, the law of the country applies where the entity's establishment, to which the contract relates, is situated (cf art 1(1)(g) and (c) Fourth Life Assurance Directive; art 13(14)(a) Solvency II Directive; see as to the details *supra* II.3.).

The wording of art 7(3)(3) Rome I Regulation implies the possibility of → *dépeçage*: the law of the Member State in which the risk is situated only governs the contract to the extent that the parties have not chosen the law applicable to the policy. Where the parties have selected the law only for a part of the life insurance policy according to art 3(1), the rest of the contract will be governed by the law applicable by virtue of art 7(3)(3) Rome I Regulation.

IV. Risks situated outside the EU/EEA: arts 3, 4, 6 and art 23 Rome I Regulation

With regard to life insurance policies covering risks situated outside the EU/EEA, different choice-of-law provisions may apply depending on the nature of the contract and the parties involved. This concerns, in particular, life insurance contracts entered into by a consumer: first, since art 23 gives precedence to certain choice-of-law rules set out in consumer Directives, the Rome I Regulation yields to national provisions transposing the respective Directives in this field. Second, art 6 Rome I Regulation provides for a special choice-of-law regime for consumers (→ Consumer contracts). Only where neither of the aforementioned rules applies may the law governing the life insurance contract be determined pursuant to the general provisions in arts 3 and 4 Rome I Regulation.

1. Choice-of-law provisions in Directives: art 23 Rome I Regulation

With regard to life insurance contracts covering risks situated outside the EU/EEA, art 23 Rome I Regulation gives precedence to the choice-of-law regime contained in certain consumer Directives. Although art 23 Rome I Regulation only opens the way for these special rules '[w]ith the exception of Article 7', this does not bar the application of special choice-of-law rules from European Directives to insurance contracts that are excluded from the scope of art 7 Rome I Regulation. Choice-of-law rules stemming from European Directives relevant in the context of life insurance contracts are, first and foremost, art 6(2) Unfair Terms Directive (Council Directive 93/13/EEC of 5 April 1993 on unfair terms in consumer contracts, [1993]

OJ L 95/29) and art 12 (2) Directive on distance marketing of consumer financial services (Directive 2002/65/EC of the European Parliament and of the Council of 23 September 2002 concerning the distance marketing of consumer financial services and amending Council Directive 90/619/EEC and Directives 97/7/EC and 98/27/EC, [2002] OJ L 271/16). The application of the said provisions requires, *inter alia*, that the parties to the contract have chosen the law of a third country and that the life insurance policy presents a strong connection to the territory of the EU/EEA Member States.

2. Consumer contracts: art 6 Rome I Regulation

If a life insurance contract does not satisfy the aforementioned criteria, the policyholder may still benefit from special choice-of-law provisions for consumers found in art 6 Rome I Regulation, provided that its requirements are met. Recital (32) only excludes the applicability of the consumer regime to life insurance contracts that fall within the scope of art 7 Rome I Regulation. Hence, with regard to life insurance policies covering risks situated outside the EU/EEA, art 6 Rome I Regulation remains applicable (see as to the details of this conflict-of-law provision → Consumer contracts). Moreover, a life insurance contract entered into by a consumer is generally not excluded by virtue of art 6(4): first, the carve-out in art 6(4)(a) Rome I Regulation relates only to contracts for the supply of services in a country other than that where the consumer has his habitual residence. Under a life insurance policy, however, the insurer will usually have to provide services such as, for example, payments in the consumer's country of residence (see eg Jürgen Basedow and Wolfgang Drasch, 'Das neue Internationale Versicherungsvertragsrecht' [1991] NJW 785, 789; Christian Heinze, 'Insurance Contracts under the Rome I Regulation' [2009] NIPR 445, 450). Furthermore, even life insurance policies in which the payment structure is tied to the performance of certain → financial instruments may typically be regarded as not being 'rights and obligations which constitute a financial instrument' within the meaning of art 6(4)(d) Rome I Regulation. This construction is in line with recent ECJ case-law on the distinction between life insurance and financial instruments (cf Case C-166/11 *Ángel Lorenzo González Alonso v Nationale Nederlanden Vida Cia De Seguros y Reaseguros SAE* [2012] OJ C 118/7, para 25).

3. Arts 3 and 4 Rome I Regulation

The parties to a life insurance contract covering risks outside the EU/EEA may choose the law applicable to the policy pursuant to art 3 Rome I Regulation within the limitations of party autonomy set out in art 3(3), (4) (→ Party autonomy), art 9 (→ Overriding mandatory provisions) and art 21 Rome I Regulation (→ Public policy (*ordre public*)).

Insofar as the parties have not made a choice under art 3, the law applicable to the life insurance policy must be determined in accordance with art 4 Rome I Regulation. In most cases, art 4(1)(b) Rome I Regulation will apply given that life insurance contracts are 'contracts for the provision of services'. This follows from the reference in Recital (17) Rome I Regulation according to which the concept of 'provision of services' should be interpreted in the same way as when applying art 7 Brussels I Regulation (recast). Therefore art 4(1)(b) Rome I Regulation requires, at the least, that the party who provides the service carries out a particular activity in return for remuneration (cf Case C-533/07 *Falco Privatstiftung, Thomas Rabitsch v Gisela Weller-Lindhorst* [2009] ECR 2009 I-3327, para 29). Life insurance contracts meet these requirements because the insurer's → contractual obligations consist of organizing the collective of the insured, taking over the specific risk and providing insurance cover defined in the policy in return for payment of the insurance premium. This reading of art 4(1)(b) Rome I Regulation is supported by other fields of European Union law where insurance policies are similarly treated as contracts for the provisions of services (cf eg Recital (20) Council Directive 2004/113/EC of 13 December 2004 implementing the principle of equal treatment between men and women in the access to and supply of goods and services, [2004] OJ 2004 L 373/37; art 2 lit. b Directive on distance marketing of consumer financial services).

Article 4(1)(b) Rome I Regulation leads to the application of the law of the country where the service provider has his habitual residence. The law applicable to life insurance contracts is therefore the law at the insurer's habitual residence (cf eg Jürgen Basedow and Jens Scherpe, 'Das internationale Versicherungsvertragsrecht und "Rom I"' in Stephan Lorenz (ed), *Festschrift für Andreas Heldrich zum 70. Geburtstag* (CH Beck 2005) 511, 515; Christian Heinze, 'Insurance Contracts under the Rome I Regulation' [2009] NIPR 445, 450). Since the insurer is a legal person, the habitual residence must be determined according to art 19 Rome I Regulation (→ Domicile, habitual residence and establishment). The → escape clause in art 4(3) may only be drawn upon where the life insurance contract is 'manifestly more closely connected' with another state than the country of habitual residence of the insurer indicated in art 4(1)(b) Rome I Regulation. The mere fact that the risk covered by the insurance policy is located in a state other than the habitual residence may in itself, therefore, never justify the operation of the escape clause.

V. Recognition and enforcement

Within the scope of application of the Brussels I Regulation (recast) (→ Brussels I (Convention and Regulation)), the rules on jurisdiction in art 8 *et seq* apply to disputes in matters relating to life insurance. Recital (13) justifies these special rules for insurance contracts by stating that the 'weaker party should be protected by rules of jurisdiction more favourable to his interests than the general rules provide for'. In light of this, pursuant to art 14(1) Brussels I Regulation (recast), the insurer may usually bring proceedings only in the courts of the Member State in which the defendant (ie the policyholder, insured or beneficiary) is domiciled. Moreover, art 15 Brussels I Regulation (recast) imposes severe restrictions on choice-of-jurisdiction clauses in life insurance contracts (see as to the details Helmut Heiss, 'Article 13' in Ulrich Magnus and Peter Mankowski (eds), *Brussels I Regulation* (2nd edn, Sellier 2012) para 1 ff). Under the Brussels I Regulation (recast), recognition and enforcement of foreign judgments is subject to the rules in art 36 *et seq*.

Particular problems arise in the context of international life insurance contracts and English solvent schemes of arrangement. The latter instrument is used in the (re)insurance business not only with regard to run-off but also in connection with active life insurance portfolios. The German Federal Court of Justice has recently refused to recognize an English scheme under the Brussels I Regulation that would have affected a German life insurance policyholder who contracted with an English insurer (German Federal Court of Justice (BGH), 15 February 2012 [2012] NJW 2113. See also Higher Regional Court (OLG) of Celle, 8 September 2009, [2010] VersR 612. *Contra*, however, Regional Court (LG) Rottweil [2010] BeckRS 13330).

VI. Need for review and possible future developments

The choice-of-law regime for insurance contracts under the Rome I Regulation was in need of reform already at the time it was promulgated: having retained the distinction between mass risks located inside and outside the Member States, art 7 Rome I does not cover all life insurance contracts. Instead, different choice-of-law rules apply: whereas art 7 covers only insurance contracts relating to risks inside the EU, arts 3, 4, 6 and art 23 Rome I Regulation have to be drawn upon for all non-EU risks. In view of the wording of art 1(4), it is uncertain whether art 7 Rome I Regulation is applicable to risks situated in EEA Member States. Finally, where life insurance contracts fall inside the scope of art 7, party autonomy remains limited pursuant to art 7(3) Rome I Regulation. This is true even for experienced parties such as multinational corporations contracting group life insurance for their employees: the exclusion of life insurance from the concept of 'large risks' by virtue of art 7(1), (2) Rome I Regulation prevents these entities from enjoying an adequate level of freedom of choice.

The complex and incongruous nature of European private international law in the field of insurance may, at least in part, explain why the Common Market for life insurance has gained but little practical relevance. Contracting across borders still implies many hurdles for insurers and insured alike. For example, given the constraints under art 7(3) Rome I Regulation, life insurance companies may find it hard to subject policies with insured from different Member States to a single law (cf Louise Merrett, 'Choice of Law in Insurance Contracts under the Rome I Regulation' (2009) 5 J Priv Int L 49, 60). But since the substantive laws of the Member States still reflect considerable differences with regard to life insurance (cf Jürgen Basedow and Till Fock (eds), *Europäisches Versicherungsvertragsrecht*, vol 1–2 (Mohr Siebeck 2002)), calculating and marketing a uniform life insurance policy that may be offered in all EU jurisdictions appears neither legally possible nor economically viable.

JAN D LÜTTRINGHAUS

This is regrettable since a true Common Market for life insurance seems to be desirable from both the insurers' and the insured's perspectives: actuarial science and hence life insurance business relies on the law of large numbers and the diversification of risk. It might therefore be more efficient – and less costly in terms of premiums – if a single 'European' tariff could be developed. This holds especially true for policyholders who make use of the Common Market freedoms and move across borders. In light of this, the creation of a uniform substantive legal regime presents many advantages: the PEICL contain a separate section on the insurance of fixed sums and therefore also apply to life insurance contracts (see art 13:101 PEICL; Jürgen Basedow and others (eds), *Principles of European Insurance Contract Law* (Sellier 2009) 281 *et seq*). Against this backdrop, the European Commission has already explored the need for removing contract law-related obstacles to the design and distribution of life insurance products' and has set up an Expert Group on a European Insurance Contract Law (cf Commission, 'White Paper – An Agenda for Adequate, Safe and Sustainable Pensions' COM(2012) 55 final, 18 and Commission decision of 17 January 2013 on setting up the Commission Expert Group on a European Insurance Contract Law, [2013] OJ C 16/6).

JAN D LÜTTRINGHAUS

Literature

Jürgen Basedow, 'Internal Market (Insurance)' in Jürgen Basedow and others (eds), *The Max Planck Encyclopedia of European Private Law*, vol 1 (OUP 2012) 955; Jürgen Basedow and Wolfgang Drasch, 'Das neue Internationale Versicherungsvertragsrecht' [1991] NJW 785; Jürgen Basedow and Till Fock (eds), *Europäisches Versicherungsvertragsrecht*, vol 1–2 (Mohr Siebeck 2002); Jürgen Basedow and Jens Scherpe, 'Das internationale Versicherungsvertragsrecht und "Rom I"' in Stephan Lorenz (ed), *Festschrift für Andreas Heldrich zum 70. Geburtstag* (CH Beck 2005) 511; Enrico Bensa, *Il Contratto di Assicurazione nel Medio Evo* (Tipografia Maritima Editrice 1884); Christian Heinze, 'Insurance Contracts under the Rome I Regulation' [2009] NIPR 445; Helmut Heiss, 'Versicherungsverträge in "Rom I": Neuerliches Versagen des europäischen Gesetzgebers' in Dietmar Baetge, Jan von Hein and Michael von Hinden (eds), *Festschrift für Jan Kropholler zum 70. Geburtstag* (Mohr Siebeck 2008) 459; Helmut Heiss, 'Article 8; Article 9' in Ulrich Magnus and Peter Mankowski (eds), *Brussels I Regulation* (2nd edn, Sellier 2012); Peter Koch, *Geschichte der Versicherungswirtschaft in Deutschland* (VVW 2012); Jan D Lüttringhaus, 'Art. 1' in Franco Ferrari (ed), *Rome I Regulation* (Sellier 2014) Jan D Lüttringhaus, 'Art. 7 Rom I-VO Versicherungsverträge' in *beck-online. GROSSKOMMENTAR* (CH Beck 2016); Louise Merrett, 'Choice of Law in Insurance Contracts under the Rome I Regulation' (2009) 5 J Priv Int L 49; Stefan Perner, 'Das Internationale Versicherungsvertragsrecht nach Rom I' [2009] IPRax 218.

Lis alibi pendens

I. Concept and notion

Lis alibi pendens (meaning 'dispute elsewhere pending', and more commonly shortened to '*lis pendens*') is a legal rule that allows a court to refuse to exercise jurisdiction when there is parallel litigation already pending in another forum. In some versions of the principle, notably in the EU (per the Brussels Convention (Brussels Convention of 27 September 1968 on jurisdiction and the enforcement of judgments in civil and commercial matters, [1972] OJ L 299/32, consolidated version, [1998] OJ C 27/1), the Brussels I Regulation (Regulation (EC) No 44/2001 of 22 December 2000 on jurisdiction and the recognition and enforcement of judgments in civil and commercial matters, [2001] OJ L 12/1) and the Brussels I Regulation (recast) (Regulation (EU) No 1215/2012 of the European Parliament and of the Council of 12 December 2012 on jurisdiction and the recognition and enforcement of judgments in civil and commercial matters (recast), [2012] OJ L 351/1) (→ Brussels I (Convention and Regulation))), *lis pendens* operates as a strict 'first in time' rule; in that version, once a forum is seized of an action, a court that is subsequently seized of a parallel case must stay its jurisdiction until the court first seized determines it has jurisdiction over the parties and cause of action, at which point the second court must dismiss the action. In cases not covered the Convention and Regulation, most civil law countries give the judge discretion to decline jurisdiction where the priority condition of *lis pendens* is met. The *lis pendens* rule can also encompass related cases rather than just the 'same case', and in such situations, courts are generally given discretion to stay or dismiss the action. Common law countries generally have not adopted a formal *lis pendens* rule but incorporate the fact of a prior pending action into their application of the related doctrine of → *forum non conveniens*.

II. Purpose and function

Lis pendens is closely allied with judgment recognition. Both concepts promote international comity by attempting to avoid or restrict parallel litigation. Indeed, *lis pendens* operates as a preemptive corollary to the *res judicata* effect of foreign judgments. Where a court will render a judgment that will determine an issue between the parties so as to preclude further litigation by application of the rule of *res judicata*, *lis pendens* anticipates the result by preventing the parallel proceeding. Indeed, in some jurisdictions, application of a *lis pendens* priority rule is expressly conditioned upon the likely enforceability of a resulting foreign judgment within the requested forum (eg art 9 Swiss Private international law Act (Bundesgesetz über das Internationale Privatrecht of 18 December 1987, 1988 BBl. I 5, as amended)). That approach has recently been adopted in the Brussels I Regulation (recast) with respect to parallel proceedings in non-Member States (arts 33, 34 Brussels I Regulation (recast)).

Although parallel litigation is often a function of each of the respective parties' assessment of the relative advantages of a particular forum, significant negative consequences often flow from duplicative lawsuits. Parallel litigation may lead to different and/or inconsistent judgments, wastes resources of both the parties and the courts, and creates tensions between governments. In some instances, multiple suits may be filed primarily for harassment and vexatious purposes.

Adoption of a *lis pendens* rule is only one alternative for dealing with parallel litigation, but is the primary approach taken in civil law jurisdictions. Common law jurisdictions are more likely to use the doctrine of → *forum non conveniens* to determine the most appropriate forum for the litigation. Courts invoking *forum non conveniens* will dismiss a case when there is a more appropriate alternative forum, whether or not a parallel lawsuit has been instituted. Thus *forum non conveniens* often negates parallel litigation even before it starts. Where a parallel lawsuit has in fact begun, that factor will be an additional one to be included in the assessment of the more appropriate forum. Common law jurisdictions also have authority to issue → anti-suit injunctions against a party who undertakes parallel litigation, but that remedy is usually limited to situations where an → injunction is necessary to prevent harassment, to prevent evasion of a forum's important public policies or to avoid unnecessary delay, inconvenience and expense.

Although a *lis pendens* rule is intended to avoid the problems associated with parallel proceedings, its requirements present their own set of issues and create other possibilities for strategic behaviour. For many applications of *lis pendens*, the determination of whether proceedings are 'parallel' requires a court to determine whether (i) the parties are sufficiently the same and (ii) whether the proceedings are based on the same cause of action (which itself implicates both the same subject matter and relief sought). In systems that authorize a broader application of *lis pendens* that encompasses 'related actions', the inquiry is more relaxed. The question of whether the causes of action are the 'same' may be straightforward when the proceedings are in the same legal system, but in the transnational context a court will have to compare laws and causes of action from different contexts. The Canadian Supreme Court, in its application of the Quebec Code of Civil Procedure's (RSQ c. C-25, art 165) *lis pendens* rule, offered the following analysis: determine whether the causes of action in the two proceedings are based on the same legal principle, and whether on application they would result in the same effects on the parties' rights and obligations (see *Rocois Construction Inc v Québec Ready Mix Inc and Others* [1990] 2 SCR 440). The EU applies its own standard for categorizing and differentiating between proceedings based on the exact same cause of action, for which its *lis pendens* rule is obligatory, and proceedings based on 'related' actions, for which the rule is discretionary.

A more challenging problem faced by jurisdictions with a *lis pendens* rule is the incentive it creates for parties' strategic pre-litigation behaviour. Under a strict *lis pendens* regime, parties have an incentive to be the first to file (in order to secure the forum they prefer), thereby increasing the likelihood of litigation and decreasing the likelihood of pre-litigation settlement. This 'race to file' often leads a party to pre-empt any possibility of negotiation and to file first in a forum with perceived procedural advantages and/or more favourable law. A strict first-to-file rule has the potential to exacerbate forum shopping (→ Forum (and law) shopping) between national courts as well as international courts and tribunals. On the other hand, although a *lis pendens* rule may encourage a race to file an action, the lack of such a rule increases the risk of a 'race to judgment', where both parties initiate proceedings and then try to obtain the first judgment so as to assert its preclusive effect in the other proceeding.

A final concern relating to parallel litigation – and the application of *lis pendens* – in private international law (outside the EU system) is the lack of a supranational tribunal to standardize how parallel litigation should be handled. No single legal regime has priority over any other, and thus different legal systems take a variety of approaches to parallel litigation leading to the possibility of even greater conflict.

III. Historical development

At its foundation, the doctrine of *lis pendens* initially developed within the internal civil procedure rule of civil law countries and was closely linked to the rules on the recognition of the preclusive effect of judgments, or *res judicata*. Discussion of *lis pendens* can be traced to 17th-century Dutch legal scholarship that developed principles that would be the foundation for the modern study of the conflict of laws and of private international law more generally (see Campbell McLachlan, '*Lis Pendens* in International Litigation' (2009) 336 Rec. des Cours 199). The principles of *lis pendens* and *res judicata* reflected the interest in → comity in a new post-Westphalian reality of separate jurisdictions with different legal systems. The internal civil procedures of civil law European countries began to include *lis pendens* rules, but the extension of these internal *lis pendens* rules to the international level was not self-evident and did not happen quickly. In tension with the idea of an international *lis pendens* was a state's interest in ensuring that its courts not be prevented from hearing cases potentially implicating its own interests. France was one such example. For a century and a half, France's procedural *lis pendens* rule was not accepted by French courts as applicable to foreign proceedings, except in the case of express treaty provisions. Just prior to the time when the 1968 Brussels Convention – which included a strict first-in-time uniform *lis pendens* rule for Member States of the EU – entered into force in France (1973), the Cour de Cassation finally accepted the *lis pendens* doctrine as applicable to other international cases (see *Soc Miniera de Fragne c. Cie européenne d'équipement industriel*, Cass. Civ., 26 November 1974). Italy was even more resistant. Until a 1995 revision to Italian law, art 3 of the Italian Code of Civil Procedure (Codice di procedura civile of 21 April 1942, R.D., 28 October 1940, No 1443 Gazz.Uff. No 253) provided: 'the competence of the Italian courts is not excluded by the fact that the same case or a connected claim is pending elsewhere before a foreign judge' (see Gerhard Walter, '*Lis Alibi Pendens* and *Forum Non Conveniens*: From Confrontation via Co-ordination to Collaboration' (2002) 4 E.J.L.R. 69).

The reluctance to extend *lis pendens* internationally has been tied to the larger question of whether one national order is prepared to recognize and give priority to judicial processes in other systems in the interests of the larger purpose of creating an international and harmonized civil procedure. Even without acceptance of that broader goal, the desire to control forum shopping, to promote judicial efficiency and to avoid multiple and inconsistent judgments has led many jurisdictions to extend their internal *lis pendens* rule covering the 'same cause of action' to international cases. One of the earliest was art 9 of the Swiss PILA which provided: 'If a lawsuit on the same matter between the same parties is already pending abroad, the Swiss court must stay the proceedings if it is to be expected that the foreign court will, within a reasonable time, render a judgment recognizable in Switzerland.'

Lis pendens (a strict priority in time rule of the 'same action' and a discretionary rule for 'related cases') was included in the original Brussels Convention of 1968. The geographic scope was enlarged with ratification of the Lugano Convention of 1988 (Lugano Convention of 16 September 1988 on jurisdiction and the enforcement of judgments in civil and commercial matters, [1988] OJ L 319/9) and with the addition of Member States to the EU. Although the Conventions' rules applied only to proceedings in other Member States where uniform rules for jurisdiction and the recognition of judgments were also required, a more expansive use of *lis pendens* was found in the national laws of many of those countries. As of 2007, 19 Member States of the EU had adopted *lis pendens* for international non-EU cases (Arnaud Nuyts and others, *Study on Residual Jurisdiction – General Report* (Brussels 2007)). In most of those states, the *lis pendens* rule for the 'same cause of action' is one of discretion and not the strict first-in-time rule of the EU regime. A *lis pendens* rule in cases of related proceedings was much slower to expand internationally, and only → France of the EU Member States extended its 'related proceedings' *lis pendens* rule to cover international cases. However, since 2015, with the introduction in arts 33 and 34 of the Brussels I Regulation (recast), Member States of the EU will now apply a discretionary *lis pendens* rule to both the 'same' and 'related' causes of action when there is a proceeding in a third state if it is expected that the court of the third state will give a judgment capable of recognition and/or enforcement in that Member State.

The extension of *lis pendens* rules to private international litigation opened the door, particularly within the EU system, for strategic behaviour by litigants in various 'race-to-file' scenarios. Court backlogs in countries such as Italy and Greece gave rise to new forum-shopping and gamesmanship opportunities through use of *lis pendens*. For example, in intellectual property cases, a potential infringer, taking advantage of the delay in the Italian courts, could commence proceedings in Italy for a declaration of non-infringement, thereby preventing the patent holder from bringing its own suit elsewhere. With such delay postponing even a decision on jurisdiction for years, this 'Italian torpedo' became a popular strategy. In another scenario, borrowers could gain an advantage by bringing a first proceeding in slower and potentially sympathetic courts, regardless of whether a more appropriate forum for the proceeding existed elsewhere. Even if unlikely to be successful on the merits at the end of the litigation, the borrower could drag the case out for many years, during which time the lender was unable to sue in any other EU country. One possible escape from such tactics was the use of an exclusive forum-selection agreement between the parties (see *Continental Bank v Aeakos SA* [1994] 1 WLR 588 (CA)). However, this option was rendered ineffective when the EU Court of Justice ruled in Case C-116/02 *Erich Gasser GmbH v MISAT Srl* ([2003] ECR I-14693) that the absolute priority rule of the court first seized applied, irrespective of either an exclusive jurisdiction clause or the prospect of delay. However, art 31(2) in the revision of the Brussels I Regulation (recast) has reversed the result in *Gasser* by expressly providing that where a court of a Member State has exclusive jurisdiction by virtue of a forum-selection agreement, courts of other Member States must stay proceedings until that court declares it has no jurisdiction under the agreement.

Parallel to the development of *lis pendens* rules in civil law countries was the development of anti-suit injunctions and the → *forum non conveniens* doctrine in common law countries as the primary tools for addressing parallel litigation. Anti-suit injunctions are not used in civil law countries, and have been described as infringements of the sovereignty of other nations (see *Re the Enforcement of an English Anti-suit Injunction*, Higher Regional Court (OLG) of Düsseldorf, [1997] ILPr 320). Nor are anti-suit injunctions appropriate under the Brussels Convention, the Brussels I Regulation and the Brussels I Regulation (recast) even when sought in support of its own *lis pendens* rule. In Case C-159/02 *Gregory Paul Turner v Felix Fareed Ismail Grovit, Harada Ltd and Changepoint SA* [2004] ECR I-3565, the ECJ held that an English anti-suit injunction, issued to restrain Spanish proceedings 'related to' to an earlier filed English action, constituted an unjustifiable interference with the court of another Member State and was inconsistent with the principle of mutual trust underlying the Brussels Convention. The anti-suit injunction in England was first used primarily in cases where an English judgment had already been rendered, thereby protecting the *res judicata* effect of a judgment. It later developed as a remedy in the context of parallel pending proceedings with a two-step requirement: that the present forum was the most appropriate for the trial of the action and that the pursuit of the foreign action was perceived as oppressive (*Societé Nationale Industrielle Aerospatiale v Lee Kui Jak* [1987] AC 871 (Privy Council)). Other common law countries, such as → Canada and → Australia have also used the remedy of an anti-suit injunction to control transnational parallel litigation. Courts in the → USA are generally reluctant to issue anti-suit injunctions to restrain parallel proceedings except when necessary to protect the court's jurisdiction or to prevent the evasion of important public policies.

In common law countries, *lis pendens* has not emerged as an independent basis for controlling parallel litigation. Rather, the existence and effect of foreign proceedings has been an additional factor as part of a *forum non conveniens* inquiry. In England, case-law holds that 'the existence of simultaneous proceedings is no more than a factor relevant to the determination of the appropriate forum' (Lord Collins of Mapesbury and others (eds), *Dicey, Morris & Collins on the Conflict of Laws* (15th edn, Sweet & Maxwell 2012) 12–043). In other countries, the fact of a prior pending proceeding may be given more substantial weight.

IV. Legal sources and regulation

1. Civil law regimes

Many civil law countries included a *lis pendens* rule in their procedural codes that applied to domestic cases and now have extended that rule to transnational litigation. For example: the French Code of Civil Procedure ((Nouveau) Code de Procédure Civile of 1 January 1976, décret No 75–1123, 5 December 1975), art 100, states:

> Where the same cause of action is pending between two courts of the same level, which are equally competent to handle the matter, the last court informed shall decline jurisdiction in favour of the first one informed if one of the parties so requests. In the absence of such a request, the court may do so of its own motion.

In the international context outside of the EU context, the application of the French rule gives the judge discretion to decline jurisdiction. This discretionary application of *lis pendens* appears to be characteristic of EU countries' applications of the concept to proceedings in non-Member States (Campbell McLachlan, '*Lis Pendens* in International Litigation' (2009) 336 Rec. des Cours 199). In a number of countries, there is no explicit statutory or code provision for the application of *lis pendens* in international cases, but analogies are drawn to *lis pendens* for domestic cases ('General Report' in JJ Fawcett, *Declining Jurisdiction in Private international law* (Clarendon 1995) 31–2). Statutory provisions in several states tie the extension of *lis pendens* in international cases to the larger issue of recognition of judgments. Article 9 Swiss PILA requires a stay of prior proceedings in favour of a foreign court only where that court's judgment would be recognized in the forum. The Italian code provision (art 7 Legge di diritto internazionale privato e processuale, part of the Italian Private international law Act (Riforma del Sistema italiano di diritto internazionale private, Act No 218 of 31 May 1995 in Gazz. Uff., Supplemento Ordinario No 128 of 3 June l995, as amended)) requires Italian courts to stay proceedings if a prior lawsuit about the same subject matter and right between the same parties is before a foreign court, provided they consider that the foreign decision can have an impact in the Italian legal order (Gerhard Walter, '*Lis Alibi Pendens* and *Forum Non Conveniens*: From Confrontation via Co-ordination to Collaboration' (2002) 4 E.J.L.R. 69). Other countries, such as → Sweden, → Germany and the → Netherlands, appear to tie a discretionary application of *lis pendens* to a prognosis of recognition of the judgment (JJ Fawcett, *Declining Jurisdiction in Private international law* (Clarendon 1995) 36–8).

2. Common law regimes

In Common law jurisdictions, *lis pendens* has not emerged as an independent basis for staying or dismissing an action. Rather, the doctrine of → *forum non conveniens*, which can apply even when no prior proceeding is pending, considers the fact of an earlier-filed action as one of the factors to be taken into account, and that factor may tip the balance in favour of staying or dismissing the action. In the USA, an additional doctrine of 'international abstention' has sometimes been invoked in situations of foreign parallel proceedings.

a) United States

No federal statutory or constitutional provision governs parallel proceedings in US and foreign courts. A few states in the USA have explicit statutory or rule provisions for stays or dismissals in deference to parallel actions, but such provisions often operate only domestically and do not always apply to actions in foreign courts. State courts have generally relied on principles of *forum non conveniens* to deal with parallel litigation in both domestic and foreign courts. The federal courts, in addition to relying on general principles of *forum non conveniens*, have sometimes followed approaches adopted for dealing with problems that arise domestically from a dual system of state and federal courts with concurrent jurisdiction over many matters. The issue of how to deal with prior foreign parallel litigation is often characterized as one of 'international abstention'.

One form of domestic parallel litigation within the USA results from its dual system of state and federal courts. In *Colorado River Water Conservations District v United States*, 424 U.S. 800 (1976), the Supreme Court, in a case involving state-federal proceedings relating to water rights held by the US government, stated that jurisdiction can be declined by a federal court only in 'exceptional circumstances'.

The Court emphasized the 'unflagging obligation' of the federal courts to exercise the jurisdiction given to them. A subsequent Supreme Court decision, *Quackenbush v Allstate Ins Co*, 517 U.S. 706 (1996), reaffirmed that principle, stating that federal courts had authority to abstain only where the relief being sought was 'equitable or discretionary'. A different view was taken in an earlier Supreme Court decision, *Landis v North American Co*, 299 U.S. 248 (1936), a case involving parallel proceedings in two different federal courts. There, the Court permitted a stay on the grounds that it was within the district court's discretion, without any requirement of 'exceptional circumstances'. For parallel litigation pending in two federal courts, the preference is in favour of the first-filed case, creating something very close to a system of *lis pendens*. In such cases, a federal court other than the first seized may stay the parallel proceeding or the court first seized may issue an anti-suit injunction (see, eg, *National Equipment Rental, Ltd v Fowler*, 287 F.2d 43 (2d Cir 1961)).

Because no Supreme Court case has addressed the issue of parallel proceedings in international cases, the dual line of domestic cases continues to influence how lower courts deal with the question in transnational litigation. The *Landis* line of authority has led courts to find that it has 'inherent power to dismiss or stay' an action in light of pending litigation in a foreign court. One such case is *Turner Entertainment Co v Degeto Film Gmbh*, 25 F.3d 1512 (11th Cir 1994), which identified three goals in addressing concurrent international jurisdiction: a sense of comity, fairness to litigants and efficient use of judicial resources. In assessing fairness, the court considered the order of filing, the convenience of the forum and the possible prejudice to the parties. Also, in *Posner v Essex Insurance Co*, 178 F.3d 1209 (11th Cir 1999), the Court of Appeals concluded that a stay of federal-court proceedings was appropriate where a prior action with significantly common issues and parties had been filed in Bermuda almost a year prior to the US action and where the Bermuda court was competent to hear the claims and would use fair and just proceedings to decide the case.

Other courts, relying on *Colorado River*, have allowed parallel litigation to proceed, concluding that a federal court owes no greater deference to foreign courts than to its own state courts (*Neuchatel Swiss General Ins Co v Lufthansa Airlines*, 925 F.2d 1193 (9th Cir 1991)). Such cases reflect the view that a plaintiff has a right to choose its own forum permitting each sovereign to reach a judgment and apply the findings of one to the other.

Without a uniform *lis pendens* rule in the USA, the result of parallel litigation is often a race to judgment, since the case that reaches judgment will have preclusive effects. Additionally, because the USA is relatively liberal regarding the recognition and enforcement of foreign judgments, a foreign case (even if initiated later) may control and have preclusive effects in the USA if the foreign court reached judgment first. A 2005 proposal by the American Law Institute (ALI) for a US federal statute on foreign judgment recognition included a provision for 'Declination of Jurisdiction When Prior Action is Pending'. The proposal provided for a declination of jurisdiction when an action concerning the same subject matter and including the same or related parties had previously been brought in a foreign court if the foreign court had an acceptable basis of jurisdiction and the foreign court was likely to render recognizable judgment. It also identified several situations – such as an attempt to frustrate an action in the more appropriate forum or the bringing of vexatious or frivolous proceedings – as exceptions to the rule of priority (Linda Silberman, 'A Proposed *Lis Pendens* Rule for Courts in the United States: The International Judgments Project of the American Law Institute, in Intercontinental Cooperation through Private international law' in Talia Einhorn and Kurt Siehr (eds), *Intercontinental Cooperation through Private international law* (TMC Asser Press 2004)).

b) Other common law jurisdictions
Historically, the English courts had taken the position that where two opposing parties had begun rival proceedings, the doctrine of *lis pendens* was 'no part of the law of England' (Campbell McLachlan, '*Lis Pendens* in International Litigation' (2009) 336 Rec. des Cours 199). However, subsequent cases adopted an approach that used *forum non conveniens* principles, accepted by the House of Lords in England in the *Spiliada Maritime Corp v Cansulex Ltd* case (*Spiliada Maritime Corp v Cansulex Ltd* [1987] AC 460 (HL)) to consider the impact of pending foreign litigation as part of that inquiry. However, the existence of simultaneous proceedings is only one factor

LINDA SILBERMAN

relevant to the determination of the appropriate forum in the application of *forum non conveniens* (Lord Collins of Mapesbury and others (eds), *Dicey, Morris & Collins on the Conflict of Laws* (15th edn, Sweet & Maxwell 2012) 12-044). For example, foreign litigation may be of no relevance if one party has commenced proceedings for tactical purposes, as in the case of a negative declaration, or if the proceedings are only at an initial stage. On the other hand, if the foreign proceedings are far advanced and likely to determine the entire dispute, the parallel proceedings will be given substantial (but not decisive) weight (Campbell McLachlan, '*Lis Pendens* in International Litigation' (2009) 336 Rec. des Cours 199). Canada, too, appears to have merely recalibrated its doctrine of → *forum non conveniens* to take into account the special factual conditions raised by the existence of an earlier-filed parallel case. Australia, among common law countries, applies a more restrictive standard in determining whether a case should be stayed or dismissed on *forum non conveniens* grounds, reflecting a principle that a plaintiff's choice of forum ought not to be lightly disturbed when no other proceedings are underway. However, in cases where foreign parallel proceedings are underway, courts in Australia are also more likely to stay or dismiss the action.

3. *European Union*

In the EU legal regime, the *lis pendens* rule was first laid out in arts 21-3 of the Brussels Convention (which for purposes of *lis pendens* is identical to the 1988 Lugano Convention). It was amended by arts 27-30 of the Brussels I Regulation, and then again by arts 29-30 of the Brussels I Regulation (recast). The substance of the *lis pendens* rules for Member States in the Convention and Regulation is substantially the same, although the Brussels I Regulation (in art 30) introduced a European definition for when a court shall be deemed to be seized. Broadly speaking, the EU *lis pendens* regime differentiated between proceedings based on the same cause of action (art 21 Brussels Convention, art 27 Brussels I regulation, art 29 Brussels I Regulation (recast)) and those based on related actions (art 22 Brussels Convention, art 28 Brussels I Regulation, art 30 Brussels I Regulation (recast)).

If the causes of action are determined to be the same, then the *lis pendens* rule is obligatory and any court other than the first seized must decline jurisdiction. Further clarifying, the ECJ ruled in the 1991 Case C-351/89 *Overseas Union Insurance Ltd and Others v New Hampshire Insurance Company* [1991] ECR I-3317 that the 'same cause of action' obligation applies to all proceedings commenced in the EU regardless of where the parties come from. In Case C-144/86 *Gubisch Maschinenfabrik KG v Giulio Palumbo* ([1987] ECR 4861) and Case C-406/92 *The owners of the cargo lately laden on board the ship 'Tatry' v the owners of the ship 'Maciej Rataj'* ([1994] ECR I-5439), the ECJ determined that the 'same cause of action' test is whether the factual basis of the claim and the laws to be applied are the same with a view to obtaining the same basic outcome. The 'same cause of action' mandatory first-filed rule also requires the parties in both proceedings to be substantially the same. The Court in *The Tatry* determined that *lis pendens* would not apply if there are two completely different parties bringing the actions. If the parties are closely related, they may be considered the same for purposes of the rule if they have 'dissociable interests' (see Case C-351/96 *Drouot Assurances SA v Consolidated Metallurgical Industries and others* [1998] ECR I-3075). An example is a judgment against one party that would have the force of *res judicata* as against the other, as when, for example, an insurer exercises its right of subrogation to sue in the name of its insured. If the causes of action in parallel proceedings are only determined to be related, the *lis pendens* rule is discretionary (courts other than the first seized 'may' stay their proceedings). Additionally, a court other than the court first seized may decline jurisdiction upon application of a party if the court first seized has jurisdiction over both related actions and consolidation is permitted (Stephen B Burbank, 'Jurisdictional Equilibrium, The Proposed Hague Convention and Progress in National Law' (2001) 49 Am.J.Comp.L. 203, 217). The Brussels I Regulation (recast) (art 31(2)) introduced an important exception to the strict EU first-in-time rule for situations in which the parties have agreed to an exclusive choice-of-forum clause. Article 31(2) provides that a court of a Member State shall stay proceedings until such time as the court seized on the basis of such agreement declares that it has no jurisdiction under the agreement, and once it does so, art 31(3) mandates that the non-chosen court dismisses the action. The provision overruled the earlier Court of Justice case (Case C-116/02 *Erich Gasser GmbH v MISAT Srl* [2003] ECR I-14693), which had been heavily criticized in commentary.

4. International regimes

a) Public international law

Due to the relatively limited number of international courts and tribunals, parallel proceedings on the level of public international law (ie involving two international judicial organs) are rare, and consequently the use of *lis pendens* rules has been rare as well. Debate continues as to whether *lis pendens* is recognized as a general rule or principle in international law in the relations between international courts and tribunals. As early as 1925, the PCIJ noted in *Certain German Interests in Polish Upper Silesia ((Germany v Poland)*, 1925 PCIJ (Ser. A) No. 6), that 'It is a much disputed question in the teachings of legal authorities and in the jurisprudence of the principal countries whether the doctrine of litispendance, the object of which is to prevent the possibility of conflicting judgments, can be invoked in international relations . . .' However, the principle of *lis pendens* can be found in a number of international conventions. For example, art 35 of the ECHR (European Convention of 4 November 1950 for the Protection of Human Rights and Fundamental Freedoms, 213 UNTS 221), provides that '[t]he Court shall not deal with any application submitted under Art. 34 that is substantially the same as a matter that . . . has already been submitted to another procedure of international investigation or settlement and contains no relevant new information'. Nonetheless, the potential for conflict among public international tribunals is less likely than in private international law since international tribunals are limited to disputes arising under its constitutive treaty (Campbell McLachlan, '*Lis Pendens* in International Litigation' (2009) 336 Rec. des Cours 199).

b) Private international law

Proposals for international *lis pendens* rules have been made by a number of institutions, such as the Institut de Droit International in its 'Principles for Determining When the Use of the Doctrine of Forum Non Conveniens and Anti-Suit Injunctions is Appropriate' ((Collins and Droz, Rapporteurs) (2002–2003) 70-II Annuaire 252), the American Law Institute and → UNIDROIT in its Principles of Transnational Civil Procedure (ALI/UNIDROIT Rules of Transnational Civil Procedure (text of the Principles and the accompanying commentary were adopted by the American Law Institute (ALI) in May 2004 and by the International Institute for the Unification of Private Law (UNIDROIT) in April 2004, (2004) 4 Unif.L.Rev. 758)), and the International Civil and Commercial Litigation Committee of the International Law Association in its Leuven/London Principles on Declining and Referring Jurisdiction in International Civil and Commercial Litigation (Res. 1/2000). In addition, the → Hague Conference on Private International Law proposed a Preliminary Draft Convention on Jurisdiction and Foreign Judgments in Civil and Commercial Matters (adopted by the Special Commission, Preliminary Document No 11 of August 2000)that included provisions for a *lis pendens* rule mitigated by *forum non conveniens* flexibility in the first-seized court.

In 2004, the Institut de Droit, addressing issues of → *forum non conveniens* and anti-suit injunctions, adopted a Report stating that parallel litigation between the same or related parties should be discouraged. The UNIDROIT/ALI Principles included both a *forum non conveniens* provision (for a manifestly inappropriate court) and a *lis pendens* provision (for a prior pending action). The latter provided: the court should decline jurisdiction or suspend the proceeding when the dispute is previously pending in another court competent to exercise jurisdiction, unless it appears that the dispute will not be fairly, effectively and expeditiously resolved in that forum (Principle 2.6). The Leuven/London Principles combined an obligation of a second-seized court to stay proceedings involving the same parties and the same subject matter of a prior proceeding with an obligation by the first-seized court to consider whether the second-seized court was a 'manifestly more appropriate forum for the determination of the merits of the matter' (Principles 4.1 and 4.3). The 1999 Hague Draft Convention on Jurisdiction and Judgments, which ultimately did not go forward, included provisions on *lis pendens* (art 21) and *forum non conveniens* (art 22) that reflected both civil and common law experiences with parallel litigation as well as the influence of the Leuven/London Principles. In addition to various tweaks of the *lis pendens* provision in the Brussels Convention and the Brussels I Regulation with respect to the scope of the proceedings, the time reference for the court first seized, and a safeguard for delay in proceedings in the first-filed court, the Hague Draft Convention included two limitations on a strict *lis pendens* rule. The first was to exclude the application of *lis pendens* when the first-filed action was a negative declaration. The second was to introduce a limited type of *forum non conveniens* to avoid the first-in-time rule if the court first seized determined that the court second seized is clearly more appropriate to resolve the dispute. The criteria for that determination are found in art 22, which provided a general rule for declining jurisdiction in 'exceptional circumstances', reflecting a more restrictive version of the traditional common-law *forum non conveniens* doctrine (Linda Silberman, 'A Proposed *Lis Pendens* Rule for Courts in the United States: The International Judgments Project of the American Law Institute, in Intercontinental Cooperation through Private international law' in Talia Einhorn and Kurt Siehr (eds), *Intercontinental Cooperation through Private international law* (TMC Asser Press 2004) 354–5).

LINDA SILBERMAN

Literature

ALI/UNIDROIT, *Principles of Transnational Civil Procedure* (CUP 2004); Stephen B Burbank, 'Jurisdictional Equilibrium, The Proposed Hague Convention and Progress in National Law' (2001) 49 Am.J.Comp.L. 203; Lord Collins of Mapesbury and others (eds), *Dicey, Morris & Collins on the Conflict of Laws* (15th edn, Sweet & Maxwell 2012); Louis F Del Duca and George A Zaphiriou, 'Rules for Declining Jurisdiction in Civil and Commercial Matters: *Forum Non Conveniens, Lis Pendens*' (1994) 42 Am.J.Comp.L. Sup. 245; JJ Fawcett, *Declining Jurisdiction in Private international law* (Clarendon Press, Oxford Private international law Series 1995); James P George, 'International Parallel Litigation: A Survey of Current Conventions and Model Laws' (2002) 37 Tex.J.Int'l L. 499; Trevor Hartley, 'How to Abuse the Law and (Maybe) Come Out on Top: Bad-Faith Proceedings Under the Brussels Jurisdiction and Judgments Convention' in James AR Nafziger and Symeon C Symeonides (eds), *Law and Justice in a Multistate World: Essays in Honor of Arthur T. Von Mehren* (Martinus Nijhoff 2002) 73–81; Campbell McLachlan, '*Lis Pendens* in International Litigation' (2009) 336 Rec. des Cours 199; Arnaud Nuyts and others, *Study on Residual Jurisdiction: General Report* (Brussels 2007); August Reinisch, 'The Use and Limits of *Res Judicata* and *Lis Pendens* as Procedural Tools to Avoid Conflicting Dispute Settlement Outcomes' (2004) 3 Law & Prac. Int'l Cts. & Tribunals 37; Rolf A Schütze, '*Lis Pendens* and Related Actions' (2002) 4 E.J.L.R. 57; Linda Silberman, 'The Impact of Jurisdictional Rules and Recognition Practice on International Business Transactions: The U.S. Regime' (2003) 26 Hous.J.Int'l L. 327; Linda Silberman, 'A Proposed *Lis Pendens* Rule for Courts in the United States: The International Judgments Project of the American Law Institute, in Intercontinental Cooperation through Private international law' in Talia Einhorn and Kurt Siehr (eds), *Intercontinental Cooperation through Private international law* (TMC Asser Press 2004); Louise E Teitz, 'Both Sides of the Coin: A Decade of Parallel Proceedings and Enforcement of Foreign Judgments in Transnational Litigation' (2004) 10 Roger Williams U.L.Rev. 1; Gerhard Walter, '*Lis Alibi Pendens* and *Forum Non Conveniens*: From Confrontation via Co-ordination to Collaboration' (2002) 4 E.J.L.R. 69.

Local data

I. Introduction: background and context

The concept of '*datum*' was first mentioned by *Brainerd Currie* (Brainerd Currie, 'On the Displacement of the Law of the Forum' (1958) 58 Colum.L.Rev. 964, reprinted in Brainerd Currie, *Selected Essays on the Conflict of Laws* (Duke University Press 1963) 66 ff) (→ Currie, Brainerd) and was further developed by *Albert A Ehrenzweig* in his theory of local and moral data (Albert Ehrenzweig, 'Local and Moral Data in the Conflict of Laws: Terra Incognita' (1966) 16 Buff.L.Rev. 55 ff) (→ Ehrenzweig, Albert A). For moral data, application of the → *lex fori* is mandatory, notwithstanding the existence of foreign elements that would otherwise suggest the application of foreign law. These are cases where justice or equity require reliance on the law of the forum – hence, moral *datum*. The theory of local data, by contrast, contains an 'automatic reference to foreign rules' (Albert Ehrenzweig, 'Local and Moral Data in the Conflict of Laws: Terra Incognita' (1966) 16 Buff.L.Rev. 55, 56). There is no rejection of foreign law; on the contrary, foreign law is generally openly admitted. Local data in this sense mainly concern local rules of administration and security regulating individual activities. Under the → Rome II Regulation (Regulation (EC) No 864/2007 of the European Parliament and of the Council of 11 July 2007 on the law applicable to non-contractual obligations (Rome II), [2007] OJ L 199/40), these norms are called 'rules of safety and conduct' (art 17). The Swiss Private international law Act (Bundesgesetz über das Internationale Privatrecht of 18 December 1987, BBl. I 5) uses a similar definition in art 142(2). Further examples can be found in international conventions, notably the Hague Traffic Accident Convention (Hague Convention of 4 May 1971 on the law applicable to traffic accidents, 965 UNTS 415) (→ Traffic accidents) and the Hague Products Liability Convention (Hague Convention of 2 October 1973 on the law applicable to products liability, 1056 UNTS 191) (→ Products liability). Regard to local data is given whenever the *lex causae* is not the law of the place of conduct. This may be the case if conduct and injury diverge and the *lex loci damni* applies. Also, application of the *lex domicilii communis*, or of a law determined under an escape clause (see, eg art 4(3) Rome II Regulation), may lead to such a divergence. In these cases, the question arises whether and how the law of the place of conduct should be considered or applied – after all, it may both determine the parties' expectations and activities, on the one hand, and express local lawmakers' interest in regulating the socio-economic circumstances in their territory, on the other hand.

II. Distinction: two variants of local data

1. Overriding mandatory provisions

Friedrich Carl von Savigny explained tort liability rules as part of the local *ordre public* (→ Savigny, Friedrich Carl von; → Public policy (*ordre public*)). The → *lex fori* would always govern tort claims (Friedrich Carl von Savigny, *System des heutigen römischen Rechts*, vol 8 (2nd reprint of ed Berlin 1849, Scientia Verlag 1981) s 374). This approach illustrates policy makers' special interest in tort liability at the time. The *lex fori* was to be applied without regard to the law that may have otherwise been applicable. Even though tort liability, in general, is no longer strictly characterized as an issue of public policy (→ Torts), a category of invariably applicable norms can also be found in modern → choice of law, particularly in art 16 of the → Rome II Regulation. A similar reference is made in art 9 of the Rome I Regulation (Regulation (EC) No 593/2008 of the European Parliament and of the Council of 17 June 2008 on the law applicable to contractual obligations (Rome I), [2008] OJ L 177/6; → Rome Convention and Rome I Regulation (contractual obligations)). This is the category of so-called → overriding mandatory provisions (*lois d'application immédiate*, or *Eingriffsnormen*). Two scenarios can be distinguished with respect to the practical implementation of foreign mandatory provisions. First, a foreign norm may be applied as a rule of law or it may be considered when applying the *lex causae* with special regard to effectuating the underlying foreign policy. Second – and of interest to local-data theory – a foreign norm, instead of being applied as law, may be considered only with respect to its actual consequences. In this case, the effects of a foreign law's enforcement (or potential enforcement) are treated as a factual component of the case – hence, not as 'law' but as 'data'. Such regard for local data is particularly evident in international contract law, where a foreign norm may be deemed to effectuate an impossibility of performance on the side of one party. Such consideration of local data accommodates individual parties' interests. In addition, even though the forum does not apply or expressly endorse the foreign norm at issue, it comes close to enforcing its policy.

2. Rules of safety and conduct

The second variant of local data is of large relevance in tort law theory and practice. It concerns the application or consideration of rules on safety and conduct of the *lex loci actus* in cases where → choice of law has determined a different law to be applied. An oft-enunciated hypothetical situation is a → traffic accident between two French tourists in England. While the *lex domicilii communis* (see, eg art 4(2) Rome II Regulation) may be applied with respect to the liability of the tortfeasor, it is the English rule of driving on the left side of the street that provides for the 'local data'. Consideration of this rule is mandatory when assessing the tortfeasor's negligence in driving the car. Hence, the French tortfeasor cannot claim, for instance, that he was acting in accordance with French law while driving his car on the right side of the street.

The *raison-d'être* of local-data considerations is often described as a matter of fact, or a logical necessity (see, eg German Federal Court of Justice (BGH), 57 BGHZ 265, 268 ('*Natur der Sache*')). Virtually universal agreement exists that considering local data accommodates the interests of foreign lawmakers in controlling local socio-economic transacting (German Federal Court of Justice (BGH), 57 BGHZ 265, 268; Hans Stoll, 'Deliktstatut und Tatbestandswirkung ausländischen Rechts' in Peter Feuerstein (ed), *Multum non multa: Festschrift für Kurt Lipstein aus Anlass seines 70. Geburtstages* (CF Müller 1980) 259, 261). With respect to its doctrinal implementation, however, two opposing camps exist. The dominant opinion puts forth a substantive-law approach (*sachrechtliche Lösung*). Its proponents explain that local rules are not 'applied' as law but merely taken account of 'as a matter of fact'. The violation of a foreign rule will thus be taken as a given by the trier of facts when applying the *lex causae* to the dispute at bar (see generally Hans Stoll, 'Die Behandlung von Verhaltensnormen und Sicherheitsvorschriften' in Ernst von Caemmerer (ed), *Vorschläge und Gutachten zur Reform des deutschen internationalen Privatrechts der außervertraglichen Schuldverhältnisse* (Mohr 1983) 160, 174–5). This perspective also governs under the Rome II Regulation. In the words of the European Commission, 'Taking account of foreign law is not the same thing as applying it: the court will apply only the law that is applicable under the conflict rule, but it must take account of another law as a point of fact . . .' Accordingly, foreign rules are treated as law only with respect to the standard of proof (Commission, 'Proposal for the Rome II Regulation' COM(2003) 427 final, 25; Andrew Dickinson, *The Rome II Regulation: The Law Applicable to Non-contractual Obligations* (OUP 2008) [15.33]; James J Fawcett, Janeen M Carruthers and Peter M North, *Cheshire, North & Fawcett Private international law* (14th edn, OUP 2008) 855). The contrary opinion, though hardly defensible in light of the Rome II Regulation, demands the 'application' of local law 'as law' (eg Heinrich Dörner, 'Alte und neue Probleme des Internationalen Deliktrechts' in Gerhard Hohloch (ed), *Festschrift für Hans Stoll zum 75. Geburtstag* (Mohr Siebeck 2001) 491, 497; Heinrich Dörner, 'Neue Entwicklungen im Internationalen Verkehrsunfallrecht' [1994] JR 6, 9–10). This approach requires that different issues of the case be governed by different laws. The question whether a rule of safety or conduct has been violated will be answered by direct reference to the *lex loci actus* (eg Christian von Bar, 'Grundfragen des Internationalen Deliktrechts' [1985] JZ 961, 968; William A Reppy, Jr, 'Eclecticism in Methods for Resolving Tort and Contract Conflict of Laws: The United States and the European Union' (2008) 82 Tul.L.Rev. 2053, 2086 (arguing that taking account of local law instead of applying it is 'bizarre')).

III. Foundation

1. The traditional approach

In European → choice of law, notably under the Rome II Regulation, the *lex causae* is determined in accordance with party interests, among other things (see, eg Recitals (16), (33), (34)). Other concerns of so-called conflicts justice are the predictability of the outcome of litigation, certainty regarding the applicable law, and the free movement of judgments, as well as harmony of decision making (see Recitals (6), (14), (16); see also generally Jan Kropholler, *Internationales Privatrecht* (6th edn, Mohr Siebeck 2006) ss 3 ff). As it seems, the civil-law doctrine of private international law barely allows for a consideration of state interests (Christian von Bar, 'Grundfragen des Internationalen Deliktrechts' [1985] JZ 961, 964 ff; Symeon C Symeonides, 'Rome II and Tort Conflicts: A Missed Opportunity' (2008) 56 Am.J.Comp.L. 173, 183, 214 *et passim*). It thus also seems to largely disregard substantive-law policies. And even though recent black-letter choice-of-law rules accommodate for substantive policies (for Rome II Regulation see eg Gerhard Wagner, 'Die neue Rom II-Verordnung' [2008] IPRax 1, 15), the strictness of many norms still does not offer much flexibility to the trier of facts.

These characteristics are combined with another fundament of traditional choice-of-law technique: the Rome II Regulation, by and large, does not provide for an issue-by-issue analysis. There is generally no → *dépeçage* in conflicts law (Symeon C Symeonides, 'Rome II and Tort Conflicts: A Missed Opportunity' (2008) 56 Am.J.Comp.L. 173, 185; Hans Stoll, 'Zur Flexibilisierung des europäischen internationalen Deliktsrechts – Vermittelnde Kritik aus Amerika an der "ROM II-VO"' in Peter Jarbonegg, Ferdinand Kerschner and Andreas Riedler (eds), *Haftung und Versicherung: Festschrift für Rudolf Reischauer* (Verl Österreich 2010) 389, 393). This is lucidly illustrated by art 15 of the Rome II Regulation, which provides that, in general, all issues of a case are to be governed by a single law.

2. Disentangling expectations and policies

But the picture is no longer so black and white. Modern European choice of law has actually come a long way toward a more policy-oriented analysis. It is for this reason, however, that upon a closer look, the theory of local data can still be characterized as a sore spot in theory and practice. Giving regard to rules of safety and conduct actually illustrates that the paradigm shift in Europe has come only halfway. European doctrine still adheres to a largely formal analysis of private parties' concerns, notably their expectations. Yet giving regard to expectations, albeit often an adequate aspect of conflicts analysis, does not always provide for a valid and consistent instrument. An additional look at the substantive policies at play in international tort scenarios is required.

a) A modest change of paradigms

It is important to keep in mind that the once-deemed 'apolitical' nature of *Savignian* → choice of law has never in fact been reality. In addition to the concern for private-party interests, modern European choice of law under the Rome II Regulation also contains entry points for a consideration of substantive policies (see, eg Recitals (20), (21); see also arts 14(2), 14(3), 16, 26). One of these entry points is the provision on local rules of conduct and security contained in art 17. The theory of local data is deemed to emanate from substantive-law purposes: as dominant commentary contends, tort-law policies (→ Torts) of deterrence and coordination could not effectively be enforced if choice of law did not give regard to local regulations (see generally Abbo Junker, 'Art. 17 VO (EG) 864/2007' in Franz Jürgen Säcker and Roland Rixecker (eds), *Münchener Kommentar zum Bürgerlichen Gesetzbuch*, vol 20 (6th edn, CH Beck 2015) para 1). In addition, the implementation of local-data theory in the Rome II Regulation invites further doubts about the civil-law phobia of *dépeçage*. Indeed, art 17 of the Rome II Regulation has also laid out something that comes close to an issue-selecting choice-of-law rule. This change of fundamentals suggests that modern European choice of law is no longer caught in the straightjacket of traditional doctrine. It may thus allow for – if not require – a consideration of substantive policies. At the same time, it suggests a moderate issue-by-issue analysis.

b) Parties' expectations and substantive-law policies

In addition to predictability and legal certainty, parties' interests are identified as a relevant concern under the Rome II Regulation. This orientation often clearly points towards the application of certain rules on safety and conduct. Sometimes, however, it may also leave the decision maker without guidance.

(1) *General scope of balancing* The general provision on the *lex loci delicti commissi* in art 4 of the Rome II Regulation is intended to guarantee certainty and to strike a 'reasonable balance between the person claimed to be liable and the person sustaining the damage' (Commission, 'Proposal for the Rome II Regulation' COM(2003) 427 final, 11; Recital (16)) (→ Torts). The European Commission expressly rejected the implementation of a *favor laesi* rule giving the victim a choice between different laws, since this would have gone beyond his expectations (Commission, 'Proposal for the Rome II Regulation' COM(2003) 427 final, 12). The concern for balancing parties' interests with respect to their expectations also underlies the rule on local data in art 17. As Recital (34) states, '[i]n order to strike a reasonable balance between the parties, account must be taken, in so far as appropriate, of the rules of safety and conduct in operation in the country in which the harmful act was committed . . . .'. The commission's explanation seems to express an intention to emphasize tortfeasor expectations (Commission, 'Proposal for the Rome II Regulation' COM(2003) 427 final, 25). Yet it does not require disregarding the victim's expectations, nor does it set a hierarchy among parties' interests or expectations (Symeon C Symeonides, 'Rome II and Tort Conflicts: A Missed Opportunity' (2008) 56 Am.J.Comp.L. 173, 213 ff). The benefit accorded to the victim through the implementation of the *lex loci damni* as a general rule in art 4(1) of the Rome II Regulation may be counterbalanced by the consideration of the *lex loci actus* in favour of the tortfeasor. But this trade-off does not mean that, in local-data analysis, the victim's expectations must be disregarded *per se*. On the contrary: considering the generally victim-friendly attitude of the regulation (notably reflected in art 4(1)), it must be assumed that the benefits of art 17 should be available not only for the tortfeasor but also for the victim (Phaedon John Kozyris,

'Rome II: Tort Conflicts on the Right Track! A Postscript to Symeon Symeonides' "Missed Opportunity"' (2008) 56 Am.J.Comp.L. 471, 483). In sum, local-data analysis, both in general and under the Rome II Regulation, requires a reasonable balancing between tortfeasor *and* victim expectations with respect to the standard of safety and conduct that is relevant for the liability at issue.

(2) *Intra-state torts* In order to determine what is 'appropriate' when considering party expectations under art 17 of the Rome II Regulation, it is important to distinguish between two types of tort. First, there are → torts where conduct and injury occur at the same place (ie in the same state). Under the conditions of art 4(2) or 4(3) of the Rome II Regulation, the *lex causae* may then differ from the *lex loci actus* that provides for the *local* rules of safety and conduct. Second, there are cases where the tortfeasor's conduct takes place in a state different from where the injury occurs; then, application of the general rule in art 4(1) leads to a divergence between the *lex causae* and the local law accounting for the rules of safety and conduct (see *infra* III.2.b)(3)).

For the first type of tort, parties' expectations will often converge and point towards the application of the local standard of safety and conduct. Then, art 17 of the Rome II Regulation may truly alleviate the tortfeasor's dilemma regarding the predictability of the applicable law. If he cannot be expected to foresee the applicable regime, he should at least be allowed to refer to local rules of conduct (Commission, 'Proposal for the Rome II Regulation' COM(2003) 427 final, 25; Recital (34); Jan von Hein, 'Die Behandlung von Sicherheits- und Verhaltensregeln nach Art. 17 der Rom-II Verordnung' in Herbert Kronke and Karsten Thorn (eds), *Grenzen überwinden – Prinzipien bewahren: Festschrift für Bernd Hoffmann zum 70. Geburtstag am 28. Dezember 2011* (Gieseking 2011) 139 ff). Similarly, the victim's expectations are protected to the extent that he can reasonably trust the protective regime of the place where his rights and entitlements are located. In some cases, however, party expectations may point towards a regime different from the local law. The question is what quality and quantity of foreign contacts is required to indicate such a divergence. Here, the existence of a pre-tort relationship between the parties is crucial. Examples include husband and wife, worker and patron, and relationships between colleagues or other primarily social relationships (eg automobile trips or travel groups). Depending on the circumstances, the tortfeasor and/or the victim may expect a regime other than the local law – particularly the law of the parties' common residence – to be applied. But it is questionable whether such a 'transfer' of the parties' home regime to a different jurisdiction should also be possible with respect to rules of safety and conduct. Looking at the problem from the perspective of party expectations, it is not necessarily the concrete situation of a shared habitual residence (→ Domicile, habitual residence and establishment) but the actual or potential socio-economic embedding at the place of conduct that matters. → Traffic accidents are illustrative: foreign parties who share the same habitual residence may travel alone in a single car and thus appear somewhat secluded from the public. Yet compliance with local traffic rules is not only an issue between tortfeasor and victim. Any car ride on public streets implies potential contact with third parties. The tortfeasor must thus be expected to comply with local traffic rules – and such an expectation will also reasonably be present for the victim. The only exception where such actual or potential contact with the socio-economic environment may be denied is in cases where the tort has truly 'occurred in an "insulated environment"' (Otto Kahn-Freund, 'Delictual Liability and the Conflict of Laws' [1968] Rec. des Cours 1, 81 ff). An oft-quoted example is *inter se* liability of the members of a travel group. If, for example, one of the travellers is a physician who negligently treats one of his fellow travellers, reasonable expectations seem to allow for reference to the *lex communis*. At first glance, there is no relevant 'local contact'. However, the physician's conduct, as in traffic accidents, may ultimately also affect the local public. It is highly doubtful whether the parties' expectations can then still be interpreted as concerning their inter-party interactions only. If, for instance, the physician overlooks a contagious disease (risking its spread beyond the group), he should not be shielded from the application of local laws. Often, as in this example, at least the tortfeasor will be expected to be aware of potential external effects. In essence, therefore, an expectation-oriented perspective requires that giving regard to local rules of safety and conduct be the rule rather than the exception.

(3) *Cross-border torts* Conduct and injury may diverge in cases – known as *Distanzdelikt* – where

an activity (eg blasting) takes place in one state but causes damage to parties in another (see Symeon C Symeonides, 'Rome II and Tort Conflicts: A Missed Opportunity' (2008) 56 Am.J.Comp.L. 173, 187). Under art 4(1) of the Rome II Regulation, the *lex loci damni* applies – in other words, the rules of safety and conduct of the place of conduct are disregarded. The balancing of party interests here is more complicated than in the first category of intra-state torts (see *supra* III.2.b)(2)). Two scenarios must be distinguished.

If the rules of safety and conduct are stricter under the *lex loci damni* than under the *lex loci actus*, art 17 of the Rome II Regulation seems to fulfil its intended purpose. As is argued, unless the tortfeasor had to reasonably expect the injury to occur in a different jurisdiction, he will be allowed to rely on local law. This seems to be the obvious conclusion to draw from Recital (34), which provides for a balancing of the parties' interests – local-law theory notably is the counterbalance to art 4(1) that generally prefers the victim over the tortfeasor (Jan von Hein, 'Die Behandlung von Sicherheits- und Verhaltensregeln nach Art. 17 der Rom-II Verordnung' in Herbert Kronke and Karsten Thorn (eds), *Grenzen überwinden – Prinzipien bewahren: Festschrift für Bernd Hoffmann zum 70. Geburtstag am 28. Dezember 2011* (Gieseking 2011) 139, 140).

The question is more complex if the rules of safety and conduct are stricter under the *lex loci actus* than under the *lex loci damni*. In this case, giving regard to local standards at the place of acting cannot work in favour of the tortfeasor. As dominant opinion regarding art 17 of the Rome II Regulation contends, the provision should therefore remain unapplied. This is intended to account for its narrow aim to eliminate unfair surprise for the defendant only. In addition, as dominant opinion further argues, expectations of the victim that go beyond the standard of safety and conduct in the state where the injury occurs are 'not worthy of protection' (eg Gerhard Wagner, 'Die neue Rom II-Verordnung' [2008] IPRax 1, 6; Ivo Bach, 'Art. 17 Rome II' in Peter Huber (ed), *Rome II Regulation: Pocket Commentary* (Sellier 2010) para 11). Under this perspective, however, both tortfeasor expectations and substantive policies are neglected. This is where a more policy-oriented choice-of-law analysis is indicated.

A closer look at the substantive-law basis of tort conflicts doctrine is revealing. As the Rome II Regulation's Recital (16) clarifies, the *lex loci damni* rule in art 4(1) not only strikes a 'fair balance' between the interests of the tortfeasor and the victim but 'also reflects the modern approach to civil liability and the development of systems of strict liability'. While the European Commission's explanation is focused on the 'compensation function' of tort law (Commission, 'Proposal for the Rome II Regulation' COM(2003) 427 final, 12), scholarly commentary correctly argues that the functions of conduct coordination and admonition that tort law is supposed to fulfil would be distorted if the applicable rules of safety and conduct come from a regime different than the one in force at the place and time of the delictual conduct (see, eg Gerhard Wagner, 'Die neue Rom II-Verordnung' [2008] IPRax 1, 5; Abbo Junker, 'Art. 17 VO (EG) 864/2007' in Franz Jürgen Säcker and Roland Rixecker (eds), *Münchener Kommentar zum Bürgerlichen Gesetzbuch*, vol 20 (6th edn, CH Beck 2015) para 1). If this avowal to a tort policy of conduct regulation and prevention is supposed to be more than mere lip service, the incentive structure of substantive law must be transferred to the level of choice of law. And party expectations serve as a transmission instrument.

Such a correlation between substantive policy and → choice of law is not unknown. For instance, this correlation is acknowledged – albeit often only implicitly – in German doctrine, where the dividing line between local-data rules and norms of the *lex causae* has been described as demarcating the national categories of *Haftungsbegründung* and *Haftungsausfüllung* (Gerhard Wagner, 'Die neue Rom II-Verordnung' [2008] IPRax 1, 5). Alternatively, US doctrine (→ USA) suggests differentiating between conduct-regulating and loss-allocating norms. The first category is described as constituting the territorial regulation of human activities akin to the group of local-data rules. The second category, by contrast, is principally non-territorial and therefore equivalent to the European categorization of rules of the *lex causae* (Symeon C Symeonides, 'Rome II and Tort Conflicts: A Missed Opportunity' (2008) 56 Am.J.Comp.L. 173, 189–90, 212). Yet it is questionable whether national concepts can provide for an internationally uniform characterization. And the US approach, in particular, fails to clearly categorize many tort rules as either conduct regulating or loss allocating (eg Peter Hay, Patrick J Borchers and Symeon C Symeonides,

Conflict of Laws (5th edn, West 2010) s 17.37). Thus, a more universal perspective is required:

Essential for the ordering function of private law is a → prescription of activities that are legitimate and of those that are prohibited. In other words, certain norms of private law – together with public-law norms – provide the setting and framework in which individual socio-economic transacting may evolve. By establishing the basis for liability and thus prohibiting certain kinds of conduct, they constitute the *Magna Carta* of freedom of activities. In terms of individual rights, such norms circumscribe the scope of subjective entitlements that are protected under the private-law regime (Heinrich Dörner, 'Neue Entwicklungen im Internationalen Verkehrsunfallrecht' [1994] JR 6, 10). This category of primary-order norms is the domain of local data. Individual conduct will be most directly determined by easily identifiable and transparent norms on local safety and conduct (see David Cavers, *The Choice-of-Law Process* (University of Michigan Press 1965) 143–4). Above all, this group of norms contains rules on the basis for liability – in other words, these norms prescribe whether the alleged tortfeasor has breached a duty and whether he acted with the necessary state of mind. This is the foundation of both run-of-the-mill negligence and intentional torts. For particularly hazardous activities, the legal system may also decide in favour of liability on the basis of the creation of a certain risk, regardless of fault (eg strict liability). Further, the category covers questions regarding whether victim conduct eliminates liability (eg contributory negligence). And it covers the issue of delictual capacity (see Christian von Bar, 'Grundfragen des Internationalen Deliktrechts' [1985] JZ 961, 967; but see Higher Regional Court (OLG) of Celle, 12 July 1965 [1966] NJW 302), as well as the question whether the tortfeasor can rely on a justifying cause for his wrong (Heinrich Dörner, 'Neue Entwicklungen im Internationalen Verkehrsunfallrecht' [1994] JR 6, 11).

The second category of tort-liability rules contains norms concerning the consequences of a primary-order norm violation. These norms are to be chosen from the *lex causae*. In choice of law, they can be substituted with a different law's provisions. Of course, such a substitution may ultimately also affect the local policy at issue, particularly with regard to the concrete level of enforcement (eg with respect to the amount of damages). Yet the influence of such substitution on the private-law order is less intense. In other words, substitution of a primary-order norm will directly alter the system of dos and don'ts under local law. The exchange of rules of the secondary order, however, has minor effects that only indirectly signal the inadmissibility of certain activities. Such norms, for instance, concern the definition of the harm for which compensation can be claimed, as well as the determination of eligible claim holders. Further, they concern → remedies and their qualitative and quantitative features (eg injunctive relief or damages). And they also provide for deduction from (eg insurance payments) or caps on the amount of damages.

IV. Application: Rome II Regulation

The handling of local data under modern doctrine, particularly under art 17 of the Rome II Regulation, poses a number of questions regarding the theory 'in action'. Taking account of the discussion above helps resolve some of the ongoing disputes.

1. The nature of local data

Commentary used to suggest that only public-law norms should be treated as local data (eg Michael Schwimann, 'Vor einer Wende in der Rechtsprechung zum Schadenersatz nach Auslandsunfällen?' [1973] ZVR 370, 375; see also Ernst Rabel, *The Conflict of Laws: A Comparative Study*, vol 2 (2nd edn, University of Michigan Press 1960) 245 ff, 'local administrative and insurance policies'). While it is true that such policies signal a stronger interest in upholding and enforcing on the side of the policy maker, modern practice correctly rejects such a limitation (Hans Stoll, 'Deliktstatut und Tatbestandswirkung ausländischen Rechts' in Peter Feuerstein (ed), *Multum non multa: Festschrift für Kurt Lipstein aus Anlass seines 70. Geburtstages* (CF Müller 1980) 259, 264; Andrew Dickinson, *The Rome II Regulation: The Law Applicable to Non-contractual Obligations* (OUP 2008) paras 15.30 ff). Local data comprise norms of public, penal and private law, regardless of whether the norm is statutory or judge-made (German Federal Court of Justice (BGH), 10 February 2009 [2009] NJW 1482, 1485). This corresponds to the general characterization of local data as norms of the primary order. Accordingly, the category also comprises the general standard of care (eg under § 276 of the German Civil Code

(Bürgerliches Gesetzbuch of 2 January 2002, BGBl. I 42, as amended); Andrew Dickinson, *The Rome II Regulation: The Law Applicable to Non-contractual Obligations* (OUP 2008) para 15.32; see Gerhard Wagner, 'Die neue Rom II-Verordnung' [2008] IPRax 1, 6; but cf Abbo Junker, 'Art. 17 VO (EG) 864/2007' in Franz Jürgen Säcker and Roland Rixecker (eds), *Münchener Kommentar zum Bürgerlichen Gesetzbuch*, vol 20 (6th edn, CH Beck 2015) para 16). Indeed, local data need not even be law in the formal sense. Customary law may qualify; it suffices that there exists an actual practice – such as for sports activities – to which all participants adhere (Hans Stoll, 'Die Behandlung von Verhaltensnormen und Sicherheitsvorschriften' in Ernst von Caemmerer (ed), *Vorschläge und Gutachten zur Reform des deutschen internationalen Privatrechts der außervertraglichen Schuldverhältnisse* (Mohr 1983) 160, 173–4).

2. *The territoriality of local data*

For traffic laws in particular, commentary and practice distinguish between rules that are 'strictly territorial' and rules that are deemed to allow for a 'more flexible' application. Strictly territorial, for instance, are rules concerning the correct side of the road to use. Such rules are supposed to apply regardless of the situation – for example, they would also apply in two-party scenarios concerning a locally committed tort between foreigners sharing the same habitual residence (Jan von Hein, 'Die Behandlung von Sicherheits- und Verhaltensregeln nach Art. 17 der Rom-II Verordnung' in Herbert Kronke and Karsten Thorn (eds), *Grenzen überwinden – Prinzipien bewahren: Festschrift für Bernd Hoffmann zum 70. Geburtstag am 28. Dezember 2011* (Gieseking 2011) 139, 145). The second category covers, *inter alia*, obligations to use a seatbelt or regulations on alcohol limits. These rules are supposed to be more flexible insofar as individuals with a habitual residence in the same country may 'carry' their *lex communis* with them to foreign jurisdictions. The local law is then disregarded (Hans Stoll, 'Zur Flexibilisierung des europäischen internationalen Deliktsrechts – Vermittelnde Kritik aus Amerika an der "ROM II-VO"' in Peter Jarbonegg, Ferdinand Kerschner and Andreas Riedler (eds), *Haftung und Versicherung: Festschrift für Rudolf Reischauer* (Verl Österreich 2010) 389, 408). With respect to alcohol limits, for instance,

courts have found a more liberal *lex communis* to prevail over a stricter regime at the place of conduct (German Federal Court of Justice (BGH) [1978] VersR 541, 542). Yet, conversely, it has also been argued that the judge should take account of rules under the *lex causae*, if the law of the place of conduct is less strict (Hans Stoll, 'Die Behandlung von Verhaltensnormen und Sicherheitsvorschriften' in Ernst von Caemmerer (ed), *Vorschläge und Gutachten zur Reform des deutschen internationalen Privatrechts der außervertraglichen Schuldverhältnisse* (Mohr 1983) 160, 175; Jan von Hein, 'Die Behandlung von Sicherheits- und Verhaltensregeln nach Art. 17 der Rom-II Verordnung' in Herbert Kronke and Karsten Thorn (eds), *Grenzen überwinden – Prinzipien bewahren: Festschrift für Bernd Hoffmann zum 70. Geburtstag am 28. Dezember 2011* (Gieseking 2011) 139, 146). One real-world example is the case of a German couple who suffered an accident while driving a car in France. One member of the couple, the passenger, had been sleeping in the car's front seat without having buckled up. The other, the driver, had failed to ensure that the passenger had fastened her seatbelt before the accident happened. According to the court, French seatbelt regulations were irrelevant; violation of the German duty was sufficient to find the driver liable (Higher Regional Court (OLG) of Karlsruhe [1985] r+s 171, 172; see also Kammergericht (KG) Berlin [1982] VersR 1199). Further, it is debated whether local law should only provide for the rule of conduct or whether it should also set the standard of reasonable care. As German practice holds, local law is the basis for assessing whether a party has violated a rule of conduct (German Federal Court of Justice (BGH) [1996] NJW-RR 732, 733). In addition, local law may determine whether the alleged tortfeasor failed to exercise reasonable care. This applies when two people hailing from the same country, but who lack a pre-existing relationship, are involved in an accident in a foreign country (German Federal Court of Justice (BGH) [1996] NJW-RR 732, 733). This is supposed to differ, however, in isolated two-party situations. Foreigners sharing the same habitual residence who find themselves travelling in the same car may be held accountable under local rules of conduct. Yet with respect to the standard of care (negligence), they are considered to have 'brought' their *lex communis* with them (German Federal Court of Justice (BGH), 10

February 2009 [2009] NJW 1482, 1485; see also Otto Kahn-Freund, 'Delictual Liability and the Conflict of Laws' [1968] Rec. des Cours 1, 96). In the same vein, if the *lex causae* prescribes a standard of strict liability, the tortfeasor's local conduct is deemed irrelevant. Accordingly, art 17 of Rome II Regulation remains without effect (Francisco J Garcimartín Alférez, 'The Rome II Regulation: On the Way towards a European Private international law Code' (2007) 3 EuLF-I 77, 90; Andrew Dickinson, *The Rome II Regulation: The Law Applicable to Non-contractual Obligations* (OUP 2008) para 15.33).

Looking at local data under the distinction between conduct rules and sanction-determining norms, these doctrines are questionable. Rules of conduct are designed to concern the external effects of human activities. Traffic regulations in particular are oriented towards the public. This concern for the public is also reflected in party expectations. Drivers will take care not to exceed the intoxication threshold for fear of criminal sanctions, and they must be expected to consider that their intoxication may cause injury to third parties. Rules regarding seatbelts are not much different. First, administrative sanctions may result from a violation. And even though no immediate third-party injury may result from a person's failure to buckle up, it is hardly questionable that seatbelt regulations also protect third parties by reducing the liability of the other side in the case of an accident.

Finally, the distinction between rules of conduct and standards of care is also problematic. This ensues from the analysis of party expectations and of substantive policies. Compliance with a certain order of socio-economic transacting also means accommodating the standard of care. No one driving a car in Manhattan will reasonably expect to be held to the standard of, for instance, rural Bavaria or the Scottish Highlands. Holding a driver to such a standard would be to create an artificial distinction between two categories that are inseparably intertwined.

3. Scope of application

Due to art 17's systematic location within the Rome II Regulation (in ch V: 'Common Rules'), it applies to the special torts in ch II (arts 5–9) and to other non-contractual obligations in ch III (arts 10–12). It also applies in cases where the parties have chosen the applicable law pursuant to art 14 (Jan von Hein, 'Die Behandlung von Sicherheits- und Verhaltensregeln nach Art. 17 der Rom-II Verordnung' in Herbert Kronke and Karsten Thorn (eds), *Grenzen überwinden – Prinzipien bewahren: Festschrift für Bernd Hoffmann zum 70. Geburtstag am 28. Dezember 2011* (Gieseking 2011) 139, 144; but see Regional Court (LG) of Traunstein, [2002] SpuRt 20). The debate over whether the provision applies to acts of unfair competition is particularly illustrative for the role of party expectations and substantive policies in local-data theory. Rather imprecisely, current doctrine interprets the law determined under art 6(1) as providing for 'conduct' regulation with respect to fair competition. Yet, in essence, it is market effects that provide the relevant point of attachment. Thus, if the defendant has not acted in the state of the marketplace (eg in the case of Internet advertising), consideration of the law of the place of actual conduct is problematic. It may provide opportunities to circumvent market regulation. This problem must be resolved by a look at expectations and policies. First, the foreseeability of effects on the marketplace (under art 6(1)) is crucial: a competitor will be held liable under the marketplace regime if the effects of his conduct (undertaken in a different state) were or could have been expected; art 17 will then not apply. Under a policy-oriented analysis, the same result ensues. This is the only interpretation that avoids distortion of the *par conditio concurrentium* in the marketplace regulated by the *lex causae*. However, under art 6(2), in cases where the *lex communis* applies, local standards of the place of actual conduct may be considered (Jan von Hein, 'Die Behandlung von Sicherheits- und Verhaltensregeln nach Art. 17 der Rom-II Verordnung' in Herbert Kronke and Karsten Thorn (eds), *Grenzen überwinden – Prinzipien bewahren: Festschrift für Bernd Hoffmann zum 70. Geburtstag am 28. Dezember 2011* (Gieseking 2011) 139, 156).

4. Reverse application: contributory negligence

Per se, art 17 concerns only 'the conduct of the person claimed to be liable'. Accordingly, one could assume that giving regard to local law is indicated for tortfeasor conduct only. Considering the fact that the local regime as the primary order for individual activity determines not only tortfeasor conduct but victim conduct, a different result ensues with regard to contributory negligence (Andrew Dickinson, *The Rome II Regulation: The Law Applicable to Non-contractual Obligations* (OUP 2008) para 15.34; Gerhard Wagner, 'Die neue Rom II-Verordnung' [2008] IPRax 1, 6).

TIM W DORNIS

Literature

Ivo Bach, 'Art. 17 Rome II' in Peter Huber (ed), *Rome II Regulation: Pocket Commentary* (Sellier 2010); Christian von Bar, 'Grundfragen des Internationalen Deliktrechts' [1985] JZ 961; David Cavers, *The Choice-of-Law Process* (University of Michigan Press 1965); Brainerd Currie, 'On the Displacement of the Law of the Forum' (1958) 58 Colum.L.Rev. 964, r"eprinted in Brainerd Currie, *Selected Essays on the Conflict of Laws* (Duke University Press 1963) 66 ff; Albert Venn Dicey and John Humphrey Carlile Morris (eds), *Dicey and Morris on the Conflict of Laws* (13th edn, Sweet & Maxwell 2000); Andrew Dickinson, *The Rome II Regulation: The Law Applicable to Non-contractual Obligations* (OUP 2008) 491; Heinrich Dörner, 'Alte und neue Probleme des Internationalen Deliktrechts' in Gerhard Hohloch (ed), *Festschrift für Hans Stoll zum 75. Geburtstag* (Mohr Siebeck 2001) 491; Heinrich Dörner, 'Neue Entwicklungen im Internationalen Verkehrsunfallrecht' [1994] JR 6; Tim W Dornis, "'Local Data' in European Choice of Law: A Trojan Horse from Across the Atlantic?" 44 Ga.J.Int'l & Comp.L. (forthcoming 2017); Tim W Dornis, "Die Theorie der 'local data' – domatische Bruchstelle im klassischen IPR," 2015 SZIER/RSDIE, 183; Albert A Ehrenzweig, 'Local and Moral Data in the Conflict of Laws: Terra Incognita' (1966–67) 16 Buff.L.Rev. 55; James J Fawcett, Janeen M Carruthers and Peter M North, *Cheshire, North & Fawcett Private international law* (14th edn, OUP 2008); Francisco J Garcimartín Alférez, 'The Rome II Regulation: On the Way towards a European Private international law Code' (2007) 3 EuLF-I 77; Peter Hay, Patrick J Borchers and Symeon C Symeonides, *Conflict of Laws* (5th edn, West 2010); Jan von Hein, 'Die Behandlung von Sicherheits- und Verhaltensregeln nach Art. 17 der Rom-II Verordnung' in Herbert Kronke and Karsten Thorn (eds), *Grenzen überwinden – Prinzipien bewahren: Festschrift für Bernd Hoffmann zum 70. Geburtstag am 28. Dezember 2011* (Gieseking 2011) 139; Erik Jayme, 'Ausländische Rechtsregeln und Tatbestand inländischer Sachnormen – Betrachtungen zu Ehrenzweigs Datum-Theorie –' in Erik Jayme (ed), *Gedächtnisschrift für Albert A. Ehrenzweig* (Müller 1976) 36–49; Abbo Junker, 'Das Internationale Privatrecht der Straßenverkehrsunfälle nach der Rom II-Verordnung' [2008] JZ 169; Abbo Junker, 'Art. 17 VO (EG) 864/2007' in Franz Jürgen Säcker and Roland Rixecker (eds), *Münchener Kommentar zum Bürgerlichen Gesetzbuch*, vol 20 (6th edn, CH Beck 2015); Otto Kahn-Freund, 'Delictual Liability and the Conflict of Laws' [1968] Rec. des Cours 1; Herma Hill Kay, 'Conflict of Laws: Foreign Law as Datum' (1965) 53 Cal.L.Rev. 47; Phaedon John Kozyris, 'Rome II: Tort Conflicts on the Right Track! A Postscript to Symeon Symeonides' "Missed Opportunity"' (2008) 56 Am.J.Comp.L. 471; Jan Kropholler, *Internationales Privatrecht* (6th edn, Mohr Siebeck 2006); Ernst Rabel, *The Conflict of Laws: A Comparative Study*, vol II (2nd edn, University of Michigan Press 1960); Rolf C Radtke, 'Schuldstatut und Eingriffsrecht' (1985) 84 ZVglRWiss 325; William A Reppy, Jr, 'Eclecticism in Methods for Resolving Tort and Contract Conflict of Laws: The United States and the European Union' (2008) 82 Tul.L.Rev. 2053; Friedrich Karl von Savigny, *System des heutigen römischen Rechts*, vol 8 (2nd reprint of ed Berlin 1849, Scientia Verlag 1981); Klaus Schurig, 'Zwingendes Recht, "Eingriffsnormen" und neues IPR' (1990) 54 RabelsZ 217; Michael Schwimann, 'Vor einer Wende in der Rechtsprechung zum Schadenersatz nach Auslandsunfällen?' [1973] ZVR 370; Hans Stoll, 'Deliktstatut und Tatbestandswirkung ausländischen Rechts' in Peter Feuerstein (ed), *Multum non multa: Festschrift für Kurt Lipstein aus Anlass seines 70. Geburtstages* (CF Müller 1980) 259; Hans Stoll, 'Die Behandlung von Verhaltensnormen und Sicherheitsvorschriften' in Ernst von Caemmerer (ed), *Vorschläge und Gutachten zur Reform des deutschen internationalen Privatrechts der außervertraglichen Schuldverhältnisse* (Mohr 1983) 160; Hans Stoll, 'Zur Flexibilisierung des europäischen internationalen Deliktsrechts – Vermittelnde Kritik aus Amerika an der "ROM II-VO"' in Peter Jarbonegg, Ferdinand Kerschner and Andreas Riedler (eds), *Haftung und Versicherung: Festschrift für Rudolf Reischauer* (Verl Österreich 2010) 389–427; Symeon C Symeonides, 'Rome II and Tort Conflicts: A Missed Opportunity' (2008) 56 Am.J.Comp.L. 173; Gerhard Wagner, 'Die neue Rom II-Verordnung' [2008] IPRax 1.

Lugano Convention

I. Introduction

The 2007 Lugano Convention (Lugano Convention of 30 October 2007 on jurisdiction and the recognition and enforcement of judgments in civil and commercial matters, [2007] OJ L 339/3) is an international instrument signed on 30 October 2007 in Lugano, Switzerland, aimed at unifying the rules on jurisdiction in → civil and commercial matters and to facilitate the recognition and enforcement of foreign decisions, authentic instruments and court settlements among its contracting parties which are the

European Union, → Denmark, → Iceland, → Norway and → Switzerland. As such, it is a parallel instrument to the Council Regulation (EC) 44/2001 of 22 December 2000 on Jurisdiction and the Recognition and Enforcement of Judgments in Civil and Commercial Matters (Brussels I Regulation), [2001] OJ L 12/1 (→ Brussels I (Convention and Regulation)).

II. Background

1. The 1988 Lugano Convention

The Lugano Convention is the successor to the Lugano Convention of 16 September 1988 on jurisdiction and the enforcement of judgments in civil and commercial matters, [1988] OJ L 319/9 (1988 Lugano Convention), and is often referred to as the 'revised Lugano Convention'. The 1988 Lugano Convention is in turn a parallel agreement to the Brussels Convention (Brussels Convention of 27 September 1968 on jurisdiction and the enforcement of judgments in civil and commercial matters, [1972] OJ L 299/32, consolidated version, [1998] OJ C 27/1) signed between the six original Member States of the European Community and successively by the new states that acceded to the EC, along with certain members of the European Free-Trade Association (EFTA), namely Iceland, Norway and Switzerland.

2. The revision of the 1988 Lugano and Brussels Conventions

In 1997, the EU Council launched a simultaneous revision of the Brussels Convention and the 1988 Lugano Convention with the aim of fully harmonizing the two instruments and resolving some of the issues that had emerged in the course of their application. The goal was *inter alia* to reflect the internationalization of commercial relations and the new developments in technology such as the Internet, to simplify issues of jurisdiction and coordination between jurisdictions, to accelerate the enforcement of foreign judgments, to clarify some of the provisions and to take into account some of the case-law of the European Court of Justice (ECJ) – now the → Court of Justice of the European Union – as well as certain decisions by national courts referred to in Protocol 2 to the 1988 Lugano Convention.

A joint *ad hoc* working group was set up with EU and EFTA representatives of the 1988 Lugano Convention to draw up a draft convention that would improve and harmonize the texts of the Brussels and the 1988 Lugano Conventions. By the end of April 1999, the working group had drafted the substantive part of the revision. However, shortly afterwards, in May 1999, the Treaty of Amsterdam (Treaty of Amsterdam amending the Treaty on the European Union, the Treaties establishing the European Communities and certain related acts (consolidated version), [1997] OJ C 340/01) came into force establishing the EU's competence regarding cooperation in civil matters of which the Brussels and Lugano Conventions are part. The revised text of the new Brussels-Lugano Convention was therefore moulded into an EC regulation, namely the Brussels I Regulation, without any substantial effect on the draft prepared by the working group.

The Brussels I Regulation entered into force on 1 March 2002 and replaced the Brussels Convention for EU Member States, except for → Denmark which is subject to a different regime regarding Title IV of the EC Treaty (visas, asylum, immigration and other policies related to the free movement of persons) that includes judicial cooperation in civil matters. Accordingly, a separate instrument had to be negotiated with Denmark and was signed in 2005.

As a result of the entry into force of the Treaty of Amsterdam and the negotiation of a separate instrument with Denmark, the finalization of the Lugano Convention and its ratification were delayed by almost ten years. Another reason for the delay was the uncertainty regarding the question of whether the European Commission had exclusive or shared competence to conclude the Lugano Convention or whether this competence still belonged to each EU Member State. This was clarified on 7 February 2006 when the ECJ affirmed the European Commission's exclusive competence (Opinion 1/03 Competence of the Community to Conclude the New Lugano Convention on Jurisdiction and the Recognition and Enforcement of Judgments in Civil and Commercial Matters [2006] ECR I-1145). It ensued that Switzerland, Norway and Iceland had only one single contracting party, namely the EU acting through the European Commission, whilst the Member States enjoyed observer status.

The final negotiations concerning the formal revision of the Lugano Convention took place in Lugano in October 2006 where nearly all controversial issues were resolved. The remaining issues were settled in the course of subsequent informal negotiations. In March 2007, a final text was agreed upon, which was signed in Lugano, Switzerland, on 30 October 2007.

3. The Brussels/Lugano regime

Pursuant to the Preamble of the Lugano Convention, the aim of the Convention is 'to strengthen in the territories of the contracting parties the legal protection of the persons therein established' and, 'for this purpose, to determine the international jurisdiction of the courts, to facilitate the recognition, and to introduce an expeditious procedure for securing the enforcement of judgments, authentic instruments and court settlements'. The Preamble further stresses the wish of the contracting parties to extend the principles of the Brussels I Regulation to them in order to strengthen their legal and economic cooperation, thus reaffirming the principle of parallelism which has been prevailing over the evolution of the Lugano and Brussels instruments. Together, the Brussels Convention, the 1988 Lugano Convention, the Brussels I Regulation and the Lugano Convention have been dubbed the 'Brussels/Lugano regime'.

III. Overview of the substantive rules of the Lugano Convention

1. Structure and form of the Lugano Convention

The Lugano Convention is structured in one main document divided into eight Titles (Title I: Scope; Title II: Jurisdiction; Title III: Recognition and Enforcement; Title IV: Authentic Instruments and Court Settlements; Title V: General Provisions; Title VI: Transitional Provisions; Title VII: Relationship to Council Regulation (EC) No 44/2001 and Other Instruments; Title VIII: Final Provisions), three Protocols (Protocol 1 on Certain Questions of Jurisdiction, Procedure and Enforcement; Protocol 2 on the Uniform Interpretation of the Convention and on the Standing Committee; Protocol 3 on the Application of art 67 of the Convention), and nine Annexes. The Protocols and Annexes form an integral part of the Convention (art 75).

The Lugano Convention is so deeply rooted into the legal systems of its original contracting parties that it has been drawn up in a single original in each of their languages – Bulgarian, Czech, Danish, Dutch, English, Estonian, Finnish, French, German, Greek, Hungarian, Icelandic, Irish, Italian, Latvian, Lithuanian, Maltese, Norwegian, Polish, Portuguese, Romanian, Slovak, Slovenian, Spanish and Swedish – all texts being equally authentic (art 79). The Swiss Federal Council acts as Depositary (art 69).

2. Territorial scope of the Lugano Convention

The Lugano Convention applies to the territory of all its contracting parties, ie the EU, Denmark, Iceland, Norway and Switzerland. The Convention refers to 'State[s] bound by this Convention' rather than mere contracting parties. This expression means any state that is a contracting party to the Convention or an EU Member State but also the EU itself (art 1(3)). This reflects the fact that the Treaty of Amsterdam granted the EU exclusive power to conclude the Lugano Convention with the result that the Convention is not an agreement between the EU Member States and other states.

The Lugano Convention is open for accession to future EFTA members, EU Member States acting on behalf of certain non-European territories that are part of their territory or for whose external relations they are responsible, and to any other state, subject to the unanimous agreement of all the contracting parties (arts 70–72).

3. Material scope of the Lugano Convention

Like earlier instruments of the Brussels/Lugano regime, the Lugano Convention applies to proceedings and judgments related to international legal relationships, including relationships that do not involve two contracting parties but one contracting party and a third state (Case 281/02 *Andrew Owusu v NB Jackson, trading as 'Villa Holidays Bal-Inn Villas', Mammee Bay Resorts Ltd, Mammee Bay Club Ltd, The Enchanted Garden Resorts & Spa Ltd, Consulting Services Ltd, Town & Country Resorts Ltd* [2005] ECR I-1445, paras 25–6).

The scope of the Lugano Convention covers all → civil and commercial matters regardless of the nature of the court or tribunal (art 1). The Lugano Convention, however, does not apply to (i) revenue, customs or administrative matters, (ii) the status or legal capacity of natural persons (→ Capacity and emancipation), matrimonial matters, wills and → succession,

(iii) bankruptcy, proceedings relating to the winding-up of insolvent companies or other legal persons, judicial arrangements, compositions and analogous proceedings, (iv) social security and (v) arbitration.

Although arbitration remains excluded from the Convention, as from the 1988 Lugano Convention and the Brussels I Regulation, its interaction with the Brussels/Lugano regime has nonetheless been the object of much debate further to the EJC ruling in *West Tankers* (Case C-185/07 *Allianz SpA and Generali Assicurazioni Generali SpA v West Tankers Inc* [2009] ECR I-663). In that case, the ECJ gave precedence to the Brussels/Lugano regime over arbitration, stating that an order restraining a person from commencing or continuing proceedings before the courts of another Member State, on the ground that such proceedings would be contrary to an arbitration agreement, was incompatible with the Brussels I Regulation. This issue was addressed in more detail in several reports and later in the context of the Recast of the Brussels I Regulation (Regulation (EU) No 1215/2012 of the European Parliament and of the Council of 12 December 2012 on jurisdiction and the recognition and enforcement of judgments in civil and commercial matters (recast), [2012] OJ L 351/1; → Brussels I (Convention and Regulation)), which maintains the arbitration exception as such in the text but clarifies its meaning in the Preamble, stressing that the Brussels I Regulation does not apply to arbitration (para 12 Preamble of the Brussels I Regulation (recast)). Although the amendments provided in the Brussels I Regulation (recast) do not extend to the Lugano Convention, the interpretation of the arbitration exception inscribed in the Preamble of the Brussels I Regulation (recast) may apply indirectly to the states bound by the Lugano Convention given that the substantive norm of the arbitration exception remains unchanged and that it is still subject to uniform interpretation by the courts of the contracting parties to the Lugano Convention (art 1 Protocol 2). In *Gazprom OAO* (Case C-536/13 "*Gazprom*" *OAO v Lietuvos Respublika* [2015] EU:C:2015:316), the ECJ further considered the issue and, while it did not revisit the *West Tankers* case law, it considered that the Brussels I Regulation did not "preclud[e] a court of a Member State from recognising and enforcing, or from refusing to recognise and enforce, an arbitral award prohibiting a party from bringing certain claims before a court of that Member State, since that regulation does not govern recognition and enforcement, in a Member State, of an arbitral award issued by an arbitral tribunal in another Member State".

4. General provisions

The Lugano Convention contains several general provisions (art 59–62). As under the 1988 Lugano Convention, the domicile of natural persons under the Lugano Convention continues to be determined by the domestic law in which they are domiciled (art 59) (→ Domicile, habitual residence and establishment). The Lugano Convention, however, departs from the 1988 Lugano Convention regarding the domicile of legal persons, which was previously determined by reference to the rules of private international law of the state whose courts had been seized. This dynamic definition, difficult to apply in practice, was replaced by a common definition which lists as alternatives the statutory seat, the place of central administration or the principal place of business of the company or other legal entities (art 60).

5. Jurisdiction

a) General rule of jurisdiction

As under the 1988 Lugano Convention, the general rule concerning jurisdiction under the Lugano Convention remains anchored to the domicile of the defendant in a state bound by the Convention. Accordingly, persons domiciled in a state bound by the Convention are sued in that state, irrespective of their → nationality (art 2). However, arts 5–24 allow exceptions to this rule (see below III.5.b)). Article 3(2) gives further guidance on the matter by specifically preventing the rules of national jurisdiction set out in Annex 1 from being invoked under the Lugano Convention.

By contrast, when the defendant is not domiciled in a state bound by the Lugano Convention, the jurisdiction of the courts of each state bound by the Convention is determined by the law of that state (art 4), save in cases falling under the rules laid down directly by the Lugano Convention irrespective of the defendant's domicile, such as the rules on exclusive jurisdiction (art 22) and prorogation of jurisdiction (art 23).

b) Special rules of jurisdiction

As under the 1988 Lugano Convention, the Lugano Convention provides for special rules of jurisdiction alternatively to the general rule of the domicile of the defendant. Pursuant to these rules, the plaintiff may bring the action in another state bound by the Convention (arts 5–7). This freedom of choice was introduced to take into account, in certain clearly defined circumstances, the existence of a particularly close → connecting factor between a dispute and the court which may be called upon to hear it, in order to support the efficacious conduct of the proceedings (Case 21/76 *Handelskwekerij GJ Bier BV v Mines de potasse d'Alsace SA* [1976] ECR 1735, para 11).

Accordingly, special jurisdiction is vested, in relation to contractual matters, in the courts of the → place of performance of the obligation (art 5(1)); in matters relating to maintenance, in the courts of the place where the maintenance creditor is domiciled or habitually resident (art 5(2)); in matters relating to tort, delict or quasi-delict, in the courts of the place where the harmful event occurred or may occur (art 5(3)); as regards a civil claim for → damages or restitution based on an act giving rise to criminal proceedings, in the court seized of those proceedings, to the extent that that court has jurisdiction under its own law to entertain civil proceedings (art 5(4)); as regards a dispute arising out of the operations of a branch, → agency or other establishment, in the courts for the place in which the branch, agency or other establishment is situated (art 5(5)); as settlor, trustee or beneficiary of a → trust created by the operation of a statute, or by a written instrument, or created orally and evidenced in writing, in the courts of the state bound by the Convention in which the trust is domiciled (art 5(6)); as regards a dispute concerning the payment of remuneration claimed in respect of the → salvage of a cargo or freight, in the court under the authority of which the cargo or freight in question (i) has been arrested to secure such payment, or (ii) could have been so arrested, but bail or other security has been given, provided that this provision shall apply only if it is claimed that the defendant has an interest in the cargo or freight or had such an interest at the time of salvage (art 5(7)).

To remedy practical difficulties in determining the → place of performance of the contractual obligation in dispute under the 1988 Lugano Convention, the Lugano Convention clarifies the rule of jurisdiction regarding contracts of sale and contracts for the provision of services by laying down their place of performance. Accordingly, the place of performance of the obligation is deemed to be, in relation to the sale of goods (→ Sale contracts and sale of goods), the place in a state bound by the Lugano Convention where, under the contract, the goods were delivered or should have been delivered (art 5(1)(b) first para), and in relation to the provision of services, the place in a state bound by the Lugano Convention where, under the contract, the services were provided or should have been provided (art 5(1)(b) second para). This amendment excludes any reference to the place of payment under such contracts, while leaving the existing provision unchanged for all other contracts (art 5(1)(a) and (c)).

The Lugano Convention also provides for specific rules in cases involving several defendants (art 6(1)), specific procedural actions such as third party proceedings (art 6(2)), counterclaims (art 6(3)) and in contractual matters, where the action may be combined with an action against the same defendant in respect of rights *in rem* in immovable property (art 6(4)) (→ Property and proprietary rights).

c) Protective rules of jurisdiction
Additional protection is afforded to weaker parties in matters relating to insurance (arts 8–14), → consumer contracts (arts 15–17) and individual contracts of employment (arts 18–21) (→ Employment contracts, jurisdiction). Specifically, the Lugano Convention generally guarantees a forum at the place of domicile of the weaker party (arts 9, 16 and 19) and excludes any prorogation of jurisdiction in relation to these contracts except when they are entered into after the dispute has arisen or if made in favour of a jurisdiction more advantageous to the weaker party (arts 13, 17 and 21).

Contracts concluded by consumers have been redefined so as to encompass those concluded in digital form. Referring to contracts concluded by a person with a professional for a purpose outside their own trade or profession, consumer contracts under the Lugano Convention include contracts for the sale of goods or instalment credit terms, contracts for a loan repayable by instalments, or for any other form of credit granted to finance the sale of goods or all other contracts concluded with a person who pursues commercial or professional activities in the state bound by the Lugano Convention where the consumer is domiciled or by any means, directs such activities to that state and the contract falls within the scope of such activities. The connection arising from a commercial activity directed to the state of domicile of the consumer – a novelty of the Lugano

Convention – aims at providing sufficient protection to consumers in → electronic commerce. Contracts of transport are, however, excluded from the definition of consumer contracts, save for those combining travel and accommodation for an inclusive price (art 15(3)).

d) Exclusive rules of jurisdiction
The Lugano Convention lays down exclusive jurisdiction rules in relation to specific subject matters due to the perceived closeness between the court and the relevant circumstances (art 22). The rules of exclusive jurisdiction apply regardless of where the parties are domiciled in the states bound by the Convention and cannot be departed from by agreement between the parties (art 23) or by implied submission to jurisdiction (art 24). A court must decline jurisdiction of its own motion if exclusive jurisdiction is vested in the courts of another state bound by the Convention (art 25). Moreover, a judgment rendered in violation of a rule of exclusive jurisdiction will not be recognized (art 35) and may not be enforceable (art 45).

Such exclusive jurisdiction exists in relation to proceedings which have as their object rights *in rem* in → immovable property or tenancies of immovable property (art 22(1)); proceedings regarding the validity of the constitution, the nullity or the dissolution of → companies or other legal persons or associations of natural or legal persons, or of the validity of the decisions of their organs (art 22(2)); proceedings which have as their object the validity of entries in public registers (art 22(3)); proceedings concerned with the registration or validity of patents, trademarks, designs or other similar rights required to be deposited or registered, irrespective of whether the issue is raised by way of an action or as a defence (art 22(4)); and proceedings concerned with the enforcement of judgments (art 22(5)).

e) Prorogation of jurisdiction and implied submission to jurisdiction
A parties' choice of jurisdiction must be respected (art 22) subject to the exclusive grounds of jurisdiction laid down in the Lugano Convention and to the exclusion of insurance, consumer or employment contracts in respect to which only limited autonomy to determine the courts having jurisdiction is allowed (art 23(5)). Such prorogation of jurisdiction is exclusive unless the parties have agreed otherwise.

To be valid, a prorogation of jurisdiction must be made or evidenced in writing, or in a form which accords with the practices which the parties have established amongst themselves. In international trade or commerce, prorogations of jurisdiction may be made in accordance with any usage of which the parties are or ought to have been aware and which in such trade or commerce is widely known to, and regularly observed by, parties to contracts of the type involved in the relevant trade or commerce.

Under the Lugano Convention, prorogations of jurisdiction apply exclusively to relationships with an international element and only if at least one of the parties is domiciled in a state bound by the Lugano Convention. If neither of the parties is domiciled in such a state, a court of a state bound by the Lugano Convention which has been designated in a prorogation of jurisdiction clause may examine the validity of the clause on the basis of its national laws, while the courts of the other states bound by the Lugano Convention have no jurisdiction over a dispute between the parties to the prorogation of jurisdiction unless the court chosen has declined jurisdiction.

The Lugano Convention also provides for a specific ground of jurisdiction in case of implied submission to jurisdiction (art 24). Accordingly, a court of a state bound by the Lugano Convention before which a defendant appears shall have jurisdiction except where appearance was entered to contest the jurisdiction, or where another court has exclusive jurisdiction under the exclusive rules of jurisdiction provided by the Convention (art 22).

f) Lis pendens and related actions
In the interest of the harmonious administration of justice, the Lugano Convention aims at minimizing the possibility of concurrent proceedings (→ *Lis alibi pendens*) and at ensuring that irreconcilable judgments will not be rendered by courts in two states bound by the Convention (related actions). Thus, where proceedings involving the same cause of action and between the same parties are brought before the courts of different states bound by the Convention, any court other than the court first seized has the obligation, of its own motion, to stay the proceedings until such time as the jurisdiction of the court first seized is established (art 27). By contrast, in the case of related actions, the court first seized may stay the proceedings but has no obligation to do so (art 28).

As an improvement from the previous instruments of the Brussels/Lugano regime, the Lugano Convention provides an autonomous definition for determining when an action shall be considered pending before a court mainly at the time when the document instituting the proceedings is served on the defendant or at the time when the complaint is lodged with the court (art 30).

g) Provisional and protective measures

The Lugano Convention allows the application to the courts of a state bound by the Convention for provisional, including protective, measures as may be available under the → *lex fori*, even if another state bound by the Convention would have jurisdiction as to the substance of the matter (art 31). In *Van Uden*, the ECJ ruled that the granting of such → provisional measures is conditional upon *inter alia* the existence of an actual connecting link between the subject matter of the measures sought and the territorial jurisdiction of the state of the court before which the measures are sought (Case 391/95 *Van Uden Maritime BV, trading as Van Uden Africa Line v Kommanditgesellschaft in Firma Deco-Line and Another* [1998] ECR I-7122).

Although provisional measures can be recognized and enforced under the general regime of recognition and enforcement provided by the Lugano Convention, it is worth noting that the recognition and enforcement of *ex parte* provisional measures requires the defendant to have been granted the right to be heard in the underlying proceedings within a reasonable time and prior to the application for recognition and enforcement in another state bound by the Convention (Case 125/79 *Bernard Denilauler v SNC Couchet Frères* [1980] ECR 1553).

6. Recognition and enforcement

a) Recognition

Mutual trust in the administration of justice is the underlying principle of the Brussels/Lugano regime. This principle is reflected in a system of automatic recognition of judgments among states bound by the Convention without the need for any procedure except in cases of dispute (art 33). Accordingly, any interested party may apply for a decision to have a judgment rendered in another state bound by the Convention recognized (art 33(2)). 'Judgment' means any judgment given by a court or tribunal of a state bound by the Convention, whatever the judgment may be called, such as a decree, order, decision or writ of execution, as well as the determination of costs or expenses by an officer of the court (art 32).

The Lugano Convention provides a comprehensive list of grounds for the non-recognition of judgments, but courts are not to raise them of their own motion (arts 34–5). Accordingly, a judgment will not be recognized (i) if such recognition is manifestly contrary to → public policy in the state in which recognition is sought (art 34(1)); (ii) where it was given in default of appearance, if the defendant was not served with the document which instituted the proceedings or with an equivalent document in sufficient time and in such a way as to enable him to arrange for his defence, unless the defendant failed to commence proceedings to challenge the judgment when it was possible for him to do so (art 34(2)); (iii) if it is irreconcilable with a judgment given in a dispute between the same parties in the state in which recognition is sought (art 34(3)); (iv) if it is irreconcilable with an earlier judgment given in another state bound by the Convention or in a third state involving the same cause of action and between the same parties, provided that the earlier judgment fulfils the conditions necessary for its recognition in the state addressed (art 34(4)).

In addition, a judgment will not be recognized if it conflicts with the protective rules regarding insurance, consumer contracts or contracts of employment, or in specific cases resulting from the interaction of the Lugano Convention with other international or bilateral instruments (art 35 with reference to arts 68, 64(3) and 67(4)). In its examination of the above-mentioned grounds of jurisdiction, the court seized is bound by the findings of fact on which the court of the state of origin based its jurisdiction (art 35(2)). Moreover, the court seized may under no circumstances review the substance of the foreign judgment (art 36).

b) Enforcement

Another implementation of the principle of mutual trust is the facilitated enforcement system for judgments issued by courts of states bound by the Convention in another state bound by the Convention when, on the application of any interested party, such judgments have been declared enforceable there.

A declaration that a foreign judgment is enforceable is to be issued after purely formal checks of the documents supplied (art 38), without any possibility for the court seized to raise, of its own motion, any of the grounds for non-enforcement provided by the Lugano Convention. The party against whom enforcement is sought is not entitled at this stage of the proceedings to make any submissions on the application for enforcement (art 41). The parties may then appeal against a decision on an application for a declaration of enforceability before the court indicated in Annex III of the Lugano Convention (art 43). The judgment given on the appeal may further be challenged before another body set out in Annex IV (art 44).

Provisional, including protective, measures may be requested prior to a declaration of enforceability, pursuant to the law of the state requested (art 47(1)), or together with such declaration (art 47(2)). The Lugano Convention also provides for → legal aid or exemption from costs for the enforcement procedure, provided that such aid or exemption was granted in the state of origin (art 50). In addition, the Convention excludes the request of any *cautio judicatum solvi* (art 51).

c) Formalities

The recognition and enforcement of a judgment under the Lugano Convention is subject to several formalities (art 53). In particular, a party seeking recognition or enforcement of a judgment must produce an authentic copy of the judgment, together with a specific certificate established using a standard form included in Annex V of the Lugano Convention (art 54) or an equivalent document (art 55). While a certified translation of the above-mentioned documents may be required (art 55), no legalization or other similar formality is needed (art 56).

d) Authentic instruments and court settlements

The recognition and enforcement procedure provided by the Lugano Convention (arts 38 ff) also applies to authentic instruments (art 57) and court settlements (art 58).

7. *Transitional provisions*

The Lugano Convention applies only to legal proceedings instituted and to documents formally drawn up or registered as authentic instruments after its entry into force in the state of origin and, where recognition or enforcement of a judgment or authentic instruments is sought, in the state addressed (art 63(1)). However, if the proceedings in the state of origin were instituted before the entry into force of the Convention, judgments rendered after that date will be recognized and enforced in accordance with Title III (i) if the proceedings in the state of origin were instituted after the entry into force of the 1988 Lugano Convention both in the state of origin and in the state addressed, and (ii) in all other cases, if jurisdiction was founded upon rules which accorded with those provided for either in Title II or in a convention concluded between the state of origin and the state addressed which was in force when the proceedings were instituted (art 63(2)).

8. *Relationship with other legal instruments*

The Lugano Convention contains specific provisions regarding its relationship with other legal instruments, including the Brussels I Regulation (arts 64–8). Accordingly, the Convention will not prejudice the application by the EU Member States of the Brussels I Regulation, the Brussels Convention and the corresponding agreement signed with Denmark (art 64(1)). However, the Lugano Convention will in any event apply in the situations listed in art 64(2) regarding matters of jurisdiction, *lis pendens* and related actions, and recognition and enforcement. Furthermore, the Lugano Convention will supersede the conventions concluded between two or more of the states bound by the Convention that cover the same matters as those to which the Lugano Convention applies (art 65).

As to the Brussels I Regulation (recast), it provides specifically that it does not affect the application of the Lugano Convention (art 73) which thus remains in force for its contracting parties.

IV. Protocols to the Lugano Convention

1. *Protocol 1 on certain questions of jurisdiction, procedure and enforcement*

Protocol 1 of the Lugano Convention covers various procedural issues to accommodate specificities encountered in the legal systems of some states bound by the Convention. Hence, art 1 regulates the issue of service whereby judicial and extrajudicial documents are to be served in accordance with the procedures laid down in the conventions and agreements applicable between the states bound by the Convention. Save for a derogatory declaration, this provision also foresees direct service via the public officers of each of the states concerned. Article 2 then provides for a derogatory regime with respect to the jurisdictional rules set out in arts 6(2) and 11 of the Convention in relation to actions on a warranty or guarantee or third-party proceedings which applies in specific states as listed in Annex IX. Finally, art 3 provides the legal basis for Switzerland's reservation to part of art 34(2) of the Convention regarding the refusal of the recognition of a judgment given in default of appearance. By contrast to the 1988 Lugano Convention, the Lugano Convention eliminates purely formal grounds for refusal and so recognizes a judgment rendered in default if the defendant, despite not being formally served with the documents which instituted the proceedings in sufficient time and in such a way as to enable him to arrange for his defence, failed to commence the proceedings to challenge the judgment when it was possible for him to do so. Considering that this situation would infringe too heavily the due process rights of the defendant, Switzerland made a reservation in that respect. All the declarations referred to in this Protocol may be withdrawn at any time by notification to the Depositary (art 4).

2. Protocol 2 on the uniform interpretation of the Convention and on the Standing Committee

Protocol 2 of the Lugano Convention lays down a specific mechanism to ensure similar interpretations of the Lugano and Brussels instruments. Protocol 2 not only commands a uniform interpretation of the 1988 Lugano Convention and the Lugano Convention among their contracting parties, but also calls for a coordinated interpretation of the Lugano Convention and the Brussels I Regulation. Protocol 2 is only one illustration of the principle of parallelism that has guided the parties to the Brussels/Lugano regime to ensure the conformity between the Brussels and the Lugano instruments.

First, the contracting parties to the Lugano Convention must 'be aware' of the ECJ's case-law regarding the Brussels Convention and the Brussels I Regulation as of 30 October 2007 (date of signature of the Lugano Convention) as well as the case-law of the courts of the contracting parties to the 1988 Lugano Convention until that date – in particular that of the EFTA Member States (Preamble Protocol 2). These decisions must be deemed authentic interpretation of the Lugano Convention. Additionally, art 1(1) of Protocol 2 foresees that, from the date of signature of the Convention, the adjudicating authorities of the EFTA Member States as well as the ECJ have the obligation to demonstrate a reciprocal consideration of their courts.

As under the 1988 Lugano/Brussels Conventions, the new system places no importance on the hierarchical rank of the adjudicating authority or on the size of a state. What matters is the strength of the arguments brought forward. In this respect, it is worth mentioning that art 2(2) of Protocol 2 in connection with art 23 of the Protocol on the Statute of the CJEU (Protocol (No 3) on the statute of the Court of Justice of the European Union to the Consolidated versions of the Treaty on European Union and the Treaty on the Functioning of the European Union, [2010] C 83/210) gives a right of intervention before the ECJ to non-EU Member States in specific cases. To a certain extent, this can be considered a balancing mechanism to the direct jurisdiction of the ECJ to issue case-law.

To ensure harmonization of the case-law, art 3 provides for the setting-up of a system of exchange of information concerning relevant judgments under the Lugano Convention, the 1988 Lugano Convention and the other Brussels instruments listed in art 64(1). The Lugano Convention also foresees the establishment of a Standing Committee *inter alia* to consult on the relationship of the Lugano Convention and other international instruments, to consider the accession of new states or the revision of the Lugano Convention (art 4 Protocol 2), as well as the convening of a meeting of experts whenever necessary to exchange views on the functioning of the Convention (art 5 Protocol 2).

3. Protocol 3 on the application of art 67 of the Convention

Protocol 3 of the Lugano Convention regulates the interaction between the Lugano Convention and other community provisions concerning jurisdiction or the recognition or enforcement of judgments which should remain unaffected by the operation of the Convention (art 1 Protocol 3 by reference to art 67).

As to the future, in accordance with art 2 of Protocol 3, an amendment of the Lugano instrument must be contemplated as soon as the organs of the EU envisage the adoption of a legislative act which entails provisions that contradict the revised Lugano Convention (art 2 Protocol 3). In particular, the Standing Committee (art 4 Protocol 2) or the meeting of experts (art 5 Protocol 2) are competent to give advice on a possible revision. Despite the strong willingness to maintain parallelism among the Brussels/Lugano regime, the last word still belongs to the Lugano states which remain free to incorporate the corresponding amendments of the Brussels I Regulation within the Lugano Convention (art 3 Protocol 3).

V. Conclusion

For more than two decades, the Lugano Convention, in line with the Brussels/Lugano regime, has effectively contributed to the harmonization of private international law rules regarding jurisdiction as well as the recognition and enforcement of judgments, and, consequently, to the development of a European judicial territory in its geographic sense. Yet, the principle of parallelism which has prevailed so far in relation to the Lugano and Brussels instruments is a fragile construction, constantly tested by the evolution of each of their respective contracting parties' legal systems. In particular, it remains to be seen whether the Lugano Convention will be amended in accordance with the Brussels I Regulation (recast). But regardless of what the future will bring, the Convention will remain a great achievement for having increased legal certainty of cross-border transactions among the EU and EFTA states and a model for the international development of private international law.

SANDRINE GIROUD

Literature

Andrea Bonomi, Eleanor Cashin Ritaine and Gian-Paolo Romano (eds), *La Convention de Lugano: Passé, présent et devenir* (Schulthess 2007); Andrea Bonomi and Christina Schmid (eds), *La révision du Règlement 44/2001 (Bruxelles I). Quelles conséquences pour la Convention de Lugano? Actes de la 23e Journée de droit international privé du 8 avril 2011 à Lausanne* (Schulthess 2011); Andreas Bucher (ed), *Commentaire romand: Loi sur le droit international privé: Convention de Lugano* (Helbing Lichtenhahn 2011); Felix Dasser and Paul Oberhammer (eds), *Lugano-Übereinkommen (LugÜ). Übereinkommen über die gerichtliche Zuständigkeit und die Anerkennung und Vollstreckung von Entscheidungen in Zivil- und Handelssachen vom 30. Oktober 2007. Kommentar* (2nd edn, Stämpli 2011); Hélène Gaudemet-Tallon, *Compétence et exécution des jugements en Europe: règlement 44/2001: Conventions de Bruxelles (1968) et de Lugano (1988 et 2007)* (4th edn, LGDJ 2010); Sandrine Giroud, Niklaus Meier and Rodrigo Rodriguez, '"Bruxelles I bis", un modèle pour une nouvelle Convention de Lugano?' in Emmanuel Guinchard (ed), *Le nouveau règlement Bruxelles I bis: Règlement n° 1215/2012 du 12 décembre 2012 concernant la compétence judiciaire, la reconnaissance et l'exécution des décisions en matière civile et commerciale* (Bruylant 2014); Jan Kropholler and Jan von Hein (eds), *Europäisches Zivilprozessrecht: Kommentar zu EuGVO, Lugano-Übereinkommen 2007, EuVTVO, EuMVVO und EuGFVO* (9th edn, Verl Recht und Wirtschaft 2011); Fausto Pocar, 'La Convention de Lugano révisée et l'espace judiciaire européen: passé, présent et devenir' in Andrea Bonomi and others (eds), *Nouvelle procédure civile et espace judiciaire européen: actes du colloque de Lausanne du 27 janvier 2012* (Droz 2012); Rodrigo Rodriguez and Sandrine Roth, 'Table de concordance commentée de la Convention de Lugano révisée du 30 octobre 2007 et de la Convention de Lugano du 16 septembre 1988' (2007) Jusletter (<http://jusletter.weblaw.ch>, last accessed on 2 March 2014); Anton K Schnyder, *Lugano-Übereinkommen (LugÜ) zum internationalen Zivilverfahrensrecht: Kommentar* (Dike 2011).

Maintenance obligations

I. The legislative framework

On 18 December 2008 the Council adopted the EU Maintenance Regulation (Council Regulation (EC) No 4/2009 of 18 December 2008 on jurisdiction, applicable law, recognition and enforcement of decisions and cooperation in matters relating to maintenance obligations, [2009] OJ L 7/1). Its provisions came into application on 18 June 2011 and they constitute a comprehensive legislative framework for all private international law aspects of family law maintenance. The Maintenance Regulation contains universally applicable rules on jurisdiction and applicable law – the latter through a reference to the Hague Maintenance Protocol 2007 (Hague Protocol of 23 November 2007 on the law applicable to maintenance obligations, [2009] OJ L 331/19). It also regulates the question of recognition of enforcement of decisions as between Member States as well as administrative cooperation between central authorities of Member States in matters relating to maintenance obligations. This leaves room for further legislation concerning the recognition and enforcement of judgments from third states (ie states that are not members of the European Union) as well as cooperation with central authorities in such countries. What is more, the Maintenance Regulation allows the continued application of the 1962 Nordic Convention (Convention of 23 March 1962 between Sweden, Denmark, Finland, Iceland and Norway on the recovery of maintenance (never officially translated to English)), not only in relation to third country parties (→ Iceland and → Norway) but also between those Member States that are parties to it (→ Denmark, → Finland and → Sweden).

The main instrument dealing with the issues of administrative cooperation with central authorities of third states and recognition and enforcement of judgments from such states will be the Hague Maintenance Convention 2007 (Hague Convention of 23 November 2007 on the international recovery of child support and other forms of family maintenance, [2011] OJ L 192/51). This convention was ratified by the European Union on 9 April 2014 and entered into force 1 August 2014. Since at the time of writing this entry only four other members of the Hague Conference have ratified the convention, older conventions will continue to play a role for the foreseeable future.

The major conventions that will continue to be applicable are: in the area of administrative cooperation – the UN Maintenance Convention 1956 (United Nations Convention of 20 June 1956 on the recovery abroad of maintenance, 268 UNTS 3) – the Hague Child Maintenance Convention 1958 (Hague Convention of 15 April 1958 concerning the recognition and enforcement of decisions relating to maintenance obligations towards children, 539 UNTS 27) and the Hague Maintenance Recognition and Enforcement Convention 1973 (Hague Convention of 2 October 1973 on the recognition and enforcement of decisions relating to maintenance obligations, 1021 UNTS 209). As many as 16 Member States and five other states or territories are parties to the Hague Child Maintenance Convention 1958 but this convention is largely superseded by the Hague Maintenance Recognition and Enforcement Convention 1973, to which 17 Member States and seven other states are parties. In addition to these conventions there are several other bilateral and multilateral treaties that cover the area of maintenance, as well as → reciprocity arrangements.

II. Pre-litigation measures

1. Agreements on jurisdiction and applicable law

For various different reasons a maintenance debtor and creditor may want to enter into agreements concerning which court shall be competent to hear maintenance claims arising between them and/or which law should be applied (at the time of contracting it might not be possible to foresee which one of the parties will be the creditor and which one will be the debtor). The typical situation would be a married couple that in a → marriage contract or a similar document want to subject all pecuniary issues that might arise out of their marriage to the jurisdiction of one court and one law, with which they are familiar. Another situation, that in practice also is most likely to involve spouses or ex-spouses, arises when debtor and creditor have agreed on a specific maintenance and include choice-of-court and -law clauses in their agreement.

In comparison to questions of matrimonial property the right of parties to contract is, if one makes a comparison of substantive laws, more limited in the area of maintenance. First, an agreement concerning matrimonial property is entered into between two adults. The most common form of maintenance is from a parent to an underage child. Second, even if most legal systems allow spouses to agree on the division of matrimonial property, they are often more restrictive when it comes to advance agreements concerning maintenance. Maintenance, unlike the division of matrimonial property, generally presupposes that the creditor is in economic need. As we will see, this more restrictive attitude in the area of maintenance is also reflected in the private international law rules.

a) Choice-of-court agreements

The Maintenance Regulation allows for choice-of-court agreements (art 4 Maintenance Regulation). Such agreements may be entered into in connexion with a particular dispute or well in advance, for instance in a marriage contract. In order to be formally valid the agreement must be in writing or in an electronic forum equivalent to writing.

The parties may chose a court of either a Member State in which one of the parties is habitually resident or is a national at the time the agreement is concluded or the court is seized. There is a presumption that the agreement confers exclusive jurisdiction on the court chosen unless otherwise indicated.

In case the agreement is concluded between spouses of former spouses they may agree to submit any disputes concerning maintenance to 'the court which has jurisdiction to settle their dispute in matrimonial matters'. Spouses or former spouses may also choose a court or the courts of the Member State, which was the Member State of the spouses' last common habitual residence for a period of at least one year. This enables a couple that has moved but has forgotten to write a choice-of-court agreement in favour of the courts in their old home country (of which none of them has to be a national) to do so. There is no time limit within which the choice of court must be made.

It is not possible to enter into a choice-of-court agreement concerning maintenance towards a child under the age of 18. It is irrelevant if the agreement is entered into with a custodian or other legal representative of the child or even if it would be in the best interests of the child. However, the language used would indicate that it is possible to enter into a choice-of-court agreement with a minor (through its legal representative) concerning maintenance due after the child has reached the age of 18 although it could be said to contradict the purpose of the rule. It should be noted that so-called vulnerable adults may enter into choice-of-court agreements but – as we shall see – not choice-of-law agreements.

It is not entirely clear what law should be applied to issues of substantial validity of the choice-of-court agreement if it is contested on grounds of lack of consent, fraud, duress etc. There are basically four alternatives: (i) the matter should be given an autonomous interpretation (→ Interpretation, autonomous) independent of national law and we will have to await the development of case-law from the Court of Justice. (ii) The law of the forum should be applied. This is the solution chosen in art 25 of the Brussels I Regulation (recast) (Regulation (EU) No 1215/2012 of the European Parliament and of the Council of 12 December 2012 on jurisdiction and the recognition and enforcement of judgments in civil and commercial matters (recast), [2012] OJ L 351/1; → Brussels I (Convention and Regulation)). (iii) The law applicable to the maintenance obligation in question at the time of the choice should be applied. (iv) The law applicable to the maintenance obligation in question at the time the court is seized should be applied. For reasons of simplicity and uniformity we would advocate the *lex fori* solution.

b) Choice-of-law agreements

Through a reference in art 15 of the Maintenance Regulation the law applicable to maintenance obligations is to be determined subject to the Hague Maintenance Protocol 2007 on the law applicable to maintenance in the Member States bound by that instrument. All Member States with the exception of → Denmark and the → United Kingdom are bound by the Hague Maintenance Protocol 2007.

Article 8 of the Hague Maintenance Protocol 2007 allows choice-of-law agreements that are not connected to specific proceedings. As a result of a wish to protect weaker parties it is not possible to enter into such choice-of-law agreements in respect of maintenance to a person under the age of 18 years or 'an adult who, by reason of an impairment or insufficiency of his or her personal faculties, is not in a position to protect his or her interest' – a so-called 'vulnerable adult'. It is irrelevant whether the agreement is to the advantage or disadvantage of the child or the vulnerable adult.

In practice, such choice-of-law agreements will most frequently be entered into between spouses or former spouses, but there is nothing in the Maintenance Regulation that prevents agreements between other adults such as between a grown child and its parents.

The choice is limited to a number of laws with which the parties can be assumed to have a close connexion: (i) the law of a state in which one of them is a national at the time of designation, (ii) the law of a state in which one of them is habitually resident at the time of designation, (iii) the law designated as applicable, or in fact applied, to their matrimonial property regime, (iv) the law designated as applicable, or in fact applied, to their divorce or legal separation.

Whether and to what extent the parties may chose the law applicable to their → matrimonial property regime is still a matter for national law but the Commission, 'Proposal of 16 March 2011 for a Council Regulation on jurisdiction, applicable law and the recognition and enforcement of decisions in matters of matrimonial property regimes' ((COM 2011), 126 final) foresees a possibility to choose either the law of the habitual residence or nationality of one of the parties at the time of designation. In those 15 Member States that are parties to the → Rome III Regulation (Council Regulation (EU) No 1259/2010 of 20 December 2010 implementing enhanced cooperation in the area of the law applicable to divorce and legal separation, [2010] OJ L 343/10) the parties may designate the law applicable. In the remaining 13 Member States this is a matter to be decided by national law.

A choice is formally valid if it is in writing and signed by the parties. Electronic equivalents to writing are also accepted. There is no requirement that the choice be express. It would therefore appear to be sufficient that it is demonstrated by the terms of agreement, for example through a reference to specific provisions of a particular national law.

There is no explicit rule concerning the substantive validity of the agreement, ie questions of consent, fraud, duress etc. However, the explanatory report to the Protocol, written by professor *Andrea Bonomi* (Explanatory Report to the Protocol of 23 November 2007 on the Law Applicable to Maintenance Obligations, drawn up by Andrea Bonomi, para 151, <www.hcch.net>), makes it clear that the law applicable to questions of substantive validity should be the law chosen by the parties. Since the report has been circulated among the states that participated in the negotiations and none of them has protested against this conclusion, it would appear that this is the preferred interpretation.

Article 8 Hague Maintenance Protocol 2007 contains two protective rules that seek to mitigate the result of unfair or ill-advised choices of law. Article 8(4) Hague Maintenance Protocol 2007 stipulates that, regardless of the law chosen by the parties, the question of whether a right to maintenance can be renounced or not shall be determined by the law of the state in which the creditor is habitually resident at the time of designation.

What is more, art 8(5) Hague Maintenance Protocol 2007 protects the ignorant party. If he or she was not fully informed and aware of the consequences of the → choice of law, that law shall not apply where the application of that law would lead to manifestly unfair or unreasonable consequences. The provision applies to debtors and creditors alike. In other words – save for the protection given in art 8(4) Hague Maintenance Protocol 2007 – so long as the party is well informed a choice of law leading to manifestly unfair or unreasonable consequences will be upheld. There is very little room left for public policy in such a case. One can only speculate on the meaning of 'fully informed and aware' but at least if there were full disclosure of the financial circumstances of the parties and both had access to independent legal advice or if a notary advised both of them, it would be very difficult to plead this exception.

2. Specific requests

Before bringing an action for the establishment of maintenance, the creditor will want some basic information. He or she will first of all need to locate the debtor. Even if it might be possible to bring an action against a person without a known address, the litigation might not prove worthwhile if the creditor does not know where to enforce it. Along the same lines, the creditor contemplating litigation will be interested in information about the financial circumstances of the debtor and the location of assets.

Such pre-litigation requests for information and assistance are made possible by both the Maintenance Regulation and, in relation to third states, the Hague Maintenance Convention 2007. Article 53 of the Maintenance Regulation allows a Central Authority to make a request for so-called specific measures to the Central Authority of another Member State. Article 7 of the Hague Maintenance Convention 2007 contains a similar rule. These provisions can also be used to facilitate the obtaining of evidence, to provide assistance in establishing parentage, to initiate or facilitate provisional measures and to facilitate the → service of documents.

III. Jurisdiction to litigate

The rules in the Maintenance Regulation are of universal application and leave no room for national rules on jurisdiction (Recital (15)). As a consequence of this, the Regulation contains rules on subsidiary jurisdiction and a rule on *forum necessitatis* in order to avoid situations of *déni de justice*.

The Hague Conventions contain no direct rules on jurisdiction, only so-called indirect rules. The conventions do not impose particular rules on jurisdiction on those states that are parties, but only if jurisdiction has been assumed on one of the approved grounds of jurisdiction listed in the conventions – the so-called 'white list' – is a judgment entitled to recognition and enforcement in other convention states. States are free to enact their own rules on jurisdiction; the only consequence is that if a national ground of jurisdiction is not on the approved 'white list' there will be no right under the conventions to recognition and enforcement of such judgments. One might say that all other – non-approved – national grounds of jurisdiction are on the 'grey list'. It is up to national law to determine whether such a judgment will be enforced. However, there is one exception to what has been said. Article 18 of the Hague Maintenance Convention 2007 grants exclusive jurisdiction to modify this judgment to the courts of the creditor's habitual residence in cases where jurisdiction was assumed by a court when maintenance was established. One might refer to this negative ground of jurisdiction as the 'black list' (see *infra*) since, if jurisdiction has been assumed contrary to this provision, it will not be enforced in other states that are parties to the Hague Maintenance Convention 2007.

1. Choice-of-court agreements

a) Express agreements

Article 4 of the Maintenance Regulation allows choice-of-court agreements concerning not only disputes that may arise in the future but also disputes that have arisen. For more information concerning this provision see *supra* section II.1.a).

A choice-of-court agreement is an approved ground of jurisdiction in all the three Hague Conventions from 1958 (arts 2(1) and 3(3) Hague Child Maintenance Convention 1958), 1973 (arts 4(1) and 7(3) Hague Maintenance Recognition and Enforcement Convention 1973) and 2007 (art 20(1)(e) Hague Maintenance Convention 2007). If the defendant expressly has submitted to the jurisdiction of the court, the judgment will be entitled to recognition and enforcement. It is worth noting that in the case of the Hague Child Maintenance Convention 1958 and the Hague Maintenance Recognition and Enforcement Convention 1973 this applies even if the agreement concerned maintenance to a child under the age of 18. Under the Hague Maintenance Convention 2007, art 20(1)(e) relieves Convention states from a duty to enforce such judgments if they relate to maintenance obligations in respect of children.

b) Tacit prorogation

Article 5 of the Maintenance Regulation allows a court to assume jurisdiction based on the appearance of the defendant – tacit prorogation – even if the defendant is a minor or a vulnerable adult. To which extent the court should inform the defendant of the fact that the court might not have jurisdiction should the defendant chose to contest it would appear to be a matter for the law and practices of the forum.

The Hague Child Maintenance Convention 1958 (arts 2(1) and 3(3)), the Hague Maintenance Recognition and Enforcement Convention 1973 (arts 4(1) and 7(3)) and the Hague Maintenance Convention 2007 (art 20(1)(b)) all have tacit prorogation on their 'white lists'. Hence, if the defendant has entered into appearance without contesting jurisdiction a judgment will be entitled to recognition and enforcement in other Convention states.

2. Jurisdiction when there is no agreement

a) Habitual residence of either of the parties

As is the norm, the Maintenance Regulation confers jurisdiction on the court for the place of habitual residence of the defendant (art 3(a) Maintenance Regulation). In order to protect weaker parties it is sometimes customary to give that party the right to bring an action at his or her habitual residence. In the Maintenance Regulation (art 3(b)), maintenance creditors, who are generally considered to be the weaker party, are given this advantage. It is up to them to decide whether making use of this possibility is to their advantage or not. This is also an approved ground of jurisdiction in all three Hague Conventions – see arts 2(1), 3(1) and (2) of the Hague Child Maintenance Convention 1958; arts 4(1) and 7(1) of the Hague Maintenance Recognition and Enforcement Convention 1973 and art 20(1)(a) and (c) of the Hague Maintenance Convention 2007. However, according to art 20(2) of the latter a state may enter a reservation against jurisdiction based on the creditor's habitual residence.

b) Court competent to decide on personal status or parental responsibility

In addition, the Maintenance Regulation grants jurisdiction to the court that has jurisdiction to decide on matters of → personal status – in this context matrimonial matters or parentage – or parental responsibility (→ Guardianship, custody and parental responsibility), so long as that jurisdiction is not solely based on the nationality of one of the parties, see art 3(c) and (d) Maintenance Regulation. Article 20(1)(f) of the Hague Maintenance Convention 2007 would accept such jurisdiction, also on the condition that it is not based on nationality alone. However, art 20(2) Hague Maintenance Convention 2007 gives states a possibility to enter a reservation against such jurisdiction. The Hague Child Maintenance Convention 1958 will not grant recognition to a judgment where maintenance is granted in connexion with a decision on personal status or parental responsibility, whereas the Hague Maintenance Recognition and Enforcement Convention 1973 will do so for spousal maintenance granted in connexion with matrimonial proceedings.

c) *Subsidiary jurisdiction and forum necessitatis*
Since the Maintenance Regulation leaves no room for the application of national rules on jurisdiction (see Recital (15) Maintenance Regulation), it is important that the Maintenance Regulation leave no gaps leading to negative jurisdiction conflicts, ie when no court is available to the applicant. In order to replace national rules on jurisdiction, which would prior to the adoption of the Maintenance Regulation have been applicable if the defendant were habitually resident in a third state, art 6 Maintenance Regulation on 'subsidiary jurisdiction' was adopted. According to this provision, when no court of a Member State has jurisdiction according to the harmonized rules described above and no court of a state that is a party to the Lugano Convention (Lugano Convention of 30 October 2007 on jurisdiction and the recognition and enforcement of judgments in civil and commercial matters, [2007] OJ L 339/3) has jurisdiction according to that convention, the courts of the Member State of the common nationality of the parties has jurisdiction. In case C-168/08 *Hadadi v Hadadi* [2009] ECR I-6871, which concerned a similar provision of the Brussels II Regulation (Council Regulation (EC) No 1347/2000 of 29 May 2000 on jurisdiction and the recognition and enforcement of judgments in matrimonial matters and in matters of parental responsibility for children of both spouses, [2000] OJ L 160/19), the ECJ held that holders of multiple nationalities could avail themselves of the nationality of their choice. It is safe to assume that the Maintenance Regulation should be interpreted in the same manner. Such a judgment will be recognized and enforced according to arts 4(1) and 7(3) of the Hague Maintenance Recognition and Enforcement Convention 1973 but not according to the Hague Child Maintenance Convention 1958 and the Hague Maintenance Convention 2007.

Also in order to avoid *déni de justice*, a provision on *forum necessitatis* was included in the Maintenance Regulation in art 7. If no court has jurisdiction under the other rules of the regulation and 'if proceedings cannot reasonably be brought or conducted or would be impossible in a third state with which the dispute is closely connected' and, what is more, if there is a sufficient connection between the dispute and the court seized, a court of a Member State may assume jurisdiction. The obvious situation in which this rule would grant jurisdiction to a court is when no court in a third country is available to the applicant due to lack of jurisdiction. The rule would also be applicable if, in theory, a court of a third country would be available but due to the political situation in that country it would not be safe for the applicant to go there or if a fair trial could not be expected. Finally, even if a court that would offer a fair trial is available to the applicant it would amount to a denial of justice if the judgment that would be the result of proceedings there would not be enforceable where assets are located. In such cases the *forum necessitatis* rule must be used if there are assets in a Member State. Needless to say, a judgment given by a court that bases its jurisdiction on *forum necessitatis* is not enforceable under the Hague Child Maintenance Convention 1958, the Hague Maintenance Recognition and Enforcement Convention 1973 or the Hague Maintenance Convention 2007.

3. *Negative rule on jurisdiction*
Article 18 of the Hague Maintenance Convention 2007 and art 8 of the Maintenance Regulation both contain a rule that bars the debtor from bringing an action for modification at the courts of any other contracting state than that in which the maintenance decision was first taken, provided that at that time the debtor was habitually resident in that country. There are certain exceptions to this rule: (i) if the creditor is an adult and has agreed to the jurisdiction of the courts of another contracting state in writing, (ii) tacit prorogation, including cases of child support, (iii) in

order to avoid *déni de justice*, if the courts in the state of origin are not available, (iv) where a decision from the state of origin would not be recognized in a contracting state where an action for modification is brought. This rule only imposes limitations for debtors. Creditors are free to bring an action for modification elsewhere.

IV. Applicable law

If the parties have made a valid → choice of law as described above under section II of this entry, this choice will naturally be upheld in litigation. Important aspects that will not be affected by the parties' choice of law are questions of proof, costs etc where the standards and rules of the forum will apply.

1. Designation of the law applicable for particular proceedings

Article 7 of the Hague Maintenance Protocol 2007 contains a particular rule concerning a choice of law made for the purposes of particular proceedings. This rule will normally apply to court litigation but in some countries decisions of maintenance are taken by an administrative authority. The rule permits a choice of the law of the forum. Unlike what is the case for agreements on applicable law that are entered into without a view to particular proceedings (art 8 of the Hague Maintenance Protocol 2007), art 7 Hague Maintenance Protocol 2007 permits agreements concerning maintenance to vulnerable adults and minors.

The relatively liberal attitude towards party autonomy expressed in art 7 Hague Maintenance Protocol 2007 corresponds to the view taken in the → Rome II Regulation (Regulation (EC) No 864/2007 of the European Parliament and of the Council of 11 July 2007 on the law applicable to non-contractual obligations (Rome II), [2007] OJ L 199/40). Article 14 Rome II Regulation allows for choice-of-law agreements with parties that do not pursue a commercial activity only if the agreement has been entered into after the event giving rise to the damage has occurred. The same philosophy underlies the rules on protective jurisdiction in the Brussels I Regulation, where agreements on jurisdiction may be entered into with typically weaker parties such as insurance policyholders, consumers and workers if they are entered into after the dispute has arisen. In such a situation, the weaker party – here, the maintenance creditor – will normally be in a stronger position than if the agreement had been entered into in advance and also often have legal representation. Nevertheless, an agreement under art 7 Hague Maintenance Protocol 2007 is valid even if it turns out to be detrimental to the maintenance creditor.

If the agreement is entered into after proceedings have commenced the only formal requirement (→ Formal requirements and validity) is that it be express. This requirement bars the court from concluding from the behaviour of the parties that they intend for the law of the forum to be applied. However, if a judge asks the parties if they are in agreement on the application of the law of the forum, oral statements made before the court are sufficient. Should the agreement be entered into before proceedings have been instituted, the agreement must be in writing and signed or in an electronic equivalent.

2. Applicable law in the absence of choice

The choice-of-law rules in the Hague Maintenance Protocol 2007 separate between four different categories of maintenance creditors, which are all subject to different choice-of-law rules. We could speak of: (i) a 'favoured group' consisting of children asking for maintenance from their parents, (ii) the 'neutral group' consisting of children under the age of 21 asking for maintenance from persons other than their parents and parents asking for maintenance from their children, (iii) spouses, (iv) 'the disfavoured group' consisting of adults asking for maintenance from persons other than their parents, spouses or children.

a) The 'favoured group'

The general point of departure for all categories is the application of the law of the habitual residence of the maintenance creditor (art 3 Hague Maintenance Protocol 2007). In case of a *conflit mobile*, ie if the creditor changes his or her habitual residence, the applicable law will change with that (art 3(2) Hague Maintenance Protocol 2007). However, according to the so-called 'cascade rule' in art 4 Hague Maintenance Protocol 2007 the 'favoured group' gets three shots at obtaining maintenance. The 'cascade rule' appears in two different versions depending on where the creditor brings proceedings. According to the standard version of the rule, if the creditor is unable to obtain maintenance according to the law of his or her habitual residence, the law of the forum shall apply. If the application of this law also results in the creditor's being unable to obtain maintenance, the law of the common nationality – provided that there is one – of the creditor and the debtor shall apply.

The second version of the 'cascade rule' applies if the creditor brings proceedings in the country in which the debtor has his or her habitual residence. In this case the order is reversed into (i) the law of the forum, (ii) the law of the habitual residence of the creditor and finally (iii) the law of the common nationality – if there is one.

b) The 'neutral group'

Here, the point of departure is again art 3 Hague Maintenance Protocol 2007 and the 'cascade rule' in art 4 Hague Maintenance Protocol 2007 as described above. The difference between the 'neutral group' and the 'favoured group' lies in the availability of a rule of defence contained in art 6 Hague Maintenance Protocol 2007 in relation to the former. This rule allows a maintenance debtor to contest a claim on the grounds that there is no such obligation according to both the law of his or her habitual residence and the law of the common nationality – if there is one.

c) Spouses

The third group consists of spouses, ex-spouses and parties to a → marriage which has been annulled. The main rule in art 3 Hague Maintenance Protocol 2007, ie the law of the habitual residence of the maintenance creditor, applies. However, the 'cascade rule' in art 4 Hague Maintenance Protocol 2007 is not available. What is more, either of the spouses can invoke the special rule in art 5 Hague Maintenance Protocol 2007 according to which the law of another state shall apply if there is a closer connection between that state and the marriage. There are no fixed rules as to what would constitute a closer connection but according to the article, the last common habitual residence of the parties is an example of a state to which there might be a closer connection. Another example of when there might be a closer connection to a particular state is if the spouses have had a long-standing habitual residence, perhaps coupled with nationality, in a state and have only recently acquired a new common habitual residence.

d) The 'disfavoured group'

This final group consists of requests for maintenance that, to some, appear exotic. Some legal systems provide for maintenance in such cases and some do not. Examples of types of maintenance that would fall into this group are maintenance to siblings, grandparents, parents-in-law, cousins, uncles and aunts. Here, the main rule in art 3 Hague Maintenance Protocol 2007 pointing to the law of the habitual residence of the maintenance creditor is applicable. There is no 'cascade' and the special rule of defence in art 6 Hague Maintenance Protocol 2007 is applicable.

V. Recognition and enforcement

The rules in the Maintenance Regulation on recognition and enforcement apply to judgments and administrative decisions on maintenance given in other Member States. What is more, authentic instruments and court settlements may be the subject of enforcement but not recognition. The difference is that an authentic instrument or a court settlement may not acquire the force of *res judicata* and does not prevent new litigation about the same maintenance obligation (unless a modification is sought) and is not binding to a court of another Member State should the issue of maintenance arise as a preliminary issue. It should be noted that in most Member States court settlements that are approved by a court result in a judgment, which as such is entitled to recognition. According to art 2(3) of the Maintenance Regulation an arrangement/agreement concluded with (before?) the administrative authorities of the Member State of origin or authenticated by them counts as an authentic instrument.

Concerning judgments from third countries the main instruments are the Hague Child Maintenance Convention 1958, the Hague Maintenance Recognition and Enforcement Convention 1973 and the Hague Maintenance Convention 2007. In addition, there are numerous bilateral and multilateral conventions and agreements to which one or more Member States are parties. Member States may continue to apply such international instruments in relation to third countries so long as they do not prejudice the application of the Maintenance Regulation. What is more, art 69(3) Maintenance Regulation allows the continued application of the 1962 Nordic Convention on the recovery of maintenance also in the relationship between Denmark, Finland and Sweden.

MICHAEL HELLNER

It follows from art 30 of the Hague Maintenance Convention 2007 that not only judgments but also 'maintenance arrangements', which includes both authentic instruments and agreements that have been 'authenticated by, concluded, registered or filed with a competent authority and may be the subject of review or modification by a competent authority', are capable of both recognition and enforcement. According to art 30(7) Hague Maintenance Convention 2007 states may make a declaration that an application for the recognition and enforcement of such an arrangement may only be made through Central Authorities. Thus far no states have made such declarations.

1. Judgments from other Member States

For the purposes of recognition and enforcement the Maintenance Regulation distinguishes between judgments from states that are bound by the Hague Maintenance Protocol 2007 on the law applicable to maintenance obligations and from states that are not. All Member States with the exception of Denmark and the United Kingdom are bound by the Hague Maintenance Protocol 2007. The 'standard' procedure, which is applied in relation to states applying the Hague Maintenance Protocol 2007, does not foresee any *exequatur* procedure whereas the 'non-standard' procedure applied to judgments from Denmark and the United Kingdom does. The official reasoning behind this differentiation is that in relation to states that do not apply the uniform choice-of-law rules, including the rule of defence against 'exotic' maintenance claims in art 6 of the Hague Maintenance Protocol 2007, the public policy exception available under the *exequatur* procedure was still necessary (see Recital (24) of the Protocol). It should be noted that in Denmark and the United Kingdom, no *exequatur* procedure will be applied concerning the recognition and enforcement of judgments from Member States applying the Hague Maintenance Protocol 2007.

The *exequatur* procedure that is used in relation to judgments from Denmark and the United Kingdom is modelled on that of the 'old' Brussels I Regulation with a few minor modifications in order to speed up the procedure. In all other cases, for which the *exequatur* procedure has been abolished, a judgment from another Member State is to be treated as a domestic judgment and an application for enforcement can be sent to the local enforcement authority.

In order to simplify the application procedure – regardless of whether the *exequatur* procedure is used or not – it is not necessary that the request for enforcement or application for a declaration of enforceability contain a full translation of the judgment. According to arts 20(1) and 28(2) Maintenance Regulation it is sufficient that an extract following the form contained in Annex II of the Maintenance Regulation be provided in addition to a certified copy of the judgment. The Member State of enforcement may require that this standardized form be translated. Only if the enforcement decision or the decision to grant a declaration of enforceability is challenged or appealed may the receiving state require translation of the judgment.

Unlike the case under the Brussels I Regulation (recast), where *exequatur* has also been abolished, there are no grounds of refusal in the Maintenance Regulation when 'non-*exequatur*' enforcement is sought. Instead, a right of review in the Member State of origin has been introduced in art 19 Maintenance Regulation for the cases in which the defendant did not enter an appearance and was unable to do so. What is more, art 21 Maintenance Regulation empowers the enforcement authority or court of the Member State of enforcement to refuse or suspend enforcement for reasons of prescription or limitation, or irreconcilable judgments. National grounds of refusal, such as debtor's lack of means or payment of the debt, continue to apply. If the '*exequatur* track' is followed, the grounds of refusal are the same as those under the 'old' Brussels I Regulation.

2. Judgments from third states

Where the Maintenance Regulation goes into detail, the Hague Child Maintenance Convention 1958 and the Hague Maintenance Recognition and Enforcement Convention 1973 largely leave the manner of recognition and enforcement to national law, see arts 6 and 13 Maintenance Regulation respectively. So long as the foreign judgment comes from a country that has assumed jurisdiction under one of the approved grounds (see above under III.) and the required documents are submitted, the judgment should be recognized and enforced unless there is ground for refusal. These grounds can be found in art 2 of the

Hague Child Maintenance Convention 1958 and arts 5 and 6 of the Hague Maintenance Recognition and Enforcement Convention 1973 and are quite standard: (i) public policy, (ii) fraud, (iii) incompatibility of decisions and (iv) lack of service or possibility for defendant to prepare his defence.

The Hague Maintenance Convention 2007 is quite different in that it contains rules on the *exequatur* procedure. In this aspect it is similar to the Maintenance Regulation (for judgments from states that are not bound by the Hague Maintenance Protocol 2007) and the 'old' Brussels I Regulation. What is more, the Convention contains two different *exequatur* procedures. The standard procedure is modelled on the 'old' Brussels I Regulation, in that at the first step the defendant is not heard – it is an *ex parte* procedure, see art 23(4) Brussels I Regulation. If the defendant has objections against the enforceability of the foreign decision he will have to appeal. The non-standard procedure (art 24 Brussels I Regulation) is based on the older *exequatur* procedure contained in the predecessor to the Brussels I Regulation – the Brussels Convention (Brussels Convention of 27 September 1968 on jurisdiction and the enforcement of judgments in civil and commercial matters, [1972] OJ L 299/32, consolidated version, [1998] OJ C 27/1). According to this procedure, the defendant is notified of the application for *exequatur* and is permitted to submit objections already at the first step of the procedure. This procedure was added since certain states felt that the *ex parte* procedure violated their concept of due process and defendant's right to be heard. States that wish to apply this procedure must make a declaration to this purpose. At the time of writing (February 2015) such a declaration had been made by → Ukraine alone.

VI. Administrative cooperation

Even though we can read in the press about the high sums of maintenance that are paid by this or that celebrity to a former spouse, most maintenance cases involve people of limited resources and concern relatively low amounts. In such cases it is simply not realistic to expect applicants to go about and establish or enforce maintenance in foreign countries entirely left to themselves. In order to strengthen access to justice both the Hague Maintenance Convention 2007 and the Maintenance Regulation build upon the system established by the UN Maintenance Convention 1956 and provide for a system of Central Authorities, very much like the other Hague and EU instruments for the protection of children.

The Central Authorities are to cooperate with each other and promote cooperation between other competent authorities in their home states in order to achieve the purposes of the Convention and the Maintenance Regulation respectively and to seek as far as possible solutions to difficulties that arise in the application of the two instruments (see art 5 of the 2007 Hague Convention and art 50 of the Maintenance Regulation). This provision mirrors similar provisions in the 1980 Hague Child Abduction Convention (Hague Convention of 25 October 1980 on the civil aspects of international child abduction, 1343 UNTS 89), the 1993 Hague Adoption Convention (Hague Convention of 29 May 1993 on protection of children and cooperation in respect of intercountry adoption, 32 ILM 1134), the 1996 Hague Child Protection Convention (Hague Convention of 19 October 1996 on jurisdiction, applicable law, recognition, enforcement and cooperation in respect of parental responsibility and measures for the protection of children, 35 ILM 1391), the 2000 Hague Adult Protection Convention (Hague Convention of 13 January 2000 on the international protection of adults, Hague Conference of Private international law (ed), *Collection of Conventions (1951–2009)* (Intersentia 2009) 426) and the Brussels II Regulation.

One major function of Central Authorities is to transmit and receive applications for the establishment or enforcement of maintenance. Indeed, even though direct applications that go directly to a court or an enforcement authority are possible under both instruments, the foreseen method is via a Central Authority. The Central Authorities may also be of assistance in a number of related matters such as facilitating the provision of legal aid, finding the debtor or creditor, encouraging amicable solutions etc (see art 6 of the Hague Maintenance Convention 2007 and art 51 of the Maintenance Regulation). The practical importance of the rules on administrative cooperation for the recovery of maintenance cannot be overestimated!

MICHAEL HELLNER

Literature

Paul Beaumont and others (eds), *The Recovery of Maintenance in the EU and Worldwide* (Hart Publishing 2014); Dagmar Coester-Waltjen and others (eds), *Europäisches Unterhaltsrecht, 8. Göttinger Workshop zum Familienrecht 2009* (Universitätsverlag Göttingen 2010); Hague Conference on Private International Law (ed), *Practical Handbook for Caseworkers under the 2007 Child Support Convention* (Permanent Bureau 2013); Eimear Long, 'The New Hague Maintenance Convention' (2008) 57 ICLQ 984; Lara Walker, *Maintenance and Child Support in Private international law* (Hart Publishing 2015).

Mancini, Pasquale Stanislao

Pasquale Stanislao Mancini was among the most influential conflicts lawyers in the 19th century, who established a unique conflicts system based on the principle of nationality.

I. Life and work

Pasquale Stanislao Mancini was born on 17 March 1817 in Castel Baronia, near Ariano in the province of Avellino in → Italy. Italy was then politically divided into various states and regions and dominated by → France, → Austria and → Spain. As an only child, born into an aristocratic lawyer's family, *Mancini* received a sophisticated humanistic education in his early years and was reputed to be a genius for his omnitalents in music, poetry, philosophy, law and other human and natural sciences. After legal studies at the University of Naples, he soon achieved fame as a lawyer, outstanding in his extraordinary forensic eloquence and power of argument. At the same time, he moved in prominent intellectual circles, editing a journal *Le Ore Solitarie* and participating in prestigious academies. His wife, *Laura Beatrice Oliva*, served as a constant source of inspiration. To sway young people toward liberal ideas, *Mancini* provided private lectures at his home (approximately 1843–47). He was then appointed substitute professor of natural law at the University of Naples in 1847. His field of interests comprised not only public and private international law, but ranged over legal philosophy, civil law, commercial law, criminal law, procedural law and even copyright law. His first notable contribution to private international law was a lecture held in 1843 to review *Rocco's* work 'Dell'uso e autorità delle leggi del Regno delle Due Sicilie considerate nelle relazioni con le persone e col territorio degli stranieri' (Niccola Rocco, *Dell'uso e autorità delle leggi del Regno delle Due Sicilie considerate nelle relazioni con le persone e col territorio degli stranieri* (1st edn, Tipografia del Guttenberg 1837)). This was subsequently published as 'Esame dell'opera di Niccola Rocco' in the 2nd edition of *Rocco's* work (Pasquale Stanislao Mancini, 'Esame di un' opera di diritto internazionale pubblicata da Niccola Rocco, e del rapporto fatto dal Portalis sulla stessa all'Accademia delle Scienze morali e politiche di Francia' in Niccola Rocco (ed), *Dell'uso e autorità delle leggi del Regno delle Due Sicilie considerate nelle relazioni con le persone e col territorio degli stranieri ossia Trattato di diritto civile internazionale*, vol 1 (2nd edn, Giuliano 1843) XLV–LXVI). In 1848, *Mancini* was elected to the new parliament of the Kingdom of Two Sicilies. However, political turmoil following King *Ferdinando II's* dissolution of parliament in March 1849 forced him into exile (Erik Jayme, 'Pasquale Stanislao Mancini. IPR zwischen Risorgimento und praktischer Jurisprudenz' in Erik Jayme, *Gesammelte Schriften, vol 4: Internationales Privatrecht. Ideengeschichte von Mancini und Ehrenzweig zum Europäischen Kollisionsrecht* (Müller 2009) 20–28; Emilia Morelli, *Tre profili: Benedetto XIV, Pasquale Stanislao Mancini, Pietro Roselli* (Edizioni dell'Ateneo 1955) 49–65; Yuko Nishitani, *Mancini und die Parteiautonomie im Internationalen Privatrecht* (Winter 2000) 33–7).

Mancini took refuge in Turin, capital of the Kingdom of Sardinia. The king, *Vittorio Emanuele II*, welcomed him and in 1850 the parliament approved a chair of international law for him personally at the University of Turin (Emilia Morelli, *Tre profili: Benedetto XIV, Pasquale Stanislao Mancini, Pietro Roselli* (Edizioni dell'Ateneo 1955) 67–75). In his inaugural lecture a year later, *Mancini* presented the principle of nationality. He characterized nations in terms of both objective elements – such as a region, race, language, customs, history, laws and religion – as well as a subjective element, ie consciousness of nationality. *Mancini* asserted that nations created by God's providence were to be seen as the constituent element ('*monad*') in international law, rather than states as a human invention (Pasquale Stanislao Mancini, 'Della nazionallità come fondamento del diritto delle genti. Prelezione al corso di diritto internazionale e marittimo pronunziata nella R. Università di Torino nel dì 22 gennaio 1851' in Pasquale Stanislao Mancini, *Diritto internazionale. Prelezioni con un saggio sul Machiavelli* (Marghieri 1873) 1–64). He implied in this statement a call for states within the fragmented Italy, oppressed as it was by foreign empires, to become independent and unify as a nation. The concept immediately found enthusiastic response and served as an inspiration for the *Risorgimento* (Erik Jayme, 'Pasquale Stanislao Mancini. IPR zwischen Risorgimento und praktischer Jurisprudenz' in Erik Jayme, *Gesammelte Schriften, vol 4: Internationales Privatrecht. Ideengeschichte von Mancini und Ehrenzweig zum Europäischen Kollisionsrecht* (Müller 2009) 29–31). As his lectures addressed both public and private international law, *Mancini* also derived from the principle of nationality choice-of-law rules that bilaterally point to the law of the state to which the individual belongs. Moreover, *Mancini* thoroughly researched and criticized existing academic opinions and established his own conflict-of-laws system by the academic year 1854/55 (Yuko Nishitani, *Mancini und die Parteiautonomie im Internationalen Privatrecht* (Winter 2000) 99–130). This was much earlier than under the previous prevailing opinion, which supposed completion of his conflict-of-laws doctrine only in the 1870s.

Parallel to the development of political unification, *Mancini* aspired to establish a uniform legal system, initially in the Kingdom of Sardinia but then throughout Italy (Giuliana d'Amelio, 'Pasquale Stanislao Mancini e l'unificazione legislativa nel 1859–61' (1961/62) 5/6 *Annali di Storia del Diritto* 159–220). His influential commentary on civil procedure law (Pasquale Stanislao Mancini, Giuseppe Pisanelli and Antonio Scialoja, *Commentario del Codice di procedura civile per gli Stati sardi con la comparazione degli altri Codici italiani, e delle principali Legislazioni straniere*, vol 1–6 (Unione Tipografica, Amministrazione della Società Editrice 1855–63)) was edited with a view to preparing uniform rules in Italy, independent of French influence (Emilia Morelli, *Tre profili: Benedetto XIV, Pasquale Stanislao Mancini, Pietro Roselli* (Edizioni dell'Ateneo 1955) 73). After the foundation of the Kingdom of Italy in 1861, new legislative work was instituted to replace eight distinct codes in Italy. Elected to the parliament, *Mancini* served on the legislative commission and was in charge among others of drafting choice-of-law rules in the Preliminary Dispositions (*Disposizioni sulla pubblicazione, interpretazione ed applicazione delle leggi in generale*) of the 1865 Italian Civil Code (Codice civile del Regno d'Italia of 2 April 1865, no 2215) (henceforth PDCC). The draft was adopted with minor modifications in 1865, so that *Mancini* succeeded in implementing his own ideas and conflict-of-laws system in this first comprehensive and independent private international law legislation (Erik Jayme, 'Considérations historiques et actuelles sur la codification du droit international privé' (1982) 177 Rec. des Cours 9, 40–49). In the course of his political career, *Mancini* served as Minister of Justice (1876–78) and Minister of Foreign Affairs (1881–85). He bore particular responsibility for concluding the Triple Alliance in 1882, working closely with *Bismarck* (Erik Jayme, 'Pasquale Stanislao Mancini. IPR zwischen Risorgimento und praktischer Jurisprudenz' in Erik Jayme, *Gesammelte Schriften, vol 4: Internationales Privatrecht. Ideengeschichte von Mancini und Ehrenzweig zum Europäischen Kollisionsrecht* (Müller 2009) 22).

On the other hand, *Mancini* actively practised law as well as serving as a professor of international law at the University of Rome from 1872. An important work on private international law was written in 1879 in the form of an expert opinion for the *Samama* case on inheritance (Pasquale Stanislao Mancini, 'Per gli eredi testamentari del fu Conte Caid Nissim Samama contro i pretendenti alla sua eredità ab intestato. Ricerca della legge regolatrice della successione del testatore' in Pasquale Stanislao Mancini, *Quistioni di Diritto*, vol 2 (Marghieri 1880) 211–473; for detail of the case, Erik Jayme, 'Pasquale Stanislao Mancini. IPR zwischen Risorgimento und praktischer Jurisprudenz' in Erik Jayme, *Gesammelte Schriften, vol 4: Internationales Privatrecht. Ideengeschichte von Mancini und Ehrenzweig zum Europäischen Kollisionsrecht* (Müller 2009) 35–9). Further, *Mancini* became the first president of the Institute of International Law in 1873 and in the following year at its Geneva Session presented his famous report 'De l'utilité de rendre obligatoires pour tous les États, sous la forme d'un ou de plusieurs traités internationaux, un certain nombre de règles générales du droit international privé pour assurer la décision uniforme des conflits entre les différentes législations civiles et criminelles' ((1874) 1 J.Dr. Int'l 221–39, 285–304). This address materializes *Mancini's* aspiration to unify private international law through multilateral treaties so as to render its application obligatory and thereby achieve international harmony. To promote his idea, *Mancini* negotiated with the French, Belgian, Austrian, German and Russian governments (Pasquale Stanislao Mancini, 'De l'utilité de rendre obligatoires pour tous les États, sous la forme d'un ou de plusieurs traités internationaux, un certain nombre de règles générales du droit international privé pour assurer la décision uniforme des conflits entre les différentes législations civiles et criminelles' (1874) 1 J.Dr.Int'l 221, 235–9). However, he failed to attain his objective prior to resigning from the Ministry of Foreign Affairs in 1885 as a result of disagreements on colonial policy in Africa. *Mancini* passed away soon after on 26 December 1888. After his death, his ideals were endorsed and promoted by *Asser*, eventually resulting in the founding of the → Hague Conference on Private International Law, thanks to the initiative of the Dutch government in 1893 (Erik Jayme, 'Pasquale Stanislao Mancini. IPR zwischen Risorgimento und praktischer Jurisprudenz' in Erik Jayme, *Gesammelte Schriften, vol 4: Internationales Privatrecht. Ideengeschichte von Mancini und Ehrenzweig zum Europäischen Kollisionsrecht* (Müller 2009) 22).

II. *Mancini's* contribution to private international law

1. Conflict-of-laws system

Mancini established a unique conflict-of-laws system on the basis of the principle of nationality. He held that the law of nationality was applicable in 'private law', while reserving the authority of the nation to govern all individuals within its territory in 'public law'. Transposing this two-tier system into choice-of-law rules, *Mancini* subdivided private law into a mandatory part and a dispositive part. They were governed respectively by (i) the principle of 'nationality' and (ii) the principle of 'freedom'. Public law, on the other hand, was governed by (iii) the principle of 'sovereignty and political independence' (Pasquale Stanislao Mancini, 'De l'utilité de rendre obligatoires pour tous les États, sous la forme d'un ou de plusieurs traités internationaux, un certain nombre de règles générales du droit international privé pour assurer la décision uniforme des conflits entre les différentes législations civiles et criminelles' (1874) 1 J.Dr.Int'l 285, 295–304).

2. Individual conflict-of-laws rules

a) Principle of nationality

In *Mancini's* conflict-of-laws system, the mandatory part of private law relates to the legal status and capacity of individuals (→ Capacity and emancipation), family relations and → succession, which was governed by the law of → nationality (arts 6 and 8 PDCC). Personal law was customarily determined by domicile (→ Domicile, habitual residence and establishment) among statutists, but this began to be substituted by nationality at the beginning of the 19th century. Indeed, it was a natural development to focus on nationality once the notion of citizenship was established through the foundation of modern sovereign states in Europe. However, the first codified rules in this respect, ie art 3(3) French Civil Code (Code Civil of 21 March 1804) and arts 4 and 34 Austrian Civil Code (Allgemeines Bürgerliches Gesetzbuch of 1 June 1811, JGS No 946/1811, as amended), provided solely for the unilateral application of the law of nationality to their own nationals, not to foreigners as a principle. In contrast, *Mancini* put forth bilateral conflicts rules, asserting that each individual was imprinted with characteristics of the nation to which they belonged. Citing *Montesquieu*, *Mancini* contended that persons in the cold zone grow to adulthood more slowly than in the warm zone, so that their age of majority was set higher in the cold zone. Since a person from the cold zone could not suddenly mature by moving to the warm zone, they should be subject to the law of their nationality (the 'climate' argument). Hence, sovereign states were considered under an obligation to accept foreigners with the status provided by their law of nationality. States were held apply the law of nationality to both their own nationals and to foreigners and reciprocate in honouring the rights of individuals belonging to other states (Pasquale Stanislao Mancini, 'De l'utilité de rendre obligatoires pour tous les États, sous la forme d'un ou de plusieurs traités internationaux, un certain nombre de règles générales du droit international privé pour assurer la décision uniforme des conflits entre les différentes législations civiles et criminelles' (1874) 1 J.Dr. Int'l 285, 293). As a consequence, *Mancini* was able to provide the principle of nationality with theoretical foundations and supported its subsequent expansion in civil law jurisdictions worldwide (Heinz-Peter Mansel, *Personalstatut,*

Staatsangehörigkeit und Effektivität (CH Beck 1988) 15–25).

However, *Mancini's* concept of nationality was not unequivocal. He defined the nation as a cultural nation that is strictly distinguished from the state. In fact, he never denied the existence of states, but rather presupposed that nations develop and attain the status of sovereign state as legitimate subjects under public international law capable of negotiating and signing treaties (Pasquale Stanislao Mancini, 'Della nazionalità come fondamento del diritto delle genti. Prelezione al corso di diritto internazionale e marittimo pronunziata nella R. Università di Torino nel dì 22 gennaio 1851' in Pasquale Stanislao Mancini (ed), *Diritto internazionale. Prelezioni con un saggio sul Machiavelli* (Marghieri 1873) 1, 23–61; Pasquale Stanislao Mancini, 'La vita de'popoli nell'umanità' in Pasquale Stanislao Mancini, *Diritto internazionale. Prelezioni con un saggio sul Machiavelli* (Marghieri 1873) 163, 195–7). While he clearly separated the concepts of state and nation in public international law, *Mancini* understood nationality in private international law in the sense of belonging to the state. One author explained it as a compromise with the reality that states did not yet coincide with nations in Europe (Heinz-Peter Mansel, *Personalstatut, Staatsangehörigkeit und Effektivität* (CH Beck 1988) 25–7). Another author analysed it as a necessity in private international law that a connecting factor refers to states provided with legislative authority to constitute the source of law (Yuko Nishitani, *Mancini und die Parteiautonomie im Internationalen Privatrecht* (Winter 2000) 82–5). The concept of nationality left ambiguity in *Mancini's* doctrine, which was subsequently criticized by a number of authors.

Among the issues governed by the law of nationality, *Mancini* particularly advocated the innovative uniformity principle in inheritance law following *Mittermaier* and *Savigny*, thereby pointing to the law of nationality of the deceased both for movables and immovables (Erik Jayme, 'Pasquale Stanislao Mancini. IPR zwischen Risorgimento und praktischer Jurisprudenz' in Erik Jayme, *Gesammelte Schriften, vol 4: Internationales Privatrecht. Ideengeschichte von Mancini und Ehrenzweig zum Europäischen Kollisionsrecht* (Müller 2009) 16–17). However, *Mancini* later restricted this principle by giving priority to the law of domicile, insofar as the home country of the deceased still followed the traditional principle of domicile (Pasquale Stanislao Mancini, 'Per gli eredi testamentari del fu Conte Caid Nissim Samama contro i pretendenti alla sua eredità ab intestato. Ricerca della legge regolatrice della successione del testatore' in Pasquale Stanislao Mancini, *Quistioni di Diritto*, vol 2 (Marghieri 1880) 320–22). This meant permitting → renvoi, in consequence, as practised in several existing Swiss legislations at that time (Heinz-Peter Mansel, *Personalstatut, Staatsangehörigkeit und Effektivität* (CH Beck 1988) 23).

b) Principle of freedom

According to *Mancini*, the facultative part of private law relates to assets, property, contracts and obligations (arts 7 and 9 PDCC). *Mancini* held that parties were free to subject their relevant legal relationship to the law of their nationality or another law, unless it ran counter to public policy (Pasquale Stanislao Mancini, 'De l'utilité de rendre obligatoires pour tous les États, sous la forme d'un ou de plusieurs traités internationaux, un certain nombre de règles générales du droit international privé pour assurer la décision uniforme des conflits entre les différentes législations civiles et criminelles' (1874) 1 J.Dr.Int'l 285, 295). In reality, however, the parties' freedom to deviate from objective connecting factors was only granted for → contractual obligations, whereas rights *in rem* in movables were subject to the law of the owner's nationality and those in immovables to the *lex rei sitae*. This inconsistency presumably derived from the fact that *Mancini* classified legal relationships according to whether or not parties have free disposition in substantive law, not in conflict of laws (Yuko Nishitani, *Mancini und die Parteiautonomie im Internationalen Privatrecht* (Winter 2000) 209–10).

With regard to the history of party autonomy, it remains controversial whether *Dumoulin* in the 16th century already allowed parties to choose their applicable law or solely relied on their hypothetical intent. *Savigny* objectively pointed to the → place of performance as the 'seat' of → contractual obligations, pursuant to the parties' 'voluntary submission'. In contrast, *Mancini* expressly maintained that party intent was superior in contracts, so that parties could depart from objective connecting factors fixed by the legislator. The objective connecting factors, ie the common nationality of the parties, otherwise the *locus contractus* (art 9 PDCC), were understood as solely embodying the parties' putative intent. Since public policy was the only restriction on the parties' freedom (art 12 PDCC), parties could indeed designate a foreign law including its mandatory rules. This meant granting party autonomy as a contractual conflicts rule, even though it was justified by a mere extension of freedom of contract in substantive law to conflict of laws and still lacked theoretical refinement (Yuko Nishitani, *Mancini und die Parteiautonomie im Internationalen Privatrecht* (Winter 2000) 176–246).

c) Principle of sovereignty and political independence

In *Mancini's* conflicts system, the state was obliged to respect private rights of both nationals and foreigners, but could subject all persons in the territory to its sovereignty with a view to ensuring its political independence and upholding the social order. Hence, the law of public policy and public law were always unilaterally applicable within the territory of the forum state (arts 10–12 PDCC). This concept of 'positive public policy', justifying unilateral and territorial application of mandatory rules, differs from today's notion of 'negative public policy', which is geared toward excluding the application of foreign law or the recognition of foreign judgments as a final resort so as to uphold the fundamental principles of the forum state.

3. Methods of conflict of laws

As mentioned above, *Mancini* maintained that the law of nationality was applicable in 'private law', whereas he reserved authority of the nation to govern all individuals within its territory in 'public law'. In this respect, conflicts of laws were solved by determining the territorial scope of application of law, that is with public law being territorial and private law extraterritorial. This is generally regarded as reminiscent of the statutist theories, which distinguished between *statuta personalia*, *statuta realia* and possibly *statuta mixta* in order to determine the territorial scope of application for each category of statute. *Mancini's* standpoint may well be a corollary of viewing conflict of laws as a branch of public international law. In fact, it accords with the method of *Zitelmann*, *Ludwig von Bar* and other authors, who sought to delineate the territorial reach of state legislative jurisdiction to resolve conflicts of laws.

However, *Mancini* notably departed from statutist theories in several respects. To determine personal law, he pointed to the law of nationality, not domicile (→ Domicile, habitual residence and establishment). Rejecting the *comitas doctrine* of the Dutch school, he also assumed an obligation of the state to apply foreign law. Moreover, in his conflicts system he espoused party autonomy and positive public policy, as yet unknown to statutists (Yuko Nishitani, *Mancini und die Parteiautonomie im Internationalen Privatrecht* (Winter 2000) 138–45). From the methodological viewpoint, *Mancini* did not in fact always seek to identify the territorial reach of relevant laws, but rather took the 'legal relationship' as a starting point to determine the applicable law in relation to (i) the principle of 'nationality' and (ii) the principle of 'freedom'. This accords with *Savigny's* method to look for the 'seat' of the legal relationship, even if *Mancini* himself criticized it as a *petitio principii* (Pasquale Stanislao Mancini, 'De l'utilité de rendre obligatoires pour tous les États, sous la forme d'un ou de plusieurs traités internationaux, un certain nombre de règles générales du droit international privé pour assurer la décision uniforme des conflits entre les différentes législations civiles et criminelles' (1874) 1 J.Dr.Int'l 285, 287). Moreover, the doctrines of *Savigny* and *Mancini* share common features that reflect their *Zeitgeist*. They both contrasted private law with public law in establishing their conflicts system. Private law was viewed as neutral and devoid of policy considerations of the relevant state. Thus, domestic and foreign private laws were considered as interchangeable. In addition, both authors upheld international harmony of decisions as the primary objective of conflict of laws, presupposing the existence of an international community of sovereign states in Europe (Heinz-Peter Mansel, 'Mancini, v. Savigny und die Kodifikation des deutschen internationalen Privatrechts von 1896' in Reiner Schulze (ed), *Deutsche Rechtswissenschaft und Staatslehre im Spiegel der italienischen Rechtskultur während der zweiten Hälfte des 19. Jahrhunderts* (Duncker & Humblot 1990) 245, 268–83).

III. Mancini's influence on private international law

1. General remarks

Mancini is generally considered the founder of the (modern) Italian school of private international law. His adherents were, in particular, *Esperson*, *Fiore*, *Lomonaco*, *Diena*, *Durand*, *Fusinato*, *Weiss* and *Laurent*, who largely relied on *Mancini's* conflict-of-laws system with minor deviations. In most civil law jurisdictions nowadays, however, the prevailing conflict-of-laws method consists in pointing to the law that is most closely connected with the legal relationship, an approach which goes back to *Savigny*. In this respect, the influence of the Italian school on private international law was rather limited to the selection of individual connecting factors or underlying ideas in determining the applicable law.

2. Principle of nationality

The principle of → nationality was adopted and developed by *Mancini's* adherents. The broad scope of personal law in *Mancini's* conflict-of-laws system, which comprised not only individual capacity and status but also contracts and rights *in rem* in movables, was even extended by *Laurent* to also include immovables. At the turn of the 20th century, the principle of nationality penetrated legislation and doctrines in civil law jurisdictions in Europe, Latin America and Asia. Because pointing to the nationality serves to uphold the tie of nationals with their home country wherever they go, it was attractive for newly established modern states as well as for states that had overseas territories or numerous out-bound emigrants.

The tide turned in around the 1930s, when the appropriacy of the principle of nationality began to be questioned. Not only was *Mancini's* 'climate' argument criticized for its fictitious nature, some authors also doubted the legitimacy of the principle of nationality, contending that nationality as a public law notion was inapt to determine the applicable law in family relations and succession, or failed to always reflect the person's closest connection. In addition, nationality requires supplementary connecting factors in the event of dual nationality and statelessness, or cascading connecting factors for spouses of different nationality so as to respect gender equality. Other authors, by contrast, supported the principle of nationality in the light of its functionality or the possibility to duly honour the individual's cultural identity. While some civil law jurisdictions continue to uphold the principle of nationality (eg → Japan, → Korea and → Turkey), EU regulations have clearly turned to the principle of habitual residence, following the model of the Hague Conventions, even though nationality serves as a subsidiary connecting factor or may be chosen by the parties.

Mancini's espousal of *renvoi* remained unnoticed. After the *Forgo* case of the French Cour de cassation (Cour de Cassation France, 24 June 1878, *Forgo*, Sirey 1878.1.429; Cour de Cassation France, 22 February 1882, *Forgo*, Sirey 1882.1.393) aroused debates on the admissibility of *renvoi*, the Italian legislature rejected it in 1942, but reintroduced it in 1995.

3. Party autonomy

As mentioned above, the initial form of → party autonomy was granted by *Mancini* and the Italian school by extending freedom of contract in substantive law to conflict of laws. At the turn of the 20th century, while court decisions in various jurisdictions favoured the parties' freedom to designate the applicable law, leading authors began to denounce party autonomy due to insufficient justifications provided by the Italian school.

The principal arguments against party autonomy were the following. First, the parties' freedom of contract cannot go beyond dispositive norms of the relevant substantive law, as otherwise the parties could have excessive power to circumvent any mandatory rules. Second, the existence and validity of the parties' consent to the → choice of law must be governed by a certain law. However, this cannot be the law chosen by the parties, as this would constitute a *petitio principii*. Nor can the governing law be the *lex fori*, due to its contingency, or even the law determined by an objective → connecting factor, as that would render party autonomy meaningless. It was not until the 1930s that these criticisms were overcome. As to the first argument based on freedom of contract, it was clarified that the authors did not appropriately distinguish freedom of contract in substantive law from party autonomy in conflict of laws. Party autonomy indeed could be justified by taking the parties' intent as an independent criterion in conflict of laws, which serves to determine the applicable law including mandatory rules. In relation to the second criticism based on the parties' consent, it was asserted that the existence and validity of the parties' consent to the choice of law could logically be governed by the law designated by the parties, since their intent is solely referred to as a specific connecting factor at the level of conflict of laws.

Following these developments, party autonomy has been recognized as a legitimate conflict-of-laws rule in contracts worldwide,

YUKO NISHITANI

except in a limited number of jurisdictions in Latin America and the Middle East that exclude or restrict the parties' choice of law. In recent legislation in Europe, the scope of party autonomy is extended to extra-contractual obligations, name, family relations and succession, and partly even to rights *in rem* in movables

4. *Positive public policy*

In *Mancini's* system, the application of laws of public policy and public law was not an exception but a principle, constituting one of the three pillars. His adherents of the Italian school sought to clarify this notion by distinguishing between internal and international public policy or considering law of public policy and public law as grounded on state authority, without being able to agree on a uniform definition. In contemporary private international law systems, the notion of 'positive public policy' instituted by the Italian school is generally not adopted. The idea, however, has been incorporated as a unilateral, territorial application of 'overriding' or 'internationally' mandatory rules that are applicable irrespective of the law governing the legal relationship concerned. In this respect, some indirect influence of the Italian school can be observed.

YUKO NISHITANI

Literature

Giuliana d'Amelio, 'Pasquale Stanislao Mancini e l'unificazione legislativa nel 1859–61' (1961/62) 5/6 *Annali di Storia del Diritto* 159; Erik Jayme, *Pasquale Stanislao Mancini. IPR zwischen Risorgimento und praktischer Jurisprudenz* (Gremer 1980; reprinted in Erik Jayme, *Gesammelte Schriften, vol 4: Internationales Privatrecht. Ideengeschichte von Mancini und Ehrenzweig zum Europäischen Kollisionsrecht* (Müller 2009) 8; translated into Italian by Antonio Ruini, *Pasquale Stanislao Mancini. Il diritto internazionale privato tra Risorgimento e attività forense* (CEDAM 1988)); Erik Jayme, 'Considérations historiques et actuelles sur la codification du droit international privé' (1982) 177 Rec. des Cours 9; Erik Jayme, *Gesammelte Schriften, vol 4: Internationales Privatrecht. Ideengeschichte von Mancini und Ehrenzweig zum Europäischen Kollisionsrecht* (Müller 2009); Pasquale Stanislao Mancini, 'Esame di un' opera di diritto internazionale pubblicata da Niccola Rocco, e del rapporto fatto dal Protalis sulla stessa all'Accademia delle Scienze morali e politiche di Francia' in Niccola Rocco (ed), *Dell'uso e autorità delle leggi del Regno delle Due Sicilie considerate nelle relazioni con le persone e col territorio degli stranieri ossia Trattato di diritto civile internazionale*, vol 1 (2nd edn, Giuliano 1843) XLV–LXVI (lecture held in 1837); Pasquale Stanislao Mancini, 'Della nazionallità come fondamento del diritto delle genti. Prelezione al corso di diritto internazionale e marittimo pronunziata nella R. Università di Torino nel dì 22 gennaio 1851' in Pasquale Stanislao Mancini, *Diritto internazionale. Prelezioni con un saggio sul Machiavelli* (Marghieri 1873) 1; Pasquale Stanislao Mancini, 'La vita de'popoli nell'umanità' in Pasquale Stanislao Mancini, *Diritto internazionale. Prelezioni con un saggio sul Machiavelli* (Marghieri 1873) 163; Pasquale Stanislao Mancini, 'De l'utilité de rendre obligatoires pour tous les États, sous la forme d'un ou de plusieurs traités internationaux, un certain nombre de règles générales du droit international privé pour assurer la décision uniforme des conflits entre les différentes législations civiles et criminelles' (1874) 1 J.Dr.Int'l 221–39, 285–304; Pasquale Stanislao Mancini, 'Per gli eredi testamentari del fu Conte Caid Nissim Samama contro i pretendenti alla sua eredità ab intestato. Ricerca della legge regolatrice della successione del testatore' in Pasquale Stanislao Mancini, *Quistioni di Diritto*, vol 2 (Marghieri 1880) 211; Pasquale Stanislao Mancini, Giuseppe Pisanelli and Antonio Scialoja, *Commentario del Codice di procedura civile per gli Stati sardi con la comparazione degli altri Codici italiani, e delle principali Legislazioni straniere* (Unione Tipografica, Amministrazione della Società Editrice 1855–63); Heinz-Peter Mansel, *Personalstatut, Staatsangehörigkeit und Effektivität* (CH Beck 1988); Heinz-Peter Mansel, 'Mancini, v. Savigny und die Kodifikation des deutschen internationalen Privatrechts von 1896' in Reiner Schulze (ed), *Deutsche Rechtswissenschaft und Staatslehre im Spiegel der italienischen Rechtskultur während der zweiten Hälfte des 19. Jahrhunderts* (Duncker & Humblot 1990) 245; Emilia Morelli, *Tre profili: Benedetto XIV, Pasquale Stanislao Mancini, Pietro Roselli* (Edizioni dell'Ateneo 1955) 47; Yuko Nishitani, *Mancini und die Parteiautonomie im Internationalen Privatrecht* (Winter 2000); Niccola Rocco, *Dell'uso e autorità delle leggi del Regno delle Due Sicilie considerate nelle relazioni con le persone e col territorio degli stranieri* (1st edn, Tipografia del Guttenberg 1837; 2nd edn, Giuliano 1843).

Marine insurance

I. Background

1. Definition

A policy of marine insurance can be defined as a contract by which the insurer undertakes, pursuant to the specific terms of the agreement, to indemnify the assured for losses incurred in connection with an insurable interest involved in a marine adventure. There must be a relevant legal relationship between the assured, ie the person benefiting from the indemnity, and the insurable interest covered by the contract; such property can be a ship, goods or other movables (eg containers), freight, profit or other pecuniary benefit. Marine insurance contracts may also cover the interest for security for a loan or similar arrangements and any liability to a third party incurred by the owner of, or other person interested in or responsible for, the insurable property. Although the main risks against which the insurance cover is granted usually fall within the concept of marine perils (ie the perils consequent on, or incidental to, the navigation of the sea), the terms of the policy can extend the scope of the same as to protect the assured against losses in inland waters or on any land risk which may be incidental to any sea voyage. Although marine insurance contracts are fully within the general legal definition of → insurance contracts, for historical reasons in several countries they are governed by special law rules which apply only to them. In several maritime nations, standard policy forms have been developed to be used in commercial practice to obtain cover related to maritime trade and activities.

2. International character of marine insurance

A distinctive feature of marine insurance is its internationality, which depends on the inherent characteristics of the contract, the structure of the shipping industry and the marine insurance market. As for the first aspect, most marine insurance contracts cover the insured property for risks which can occur in different areas of the world, it being a normal situation that a ship would navigate between ports of different countries, that goods would be carried from one country to another, and that marine incidents would occur anywhere that the insured property is located around the world, thus causing the assured to suffer losses or incur liability for events occurred in different countries.

In addition, taking into consideration the most common types of marine insurance contracts, it is a usual feature that for a single insured ship there can be a variety of potentially interested parties, such as the registered owner, the bare boat charterer, the charterer, the managing company or the mortgagee, all of whom can be domiciled in different countries and whose legal relationship with the same insured property can be relevant for the purposes of the insurance cover. Similarly, marine cargo insurance is usually stipulated in respect of goods being sold by a seller who in most cases has a different nationality or domicile from the buyer.

Furthermore, a common feature of the marine insurance market is its international character, so that it is not unusual that the insurer and the assured are domiciled in different countries, that a single insurance contract is concluded by several co-insurers domiciled in different countries, and that the underlying insurance contract is re-insured with re-insurers domiciled in a country different from that of the insurer. Finally, marine insurance contracts frequently adopt standard forms used in the most important marine insurance markets, even when neither the insurer nor the insured are domiciled in such countries, those being standard forms internationally well known in their scope of cover and therefore more easily accepted in international trade.

Given their inherent international character and the peculiar structure of both the contract arrangements and the relevant market, marine insurance contracts can give rise to some specific issues in terms of choice-of-law and jurisdiction rules.

II. Private international law

1. Marine insurance and large risks

The concept of large risks was originally developed in the (then) European Community law in the context of the implementation of the freedom to provide cross-border insurance services, in order to distinguish insurance contracts for mass risks, for which there was an overriding public interest to grant a proper level of protection to the assured (considered as the weaker party), from the insurance contracts for which no such interest was present. As a result, the Second Insurance Directive (Directive 88/357/EEC of 22 June 1988 on the coordination of laws, regulations and administrative provisions relating to direct insurance other than life assurance and laying down provisions to facilitate the effective exercise of freedom to provide services and amending Directive 73/239/EEC, [1988] OJ L 172/1), amended art 5(d) of the

First Insurance Directive (Directive 73/239 of 24 July 1973 on the coordination of laws, regulations and administrative provisions relating to the taking-up and pursuit of the business of direct insurance other than life assurance, [1973] OJ L 228/3), and set out the legal definition of large risks, which were subject to a more liberal regime in the case of cross-border business. However, the distinction was also relevant for private international law purposes, since the Second Insurance Directive established a different regime for → choice of law involving → insurance contracts for mass risks from that for the conflict rules involving insurance contracts for large risks, the rationale again being the need to protect the position of the assured in contracts of the former type.

At present, the legal definition of large risks is set out in art 13(27) of the Solvency II Directive (Directive 2009/138/EC of the European Parliament and of the Council of 25 November 2009 on the taking-up and pursuit of the business of Insurance and Reinsurance (Solvency II), [2009] OJ L 335/1, as amended), and it has the peculiar feature of using different criteria in order to identify such large risks. In fact, there are specific risks which are *per se* considered to be part of such a category by virtue of their objective qualification, irrespective of any consideration of the quality of the parties to the contract to which the risks pertain (art 13(27)(a)), whilst other risks are considered to be large if the parties to the relevant contract are of the required minimum size in accordance with the features set forth in art 13(27)(b)(c).

It is usually argued that in marine insurance, given the structure of the relevant market and of related agreements, there is no specific public interest in the protection of the assured, so that it is generally understood that marine insurance contracts refer *per se* to large risks; however, this understanding must be verified in respect of the specific legal criteria to define large risks. In fact, according to art 13(27)(a) of the Solvency II Directive the legal concept of large risks includes the risks classified under classes 4 (railway rolling stock), 5 (aircraft), 6 (ships, including sea, lake and river and canal vessels), 7 (goods in transit, including merchandise, baggage and all other goods), 11 (aircraft liability) and 12 (liability for ships, including sea, lake and river and canal vessels) as defined in Part A of Annex I to the Solvency II Directive, irrespective of the quality of the parties to the contract. Focusing on classes 6, 7 and 12 it is therefore clear that marine insurance contracts – for damage to or loss of river and canal vessels, lake vessels, and sea vessels; damage to or loss of goods in transit or baggage; and for all liability arising out of the use of ships, vessels or boats on the sea, lakes, rivers or canals, including carrier's liability (being generally referred to as Hull and Machinery covers, Cargo covers, and Protection and Indemnity covers, respectively), all of which form the largest part of a typical marine insurance business – are considered as large risks *per se*.

However, there can be some dubious cases; for example, insurance contracts in respect of a ship under construction are usually considered to be part of the marine insurance genus, but do ships under construction fall within the definition of ship relevant to the purposes of art 13(27) of the Solvency II Directive? Other dubious cases might be the shipbuilders' liability and ship repairs' liability covers, which *prima facie* can hardly be considered as referring to liabilities arising from the use of the ship (as required for class 12 risks), or to the specific cover provided by marine cargo insurance contract in respect of the cargo contribution for General Average or Salvage, which might be considered as not referring to a loss or damage to the insured goods in transit (as required by class 7), it being more properly classified a financial loss. It is even more difficult to assume that loss of hire or freight insurance, another traditional marine insurance cover, falls within the above-mentioned classes.

Some of these dubious cases can be resolved by applying the other criteria set out by the Solvency II Directive, under which the quality of the contracting parties must be taken into consideration. For example, even if it might be dubious whether a marine insurance policy covering the mortgagees' interest on a ship pertains to class 6 (which would be the most obvious conclusion taking into consideration the market practice), it should nonetheless be considered part of class 14 (insolvency in general, export credit, instalment credit, mortgages, agricultural credit), so that pursuant to art 13(27)(b) it could still be regarded a large risk, albeit only where the policyholder is engaged professionally in an industrial or commercial activity, or in one of the liberal professions and the risks relate to such activity, which in fact is a usual feature for such cover. Another example might be to consider the already mentioned marine insurance for loss of hire or freight and for contribution to General Average or Salvage as within class 16 (miscellaneous financial loss) and the shipbuilders' and ship repair liability cover as within class 13 (general liability), both of which are considered by art 13(27)(c) of the Solvency II Directive as large risks so far as the policyholder exceeds the limits of at least two of the following criteria: (i) a balance-sheet total of EUR 6.2 million, (ii) a net turnover of EUR 12.8 million, (iii) an average number of 250 employees during the financial year.

In some other dubious cases it seems difficult to find a way out: for example, the risks pertaining to class 17 (legal expenses and costs of litigation) are outside the legal definition of large risks, albeit in market practice the defence cover is usually provided (at an additional cost) in the context of the protection and indemnity insurance which is considered as pertaining to large risks (class 12). On the other hand, there are cases which fall within the legal definition of large risks, yet they would seem to be more properly related to mass risks, such as the hull insurance of yachts and sailing boats, usually involving consumers.

The construction of legal terms adopted in EU legal instruments is generally an autonomous one, so that it is generally irrelevant whether under national laws such risks are considered marine ones or not, thus creating the possibility of some difference between the market notion of marine risks and the legal definition of large risks pursuant to the Solvency II Directive. However, it is suggested that, in order to give an *effet utile* to the Solvency II Directive definitions, the actual market practice should be taken into consideration in order to assess whether some specific risks fall within the above-mentioned classes, in order not to place an undue burden on the marine insurance sector where the issue of protection of the assured is less relevant, since it mostly involves business-to-business services; in addition, it could be argued that ancillary risks which are closely related to the large risks for which the main cover is granted should fall within the same category.

The concept of large risk is still relevant to establish the private international law regime applicable to marine insurance contracts, since pursuant to art 7 of the Rome I Regulation (Regulation (EC) No 593/2008 of the European Parliament and of the Council of 17 June 2008 on the law applicable to contractual obligations (Rome I), [2008] OJ L 177/6; → Rome Convention and Rome I Regulation (contractual obligations)), an insurance contract covering a large risk as defined in art 5(d) of the First Insurance Directive (now replaced by art 13(27) of the Solvency II Directive) is subject to conflict rules different from those applicable to insurance contracts referring to other risks.

2. Marine insurance and the localization of the risks

At present, the Solvency II Directive (art 13(13)) defines the Member State of localization of the risk as: (a) the Member State in which the property is situated, where the insurance relates either to buildings or to buildings and their contents, insofar as the contents are covered by the same insurance policy, (b) the Member State of registration, where the insurance relates to vehicles of any type, (c) the Member State where the policyholder took out the policy in the case of policies of a duration of four months or less covering travel or holiday risks, whatever the class concerned, (d) in all cases not explicitly covered by points (a), (b) or (c), the Member State in which either of the following is situated: (i) the habitual residence of the policyholder or (ii) if the policyholder is a legal person, that policyholder's establishment to which the contract relates.

Such legal criteria have no connection with the concept of localization of the risk as in the territorial scope of application of an insurance contract; a feature invariably present in marine insurance contracts to exclude from the cover the accident occurring outside such agreed area. These criteria refer to all insurance contracts, thus creating some specific issues when they are to be applied to even the most common types of marine insurance contracts.

Starting from marine insurance contracts relating to ships, it seems proper to consider them as localized in the state where the vessel is registered, ie the state of the flag, since a ship falls within the definition of vehicle relevant to EU law; in addition, the term 'relates' can be given a sufficiently wide meaning, thus avoiding most of the doubts already mentioned when discussing the classification of some specific covers as large risks. However, a number of issues might still arise. In today's shipping industry the link between the state of the → flag and those interested in the vessel can be very tenuous, since the choice of the place of registration of the ship may depend on a number of commercial considerations (such as the possibility to choose the nationality of the crew members, the existence of flag restrictions for the use of the ship in given trades, the availability of specific financial schemes depending on the flag of the vessel to be built or purchased), so that such a link may not really be relevant to localizing the actual underlying interests in the vessel. However, it must be recalled that referring to the place of registration has the benefit of making the place where the risk is localized certain and foreseeable and, given the purposes for which such a rule is adopted, ie to identify the scope of application of EU law, such an advantage should outweigh the potential shortcomings. For the sake of completeness, it should be noted that it is possible for a ship to be registered in two separate states, as in the case of suspension of the registration due to the transfer of the vessel to a bare-boat register or due to the temporary registration of the vessel under the flag of another state. In such cases, the state of registration should be considered to be the state of the temporary flag, irrespective of the fact that the same ship is still registered (albeit under suspension) in the original register of a different state.

As for marine cargo insurance, it cannot be considered as 'covering travel or holiday risks', since such terms clearly refer to personal covers and not insurance for goods in transit, so that they are to be localized in the Member State in which the habitual residence of the policyholder or, if the policyholder is a legal person, that policyholder's establishment to which the contract relates, is situated. Given the fundamental principle of insurance law for which there must be a relevant legal relationship between the person benefiting from the indemnity and the property covered by the insurance contract, it seems quite logical that the residence of the latter person be used for the purposes of risk localization. However, it should be noted that art 13(13)(c) of the Solvency II Directive does not literally refer to the assured, but to the policyholder, which seems to imply that there might be a difference between these two concepts. As a matter of fact, in marine cargo insurance the situation is made also more complex because it is a standard term of trade, incorporated in most of the relevant policies, that the cover is stipulated 'on behalf of whom it may concern', since at the time of the agreement it might be still not known who will be the person vested with the legal relationship in respect of the property at the time of the entry into force of the insurance cover or because the policy is taken by a freight forwarder in its own name but on behalf of an undisclosed principal. In addition, it is also contemplated that such a person might possibly change during the duration of the insurance contract, as a result of the sale of the goods. In fact, in case of a casualty the insurance indemnity will be ultimately paid to the person at risk at the time of the accident, although since the goods can be sold and purchased several times during the sea passage, the identity of the person cannot be known to the insurers at the time of the issuing of the policy. As a result, in the context of marine cargo insurance, it could be unclear if – for the purposes of the localization of the risks – the habitual residence of the person who originally concluded the contract with the insurer must be used, irrespective of whether such person also is or will be the assured under the terms of the policy, or rather whether the habitual residence of the actual assured should be used, even though in some cases the actual assured's identity, and therefore its residence, cannot be known at the time of the issuing of the policy. Given the importance of properly localizing the risk from the beginning of the contractual relationship, the former solution seems to better ensure the *effet utile* of the relevant rule.

As for protection and indemnity insurance, it seems proper to give more weight to the circumstance that the scope of such cover is the liability relating to the use of the vessel, to be construed in very wide terms, thus making it possible to consider such a contract as relating to the ship and therefore to apply art 13(13)(b) of the Solvency II Directive, with the benefit of legal certainty.

The concept of localization of the risk is still marginally relevant to establish the private international law regime applicable to marine insurance contracts, not only in the (arguably very limited) cases when some specific marine insurance covers might be considered as small or medium risks, but also since it could be a relevant → connecting factor even if the contract is considered as referring to large risks.

3. Choice-of-law rules and marine insurance contracts

Pursuant to art 7 of Rome I Regulation, an insurance contract covering a large risk, defined as above, shall be governed by the law chosen by the parties in accordance with art 3 of the same Regulation, irrespective of where the risks are localized. Since most marine insurance contracts cover large risks, the parties to the same have a high degree of freedom to choose the law applicable to the contract, within the general limits of the Rome I Regulation; in fact, most marine insurance policies and standard forms do incorporate express choice-of-law clauses, which usually refer to the law of the insurer. Moreover, according to art 3, in the absence of an express choice-of-law clause, the parties' intention in respect of the applicable law can be clearly demonstrated by the terms of the contract or the circumstances of the case. In this connection, it has been debated whether the parties' decision to adopt a standard form can be considered as an indication of a tacit choice of the law of the state where such a standard form was created as the governing law of the contract. It is quite common for marine insurance contracts to adopt standard forms which are widely used in international trade, even though the same have been elaborated in states which have no direct connection with the insurer or the assured, for a variety of reasons.

For example, in marine cargo insurance the use of such standard forms makes it easier for the CIF seller to comply with its obligation under the terms of the contract of sale to provide for a specific insurance cover, since the actual extent of the cover granted under such internationally accepted standard forms is well known to the buyer. In hull and machinery insurance, the use of an internationally accepted standard form makes it possible for the shipowners to compare the contractual offer made by insurers which might be localized in different jurisdictions, by referring to the same cover, whose scope of application is well known, instead of having to assess case by case the actual scope of application of each different cover, if provided under different, national forms. In addition, the use of an internationally accepted standard form can make it easier for the insurer to find proper reinsurance, since the actual extent of the cover granted under such a form is well known to the reinsurer as well. In consideration of the above, in the absence of an express choice-of-law clause, the use of such internationally accepted standard forms does not necessarily reflect the intention of the parties to submit the whole insurance agreement to the law of the state where such standard forms were developed (even though it can be a significant indication, among others, of the existence of such intention). On the other hand, the use of such a form clearly indicates the willingness of the parties to ensure, for their specific contract, the same kind of insurance cover resulting from the adoption of such form, so that its wording and legal concepts usually are to be construed taking into consideration the legal environment in which such terms have been developed.

As a result, where the contract is composed of a main policy cover incorporating the fundamental terms of the agreement, and one or several standard forms relating to the specific risks covered, the tacit choice referred to in the previous paragraph arguably is confined to the risk covered by the respective standard form while other parts of the contract are not affected by that choice. This may amount to a → *depeçage* as permitted under art 3(1), 3rd sentence of the Rome I Regulation. The benefit of such solution is the possibility to have the terms of such a standard form construed and applied taking into consideration the internationally accepted meaning and scope of application of the same, as resulting from insurance trade practice and relevant precedents. Therefore, the parties can be considered at least as having tacitly chosen the law of the state where the form has been developed as the governing law of one part of the insurance contract, ie only for the issues related to the construction of the policy terms used in such a form.

As pointed out, the principle of the freedom of choice of the applicable law is the cornerstone of the Rome I Regulation, so that it must be ensured that the choice freely made by the parties as regards the law applicable to their contractual relationship is respected (Case C-184/12 *United Antwerp Maritime Agencies (Unamar) NV v Navigation Maritime Bulgare* [2013] OJ C 367/12, para 49). As a result, in adopting a similar approach in the course of the assessment on whether mandatory rules established by any law, other than the one chosen by the parties, can be applied to a marine insurance contract pursuant to art 9 Rome I Regulation, it must be considered that the whole structure of the insurance directives and the choice-of-law rules applicable to large risks are based on the assumption that for such insurance contracts there is no overriding public interest to protect the assured, so that, in order not to compromise the harmonizing effect intended by such EU instruments, the possibility that rules aimed at the protection of the weaker party may be applied as mandatory rules to such a contract, and to restrict the applicability of the law freely chosen by the parties, should be excluded.

To the extent that the applicable law has not been chosen by the parties, marine insurance contracts are to be governed by the law of the country where the insurer has its habitual residence (Rome I Regulation, art 7(2)(2)). The reference to this → connecting factor seems to overlook the fact that in most cases marine policies are concluded by a number of co-insurers, who can have their habitual residence in different countries. In such cases, it seems more appropriate to refer only to the residence of the leading insurer. However, when it is clear from all the circumstances of the case that the contract is manifestly more closely connected with another country, the law of that other country should apply. In establishing this closer connection, it is suggested that the localization of the risks should play a minimal role, since as mentioned above there is no real substantive significance in establishing where the interests underlying marine insurance are localized. On the other hand, proper weight should be given in such an assessment to those elements which, as per market practice, tend to indicate the centre of gravity of the contractual relationship. Such indications include the domicile of the brokers, the use of specific standard forms and clauses or the incorporation of follow clauses connecting the contract to a lead policy, and thereby referring to the latter's insurance market of origin.

In conclusion, as discussed above, although marine insurance contracts should be considered as mostly referring to large risks, such a conclusion depends on the actual construction of such a legal concept. The possibility cannot be excluded that some specific risks, albeit usually covered by marine policies, might be considered as mass risks for the purposes of choice-of-law rules and, therefore, be subject to the general rules established by art 7 Rome I Regulation for insurance contracts referring to such other risks.

4. *Jurisdiction*

Jurisdiction rules applicable to marine insurance contracts are basically the same as those applicable to general insurance contracts, yet in the context of the Brussels Convention (Brussels Convention of 27 September 1968 on jurisdiction and the enforcement of judgments in civil and commercial matters, [1972] OJ L 299/32, consolidated version, [1998] OJ C 27/1), as amended by the Convention of Accession of 9 October 1978 of the Kingdom of Denmark, of Ireland and of the United Kingdom of Great Britain and Northern Ireland to the Convention on jurisdiction and enforcement of judgments in civil and commercial matters and to the Protocol on its interpretation by the Court of Justice (78/884/EEC), [1978] OJ L 304/1, special prorogation of jurisdiction rules were applicable only to some specific marine insurance policies (art 12(5) and 12(A)).

In the context of the Brussels I Regulation (Regulation (EC) No 44/2001 of 22 December 2000 on jurisdiction and the recognition and enforcement of judgments in civil and commercial matters, [2001] OJ L 12/1) and of the Brussels I Regulation (recast) (Regulation (EU) No 1215/2012 of the European Parliament and of the Council of 12 December 2012 on jurisdiction and the recognition and enforcement of judgments in civil and commercial matters (recast), [2012] OJ L 351/1) (→ Brussels I (Convention and Regulation)) reference to some specific marine insurance contracts has been kept, yet the special regime for prorogation of jurisdiction has been extended to all large risks too.

In fact, pursuant to art 15(5), of the Brussels I Regulation (recast) the provisions of the section on insurance may be departed from by an agreement of the parties which relates to a contract of insurance insofar as it covers one or more of the risks set out in art 16 Brussels I Regulation (recast). Such risks are thus defined as those related to (1) any loss of or damage to: (a) seagoing ships, installations situated offshore or on the high seas, or aircraft, arising from perils which relate to their use for commercial purposes, (b) goods in transit other than passengers' baggage where the transit consists of or includes carriage by such ships or aircraft; (2) any liability, other than for bodily injury to passengers or loss of or damage to their baggage: (a) arising out of the use or operation of ships, installations or aircraft as referred to in point 1(a) insofar as, in respect of the latter, the law of the Member State in which such aircraft are registered does not prohibit agreements on jurisdiction regarding insurance of such risks, (b) for loss or damage caused by goods in transit as described in point 1(b); (3) any financial loss connected with the use or operation of ships, installations or aircraft as referred to in point 1(a), in particular loss of freight or charter-hire; (4) any risk or interest connected with any of those referred to in points 1-3.

However, the special rule on prorogation applies also to insurance contracts relating to all large risks (art 16(5) Brussels I Regulation (recast)), so that by comparing the two sets of definitions it appears that most of the cases of marine insurance contracts expressly excluded by art 16 of Brussels I Regulation (recast) in points 1-3 are nevertheless large risks, either *per se*, or by applying the other criteria mentioned by art 13(27) of the Solvency II Directive; as a result, it is also suggested that even the contracts for risks expressly excluded by the same art 16(1)-(3), eg loss or damage to passengers' baggage and liability for bodily injury to passengers or loss of or damage to their baggage, are nonetheless to be considered as subject to art 15(5) of the Brussels I Regulation (recast), those being large risks, pursuant to art 16(5) of the same.

In consideration of the above, it is worthwhile mentioning that art 16(4) states that any risk or interest connected with any of those expressly considered as within the special regime for prorogation of jurisdiction by art 16(1)-(3) are to be considered as subject to the same regime; it is suggested that the same approach could be adopted for art 16(5), so that also any risk or interest connected with a large risk and covered by the same policy should fall into the special regime, and this seems to support the argument that such an approach should be used only in construing the definitions of large risks in art 13(27) of the Solvency II Directive, so that ancillary risks which are closely related to the large risks should still be considered as part of the large risks. In addition, if a single insurance policy covers marine and/or large risks, and other risks which are to be qualified as mass risks, the applicability of the special regime should be evaluated on the basis of the specific cause of action, so that it is possible that claims brought under the same policies might be subject to different rules concerning the validity of the prorogation of jurisdiction clause.

As stated in many ECJ cases, the insurance section of Brussels I Regulation reflects an underlying concern to protect the assured (eg Case C-77/04 *Groupement d'intérêt économique (GIE) Réunion européenne v Zurich España and Société pyrénéenne de transit d'automobiles* [2005] ECR I-4522, para 17) and must be given a teleological interpretation with the aim of guaranteeing better protection of the weaker party than the general rules of jurisdiction (eg Case C-463/06 *FBTO Schadeverzekeringen NV v Jack Odenbreit* [2007] ECR I-11323, para 28). This approach is applicable also to the Brussels I Regulation (recast), so that the aim of protecting the economically weaker party must be also considered in construing the rules concerning the autonomy of the parties in relation to a jurisdiction clause; it can be thus argued that a jurisdiction clause, stipulated by the policyholder and conforming with art 15(1)-(4) of the Brussels I Regulation (recast), cannot be relied on against a beneficiary under that contract who has not expressly subscribed to that clause and is domiciled in a Member State other than that of the policyholder and the insurer (as it was upheld under the 1968 Brussels Convention, see Case C-112/03 *Société financière et industrielle du Peloux v Axa Belgium and others, Gerling Konzern Belgique SA, Établissements Bernard Laiterie du Chatelard, Calland Réalisations SARL, Joseph Calland, Maurice Picard, Abeille Assurances Cie, Mutuelles du Mans SA, SMABTP, Axa Corporate Solutions Assurance SA, Zuroch International France SA* [2005] ECR I-3727, paras 31 ff).

On the other hand, it should be considered that in the context of EU law, insurance contracts relating to large risks (including marine insurance policies) are in fact considered as not involving issues of protection of the weaker party and in the context of the Brussels I Regulation (recast) such difference is reflected in the special regime for prorogation of jurisdiction. It is therefore suggested that for insurance contracts relating to large risks, including marine insurance policies, the forum selection clauses agreed upon by the insurer and the policyholder should also be valid as against the assured and beneficiaries of such policies, there being no overriding need to protect them.

For sake of completeness, it should be mentioned that insurance contracts are included in the scope of application of Hague Convention of 30 June 2005 on-choice of-court agreements (44 ILM 1294), so that such Convention might interfere with the application of Brussels I Regulation (recast) rules on choice-of-court agreements in insurance matters. In such respect, it should be noted that – even though most marine matters are excluded from the scope of application of the Hague Choice of Court Convention – marine insurance contracts are nevertheless included (art 17.1); however, for the reasons stated above, art 15(5) of the Regulation applies to most marine insurance contracts, so that in case of choice-of-court agreements in such contracts, it is submitted that there is no incompatibility between the regime of the Brussels I Regulation (recast) and the regime of the Hague Choice of Court Convention.

III. Compulsory marine insurance

1. Background

An emerging feature of marine insurance is the introduction of several international conventions providing for the compulsory financial security – usually provided by the stipulation of specific insurance policies – covering the special risks involved in the use of the vessel and regulated by those conventions (1969 CLC (International Convention on Civil Liability for Oil Pollution Damage of 29 November 1969, 973 UNTS 3), as amended by the 1992 CLC (International Convention of 27 November 1992 on civil liability for oil pollution damage, 1956 UNTS 255), art VII; HNS Convention (International Convention of 3 May 1996 on liability and compensation for damage in connection with the carriage of hazardous and noxious substances by sea, 35 ILM 1406; as amended by the Protocol of 20 April 2010 to the International Convention on liability and compensation for damage in connection with the carriage of hazardous and noxious substances by sea, IMO Doc LEG/CONF.17/DC/1 (29 April 2010)), art 12; Bunker Convention 2001 (International Convention of 23 March 2001 on civil liability for bunker oil pollution damage, IMO Doc LEG/CONF 12/19, 40 ILM 1406), art 7; Athens Convention 2002 (Athens Convention of 1 November 2002 relating to the carriage of passengers and their luggage by sea, IMO Doc LEG/CONF.13/20 (19 November 2002)), art 4bis; see also the amendments to the Code implementing Regulations 2.5 and 4.2 and appendices of the MLC 2006 (Maritime Labour Convention of 23 February 2006, official text available on the website of the International Labour Organization <www.ilo.org>, last accessed on 26 February 2014), adopted by the Special Tripartite Committee on 11 April 2014 and approved at the 103th Conference on 11 June 2014). The general scheme adopted in such regulations is rather similar and the main features are that (i) the stipulation of the insurance cover must be made compulsory by the contracting states for the vessels flying their own → flag pursuant to the terms of the convention; (ii) some terms of the cover are mandatory as set out by the convention (eg the minimum amount for which the cover must be stipulated); (iii) some aspects of the legal regime applicable to the insurance contract are set out by the convention (eg the effects of the termination of the contract), whilst other terms are left to the law of the state of the vessel's flag (eg conditions of issue and terms of validity); (iv) the aim of the insurance cover is to enable the damaged party to obtain the compensation, so that such a party has a → direct action against the insurer and the regime of the defences which can be raised by the latter against such a claim is set out by the convention (eg the opposability of the limitation of liability in the case of wilful misconduct by the assured); (v) there are special rules on jurisdiction for actions for compensation under the terms of the convention, which also apply to the direct action of the damaged party against the insurer; (vi) contracting states must ensure the compliance of the insurance requirements in respect of any ship, wherever registered, entering or leaving a port in its territory.

2. Impact of choice-of-law and jurisdiction rules

The marine insurance contracts stipulated to comply with such insurance requirements are subject to mandatory rules to be implemented by the state of the → flag of the vessel and enforced also by the other contracting states pursuant to the terms of such conventions, which refer also to some aspects involving applicable law and jurisdiction.

As concerns choice-of-law rules, it should be noted that according to art 7(4) Rome I Regulation for insurance contracts covering risks for which a Member State imposes an obligation to take out insurance, Member States may lay down that such insurance contracts shall be governed by the law of the Member State that imposes the obligation. In any case, the insurance contract shall not satisfy the obligation to take out insurance unless it complies with the specific provisions relating to that insurance laid down by the Member State that imposes the obligation and the law of such Member State shall prevail over other laws applicable to the contract. In order to give an *effet utile* to the mandatory rules of the relevant international convention, it is suggested that such overriding application of the terms of the insurance cover set out in the relevant international convention is to be given full effect by a Member State which is also a contracting state. This can be put into effect pursuant to art 7(4) Rome I Regulation, when the vessel is flying the flag of another Member State which is also a contracting state, and pursuant to art 9(1) Rome I Regulation (relating to overriding mandatory provisions which are regarded as crucial for safeguarding its public interests) in all other cases, given the obligation for the contracting state to enforce the convention provisions also in respect of vessels flying another flag.

As concerns the special rules on jurisdiction set out in such international conventions, it should be noted that although art 7(1) Rome I provides, in relation to matters governed by specialized conventions, for the application of those conventions, such application cannot compromise the principles which underlay judicial cooperation in civil and commercial matters in the European Union (Case C-452/12 *Nipponkoa Insurance Co (Europe) Ltd v Inter-Zuid Transport BV* [2014] OJ C 52/19, para 36). However, it must be noted that, when dealing with the accession to the Athens Convention 2002 (Council decision of 12 December 2011 concerning the accession of the European Union to the Protocol of 2002 to the Athens Convention relating to the Carriage of Passengers and their Luggage by Sea, 1974, as regards Articles 10 and 11 thereof (2012/23/EU), [2012] OJ L 8/13), it has been decided that the Brussels I (recast) rules on recognition and enforcement of judgments should prevail over the corresponding convention rules when the matter is within the scope of application of any relevant European Union instrument, whilst no similar reservation has been made in respect of the convention rules on jurisdiction. As a result, it is suggested that pursuant to art 71(1) Brussels I Regulation (recast) it should still be possible to apply the special rules on jurisdiction and on recognition and enforcement of judgments, if any, set out by the international conventions, subject to a case-by-case assessment of their compatibility with the principles which underlie judicial cooperation in → civil and commercial matters in the EU (eg predictability as to the courts having jurisdiction and therefore legal certainty for litigants; see Case C-157/13 *Nickel & Goeldner Spedition GmbH v 'Kintra' UAB* [2013] OJ C 156/23). This test is required with regards to the possibility to either apply the special rules of the convention on recognition and enforcement of judgments, if any, or the provisions of the Brussels I Regulation (recast).

Article 7(4) Rome I Regulation also applies in respect of the compulsory marine insurance imposed by the Directive 2009/20/EC of the European Parliament and of the Council of 23 April 2009 on the Insurance of Shipowners for Maritime Claims ([2009] OJ L131/128), so that – irrespective of the applicable law of the contract – the actual compliance of the insurance cover must be evaluated taking into consideration the requirements relating to such compulsory cover set out in the Directive, as implemented in the law of the flag state or of the port state.

PIERANGELO CELLE

Literature

Yvonne Baatz, 'Jurisdiction in Contractual Disputes on Marine Insurance and Reinsurance Contracts to which the EC Jurisdiction Convention Applies' in David Rhidian Thomas (ed), *The Modern Law of Marine Insurance*, vol 2 (LLP 2002); Yvonne Baatz, 'Recent Developments in Party Choice of the Applicable Law and Jurisdiction in Marine Insurance and Reinsurance Contracts' in David Rhidian Thomas (ed), *The Modern Law of Marine Insurance*, vol 3 (LLP 2009); Gralf-Peter Calliess (ed), *Rome Regulations: Commentary on the European Rules of the Conflict of Laws* (Kluwer Law International 2011); Raymond Cox, Louise Merrett and Marcus Smith, *Private international law of Reinsurance and Insurance* (Informa Law 2006); Urs Peter Gruber, 'Insurance Contracts' in Franco Ferrari and Stefan Leible (eds), *Rome I Regulation: The Law Applicable to Contractual Obligations in Europe* (Sellier de Gruyter 2009); Helmut Heiss, 'Insurance Contracts in Rome I: Another Recent Failure of the European Legislator' [2009] EJCCL 61; Xandra Ellen Kramer, 'Conflict of Laws on Insurance Contracts in Europe: The Rome I Proposal – Towards Uniform Conflict Rules for Insurance Contracts?' in Marc L Hendrikse and Jacques GJ Rinkes (eds), *Insurance and Europe* (Uitgeverij Paris 2007); Xandra Ellen Kramer, 'The New European Conflict of Law Rules on Insurance Contracts in Rome I: A Complex Compromise' [2008] *The ICFAI University Journal of Insurance Law* 23; Francesco Seatzu, *Insurance in Private international law: A European Perspective* (Hart Pub 2003).

Maritime law (uniform law)

I. Justifications for seeking uniformity

Maritime law has been the subject of more extensive efforts to promote uniformity, and over a longer period of time, than almost any other field of law. Broadly referred to here as encompassing laws regulating seagoing vessels and the goods and passengers carried within them, it is an area that lends itself naturally to such efforts given the universal challenges that confront those involved in sea transport, and the international nature of much maritime trade. Although complete uniformity will always remain an ideal rather than an achievable reality, there are certainly some facets of maritime law (notably those involving basic safety and environmental shipping standards) where it can be stated with confidence that the same laws have been adopted throughout the world.

Sea travel has always carried risks, whether from weather and sea conditions, unsafe vessels or human error. Cargoes are lost, damaged, or arrive late. People are injured, ships collide. Moreover, these risks are not just faced by persons operating within a single jurisdiction. The enormous quantity of goods moved between ports by ships on a daily basis passes not only through the geographical borders of different jurisdictions, but may also be subjected to a range of different legal systems including the law governing any contract under which the vessel has been chartered, the law governing various contracts of carriage and the law of the national → flag under which the vessel is operating.

As such incidents have always occurred in connection with maritime transport, regardless of the nationality of the ship, cargo or persons involved, the international community is well placed to pursue a uniform legal response to a common set of readily identifiable problems. This line of reasoning is particularly strong in relation to safety issues. For example, '[o]ne can imagine the utter confusion that would result if the law of some flag states required a red light on the port side of a vessel and a green light on the starboard side, while under the law of others the rule was reversed' (Nicholas J Healy, 'International Uniformity in Maritime Law: The Goal and the Obstacles' (1979) 9 Cal.W.Int'l L.J. 494, 498). As maritime disasters can occur involving a vessel operating under the flag of one state in the territorial sea of another, it makes sense to establish at an international level the safety rules and standards that should be applied to prevent such disasters, and the liability regimes that will apply if preventative measures fail.

As the discussion below will demonstrate, maritime law has achieved a higher level of uniformity when it comes to regulatory matters addressing safety and the environment than it has in relation to rules on cargo liability or procedural issues. Nonetheless, there are still strong considerations supporting moves to unify the aspects of maritime law that primarily affect the commercial side of shipping. Merchants trading across borders (and their insurers) have an understandable commercial interest in being able to predict with a reasonable level of certainty what legal rules will apply to the shipment, and what the outcome is likely to be should something go wrong *en route*. Such parties will want to know the substantive law governing their contracts of carriage, the forum in which any dispute will be determined and whether a judgment obtained in one country would be enforceable in another (Athanassios N Yiannopoulos, 'The Unification of Private Maritime Law by International Conventions' (1965) 30 LCP 370). Some of these issues can be resolved by uniform rules of private international law, but uniform substantive law makes it easier for the parties to determine their obligations towards one another from the outset (→ Private international law, concept and purpose; → Uniform substantive law and private international law). This can in turn promote the speedy settlement of disputes, while a clearer knowledge of parties' potential liability helps insurers to set premiums with more accuracy (Nicholas J Healy, 'International Uniformity in Maritime Law: The Goal and the Obstacles' (1979) 9 Cal.W.Int'l L.J. 494, 499 f). While these considerations may not be unique to maritime law, they are strengthened by the justifications for uniformity stemming from the context of maritime transport, described above.

II. Historical narrative of uniformity

1. Early maritime codes

Authors addressing the topic of uniform maritime law frequently refer back to several stages of European legal history in support of the argument that maritime law was once relatively uniform. They argue that the apparent acceptance of earlier maritime codes, at various times, across wide areas of the Mediterranean as well as western and northern Europe, means that merchants could trade in the knowledge that the maritime laws in their ports of loading and unloading would be uniform. The earliest known example of such a code is the Rhodian Sea Law, which developed as an unwritten body of law in Ancient Greece around the 8th or 9th century BC, before lending its name to a written code emanating from Byzantium in the 7th or 8th century BC. Later examples include the Roles of Oleron (appearing in 12th-century France), the Consolat del Mar (14th century, western Mediterranean) and the Laws of Visby and those of the Hanseatic League (both 16th century, Baltic). Some of these bodies of law appear to have been accepted by merchants and courts across wide areas of Europe and the Mediterranean. The Roles of Oleron, for instance, were relied on from the Atlantic coast of Spain to Scandinavia, and were highly influential in the development of later codes.

These older laws are usually drawn on to illustrate the evolution of a common → *lex maritima* on which much of current maritime law is based. From what records we have of these earlier laws they were nowhere near as extensive as contemporary maritime law, but nonetheless contained the sources of many concepts still relied upon in the 21st century such as ships' mortgages, maritime liens (a form of privileged claim attaching to maritime property) and general average (rules that determine contributions between shipowners and cargo interests in the event that loss is suffered from an event such as the jettisoning of cargo). Some authors have also discussed the existence of a 'general maritime law' stemming from a combination of the → *lex maritima* and the common practices of the shipping industry, arguing that it continues to apply to maritime disputes before courts in common law jurisdictions such as the USA and Canada. Their position is that this unwritten general maritime law is able to fill any gaps left by statutes or international conventions when such disputes arise (see William Tetley, 'The General Maritime Law: The Lex Maritima' (1994) 20 Syracuse J.Int'l L.& Com. 105). A more sceptical view of this approach is that this notion of a 'general maritime law' is merely descriptive of the national law of the jurisdiction in question, which may draw upon sources of considerable antiquity, but nonetheless does not represent a form of international uniform law.

Despite the consistency achieved among the early codes of maritime law, the history of maritime law has not been one of consistent progress towards uniformity. *Paulsen* has argued that 'the rise of nationalism over the centuries destroyed the uniformity of maritime law, which had been established by commercial traders from time immemorial' (Gordon W Paulsen, 'An Historical Overview of the Development of Uniformity in International Maritime Law' (1983) 57 Tul.L.Rev. 1065). In particular scholars highlight a period during the 18th and 19th centuries during which European countries enacted various pieces of national legislation designed to favour national fleets at the expense of foreign competition.

2. 19th-century moves towards uniformity

By the late 19th century various European powers saw the desirability of promoting a greater degree of uniformity in maritime law, and began a programme of law reform that has not ceased since. One of the earliest examples was an 1864 attempt to codify the rules on general average, undertaken by the British National Association for the Promotion of Social Science in York, while in 1885 and 1888 two Belgian-sponsored conferences were held with the aim of codifying all of maritime law (an over-ambitious project that was doomed to fail) (Albert Lilar and Carlo van den Bosch, *Le Comité Maritime International 1897–1972* (Le Comité Maritime International 1972) 7 f). At a more formal diplomatic level the first successful steps towards uniform law were taken in the field of collision regulations (so-called 'rules of the road') with the USA hosting a conference that led to the Convention on the International Regulations for Preventing Collisions at Sea, adopted in 1889 (Frank Lawrence Wiswall, 'Uniformity in Maritime Law: The Domestic Impact of International Maritime Regulation' (1983) 57 Tul.L.Rev. 1208, 1215 f).

The first international organization to begin working on a programme of harmonizing maritime law was the International Law Association (founded in 1873), whose members drafted the York-Antwerp Rules on general average in 1890 (N Geoffrey Hudson and Michael D Harvey, *The York-Antwerp Rules* (3rd edn, Routledge 2010) appendix 2), providing commercial parties with a set of rules they could incorporate into their contracts of carriage. However, it became apparent that the breadth and complexity of maritime law warranted a specialist organization, and in 1897 the Comité Maritime International (CMI) was established in Antwerp. The CMI fast became the driving force behind a number of early maritime conventions, including work in the field of → salvage, collisions and cargo liability. Comprising volunteers from different areas of the shipping world, such as legal experts, shipowners, merchants and insurance industry representatives, the CMI relied on branches in different countries feeding information and views back to a central body that could undertake the difficult task of drafting a convention and attempting to convince states to ratify it.

3. The 20th century and beyond

Before 1968 the Belgian government would assist with the final stage of the CMI's process by hosting diplomatic conferences for the purpose. But by this time the United Nations body responsible for maritime affairs, the International Maritime Organization (→ IMO) (originally named the Inter-Governmental Maritime Consultative Organization) had been established for 20 years and there was greater scope for UN-led international agreements in relation to which the CMI would play a supporting, advisory role (Albert Lilar and Carlo van den Bosch, *Le Comite Maritime International 1897–1972* (Le Comité Maritime International 1972) 98–101).

As a result it has been various UN bodies that have promoted much of our current uniform maritime law. The → IMO facilitates cooperation between states in the fields of maritime safety, efficiency of navigation, and the prevention and control of marine pollution. Headquartered in London, much of its work is carried out by specialist committees of experts, notably in this context its Legal Committee. The bulk of the IMO's output is of a regulatory nature (as opposed to governing matters of purely private law), and a number of the international conventions for which it is responsible, outlined below, have achieved near-universal adoption.

Matters of a more commercial nature have been addressed by the UN Conference on Trade and Development (UNCTAD) and the UN Commission on International Trade Law (→ UNCITRAL), both of which have been involved in promoting conventions on carriers' liability, for example (also outlined below).

The former body was established in 1964 to promote trade and development by producing analyses and recommendations for economic policymakers in UN Member States, facilitating intergovernmental conferences to discuss the global economy and providing technical assistance to developing countries. The latter is a specialist legal body established in 1966, responsible for the examination of legislation regulating international trade and which works to promote wider participation in international conventions in this area, as well as uniform and model laws.

III. Avenues for promoting uniformity

With UN bodies such as the → IMO, UNCTAD and → UNCITRAL able to capture the attention of the international community, and independent organizations of experts ready to provide them with advice such as the CMI and → UNIDROIT (an independent agency based in Rome that works towards the harmonization of private law), the unification of maritime law at the international level remains in good hands. However, not all moves towards uniformity need to be taken in the form of an international convention. The efforts of commercial people and organizations such as the Baltic and International Maritime Council (BIMCO) in developing and updating the standard-form contracts that are used throughout the shipping sector as the basis for charter parties, the carriage of goods, salvage operations and other fields should not be overlooked. Nor should the role of uniform rules, which parties can incorporate into their contracts. An example of such rules are the Uniform Rules for Sea Waybills 1990 (CMI Uniform Rules for Sea Waybills 1990, Comitè Maritime International (CMI), *CMI Yearbook 1990*) developed by the CMI, which parties can use to clarify their obligations when using this form of transport document (→ Sea waybills and other transport documents).

Regional bodies such as the European Union can also promote steps towards greater international uniformity, for instance by having members adopt internationally agreed uniform law on a regional basis. An example of this in the maritime law context is when the EU essentially put the rules on liability for the carriage of passengers established by the Athens Carriage of Passengers Convention (Athens Convention of 13 December 1974 relating to the carriage of passengers and their luggage by sea, 1463 UNTS 20; as amended by the Athens Convention of 1 November 2002 relating to the carriage of passengers and their luggage by sea, IMO Doc LEG/CONF.13/20 (19 November 2002)) into force for all its Member States (Regulation (EC) No 392/2009 of the European Parliament and of the Council of 23 April 2009 on the liability of carriers of passengers by sea in the event of accidents, [2009] OJ L 131/24; → Carriage of passengers). Less extensive measures can also be taken, as for example when the Member States adopted a statement recognizing the importance of ratifying the 1996 Protocol (35 ILM 1433) to the 1976 Convention on Limitation of Liability for Maritime Claims of 19 November 1976 ('1976 LLMC', 1456 UNTS 221) (Recital (3) Directive 2009/20/EC of the European Parliament and of the Council of 23 April 2009 on the insurance of shipowners for maritime claims, [2009] OJ L 131/128), and then based a regional liability insurance regime upon that convention (→ Liability, limitation of maritime).

Where international conventions have been used in the maritime context, parties have tended to focus on achieving uniformity in only certain aspects of one area of maritime law (hence the phrase 'international convention on the unification of certain rules of law' that precedes many of the early CMI conventions). Rules of procedure, for example, are frequently left to national law, with the negotiators instead focusing on controversial details such as the maximum amount for which a shipowner will be held liable if a defined claim arises. As with any international agreement, uniformity can be diluted by the introduction of articles to a convention permitting States Parties to enter reservations, or simply giving them the option to use national law in certain situations. For example, the 1976 Limitation Convention, which deals with shipowners' liability for a broad range of claims that may be made against them, permits States Parties to enter a reservation removing limitation from claims associated with wreck removal (art 18), and permits States Parties to apply national law to vessels under 300 tons, and situations that do not involve parties from any other jurisdiction (art 15).

As is well known, the adoption of a convention does not necessarily mean it will achieve wide ratification, or even enter into force. Of the conventions outlined below, some have been highly successful while others have failed to attract more than a handful of ratifying states. These less successful conventions should not be ignored, as they still serve to highlight areas of maritime law that may warrant future efforts to promote uniformity.

IV. Examples of uniform laws

It would be overly simplistic to say that some uniform rules in the maritime sphere cover private maritime law matters, and others public maritime law. Instead this area presents a much more complex blend of international, domestic, public and private factors as illustrated by the 1989 Salvage Convention (International Convention of 28 April 1989 on salvage, 1953 UNTS 165), an agreement with 64 States Parties representing half of the world's shipping tonnage (information on the status of most maritime conventions is maintained on the IMO's website, available at <www.imo.org>). First, it is an international agreement within the realm of public international law. States that become parties to it take on obligations to other contracting states to implement it within their domestic legal orders. However, the purpose of the Convention is primarily aimed at disputes between private parties who may rely on its rules (once incorporated into a State Party's domestic law) to have a local court determine, for example, the appropriate level of reward for a salvor who successfully salvages a vessel in distress. The Convention also represents a mixture of public and private law ideas. On the one hand a party might complain that a contract in the salvage context was agreed to on unfair terms, and seek a court order amending that agreement (art 7 1989 Salvage Convention). On the other hand the Convention contains an article on the rights of coastal states to take measures to protect their coastlines from pollution (art 9 1989 Salvage Convention).

Although some maritime instruments are more clear-cut than the 1989 Salvage Convention, the example is raised here to demonstrate that there is no easy way to pigeonhole efforts at uniformity in maritime law. Accordingly the best means of identifying the principal categories where uniformity has been attempted is to divide them broadly by subject matter. The following discussion of uniform maritime law instruments is intended to provide only an overview of the extensive body of material in existence. More detailed information is available on the websites of the organizations mentioned in the previous section, or in specialist publications in the areas of maritime law highlighted below.

1. Safety regulations and liability

Rules promoting uniformity in respect of safety of life at sea have been the subject of several highly successful international conventions. Starting with the rules on avoiding collisions agreed to in the 19th century, the international community has shown a particular willingness to cooperate in this area. The rules devised have related not only to the safety practices and standards that vessels should meet in order to operate internationally, but also liability rules determining the financial outcome for parties who fail to observe them.

For example, the current navigational rules on avoiding collisions were agreed to in 1972, and are one of the IMO's most successful conventions with 156 States Parties representing 99 per cent of the world's tonnage. These are complemented by the Collision Convention (International Convention of 23 September 1910 for the Unification of certain Rules of Law related to Collision between Vessels, in K Zweigert and J Kropholler, *Sources of International Uniform Law*, vol 2 (AW Sijthoff 1972) 3), promoted by the CMI and in force to this day with 86 States Parties, which sets out rules on liability where ships do collide. In addition this Convention provides an example of uniformity being agreed to as between common law and civilian legal systems. The parties agreed to adopt the civilian law approach to liability for collisions in which both ships were partly to blame, dividing damages proportionately according to the degree of responsibility, as opposed to the common law rule of having losses lie where they fell (HM Cleminson, 'International Unification of Maritime Law' (1941) 23 J.Comp.Leg. 164, 165).

The standards a vessel must meet in relation to lifesaving apparatus, fire-fighting equipment, stability and so on are governed by a series of Safety of Life at Sea (SOLAS) conventions, the first of which was negotiated in 1912 following the Titanic disaster. The outbreak of the First World War stalled progress on this agreement, and the issue had to be revisited in 1929. The current version of SOLAS (International Convention of 1 November 1974 for the safety of life at sea, 1184 UNTS 278) has 162 States Parties representing 99 per cent of the world's tonnage. The two protocols to SOLAS and the related 1966 safety convention on vessels' load lines (Load Lines Convention (International Convention on Load Lines of 5 April 1966, 640 UNTS 133); indicating minimum safe freeboard when a ship is loaded) have been similarly successful.

The high degree of uniformity achieved in this area is bolstered by a common enforcement regime known as port state control (see the Paris Memorandum of Understanding on Port State Control of 26 January 1982, 21 ILM 1, available at <www.parismou.org/about-us/memorandum>). Through this system, organized on a regional basis, state officials inspect the vessels visiting their ports (regardless of the flag under which the vessel is operating) to see whether they meet the relevant safety, environmental and other regulatory standards agreed to in the most successful of the international agreements. This information, including the need for any remedial action, is then shared with other states in the regional group, who can target their inspections according to the risk profile of visiting vessels.

2. Environmental regulations and liability regimes

The environmental counterpart to SOLAS is the MARPOL (International Convention on the prevention of pollution from ships 1973, 1340 UNTS 184, as modified by the Protocol of 1978 relating thereto, adopted 2 November 1973 and 17 February 1978 respectively, 1340 UNTS 61), which dates from the 1970s and has been added to throughout the decades by way of protocols dealing with issues such as sewage and air pollution from ships. As with SOLAS, MARPOL and its protocols have had great success internationally with States Parties representing between 90 per cent and 99 per cent of international tonnage. MARPOL contains a large number of technical requirements that marine surveyors and other experts can use to determine whether a ship meets minimum environmental standards, including limits on the amount of oily waste a ship can discharge into the ocean. Even though the technical rules contained in SOLAS and MARPOL are not of a private international law nature, in that they are unlikely to form the basis of disputes between private parties, they nonetheless establish the regulatory standards private parties must meet in order to operate vessels safely and without incident in the international environment.

Failure to comply with these standards before departure from port could see a commercial operation held up for a significant period of time until any deficiencies are remedied, whereas if preventive measures fail and a pollution event occurs a series of international conventions dealing with the liability of shipowners for marine pollution may come into play. Starting with a 1969 convention on liability for pollution from oil tankers (1969 CLC (International Convention on Civil Liability for Oil Pollution Damage of 29 November 1969, 973 UNTS 3)), now replaced by a 1992 Protocol (1992 CLC (International Convention of 27 November 1992 on civil liability for oil pollution damage, 1956 UNTS 255)), negotiated in the wake of the *Torrey Canyon* disaster, conventions have emerged on pollution from nuclear material (1971 Brussels Civil Liability Convention (Convention Relating to Civil Liability in the Field of Maritime Carriage of Nuclear Material of 17 December 1971, 974 UNTS 255)), hazardous and noxious substances (HNS Convention (International Convention of 3 May 1996 on liability and compensation for damage in connection with the carriage of hazardous and noxious substances by sea, 35 ILM 1406; as amended by the Protocol of 20 April 2010 to the International Convention on liability and compensation for damage in connection with the carriage of hazardous and noxious substances by sea, IMO Doc LEG/CONF.17/DC/1 (29 April 2010))) and ships' bunkers (fuel) (Bunker Convention 2001(International Convention of 23 March 2001 on civil liability for bunker oil pollution damage, IMO Doc LEG/CONF 12/19, 40 ILM 1406)). Not all of these have achieved a high level of international acceptance, but where pollution from oil or bunkers is concerned tonnage coverage is over 90 per cent. These rules have the effect of making shipowners strictly liable for pollution incidents, but subject to a cap on liability (→ Liability, limitation of maritime). They also put into effect compulsory insurance requirements with rights of → direct action against the insurer and, in the case of oil tankers, give claimants access to a separate compensation fund maintained by levies on the oil industry.

3. Carriage of goods and passengers

While international uniformity in the areas of safety and the environment has largely been promoted by way of international conventions, the commercially-focused subject of the carriage of goods and passengers by ship has been approached with a wider range of legal tools (→ Carriage of goods by sea; → Carriage of passengers). For example, shippers and carriers can negotiate their contracts of carriage using a standard form contract from an organization like the Baltic and International Maritime Council (BIMCO), tailored to the needs of their trade (GRAINCON for voyage charters for the carriage of grain, for example ('BIMCO Standard Grain Voyage Charterparty' (May 2003)) and incorporating model clauses such as the BIMCO dispute resolution clauses. A large liner shipping company such as *Hapag Lloyd* can use the York Antwerp Rules on general average by incorporating them by reference into its standard → bill of lading terms and conditions (cl 22). As noted above, these Rules, which have been updated over the decades since they were first set down, represent uniform model rules of a non-binding, opt-in nature.

It is in the interests of shippers and carriers to know what the legal outcome will be if cargo is lost, damaged or delayed. If all parties are operating within the same legal system then this information should be readily available. On the other hand, if a German seller is relying on a Danish carrier's Liberian-flagged vessel to carry its goods to a New Zealand buyer, then it is in the parties' best interests for the contract of carriage to set out a regime for allocating liability should the shipment go awry. Although such a regime could be left to the contracting parties to negotiate, past experience suggests that, left to their own devices, carriers will exclude virtually all liability leaving shippers without adequate protection. This in turn led to conflicting decisions in various jurisdictions as to whether such clauses were enforceable (Athanassios N Yiannopoulos, 'The Unification of Private Maritime Law by International Conventions' (1965) 30 LCP 370, 386).

In a series of attempts to reach a uniform position allocating the risks of carriage between shippers and carriers several international conventions have been adopted. The earliest was the Hague Rules of 1924 (International Convention of 25 August 1924 for the unification of certain rules relating to bills of lading, 120 LNTS 155), initially promoted by the International Law Association and later the CMI. These were amended by protocols in 1968 (1968 Visby Protocol (Protocol of 23 February 1968 to amend the International Convention for the unification of certain rules of law relating to bills of lading signed at Brussels on 25 August 1924 (Hague Rules), 1412 UNTS 128)) and 1979 (Protocol of 21 December 1979 to amend the International Convention for the unification of certain rules to bills of lading (Hague Rules) as modified by the Amending Protocol of 23 February 1968 (Visby Protocol), 1412 UNTS 146), with the updated result being renamed the Hague-Visby Rules. Next came the Hamburg Rules in 1978 (United Nations Convention of 31 March 1978 on the carriage of goods by sea, 1695 UNTS 3), and most recently the Rotterdam Rules (United Nations Convention of 11 December 2008 on contracts for the international carriage of goods wholly or partly by sea, UN Doc A/RES/63/122, 63 UNTS 122) adopted in 2009 but not yet in force (both negotiated through → UNCITRAL). These conventions vary in terms of their 'carrier-friendliness', with the Hague Rules broadly regarded as the most favourable to carriers and the Hamburg Rules most favourable to shippers. They also differ in terms of the maximum amount payable by the carrier for lost or damaged goods, and in the range of defences available to carriers. The most notorious of these is the so-called 'nautical fault' defence, under which a carrier is not liable for damage resulting from the negligent navigation or management of the ship.

Taking the *Hapag Lloyd* standard bill of lading terms (as of November 2008) as an example, most carriers will state that carriage is subject to the Hague Rules, or the Hague-Visby Rules if these are compulsorily applicable to the contract (cl 7). In other words, they will frame their standard contracts so as to apply the most carrier-favourable terms possible. Both sets of Rules mandatorily apply to contracts of carriage evidenced by bills of lading (→ Bill of lading), but even if a different shipping document is used parties may apply them to the contract voluntarily, as for example when parties adopt the CMI's Uniform Rules for Sea Waybills (cl 4(i), → Sea waybills and other transport documents).

This situation permits a degree of uniformity, but not to the level found in relation to the safety- and environmental-related conventions discussed above. Some states use the Hague Rules, some the Hague-Visby Rules, some the Hamburg Rules, while the Rotterdam Rules have not entered into force and have received only three ratifications to date (→ Spain, Togo and the Republic of the Congo). In addition some states have adopted more than one of these instruments without denouncing the older one, while others have developed their own carriage liability regimes (notably the United States Carriage of Goods by Sea Act, 46 U.S.C. § 30702) and others such as Germany have adopted an international regime but altered aspects of it (the provisions of the German Commercial Code (Handelsgesetzbuch of 10 May 1897, RGBl. 219, as amended) are modelled on the Hague-Visby Rules, but remove the nautical fault defence among other amendments).

Shipowners' liability for accidents involving passengers and their luggage is dealt with by the Athens Convention of 1974, and the Athens Convention 2002. However, this convention has attracted only 35 States Parties to date, representing 46 per cent of world tonnage. The 2002 Protocol, which introduces compulsory insurance among other amendments, has 14 parties and entered into force in April 2014.

4. Global liability, maritime claims and procedure

As with the more private-law-orientated regimes on liability for carriage of goods, attempts at uniform law in the field of maritime claims and procedure have been less successful in securing a high degree of international uniformity. This can be seen as unfortunate, as the international nature of maritime transport means that, for example, a legal dispute arising in relation to a Swedish cargo-owner's contract with a Swiss company's Norwegian-flagged vessel can end up before the courts of Australia, Japan or some equally distant country in which the vessel happens to be visiting port. Maritime law proceedings are often commenced by the arrest of the defendant's vessel as security for the claim, meaning the choice of forum (→ Choice of forum and submission to jurisdiction) can be dependent upon the geographical location of that vessel, as opposed to the forum selected by the parties to any relevant contracts.

Furthermore, once a claim is made and a vessel is arrested other claimants might appear. For example the mortgagee of the ship might claim alongside the party that supplied the ship's bunkers, various cargo-owners, and the crew whose wages have not been paid. Rules on the ranking of claims are therefore required, including those relating to competing claims between the holders of such maritime liens (or comparable interests) as the court is able to recognize. The key advantage of achieving international uniformity in this area of law would be that litigants would know in advance the kinds of disputes in relation to which a vessel could be arrested, and how claims against that ship would rank. However, conventions on the recognition and ranking of maritime liens and mortgages adopted in 1926 (International Convention of 10 April 1926 for the unification of certain rules relating to maritime liens and mortgages, 120 LNTS 187), 1967 (International Convention for the Unification of Certain Rules of Law relating to Maritime Liens and Mortgages (adopted 27 May 1967, not yet in force, reproduced in: United Nations, *Register of Texts of Conventions and other Instruments Concerning International Trade Law*, vol 1 (1971) 268)) and 1993 (International Convention of 6 May 1993 on maritime liens and mortgages, 2276 UNTS 39), and conventions on arrest adopted in 1952 (International Convention of 10 May 1952 relating to the Arrest of Seagoing Ships, 439 UNTS 193) and 1999 (International Convention of 12 March 1999 on Arrest of Ships, 2797 UNTS I-44196), have achieved mixed results. The 1926 Maritime Liens and Mortgages Convention had just over 20 States Parties, the 1967 version never entered into force, and the 1993 attempt has only 17 States Parties. The 1952 Arrest Convention was quite successful with over 70 States Parties, as well as some jurisdictions that have based their arrest laws on its text despite not having signed the agreement itself (see New Zealand Admiralty Act 1973 (Public Act No 119 of 23 November 1973), but the 1999 Arrest Convention currently has only 11 States Parties.

Uniformity is not much greater in respect of global limitation regimes, which provide a maximum cap on liability for shipowners arising from any distinct occasion. For example, if a ship was lost along with its cargo the Hague Rules might determine how much the shipowner owed each cargo-owner, but any applicable rules on global liability would determine how much that shipowner owed all cargo claimants along with any other parties seeking redress. Although forms of global limitation of liability appeared in various national laws much earlier, the first attempts at a uniform approach were in the early 20th century with international conventions adopted in 1924 (International Convention of 25 August 1924 for the unification of certain rules relating to the limitation of the liability of owners of seagoing vessels, 120 LNTS 123), 1957 (International Convention of 10 October 1957 relating to the limitation of the liability of owners of sea-going ships, 1412 UNTS 73) and 1976 (1976 LLMC). As an illustration of their success rate the most recent of these has 54 States Parties representing 55 per cent of world tonnage. The benefits of uniformity in this area, and even the existence of such rules at all, is a controversial topic in maritime law (→ Liability, limitation of maritime).

V. Prospects for future uniform law efforts

As the above survey suggests, the idea of uniformity in maritime law has had its share of successes and failures. In some areas, notably those of a regulatory nature addressing safety and environmental issues, an impressive level of international cohesion has been achieved. In other areas, particularly those of a more private law nature dealing with cargo liability and matters surrounding claims and procedure, efforts at an international level have seen only limited progress.

One of the impressive aspects of the international maritime regulatory field has been the manner in which the international community has maintained uniformity in the face of rapid technological change. After all, a uniform legal position that is lagging well behind industry practice may do more harm than good. Instead of having to adopt a new protocol to SOLAS or MARPOL every time new technology becomes standard, the → IMO's conventions use a 'tacit acceptance' procedure to keep amendments entering into force in a timely fashion. Essentially, amendments enter into force for a State Party unless that state expressly objects, removing the need for states to constantly sign and ratify new protocols. This has not been replicated in other areas of maritime law, meaning that while some topics have been addressed with a high level of uniformity, such as oil tanker pollution liability, others discussed above have failed to achieve anything approaching a level that could be described as international uniformity.

In fact, as states agree to new conventions in the hope of addressing the problems identified in earlier efforts, a splintering effect can occur whereby older conventions lose some (but not all) support, new conventions fail to gain wide-scale support, and the area ends up less uniform than it was to begin with. The most notable example of this has been in the cargo liability context (compare the more successful efforts of the air transport sector in this regard → Air Law (uniform law)). In perhaps no other area has so much hope been held out for the development of new rules, with former CMI president *Patrick Griggs* describing the process leading to the 2009 Rotterdam Rules as 'the best, and probably the last, chance of restoring international uniformity' (Patrick JS Griggs, 'Obstacles to Uniformity of Maritime Law: The Nicholas J Healy Lecture' (2003) 34 J.Mar.L.& Com. 191, 195). However, the Rules have had little success to date.

This splintering effect is not an issue where uniform positions reached by commercial operators by way of model rules and standard form contracts are concerned, as these can be modified by such operators as and when the need arises. This suggests that where uniformity is to be sought by international conventions it would be wise for governments to listen to the needs of these operators and try to implement reforms that they express a desire for: 'that in the final analysis, the jurist must hold the pen and that it is the man with the experience who must dictate the solution' (Albert Lilar and Carlo van den Bosch, *Le Comité Maritime International 1897–1972* (Le Comité Maritime International 1972) 12–13). To this a note of caution could be added that such suggestions are more likely to favour carriers and parties closely involved in the shipping world over cargo-owners and others who use their services only from time to time.

Furthermore, there is always a political aspect to such matters, and different states will inevitably have different priorities, making it difficult to reach compromises that will be ratified by a large number of states. For example, a country with a strong shipowning lobby and applying the Hague Rules may want nothing to do with a convention that improves the lot of cargo-owners. Added to this is simply the fact that there are few votes in any country resting on maritime law reform, especially commercial maritime law, so it is hard to get such reform on to a government's agenda (William Tetley, 'Uniformity of International Private Maritime Law – The Pros, Cons, and Alternatives to International Conventions: How to Adopt an International Convention' (2000) 24 Tul. Mar.L.J. 775, 805 ff). A lack of political support for change has been particularly acute in the case of the USA which, with the exception of SOLAS, MARPOL and the 1989 Salvage Conventions, has largely declined to ratify the international maritime conventions outlined above. The → USA has its own liability regimes for pollution, cargo and global liability, for example, and a common call from scholars throughout previous decades has been for this major jurisdiction to make a greater effort to join the international position (Athanassios N Yiannopoulos, 'The Unification of Private Maritime Law by International Conventions' (1965) 30 LCP 370, 382; Nicholas J Healy, 'International Uniformity in Maritime Law: The Goal and the Obstacles' (1979) 9 Cal.W.Int'l L.J. 494, 501 f; Patrick JS Griggs, 'Obstacles to Uniformity of Maritime Law: The Nicholas J Healy Lecture' (2003) 34 J.Mar.L.& Com. 191, 207 f).

Despite these obstacles the proponents of uniformity persevere with their agenda, relying on advances in communication technology to advance their efforts. For example, an ongoing CMI project is the collection of decisions from national courts throughout the world commenting on and interpreting international maritime conventions. Similar work is carried out by the UNCITRAL secretariat. This enables a lawyer in the → United Kingdom to quickly ascertain what a court in → Germany has said about the same provision of international law, and represents one of the most promising avenues for the promotion of uniformity. After all, it is not satisfactory for different states to simply adopt the same rules: true uniformity is only achieved when those rules are interpreted and applied in a uniform manner.

BEVAN MARTEN

Literature

Francesco Berlingieri, 'Unification and Harmonisation of Maritime Law Revisited' (2006) 59 R.H.D.I. 603; HM Cleminson, 'International Unification of Maritime Law' (1941) 23 J.Comp. Leg. 164; John C Colombos, 'The Unification of Maritime International Law in Time of Peace' (1944) 21 BYIL 96; Patrick JS Griggs, 'Uniformity of Maritime Law: An International Perspective' (1999) 73 Tul.L.Rev. 1551; Patrick JS Griggs, 'Obstacles to Uniformity of Maritime Law: The Nicholas J Healy Lecture' (2003) 34 J.Mar.L.& Com. 191; Nicholas J Healy, 'International Uniformity in Maritime Law: The Goal and the Obstacles' (1979) 9 Cal.W.Int'l L.J. 494; Albert Lilar, 'L'Unification Internationale du Droit Maritime' (1955) 1 *Rivista del Diritto della Navigazione* 3; Albert Lilar and Carlo van den Bosch, *Le Comité*

Maritime International 1897–1972 (Le Comité Maritime International 1972); Gordon W Paulsen, 'An Historical Overview of the Development of Uniformity in International Maritime Law' (1983) 57 Tul.L.Rev. 1065; Ulfred Sieveking, 'Internationale Bestrebungen zur Vereinheitlichung des Seerechts' [1921] *Hanseatische Rechts-Zeitschrift* 945; William Tetley, 'The General Maritime Law: The Lex Maritima' (1994) 20 Syracuse J.Int'l L.& Com. 105; William Tetley, 'Uniformity of International Private Maritime Law – The Pros, Cons, and Alternatives to International Conventions: How to Adopt an International Convention' (2000) 24 Tul. Mar.L.J. 775; Frank Lawrence Wiswall, 'Uniformity in Maritime Law: The Domestic Impact of International Maritime Regulation' (1983) 57 Tul.L.Rev. 1208; Hans Wüstendörfer, 'Leistungen und Grenzen der internationalen Vereinheitlichung des Seerechts' (1951) 8 MDR 449; Athanassios N Yiannopoulos, 'The Unification of Private Maritime Law by International Conventions' (1965) 30 LCP 370.

Maritime torts

I. Background and outline

Legal obligations that occur in the maritime domain have traditionally been subject to a distinct body of rules for a number of reasons, including the technical peculiarities of the sector to which they refer and the operating structure which is typical of the shipping business.

In addition, due to the intrinsically international character of the maritime industry, such rules – especially since the second half of the 20th century – have progressively been embodied into uniform law instruments of a substantive nature, adopted with a view to overcoming discrepancies between national legal systems that may otherwise impair the orderly conduct of trade on an international scale.

The effects of such a unification process have been felt in the areas of contractual and non-contractual liability alike. With regard to non-contractual liability – to which the present entry is devoted – it is worth noting that vessels flying the → flag of a given state are typically engaged in navigation in maritime zones that are subject to other states' sovereignty or jurisdiction, and that the activities they carry out may have an adverse impact on ships of different nationalities (eg in case of a collision) as well as on third-state waters (eg when polluting substances are spilled into the sea).

Given the intricacy of choice-of-forum and choice-of-law issues that are likely to arise under such circumstances, it is not surprising that the international community (with the proactive support of the shipping world) has gone to great lengths to eliminate, or at least to a large extent reduce, the uncertainties implied in the selection of the competent court and the applicable law. This has involved establishing a number of regulatory frameworks providing for uniform rules on standards of liability, available defences, recoverable damage and other relevant matters.

It is noteworthy in this connection that varying approaches have been adopted in ostensibly similar contexts, as attested for instance by the Hague Traffic Accidents Convention (Hague Convention of 4 May 1971 on the law applicable to traffic accidents, 965 UNTS 415), a prominent example of a unification exercise which has focused on choice-of-law provisions rather than on substantive law.

Against this background, the following three sections will address in turn the content of some of the most significant instruments that have established uniform compensation and liability regimes applicable to specific maritime torts (see II. below), the issue of jurisdiction, recognition and enforcement of judgments rendered in the field of maritime torts according to the Brussels I Regulation (Regulation (EC) No 44/2001 of 22 December 2000 on jurisdiction and the recognition and enforcement of judgments in civil and commercial matters, [2001] OJ L 12/1 (→ Brussels I (Convention and Regulation)); see III. below), and finally the issue of the law applicable to maritime torts, with particular regard to the solutions provided by the → Rome II Regulation (Regulation (EC) No 864/2007 of the European Parliament and of the Council of 11 July 2007 on the law applicable to non-contractual obligations (Rome II), [2007] OJ L 199/40; see IV. below).

II. Uniform law

The Collision Convention (International Convention of 23 September 1910 for the Unification of certain Rules of Law related to Collision between Vessels, in K Zweigert and J Kropholler, *Sources of International Uniform Law*, vol 2 (AW Sijthoff 1972) 3), with a view to apportioning liability between the vessels involved in a collision, undoubtedly represented a significant model for the developments that occurred in the field of unification of substantive maritime tort law throughout the 20th century. Such developments, however, have also been strictly intertwined with the occurrence of severe maritime casualties.

It was in fact the grounding of the *Torrey Canyon* oil tanker off the southwest coast of England on 19 March 1967, that prompted the diplomatic process which eventually led to the adoption of the 1969 CLC (International Convention on Civil Liability for Oil Pollution Damage of 29 November 1969, 973 UNTS 3) and the 1971 Fund Convention (International Convention on the Establishment of an International Fund for Compensation for Oil Pollution Damage of 18 December 1971, 1110 UNTS 57).

These two instruments, as is well known, have subsequently been amended and, as a matter of fact, replaced by their 1992 counterparts (the 1992 CLC (International Convention of 27 November 1992 on civil liability for oil pollution damage, 1956 UNTS 255) and the 1992 Fund Convention (Protocol to the International Fund for Compensation for Oil Pollution Damage of 27 November 1992, 1956 UNTS 255, later amended by the Protocol of 27 September 2000, and the Protocol of 16 May 2003, [2004] OJ L 78/24), which both entered into force on 30 May 1996 (of the two 'old' conventions, only the 1969 CLC remains in force and for a limited number of states, whereas the 1971 Fund Convention ceased to be in force in 2002, when the number of contracting parties fell under 25).

The 1992 CLC and the 1992 Fund Convention, which share the same definition of 'pollution damage', aim at ensuring that any loss or damage caused by the escape or discharge of oil from a tanker (including the cost of preventive measures and further loss or damage caused by preventive measures) is adequately compensated, provided that compensation for impairment of the environment other than loss of profit from such impairment 'shall be limited to costs of reasonable measures of reinstatement actually taken or to be undertaken' (art I.6 CLC).

Leaving aside the criticism that the above caveat has attracted (as it renders it impossible to recover any damage that cannot be remediated or can only be remediated at an unreasonable expense), it is important to note that the two Conventions promote a significantly wide geographical scope of application. This is because they cover pollution damage occurring in the territory of contracting states (including the territorial sea) and the exclusive economic zone (EEZ) (or if no exclusive economic zone has been established in accordance with international law, an equivalent area to be proclaimed by the contracting state), as well as preventive measures, wherever taken, to prevent or minimize such damage.

Considered as a whole, the 1992 CLC and the 1992 Fund Convention constitute a single legal regime which is founded primarily on the principle of the registered owner's strict liability vis-à-vis the victims of the oil spill, since only exceptional circumstances may discharge its liability, such as an act of war or the act or omission of a third party done with the intent to cause damage. Liability is therefore in principle 'channelled' towards the shipowner to the exclusion of other potentially responsible subjects, but is not unlimited, as thresholds apply which vary depending on the ship's tonnage up to a maximum amount. When the owner of the ship benefits of one of the few defences available to him, is incapable of meeting its obligations in full or the damage caused exceeds the applicable limit, the liability of the International Oil Pollution Compensation (IOPC) Fund is triggered. Once again this liability is up to a maximum amount which is currently set at 300 million Special Drawing Rights (SDR) of the International Monetary Fund (IMF), this after several amendments passed to take into account the increased damaging potential of maritime casualties as demonstrated by accidents such as those occurred to the *Erika* (1999) and the *Prestige* (2002). A Supplementary Fund was also created in 2003, to which States Parties to the 1992 Fund Convention can accede on a voluntary basis, ensuring compensation of up to 750 million SDR for any single accident. The system is remarkably complemented by a duty for the shipowner to take out insurance coverage up to its possible maximum liability.

Since the IOPC Fund as well as the Supplementary Fund are financed by contributions paid annually by receivers of oil located in contracting states, it appears that the legal regime under consideration has been capable not only of ensuring adequate compensation for pollution damage suffered in connection with the carriage of oil by sea, but also of equitably apportioning the financial burden between the shipping industry on the one hand and oil importers, manufacturers and distributors on the other.

Crucially, the 1992 CLC also caters for those jurisdiction and enforcement aspects that necessarily arise from an oil spill with transnational implications.

CLC art IX in particular provides that actions for compensation may only be brought in the contracting state or states in whose territory, territorial sea, EEZ or equivalent zone the relevant pollution damage has either been suffered or prevented or minimized by virtue of the successful adoption of preventive measures.

According to art X, a judgment delivered by one of the courts indicated by art IX will be recognized in other contracting states when it is 'enforceable in the state of origin where it is no longer subject to ordinary forms of review', unless the judgment was obtained by fraud or the defendant was denied reasonable notice or a fair opportunity to present its case. In addition judgments will be enforceable in each contracting state 'as soon as the formalities required in that State have been complied with', without the possibility for such formalities to permit the merits of the case to be re-examined.

Leaving aside for the time being the relationship between ordinary conflict-of-jurisdiction and choice-of-law rules on the one hand, and uniform conventions such as the CLC and the Fund Convention on the other (as this will be discussed below in sections III. and IV. respectively), it is important to point out that the rationale of a self-contained body of norms, providing not only for substantive measures but also for jurisdiction and enforcement rules, is precisely to prevent private international law 'intricacies' from hindering a prompt and predictable compensation process.

This is perhaps best illustrated by a judgment recently rendered by the United States Court of Appeals for the Second Circuit in a case brought by the Kingdom of Spain against the American Bureau of Shipping (ABS) as a consequence of the sinking of the *Prestige* off the northwest coast of Spain (*Reino de España on its own behalf and as trustee v American Bureau of Shipping*, 691 F.3d 461 (2nd Cir 2012)). The tanker had been inspected and classed by ABS, a leading classification society, 'for its entire working life until its casualty' and Spain's argument was that the relevant action should be governed by the law of the USA, which is not party to any of the CLC or the Fund Conventions, as opposed to the uniform regime. This was, at least presumably, an attempt to circumvent the principle of liability channelling, which in turn would have precluded the possibility of holding liable someone other than the shipowner. Spain was in theory successful, since, on weighing the so-called '*Lauritzen* factors' developed by the USA Supreme Court (*Lauritzen v Larsen*, 345 U.S. 571 (1953)), the Court of Appeals deemed US law applicable, largely because 'the domicile of defendants and the place of the wrongful act' clearly favoured the application of American law. However, the case failed on the merits due to the claimant's inability to prove that ABS and its subsidiaries had in fact recklessly breached any duty they might owe to Spain.

While the CLC-Fund Convention regime is rightly regarded as a successful example of uniform legislation, attempts to export some of its key features to other areas have delivered mixed results.

On the one hand, the HNS Convention (International Convention of 3 May 1996 on liability and compensation for damage in connection with the carriage of hazardous and noxious substances by sea, 35 ILM 1406; as amended by the Protocol of 20 April 2010 to the International Convention on liability and compensation for damage in connection with the carriage of hazardous and noxious substances by sea, IMO Doc LEG/CONF.17/DC/1 (29 April 2010)), adopted in 1996 with a view to ensuring compensation for damage resulting from the maritime transport of hazardous and noxious substances and largely modelled on the oil pollution regime described above, in the event failed to collect the number of ratifications required for its entry into force. With a view to attracting sufficient ratifications (12 are needed for its entry into force, eight of which have been filed so far, the Convention was amended in 2010 in an effort to resolve 'certain issues . . . inhibiting the entry into force of the Convention and . . . the implementation of the international regime contained therein'. These issues related mainly to the reporting obligations of States Parties and the definition of contributing cargo).

On the other hand, the Bunker Convention 2001 (International Convention of 23 March 2001 on civil liability for bunker oil pollution damage, IMO Doc LEG/CONF 12/19, 40 ILM 1406), adopted in 2001 and once again modelled on the CLC, entered into force in 2008, ensured compensation to those suffering damage caused by spills of oil carried as fuel in ships' bunkers.

Before moving to the jurisdiction, recognition and enforcement aspects of maritime torts, the uniform rules that apply to limitation of liability in general must also be recalled. These are nowadays contained in the 1976 LLMC, originally adopted in 1976, entered into force in 1986 and subsequently amended in 1996 (Convention of 19 November 1976 on limitation of liability for maritime claims, 1456 UNTS 221, as amended by the 1996 Protocol, 35 ILM 1433, Protocol entered into force in 2004) and again in 2012 (amendment adopted by the Legal Committee of IMO at its ninety-ninth session (April 2012) by resolution LEG.5(99), entered into force on 8 June 2015).

Under the 1976 LLMC, distinct limits per ton are provided with regard to loss of life or personal injury on the one hand and property claims on the other, including damage to other ships or third-party property in general. Such claims are said to be almost 'unbreakable' due to the fact that shipowners and salvors to whom the 1976 LLMC applies will be able to avail themselves of the limits that are set thereby, unless it is demonstrated that the loss resulted from their personal act or omission committed with the intent to cause such a loss, or recklessly and with knowledge that such loss would probably result.

The relevant limits were raised in 1996 and again in 2012, while since 2004 their revision is subject to the so-called 'tacit amendment' procedure, typical of the conventions adopted under the auspices of the International Maritime Organization (→ IMO), which itself allows an amendment to an existing convention to enter into force for any contracting state that raises no specific objection.

III. Jurisdiction, recognition and enforcement of judgments

As recalled in the previous section, uniform legal systems on liability and compensation such as the CLC-Fund Convention provide for *ad hoc* rules on jurisdiction, recognition and enforcement, as is also the case for those regimes relating to damage caused by the HNS Convention (arts 38–40) and oil transported as bunker (arts 9 and 10).

By their very nature, such bodies of rules might at first sight appear intended to prevail as a matter of principle over domestic 'general' conflict-of-jurisdiction solutions, But this is not necessarily so, at least not without exception or qualification.

An appropriate case in point is provided by the Brussels I Regulation, whose art 71 contains a rather complex coordination provision relating to the relationship of the Regulation itself with conventions to which Member States are parties, and which, in relation to 'particular matters', governs jurisdiction or the recognition or enforcement of judgments.

As a matter of principle, the Regulation does not 'affect' such conventions (art 71(1)). However, this does not mean that application of the Regulation is prevented generally. On the contrary, as far as jurisdiction is concerned, art 71(2)(a) provides for the seizure of a Member State court pursuant to a convention on a particular matter to which that Member State is a party, 'even where the defendant is domiciled in another Member State which is not party to that convention', provided that the Regulation's art 26 (on the defendant's right to be given the opportunity to appear and be heard) is applied.

With regard to recognition and enforcement, art 71(2)(b) further provides that judgments delivered in a Member State by a court 'in the exercise of jurisdiction provided for in a convention on a particular matter' will be recognized and enforced in the other Member States in accordance with the Brussels I Regulation. In an attempt to shed light on the meaning of this apparently contradictory requirement, the closing paragraph of art 71 specifies that, if the relevant convention is binding on both the Member State of origin and the Member State addressed and lays down conditions for the recognition or enforcement of judgments, then those conditions will apply even though 'the provisions of [the] Regulation which concern the procedure for recognition and enforcement of judgments may [also] be applied'.

It emerges from the wording of art 71, as well as from the relevant ECJ case-law (see in particular Case C-406/92 *The owners of the cargo lately laden on board the ship 'Tatry' v the owners of the ship 'Maciej Rataj'* [2004] ECR I-5439 and Case C-148/03 *Nürnberger Allgemeine Versicherungs AG v Portbridge Transport International BV* [2004] ECR I-10327), that the Regulation does not aim at ensuring the primacy of international conventions on particular matters at all costs and under any circumstance. On the contrary it is evident that the underlying rationale of art 71 is rather that of mutual integration, so that the Regulation should indeed maintain a residual scope of application to coincide with specific aspects covered by the Regulation but not governed by the relevant particular convention on the one hand, and matters in relation to which no inconsistency exists between the two 'competing' instruments on the other. This is what is arguably meant by the final paragraph of art 71, where it is stated that the relevant provisions of the Regulation 'may be applied' presumably if they are not in contradiction with the relevant convention, when it comes in particular to the procedure for the recognition and enforcement of judgments. It must be noted, incidentally, that the provision at issue underwent no material change in the revision process leading to the adoption of the Brussels I Regulation (recast) (Regulation (EU) No 1215/2012 of the European Parliament and of the Council of 12 December 2012 on jurisdiction and the recognition and enforcement of judgments in civil and commercial matters (recast), [2012] OJ L 351/1; → Brussels I (Convention and Regulation)), a version which has replaced its 2001 predecessor since 10 January 2015.

In those areas where no uniform convention exists, 'ordinary' rules on conflict of jurisdiction will come into play.

With regard to the Brussels I Regulation, which covers → civil and commercial matters in general, no question can be raised as to its applicability to maritime torts. It follows that as a general rule in connection with such torts, a person domiciled in a Member State will be sued (regardless of their nationality) in the courts of that Member State (art 2(1)) and art 4(1) of the Regulation recast where no jurisdiction clause has been agreed by the parties pursuant to art 23.

Among the special jurisdiction clauses, particular attention has to be paid to art 5, para 3, covering obligations deriving from → torts, delicts or quasi-delicts, which provides that in such matters a person domiciled in a Member State may be sued in another Member State 'in the courts for the place where the harmful event occurred or may occur'. Here it should be considered that according to relevant case-law the phrase 'the place where the harmful event occurred' implies 'that the plaintiff has an option to commence proceedings either at the place where the damage occurred or the place of the event giving rise to it'. This is based on the assumption, shared by the ECJ, that both the place of the event giving rise to the damage and the place where the damage occurred can constitute a significant connecting factor from a jurisdiction standpoint, so that 'it does not appear appropriate to opt for one of the two connecting factors mentioned to the exclusion of the other, since each of them can, depending on the circumstances, be particularly helpful from the point of view of the evidence and of the conduct of the proceedings' (Case 21/76 *Handelskwekerij GJ Bier BV v Mines de potasse d'Alsace SA* [1976] ECR 1735).

In this respect, and with a view to clarifying the respective scopes of application of contractual and non-contractual obligations in the maritime area, the ECJ has also held that art 5(3) (but not art 5(1), on contract matters) will govern an action brought by the consignee of goods damaged on completion of a transport operation, on the basis of the → bill of lading covering the maritime transport, not against the person who issued the bill of lading, but against the person whom the plaintiff considers to be the actual maritime carrier (Case C-51/97 *Réunion européenne SA and Others v Spliethoff's Bevrachtingskantoor BV and the Master of the vessel Alblasgracht V002* [1998] ECR I-6511).

The ECJ subsequently also held that art 5(3) applied to a case concerning the legality of industrial action and that, in that context, the place of the event giving rise to the damage was to be considered as where the notice of industrial action had been given and publicized. However, it was for the national court to identify the place where the damage had occurred, depending on the location where the financial loss may be regarded as having arisen (Case C-18/02 *Danmarks Rederiforening, acting on behalf of DFDS Torline A/S v LO Landsorganisationen i Sverige, acting on behalf of SEKO Sjöfolk Facket för Service och Kommunikation* [2004] ECR I-1417).

IV. Applicable law

Traditionally, ships have been qualified as part of the territory of the state of their nationality (*territoire flottant*), so that in consequence non-contractual obligations arising out of events occurring on board ships have been regarded as subject to the law of their flag.

The assimilation between a ship and the territory of the state of registration has attracted increasing criticism and is nowadays regarded by leading commentators as no more than a metaphor, which is nonetheless useful to ensure application of the law of the → flag to maritime torts whose consequences are felt exclusively on board.

In fact, while cases such as the historical and often cited *R v Anderson* (11 Cox Crim. Cases 198) have been taken as authority for the principle according to which the flag law will apply to acts taking place on board a ship on the high seas in general, the fact nevertheless remains that non-contractual obligations arising out of such acts are still subject to the flag law at least where there has been no impact outside the ship, as under those circumstances that law will coincide without room for uncertainty with the *lex loci commissi delicti*.

In this respect, American case-law provides significant examples. On the one hand, as already anticipated, see section II. above, according to the Supreme Court ruling in *Lauritzen v Larsen* (345 U.S. 571 (1953)), maritime choice of law in the USA involves eight possible factors: (i) the place of the wrongful act, (ii) the law of the ship's flag, (iii) the domicile (→ Domicile, habitual residence and establishment) of the injured party, (iv) the domicile of the shipowner, (v) the place of the contract, (vi) the inaccessibility of the foreign forum, (vii) the law of the forum, (viii) the shipowner's base of operations. Despite this, in *Klinghoffer v SNC Achille Lauro* the New York Southern District Court, confronted with the murder of an American citizen committed on board an Italian-flagged cruise ship, expressly recognized 'the strong deference accorded the law of the flag', and ruled on balance in favour of the application of Italian law (795 F.Supp. 112 (SDNY 1992)).

Other national legal systems, including civil law jurisdictions, have adopted similar approaches. This is demonstrated, for example, by arts 4 and 5 of the Italian Codice della navigazione (Regio decreto-legge 30 marzo 1942, n 327) which, respectively, state that Italian ships on the high seas are to be considered as Italian territory, and that acts and events occurring on board a ship in the sovereign waters of a foreign state will be governed by the national law of the ship whenever the applicable law is that of the place where the act or event has occurred.

As has been authoritatively observed, this result will not be reached and the law of the flag will give way to alternative solutions, including (even) when the relevant events have occurred on the high seas, whenever a stronger link can be established leading to a different legal system. Examples here are where a state property (eg a submarine pipeline or cable) is damaged as a consequence of a tortious act, or where there is a pre-existing link (eg in the form of a contractual relationship) between the tortfeasor and the injured party.

What follows is that the law of the flag tends to be applied to non-contractual liability instances, including torts, which arise in waters subject to another state's sovereignty or jurisdiction, as long as the relevant events raise the exclusive interests of the ship's state of registration or of the subjects involved in the maritime voyage. In other words there may be no interference whatsoever with the orderly course of life within the state in whose maritime area such events have occurred.

Interestingly, in connection with the discussion so far, in the area of → contractual obligations, when adopting the Rome I Regulation (Regulation (EC) No 593/2008 of the European Parliament and of the Council of 17 June 2008 on the law applicable to contractual obligations (Rome I), [2008] OJ L 177/6; → Rome Convention and Rome I Regulation (contractual obligations)), the European legislator opted for the introduction of an *ad hoc* rule governing the law applicable to contracts of carriage of goods and passengers (art 5). By contrast, the → Rome II Regulation (Regulation (EC) No 864/2007 of the European Parliament and of the Council of 11 July 2007 on the law applicable to non-contractual obligations (Rome II), [2007] OJ L 199/40) contains no *ad hoc* choice-of-law rule dealing with maritime or transport-related torts, so that such disputes are subject to the general rule embodied in art 4, with the exception, of course, of those instances that might fall within the scope of application of other 'special' rules, such as art 7 on environmental liability.

One important consequence that follows from the above-mentioned policy choice is clearly the absence of any reference in the Rome II Regulation to specific maritime zones, or more precisely the fact that the exact location of the tortious behaviour in one or another maritime zone appears to lose importance.

However, this corresponds entirely with the trend highlighted earlier with regard to the decreasing importance of the flag law as the law applicable to maritime torts. What actually emerges from art 4 of the Regulation is that the focus for the purpose of determining the law applicable to a (maritime) tort has to be placed on the country 'in which the damage occurs' rather than on the country in which the event giving rise to the damage has taken place. This has the effect that, whenever such damage occurs in waters that are subject to the sovereignty or the jurisdiction of a coastal state, then the law of that state will in principle apply. The so-called → 'escape clause' provided by art 4(3) may in addition come into play where it is 'clear from all the circumstances of the case' that the tort is 'manifestly more closely connected' with a different country, for example because of a pre-existing relationship between the parties, such as a contract closely connected with the tort in question. This may lead, for example, to application of the law governing → contractual obligations relevant to a maritime venture also to non-contractual liability arising from that venture.

In this respect, and returning briefly to contractual matters, it should be recalled that the already mentioned art 5 of the Rome I Regulation provides that, absent an agreement on the applicable law, carriage of goods contracts will be governed by the 'law of the country of habitual residence of the carrier, provided that the place of receipt or the place of delivery or the habitual residence of the consignor is also situated in that country', while carriage of passengers contracts will be governed by the 'law of the country where the passenger has his habitual residence, provided that either the place of departure or the place of destination is situated in that country'. Such rules are subject to derogations (eg the manifestly closer connection clause applies, see art 5(3)) and qualifications (eg the choice available to the parties regarding the law applicable to a contract for the carriage of passengers is more limited than under general circumstances, see art 5(2)). However, from a general standpoint, the rules attest to the fact that, unlike in the area of torts, the general rules on the law applicable to contractual obligations as provided for by the Rome I Regulation were seen by the European legislator as unsuitable to govern transport contracts.

By way of an exception, a departure from the general rule set by the Rome II Regulation may theoretically appear proper in those cases where the damage is suffered in a location that the tortfeasor could not reasonably have foreseen. This occurred for example in *Bureau Veritas SA v Groupama Transport*, decided by the French Cour de Cassation on 27 March 2007, ie before entry into force of the Regulation. Here French law was deemed applicable to a claim brought against a French-based classification society as a consequence of the grounding of a ship, regardless of the location both of events giving rise to the damage (visits made in Singapore and China) and of the damage itself (Madagascar waters). Under the circumstances, the *'fait générateur du dommage'* was in fact assumed to be located at the place not only where the defendant was based but also where the pertinent decisions had been taken and the relevant documents kept. While it remains to be seen whether the same approach could be taken under the Regulation, the 'unforeseeability test' set by the French Supreme Court remains a high hurdle in all cases where the responsible party has some knowledge of the ship's operations.

On a conclusive note, it may be appropriate to clarify the relationship between the Rome II Regulation and the international instruments providing for substantive solutions that have been examined above, see section II. Interestingly, Recital (36) of the Regulation reminds that '[r]espect for international commitments entered into by the Member States means that [the] Regulation should not affect international conventions to which one or more Member States are parties at the time [the] Regulation is adopted', and does so without restricting such requirement to any particular category of international conventions. Conversely, its art 28(1) provides that the Regulation 'shall not prejudice the application of international conventions to which one or more Member States are parties at the time when this Regulation is adopted *and which lay down conflict-of-law rules relating to non-contractual obligations*' (emphasis added).

Three different arguments can be made with a view to ensuring the uniform interpretation and application of the substantive law Conventions under consideration. First, while it is true that conventions such as the CLC-Fund Convention cannot be said to 'lay down conflict of laws rules' as such, it must nevertheless be conceded that, as pointed out by authoritative commentators, they are indeed intended to determine by themselves the scope of application of the substantive rules (of non-derogable nature) for which they provide. Second, in order to ensure an interpretation of the Regulation coherent with its Recital (36), the substantive law conventions that are part of the law of the forum may be qualified as overriding mandatory provisions within the meaning of art 16 of the Regulation, as they in any case are intended to be applied 'irrespective of the law otherwise applicable to the non-contractual obligation' at stake. Third and finally, one could also take the more radical view that the fact that a uniform law convention is applicable to a given set of facts would fundamentally preclude the existence of a 'situation . . . involving a conflict of laws' (art 1(1)), thus also excluding application of the Rome II Regulation.

LORENZO SCHIANO DI PEPE

Literature

Yvonne Baatz, 'The Conflicts of Laws in Institute of Maritime Law' in Maritime Law Institute, *Southampton on Shipping Law* (Informa 2008) 1; Jürgen Basedow, 'Rome II at Sea: General Aspects of Maritime Torts' (2010) 74 RabelsZ 118; Sergio M Carbone, *Legge della bandiera e ordinamento italiano* (Giuffrè 1970); Sergio M Carbone, 'La réglementation du transport et du trafic maritimes dans le développement de la pratique internationale' (1980) 166 Rec. des Cours 251; Sergio M Carbone, 'Conflits de lois en droit maritime' (2009) 340 Rec. des Cours 63; Sergio M Carbone and Lorenzo Schiano di Pepe, *Conflitti di sovranità e di leggi nei traffici marittimi tra diritto internazionale e diritto dell'Unione europea* (Giappichelli 2010); Sergio M Carbone and Lorenzo Schiano di Pepe, 'Uniform Law and Conflicts in Private Enforcement of Environmental Law: The Maritime Sector and Beyond' in Jürgen Basedow, Ulrich Magnus and Rüdiger Wolfrum (eds), *The Hamburg Lectures on Maritime Affairs 2007 and 2008* (Springer 2010) 21; Timothy B De Sieno, 'Choice of Law in Maritime Torts: An Analysis of a Recent Trend' (1989) 20 J.Mar.L.& Com. 387; Martin P George, 'Choice of Law in Maritime Torts' (2007) 3 J Priv Int L 137; Paola Ivaldi, *Inquinamento marino e regole internazionali di responsabilità* (CEDAM 1996); Luke T Lee, 'Jurisdiction over Foreign Merchant Ships in the Territorial Sea: An Analysis of the Geneva Convention on the Law of the Sea' (1961) 55 Am.J.Int'l L. 77; Francesco Munari and Lorenzo Schiano di Pepe, 'Liability for Environmental Torts in Europe: Choice of Forum, Choice of Law and the Case for Pursuing Effective Legal Uniformity' in Alberto Malatesta (ed), *The Unification of Choice of Law Rules on Torts and Other Non-Contractual Obligations in Europe* (CEDAM 2007) 173; Symeon C Symeonides, 'Cruising in American Waters: Spector, Maritime Conflicts, and Choice of Law' (2006) 37 J.Mar.L.& Com. 491; Symeon C Symeonides, 'Rome II and Tort Conflicts: A Missed Opportunity' (2008) 56 Am.J.Int'l L. 173; Haijiang Yang, *Jurisdiction of the Coastal State over Foreign Merchant Ships in Internal Waters and the Territorial Sea* (Springer 2006).

Marriage

I. Background and concept

According to the prevailing view in many legal systems, marriage is a contract or sacrament on the one hand and a status on the other. Thus, the question of which laws are to govern the formation of a marriage has to be answered. Private international law is also at issue if the validity of an already concluded marriage is at stake, especially if this marriage has been celebrated abroad. Finally, the laws applicable to the consequences of the status 'marriage' have to be determined.

All these private international law questions concern a number of issues: formal validity of a marriage may be governed by a law other than that applicable to the capacity of the future spouses to marry each other. Other conflict rules might apply to both of these aspects if the marriage was formed abroad. The consequences of marriage as a status are manifold. They include → matrimonial property regimes, mutual → maintenance obligations, rules on mutual respect, trust, fidelity, moral support or issues such as names (→ Names of individuals), citizenship (→ nationality), parentage (→ Kinship and legitimation), parental authority (→ Guardianship, custody and parental responsibility) etc. Such effects may be governed by a number of choice-of-law rules. The following remarks will concentrate on the first two issues, namely the laws applicable to the formation of the marriage and the laws which govern the validity of a marriage contracted abroad (II.–IV.) and finally take a glance at those (general) effects of marriage which are not subject to the special conflict rules concerning the specific matters named above (V.).

Although certain trends in substantive marriage laws as well as in the respective conflict laws are common to most of the European legal systems, the applicable rules vary considerably in detail.

II. Purpose and function of conflict rules

One important function of private international law rules is to designate the applicable law in such a way that the results are predictable and foreseeable and that legal security is provided for all persons concerned (Peter M North, 'Development of Rules of Private international law in the Field of Family Law' (1980) 166 Rec. des Cours 9, 43 ff; Trevor C Hartley, 'The Policy Basis of English Conflict of Laws on Marriage' (1972) 35 MLR 571). In the field of marriage, these issues should be of paramount consideration: the persons getting married should be able to know which requirements have to be fulfilled in order to contract a valid marriage at the time of formation. They should also be able to ascertain whether or not this marriage will be regarded as valid in this and in any other jurisdiction. In a mobile society, it seems of great importance that marriages validly contracted in one legal system will be honoured in other legal systems alike. So-called 'limping marriages', ie a marriage validly concluded in one jurisdiction but not regarded as valid in another, are only a 'second choice' and should be avoided wherever possible. However, legal systems may have (policy-related) concerns which present an obstacle to achieving these goals.

On the one hand, → public policy issues play an especially important role in marriage law. The concepts and goals of the relevant national (substantive) law rules on marriage influence the respective conflict rules. Thus, private international law on marriage very often concerns and pursues substantive law issues. The conflict rules get 'materialized' (*Materialisierung des internationalen Privatrechts*). One of these concerns is the *favor matrimonii*. This means that access to marriage should not be unduly restricted. It may also indicate that, at least in some situations, a marriage validly concluded under one law shall not be invalidated by another law even though the latter may have been applicable if the marriage had been concluded in that jurisdiction (Trevor C Hartley, 'The Policy Basis of English Conflict of Laws on Marriage' (1972) 35 MLR 571, 572; Ian Sumner, 'Registered Partnerships and Private international law: Great Britain and the Netherlands Compared' in Andrea Bonomi and Bertil Cottier (eds), *Aspects de droit international privé des partenariats enregistrés en Europe* (Schulthess 2004) 29, 45). Further, under certain circumstances and conditions, access to marriage will be allowed or a concluded marriage will be regarded as valid, despite the fact that the law called upon to govern the validity would not grant access to, or validity of, that marriage. Examples of this concern are art 13(2) Introductory Act to the German Civil Code (Einführungsgesetz zum Bürgerlichen Gesetzbuch of 21 September 1994, BGBl. I 2494, as amended, henceforth EGBGB), art 43(3) Swiss Private international law Act (Bundesgesetz über das Internationale Privatrecht of 18 December 1987, 1988 BBl. I 5, as amended, henceforth Swiss PILA), art 5 Hague Marriage Convention 1978 (Hague Convention of 14 March 1978 on celebration and recognition of the validity of marriages, 1901 UNTS 131). For the same reason, impediments of the applicable marriage law may be disregarded if these impediments violate fundamental principles of marriage law of the jurisdiction where the couple seeks to marry or where the marriage whose validity is questioned was concluded. For instance, the constitutionally guaranteed freedom to marry in German law allows – even requires – that fundamental intrusions into this right (such as forbidding divorced persons to marry) be disregarded. The *favor matrimonii* may also influence the designation of the law applicable to the formalities for celebrating a marriage or may require a departure from the normally applicable rules on the recognition of a marriage.

At the other end of the spectrum, public policy issues may also influence private international law by prohibiting the formation or recognition of certain marriages, such as bigamous or child marriages, forced marriages and → same-sex marriages (Sharon Shakargy, 'Marriage by the State or Married to the State? On Choice of Law in Marriage and Divorce' (2013) 9 J Priv Int L 499, 501, 510, 515). This might be a general prohibition, or it may apply only to marriages of the country's nationals or inhabitants, or to marriages concluded within that jurisdiction. Thus, the normal conflict rules might be supplemented by special rules pertaining to certain issues. Another option is to suspend the application of the normally applicable conflict rules for public policy reasons – either generally or in specific situations.

These restrictions on the 'normal' choice-of-law rules might achieve a certain (although by far not complete) uniformity of the applicable laws on the formation of marriage within one legal system. But then again these inroads into the normal conflict rules risk impairing predictability and foreseeability of the results and may lead to limping marriages. There is a considerable tension between the *favor matrimonii* on the one hand and legal security on the other. The enforcement of national fundamental values is, at least to a certain extent, incompatible with the respect of other legal systems.

III. Legal sources

In light of this background and the different aims pursued, it should be of little surprise that private international law rules on marriage vary considerably within the legal systems. In most jurisdictions outside the common law world, these conflict rules are of statutory nature. Even many jurisdictions within the USA have enacted statutes on conflict rules for the validity of marriages. Special statutes might designate the applicable law for certain types of marriage ceremonies abroad. English law, however, still adheres mainly to the common law principles.

Some regional treaties, like the Inter-Nordic Rules on International Private and Procedural Law have promoted a unified approach. Others, like the Código Bustamante of 1928 (Convention on Private international law (Bustamante Code), adopted at Havana on 20 February 1928 at the Sixth International Conference of American States; OAS, Law and Treaty Series, No 34; art 2) have enjoyed little acceptance or are outdated today. The German-Persian Treaty (of 17 February 1929, RGBl. 1930 II, 1006) deals only with the general application of the law of nationality (art 4(3)). International conventions aiming at a unification of conflict rules (the Hague Marriage Convention of 1902 (Hague Convention of 12 June 1902 relating to the settlement of the conflict of the laws concerning marriage) and the Hague Marriage Convention of 1978 (Hague Convention of 14 March 1978 on Celebration and Recognition of the Validity of Marriages, 1901 UNTS 131), see Christian von Bar, 'Die eherechtlichen Konventionen der Haager Konferenz(en)' (1993) 57 RabelsZ 63) have not attracted many contracting states (only → Germany and → Italy in the case of the 1902 Convention and → Australia, → Luxembourg and the → Netherlands in that of the 1978 Convention). Some international treaties set standards with regard to the substantive validity (such as the United Nations Convention of 10 December 1962 on Consent to Marriage, Minimum Age for Marriage and Registration of Marriages, 521 UNTS 231) or provide for the issuance of certain documents facilitating marriage abroad (CIEC/ICCS Convention to Facilitate the Celebration of Marriages Abroad of 10 September 1964, 932 UNTS 109; → CIEC/ICCS (International Commission on Civil Status)), rather than dealing with conflict rules.

So far the European Union has been reluctant to produce legislation on the applicable law concerning the formation of marriages. Only procedural questions on annulment of marriage are dealt with in the → Brussels IIa Regulation (Council Regulation (EC) No 2201/2003 of 27 November 2003 concerning jurisdiction and the recognition and enforcement of judgments in matrimonial matters and the matters of parental responsibility, repealing Regulation (EC) No 1347/2000, [2003] OJ L 338/1). The European Commission is considering whether or not to address the problems by proposing rules on the recognition of marriages evidenced by documents issued in one of the member states (→ Recognition of legal situations evidenced by documents) but has not yet come forward with a draft.

IV. Current state of law

If one wants to depict the various national conflict rules and the proposals on the international scene, it seems advisable to first distinguish between the conflict rules on the formal validity and those on the substantive validity of a marriage.

1. Formal validity

Like the Hague Marriage Conventions of 1902 and 1978, most legal systems apply – at least in principle – the *lex loci celebrationis* to the formal requirements of a marriage (for English law: *Scrimshire v Scrimshire* (1752) 2 Hag Con 395, 161 ER 782; *McCabe v McCabe* (1994) 1 FCR 257; for Scottish Law: s 38 (1) Family Law (Scotland) Act 2006 (2006 asp 2); for French Law: art 171-1 Civil Code (Code Civil of 21 March 1804); for Dutch Law: art 28 seq Dutch Civil Code Book 10 (New Civil Code (Nieuw Burgerlijk Wetboek) of 1 January 1992); for German Law: art 11 EGBGB; for Swiss Law: art 45 Swiss PILA; see also art 2 Hague Marriage Convention 1978; art 5(1) Hague Marriage Convention 1902 with reservations in art 5(2) where the home state requires a religious ceremony for its nationals). The same is true with regard to non-European jurisdictions (art 132 Paraguay Civil Code (Civil Code of Paraguay as revised by Law No. 1183 of 18 December 1985); art 239 Uruguay Civil Code (Código Civil de la República Oriental del Uruguay as of 26 February 2010); art 159, 161 Argentinian Civil Code (Código Civil de la República Argentina of 25 September 1869, by the passage of Law 340, entry into force 1 January 1871, henceforth Argentinian CC); s 283(2) Restatement (Second) of Conflict of Laws (American Law Institute, Restatement of the Law, Second: Conflict of Laws 2d, St. Paul 1971; → Restatement (First and Second) of Conflict of Laws)).

This conflict rule minimizes the formal difficulties for spouses who wish to get married outside their home state and provides legal security to those who have been married abroad with regard to the formal validity of their marriage. It cuts back the formalities in the case of transnational relationships and offers a free choice of the place where the celebration of the marriage takes place. Especially in a global society, the choice of the place of celebration seems to be important to the persons concerned from an emotional point of view. From the conflict-of-law perspective on the other hand, the place of celebration may bear very little relationship to the persons involved and the marriage contracted – except for the celebration itself. However, a misuse or a *'fraude à la loi'* (→ Evasion of laws (*fraus legis*)) in choosing the place of celebration is very unlikely if only formal validity is concerned. Nevertheless, it has to be borne in mind that the question of where to draw the line between rules on formal validity and those on essential validity might be answered differently in the various legal systems. Generally, the formalities of the ceremony itself, as well as the preparatory requirements such as licences, publication etc and the registration of the marriage act, are regarded as formal issues. On the borderline are questions such as whether parental consent or judicial approval are required or whether the future spouses must be present at the ceremony. German law regards the consent of parents or third persons and the judicial approval as of a substantive nature. It accepts the representation of future spouses at the ceremony as a formal matter only if the proxy merely declares the consent of the future spouse (marriage by proxy, *Handschuhehe*), but not if the proxy decides whether to consent or not. By contrast, English and Scottish law classify the rules on these issues as formal (for marriage by proxy, see *McCabe v McCabe* (1994) 1 FCR 257; *Ponticelli v Ponticelli* [1958] P. 204; for parental consent: *Ogden v Odgen* [1908] P. 46); consequently before the Marriage (Scotland) Act 1977 some German youngsters would celebrate a marriage ceremony at the Scottish border and enter into a so-called Gretna Green marriage which was defective (voidable) under German law.

Besides differences in the precise boundaries between formal and substantive rules, the place of celebration may cause difficulties and result in different answers, especially if a marriage is not concluded in the presence of both future spouses (or their proxies) and the relevant person for the marriage ceremony. According to the prevailing view, the law of all places where constituting acts have taken place will have to be complied with. Consulates or diplomatic missions are, in principle, not extraterritorial units. Thus, marriages celebrated in a foreign consulate or embassy etc have to conform to the formal rules of the host state, except where a treaty between the states concerned or a special rule of the host state provide otherwise (see, for example, art 23 German-Russian Treaty of 1958 for future spouses of Russian nationality; for Dutch law: art 30, 31(2) Dutch Civil Code Book 10; for the UK: s 11 Foreign Marriage Act 1892 (1892 c 23 (Regnal. 55_and_56_Vict)) in connection with s 3 Foreign Marriage Order 1970 (no 1539); for French law: Decree of 20 October 1939, Decree of 15 December 1958; art 9 Hague Marriage Convention 1978). If the marriage ceremony takes place on a ship on the high seas by the captain of the ship, the law of the → flag is regarded as the *lex loci celebrationis*. For the celebration of a marriage on an aircraft by the captain, the law of the place of registration of the aircraft is usually the *lex loci celebrationis*.

In many legal systems, a reference to the *lex loci celebrationis* is a reference to the internal law of the place of celebration. But even if the reference includes private international rules, the law referred to will nearly always accept this reference. Thus, → renvoi does not play an important role in these formal questions.

However, many legal systems supplement the reference to the *lex loci celebrationis* by additionally calling upon another law. This might be the law of the home state of one or both spouses or the → *lex fori*. The 'home state law' may be determined by → nationality (for example in German (→ Germany), French (→ France), Italian (→ Italy) law), domicile (English law), habitual residence (Dutch law) or registered residence of the future spouses (→ Domicile, habitual residence and establishment). The law additionally called upon may be applied cumulatively or alternatively. If the validity of a marriage already concluded is at issue, the alternative reference to another law promotes the *favor matrimonii*: the marriage, although not concluded according to the rules of the *lex loci celebrationis*, might be regarded as valid under the other law or laws such as the rules of the home state of both spouses. However, at the same time, a limping marriage may result if the law at the place of celebration insists on the application of its own rules on the formalities of marriages concluded within its territories (see, eg German law: art 13(3) EGBGB; for English law: Geoffrey Chevalier Cheshire, Peter M North and James J Fawcett, *Private international law* (13th edn, Butterworth 1999) 709; for Dutch law: art 30 Dutch Civil Code Book 10).

The cumulative reference to the → *lex fori* (art 45 Swiss PILA) safeguards the application of all internal rules on formalities even beyond issues of public policy. In order not to impair access to marriage in an undue way, the cumulative reference is often limited to cases which potentially involve *fraus legis* (art 45(2) Swiss PILA) (→ Evasion of laws (*fraus legis*)) or public policy (art 32 Dutch Civil Code Book 10). The cumulative reference to the *lex fori* may include the conflict rules of that law (art 31(3) Dutch Civil Code Book 10). A cumulative reference to the law of the home state(s) aims at avoiding limping marriages; on the other hand, it may unduly impair access to marriage, especially if the spouses do not intend to return and live in their (former) home states.

Many legal systems provide certain exceptions to the rules discussed – either for certain forms of marriage (common law marriage, marriage on vessels etc) or for certain situations (especially if sufficient facilities at the place of celebration were lacking because of war or other incidents).

2. *Substantive validity*

a) Structures
The situation is even more complicated when it comes to conflict rules on the substantive validity of a marriage. There is, on the one hand, again the consideration of favouring access to, and the validity of, marriages by broad choice-of-law rules. On the other hand, the acceptability of foreign rules on the personal conditions of future spouses is a very delicate matter. Although it is true that marriage impediments have been reduced in many states around the world and in almost all European states to very basic issues, there are still some aspects of substantive family law which seem to be of paramount consideration for national legislators and national courts. This concerns especially – as already mentioned above – free consent, age of spouses and monogamy.

Most of the legal systems deal with these very delicate issues under the heading of public policy and do not provide special conflict rules in this respect. The public policy issue might play a different role if the marriage has been concluded abroad and if none of the spouses had the nationality of, or is a habitual resident or domiciled in, the state where the validity is at stake. Openness and the respect for foreign law will be greater in these situations than when a marriage is celebrated within this state or by its nationals or inhabitants (for polygamous marriages in English law: *Radwan v Radwan No 2* [1973] Fam 35; *Dhaka v Ranu Begum* [1986] Imm AR 460; in German law: Tobias Helms, 'Im Ausland begründete – im Inland unbekannte Statusverhältnisse' [2012] StAZ 2, 3; Federal Court on Social Law (BSozG), 30 August 2000 [2003] IPRax 267; State Social Insurance Court (LSG) Darmstadt, 29 June 2004 [2005] IPRax 43). Other jurisdictions provide special rules barring such marriages even if the applicable law would allow them (see art 29 Dutch Civil Code Book 10), or shape their conflict-of-law rules in such a way that the impediments of the *lex fori* must always be respected alongside the applicable law when a marriage is celebrated there (see Swedish law 26 s 1, Chapter 1 § 1 (Act No 1904:26 on certain International Legal Conditions Regarding Marriage and Guardianship)) or when a citizen or a person habitually resident in this state is involved (see art 44(1), (2) Swiss PILA; art 1.25 Lithuanian Civil Code (of 6 September 2000)). In consequence, some legal systems (→ Switzerland, → Sweden, the → Netherlands, → Lithuania) and the Hague Marriage Convention 1978 provide different rules for the celebration of a marriage within the state and for the recognition of a marriage celebrated abroad. When a marriage is celebrated abroad, two different approaches may be followed: either the law provides conflict rules designating the substantive law or laws governing the validity (private international law solution (art 31(1), (3) Dutch Civil Code Book 10)) or, alternatively, the marriage is recognized if it is regarded as valid at the place of celebration irrespective of the law applied (recognition instead of private international law rules) (→ Recognition of legal situations evidenced by documents) (art 45 Swiss PILA; art 1.25 (4) Lithuanian Civil Code; art 9 Hague Marriage Convention 1978).

b) Connecting factors
Traditionally in continental Europe, nationality of the spouses has been the decisive → connecting factor for many decades. Whereas originally, sometimes the nationality of the future husband (only) was decisive (Hungarian Marriage Law of 1894 (Act No XXXI 1894) §§ 110, 111), today the respective law of both future spouses normally has to be applied. This means that it is necessary to examine the national laws of each future spouse; each party must have the capacity (→ Capacity and emancipation) to marry the other according to his or her national law (see art 13(1) EGBGB; art 27 Italian Private international law Act (Riforma del Sistema italiano di diritto internazionale private, Act No 218 of 31 May 1995 in Gazz.Uff., Supplemento Ordinario No 128 of 3 June l995, as amended) and art 115 Italian Civil Code (Codice Civile of 4 April 1942 (Gazz. Uff. No 79 and 79bis; edizione straordinaria)); art 37 Hungarian Private international law (Law-decree No 13 of 1979 on Private international law); art 48 Czech Private international law (91/2012 Coll. Act of 25 January 2012 on Private international law); art 17(1) Austrian Federal Code on Private international law (Bundesgesetz über das internationale Privatrecht of 15 June 1978, BGBl. No 304/1978, as amended); art 3 French Civil Code (implicitly)). Similarly, English courts traditionally apply the dual domicile test (Albert Dicey, *Conflict of Laws* (8th edn, Stevens 1967); Peter M North, 'Development of Rules of Private international law in the Field of Family Law' (1980) 166 Rec. des Cours 9, 69). The capacity (→ Capacity and emancipation) to marry is governed by the law of the prenuptial domicile of each future spouse (→ Domicile, habitual residence and establishment).

Both these approaches rely on 'a real and substantive' relationship between the applicable law and the future spouses at the time of the celebration. The relationship is (relatively) easy to ascertain and therefore promotes certainty as to the applicable law (Trevor C Hartley, 'The Policy Basis of English Conflict of Laws on Marriage' (1972) 35 MLR 571, 576). It might also ensure some certainty with regard to the respect for the validity of this marriage abroad, because the state of the spouse's nationality or their domicile might have a similar interest in applying their laws to the validity of the marriage. Thus, it seems that limping marriages are avoided (Law Commission Working Paper No 89, Private international law: Choice of Law Rules in Marriage (1985) para 3.36).

However, there are a number of substantial disadvantages to this approach. First, → nationality (or domicile in English law) does not always indicate a real connection between the applicable law and the legal situation. The spouses may never have lived or may not be willing to spend their marital life in the respective jurisdictions (Alan Reed, 'Essential Validity of Marriage: The Application of Interest Analysis and Depeçage to Anglo-American Choice of Law Rules' (2000) 20 N.Y.Sch.J.Int'l.& Comp.L. 387, 394). Both concepts have lost at least some significance in conflict of laws, even for determining the law applicable in family law matters. In addition, the accumulation of impediments of two laws contravenes the *favor matrimonii*. The bars to marriage are less justified if they result from the application of a law which bears very little connection to the marriage (Trevor C Hartley, 'The Policy Basis of English Conflict of Laws on Marriage' (1972) 35 MLR 571, 577; Sharon Shakargy, 'Marriage by the State or Married to the State? On Choice of Law in Marriage and Divorce' (2013) 9 J Priv Int L 499, 504, 510). Finally, if the reference is made to the substantive law directly (excluding its private international law rules) this approach cannot prevent 'limping marriages' in case the national laws of the spouses or the laws of their domiciles designate other laws to govern the validity of the marriage. This is especially true since many jurisdictions have substituted nationality with habitual residence as a jurisdiction selection test or – within the Anglo-American world – have changed the concept of domicile to come close to the notion of habitual residence (for critics of the English domicile concept, see Richard Fentiman, 'Domicile Revisited' (1991) 50 CLJ 445). The same problem of a limping marriage arises if according to the law of celebration another law than that of the nationality or domicile of the spouses has been applied.

Habitual residence as a → connecting factor in private international law and in international civil procedure has become common and can also be found in modern Hague conventions and EU legislation (→ Domicile, habitual residence and establishment). Some uncertainties remain about borderline cases and specific situations, but in general, habitual residence has been accepted even in family law matters. But if the laws of the prenuptial habitual residences of both spouses have to be examined to determine their capacity to marry, the accumulation of laws might again unduly impair access to marriage. Once again, the law of the prenuptial habitual residence might have a very spurious connection to this marriage, as the spouses might spend all of their marital life in another jurisdiction.

Therefore, it has been suggested that the capacity to marry should be determined by the law of the intended matrimonial home (in English law relying on Friedrich Carl von Savigny, *System des heutigen römischen Rechts*, vol 8 (Veit 1849) 397; by Geoffrey Chevalier Cheshire, *Private international law* (5th edn, Clarendon Press 1957) 310; *Radwan v Radwan No 2* [1973] Fam 35; Charles Taintor, 'Marriage in the Conflict of Laws' (1956) 9 Vand.L.Rev. 607) as this legal system will have a close and real connection to the marriage. However, because of the prospective character of the connecting factor, determination of the applicable law in this way causes some difficulties at the time of celebration of the marriage, especially for the officials involved in the marriage ceremony (Alan Reed, 'Essential Validity of Marriage: The Application of Interest Analysis and Depeçage to Anglo-American Choice of Law Rules' (2000) 20 N.Y.Sch.J.Int'l.& Comp.L. 387, 398). Such a conflict rule could, in addition, invite false statements by the future spouses in order to obtain access to marriage. After the marriage, the *ex post* retrospective examination of the intended marital home might be disputed.

Influenced by modern US conflict-of-law theories (→ Restatement (First and Second) of Conflict of Laws), it has been suggested that the law of the jurisdiction with the 'most real and substantial connection' should govern the (substantive) validity of a marriage (Edward Sykes, 'The Essential Validity of Marriage' (1955) 4 ICLQ 159, 165; *Vervaeke v Smith* [1983] AC 145, 166 *obiter*; § 283(1) Restatement (Second) of Conflict of Laws; Willis Reese, 'The Hague Convention on the Celebration and Recognition of the Validity of Marriages' (1979) 20 Va.J.Int'l L. 25, 30, 36). Due to the lack of certainty, this approach did not find many followers. The same is true with regard to the proposal of a detailed interest-analysis (→ Interest and policy analysis in private international law) test concerning the various impediments to marriage (Alan Reed, 'Essential Validity of Marriage: The Application of Interest Analysis and Depeçage to Anglo-American Choice of Law Rules' (2000) 20 N.Y.Sch.J.Int'l.& Comp.L. 387, 408 ff).

Finally, conflict rules designate the application of the *lex loci celebrationis* not only to the formal validity of a marriage but also to the capacity of the spouses to marry (art 132 Paraguay Civil Code; art 239 Uruguay Civil Code; art 159, 161 Argentinian CC and the traditional conflict rule of the Restatement (First) of Conflict of Laws (American Law Institute, Restatement of the Law, First: Conflict of Laws, St. Paul 1934; → Restatement (First and Second) of Conflict of Laws), s 121; art 9 Hague Marriage Convention 1978). This approach has the advantage that the content of the applicable law is easy to ascertain for the officials involved in the conclusion of a marriage. For the future spouses, this conflict rule guarantees certainty as to the rules applicable at the time of formation of the marriage as well as to the validity of the marriage in the future. If it were a globally accepted conflict rule, the validity of the marriage would be guaranteed wherever the question arises. Only → public policy arguments would impair this result (Dagmar Coester-Waltjen, 'Reform des Art. 13 EGBGB?' [2013] StAZ 10).

But the *lex loci celebrationis* approach has some disadvantages too. The place of celebration may have been chosen simply for touristic reasons and thus have no connection to the parties and their marriage. There is also the danger that future spouses want to escape marriage impediments imposed by the laws of the state where they live or to which they 'belong'. To address the first problem, some jurisdictions reduce the application of their own marriage impediments to very basic issues and dispense with other impediments if either the national law of one of the parties or the law of one party's domicile (→ Domicile, habitual residence and establishment) allow such marriage (Swedish Law Statute 1904: 26 s 1 Ch 1 § 1; see also art 3 Hague Marriage Convention 1978). In order to address evasion strategies employed by the parties and to prevent limping marriages, legal systems require for the conclusion of the marriage, in addition to the *lex loci celebrationis*, the application of the national or domiciliary law of at least one spouse or the recognition of that marriage in the home state of one or both spouses (see also art 3 Hague Marriage Convention 1978). This combination of the *lex loci celebrationis* with another law having some connection with the parties might be required only if there is suspicion of a *fraus legis* (art 45(2) Swiss PILA; → Evasion of laws (*fraus legis*)) or if there is no real connection to the place of celebration (art 43(2) Swiss PILA; Swedish Law Statute 1904:26 s 1 Ch.1 § 1 (2)) or always if the state's own citizens are involved (arts 115, 116 Italian Civil Code).

If the validity of the marriage concluded elsewhere is at issue, legal systems tend to uphold that marriage (*In re May's Estate*, 114 N.E.2d 4 (N.Y.1953)), except where → public policy issues either especially enunciated or included in general public policy considerations exist. This is notably the approach of the Hague Marriage Convention 1978 (art 7 *et seq*), which provides for recognition of a validly concluded marriage, regardless of which law has been applied. States which have ratified the Convention follow this approach (art 47 Luxembourg Civil Code (Code Civil of 5 March 1803); see also although not a contracting state Swedish Law Statute 1904:26 s 1 Ch 1 § 1), sometimes with some variations (see art 31(3) Dutch Civil Code Book 10).

V. Effects of marriage (general)

1. The problems of definition and demarcation

In all legal systems, a validly concluded marriage has certain legal effects with regard to personal, pecuniary and proprietary relations between the spouses and, in some respects, between them and third parties. Most of these issues are dealt with by specific conflict rules, which are sometimes the subject of international conventions (such as the Hague Convention on Matrimonial Property) or – in modern times – of European regulations (for instance, the Maintenance Regulation). However, there remain certain areas in substantive family law which cannot be classified under the specific headings of matrimonial property, maintenance (→ Maintenance obligations) and so on. These substantive rules are likely to vary greatly in nature, including, for example, increased or reduced legal capacity of a married person, interspousal contracts and → torts, consequences for breach of conjugal rights, the right to conduct the household, presumptions of ownership or the right to pledge the other spouse's credit. One might consider these different rules as being part of the general (personal) effects of marriage.

The question of which rules should be treated as falling under this heading and which should be classified as a special topic, will be answered differently in the various legal systems. It might be especially difficult to draw the borderline between these general effects and the matrimonial property regime when pecuniary matters are at stake. But with the development of more and more conflict rules for specific family law issues in recent decades, the general effects of marriage have now been reduced to residual norms of marriage law. Thus, the respective conflict rule is of a subsidiary nature. In addition, many of the traditional substantive rules – such as reduced legal capacity, prohibition of interspousal contracts, claims for restitution of conjugal rights – have been abolished or have lost their significance due to the principle of equality of spouses. Finally, many of the remaining rules will rarely lead to litigation, but mostly concern internal family matters. They are to apply predominantly to existing and well-functioning marriages. The practical impact of private international law is therefore very limited in this area.

2. Connecting factors

International conventions seldom take account of these subject matters. The Hague Convention on the Effects of Marriage of 1905 (art 1) and the Código Bustamante of 1928 refer briefly to these issues but have not had any practical significance, especially as their scope of application has remained uncertain (Christian von Bar (1993) 57 RabelsZ 63, 77, 110).

Both referred to the national laws of the spouses. As it has become more common for spouses to not share the same → nationality (especially since, in most legal systems, the wife no longer automatically acquires the nationality of the husband on marriage) and as the dominance of the husband's nationality is regarded as discriminatory, nationality as a → connecting factor is of relevance today only if both spouses possess that same nationality (Nadine Watté, *Les droits et devoirs respectifs des époux en droit international privé* (Larcier 1987) 123).

Despite the general trend towards habitual residence or domicile as a connecting factor in private international law (→ Domicile, habitual residence and establishment), many continental European jurisdictions (→ Germany, → Italy,

→ Austria, → France, → Greece, → Bulgaria, → Portugal) still refer to nationality. Only if spouses do not have the same nationality is the common habitual residence decisive. Other legal systems apply the law of the (first) marital (habitual) residence (→ Brazil, → Belgium, → Finland, → Switzerland). In some – but only a few – states, the spouses may designate the applicable law (→ Germany, → Spain). As a default rule, the law with the most significant relationship may have to be determined (→ Switzerland, → Germany) or the → *lex fori* might apply. Very often, a series of connecting factors with cascading effect are provided. In the Anglo-American world, the *lex fori* seems to be preferred, although many of these questions might be dealt with as contractual, tortious or property issues (Christian von Bar, 'Personal Effects of Marriage' in Konrad Zweigert and Ulrich Drobnich (chief eds), *International Encyclopedia of Comparative Law*, vol 3 (Mohr 1986) ch 17 paras 19, 24).

3. Harmonization with other family law matters

As the demarcation between the general and special effects of marriage can prove very difficult, choosing a single law to govern all or almost all family relations would avoid clashes between different applicable laws and the need for adaptation and characterization. Some legal systems therefore have identical conflict rules for several of the effects of marriage. In particular, the law applicable to the matrimonial property regime is very often called upon to also govern the general (personal) effects of marriage. Sometimes, this implies that the principle of immutability applies to all issues, though this is not always the case. But the application of a single law to all family law matters is very difficult to achieve, because in most legal systems special conflict rules focus on specific aspects of family law. The nationality of the husband as the overriding principle has lost its significance. Thus, it seems unavoidable that the legal systems applicable to all the effects of one single marriage might form a colourful mosaic indeed.

VI. Modern trends

Although some national legislators continue to express concerns about the concept of marriage for their own nationals and inhabitants, there seems to be a clear trend to respect the validity of marriages already concluded elsewhere as long as basic issues of public policy are not impaired. Whether this result will be reached by the general application of the *lex loci celebrationis* combined with the laws of the home state in certain situations only, or whether legislators will provide for a marriage to be recognized simply if it is evidenced by documents, remains to be seen.

DAGMAR COESTER-WALTJEN

Literature

Geoffrey Chevalier Cheshire, Peter M North and James J Fawcett, *Private international law* (13th edn, Butterworth 1999); Dagmar Coester-Waltjen, 'Reform des Art. 13 EGBGB?' [2013] StAZ 10; Albert Dicey, *Conflict of Laws* (8th edn, Stevens 1967); Richard Fentiman, 'Domicile Revisited' (1991) 50 CLJ 445; Trevor C Hartley, 'The Policy Basis of English Conflict of Laws on Marriage' (1972) 35 MLR 571; Tobias Helms, 'Im Ausland begründete – im Inland unbekannte Statusverhältnisse' [2012] StAZ 2; Peter M North, 'Development of Rules of Private international law in the Field of Family Law' (1980) 166 Rec. des Cours 9; Alan Reed, 'Essential Validity of Marriage: The Application of Interest Analysis and Depeçage to Anglo-American Choice of Law Rules' (2000) 20 N.Y.Sch.J.Int'l.& Comp.L. 387; Willis Reese, 'The Hague Convention on the Celebration and Recognition of the Validity of Marriages' (1979) 20 Va.J.Int'l L. 25; Sharon Shakargy, 'Marriage by the State or Married to the State? On Choice of Law in Marriage and Divorce' (2013) 9 J Priv Int L 499; Ian Sumner, 'Registered Partnerships and Private international law: Great Britain and the Netherlands Compared' in Andrea Bonomi and Bertil Cottier (eds), *Aspects de droit international privé des partenariats enregistrés en Europe* (Schulthess 2004) 29; Edward Sykes, 'The Essential Validity of Marriage' (1955) 4 ICLQ 159; Charles Taintor, 'Marriage in the Conflict of Laws' (1956) 9 Vand.L.Rev. 607; Christian von Bar, 'Personal Effects of Marriage' in Konrad Zweigert and Ulrich Drobnig (chief eds), *International Encyclopedia of Comparative Law*, vol 3 (Mohr 1986) ch 17; Nadine Watté, *Les droits et devoirs respectifs des époux en droit international privé* (Larcier 1987).

Matrimonial property

I. Concept and notion

Matrimonial property law regulates the proprietary and related financial consequences of →

marriage. By the act of marriage all spouses in civil law jurisdictions are subject to a matrimonial property regime. Unlike the law of property this regime relates, not to the single asset, but to the spouses' assets as a whole, with possible repercussions on their proprietary rights in single assets (→ Property and proprietary rights). Two basic approaches can be distinguished in the European civil law jurisdictions: either through the act of marriage some form of community of property (full or partial) is created, or marriage itself has no immediate proprietary consequences. In the latter case there then are legal mechanisms which ensure a participation in the property as well. Irrespective of the basic approach taken, the matrimonial property will be divided between the spouses according to the applicable matrimonial property regime should the marriage end in divorce (→ Divorce and personal separation). If the marriage ends by the death of one of the spouses, the matrimonial property regime determines which property was owned by the deceased for the purposes of → succession law.

In addition, most legal systems also have provisions relating to specific aspects of the general law on marriage as, for example, rules governing the protection of the family or the liability for household debts (see Walter Pintens, 'Matrimonial Property Law' in Jürgen Basedow and others (eds), *The Max Planck Encyclopedia of European Private Law*, vol 2 (OUP 2012) 1158). This structure is also reflected in private international law, where the → connecting factor often only applies to the matrimonial property regime as such but where specific exceptions exist for the family home mostly governed by the *lex rei sitae*. Furthermore it is important to note that some financial consequences of marriage and divorce are subject to different private international law rules, particularly maintenance (→ Maintenance obligations).

By contrast, there are no matrimonial property regimes in the European common law jurisdictions, and indeed even the concept of 'matrimonial property' only very recently was considered by the courts (see eg *Miller v Miller; McFarlane v McFarlane* [2006] UKHL 24). Hence marriage here also does not change the proprietary relationships of the spouses; in case of divorce the courts have a very wide discretion to re-allocate property and award other remedies, taking a holistic view of the financial consequences of divorce.

Substantive law guarantees the autonomy of the spouses to a large extent. In almost all European civil law jurisdictions the spouses enjoy a broad liberty and can freely choose their matrimonial property regime by entering into a marital agreement. Consequently, international matrimonial property law reflects the dichotomy between default regime and optional regimes and devotes extensive rules to the *professio iuris*. In the common law jurisdictions the autonomy of the spouses at first glance appears to be more restricted (see below and Jens M Scherpe, 'Marital Agreements' in Jürgen Basedow and others (eds), *The Max Planck Encyclopedia of European Private Law*, vol 2 (OUP 2012) 1124; Jens M Scherpe (ed), *Marital Agreements and Private Autonomy in Comparative Perspective* (Hart 2012)).

II. Purpose and function

Given that 16 million out of 122 million married couples in the European Union do not have the same nationality or live in a state other than their state of origin (Commission, 'Communication from the Commission to the European Parliament, the Council, the European Economic and Social Committee and the Committee of the Regions, bringing legal clarity to property rights for international couples' COM(2011) 125 final, p 2), choice-of-law rules have to guarantee the stability and predictability of the matrimonial property regime and to avoid that a change of nationality, domicile or habitual residence leads by operation of law to a change of matrimonial property regime. It is of the utmost importance for spouses in a mobile society that a regime entered into in a jurisdiction is recognized in other jurisdictions. This concern has inspired many legislatures to introduce the principle of the immutability of the regime both in substantive law and in → choice of law. In cross-border cases immutability may be at risk. But private international law can bridge the gap between different substantive legal systems, although different public policy approaches can still be an impediment. Therefore, harmonization of conflict rules should be high on the agenda.

III. Historical development

The history of international matrimonial property law is characterized by two major developments. The first one concerns the conflict rules and especially the → connecting factor. Traditionally the nationality of the husband was used as the connecting factor. For a long period this was not seen as discriminatory. Many authors opined that a connecting factor as such was neutral, and that it was the applicable law that should take fundamental rights into account and realize the equality of husband and wife. But already in the 1950s it was argued that private international law was bound by constitutional law (→ Constitutional law and private international law) and fundamental rights in the same way as substantive law (Aleksandr N Makarov, 'Die Gleichberechtigung der Frau und das internationale Privatrecht' (1952) 17 RabelsZ 382). In 1971 the Federal Constitutional Court of Germany ruled that for private international law the same principles as for every other branch of the law should apply and that the choice of a connecting factor should be in accordance with fundamental rights (German Federal Constitutional Court (BVerfG), 31 BVerfGE 58). But it took several years before legislators and courts applied those principles and the common nationality or, in case of different nationalities, the habitual residence of the spouses replaced the nationality of the husband as connecting factor. That said, as in other fields of private international law the use of nationality as → connecting factor is losing ground and increasingly is replaced by habitual residence even when the spouses have a common → nationality. As early as in the 16th century, Charles Dumoulin in France advocated greater autonomy with regard to → choice of law and matrimonial property. This was accepted by the courts and has been established legal practice ever since. Only if the parties did not choose the law applicable to their matrimonial property regime, it was the law of the domicile which governed the property relations of the spouses, and not the law of the nationality of the spouses (see Pierre Bourel, Pascal de Vareilles-Sommières and Yvon Loussouarn, *Droit international privé* (10th edn, Dalloz 2013) no 386 ff). Comparable developments took place in Belgium and the Netherlands (see Georges van Hecke and Koenraad Lenaerts, *Internationaal privaatrecht* (2nd edn, Story-Scientia 1989) 271). This is the historical background against which the Hague Matrimonial Property Convention (Hague Convention of 14 March 1978 on the law applicable to matrimonial property regimes, 16 ILM 14) needs to be understood and which now also appears to be the foundation of the approach of the Council Regulation (EU) 2016/1103 of 24 June 2016 implementing enhanced cooperation in the area of jurisdiction, applicable law and the recognition and enforcement of decisions in matters of matrimonial property regimes, OJ L183/1 of 8 July 2016. The Regulation is in force as of 28 July 2016 and will be applicable from 29 January 2019 (on this see Anatol Dutta, 'Das neue internationale Ehegüterrecht der Europäischen Union', [2016] FamRZ 1973 and Christian Kohler and Walter Pintens, 'Entwicklungen im europäischen Personen- und Familienrecht 2015–2016', [2016] FamRZ 1509).

The second development is the introduction of private autonomy by allowing the spouses to choose the applicable law. There is a growing awareness that national choice-of-law rules are still too diverse to guarantee stability and predictability and that there is a need for unification. A first step was the Hague Matrimonial Property Convention. But this initiative was not very successful. Today the Convention only is in force for → France, → Luxembourg and the → Netherlands. The EU Regulation therefore allows for the *professio juris*.

IV. Legal sources

1. National

Notwithstanding certain common tendencies there is still a great variance between the legal systems, even though international matrimonial property law is codified in many but not all European legal systems. However, the rules on connecting factors, → renvoi and *professio iuris* differ in detail, and the common law jurisdictions of Europe generally favour a → lex fori approach in any event.

2. International

A first initiative on an international level was the Hague Convention of 17 July 1905 (Hague Convention of 17 July 1905 concernant l'interdiction et les mesures de protection analogues, Georges Frédéric de Martens, *Nouveau*

Recueil Général de Traités et autres actes relatifs aux rapports de droit international. Troisième série, vol 6 (39th edn, Scientia-Verlag 1942) 490, available at <www.hcch.net>) relating to conflict of laws with regard to the effects of → marriage on the rights and duties of the spouses in their personal relationship and with regard to their estates, dealing *inter alia* with the marital property regime and marital agreements and using the nationality of the husband as connecting factor. The latter was one of the reasons that most contracting parties later denounced the Convention. The second initiative was the Hague Matrimonial Property Convention, which replaced the nationality of the husband by the first habitual residence of the spouses after the marriage as main connecting factor but leaving some room for nationality as connecting factor.

3. European

Until recently there was little European cooperation in this field. The Nordic countries adopted the 1931 Nordic Convention containing certain provisions of private international law on marriage, adoption and guardianship (Convention of 6 February 1931 containing certain Provisions of Private international law regarding Marriage, Adoption and Guardianship, with final Protocol, 126 LNTS 121) which was amended on 26 January 2006 (see Elisabeth Meurling, 'Less Surprise for Spouses Moving within the Nordic Countries? Amendment to the 1931 Nordic Convention on Marriage' (2009) 11 YbPIL 385 and Maarit Jänterä-Jareborg, 'Inter-Nordic Exceptions in EU Regulations on Matters of Family and Inheritance Law' in Alain-Laurent Verbeke and others (eds), *Confronting the Frontiers of Family and Succession Law: Liber amicorum Walter Pintens* (Intersentia 2012) 748), but it only applies if a combination of nationality of one of the Nordic Countries and residency requirements are met (see below). It is also worth mentioning here the Franco-German Treaty (Abkommen zwischen der Bundesrepublik Deutschland und der Französischen Republik über den Güterstand der Wahl-Zugewinngemeinschaft (BGBl. 2012 II, 178) / Accord entre la République fédérale d'Allemagne et la République Française instituant un régime matrimonial optionnel de la participation aux acquêts (available at <www.dnoti.de>)) introducing a common optional regime on the basis of the German community of accrued gains (*Zugewinngemeinschaft*) and the French participation in *acquests* (*participation aux acquêts*) in the civil codes of both countries. But this regime concerns substantive legislation, is neutral in respect of private international law and is available to couples regardless of their nationality, domicile or habitual residence (see Dieter Martiny, 'Der neue deutsch-französische Wahlgüterstand' [2011] ZEuP 577).

The EU Regulation is the outcome of enhanced cooperation and will only be applicable in the following Member States: Austria, Belgium, Bulgaria, Cyprus, Croatia, the Czech Republic, Finland, France, Germany, Greece, Italy, Luxembourg, Malta, the Netherlands, Portugal, Slovenia, Spain and Sweden. The Nordic Convention will take precedence over the Regulation insofar as this Convention provided for more simplified and more expeditious procedures for the recognition and enforcement of decisions. Seeing the lack of unanimity in the Council, the applicability depends on the outcome of an enhanced cooperation.

V. Current (and future) regulation

1. Jurisdiction

In most European legal systems the courts having jurisdiction in divorce cases (→ Divorce and personal separation) are also competent for the liquidation and distribution of the matrimonial property as in → Belgium, → France, → Germany, → Hungary, → Luxembourg, the → Netherlands, → Slovakia, → Switzerland and → Sweden. In some of these countries the court will appoint a notary for this task (eg in Belgium, France and Luxembourg). In the Member States of the European Union with the exception of → Denmark the → Brussels IIa Regulation (Council Regulation (EC) No 2201/2003 of 27 November 2003 concerning jurisdiction and the recognition and enforcement of judgments in matrimonial matters and the matters of parental responsibility, repealing Regulation (EC) No 1347/2000, [2003] OJ L 338/1) applies to divorce proceedings, if the defendant has his habitual residence in a Member State or has the nationality of a Member State or, in the cases of Ireland and the United Kingdom, his habitual residence in one of those states (art 6 Brussels IIa Regulation). Otherwise the national rules concerning jurisdiction apply (art 7 Brussels IIa Regulation). Comparable rules exist in many countries for courts having jurisdiction in succession cases as for example in

Switzerland (art 51 Swiss Private international law Act (Bundesgesetz über das Internationale Privatrecht of 18 December 1987, 1988 BBl. I 5, as amended, henceforth Swiss PILA)). In the Member States of the European Union (with the exception of Denmark, Ireland and the United Kingdom) the Succession Regulation's (Regulation (EU) No 650/2012 of the European Parliament and of the Council of 4 July 2012 on jurisdiction, applicable law, recognition and enforcement of decisions and acceptance and enforcement of authentic instruments in matters of succession and on the creation of a European Certificate of Succession, [2012] OJ L 201/107) main jurisdiction ground is the last habitual residence of the deceased (art 4 Succession Regulation).

In case of other property disputes not connected to divorce proceedings, so for example in the important case of factual separation, a wide variety exists mostly on the basis of general jurisdiction rules or more exceptionally on the basis of specific rules for matrimonial property cases as in Belgium and Spain. Some systems are very liberal and accept jurisdiction if one of the spouses has habitual residence or is domiciled in the country as for example in Denmark and Hungary (art 59 Hungarian Private international law Act (Law-decree No 13 of 1979 on Private international law, henceforth Hungarian PILA)) or England (s 15 Matrimonial Proceedings Act 1984 (c 42)). In Ireland domicile or habitual residence of one year is required, in Cyprus a habitual residence of three months is sufficient. However, it is important to note that in the common law jurisdictions the doctrine of → *forum non conveniens* is used as a correction mechanism and the court can thus refuse jurisdiction. Some jurisdictions accept jurisdiction on the basis of habitual residence or nationality of one of the spouses as in → Austria (§ 114a(4) Jurisdiktionsnorm (BGBl. Nr 111/1895)) and → Bulgaria (art 7 Bulgarian Private international law Code (Law No 42 of 17 May 2005, as amended, henceforth Bulgarian PILA)). Also in France the French nationality of one of the spouses suffices (arts 14 and 15 French Civil Code (Code Civil of 21 March 1804)) but other grounds are determined by extension of the rules on internal jurisdiction. In Lithuania the Lithuanian nationality of one of the spouses is necessary, but for jurisdiction on the basis of domicile a Lithuanian domicile of both spouses is required (art 784 Lithuanian Civil Procedure Code (Civilinio proceso kodeksas of 28 February 2002, Official Journal, 2002, No 36–1340)). In Italy (art 3 Italian Private international law Act (Riforma del Sistema italiano di diritto internazionale private, Act No 218 of 31 May 1995 in Gazz. Uff., Supplemento Ordinario No 128 of 3 June l995, as amended, henceforth Italian PILA)), the Netherlands (art 2 Dutch Code of Civil Procedure (Wetboek van Burgerlijke Rechtsvordering, available at <http://wetten.overheid.nl>, last accessed on 25 November 2014)) and Portugal (art 75 Portuguese Code of Civil Procedure (Código do Processo Civil of 28 December 1961, Decreto Lei No 44129)) the habitual residence of the defendant is the decisive ground. German courts have international jurisdiction when they have territorial jurisdiction (§ 105 German Law on the Procedure in Family Matters (Gesetz über das Verfahren in Familiensachen und in den Angelegenheiten der freiwilligen Gerichtsbarkeit of 17 December 2008, BGBl. I 2586, as amended, henceforth FamFG)). The main criterion is the habitual residence of the defendant (§ 262 FamFG). In Greece the main ground is the habitual residence of the defendant, but other grounds are the spouses' last common habitual residence and the common Greek nationality of the spouses (arts 611 and 612 Greek Code of Civil Procedure (Presidential Decree 503/1985, Government Gazette A 182/1985)). Some systems use the nationality of a spouse as a ground, but impose conditions on the use of the habitual residence. In the → Czech Republic (§§ 37 and 38 Private international law Act (Act No 91/2012 Sb, on private international law, henceforth Czech PILA)) and Slovakia (§ 38 PILA (Act No 97 of December 1993)) the habitual residence is only a sufficient ground for jurisdiction if the decision could be recognized in the states of the nationality of the spouses or if at least one spouse resided in the country for a longer period of time. In Sweden the habitual residence of the defendant is a ground, the habitual residence of the claimant only if Swedish law is applicable (§ 2 Law 1990/:272). In Belgium the domicile or the habitual residence of the defendant and the common nationality of the spouses are grounds (arts 5 and 42 Belgian Code of Private international law (Code de Droit International Privé, Loi du 16 juillet 2004 portant le Code de droit international privé, MB 27 July 2004, 57344, as amended, henceforth Belgian PILA)). The spouses' last common habitual residence is only a ground if they had their habitual residence in Belgium less than 12 months before filing the claim. The claimant's habitual residence is a ground if he or she had residence in Belgium for at least 12 months at the time of the introduction of the claim (art 42 Belgian PILA). In Spain, besides the common Spanish nationality of the spouses in case of a joint petition, the Spanish habitual residence of both spouses is sufficient as well as the Spanish habitual residence of a Spanish claimant (art 22, 3° Spanish Organic Law on the Judiciary (Organic Law 6/1985, of 1 July, on the Judiciary, Official State Gazette No 157, of 2 July 1985)). Similarly, Finnish and Polish law impose certain conditions on the domicile or habitual residence (§ 127 Finnish Marriage Act (Avioliittolaki (1929/234)); art 1103/1 Polish Code of Civil Procedure (Official Journal 1964 No 43, pos. 296)).

The EU Regulation makes a distinction between international jurisdiction in the event of death and in cases of divorce, legal separation or marriage annulment (arts 4 and 5 EU Regulation) (→ Divorce and personal separation). A court seized in matters of succession under the Succession Regulation has also jurisdiction to rule on matters of the matrimonial property regime in connection with that succession case. The same principle applies for a court seized under the Brussels IIa Regulation. But given that the very broad jurisdiction rules in the Brussels IIa Regulation make forum shopping (→ Forum (and law) shopping) quite easy, the jurisdiction is in some cases subject to a spousal agreement. If no court has jurisdiction in connection with death or divorce (→ Divorce and personal separation), jurisdiction lies with the courts of the Member State (i) in whose territory the spouses are habitually resident at the time the court is seized, or failing that, (ii) in whose territory the spouses were last habitually resident, insofar as one of them still resides there at the time the court is seized, or failing that, (iii) in whose territory the respondent is habitually resident at the time the court is seized, or failing that, (iv) of the spouses' common nationality at the time the court is seized (art 5 Brussels IIa Regulation).

In almost all legal systems and in the EU Regulation a plenitude of courts can have jurisdiction with the result that the place of the proceedings and the applicable law are uncertain (Andrea Bonomi, 'Les propositions de règlement de 2011 sur les regimes matrimoniaux et les effets patrimoniaux des partenariats enregistrés' in Andrea Bonomi and Christina Schmid (eds), *Droit international privé de la famille* (Schulthess 2013) 61). Therefore, some legal systems allow the spouses a choice of court. An example can be found in Swiss law (art 5 Swiss PILA). Also under the EU Regulation such a choice is possible but only in favour of the courts of the state whose law is applicable (art 17 EU Regulation).

2. Applicable law

a) Choice of law

(1) *National laws and the Hague Matrimonial Property Convention* Many jurisdictions in principle exclude any → choice of law. Examples are Cyprus, the Czech Republic, Denmark (unless the Nordic Convention is applicable), Greece, Hungary, Latvia, Malta and Slovakia. But an indirect choice of substantive law is possible if the applicable law allows the couple to enter into a marital agreement and to choose a foreign matrimonial regime. Other systems allow a choice of law only under certain conditions (for France see above III.). In Portuguese law a choice of law is only possible if a foreign law is applicable under the objective connecting factor and one of the spouses has his or her habitual residence in Portugal. In this case the spouses may choose a regime from the Portuguese Civil Code (art 53(3) Portuguese Civil Code (Código Civil of 25 November 1966, Decreto Lei No 47–344, henceforth Portuguese CC)). In Spain only spouses of different nationality can make a choice of law. They may choose the law of the state of the nationality or of the habitual residence of either spouse (art 9(2) Spanish Civil Code (Código Civil of 24 July 1889, Geceta de Madrid No 206, 25 July 1889, henceforth Spanish CC)). In Bulgaria, Croatia and Slovenia a choice of law is only possible, if the applicable law allows it (art 79 Bulgarian PILA; art 37 Croatian Private international law Act (Act Concerning the Resolution of Conflicts of Laws with the Provisions of Other States in Certain Matters of 1991 (Zakon o rješavanju sukoba zakona s propisima drugih zemalja u određenim odnosima, henceforth Croatian PILA)); art 39 Slovenian PILA (Zakon o mednarodnem zasebnem pravu in postopku, ZMZPP, Url.l RS, No 56/99)). Under English law a choice of law technically is not excluded, but the judge will apply the *lex fori* in any event; the outcome under the chosen law will apparently merely be taken into account to determine

the intention of the parties to be bound, and, perhaps, under the overarching principle of fairness which governs the court's discretion (*Radmacher v Granatino* [2010] UKSC 42; see also *Z v Z (No 2)* [2011] EWHC 2878 (Fam)).

But in many legal systems there is a strong development towards allowing a choice of law. Some systems such as Austria are very liberal. The spouses can choose a law without any connection with the nationality, the domicile or the habitual residence (→ Domicile, habitual residence and establishment) of the spouses, the only restriction being that this law may not violate public policy (§ 19 Austrian Federal Code on Private international law (Bundesgesetz über das internationale Privatrecht of 15 June 1978, BGBl. No 304/1978, as amended, henceforth Austrian PILA); Scotland also permits an unrestricted choice of law (s 39(6)(b) Family Law (Scotland) Act 2006 (2006 asp 2)). But most systems restrict the choice of law in order to avoid that the spouses designate the law of a state without any connection to the marriage. The Hague Matrimonial Property Convention restricts the choice prior to the marriage to (i) the law of the state of which either spouse is a national at the time of choice, (ii) the law of the state of which either spouse has his or her habitual residence at the time of choice and (iii) the law of the first state where one of the spouses establishes a new habitual residence after marriage (art 3(1), (2) Hague Matrimonial Property Convention). → *Dépeçage* is allowed for present and future immovable property. The spouses may submit all or some of the immovables to the *lex rei sitae* (art 3(3) Hague Matrimonial Property Convention). In most systems the choice is restricted to the law of the state of domicile or habitual residence and nationality of either spouse as in Estonia (§ 58(1) Estonian Private international law Act of 27 March 2002 (effective 1 July 2002, The State Gazette, 'Riigi Teataja' I 2002, 35, 217, henceforth Estonian PILA)), Finland (§ 130 Marriage Act), Germany (with *dépeçage* for immovable property; art 15(2) Introductory Act to the German Civil Code (Einführungsgesetz zum Bürgerlichen Gesetzbuche of 21 September 1994, BGBl. I 2494, as amended, henceforth EGBGB)), Italy (art 30 Italian PILA), Poland (art 52(1) Polish Private international law Act (Official Journal 2011 No 80, pos. 432, henceforth Polish PILA)), Romania (art 2590(2) Romanian Civil Code (Law 287/2009, published in the Official Gazette No 511 of 24 July 2009, and subsequently amended and supplemented by Law 71/2011, published in the Official Gazette No 409 of 10 June 2011, henceforth Romanian CC)) and Sweden (§ 3 Act 1990:272). In Belgium and Romania an additional choice of the law of the state of the first common habitual residence of the spouses is possible. In Finland the law of the state of the last common domicile can additionally be chosen. In Lithuania the law of the state of the present or future domicile of both spouses, the law of the state in which the marriage was entered into and the law of the state of the nationality of either spouse may be chosen (art 1.28(2) Lithuanian CC (Civil Code of the Republic of Lithuania of 18 July 2000, Law No VIII-1864 (Last amended on 12 April 2011, No XI-1312))). In Switzerland the law of the state of the present or future domicile of both spouses or the law of the state of nationality of one of the spouses may be chosen (art 52 Swiss PILA).

Most legal systems not only allow a choice before but also during the marriage as in Austria, Germany, Italy and Switzerland. The same applies according to the Hague Matrimonial Property Convention, limiting this choice to (i) the law of the state of which either spouse is a national at the time of choice and (ii) the law of the state of which either spouse has his or her habitual residence at the time of choice. Portuguese and Spanish law exclude a choice during marriage. In some legal systems the choice made during the marriage has no retroactive effect; but the spouses expressly can decide that the effect should be retroactive, as for example in Belgium (art 50(3) Belgian PILA), Germany or Romania. In other systems as in Swiss law (art 53(2) Swiss PILA) and under the Hague Matrimonial Property Convention (art 7) the choice has retroactive effect but the spouses can decide otherwise. The retroactive effect cannot infringe the rights of third parties.

In most systems the formal requirements for a → choice of law are governed by the *lex causae* or the *lex loci actus* as in Belgium (arts 50(2) and 52(1) Belgian PILA), Italy (art 30 Italian PILA), Poland (art 52(3) Polish PILA) and Romania (art 2590 Romanian CC). In Bulgaria the formal requirements of the chosen law are applicable (art 80 Bulgarian PILA). But certain minimal requirements exist in several other countries. In Finland (§ 130 Finnish Marriage Act) and Italy the choice should be in writing; in Belgium (art 52(1) Belgian PILA), Bulgaria (art 80 Bulgarian PILA) and Romania (art 2590 Romanian CC) the choice should be in writing, dated and signed. In Germany a notarial deed is necessary, but for a choice made abroad the formal requirements of the *lex causae* or the *lex loci actum suffice* (art 17(4) German EGBGB). Also in Estonia a notarial deed is required; for a choice of law made abroad the requirements of the *lex causae* are prescribed (§ 58(2) Estonian PILA).

Renvoi generally is excluded.

(2) *Nordic Convention* Provided that the 1931 Nordic Convention containing certain provisions of private international law on marriage, adoption and guardianship is applicable to the spouses (determined by art 3, see below), according to the new art 3a of the Nordic Convention the spouses can choose the law of a contracting state provided one of them is a national of that state or has habitual residence there at the time the agreement is concluded. Such a choice can also be made before the → marriage. If one or both spouses move to another contracting state and they were both habitually resident there, they can also choose the law of that state.

Such a choice of law according to art 4 of the Nordic Convention is formally valid if the form required: (i) by the law which is applicable to the spouses' financial relations at the time (following art 3 and 3a Nordic Convention), or (ii) by the law of the contracting state of which one or both of the spouses were nationals at the time was met. If the law so designated does not contain specific formalities for choice of law, the form requirements for marital agreements apply (art 4(2) Nordic Convention).

(3) *The EU Regulation* Under the EU Regulation the spouses or future spouses may agree to designate or to change the applicable law but their choice is restricted to: (i) the law of the state where the spouses or future spouses, or one of them, is habitually resident at the time the agreement is concluded, or (ii) the law of a state of → nationality of either spouse or future spouse at the time the agreement is concluded (art 22 EU Regulation). Contrary to the Succession Regulation, this Regulation does not offer a solution in case of multiple nationalities. Taking into account the case-law of the European Court of Justice there should be no preference for the nationality of the forum or for the effective one. Each nationality should be eligible. (Case C-148/02 M *Carlos Garcia Avello v Belgium* [2003] ECR I-11635, para 28; Case C-168/08 *Laszlo Hadadi (Hadady) v Csilla Marta Mesko, married name Hadadi (Hadady)* [2009] ECR I-06871, paras 41 ff).

Unless the spouses agree otherwise, a choice of the applicable law made during the marriage has no retroactive effect. A retroactive change cannot affect the rights of third parties.

As a minimum form requirement, the agreement has to be made expressly, in writing, dated and signed by both spouses (art 23 EU Regulation). This rule differs from the Succession Regulation which allows an implicit choice. But unfortunately the relatively straightforward rules just described are not all that needs to be considered. Rather complicated additional requirements apply (see Walter Pintens, 'Formerfordernisse in dem Vorschlag für eine EU-Verordnung im Bereich des Ehegüterrechts' in Dieter Schwab and Hans-Joachim Dose (eds), *Familienrecht in Praxis und Theorie: Festschrift für Meo-Micaela Hahne zum 65. Geburtstag am 18. März 2012* (Gieseking 2012) 99):

(i) if the law of the Member State in which both spouses have their habitual residence at the time the agreement is concluded lays down additional formal requirements (→ Formal requirements and validity) for matrimonial property agreements, those requirements must be complied with;
(ii) if the spouses are habitually resident in different Member States at the time the agreement is concluded and the laws of those States provide for different formal requirements for matrimonial property agreements, the agreement shall be formally valid if it satisfies the requirements of either of those laws;
(iii) if only one of the spouses is habitually resident in a Member State at the time the agreement is concluded and that State lays down additional formal requirements for matrimonial property agreements, those requirements shall apply (art 23(2)-(4) Regulation).

Those additional requirements will often necessitate a notarial deed. Somewhat worryingly, additional requirements from third states are disregarded under the Regulation, although it is not apparent why spouses with habitual residence in a third state deserve less protection than spouses with habitual residence in a Member State.

WALTER PINTENS AND JENS M SCHERPE

b) Absence of choice of law

(1) The Hague Matrimonial Property Convention The Hague Matrimonial Property Convention applies to all spouses who married on or after 1 September 1992. The Convention applies even if the nationality or the habitual residence of the spouses or the law to be applied is not that of a contracting state (art 2 Hague Matrimonial Property Convention). If the spouses, before marriage, have not designated the applicable law, their matrimonial property regime is governed by the internal law of the state in which both spouses establish their first habitual residence after marriage (art 4(1) Hague Matrimonial Property Convention). Nonetheless, the matrimonial property regime is governed by the internal law of the state of the common nationality of the spouses: (i) where a declaration in accordance with art 5 has been made by that state and its application to the spouses is not excluded by the provisions of the second paragraph of that Article; (ii) where that state is not a party to the Convention and according to the rules of private international law of that state its internal law is applicable, and the spouses establish their first habitual residence after marriage in a state which has made a declaration in accordance with art 5, or in a state which is not a party to the Convention and whose rules of private international law also provide for the application of the law of their nationality; (iii) where the spouses do not establish their first habitual residence after marriage in the same state (art 4(2) Hague Matrimonial Property Convention).

With this solution the Hague Conference has found a compromise between nationality and habitual residence. If the spouses do not have their habitual residence in the same state, nor have a common nationality, their matrimonial property regime is governed by the internal law of the state with which, taking all circumstances into account, it is most closely connected (art 4(3) Hague Matrimonial Property Convention). → Renvoi is excluded. In principle, the applicable law continues to apply as long as the spouses have not designated a different applicable law and notwithstanding any change of their nationality or habitual residence (art 7(1) Hague Matrimonial Property Convention). But if the spouses have neither designated the applicable law nor concluded a marital agreement, the law of the state of a new habitual residence under certain conditions becomes applicable in place of the law previously applicable, eg when the new habitual residence has endured for a period not less than ten years (art 7 Hague Matrimonial Property Convention). This creates a degree of instability of the matrimonial property regime and presumably is one of the reasons why the Hague Matrimonial Property Convention was not very successful.

The effects of the matrimonial property regime on the legal relations between a spouse and a third party are governed by the law applicable to the matrimonial property regime in accordance with the Convention (art 9(1) Hague Matrimonial Property Convention). Nonetheless, the law of a contracting state may provide that the law applicable to the matrimonial property regime may not be relied upon by a spouse against a third party where either that spouse or the third party has his habitual residence in its territory, unless any requirements of publicity or registration specified by that law have been complied with, or the legal relations between that spouse and the third party arose at a time when the third party either knew or should have known of the law applicable to the matrimonial property regime (art 9(2) Hague Matrimonial Property Convention). The law of a contracting state where an immovable is situated may provide an analogous rule for the legal relations between a spouse and a third party as regards that immovable (art 9(3) Hague Matrimonial Property Convention).

The application of the law determined by the Convention may be refused only if it is manifestly incompatible with public policy (art 14 Hague Matrimonial Property Convention).

(2) Nordic Convention According to the revised art 3(1) of the 1931 Nordic Convention containing certain provisions of private international law on marriage, adoption and guardianship, the law governing the financial relations of the spouses is the law of the state in which they were resident at the time of the marriage, provided they both are nationals of a contracting state. If the spouses later move to a different contracting state and have lived there for at least two years, the law of that state becomes applicable instead; however, if the spouses previously have lived in that state together or are nationals of that state, the law of that state becomes applicable immediately (art 3(2) Nordic Convention).

Importantly, if the spouses fall under the provisions of art 3 Nordic Convention in principle but later move to a non-contracting state, the

Convention is not applicable to their financial relations (art 4a Nordic Convention). In any event, if the requirements just outlined are not met, the applicable law is determined by the national law of the respective state instead.

(3) *National laws* A large majority of the legal systems apply a form of cascade connection (German: *Kegelsche Leiter*) to determine the applicable matrimonial property law, based on the idea of identifying a law with a close connection to the spouses. This → connecting factor may be the common nationality or the habitual residence in combination with other subsidiary factors. In Austria (§ 19 and 18(1) Austrian PILA), Bulgaria (art 79 Bulgarian PILA), Croatia (art 36 Croatian PILA), Czech Republic (§ 21(1) Czech PILA), Germany (arts 15 and 14 German EGBGB), Spain (art 9.2 Spanish CC), Greece (art 15 Greek Civil Code (Astikos Kodikas of 23 February 1946, A.N. 2250/1040; FEK A 91/1940, 597, henceforth Greek CC)), Hungary (art 12(1) Hungarian PILA), Italy (arts 30 and 29 Italian PILA), Poland (art 51(1) Polish PILA), Portugal (art 53 Portuguese CC), Slovakia (§ 21 Slovakian PILA) and Slovenia (art 38(1) Slovenian PILA) the common nationality of the spouses is the main connecting factor. The nationality is a rather stable factor since a change of nationality still is more exceptional than a change of habitual residence. But the use of the nationality has the disadvantage that spouses living in another state than the state of their nationality are submitted to a law which has perhaps no significant meaning for them and the way they live their marriage (Andrea Bonomi, 'Les propositions de règlement de 2011 sur les régimes matrimoniaux et les effets patrimoniaux des partenariats enregistrés' in Andrea Bonomi and Christina Schmid (eds), *Droit international privé de la famille* (Schulthess 2013) 61, 67). Therefore, many jurisdictions prefer the habitual residence as main connecting factor; examples for this are Belgium (art 51 Belgian PILA), Estonia (§ 57 Estonian PILA) and Switzerland (art 54 Swiss PILA). Systems using the common nationality of the spouses or domicile or residence as the main connecting factor then use domicile or habitual residence or common nationality as secondary factors (eg Austria, Belgium, Bulgaria, Croatia, Estonia, Germany, Greece, Poland, Slovenia, Spain and Portugal).

For the exceptional cases of spouses without common nationality and/or habitual residence in the same state, the legal systems mainly use the law of the state with which the spouses have the closest link (eg Germany, Greece and Slovenia), but for example Belgium and Spain apply the law of the state where the marriage has been celebrated. Croatia then applies the *lex fori*. Switzerland solves the problem by the application of a rule of substantive law and applies the Swiss regime of separation of property (art 54(3) Swiss PILA).

Renvoi is excluded in Belgium (art 16 Belgian PILA), Greece (art 32 Greek CC) and Switzerland (art 14(2) Swiss PILA), whereas Austria (§ 5 Austrian PILA), Germany (art 4(1) German EGBGB), Italy (art 13 Italian PILA) and Spain accept *renvoi*, in some systems only under certain conditions. All those rules are rather rigid. A correction by an exception clause in case of an unsatisfactory outcome is rather rare, eg when the spouses only have a weak link with the state of the applicable law and a much stronger link with another state. Examples are Belgium (art 19 Belgian PILA) and Switzerland (art 15 Swiss PILA). But in practice those clauses are only applied in exceptional cases.

By contrast, Czech (§ 21 Czech PILA), Hungarian (art 12 Hungarian PILA) and Slovakian law (§ 21 Slovakian PILA) apply the → *lex fori*, as do the common law jurisdictions of Europe. In most legal systems the answer to the *conflit mobile* is the immutability of the applicable law. A change of → nationality, domicile or habitual residence has no effect (→ Domicile, habitual residence and establishment). Most legal systems after such a change still apply the law of the common nationality at the celebration of the marriage or the law of the first domicile or habitual residence after the marriage (eg Austria (§ 19 Austrian PILA), Belgium (art 51 Belgian PILA), Germany (art 15(1) German EGBGB), Greece (art 15 Greek CC), Spain (art 9.2 Spanish CC) and Portugal (art 53 Portuguese CC)). However, in Hungary (§ 39 Hungarian PILA), Italy and Switzerland (art 55(1) Swiss PILA) the mutability of the matrimonial property regime is accepted, even with retroactive effect. But the rights of third persons are protected. The Hague Matrimonial Property Convention has reached a compromise solution. The mutability is accepted but without any retroactive effect (art 8 Hague Matrimonial Property Convention).

(4) *EU Regulation* If under the EU Regulation no → choice of law is made, three

connecting factors with subsidiary character apply (art 26 EU Regulation). The primary applicable law is the law of the state of the spouses' first common habitual residence after their → marriage. The habitual residence thus takes precedence over the spouses' common nationality. But this is in accordance with the Hague Matrimonial Property Convention, the Regulations on divorce and succession and recent national codifications in Belgium and Switzerland. Still, this rule would be a major change for many legal systems, including Germany and Italy, which are still primarily relying on the spouses' common nationality. There also is some criticism that the first habitual residence determines the applicable law under the EU Regulation and not the last one. However, using the last habitual residence would imply that the applicable law changes each and every time the spouses move to another country, hence the EU Regulation is making the right choice if the aim (as per the Stockholm Programme (The Stockholm Programme – An open and secure Europe serving and protecting citizens, [2010] OJ C 115/ 1–38)) is to have certainty and stability as to the matrimonial property regime and avoid a potential loss of rights.

That said, as other Regulations this Regulation does not define the concept of habitual residence. An autonomous interpretation therefore is necessary (Case C-443/03 *Götz Leffler v Berlin Chemie AG* [2005] ECR I-9637, para 45). All factual circumstances have to be taken into account, and the social integration of the persons concerned is an important element (Case C-497/10 *Barbara Mercredi v Richard Chaffe* [2010] ECR I-14309, para 47).

Hence under the EU Regulation the applicable law has a permanent character and is not changed when a new habitual residence is established, even if this residence lasts for many years. The only possibility to change the applicable law is an express choice of law by the couple.

If there is no common habitual residence, the law of the state of the spouses' common nationality at the time of their marriage applies. However, if the spouses have more than one common nationality at the time of the marriage this → connecting factor does not apply. If the spouses have no common nationality (or in case of multiple nationalities), the law of the state with which the spouses jointly have the closest connection at the time of the conclusion of the marriage applies. To determine the 'closest connection' all circumstances and especially the place of celebration of the marriage should be taken into account. But nevertheless, the notion of the closest connection is vague and will presumably cause interpretation problems. Therefore it could be argued that using the *lex fori* as final possibility (as eg in the → Rome III Regulation (Council Regulation (EU) No 1259/2010 of 20 December 2010 implementing enhanced cooperation in the area of the law applicable to divorce and legal separation, [2010] OJ L 343/10)) would be the better choice.

By way of exception, where it is clear from all the circumstances of the case that a state other than the state whose law is applicable under art 26(1)(a) has a longer and manifestly closer connection with the spouses, and that the spouses had relied on the law of that other state, the court may apply the law of that other state. The combination of all the circumstances in the following example could justify the application of the exception clause: the first habitual residence was of an extremely short duration; the spouses do not have any links with the state of their first habitual residence; the spouses have resided for decades in another state where they are socially integrated and where they have all their assets; they have relied on the law of that state. The application of the exception clause has retroactive effect, but the change of the applicable law shall not affect the rights of third parties.

Needless to say, the exception clause can only apply in the absence of choice of law. If the spouses have explicitly chosen the applicable law, a new explicit choice is necessary to change the applicable law.

3. Marital agreements

In many European jurisdictions there are no specific private international law rules on the applicable law concerning marital agreements (eg Austria, Germany, the Netherlands), and then the general law applicable to the financial relations of the spouse will apply. Hence marital agreements will be generally considered binding in the civil law jurisdictions if they are valid and binding according to the law of the jurisdiction in which they were concluded (unless contrary to public policy); however, some jurisdictions (eg Belgium, art 27 Belgian PILA) in addition require that the validity is established according to the law designated by the relevant national private international law rules. That said, several civil law jurisdictions have express provisions on whether a foreign matrimonial property regime may be chosen, and some jurisdictions (eg Germany, § 1409 German Civil Code (Bürgerliches Gesetzbuch of 2 January 2002, BGBl. I 42, as amended); Spain, art 9 Spanish CC)) do not allow the spouses to choose foreign law if according to the relevant conflict rules their national law is applicable; however, if relevant provisions allow the spouses a choice of law for their matrimonial property regime (eg because of the nationality of habitual residence of the spouses) then of course a foreign matrimonial property regime can be chosen as well.

Regarding the formalities it is usually sufficient for a marital agreement to be valid in principle if the formalities required by the *lex loci contractus* were met; in some jurisdictions (eg Sweden) it additionally also suffices that the formalities required by the law of the state in which both spouses are habitually resident were fulfilled.

However, the common law jurisdictions are an exception here since neither foreign nor domestic marital agreements are binding on the parties. They merely are a factor to be taken into account by the court when exercising its discretion, although in that they are increasingly given weight (cf *Radmacher v Granatino* [2010] UKSC 42). Therefore there are no rules as such on applicable law or formalities. Once a court has accepted jurisdiction, the *lex fori* will be applied in the European common law jurisdictions to all aspects concerning matrimonial property, including any marital agreements.

The Nordic Convention in art 3c(2) contains a specific rule regarding the validity of marital agreements, namely that this to be determined according to the law applicable to the financial relations of the spouses at the time the question regarding the validity arises.

The formal requirements for 'marriage contracts' under the EU Regulation in art 25 mirror those described above for art 23.

4. Recognition and enforcement

There currently are no specific international or European instruments on enforcement or recognition of decisions concerning matrimonial property, so the national rules in the respective jurisdiction apply. However, in most legal systems there are no special rules dealing with enforcement or recognition of judgments concerning matrimonial property law, so that the general rules on this apply (→ Recognition and enforcement of judgments (civil law); → Recognition and enforcement of judgments (common law)).

However, Chapter IV of the EU Regulation deals with the recognition, enforceability and enforcement of decisions and authentic instruments, and the proposed provisions essentially correspond to those in the Succession Regulation. Hence decisions from another Member State should in principle be recognized in other Member States without any special procedure being required (art 36 EU Regulation), unless manifestly contrary to public policy, the defendant was not served with the document in sufficient time or in such a way that a defence against the claim was possible, the decision is irreconcilable with a decision given in the matter between the same parties in the Member State addressed, or it is irreconcilable with an earlier decision involving the same cause of action between the same parties (art 23 EU Regulation). In any event, the jurisdiction of the court of the Member State in which the decision was taken is not to be reviewed (art 39 EU Regulation) and under no circumstances is the decision to be reviewed as to its substance (art 40 EU Regulation). The enforcement of decisions is to take place in accordance with the provisions of the Brussels I Regulation (Regulation (EC) No 44/2001 of 22 December 2000 on jurisdiction and the recognition and enforcement of judgments in civil and commercial matters, [2001] OJ L 12/1; → Brussels I (Convention and Regulation)) (art 42 EU Regulation).

Authentic instruments drawn up in a Member State are to be accepted in other Member States and shall have the same evidentiary effects as in the state of origin, provided such acceptance is not contrary to public policy in the Member State concerned. The authenticity of such instrument can only be disputed before the courts of the Member State of origin and decided under the law of that state. The legal acts recorded in the instrument are to be disputed before the courts having jurisdiction under the Regulation and shall be decided under the applicable law pursuant to the Regulation. If such instruments are drawn up and enforceable in one Member State, they can be declared enforceable in another Member State following the procedures set out in the Brussels I Regulation (art 58 EU Regulation). Court settlements are to be recognized and declared enforceable under the same conditions as authentic instruments (art 60 EU Regulation).

VI. Modern trends

There hardly are any 'modern trends' concerning the international matrimonial property law since the move away from nationality towards habitual residence/domicile as a connecting factor started decades ago. A perhaps more modern issue concerns the follow-up question: which habitual residence – the first or last common residence of the spouses?

Utilizing the last common residence as the connecting factor might have the advantage of better reflecting the understanding the spouses have of their financial relations at the time. But the mutability of the law applicable to the property relations of the spouses carries with it great risks that often cannot be understood by laypersons who therefore cannot effectively exercise the autonomy that many instruments give them. For example, if a couple from a jurisdiction where a separation of property is the default matrimonial property regime moves to a jurisdiction where a (full) community of property regime is the default one applying and they have not entered into a marital agreement, their property relations might change dramatically towards sharing more property. The reverse of course applies for a move in the other direction. This can have a very serious impact not only on the spouses (and their estate and tax planning) but also on third parties such as creditors etc and might even lead very shrewd or well-advised debtors to go forum/residence shopping. In any event, the mutability leads to considerable uncertainty, which arguably is one of the reasons the Hague Matrimonial Property Convention was not particularly successful – and why the EU Regulation opted for the first common habitual residence as connecting factor instead.

WALTER PINTENS AND JENS M SCHERPE

Literature

Alexander Bergmann, Murad Ferid and Dieter Henrich (eds), *Internationales Ehe- und Kindschaftsrecht* (6th edn, Verlag für Standesamtwesen 1983); Katharina Boele-Woelki, 'Property Relations of International Couples in Europe' in Herbert Kronke and Karsten Thorn (eds), *Grenzen überwinden – Prinzipien bewahren: Festschrift für Bernd von Hoffmann zum 70. Geburtstag am 28. Dezember 2011* (Gieseking 2011) 63; Andrea Bonomi, 'Les propositions de règlement de 2011 sur les regimes matrimoniaux et les effets patrimoniaux des partenariats enregistrés' in Andrea Bonomi and Christina Schmid (eds), *Droit international privé de la famille* (Schulthess 2013) 53; Andrea Bonomi and Marco Steiner, *Les Régimes Matrimoniaux en Droit Comparé et en Droit International Privé* (Droz 2006); Nina Dethloff, 'Güterrecht in Europa' in Herbert Kronke and Karsten Thorn (eds), *Grenzen überwinden – Prinzipien bewahren: Festschrift für Bernd von Hoffmann zum 70. Geburtstag am 28. Dezember 2011* (Gieseking 2011) 73; Dieter Henrich, 'Auf dem Weg zu einem europäischen internationalen Ehegüterrecht' in Isabell Götz (ed), *Familie – Recht – Ethik: Festschrift für Gerd Brudermüller zum 65. Geburtstag* (Beck 2014) 311; Jacqueline Gray and Pablo Quinzá Redondo, 'Stress-Testing the EU Proposal on Matrimonial Property Regimes' (2013) 11 *Familie & Recht*, DOI:10.5533/FenR/000011; Dieter Martiny, 'Die Kommissionsvorschläge für das international Ehegüterrecht sowie für das Güterrecht eingetragener Partnerschaften' [2011] IPRax 437; Jens M Scherpe (ed), *Marital Agreements and Private Autonomy in Comparative Perspective* (Hart 2012); Rembert Süß and Gerhard Ring, *Eherecht in Europa* (2nd edn, Zerb 2012); Bea Verschraegen (ed), 'Private international law' in Roger Blanpain and Michele Colluci (eds), *International Encyclopaedia of Laws* (Kluwer 2004); Ilaria Viarengo, 'The EU Proposal on Matrimonial Property Regimes' (2011) 13 YbPIL 199; generally: <www.coupleseurope.eu>.

Mediation

I. Background and context

Modern societies are very much linked to the idea of litigation. Nowadays the volume of disputes brought before state courts increases, the proceedings become lengthier and the costs incurred by the parties in such proceedings also greatly increase. The aim of tackling this situation underpins the growing support for ADR – especially mediation – in many countries to the extent that ADR devices are said to no longer be an 'alternative' to litigation but are 'increasingly becoming a mainstream and integrated part of many legal systems' (Nadja Alexander, 'Four Mediation Stories from Across the Globe' (2010) 74 RabelsZ 732 f).

Mediation is a legal institution that has historically been present in many legal systems of the world; however, specific solutions embodied and the extent of its acceptance vary from country to country. Additionally, some cases exist in which certain institutions are named as mediation although they are not – eg the institution of the *médiateur de la République* in some

French African countries – or the institution overlaps with others like transaction or conciliation (Christian Bühring-Uhle, Lars Kirchhoff and Gabriele Scherer, *Arbitration and Mediation in International Business* (Kluwer 2006) 176).

Nowadays mediation occupies a very important position within ADR. It is a flexible and easily tailored way for parties to work out solutions to their disputes allowing the continuance of their relationships at the same time. However, despite all its benefits and with the exception of some countries like the USA where a 'sophisticated, skilled and rule-oriented practice' is said to exist (Shanin Specter and Jason L Pearlman, 'United States: Mediation' in Carlos Esplugues and Silvia Barona (eds), *Global Perspectives on ADR* (Intersentia 2014) 538), the use of mediation is still very scarce in some areas of the world – eg the EU or Latin-America – whereas in other areas it seems to be very much linked to the court – eg Asia where a sort of judicial conciliation procedure exists in many countries.

II. The European Union: Directive 2008/52/EC

Europe is not strange to this move. The enactment of Directive 2008/52/EC of the European Parliament and of the Council of 21 May 2008 on certain aspects of mediation in civil and commercial matters ([2008] OJ L 136/3) reflects the quest to reach a common minimum legal framework in Europe as a necessary tool for enhancing the use of the institution by EU citizens (Carlos Esplugues, 'Civil and Commercial Mediation in the EU after the Transposition of Directive 2008/52/EC' in Carlos Esplugues (ed), *Civil and Commercial Mediation in Europe. Vol. II, Cross-Border Mediation* (Intersentia 2014) 485, 493 ff).

1. Goals of the Directive

The 2008/52/EC Directive aims to introduce a highly predictable and harmonized set of rules on mediation as a way to foster its use in Europe. Nevertheless, as the 2008 Directive's title makes clear, this framework legislation only covers matters considered to be essential by the EU legislator. Specifically, voluntariness of the mediation (art 3), enforceability of the agreement reached by the parties (art 6), confidentiality of the mediation and mediation process (art 7) and effect of mediation in limitation and → prescription periods (art 5). Besides, certain rules as to the training of mediators and publicity regarding this institution are also included in the 2008 Directive (arts 4, 9)

2. Transposition of the Directive

The 2008/52/EC Directive had to be transposed in all Member States but → Denmark, which remains outside its scope of application, no later than 21 May 2011, although this was finally accomplished at the end of 2012. Social and legal realities on which the 2008 Directive rests are very different throughout the EU Member States. In some Member States there is a longstanding culture of pact and negotiation (eg in → Ireland and → Sweden), whereas in others this culture is lacking (eg → Italy or → Spain). In several countries a clearly mediation-friendly atmosphere exists (eg → Austria, England and Wales or the → Netherlands), whereas in others a sort of prevention against mediation still remains (eg → Hungary). Finally, and among some other facts, in many Member States differences between mediation, conciliation and other ADR schemes are still not clearly stated (eg in the Baltic countries), or direct confusion between them existed and seems to remain (eg in the → Czech Republic, → France or → Italy).

The combination of all these different approaches to, and understandings of, mediation and conflict resolution has not facilitated an easy implementation of the 2008/52/EC Directive nor a fully clear and common framework for mediation in Europe. In fact some attempts to reconsider the Directive exist nowadays.

3. Scope

The Directive applies to mediation 'in cross-border disputes, to civil and commercial matters' regarding rights and obligations on which the parties are free to decide themselves (art 1(2) and Recital (10)). The Directive embodies a functional uniform notion of mediation in art 3(a)(I).

A broad number of Member States have accepted the 2008 Directive's invitation to regulate both internal and cross-border disputes (Recital (8)). In contrast, in other Member States no specific solutions as regards mediation in cross-border disputes are said to exist (Czech Republic or → Finland). On the contrary, some countries like Scotland or England and Wales solely enacted legislation on cross-border mediation, leaving untouched and fully applicable current legal solutions on internal mediation. Also in the Netherlands, the Mediation Act (Wet implementatie richtlijn nr. 2008/52/EG betreffende bepaalde aspecten van bemiddeling/mediation in burgerlijke en handelszaken, Official Journal No 570 of 20.12.2012, available at <http://njb.nl/Uploads/2013/10/stb12_570.pdf>) applies only to cross-border mediation.

Additionally, the scope awarded to cross-border mediation also varies from country to country in the EU. In coherence with the Directive, mediations lacking an EU dimension would be left outside the legislation implementing it and have to be governed by national legislation. Many Member States' Acts on mediation are silent on this relevant issue whereas some national legislations – eg Cyprus, → Estonia, → Hungary, → Lithuania, → Poland, → Slovenia or → Spain – explicitly cover both EU and non-EU cross-border mediations.

Another important issue regarding the scope of the regulations enacted in the Member States refers to the kind of disputes covered by the legislation implemented. The general reference to 'civil and commercial' disputes on disposable rights and matters is accompanied in many EU Member States by some debate and exceptions to the general rule: for instance, discussion regarding the potential submission of family disputes to mediation exists in countries like Cyprus, → Greece or → Italy. Conversely, a potential reference of some public law disputes to mediation is accepted in certain Member States: criminal law (eg → Austria or → Romania) or tax law (eg → Croatia).

4. The notion of mediation: mediation and party autonomy

In line with the notion of mediation provided by the Directive of 2008 almost all Member States now embody a common notion of mediation explicitly supporting its voluntary nature. The existing link between mediation and party autonomy implies that it is for the parties to decide to take their dispute to mediation, to organize the proceeding the way they wish and to be involved in the proceeding or to withdraw from it whenever they wish or to reach or not a settlement on the dispute at stake. In these tasks the mediator will of course support them, but it is for the parties to decide.

This full link of mediation to party autonomy can be carried to its logical end by accepting that this dependence may encompass the parties' right to undertake the mediation outside the scope of the several national regulations governing the institution. Of course this possibility will raise, among other questions, that of the enforceability of the settlement reached by the parties during the mediation process, which seems unlikely in countries like → Belgium or → Austria.

This apparently unanimous approach in favour of the voluntary nature of mediation encounters certain qualifications in some countries. The 2008 Directive permits compulsory mediation schemes to remain. In certain countries general compulsory pre-trial mediation schemes have existed or still exist: eg Italy grants mandatory condition to mediation. Additionally, some limited mandatory mediation schemes are encountered in the Member States in relation to certain disputes or areas of law, or types of persons involved in disputes: eg traineeships (→ Austria), small civil law disputes (→ Germany), family disputes (→ Malta) or labour (→ Croatia).

Nevertheless some debate exists as to the compatibility of mandatory schemes with the voluntary basis on which mediation stands. Compulsory mediation as condition for court proceedings also raises the question of its compatibility with art 6 ECHR and EU law. The English Court of Appeal in *Halsey v Milton Keynes General NHS Trust and Steel* ([2004] EWCA Civ 576, [2004] WLR 3002, [13]) responded in the negative. Also the Italian Constitutional Court in its Judgment 272/2012, of 24 October 2012 (Gazz.Uff., No 49, of 12 December 2012) rejected, among other questions, the 'Compulsory Mediation' procedure for the resolution of certain disputes designed in art 5(1) of the Legislative Decree No 28 of 4 March 2010 which had implemented the 2008/52/EC Directive (Gazz.Uff., of 5 March 2010), although on grounds different to its incompatibility with party autonomy.

On the contrary, the judgment rendered by the ECJ on 8 March 2010, on the Joined Cases C-317/08, C-318/08, C-319/08 and C-320/08 *Rosalba Alassini and Others v Telecom Italia SpA and Others* ([2010] ECR I-213) granted a positive response to this issue. Also, a somewhat positive attitude towards the existence of these schemes underlies the European Parliament's

Resolution of 13 September 2011 (2011/2026(INI), [2013] OJ C 51E/17, paras 5, 10).

5. *Referral of the dispute to mediation*

The 2008 Directive is applicable to all types of mediation. That is, to out-of-court mediation as well as to court-annexed mediation.

a) Out-of-court mediation

The dependence of mediation on party autonomy affects every single aspect of the mediation process. Because of this direct link it is essential to ascertain the existence of a free decision of the parties to submit their dispute to mediation prior to the rise of the dispute or posterior to it for mediation to be possible, valid and effective.

From a legal standpoint this generates the question of how to determine whether the will of each party is actually ascertained and granted legal effectiveness. As a matter of principle, the parties' common desire to submit their dispute to mediation should be documented into a 'mediation agreement' or 'mediation clause' – whatever it is called – which may be included in the contract or have the form of an independent agreement. The Member States often do not have rules for mediation clauses. In some cases there is not even a clear understanding as regards its nature (eg → Spain).

Taking into account the voluntary condition of mediation, the final content of the mediation clause will be dependent on the will of the parties, although some minimum information can be encountered in each clause: parties to the mediation, how and when mediation is to be initiated and its duration, scope of mediation, applicable procedural and substantive law, venue, language, method for the selection mediators and any other representative or methods for specifying cost or fees and other charges.

Nevertheless, this general rule may have some exceptions as regards specific areas of law in which some special interests are safeguarded by the legislator and certain explicit requirements may be requested. The case of consumer disputes and the newly enacted Directive 2013/11/EU of the European Parliament and of the Council of 21 May 2013 on alternative dispute resolution for consumer disputes and amending Regulation (EC) No 2006/2004 and Directive 2009/22/EC ((Directive on consumer ADR), [2013] OJ L 165/63) is paradigmatic to this respect.

The will of the parties expressed through the drafting of a mediation clause is the basis on which any mediation stands. But this mediation clause tends to be accompanied in many EU Member States – at a certain point – by the drafting of an agreement to mediate. The agreement to mediate is usually concluded by the parties and generally also the mediator once the dispute has arisen or just before the effective commencement of the mediation procedure. Through this agreement the parties and the mediator set forth the general framework for the mediation to be developed and the route to be followed by the mediation.

The absence of a proper regulation of the mediation clause in many EU Member States is also reproduced to some extent as regards the agreement to mediate and its requirements, content and meaning.

Across the Member States mediation clauses and agreements to mediate have different kinds of effects. It also needs to be ascertained to what extent they are really requirable and on what grounds.

b) Court-annexed mediation

Court-annexed mediation is mediation developed in the frame of or in connection with a judicial procedure. Overall a mixed attitude towards court-annexed mediation exists in Europe. Only in very few countries is court-annexed mediation not accepted or envisaged at all (eg → Austria or, formerly, → Hungary); mostly it is fully accepted by the law.

Reasons for the judge to refer parties to mediation vary from country to country. Additionally, legislation of the Member States envisage different positions as regards the resource to mediation by the parties after the invitation was made by the judge. Although in most countries it is up to the parties to accept the invitation of the court, some cases of mandatory referral to mediation without consent of the parties or at least of both parties are envisaged (eg → Bulgaria or → Germany). In addition, some situations in which a *de facto* compulsory situation exists in so far as fees to be paid by the party who refused to refer his dispute to mediation are increased or no reduction of the costs to be paid is granted (eg Baltic countries, → Czech Republic or → Slovenia among many others).

6. Mediation and access to justice: the regulation of prescription and limitation periods

Mediation is an opportunity for the parties to settle their dispute, but an opportunity that in no case can undermine their right to refer any dispute arising among them to national courts or arbitration. Parties must be assured full rights to refer their dispute to national courts or arbitration in case of the failure of mediation.

The 2008 Directive does not harmonize the different national rules on prescription and limitation periods (art 8(1)) but it explicitly compels Member States to ensure access to state courts or arbitration in case of failure of the mediation process.

7. Participants in the mediation

a) The mediator

In accordance with the principle of party autonomy on which mediation stands, the parties are usually free indirectly or directly to choose their mediator for the dispute, the number of mediators and, if they so wish, to fix a general framework or some limits for the mediator's activities.

Despite the broad recognition of party autonomy, some countries require the mediator to be accredited. This condition is relevant in some countries at least on two issues: the organization of the mediation procedure and the enforceability of the settlement potentially reached (eg → Austria and → Belgium). In addition to this, some countries set forth some mandatory limits as regards the selection of mediators and their pertinence to a mediation centre (→ Italy) or the ability of some legal professions to act as mediators. In Greece, for instance, the mediator must be a lawyer accredited as mediator and in other Member States court-annexed mediations may be provided by judges too (eg Baltic countries, → Greece, → Finland or → Croatia). Conversely, some legal professions are excluded from serving as mediators: notaries (eg → Lithuania) or judges and persons belonging to the administration of justice (eg → Bulgaria).

Mediators have certain obligations regarding the mediation in general, and to the parties to it in particular. These obligations are independent from each other but remain fully interrelated. As a matter of principle, the mediator must, among other things, conduct the mediation in a neutral, impartial and competent manner, create favourable conditions for the parties to settle their dispute, assist the parties to communicate, facilitate the parties' negotiations and encourage settlement. However, the final outcome of the mediation solely depends on the parties' decision. He or she also has a duty of disclosure towards the parties involved in the mediation before and throughout the procedure. Additionally he or she must honour confidentiality.

The dependence of the success of mediation on mediators makes him or her liable for his or her work. Nevertheless it is not always easy to assess the liability of a person whose only activity is to maintain a facilitative conduct towards the parties.

Mediation is a private justice device that entails some costs for those using it. This fact, and the desire of the Member States to foster resource to mediation, raises the issue of the availability of → legal aid for the parties involved in the mediation – mainly as regards court-annexed mediation (eg → Belgium, the → Netherlands, → France, → Germany or → Austria) – and, also, of the existence of any scheme to encourage the dispute to be taken to mediation and of sanctions for not doing so. Thus, some rules encouraging resource to mediation by way of lowering judicial costs exist basically, again, regarding court-annexed mediation (eg → Hungary, → Germany, → Slovakia, → Poland, → Romania, → Spain or → Italy). Furthermore, adverse costs are foreseen in other EU Member States like England and Wales (note, *Halsey v Milton Keynes General NHS* [2004] EWCA Civ 576; [2006] EWHC 2924 (TCC)).

b) The parties

As stated, mediation is directly linked to the will of the parties. It is up to them to start the mediation, to withdraw from it or to reach an agreement.

8. The mediation proceeding

Most of the EU Member States consider that it is for the parties to draft the mediation proceeding either directly or indirectly. This means that many EU Member States' legislation embody only some basic, rudimentary rules on the mediation proceeding, mostly directed at establishing the very basic principles of mediation and to ensure a certain level of information for the potential parties to the mediation.

The duration of the mediation is a very relevant topic for the parties (who want to have their dispute settled as soon as possible), for the mediator (who must ascertain whether it is worthwhile to continue with the mediation), and for courts and arbitrators insofar as limitation and → prescription periods are suspended while mediation is pending.

9. Termination of the mediation

Any mediation, both out-of-court and court-annexed mediation, may finish in two ways: either successfully – that is, where a settlement is reached by the parties – or unsuccessfully – in those cases where the mediation did not start, or no agreement was reached by the parties in the course of the procedure. Whatever the outcome may be, a general exigency of recording of the development of the mediation exists in many countries within and outside the EU. This exigency creates some tension for the mediator as regards the principle of confidentiality. What he or she may record and what could entail a breach of the principle is something to be specified on a case-by-case basis.

a) Unsuccessful termination

Unsuccessful termination of the mediation takes place when mediation proceedings end up without a settlement between the parties having been reached.

The unsuccessful termination of mediation is treated in different ways in the Member States. Many Members States consider that the termination of the mediation depends on the will of the parties who at any stage of the procedure may manifest their will to withdraw from it or simply because an agreement is not reached (eg → Austria, → Belgium, → Croatia, → Germany or → Poland). In some countries, on the contrary, and despite recognition of the link between the will of the parties and the mediation, a more detailed rule is embodied (eg → Bulgaria, → Latvia or → Lithuania). Finally, other Member States make the termination of the mediation fully or partially dependent on the perception of the mediator as regards the suitability of the settlement (eg → Greece or → Spain).

b) Successful termination

Mediation is considered to be successfully concluded in those cases in which the parties reach a settlement on the dispute referred to mediation. This settlement may be full or partial. The settlement reached by the parties ends the dispute and has a direct effect on the duties and obligations of the parties, although as a matter of principle it is generally considered in Europe to have a contractual nature and to be binding solely upon the parties.

The settlement reached by the parties raises some questions regarding the formal requirements for the agreement reached to be valid (→ Formal requirements and validity). Several degrees of formal exigencies exist in Europe to this respect. Some countries which have a very flexible approach to this issue (eg → Austria, → Germany, → Poland, → Slovenia, the → United Kingdom or the → Netherlands) coexist with other Member States which require certain formal conditions for the settlement to be considered valid and effective (eg → Belgium, → Czech Republic, → Lithuania, → Estonia, → Luxembourg or → Slovakia). Additionally, some countries only specify the minimum content of the agreement reached (eg → Bulgaria or → Hungary).

In addition to the formal requirements of the settlement, the law applicable to the substance of the dispute is also relevant. Depending on the specific matter to be dealt with, the solution provided may or may not be based on legal arguments.

Enforceability of the settlement reached constitutes one of the most relevant issues in relation to mediation. This enforceability must be ensured both as regards purely internal agreements and as to agreements reached in cross-border disputes (Recital (20) Directive 2008/52/EC). But, at the same time, it needs to be combined with the protection of confidentiality.

The analysis of the several legal solutions existing in Europe shows the presence of two ideas on which the solution provided to this issue rest. First, the agreement reached – with some minor exceptions in → Hungary, → Croatia or → Portugal – is almost broadly considered to be a contract binding on the parties. Its absence of voluntary fulfilment must be requested before national courts or, where applicable, arbitration. Second, as a general rule, for the settlement to be fully enforceable a certain level of homologation by a public authority is required throughout the EU: either judges (eg → Bulgaria, → France, → Finland, → Greece, → Hungary, → Luxembourg, → Poland or → Sweden) or any other public authority, mainly notaries (eg → Austria, → Czech Republic, → Estonia, Scotland, → Slovakia, → Slovenia or → Spain). Who will homologate the agreement reached, how will this be done and on what grounds the homologation will be granted varies from country to country.

In any case settlements reached by non-accredited mediators lack enforceability in → Belgium or → Italy.

III. Cross-border mediation in civil and commercial matters

In a purely ideal scenario, no reference to any law or private international law rule should be made insofar as the settlement reached by the parties would be honoured on a voluntary basis. But this seems unrealistic. In the current situation of growing cross-border litigation and of a foreseeable increase in the use of mediation to solve this kind of dispute problems will surely arise in the future and they will be specially complicated in cross-border situations.

In general terms, the Directive has been successful in raising a general awareness of the necessity of ensuring the free circulation of settlements arising out of mediation in the EU. Nevertheless, this growing concern has not been accompanied by the designation of a comprehensible and clear common legal framework for cross-border mediation in the Member States. This negative situation may also have some collateral negative consequences; it gives rise to a somewhat risky extrapolation by analogy of the rules on international commercial arbitration and the philosophy underlying them to cross-border mediation in order to fill existing legal gaps (eg → Czech Republic, → Italy, → Poland or → Slovakia).

1. The law applicable to the mediation clause

With the exception of → Greece, EU national legal systems on mediation are habitually silent as regards the law applicable to the mediation clause or the agreement to mediate in cross-border mediation. This lack of explicit response is exacerbated by the absence of a unanimous understanding of the nature of the mediation clause and of the agreement of the plural number of relationships that arise out of the mediation clause and of the agreement to mediate.

As a matter of principle the mediation clause and the agreement to mediate are broadly considered in several EU Member States to have a contractual nature; consequently it is accepted that rules on determination of the law applicable to contracts should be applicable to them. That means that the Rome I Regulation (Regulation (EC) No 593/2008 of the European Parliament and of the Council of 17 June 2008 on the law applicable to contractual obligations (Rome I), [2008] OJ L 177/6; → Rome Convention and Rome I Regulation (contractual obligations)) would govern the law applicable to the consent to mediate, the substantive and formal validity of the agreement or agreements reached, the contractual liability arising out of the lack of fulfilment of the obligations entered into, and any other aspects of the agreement falling under its material scope of application. Conversely, all those issues not covered or dealt with by the Regulation will be governed by the existing national private international law rules, whatever their origin – international or domestic – may be: eg capacity (→ Capacity and emancipation) to enter into a mediation clause or agreement to mediate.

2. The role played by the mediator

No special regulation as regards foreign mediators is enacted in most EU Member States. Nevertheless, as a matter of principle no discrimination by reason of nationality is envisaged in the Member States, even in some countries in relation to non-EU citizens. The application of the national general legal framework regarding foreign mediators also relates to countries which distinguish between registered and non-registered mediators.

Some questions as regards the determination of the law governing the status of the mediator in relation to his or her duties on confidentiality and independence in accordance with the mediation clause or the agreement to mediate are also said to exist in certain EU Member States. In any case, liability of the mediator in cases of cross-border mediation should be governed by Regulations Rome I or Rome II (Regulation (EC) No 864/2007 of the European Parliament and of the Council of 11 July 2007 on the law applicable to non-contractual obligations (Rome II), [2007] OJ L 199/40), depending on the specific relationship at stake and on whether contractual or non-contractual liability is claimed.

3. The law applicable to the procedure

National rules on mediation tend to make the development of the proceeding dependent on the will of the parties in cases of private mediation. That means that it would be for them to fix the rules of the proceeding, venue, language or seat in accordance with the law of the place where the mediation takes place.

The only limits stressed are those related to the preservation of some basic principles like the maintenance of confidentiality, impartiality, equal treatment of the parties and so on, in accordance with the law of the seat of the mediation. Because of the monistic position maintained in many EU Member States, these principles are applicable both to internal and cross-border mediations in that country. This is even clearer for court-annexed mediation.

4. The law applicable to the content of the settlement reached

Settlements reached by the parties will deeply vary depending on the specific dispute at stake. In certain cases the agreement will be limited to the detailed factual outcome without any reference to, even any room for, the law. In other cases, it may be necessary to determine the applicable law and here choice-of-law rules may have a role to play in cross-border disputes.

Nothing is said as regards the law applicable to the agreement reached in most EU national legislations, in relation to either its existence or content. The law applicable to the content of the settlement is directly dependent on the nature of the dispute at stake and the content of the agreement reached by the parties. The law applicable to it will be determined in accordance with the existing rules of private international law in relation to the merits of the dispute at stake, not those applicable to the mediation. This is broadly understood as meaning that in those cases falling fully or partially within the scope of the Rome I Regulation, it will be applicable to those issues to be settled that are covered by it. Some isolated national case-law upholds this possibility (in → France, C.Cass.Soc., 29 January 2013, No 11-28041, <http://legimobile.fr/fr/jp/j/c/civ/soc/2013/1/29/11-28041/>, last accessed on 10 February 2014). In the case of disputes over family matters or successions, relevant EU instruments on private international law should also be taken into account. Otherwise national private international law rules will apply as regards the determination of the law governing the merits of the settlement, if any such a law exists or is necessary, taking into account the specific settlement reached by the parties.

5. Enforcement of foreign settlements

The settlement reached by the parties is considered a contract that is expected to be voluntarily honoured by them. In the event of a lack of fulfilment by the parties, the settlement will have to be ensured through court actions. No direct enforceability is sought as a general rule.

Within the EU legal instruments on recognition and enforcement a single reference to the direct enforcement of settlements reached in the framework of a mediation proceeding may be found at arts 55(e) and 46 of → Brussels IIa Regulation (Council Regulation (EC) No 2201/2003 of 27 November 2003 concerning jurisdiction and the recognition and enforcement of judgments in matrimonial matters and the matters of parental responsibility, repealing Regulation (EC) No 1347/2000, [2003] OJ L 338/1) in relation to the cooperation between central authorities in matters of parental responsibility.

The direct enforceability of the settlement reached by the parties within a mediation proceeding is usually made dependent on its homologation by a public authority, generally notaries or judges. This fact is very relevant in cross-border disputes in relation to agreements entered into in an EU Member State for which enforcement is sought abroad. As a matter of fact, only settlements that are considered enforceable in the country of origin will be recognized and enforced abroad. Logically, the legal regime applicable to this recognition will vary if the enforcement is sought in another EU Member State or outside the EU. And of course, a different situation will exist when recognition of settlements reached outside the EU is sought in a specific EU Member State.

(i) The enforcement of settlements reached within the EU in another Member State is broadly made dependent on the participation of national courts. As a general rule no direct enforceability is envisaged: an isolated exception to this position is found in → Portugal (art 9(4) of Act 29/2013, D.R. Serie 1, No 77 of 19 April 2013). Leaving aside this unique case, regarding the recognition and enforcement in one Member State of a settlement reached in another Member State there are two options depending on whether or not an EU legal instrument exists that covers the subject matter of the dispute and taking into account the specific legal instrument in which this settlement has been embodied.

In the case of settlement reached in a certain Member State within the EU, the settlement reached by the parties on a topic covered by the existing EU legal instruments on recognition and enforcement of judgments which is embodied in a judgment, an authentic instrument – eg a notarial deed – or a court settlement which are enforceable in accordance to the law of the country where these instruments have been rendered will be subject to the system of recognition and enforcement system designed by the EU.

If the settlement fully or partially falls outside the scope of any of the existing EU Regulations, international conventions and national rules on recognition and enforcement of foreign judgments and decrees existing in every EU Member State would be applicable. In most cases not only judgments but also other authentic documents are covered by these provisions.

(ii) Regarding settlements reached outside the EU to be enforced in an EU Member State, because most of the Member States have enacted legislation on cross-border mediation as a consequence of the implementation of the 2008/52/EC Directive, the scope of application of this legislation tends to be limited to purely EU cross-border situations and therefore no special rules as regards the recognition of non-EU settlements exist. Logically the general rules on recognition and enforcement applicable in the country where enforcement is sought will apply. Moreover, even in cases of enactment of specific legislation on the recognition and enforcement of settlements reached outside the EU (eg → Spain), this fact logically does not alter the scope of application of the existing EU instruments and a reference to national solutions is made.

(iii) In the event of lack of fulfilment of a settlement reached in cross-border mediation (carried out within or outside the EU) lacking enforceability in their country of origin, any of the parties may at any time lodge a claim for breach of contract before the competent court of any EU Member State and ask for its compulsory enforcement. The jurisdiction of that court will be determined in accordance with the existing EU Regulations, basically of Brussels I Regulation (Regulation (EC) No 44/2001 of 22 December 2000 on jurisdiction and the recognition and enforcement of judgments in civil and commercial matters, [2001] OJ L 12/1; → Brussels I (Convention and Regulation)) or, as the case may be, following national rules.

Other cases may exist in which the parties want to enforce in one Member State an agreement entered into in another Member State, or indeed outside the EU, that has not been homologated by any public authority and that consequently lacks enforceability. Some EU Member States approach this matter explicitly (eg → Spain), but most extrapolate the approach in purely domestic disputes to such cross-border situations. Responses provided tend to be similar. The settlement should gain enforceability in the country where enforcement is sought and this should generally be done either by way of having the settlement notarized or by having it embodied in a judicial resolution in accordance with the law of the place where this is done.

CARLOS ESPLUGUES

Literature

Nadja Alexander, *International and Comparative Mediation: Legal Perspectives* (Wolters Kluwer 2009); Nadja Alexander, 'Four Mediation Stories from Across the Globe' (2010) 74 RabelsZ 732; Neil Andrews, *The Three Paths of Justice: Courts Proceedings, Arbitration and Mediation in England* (Springer Science 2012); Silvia Barona and Carlos Esplugues, 'ADR Mechanisms and their Incorporation into Global Justice in the Twenty-first Century: Some Concepts and Trends' in Carlos Esplugues and Silvia Barona (eds), *Global Perspectives on ADR* (Intersentia 2013) 1; Jacob Bercovith and Scott Sigmund Gartner, *International Conflict Mediation: New Approaches and Findings* (Routledge 2009); Beatrice Brenneur, *Overview of Judicial Mediation in the World: Mediation, the Universal Language of Conflict Resolution* (L'Harmattan 2010); Christian Bühring-Uhle, Lars Kirchhoff and Gabriele Scherer, *Arbitration and Mediation in International Business* (Kluwer 2006); Giuseppe de Palo and Mary B Trevor, *EU Mediation Law and Practice* (OUP 2012); Carlos Esplugues, 'Access to Justice or Access to States Courts' Justice in Europe? The Directive 2008/52/EC on Civil and Commercial Mediation' (2013) *Revista de Processo* 221 (July) 303; Carlos Esplugues (ed), *Civil and Commercial Mediation in Europe Cross-Border Mediation* (Intersentia 2014); Carlos Esplugues, José L Iglesias and Guillermo Palao (eds), *Civil and Commercial Mediation in Europe: National Mediation Rules and Procedures* (Intersentia 2012); Christopher Hodges, Stefan Vogenauer and Magadalena Tulibacka, *The Cost and Funding of Civil Litigation: A Comparative Perspective* (Hart 2010); Klaus J Hopt and Felix Steffek (eds), *Mediation Principles and Regulation in Comparative Perspective* (OUP 2013); Jacqueline M Nolan-Haley, 'Is Europe Headed Down the Primrose Path with Mandatory Mediation?' (2012) 32, N.C. J. Int'L L. & Com. Reg. 981; Vincent Tilman, *Lessons Learnt from the Implementation of the EU Mediation Directive: The Business Perspective, Directorate General for Internal Policies. Policy Department C: Citizens' Rights and Constitutional Affairs* (Legal Affairs 2011).

Money and currency

I. Concept

1. In general

Despite difficulties of definition, the terms 'money' and 'currency' should be distinguished, in that money (*argent, Geld, dinero*) is an abstract concept denoting possession of purchasing power, whereas currency (*monnaie, Währung, moneda*) denotes a concrete means of exchange, issued by a state which uses it as the blood of the economy. Seen in this way, the concept of money is broader than that of currency. It has been stated that 'Money is a term so frequently used and of such importance that one is apt to overlook its inherent difficulties, and to forget that the multitude of its functions necessarily connotes a multitude of meanings in different legal situations' (Charles Proctor, *Mann on the Legal Aspects of Money* (7th edn, OUP 2012) N.1.01). In other words, it is necessary to look at the functions fulfilled by money to define it as a legal concept.

The concept of money may be reduced to three different functions: (i) a unit designed to measure value characterized by a specific name (the abstract aspect of money), as well as (ii) the representation of purchasing power and (iii) a means of payment, both of which represent the concrete aspect money (Stephen A Silard, 'Money and Foreign Exchange', *International Encyclopedia of Comparative Law XXVIII* (1975) ch 20, 20–22).

2. Money in public international law

Money in public international law is described as a part of the sovereign monetary power of the state. The state's sovereign power to define its own currency was first recognized in England (*Emperor of Austria v Day and Kossuth* [1861] 3 DeG F&J 217), when Lord Justice *Turner* stated

[t]he regulation of the coin and currency of every State is a great prerogative right of the sovereign power . . . Money is the medium of commerce between all civilized nations; therefore the prerogative of each sovereign State as to money is but a great public right recognized and protected by the law of nations.

The PCIJ affirmed this view in the Serbian and Brazilian loans cases in 1929 (*Case concerning the Payment of various Serbian Loans issued in France/Case concerning the Payment in Gold of the Brazilian Federal Loans issued in France*, PCIJ series A Nos 20/21). The Swiss Private international law Act (Bundesgesetz über das Internationale Privatrecht of 18 December 1987, 1988 BBl I 5, as amended, henceforth Swiss PILA) has enshrined this principle in art 147(1): 'Currency is defined by the law of the State issuing the currency'. This internal aspect of monetary sovereignty has been perpetuated in the creation of the Euro, in that those EU Member States within the euro zone have remitted their sovereign monetary power to the EU, which accordingly has exclusive competence over monetary policy in those states (art 3 TFEU (The Treaty on the Functioning of the European Union (consolidated version), [2012] OJ C 326/47)). Meanwhile, the German Federal Constitutional Court has confirmed that this transfer of competence was compatible with the German Constitution (Grundgesetz für die Bundesrepublik Deutschland, 23 May 1949, BGBl. p 1) in the *Maastricht Judgment* of 12 October 1993 (Federal Constitutional Court of Germany (BVerfG), 89 BVerfGE 155).

Monetary sovereignty also exhibits an external character, in that external monetary sovereignty entitles the state to impose its own statutory system of exchange control to protect its currency vis-à-vis other states. However, for States Party to the IMF, the Bretton Woods Agreement (Articles of Agreement of 27 December 1945 of the

International Monetary Fund, adopted in Bretton Woods on 22 July 1944, 2 UNTS 39) restricts that protective right through an international exchange control system, although rather than prohibiting national exchange control statutes, the Agreement sets strict legal requirements for them.

3. Private international law

From a private international law perspective, money should be studied both as a unit of value (currency of account) and a means of payment (currency of payment). The use of a foreign currency (ie a currency which is not the one of the forum) entails questions of applicable law, jurisdiction and enforcement of foreign decisions.

II. Historical development

1. The gold era

The existence of metallic coins circulating as means of payment is as ancient as the first codification of law. A reference to metallic coins is found in the Hammurabi Code (around 1760 BC). For centuries, currencies were defined with reference to a certain weight of silver and/or gold. Each country decided for itself the definition of its currency, without regard to the definition of other currencies. Monetary legislation existed only at the national level. At the end of the 19th century, gold became the common reference for national currencies. Countries which previously had adopted a bimetallism definition of their currencies, using gold and silver, waived their reference to silver. Within such a system, the exchange rate between currencies was fixed, the common denomination being gold.

However, the 'gold standard' was abandoned after the First World War, because the system could not meet the monetary needs of reconstruction and payment of war reparation debts. In its place came the 'gold exchange standard', whereby central bank reserves could be made not only in gold but also in currencies exchangeable for gold (mainly the US dollar and the pound sterling) (Benvenuto Griziotti, 'L'évolution monétaire dans le monde depuis la guerre de 1914' (1934) 49 Rec. des Cours 70). These measures were accompanied by national legislation prohibiting payment in gold, in order to protect national gold reserves. At the same time, in the 1920s the first international conventions were concluded between states and the League of Nations in order to save the currencies of European states (Boris Nolde, 'La monnaie en droit international public' (1929) 27 Rec. des Cours 322). This regime of fixed exchange rates, based upon a ratio between currencies and gold and dependant solely on the will of governments, disappeared after the Second World War.

2. The Bretton Woods system

After the period before the Second World War of national currency instability in Europe, an agreement was reached in July 1944 to establish an international monetary system which would promote currency stability through fixed rates of exchange. The Bretton Woods agreements became effective on 27 December 1945. A par value was fixed in terms of gold as the common denominator of the par value system. A par value could be expressed directly in terms of gold of the weight and fineness in effect on 1 July 1944, or indirectly in relation to the US dollar. Consultation with the Fund was necessary before a member made any alteration to its par value. Most countries opted for the second indirect (dollar-based) option, with the result in effect that the common denominator of monetary systems shifted from gold to the US dollar. During the subsequent two-and-a-half decades, national currencies benefitted from a remarkable degree of stability, allowing international trade to flourish.

3. The post-Bretton Woods system

The period of post-war stability ended in 1971, when the then President of the United States, Richard Nixon, decided on 15 August that the USA would no longer undertake to maintain a specific external value for the US dollar. Since then the international monetary system has undergone radical changes. The 1971 decision led to the Second Amendment of the IMF Articles of Agreement on 30 April 1976, which became effective on 1 April 1978 (15 ILM 546). This amendment abandoned the fixed exchange rate system, and allowed national currencies to fluctuate. State members were then free to choose their exchange rate regime, subject to one exception of the prohibition against maintaining the external value of their currencies in terms of gold. Basically, three exchange rate regimes may be distinguished: (i) what economists call 'hard peg', where a state introduces the currency of a more developed country rather than having an own currency (phenomenon of 'dollarization'), (ii) 'soft peg' (or intermediate) where a state pegs its own currency to the currency of a more developed country (or to a composite of currencies) and (iii) the floating exchange rate, where countries decide not to interfere with market forces and leave the exchange rate to the interaction of supply and demand.

III. Legal sources

1. National

Very few European countries have adopted private international law rules on money or currency. Noteworthy exceptions are the Swiss PILA, art 147 of which addresses currency issues in private international law, and the Romanian Civil Code (Law 287/2009, published in the Official Gazette No 511 of 24 July 2009, and subsequently amended and supplemented by Law 71/2011, published in the Official Gazette No 409 of 10 June 2011), whose provisions on private international law (Book 7) contain art 2.646 on the currency of payment, a provision similar to art 147 Swiss PILA. The Polish Private international law Act (Official Journal 2011 No 80, pos. 432, henceforth Polish PILA) also contains an article on currency (art 38).

As far as substantive rules on currency or monetary obligations are concerned, some legal systems contain specific rules on the payment of monetary obligations and usually offer the possibility to the debtor to perform its obligation by paying with the local currency, ie the currency of the state where the payment shall take place (see for instance § 244 German Civil Code (Bürgerliches Gesetzbuch of 2 January 2002, BGBl. I 42, as amended); art 1277 ff Italian Civil Code (Codice Civile, Gazz.Uff. 4 April 1942, No 79 and 79bis; edizione straordinaria) and art 84 Swiss Code of Obligations (Bundesgesetz betreffend die Ergänzung des Schweizerischen Zivilgesetzbuches (Fünfter Teil: Obligationenrecht) of 14 June 1881, SR 220)). The French Monetary and Financial Code (Code monétaire et financier, 2000 (available at <www.legifrance.gouv.fr>)) seems to be the sole piece of codification on monetary legislation in Europe. The first book is dedicated to the law of currency.

2. International

The Articles of Agreement of the International Monetary Fund are the central legal instrument of the international monetary system and of international monetary law.

3. European

The euro is regulated by various European texts. Among the most important are Regulations 1103/97 (Regulation (EC) No1103/1997 of the European Council of 17 June 1997 on certain provisions relating to the introduction of the euro, [1997] OJ L 162/1) and 974/98 (Regulation (EC) No 974/1998 of the European Council of 3 May 1998 on the introduction of the euro, [1998] OJ L 139/1), which created the euro, while Regulation 260/2012 (Regulation (EU) No 260/2012 of the European Parliament and of the Council of 14 March 2012 establishing technical and business requirements for credit transfers and direct debits in euro and amending Regulation (EC) No 924/2009, [2012] OJ L 94/22) regulates credit transfers and direct debits in euro.

There are no specific texts on the conflict of laws on monetary obligations in the EU. However, art 12 Rome I Regulation (Regulation (EC) No 593/2008 of the European Parliament and of the Council of 17 June 2008 on the law applicable to contractual obligations (Rome I), [2008] OJ L 177/6; → Rome Convention and Rome I Regulation) and art 15 Rome II Regulation (Regulation (EC) No 864/2007 of the European Parliament and of the Council of 11 July 2007 on the law applicable to non-contractual obligations (Rome II), [2007] OJ L 199/40) address the law to be taken into consideration for payment. Incidentally, a European Convention on Foreign Money Liabilities (60 ETS) was adopted on 11 December 1967 in Paris. Four Member States of the European Council signed it but only Luxembourg ratified it, so that the Convention has never entered into force.

IV. Current issues implying the use of foreign currency in private international relationships

1. Determination of the currency of account in a contractual relationship

Most legal systems provide that, in case of an absent or ambiguous currency denomination, the determination of the currency of account is a question of interpretation to be solved by the *lex causae*. Thus, the designation of the currency of account is a two-step process. First, it is necessary to determine the legal system governing the construction of the contract. Second, the domestic rules of the applicable law will be used to ascertain the currency of account (Charles Proctor, *Mann on the Legal Aspects of Money* (7th edn, OUP 2012) N. 5.08; Albert Venn Dicey, John Humphrey Carlile Morris and Lawrence Collins (eds), *Dicey, Morris and Collins on the Conflict of Laws* (14th edn, Sweet & Maxwell 2006) rule 209: 'Where there is doubt as to the currency in which a debt is expressed (money of account), and especially where the expression used for the denomination thereof connotes the currencies of two or more States . . . the money of account must be ascertained by construing the contract in accordance with the law applicable to it'). In case of → damages, a more direct rule might be used to designate the most relevant currency to be used for the assessment of damages, without having regard to a specific applicable law but by using a → connecting factor (the habitual residence of the creditor) (Caroline Kleiner, *La monnaie dans les relations privées internationales* (LGDJ 2010) 218). This connecting factor method is used in the UNIDROIT Principles (International Institute for the Unification of Private Law/Institut international pour l'unification du droit privé (ed), *UNIDROIT Principles of International Commercial Contracts 2010* (3rd edn, UNIDROIT 2010)). Article 7.4.12 states that 'damages are to be assessed either in the currency in which the monetary obligation was expressed or in the currency in which the harm was suffered, whichever is more appropriate'. The same method has also been applied in various court decisions in → France, Scotland and → Germany concerning the choice of currency of account of damages (Oliver Remien, 'Schadensersatzwährung im Deliktrecht' [1995] ZEuP 119).

2. Debt labelled in foreign unit of account

Contracting parties may agree to assess their obligations in a currency of account which is neither the one used in their domicile state, nor that of the state of the place of payment, nor that of the state whose law governs their contract. Instead parties use a foreign unit of account. Whether that choice is permitted depends on the law applicable to the contract, as it is an issue pertaining to the determination of the obligation itself. However, not all European legal systems follow this approach. For example, according to French case-law, monetary clauses included in international contracts, defined as contracts implying a movement of monetary flow from and into the country, are valid, notwithstanding their invalidity according to the *lex contractus* (Cass. civ., 21 June 1950, *Messageries maritimes*, Bertrand Ancel and Yves Lequette, in *Les grands arrêts de la jurisprudence française de droit international privé* (5th edn, Dalloz 2006) N.22).

If such choice of currency is lawful, then the issue arises of the value of the chosen currency. This in turn raises the issue of whether the 'nominalism' principle should be applied. Some scholars argue that the nominalism principle applies as a principle of international law, regardless of the applicable law (Frederick Alexander Mann, 'Money in Public International Law' (1959) 96 Rec. des Cours 1, 106–8 and 115–17; Dominique Carreau, *Souveraineté et coopération monétaire* (Julliard 1974) 62). However, the predominant approach consists in regarding nominalism as an implicit term of a contract. Consequently, when parties omit to safeguard themselves by appropriate protective clauses, they must be considered to have accepted the risks of depreciation of the monetary unit they have chosen for their relations. According to this view, application of the nominalism principle should be governed by the proper law of the contract or the law applicable to the relationship to which the monetary obligation is attached. English scholars have thus formulated the following rule:

> In whatever currency a debt is expressed, it is for the law governing the transaction from which the debt arises, eg in the case of a contractual debt for the law applicable to the contract, to determine whether and to what extent the debtor is liable, in the event of a depreciation of the currency, to make additional payment to the creditor by way of revalorization. (Albert Venn Dicey, John Humphrey Carlile Morris and Lawrence Collins (eds), *Dicey, Morris and Collins on the Conflict of Laws* (14th edn, Sweet & Maxwell 2006) rule 207, No. 36-015)

The same rule is enshrined in art 147(2) Swiss PILA, which states that 'the effect that currency exerts on the amount of a debt shall be governed by the law applicable to the debt', as well as in art 2.646(2) Romanian Civil Code and art 38 Polish PILA. However, this solution ignores the principle that only the issuing state is empowered to define the value of its currency, according to the *lex monetae* principle. In other words, the value of a currency and its effects on the obligation depends on the law of the state which enacted that currency (Helmut Grothe, *Fremdwährungsverbindlichkeiten, das Recht der Geldschulden mit Auslandsberührung Kollisionsrecht – Materielles Recht – Verfahrensrecht* (Walter de Gruyter 1999) 158; Tullio Treves, 'Les effets de la dépréciation monétaire sur les rapports juridiques contractuels en droit international privé italien' in *Les effets de la dépréciation monétaire sur les rapports juridiques contractuels, Travaux de l'association Henri Capitant, tome XXIII Journées d'Istambul* (Economica 1973) 213, 215 and 221).

3. *Payment of a debt with a foreign currency*

The distinction between currency of account and currency of payment includes the assumption that, although a monetary obligation is assessed in a particular currency, payment will not necessarily be made in that specific currency. Parties may have agreed that the payment of their contractual obligation should be paid in another currency than that they have chosen for their obligation. Absent an express choice, it is necessary to determine the currency of payment and whether payment in a foreign currency is valid. Both questions raise private international law issues, since the payment in a foreign currency implies the application of at least one foreign legal system, that of the currency of payment, the *lex monetae*.

Determination of the currency of payment and whether an obligation may be discharged by payment in a foreign currency may depend on different legal systems. First, as these questions concern the performance of an obligation, they should probably be governed by the *lex causae*. However, art 10(2) Rome Convention (Rome Convention on the law applicable to contractual obligations (consolidated version), [1998] OJ C 27/34) as well as art 12(2) Rome I Regulation provide that 'in relation to the manner of performance and the steps to be taken in the event of defective performance, regard shall be had to the law of the country in which performance takes place'. According to this provision, the law of the country where payment is to be made (the *lex loci solutionis*) will be taken into account, the manner of performance being understood by the Convention drafters as encompassing determination of the currency of payment (Mario Giuliano and Paul Lagarde, 'Report on the Convention on the law applicable to contractual obligations by Mario Giuliano, Professor, University of Milan, and Paul Lagarde, Professor, University of Paris I' [1980] OJ C 282/1, 33). The same solution, but framed in clearer words, has been adopted in Switzerland. Article 147(3) Swiss PILA provides that '[t]he law of the State in which payment must be made shall determine in which currency the payment is to be made'. In the same vein, art 2.646(3) Romanian Civil Code provides that 'the law of the State in which payment must be made shall determine in which currency the payment is to be made, unless the parties, in the private international law relationships resulting from the contract, have agreed on another currency of payment'. At first sight, the solution is simple. However, when the parties omit to determine the place of payment, the *lex loci solutionis* will depend on the designation of the place of payment, which depends in turn on the *lex causae* according to the ECJ (Case 12/76 *Industrie Tessili Italiana Como v Dunlop AG* [1976] ECR 1473).

Certain legal systems provide for substantive rules related to the currency of payment in case of a local payment. In Germany, § 244 Civil Code offers the debtor the possibility to discharge its obligation in local currency (in euro) when the debt is payable within the country, unless payment in another currency has been expressly agreed (Helmut Grothe, *Fremdwährungsverbindlichkeiten, das Recht der Geldschulden mit Auslandsberührung Kollisionsrecht – Materielles Recht – Verfahrensrecht* (Walter de Gruyter 1999) 131). Similarly, art 84 Swiss Code of Obligations provides that the debtor may offer a payment in Swiss francs if the payment takes place in Switzerland, but only if parties had not foreseen a compulsory payment in the agreed currency of payment. The UNIDROIT Principles lay down the same rule in art 6.1.9, but add more precise rules applicable where the currency of payment cannot be obtained because of its inconvertibility. The article also stipulates that

> the payment in the currency of the place for payment is to be made according to the applicable

rate of exchange prevailing there when payment is due. However, if the obligor has not paid at the time when payment is due, the obligee may require payment according to the applicable rate of exchange prevailing either when payment is due or at the time of actual payment.

In France, the seminal distinction is that drawn between domestic and international contracts. With domestic contracts, payment made in France should always be made in the French currency, whereas payment in international contracts should be discharged in the agreed currency (art 1343-3 of the French civil code).

In Germany, there is a debate on whether such substantive rules should be applied as part of the *lex causae* or as *lois d'application immediate*. For the *lex causae* it is argued that since choice of the currency of payment is a party right, § 244 German Civil Code should be applied only when German law governs the contract (Helmut Grothe, *Fremdwährungsverbindlichkeiten, das Recht der Geldschulden mit Auslandsberührung Kollisionsrecht – Materielles Recht – Verfahrensrecht* (Walter de Gruyter 1999) 131). But other scholars argue that this stipulation applies whenever payment is due in Germany, whatever the applicable law (Karsten Schmidt, '§ 244 BGB' in Christian Baldus and others (eds), *J. von Staudingers Kommentar zum Bürgerlichen Gesetzbuch* (Sellier-de Gruyter 1997) para 77; Georg Maier-Reimer, 'Fremdwährungsverbindlichkeiten' [1985] NJW 2049). In Switzerland, the rationale for application of art 84 Code of Obligations has led to no such doctrinal split, so that art 84 is considered applicable whenever a payment is to be discharged in Switzerland, irrespective of whether Swiss law is the *lex contractus* (Denis Loertscher, *Commentaire Romand, Code des obligations I* (2nd edn, Helbing & Lichtenhahn 2012) art 84, para 14).

4. Judgment or arbitral award in foreign currency

Municipal courts are confronted with the problem of designation of the unit of account only where they have the right to choose the money of account in their judgment. That is to say, the issue arises only when courts are not compelled to use the monetary unit of the forum (the so-called *moneta fori*). Whether a foreign unit of account may be used is a procedural issue, which should therefore be governed by procedural law, ie the → *lex fori*. The current state of law in most countries is that municipal courts enjoy a degree of liberty to render their judgments in a foreign currency. However, in England, the law changed with the *Milangos case* (*Miliangos v George Frank Ltd* [1976] AC 443; Vaughan Black, *Foreign Currency Claims in the Conflict of Laws* (Hart Publishing 2010) 25). In France, courts may assess the damages awarded in a foreign currency since the 1920s (Caroline Kleiner, *La monnaie dans les relations privées internationales* (LGDJ 2010) 197). In the → USA, the Restatement (Third) on Foreign relations (American Law Institute, Restatement of the Law, Third: The Foreign Relations Law of the United States, St. Paul 1987) suggests in its § 823 (Judgments on Obligations in Foreign Currency: Law of the United States) that US courts ordinarily give judgment on causes of action arising in another state, or denominated in a foreign currency, in US dollars. However, they are not precluded from giving judgment in the currency in which the obligation is denominated or the loss was incurred.

The situation is different for choice of currency in arbitral awards. Arbitrators have no forum and are bound only by party autonomy, so that arbitration laws are generally silent on the currency issue. An exception is art 48(4) English Arbitration Act 1996 (ch 23), which provides that '[t]he tribunal may order the payment of a sum of money, in any currency'. This freedom of choice entails that the currency of account should be determined according to a specific method, either by referring to the *lex causae* (traditional approach) or to a direct method using a connecting factor (see IV.1.).

5. Recognition of foreign judgment labelled in a foreign currency

When enforcement of a judgment is sought abroad, the issue arises of whether the national court where enforcement is sought can adjust the quantum of → damages awarded to take into account any depreciation of the currency used in the judgment. To re-evaluate the quantum awarded by a foreign court clearly conflicts with the principle denying substantive review of judgments. Where a foreign judgment requires a party to pay a certain amount of damages expressed in a foreign currency, French case-law refuses to reassess the quantum of damages, even when the currency has been devalued

(Cass civ (1), 11 June 2002, *Molinari*, Rev.crit. DIP 2003, 318, with observations by *Horatia Muir Watt*).

Whenever damages in a judgment are expressed in a foreign currency, be it a local or a foreign judgment to be enforced, the enforcement needs to go through a conversion process. Indeed, most countries apply the rule that enforcement of judicial decisions should be discharged in local currency (Frank Vischer, *Geld- und Währungsrecht im nationalen und internationalen Kontext* (Helbing Lichtenhahn 2010) 30). Consequently, the debt must be converted into the local currency at the rate of exchange on the day of payment. Thus the Restatement (Second) on Conflict of Laws (American Law Institute, Restatement of the Law, Second: Conflict of Laws 2d, St. Paul 1971; → Restatement (First and Second) of Conflict of Laws) suggests in § 144 that when enforcement of a foreign judgment expressed in foreign currency is sought in the USA, 'the forum will convert the currency as of the date of the award'.

6. Exchange control provisions

Exchange control regulations are intended to safeguard a country's balance of payments (George Van Hecke, 'Currency', *International Encyclopedia of Comparative Law III* (1972) ch 36, 36 N.15). The adoption of such measures is subject to certain conditions for states that are parties to the IMF (see I.2.). When Member States comply with the IMF Agreement requirements, their exchange control regulations are granted recognition in other member countries according to art VIII-2 b) of the Agreement, which states that '[e]xchange contracts which involve the currency of any member and which are contrary to the exchange control regulations of that member maintained or imposed consistently with this Agreement, shall be unenforceable in the territories of any member'. An authoritative interpretation of art VIII-2 b) was delivered by the Fund's Board of Executive Directors on 14 June 1949, according to which the prohibition of enforcement means that 'the obligations of such contracts will not be implemented by the judicial or administrative authorities of member countries, for example, by decreeing performance of the contracts or by awarding damages for non-performance'.

V. Modern trends

The legal concept of money has been consistently challenged since the creation of so called 'private money', such as the bitcoin in 2008. What is challenged is the state monopoly over the creation of a monetary unit. From a legal point of view, this phenomenon cannot be qualified as money, since the essence of money is to permit and facilitate exchanges. Hence an instrument may be qualified as money only to the extent it is an officially accepted media for exchanges. In other terms, 'money is that which serves as a means of exchange – subject to the crucial proviso that its functions must have the formal and mandatory backing of the domestic legal system in the State or area in which it circulates' (Charles Proctor, *Mann on the Legal Aspects of Money* (7th edn, OUP 2012) N1.15). So far, no monetary legislation applies to relationships labelled in bitcoins. However, the ECJ decided that exchanges of traditional currencies for units of the "bitcoin" virtual currency and vice and versa constitute the supply of services exempted from VAT since they concern transactions concerning currency, bank notes and coins used as legal tender (ECJ, C-264/14, Skatteverket v. David Hedqvist). In a few states, specific legislation has been drafted and adopted to regulate the use of bitcoins in payments, which shows that they do not fit in the existing legislation. Bitcoins cannot be compared with other currencies, whose use requires no specific legislation.

CAROLINE KLEINER

Literature

Vaughan Black, *Foreign Currency Claims in the Conflict of Laws* (Hart Publishing 2010); Geneviève Burdeau, 'L'exercice des competences monétaires par les Etats' (1988) 212 Rec. des Cours 211; Dominique Carreau, 'Le système monétaire international privé (UEM et Euromarchés)' (1998) 274 Rec. des Cours 311; François Gianviti, 'Réflexions sur l'art VIII, section 2 b des Statuts du FMI' [1973] Rev.crit.DIP 471; Helmut Grothe, *Fremdwährungsverbindlichkeiten, das Recht der Geldschulden mit Auslandsberührung Kollisionsrecht — Materielles Recht — Verfahrensrecht* (Walter de Gruyter 1999); Hugo J Hahn and Ulrich Häde, *Währungsrecht* (CH Beck 2010); George Van Hecke, 'Currency', *International Encyclopedia of Comparative Law III* (1972) ch 36; Hideki Kanda and Kazuaki Sono, 'The Future of Lex Monetae' in Mario Giovanoli and Diego Devos (eds), *International Monetary and Financial Law: The Global Crisis* (OUP 2011) 506; Frédéric-Edouard Klein, 'De l'application de l'Article VIII 2 (b) des Statuts du Fonds Monétaire International en Suisse' in Christian Dominicé, Robert Patry and Claude Reymond (eds), *Études de droit international en l'honneur de Pierre Lalive* (Helbing & Lichtenhahn 1993) 261; Caroline Kleiner, 'Money in Private international law: What Are the Problems? What Are the Solutions?' [2009] YbPIL 565; Caroline Kleiner, *La monnaie dans les relations privées internationales* (LGDJ 2010); Elias Krispis, 'Money in Private international law' (1967) 120 Rec. des Cours 191; Denis Loertscher, *Commentaire Romand, Code des obligations I* (2nd edn, Helbing & Lichtenhahn 2012); Georg Maier-Reimer, 'Fremdwährungsverbindlichkeiten' [1985] NJW 2049; Frederick Alexander Mann 'Money in Public International Law' (1959) 96 Rec. des Cours 1; Charles Proctor, *Mann on the Legal Aspects of Money* (7th edn, OUP 2012); Luca Radicati di Brozolo, 'International Payments and Conflicts of Laws' (2000) 48 Am.J.Comp.L. 307; Oliver Remien, 'Schadensersatzwährung im Deliktrecht' [1995] ZEuP 119; Karsten Schmidt, '§ 244 BGB' in Christian Baldus and others (eds), *J. von Staudingers Kommentar zum Bürgerlichen Gesetzbuch* (Sellier-de Gruyter 1997); Karsten Schmidt, 'Schuldwährung, Zahlungwährung und Zahlungsort. Eine Skizze zu Art. 84 OR, § 361 HGB und §§ 244, 270 BGB' in Heinrich Honsell (ed), *Privatrecht und Methode Festschrift für Ernst A. Kramer* (Helbing & Lichtenhahn 2004) 684; Stephen A Silard, 'Money and Foreign Exchange', *International Encyclopedia of Comparative Law XXVIII* (1975) ch 20; Tullio Treves, 'Les effets de la dépréciation monétaire sur les rapports juridiques contractuels en droit international privé italien' in *Les effets de la dépréciation monétaire sur les rapports juridiques contractuels, Travaux de l'association Henri Capitant, tome XXIII Journées d'Istambul* (Economica 1973) 213; Frank Vischer, *Geld- und Währungsrecht im nationalen und internationalen Kontext* (Helbing Lichtenhahn 2010).

Multimodal carriage contracts

I. Definition and concept

Multimodal transport is the carriage of goods by at least two different modes of transport based on a contract pursuant to which the carrier (ie the multimodal transport operator) undertakes the responsibility for the performance of the entire carriage. As has been pointed out, what truly constitutes multimodal transport is not the mere fact that different modes of transport are combined but the fact that a single contract of carriage includes carriage by different modes of transport and provides for the responsibility of a single carrier who is not necessarily the actual carrier of the single segment of transport (Ignacio Arroyo, 'Ambito de applicacion de la normativa uniforme: su extensiòn al transporte da puerta a puerta' [2001] Dir Marit 534; Jan Ramberg, 'Is Multimodal Transport a Contract sui generis also within the Field of EU Competition?' in Mario Riccomagno (ed), *Il trasporto multimodale nella realtà giuridica odierna* (Giappichelli 1997) 7).

However, it is clear that the obligation undertaken pursuant to a multimodal transport contract by the carrier is different from that assumed by a freight forwarder, because the latter is only obliged 'to arrange for the carriage of goods', whereas the former assumes the obligation 'to carry the goods' (Ralph De Wit, *Multimodal Transport* (LLP 1995) 19).

The economic relevance of multimodal transport is a consequence of the integration of transport operations which is the result of the so-called container revolution. In this respect, before analysing the issues related to the carrier's liability in multimodal transport, it is fundamental to consider the evolution of the regulation of the international transport of goods by sea from the Hague Rules (International Convention of 25 August 1924 for the unification of certain rules relating to bills of lading, 120 LNTS 155) to the Rotterdam Rules (United Nations Convention of 11 December 2008 on contracts for the international carriage of goods wholly or partly by sea, UN Doc A/RES/63/122, 63 UNTS 122), all the more so because the major part of multimodal transport includes sea segments. As a matter of fact, international maritime transport appears with more frequency as a mere phase of a multimodal transport.

II. Historical background: the evolution of the regulation of the international transport of goods by sea

The 1924 Hague Rules were conceived in order to compromise the interests of maritime carriers with those of shippers with the aim of limiting the abuse of freedom of contract (Guenter Treitel and Francis Martin Baillie Reynolds, *Carver on Bill of Lading* (Sweet & Maxwell 2001) § 9–062; Hakan Karan, *The Carrier's Liability under International Maritime Conventions: The Hague, Hague-Visby, and*

Hamburg Rules (Edwin Mellen Press 2004) 21; Sergio Maria Carbone, *Contratto di trasporto marittimo di cose* (2nd edn, in cooperation with Andrea La Mattina, Giuffrè 2010) 251). This conception was carried over to the 1968 Visby Protocol (Protocol of 23 February 1968 to amend the International Convention for the unification of certain rules of law relating to bills of lading signed at Brussels on 25 August 1924 (Hague Rules), 1412 UNTS 128) and the 1979 Brussels Protocol (Protocol of 21 December 1979 to amend the International Convention for the unification of certain rules to bills of lading (Hague Rules) as modified by the Amending Protocol of 23 February 1968 (Visby Protocol), 1412 UNTS 146), both amending the 1924 Hague Rules with the sole intent of clarifying certain matters already regulated by the Convention (all three instruments together will be henceforth referred to as Hague-Visby Rules).

The Hamburg Rules (United Nations Convention of 31 March 1978 on the carriage of goods by sea, 1695 UNTS 3) had the aim of defending cargo interests in a stronger way than provided for by the Hague Rules and its amendments. But, despite their promoters' intention, the Hamburg Rules – aside from their drafting style – have been viewed largely in the same vein as the Hague-Visby Rules: indeed, carriers' liability has not been significantly enhanced (Regina Asariotis, 'Allocation of Liability and Burden of Proof in the Draft Instrument on Transport Law' [2002] LMCLQ 388; Sergio Maria Carbone, *Contratto di trasporto marittimo di cose* (2nd edn, in cooperation with Andrea La Mattina, Giuffrè 2010) 251; Andrea La Mattina, 'Le prime applicazioni delle Regole di Amburgo tra autonomia privata, diritto internazionale privato e diritto uniforme dei trasporti' [2004] Riv.Dir.Int'le Priv. & Proc. 597; Marco Lopez de Gonzalo, 'Operatività e limiti delle regole di diritto uniforme relative al trasporto marittimo' in Manuel Januário da Costa Gomes (coordinator), *Jornadas de Lisboa de Direito Marìtimo – O contrato de transporte marìtimo de mercadorias* (Almedina 2008) 80–81; William Tetley, *Marine Cargo Claims* (4th edn, Editions Yvon Blais 2008) 936–7).

The new approach adopted in the Rotterdam Rules is also substantially consistent with the above-mentioned uniform maritime transportation law currently in force, even if it better defines some of its aspects. The drafters of the Rotterdam Rules have taken into account the reasons why the Hamburg Rules have failed to reach sufficient international consensus, and have returned to a carrier liability scheme similar to that adopted by the Hague-Visby Rules (Regina Asariotis, 'Allocation of Liability and Burden of Proof in the Draft Instrument on Transport Law' [2002] LMCLQ 388; Anthony Diamond, 'The Next Sea Carriage Convention?' [2008] LMCLQ 149). In particular, the 'presumed fault' of the carrier, established by art 17.2 of the Rotterdam Rules, is based on some fundamental obligations (established by Articles 11, 13 and 14) with which the carrier must comply, coupled with a complex (and more precise) *onus probandi* scheme, which is modelled on an amended version of the traditional 'excepted perils' system (Kofi Mbiah, 'The Convention on Contracts for the International Carriage of Goods Wholly or Partly by Sea: The Liability and Limitation of Liability Regime' [2007–2008] CMI Yearbook 289).

However, it would be a mistake to consider the Rotterdam Rules as a mere update of the Hague-Visby Rules (Anthony Diamond, 'The Next Sea Carriage Convention?' [2008] LMCLQ 149). As a matter of fact, the new 2008 Convention (ie, the Rotterdam Rules) modifies the carrier liability regime currently in force, and takes into account both the technical evolution of sea transport and a full-fledged assessment of the duties which a modern carrier should fulfil (Michael Sturley, 'The UNCITRAL Carriage of Goods Convention: Changes to Existing Law' [2007–2008] CMI Yearbook 255).

In short, the Rotterdam Rules reflect the regime of traditional carrier liability schemes, and yet provide important clarification, as well as innovations with respect to those parts of the Hague-Visby Rules that are no longer consistent with the evolution of the practical needs of maritime transport. In this sense, we agree with the definitions of the Rotterdam Rules, which have been baptized as 'evolutionary and not revolutionary' (Michael Sturley, 'The UNCITRAL Carriage of Goods Convention: Changes to Existing Law' [2007–2008] CMI Yearbook 255) as well as a fair compromise between 'tradition and modernity' (Philippe Delebecque, 'The New Convention on International Contract of Carriage of Goods Wholly or Partly by Sea: A Civil Law Perspective' [2007–2008] CMI Yearbook 264).

III. The need for a regulation of multimodal transport

An important new element of the Rotterdam Rules is established in Article 26, where a specific regime has been introduced for multimodal transport in particular cases. As a matter of fact, this provision extends – under certain conditions – the period of liability of the maritime carrier to non-sea legs of a certain multimodal maritime transport (Sergio Maria Carbone and Andrea La Mattina, 'L'ambito di applicazione del diritto uniforme dei trasporti marittimi internazionali: dalla Convenzione di Bruxelles alla UNCITRAL Convention' [2008] Riv.Dir.Int'le Priv. & Proc. 981; David A Glass, *Freight Forwarding and Multimodal Transport Contracts* (2nd edn, Informa 2012) 355–6; Andrea La Mattina, 'Le Regole di Rotterdam e il trasporto multimodale' in Giorgio Berlingieri (ed), *Scritti in onore di Francesco Berlingieri* (Il Diritto Marittimo 2010) 647; Theodora Nikaki, 'Conflicting Laws in "Wet" Multimodal Carriage of Goods: The UNCITRAL Draft Convention on the Carriage of Goods [wholly or partly] [by sea]' [2006] J.Mar.L.& Com. 521; Gertjan Van der Ziel, 'Multimodal Aspects of the Rotterdam Rules' [2009] CMI Yearbook 301).

As has been already pointed out, in the current economic context, international maritime transport appears with more frequency as a mere phase of a multimodal transport. But this kind of transport is not specifically regulated by any international convention, the Geneva Multimodal Transport Convention (United Nations Convention of 24 May 1980 on international multimodal transport of goods, UN Doc TD/MT/CONF/16) never having entered into effect. In this situation, Italian and foreign judges have attempted to determine the legal regime which is applicable to multimodal transport (especially to multimodal maritime transport), in some cases extending the international maritime transport rules currently in force to all (or to part) of the phases of multimodal transport (Andrea La Mattina, 'Il trasporto multimodale nei leading cases italiani e stranieri' [2007] Dir Marit 1010). In particular, where the maritime segment of the carriage was the 'prevailing route', the Hague-Visby Rules have often been applied to the entire sequence of multimodal transport and, therefore, even to the non-maritime phases of such multimodal transport (Trib Genova, 12 March 1992, [1993] Dir Marit 430; *Moore-McCormack Lines, Inc v International Terminal Operating Co*, 619 F.Supp. 1406 (SDNY 1983); *Hoogovens Estel Verkoopantoor v Ceres Terminals, Inc*, [1984] AMC 1417; *Marubeni-Iida, Inc v Nippon Yusen Kaisha*, [1962] AMC 1082; *Berkshire Fashions Inc v MV Hakusan II*, 954 F.2d 874, 881 (3d Cir 1992); *Hartford Fire Ins Co v Orient Overseas Container Lines*, 230 F.3d 549, 555 f (2nd Cir 2000); App Aix-en-Provence, 10 July 1984, [1987] DMF 84). On the contrary, in other cases the decision is based on the so-called 'network liability system', thereby splitting the liability regime of the multimodal carrier and affirming that such a regime varies on the basis of the place where the damage to the goods occurs. In these cases, the Hague-Visby Rules have only been applied if the damage is caused during the maritime phase of a certain multimodal transport (App Roma, 5 January 1948 [1948] Foro it. I 697; Trib Genova, 15 April 1950 [1950] Dir Marit 576; App Milano, 7 November 1950 [1951] Foro it. I 76; Trib Milano, 26 February 2004 [2006] Dir Marit 1220; Cass (IT), 6 June 2006, n 13253 [2007] Riv.Dir.Int'le Priv. & Proc. 407; *Reider v Thompson*, 339 U.S. 113, [1951] AMC 38; *Compagnie Française de Navigation à Vapeur v Bonnasse*, 19 F.2d 777, 779 f, [1927] AMC 1325, 1329 (2d Cir 1927); *HSBC Insurance Ltd v Scanwell Container Line Ltd*, [2001] Eur.T.L. 358; App Versailles, 25 May 2000, *Merz Conteneurs v Brambi Fruits et al*, <www.legifrance.gouv.fr>; App Rouen, 13 November 2001, *Via Assurance v Gefco*, [2002] Revue Scapel 30; *Mayhew Foods Ltd v Overseas Containers Ltd* (1984) 1 Lloyd's Rep. 317; Higher Regional Court (OLG) of Hamburg, 19 August 2004 [2004] TranspR 403. *Contra* see Trib. Genova, 11 January 2011, unpublished, where it was affirmed that multimodal transport is a '*sui generis*' kind of carriage to which the system of liability provided for by the regulation of each segment of the carriage is not applicable).

Both of these trends are positive as well as negative. On the one hand, the application of the Hague-Visby Rules to multimodal transport where the maritime leg is prevailing over the other segments, irrespective of the localization of the damage to the goods, eliminates all doubts concerning the notion of 'non-localized' damages (meaning those damages that arise from an unknown route) (Lord Kenneth Diplock, 'A Combined Transport Document: The Genoa Seminar on Combined

Transport' [1972] JBL 273), but it does not seem at all convincing, because (a) it 'strains' the application of the Hague-Visby Rules, which do not take into consideration the specific features of the routes other than the maritime one (Francesco Berlingieri, *Le convenzioni internazionali di diritto marittimo e il codice della navigazione* (Giuffrè 2009) 33) and (b) it casts doubt on the notion of 'prevailing route'.

On the other hand, recourse to the 'network liability system' does not create compatibility problems with the application of the international 'unimodal' conventions and, in particular, with the Hague-Visby Rules, but it does create uncertainty concerning the applicable regime of responsibility which is unpredictable before the damage occurs and which may not be determined at all in the case of 'non-localized' damage. Such uncertainty may not only increase litigation, but may also result in increased insurance costs connected with multimodal transport. In short, as has been said, 'a network system of liability is too complex, gives the cargo interest too little notice of what rules will govern the carriage and provides too much scope for litigation, particularly in respect of the points of demarcation between the modes which constitute the relevant multimodal transport' (David A Glass, *Freight Forwarding and Multimodal Transport Contracts* (2nd edn, Informa 2012) 327). In this respect, among other things, it is extremely difficult to determine when (and where) a single stage of a multimodal transport precisely ends and another begins and, consequently, which regulation applies to a particular stage.

In light of such uncertainties, the Supreme Court of the United States in the Kirby case (*Norfolk Southern Railway Co v James N Kirby, Pty Ltd*, 543 U.S. 14 (2004)) inaugurated what has been defined as a 'conceptual approach' (Michael Sturley, 'An Overview of the Latest Developments in Cargo Liability Law at the United States Supreme Court' [2005] Dir Marit 358) affirming that a multimodal transport contract that includes a maritime route and a 'shorter', but not necessarily 'incidental', land route has a maritime nature (unless the will of the parties to such a contract indicates otherwise). Therefore – independently from the identification of the place where eventual damage to the goods occurs – such a multimodal transport contract has to be regulated by the COGSA (Carriage of Goods by Sea Act (1936) 46 U.S.C. §§ 1300–1315, ie the Federal legislation on maritime transport where the Hague Rules have been implemented). In the case in question, the Supreme Court (i) completely overrides the 'network liability system' (that – as was said by the Court – may cause 'confusion and inefficiency'), as it is not relevant in determining where the damage to the goods occurred, and (ii) grants more certainty and predictability to the conclusions of the case-law trend indicated above, making it unnecessary to measure to an acute degree of precision which is the 'prevailing' route of a certain multimodal maritime transport in order to determine its applicable legal regime.

From the same perspective, in the *Kawasaki* case, the Supreme Court has recently affirmed that a through → bill of lading issued abroad by an ocean carrier can apply to the domestic, inland portion of multimodal transport (providing both for sea and rail carriages), with the consequence that not only the ocean carriage but also the inland carriage will be governed by the COGSA (*Kawasaki Kisen Kaisha Ltd. v Regal-Beloit Corp.*, 130 S. Ct. 2433 (2010)).

It is still not possible to verify what the impact of the *Kirby* and *Kawasaki* cases will be on the decisions of other non-American judges. Furthermore, at present we cannot ignore the situation of uncertainty that still characterizes the rules which are applicable to multimodal transport due to the absence of unequivocal case-law or a uniform regime in the various jurisdictions.

Only a specific regulatory intervention that is desired by most parties, and that has being the subject of interest by → UNCITRAL, would solve the problem (Andreas Furrer and Michael Schürch, 'Cross-border Multimodal Transport: Problems and Limits of Finding an Appropriate Legal Regime' in Katharina Boele-Woelki and others (eds), *Convergence and Divergence in Private international law: Liber Amicorum Kurt Siehr* (Schulthess Verlag 2010)).

IV. The multimodal transport regulation provided for by the Rotterdam Rules and its limitations

From this perspective, the drafters of the Rotterdam Rules (and before them, the drafters of the CMI Draft Instrument on Transport Law, on which the Rotterdam Rules are based) intended to specify the extension, in certain cases, of their application to multimodal transport (door-to-door) that include a maritime route. In short, the new convention elaborated on behalf of the UNCITRAL does not have the aim of regulating multimodal transportation *tout court*, but – under certain conditions and in the presence of certain circumstances – only to extend its scope of application to the land and/or air and/or internal waterways route (if any) prior and/or subsequent to maritime transport. Therefore, the Rotterdam Rules are a little less of a 'true' multimodal convention (such as the Geneva Multimodal Transport Convention) but a little more of a convention on maritime transport: correctly, in fact, a 'multimodal maritime approach' has been referred to (Michael Sturley, 'Scope of the Coverage under the UNCITRAL Draft Instrument' [2004] JIML 138, 146). As has been said, whilst this (partial) approach might seem to be 'a retrograde step' in respect of the Geneva Multimodal Transport Convention, 'it reflects the current reality of logistics at a global level since much of the global pattern of trade can be distinguished between sea-based logistics and air-based logistics' (David A Glass, *Freight Forwarding and Multimodal Transport Contracts* (2nd edn, Informa 2012) 356). Hence, the Rotterdam Rules have the intention of satisfying the needs of the regulation of sea-based logistics.

In this sense, the Rotterdam Rules, firstly, extend the definition of a 'contract of carriage' relevant to its proper scope of application and affirm in art 1.1 that such a contract shall provide for carriage by sea and may provide for carriage by other methods of transport in addition to the sea carriage; also the combined provisions of art 5 (entitled 'General scope of application') and art 12 (entitled 'Period of responsibility of the carrier') provide that the period of responsibility of the carrier includes the moment from the receipt of the goods until the moment of the delivery of the same goods to the consignee, and that the responsibility of the carrier is not necessarily limited to the phase when the goods are placed on the ship. Furthermore, from art 5 of the Rotterdam Rules it is possible to deduce that the places of the receipt/delivery of the goods may in certain cases not coincide with the ports of loading/unloading.

Therefore, as has been observed, the Hague Rules, in its original formulation, was a 'tackle-to-tackle' convention, the Hague-Visby Rules and the Hamburg Rules were 'port-to-port' conventions, and, finally, the Rotterdam Rules are drafted to become a 'door-to-door' convention, even if they merely concern 'wet' multimodal transport, ie multimodal maritime transport (Francesco Berlingieri, 'Multimodal Aspects of the Rotterdam Rules' <www.rotterdamrules2009.com>). In reality, as already observed above, the text in question is not really a 'door-to-door' convention because the scope of application of the Rotterdam Rules is limited under both the 'subjective' profile and the 'objective' one.

The scope of application of the Rotterdam Rules is characterized by a 'subjective' approach because, once the convention is in force, they will regulate the liability of (i) the 'contractual' maritime carrier – and this (subject to the 'objective' limits mentioned further on) with reference to the services that the carrier provides, directly or indirectly, on the maritime route as well as on the land or air or internal waterways route – and (ii) the so-called 'maritime performing parties', meaning those individuals who are charged by the same contractual carrier to execute – 'during the period between the arrival of the goods at the port of loading of a ship and their departure from the port of discharge of a ship' (art 17) – 'any of the carrier obligations under a contract of carriage with respect to the receipt, loading, handling, stowage, carriage, care, unloading or delivery of the goods' (art 1.6.a). In other words, the Rotterdam Rules – as implicitly stated in art 4.1.a – shall not cover the liability of any other 'non-maritime carrier', unless it operates 'exclusively within a port area' (art 1.7). This limitation has been criticized by some US scholars, who have highlighted the fact that the Rotterdam Rules are not able to attain the results that were recently reached by the Supreme Court in the *Kirby* case, therefore obliging operators to utilize the 'Himalaya Clause' in order to allow a voluntary extension of the regulation for maritime transport to land carriers (Michael E Crowley, 'The Limited Scope of the Cargo Liability Regime Covering Carriage of Goods by Sea: The Multimodal Problem' [2005] Tul.L.Rev. 1461, 1502).

The Rotterdam Rules are also limited under the 'objective' profile as they do not provide a uniform regime for all the phases of a multimodal transport but by adopting the so-called 'network liability system' only in cases of loss or damage to the goods occurred exclusively on one route. As a matter of fact, art 26 determines the prevailing application of any other relevant 'international instrument' (but not any state legislation) specifically shaped for each relevant non-maritime phase if the interested party would have concluded a separate transportation contract and if the relevant applicable instrument imperatively determines the compulsory application of its provisions ('either at all or to the detriment of the shipper') concerning the responsibility of the carrier, the limitation of liability and a time bar. Hence, from an 'objective' point of view, the Rotterdam Rules may only be applied with regard to non-maritime routes if: (i) damage to the goods occurs exclusively on a non-maritime route or the damage is not localized (meaning that the route of the transport where the damage occurs is unknown) and (ii) there is no mandatory uniform regime of the non-maritime route concerning the responsibility of the carrier, the limitation of liability and a time bar, or, if there is such a regime, the Rotterdam Rules do not clash with the corresponding provisions of it (in this respect, please consider UNCITRAL Doc A/CN.9/WG.III/WP. 78, para 18, pursuant to which 'the limited network system only comes into play in situations where . . . there might be a conflict between the liability provisions of the [draft] convention and the liability provisions of the relevant unimodal transport conventions').

The rationale of this regulation resides in the will to avoid any conflict between the Rotterdam Rules (in the part where it extends its proper scope of application to the non-maritime route) and the 'unimodal' conventions which regulate land, air and internal waterway transportation.

Concerning this last proposal, moreover, the superfluous nature of such a rule has been affirmed considering that there is no conflict amongst the multimodal provisions of the Rotterdam Rules and the scope of application of the 'unimodal' conventions, in so far as these – with the exception of what we will state further on – do not cover the regulation of multimodal transport (Ignacio Arroyo, 'Ambito de applicacion de la normativa uniforme: su extensiòn al transporte da puerta a puerta' [2001] Dir Marit 534).

Furthermore, the fact that art 26 of the Rotterdam Rules provides for the compulsory application of another 'international instrument' to non-maritime routes (but only with reference to the responsibility of the carrier, the limitation of liability and the time bar) implies that for those routes two different regimes may be contemporaneously applicable: (i) the one that belongs to the route if a 'unimodal' transport contract were to have been executed for that route (ie the regime provided for by CMR (Convention of 19 May 1956 on the contract for the international carriage of goods by road, 399 UNTS 189), COTIF (Convention of 9 May 1980 concerning international carriage by rail, 1396 UNTS 2, in the version of the Protocol of Modification of 3 June 1999, available at <www.otif.org>), CMNI (International Convention of 22 June 2001 on the contract of carriage of goods by inland waterway, UN Doc A/CN.9/645) or the Montreal Convention (Convention of 28 May 1999 for the unification of certain rules relating to international carriage by air, 2242 UNTS 309)), but limited to the above-mentioned aspects of the responsibility of the carrier, the limitation of liability and the time bar, and (ii) that of the Rotterdam Rules, with reference to all of the other aspects of the multimodal transport contract (amongst these, for example, are the obligations of the shipper, the transport documents, the delivery, the 'right of control', and the transfer of the rights that arise from the contract) (Mahin Faghfouri, 'International Regulation of Liability for Multimodal Transport: In Search of Uniformity' [2006] WMU J Mar affairs 95). From this, 'an obscure patchwork of different regimes which were not designed to complement each other' arises (UNCTAD doc. A/CN.9/WG.III/WP.21/Add. 1, Annex II, para 44), that, in any case, does not resolve all the potential conflicts between the new Convention and the other applicable instruments with regard to non-maritime transport, thereby not solving the problem of an 'overlap' with reference to that which is indicated under point '(ii)' above (David A Glass, 'Meddling in Multimodal Muddle? A Network of Conflict in the UNCITRAL Draft Convention on the Carriage of Goods [wholly or partly] [by sea]' [2006] LMCLQ 306).

Lastly, with the aim of preventing possible conflicts with other 'unimodal' conventions, art 82 of the Rotterdam Rules – similar to art 25 of the Hamburg Rules, but with more specific wording – contains a safeguard clause concerning the scope of application of the multimodal transport regulations provided for by other 'unimodal' conventions in force at the time the Rotterdam Rules would enter into force, provided that no subsequent 'replacement conventions' can be taken into account (David A Glass, *Freight Forwarding and Multimodal Transport Contracts* (2nd edn, Informa 2012) 367). Article 82 therefore provides that the Rotterdam Rules do not affect the application of multimodal transport regulations laid down by other conventions to maritime routes (in particular, the Rotterdam Rules do not affect the application of the following provisions: (a) art 18.3 of the Warsaw Convention (Convention of 12 October 1929 for the unification of certain rules relating to international carriage by air, 137 LNTS 11) and art 18.4 of the Montreal Convention on air transport; (b) art 2 of the CMR Convention on road transport; (c) art 1.3 and art 1.4 of the CIM – COTIF Convention on railway transport; (d) art 2.2 of the CMNI Convention on internal waterways transport (Cecile Legros, 'Relations between the Rotterdam Rules and the Convention on the Carriage of Goods by Road' [2012] Tul.Mar.L.J. 725; Bevan Marten, 'Multimodal Transport Reform and the European Union: A Minimalist Approach' [2012] Eur.T.L. 129; Eric Røsaeg, 'Conflicts of Conventions in the Rotterdam Rules' [2009] JIML 238)).

V. The period of liability of the (multimodal) carrier under the Rotterdam Rules

As already said, even though the Rotterdam Rules are not a 'multimodal convention' *tout court*, they do provide that the maritime carrier is responsible for the whole period during which it has custody of the goods, not only regardless of the fact that such goods are loaded on board the ship, but also (and above all) regardless of the fact that the receipt of those goods occurs in a maritime port (Sergio Maria Carbone, *Contratto di trasporto marittimo di cose* (2nd edn, in cooperation with Andrea La Mattina, Giuffrè 2010) 500).

Furthermore, the Rotterdam Rules provide for important clarifications in order to determine more effectively the period of liability of the carrier and, in particular, in order to resolve certain doubts regarding their extension which have arisen in the case-law applying the Hague-Visby Rules.

First, the Rotterdam Rules have confirmed that (as already specified by the Hamburg Rules) if a public law provision of the *lex loci* of the state where the goods are loaded (or unloaded) compels the carrier to receive such goods from (or to deliver to) a special purpose public enterprise, the period of the carrier's responsibility will start (or will end) only when the goods are actually received from (or are delivered to) this entity (art 12.2).

Second, pursuant to the combined effect of art 12.3 and art 17.1 of the Rotterdam Rules, the period of liability of the maritime carrier can be potentially reduced through an agreement between the parties to the contract of carriage, provided that – in any case – such period cannot start after the loading operations onto a ship have commenced and cannot end before the unloading operations from a ship have been completed. Bearing this provision in mind, it is clear that the Rotterdam Rules essentially have a 'maritime' (not multimodal) nature, because their 'core' mandatory regulation applies only to the 'maritime' route. That is even more evident considering that art 13.2 of the Rotterdam Rules – implementing the solutions reached by English case-law in respect of f.i.o. and f.i.o.s.t. clauses under the Hague-Visby Rules (Anthony Diamond, 'The Next Sea Carriage Convention?' [2008] LMCLQ 149) – provides that the carrier and the shipper may agree that the operations of loading, handling, stowing or unloading can be performed by the shipper himself (or by the documentary shipper or by the consignee): in such a case, the carrier is not liable for any damage to the goods caused by these operations, unless they are performed by a performing party (art 17.3, point 'i' of the Rotterdam Rules).

In short, since the Rotterdam Rules '[do] not seek to control the contractual scope of the carriage, the parties are free to determine the point at which the takeover of the goods or the delivery of the goods occurs'. Consequently, the carrier's liability would depend on the provisions of the relevant contract of carriage and, in particular, on the scheme on which such a contract is based (door to door, depot to depot, terminal to terminal or port to port). However, 'any clause which seeks to indicate that receipt takes place after the beginning of initial loading or that delivery takes place before the completion of final unloading is void (David A Glass, *Freight Forwarding and Multimodal Transport Contracts* (2nd edn, Informa 2012) 359).

Finally, the Rotterdam Rules provide a detailed regulation of the parties' rights and duties regarding the termination of the maritime carrier's period of liability. In particular, art 48 regulates the consequences of the impossibility for the carrier to deliver the goods to the relevant cargo-interested parties. In such a case, the carrier must promptly inform the cargo-interested parties who are indicated in the contract of carriage and, afterwards, if they do not accept delivery, the carrier may, 'at the risk and expense of the person entitled to the goods, take such action in respect of the goods as circumstances may reasonably require'.

VI. The multimodal transport regulation provided for by Dutch and German law

The Rotterdam Rules have not yet entered into force and – as has been said – at present there is no uniform regulation of multimodal transport. In this context, it seems useful to make reference to some national legislation which has tried to regulate multimodal transport.

From a European perspective, we have to consider, in particular, Dutch and German law.

Of course, such national legislation may regulate a single multimodal transport if it is the applicable law pursuant to the relevant conflict-of-laws rules. In this respect, Regulation (EC) No 593/2008 of the European Parliament and of the Council of 17 June 2008 on the law applicable to contractual obligations (Rome I), [2008] OJ L 177/6, which is applicable in all Member States except Denmark, provides for a specific conflict of laws rule concerning contracts of carriage of goods, regardless of the chosen means of transportation (see Article 5(1) and (3)).

Article 5 provides, as a general → connecting factor, (i) the law chosen by the parties according to Article 3 of the same instrument, which is expressly referred to by the rule at issue.

As long as the parties have not chosen the applicable law, Article 5 provides for (ii) the application of the law of the country of habitual residence of the carrier, provided that, however, the place of receipt or the place of delivery or the habitual residence of the consignor is also situated in that country. Whenever such coincidence does not take place, Article 5 indicates that the applicable law is (iii) the law of the country where the place of delivery as agreed by the parties is situated.

Finally, in the absence of a choice-of-law agreement, according to Article 3 of the Regulation, the rule at issue allows the judge to apply the law of a country other than that indicated by the aforementioned provisions (*supra* under (ii) and (iii)), as long as it is clear that the contract is manifestly more closely connected with such a country.

With reference to Dutch law, the relevant multimodal transport regulation was introduced in the Dutch Civil Code (now the Dutch New Civil Code (Nieuw Burgerlijk Wetboek of 1 January 1992)) in 1991. In particular, Book 8, Section 8.2.2 provides for the law applicable to a 'Contract of combined carriage of goods', which is defined by Article 8:40 of the Dutch Civil Code as 'the contract of carriage whereby the carrier (combined carrier) engages himself under one single contract towards the consignor to perform the transport in part by sea, inland waterway, road, railway, air, pipeline or by means of any other mode of transport'. This definition makes clear that the law has the aim of regulating all kinds of multimodal transport (Aliki Kiantou-Pampouki, 'The General Report' in Aliki Kiantou-Pampouki (ed), *Multimodal Transport: Carrier Liability and Issues Related to the Bills of Lading* (Bruylant 2000) 19). In principle, Dutch law is based on a network liability scheme, providing in Article 8:41 that 'each part of the transport shall be governed by the rules of law applicable to that part'. But in the case of non-localized → damages a uniform regime of liability is provided for by Article 8:43, which calls for the application of the claimant's most favourable regime, affirming that – in that case – the liability of the multimodal transport operator 'is determined according to the rules of law applicable . . . from which results the highest amount of damages'.

With reference to German law, the 'Transportrechtsreformgesetz' of 25 June 1998 (BGBl. I 1588) has significantly modified the law of transport of goods and, in particular, the relevant provisions of the German Commercial Code (Handelsgesetzbuch of 10 May 1897, RGBl. 219, as amended), submitting the various modes of transport of goods – with the exception of the → carriage of goods by sea – to the same legal regime and providing for specific rules regulating multimodal transport contracts (Rolf Herber, 'The New German Transport Legislation' [1998] 33 Eur.T.L. 591). The multimodal transport regulation provided for by §§ 452–452d of the German Commercial Code can be summarized as follows:

(a) in case of localized damage, the liability of the multimodal carrier shall be based on a 'network system', provided that the parties to the multimodal transport contract may choose the application of the general regime of the carrier's liability under §§ 407 ff of the German Commercial Code;

(b) in case of non-localized damage, there are two possibilities: (i) if the multimodal transport does not include a sea route, the liability of the multimodal carrier shall be based on the general regime of the carrier's liability under the German Commercial Code; (ii) if the multimodal transport includes a sea route, the liability of the multimodal carrier shall be based on the same regime as under point (i), provided that the parties may invoke the relevant (international or national) rules of liability applicable to the transport of goods by sea, where each of them, having a legitimate interest, is in a position to give evidence that the specific damaging event occurred during the national phase of the transport.

VII. Conclusions

Although they are not revolutionary, the Rotterdam Rules for the first time provide a regime concerning the liability of the sea carrier which specifically takes into consideration the development of sea transport from a 'multimodal perspective'. The new convention does not directly regulate any kind of multimodal transport, but – subject to certain conditions – it merely extends its scope of application to non-maritime routes involving the so-called 'wet' multimodal transport for the maritime characterization of the prevailing part of it. In other words, the Rotterdam Rules do not provide a 'uniform' regime of responsibility concerning the multimodal carrier, but – by applying a sort of 'network liability system' – they try to fill the gaps left open by the 'unimodal' conventions currently in force and, in particular, by the Hague-Visby Rules.

Of course, we think that it would have been better to have a complete regulation of multimodal transport (Andrea La Mattina, 'La responsabilità del vettore multimodale: profili ricostruttivi e de iure condendo' [2005] Dir Marit 3) and we hope that one day it will be possible to have a truly 'uniform' system of international transport, common to all phases of carriage and based upon a sole convention *in lieu* of several 'unimodal' instruments, but at present it seems that the ratification of the Rotterdam Rules by the major maritime states, with a view to replacing all the international conventions on the transport of goods by sea currently in force, could be the first reasonable step in order to (partially) resolve the uncertainty that characterizes the subject of multimodal transport.

SERGIO M CARBONE

Literature

Ignacio Arroyo, 'Ambito de applicacion de la normativa uniforme: su extensiòn al transporte da puerta a puerta' [2001] Dir Marit 534; Regina Asariotis, 'Allocation of Liability and Burden of Proof in the Draft Instrument on Transport Law' [2002] LMCLQ 388; Francesco Berlingieri, *Le convenzioni internazionali di diritto marittimo e il codice della navigazione* (Giuffrè 2009); Francesco Berlingieri, 'Multimodal Aspects of the Rotterdam Rules' <www.rotterdamrules2009.com>, last accessed on 3 January 2013; Sergio Maria Carbone, *Contratto di trasporto marittimo di cose* (2nd edn, in cooperation with Andrea La Mattina, Giuffrè 2010); Sergio Maria Carbone and Andrea La Mattina, 'L'ambito di applicazione del diritto uniforme dei trasporti marittimi internazionali: dalla Convenzione di Bruxelles alla UNCITRAL Convention' [2008] Riv.Dir. Int'le Priv. & Proc. 981; Michael E Crowley, 'The Limited Scope of the Cargo Liability Regime Covering Carriage of Goods by Sea: The Multimodal Problem' [2005] Tul.L.Rev. 1461; Philippe Delebecque, 'The New Convention on International Contract of Carriage of Goods Wholly or Partly by Sea: A Civil Law Perspective' [2007–2008] CMI Yearbook 264; Ralph De Wit, *Multimodal Transport* (LLP 1995); Anthony Diamond, 'The Next Sea Carriage Convention?' [2008] LMCLQ 149; Lord Kenneth Diplock, 'A Combined Transport Document: The Genoa Seminar on Combined Transport' [1972] JBL 273; Mahin Faghfouri, 'International Regulation of Liability for Multimodal Transport: In Search of Uniformity' [2006] WMU J Mar affairs 95; Andreas Furrer and Michael Schürch, 'Cross-border Multimodal Transport: Problems and Limits of Finding an Appropriate Legal Regime' in Katharina Boele-Woelki and others (eds), *Convergence and Divergence in Private international law: Liber Amicorum Kurt Siehr* (Schulthess Verlag 2010); David A Glass, 'Meddling in Multimodal Muddle? A Network of Conflict in the UNCITRAL Draft Convention on the Carriage of Goods [wholly or partly] [by sea]' [2006] LMCLQ 306; David A Glass, *Freight Forwarding and Multimodal Transport Contracts* (2nd edn, Informa 2012); Hakan Karan, *The Carrier's Liability under International Maritime Conventions: The Hague, Hague-Visby, and Hamburg Rules* (Edwin Mellen Press 2004); Aliki Kiantou-Pampouki, 'The General Report' in Aliki Kiantou-Pampouki (ed), *Multimodal Transport: Carrier Liability and Issues Related to the Bills of Lading* (Bruylant 2000); Andrea La Mattina, 'Le prime applicazioni delle Regole di Amburgo tra autonomia privata, diritto internazionale privato e diritto uniforme dei trasporti' [2004] Riv.Dir. Int'le Priv. & Proc. 597; Andrea La Mattina,

'La responsabilità del vettore multimodale: profili ricostruttivi e de iure condendo' [2005] Dir Marit 3; Andrea La Mattina, 'Il trasporto multimodale nei leading cases italiani e stranieri' [2007] Dir Marit 1010; Andrea La Mattina, 'Le Regole di Rotterdam e il trasporto multimodale' in Georgio Berlingieri (ed), *Scritti in onore di Francesco Berlingieri* (Il Diritto Marittimo 2010); Cecile Legros, 'Relations between the Rotterdam Rules and the Convention on the Carriage of Goods by Road' [2012] Tul.Mar.L.J. 725; Marco Lopez de Gonzalo, 'Operatività e limiti delle regole di diritto uniforme relative al trasporto marittimo' in Manuel Januário da Costa Gomes (coordinator), *Jornadas de Lisboa de Direito Marìtimo – O contrato de transporte maritimo de mercadorias* (Almedina 2008); Bevan Marten, 'Multimodal Transport Reform and the European Union: A Minimalist Approach' [2012] Eur.T.L. 129; Kofi Mbiah, 'The Convention on Contracts for the International Carriage of Goods Wholly or Partly by Sea: The Liability and Limitation of Liability Regime' [2007–2008] CMI Yearbook 289; Theodora Nikaki, 'Conflicting Laws in "Wet" Multimodal Carriage of Goods: The UNCITRAL Draft Convention on the Carriage of Goods [wholly or partly] [by sea]' [2006] J.Mar.L.& Com. 521; Jan Ramberg, 'Is Multimodal Transport a Contract sui generis also within the Field of EU Competition?' in Mario Riccomagno (ed), *Il trasporto multimodale nella realtà giuridica odierna* (Giappichelli 1997); Eric Røsaeg, 'Conflicts of Conventions in the Rotterdam Rules' [2009] JIML 238; Michael Sturley, 'Scope of the Coverage under the UNCITRAL Draft Instrument' [2004] JIML 138; Michael Sturley, 'An Overview of the Latest Developments in Cargo Liability Law at the United States Supreme Court' [2005] Dir Marit 358; Michael Sturley, 'The UNCITRAL Carriage of Goods Convention: Changes to Existing Law' [2007–2008] CMI Yearbook 255; William Tetley, *Marine Cargo Claims* (4th edn, Editions Yvon Blais 2008); Guenter Treitel and Francis Martin Baillie Reynolds, *Carver on Bill of Lading* (Sweet & Maxwell 2001); Gertjan Van der Ziel, 'Multimodal Aspects of the Rotterdam Rules' [2009] CMI Yearbook 301.

Multiple defendants and joint liability

The widespread division of labour in modern economies leads to a multiplication of liability for potential damages. For private international law, this raises the question under which circumstances the cooperation of several participants translates into a common place of jurisdiction and a common applicable law for all potentially liable persons. As the noble oath *'Tous pour un, un pour tous'* is more commonly encountered in literature than in litigation, co-defendants which are to be joined in a single forum may try to avoid being found liable by challenging the jurisdiction of the court, raising the issue of jurisdiction over multiple defendants (see I. below). Moreover, in such cases the question of the law applicable to joint liability arises, in particular if one tortfeasor has compensated the victim and seeks contribution from another tortfeasor (see II. below).

As the term 'joint liability' makes clear, this entry is concerned with the scenario of several debtors who are liable for the same claim ('multiple liability' in the parlance of art 20 Rome II Regulation (Regulation (EC) No 864/2007 of the European Parliament and of the Council of 11 July 2007 on the law applicable to non-contractual obligations (Rome II), [2007] OJ L 199/40) and art 16 Rome I Regulation (Regulation (EC) No 593/2008 of the European Parliament and of the Council of 17 June 2008 on the law applicable to contractual obligations (Rome I), [2008] OJ L 177/6). This entry does not cover the scenario where a third party who is not liable for the same claim, but who has a duty arising from a separate legal basis (typically an insurance contract) to satisfy the creditor, wishes to exercise against the debtor the creditor's rights against the debtor ('subrogation' in the terminology of art 19 Rome II Regulation and art 15 Rome I Regulation). Moreover, this entry is not concerned with collective litigation involving a larger number of plaintiffs and/or defendants. Finally, the specific rules for reimbursement of benefits paid by public bodies in place of maintenance (art 64(2) Maintenance Regulation (Council Regulation (EC) No 4/2009 of 18 December 2008 on jurisdiction, applicable law, recognition and enforcement of decisions and cooperation in matters relating to maintenance obligations, [2009] OJ L 7/1); art 10 Hague Maintenance Protocol 2007 (Hague Protocol of 23 November 2007 on the law applicable to maintenance obligations, [2009] OJ L 331/19)) and maintenance contribution claims between private parties are beyond the ambit of this entry.

SERGIO M CARBONE / CHRISTIAN HEINZE

I. Jurisdiction over multiple defendants

1. Concept

The jurisdictional rules on multiple defendants (sometimes also called subjective joinder) define the circumstances under which actions against two or more defendants may be joined in the forum where one of the defendants, often referred to as 'anchor defendant' (for this term *Canada Trust Company and Others v Stolzenberg and others (No 2)* [2002] 1 AC 1, 6), is resident or otherwise liable to jurisdiction. A related phenomenon is jurisdiction granted in the court of the main proceedings for an action on a warranty, guarantee or another indemnification claim of the defendant against a third party (see art 8(2) Brussels I Regulation (recast) (Regulation (EU) No 1215/2012 of the European Parliament and of the Council of 12 December 2012 on jurisdiction and the recognition and enforcement of judgments in civil and commercial matters (recast), [2012] OJ L 351/1)). In these cases, it is not the plaintiff but rather the defendant who seeks to join a third party to the proceedings to secure indemnification for any costs or damages incurred in the main proceedings between plaintiff and defendant. Apart from the rules on multiple defendants, a consolidation of actions against several defendants may also be possible under other heads of jurisdiction, provided that all defendants meet the requirements of the provision in question. For example, tort jurisdiction may allow suing several defendants in the state where the tort occurred if all defendants have participated in the tort in the respective country. The rules on jurisdiction over multiple defendants can be distinguished from such other heads of jurisdiction in that they establish jurisdiction over the co-defendants *only* on the basis of a certain relationship between the co-defendants and the anchor defendant. Other grounds of jurisdiction, such as tort jurisdiction, may also lead to several defendants being subject to jurisdiction in the same court, but in these cases the jurisdiction over the co-defendants is not based on their relationship with the anchor defendant (alone), but rather on the fact that each co-defendant fulfilled the requirements of the jurisdiction ground in question, eg committed a tort in the country of the court seized with the action.

a) Neighbouring national procedural law
Depending on national procedural law, further defendants may either be joined initially, ie in the initial complaint, or in the course of the proceedings, the latter normally being subject to stricter requirements. Moreover, national procedural law may provide for mandatory (compulsory) joinder (for example for indivisible obligations or for actions against a group of debtors, eg hereditary debts, where joinder of actions is required in order to avoid contradictory judgments) as well as for voluntary (permissive) joinder of actions against several defendants (which is often motivated by considerations of procedural economy). In cases of mandatory joinder, national procedural law will normally render it inadmissible to sue only a single defendant without the mandatory co-defendants. On the other hand, in such cases the defence of a single co-defendant will often be attributed to the entire group of defendants, which will normally not apply for the simple permissive joinder.

b) Neighbouring jurisdictional rules
The rules on multiple defendants or subjective joinder need to be distinguished from objective joinder where multiple claims, for example based in contract and in tort, are joined against a single defendant. The jurisdiction open to the plaintiff to sue several defendants in the same court also needs to be distinguished from the discretionary power of the judge to join two or more separate (but related) proceedings which are already pending. The discretionary power of the judge to join related actions may be wider than the jurisdiction rules on multiple defendants, because the decision to consolidate the actions is made not by the plaintiff but by the impartial judge. Finally, jurisdictional rules on multiple defendants may be distinguished from the non-recognition ground of irreconcilable judgments (eg art 45(1)(c), (d) Brussels I Regulation (recast)), in that the notion of irreconcilable judgments in the non-recognition grounds is narrower than in the jurisdiction provision for multiple defendants as it refers only to judgments 'between the same parties'. As with all rules of special jurisdiction, the rules on multiple defendants are subject to exclusive jurisdiction. It is accordingly not possible to join a defendant if the action against that defendant falls within the scope of a ground of exclusive jurisdiction or an exclusive jurisdiction agreement with the plaintiff (Case 23/78 *Meeth v Glacetal* [1978] ECR 2133, para 5; see also Case C-352/13 *Cartel Damage Claims Hydrogen Peroxide SA (CDC) v Evonik Degussa GmbH and others* (CJEU, 21 May 2015) para 61, for limits paras 68–71).

2. Purpose

Generally speaking, the jurisdiction rules on multiple defendants can be justified on two grounds. The primary purpose of such rules, eg art 8(1) Brussels I Regulation (recast), is to avoid irreconcilable judgments in respect of different defendants on claims which are closely connected (Jenard Report (Paul Jenard, 'Report on the Convention on jurisdiction and the enforcement of judgments in civil and commercial matters' [1979] OJ C 59/1) 27; Case C-145/10 *Eva-Maria Painer v Standard Verlags GmbH and others* [2011] ECR I-12533, para 77). A second, less important justification is fostering procedural economy by consolidating related actions with similar facts and evidence. While procedural economy may militate in favour of a broad understanding of the rules on multiple defendants, in the interest of predictability for each co-defendant it should nevertheless only be regarded as a secondary justification for such provisions which cannot justify an interpretation going beyond the limits defined by the interest to avoid irreconcilable judgments (for a strict interpretation of art 8(1) Brussels I Regulation (recast) see Case C-145/10 *Eva-Maria Painer v Standard Verlags GmbH and others* [2011] ECR I-12533, para 74).

3. Current regulation

a) EU law

For defendants domiciled in an EU Member State (non-EU domiciled defendants fall under national jurisdiction rules, Case C-645/11 *Land Berlin v Ellen Mirjam Sapir and others* [2013] OJ C 156/11, para 55), art 8(1) Brussels I Regulation (recast) permits to sue a person who is 'one of a number of defendants, in the courts for the place where any one of them is domiciled, provided the claims are so closely connected that it is expedient to hear and determine them together to avoid the risk of irreconcilable judgments resulting from separate proceedings'. The close connection which forms the basis of jurisdiction under art 8(1) Brussels I Regulation must exist between the claim against the anchor defendant domiciled in the forum state and each claim against another defendant that is to be joined to the action. It is not sufficient for a joinder of claims that the claim against a co-defendant is closely connected with the claim against another co-defendant who is not the anchor defendant.

The definition of 'close connection' in art 8(1) Brussels I Regulation (recast) was modelled on the definition of 'related actions' in what is today art 30(3) Brussels I Regulation (recast) (see Case 189/87 *Athanasios Kalfelis v Bankhaus Schröder, Münchmeyer, Hengst and Co and others* [1988] ECR 5565, para 12; Case C-98/06 *Freeport v Arnoldsson* [2006] ECR I-8319, para 53). This parallel is unfortunate, as art 8(1) and art 30(3) Brussels I Regulation (recast) serve different purposes: whereas art 30 Brussels I Regulation (recast) allows consolidation of related actions by an (impartial) judge, art 8 Brussels I Regulation (recast) gives the plaintiff the choice of an additional forum. In view of this difference, the 'close connection' in art 8(1) Brussels I Regulation (recast) should be interpreted more narrowly than the same words in art 30(3) Brussels I Regulation (recast). The key question thus becomes what is meant by 'close connection' in art 8(1) Brussels I Regulation (recast). According to the ECJ, in order for decisions to be regarded as 'irreconcilable', 'it is not sufficient that there be a divergence in the outcome of the dispute, but that divergence must also arise in the context of the same situation of law and fact' (Case C-539/03 *Roche Nederland BV and Others v Frederick Primus and Milton Goldenberg* [2006] ECR I-6535, para 26; Case C-645/11 *Land Berlin v Ellen Mirjam Sapir and others* [2013] OJ C 156/11, para 43; Case C-352/13 *Cartel Damage Claims Hydrogen Peroxide SA (CDC) v Evonik Degussa GmbH and others* (CJEU, 21 May 2015) para 20). Jurisdiction under art 8(1) Brussels I Regulation (recast) is thus only available if a risk of divergence in the outcome of the dispute exists. It is insufficient that a joint hearing would help to save time and cost. Moreover, this risk of divergence is qualified in that it must 'arise in the context of the same situation of law and fact'.

(1) Same factual situation As regards the same factual situation, the ECJ has held that in a scenario where 'the defendants are different and the [patent] infringements they are accused of, committed in different Contracting States, are not the same', then 'possible divergences between decisions . . . would not arise in the context of the same factual situation'. On the other hand the Court indicated in the same decision that the factual situation would be the same 'where defendant companies, which belong to the same group, have acted in an identical or similar manner

in accordance with a common policy elaborated by one of them' (Case C-539/03 *Roche Nederland BV and Others v Frederick Primus and Milton Goldenberg* [2006] ECR I-6535, paras 28, 34). In a later decision, the ECJ confirmed that the 'fact that defendants against whom a copyright holder alleges substantially identical infringements of his copyright did or did not act independently may be relevant' for the finding of the same factual situation (Case C-145/10 *Eva-Maria Painer v Standard Verlags GmbH and others* [2011] ECR I-12533, para 83). As the law stands today, *Roche* and *Painer* suggest that the same factual situation can be established if – cumulatively – the co-defendants acted in an identical or at least similar manner and in accordance with a common policy. However, both elements serve different purposes. While the 'identical or at least similar manner' may be justified from the viewpoint of procedural economy and the notion of irreconcilable judgments – diverging judgments about different conduct of defendants are simply not contradictory – the 'common policy' seeks to ensure legal certainty and predictability as to the jurisdiction of the courts for the non-domiciled defendants (see Recitals (15) and (16) Brussels I Regulation (recast); Case C-145/10 *Eva-Maria Painer v Standard Verlags GmbH and others* [2011] ECR I-12533, paras 75, 81). In requiring a common policy, it can be ensured that each co-defendant joined on the basis of art 8(1) Brussels I Regulation (recast) knew of the conduct of their co-defendants and was in some way linked to their activities. Examples for a common policy situation are infringements of the same or parallel right(s) by different entities belonging to the same corporate group, joint infringement where each co-defendant is aware of the conduct of their fellow infringers as part of a common plan, or the actions of co-defendants in a chain of infringers, provided that the actions of each co-defendant complement each other in establishing a distribution system known to all co-defendants (for more details Christian Heinze, 'Article 2:206: Multiple Defendants' in European Max Planck Group on Conflict of Laws in Intellectual Property (ed), *Conflict of Laws in Intellectual Property: The CLIP Principles and Commentary* (OUP 2013) 2:206.C08–2:206.C15, pp 103, 106–10). By contrast, a finding of the same factual situation will normally be excluded where the claims against the anchor defendant and against the non-domiciled co-defendants infringed the same or a similar right, but where the infringements occurred 'independently and without knowledge of one another' as unconcerted, parallel conduct (Case C-145/10 *Eva-Maria Painer v Standard Verlags GmbH and others* [2011] ECR I-12533, Opinion of 12 April 2011 of AG Trstenjak, para 92). If jurisdiction could be based on mere parallel but unconcerted conduct, a co-defendant could be sued in the courts of a country where someone else entirely unknown, possibly only by coincidence, may have committed the same infringement, which is difficult to reconcile with the requirement of foreseeability of jurisdiction to the defendant. Having thus identified 'common policy' and 'parallel but unconcerted conduct' as the two counterpoints of the same factual situation, the difficult question becomes how common the policy must have been. Is it sufficient to establish a partially common policy consisting of a common (eg competition law) infringement, even if the implementation of that common policy diverged (ie the defendants participated in different ways, in different places, at different times and claimed a different sale price from customers), or alternatively must the entire policy including the damage caused be common? Case C-352/13 *Cartel Damage Claims Hydrogen Peroxide SA (CDC) v Evonik Degussa GmbH and others* (CJEU, 21 May 2015) paras 21–5 held that a finding of a single infringement of EU competition law suffices to establish a close connection in the sense of art 8(1) Brussels I Regulation (recast), even if the implementation of that common infringement diverged.

(2) Same situation in law As regards the second element of an irreconcilable decision in the sense of art 8(1) Brussels I Regulation (recast), it seems useful to distinguish between two cases. First, a divergence in law may be caused by the applicability of different substantive laws on the claims against the anchor defendant and the co-defendant (eg a tort law claim based on English law against the anchor defendant and French law against the co-defendant). Second, a divergence in law may also be caused by different legal bases for the actions against the anchor defendants and the co-defendant (eg one claim based on contract and the other on tort).

For a divergence due to the applicability of different substantive laws, the ECJ originally took the view that the application of different national laws to claims against co-defendants necessarily excludes a finding of the same situation in law, as potentially diverging judgments will be based on different substantive laws (Case C-539/03 *Roche Nederland BV and Others v Frederick Primus and Milton Goldenberg* [2006] ECR I-6535, paras 30, 31, 35). However, such a formalistic view disregards that the applicable laws may be fully or at least partially harmonized. Moreover, it fails to take into account that inconsistencies between two judgments may result not from the different applicable substantive laws (which may use comparable or even identical concepts), but rather from a different appraisal of the facts by two distinct courts. Accordingly, it seems more convincing to say that different national laws being applicable to claims against co-defendants should not in itself be an obstacle to invoking jurisdiction under art 8(1) Brussels I Regulation (recast). Rather, whether the application of different national laws against various co-defendants excludes the finding of the same situation in law will depend on an analysis of the individual case, with 'substantially identical' national laws on which the claims are based against the co-defendants supporting the finding of the same situation in law (Case C-145/10 *Eva-Maria Painer v Standard Verlags GmbH and others* [2011] ECR I-12533, paras 80–82. For examples where identity may be presumed see Christian Heinze, 'Article 2:206: Multiple Defendants' in European Max Planck Group on Conflict of Laws in Intellectual Property (ed), *Conflict of Laws in Intellectual Property: The CLIP Principles and Commentary* (OUP 2013) 2:206.C17–2:206.C18, pp 103, 110–11). In its most recent Case C-352/13 *Cartel Damage Claims Hydrogen Peroxide SA (CDC) v Evonik Degussa GmbH and others* (CJEU, 21 May 2015) paras 23–4, the ECJ went still further and held that

> even in the case where various laws are, by virtue of the rules of private international law of the court seised, applicable to the actions . . . , such a difference in legal basis does not, in itself, preclude the application of [art 8(1) Brussels I Regulation (recast)], provided that it was foreseeable by the defendants that they might be sued in the Member State where at least one of them is domiciled.

The latter condition of foreseeability 'is fulfilled in the case of a binding decision of the Commission finding there to have been a single infringement of EU law'.

A similar flexibility can be observed in the second category of possible legal divergences, ie in the scenario where the actions against anchor defendant and co-defendants are founded on different bases in substantive law (eg claims in contract and tort). For such a scenario, the ECJ has held that the identity of legal bases of action against the co-defendants 'is only one relevant factor among others' (Case C-645/11 *Land Berlin v Ellen Mirjam Sapir and others* [2013] ECLI:EU:C:2013:228, para 44; contra Case C-51/97 *Réunion européenne SA v Spliethoff's Bevrachtingskantoor BV* [1998] ECR I-6511, para 50). Even if the claims are based on different legal bases, such as tort and → unjust enrichment, the same situation in law may be found if all claims against the co-defendants 'are directed at the same interest', such as the repayment of an erroneously transferred surplus amount (Case C-645/11 *Land Berlin v Ellen Mirjam Sapir and others* [2013] ECLI:EU:C:2013:228, para 47). Other often-cited (but not automatic) examples of the same situation in law are co-defendants who are jointly liable or a situation where the outcome of one claim is dependent on the outcome of the other (eg secondary liability).

(3) Limits Finally, art 8(1) Brussels I Regulation (recast) does not 'allow a plaintiff to make a claim against a number of defendants for the sole purpose of removing one of them from the jurisdiction of the courts of the Member State in which that defendant is domiciled' (Case C-103/05 *Reisch Montage v Kiesel Baumaschinen* [2006] ECR I-6827, para 32; Case C-145/10 *Eva-Maria Painer v Standard Verlags GmbH and others* [2011] ECR I-12533, para 78). While the contours of this exception are not fully clear, it seems to cover in particular cases where the jurisdiction based on art 8(1) Brussels I Regulation (recast) derives from an abuse of rights, such as deliberately delaying the formal conclusion of an out-of-court settlement with the anchor defendant until after proceedings have been instituted against the non-domiciled co-defendants (for discussion of such a scenario see Case C-352/13 *Cartel Damage Claims Hydrogen Peroxide SA (CDC) v Evonik Degussa GmbH and others* (CJEU, 21 May 2015) paras 26–32).

CHRISTIAN HEINZE

(4) Scope of jurisdiction Provided that the actions against the co-defendants are closely connected, according to a widely-held view art 8(1) Brussels I Regulation (recast) allows bringing proceedings against all co-defendants in the court where any one of them is domiciled. If this general rule were applied without any restriction, it could lead to overly broad jurisdiction over non-resident co-defendants where the action against the resident anchor defendant may be manifestly inadmissible. In the scenario of procedural inadmissibility of the action against the anchor defendant, a risk of irreconcilable judgments simply does not arise because the action against the anchor defendant will be judged inadmissible and thus rejected for (procedural) reasons unrelated to the other actions. Contrary to what the ECJ seems to suggest (Case C-103/05 *Reisch Montage v Kiesel Baumaschinen* [2006] ECR I-6827, para 31), jurisdiction under art 8(1) Brussels I Regulation (recast) should thus be excluded if the anchor claim is manifestly inadmissible (Christian Heinze, 'Article 2:206: Multiple Defendants' in European Max Planck Group on Conflict of Laws in Intellectual Property (ed), *Conflict of Laws in Intellectual Property: The CLIP Principles and Commentary* (OUP 2013) 2:206. C23, pp 103, 114–15).

b) Other jurisdictions
(1) Japan A rule very similar to art 8(1) Brussels I Regulation (recast) can be found in → Japan. Arts 3–6 of the Japanese Civil Procedure Code (Act No 109 of 26 June 26 1996) as amended by the new Japanese Act on International Jurisdiction 2011 (Japanese Act on International Jurisdiction, 'Act for the Partial Amendment of the Code of Civil Procedure and the Civil Interim Relief Act', adopted on 28 April 2011 and promulgated on 2 May 2011) states that where 'two or more claims are made jointly in a single action and the courts of Japan have jurisdiction over only one of them, then the action may be filed with the courts of Japan only if that particular claim over which the jurisdiction exists has a close connection with the other claims'. For actions against different defendants, this jurisdiction is subject to 'cases described in the first sentence of article 38'. This provision, in turn, sets out that

> two or more persons may sue or be sued as joint parties where the rights or obligations which constitute the subject matter of the action are common to all of them or are based on the same legal and factual grounds. The same shall apply where the rights or obligations which constitute the subject matter of the action are of the same type and are based on the same type of legal and factual grounds. (Koji Takahashi, *Japan's New Act on International Jurisdiction* (Smashwords 2011) 9)

Furthermore, a commentator explains that a joint and several obligation is an example of 'obligations which . . . are common to all of [the parties]' (art 38 Japanese Act on International Jurisdiction) and an obligation of joint tortfeasors is an example of 'obligations which . . . are based on the same legal and factual grounds' (art 38 Japanese Act on International Jurisdiction; Koji Takahashi, *Japan's New Act on International Jurisdiction* (Smashwords 2011) 9).

(2) USA By contrast, US law seems reluctant to conclude that a non-resident defendant without an affiliation to a forum state should be subject to personal jurisdiction in that state on the basis of a close connection between a claim against the non-resident defendant and a claim against a resident defendant. This reluctance is grounded in the understanding that the due process requirements of *International Shoe Co v Washington*, 326 U.S. 310, 316 (1945) – ie that 'in order to subject a defendant to a judgment in personam . . . he have certain minimum contacts with it' – 'must be met as to each defendant over whom a state exercises jurisdiction' (*Rush v Savchuk*, 444 U.S. 320, 332 (1980)). For instance, in *Asahi Metal Industries Co v Superior Court* (480 U.S. 102 (1987)), the Supreme Court denied jurisdiction of the Californian courts for an indemnification action between Taiwanese and Japanese companies, which originated from a product liability claim for an accident in California. More recently, the Court stated in *J McIntyre Machinery Ltd v Nicastro* (564 U.S. (2011), No 09-1343 (27 June 2011)) that there will be no exercise of judicial power 'unless the defendant purposefully avails itself of the privilege of conducting activities within the forum State, thus invoking the benefits and protections of its laws', while 'it is the defendant's actions, not his expectations, that empower a State's courts to subject him to judgment' (*J McIntyre Machinery Ltd v Nicastro*, 564 U.S. (2011), No 09-1343 (27 June 2011) p 8). Seemingly, this is

a more stringent standard than European law requires, where mere foreseeability of jurisdiction for the defendants arguably suffices. In consequence, the concept of jurisdiction based on a 'conspiracy theory' or other forms of pendent party personal jurisdiction is largely seen with scepticism, arguing that 'the theory looks to the contacts of the conspiracy, rather than to the contacts of each conspirator' (Stuart M Riback, 'The Long Arm and Multiple Defendants: The Conspiracy Theory of In Personam Jurisdiction' (1984) 84 Colum.L.Rev. 506, 510; see also Peter Hay, Patrick Borchers and Symeon Symeonides, *Conflict of Laws* (5th edn, West Academic Publishing 2010) 523).

II. Law applicable to joint liability

1. Concept

In the following, the term 'joint liability' will be understood in a broad sense, comprising both liability of joint tortfeasors for a jointly committed tort (joint liability) and liability of tortfeasors acting independently who are concurrently liable for the same damage (joint and several liability, for the traditional distinction see Simon Deakin, Angus Johnston and Basil Markesinis, *Tort Law* (7th edn, Clarendon Press 2013) 880). For the purposes of choice of law, joint liability raises essentially two issues. First, it has to be decided whether more than one person is liable for the damage caused to the victim, ie whether joint liability exists, and whether the victim is entitled to claim the whole compensation from a single co-tortfeasor. This issue, ie the external relationship of the group of tortfeasors in relation to the victim(s), is governed by the same law which governs the liability of each individual tortfeasor. Once liability of the group of tortfeasors is established, a second issue arises, namely which law is to govern the internal relationship between the joint tortfeasors. This issue arises most commonly when one tortfeasor has compensated the victim and seeks to claim contribution from the fellow tortfeasors. The doctrinal instrument for such contribution may vary, depending on the tort in question and the national law applicable to it (in detail Koji Takahashi, *Claims for Contribution and Reimbursement in an International Context* (OUP 2000) 7–18). For instance, contribution between fellow tortfeasors may be effected via a → *cessio legis* (ie an *ex lege* assignment of the victim's claim against the co-tortfeasors to the tortfeasor who has paid the victim).

Alternatively contribution may be effected in the form of a right of the co-tortfeasor who has paid the victim to claim from the victim assignment of the victim's claims against the co-tortfeasors. This leads to a substitution of the victim as creditor of the claim by the paying co-tortfeasor, ie to subrogation whereby the paying tortfeasor acquires the right to enforce the victim's right. Moreover, contribution may also be achieved by creating a separate cause of action which is unrelated to the original tort claims of the victim against the other co-tortfeasors, and arises either by virtue of the fact that one co-tortfeasor has compensated the victim, or by the general law of restitution or → *negotiorum gestio*.

2. Purpose

The rules on joint liability are a necessary consequence of the fact that more than one party may be liable for the same damage. In such a situation, the law has to determine whether the entire damage may be claimed from each single tortfeasor and what effect payment of one co-tortfeasor has on the obligation of the fellow perpetrators. More specifically, the rules on contribution seek to ensure that the burden of compensating the victim does not fall arbitrarily on the co-tortfeasor the victim happens to pursue first. Rather, by creating a right of contribution between the co-tortfeasors, it is ensured that the burden of compensation is distributed according to their respective share in causing or bearing responsibility for the damage.

3. Current regulation

a) EU law

For EU private international law, art 15(a) Rome II provides that '[t]he law applicable to non-contractual obligations under this Regulation (as determined by arts 4–14 Rome II) shall govern in particular: (a) the basis and extent of liability, including the determination of persons who may be held liable for acts performed by them'. Article 15(a) Rome II Regulation thus makes clear that the law applicable to the external relationship between each debtor (typically each co-tortfeasor) and the creditor (typically the victim) is the law applicable under the general conflict rules of arts 4–14 Rome II Regulation. This not only concerns the existence of liability in the relationship of tortfeasor and victim, but the expression 'extent of liability' in art 15(a)

Rome II Regulation 'also includes division of liability between joint perpetrators' (European Commission, 'Proposal for a Regulation of the European Parliament and the Council on the Law Applicable to Non-Contractual Obligations ("Rome II")' COM(2003) 427 final, 23; see also art 15(b) Rome II Regulation 'division of liability' and art 15(g) Rome II Regulation 'liability for the acts of another person'). Thus, art 15 Rome II Regulation makes clear that the existence of liability ('persons . . . liable') and the question whether liability is joint and several or merely several and, if so, to which extent each debtor is liable to the victim ('division of liability') is governed by the law applicable to the non-contractual obligation between creditor and each debtor (eg victim and each co-tortfeasor) as determined by arts 4–14 Rome II Regulation (Andrew Dickinson, *The Rome II Regulation: The Law Applicable to Non-Contractual Obligations* (OUP 2008) para 14.17).

(1) External relationship as towards the creditor   In most cases, the application of the law as determined by arts 4–14 Rome II Regulation to existence and division of liability between co-tortfeasors will be unproblematic, as the law applicable to the claims against all co-tortfeasors will be governed by the same law because the relevant → connecting factor is the same for each claim. If an accident occurred in state A in which both B and C injured D, then the law of the country A where the damage occurred (art 4(1) Rome II Regulation) will govern both the existence and the extent of liability of B and C as towards D. However, the situation becomes more complicated if the law applicable to the claims against each co-tortfeasor is different because conflict rules apply a connecting factor different from the (common) place of the injury (eg art 4(2), (3) Rome II Regulation). If, in our example, both tortfeasor B and victim D are habitually resident in state S, but co-tortfeasor C is not, then the law applicable to the delictual claim of victim D against B is governed by the law of state S (art 4(2) Rome II Regulation), whereas the claim against C is still governed by the law of the place of damage, ie the law of state A. In such a scenario, the question arises whether potential privileges of tortfeasor B against victim D under the law of state S should also affect the rights of victim D against tortfeasor C under the law of state A.

Whereas privileges of single debtors will normally only have effect on the level of substantive law and thus not influence the rights of the victim against a co-tortfeasor under a different law, it is debatable whether some substantive law privileges should be effective already on the level of choice of law. In the field of intellectual property law, for example, such an effect has been proposed for the safe harbour provisions for certain intermediaries under arts 12–15 of the e-Commerce Directive (Directive 2000/31/EC of the European Parliament and of the Council of 8 June 2000 on certain legal aspects of information society services, in particular electronic commerce, in the Internal Market (Directive on electronic commerce) [2000] OJ L178/1) or 17 U.S.C. § 512 (see art 3:604 of the CLIP Principles (European Max Planck Group on Conflict of Laws in Intellectual Property, *Conflict of Laws in Intellectual Property: The CLIP Principles and Commentary* (OUP 2013)). As a result of the application of the law of the country for which protection is claimed (art 8(1) Rome II Regulation), intermediaries such as Internet service providers, in scenarios where an infringement occurs in ubiquitous media and protection may be claimed for several countries, may find themselves confronted with a multitude of different laws, which may make it difficult to ascertain the limits of their potential secondary liability. For this reason, art 3:604(2) CLIP Principles, subject to certain substantive minimum standards (art 3:604(3) CLIP Principles: liability for failure to react in case of actual knowledge or a manifest case of infringement and liability for active inducement), provides the following:

> [i]n case of facilities or services being offered or rendered that are capable of being used for infringing and non-infringing purposes by a multitude of users without intervention of the person offering or rendering the facilities or services in relation to the individual acts resulting in infringement, the law applicable to the liability of that person is the law of the State where the centre of gravity of her/his activities relating to those facilities or services is located.

In view of the ever-increasing delocalization of computing processes and the importance of the services of Internet intermediaries, it remains to be seen whether this or similar proposals for a concentration on single law will mature into binding choice-of-law rules.

(2) Internal relationship between co-debtors   While the external relationship of each joint debtor as towards the creditor is governed by

the law applicable to their relationship under arts 4–14 Rome II Regulation, the law which governs the internal relationship between several debtors who are liable for the same claim is determined by art 20 Rome II Regulation (for non-contractual claims) and art 16, 1st sentence Rome I Regulation (for contractual claims). Under the heading 'Multiple Liability', art 20 Rome II Regulation provides:

> [i]f a creditor has a claim against several debtors who are liable for the same claim, and one of the debtors has already satisfied the claim in whole or in part, the question of that debtor's right to demand compensation from the other debtors shall be governed by the law applicable to that debtor's non-contractual obligation towards the creditor.

As the difference in wording between art 20 Rome II Regulation (art 16, 1st sentence Rome I Regulation) and its predecessor in art 13(2) Rome Convention on the law applicable to contractual obligations (consolidated version), [1998] OJ C 27/34 (which had been the original model for the Rome II Regulation in the European Commission, 'Proposal for a Regulation of the European Parliament and the Council on the Law Applicable to Non-Contractual Obligations ("Rome II")' COM(2003) 427 final) makes clear, the provisions cover all possible forms of contribution between jointly liable debtors ('debtor's right to demand'), irrespective of their legal basis (eg → *cessio legis*, subrogation, separate cause of action, restitution or → *negotiorum gestio*), and not only – as under art 19 Rome II (art 15 Rome I) – those 'rights which the creditor had against the debtor' (see the clarifying proposal by the Hamburg Group for Private international law, 'Comments on the European Commission's Draft Proposal for a Council Regulation on the Law Applicable to Non-Contractual Obligations' (2003) 67 RabelsZ 1, 49–50). Therefore, art 20 Rome II (art 16 Rome I) is *lex specialis* to arts 10, 11 Rome II Regulation for compensation claims based on restitution or → *negotiorum gestio* (Tim W Dornis, 'Contribution and Indemnification among Joint Tortfeasors in Multi-State Conflict Cases: A Study of Doctrine and the Current Law in the US and Under the Rome II Regulation' (2008) 4 J Priv Int L 237, 244). Moreover, the existence of a specific provision for compensation claims in art 20 Rome II rules out that such claims can generally be regarded as internationally mandatory provisions in the sense of art 16 Rome II Regulation (Andrew Dickinson, *The Rome II Regulation: The Law Applicable to Non-Contractual Obligations* (OUP 2008) para 14.120).

Article 20 Rome II Regulation states that the right of the debtor (co-tortfeasor) who first paid the creditor (victim) to demand compensation from the other debtors is governed by the same law which governs the first payer's non-contractual obligation towards the creditor under arts 4–14 Rome II Regulation, in short: the (first) payer's law applies. The application of the payer's law is commonly justified by the fact that debtors who pay first are in a worse position than the other debtors because they run the risk of non-payment on their contribution claims. Moreover, the application of the payer's law may even result in a 'race to payment', which would be beneficial for the creditor. Furthermore, it may be argued that '[c]ontribution between several debtors is only a question of distributing non-contractual liability towards the creditor' and thus 'closely related to that liability' (Hamburg Group for Private international law, 'Comments on the European Commission's Draft Proposal for a Council Regulation on the Law Applicable to Non-Contractual Obligations' (2003) 67 RabelsZ 1, 49–50; critical as to these justifications Tim W Dornis, 'Contribution and Indemnification among Joint Tortfeasors in Multi-State Conflict Cases: A Study of Doctrine and the Current Law in the US and Under the Rome II Regulation' (2008) 4 J Priv Int L 237, 252–3, 264). Article 20 Rome II Regulation therefore departs from other approaches to contribution claims which were proposed prior to the Rome II Regulation, namely the general application of the law of the place of the damage (*lex loci delicti*) or the application of the non-paying debtor's law (at least for the content, defences and discharges for reasons of debtor protection) or even a cumulative application of all laws applicable to the non-contractual obligation of the joint debtors (for references on these approaches in older case-law and doctrine see Tim W Dornis, 'Contribution and Indemnification among Joint Tortfeasors in Multi-State Conflict Cases: A Study of Doctrine and the Current Law in the US and Under the Rome II Regulation' (2008) 4 J Priv Int L 237, 251–5; Anna-Lisa Kühn, *Die gestörte Gesamtschuld im Internationalen Privatrecht* (Mohr Siebeck 2008) 143–9).

In order to arrive at the application of the 'first payer's law', two conditions must be met.

First, all debtors between which contribution is claimed must be liable for the 'same claim', and second, the debtor claiming contribution must have 'already satisfied the claim [of the creditor] in whole or in part'. As the words 'debtors who are liable for the same claim' make clear, art 20 Rome II Regulation applies only to cases where the debtors are directly and jointly liable to the creditor (Ivo Bach 'Art. 20' in Peter Huber (ed), *Rome II Regulation: Pocket Commentary* (Sellier European Law Publishers 2011) para 3). The provision covers neither the rights for payment on the claim of a third party who is not a debtor of the original claim (this scenario falls under art 19 Rome II Regulation), nor is art 20 Rome II Regulation concerned with only several liability. Liability for the 'same claim' does not require that the same law governs the claims against all debtors (in such a situation, art 20 Rome II Regulation is not needed; see also art 16, 2nd sentence Rome I Regulation). Rather, 'same claim' means that the obligations of the individual debtors are on equal footing (not one debtor being primarily liable, such as tortfeasor and insurer, a scenario which falls under art 19 Rome II Regulation) and that the 'creditor's interest [can be] discharged by one of them' (see Report on the Convention on the law applicable to contractual obligations by Mario Giuliano, Professor, University of Milan, and Paul Lagarde, Professor, University of Paris I, [1980] OJ C 282/1 35), ie the creditor can only claim payment once because the debtors are liable for the same damage (Abbo Junker, 'Art 20 VO (EG) 864/2007' in Franz Jürgen Säcker and Roland Rixecker (eds), *Münchener Kommentar zum Bürgerlichen Gesetzbuch*, vol 10 (6th edn, CH Beck 2015) para 11).

The second condition, namely that the debtor has 'already satisfied the claim in whole or in part' raises the issue which law applies to a right of contribution prior to payment of a debtor. While it may be conceivable to treat a claim to contribution before payment as an aspect of 'division of liability' in the sense of art 15(b) Rome II Regulation, and therefore apply the same law which governs the non-contractual obligation towards the creditor (victim) (Andrew Dickinson, *The Rome II Regulation – The Law Applicable to Non-Contractual Obligations* (OUP 2008) para 14.119), the distinction between the external and internal relationship of co-tortfeasors and the proximity to art 19 Rome II Regulation argues in favour of applying art 20 Rome II Regulation by analogy (Abbo Junker, 'Art 20 VO (EG) 864/2007' in Franz Jürgen Säcker and Roland Rixecker (eds), *Münchener Kommentar zum Bürgerlichen Gesetzbuch*, vol 10 (6th edn, CH Beck 2015) para 12). In consequence, a claim to contribution which arises already before one debtor has partially satisfied the creditor should be governed by the same law which would apply if the debtor had already paid (Ivo Bach 'Art. 20' in Peter Huber (ed), *Rome II Regulation: Pocket Commentary* (Sellier European Law Publishers 2011) para 9 proposes to apply the law of the debtor 'most likely [to] be the one who satisfies the creditor', eg because this debtor has already been sued by the creditor). If compensation claims are pursued successively, eg first debtor A pays full compensation to victim V, then seeks compensation from debtor B and debtor B from debtor C, both debtors A and B have 'satisfied' the creditor, leading to the law governing the obligation V – A being applicable to A's compensation claim against B, and the law governing the obligation between A and B (the same as V – A) governing the compensation claim between B and C (Ivo Bach 'Art. 20' in Peter Huber (ed), *Rome II Regulation: Pocket Commentary* (Sellier European Law Publishers 2011) para 11).

(3) Choice of law and escape clause As a result of the application of the first payer's law under art 20 Rome II Regulation (art 16 Rome I Regulation), a → choice of law between creditor and paying debtor under art 14 Rome II Regulation would also change the law applicable to the contribution claims against the co-debtors. However, as an agreement under art 14 Rome II Regulation 'shall not prejudice the rights of third parties' (art 14(1), 2nd sentence Rome II Regulation), the position of the other co-debtors may not be adversely affected by a choice of law between creditor and paying debtor. In contrast to proposals made during the legislative debates on Rome II Regulation (see Hamburg Group for Private international law, 'Comments on the European Commission's Draft Proposal for a Council Regulation on the Law Applicable to Non-Contractual Obligations' (2003) 67 RabelsZ 1, 49–50), art 20 Rome II does not provide for an → escape clause (Tim W Dornis, 'Contribution and Indemnification among Joint Tortfeasors in Multi-State Conflict Cases: A Study of Doctrine and the Current Law in the US and Under the Rome II Regulation' (2008) 4 J Priv

Int L 237, 276 argues in favour of an application of art 4(2) and (3) Rome II Regulation by analogy). This omission can become acute if there is a special relationship between the co-debtors (eg contract, liability of company and director as towards third parties). However, such a special relationship is not entirely irrelevant, in that even if it fails to meet the requirements for a choice of law agreement under art 14 Rome II Regulation, it might still be of relevance on the level of applicable substantive law (see Manfred Wandt, 'Zum Rückgriff im Internationalen Privatrecht' (1987) 86 ZVglRWiss 272, 287–9).

(4) Privileges of a single debtor A particular problem arises if one of several 'jointly' liable debtors is by law exempt from or privileged in liability as towards the creditor (eg an employee as towards employer) under the law applicable to their non-contractual obligation as towards the creditor. In such a situation, basically two questions need to be answered: (i) is this privilege also effective for the contribution claim of the (first) paying debtor against the non-paying (privileged) debtor, and (ii) does the privilege, provided that it is effective, have any effect on the claims of the creditor against the (first) paying (non-privileged) debtor? For question (i), art 16, 2nd sentence Rome I Regulation seems to offer a solution, preserving the defences of the non-paying debtor applicable under the law governing their obligation as towards the creditor also against the contribution claim, when it states '[t]he other debtors may rely on the defences they had against the creditor to the extent allowed by the law governing their obligations towards the creditor'. Unfortunately, the wording of art 20 Rome II Regulation has not been aligned with art 16 Rome I Regulation, raising uncertainty whether the same solution may be applied to the Rome II Regulation (Tim W Dornis, 'Contribution and Indemnification among Joint Tortfeasors in Multi-State Conflict Cases: A Study of Doctrine and the Current Law in the US and Under the Rome II Regulation' (2008) 4 J Priv Int L 237, 275 argues for an application of the non-paying tortfeasor's law to bars to tort liability and/or contribution which is to be achieved by 'thoughtful construction'). Provided that question (i) is answered in the affirmative, ie if the privileged debtor may rely on their defence against the contribution claim of the paying debtor, then the question arises whether the liability of the first paying debtor as towards the creditor ought to be reduced. This, it would seem, is difficult in most cases as the law stands today, because the external liability of the first paying debtor as towards the creditor is governed by the law determined under arts 4–14 Rome II Regulation between these two parties, while the privilege of the other debtor derives from the law governing his obligation as towards the creditor. Thus, the privilege between the non-paying debtor and the creditor does not apply to the relationship between paying debtor and creditor. Nevertheless, a reduction in liability even of the paying (non-privileged) debtor as towards the creditor might come into play if the applicable law between creditor and paying debtor allows for a comparable reduction of the debtor's liability towards the creditor where the contribution claim of the paying debtor is (partially) barred.

b) US law
Until the 1960s, it was almost the unanimous view in the USA that the claim to contribution between joint tortfeasors should be governed by the *lex loci delicti* (see *Cooney v Osgood Machinery, Inc*, 81 N.Y.2d 66, 71–2 (1993) with references). In a similar manner, § 173 Restatement (Second) of Conflict of Laws (American Law Institute, Restatement of the Law, Second: Conflict of Laws 2d, St. Paul 1971; → Restatement (First and Second) of Conflict of Laws) confirmed that the contribution claims are governed by the same law which applies to the tort claims when it states '[t]he law selected by application of the rule of § 145 Restatement (Second) of Conflict of Laws [ie the general principle on the law applicable to torts] determines whether one tortfeasor has a right to contribution or indemnity against another tortfeasor'. However, the comments on § 173 Restatement (Second) of Conflict of Laws already take a slightly different stance: while comment a to § 173 Restatement (Second) of Conflict of Laws confirms that – to date (1971/72) – most courts 'have held that the question of contribution between joint tortfeasors is determined by the local law of the state of conduct and injury', the comment proposes also to apply in the future the 'local law of this state . . . unless some other state has a greater interest in the determination of the particular issue'. Such a 'greater interest' may exist if both tortfeasors are domiciled in the same state or 'if this state would have the greatest interest in the issue of

contribution and that its local law should be applied'. This more flexible analysis of state and party interests in conflict-of-laws cases had consequences for contribution claims. For example, New York courts began to distinguish between conduct-regulating rules, which continued to be governed by the *lex loci delicti*, and loss-allocating rules for the situation after a tort had occurred which were subjected to a different regime, the so-called *Neumeier-rules* (*Neumeier v Kuehner*, 31 N.Y.2d 121, 128 (1972); for the New York conflict rule *Allianz Insurance Company v Otero*, 353 F.Supp.2d 415, 422–3 (SDNY 2004)). The conflict rules on contribution between co-tortfeasors were characterized as loss-allocating rules, making it necessary to engage in an evaluation of the 'relative interests of jurisdictions with conflicting laws' (*Cooney v Osgood Machinery, Inc*, 81 N.Y.2d 66, 75 (1993)). If the parties share the same domicile, such an evaluation points to the application of their common domicile's loss distribution law, including the rules on contribution (*Cooney v Osgood Machinery, Inc*, 81 N.Y.2d 66, 74 (1993)). If, however, the parties lack a common domicile, the matter becomes more complicated, in particular if the interests of the respective jurisdictions involved diverge. In a case where an accident occurred to a Missouri employee in a Missouri plant, the New York Court of Appeals turned to the criterion of 'protection of the reasonable expectations' of both parties. The court held that the supplier of deficient products from New York who has been held liable by the employee cannot reasonably expect that contribution will be available against his co-tortfeasor, the employer of the injured employee. This is because the employer is shielded under Missouri law from liability as towards his employee if the employee obtained workers' compensation benefits (*Cooney v Osgood Machinery, Inc*, 81 N.Y.2d 66, 77–8 (1993)). In sum, it seems that conflict rules of US states on tort contribution claims apparently refer in the majority of cases still to the *lex loci delicti* as a default rule. An exception is made if the co-tortfeasors have a common domicile or if 'extraordinary substantive law purposes require a different finding' (Tim W Dornis, 'Contribution and Indemnification among Joint Tortfeasors in Multi-State Conflict Cases: A Study of Doctrine and the Current Law in the US and Under the Rome II Regulation' (2008) 4 J Priv Int L 237, 250 with further references).

CHRISTIAN HEINZE

Literature

Jürgen Basedow and Christian Heinze, 'Kartellrechtliche Schadensersatzklagen im europäischen Gerichtsstand der Streitgenossenschaft (Art. 6 Nr. 1 EuGVO)' in Stefan Bechtold and others (eds), *Festschrift zum 70. Geburtstag von Wernhard Möschel* (Nomos 2011) 63; Andrew Dickinson, *The Rome II Regulation: The Law Applicable to Non-Contractual Obligations* (OUP 2008); Tim W Dornis, 'Contribution and Indemnification among Joint Tortfeasors in Multi-State Conflict Cases: A Study of Doctrine and the Current Law in the US and Under the Rome II Regulation' (2008) 4 J Priv Int L 237; Hamburg Group for Private international law, 'Comments on the European Commission's Draft Proposal for a Council Regulation on the Law Applicable to Non-Contractual Obligations' (2003) 67 RabelsZ 1; Peter Hay, Patrick Borchers and Symeon Symeonides, *Conflict of Laws* (5th edn, West Academic Publishing 2010); Christian Heinze, 'Article 2:206: Multiple Defendants' in European Max Planck Group on Conflict of Laws in Intellectual Property (ed), *Conflict of Laws in Intellectual Property: The CLIP Principles and Commentary* (OUP 2013) 103; Abbo Junker, 'Art 20 VO (EG) 864/2007' in Franz Jürgen Säcker and Roland Rixecker (eds), *Münchener Kommentar zum Bürgerlichen Gesetzbuch*, vol 10 (6th edn, CH Beck 2015); Anna-Lisa Kühn, *Die gestörte Gesamtschuld im Internationalen Privatrecht* (Mohr Siebeck 2008); Nils Lund, *Der Gerichtsstand der Streitgenossenschaft im europäischen Zivilprozessrecht* (Mohr Siebeck 2014); Stuart M Riback, 'The Long Arm and Multiple Defendants: The Conspiracy Theory of In Personam Jurisdiction' (1984) 84 Colum.L.Rev. 506; Koji Takahashi, *Claims for Contribution and Reimbursement in an International Context* (OUP 2000); Koji Takahashi, *Japan's New Act on International Jurisdiction* (Smashwords 2011); Zheng Sophia Tang, 'European Jurisdiction in Multiple Defendant Litigation' (2009) 34 E.L.Rev. 80; Matthias Weller, 'Kartellprivatrechtliche Klagen im Europäischen Prozessrecht: "Private Enforcement" und die Brüssel I-VO' (2013) 112 ZVglRWiss 89.

Names of individuals

I. Background and justification

A person's name is a constituent element of their identity and their private life (Case C-208/09 *Ilonka Sayn-Wittgenstein v Landeshauptmann von Wien* [2010] ECR I-13693, henceforth C-208/09 *Sayn-Wittgenstein*). At the European level, a person's name is protected by art 7 EU Charter of Fundamental Rights (Charter of Fundamental Rights of the European Union of 18 December 2000, [2000] OJ C 364/1 (consolidated version 2012/C 326/02, [2012] OJ C 326/391)) and by art 8 ECHR (European Convention of 4 November 1950 for the Protection of Human Rights and Fundamental Freedoms, 213 UNTS 221). Note that art 8(1) ECHR refers only in general terms to the right of a person's 'private life', without providing for any specific definition ('Everyone has the right to respect for his private and family life, his home and his correspondence'). In *Niemietz v Germany* ((1992) Series A no 251-B, para 29), the ECHR stated that the notion of 'private life' should not be restricted to an 'inner circle' but also comprise to a certain degree the right to establish and develop relationships with other human beings. Regarding names, the ECHR in *Burghartz v Switzerland* ((1994) Series A no 280-B, para 24; *Guillot v France* (1996-V) 1593, para 21) clarified that a person's name as 'a means of personal identification and of linking to a family concerns their private and family life'. This notion was not excluded by the fact that both society and the state have an interest in regulating the use of names, 'since these public-law aspects are compatible with private life conceived of as including ... the right to establish and develop relationships with other human beings, in professional or business contexts as in others'. However, noting that names retain a crucial role in the identification of people, the ECHR accepted that there may be reasons resulting from public interests that force states to restrict the right of names (see *Stjerna v Finland* (1994) Series A no 299-B, para 39).

II. Conflict of laws

Unlike certain matters concerning family law, eg divorce (→ Divorce and personal separation), maintenance, → matrimonial property regimes as well as the law of → succession, the law of names has not so far been the subject of 'measures for the approximation of the laws and regulations of the Member States' according to art 81(1), (2) TFEU (The Treaty on the Functioning of the European Union (consolidated version), [2012] OJ C 326/47). As the ECJ stated in *Garcia Avello* (Case C-148/02 *Carlos Garcia Avello v Belgian State* [2003] ECR I-11613, henceforth C-148/02 *Garcia Avello*), national rules governing a person's name are still matters falling within the Member State competence.

Regarding Member State choice-of-law rules, four different types of → connecting factors may be distinguished. First, for reasons of legal certainty, stability and the regulatory function of a person's name, most European countries, such as → Belgium, → Germany, → Luxembourg, the → Netherlands, → Austria and → Spain, take as the primary connecting factor a person's → nationality or, in the case of spouses, their respective nationalities. The nationality approach is supported by the assumption that a person has the closest connection with the laws of their home country. Second, a small number of states, for example the Nordic countries as well as → Switzerland, take as the leading connecting factor a person's habitual residence or, in the case of spouses, their respective first common habitual residence. Where the habitual residence is concerned, the primary policy objective is integration of a person into the society of their whereabouts and a new environment. It is considered highly likely that a person has the closest ties with the country in which he or she is actually living. Third, there are the common law countries, to be considered separately as falling outside the conflict-of-law systems mentioned so far. Given the absence of substantive law rules pertaining to names, choice-of-law rules that provide how foreign names or the names of foreigners living in Britain are to be dealt with are also lacking. Fourth, some Member States belonging to the Romanic legal sphere, such as → Italy, → France and → Greece, prefer a qualification of names in accordance with family law. That means that a specific operation that is relevant for a change of name due to substantive family law is taken as the primary connecting factor in choice-of-law rules regarding names. Since under substantive law issues regarding the change of names largely arise in family matters, it is considered preferable if connecting factors in those areas are consistent with each other.

As far as → party autonomy is concerned, there are only few states, such as → Germany, → Finland, → Spain and → Switzerland that provide for the, albeit limited, freedom of an individual or spouses to choose the applicable law to their name. Under German law for instance, only spouses are given the possibility to choose the applicable law (art 10(2), (3) Introductory Act to the German Civil Code (Einführungsgesetz zum Bürgerlichen Gesetzbuche of 21 September 1994,

BGBl. I 2494, as amended, henceforth EGBGB)). However, the freedom of the spouses to choose the law applicable to their married name is limited to a number of connecting factors with which they have a close connection. Article 10(2) EGBGB provides that the spouses may designate only the law of any state of which either spouse is a national (no 1) or German law provided that one of them has their habitual residence in Germany (no 2). If spouses adopted a married name and only one of them has the right of custody of a common child (→ Guardianship, custody and parental responsibility), then art 10(3) EGBGB offers this parent the right to confer the married name on the child pursuant to the law of any state of which either parent is a national (no 1) or in accordance with German law, provided that one parent has habitual residence in Germany (no 2) or with the law of any state of which either parent who conferred the name is a national. Allowing spouses to choose the applicable law is deemed to be an adequate solution taking into account the legitimate interests of cross-border couples. It grants spouses the possibility to reconcile the applicable law with their individual circumstances, thereby enhancing legal certainty and foreseeability. Provided they are habitually resident in Germany, couples with foreign nationality may also benefit from the freedom to choose the applicable law pursuant to art 10(2) EGBGB. However, spouses are not allowed to choose the law of the state of their habitual residence.

III. Relationship with other international instruments and EU law

1. International instruments

Regarding international instruments, the Hague Child Protection Convention (Hague Convention of 19 October 1996 on jurisdiction, applicable law, recognition, enforcement and co-operation in respect of parental responsibility and measures for the protection of children, 35 ILM 1391), according to its art 4(c), is notably not applicable to the name and forenames of a child. Furthermore, since 1956 the International Commission on Civil Status (ICCS, → CIEC/ICCS (International Commission on Civil Status) has produced several conventions regarding the law of names. However, concerning conflict of laws, the ICCS Convention of 5 September 1980 on the law applicable to surnames and given names, 1553 UNTS 7 has taken effect only in → Italy, → Portugal, → Spain and the → Netherlands.

2. EU law

a) Preliminary remarks

First, the ECJ in *Garcia Avello* notably stated (C-148/02 *Garcia Avello*, para 25) that the rules governing a person's name are matters falling under current Community law within Member State competence. Moreover, the European legislature has so far adopted no measures in the field of private international law concerning names. However, when exercising their competence Member States must comply with EU law.

Concerning conflict of laws in the field of names, two main principles in the TFEU may be affected: that of non-discrimination (art 18 TFEU) and the right of free movement of EU citizens (art 21 TFEU). The ECJ has issued a number of decisions on both (see below). As far as art 18 TFEU is concerned, its first paragraph provides that '[w]ithin the scope of application of the Treaties, and without prejudice to any special provisions contained therein, any discrimination on grounds of nationality shall be prohibited'. According to settled ECJ case-law 'the principle of non-discrimination requires that comparable situations must not be treated differently and that different situations must not be treated in the same way' (C-148/02 *Garcia Avello*, para 31). Any justification must be based on 'objective considerations' that are independent of a person's nationality and must be proportionate to the objective being legitimately pursued (C-148/02 *Garcia Avello*, para 31; Case C-224/98 *Marie-Nathalie D'Hoop v Office national de l'emploi* [2002] ECR I-6191, para 36). Article 18 TFEU includes both direct discrimination based on nationality and indirect discrimination based on different criteria that, as a result, leads to a factual discrimination of Member State citizens. What is crucial for the application of art 18 TFEU is that the situation concerned falls within the scope of application of the Treaties. The freedom to move and reside within the territory of the Member States, as provided by art 21 TFEU, is of considerable importance in this regard (see C-148/02 *Garcia Avello*, para 24). That does not mean that the scope of art 18 TFEU is extended to pure internal situations. However, as the ECJ clarified in *Garcia Avello*, the necessary link to EU-law at least exists in regard to persons who are nationals of one Member State and who lawfully reside in the territory of another Member State (C-148/02 *Garcia Avello*, para 27).

Regarding the freedom of movement, one has to note that there is a prohibition of restriction laid down in art 21 TFEU. The purpose of art 21 TFEU is the removal of obstacles to the freedom of movement of EU citizens. In this regard, it completes the aim of the EU to build up a European internal market for goods and services. Concerning the law of names, the ECJ in its case-law mainly deals with the issue of whether the refusal by a Member State to recognize the name of a person who is a citizen of another Member State infringes art 21 TFEU.

b) Case-law of the ECJ in the field of a person's name
In its first decision concerning the law of names of individuals (Case C-168/91 *Christos Konstantinidis v Stadt Altensteig – Standesamt and Landratsamt Calw – Ordnungsamt* [1993] ECR I-1191, henceforth C-168/91 *Christos Konstantinidis*), the ECJ had to decide how a Member State which uses the Roman alphabet may transcribe a Greek name in Roman characters in its registers of civil status. The ECJ held that transliteration rules are incompatible with the freedom of establishment (→ Freedom of establishment/persons (European Union) and private international law) laid down in art 52 EEC Treaty (Treaty of 25 March 1957 establishing the European Economic Community, 294–8 UNTS) in so far 'as their application causes a Greek national such a degree of inconvenience as in fact to interfere with his freedom to exercise the right of establishment' (C-168/91 *Christos Konstantinidis*, para 15). In the case at hand *Mr Konstantinides*, a self-employed masseur, was obliged to spell his name, in his business advertisements, in accordance with the transliteration rules used in the registers of civil status, which in turn exposed him to the risk that potential clients might confuse him with other persons. *Konstantinides* remains the sole case where the law of names was assessed in the light of the four fundamental freedoms laid down in the provisions which are now numbered as arts 39 *et seq* TFEU.

The second case of 2003 (C-148/02 *Garcia Avello*) dealt with the name of children of dual nationality. The children of *Mr Garcia Avello* and *Mrs Weber*, born and living in Belgium, had dual Spanish and Belgian nationality. The children had been registered in Belgium under the name of their father, '*Garcia Avello*'. The parents requested the Belgian authorities to change their children's patronymic surname to '*Garcia Weber*', a name composed of the father's and the mother's surname in accordance with well-established practice under Spanish law. By referring to Belgian law, which confers the father's surname on children, the Belgian authorities rejected that suggestion. In the ensuing proceedings, the Conseil d'Etat asked the ECJ whether arts 17 and 18 TEC (Consolidated version of the Treaty establishing the European Community (2002) [2002] OJ C 325/33; arts 18 and 21 TFEU) are to be interpreted as precluding the Belgian administrative authority from refusing that change. Before answering the question for a preliminary ruling, the ECJ made some general observations concerning the scope of the Treaties. The ECJ stated that in the situation at hand the necessary links with EU-Law 'exist in regard to persons in a situation such as that of the children of *Mr Garcia Avello*, who are nationals of one Member State lawfully resident in the territory of another Member State' (C-148/02 *Garcia Avello*, para 27). Concerning the non-discrimination principle laid down in art 18 TFEU, the ECJ pointed out that those Belgian nationals who in addition have the nationality of another Member State are treated differently, under the two legal systems concerned, from persons who have only the Belgian nationality. According to the Court, persons with dual nationalities are often confronted with 'serious inconvenience . . . at both professional and private levels' resulting from the discrepancy in surnames (C-148/02 *Garcia Avello*, para 36). They face considerable difficulties in benefiting, in one of the Member States of which they are a national, from the legal effects of diplomas or documents drawn up in the surname recognized in the other Member State of which they have an additional nationality.

In the wake of *Garcia Avello*, Belgium opted for a purely administrative implementation of the Court's ruling rather than undertaking fundamental legislative reform of its law of names. Such a decision is fully in accordance with European requirements for the following reasons: First, the ECJ decided neither on the Belgian choice-of-law rules nor on the Belgian law of names itself. Instead, the Court only declared an unequal treatment of citizens with dual nationality based on the application of Belgian law to be incompatible with EU law. The question of how to address this matter was left to the discretion of the Belgian state. Second, taking these aspects into consideration, there was no need to give dual nationals a *de facto* right to choose between their respective national laws (note that Spain took the *Garcia*

Avello-judgment as an opportunity to offer individuals with dual nationality such a right to choose). There is no doubt that such a right to choose would be the most suitable way to reconcile the applicable law with the individual circumstances of a person and, therefore, to provide for legal certainty, predictability and flexibility. However, apart from the political significance of the principle of party autonomy in European conflict of laws, it should be borne in mind that the ECJ in *Garcia Avello* did not vote for such a solution.

The decision in *Grunkin and Paul* of 2008 (Case C-353/06 *Stefan Grunkin and Dorothee Regina Paul* [2008] ECR I-7639, henceforth C-353/06 *Grunkin and Paul*) once again dealt with Member State refusal to recognize a child's surname determined and registered in another Member State. The person concerned was born in → Denmark as the German child of two Germans who wanted the child to bear a family name composed of the surnames of both parents (*Grunkin-Paul*). This name was entered into the Danish birth certificate. However, the German authorities refused to recognize that name; relying both on German choice-of-law rules designating the national law of the child, ie German law as the applicable law (art 10 EGBGB), and also on the German law of names (§ 1617(1) German Civil Code (Bürgerliches Gesetzbuch of 2 January 2002, BGBl. I 42, as amended)) that does not provide for surnames composed of the family names of the parents. In the course of the following proceedings, the competent national court decided to stay proceedings asking the ECJ whether, in light of the prohibition on discrimination set out in art 12 TEC (art 18 TFEU) and having regard to the right to the freedom of movement laid down by art 18 TEC (art 21 TFEU), the German provision in art 10 EGBGB was valid in so far as it provides that the law relating to names is governed by nationality alone. Notwithstanding the question for a preliminary ruling, the ECJ did not decide on the German choice-of-law rule as such but rather focused on the non-acceptance of the name *Grunkin-Paul* as being determined and registered in Denmark by the German authorities. Concerning this matter, the ECJ first clarified that the child in question was not being discriminated against on the grounds of nationality (art 18 TFEU). This was because the child and its parents had only German nationality and art 10 EGBGB refers to German substantive law on surnames, so that the determination of the child's surname in Germany was in accordance with German legislation and thus could not constitute discrimination on nationality grounds (C-353/06 *Grunkin and Paul*, paras 20, 21). Dealing with the freedom of movement in art 21 TFEU, the ECJ referred to its judgment in *Garcia Avello* and stated that

> having to use a surname, in the Member State of which the person concerned is a national, that is different from that conferred and registered in the Member State of birth and residence is liable to hamper the exercise of the right, established in [art 21 TFEU], to move and reside freely within the territory of the Member States. (C-353/06 *Grunkin and Paul*, para 22)

Like the child in *Garcia Avello* the child in the present case had to suffer 'serious inconveniences' arising from the discrepancy in surnames that resulted from the fact that it had to bear a different surname in its state of birth and residence and in the state of which it was a national (C-353/06 *Grunkin and Paul*, para 24). The court clarified that every time the child concerned had to prove its identity in Denmark, it risked having to dispel doubts concerning its identity (C-353/06 *Grunkin and Paul*, para 26). The court stressed that in this context it was immaterial that the child concerned had so far suffered no such disadvantages but rather that he could expect such disadvantage in the future. In the wake of this decision, the German legislature, as in Belgium after *Garcia Avello*, initially opted for a purely administrative solution in order to prevent a conflict between EU law and national law. Pursuant to art 21 TFEU, German authorities were obliged to recognize a child's surname that had been determined and registered in another Member State. However, the German legislature established the new art 48 EGBGB with effect from 29 January 2013 (Gesetz zur Anpassung der Vorschriften des Internationalen Privatrechts an die Verordnung (EU) Nr. 1259/2010 und zur Änderung anderer Vorschriften des Internationalen Privatrechts of 23 January 2013, BGBl. I 101), whereby, assuming that German law is applicable, a person has the right to choose a name determined and registered during a period of habitual residence in another Member State, provided that the choice would not be manifestly contrary to → public policy. The declaration made before the registrar must be publicly certified. Note that due to the requirement of the application of German law in many cases, EU citizens without German nationality are unlikely to be able to benefit from that rule.

In its judgment of 22 December 2010 (C-208/09 *Sayn-Wittgenstein*), the ECJ continued to develop its case-law regarding the acceptance of names determined and recognized in other Member States. In the case at hand, an Austrian national living in Germany had acquired the name of *Fürstin von Sayn-Wittgenstein* by adoption. As ever since the end of the Habsburg Monarchy Austrians have been prohibited from bearing noble titles, the Austrian authorities informed the applicant in the main proceedings that her surname had to be corrected in the register of civil status to *Sayn-Wittgenstein*. During the course of review proceedings initiated by the applicant against that decision, the Austrian Verwaltungsgerichtshof referred the following question to the ECJ for a preliminary ruling:

[d]oes Article [21 TFEU] preclude legislation pursuant to which the competent authorities of a Member State refuse to recognise the surname of an (adult) adoptee, determined in another Member State, in so far as it contains a title of nobility which is not permissible under the (constitutional) law of the former Member State?

With regard to the question for a preliminary ruling, the ECJ turned principally to its *Grunkin and Paul* decision (see above). The ECJ held that the case at hand could not be distinguished from the *Grunkin and Paul* judgment in that the applicant in the main proceedings had to suffer the same 'serious inconveniences' within the meaning of *Grunkin and Paul* that result 'from having to alter all the traces of a formal nature of the name *Fürstin von Sayn-Wittgenstein* left in both the public and the private spheres, given that her official identity documents currently refer to her by a different name' (C-208/09 *Sayn-Wittgenstein*, para 67).

Interestingly the applicant in the main proceedings, during the 15 years between the first registration of her surname (following the adoption) in Austria and the decision to correct the name, had been issued in Germany with several official documents, eg a driving licence, and owned a company registered there under the name *Fürstin von Sayn-Wittgenstein*. Moreover, her Austrian passport was extended under the same name during those years. According to the Court, it was accordingly probable that the applicant would be required to produce documents issued or drawn up before the alteration, which show a different surname from that appearing in her new identity documents (C-208/09 *Sayn-Wittgenstein*, para 67). The court pointed to its judgment in *Grunkin and Paul* where in para 28 it had stated that a difference in surnames was liable to give rise to doubts as to the person's identity and the authenticity of the documents submitted or the veracity of their content, and that that risk was such as to hinder the exercise of the right conferred by art 21 TFEU. Even if that risk might not be as grave in the present case as the feared serious inconvenience for the child involved in *Grunkin and Paul*, the ECJ was of the opinion that 'the real risk, in circumstances such as those in the main proceedings, of being obliged because of the discrepancy in names to dispel doubts as to one's identity is such as to hinder the exercise of the right which flows from Art 21 TFEU' (C-208/09 *Sayn-Wittgenstein*, para 70).

However, the ECJ assumed that the restriction on the freedom enjoyed by EU citizens of movement and residence was justified by objective considerations relating to → public policy. In that regard, the ECJ accepted that the Austrian Law on the abolition of the nobility, as an element of national identity, has to be taken into consideration when striking a balance between legitimate interests and the right of free movement of persons recognized under European Union law (C-208/09 *Sayn-Wittgenstein*, para 83). According to the Court, by refusing to recognize the nobility elements of a name such as that of the applicant in the main proceedings, the Austrian authorities 'did not appear to have gone further than is necessary in order to ensure the attainment of the fundamental constitutional objective pursued by them' (C-208/09 *Sayn-Wittgenstein*, para 93).

In its decision *Runevič-Vardyn* (Case C-391/09 *Runevič-Vardyn and Wardyn* [2011] ECR I-3787, henceforth C-391/09 *Runevič-Vardyn*), 18 years after *Konstantinides*, the ECJ again had to deal with the phonetic spelling of a name. A Lithuanian national married a Polish national, and the competent Lithuanian authorities issued a marriage certificate in which the husband's name (*Łukasz Paweł Wardyn*) was transcribed as *Lukasz Pawel Wardyn* by using the characters of the Lithuanian version of the Roman alphabet. His wife's name appears in the form *Malgožata Runevič-Vardyn*, ie also only Lithuanian characters were used and her husband's surname was added to her own surname. Both applicants in the main proceedings submitted requests to the Lithuanian authorities in order to change the entries on the certificates of civil status in question. In doing so, the husband asked to transcribe his forenames on the marriage certificate in a form which complied with the rules governing Polish spelling. The Lithuanian authorities refused this request. In the course of the following proceedings, the First District Court of the City of Vilnius referred several questions to the ECJ for a preliminary ruling. The court wanted to know among others whether in light of art 21(1) TFEU and art 18(1) TFEU Member States were prohibited from providing in national legal rules that forenames and surnames may be written on certificates of civil status using only the characters of the national language of the country of certification. Furthermore, it asked the ECJ whether Member States are precluded from providing in national legal rules that the forenames and surnames of individuals of different origin or nationality must be written on certificates of civil status using just the basic Roman characters and not employing diacritical marks, ligatures or other modifications to the characters of the Roman alphabet which are used in other languages.

Referring to its previous judgments, the ECJ first stated that the rules governing the way in which a person's surname and forename are entered on certificates of civil status are matters

> coming within the competence of the Member States[.] [T]he latter must none the less, when exercising that competence, comply with European Union law, and in particular with the Treaty provisions on the freedom of every citizen of the Union to move and reside in the territory of the Member States. (C-391/09 *Runevič-Vardyn*, para 63)

However, the ECJ eventually denied a restriction of the freedom of movement as provided by art 21 TFEU on a number of grounds. First, concerning the wife's request for her forename and maiden name to be changed on the birth and marriage certificates, the ECJ held that every time a citizen of the EU moves to another Member State and marries a national of that state,

> the fact that the surname which that citizen had prior to marriage, and her forename, cannot be changed and entered in documents relating to civil status issued by her Member State of origin except using the characters of the language of that latter Member State cannot constitute treatment that is less favourable than that which she enjoyed before she availed herself of the opportunities offered by the Treaty in relation to free movement of persons. (C-391/09 *Runevič-Vardyn*, para 69)

Consequently, the absence of such a right cannot be regarded as a restriction of art 21 TFEU. Second, with regard to the couple's request to add, on the marriage certificate, the husband's surname to the maiden name of his wife, the ECJ acknowledged that the fact that, on the marriage certificate, the husband's surname is added to the wife's maiden name in a form which does not correspond to the husband's surname as registered in his Member State of origin might be liable to cause 'serious inconvenience for those concerned at administrative, professional and private levels', according to the ECJ's case-law in *Garcia Avello*, *Grunkin and Paul* and *Sayn-Wittgenstein* (C-391/09 *Runevič-Vardyn*, para 74). However, whether such serious inconveniences arise from the refusal of the competent authorities to amend the husband's surname is a question for the competent national court (C-391/09 *Runevič-Vardyn*, paras 74, 75). Third, regarding the husband's request to have his forenames entered on the marriage certificate in a form compliant with the rules governing Polish spelling, the ECJ was of the opinion that the omission of diacritical marks could 'in itself, cause actual and serious inconvenience for the person concerned, within the meaning of the [court's] case-law . . . as to give rise to doubts as to her identity and the authenticity of the documents submitted by her, or the truthfulness of their content' (C-391/09 *Runevič-Vardyn*, para 81). However, the refusal of the competent authorities of a Member State to amend the marriage certificate of a national of another Member State, in such a way that the forenames of that citizen are entered on that certificate with diacritical marks in the form in which they were entered on the certificates of civil status issued by his Member State of origin, was not seen by the ECJ as a restriction on the freedoms conferred on all EU citizens by art 21 TFEU (C-391/09 *Runevič-Vardyn*, para 82). The latest decision on the law of names is Bogendorff von Wolffersdorff (Case C-438/14 [2014] ECHR) of 2 June 2016. In this decision the ECJ ruled that "art 21 TFEU must be interpreted as meaning that the authorities of a Member State are not bound to recognise the name of a citizen of that Member State when he also holds the nationality of another Member State in which he has acquired that name which he has chosen freely and which contains a number of tokens of nobility, which are not accepted by the law of the first Member State, provided that it is established, which it is for the referring court to ascertain, that a refusal of recognition is, in that context, justified on public policy grounds, in that it is appropriate and necessary to ensure compliance with the principle that all citizens of that Member State are equal before the law".

In summarizing the ECJ's case-law on the law of names, it is apparent that conflicts between national choice-of-law rules on the one hand and EU law on the other hand can hardly be eliminated on a purely case-by-case basis. As far as the principles of legal certainty and predictability are concerned, creating uniform conflict rules for the law of names in Europe would be a preferable solution. Just as the European legislature has already dealt with private international law in the field of maintenance, property regimes divorce and succession law, it should endeavour to find the most suitable way to reconcile the applicable law with the individual circumstances of the person concerned. This result can be achieved by granting individuals a right to choose the applicable law and, in the absence of choice, by pursuing the habitual residence approach.

KATHRIN KROLL-LUDWIGS

Literature

Thomas Ackermann, 'Case C-148/02, Carlos Garcia Avello v. État Belge, Judgment of the Full Court of 2 October 2003, [2003] ECR I-11613' (2007) 44 CMLR 141; Alexander Bergmann, Murad Ferid and Dieter Henrich (eds), *Internationales Ehe- und Kindschaftsrecht*; Christof Böhmer, 'Die Transliteration ausländischer Namen' [1994] IPrax 80; Eric Cusas, 'Arrêt "Sayn-Wittgenstein": la libre circulation et les titres de noblesse' (2011) 178 J.D.E. 100; Anatol Dutta and others, 'Ein Name in ganz Europa – Entwurf einer Europäischen Verordnung über das Internationale Namensrecht' [2014] StAZ 33; Rainer Frank, 'Die Entscheidung des EuGH in Sachen Garcia Avello und ihre Auswirkung auf das internationale Namensrecht' [2005] StAZ 161; Katja Funken, 'Anmerkung zu EuGH, Urt. v. 14.10.2008, C-353/06 – Grunkin und Paul' [2008] FamRZ 2091; Tobias Helms, 'Europarechtliche Vorgaben zur Bestimmung des Namensstatuts von Doppelstaatern: Anmerkung zu EuGH, Urteil vom 2.10.2003, C-148/02 – Garcia Avello' [2005] GPR 36; Reinhard Hepting and Rainer Hausmann, 'Vorbemerkung zu Art. 10 EGBGB' in *Julius von Staudingers Kommentar zum Bürgerlichen Gesetzbuch: Einführungsgesetz zum Bürgerlichen Gesetzbuche/IPR; Art 7, 9–12, 47 (Internationales Recht der natürlichen Personen und der Rechtsgeschäfte)* (Sellier-de Gruyter 2013) no 182 ff; Marion Ho-Dac, 'Commentaire de l'arrêt de la CJUE, du 12 mai 2011, Małgożata Runevič-Vardyn, C-391/09' [2011] GPR 317; Philipp Kubicki, 'Kurze Nachlese zur Rechtssache Grunkin-Paul – Art. 18 EG und die Rechtsfolgen eines Verstoßes' [2009] EuZW 366; Kathrin Kroll-Ludwigs, 'Hinkende Namensrechtsverhältnisse im Fokus der gemeinschaftsrechtlichen Freizügigkeit' (2008) 107 ZVglRWiss 320; Kathrin Kroll-Ludwigs, 'Anmerkung zu EuGH, Rs. C-353/06 – Grunkin und Paul' [2009] JZ 153; Kathrin Kroll-Ludwigs, 'Anmerkung zu EuGH, Urt. v. 22.12.2010, Rs. C-208/09 – Sayn-Wittgenstein' [2011] GPR 242; Kathrin Kroll-Ludwigs, *Die Rolle der Parteiautonomie im europäischen Kollisionsrecht* (Mohr Siebeck 2013); Volker Lipp, 'Namensrecht und Europarecht – Die Entscheidung Grunkin-Paul II und ihre Folgen für das deutsche Namensrecht' [2009] StAZ 1; Johan Meeusen, 'The Grunkin and Paul Judgment of the ECJ, or How to Strike a Delicate Balance between Conflict of Laws, Union Citizenship and Freedom of Movement in the EC' [2010] ZEuP 189; Juliana Mörsdorf-Schulte, 'Europäische Impulse für Namen und Status des Mehrstaaters' [2004] IPRax 315; Clíodhna Murphy, 'La jurisprudence de la Cour de justice et du Tribunal de première instance. Commentaires des arrêts. Arrêt «Sayn-Wittgenstein»' (2011) 1 R.D.U.E. 131; Walter Pintens, 'Der Fall Konstantinidis. Das Namensrecht als Beispiel für die Auswirkungen des Europäischen Gemeinschaftsrechts auf das Privatrecht' [1995] ZEuP 92; Jürgen Rieck, 'Anerkennung des Familiennamens in Mitgliedstaaten – Grunkin-Paul' [2009] NJW 125; Gabriel Toggenburg, 'Die "falsche" Fürstin: Zum grenzüberschreitenden Verkehr von Adelstiteln vor dem Hintergrund der Unionsbürgerschaft' [2011] EuLR 78; Hanneke Van Eijken, 'Case C-391/09, Malgozata Runevic-Vardyn and Lukasz Pawel Wardyn v. Vilniaus miesto savivaldybes administracija and Others, Judgment of the Court (Second Chamber) of 12 May 2011' [2012] CMLR 809; Fabian Wall, 'Keine Adelsprädikate für Österreicher durch Adoption in Deutschland – Schlussfolgerungen aus den Schlussanträgen und dem Urteil des EuGH in der Sache "Sayn-Wittgenstein"' [2011] StAZ 203.

Nationality

I. Concept and notion

1. Nationality and citizenship

The term 'nationality' carries two meanings. First, 'nationality' describes the formal legal belonging of a natural person to a state. In this meaning, it is synonymous with the term 'citizenship' (*Staatsbürgerschaft, Staatsangehörigkeit; citoyenneté; cittadinanza; cidadania; ciudadanía*). A condition for the formation and existence of a state is the existence of people of a polity (or state) – that is, citizens. Citizenship of a state carries certain rights and obligations between the citizen and the state with it; in democracies, for example, one instance of this is the right to vote. Second, 'nationality' can also describe the belonging of a person to a 'nation' (derived from the Latin term *natio*). In this meaning, 'nation' can be understood as a collective of people of a shared cultural and historic origin and, often, of a common language. The meaning of the term is not defined by reference to the notion of 'state'; rather, it is an anthropologic notion. In the case of a 'nation state', the two groups 'nation' and 'people of the polity (or state)' overlap completely.

In modern private international law and international procedural law, 'nationality' always refers to the formal legal status of citizenship. Thus the terms 'nationality' and 'citizenship' are used synonymously with this meaning from here on, unless indicated otherwise.

2. Meaning in conflict of laws

In conflict of laws, the use of nationality as a connecting factor is called the 'nationality principle'. The natural person's nationality is used as a connecting factor to determine predominantly the law applicable to the → personal status (see II.). The law of the state of a person's citizenship is also called '*lex patria*' (national law). For example, art 37(2) Swiss Private international law Act (Bundesgesetz über das Internationale Privatrecht of 18 December 1987, 1988 BBl I 5, as amended) states: 'A person can nevertheless demand that his name is governed by the laws of its home state.' Citizenship plays a limited role in international procedural law (see VII.). For example, art 8(c) → Rome III Regulation (Council Regulation (EU) No 1259/2010 of 20 December 2010 implementing enhanced cooperation in the area of the law applicable to divorce and legal separation, [2010] OJ L 343/10) – albeit only subsidiarily – renders the law of the state 'of which both spouses are nationals at the time the court is seized' applicable in the event of a divorce (→ Divorce and personal separation). At the same time, according to art 3(1)(b) → Brussels IIa Regulation (Council Regulation (EC) No 2201/2003 of 27 November 2003 concerning jurisdiction and the recognition and enforcement of judgments in matrimonial matters and the matters of parental responsibility, repealing Regulation (EC) No 1347/2000, [2003] OJ L 338/1), jurisdiction in matters relating to divorce, legal separation or marriage annulment shall lie *inter alia* with the courts of the Member State of the nationality of both spouses. A dichotomy exists between the use of citizenship on the one hand and the use of spatial connecting factors such as residence or domicile on the other. Generally, citizenship does not play a major role as a → connecting factor in common law jurisdictions. Traditionally, at common law, 'domicile' is used as the connecting factor rather than citizenship (→ Domicile, habitual residence and establishment). Thus, in EU law, art 3(1)(c) Brussels IIa Regulation provides a → substitution. In the case of the → United Kingdom and → Ireland, the aforementioned international jurisdiction in divorce matters of the courts of the state of the spouses' common nationality is replaced by the jurisdiction of the courts of the state of common domicile. For the purpose of the regulation, 'domicile' has the same meaning as it has under the legal systems of the United Kingdom and Ireland (art 3(2) Brussels IIa Regulation).

In most legislations, nationality is used as a connecting factor in the form of multilateral conflict rules. In this way, the different legal systems are treated equally in conflict of laws. Unilateral rules that combine the nationality principle with the use of residence as a connecting factor in cases of domestically-resident aliens (eg art 1195(1), (3) Civil Code of the Russian Federation (as amended by Federal Law No 260-FZ on 30 September 2013)) are a rare exception. This is because such unilateral connections go against the conflict-of-laws principle of equal treatment of legal systems.

3. Acquisition and loss of citizenship

Each state decides under which conditions its citizenship is acquired (Case C-135/08 *Rottmann v Bavaria* [2010] ECR I-1449, para 39; art 3(1) Strasbourg European Convention on Nationality of 6 November 1997 (ETS No 166)). Thus, any issue of family law raised in the proceedings leading to the conferral of citizenship by a country must be resolved as it would be by the courts of this state. This means that incidental questions (→ Incidental (preliminary) question) relating to family law are to be resolved by referring to the laws of the legal system which has already been selected to govern the principal issue. This includes the foreign conflict-of-laws rules.

General public international law only rarely limits states' authority to shape their citizenship laws. In the *Nottebohm* case (*Liechtenstein v Guatemala* (1955) 1 I.C.J. Rep 4, para 24 ff), the ICJ held that a person can only be considered a citizen of a certain state if he has a factual, genuine link to this state. However, the threshold for meeting the conditions of such a genuine connection is very low. The decision was rendered in the field of diplomatic protection; whether it contains a general rule of law is open to debate. At any rate, the decision has no impact on the conflict of laws.

Every national of a Member State also has EU citizenship (art 20 TFEU (The Treaty on the Functioning of the European Union (consolidated version), [2012] OJ C 326/47)). This allows the CJEU to review the compatibility of Member States' citizenship laws and of their application; for example, the Court reserves the right to check whether the denaturalization of an EU citizen is proportional and legal (Case C-135/08 *Rottmann v Bavaria* [2010] ECR I-1449, para 45, 55 ff). The ECtHR checks whether the national citizenship laws of an ECHR Member State are consistent with ECHR requirements – for example, if, in citizenship law, children born in wedlock are treated the same as those born out of it (*Genovese v Malta*, no 53124/09 (ECtHR, 11 October 2011)), or whether men and women are treated equally.

Some bi- or multilateral treaties stipulate requirements regarding national citizenship law in order to prevent results such as multiple citizenship, statelessness, or discrimination against married women (see the UN Convention of 29 February 1957 on the nationality of married women, 309 UNTS 65). According to this convention, for women, marriage entails neither a loss of citizenship, nor the *ipso iure* acquisition of the husband's citizenship. Rather, as a general rule, it creates a right to naturalization in the spouse's country of citizenship. The Strasbourg European Convention on Nationality of 6 November 1997 (ETS No 166) favours multiple citizenship in various cases.

Citizenship is acquired by virtue of law or through a sovereign act (for an overview: Oliver Dörr, 'Nationality' in Rüdiger Wolfrum (ed), *Max Planck Encyclopedia of Public International Law* (OUP 2012) paras 11 ff, 18 ff; Olivier Vonk, *Nationality Law in the Western Hemisphere* (Brill/Nijhoff 2014) 3 ff, 384 ff).

a) Acquisition by birth
The most important reason for acquisition is acquisition by birth *ex lege*. Two principles of acquisition by birth can be distinguished: the *ius soli* and the *ius sanguinis* principle.

(1) Acquisition by virtue of birth within state territory According to the *ius soli* principle, birth within a state's territory confers the citizenship of that state to the person born. The *ius soli* principle is prevalent in Latin America and Anglo-Saxon countries. Generally, it is more common in traditional immigration countries because, starting from the second generation of immigrants, it leads to a greater congruity of resident population and people of the polity.

(2) Acquisition by virtue of birth through descent The second principle is the principle of *ius sanguinis*, which still prevails in continental Europe. According to this principle, citizenship is conferred by descent from a citizen. Countries that were traditional emigration countries at the beginning of the 20th century prevalently follow the *ius sanguinis* principle. Some of these countries, which have by now become immigration countries, have complemented their citizenship laws with variations of *ius soli* acquisition rules. One example that comes to mind is Germany, which reformed its citizenship laws in this sense in 2000 and further extended its citizenship laws in 2014. Nowadays, the equal treatment of women and men in nationality law is the international standard. But up until the middle of the 20th century, only the father could confer citizenship on the child. Today this is the case in only a few countries, particularly those influenced by Islamic law (eg Abu Dhabi, Bahrain, Oman, → Saudi Arabia, Senegal, Somalia, Syria and the United Arab Emirates). In some countries which follow the *ius soli* principle, citizenship is conferred by patrilineal descent alone in the event of births abroad (eg the Bahamas,

Barbados, → India, → Iran, Jordan, Kuwait, Lebanon, Liberia and Niger).

b) Acquisition ex lege on other grounds

→ Adoption, legitimation, → marriage and other changes in the civil status of a natural person can lead to the acquisition of the citizenship of a state to which another person – for instance, the adopting party or spouse – belongs. But according to modern conventions (see for example UN Convention of 29 February 1957 on the nationality of married women), for women, → marriage or divorce (or other dissolution of marriage; → Divorce and personal separation) entails neither a loss of citizenship, nor the *ipso iure* acquisition of the husband's citizenship (same rule for both spouses: Strasbourg European Convention on Nationality of 6 November 1997). Rather, as a general rule, it creates a right to naturalization in the spouse's country of citizenship.

c) Acquisition by naturalization

Citizenship can also be awarded through a sovereign act (naturalization). Nowadays, the laws of many nations recognize the right to naturalization of spouses, registered partners, or children of their citizens; the right to naturalization of domestically-born foreigners may also be recognized if certain further conditions are met. Within the EU, the possibility of dual citizenship of two Member States is promoted. In some countries, the acquisition of citizenship a declaration addressed to the relevant state (eg in the event of aliens born inside that state) is equivalent to naturalization.

d) Loss

Loss of citizenship can occur through a sovereign act (denaturalization by legislative act, administrative act or – rarely – judicial act of state) or by operation of law. According to customary international law, no one shall be arbitrarily deprived of his nationality (see also art 15(2) Universal Declaration on Human Rights of 10 December 1948, Resolution 217 A (III) General Assembly (1948–49) U.N.Y.B. 535; see Oliver Dörr, 'Nationality' in Rüdiger Wolfrum (ed), *Max Planck Encyclopedia of Public International Law* (OUP 2012) paras 32 ff). Nowadays, only a few countries provide for a loss of citizenship in the event of marriage to a foreign spouse; this is particularly common if the citizen in question is a woman (for example, with varying other requirements, according to the laws of Afghanistan, the People's Republic of → China, → Indonesia, → Iran, the Republic of → Korea (South Korea), Kuwait, Libya, Madagascar, etc.).

4. Citizenship of tangible movables and legal persons

Public international law sometimes makes reference to the concept of 'nationality' of legal persons. Similarly, nationality is also ascribed to tangible movables, particularly ships and aircraft (see on this point Oliver Dörr, 'Nationality' in Rüdiger Wolfrum (ed), *Max Planck Encyclopedia of Public International Law* (OUP 2012) para 24). Pursuant to art 17 of the Convention of 7 December 1944 on International Civil Aviation (15 UNTS 295), aircraft have the nationality of the state in which they are registered. In private international law, some jurisdictions explicitly use the nationality of means of transport as a connecting factor. For example, art 45(1) no 1 of the Introductory Act to the German Civil Code (Einführungsgesetz zum Bürgerlichen Gesetzbuche of 21 September 1994, BGBl. I 2494, as amended, henceforth EGBGB) provides that interests in aircraft are governed by the law of the country of origin. This is the country of the aircraft's nationality. The rules that govern the nationality of legal persons and mobile assets such as ships are very different from those that govern natural persons. This entry deals only with the latter.

II. Purpose and function

1. Personal status

Private international law sees citizenship as the → connecting factor predominantly to determine → personal status. The term 'personal status' has different meanings (Heinz-Peter Mansel, *Personalstatut, Staatsangehörigkeit und Effektivität* (CH Beck 1988) 42–3). One of these meanings is to refer to the law that governs certain legal questions intrinsically linked to a person, such as personal law (name, legal capacity (→ Capacity and emancipation) and contractual capability etc), family law or the law of successions.

In many states, personal status is determined by a person's domicile or habitual residence; in others, nationality is used as the connecting factor (see I.2., IV.). The nationality principle was not developed as a means of indicating the applicable law in matters relating to personal status until the 19th century. Nowadays, it is explained by referring to four arguments, which are widely used in legislative materials, doctrine and case-law. These different legal policy accounts are not mutually exclusive; instead, they complement one another. They have different strengths and weaknesses. Based on factors such as the historical state of the legislator at the time the rule was postulated, or the percentage of alien residents, one reason or another will be more important to the legislator. In liberal democracies, justification by reference to a democratic theory might be of importance (see II.4.). In non-democratic states, on the other hand, the legislator's decision to follow the nationality principle is more likely to be based on considerations of state sovereignty over their subjects, given that the individual is seen less as an autonomous person and more as an object of the law (see II.3.) In societies with a homogenous resident population and a low percentage of foreigners, justification by reference to cultural identity is accorded greater weight (see II.2.). Pragmatic arguments are commonly used (see II.5.).

2. Closest connection of a person to a state

The nationality principle is still being justified by referring to the hypothesis that, in an ideal situation, the law to which a person has the strongest link is the law of his nationality. This is because, from a generalized perspective, nationality documents a lasting, personal link between persons and the state whose citizenship they hold. Its laws are the ones which the national knows best (Federal Constitutional Court of Germany (BVerfG), 18 July 2006, [2007] IPRax 217, 222 ff; see Heinz-Peter Mansel, 'Die kulturelle Identität im internationalen Privatrecht' in Georg Nolte and others (eds), *Pluralistische Gesellschaften und Internationales Recht* (CF Müller 2008) 137, 156 with further references). This state is thus generally called the 'home state'. According to the doctrine of conflict interests established by *Gerhard Kegel* (→ Kegel, Gerhard) the use of nationality as a connecting factor respects the continuity interest of the person in question. They are permanently subject to the same personal laws, regardless of location or jurisdiction (Alexander Lüderitz, 'Anknüpfung im Parteiinteresse' in Alexander Lüderitz and Jochen Schröder (eds), *Internationales Privatrecht und Rechtsvergleichung im Ausgang des 20. Jahrhunderts. Bewahrung oder Wende? Festschrift für Gerhard Kegel* (Metzner 1977) 31, 33 ff).

Erik Jayme in particular argues for the existence of the subjective right, based on human rights (→ Human rights and private international law) and constitutional rights, to the recognition of the cultural identity of the individual, which is shaped by the common history and culture of all citizens of a state (Erik Jayme, 'Identité culturelle et intégration: le droit international privé postmoderne' (1995) 251 Rec. des Cours 9, 11 f, 167 f; see also Hélène Gaudemet-Tallon, 'Nationalité, statut personnel et droit de l'homme' in Heinz-Peter Mansel and others (eds), *Festschrift für Erik Jayme* (Sellier European Law Publishers 2004) 205 ff; Yuko Nishitani, 'Global Citizens and Family Relations' [2014] ELR 134, 137). The concept of basing the nationality principle on the notion of cultural identity has found increasing acceptance in the scholarly community. The *Institute de Droit international*, in its resolution of 25 August 2005 on 'Différences culturelles et ordre public en droit international privé de la famille' ((2006) 71:2 *Annuaire de l'Institut de Droit international* 291, 292, [2005] IPRax 559, 560; Rapporteur: Paul Lagarde), has recognized the use of nationality as an expression of the law's cultural orientation, but has also proposed giving a person the right to choose between the laws of his home state and the laws of his domicile state.

This justification of the nationality principle by reference to the person is a genuine private law justification. Thus, it is appropriate to the conflict of laws. However, it has the disadvantage of only being appropriate in ideal cases. In mobile societies, a large percentage of residents can be foreigners who have become alienated from their home jurisdiction and are now rooted in the legal order of their host state. The interest to adapt – leading to an application of the laws of residence – can thus outweigh the aforementioned continuity interest (see Alexander Lüderitz, 'Anknüpfung im Parteiinteresse' in Alexander Lüderitz and Jochen Schröder (eds), *Internationales Privatrecht und Rechtsvergleichung im Ausgang des 20. Jahrhunderts. Bewahrung oder Wende? Festschrift für Gerhard Kegel* (Metzner 1977) 31, 33). On the other hand, in large, culturally diverse societies, greater groups of foreigners might exist in which the continuity interest outweighs the adaption interest, for example because they live in the host state as immigrants for economic reasons or for a limited period of time as skilled workers, and continue to have stronger ties to their origin state than to their host state. In certain circumstances, this could also affect second- and third-generation immigrants (for numbers on the impressive share of first- and second-generation migrants within the resident population of European countries see Eurostat, European Commission, *Migrants in Europe: A Statistical Portrait of the First and Second Generation* (2011)). Nowadays, thanks to modern means of communication, keeping ties to one's home society has become much easier.

3. Sovereignty over subjects and state sovereignty

A second line of reasoning is based on state interests. The use of nationality as a connecting factor protects the state's sovereignty over its subjects as well as home state sovereignty. Furthermore, the nationality principle respects the sovereignty of other states, as well as the independence of those states' legal systems (Federal Constitutional Court of Germany (BVerfG), 18 July 2006, [2007] IPRax 217, 222 ff). The UN Administrative Tribunal (*Adrian v The Secretary-General of the United Nations*, Judgment No 1183, Case No 1276 dated 30 September 2004) points to cultural identity, but particularly to state sovereignty with regards to the shape of the state's own legal order when justifying the nationality principle. The application of the *lex patria* to questions relating to an individual's personal status respects the cultural and religious diversity of different legal systems. In the *Adrian* decision, this principle became relevant in the context of the recognition of → same-sex marriages by the UN. The tribunal held that the question as to whether or not a UN civil servant had certain spousal benefits if both spouses are men depended on the recognition of this marriage by the home state; it should be noted that the UN has reversed its administrative policy and now recognizes any same-sex marriage that was valid according to the laws at the place it was entered into. The UN tribunal also emphasized the point of state sovereignty protection through this measure.

This line of reasoning is based on considerations of public law alone, referring to the state only. It takes a state-centric approach and neglects the specific conflicts interest: determination of the applicable law with which the person has the closest connection in the interest of this person. It might have more importance for a UN court because of its deference to the interest of the UN member states.

Reversely, the nationality principle in conflict of laws cannot be justified by the assumption that a citizen living abroad has a right against his host state to ensure the application of his home laws in personal matters. This right does not derive from general international law. Presumably, it is unknown to most national constitutions; at any rate, it does not derive from the general equality principle. The determination of an individual's personal status by his nationality, habitual residence or domicile is not a function of human rights (on this see Heinz-Peter Mansel, 'Die kulturelle Identität im internationalen Privatrecht' in Georg Nolte and others (eds), *Pluralistische Gesellschaften und Internationales Recht* (CF Müller 2008) 137, 156 with further references) (→ Constitutional law and private international law).

4. Open societies and democratic participation

Modern liberal-pluralistic democracies are shaped by their constitution and the idea of human rights. Constitutional patriotism replaces a common culture shared by all members as the link between state and polity (constitutional patriotism as described by *Dolf Sternberg* and expanded to include the political idea of the EU by Jürgen Habermas, 'Citizenship and National Identity' in Bart Van Steenbergen (ed), *The Condition of Citizenship* (Sage 1994) 20 ff; for constitutional patriotism in civil society see Jürgen Habermas, *Faktizität und Geltung* (Suhrkamp 1992) 633 ff). This approach might be more suitable for explaining the new orientation of Western mobile societies open to immigration than merely culturally determined concepts. This also gives rise to another basis of legitimacy for the nationality principle. It means that private law is made by parliaments. The right to elect the parliament is tied to citizenship in most countries on earth. In an idealized, ordinary situation, the possibility of influencing law through political participation in parliamentary elections allows citizens to identify themselves with the laws of their country and to accept them as their own laws (Heinz-Peter Mansel, 'Die kulturelle Identität im internationalen Privatrecht' in Georg Nolte and others (eds), *Pluralistische Gesellschaften und Internationales Recht* (CF Müller 2008) 137, 165–6).

But nationality is used as a connecting factor regardless of the right to vote; people lacking the right to vote are subjected, with regards to personal status, to the laws of their home state as well. Claims have been made that the element of potential political participation is fictitious (see *inter alia* Louis d'Avout, 'La lex personalis entre nationalité, domicile et résidence habituelle' in *Mélanges en l'honneur du Professeur Bernard Audit* (L.G.D.J. 2014) 17, 22 no 13; Yuko Nishitani, 'Global Citizens and Family Relations' [2014] ELR 134, 138). However, the democratic theory argument does not depend on the concrete influence of voting decisions on the legal system. Rather, the opportunity of political participation in modern, democratic-liberal and culturally divergent societies appears to be a suitable and rational means of establishing a connection between a person and the legal order of a state. Against it, it is argued that there are no elections in many of the states which follow the nationality principle. In these states, the connecting factor is mostly based on a different foundation, state sovereignty being the most common. For democratic states, the constitutional state of active citizens remains a valid legal policy model for the use of nationality as a → connecting factor (see Heinz-Peter Mansel, 'Die kulturelle Identität im internationalen Privatrecht' in Georg Nolte and others (eds), *Pluralistische Gesellschaften und Internationales Recht* (CF Müller 2008) 137, 165–6).

5. Legal certainty and pragmatism

Use of nationality as a connecting factor can be justified by referring to pragmatic reasoning. In regular cases, nationality is more secure and easier to determine than domicile or habitual residence (→ Domicile, habitual residence and establishment). Due to the fact that nationality cannot be changed quickly, manipulation of the connection is not as easy as it would be if (habitual) residence were used. Thus, while it is still a connecting factor which is subject to change, it creates fewer changes of applicable law (see The Law Commission and The Scottish Law Commission, *Private international law: The Law of Domicile* (Law Com No 168, 1987, Scot Law Com No 107, 1987) para 3.9). On the other hand, use of nationality as a connecting factor leads to an increased application of foreign laws in a heterogeneous society. This, in turn, leads to a more difficult application of the laws and an increase in costs of determining the content of foreign laws. It might also result in triggering the *ordre public* more frequently.

III. Historical development

The nationality principle was not developed in Continental Europe as a means of indicating the law applicable in matters relating to personal status until the 19th century. At that time, the political purpose of citizenship was a central topic. The state's sovereignty over its subjects gained importance; thus, to the legislators of the national statutes that evolved during the 19th century, subduing all of their citizens under their laws seemed legitimate. For them, this was an expression of state sovereignty. The French Civil Code (Code Civil of 21 March 1804; henceforth French CC) (in art 3(3)) followed by the Austrian Civil Code (Allgemeines Bürgerliches Gesetzbuch of 1 June 1811, JGS No 946/1811, as amended) (in art 4, 34) began this trend by stipulating unilateral conflict-of-laws rules for their own nationals. The civil code of the Kingdom of Saxony of 1863 (in § 7 Bürgerliches Gesetzbuch) and the Italian Codice civile of 1865 then introduced the multilateral use of nationality as a connecting factor. The Italian civil code was based on the works of *Pasquale Stanislao Mancini* (1817–88; → Mancini, Pasquale Stanislao). His famous speech of 1851 about *nazionalità* as the foundation of international law ('Della nazionalità come fondamento del dritto delle genti: prelezione al corso di dritto internazionale e marittimo pronunziata nella R. Università di Torino nel dì 22 gennaio 1851' in Pasquale Stanislao Mancini, *Diritto internazionale* (Marghieri 1873)) is considered to be the theoretical underpinning for the success of the use of nationality as a connecting factor in 19th-century private international law (Erik Jayme, 'Identité culturelle et intégration: le droit international privé postmoderne' (1995) 251 Rec. des Cours 9, 174 f). *Mancini* put private international law on an international law foundation. He viewed the use of nationality as a connecting factor as an expression of the state's responsibility for its citizens. The *Institut de Droit international* – established in 1873 by *Mancini* and *Johann Caspar Bluntschli* – recommended the use of nationality as a connecting factor in its resolutions. The national legislators of → Spain, → Portugal, → Hungary, → Romania, → Sweden, → Turkey, the → Netherlands, → Japan, → China, → Chile, → Colombia, →

Peru and → Venezuela followed this recommendation (Heinz-Peter Mansel, *Personalstatut, Staatsangehörigkeit und Effektivität* (1988) 25 ff), but the principle was not fully adopted in all jurisdictions. For example, French conflict of laws – and, after it, the legal systems that were based on French law – provided for the use of domicile as a connecting factor with regard to questions relating to the laws of → successions and → matrimonial property. The later codification of German private international law (the EGBGB of 18 August 1896 (RGBl. 604), which entered into force on 1 January 1900) used nationality as the sole connecting factor and replaced the domicile principle, which had previously been in place throughout almost all parts of Germany. Further codifications during the first half of the 20th century (eg the Greek conflicts codification of 1940 and the Italian codification of 1942, as well as codifications in Finland and Poland) used nationality as a connecting factor for determining personal status. Twenty-first-century codifications followed (eg Japan, the Republic of Korea (South Korea), the Republic of China (Taiwan) etc, see Yuko Nishitani, 'Gobal Citizens and Family Relations' [2014] ELR 134, 137). It is worth noting that the Asian countries listed here have only a small percentage of foreigners among the resident population (Yuko Nishitani, 'Gobal Citizens and Family Relations' [2014] ELR 134, 137). Throughout the common law world, the Scandinavian legal family, the laws of → Estonia and → Latvia in the Baltic states, and → Switzerland, nationality has never achieved significant importance (see the overview in Louis I de Winter, 'Nationality or Domicile? The Present State of Affairs' (1969) 128 Rec. des Cours 344–503).

IV. Modern trends

1. Equality

Since the middle of the 20th century, the use of nationality as a connecting factor has been declining internationally. While personal status is still often determined by referring to nationality in national conflicts codifications (see V.1.), it is no longer the sole connecting factor. In international family law, this is because a connection with regard to family relations using nationality will fail if the family members have different nationalities. Using the nationality of the male alone (ie in his role as the husband or father) would be a clear breach of the equality principle. After some hesitation, this was confirmed by courts in the 1990s at the latest (see for Germany: Federal Constitutional Court of Germany (BVerfG), 4 May 1971, 31 BVerfGE 58; 22 February 1983, 63 BVerfGE 181; 8 January 1985, 68 BVerfGE 384; for Italy: Corte di Cassazione, 26 February 1987 n 71, [1987] Foro italiano I 2317; 25 November 1987 n 477, [1988] Foro italiano I 1455) (→ Constitutional law and private International Law).

2. Integration

In those European legal systems that turned to the nationality principle in the 19th century, the integration of immigrants who arrive in the country due to work migration or as refugees is becoming the policy goal of law more and more often. Using habitual residence as a connecting factor is seen as a means of achieving this goal. It leads to the equal treatment of the entire resident population; in addition, it makes the courts' work easier since it leads to a more frequent application of the municipal laws of the forum. This idea of integration – and because of the participation of the → United Kingdom, → Ireland, → Malta and Cyprus in legislation – EU conflict of laws relies on nationality only exceptionally (see V.3.). It has not played a significant role in treaties created by the → Hague Conference on Private International Law since 1957 (see V.2.).

3. Self-determination

There is a tendency in recent decades to give citizens a choice in matters of personal status between the laws determined by reference to nationality on the one hand, and the laws determined by reference to habitual residence (or domicile) on the other (→ Domicile, habitual residence and establishment). This accords adequate weight to the ever more important right of self-determination. The citizen himself solves the dilemma of determining the applicable personal status law. This solution was recommended by the *Institut de Droit international* several times (resolution of 25 August 2005 on 'Différences culturelles et ordre public en droit international privé de la famille' ((2005) 71:2 *Annuaire de l'Institut de Droit international* 291, 292, [2005] IPRax 559, 560, Rapporteur: Paul Lagarde); resolution of September 1989 on 'La dualité des principes de nationalité et de domicile en droit international privé' ((1987) 62:2

Annuaire de l'Institut de Droit international 127, [1988] IPRax 65, 66, Rapporteur: Yvon Loussouarn); for more details see Christian Kohler, 'L'autonomie de la volonté en droit international privé: un principe universel entre libéralisme et étatisme' (2013) 359 Rec. des Cours 285, 416 ff). Such a right to choose (→ Party autonomy) is provided for in particular by the Italian Private international law Act (Riforma del Sistema italiano di diritto internazionale private, Act No 218 of 31 May 1995 in Gazz.Uff., Supplemento Ordinario No 128 of 3 June l995, as amended, henceforth Italian PILA) in art 46(1), (2) and art 21, 22 Succession Regulation (Regulation (EU) No 650/2012 of the European Parliament and of the Council of 4 July 2012 on jurisdiction, applicable law, recognition and enforcement of decisions and acceptance and enforcement of authentic instruments in matters of succession and on the creation of a European Certificate of Succession, [2012] OJ L 201/107; → Rome IV Regulation). In the Italian PILA, as a rule, nationality is used as the connecting factor. Connection by means of residence can only exceptionally be achieved by → choice of law. This rule-exception relationship is reversed in the Succession Regulation. A similar trend is starting to become apparent in matrimonial property law. According to art 15(1), referring to art 14(1) no 1 EGBGB, the matrimonial property regime is constituted by the shared home laws of the spouses. However, they can make a choice of law, thus rendering the laws at the place of residence of one of the spouses applicable (art 15(2) no 2 EGBGB). In a similar vein, spouses who do not share a common nationality can elect the law governing general effects of marriage under art 9(3) of the Spanish Civil Code (Código Civil of 24 July 1889, Geceta de Madrid No 206, 25 July 1889; henceforth Spanish CC). Articles 16 lit a), 17(1) lit a) Commission Proposals for the Matrimonial Property Regulations (Proposal for a Council Regulation on jurisdiction, applicable law and the recognition and enforcement of decisions in matters of matrimonial property regimes (COM(2011) 126/2)) reverse this rule-exception relationship. The matrimonial property regime is the law of the state of the spouses' habitual common residence; however, the spouses can elect the law of the state of their first common habitual residence after they got married. According to art 10(2), (3), 17b(2) EGBGB, spouses, registered partners or parents can decide whether their name or their child's name should be governed by the laws of nationality or of residence. The possible examples are legion.

4. New rule-exception relationship

Use of nationality is becoming a subsidiary or alternative → connecting factor besides the habitual residence rather than the main principle – or so seems to be the trend in Europe. For instance, art 17(1) lit a), b) of the aforementioned Commission Proposals for the Matrimonial Property Regulations provides that, when no choice of law is possible, the law of the common residence governs questions of → matrimonial property. Only in the absence of this connection is nationality relied upon to determine the applicable law. The same hierarchy is applied by art 8 Rome III Regulation. The so-called '*Kegel's* ladder' (→ Kegel, Gerhard) is thus turned upside-down (cf art 14(1) nos 1, 2 EGBGB).

V. Current regulation

1. National

A number of legal systems use nationality as either the sole connecting factor or as one of several connecting factors. As of yet, the nationality principle has neither declined in nor disappeared from national codifications; rather, it has merely decreased in relative importance. This is because in more recent European codifications, residence has partially replaced nationality as a connecting factor. In Europe, the following examples can be given of countries which use nationality as a connecting factor when determining personal status laws (this information was taken from the country reports in Rainer Hausmann 'Anhang zu Art 4 EGBGB, Länderberichte' in Dieter Henrich and others (eds), *Julius von Staudingers Kommentar zum Bürgerlichen Gesetzbuch: Einführungsgesetz zum Bürgerlichen Gesetzbuche/IPR Art 3–6 (Internationales Privatrecht – Allgemeiner Teil)* (Sellier – de Gruyter 2013)): → Albania, → Belgium, → Bosnia and Herzegovina, → Bulgaria, → Germany, → France, → Greece, → Italy, → Liechtenstein, → Luxembourg, → Macedonia, FYR, → Montenegro, the → Netherlands, → Poland, → Portugal, → Romania, → Serbia, → Slovakia, → Slovenia, → Spain, → Turkey and → Hungary, as well as the → Russian Federation and the other successor states of the Soviet Union (ie Armenia,

→ Belarus, → Georgia, → Kazakhstan, Kyrgyzstan, Moldova, Tajikistan, Turkmenistan, → Ukraine and Uzbekistan). The *lex patriae* was also applicable in → Lithuania, although only for a limited time (from 1994 to 2001). In Asia, the following countries use the nationality principle; particular examples include: → Japan, the Republic of → China (→ Taiwan), the Republic of → Korea (South Korea), and → Thailand. In Latin America, some countries follow the nationality principle (eg Cuba) and some apply it unilaterally to their nationals (→ Chile, → Ecuador, → Colombia); there are also some which have rejected it in favour of the domicile principle (eg → Brazil in 1999, → Venezuela etc) or which have always followed the domicile principle (eg → Paraguay, → Peru, → Uruguay etc). Most conflict of laws systems in the North African and Arabic region follow the nationality principle (eg → Egypt, Algeria, Iraq, → Iran, Jordan, Libya, Morocco, Somalia, Sudan, Syria, → Tunisia etc), as do → Angola, Gabon, → Mozambique, Senegal and Togo.

2. International

A number of older treaties dealing with personal status matters use nationality as a connecting factor. However, nationality ceased to play a significant role as of the mid-20th century; this is revealed by an analysis of the treaties of the Hague Conference on Private International Law (see Jürgen Basedow, 'The Law of Open Societies: Private Ordering and Public Regulation of International Relations. General Course on Private international law' (2013) 360 Rec. des Cours 249). The Latin American Código de Derecho Internacional Privado of 20 February 1928 (Código Bustamante, Bustamante Code on Private international law of 20 February 1928, OAS, Law and Treaty Series, no 34) left it to the treaty states to decide whether personal status laws were to be determined by referring to domicile or to nationality (→ Domicile, habitual residence and establishment).

3. European

According to art 20 TFEU, citizenship of a Member State confers Citizenship of the Union. However, this is not a conflict-of-laws connecting factor. In European conflict of laws, the law pertaining to → personal status matters is generally determined by reference to habitual residence. Even though the EU regulations are uniform law and thus govern all situations, not just those with a connection to the Internal Market, the idea of integration leads to the replacement of the nationality principle. Nevertheless, through a special choice of law, one may usually elect the law of one's home state (Succession Regulation; Commission Proposals for the Matrimonial Property Regulations, see IV.2.; art 5(3) lit c) Rome III Regulation; art 15 Maintenance Regulation with art 8(1) lit c) Hague Maintenance Protocol 2007 (Hague Protocol of 23 November 2007 on the law applicable to maintenance obligations, [2009] OJ L 331/19)). According to art 8 lit c) Rome III Regulation, in the absence of a choice of law, the third subsidiary connection is that the law governing divorce will be determined by referring to the law of the state of which both spouses are nationals at the time the court is seized. According to art 7(3) lit c) Rome I Regulation (Regulation (EC) No 593/2008 of the European Parliament and of the Council of 17 June 2008 on the law applicable to contractual obligations (Rome I), [2008] OJ L 177/6; → Rome Convention and Rome I Regulation (contractual obligations)), in the case of life assurance, the law of the Member State of which the policyholder is a national can be elected as the law governing the contract.

Article 18 TFEU prohibits any discrimination based on nationality. With regard to conflict of laws, this only means that the unilateral use of nationality as a connecting factor is not allowed within the TFEU's sphere of application. Multilateral conflict rules using nationality as a connecting factor are not discriminatory (see Jürgen Basedow, 'Das Staatsangehörigkeitsprinzip in der Europäischen Union' [2011] IPRax 109; Heinz-Peter Mansel, 'The Impact of the European Union's Prohibition of Discrimination and the Right of Free Movement of Persons on the Private international law Rules of Member States' in Katharina Boele-Woelki and others (eds), *Convergence and Divergence in Private international law: Liber Amicorum Kurt Siehr* (Eleven International Publishing 2010) 289, 296 ff). The Union itself uses this connecting factor in its capacity as legislator in art 8 lit c) Rome III Regulation. Furthermore, using the nationality of the person concerned can regularly be justified (see Heinz-Peter Mansel, 'The Impact of the European Union's Prohibition of Discrimination and the Right of Free Movement of Persons on the Private international law Rules of Member States' in Katharina Boele-Woelki and others (eds), *Convergence and Divergence in Private international law: Liber Amicorum Kurt Siehr* (Eleven International Publishing 2010) 289, 297 f). For people holding multiple citizenships, see VI.3.

VI. Particular problems in practice

1. Failure in individual cases

Using nationality as a connecting factor may lead to a system of laws to which the person concerned has no connection and which appears culturally foreign to him; the same problem might occur when using habitual residence: 'As determinants of the personal law, nationality yields a predictable but frequently an inappropriate law; domicile yields an appropriate but frequently an unpredictable law' (James Fawcett, Janeen Carruthers and Peter North, *Cheshire, North & Fawcett's Private international law* (14th edn, OUP 2008) ch 9, 7(a)(ii)). Suggestions have been made to use ordinary residence rather than nationality as the connecting factor if the person concerned obviously and clearly only has ties to the country that has been his country of residence for a period of years (on this see Heinz-Peter Mansel, *Personalstatut, Staatsangehörigkeit und Effektivität* (CH Beck 1988) 466 ff with further references). This suggestion has not been well-received due to the legal uncertainty created by having to make case-by-case decisions. General → escape clauses, such as the one found in art 8 Book 10 Dutch New Civil Code (Nieuw Burgerlijk Wetboek of 1 January 1992, henceforth Dutch CC) or art 19 of the Belgian Code of Private international law (Code de Droit International Privé, Loi du 16 juillet 2004 portant le Code de droit international privé, MB 27 July 2004, 57344, as amended, henceforth Belgian PILA), are rarely used to this end.

2. Composite legal systems

Nationality itself is not a sufficiently clear connecting factor in cases of states with composite legal systems (eg → Canada, → Iran, Iraq, → Israel, → Spain, the → United Kingdom, the → USA etc). An additional connection needs to be made at a lower level. However, this is not a specific problem of use of nationality as the connecting factor. Individual national conflicts laws, treaties and EU regulations contain provisions for such lower level connections. Examples include: art 14 Rome III Regulation, art 36 Succession Regulation, art 16 Hague Maintenance Protocol 2007 (interlocal conflict of laws), art 15 Rome III Regulation, art 37 Succession Regulation, art 16 Hague Maintenance Protocol 2007 (interpersonal conflict of laws).

3. Multiple nationalities

The number of people holding multiple nationalities is constantly rising due to the fact that it is more and more common nowadays for both parents to be able to confer their citizenship (see I.3.a)). If a person has more than one nationality, a decision has to be made as to which one is decisive. Most national laws contain provisions for such cases and either (i) favour the laws of the home state in which the person is ordinarily resident or, subsidiarily, the home state to which the person actually has the closest ties (eg art 19 Chinese Statute of Application of Law to Foreign Civil Relations (adopted at the 17th session of the Standing Committee of the 11th National People's Congress on 28 October 2010, effective 1 April 2011, henceforth Chinese PILA); art 11(1) Book 10 of the Dutch CC, etc), or (ii) only use actual ties (eg art 5(1) German EGBGB; art 2(1) Polish Private international law Act (Official Journal 2011 No 80, pos 432, henceforth Polish PILA), etc).

If a person holds the nationality of the forum state, most laws only use this nationality (eg art 9(1) Austrian Federal Code on Private international law (Bundesgesetz über das internationale Privatrecht of 15 June 1978, BGBl. No 304/1978, as amended, henceforth Austrian PILA); art 3, § 2 no 1 Belgian PILA; art 5(1) German EGBGB; art 19(2) Italian PILA; art 2(1) Polish PILA; art 27 Portuguese Código civil (Direitos dos estrangeiros e conflitos de leis); art 9, § 9 Spanish CC etc). Non-codification of the preference of the forum's nationality is rare (examples include art 1262(1) Armenian Civil Code (Civil code of Armenia as adopted in 1998, Division 12, art 1253–93); art 19 Chinese PILA; art 11(1) Book 10 of the Dutch CC). Under the former, unwritten German conflict laws, the effective nationality – meaning the nationality of the state to which the person has the closest connection – was also determinative in cases of people holding German nationality and at least one other nationality (see German Federal Court of Justice (BGH), 20 June 1979, [1979] NJW 2468). Conflicts rules that allow a choice between home laws often permit the person holding multiple nationalities to choose any of their home laws (see art 22 Succession Regulation). The same applies in cases where nationality establishes the jurisdiction of one of the home states' courts. The ECJ made a similar decision with regards to jurisdiction for recognition in *Hadadi v Hadadi* (C-168/08, [2009] ECR I-6871). If the applicable law is to be determined through nationality and there is a contest between the nationalities of different Member States, according preference to the forum's nationality might be a breach of art 18 TFEU (in this sense Jürgen Basedow, 'Das Staatsangehörigkeitsprinzip in der Europäischen Union' [2011] IPRax 109, 114; Heinz-Peter Mansel, 'The Impact of the European Union's Prohibition of Discrimination and the Right of Free Movement of Persons on the Private international law Rules of Member States' in Katharina Boele-Woelki and others (eds), *Convergence and Divergence in Private international law: Liber Amicorum Kurt Siehr* (Eleven International Publishing 2010) 291, 298 with further references). The German Federal Court of Justice did not have to take a position on this question and could leave it unanswered (German Federal Court of Justice (BGH), 19 February 2014 [2014] NJW 1381, 1384). The ECJ did not have to take an explicit position either. However, it has implicitly indicated that preference for the forum state might be discriminatory in certain circumstances. In *Garcia Avello* (Case C-148/02 *Carlos Garcia Avello v Belgian State* [2003] ECR I-11613) the Court held that, with regard to a Spanish-Belgian national who ordinarily resided in Belgium, the application of Belgian name laws would be discriminatory if the parents wanted to give the child a name according to the laws and traditions of Spain. In effect, the CJEU held that the preference for the forum state's nationality or effective nationality was discriminatory; the Court allowed a choice of law between the two home laws. Where there is no choice of law, or where there are multiple people involved and they do not all make the same choice, a decision has to be made on a case-by-case basis. The *Garcia Avello* decision at least shows that a mechanical application of a preference rule violates art 18 TFEU (Jürgen Basedow, 'Das Staatsangehörigkeitsprinzip in der Europäischen Union' [2011] IPRax 109, 114).

4. *Stateless people, refugees and asylum-seekers*

The personal status of stateless people and refugees is primarily governed by treaties. In most cases, residence is used to determine the personal status. Of particular importance for stateless people is the United Nations Conventions relating the Status of Stateless Persons of 28 September 1954 (360 UNTS 117); for refugees, the most important treaty is the Geneva Convention of 22 April 1951 relating to the Status of Refugees (189 UNTS 137).

The treaty rules are reflected in national legislation. For people who are stateless, most national laws apply either (i) the laws of the place of habitual residence and, occasionally, subsidiarily, the laws of the place of simple residence (eg art 9(1) Austrian PILA; art 3, § 3 (refugees) § 4 (stateless) Belgian PILA; art 5(2) EGBGB etc) or (ii) the laws of the place of registered residence and, subsidiarily, the laws of the place of simple residence (eg art 1262(2) Armenian Civil Code; art 19(1) Italian PILA; art 3 Polish PILA etc). Occasionally, the same laws are applied in cases where the nationality of a person cannot be determined (eg art 3, § 4 Belgian PILA; art 5(2) EGBGB; art 3 Polish PILA).

Asylum-seekers and those who have already received asylum are treated as refugees within the meaning of the Refugee Convention under some national laws even though they do not meet the criteria of the convention (eg § 2(2) Asylum Procedure Act (Asylverfahrensgesetz (AsylVfG) of 2 September 2008, BGBl. I 1798, as amended)). In other countries, however, for such individuals, the laws of the asylum state are applied to personal status matters (art 1262(3) Armenian Civil Code).

5. *Changes of home state in public international law*

If a new government is exercising sovereignty in a person's home state – either because of an annexation, occupation, putsch, revolution or a collapse of the old government – and the forum state does not recognize this change, it is uncertain if a new nationality introduced by the new government has any effect in conflict of laws. It is mostly accepted in cases in which the new government effectively exercises a law-controlling power in the territory (see Joe Verhoeven, 'Relations internationales de droit privé en l'absence de reconnaissance d'un Etat, d'un gouvernement ou d'une situation' (1985-II) 192 Rec. des Cours 9, 158 ff and 179 ff).

VII. Jurisdiction

A lot of states provide for a so-called 'home jurisdiction' in matters of personal law, family law and the laws of succession. The courts of these states have international jurisdiction for any lawsuit or motion brought by their nationals. In particular, a person can have matters relating to personal status (eg divorce (→ Divorce and personal separation), descent, → adoption etc) resolved with immediate binding effect for his home state and its administrative agencies. Article 14, 15 French CC and the legal systems that have adopted this rule provide for an even more comprehensive home jurisdiction. According to this rule, a French national can sue a foreigner in a French court. At the same time, a foreigner can sue a French national in a French court. The wording of this rule is limited to contractual matters, but French courts have extended it to all types of legal disputes.

Home jurisdiction rules extend the duty of other parties to appear in front of a court. Thus, the jurisdiction under art 14, 15 French CC is deemed to be exorbitant under art 3(1) Brussels I Regulation (art 5(2) and art 76(1) lit a) Brussels I Regulation (recast)). That notwithstanding, a claimant residing in France can rely on it with regard to a defendant residing outside the EU, according to art 4(2) Brussels I Regulation (art 6(2) Brussels I Regulation (recast)). Due to their potentially discriminatory effect, home jurisdiction rules are rarely used in EU legislation; a limited example can be found in the Brussels IIa Regulation (see for an example I.2.), art 6 Maintenance Regulation (common nationality as a means of determining subsidiary jurisdiction), and art 10 Succession Regulation (subsidiary jurisdiction of the home state when the habitual residence of the deceased at the time of death is not located in a Member State).

HEINZ-PETER MANSEL

Literature

Louis d'Avout, 'La lex personalis entre nationalité, domicile et résidence habituelle' in *Mélanges en l'honneur du Professeur Bernard Audit* (L.G.D.J. 2014) 17; Jürgen Basedow, 'Das Staatsangehörigkeitsprinzip in der Europäischen Union' [2011] IPRax 109; Oliver Dörr, 'Nationality' in Rüdiger Wolfrum (ed), *Max Planck Encyclopedia of Public International Law* (OUP 2012); Hélène Gaudemet-Tallon, 'Nationalité, statut personnel et droit de l'homme' in Heinz-Peter Mansel and others (eds), *Festschrift für Erik Jayme* (Sellier European Law Publishers 2004) 205 ff; Jürgen Habermas, 'Citizenship and National Identity' in Bart Van Steenbergen (ed), *The Condition of Citizenship* (Sage 1994) 20ff; Erik Jayme, 'Identité culturelle et intégration: le droit international privé postmoderne' (1995) 251 Rec. des Cours 9; Christian Kohler, 'L'autonomie de la volonté en droit international privé: un principe universel entre libéralisme et étatisme' (2013) 359 Rec. des Cours 285; Alexander Lüderitz, 'Anknüpfung im Parteiinteresse' in Alexander Lüderitz and Jochen Schröder (eds), *Internationales Privatrecht und Rechtsvergleichung im Ausgang des 20. Jahrhunderts. Bewahrung oder Wende? Festschrift für Gerhard Kegel* (Metzner 1977) 31; Pasquale Stanislao Mancini, 'Della nazionalità come fondamento del dritto delle genti: prelezione al corso di dritto internazionale e marittimo pronunziata nella R. Università di Torino nel di 22 gennaio 1851' published by Erik Jayme (G Giappichelli 1994; first published by Botta 1851; later in Diritto internazionale, Marghieri 1873) 19; Heinz-Peter Mansel, *Personalstatut, Staatsangehörigkeit und Effektivität* (CH Beck 1988); Heinz-Peter Mansel, 'Die kulturelle Identität im internationalen Privatrecht' in Georg Nolte and others (eds), *Pluralistische Gesellschaften und Internationales Recht* (CF Müller 2008) 137; Heinz-Peter Mansel, 'The Impact of the European Union's Prohibition of Discrimination and the Right of Free Movement of Persons on the Private international law Rules of Member States' in Katharina Boele-Woelki and others (eds), Convergence and Divergence in Private international law: *Liber Amicorum Kurt Siehr* (Eleven International Publishing 2010) 291; Yuko Nishitani, 'Gobal Citizens and Family Relations' [2014] ELR 134; Joe Verhoeven, 'Relations internationales de droit privé en l'absence de reconnaissance d'un Etat, d'un gouvernement ou d'une situation' (1985-II) 192 Rec des Cours 9; Olivier Vonk, *Nationality Law in the Western Hemisphere* (Brill/Nijhoff 2014); Louis I de Winter, 'Nationality or Domicile? The Present State of Affairs' (1969-III) 128 Rec. des Cours 344.

Negotiorum gestio

I. Generalities

Negotiorum gestio is a specific kind of extracontractual obligation. Accordingly, it is governed by the → Rome II Regulation (Regulation (EC) No 864/2007 of the European Parliament and of the Council of 11 July 2007 on the law applicable to non-contractual obligations (Rome II), [2007] OJ L 199/40), of which art 11 concerns this topic. The fact that a single article is deemed sufficient, reflects the lack of genuine relevance and importance *negotiorum gestio* enjoys both in the academic treatment of private international law and in practice. To some extent, *negotiorum gestio* is a step-child of the Rome II Regulation. Generally, the topic has generated relatively little excitement and academic treatment, and the number of rules devoted to issues of *negotiorum gestio* in national private international law codifications is limited if not scarce. For instance, the Turkish Private international law Code (Code on Private International and International Civil Procedure Law of 27 November 2007 (Act No 5718) (Milletlerarası Özel Hukuk ve Usul Hukuku Hakkında Kanun), Resmî Gazete No 26728 of 12 December 2007), although generally borrowing heavily from the Rome II Regulation, contains no rule on *negotiorum gestio*. Nor do the Swiss Private international law Act (Bundesgesetz über das Internationale Privatrecht of 18 December 1987, 1988 BBl I 5, as amended) and § 31.850 (5) Or.Rev.Stat. Article 14 new Japanese Private international law Act (Japanese Act on General Rules for Application of Laws (Hōno Tekiyō ni Kansuru Tsūsokuhō, Law No 10 of 1898, as newly titled and amended by Act No 78 of 21 June 2006)) treats *negotiorum gestio* and → unjust enrichment alike in a rather brush-stoke rule, without further differentiation and summarizing them under the common heading of 'non-contractual obligations other than tort'. Article 47 Chinese Statute of Application of Law to Foreign Civil Relations (adopted at the 17th session of the Standing Committee of the 11th National People's Congress on 28 October 2010, effective 1 April 2011, henceforth Chinese PILA) on its wording also treats *negotiorum gestio* together with unjust enrichment, although this rule is more elaborate than the Japanese provision. By contrast art 30 Korean Private international law Act (Law 6465 of 7 April 2001, Amending the Conflict of Laws Act of the Republic of Korea, henceforth Korean PILA) addresses *negotiorum gestio* in a separate Article devoted entirely to the topic.

The main reason for the relative lack of even modern legislation on *negotiorum gestio* might be that the topic is not germane to the substantive law of many legal orders. Where the own substantive law of a forum is silent regarding *negotiorum gestio*, that form state can hardly be expected to deal with *negotiorum gestio* in its private international law. A second reason might be that *negotiorum gestio* covers a vast array of possible cases and scenarios which have little in common and which do not lend themselves to a uniform private international law approach, particularly from a comparative law perspective (→ Comparative law and private international law). *Negotiorum gestio* cannot be conclusively and exhaustively described as benevolent intervention in another's affairs. In some jurisdictions it might serve as a form of default regulation for void or invalid contracts, while in others it might function as a regulatory instrument for re-allocating and re-distributing by private enforcement.

The lack of intensity and specific care in the treatment which the Rome II Regulation administers to *negotiorum gestio* might indicate the lack of practical relevance in private international law of *negotiorum gestio*. There are only very few decided cases and beyond that a dearth of potential factual scenarios.

The principle example which comes to mind, that of assistance rendered by one ship to another on the high seas with consequential → salvage is governed by a special convention, the 1989 Salvage Convention (International Convention of 28 April 1989 on Salvage, 1953 UNTS 165), successor to the 1910 Salvage Convention (International Convention of 23 September 1910 for the Unification of certain Rules of Law related to Assistance and Salvage at Sea, in K Zweigert and J Kropholler, *Sources of International Uniform Law*, vol 2 (AW Sijthoff 1972) 7; 206 LNTS 220), and accordingly is outside the application of general conflict rules. Further in practice, most salvage cases involve salvors, who simply do not render their services without having obtained a proper contract in advance. Generally, in most instances where assistance of any kind or specific services are required, parties will conclude appropriate contracts, whereupon the case is no longer one of *negotiorum gestio*.

II. Characterization issues

1. In general

The basic characterization of *negotiorum gestio* is to be found in art 11(1) *principio* Rome II Regulation, which covers non-contractual obligations arising out of an act performed without due authority in connection with the affairs of another person. This is a rather broad notion, and the Regulation correctly refrains from introducing benevolence as a prerequisite. By contrast, investigating the intervener's motives and requiring the intervener to act out of altruistic, not egotistic motives as proposed by art V-1:101 DCFR (Study Group on a European Civil Code/ Research Group on EC Private Law (Acquis Group) (ed), Principles, Definitions and Model Rules of European Private Law, Draft Common Frame of Reference (DCFR), Outline Edition 2009), would introduce additional limitations and unduly burden the characterization process through looking *ex post* into a person's mind. Article 11(1) Rome II Regulation must attempt to cover divergent approaches by on the one hand those Member States whose legal systems, rooted in Roman law, recognize the institution of *negotiorum gestio*, and other Member States from whose substantive laws the institution is absent. Furthermore, the Regulation must govern both claims by the intervener against the principal and claims by the principal against the intervener, the latter for recovery of damage caused or benefits received. Finally, for the applicability of art 11 Rome II Regulation it is immaterial whether a *negotiorum gestio* is justified or unjustified, since both categories of *negotiorum gestio* receive equal treatment. The issue of whether a justification exists is left to the law applicable to the concrete *negotiorum gestio*. Recital (11) Rome II Regulation calls for an autonomous concept for the term 'non-contractual obligation', whereas Recital (29) Rome II Regulation mentions *negotiorum gestio* only in passing without further exploration or explanation.

2. Specific issues

The specific issues of characterization of *negotiorum gestio* have been less intensively discussed than → torts in general. This is evidenced by art 15 Rome II Regulation, in that it is formulated in terms specific for torts, eg liability, damage or compensation for damage, whereas *negotiorum gestio* would require the use of a different terminology. It would have been appropriate to insert a separate characterization rule specifically designed for *negotiorum gestio*, as generally providing parallel systematic treatment of *negotiorum gestio* to that of tort through a separate, complete and comprehensive chapter would have put both topics on an equal footing at least with regard to systematic weight.

III. Connecting factors

Article 11 Rome II Regulation would seem as suitable as any rule to regulate the private international law of *negotiorum gestio* in that it takes the most elaborate approach currently visible in the market of conflict laws. The art 11 provision employs a five step-approach to ascertaining the law applicable to a certain *negotiorum gestio*.

1. Parties' choice of law

The first step is covert as regards the Regulation, in that creditor and debtor may chose the applicable law pursuant to art 14 Rome II Regulation and under the ramifications enshrined in that rule. Party autonomy is not expressly granted in art 11 Rome II Regulation, since that would have been an unnecessary reduplication, given the overall structure of the Regulation with its art 14 covering all kinds of non-contractual obligations including *negotiorum gestio*. Applying art 14 Rome II Regulation includes all restrictions placed by the provision on party autonomy, particularly its severe limitations on B2C relationships. If judged only on its wording, art 47 cl 1 Chinese PILA also grants the parties unrestricted autonomy to choose the law applicable to a *negotiorum gestio*.

2. Accessory connection to a leading relationship

The second step establishes an accessory connection by virtue of art 11(1) Rome II Regulation:

> [i]f a non-contractual obligation arising out of act performed without due authority in connection with affairs of another person concerns a relationship between the parties, such as one arising out of a contract or a tort/delict, that is closely connected with that non-contractual obligation, it shall be governed by the law that governs that relationship.

Article 30(1) cl 2 Korean PILA provides to the same effect.

However, some cautionary remarks might be appropriate. First, under art 11 the contract must contain no contractual obligation of one party to act on the other's behalf and in its interest, as otherwise no *negotiorum gestio* could exist. This is because a *negotiorum gestio* can only properly be said to exist where a contractual obligation is absent. Second, there is some doubt regarding whether the governing relationship must be a pre-existing one, as is of particular importance with regard to torts committed *uno actu* with the *negotiorum gestio*.

Contracts and torts expressly listed as potential candidates for constituting a leading relationship are only examples. Relationships stemming from family law are equally feasible if relationships are disregarded arising out of family relations, matrimonial property regimes or → successions as excluded from the scope of the Rome II Regulation pursuant to its art 1(2)(a) and (b). It is irrelevant whether the law applicable to the leading relationship is determined following the parties' choice of law in turn recognized under the relevant private international law rules, or alternatively ascertained by an objective determination. This means in particular that the greater extent of party autonomy granted in the realm of contracts by arts 3–9 Rome I Regulation (Regulation (EC) No 593/2008 of the European Parliament and of the Council of 17 June 2008 on the law applicable to contractual obligations (Rome I), [2008] OJ L 177/6; → Rome Convention and Rome I Regulation (contractual obligations)) also gains importance in the field of *negotiorum gestio*.

3. Parties' common habitual residence

The third step is to be found in art 11(2) Rome II Regulation: '[w]here the law applicable cannot be determined on the basis of paragraph 1, and the parties have their habitual residence in the same country when the event giving rise to the damage occurs, the law of that country shall apply'. Hence, the law of the parties' common habitual residences in the same country, not necessarily the same place, is to be applied. However, if the parties reside in different countries, under art 11(2) Rome II Regulation the required connecting factor is expressly a particularly strong connection, reflecting the same idea as under art 4(2) for tort.

Article 47 cl 2 Chinese PILA seizes on the parties' common habitual residence on the second tier.

4. Performance of the act

The fourth step contains the most specific and perhaps even the principal rule. Article 11(3) Rome II Regulation reads: '[w]here the law applicable cannot be determined on the basis of paragraph 1 or 2, it shall be the law of the country in which the act was performed'. This clearly is both a default and a catch-all rule. Article 30(1) cl 1 Korean PILA refers to the place where the management of another's affairs was done. Article 47 cl 3 Chinese PILA seizes on the place where the *negotiorum gestio* occurs.

Nevertheless, the connecting factor employed raises a number of notional issues. The first is to decide whether the event as such matters or its consequences. The wording would tentatively lead to emphasizing the act, whereas consistency with art 4(1) Rome II Regulation, the basic conflicts rule for torts, strongly militates in favour of the consequences. Congruency and consistency with the approach taken as to torts may be of the essence in the frequent cases where claims in tort and in *negotiorum gestio* happen to coincide. In addition, if one emphasizes the activity as the predominant element, the consequential issue of identifying the relevant activity ensues, and in particular whether commencement of the activity is decisive, or each single act of activity, or the culminating activity. Referring to the drafting process, it is at least clear that performance of the act leads to the *locus gestionis* as promoted by the European Parliament (Legislative Resolution P6_TA(2005)0284 p 14), and that the Commission Proposal in favour of the *lex domicilii gestoris* (European Commission, 'Proposal for a Regulation of the European Parliament and of the Council on the Law Applicable to Non-Contractual Obligations ("Rome II")' COM(2003) 427 final p 35 *et seq*) was ultimately rejected.

Article 30(2) Korean PILA opts for the *lex causae* of the respective obligation if the gestor performs and fulfils another's obligation.

5. Escape clause

The fifth step consists of an escape clause as laid down in art 11(4) Rome II Regulation:

> [w]here it is clear from the circumstances of the case that the non-contractual obligation arising out of act performed without due authority in connection with affairs of another person is manifestly more closely connected with a country other than that indicated in paragraphs 1, 2 and 3, the law of that other country shall apply.

As with all escape clauses, this rule has to be employed with extreme caution and must not be misunderstood as a backdoor device granting the liberty to deviate at will from the preceding rules.

PETER MANKOWSKI

Literature

Saverio de Bellis, 'La negotiorum gestio nel Regolamento (CE) n. 864/2007' in Gabriella Venturini and Stefania Bariatti (eds), *Liber Fausto Pocar – Volume II – Nuovi strumenti del diritto internazionale private* (Giuffré 2009) 245; Gralff-Peter Calliess (ed), *Rome Regulations* (Kluwer 2011); Andrew Dickinson, *The Rome II Regulation* (OUP 2008); Tim Q. Dornis, 'Die Erbensuche im Kollisionsrecht – Von grenzüberschreitender "Menschenhülfe" zu internationaler Marktregulierung', [2015] ZfPW 376; Tim W. Dornis, 'Das Kollisionsrecht der auftragslosen Geschäftsführung – Ein Beispiel für Materialisierung und Typisierung im modernen europäischen IPR', (2016) 80 Rabels Zeitschrift 543; Gerfried Fischer, 'Ungerechtfertigte Bereicherung und Geschäftsführung ohne Auftrag im europäischen Internationalen Privatrecht' in Jörn Bernreuther and others (eds), *Festschrift für Ulrich Spellenberg zum 70. Geburtstag* (Sellier 2010) 151; Felix Hartmann, 'Von der negotiorum gestio zur Benevolent Intervention in Another's Affairs' in Thomas Lobinger (ed), *Festschrift für Eduard Picker zum 70. Geburtstag am 3. November 2010* (Mohr Siebeck 2010) 341; Peter Huber, *Rome II Regulation* (Sellier 2011); Timo Nehne, 'Die internationale Geschäftsführung ohne Auftrag nach der Rom II-Verordnung – Anknüpfungsgegenstand und Anknüpfungspunkte' [2012] IPRax 136; Franz Jürgen Säcker and Roland Rixecker (eds), *Münchener Kommentar zum BGB, Bd. 10: Rom I-VO; Rom II-VO; Art. 1–24 EGBGB* (5th edn, CH Beck 2010); Christian von Bar (ed), *Benevolent Intervention in Another's Affairs* (Sellier 2006); Manfred Wandt, *Die Geschäftsführung ohne Auftrag im internationalen Privatrecht* (Duncker & Humblot 1989); Christoph Wendelstein, 'Das Statut der Geschäftsführung ohne Auftrag in Nothilfefällen – "Wechselwirkungen" zwischen Kollisionsrecht und Sachrecht' [2014] GPR 46.

Nuclear liability

I. Justifications for seeking uniformity

More and more countries in Europe and around the world use nuclear energy or are engaged in building new installations as means to satisfy their growing energy needs and to fulfil their commitments to reduce carbon dioxide emissions. The proliferation of nuclear technology around the globe and its intensified use has increased the risk of accidents at a nuclear installation or during the transport of nuclear substances. Major accidents may cause severe damage as the 1986 Chernobyl and the 2011 Fukushima incidents have shown: there is not only direct and immediate damage to property. Even years after the accident victims may suffer damage to health due to the long-term effects of ionizing radiation on the human body. In addition people may need to be relocated to new homes, measures to reinstate an impaired environment have to be taken and farmers and fishermen must be compensated for economic loss resulting from bans on the sale of agricultural products or fish. Nuclear damage will often not be confined to the country in which the accident took place as wind or water spread releases radiation to neighbouring or even more remote countries. The 1986 Chernobyl incident for example caused damage not only in the → Ukraine where the power plant was located, but also in → Austria, → Belarus, → Finland, → Germany, → Poland, → Sweden, Russia (→ Russian Federation) and elsewhere. Therefore even countries without nuclear installations on their territory must consider issues of jurisdiction and applicable tort law to ensure an adequate protection of their citizens.

Since the beginning of the commercial use of nuclear technology in the mid-1950s many states were aware of the nuclear risk and the trans-boundary nature of damage caused by major accidents. In addition the view was widespread that the particularities of the nuclear risk calls for an international liability regime which not only unifies the general standards of liability but also addresses the issues of jurisdiction for actions for → damages as well as the recognition and enforcement of judgments abroad (Carlton Stoiber and others, *Handbook on Nuclear Law* (IAEA 2003) 107).

The drafting of a uniform liability regime involves, however, crucial policy choices: as the damages resulting from a major accident can be of a very high magnitude, the operator of a nuclear installation will not have sufficient funds to fully indemnify all victims. This raises the question as to the amount of his liability. Moreover, an international insurance system has to be organized to increase the amount of available funds for compensation. Finally, the salient question has to be answered if and under which circumstances the taxpayers, either in the state in which the incident took place and/or in the state(s) where the damage occurred, will provide additional funds for the compensation of victims. Against this background the design of a uniform liability law thus depends on various factors. One important factor is the willingness of a society to support the growth of the nuclear industry. The higher the support of the state for its nuclear industry, the lower will be the burden of liability for operators of nuclear installations. This is a form of subsidy to the nuclear industry. Another important factor is the general economic situation of a state. For developed states it is for example less burdensome to promise the supply of additional public funds for the compensation of losses than for developing states. Therefore it does not come as a surprise that over the course of the years a variety of international nuclear liability conventions have been concluded.

II. Avenues for promoting uniformity

1. International Atomic Energy Agency

The main body for the unification of nuclear liability law is the International Atomic Energy Agency (IAEA) in Vienna, which was established in 1957. Under the auspices of this organization various international conventions have been negotiated, namely the Vienna Nuclear Liability Convention (Vienna Convention on Civil Liability for Nuclear Damage of 21 May 1963, 1063 UNTS 265) revised by a protocol in 1997 (Protocol to amend the Vienna Convention on Civil Liability for Nuclear Damage of 12 September 1997, 2241 UNTS 270) and the Nuclear Supplementary Compensation Convention (Convention on Supplementary Compensation for Nuclear Damage of 12 September 1997, INFCIRC/567, henceforth SC Convention).

The Vienna Nuclear Liability Convention establishes the liability of the operator of a nuclear installation. The 1997 Protocol broadens the scope of liability, increases the amount of liability of the operator of a nuclear installation and shall provide for enhanced means to secure adequate and equitable compensation (cf preamble of the 1997 Protocol).

The SC Convention supplements the liability system laid down in the Vienna Nuclear Liability Convention with the aim of increasing the amount of compensation for nuclear damage. It establishes a second tier of compensation to complement the operator's liability so that victims may be compensated out of additional funds provided by the contracting states. Moreover, the SC Convention is designed to link (and in part even to supersede) different (national or regional) liability regimes.

The Vienna Nuclear Liability Convention and the SC Convention are open to all states in the world and could thus serve as a basis for a unification of the law at the global level. Compared to nuclear agreements for specific nuclear matters such as the Convention on the Early Notification of a Nuclear Accident of 26 September 1986 (1439 UNTS 276) and the Convention on Assistance in the Case of a Nuclear Accident or Radiological Emergency of 26 September 1986 (1457 UNTS 133), which have both been ratified by over 100 states, the unification effect reached so far by the liability conventions is rather limited (Norbert Pelzer, 'On Global Treaty Relations: Hurdles on the Way towards a Universal Civil Nuclear Liability Regime' (2008) 6 EurUP 268, 270 f). The Vienna Nuclear Liability Convention has 40 contracting parties, including → Argentina, Belarus, → Brazil, → Egypt, Russia, → Saudi Arabia and the Ukraine. Of the EU Member States, ten have joined this convention (→ Bulgaria, → Croatia, → Czech Republic, → Estonia, → Hungary, → Latvia, → Lithuania, Poland, → Romania and → Slovakia). The 1997 Protocol has so far been ratified by only 13 states, amongst them three EU states (Latvia, Poland and Romania). The SC Convention has thus far been ratified by nine states in the world (Argentina → Ghana, → India, → Japan, → Montenegro, Morocco, Romania, the United Arab Emirates and the → USA) and is in force since 15 April 2015 (the latest status of both conventions and the 1997 Protocol to the Vienna Nuclear Liability Convention is available at <www.iaea.org>).

It is important to note that not all nuclear power states in the world are bound by international conventions. → Canada, → China, → India, → Japan, both Koreas, Pakistan and → South Africa for example have so far not joined any of the international liability regimes. Some states have, however, aligned their national laws in part with selected liability standards laid down in the Vienna Nuclear Liability Convention. Also the USA did not adhere to an international treaty system for a long time as it was the first state that had codified a comprehensive nuclear liability regime, the Price-Anderson Act of 1957 (Price-Anderson Nuclear Industries Indemnity Act, 42 U.S.C. ch

23; revised in 2005). This changed in 2008, when the USA joined the SC Convention, which came into force on 15 April 2015

2. Organisation for Economic Co-operation and Development

The second international organization active in the field of uniform liability rules is the Organisation for Economic Co-operation and Development (OECD) in Paris. The debates on the elaboration of a nuclear liability convention started at the end of the 1950s under the auspices of its forerunner, the Organisation for European Economic Co-operation (OEEC). As the OEEC was established as a body for the administration of the Marshall Plan for the reconstruction of Europe after the Second World War (which was opposed by the Soviet Union and the states within its zone of influence), from the outset the focus of the negotiations was on the creation of a regional system primarily for Western European states. Within the framework of the OEEC/OECD the Paris Convention on Third Party Liability in the Field of Nuclear Energy of 29 July 1960 (956 UNTS 263) was adopted which was later amended by the Additional Protocol of 1964 (Additional Protocol of 28 January 1964 to the Convention of Third Party Liability in the Field of Nuclear Energy, 956 UNTS 335), the Protocol of 1982 (Protocol of 16 November 1982 to amend the Convention on third party liability in the field of nuclear energy, as amended by the Additional Protocol of 28 January 1964, 1519 UNTS 329) and the Protocol of 2004 (Protocol of 12 February 2004 to amend the Convention on Third Party Liability in the Field of Nuclear Energy, as amended by the Additional Protocol of 28 January 1964 and by the Protocol of 16 November 1982, <www.oecd-nea.org/law/paris_convention.pdf>) (henceforth Paris Nuclear Liability Convention). This liability regime was strengthened by the Brussels Convention Supplementary to the Paris Convention (Convention of 31 January 1963 Supplementary to the Convention on Third Party Liability in the Field of Nuclear Energy, 1041 UNTS 358), which was revised by Protocols of 1964 (Additional Protocol of 28 January 1964 to Amend the Convention of 31 January 1963 Supplementary to the Convention on Third Party Liability in the Field of Nuclear Energy of 29 July 1960, 956 UNTS 335), 1982 (Protocol of 16 November 1982 to Amend the Convention of 31 January 1963 Supplementary to the Convention on Third Party Liability in the Field of Nuclear Energy of 29 July 1960 as amended by the Additional Protocol of 28 January 1964, 1650 UNTS 446) and 2004 (Protocol of 12 February 2004 to Amend the Convention of 31 January 1963 Supplementary to the Paris Convention on Third Party Liability in the Field of Nuclear Energy of 29 July 1960, as amended by the Additional Protocol of 28 January 1964 and by the Protocol of 16 November 1982, <www.oecd-nea.org/law/brussels_supplementary_convention.pdf>). These conventions are open to OECD states only. Other states may join if all contracting parties agree to an accession.

The unifying effect of these regional conventions is also of a limited nature. The 1960 Paris Nuclear Liability Convention and its revisions through the protocols of 1964 and 1982 have been ratified by 16 states, including all Western European countries except Austria, → Luxembourg, → Ireland, Cyprus and → Malta. These states consider their national laws to provide a better compensation scheme for victims of nuclear accidents than the international liability regime. The 2004 Protocol to amend the Paris Nuclear Liability Convention is not yet in force as the necessary amount of ratifications has not been reached (the latest status of the amended Paris Convention and the 2004 Protocol is available at <www.oecd-nea.org>). It was negotiated in the aftermath of the 1986 Chernobyl disaster, an incident that demonstrated clearly that the Paris Nuclear Liability Convention's liability system does not provide sufficient and adequate compensation for nuclear damage suffered in major nuclear incidents. The 2004 Protocol therefore substantially increases the liability caps and enlarges the Convention's scope of application to nuclear installations for the disposal of waste and installations that are in the course of being decommissioned. Moreover it broadens the types of damages for which victims are entitled to claim compensation. In addition to personal injury and damage to property, the 2004 Protocol entitles victims *inter alia* to claim compensation for measures to reinstate a significantly impaired environment and for loss of income deriving from a direct economic interest in any use or enjoyment of the environment. These amendments convinced Switzerland to join the Paris Nuclear Liability Convention in 2009. Its accession will become effective when the 2004 Protocol comes into force.

The 1963 Brussels Supplementary Convention bolsters the Paris Nuclear Liability Convention's regime by stipulating that the contracting states have to provide for additional funds in cases where the amounts of compensation to be paid by the installation's operator under the Paris Convention are insufficient. To keep the Brussels Supplementary Convention and the Paris Nuclear Liability Conventions synchronized, each revision of the Paris Convention went hand in hand with a revision of the Brussels Supplementary Convention (1964 and 1982 Protocols). The 'post-Chernobyl' protocol to the Brussels Supplementary Convention of 2004, which increases the amounts of compensation considerably, is not yet in force. The Brussels Supplementary Convention and its 1964 and 1982 amending protocols have been adopted so far by 12 states, most of which belong to the EU (Belgium, Denmark, Finland, France, Germany, Italy, the Netherlands, Norway, Slovenia, Spain, Sweden and the → United Kingdom). From the EU Member States that adhere to the Paris Nuclear Liability Convention, only → Greece and → Portugal have not joined the Brussels Supplementary Convention. Recently Switzerland has also ratified the Brussels Supplementary Convention including all protocols. Its ratification will become effective when the 2004 Protocol to the Brussels Supplementary Convention will enter into force (the latest status of the amended Brussels Supplementary Convention and its 2004 Protocol is available at <www.oecd-nea.org>).

3. International Maritime Organization

For the field of maritime law, a third actor has to be mentioned: the International Maritime Organization (→ IMO). In a joint effort, the IAEA, the OECD and the IMO hosted in 1971 an international conference in Brussels, which adopted the 1971 Brussels Civil Liability Convention (Convention Relating to Civil Liability in the Field of Maritime Carriage of Nuclear Material of 17 December 1971, 974 UNTS 255).

This convention in essence exonerates maritime players from liability for nuclear damage to ensure that maritime liability rules do not interfere with the liability regime set forth by the Paris and Vienna Nuclear Liability Conventions. One common feature of the Paris and Vienna Nuclear Liability Conventions is the channelling of liability onto the operator of the nuclear installation (*infra* III.1.). Therefore the 1971 Brussels Civil Liability Convention exempts those persons from liability who by virtue of an international convention or of national maritime transport law rules might be held liable for damage caused by a nuclear incident. The exemption applies if the operator of a nuclear installation is also liable for that damage, be it according to the Paris Nuclear Liability Convention, the Vienna Nuclear Liability Convention or by provisions of national law that correspond to the rules of these conventions (art 1 1971 Brussels Civil Liability Convention). Therefore the shipowner is never liable for nuclear damage caused by the transport of nuclear material unless he caused the damage intentionally. This exoneration from liability does not affect the liability of the operator of a nuclear ship for damage caused by nuclear fuel or radioactive waste produced in such ship (art 3 1971 Brussels Civil Liability Convention). The 1971 Brussels Civil Liability Convention entered into force on 15 July 1975. Today 17 states have joined this convention: Argentina, Belgium, Bulgaria, Denmark, Dominican Republic, Finland, France, Gabon, Germany, Italy, Latvia, Liberia, the Netherlands, Norway, Spain, Sweden and Yemen.

An earlier attempt to unify the law of the liability of operators of nuclear ships was not successful. The Convention on the Liability of Operators of Nuclear Ships of 25 May 1962 ((1963) 57 Am.J.Int'l L. 268) has not yet entered into force and it is very unlikely that this will change in the near future. Under this Convention the operator of a nuclear ship is strictly liable for nuclear damage caused by the ship up to a certain liability cap. Some states, for example Germany, have, however, transposed the general principles of this Convention into their national tort law.

4. Towards a global or at least a European liability regime?

This brief overview of the international treaty law has shown that it is very difficult to create a truly uniform solution at the global level. As not even all major nuclear power states have joined one of the major two liability regimes, the Vienna and the Paris regime, there is little hope that considerable progress will be made in the near future to unify the law substantively. It is, however, expected that the number of states joining the international regime will slowly increase over the coming years. There is hope that the recent ratification of the Nuclear Supplementary Compensation

Convention by the United States will encourage other states to join this convention, which is open to all states regardless of whether they are parties to any other international nuclear liability regime (Norbert Pelzer, 'On Global Treaty Relations: Hurdles on the Way towards a Universal Civil Nuclear Liability Regime' (2008) 6 EurUP 268, 272). If a state that is not a party to the Paris or the Vienna Nuclear Liability Convention wants to join the Nuclear Supplementary Compensation Convention it must, however, ensure that its national legislation is consistent with certain minimum standards laid down in the annex to the SC Convention as far as those provisions are not directly applicable in that contracting state.

Given that the major effects of most nuclear accidents usually occur on the continent where the nuclear facility or installation is located, there might be better chances to unify the law on a regional basis. A regionalized system would facilitate compromises with regard to liability caps and additional funds as such policy choices are often based on the standard of economic development of a state or a region. It remains doubtful, however, even within the European Union, whether more uniformity may be reached through international conventions. The current system still reflects the old dividing line of the Cold War: most (but not all) Western European states are party to the Paris Nuclear Liability Convention, whereas many Eastern European states still adhere to the Vienna Nuclear Liability Convention. There is little hope that the European states belonging to one of these conventions will withdraw from it and join the alternative system in the near future (Ulrich Magnus, 'Probleme des internationalen Atomhaftungsrechts' in Dietmar Baetge, Jan von Hein and Michael von Hinden (eds), *Die richtige Ordnung: Festschrift für Jan Kropholler zum 70. Geburtstag* (Mohr Siebeck 2008) 595, 601).

To link the Vienna and the Paris regime, the Joint Protocol (Joint Protocol relating to the application of the Vienna Convention on Civil Liability for Nuclear Damage and the Paris Convention on Third Party Liability in the Field of Nuclear Energy of 21 September 1988, 1672 UNTS 293) was elaborated. This protocol 'bridges' the gap between both liability conventions by mutually extending the benefits of one convention to victims located in states of the other convention and by providing for rules that shall limit the simultaneous application of both Conventions. This 'bridging' was necessary to close a severe gap in the law. Put simply, the Paris Nuclear Liability Convention applies to nuclear incidents occurring in the territory of a contracting state and to damage suffered in such territory (art 2 Paris Nuclear Liability Convention). The Vienna Nuclear Liability Convention is based on the same principle even if there is no explicit rule on its geographical scope of application. As a consequence, a nuclear incident caused in a Vienna state that caused damage in a Paris state is not covered by either of the conventions and *vice versa* (Norbert Pelzer, 'Conflict of Laws Issues under the International Nuclear Liability Conventions' in Jürgen F Baur and others (eds) *Festschrift für Gunther Kühne zum 70. Geburtstag* (Verlag Recht und Wirtschaft 2009) 819, 836f). Through the Joint Protocol, victims of a nuclear accident occurring in a Paris state that has caused damage in a Vienna state can be compensated under the Paris regime and *vice versa*, provided that both states have ratified the Joint Protocol. Thus far 28 states have ratified the Joint Protocol, among them 19 EU Member States (Bulgaria, Czech Republic, Denmark, Estonia, Finland, France Germany, Greece, Hungary, Italy, Latvia, Lithuania, the Netherlands, Poland, Romania, Slovakia, Slovenia, Sweden) (the latest status of the Joint Protocol is available at <www.iaea.org>). Given that not all EU states adhering to one of the basic liability conventions have ratified the Joint Protocol, even this instrument does not ensure uniformity within the EU.

Against this background the European Commission in its Nuclear Illustrative Programme of 2007 raised the idea of 'developing a harmonised liability scheme and mechanisms to ensure the availability of funds in the event of damage caused by a nuclear accident' (Commission of the European Communities, 'Communication from the Commission to the Council and the European Parliament: Nuclear Illustrative Programme' COM(2007) 565 final, p 23). Until now, the Commission has, however, not pursued this idea further (on a European nuclear liability instrument *de lege ferenda* Monika Hinteregger, 'Atomhaftung in Europa – Bestand und Perspektiven' in Peter Apathy and others (eds), *Festschrift für Helmut Koziol zum 70. Geburtstag* (Jan Sramek Verlag 2010) 667, 676f).

III. Uniform law and private international law

1. No comprehensive international liability system

To understand the interplay between the international liability conventions and the principles of private international law, it is important to note that none of the main international liability regimes (Paris Regime, Vienna Regime and the SC Regime) provides for a comprehensive regime covering all aspects of liability towards third parties for nuclear damage. These instruments merely unify the core elements of liability. The regime set forth by the various conventions rests on the following key principles (Susanne Kissich, *Internationales Atomhaftungsrecht: Anwendungsbereich und Haftungsprinzipien* (Nomos 2004) 62–86; Carlton Stoiber and others, *Handbook on Nuclear Law* (IAEA 2003) 109–16; Tom Vanden Borre, 'Shifts in Governance in Compensation for Nuclear Damage, 20 Years after Chernobyl' in Michael Faure and Albert Verheij (eds), *Shifts in Compensation for Environmental Damage* (Springer 2007) 261, 271–8):

- The liability of the operator of a nuclear installation is designed as strict liability (ie regardless of fault) with few defences for exoneration from liability. The operator is for example not liable if the nuclear accident results from an armed conflict (arts 3, 9 Paris Nuclear Liability Convention; art IV(1), (3) Vienna Nuclear Liability Convention; art 3(3), (5) Annex to SC Convention).
- The liability for nuclear damage is 'channelled' to the operator of the nuclear installation that is the cause of the damage (art 6 Paris Nuclear Liability Convention; art II(5) Vienna Nuclear Liability Convention; art 3 Annex to SC Convention). Thus third parties are for example prevented from suing the supplier of nuclear technology for damages.
- The liability of the operator is capped (art 7 Paris Nuclear Liability Convention; art V Vienna Nuclear Liability Convention; art 4 Annex to SC Convention). So beyond a certain point the risks of a nuclear accident are socialized.
- It is compulsory for operators to insure against liability risks to ensure that funds will be made available to third parties (art 10 Paris Nuclear Liability Convention; art VII Vienna Nuclear Liability Convention; art 5 Annex to SC Convention).
- Jurisdiction for damages actions is exclusively conferred upon the courts of the contracting party within whose territory the nuclear accident occurred (art 13(a) Paris Nuclear Liability Convention; art XI(1) Vienna Nuclear Liability Convention; art XIII(1) SC Convention).
- In addition the conventions define the losses for which compensation can be claimed (art 3(a) Paris Nuclear Liability Convention; art I(1)(k) Vienna Nuclear Liability Convention; art I(f) SC Convention) and set forth limitation periods (art 8 Paris Nuclear Liability Convention; art VI Vienna Nuclear Liability Convention; art 9 Annex to SC Convention).

Certain issues are not governed by the international regime set forth by the conventions. There is for example no general definition of the legal term 'operator'. Further, all conventions recognize that 'the nature, form and extent of the compensation' as well as the 'equitable distribution' of the funds shall be governed by national law (art 11 Paris Nuclear Liability Convention; art VIII Vienna Nuclear Liability Convention; art 11 Annex to SC Convention). Moreover, the contracting states may deviate to a certain extent with regard to the rules harmonized by the Conventions (for example by fixing different liability caps or limitation periods). Finally, states may declare reservations with regard to certain provisions which curtail the unifying effect even further. Germany, for example, has declared that the exoneration of the operator in cases of armed conflicts or similar circumstances will not apply with respect to damage occurring within Germany (§ 25(3) German Law on Nuclear Energy (Gesetz über die friedliche Verwendung der Kernenergie und den Schutz gegen ihre Gefahren (Atomgesetz) of 23 December 1959, BGBl. I 1565, as amended, henceforth AtG).

Given that the various conventions harmonize the law only partially and that each regime has only attracted a limited number of states so far, the current system can be described as patchwork legislation or as a 'labyrinth' of treaty law (Tom Vanden Borre, 'Shifts in Governance in Compensation for Nuclear Damage, 20 Years after Chernobyl' in Michael Faure and Albert Verheij (eds), *Shifts in Compensation for Environmental Damage* (Springer 2007) 261, 268). The coexistence of various conventions whose rules are supplemented by national law may lead in trans-boundary cases to different treatment of the victims of nuclear damage as a closer look at the issues of jurisdiction and applicable law shall demonstrate. For reasons of space, the focus below will be on the application of the liability regimes that are in force for EU Member States.

2. Jurisdiction

All conventions provide that jurisdiction for actions for compensation for nuclear damage lies exclusively with the courts of the contracting party within whose territory the nuclear incident occurred (art 13(a) Paris Nuclear Liability Convention; art XI(1) Vienna Nuclear Liability Convention). If the nuclear incident has occurred outside the territory of the contracting parties or if the place of the nuclear incident cannot be determined with certainty, jurisdiction over such actions shall lie exclusively with the courts of the contracting party in whose territory the nuclear installation of the operator allegedly liable is situated (art 13(b) Paris Nuclear Liability Convention; art XI(2) Vienna Nuclear Liability Convention). If, according to these rules, courts of more than one contracting party have jurisdiction, the conventions provide for mechanisms to identify an exclusive forum for all claims against the operator (art 13(c) Paris Nuclear Liability Convention; art XI(3) Vienna Nuclear Liability Convention). Courts in other contracting states must dismiss the action for damages. Thus in cases of damage abroad, victims might have to litigate outside their home state.

The rationale behind the concentration of all proceedings arising out of the same nuclear incident against the operator (or a direct claim against its insurer or guarantor) 'is the need for a single legal mechanism to ensure that the limitation on liability is not exceeded. Moreover, if suits arising out of the same incident were to be tried and judgments rendered in the courts of several different countries, the problem of assuring equitable distribution of compensation might be insoluble' (Revised *Exposé des Motifs* of the Paris Convention, available at <www.oecd-nea.org/law/nlparis_motif.html>, para 54).

Given the coexistence of different instruments, such a concentration of proceedings is, however, not always ensured. Each convention binds only the courts of the contracting states. Victims in non-contracting states or states adhering to another convention that have not ratified the Joint Protocol are not bound by the exclusive jurisdiction rule and may bring their actions for damages before a court that has jurisdiction according to its own procedural law. The following hypothetical examples shall demonstrate the consequences of this position.

Assume that a nuclear accident takes place in Romania and also causes damage in Belgium. In this scenario Belgian victims are entitled to sue either in Belgium or in Romania. As Belgium is a Paris state and Romania is a Vienna state, neither convention applies to the case (both conventions apply only to accidents that occurred in the territory of a contracting state). The Joint Protocol (which mutually enlarges the benefits of one convention to victims located in a contracting state of the other convention) does not apply either, as Romania has ratified it but not Belgium. A court would thus rely on its general procedural law to determine its jurisdiction. As the defending operator of the nuclear installation is domiciled in an EU Member State, the Brussels I Regulation applies, which allows the Belgian victims to sue the operator either at his domicile in Romania (art 2 Brussels I Regulation (Regulation (EC) No 44/2001 of 22 December 2000 on jurisdiction and the recognition and enforcement of judgments in civil and commercial matters, [2001] OJ L 12/1)/art 4 Brussels I Regulation (recast) (Regulation (EU) No 1215/2012 of the European Parliament and of the Council of 12 December 2012 on jurisdiction and the recognition and enforcement of judgments in civil and commercial matters (recast), [2012] OJ L 351/1; → Brussels I (Convention and Regulation))) or at the place where the harmful event occurred (art 5(3) Brussels I Regulation/art 7(2) Brussels I Regulation (recast)). The ECJ has ruled that the place where the harmful event took place covers both, the place where the damage occurred as well as the place of the event giving rise to the damage, so that the defendant may be sued at the choice of the plaintiff in one of those two places (Case C-21/76 *SCJEC Handelskwekerij GJ Bier BV v Mines de Potasse d'Alsace SA* [1976] ECR 1735, paras 24–5). The victims could therefore bring the action either in Romania (place of the event giving rise to the damage) or in Belgium (place where the damage occurred). It is very likely that the Belgian victims would bring their action before a court in Belgium to avoid out-of-state litigation.

If in the same hypothetical, persons residing in Germany would suffer damage, those victims could only sue in Romania. Germany (Paris Nuclear Liability Convention state) and

Romania (Vienna Nuclear Liability Convention state) are parties to different liability regimes. Nevertheless as both states have ratified the Joint Protocol, the Vienna Nuclear Liability Convention would apply as Romania was the territory in which the accident took place (art III(2) Joint Protocol). Therefore victims in Germany are compensated under the liability regime of the Vienna Nuclear Liability Convention including its jurisdiction rule. If one widens the lens even further and assumes that the accident also caused damage in Austria and Luxembourg, the operator might face actions before courts of these countries, neither of which are bound by the Paris or the Vienna Nuclear Liability Convention meaning that plaintiffs could rely on art 5(3) Brussels I Regulation/ art 7(2) Brussels I Regulation (recast) to sue in their home countries (all examples by Ulrich Magnus, 'Probleme des internationalen Atomhaftungsrechts' in Dietmar Baetge, Jan von Hein and Michael von Hinden (eds), *Die richtige Ordnung: Festschrift für Jan Kropholler zum 70. Geburtstag* (Mohr Siebeck 2008) 595, 606–7). Against this background, a further unification of jurisdiction rules is warranted to avoid forum shopping, which might distort the aim of an equitable distribution of compensation amongst different classes of victims.

3. *Applicable law*

Issues not governed by the rules laid down in the Paris or Vienna Nuclear Liability Convention must be decided according to national law. The conventions explicitly provide that the nature, form and extent of the compensation shall be governed by the law of the court that has jurisdiction under the respective Convention (art 14(b) Paris Nuclear Liability Convention; arts I(1)(e) VIII Vienna Nuclear Liability Convention). This is usually the court of the country in which the accident took place. The reference to the national law includes the rules of private international law of that state (Revised *Exposé des Motifs* of the Paris Nuclear Liability Convention, available at <www.oecd-nea.org/law/nlparis_motif.html>, para 60). Thus the competent court will apply its choice-of-law rule for general tort cases or nuclear accidents that it would also apply to cases not covered by the Convention (Ulrich Magnus, 'Probleme des internationalen Atomhaftungsrechts' in Dietmar Baetge, Jan von Hein and Michael von Hinden (eds), *Die richtige Ordnung: Festschrift für Jan Kropholler zum 70. Geburtstag* (Mohr Siebeck 2008) 595, 610).

Within the EU, the → Rome II Regulation (Regulation (EC) No 864/2007 of the European Parliament and of the Council of 11 July 2007 on the law applicable to non-contractual obligations (Rome II), [2007] OJ L 199/40) lays down unified conflict rules for non-contractual obligations. The Regulation's scope does not, however, cover non-contractual obligations arising out of nuclear damage (art 1(2)(f) Rome II Regulation). The drafters of the Rome II Regulation were of the opinion that there was no need of a harmonization of the choice-of-law rules for nuclear damage as this area of law is dominated by uniform law. Moreover, the European Commission seemed to fear that no agreement could be reached on the design of a conflict rule. The exclusion of non-contractual obligations arising out of nuclear damage was therefore explained with 'the importance of the economic and State interests at stake' (European Commission, 'Proposal for a Regulation of the European Parliament and the Council on the Law Applicable to Non-Contractual Obligations ("Rome II")' COM(2003) 427 final, p 9). In light of the gaps within the international conventions and the fact that those conventions do not cover all varieties of damage caused by nuclear technology (they do not apply to damage caused by the use of radioactive substances for medicinal purposes), the exemption of nuclear damage in its entirety is not justified and has been rightly criticized (Abbo Junker, 'Die Rom II-Verordnung: Neues Internationales Deliktsrecht auf europäischer Grundlage' [2007] NJW 3675, 3677; Ulrich Magnus, 'Probleme des internationalen Atomhaftungsrechts' in Dietmar Baetge, Jan von Hein and Michael von Hinden (eds), *Die richtige Ordnung: Festschrift für Jan Kropholler zum 70. Geburtstag* (Mohr Siebeck 2008) 595, 601 and 610).

Without harmonization each court in the EU applies its national choice-of-law rules. The design of these rules differs considerably. Whereas some courts would apply the law of the place of the damage (*lex damni*), other courts would resort to the law of the place of the dangerous activity or would even allow the plaintiff to unilaterally choose between the law in the country in which the damage occurred or the law of the country in which the action giving rise to the damage took place (see the general overview on trans-boundary environmental damage provided by Thomas Kadner Graziano, *Gemeineuropäisches Internationales Privatrecht* (Mohr Siebeck 2002) 236–57; Christophe Bernasconi, 'Civil Liability Resulting from Transfrontier Environmental Damage: A Case for the Hague Conference?' (1999) 12 Hague Yrbk Intl L 35, 74–84).

The *lex damni* could be applied by English courts (Private international law (Miscellaneous Provisions) Act 1995 (c 42)) as well as by Irish courts (Paul O'Higgins and Patrick McGrath, 'Third Party Liability in the Field of Nuclear Law: An Irish Perspective' (2002) 70 *Nuclear Law Bulletin* 7, 18). The general choice of law rule for tort cases in Austria calls for the application of the law of the country in which the event giving rise to the nuclear damage occurred, ie where the nuclear accident took place (§ 48(2) Austrian Federal Code on Private international law (Bundesgesetz über das internationale Privatrecht, BGBl. No 304/1978, as amended)). If the injured party requested it, the court may also apply the *lex damni* in case the damage occurred in Austria (§ 23(1) Austrian Law on Nuclear Liability (Bundesgesetz über die zivilrechtliche Haftung für Schäden durch Radioaktivität, BGBl. No 170/1998, henceforth AtomHG)). In case the damage has occurred outside Austria but is to be judged under Austrian law, an indemnification is only possible as far as the personal statute of the plaintiff allows so (§ 23(2) AtomHG).

The law to be applied by a German court depends on the fact where the accident occurred: in a situation where the action is directed against the operator of the nuclear installation causing the damage who is domiciled in another Paris Nuclear Liability Convention state, German law as the *lex fori* applies (§ 40(1) AtG). Certain legal issues have, however, to be judged according to the law of the contracting state on whose territory the installation is located, eg the questions of who is to be regarded as the operator of the nuclear installation, to which maximum amount this person can be made liable or the length of the limitation period (§ 40(2) AtG). In cases where German courts have jurisdiction to rule on claims for nuclear damage caused by an installation located in a state that is not party to the Paris Nuclear Liability Convention, the general choice-of-law rule for tort claims applies (art 40 Introductory Act to the German Civil Code (Einführungsgesetz zum Bürgerlichen Gesetzbuche of 21 September 1994, BGBl. I 2494, as amended)). According to this rule tort claims are governed by the law of the country in which the liable party has acted, ie the law of the country in which the nuclear accident took place. At the demand of the injured party, the court may also apply the law of the country in which the damage occurred, ie German law.

In summary the lack of harmonized conflict rules for nuclear damage at the EU level does not foster legal clarity and creates too much room for forum shopping to influence the applicable law of damages. When revising the Rome II Regulation, the EU should strike down the exception for non-contractual claims arising out of nuclear damage and introduce a choice-of-law rule that will apply in situations where the claim is not governed by an international liability convention.

4. Recognition and enforcement of judgments

All conventions provide for some general rules to ensure that a judgment rendered in one contracting state that has acquired the effect of *res iudicata* may be recognized and enforced in another contracting state (art 13(d) Paris Nuclear Liability Convention; art XII Vienna Nuclear Liability Convention). The rules on enforcement apply only to contracting states or non-contracting states that have ratified the Joint Protocol. All other states may determine the recognition and enforcement of foreign judgments according to their *lex fori* (including EU law). Thus a judgment rendered by a German court that is to be enforced in Austria (which has ratified neither the Paris nor the Vienna Nuclear Liability Convention) will be based on the regime set forth by the Brussels I Regulation, whereas the enforcement of the same judgment in France, which is party to the Paris Nuclear Liability Convention, would be governed by this convention.

WOLFGANG WURMNEST

Literature

Christophe Bernasconi, 'Civil Liability Resulting from Transfrontier Environmental Damage: A Case for the Hague Conference?' (1999) 12 Hague Yrbk Intl L 35; Monika Hinteregger, 'Atomhaftung in Europa – Bestand und Perspektiven' in Peter Apathy and others (eds), *Festschrift für Helmut Koziol zum 70. Geburtstag* (Jan Sramek Verlag 2010) 667; Abbo Junker, 'Die Rom II-Verordnung: Neues Internationales Deliktsrecht auf europäischer Grundlage' [2007] NJW 3675–82; Thomas Kadner

Graziano, *Gemeineuropäisches Internationales Privatrecht* (Mohr Siebeck 2002); Susanne Kissich, *Internationales Atomhaftungsrecht: Anwendungsbereich und Haftungsprinzipien* (Nomos 2004); Ulrich Magnus, 'Probleme des internationalen Atomhaftungsrechts' in Dietmar Baetge, Jan von Hein and Michael von Hinden (eds), *Die richtige Ordnung: Festschrift für Jan Kropholler zum 70. Geburtstag* (Mohr Siebeck 2008) 595; Paul O'Higgins and Patrick McGrath, 'Third Party Liability in the Field of Nuclear Law: An Irish Perspective' (2002) 70 *Nuclear Law Bulletin* 7; Norbert Pelzer, 'On Global Treaty Relations: Hurdles on the Way towards a Universal Civil Nuclear Liability Regime' (2008) 6 EurUP 268; Norbert Pelzer, 'Conflict of Laws Issues under the International Nuclear Liability Conventions' in Jürgen F Baur and others (eds), *Festschrift für Gunther Kühne zum 70. Geburtstag* (Verlag Recht und Wirtschaft 2009) 819; Carlton Stoiber and others, *Handbook on Nuclear Law* (IAEA 2003); Tom Vanden Borre, 'Shifts in Governance in Compensation for Nuclear Damage, 20 Years after Chernobyl' in Michael Faure and Albert Verheij (eds), *Shifts in Compensation for Environmental Damage* (Springer 2007) 261.

Online dispute resolution

I. Concept and function

Online dispute resolution (ODR) is a (1.) virtual process of (2.) alternative dispute resolution that is (3.) technology-facilitated. Its function is to provide effective access to justice at reasonable cost, in particular for (4.) online disputes that often are of a (5.) 'low-value, high-volume' type and/or have a (6.) 'cross-border' dimension.

1. Virtual process

ODR is 'online', because it is a service provided on the Internet using means of information and communication technology (henceforth ICT). While some ODR procedures employ ICT such as e-mail, chats or videoconferencing, others are integrated into so-called 'ODR platforms'. An ODR platform is essentially a software tool, accessible through a password-protected webpage or by a software application. The ODR platform allows for asynchronous electronic communication, to share digital documents, pictures and videos, and to create an electronic case file ('written proceedings'). In addition, the ODR platform may also provide for simultaneous exchange of text, voice and video to enable live negotiations and consultations ('quasi hearings'). Thus, the parties to the dispute and the neutral third party are not physically present at the same place and not necessarily at the same time. The same applies to witnesses, documentary evidence or any other form of proof, which is usually allowed in digitized form only. As a result, the ODR process can be qualified as 'virtual'.

2. Alternative dispute resolution

In principle, any kind of dispute resolution service can be provided online, including litigation. To meet the formal requirements of litigation in a completely digitized process, however, is either impossible or very costly. Consequently ODR providers tend to use the less formal mechanisms of alternative dispute resolution (ADR; → Alternative dispute resolution). Under the acronym ODR, the entire range of traditional ADR procedures are discussed, *inter alia* informal assisted negotiation, → mediation, conciliation, ombudsman and formal arbitration. If provided online, these mechanisms are also referred to as 'electronic ADR' (eADR). Thus, the distinction between ADR and ODR has been somewhat blurred, as many traditional providers of ADR operate a webpage and make use of e-mail communication. However, the term 'ODR' extends to dispute resolution mechanisms beyond traditional ADR, such as 'virtual juries' or 'blind bidding' procedures. Consequently, ODR is distinct from traditional ADR in that ICT is involved as a 'fourth party'.

Like ADR, ODR is often discussed in relation to access to justice. This principle received the status of a human right when states acquired a monopoly in the legitimate use of force. It is enshrined in art 6(1) ECHR (European Convention of 4 November 1950 for the Protection of Human Rights and Fundamental Freedoms, 213 UNTS 221) and art 47 EU Charter of Fundamental Rights (Charter of Fundamental Rights of the European Union of 18 December 2000, [2000] OJ C 364/1 (consolidated version 2012/C 326/02, [2012] OJ C 326/391)). In the context of ODR, access to justice means that everyone involved in a dispute is entitled to an easily accessible redress mechanism that provides for a timely resolution and effective remedies at reasonable cost. It is argued that a modern understanding of the rule of law requires not only access to courts but also access to ADR and increasingly ODR.

Recently, there is a trend to link ODR with the use of ICT in litigation. The Canadian province of British Columbia, for example, is establishing a so-called 'Civil Resolution Tribunal', making it mandatory for certain disputes to go through an ODR procedure before being admitted to court (see Darin Thompson, 'The Growth of Online Dispute Resolution and Its Use in British Columbia' (2014) available at <www.cle.bc.ca/ PracticePoints/LIT/14-GrowthODR.pdf>). Moreover, in the UK the Civil Justice Council recently recommended creating an Internet-based ODR-like court service (see Civil Justice Council – Online Dispute Resolution Advisory Group, Online Dispute Resolution for Low Value Civil Claims (February 2015) available at <www.judiciary.gov.uk/wp-content/uploads/ 2015/02/Online-Dispute-Resolution-Final-Web-Version1.pdf>).

3. Technology-facilitated

There are many possible ways for ICT to enable the ODR process. While in some ODR procedures technology merely facilitates the communication process, in other instances such as assisted or automated negotiations technology is incorporated into the actual dispute resolution process. Hence, technology is said to participate in ODR as a 'fourth party' (Ethan Katsh and Janet Rifkin, *Online Dispute Resolution: Resolving Conflicts in Cyberspace* (Jossey-Bass 2001) 93 *et seq*).

In 'assisted negotiations' the ODR procedure entails a software-assisted negotiation stage that facilitates consensual solutions based on prior experience in the resolution of disputes or computerized expert systems. Via menu-driven input masks, the parties define the object of the dispute, determine their aims, deduce their willingness to compromise and reach voluntary settlement supported by standardized information about possible solutions (see Arno R Lodder and Ernest M Thiessen, *The Role of Artificial Intelligence in Online Dispute Resolution*, available at <www.mediate.com/ Integrating/docs/lodder_thiessen.pdf>). Only where necessary is a neutral third party subsequently involved in order to mediate, or as a matter of escalation to adjudicate or even arbitrate.

A more extensive incorporation of ICT into the dispute resolution process can be found in 'automated negotiations'. A well-known example is the so-called (parallel online) 'blind bidding' process. As part of this automated process the parties submit (in successive rounds) offers that they are willing to pay or receive to settle the claim. These settlement offers are shared with a computer only, but not with the other party (hence blind bidding). If the parties' offers are too far apart, the computer asks for improved offers. If the parties' offers reach a previously defined corridor (eg a deviation of the offers of 30 per cent), the computer program splits the remaining difference and sets a binding settlement amount. The parties are deemed to have settled. Starting from this simple model, advanced software solutions have been developed, which are based on complex game theoretical models. However, these automated processes of 'blind bidding' are suitable only where the definite amount of damages due as opposed to the actual liability of a party as such is under dispute, eg the amount of the reduction on a defective good or an insurance sum to be paid.

Technological components can also allow 'virtual juries' to decide cases by reviewing and voting online on a case. These 'virtual juries' are often composed of fellow users of a service, eg the Community Court of eBay India that consists of 21 randomly picked volunteers. In addition, the question arises of whether and how artificial intelligence can contribute to the ODR process (see Davide Carneiro and others, 'Online Dispute Resolution: An Artificial Intelligence Perspective' (2012) 41 Artif.Intell. Rev. 211; Anjanette H Raymond and Scott J Shackelford, 'Technology, Ethic, and Access to Justice: Should an Algorithm Be Deciding Your Case?' (2014) 35 Mich.J.Int'l L. 485).

The type and extent of the use of ICT depend not only on their spread among potential users, but also on the aim and type of the dispute resolution process. When for example in international (commercial) arbitration the formal requirements of the New York Convention (New York Convention of 10 June 1958 on the recognition and enforcement of foreign arbitral awards, 330 UNTS 3) have to be met, high technical standards are required, while in more informal dispute resolution procedures easily accessible and inexpensive solutions will prevail.

4. Online disputes

ODR is predominantly concerned with conflicts arising from the use of the Internet, such as disputes over e-commerce transactions (→ Electronic commerce) or domain names, which will be discussed briefly. The key to the success of ODR providers in the mentioned areas is that they not only offer an easily accessible, quick, effective and low-cost dispute resolution process, but that they have also succeeded in integrating their offer to the primary markets for e-commerce and domain name registration respectively, where the online disputes arise. This integration is brought about in both cases by cooperation agreements with the primary market makers, and by creating socio-legal bonds for potential dispute parties to commit to the process.

In the long run, however, ODR may extend to disputes that have their origin offline and are of a more complex nature. A current example is the Dutch ODR provider *Rechtwijzer 2.0* that deals with family matters.

a) eBay
The dispute resolution service for the online market place *eBay* is currently provided by the online payment system *PayPal* and was previously operated by *SquareTrade*.

The *eBay* buyer protection is available for parties that either paid the *eBay* transaction using *PayPal* or chose a transaction secured by the *eBay* Guarantee. The *PayPal* dispute resolution procedure is arranged in two stages. First, there is a software-assisted negotiation stage between the involved parties via a secured webpage. The automated multiple choice questionnaires, posed to the parties while filing or responding to the complaint, are based on the experience of typical *eBay* buyer–seller disputes such as 'item not paid', 'item not delivered', 'item defective' or 'item substantially not as described'. In this stage the process is fully automated, in that parties are guided by customized multiple choice suggestions of how their dispute might be resolved. In the majority of cases, the involved parties (are expected to) arrive at a settlement themselves. Second, in the adjudication stage each party may ask *PayPal* to decide the case, provided that consensus was not achieved in the first stage. Based on the electronic case file produced in the negotiation stage, and where necessary additional evidence submitted by the parties, *PayPal* decides the case free of charge. During the ODR procedure *PayPal* suspends the accounts of the parties, so that the consensual solution resulting from the negotiation stage or the decision resulting from the adjudication stage may be 'enforced' by a *PayPal* chargeback.

Before the takeover of *PayPal*, *eBay* provided ODR on the basis of a cooperation agreement with *SquareTrade*, which from 2000 through 2008 dealt with over one million *eBay*-related conflicts linked to 120 countries in five languages. *SquareTrade*'s ODR process was similarly divided into two stages, with the first stage being a software-assisted negotiation stage. The second stage, however, entailed a mediation phase. On request by the parties, the mediator was allowed to make a non-binding suggestion for a settlement, but for a lack of an enforcement mechanism adjudication was not provided. Overall, 80 per cent of the cases could be resolved by a consensual settlement, which was observed in 98 per cent of cases. The average duration of a procedure was two weeks. In addition, *SquareTrade* offered a trustmark for sellers who, on the basis of a code of conduct, pre-committed to solve problems through the *SquareTrade* procedure, promised to act in good faith in order to reach a compromise, and to adhere to any agreement reached. The *SquareTrade* mediation process was backed by reputation, since non-cooperative behaviour could be sanctioned with negative feedback on *eBay*. In 2008, however, *SquareTrade* stopped providing ODR services because *eBay* changed its feedback policy. Sellers could no longer leave feedback on buyers, so there was no mutuality, and hence, nothing to mediate.

b) Uniform Domain Name Dispute Resolution Policy
Another example of a successful ODR process is the Uniform Domain Name Dispute Resolution Policy (UDRP) of the Internet Corporation for Assigned Names and Numbers (henceforth ICANN) (see Andrew F Christie, 'Online Dispute Resolution: The Phenomenon of the UDRP' in Paul Torremans (ed), *Research Handbook on the Cross-Border Enforcement of Intellectual Property* (Edward Elgar 2014) 642). ICANN accredits ODR providers to conduct dispute resolution under the UDRP. Currently there are five providers, among which the WIPO Arbitration and Mediation Centre is dominant, resolving since 1999 over 30,000 domain name disputes from over 175 countries.

The UDRP is part of the adhesion contract domain name holders submit to when registering a domain name. It is aimed at protecting against abusive domain name registrations containing trademarks – the so-called 'cybersquatting'. Thus, it is a mandatory administrative procedure to domain name holders, although its results are not legally binding. A complaint by a trademark holder is deemed served on the holder of the domain in dispute, if it is sent to their registered e-mail address. The holder of the domain name can defend against the claim by demonstrating their rights to and the legitimate interest in it. If the holder of the domain name fails to respond to a complaint, a default judgment will be rendered. In addition, time limits are extremely tight and the procedural costs relatively low. Altogether, the ODR service offered by WIPO (→ WIPO and private international law) to trademark holders under the UDRP is highly competitive when compared to the alternatives, eg court or traditional ADR proceedings. Moreover, the panel decisions are 'electronically enforced' on domain name holders by virtue of ICANN's monopoly power over the registration process in generic top-level domains (dotcom, dotorg etc). If the respondent fails to file an appeal to a competent court within a ten-day period, the registrar will disconnect the domain name from the IP number of the respondent and transfer it to the trademark holder.

5. 'Low-value, high-volume' disputes

A huge potential for ODR services is seen in 'low-value, high-volume' disputes, ie where a large number of cases with a rather low value at dispute occur. In particular in the rapidly growing area of business-to-consumer (B2C) e-commerce, ODR is perceived as a viable alternative to the court system. Litigation in these cases is not only burdensome, but legal costs may very well prove to be higher than the amount at stake. This often leads to 'rational apathy' on the part of the consumer, who would rather write-off the loss than engage in litigation (Fernando Gascón Inchausti, 'Specific Problems of Cross-border Consumer ADR: What Solutions?' (2014) 11 GPR 197, 200). Thus, such disputes often remain unresolved. ODR could help consumers to obtain access to justice under these circumstances.

The attribute of 'low-value, high-volume' is nevertheless problematic. On the one hand, the issue of what constitutes a 'low-value' dispute is quite controversial. The concept not only varies in relation to GDP *per capita*, but also depends on the availability of small-claims courts. Thus, in continental Europe an amount below EUR 1,000 is discussed, while the USA estimates the limit to be around USD 10,000. On the other hand, the characterization of a dispute as 'high-volume' may imply that unfair contract terms in contracts of adhesion are a problem involved in the dispute, but apart from that does not add anything of value to the definition of ODR regarding the single dispute at hand. It follows that the formula of 'low-value, high-volume' disputes has to be seen as a merely descriptive rather than a defining element of ODR, applicable in many but certainly not all cases.

6. 'Cross-border' dimension

The impediments to judicial redress are even more severe in cross-border cases. A case has a 'cross-border' dimension if the parties to the dispute have their seat, place of business or habitual residence in different countries. These traditional connecting factors lose much of their persuasive power in e-commerce, since they are no longer easily verifiable, but quite easy to shift to favourable jurisdictions. The ubiquitous nature of the Internet facilitates not only communication, but also transaction across borders. As a result, a growing number of disputes have a 'cross-border' dimension.

Multi-jurisdictional litigation in state courts involves highly complicated questions of jurisdiction, → choice of law, and mutual recognition and enforcement. The applicable consumer protection regimes diverge considerably among nations. It follows that international litigation is complex, expensive and slow, and accordingly even less suitable than domestic litigation for the resolution of the above discussed disputes. In the long run, the creation of accessible and transparent ODR services may also have the beneficial economic effect of increasing the number of consumers and businesses that are willing to engage in cross-border e-commerce.

II. Historical development

The notion that the Internet's communicative potential can be used to establish alternative forms of dispute resolution procedures in the form of ODR dates back to the mid-1990s (see *inter alia* Martin C Karamon, 'ADR on the Internet' (1996) 11 Ohio St. J. on Disp. Resol. 537, Alejandro E Almaguer and Roland W Baggott, 'Shaping New Legal Frontiers: Dispute Resolution for the Internet' (1998) 13 Ohio St. J. on Disp. Resol. 711; Robert C Bordone, 'Electronic Online Dispute Resolution: A Systems Approach – Potential, Problems, and a Proposal' (1998) 3 Harv. Negotiation L. Rev. 175).

But is there a case for regulating ODR? Litigation is highly regulated since – besides a fictitious social contract – there is no consent required in the process. ADR comprises various forms of out-of-court dispute resolution that are regulated depending on the degree of party consent involved: negotiation needs no specific regulation next to general contract law, as parties have to consent on the result of the process; the same holds true for the mediation process, which may or may not need some legal guidance regarding pre-contractual information, the neutrality of the mediator, or effects of the process on limitation or → prescription periods. Arbitration, in turn, is quite formal and regulated, as parties agree on the process rather than on the result, and access to courts is restricted. Somewhere in between are non-mandatory and/or non-binding forms of arbitration, adjudication or conciliation, which in connection with socio-economic sanctions may reverse the risk of litigation between the involved parties, but do not exclude access to court. As ODR is not only a new phenomenon, but entails – as the above described successful instances of ODR show – negotiations and mediations rather than mandatory and binding arbitration, ODR was for a long time and remains even today predominantly free of binding state regulation.

In 1999, however, the Organisation for Economic Co-operation and Development (OECD) released its 'Guidelines for Consumer Protection in the Context of Electronic Commerce', which included a call for self-regulation. Businesses, consumer representatives and governments should work together to develop fair, effective and transparent self-regulatory procedures, including alternative dispute resolution mechanisms, to resolve consumer disputes arising from B2C e-commerce, with special attention to cross-border transactions. Against this backdrop genuine efforts of self-regulation developed with a view to rendering the market for ODR services more transparent and to creating trust among potential users. These efforts concerned on the one hand the establishment of certain minimum standards for ODR providers and on the other hand various measures in order to guarantee compliance with these principles.

One has to bear in mind that a number of principles for traditional ADR procedures in consumer affairs already existed, eg the 15 principles of the American Arbitration Association's (AAA) 'Due Process Protocol for Mediation and Arbitration of Consumer Disputes' of 1998 (see Lucille M Ponte, 'Boosting Consumer Confidence in E-Business: Recommendations for Establishing Fair and Effective Dispute Resolution Programs for B2C Online Transactions' (2002) 12 Alb. L.J. Sci. & Tech. 441 for the necessity to adopt the protocol to the Internet). Thus, special guidelines for ODR procedures for B2C e-commerce disputes could build upon these principles. Based on extensive consultation, the Task Force on Electronic Commerce and Alternative Dispute Resolution of the American Bar Association (ABA) published 'Recommended Best Practices by Online Dispute Resolution Service Providers' in September 2002. These were intended as a non-binding point of orientation for ODR service providers, consumers and trustmark providers. In November 2003 the Task Force on Consumer Policy for e-Business of the International Chamber of Commerce (ICC) published 'Best Practices for Online Dispute Resolution (ODR) in B2C and C2C transactions', which contained guidelines both for enterprises handling B2C e-commerce and for ODR service providers. At the same time, the Global Business Dialogue on E-Commerce (GBDe) and Consumers International (CI) agreed on common 'Alternative Dispute Resolution Guidelines' for B2C e-commerce, which contained recommendations for enterprises, ODR service providers and governments.

To implement the mentioned standards for ODR providers, a number of measures were discussed, ranging from self-regulation to national (outline) legislation. In the context of ODR the role of the state tends to be more emphasized than is usually the case for ADR (see Thomas Schultz 'An Essay on the Role of Government for ODR' (2003) available at <www.mediate.com/Integrating/docs/Schultz.pdf>; Julia Hörnle, *Cross-Border Internet Dispute Resolution* (CUP 2009) 246). It is argued that procedural standards for ODR have to be developed and disseminated by institutions that leave no doubt regarding their neutrality in the face of conflicting interests and thus enjoy the unreserved confidence of all involved. Initiatives for self-regulation, led by industry and commerce such as the GBDe or the ICC, do not meet these criteria on their own. Also, ODR standards that would be developed with the support of states could be advantageous, as they could work as guidelines for judicial review in particular cases. For example, the terms of trade of ODR service providers as well as terms of trade clauses concerning dispute settlement in consumer contracts cannot easily be declared ineffective if they are perceived as complying with nationally, regionally or globally accepted ODR standards.

Another way to safeguard the compliance with ODR standards would be to create an accreditation association that grants trustmarks to ODR providers and is also able to withdraw them. But such an accreditation of ODR providers with a global ODR trustmark would require substantial financial and personal resources, which although desirable seem unachievable.

The problem with the established trustmark schemes and ODR systems is that they predominantly work on the domestic level and that a proliferation of trustmarks has a negative effect on their impact. Also, trustmark initiatives aiming at cross-border cooperation on the basis of common minimum standards such as the 'BBBOnLine Reliability Seal' in the USA and Canada, the Asia Trustmark Alliance (ATA) or Online Confidence (OC) by the Association of European Chambers of Commerce (Eurochambres) were not successful on a regional level. The same can be stated for the Global Trustmark Alliance Organizing Committee, founded in 2004.

Nevertheless, the self-regulatory guidelines by highly reputable organizations gave evidence of a certain global consensus on minimum principles, which emerged beyond traditional international public law negotiations between states. But in the following years none of the aforementioned self-regulatory instruments succeeded in becoming a generally-accepted standard, giving rise to the current regulatory efforts.

III. Current regulation

After a phase of self-regulatory attempts in ODR, there is currently a trend towards state regulation on various levels.

1. National

There is hardly any regulation of ODR mechanisms on the domestic level. Only very few nations attempt to regulate ODR or to implement it in the judicial process (see I.2. above). But since ODR procedures are broadly considered to be a subcategory of ADR mechanisms, they have to meet the existing national regulations for the respective ADR procedures. As arbitral proceedings are subject of domestic arbitration laws, an online arbitration would have to comply with these regulations if the parties were to enjoy the advantages of an arbitral award, ie state recognition and international enforcement under the New York Convention, which currently has 156 parties (→ Arbitration, recognition of awards). The same applies where there are national regulations concerning, for example, mediation or ombudsman schemes.

Many countries are currently introducing ICT in their judicial process in the form of e-justice projects, eg electronic legal communication, case files or registers. Therefore, an increasing willingness by lawmakers to regulate the electronic form of ADR, namely ODR, as well can be assumed.

2. Regional

a) European Union

The EU's endeavour to facilitate the use of ADR and ODR is embedded in an overall strategy to increase consumer access to justice and to establish the European (Digital) Single Market. In its effort to increase citizen access to justice, the EU has consistently adopted a two-fold approach: on the one hand strengthening cross-border judicial cooperation (→ Small Claims Regulation (2007), → Payment Order Regulation) and on the other hand promoting ADR (→ Alternative dispute resolution) mechanisms. The EU's efforts towards the creation of a regulatory framework for ADR services date back to the 1970s. But until 2013 binding quality standards for ADR – and thus also for ODR – procedures were missing at the European level.

In a first stage, the regulatory framework for ADR services consisted only of two non-binding recommendations by the European Commission from 1998 (Commission Recommendation 98/257/EC of 30 March 1998 on the principles applicable to the bodies responsible for out-of-court settlement of consumer disputes, [1998] OJ L 115/31) and 2001 (Commission Recommendation 2001/310/EC of 4 April 2001 on the principles for out-of-court bodies involved in the consensual resolution of consumer disputes, [2001] OJ L 109/56). These recommendations established a set of guidelines for ADR procedures, which were non-binding, but nevertheless a precondition for participation in the EEJ-Net (European

Extra Judicial-Network), which is now the ECC-Net (European Consumer Centres-Network). These networks assist consumers in cross-border disputes to identify and access the competent ADR entity. The 2004 'European Code of Conduct for Mediators' (available at <http://ec.europa.eu/civiljustice/adr/adr_ec_code_conduct_en.pdf>) contained a number of non-binding ethical principles for mediators and institutional providers of mediation procedures. Also, the European Mediation Directive of 2008 (Directive 2008/52/EC of the European Parliament and of the Council of 21 May 2008 on certain aspects of mediation in civil and commercial matters ([2008] OJ L 136/3); → Mediation) did not fix the lack of binding quality standards, as it focused rather on the coordination and interconnection of mediation and court procedures than on the quality and the proper functioning of out-of-court mediation procedures.

A new stage of the regulatory development has been introduced by the 2013 legislative package consisting of the ADR Directive (Directive 2013/11/EU of the European Parliament and of the Council of 21 May 2013 on alternative dispute resolution for consumer disputes and amending Regulation (EC) No 2006/2004 and Directive 2009/22/EC (Directive on consumer ADR), [2013] OJ L 165/63) and the ODR Regulation (Regulation (EU) No 524/2013 of the European Parliament and of the Council of 21 May 2013 on online dispute resolution for consumer disputes, [2013] OJ L 165/1). The ADR Directive and the ODR Regulation are strongly interconnected and can only be understood as a unit.

The ADR Directive, which Member States had to transpose into national law by 9 July 2015, concerns the establishment, the quality and the supervision of ADR providers. Thereby, it addresses the three main problems of the current ADR landscape in the EU, identified by the European Commission: (i) the existence of gaps in the sectoral and geographical coverage by ADR, (ii) the low use of ADR bodies by consumers and businesses due to a lack of awareness and a lack of information, (iii) disparities in the quality of ADR services.

The ADR Directive applies to all providers of B2C ADR services, and therefore extends also to ODR providers. ADR and ODR providers must be in conformity with the quality standards defined by the ADR Directive if they wish to be publicly listed with the Member States and the EU and benefit from the European ODR platform created in accordance with the ODR Regulation. Nevertheless, if the ADR and ODR providers fail to conform to the quality standards, their services are not restricted. The uniform quality requirements established by the ADR Directive are: access to ADR entities and procedures, expertise, independence and impartiality, transparency, effectiveness, fairness, liberty to act, legality and the effect of ADR procedures on limitation and prescription periods.

The ADR Directive is complemented by the ODR Regulation. The ODR Regulation considers ODR as offering a 'simple, efficient, fast and low-cost out-of-court solution to disputes arising from online transactions'. Thus, the ODR Regulation aims to facilitate access to ADR and ODR providers by creating a European ODR platform to be run by the European Commission. As of January 2016 the ODR platform is available to consumers and businesses in all official EU languages for complaints concerning online sales or service contracts in the EU see https://webgate.ec.europa.eu/odr/. The European ODR platform provides an electronic complaint form which enables the parties to identify a competent ADR or ODR provider to deal with the complaint. If the parties cannot agree on a competent provider, the claim is not processed further. Therefore the European ODR platform does not itself act as a dispute resolution service, but merely as a 'clearing house' that brings together consumers, businesses and ADR and ODR providers. The European approach puts its focus on B2C procedures and envisions complaints brought by a consumer against a business to be the default case. But the ODR platform also makes its services available to businesses filing complaints against consumers provided Members States enact the appropriate national legislation. Not covered by the ODR Regulation are complaints between consumers (C2C) or businesses (B2B).

The ODR Regulation contains no detailed requirements for the dispute resolution procedure itself. However, considering that the ODR platform may only forward the complaint to an ADR or ODR provider that meets the quality requirements of the ADR Directive, any ODR process initiated through the EU ODR platform must comply with the procedural quality standards of the ADR Directive. The ODR Regulation expressly allows for the subsequent procedure to be conducted as any possible

ADR scheme, including mediation, conciliation or arbitration. Remarkably, the procedure following the online determination of the provider need not be an online process, but could be conducted entirely offline, eg by regular mail. Also, the ODR Regulation determines that a provider may not require the parties to be physically present and will have to conclude the procedure within 90 calendar days.

In addition to the described 'clearing house' function, the European ODR platform shall offer a so-called 'case management tool' for ADR and ODR providers. However, it remains unclear what functions will be covered by that tool, while at the same time ADR and ODR providers will not be obliged to use it. The European ODR platform shall also provide a translation function – the extent of which is also unclear. Even if the case management tool and the translation function were elaborately designed, the ODR platform will not function as an ODR provider itself, therefore departing from the approach the EU pursued with its ECODIR (Electronic Consumer Dispute Resolution) project.

The EU's package of the ADR Directive and the ODR Regulation constitutes an overall shift from ADR to ODR, since substantial ICT elements are incorporated. For example, the ADR Directive stipulates that ADR providers have to maintain an up-to-date website and must make the procedure easily accessible online. Also, the ODR Regulation strives for a full coverage for the online out-of-court resolution of disputes arising from online contracts by ensuring that all ADR entities listed in accordance with the ADR Directive are registered with the ODR platform. The EU's advancements in ODR will be accompanied by extensive information duties of businesses and ODR providers alike. Additionally every Member State will have to provide ODR contact points with ODR advisors.

b) Organization of American States
In 2003 the Organization of American States (OAS) dealt with the topic of ODR on the 'Seventh Inter-American Specialized Conference on Private international law' (CIDIP-VII). During the conference and in its aftermath various soft and hard law approaches to the resolution of cross-border e-commerce complaints were discussed (see Colin Rule, Louis F Del Duca and Daniel Nagel, 'Online Small Claim Dispute Resolution Developments: Progress on a Soft Law for Cross-Border Consumer Sales' (2011) 29 Penn St. Int'l L. Rev. 651; Colin Rule, Vikki Rogers and Louis F Del Duca, 'Designing a Global Consumer Online Dispute Resolution (ODR) System for Cross-Border Small Value – High Volume Claims – OAS Developments' (2010) 42 UCC L.J. 221). Eventually the regulatory efforts of the OAS seized without tangible results.

3. International

On the international level there have been efforts under the umbrella of the United Nations to contribute to the development of global ODR standards. In cooperation with academic institutions the UNECE (United Nations Economic Commission for Europe) and UNESCAP (United Nations Economic and Social Commission for Asia and the Pacific) organized conferences called 'UN-Forum on Online Dispute Resolution'.

In 2010 UNCITRAL (United Nations Commission on International Trade Law, → UNCITRAL) established Working Group III in order to undertake work in the field of ODR concerning cross-border e-commerce. The Working Group's original mission was to create a uniform set of rules for ODR on a global level, comprising guidelines and minimum requirements for ODR platforms and providers, guidelines and minimum requirements for neutrals, substantive legal principles for resolving disputes, and rules for a cross-border enforcement mechanism.

While the EU's ADR and ODR package is in principle limited to disputes with consumer participation, UNCITRAL restricts its scope by referring to 'low-value, high-volume' disputes. The Working Group's mandate therefore covered B2B, B2C, C2B as well as C2C transactions. Also, the Working Group was intended to focus on the needs of developing countries and countries facing a post-conflict situation. By aiming to create not an international treaty or model rules but rather merely soft law instruments that the parties will have to consent to in their individual contract, UNCITRAL laid an emphasis on → party autonomy (see Ronald A Brand, 'Party Autonomy and Access to Justice in the UNCITRAL Online Dispute Resolution Project' (2012) 10 Loy.U.Chi.Int'l.L.Rev. 11, 16 *et seq*).

The Working Group started negotiations on a set of procedural rules, but soon it turned out that a consensus was difficult to reach. The draft rules provided for a three-stage ODR process.

While the first two stages of direct negotiations between the parties and negotiations facilitated by a neutral were fairly undisputed, the final stage of the ODR procedure was at the centre of debate. Broadly speaking two conflicting positions appeared in the Working Group. While some delegations (→ USA, → Colombia, Honduras and Kenya) argued in favour of an ODR procedure that leads to a binding arbitration stage, especially European delegations proposed a non-binding recommendation stage as the only or at least default procedure.

The proponents of an arbitration stage argued that only a binding arbitration stage can satisfy the requirement of a final resolution of a dispute. Particularly parties in developing countries and countries facing post-conflict situations would often have no access to a functioning justice system, thus leaving ODR as the only efficient means of redress. Also, an efficient ODR procedure should lead to an award that is enforceable according to the New York Convention (→ Arbitration, recognition of awards).

The proponents of a recommendation stage emphasized that enforceability according to the New York Convention is not worthwhile for several reasons. First, pre-dispute agreements between consumers and businesses concerning ODR procedures that lead to binding results, like arbitration, are in several jurisdictions considered to be invalid for consumers (see Ronald A Brand, 'Party Autonomy and Access to Justice in the UNCITRAL Online Dispute Resolution Project' (2012) 10 Loy.U.Chi.Int'l.L.Rev. 11). Additionally, any need for enforcement by a state would be unsuitable for 'low-value, high-volume' disputes. Hence, the Working Group should rather focus on creating incentives for parties to comply voluntarily with the outcome of ODR procedures (for example by trustmarks).

An amended draft sought to solve the described conflict by including both the arbitration and the recommendation stage in the draft procedural rules. By establishing the duty of the ODR provider to inform the parties of the two possible alternatives before entering the final stage, the Working Group tried to find a solution agreeable to all delegations. The recommendation stage was intended to be the default procedure. However, to reach a consensus turned out to be impossible due to irreconcilable attitudes towards consumer arbitration. While the EU prefers to limit arbitration to B2B disputes and regards out-of-court procedures as supplementing state litigation, the USA shows a traditional affinity with consumer arbitration that aims to substitute forms of judicial redress.

While a termination of the mandate was already debated, in July 2015 UNCITRAL instructed the Working Group to provide a non-binding descriptive document reflecting those elements of an ODR process, on which consensus had already been reached, excluding the nature of the final stage (arbitration/non-arbitration). A time limit of one year (two sessions) was set. In 2016, the Working Group finally agreed on 'Technical Notes on ODR', which were adopted by UNCITRAL in July (see: http://www.uncitral.org/uncitral/en/uncitral_texts/odr/2016Technical_notes.html). The impact of these Technical Notes is quite questionable, as they are not suitable to be used as rules for any ODR proceeding and do not impose any legal requirement binding on theparties or any persons and/or entities administering or facilitating an ODR proceeding.

IV. Modern trends of ODR: an outlook on global justice

The future relevance of ODR has yet to be decided. Certain aspects may be emphasized. One might wonder whether the (planned) regulations of ODR on the regional and global level will be able to reach their goal of increasing trust in ODR procedures. The consequence could be quite the opposite. In particular the consumer could be confused by the multiplicity of ODR services – those that comply with the ADR Directive, those in accordance with the UNCITRAL Technical Notes, those with their own or no defined quality standards.

Also ODR providers still have to show that they can be viable outside closed online markets (like *eBay*) or special areas (like the ICANN UDRP). ODR providers have so far only succeeded when integrating their services very closely into the primary markets, where goods and services were traded and conflicts evolved, and if socio-legal bonds were created, which ensured that conflict parties actually participate in the procedure as well as adhere to the results. While a 2004 survey accounted for 115 ODR providers worldwide (see Melissa Tyler, '115 and Counting: The State of ODR 2004' in Melissa C Tyler, Ethan Katsh and Daewon Choi (eds), *Proceedings of the Third Annual Forum on Online Dispute Resolution* (Melbourne 2004), 11 years later only a few ODR are (still) operating (see Graham Ross, *Civil Justice*

Council: ODR Advisory Group First Draft Paper on ODR Case Studies (2015) available at <www.judiciary.gov.uk/publications/case-studies/>).

While the regulatory efforts of the EU or UNCITRAL could lead to higher quality standards of ODR procedures, these still do not suffice to guarantee due process – particularly in cases involving consumers. While ODR providers rely heavily on their ICT components, technical aspects are not addressed in the EU's and UNCITRAL's work respectively. Because ODR providers offer technology-based legal services, their due process is determined not only by legal but also by technological aspects. Therefore a more technological approach to the regulation of ODR is necessary. For example, technical regulations should safeguard the quality standard of impartiality and independence if the dispute resolution process is supported not by a human neutral but by an assisted negotiations technology that suggests possible solutions to the parties. Also, the quality requirements of the European ADR Directive are in many instances quite vague. A solution to these shortcomings could be seen in uniform technical standards for ODR services. These standards could specify both the legal and the technological requirements for the quality of ODR services and serve as a complementary regulatory tool when drafted under the auspices of the European Committee for Standardization (CEN) or the International Organization for Standardization (ISO) (see Christoph Busch and Simon Reinhold, 'Standardisation of Online Dispute Resolution Services: Towards a More Technological Approach' (2015) 1 EuCML 50).

While technology as the 'fourth party' already plays a major role in ODR, its future significance cannot be underestimated. ODR procedures will benefit from an increasing utilization of artificial intelligence (see Davide Carneiro and others, 'Online Dispute Resolution: An Artificial Intelligence Perspective' (2012) 41 Artif.Intell. Rev. 211) and other ICT-elements like Big Data. One just has to imagine what would happen to the field of dispute resolution, if one day *Amazon, Google, Apple, Facebook* or the like were to take over the industry. Would a dream (of ubiquitous access to justice) come true, or prove a nightmare? However, the political actors at UNCITRAL, including the European Commission, seem not to have learnt their lesson from *Lawrence Lessig*, who taught us that 'Code is Law' (Lawrence Lessig, *Code, Version 2.0* (Basic Books 2006)).

After some 20 years, the field of ODR is about to come of age. Despite a considerable amount of sophisticated ODR scholarship, a number of pressing issues remain to be addressed in a continuously developing field. Thus, it will be necessary to discuss ethical considerations of ODR procedures (see Scott J Shackelford and Anjanette H Raymond, 'Building the Virtual Courthouse: Ethical Considerations for Design, Implementation, and Regulation in the World of ODR' (2014) 3 Wis.L.Rev. 615) as well as to adapt the solutions of well-known ADR problems to the context of ODR (see Brian Farkas, 'Old Problem, New Medium: Deception in Computer-facilitated Negotiation and Dispute Resolution' (2012) 14 Cardozo J. Confl. Res. 161; Anjanette H Raymond, 'Yeah, But Did You See the Gorilla? Creating and Protecting an Informed Consumer in Cross-Border Online Dispute Resolution' (2014) 19 Harv.Negot.L. Rev. 129).

If the resolution of (cross-border) disputes were increasingly shifted into private ODR procedures, the issues will arise of which substantive rules should be applied to reach the decision or recommendation for the complaint. In order to achieve legal certainty, disregarding national law and applying codes of conduct, equity or ultimately transnational law are options, which may emerge. Such a privatization of private (international) law would liberate ODR providers from engaging in the ultimately cumbersome conflict of (consumer protection) laws. Only time will tell whether or not such a transnational legal regime will be able to not merely satisfy market actors but also fulfil the promises once given by the first consumer protection laws, ie to provide for fairness in B2C transactions. However, when compared to the disappointing results of more than a hundred years of harmonization endeavours with respect to the private laws of the nation states, the idea of implementing a truly transnational regime for cross-border consumer contracts based on private codes and decisions in equity within a global ODR system seems to be quite promising when compared to the *rigor iuris* of the current EU consumer protection regime.

GRALF-PETER CALLIESS AND
SIMON JOHANNES HEETKAMP

Literature

Julio César Betancourt and Elina Zlatanska, 'Online Dispute Resolution (ODR): What Is It, and Is It the Way Forward?' (2013) 79 *International Journal of Arbitration, Mediation and Dispute Management* 256; Richard C Bordone, 'Electronic Online Dispute Resolution: A Systems Approach – Potential, Problems and a Proposal' [1998] Harv.Neg.L.Rev. 175; Christoph Busch and Simon Reinhold, 'Standardisation of Online Dispute Resolution Services: Towards a More Technological Approach' (2015) 1 EuCML 50; Gralf-Peter Calliess, 'Online Dispute Resolution: Consumer Redress in a Global Market Place' (2006) 7 GLJ 647; Gralf-Peter Calliess and Peer Zumbansen, *Rough Consensus and Running Code: A Theory of Transnational Private Law* (Hart Publishing 2010) ch 3; Davide Carneiro and others, 'Online Dispute Resolution: An Artificial Intelligence Perspective' (2012) 41 Artif. Intell.Rev. 211; Andrew F Christie, 'Online Dispute Resolution: The Phenomenon of the UDRP' [2015] Melbourne Law School Legal Studies Research Paper No. 681, available at <http://papers.ssrn.com/sol3/papers.cfm?abstract_id=2433380>; Pablo Cortés, *Online Dispute Resolution for Consumers in the European Union* (Routledge 2011); Pablo Cortés, 'Online Dispute Resolution Services: A Selected Number of Case Studies' [2014] C.T.L.R. 172; Pablo Cortés and Fernando Esteban de la Rosa, 'Building a Global Redress System for Low-Value Cross-Border Disputes' (2013) 62 ICLQ 407; Pablo Cortés and Arno R Lodder, 'Consumer Dispute Resolution Goes Online: Reflections on the Evolution of European Law for Out-of-Court Redress' (2014) 21 MJ 14; Julia Hörnle, *Cross-Border Internet Dispute Resolution* (CUP 2009); Julia Hörnle, 'Encouraging Online Dispute Resolution in the EU and Beyond: Keeping Costs Low or Standards High' (2013) 38 E.L.Rev. 187; Ethan Katsh and Janet Rifkin, *Online Dispute Resolution: Resolving Conflicts in Cyberspace* (Jossey-Bass 2001); Gabrielle Kaufmann-Kohler and Thomas Schultz, *Online Dispute Resolution: Challenges for Contemporary Justice* (Kluwer Law International 2004); Arno R Lodder and John Zeleznikow, *Enhanced Dispute Resolution through the Use of Information Technology* (CUP 2010); Mirèze Philippe, 'ODR Redress System for Consumer Disputes Clarifications, UNCITRAL Works and EU Regulation on ODR' [2014] IJODR 57; Lucille M Ponte and Thomas D Cavenagh, *Cyberjustice: Online Dispute Resolution* (Prentice Hall 2004); Susan S Raines and Melissa C Tyler, 'From e-Bay to Eternity: Advances in Online Dispute Resolution' [2007] Melbourne Law School Legal Studies Research Paper No. 200, available at <http://papers.ssrn.com/sol3/papers.cfm?abstract_id=955968>; Graham Ross, 'The Possible Unintended Consequences of the European Directive on Alternative Dispute Resolution and the Regulation on Online Dispute Resolution' (2014) 10 *Democracia Digital e Governo Eletrônico* 206; Colin Rule, *Online Dispute Resolution for Business: B2B, E-Commerce, Consumer, Employment, Insurance, and other Commercial Conflicts* (Jossey-Bass 2002); Scott J Shackelford and Anjanette Raymond, 'Building the Virtual Courthouse: Ethical Considerations for Design, Implementation, and Regulation in the World of ODR' (2014) 3 Wis.L.Rev. 615; Mohamed S Abdel Wahab, Ethan Katsh and Daniel Rainey (eds), *Online Dispute Resolution: Theory and Practice – A Treatise on Technology and Dispute Resolution* (Eleven International Publishing 2011).

Optional (facultative) choice of law

I. Concept

The rules of → choice of law select from the international multitude of legal systems the one law to be applied to a specific social situation, transaction or occurrence. In litigation, the legal system so designated may be the domestic law of the court seized (the → *lex fori*) or the law of some other jurisdiction. The same choice-of-law rule may thus have a different effect depending on where proceedings are brought. Where the rule points to the court's domestic law, the professionals acting in the litigation (judges, attorneys) are familiar with 'their' system. However, where the rule points to a law 'foreign' in the court resorted to, the law to be applied is generally more difficult to find, ascertain, understand and apply so that the involved legal practitioners and judges may need the help of outside experts. All in all, applying foreign law is more cumbersome, costly, time consuming and less reliable than applying the substantive law of the forum.

Under these circumstances, the participants in the proceedings (parties, counsel, judges) may wish to avoid application of the foreign law designated by the choice-of-law rule and rather to have the case decided according to the substantive law of the court seized. Where the law allows the parties or court such resort to the *lex fori*, the choice-of-law rule departed from is termed optional or facultative, because its reference to a foreign law will be followed only when the court or parties opt for, or fail to opt against, that reference. Looking to the substantive laws offered for application, one could also say that the option is between the referred to foreign substantive law and the court's domestic substantive law. Where the law allows no departure from the foreign law reference, the pertinent choice-of-law rule is absolutely binding and it may be termed mandatory or imperative.

II. Models

Optional choice of law may exist in various forms. It may require a party to invoke application of the foreign law to which the choice-of-law rule refers. The option in this case is to opt in to the working of the choice-of-law rule and thereby to the application of the designated foreign law. The domestic law of the court in this case functions as a subsidiary rule, ie a 'default rule', and is there to intervene when the choice-of-law rule has not been invoked, that is the designated foreign law option has been declined. On the other hand, the option may be there to exclude the working of the choice-of-law rule referring to foreign law. In this case the option is to opt out from that referral. If the option is not exercised, the choice-of-law rule and the referred to foreign law will simply have to be applied.

The option whether or not to have the choice-of-law rule and its referral to foreign law applied may lie in the hands of the court or the parties. In the case of the court, the court determines and thereby imposes the applicable law, be it foreign or domestic. With the parties, the option resembles the rules of private international law allowing → party autonomy, that is rules enabling the parties to select the law applicable to a transaction or other occurrence with binding force on the parties and court. There is indeed an implicit understanding of many such rules that the parties may choose the applicable law even during a pending litigation and even replace a previous choice they have made within or before the litigation.

The concept of optional choice of law is narrower than the rules allowing party autonomy in a number of respects. The option applies only to the pending litigation, it can bring into play (as an alternative to the designated foreign law) only the domestic law of the forum and not some other eligible law, and it will be binding on the parties, the court and other seized institutions only within the limits of *res iudicata* in the pending proceeding. On the other hand, the concept extends the party options by allowing parties recourse to the law of the forum even where the otherwise applicable choice-of-law rule does not expressly grant party autonomy or where the parties have previously exercised their autonomy and chosen some other law to govern their relationship. It is thus an option complementing any other choice-of-law rule, whether optional or mandatory.

III. Law and practice

Optional choice of law as described here is a profoundly accepted part of the law in many jurisdictions but is disapproved of in many others.

1. Optional law

An opt-in variant of optional choice of law is most prominently practised in England, albeit under a different name. The English rule is that foreign law must be pleaded and proved by the party relying on it for support of the claim or defence. Relying on foreign law implies that it is alleged to be applicable under a choice-of-law rule to be followed in the jurisdiction. By this way, actual application of the choice-of-law rule depends on whether a party wishes to plead and prove the designated foreign law. Thus, that law and the reference rule itself are optional.

The English model is followed in all common law jurisdictions, including the → USA, and also in → Luxembourg. In → Finland and → Latvia it is practised except in matters of family and → succession law and matters concerning personal status (capacity (→ Capacity and emancipation), guardianship (→ Guardianship, custody and parental responsibility)).

For an opt-out variant, → France is the most prominent example. When the facts pleaded by the parties show international elements calling for application of choice-of-law rules, and if those rules require the application of foreign law to the litigation (→ Foreign law, application and ascertainment), the court must follow this referral on its own motion, an express or implied demand by the parties being unnecessary. The parties may, however, by procedural accord (express or implied) renounce application of the designated foreign law in favour of French substantive law. The court has to follow this consensual choice-of-forum law if, under the procedural rules, the parties are free to dispose over the litigated right, for instance by acknowledgement, disclaimer or settlement.

In Europe, the opt-out version is followed (apart from France) in → Belgium and → Hungary. It is also practised in Scandinavia, with the exception of proceedings concerning the family status of persons (divorce, establishment of parenthood, guardianship (→ Guardianship, custody and parental responsibility)).

It may be difficult at times to distinguish between the opt-in and the opt-out variant. Where an agreement of the parties for application of the *lex fori* can be accepted by the court even as a merely tacit one and the parties plead only the court's domestic law, the court may either find such opt-out agreement in their procedural conduct, or it may apply forum law on the ground that the parties have failed to opt in to the choice-of-law rule referring to foreign law.

2. Mandatory law

The opposite principle is mandatory → choice of law. This means that the parties cannot escape by agreement or simply by inaction from application of the foreign law as designated by the pertinent choice-of-law rule, unless that rule itself or some special rule allows the parties to choose an alternative law to apply, including forum law. If no such party choice is allowed, the pertinent rule is deemed mandatory.

Mandatory choice of law is the rule in most jurisdictions of central, eastern and southern Europe. It is often seen as a civil law concept, contrasting with the optional concept of the common law. It has apparently also been followed in the recent codifications in Russia (→ Russian Federation) and → China (with two interesting exceptions, see V. below).

3. European Union

In the EU, a resort to the *lex fori* is expressly provided for by the Maintenance Regulation (Council Regulation (EC) No 4/2009 of 18 December 2008 on jurisdiction, applicable law, recognition and enforcement of decisions and cooperation in matters relating to maintenance obligations, [2009] OJ L 7/1) (art 15, referring to art 7 of the Hague Maintenance Protocol 2007 (Hague Protocol of 23 November 2007 on the law applicable to maintenance obligations, [2009] OJ L 331/19)) and in the → Rome III Regulation (Council Regulation (EU) No 1259/2010 of 20 December 2010 implementing enhanced cooperation in the area of the law applicable to divorce and legal separation, [2010] OJ L 343/10); art 5 para 1). Moreover, the Rome I and II Regulation (Regulation (EC) No 593/2008 of the European Parliament and of the Council of 17 June 2008 on the law applicable to contractual obligations (Rome I), [2008] OJ L 177/6, and Regulation (EC) No 864/2007 of the European Parliament and of the Council of 11 July 2007 on the law applicable to non-contractual obligations (Rome II), [2007] OJ L 199/40), where they provide for party autonomy, expressly allow such party choice during litigation and thereby, of course, also for choice of the *lex fori* (art 3(2) Rome I Regulation, art 14(2) Rome II Regulation). But apart from those instances, the EU has as yet to take a general view on the optional or mandatory character of choice of law regarding its own enactments. The European Commission is considering whether to propose rules on the subject and has obtained expert reports and advice (Carlos Esplugues, José Iglesias and Guillermo Palao (eds), *Application of Foreign Law* (Sellier 2011); Swiss Institute of Comparative Law, *The Application of Foreign Law in Civil Matters in the EU Member States and its Perspectives for the Future*, JLS/2009/JCIV/PR/0005/E4, Part I: Legal Analysis, July/September 2011, available at <http://ec.europa.eu/justice/civil/files/foreign_law_en.pdf>, last accessed on 31 January 2014).

IV. Debate

Optional choice of law in the opt-in variant seems to be firmly established in England and other common law jurisdictions. In other countries, the merits and demerits of optional choice of law have been subject to debate over the past four or five decades.

Proponents of optionality point to how the nature of adjudication changes markedly when a court proposes to apply a foreign law which is less familiar to the court than its domestic law. Under that view, parties (and within limits also courts) in civil litigation should have the choice of whether to evade the difficulties, delay, costs and uncertainty of adjudication under foreign law or rather to enjoy the promised benefit of having the foreign law applied which a relatively well-considered choice-of-law rule has in store.

The main objection of the optionality opponents is that, when parties are allowed to evade the carefully devised international system by an easy retreat to the *lex fori*, it would undermine the overall authority of private international law, and the desired coordination of substantive legal systems in the interests of international uniformity of decisions irrespective of the forum seized would be compromised and disturbed. Further, it is argued, law shopping would be added to the evils of forum shopping

(→ Forum (and law) shopping). In the EU, after the enactment of various choice-of-law instruments (the 'Rome Regulations'), the question also arises whether optionality of those rules in the Member State courts would be compatible with the binding force of EU law in the Member States and with the principle of practical effectiveness (*effet utile*) traditionally claimed for EU law.

The legal debate in Europe has been most lively in France, Germany and the Netherlands. In Germany and the Netherlands, it has yet to influence statutory or case-law while the legislatures and higher courts still adhere to mandatory → choice of law. In France, the debate was triggered by an apparently unsteady course of the *Cour de cassation*, which only recently can be regarded as settled in favour of the described opt-out character of choice of law. As to the new EU choice-of-law regulations, insofar as they are not expressly declared to be optional (see III. above), the debate remains open, and the European Commission is mandated to consider the issue. Together with private international law party autonomy, optional choice of law may be seen as part of the broader freedom of persons (→ Freedom of establishment/persons (European Union) and private international law) to arrange their affairs by themselves that is fundamental to much of private law and to European law, and accordingly may be viewed as favourably in Europe as that broader principle.

V. Court options

Optional choice of law is debated primarily as serving party interests. However, interests of a jurisdiction's administration of justice are also involved. The application of foreign law (→ Foreign law, application and ascertainment) is generally an added demand on the resources of a court system. An option for the court seized to depart in favour of its domestic law from application of the designated foreign law might be a remedy to save judicial time, money and endeavour. This may be particularly welcome in small claims cases and in summary proceedings.

It seems that in Scandinavia, courts have been allowed discretion to abstain from applying foreign law where the amount in dispute did not justify the endeavour. Also in France and Luxembourg, the court may at its discretion apply domestic law instead of foreign law referred to by the choice-of-law rule as long as the parties fail to invoke the foreign law's application. In Switzerland, the court may oblige the parties to prove the content of the referred to foreign law in litigation on claims with a financial value (art 16 para 1 Swiss Private international law Act (Bundesgesetz über das Internationale Privatrecht of 18 December 1987, 1988 BBl I 5, as amended)). The Swiss model has been followed in Russia for claims relating to the parties' business (art 1191 no 2 para 3 of the Civil Code of the Russian Federation (as amended by Federal Law No 260-FZ on 30 September 2013)); in China, in cases where the parties themselves by a choice-of-law clause have made foreign law apply to their relationship, the Statute of Application of Law to Foreign Civil Relations (adopted at the 17th session of the Standing Committee of the 11th National People's Congress on 28 October 2010, effective 1 April 2011) itself renders them liable to provide the court with the foreign legal information (§ 10 para 1 sentence 2).

Evidently, court discretion as to the applicability of foreign law or as to the burden of proving it threatens to impair legal certainty, improvement of which in international legal intercourse is a frequently declared objective of choice-of-law rules. Therefore, granting discretion on a broad scale for the sake of the forum's judicial resources is nowhere found in statutory choice-of-law rules, but is rather justified occasionally in case-law and the commenting literature.

Moreover, there are less visible means by which a court may at its discretion find an acceptable way to its domestic substantive law. It is notorious that judges generally dislike applying foreign law unfamiliar to them, particularly if written in a foreign language. This psychological sub-current explains the 'homeward trend' of courts so often noted by observers. Thus, a court may wittingly or unwittingly overlook the international element in a case which might otherwise have referred to a foreign law. Absent objection or appeal by the parties, the court has in effect independently evaded the foreign law, and even if a party then appeals against non-application of the choice-of-law rule, it may be barred from raising this point following its silence in the instance below. Another such way is offered by → escape clauses which choice-of-law statutes here and there add to their stricter primary rules, such as art 4(3) of the Rome I Regulation and arts 4(3), 10(4) and 11(4) of the Rome II Regulation. The escape clause may pave the way to the *lex fori*, if only by the simple argument that the very fact of the case legitimately pending in the forum makes it 'more closely connected' with the forum's law rather than with the foreign law designated in the primary rule.

Finally, there is discretionary potential in favour of the *lex fori* in the process of ascertaining foreign law. In most jurisdictions, the *lex fori* is deemed the applicable law of last resort if the foreign law invoked by the choice-of-law rule cannot be established (by the court) or proved (by the parties) with sufficient certainty. In the process of finding out the applicable foreign rules, there is unavoidably a margin of court discretion in forming its opinion, and this margin may also be used by the court to fall back on its domestic law because of an alleged lack of ascertainment of the referred to foreign law. Discretion can be used all the more readily in summary proceedings for provisional and expeditious relief. In many jurisdictions, forum law in such proceedings will be resorted to from the outset. In others, the choice-of-law rule referring to foreign law will be principally respected, whereas the court is expected to accommodate its investigation with the need for a timely decision. In other words, the court is to retreat to the *lex fori* when, in its discretion, further investigation would run counter to the summary and provisional character of the proceeding.

All in all, there are discretionary devices in every choice-of-law system, whether mandatory or optional, for the court in fact to 'opt' for the *lex fori*. However, in the jurisdictions described above the devices will less explicitly be used than the choice-of-law option accorded the parties.

VI. Requirements and effects

Optional choice of law can be regarded as a device of either private international law or procedural law, or alternatively as pertaining to both fields, or finally can be regarded as a separate element linking them. In the jurisdictions where optional choice of law is practised it is primarily regarded as a procedural device. In the legal debate on its merits, private international law experts generally discuss it as a specific (welcome or unwelcome) aspect of private international law.

The procedural view implies that exercise of the option is subject to the forum's pleading rules. It is thus the forum's law of civil procedure that decides on where to exercise the option (in the court or outside), in what form (orally, written, expressly or also impliedly), by whom (parties or only their counsel), at which stage (before or after the trial, also on appeal), whether it can be revoked, as well as its remaining consequences after an eventual judgment or court settlement. The leading idea for all these issues is that the option, as a procedural device in a particular litigation, must conform with and be confined to the ends to be gained by that litigation.

The discussion by private international law experts, on the other hand, is less concerned with practical details than with the question of whether the claimed optionality of choice of law serves legitimate interests or rather impairs them and the orderly administration of private international law justice.

VII. Other optional devices

There may be other means for party retreat to the *lex fori* but with slightly different preconditions and effects.

1. Choice-of-law agreements

Where private international law expressly allows party choice of law, such as in the Rome Regulations of the European Union (see III.3.), the parties may from the outset choose the *lex fori* to apply to their relationship. If they do so outside and before any litigation, that choice of law is a 'floating' one, in that it refers to the domestic law of whichever court to which a future dispute arising from that relationship might be taken. If the parties choose during a pending dispute, the agreement refers to the domestic law of the actually seized court, and will be honoured by the court provided the applicable choice-of-law rule allows for subsequent choice-of-law agreements and even for agreements after the start of litigation. Examples of such rules are art 3(2) Rome I Regulation, art 14(1) Rome II Regulation, art 3(4) Rome III Regulation, arts 7 and 8 Hague Maintenance Protocol 2007 (see III.3.).

Choice-of-law agreements on the basis of private international law rules are, however, distinct in many respects from procedurally opting for the *lex fori* in that (i) such agreements are concluded between the parties, inside or outside the court, (ii) they may be subject to separate formal and substantive requirements, (iii) they generally cover the entire legal relationship between the parties and thus may also have effect in other disputes arising from the relationship and in possibly other courts and finally (iv) they generally cannot be revoked unilaterally. By contrast the exercise of the procedural option is (i) a unilateral declaration by either party to the court, and in the opt-out version away from foreign law, it need not be agreed between the parties but only be declared concurrently to the court, (ii) it is subject only to the procedural pleading rules, (iii) it covers only the pending dispute and (iv) it can be revoked unilaterally at some later stage if the procedural rules allow an amendment to a previous pleading.

2. *Dressing the case*

It is often pointed out in the literature that the parties can reach the desired *lex fori* by simply not dressing their case as an international one. In civil litigation, as a rule, the court can rely on the facts alleged by the parties and need not, even must not, go behind their factual allegations by independently seeking information unrelated to the facts alleged, with the possible exception of cases where the public interest or interests of third parties are involved. In this pleading system, the parties can make their case appear as purely domestic in nature, not requiring any choice-of-law consideration by the court, with the rules of domestic law thus applying as a matter of course. This kind of procedural behaviour could open the way to the *lex fori* even in those jurisdictions which do not officially recognize optional choice of law (see III.2. above).

Nevertheless the dressing 'option' seems to be largely theoretical. In practice the parties will rarely be able to conceal from the court the international elements of their case. If the parties are located in different jurisdictions, the international element will appear already in the documents deriving from and to be served in another jurisdiction. Even if the parties reside in the same jurisdiction, it will be difficult to state the relevant facts without mentioning where they have or should have occurred, such as where the contract was concluded and should have been performed, where the accident occurred or the damage should have been avoided, where the will was made, the trust settled, the assets located and the beneficiaries are resident, or corporations are registered. It is difficult to contrive a supposed purely domestic case leaving the court completely unaware of a potential application of choice-of-law rules. Further, the threat of uncovering such a manoeuvre by one of the parties apprehending an unfavourable outcome under the *lex fori* is present throughout the proceedings.

3. *Proof of foreign law*

Where the law relies on the parties to prove the applicable foreign law, the parties may at their will abandon their investigations and return without a presentable result in the hope of having the court apply its domestic law as the subsidiary rule. However, this road to the *lex fori* is not available in jurisdictions with mandatory choice of law, in which it is for the court, either alone or besides the parties, to look for the designated foreign law (see III.2.). When abandoning further enquiries, the parties in these jurisdictions could hope for application of the *lex fori* only when the court would also abstain from further investigation. To the extent the court has discretion, it is then rather the court's than the parties' option to resort to the *lex fori*.

VIII. Non-contentious proceedings and non-judicial authorities

Optional choice of law has developed in, or is proposed for, civil litigation, that is for disputes over private rights and duties for which a court decision is sought by the parties. However, choice of law may also become necessary in non-contentious matters that in many jurisdictions are entrusted to the courts; such as guardianship over minors and handicapped persons (→ Guardianship, custody and parental responsibility), → adoption, registration of wills, certification of → succession rights, keeping land as well as commercial registers. It may also become relevant for non-judicial authorities, such as those administering taxation, social welfare, immigration, or for notaries when drawing up formal documents, for civil registries when celebrating → marriages and issuing certificates of birth and kinship, marriage and death.

Theoretically, applicants in such proceedings and at such authorities could also here be given the option to fall back on the domestic law of the court or other agency, although the choice-of-law rule refers to a foreign law. Practically, however, such an option would be superfluous where the courts in non-contentious proceedings are in any case unwilling to apply foreign law and will rather decline jurisdiction from the outset than make findings on a law other than their own. This attitude prevails for non-contentious proceedings in common law countries.

In other countries, giving the parties the right to retreat from the designated foreign law to the *lex fori* would run counter to, or overstep, the purpose of the proceedings or frustrate the function of the → agency concerned. For example, guardianship (→ Guardianship, custody and parental responsibility) is in the interest of the person to be cared for and in the public interest rather than that of an actual applicant. Adoption decrees and succession certificates may concern third persons under the applicable foreign law and not only the persons openly participating in the proceedings. The tax authority, when it finds foreign law to be applicable to a preliminary private law issue relevant for the tax assessment (for instance ownership, heirship, claims and liabilities of the deceased), must apply the law regardless of taxpayer wishes.

For these reasons, optional choice of law is generally not practised in non-contentious proceedings and is rarely proposed for them. Even advocates of optional choice of law restrict it to proceedings where only the interests of the applicants are involved and can be protected by the court's active attention in the proceedings.

AXEL FLESSNER

Literature

Sabine Corneloup, 'Rechtsermittlung im Internationalen Privatrecht der EU: Überlegungen aus Frankreich' (2014) 78 RabelsZ 844; Theodorus M de Boer, 'Facultative Choice of Law: The Procedural Status of Choice of Law Rules and Foreign Law' (1996) 257 Rec. des Cours 225; Theodorus M de Boer, 'Facultative Choice of Law in Extrajudicial Proceedings' in Faculté de Droit de Lausanne (ed), *Mélanges Fritz Sturm* (Editions Juridiques de l'Université de Liège 1999) 1409; Bénédicte Fauvarque-Cosson, *Libre disponibilité des droits et conflits de lois* (LGDJ 1996); Richard Fentiman, *Foreign Law in English Courts: Pleading, Proof and Choice of Law* (OUP 1998); Axel Flessner, 'Fakultatives Kollisionsrecht' (1971) 34 RabelsZ 547; Axel Flessner, *Interessenjurisprudenz im internationalen Privatrecht* (Mohr Siebeck 1990); Axel Flessner, 'Das Parteiinteresse an der Lex fori nach europäischem Kollisionsrecht' in Alain-Laurent Verbeke and others (eds), *Confronting the Frontiers of Family and Succession Law: Liber Amicorum Walter Pintens* (Intersentia 2012) 593; Maarit Jänterä-Jareborg, 'Foreign Law in National Courts: A Comparative Perspective' (2003) 304 Rec. des Cours 181; Stephan Lesage-Mathieu, *Dispositives Kollisionsrecht im prozessualen Kontext* (Peter Lang 2005); PMM Mostermans, *De processuele behandeling van het conflictenrecht* (Tjeenk Willink 1996); Peter-Christian Müller-Graff, 'Fakultatives Kollisionsrecht im internationalen Wettbewerbsrecht?' (1984) 48 RabelsZ 289; Daniel Reichert-Facilides, *Fakultatives und zwingendes Kollisionsrecht* (Mohr Siebeck 1995); Giesela Rühl, *Statut und Effizienz: Ökonomische Grundlagen des Internationalen Privatrechts* (Mohr Siebeck 2011); Hans Jürgen Sonnenberger, 'Internationales Privatrecht: Einleitung' in Hans Jürgen Sonnenberger (ed), *Münchener Kommentar zum Bürgerlichen Gesetzbuch*, vol 10 (5th edn, CH Beck 2010) paras 227, 617; Fritz Sturm, 'Fakultatives Kollisionsrecht: Notwendigkeit und Grenzen' in Herbert Bernstein, Ulrich Drobnig and Hein Kötz (eds), *Festschrift für Konrad Zweigert* (Mohr Siebeck 1981) 329; Clemens Trautmann, *Europäisches Kollisionsrecht und ausländisches Recht im nationalen Zivilverfahren* (Mohr Siebeck 2011); Gerhard Wagner, 'Fakultatives Kollisionsrecht und prozessuale Parteiautonomie' [1999] ZEuP 6.

Overriding mandatory provisions

I. Introduction

Overriding mandatory provisions (internationally mandatory provisions, *lois de police*, *lois d'application immédiate*, international zwingende Normen, Eingriffsnormen) are those rules that are applicable to a situation irrespective of the *lex causae*. They oust the normally applicable law, or at least certain parts of it, and, in so doing, they upset the normal operation of conflict-of-law rules. Furthermore, where the parties have themselves chosen the applicable law, they impinge upon party autonomy. To give an example, let us suppose that a contract, governed by the law of country A, which provides for the services of an architect to be rendered in country B, stipulates that the architect is to receive a certain amount of money in fees; the stipulated fee is in conformity with the rules of country A, the *lex causae*, but exceeds the amount allowed by the law of country B. Under the normal principles of private international law, the validity of the terms of the contract is a matter for the applicable law. However, country B may intend that its rule that sets a ceiling on architects' fees is to be applicable to any contract that is performed on its territory, irrespective of the contract's governing law. If this is the case, then that rule is an overriding mandatory rule. If an action for recovery of fees is brought in the courts of country B, that rule will be applied there as a mandatory rule of the *lex fori*; if the action is brought in another country, it will be for that country to decide whether or not to give effect to that mandatory rule.

Normally, rules will be held to be overriding mandatory provisions only if they are judged necessary for the maintenance or protection of some extremely important interest of the state that enacted them and they will apply only if the situation has some connection with that state. The classic definition of the nature of such rules was laid down by *Phocion Franceskakis* in 1966 as being 'rules compliance with which is necessary for the protection of the political, social and economic organisation of the country'. This definition of overriding mandatory rules was adapted and applied by the European Court of Justice in 1999 in the *Arblade* judgment (Joined cases C-369/96 and C-376/96 *Criminal proceedings against Jean-Claude Arblade and Arblade & Fils SARL* and *Bernard Leloup, Serge Leloup and Sofrage SARL* [1999] ECR I-8453) to public order legislation: in this context, the significance of being classified as public order legislation meant that a particular Belgian law was applicable to all persons present on Belgian territory. The Court held as follows: 'public order legislation . . . [means] national provisions compliance with which has been deemed to be so crucial for the protection of the political, social or economic order in the Member State concerned as to require compliance therewith by all persons present on the national territory'. This description is not entirely accurate since it blurs the distinction between the mandatory nature of a rule and the spatial application of that rule. As we shall see, rules may have an overriding mandatory nature in a number of situations, and their application is not necessarily dependent on the persons affected being present on the territory of the state concerned. Nevertheless, the Court's *dictum* in *Arblade* has served as the basis for an attempt at a statutory definition in the Rome I Regulation (Regulation (EC) No 593/2008 of the European Parliament and of the Council of 17 June 2008 on the law applicable to contractual obligations (Rome I), [2008] OJ L 177/6; → Rome Convention and Rome I Regulation (contractual obligations)) on the law applicable to → contractual obligations.

It is also important to bear in mind the context of the *Arblade* judgment, which had nothing to do with the conflict of laws but was, in fact, a criminal prosecution. In the judgment, the European Court reiterated the axiomatic point that, merely because legislation may be characterized by the Member State that enacted it as *ordre public* legislation, that does not exempt it from scrutiny under the basic principles of EU law. In particular, a rule of such legislation may have to be set aside if, concretely, it impedes the exercise of EU Treaty freedoms.

II. Overriding rules distinguished from non-derogable rules

It is important to distinguish both on a conceptual and a practical level between 'provisions which cannot be derogated by agreement' (or, more simply, 'non-derogable rules') and overriding mandatory rules. The first category comprises rules from which the parties, in a purely domestic context, may not depart; such rules are typically to be found in employment, consumer and insurance legislation and their function is to restrict party autonomy in order to protect the weaker party (namely the employee, consumer or policyholder/assured). Subject to certain limited and well-defined exceptions in the Rome I Regulation (arts 3(3), 3(4), art 6(2) and art 8(1)), such rules will not be applicable in an international context where the rules in question do not form part of the applicable law (*lex causae*). Overriding mandatory provisions are rules that are applied to a given situation whatever the law designated by the forum's conflict rules. In the Rome Convention (Rome Convention on the law applicable to contractual obligations (consolidated version), [1998] OJ C 27/34), the same expression 'mandatory rules' is used to designate both concepts, which was a source of confusion, but, in the Rome I Regulation the distinction is drawn more clearly between the two concepts.

III. Approaches in different Member States of the EU

There is a strong link between public law and overriding mandatory rules. Thus, for example, a law of the forum that outlaws the performance of a contract irrespective of whether it is valid under its applicable law and which, on its own terms, applies to the situation will almost

Michael Wilderspin

invariably have the effect of rendering the contract invalid or, at least, unenforceable.

The extent to which a rule must serve a public interest goal before it can be treated as an overriding mandatory rule varies very much in the Member States. In → Germany, for example, the approach is strict; where the legislature has not expressly stipulated that a provision must be applied irrespective of the governing law, in order for the courts to accept that it is an overriding mandatory rule, the rule in question must exercise a regulatory function and be, at least primarily, for the protection of the public interest. In this respect, rules on antitrust, currency control (→ Money and currency), trade restrictions, criminal law and financial markets are treated as paradigm examples of overriding mandatory rules. Conversely, rules that are primarily for the balancing of private interests (such as rules on employees' rights and consumer protection) have been treated as merely non-derogable (see II.). Nevertheless, the dividing line may be difficult to draw; for example, rules for the protection of disabled employees and the conferral of maternity entitlements have been held to be overriding mandatory rules. The German approach has the advantage of minimizing the risk that a particular provision may be simultaneously a non-derogable rule and an overriding rule, which helps to avoid difficult questions of articulation between the appropriate provisions of the Rome I Regulation.

In → France, however, such a sharp distinction is not drawn and the protection of weaker parties is regarded as a legitimate reason to confer overriding status on a rule; thus, rules for the protection of consumers, employees and sub-contractors have been held to be overriding mandatory rules.

Similarly, in the → United Kingdom, public law rules have the status of overriding rules (for example, in one case, one party borrowed money from another in breach of exchange control legislation; it was held that the contract was unenforceable with the effect that the lender was unable to obtain repayment of the loan (*Boissevain v Weil* [1950] 1 All ER 728). However, there is no particular objection to conferring overriding status on laws whose primary purpose is to protect private interests: whether such rules have overriding effects is seen largely as a question of statutory interpretation. Indeed, the legislature has, by stipulating that their provisions apply irrespective of the applicable law, explicitly conferred overriding status on a number of rules in the field of employee protection (see s 204 of the Employment Rights Act 1996 (c 18)) and consumer protection (see the Consumer Credit Act 1974 (c 39)).

Lastly, it needs to be borne in mind that, in *Arblade*, the European Court accepted that in principle provisions for the protection of employees' rights could qualify as overriding mandatory rules and, more recently in *Unamar v NMB* (Case C-184/12 *United Antwerp Maritime Agencies (UNAMAR) NV v Navigation Maritime Bulgare* [2013] OJ C 367/12) it did the same with regard to national rules for the protection of commercial agents. The approach of the European Court to this question tends to suggest that European law does not require Member States to be as strict in this respect as → Germany.

IV. The Rome Convention on the law applicable to contractual obligations

The Rome Convention provides that nothing in the Convention restricts the application of the rules of the forum where they are mandatory irrespective of the law otherwise applicable to the contract (art 7(2)). Article 7(1) of the Convention permits effect to be given to the mandatory rules of the law of another country with which the situation has a close connection. Given its very open ended wording, the perceived uncertainty of the close connection test and the potential interference with party autonomy, art 7(1) was very controversial and contracting states were permitted to reserve the right not to apply it. Seven contracting states (→ Germany, → United Kingdom, → Portugal, → Ireland, → Latvia, → Luxembourg and → Slovenia) availed themselves of this right.

The Rome Convention did not make any attempt to define what kind of rules might fall within the scope of art 7, albeit the Giuliano-Lagarde Report (Report on the Convention on the law applicable to contractual obligations by Mario Giuliano, Professor, University of Milan, and Paul Lagarde, Professor, University of Paris I, [1980] OJ C 282/1) gave as examples rules on cartels, competition and restrictive practices, consumer protection and rules concerning carriage. However, guidance in this respect was given by the European Court in *Unamar v NMB*. In that judgment, the Court held that the concept of mandatory rules within the meaning of art 7 of the Rome Convention (ie overriding mandatory rules) should be interpreted strictly. Thus, where a national law does not specifically state that it is to have overriding effect, a court should be very cautious before attributing that effect to it. It also seems to be implicit in the *Unamar* judgment that a simple statement by the national legislature that the rule is to have overriding effect does not necessarily suffice in this regard; in addition, the national court must examine the general structure and circumstances of adoption of the rule in order to determine 'whether it is mandatory in nature'. Crucial passages of this important judgment are obscurely worded, but it implies that, while it is for the national decision maker to determine what interests are judged so essential as to merit protection by an overriding mandatory rule, it must nevertheless give reasons for its choice. It remains to be seen how national courts interpret this requirement and whether they will be prepared to set aside a rule to which the national legislature has made it clear that it wants to confer overriding effect. At the same time, the Court accepted in principle that a national rule might fall within the scope of art 7 of the Rome Convention even if it aimed to protect weaker parties and thus to balance the interests of private parties (as opposed to the public interest).

V. The Rome I Regulation

Unlike the Rome Convention, the Rome I Regulation contains a conceptual definition, in art 9(1), of overriding mandatory provisions. They are 'provisions the respect for which is regarded as crucial by a country for safeguarding its public interests, such as its political, social or economic organisation' to such an extent that they apply irrespective of the applicable law. Recital (37) of the preamble to the Regulation specifically draws attention to the distinction between overriding mandatory rules and non-derogable rules and opines that the former concept should be interpreted more restrictively than the latter.

As to the interpretation of this provision, there is on the one hand a subjective element: overriding provisions are provisions regarded as crucial 'by a country', which grants states a certain amount of leeway. On the other hand, the use of the word 'crucial', as opposed to a less strong word, indicates that a country should not lightly characterize rules as overriding. The definition in art 9(1) is clearly based on the description of *ordre public* rules given by the European Court in *Arblade*. However, one significant difference is the addition in the Rome I Regulation of the words 'its public interests, such as . . .' before the words 'its political, social or economic organisation'. One possible interpretation for the addition of these words is that they simply underline that henceforth the political, social and economic organization of a country are merely examples of the kinds of interests that may legitimately be protected by overriding mandatory rules; on this view, the addition of these words loosens the definition in *Arblade* in that art 9 does not contain an exhaustive list of the categories of such interest. However, another possible, and diametrically opposed, view is that the addition of these words makes the definition more restrictive, in that the addition of these words excludes rules that aim primarily to balance competing private interest. If this view is correct, it means, as certain commentators have concluded, that the Union legislature has adopted in the Rome I Regulation the stricter German approach. Given this divergence of views, it is likely that courts in the various Member States will simply see in the new wording an endorsement of their existing practice.

It is thought that the correct position is that the addition of the words 'public interests' is not to be interpreted so strictly as to exclude at the outset all rules that are designed primarily to protect private interests. Nevertheless, it seems to be the case that, in setting out this *ex ante* definition in the text, the legislature intended to provide some limits on the Member States' discretion. Thus the notion of overriding provisions is to be interpreted restrictively. Read in conjunction with the *Unamar* judgment, it is thought that the effect of the definition in art 9(1) Rome I is that, where a rule does not expressly state that it is intended to have overriding effect, courts should be extremely cautious in ascribing such an effect and, even where the legislature has expressly declared that such a rule is to have overriding effect, the courts must, before accepting such an effect, nevertheless examine closely the interests at stake and determine whether the legislature has given adequate reasons for its choice. Despite the fact that art 9(1) restricts to a certain extent the freedom of the Member States to determine which of its rules may be overriding mandatory rules, it is important to bear in mind that the wording ('provisions the respect for which is regarded as crucial by a country') does not attempt to provide a comprehensive definition that will lead to a harmonized approach in all Member States.

VI. Application of overriding mandatory rules of the forum

Article 9(2) of the Rome I Regulation provides that nothing in the Regulation 'shall restrict the application of the overriding mandatory provisions of the law of the forum'. In substance, this rule replicates art 7(2) of the Rome Convention. Thus, once the forum has determined that (i) the national legislature intended a given rule to have overriding effect and (ii) that the rule in question corresponds to the definition in art 9(1), the Rome I Regulation does not prevent the forum from applying that rule irrespective of the relevant rules of the *lex causae*.

Notwithstanding the unconditional wording of art 9(2), the forum may nevertheless, as stated above, in an extreme case, be required to set aside a rule if it constitutes an impediment to the free movement of goods or persons or capital or the free provision of services within the Internal Market (*Arblade*). This principle flows directly from the Treaty and is unaffected by the Rome I Regulation.

VII. Giving effect to overriding rules of the place of performance

In its proposal for the Rome I Regulation, the Commission had originally proposed to maintain the substance of art 7(1) of the Rome Convention. Given the large number of reservations to that provision, the proposal proved so controversial that the debate attained an intensity that was out of all proportion to the impact that the application of the proposed rule was likely to produce. In the event, a compromise was reached (art 9(3)) whereby 'effect may be given to the overriding mandatory provisions of the law of the country where the obligations arising out of the contract have to be or have been performed, in so far as those . . . provisions render the performance of the contract unlawful'. Article 9(3) merely gives a discretion, rather than an obligation, to the forum to give effect to such a rule of the country of performance, and thus creates some uncertainty as to when it will be applied. It has nevertheless replaced the somewhat loose connecting factor of the country with which a situation has a close connection (which featured in its predecessor, art 7(1) of the Rome Convention) by the more precise criterion of the country of performance. In doing this it has removed many of the objections that were levelled against its predecessor. Although art 9(3) merely grants discretion, the conditions for its application are nevertheless strict. In the first place, the rules of the country of performance must make performance unlawful; it does not suffice that those rules are simply overriding. Thus, for example, if we take the example of the contract with the architect in section I., if an action for recovery of fees is brought by the architect before the courts of country A, whether effect may be given to the law of country B, which sets a ceiling on architects' fees, will depend on whether payment of the portion of the fee exceeding the statutory ceiling fee is unlawful or merely unenforceable according to the law of country B. Furthermore, art 9(3) applies only if the obligations that make the contract unlawful are to be or have been performed in the country whose legislation is sought to be given effect. It does not apply if the obligation can be performed elsewhere. Thus, in the above example, unless by virtue of the contract the fees had to be paid in country B, art 9(3) would not apply (see by analogy *Kahler v Midland Bank* [1950] AC 24; the law of the habitual residence of one of the parties that made performance illegal did not need to be taken into account since the contract did not have to be performed in that country). It has been noted that this provision is very similar to the rule of English law that an English (and possibly a foreign) contract will not be enforced if its performance would be illegal under the law of the place of performance, even if the illegality has supervened after the contract has been concluded (*Ralli Bros v Compania Naviera Sota y Anzar* [1920] 2 KB 287).

VIII. The Rome II Regulation

Article 16 of the → Rome II Regulation (Regulation (EC) No 864/2007 of the European Parliament and of the Council of 11 July 2007 on the law applicable to non-contractual obligations (Rome II), [2007] OJ L 199/40) provides that nothing in the Regulation is to restrict the application of provisions of the law of the forum where they are mandatory irrespective of the law otherwise applicable to the non-contractual obligation. This provision corresponds *mutatis mutandis* to art 7(2) of the Rome Convention, *supra*. In particular, it is clear that it is referring to overriding mandatory rules (as opposed to non-derogable rules). However, unlike its counterpart in the Rome I Regulation it contains no conceptual definition of overriding mandatory rules and nor does it permit the forum to give effect to the overriding mandatory rules of a country other than the forum with which the situation has a close connection. However, it is likely, given the relationship between the Rome I and Rome II Regulations, that the concepts in both Regulations will be interpreted the same way.

IX. Overriding mandatory rules in EU legislation

Lastly, it is important to bear in mind that a number of EU Directives in notably the area of consumer protection contain articles that, in effect, confer the status of overriding provisions on some or all of the substantive provisions of the Directive in question (or, put more correctly, such articles require the Member States, when transposing the Directive, to confer such status on the national transposition measures). For example, the Unfair Terms Directive (Council Directive 93/13/EEC of 5 April 1993 on unfair terms in consumer contracts, [1993] OJ L 95/29) contains a provision (art 6(2)) that requires Member States to ensure that consumers are not deprived of the protection conferred by the Directive by the choice of the law of a third country if the contract has a close connection with the territory of the Member States. Thus, if the parties have chosen to have their contract governed by the law of a third country, the provisions of the Directive apply, provided that there is a close connection with the territory of the Member States. Such rules are poorly articulated with art 3(4) of the Rome I Regulation (which provides that the choice of the law of a third country is without prejudice to the non-derogable rules of Union law only if the chosen law has no connection with the situation). Furthermore, even if a Directive does not explicitly state that its provisions are to have the status of overriding mandatory rules, the provisions may nevertheless be interpreted as such. For example, in *Ingmar v Eaton Leonard Technologies* (Case C-381/98 *Ingmar GB Ltd v Eaton Leonard Technologies Inc* [2000] ECR I-9325) the European Court held that provisions in the Commercial Agents Directive (European Council Directive (86/653/EEC) of 18 December 1986 on the coordination of the laws of the Member States relating to self-employed commercial agents, [1986] OJ L 382/17) which, on the face of it, appeared to confer only the status of non-derogable rules, had to be applied by the forum whenever the situation had a close connection with the territory of the Member States even where the parties had chosen the law of a third country as applicable law.

MICHAEL WILDERSPIN

Literature

Andrea Bonomi, 'Le régime des règles impératives et des lois de police dans le Règlement Rome I sur la loi applicable aux contrats' in Eleanor Cashin Ritaine and Andrea Bonomi (eds), *Le nouveau règlement européen Rome I sur la loi applicable aux obligations contractuelles* (Schulthess 2008); Adeline Chong, 'The Public Policy and Mandatory Rules of Third Countries in International Contracts' [2006] J Priv Int L 27; Lord Collins of Mapesbury and others (eds), *Dicey, Morris & Collins on the Conflict of Laws* (15th edn, Sweet & Maxwell 2012); Stéphanie Francq and Fabienne Jault-Seseke, 'Les lois de police, une approche de droit comparé' in Sabine Corneloup and Natalie Joubert (eds), *Le règlement communautaire Rome I et le choix de loi dans les contrats internationaux* (Litec 2011); Robert Freitag, 'Die kollisionsrechtliche Behandlung ausländischer Eingriffsnormen nach Art. 9 Abs. 3 Rom I-VO' [2009] IPRax 109; Jonathan Harris, 'Mandatory Rules and Public Policy under the Rome I Regulation' in Franco Ferrari and Stefan Leible (eds), *Rome I Regulations* (Sellier 2009); Trevor C Hartley, 'Mandatory Rules in International Contracts: The Common Law Approach' (1998) 266 Rec. des Cours 337; Michael Hellner, 'Third Country Overriding Mandatory Rules in the Rome I Regulation: Old Wine in New Bottles?' [2009] J Priv Int L 447; Andreas Köhler, *Eingriffsnormen-Der unfertige Teil des europäischen IPR* (Mohr Siebeck 2013); Felix Maultzsch, 'Rechtswahl und ius cogens im Internationalen Schuldvertragsrecht' (2011) 75 RabelsZ 60; Horatia Muir Watt, 'Les limites du choix: Dispositions impératives et internationalité du contrat' in Sabine Corneloup and Natalie Joubert (eds), *Le règlement communautaire Rome I et le choix de loi dans les contrats internationaux* (Litec 2011); Richard Plender and Michael Wilderspin, *The European Private international law of Obligations* (3rd edn, Sweet & Maxwell 2009); Allan Philip, 'Mandatory Rules, Public Law and Choice of Law' in Peter North (ed), *Contract Conflicts* (North-Holland Publishing 1982) 81; Christoph Reithmann and Dieter Martiny, *Internationales Vertragsrecht* (7th edn, Otto Schmidt 2010); Oliver Remien, 'Variationen zum Thema Eingriffsnormen nach Art. 9 Rom I-VO and Art. 16 Rom II-VO unter Berücksichtigung neuerer Rechtsprechung zu Art. 7 Römer Übereinkommen' in Herbert Kronke and Karsten Thorn (eds), *Grenzen überwinden-Prinzipien bewahren – Festschrift für Bernd von Hoffmann zum 70. Geburtstag* (Gieseking Verlag 2011); Moritz Renner 'Kommentierung der Art. 9 und 21 Rom I-VO' in Gralf-Peter Callies (ed), *The Rome Regulations* (Kluwer Law International 2011).

Party autonomy

I. Overview: the political economy of private ordering

Now enshrined in art 3 of the Rome I Regulation (Regulation (EC) No 593/2008 of the European Parliament and of the Council of 17 June 2008 on the law applicable to contractual obligations (Rome I), [2008] OJ L 177/6; → Rome Convention and Rome I Regulation (contractual obligations)), the principle that has come to be known as 'party autonomy', according to which parties to an international business contract are free to choose the governing law, emerged as a key methodological concept in the course of the 20th century. It served the progressive liberalization of cross-border markets, which broke the frames of protectionist regulatory schemes, emancipating international flows of capital, goods and services from the claims of → territoriality. Through a series of technical moves which will be described below, the law has accredited freedom of choice as the foundation of a whole parallel world of private transnational ordering, complete with its own institutions and governing principles (→ Choice of law). Indeed, from the resulting representation of the relationship between free choice of law and sovereign authority stems the fiction of an autonomous private transnational legal order, widely accepted as the source of regulation, conceded by the various states, of cross-border relationships between economic actors. In this perspective, party autonomy is to a large extent the expression, within the confines of private international contract law, of a wider political economy which serves the global expansion of the neoliberal market. As such, it fulfils a significant function in creating an enabling environment for private sector activity in the context of a globally integrated economy.

II. Theoretical representations of party autonomy

Under the classical liberal paradigm, party autonomy was designed to be exercised within a political framework which ensured the ultimate primacy of public market regulation. This scheme owes as much to domestic contract theory as to the Westphalian model of the public international legal order, composed (exclusively) of equal and sovereign states. Together, state sovereignty and freedom of contract combined to produce a view of the relationship between law and market in the transnational economic sphere according to which the empowerment of private actors was subject to limits imposed in the name of the general interest. Whether framed in terms of public policy or overriding mandatory rules, such restrictions imposed upon the conduct of private transnational trade are set by a presumptively like-minded community of sovereign states similarly desirous of promoting the reciprocal benefits of international trade.

Within such a scheme, the reasons for which any sovereign state would allow parties to contract out of its own rules and substitute those of a neighbouring community, were to be found in both the purported special needs of cross-border transactions and the dilution of the claim of any one state to regulate them exclusively. This implied in turn that sovereign states were deemed to be unconcerned, or their polities less affected, by transactions which did not directly involve their domestic economy; in a world where market was coextensive with territory, this idea translated methodologically into a presumption of territoriality of national regulation. And indeed, this separation of the two worlds of domestic and international transactions had a functional justification: social and economic policies were non-negotiable in homogeneous cases which fell clearly within their regulatory ambit; on the other hand such policies were not endangered by contracting-out when the relationship, bearing foreign elements, was not perceived to 'belong' to the local economy.

However, while contractual choice of law might be encouraged in the interests of cross-border commerce, its corollary was the assumption that the community of states – specifically, those which were sufficiently closely connected to the parties to justify the jurisdiction of their courts – would moderate private autonomy to accommodate the requirements of the common good. No unbridled '*contrat sans loi*', then, but a regulated freedom to be subject to the sovereign legal order of one's choice. Like international commercial arbitration (→ Arbitration, international commercial), whose growth followed on the generalization of party autonomy as a foundational principle of choice of law, the empowerment of private actors is supposed to cater to the special needs of international economic intercourse.

The notion that party autonomy in the international arena, like freedom of contract in the domestic context, is a measured concession by the liberal state to private ordering, rests on theoretical premises which are also to be found, outside the field of contract, at the heart of multilateral conflicts methodology. Thus, the very representation of the conflict between laws within the continental *savignian* tradition presupposes a certain commonality of normative preferences among like-minded (and pre-regulatory) sovereigns. Indeed, private law – of which the province is that of horizontal relationships between non-state actors – is perceived to be largely facilitative of private transactions, so that a conflict of laws may be seen essentially as the virtual availability of as many interchangeable sets of rules as there are connections between a given set of facts and different legal systems. Conversely, any given legal system is assumed to provide a set of rules of contract law that can suitably – that is, rationally – be applied in any geographical context.

This double, liberal, representation of the relationship between state and market, law and territorial polity, had, however, to adjust to the rapid growth (in Europe, largely in the second half of the 20th century) of public economic regulation affecting the market (such as competition, securities, consumerism) or society (health, environmental, social protection (→ Social protection and private international law)), as well as the rise of fundamental rights in fields of private law previously considered to be immune from constitutionalization. Public policy concerns, social rights, or *lois de police* ('overriding provisions') in the legislation of closely connected states, frequently endowed with 'extraterritorial' scope, narrowed the expanse of private empowerment (→ Overriding mandatory provisions). Importantly, such concerns were relevant both to judicial proceedings within the forum state, or in respect of foreign judgments and awards at the enforcement stage.

Thus, in a European setting, first in the Rome Convention (art 7) (Rome Convention on the law applicable to contractual obligations (consolidated version), [1998] OJ C 27/34) and now in the Rome I Regulation (art 9), room was made for 'provisions the respect for which is regarded as crucial by a country for safeguarding its public interests, such as its political, social or economic organisation, to such an extent that they are applicable to any situation falling within their scope, irrespective of the law otherwise applicable to the contract'. Such rules may override the otherwise applicable law when a court thinks this makes sense in terms of the policies they express.

Beyond this adjustment, however, private international law did not proceed to revisit the conceptualization of party autonomy in the light of the intensive growth of market and social regulation in the domestic sphere, with its transformation of the nature and function of private law; nor did its methods appear to evolve in response to the decline of the Westphalian model in international relations and the tectonic upheavals induced by globalization within both the theory of law and sovereignty and the reality of cross-border trade and investment. Yet within the changed normative, political and economic environment, party autonomy can no longer be represented as a carefully monitored concession of the liberal sovereign state. Philosophically, the shift from obligation to empowerment can be described in *Foucauldian* terms as a move to a neoliberal model of private governance. Technically, it involves what might be called 'methodological slippage'.

III. 'Private legislation' and technical design

Unquestioning acceptance of the principle of party freedom points to its status as a foundational myth of private international economic law. Indeed, its success has been unimpeded by the fact that significant issues as to its real ambit remain unsettled, as will be shown below. Nor does it seem to matter that despite its *Kantian* pedigree, its dominant justification is essentially utilitarian, linked to the needs of international trade. Although methodological, political and economic objections do appear from time to time, albeit outside mainstream doctrine, they remain largely unheeded; thus, neither the functionalist arguments drawn from governmental interests analysis, nor the potential democratic deficit resulting from the permission to contract out of local rules, nor indeed the uncertain economic rationality underlying the apparent indifference of states to free-riding by foreign parties on proven or novel regulatory models, detract from its remarkable success. The latter is, most recently, illustrated by the Hague Principles on the Choice of Law in International Contracts (Hague Principles on Choice of Law in International Commercial Contracts (approved on 19 March 2015, available at <www.hcch.net>)), which 'sets forth general principles concerning choice of law in international commercial contracts. They affirm the principle of party autonomy with limited exceptions'.

The power thus conceded to private actors to harness available state legislation to the needs of their cross-border transaction was, and still is, perceived as doubly conditional to the requirements of the rule of law. The first perceived expression of the latter is a condition of internationality, which is supposed to prevent domestic contracts from circumventing local public policy; the second is the requirement of the public (meaning state) origin of the chosen law, so as to prevent parties from cherry-picking or resorting to wholly private rules. Neither, in the contemporary legal context, fulfils the function of safeguarding the public interest for which it was initially designed. On the contrary, as currently framed, they create a hiatus between the rules and practice of international contracting; hence, a sense of methodological misfit. Furthermore, both serve to perpetuate a vision of the world, including the relationship between regulation and party autonomy, on the foundations of which the myth of autonomous private ordering was constructed.

The first condition (which, in a European setting, was already enshrined in the Rome Convention), restricts the exercise of free → choice of law to international contracts – or rather, due to the extraordinary difficulty of defining this cardinal requirement, to contracts of which all the elements relevant to the situation at the time of the choice were not located within one state. The Rome I Regulation introduces, in addition, the idea that, for the purposes of European legislation, a domestic contract is one which is connected solely to Member States' territories as a whole (art 3(4)). However, whether the perspective adopted is national or, now, European, it presupposes a bright line separating the closely regulated world of the domestic (or intra-European) economy, from the area of freedom where, beyond national (or European) frontiers, state policies relax their grip. The rise of the regulatory state, entailing the multiplication of overriding mandatory rules or '*lois de police*' with extraterritorial thrust (as seen above), has made it difficult to maintain the bright line between domestic and international spheres in terms of the respective intensity of state interests. In other words, the idea that sovereign regulatory concerns stop at national borders could not survive either the appearance of new forms of market regulation or the growing interconnectedness of local economies.

Across the Atlantic, attempts were made to adjust methodology to the increasingly regulatory function of private law. Although these attempts were not always successful in the long run, the important lesson of the American realist revolution was that multilateralism was unworkable in a world where private law is neither purely facilitative nor indeed interchangeable. In a functionalist perspective, conflicts of laws arise from the existence of contradictory regulatory interests, identified by sounding out the policies of the states involved. However, they are considered strictly derogatory, in the sense that they do not represent the 'normal' way of reasoning in the conflict of laws. Therefore, they do not affect the initial requirement that the contract be international, or non-domestic, for the principle of party choice to come into play as a choice of law rule, accrediting in turn the distinctiveness of the world of international transactions. Maintaining this multilateralist fiction contributes to perpetuate the underlying world-view of a community of states conceding an area of party freedom beyond their frontiers, but over which they retain the ultimate control.

This representation of an orderly world in which benign liberal states determine the outer limits of private economic activity is also linked to the second limitation to free choice. Today, within the Rome I Regulation, like half a century ago in national case-law, although parties may choose any law in the world, with no requirement as to geographical linkage to the state whose law is thus chosen and no condition as to the completeness, modernity or democratic legitimacy of its legal system, their freedom nevertheless stops short of non-state norms such as the → *lex mercatoria* or the UNIDROIT rules for international contracts. These, according to Recital (13) of the Rome I Regulation, may merely be 'incorporated by reference' into the contract, where they are necessarily subject to the contrary provisions of the governing law. Underlying this second restriction is the idea that the contract law of liberal states is presumptively interchangeable, because it is deemed to be based on a shared conception of societal needs (albeit largely facilitative and exclusive of specific regulatory interference), whereas norms of purely private origin cannot be supposed to implement similar conceptions. In other words, according to this vision, it was important that the parties should not escape the network of state regulation.

The fear inspired by the concept of 'private legislation' – or, even more forbidding, '*le contrat sans loi*' – may or not be justified: it could well be, as frequently argued, that the content of the new law merchant has now developed sufficiently so as to present a coherent, reasonably complete and generally acceptable set of operative principles; it is also arguable that carefully thought out principles of substantive contract law drafted at an international level may be more valuable and adjusted to the needs of cross-border trade than many state laws which might be less progressive, less clear, more parochial etc. In economic terms, the burden of over-regulation could be an evil greater than excessive freedom in the international sphere. But the point here is that if the mandatory social and economic policies of connected states are implemented whenever it makes sense to do so in functional terms, then the quality of whatever non-state contract norms the parties may have chosen – in the unlikely event they have committed themselves to incomplete, incoherent or non-progressive principles – hardly matters. In the absence of a specific regulatory interest, which would trump any other chosen rule anyway, the choice of non-state law does not endanger the public policies of potentially concerned states, of which, on the other hand, the protection is inadequately ensured by the sole requirement that the parties choose a state law. Excessive focus on the latter has signified, paradoxically, that party autonomy has ceased to imply subordination of private actors to state authority.

IV. Changes of state: the reversal of the relationship between law and market

Private actors are empowered to attain 'regulatory lift-off' because the liberal state has renounced – or has been constrained by competitive economic forces to give up – the means to ensure the primacy of its own – or another's – public policy regulation over 'private legislation'. Indeed, the changing global context in which party autonomy is exercised, and to which it has largely contributed as both a foundational myth and a methodological tool, has induced two significant functions for which it was not initially designed. These 'changes of state' are directly linked to those which affect the relationship between law and market. By allowing parties to cross jurisdictional barriers unhindered, the principle of free choice reverses the relationship between public regulation and private choice and generates a competitive market for legal products and judicial services.

The first symptom of a reversal of the status of regulation in respect of party → choice of law, jurisdictional barrier-crossing, results from the combined effect of choice of forum, choice of law and free movement of decisions or awards. The general acceptance of free choice of forum in cross-border litigation (→ Choice of forum and submission to jurisdiction), in the name of party autonomy, along with the spectacular rise of arbitration (→ Arbitration, international commercial), is traditionally justified in terms of the promotion of international commerce through the benefit of predictability, procedural economy and litigation risk management. Such concerns hold true even when internationally mandatory provisions are at stake: there is no particular reason why courts should not be trusted mutually to uphold the interests of the members of a benign community of states and indeed, the Rome Convention (art 7-1) and Regulation Rome I (art 9-3) have gone a long way down this path. Reputedly more flexible, international commercial arbitration presents all these advantages, with the added attraction of confidentiality; furthermore, when political stakes are high, such as in state investment contracts (→ Arbitration, investment), it offers an appearance of neutrality, its legitimacy being enhanced by increasing institutionalization. Increasingly commonplace in practice, such agreements have thrived as initial doubts as to the desirability of allowing private actors to appropriate access to the courts have dwindled.

Free choice of forum obviously impacts upon the applicability, and thereby the imperativity, of the mandatory rules of any state other than the chosen forum (which in the case of arbitration means practically none at all). This is why the liberal scheme on which party autonomy rests presupposes that any extension of the scope of party choice of court, or the enlargement of arbitrability, is compensated by the right to a 'second look' by the supervising or enforcing state over the judgments or awards issuing from the chosen forum. This scheme is apparent in the Supreme Court of the United States' famous *dictum* in the *Mitsubishi* case, whereby 'in the event that choice-of-law forum and the choice-of-law clauses operated in tandem as a prospective waiver of a party's right to pursue statutory remedies for antitrust violations, we would have little hesitation in condemning the agreement as against public policy' (*Mitsubishi Motors Corp v Soler Chrysler-Plymouth, Inc*, 473 U.S. 614 (1985), the 'prospective waiver' footnote, no 19). But it rapidly became apparent that the 'second look' was, in many instances, either unrealistic (when no enforcement was required, the parties having settled, for instance), or problematic (when the supervising court is not better equipped than the arbitrator to make an assessment on the merits in economic terms), or indeed practically excluded through deference to the chosen forum (as in cases as notorious as the *Lloyd's* litigation (see *Roby v Corporation of Lloyd's*, 996 F.2d 1353 (2d Cir 1993); *Bonny v Society of Lloyd's*, 3 F.3d 156 (7th Cir 1993)). A powerful economic incentive for states to renounce their 'second look' has been to provide a free zone for the arbitration industry.

Indeed, and second, the generalization of choice-of-court agreements, along with the parallel growth of international arbitration, is now understood as giving rise to a worldwide market in adjudication or dispute resolution. Enhancing global jurisdictional competition would supposedly reap benefits in terms of the improvement of the quality of courts worldwide. However, the real problem lies in the fact that when court access is thus privatized, there is a correlative absence of judicial (or arbitral) regulation of interests beyond those of the parties to the dispute. In this respect, it is instructive to turn to the conclusion, which can hardly be suspected of anti-libertarian bias, reached by *Landes* and *Posner* using economic analysis (→ Economic analysis and private international law) of justice in respect of the domestic judicial system: privately designated judges lack both the legitimacy (conferred by public investiture) and the (private financial) incentive to take account of societal interests in their decision-making process. This conclusion certainly plays out, for instance, in respect of the impact of human rights in investment arbitration (→ Arbitration, investment), where contractual mandate and choice of law pre-empt any consideration of wider public or third-party interests. Although of course the public financing of the court system establishes both the legitimacy and the incentive which arbitration lacks in protecting societal interests beyond those of the parties to the litigation, the tendency of courts designated by choice-of-forum agreements to act 'as if they were arbitrators' obviously detracts from this particular regulatory function.

V. Distributional effects of party autonomy: horizons

The centrality of private → choice of law in the European tradition is so taken for granted, or at least, appears to be so solidly rooted in the history of Western private international law, that astonishingly little attention has been paid to the function it fulfils within the changing economic and political environment induced by globalization. The cloak of tradition is reinforced by more recent law and economics doctrines, which tend to promote party autonomy as efficiency, in the form of predictability, reduced transaction costs or facilitated risk-management. No doubt these virtues exist, at least for the party whose skills in contract negotiation and drafting are strongest. It is highly probable, however, that the interests purportedly served by unbridled freedom of choice, whether cast as those of the market or of a purported community of merchants, do not allow for adequate governance of the cross-border activities of private actors. In this respect, the (in)famous *Lloyd's* litigation serves as a cautionary illustration of the cumulative effect of contract doctrine and private international law theory. Thus, under a wider perspective than that offered by various dimensions of private law doctrine, it becomes clear that party autonomy no longer serves to free private enterprise from entrenched parochial constraints under the benign supervision of a community of liberal states, but works to transform national public regulation into a disposable private good in a deregulated economy. This holds true even after the various recent financial crises and the disastrous role played by self-regulation in subordinating wider public concerns to speculative interests.

In this respect, the implications of party autonomy for what has been aptly described as 'regulatory lift-off' must be seen in the context of the various legal tools which provide the private legal infrastructure of global markets and foreign investment. Among these, within the European context, free movement of goods and services entertains a symbiotic relationship with party choice, the latter being the metaphorical expression of cross-border mobility and regulatory arbitrage. While consumer protection has found its place here, neither social rights nor the production chains which supply the European consumer market benefit from similar solicitude. Indeed, more globally, party autonomy also structures transnational production and supply chains (generating what has been described as a 'plug-in effect' in respect of sub-contractors and suppliers), and can moreover be linked in this context to direct investment, of which it supports the international (contractual) regime. The private legal regime thus created is reinforced, on the one hand, by private international law rules in tort, when they work to keep any obligation to pay attention to third party interests under the sway of local law, itself often constrained to lower the level of reparation by reason of competition to attract foreign investment. On the other hand and furthermore, the private international law regime governing the structure of multinational enterprise reinforces the autonomy of corporate entities when it comes to the duty to care or repair in respect of industrial accidents, environmental damage or human rights abuse (→ Human rights and private international law).

At the same time, however, various countervailing tendencies have appeared. Technically, in the current state of the law, the only obvious way of ensuring that law retains its authority when parties have the licence to cross barriers is to make the 'second look' effective at the enforcement stage. This has been made possible within the European Union, where Member States have the obligation to refuse recognition to arbitral awards given in violation of European competition and consumer law, and presumably of those fundamental rights which are part of the Union legal order (→ Arbitration, recognition of awards). Another notable development in the same context is the progressive mainstreaming of consumer protection, which – through the leverage provided by principles imported from outside contract theory, such as non-discrimination – has been evolving from the status of exception to the rule in respect of cross-border provision of goods and services (→ Consumer contracts). Party autonomy is therefore severely curtailed in an increasing number of circumstances, albeit within the safe confines of the European consumer market. However, it may well be that there is a need for a more radical reformulation of the issues at stake. In the rapidly changing context of global economy, the real difficulties are not (merely) market practices shaped by stronger parties through free choice of law and forum, but the implications of the growth of (hitherto) unaccountable private authority. The role played by party autonomy in this evolution needs to be acknowledged before appropriate models of social justice can be imagined in the unchartered legal environment beyond the state.

Horatia Muir Watt

Literature

Henri Batiffol, 'Subjectivisme et objectivisme en droit international privé des contrats' in Université de Toulouse Faculté de droit et des sciences économiques (ed) *Mélanges offerts à Jaques Maury*, vol 1 (Dalloz/Sirey 1960) 39; Adrian Briggs, *Agreements on Jurisdiction and Choice of Law* (OUP 2008); Phocion Francescakis, 'Quelques précsions sur les lois d'application aimmédiate et leurs rapports avec les règles de conflit de lois' [1966] Rev.crit.DIP 1; Nils Jansen and Ralf Michaels, 'Private Law beyond the State? Europeanization, Globalization, Privatization' (2006) 54 Am.J.Com.L. 843; Horatia Muir Watt, 'Aspects économiques de droit international privé (Réflexions sur l'impact de la globalisation économique sur les fondements des conflits de lois et de juridictions' (2005) 307 Rec. des Cours 25; Jean Paulin Niboyet, 'La théorie de l'autonomie de la volonté' (1927) 16 Rec. des Cours 1; Peter Nygh, *Autonomy in International Contracts* (Clarendon Press 1999); Larry Ribstein, 'From Efficiency to Politics in Contractual Choice of Law' (2003) 37 Ga.L.Rev. 363; Gian Paolo Romano, 'Règles internationalement supplétives et règles internationalement disponibles' in Andrea Bonomi and others (eds) *Regards comparatistes sur le phénomène contractuel* (PUAM 2009); Robert Wai, 'Transnational Liftoff and Juridical Touchdown: The Regulatory Function of Private international law in a Global Age' (2002) 40 Colum.J.Transnat'l L. 209.

Payment Order Regulation

I. Background and context

Particularly the Brussels I Regulation (Regulation (EC) No 44/2001 of 22 December 2000 on jurisdiction and the recognition and enforcement of judgments in civil and commercial matters, [2001] OJ L 12/1) (→ Brussels I (Convention and Regulation)) and the European Enforcement Order Regulation (Regulation (EC) No 805/2004 of the European Parliament and of the Council of 21 April 2004 creating a European Enforcement Order for uncontested claims, [2004] OJ L 143/15) have facilitated cross-border debt recovery within Europe (→ Debt recovery, cross-border). The European Commission indicated, however, already in its Green Paper of 20 December 2002 (Commission, 'Green Paper on a European order for payment procedure and on measures to simplify and speed up small claims litigation' COM(2002) 746 final) that there is need for further action: the aim was not only to unify the rules on free movement of enforcement titles, but to create a unified European procedure leading to an enforceable judgment. The result was the creation of the European Payment Order Regulation (Regulation (EC) No 1896/2006 of the European Parliament and of the Council of 12 December 2006 creating a European order for payment procedure, [2001] OJ L 399/1) (see below) and later on the European Small Claims Procedure Regulation (Regulation (EC) No 861/2007 of the European Parliament and of the Council of 11 July 2007 establishing a European Small Claims Procedure, [2007] OJ L 199/1) (→ Small Claims Regulation).

On 12 December 2006, the European Payment Order Regulation was adopted (preliminary materials: Commission, 'Proposal for a Regulation of the European Parliament and of the Council creating a European order for payment procedure' COM(2004) 173 final and Commission, 'Amended Proposal for a Regulation of the European Parliament and of the Council creating a European order for payment procedure' COM(2006) 57 final). The legislative competence was founded on art 61(c), 65(c), 67 EEC Treaty (Treaty of 25 March 1957 establishing the European Economic Community, 294–8 UNTS). The relevant provisions in practice entered into force on 12 December 2008 (art 33(2) European Payment Order Regulation). By using this procedure a judgment on uncontested pecuniary claims can be obtained in the form of a so-called European Order for Payment. The new procedure provides a simple and cost-effective means of enforcing cross-border pecuniary claims. The European Order for Payment is the first genuine European enforcement order in the history of European civil procedure legislation (the older 'European Enforcement Order' does not deserve this attribute, because the European Enforcement Order Regulation only establishes a procedure whereby national enforcement orders attained in accordance with national procedure law are simply 're-labelled' as 'European orders'). The European Order for Payment Regulation can be regarded as the procedural supplement to the Directive No 2000/35/EC of the European Parliament and of the Council of 29 June 2000 on combating late payment in commercial transactions, [2000] OJ L 200/35.

II. Scope of application

The European Order for Payment Procedure is akin to fast-track procedures leading to an enforceable order, as provided for in many national legal systems of the Member States. These simplified national procedures are not superseded by the European Order for Payment Procedure (art 1(2) European Payment Order Regulation). While such national procedures are outside the framework of the European Payment Order Regulation, the Member States must nevertheless take account of the principles of equivalence and effectiveness as required by European Union law (cf ECJ Case C-618/10 *Banco Español de Crédito SA v Joaquín Calderón Camino* [2012] OJ C 227/5).

Although the Commission initially had more ambitious plans, the European Payment Order Regulation applies only to cross-border cases (cf art 2(1)). A cross-border case is one in which at least one of the parties is domiciled or habitually resident in a Member State other than the Member State of the presiding court (art 3). If, for example, the proceedings are initiated in Germany, the European Payment Order Regulation is applicable where: (1) the claimant is domiciled in Germany and the defendant in Austria; (2) the claimant is domiciled in Austria and the defendant in Germany; (3) both parties are domiciled in Austria; (4) one party is domiciled in Austria and the other in France; or (5) one party is domiciled in Austria and the other in a third state (eg Switzerland). In contrast, art 3(1) European Payment Order Regulation does not apply where both parties are domiciled in a third state, both parties are domiciled in the forum state or one of the parties is domiciled in the forum state and the other in a third state, which may seem inadequate if enforceable assets are located in another Member State. A question to be answered separately from the aforementioned scope of the European Payment Order Regulation is the international jurisdiction of the Member State issuing the enforcement order (see below).

The European Payment Order Regulation applies to the collection of pecuniary claims for a specific amount that have fallen due at the time of application (art 4) and arise out of any civil or commercial matter with the exception of those mentioned in art 2(1) and art 2(2). These rules mainly correspond to the standards found in the context of art 1 Brussels I Regulation (→ Civil and commercial matters). Nonetheless, it is noteworthy that the European Payment Order Regulation covers non-contractual obligations only by way of exception and under certain circumstances (art 2(2)(d)). Whether the claim to be enforced arises out of a consumer or a business transaction is irrelevant. Unlike the European Small Claims Procedure, the European Payment Order Regulation is therefore applicable to claims of unlimited amount.

III. Procedure

Proceedings are initiated by submission of an application for a European Order for Payment to a competent court. Pursuant to art 6(1) European Payment Order Regulation, international jurisdiction is in general determined in accordance with the relevant provisions of the Brussels I Regulation (now: Regulation (EU) No 1215/2012 of the European Parliament and of the Council of 12 December 2012 on jurisdiction and the recognition and enforcement of judgments in civil and commercial matters (recast), [2012] OJ L 351/1; → Brussels I (Convention and) Regulation (recast)). This is why generally the courts of the Member State in which the defendant is domiciled have jurisdiction unless the claimant has opted for one of the specific jurisdictions provided in art 5 *et seq* of the Brussels I Regulation (art 7 *et seq* Brussels I Regulation (recast)); however, if the defendant is a consumer, the jurisdiction of the defendant's domicile is exclusive, so that no other Member State may issue a European Order for Payment (art 6(2) European Payment Order Regulation).

For the initiation of proceedings it is mandatory to use a standard form (art 7 European Payment Order Regulation). The requirements for an application for a European Order for Payment are exclusively determined by art 7 and may not be extended by national law (ECJ Case C-215/11 *Iwona Szyrocka v SiGer Technologie GmbH* [2013] OJ C 38/5, regarding a Polish provision that mandates the specification of the disputed amount). The application shall be submitted in paper form or by any other means of communication accepted by the Member State of origin and available to the court of origin (art 7(5) European Payment Order Regulation). A description of evidence supporting the claim is sufficient (art 7(2)(e) European Payment Order Regulation); documents or other means of evidence therefore need not be attached. However, the claimant must declare that the information provided is true to the best of his knowledge and belief and he must acknowledge that any deliberate false statement could lead to appropriate penalties under the law of the Member State of origin (art 7(3) European Payment Order Regulation). Representation by a lawyer or another legal professional is not mandatory (art 24 European Payment Order Regulation). Whether → agency (eg through debt collection firms) is permissible, must be answered according to national law.

The examination of the application by the court is limited to the scope of the European Order for Payment Regulation, the existence of a cross-border case, the jurisdiction of the court and the formal requirements of the application (art 8 European Payment Order Regulation). Regarding the merits of the claim, the court (not necessarily a judge; cf Recital (16)) only assesses whether the claim appears to be founded based on the allegations of the claimant. The Regulation expressly provides that this examination may be conducted in the form of an automated procedure (art 8(2)). In the event of formal deficiencies of the application, further proceedings are governed by art 9 European Payment Order Regulation or, in the event of wholly or partly meritless claims, by arts 10 and 11. There is no right of appeal against the rejection of the application (art 11(2)) and no need, since the rejection does not have *res-judicata* effect (art 11(3)).

If all requirements are met, the court issues a European Order for Payment using a standard form (art 12(1)). The European Order for Payment, together with a copy of the application form and further information on the legal remedies available, shall be served on the defendant (art 12(2)–(5)). The details of service are governed by the European Service Regulation (Regulation (EC) No 1393/2007 of the European Parliament and of the Council of 13 November 2007 on the service in the Member States of judicial and extrajudicial documents in civil or commercial matters (service of documents), and repealing Council Regulation (EC) No 1348/2000, [2007] OJ L 324/79) or the national service rules which must meet the minimum standards laid down in art 13 *et seq* European Payment Order Regulation (art 12(5) European Payment Order Regulation). Within 30 days of service of the European Order for Payment, the defendant may lodge a statement of opposition with the court of origin (art 16(1) and (2) European Payment Order Regulation); neither the use of the supplied standard form nor any statement of reasons is mandatory. If the statement of opposition is entered within the time limit, the proceeding continues before the competent courts of the Member State of origin in accordance with the rules of ordinary civil procedure unless the claimant has explicitly requested that the proceedings be terminated in that event (art 17 European Payment Order Regulation). According to the ECJ, a statement of opposition to a European Order for Payment cannot be regarded as constituting the entering of an appearance within the meaning of art 24 Brussels I Regulation (now: art 26 Brussels I Regulation (recast)), even if the defendant in the statement of opposition puts forward arguments relating to the substance of the case without challenging the jurisdiction of the Member State of origin (cf Case C-144/12 *Goldbet Sportwetten GmbH v Massimo Sperindeo* [2013] OJ C 225/29).

If no statement of opposition has been lodged with the court of origin within the time limit laid down in art 16(2) European Payment Order Regulation, the court of origin shall, after having verified the date of service, declare the European Order for Payment enforceable using a standard form (art 18). The order shall be directly recognized and enforced in every Member State without the need for a declaration of enforceability (see below). Review of the European Order for Payment before the competent court in the Member State of origin remains possible only in exceptional cases and under strict preconditions (cf ECJ Case C-324/12 *Novontech-Zala kft. v Logicdata Electronic & Software Entwicklungs GmbH* [2013] OJ C 225/45: no review for failure to observe the time limit by reason of the negligence of the defendant's representative). According to the ECJ, the procedures laid down in art 16 *et seq* are not applicable where it appears that a European Order for Payment has not been served in a manner consistent with the minimum standards laid down in art 13 *et seq*; however, where it is only after a European Order for Payment has been declared enforceable that such an irregularity is exposed, the defendant must have the opportunity to raise that irregularity, which, if it is duly established, will invalidate the declaration of enforceability (ECJ Case C-119/13 & C-120/13 *eco cosmetics & Raiffeisenbank St. Georgen* [2014] OJ C 395/10).

The court fees of a European Order for Payment Procedure and of the ordinary civil proceedings that ensue in the event of a statement of opposition are governed by national law (art 26 European Payment Order Regulation). However, national law must ensure that the initiation of a European Order for Payment Procedure may not cause the claimant additional costs (art 25(1)).

IV. Enforcement

Once the claimant has obtained a European Order for Payment, this order is enforceable in every Member State (with the exception of Denmark, art 2(3) European Payment Order Regulation). The requirements of enforcement and the possibilities of review in the state of enforcement are designed in accordance with the corresponding rules in the European Enforcement Order Regulation and the European Small Claims Procedure Regulation: a European Order for Payment shall be enforced under the same conditions as an enforceable decision issued in the Member State of enforcement (art 21(1)(2) European Payment Order Regulation). A declaration of enforceability (*exequatur*) is not required (art 19 European Payment Order Regulation). The documents to be provided by the claimant are listed in art 21(2) European Payment Order Regulation. Where necessary, a certified translation of foreign-language documents into the official language of the Member State of enforcement shall be provided. The enforcement in the Member State of enforcement may only be refused, stayed or limited in accordance with art 22 and art 23 European Payment Order

Regulation. A review as to the substance of the European Order for Payment in the Member State of enforcement ('*révision au fond*') is explicitly prohibited (art 22(3)), nor is a review with regard to the *ordre public* allowed.

V. Significance

Since its coming into force, the European Order for Payment Procedure has gained considerable practical importance in cross-border cases, much more so than the European Small Claims Procedure. This may be due to the fact that the European Order for Payment Procedure is not limited by a maximum monetary amount and that claimants will most likely make an effort to enforce their rights in cross-border cases when a significant amount of money is at stake. That is why, presumably, an 'ordinary lawsuit' in accordance with national law and based on the Brussels I jurisdiction rules will continue to play a major role alongside the European Order for Payment in cross-border enforcement cases. In order to increase the European Order for Payment Procedure's public recognition, the European Commission published a Practice Guide in 2011. The report reviewing the operation of the European Order for Payment Procedure was published on 13 October 2015 (Com (2015) 495 final), but it proposes only marginal reforms.

WOLFGANG HAU

Literature

Mikael Berglund, *Cross Border Enforcement of Claims in the EU: History, Present Time and Future* (Wolters Kluwer 2009); Carla Crifò, *Cross-Border Enforcement of Debts in the European Union, Default Judgments, Summary Judgments and Orders for Payment* (Wolters Kluwer 2009); Carla Crifò, 'Civil Procedure in the European Order' in Déirdre Dwyer (ed), *The Civil Procedure Rules Ten Years On* (OUP 2010); Michel Défossez, 'Titre exécutoire européen, injonction de payer européenne et procédure européenne de règlement des petits litiges' in Michel Défossez and Juliette Sénéchal (eds), *Enforcing Contracts: Aspects procéduraux de l'exécution des contrats transfrontaliers en droit européen et international* (Larcier 2008); Anna Katharina Fabian, *Die Europäische Mahnverfahrensverordnung im Kontext der Europäisierung des Prozessrechts* (Jenaer Wissenschaftliche Verlagsgesellschaft 2010); Aude Fiorini, 'Facilitating Cross-border Debt Recovery: The European Payment Order and Small Claims Regulations' (2008) 57 ICLQ 449; Emmanuel Guinchard, 'L'Europe, la procédure civile et le créancier: l'injonction de payer européenne et la procédure européenne de règlement des petits litiges' (2008) R.T.D.C. 465; Barbara Kloiber, 'Das Europäische Mahnverfahren' (2009) ZfRV 68; Johannes Maximilian Kormann, *Das neue Europäische Mahnverfahren im Vergleich zu den Mahnverfahren in Deutschland und Österreich* (Jenaer Wissenschaftliche Verlagsgesellschaft 2007); Xandra E Kramer, 'Enhancing Enforcement in the European Union: The European Order for Payment Procedure and Its Implementation in the Member States, Particularly in Germany, the Netherlands, and England' in Cornelis Hendrik van Rhee and Alan Uzelac (eds), *Enforcement and Enforceability: Tradition and Reform* (Intersentia 2010); Maria Lopez de Tejada and Louis d'Avout, 'Les non-dits de la procédure européenne d'injonction de payer' (2007) Rev.crit.DIP 717; Marco Mellone, 'Legal Interoperability in Europe: An Assessment of the European Payment Order and the European Small Claims Procedure' in Franceso Contini and Giovan Francesco Lanzara (eds), *The Circulation of Agency in E-Justice: Interoperability and Infrastructures for European Transborder Judicial Proceedings* (Springer 2014); Melanie Meyer-Berger, *Mahnverfahren und Vollstreckung: Probleme und Entwicklungen aus nationaler und europäischer Sicht* (Dr. Kovač 2007); Gar Yein Ng, 'Testing Transborder Civil Procedures in Practice: Findings from Simulation Experiments with the European Payment Order and the European Small Claims Procedure' in Franceso Contini and Giovan Francesco Lanzara (eds), *The Circulation of Agency in E-Justice: Interoperability and Infrastructures for European Transborder Judicial Proceedings* (Springer 2014); Alvaro Pérez-Ragone, *Europäisches Mahnverfahren: Ein prozesshistorischer, -vergleichender und dogmatischer Beitrag zur Vergemeinschaftung der Inkassoverfahrensnormen in der Europäischen Union* (Carl Heymanns 2005); Andreas Pernfuß, *Die Effizienz des Europäischen Mahnverfahrens* (Nomos 2009); Nicola Preuß, 'Erlass und Überprüfung des Europäischen Zahlungsbefehls' (2009) 122 ZZP 3; Walter H Rechberger, 'Die neue Generation: Bemerkungen zu den Verordnungen Nr. 805/2004, Nr. 1896/2006 und Nr. 861/2007 des Europäischen Parlaments und des Rates' in Rolf Stürner and others (eds), *Festschrift für Dieter Leipold zum 70. Geburtstag* (Mohr Siebeck 2009); Anne Röthel and Ingo Sparmann, 'Das europäische Mahnverfahren' (2007) WM 1101; Eva Storskrubb, *Civil Procedure and EU Law: A Policy Area Uncovered* (OUP 2008); Bartosz Sujecki, *Das elektronische Mahnverfahren: Eine rechtsvergleichende und europarechtliche Untersuchung* (Mohr Siebeck 2008); Dimitrios Tsikrikas, 'L'injonction de payer européenne' (2009) 14 ZZPInt 221.

Personal status

I. Notion and relevance

The personal status of a natural person describes that person's position in the legal order. It is largely defined by family law and the law of persons. As personal status refers exclusively to natural persons, it has to be distinguished from the status of juridical persons, which in the conflict of laws is subject to the law governing that person, for example, the applicable company or foundation law. The personal status of a natural person encompasses not only legal personality and capacity (→ Capacity and emancipation), but also the filiation of that person as a descendant of a certain father and mother, the marital status as a spouse or registered partner and, at least in continental systems, the person's name (see, for example, the definition of personal status in § 1 of the German Personal Status Act (Personenstandsgesetz of 19 February 2007, BGBl. I 112, as amended). An element of personal status which traditionally was rather fact-oriented but which is increasingly expressed in law is a person's gender: many jurisdictions have introduced a possibility for transgender persons to obtain gender recognition and hence a change of their legal sex (→ Transsexual and transgender persons). In some countries for intersexual persons a new gender status ('X gender') has been introduced. Interlinked with, but not part of the personal status is a person's nationality; nevertheless, in many jurisdictions private international law uses nationality as the main connecting factor for personal status matters (see IV. below). As personal status has important implications in family law but also in other areas of law, such as taxes, nationality, immigration or social security, the elements of personal status are in most jurisdictions registered by the state in civil status registers which publicly document the personal status of its citizens.

In cross-border cases, international cooperation in personal status matters is paramount. In particular, a harmonization of the conflict rules relevant for personal status is of great importance in order to create a harmony of decision in terms of a person's status and avoid 'limping' status relations. If the legal personality, capacity (→ Capacity and emancipation), marital status, filiation, name or gender of a person is differently defined by different states due to divergent conflict rules, the consequences for a person can be harsh. Many practical problems in cross-border cases can be solved by introducing common documentation standards, for example by creating standard forms for civil status documents. In the past, the *Commission Internationale de l'Etat Civil* (→ CIEC/ICCS (International Commission on Civil Status)) was one of the main actors in the field of cross-border personal status matters; however, the efforts of the CIEC at least within Europe will in the near future be increasingly superseded by those of the European Union (see V. below).

II. From the *statuta personalia* to differentiated conflict rules

The concept of personal status concerns a range of legal issues and relationships. Nevertheless, since the beginning of private international law doctrine in many jurisdictions, the idea has persisted that personal status should be comprehensively governed by a single legal system. For example, the doctrine of *statuta* in the Northern Italian cities of the 13th century broadly distinguished between three kinds of legal regime: the *statuta realia* applicable to all → immovable property situated in the territory of the city, the *statuta mixta* applicable to legal transactions concluded in the territory of the city, and the *statuta personalia* applicable to the personal status of a citizen irrespective of where the citizen resided. Hence, the law comprehensively governing the personal status of a citizen remained stable. The doctrine of *statuta* in general has gradually been displaced by modern private international law theory. However, on the Continent, influenced by Friedrich Carl von Savigny (→ Savigny, Friedrich Carl von) and his classic choice of law model, which focused on the 'seat of the legal relationship' rather than a private law provision and its geographic scope, the idea of a general regime governing personal status as a '*statut personnel*' or '*Personalstatut*' has survived. For example, the Spanish and Portuguese Código civil still determine the '*ley personal*' or '*lei pessoal*' as a law generally governing personal status (see art 9(1) of the Spanish Civil Code (Código Civil of 24 July 1889, Geceta de Madrid No 206, 25 July 1889): '*La ley personal correspondiente a las personas físicas es la determinada por su nacionalidad. Dicha ley regirá la capacidad y el estado civil, los derechos y deberes de familia y la sucesión por causa de muerte*'; art 25 of the Portuguese Civil Code 1966 (Código Civil approved by Decreto-Lei No 47.344, of 25 November 1966, [1966]

DG I série 274/1883, with subsequent amendments): '*O estado dos indivíduos, a capacidade das pessoas, as relações de família e as sucessões por morte são regulados pela lei pessoal dos respectivos sujeitos...*'). The French Civil Code (Code Civil of 21 March 1804) also still provides in its famous art 3(3): '*Les lois concernant l'état et la capacité des personnes régissent les Français, même résidant en pays étranger*'. The idea of a general personal status regime can also partly be traced in modern private international law codifications. The Austrian Federal Code on Private international law (Bundesgesetz über das internationale Privatrecht of 15 June 1978, BGBl. No 304/1978, as amended, henceforth Austrian PILA) defines in its § 9 a general personal statute ('*Personalstatut*') to which the conflict rules for personality and capacity, names, → marriage and filiation refer (see §§ 12 *et seq*, § 16(2), § 17(1), §§ 21 *et seq* of the Austrian PILA). The same general notion of the personal status regime can also be found in some of the older treaties, such as in art 8(3) of the German-Persian Establishment Treaty of 1929. It appears that only in the common law such a general notion of a law governing the personal status never existed.

Nowadays, however, the general notion of a law governing the personal status of natural persons is dissipating, even in continental systems. Personal status on the choice of law level requires differentiated conflict rules rather than a 'one-size-fits-all' approach (see for details IV. below). It is accordingly no surprise that in most legal systems at least filiation (→ Kinship and legitimation), → marriage, partnership (→ Registered partnerships) and names (→ Names of individuals) are subject to special choice-of-law rules, as for example the separate entries for these areas of law in this Encyclopedia show. Only legal personality and capacity of natural persons and partly the name of persons as a core area of personal status are on the Continent often still subject to a general personal status regime (see eg art 7 of Introductory Act to the German Civil Code (Einführungsgesetz zum Bürgerlichen Gesetzbuche of 21 September 1994, BGBl. I 2494, as amended, henceforth EGBGB); arts 5 *et seq* of the Greek Civil Code (Astikos Kodikas of 23 February 1946, A.N. 2250/1040; FEK A 91/1940, 597); §§ 10 *et seq* of the Hungarian Private international law (Law-decree No 13 of 1979 on Private international law, henceforth Hungarian PILA); arts 20 *et seq* of the Italian Private international law Act (Riforma del Sistema italiano di diritto internazionale private, Act No 218 of 31 May 1995 in Gazz. Uff., Supplemento Ordinario No 128 of 3 June 1995, as amended, henceforth Italian PILA); arts 11 *et seq* of the Polish Private international law Act (Official Journal 2011 No 80, pos 432)). However, even this core area is constantly eroding, in particular in terms of capacity. In common law jurisdictions, capacity was generally not regarded as forming part of a general law governing personal status. Rather capacity was traditionally conceived as a special issue subject to the choice-of-law rules for the field of law in which the issue of capacity arises, for example the law applicable to marriage, → succession or contract (see eg Lord Collins of Mapesbury and others (eds), *Dicey, Morris & Collins on the Conflict of Laws* (15th edn, Sweet & Maxwell 2012) rules 74, 151, 228). A similar tendency can now be observed in the private international law of the EU. Although capacity is excluded from the scope of most instruments, special occurrences of capacity are, at least partly, covered by the special conflict rules. For example, art 1(2)(b) of the Succession Regulation (Regulation (EU) No 650/2012 of the European Parliament and of the Council of 4 July 2012 on jurisdiction, applicable law, recognition and enforcement of decisions and acceptance and enforcement of authentic instruments in matters of succession and on the creation of a European Certificate of Succession, [2012] OJ L 201/107; → Rome IV Regulation) clarifies that the Regulation does not apply to legal personality and capacity. However, art 23(2)(c) and art 26(1)(a) and (2) of the Succession Regulation show that the capacity to inherit or to testate is indeed part of the European *lex hereditatis*. Special provisions for legal personality and capacity regarding → contractual obligations can also be found in art 13 of the Rome I Regulation (Regulation (EC) No 593/2008 of the European Parliament and of the Council of 17 June 2008 on the law applicable to contractual obligations (Rome I), [2008] OJ L 177/6; → Rome Convention and Rome I Regulation (contractual obligations)).

III. The relevance of status decisions and documents

It should not be overlooked that regarding the personal status of a person the choice of law process is often ousted by decisions of courts or other authorities. Such status decisions cannot only establish a given status of a natural person which already exists by the operation of law, but they might also change that status, in particular as far as filiation and marriage (divorce (→ Divorce and personal separation)) are concerned. In such situations, the question of the applicable law does not arise. Rather – as domestic decisions are of course binding for domestic civil status registers – foreign status decisions might have to be recognized.

Within the EU only the rules on the recognition of divorce decisions are widely harmonized by the → Brussels IIa Regulation (Council Regulation (EC) No 2201/2003 of 27 November 2003 concerning jurisdiction and the recognition and enforcement of judgments in matrimonial matters and the matters of parental responsibility, repealing Regulation (EC) No 1347/2000, [2003] OJ L 338/1), which provides for a swift and simple procedure to recognize divorce decisions from other Member States. The recognition of those decisions is facilitated by forms which standardize the content of divorce decisions and allow authorities – usually civil status officers – to register a foreign divorce decree without an official translation. By contrast to some national laws, under the Brussels IIa Regulation no special recognition procedure is required, but rather divorce decisions are to be recognized *ex lege*.

Some legal systems even go a step further and additionally weaken the relevance of the conflict of laws in civil status matters. For example, in → France, the → Netherlands or → Switzerland, foreign civil status documents have the same effects as civil status decisions of the domestic courts, irrespective of the law applicable from a domestic perspective (see art 47 French Civil Code; art 10:24(1)1 Dutch New Civil Code (Nieuw Burgerlijk Wetboek of 1 January 1992, henceforth Dutch CC); art 32 of the Swiss Private international law Act (Bundesgesetz über das Internationale Privatrecht of 18 December 1987, 1988 BBl I 5, as amended, henceforth Swiss PILA)). Once an individual's personal status is documented abroad, little remains of the law governing that status – a legal technique which might also inspire the European legislature when enhancing the international cooperation in civil status matters within the EU (see V. below).

IV. The relevant connecting factors

What are the reasons for the gradual breakup of the comprehensive notion of a law governing the personal status of natural persons? The main reason for this development lies in the fact that the classic → connecting factor for status matters is no longer regarded as appropriate for all elements of personal status. Traditionally, systems with a comprehensive personal status regime followed – as proposed by the 19th-century Italian private international lawyer *Pasquale Stanislao Mancini* (→ Mancini, Pasquale Stanislao) – the nationality principle by stressing the stability of a person's connection with his or her home state. As under the doctrine of *statuta* (see II. above) the law governing personal status remained stable wherever the individual resided. Independent of the general discussion on the appropriate personal connecting factor in the conflict of laws (→ nationality versus habitual residence (→ Domicile, habitual residence and establishment)), in terms of status matters nationality has one advantage. Subjecting personal status matters to the law of the person's nationality secures a harmony with the personal identification documents which are mainly issued and administrated by the state of nationality.

However, private international law lawmakers have increasingly noticed that nationality as a general → connecting factor is not appropriate for all status issues. First, there is a need for a connecting factor distinct from nationality for status relationships, for example marriage, if the nationalities of the persons party to that relationship diverge. Submitting the validity of such status relationships to the parties' nationalities cumulatively might be possible (see eg for the substantive validity of a marriage § 17(1) Austrian PILA; art 13(1) EGBGB; § 37(1) Hungarian PILA; art 27 Italian PILA). However, such a solution is prone to invalidating status relationships and accordingly requires special public policy clauses (see § 17(2) Austrian PILA; art 13(2) EGBGB). Far more favourable for the validity of the status relationship or a status transaction is an approach which, at least in the case of diverging nationalities of the parties, submits the status issue to a common connecting factor, such as a past or present habitual residence (see eg for marriage art 44 Swiss PILA; for divorce art 8 → Rome III Regulation (Council Regulation (EU) No 1259/2010 of 20 December 2010 implementing enhanced cooperation in the area of the law applicable to divorce and legal separation, [2010] OJ L 343/10)) or the nationality or habitual residence of one of the spouses (see the solution in art 3(1) Hague Convention of 14 March 1978 on Celebration and Recognition of the Validity of Marriages, 1901 UNTS 131).

Second, in status matters nationality has been partly overturned as the modern personal connecting factor by other connecting factors, such as habitual residence. Also in the area of personal status legislators have recognized that not only the stability interests of the person to his or her home state should be protected but also the interest of integrating into the system where the person factually resides. This for example relates to filiation, where some systems now primarily point to habitual residence (see eg art 19 EGBGB; see also art 10:92 Dutch CC). In rare instances the residence principle is followed even regarding a person's name (see eg art 37(1) Swiss PILA; the same applies in → Denmark by customary law). Swiss law even for the core area of the personal status – legal personality and capacity – mainly refers to the law of the residence ('*Wohnsitz*') of the relevant person (see arts 33 *et seq* Swiss PILA). In addition, for the validity of → registered partnerships or other new status relationships (eg → same-sex marriages), nationality would not be an appropriate connecting factor even if it were used for the validity of the traditional marriage. A number of legal systems continue not to provide for such new status relationships. Hence, referring to nationality would risk invalidating such partnerships where one of the partners' law of nationality does not permit such a status relationship. It accordingly makes sense that – rather than applying a law generally governing the personal status of the person – most systems providing for registered partnerships refer to the law where the partnership is registered (see § 27a Austrian PILA; arts 10:60 *et seq* Dutch CC; art 17b EGBGB; see however, § 41/A Hungarian PILA). Departing from the nationality principle in status matters might even have a human rights dimension: the Federal Constitutional Court of Germany stressed that the practice under the original version of the German Transsexuals Act (Gesetz über die Änderung der Vornamen und die Feststellung der Geschlechtszugehörigkeit in besonderen Fällen (Transsexuellengesetz of 10 September 1980, BGBl. I 1654, as amended) of referring transgender persons for gender recognition to their home states would violate the equality principle (→ Transsexual and transgender persons), at least if the legislator refused to recognize the preferred gender of foreigners who legally, and not merely temporarily, reside in → Germany and whose law of nationality does not provide for the legal recognition of gender (Federal Constitutional Court of Germany (BVerfG) 18 July 2006, 116 BVerfGE 243).

A third reason for the erosion of the general personal status regime referring exclusively to nationality is the strengthening of party autonomy in private international law. Some systems have retained nationality as the primary connecting factor for status questions while nevertheless allowing the person a limited choice of law. Under German law, for example, the name of a person is still subject to the law of his or her nationality (see art 10(1) EGBGB). However, by breaking up the general personal statute, German law allows a person to submit his or her name to certain other laws which are connected to that person (see the options in art 10(2) and (3) EGBGB). Also Swiss law – following for status matters mainly the residence principle – allows a restricted freedom of choice regarding a person's name in favour of nationality (art 37(2) of the Swiss PILA).

V. Personal status and EU citizenship

Personal status is also of particular importance for a European 'area of freedom, security and justice' – an area whose creation the EU promises its citizens since the Treaty of Amsterdam (Treaty of Amsterdam amending the Treaty on the European Union, the Treaties establishing the European Communities and certain related acts (consolidated version), [1997] OJ C 340/01). The relevance of the law governing the personal status has been shown by the case-law of the ECJ regarding names. In a number of decisions the ECJ concluded that the lack of a harmony of decision regarding the names of persons within the EU can violate the principle of non-discrimination and the freedom of movement and residence, today both enshrined in the TFEU (The Treaty on the Functioning of the European Union (consolidated version), [2012] OJ C 326/47) in arts 18 and 21. The ECJ ruled that a name which has been acquired in one Member State has to be recognized in the other Member States (see Case C-353/06 *Stefan Grunkin and Dorothee Regina Paul* [2008] ECR I-7639; see also ECJ, Case C-208/09 *Ilonka Sayn-Wittgenstein v Landeshauptmann von Wien* [2010] ECR I-13693; cf also Case C-148/

02 Carlos Garcia Avello v Belgian State [2003] ECR I-11613). The precise preconditions for, and the consequences of, this recognition duty based on primary EU law are still debated. It is, for example, unclear whether this principle also applies outside the law of names regarding the other elements of personal status. The European legislature should use its comprehensive competence in the area of private international law in order to create a harmony of decision in personal status matters and to avoid 'limping' status relations. If common choice-of-law principles are established within the EU, little is left for a recognition duty based on primary EU law. Nevertheless, it could be sensible to introduce, as a secondary measure alongside the harmonization of the conflict rules, such a duty to recognize foreign civil status documents, as has been done in the private international laws of some states (see III. above).

Harmonization of the law governing personal status matters within the EU has not yet been addressed; most EU private international law instruments expressly exclude personal status matters from their substantive scope (see eg art 1(2)(a) Succession Regulation). The European legislature has only begun to enhance cooperation between the Member State's civil status officers. The European Commission has proposed a Regulation on promoting the free movement of citizens and businesses by simplifying the acceptance of certain public documents in the EU (European Commission, 'Proposal for a Regulation of the European Parliament and of the Council on promoting the free movement of citizens and businesses by simplifying the acceptance of certain public documents in the European Union and amending Regulation (EU) No 1024/2012 of 24 April 2013' COM(2013) 228 final) which should allow the 'acceptance' of public documents without recognizing their content. Furthermore, the Commission suggests introducing multilingual standard forms concerning birth, death, marriage, registered partnership and legal status – the most important civil status documents.

ANATOL DUTTA

Literature

Jean-Yves Carlier, *Autonomie de la volonté et statut personnel* (Bruylant 1992); Lord Collins of Mapesbury and others (eds), *Dicey, Morris & Collins on the Conflict of Laws* (15th edn, Sweet & Maxwell 2012); Richard Fentiman, 'Activity in the Law of Status: Domicile, Marriage and the Law' 6 (1986) Oxford J.Leg.Stud. 353; Myriam Hunter-Henin, *Pour une redéfinition du statut personnel* (Pu aix marseill 2004); Alexander Makarov, 'Personalstatut und persönlicher Status' in Eduard Wahl, Rolf Serick and Hubert Niederländer (eds), *Rechtsvergleichung und Rechtsvereinheitlichung – Festschrift zum fünfzigjährigen Bestehen des Instituts für ausländisches und internationales Privat- und Wirtschaftsrecht der Universität Heidelberg* (Winter Universitätsverlag 1967) 115; Heinz-Peter Mansel, *Personalstatut, Staatsangehörigkeit und Effektivität* (CH Beck 1996); Eduard-Maurits Meijers, 'L'historie des principes fondamentaux du droit international privé à partir du moyen âge, spécialement dans l'Europe occidentale' (1934) 49 Rec. des Cours 543; Cafari Panico, *Lo stato civile ed il diritto internazionale privato* (CEDAM 1992); Walter Pintens, 'Familienrecht und Personenstand – Perspektiven einer Europäisierung' (2009) StAZ 97; Walter Pintens, 'Civil Status Registration' in Jürgen Basedow and others (eds), *The Max Planck Encyclopedia of European Private Law* (OUP 2012) 198; Christian Rochat, *La dislocation du statut personnel* (Imprimerie vaudoise 1986); Giulia Rossolillo, *Identità personale e diritto internazionale privato* (CEDAM 2009); Kurt Siehr, 'Personal Law' in Jürgen Basedow and others (eds), *The Max Planck Encyclopedia of European Private Law* (OUP 2012) 1269; Guido Tedeschi, 'Personal Status and Statut Personnel' (1969) 15 McGill L.J. 452; Benedetta Ubertazzi, *La capacità delle persone fisiche nel diritto internazionale privato* (CEDAM 2006); Louis Isaac de Winter, 'Nationality or Domicile: The Present State of Affairs' (1969) 128 Rec. des Cours 347.

Personality rights

I. Concept and notion

Personality rights are the rights related to the protection of the integrity and inviolability of the person. These rights include the right to respect of one's name, reputation and privacy. Despite this concise definition, there is no common consensus in Europe on the nature and the scope of personality rights. English law, for example, does not recognize a general personality right. Common law and equity provide instead for a patchwork of different remedies for specific breaches of a personality right, such as the tort of defamation, malicious falsehood, passing-off and breach of confidence. On the other hand, German law does recognize a general personality right. This right, derived from the fundamental right of personality as enshrined in the

Basic Law for the Federal Republic of Germany (Grundgesetz of 23 May 1949, BGBl. 1, as amended), can be relied on both against the state as well as another private individual.

The constitutional protection of personality rights in → Germany demonstrates that these rights have a dimension in both public and private law. The right to integrity and inviolability of the person is guaranteed by the fundamental right to a private life. However, any claim for the violation of a personality right, even if that right is considered to be part of the constitutional heritage, still has to be shoehorned in a civil claim. Personality rights are thus in the grey area between public and private law. This may be particularly problematic when the infringement of personality rights has a cross-border dimension. The constitutional dimension of personality rights makes the application of private international law to a cross-border infringement of personality rights an extremely delicate exercise.

Globalization (→ Globalization and private international law) and the emergence of the Internet in the last two decades have significantly increased the potential for cross-border infringements of personality rights. The diverging national conceptions of personality rights have proven to be a significant barrier to international cooperation in this area. This has particularly been the case because the right to private life often clashes with another fundamental right, the freedom of expression. The reaction of national courts has been primarily to stress the importance of their own fundamental values. In order to properly understand these sensitivities, sections II. and III. will highlight the purpose and function of personality rights and their historical development in substantive law. Section IV. will analyse the current private international law rules on the cross-border infringement of personality rights.

II. Purpose and function

General tort law protects the psycho-physical integrity and the bodily aspects of the person. Personality rights protect the non-bodily aspects of a person, such as a person's honour and dignity. The function of personality rights is to provide a (potential) victim of an infringement of their honour and dignity with a remedy to prevent or stop an infringement of the personality right, or when appropriate, to claim → damages *ex ante*. In some common law jurisdictions, a victim may also claim punitive damages. It should moreover be borne in mind that the private remedies against a violation of personality rights do not represent the entire picture, in that violation of certain personality rights, as with defamation, also constitutes in many civil and common law countries an offence under criminal law.

III. Historical development

The answer to the question what constitutes an affront to the reputation or dignity of a person is socio-cultural and entirely depends on place and time. Personality rights inherently evolve according to the needs of every jurisdiction. The account of the historical development of personality rights provided by the present section can therefore only scratch the surface.

The historical antecedents of personality rights can be traced back to Roman law. The general principle of *neminem laedere* provided that no one could cause harm to another person. Each person was accordingly free to act only insofar as the equal rights of others were not infringed. What is currently known as personality rights was addressed by the *actio iniuriarum*. This *actio* provided a remedy for harm or loss related to the *corpus* (bodily integrity), *fama* (reputation) or *dignitas* (dignity).

The *ius commune* inspired the drafters of the Code Napoléon (1804) to introduce a general clause in the law of delict. Contrary to Roman law, the Code Napoléon was based on the principle of equal treatment in the law of damages of compensation of economic and non-economic loss. The compensation of a violation of a personality right was thus brought within the realm of general tort law. In Germany, the law developed in the 19th century in a different direction. German scholars proposed a rigid separation between public and private law. The violation of the honour and dignity of another person was considered to be a matter of criminal law. Consequently, there was no civil remedy against the violation of a personality right.

In England, the protection of the honour and reputation of a person was long restricted to the tort of defamation. Although common law and equity have distinct remedies for malicious falsehood, passing-off and breach of confidence law, personality rights beyond defamation remain relatively underdeveloped. For example, English law still does not recognize a general right to privacy.

JAN-JAAP KUIPERS

The historical differences between the European legal systems have largely been overtaken by a different development. Primarily under the influence of the ECHR (European Convention of 4 November 1950 for the Protection of Human Rights and Fundamental Freedoms, 213 UNTS 221), the legal systems in Europe are increasingly converging. Although fundamental rights historically came into existence to protect an individual against state intervention, it was gradually accepted that they could also be indirectly applicable to horizontal relations. Couched in terms of fundamental rights, the infringement of a personality right becomes a conflict between the right to private life and the freedom of speech which can only be resolved by performing a balancing exercise. There are two sides to this development. The creation of a common core of European (personality) rights has eliminated the most dramatic differences between the substantive laws. On the other hand, the gradual constitutionalization of private law has also made the regulation of cross-border infringements of personality rights an extremely sensitive issue.

IV. Current regulation

In Europe, the rules relating to the cross-border infringement of personality rights are derived from sources on at least three different levels. The EU has enacted regulations dealing with cross-border proceedings in → civil and commercial matters. These rules are relevant with regard to jurisdiction as well as recognition and enforcement. The law applicable to the cross-border infringement of personality rights is primarily determined by national law. Fundamental rights, as enshrined most notably in the ECHR, constitute a third category. Fundamental rights may directly or indirectly, via the public policy exception, correct the applicable law or be the basis for the refusal to recognize and enforce a foreign decision.

1. Jurisdiction

a) European

The Brussels I Regulation (Regulation (EC) No 44/2001 of 22 December 2000 on jurisdiction and the recognition and enforcement of judgments in civil and commercial matters, [2001] OJ L 12/1; → Brussels I (Convention and Regulation)) applied to → civil and commercial matters with a cross-border dimension, including claims arising out of an infringement of personality rights brought before 10 January 2015. The Brussels I Regulation (recast) (Regulation (EU) No 1215/2012 of the European Parliament and of the Council of 12 December 2012 on jurisdiction and the recognition and enforcement of judgments in civil and commercial matters (recast), [2012] OJ L 351/1) applies to proceedings instituted on or after 10 January 2015. Although certain provisions have been renumbered, the jurisdictional rules relating to claims arising out of an infringement of personality rights have not materially changed.

The overarching objective of the Brussels I Regulation is to strengthen the legal protection of persons established in the EU by enabling the applicant to easily identify the court before which he may bring a proceeding and, on the other hand, to allow the defendant to reasonably foresee before which court he may be sued. The general rule is therefore that a defendant should be sued in the courts of the Member State of his domicile (art 2 Brussels I Regulation; art 4(1) Brussels I Regulation (recast)). However, in a few well-defined situations there is the concurrent jurisdiction of another court because of a particularly close connection between that court and the dispute. In such a situation, the applicant may choose between the competent courts.

One of these special situations has a particular importance for the cross-border infringement of personality rights. Article 5(3) Brussels I Regulation (art 7(2) Brussels I Regulation (recast)) provides that in matters relating to a tort, delict or quasi-delict, the defendant may also be sued in the courts of the place where the harmful event occurred. In *Mines de Potasse* (Case C-21/76 *SCJEC Handelskwekerij GJ Bier BV v Mines de Potasse d'Alsace SA* [1976] ECR 1735), the ECJ held that the place where the harmful event occurred could be both the place of the event giving rise to the damage (*Handlungsort*) as well as the place where the damage occurred (*Erfolgsort*). In defamation cases, the unqualified possibility to choose between those two forums would unduly strengthen the applicant's position. The ECJ therefore in *Shevill* (Case C-68/93 *Fiona Shevill, Ixora Trading Inc, Chequepoint SARL and Chequepoint International Ltd v Presse Alliance SA* [1995] ECR I-415) limited the international jurisdiction of the court of the *Erfolgsort*.

The facts of the *Shevill* case were as follows. A British citizen was accused in a French newspaper of being involved in criminal activities. Although at the time when the article was published the British citizen was domiciled in England, the alleged criminal activity had taken place in France. The newspaper was predominantly distributed in France and only a few copies had been shipped to England. The ECJ first confirmed the right of the applicant under art 5(3) to choose between the *Handlungsort* and *Erfolgsort*. The ECJ subsequently introduced the so-called 'mosaic principle', whereby an applicant may only bring proceedings before the courts of the *Erfolgsort* to the extent the damage actually occurred within the relevant forum. Should the claimant desire to concentrate all proceedings before a single court, he would have to address either the courts of the place where the harmful event giving rise to the liability occurred or the courts of the place where the defendant is domiciled. Hence, a court may derive international jurisdiction from art 5(3) provided that (i) the publication was distributed in the forum and (ii) the applicant enjoyed a personal reputation there.

Shevill leaves the victim of a cross-border infringement of a personality right with an important strategic choice. The applicant may either bring proceedings before the court of the place where the publisher is established, and seek recovery of the prejudice suffered worldwide, or enjoy the benefit of suing locally, but having to restrict the claim to the → damages sustained within that forum. In that way, *Shevill* strikes a balance between interests of the publisher and the alleged victim. If too many national courts were to have jurisdiction, it would become completely unpredictable for the defendant to identify in advance before the courts of which Member State he may be sued. Moreover, a multitude of competent courts could lead to forum shopping, or 'libel tourism'. The mere threat of having to face legal proceedings abroad may already in itself have a chilling effect upon the freedom of expression. On the other hand, the potential victim of defamation should be provided with an effective remedy to guarantee the right to private life. The reconciliation of those competing fundamental rights in *Shevill* is largely based on the distribution of the publication. By distributing the publication in a specific Member State, the publisher may reasonably foresee the jurisdiction of the courts of that Member State.

Shevill was decided in 1993, and hence in a period predating the digital age. In particular the emergence of the Internet has made many question whether the balance struck by *Shevill* was still appropriate. The digital world functions in a way fundamentally different from the analogue world. In the first place, on the Internet information is not actively made available by a publisher in a specific Member State, but only passively by allowing Member State citizens to visit the relevant website. Moreover, since information circulates on the web perpetually, the affront to the personal reputation of the victim by online defamation may potentially be much more severe.

In *eDate Advertising* (Joined Cases C-509/09 and C-161/10 *eDate Advertising GmbH v X, Olivier Martinez, Robert Martinez v MGN Limited* [2011] ECR I-10269), the ECJ recognized that the reduced importance of the distribution criterion necessitated a change in the *Shevill* doctrine. According to the ECJ, the court of the place where the alleged victim has his centre of interests will be in the best position to assess the potential impact of the publication on the concerned individual's personality rights. The applicant should therefore be entitled to bring a claim relating to all → damages suffered worldwide with that court. The place of a person's centre of interests will often correspond with the place of the concerned person's habitual residence. However, the presumption can be rebutted by other indications such as the pursuit of a professional activity in a specific jurisdiction.

The ECJ thus supplemented the *Shevill* doctrine by reading a third → connecting factor into art 5(3) Brussels I Regulation. Hence, in the case of a personality right violation *via* the Internet, the applicant may choose between (i) the court of the place where the publisher is domiciled, (ii) the court of the place where the alleged victim has its centre of interests and (iii) the courts of each Member State from where the information has been accessible provided that the victim enjoys a personal reputation there. In addition, the applicant may always bring proceedings before the court of the place where the defendant is domiciled (art 2).

eDate Advertising is a very peculiar judgment. If the reduced importance of the element of distribution is the justification for the reconsideration of the *Shevill* doctrine, one would expect the ECJ to introduce a requirement aimed at guaranteeing foreseeability of the jurisdiction of national courts. However, the ECJ reached precisely the opposite conclusion. If we assume that the place of the centre of interest of the alleged victim will often correspond with his habitual place of residence, then the alleged victim will have the possibility to litigate at home, and the ECJ essentially introduced a forum *actoris*. The ECJ has, however, consistently ruled that the existence of a forum *actoris* was incompatible with the structure of Brussels I Regulation, since this would not guarantee foreseeability for the defendant. In fact, with regard to art 5(3), the ECJ has consistently refused to take the habitual residence of the alleged victim into account. Finally, the ECJ has complicated art 5(3) by introducing a distinction between personality rights violations in the real and the digital world. Such a rigid distinction cannot function in practice. For example, many newspapers are republished online, so that the question immediately arises of how art 5(3) should be interpreted when the same article is published in the printed and digital edition of a newspaper.

It is therefore unlikely that *eDate Advertising* will be the last case decided by the ECJ on the cross-border infringement of personality rights *via* the Internet. If the decision in *eDate Advertising* is indicative, the ECJ is likely to strengthen the position of the alleged victim of a violation of personality rights.

b) National

Brussels I Regulation (recast) applies to all defendants domiciled in a Member State. Despite recent efforts to extend the scope of application of Brussels I Regulation (recast), the jurisdiction over defendants domiciled in a third country remains largely a matter of national procedural law. In addition since defamation may give rise to criminal proceedings, the court may also base its jurisdiction on criminal law. Certain Member States allow the victim to lodge an accessory civil claim in the criminal proceedings. A notorious example occurred in France where an Israeli resident filed in France for the criminal prosecution of a New York professor for publication of a negative book review, written by a German law professor, on a US website. Although the French court declined jurisdiction and awarded → damages against the plaintiff on the grounds of abuse of procedure, the example demonstrates the dangerous potential of criminal law for forum shopping (Tribunal de Grande Instance de Paris, 3 March 2011, Case No 0718523043).

To return to civil law, a number of Member States, such as the → Netherlands, have adopted jurisdictional rules that largely mirror Brussels I Regulation (recast). In such Member States, it is less relevant for the purposes of international jurisdiction whether a defendant is domiciled in a Member State or not. Even if the defendant is domiciled in a third country, national procedural laws will lead in the far majority of cases to similar outcomes.

A particular position is taken by the United Kingdom (→ United Kingdom). Much has been said about the 'systematic dismantling' of the common law of conflict of laws by the EU. Brussels I Regulation and the relevant common law rules indeed seem to be based on partly different paradigms. If a defendant is not domiciled in a Member State, the common rules apply in full force. In recent years, London has acquired the reputation of being 'the libel capital of the world'. The truth of the matter is that the English rules on jurisdiction are not fundamentally more exorbitant than art 7(2) Brussels I Regulation (recast) (art 5(3) Brussels I Regulation). Rule 3(1)(9) of the Civil Procedure Rules, and Practice Direction constitutes effectively codification of the ECJ decision in *Mines de Potasse*. Moreover, English courts can rely upon the doctrine of *forum non conveniens* to strike out actions that have a manifestly closer connection with another jurisdiction.

There may be different reasons why England is such a popular destination for libel tourists. For instance, the damages awarded to a successful plaintiff are generally higher compared to other European jurisdictions. Others reasons could be that because of the absence of a language barrier, Americans may more easily find their way in English courts. Finally, it is relatively expensive to litigate in England. The high court fees could be a tactical advantage for a wealthy plaintiff, who may seek to bully an impecunious defendant out of his day in court. Until very recently, the effectiveness of the *forum non conveniens* to strike such cases out was significantly undermined by application of the multiple-publication rule. This rule provides that each publication of the offending material constitutes a separate tort. The strategic plaintiff will accordingly limit the action to all publications in England. Since there is in such circumstances no clearly more appropriate forum than England, the *forum non conveniens* is essentially neutralized. This problem has now been remedied by the Defamation Act 2013 (2013 ch 26), section 9(2) of which provides that

> a court does not have jurisdiction to hear and determine an action to which the section applies unless it is satisfied that, of all the places in which the statement complained of has been published, England and Wales is clearly the most appropriate place in which to bring an action in respect of the statement.

2. Applicable law

a) European

Although the initial Commission proposal for a Rome II Regulation (European Commission, 'Proposal for a Regulation of the European Parliament and the Council on the Law Applicable to Non-Contractual Obligations ("Rome II")' COM(2003) 427 final) laid down a specific conflict-of-laws rule relating to the infringement of personality rights, the issue proved too controversial for its inclusion in a general codification of conflict-of-laws rules. After intensive lobbying of the press and media, it was ultimately decided to exclude from the scope of Regulation determination of the law applicable to non-contractual obligations arising out of violations of privacy and rights relating to personality, including defamation (art 1(2)(g)).

The exclusion of personality rights from the scope of → Rome II Regulation (Regulation (EC) No 864/2007 of the European Parliament and of the Council of 11 July 2007 on the law applicable to non-contractual obligations (Rome II), [2007] OJ L 199/40) is regrettable. The objections of the media lobby are somewhat misplaced. The current patchwork of conflict-of-laws rules in force in the Member States only perpetuates the gaps and inconsistencies between the jurisdictions. More than anything, this conflict-of-laws spaghetti strengthens the position of the unscrupulous applicant since it opens up more possibilities to shop in the different jurisdictions. Since claims relating to personality rights are not excluded from the scope of Brussels I Regulation (recast), a court may only refuse the recognition and enforcement of a judgment pronounced by the courts of another Member State on the narrow grounds specifically provided for by art 34. This means, for example, that an English court may on the basis of the double actionability rule refuse the application of French defamation law, but if in the same factual pattern the applicant decides to bring proceedings in France, and the French court applies French law, there will only be limited possibilities for the defendant to oppose the subsequent enforcement of that judgment in the United Kingdom. If confronted with such a scenario, it is not hard to imagine which choice the strategic applicant will make.

The issue of personality rights was included in the review clause contained in art 30 Rome II Regulation. The Commission presented accordingly a comparative study on the situation in the (at the time) 27 Member States as regards the law applicable to non-contractual obligations arising out of violations of privacy and rights relating to personality (the 'Mainstrat Study', Comparative study on the situation in the 27 Member States as regards the law applicable to non-contractual obligations arising out of violations of privacy and rights relating to personality (JLS/2007/C4/028)) in February 2009. Despite repeated calls from the European Parliament, the Commission entirely omitted to react to the study, and the issue seems not to be on the political agenda. Be that as it may, at least for the moment, the determination of the law applicable to personality rights is nearly exclusively governed by national law.

b) National

The controversy surrounding Rome II Regulation provides evidence that the determination of the law applicable to a cross-border infringement of personality rights is an extremely sensitive issue. Some Member States have therefore introduced a double actionability rule. This rule entails that, for the purpose of determining whether a tort or delict is actionable, the tort or delict should give rise to a cause of action under both the *lex fori* and the law of the other country concerned. For example in the UK, the Private international law (Miscellaneous Provisions) Act 1995 (ch 42) abolished the double actionability rule, but it was feared that publishers or broadcasters established in the UK would be subjected to defamation proceedings under a repressive foreign law. Defamation was therefore entirely excluded from the scope of the 1995 Act. The double actionability rule accordingly still applies in the UK. Other examples of Member States that apply a double actionability rule are Cyprus and → Malta.

The 1995 Act has added another layer of complexity to the conflict of laws. For privacy claims, such as breach of confidence, the provisions of the 1995 Act will apply. However, in view of the exclusion of defamation the scope of the 1995 Act, common law rules, including the double actionability rule and the multiple-publication rule, continue to be applicable to defamation claims. The multiple-publication rule impacts upon, amongst others, the applicable law. Since under the multi-publication rule each publication of defamatory material gives rise to a separate cause of action, the applicable law should be separately established for each occasion the information is published. If a plaintiff has limited his claim to all publications in England, English law will apply.

In the majority of Member States, the infringement of personality rights is governed by the general conflict-of-laws rules on the law applicable to non-contractual obligations. The most commonly used → connecting factor is the *lex loci delecti*, leading to the application of the law of the place where the harmful event occurred. In the event where the place giving rise to the damage and the place where the damage occurred diverge, the conflict-of-laws rules of some Member States formally favour the former, but the result is in practice more ambiguous. For example in → Austria, absent a choice of law by the parties, disputes relating to non-contractual obligations are governed by the law of the country where the harmful conduct takes place (art 35 and 48 Law on Private international law (IPR-Gesetz of 15 June 1978), BGB für die Republik Österreich No 304/1978). With regard to defamation, Austrian courts have interpreted the *lex loci delecti* to be the place where the injured party has suffered the affront and where the effects are felt most deeply. That place will often coincide with the place of habitual residence of the victim. Germany and Italy have incorporated the principle of ubiquity. According to art 40 Introductory Act to the German Civil Code (Einführungsgesetz zum Bürgerlichen Gesetzbuche of 21 September 1994, BGBl. I 2494, as amended) and art 62(1) Italian Private international law Act (Riforma del Sistema italiano di diritto internazionale private, Act No 218 of 31 May 1995 in Gazz.Uff., Supplemento Ordinario No 128 of 3 June 1995, as amended) the *lex loci delecti* refers, in the case of a tortious act committed at a distance, both to the law of the place where the harmful event giving rise to the damage occurred as well as to the law of the place where the damage was sustained. The applicable law will in principle be the law of the country in which the liable party has acted. However, the plaintiff may instead require the application of the law of the place where the event giving rise to the harmful event occurred.

Only five Member States have adopted a special conflict-of-laws rule dealing with defamation. These Member States are → Belgium (art 99 (2(1)) Code of Private international law (Code de Droit International Privé, Loi du 16 juillet 2004 portant le Code de droit international privé, MB 27 July 2004, 57344, as amended)), → Bulgaria (art 108 International Private Law Code (Кодекс на международното частно право of 17 May 2005) 17 May 2005, Prom. SG. 42, as amended), → Hungary (art 10 Decree-Law No 13 of 1979 on International Private Law), → Lithuania (art 1.45 Lithuanian Civil Code of 18 July 2000 (Lietuvos Respublikos civilinis kodeksas) Law No XI-1312, as amended) and → Romania (art 112 Law No 105 on the Settlement of the Private international law Relations of 22 September 1992 (Legea nr. 105/1992 cu privire la reglementarea raporturilor de Drept International Privat). These conflict-of-laws rules generally favour the alleged victim of the infringement of personality rights, in that they either give the victim the option to choose between certain laws (Belgium, Bulgaria, Lithuania, Romania) or require the application of the *lex fori* provided that is more favourable to the victim (Hungary). Worth mentioning is that the victim may in Belgium, Bulgaria and Romania only opt for the application of the law of the place where damage occurred provided that the person potentially liable could have reasonably foreseen that harm would occur in that country. Such a requirement of foreseeability is also applicable in → Slovenia via the general conflict-of-laws rules (art 30 Private international law and Procedure Act of 13 July 1999 (Zakon o mednarodnem zasebnem pravu in postopku), Url.l RS, No 56/99).

c) International

There is no international convention laying down conflict-of-laws rules with regard to disputes arising out of the infringement of a personality right. Nevertheless, the ECHR has had a profound impact on the law applicable to cross-border infringements of personality rights. The protection of personality rights is deeply rooted in the national legal cultures. The balance between the freedom of speech and the right to private life, or the amount of intrusion into his private life that an individual has to tolerate in the name of public debate, is essentially the reflection of a particular view on how a democracy should operate. Until very recently, the outcome of that balancing exercise was primarily determined by the historical-political developments in the jurisdiction concerned. In recent years, largely under the influence of the ECHR the European legal systems are increasingly converging.

Article 8 ECHR provides that everyone has the right to respect for his private and family life. The ECtHR has made a distinction between personal integrity rights, seen as inalienable, and reputation, seen as linked to the external evaluation of the individual by society. The rights relating to personal integrity will therefore always fall within the ambit of art 8 (*von Hannover v Germany* App no 5932/00 (ECtHR, 24 June 2004)), while the right to reputation has only sporadically been deemed to be an independent right (*Karakó v Hungary* App no 39311/05 (ECtHR, 28 April 2009) paras 22–3). The discrediting of someone's reputation will result in an infringement of art 8 only if the factual allegations are of such a seriously offensive nature that their publication has an inevitable effect on the private life of the individual concerned. Once an infringement of art 8 is established, it is for the high contracting party to demonstrate that the intrusion (i) is prescribed by law, (ii) serves a legitimate aim and (iii) is necessary in a democratic society.

The majority of cases decided by the ECtHR on personality rights concern news reports where sensitive information about a private person was published in the mass media. The applicant is then either the private individual who alleges that the high contracting party has not sufficiently protected their right to private life, or the press agency, which alleges that the measures taken by the high contracting party violate the freedom of expression. Rather than testing whether the infringement may be justified by an overriding public interest, the ECtHR balances the fundamental rights against one another. Although the ECHR is merely an instrument of subsidiary protection and national authorities have a margin of appreciation, the ECtHR has identified a number of relevant factors that a national court should take into account. Particularly relevant are: (i) whether the publication is a contribution to a debate of general interest, (ii) the degree to which the person concerned is known, (iii) the content, form and consequences of the publication and (iv) the circumstances under which the information is gathered. If the person had a legitimate expectation for the protection of their private life and the publication contributes little to a debate of general interest, then the balance will generally tilt in favour of the protection of personality rights. If the person lives a more exposed life and the publication is in the interest of the public, the balance will generally tilt in favour of the protection of the freedom of expression.

The decisions whether the balance should be struck in favour of the right to private life or the freedom of speech is often a largely factual issue. The ECtHR will therefore only exceptionally review whether a particular rule of national law is compatible with the ECHR. The ECtHR will only step in when the national legal framework is manifestly insufficient to arrive at a well-balanced solution. Such for example is the case when national law excludes altogether, subject to some minor exceptions, the protection of the right to private life with regard to persons of contemporary society (*von Hannover v Germany* App no 5932/00 (ECtHR, 24 June 2004)). On the other hand, the ECtHR has refused to accept that art 8 requires the introduction into national law of an obligation to notify the subject of publication of the intent to publish certain information (*Mosley v United Kingdom* App no 480009/08 (ECtHR 10 May 2011)).

The ECHR predominantly affects substantive law. Nevertheless, ECtHR case-law also has significance for private international law. In the first place, the introduction of a common core of personality rights and the development of minimum safeguards has taken away the most dramatic differences between European national laws. As a consequence, the outcome of any given case will depend much less on the substantive law found applicable. At least in theory, this should reduce the risk of forum shopping (→ Forum (and law) shopping). Moreover, the introduction of a minimum floor of protection makes it less likely that the application of a foreign law, or the recognition and enforcement of a foreign judgment, will be refused on the basis of → public policy.

3. Recognition and enforcement

a) European
The recognition and enforcement of a decision rendered by a court in another Member State is governed by the Brussels I Regulation, or with regard to legal proceedings instituted on or after 10 January 2015, the Brussels I Regulation (recast). Under the Brussels I Regulation, a court has only limited possibilities to refuse the recognition and enforcement of a judgment pronounced by the courts of another Member State. The Brussels I Regulation (recast) offers an even more enhanced scheme for the recognition and enforcement of a decision by a court in another Member State (→ Brussels I (Convention and Regulation)).

b) National
Brussels I Regulation (recast) only applies to judgments rendered by the courts of other Member States. The recognition and enforcement of a judgment rendered by the court of a third country is governed by national law.

Applicants seeking to obtain judgment in a European jurisdiction against a defendant domiciled in the USA should be aware that recognition and enforcement of that decision in the USA is virtually impossible. US substantive law differs significantly from that of the Member States. Under the First Amendment of the US Constitution, freedom of speech enjoys a nearly absolute protection. Some applicants have attempted to get around the application of the First Amendment by bringing an action for the infringement of a personality right against a US domiciled defendant in courts outside the USA, most notably in London. This has triggered severe public debate in the USA, in particular where the action against the US defendant was brought by a compatriot. In August 2010, the US Congress adopted the Securing the Protection of our Enduring and Established Constitutional Heritage Act (124 Stat. 2480–84, henceforth SPEECH Act). The SPEECH Act basically requires that, if a plaintiff seeks enforcement of a foreign judgment in the USA, the foreign court must guarantee the freedom of speech to an extent at least equivalent to the First Amendment. Insofar as enforcement of the foreign judgment would be necessary in the USA, the observance of the First Amendment is in this way factually imposed upon a foreign court. The SPEECH Act has been severely criticized, including in the USA, and does not appear to be entirely free of the cultural imperialism it sought to redress.

c) International
The recognition and enforcement of a foreign judgment dealing with the infringement of a personality right falls within the scope of the Hague Recognition and Enforcement Convention (Hague Convention of 1 February 1971 on the recognition and enforcement of foreign judgments in civil and commercial matters, 1144 UNTS 258). The practical relevance of this Convention is marginal, since it has only been ratified by → Albania, Cyprus, Kuwait, the Netherlands and → Portugal and the scheme of recognition and enforcement provided for by the Convention will only be applicable after the contracting parties have concluded a (bilateral) Supplementary Agreement to this effect.

The recognition and enforcement of a foreign judgment is thus a matter primarily governed by national law. The recognition and enforcement of a judgment is not excluded from the scope of the ECHR, however. This has particular relevance if the recognition and enforcement is sought of a judgment emanating from a court in a country that has not ratified the ECHR. In *Pellegrini v Italy* (App no 30882/89 (ECtHR, 20 July 2001)), the ECtHR accepted that Italy was in breach of its obligations under the ECHR because the Italian courts had failed to verify whether the proceedings before the ecclesiastical courts of the Holy See were in compliance with the right to a fair trial (art 6 ECHR). It remains to be seen whether the obligation to verify the observance by the court of origin of fundamental rights is limited to the procedural right to a fair trial or also extends to the substantive rights protected by the ECHR, such as the right to private life. If that were to be the case, a high contracting party would at the stage of recognition and enforcement be obliged to scrutinize whether the foreign judgment complies with the minimum safeguards as provided for by arts 8 and 10 ECHR. The application of the ECHR would then enter via the backdoor, in a way similar to the criticized SPEECH Act.

V. Modern trends

The constitutionalization of personality rights has brought greater convergence in Europe, but caused transatlantic polarization. That may be changing. The criticism of the other side of the Atlantic of being too 'plaintiff-friendly' was one of the reasons triggering reform in England. As was discussed above, the Defamation Act 2013 (2013 ch 26) attempts to discourage forum shopping amongst others by requiring the court addressed to verify whether of all the places in which the statement complained of has been published, England and Wales is clearly the most appropriate place in which to bring legal proceedings in respect of the statement.

Reform may also be underway in the EU. The European Parliament in May 2012 called upon the Commission to submit a proposal amending the Rome II Regulation and add a separate conflict-of-laws rule dealing with the infringement of personality rights. As a basic rule, the law governing the non-contractual obligation arising out of a violation of personality right would be the law of the country in which the most significant element or elements of the loss or damage occur or are likely to occur, unless the putative tortfeasor could not have reasonably foreseen substantial consequences of their act occurring in that country. The right to reply and preventive measures are addressed separately, whereby the applicable law will be the law of the country in which the publisher, broadcaster or handler has its habitual residence.

The proposed conflict-of-laws rule is well-balanced and stands out for leaving it up to substantive law to strike the appropriate balance between the protection of personality rights and the safeguard of the freedom of speech. Although it is unlikely that all the issues surrounding the cross-border infringement of personality rights will be resolved in the foreseeable future, the resolution of the European Parliament and the larger restraint exercised by European courts towards international disputes is certainly a step towards a workable solution.

JAN-JAAP KUIPERS

Literature

William Bennett, 'New Developments in the United Kingdom: The Defamation Act 2013' (2012/13) 14 YbPIL 173; Gert Brüggemeier, Aurelia Colombi Ciacchi and Patrick O'Callaghan (eds), *Personality Rights in European Tort Law* (CUP 2010); Matthew Collins, *The Law of Defamation and the Internet* (OUP 2010); Richard Garnett and Megan Richardson, 'Libel Tourism or Just Redress? Reconciling the (English) Right to Reputation with the (American) Right to Free Speech in Cross-Border Libel Cases' (2009) 5 J Priv Int L 471; Trevor Hartley, '"Libel Tourism" and Conflict of Laws' (2010) 59 ICLQ 25; Jan-Jaap Kuipers, 'Towards a European Approach in the Cross-Border Infringement of Personality Rights' (2009) 12 GLJ 1681; Laura E Little, 'Internet Defamation, Freedom of Expression, and the Lesson of Private international law for the United States' (2012/13) 14 YbPIL 181; A. Mills, *The Law Applicable to Cross-border Defamation on Social Media: Whose Law Governs Free Speech in 'Facebookistan'?*, (2015) 1 Journal of Media Law, 1; Csongor Istvàn Nagy, 'The Word is a Dangerous Weapon: Jurisdiction, Applicable Law and Personality Rights in EU Law: Missed and New Opportunities' (2012) 8 *J Priv Int L* 251; Peter Arnt Nielsen, 'Libel Tourism: English and EU Private international law' (2013) 9 *J Priv Int L* 269; Thomas Thiede, *Internationale -Persönlichkeitsrechtsverletzungen durch Massenmedien* (Jan Sramek Verlag 2010); Gerhard Wagner, 'Article 6 of the Commission Proposal: Violation of Privacy-Defamation by Mass Media' (2005) 13 *ERPL* 21.

Place of performance

The place of performance of a contractual obligation is the place where the debtor is required to perform the acts necessary for honouring his obligation in order for his promise to be fulfilled. In the case of negative obligations, it is the place or places where the debtor must refrain from a given conduct. The place of performance may be relevant to private international law in a variety of ways, in connection with rules governing jurisdiction, the recognition and enforcement of judgments and choice of law.

I. The significance of the place of performance to private international law: an overview

As far as adjudicatory jurisdiction is concerned, the place where a contractual obligation is to be performed (*locus destinatae solutionis*) is often employed to localize the contract and to identify, on that basis, the court entitled to hear the claims that may arise in connection therewith. Several provisions, both domestic and uniform, follow this pattern, albeit with some variations. Thus, for example, art 29(1) of the German Code of Civil Procedure (*Zivilprozessordnung* of 5 December 2005, BGBl. I 3202, as amended), which regulates both venue and the jurisdiction of German courts in cross-border cases, provides that disputes arising from a contractual relationship, including those regarding the existence of the relationship at stake, may be decided by the court for the place where the obligation in question is to be performed. Similarly, art 7(1)(a) of the Brussels I Regulation (recast) (Regulation (EU) No 1215/2012 of the European Parliament and of the Council of 12 December 2012 on jurisdiction and the recognition and enforcement of judgments in civil and commercial matters (recast), [2012] OJ L 351/1; → Brussels I (Convention and Regulation)), grants special jurisdiction over 'matters relating to a contract' to 'the court for the place of performance of the obligation in question'.

The *locus destinatae solutionis* may have a role to play in the recognition of foreign judgments, in particular when it comes to verifying whether the requirement of jurisdiction of the court of origin, where relevant, has been met in a given case. Several bilateral agreements on matters of judicial cooperation include rules to this effect. This is the case, for instance, of a Convention of 9 December 1987 between Argentina and Italy on judicial assistance and the recognition of judgments (Rome Convention of 9 December 1987 between the Republic of Italy and the Republic of Argentina on judicial assistance and the recognition of judgments, available through the Treaty Database of the Ministry of Foreign Affairs of the Republic of Italy, available at <http://itra.esteri.it>). The Convention, having stated in art 22(1) that decisions emanating from one contracting party shall be recognized in the legal order of the other contracting party provided *inter alia* that they have been rendered by a court possessing jurisdiction in conformity with the Convention itself, establishes in art 22(2)(c) that, in matters relating to a contract, the court of origin shall be deemed to have jurisdiction if it is the court of the contracting state where the parties had agreed, either explicitly or tacitly, that the obligation in dispute was to be performed.

Rules relating to → choice of law, too, frequently refer to the place of performance as a means to localize a contract and identify its governing law. For instance, art 8(2) of the Rome I Regulation (Regulation (EC) No 593/2008 of the European Parliament and of the Council of 17 June 2008 on the law applicable to contractual obligations (Rome I), [2008] OJ L 177/6; → Rome Convention and Rome I Regulation (contractual obligations)) provides that, absent a choice of the parties, an individual contract of employment 'shall be governed by the law of the country in which ... the employee habitually carries out his work in performance of the contract'. Under the same regulation, the place of performance of an obligation may be relevant to the operation of the general provision of art 4 on the law applicable in the absence of choice, namely when the → escape clauses in art 4(3) or the residual provision in art 4(4) are called into question: the place of performance of the obligations arising from a contract is among the elements that may be relied upon to determine the country with which the contract in question features in fact a particularly close connection.

In → choice of law, the place of performance may also be relevant to determining whether individual rules of a law other than the *lex causae* and the *lex fori* may affect the substantive regulation of the contract, or may have a bearing on the way in which specific issues relating thereto should be decided. Under art 9(3) of the Rome I Regulation, 'effect may be given' to the overriding mandatory provisions of a third country, provided that they belong to 'the law of the country where the obligations arising out of the contract have to be or have been performed' and that they 'render the performance of the contract unlawful'. On a different note, art 12(2) of the Regulation provides that, in determining 'the manner of performance and the steps to be taken in the event of defective performance' of a contractual obligation, 'regard shall be had to the law of the country in which performance takes place'.

Various reasons explain why rules of private international law refer to the place of performance of a contractual obligation, instead of other occurrences relating to the contract, for the purposes indicated above. On the one hand, the *locus solutionis* is a place where the relationship between the parties is likely to undergo a number of substantively significant developments (see further below, section II.). It is thus reasonable to assume that using the place of performance as a pinpoint to localize the contract will often lead to sensible and foreseeable results, consistent with the principle of proximity and predictability. On the other hand, the place where a contractual obligation must be performed is typically one of the places where a contract becomes 'tangible', ie where the economic and social implications of the parties' transaction may be perceived in a particularly clear way. It may thus be assumed that the state on whose territory (or market) the said implications become apparent is particularly interested in regulating the contract (or certain specific aspects of it), either through the intervention of its courts pursuant to the relevant rules on jurisdiction, or through the application (or consideration) of its substantive rules in accordance with the relevant choice-of-law provisions.

II. Identifying the place of performance for the purposes of private international law: the problem stated

In the substantive law of contracts, determining where an obligation is to be performed is a practically important issue. Geographical factors are likely to affect the ability of performance to satisfy the interests of the creditor.

In principle, a failure on the part of the debtor to discharge his obligations at the place where performance is to be effected entitles the creditor to resort to the appropriate remedies for defective performance, including the right to claim → damages. In contracts for the sale of goods (→ Sale contracts and sale of goods), in particular where the contract is one involving the carriage of the goods, the place of delivery has an influence on the allocation as between the parties of the costs of the transaction: as a matter of fact, should delivery be effected at an improper place, extra costs might be incurred to transfer the goods on to the 'right' place, and delays may ensue.

Similar remarks, *mutatis mutandis*, apply to money obligations (→ Money and currency). In the place where the amount is actually made available to the payee rules may exist restricting the ability of the latter to make use of the sum received, or otherwise adversely affecting the interests of the creditor (eg limiting the conversion of the sum into a foreign currency).

1. The rules determining the place of performance for substantive purposes

It is not surprising, in light of the foregoing, that domestic legal orders and uniform texts dealing with contracts almost invariably include substantive rules regulating precisely the place of performance of obligations.

Normally, these rules refer in the first place to the agreement of the parties. Where the parties have not themselves designated the place of performance in a manner consistent with the applicable law (ie in the particular form, if any, required for the validity of the agreement, or in conformity with the substantial requirements, if any, prescribed with respect to particular obligations), a more or less developed set of default rules is usually meant to apply.

The layout and content of these rules may vary significantly from country to country and from one uniform legal instrument to another (for a comparative overview, see Ole Lando and Hugh Beale (eds), *Principles of European Contract Law – Parts I and II Combined and Revised* (Kluwer Law International 2000) 331). Some common features, however, may be detected.

It is frequently provided that, in determining the place of performance of a given obligation, regard must be had to the nature of the obligation and its object. Thus, if a contract has been concluded for the restoration of a building, the contractor's obligations will obviously need to be performed, both in fact and at law, where the building is located. The nature and object of the obligation may either be regarded as evidence of a tacit will of the parties or as legal factors objectively supplementing the content of the relationship, based on standards of reasonableness.

For obligations that are not univocally attached to one or more particular places, default rules exist indicating the relevant locality. Similar indications are usually needed, in particular, to determine the place of performance of money obligations. As means of payment become thoroughly incorporeal, objective factors of localization tend to lose ground to personal ones. In practice, depending on the substantive policies inspiring the legislator in question (or the authors of the uniform text considered), payment shall usually be required to take place at the domicile (or the residence) of either the creditor or the debtor (→ Domicile, habitual residence and establishment).

The first option, based on the idea that it is for the debtor to seek the creditor (ie, that money obligations are normally *portables*), represents the rule, *inter alia*, under English, Italian and Swiss law, as well as under the → CISG (United Nations Convention of 11 April 1980 on Contracts for the International Sale of Goods, 1489 UNTS 3; art 57(1)) and the UNIDROIT Principles (International Institute for the Unification of Private Law/Institut international pour l'unification du droit privé, *UNIDROIT Principles of International Commercial Contracts 2010* (3rd edn, UNIDROIT 2010); art 6.1.6(1)). The same solution is adopted by the European Convention of 16 May 1972 on the place of payment of money liabilities (CETS No 75), the single most remarkable, yet ultimately unsuccessful, attempt to unify the law in respect of this specific issue (the Convention has never entered into force, as the prescribed number of ratifications and accessions has never been reached). The second option, founded on the assumption that money obligations are in principle *quérables*, is followed by French, Belgian and Spanish law, among others. Other schemes exist in some legal systems, namely in → Austria and → Germany, whereby the residence of the debtor is legally considered to be the place of payment, but the money has to be sent, at the debtor's cost and risk, to the creditor's residence.

Further specifications are normally needed to ensure the proper operation of the preceding rules, in particular in light of the fact that the domicile or the residence of the parties may change during the life of the contract. In practice, it remains to be seen whether the relevant moment in time for determining the domicile (or residence) of the relevant contracting party should be the moment when the obligation has arisen, ie the moment in which the contract was concluded (as it is established, eg, under English and German law), or rather the moment at which the obligation becomes due (as provided, eg, under Dutch law). Some legal texts, after stating that payment must be made at the domicile (or the residence) of the creditor at the time of the conclusion of the contract, specify that subsequent changes in the creditor's domicile (or residence) shall not result in a change of the place of performance, but rather require the creditor to bear any increase in the expenses incidental to payment as may be caused by the change itself (this is notably the case of the CISG and the UNIDROIT Principles).

Special provisions may be found in some legal systems, supplementing the rules described so far in light of the peculiar features of particular types of contracts. Thus, for example, French law has it that if the price for goods is payable on delivery, payment shall be made at the place of delivery.

2. The determination of the place of performance for private international law purposes, between autonomy and dependence

Basically, two opposing approaches may be followed when the need arises to identify the place of performance of an obligation for the purposes of private international law.

According to the 'autonomous' solution, the place of performance is to be identified in accordance with standards and criteria established by the concerned rule of private international law itself or by some other rules ancillary to the latter. By contrast, following the 'dependent' approach, the place of performance must be determined in accordance with the same standards that need to be employed, in the circumstances, for substantive purposes, ie, typically, the standards provided for by the *lex causae*. Incidentally, the point has sometimes been made that the relevant standards should rather be looked for in the *lex fori*. The latter solution, occasionally followed with regard to domestic rules on jurisdiction (see, eg, concerning art 113 of the Swiss Private International Act (*Bundesgesetz über das Internationale Privatrecht*) of 18 December 1987, 1988 BBl I 5, as amended), the opinion reported by Bernard Dutoit, *Droit international privé suisse* (4th edn, Helbing & Lichtenhan 2005) 366), reflects the idea that the language of rules should be assumed to be consistent with the concepts and categories of the legal system to which the rules themselves belong, as suggested by the *lex fori* approach to characterization. If the said solution were to apply to uniform rules, however, the goal of uniformity would in fact be frustrated.

The key argument in favour of autonomy rests on the consideration that substantive and private international law rules perform different functions and underlie different policies. Thus, the fact that certain notions employed in private international law rules might originate in substantive law does not imply that the said notions should necessarily be interpreted, for private international law purposes, in the same way as they would be interpreted in substantive law. The argument proves particularly persuasive when the identification of the place of performance is relevant to the operation of jurisdictional rules, more particularly to the operation of rules of 'special' jurisdiction. The goals pursued by the latter rules, eg proximity and predictability in the identification of the competent court, may in fact have little in common with the policy considerations – the protection of either the creditor or the debtor of a given obligation, the safeguard of expectations relied upon at the moment of the conclusion of the contract as regards the costs of the transaction etc – that explain the design of the corresponding substantive rules (Walter A. Stoffel, 'Place of Performance-Jurisdiction and Plaintiff's Interests in Contemporary Societies' (2002) 4 E.J.L.R. 195 ff).

The following arguments may, instead, be put forward in favour of the *lex causae* approach. When dealing with the intricacies of cross-border relationships, the law should in principle be maintained as simply as possible. Thus, since the identification of the *locus solutionis* is already ensured by specialized rules of substantive law, the latter should be used to the widest possible extent and no further (and possibly duplicate) rules should be elaborated. Indeed, this way of proceeding may require some extra work from the interpreter, since the latter, instead of directly determining the place of performance of a particular obligation, must engage in a two-step process implying the identification of the substantive rules applicable to the circumstances and the application of such rules to the case at hand. In spite of this, the dependent solution is likely to bring some practical advantages. On the one hand, it provides the parties with a significant degree of certainty, as the things they know (or should know) with regard to the substantive content of their relationship, ie their rights and obligations in respect of performance (including the localization thereof), will ultimately hold valid for private international law purposes, too. On the other hand, the *lex causae* approach allows the interpreter to address the niceties and subtleties of the identification of the place of performance through a sophisticated legal toolbox, ie the one provided by the substantive rules of the national legal order in question, as possibly clarified and refined by the case-law developed in connection therewith. As a matter of fact, identifying the place of performance of an obligation may sometimes imply the decision of rather complex legal issues: for example, it is normally accepted that the place of performance may be determined by the agreement of the parties (both for substantive and for private international law purposes), but in some circumstances it may be unclear whether an agreement has actually been concluded (eg where it appears that the originally agreed terms of the contract have been modified by the practice of the parties), or what the precise meaning of the agreement should be understood to be. Substantive rules are often well equipped to deal with these 'hard' cases (including through general rules on the formation and interpretation of contracts, as the case may be), whereas autonomous rules, which only seldom feature an elaborate design, may appear to lack the desired degree of precision and technical refinement.

III. Some actual solutions, as embodied in present-day rules

There is no general, let alone universally accepted, answer to the problem of whether, for private international law purposes, the place of performance should better be identified autonomously or by reference to the *lex contractus*.

1. In the conflict of laws

The issue has apparently given rise to little discussion in respect of cases where the identification of the *locus solutionis* of a given obligation is required to identify the governing law of a contract or is otherwise relevant to the operation of conflict-of-laws provisions *stricto sensu*. By the way, the situations where the matter is practically relevant are not numerous. However, where doubts arise, the preference, it is submitted, should be accorded to the dependent solution.

It is worth recalling in this respect that substantive issues relating to the performance of contractual obligations are to be decided in accordance with the law applicable to the contract, as identified through the relevant connecting factors. This almost undisputed statement finds explicit support, among others, in various legal instruments laying down uniform rules on contracts conflicts, such as art 12(1)(b) of the Rome I Regulation, art 14(c) of the Inter-American Contracts Convention (Inter-American Convention of 17 March 1994 on the Law Applicable to International Contracts, 33 ILM 732) and art 8 of the Hague Agency Convention (Hague Convention of 14 March 1978 on the law applicable to agency, Hague Conference of Private international law (ed), *Collection of Conventions (1951–2009)* (Intersentia 2009) 268). It is reasonable to assume that where provisions intended to operate in conjunction with such connecting factors make reference, for their own purposes, to the place of performance of a given obligation, the said place should be identified in conformity with the substantive rules of the *lex contractus*. Thus, for example, the overriding mandatory provisions of a third country to which a court may 'give effect' pursuant to the rule in art 9(3) of the Rome I Regulation, mentioned above, should be understood to be the mandatory rules of the country where performance is to be effected in accordance with the law applicable to the contract.

2. In respect of rules on the recognition and enforcement of judgments

The issue of how the place of performance should be identified for the purposes of rules on the recognition and enforcement of judgments has seemingly attracted little discussion, although probably for different reasons.

The requirement of jurisdiction of the court of origin, where relevant, reflects the intention of the requested state to avoid the recognition of judgments resulting from unfair proceedings, in particular when the defendant has been attracted before the courts of the country of origin on the ground of a head of jurisdiction that the requested state considers to be exorbitant. Accordingly, it is contended that in determining whether the obligation in dispute had to be performed in the country of origin of the judgment, the core issue is not whether the technicalities of the *locus destinatae solutionis* have been observed, but rather whether a reasonable connection existed between the subject matter of the dispute and the country where the judgment has been rendered. The relevant rules on recognition, by the way, do not generally require that the court of origin asserted its jurisdiction on precisely the same grounds as would have been available in the circumstances to the courts of the requested state, but rather that jurisdiction, in the two countries, depends on substantially equivalent standards.

3. With respect to rules governing jurisdiction to adjudicate

It is in the field of adjudicatory jurisdiction where the debate on the standards and criteria relevant to identifying the place of performance of obligations has featured sharply opposing views (→Jurisdiction, contracts and torts). As it is rare to find jurisdictional rules laying down explicit criteria for localizing obligations (one notable example of precision in this respect is art 8(2) of the MERCOSUR Protocol of Buenos Aires on International Jurisdiction in Contractual Matters (MERCOSUR/CMC/DEC. No 1/94, signed at 5 August 1994, available at <www.mre.gov.py>), but the criteria there are far from being unproblematic), the issue at stake is essentially one of interpretation.

The case of the European unified rules on jurisdiction and the recognition and enforcement of judgments in → civil and commercial matters, as inaugurated by the Brussels Convention (Brussels Convention of 27 September 1968 on jurisdiction and the enforcement of judgments in civil and commercial matters, [1972] OJ L 299/32, consolidated version, [1998] OJ C 27/1) (→ Brussels I (Convention and Regulation)), is particularly significant in this respect and deserves to be analysed in some detail.

For a long time, the *lex causae* approach has been the key reference in this context, following a seminal decision by the Court of Justice of the European Communities (as it was named then). In *Tessili* (Case 12/76 *Industrie Tessili Italiana Como v Dunlop AG* [1976] ECR 1473), the Court was asked to clarify the meaning of the expression 'place of performance of the obligation in question', as employed in art 5(1) of the Brussels Convention. The Court began by observing that the Convention frequently uses words and legal concepts drawn from civil, commercial and procedural law and capable of a different meaning from one Member State to another, and acknowledged that the question arises whether these words and concepts must be regarded as having their own independent meaning or as referring to substantive rules of the applicable law, as specified by the rules of conflict of laws of the forum. That said, having regard to the differences between national laws and 'to the absence at this stage of legal development of any unification in the substantive law applicable', the Court found that it was impossible to give 'any more substantial guide' to the interpretation of the notion of 'place of performance', adding that this was 'all the more true since the determination of the place of performance of obligations depends on the contractual context to which these obligations belong'. In the end, it held that the concept of place of performance 'cannot be understood otherwise than by reference to the substantive law applicable under the rules of conflict of laws of the court before which the matter is brought'. In practice, according to the Court of Justice, the national court seized of the matter should first determine, in conformity with the conflict-of-laws rules of the forum, the law applicable to the substance of the case; then, in order to ascertain its entitlement to decide the case on the merits, it should verify whether, in accordance with that law, the obligation in dispute was to be performed within its jurisdiction.

The solution has been the object of strong criticism. The *Tessili* approach, apart from being practically complicated, was felt by many to be at odds with two basic policies underlying the Brussels regime. On the one hand, the Court's solution was considered to jeopardize the goal of uniformity by making the identification of the competent court ultimately contingent on rules that may vary from country to country: the conflict-of-laws rules of the forum (which had not yet been unified in Europe at the time of the Court's judgment) and the substantive rules on performance, as laid down in the *lex causae*. On the other, especially as far as money obligations were concerned, *Tessili* was considered to be likely to give rise to 'abstract' results, ie to allow jurisdiction to be granted to courts displaying a tenuous, if not fortuitous, connection with the subject matter of the dispute, or at least to allow jurisdiction to be conferred upon courts other than those featuring the most significant connection with the case at hand, whereas the opposite should happen under the principles of proximity and predictability on which 'special' jurisdiction is meant to be based.

Although these arguments have lost some of their weight over time, namely due to the unification of conflict-of-laws rules on → contractual obligations performed by the Rome Convention (Rome Convention on the law applicable to contractual obligations (consolidated version), [1998] OJ C 27/34), the predecessor of the Rome I Regulation (and, on a different note, by the Court's opinion whereby the place of performance shall be identified for the purpose of jurisdiction in accordance with internationally uniform rules of substantive law, where applicable in the forum to the case at hand: Case C-288/92 *Custom Made Commercial Ltd v Stawa Metallbau GmbH* [1994] ECR I-2913), the defects of *Tessili* became a serious concern for the European legislator and an autonomous solution was sought.

In 2000, when the Convention was replaced by the Brussels I Regulation (Regulation (EC) No 44/2001 of 22 December 2000 on jurisdiction and the recognition and enforcement of judgments in civil and commercial matters, [2001] OJ L 12/1; → Brussels I (Convention and Regulation)), the rule on special jurisdiction in contracts was amended. A compromise was reached between those advocating the pure and simple deletion of the old rule and those persuaded that the rule still served an important practical need and changes would have hardly made it better. The resulting provision, almost left unchanged by the recast brought about by the Brussels I Regulation (recast), establishes that jurisdiction in contracts is still granted, as a rule, to 'the courts for the place of performance of the obligation in question' (art 5(1)(a) of the Brussels I Regulation, corresponding to art 7(1)(a) of the Brussels I Regulation (recast)). However, it is now specified that, unless otherwise agreed, the place of performance of the obligation in question shall be, 'in the case of the sale of goods, the place in a Member State where, under the contract, the goods were delivered or should have been delivered', and, 'in the case of the provision of services, the place in a Member State where, under the contract, the services were provided or should have been provided': art 5(1)(b) of the Brussels I Regulation, corresponding to art 7(1)(b) of the Brussels I Regulation (recast).

While the 'traditional' interpretation of the rule remains in force for cases falling solely under the 'old' rule in (a) (as the Court of Justice explicitly confirmed in *Falco*: Case C-533/07 *Falco Privatstiftung and Thomas Rabitsch v Gisela Weller-Lindhorst* [2009] ECR I-3327), a two-fold innovation has been introduced for cases covered by (b). On the one hand, contrary to the 'analytical' approach followed by the Court of Justice since its early case-law, the only relevant obligation for jurisdictional purposes is now – in disputes relating to a sale of goods or a provisions of services – the 'characteristic' obligation of the contract (respectively, the obligation to supply the goods or to provide the services). This way, the difficulties caused by the 'abstract' character of the criteria used for the identification of the place of performance of money obligation have no longer reasons to arise. On the other hand, the place of performance of the characteristic obligation itself is no longer to be determined, in cases falling under (b), in accordance with the *lex causae*. The place of delivery and the place of the provision of services, as the Court clarified, must be treated as a factual notion, calling for a 'pragmatic' assessment. Thus, in determining the place where the goods should be delivered to the buyer in the case of a sale involving the carriage of the goods by an independent carrier, one should not look at the rules indicating where delivery is to be effected for substantive purposes (eg, art 31(a) of the → CISG on contracts for the international sale of goods, providing that, absent an agreement by the parties, delivery shall consist in handing the goods over to the first carrier for transmission to the buyer'; see also, for a similar solution, art 93(1)(b)(i) of the proposed Common European Sales Law (CESL-D, Proposal of 11 October 2011 for a Regulation of the European Parliament and of the European Council on a Common European Sales Law COM(2011) 635 final)); rather, one should consider the delivery to be due at the place 'where the physical transfer of the goods took place, as a result of which the purchaser obtained, or should have obtained, actual power of disposal over those goods at the final destination of the sales transaction' (Case C-381/08 *Car Trim GmbH v KeySafety Systems Srl* [2010] OJ C 100/4).

It is debatable whether the new approach is entirely satisfying. Simple cases are now likely to receive clear and 'direct' answers, but where hard cases arise a rather 'creative' attitude is apparently required from the interpreter. As a matter of fact, while the possibility of relying on the applicable substantive law is formally excluded by the Court, the Regulation (as well as EU law at large) still lacks a complete set of autonomous standards capable of determining the place of performance in the diverse scenarios that may actually arise in practice.

One example of the kind of creativity required to address the subtleties of the localization of performance is represented by the judgment of the Court of Justice in *Wood Floor Solutions* (Case C-19/09 *Wood Floor Solutions Andreas Domberger GmbH v Silva Trade SA* [2010] OJ C 113/14). The Court had been asked to clarify how the place of performance of the relevant obligation should be determined in a case relating to a commercial agency agreement (→ Commercial agency, franchise and distribution contracts) under which the agent had undertaken to provide his services in more than one country. In the Court's view, the place of the main provision of services by the agent, as it appears from the provisions of the contract, should be regarded as decisive. In this connection, if the provisions of a contract do not enable the place of the main provision of services to be determined, but the agent has already provided such services, it is appropriate, in the alternative, to take account of the place where he has in fact for the most part carried out his activities in the performance of the contract, provided that the provision of services in that place is not contrary to the parties' intentions as it appears from the provisions of the contract. For that purpose, the factual aspects of the case may be taken into consideration, including the time spent in those places and the importance of the activities carried out there. However, if the place of the main provision of services cannot be determined on that basis, it must be regarded as the place where the commercial agent is domiciled: that place can always be identified with certainty and has a link of proximity with the dispute, since the agent will in all likelihood provide a substantial part of his services there. The Court's instructions, far from being a 'neutral' narration of the relevant facts, are very similar to a set of rules: they may not formally qualify as rules, but their nature is in fact that of 'normative' standards. By the way, the transition from 'dependency' to 'autonomy' could hardly be achieved without setting new norms: what is at stake, in spite of the modesty and understatement of the Court, is not in fact a shift from 'rules' to 'facts', but rather a shift from national rules – those of the *lex causae* – to uniform standards, ie those 'discovered' by the Court of Justice in the laconic wording of the Regulation (Pietro Franzina, 'Struttura e funzionamento del foro europeo della materia contrattuale alla luce delle sentenze Car Trim e Wood Floor della Corte di giustizia' (2010) 46 Riv.Dir.Int'le Priv. & Proc. 669 ff).

One would be tempted to say that difficulties of this kind are confined to the cases where no agreement has been entered into by the parties regarding the place of performance of the relevant obligation. In reality, while it is true that agreed solutions will often make the picture significantly clearer for jurisdictional purposes, delicate issues are likely to arise in some instances that require to be decided, here too, in accordance with normative standards. In particular, the validity of the agreement on the *locus solutionis* may be challenged, and doubts may exist as to the precise interpretation of ambiguous expressions used by the parties. Here, too, the case-law of the Court of Justice reflects the difficulty of abandoning the old paradigm of the *lex causae* in favour of autonomy. The initial view of the Court, at least as far as validity is concerned, was that the *Tessili* approach should be followed: in *Zelger* (Case 56/79 *Siegfried Zelger v Sebastiano Salinitri* [1980] ECR 89), the Court acknowledged that an agreement on the place of performance 'is sufficient to found jurisdiction in that place', but added that this may happen only where the parties 'are permitted by the law applicable to the contract, subject to any conditions imposed by that law, to specify the place of performance of an obligation without satisfying any special condition of form'. More recently, however, in a case falling under the 'innovative' rules on contracts for the sale of goods and the provision of services, the Court, faced with a problem of interpretation of an agreement relating to the place of delivery (allegedly made by way of incorporation in the contract of sale at hand of terms generally recognized and applied through the usages of international trade or commerce), avoided referring to the law applicable to the substance of the contract (although this represents the obvious reference when deciding issues of contract interpretation: see, *inter alia*, art 12(1)(a) of the Rome I Regulation), and rather suggested the use of autonomous standards aimed at establishing whether the trade terms employed by the parties are capable of 'clearly' identifying the place of delivery (Case C-87/10 Electrosteel Europe SA v Edil Centro SpA [2011] OJ C 226/6).

Pietro Franzina

Literature

Yeşim M. Atamer, 'Performance and its Modalities' in Jürgen Basedow and others (eds), *Max Planck Encyclopedia of European Private Law* (OUP 2012); Dagmar Coester-Waltjen, 'Der Erfüllungsort im internationalen Zivilprozessrecht' in Reinhold Geimer and Rolf A Schütze (eds), *Recht ohne Grenzen – Festschrift für Athanassios Kaissis zum 65. Geburtstag* (Sellier 2012) 91; Hortense Fabre-Dubout, *La localisation du contrat entre lieux et espace* (Presses Universitaires d'Aix-Marseille 2007); Franco Ferrari, 'Remarks on the Autonomous Interpretation of the Brussels I Regulation, in Particular of the Concept of "Place of Delivery" under Article 5(1)(b), and the Vienna Sales Convention (on the Occasion of a Recent Italian Court Decision)' [2007] Rev.Droit.Aff.Int'les 83; Thomas Kadner Graziano, 'Jurisdiction Under Article 7 No. 1 of the Recast Brussels I Regulation: Disconnecting the Procedural Place of Performance From Its Counterpart in Substantive Law. An Analysis of the Case Law of the ECJ and Proposals *De Lege Lata* and *De Lege Ferrenda*' (2014–15) 16 YBPIL 167; Stefan Leible, 'Der Erfüllungsort iSv Art. 5 Nr. 1 lit. b Brüssel I-VO: ein Mysterium?' in Jörn Bernreuther and others (eds), *Festschrift für Ulrich Spellenberg* (Sellier 2010) 451; Chengwei Liu, 'Place of Performance: Comparative Analysis of Article 31 and 57 of the CISG and Counterpart Provisions in Article 7:101 of the PECL' in John Felemegas (ed), *An International Approach to the Interpretation of the United Nations Convention on Contracts for the International Sale of Goods (1980) as Uniform Sales Law* (CUP 2007) 346; Gian Paolo Romano, 'Le for au lieu de l'exécution dans la jurisprudence récente de la Cour de Justice de l'Union européenne' in Andrea Bonomi and others (eds), *Nouvelle procédure civile et espace judiciaire européen – Actes du Colloque de Lausanne du 27 janvier 2012* (Librairie Droz 2012) 63; Haimo Schack, *Der Erfüllungsort im deutschen, ausländischen und internationalen Privat- und Zivilprozessrecht* (Metzner 1985); Walter A. Stoffel, 'Place of Performance-Jurisdiction and Plaintiffs Interests in Contemporary Societies' (2002) 4 E.J.L.R. 185.

Prescription

I. Concept and notion

1. Prescription as the extinction of a right or as a bar to a remedy and related notions

Prescription is an area of law with a widely divergent terminology between legal systems. The purpose of this short introduction is to establish the terminology used in this entry.

a) Prescription (or limitation)
'Prescription' (also called 'limitation') limits the amount of time during which a claim can be pursued by means of a court order. The notion of prescription is known in all legal systems. Some legal systems limit its scope to claims stemming from the law of obligations; consequently their choice-of-law rules are limited in scope as well. In other national private law systems, all claims are subject to prescription. This includes claims that arise in family law, the law of succession, property law (→ Property and proprietary rights), etc. Some frameworks extend the notion of prescription to apply to rights to alter a legal relationship and to defences as well (eg art 10.1(1) UNIDROIT Principles (International Institute for the Unification of Private Law/Institut international pour l'unification du droit privé (ed), *UNIDROIT Principles of International Commercial Contracts 2010* (3rd edn, UNIDROIT 2010)).

In continental legal systems, prescription (Dutch: *verjaring*, French: *prescription*, German: *Verjährung*, Italian: *prescrizione*, Portugese: *prescrição*, Spanish: *prescripción*) in this sense does not extinguish a right; it only restricts the exercise of the right (see for a comparison with the common law approach *Don v Lippmann* [1837] 5 Cl.& F. 1, 19, 20 (HL); see also Alexander Anton, Paul Beaumont and Peter McEleavy, *Private international law* (3rd edn, W. Green 2011) 27.23; on the distinction see Ernst Rabel, *The Conflict of Laws: A Comparative Study*, vol 3 (2nd edn, University of Michigan Press 1964) 500). The debtor receives a right to refuse performance (for a comparative perspective, see Reinhard Zimmermann, *Comparative Foundations of a European Law of Set-Off and Prescription* (CUP 2002) 62 f; Bénédicte Fauvarque-Cosson, 'Aspects de droit comparé de la prescription' in Patrick Courbe, *Les désordres de la prescription. Colloque tenu au Palais de justice de Rouen, 4 février 1999* (Publications de l'Université de Rouen et du Havre 2000) 45; on soft law (DCFR (Study Group on a European Civil Code and Research Group on EC Private Law (Acquis Group) (ed), *Principles, Definitions and Model Rules of European Private Law, Draft Common Frame of Reference (DCFR)* (Full Edition, Sellier 2009), PECL (Ole Lando and Hugh Beale, *Principles of European Contract Law* (Parts I and II, Kluwer Law International 1999)), UNIDROIT Principles; on uniform law: Reinhard Zimmermann, 'Prescription' in Jürgen Basedow and others (eds), *Max Planck Encyclopedia of European Private Law* (OUP 2012) 1308–9; on limitation in the CESL see Jens Kleinschmidt, 'Einheitliche Verjährungsregeln für Europa? Zu den Gewährleistungsfristen im Vorschlag für ein Gemeinsames Europäisches Kaufrecht' (2013) 213 AcP 538).

b) Praescriptio acquisitiva and extinctiva
Modern private law has long distinguished between *praescriptio acquisitiva* (adverse possession, acquisitive prescription) and *extinctiva* (prescription) (see Andreas Piekenbrock, *Befristung, Verjährung, Verschweigung und Verwirkung* (Mohr Siebeck 2006) 138–42). The term 'extinctive prescription' does not necessarily imply that the claim is extinguished. It equally encompasses cases where prescription works as a bar to a remedy (cf art 2921 Civil Code of Québec (L.Q. 1991, ch 64)). Both varieties of prescription are still commonly treated together. Acquisition by prescription is nowadays a question of property law. In conflict of laws, it is a question of international property law (→Property and proprietary rights; see especially Guido Carducci, 'Acquisition a non domino, prescription acquisitive, possession vaut titre, conflit mobile et circulation d'une res extra commercium' in *Travaux du Comité Français de Droit International Privé, 2013–14* (Comité Français de Droit International Privé 2015) 137 ff). This entry deals with extinctive prescription and the term 'prescription' is used to denote this notion.

c) Estoppel and Verwirkung
The lapse of the relevant time period is sufficient for the prescription to take effect. No further requirements apply. This distinguishes prescription from the notion of *Verwirkung* that is known in legal systems such as German law. The latter notion refers to the extinction of the right in cases where the claimant is said to act disloyally in bringing his claim too late; this is a manifestation of the principle of good faith. Equity's notion of → estoppel by laches is similar (Peter Hay, 'Die Qualifikation der Verjährung im US-amerikanischen Kollisionsrecht' [1989] IPRax

197 with fn 1) (*infra* II.4.). Romanic legal systems have the notion of the *rinuncia tacita* or *renoncation tacite* (for a comparative overview see Michael Will, 'Verwirkung im internationalen Privatrecht' (1978) 42 RabelsZ 211; Gerhard Kegel, 'Verwirkung, Vertrag, Vertrauen' in Paul Hofmann, Ulrich Meyer-Cording and Herbert Wiedemann (eds), *Festschrift für Klemens Pleyer* (Carl Heymanns 1986) 513, 528 f).

d) Preclusion
Other than the periods of prescription, there are periods that extinguish a right once the period has lapsed (Ernst Rabel, *The Conflict of Laws: A Comparative Study*, vol 3 (2nd edn, University of Michigan Press 1964) 500 f). Within the Germanic legal family, these are known as *Ausschlussfristen*; in French law, they are called *délai préfix, forclusion* (Daniel Girsberger, *Verjährung und Verwirkung im internationalen Obligationenrecht* (Schulthess 1989) 30; Ernst Rabel, *The Conflict of Laws: A Comparative Study*, vol 3 (2nd edn, University of Michigan Press 1964) 500) or *déchéances fondées sur l'expiration d'un délai*. In Spanish, they are referred to as *caducidad basadas en la expiracion de un plazo* (see art 12(1)(d) Rome I Regulation (Regulation (EC) No 593/2008 of the European Parliament and of the Council of 17 June 2008 on the law applicable to contractual obligations (Rome I), [2008] OJ L 177/6; → Rome Convention and Rome I Regulation (contractual obligations)). In Anglo-American law, no term has been established unanimously to correspond to *Ausschlussfristen*. The expressions 'preclusion' (Ernst Rabel, *The Conflict of Laws: A Comparative Study*, vol 3 (2nd edn, University of Michigan Press 1964) 500) and 'substantive time limit' or 'statutes of response' are used; only occasionally the term 'prescription' is utilized (Daniel Girsberger, *Verjährung und Verwirkung im internationalen Obligationenrecht* (Schulthess 1989) 30).

e) Statutory use of the terminology
International use of the terms 'prescription' and 'limitation' is not always unambiguous. In art 12(d) Rome I Regulation and art 15(h) → Rome II Regulation (non-contractual obligations) (Regulation (EC) No 864/2007 of the European Parliament and of the Council of 11 July 2007 on the law applicable to non-contractual obligations (Rome II), [2007] OJ L 199/40) as well as in art 11(e) Hague Maintenance Protocol 2007 (Hague Protocol of 23 November 2007 on the law applicable to maintenance obligations, [2009] OJ L 331/19), 'prescription' refers to *Verjährung* – that is, the defence against a claim being made, but not the extinction of an obligation (on this distinction see further Lord Collins of Mapesbury and others (eds), *Dicey, Morris & Collins on the Conflict of Laws* (15th edn, Sweet & Maxwell 2012) 7.55–7.57). The term 'prescription' is used in this sense here as well.

In both regulations, 'limitation', on the other hand, refers to preclusions. The German and the French versions of art 12(1)(d) Rome I Regulation are not phrased in terms of 'limitation of actions', but speak of *'Rechtsverluste[e], die sich aus dem Ablauf einer Frist ergeben'* and *'déchéances fondées sur l'expiration d'un délai'*, respectively.

In art 15(h) Rome II Regulation, the German version translates 'limitation' as *'Rechtsverluste'* and the French version translates it as *'déchéance fondées sur l'expiration d'un délai'* (see I.1.). Similarly, art 11(e) Hague Maintenance Protocol 2007 uses *'les délais pour intenter une action'* in French and *'die für die Einleitung eines Verfahrens geltenden Fristen'* in German. This refers to substantive periods of preclusion (Kurt Siehr, 'art 11 Unterhaltsprotokoll' in Jan von Hein (ed), *Münchener Kommentar zum Bürgerlichen Gesetzbuch, Band 10: Internationales Privatrecht I, Europäisches Kollisionsrecht, Einführungsgesetz zum Bürgerlichen Gesetzbuche (Art 1–24)*, vol 10 (6th edn, CH Beck 2015) para 104). The laws applicable to prescription, *Ausschlussfristen*, and *Verwirkung* should be determined using the same connecting factor to avoid problems of classification (*infra* II.4.; → Classification (characterization)).

2. Procedural understanding: limitation of action

Prescription was originally a notion of procedural law. An action could only be brought within a certain deadline. If the period had lapsed, an action could not be brought, but the suit would be dismissed without prejudice (Peter Hay, 'Die Qualifikation der Verjährung im US-amerikanischen Kollisionsrecht' [1989] IPRax 197 f; Daniel Girsberger, *Verjährung und Verwirkung im internationalen Obligationenrecht* (Schulthess 1989) 29); if another action was brought, the defence of *res iudicata* is unavailable (see for example Restatement (Second) of Conflict of Laws (American Law Institute, Restatement of the Law, Second: Conflict of Laws 2d, St Paul 1971) (→ Restatement (First and Second) of Conflict of Laws) § 110; *Keeton v Hustler* 465 U.S. 770 (1984)). While this is no longer uniformly the Anglo-American position, many jurisdictions still follow this rule. They deem a limitation of action to be a matter of procedural law if the modern statute law does not provide otherwise (on this and on reform approaches see Peter Hay, 'Die Qualifikation der Verjährung im US-amerikanischen Kollisionsrecht' [1989] IPRax 197 f; Daniel Girsberger, *Verjährung und Verwirkung im internationalen Obligationenrecht* (Schulthess 1989) 29).

3. Substantive law understanding: prescription of claim

The civil law initially shared this procedural understanding (*supra* I.2.). Only under the influence of *Bernhard Windscheid* (*Die actio des römischen Civilrechts vom Standpunkte des heutigen Rechts* (1856)) has the substantive classification of prescription replaced this procedural understanding, first in Germany, then in most other continental legal systems (see Ernst Rabel, *The Conflict of Laws: A Comparative Study*, vol 3 (2nd edn, University of Michigan Press 1964) 492; Reinhard Zimmermann, 'Prescription' in Jürgen Basedow and others (eds), *Max Planck Encyclopedia of European Private Law* (OUP 2012) 1306–10) and, subsequently, in many legal systems throughout Latin America, Asia, and Africa that descend from continental legal systems. Under this → classification (characterization), prescription results in a substantive defence against the enforceability of a substantive claim. This is also called 'liberative prescription'. The claim continues to exist (*supra* I.1.), but an order requiring performance of the obligation would be without merit on the level of substantive law. Understood this way, 'liberative prescription' is synonymous with 'extinctive prescription' (*supra* I.1.b)) and unless otherwise indicated, the term 'prescription' alone is meant to denote this variety of prescription.

II. Determining the law applicable to prescription

1. The general principle in civil law jurisdictions

a) Principle: prescription follows the claim

The law governing a claim or a right, referred to as the 'proper law', also governs its prescription. This is nowadays a generally accepted connection principle in civil law jurisdictions.

Therefore, the law governing a contract also governs prescription of the contractual claim, the applicable property law governs prescription in property law (→ Property and proprietary rights), the law governing a family law claim governs its prescription, and so forth. This expresses a just balance of interests; because of the close connection between the creation of a right and the content of this right, the laws of the jurisdiction that governs the creation of a claim or a right should also govern its temporal limit.

Friedrich Carl von Savigny (→ Savigny, Friedrich Carl von) already made the same proposition in the seventh volume of his 'System of the Modern Roman Law' with regards to the law of obligations and was able to assert that this position was 'acknowledged as the right one at all times by a not insignificant number of jurists' (Friedrich Carl von Savigny, *System des heutigen römischen Rechts* (Veit und Comp 1849) § 374 III ('Obligationenrecht') – for particular questions see pages 273–5). He explicitly rejected the other, older position that would have resulted in an application of the → *lex fori* because it classified the rules of prescription as 'procedural rules'. Furthermore, the application of the proper law over the *lex fori* approach entailed the additional advantage of avoiding both arbitrary forum shopping by claimants wanting to avail themselves of a longer period of prescription, and a change of residence by defendants willing to submit to the personal jurisdiction of courts with a short period of prescription (Friedrich Carl von Savigny, *System des heutigen römischen Rechts* (Veit und Comp 1849) 274 f).

b) Current rules in national statutes

Against this historical background it is not surprising that in civil law jurisdictions, the proper law of the claim or right also governs prescription. In most national conflict of laws codifications, this is laid down in a discrete rule. The following rules can be listed as examples: art 2671 Argentine Civil and Commercial Code (enacted by Law of Congress No 29.994 of 1 October 2014, signed into law on 7 October 2014, Official Gazette No 32.985); art 1283 Armenian Civil Code (Civil Code of Armenia as adopted in 1998, Division 12, arts 1253–93, [2009] IPRax 99); art 19(1) Act of the Republic of Azerbaijan on Private international law ([2003] IPRax 389); art 40 Civil Code of Angola (Jan Kropholler and others (eds), *Außereuropäische IPR-Gesetze* (Deutsches Notarinstitut 1999) 50); art 1012 Act on Civil Status and Family of Burkina Faso (Jan Kropholler and others (eds), *Außereuropäische IPR-Gesetze* 139); art 7 Chinese Statute of Application of Law to Foreign Civil Relations (adopted at the 17th session of the Standing Committee of the 11th National

People's Congress on 28 October 2010, effective 1 April 2011, [2011] IPRax 203); art 1106(1) Civil Code of the Republic of Kazakhstan; art 1.59 Civil Code of the Republic of Lithuania ([2003] IPRax 305); art 8 Macedonian Law on Private international law ([2008] IPRax 158); art 542 Mongolian Civil Code ([2003] IPRax 382); art 25 (general rule), art 48(no 5) (contract), art 64(no 8) (involuntary obligations), and art 97(no 5) Montenegrin Act of 23 December 2013 on Private international law ([2014] IPRax 558, 561, 563, 566); art 40 Civil Code of Mozambique (Jan Kropholler and others (eds), *Außereuropäische IPR-Gesetze* 587); art 14 Book 10 Dutch New Civil Code (Nieuw Burgerlijk Wetboek of 1 January 1992, [2013] IPRax 585); art 14 Código de Derecho Internacional Privado de la República de Panamá (Ley 7 de 8 mayo de 2014 que adopta el Código de Derecho Internacional Privado de la República de Panamá, Gaceta Oficial Digital (available at <www.gacetaoficial.gob.pa>) No 27530 of 8 May 2014); art 26 Polish Private international law Act (Official Journal 2011 No 80, pos 432, [2011] IPRax 611); art 2099 Civil Code of Peru (Jan Kropholler and others (eds), *Außereuropäische IPR-Gesetze* 701); art 3131 Civil Code of Québec (L.Q. 1991, ch 64; Jan Kropholler and others (eds), *Außereuropäische IPR-Gesetze* 371); art 1208 Civil Code of the Russian Federation (as amended by Federal Law No 260-FZ on 30 September 2013, [2002] IPRax 329); art 148(1) Swiss Private international law Act (Bundesgesetz über das Internationale Privatrecht of 18 December 1987, 1988 BBl I 5, as amended); art 8 Slovenian Private international law Act 1999 (Zakon o mednarodnem zasebnem pravu in postopku, Uradni list Republike Slovenije, No 56/1999 of 13 July 1999, [2003] IPRax 163); art 46 Czech Private international law Act (Act No 91/2012 Sb, on private international law, [2014] IPRax 97); art 8 Turkish Private international law Code (Code on Private International and International Civil Procedure Law of 27 November 2007 (Act No 5718), Resmî Gazete No 26728 of 12 December 2007, [2008] IPRax 254); art 1183(1) Civil Code of the Republic of Uzbekistan (Jan Kropholler and others (eds), *Außereuropäische IPR-Gesetze* 937); and art 1118(1) Civil Code of Belarus (Law No 218-Z of 7 December 1998, [2000] IPRax 152). Both the previous French law (Bénédicte Fauvarque-Cosson, 'La prescription en droit international privé' in *Travaux du Comité Français de Droit International Privé* (LGDJ 2004) 235, 239 ff) and the current one (art 2221 Code civil des Français, reformed in 2016) subject prescription to the law governing the claim or right in question (Bernard Audit and Louis d'Avout, *Droit International Privé* (7th edn, Economica 2013) 502).

The South American codifications are often influenced – and occasionally superseded – by the Montevideo Treaty on International Civil Law (Treaty of Montevideo of 12 February 1889 on international civil law (Germán Cavelier Gaviria, *Tratados de Colombia*, vol 2 (Kelly 1984) 111–28) amended by the treaty of 19 March 1940). According to this treaty, the proper law governs prescription, because the law governing contractual and extra-contractual obligations governs prescription of these claims, while property claims are governed by the *lex rei sitae* (art 51, 52). Articles 229, 230 Bustamante Code (Convention on Private international law (Bustamante Code), adopted at Havana on 20 February 1928 at the Sixth International Conference of American States; OAS, Law And Treaty Series, No 34) had established a similar rule before the Montevideo Treaty on International Civil Law was amended in 1940.

The national conflict rules are often included in the section governing general questions of private international law (eg the conflict of law rules of → China, the → Netherlands, → Poland and → Slovenia). Occasionally, the scope of these rules is limited to contractual claims or claims within the law of obligations (see for example → Lithuania's private international law codification).

c) Current rules in European law: scope of application rather than separate connection
The rule determining the applicable prescription law can be understood as not being a discrete conflict rule in the form of an accessory connection (→ Connecting factor), linking the applicable prescription law with the law governing the claim or right (despite the fact that it commonly takes this form in most laws); instead, this rule for prescription describes the substantive scope of application (German: *Anknüpfungsgegenstand*) of the connection that establishes the proper law of the claim or right. This has been recognized by → Kegel, Gerhard (Gerhard Kegel, *Die Grenze von Qualifikation und Renvoi im internationalen Verjährungsrecht* (Westdeutscher Verlag 1962) 13). Similarly, → *Savigny, Friedrich Carl von* emphasized that the proper law of the obligation should also govern prescription because prescription and the object of prescription are closely connected (*supra* II.1.a)).

It thus follows that the Rome I (→ Rome Convention and Rome I Regulation (contractual obligations)) and → Rome II Regulation (non-contractual obligations) provide that the law applicable to a contract or to non-contractual obligations under the respective Regulation shall govern in particular 'the various ways of extinguishing obligations, and prescription and limitation of actions' (art 12(1)(d) Rome I Regulation) and 'the manner in which an obligation may be extinguished and rules of prescription and limitation, including rules relating to the commencement, interruption and suspension of a period of prescription or limitation' (art 15(h) Rome II Regulation). The conflict of laws question of how to connect prescription is framed in terms of the scope of the proper law of the obligation. Similarly, art 11(e) Hague Maintenance Protocol 2007 provides that the law applicable to the → maintenance obligations shall determine prescription or limitation periods. Similarly, art 8(8) Hague Traffic Accident Convention (Hague Convention of 4 May 1971 on the law applicable to traffic accidents, 965 UNTS 415) provides the law governing the tort claim governs rules of prescription and limitation.

In a similar way, a few national laws determine the applicable prescription laws by defining the scope of application of the proper law of the claim or right. The Montenegrin Act of 23 December 2013 on Private international law is structured this way. A general rule on prescription (art 25) is complemented by special rules that incorporate art 12(1)(d) Rome I Regulation, art 15(h) Rome II Regulation and art 11(e) Hague Maintenance Protocol 2007 into national law. See art 48 no 5 (contract), art 64 no 8 (involuntary obligations) and art 97 no 5 of the Montenegrin Act.

d) Particular rules
Some national codifications provide special rules complementing the general rules described in section II.1.b). For example, there are particular → public policy (*ordre public*) rules. The connection with the forum state – which is a necessary condition for the *ordre public* to apply – is codified. For example, art 1118(2) Civil Code of → Belarus provides that claims that never expire according to the law applicable on prescription do expire according to the laws of Belarus if one party of the legal relationship is a national of Belarus or a comparable legal person. A comparable rule is contained in art 1106(2) Civil Code of the Republic of Kazakhstan. Article 19(2) of the Act of the Republic of Azerbaijan on Private international law ([2003] IPRax 388) ensures the non-expiry of a claim if the aforementioned domestic connection exists. A similar rule can be found in art 1183(2) Civil Code of the Republic of Uzbekistan (Jan Kropholler and others (eds), *Außereuropäische IPR-Gesetze* 937).

Different connections are rarely codified in civil law jurisdictions, but an example that can be given is art 26 Civil Code of Costa Rica (Jan Kropholler and others (eds), *Außereuropäische IPR-Gesetze* 207): where the obligation is to be fulfilled in Costa Rica, the prescription law of Costa Rica applies.

The EU Commission announced an initiative to change the → Rome II Regulation (non-contractual obligations) in 2011 (European Commission, 'Communication from the Commission to the European Parliament, the Council, the Economic and Social Committee and the Committee of Regions: Strengthening Victims' Rights in the EU' COM(2011) 274 final, p 7). The Commission is concerned that victims of → traffic accidents are unable to pursue their claims for compensation because they are surprised by the 'particularly short limitation or prescription periods in the Member State[s] where the accident[s] occurred'. Therefore, the Commission intends to amend the Rome II Regulation for the benefit of the victims, to the effect that the 'limitation periods of their home countr[ies]' shall apply. To date, this initiative has not been pursued further. Using the habitual residence of a victim as a connecting factor could be problematic because it would not be foreseeable for the tortfeasor; it would also subject the claims of victims residing in different countries to different prescription regimes.

2. Principle in common law jurisdictions

a) Prescription follows the lex fori
The common law has traditionally perceived prescription as a concept of procedural law (*supra* I.2.). As a result, the prescription laws of the → *lex fori* have been and predominantly continue to be applied today (on English law see Lord Collins of Mapesbury and others (eds), *Dicey, Morris & Collins on the Conflict of Laws* (15th edn, Sweet & Maxwell 2012) 7.45; on American law see Peter Hay, 'Die Qualifikation der Verjährung im US-amerikanischen Kollisionsrecht' [1989] IPRax 197 f; on the history of the *lex fori* connection in international prescription law see Margaret R. Grossman, 'Statutes of Limitations and the Conflict of Laws: Modern Analysis' [1980] Ariz.St.L.J. 1; Gerhard Kegel, *Die Grenze*

von Qualifikation und Renvoi im internationalen Verjährungsrecht (Westdeutscher Verlag 1962) 19–22, 27 f (both with further references)). But calls for a substantive law classification – and consequently an application of the prescription laws of the proper law of the claim or right – have been voiced by a number of courts in common law jurisdictions, particularly → Australia, → Canada, England and the → USA (Lord Collins of Mapesbury and others (eds), *Dicey, Morris & Collins on the Conflict of Laws* (15th edn, Sweet & Maxwell 2012) 7.45, 7.47; Peter Hay, 'Die Qualifikation der Verjährung im US-amerikanischen Kollisionsrecht' [1989] IPRax 197 f).

b) Developments in statutory law: prescription follows the proper law of the claim or right
The last few decades have seen a change in statutory law. In the conflict of laws regimes of the → United Kingdom of Great Britain and Northern Ireland and the → USA, new statutory prescription rules for statutory rights of actions (ie causes of action created by statute) are usually characterized as being rules of substantive law (for the UK see Lord Collins of Mapesbury and others (eds), *Dicey, Morris & Collins on the Conflict of Laws* (15th edn, Sweet & Maxwell 2012) 7.45; for the USA see Peter Hay, 'Die Qualifikation der Verjährung im US-amerikanischen Kollisionsrecht' [1989] IPRax 197, 198; for an analysis as to whether the Belgian law of prescription is procedural law or substantive law see *Ramsay v Boeing Co*, 432 F.2d 592, 599 (5th Cir 1970); see also Peter Hay, Patrick Borchers and Symeon Symeonides, *Conflict of Laws* (5th edn, West Academic Publishing 2010) 156))). An important change was brought about by the UK Foreign Limitation Periods Act 1984 (c 16); the act provides 'for any law relating to the limitation of actions to be treated, for the purposes of cases in which effect is given to foreign law or to determinations by foreign courts, as a matter of substance rather than as a matter of procedure' (Foreign Limitation Periods Act 1984, preamble). This brought British law in line with the substantive classification provided by art 10(1)(d) Rome Convention (Rome Convention on the law applicable to contractual obligations (consolidated version), [1998] OJ C 27/34), which has been replaced by art 12(1)(d) Rome I Regulation. The Foreign Limitation Periods Act 1984 has been adopted by the legislators in New Zealand (New Zealand Limitations Amendment Act (1996, no 131)) and in the Australian state of New South Wales (Limitation Periods) Act (1993, no 94).

The procedural classification prevails in the US, but is questioned occasionally. The National Conference of Commissioners on Uniform State Laws passed a model law on international prescription law in 1982. This Uniform Conflict of Laws – Limitations Act (1982) (see 12 ULA, Uniform Conflict of Laws – Limitations Act) follows the proper law principle (→ Proper law (doctrine)). Section 4 Uniform Conflict of Laws – Limitations Act contains a kind of escape provision, in the form of a particular *ordre public* provision. According to this provision, the prescription law of the → *lex fori* can be applied if the proper law of the claim or right does not allow a fair pursuit of the claim. This model law is, however, far from being successful. Only Colorado (1984, Colo. Rev. Stat. § 13-82-101 to 13-82-107), Minnesota (2004, s 541.31 Minnesota Statutes), Montana (Mont. Code § 27-2-501 *et seq*), Nebraska (2006, LB 1115), North Dakota (1985, N.D. Cent. Code §§ 28-01.2-01 to 28-01.2-05), Oregon (1987, Or. Rev. Stat. § 12.410 ff) and Washington (1983, Wash. Rev. Code § 4.18.010 to 4.18.904) have adopted the model law. Arkansas adopted it in 1985 (Ark. Stat. Ann. §§ 37–301 to 37–307), but repealed it in 1999 (see <www.uniformlaws.org/Legislation.asp>; Peter Hay, Patrick Borchers and Symeon Symeonides, *Conflict of Laws* (5th edn, West Academic Publishing 2010) 154 f).

The new version of the § 142 Restatement (Second) of Conflict of Laws, which was adopted in 1988, has opted for a varied rule which favours the → *lex fori* over the → proper law (doctrine) of the claim or right (see Peter Hay, 'Die Qualifikation der Verjährung im US-amerikanischen Kollisionsrecht' [1989] IPRax 197, 200 ff; Peter Hay, Patrick Borchers and Symeon Symeonides, *Conflict of Laws* (5th edn, West Academic Publishing 2010) 154 f). The Louisianan regime of conflict of laws in the differentiated art 3549 Louisiana regime of Civil Code (Acts 1991, No 923, §1, effective 1 January, 1992; Acts 2005, No 213, § 1) favours the application of the *lex fori* as well.

c) Borrowing statutes
Because most US jurisdictions subject prescription to the *lex fori*, there can be 'forum shopping' (→ Forum (and law) shopping). The courts in Mississippi and New Hampshire are called

'statute of limitations havens' because they apply the prescription laws of their → *lex fori* even when the connection between the facts of the case and the forum is relatively weak; additionally, the limitation periods in both jurisdictions are fairly long (see Sam Walker, 'Forum Shopping for Stale Claims: Statutes of Limitations and Conflict of Laws' (1989) 23[1] Akron Law Review 19 f; on the laws of New Hampshire see *New Hampshire Keeton v Hustler Magazine* 465 U.S. 770 (1984)). To ensure that the forum is not selected for the length of its prescription period, a number of US states have adopted so-called 'borrowing statutes'. According to these statutes, the laws of a different jurisdiction are to be applied instead of the *lex fori* if according to these other laws prescription did not occur in the case at hand. Most states borrowing statutes apply the law of the jurisdiction in which the claim arose, but some apply the law at the residence of the debtor (Alejo de Cervera, *The Statute of Limitations in American Conflicts of Laws* (University of Puerto Rico Press 1966) 69 ff; Peter Hay, Patrick Borchers and Symeon Symeonides, *Conflict of Laws* (5th edn, West Academic Publishing 2010) 157–60; Gerhard Kegel, *Die Grenze von Qualifikation und Renvoi im internationalen Verjährungsrecht* (Westdeutscher Verlag 1962) 22–4; Dana Patrick Karam, 'Conflict of Laws – Liberative Prescription' (1987) 47 La.L.Rev. 1153, 1159 f; Sam Walker, 'Forum Shopping for Stale Claims: Statutes of Limitations and Conflict of Laws' (1989) 23[1] Akron Law Review 19, 24 f). In order to 'prevent forum shopping by nonresidents attempting to take advantage of a more favorable statute of limitations in this state', New York's borrowing statute (s 202 New York Civil Practice Law and Rules, available at <http://public.leginfo.state.ny.us/lawssrch.cgi?NVLWO> under 'Laws', 'Laws of New York') requires that '[a]n action based upon a cause of action accruing without the state cannot be commenced after the expiration of the time limited by the laws of either the state or the place without the state where the cause of action accrued ...' (*Global Fin Corp v Triarc Corp* 93 N.Y.2d 525, 528 (1999)). In cases involving a purely economic loss a cause of action usually accrues in the sense of section 202 New York Civil Practice Law and Rules 'where the plaintiff resides and sustains the economic impact of the loss' (*Global Fin Corp v Triarc Corp* 93 N.Y.2d 525, 529 (1999); *Portfolio Recovery Assocs LLC v King* 14 N.Y.3d 410, 416 (2010); on the conflict of laws impact of borrowing statues see Peter Hay, Patrick Borchers and Symeon Symeonides, *Conflict of Laws* (5th edn, West Academic Publishing 2010) 157–60; Peter Hay, 'Die Qualifikation der Verjährung im US-amerikanischen Kollisionsrecht' [1989] IPRax 197, 198). A corporation resides in either its principal place of business or its place of incorporation (*Oxbow Calcining USA Inc v American Industrial Partners* 948 N.Y.S. 2d 24, 30 (1st Dep't 2012)). The borrowing statutes of the different American states are not uniform. For example, the location where the claim arose can be determined using different criteria, or the connecting factor determining the subsidiary prescription law can be different.

3. Islamic legal system

In Islamic jurisdictions, the application of the → *lex fori* is said to prevail (see Bénédicte Fauvarque-Cosson, 'La prescription en droit international privé' in *Travaux du Comité Français de Droit International Privé* (LGDJ 2004) 235, 260 there no 55).

4. Uniform connection of prescription, preclusion, and estoppel and related notions

The uniform connection of the legal notions 'prescription', 'preclusion' and 'estoppel by laches' (or its civilian counterpart *Verwirkung*) (*supra* I.1.) is advantageous because the distinction between these notions is not always clear on the level of substantive law. This could lead to problems of → classification (characterization), but in an area of law that is very much guided by the principles of legal certainty and clarity – such as the area of law being discussed – such problems of connection should be avoided (see also Andreas Piekenbrock, *Befristung, Verjährung, Verschweigung und Verwirkung* (Mohr Siebeck 2006) 491). The uniform or parallel connection of these different legal notions is often achieved in civilian conflict of laws systems. For example, art 12(1)(d) Rome I Regulation and art 15(h) Rome II Regulation both encompass prescription and preclusion (*supra* I.1.).

The preclusion of contractual claims or claims for extra-contractual liability is classified as a question of substantive law in national civil law conflict of laws systems (Daniel Girsberger, *Verjährung und Verwirkung im internationalen Obligationenrecht* (Schulthess 1989) 73 f). They are subjected to the proper law (→ Proper law (doctrine)) of the claim or right. An example for a statute which explicitly operates in this manner is art 27 of the Polish Private international law Act. It extends the scope of the conflict rule regarding prescription to other legal notions dealing with a lapse of time. Where preclusion and prescription relate to statutory causes of actions (*supra* II.2.), the proper law of the claim or right applies to them in Anglo-American legal systems as well (Frank Vischer, David Oser and Lucius Huber, *Internationales Vertragsrecht* (2nd edn, Stämpfli 2000) § 6 I, page 522 f; Lord Collins of Mapesbury and others (eds), *Dicey, Morris & Collins on the Conflict of Laws* (15th edn, Sweet & Maxwell 2012) 7.47 f; see Peter Hay, 'Die Qualifikation der Verjährung im US-amerikanischen Kollisionsrecht' [1989] IPRax 197 f; on the different classification of rules of prescription in Anglo-American law *supra* II.2.).

5. *Classification and* renvoi

a) *Different classifications in civil law and common law*

(1) *The problem* The international law of prescription gives rise to a traditional problem of → classification (characterization). This problem stems from different schemes of classification of prescription in common law and civil law. It is often illustrated by referring to a famous (incorrect) decision by the German *Reichsgericht* (Imperial Court of Justice, 4 January 1882, 7 RGZ 21): the plaintiff brought an action in Germany arising from a promissory note issued in Tennessee. The defendant raised the prescription defence. According to the German conflict of laws rules, Tennessean law would have governed prescription. At the outset, the *Reichsgericht* correctly concluded that the substantive law of Tennessee does not contain any rules for prescription because the relevant question – when does a claim become subject to prescription? – was (and still is) governed by a procedural statute of limitations. The *Reichsgericht* deemed itself unable to apply the prescription rules of the procedural statute of limitations because a German court could only apply the German rules of civil procedure. It furthermore held that Tennessean regime of conflict of laws does not contain a rule which would refer back to the application of substantive German law as the *lex fori*, even though Tennessean law follows the rule that the law of procedure is always the forum's law. As result of the *Reichsgericht*'s approach, the claim could not be subject to prescription. The *Reichsgericht* later described its holding as incorrect (see Imperial Court of Justice (Reichsgericht), 12 November 1932, 145 RGZ 121, 130 = [1911] Juristische Wochenschrift 148) – a view which is the modern consensus. The *Reichsgericht* had ignored the double role conflict of laws rules play.

(2) *The conflict rule's double role in cases of exclusion of renvoi*

First, each conflict rule establishes for which categories of legal questions it determines the applicable law; therefore, it defines its own scope of application (German: *Anknüpfungsgegenstand*) (→ Connecting factor) and what distinguishes it from the other conflict rules. For example, art 12(1)(d) Rome I Regulation determines the applicable law primarily for questions of prescription, preclusion and *Verwirkung*. Second, where a conflict rule refers to the substantive law of a different jurisdiction – and not to the foreign conflict of laws – it also determines which substantive rules apply. It selects the applicable rules from among the legal rules of the determined jurisdiction. All substantive rules which serve the purpose and function that fall under the conflict rule's scope of application are included in the conflict rule's determination of the applicable law, notwithstanding their taxonomic place in the foreign legal system. This is why the *Reichsgericht* could have classified – and consequently applied – the Tennessean procedural prescription rules as being substantive from the point of view of German conflict of laws to the extent that they were functionally equivalent to the substantive rules of the German law of prescription, which in turn influenced the classification and scope of application of the German conflict of laws rule on prescription.

The Rome I and Rome II Regulations only refer to substantive laws (see art 20 Rome I Regulation and art 24 Rome II Regulation) (→ *Renvoi*). The scopes of application of art 12(1)(d) Rome I Regulation and art 15(h) Rome II Regulation are to be determined by their autonomous interpretation (→ Interpretation, autonomous). An autonomous interpretation also reveals which prescription rules of the proper law of obligations fall within the scope of these two conflict rules. It is commonly accepted that the procedural limitation rules in common law fall within the scope of art 12(1)(d) Rome I Regulation and art 15(h) Rome II Regulation if and to the extent that they are functionally equivalent to the substantive prescription rules envisaged by the Rome regulations (see Ulrich Magnus, 'art 12 Rome I Regulation' in *Julius von Staudingers Kommentar* zum Bürgerlichen Gesetzbuch: Staudinger BGB – EGBGB/IPR Einführungsgesetz zum Bürgerlichen Gesetzbuche/IPR, Einleitung zur Rom I-VO; Art 1–10 Rom I-VO (Internationales Vertragsrecht 1) (14th edn, Sellier-de Gruyter 2011) para 71 with further references; on the earlier German law see German Federal Court of Justice (BGH), 9 June 1960 [1960] NJW 1720–2).

American courts have clearly recognized that the classification of foreign prescription rules has to be done according to domestic criteria if they have to decide whether their own conflict rules also invoke the foreign prescription rules. For example, the United States Court of Appeals (5th Circ) held in *Ramsay v Boeing Company* (432 F.2d 592, 599 (5th Cir 1970)):

> ... a civil law jurisdiction seldom finds it necessary to construe its prescription statutes in such a way to make it easily apparent to a common law court whether the statute is considered substantive or procedural in the common law conflict of laws sense. The test adopted by *Davis v Mills*, [194 U.S. 451, 24 S.Ct. 692, 48 L.Ed. 1067 (1904)], and said to be the usually applied test, Reporter's Notes, Comment c, 143, Restatement (Second) of Conflict of Laws [(Proposed Official Draft, Adopted May 24, 1968)], is whether the statute is 'directed to the newly created liability so specifically as to warrant saying it qualified the right'. This test, however, lacks the clarity necessary for facile application. ... A more satisfactory approach in this situation is to determine whether the Belgian prescription statute has attributes under Belgian law which Mississippi would characterize as substantive.

(3) Renvoi *resulting from a different classification* Rome I and Rome II exclude the *renvoi* (*supra* II.5.a)(2)). Also, the Hague Maintenance Protocol 2007 only refers to substantive laws as far as prescription of maintenance claims under the applicable law is concerned (art 12 Hague Maintenance Protocol 2007; also *supra* II.1.c)). The prescription of succession claims is subjected to the proper law of the → succession when the Succession Regulation (Regulation (EU) No 650/2012 of the European Parliament and of the Council of 4 July 2012 on jurisdiction, applicable law, recognition and enforcement of decisions and acceptance and enforcement of authentic instruments in matters of succession and on the creation of a European Certificate of Succession, [2012] OJ L 201/107; → Rome IV Regulation (succession)) applies. A *renvoi* is only possible if the conditions of art 34 are met (art 34 generally only permits a *renvoi* in certain circumstances). Questions of *renvoi* can arise in connection with other conflict rules – particularly national conflict rules – such as the prescription of property law claims or of family law claims. Specific problems of *renvoi* arise where, for example, the German autonomous international law of prescription refers to the law of an American state, including its conflict of laws, and this jurisdiction places prescription within its procedural law. In the situation where the courts of the American state only apply the prescription law of their own → *lex fori*, there are two possible ways to solve this problem:

(i) the first option consists of arguing that because the courts of the American state only apply the prescription laws of their own country, their conflict of laws regime accepts that the law of their country is being invoked. Thus, there is no *renvoi*. This is an often-taken position (Ernst Rabel, *The Conflict of Laws: A Comparative Study*, vol 3 (2nd edn, University of Michigan Press 1964) 534 f; *Perrot v Suchard*, Swiss Federal Court, 15 March 1949, BGE 75 II 57, 66; German Federal Court of Justice (BGH), 9 June 1960 [1960] NJW 1720–2; Daniel Girsberger, *Verjährung und Verwirkung im internationalen Obligationenrecht* (Schulthess 1989) 49, 70; Hans Jürgen Sonnenberger, 'art 4 EGBGB' in Franz Jürgen Säcker und Roland Rixecker (eds), *Münchener Kommentar BGB*, vol 11 (5th edn, C.H. Beck 2010) para 40; Ulrich Magnus, 'art 12 Rome I Regulation' in *Julius von Staudingers Kommentar zum Bürgerlichen Gesetzbuch: Staudinger BGB – EGBGB/IPR Einführungsgesetz zum Bürgerlichen Gesetzbuche/ IPR, Einleitung zur Rom I-VO; Art 1–10 Rom I-VO (Internationales Vertragsrecht 1)* (14th edn, Sellier – de Gruyter 2011) paras 19, 71; see also

Cour d'appel de Paris, 3 March 1994, [1994] Rev.crit.DIP 532 with a note by *Bertrand Ancel*; *Cour de cassation Ci. 1er*, 11 March 1997, [1997] Rev.crit.DIP 202 with a note by *Bertrand Ancel*).

(ii) the second position advanced by parts of doctrine assumes that a difference in classification results in a *renvoi*. The fact that the American forum state always applies the domestic prescription law of its own *lex fori* is generalized and a hypothetical rule is postulated to the effect that the prescription law of the actual *lex fori* applies; in the example given above, this would be the prescription law of the German forum state (see eg Gerhard Kegel, *Die Grenze von Qualifikation und Renvoi im internationalen Verjährungsrecht* (Westdeutscher Verlag 1962) 40–3; Gerhard Kegel and Klaus

Schurig, *Internationales Privatrecht* (9th edn, C.H. Beck 2004) § 10 VI, § 17 VI 1). According to *Kegel*, this is a reference that excludes the conflict of laws (Gerhard Kegel, *Die Grenze von Qualifikation und Renvoi im internationalen Verjährungsrecht* (Westdeutscher Verlag 1962) 42). The majority of proponents of this doctrine accepts the → *renvoi* in principle, but argues that it does not have to be followed for a variety of reasons (further with references Jan von Hein, 'art 4 EGBGB' in Jan von Hein (ed), *Münchener Kommentar zum Bürgerlichen Gesetzbuch, Band 10: Internationales Privatrecht I, Europäisches Kollisionsrecht, Einführungsgesetz zum Bürgerlichen Gesetzbuche (Art 1–24)*, vol 10 (6th edn, C.H. Beck 2015) para 75).

b) Delimiting substantive and procedural legal concepts

Before the British Foreign Limitation Periods Act (*supra* I.2.) entered into force, the House of Lords (the precursor of the Supreme Court) would classify a limitation period as procedural rather than substantive if its lapse resulted in an unenforceable, but not extinguished, claim (*Black Clawson International Ltd v Papierwerke AG* [1975] AC 591 per Lord Wilberforce):

> One of the rules ... relates to the distinction made in English Private international law between matters of substance and matters of procedure, and, within that, the classification of limitation as a matter of procedure. Classification of limitation as procedural means that in proceedings in an English Court, English law, as the *lex fori*, will apply its domestic law to limitation and will not apply foreign limitation provisions even if the foreign law is the proper law, unless, at least, they extinguish the right.

This meant that the prescription law in the German Civil Code (§ 194 ff German Civil Code (*Bürgerliches Gesetzbuch* of 2 January 2002, BGBl. I 42, as amended, henceforth German CC)) was classified as being procedural (on this see Rudolf Edler, 'Verjährung und res iudicata im englischen internationalen Privatrecht' [1976] 40 RabelsZ 43, 51 f) because it only created a defence; it did not extinguish the claim (see § 214(1) German CC: 'After limitation occurs, the obligor is entitled to refuse performance'). Nowadays, the UK Foreign Limitation Periods Act 1984 has rendered this distinction obsolete, because according to section 4, the 'relevant law' of any country (including England and Wales) relating to limitation means the procedural and substantive law applicable. Nevertheless, the distinction between prescription and mere procedural deadlines, which serve another function, remains important.

The question of the distinction between (substantive) periods of prescription or preclusion on the one hand and purely procedural periods on the other arises in each conflict system. In principle, conflict rules only apply to notions of substantive law, not to notions of procedure. This principle is found for example in art 12(1)(d) Rome I Regulation, art 15(h) Rome II Regulation and art 11(e) Hague Maintenance Protocol 2007. As shown above (*supra* II.5.a)b)), classification has to take place based on the point of view of the relevant conflict rule; the test is whether the period is functionally equivalent to a substantive period of prescription or preclusion. The terms 'prescription' and 'preclusion' are to be defined by reference to the conflict rule. Where the rule is contained in a European regulation, the interpretation has to be autonomous, taking the regulation as the basis; where the conflict rule is one of national law, classification depends on the functional equivalency of the foreign rules to the national rules.

From a comparative law standpoint (→ Comparative law and private international law), certain similarities can be noted with regards to the use of distinguishing criteria. For example, periods that presuppose that court proceedings have started and whose primary purpose is to regulate these proceedings are usually not classified as prescription periods (Daniel Girsberger, *Verjährung und Verwirkung im internationalen Obligationenrecht* (Schulthess 1989) 217 f, 128 f).

6. Scope of reference

The law applicable to prescription has a wide scope of application in order to avoid conflicts that could occur when the legal framework for prescription is split among different applicable laws. All matters related to prescription are included in the reference made by international prescription law, even where this is not explicitly stated in the conflict rule. Some conflict rules indicate their scope of application through examples. For instance, the reference in art 15(h) Rome II Regulation explicitly includes 'rules relating to the commencement, interruption and suspension of a period of prescription or limitation' (as does art 8(8) Hague Traffic Accident Convention).

Section 4(1) UK Foreign Limitation Periods Act 1984 refers to the applicable prescription law for rules 'to the effect of, the application, extension, reduction or interruption of that period; and where under that law there is no limitation period which is so applicable, to the rule that such proceedings may be brought within an indefinite period'. Generally, one can say that the law applicable to prescription includes 'the commencement, the computation, the extension, (suspension, postponement of expiry, renewal of period) of the prescription as well as the effects of prescription (right of the debtor to refuse performance, right to the creditor to keep hold of performance)' (see Götz Schulze, 'art 12 Rome I Regulation' in Gralf-Peter Callies (ed), *Rome Regulations* (Kluwer Law International 2011) para 29 with further references). The question whether the application of the rules of prescription is mandatory as a matter of law or whether the courts only need to apply them where the parties plead them is answered by the applicable prescription law as well.

III. General questions

1. Choice of law

To the extent that questions of prescription or preclusion are subjected to the proper law of the claim or right (*supra* II.1.a)–c)), a → choice of law concerning the main obligation includes prescription. If only the applicable prescription law is chosen, then this is a partial choice of law concerning the proper law, but restricted in scope to questions of prescription. Whether such a partial choice of law (leading to a → *dépeçage*) is permissible depends on the conflict rule relating to the proper law of the claim or right. A partial choice of law relating only to the applicable prescription law is permissible under art 3(3)(3) Rome I Regulation (see Ulrich Magnus, 'art 12 Rome I Regulation' in *Julius von Staudingers Kommentar zum Bürgerlichen Gesetzbuch: Staudinger BGB – EGBGB/ IPR Einführungsgesetz zum Bürgerlichen Gesetzbuche/IPR, Einleitung zur Rom I-VO; Art 1–10 Rom I-VO (Internationales Vertragsrecht 1)* (14th edn, Sellier – de Gruyter 2011) para 22 with further references). The same is said to be impermissible in Swiss international contract law (Kurt Siehr, *Das Internationale Privatrecht der Schweiz* (Schulthess 2002) § 19 VIII 1 c, page 347; contra Daniel Girsberger, *Verjährung und Verwirkung im internationalen Obligationenrecht* (Schulthess 1989) 119 ff with further references). Where prescription is mentioned as being one application of the proper law of the claim or right in a conflict statute, the specific mention of prescription combined with a general permissibility of a partial choice of law indicates that the partial choice of law of the applicable prescription law is permissible (similarly see Erik Jayme, 'Betrachtungen zur dépeçage im internationalen Privatrecht' in Hans-Joachim Musielak and Klaus Schurig (eds), *Festschrift für Gerhard Kegel* (Kohlhammer 1987) 253, 263; Daniel Girsberger, *Verjährung und Verwirkung im internationalen Obligationenrecht* (Schulthess 1989) 120).

2. Change of applicable law

In situations where the applicable law changes while the prescription period is still running, one needs to determine whether prescription is governed by the previous prescription law or the new one. In the international law of obligations, a change of the applicable law rarely occurs because the → connecting factor (*supra* II.6.) is fixed. The exception to this rule is a subsequent → choice of law (eg art 3(2) Rome I Regulation, art 14 Rome II Regulation). Where the claim is to be classified as a property law claim for the purpose of conflict of laws, the common application of the *lex rei sitae* for movables (→ Property and proprietary rights) can result in a change of applicable law if the property is moved to another jurisdiction. In such cases, the general rules on *conflits mobiles* apply (→ Connecting factor), *supra* II.6.). There are instances where conflict of laws regimes explicitly require prescription to be governed by the laws of the location of the thing at the time the 'prescription period lapses' (see art VII (16) Introductory Title of the Civil Code of Nicaragua (Jan Kropholler and others (eds), *Außereuropäische IPR-Gesetze* 615); similarly art 2091 Civil Code of Peru (Jan Kropholler and others (eds), *Außereuropäische IPR-Gesetze* 697). The new property law of the property's location at the time when a property law claim expires is also relevant regarding the question whether a time period that was elapsing while the previous law was applicable is taken into account when deciding whether the current prescription period has lapsed. In German conflict of laws, this rule can be derived from art 43(1) Introductory Act to the German Civil Code (*Einführungsgesetz zum Bürgerlichen*

Gesetzbuche of 21 September 1994, BGBl. I 2494, as amended, henceforth EGBGB). The rule is implicitly presupposed in art 43(3) EGBGB (see Heinz-Peter Mansel 'art 43 EGBGB' in *Julius von Staudingers Kommentar zum Bürgerlichen Gesetzbuch: Staudinger BGB – EGBGB/IPR Einführungsgesetz zum Bürgerlichen Gesetzbuche/IPR, Artikel 43–6 EGBGB (Internationales Sachenrecht)* (14th edn, Sellier – de Gruyter 2015) paras 745–62; on Swiss law and comparative law see Daniel Girsberger, *Verjährung und Verwirkung im internationalen Obligationenrecht* (Schulthess 1989) 92 f).

3. Ordre public

Discrete rules of prescription or preclusion can violate the *lex fori*'s → public policy (*ordre public*). In principle, the general *ordre public* provision is applicable (eg art 21 Rome I Regulation or art 26 Rome II Regulation). The case-law on *ordre public* in questions of prescription is abundant and depends on many national particularities (for a comprehensive overview see Daniel Girsberger, *Verjährung und Verwirkung im internationalen Obligationenrecht* (Schulthess 1989) 85–92; Frank Vischer, David Oser and Lucius Huber, *Internationales Vertragsrecht* (2nd edn, Stämpfli 2000) § 6 I, page 523 f).

Some national conflict of laws codifications contain either special *ordre public* provisions that are meant to protect the state's citizens according to the domestic standard relating to prescription and exclusion of prescription set by the legislature (*supra* II.1.a)) or provisions that in other ways deviate from the general *ordre public* clause (see s 2 UK Foreign Limitation Periods Act 1984; see also s 4 Uniform Conflict of Laws – Limitations Act, *supra* II.2.); the latter category is meant to ensure that the claimant is allowed to liquidate their claim in a fair manner even if, for example, the claimant is absent. In general, the *ordre public* escape clause should be used sparingly in the prescription and preclusion context, because a number of legislative rules, particularly those that concern period lengths, are more historical than really mandatory (on s 2 UK Foreign Limitation Periods Act 1984 see *City of Gotha and Federal Republic of Germany v Sotheby's and Cobert Finance SA* [1998] 1 WLR 114; on this see Kurt Siehr 'Verjährt ein Anspruch auf Herausgabe des Eigentums? – Deutsches Verjährungsrecht vor englischem Gericht' in Michael Carl, Herbert Güttler and Kurt Siehr, *Kunstdiebstahl vor Gericht: City of Gotha v Sotheby's/Cobert Finance S.A.* (de Gruyter 2001) 53 ff).

Furthermore, prescription and preclusion call for clear, general and precise rules in order to safeguard legal certainty and clarity. One should operate on the assumption that this goal is endangered by an individual application of the *ordre public* escape clause.

4. Suspension of the prescription period by procedural acts

When prescription laws are substantive, they often contain a rule stipulating that bringing proceedings or other procedural acts (for instance, opening separate evidence proceedings) will prevent the prescription period from lapsing. In international cases, this raises the question whether bringing proceedings in a forum whose prescription laws are not applicable will trigger the same consequences. This is an issue of applying the substantive prescription laws; they decide whether the same consequence that would arise from bringing domestic proceedings will also arise where the procedural act is undertaken in another country. This is a question of → substitution. Particularly important is the question whether the relevant prescription law reply is triggered by the action of 'bringing a lawsuit in another country' (for Austrian law affirmative in principle just see Georg E. Kodek, 'Auslandsklage und Verjährung: Zum Zusammenspiel von materiellem Recht und Prozessrecht bei § 1497 ABGB' in Reinhold Geimer and others (eds), *Ars aequi et boni in mundo: Festschrift für Rolf A. Schütze zum 80. Geburtstag* (C.H. Beck 2014) 259–77; contra for English law Mary-Rose McGuire, *Verfahrenskoordination und Verjährungsunterbrechung im Europäischen Prozessrecht* (Mohr Siebeck 2004) 280–3) and whether it is a further condition of the substitution that the expected judgment is able to be recognized in the jurisdiction whose prescription laws apply (this is the subject of debate in German law, where the majority of writers in doctrine would seem to answer the question in the affirmative; see pro Götz Schulze, 'art 12 Rome I Regulation' in Gralf-Peter Callies (ed), *Rome Regulations* (Kluwer Law International 2011) para 30 with further references; contra Stefan Leible, 'Verjährung im Internationalen Vertragsrecht' in Ulrich Hösch (ed), *Zeit und*

Ungewissheit im Recht: Liber amicorum für Wilfried Berg (Boorberg 2011) 234, 243 f with further references; contra for English law Mary-Rose McGuire, *Verfahrenskoordination und Verjährungsunterbrechung im Europäischen Prozessrecht* (Mohr Siebeck 2004) 283–5). These questions are answered differently in different legal systems and are debated particularly fiercely (see for an overview Mary-Rose McGuire, *Verfahrenskoordination und Verjährungsunterbrechung im Europäischen Prozessrecht* (Mohr Siebeck 2004) 212–314).

HEINZ-PETER MANSEL

Literature

Alejo de Cervera, *The Statute of Limitations in American Conflicts of Laws* (University of Puerto Rico Press 1966); Patrick Courbe, 'La prescription en droit international privé' in Patrick Courbe, *Les désordres de la prescription. Colloque tenu au Palais de justice de Rouen, 4 février 1999* (Publications de l'Université de Rouen et du Havre 2000) 65; Lord Collins of Mapesbury and others (eds), *Dicey, Morris & Collins on the Conflict of Laws* (15th edn, Sweet & Maxwell 2012); Bénédicte Fauvarque-Cosson, 'Aspects de droit comparé de la prescription' in Patrick Courbe, *Les désordres de la prescription. Colloque tenu au Palais de justice de Rouen, 4 février 1999* (Publications de l'Université de Rouen et du Havre 2000) 45; Bénédicte Fauvarque-Cosson, 'La prescription en droit international privé' in *Travaux du Comité Français de Droit International Privé* (LGDJ 2004) 235; Daniel Girsberger, *Verjährung und Verwirkung im internationalen Obligationenrecht* (Schulthess 1989); Peter Hay, 'Die Qualifikation der Verjährung im US-amerikanischen Kollisionsrecht' [1989] IPRax 197; Gerhard Kegel, *Die Grenze von Qualifikation und Renvoi im internationalen Verjährungsrecht* (Westdeutscher Verlag 1962); Jan Kropholler and others (eds), *Außereuropäische IPR-Gesetze* (Deutsches Notarinstitut 1999); Mary-Rose McGuire, *Verfahrenskoordination und Verjährungsunterbrechung im Europäischen Prozessrecht* (Mohr Siebeck 2004); Ernst Rabel, *The Conflict of Laws: A Comparative Study*, vol 3 (2nd edn, University of Michigan Press 1964); Frank Vischer, David Oser and Lucius Huber, *Internationales Vertragsrecht* (2nd edn, Stämpfli 2000); Reinhard Zimmermann, *Comparative Foundations of a European Law of Set-Off and Prescription* (CUP 2002); Reinhard Zimmermann, 'Prescription' in Jürgen Basedow and others (eds), *Max Planck Encyclopedia of European Private Law* (OUP 2012); Peter Hay, Patrick Borchers and Symeon Symeonides, *Conflict of Laws* (5th edn, West Academic Publishing 2010).

Private international law, foundations

I. Introduction

The modern legal world is characterized by the parallel existence of multiple, variously calibrated legal systems. Usually, this multitude of laws is of little consequence. Even today, most transactions are entirely national with accordingly connections to one legal system only. However, for the increasing number of cross-border transactions the multiplicity of laws provides serious problems: for example, a contract may be valid under the law of one of the states involved but invalid under the law of the other. Proof of a breach of contract may be adduced with means in one state that would have no evidentiary value in the other. Or, a judgment that requires a contracting party to compensate the other might be enforceable in one state without being enforceable in the other. Clearly, the connection to multiple private and procedural legal systems that potentially structure and protect property rights in different ways results in uncertainties that are unknown to national transactions and that render international transactions risky undertakings. Private international law is one means to deal with and, arguably, to mitigate such uncertainties.

II. Terminology

To this day and despite its widespread use, there is no consensus regarding the precise meaning of the term 'private international law'. In fact, as *Lord Mance* recently pointed out 'dispute starts from the title page' (Jonathan Mance, 'The Future of Private international law' (2005) 1 J Priv Int L 185). In some countries, notably → Germany, private international law comprises (only) those rules that determine, in cases with connections to various countries, the applicable law (see art 3 of the Introductory Act to the German Civil Code (*Einführungsgesetz zum Bürgerlichen Gesetzbuche* of 21 September 1994, BGBl. I 2494, as amended, in the following EGBGB). In other countries, notably England, private international law also covers issues of international civil procedure, notably jurisdiction and recognition and enforcement of foreign judgments (→ United Kingdom). Again in other countries, notably → Belgium → France and → Italy, private international law (*droit international privé, diritto internazionale privato*) encompasses all of the aforementioned aspects, ie choice of law, jurisdiction and recognition and enforcement of judgments, plus the law of → nationality and citizenship as well as the rules regulating the condition of aliens (→ Aliens law) (Dominique Bureau and Horatia Muir Watt, *Droit international privé*, vol 1 (3rd edn, Presses Universitaires de France 2014) para 1 ff). Finally, there are countries that make no use of the term private international law at all. Examples include the → USA where courts and scholars refer to 'conflict of laws' when talking about the legal field dealing with jurisdiction, choice of law and recognition and enforcement of foreign judgments (Peter Hay, Patrick J Borchers and Symeon C Symeonides, *Conflict of Laws* (5th edn, West 2010) 1 ff). The latter is of course an irony of history because the term 'private international law' was coined in the USA when the US-American judge and scholar *Joseph Story* wrote in his *Commentaries on the Conflict of Laws* that 'that branch of public law may be fitly denominated private international law' (Joseph Story, *Commentaries on the Conflict of Laws* (Billard 1834) 9) (→ Story, Joseph).

The lack of a clear nomenclature continues on the level of the European Union: art 81(2)(c) TFEU (The Treaty on the Functioning of the European Union (consolidated version), [2012] OJ C 326/47) refers to 'conflict of laws' to determine the European legislature's competence to adopt coordinating measures in civil matters with cross-border implications. However, according to art 81(2)(a) and (c) TFEU the European legislature's competence also, and alongside 'conflict of laws', covers jurisdiction as well as recognition and enforcement of foreign judgments. Conflict of laws within the meaning of art 81(2)(c) TFEU is accordingly limited to those rules that determine the applicable law and thus corresponds to the narrow German notion of private international law. In contrast, in the literature on European Union law the term 'conflict of laws' is not commonly used. Leading treatises rather resort to 'private international law' when they describe the European legislature's activities in the area of jurisdiction, choice of law and recognition and enforcement (Michael Bogdan, *Concise Introduction to European Private international law* (3rd edn, European Law Publishers 2016); Geert van Calster, *European Private international law* (2nd edn, Hart 2015); Richard Plender and Michael Wilderspin, *The European Private international law of Obligations* (4th edn, Sweet & Maxwell 2015); Peter Stone, *EU Private international law* (3rd edn, Edward Elgar 2014)).

Against this background, the notion 'private international law' is neither clear nor does it enjoy global recognition. In addition, the term is also misleading in that private international law is for the most part neither international in nature nor contains any rules of substantive private law. However, the notion is used in many countries and regions of the world, including the European Union. This is why it is also applied in this Encyclopedia, and why it will be applied in the remainder of this entry. Unless otherwise specified the term is understood to cover all aspects of choice of law, jurisdiction as well as recognition and enforcement of foreign judgments and, hence, seen as equivalent to the notion of conflict of laws.

III. Significance

The practical significance of private international law has grown substantially over the last decades. For the USA, this finding has been described and detailed by *Symeon C Symeonides*, in his annual reports on → choice of law: for his first study, conducted in 1988, he had to analyse a total of 1,247 cases decided in American courts (Symeon C Symeonides, 'Choice of Law in the American Courts in 1988' (1989) 37 Am.J.Comp.L. 457). By 2015 the number of choice-of-law cases he had to account for had risen to 4,665 (Symeon C Symeonides, 'Choice of Law in the American Courts in 2015: Twenty-ninth Annual Survey' (2016) 64 Am.J.Comp.L. 221). Unfortunately, no comparable data are readily available for Europe and other parts of the world. However, there can be little doubt that any study would show a similar rise in private international law cases tried in national courts: to begin with, the volume of international trade has increased dramatically in recent decades. In fact, as a result of globalization and increased regional integration, businesses and firms buy and sell ever more across borders (see, for example, World Trade Organization, *International Trade Statistics* 2015 (WTO Geneva 2015) available at <www.wto.org>). However, it is not only corporate and business entities that increasingly engage in cross-border activity, but also private individuals.

GIESELA RÜHL

Take for example cross-border online shopping. According to a recent study the number of consumers who buy from foreign websites and the amount of money they spend online is huge (The Nielsen Company, *Modern Spice Routes: The Cultural Impact and the Economic Opportunity of Cross-Border Shopping* (2014)). In → Germany, for example, 14.1 million consumers engaged in online cross-border shopping in 2013, spending approximately 7.6 billion Euros on foreign websites. In the → United Kingdom and in the → USA numbers buying online and across borders were even higher: 15.9 million consumers spending 11 billion Euros (8.5 billion GBP) and 34.1 million consumers spending 36 billion Euros (40.6 billion USD) respectively. In addition to online shopping, private individuals also engage in more and more cross-border conduct when it comes to their personal life: a substantial number of → marriages, for example, are international in nature, meaning that spouses are of different nationalities, are living in different states or are living together in a state other than their home country. Furthermore, children are adopted from foreign countries (→ Adoption). And finally, foreign countries are becoming increasingly popular holiday destinations. Cross-border mobility thus plays an ever growing role in the lives of an ever growing number of people.

IV. Sources

Private international law deals with and coordinates the multitude of legal systems. It falls into two different sub-fields: choice of law and international civil procedure (⇒ Choice of law). Choice of law determines which law applies in international situations. International civil procedure determines which national court is competent to hear a dispute (→ Jurisdiction, foundations) and how foreign judgments may be recognized and enforced domestically (→ Recognition and enforcement of judgments). Furthermore, international civil procedure governs how international legal issues should be handled procedurally speaking. It conditions, for example, how foreign law is to be applied and ascertained (→ Foreign law, application and ascertainment). In addition, international civil procedure contains rules as to the position of foreigners before national courts. Finally, international civil procedure also regulates the production of documents and the procurement of evidence abroad (→ Evidence, procurement of).

Despite their international subject matter, both sub-fields of private international law are to a large extent rooted in domestic law. However, the number of international frameworks has increased during recent decades. Ever since the beginning of the 20th century the → Hague Conference on Private International Law has adopted an ever growing number of international treaties relating to almost all areas of private international law (→ Treaties in private international law). Ever since the 1950s the development of private international law has additionally been defined by efforts to Europeanize the field. From a historic perspective, this of course is nothing new. Prior to the integration of private international law into national codes in the course of the 19th century codification movement, legal scholars across Europe had spent many years attempting to develop a unified regime of choice-of-law rules on the basis of the so-called statute theory (→ Private international law, history of). However, these efforts proved fruitless, and despite intensive discussions, only few rules and principles could command a consensus. Renewed attempts to unify private international law at the European level in the middle of the 20th century suffered the same fate: since the Community's founding treaties neglected to bestow European lawmakers with a specific legislative competence in the area of private international law, Member States were compelled to pursue consensus solutions in the form of public international law treaties. As a consequence, Europeanization was achieved only in a fragmented fashion, merely encompassing rules on jurisdiction, recognition and enforcement of judgments in → civil and commercial matters as well as rules on determination of the applicable law in contractual matters. Only at the end of the 1990s did the Member States confer upon European lawmakers a specific competence as regards private international law – and in so doing laid the groundwork for an unprecedented series of legislative measures that has in just over ten years led to the very first true Europeanization of the relevant rules (→ European Union and private international law). Today, private international law is embodied in an ever growing number of European Union Regulations, the most important and well known being the Brussels

I Regulation (recast) (Regulation (EU) No 1215/2012 of the European Parliament and of the Council of 12 December 2012 on jurisdiction and the recognition and enforcement of judgments in civil and commercial matters (recast), [2012] OJ L 351/1), the Brussels IIa Regulation (Council Regulation (EC) No 2201/2003 of 27 November 2003 concerning jurisdiction and the recognition and enforcement of judgments in matrimonial matters and the matters of parental responsibility, [2003] OJ L 338/1), the Rome I Regulation (Regulation (EC) No 593/2008 of the European Parliament and of the Council of 17 June 2008 on the law applicable to contractual obligations (Rome I), [2008] OJ L 177/6), the Rome II Regulation (Regulation (EC) No 864/2007 of the European Parliament and of the Council of 11 July 2007 on the law applicable to non-contractual obligations (Rome II), [2007] OJ L 199/40), the Rome III Regulation (Council Regulation (EU) No 1259/2010 of 20 December 2010 implementing enhanced cooperation in the area of the law applicable to divorce and legal separation, [2010] OJ L 343/10), the Succession Regulation (Regulation (EU) No 650/2012 of the European Parliament and of the Council of 4 July 2012 on jurisdiction, applicable law, recognition and enforcement of decisions and acceptance and enforcement of authentic instruments in matters of succession and on the creation of a European Certificate of Succession, [2012] OJ L 201/107), the Maintenance Regulation (Council Regulation (EC) No 4/2009 of 18 December 2008 on jurisdiction, applicable law, recognition and enforcement of decisions and cooperation in matters relating to maintenance obligations, [2009] OJ L 7/1) as well as the Evidence Regulation (Council Regulation (EC) No 1206/2001 of 28 May 2001 on cooperation between the courts of the Member States in the taking of evidence in civil or commercial matters, [2001] OJ L 174/1) and the European Service Regulation (Regulation (EC) No 1393/2007 of the European Parliament and of the Council of 13 November 2007 on the service in the Member States of judicial and extrajudicial documents in civil or commercial matters (service of documents), [2007] OJ L 324/79). Outside Europe, however, national legislation is still the dominant source of private international law. This becomes clear when looking to the large number of national codifications enacted or reformed around the globe in recent years (see, for example, → Albania, → Belgium, → Bulgaria → China, → Czech Republic, → Dominican Republic, → Estonia, → Georgia, → Japan, → Liechtenstein, → Macedonia, → Montenegro, → Poland, → Slovenia, → South Korea, → Taiwan, → Tunisia, → Turkey, → Ukraine, → Venezuela).

V. A closer look: choice of law

The traditional core of private international law is → choice of law. Understood as the collectivity of provisions and principles that determine, in cases with connections to foreign legal systems, the applicable law, its purpose is the focal point of vigorous debates. By contrast, the modern concept of choice of law as such enjoys broad recognition and application today.

1. Concept

The modern concept of → choice of law has emerged from century-long debates. It is applied today in virtually all international treaties and European regulations as well as in countries that recognize the concept of private international law. It can be characterized as cosmopolitan, selectivist and multilateralist.

a) Cosmopolitan: application of foreign law
The first characteristic feature of modern choice-of-law systems is their lack of a requirement that courts apply the law of the forum (→ *Lex fori*) when faced with international cases. In a cosmopolitan manner they allow courts to apply some other law, notably the law of a foreign country. The openness towards the application of a law other than the *lex fori*, however, is not a matter of course. In fact, the very first attempts to resolve cases with cross-border elements were characterized by application of the *lex fori* (→ Private international law, history of): when Greek city-states began to engage in trade with one another in the 4th century BC courts had to deal increasingly often with disputes involving members of different city-states. In order to deal with these disputes the Greeks developed several strategies, among them the conclusion of treaties between the city-states and the creation of special courts for commercial and maritime matters. However, due to the basic unity of Greek law, the dominant strategy was a *lex fori*

approach that provided for application of each city-state's law in its own courts. Application of forum law was also the dominant strategy for cross-border transactions in England in the aftermath of the Norman Conquest. The English common law courts – that existed alongside specialized maritime and commercial courts, which had their own way of dealing with multistate cases – refused to apply the law of a different country and instead applied their own law, the common law. The reason for this practice was procedural rather than doctrinal. Under the English rules of civil procedure a suit had to be filed in the jurisdiction in which the action had arisen. Therefore, a suit could only be brought in an English court if the action had arisen in England. If this was the case, however, it meant that the rules of the common law applied. At first, English courts stood strictly by these procedural rules: cases that involved foreign facts were dismissed for lack of jurisdiction and the plaintiff, whether foreign or English, was forced to litigate abroad. After some time, however, English courts perceived the denial of jurisdiction in these cases as unjust. Therefore, they eventually allowed plaintiffs to assert that a foreign place such as Hamburg, Brussels or Paris actually was located in England. This, in turn, allowed the courts to hear the case and to apply the common law. Objections raised by defendants against this practice were dismissed by pointing to the fact that the law had invented a fiction for the 'furtherance of justice'.

The origins of the modern, cosmopolitan system of → choice of law are usually assigned to the 12th century. Back then, Italian scholars faced the problems arising from the co-existence of different local laws in the city-states of Upper Italy. In answering the question of which law to apply in cases involving members from different city-states, they decided to apply the law of one of the city-states involved. By allowing and at times even requiring courts to apply the law of another city-state, the Italian scholars as well as their French and Dutch successors – who were later called statutists – invented the cosmopolitan *lex causae* approach, which has dominated the choice-of-law scene ever since. It has survived all attacks by academics, notably those of *Carl Georg von Wächter* (→ Wächter, Carl Georg von). In a seminal series of articles published in 1841 and 1842 (Carl Georg von Wächter, 'Ueber die Collision der Privatrechtsgesetze verschiedener Staaten'

(1841) 24 AcP 230, (1842) 25 AcP 1, (1842) 25 AcP 161 and (1842) 25 AcP, 361) *von Wächter* analysed the statutists' method and concluded that they had not succeeded in developing consistent and generally accepted solutions for problems of cross-border transactions. He therefore proposed discarding the statutists' *lex causae* approach in favour of a *lex fori* theory that required judges to apply forum law in most of the cases. The immediate impact of his writings, however, was marginal as he gained few followers in his lifetime.

The fact that *Wächter*'s *lex fori* theory was not applied in practice during the 19th century does not mean that he had no influence on the development of → choice of law theory. On the contrary, his ideas underwent a remarkable revival during the 20th century, when American scholars rebelled against the then leading American approach to choice of law – the → vested rights theory as incorporated in the Restatement (First) of Conflict of Laws (American Law Institute, Restatement of the Law, First: Conflict of Laws, St Paul 1934). Under the impression of the perceived arbitrary results of the vested rights theory – which followed a *lex causae* approach – several scholars, notably *Albert A Ehrenzweig* (→ Ehrenzweig, Albert A), asked courts to apply and interpret their own law only. By the same token, *Brainerd Currie* (→ Currie, Brainerd) favoured application of forum law, even though his governmental interest analysis did not openly advocate a *lex fori* approach (→ Interest and policy analysis in private international law). Today, however, a *lex fori* approach is not widely used in practice (→ *Lex fori*).

b) Selectivist: choice between existing legal systems
The second characteristic feature of modern choice-of-law systems is that they require courts to apply the law of the forum or the law of a foreign country when faced with an international case. By contrast, they do not allow courts to create new substantive laws applicable only in international cases and specifically tailored to their particular needs. As a result, modern choice-of-law systems follow a selectivist, and not a substantivist approach. The latter, however, was popular throughout history, notably in Roman times (→ Private international law, history of). It emerged when Romans increasingly engaged in international trade and therefore had to face growing numbers of legal disputes involving members of foreign countries. To

deal with these disputes Romans created a new institution empowered to conduct litigation involving non-Romans: the *praetor peregrinus*. Drawing on general legal principles, the notion of good faith as well as his own legal imagination, he solved multistate cases by *ad hoc* crafting new substantive rules especially designed for cross-border transactions. These new substantive rules gradually developed into a separate body of norms, the → *ius gentium*, which applied to international disputes only, and was distinct from the *ius civile* that regulated disputes between Roman citizens.

The Roman substantivist method invented by the *praetor peregrinus* died out when the *ius gentium* was incorporated into the *ius civile* and codified in the *Corpus Juris Justinianus*. However, it had a revival in the English commercial and maritime courts several centuries later. These courts, which existed alongside the forum-oriented common law courts, declined to apply the common law, which had been developed to meet the needs of a rural society. Instead they referred to the Roman *praetor peregrinus* and engaged in the *ad hoc* development of a set of new substantive rules especially designed for commercial and maritime cases. These rules that later became known as law merchant and maritime law drew on different historic and geographical sources and claimed universal application. However, they met the same fate as the *ius gentium* in that they were eventually absorbed by the English common law courts and incorporated indistinguishably into the common law (→ Private international law, history of).

Modern → choice of law systems are without exception based on the selectivist method, which again goes back to the statutists' method developed by 12th century Italian scholars (→ Unilateralism). When faced with the question how to solve disputes between members of different city-states they did not develop a new set of substantive rules as the Romans had. Instead, they applied the law of one or the other city-state and thus made a choice between existing laws rather than blending them. In practice, this method of choosing the applicable law from existing laws has prevailed until today. Even *Friedrich Carl von Savigny* (→ Savigny, Friedrich Carl von), who criticized the workings of the statutists' method insofar as it amounted to a unilateral choice-of-law theory, accepted without question that international disputes had to be solved by applying the laws of one of the states involved. However, the substantivist approach formed the basis for some of the most important American approaches to choice of law in the 20th century, notably *Friedrich K Juenger*'s best law approach. As a reaction to the perceived arbitrariness of the Restatement (First) of Conflict of Laws, *Juenger* suggested that courts should not choose between application of existing laws but strive for the application of the best law. Arguing that national laws were not suited for the resolution of international disputes, he granted courts the right to construct new *ad hoc* substantive rules especially designed for international cases. *Juenger*'s writings were embraced and enhanced by a number of American scholars, notably *Luther M McDougal, Arthur T von Mehren* and *Donald T Trautmann* as well as – in Europe – *Ernst Steindorff*. They all promoted – to different degrees and according to different guidelines – the *ad hoc* crafting and application of new substantive law rules for international cases. However, the response from practice was faint. In the USA, a substantivist approach was finally rejected in 1969 when the Restatement (Second) of Conflict of Laws (American Law Institute, Restatement of the Law, Second: Conflict of Laws 2d, St Paul 1971) was adopted (→ Restatement (First and Second) of Conflict of Laws). In Europe, it was never seriously considered as a relevant approach to choice of law.

c) Multilateralist: use of choice-of-law rules
The third characteristic feature of modern choice-of-law systems is that they apply choice-of-law rules and → connecting factors to determine the applicable law. They assign a legal relationship to a legal order with the help of predefined criteria, and hence apply what has become known as the multilateralist method of → choice of law. By contrast, in determining the applicable law these systems make no use, at least not as a matter of principle, of the unilateralist method that defines the reach of legal norms according to their intended geographical scope. However, the unilateralist method played a crucial role in the history of choice of law and continues to be influential (→ Unilateralism). It goes back to the Italian scholars of the 12th century. When addressing the question of which city-state's law to apply in a particular case they decided to approach the problem by defining the intended spatial reach of the conflicting local laws. To this end, they divided the respective provisions into two basic

categories – personal and territorial. Rules that were considered personal applied to cases involving the citizens of that city-state no matter where they were, whereas territorial rules claimed application to anyone, whether citizen or foreigner, who was resident within the city boundaries. To decide which local law fell into which category the Italian scholars – and their French and Dutch successors – initially relied on the wording of the particular substantive rule. Later on, they based the classification on the presumed or apparent legislative intent. However, no matter which criteria the statutists applied to discern the spatial reach of local laws, they failed to develop generally accepted solutions for cross-border cases. In 1841 *Carl Georg von Wächter* (→ Wächter, Carl Georg von) therefore opened his attack on the statutists' method with the observation that 'some of these older writings presented the matter so as if there was agreement over the most points: but on closer inspection of the literature one becomes convinced that the latter is by no means the case. ... Furthermore, long standing principles were gradually attacked and robbed of their application ... – and the more lively the question was discussed the further estranged the views.' (Carl Georg von Wächter, 'Ueber die Collision der Privatrechtsgesetze verschiedener Staaten' (1841) 24 AcP 230, 233 f).

Wächter's observations paved the way for *Friedrich Carl von Savigny* (→ Savigny, Friedrich Carl von), who is generally regarded as the founder of the multilateral method. In line with the general spirit of the 19th century, *Savigny* considered private law to be the product of civil society rather than a subset of state law and an expression of state power. The determination of the applicable law could therefore not start from the local laws in question, but had to emanate from the legal relationship. Since private law was neither part of the state order nor an expression of state power, but rather an expression of the people and of individual will, conflicts between legal orders appeared to *Savigny* not as conflicts between sovereign states, but rather as conflicts between areas of individual will or spheres of freedom. And since law was an expression of the people and of individual will, legal relationships had to fit spatially into a particular legal area. In *Savigny's* words they had to have – a 'natural home' (*natürliche Heimat*), a 'seat' (*Sitz*). It was, hence, for choice of law 'to discover for every legal relation (case) that legal territory to which, in its proper nature, it belongs or is subject in (in which it has its seat)' (Friedrich Carl von Savigny, *Das System des heutigen römischen Rechts*, vol 8 (1849) 108, translated by W Guthrie, *Private international law. A treatise on the conflict of laws and the limits of their operation in respect of place and time* (1869) 89). This seat, in turn, had to be identified by classifying legal relationships into broad categories and then linking those categories with a legal order by means of connecting factors such as the domicile (→ Domicile, habitual residence and establishment) of a person or the place of a transaction. *Savigny* hence developed a system of choice-of-law rules that assigned a legal relationship to one particular legal order regardless of whether that legal order had expressed a wish to be applied. In doing so, he rejected the statutists' unilateral method of defining the spatial reach of legal rules and promoted what later became known as the modern method of choice of law.

The fact that the unilateral method was replaced by *Savigny's* multilateral method does not, however, mean that the unilateral method simply vanished from the choice-of-law scene. On the contrary, it continued to form the basis for the most influential approach that arose in the course of the → (American) conflict of laws revolution: *Brainerd Currie's* governmental interest analysis (→ Interest and policy analysis in private international law). *Currie* advanced a modern form of the unilateralist choice-of-law method in that, just like the statutists, he set out to determine the applicable law by defining the spatial reach of substantive laws. However, instead of classifying laws according to their personal or territorial purport, *Currie* advocated an *ad hoc* judicial interpretation of the involved substantive laws based on the policies underlying those laws. Such an interpretation, he argued, would determine a state's interest in having its law applied in a certain case – the 'governmental interest' – which in turn would define the laws' intended sphere of operation in terms of space and designate the applicable law.

Without exaggeration, *Currie's* governmental interest analysis can be classified as the most important and most influential modern approach to → choice of law. In fact, even though a multilateralist approach has prevailed on a large scale both in the USA and Europe, unilateralists elements are present in virtually all contemporary choice-of-law systems (→ Unilateralism). This becomes particularly evident when looking at the

Restatement (Second) of Conflict of Laws, which is followed by most of the jurisdictions in the USA (→ Restatement (First and Second) of Conflict of Laws). Although it essentially adopts a multilateralist approach by advocating the application of the law of the state with the most significant relationship with the case in question, it also recognizes the concept of state interests as an important factor for the choice of law. Indeed, the process of identifying the state with the most significant relationship comprises, among others, the examination of the relevant policies of both the forum and other interested states. In Europe, while it remains faithful to multilateralism in general, unilateralist elements can be found for example in the form of → overriding mandatory provisions. According to art 9 (3) Rome I Regulation, for example, when applying the law of a country, effect may be given to the overriding mandatory provisions of the → place of performance. Similar provisions are to be found in art 16 Rome II Regulation and art 30 of the Succession Regulation.

2. *Purpose*

In contrast to the concept of → choice of law, its very purpose is still subject to debate. Two questions may be distinguished: first, whether choice of law concerns enforcement of individual (private) or state (public) interests, and second whether choice of law concerns justice on the level of choice of law ('conflicts justice') or substantive law ('material justice'). Basically, two schools of thought provide answers. According to the (classical) school of thought that prevails in Europe and most national choice-of-law regimes, choice of law serves to solve conflicts between private individuals and aims at conflicts justice, notably international uniformity of decisions and legal certainty. According to the arguably more political school of thought that dominates the discussion in the USA choice of law serves to solve conflicts between states and aims at material justice.

a) The classical school

The classical school of thought can be traced back to *Friedrich Carl von Savigny*, the acknowledged founder of the multilateral method of choice of law (⇒ Savigny, Friedrich Carl von). As indicated earlier he considered private law to be an expression of civil society and the people rather than an expression of states. He therefore advanced the idea that every legal relationship had to have a 'rightful place' or 'seat' and that it was for choice of law to determine that place or seat. Since each legal relationship had exactly one 'rightful place' or 'seat' *Savigny* also promoted the idea that the applicable law had to be the same irrespective of where an action was brought. The search for the seat of the legal relationship was therefore intended to guarantee international uniformity of decisions by ensuring that 'the same legal relations (cases) have to expect the same decision, whether the judgment be pronounced in this state or in that' (Friedrich Carl von Savigny, *System des heutigen römischen Rechts*, vol 8 (1849) 27; translated by W Guthrie, *Private international law. A treatise on the conflict of laws and the limits of their operation in respect of place and time* (1869) 27). Unfortunately, *Savigny* made no attempt to explain in detail how to find the one 'rightful place' or 'seat' of a legal relationship. Even though he suggested a number of choice-of-law rules for example for contracts and → torts, he remained silent as to the precise factors to be taken into account. However, he made clear that territorial aspects as well as legal certainty and predictability played an important role. By the same token, he made clear that the content or the function of the local laws in question as well as the substantive outcome in individual cases were immaterial. He thereby invented the classical school of choice of law that focuses on what was later by American writers termed 'conflict justice'.

Today, *Savigny*'s ideas form the basis of most modern choice-of-law systems including notably the choice-of-law system of the European Union. In fact, there is broad agreement that the applicable law has to be determined by finding the law of the closest connection – an expression which clearly mirrors *Savigny*'s search for the seat of the legal relationship (see art 4(3) Rome I Regulation, art 4(3) of the Rome II Regulation, § 1 Austrian Federal Code on Private international law (*Bundesgesetz über das internationale Privatrecht* of 15 June 1978, BGBl. No 304/1978, as amended), art 15 Swiss Private international law Act (*Bundesgesetz über das Internationale Privatrecht* of 18 December 1987, 1988 BBl I 5, as amended), arts 41 and 46 EGBGB). In addition, there is broad agreement that the choice-of-law process is about ensuring international harmony of decisions as well as legal certainty and predictability. According to Recital (6) of both the Rome I Regulation and the Rome II Regulation, for example, '[t]he proper functioning of the internal market creates a need, in order to improve the predictability of the outcome of litigation, certainty as to the law applicable and the free movement of judgments, for the conflict-of-law rules in the Member States to designate the same national law irrespective of the country of the court in which an action is brought'. Finally, it is also broadly agreed that, as a matter of principle, the content and the function of the private laws in question do not have to be taken into account when determining the applicable law.

The fact that most modern choice-of-law systems and the European choice-of-law system in particular are still based on *Savigny*'s ideas does not, however, mean that choice-of-law theory has not progressed ever since the 19th century. In fact, the design of choice-of-law rules and the type of connecting factors used have undergone tremendous change under the influence of modern American writers (Marc-Philippe Weller, 'Anknüpfungsprinzipien im Europäischen Kollisionsrecht: Abschied von der klassischen IPR-Dogmatik?' [2011] IPRax 429). For example, the principle of → party autonomy that allows parties to choose the applicable law plays a central role today whereas it was strikingly absent from *Savigny*'s concept of choice of law (Jürgen Basedow, 'The Law of Open Societies – Private Ordering and Public Regulation of International Relations' (2013) 360 Rec. des Cours 1, 164 ff). Also, substantive policies, such as the protection of consumers, employees and other weaker parties, plays an ever more important role when framing choice-of-law rules (Giesela Rühl, 'The Protection of Weaker Parties in the Private international law of the European Union: A Portrait of Inconsistency and Conceptual Truancy' (2014) 10 J Priv Int L 335). However, just as in the 19th century, current (European) choice-of-law theory is still firmly rooted in the belief that choice of law solves conflicts between private individuals rather than states and that it aims at conflicts rather than material justice.

b) The political school
The second school of thought that elaborates on the purpose of → choice of law is rooted in the → USA of the 20th century and emerged during the so-called → (American) Conflict of Law Revolution. Rightly called the 'political' school of choice of law (Eckart Rehbinder, 'Zur Politisierung des Internationalen Privatrechts' [1973] JZ 151) it focuses not on assigning a legal relationship to the most appropriate legal order but on reaching the most appropriate results in individual cases and hence material justice. The basis for this proposition is an alternative view of private law. Unlike the classical school of thought, the political school does not see private law as a neutral and apolitical legal zone, free of state interests and social functions. Under the influence of American legal realism, it rather emphasizes its socially formative and purposive character, which assists states in realizing their interests and intentions. For choice of law, this understanding of private law means that conflicts between various legal orders are conceived of as conflicts between various states and their interests. The central problem that choice of law must solve is therefore not the finding of the legal order in which the legal relationship has its 'seat'. Rather, the concern is the discovery of the legal order with the largest interest in the application of its substantive norms. In the words of *Lea Brilmayer*: 'the central thesis of the modern approaches to choice of law is that law-making is an instrumental activity. A legislator or common law judge formulates norms in order to achieve some social purpose, choice of law, the modern theorists claim, should reflect this focus as much as any other area of law. In deciding whether a particular law applies in a case with interstate connections, the judge should analyse the purposes underlying the competing legal norms. What benefits were the rules designed to achieve, or what evils were they designed to avert?' (Lea Brilmayer, 'Rights, Fairness, and Choice of Law' (1989) 98 Yale L.J. 1227, 1284). For the political school the determination of the applicable law, as with the medieval statutists' theory, is therefore dependent on an assessment of the intention of the relevant substantive norms. However, unlike the statutists' theory, which divided the respective provisions into two and later three basic categories, the political school requires courts to determine, weigh and compare the affected substantive policies or governmental interests in each case. How exactly this has to be done has been controversially debated for decades and different proponents of the political school – *David F Cavers, Brainerd Currie, Robert A Leflar*,

Albert A Ehrenzweig, Arthur T von Mehren, Donald T Trautman and *Russel J Weintraub* to name just a few – provide markedly different answers (→ Interest and policy analysis and private international law). The details, however, are of no consequence for the purpose of this entry. What matters is the fact that all of the above-mentioned writers conceptualize conflicts between different legal systems as conflicts between states. In consequence, they determine the applicable law with a view to the content and the function of the competing state laws as well as the outcome of their application in individual cases. Their focus is thus material as opposed to conflicts justice.

Today, the political school of → choice of law still plays an important role in the → USA. When determining the applicable law § 6(2) of the Restatement (Second) of Conflict of Laws, for example, requires courts to consider among others the relevant policies of the forum, the relevant policies of other interested states and the relative interests of those states in the determination of the particular issue as well as the basic policies underlying the particular field of law. In Europe, by contrast, the political school never gained ground. Even though it had a number of influential followers including, for example, *Peter M Gutzwiller, Christian Joerges, Heinrich Kronstein* and *Rudolf Wiethölter*, it never made its way into legislation or court decisions. Nonetheless, the political school had an influence on the development in Europe. Most importantly and as indicated earlier, European choice-of-law rules account today more intensively for substantive policies than at the beginning of the 20th century (Marc-Philippe Weller, 'Anknüpfungsprinzipien im Europäischen Kollisionsrecht: Abschied von der klassischen IPR-Dogmatik?' [2011] IPRax 429).

3. Modern trends

In addition to the two above-outlined schools of thought, a number of writers have recently advocated approaches that enrich the current debate on the concept and the purpose of choice of law. These approaches are interdisciplinary in nature, drawing on insights from other social sciences. One approach, for example, draws inspiration from economic theory and focuses on the effects of choice-of-law rules. Rejecting the idea that choice of law is about finding the legal order with the closest connection or the greatest interest in deciding the case, it argues that choice of law is rather a matter of identifying the legal order that sets incentives for efficient individual and state behaviour. The details are discussed elsewhere in this Encyclopedia (→ Economic analysis and private international law). For the purposes of this entry suffice it to say that an economic theory does not fundamentally question the conceptual ability of choice of law to deal with the problems of international transactions in an increasingly interconnected world. It therefore contrasts with other modern approaches that consider choice of law to be ill-equipped to deal with new phenomena brought about by globalization such as the rise of transnational private law regimes and the rise of non-state actors. The details are, again, discussed elsewhere (→ Globalization and private international law).

VI. Conclusion

Private international law plays a key role in solving the problems that flow from the coexistence of differently calibrated legal systems. Broadly understood as the law of private international legal relationships, it helps to deal with the uncertainties associated with the ever growing number of international transactions. Whether it will manage to deal with all challenges that accompany globalization and increased regional integration only time will tell. However, over the centuries private international law has proved to be open and flexible enough to react to fundamental economic and social change. We may therefore expect that private international law will be able to maintain its place in the overall governance structure for cross-border transactions.

GIESELA RÜHL

Literature

Jürgen Basedow, 'The Law of Open Societies – Private Ordering and Public Regulation of International Relations' (2013) 360 Rec. des Cours 1; Lea Brilmayer, 'Rights, Fairness, and Choice of Law' (1989) 98 Yale L.J. 1227; Brainerd Currie, *Selected Essays on the Conflict of Laws* (Duke University Press 1963); Christian Joerges, *Zum Funktionswandel des Kollisionsrechts* (Mohr Siebeck 1971); Gerhard Kegel, 'Introduction' (Chapter 1) and 'Fundamental Approaches' (Chapter 3) in *International Encyclopedia of Comparative Law*, vol 8 *(Private international law)* (Mohr Siebeck 1986); Egon Lorenz,

Zur Struktur des Internationalen Privatrechts (Duncker & Humblot 1977); Ralf Michaels, 'The New European Choice-of-Law Revolution' (2008) 82 Tul.L.Rev. 1607; Horatia Muir Watt, 'Private international law' in Jan Smits (ed), *Elgar Encyclopedia of Comparative Law* (Edward Elgar 2012) 701; Giesela Rühl, *Statut und Effizienz. Ökonomische Grundlagen des Internationalen Privatrechts* (Mohr Siebeck 2011); Giesela Rühl, 'Methods and Approaches in Choice of Law: An Economic Perspective' (2006) 24 Berkeley J.Int'l L. 801; Symeon C Symeonides, *Codifying Choice of Law Around the World – An International Comparative Analysis* (OUP 2014); Marc-Philippe Weller, 'Anknüpfungsprinzipien im Europäischen Kollisionsrecht: Abschied von der klassischen IPR-Dogmatik?' [2011] IPRax 429.

Private international law, history of

For over three thousand years private international law was largely national law before becoming increasingly unified by international conventions, treaties and regional regulations. During this period of early development, the history of private international law was predominantly national in character, while following certain international trends and theories. The following is devoted to such international trends, theories and models rather than to national law of individual nations or countries.

Another issue to be determined as a preliminary is the precise definition of: private international law. It could constitute conflicts law in the modern sense or any addressing of problems involving different sets of laws for different types of person. The present author prefers the second broader approach and the conviction that private international law may even have existed, and its associated problems may have been resolved by various methods, before the development of modern bilateral conflict rules.

I. Ancient times

Four distinct models for dealing with foreign claims of protection in local institutions may be distinguished: no protection, special courts, special law and protection by national or state law.

1. No protection at all

In early times, any law, whether codified as the Code of Hammurabi (18th century BC), the Hebrew law of the Pentateuch (9th–5th century BC) or the law of Athens (Dracon of 621 and Solon of 594 BC) or Rome (Twelve Tables, 450 BC) or uncodified, constituted a covenant of peace and was strictly limited to the free citizens of the respective community, unless a host protected a foreign guest or a treaty with the foreign community guaranteed protection of the foreigner. These laws applied only to local citizens within the local territory and as such – in modern terms – they were mandatory in nature. Foreign law was ignored.

2. Special courts in foreign countries

According to reliable sources there were in ancient Egypt some courts or judicial bodies which administered Greek law in a territory governed by Egyptian law (Erich Berneker, *Die Sondergerichtsbarkeit im griechischen Recht Ägyptens* (Beck 1935) 144–53; Hans Lewald, 'Conflits de lois dans la monde grec et romain' (1968) 57 Rev.crit.DIP 419, 437; Michael Rostovtzeff, *The Social and Economic History of the Hellenistic World* (OUP 1941) 324; Hans Julius Wolff, *Das Problem der Konkurrenz von Rechtsordnungen in der Antike* (Winter 1979) 57 ff). These chrematist courts may have been the forerunners of later special courts for foreigners in a host state.

3. Special substantive law for foreigners

The *ius civile* of Roman law applied exclusively to Roman citizens, and did not extend to foreign people or to relations of Roman citizens with foreigners (*peregrini*). For these relations the Romans, especially the *praetor peregrinus*, applied the → *ius gentium* (Max Kaser, *Ius gentium* (Böhlau 1993) 4 ff; Moritz Voigt, *Die Lehre vom jus naturale, aequum et bonum und jus gentium der Römer*, vol 1 (Voigt & Günther 1856) 64, 399 ff, vol 2 (Voigt & Günther 1858) 268 ff). This *ius gentium* can be characterized by four distinctive features. First, the *ius gentium* was also Roman substantive law. It was created by Roman authorities (*praetor peregrinus*) who – apart from the modern term *ius gentium* as law between states – applied that law in cases with and between foreigners. Second, the *ius gentium* was not based on comparative research, but rather on traditional knowledge and general experience which requires no proof or evidence. It was a kind of customary law (Max Kaser, *Ius gentium* (Böhlau 1993) 6). Third, the *ius gentium* was less rigid and formalistic than the *ius civile*. It was more equitable and akin to natural justice (*ius naturale*). Finally, the *ius gentium* was not law for foreigners (*Fremdenrecht, conditions des étrangers*) since it also applied to Romans when they entered into legal relations with foreigners.

4. Protection by national or state law

Before the *Constitutio Antoniniana* (*ca* 212 AD) was given and Roman citizenship was awarded to everybody living in the Roman Empire (apart from certain subjugated tribes or nations) the personal principle prevailed (Greek law for Greek citizens, Roman law for Romans, Jewish law for Jews), and the principle of → choice of law or of the → *lex fori* is likely to have protected also foreigners living in the Eastern or Western part of the Roman Empire (Barbara Pferdehirt, 'Neubürger mit Begeisterung? Die Auswirkungen der Constitutio Antoniniana auf das Individuum' in Barbara Pferdehirt and Markus Scholz (eds), *Bürgerrecht und Krise. Die Constitutio Antoniniana 212 n. Chr. und ihre innenpolitischen Folgen* (RGZM 2012) 59 ff). Late in antiquity the *Codex Theodosianus* was published in 438 AD. The vulgar Roman law lost its formal rigour and could be administered by local judges. Also regional codes (eg *Lex Romana Visigothorum, Lex Burgundionum*) provided protection until in the Middle Ages conflicts between city statutes and the common Roman law had to be decided.

II. Middle Ages

The development of private international law in the Middle Ages can only be understood by realizing the potential conflicts to be resolved or ignored.

1. Conflicts with the person's law of origin

Having conquered certain regions, the Roman Empire tended not to alter the indigenous law. Rather the inhabitants of such regions continued to be governed by their law of origin. If seized by a court of Roman law, a party could plead that application of their law of origin by making a *professio iuris* like this: *professo sum ex natione mea lege vivere langobarda* (Karl Neumeyer, *Die gemeinrechtliche Entwicklung des internationalen Privat- und Strafrechts bis Bartol*us (Schweitzer 1901 and 1916) I 98). But this system of personality could not last indefinitely as it was complained that 'it does happen that five men walk or are seated together and that no one has the same law as another of his brothers' (Bishop Agobard of Lyon, *ca* 770–840). After a considerable period this personality system vanished (Simeon L. Guterman, 'The Principle of the Personality of Law in the Early Middle Ages: A Chapter in the Evolution of Western Institutions and Ideas' (1966) 21 U.Miami L.Rev. 259 ff; Karl Neumeyer, *Die gemeinrechtliche Entwicklung des internationalen Privat- und Strafrechts bis Bartolus* (Schweitzer 1901 and 1916) I 22 ff; Louis Stouff, 'Il principio della personalità delle leggi dalle invasioni barbariche al secolo XII' (1967) 21 Dir.internaz. 80 ff) to be revived in the 19th century by *Pasquale Stanislao → Mancini* (1817–1888) and the principle of nationality.

2. Conflicts with local statutes

A form of interstate conflict or conflict of hierarchy arose with respect to local statutes, principally in Italian towns which were permitted to modify the common Roman law (*ius commune*). According to medieval constitutional law, cities were allowed to do so but the issue arose of whether all assets wherever located, and all persons whether or not citizens, were bound by these statutes, called *statuta*. One would imagine that the *statuta* stipulated their territorial and personal dimensions. But they incorporated no specific term from which the applicability of the statute could be determined by interpretation. This task of interpreting the local *statuta* was taken up by the jurists of Italian universities, founded in the 11/12th centuries. These jurists wrote a Gloss and commentaries on the *Corpus iuris civilis* (henceforth CIC) and tried to systematize Roman law contained in the CIC as a collection of single questions answered by Roman jurists such as *Papinian* or *Ulpian*. In the CIC there is no special part, chapter or questions on conflicts law. Thus the early jurists (→ *Aldricus* of the 12th century, *Accursius* of the early 13th century, *Bartolus of Sassoferrato* of the early 14th century (→ Bartolus), his pupil *Baldus* of the late 14th century and other scholars of → France and → Italy) chose as the starting point for their ideas on conflicts law the beginning of the *Codex Iustiniani* (Codex

I, 1 on '*Cunctos populos*' of 529 AD), repeating the Edict of Thessalonica of 380 AD, which introduced Christianity into the entire Roman Empire (Max Gutzwiller, *Geschichte des Internationalprivatrechts. Von den Anfängen bis zu den großen Privatrechtskodifikationen* (Helbing & Lichtenhahn 1977) 16 ff). These jurists were called glossators and commentators, and developed a certain system according to which local statutes should be interpreted if they were silent regarding their territorial and personal applicability. The scholars finally agreed that local statutes are either *statuta personalia*, *statuta realia* or *statuta mixta*, ie the statutes applied only to certain people, exclusively to certain assets or to certain acts which should be qualified neither as personal nor as acts in rem (Max Gutzwiller, *Geschichte des Internationalprivatrechts. Von den Anfängen bis zu den großen Privatrechtskodifikationen* (Helbing & Lichtenhahn 1977) 93 ff). Whether these *statuta* were to be qualified as *personalia*, *realia* or *mixta*, the scholars sought to ascertain whether the statutes were prohibitive (*statuta prohibitive, applicable to all persons*), permissive (*statuta permissive, applicable to all persons*), favourable (*statuta favorabiles, applicable to all persons*) or odious (*statuta odiosa*, restricted to the *lex fori*). Ultimately *Bartolus* decided the qualification according to the formulation of a statute (see II.4.b below).

3. Conflicts between general local and common Roman law

The Roman Empire extended in 100 AD to all countries around the Mediterranean Sea and to more than 40 different modern states. Although Roman law was or became applicable in most of these territories, local law was applied to local matters and even to matters having some contacts with a different foreign local law. This law was not the so-called vulgar Roman law but rather local law, in many cases Hellenic law particularly in the Eastern territories of the Roman Empire. Here also interstate conflicts could arise and had to be resolved, but no special rules applied except the principles of *ius gentium*, special statutes of limited applicability, and distorted 'vulgar local law' (Ludwig Mitteis, *Reichsrecht und Volksrecht in den östlichen Provinzen des römischen Kaiserreichs* (Teubner 1891)). Roman law proper applied particularly when the Emperor issued an edict (generally applicable regulation) or gave a *rescriptio* (binding answer) to specific local questions to be answered in the name of the Roman Emperor.

4. Conflicts with the law of foreign countries

With respect to the law of foreign countries two different methods have to be distinguished.

a) Lex mercatoria

In the Middle Ages (particularly at the time of the Hanseatic League) a certain → *lex mercatoria* was applied by fair and market courts but not by ordinary state courts (Alice Beardwood, *Alien Merchants in England 1350–1377* (Medieval Academy of America 1931) 76 ff; Wyndham Beawes, *Lex mercatoria* (6th edn, Rivington 1813); Wyndham Anstis Bewes, *The Romance of the Law Merchant* (Sweet & Maxwell 1923); Frank Eichler, *Lex mercatoria – das englische Marktrecht des Mittelalters* (Mauke 2008); William Mitchell, *Essay on the Early History of the Law Merchant* (CUP 1904); Derek Roebuck, *Mediation and Arbitration in the Middle Ages, England 1154–1558* (Holo Books 2013) 70 ff).

b) Solution by some rules of delimitation

Apparently also with respect to international conflicts, courts and scholars applied the same statutist method as developed for interstate or interregional conflicts. This can be shown by the famous '*quaestio angelica*' (English question) discussed by *Bartolus* in Commentaries to Codex 1.1.1. under no 42 (= Friedrich Meili, 'Die theoretischen Abhandlungen von Bartolus und Baldus' (1894) 4 NiemZ 340, 345 ff, and Joseph Henry Beale, *Bartolus on the Conflict of Laws* (Harvard University Press 1914) 44 ff). *Bartolus* asked for the governing succession law if a person died in Italy (with no primogeniture succession) and also bequeathed property in England (with primogeniture succession) to the English estate. *Bartolus*' response is highly formalistic and hardly satisfactory: if the statute reads '*bona decedentium veniant ...*', then the statute is a real one and the respective *lex rei sitae* applies, whereas if the statute reads '*primogenitus succedat ...*', then the statute must be personal and the law of the deceased person applies.

III. Development from the 16th to the 18th century

Although literature on conflicts law was written everywhere in Latin as the scientific *lingua franca*, the development in some European regions diverged due to political and social factors.

1. Development in France

→ France was a centrally organized state but still lacked uniform private law until it was consolidated in the Code civil of 1804. France was divided into two major parts. The North was called *pays de coutume* based on regional customs (eg *Coutume de Paris* or *Coutume de Bretagne*), local statutes and subsidiarily Roman law, whereas the South was *pays de droit écrit* based principally on Roman law. Conflicts arose between these two parts as well as between different *coutumes*. These problems were discussed very early by two scholars: Charles Dumoulin (*Carolus Molinaeus*: 1500–66) and Bertrand d'Argentré (*Argentraeus*: 1519–90). Dumoulin still adhered to the Italian statutists and further developed this method, introducing → party autonomy as a → connecting factor (Franz Gamillscheg, *Der Einfluss Dumoulins auf die Entwicklung des Kollisionsrechts* (De Gruyter/Mohr Siebeck 1955) 110 ff; Max Gutzwiller, *Geschichte des Internationalprivatrechts. Von den Anfängen bis zu den großen Privatrechtskodifikationen* (Helbing & Lichtenhahn 1977) 69 ff; Armand Lainé, *Introduction au droit international privé contenant une étude historique et critique de la théorie des statuts* (Pichon 1888 and 1892) I 294 ff). Dumoulin was an open minded person, a fervent Calvinist and proponent of the unification of French private law. Argentré was quite different, an ardent citizen of Brittany and known for his espousal of the famous assertion '*les coutumes sont réelles*'. This, however, did not mean that, in Argentré's view, the *coutumes* were restricted to local matters, but rather also exerted certain extraterritorial effects, as developed by Argentré himself and by his followers in later centuries (Max Gutzwiller, *Geschichte des Internationalprivatrechts. Von den Anfängen bis zu den großen Privatrechtskodifikationen* (Helbing & Lichtenhahn 1977) 81 ff; Armand Lainé, *Introduction au droit international privé contenant une étude historique et critique de la théorie des statuts* (Pichon 1888 and 1892) I 311 ff).

French practice and theory before 1804 are dealt with extensively by George-René Delaume.

2. Development in the Netherlands

While the situation in the Netherlands was quite different from that in France, it nevertheless bore certain comparisons. From 1568 until 1648 the Low Countries fought for their independence until they were recognized by the Peace Treaty of Westphalia (1648) as a Dutch Republic consisting mainly of Calvinist inhabitants. Law in the Netherlands was not unified until 1838 when the *Burgerlijk Wetboek* (a Dutch version for the French Code civil) entered into force. In various regions different laws applied, and hence many conflicts arose in interregional and international cases, eg in the case of the '*famosissima quaestio*' (Daniel Josephus Jitta, *Die 'famosissima quaestio' von 1693* (Enke 1909); Alfred E. von Overbeck, 'La famosissima quaestio resolue?' in *Comparability and Evaluation, Essays Dimitra Kokkini-Iatridou* (Nijhoff 1994) 251 ff).

A couple was domiciled in Bruxelles at the time of marriage and subsequently. The wife died leaving real estate located in Bergen-op-Zoom (North of Antwerp in North Brabant). The wife had already owned the property at the time of marriage and she bequeathed it by a duly written will to her sisters. Matrimonial property in Bruxelles did not comprise pre-marital property, so that the wife could dispose of her pre-marital property without limitation. In Bergen-op-Zoom, however, *communio universalis* (community property) governed as the → matrimonial property regime of spouses, according to which the deceased wife could only dispose of half of her property located in Bergen-op-Zoom. The husband challenged the will, claiming one half of the estate in Bergen-op-Zoom. Ultimately the *Suprema Curia Brabantiae* in The Hague ruled in favour of the husband, holding that the *lex rei sitae* governed, as opposed to the law of the spouses' domicile.

More significant are the discussions of Paul Voet (1619–67), his son Johannes Voet (1647–1714) (→ Voet, Paulus and Johannes) and Ulrich Huber (1636–94) (→ Huber, Ulrik). These scholars, proud of this recently recognized independence of the Netherlands, accepted Argentré's theory of → territoriality but added an important factor of great influence. They held the view that rights acquired abroad should be recognized as vested rights by *comitas gentium* (→ comity of nations), and be enforced by local courts or agencies (Roeland Duco Kollewijn, *Geschiedenis van de Nederlandse wetenschap van het internationaal privaatrecht tot 1880* (Noord-Hollandsche Uitg. 1937) 78 ff; Eduard Maurits Meijers, 'L'histoire des principes fondamentaux du droit international privé à partir du Moyen Age, spécialement dans Europe occidentale' (1934) 49 Rec. des Cours 543, 653 ff; Friedrich Meili, 'Ein Specimen aus der holländischen Schule de internationalen Privatrechts: (Ulricus Huber 1636–1694)' (1898) 8 NiemZ 189 ff; Johannes Marinus Bernardus Scholten, *Het begrip comitas in het internationaal privaatrecht van de Hollandse Juristenschool der zeventiende eeuw* (Dekker & van de Vegt 1949) 11 ff). Here we find one of the first influences of public international law on conflicts law, perhaps inspired by *Hugo Grotius* (1583–1645) and his work *De iure belli et pacis* (1625).

3. Development in German-speaking countries

Also the German speaking countries of → Austria, → Germany, → Liechtenstein and → Switzerland lacked a unified written private law. Law was to a large extent local law with Roman common law as subsidiarily applicable law. Unification came later: in Austria and Liechtenstein the ABGB of 1811, in Switzerland the Code of Obligations of 1881 and the Civil code of 1907 and in Germany the BGB of 1896. Hence, most of the conflicts cases arising in these countries were interregional, rather than international conflicts cases.

The scholars from German-speaking countries contributed to conflicts law in Latin, as did most European authors before 1800. The most significant individuals were *Benedict Carpzov* (1595–1666, judge in Saxony), *David Mevius* (1609–70, practising jurist and professor in Swedish Pomerania), *Samuel Stryk* (1640–1710, judge and professor in Saxony), *Heinrich von Cocceji* (1644–1719, professor in Heidelberg, Utrecht and Frankfurt/Oder) and *Johann Nikolaus Hert* (1651–1710, professor in Giessen). When consulted, these scholars supplied answers to practical cases, while seeking to generalize their opinions in their treatises on conflict of laws. *Mevius* supervised the first book on bankruptcy (with international dimensions) and *Hert* coined the expression *collisio legum* in his book *De collisione legume dissertatio* (1688). All of these scholars sought to escape the rigid rules of the Italian medieval statutist and proposed reasonable solutions for cases of daily practice (Christian von Bar and Peter H. Dopffel, *Deutsches Internationales Privatrecht im 16. und 17. Jahrhundert*, 2 vols (Mohr Siebeck 1995 and 2001) I and II).

4. Development in Great Britain

England took no part in the continental discussion of conflicts problems. *William Blackstone* (1723–80), in his *Commentaries of the Laws of England* (1st edn, 1765–9), wrote that relations between foreigners are subject to the law merchant (see II.4. above) as part of the law of nations (vol IV, 9th edn, 1783, 67). In all other cases the *lex fori* is applied by local courts with jurisdiction, and occasionally the judges referred to foreign, mostly Dutch authorities (D.J. Llewellyn Davies, 'The Influence of Huber's *De Conflictu Legum* on English Private international law' (1937) 18 BYIL 49).

The situation was quite different in Scotland. United with England since 1707 to form part of the Kingdom of Great Britain, Scotland traditionally had close contacts with the Netherlands. Students went to Leiden and Utrecht and brought with them new Dutch ideas about conflicts law. *Lord Kames* (1696–1782), a contemporary of *Blackstone*, devoted an entire chapter in his 'Principles of Equity' to 'foreign matters' (Henry Home Lord Kames, *Principles of Equity* (Millar 1760) 265 ff).

5. Summary

At the end of the 18th century conflicts law was still rather primitive in form. Parties, courts and lawyers tended to muddle through a bulk of learned writings, attempting to find an appropriate solution for their cases at issue. There was hardly any guiding principle or convincing theory to assist private parties involved in an interregional or international dispute. Evidence for this lack is provided by the codifications in the late 18th century and the early 19th century. Neither the Prussian ALR of 1794 nor the French Code civil of 1804 or the Austrian ABGB of 1811 contained a comprehensive chapter on private international law. Only isolated provisions vaguely indicated the spatial and personal dimension of their contents.

IV. Private international law in the 19th century

Modern private international law commenced in the 19th century. In many countries, scholars discussed the problems, found new solutions and occasionally went astray. Most scholars were also practitioners, giving guidance to the courts and the legislatures of their respective countries, as well as contributing to multilateral international conventions which originated in the 19th century.

1. Literature on private international law

National languages have now supplanted Latin in writings on private international law intended for students and practitioners of the bar and judges in courts (see the bibliography with Joseph Henry Beale, *A Treatise on the Conflict of Laws*, vol I/1 (Harvard University Press 1916) XVII–LXX). Many books have been translated into English (eg the Germans *Ludwig von Bar* and *Friedrich Carl von → Savigny, Friedrich Carl von*), French (eg the Dutch author *Tobias Michael Carel Asser*, the Italian scholar *Pasquale Fiore*), Italian (eg the Belgian *François Laurent* and the German author *Friedrich Carl von Savigny*) and Spanish (eg the French author *Jean Jacques Gaspard Foelix* and the Italian scholar *Pasquale Fiore*). Apart from this formality, scholars concentrated on all problems of private international law and their works can be characterized in three respects.

a) From Bartolus *and* Huber *to national conflicts law*

In the early 19th century authors continued to cite and argue with the old authorities of the Middle Ages and the early modern times, seeking to rationalize or criticize their ideas (Nicola Rocco, *Dell'uso e autorità delle leggi del Regno delle Due Sicilie* (Guttemberg 1837) 121 ff). In English-speaking countries in particular a following developed for → *Huber, Ulrik*, with scholars accepting and basing their research on *Huber*'s theory of comity and vested rights (Samuel Livermore, *Dissertation on the Questions which Arise from the Contrariety of the Positive Laws of Different States and Nations* (Levy 1828) 21 ff; Joseph Story, *Commentaries on the Conflict of Laws* (Billiard, Gray 1834) 37 ff; D.J. Llewellyn Davies, 'The Influence of Huber's De Conflictu legum on English Private international law' (1937) 18 BYIL 49). In continental European countries, writers on private international law concentrated increasingly on national conflicts law as soon as conflicts law became codified, particularly in Italy (1865), Switzerland (1891) and Germany (1896). This form of 'nationalization' of conflicts doctrine continued once conflicts law was codified in national statutes on private international law in the 20th century.

b) Bases of private international law in public international law

Since the middle of the 19th century certain authors have based their ideas about private international law on public international law. In 1851 *Pasquale Stanislao Mancini* → (*Mancini, Pasquale Stanislao* (1817–88)), scholar, politician and ardent Italian patriot, delivered his famous inaugural speech (*Prelezione*) at the University of Torino on *Della nazionalità come fondamento del diritto delle genti* (Botta 1851). He was of the opinion that nationality (not citizenship) of people with the same language and customs should be the foundation of modern states, as opposed to territories created as states by conventions, treaties or international pacts. The Kingdom of Savoy at that time was fighting the Austrians as the occupying power in Italy. This nationality theory persisted for a considerably long time until it declined in the 20th century (Arthur Nussbaum, 'Rise and Decline of the Law-of-Nations Doctrine in the Conflict of Laws' (1942) 42 Colum.L.Rev. 189–208).

c) New directions for modernization

Among the many new ideas of conflicts law three most important developments should be mentioned: the shift from statutes to relationship, nationality or citizenship as → connecting factor and internationalization of conflicts law by international conventions.

(i) The German law professor, historian and Prussian minister *Friedrich Carl von Savigny* → (*Savigny, Friedrich Carl von* (1779–1861)) contributed immensely to conflicts law in the last vol 8 of his work *System des heutigen Römischen Recht* published in 1849 and translated into English by *William Guthrie* in 1869 and 1880 (2nd edn). *Savigny* no longer relied on statutes and their interpretation but rather on the legal relationship in question. For *Savigny*, every legal relationship should be examined for that 'legal territory to which, in its proper nature, it belongs or is subject (in which it has its seat)' (Savigny 108; Savigny, *A Treatise on the Conflict of Laws and the Limits of their Operation in Respect of Place and Time*, translated by William Guthrie (Clark 1880) 89). As soon as law became comprehensively codified in many countries (Prussia: 1794, France: 1804, Austria: 1811;

Baden: 1809/10; Netherlands: 1838; Canton Zürich: 1854, Saxony: 1863; Baltic States: 1864; Italy: 1865), not the single article determined its spatial and personal applicability, but rather the introductory norms placed either at the beginning of the code (eg art 1 *Privatrechtliches Gesetzbuch* (PGB) Canton Zürich) or contained in a separate statute (eg EGBGB).

This search for the law governing a legal relationship became the guiding feature for future research, case-law and codification of private international law (Max Gutzwiller, *Der Einfluß Savignys auf die Entwicklung des Internationalprivatrechts* (Freiburg 1923)). We still use this notion when looking for the 'closest connection' in the EU Rome Regulations and other regulations.

(ii) *Pasquale Stanislao Mancini* → (*Mancini, Pasquale Stanislao*), as already mentioned (see IV.1.b) above), advocated that '*nazionalità*' should be the basis of the law of nations. Accordingly it was no surprise that he influenced the Italian legislature of 1865 to provide '*nazionalità*' of persons as → connecting factor for international (not interstate) family and succession law of conflicts law (arts 6, 8 Codice civile 1865). This example was sufficiently persuasive to be imitated by legislatures of other countries and in early Hague conventions.

(iii) It was also *Pasquale Stanislao Mancini* who advocated that international conventions should be concluded in order to achieve uniformity and harmony in the application of conflicts rules (Mancini, 'De l'utilité de rendre obligatoires pour tous les Etats, sous la forme d'un ou de plusieurs traités internationaux, un certain nombre de règles générales du Droit international privé pour assurer la décision uniforme des conflits entre les différentes législations civiles et criminelles' (1874) 1 Clunet 221 ff, 285 ff). *Mancini* died in 1888, but some years later *Tobias Michael Carel Asser* (1838–1913) succeeded in convening the first session of the Hague Conference on Private International Law in 1893. Since then the Hague Conference has prepared many conventions on private international law, civil procedure and legal assistance (see IV.3. below).

2. *Case-law of national court*

Since antiquity, cases have been the essential arena of private international law, and this has not changed until today. Courts face the conflicts problem, rely on able attorneys and consult the treatises of learned scholars.

a) Bilateral rules of conflict of laws
With the statutists it was merely necessary to determine whether a specific local statute applied. However, as soon as this approach was abandoned in a search for the legal system with the closest connection, bilateral conflict rules were formulated indicating the governing law, be it local or foreign law. The courts of many countries assumed this task, and by interpretation ruled that a uniform conflicts rule on the applicable law of the forum should be extended by analogy to a bilateral rule, applying foreign law on the same basis of the applicable → connecting factor (see for Germany Hans Lewald, *Das deutsche internationale Privatrecht* (Tauchnitz 1931) 6 ff).

b) Qualification of legal problems
Bilateral conflicts rules do not prevent all legal problems being treated similarly in conflicts cases. These problems also arose first in the courts, for example in the issue of how English or American statutes of limitation should be qualified – whether as matters of substantive law subject to the substantive law governing the lawsuit, or as a matter of procedural law subject to the law of the forum. At first the courts were unsure and decided that a claim does not become statute-barred because the law governing the claim is silent regarding limitation and because the law of the forum qualifies limitation as a matter of substance as opposed to procedure (German Imperial Court of Justice (Reichsgericht) of 4 January 1882, (1882) 7 RGZ 21). Very soon, however, the problem of qualification or characterization (→ Classification (characterization)) was 'discovered' by *Franz Kahn* → (Kahn, Franz) and *Étienne Bartin* → (Bartin, Étienne).

c) Renvoi of the law applicable
Over 150 years ago in 1841, one of the first cases of → *renvoi* was decided in the English case *Collier v Rivaz* (163 ER 608). The English court was seized with the case of a British subject who died domiciled in → Belgium leaving codicils in a form which were valid under English law but invalid under Belgian law. The English court accepted a *renvoi* of Belgian private international law (applicable as the laws of the deceased's last domicile) to the English *lex patriae* and deemed the codicils valid.

3. National statutes on private international law

National legislation began to develop in the late 18th century. The early focus of codification was not on private international law but on substantive private law (Prussian ALR of 1794, French Code civil of 1804 and Austrian ABGB of 1811) with a few scattered provisions on conflicts problems. This changed half a century later. New codifications of private law were launched and – remarkably – a number of introductory provisions on the conflicts issue were at the head of the codifications: §§ 1 ff PGB of the Swiss Canton Zürich of 1854; art 14 ff Código civil of 1855 of Chile; art XXVII ff Baltic Civil Code of 1864; art 6 ff Codice civile of Italy of 1865; art 1 ff Código civil of Argentine of 1871; and Swiss Statute on Domiciliaries and Residents of 1891.

Nevertheless these introductory provisions were also incomplete and gave no guarantee of international harmony or unification. This could only be achieved by international conventions as advocated by → *Mancini, Pasquale Stanislao*.

4. International conventions

In 1889 a congress of delegates from Argentina, Bolivia, Brazil, Chile, Paraguay, Peru and Uruguay convened in Montevideo and prepared drafts of international conventions on International Civil Law and on International Commercial Law. This unification was limited to American counties, but was later continued by the Inter-American Council of Jurists, which drafted the Código Bustamante of 1928 (Convention on Private international law (Bustamante Code), adopted at Havana on 20 February 1928 at the Sixth International Conference of American States; OAS, Law and Treaty Series, No 34; → *Bustamante, Antonio Sánchez de*) accepted by several Latin-American countries (see Jürgen Samtleben, *Internationales Privatrecht in Lateinamerika*, vol 1 (Mohr Siebeck 1979) 13 ff).

In 1893 the first session of the → Hague Conference on Private International Law took place in The Hague. *Tobias Michael Carel Asser*, a founding member of the *Institut de droit international*, founded in Gent/Belgium in 1873, succeeded in persuading the Dutch government to invite state delegates to The Hague with a view to achieving the goal declared in the Dutch Government Memorandum of 1893 and addressed to the invited powers: 'In no other way, than by international agreement, cast in the form of conventions or harmonized legislation, can conflicts of law be resolved in a truly effective way' (Memorandum addressed by the Government of the Netherlands to the Powers invited to the Conference on Private international law (1893), (1993) 40 NILR XV, XVI).

5. Summary

Most problems of private international law were already subject to discussion in the 19th century. Only few novel problems arose later for resolution (eg mandatory rules of third states). Conflicts law was still rather rigid and – as considered by most scholars – apolitical and neutral. This changed some 100 years later in the late 20th century.

V. Recent developments since 1900

Two world wars plunged most European countries into post-war financial and economic crises. After the Second World War the so-called Cold War prevailed for over 40 years. The EU was founded and began to integrate European Member States. In 1990 the Balkan War broke out and Yugoslavia collapsed and split into several independent states. Finally, globalization got under way with rapid information, increased international trade and considerable personal mobility between states. These factors also impacted on private international law.

1. Nationalization by statutory law, literature and case-law

Despite unification by Hague conventions, private international law became generally national in character. Conflicts law was incorporated into national statutory provisions as soon as new civil codes were introduced (eg Greek Civil code 1940 (Astikos Kodikas of 23 February 1946, A.N. 2250/1040; FEK A 91/1940, 597), Italian Civil Code (Codice Civile, Gazz.Uff. 4 April 1942, no 79 and 79bis; edizione straordinaria), Egypt 1948 (Law No 131/1948 of 16 July 1948, al qānūn al madanī), Portuguese Código civil 1966 (Código Civil of 25 November 1966, Decreto Lei No 47–344)) or once obsolete statutory provisions became so unsatisfactory that a jurist could be persuaded to draft a fresh statute on private international law (eg Austrian Federal Code on Private international law (Bundesgesetz über das internationale

Privatrecht of 15 June 1978, BGBl. No 304/1978), Turkey 1982 (Law No 2675 of 1982 on Private international law and Procedure), Swiss Private international law Act (Bundesgesetz über das Internationale Privatrecht of 18 December 1987, 1988 BBl II 5 = AS 1988, 1776); Italian Private international law Act (Riforma del Sistema italiano di diritto internazionale privaté, Act No 218 of 31 May 1995 in Gazz.Uff, Supplemento Ordinario No 128 of 3 June l995), Belgian Private international law Act (Wet houdende het Wetboek von international privaatrecht/Code de droit international privé of 16 July 2004, BS 27 July 2004, pp 57344, 57366), Polish Private international law Act (Official Journal 2011 No 80, pos 432), the Netherlands 2011 (Book 10 of the Dutch New Civil Code (Nieuw Burgerlijk Wetboek of 1 January 1992) and the Czech Republic 2012 (Act No 91/2012 Sb, on private international law)). Since 1963, East European socialist countries introduced special statutes on private international law (eg Soviet Union 1961, Czechoslovakia 1963, Poland 1965 and the German Democratic Republic 1975). These sources had to be explained in treatises and commentaries in order to provide guidance for courts, lawyers and students. Case-law was compiled and served as precedent for daily practice. Hardly any foreign sources or authorities were cited in national judgments or legal literature. Courts and scholars dealt with certain national specialties, for example England with the 'double *renvoi*' (Lord Collins of Mapesbury and others (eds), *Dicey, Morris & Collins on the Conflict of Laws*, vol 1 (15th edn, Sweet & Maxwell 2012) no 4-001), France with '*lois d'application immediate*' (Phocion Francescakis, *La théorie du renvoi et les conflits de systèmes en droit international privé* (Sirey 1958) 11 ff), Germany with the '*Vorfrage*' (George Melchior, *Die Grundlagen des deutschen IPR* (De Gruyter 1932) 245 ff) and Italy with the '*rinvio recettizio*' (Rodolfo De Nova, 'New Trends in Italian Private international law' (1963) 28 LCP 808, 810–13).

2. *Constitutionalization*

Once constitutional law (→ Constitutional law and private international law) became directly enforceable after World War II, it also affected private international law. National constitutional law as well as the European Convention for the Protection of Human Rights and Fundamental Freedoms (ECHR, European Convention of 4 November 1950 for the Protection of Human Rights and Fundamental Freedoms, 213 UNTS 221) and the Treaty of the European Economic Community (Treaty of 25 March 1957 establishing the European Economic Community, 294–298 UNTS, later EU) had an enormous influence on conflicts law.

a) National constitutional law
Particularly in Germany, but also in other countries, the issue arose whether conflicts law determines not only the applicable private law but also the pertinent constitutional law (Murad Ferid, 'Wechselbeziehungen zwischen Verfassungsrecht und Kollisionsnormen' in *Vom deutschen zum europäischen Recht. Festschrift Hans Dölle*, vol 2 (Mohr Siebeck 1963) 119–48, 143) or whether national conflicts law itself has to be compatible with standards of the constitutional law of the forum state. More than 20 years after entry into force of the new Basic Law for the Federal Republic of Germany (Grundgesetz of 23 May 1949, BGBl. 1, as amended) the Federal Constitutional Court decided that all German rules on private international law have to be compatible with the constitutional requirement of basic rights as provided by the German constitution (Federal Constitutional Court of Germany (BVerfG), 4 May 1971, 31 BVerfGE 58, with comment by Friedrich K. Juenger, 'The German Constitutional Court and the Conflict of Laws' (1972) 20 Am.J.Comp.L. 290–8). The case concerned the question whether a woman validly divorced under German law can legally marry a foreigner whose national law does not recognize the divorce and therefore prohibits the new marriage. It was held that declining such a marriage by German civil registrars would violate the basic right to remarry (art 6(1) Basic Law for the Federal Republic of Germany) after the previous marriage has been dissolved. Accordingly a new marriage cannot be declined by German civil registrars. One month later the Swiss Federal Court decided the same problem the same way (Federal Court of Switzerland (*Schweizerisches Bundesgericht*), 3 June 1971, BGE 97 I 389).

The following years the inequality of man and women, husband and wife was declared unconstitutional (Federal Constitutional Court of Germany (BVerfG), 22 February 1983, 63 BVerfGE 181, Corte cost 5 March 1987, n 71, 23 Riv.Dir.Int'le Priv. & Proc. 297 (1987)) and a number of states soon passed legislation abolishing such inequalities (Austria: 1978; Germany: 1986; Switzerland: 1987; Italy: 1995).

b) European Convention on Human Rights
All 47 Member States of the Council of Europe are state parties to the ECHR. They submitted to the jurisdiction of the European Court of Human Rights (ECtHR) in Strasbourg and this Court may be referred to on potential human rights violations in specific cases (→ Human rights and private international law). Such a violation has been assumed in several international cases. For example, the father of an illegitimate child has a right to contact his child and such a contact cannot be opposed without reason by the child's mother (*Görgülü v Germany* App no 74969/01 (ECtHR 26 February 2004), 2004 HRLJ 93); a child lawfully adopted abroad has to be treated as an adopted child after a certain period (14 years) even if the foreign → adoption is not recognized (*Negrepontis-Giannisis v Greece* App no 56759/08 (ECtHR, 3 May 2011)); and an abducted child should not be returned to the country of abduction if such return would be adverse to the child's welfare (*Neulinger v Switzerland* App no 41615/07 (ECtHR 6 July 2010)). Not all of these decisions have met with approval. The ECtHR is criticized for paying insufficient respect to special international agreements which are concluded in order to combat abuses and international fraud (see now *Povse v Austria* App no 3890/11 (ECtHR, 18 June 2013) also published in 2013 FamRZ 1793).

c) Treaty of the European Union: Europeanization of European private international law
The Treaty of the European Union (TEU, Consolidated Version of the Treaty on European Union [2012] OJ C 326/13) with its guaranteed freedoms may also impose limits on national legislators of private international law, as for example in the company law field with respect to cross-border movement of → companies and the maintenance of legal capacity (→ Capacity and emancipation). With respect to company law the ECJ favoured the theory of the law of foundation to govern also the company's capacity to sue and to be sued: ECJ 3 November 2002 in the case of *Überseering* (Case C-208/00 *Überseering BV v Nordic Construction Company Baumanagement GmbH* [2002] ECR I-9919) (→ Companies).

In the law of personal names the ECJ favoured the parents' choice of a different → nationality to choose the name of their child according to either nationality: ECJ of 2 October 2003 in the case of *Garcia Avello* (Case C-148/02 *Carlos Garcia Avello v Belgian State* [2003] ECR I-11613), and with respect to change of the parents' domicile the ECJ was in favour of the law of first domicile and registration of the child with the civil registrar: Case C-353/06 *Stefan Grunkin and Dorothee Regina Paul* [2008] ECR I-7639) in the case of *Grunkin Paul* (→ Names of individuals). The ECJ only decided that a certain result is incompatible with the TEU, but failed to mention how European private international law should be properly formulated.

Today, private international law in Europe has become almost completely European law. Over ten regulations and directives with over 500 articles apply. In the near future these individual sources will be merged into a comprehensive European Code of Private international law, thereby completing the process of the Europeanization of private international law within the EU.

3. Policy-orientated conflicts law, mandatory rules

In the past private international law was thought to be rather formalistic and strict. Justice had to be administered under substantive law to be applied by the competent forum. This attitude has changed since the Second World War. Three phases can be distinguished.

a) Overriding mandatory provisions, especially of third countries
One purpose of private international law is to select the applicable private law system which governs an international dispute. Public law is, however, not selected by private international law. But foreign → overriding mandatory provisions can be given effect in private law disputes.

b) Habitual residence and party autonomy
Since the 19th century many continental European, Latin American and Asian countries supported → *Mancini, Pasquale Stanislao* and his plea for *nazionalità* as the primary → connecting factor in matters of family and succession law (see IV.1.b) above). This has changed considerably and the habitual residence (→ Domicile, habitual residence and establishment) of the respective person has been favoured as connecting

factor for almost 60 years and party autonomy is recognized more often.

c) Protection of the weaker party

To protect the normally weaker party is one of the most important examples of modern policy-oriented conflicts law. Apart from the protection of children and adults, the consumer, employee and insured person are protected not only in substantive law but also in conflicts law by three kinds of provision. (i) The weaker party may bring a lawsuit against the supplier to a consumer, against the employer or the insurance company, including at the weaker party's place of habitual residence. (ii) Any choice of court agreement is invalid if contracted before the action arose. (iii) The governing law is that of the weaker party's habitual residence unless the chosen law is more favourable to that party (→ Consumer contracts; → Employment contracts, applicable law; → Insurance contracts).

4. Traditional private international law or also 'recognition' of situations created abroad

Hitherto EU law has provided traditional bilateral rules of reference of universal character and avoided the limitation of the rules to domestic disputes and a resulting unilateral character of the rules. Whether this system will prevail, however, remains controversial. Especially French scholars want to limit European private international law to the 'recognition' of disputes arising abroad, leaving domestic disputes to national private international law (Paul Lagarde, 'Développements futurs du droit international privé dans une Europe en voie d'unification: quelques conjectures' (2004) 68 RabelsZ 225, 229 ff; Paul Lagarde (ed), *La Reconnaissance des situations en droit international privé* (Pedone 2013); Pierre Mayer, 'La méthode de la reconnaissance en droit international privé' in Bertrand Ancel and others, *Le droit international privé. Etudes et méthodes. Mélanges en honneur de Paul Lagarde* (Dalloz 2005) 547 ff). German scholars prefer the traditional system consisting of bilateral rules of reference and the recognition of foreign judgments and decisions of courts and other public authorities (Hans Jürgen Sonnenberger, 'Anerkennung statt Verweisung? Eine neue internationalprivatrechtliche Methode?' in Jörn Bernreuther and others (eds), *Festschrift für Ulrich Spellenberg* (Sellier 2010) 371 ff; Michael Grünberger, 'Alles obsolet? – Anerkennungsprinzip vs. Klassisches IPR' in Stefan Leible and Hannes Unberath (eds), *Brauchen wir eine Rom O – Verordnung* (Jenaer Wissenschaftliche Verlagsgesellschaft 2013) 81 ff). It remains to be seen which method will ultimately prevail in European private international law (Katja Funken, *Das Anerkennungsprinzip im internationalen Privatrecht* (Mohr Siebeck 2009); Janis Leifeld, *Das Anerkennungsprinzip im Kollisionsrechtssystem des internationalen Privatrechts* (Mohr Siebeck 2010); Julia Rieks, *Anerkennung im Internationalen Privatrecht* (Nomos 2012)).

5. From national to regional and globalized private international law

The dream of → Mancini, Pasquale Stanislao that private international law will be universally unified in international conventions (Mancini, 'De l'utilité', *supra* IV.1. c)(iii), (1874) 1 Clunet 221 ff, 285 ff) has not been realized. The Hague Conference, which started in 1893, had only limited success because the English-speaking countries took no part until they joined the Conference after the Second World War, while many other countries, although members, did not ratify the conventions prepared by the sessions of the Hague Conference. Other universally acting bodies (specialized agencies of the United Nations, such as the International Labour Organization in Geneva, UNESCO in Paris, → UNCITRAL in Vienna; World Intellectual Property Organization in Geneva) and independent agencies (as, eg, *Commission International de l'État Civil* in Strasbourg or UNIDROIT in Rome) sought less to unify private international law, instead preparing conventions on substantive law in their respective fields of activity (see Jan Kropholler, *Internationales Einheitsrecht* (Mohr Siebeck 1975) 43 ff).

The Hague Conference was not the only international organization preparing international conventions unifying private international law. Several regional bodies also sought to unify conflicts law at least on a regional basis. In Latin America the South American congresses and the Pan-American Conference started as early as the 19th century reaching their highest point in 1928 when the *Código Bustamante* was created in Havana (see Jürgen Samtleben, *Internationales Privatrecht in Lateinamerika* (Mohr Siebeck 1979) 6 ff). In Europe the Scandinavian States cooperated very early until they formalized their cooperation in the

Nordic Council of 1952. The Benelux States started to draft a project on private international law but abandoned it in favour of the unification of law by the European Economic Community, the forerunner of the EU, today the main actor in regional unification of private international law in Europe. In Eastern Europe the Comecon (Council for Mutual Economic Assistance) existed from 1949 until 1991 and tried to regulate trade between the Socialist countries through special treaties and international arbitration.

Globalization of sources of private international law has not yet been achieved. Private international law is still national or regional law and we have to wait for a universal unification of this field of law.

KURT SIEHR

Literature

Christian von Bar and H. Peter Dopffel, *Deutsches Internationales Privatrecht im 16. und 17. Jahrhundert* (2 vols, Mohr Siebeck 1995 and 2001); Joseph Henry Beale, *Bartolus on the Conflict of Laws* (Harvard University Press 1914); Enrico L. Catellani, *Il diritto internazionale privato e i suoi recenti progressi* (2nd edn, UTET 1895 and 1902); Georges-René Delaume, *Les conflits de lois à la veille du Code civil* (Sirey 1947); Franz Gamillscheg, *Der Einfluss Dumoulins auf die Entwicklung des Kollisionsrechts* (De Gruyter/Mohr Siebeck 1955); Max Gutzwiller, *Geschichte des Internationalprivatrechts. Von den Anfängen bis zu den großen Privatrechtskodifikationen* (Helbing & Lichtenhahn 1977); Max Kaser, *Ius gentium* (Böhlau 1993); Roeland Duco Kollewijn, *Geschiedenis van de Nederlandse wetenschap van het internationaal privaatrecht tot 1880* (Noord-Hollandsche Uitg. 1937); Armand Lainé, *Introduction au droit international privé contenant une étude historique et critique de la théorie des statuts* (Pichon 1888 and 1892); Hans Lewald, 'Conflits de lois dans la monde grec et romain' (1968) 57 Rev.crit.DIP 419–440, 615–639; Eduard Maurits Meijers, 'L'histoire des principes fondamentaux du droit international privé à partir du Moyen Age, spécialement dans Europe occidentale' (1934) 49 Rec. des Cours 543; Friedrich Meili, 'Die theoretischen Abhandlungen von Bartolus und Baldus' (1894) 4 NiemZ 258–69, 340–6, 446–73; Friedrich Meili, 'Ein Specimen aus der holländischen Schule des internationalen Privatrechts: Ulricus Huber 1636–1694' (1898) 8 NiemZ 189–200; Karl Neumeyer, *Die gemeinrechtliche Entwicklung des internationalen Privat- und Strafrechts bis Bartolus* (Schweitzer 1901 and 1916); Michael Rostovtzeff, *The Social and Economic History of the Hellenistic World* (OUP 1941); Johannes Marinus Bernardus Scholten; *Het begrip comitas in het internationaal privaatrecht van de Hollandse Juristenschool der zeventiende eeuw* (Dekker & van de Vegt 1949); Hans Julius Wolff, *Das Problem der Konkurrenz von Rechtsordnungen in der Antike* (Winter 1979).

Private international law, methods of

I. Methods and purposes of private international law

The choice of a method follows from the purpose pursued by the conflicts analysis. Since there is no general agreement on that purpose (→ Private international law, Concept and Purpose), the methods employed differ likewise. The purposes may be classified as unilateralist, comparativist (referring to substantive law) or coordination-oriented.

The unilateralist approaches are exclusively or primarily interested in the scope of application of the forum's own law (→ Unilateralism); their starting point is the application of the → lex fori as has been advocated most clearly by Albert A Ehrenzweig (Albert A Ehrenzweig, *Private international law* (3rd edn, Sijthoff 1974) 51; → Ehrenzweig, Albert A). Determining the scope of the *lex fori* is a matter of its interpretation. It is one issue among other similar issues which are resolved by way of interpreting the substantive rule in question, eg by assessing its dispositive or mandatory character. The answers follow from the text, context, and purpose of the substantive rule. There is nothing specific about the conflicts analysis. The peculiar nature of the choice of law, ie the coordination of the law of the forum with other legal systems, has a bearing only at a secondary stage: depending on the specific approach taken it may serve either as a corrective or as the basis for a further unilateral conflict rule dealing with the effects to be given to foreign legal rules in domestic courts. Unilateralist approaches are inescapable in certain areas where the law uncompromisingly commands its own enforcement. But they are not suited to resolve the basic problem that arises from the coexistence of numerous jurisdictions with limited territorial effects in a world of open frontiers where the cross-border flow of humans, capital, goods, and services is a global reality and nearly constitutionally ensured. Since there is nothing specific about the methods employed in private international law through the unilateralist approaches, they will not be pursued here in detail.

For others, the main purpose of private international law is the furtherance of certain substantive policies. One variant pursues such material objectives through multiple connections (→ Choice of law, section IV.2.). They are the yardstick for the selection, from several jurisdictions involved, of the one that is preferred for coordination purposes. This is different in the case of the better rule approach (→ Better law approach). Here, from several laws involved, the judge is supposed to choose the law which is more appropriate to resolve a given issue, the law which may thus be said to be more modern and better in this respect. There is neither a clear identification of the laws that may be considered as involved nor a pre-establishment of a given substantive policy. The choice is one made on the basis of comparative law (→ Comparative law and private international law). The resulting methods are not specific to private international law and need not be discussed in this context.

An objective that has no counterpart in domestic law and which is thus characteristic of private international law is the coordination or, as it was put by *Lord Mance*, 'the smooth interaction of different legal systems' (Jonathan Mance, 'The Future of Private international law' (2005) 1 J Priv Int L 185, 185). Private international law typically deals with fact situations comprising foreign elements which may provoke the expectation of the private actors involved that their legal relations be subject to a law other than that of the forum; in addition, the states involved may claim the application of their respective laws. It is the task of private international law to cope with the divergent expectations and claims. Thus, the point of departure of private international law is not the protection of the forum state's legal order; this is only one of the various expectations and claims that have to be balanced. Rather, the starting point of private international law is the coexistence of several legal orders which, pursuant to the principle of sovereign equality of states, are basically placed on an equal footing. This situation gives rise to the problem of coordination. The task can easily be performed 'from above', ie in a federal entity such as the European Union by the European Court of Justice. It is much more difficult for a court sitting within one of the states whose law is involved in the resolution of the dispute, since the court in that case has to perform a dual task: alongside the coordination with other legal systems – which requires a certain degree of self-containment – the court shall also protect the fundamental principles of its own legal order. The coordination of legal systems is not a goal in itself. It is rather meant to enable private actors to carry out their cross-border activities in a multi-jurisdictional world. A major consequence is the protection of rights acquired under a foreign law (→ Vested rights theory).

Several methods dealing with the coordination of the diverse legal orders and their accommodation by private actors have emerged from this background (Paolo Picone, *Ordinamento competente e diritto internazionale privato* (CEDAM 1986) 14–19; Paolo Picone 'Les méthodes de coordination entre ordres juridiques en droit international privé' (1999) 276 Rec. des Cours 9, 25): (i) A simple solution, that is viable, however, only in few situations, is the assertion of exclusive jurisdiction by the courts of a country which will apply their own law and expect their decision to be recognized in all other states. (ii) Where courts in several countries have jurisdiction, the traditional method is the localization of a fact situation and its assignment to one of them, mainly the country most closely connected whose law will then be applied to the international fact situation as if it were of a purely national dimension. (iii) A compromise solution is the combination of the two previous methods; it acknowledges the concurrent jurisdiction of courts in different countries, but subjects it to the condition of the prospective recognition of the future judgment in the country whose law is to govern the merits under the conflict rules of the forum. (iv) A further intermediate approach determines the applicable law in light of substantive values such as the validation of a will or transaction, instead of looking for the closest connection. (v) While it is up to the court first seized of a case to apply methods (i) to (iv), a judge later seized of a case in a different country could also contribute to coordination by simply recognizing judicial and extrajudicial decisions that have been taken abroad and legal situations or relations that have been perfected in other countries. These methods will now be discussed in greater detail.

II. Exclusive jurisdiction

An easy solution for the problem of coordination appears to be the assignment, to every legal relation under the sun, of a single court that would have exclusive jurisdiction and apply its own law. Where the resulting judgment is recognized everywhere else, the coordination of legal systems would be perfect. An authoritative textbook on public international law in fact hints at this solution; noting that it is, however, not in line with the practice of private international law, it offers an unexpected reason for that divergence from what appears to be mandated by common sense: 'If a judge in state X is trying a case which has more connection with state Y than with state X, he is likely to feel that the case should have been tried in state Y, or (since some judges are reluctant to forego the sense of self-importance which comes from trying cases) that he himself should try the case in accordance with the law of state Y. Feelings of this sort have produced a complicated set of rules in almost every country...' (Peter Malanczuk, *Akehurst's Modern Introduction to International Law* (7th edn, Routledge 1997) 71). But is the solution of a single court having exclusive jurisdiction and applying its own law really that simple? Is the application of foreign law only the result of a judge's 'sense of self-importance'?

It is true that exclusive jurisdiction has been acknowledged as a means for the coordination of divergent legal systems in situations which are by necessity and inseparably connected to a single state, eg where proprietary rights (→ Property and proprietary rights) in immovable property or entries in national public registers for companies or intellectual property rights are at stake (see art 24 of the Brussels I Regulation (recast) (Regulation (EU) No 1215/2012 of the European Parliament and of the Council of 12 December 2012 on jurisdiction and the recognition and enforcement of judgments in civil and commercial matters (recast), [2012] OJ L 351/1); → Brussels I (Convention and Regulation)). The fact situations involved in these cases are inescapably linked to a single jurisdiction, but all attempts to extend this mechanism to other, more mobile or even dynamic legal relations, have failed. In matters of contracts, torts, family relations or succession, the recognition of the concurrent jurisdiction of several courts located in different jurisdictions is often inevitable. Concentrating all possible disputes within a single state might lead to an outright denial of justice for certain parties involved.

In this respect, the development of the law relating to international divorce proceedings in England in the 19th and 20th centuries provides a telling example. In the second half of the 19th century, English courts increasingly took the view that only the court of the spouses' common domicile could issue a divorce decree, see *Pitt v Pitt* [1864] 141 RR 752; *Harvey v Farnie* [1882] 8 AC 43. This trend ultimately culminated with the Privy Council holding that any other connecting factor was detrimental to the harmony of decisions and contrary to international law, *LeMesurier v LeMesurier* [1895] AC 517, 540 (PC). The tacit understanding flowing from this reasoning was that a judgment rendered in the court having exclusive jurisdiction would be recognized in all other countries, thus producing a global uniformity of the legal assessment. This theory of jurisdiction and recognition was based on the English law of domicile as applied in those days. The English-style domicile could be far away from the actual residence of the persons involved. It could be, for example, in England, while the individuals in question had been living in India for 20 years. Moreover, every person could have only a single domicile and wives shared the domicile determined by the husband. Therefore, the said English court practice amounted to the exclusive divorce jurisdiction of the courts of a single country for every couple in the world irrespective of the spouses' habitual residence. For persons residing far away from the country of their domicile, this could amount to a great hardship and even to an outright denial of justice. A divorce application in an English court might have been simply unaffordable for a spouse living in Burma or South Africa. The idea of exclusive divorce jurisdiction therefore had to be abandoned over time, see *Travers v Holley* [1953] P 246 (CA); *Indyka v Indyka* [1969] 1 AC 33 (HL); art 3, 22 and 24 → Brussels IIa Regulation (Council Regulation (EC) No 2201/2003 of 27 November 2003 concerning jurisdiction and the recognition and enforcement of judgments in matrimonial matters and the matters of parental responsibility, repealing Regulation (EC) No 1347/2000, [2003] OJ L 338/1).

The English example amounts to the use of identical connecting factors for jurisdiction and the choice of the applicable law. The same idea has been espoused under the designation of *lex fori in foro proprio* or *Gleichlauf* in a number of other countries and areas of the law. To the extent that it results in the assignment of exclusive jurisdiction, it has progressively lost significance, despite the apparent appeal of simplicity. Thus, the long-standing German practice of assigning exclusive jurisdiction in matters of → succession to the state of the decedent's citizenship whose law was applicable under rules of German private international law had already been given up prior to the European succession regulation (Kurt Siehr, *Internationales Privatrecht* (CF Müller 2001) 113 ff, 364). In the field of jurisdiction for general → civil and commercial matters, modern instruments such as the Brussels I Regulation (Regulation (EC) No 44/2001 of 22 December 2000 on jurisdiction and the recognition and enforcement of judgments in civil and commercial matters, [2001] OJ L 12/1; → Brussels I (Convention and Regulation)) or the → Lugano Convention (Lugano Convention of 30 October 2007 on jurisdiction and the recognition and enforcement of judgments in civil and commercial matters, [2007] OJ L 339/3) clearly demonstrate that procedural convenience and justice in many situations require the coexistence of several heads of competence potentially located in as many states. The assignment of exclusive jurisdiction has been maintained only for a few fact situations such as those mentioned above.

III. Choice of law by localization

Given the concurrent jurisdiction of courts in different countries in cases having a cross-border dimension, legal certainty is seriously imperilled if the competent courts can be expected to apply their own laws, unless those laws lead to the same result; in the latter case nothing turns on the selection of a specific law, but where the application of the various laws involved results in different outcomes, legal certainty is lost. It can be regained by private parties through either a choice of a forum that is intended to have exclusive jurisdiction (→ Choice of forum and submission to jurisdiction) or an agreement on the applicable law which will be respected in all competent courts and entail the adjudication of the case under the same substantive rules by all courts (→ Party autonomy).

However, these instruments of private ordering are not available everywhere, and where they are, parties often do not make use of them. It is even fair to say that private international law mainly developed in cases where no such choice was made. It would be incompatible with the commands of justice and the expectations of the parties if the outcome of the case entirely depended, in the absence of choice, on the court seized of the case and on its *lex fori*. As it was put already by *Savigny*: 'Legal relations must respect, in cases of a conflict of laws, the same adjudication irrespective of whether the judgment will be handed down in this or in that state' (Friedrich Carl von Savigny, *System des heutigen römischen Rechts*, vol 8 (Veit & Co 1849) 27; → Savigny, Friedrich Carl von). As a consequence, the courts of the various countries involved are supposed, at least in theory, to apply one and the same substantive law to a cross-border case. This includes, for some of the courts, the basic willingness to apply foreign law, a fundamental precondition for attaining the uniformity of outcome. For identifying the law that would ideally be applicable in all courts of the world, *Savigny* suggested to localize the legal relation in question and to look for the jurisdiction where, according to its nature, it is rooted (Friedrich Carl von Savigny, *System des heutigen römischen Rechts*, vol 8 (Veit & Co 1849) 28). In more recent times, this principle has been revitalized under the name of closeness or proximity between the case and a jurisdiction (Paul Lagarde, 'Le principe de proximité dans le droit international privé contemporain' (1986) 196 Rec. des Cours 9); the assessment of these criteria is not confined to local elements but includes also aspects relating to the substance of the legal relation in question.

In the years following the Second World War, the goal enunciated by *Savigny* has been heavily criticized. It was said to be utopian and the efforts made to achieve it to be futile and even harmful, since interests of the parties and legitimate policy considerations would often be ignored (Trevor Hartley, 'The Modern Approach to Private international law: International Litigation and Transactions from a Common Law Perspective' (2006) 319 Rec. des Cours 9, 29–30). The → (American) Conflict of laws revolution almost abandoned the objective of coordination and replaced the choice-of-law method with all kinds of unilateralist and comparativist approaches. The resulting situation has been characterized as 'chaotic' (Peter Nygh, 'Reform of Private international law in Australia' (1994) 58 RabelsZ 727–740, 739). In Europe, scholars and legislation have essentially adhered to the *Savignian* model, but have accommodated the criticism with a progressive differentiation, flexibilization and materialization of choice-of-law rules. The more recent developments outside Europe, in particular legislation in countries such as → China, → Japan, and → Korea or → Turkey, → Russia, → Tunisia, and → Venezuela demonstrate an almost worldwide approval of the European response.

It is nevertheless true that the *Savignian* model of bilateral conflict rules should not be overrated. Since bilateral conflict rules do not relate to procedure, which is always governed by the *lex fori*, divergent procedural laws, relating to evidentiary matters for example, may still have a distortionary effect on the outcome of a case, depending on the jurisdiction seized, even if adjudication is subject to the same substantive law in the courts of the various countries involved. Moreover, bilateral conflict rules are only suited for those parts of a legal system which are not impregnated by the growing regulatory ambitions of the modern welfare state. In the latter areas, unilateral approaches appear to follow from the regulatory policies. But even in these areas, for example in employment law or market regulation, the goal of coordination subsists. It requires the use of bilateralism wherever possible whereas in other areas, the drafting of unilateral conflict rules including those which give effect to mandatory laws of foreign countries is required.

IV. Jurisdiction dependent on prognosticated recognition

Both methods discussed so far have one thing in common: they implicitly recognize the claim that a single jurisdiction should have applicability for a given case – the 'single competent law'. The idea of the single competent law is also echoed where the – concurrent – jurisdiction of a court depends on the forecast that a resulting decision will be recognized in the country whose law governs the legal relation in question in accordance with the choice-of-law rules of the forum.

An example can still be found in § 98(1) of the German Law on the Procedure in Family Matters (*Gesetz über das Verfahren in Familiensachen und in den Angelegenheiten der freiwilligen Gerichtsbarkeit* of 17 December 2008, BGBl. I 2586, as amended). The provision lays down the conditions of jurisdiction of German courts in matrimonial matters. If both spouses are foreign nationals and only one of them is habitually resident in Germany, German courts will have jurisdiction 'unless the resulting decision will obviously not be recognized by the national law of either spouse', see § 98(1) no 4. For the major part of its scope of application this provision has been superseded by the Brussels IIa Regulation, but it has arguably kept its significance for proceedings aiming at a mere declaration that a marriage exists or does not exist. Confined to its limited remaining scope, the provision gives evidence of the respect for the 'single competent law' and its leading role.

On the other hand it is also clear that rules of this kind give rise to considerable difficulties in legal practice since they require an investigation into foreign law already at an early stage of the proceedings when the jurisdiction of the court has to be ascertained. It is true that the German provision cited above reduces these difficulties by requiring an 'obvious' non-recognition of the foreign judgment. However, even a superficial assessment, such as the one that appears to be required here, is not possible without a look into the foreign law, an inquiry which may be costly and time-consuming. It is therefore unsurprising that jurisdictional rules of this type are very rare and that they can hardly be recommended.

V. Choice of law by multiple connections

In the more recent history of private international law, a method has come to the fore that no longer aims at the identification of the 'single competent law', but employs multiple connections to sort out several laws which are more or less closely linked to a legal situation or relation. The various laws may then be applied to the case by accumulation or by alternation in light of certain substantive policies. A third alternative that equally serves material objectives is the ranking of the laws as primary and residual (→ Choice of law, section IV.2.). In all these cases the choice-of-law analysis is made in two stages, the first selecting the laws in question, and the second determining their relation to each other in light of certain substantive policy goals.

Just like the single connection choice-of-law method (above III.), the methods employing multiple connections aim at coordinating the law of the forum with that of foreign legal systems. The cumulative application purports even a very far-reaching coordination with several legal systems while alternative and residual connections pursue a more modest objective, namely the coordination with a single one of the relevant legal orders. The shortcomings in terms of coordination are compensated by the achievement of a given substantive aim. For example, the validation of a contract is favoured where the conflict rule allows the formal validity to be achieved by either the law applicable to the contract itself or by the law of the place of contracting. As regards the formal validity of wills, the Hague Testamentary Dispositions Convention (Hague Convention of 5 October 1961 on the conflicts of laws relating to the form of testamentary dispositions,

510 UNTS 175) lists not less than five different laws; compliance with the formal requirements (→ Formal requirements and validity) established by any one of them would be sufficient. In a similar vein, the welfare of a child is served where its descent from an alleged father may be proved under several laws, eg the law of the child's habitual residence, the mother's national law or the law governing the effects of the mother's marriage. The laws in question are compared in view of the substantive policy pursued. This substantive policy has been pre-established by legislation or other legal rules. It is the yardstick for the selection, from several jurisdictions involved, of the one that is preferred for coordination purposes.

As demonstrated by these examples, the methods of multiple connections pursue a mix of purposes: while the coordination element originates in traditional private international law, the substantive policies are identified from a comparison of substantive laws. Some of them, such as the child's welfare or the rule of validation, might be considered as belonging to the common core of modern legal development. It is this element of substantive policy that has brought about a certain materialization of the choice of law in more recent times.

VI. Recognition

Courts are often confronted with cross-border legal relations that have already been submitted to a court or agency in a foreign country or that somehow appear to have been finalized abroad. What has emerged from the foreign proceedings may be called a crystallization of the law: either a judicial decision or a registration, certification or similar official act that is based upon the application of law. In domestic proceedings this will raise the question whether the court can simply recognize the foreign crystallization of the law and thereby import the effects it is intended to have in the country of origin without addressing the merits of the legal relation in question.

The → Full Faith and Credit Clause of the US Constitution provides an example of this approach (art IV, s 1 of the US Constitution). It demonstrates the strength of the principle, but also the vagueness of the requirements that have to be met for its operation. In the past, the US Supreme Court sometimes relied on the clause in order to ensure that the interests of the sister states be given regard, or even to impose on one state the application of another's law, apparently considering these laws as 'public acts' entitled to be respected under the Full Faith and Credit Clause. The current significance of the clause seems, however, to be much more limited and mainly confined to the recognition of judicial records and decisions (Peter Hay, Patrick Borchers and Symeon Symeonides, *Conflict of Laws* (5th edn, Thomson Reuters 2010) 175–6 and 186 ff). In the European Union the principle of recognition may play an important role in the future. Legislation on private international law is to be 'based on the principle of mutual recognition of judgments and of decisions in extra judicial cases', art 81 TFEU (Treaty on the Functioning of the European Union (consolidated version), [2012] OJ C 326/47). The explicit reference to judgments and decisions in extrajudicial cases appears to exclude recourse to the principle of mutual recognition for the purposes of → choice of law. But the bearing of the principle is still unclear and will have to be determined by future legislation and case-law.

While the principle of mutual recognition undoubtedly plays an important function in private international law, it is confined to an extension of the effects of acts issued by the administrative authorities and courts of foreign jurisdictions. Where a legal situation or relation, such as a will or a contract, is perfected in a foreign country exclusively by private action, recognition as such does not help (→ Recognition of legal situations evidenced by documents). We can only recognize what has a legal existence. Only a valid contract and a valid will are susceptible of being recognized. In order to find out whether the contract or the will is valid, it is indispensable first to identify the applicable law. But once we have determined that law and found out that the will or the contract in question is valid, there is no room left for a separate operation of recognition; the validity in domestic proceedings already follows from the application of the law resulting from the conflicts rule. Thus, recognition is by necessity confined to what has been called crystallizations of the law brought about by some kind of law-oriented proceeding of a foreign court or state agency.

But even within these limitations, recognition is only a supplement to, and not a substitute for, → choice of law. Recognition only addresses the second state dealing with the legal relation, not the first country. One might perhaps assume that a liberal regime of recognition would enable the courts and agencies of the first country simply to apply their own law, relying on a later recognition in other countries. But other countries are not always involved. Assume for example, a case where a European traveller dies in a road accident in Canada and that certain assets located in a bank in Toronto form part of the decedent's estate. Should the succession in those assets really be governed by the laws of Ontario despite the decedent having been a habitual resident and national of a European country? Should a will drafted by that traveller under the laws of his European country of origin be quashed under the laws of Ontario because it is not in line with its mandatory rules? If a Canadian court has to deal with the matter, it would likely find that idea repugnant to justice and would rather determine the succession in accordance with the law more closely connected with the decedent.

VII. Conclusion

It follows from the discussion of the various methods of private international law outlined in this entry that each of them, perhaps with the exception of the third method, has its appropriate place where it is superior to the other methods. Moreover, in some areas they supplement each other while in others they are rivals.

JÜRGEN BASEDOW

Literature

Albert A Ehrenzweig, *Private international law* (3rd printing, Sijthoff 1974); Trevor Hartley, 'The Modern Approach to Private international law: International Litigation and Transactions from a Common Law Perspective' (2006) 319 Rec. des Cours 9; Peter Hay, Patrick Borchers and Symeon Symeonides, *Conflict of Laws* (5th edn, Thomson Reuters 2010); Paul Lagarde, 'Le principe de proximité dans le droit international contemporain' (1986) 196 Rec. des Cours 9; Kurt Lipstein (ed), *International Encyclopedia of Comparative Law*, vol III/1 and 2 (Mohr Siebeck and Martinus Nijhoff 2011); Peter Malanczuk, *Akehurst's Modern Introduction to International Law* (7th edn, Routledge 1997); Jonathan Mance, 'The Future of Private international law' (2005) 1 J Priv Int L 185; Heinz-Peter Mansel, 'Anerkennung als Grundprinzip des europäischen Rechtsraums'(2006) 70 RabelsZ 651; Pierre Mayer, 'Les méthodes de reconnaissance en droit international privé' in *Le droit international privé – esprit et méthodes. Mélanges en l'honneur de Paul Lagarde* (Dalloz 2005) 547; Ralf Michaels, 'EU Law as Private international law? Reconceptualising the Country-of-origin Principle as Vested Rights Theory' (2006) 2 J Priv Int L 195; Paul Heinrich Neuhaus, *Die Grundbegriffe des Internationalen Privatrechts* (2nd edn, Mohr Siebeck 1976); Paolo Picone, *Ordinamento competente e diritto internazionale privato* (CEDAM 1986); Paolo Picone, 'Les méthodes de coordination entre ordres juridiques en droit international privé' (1999) 276 Rec. des Cours 9; Friedrich Carl von Savigny, *System des heutigen römischen Rechts*, vol 8 (Veit & Co 1849); Kurt Siehr, *Internationales Privatrecht* (CF Müller 2001).

Proceedings, law governing

I. Concept and context

'One of the eternal truths of every system of private international law is that a distinction must be made between → substance and procedure, between right and remedy. The substantive rights of the parties to an action may be governed by a foreign law, but all matters appertaining to procedure are governed exclusively by the law of the forum.' – This paradigmatic quote by James Fawcett, Janeen Carruthers and Peter North, *Cheshire, North & Fawcett's Private international law* ((14th edn, OUP 2008) 75) outlines the topic of this entry. It does not, however, concern the question, how the often very subtle distinction between substance and procedure can be drawn (cf the corresponding entry), but rather whether and in how far it can be said that all procedural matters are governed exclusively by the *lex fori*. Quite a few entries in this encyclopedia have connections to the subject 'law governing proceedings' being addressed here. Note especially the entries → Choice of law, → Foreign law, application and ascertainment, → Forum (and law) shopping, → *Lex fori* and → Party autonomy.

II. Court proceedings

1. Lex fori rule

At its core, the *lex fori* rule conveys that the court applies the procedural rules *ad ordinem litis* from the procedural law (including, where relevant, EU and Convention law) applicable in the forum. This also applies when the parties are foreigners or when the case involves other cross-border implications. By contrast, in such international cases the court must determine the rules *ad decisionem* applicable with regard to the substance of the case on the basis of a → choice of law analysis.

JÜRGEN BASEDOW / WOLFGANG HAU

The principle '*forum regit processum*' is very old. Early academic authority is provided, for example, by *Bartolus* (cf entry → Bartolus), but also by *Johannes Voet* (cf entry, → Voet, Paulus and Johannes) who stated in his *Commentarius ad Pandectas*, vol 1 ((Leiden 1698) Lib V Tit I 51):

> *Quia vero regionum, civitatum, vicorum varia imo contraria saepe jura sunt, observandum est, quantum quidem ad ordinem judicii formamque attinet, judicem nullius alterius sed sui tantum fori leges sequi* (translated by *Erwin Spiro* as follows: 'Where the laws of the various countries and communities differ, a judge will always apply his law to procedural questions').

The → *lex fori* rule has been laid down to the same effect by the *Institut de droit international* in its Zurich Resolution of 1877 (Institut de droit international, Résolution 'Règles internationales proposées pour prévenir des conflits de lois sur les formes de la procédure', Zurich 11 September 1877) (art 2: *Les formes ordinatoires de l'instruction et de la procédure seront régies par la loi du lieu où le procès est instruit. Seront considérées comme telles, les prescriptions relatives aux formes de l'assignation (sauf ce qui est proposé ci-dessous, 2e al.), aux délais de comparution, à la nature et à la forme de la procuration ad litem, au mode de recueillir les preuves, à la rédaction et au prononcé du jugement, à la passation en force de chose jugée, aux délais et aux formalités de l'appel et autres voies de recours, à la péremption de l'instance*), in the Bustamante Code of 1928 (Convention on Private international law (Bustamante Code), adopted at Havana on 20 February 1928 at the Sixth International Conference of American States; OAS, Law and Treaty Series, No 34) (art 314: 'The law of each contracting state determines the competence of courts, as well as their organization, the forms of procedure and of execution of judgments, and the appeals from their decisions'), and the American Law Institute in its Restatement (Second) of Conflict of Laws of 1971 (American Law Institute, Restatement of the Law, Second: Conflict of Laws 2d, St Paul 1971; → Restatement (First and Second) of Conflict of Laws; § 122: 'A court normally applies its own local law rules prescribing how litigation shall be conducted even when it applies the local law rules of another state to resolve other issues in the case', but see also §§ 123–43 for special applications and some modifications of the general principle).

Furthermore, the rule is well-settled in most, if not all, national legal systems, sometimes regarded as a matter of customary law, sometimes codified (cf eg art 12 of the Italian Private international law Act (Riforma del Sistema italiano di diritto internazionale private, Act No 218 of 31 May 1995 in Gazz.Uff, Supplemento Ordinario No 128 of 3 June l995, as amended), and for a recent example art 3 of the Dutch Law on Private international law (Dutch Law on Private international law: Wet 19 mei 2011 tot vaststelling en invoering van Boek 10 (Internationaal privaatrecht) van het Burgerlijk Wetboek)). The European instruments on international civil litigation do not expressively state the principle '*forum regit processum*' as a general rule. However, art 1(3) Rome I Regulation (Regulation (EC) No 593/2008 of the European Parliament and of the Council of 17 June 2008 on the law applicable to contractual obligations (Rome I), [2008] OJ L 177/6; → Rome Convention and Rome I Regulation (contractual obligations)) and art 1(3) → Rome II Regulation (non-contractual obligations) (Regulation (EC) No 864/2007 of the European Parliament and of the Council of 11 July 2007 on the law applicable to non-contractual obligations (Rome II), [2007] OJ L 199/40) make clear that their choice-of-law rules do not apply to procedural matters. In principle, there is no reason to believe that the *lex fori* rule as such could be inconsistent with European law. In particular, as a general rule, a party cannot insist on the application of the procedural law of her Member State of origin. This of course must be distinguished from the obvious point that European law prohibits national procedural law to discriminate against foreign parties.

The *lex fori* (including the Regulations and Conventions applicable in the forum) also decides on the extent to which the parties are free to modify procedural rules by agreeing, for example, on the place of the court proceedings (cf entry → Choice of forum and submission to jurisdiction), and further aspects of the conduct and/or the termination of the proceedings.

A different question is whether the parties enjoy autonomy in the strict sense to decide which national procedural regime should apply, hence, whether they can bind the court by opting for the applicability of foreign procedural law. It is one of the important and today still hardly doubted consequences of the *lex fori* rule that this question is to be answered in the negative. In particular, it cannot be argued that the parties' ability to contract out of a procedural system by agreeing on a choice of court or an arbitration clause (cf *supra* III.5.) necessarily entails the lesser power to opt for a foreign procedural regime.

2. Rationale

The *lex fori* rule used to be based on a variety of reasons. Courts and academics have referred to the principle of territorial sovereignty, to the public law nature of procedural law as a matter of administration of justice entrusted to the courts, to the principle '*locus regit actum*' or to the doctrine of → public policy (*ordre public*). All of these arguments are less than convincing. Today, reference is primarily made to the practicability, respectively convenience, of a court applying its own procedural law. Indeed, courts are familiar with their own procedural law, and it seems sensible that the constitution and competence of the courts on the one hand and the conduct of the proceedings on the other hand be attuned to one another.

Practicability alone can, however, not justify the principle (since otherwise the application of foreign substantive law would have to be avoided too), but only in combination with the argument of neutrality: since the procedural law only contains provisions governing the behaviour of the court and the parties, but does not predetermine the decision on the merits, international uniformity of decisions is not disturbed if each court applies, in general, its own procedural rules. If the validity of the *lex fori* rule is based on the neutrality of procedural law with regard to the decision on the merits, it must be ensured that provisions relevant for the outcome of the lawsuit are not ascribed to the *lex fori* simply because they are part of foreign procedural law. Therefore, the often difficult and controversial distinction between procedural and substantive law seems crucial (cf the corresponding entry, → Substance and Procedure). The decisiveness of the *lex fori* is at least widely acknowledged with regard to questions such as the constitution and competence of courts, commencement of proceedings, forms of action, court powers to manage and conduct proceedings, mandatory representation by counsels, pleading requirements, public hearings, costs, forms and requirements of judgments, and appeals.

The doctrinal classification of the *lex fori* principle has been much discussed. There are plenty of more or less extensive theoretical approaches, according to which the procedural law applicable in a single case shall be determined – just as the applicable substantive law – on the basis of a choice-of-law analysis. None of these approaches has gained general acceptance. But it would also be misguided to claim a categorical difference between private international law on the one hand and international civil procedure law on the other hand; rather, the *lex fori* principle and its exceptions are, from a technical perspective, indeed choice-of-law principles, but in the fields of international civil procedure law.

3. Incidental questions

While there is no general confirmation of the rule '*forum regit processum*' under European law, there are provisions which can be understood as isolated choice-of-law rules for incidental questions (→ Incidental (preliminary) question) referring to the *lex fori*. One example is art 61(1) Brussels I Regulation (recast) (Regulation (EU) No 1215/2012 of the European Parliament and of the Council of 12 December 2012 on jurisdiction and the recognition and enforcement of judgments in civil and commercial matters (recast), [2012] OJ L 351/1; → Brussels I (Convention and Regulation)): 'In order to determine whether a party is domiciled in the Member State whose courts are seized of a matter, the court shall apply its internal law.'

Further examples can be found in provisions concerning international jurisdiction, such as art 7 no 3 Brussels I Regulation (recast) ('to the extent that that court has jurisdiction under its own law to entertain civil proceedings') and art 3 lit c) and d) Maintenance Regulation (Council Regulation (EC) No 4/2009 of 18 December 2008 on jurisdiction, applicable law, recognition and enforcement of decisions and cooperation in matters relating to maintenance obligations, [2009] OJ L 7/1) ('the court which, according to its own law, has jurisdiction to entertain proceedings').

However, European regulations on international civil procedure also contain provisions referring to foreign law, eg art 61(2) Brussels I Regulation (recast):

> If a party is not domiciled in the Member State whose courts are seised of the matter, then, in order to determine whether the party is domiciled

in another Member State, the court shall apply the law of that Member State.

or provisions referring to national law which is not necessarily the *lex fori* of the court invoked, cf art 25(1) Brussels I Regulation (recast):

> If the parties ... have agreed that a court or the courts of a Member State are to have jurisdiction to settle any disputes ..., that court or those courts shall have jurisdiction, unless the agreement is null and void as to its substantive validity under the law of that Member State.

National procedural law, too, can contain provisions which might be understood as isolated choice-of-law rules for incidental questions, cf, for example, § 55 of the German Code of Civil Procedure (*Zivilprozessordnung* of 5 December 2005, BGBl. I 3202, as amended, henceforth German CCP):

> A foreigner who, according to the laws of his country, lacks the capacity to sue and be sued, shall be deemed to have such capacity if, pursuant to the laws to which the court hearing the case is subject, he is entitled to such capacity to sue and be sued.

4. Relevance of foreign procedural law

Today, it is widely acknowledged that the main structure of the conduct of proceedings is determined to a great extent by the *lex fori*, but that the functional or teleological nexus between individual procedural questions and a subjective substantial legal position, whose enforcement the proceedings are designed to achieve, can require the selective application of foreign procedural law. Thus, where foreign procedural law is, by way of exception, applied or at least taken into account, it is normally taken from the legal system from which the provisions applicable in substance also come, ie the *lex causae*. When the *lex fori* doctrine is viewed as a flexible principle rather than a dogma, cases in which foreign procedural law is applied appear to be justified exceptions.

Indeed, substantive law can influence the organization of the proceedings in some contexts so significantly that it seems imperative that domestic procedural law be adapted to the applicable foreign substantive law. Thus, foreign procedural provisions supplementing the substantive law can be applicable or, conversely, some regulatory provisions of the domestic procedural law, which are unknown to the foreign substantive law, can be adapted or even disapplied. The objective of this is, on the one hand, to meet the right to legal protection within the forum state and, on the other hand, to ensure the recognition of a judgment in a foreign legal system which requires observance of certain procedural rules. For example, a German family court may – in deviation from German law – undertake a special attempt at reconciliation, consult a public prosecutor, or include the reason for divorce in the operative part of the decision if this is mandatory according to the foreign divorce law (→ Divorce and personal separation).

III. Special issues

1. Uniform and model laws on civil procedure

With the European Payment Order Regulation (Regulation (EC) No 1896/2006 of the European Parliament and of the Council of 12 December 2006 creating a European order for payment procedure, [2006] OJ L 399/1) and the European Small Claims Procedure Regulation (Regulation (EC) No 861/2007 of the European Parliament and of the Council of 11 July 2007 establishing a European Small Claims Procedure, [2007] OJ L 199/1), two unified procedural systems were established within the European Union. While both procedures have to be interpreted autonomously as far as possible, the regulations cannot address every procedural aspect. Rather, they leave some important gaps, which need to be supplemented by national procedural law. Hence, art 26 European Payment Order Regulation reads: 'Relationship with national procedural law: All procedural issues not specifically dealt with in this Regulation shall be governed by national law.'

Although this provision does not clarify which national regime is to be applied, it seems obvious that the *lex fori* is meant. In this sense, art 19 European Small Claims Procedure Regulation reads explicitly:

> Applicable procedural law: Subject to the provisions of this Regulation, the European Small Claims Procedure shall be governed by the procedural law of the Member State in which the procedure is conducted.

Similar provisions are contained in further uniform or model rules in the field of international civil procedure. One example of this is Rule 1.2 ALI/UNIDROIT Rules of Transnational Civil Procedure (text of the Principles and the accompanying commentary were adopted by the

American Law Institute (ALI) in May 2004 and by the International Institute for the Unification of Private Law (→ UNIDROIT) in April 2004, (2004) 4 Unif.L.Rev. 758): 'The procedural law of the forum governs matters not addressed in these Rules.'

2. International judicial cooperation

International instruments on international judicial cooperation can refer to the law of the requesting court or to the law of the requested court. Art 10 Evidence Regulation (Council Regulation (EC) No 1206/2001 of 28 May 2001 on cooperation between the courts of the Member States in the taking of evidence in civil or commercial matters, [2001] OJ L 174/1) provides an example:

2. The requested court shall execute the request in accordance with the law of its Member State.
3. The requesting court may call for the request to be executed in accordance with a special procedure provided for by the law of its Member State ... The requested court shall comply with such a requirement unless this procedure is incompatible with the law of the Member State of the requested court or by reason of major practical difficulties. ...

Similar provisions are contained in art 9 Hague Evidence Convention (Hague Convention of 18 March 1970 on the taking of evidence abroad in civil or commercial matters, 847 UNTS 241), art 5(1) Hague Service Convention (Hague Convention of 15 November 1965 on the service abroad of judicial and extrajudicial documents in civil or commercial matters, 658 UNTS 163), and art 7 European Service Regulation (Regulation (EC) No 1393/2007 of the European Parliament and of the Council of 13 November 2007 on the service in the Member States of judicial and extrajudicial documents in civil or commercial matters (service of documents), and repealing Council Regulation (EC) No 1348/2000, [2007] OJ L 324/79). In some cases both legal regimes are decisive, for example, according to art 14(1) Evidence Regulation:

A request for the hearing of a person shall not be executed when the person concerned claims the right to refuse to give evidence or to be prohibited from giving evidence,

(a) under the law of the Member State of the requested court; or
(b) under the law of the Member State of the requesting court, and such right has been specified in the request, or, if need be, at the instance of the requested court, has been confirmed by the requesting court.

The same applies according to the Hague Evidence Convention (art 11(1)), which provides further that even the right of a third state can be authoritative, art 11(2):

A Contracting State may declare that, in addition, it will respect privileges and duties existing under the law of States other than the State of origin and the State of execution, to the extent specified in that declaration.

3. Enforcement proceedings

In the field of civil enforcement regimes, the validity of the rule *'forum regit processum'* is even more obvious than in the field of proceedings leading to a judgment. Therefore, special questions, such as which modes of execution and remedies are available, or whether personal constraint is permissible, are determined by the *lex loci executionis* (see, eg, § 131 Restatement (Second) of Conflict of Laws, but also § 132 for an exception regarding property exempt from execution). This becomes especially important with regard to foreign execution orders, to which, in principle, the same rules should apply as to domestic ones. This is, for example, clarified in art 41(1) Brussels I Regulation (recast), which reads:

Subject to the provisions of this Section, the procedure for the enforcement of judgments given in another Member State shall be governed by the law of the Member State addressed. ...

Similar provisions are contained in art 41(1) Brussels I Regulation (recast), art 47(1) → Brussels IIa Regulation (Council Regulation (EC) No 2201/2003 of 27 November 2003 concerning jurisdiction and the recognition and enforcement of judgments in matrimonial matters and the matters of parental responsibility, repealing Regulation (EC) No 1347/2000, [2003] OJ L 338/1), art 21(1) European Payment Order Regulation as well as art 21(1) European Small Claims Procedure Regulation. Hence, there is no two-tier enforcement regime for foreign and domestic judgments. However, it is recognized that foreign law can be relevant to certain incidental questions (→ Incidental (preliminary) question). This is shown by art 39 Brussels I Regulation (recast), which reads:

A judgment given in a Member State which is enforceable in that Member State shall be enforceable in the other Member States without any declaration of enforceability being required.

Further similar provisions are contained in art 58 and 59 Brussels I Regulation (recast), art 17(2) and art 26 European Payment Order Regulation, art 28(1) Brussels IIa Regulation, and also in national law, cf, for example, § 723(2) German CCP:

> The judgment for enforcement is to be delivered only once the judgment handed down by the foreign court has attained legal validity pursuant to the laws applicable to that court.

4. Insolvency proceedings

In the field of insolvency law, it can be especially difficult to distinguish between → substance and procedure. So far as procedural questions are concerned, the validity of the *lex fori concursus* is acknowledged. In this sense, art 7 Insolvency Regulation (recast) (Regulation (EU) No 2015/848 of the European Parliament and of the Council of 20 May 2015 on insolvency proceedings (recast), [2015] OJ L 141/19) provides:

> 1. Save as otherwise provided in this Regulation, the law applicable to insolvency proceedings and their effects shall be that of the Member State within the territory of which such proceedings are opened (the 'State of the opening of proceedings').
> 2. The law of the State of the opening of proceedings shall determine the conditions for the opening of those proceedings, their conduct and their closure. It shall determine in particular: ...

A similar rule is contained in art 35 Insolvency Regulation (recast) relating to secondary proceedings. By contrast, arts 8–17 Insolvency Regulation (recast) deal with special rules on the applicable law in the case of issues classified as substantive, not procedural. Noteworthy is art 18 Insolvency Regulation (recast), which provides that the effects of insolvency proceedings on a pending lawsuit concerning an asset or a right of which the debtor has been divested shall be governed solely by the law of the Member State in which that lawsuit is pending (ie the *lex fori* of the lawsuit, which is not necessarily the *lex fori concursus*).

5. Arbitration

Differently to state courts, arbitration tribunals do not have a *lex fori*. Nonetheless, it must be determined which legal system's provisions on arbitration apply. In this regard, the application of the *lex fori* – respectively the *lex loci arbitri* – is accepted in principle. Accordingly, art 1(2) UNCITRAL Arbitration Model Law (United Nations Commission on International Trade Law, UNCITRAL Model Law on International Commercial Arbitration as adopted on 21 June 1985, and as amended on 7 July 2006, UN Doc A/40/17 and A/61/17; → Arbitration, (UNCITRAL) Model Law) reads: 'The provisions of this Law, except articles 8, 9, 17 H, 17 I, 17 J, 35 and 36, apply only if the place of arbitration is in the territory of this State.'

To be distinguished from this is the question, which procedural rules the arbitral tribunal shall apply within the limits prescribed by the *lex fori*. Concerning this matter, art V(1)(a) New York Convention (New York Convention of 10 June 1958 on the recognition and enforcement of foreign arbitral awards, 330 UNTS 3) establishes that it is primarily up to the parties to agree on the arbitral procedure and that, failing such agreement, the law of the country where the arbitration took place applies. Accordingly, art 19 UNCITRAL Arbitration Model Law suggests that in principle the parties respectively the arbitral tribunal should enjoy autonomy regarding the conduct of the arbitral proceedings:

> 1. Subject to the provisions of this Law, the parties are free to agree on the procedure to be followed by the arbitral tribunal in conducting the proceedings.
> 2. Failing such agreement, the arbitral tribunal may, subject to the provisions of this Law, conduct the arbitration in such manner as it considers appropriate.

The conduct of the arbitral proceedings must not follow the same rules as the arbitration agreement. It is also possible that individual aspects – for example, the constitution of the arbitral tribunal, the making of the award and the termination of proceedings – be governed by different rules and legal regimes.

WOLFGANG HAU

Literature

Anne Kathrin Arnold, *Lex fori als versteckte Anknüpfung* (Duncker & Humblot 2009); Jürgen Basedow, 'Qualifikation, Vorfrage und Anpassung im Internationalen Zivilverfahrensrecht' in Peter Schlosser (ed), *Materielles Recht und Prozessrecht* (Gieseking 1992) 131; Peter Böhm, 'Die Rechtsschutzformen im Spannungsfeld von lex fori und lex causae' in Richard Holzhammer, Wolfgang Jelinek and Peter Böhm (eds), *Festschrift für Hans W. Fasching zum 65. Geburtstag* (Manz 1988) 107; Dagmar Coester-Waltjen, *Internationales Beweisrecht – Das auf den Beweis anwendbare Recht in Rechtsstreitigkeiten mit Auslandsbezug* (Gremer 1983); Jacob Dolinger and Carmen Tiburcio, 'The Forum Law Rule in International Litigation' (1998) 33

Tex.Int'l L.J. 425; James Fawcett, Janeen Carruthers and Peter North, *Cheshire, North & Fawcett's Private international law* (14th edn, OUP 2008); Richard Garnett, *Substance and Procedure in Private international law* (OUP 2012); Wolfgang Grunsky, 'Lex fori und Verfahrensrecht' (1976) 89 *ZZP* 241; Fritz Jaeckel, *Die Reichweite der lex fori im internationalen Zivilprozessrecht* (Duncker & Humblot 1995); Karl-Georg Loritz, 'Ausländisches Verfahrensrecht im deutschen Zivilprozess' in Forschungsinstitut für prozessrechtliche Studien (ed), *Essays in Honor of Areios Pagos 150th Anniversary*, vol 1 (Ekdoseis Ant Sakkoula 2007) 121; Marie-Laure Niboyet, 'Contre le dogme de la lex fori en matière de procédure' in *Vers de nouveaux équilibres entre ordres juridiques – Mélanges en l'honneur de Hélène Gaudemet-Tallon* (Dalloz 2008) 363; Hubert Niederländer, 'Materielles Recht und Verfahrensrecht im Internationalen Privatrecht' (1955) 20 RabelsZ 1; George Panagopoulos, 'Substance and Procedure in Private international law' (2005) 1 J Priv Int L 69; Georgios Petrochilos, *Procedural Law in International Arbitration* (OUP 2004); Herbert Roth, 'Die Reichweite der lex fori-Regel im internationalen Zivilprozeßrecht' in Wilfried Küper and Jürgen Welp (eds), *Festschrift für Walter Stree und Johannes Wessels zum 70. Geburtstag* (CF Müller 1993) 1045; Erwin Spiro, 'Forum Regit Processum (Procedure is Governed by the Lex Fori)' (1969) 18 ICLQ 949; Stacie Strong, 'Limits of Procedural Choice of Law' (2014) 39 Brooklyn J.Int'l L. 1027; Anna Sussarova, 'La portée du principe "forum regit processum" dans la pratique judiciaire belge' (2012) RDC/TBH 156; Stephen Szászy, 'The Basic Connecting Factor in International Cases in the Domain of Civil Procedure' (1966) 15 ICLQ 436; Jacob Van de Velden, 'The "Cautious Lex Fori" Approach to Foreign Judgments and Preclusion: Yukos Capital Sarl v OJSC Rosneft Oil Co' (2012) 61 ICLQ 519; Gerhard Wagner, *Prozessverträge – Privatautonomie im Verfahrensrecht* (Mohr Siebeck 1998).

Products liability

I. Introduction

Products liability is the field of law that deals with the extra-contractual liability of manufacturers, distributors, suppliers, retailers, and other persons for damage caused by products they have made available to the public. The answer to the question of which person in a chain of distribution is ultimately responsible for the damage caused by a defective product depends on the applicable law.

In products liability cases the person claimed to be liable has often acted in a place that is different from the place where the person claiming compensation has suffered injury: a product is designed and manufactured in one place and marketed and purchased in others. Once acquired, the product is carried to yet other places where it ultimately causes damage to the person who acquired it, to persons close to the purchaser, or to third parties (so-called 'innocent bystanders'). Given the high mobility of many products, the place of manufacturing, purchase and injury may be located in two or more countries. Hence the great potential for complex transnational torts scenarios in the field of products liability (for other complex torts see → Torts).

In the EU, the substantive law on products liability is to some extent harmonised by the Products Liability Directive (Council Directive 85/374/EEC of 25 July 1985 on the approximation of the laws, regulations and administrative provisions of the Member States concerning liability for defective products [1985] OJ L210/29). The harmonising effect of this Directive is however limited, in that according to art 9 Products Liability Directive, damage to property is covered only if the product was intended for private use, and pure economic loss is not covered at all. Cases that are beyond the scope of application of the Directive continue to be governed by national liability laws that differ from each other in many respects. Consequently, the outcome in a given case often depends on the applicable law.

In Europe, the law applicable to products liability cases that present a foreign element is determined either by the → Rome II Regulation (Regulation (EC) No 864/2007 of the European Parliament and of the Council of 11 July 2007 on the law applicable to non-contractual obligations (Rome II), [2007] OJ L 199/40) or by the Hague Products Liability Convention (Hague Convention of 2 October 1973 on the law applicable to products liability, 1056 UNTS 191). In countries that are neither EU Member States nor contracting states to the Hague Products Liability Convention (such as → Switzerland), the law applicable to products liability is determined by their domestic private international law.

Given the limited number of contracting states to the Hague Products Liability Convention (see below III.1.), the Rome II Regulation is by far the most important instrument in Europe when it comes to determining the law applicable to products liability.

Before entry into force of the Rome II Regulation, there was a broad variety of solutions in Europe regarding the law applicable to products liability (see the overview in Thomas Kadner Graziano, 'The Law Applicable to Product Liability: The Present State of the Law in Europe and Current Proposals for Reform' (2005) ICLQ 475, 478–9). Given the mobility of many products, there has however been a widespread consensus that applying the law of the place where the injury occurred, ie the *lex loci delicti* (→ Torts), would often be inadequate and lead to fortuitous results in products liability scenarios. Thus persons living in country A might buy a product in country B and take it to country C (on vacation or on a business trip) which might be any (distant) country in the world. While using it there, they might suffer damage due to a defect of the product. To apply the law of country C where the injury occurred would often not constitute a sensible solution for the manufacturer of the product, who would not know in advance to which country in the world the user might carry the product before the damage occurs, or for the victim who will, in general, expect the application of the law of a country with which they have a closer connection.

II. The applicable law according to the Rome II Regulation

Faced with the difficulty of finding a satisfactory solution for the applicable law in products liability cases, art 5 Rome II Regulation combines various criteria which achieve a finely tuned determination of the applicable law. The criteria are arranged in a hierarchy or cascading system of connecting factors, so that if the criteria for applying the first rule are not met, then the second applies (and so on). These steps will now be analysed in sequence.

1. Party autonomy (art 14)

Under the Rome II Regulation, it first needs to be determined whether the parties have agreed on the applicable law: art 14(1) allows for a choice of the applicable law in torts *ex post* and, under certain conditions, also *ex ante* (→ Torts).

In the case-law on products liability dating from before the Rome II Regulation, when the parties pleaded in court proceedings according to the law of the forum, the courts occasionally deduced that they thereby impliedly chose the law of the forum as the applicable law (see eg the German case: German Federal Court of Justice (BGH), 17 March 1981 *Apfelschorf (apple scrap)* [1982] IPRax 13).

According to art 14(1) 2nd sentence Rome II Regulation '[t]he choice [of law] shall be expressed or demonstrated with reasonable certainty by the circumstances of the case'. Contrary to the above case-law, mere silence is thus insufficient, and the Rome II Regulation requires that the parties either make an express choice of applicable law or make an implied choice which is however 'demonstrated with reasonable certainty by the circumstances'.

2. Pre-existing relationship – rattachement accessoire (art 5(2))

If the parties have not chosen the applicable law but are in a pre-existing relationship with each other, such as a contractual relationship that is closely connected with the tort or delict in question, then the law applicable to this relationship will also apply to the tort claim (so-called *rattachement accessoire*). Article 5(2) Rome II Regulation thus restates a principle that is already expressed more generally in art 4(3) Rome II Regulation (for the rationale of *rattachement accessoire* see → Torts).

3. Application of the law of the parties' common habitual residence (art 5(1) in conjunction with art 4(2) Rome II Regulation)

The next step on the cascade of connecting factors is art 5(1), 1st part, in conjunction with art 4(2) Rome II Regulation: if 'the person claimed to be liable and the person sustaining damage both have their habitual residence in the same country at the time when the damage occurs', then the law of this country applies (for the reasons behind applying the law of the parties' common habitual residence see → Torts).

4. Application of the law of the injured party's habitual residence (art 5(1)(a))

The next step, often relevant in practice, is found in art 5(1)(a) Rome II Regulation: 'the law of the country in which the person sustaining the damage had his or her habitual residence when the damage occurred' applies, providing that 'the product was marketed in that country'.

The Rome II Regulation contains no definition of the notion of marketing. However, according to ECJ case-law a product is marketed when it is offered to the public for use or consumption (ECJ C-127/04 *Declan O'Byrne v Sanofi Pasteur and others* [2006] ECR I-1313). The ECJ held in relation to the interpretation of the Products Liability Directive that 'a product is put into circulation when it is taken out of the manufacturing process operated by the producer and enters a marketing process in the form in which it is offered to the public in order to be used or consumed'.

For art 5(1)(a) Rome II Regulation to be applicable, it is not necessary that the precise product that caused the damage was actually bought in the country of the injured person's habitual residence, but rather it is sufficient that this line of products was marketed in that country (see art 5(1), 2nd sentence Rome II Regulation: 'the marketing of the product, or a product of the same type'). This is particularly relevant for bystanders injured by a product that they did not purchase.

Article 5(1)(a) applies both in situations where the persons whose liability is claimed have marketed the product in this country themselves, and where it was marketed there by an independent retailer or distributor. This follows among others from the fact that the Rome II Regulation requires that the marketing of the product in the country in question must have been foreseeable, as opposed to requiring that the persons alleged to be liable must themselves have marketed it there, or that they had been in control of the marketing process there (see the 2nd sentence of art 5(1) Rome II Regulation).

Given that the Rome II Regulation applies both to victims domiciled in the EU and those domiciled in third countries, the law of the country of the injured party's habitual residence applies irrespective of whether this is an EU Member State or a third country.

Article 5(1)(a) Rome II Regulation aims at protecting the person sustaining damage. Application of the law of the victim's habitual residence is the simplest and, in principle, the least costly solution for the person having suffered damage. It is also fair for the persons claimed to be liable, in that these persons are making a profit from the distribution of their products in this country and ought reasonably to expect the law of a country in which their products are distributed to apply when these products cause damage there (see European Commission, 'Proposal for a Regulation of the European Parliament and the Council on the Law Applicable to Non-Contractual Obligations ("Rome II")' COM(2003) 427 final, p 16, and Thomas Kadner Graziano, *Gemeineuropäisches Internationales Privatrecht – Harmonisierung des IPR durch Wissenschaft und Lehre (am Beispiel der ausservertraglichen Haftung für Schäden)* (Mohr Siebeck 2002), 278 *et seq*).

A particular strength of art 5(1)(a) Rome II Regulation is that it is effective for both new and second-hand products. In addition, the rule applies and achieves reasonable results, both in proceedings brought by the purchaser of a product and those brought by third parties that are not in relationship with the buyer but suffered damage from the product (so-called 'innocent bystanders').

5. *Application of the law of the place of marketing and purchase (art 5(1)(b))*

If products such as the one that caused the damage were not marketed in the country in which the injured person had her habitual residence, then pursuant to art 5(1)(b) Rome II Regulation, 'the law of the country in which the product was [actually] acquired' will apply 'if the product was marketed in that country'.

There are numerous arguments for applying the law of the country of marketing and acquisition. Manufacturers who have their products sold in a foreign country must take into account the potential for their products to cause damage there, and that an injured person would expect the law of this country to apply. Additionally, applying the law of the place of acquisition makes the same rules applicable to all suppliers that have their products sold there, thereby favouring equality between competitors in this market. Using the law of the place of marketing and of acquisition also promotes legal certainty, and finally, applying this law is equally acceptable for both the manufacturer and the purchaser and it is in conformity with their expectations. Consequently, academic opinion in Europe has long argued for the application of the law of the place of acquisition of the product, see eg Harry Duintjer Tebbens, *International Product Liability* (Kluwer 1981) 381 *et seq*; Alberto Saravalle, *Responsabilità del produttore* (CEDAM 1991) 217 *et seq*; Manfred Wandt, *Internationale Produkthaftung* (Fachmedien Recht und Wirtschaft in Deutscher Fachverlag GmbH 1995) no 1086 *et seq*, 1100, 1231; Thomas Kadner Graziano (2005) ICLQ

475; id, *Gemeineuropäisches Internationales Privatrecht* (Mohr Siebeck 2002) 278 ff.

However, using the place of acquisition may not be appropriate where the damage was suffered by an innocent bystander who has not acquired the product. Instead, the next rule on the cascade of connecting factors, ie the place of injury rule set out in art 5(1)(c) Rome II Regulation should apply to damage suffered by bystanders (if the case does not fall under art 5(1)(a) already).

6. Application of the law of the place of injury (art 5(1)(c))

As provided by art 5(1)(c) Rome II Regulation, if the product was neither marketed in the injured person's country of habitual residence nor in the country in which it was actually bought, products liability will be governed by 'the law of the country in which the damage occurred, if the product was marketed in that country'.

Under the Rome II Regulation, the place of damage thus occupies a merely subsidiary position in the list of connecting factors for determining the applicable products liability law, and rightly so. In fact, given the high mobility of many products, the risk of reaching fortuitous and arbitrary results is considerable when the law of the place of injury is used with respect to persons who have purchased the product in another country. The application of the law of the place of injury, if not accompanied by other factors, may often be neither in the interest of the person whose liability is claimed nor in the interest of the injured person (see the example above I. *in fine*). On the other hand, the place of injury rule often works well where the damage was suffered by an innocent bystander.

7. Foreseeability clause

According to art 5(1) *in fine* Rome II Regulation, 'the law applicable shall be the law of the country in which the person claimed to be liable is habitually resident if he or she could not reasonably foresee the marketing of the product, or a product of the same kind, in the country the law of which is applicable under (a), (b) or (c)'.

Article 5(1) *in fine* provides the only 'foreseeability clause' in the Rome II Regulation. In the European case-law on international torts dating from the period before entry into force of the Rome II Regulation, there is no single published case in which a court concluded that the injury in the country in which it occurred was not reasonably foreseeable for the person claimed to be liable (compare Thomas Kadner Graziano, *Gemeineuropäisches Internationales Privatrecht – Harmonisierung des IPR durch Wissenschaft und Lehre (am Beispiel der ausservertraglichen Haftung für Schäden)* (Mohr Siebeck 2002) 224). In fact, most products are today distributed on an international or even global scale, and can freely circulate across borders, as is well known to manufacturers and distributors. The foreseeability clause in art 5(1) Rome II Regulation *in fine* will thus rarely if ever be relevant in practice.

III. The 1973 Hague Convention on the law applicable to products liability

1. Relationship between the Rome II Regulation and the Hague Products Liability Convention

Products liability is the subject matter of a second Hague Convention in the field of torts, namely the Hague Products Liability Convention (text and status table available at <www.hcch.net>). The Convention is currently in force in 11 countries, including seven EU Member States (→ France, the → Netherlands, → Luxembourg, → Finland, → Spain, → Slovenia and → Croatia; it is also in force in → Norway, → Macedonia, FYR, → Serbia and → Montenegro).

As with the Hague Traffic Accident Convention (Hague Convention of 4 May 1971 on the law applicable to traffic accidents, 965 UNTS 415), the Rome II Regulation does not affect application of the Hague Products Liability Convention, pursuant to its art 28(1). In the EU Member States in which the Convention is in force, the applicable law in products liability cases will thus be determined by the Hague Products Liability Convention, as opposed to the Rome II Regulation. As with traffic accidents, this may be seen as an unsatisfactory situation which could very well be remedied (→ Traffic accidents).

2. The applicable law according to the Hague Products Liability Convention

Just like the Hague Traffic Accident Convention, the Hague Products Liability Convention provides no rules on → choice of law by the parties (→ party autonomy) nor on pre-existing relationship (*rattachement accessoire*). Neither were on the agenda in the early 1970s.

The Hague Products Liability Convention combines four criteria, of which two generally need to be met in order to find the applicable law. The different combinations of criteria apply in a hierarchical order.

First, the law of the country of habitual residence of the party having suffered the damage applies, provided that the person claimed to be liable is also established there or the claimant has purchased the product in this country (art 5 Hague Products Liability Convention). The first of these two alternatives corresponds to a widespread rule in the private international law of torts, ie to apply the law of the country where both parties have their habitual residence or establishment. Incidentally the Rome II Regulation uses the same criterion, provided there is no choice of law by the parties and no case for an accessory connection, see art 5(1) with art 4(2) Rome II Regulation, and II.3. above. The second alternative corresponds largely to art 5(1)(a) Rome II Regulation. However, under Rome II it is sufficient that the product was marketed in the country of the injured person's habitual residence, whereas the Hague Products Liability Convention requires a purchase by that person in this country.

Second, the law of the country where the injury occurred, ie where the legally protected interest was initially harmed, applies, provided that this is also 'a) the place of the habitual residence of the person directly suffering damage, or b) the principal place of business of the person claimed to be liable, or c) the place where the product was acquired by the person directly suffering damage' (art 4 Hague Products Liability Convention). The place of injury thus appears at an earlier stage than in the Rome II Regulation. However, the law of the place of injury applies only when this place coincides with the place of the injured party's habitual residence, which might frequently be the case, or with the principal place of business of the person claimed to be liable, or with the place where the victim has purchased the product (the Rome II Regulation focuses instead on the place of marketing and purchase, and has recourse to the place of injury only as a last resort in products liability cases, see II.6. above).

Finally, where the conditions of none of the above rules are met, the law of the country of the principal place of business of the person claimed to be liable applies, but the victim may opt instead for the law of the country where the injury occurred (art 6 Hague Products Liability Convention).

IV. Private international law rules on products liability in other jurisdictions

Further specific rules on the law applicable to products liability are found in the private international law acts of → Switzerland (Swiss Private international law Act (*Bundesgesetz über das Internationale Privatrecht* of 18 December 1987, 1988 BBl I 5, as amended, henceforth Swiss PILA)) and → Tunisia (Code of Private international law (Law No 98-97 of 27 November 1998), Official Journal of the Republic of Tunisia, 1 December, p 2332, henceforth Tunisian PILA))), in the Civil Codes of Québec (L.Q. 1991, ch 64), Russia (Civil Code of the → Russian Federation (as amended by Federal Law No 260-FZ on 30 September 2013, henceforth Russian CC)) and → Belarus (Law No 218-Z of 7 December 1998), in the Japanese Act on General Rules for Application of Laws (Hōno Tekiyō ni Kansuru Tsūsokuhō, Law No 10 of 1898, as newly titled and amended by Act No 78 of 21 June 2006, henceforth Japanese PILA) and the Chinese Statute of Application of Law to Foreign Civil Relations (adopted at the 17th session of the Standing Committee of the 11th National People's Congress on 28 October 2010, effective 1 April 2011, henceforth Chinese PILA).

Once the injury has occurred, most of these instruments (with the exception of the Civil Codes of Québec and Belarus) leave it to the parties to determine the applicable law if they wish to do so (art 133 section 1 Swiss PILA; art 1219 section 3 Russian CC; art 21 Japanese PILA; art 44 2nd sentence Chinese PILA, art 71 Tunisian PILA). They all permit a choice *ex post*, which is limited to the *lex fori* in Switzerland, Russia and Tunisia.

In the absence of a choice by the parties, the law of the parties' domicile or residence (→ Domicile, habitual residence and establishment) is applicable provided both parties are domiciled in the same country (art 133 section 1 Swiss PILA; art 3126 section 2 Civil Code of Quebec; art 1219 section 2 *in fine* Russian CC; art 20 Japanese PILA; art 44 2nd alternative Chinese PILA; art 70 section 3 Tunisian PILA). Some codes or statutes provide for the application of the law governing a pre-existing relationship between the parties, in particular where they are in a contractual relationship (art 133 section 3 Swiss PILA; art 3127 Civil Code of Québec; art 20 Japanese PILA).

All of the above-mentioned codes and acts further contain specific rules with objective connecting factors for products liability claims. Absent an agreement on the applicable law, the person having suffered damage can choose between the law of the state where the manufacturer has its establishment or residence and the law of the state where the good was acquired, art 135 Swiss PILA, art 3128 Civil Codes of Québec, art 1221 section 1 Russian CC, art 1130 Civil Code of Belarus, art 72 of the Tunisian PILA. Under the Swiss PILA and the Russian CC, applying the law of the place of acquisition is excluded if the persons held liable prove that the product was marketed there without their consent. The Civil Codes of Russia, Belarus, and Tunisia further allow the choice of the law of the country where the injured party is domiciled or has its principal activity.

Under art 45 Chinese PILA, the law of the country of the habitual residence of the person having suffered the damage applies to product liability, without further requirements. The victim may instead choose the law applicable at the principal place of business of the person claimed to be liable or at the place where the injury occurred. The law of the place of injury can also be chosen by the victim under art 72 no 2 of the Tunisian PILA.

In contrast, according to art 18 Japanese PILA, a claim against the producer following an injury to life, body, or property 'caused by the defect of a delivered product ... shall be governed by the law of the place where the injured person has been delivered the product. However, where the delivery of the product to that place could not usually be foreseen, the law of the principal place of business of the producer applies'.

In products liability, in order to facilitate compensation, the courts in the → USA tend to focus on the law most favourable to the victim. Some courts applied the law in force at the consumer's domicile even in cases in which neither the injury was suffered nor the product sold there, see eg *Phillips v General Motors Corp.*, 995 P.2d 1002 (Montana 2000); *Kasel v Remington Arms Co*, 24 Cal.App. 3d 711 (California 1972); *Stephen v Sears, Roebuck & Co*, 266 A. 2d 855 (New Hampshire 1970). These courts emphasized the interest in protecting the consumer or any other user, and they assumed that the state of the consumer's domicile had the most significant contact and interest in having its law applied, at least when this facilitated recovery.

Other courts in the USA applied the law of the manufacturer's federal state, which was often particularly favourable to foreign victims. In these decisions the courts emphasized the interest in deterring a manufacturer's improper conduct and/or the interest in providing incentives for producing the safest products possible, *Reyno v Piper Aircraft Corp*, 639 F.2d 149, 168 (3d Cir 1980), reviewed on another issue, 454 U.S. 235, 102 S.Ct. 252; *Gantes v Kason Corp*, 145 N.J. 478. 679 A.2d 106 (1996); *Baird v Bell Helicopter Textron*, 491 F.Supp. 1129, 1141 (ND Texas 1980); *Johnson v Spider Staging Corp*, Wash. 2d 577, 555 P.2d 997, 1002 (1976).

In other cases the courts applied the law of the victim's country of domicile even though it was less favourable to the plaintiff, *Harrison v Wyeth Laboratories*, 510 F.Supp. 1 (E D Pennsylvania 1980), affirmed 676 F.2d 685 (3d Circ 1982). In this case, a woman was injured in the United Kingdom by oral contraceptives manufactured there under the licence of a Pennsylvania-based company. The court reasoned that the UK had a greater interest than Pennsylvania in the control of drugs distributed and consumed in the UK. This led to the application of English law, less favourable to the claimant than that of Pennsylvania.

V. Case scenarios

In the following chapter, the rules presented above will be illustrated using selected case scenarios:

Scenario 1

A product (eg a bicycle) is designed and manufactured by X in country A and dispatched from its factory. The product is then distributed through an independent chain of distribution in countries A, B, C. Y purchases the product in country B, where he has his habitual residence. Due to a defect in the product (eg a defective bicycle fork) it causes physical injury and damage to property

(i) to Y in country B where he has his habitual residence;
(ii) to Y in country C where he spent his vacation taking the product with him;
(iii) to Z1, a family member of Y, in country B;
(iv) to Z2, an innocent bystander in country C

where he has his habitual residence.
(v) Variation: Y with domicile/habitual residence in country B purchases the product in country C but suffers damage in B.

In Scenario 1(i) the parties have not chosen the applicable law, they are not in a contractual relationship with each other, and they have their habitual residence in different countries. According to all of the above-mentioned instruments, as well as some US American case-law, the law of country B, where Y has his habitual residence and where he has purchased the product would ultimately be applicable (references above, II.–IV.). Under the rules applicable in → Switzerland, Russia (→ Russian Federation), → Belarus, Québec, → China and → Tunisia the victim could instead choose the law of country A where the manufacturer is established.

In Scenario 1(ii) the injury occurred in a country which is different from the one where the injured person is habitually resident and where the product was purchased. In none of the above-mentioned private international law systems does the place of injury play a central role in product liability. This scenario would thus be solved in the same way as the first scenario, and the law of country B, where Y has his habitual residence and where he has purchased the products would be applicable. Under the rules applicable in Switzerland, Québec, Russia, Belarus and China the victim could choose the law of country A instead of where the manufacturer is established. It is only under the Chinese Act and under the Tunisian Act that the victim would have a further option in favour of the law of the country of injury, ie country C (see II.–IV. above).

The same solution as in Scenario (i) should arguably apply in Scenario 1(iii) where the victim is a person who is close to the purchaser of the defective product.

In Scenario 1(iv) the damage is suffered by an innocent bystander. He has his habitual residence in country C where products such as the one that caused the damage were marketed. According to art 5(1)(a) Rome II Regulation, the law of country C thus applies. The same is true under the Hague Products Liability Convention, since C is the country where the injury occurred and where Z2 has his habitual residence (art 4 Hague Products Liability Convention). According to the Chinese PILA, the law of country C would also apply given that the victim has his habitual residence there; under Chinese law the person having suffered the injury could however opt for the law of country A where the manufacturer is established.

Under the other systems, the law applicable to claims brought by bystanders is less clear: applying the law of the country of purchase is not appropriate for claims by bystanders, and applying the law of the principal place of business of the manufacturer arguably does not suit either for victims who are not involved in the purchasing process (and are not closely related to the purchaser). According to the rules applicable in → Russia, → Belarus and → Tunisia, C could however opt for the law of country C where he is domiciled.

In Scenario 1(v) Y purchases the product in country C but suffers damage in B, the country of his habitual residence where the product was also marketed: according to art 5(1)(a) Rome II Regulation, the law of country B would apply, given that Y has his habitual residence there and products such as the one that caused the damage are marketed there. Under art 4 Hague Products Liability Convention, the law of country B would also apply since Y has his habitual residence and suffered the damage there. Under the Chinese PILA, Y would have the choice between the laws of country A (principal place of business of the manufacturer) and B (Y's habitual residence; place where the injury occurred).

Under the rules applicable in Switzerland, Québec, Russia, Belarus and Tunisia, the victim would have the choice between the laws of countries A (the country of establishment of the manufacturer) and C (the country of purchase). Under the Civil Codes of Russia, Belarus and Tunisia, he would additionally have the option to choose the law of country B (where he, the injured party, was domiciled). Finally, under the Japanese PILA, the law of country C where the product was delivered would arguably apply.

Scenario 1(v) illustrates that in cases where the places of purchase on the one hand and of the victim's habitual residence and of injury on the other are located in different countries, the solutions vary considerably. However, Scenarios 1(i)–(iv) show that in many standard cases, the rules presented above often eventually lead in principle to similar results, but in some jurisdictions with different options for the person who suffered injury.

Scenario 2

X, a company established in country A, designs and manufactures prosthetic hips or breast implants there. They are distributed to doctors and hospitals through independent chains of distribution in countries A, B and many others. Y has an implant in country B. Due to defects of the implant, Y suffers damage and brings a claim against the manufacturer X.

Given that Y has her habitual residence in country B and that the defective implants were marketed to hospitals and doctors there, art 5(1)(a) Rome II Regulation leads directly to the application of the law of country B. Under this rule, it is immaterial that it was not Y, but her doctors or the hospital, who purchased the defective product in country B. On the other hand, under the Hague Products Liability Convention, in order to apply the law of the country of the victim's habitual residence, it is in principle required that the claimant herself purchased the product in this country (art 5 and above, III.2.). However, art 4 of the Hague Products Liability Convention would eventually also lead to the application of the law of country B since Y suffered the injury in country B and had her habitual residence there. In systems that focus exclusively on the country where the victims themselves purchased the defective product, such as the Japanese PILA, the solution to Scenario 2 is less clear.

Scenario 3

A product is manufactured by a US American company and marketed eg in → France, but not eg in → Belgium. One item is sold in France to X, who is not a retailer. He takes it to Belgium and there sells it to Y. Y is injured in Belgium and brings a claim there against the US American manufacturer.

Belgium is not a contracting state to the 1973 Hague Convention. Belgian courts will thus determine the applicable law according to the Rome II Regulation. The parties have not chosen the applicable law and they are not in a contractual relationship, so there is no case for accessory connection. Neither art 5(1)(a) nor (b) Rome II Regulation lead to the applicable law, in that Y is habitually resident in Belgium but the product was not marketed there, and it was not marketed in Belgium where Y acquired it from X. Finally, art 5(1)(c) Rome II Regulation does not determine the applicable law either: Y suffered injury in Belgium but the product was not marketed there.

The Rome II Regulation thus does not provide a rule for cases where the product was not marketed in the country of the victim's habitual residence, of purchase, or of injury. In legal doctrine it is suggested that the law of the place of injury be applied in such scenarios (in Scenario 3: Belgian law) under the general rule in art 4(1) Rome II Regulation (Trevor Hartley, 'Choice of Law for Non-contractual Liability: Selected Problems under the Rome II Regulation' (2008) ICLQ 899, 906; Adam Rushworth and Andrew Scott, 'Rome II Regulation: Choice of Law for Non-contractual Obligations' (2008) LMCLQ, 274 at 284). However, in order to apply the law of the country where the injury occurred, Rome II expressly requires in art 5(1)(c) Rome II Regulation that the product was marketed there. It is therefore suggested to fill the gap by applying the law of the place of marketing that has the closest connection to the facts of the case. This would be in line with the fact that the European legislator used the place of marketing in art 5(1)(a), (b) and (c) Rome II Regulation as a central and indispensable connecting factor. In Scenario 3 this should arguably lead to the application of French law. The same outcome could be reached under art 5(1)(b) Rome II Regulation if the original acquisition by X (instead of Y) were regarded as the relevant purchase in Scenario 3.

If this case were brought before the courts of a contracting state to the Hague Products Liability Convention, art 5 Hague Products Liability Convention might lead to the application of Belgian law: Belgium was the country of the habitual residence of the victim, who had purchased the product there. If, however, a purchase in a professional chain of distribution were required, art 5 Hague Products Liability Convention would not apply. Then art 4 Hague Products Liability Convention would also lead to Belgian law, since this was the country where the injury occurred and where the person directly suffering damage had his or her habitual residence.

VI. Jurisdiction

In EU Member States, jurisdiction in product liability cases is governed by the Brussels I Regulation (recast) (Regulation (EU) No 1215/2012 of the European Parliament and of the Council of 12 December 2012 on jurisdiction and the recognition and enforcement of judgments in civil and commercial matters (recast), [2012] OJ L 351/1; → Brussels I (Convention and Regulation)) or, where applicable, by the → Lugano Convention (Lugano Convention of 30 October 2007 on jurisdiction and the recognition and enforcement of judgments in civil and commercial matters, [2007] OJ L 339/3). According to art 4(1) Brussels I Regulation (recast)/2(1) Lugano Convention, persons domiciled in a Member/contracting State will be sued in the courts of that Member/contracting State. A claim for products liability can also be brought, if the claimant so chooses, 'in the courts for the place where the harmful event occurred or may occur' (art 7(2) Brussels I Regulation (recast)/art 5(3) Lugano Convention). According to well-established ECJ case-law, this special jurisdiction is available both at the place where the person claimed to be liable acted and the place where the damage occurred (ie where the protected interest was initially harmed), ECJ C-21/76 *SCJEC Handelskwekerij GJ Bier BV v Mines de Potasse d'Alsace SA* [1976] ECR 1735 (→ Torts).

1. Place of acting of the person claimed to be liable

With respect to the 'place of acting' in products liability claims, the ECJ decided that 'in the case where a manufacturer faces a claim of liability for a defective product, the place of the event giving rise to the damage is the place where the product in question was manufactured', ECJ C-45/13 *Andreas Kainz v Pantherwerke AG* [2014] OJ C 85/10. The ECJ reasoned with regard to the rationale of this special jurisdiction that a forum at the place where the product was manufactured 'facilitates, on the grounds of, *inter alia*, the possibility of gathering evidence in order to establish the defect in question, the efficacious conduct of proceedings and, therefore, the sound administration of justice'.

It should be noted that the ECJ did not locate the place of acting at the place where the product was marketed, although this would have been in line with the central role that the place of marketing plays (as 'place of acting') under the Rome II Regulation. The *Kainz* decision thus confirms the restrictive interpretation and the exceptional character of the rules on special jurisdiction in art 7 Brussels I Regulation (recast)/art 5 Lugano Convention. It also emphasizes the independent interpretation of the same legal terms (in the present case: the 'place of acting') for purposes of jurisdiction on the one hand and for purposes of determining the applicable law on the other.

2. Place where the damage occurred

The leading products liability case concerning the location of the place of damage under the Brussels I Regulation/Lugano Convention is ECJ C-189/08 *Zuid-Chemie v Philippo's Mineralenfabriek NV/SA* [2009] ECR I-6917: a Dutch company *Zuid-Chemie* used ingredients in its factory in the Netherlands to produce fertilizer, which it then sold and delivered to its customers. *Zuid-Chemie* had purchased the ingredients from another company which in turn had acquired them from a third company, *Philippo's*. *Philippo's* had ordered some raw materials for producing the ingredients from a fourth company. All companies were established in the Netherlands.

Philippo's manufactured the ingredients in its factory in Belgium where the final purchaser, *Zuid-Chemie*, came to take delivery of them. It transpired that the raw materials *Philippo's* had purchased from the fourth company were defective, rendering the ingredients produced by *Philippo's* in Belgium, and ultimately the fertilizer produced by *Zuid-Chemie* in the Netherlands, unusable. *Zuid-Chemie* accordingly claimed → damages for the resulting loss from *Philippo's* on an extra-contractual basis.

The parties did not dispute that the place of acting of *Philippos's* was to be located in Belgium, where this company had manufactured the defective ingredient and where it had been delivered to the claimant. The question was rather where to locate the place where the claimant's damage had occurred.

The ECJ held that 'the place where the damage occurred cannot be any other than Zuid-Chemie's factory in the Netherlands where the [ingredient], which is the defective product, was processed into fertiliser, causing substantial damage to that fertiliser which was suffered by Zuid-Chemie and which went beyond the damage to the [ingredient] itself'.

VII. Conclusions

Designating the applicable law in product liability cases has always been regarded as particularly difficult, and the range of solutions that were applied in the different jurisdictions before the entry into force of the Rome II Regulation was particularly broad. Article 5 of the Rome II Regulation combines several criteria that must be fulfilled in order to arrive at the applicable law and thereby reaches finely tuned and well-balanced results. In the field of products liability, as in many others, the Rome II Regulation has thus brought much needed clarifications thereby contributing to legal certainty and predictability of the applicable law.

THOMAS KADNER GRAZIANO

Literature

(see also → Torts; → Rome II Regulation (non-contractual obligations))
James J Fawcett, 'Products Liability in Private international law: A European Perspective' (1993-I) 238 Rec. des Cours 9; Trevor Hartley, 'Choice of Law for Non-contractual Liability: Selected Problems under the Rome II Regulation' (2008) ICLQ 899; Martin Illmer, 'The New European Private international law of Product Liability – Steering Through Troubled Waters' (2009) 73 RabelsZ 269; Thomas Kadner Graziano and Matthias Erhardt, 'Cross-Border Damage Caused by Genetically Modified Organisms: Jurisdiction and Applicable Law' in Bernhard Koch (ed), *Damage Caused by Genetically Modified Organisms* (De Gruyter 2010) 784; Thomas Kadner Graziano, 'The Law Applicable to Product Liability: The Present State of the Law in Europe and Current Proposals for Reform' (2005) ICLQ 475; Thomas Kadner Graziano, 'Le nouveau droit international privé communautaire en matière de responsabilité extracontractuelle' (2008) Rev. crit.DIP 445; Thomas Kadner Graziano, *La responsabilité délictuelle en droit international privé européen* (Helbing Lichtenhahn – Bruylant – L.G.D.J. 2004) 61; Thomas Kadner Graziano, *Europäisches Internationales Deliktsrecht* (Mohr Siebeck 2003) 63; Thomas Kadner Graziano, *Gemeineuropäisches Internationales Privatrecht – Harmonisierung des IPR durch Wissenschaft und Lehre (am Beispiel der ausservertraglichen Haftung für Schäden)* (Mohr Siebeck 2002) 258; P John Kozyris, 'Values and Methods in Choice of Law for Products Liability: A Comparative Comment on Statutory Solutions' (1990) 38 Am.J.Comp.L. 475; Jan Kropholler and others, *Aussereuropäische IPR-Gesetze*, (Deutsches Notarinstitut/Max-Planck-Institut für ausländisches und internationales Privatrecht 1999); Willis LM Reese, 'The Hague Convention on the Law Applicable to Products Liability' (1974) 8 Int'l Law. 606; Willis LM Reese, 'Further Comments on The Hague Convention on the Law Applicable to Products Liability' (1978) 8 Ga.J.Int'l.& Comp.L. 311; Symeon C Symeonides, 'Choice of Law for Products Liability: The 1990s and Beyond' (2004) Tul.L.Rev. 1247; Symeon Symeonides, 'Party Choice in Product-Liability Conflicts' (2004) Willamette J. Int'l L. & Disp. Resol. 263; Russel Weintraub, *Commentary on the Conflict of Laws* (6th edn, Foundation Press/ThomsonReuters 2010) § 6.31 *et seq*; see also the references in <www.hcch.net/index_de.php?act=conventions.publications&dtid=1&cid=84>.

Proper law (doctrine)

I. Introduction

The term 'proper law' has been, and to a reduced extent still is, used in English private international law to refer to the system of law which, as a result of the application of choice-of-law rules, is the law which applies to a particular issue or to a particular relationship (→ United Kingdom). It was – and is – frequently used synonymously with 'governing law' or, more recently, with 'applicable law'.

The term 'proper law' was most widely used in England to denote the law applicable to a contract; its origins in this context can be traced to the writings of *John Westlake* (1828–1913) in the 19th century, to whom the term is attributed (Lord Collins of Mapesbury and others (eds), *Dicey, Morris & Collins on the Conflict of Laws*, vol 2 (15th edn, Sweet & Maxwell 2012) 1777 para 32-006).

The meaning of what was described by the term, 'proper law', developed, however, over time. The term itself first appeared in an English case in 1922 to explain the choice-of-law rule for contract, where the Privy Council cited *Dicey's Conflict of Laws* (3rd edn, 1922), in which *Dicey* had explained that when a contract was made in one country and was to be performed in another, 'the proper law of the contract, especially as to the mode of performance, may be presumed to be the law of the country where the performance is to take place (lex loci solutionis)' (*Benaim and Co v Debono* [1924] AC 514, 520).

That statement of law was later criticized. Indeed, in 1937, again invoking the term 'proper law' as the law which the court is to apply to determine the obligations under a contract, the Privy Council explained that 'English law in deciding these matters has refused to treat as conclusive, rigid or arbitrary, criteria such as the lex loci contractus or lex loci solutionis, and has treated the matter as depending on the intention of the parties to be ascertained in each case on a consideration of the terms of the contract, the situation of the parties, and generally on all the surrounding factors' (*Mont Albert Borough Council v Australasian Temperance and General Mutual Life Assurance Society Limited* [1938] AC 224, 240).

This reflected a reluctance on the part of English judges to adopt a clear but rigid choice-of-law rule for contract and a preference for a rule reflecting → party autonomy. But this was not new. Indeed, as early as 1760, in *Robinson v Bland* (1760) 97 ER 717, 718; 2 Burr 1077, 1078, *Lord Mansfield* rejected the previous approach of applying the law of the place of contracting (already by then, in his view, outdated), explaining the 'law of the place can never be the rule, where the transaction is entered into with an express view to the law of another country, as the rule by which it is to be governed'. As *Dicey, Morris* and *Collins* explain, the trend towards recognition of party autonomy as the basis for → choice of law reflected the fact that, increasingly, goods were being bought and sold by people in different countries and, therefore, the place of contracting could be fortuitous, depending on the location of the offeror and offeree, and, indeed, might bear no relationship to the → place of performance (Lord Collins of Mapesbury and others (eds), *Dicey, Morris & Collins on the Conflict of Laws*, vol 2 (15th edn, Sweet & Maxwell 2012) 1777 para 32-004). In 1950, the Privy Council, considering what the proper law of a contract was, had said, '[o]n the assumption that express reference is made to none, the question becomes a matter of implication to be derived from all of the circumstances of the transaction' (*Bonython v Commonwealth of Australia* [1951] AC 201, 221). This description of the approach of the common law is consistent with the rule which later came to be refined as the common law choice of rule in England: see, especially, *Amin Rasheed Shipping Corporation v Kuwait Insurance Co* [1984] AC 50.

More recently, the introduction of the Rome Convention (Rome Convention on the law applicable to contractual obligations (consolidated version), [1998] OJ C 27/34) and its enactment into English law saw the rise of the term 'applicable law' which, at least in relation to contract, is now the prevalent term. (As to an explanation of the 'applicable law', and the differences between it and the 'proper law', see Anthony Jaffey 'The English Proper Law Doctrine and the EEC Convention' (1984) 33 ICLQ 531. Some such differences are explained below.)

The term, 'proper law', however, remains used in some circumstances, especially in fields outside the scope of the European instruments of private international law. For a time it was also suggested that there was a 'proper law' of tort, and it is also used in other contexts, some of which are mentioned here.

It is perhaps unsurprising, in these circumstances, that there is no definition of the term that may be applied generally, let alone a coherent, unified theory of 'proper law' and an entry on the topic runs the risk of being an exploration of choice of law generally, particularly in relation to contract. It is nevertheless possible to identify the use of the term in various areas of private international law.

II. Contract

The common law of England applies to determine the 'proper law' of a contract entered into before 1 April 1991. Since then, either the Rome Convention or the Rome I Regulation (Regulation (EC) No 593/2008 of the European Parliament and of the Council of 17 June 2008 on the law applicable to contractual obligations (Rome I), [2008] OJ L 177/6) applies (→ Rome Convention and Rome I Regulation (contractual obligations)). The former applies to contracts entered into on or after 1 April 1991 and before 17 December 2009; the latter applies to contracts entered into on or after 17 December 2009. As will be seen, there are methodological differences between the inquiry made under the Rome I Regulation (and before it, the Rome Convention) as to the 'applicable law' of a contract and the common law's inquiry as to the proper law. While the 'proper law' asks, in the absence of choice, the identity of 'the system of law by reference to which the contract was made or that with which the transaction has its closest and most real connection (*Bonython v Commonwealth of Australia* [1951] AC 201, 219), the 'applicable law' in those circumstances is determined in accordance with a scheme based on primary principles; exceptions to those principles and rules of displacement for circumstances in which the principles and exceptions do not, or should not, apply. Hence, for example, in the absence of choice by the parties, a contract for the sale of goods (→ Sale contracts and sale of goods) is governed in principle by the law of the country where the seller has his or her habitual residence (art 4(1)(a) Rome I Regulation) and a contract relating to a right *in rem* in immovable property is governed by the law of the country where the country is situated (art 4(1)(c) Rome I Regulation). But as an exception to those principles, or if they point one to more than one country, the contract is to be governed by the law of the country of the habitual residence of the party required to give 'characteristic performance' (a term previously unknown to the English 'proper law' approach) (art 4(2) Rome I Regulation). But a rule of displacement may then apply, in favour of the law of a country which is manifestly more closely connected with the contract (art 4(3) Rome I Regulation), or a default rule which if none of the otherwise applicable rules apply, selects the law of the country with which the contract is most closely connected (art 4(4) Rome I Regulation). Hence the rule of last resort under the Rome Regulation is practically the same as the English common law rule; but the application of the structured rules in the Rome I Regulation is likely in most cases to produce the same answer as the proper law rule. The differences in outcome, rather than methodology, are likely to be exceptions, in practice.

The English common law, which asks what is the proper law of the contract, continues to apply in circumstances excluded from the Rome I Regulation, most significantly in relation to jurisdiction and arbitration agreements. Consequently the interpretation of (for example) jurisdiction or arbitration agreements is still subject to the common law rules, subject, in the case of jurisdiction agreements, to art 25 of the Brussels I Regulation (recast) (Regulation (EU) No 1215/2012 of the European Parliament and of the Council of 12 December 2012 on jurisdiction and the recognition and enforcement of judgments in civil and commercial matters (recast), [2012] OJ L 351/1; → Brussels I (Convention and Regulation)).

The concept of the proper law of the contract also applies in other common law jurisdictions such as → Canada and → Australia. Indeed, the English proper law approach derives, at least in part, from Canadian and Australian cases at a time when appeals from those jurisdictions still lay to the Privy Council: see, respectively, *Vita Food Products Inc v Unus Shipping Co* [1939] AC 277 and *Bonython v Commonwealth of Australia* [1951] AC 201. In those jurisdictions, the proper law continues to be applied in the manner that can be traced to its English heritage, unaffected by subsequent European developments (*Akai Pty Ltd v The People's Insurance Co* (1996) 188 CLR 418, 440).

At common law, the 'proper law' of a contract was, or is, the law that governs the interpretation and validity of the contract, the mode of performance and the consequences of breaches of the contract (*Compagnie Tunisienne de Navigation SA v Compagnie d'Armement Maritime SA* [1971] AC 572, 603; *Amin Rasheed Shipping Corporation v Kuwait Insurance* [1984] AC 50, 60). In the 11th edition of *Dicey and Morris on the Conflict of Laws*, vol 2 ((11th edn, Sweet & Maxwell 1987) 1161) it was described as follows: the term 'proper law of a contract' means the system of law by which the parties intended the contract to be governed, or, where their intention is neither expressed nor to be inferred from the circumstances, the system of law with which the transaction has its closest and most real connection.

The 'proper law' is discerned by asking, successively, whether there is an express → choice of law, whether there is an implied choice, and, in the absence of either of the two previous alternatives, to consider the law with which the contract has its closest and most real connection. In practice, the latter two questions are often elided, largely because the same or similar factors are considered in applying both questions, but they remain conceptually distinct. Thus, '[i]f it is apparent from the terms of the contract itself that the parties intended it to be interpreted by reference to a particular system of law, their intention will prevail and the latter question as to the system of law with which, in the view of the court, the transaction to which the contract relates would, but for such intention of the parties, have had the closest and most real connection, does not arise' (see *Amin Rasheed Shipping Corp v Kuwait Insurance Co* [1984] AC 50, 61). The focus is, and has been, on the autonomy of persons to determine the law applicable to their own dealings, subject only to mandatory laws of the forum, the public policy of the forum and other such exceptions (→ Overriding mandatory provisions; → Public policy (*ordre public*)). In this respect, the proper law rules and the rules of the Rome I Regulation (art 3(1)) are similar, and perhaps even identical.

The most common, and straightforward, manner in which the parties may make the proper law of the contract clear is to provide, as a clause in their written agreement, that they agree that a particular system of law is to apply to the interpretation of, and to any dispute in relation to, the contract (→ Choice of law; → Party autonomy). Most obviously, a simple statement that the 'contract shall be governed by X law' will suffice.

If there is no express choice, the court will look to see whether there is an implied choice of law. Various factors have been identified in the English judicial authorities as demonstrating such a choice. A choice of the jurisdiction of a particular country, or arbitration in that country, often, but not always, brings with it an implied choice to apply the law of that country. But the other terms and the nature of the contract, as well as the general circumstances of the case, may also inform whether there is an implied choice.

The proper law's search for an express or implied choice, although traditionally seen as two conceptually distinct phases in the contractual choice-of-law methodology has been described as being 'but species of the one genus, that is concerned with giving effect to the intention of the parties' (*Akai Pty Ltd v The People's Insurance Co* (1996) 188 CLR 418, 440).

In the absence of a choice (whether express or implied), in order to find the 'proper law', the court asks which system of law has the closest and most real connection with the contract. That law may be discerned by reference to, for example, where the contract was made, the → nationality or residence of the contracting parties and the → place of performance of the contract, with such factors being given the degree of weight which is appropriate in all the circumstances.

As noted above, where there was no express choice of law, the determination of the 'proper law' by reference to either the implied choice of the parties or the 'closest and most real connection' often requires regard to be had to the same matters. The difference was said to be that, in relation to the former, the relevant inquiry is what the imputed intention of the parties was (namely, what would they have said as to the choice of law if they had been asked at the time) while, in relation to the latter, one objectively (and irrespective of the parties' intention) decides which system of law has the closest and most real connection (see *The Komninos S* [1991] 1 Lloyd's Rep 370, 374). The contrast is between contractual interpretation and application of a rule of law.

But what is applied by an English court when it applies the 'proper law'? It means the law so chosen or that with which the contract has its closest and most real connection, but excluding the choice-of-law rules of that country's law. That is, the parties' legal rights in respect of their contractual relationship are to be determined by the 'proper law', namely the rules of domestic law of the relevant country, excluding any → *renvoi*.

III. Tort

Since 1 January 2009 the choice-of-law rule for tort in England, as in the rest of the European Union, is determined by the rules in the → Rome II Regulation (non-contractual obligations) (Regulation (EC) No 864/2007 of the European Parliament and of the Council of 11 July 2007 on the law applicable to non-contractual obligations (Rome II), [2007] OJ L 199/40), except for a limited range of matters which fall outside its scope as defined by art 1, notably defamation. As explained elsewhere, this involves the application of the rules found in art 4 of that Regulation. Put simply, the general rule is that the law applicable to the tort or delict is the law of the country in which the damage occurs irrespective of the country in which the event giving rise to the damage occurred and irrespective of the country or countries in which the indirect consequences of that event occur. There are exceptions: first, if the person claimed to be liable and the person sustaining damage both have their habitual residence in the same country, the law of that country applies; and second, where it is clear from all the circumstances of the case that the tort is manifestly more closely connected with a country other than that which the general rule identifies, or which applies by application of the preceding exception, the law of that country applies.

But (again) it has not always been so. Before the Rome II Regulation came into effect, the choice-of-law rules in English law for most torts were those laid down by the Private international law (Miscellaneous Provisions) Act 1995 (c 42), which came into effect on 1 May 1996 and which largely follow the recommendations of the Law Commission (Consultative Memorandum No 62, 1984). This Act provided for the *lex loci delicti* as a general rule, but contained a displacement rule which weighed conflicting factors if they made it 'substantially more appropriate' for another system of law to apply to any given issue (→ United Kingdom). This law, which was itself subject to exceptions and qualifications, notably the exclusion of defamation, replaced the previous common law rule, although the latter retains a vestigial applicability for cases outside the subject matter scope of both the 1996 Act and the Rome II Regulation. The common law rule also continues to apply in various common law countries which follow English law (for example, in Bermuda), although its acceptance in major common law jurisdictions is much more limited than in the case of the proper law of contract.

It is in the context of the common law choice-of-law rules for tort, that there had been reference to a 'proper law' of tort. Indeed, *John Morris*, one of the most famous writers on private international law in England, advocated the adoption of such a 'proper law of the tort'. He wrote that the proper law of tort would enable a court to choose 'the law which, on policy grounds, seems to have the most significant connection with the chain of acts and consequences in the particular situation' before it (John Morris, 'The Proper Law of a Tort' (1951) 64 Harv.L.Rev. 881, 888). It underlies the approach of some of the United States courts on this question (eg, *Wilcox v Wilcox*, 133 N.W.2d 408 (Wis. 1965); *Freund v Spencer*, 260 N.Y.S.2d 149 (N.Y. Sup. Ct. 1965)).

But this approach was never embraced by the English courts. Indeed, by the time the 1996 Act was passed, the so-called rule of 'double actionability' had been developed as the relevant English rule: the alleged wrong must have been actionable if committed in England and must not have been justified by the law of the place where it was done (*Phillips v Eyre* (1870) LR 6 QB 1). To some extent this involved a compromise between the two competing possible rules, namely the → *lex fori* (law of the forum) and the *lex loci delicti* (the law of the place of the tort). The double actionability rule was approved in 1970 by the House of Lords in *Boys v Chaplin* [1971] AC 356, but with an exception such that 'a particular issue between the parties may be governed by the law of the country which, with respect to that issue, has the most significant relationship with the occurrence and the parties'. In that exception, one finds aspects of *Morris*' theory of the 'proper law of tort'. That is, in determining whether an issue may be governed by another law, one is to have regard to whether an issue has more significant connections with another law.

In *Boys v Chaplin*, it had been argued that the English common law should adopt the 'proper law of the tort'. The existence of a 'proper law of contract' was called in aid, as was various United States authority. But it was rejected by the House of Lords. Indeed, the United States authorities were said to have led to uncertain results and the analogy of the 'proper law of the contract' was not useful since the parties to a contract usually have the opportunity to choose the law beforehand. *Lord Donovan* went so far as to say that reference to public policy, as was encouraged by the 'proper law of the tort' was 'to mount an "unruly horse"'.

Unlike its contractual brother, the tortious 'proper law' rule never assumed support in the English courts, save that its underlying rationale could be seen in the so-called flexible exception to the double actionability rule.

IV. Unjust enrichment

At common law, before the Rome II Regulation, the obligation to restore the benefit of an enrichment obtained at another person's expense was governed by the 'proper law' of the obligation (see generally *Fibrosa Spolka Akcyjna v Fairbairn Lawson Combe Barbour Ltd* [1943] AC 32; *Dimskal Shipping Co SA v International Transport Workers Federation* [1992] 2 AC 152) (→ United Kingdom). The proper law of the obligation was discerned by asking, first, whether the obligation arose in connection with a contract. If so, the proper law was the law applicable to the contract. If the obligation arose in connection with a transaction concerning land, its proper law was the law of the country where that land was situated (namely, the *lex situs*). If it arose in other circumstances, the proper law was the law of the country where the enrichment occurred.

V. Marriage

A further area in which one sees reference to the 'proper law' is in the common law rule applicable to the validity of a → marriage contract or settlement. The Rome I Regulation specifically excludes from its operation rights in property (→ Property and proprietary rights) arising out of a matrimonial relationship. It falls then to the common law. In principle, there is no reason why the 'proper law' of the (marriage) contract should not be determined by the common law rules identified above in relation to contract, which applied before the advent of the Rome Convention and, later, the Rome I Regulation, and which continue to apply where the Regulation has no operation. But the subject matter of a marriage contract is obviously different from the generality of contracts which are within the scope of the Rome I Regulation. So, while the common law will still look to whether there is an express or implied choice of law, in the absence of a reason to the contrary, the 'proper law' of a marriage contract or settlement is the law of the matrimonial domicile (see, eg, *Duke of Marlborough v Attorney-General* [1945] Ch 78).

VI. Trusts

Until the advent of the Hague Trusts Convention (Hague Convention of 1 July 1985 on the Law Applicable to Trusts and on their Recognition, 1664 UNTS 311) (→ Hague Conference on Private International Law; → Trust), which was given the force of law in England from 1 August 1987 by the Recognition of Trusts Act 1987 (c 14), a trust was also said to have a 'proper law', being the law that applies to determine the rights and obligations of the trustees and beneficiaries of the trust (→ United Kingdom). Unlike a contract, which is an inter partes agreement, a trust created by settlement is not the subject of an agreement from which the 'proper law' is to determined. But the principle as to the determination of the 'proper law' of the trust is relevantly identical. It was determined by asking whether the settlor had expressly or impliedly chosen the system of law which was to govern the settlement, and if not by finding the law with which the trust has the closest or most real connection. The Hague Trusts Convention, by arts 6 and 7, applies the same test, albeit referring, as with the European instruments, to the 'applicable law'.

VII. Other instances of the 'proper law'

The use of the term 'proper law' can also been seen in suggestions for law reform in diverse areas of → choice of law. The editors of *Dicey, Morris & Collins* suggest, for example, that, at common law, a possible rule for determining the uniformly applicable rule for the assignment of intangible things could be achieved by a 'proper law of the underlying obligation' (Lord Collins of Mapesbury and others (eds), *Dicey, Morris & Collins on the Conflict of Laws*, vol 2 (15th edn, Sweet & Maxwell 2012) 1357 para 24–053). That is, rather than focussing on the choice-of-law rules for contract, or for those governing the right to which an intangible relates, the authors suggest the possibility of formulating a 'proper law' by reference to which a dominant role is ascribed to one such law, which then becomes the proper law applicable to the underlying obligation.

Further, in some cases, one finds reference to the 'proper law' as being the equivalent of the *lex causae*, namely the law which applies to the particular cause of action, or particular issue. For example, in *Hardwick Game Farm v Suffolk Agricultural Poultry Producers Association* [1966] 1 WLR 287, 330, Diplock LJ explained that '[t]he proper law governing the transfer of corporeal movable property is the lex situs'. When used in this context, it is intended to be a reference to the applicable law; it does not, in contradistinction to the common law choice-of-law rule for contract, seek to identify rules by which to determine the applicable law.

VIII. Conclusion

The term 'proper law' is encountered in different contexts in private international law. Its prevalence in English law is declining now that many areas are governed by European instruments where the term is not found. While it is not possible to find an overarching theme in the use of the term, its use, particularly in the context of common law choice-of-law rules, remains an important one.

ALEXANDER LAYTON AND ALBERT DINELLI

Literature

Lawrence Collins and others (eds), *Dicey and Morris on the Conflict of Laws*, vol 2 (11th edn, Sweet & Maxwell 1987); Albert Venn Dicey and Arthur Barriedale Keith, *Conflict of Laws* (3rd edn, Sweet & Maxwell 1922); Anthony Jaffey 'The English Proper Law Doctrine and the EEC Convention' (1984) 33 ICLQ 531; John Morris, 'The Proper Law of Tort' (1951) 64 Harv.L.Rev. 880.

Property and proprietary rights

An ancient customary rule in conflict of laws is that a territorial regime applies to tangible property-related issues, with the applicable law called in practice *lex situs* or *lex rei sitae*. A brief survey of history and methodology illuminates current rules of private international law in Europe. Moreover, the *lex rei sitae* is considered by some to be applicable to certain aspects of intangible property (transfer or pledge).

I. History and methodology (12th–19th century)

1. 'Status rerum' and 'statutum reale'

In the middle ages, when territoriality first applied to immovables, two ways of conceiving the territoriality rule emerged. First, → territoriality was considered as giving an objective status to things involved in international relationships, and second, it was understood in those times as the category of mandatory laws applying to certain individual real rights.

In the first meaning, which stressed the importance of the object of property, it was the role of law to give an objective status to the property. Due to this *status rerum*, all questions of public and private law relating to individual or collective entitlement to possession or ownership were resolved, and it was seen as natural that this status extensively applied to all immovables located on the territory of the sovereign. In this very old understanding, we can see the roots of the positive multilateral choice-of-law rule, connecting real rights to the *lex rei sitae*. Many 20th century European scholars, espousing the Savignian theory, take as a logical starting point that the *res* is the object of the connecting rule and that it cannot be assigned to a non-territorial regime.

The second way of conceiving territoriality echoes the old statutory methodology. Its starting point is the law actually involved in international conflicts. Local law was always preferred to foreign statutes because of its content. Considerations of public interest justified the rules applying to real rights and their transfer (*inter vivos* or mostly *post mortem*). The feudal system was largely based on the regime of → immovable property, so that the acquisition of an individual interest in it whether by citizens or foreigners was mandatorily subject to the local law. This could be seen as a very early method of applying overriding mandatory rules (*lois de police*, *Eingriffsnormen*; → Overriding mandatory provisions).

From 1200 to 1900, there was no point in distinguishing between the two approaches. Indeed, territoriality had a broad scope of application as regards immovables, such as issues of capacity to transfer, matrimonial regimes and of course → successions. Nowadays, the principle of territoriality is declining. Accordingly, the second approach is more appropriate when there are certain real rights relating to the same property and partly subject to a foreign law.

In the ancient customs of European conflict of laws, movables were generally considered as forming a sub-category of the personal status (*mobilia sequuntur personam*, *mobilia ossibus inhaerent*). This changed in the second half of the 19th century when judges were called upon to apply certain mandatory laws to movable property and accordingly began to take the territoriality principle into account. The *lex situs* progressively became a rule of case-law. Between 1900 and 1950, it became a general European rule that tangible property (both immovable and movable) was subject to the law of the place where the thing was located. Nevertheless, this rule then came to be seen as excessive, particularly in matters of securities on movables (see below II.2.).

2. Unilateralist methodology in choice of laws and international civil procedure

Due to statutist methodology, *lex rei sitae* applied on a unilateral basis to tangibles located on the territory. Immovables in particular have always received a specific treatment in international litigation. Indeed, there was a special link between jurisdiction and applicable law for reasons of convenience and public policy. The local forum could hardly allow a foreign judge to address matters of public interest relating to local property. Territorial power to adjudicate disputes was often considered as exclusive. Moreover, territorial power to enforce local and foreign acts or judgments rendered the forum ideally placed to determine the scope of the mandatory regime of local things. A late German author described the *lex situs* as a 'strongest State principle' (*Wilhelm Wengler*). For a foreign state seeking to resolve conflicts of laws relating to real property in another country, *lex situs* can be used as an application of the theory of the 'competent legal order' (*Paolo Picone*). Under this theory, the territorial → connecting factor not only helps determine the law; but also indicates the overall perspective that should be adopted by every foreign judge or authority on questions relating to jurisdiction and power to adjudicate the case. In other words, that authority should act in compliance with all mandatory requirements of the *situs forum* (including those relating to jurisdiction and civil procedure). These solutions enable judges to achieve international harmony (eg, art 12(1) Succession Regulation (Regulation (EU) No 650/2012 of the European Parliament and of the Council of 4 July 2012 on jurisdiction, applicable law, recognition and enforcement of decisions and acceptance and enforcement of authentic instruments in matters of succession and on the creation of a European Certificate of Succession, [2012] OJ L 201/107; → Rome IV Regulation (succession)); other significant example in: art 108 Swiss Private international law Act (*Bundesgesetz über das Internationale Privatrecht* of 18 December 1987, 1988 BBl I 5, as amended, henceforth Swiss PILA)). A foreign judge can hardly violate the *lex situs* when acting like a judge hypothetically sitting in the country of physical location of the property. For this reason the territoriality principle was soon perceived as covering not only all issues of conflict of laws, but also certain questions of international civil procedure.

In the interests of encouraging international harmony today's judges can apply original methods for determining the law relating to tangible property. They can characterize claims to title in property under the *lex situs*, despite the fact that the *lex fori* generally applies to characterization in international matters. When useful, for example in successions, the distinction between movables and immovables under the *lex situs* increases the likelihood of the judgment being compatible with the public policy of the *situs*. This can be said for many national systems during the 20th century. However, the *lex situs* characterization was strongly criticized by scholars, to the extent that it became uncertain. Identifying with the *situs* judge can also be helpful in resolving the classic difficulties of → '*renvoi*' as well as 'preliminary' or 'incidental' questions (→Incidental (preliminary) question).

Certain original solutions to conflict of laws in property are still the result of → unilateralism. As has been shown, the territoriality principle not only works as a classic rule of conflict of laws but the universal connecting factor to *lex situs* also operates as a principle of meta-conflict of laws. Judges at times have to relinquish their own approach and adopt that of a more appropriate foreign forum. This way of determining the primary regime of rights *in rem*, based not on public international law but rather on traditional considerations of practical convenience, is nevertheless specific to tangible property and cannot be transposed to modern intangible property.

II. Tangible property

Rules relating to jurisdiction will not be developed here. The local or foreign *situs* judge may have exclusive jurisdiction by operation of statute (eg for immovable property art 22(1) Brussels I Regulation (Regulation (EC) No 44/2001 of 22 December 2000 on jurisdiction and the recognition and enforcement of judgments in civil and commercial matters, [2001] OJ L 12/1), which now is art 24 Brussels I Regulation (recast) (Regulation (EU) No 1215/2012 of the European Parliament and of the Council of 12 December 2012 on jurisdiction and the recognition and enforcement of judgments in civil and commercial matters (recast), [2012] OJ L 351/1) (→ Brussels I (Convention and Regulation))) or case-law. International litigation relating to movables is ordinarily not subject to specific rules, except for cultural property matters (see for example art 7(4) Brussels I Regulation (recast)).

Conflict of laws *stricto sensu* may be divided into two types, those governed by general rules and those governed by specific ones.

1. Principles that are common to movables and immovables

a) Regime of property and other rights in rem

The *lex situs* applies to proprietary and other real rights relating to tangible objects (mobility will be addressed below). Nowadays, although the basic principle is rarely questioned, the scope of the *lex situs* can vary widely between states. In some countries, for reasons of → public policy (*ordre public*) and creditor protection, a judge may be required to apply the *lex situs* both to the content of the real right and to its acquisition. Extinction of the real right, proof of it and responsibility of third parties for specific infringement are also commonly assessed under the *lex situs*. Where there are conflicting real rights, in particular pledges or other security rights, the common principle is that the current *lex situs* determines the effects of each right and its priority.

Legal orders such as → France or England (→ United Kingdom), which admit flexibility in their internal property laws, might recognize a scope of application for the law of autonomy, ie the law chosen by the parties to an international transaction. If there is nothing in the *lex situs* to prevent the reduction of its scope of application, then the foreign law chosen by the interested parties may apply, even to third parties. This system is useful in matters of trusts. As the Hague Trust Convention (Hague Convention of 1 July 1985 on the Law Applicable to Trusts and on their Recognition, 1664 UNTS 311) suggests, a trust created under a foreign law can be recognized in respect of local property. In addition to the law of the trust itself, only the overriding mandatory rules of the *lex situs* apply for the protection of third parties or public interests (see more generally → Trust). By contrast, certain European legal systems have a *numerus clausus* of real rights and a restrictive conception of freedom as applied to transactions relating to such rights. Consequently, in international matters these systems tend to apply only the *lex situs* and disregard the chosen law.

b) Transfer of property
The validity and effects of any transfer of property must be judged under the *lex situs*. This basic rule applies to all items of tangible property, whether the transfer results from the consent of the owner (voluntary transfer) or not (involuntary transfers, in cases of enduring possession or *bona fide* purchase). Interested and third parties may rely on the operation of the current *lex situs* rule when dealing with tangible property. Local law may provide for organized public registers and notices that will bind all those attempting to acquire property or any other real right. Even in the absence of such an organization, the mere idea of publicity may have legal consequences for the transfer and lead to additional formal requirements, such as delivery in possession. The German principle of abstract transfer of property, which distinguishes between the underlying contract and the legal act of transfer, should also be applied as a territorial rule to local property. We see here that both the prerequisites of the transfer and its consequences may vary between countries. That being said, in all European systems the contractual obligation to transfer is not mandatorily subject to *lex situs*, but rather falls under the law of the contract itself (see arts 3 and 4 Rome I Regulation (Regulation (EC) No 593/2008 of the European Parliament or the Council of 17 June 2008 on the law applicable to contractual obligations (Rome I), [2008] OJ L 177/6; → Rome Convention and Rome I Regulation (contractual obligations))); and that law should also be applied to transfer of risks (fortuitous loss or alteration of property).

In an actual conflict of laws, there can be doubts as to the precise line to be drawn between *lex situs* and the law of the contract. There is no general rule here, except for the principle that it is for the *lex situs* of the property to determine the precise scope of its law. It may be judicious for the afore-mentioned forum to decide not to apply *lex situs* extensively and to allow some leeway to another law, especially *lex contractus*. Some European systems, such as → France and → Italy (see in particular art 51 of the Italian Private international law Act (*Riforma del Sistema italiano di diritto internazionale privato*, Act No 218 of 31 May 1995 in Gazz.Uff, Supplemento Ordinario No 128 of 3 June l995, as amended)), even decide that the principle of a voluntary transfer must derive from the *lex contractus*, whereas the *lex situs* only applies to some effects *erga omnes*. However, while it is convenient to apply this principle to local property, it would not be effective with foreign property. Once again, unilateralist methodology is helpful here in order to resolve the specific conflicts arising from this diversity of conceptions (see I.2. above).

In contractual relationships, there may be doubts as to the law applicable to retention rights or clauses, in that the *lex situs* does not necessarily apply. Such rights can be subject to the law of the cause for retention (eg the law of contract), provided the current *lex situs* recognizes the retention (see recently art 10–129 Book 10 Dutch New Civil Code (Nieuw Burgerlijk

Wetboek of 1 January 1992, <wetten.overheid.nl>, henceforth Dutch CC)). This kind of legal issue may fall under two different laws. This may appear overly complex, but the *lex contractus* serves continuity, whereas the *lex situs* is necessary for third party protection.

Involuntary transfers may result from the *lex situs* or from the *lex loci actus*, ie the law of the country where the individual act that is the cause of acquisition occurred (see specifically art 87 Belgian Code of Private international law (*Code de Droit International Privé*, Loi du 16 juillet 2004 portant le Code de droit international privé, MB 27 July 2004, 57344, as amended, henceforth Belgian PILA)). When this event is instantaneous, no difficulty arises unless the action occurs on the high sea or in space (ie in sovereignty-free areas). In this case, the law of the vessel or the law of the first *situs* after seizure may apply. A more difficult case is that of an involuntary transfer being the consequence of long-lasting possession, where a specific problem may arise due to a change of applicable law during the period of acquisition. In the case of immovables, this can only happen in cases of change of sovereignty. In the case of movables, it happens more frequently by virtue of change of physical location. In both cases, it is the role of the last *lex situs* to decide the acquisition of property. However, the last *lex situs* can be combined with the previous one, to take account of the previous circumstances and time period.

Expropriations and nationalizations can be special grounds for involuntary transfers in international matters. Territoriality allows the local forum to decide a change of ownership. But sometimes an issue of extraterritoriality arises when a given statutory or governmental regulation provides for a transfer of property abroad. In principle, public international law does not prohibit extraterritoriality, but the judge or the law of the actual place of location of a property can accept or refuse it on specific grounds (eg payment of insufficient compensation to the previous owner). It is not surprising that, here also the relevant legal order has a right of veto (see also → Expropriation).

2. Specific rules for movables

Specific rules apply to certain mobile objects or to particular transactions relating to them, such as securitization.

a) Real rights in cases of mobility
Each European system of private international law has developed rules or techniques for resolving the problem arising from the mobility of the object. French authors speak of 'mobile conflict' (*conflit mobile*), whereas German literature uses the formula 'change of status' (*Statutenwechsel*). In fact, there is a chronological change of applicable law, in cases where the *res* moves from one *situs* to another. There is a gap between theories and practical ways to resolve the problem.

The radical solution is in theory to apply the new *lex situs* to the future treatment of the *res* and the real rights relating thereto. Thus, all rights that were previously valid under another law must be transposed in order to be compatible with the admitted forms of the current *lex situs*. If such an 'adaptation' or 'transposition' is not possible, then the acquired rights disappear fortuitously. Certain legal systems (eg → Switzerland, see art 102 Swiss PILA) have provided for a specific delay for transposition, whereby the old right remains valid on the new territory for an interim period but then must be converted into an equivalent local right in order to remain effective.

Some might observe that the radical solution, still practised by some legal systems such as → France, is mechanical and inflexible. In individual cases, a single *res* can travel in different directions and therefore become subject to a double 'mobile conflict' (multiple change of location of the property). For example imagine a painting located in France, moved for a time to → Italy and then returned to France. In this kind of situation, France will be sovereign to decide the treatment of the *res*, even during the Italian period. It would be an abuse of abstractions to solve the conflict by a strict chronological distinction: French law, then Italian law, then again French law. French law applies in principle to such kinds of property; but the judge and the law of the French *situs* may take the Italian law and facts into consideration, especially where third party rights were acquired during the Italian period.

→ Unilateralism and functional methodology offer an alternative to the mechanical and chronological solution. Change of *situs* does not necessarily change the law or complete treatment of the movable, but rather first displaces the appropriate perspective for solving the conflicts and second brings into play

Louis d'Avout

some of the overriding mandatory rules of the new legal order. That being said, a modern and convenient solution to mobile conflicts is to state that the previously constituted rights remain valid, unless they encroach upon a specific interest protected by the laws of the new *situs*. This is the significant, recently codified German solution (art 43(2) Introductory Act to the German Civil Code (*Einführungsgesetz zum Bürgerlichen Gesetzbuche* of 21 September 1994, BGBl. I 2494, as amended, henceforth EGBGB)), which recalls the historical and theoretical bases of territoriality in matters of private property.

b) Fictions for vessels, res *in transit and cultural property*
In export transactions, the future location can be anticipated by the parties. The seller and buyer, acting under a reservation of title clause, may decide in advance to respect the rules of the future country of location and ignore those of the location at the time of transaction. Most written rules of private international law accept this anticipation for *res* in transit. The only practical limit would be a stoppage during transportation, in which case the *lex situs* of the place of stoppage might apply contrary to the parties' intention.

A similar fiction is used for transport vessels, such as ships, planes, trains and vehicles. Today, many international conventions have superseded the customary rules and have helped to achieve a reliable international property regime (security rights which are subject to international registration, see → Security interests in mobile equipment (uniform law), → Flag, → Air law (uniform law), → Maritime law (uniform law)). Instead of applying the law of the place of location, which can vary, a European judge would as a matter of principle first consider the organized property regime of the country where the vessel is registered (→ Property and proprietary rights in vessels). A ship's flag, also considered as a sign of nationality, shows the relevant legal order to all. This early rule of shipping law now applies to all international transport vessels, and it should also reasonably apply to personal vehicles. Nevertheless, in every case there is one practical limit, in that for cases of seizure or similar proceedings abroad, local law must first be checked because it may refuse to recognize the property regime of the country of registration. Registration is a kind of fictitious localization, and international practice dislikes fictions. This is why the true location of the *res* sometimes takes precedence over registration (particularly for statutory security interests, eg maritime liens, and the ranking of diverse real rights on the vehicle; see art 45(2) EGBGB, similar to the English and French case-law).

An equivalent reasoning should apply to the protection of cultural property moved abroad. Claims from the state of origin, based on standards of public law, can be heard before the courts of the country of new location, provided there is nothing in the *lex situs* to prevent restitution to the previous owner. Nowadays special rules of uniform law apply at the international or European level, to facilitate such restitutions and more generally the return of cultural property to its country of origin (see Council Directive 93/7/EEC of 15 March 1993 on the return of cultural objects unlawfully removed from the territory of a Member State, [1993] OJ L 74/74, revised by Directive 2014/60/EU of the European Parliament and of the Council of 15 May 2014 on the return of cultural objects unlawfully removed from the territory of a Member State and amending Regulation (EU) No 1024/2012 (Recast), [2014] OJ L 159/1).

c) Real rights, in particular securities, in insolvency cases
When combining applicable laws, most European judges find that insolvency cases are the most difficult. No great difficulty arises when the insolvency proceedings take place in the country of current location, since any real right in the proceedings automatically falls under that law. The law of contract or that of the place of location at the time of creation of the right may also apply to questions of validity. On the other hand, however, when the *situs* is outside the country of the insolvency proceedings, two alternative principles may apply. The first is to decide to apply both the law governing the insolvency and that of the location of the *res*; the practical difficulty being the recognition of the insolvency proceedings in the country of location. The second principle is to declare the real right unaffected by any extraterritorial effect of the insolvency proceedings. This is the principle adopted in the Insolvency Regulation (Council Regulation (EC) No 1346/2000 of 29 May 2000 on insolvency proceedings, [2000]

OJ L 160/1) (→ Insolvency, applicable law). The relevant time factor here is the date the insolvency proceedings opened, since at that date, all things situated in the territory are affected, all things outside may remain unaffected (unless a secondary insolvency proceeding is opened in the country of location).

Certain of these principles are nowadays transposed to intangible property.

III. Intangible property

1. 'Situs' as a connecting factor for intangibles?

Intangible property is not a homogenous category. Specific connecting rules apply to all rights other than rights in *rem* (→ Cheques, → Contractual obligations, → Companies, → Bonds and loans, → Intellectual property, applicable law, → Intellectual property, jurisdiction). The governing law, which can generally be called *lex creationis*, defines the content of the right, and at times the conditions of its creation and transfer. In this respect, the *lex creationis* plays a role that is similar to that of *lex rei sitae* for tangibles. In specific cases of involuntary transfers or seizure of the property rights, a different law may apply that some believe to be the *lex rei sitae*. This *lex situs* as applied to intangibles is determined by way of analogy rather than by natural localization. For purposes of creation of security rights, for example, an intangible asset is sometimes deemed to be located in the country where the debtor/the creditor is established.

a) Debts

Generally speaking, debts or obligations, contractual or otherwise, are not subjected to a *lex situs* rule under European law. For purposes of assignment and securitization, the Rome I Regulation (art 14 and Recital (38)) provides that both the *lex contractus* and the *lex creationis* apply between the debtor, the creditor and the assignee. However neither has the power to have a negative effect on third parties. Various solutions are being studied to find a uniform rule applicable to third party effects of such an assignment. Whereas the application of the law where the debtor is established is the traditional rule in some Member States, a newer rule consists in applying the law of the place where the creditor/assignor is established. This may facilitate assignments of receivables in bulk (see UNCITRAL Assignment of Receivables Convention (United Nations Convention on the Assignment of Receivables in International Trade, concluded 12 December 2001, adopted by resolution A/RES/56/8)).

The Insolvency Regulation offers a specific solution for insolvency proceedings. Pursuant to art 5, real rights on property located outside of the Member State where the proceedings opened remain unaffected. This rule also applies to claims and debts. Under art 2(g), the assets are located on the territory of the Member State where the debtor is established.

In this regard, the European rule recalls older case-law rules of the Member States. During the 20th century, judges were called to decide upon seizure or expropriations of debts. They applied varied reasoning whereby the intangible asset was at times considered as located at the place of its debtor or in the country where it was lawfully created; and at other times it was deemed located in any country where it could produce effects.

b) Intellectual property rights

In the Insolvency Regulation, intellectual property rights are not subjected to a specific rule of localization. Rather they are treated like other registered rights, to the extent they are registered (see c)).

In the absence of special regulations, intellectual property rights are deemed located in any country where they are protected. This composite solution – one location per country of recognition – is applicable at both the international level (art 2(1) Paris Industrial Property Convention (Paris Convention for the Protection of Industrial Property, 20 March 1883, with later amendments, 828 UNTS 305); art 5 Berne Convention (Berne Convention for the Protection of Literary and Artistic Works of 9 September 1886, completed at Paris on 4 May 1896, revised at Berlin on 13 November 1908, completed at Berne on 20 March 1914, revised at Rome on 2 June 1928, revised at Brussels on 26 June 1948, revised at Stockholm on 14 July 1967 and revised at Paris on 24 July 1971, 1161 UNTS 3 and amended in 1979 Treaty Doc no 99-27, and 1985, 828 UNTS 221)) and the state level, but unfortunately it is ineffective for regional titles of intellectual property. This is the case for Community Trademarks and Designs, and might become that of the European Unitary Patent. According to the Regulations that are respectively applicable, a single place of location is determined within the European territory. It indicates the legal system that has jurisdiction over the assets for questions of property or seizure. According to art 16 Community Trade Mark Regulation (Council Regulation (EC) No 207/2009 of 26 February on the Community trade mark, [2009] OJ L 78/1), the Community trademark is located: (i) in the Member State where its owner has its seat or domicile; (ii) absent a European seat or domicile, in the Member State where the owner is established; (iii) absent any establishment in Europe, in the Member State where the Registration office is located. A similar rule is applied in the other Regulations enacting unitary European titles of intellectual property.

This kind of rule should not be interpreted broadly. They are highly functional and should not be the subject of analogical reasoning.

c) Shares, negotiable and other registered rights

Under arts 5 and 2 of the Insolvency Regulation, proprietary rights that must be entered in a public register are deemed located in the Member State 'under the authority of which the register is kept'. This is a modern solution, which is limited to insolvency cases and does not apply to any modern incorporeal property titles.

European Directives also lay down a special *lex situs* rule for financial assets that are the object of transactions on organized markets. Directive 98/26/EC on settlement finality in payment and securities settlement systems (Directive 98/26/EC of the European Parliament and of the Council of 19 May 1998 on settlement finality in payment and securities settlement systems [1998] OJ L166/45) provides for a uniform substantive rule, according to which the security rights are not affected by the insolvency proceedings concerning the settler. Article 9(2) of the Directive follows with a rule of conflict of laws according to which, when the object of security 'is legally recorded on a register, account or centralised deposit system located in a Member State, the determination of the rights [thereon] shall be governed by the law of that Member State'. A similar rule is to be found in other Directives in the field of bank regulation and financial markets. In Directive 2002/47/EC of the European Parliament and of the Council of 6 June 2002 on financial collateral arrangements ([2002] OJ L 168/43), Recital (8) states: '[t]he *lex rei sitae* rule, according to which the applicable law for determining whether a financial collateral arrangement is properly perfected and therefore good against third parties, is the law of the country where the financial collateral is located, is currently recognised by all Member States'. Consequently, art 9 of the Directive provides that: '… book entry securities collateral shall be governed by the law of the country in which the relevant account is maintained'.

For many European countries, these modern rules are quite new (indeed, they come from the USA and were recommended at supranational level, see Hague Securities Convention (Hague Convention of 5 July 2006 on the law applicable to certain rights in respect of securities held with an intermediary, 46 ILM 649) and UNIDROIT Convention on Substantive Rules for intermediated Securities of 9 October 2009, available at <www.unidroit.org/english/conventions/2009intermediatedsecurities/convention.pdf>). From an examination of national laws, it appears that the primary connecting rule goes for the *lex creationis*. Under this rule, an intangible right is first governed by the law under which it was created (ie the law of the corporation in cases where shares or other securities are issued). This law governs the question of assignability (→ Assignability/Assignment of claims) of the asset and the technique of assignment. When the law provides for a document permitting the transfer (bearer or negotiable bonds) or if the security is held in a bank account, then the *lex situs* of the document or the law of the place of the account will govern the transfer (see recently: art 91-1 Belgian PILA; art 137 s Book 10 of the Dutch CC).

In the case of bank accounts, the account of the current owner is relevant, but it remains uncertain whether the law of the relevant account is determined in an objective or subjective manner. An objective determination would lead to the law of the place of establishment of the account manager. A subjective determination would be the law of the bank account, which leads in practice to the law chosen by the account manager. More recently, a tendency by the European legislature can be discerned to reject the subjective determination as applied to proprietary questions and to show favour to the objective determination of the place of the account (see the Insolvency Regulation (recast) (Regulation (EU) No 2015/848 of the European Parliament and of the Council of 20 May 2015 on insolvency proceedings (recast), [2015] OJ L 141/19)).

Traditionally, negotiable instruments issued in international transport transactions are handled in the same way. A distinction is made between the law governing the transferred right and the law applicable to its transfer. The latter can be either the *lex situs* when there is a tangible negotiable title, or the law applicable to the issuance of the negotiable instrument when it is intangible.

2. Principles that are applicable to the individual and collective regime of intangibles

a) Multiplicity of connecting factors

Despite the European tendency to consider intangible assets as located in a single country for purposes of conflict of laws (for matters of jurisdiction, IP and rights that are held in public registers are the subject of specific rules, see art 22 Brussels I Regulation, art 24 Brussels I Regulation (recast)), it should be remembered that the connecting factors differ fundamentally from those applicable to tangibles. In one case, there is a natural asset subject to the direct power of the territorial sovereign state (this power is at the origin of the *lex situs*, see I. above). In the other, there is an intangible asset that has no exclusive and physical location because it is a pure creation of law. For a given case of transfer of property or creation of a real right on intangibles, *lex creationis* can be considered as synonymous with *lex situs*; but it is not the only law applying to the effects as against third parties. When there is an organized system of public notices (registers, mandatory or not, held by a public or a private authority), the rules of the law applicable to the system are of immediate and mandatory application. In international cases, they then take precedence over the *lex creationis* or the *lex contractus*.

The various laws which apply at any given time to incorporeal assets might be curtailed by legislation. One way of doing this is to choose a place of localization of the asset. However, nowadays these specific localization rules for incorporeal are exceptions and they fail to achieve international harmony. Accordingly they should be applied with care and restraint.

b) Methodology for groupings of assets

A final issue is at times provided for in the law of modern European states, namely the law applicable to groups of assets or organized funds that lack legal personality. A → trust is a good example that has already been mentioned. Its assets can be solely tangible or else mixed tangible and intangible. Another example is the 'business unit' when it is considered as separate from the owner's other assets (goodwill, *fonds de commerce*, *Zweckvermögen*). What is the law applicable to the transfer of property or the creation of a security right relating to it? In fact there is little experience in addressing these issues in cross-border cases, except for questions of expropriations in times of unrest. Current rules of conflict of laws casuistically lay down that the law governing such ownership issues is that manifesting the closest connection to the facts. Applying the classical reasoning to the 'envelope' (ie the fund considered as a property, containing other properties), two assertions can be made. First, there is no natural *situs* for such a creation of law. Second, a fictitious location can be fixed in the country of principal operation, provided that the specific status of the properties contained in the fund remains unaffected. In these cases, the consequences of a transfer of property or pledge of the entire fund in respect of its individual parts are governed by two laws – the law applicable to the fund and that applicable to the individual piece of corporeal or incorporeal property. As could be stated in accordance with the German tradition, the individual status of a piece of property always takes precedence over the collective status subjected to another law (art 3a(2) EGBGB, art 30 Succession Regulation).

Louis d'Avout

Literature

Louis d'Avout, *Sur les solutions du conflit de lois en droit des biens* (Economica 2006); Louis d'Avout, 'Property Law (Europe)' in Jürgen Basedow and Knut Pissler (eds), *Private international law in Mainland China, Taiwan and Europe* (Mohr Siebeck 2014); Janeen M Carruthers, *The Transfer of Property in the Conflicts of Laws* (OUP 2005); Lord Collins of Mapesbury and others (eds), *Dicey, Morris & Collins on the Conflict of Laws* (15th edn, Sweet & Maxwell

2012); Giulio Diena, *I diritti reali considerati nel diritto internazionale privato* (Unione Tip-Editrice Torinese 1895); Giulio Diena, 'Les conflits de lois en matière de droits réels à l'Institut de droit international' [1911] Rev.crit.DIP 561; Ulrich Drobnig, 'The Recognition of Non-Possessory Security Interest Created Abroad in Private international law' in Zoltán Pétery and Vanda Lamm (eds), *General Report to the 10th International Congress of Comparative Law (Budapest 1978)* (Akadémiai Kiadó 1981); Ulrich Drobnig, 'A Plea for European Conflict Rules on Proprietary Security' in Michael Joachim Bonell and Marie-Louise Holle (eds), *Liber Amicorum Ole Lando* (Djofpublishing 2012); Axel Flessner, 'Rechtswahl im internationalen Sachenrecht-neue Anstösse aus Europa' in Peter Apathy and others (eds), *Festschrift für Helmut Koziol* (Jan Sramek Verlag KG 2010) 125; Eva-Maria Kieninger, *Mobiliarsicherheiten im Europäischen Binnemarkt* (Nomos 1996); Eva-Maria Kieninger, 'Property Law (International)' in Jürgen Basedow and others (eds), *The Max Planck Encyclopedia of European Private Law* (OUP 2012); Karl Kreuzer, 'La propriété mobilière en droit international privé' (1996) 229 Hague Lectures 9; Karl Kreuzer, 'Conflict-of-Laws Rules for Security Rights in Tangible Assets in the European Union' in Horst Eidenmüller and Eva-Maria Kieninger (eds), *The Future of Secured Credit in Europe* (de Gruyter 2008) 297; Paul Lagarde, 'Sur la loi applicable au transfert de propriété…' in Alegria Borras and others (eds), *E Pluribus Unum, Liber Amicorum Georges Droz* (Martinus Nijhoff 1996) 151; Pierre A Lalive, *The Transfer of Chattels in the Conflict of Laws: A Comparative Study* (Clarendon Press 1955); Dieter Martiny, 'Lex rei sitae as a connecting factor in EU Private international law' [2012] IPRax 119; Jean-Paulin Niboyet, *Des conflits de lois relatifs à l'acquisition de la propriété et des droits sur les meubles corporels à titre particulier* (Sirey 1912); Jean-Paulin Niboyet, *Traité de droit international privé français, tome IV, La territorialité* (Sirey 1947); Maisie Ooi, *Shares and other Securities in the Conflict of Laws* (OUP 2003); Ernst Rabel, *The Conflict of Laws: A Comparative Study*, vol 4 (Ann Arbor 1958); Ann-Christin Ritterhoff, *Parteiautonomie im internationalen Sachenrecht* (Duncker und Humblot 1999); Pippa Rogerson, 'The Situs of Debts in the Conflict of Laws: Illogical, Unnecessary and Misleading' (1991) 49 CLJ 441; Hans Stoll, 'Internationales Sachenrecht' in Jan Kropholler (ed), *Julius von Staudingers Kommentar zum Bürgerlichen Gesetzbuch mit Einführungsgesetz und Nebengesetzen* (13th edn, Sellier-de Gruyter 1996); Gian C Venturini, 'Property' in Ulrich Drobnig and others (eds), *International Encyclopedia for Comparative Law, vol. III, Private international law* (Mohr Siebeck 1976) ch 21; Celia Wasserstein-Fassberg, 'On Time and Place in Choice of Law for Real Property Conflicts' [2002] ICLQ 385; Wilhelm Wengler, *Internationales Privatrecht, 2 Volumes* (Sellier 1981); Roel Westrick and Jeroen van der Weide (eds), *Party Autonomy in International Property Law* (Sellier 2011).

Property and proprietary rights in vessels

I. Concept and function

1. Ownership of the vessel: acquisition

In order to define the owner's rights with reference to the vessel it is necessary at the outset to clarify the notion of 'vessel' or 'ship' and that of 'ownership' as specifically related to vessels.

Absent a commonly accepted definition of 'ship', its meaning must be illustrated by reference to the relevant applicable law, at both the national and international levels. Thus, the Italian *Codice della Navigazione* (art 136 Regio decreto 30 March 1942, no 327, in Gazz.Uff. No 93 of 18-4-1942) defines a ship as every floating and movable construction to be used for transport on maritime or inner waters, even for towage, fishing, amusement or other purposes; the UK Merchant Shipping Act 1995 (c 21) defines a 'ship' as every description of vessel used in navigation, while in France a 'ship' is described as a vessel ordinarily exposed to the perils of the sea. At the international level, art 1 of the 1992 CLC (International Convention of 27 November 1992 on civil liability for oil pollution damage, 1956 UNTS 255) refers to any seagoing vessel and seaborne craft of any type whatsoever constructed or adapted for the carriage of oil in bulk as cargo, while art 1 of the 1989 Salvage Convention (International Convention of 28 April 1989 on Salvage, 1953 UNTS 165) defines the vessel as any ship or craft or any structure capable of navigation.

The feature common to all definitions, however, is that a 'ship' is a *res* uniquely composed of many constitutive parts (such as the engine, the hull) the propriety of which cannot be separated from the property as a whole.

On the meaning of 'ownership', much debate has arisen as to the content of the property rights, since each national legal order provides for a different definition of 'property' (→ Property and proprietary rights). However, it can be stated that property gives the owner the right to enjoy quiet and uninterrupted possession of the ship as well as the absolute right to sell it or to appoint a third party to operate it.

Regarding the specific ownership of a vessel, the relationship between the person that legally owns the vessel and the person who operates it ought to be analysed. The distinction between those two figures dates back to the Roman era, where the *exercitor* would perform his tasks with a vessel owned by another person, the *dominus*. After centuries of confusion between the two terms (see the 1808 Code Napoléon and the 1865 and 1886 Commercial Code) the Italian *Codice della Marina Mercantile* (1877) introduced once again the distinction between ownership and operation of the vessel. All the same, it cannot be maintained either that this differentiation became common to all national legal orders or that international instruments dealing with ships and shipowners incorporated such a distinction.

In fact, even if rights accorded to the owner are usually conceptually distinct from those granted to the person operating the ship, international conventions often either extend proprietary rights to both categories (1957 Limitation Convention (International Convention of 10 October 1957 relating to the limitation of the liability of owners of seagoing ships, 1412 UNTS)), or alternatively adopt a broad definition of 'shipowner' which includes also other subjects having no proprietary rights over the ship, such as charterers, managers and operators (Comité Maritime International, *The Travaux Preparatoies of the LLMC Convention, 1976 and of the Protocol of 1996* (Comité Maritime International 1997)). An exception to this trend is represented by the 1992 CLC, which refers only to the person (or persons) registered as the owner of the ship.

Both approaches are followed at the national level, so that while some legal orders distinguish between the shipowner and other persons operating the ship (→ Switzerland, → Italy), others adopt a broader definition of ownership, which also includes the rights of the person who runs the vessel (→ France, → Germany, the → Netherlands, → United Kingdom). This latter position is usually justified in the light of the fact that the same responsibility regime is applicable to both subjects. This renders the distinction between them merely formal, with no substantive effects stemming from it.

Turning to the acquisition of the ownership of the vessel, this can be obtained following the set of rules applicable to the acquisition of property (either movable or immovable depending on the qualification given by each national legal order), which may vary, however, depending on national legislations. As a general rule, we can state that property can be acquired either (i) originally, meaning without any relationship among the owner and the previous owner, such as in cases of conclusion of a contract of construction of the ship, confiscation; usucaption (depending on national legal orders), or (ii) in a derivative manner, whereby the relationship between the old and the new proprietary is a requisite, such as in cases of conclusion of a sale contract of the vessel.

2. Proprietary rights and obligations: definition

The term 'Proprietary Right' has no unique or clear-cut meaning, but rather seems to be related to the rights that are part of a person's estate, assets or property (ie the vessel), as opposed to a right arising from a person's legal status.

Concomitant with proprietary rights stand proprietary duties, one of which is fundamental whenever the object of the right is the vessel: the owner is to register the ship within a national register, ie entering some information in the public records.

This duty has a dual function: on the one hand the purpose of demonstrating the ownership of the ship, as it is required under national rules, while on the other hand, registration creates a relevant link between a state and a ship, providing the vessel with the nationality of the state of registration.

In other words, the owner is usually responsible for registration of the ship within a national register, with national legal systems for certainty purposes requiring transcription in the register of all acts which constitute, transfer or extinguish the ownership of the vessel, while the record of the vessel created following the rules of the state where registration is sought has the aim of granting a nationality to the ship.

From another perspective, we can identify public law and private law functions of registration. Public law functions include (i) allocation of a vessel to a specific state; (ii) conferment of the right to fly the national → flag, and (iii) publicity, while among the private functions we may cite (i) protection of the registered owner's title, and (ii) protection of the title and the preservation and ranking of priorities between persons holding a security interest in the vessel.

In order to comply with this registration duty, and in accordance with the general principle of international law following which each state is free to determine the conditions for the concession of its → nationality to a ship, states have laid down rules allowing a shipowner to register his vessel within their national registers. There are neither uniform rules concerning the attribution of nationality of the ship, nor common principles stating that a certain degree of connection between the state and the ship must exist. Consequently, the nationality accorded by a state to a ship in compliance with its national law has to be recognized and given effect in other states without considering or contesting the basis upon which the nationality is accorded. According to this principle, the Permanent Court of Arbitration in the *Muscat Dhows* case of 1905 stated that a state conferring a → flag to a vessel 'is only bound by its own legislation and administrative rules'.

Despite the debate that has arisen on the existence of an international rule imposing a qualified link between the state and the ship (or the shipowner), it is well established that the full freedom of states in this matter can only be limited by the operation of two other principles affirmed in international law: (i) the ship can only have one nationality (see art 92 of the UNCLOS (United Nations Convention of 10 December 1982 on the Law of the Sea, 1833 UNTS 396) 'ships shall sail under the flag of one State only and, save in exceptional cases expressly provided for in international treaties or in this Convention, shall be subject to its exclusive jurisdiction on the high seas' and art 4 of the United Nations Convention of 7 February 1986 on conditions for registration of ships (UN Doc. TD/RS/CONF/19/Add.1) 'ships shall sail under the flag of the State only. No ship shall be entered in the registers of ships of two or more States at time'); and (ii) there should be a genuine link between the state and the ship flying its flag (art 91 of the UNCLOS 'every State shall fix the conditions for the grant of its nationality to ships, for the registration of ships in its territory, and for the right to fly its flag. Ships have the nationality of the state whose flag they are entitled to fly. There must exist a genuine link between the state and the ship' and arts 7, 8, 9 and 10 of the United Nations Convention of 7 February 1986 on conditions for registration of ships (UN Doc. TD/RS/CONF/19/Add.1), which make reference to the economic aspect of the genuine link, providing for the participation by nationals of the flag state in the ownership, manning and management of the vessel).

According to this principle, however, states are not required to follow precise and pre-established rules for the attribution of their nationality. The principle is rather a recommendation directed to states party to the Convention. In line with this interpretation, the United Nations Convention of 7 February 1986 on conditions for registration of ships acknowledges the freedom of states to give vessels their own nationality and only requires flag states to carry out proper controls aimed at verifying whether the ship complies with international standards (largely security standards).

In the same vein, international courts recognize the freedom of states to allow the registration of a ship in their national registers in accordance with their own proper rules and irrespective of the existence of a specific link between the ship and the national legal order: see the 1953 US Supreme Court *Lauritzen v Larsen* case – where it is stated that 'each State under international law may determine for itself the conditions on which it will grant its nationality to a merchant ship' (*Lauritzen v Larsen* 345 U.S. 571 (1953)); as well as the 1960 ICJ advice, following which the duty to ascertain the genuine link is not established in international law; and more recently the 1992 ECJ decision in case C-286/90 confirming that

> under international law a vessel in principle has only one nationality, that of the State in which it is registered ... the fact that the sole link between a vessel and the State of which it holds the nationality is the administrative formality of registration cannot prevent the application of that rule. It was for the State that conferred its nationality in the first place to determine at its absolute discretion the conditions on which it would grant its nationality (Case C-286/90 *Anklagemyndigheden v Peter Michael Poulsen and Diva Navigation Corp* [1992] ECR I-6019).

With reference to EU law and the recording of ships in national registers, a mention is due to ECJ case-law on compatibility between national rules allowing the record of a vessel within a national register and EU law concerning freedom of establishment and freedom to provide services. In effect, since the 1991 *Factortame I* judgment (ECJ, Case C-221/89 *The Queen v Secretary of State for Transport, ex parte Factortame* [1991] ECR I-3905) the ECJ stated that it is contrary to the provisions of EU law, and in particular to art 52 TFEU (The Treaty on the Functioning of the European Union (consolidated version), [2012] OJ C 326/47), for a Member State to enact legislation stipulating as conditions for the registration of a vessel in its national register: (i) that the owners and the charterers, managers and operators of the vessel must be nationals of that Member State or → companies incorporated in that Member State; (ii) that the said owners, charterers, managers, operators, shareholders and directors, as the case may be, must be resident and domiciled in that Member State. However, this does not mean that it is contrary to EU law for a Member State to stipulate as a condition for the registration of a vessel in its national register that the vessel in question must be managed and its operations directed and controlled from within that Member State.

Moreover, it has to be noted that the registry in which record of the ship is kept is always a national or domestic one, as operated by most maritime nations, that in accordance with national law can require strict or weak conditions for access. This raises the problem of open registries and flags of convenience. However, in parallel with such a registration another record is requested whenever the vessel, owned and registered by the shipowner, is leased to a third party, the lessee, for a stipulated period during which that party has complete possession and control of the ship (bareboat charter party). In this case a secondary registration is required in the bareboat charter ship registries (BBC), also called dual registries, following the nationality of the lessee. But such a registration is limited in time, since it ends when the charter contract terminates. Once this happens the first registration again becomes effective, giving nationality and the flag to the vessel.

II. Current regulation

1. Survey

Given the lack of uniform private international law rules concerning property and proprietary rights (at both the international and the European level), it can be maintained that the law applicable to those issues is in principle the law of the state where the object is located – *lex rei sitae* or *lex situs* (→ Property and proprietary rights).

If it is true that this principle has been codified and followed by most states of the international community, it is also true that all of them make an exception when it comes to vehicles, and in particular to ships and aircraft, whereby following many national private international law rules the law governing property is the law of the flag state.

Examples can be found in: art 45(1) of the Introductory Act to the German Civil Code (*Einführungsgesetz zum Bürgerlichen Gesetzbuche* of 21 September 1994, BGBl. I 2494, as amended), which appoints the law of the place of origin as the connecting factor in identifying the law applicable to property of vessels; the Spanish Civil Code (art 10(2) Código Civil of 24 July 1889, Geceta de Madrid No 206, 25 July 1889) which chooses the law of the state of the register where the ship is recorded in light of the stability characterizing this connection; section 22 of the Estonian Private international law Act of 27 March 2002 (effective 1 July 2002, The State Gazette, 'Riigi Teataja' I 2002, 35, 217), art 22 of the Turkish Private international law Code (Code on Private International and International Civil Procedure Law of 27 November 2007 (Act No 5718) (*Milletlerarası Özel Hukuk ve Usul Hukuku Hakkında Kanun*), Resmî Gazete No 26728 of 12 December 2007); and the Belgian Private international law Act (art 89 *Wet houdende het Wetboek von international privaatrecht/Code de droit international privé* of 16 July 2004, BS 27 July 2004, pp 57344, 57366), which provides that the law of the state of registration applies to all means of transport for which a record in the public register is required.

In a similar vein, the Italian *Codice della navigazione* (art 6) stipulates that property (as well as other real rights to the vessel) is regulated by the national law of the vessel. Despite the wording of this rule, which seems to require a fixed private international law → connecting factor derogating from the general criterion established in arts 51 and 55 of the Italian Private international law Act (*Riforma del Sistema italiano di diritto internazionale private*, Act No 218 of 31 May 1995 in Gazz.Uff, Supplemento Ordinario No 128 of 3 June 1995, as amended) scholars have interpreted it as being applicable only when the *lex rei sitae* criterion cannot be used because no state has jurisdiction over the area where the vessel is located.

The United Kingdom and France have also created a special conflict of laws rule related to ships, whose scope of application is limited to cases of impossibility of determining of a state where 'the object is located'. In particular, the rule provides that if the ship is sailing the high seas, the law applicable is the law of the state of registration, while if the ship is located on any state's territory or within its national waters, that state's law will apply. The UK and France therefore combine the *lex rei situs* connecting factor with the country of origin criterion, which acquires a residual role in cases where no national law can be applied.

2. The law of the flag as a residual private international law rule

As far as private international law rules rely on the ship's → nationality as a → connecting factor, they refer to a public international law concept (→ Public international law and private international law), that – as already mentioned – is connected to the registration in national territories as well as to the attribution of a → flag to the vessel.

During the first half of the 20th century, the nationality of a ship constituted a highly significant factor linked to the exercise of the states' jurisdiction and sovereignty over the vessel, its owner or its operator.

The socio-economic evolution of maritime commerce and navigation has entailed a weakening of the necessary link between states and vessels flying their flags. Indeed, the ownership of the vessel often holds no connection with the state that has been chosen as a country for registration in the light of its (favourable) rules concerning controls and public authoritative powers over the ship. Since the second half of the last century, the phenomenon of the so-called 'flags of convenience' has developed, and as mentioned (see above) neither public international law instruments, including treaties suggesting the need for a 'genuine link' between the vessel and the state of registration, nor customary law have been able to limit the dissemination of this practice.

This phenomenon gave rise to a debate concerning the coordination between powers granted to flag states and those afforded to port and coastal states, which has led to the limitation of the powers of flag states in favour of states holding a closer connection with the ship.

Moving from the public international law level to that of private international law (→ Public international law and private international law), the weakened role of the flag state has also impacted upon the potency of the ship's nationality as a connecting factor. In national case-law we find decisions affirming that the connecting factor of the nationality of the vessel is a subsidiary one, meaning that it can be used only when other connecting factors cannot assess rights and obligations of the involved actors in a proper way (Italian Corte di Cassazione, Sezioni Unite, 18 October 1993, No 10293).

Nevertheless the judge may not be prevented from making use of the special connecting factor related to the nationality of the vessel also when either the criteria used by the state of nationality in order to allow registration within the national register are not the same as those used by the state of the forum, or when the state of the forum does not recognize the existence of a 'genuine link' between the state and the ship. Accordingly, the nationality of the vessel has to be determined by using the substantive laws of the foreign state that presumably granted its flag to the vessel.

Such an application of the private international law method of recognition of the competent legal order allows a uniform treatment of property rights in connection with the ship, giving relevance to a fixed substantive element that cannot be considered and evaluated by the legal order and legal institutions of the forum.

3. Scope of application of the law governing property

In order to limit the scope of application of the special rule laid down for property over vessels, and in connection with the tendency to interpret restrictively the exception to general private international law principles, a distinction must be drawn between the property right and acts or facts giving rise to the right. In other words, the ship's nationality will govern property and proprietary rights but need not be used as a connecting factor with regard to elements falling outside the strict definition of property and proprietary rights.

Accordingly, the law of the flag state will regulate all aspects that, according to general private international law principles, are subject to the *lex rei sitae* rule. This means that the following will fall within the scope of the special rule regulating the property of vessels: (i) the conditions for acquisition of property; (ii) the identification and protection of the person having the propriety right as well as the qualification of the vessel as such; and (iii) the evidence of the acts that constitute, transfer or extinguish the proprietary right.

Conversely, there are several aspects that are covered by a different law, in particular by the law applicable to the relationship which legitimates the entitlement of the right. More precisely, the effects and conditions of all acts transferring the ownership of the vessel to another subject are regulated by the law applicable pursuant to the conflict of laws rule connected with the specific act or relationship. This means that if the property is transferred by contract, the validity and the effects of the contract will be governed by the law applicable to the contractual obligation itself, while the remaining aspects related to the property in the ship will follow the law of the flag state.

In the leading case *Lauritzen v Larsen*, the Supreme Court of the US stated that

> maritime law, like our municipal law, has attempted to avoid or resolve conflicts between competing laws by ascertaining and valuing points of contact between the transaction and the states or governments whose competing laws are involved. The criteria, in general, appear to be arrived at from weighing of the significance of one or more connecting factors between the shipping transaction regulated and the national interest served by the assertion of authority (*Lauritzen v Larsen* 345 U.S. 571 (1953)),

pointing out several connecting factors which, in the case specifically connected to tort claims, can create a valuable link between the case and a national law. The statement specifically describes seven 'contacts' for a tort case where two foreign nations were involved: → Denmark, because the ship and the seaman involved were Danish nationals; → Cuba, because the tortious conduct occurred and caused injury in Cuban waters; the → United States because the seaman had been hired in and was returned to the United States, which also is the state of the forum.

The seven connecting factors described by the court were, therefore, (i) the place of the wrongful act; (ii) the law of the → flag; (iii) the allegiance or domicile of the injured person; (iv) the allegiance of the defendant shipowner; (v) the place of the contract; (vi) the inaccessibility of the forum; (vii) the law of the forum.

In deciding the case, the US Supreme Court took into consideration all these → connecting factors, drawing a most relevant link within Danish law, since many of the factual elements recalled by the criteria are located in Denmark (the parties were both Danish subjects, the events took place on a Danish ship, not within US territorial waters).

MARIA ELENA DE MAESTRI

Literature

Ademun Ademun-Odeke, 'An Examination of Bareboat Charter Registries and Flag of Convenience Registries in International Law' (2005) 36 *Ocean Development & International Law* 339; Jürgen Basedow, 'Billigflaggen, Zweitregister und Kollisionsrecht in der deutschen Schiffahrtspolitik' in Ulrich Drobnig, Jürgen Basedow and Rüdiger Wolfrum (eds), *Recht der Flagge und "billige Flaggen". Neuere Entwicklungen im internationalen Privatrecht und Völkerrecht* (Müller Juristischer Verlag 1990) 75; Pierre Bonassies, 'La loi du pavillon et les conflits de droit maritime' (1979) 125 Rec. des Cours 505; Sergio Maria Carbone, *Conflits de lois en droit maritime* (Martinus Nijhoff Publishers 2010); Sergio Maria Carbone and Lorenzo Schiano di Pepe, *Conflitti di sovranità e di leggi nei traffici marittimi tra diritto internazionale e diritto dell'Unione europea* (Giappichelli 2010); Richard Coles and Edward Watt, *Ship Registration: Law and Practice* (2nd edn, Informa 2009); Ulrich Drobnig, 'Billige Flaggen im Internationalen Privatrecht' in Ulrich Drobnig, Jürgen Basedow and Rüdiger Wolfrum (eds), *Recht der Flagge und "billige Flaggen". Neuere Entwicklungen im internationalen Privatrecht und Völkerrecht* (Müller Juristischer Verlag 1990) 31; Carlos Esplugues Mota, José Luis Iglesias Buhigues, Guillermo Palao Moreno, *Derecho Internacional Privado* (Tirant Lo Blanch 2016); James Fawcett and Janeen M Carruthers, *Private international law* (OUP 2008); Christopher Hill, *Maritime Law* (LLP 2003); Eva-Maria Kieninger, 'Property Law (International)' in Jürgen Basedow and others (eds), *The Max Planck Encyclopedia of European Private Law* (OUP 2012); Eva-Maria Kieninger, 'Security Interests in Transport Vehicles' in Jürgen Basedow and others (eds),

The Max Planck Encyclopedia of European Private Law (OUP 2012); John NK Mansell, *Flag State Responsibility. Historical Development and Contemporary Issues* (Springer 2009); Giorgio Righetti, *Trattato di diritto marittimo*, Part *I*, vol III (Giuffré 1987); Lorenzo Schiano di Pepe, *Inquinamento marino da navi e poteri dello Stato costiero. Diritto internazionale e disciplina comunitaria* (Giappichelli 2007); William Tetley, International Conflict of Laws (*Common Civil and Maritime*) (Blais 1994).

Provisional measures

I. Concept and context

Most legal systems take account of a creditor's need to obtain interim relief pending final determination of a lawsuit. In complex or protracted cross-border disputes, the interest of the creditor (claimant) seeking protection by such provisional measures is even more important than in purely domestic cases. Equally important is the interest of the debtor (respondent) in an irrevocable decision not being reached through accelerated proceedings with limited opportunities for defence, or at least his interest in holding the claimant liable for damage arising therefrom.

In this context, questions arise on different levels. Before a provisional measure is issued, first and foremost the international jurisdiction of the court must be clarified (see II.), but there are also other procedural aspects at stake (see III.). Questions of cross-border recognition and, where necessary, enforcement of provisional measures should also be considered when determining what court to seize for the purpose of rendering a decision on provisional measures, rather than post-issuance. The ALI/UNIDROIT Rules of Transnational Civil Procedure (text of the Principles and the accompanying commentary were adopted by the American Law Institute (ALI) in May 2004 and by the International Institute for the Unification of Private Law (UNIDROIT) in April 2004, (2004) 4 Unif.L.Rev. 758) deal with provisional measures and thereby give a meaningful account of the core questions, namely in Principle 8 and in Rule 17. The latter reads:

17.1 The court may grant provisional relief to restrain or require conduct of a party or other person when necessary to preserve the ability to grant effective relief by final judgment or to maintain or otherwise regulate the status quo. The grant or extent of the remedy is governed by the principle of proportionality. Disclosure of assets wherever located may be ordered.

17.2 The provisional relief may be issued before the opposing party has an opportunity to respond only upon proof of urgent necessity and preponderance of considerations of fairness. The applicant must fully disclose facts and legal issues of which the court properly should be aware.

17.3 A person against whom an ex parte order is directed must have an opportunity at the earliest practicable time to respond concerning the appropriateness of the order.

17.4 The court may, after hearing those interested, issue, dissolve, renew, or modify an order.

17.5 An applicant for provisional relief is liable for compensation of a person against whom an order is issued if the court thereafter determines that the relief should not have been granted.

17.5.1 The court may require the applicant for provisional relief to post a bond or formally to assume a duty of compensation.

17.6 The granting or denial of provisional relief is subject to immediate appellate review.

The following entry puts emphasis on the legal situation within the European Union; in addition, important Hague Conventions are taken into consideration. Special provisions applying in various fields of law, like international transport law (as, for example, by virtue of the 1952 Arrest Convention (International Convention of 10 May 1952 relating to the Arrest of Seagoing Ships, 439 UNTS 193)), are not addressed. A number of entries in this encyclopedia refer entirely or mainly to special aspects of provisional measures and are thus not looked at closely in this entry. Note particularly the entries → European Account Preservation Order Regulation, → Anti-suit injunctions, → Arrest of vessels, → Child abduction, → Freezing injunctions and search orders, and → Injunction. For an overview on the special topic of interim measures and preliminary orders ordered by an arbitration tribunal or a court in relation to arbitration proceedings reference is made to art 17 *et seq* UNCITRAL Arbitration Model Law (United Nations Commission on International Trade Law, UNCITRAL Model Law on International Commercial Arbitration as adopted on 21 June 1985, and as amended on 7 July 2006, UN Doc A/40/17 and A/61/17; → Arbitration, (UNCITRAL) Model Law) and to the 1990 ICC Pre-Arbitral Referee Rules (International Chamber of Commerce: Pre-Arbitral Referee Rules – Rules for a Pre-Arbitral Referee Procedure of the International Chamber of Commerce, in force as from 1 January 1990).

II. Jurisdiction

The need for effective legal protection mandates corresponding international jurisdiction, including outside the state in which proceedings have been or will be brought.

1. European Union

Under European law, international jurisdiction for provisional measures is in principle determined by the general rules. However, courts lacking jurisdiction according to the general rules are, in addition, allowed to revert to the jurisdictional provisions of the *lex fori*, in order to avoid gaps in legal protection. Art 31 Brussels I Regulation (Regulation (EC) No 44/2001 of 22 December 2000 on jurisdiction and the recognition and enforcement of judgments in civil and commercial matters, [2001] OJ L 12/1; → Brussels I (Convention and Regulation)) (respectively art 31 → Lugano Convention (Lugano Convention of 30 October 2007 on jurisdiction and the recognition and enforcement of judgments in civil and commercial matters, [2007] OJ L 339/3)) and now also art 35 Brussels I Regulation (recast) (Regulation (EU) No 1215/2012 of the European Parliament and of the Council of 12 December 2012 on jurisdiction and the recognition and enforcement of judgments in civil and commercial matters (recast), [2012] OJ L 351/1) are to be understood in this two-fold sense. They read: 'Application may be made to the courts of a Member State for such provisional, including protective, measures as may be available under the law of that Member State, even if the courts of another Member State have jurisdiction as to the substance of the matter.'

First, according to this provision, the general rules on jurisdiction provided for in art 2 *et seq* Brussels I Regulation/Lugano Convention (respectively art 4 *et seq* Brussels I Regulation (recast)) are also applicable for provisional measures. Second, as an exception, recourse to national rules on jurisdiction remains possible, provided that the unified grounds of jurisdiction cannot be established and there is, nevertheless, the need for an interim ruling or protection in a given Member State.

The rule that the Brussels I Regulation allows application of the national provisions on jurisdiction for provisional measures, should even apply where art 22 Brussels I Regulation (art 24 Brussels I Regulation (recast)) provides for an exclusive jurisdiction in the main proceedings (cf ECJ Case C-616/10 *Solvay SA v Honeywell Fluorine Products Europe BV* [2012] OJ C 287/7: art 24 no 4 Brussels I Regulation takes no priority over art 31 Brussels I Regulation). Courts are even allowed to draw on the so-called exorbitant jurisdictions as excluded by art 3(2) Brussels I Regulation, namely on the rules which establish jurisdiction based on the mere presence of the defendant's assets in the forum (for → Germany: § 23 German Code of Civil Procedure (*Zivilprozessordnung* of 5 December 2005, BGBl. I 3202, as amended, henceforth German CCP)). However, the ECJ has ruled that recourse to the national laws of jurisdiction is only permissible when there is a real connecting link between the object of the provisional measure applied and the territory of the Member State (cf ECJ Case C-391/95 *Van Uden Maritime BV, trading as Van Uden Africa Line v Kommanditgesellschaft in Firma Deco-Line* [1998] ECR I-7091; ECJ Case C-99/96 *Hans-Hermann Mietz v Intership Yachting Sneek BV* [1999] ECR I-2277). What this means in detail remains unsettled.

Sometimes it is doubtful whether a choice of court agreement also affects jurisdiction for provisional measures. Regarding the prorogation effect, it can be assumed that the court of choice should also become competent to issue provisional measures. On the other hand, it needs clear words to derogate from the competence based on art 31 Brussels I Regulation/Lugano Convention 2007 respectively art 35 Brussels I Regulation (recast). Where the subject matter of an application for provisional measures relates to a question falling within the scope *ratione materiae* of the Brussels I Regulation or the Brussels I Regulation (recast), the above-mentioned rules conferring jurisdiction on the court can apply notwithstanding the fact that proceedings have already been, or may be, commenced on the substance of the case before an arbitration tribunal (cf ECJ Case C-391/95 *Van Uden Maritime BV, trading as Van Uden Africa Line v Kommanditgesellschaft in Firma Deco-Line* [1998] ECR I-7091 and entry → Brussels I (Convention and Regulation)).

Some legal systems classify the preservation of evidence as a question of interim relief. Against this backdrop, the relationship between the Evidence Regulation (Council Regulation (EC) No 1206/2001 of 28 May 2001 on cooperation between the courts of the Member States in the taking of evidence in civil or commercial matters, [2001] OJ L 174/1) and the Brussels I rules on jurisdiction has to be determined. According to the ECJ, art 24 of the former Brussels Convention (Brussels Convention of 27 September 1968 on jurisdiction and the enforcement of judgments in civil and commercial matters, [1972] OJ L 299/32, consolidated version, [1998] OJ C 27/1) did not apply to independent proceedings for the taking of evidence, ie proceedings which are conducted separately from the main proceedings (*in casu*: a pre-trial examination of witnesses according to Dutch Law; ECJ Case C-104/03 *St Paul Dairy Industries NV v Unibel Exser BVBA* [2005] ECR I-3481). This caselaw seems to remain relevant regarding art 31 Brussels I Regulation and henceforth art 35 Brussels I Regulation (recast). Note hereto also entry → Evidence, procurement of.

With regard to International Family and Succession Law, art 20 → Brussels IIa Regulation (Council Regulation (EC) No 2201/2003 of 27 November 2003 concerning jurisdiction and the recognition and enforcement of judgments in matrimonial matters and the matters of parental responsibility, repealing Regulation (EC) No 1347/2000, [2003] OJ L 338/1), art 14 Maintenance Regulation (Council Regulation (EC) No 4/2009 of 18 December 2008 on jurisdiction, applicable law, recognition and enforcement of decisions and cooperation in matters relating to maintenance obligations, [2009] OJ L 7/1) and art 19 Succession Regulation (Regulation (EU) No 650/2012 of the European Parliament and of the Council of 4 July 2012 on jurisdiction, applicable law, recognition and enforcement of decisions and acceptance and enforcement of authentic instruments in matters of succession and on the creation of a European Certificate of Succession, [2012] OJ L 201/107; → Rome IV Regulation (succession)) contain provisions which correspond to art 31 Brussels I Regulation, respectively art 35 Brussels I Regulation (recast). They, too, are commonly interpreted in the double sense that on the one hand international jurisdiction for provisional measures is ordinarily determined by the general rules, but that on the other hand a court lacking jurisdiction according to those rules may, as an exception, take recourse to the jurisdictional provisions of the *lex fori*. While art 20 Brussels IIa Regulation is of little relevance in matrimonial matters in the sense of art 1(1)(a) Brussels IIa Regulation, it is very significant in matters concerning child protection: for this purpose, art 20 Brussels IIa Regulation establishes jurisdiction in urgent cases to order provisional measures independently from art 8 *et seq* Brussels IIa Regulation in the state where the child is present. With regard to the conditions under which those provisional measures may be issued, the ECJ has already provided some important clarifications (cf ECJ Case C-523/07 *A* [2009] ECR I-2805; ECJ Case C-403/09 *Jasna Detiček v Maurizio Sgueglia* [2009] ECR I-12193). Art 20(2) Brussels IIa Regulation explicitly states that the judgment in the main proceedings prevails over the preliminary ruling. It reads: 'The measures referred to in paragraph 1 shall cease to apply when the court of the Member State having jurisdiction under this Regulation as to the substance of the matter has taken the measures it considers appropriate.'

2. Hague Conventions

Some Hague Conventions contain special provisions on international jurisdiction for provisional measures. Article 11 Hague Child Protection Convention (Hague Convention of 19 October 1996 on jurisdiction, applicable law, recognition, enforcement and cooperation in respect of parental responsibility and measures for the protection of children, 35 ILM 1391), for instance, authorizes the authorities of any contracting state in whose territory the child or property belonging to the child is present to take any necessary measures of protection 'in all cases of urgency'. Even if there is no urgency, art 12 Hague Child Protection Convention allows the authorities of a contracting state in whose territory the child or property belonging to the child is present to take measures of a provisional character for the protection of the person or property of the child which have a territorial effect limited to the state in question, insofar as such measures are not incompatible with measures already taken by authorities which have jurisdiction under the general rules. It is explicitly pointed out that the provisional measures taken shall lapse as soon as the authorities have taken the measures required by the situation in the main proceedings (art 11(2) and (3) respectively art 12(2) and (3) Hague Child Protection Convention). Provisions similar to art 11 and 12 Hague Child Protection Convention are contained in art 10 and 11 Hague Adult Protection Convention (Hague Convention of 13 January 2000 on the international protection of adults, Hague Conference of Private international law (ed), *Collection of Conventions (1951–2009)* (Intersentia 2009) 426).

By contrast, art 7 Hague Choice of Court Convention (Hague Convention of 30 June 2005 on choice of court agreements, 44 ILM 1294) makes clear that it does not govern interim measures of protection, rather that this Convention neither requires nor precludes the grant, refusal or termination of interim measures of protection by a court of a contracting state and does not affect whether or not a party may request or a court should grant, refuse or terminate such measures. In consequence, the general rules are applicable whereby the scope of the choice of court agreement with respect to provisional measures has to be carefully examined (provided that the *lex fori* acknowledges such agreements regarding interim relief at all).

III. Procedural matters

If there is international jurisdiction to order provisional measures, the individual prerequisites are to be determined according to the provisions of the respective *lex fori*. However, the ECJ has pointed out that the relevant national rules must be in accordance with European law and must not, in particular, result in a violation of EU primary law. Hence, the ECJ objected to a former German provision, whereby the claimant could obtain a writ of seizure against the assets of a potential debtor based on the mere fact that the expected judgment in the main proceedings would have to be enforced abroad (§ 917(2) German CCP in the version valid until 1998). The ECJ rightly assumed a discrimination of debtors residing abroad irreconcilable with art 18 TFEU (the Treaty on the Functioning of the European Union (consolidated version), [2012] OJ C 326/47).

In order to preserve a surprise effect, it can be appropriate to order provisional measures without any oral hearing or any consultation with the defendant. Again, the prerequisites for the admissibility of such an *ex parte* procedure follow the *lex fori*. It should however be borne in mind that provisional measures issued in such procedure will not be recognized or enforced under the Brussels I rules (see below). An applicant not willing to take any risks should therefore only follow this path in the Member State in which the provisional measure can be enforced.

When ordering provisional measures, the court must also observe the principles on immunity under public international law (cf entry → Immunity). A violation of foreign sovereignty impends, for example, in the case of a writ of seizure against the assets of an embassy or the shares of a company owned by a foreign state (cf Federal Constitutional Court of Germany (BVerfG) *National Iranian Oil Company* (1983) 64 BVerfGE 1, 36 ff.).

Frequently, provisional measures are initiated simultaneously in several states or parallel to main proceedings in another jurisdiction (cf entry → *Lis alibi pendens*). In general, this does not give rise to concern. In particular, such parallel proceedings are in line with art 27 Brussels I Regulation (respectively art 29 Brussels I Regulation (recast)), because the subject matters of the disputes in the main proceedings and in the provisional proceedings are not identical. With regard to the competition between a provisional proceeding according to art 20 Brussels IIa Regulation and main proceedings regarding child protection pending in another Member State, the ECJ has held that no *lis pendens* (→ *Lis alibi pendens*) arises out of proceedings relating exclusively to a provisional measure, even if these have been commenced prior to any other proceedings (ECJ Case C-296/10 *Bianca Purrucker v Guillermo Vallés Pérez* [2010] ECR I-11163).

In practice, cases may cause significant problems where the claim to be secured by provisional measures is to be determined according to foreign law. This raises the question whether or to what extent it is necessary to determine the applicable foreign law in accelerated proceedings for interim relief (cf entry → Foreign law, application and ascertainment). In → Germany, a widespread view generally limits the judge's duty of inquiry to presently available sources of information. The applicability of foreign law in provisional proceedings is thus made contingent upon the applicant's submission to the court. This approach is, however, just as misguided as general recourse to the substantive law of the *lex fori*. Only if it is not possible to gain sufficient knowledge of the foreign law in a proportionate period of time, should recourse be made to the substantive law of the *lex fori*. Rejection of an application for interim relief should also be considered, where its *lex causae* justification appears dubious, even though it would be permitted under German law.

IV. Recognition and enforcement

In principle, provisional measures which have been issued in summary proceedings are recognized under the general rules. In European law, this follows from art 32 Brussels I Regulation (art 32 Lugano Convention) respectively art 36 Brussels I Regulation (recast), art 21 Brussels IIa Regulation, art 17 and 23 Maintenance Regulation, and art 39 Succession Regulation. By the same token, the normal grounds for refusing recognition or enforcement also apply to foreign provisional measures (cf ECJ Case C-80/00 *Italian Leather SpA v WECO Polstermöbel GmbH & Co* [2002] ECR I-4995), regarding the question whether a foreign decision on interim measures ordering an obligor not to carry out certain acts is irreconcilable with a decision on interim measures refusing to grant such an order in a dispute between the same parties in the state where recognition is sought.

The ECJ has derived the rule from art 27 no 2 of the former Brussels Convention that only decisions emerging from an adversarial procedure (even if it may have remained unilateral through default by the defendant) can be recognized and enforced, but not decisions deriving from so-called *ex parte* procedures (ECJ Case C-125/79 *Bernard Denilauler v SNC Couchet Frères* [1980] ECR 1553). Even though this case-law is sometimes criticized as being outdated since the entry into force of the Brussels I Regulation, the prevailing opinion regards it as still applicable under the Brussels I Regulation. In the context of the Brussels I Regulation (recast), the legislator has ruled in favour of this view, namely by including a new definition of the term 'judgment' in art 2 lit a) subparagraph 2 Brussels I Regulation (recast), which reads as follows:

> For the purposes of Chapter III, 'judgment' includes provisional, including protective, measures ordered by a court or tribunal which by virtue of this Regulation has jurisdiction as to the substance of the matter. It does not include a provisional, including protective, measure which is ordered by such a court or tribunal without the defendant being summoned to appear, unless the judgment containing the measure is served on the defendant prior to enforcement;

In consequence, only such provisional measures are unconditionally subject to recognition as have been issued by a court having jurisdiction by virtue of art 4 *et seq* Brussels I Regulation (recast), provided that the respondent was granted the right to be heard before the measure was issued or that the provisional measure is served upon him before it is enforced. In contrast, Recital (33) points out, oddly enough, that the new rules 'should not preclude the recognition and enforcement of such measures under national law'. In the end, the recast does not therefore prevent the possibility of forum shopping (→ Forum (and law) shopping), rather it creates additional confusion through the possibility of recourse to national provisions on recognition and, hence, endangers desirable legal clarity.

A similar caveat to recognition has previously been developed by the ECJ with regard to matters concerning children: art 21 *et seq* Brussels IIa Regulation shall not be applicable to provisional measures relating to parental responsibility under art 20 Brussels IIa Regulation, where the relevant court would, in the main proceedings, lack jurisdiction by virtue of art 8 *et seq* Brussels IIa Regulation (ECJ Case C-256/09 *Bianca Purrucker v Guillermo Vallés Pérez* [2010] ECR I-7353).

Recognition and enforcement throughout Europe is, naturally, not a problem when provisional measures are not based on national procedural law but derive from European law. This will become relevant under the EAPO Regulation (Regulation (EU) No 655/2014 of the European Parliament and of the Council of 15 May 2014 establishing a European Account Preservation Order procedure to facilitate cross-border debt recovery in civil and commercial matters, [2014] OJ L 189/59) (→ European Account Preservation Order Regulation).

Generally, the rules on recognition contained in the Hague Child Protection Convention and the Hague Adult Protection Convention, as well as on maintenance law (such as the Hague Child Maintenance

Convention 1958 (Hague Convention of 15 April 1958 concerning the recognition and enforcement of decisions relating to maintenance obligations towards children, 539 UNTS 27), the Hague Maintenance Recognition and Enforcement Convention 1973 (Hague Convention of 2 October 1973 on the recognition and enforcement of decisions relating to maintenance obligations, 1021 UNTS 209) and the Hague Maintenance Convention 2007 (Hague Convention of 23 November 2007 on the international recovery of child support and other forms of family maintenance, [2011] OJ L 192/51)), also refer to provisional measures. This, of course, only applies for measures intended to have a transnational effect; this requirement is, for instance, not fulfilled in the cases of art 12 Hague Child Protection Convention and art 11 Hague Adult Protection Convention ('measures ... which have a territorial effect limited to the State in question'). An expert group in The Hague is currently discussing the possibility of a new convention on the recognition and enforcement of foreign protection orders. It concerns 'protection orders, in the cross-border context, that are used to prevent harmful behaviours where an individual's life, physical or psychological integrity, personal liberty, security or sexual integrity is at risk'.

A separate question is that dealt with in provisions such as art 40 Brussels I Regulation (recast) and art 18 Maintenance Regulation: an enforceable judgment shall carry with it by operation of law the power to proceed to any protective measures which exist under the law of the Member State addressed. This provides protection for the creditor when there is a risk that recognition or enforcement of a judgment rendered abroad could be challenged by the debtor.

WOLFGANG HAU

Literature

Ingemar Carl, *Einstweiliger Rechtsschutz bei Torpedoklagen* (Peter Lang 2007); Claudio Consolo, 'The Subtle Interpretation of the Case Law of the European Court on Provisional Remedies' [2005] ZSR 359; Andrew Dickinson, 'Provisional Measures in the "Brussels I" Review – Disturbing the Status Quo?' [2010] IPRax 203; Thomas Garber, *Einstweiliger Rechtsschutz nach der EuGVVO* (BWV 2011); Trevor Hartley, 'Interim Measures under the Brussels Jurisdiction and Judgments Convention' (1999) 24 E.L.Rev. 674; Christian Heinze, 'Internationaler einstweiliger Rechtsschutz' [2003] RIW 922; Christian Heinze, 'Choice of Court Agreements, Coordination of Proceedings and Provisional Measures in the Reform of the Brussels I Regulation' (2011) 75 RabelsZ 581; Konstantinos Kerameus, 'Provisional Remedies in Transnational Litigation' in International Association of Procedural Law (ed), *Trans-National Aspects of Procedural Law*, vol 3 (Giuffrè 1998) 1169; Maximiliane Kimmerle, *Befriedigungsverfügungen nach Art. 24 EuGVÜ/ Art. 31 EuGVO* (Mohr Siebeck 2013); Sabine Kofmel Ehrenzeller, *Der vorläufige Rechtsschutz im internationalen Verhältnis* (Mohr Siebeck 2005); Thalia Kruger, 'Provisional and Protective Measures' in Arnaud Nuyts and Nadine Watté (eds), *International Civil Litigation in Europe and Relations with Third States* (Bruylant 2005) 311; Georges de Leval, 'La notion de mesures conservatoires ou provisoires' in Jacques Isnard and Jacques Norman (eds), *Nouveaux droits dans un nouvel espace européen de justice: Le droit processuel et le droit de l'exécution, Colloque international, Paris les 4 et 5 juillet 2001* (Editions juridiques et techniques 2002) 383; Stephen C McCaffrey and Thomas O Main, *Transnational Litigation in Comparative Perspective: Theory and Application* (OUP 2010); Marie Nioche, *La décision provisoire en droit international privé européen* (Bruylant 2012); Lennart Pålsson, 'Interim Relief under the Brussels and Lugano Conventions' in Jürgen Basedow and others (eds), *Private Law in the International Arena – Liber Amicorum Kurt Siehr* (TMC Asser Press 2000) 621; Alvaro Pérez-Ragone and Wei-Yu Chen, 'Europäischer einstweiliger Rechtsschutz – eine dogmatische Systembildung im Lichte der EuGH-Entscheidungen' (2012) 17 ZZPInt 231; Thomas Pfeiffer and Hannes Wais, 'Einstweilige Maßnahmen im Anwendungsbereich der EuGVO' [2012] Int J Proc Law 274; Peter Schlosser, 'Aus Frankreich Neues zum transnationalen einstweiligen Rechtsschutz in der EU' [2012] IPRax 88; Félicie Schneider, *Die Leistungsverfügung im niederländischen, deutschen und europäischen Zivilprozessrecht* (Mohr Siebeck 2013); Rolf Stürner, 'Der einstweilige Rechtsschutz in Europa' in Hans Erich Brandner (ed), *Festschrift für Karlmann Geiß* (Heymann 2000) 199; Rolf Stürner and Masanori Kawano, *Comparative Studies on Enforcement and Provisional Measures* (Mohr Siebeck 2011); Dimitrios Tsikrikas, 'Internationale Zuständigkeit zum Erlass einstweiliger Maßnahmen nach den Regeln der EuGVO' (2012) 17 ZZPInt 293; Dorothea van Iterson, 'Recognition and Enforcement of Foreign Civil Protection Orders – a Topic for the Hague Conference?' in The Permanent Bureau of the Hague Conference on Private International Law (ed), *A Commitment to Private international law: Essays in Honour of Hans van Loon* (Intersentia 2013) 609; Mirko Weinert, *Vollstreckungsbegleitender einstweiliger Rechtsschutz* (Mohr Siebeck 2007); Christian Wolf and Sonja Lange, 'Das Europäische System des einstweiligen Rechtsschutzes – doch noch kein System?' [2003] RIW 55.

Public international law and private international law

I. Introduction

The relationship between public and private international law is a topic which has long been debated, and which remains controversial. Many modern private international lawyers would doubt that any deep relationship exists between the two subjects. At least formally, rules of private international law are often considered to be ordinary rules of national law, or even rules of national procedural law, made by national courts or legislatures. There is significant variation between the rules of private international law adopted in different states, and it would be very difficult to argue that, at least under current international law, any particular rules of private international law are mandated (with the possible exception of a state's exclusive authority over questions of title to its land).

It is true, of course, that rules of private international law may be (and perhaps increasingly are) harmonized through treaties, and thus take the form of rules which are part of and governed by public international law, including its rules on the formation, validity and interpretation of treaties. Such treaties are commonly negotiated under the auspices of an international organization, the → Hague Conference on Private International Law (discussed further below), but may also be established by regional organizations as part of economic integration efforts. The Brussels Convention (Brussels Convention of 27 September 1968 on jurisdiction and the enforcement of judgments in civil and commercial matters, [1972] OJ L 299/32, consolidated version, [1998] OJ C 27/1; → Brussels I (Convention and Regulation)), Rome Convention (on the law applicable to contractual obligations (consolidated version), [1998] OJ C 27/34; → Rome Convention and Rome I Regulation (contractual obligations)) and → Lugano Convention (of 30 October 2007 on jurisdiction and the recognition and enforcement of judgments in civil and commercial matters, [2007] OJ L 339/3) are European illustrations of this practice – while the former two Conventions have now been replaced with European Regulations, the Lugano Convention is essentially designed to apply to non-EU Member States, and thus continues to function as a separate treaty. There are numerous other examples of such practices around the world, including the Protocol of Las Leñas (of 27 June 1992 on Judicial Cooperation and Assistance in Civil, Commercial, Labour and Administrative Matters, 2145 UNTS 421) and the Protocol of Buenos Aires (on International Jurisdiction in Contractual Matters, signed on 5 August 1994, available at <www.sice.oas.org/trade/mrcsrs/decisions/AN0194_e.asp) adopted by Mercosur in South America. Where such treaties are not directly enforceable as a matter of national constitutional law (→ Constitutional law and private international law), national rules may also be necessary in order to implement the public international law obligations of the state. In any case, states may thus owe obligations of private international law to each other as a matter of public international law. It is further possible that, for example, the International Court of Justice might be seized with a dispute concerning the interpretation of a private international law treaty. This indeed occurred in relation to a dispute between → Belgium and → Switzerland regarding the → Lugano Convention, submitted to the ICJ in 2009, although the proceedings were discontinued in 2011. But no particularly deep connection between public and private international law is necessarily established through these possibilities or practices. A treaty harmonizing national rules of contract law would not make contract law 'international' in character – the international harmonization of private international law through treaties does not, on its own, give private international law a distinct character from other rules of national law.

A stronger connection between public and private international law is suggested through the central role played by the doctrine of → comity in private international law. Rules of private international law are at least partially based around ideas of respectful relations between states. A state should only impose its law or exercise its judicial authority in relation to a dispute where it has a 'legitimate' claim to do so; otherwise the proper course of action, motivated by comity, is to defer to another court's jurisdiction, apply another state's law, or recognize and enforce the judgment of another state. Scholars and national courts frequently refer to the concept of comity as a motivating force behind private international law, but the classic definition that it is 'neither a matter of absolute obligation, on the one hand, nor of mere courtesy and goodwill, upon the other' (*Hilton v Guyot* 159 US 113, 163–4 (1895)) captures its inherent ambiguity or tension. The term comity is generally used to suggest that these principles of deference and respect are not required as part of public international law, even if they are more than a matter of courtesy, thus again suggesting (although not without ambiguity) that there is only a shallow connection between public and private international law.

This entry explores the contention that the connections between public and private international law are deeper than the above would suggest. It examines the historical relationship between the two areas of law, their overlap in terms of regulatory function, and an increased openness within both disciplines to the possibility of a connection between them. In so doing, it examines a range of ways in which public and private international law are mutually influential.

II. A brief history of public and private international law

The earliest origins of private international law are generally considered to be around the time of the Italian renaissance – a time when an expansion of international trade and commerce led to an increase in disputes with significant foreign elements (→ Private international law, history of). The idea of private international law emerged to respond to these problems, as a mechanism to address the risk of conflicting legal treatment of private disputes, while accepting a degree of pluralism in substantive private law. Private international law rules were developed as a distinct part of the universal natural law, 'secondary' norms which facilitated and supported the existence of diverse local legal systems by coordinating legal diversity. Private international law was thus first conceived of not as part of the local law which differed from city-state to city-state, but as part of a universal (natural) international law system – the 'law of nations' – which encompassed the modern territory of both public and private international law.

This idea of private international law has sustained and defined the discipline throughout most of its history. Under the statutist approach (→ Unilateralism), perhaps the earliest idea of private international law, the potential for conflict between legal systems was addressed by attempting to develop a principled and analytical way of determining the scope or the effect of different laws. This was based on the idea that each statute 'naturally' belongs to one of two categories of laws, either 'personal' or 'territorial'. The distinction between these types of laws was intended to reflect a natural division operating in all legal systems, thus again conceiving of private international law as part of a universal and international system of law.

Later scholars adopted different methods of defining this distinction, variously emphasizing the importance of territorial or personal characteristics, while retaining the essentially internationalist character of the discipline. The two dominant 19th century figures in private international law, at least outside the Anglo-American tradition, may be singled out as influential archetypes. In the early 19th century, the German scholar *Savigny* (→ Savigny, Friedrich Carl von) rejected the statutist focus on the characterization of the laws themselves, arguing for an account of private international law in which the basic unit of analysis is the 'legal relation'. For *Savigny*, the role of private international law was thus to find the law to which each relation 'belongs', to 'ascertain the seat (the home) of every legal relation'. It is central to *Savigny*'s approach that the private international law rules he developed were higher level, universal norms – part of an international system of law, derived from the fact of a community of territorial states.

The Italian scholar and political figure *Mancini*, (→ Mancini, Pasquale Stanislao) working later in the 19th century, shared much of *Savigny*'s approach, but adopted → nationality as the founding concept and the key determinant in attributing regulatory authority to states. This was based on a conception of the nation as founded on personal connections (embodying the people and their history and culture) rather than territorial power. On the basis of this approach, *Mancini* argued that the applicable law in a private international law dispute should (generally) be determined by the nationality of the parties. Like *Savigny*, *Mancini* viewed private international law rules as 'secondary norms' which are essentially part of a broader system of law – in his case, the law of a community of nations rather than *Savigny*'s community of territorial states. In both cases, rules of private international law were essentially characterized as serving an international function of global ordering or governance, co-ordinating relations between different legal orders.

This close relationship between public and private international law, viewed as integral parts of a broadly defined 'law of nations', faded in both theory and practice over the course of the 19th century. By the end of the 19th century, there was an increasing view that rules of private international law were not inherent parts of international law, because international law was concerned only with the 'public' relations between states. This theoretical development corresponded with an increased diversity of private international law rules in practice (partly prompted by divisions over the use of 'nationality' as a connecting factor), which made the view of private international law as fundamentally international in character increasingly seem untenable. In federal systems, such as the United States (→ USA), the analysis and development of private international law increasingly focused on problems arising within the system, involving its constituent states. Their resolution increasingly drew on national policies and constitutional concerns, and a lack of distinction between the interstate and foreign contexts shifted the focus away from the traditional 'international' perspective on private international law.

In response and reaction to these developments, a series of Hague Conferences on Private international law were held between 1893 and 1904, to work towards the harmonization of Private International Law (→ Hague Conference on Private International Law). While these conferences had only limited success, they were nevertheless greatly significant in maintaining the idea that private international law was a subject which should be dealt with at the international level. The tradition of internationalism which they established was the direct antecedent of the Hague Conference on Private International Law, founded as an international institution in 1955.

III. Functional and doctrinal connections between public and private international law

In the early parts of the 20th century, the idea that public and private international law were entirely separate disciplines appeared to become established. This was a product both of a narrowing of the domain of public international law, to exclude 'private' actors and their relations, and of the reconceptualization of private international law itself as national law. This theoretical separation has, however, tended to mask a range of functional connections between the two subjects, which have long been evident to practitioners whose work has cut through the artifice of academic disciplinary boundaries. The rules of public international law include rules of 'jurisdiction', which determine the permitted scope of a state's exercise of regulatory authority (→ Jurisdiction, foundations). A state may, for example, criminalize conduct in its territory, or the conduct of its nationals outside its territory. Each act of regulation must be justified by one of the accepted grounds of jurisdiction in order to comply with public international law. Because of the exclusion of 'private' concerns from public international law, doubts have sometimes been expressed as to whether these rules apply to private law regulation or disputes. There is, however, little in principle to support such a distinction. Rules of private law are exercises of 'public' governmental authority as much as rules of criminal law, and they are ultimately sanctioned through coercive judicial and executive powers. If a court orders that a party is liable to pay → damages or face seizure of their property because they have breached tort law, this is not characteristically different from an order that they are liable to pay a fine or face seizure of the same property because they have breached criminal standards. The ultimate recipient of the penalty may differ, but the state power which is exercised to compel payment does not. Public and private law remedies indeed often overlap, and may be interchangeable. In different legal systems, different approaches may notably be taken to regulating particular issues – for example, competition law may be approached through public or private enforcement, or a combination of both. The distinction between public and private law has long been criticized as a legal artifice, and in any case does not appear materially relevant to the question of whether state regulatory power is implicated. A state's contract law, no less than its criminal law, pursues national policy objectives. Public international law scholarship has, in recent years, re-opened its attention to a range of matters traditionally characterized as 'private' and thus as falling outside the scope of the discipline, recognizing that they have important 'public' governance implications and effects.

The recognition that public international law rules of jurisdiction apply to matters of private law reveals a functional commonality between public and private international law rules. Both impose limits on the circumstances in which a state may assert its regulatory authority over a particular person, relationship or event. Public international law establishes that a state may not impose its regulation in the absence of a recognized justification, but does not (at least generally) mandate that state regulation be imposed where such a recognized justification exists. Principles of 'access to justice', developing particularly in the context of human rights law (→ Human rights and private international law), may in future have an increased role in requiring states to expand their grounds of civil jurisdiction, but at present they have had a limited influence. The implication of this is that there is a great deal of scope for different rules of private international law to function compatibly with public international law. Public international law defines the outer limits within which national rules of private international law must operate. Those national rules are then an implementation of both public international limits, and, within those limits, national policies concerning matters of private international law. This is not to say that private international law is 'subsumed' by public international law. Private international law has its own policy concerns and interests, which operate within the public international law framework. The rules of private international law are also some of the strongest evidence of what states view as accepted grounds of public international law jurisdiction, and what they view as 'exorbitant'. Private international law sources were indeed historically one of the strongest influences on the development of public international law jurisdictional rules. The functional commonality between the two disciplines highlights the importance of recognizing that they are in a relationship of mutual influence.

Private international law rules are shaped by rules of public international law, but rules of public international law are also shaped by the practices of states in the context of private international law.

An additional distinct influence of public international law on private international law may be observed in the development of rules of → public policy (*ordre public*), as a defence against the recognition and enforcement of a foreign judgment, or an exception from the application of foreign law (→ Foreign law, application and ascertainment). Public policy is the means through which states may determine that other policy considerations outweigh those of private international law itself – that the usual obligations to recognize a foreign judgment or apply a foreign law are trumped by the harm which would be caused in doing so in the particular circumstances, because the judgment or law offends against important principles of domestic law. For this reason, however, public policy must be construed narrowly, otherwise it would risk undermining private international law altogether – a foreign judgment or law must not be rejected simply because it is different, but only where that difference is fundamentally objectionable. Different considerations apply, however, where the public policy concerned is not derived from national interest, but from public international law such as international human rights law – sometimes referred to as 'truly international' public policy. In these circumstances, the application of public policy is not a projection of one state's norms on matters which would otherwise be governed by the other state, but rather a recognition and enforcement of norms which bind both states. National courts have rightly suggested that they should be readier to apply public policy in such circumstances – for example, refusing to apply Iraqi law which purported to nationalize property seized in the 1990 invasion of Kuwait, contrary to the UN Charter and resolutions of the Security Council (*Kuwait Airways v Iraqi Airways* [2002] UKHL 19). In such cases, giving effect to norms of international law by refusing to apply foreign law or recognize a foreign judgment essentially involves prioritizing other rules of public international law over the rules of 'jurisdiction' which provide the foundations of private international law (→ Private international law, foundations) – but such a prioritization may well be demanded by public international law itself. In any case, an internationalized public policy does not challenge the connection between public and private international law, but rather strengthens it.

A further element to the 'internationalism' of private international law may be found in its policy objectives. As noted above, private international law has its own policy concerns and interests. Like public international law, it governs the allocation of regulatory authority between states, relying traditionally on territorial or personal connections to justify regulation. But within the discipline of private international law, there are also policy goals which relate to how this regulation should function. Rules of private international law have traditionally (through choice-of-law rules in particular) sought to achieve objectives of decisional harmony, ensuring that the same decision is reached wherever in the world a dispute is litigated. Together with rules limiting overlapping jurisdiction and requiring the recognition and enforcement of foreign judgments, this minimizes the risk that parties may be subject to inconsistent regulation, leading to potentially conflicting exercises of state enforcement powers. Another related principle is that incentives and opportunities for forum shopping should be reduced (through both choice-of-law rules and jurisdictional rules), and thus litigation should take place in the most appropriate forum rather than the forum which most favours the claimant – risking again parallel proceedings and inconsistent regulation, as well as inefficient dispute resolution. To put these policy goals another way, private international law has long been concerned, among other things, with coordinating the peaceful coexistence of sovereign states, by striving to reduce the 'conflict of laws between them'.

These are not objectives which can be reached by each state acting unilaterally in adopting its own national rules of private international law, in pursuit of its own policies. They require a process of formal or informal coordination, the recognition by states that they have collective interests and goals which may be best served through rules of private international law which are, at least to some extent, internationally harmonized. This 'internationalist' perspective on private international law is exemplified by the work of the Hague Conference on Private international law. According to this tradition, part of the function of rules of private international law is fundamentally 'public' and 'international' in character – it has at least a relationship of functional equivalence to the global governance ambitions of public international law. Similar 'public' functions of private international law rules may be observed in federal or similar systems in which private international law rules serve the function of ordering the distribution of regulatory authority, a role which private international law has increasingly played in the European Union, → Australia and → Canada. While as noted above these developments have in the past discouraged thinking about private international law from an international perspective (by instead increasing focus on such issues as they arise within the federal system), ironically they illustrate the way in which private international law might be applied to achieve public, systemic objectives, closely aligned to those of public international law. An internationalist vision of the character and objectives of private international law has been strongly influential in the history of the discipline, and could well remain central to its future.

ALEX MILLS

Literature

Adrian Briggs, 'The Principle of Comity in Private international law' (2012) 354 Rec. des Cours 65; Stéphanie De Dycker, 'Private international law Disputes before the International Court of Justice' (2010) 1 JIDS 475; Edward Hambro, 'The Relations Between International Law and Conflict Law' (1962-I) 105 Rec. des Cours 1; Erik Jayme, *Internationales Privatrecht und Völkerrecht* (CF Müller 2003); Stefan Leible and Matthias Ruffert (eds), *Völkerrecht und IPR* (Jenaer Wissenschaftliche Verlagsgesellschaft 2006); Andreas F Lowenfeld, 'Public Law in the International Arena: Conflict of Laws, International Law, and Some Suggestions for Their Interaction' (1979-II) 163 Rec. des Cours 311; Campbell McLachlan, 'The Influence of International Law on Civil Jurisdiction' (1993) 6 Hague Yrbk Intl L 125; Francis A Mann, 'The Doctrine of Jurisdiction Revisited After Twenty Years' (1984-III) 186 Rec. des Cours 19; Pierre Mayer, 'Droit international privé et droit international public sous l'angle de la notion de compétence' (1979) 68 Rev.crit.DIP 1, 349 and 537; Ralf Michaels, 'Public and Private international law:

German Views on Global Issues' (2008) 4 J Priv Int L 121; Alex Mills, 'Rethinking Jurisdiction in International Law' (2014) 84 BYIL 187; Alex Mills, *The Confluence of Public and Private international law* (CUP 2009); John R Stevenson, 'The Relationship of Private international law to Public International Law' (1952) 52 Colum.L.Rev. 561; Pascal de Vareilles-Sommières, *La Compétence Internationale de L'État en Matière de Droit Privé* (LGDJ 1997); Ben Atkinson Wortley, 'The Interaction of Public and Private international law Today' (1954-I) 85 Rec. des Cours 237.

Public policy (*ordre public*)[1]

I. *Ordre public*: an exception clause

The participation of states in the community of nations is coupled with the prerequisite of acknowledging that cases involving foreign elements may have consequences in more than one jurisdiction. This is why nations developed the rules of private international law/conflict of laws – in order to determine the applicable law in cross-border legal relationships and facilitate the pursuit of such relationships. Private international law is premised on international → comity. International comity is demonstrated in the principle that foreign law should be given fair and just consideration and that rights acquired in foreign jurisdictions should be acknowledged by a forum to the greatest extent possible. However, the commitment in any given forum to apply the law of another jurisdiction or to recognize and enforce a foreign judgment or arbitral award has its limits. These limits are in broad terms local morality and social order. A foreign rule, a judgment or a decree have no effect in the domestic legal system if they are deemed contrary to that system's public policy or *ordre public* (both terms will be used here interchangeably). *Ordre public* can thus operate both as a sword and as a shield (see section IV. below the distinction between positive and negative *ordre public*). In activating its *ordre public*, the forum does not reject the content of foreign law as such, but merely denies the consequences flowing from the application of foreign law or the recognition and enforcement of a foreign judgment or arbitral award in the forum. The rationale is simple: in the particular case foreign law, judgments or arbitral awards are regarded as harmful or offensive for the forum while at the same time the values and principles enshrined in the *lex fori* are too fundamental to be ousted. *Ordre public* is a general and abstract notion that is specified by the judge.

II. *Ordre public* in the two main legal traditions: common law and continental law

In the common law legal systems, *ordre public* is termed public policy and its ambit, extent and manner of application is defined through the evolution of case-law. In English law, the first seeds of the concept of public policy appeared in the 15th century and by the 18th century it had developed into the notion we know today. There is evidence that by the early 20th century, public policy was applied in an expansive manner. Since then, there has been a shift in the development of the concept towards a clearer distinction between domestic public policy and international public policy. The latter is relevant for cross-border legal relationships and applies only in extremely rare instances.

Under American law, public policy is invoked in intra-state, interstate and international legal relationships. Intra-state public policy corresponds to the English domestic public policy and ensures that the laws of any given state are applied in a uniform way. Interstate and international public policy become relevant where conflicts of norms either from different US states or from other countries occur. According to the US Supreme Court, the full faith and credit clause requires states within the US to distinguish the way they treat conflicts of applicable laws among the various sister states from the recognition of judgments rendered by courts in other US states. Considerations of public policy in one US state may override the policies underlying the application of another state's law. However, no public policy exception can be invoked by a court of a US state vis-à-vis the recognition and enforcement of judgments originating from other US states (*Franchise Tax Board v Hyatt* 538 U.S. 488, 494 (2003)). International public policy is applied by American courts in a restricted manner, and is underpinned by the consideration that the consequences derived from its

---

[1] This contribution reflects the personal views of the author and does not represent in any way the position of the past, present or future insititutions with which the author was/is/will be affiliated.

application should be just and predictable for those involved in interjurisdictional relationships. As a result, the international public policy prevailing in international transactions is narrower in scope than that in intra-state and interstate transactions (→ Interregional/ Interstate law).

In most continental legal systems, one finds statutory provisions in national codified legislations that define the conditions for the application of *ordre public*. For example, the present wording of the provision addressing *ordre public* in German private international law (art 6 Introductory Act to the German Civil Code (*Einführungsgesetz zum Bürgerlichen Gesetzbuche* of 21 September 1994, BGBl. I 2494)) requires that the concrete application of a foreign law should lead to 'a result manifestly (*offensichtlich*) incompatible with the fundamental principles of the German legal order', for it to be ousted. In the second sentence of the same article, it is *expressis verbis* stated that the same rule applies when the said application would constitute a violation against '*Grundrechte*', ie fundamental rights or human rights. A requirement for the operation of *ordre public* is the '*Inlandsbeziehung*', ie proximity (spatial, personal or temporal) to the forum.

Most codifications make general reference to *ordre public*: see art 16 Italian Private international law Act (*Riforma del Sistema italiano di diritto internazionale private*, Act No 218 of 31 May 1995 in Gazz.Uff, Supplemento Ordinario No 128 of 3 June l995, as amended); art 17 Swiss Private international law Act (*Bundesgesetz über das Internationale Privatrecht* of 18 December 1987, 1988 BBl I 5, as amended); art 3081 of the Code civil of Quebec (L.Q. 1991, ch 64); art 5 Turkish Private international law Code (Code on Private International and International Civil Procedure Law of 27 November 2007 (Act No 5718) (*Milletlerarası Özel Hukuk ve Usul Hukuku Hakkında Kanun*), Resmî Gazete No 26728 of 12 December 2007). In other legislative codifications, *ordre public* is combined with good morals, as in art 28 of the Egyptian Civil Code (Law No 131/1948 of 16 July 1948, *al qānūn al madanī*); art 30 of the Japanese Act on General Rules for Application of Laws (*Hōno Tekiyō ni Kansuru Tsūsokuhō*, Law No 10 of 1898, as newly titled and amended by Act No 78 of 21 June 2006); art 33 of the Greek Civil Code (*Astikos Kodikas* of 23 February 1946, A.N. 2250/1040; FEK A 91/1940, 597). Furthermore, codifications may also include references to the public law of the forum (art 14 of the Argentine Civil Code (*Código Civil de la República Argentina* of 25 September 1869, by the passage of Law 340, entry into force 1 January 1871) or the basic tenets and values of the legal order of the state concerned (art 6 of the Austrian Federal Code on Private international law (*Bundesgesetz über das internationale Privatrecht* of 15 June 1978, BGBl. No 304/1978, as amended)). Finally, explicit reference to the 'international *ordre public*' is also found (art 22 of the Portuguese Civil Code 1966 (*Código Civil* approved by Decreto-Lei No 47.344, of 25 November 1966, [1966] DG I série 274/1883, with subsequent amendments; consolidated version available at (<www.pgdlisboa.pt>)).

Turning to French law, art 6 of the French Civil Code (Code Civil of 21 March 1804; henceforth French CC) provides that statutes relating to public policy and morals may not be derogated from by private agreement. This provision concerns French internal public policy and not the mechanism intended to oust the application of foreign law. On the other hand, the concept of public policy in private international law is developed by case-law and legal doctrine. It connotes the principles of universal justice considered by public opinion as having absolute value, the fundamental principles of the French legal system, as well as provisions relating to the political, social and economic structure of the country. Certain core elements mentioned above of the public policy and morals, as stipulated in art 6 French CC, thus form an integral part of the French *ordre public* international. French law clearly distinguishes *ordre public* from the '*lois d'application immédiate*' which are directly applicable – regardless of the conflict of laws provisions – and which must be observed for the protection of the country's political, social or economic order.

One observation relating to the development and role of the exception clause in the common and continental legal systems concerns the terminology of the words 'policy' and '*ordre*'. The two terms are by no means equivalent. 'Policy' suggests that the principles concerned are enshrined in wider societal and political ideas, whereas '*ordre*' is closer to the English term 'law and order' and has fewer political connotations compared to policy.

III. *Ordre public* in international and European legal instruments

References to the exception clause of *ordre public* are found in a number of international codifications of private international law as well as in the legal instruments of the EU. The list set out below is by no means exhaustive, but is indicative of the widespread recognition of the role and importance attributed by states to this mechanism.

1. *European Union legal instruments*

The European instruments implementing uniform rules of private international and international procedural law within the EU frequently include *ordre public* as an exception clause to the otherwise applicable law or as a ground for refusing recognition and enforcement of a judgment issued by the courts of another Member State. These clauses share an emphasis of the fact that the contrariness to the '*ordre public*' of the forum – also understood as the place where recognition of a judgment is sought – should be manifest. In addition, there are two examples where the exception clause is further qualified as demonstrated below:

- art 21 Rome I Regulation (Regulation (EC) No 593/2008 of the European Parliament and of the Council of 17 June 2008 on the law applicable to contractual obligations (Rome I), [2008] OJ L 177/6; → Rome Convention and Rome I Regulation (contractual obligations));
- art 26 → Rome II Regulation (non-contractual obligations) (Regulation (EC) No 864/2007 of the European Parliament and of the Council of 11 July 2007 on the law applicable to non-contractual obligations (Rome II), [2007] OJ L 199/40);
- art 12 → Rome III Regulation (divorce) (Council Regulation (EU) No 1259/2010 of 20 December 2010 implementing enhanced cooperation in the area of the law applicable to divorce and legal separation, [2010] OJ L 343/10);
- art 35 Succession Regulation (Regulation (EU) No 650/2012 of the European Parliament and of the Council of 4 July 2012 on jurisdiction, applicable law, recognition and enforcement of decisions and acceptance and enforcement of authentic instruments in matters of succession and on the creation of a European Certificate of Succession, [2012] OJ L 201/107; → Rome IV Regulation (succession));
- art 34(1) Brussels I Regulation (Regulation (EC) No 44/2001 of 22 December 2000 on jurisdiction and the recognition and enforcement of judgments in civil and commercial matters, [2001] OJ L 12/1) and art 45(1)(a) Brussels I Regulation (recast) (Regulation (EU) No 1215/2012 of the European Parliament and of the Council of 12 December 2012 on jurisdiction and the recognition and enforcement of judgments in civil and commercial matters (recast), [2012] OJ L 351/1) (→ Brussels I (Convention and Regulation)): in the Brussels I Regulation (recast), *ordre public* remains in place as a ground for refusal of recognition and enforcement of judgments issued within the EU, but it is noted that, on the occasion of revision of the text by the European Commission, deletion of the clause had been proposed.
- art 23(a) → Brussels IIa Regulation (Council Regulation (EC) No 2201/2003 of 27 November 2003 concerning jurisdiction and the recognition and enforcement of judgments in matrimonial matters and the matters of parental responsibility, repealing Regulation (EC) No 1347/2000, [2003] OJ L 338/1), where the court of the forum must have regard to the best interests of the child when considering activation of the mechanism of *ordre public*. This means that in specifying the content of the forum's *ordre public*, the court must gauge the effects that the legal conclusion will have on the child's best interests. The analysis may thus lead to application of a law other than the otherwise applicable law or law of the forum;
- art 26(6) Insolvency Regulation (Council Regulation (EC) No 1346/2000 of 29 May 2000 on insolvency proceedings, [2000] OJ L 160/1), where the content of *ordre public* encompasses in particular the fundamental principles of the forum or the constitutional rights and liberties of the individual.

On the other hand, the exception of *ordre public* does not appear in: European Enforcement Order Regulation (Regulation (EC) No 805/2004 of the European Parliament and of the Council of 21 April 2004 creating a European Enforcement Order for uncontested claims, [2004] OJ L 143/15); European Payment Order Regulation (Regulation (EC)

No 1896/2006 of the European Parliament and of the Council of 12 December 2006 creating a European order for payment procedure, [2006] OJ L 399/1); and European Small Claims Procedure Regulation (Regulation (EC) No 861/2007 of the European Parliament and of the Council of 11 July 2007 establishing a European Small Claims Procedure, [2007] OJ L 199/1).

2. *International codifications*

A number of conventions, model laws and sets of uniform rules developed within the framework of the Hague Conference on Private International Law, → UNIDROIT and → UNCITRAL provide for a reservation of the *ordre public*. For example:

- art 6 Hague Sales Convention (Hague Convention of 15 June 1955 on the law applicable to international sales of goods, 510 UNTS 147);
- art 4 Hague Child Maintenance Convention 1956 (Hague Convention of 24 October 1956 on the law applicable to maintenance obligations towards children, 510 UNTS 161);
- art 2(5) Hague Child Maintenance Convention 1958 (Hague Convention of 15 April 1958 concerning the recognition and enforcement of decisions relating to maintenance obligations towards children, 539 UNTS 27);
- art 16 Hague Infant Protection Convention (Hague Convention of 5 October 1961 concerning the powers of authorities and the law applicable in respect of the protection of infants, 658 UNTS 143);
- art 7 Hague Testamentary Dispositions Convention (Hague Convention of 5 October 1961 on the conflicts of laws relating to the form of testamentary dispositions, 510 UNTS 175);
- art 10 Hague Divorce and Separation Convention (Hague Convention of 1 June 1970 on the recognition of divorces and legal separations, 978 UNTS 399);
- art 5(1) of the Hague Maintenance Recognition and Enforcement Convention 1973 (Hague Convention of 2 October 1973 on the recognition and enforcement of decisions relating to maintenance obligations, 1021 UNTS 209);
- art 11 Hague Maintenance Applicable Law Convention 1973 (Hague Convention of 2 October 1973 on the law applicable to maintenance obligations, 1056 UNTS 204);
- art 24 Hague Adoption Convention (Hague Convention of 29 May 1993 on protection of children and cooperation in respect of inter-country adoption, 1870 UNTS 167; 32 ILM 1134);
- art 23(2)(d) Hague Child Protection Convention (Hague Convention of 19 October 1996 on jurisdiction, applicable law, recognition, enforcement and cooperation in respect of parental responsibility and measures for the protection of children, 35 ILM 1391);
- art 13 Hague Maintenance Protocol 2007 (Hague Protocol of 23 November 2007 on the law applicable to maintenance obligations, [2009] OJ L 331/19);
- § 30B of UNIDROIT Principles of Transnational Civil Procedure (ALI/UNIDROIT Rules of Transnational Civil Procedure (text of the Principles and the accompanying commentary were adopted by the American Law Institute (ALI) in May 2004 and by the International Institute for the Unification of Private Law (UNIDROIT) in April 2004, (2004) 4 Unif.L.Rev. 758));
- art V (2)(b) 1958 New York Convention (New York Convention of 10 June 1958 on the recognition and enforcement of foreign arbitral awards, 330 UNTS 3);
- art 34(2)(b)(ii) 1985 UNCITRAL Arbitration Model Law (United Nations Commission on International Trade Law, UNICITRAL Model Law on International Commercial Arbitration as adopted on 21 June 1985, and as amended on 7 July 2006, UN doc A/40/17 and A/61/17; → Arbitration, (UNCITRAL) Model Law);
- art 23 UNCITRAL Assignment of Receivables Convention (United Nations Convention on the Assignment of Receivables in International Trade, concluded 12 December 2001, adopted by resolution A/RES/56/8) (which makes reference both to *ordre public* and mandatory rules);
- art 6 UNCITRAL Model Law on Cross-Border Insolvency with Guide to Enactment, 1997 (UNCITRAL (ed), Model Law on Cross-Border Insolvency with Guide to Enactment (1997): Model Law on Cross-Border Insolvency of the United Commission on International Trade Law, Resolution 52/158 adopted by the General Assembly, 30 January 1998, No E.99.V.3, General Assembly Resolution 52/158 of 15 December 1997).

IV. **Sub-divisions of the concept of** *ordre public*

The concept of *ordre public* has been significantly fragmented and sub-divided into various categories in the legal doctrine. A first division is made between negative and positive *ordre public*. The negative function consists in denying the effects resulting from the application of foreign law or from the recognition and enforcement of a foreign judgment/arbitral award. Family, → succession, personal as well as contract law are the main fields where the mechanism of negative *ordre public* is usually activated. On the other hand, concerning the matter of *ordre public positif*, a long debate has been conducted in legal scholarship. Various terms have been used to signify its function: *lois d'application immédiate*, *Eingriffsnormen*, internationally mandatory rules or specially mandatory rules. Distinctions among these various terms have been argued by private international law scholars. In general, rules of positive *ordre public* relate to the functioning of the state and the economy. For the purpose of this encyclopedic entry, the positive function of *ordre public* will mean the mechanism by which certain substantive rules – generally but not necessarily of the *lex fori* – apply directly under certain conditions and thus interfere with the operation of the conflict of laws rules.

Ordre public is also divided into domestic and international as was mentioned in the section dealing with the historical evolution of the concept (see section II. above). The domestic version of *ordre public* concerns all those peremptory rules from which legal persons cannot deviate by way of agreement. On the other hand, the international – otherwise known as 'transnational' or 'truly international' – *ordre public* operates in a transnational context with a view to preserving the principal values of the forum vis-à-vis insulting and intolerable interferences resulting from the application of a foreign law or the enforcement of a foreign judgment/arbitral award. Not all rules of domestic *ordre public* amount to rules of international *ordre public*. On the contrary, only a small number of mandatory domestic provisions are deemed to implement moral, societal, political or economic principles as well as values which are so fundamental as to justify the ousting of otherwise applicable foreign norms. The international *ordre public* has a far more limited content and a narrower scope of application than the domestic *ordre public*.

A further sub-categorization of the concept is substantive (*ordre public matériel*) versus procedural *ordre public*. This classification focuses on the source, content and type of the rules concerned. The former encompasses all rules setting out the rights and obligations deriving from a legal relationship, while the latter concerns the procedural rules established for the enforcement of such rights and obligations before courts and arbitral tribunals. Further, when *ordre public* operates as a barrier to the application of foreign law, the court of the forum always applies the *lex fori* for the procedural matters, so that *ordre public* addresses only substantive law issues. Conversely, when *ordre public* operates as a barrier to the recognition and enforcement of foreign judgments and arbitral awards, it includes both substantive and procedural considerations.

A norm classified as forming part of the *ordre public* can at any time fall under one or more of the categories mentioned in this section; for example it can be international, negative and substantive at the one and same time.

V. Relativity of *ordre public*

Ordre public is a relative notion. It changes through time and place. Its content is subject to constant evolution and reflects the current state of values and morality in a given society. The relative character of *ordre public* is further demonstrated by the fact that the court has to take into account all the specific circumstances of the case before dismissing a foreign law on the grounds of *ordre public*. The logic behind the relative operation of *ordre public* can be summarized as follows: while in abstract terms a foreign law provision may run counter to the principles reflected in the *lex fori*, its application in the light of the specific circumstances of the case may nevertheless be compatible with it. Conversely, the abstract rule of a foreign legal system may be fully aligned with the fundamental values of the forum while under specific circumstances the result of its application may lead to constitute a flagrant violation of the forums *ordre public*.

In Germany, this feature of *ordre public* is called '*Inlandsbeziehung*' (literally meaning connection with the country') and in France it is known as *effet atténué*. While the two notions are not identical in meaning, the logic underpinning them is premised on the same idea: it signifies the proximity, spatial and temporal, that the facts of the legal relationship in question have with the forum.

Inlandsbeziehung is not an additional → connecting factor of the private international law rule; it rather sheds more light on the degree of violation of the *ordre public* of the forum. When the violation deriving from the application of a foreign law is particularly flagrant and intense, a minor *Inlandsbeziehung* of the set of facts to the forum suffices and vice versa. Domicile, residence (→ Domicile, habitual residence and establishment) and nationality are recurring factors of proximity for *Inlandsbeziehung*. If the violation of the *ordre public* consists in the disregard of the essence of fundamental principles for the protection of human rights (→ Human rights and private international law), it does not seem pertinent to adapt the effect of the mechanism in accordance with the *Inlandsbeziehung*, and in particular nationality. However, this statement has to be qualified. For example, in Europe it is considered that polygamous marriages (one man married to several women) violate gender equality and lead to discrimination on the grounds of gender. Accordingly, the celebration of such marriages in Europe is considered contrary to *ordre public*. Conversely, European courts tend to recognize the validity of such marriages when celebrated outside Europe. However, recognition of the legal effects deriving from such marriages between spouses living in the territory of a European state (such as for maintenance claims, residence permit) gives rise to more complicated considerations. In those instances, the courts around Europe have taken differing positions and various opinions are debated in legal scholarship as to how to tackle this issue. The diversity in the approaches adopted by the various national European courts provides a clear evidence of the relativity of the notion of *ordre public*.

In a similar vein and with regard to the recognition and enforcement of decisions, the attenuated effect of *ordre public* makes a distinction between, on the one hand the reaction of *ordre public* in the case of acquisition of a right in the forum and, on the other hand giving effect in the forum to a right acquired abroad without fraud according to a law which is applicable based on the French rules of private international law. *Ordre public* reacts more strongly for rights acquired domestically compared to rights legitimately acquired abroad.

The proximity to the forum here is of a temporal character in that the *ordre public* mechanism is activated in a different way depending on whether the rights are acquired for the first time when the forum is seized of the case or whether they have already been acquired and the forum is called upon to assess and give effect to the consequences deriving from their acquisition. The main idea behind the attenuated effect relates to the justified expectations of the parties. A judicial pronouncement, produced at a given time and in a certain place, develops legal repercussions before the stage of its recognition and enforcement by a foreign court. Legal certainty and respect for public international law principles of comity and sovereignty impose a lenient, as well as narrow control of the foreign decision.

VI. Legal consequences and effects

Once the application of the foreign law is rejected, the need emerges to identify an applicable law in order to govern the legal relationship. Most private international law statutes do not provide for the subsidiarily applicable law and leave the task of identifying it to the judge. Others explicitly provide the → substitution by the *lex fori*. In some jurisdictions, a middle path is adopted, according to which the *lex fori* is applicable to the extent necessary.

When the *lex fori* substitutes foreign law it does so to a limited extent; only a highly specific provision of the *lex fori* replaces the provision of the foreign *lex causae* which is rejected by the *ordre public*. However, there may be instances where it is possible to apply other more appropriate rules of the applicable foreign legislation. In such instances, substitution of the applicable foreign legislation by the *lex fori* may not be the most appropriate step.

When the *ordre public* is applied in the context of recognition and enforcement of a foreign judgment or arbitral award, it results in the rejection of absorption in the forum of the legal effects deriving from such judgment or arbitral award. There is no further impact than this.

VII. Europeanization of *ordre public*

In the European legal order, several types of *ordre public* coexist. First, *ordre public*/public policy is one of the permissible limitations – the other two being public morality and public security – to the fundamental economic freedoms enjoyed within the EU market. In this context the clause is of national origin and restricts the exercise of rights having an economic content. EU law does not provide a definition for these clauses. In ECJ case-law it has been recognized, for example, that the various EU Member States can have different standards and thresholds when it comes to fundamental values and rights, including human dignity (Case C-36/02 *Omega Spielhallen- und Automatenaufstellungs-GmbH v Oberbürgermeisterin der Bundesstadt Bonn* [2004] ECR I-9609). The content and operation of this type of public policy is not relevant for private international law.

Furthermore, there are the rules for the protection of fundamental rights guaranteed under the ECHR (European Convention of 4 November 1950 for the Protection of Human Rights and Fundamental Freedoms, 213 UNTS 221). The system of the Convention aspires to transcend the legal boundaries of national sovereignty, establish common minimal standards among its contracting states while guaranteeing cultural legal pluralism. Those minimal standards serve as a constitutional instrument of a 'European public order' according to the Court (*Loizidou v Turkey* App no 15318/89 (ECtHR, 23 March 1995) Series A no 310).

At the same time, there exist mandatory rules of EU law that have to be applied mandatorily – irrespective of the applicable law – by all Member States, an example of which is fundamental procedural rights such as the right to a fair hearing, competition law rules and provisions aimed at the protection of a weaker party in a legal relationship such as consumers and employees. In particular and with respect to fundamental rights it is noted that the Treaty of Lisbon (Treaty of Lisbon amending the Treaty on European Union and the Treaty establishing the European Community, signed at Lisbon, 13 December 2007, [2007] OJ C 306/1, consolidated version, [2012] OJ C 326/1) rendered legally binding the EU Charter of Fundamental Rights (Charter of Fundamental Rights of the European Union of 18 December 2000, [2000] OJ C 364/1, (consolidated version 2012/C 326/02, [2012] OJ C 326/391)) and also made possible the accession of the EU to the ECHR. In the meantime, states have an obligation to respect the ECHR even when they are applying or implementing EU law. The cluster of those EU mandatory rules, which incorporate the human rights standards of the ECHR, can be labelled as '*ordre public communautaire*'.

The Europeanization of domestic private international law by way of implementing rules for a EU private international law was accelerated by the Treaty of Amsterdam (Treaty of Amsterdam amending the Treaty on the European Union, the Treaties establishing the European Communities and certain related acts (consolidated version), [1997] OJ C 340/01), which transferred competence in the field of judicial cooperation in → civil and commercial matters from the third to the first pillar. However, it is not yet possible today to speak of a unified European private international law that renders the national legislations in this field obsolete. The content and mechanism of *ordre public* have followed suit. *Ordre public* was considered to be the bastion of a state's legal system that allowed it to oppose the application of a foreign law, including the law of other EU Member States. In the meantime, within the community of Member States of the EU and signatory parties to the ECHR certain minimal standards and mandatory pieces of legislation have emerged. These elements deploy two functions: (i) they harmonize in specific matters the defence of *ordre public* that the EU Member States will have to oppose vis-à-vis third states; and (ii) they reduce the chances that the Member States will raise among themselves objections on the ground of *ordre public* for such matters.

IOANNA THOMA

Literature

Jürgen Basedow, 'Die Verselbständigung des europäischen ordre public' in Michael Coester, Dieter Martiny and Karl August Prinz von Sachsen Gesaaphe (eds), *Privatrecht in Europa – Vielfalt, Kollision, Kooperation, Festschrift für Hans Jürgen Sonnenberger zum 70. Geburtstag* (Beck 2004) 291; Jean-Paul Costa, 'La Cour européenne des droits de l'homme: vers un ordre juridique européen?' in *Mélanges en hommage à Louis-Edmond Pettiti* (Bruylant 1998) 165; Jochen A Frowein, 'La convention européenne des droits de l'homme comme ordre public de l'Europe' in *Collected Courses of the Academy of European Laws*, 12 *Collected Courses of the Academy of European Law* (Martinus Nijhoff Publishers, 1990) 267; Jan Kropholler,

Internationales Privatrecht (6th edn, Mohr Siebeck 2006); Paul Lagarde, 'Public Policy' in *International Encyclopedia of Comparative Law*, vol 3 (Mohr Siebeck 1994) ch 11; Franco Mosconi, 'Exceptions to the Operation of Conflict of Laws Rules' (1989) 217 Rec. des Cours 202; Kent Murphy, 'The Traditional View of Public Policy and *Ordre Public* in Private international law' (1981) 11 Ga.J.Int'l.& Comp.L. 591; Andreas Spickhoff, *Der ordre public im internationalen Privatrecht, Entwicklung – Struktur –Konkretisierung* (Metzner 1989); Ioanna Thoma, *Die Europäisierung und Vergemeinschaftung des nationalen ordre public* (Mohr Siebeck 2007).

Rabel, Ernst

Ernst Rabel has been the most influential promoter of the use of comparative law (→ Comparative law and private international law) in general and in the conflict of laws in particular.

I. Life and work

Ernst Rabel was born on 28 January 1874 in Vienna, which at the time was the cosmopolitan capital of a multinational empire, a place at the crossroads of Slavonic, Germanic, Romanic, and Hungarian cultural traditions. His parents were of Jewish descent and had converted to Catholicism. His father was a distinguished advocate and member of the Vienna bar. *Ernst Rabel* received a humanistic education that was common in the upper middle-class of his time. But he also learned to read and write three modern languages – English, French, and Italian – which was much less typical in those days and became the basis for his later studies of comparative law (Rolf-Ulrich Kunze, *Ernst Rabel und das Kaiser-Wilhelm-Institut* (Wallstein 2004) 32). At the age of 21 he graduated from Vienna Law School with an unpublished doctoral dissertation written under the supervision of the legal historian *Ludwig Mitteis* (Ulrich Drobnig, 'Die Geburt der modernen Rechtsvergleichung – Zum 50. Todestag von Ernst Rabel' [2005] ZEuP 821). For some time he stayed in Vienna and worked in his father's law firm before following *Mitteis* to Leipzig, where he was awarded the *Habilitation* (postdoctoral lecture qualification) on the basis of a Romanist investigation into the seller's liability for defects of title (Ernst Rabel, *Die Haftung des Verkäufers wegen Mangels im Rechte* (Veit 1902)). He continued to assist *Mitteis* before being appointed as an extraordinary professor in Leipzig in 1904. In 1906 he was called to a chair at the University of Basle in Switzerland where he also served as a judge on the appellate court of the canton (Ernst Rabel, 'Vorträge – Unprinted Lectures' (1986) 50 RabelsZ 282, 287). Appointments to the Universities of Kiel (1910) and – only one year later – Göttingen (1911) ensued.

In the middle of the First World War, *Rabel* received an offer for an appointment from the University of Munich, which he accepted on condition that an Institute of Comparative Law would be set up. This was the first institute of the kind worldwide. It gives evidence of a new orientation of *Rabel*'s interest: while he continued his activities in Roman law and legal history, he now started to explore a new field of legal scholarship (Ulrich Drobnig, 'Die Geburt der modernen Rechtsvergleichung – Zum 50. Todestag von Ernst Rabel' [2005] ZEuP 821; Rolf-Ulrich Kunze, *Ernst Rabel und das Kaiser-Wilhelm-Institut* (Wallstein 2004) 33). Due to the shortcomings of the time, the Institute was a small one and when talking about it a couple of years later *Rabel* was still of the opinion that 'the ambitious name of an "Institute" requires an explanation which, for the time being, is not justified by impressive rooms or facilities' (Ernst Rabel, 'Das Institut für Rechtsvergleichung an der Universität München' (1919), in Hans G. Leser (ed), *Ernst Rabel – Gesammelte Aufsätze*, vol 3 (Mohr Siebeck 1967) 22, 27). But at the same time, he designed and presented a comprehensive Institute programme which aimed to serve students, scholars, and practitioners principally through a library which should collect books and other material from all jurisdictions across the globe.

The peace treaties terminating the First World War which gave rise to new states, to cessions of territory, to dual citizenship, and to the creation of several international tribunals stimulated many activities in the field of comparative and international law. *Rabel*, a pioneer in the field, was a member of the German-Italian Mixed Arbitral Tribunal, one of several similar institutions that owed their existence to the Versailles Peace Treaty (Treaty of Peace between the Allied and

Associated Powers and Germany of 28 June 1919, 225 CTS 188); he belonged to that tribunal from 1921 to 1927 (Rolf-Ulrich Kunze, *Ernst Rabel und das Kaiser-Wilhelm-Institut* (Wallstein 2004) 38). He was also a judge *ad hoc* in five lawsuits between Germany and Poland conducted at the Permanent Court of International Justice at The Hague which, in his own words, 'took me the better part of the years 1925 to 1928' (Ernst Rabel, 'Vorträge – Unprinted Lectures' (1986) 50 RabelsZ 282, 288). For the holders of such offices, comparative and international law became the everyday reality, and the observers could witness the first heyday of these legal disciplines. It was in those years that *Rabel* was appointed, in 1925, to a chair at the Faculty of Law of what is now the Humboldt University of Berlin and to the position as the founding Director of the Institute for Foreign Private Law and Private international law affiliated to the Kaiser-Wilhelm-Gesellschaft. The Institute soon became the centre of comparative legal research in Europe. It was evacuated from Berlin in 1944 and moved, after an intermediate period at Tübingen, to Hamburg in 1956, where it is now the Max Planck Institute for Comparative and International Private Law.

At the Institute, *Rabel* began a number of activities which remained influential over many years, some until the present time: alongside several programmatic lectures and articles, he put on track a book series, a law journal which has borne his name since 1961 (*Rabels Zeitschrift für ausländisches und internationales Privatrecht – RabelsZ*), a systematic collection of German case-law on private international law (*Die deutsche Rechtsprechung auf dem Gebiet des Internationalen Privatrecht – IPRspr*), and numerous German reports to the International Congresses of Comparative Law.

Moreover, he was responsible for initiating the education of a large number of young scholars, many of whom later became top-ranking practitioners, professors of law, and leading politicians. In those years, he also started the outstanding comparative research project on the law of sales (Ernst Rabel, *Das Recht des Warenkaufs* (de Gruyter 1936 and 1958)); as a member of the Governing Council of the UNIDROIT International Institute for the Unification of Private Law at Rome he convinced that body to put the unification of the law of sales on the agenda of that organization. The UNIDROIT project ultimately led to the → CISG (United Nations Convention on the International Sale of Goods of 11 April 1980, 1489 UNTS 3) which is now in force in about 80 countries worldwide.

Being of Jewish descent, *Rabel* could not keep his position in Nazi Germany. While the expulsion of Jews from public office had started already in 1933 (*Gesetz zur Wiederherstellung des Berufsbeamtentums* of 7 April 1933, RGBl. I, 175), Rabel remained unaffected over some years due to his international reputation and to his prominent position in the Kaiser-Wilhelm-Gesellschaft, but he was finally compelled to step down as a director in February 1937 (Rolf-Ulrich Kunze, *Ernst Rabel und das Kaiser-Wilhelm-Institut* (Wallstein 2004) 167). Being tolerated as a guest of the library of the Institute, he stayed in Germany until the November pogroms of 1938, which convinced him that emigration was necessary to save his life. He left Germany for the United States in summer 1939 (March 1939 according to Jürgen Thieme, 'Ernst Rabel (1874–1955) – Schriften aus dem Nachlaß. Einführung' (1986) 50 RabelsZ 251, 266, fn 78; but see Rolf-Ulrich Kunze, *Ernst Rabel und das Kaiser-Wilhelm-Institut* (Wallstein 2004) 169).

Thus, when *Rabel* had almost reached the age of retirement, he started a new life in the US, first in Chicago and from 1942 onward in Ann Arbor, Michigan. Together with his former assistant, *Max Rheinstein*, a professor at the University of Chicago, he started to work on 'European Annotations' to the Restatement (First) of Conflict of Laws (American Law Institute, Restatement of the Law, First: Conflict of Laws, St. Paul 1934; → Restatement (First and Second) of Conflict of Laws), which had been adopted by the American Law Institute in 1934. *Rabel* soon convinced the ALI, which had commissioned this work, that its scope was too narrow. What was needed was a universal, not a European approach, and, moreover, he favoured a comparative treatise rather than annotations accompanying the restatement (Jürgen Thieme, 'Ernst Rabel (1874–1955) – Schriften aus dem Nachlaß. Einführung' (1986) 50 RabelsZ 251, 266, 267–8). Funded by the Law School of the University of Michigan and by the Harvard Law School, *Rabel*'s work on the four volumes of 'The Conflict of Laws' took most of his time

Jürgen Basedow

during the Second World War and the post-war period; the books were published in 1945, 1947 and 1950, the last volume only posthumously in 1958. In 1948, the newly established Free University of Berlin reinstated him in his rights as an emeritus professor. He was also invited to serve as an academic advisor to the Max Planck Institute, as it was now called, in Tübingen, where he spent much time in completing his work on comparative sales law with the assistance of young scholars of the Institute. In the early 1950s, a second edition of 'The Conflict of Laws' was started, again with the support of young assistants from Germany, *Ulrich Drobnig* and *Herbert Bernstein* (Ulrich Drobnig, 'Die Geburt der modernen Rechtsvergleichung – Zum 50. Todestag von Ernst Rabel' [2005] ZEuP 821. 823 f). *Rabel* died in Zurich at the age of 81 on 7 September 1955.

II. *Rabel*'s contribution to private international law

Rabel's academic work is characterized by a gradual transgression from Roman law to comparative law (→ Comparative law and private international law) and, further, to private international law. He published his first major piece on private international law rather late, namely in 1931 at the age of 57 years (Ernst Rabel, 'Das Problem der Qualifikation' (1931) 5 RabelsZ 241). To understand this universal mind and his contribution to private international law, it is necessary to take a closer look at the previous stages of his scholarly interest dedicated to Roman law, to comparative law, and to the development of international law.

1. *From Roman law to comparative law*

When *Rabel* studied law at the University of Vienna, the Roman Digest was no longer effective law in the Austro-Hungarian Empire, as the General Civil Code had been enacted in 1811. But Roman law had kept its function as the universal framework of legal concepts and categories, rules, and principles in Germany with its Pandectist School, which at the time played a leading role in European scholarship and attracted the interests of academics in the German-speaking countries and beyond. Roman law was considered as a kind of legal grammar that allowed scholars and lawyers from across the continent to discuss issues of common interest. Where it had residual effect next to the local laws of the respective jurisdiction, the determination of the applicable law was often believed to be redundant, since the body of rules and principles of ancient origin was assumed to be of general and universal acceptance (Reinhard Zimmermann, '"In der Schule von Ludwig Mitteis" – Ernst Rabels rechtshistorische Ursprünge' (2001) 65 RabelsZ 1, 27).

The enactment of the German Civil Code (*Bürgerliches Gesetzbuch* of 18 August 1896, RGBl. 195, entered into force on 1 January 1900) struck a heavy blow to this perception of the legal landscape. The law schools of German universities were compelled to change focus: instead of primarily teaching Roman law as a general framework of all German jurisdictions, they now had in the first instance to teach the positive law of the new Civil Code. Likewise, the research activities of German law professors had to shift towards textbooks, commentaries, and articles explaining the new law. Roman law was relegated to legal history; the leading scholars of the discipline could still provide foundational knowledge to the students, but they were no longer regarded as influential experts of the living law. University chairs and research funds which had been reserved for the study of Roman law for decades were reallocated to modern law. It was a period when many young Romanists were looking for a new orientation of their own research agenda. Some of them continued Romanist studies, widening however the perspective and including the economic and social background. Others, without abandoning their interest in Roman law, realized that the future legal landscape of Europe would be characterized by national legal systems and their coexistence; these individuals would either directly move into private international law, as was the case with *Hans Lewald* and *Leo Raape*, or they would go into comparative law which, according to a belief widespread in Europe and in particular in France around 1900 (*Saleilles*), promised to bring to light a set of general principles recognized by all nations, a common core or *droit commun législatif*. The latter choice was made by *Ernst Rabel*; he did not want, however, to confine comparative research to the identification of a common core or the best possible solution, wanting instead to include the 'vibrant bodies of all laws under the sun into his reflection on law' (Ernst Rabel, 'Aufgabe und Notwendigkeit der Rechtsvergleichung' in Hans G Leser (ed), *Ernst Rabel – Gesammelte Aufsätze*, vol 3 (Mohr Siebeck 1967) 1, 5–6).

2. From Roman law and comparative law to international law

Rabel's first contacts with the legal frame of cross-border legal relations were apparently due to his practical work as a judge in international tribunals. The need to convince foreign-bred lawyers sitting on those tribunals posed problems which could not be solved from a positivistic perspective rooted in a single national legal system. Rather, both Roman law and comparative law (→ Comparative law and private international law) proved of fundamental significance. In an article published in 1944, he pointed out in retrospect: 'It was plain, indeed, after the First World War, in innumerable diplomatic conferences, in the numerous international tribunals of that time, in a rapidly growing literature fighting for vital interests of the various countries, that Roman law culture proved the only common language and the only undoubted measure of justice. We Romanists, for this reason had, per force, to become practitioners of jus gentium' (Ernst Rabel, 'On Comparative Research in Legal History and Modern Law' in Hans G Leser (ed), *Ernst Rabel – Gesammelte Aufsätze*, vol 3 (Mohr Siebeck 1967) 247, 254; Reinhard Zimmermann, '"In der Schule von Ludwig Mitteis" – Ernst Rabels rechtshistorische Ursprünge' (2001) 65 RabelsZ 1, 20). And in 1927 he reflects on the experience gathered in his judicial practice. He points to the 'conspicuous and significant comparative law reasoning that the international judge has to carry out nowadays in almost every case' (Ernst Rabel, 'Rechtsvergleichung und internationale Rechtsprechung' in Hans G Leser (ed), *Ernst Rabel – Gesammelte Aufsätze*, vol 2 (Mohr Siebeck 1965) 1, 7). The obligation of the international tribunals to take some kind of decision and the gaps existing in international law produce the need to have recourse, under art 38 of the PCIJ Statute (Statute of the Permanent Court of International Justice of 16 December 1920, 6 LNTS 380), to the 'general principles recognised by civilised nations'; their ascertainment requires 'an application of comparative law of the most exquisite kind' (Ernst Rabel, 'Rechtsvergleichung und internationale Rechtsprechung' in Hans G Leser (ed), *Ernst Rabel – Gesammelte Aufsätze*, vol 2 (Mohr Siebeck 1965) 1, 15, 17).

Uniform law arises from the identification of general principles by international tribunals, but in a more consistent and comprehensive way by means of legislative texts which, at the time of *Rabel*, were usually adopted the form of an international convention. Connecting to his early research in the law of sales, he devoted much of his time as a director of the Institute in Berlin to the comparative law of the sale of goods (→ Sale contracts and sale of goods). Long after *Rabel*'s death, these efforts, which will not be described here in further detail, led to one of the most successful international conventions in the field of uniform private law (→ CISG). An early draft of 1935 had already limited the scope of the project to cross-border sales, thereby connecting to the domain of private international law. But *Rabel* leaves no doubt that this is a regrettable limitation: 'If we succeed to convince lawyers and merchants of a country of the progress brought about by the new law, would they not find it even more reasonable that the old law should be abandoned entirely instead of remaining in force alongside the new one?' (Ernst Rabel, 'Der Entwurf eines einheitlichen Kaufgesetzes' in Hans G Leser (ed), *Ernst Rabel – Gesammelte Aufsätze*, vol 3 (Mohr Siebeck 1967) 522, 553 f). *Rabel*'s remarks leave little doubt that he considered the choice-of-law process as second best in comparison with uniform law.

3. From comparative law to private international law

But *Rabel* was both a realist and practice minded. He knew that differences between national legal systems were a reality of cross-border trade and could not be overcome by the dreams of uniform law. Nevertheless, his approach to private international law was somehow hesitant (Gerhard Kegel, 'Ernst Rabel – Werk und Person' (1990) 54 RabelsZ 1, 14). It is noteworthy that his comprehensive report on the research areas of the Institute published in 1937 explicitly refers to the assistance provided by *Wilhelm Wengler*, research associate of the Institute, in respect of the part on private international law, whereas *Rabel* drafted the first part on comparative law and foreign law apparently without such assistance (Ernst Rabel, 'Die Fachgebiete des

Kaiser-Wilhelm-Instituts für ausländisches und internationales Privatrecht (gegründet 1926)' in Hans G Leser (ed), *Ernst Rabel – Gesammelte Aufsätze*, vol 3 (Mohr Siebeck 1967) 180, 213).

Although *Rabel* did not devote much time to private international law during his Berlin years, he published his groundbreaking article on characterization in that period. Maybe the treatment of the subject was again primarily due to his wish to demonstrate the practical usefulness of comparative law, similar to his previous publications on international jurisprudence and general principles of law. But in respect of his methodology the article undoubtedly paves the way for the later *opus magnum* on the conflict of laws. *Rabel* identifies two objectives of characterization: according to the first, an issue covered by a conflict rule must receive an answer from the legal order designated by that conflict rule, and the second requires that conflict rules must be susceptible of covering all legal phenomena of the world, even those which are inexistent in the law of the forum (Ernst Rabel, 'Das Problem der Qualifikation' (1931) 5 RabelsZ 241, 263). In respect of characterization, he consequently postulates the 'important task of assigning the legal phenomena to conflict rules on the basis of comparative law' (Ernst Rabel, 'Das Problem der Qualifikation' (1931) 5 RabelsZ 241, 268). The common identification of concepts used in conflict rules with the same concepts employed in other parts of the same legal system, ie the characterization *lege fori* is rejected. While *Rabel* considers private international law as a part of national law, he nevertheless points to the basic task of the discipline, which is 'to serve the co-existence of the peoples in the world and the international interests of a state, its society and its national economy. The territorial boundaries of legal systems must be established by national sources of law and, in spite of domestic interests, in *growing conformity* (*Rabel's* emphasis). 'This requires taking account of the substantive foreign law, but also a comparative ascertainment of conflict rules. (Ernst Rabel, 'Die Fachgebiete des Kaiser-Wilhelm-Instituts für ausländisches und internationales Privatrecht (gegründet 1926)' in Hans G Leser (ed), *Ernst Rabel – Gesammelte Aufsätze*, vol 3 (Mohr Siebeck 1967) 224). Thus, the objective of → choice of law is not so much the territorial confinement of the laws of the forum state, it is rather and primarily intended to enable the co-existence of different societies and economies. It is viewed, not from inside a single legal system, but from above the various laws. Consequently, it is inseparable from comparative law, both in substance and in methodology.

These views have guided *Rabel's opus magnum* on the conflict of laws. The four volumes deal with the specific parts of private law, ie with family law, succession, property, contracts, etc. Contrary to the typical treatment of private international law (and of so many other areas of the law) by German authors, they do not sort out the general issues such as incidental questions (→ Incidental (preliminary) question), characterization (→ Classification (characterization)) or → *renvoi* in a separate general part; only short sections placed at the beginning and at the end of the treatise are dedicated to general aspects such as the structure of the conflict rule or the application of foreign law. The treatment of the subjects often starts with a short survey over the differences in substantive law; its comparative character also results from the consideration of the conflict rules of different jurisdictions. While the treatise thus espouses a comparative approach to the various topics, it focuses on what may be called model solutions of the individual issues. Consequently, it does not contain a comprehensive account of any single national system of private international law. As compared with other comparative books on the conflict of laws which prefer the method of the national reports on some legal systems, *Rabel's* treatise has therefore been held to be 'less valuable as a reference book' (Ole Lando, 'Ernst Rabel (1874–1955)' in Stefan Grundmann and others (eds) *Festschrift 200 Jahre Juristische Fakultät der Humboldt-Universität zu Berlin* (De Gruyter 2010) 605, 621). On the other hand, due to the very comprehensive treatment of the discipline, the treatise has been praised as the culmination and apogee of private international law in the 20th century (Gerhard Kegel, 'Ernst Rabel – Werk und Person' (1990) 54 RabelsZ 1, 17). Both assessments contain accurate descriptions of different aspects: the first as relates to the practical usefulness, the second in respect of the depth of the scholarly reflection.

III. *Rabel's* influence on private international law

Rabel's ambitious research programme has had a clearly perceptible impact on the discipline of private international law, both in the short run and in the long run. This impact primarily concerns the methodology of legal reasoning. 'In Germany, the country of dogmatism, *Rabel* made it a virtue to be undogmatic' (Ole Lando, 'Ernst Rabel (1874–1955)' in Stefan Grundmann and others (eds) *Festschrift 200 Jahre Juristische Fakultät der Humboldt-Universität zu Berlin* (De Gruyter 2010) 605, 612). At a time when aprioristic thinking was very common among German conflict law professors, he advocated what may be called a German variant of legal realism, namely a close look at jurisprudence and in particular at the issues arising in legal practice as well as the solutions and arguments made by the courts. According to *Rabel*, 'a statute without the related case law is like a skeleton without muscles' (Ernst Rabel, 'Aufgabe und Notwendigkeit der Rechtsvergleichung' in Hans G Leser (ed), *Ernst Rabel – Gesammelte Aufsätze*, vol 3 (Mohr Siebeck 1967) 4). In respect of private international law in particular, he favoured the 'inductive method that would help to draft an appropriate network of conflict rules' (Ernst Rabel, 'Die Fachgebiete des Kaiser-Wilhelm-Instituts für ausländisches und internationales Privatrecht (gegründet 1926)' in Hans G Leser (ed), *Ernst Rabel – Gesammelte Aufsätze*, vol 3 (Mohr Siebeck 1967) 224). In line with such postulates, he initiated a systematic collection of the German case-law on private international law once he had the means to do so at the Kaiser-Wilhelm-Institut; the annual volumes of *Die deutsche Rechtsprechung auf dem Gebiet des internationalen Privatrechts* have been published for over 90 years and still provide an almost complete coverage of German case-law. The lengthy commentaries which discuss statutes article by article – and which are characteristic of German legal culture – equally exist for private international law codified in the Introductory Act to the German Civil Code (*Einführungsgesetz zum Bürgerlichen Gesetzbuche* of 21 September 1994, BGBl. I 2494, as amended); they give evidence of the great attention which the case-law receives in scholarly legal writings at present.

Rabel's comparative approach to private international law has likewise had a clearly perceptible impact both in an institutional sense in Germany and in an academic sense worldwide. It is true that courts will rarely undertake the comparative characterization advocated by *Rabel*; they simply do not have the means required for that. But when it comes to academic disputes on the classification of a given legal phenomenon unknown to the *lex fori*, scholarly writing will often explore the role of that phenomenon in its legal system of origin and compare its functions with those known to the law of the forum state. This approach is of course much easier to handle for international tribunals than for a domestic court. It is therefore unsurprising that the → Court of Justice of the European Union has in fact espoused and used *Rabel*'s method (Ole Lando, 'Ernst Rabel (1874–1955)' in Stefan Grundmann and others (eds) *Festschrift 200 Jahre Juristische Fakultät der Humboldt-Universität zu Berlin* (De Gruyter 2010) 605, 609): While in the early days the conclusions of the Advocates General contained many comparative references to the national laws of the Member States, the Court has gradually moved from a comparative to an autonomous interpretation of EU law (→ Interpretation, autonomous).

Moreover, the comparative approach has left many traces in legal scholarship. Large treatises of private international law take account of the conflict rules of foreign nations. The progressive codification of private international law that has taken place in dozens of countries over the last decades has often been prepared by legal scholars who commonly make use of comparative investigations. The most monumental piece of evidence of the search for model solutions is the International Encyclopedia of Comparative Law (IECL), which is intended to cover all areas of private law; the two half-bindings of Volume 3 on private international law are the most comprehensive treatment of our discipline, inspired by *Rabel*'s methodological ideas. In 1948, *Zweigert* referred to these ideas as foundational for a new approach to the conflict of laws. After the aprioristic and the positivistic schools, he called this new approach the 'third school of private international law' (Konrad Zweigert, 'Die dritte Schule im internationalen Privatrecht' in Hans-Peter Ipsen (ed), *Festschrift für Leo Raape* (Rechts- und Staatswissenschaftlicher Verlag 1948) 35, 40 f). Taking into account this impressive shift in legal scholarship, the designation of the new current of legal thinking as a 'school' was not exaggerated.

JÜRGEN BASEDOW

Rabel's ideas have also been influential in respect of the institutional structure of comparative legal research in Germany and some neighbouring countries. The scholarly interest in comparative law initially arose in diverse areas: scholars specializing in areas such as maritime law, copyright law or, later on, commercial law, civil law or criminal law tried to improve their understanding of the discipline by enquiries into the law of foreign countries in their respective fields. When *Rabel* established the Munich Institute which was exclusively dedicated to comparative law, this still appears to have been the general background. After the First World War, however, the need of legal practitioners for information on foreign law and the application of foreign law in the courts became of paramount importance, and it emerged that the discipline of private international law was rather undeveloped. The intellectual merger of comparative law and international private law advocated by *Rabel* led to the institutional merger of both disciplines in the form of the Kaiser-Wilhelm-Institut for Foreign Private Law and Private international law and in the many chairs in German universities which are dedicated to education and research in comparative law and private international law. This combination is rather infrequent in other countries.

As to the substance of *Rabel*'s views on private international law, one could equally trace some modern trends of legal development to his writings. But both the progressive recognition of party autonomy as well as the gradual replacement of the nationality principle by habitual residence as the primary connecting factor for personal status have been 'in the air' anyway. In this respect, *Rabel* was perhaps less a preacher and missionary than the messenger of coming changes.

JÜRGEN BASEDOW

Literature

Ulrich Drobnig, 'Die Geburt der modernen Rechtsvergleichung – Zum 50. Todestag von Ernst Rabel' [2005] ZEuP 821; Gerhard Kegel, 'Ernst Rabel – Werk und Person' (1990) 54 RabelsZ 1; Rolf-Ulrich Kunze, *Ernst Rabel und das Kaiser-Wilhelm-Institut für ausländisches und internationales Privatrecht 1926– 1945* (Wallstein 2004); Ole Lando, 'Ernst Rabel (1874–1955)' in Stefan Grundmann and others (eds), *Festschrift 200 Jahre Juristische Fakultät der Humboldt-Universität zu Berlin* (De Gruyter 2010) 605; Hans G Leser (ed), *Ernst Rabel – Gesammelte Aufsätze*, vols 2 and 3 (Mohr Siebeck 1965 and 1967); Ernst Rabel, *Die Haftung des Verkäufers wegen Mangels im Rechte* (Veit 1902); Ernst Rabel, 'Das Problem der Qualifikation' (1931) 5 RabelsZ 241; Ernst Rabel, *Das Recht des Warenkaufs* (de Gruyter 1936 and 1958); Ernst Rabel, 'Vorträge – Unprinted Lectures' (1986) 50 RabelsZ 282; Jürgen Thieme, 'Ernst Rabel (1874–1955) – Schriften aus dem Nachlaß. Einführung' (1986) 50 RabelsZ 251; Reinhard Zimmermann, '"In der Schule von Ludwig Mitteis" – Ernst Rabels rechtshistorische Ursprünge' (2001) 65 RabelsZ 1; Konrad Zweigert, 'Die dritte Schule im Internationalen Privatrecht' in Hans Peter Ipsen (ed), Festschrift für Leo Raape (Rechts- und Staatswissenschaftlicher Verlag 1948) 35.

Reciprocity

I. Concept and origin

'Reciprocity' – a basic means of influencing the behaviour of other actors – is a fundamental element of human interaction. Conduct in society is widely motivated by the expectation, be it communicated or tacit, that another member of society will react in an equivalent manner. Nevertheless, within legal relations between individuals, reciprocity has lost its force as the primary mechanism to affect the conduct of others. Instead, behaviour is significantly determined by state enforced legal rules, in particular by criminal and private law. However, apart from the use of force, reciprocity remains a powerful tool of conduct control in areas where relations are not comprehensively regulated or the relevant rules are not enforced by independent institutions. As this is still the case in the relations between sovereign states, it is inevitable that the legal aspects of reciprocity are mainly discussed in the area of public international law (→ Public international law and private international law).

Private international law primarily deals with the relations between individuals in cross-border situations, so that little room should be left for reciprocity. However, at the same time private international law also touches at least indirectly upon the relations of the states connected with a case at issue, whose respective legal spheres have to be delineated and coordinated. In consequence, reciprocity remains relevant to the extent a certain state behaviour in matters of private international law not only administers private justice between individuals but also, as an indirect response, concerns the relationship between the states involved. At least at first sight, the role of reciprocity is also demonstrated by the fact that the rules of private international law are to a considerable extent the object of international conventions, instruments which are regarded from a public international law perspective as institutions where 'reciprocity produces its most profound effects' (Bruno Simma, 'Reciprocity' in *Max Planck Encyclopedia of Public International Law* (OUP 2008) para 4, regarding treaties). Hence, focussing on the intra-state perspective, each private international law rule in an international instrument is potentially governed by the idea of reciprocity, at least as far as it deviates from the national private international law of the participating states. Even unilaterally in their national private international laws, states partly require reciprocity for the administration of private justice in cross-border cases, particularly regarding the recognition and enforcement of foreign judgments (see V. below).

The drawbacks of reciprocity in private international law are evident. Reciprocity as a guideline for administrating private justice in cross-border cases is both unjust and ineffective. Reciprocity allows the interstate relations to impact on private rights and their realization. Private interests are subjected to state interests. Furthermore, requiring reciprocity by other states in advance, ie only acting if the other actor has already counter-acted, is not conducive to international cooperation. Game theory (see in particular, Robert Axelrod, *The Evolution of Cooperation* (Basic Books 1984))), which can be used as a model to analyse the interaction between states (see eg Thomas Pfeiffer, 'Kooperative Reziprozität' (1991) 55 RabelsZ 734, 742; → Game theory and private international law), demonstrates that a 'tit for tat' strategy is far more promising than demanding reciprocity in advance. It is most advantageous for each player to assume cooperative behaviour on the part of the other players. The optimum strategy is to be cooperative and only react with uncooperative behaviour if the other player fails to cooperate. Accordingly, it is only to be expected that reciprocity requirements have not increased international cooperation in private international law (see in particular V. below).

II. Application of foreign law

Regarding the application of foreign law (→ Foreign law, application and ascertainment), reciprocity does not play a major role. A reciprocity rule would require the judge to consider a kind of indirect *renvoi* before applying foreign law. A court could only apply a foreign *lex causae* if the foreign conflict rules (of the *lex causae*) pointed in a similar situation to the *lex fori* (see Jürgen Basedow, 'Gegenseitigkeit im Kollisionsrecht' in Katharina Hilbig-Lugani and others (eds), *Festschrift für Dagmar Coester-Waltjen* (Gieseking, 2015, 335, 336 *et seq*))). Such a – rather complex – reciprocity requirement is lacking in most private international laws. Only rarely is reciprocity mentioned in the context of the choice-of-law process. A notable exception, where the reciprocity idea becomes visible at least rudimentarily, is art 1089(1) of the General Part of the Civil Code of the Republic of Kazakhstan (introduced by the Enactment of the Supreme Council of the Republic of Kazakhstan, No 269-XIII, 27 December 1994, as amended), where special provisions are reserved which provide that foreign law is only applied on the basis of mutuality.

The lack of reciprocity requirements regarding the application of foreign law is rather easy to explain. The application of foreign law is not rooted in the relationship between the forum state and the state whose law is to be applied, and in particular, such application is not a matter of → comity towards other states. Rather, at least in the *Savignyan* tradition, foreign law is applied in order to implement best the private interests of the individuals concerned, for example their party autonomy or their expectation that a law closely connected to the parties governs their relations. The fact that in almost no system is the application of foreign law subject to reciprocity is also an indication that state interests probably play a significantly smaller role in the choice-of-law process than some would claim, in particular proponents of the governmental interest theory (as Brainerd Currie, 'Notes on Methods and Objectives in the Conflict of Laws' (1959) Duke L.J. 171).

The question remains whether the application of foreign law based on international conventions or other supranational instruments can be explained by reciprocity. In the past some of the conventions drafted by the → Hague Conference on Private International Law restricted the duty to apply foreign law to the law of other contracting states, see for example art 8(2) of the Hague Convention of 12 June 1902 relating to the settlement of the conflict of the laws concerning marriage, and art 9(2) of the Convention of 12 June 1902 relating to the settlement of the conflict of laws and jurisdictions concerning divorce and separation. The modern Hague Conventions, however, at least since the Hague Testamentary Dispositions Convention (Hague Convention of 5 October 1961 on the conflicts of laws relating to the form of testamentary dispositions, 510 UNTS 175) (see art 6), generally contain universal conflict rules which apply even if they refer to the law of a non-contracting state. This universal application excludes any notion of reciprocity. Also the private international law of the EU designs its conflict rules as *loi uniforme*, see art 2 of the Rome I Regulation (Regulation (EC) No 593/2008 of the European Parliament and of the Council of 17 June 2008 on the law applicable to contractual obligations (Rome I), [2008] OJ L 177/6; → Rome Convention and Rome I Regulation (contractual obligations)), art 3 of the → Rome II Regulation (non-contractual obligations) (Regulation (EC) No 864/2007 of the European Parliament and of the Council of 11 July 2007 on the law applicable to non-contractual obligations (Rome II), [2007] OJ L 199/40), art 4 of the → Rome III Regulation (divorce) (Council Regulation (EU) No 1259/2010 of 20 December 2010 implementing enhanced cooperation in the area of the law applicable to divorce and legal separation, [2010] OJ L 343/10), and art 20 of the Succession Regulation (Regulation (EU) No 650/2012 of the European Parliament and of the Council of 4 July 2012 on jurisdiction, applicable law, recognition and enforcement of decisions and acceptance and enforcement of authentic instruments in matters of succession and on the creation of a European Certificate of Succession, [2012] OJ L 201/107; → Rome IV Regulation (succession)). Hence, the existence of international instruments obliging states to apply foreign law cannot be characterized as an expression of reciprocity regarding the application of foreign law. Rather the harmonization of the conflict rules as such is the main purpose, in order to protect the private interests of individuals by safeguarding a harmony of decision also with respect to third states. States mutually bind each other to apply a certain law – be it foreign or not – in order to guarantee that the rights and duties of private parties are within the participating states subject to the same substantive law. Consequently, only the duty to safeguard this harmony of decision can be the object of reciprocity, but not a duty to apply foreign law.

Exceptions of the *loi uniforme* approach in international instruments are rare but they still exist. For example, the private international law conventions within the Commonwealth of Independent States (→ Commonwealth of Independent States and private international law) adopted in the 1990s, in principle merely establish a duty to apply the law of one of the Member States, see eg art 11 of the Kiev Agreement of 20 March 1992 concerning the procedure for resolution of disputes related to conducting an economic activity. However, also the modern Hague Conventions contain exceptions restricting the duty to apply foreign law to the laws of contracting states. A rather surprising example is the Hague Trust Convention (Hague Convention of 1 July 1985 on the Law Applicable to Trusts and on their Recognition, 1664 UNTS 311). Article 21 of the Convention allows the contracting states to refuse the recognition of foreign → trusts the validity of which is not governed by the law of a contracting state. This restriction relates to the application of foreign law, whereby the 'recognition' of trusts under the Hague Trust Convention obliges the contracting states to award certain minimum effects to a trust according to its applicable law, see art 11 *et seq* of the Convention.

The application of foreign law (→ Foreign law, application and ascertainment) does not touch the interests of the states involved as far as their private law is concerned. The situation might be different when it comes to the enforcement of public interests of foreign states, for example, when the application of foreign public law is in question. In that context, the courts – following the universally accepted revenue rule – normally deny the application of foreign criminal, tax and other public law, in part explicitly by reference to the lack of reciprocity in that area (see eg the reasoning in *Her Majesty the Queen in Right of the Province of British Columbia v Gilbertson*, 597 F.2d 1161 (9th Cir 1979)). In principle, private international law does not address the application of foreign public law. Nevertheless, also in the context of private international law, the application of foreign law can enforce the public interests of other states in certain situations, in particular regarding the application of → overriding mandatory provisions. The application of such provisions by definition lies in the interest of the state because they are 'safeguarding its public interests, such as its political, social or economic organisation' (see the definition in art 9(1) Rome I Regulation). Accordingly, it is natural that two of the fathers of the doctrine that overriding mandatory provisions have to be recognized by other states argue in part on the basis of reciprocity, stating that foreign public interests are enforced in the expectation that other states also enforce our public interests (see Wilhelm Wengler, 'Die Anknüpfung zwingenden Schuldrechts im internationalen Privatrecht' (1941) 54 ZVglRWiss 168, 181 *et seq*; Konrad Zweigert, 'Nichterfüllung auf Grund ausländischer Leistungsverbote' (1942) 14 RabelsZ 283, 290 *et seq*). Therefore, reciprocity might be one factor when deciding on the application of foreign internationally mandatory provisions, for example within the discretion granted by art 9(3) Rome I Regulation.

III. Respecting and enforcing foreign jurisdiction

Whereas the idea of reciprocity is alien to the conflict of laws, it can still be traced in international procedural law. This first relates to the jurisdiction of foreign states, which is often respected by other states to a greater extent in situations where reciprocity is guaranteed, in particular by international instruments. One example concerns exorbitant jurisdictions. The states are often only willing to waive an exorbitant jurisdiction in favour of the jurisdiction of other states if those other states are prepared to respond reciprocally, see within the EU art 5(2) Brussels I Regulation (recast) (Regulation (EU) No 1215/2012 of the European Parliament and of the Council of 12 December 2012 on jurisdiction and the recognition and enforcement of judgments in civil and commercial matters (recast), [2012] OJ L 351/1; → Brussels I (Convention and Regulation)), which clarifies that the Member States may not engage exorbitant heads of jurisdictions regarding defendants domiciled within the EU. Also the notion that certain states, which are bound by common jurisdictional rules, will mutually trust each other in the application of those provisions can be regarded as an expression of reciprocity. The states normally only relinquish the right to refuse a foreign jurisdiction if it is safeguarded that their jurisdiction is similarly respected. Hence, it is consistent that the ECJ bases the prohibition of anti-suit injunctions (→ Anti-suit injunctions) within the EU or the duty to recognize a foreign *lis pendens* (even if in contradiction with an express choice of court agreement; → *Lis alibi pendens*) on the idea of mutual trust, and hence on reciprocity between the Member States (see ECJ, Case C-159/02 *Gregory Paul Turner v Felix Fareed Ismail Grovit, Harada Ltd and Changepoint SA* [2004] ECR I-3565 and ECJ, Case C-116/02 *Erich Gasser GmbH v MISAT Srl* [2003] ECR I-14693).

On the basis of reciprocity, states are even willing to enforce foreign jurisdiction, as happens within the Hague Child Abduction Convention (Hague Convention of 25 October 1980 on the civil aspects of international child abduction, 1343 UNTS 89). This Convention obliges the contracting states to return children swiftly to the state of origin if wrongfully removed or retained abroad. This effective mechanism is only indirectly aimed at protecting private interests, in particular the best interests of the child. The principal objective of the Hague Child Abduction Convention is to protect the jurisdiction of the state of origin on the basis of the child's presence in that jurisdiction, by restoring the status quo *ante* even if the return order is not in the child's best interest, see art 13(b) of the Convention *e contrario*, which is even further restricted between the Member States of the EU by art 11(4) → Brussels IIa Regulation (Council Regulation (EC) No 2201/2003 of 27 November 2003 concerning jurisdiction and the recognition and enforcement of judgments in matrimonial matters and the matters of parental responsibility, repealing Regulation (EC) No 1347/2000, [2003] OJ L 338/1). Without reciprocity, most states would be unwilling to disregard private interests to such an extent in favour of the protection of a foreign state's jurisdiction.

IV. Equal treatment of foreigners in civil proceedings

A second area where in international procedural law the idea of reciprocity becomes visible concerns the rules on the position of foreigners in civil proceedings, one of the last resorts of the law relating to aliens in the area of private law (→ Aliens law (*Condition des étrangers, Fremdenrecht*)). In the meantime, almost all states open their courts to foreigners in order to enforce their private rights within their jurisdiction. Provisions have been repealed like the old art 65(1)(c) Portuguese Code of Civil Procedure (*Código do Processo Civil*, Decreto Lei No

44129), which provided that foreigners can only avail themselves of the jurisdiction of the Portuguese courts against Portuguese nationals if the state of the claimant's → nationality would also open its courts *mutatis mutandis*. Also discrimination of foreigners in civil proceedings regarding → legal aid or the duty to bail for legal costs have been abolished in many jurisdictions irrespective of any reciprocity regarding the position of the own nationals in foreign civil proceedings. The reason for this decline of reciprocity again lies in the fact that the states increasingly recognize that the protection of private interests should not depend on the relationship between the states involved, in particular if, as is the case regarding legal aid, the individual's human rights and access to justice are at stake.

V. Recognition and enforcement of foreign decisions and other forms of judicial cooperation

A third and final resort of reciprocity within private international law remains the judicial cooperation between states, which often depends on reciprocity. Reciprocity in this area is guaranteed in particular by conventions or other international instruments which oblige the participating states to cooperate mutually. Outside international instruments, judicial cooperation between states is often linked to reciprocity. For example, the German Code of Civil Procedure (*Zivilprozessordnung* in the version of 5 December 2005, BGBl. I 3202, as amended) in § 328(1) no 5 still expressly refuses recognition of foreign judgments if reciprocity is not guaranteed, at least regarding general → civil and commercial matters. However, the reciprocity requirement only partly applies to the recognition of decisions in family matters, see § 109(4) German Law on the Procedure in Family Matters (*Gesetz über das Verfahren in Familiensachen und in den Angelegenheiten der freiwilligen Gerichtsbarkeit* of 17 December 2008, BGBl. I 2586, as amended).

However, reciprocity regarding the recognition of foreign decisions appears to be no more than a last '*pièce de résistance*' (Jürgen Basedow, 'Gegenseitigkeit im Kollisionsrecht' in Katharina Hilbig-Lugani and others (eds), *Festschrift für Dagmar Coester-Waltjen* (Gieseking 2015 335, 348)). The number of jurisdictions which have abolished reciprocity requirements regarding the recognition of judgments is increasing.

Traditionally, some systems regarded the recognition and enforcement of foreign decisions solely as an enforcement of private rights based on the doctrine of obligation (see eg for England and Wales *Schibsby v Westenholz* [1870] LR 6 QB 155), leaving little scope for reciprocity. Furthermore, the protection of human rights (→ Human rights and private international law) could also force the states to rethink reciprocity as a precondition for the recognition and enforcement of decisions and other forms of legal assistance. In particular, the ECHR (European Convention of 4 November 1950 for the Protection of Human Rights and Fundamental Freedoms, 213 UNTS 221) could compel the contracting states to recognize foreign decisions without reciprocity requirement if the recognition is necessary to protect the parties' rights to fair a trial (see as to art 6 ECHR *Sholokhov against Armenia and Republic of Moldova* [2012] App No 40358/05 (ECtHR, 31 July 2012)). Finally, in particular regarding the recognition and enforcement of decisions, the experience of the last decades have been that reciprocity requirements do not influence the behaviour of other states towards international cooperation (see for example the recent study of John F Coyle, 'Rethinking Judgments Reciprocity' (2014) 92 N.C.L.Rev. 1109). However, it should be noted that the reciprocity idea is far from dead. In 2006, the American Law Institute proposed reintroducing the reciprocity requirement in a new Foreign Judgments Recognition and Enforcement Act – honouring 19th century case-law of the US Supreme Court (*Hilton v Guyot*, 159 US 113 (1895)). This case-law had not been adopted by state law, and hence, after *Erie*, also not by the federal courts. The ALI is relying on well-tried but unconvincing arguments when it states that the reciprocity requirement proposed should not 'make it more difficult to secure recognition and enforcement of foreign judgments, but rather to create an incentive to foreign countries to commit to recognition and enforcement of judgments rendered in the USA'.

ANATOL DUTTA

Literature

Jürgen Basedow, 'Gegenseitigkeit im Kollisionsrecht' in Katharina Hilbig-Lugani and others (eds), *Festschrift für Dagmar Coester-Waltjen* (Gieseking 2015) 335; Louisa Childs, 'Shaky Foundations: Criticism of Reciprocity and the Distinction Between Public and Private international law' (2005) 38 N.Y.U.J.Int'l Law & Pol. 221; John Coyle, 'Rethinking Judgments

Reciprocity' (2014) 92 N.C.L.Rev. 1109; Alfred Ernst, *Gegenseitigkeit und Vergeltung im internationalen Privatrecht* (Pfäffikon-Zürich 1950); Richard Hulbert, 'Some Thoughts on Judgments, Reciprocity, and the Seeming Paradox of International Commercial Arbitration' (2008) 29 U.Pa.J.Int'l L. 641; Paul Lagarde, 'La réciprocité en droit international privé' (1977) 154 Rec. des Cours 102; Arthur Lenhoff, 'Reciprocity: The Legal Aspect of a Perennial Idea' (1954–5) 49 Northwest.U.L.Rev. 619 and 752; Arthur Lenhoff, 'Reciprocity and the Law of Foreign Judgments: A Historical–Critical Analysis' (1956) 16 La.L.Rev. 465; Jean Paulin Niboyet, 'La notion de réciprocité dans les traités diplomatiques de droit international privé' (1935) 52 Rec. des Cours 253; Andreas Paulus, 'Reciprocity Revisited' in Ulrich Fastenrath and others (eds), *From Bilateralism to Community Interest: Essays in Honour of Bruno Simma* (OUP 2011) 113; Thomas Pfeiffer, 'Kooperative Reziprozität' (1991) 55 RabelsZ 734; Bruno Simma, 'Reciprocity' in *Max Planck Encyclopedia of Public International Law* (OUP 2008).

Recognition and enforcement of judgments (civil law)

I. Underlying ideas

The debate on the recognition and enforcement of foreign judgments revolves around two approaches. Some concentrate on the interests of the states involved while others place more emphasis on the interests of the private individuals whose rights and obligations are at stake. Though the vantage points of these approaches differ, their proponents often arrive at similar results. It seems undisputed that there is no obligation under international law to recognize and enforce foreign judgments. Only on the basis of a sovereign decision of the receiving state can judgments have any effects outside the jurisdiction where they originated. There is, however, broad consensus today that it is in the public interest as well as in the interests of the private parties involved that foreign judgments are, in principle, recognized and enforced. Followers of both approaches also agree that recognition and enforcement ought to be refused if they conflict with significant public or private interests (the strongest point of disagreement perhaps being whether recognition and enforcement should depend on → reciprocity). Nevertheless, national laws still often make it difficult to recognize and enforce foreign judgments outside the scope of EU legislative acts and international treaties.

1. Scope of application of national laws

In the EU, recognition and enforcement of judgments from other Member States is increasingly governed by EU law, as the gaps in the scope of application *ratione materiae* of EU instruments in this field are closing. The delineation of the geographical scope of application of EU law and national law is more straightforward in matters of recognition and enforcement than in the field of jurisdiction. EU law only applies to judgments originating from Member State courts, while recognition and enforcement of third-state judgments is governed by national law (or international treaty, as appropriate). In many jurisdictions, the prerequisites and procedures provided for under national law have been influenced by the Brussels I Regulation (Regulation (EC) No 44/2001 of 22 December 2000 on jurisdiction and the recognition and enforcement of judgments in civil and commercial matters, [2001] OJ L 12/1) (and, before that, the Brussels Convention (Brussels Convention of 27 September 1968 on jurisdiction and the enforcement of judgments in civil and commercial matters, [1972] OJ L 299/32, consolidated version, [1998] OJ C 27/1) (→ Brussels I (Convention and Regulation)), as well as other European legislative instruments in the field. Nevertheless, considerable differences between the EU regimes and the national regimes remain. This is at least partly because the principle of mutual trust permeating the EU system of free movement of judgments does not operate in the relationship with third states.

As EU law overrides national law, national rules on recognition and enforcement conflicting with EU law must be disapplied. In the relationship between international treaties and national law, national provisions that are more favourable to recognition and enforcement often take precedence over more restrictive treaty provisions. However, matters are somewhat different in the relationship between EU law and Member State law. Legislative acts enacted by the EU in this field are based on a balancing of party interests. They not only serve to protect the judgment creditor but also contain safeguards in favour of the judgment debtor. This delicate balance might be disturbed were one to give precedence to a more recognition-friendly national law. Outside the scope of application of EU law, however, recognition and enforcement of judgments from other EU Member States is still a matter of national law. It is not always easy to determine to what extent EU law leaves it to national law to decide whether certain acts should be recognized and enforced. In some cases, the EU legislature has sought to clarify matters. According to Recital (33) of the Brussels I Regulation (recast) (Regulation (EU) No 1215/2012 of the European Parliament and of the Council of 12 December 2012 on jurisdiction and the recognition and enforcement of judgments in civil and commercial matters (recast), [2012] OJ L 351/1; → Brussels I (Convention and Regulation)), the limits to the recognition and enforcement of → provisional measures issued *ex parte* that are provided for in the Regulation 'should not preclude the recognition and enforcement of such measures under national law'. However, in other fields where EU law does not provide for the recognition and enforcement of certain types of judicial act, it remains an open issue whether this is to be understood as a prohibition of the cross-border circulation of such acts or whether it remains for national law to determine recognition or enforcement issues. In particular, there is considerable uncertainty in this regard in certain family law matters (see Christoph Thole, 'Die Entwicklung der Anerkennung im autonomen Recht in Europa' in Burkhard Hess (ed), *Die Anerkennung im Internationalen Zivilprozessrecht – Europäisches Vollstreckungsrecht* (Gieseking 2014) 25, 29). There seems to be no general answer to this problem. It is a matter of interpreting each provision excluding certain types of acts from the free movement of judgments under EU law so as to determine whether national law may grant recognition and enforcement to such acts.

Most European states have entered into a significant number of bilateral and/or multilateral treaties on the recognition and enforcement of foreign judgments. These treaties serve to fulfil the requirement of reciprocity (where it still exists). Usually, they also modify the prerequisites for recognition and enforcement and the grounds for refusal. Bilateral agreements between EU Member States have been superseded by the Brussels I Regulation in its scope of application (→ Brussels I (Convention and Regulation)). However, they continue to apply in matters not covered by that Regulation or other EU legislative acts taking precedence. Multilateral treaties providing for the free movement of judgments exist, eg in the fields of maintenance, child custody (→ Guardianship, custody and parental responsibility) or transport law. According to art 71 Brussels I Regulation, conventions dealing with jurisdiction or the recognition and enforcement of judgments in specific matters continue to apply in principle. However, the ECJ has held that rules of such conventions only 'apply provided that they ... ensure, under conditions at least as favourable as those provided for by the regulation, the free movement of judgments in civil and commercial matters and mutual trust in the administration of justice in the European Union (*favor executionis*)' (ECJ Case C-533/08 *TNT Express Nederland BV v AXA Versicherung AG* [2010] ECR I-4107; see also ECJ Case C-452/12 *Nipponkoa Insurance Co (Europe) Ltd v Inter-Zuid Transport BV* [2014] OJ C 52/19).

2. *Mechanisms*

Today, recognition and enforcement of foreign judgments is largely a matter between the judgment creditor and the requested state. It is for the judgment creditor to apply to the requested state's authorities. Cross-border enforcement of judgments as a matter of judicial assistance at the request of a court from another jurisdiction has become largely obsolete, apart from the enforcement of → maintenance obligations and child custody decisions.

The enforcement procedure itself is in principle a purely domestic affair of the requested state (though cross-border elements may also be present in the enforcement proceedings → Debt recovery, cross-border). Foreign judgments are enforced in the requested state in the same way as domestic ones. Meanwhile, the effects of recognition, ie the procedural effects of a recognized foreign judgment (apart from its enforceability), are widely disputed. There are two basic schools of thought. One treats the foreign judgment as if it were a domestic one. The other argues in favour of accepting the effects it would have in its home jurisdiction. Often the two approaches are combined and foreign judgments are given the effects that they would have in their home jurisdiction, but only as far as these effects are also known in (or at least are not completely alien to) the legal system of the requested state. It is usually left to case-law and legal doctrine to determine which of the approaches should be followed (see Christoph Thole, 'Die Entwicklung der Anerkennung im autonomen Recht in Europa' in Burkhard Hess (ed), *Die Anerkennung im Internationalen Zivilprozessrecht – Europäisches Vollstreckungsrecht* (Gieseking 2014) 25, 52). In some jurisdictions, however, there are explicit provisions dealing with this issue. Thus, according to § 84b Austrian Act on the Enforcement of Judgments (Exekutionsordnung of 27 May 1896, Reichsgesetzblatt No 79/1896, as amended, henceforth Austrian EO), a foreign judgment is treated like a domestic one after being declared enforceable, but cannot exercise greater effects than it would in its home jurisdiction. At least for enforcement purposes, therefore, a 'cumulation doctrine' applies in Austria.

II. Prerequisites for recognition and enforcement

1. Judgments and other titles for enforcement

The rules on recognition and enforcement discussed in this article apply only to judgments in → civil and commercial matters and not to matters of public law. In general, only decisions issued in such matters by state courts are subject to the rules on recognition and enforcement of judgments. Private acts (such as decisions rendered by association tribunals or divorces effected by declaration of one or both of the spouses) are not usually considered as judgments for recognition and enforcement purposes. It is thought to be a matter of private international law whether and to what extent the effects of such acts are recognized (Haimo Schack, *Internationales Zivilverfahrensrecht* (6th edn, CH Beck 2014) nos 900–905). However, divorces pronounced by religious functionaries or ecclesiastical tribunals are widely recognized as judgments, at least subject to certain conditions (Gerhard Walter and Samuel Baumgartner, 'General Report – The Recognition and Enforcement of Judgments Outside the Scope of the Brussels and Lugano Conventions' in Gerhard Walter and Samuel Baumgartner (eds), *Recognition and Enforcement of Foreign Judgments Outside the Scope of the Brussels and Lugano Conventions* (Kluwer Law International 2000, Supplement 2005) 1, 16).

As regards settlements, approaches vary between jurisdictions. Under German law, settlements concluded before foreign courts are in principle neither recognized nor enforced (Herbert Roth, '§ 328' in Friedrich Stein and Martin Jonas (eds), *Kommentar zur Zivilprozessordnung*, vol 5 (23rd edn, Mohr Siebeck 2015) no 58). Instead, parties have to bring an action before a German (or foreign) court on the basis of the settlement to be awarded an enforceable judgment. However, as far as a settlement is also a contract between the parties under substantive law, its effects under the applicable substantive law remain relevant, regardless of whether the procedural effects are recognized (Peter Gottwald, '§ 328' in Wolfgang Krüger and Thomas Rauscher (eds), *Münchener Kommentar zur Zivilprozessordnung*, vol 1 (4th edn, CH Beck 2013) no 74). Other jurisdictions, such as → Austria or → Switzerland, at least provide for the enforcement of foreign court settlements. Under Swiss law, other procedural effects of settlements (eg a *res judicata* effect) are also recognized subject to the same prerequisites that apply to judgments (art 30 Swiss Private international law Act (Bundesgesetz über das Internationale Privatrecht of 18 December 1987, 1988 AS 1776, as amended, henceforth Swiss PILA)). Particular challenges are presented by collective settlements. At least where such settlements are subject to judicial scrutiny, many argue that the rules on judgments rather than those on settlements should govern their recognition and enforcement (Burkhard Hess, 'Die Anerkennung eines Class Action Settlement in Deutschland' [2000] JZ 373, 377).

Only judgments directly relating to the parties' substantive rights and obligations are undoubtedly subject to the rules on recognition and enforcement. Meanwhile, it is questionable whether procedural orders (such as dismissals for want of jurisdiction, evidence orders or anti-suit injunctions) fall within the scope of these rules. In the case of *Gothaer Allgemeine Versicherung v Samskip* (Case C-456/11 *Gothaer Allgemeine Versicherung AG and Others v Samskip GmbH* [2012] ECR I-719), the ECJ took the position that a dismissal for lack of jurisdiction must be recognized under the Brussels I Regulation. However, it is open to doubt whether this approach also fits cases governed by national law. As regards decisions ordering the recognition and enforcement of foreign judgments, most civil law jurisdictions seem to follow the principle that they cannot be subject to recognition and enforcement abroad (*exequatur sur exequatur ne vaut*).

There are specific regimes for the recognition and enforcement of arbitral awards. In some jurisdictions, an arbitral award is incorporated in a judgment if the court grants leave for enforcing the award (merger doctrine). In Germany, the German Federal Court of Justice (*Bundesgerichtshof*) used to allow for the recognition and enforcement of such judgments (while still permitting the creditor to rely on the arbitral award instead). Meanwhile, however, the *Bundesgerichtshof* has abandoned its former position and has decided that in such cases, only the arbitral award itself can be recognized and enforced, and that accordingly only the rules on the recognition and enforcement of arbitral awards apply (German Federal Court of Justice (BGH), 2 July 2009 [2009] NJW 2826).

The rules on recognition and enforcement often require that the foreign judgment be final in order to qualify for recognition and enforcement. In many civil law jurisdictions, this has been understood as meaning that the judgment must have become *res judicata* before it can be recognized and enforced abroad. Besides cases where the judgment, though already enforceable in the country of origin, is still subject to review by a higher court, this can especially compromise the recognition and enforcement of provisional measures. However, there seems to be a tendency to take a more liberal stance in this regard and to only require that the judgment has become enforceable in the country of origin and (as regards recognition) that it already has effects that can be subject to recognition.

In principle, the rules on recognition and enforcement only relate to the procedural effects of judgments (such as enforceability or the *res judicata* effect). Where judgments have substantive effects (such as the immediate modification of rights or legal relationships) or where the provisions of substantive law expressly or impliedly refer to judgments, it is less clear which rules apply in cross-border cases. Some authors argue that the applicable substantive law should decide whether substantive effects of foreign judgments should be recognized or taken into consideration. Others tend to refer to the rules on recognition of the *lex fori* in all cases where the effects of foreign judgments are at stake. Some authors combine both approaches. All in all, the legal and doctrinal development in this field still seems unfinished.

2. Jurisdiction of the court of origin

One of the main differences between EU law and national rules on recognition and enforcement is that national rules generally provide for a review of the jurisdiction of the court of origin. Outside the scope of application of EU law and in particular in relation to third states, the principle of mutual trust that prohibits such a review under EU law does not apply. Nor is there a common set of jurisdiction rules to compensate for the lack of a review of jurisdiction at the recognition and enforcement stage.

In some jurisdictions, such as Germany (§ 328(1) no 1 German Code of Civil Procedure (Zivilprozessordnung of 5 December 2005, BGBl. I 3202, as amended, henceforth German CCP)) and Austria (§ 80(1) Austrian EO), the national rules on jurisdiction are 'mirrored' at the enforcement stage, ie the court of the state of enforcement examines whether the court of origin would have had jurisdiction under the law of the requested state ('mirror principle', 'Spiegelbildprinzip'). Italy follows, in principle, a similar system. Apparently, however, the scrutiny is less strict than in → Germany and → Austria, as the court only examines whether the foreign court's jurisdiction is compatible with the principles of the Italian law of jurisdiction (art 64(1)(a) Italian Private international law Act (Riforma del Sistema italiano di diritto internazionale private, Act No 218 of 31 May 1995 in Gazz.Uff, Supplemento Ordinario No 128 of 3 June1995, as amended, henceforth Italian PILA); Michele Lupoi, 'Recognition and Enforcement of Judgments Outside the Scope of Application of the Brussels and Lugano Conventions: Italy' in Gerhard Walter and Samuel Baumgartner (eds), *Recognition and Enforcement of Foreign Judgments Outside the Scope of the Brussels and Lugano Conventions* (Kluwer Law International 2000, Supplement 2005) 347, 355). In Germany, the mirror principle has been mitigated to a certain extent in family law matters (see § 109(2) and (3) German Act on Proceedings in Family Matters and in Matters of Non-contentious Jurisdiction (Gesetz über das Verfahren in Familiensachen und in den Angelegenheiten der freiwilligen Gerichtsbarkeit of 17 December 2008, BGBl. I 2586, as amended, henceforth FamFG)). Austrian law retains the mirror principle in these matters (§§ 91a(2) no 4, § 97(2) no 4, § 113(1) no 4, § 131b(4) no 4 Austrian Non-contentious Proceedings Act (Außerstreitgesetz of 13 December 2003, BGBl. I No 111/2003, as amended, henceforth Außerstreitgesetz)).

Where the mirror principle applies, the requested state's national rules on jurisdiction (and not, for example, those of the Brussels I Regulation) are generally considered to be the basis for examining the jurisdiction of the court of the state of origin. A jurisdiction rule that would be considered exorbitant under EU law may thus be a basis for the recognition and enforcement of a third-state judgment (Peter Gottwald, '§ 328' in Wolfgang Krüger and Thomas Rauscher (eds), *Münchener Kommentar zur Zivilprozessordnung,* vol 1 (4th edn, CH Beck 2013) no 88). However, some authors argue in favour of at least partially mirroring the Brussels I Regulation in such cases (see eg Christoph Kern, 'Anerkennungsrechtliches Spiegelbildprinzip und europäische Zuständigkeit' (2007) 120 ZZP 31–71).

In other jurisdictions, there is a separate set of rules for the examination of the jurisdiction of the court of origin. This is the case, for example, in → Switzerland, where the Private international law Act confers jurisdiction on the Swiss courts in a considerably more generous manner than it is willing to accept the jurisdiction of foreign courts. In particular, foreign judgments against Swiss residents are generally not recognized and enforced unless the Swiss resident voluntarily submitted to the foreign court's jurisdiction.

French case-law does not rely on a fixed set of rules when reviewing the foreign court's jurisdiction. Instead, French courts examine whether there is a characteristic link between the dispute and the state of origin (Cass. 1e civ., *Simitch* [1985] Rev.crit.DIP 369). In addition, they check whether the court of origin unduly interfered with the jurisdiction of French courts. Formerly, this used to be quite a serious obstacle in practice. Recognition and enforcement was refused in cases where the French courts would have had jurisdiction under art 14 or 15 French Civil Code (Code Civil of 21 March 1804, henceforth French CC) (ie because one of the parties was a French citizen) unless it was found that the French party had waived their application (Gilles Cuniberti, 'The Liberalization of the French Law of Foreign Judgments' (2007) 56 ICLQ 931, 934–935). However, in the *Prieur* case (Cass. 1e civ. 23 May 2006, 04-12.777), the *Cour de cassation* modified its position and decided that art 15 French CC no longer stands in the way of recognizing and enforcing a foreign judgment.

Bilateral conventions usually contain a list of grounds for jurisdiction that are accepted for the purposes of recognition and enforcement. Other conventions instead provide for a so-called 'black list', enumerating the cases where recognition and enforcement may be refused for lack of jurisdiction of the court of origin.

3. Reciprocity

In the civil law world, the traditional approach used to be to require → reciprocity as a prerequisite for recognition and enforcement (Friedrich Juenger, 'The Recognition of Money Judgments in Civil and Commercial Matters' (1988) 36 Am.J.Comp.L. 1, 7–8). This requirement has gradually been eroded in many jurisdictions in recent years. Nevertheless, a number of civil law jurisdictions still retain it at least for certain types of cases.

Some jurisdictions are particularly restrictive, only recognizing and enforcing foreign judgments on the basis of bilateral or multilateral agreements or formal declarations. This is the case in → Austria (§ 79(2) Austrian EO), → Denmark and → Finland (Arnaud Nuyts, *Study on Residual Jurisdiction – General Report. Review of the Member States' Rules Concerning the 'Residual Jurisdiction' of their Courts in Civil and Commercial Matters Pursuant to the Brussels I and II Regulations* (2007), available at <ec.europa.eu/civiljustice/news/docs/study_residual_jurisdiction_en.pdf>, no 88). Article 431 Dutch Code of Civil Procedure (Wetboek van Burgerlijke Rechtsvordering, available at <http://wetten.overheid.nl>) contains a similar rule. Apparently, however, Dutch courts treat actions upon foreign judgments generously (Rene Verschuur, 'Recognition and Enforcement of Foreign Judgments in the Netherlands' in Gerhard Walter and Samuel Baumgartner (eds), *Recognition and Enforcement of Foreign Judgments outside the Scope of the Brussels and Lugano Conventions* (Kluwer Law International 2000, Supplement 2005) 403, 409). The Swedish courts seem to follow a similar approach (Friedrich Juenger, 'The Recognition of Money Judgments in Civil and Commercial Matters' (1988) 36 Am.J.Comp.L. 1, 27). → Germany also retains the reciprocity requirement (§ 328(1) no 5 German CCP), with the exception of judgments concerning non-pecuniary claims in matters where German courts lack jurisdiction (§ 328(2) German CCP). Formal reciprocity on the basis of a treaty or declaration is not required, and German courts appear to be rather generous in assuming reciprocity. Thus, this requirement seems to be a less serious obstacle for recognition and enforcement in Germany than, for example, in Austria. In some family law matters, the reciprocity requirement is dispensed with both in Germany (see § 109(1) and (4)

FamFG) and in Austria (see §§ 91, 97, 113, 131b Außerstreitgesetz). The same is the case with regard to judgments opening insolvency proceedings (§ 343 of the German Insolvency Statute (Insolvenzordnung of 5 October 1994, BGBl. I S. 2866, as amended), and § 240 of the Austrian Insolvency Statute (Bundesgesetz über das Insolvenzverfahren of 1 January 1915, RGBl. No 337/1914, as amended)).

A number of recent codifications in various jurisdictions have entirely done away with the requirement of reciprocity. Thus, the Swiss PILA contains no such requirement (with the exception, however, of judgments opening insolvency proceedings: art 166(1)(c)). The Italian PILA and several recent Eastern European codifications (see Christa Jessel-Holst, 'Zum Gesetzbuch über internationales Privatrecht der Republik Mazedonien' [2008] IPRax 154, 157) also dispense with the requirement of reciprocity.

III. Grounds for refusal of recognition and enforcement

Recognition and enforcement is generally refused where it would be irreconcilable with certain fundamental values underlying the law of the requested state. Usually, the rules on recognition and enforcement contain a public policy exception, as well as certain additional grounds for refusal. At least some of these are specific manifestations of the public policy exception. The grounds for refusal are often understood as safeguards against impairments of the requested state's sovereignty. Increasingly, however, their function is perceived to be to protect fundamental rights and other important interests of the parties to the procedure. On the whole, there has been a tendency in recent years to reduce barriers against the recognition and enforcement of foreign judgments.

1. Substantive public policy

The review of the foreign judgment as to its substance (*révision au fond*) by the court of the requested state has generally been abandoned (Friedrich Juenger, 'The Recognition of Money Judgments in Civil and Commercial Matters' (1988) 36 Am.J.Comp.L. 1, 28–29). Nevertheless, a degree of scrutiny of the content of foreign judgments remains in the form of the substantive public policy exception. On the basis of this exception, recognition and enforcement is refused if granting it would violate the fundamental principles of the requested state's law. From today's perspective, violations of human rights (→ Human rights and private international law) perhaps play the most important role in this respect.

When examining the compatibility with the requested state's → public policy (*ordre public*), courts tend to take into account how strongly the case is connected to the requested state – the closer the connection, the stricter the examination. In general, the standards applied at the stage of recognition and enforcement are less strict than they would be if it were for the requested state's courts themselves to decide the case as to its substance and to examine whether the applicable law is compatible with that state's public policy. This is referred to as the *effet atténué* (mitigated effect) of public policy at the enforcement stage. However, it is open to doubt whether such mitigation is appropriate in cases of human rights violations.

In particular, recognition and enforcement may be refused on the basis of the substantive public policy exception if obeying the order contained in the judgment would constitute a punishable offence under the law of the requested state. Furthermore, courts in many civil law jurisdictions tend to consider orders imposing excessive punitive → damages as violations of their substantive public policy (see eg for Germany: Federal Court of Justice (BGH), 4 June 1992, 118 BGHZ 312; and for Italy: Corte di Cassazione [2007] Riv.Dir.Int'le Priv. & Proc. 777; Corte di Cassazione, *Soc Ruffinatti v Oyola-Rosado*, 8 February 2012; see also Christoph Thole, 'Die Entwicklung der Anerkennung im autonomen Rect in Europa' in Burkhard Hess (ed), *Die Anerkennung im Internationalen Zivilprozessrecht – Europäisches Vollstreckungsrecht* (Gieseking 2014) 25, 48–49).

2. Procedural public policy

Incompatibility with the fundamental principles of procedural law is also usually a ground for refusing recognition and enforcement. Meanwhile, a more detailed scrutiny of the procedure before the court of origin has generally been abandoned (for → France, see Cass. 1e civ., *Bachir* [1968] Rev.crit.DIP 98, overruling Cass. 1e civ., *Munzer* [1964] Rev.crit.DIP 344). In particular, it is usually not considered relevant whether the court of origin complied with its own rules of procedure.

The basic notions of procedural fairness are among the most important elements of procedural → public policy (*ordre public*). Today, art 6 § 1 ECHR (European Convention of 4 November 1950 for the Protection of Human Rights and Fundamental Freedoms, 213 UNTS 221) plays a predominant role in this respect (Patrick Kinsch, 'The Impact of Human Rights on the Application of Foreign Law and on the Recognition of Foreign Judgments – A Survey of the Cases Decided by the European Human Rights Institutions' in Talia Einhorn and Kurt Siehr (eds), *Essays in Memory of Peter E Nygh* (TMC Asser Press 2004) 197, 218–228). In the case of *Pellegrini v Italy* App No 30882/96 (ECtHR, 20 July 2001), the European Court of Human Rights ruled that there may even be a duty of the requested state under the Convention to refuse recognition and enforcement if the procedure in the state of origin was incompatible with the right to a fair trial guaranteed under the Convention.

In particular, a serious violation of the right to be heard constitutes a ground for refusal of recognition and enforcement. A debarment because of failure to comply with a court order may, at least in certain cases, constitute such a violation (see ECJ Case C-394/07 *Marco Gambazzi v DaimlerChrysler Canada Inc and CIBC Mellon Trust Company* [2009] ECR I-2563). Some take the questionable position that opt-out class actions are always incompatible with the civil law standards of procedural fairness. A violation of the right to an independent and impartial tribunal can also give rise to a refusal of recognition and enforcement. However, mere differences in court organization or in the systems of selection of judges are generally not considered to be matters of procedural public policy.

It is also widely considered as a ground for refusal (either as a separate ground or as a matter of public policy) if the judgment was obtained by fraud or if it was based on an abusive lawsuit (see Friedrich Juenger, 'The Recognition of Money Judgments in Civil and Commercial Matters' (1988) 36 Am.J.Comp.L. 1, 23–25).

Recognition and enforcement may also be refused on the grounds of violation of procedural public policy where the court of origin, from the requested state's point of view, unduly interfered with the authority of that state's (or a third state's) courts. In particular, anti-suit injunctions are widely considered as an improper interference with the powers of foreign courts and therefore as ineligible for recognition and enforcement. However, the French *Cour de cassation* has taken a more generous stance in this respect and has permitted the recognition and enforcement of a foreign anti-suit injunction at least in certain circumstances (Cass. 1e civ., *In Zone Brands*, 14 October 2009).

3. Lack of service of process

It is a particularly grave violation of the right to be heard if the defendant was deprived of the possibility of participating in the proceedings for lack of proper service. Many jurisdictions provide for a specific ground for refusal of recognition and enforcement in this respect. Article 45(1)(b) Brussels I Regulation also contains such a ground for refusal. However, while the Brussels I Regulation has abandoned the requirement that service of process took place in a formally correct manner, and only requires that it was effected in sufficient time and in such a way as to enable the defendant to arrange for their defence, many national laws continue to insist on a formally correct service of process. This may create considerable room for abuse, not least because of the often intricate and complicated rules in this field.

4. Conflicting judgments

The possibility of enforcing conflicting judgments in the same state would seriously compromise legal security and disturb the rule of law. It is a matter of necessity to obviate such situations. Some jurisdictions treat this as a → public policy (*ordre public*) issue, while others provide for specific rules on conflicting judgments. Often, a domestic judgment takes precedence over a foreign one regardless of their dates. In conflicts between foreign judgments, meanwhile, the civil law jurisdictions usually follow the first-in-time rule. Some jurisdictions also provide for the refusal of recognition and enforcement if the court of origin ignored parallel proceedings pending before a court in the requested state (or in a third state).

5. Incompatibility with the requested state's private international law

In some jurisdictions, recognition and enforcement used to be excluded in cases where the court of origin had applied a different substantive law than that which would have governed the matter under the requested state's choice-of-law rules. In particular, this used to be the position of the French courts (Cass. 1e civ., *Munzer* [1964] Rev.crit.DIP 344) until the choice-of-law test was abandoned by the *Cour de cassation* (Cass. 1e civ., *Avianca*, 20 February 2007). Article 25(1)(3) Belgian Private international law Act (Wet houdende het Wetboek von international privaatrecht/Code de droit international privé of 16 July 2004, BS 27 July 2004, pp 57344, 57366) still retains it (albeit in a somewhat attenuated form). Before the 1986 amendment of private international law (as of 25 July 1986, BGBl. 1142), § 328(1)(3) German CCP also used to contain a provision to this effect with respect to private international law rules concerning certain matters of family law (Haimo Schack, *Internationales Zivilverfahrensrecht* (6th edn, CH Beck 2014) no 962). Article 27 No 4 of the Brussels Convention also provided for such a ground for refusal, but it was not retained in the Brussels I Regulation.

IV. Procedure

Traditionally, many jurisdictions required a party wishing to rely on a foreign judgment to apply for recognition in a special procedure before a court or before an administrative authority (delibation or *exequatur* procedure). However, modern laws increasingly tend to provide for 'automatic' recognition, meaning that a party may use a foreign judgment before any court or other authority which will then examine, as a preliminary question, whether the judgment meets the prerequisites for recognition (see Christoph Thole, 'Die Entwicklung der Anerkennung im autonomen Recht in Europa' in Burkhard Hess (ed), *Die Anerkennung im Internationalen Zivilprozessrecht – Europäisches Vollstreckungsrecht* (Gieseking 2014) 25, 45–46). In some jurisdictions a special procedure is only required for certain types of judgments, such as divorce judgments in → Germany (§ 107 FamFG) or judgments opening insolvency proceedings in → Switzerland (arts 166–169 Swiss PILA). Many jurisdictions retain the requirement of obtaining *exequatur* as a prerequisite for the enforcement of foreign judgments. → Austria even newly introduced such a requirement in the 1990s, wishing to align its domestic procedure with the Brussels Convention and the 1988 Lugano Convention (Lugano Convention of 16 September 1988 on jurisdiction and the enforcement of judgments in civil and commercial matters, [1988] OJ L 319/9). In some jurisdictions (eg Switzerland), there is no obligatory *exequatur* procedure, but the party demanding recognition and/or enforcement may apply for a declaration of recognition and enforceability. In cases where there is a dispute about whether the prerequisites for recognition and enforcement are met, it is beneficial for the parties if they can bring about a binding decision and thus legal security in this respect.

TANJA DOMEJ

Literature

Samuel Baumgartner, 'How Well Do U.S. Judgments Fare in Europe?' (2008–2009) 40 Geo.Wash.L.Rev. 173; Gilles Cuniberti, 'The Liberalization of the French Law of Foreign Judgments' (2007) 56 ICLQ 931; Reinhold Geimer, *Internationales Zivilprozessrecht* (7th edn, Otto Schmidt 2015); Peter Gottwald, 'Grundfragen der Anerkennung und Vollstreckung ausländischer Entscheidungen in Zivilsachen' (1990) 103 ZZP 257; Friedrich Juenger, 'The Recognition of Money Judgments in Civil and Commercial Matters' (1988) 36 Am.J.Comp.L. 1; Patrick Kinsch, 'The Impact of Human Rights on the Application of Foreign Law and on the Recognition of Foreign Judgments – A Survey of the Cases Decided by the European Human Rights Institutions' in Talia Einhorn and Kurt Siehr (eds), *Essays in Memory of Peter E. Nygh* (TMC Asser Press 2004) 197; Dieter Martiny, 'Anerkennung ausländischer Entscheidungen nach autonomem Recht' in Max-Planck-Institut für ausländisches und internationales Privatrecht (ed), *Handbuch des Internationalen Zivilverfahrensrecht*, vol III/1 (Mohr Siebeck 1984); Dieter Martiny, 'Recognition and Enforcement of Foreign Money Judgments in the Federal Republic of Germany' (1987) 35 Am.J.Comp.L. 721; Franz Matscher, 'Grundfragen der Anerkennung und Vollstreckung ausländischer Entscheidungen in Zivilsachen (aus österreichischer Sicht)' (1990) 103 ZZP 294; Heinrich Nagel and Peter Gottwald, *Internationales Zivilprozessrecht* (7th edn, Otto Schmidt 2013); Arnaud Nuyts, *Study on Residual Jurisdiction – General Report. Review of the Member States' Rules Concerning the 'Residual Jurisdiction' of their Courts in Civil and Commercial Matters Pursuant to the Brussels I and II Regulations* (2007) (available at <ec.europa.eu/civiljustice/news/docs/study_residual_jurisdiction_en.pdf>, visited 4 June 2014); Haimo Schack, *Internationales Zivilverfahrensrecht* (6th edn, CH Beck 2014); Christoph Thole, 'Die Entwicklung der Anerkennung im autonomen Recht in Europa' in Burkhard Hess (ed), *Die Anerkennung im Internationalen Zivilprozessrecht – Europäisches Vollstreckungsrecht* (Gieseking 2014) 25; Hans

Ulrich Walder, 'Grundfragen der Anerkennung und Vollstreckung ausländischer Urteile unter besonderer Berücksichtigung schweizerischer Sicht' (1990) 103 ZZP 322; Gerhard Walter and Samuel P Baumgartner (eds), *Recognition and Enforcement of Foreign Judgments Outside the Scope of the Brussels and Lugano Conventions* (Kluwer Law International 2000, Supplement 2005); Wolfgang Wurmnest, 'Recognition and Enforcement of U.S. Money Judgments in Germany' (2005) 23 Berkeley J.Int'l L. 175.

Recognition and enforcement of judgments (common law)

I. Systems for the recognition and enforcement of foreign judgments

In principle, as well as in practice, the private international law of foreign judgments needs to strike a balance between two fundamental propositions. On the one hand, a judicial order by way of adjudication is an exercise of delegated sovereign power. This means that it has unquestionable coercive force within the territory within which it was made, but none outside it, for it is only the order of a local judge that can be enforced as such within the territory of a state. On the other hand, it is in the public interest that once there has been a proper or sufficient adjudication of claims and defences, it should not be open to the parties to reopen and relitigate matters which have been (or which should have been) adjudicated by the judge. If there is no reason to confine this principle of public policy to adjudications made within the forum state, it becomes necessary to determine when and to what extent a foreign adjudication may be recognized as making the issue between the parties no longer open to dispute by reason of the principle of *res judicata*. And if this is so, it is also necessary to devise a way to allow a foreign judgment to be enforced and executed, whether directly or indirectly, within the territory of the state in which it is presented.

An initial distinction is to be drawn between the recognition of a foreign judgment as a final, conclusive and non-reviewable determination of the claim, defence or issues regarding the judgment as *res judicata* and the enforcement of that judgment by processes of execution. It is obvious that a legal system must recognize any judgment which it is prepared to enforce; it is equally clear that not all judgments which are recognized are liable to be enforced. Although we will concentrate on the enforcement of foreign judgments, it is important to understand at the outset that the conditions which determine the enforceability of a foreign judgment are, in most respects, conditions which determine its recognition as *res judicata* and that there are circumstances – such as where a defendant has prevailed against a claimant and who wishes to rely on the foreign judgment to prevent the claimant trying to sue again – in which recognition of the judgment is all that is required to settle the issue between the parties.

A practical distinction is also to be drawn between judgments in civil and commercial matters, to which general provisions for recognition and enforcement, by treaty or convention or otherwise, extend, and other judgments. This latter category in particular covers judgments in matters of status, → succession and insolvency, for which separate and particular provision is usually made, even if the matter is civil or commercial, but also judgments in matters of penal law, revenue law and public law, which are not generally thought of as civil or commercial in nature. This 'excluded' category is mentioned below, in section IV., though the details will be found under the specialist topics to which the judgments relate.

II. Recognition and enforcement according to treaty or convention: civil and commercial matters

1. General

Foreign judgments are liable to be enforced in another state ('the receiving state') according to international treaty or convention, or in accordance with the national rules of private international law. International treaties may be bilateral or multilateral in nature, stipulating the conditions under which a foreign judgment will be recognized and enforceable in the receiving state. These obviously vary from legal tradition to legal tradition, but what they have in common is the designation of rules which determine whether the judgment is in principle entitled to be enforced in the receiving state, as well as the objections or defences which may be raised by the judgment debtor to prevent such enforcement. The rules which determine the in-principle enforceability of the judgment were traditionally jurisdictional, expressed in terms of the connection between the foreign court and the parties to the litigation, normally the defendant. But where the convention or treaty in question operates (as within the EU they increasingly do) by laying down common rules of jurisdiction, there is much less room for a review in the receiving state of the jurisdiction of the adjudicating court.

As to the further defences which are permitted to be raised (that is, contentions other than a simple denial of the necessary jurisdictional connection), the admissibility of substantive defences is variable. According to the common law tradition and to many treaties, the general principle of recognition and enforcement is that the merits of the foreign judgment may not be subjected to review or, to put it another way, judgments are recognized and enforced because they are sufficient, rather than because they are, in the eyes of the receiving court, 'right'. According to this point of view, the only truly substantive defence which will be permitted is that recognition or enforcement would be contrary to public policy in the receiving state. For although such treaties and conventions which provide for recognition and enforcement usually specify that a foreign judgment is not reviewed as to its merits, they will provide for enforcement to be refused where it would offend the public policy of the receiving state. Even so, it is consistent with principle that the role of public policy be kept to a minimum. After all, as *Cardozo J* famously said in *Loucks v Standard Oil Co of New York* 224 NY 99 (1918): 'we are not so provincial as to say that every solution of a problem is wrong because we deal with it otherwise at home'. So it is with foreign judgments: the fact that a foreign court has adjudicated in a manner which differs from that which would have taken place before a local court will be of no relevance unless the high threshold of public policy in the receiving state is met. It does not matter whether this results from the application of a different rule for choice of law or from the application of a different domestic law, or from the application of procedural rules which differ from those applicable to adjudications in the courts of the receiving state, or from the fact that the court has made an order for compensation or for the payment of costs and legal expenses in a way which the courts of the receiving state would not have done. In other legal traditions, though the public policy defence is still applied, there may also be greater attention paid to whether the foreign court applied the law as a court in the receiving state would have done or otherwise disposed of the case as a court in the receiving state might have done. This does not involve a reconsideration of the merits of the judgment, but does require a closer correspondence between the legal reasoning used by the foreign court and that which would have been followed by a court in the receiving state.

No system of law can tolerate the recognition or enforcement of a foreign judgment which would require the receiving court to make an order which it would consider to be in conflict with the European Convention on Human Rights (European Convention of 4 November 1950 for the Protection of Human Rights and Fundamental Freedoms, 213 UNTS 221) or Basic Laws of a constitutional kind. More generally, therefore, greater attention is given to defences which are procedural in nature. Of these, the general principle is that if proceedings before the original court may be shown not to be in sufficient accordance with procedural standards or international norms of procedural fairness and so forth, recognition, and therefore enforcement, should not be permitted. In practice there is an overlap between these procedural objections to recognition and enforcement, and the requirements of the European Convention on Human Rights, but procedural objections to the manner in which the matter was disposed of by the foreign court pre-date the European Convention by many decades.

The procedure by which a judgment, which meets the criteria for recognition and enforcement as prescribed by treaty or convention, may be enforced varies from case to case. According to a pattern found in a number of common law jurisdictions, including the → United Kingdom, the judgment may be registered, with the judgment debtor being given a limited period within which to apply to have the registration set aside. In other systems, a judgment creditor may be required to make an application to court, which may be more or less formal in nature, for an order (frequently called *exequatur*) granting permission to enforce the judgment in the receiving state; in such a case, the judgment debtor will be permitted to appeal against the grant of *exequatur*. However, it is widely understood that enforcement by virtue of a treaty or convention is confined to proceedings to enforce an original foreign judgment, and that it is not permissible for a judgment from state A to be declared or rendered enforceable in state B and then for proceedings to be brought to enforce the 'judgment' from the courts of state B in state C: *exequatur sur exequatur ne vaut*, as it is sometimes said.

2. The Brussels Convention and the Brussels I Regulation

Within federal systems, legislative provision is usually made to ensure the enforcement, more or less automatically, of judgments from courts from other jurisdictions within the federation. The 'full faith and credit' provisions of the constitution of the USA and the corresponding standards in → Australia, → Canada, → Switzerland and the → United Kingdom (or legislation made to give specific effect to those constitutional imperatives), for example, will usually provide for the mutual recognition and enforcement of judgments from courts in other parts of the federal structure. The most ambitious by far of the legislative systems for the mutual recognition and enforcement of judgment from courts of sister states has been developed in the EU by a series of Conventions dating from 1968 (the 'Brussels Convention' (Brussels Convention of 27 September 1968 on jurisdiction and the enforcement of judgments in civil and commercial matters, [1972] OJ L 299/32, consolidated version, [1998] OJ C 27/1)) as periodically updated and amended, and more recently a successor European Regulation (the 'Brussels I Regulation' (Regulation (EC) No 44/2001 of 22 December 2000 on jurisdiction and the recognition and enforcement of judgments in civil and commercial matters, [2001] OJ L 12/1)). As a result of having legislated a set of directly applicable jurisdictional rules for the adjudication of → civil and commercial matters, the Conventions and the Regulation were in a position to put in place a set of rules for the near-automatic recognition and enforcement of judgments in civil and commercial matters from courts in other parts of the EU. For if a court in a receiving state is entitled, or even bound, to assume that the exercise of jurisdiction by the original court was based on and conformed to the very same jurisdictional rules and principles as the receiving court would itself have applied if it had been called upon to adjudicate, it is entirely reasonable to provide that the recognition and enforcement of the judgment be required, without review or question, in all but a narrow and defined list of circumstances. These narrow circumstances in which recognition, and hence enforcement, may be refused are of three kinds: (i) jurisdictional, where non-recognition serves the superior aim of reinforcing the rules of adjudicatory jurisdiction as these apply to certain privileged (claims by insureds, consumers and employees) or exclusive (title to land or to tenancies of land, certain fundamental matters of corporations law, entries or public registers) jurisdictional rules; (ii) procedural, where non-recognition serves the aim of protecting the defendant's right to be sufficiently notified of and heard in the proceedings, or deals with the inescapable problem created by a conflict between two or more judgments; and (iii) substantive, where non-recognition is required by the public policy of the receiving state – a single rule which covers a disparate sprinkling of unusual or extreme cases. On this point, the European Court explained in Case C-7/98 *Krombach v Bamberski* [2000] ECR I-1935 that national public policy may be used to prevent recognition and enforcement: 'where recognition or enforcement of the judgment delivered in another Contracting State would be at variance to an unacceptable degree with the legal order of the State in which enforcement is sought inasmuch as it infringes a fundamental principle'. The infringement 'would have to constitute a manifest breach of a rule of law regarded as essential in the legal order of the State in which enforcement is sought or of a right recognised as being fundamental within that legal order'. However, an objection, no matter how demonstrably well-founded, that the original court erred in finding that it had jurisdiction, or erred in finding the facts or applying the law will simply be inadmissible.

However, an arguable shortcoming in the scheme of automatic recognition of judgments is shown where a court has exercised jurisdiction over a defendant, in specific accordance with the Brussels I Regulation, on the basis of rules of national jurisdictional law which may be designated as 'residual', or 'exorbitant' or 'long-arm', in nature. The resulting judgment still qualifies for automatic recognition in the same way as does one given in proceedings in which the foreign court was bound by the uniform jurisdictional rules of the Regulation. In effect, this superficially equal treatment of judgments discriminates sharply against defendants who do not have a domicile in a Member State, who are exposed to exorbitant or eccentric rules of national jurisdiction, but who cannot invoke the corresponding national law rules which have limited the recognition of foreign judgments. The result is deeply unsatisfactory, but nobody who has the power to do anything about it seems inclined to reconsider it.

3. Simplification of the procedure for enforcement under the Brussels I Regulation

Procedurally, the Brussels Convention and the Brussels I Regulation, in their original form, required the judgment creditor to make an application to a court in the receiving state for the registration of the foreign judgment. For although enforcement was intended to be automatic, it was considered that a judgment needed to be formally taken into the legal order of the receiving state before the process of enforcement by execution could be put in hand. The judgment debtor had a limited time and right to appeal against the order for registration of the judgment so as to prevent enforcement, but in all cases, enforcement required the judgment creditor to make an application, with unavoidable expense and delay. And although the evidence for it was mostly anecdotal, there was a persistent view that even this reduced degree of formality was an impediment to the free circulation of judgments; in any case, if no formality is required before a judgment from Berlin may be enforced in Frankfurt, why should the matter stand any differently if the judgment originated from Paris or Prague? According to the Brussels I Regulation (recast) (Regulation (EU) No 1215/2012 of the European Parliament and of the Council of 12 December 2012 on jurisdiction and the recognition and enforcement of judgments in civil and commercial matters (recast), [2012] OJ L 351/1; → Brussels I (Convention and Regulation)), a judgment given in proceedings that commenced after that date will be more easily and directly enforceable by the judgment creditor. The judgment creditor will be required to assemble and compile paperwork in standard form in order to confirm that the judgment was regularly given and is enforceable in the state of origin; on submission of these documents to the appropriate office in the receiving state, the judgment will be registered for enforcement. Nothing more will be required of the judgment creditor. The judgment debtor will be notified of the fact of registration and will have a limited time within which to apply for order for refusal of enforcement. Though the grounds on which this order may be applied for and made have remained substantially unchanged from the predecessor text of the Regulation (a specific proposal to remove the public policy ground for objection to recognition not having found favour with the Member States), the fact that it is the judgment debtor rather than the judgment creditor who needs to make an application to the courts of the receiving state has a significant symbolic value as well as an economic one.

4. Recognition under the Brussels I Regulation

Where the rules for enforcement are established, directly or indirectly, by treaty or convention, the same instrument will often, though not invariably, provide the rules for the recognition of foreign judgments. Typically recognition of the judgment will not involve any procedure beyond that required to establish the authenticity of the judgment; indeed, it may be sufficient simply to plead it or put it in evidence with such proof of authenticity as the receiving state may require. In the case of judgments whose enforcement is provided for by the Brussels Convention or the Brussels I Regulation, the few jurisdictional, procedural and substantive grounds on which enforcement may be withheld are stated as grounds upon which a judgment shall not be recognized (the separate requirement that the judgment be enforceable in the state of origin being material to enforcement, but not to recognition). Yet, where the judgment is entitled to recognition, the obligation on the receiving court is in principle to accord the judgment the same effect or effects as it has or would have in the state of origin, though perhaps not to the extent that this would involve ascribing to it a significant effect which a local judgment would not have had. However, and again in principle, no special procedure is required before a foreign judgment qualifies for recognition.

III. Enforcement otherwise than in accordance with treaty or convention: civil and commercial matters

Where no international treaty or convention prescribes the rules for the recognition and enforcement of a foreign judgment, the effect of a foreign judgment in the receiving state is determined by the ordinary private international law of the receiving state. Naturally the substance of these rules will vary from state to state, but also from legal tradition to legal tradition.

1. Civil law systems

In the case of civil law jurisdictions, it is probably correct to say that the laws betray a number of approaches, but that no overarching principle is to be discerned. In some states, of which the → Netherlands and the Nordic states are examples, an extreme position is ostensibly adopted, according to which, in the absence of a treaty or a convention, a foreign judgment will neither be enforced nor recognized as *res judicata*; a similar disposition is found in Russian law (→ Russian Federation). A foreign judgment may be treated as evidence relevant to proceedings which must be brought once more upon the original claim, though there is some indication in more recent decisions of the Dutch Supreme Court, and perhaps also in the Nordic states, that the *de facto* recognition of foreign judgments may take place with the approximate result that although the judgment creditor will be required to sue again to establish his claim, the court may, in practice, not look beyond the foreign judgment in ascertaining the merits of the claim. However, the precise extent of this relaxation of an earlier clear rule is unclear.

In other civilian jurisdictions, private international law is prepared in principle to recognize foreign judgments in certain circumstances, though enforcement will still require an order of *exequatur*. Recognition will invariably require: (i) that the foreign court sufficiently respected the rights of the defence in allowing the defendant a proper right to be notified and heard (and, in an appropriate case, represented by counsel of his choice); and (ii) that the procedure before the foreign court, and maybe the foreign court itself, was sufficiently judicial, independent and impartial that its judgment should be accepted as a judicial determination; and (iii) that recognition of the judgment should not conflict with the public policy of, or other basic or essential laws in, the receiving state. In relation to this last point, judgments in which the damages awarded are considered to be excessive, or which are deliberately awarded for a sum greater than the loss which the claimant can be shown to have sustained, are sometimes problematic, especially when a court in one state allows damages to be uplifted *in lieu* of being able to make an order for the payment of costs or legal expenses. But there may be further or additional requirements, of which the following list gives an indication, such as: (i) the foreign court having exercised jurisdiction on a basis which is consistent with the rules of jurisdiction applicable in the receiving state; or (ii) the foreign court having exercised jurisdiction on a basis regarded by the law of the receiving state as sufficient to lead to recognition of the judgment; or (iii) the case not being one in which the receiving court considers its own rules of jurisdiction to be compulsory or exclusive; or (iv) the foreign court having approached any question of choice of law in a manner which corresponds to the choice-of-law rules of the receiving court; or (v) there being compliance with a principle of reciprocity, whereby a foreign judgment will not be recognized unless a court in the foreign state would recognize a judgment from the courts of the receiving state if the circumstances were to be reversed, which condition may be applied with greater or less great stringency; or (vi) any combination of these (and possibly other) factors.

In those cases in which a foreign judgment is to be enforced in the receiving state, it is usual for this to require an authenticating order, or *exequatur*, to be given by a court in the receiving state. A court will not grant *exequatur* unless the foreign judgment satisfies the criteria for recognition, whatever they may be. But there may also be further limitations upon the enforcement, which may be expressed in terms of the kinds of foreign judicial order which may be enforced, and upon whether the foreign judgment is *res judicata* in the court which gave it, or still subject to the possibility of appeal or review to a higher court, in the state of origin. It is also problematic, and may not be possible, for a court to be called upon to enforce a foreign judgment of a type or for an order which could not be made by a court in the receiving state.

2. Common law approach

It seems correct to describe the civilian approach to the private international law of foreign judgments as one which determines whether the foreign judgment should be received into the legal system as a foreign judgment, that is, as an act of foreign judicial adjudication which a court may nevertheless approve for enforcement. The common law tradition is somewhat different, placing its principal focus on whether the party that is said to be bound by the judgment of the foreign court was present within the territorial jurisdiction of the court when the proceedings were instituted or submitted to the adjudicatory jurisdiction of the foreign court.

The first of these alternatives is probably a reflection of the principles of comity and respect for territorial sovereignty. According to this, at least as the principles are understood in the Anglo-American legal systems, an act or exercise of sovereign power, conducted within the territory of a foreign sovereign, is to be recognized, respected and is not generally to be questioned. A foreign judge is entitled to adjudicate a claim against a defendant if the defendant was voluntarily present within the jurisdiction of the foreign court when proceedings were commenced, and the grounds on which he exercised jurisdiction, and the substance and application of the law by which he did it, are in general irrelevant to the recognition of the adjudication as being binding on the losing party. As to the second alternative, if the defendant was not present at the institution of proceedings, the principles of comity and sovereignty will not require the recognition of the judgment. But if there is an agreement between the claimant and the defendant, which may be express, implied or tacit, to accept and abide by the adjudication of the foreign court, as the claimant does by instituting proceedings, and as the defendant does by appearing or agreeing to appear to defend the proceedings, then the parties are mutually bound by their agreement to abide by the adjudication of the court and to accept its judgment as *res judicata*. In this case it is not so much the foreign judgment, but the private agreement of the parties which provides the basis for the acceptance of the foreign judgment as *res judicata*. Of course, any such agreement to accept a foreign adjudication as binding may be avoided if it may be shown that the judgment was obtained by fraud or malpractice, or by non-observance of the rules of natural justice, but otherwise the agreement to accept the adjudication will be binding on the parties to the agreement (and, of course, on the defendant who was present within the foreign jurisdiction when the proceedings were begun). It follows that a contention that the foreign court erred in its adjudication will be irrelevant, as this will not impeach an agreement to accept the adjudication; however, if the foreign court has adjudicated in clear breach of an agreement as to jurisdiction, or perhaps as to the law which the parties had agreed upon to govern their mutual relations, the agreement to accept the judgment may still be challenged. It is perhaps surprising that the same 'defences' to recognition are permitted where the basis for recognition is the presence of the defendant within the territorial jurisdiction of the foreign court, but this is clearly the law.

The common law is in accord with civilian systems in taking the view that, in the absence of a treaty or convention, a foreign judgment may not be enforced, or enforced without further judicial order. However, the common law does not use a procedure of *exequatur* as a precondition to enforcement by execution. Instead, it requires the judgment creditor to bring original proceedings, but these proceedings are founded on the foreign judgment as a cause of action which is sufficient by itself and conceptually independent of the original underlying claim. The aim is to obtain an English judgment which may then be enforced by execution. But the difference between this and civilian systems is more apparent than real. In the common law, as in the civilian systems, an order of the local court is required before (in countries of the civilian tradition) the foreign judgment may be enforced or (in countries of the common law tradition) a local judgment, which replicates the foreign judgment, may be enforced.

IV. Other judgments: personal status, succession, insolvency, etc

It is usual in the law relating to foreign judgments to deal separately with judgments given by courts in matters of → personal status such as a declaration, dissolution or annulment of → marriage or of civil partnership, or in matters of → succession to or of the administration of deceased estates, or in matters of bankruptcy and insolvency. The laws on the recognition and enforcement of foreign judgments in these areas are remarkably diverse, and may be thought to be peculiarly suited to reform by international agreement. In the field of family law, it is usual for judgments from the courts of the personal law to be recognized as *res judicata*, but this is subject to two big conditions. The first is that the 'personal law' is not a uniform one; in some states the law of the → nationality is dominant, in others the law of the habitual residence, and in yet others the law of the domicile (→ Domicile, habitual residence and establishment). The second is that in the context of a marriage or civil partnership, not only may the parties have separate personal laws, but there are other courts which might be thought to be proper courts before which to bring a question concerning the validity or subsistence of a marriage. When it comes to judgments concerning the welfare of children, there is no easy way to list as a matter of principle those courts whose judgments should be presumed to be internationally conclusive, for the facts of family and post-family life may be dispersed across several laws and jurisdictions, and may be as chaotic as they are unfortunate. So untidy is the effect of leaving these issues to the separate schemes of national law that only legislation can establish the certainty and stability which individuals are entitled to expect; to this end, the → Brussels IIa Regulation (Council Regulation (EC) No 2201/2003 of 27 November 2003 concerning jurisdiction and the recognition and enforcement of judgments in matrimonial matters and the matters of parental responsibility, repealing Regulation (EC) No 1347/2000, [2003] OJ L 338/1) harmonizes the recognition and enforcement of judgments from the courts of Member States. Judgments concerning succession and the administration of estates are likely to be recognized if they are given by the courts of the place whose law will be applied to the succession, but that also may vary according to the question of which court it is whose view of the personal law is taken as relevant. Once again, legislation to establish a greater degree of uniformity has been made in the form of the EU Succession Regulation (Regulation (EU) No 650/2012 of the European Parliament and of the Council of 4 July 2012 on jurisdiction, applicable law, recognition and enforcement of decisions and acceptance and enforcement of authentic instruments in matters of succession and on the creation of a European Certificate of Succession, [2012] OJ L 201/107; → Rome IV Regulation (succession)), but this will not immediately operate in all Member States.

In the context of insolvency, it was for a long time understood that insolvency was governed by the law of the forum and that there was only a limited scope for giving effect to the judgments of foreign courts in relation to the insolvency administration. But this became unsustainable in the face of large-scale international insolvencies, and a degree of coordination has been established by international agreement. Within the EU, judgments which open insolvency proceedings in respect of debtors who have their centre of main interests in a Member State will in principle be recognized by virtue of the EU Insolvency Regulation (Council Regulation (EC) No 1346/2000 of 29 May 2000 on insolvency proceedings, [2000] OJ L 160/1), as will judgments and orders made in the course of those proceedings. More generally, legislation to implement a Model Law drafted by → UNCITRAL (UNCITRAL Model Law on Cross-Border Insolvency with Guide to Enactment, 1997 (UNCITRAL (ed), Model Law on Cross-Border Insolvency with Guide to Enactment (1997): Model Law on Cross-Border Insolvency of the United Commission on International Trade Law, Resolution 52/158 adopted by the General Assembly, 30 January 1998, No E.99.V.3, General Assembly Resolution 52/158 of 15 December 1997)) allows for the recognition of judgments opening insolvency proceedings in the courts for a debtor's centre of main interests, but it does not extend to requiring the recognition of judgments, such as those requiring individuals to pay or repay sums wrongfully received into the insolvent estate.

Foreign judgments concerning criminal law and judgments enforcing revenue laws or tax claims are generally not enforceable outside the state in which they were given; if there are exceptions to this near-universal principle, they will need to be enshrined in specific legislation. A line of demarcation separates the enforcement of revenue claims from the recognition of revenue laws as forming part of a civil claim for a commercial debt; only in the former is the exclusionary rule implicated. Where the effect of enforcement of a judgment might be to give effect, directly or indirectly, to the public laws of a foreign state, or to exercises of foreign sovereign or foreign prerogative power, there is some uncertainty in the case-law and some ambiguity in the laws.

ADRIAN BRIGGS

Literature

American Law Institute, *Recognition and Enforcement of Foreign Judgments: Analysis and Proposed Federal Statute* (ALI Publishers 2006); Peter Barnett, *Res Judicata, Estoppel and Foreign Judgments* (OUP 2001); Lord Collins of Mapesbury and others (eds), *Dicey, Morris & Collins on the Conflict of Laws* (15th edn, Sweet & Maxwell 2012) ch 14; Horace Emerson Read, *Recognition and Enforcement of Foreign Judgments* (HUP 1938); Arthur Von Mehren, *Adjudicatory Authority in Private international law: A Comparative Study* (Hague Academy of International Law 2007).

Recognition of administrative acts

I. Concept, notion and historical development

The legal effects of an administrative act issued by a state are, in principle, confined to the legal system and the territory of that state. The recognition of administrative acts serves as a mechanism to overcome this limited territorial effect. In this respect, the recognition of foreign administrative acts is very much related to the field of private international law, particularly to its procedural aspects such as the recognition and enforcement of foreign judgments (→ Recognition and enforcement of judgments (civil law); → Recognition and enforcement of judgments (common law)) and the recognition and enforcement of foreign arbitral awards (→ Arbitration, recognition of awards) (Matthias Ruffert, 'Recognition of Foreign Legislative and Administrative Acts' in Rüdiger Wolfrum (ed), *Max Planck Encyclopedia of Public International Law* (2011) no 2).

The notion of recognition is widely used in various fields of the law, often with varied meanings. When it comes to the conflict of laws, the term 'recognition' is commonly used to express the extension of effects of the law occurred abroad to the domestic legal sphere and is to be distinguished from the application of foreign law (→ Foreign law, application and ascertainment). Within the terms of the definition commonly employed in the conflict of laws, the recognition of administrative acts can be described as the extension of the legal effects of an administrative act of a foreign authority to the domestic jurisdiction. As this broad definition indicates, the concept of recognition of foreign administrative acts includes a range of different meanings, depending on the type of administrative act – in particular on the legal effects it is intended to generate in the state of origin – and depending on which effects are sought to be transferred to the host state. The most far-reaching transfer of legal effects constitutes enforcement, eg of a payment order or a prohibition order, aiming at the full implementation of the foreign act in the territory of the host state, ie the recovery of money or the suppression of the prohibited activity. It is to be distinguished from mere recognition. Recognition in a strict sense may relate to foreign administrative acts providing for the certification of certain abilities, the award of entitlements or the imposition of duties which are sought to be recognized as such, eg in view of certain legal effects, and without any enforcement being applied for in the host state. Not covered by the notion of recognition, by contrast, is the taking into consideration of an administrative act as a mere matter of fact. If, for example, the competent authorities of an exporting country intervene in the performance process of an international sales contract by way of an export prohibition, such foreign act will surely be taken into consideration in civil proceedings as an impediment preventing the seller from performing its → contractual obligations. However, this constitutes a mere factual consequence of the existence of the foreign administrative act since it does not produce any legal effect outside the territory of the state of origin; it must therefore be differentiated from recognition in a strict sense.

With respect to the legal effects to be attributed to the foreign administrative act in the domestic legal sphere and corresponding to the recognition of foreign judgments in the law of civil procedure, the administrative act in question may have the same effects as it does in the state of origin (*Wirkungserstreckung*) or the administrative act may be assimilated to a respective administrative act of the host state (*Wirkungsgleichstellung*), or, thirdly, there may be a combination in the sense that the effects of an equivalent administrative act in the host state form the ceiling for the effects that may be attributed to the foreign administrative act (Christoph Ohler, *Die Kollisionsordnung des Allgemeinen Verwaltungsrechts* (Mohr Siebeck 2005) 53).

As to the recognition procedure, explicit recognition in each individual case may be required, taking the form of an administrative or judicial decision dealing exclusively with the issue of recognition in the host state, as opposed to an 'automatic' recognition in an abstract manner based on a legal provision of general application of the host state. In the latter case, the authority or court confronted with the foreign administrative act will deal with its recognition incidentally and without a separate procedure in the course of its own proceedings. An explicit recognition will, for instance, generally be required for the recognition of a professional qualification that is contingent upon the prior assessment of 'equivalence' by the competent authority in the host state. By contrast, for example, in civil proceedings on damages actions for the infringements of antitrust rules, the adjudicating court might in the course of these proceedings incidentally recognize (or treat as at least *prima facie* evidence) the prior finding of a foreign competition authority that a breach of the antitrust rules has occurred (see section V.3. below).

Where the recognition of foreign administrative acts is prescribed by EU law or public international law, scholars have stressed the transnational character of such acts, in particular in the context of recognition duties within the EU. From this perspective, foreign administrative acts recognized in such an abstract and anticipated manner are, by themselves, deemed to have effects outside the legal system they derive from and are therefore characterized as 'transnational administrative acts' (*Transnationaler Verwaltungsakt*; see eg Eberhard Schmidt-Aßmann, 'Deutsches und Europäisches Verwaltungsrecht' [1993] DVBl 924, 935; Matthias Ruffert, 'Der transnationale Verwaltungsakt' [2001] Die Verwaltung 453).

Historically, administrative law has generally been characterized as an area of law that is strictly limited to a certain state and to the territory of that state ('principle of territoriality'; → Territoriality) and, accordingly, by the strictly territorial effect of administrative acts, although exceptions to this basic premise have traditionally been acknowledged with respect to certain acts, eg the conferment of nationality, and particularly in view of certain private law effects of such acts (see also section V. below). This basic premise has been markedly loosened by recent developments, in particular within the EU. As cross-border relations have significantly increased and have become increasingly normal, cases involving the recognition of foreign administrative acts have become an everyday occurrence. Today, many international legal regimes require the recognition of foreign administrative acts, particularly in order to deal with the tasks and challenges brought about by the process of globalization (Matthias Ruffert, 'Recognition of Foreign Legislative and Administrative Acts' in Rüdiger Wolfrum (ed), *Max Planck Encyclopedia of Public International Law* (2011) no 3). The traditional view that administrative acts, in principle, only produce effects within the legal system and the territory of the state of origin has thereby gradually become less important.

II. Purpose and function

The recognition of foreign administrative acts serves as a means to achieve coordination between states and is to a large extent based on social or economic policy considerations. With respect to the recognition of administrative acts with favourable effects on the individual, eg the recognition of authorizations or professional qualifications, a lack of coordination between administrative legal orders can impair individual freedom and mobility, cross-border economic exchange and international trade: an individual or company offering certain products authorized in one country may wish to market and sell its products in other countries and will need to seek different authorizations in order to do so; an individual wishing to pursue a regulated profession in a country other than the one in which he or she has obtained his or her professional qualification may be hindered from doing so in the event that his or her professional qualification is not recognized by the host state. In addition to the harmonization of laws and regulations of the states concerned, the recognition of foreign administrative acts can help to eliminate such 'double burdens' for individuals or companies. The recognition of administrative acts can therefore be considered a means to reduce transaction costs, favouring an efficient allocation of resources (Sascha Michaels, *Anerkennungspflichten im Wirtschaftsverwaltungsrecht der Europäischen Gemeinschaft und der Bundesrepublik Deutschland* (Duncker & Humblot 2004) 140 *et seq*). With respect to professional qualifications, recognition may further be motivated by the better integration of immigrants in the host labour market and society (Werner Meng, *Extraterritoriale Jurisdiktion im öffentlichen Wirtschaftsrecht* (Springer 1994) 90). The mutual recognition of administrative acts may also facilitate the administrative decision-making process by making a separate decision in the host state simpler or even superfluous, thus reducing the administrative workload. This may be further underpinned by the fact that the state of origin is in a better factual or legal position than the host state to issue the administrative decision in question (Karl Neumeyer, *Internationales Verwaltungsrecht, IV* (Schweitzer 1936) 306). As regards the recognition of administrative acts having burdensome effects on the individual, such as prohibitions or penalties, the recognition of such acts may be based on various public interests such as public order or security. Whereas the recognition of the favourable effects of administrative acts inherently reflects a liberal tendency, the contrary is true for the burdensome effects of administrative acts: the individual may see himself or herself confronted not only with the authority of one state, but also with the authorities of potentially all states participating in the recognition of each other's burdensome administrative acts (cf Anatol Dutta, *Die Durchsetzung öffentlichrechtlicher Forderungen ausländischer Staaten durch deutsche Gerichte* (Mohr Siebeck 2006) 10 *et seq*; Markus Möstl, 'Preconditions and Limits of Mutual Recognition' [2010] 47 CMLR 405, 409).

III. Legal sources of recognition duties

Under public international and EU law, numerous rules can be ascertained that provide for the duty to recognize certain foreign administrative acts. The recognition of foreign administrative acts may further be envisaged under national law.

1. Public international law

a) General international law
Pursuant to general international law, states are not under a general obligation to recognize and enforce foreign administrative acts in their territory; at the same time, general international law does not prohibit the recognition and enforcement of foreign administrative acts. In the absence of treaty commitments, states are thus free to recognize and enforce – or not to recognize and enforce – foreign administrative acts.

However, in respect of certain foreign administrative acts having declaratory effect or establishing or altering a legal relationship, the complete non-recognition of such acts may touch upon the basic principle of non-interference in the internal affairs of states; in the event that a state is vested with exclusive jurisdiction under public international law, the non-recognition of an administrative act that derives from such exclusive jurisdiction by another state may amount to the infringement of a customary rule of public international law (Alfred Verdross and Bruno Simma, *Universelles Völkerrecht* (3rd edn, Duncker & Humblot 1984) § 1021). Accordingly, matters such as the conferment of nationality or the appointment of public officials by a state ought to be recognized by all other states (Christoph Ohler, *Die Kollisionsordnung des Allgemeinen Verwaltungsrechts* (Mohr Siebeck 2005) 51). Typically, however, more than one state will have a basis for the exercise of jurisdiction over the same matter; in the case of concurrent jurisdiction, the duty to recognize a foreign administrative act would contravene the (equal) sovereignty of other states (Alfred Verdross and Bruno Simma, *Universelles Völkerrecht* (3rd edn, Duncker & Humblot 1984) § 1021). States thus remain generally free to recognize or not to recognize foreign administrative acts.

The Act of State doctrine, based on an assumption to recognize acts by foreign governments, is not considered to be a rule of customary international law; this assessment has also been affirmed by the US Supreme Court in the famous *Sabbatino* case of 1964 (*Banco Nacional de Cuba v Sabbatino* (1964) 376 US 398, 422: 'international law does not require application of the doctrine'; see also Federal Constitutional Court of Germany (BVerfG), 15 May 1995, 92 BVerfGE 277, 321 *et seq*). The Act of State doctrine, developed in Anglo-Saxon case-law, sets out a judicial rule barring domestic courts from reviewing the validity of another government's acts done within its own territory (see § 443(1) Restatement (Third) of Foreign Relations Law (American Law Institute, Restatement of the Law, Third: The Foreign Relations Law of the United States, St Paul 1987); Maria Berentelg, *Die Act of State-Doktrin als Zukunftsmodell für Deutschland?* (Mohr Siebeck 2010) 28 *et seq*).

While there is thus no evidence of a general duty to recognize foreign administrative acts in customary international law, there is often an undeniable practical necessity for the recognition of administrative acts. States therefore often do recognize foreign administrative acts as a matter of their respective national laws, ie autonomously, or enter into particular international treaties in order to establish reciprocal recognition duties.

b) Particular international treaties
In areas where the necessity of mutual recognition is particularly striking, many international treaties have been concluded on a global level to provide for the mutual recognition of foreign administrative acts.

The field of international transport may serve as an illustrative example. As early as 1926, the contracting states of the Convention internationale relative à la circulation automobile – done at Paris on 24 April 1926 (Recueil systématique (RS) 0.741.11) and still in force in many countries – prescribed in its art 7 the recognition of driving licences issued by the authorities of other contracting states. In more recent times, the Convention on Road Traffic, concluded at Vienna on 8 November 1968 under the auspices of the Economic and Social Council of the United Nations (1042 UNTS 17), provides in its art 41 for the mutual recognition of driving permits granted in other contracting states. In a similar vein, art 33 Chicago Convention (Convention of 7 December 1944 on International Civil Aviation, 15 UNTS 295), establishing the International Civil Aviation Organization (→ ICAO) requires the contracting states to recognize 'certificates of airworthiness and certificates of competency and licences issued or rendered valid by the contracting State in which the aircraft is registered'. In the field of maritime safety, the SOLAS (International Convention of 1 November 1974 for the safety of life at sea, 1184 UNTS 278) provides for the duty to recognize certificates issued under the authority of a Contracting Government for all purposes covered by the Convention and stipulates that they 'shall be regarded ... as having the same force as certificates issued by them' (see art 17 of the Annex to the SOLAS Convention).

The core international agreement in Europe regarding the recognition of educational qualifications is the Convention on the Recognition of Qualifications concerning Higher Education in the European Region, signed in Lisbon by several European states on 11 April 1997 (2136 UNTS 3). The Convention, jointly drafted by the Council of Europe and UNESCO, stipulates that qualifications giving access to higher education and higher education qualifications (as well as periods of study) must be recognized unless 'substantial differences' can be proved by the institution of the host country that is charged with recognition.

In the field of international trade, the legal framework of the World Trade Organization may provide, at least to some degree, for the mutual recognition of foreign administrative acts. For instance, the Agreement on the Application of Sanitary and Phytosanitary Measures (SPS Agreement) (1867 UNTS 493) stipulates in its art 4(1) a duty to recognize the sanitary and phytosanitary measures of other members even if such measures differ from a member's own or from those used by other members, provided that the exporting member can objectively demonstrate that its measures achieve the importing member's appropriate level of sanitary or phytosanitary protection (the 'equivalence principle'; see Peter Stoll and Frank Schorkopf, *WTO – World Economic Order, World Trade Law* (Nijhoff 2006) 142). Article VII GATS (General Agreement on Trade in Services of 15 April 1994, 1869 UNTS 183) addresses, *inter alia*, the recognition of professional qualifications. While art VII GATS does not in any way require WTO members to recognize professional qualifications of other members, it allows members to recognize qualifications granted by some members and not others; that is, it permits members to deviate from the basic rule that treatment offered to one member must be extended to all others ('Most Favoured Nation', MFN) and, in that way, intends to encourage the conclusion of Mutual Recognition Agreements (MRAs). At the same time, art VII GATS tries, through several procedural and substantive requirements, to ensure the openness of such MRAs and to prevent members from completely undermining the MFN principle.

In the field of → nationality, the Convention on Certain Questions relating to the Conflicts of Nationality Laws, concluded at The Hague on 12 April 1930 (179 LNTS 89), provides for the duty to recognize the conferment of nationality of other contracting states 'in so far as it is consistent with international conventions, international custom, and the principles of law generally recognized with regard to nationality' (art 1). It can be assumed that to this extent the Convention reflects a rule of customary international law (see above under section III.1.a); Werner Meng, *Extraterritoriale Jurisdiktion im öffentlichen Wirtschaftsrecht* (Springer 1994) 95).

2. EU law

The duties amongst EU Member States to recognize each other's administrative acts are of quite a different scale compared to those existing between states whose relations to each other are determined solely by public international law. EU law constitutes a much more integrated legal framework providing for a wide range of recognition duties resulting from both primary EU Treaty law as well as EU secondary legislation.

a) EU primary law
Under EU primary law, duties to recognize foreign administrative acts may essentially follow from an application of the European basic freedoms (ie free movement of goods, workers, establishment and the provision of services, and capital) and the provisions on citizenship of the EU. By contrast, the principle of sincere cooperation

according to art 4(3) TEU (Consolidated Version of the Treaty on European Union [2012] OJ C 326/13) does not in itself entail a general duty of the Member States to recognize each other's administrative acts, nor can a general principle of law of such content be ascertained in EU law (Sascha Michaels, *Anerkennungspflichten im Wirtschaftsverwaltungsrecht der Europäischen Gemeinschaft und der Bundesrepublik Deutschland* (Duncker & Humblot 2004) 215).

As early as 1979, the European Court of Justice (ECJ) implemented the basic principle that compliance with the administrative regulations that govern the production, quality and marketing of goods in the country of origin will usually suffice for the admission of such products in any other Member State within the Internal Market (the 'principle of mutual recognition'; see ECJ Case 120/78 *Rewe-Zentral AG v Bundesmonopolverwaltung für Branntwein – 'Cassis de Dijon'* [1979] ECR 649, para 14 – the effects of this principle are outlined in the Commission interpretative communication on facilitating the access of products to the markets of other Member States: the practical application of mutual recognition, [2003] OJ C 265/2; for the further design of the principle in secondary legislation, see the Mutual Recognition Regulation concerning technical requirements (Regulation (EC) No 764/2008 of the European Parliament and of the Council of 9 July 2008 laying down procedures relating to the application of certain national technical rules to products lawfully marketed in another Member State and repealing Decision No 3052/95/EC, [2008] OJ L 218/21)). Apart from the defences explicitly laid down in the Treaty, limitations are only permitted in exceptional cases of 'mandatory requirements', such as environmental or consumer protection. While compliance with the administrative regulations of the Member State of origin does not necessarily depend on the issuing of an administrative act, the recognition of such acts where issued is ensured under this basic principle. The rationale of the principle of mutual recognition – as established in *Cassis de Dijon* – has in a long series of judgments successively been extended to the various European basic freedoms (Christine Janssens, *The Principle of Mutual Recognition in EU Law* (OUP 2013) 11 *et seq*). With respect to the freedom of establishment (art 49 TFEU (Treaty on the Functioning of the European Union, [2012] OJ C 326/47)), the ECJ has outlined the principle that Member State authorities have to examine the qualifications acquired by the person concerned in another Member State and must compare the knowledge and skills acquired with those required by the domestic qualification. If the qualification is found to be equivalent, the host Member State must recognize the qualification (ECJ Case C-340/89 *Vlassopoulou v Ministerium für Justiz, Bundes und Europaangelegenheiten Baden-Württemberg* [1991] ECR I-2357, paras 16 and 19; ECJ Case C-238/98 *Hugo Fernando Hocsman v Ministre de l'Emploi et de la Solidarité* [2000] ECR I-06623, para 36). In non-harmonized areas of law, where secondary legislation on the mutual recognition of administrative acts is lacking, the assessment of equivalence is thus essential for a possible recognition duty.

b) EU secondary law
Numerous EU instruments providing for the mutual recognition of administrative acts have been adopted by means of EU secondary legislation. These EU instruments typically share the characteristic that they provide for the harmonization or even unification of rules in a specific field of law, combined with an obligation of the Member States to recognize administrative acts taken in accordance with these harmonized or unified rules in the Member State of origin (Jürgen Basedow, 'Recognition of Foreign Decisions within the European Competition Network' in Jürgen Basedow, Stéphanie Francq and Laurence Idot (eds), *International Antitrust Litigation* (Hart Publishing 2012) 393, 394). While the recognition duties that may follow from an application of the European basic freedoms are by their nature – as subjective rights of the individual – confined to the favourable effects of an administrative act for the individual (Anatol Dutta, *Die Durchsetzung öffentlichrechtlicher Forderungen ausländischer Staaten durch deutsche Gerichte* (Mohr Siebeck 2006) 263; Christine E Linke, *Europäisches Internationales Verwaltungsrecht* (Peter Lang 2001) 211), EU secondary legislation also provides for the recognition of particular administrative acts that have burdensome effects on the individual, such as financial penalties (Council of the European Union, 'Council Framework Decision 2005/214/JHA of 24 February 2005 on the application of the principle of mutual recognition to financial penalties' [2005] OJ L 76/16), the expulsion of third country nationals (Council Directive 2001/40/

EC of 28 May 2001 on the mutual recognition of decisions on the expulsion of third country nationals, [2001] OJ L 149/34) or claims relating to taxes, duties and other measures (Council Directive 2010/24/EU of 16 March 2010 concerning mutual assistance for the recovery of claims relating to taxes, duties and other measures, [2010] OJ L 84/1). The principle of mutual recognition, developed under the European basic freedoms, is now firmly established in many other areas of EU law; the TFEU, for instance, refers to the principle of mutual recognition with respect to judicial cooperation in criminal matters within the 'area of freedom, security and justice' (art 82(1) TFEU). EU secondary legislation has led to an increasing number of instruments which apply the principle of mutual recognition in this area of law (for details, see Christine Janssens, *The Principle of Mutual Recognition in EU Law* (OUP 2013) 131 *et seq*). The greater part of the EU instruments providing for mutual recognition of administrative acts still relates to administrative acts favourable to the individual, particularly secondary legislation in the areas of freedom of establishment (→ Freedom of establishment/persons (EU) and private international law), free movement of goods and services, and the coordination and harmonization of standards builds on the instrument of mutual recognition of foreign administrative acts (Matthias Ruffert, 'Recognition of Foreign Legislative and Administrative Acts' in Rüdiger Wolfrum (ed), *Max Planck Encyclopedia of Public International Law* (2011) no 13).

In some economic sectors, secondary legislation provides that an authorization granted by one Member State will allow the economic operator to provide its services throughout the EU without further authorization requirements (the so-called 'single licence' or 'single passport system'). This is the case, for example, in the insurance and banking sector (for the insurance sector, see art 15(1) Solvency II Directive (Directive 2009/138/EC of the European Parliament and of the Council of 25 November 2009 on the taking-up and pursuit of the business of insurance and reinsurance, [2009] OJ L 335/1); for credit institutions, see arts 33 *et seq* Directive 2013/36/EU of the European Parliament and of the Council of 26 June 2013 on access to the activity of credit institutions and the prudential supervision of credit institutions and investment firms, [2013] OJ L 176/338).

Secondary legislation also implemented the mutual recognition of driving licences at an early stage. Directive 2006/126/EC of the European Parliament and of the Council of 20 December 2006 on driving licences ([2006] OJ L 403/18) recast the prior legislation and further harmonized the conditions for issuing national driving licences. In some instances, the regime of mutual recognition of driving licences has led to so-called 'driving licence tourism'; drivers who had lost their driving permit for driving under the influence of alcohol in their state of residence acquired driving permits in another Member State, circumventing the legislation of the state of residence. This phenomenon has given rise to several rulings of the ECJ (see eg more recently ECJ Case C-419/10 *Wolfgang Hofmann v Freistaat Bayern*, ECLI:EU:C:2012:240, with references to further case-law of the Court).

With regard to professional qualifications, there has for many years been an active programme of EU secondary legislation, accompanied by a large amount of case-law from the ECJ. The EU has moved progressively from a sectoral harmonization and coordination approach towards a comprehensive mutual recognition approach (Paul Craig and Gráinne de Búrca, *EU Law* (6th edn, OUP 2015) 842 *et seq*). In 2005 the prior legislation regarding the recognition of professional qualifications was consolidated and replaced by the umbrella Directive 2005/36/EC of the European Parliament and of the Council of 7 September 2005 on the recognition of professional qualifications ([2005] OJ L 255/22).

3. National law

In the absence of an obligation under public international or under EU law to recognize specific foreign administrative acts, states often still do so as a matter of their respective national laws, ie autonomously. For instance, the German legislator broadly provides for the application of the rules on mutual recognition of professional qualifications laid down in Directive 2005/36/EC on the recognition of professional qualifications also vis-à-vis third country nationals (Berufsqualifikationsfeststellungsgesetz of 6 December 2011, BGBl. I 2515). Third country nationals established in the EU have no general rights of mutual recognition under Directive 2005/36/EC, even if they have undergone exactly the same education as EU nationals within a Member State; they are not protected by the basic freedoms of the Treaty or by secondary legislation. It is thus a matter of national law to provide for recognition vis-à-vis third country nationals (see also Recital (10) of Directive 2005/36/EC declaring that: 'This Directive does not create an obstacle to the possibility of Member States recognising, in accordance with their rules, the professional qualifications acquired outside the territory of the European Union by third country nationals').

IV. Limits to the recognition of foreign administrative acts

The recognition of foreign administrative acts is a method to avoid situations in which the authorities of several states fully examine the same legal matter; it is the basic idea of recognition not to fully reconsider the foreign decision in the host state (Henrik Wenander, 'Recognition of Foreign Administrative Decisions' [2011] ZaöRV 755, 773). Therefore, foreign administrative acts that are to be recognized according to particular instruments may not be reassessed with regard to the legal conditions to issue them and may, in general, not be refused on the ground that they are contrary to the domestic law of the host state, unless a provision would allow for derogations (Matthias Ruffert, 'Der transnationale Verwaltungsakt' [2001] Die Verwaltung 453, 474 *et seq*). With respect to the EU instruments requiring the mutual recognition of driving licences, the ECJ has ruled in a series of judgments that it is for the issuing Member State to investigate whether the minimum conditions imposed by EU law have been satisfied and therefore whether the issuing of a driving licence is justified. Once the authorities of one Member State have issued a driving licence, the other Member States are not permitted to investigate further whether the conditions for issuing the licence have been met. The possession of a driving licence issued by one Member State has to be regarded as constituting proof that on the day on which the licence was issued, its holder satisfied those conditions (see ECJ Case C-419/10 *Wolfgang Hofmann v Freistaat Bayern* ECLI:EU:C:2012:240, paras 45 *et seq*; ECJ Case C-184/10 *Mathilde Grasser v Freistaat Bayern* [2011] ECR I-4057, paras 20 *et seq*; ECJ Case C-321/07 *Criminal Proceedings against Karl Schwarz* [2009] ECR I-1113, paras 76 *et seq*).

There are, however, important limitations to the recognition of foreign administrative acts.

As regards recognition duties which may (exceptionally) flow from customary international law, the recognition of an administrative act issued by a state in the exercise of an exclusive international competence may be refused in the event that the recognition would be contrary to the public policy of the host state, ie its *ordre public* (→ Public policy (*ordre public*)), or if the administrative act in question was rendered in violation of a rule of public international law (Alfred Verdross and Bruno Simma, *Universelles Völkerrecht* (3rd edn, Duncker & Humblot 1984) § 1021; Martin Kment, *Grenzüberschreitendes Verwaltungshandeln* (Mohr Siebeck 2010) 452 *et seq*). With respect to the recognition duties that may flow from an application of the basic freedoms of the Treaty, recognition may essentially be refused under the 'mandatory requirements' established by the ECJ. Under secondary EU law, the scope for refusing recognition depends on the specific instrument in question and the specific rules contained therein.

V. Foreign administrative acts and private international law

1. General remarks

Foreign administrative acts, such as → expropriations or authorizations, may have important repercussions on the relationship between individuals. Above and beyond the purely factual role that foreign administrative acts may have in private law matters (see section I. above), questions as to the recognition of foreign administrative acts commonly arise in the context of private international law, where the legal situation created by an administrative act is an incidental (or preliminary) question in the application of a rule of private law; furthermore, the question may occur whether or not an administrative act referred to in a rule of private law may be substituted with a foreign administrative act (question of → Substitution). For either case, it is irrelevant whether a favourable or a burdensome administrative act is in question and the private role of the foreign administrative act suggests that the act is to be recognized (Hans Jürgen Sonnenberger, 'IPR Einleitung' in Franz Jürgen Säcker and Roland Rixecker (eds), *Münchener Kommentar zum Bürgerlichen Gesetzbuch*, vol 11 (5th edn, CH Beck 2010) para 397). Because of their relevance for private law, particular interest in private international law literature is traditionally devoted to the effects of foreign expropriations (→ Expropriation) and the effects of foreign environmental authorizations in cases of civil liability. In addition, findings by foreign competition authorities in damages actions for the infringement of antitrust rules serve as an example of the private role of foreign administrative acts.

2. Foreign environmental authorizations in cases of civil liability

Regarding foreign environmental authorizations, the question whether the effects of such authorizations should be recognized (and may possibly exclude the possibility of obtaining civil law remedies for → damages or → injunctions in neighbouring countries) has proved to be an as-yet unresolved issue concerning the application of the provision in the → Rome II Regulation (Regulation (EC) No 864/2007 of the European Parliament and of the Council of 11 July 2007 on the law applicable to non-contractual obligations (Rome II), [2007] OJ L 199/40) on → environmental liability, ie art 7. The Rome II Regulation does not (explicitly) address this issue and international treaties on cross-border environmental damage are usually lacking (but see, for example, the Convention between Germany and Austria of 19 December 1967 Concerning the Effects on the Territory of the Federal Republic of Germany of the Construction and Operation of the Salzburg Airport, 945 UNTS 87). The explanatory memorandum accompanying the proposal for the Rome II Regulation by the European Commission suggests that foreign authorizations could be treated as → 'local data' under art 17 of the Rome II Regulation (European Commission, 'Proposal for a Regulation of the European Parliament and the Council on the Law Applicable to Non-contractual Obligations ("Rome II")' COM(2003) 427 final, 20).

In the past, some courts in Europe held that pursuant to the principle of territoriality, administrative authorizations deploy their effect only within the territory of the state in which they were issued, and they have consequently declined to take account of such foreign environmental authorizations under the applicable *lex fori* (German Federal Court of Justice (BGH), [1978] IPRspr. no 40; Higher Regional Court (OLG) of Saarbrücken [1958] NJW 752, 754). Other courts were more permissive and found that foreign environmental authorizations can be taken into account if the emissions are in accordance with international environmental law, if the conditions of the foreign authorization are equivalent to those existing under the *lex fori* and if the individual seeking civil remedies has had the possibility to raise objections in the administrative procedure which led to the issuing of the authorization (Higher Regional Court (OLG) Linz, [1987] JBl. 577, 579; confirmed by the Austrian Supreme Court of Justice (Oberster Gerichtshof) [1989] JBl. 239; see also Rechtbank Rotterdam [1984] Nederlandse Jurisprudentie no 341).

In line with the explanatory memorandum accompanying the proposal of the European Commission, some authors favour a solution where foreign environmental authorizations are taken into consideration as 'local data' under art 17 Rome II Regulation if certain criteria of the kind established by the aforementioned case-law are met (see eg Thomas Kadner Graziano, 'The Law Applicable to Cross-Border Damage to the Environment' [2007] 9 YbPIL 71, 79 *et seq*). Since art 17 Rome II Regulation accords some discretion to the adjudicating court ('in so far as is appropriate'), this solution would allow for flexibility as to the recognition requirements and thus would not lead to an automatic recognition in each case. Others reject the application of art 17 Rome II Regulation, which refers to 'rules of safety and conduct' such as road safety rules, but still approve the recognition of foreign environmental authorizations provided that certain requirements are met (Peter Mankowksi, 'Ausgewählte Einzelfragen zur Rom II-VO' [2010] IPRax 389, 390 *et seq*). The specific requirements for recognition still need to be clarified; a subject of particular scepticism is the requirement that the foreign public law conditions allowing authorization be 'equivalent' with those conditions existing under the *lex fori*. While the conditions under which foreign authorization can be recognized still need to be settled, the view adopted by some courts in the past that foreign authorizations can only deploy their effects in the state where they were issued and therefore cannot be recognized seems to be outdated (see also the judgment of the ECJ in Case C-115/08 *Land Oberösterreich v ČEZ as* [2009] ECR I-10265, relying on the principle of prohibition of discrimination on the grounds of nationality within the scope of application of the EAEC Treaty).

Dirk Wiegandt

3. Findings of foreign competition authorities in damages actions for infringement of antitrust rules

In civil proceedings, where victims of an infringement of the antitrust rules contained in arts 101 and 102 TFEU sue the infringers for → damages after a competition authority has found that a breach of the antitrust rules occurred (usually referred to as 'follow-on actions'), related questions arise with respect to the effects of decisions taken by national competition authorities within the 'European Competition Network'. While it follows from art 16(1) of Regulation 1/2003 (Council Regulation (EC) No 1/2003 of 16 December 2002 on the implementation of the rules on competition laid down in Articles 81 and 82 of the Treaty, [2003] OJ L 1/1) that a Commission decision finding an infringement under art 101 or 102 TFEU constitutes a binding act to which decisions by national courts must not run counter Regulation 1/2003 does not address the question of the recognition of decisions of the national competition authorities. With a view to facilitating follow-on actions, art 9 Directive 2014/104/EU of the European Parliament and of the Council of 26 November 2014 on certain rules governing actions for damages under national law for infringements of the competition law provisions of the Member States and of the European Union ([2014] OJ l 349/1) requires Member States to ensure that a prior infringement decision taken by their own national competition authority is binding on their civil courts and that an infringement decision taken in another Member State can be presented as at least *prima facie* evidence that an infringement has occurred. Some Member States were reluctant to accept the strictly binding effect of foreign infringement decisions in damages actions, while others implemented the binding effect of foreign infringement decisions quite some time before the adoption of the Directive (see § 33(4) of the German Act against restrictions of competition (Gesetz gegen Wettbewerbsbeschränkungen of 27 July 1957, BGBl. I 1081, English translation of the current version as amended available at <www.gesetze-im-internet.de/englisch_gwb/index.html>)). Whatever effect is attributed to foreign infringement decisions, it is essential to identify the precise material, personal, temporal and territorial scope of the decision in question. It is noteworthy that the effect of infringement decisions is limited to damages actions; it does not extend to other possible private law remedies resulting from an infringement of antitrust rules. Furthermore, the effect is limited to the positive finding of an infringement; not covered are further requirements of a damages action, such as the extent of the loss suffered by the victim and the causal link between the infringement and the loss or the fault of the defendant.

VI. Modern trends and perspectives

A survey of the existing recognition duties illustrates that the traditional view according to which administrative acts only produce effects within the territory of the legal system they derive from has become subject to numerous exceptions. Today, there are multiple regimes requiring the recognition of foreign administrative acts and they are likely to increase even further in the future, in particular within the integration process of the EU. The effects of foreign administrative acts in the context of private law, ie their implications on the relationship between individuals, have been studied with respect to specific types of administrative acts. By contrast, general principles on the conditions and possible limits for recognition – as they exist with respect to the recognition and enforcement of foreign judgments (see eg arts 36 *et seq* and regarding refusal of recognition art 45 Brussels I Regulation (Regulation (EU) No 1215/2012 of the European Parliament and of the Council of 12 December 2012 on jurisdiction and the recognition and enforcement of judgments in civil and commercial matters, [2012] OJ L 351/1; → Brussels I (Convention and Regulation))) – are lacking and still have to be elaborated.

DIRK WIEGANDT

Literature

Jürgen Basedow, 'Recognition of Foreign Decisions within the European Competition Network' in Jürgen Basedow, Stéphanie Francq and Laurence Idot (eds), *International Antitrust Litigation* (Hart Publishing 2012) 393; Maria Berentelg, *Die Act of State-Doktrin als Zukunftsmodell für Deutschland?* (Mohr Siebeck 2010); Giuseppe Biscottini, 'L'efficacité des actes administratifs étrangers' (1961) 104 Collected Courses of the Hague Academy of International Law 635;

Anatol Dutta, *Die Durchsetzung öffentlichrechtlicher Forderungen ausländischer Staaten durch deutsche Gerichte* (Mohr Siebeck 2006); Christine Janssens, *The Principle of Mutual Recognition in EU Law* (OUP 2013); Martin Kment, *Grenzüberschreitendes Verwaltungshandeln* (Mohr Siebeck 2010); Klaus König, *Die Anerkennung ausländischer Verwaltungsakte* (Carl Heymanns 1965); Christine E Linke, *Europäisches Internationales Verwaltungsrecht* (Peter Lang 2001); Werner Meng, *Extraterritoriale Jurisdiktion im öffentlichen Wirtschaftsrecht* (Springer 1994); Jörg Menzel, *Internationales Öffentliches Recht* (Mohr Siebeck 2011); Sascha Michaels, *Anerkennungspflichten im Wirtschaftsverwaltungsrecht der Europäischen Gemeinschaft und der Bundesrepublik Deutschland* (Duncker & Humblot 2004); Markus Möstl, 'Preconditions and Limits of Mutual Recognition' (2010) 47 CMLR 405; Karl Neumeyer, *Internationales Verwaltungsrecht, IV* (Schweitzer 1936); Christoph Ohler, *Die Kollisionsordnung des Allgemeinen Verwaltungsrechts* (Mohr Siebeck 2005); Charalambous Pamboukis, *L'acte public étranger en droit international privé* (Librairie générale de droit et de jurisprudence 1993); Matthias Ruffert, 'Der transnationale Verwaltungsakt' [2001] Die Verwaltung 453; Matthias Ruffert, 'Recognition of Foreign Legislative and Administrative Acts' in Rüdiger Wolfrum (ed), *Max Planck Encyclopedia of Public International Law* (2011); Klaus Vogel, *Der räumliche Anwendungsbereich der Verwaltungsrechtsnorm* (Metzner 1965); Henrik Wenander, 'Recognition of Foreign Administrative Decisions' [2011] ZaöRV 755.

Recognition of legal situations evidenced by documents

I. Background and concepts

When it comes to their legal situation, persons and businesses in an increasingly mobile society may face difficulties in cross-border activities or in moving from one legal system to another (for example, concerning the validity of a → marriage or of the formation of a company, of an adoption or with regard to ownership). Although these legal situations may be evidenced by documents, the documents might not be regarded as proof of the legal situation, and the legal situation recorded in the respective document might not be treated as valid beyond the borders of the state of origin.

These problems are also encountered when legal situations are evidenced by judicial decisions. For judgments, international treaties and European regulations take care of many of the transnational problems. Foreign decrees very often do not need any legalization (→ Legalization of public documents) and an Apostille may not even be required. In some international instruments, the 'authority and effectiveness' of a judgment is accorded automatically beyond the borders of the state in which it was rendered. This might be the case even without any review of the private international law or the substantive law applied and without examination of the facts. The recognition might only be subject to very few grounds of refusal, such as → public policy (*ordre public*) or the violation of the right to be heard. Outside these exceptions, the (foreign) judgment will very often have the force of *res judicata*.

According to the European regulations, this is, for example, the case for Member State judgments in → civil and commercial matters (art 33 Brussels I Regulation (Regulation (EC) No 44/2001 of 22 December 2000 on jurisdiction and the recognition and enforcement of judgments in civil and commercial matters, [2001] OJ L 12/1); art 36 Brussels Ibis Regulation (Regulation (EU) No 1215/2012 of the European Parliament and of the Council of 12 December 2012 on jurisdiction and the recognition and enforcement of judgments in civil and commercial matters (recast), [2012] OJ L 351/1) (→ Brussels I (Convention and Regulation))), for decisions of other Member States (except → Denmark) on divorce and parental authority (art 21 → Brussels IIbis Regulation (Council Regulation (EC) No 2201/2003 of 27 November 2003 concerning jurisdiction and the recognition and enforcement of judgments in matrimonial matters and the matters of parental responsibility, repealing Regulation (EC) No 1347/2000, [2003] OJ L 338/1)), on maintenance (arts 17 and 23 Maintenance Regulation (Council Regulation (EC) No 4/2009 of 18 December 2008 on jurisdiction, applicable law, recognition and enforcement of decisions and cooperation in matters relating to maintenance obligations, [2009] OJ L 7/1) (→ Maintenance obligations)) and on → succession (art 39 Succession Regulation (Regulation (EU) No 650/2012 of the European Parliament and of the Council of 4 July 2012 on jurisdiction, applicable law, recognition and enforcement of decisions and acceptance and enforcement of authentic instruments in matters of succession and on the creation of a European Certificate of Succession, [2012] OJ L 201/107; → Rome IV Regulation)). Outside the EU, some treaties provide for mutual (facilitated) recognition in specific areas of law (see, for example, the Hague Child Maintenance Convention 1958 (Hague Convention of 15 April 1958 concerning the recognition and enforcement of decisions relating to maintenance obligations towards children, 539 UNTS 27), the Hague Divorce and Separation Convention (Hague Convention of 1 June 1970 on the recognition of divorces and legal separations, 978 UNTS 399), the Hague Recognition and Enforcement Convention (Hague Convention of 1 February 1971 on the recognition and enforcement of foreign judgments in civil and commercial matters, 1144 UNTS 258) and the Hague Maintenance Recognition and Enforcement Convention 1973 (Hague Convention of 2 October 1973 on the recognition and enforcement of decisions relating to maintenance obligations, 1021 UNTS 209)). Some national legislators have also become generous in recognizing foreign judicial decisions without a *révision au fond*.

However, if a legal situation is evidenced not by a judicial decision but simply by documents, these rules on recognition hardly ever apply (for exceptions, see below, section III.1.b)). Persons and businesses might therefore be confronted with several problems: the document they produce in another jurisdiction may be of no legal relevance at all, although it has been validly established in the state of origin. The document may not furnish evidence of anything without prior legalization. Even if such legalization is carried out, the legal effects of such documents may not be recognized *per se*. Thus, two different issues are at stake: first, the authenticity and the evidential value of a foreign document; and, second, the legal effects of such document, ie the authority and effectiveness of the legal situation evidenced by this document. Both issues raise different problems and have to be treated separately.

Several international instruments deal with the evidential value of foreign documents, but most of them explicitly exclude their application to the legal effects of such documents (see art 2(14) and Recital (18) EU Regulation ('Proposal for a Regulation of the European Parliament and of the Council of 6 June 2016 on promoting the free movement of citizens and businesses by simplifying the acceptance of certain public documents in the European Union and amending Regulation (EU) No 1024/ 2012 of 24 April 2013 OJ 2016 L 200); art 4 CIEC/ICCS Convention on the Establishment of Maternal Descent of Natural Children (Convention on the Establishment of Maternal Descent of Natural Children, signed at Brussels on 12 September 1962, ICCS Convention No 6; 932 UNTS 76)). This aspect, and not the authenticity and the evidential value of foreign documents (→ Legalization of public documents), is the topic of this article.

When a legal situation has been created (eg a → marriage or a corporation), there are principally two ways to deal with the legal effects of this situation in other jurisdictions (→ Private international law, methods of, sections III. and VI.). First, the legal effects of this act or event may be determined by the law dictated by the private international law rules of the jurisdiction where the respective question arises (conflict rules of the → *lex fori*). For example, the validity and the effects of a marriage celebrated in state A will be determined in state B in accordance with the law designated by B's choice-of-law rules. If the private international law of state B applies the *lex domicilii* of the spouses to the substantive validity of a marriage, the marriage celebrated in state A will not be regarded as valid if the → marriage contravenes the imperative requirements of the *lex domicilii* of the spouses. This could be the case, for example, if state A determines these questions by reference to its own law, which does not provide any of these impediments. If, however, the marriage is valid according to the *lex domicilii* (because there are no impediments or because the *lex domicilii* refers to the *lex loci actus*), then the marriage is also regarded as valid in state B. This is a so-called 'private international law solution'.

If, however, the act or event is evidenced by a document issued in state A, a second possible solution comes into play: the legal situation evidenced by this document of state A could be recognized as valid and with all its legal consequences in other legal systems, irrespective of the law applied and irrespective of the law which should determine these questions according to the private international law rules of the other jurisdictions. The document validly established in state A could have the same legal effect in states B, C, D, etc. In the example above, the marriage certificate of state A would also prove a valid marriage in state B without further examination. This would apply even if impediments of the *lex domicilii*, applicable according to the conflict rules of state B, had been ignored. This approach may be called 'the principle of mutual recognition'.

The differences between the two approaches may be characterized as follows: according to the first approach, a legal situation is respected in another jurisdiction if it is valid according to the conflict laws of that jurisdiction. The latter approach recognizes a legal situation as valid if the document evidencing this situation was validly established in the state of origin (Paolo Picone, 'Les méthodes de coordination des ordres juridiques en droit international privé' (1999) 276 Rec. des Cours 13: 'indifférence à la loi appliquée, mais non à l'ordre juridique compétent'). Comparable to a judgment, the principle of *res judicata* may be said to apply to the document.

The result of both approaches will be the same in cases where the conflict rules of state B designate the same law as applied in state A (for example, the *lex loci actus*). But the methods in achieving this outcome differ: in the first case, private international law rules determine the result, whereas in the second, the conflict rules are of no importance whatsoever.

II. Historical development

1. Ulricus Huber and the vested right theory

It seems to be generally accepted that the idea of recognition of legal effects resulting from a legal act or event in another jurisdiction was developed by *Ulricus Huber* (→ Huber, Ulrik) (1636–1694) (Hans Jürgen Sonnenberger, 'Anerkennung statt Verweisung? Eine neue internationalprivatrechtliche Methode' in Jörn Bernreuther and others (eds), *Festschrift für Ulrich Spellenberg* (Sellier 2012) 371, 375). The concept tried to overcome the Statutists' theory and to explain at the same time why legal effects attributed by a foreign law could be recognized in another jurisdiction. Despite the (strictly) territorial approach, the legal situation is not governed by the → *lex fori*, but is 'recognized' with its effects attributed by the foreign jurisdiction.

In the Anglo-American world, *Huber's* ideas have been adopted and developed further by *Joseph* → *Story* (1797–1845) in the USA and in England (see Kurt Nadelmann, 'Introduction to Hessel E. Yntema, the Comity Doctrine' (1966) 65 Mich.L.Rev. 1, 2). The idea of the recognition of duly acquired rights culminated in *Joseph Beale's* → vested rights theory. *Beale* treated legal effects of acts and events which happened abroad as facts or as obligations not to be called into question anywhere.

Although this theory was highly influential in the US courts until the 1950s and also influenced French doctrine (*Pillet*), its impact on continental European choice-of-law rules was very limited. *Huber's* and *Story's* theories also lost their influence in England. In the USA, *Beale's* theory came to be severely criticized. However, it must be stressed that most critics regarded that theory as one of private international law and not as an alternative to choice-of-law rules. The reason for this might be that a right was regarded as vested only if 'created by the appropriate law'. In contrast, → *Rabel* clearly states that 'this theory ... is the exact antipode of private international law' (Ernst Rabel, *Conflict of Laws, Volume I* (2nd edn, UoM 1958) 14).

2. Conventions on civil status

The discussion on mutual recognition of legal situations has been revived in the process of drafting and commenting new international conventions on civil status and in relation to the ongoing process of ensuring free movement of goods, persons, services and capital within the EU. The international conventions of The Hague and the → CIEC/ICCS (International Commission on Civil Status) will be examined in detail in section III. Though the acceptance of these conventions has been very limited so far (the Convention concerning the recognition of the legal personality of foreign companies, associations and institutions of 1956 did not even enter into force), their impact on the discussion has been considerable. Some of the conventions might have been 'ahead of their time' (Hans van Loon, 'Unification and Cooperation in the Field of International Family Law: A Perspective from The Hague' in Alegría Borrás and others (eds), *E Pluribus Unum, Liber Amicorum Georges Droz* (Kluwer 1996) 173, 179), but still they provide a method which might be suitable for dealing with certain problems in a globalized society (like → surrogacy). The idea is that – provided agreement on the relevant standards can be reached – mutual recognition and cooperation may serve to overcome some problems in a globalized world.

3. Mutual recognition in the Internal Market

'Mutual recognition' as a principle of the Internal Market of the EU concerns a broader field of problems: the four fundamental freedoms of the EU have given rise to a heated discussion of 'mutual recognition as a principle of supplementing or even replacing the private international rules' (→ Freedom of establishment/persons (European Union) and private international law). Decisions of the CJEU (→ Court of Justice of the European Union) on the significance of the law of the state of origin with regard to free movements of goods and services (see below section III.1.a)) as well as on the recognition of a corporation or an individual's name registered in another Member State have been feeding this approach. In addition, the Commission has issued a Green Paper Concerning the Promotion of Free Movement of Public Documents and Recognition of the Effects of Civil Status Records (European Commission, 'Green Paper: Less bureaucracy for citizens: promoting free movement of public documents and recognition for the effects of civil status records of 14 December 2010' COM(2010) 747 final). The idea is that civil status records drawn up by the authorities of one Member State (for example, concerning birth, marriage, paternity or death) should have the same effect, ie prove the documented legal situation, in all other Member States. As this idea has met with a certain amount of criticism (Heinz-Peter Mansel and others, 'Stellungnahme im Auftrag des Deutschen Rates für Internationales Privatrecht zum Grünbuch der Europäischen Kommission – Weniger Verwaltungsaufwand für EU-Bürger: Den freien Verkehr öffentlicher Urkunden und die Anerkennung der Rechtswirkungen von Personenstandsurkunden erleichtern – KOM(2010) 747 endg' [2011] IPRax 335), the new Regulation 2016/1191 of the European Parliament and of the Council of 6 June 2016 on promoting the free movement of citizens and businesses by simplifying the acceptance of certain public documents in the European Union and amending Regulation (EU) No 1024/2012 of 24 April 2013 OJ 2016 L 200 addresses neither the effects of civil status records nor of other public documents, but leaves this topic to further discussion. Thus, the question of whether fundamental freedoms within the EU might be guaranteed more efficiently by a unification of the private international law or by a method of recognition is still an open one.

III. Contemporary significance

1. Mutual recognition within the EU

a) Primary sources of European law

The free movement of goods and services might require trading rules of the Member States (as well as EFTA states and Turkey) which do not hinder, directly or indirectly, actually or potentially, intra-community trade (Case C-8/74 of 11 July 1974, *Procureur du Roi v Dassonville* [1974] ECR 837). In the absence of (unified) Community rules, lawful production and marketing in the country of origin has to be 'recognized' in the other Member States. Other Member States may, in principle, not bar the import of these products (Case C-120/78 of 2 February 1979, *Rewe-Zentral AG v Bundesmonopolverwaltung für Branntwein (Cassis de Dijon)* [1979] ECR 649). This principle is said to arise from arts 34 and 35 TFEU (Treaty on the Functioning of the European Union (consolidated version), [2012] OJ C 326/47). The destination Member State must allow free access to its market for all EEA/Turkish products, provided that these products have an equivalent level of protection of the various legitimate interests at stake. The Commission calls this the principle of 'mutual recognition' (European Commission, 'Commission interpretative communication on facilitating the access of products to the markets of other Member States: the practical application of mutual recognition (text with EEA relevance)' [2003] OJ C265/2–16). However, although the rules of the country of origin are of considerable importance, this kind of 'mutual recognition' does not provide for the recognition of a legal situation evidenced by documents, which is the subject of this article. It is rather a result-oriented adjustment after the 'normal' rules of private international law have been applied (Pierre Mayer, 'Les méthodes de la reconnaissance en droit international privé' in *Le droit international privé: esprit et méthodes Mélanges en l'honneur de Paul Lagarde* (Dalloz 2005), 547, 549; for the principle of 'equivalence', see Hélène Gaudemet-Tallon, 'De nouvelles fonctions pour l'équivalence en droit international privé?' in Bertrand Ancel and others (eds), *Le droit international privé: esprit et méthodes. Mélanges en l'honneur de Paul Lagarde* (Dalloz 2009) 303, 309).

Nevertheless, the approach of the CJEU and the Commission has provoked and continues to provoke heated discussion on whether private international law rules have to or should be replaced or displaced by a principle of 'mutual recognition' (Erik Jayme and Christian Kohler, 'Europäisches Kollisionsrecht 2004: Territoriale Erweiterung und methodische Rückgriffe' [2004] IPRax 481, 483; Wulf-Henning Roth, 'Methoden der Rechtsfindung und Rechtsanwendung im Europäischen Kollisionsrecht' [2006] IPRax 338–347). This debate has been intensified by CJEU decisions on the freedom of establishment of corporations (Cases C-212/97 of 9 March 1999, *Centros Ltd v Erhvervs- og Selskabsstyrelsen* [1999] ECR I-1459; C-208/00 of 5 November 2002, *Überseering BV v Nordic Construction Company Baumanagement GmbH* [2002] ECR I-9919; C-167/01 of 30 September 2003, *Kamer van Koophandel en Fabrieken voor Amsterdam v Inspire Art Ltd* [2003] ECR I-10155; C-411/03 of 13 December 2005, *SEVIC Systems AG ECR* [2005] ECR I-10805; and C-210/06 of 16 December 2008, *Cartesio Oktató és Szolgáltató bt* [2008] ECR I-9641). At the start of this line of cases, some academics interpreted these decisions as requiring the application of the law of the country of registration, but the following decisions made clear that arts 49 and 54 TFEU only require the freedom of establishment across the borders of the Member States (→ Freedom of establishment/persons (European Union) and private international law). It is up to the Member States whether they ensure this freedom either by applying the law of the place of registration or by recognizing a formally registered corporation as a valid legal entity, or by a mixture of these approaches (see Heinz-Peter Mansel, 'Anerkennung als Grundprinzip des Europäischen Rechtsraums' (2006) 70 RabelsZ 651, 675, 681). Thus, recognition of the corporation evidenced by the documents of registration is only one option, but is not prescribed by EU law (arts 49 and 54 TFEU).

The same is true with regard to the recognition of individuals' names registered or acquired in one Member State (→ Names of individuals) (Case C-168/91 of 30 March 1993, *Christos Konstantinidis v Stadt Altensteig – Standesamt and Landratsamt Calw – Ordnungsamt* [1993] ECR I-1191; Case C-148/02 of 2 October 2003, *Carlos Garcia Avello v Belgian State* [2003] ECR I-11613; Case C-353/06 of 14 October 2008, *Stefan Grunkin and Dorothee Regina Paul* [2008] ECR I-7639). The Member States decide how they can ensure the free movement of citizens within the EU without causing problems with regard to the use of surnames. Several options exist, from the application of the law of the first registration to the choice of the persons concerned (Heinz-Peter Mansel, 'Anerkennung als Grundprinzip des Europäischen Rechtsraums' (2006) 70 RabelsZ 651, 690 *et seq*).

Whether the guarantee of the free movement of citizens implies the 'recognition' of a → marriage or civil partnership is also a subject of debate. Do Member States have an obligation to recognize a marriage or civil partnership evidenced by a document established within one EU Member State for all purposes as a civil status or not (see Erik Jayme, 'Das Internationale Privatrecht im System des Gemeinschaftsrechts – Tagung in Macerata' [2006] IPRax 67, 68)? The prevailing view seems to be that as long as a Member State does not deny the right to 'family life', neither art 21 TFEU nor art 2(2)(a), (b) of the Free Movement of Citizens Directive (Directive 2004/38/EC of the European Parliament and of the Council of 29 April 2004 on the right of citizens of the Union and their family members to move and reside freely within the territory of the Member States amending Regulation (EEC) No 1612/68 and repealing Directives 64/221/EEC, 68/360/EEC, 72/194/EEC, 73/148/EEC, 75/34/EEC, 75/35/EEC, 90/364/EEC, 90/365/EEC and 93/96/EEC, [2004] OJ L 158/77) requires a recognition of the civil status as such (Katja Funken, *Das Anerkennungsprinzip im Internationalen Privatrecht* (Mohr 2009) 173 *et seq*). Thus, it seems that the European primary legislation, despite its emphasis on the fundamental freedoms and the respect that Member States must pay to these principles, does not prescribe mutual recognition as the only method in dealing with cross-border activities. Nevertheless, the scholarly debate concerning whether mutual recognition should supplement or displace private international law, especially on civil status, has not yet drawn to a close (see European Commission, 'Green Paper: Less bureaucracy for citizens: promoting free movement of public documents and recognition for the effects of civil status records of 14 December 2010' COM(2010) 747 final, No 4; European Commission, 'Proposal for a Regulation of the European Parliament and of the Council on promoting the free movement of citizens and businesses by simplifying the acceptance of certain public documents in the European Union and amending

Regulation (EU) No 1024/2012 of 24 April 2013' COM(2013) 228 final No 2).

b) The role of documents in the EU Regulations concerning the recognition and enforcement of judgments

The EU Regulations providing for the recognition and enforcement of Member State judgments in certain fields of the law place authentic documents enforceable in the Member State of origin on an equal footing with foreign judgments as far as enforcement is concerned (see art 58 Brussels I Regulation, art 46 Brussels Ibis Regulation; art 48 Maintenance Regulation; arts 59 and 60 Succession Regulation). The Brussels Ibis Regulation neither provides nor implies that the respective document must be treated like a judgment, ie have the force of *res judicata* concerning the subject matter concerned (Rolf Wagner, 'Die Anerkennung von Personenstandsurkunden in Europa' [2014] NZFam 121, 122). The Succession Regulation only deals with the evidentiary value of the document (art 59(1)). The legal situation documented is determined by the applicable succession law (art 59(3), Recital (63)) and does not hinge on the question of 'recognition' (Rome IV Regulation).

The situation is slightly different with regard to the respective provisions of the Brussels IIbis Regulation and the Maintenance Regulation. Both Regulations provide that the enforceable authentic documents have to be recognized according to their rules on judgments. Does this mean that they have quasi-*res judicata* force in relation to the legal situation evidenced therein? The interpretation of these rules in legal literature differs: some authors consider the rule as negligently formulated (Reinhold Geimer and Rolf Schütze, *Europäisches Zivilverfahrensrecht* (3rd edn, Beck 2010) Art. 46 EuEheVO para 4), practically inappropriate and insignificant, and believe the wording to be mistaken (Jörg Pirrung, 'Vorbem C–H zu Art 19 EGBGB' in Dieter Henrich and Jörg Pirrung (eds), *J. von Staudingers Kommentar zum Bürgerlichen Gesetzbuch: Staudinger BGB – EGBGB/IPR Einführungsgesetz zum Bürgerlichen Gesetzbuche/ IPR (Internationales Kindschaftsrecht 2)* (Sellier/ De Gruyter 2009) C-177). Others want to interpret the rule restrictively to cover only the evidential value (Marianne Andrae, 'Art. 48 EuUntVO' in Thomas Rauscher (ed), *EuZPR/EuIPR* (4th edn, Sellier 2015) para 6). But there seems to be a majority opinion which also applies the rules on recognition of judgments to these authentic instruments (Lajos Vékás, 'Art. 46' in Ulrich Magnus and Peter Mankowski (eds), *Brussels IIbis Regulation* (Sellier 2012) para 24; Katharina Paraschas, 'Art. 46 Brussels IIbis Regulation' in Arthur Bülow, Karl-Heinz Böckstiegel, Reinhold Geimer and Rolf Schütze (eds), *Internationaler Rechtsverkehr* (Beck 2011) para 17; Thomas Rauscher, *EuZPR/EuIPR* (Sellier 2015) Art. 46 Brussels IIbis Regulation, para 2; Pascal Ancel and Horatia Muir Watt, 'La désunion europeénne: Le Règlement dit Bruxelles II' (2001) 28 Rev.crit.DIP 403, 437, 441; Peter Picht, 'Art. 48 EuUntVO' para 6 in Arthur Bülow and others (eds), *Internationaler Rechtsverkehr* (Beck 2011)). As the application of the respective rules is in any case confined to enforceable documents, the significance of such 'recognition' is limited. This is especially true as in these areas of law, a change of circumstances often allows a new decision on future obligations and rights; documents have therefore very little, if any, quasi-*res judicata* effect.

Thus far, it seems that neither the primary legal sources of the EU nor the Regulations on the recognition and enforcement of judgments in certain fields of law necessarily favour the mutual recognition of legal situations evidenced by documents.

2. International conventions

There are several international conventions, mainly drafted by the → CIEC/ICCS (International Commission on Civil Status) or in The Hague, which might serve as models for the recognition of a legal situation evidenced by documents. However, the setting of these rules is very different and not always completely clear. Thus, there is some debate as to whether these conventions follow the recognition approach at all. The Convention on the Establishment of Maternal Descent of Natural Children, signed at Brussels on 12 September 1962, ICCS Convention No 6; 932 UNTS 76, provides in art 1 that the woman registered in the birth certificate will be recognized as the mother of the child; however, the contrary may be proved (second sentence of art 1). As neither the law applied nor the law applicable according to the rules of the state of the register or of the state of recognition plays a role, one might classify this rule as one of recognition, but art 4 excludes the validity of the mother's recognition from the application of the Convention.

In any case, the details of this kind of recognition remain obscure. The Convention of 10 September 1970 on legitimation by marriage, 1081 UNTS 247 – although speaking of 'recognition' – contains only rules on the applicable law. But the International Convention No 29 on the recognition of decisions recording a gender reassignment (Convention No 29 relative à la reconnaissance des décisions constatant un changement de sexe) by the International Commission on Civil Status (Commission Internationale de l'État Civil, CIEC (→ CIEC/ICCS (International Commission on Civil Status))), adopted on 16 September 1999 in Lisbon and signed on 12 September 2000 in Vienna, the Convention on the recognition of surnames signed by the General Assembly in Antalya on 16 September 2005, ICCS Convention No 31 and the Convention on the recognition of registered partnerships opened for signature at Munich on 5 September 2007, ICCS Convention No 32 do provide for a recognition of the legal situation evidenced either by an administrative decision (sex reassignment) or by the extract of a registry (not clear with regard to *ex lege* changes of surnames). Most of these conventions either exclude certain delicate matters or provide possibilities of reservation for the contracting states (see conventions on sex reassignment and on → registered partnerships), or limit the scope to the civil status as such to allow non-recognition for certain defined reasons. The Conventions have had only limited success so far because too many important questions are left open.

The same is not true for the Hague Marriage Convention (Hague Convention of 14 March 1978 on Celebration and Recognition of the Validity of Marriages, 1901 UNTS 131), though it has not been widely ratified. Article 9 of the Convention clearly obliges the contracting states to recognize a → marriage 'validly entered into under the law of the state of celebration or which subsequently becomes valid under that law', subject to some substantive marriage impediments (art 11) and to public policy (art 14). The Convention combines this principle of recognition with conflict rules for the celebration of a marriage in the contracting states (arts 2, 3, 5 and 6). This combination of conflict rules and recognition supplemented by some substantive rules (art 11), as well as some exceptions (arts 3 (1), 9(2) and 12(2)) and limitations of the scope of the chapter on recognition (arts 8 and 12), seems to make the application of the rules of the Convention too complicated and has resulted in criticism (Peter North, 'Development of Rules of Private international law in the Field of Family Law' (1980) 166 Rec. des Cours 9, 97). In addition, in the Anglo-American world, a conflict rule providing for the application of foreign law for the celebration of a marriage has raised doubts as to its practicability (Willis Reese, 'The Hague Convention on Celebration and Recognition of the Validity of Marriages' (1979) 20 Va.L.Rev. 25, 32; Patrick Glenn, 'Conflict of Laws – The 1976 Hague Conventions on Marriage and Matrimonial Property Regimes' (1977) 55 Can. Bar Rev. 586, 590). The main objection, however, results from art 16 of the Convention, which allows contracting states to exclude the application of Chapter 1, the conflict rules for the celebration of marriage. Thus, contracting states would have to recognize marriages even if the state of celebration did not apply the conflict rules of the Convention.

On the other hand, the 'synthèse de deux systèmes' (Georges Droz, 'Cours général de droit International privé' (1991) 177 Rec. des Cours 154) – private international law rules on celebration and rules of recognition on validity – combined with enumerated grounds for refusal copies the pattern of international conventions (and EU regulations on the recognition of judgments) and may be a model for the future (Hans van Loon, 'Unification and Cooperation in the Field of International Family Law: A Perspective from The Hague' in Alegría Borrás and others (eds), *E Pluribus Unum, Liber Amicorum Georges Droz* (Kluwer 1996) 173, 179), although a number of problems still have to be dealt with.

A similar, but in some respects different, approach is taken by the Hague Adoption Convention (Hague Convention of 29 May 1993 on protection of children and co-operation in respect of intercountry adoption, 1870 UNTS 167; 32 ILM 1134): art 23(1) obliges the Contracting States to recognize *ipso iure* as → CIEC/ICCS (International Commission on Civil Status) adoption 'certified by the competent authority of the state of the adoption as having been made in accordance with the Convention'. Instead of choice-of-law rules, the Convention contains substantive and procedural rules which set standards to be applied in preparing and establishing the adoption as well as in relation to the effects of an adoption. Ensuring compliance with certain minimum standards irrespective of the applicable or applied law and legal security for the persons concerned, especially the best interests of children, is the main goal of this Convention. The Convention has been ratified by 93 states; thus, its concept seems to be convincing at least in this field of law.

Finally, it has to be mentioned that the recognition of a legal situation established in another jurisdiction might be required by art 8 ECHR (European Convention of 4 November 1950 for the Protection of Human Rights and Fundamental Freedoms, 213 UNTS 221) as far as civil status and family life is concerned, even if private international law would not lead to this result (see Patrick Kinsch, 'Recognition in a Form of a Status Acquired Abroad – Private international law Rules and European Human Rights Law' in Katharina Boele-Woelki, Talia Einhorn and Daniel Girsberger (eds), *Convergence and Divergence in Private international law, Liber Amicorum Kurt Siehr* (Schulthess 2010) 259, 22, 274).

3. National laws

Swiss and Dutch laws on the validity of a → marriage celebrated abroad are often analysed with regard to their choice-of-law approach: do they apply the concept of recognition of a legal situation or do they follow (more or less) the traditional private international law approach applying the *lex loci actus/celebrationis*? The → Netherlands have ratified the Hague Marriage Convention and have implemented the rules on the recognition (→ Human rights and private international law) of a marriage celebrated abroad (art 9 of the Convention) in Book 10 Dutch New Civil Code (Nieuw Burgerlijk Wetboek of 1 January 1992, available at <http://wetten.overheid.nl>; arts 27 *et seq*). But as art 31(3) also refers to the private international rules of the place of celebration, this approach should be classified as a private international law solution. Article 24 provides for the recognition of surnames and forenames (→ Names of individuals) recorded outside the Netherlands if the instruments have been drawn up by a competent authority in accordance with the local provisions. Is this a private international law rule referring to the *lex loci actus*?

According to art 45 Swiss Private international law Act (Bundesgesetz über das Internationale Privatrecht of 18 December 1987, 1988 BBl I 5, as amended), a → marriage validly celebrated abroad will be recognized in → Switzerland regardless of the law applied at its celebration (Switzerland is not a contracting state of the Hague Marriage Convention, but follows a comparable approach; see Pierre Lalive, 'La Convention de la Haye du 14 mars 1978 sur la célébration et la reconnaissance de la validité des mariages' (1978) 34 SchwJbIntR 31, 45). The question of which law governs the validity of the marriage is left open (Kurt Siehr, *Das Internationale Privatrecht der Schweiz* (Schulthess 2002) 22). This might be classified as the relevance of the 'ordinamento competente' 'in blocco', a theory developed by Paolo Picone (*inter alia* in Jürgen Basedow and others (eds), *Private Law in the International Arena – From National Conflict Rules Towards Harmonization and Unification – Liber Amicorum Kurt Siehr* (Asser 2000) 569, 585). This theory goes beyond the rules of reference of private international law and comes very close to the concept of 'recognition' of a legal situation.

4. Arguments in favour and against the new approach

Rules on the recognition of legal situations evidenced by documents cannot supersede and displace rules of private international law. Private international law rules are needed to determine the applicable law within a jurisdiction. Rules on recognition may only supplement choice-of-law rules.

It has been highlighted at several instances that the concept of recognition would facilitate solutions for trans-border problems and prevent 'limping' legal situations (Paul Lagarde, 'Développements futurs du droit international privé dans une Europe en voie d'unification: quelques conjectures' (2004) 68 RabelsZ 225; Dagmar Coester-Waltjen, 'Anerkennung im Internationalen Personen-, Familien- und Erbrecht und das Europäische Kollisionsrecht' [2006] IPRax 392, 394). Whereas the application of the private international law rules of the forum might produce different results in the various jurisdictions, the 'recognition approach' would allow the persons concerned to rely on a legal situation evidenced by a document wherever they are and at whatever time the question of validity arises (Paul Lagarde, 'Développements futurs du droit international privé dans une Europe en voie d'unification: quelques conjectures' (2004) 68 RabelsZ 225, 231). The institutions dealing with the document would not have to examine their own choice-of-law rules, or those of the issuing state, or the factual situation. The recognition approach could also be applied to private acts whenever they are certified by a document of a competent authority (Patrick Kinsch, 'Recognition in a Form of a Status Acquired Abroad – Private international law Rules and European Human Rights Law' in Katharina Boele-Woelki, Talia Einhorn and Daniel Girsberger (eds), *Convergence and Divergence in Private international law, Liber Amicorum Kurt Siehr* (Schulthess 2010) 259, 274; see also *Singh v Entry Clearance Officer New Delhi* [2004] EWCA Civ 1075 on adoption by private act). The threat posed by a great variety of substantive and conflict rules to transnational activities would be greatly reduced.

Nevertheless, some important counter-arguments have been brought forward against recognition as a concept for dealing with transnational problems: first, this concept is not needed because many of the problems arising from the application of the private international law rules of the forum can be avoided by the unification of those conflict rules (Hans Jürgen Sonnenberger, 'Anerkennung statt Verweisung? Eine neue internationalprivatrechtliche Methode' in Jörn Bernreuther and others (eds), *Festschrift für Ulrich Spellenberg* (Sellier 2012) 371, 389). Especially within the EU, unified private international law is needed to prevent forum shopping (→ Forum (and law) shopping). This should be the paramount consideration of the European legislator. If all EU Member States apply the same conflict rule, for instance on the formation of a marriage, the marriage validly concluded according to the applicable law will also be regarded as valid in another forum because the private international rules of the forum lead to the same law and therefore, at least in principle, to the same result. Private international law rules can even take care of changes in the → connecting factors without risking potential pitfalls to the legal situation created before the change (see art 16(3) Hague Child Protection Convention (Hague Convention of 19 October 1996 on jurisdiction, applicable law, recognition, enforcement and co-operation in respect of parental responsibility and measures for the protection of children, 35 ILM 1391)). Thus, recognition as an additional method of dealing with transnational problems might only complicate the situation.

However, outside the EU agreements on private international law, rules concerning the respective legal situations might be even more difficult to achieve than within the EU. Rules on the mutual obligation to recognize a certain status when established abroad might be easier to agree upon because they would leave the national conflict rules unchanged. Even in the French debate, the importance of saving the national traditional conflict rules from changes by the European legislator is widespread (Paul Lagarde, 'Développements futurs du droit international privé dans une Europe en voie d'unification: quelques conjectures' (2004) 68 RabelsZ 225, 226, 229). By getting around the conflict-of-law issue, the 'dogma' of applying always the → *lex fori* or the dominance of → nationality or habitual residence (→ Domicile, habitual residence and establishment) as connecting factors need not be dealt with. Another possibility would be to supplement unified conflict rules with the principle of recognition of legal situations established abroad (like the Hague Marriage Convention proposes in principle, save art 16; see above). Some propose applying the recognition concept (only) in connection with a → choice of law by the parties (Charalambos Pamboukis, 'La renaissance –metamorphose de la méthode de reconnaissance' (2008) 67 Rev.crit.DIP 513 *et seq*) or with a strict *lex fori* rule (Gian Paolo Romano, 'La bilatéralité éclipsée par l'autorité: développements récents en matière d'état des personnes' (2006) 65 Rev.crit.DIP 458, 507). Recognition on the basis of unified private international law rules will dispense with an examination of the applicable law and thus reduce the barriers to transnational activities, although it still presumes mutual trust in the authorities issuing the respective documents.

A second counter-argument is the potential distrust of the institutions issuing the documents. Did they issue a certificate which documents the legal situation correctly? Very often, foreign authorities seem even less trustworthy than foreign courts. Will they have applied a law which, from the point of view of the forum, has at least some connection to the situation evidenced? Which documents can be recognized, which institutions may issue these documents and which institutions may be regarded as competent (Pierre Mayer, 'Les méthodes de la reconnaissance en droit international privé' in Bertrand Ancel and others (eds), *Le droit international privé: esprit et méthodes Mélanges en l'honneur de Paul Lagarde* (Dalloz 2005) 547, 553)? In addition, there may also be distrust of the persons concerned: did they take advantage of a law (or institution) solely in order to escape the impediments of the normally applicable law (→ Evasion of laws (*fraus legis*))? Did they cheat when applying for the document? It might have been much easier to make false statements in a foreign jurisdiction than at home.

Recognition therefore seems only to be acceptable as long as certain minimum standards are guaranteed. This could be achieved by providing for the observance of some substantive and procedural principles irrespective of the laws applied. The success of the Hague Adoption Convention seems to speak for this solution. The distrust of foreign institutions or authorities and of the persons concerned may be overcome, notably by a limited agreement on certain principles with regard to the respect for human rights (→ Human rights and private international law). A detailed instrument on the recognition of certain legal situations evidenced by documents might allow important principles of private law (for example, no recognition of child marriages) and fundamental values that are internationally accepted (such as *favor matrimonii*, best interests of the child as paramount consideration) to also be taken into account.

Third, the concept as it stands remains more or less obscure (Heinz-Peter Mansel, 'Anerkennung als Grundprinzip des Europäischen Rechtsraums' (2006) 70 RabelsZ 651, 720). Which effects will follow from the recognition of the legal situation? Will the legal situation be accepted as to the foreign law 'in blocco'? Will the legal situation have the same effects as in the state of origin or the effects which such a legal situation would have in the state of recognition if it were established there (Pierre Mayer, 'Les méthodes de la reconnaissance en droit international privé' in Bertrand Ancel and others (eds), *Le droit international privé: esprit et méthodes Mélanges en l'honneur de Paul Lagarde* (Dalloz 2005), 547, 555)? For example, may paternity be contested in accordance with the rules of the jurisdiction where the paternity has been documented or with those of the recognizing state? Will the recognition extend to procedural issues and preliminary questions (*Vorfragen*)? However, the effects could be defined in a convention on a similar level of detail as the Hague Adoption Convention (→ Adoption) (Paul Lagarde, 'Développements futurs du droit international privé dans une Europe en voie d'unification: quelques conjectures' (2004) 68 RabelsZ 225, 235).

Finally, despite the openness towards legal situations created abroad, a refusal to recognize for → public policy reasons must be provided for. To this extent, a principle of recognition of legal situations evidenced by documents alone does not resolve all the problems of cross-border activities. A more detailed conception is needed (Christian Kohler, 'Der Einfluss der Globalisierung auf die Wahl der Anknüpfungsmomente im Internationalen Familienrecht' in Robert Freitag and others (eds), *Internationales Familienrecht für das 21. Jahrhundert, Symposion Spellenberg* (Sellier 2006) 9, 24).

The → CIEC/ICCS (International Commission on Civil Status) and the Hague Conventions as well as the Swiss and the Dutch rules may serve as a source of inspiration. But the mix of conflict rules, substantive and procedural standards, limitations on the scope of recognition with regard to the types of documents and the authorities competent to issue the respective documents, as well as the grounds for refusal of recognition ('multiplication' of the kinds of law; see Jürgen Basedow, 'The Effects of Globalisation in Private international law' in Jürgen Basedow and Toshiyuki Kono (eds), *Legal Aspects of Globalisation* (Kluwer 2002) 1, 4), make a systematic and convincing approach (acceptable as a method of private international law) very difficult.

DAGMAR COESTER-WALTJEN

Literature

Pascal Ancel and Horatia Muir Watt, 'La désunion europeénne: Le Règlement dit Bruxelles II' (2001) 28 Rev.crit.DIP 403; Jürgen Basedow, 'The Effects of Globalisation in Private international law' in Jürgen Basedow and Toshiyuki Kono (eds), *Legal Aspects of Globalisation* (Kluwer 2002) 1; Dagmar Coester-Waltjen, 'Anerkennung im Internationalen Personen-, Familien- und Erbrecht und das Europäische Kollisionsrecht' [2006] IPRax 392; Georges Droz, 'Cours général de droit International privé' (1991) 177 Rec. des Cours 154; Marc Fallon and Johan Meeusen, 'Private international law in the European Union and the Exception of Mutual Recognition' (2002) 4 YbPIL 37; Katja Funken, *Das Anerkennungsprinzip im Internationalen Privatrecht* (Mohr 2009); Hélène Gaudemet-Tallon, 'De nouvelles fonctions pour l'équivalence en droit international privé?' in Bertrand Ancel and others (eds), *Le droit international privé: esprit et méthodes. Mélanges en l'honneur de Paul Lagarde* (Dalloz 2005) 303; Patrick Glenn, 'Conflict of Laws – The 1976 Hague Conventions on Marriage and Matrimonial Property Regimes' (1977) 55 Can. Bar Rev. 586; Erik Jayme, 'Das internationale Privatrecht im System des Gemeinschaftsrechts' [2006] IPRax 67; Erik Jayme and Christian Kohler, 'Europäisches Kollisionsrecht 2001: Anerkennungsprinzip statt IPR?' [2001] IPRax 501; Patrick Kinsch, 'Recognition in a Form of a Status Acquired Abroad – Private international law Rules and European Human Rights Law' in Katharina Boele-Woelki, Talia Einhorn and Daniel Girsberger (eds), *Convergence and Divergence in Private international law, Liber Amicorum Kurt Siehr* (Schulthess 2010) 259; Christian Kohler, 'Der Einfluss der Globalisierung auf die Wahl der Anknüpfungsmomente im Internationalen Familienrecht' in Robert Freitag and others (eds), *Internationales Familienrecht für das 21. Jahrhundert, Symposion Spellenberg* (Sellier 2006) 9; Paul Lagarde, 'Développements futurs du droit international privé dans une Europe en voie d'unification: quelques conjectures' (2004) 68 RabelsZ 225; Heinz-Peter Mansel, 'Anerkennung als Grundprinzip des Europäischen Rechtsraums' (2006) 70 RabelsZ 651; Heinz-Peter Mansel and others, 'Stellungnahme im Auftrag des Deutschen Rates für Internationales Privatrecht zum Grünbuch der Europäischen Kommission – Weniger Verwaltungsaufwand für EU-Bürger: Den freien Verkehr öffentlicher Urkunden und die Anerkennung der Rechtswirkungen von Personenstandsurkunden erleichtern – KOM(2010) 747 endg' [2011] IPRax 335; Pierre Mayer, 'Les méthodes de la reconnaissance en droit international privé' in Bertrand Ancel and others (eds), *Le droit international privé: esprit et méthodes Mélanges en l'honneur de Paul Lagarde* (Dalloz 2005) 547; Peter North, 'Development of Rules of Private international law in the Field of Family Law' (1980) 166 Rec. des Cours 9; Peter Nygh, 'The Hague Marriage Convention – A Sleeping Beauty?' in Alegría Borrás and others (eds), *E Pluribus Unum. Liber Amicorum George Droz* (Kluwer 1996) 25; Charalambos Pamboukis, 'La renaissance – metamorphose de la méthode de reconnaissance' (2008) 67 Rev. crit.DIP 513; Paolo Picone, 'Les méthodes de coordination des ordres juridiques en droit international privé' (1999) 276 Rec. des Cours 13; Paolo Picone, 'Die "Anwendung" einer ausländischen "Rechtsordnung" im Forum Staat – perseverare est diabolicum' in Jürgen Basedow and others (eds), *Private Law in the International Arena – From National Conflict Rules Towards Harmonization and Unification – Liber Amicorum Kurt Siehr* (Asser 2000) 569; Willis Reese, 'The Hague Convention on Celebration and Recognition of the Validity of Marriages' (1979) 20 Va.L.Rev. 25; Gian Paolo Romano, 'La bilatéralité éclipsée par l'autorité: développements récents en matière d'état des personnes' (2006) 65 Rev.crit.DIP 458; Hans Jürgen Sonnenberger, 'Anerkennung statt Verweisung? Eine neue internationalprivatrechtliche Methode' in Jörn Bernreuther and others (eds), *Festschrift für Ulrich Spellenberg* (Sellier 2012) 371; Hans van Loon, 'Unification and Cooperation in the Field of International Family Law: A Perspective from The Hague' in Alegría Borrás and others (eds), *E Pluribus Unum, Liber Amicorum Georges Droz* (Kluwer 1996) 173; Rolf Wagner, 'Inhaltliche Anerkennung von Personenstandsurkunden – Ein Patenrezept? – Überlegungen aus international-privatrechtlicher Sicht' [2011] FamRZ 609–615; Rolf Wagner, 'Die Anerkennung von Personenstandsurkunden in Europa' [2014] NZFam 121, 122.

Registered partnerships

I. Concept and notion

Civil → marriage is a centuries-old institution whereby states attach consequences to the fact that two adults decide to live together as a couple. In recent decades, this model of family relationship has increasingly been questioned. Following the demise of marriage as an institution, with marriage rates drastically declining, states have started recognizing other institutions which give legal effect to the fact that two people live together. Registered partnership is one of the institutions which emerged from this evolution, alongside → same-sex marriage.

A registered partnership is a relationship which has been subject to registration by a public authority (or another body to which this competence has been delegated, such as a public notary), embodying the commitment between two persons to form a couple (compare the Convention on the recognition of registered partnerships opened for signature at Munich on 5 September 2007, ICCS Convention No 32, according to which a registered partnership is 'a commitment to live together, other than a marriage, entered into by two persons of the same sex or different sex, giving rise to registration by a public authority'). The name given to this institution may vary greatly: it may be called a registered partnership, civil partnership, domestic partnership, life partnership, civil solidarity pact, etc.

The shape and consequences of partnerships are not identical in the various national laws. In some countries, such as → Germany and England (→ United Kingdom), partnerships are open only to same-sex partners, while in other countries, such as → Belgium, → Luxembourg and → France, partners of different genders may also enter into a partnership.

Differences also exist regarding the content and the consequences attached to registered partnerships. The regime of such partnerships may have varying degrees of closeness to that of marriage. In Germany, the → Netherlands and Scandinavian countries, partnerships carry consequences which are closely modelled on those of marriage, even though differences remain between the institutions. In → Belgium, → France and → Luxembourg, partnerships have less significant effects than marriage. This is particularly true in relation to the effects that partnerships may have on a parental link between the partners and children born within the partnership.

The rise of registered partnerships has had important private international law consequences. In view of the ever-increasing mobility of persons within the EU and beyond, the conflict-of-laws treatment of same-sex marriages and partnerships is indeed far from a purely theoretical concern.

A different regime applies to non-registered unions. The private international law regime for such unions is in most countries not dealt with by statutory provisions.

II. Historical development

Registered partnership was first introduced as a new institution in → Denmark in 1989 (Act on Registered Partnership, No 372, 7 June 1989). As it initially stood, the Danish registered partnership was very close to marriage. It was only open for partners of the same sex. Norway followed suit in 1993 and Sweden in 1995. In all these countries, the starting point for the introduction of the registered partnership was the concern to guarantee equal treatment to same-sex couples who had no access to marriage.

Within a time span of 20 years, registered partnerships were introduced in many countries. At the end of 2014, it was estimated that at least 50 countries or sub-state entities had introduced a form of registered partnership.

Given the very specific nature of registered partnerships, states creating a regime for partnership often also adopted specific private international law provisions dealing with registered partnerships. The 1989 Danish Act included a provision governing the requirements to access partnership, under which two persons could conclude a partnership in Denmark provided at least one of the parties had their permanent residence in Denmark or was a Danish national. In other countries as well, provisions were adopted to regulate access to the partnership. The Swedish Act, for example, provided that the registration of a partnership could only take place if at least one of the partners is a Swedish citizen domiciled in Sweden (see Michael Bogdan, 'IPR-Aspekte der schwedischen eingetragenen Partnerschaft für Homosexuelle' [1995] IPRax 56).

During this initial stage, national lawmakers favoured unilateral rules for dealing with registered partnerships. The Finnish Act (Act on Registered Partnerships (*Laki rekisteröidystä parisuhteesta* No 950/2001)), for example, provided that the substantive requirements for concluding a registered partnership should always be governed by Finnish domestic law (s 11 Partnership Act 2001). The Luxembourg Act (Loi du 9 juillet 2004 relative aux effets légaux de certains partenariats, Recueil de Legislation A No 143 of 6 August 2004 page 2020, available at <www.legilux.public.lu/leg/a/archives/2004/0143/a143.pdf>) provides that its provisions only apply to partnerships concluded under Luxembourg law (art 1 Act 9 July 2004).

In some countries, the creation of a registered partnership did not lead to the adoption of specific private international law rules. Thus, Belgium created a registered partnership in 1998 (Loi du 23 novembre 1998 instaurant la cohabitation légale, MB, 12 January 1999) without adopting any specific provisions dealing with the cross-border issues.

By contrast, other lawmakers adopted specific provisions on cross-border issues. This was the case, for example, in the → Netherlands, → Germany and → Switzerland. The adoption of specific provisions was thought necessary in view of the diversity of partnerships and the lack of consensus on the content of the relationship, which made it difficult to proceed from the assumption that all relations should be treated equally.

When adopting specific private international law provisions for registered partnerships, these countries did not follow an early suggestion to borrow from the rules dealing with cross-border contracts in order to create a framework for the cross-border aspects of registered partnerships (see eg Mariel Revillard, 'Le pacte civil de solidarité en droit international privé' (2000) No 37124 Rép. Defrénois, 337 No 13). This approach started from the assumption that registered partnerships were akin to contracts, a comparison made easier by the attempts by some lawmakers to confine the partnerships they created to the realm of contracts. French law, for example, defines registered partnership as a contract (art 515-1 French Civil Code (Code Civil of 21 March 1804, henceforth French CC)).

Rejecting the contractual approach, lawmakers instead treated partnerships as family relations. Indeed, a close observation revealed the many commonalities between partnership and → marriage, such as the prohibition against entering into two partnerships simultaneously, the application of prohibitions inspired by marriage in relation to the kinship links between spouses and the application *mutatis mutandis* and to various degrees of rules relating to the effects of marriage. Further, it was found that allowing partners to benefit from the conflict-of-laws rules devised for cross-border contracts would lead to unacceptable results.

If a consensus emerged to treat registered partnerships as family relations rather than as contracts, only limited support was found for the application to partnerships of the traditional rules devised for family situations and in particular for marriages (as suggested eg by Hélène Chanteloup, 'Menus propos autour du pacte civil de solidarité en droit international privé' (2000) 275 Gaz. Pal. 4–16). Only → Switzerland used this technique to regulate the cross-border aspects of registered partnerships. The general reference in the Swiss Private international law Act (Bundesgesetz über das Internationale Privatrecht of 18 December 1987, 1988 BBl I 5, as amended, henceforth Swiss PILA) to the rules applicable to marriage was, however, qualified by specific provisions aimed at issues arising only for registered partnerships (arts 65b, 65c and 65d).

In most countries, lawmakers preferred to consider that partnerships are family relations which should, however, be subject to specific rules. Indeed, most lawmakers adopted bilateral rules which subjected partnerships to the law of the place where the partnership was registered. This was the case in the → Netherlands, → Belgium, → Germany, → France and other countries which also adopted specific private international law rules dealing with registered partnerships. Most of these rules were not limited to specific types of registered partnerships. In some jurisdictions, however, the legislature distinguished between various forms of partnerships, reserving the application of the conflict-of-laws rules aimed at registered partnerships to those partnerships which differed significantly from marriage. The other types of partnerships, which closely resembled marriage, were left out to conflict-of-laws rules aimed at marriage.

III. Legal sources

The private international law regime of registered partnerships is currently for the most part governed by national conflict rules. In most national laws, specific private international law provisions have been adopted to deal with registered partnerships. In some countries, these provisions may be found in the Act dealing specifically with registered partnerships. In other countries, such as → Germany, → Belgium and → Switzerland, the specific provisions are included in a general Act or code of private international law.

1. International conventions

The Commission internationale de l'état civil (→ CIEC/ICCS (International Commission on Civil Status)) has drafted a Convention on the recognition of registered partnerships, which was opened for signature at Munich on 5 September 2007. However, this Convention failed to attract significant support. It has been signed by only two countries (→ Spain and → Portugal) and has not yet entered into force. Leaving aside this Convention, there is no specific international instrument dealing with registered partnerships. The Hague Conference has engaged in preliminary work exploring the feasibility of an international instrument dealing with private international law aspects of registered partnerships as part of a larger project dealing with unmarried couples. However, this has not resulted in the adoption of any text (see lastly Preliminary Document No 11 for the attention of the Council of the Hague Conference of April 2008 on General Affairs and Policy).

It is thought that certain Hague Conference Conventions dealing with family law issues are not applicable to registered partnerships. This applies in particular to the Hague Marriage Convention (Hague Convention of 14 March 1978 on Celebration and Recognition of the Validity of Marriages, 1901 UNTS 131) (for more details, see Rolf Wagner, 'Das neue Internationale Privat- und Verfahrensrecht zur eingetragenen Lebenspartnerschaft' [2001] IPRax 281, 284) and the Hague Matrimonial Property Convention (Hague Convention of 14 March 1978 on the law applicable to matrimonial property regimes, 16 ILM 14). On the other hand, nothing prevents the application of the Hague Child Protection Convention

(Hague Convention of 19 October 1996 on jurisdiction, applicable law, recognition, enforcement and co-operation in respect of parental responsibility and measures for the protection of children, 35 ILM 1391) to the relationships between parents and children when the parents are bound by a registered partnership. The application of the Hague Adoption Convention (Hague Convention of 29 May 1993 on protection of children and co-operation in respect of intercountry adoption, 1870 UNTS 167; 32 ILM 1134) to the → adoption of a child by registered partners is an open question. Much will depend on the national provisions implementing this Convention in national law.

Maintenance claims between registered partners may be determined using the provisions of the Hague Maintenance Protocol 2007 (Hague Protocol of 23 November 2007 on the law applicable to maintenance obligations, [2009] OJ L 331/19). The Hague Protocol determines 'the law applicable to maintenance obligations arising from a family relationship, parentage, marriage or affinity, including a maintenance obligation in respect of a child regardless of the marital status of the parents' (art 1(1)). As explained by the general reporter, the Protocol is not intended to determine the law applicable to the family relationships from which the maintenance obligation arises (Andrea Bonomi, *Explanatory Report on the Hague Protocol of 23 November 2007 on the Law Applicable to Maintenance Obligations* (Permanent Bureau of the Conference 2013) para 23, henceforth Bonomi, *Explanatory Report*). Accordingly, each state may determine the law applicable to the relevant family relationship using its own conflict-of-laws rules. Although the Protocol does not specify whether → maintenance obligations arising out of registered partnerships are included within its scope, this omission is not an accident. It leaves open the possibility for states wishing to do so to apply the provisions of the Protocol to claims arising between registered partners (Bonomi, *Explanatory Report*, para 31). These states may even decide to apply the specific provisions of the Protocol covering the situations of spouses (such as art 5) to registered partners (Bonomi, *Explanatory Report*, para 31). States which do not recognize registered partnerships may, on the other hand, decide not to apply the Protocol to claims arising between partners if they consider that the relationships between the partners do not amount to family relationships.

2. The EU

Within the EU, no attempt has been made to produce an instrument which would cover all questions arising in relation to registered partnerships. Rather, the question is whether the existing Regulations apply to registered partnerships. There seems to be a consensus that the → Brussels IIa Regulation (Council Regulation (EC) No 2201/2003 of 27 November 2003 concerning jurisdiction and the recognition and enforcement of judgments in matrimonial matters and the matters of parental responsibility, repealing Regulation (EC) No 1347/2000, [2003] OJ L 338/1) does not apply to the dissolution of registered partnerships (Walter Pintens, 'Marriage and Partnership in the Brussels IIa Regulation' in *Liber memorialis Petar Šarčević* (Sellier 2006) 335, 339). However, it may apply to issues arising in relation to the parental responsibility concerning children whose parents are bound by a partnership. Maintenance claims between registered partners may be subject to the provisions of the Maintenance Regulation (Council Regulation (EC) No 4/2009 of 18 December 2008 on jurisdiction, applicable law, recognition and enforcement of decisions and cooperation in matters relating to maintenance obligations, [2009] OJ L 7/1). The Regulation is applicable to 'maintenance obligations arising from a family relationship, parentage, marriage or affinity' (art 1(1)). Recital (11) of the Regulation indicates that all maintenance creditors should be afforded equal treatment. Recital (21) adds that the uniform rules on conflict of laws only determine the law applicable to → maintenance obligations. These rules do not determine the law applicable to the establishment of the family relationships on which the maintenance obligations are based. Accordingly, the establishment of such family relationships 'continues to be covered by the national law of the Member States, including their rules of private international law'. Hence, there is room for application of the Maintenance Regulation to claims based on registered partnerships.

The EU has adopted a Regulation dealing specifically with registered partnerships. Regulation 2016/1104 introduces conflicts of laws rules aiming at the patrimonial relationships between registered partners. It will become fully effective starting in January 2019.

There has also been discussion whether EU action was necessary to foster mutual recognition of registered partnerships (eg Béatrice

Weiss-Gout and Marie-Laure Niboyet-Hoegy, 'La reconnaissance mutuelle des mariages entre personnes de même sexe et des partenariats entre personnes de même sexe ou de sexe opposé. La situation dans les différents Etats membres. Besoin d'une action de l'UE?' Report European Parliament, [2010] PE 432.731, p 9). At this stage, however, no such action has been undertaken. Registered partners may be able to benefit from the effects of European citizenship or the principle of non-discrimination, which were given some effect in family law matters by the ECJ (Case C-148/02 *Carlos Garcia Avello v Belgian State* [2003] ECR I-11613).

IV. Current regulation

When looking at the private international law aspects of registered partnerships, a distinction must be drawn between several aspects: alongside the issue of access to partnerships and the consequences thereof, one should also consider how to address the characterization of such relationships. Attention should also be paid to the question of recognition of registered partnerships, especially in countries which have not allowed such partnerships.

1. Characterization: which partnerships?

A first question which had to be resolved relates to the definition of the relationships covered by the private international law rules. There are as many registered partnerships as there are countries in which this institution has been adopted. The sharp differences existing between the different national versions of the partnerships make it necessary to define with precision which partnerships are included in a given rule.

Some lawmakers have neglected this issue, leaving open the question which partnerships may be covered by the rules they adopted. This is the case, for example, in → France, where art 515-7-1 French CC, as adopted in 2009, provides a bilateral conflict-of-laws rule applicable to 'registered partnerships'. However, the legislature has not indicated which relationships may be considered to be registered partnerships and whether this concept should be interpreted using the *lex fori* or another approach. Likewise, the German legislature has not provided a definition of the registered partnership when adopting art 17a Introductory Act to the German Civil Code (Einführungsgesetz zum Bürgerlichen Gesetzbuche of 21 September 1994, BGBl. I 2494, as amended, henceforth EGBGB). In these countries, a question may therefore arise when applying the specific rules to partnerships registered under a foreign law. One may indeed wonder whether all registered partnerships qualify under the local rule or whether these rules should only apply provided that the registered partnership meets certain minimum requirements (for Germany, see Dieter Martiny, 'Private international law Aspects of Same-Sex Couples under German Law' in Katharina Boele-Woelki and Angelika Fuchs (eds), *Legal Recognition of Same-Sex Relationships in Europe* (Intersentia 2012) 189, 203).

In other countries, a definition has been adopted of what constitutes a registered partnership. Article 61(5) of Book 10 Dutch New Civil Code (Nieuw Burgerlijk Wetboek of 1 January 1992, available at <http://wetten.overheid.nl>, henceforth Dutch CC) for example, provides *ex ante* the minimum content that a partnership should have in order to be treated as such. According to this provision, a foreign partnership will only be recognized as such provided that the partnership is a form of close personal relationship between two persons which has been registered by a local and competent authority. Further, the partnership must exclude the possibility of partners marrying or concluding another partnership with a third party. Finally, it must have consequences which are broadly similar to those arising from marriage. → Belgium has also reserved the application of the special rule it created for partnerships to those foreign partnerships which do not create between the partners a relationship equivalent to that created by marriage (art 58 Belgian Code of Private international law (Code de Droit International Privé, Loi du 16 juillet 2004 portant le Code de droit international privé, MB 27 July 2004, 57344, as amended, henceforth Belgian PILA)).

This approach makes it easier to apply the specific private international law provisions adopted for registered partnerships. On the other hand, the fate of a foreign partnership which falls short of the requirements is unclear. Under the distinction made by the Belgian legislature, if a partnership produces effects equivalent to those of marriage, application may be made of the choice-of-laws rules covering marriage.

The application of the conflict-of-laws rules included in the CIEC Convention is made

PATRICK WAUTELET

easier because the Convention also includes an autonomous definition of the concept of 'registered partnership' (art 1).

2. Access to registered partnerships

An important question to be addressed in relation to cross-border registered partnerships is that of access to such partnerships. From a private international law perspective, one should determine which formal and substantial requirements must be met before a registered partnership may be created.

Looking at the formal requirements (→ Formal requirements and validity), the principle as accepted in most countries does not differ from that generally used for → marriage. Indeed, local law is applied when determining which formal requirements govern the creation of a partnership. Various methods are used to that effect. In some countries, reference is made to the rules which apply to marriage (eg s 2(1) Danish Act). In other countries, a specific conflict-of-laws rule is adopted, which provides for the application of local law (eg § 11 Finnish Partnership Act; art 60(3) Book 10 Dutch CC). Some laws include no specific conflicts rule for the formal requirements. Rather, this question is taken together with all other requirements aimed at the creation of a partnership, which are governed by local law – this is the case in Belgium (art 60 Belgian PILA), France (art 515-7-1 French CC) and Germany (art 17b EGBGB). Occasionally, reference is made to the possibility for consular officers to register partnerships in accordance with the law of their countries (eg art 60(3) Book 10 Dutch CC).

The departure from principles applicable to cross-border marriage is much sharper when we look at the substantial requirements. The rule which seems to have received widespread recognition is that access to partnerships should be governed by the law of the country where the partners seek to have their union registered or otherwise formalized, the so-called *lex loci registrationis*. This rule has been adopted in → Belgium (art 60 Belgian PILA), → Germany (art 17b EGBGB), → France (art 515-7-1 French CC), → Denmark (art 3(2) Danish Registered Partnership Act) and in → Austria (art 27a of the Austrian Federal Code on Private international law (Bundesgesetz über das internationale Privatrecht of 15 June 1978, BGBl. No 304/1978, as amended)). In all these countries, the rule is drafted on a bilateral basis.

In England and in the → Netherlands, the rule is expressed unilaterally by reference only to the application of local law. Swiss law reaches the same result by declaring the rule pertaining to marriage applicable to partnerships (art 65a Swiss PILA).

Another difference with the treatment of marriage is that in some systems, no possibility is offered for those partners failing to qualify under local law to benefit from the application of the provisions of their national law as they would if they intended to get married. This is the case in the Netherlands and → Switzerland. Hence, access to partnerships is made more difficult than access to marriage.

The predominance of the *lex loci registrationis* principle means that access to registered partnerships is subject to the application of local law. The application of local law opens the way for foreigners to enter into a local partnership without any examination of the possibility for the persons concerned to enter into such a partnership under their national law. As has been done for same-sex marriage, many states have therefore imposed additional requirements which restrict access to partnerships. The goal is to avoid the creation of so-called 'registration havens' for foreigners, which could be even more prevalent than for marriage, since the prevailing view in relation to the effects of partnership is to submit the effects to the law of the country where the partnership was registered (see section IV.3. below).

In order to restrict access to partnerships, states have usually imposed a requirement that the would-be partners demonstrate the existence of a connection with the state of registration. The nature of this connection may vary and has changed over time. In many countries (such as → Belgium (art 59(2) Belgian PILA), → France (art 515-3 French CC), → Luxembourg (art 3(1) Luxembourg Registered Partnership Act) and → Switzerland (art 5(1) Swiss Federal Act on registered partnership between same-sex persons of 18 June 2004), the requirement is based on the habitual residence of the partners. In a limited number of states, access to partnerships is reserved to nationals of the state or at least requires that one of the partners is a national. This is the case in → Slovenia (art 3(2) Civil Partnership Registration Act of 22 June 2005, Uradni list RS Nos 65/2005, 55/2009) and the → Czech Republic (§ 5 Czech Act 115/2006 on Registered Partnerships).

In yet other countries, the requirements are based on a combination of the habitual residence and nationality of the partners. The combination is usually an alternative, as is the case in the → Netherlands, where partners may conclude a partnership if they reside in the Netherlands, but also if one of the partners is a Dutch national (art 80a(4) Dutch CC). In the Scandinavian countries, the same alternative system is applied, whereby registration is possible if the partners either reside in the country or are nationals of the country (§ 2(3)(1) Norwegian Law; § 10 Finnish Registered Partnership Act; § 2(2) Danish Registered Partnership Act). Finally, one should also mention the peculiar case of → Germany: it appears that Germany imposes no requirement in relation to the partners' nationality or residence. In other words, foreign nationals who do not habitually reside in Germany could apparently enter into a partnership in Germany on the occasion of a short-term visit to this country.

Taken together, the rules adopted for cross-border partnerships depart significantly from the traditional approach used for marriage; the application of the law of the nationality of the spouses has been overwhelmingly replaced by that of the law of the country where the registration takes place.

The application of local law may be explained by the concern to ease the task of public authorities, particularly in a field where legislative changes occur frequently. However, the choice for local law also embodies a substantive policy decision, in that the goal is to facilitate access to registered partnerships. The application of the law of nationality would indeed constitute an obstacle given that there are a number of countries where no registered partnership is available. The application of local law instead of the law of the nationality of the persons concerned makes it possible for non-nationals to have access to partnerships. At the same time, the application of local law helps to underline that partnerships remain different from marriage.

The choice for the application of local law creates two categories of marital union for conflict-of-laws purposes: marriage and registered partnerships. As this distinction follows the existence in substantive law of two categories, the application of different conflict-of-laws rules does not create a discriminatory.

The choice for the application of local law also has consequences for the recognition side. Since access to the partnership is not subject to the national law of the partners, it may be that the partners enter into a relationship which does not exist, or only exists in a significantly different shape in the home country. The seeds of limping relationships are therefore sown.

3. Consequences of registered partnerships

As with → marriage, a registered partnership may have consequences for both partners regarding their personal and financial relationships, and for third parties. When looking at these consequences, one notices that some countries, such as → France and → Belgium, have limited themselves to adopting one single rule, which apparently governs all the consequences of partnerships. Other countries, such as the → Netherlands, have adopted a series of detailed rules, distinguishing between the various consequences a registered partnership may have. Regardless of the model used, it is clear that no single rule may govern all the possible effects of partnerships. Rather, partners are subject to different rules depending on the consequence concerned. No doubt exists either on the fact that such issues as the majority of each partner or the relations which may be established vis-à-vis children born to the partners, remain governed by the normal conflict rules.

It is first necessary to consider the *core* consequences of partnerships, ie those flowing directly from the existence of the partnership. These consequences concern the effect of a partnership on the life of the partners, the possible existence of an obligation to live together, to care for and assist each other, the possibility for a partner to marry and also the possibility to terminate the partnership. In a following section, the attention will turn to other consequences of partnerships.

a) General consequences of registered partnerships

No consensus has appeared in private international law on the treatment of the general consequences of partnerships. It is therefore necessary to distinguish between the different approaches.

In a first group of countries, the law of the country of registration of the partnership is deemed to be relevant to govern the consequences of registered partnerships. This application of the *lex loci registrationis* has been adopted, for example, in → France (art 515-7-1 French CC), → Belgium (art 60 Belgian PILA) and Quebec (art 3090.1(2) Civil Code of Québec (S.Q., 1991, c 64)). It has also been suggested by the European Commission in the Draft Regulation on the property consequences of registered partnerships (art 15 European Commission, 'Proposal for a Council Regulation on jurisdiction, applicable law and the recognition and enforcement of decisions in matters of matrimonial property regimes' COM(2011) 126 final).

The rationale of the rule may be found in the diversity of consequences attached by national laws to partnerships. Taking this diversity into account, some states have felt that cutting the umbilical cord between the partnership and its state of origin will give rise to difficulties. Without a basic consensus on the shape and effects of partnerships, the application of a foreign law on a local partnership appears too cumbersome.

A foreign partnership will therefore be governed by foreign law, while a local partnership is subject to local law. This simple principle is only qualified by the operation of classic mechanisms, such as the public policy exception.

Applying the *lex loci registrationis* or the law of the country of origin may give rise to well-known difficulties. This will be the case when the law of the country of origin designates one of its institutions and entrusts it with a specific mission in relation to the partnership, while this institution does not exist in the country where the question arises.

States where partnerships are subject to local law will only allow for the creation of a partnership in the form they have accepted. This is important since the consequences attached to a partnership may vary greatly in the various enactments. It is enough to refer to the difference existing between countries where partnerships are open only to same-sex partners and countries where partners of different genders may also enter into a partnership. The question of where a partnership is entered into therefore remains relevant.

In another group of countries, preference is given to the exclusive application of local law, without consideration of the law of the country where the partnership was concluded.

When dealing with local partnerships, this approach makes little difference when compared with the former method. However, the difference appears when one deals with foreign partnerships. Since foreign partnerships will be governed by local law regardless of where they were concluded, this may lead to a *rewriting* of the partnership. Foreign partnerships must not have *stronger* effects than those granted to local partnerships. They may, however, be granted other consequences than those attached to the partnership in its state of origin. In all cases, the application of this mechanism entails a difficult exercise in comparing the consequences of registered partnerships under various national laws.

In some countries, the consequences flowing from registered partnerships are dealt with using the conflict-of-laws rules developed for marriages, which are applied by analogy. This is the case in → Switzerland. Instead of subjecting those effects to the law of the country of origin or to Swiss law, the Swiss legislature has chosen to apply by analogy the conflict-of-laws rules devised for marriage. Accordingly, there is no single rule governing the consequences of partnerships, but rather partners are subject to different rules depending on the effect concerned.

b) Other consequences of registered partnerships between the partners

Registered partnerships may produce legal effects going beyond the *core* consequences already examined. Partners may make maintenance claims vis-à-vis each other. They may have claims to assets acquired during the partnership. Issues could arise in relation to the name of a partner after the partnership has been terminated.

In respect of marriages, contemporary private international law has developed specific conflict-of-laws rules for all these consequences. There is therefore a sharp distinction to be made between the *core* consequences of marriage and other effects.

The situation for registered partnerships is less clear-cut. In some countries, the conflicts rule adopted specifically for registered partnerships remains vague in terms of its scope. The French text in this respect is deceptively simple, referring only to the 'effects' of the partnership, without any further indication as to the nature of the effects covered. It is therefore unclear whether such effects as property relationship, alimony claims or → succession rights are covered by the rule. The rule adopted in → Belgium goes slightly further, whereby art 60 Belgian PILA refers to the consequences of the partnership on the partners' 'assets'. This seems to exclude all other effects, such as possible maintenance claims made by one of the partners. However, art 60 must be read together with other provisions of the PILA, which provide specific solutions for other aspects not covered by art 60. Therefore, it seems that for the consequences not covered by art 60, one should apply the *normal* rules of the PILA.

The Dutch legislature went much further in devising a comprehensive system dealing with the effects of partnerships. Book 10 Dutch CC contains over 20 different provisions dealing with the various effects of partnerships, including rules for the relations with third parties. Some of these provisions allow the partners to select the law applicable to a particular question, such as that of the → matrimonial property relations (art 70) or the personal relations between partners (art 64). Failing a choice by the partners, Dutch law usually applies to the consequences of the partnership. For some issues, reference is made to international conventions, such as the Hague Maintenance Protocol 2007, which is deemed to be applicable to maintenance obligations between partners (art 90).

In general there seems to be a recognition that some of the consequences of registered partnerships may be entrusted to specific rules applicable to other family relationships. This is the case, for example, for the family name which partners may wish to adopt, the possible maintenance claims which partners may assert or the possible claims of the surviving partner to the estate of a deceased partner. It is widely accepted that these claims fall outside the *lex loci registrationis* and must be dealt with under the other conflicts rules.

As with marriages, the application of specific conflict-of-laws rules for those questions may lead to two difficulties. The first touches on the characterization of the partnership. The application to some consequences of the partnership of another law than the law of the state of origin begs the question of how to deal with the foreign partnership under the applicable law. If two same-sex partners who have concluded a partnership in the → Netherlands move to → France, where one of the partners has bought a house, French law will govern the rights and claims of the surviving partner if one of the partners dies. It will be necessary in this respect to inquire whether the Dutch law of partnership may be deemed to correspond to the French law of partnership to which the French provisions on succession refer. This question is not specific to same-sex partnerships – it also arises when dealing with foreign marriages which deviate from the local standard, such as polygamous unions.

In some countries the characterization issue is easier to deal with because an *ex ante* determination has been made of what constitutes a partnership equivalent to the local partnership. This is the case, for example, in Belgium and the Netherlands. When no such *ex ante* determination has been made, judges and practitioners alike bear the responsibility of determining whether a given foreign partnership should be recognized as the equivalent of the French PACS.

Once the hurdle of characterization is surmounted, a second difficulty may arise as the application to a specific consequence of the partnership of another law than the law of the country of origin could result in a substantial modification of the partnership as initially created. The partnership could entail fewer or more effects than were contemplated under the law of the state of origin. This may lead to a *downsizing* of the partnership or conversely may attach more rights and consequences to a partnership than was initially provided.

In an extreme case, the designated law could simply ignore the institution of the partnership, leaving the partners unprotected. Some lawmakers have provided a fallback solution. This is the case in → Germany for the issue of the succession rights of the partners. The German legislature has indeed adopted a specific rule which grants the surviving partner the benefit of the application of the law of the country of origin if the law applicable to the inheritance does not give the surviving partner any rights. The rationale of this special treatment is to guarantee that all partnerships will generate effects in those fields. As a whole, a foreign partnership may therefore generate more effects when the partners reside in Germany than in the country of origin.

c) Partners and children
Issues of parentage arising in relation to registered partnerships are usually not subject to specific rules. Rather, whether and when a partner may be considered to be the parent of a child of his or her partner is to be determined by the general conflict-of-laws rules applicable to parentage. The same applies to the name of children.

Similarly, → adoption by partners remains subject to the operation of the general conflict-of-laws rules dealing with cross-border adoptions.

PATRICK WAUTELET

4. Termination of registered partnerships

As with its formation, the dissolution of a registered partnership is governed in most countries by the law of the state where the partnership was registered. This appears to be the case in → France, → Germany, → Belgium and → Luxembourg. In the → Netherlands, another position is taken which submits termination of partnerships to Dutch law, except for foreign partnerships where the partners have chosen the law of the country of registration.

The application of the law of the country of registration differs significantly from the position in relation to marriage, where the principle is that divorce (→ Divorce and personal separation) is governed by the law of the spouses' habitual residence. Choice of law is usually not allowed in respect of the termination of registered partnerships. As with the consequences of partnerships, the preference given to the law of the country of registration can be explained by the concern to underline that partnership remains different from marriage. This rule also expresses the idea that partnerships as institutions may differ too widely between countries to allow for the severing of the termination from the country where the partnership was registered.

The application to termination of the law of the country of registration may bring about difficulties when it appears that the termination is, according to that law, the privilege of an authority which does not exist in the country where termination is sought or which lacks such competence in the country where termination is sought. This explains why in some countries, termination can only be requested for local partnerships or priority is given to local law to govern termination.

5. Recognition

How and to what extent foreign partnerships may be recognized depends in the first place on the system adopted to govern partnerships in general.

In countries where the *lex loci registrationis* principle has been adopted, no specific rule on recognition is needed. Indeed, the *lex loci registrationis* rule works both as a choice-of-law rule and as a recognition rule. Foreign partnerships are recognized provided that they comply with the requirements of the country of origin. Recognition does not therefore require a specific rule.

However, a specific rule will be needed if partnerships are subject to a unilateral rule. This is the case, for example, in → Finland, where art 12 Finnish Registered Partnership Act provides that foreign partnerships are recognized in Finland provided they are valid in the state of registration.

In some cases, the recognition of foreign partnerships is qualified in order to preserve the coherence of domestic rules. This is the case in Germany, where, for constitutional reasons, art 17b(4) EGBGB provides that the consequences of a foreign partnership may not exceed those provided by German law. The precise consequences of this mechanism are still subject to debate, in particular as regards the question of when the limitation may come into play.

In countries where partnerships are governed by local law, without consideration of the law of the country where the partnership was concluded, the recognition of foreign partnerships calls for a specific approach. Under s 215 of the 2004 Civil Partnership Act (2004 c 33) adopted in England, a registered partnership formed abroad and capable of being recognized in England will be deemed equivalent to a civil partnership, thereby generating the same effects as a civil partnership concluded in England.

When considering what effect may be given to a partnership registered abroad, one should take into account the impact of both fundamental rights and European freedoms, which may severely restrict the ability of a state to deny recognition to a foreign partnership.

PATRICK WAUTELET

Literature

Giacomo Biagioni, 'On Recognition of Foreign Same-Sex Marriages and Partnerships' in Daniele Gallo, Luca Paladini and Pietro Pustorino (eds), *Same-Sex Couples before National, Supranational and International Jurisdictions* (Springer 2014) 359; Ian Curry-Sumner, *All's Well that Ends Registered? The Substantive and Private international law Aspects of Non-marital Registered Relationships in Europe. A Comparison of the Laws of Belgium, France, the Netherlands, Switzerland and the United Kingdom* (Intersentia 2005); Meinhard Forkert, *Eingetragene Lebenspartnerschaften im deutschen IPR: art 17b EGBGB* (Mohr Siebeck 2003); Gérald Goldstein, 'La cohabitation hors mariage en droit international privé' (2006) 320 Rec. des Cours 9; Cristina Gonzalez Beilfuss, *Parejas de hecho y matrimonios del mismo sexo* (Marcial Pons 2004); Gerard-René de Groot, 'Private international law Aspects Relating to Homosexual Couples' (2007) 11 EJCL issue 3; Institut suisse de droit comparé, *Aspects de droit international privé des partenariats enregistrés en Europe* (Schulthess 2004); Christina Karakosta, 'Portability of Same-Sex Marriages and Registered Partnerships within the EU' (2013) 2 Cyprus HR Law Rev 53; Dieter Martiny, 'Private international law Aspects of Same-Sex Couples under German Law' in Katharina Boele-Woelki and Angelika Fuchs (eds), *Legal Recognition of Same-Sex Relationships in Europe* (Intersentia 2012) 189; Martina Melcher, '(Mutual) Recognition of Registered Relationships via EU Private international law' (2013) 9 J Priv Int L 149; Hélène Peroz, 'La loi applicable aux partenariats enregistrés' (2010) 137 J.Dr.Int'l 399; Ana Quinones Escamez, 'Propositions pour la formation, la reconnaissance et l'efficacité internationale des unions conjugales ou de couple' [2007] Rev.crit.DIP 357; Giulia Rossolillo, 'Registered partnerships e matrimoni tra persone dello stesso sesso: problemi di qualificazione ed effetti nell'ordinamento italiano' [2003] Riv.Dir.Int'le Priv. & Proc. 363; Roberto Virzo, 'The Law Applicable to the Formation of Same-Sex Partnerships and Marriages' in Daniele Gallo, Luca Paladini and Pietro Pustorino (eds), *Same-Sex Couples before National, Supranational and International Jurisdictions* (Springer 2014) 343; Patrick Wautelet, 'Private international law Aspects of Same-Sex Marriages and Partnerships in Europe. Divided We Stand?' in Katharina Boele-Woelki and Angelika Fuchs (eds), *Legal Recognition of Same-Sex Relationships in Europe* (Intersentia 2012) 143.

Regulatory competition

I. Notion and concept

According to traditional legal theory, law is classified as a public good provided by regulators (courts or judges) in a more or less formal (and ideally democratic) process. In recent years, however, this view of the lawmaking process has been challenged. According to the theory of regulatory competition, law is a product that comes into existence and is shaped by market forces. Based on the economic theory of jurisdictional competition (Charles Tiebout, 'A Pure Theory of Local Expenditure' (1956) 64 J.Pol.Econ. 416), the theory assumes that, just like goods and services, legal rules are traded on markets and are subject to the mechanism of supply and demand. Thus, on the demand side, businesses and consumers look for legal rules that meet their needs, while on the supply side, states endeavour to offer such rules. If there is more than one state, the theory of regulatory competition argues, market forces will eventually drive states to compete for application of their laws by adopting rules that suit the needs of businesses and consumers.

From an economic perspective, regulatory competition serves various purposes, all of which are regarded as beneficial and viable. According to neoclassical economic theory, competition for legal rules may – just like competition for goods and services – help to better satisfy individual preferences. Based on the assumption that businesses and consumers will actively shop around for legal rules and regimes, it is claimed that regulatory competition will result in better-tailored and more diverse laws that will allow businesses and consumers to choose their preferred option. According to evolutionary economic theory, regulatory competition may additionally contribute to the ongoing improvement and innovation of legal rules and the legal system as such. Based on the notion of competition as a 'discovery or learning process' (Friedrich von Hayek, 'Der Wettbewerb als Entdeckungsverfahren' in Karl Friedrich Maier (ed), *Freiburger Studien. Gesammelte Aufsätze von F. A. von Hayek* (JCB Mohr (Paul Siebeck) 1968) 249), evolutionary economic theory argues that competition is a trial-and-error process of generating knowledge and adjusting legal rules to changing social and economic realities. Finally, evolutionary economic theory also regards regulatory competition as a means to effectively control and limit the powers of regulators and interest groups. This is because competition for legal rules – just like competition for goods and services – ensures diversity and avoids a concentration of powers that might harm businesses and consumers alike.

II. Fundamental requirements

The theory of regulatory competition has recently been applied to a broad range of legal fields. These include tax law, environmental law, labour law and antitrust law, as well as corporate law, contract law, consumer protection and family law (Larry Ribstein and Erin O'Hara, *The Law Market* (OUP 2008)). To the extent that the theory is applied to private law, private international law plays a crucial role. In fact, it is fair to describe private international law as the facilitator of regulatory competition, since regulatory competition may only come into existence if on the demand side, businesses and consumers are allowed to choose between legal rules. If they are not allowed to do so, regulators have no incentive to adjust their laws and to engage in competition with others. It follows that the parties' freedom of choice granted by private international law (→ Choice of law; → Party autonomy) is what sets regulatory competition in motion and what keeps it going. However, the mere existence of freedom of choice on the level of private international law does not suffice to stir regulatory competition. Rather, a number of additional requirements relating to the demand side on the one hand and the supply side on the other hand need to be met. On the demand side, businesses and consumers must actually exercise their freedom of choice. In addition, they must exercise their choice based on the quality of the law or the legal rules in question and not, for example, on their familiarity. On the supply side, the theory further requires that regulators, notably states, are concerned about the application of their laws and are willing to adjust their laws to the perceived needs of businesses and consumers. In sum, 'for regulatory competition to work we need both responsiveness of economic actors to differences in regulation and responsiveness of regulators to any induced factor movements' (Konstantine Gatsios and Peter Holmes, 'Regulatory Competition' in Paul Newman (ed), *The New Palgrave Dictionary of Economics and the Law*, vol 3 (Palgrave Macmillan 1998) 271, 274). Unfortunately, in reality, meeting these requirements is far from a matter of course. The reasons for this are manifold.

1. The responsiveness of businesses and consumers

As regards the demand side, the responsiveness of businesses and consumers may very often be absent because choice is costly. In order to make an informed choice, businesses and consumers need to know the differences between various offers, ie the differences between legal rules or entire legal systems. Therefore, they have to gather information about the pertaining rules and regulations and to compare them in order to find out which is the best. Needless to say, this endeavour incurs considerable costs. In addition, the very exercise of a choice is costly. This holds particularly true if a legal rule or an entire legal system cannot be chosen with the help of a choice-of-law clause, but requires physical mobility. In these cases, a choice will incur not only information costs but also costs of moving, as well as costs associated with the loss of social relationships and, as the case may be, the costs of establishing new social relationships, including learning a new language. Since these costs cannot be reduced to zero, it is very unlikely that consumers and businesses will always exercise their freedom of choice. Furthermore, even if businesses and consumers decide to choose a particular law, this does not mean that this choice best matches their preferences. To begin with, legal rules and legal systems are complex phenomena that are at times hard to understand and, what is more, to compare. Businesses and consumers will therefore frequently not choose a legal rule that best satisfies their needs. At times they might not even try to find the best available legal system. Taking into account the costs associated with finding the best available law, they might rather choose a law because they know it or because it is chosen by other people. In all these cases the choice does not perfectly reflect the parties' preferences and accordingly cannot be classified as a perfect response to the quality of different laws.

2. The responsiveness of regulators

In addition to businesses' and consumers' responsiveness, doubts exist as to regulators' responsiveness (Eva-Maria Kieninger, *Wettbewerb der Privatrechtsordnungen im Europäischen Binnenmarkt* (Mohr Siebeck 2002); Stefan Vogenauer, 'Regulatory Competition through Choice of Contract Law and Choice of Forum in Europe: Theory and Evidence' (2013) 21 ERPL 13). To begin with, it is difficult to see why regulators should engage in regulatory competition at all. If businesses and consumers fail to choose legal rules either at all or for their quality, why should regulators care about changing their laws to make them more attractive to businesses and consumers? In addition, according to standard economic theory, regulators (notably states) need incentives to adjust their laws to the perceived needs of businesses and consumers. However, it is not obvious where these incentives may come from in the field of private law. Naturally, in some areas (notably corporate law) states may obtain revenue from filing fees and, as the case may be, from franchise tax. However, it is unclear how states may benefit from the application of other aspects of their private laws, notably their contract of family. The only possible source of income seems to be an increase in tax revenue resulting from more local lawyers working on international contract cases. However, it is unclear whether these additional gains, assuming they materialize at all, are sufficient to induce states to adjust their contract laws.

Furthermore, even if states have a financial incentive to adjust their laws, they might face difficulties in doing so in practice. This is because states are in no position to take note of party choice across the board and to identify the causes for the choice of a particular law. Most choice-of-law clauses are not published or publicly available, and to the extent that they are available, they fail to illuminate the reasons for a particular choice. In company law, for example, a choice of one state's company law is either effectuated through incorporation of the company or through establishment of the country's real seat in that state (→ Companies). However, the mere incorporation or relocation tells us nothing about factors that drive the choice. Therefore, the only means of obtaining the relevant information about party motivation in choosing a particular law are large-scale surveys. However, such surveys are difficult and correspondingly costly to conduct. In addition, they do not necessarily lead to useful results since businesses and consumers might have different reasons for choosing a particular law. Thus, states may experience difficulties in adjusting their laws in a targeted fashion to the preferences of private actors.

3. Empirical evidence

The above considerations shed a rather dark light on regulatory competition, its actual existence and its ability to enhance legal rules and legal systems. When looking at the empirical evidence, however, the picture is more promising. In fact, it would seem that in many areas of private law, regulatory competition can actually be observed (Larry Ribstein and Erin O'Hara, *The Law Market* (OUP 2008)). Take, for example, corporate law in the USA. Here, scholars broadly agree that states compete for corporate charters, with Delaware taking the lead (Roberta Romano, *The Genius of American Corporate Law* (Aei Press 1993)). In Europe, by contrast, scholars tend to be more sceptical (Eva-Maria Kieninger, *Wettbewerb der Privatrechtsordnungen im Europäischen Binnenmarkt* (Mohr Siebeck 2002)). However, following a number of ECJ judgments effectively allowing companies to incorporate and move freely within the EU, English limited liability companies immediately became extremely popular, prompting several European states including Germany and France to enact new corporate laws in response (Wolf-Georg Ringe, 'Corporate Mobility in the European Union – A Flash in the Pan? An Empirical Study on the Success of Law Making and Regulatory Competition' [2013] ECFR 230). Against this background, the majority view today is that there is also competition for corporate charters in Europe (Horst Eidenmüller, 'The Transnational Law Market, Regulatory Competition, and Transnational Corporations' (2011) 18 Ind.J.Global L.Stud. 707).

The position is more complicated regarding other fields of private law, notably contract law. Here, a number of prominent German scholars have recently expressed doubts as to whether states actually engage in regulatory competition (Eva-Maria Kieninger, *Wettbewerb der Privatrechtsordnungen im Europäischen Binnenmarkt* (Mohr Siebeck 2002); Stefan Vogenauer, 'Regulatory Competition through Choice of Contract Law and Choice of Forum in Europe: Theory and Evidence' (2013) 21 ERPL 13).

Regarding the demand side, these scholars argue that it is less the quality of the law that drives private actors' choice than familiarity with the chosen law. Regarding the supply side, they claim that states lack the incentives and willingness to adjust their contract laws to private actor needs. However, these arguments miss the point for two reasons (Giesela Rühl, 'Regulatory Competition in Contract Law: Empirical Evidence and Normative Implications' (2013) 9 ERCL 61). First, there is empirical evidence that the quality of the law is at least one of the factors driving party choice. Naturally, familiarity is also important and, according to some studies, even more important. But in order to stir regulatory competition, the quality of the law need not be the only or the most important factor for a choice of law; it merely needs to be a sufficiently important one for a sufficiently large number of businesses and consumers. In fact, regulatory competition would only be excluded if all parties based their choice exclusively on the familiarity of the chosen law. However, according to the studies just mentioned, this is clearly not the case. Second, there is empirical evidence that states actually have an interest in the application of their contract laws and that they are actually willing to adjust their laws to the perceived needs of businesses and consumers. To begin with, several states, including the → United Kingdom, → France and → Germany, have recently engaged in what has become known as the 'battle of the brochures'. In a series of publications they describe the advantages of their respective contract laws vis-à-vis the contract laws of other states (Law Society of England and Wales, *England and Wales: The Jurisdiction of Choice* (2008); Bundesnotarkammer and others, *Law – Made in Germany. Global. Effective. Cost-Efficient* (2009, 2012 and 2014). In addition, and more importantly, a large number of states, including → Germany, → Estonia, → Hungary, → Lithuania, the → Netherlands, → Poland and → Romania, have partly or wholly revised their contract laws over the last two decades in order to render them 'fit for Europe'. Empirical evidence thus suggests that there is also regulatory competition in contract law – and arguably beyond.

III. Potential effects

The original theory of regulatory competition assumes that competition for legal products will always enhance efficiency and thus induce what has been termed a 'race to the top'. More specifically, the theory assumes that regulatory competition will support the evolution of legal rules that satisfy business and consumer preferences, and that, in turn, the theory will also induce the evolution of new and arguably better rules. This development, however, is not a matter of course. Just like markets for goods and services, markets for laws can fail and lead to laws that prove beneficial only for some members of society and not for society at large. The reasons for the development of what is at times termed a 'race to the bottom' are again manifold. First, legal rules result from political processes that may be influenced and shaped by interest groups. It follows that there is a risk that interest groups skew state actions in a direction that proves beneficial for interest group members, but not necessarily for others.

In addition, states might actively try to cater to the interests of some members of society only at the expense of others. This may be the case if only some parties can influence the choice of the applicable law, even though the choice also affects others. Take, for example, choice-of-law clauses such as those in → consumer contracts that are negotiated by parties with unequal bargaining power. Since it is usually the professional and not the consumer who chooses the applicable law, regulators have to enact laws that cater to the preferences of professionals if they wish to have their laws applied. Finally, path dependencies may effectively prevent regulatory competition from producing rules that are universally beneficial. This is because legal change never takes place without context, but rather takes place in a pre-existing legal environment shaped by previous legislative or judicatory decisions. It follows that path dependencies will render radical changes and new beginnings difficult and unlikely – even if they represent the best course of action. This also holds true because any legal change involves costs.

Against this background, the interesting question is what actually happens in practice. Does regulatory competition induce a proverbial race to the top or the bottom? Unfortunately, there is no clear-cut answer. Take corporate law, for example, where it has long been discussed whether regulatory competition is more likely to lead to better or worse corporate laws. In the race to the bottom scenario, states compete for corporate charters by biasing their substantive corporate laws towards managers, ie those parties who take, or at least strongly influence, the decision of where to incorporate (Lucian A Bebchuk, 'Federalism and the Corporation: The Desirable Limits on State Competition in Corporate Law' (1992) 105 Harv.L.Rev 1437; Lucian A Bebchuk and Allen Ferrell, 'Federalism and Corporate Law: The Race to Protect Managers from Takeovers' (1999) 99 Colum.L.Rev. 1168). By contrast, in the race to the top scenario, states focus on management incentives to maintain equity attractiveness and compete for corporate charters by making their substantive corporate laws more beneficial for both managers and shareholders (Roberta Romano, *The Genius of American Corporate Law* (Aei Press 1993); Roberta Romano, 'Competition for Corporate Charters and the Lesson of Takeover Statutes' (1993) 61 Fordham L.Rev. 843). Unfortunately, there is also no solid empirical evidence available indicating whether the race to the top or the race to the bottom scenario prevails. Again, take corporate law, where so-called event studies show that the stock market price of a publicly held corporation increases following incorporation in Delaware (Michael Bradley and Cindy Schipani, 'The Relevance of the Duty of Care Standard in Corporate Governance' (1989) 75 Iowa L.Rev. 1; Peter Dodd and Richard Leftwich, 'The Market for Corporate Charters: "Unhealthy Competition" versus Federal Regulation' (1980) 53 JBL 259; Randall Heron and Wilbur Lewellen, 'An Empirical Analysis of the Reincorporation Decision' (1998) 33 J.Fin.Quant.A. 549; Allen Hyman, 'The Delaware Controversy – The Legal Debate' (1979) 4 J.Corp.L. 368; Jeffry Netter and Annette Poulsen, 'State Corporation Laws and Shareholders: The Recent Experience' (1989) 18 Fin.Man. 29). In addition, there are event studies indicating that a corporation's value as measured by what is referred to as 'Tobin's Q' increases upon incorporation in Delaware (Robert Daines, 'Does Delaware Law Improve Firm Value?' (2001) 62 J.Fin.Econ. 525). However, for various reasons, these studies do not allow the conclusion that regulatory competition in corporate law in the USA has induced a race to the top (Sanjai Bhagat and Roberta Romano, 'Event Studies and the Law: Part II: Empirical Studies of Corporate Law' (2002) 4 ALER 380 *et seq*; Guhan Subramanian, 'The Disappearing Delaware Effect' (2004) 20 J.L.Econ.& Org. 31).

Outside corporate law, notably in contract law, the picture is hardly better, in that here, too, there is no empirical evidence concerning the effects of regulatory competition. As regards contract law, such empirical evidence would also be difficult to find, as the quality of contract law depends on contracting party preferences. Since the parties decide whether a contract law is good or bad, it follows that the only way to determine whether regulatory competition leads to better or worse contract law is to analyse the effects of a contract law reform. If more parties decide to choose a certain contract law after it has been amended, it may safely be assumed that the reform – and thus regulatory competition – has had positive effects. Unfortunately, there are as yet no such empirical studies analysing the impact of recent contract law reforms, and such studies would also be difficult to conduct given the non-public nature of most contracts. However, there are good reasons to believe that regulatory competition in contract law, and arguably beyond, will instead induce a progressive improvement rather than deterioration in law. This is because a choice of the applicable contract law, at least as a matter of principle and in contrast to corporate law, only affects the immediate parties to the contract, ie the parties that actually agree on the choice of law. On condition that these parties' choice is voluntary and informed, states have no incentive to skew their contract laws in favour of one party or the other, but rather have an incentive to accommodate the interests of all parties involved. It follows that regulatory competition in contract law, at least as a matter of principle, is more likely to induce a race to the top than a race to the bottom. This naturally does not rule out a race to the bottom in practice. In fact, there are cases that are more likely to trigger deterioration in law as opposed to its improvement. Choice-of-law clauses in → consumer contracts or, more generally, choice-of-law clauses negotiated by parties with unequal bargaining power have already been mentioned. In addition, there are choice-of-law clauses that affect third parties who have no say during the contract drafting process, such as in contracts for the benefit of third parties. In both cases, in their wish to have their contract laws applied, lawmakers may tend to enact laws catering solely to the preferences of those parties actually choosing the applicable law. Thus, lack of equal bargaining power and lack of participation in the drafting process may lead to one-sided laws that themselves may eventually induce a race to the bottom.

IV. Normative implications

The preceding considerations hold a number of implications for private international law. The most important is that regulatory competition should be promoted if and to the extent that it is more likely to induce progressively improved law, whereas it should be regulated, ie restricted, if and to the extent that it is more likely to do the opposite. In both cases, private international law plays a crucial role because it can help both to facilitate and to regulate regulatory competition. In addition, substantive law may become relevant.

1. The role of private international law

a) The race to the top scenario
In the race to the top scenario, private international law may help to promote regulatory competition first and foremost by allowing

parties to choose the applicable law. In current private international law regimes, freedom of choice, and thus the very foundation of regulatory competition, already enjoys widespread application. In fact, if there is one concept in private international law that has steadily extended its scope over the last few years, it is freedom of choice (→ Choice of law). Such freedom takes two distinct forms – direct and indirect. It is direct if the parties may choose the applicable law via a choice-of-law clause, while it is indirect if the parties may influence facts that determine the applicable law. In corporate law, for example, many states follow the incorporation theory and apply the law of the state where the company was incorporated (→ Companies). As a result, parties may indirectly choose the applicable corporate law by choosing the state of incorporation. For the most part, however, freedom of choice is granted directly, so that parties may choose the applicable law by agreement. Its classic, and until today the least contested, area of application of direct freedom of choice is contract law. Here, with the exception of some South American and Middle Eastern countries, it claims widespread application (Jürgen Basedow, 'Theorie der Rechtswahl oder Parteiautonomie als Grundlage des Internationalen Privatrechts' (2011) 75 RabelsZ 32; Giesela Rühl, *Statut und Effizienz* (Mohr Siebeck 2011)). In other fields, direct freedom of choice has recently gained recognition. This holds particularly true for the private international law of non-contractual obligations. Here, national legal orders and international instruments commonly provide that agreements on the applicable law are permissible after the event generating the non-contractual obligation has occurred. Article 14(1) → Rome II Regulation (Regulation (EC) No 864/2007 of the European Parliament and of the Council of 11 July 2007 on the law applicable to non-contractual obligations (Rome II), [2007] OJ L 199/40), for example, allows parties to submit non-contractual obligations to the law of their choice by an agreement entered into subsequent to the event giving rise to the damage. In international family and → succession law, parties in many legal orders are now allowed to choose from a range of laws. According art 5(1) → Rome III Regulation (Council Regulation (EU) No 1259/2010 of 20 December 2010 implementing enhanced cooperation in the area of the law applicable to divorce and legal separation, [2010] OJ L 343/10), for example, spouses may designate the law applicable to their divorce or legal separation provided that it is either the law of their common habitual residence, the law of their last common habitual residence, the law of the → nationality of either spouse or the law of the forum. By the same token, art 15 Maintenance Regulation (Council Regulation (EC) No 4/2009 of 18 December 2008 on jurisdiction, applicable law, recognition and enforcement of decisions and cooperation in matters relating to maintenance obligations, [2009] OJ L 7/1) refers to art 8(1) of the Protocol to the new Hague Maintenance Convention 2007 (Hague Convention of 23 November 2007 on the international recovery of child support and other forms of family maintenance, [2011] OJ L 192/51 and Hague Protocol of 23 November 2007 on the law applicable to maintenance obligations, [2009] OJ L 331/19) that allows parties to submit their maintenance obligation to the law of either party's nationality or habitual residence (→ Maintenance obligations). Finally, art 22 Succession Regulation (Regulation (EU) No 650/2012 of the European Parliament and of the Council of 4 July 2012 on jurisdiction, applicable law, recognition and enforcement of decisions and acceptance and enforcement of authentic instruments in matters of succession and on the creation of a European Certificate of Succession, [2012] OJ L 201/107; → Rome IV Regulation) allows the (future) deceased to choose the law applicable in respect of succession rights resulting from death. Against this background, it is fair to say that freedom of choice is deeply embedded in private international law. However, it should be noted that outside Europe, freedom of choice is for the most part granted by national law. Of course, this is not a problem as long as states actually allow the parties to choose the applicable law. However, it entails the risk that individual states unilaterally do away with freedom of choice and thereby undermine the market for laws. Ideally, freedom of choice should therefore not only be enshrined in national law, but also in international law.

In addition to allowing freedom of choice, private international law may also promote regulatory competition by removing unnecessary restrictions to freedom of choice. At the moment, many national legal orders and international legal instruments restrict freedom of choice in a number of instances. According to art 3 Rome I Regulation (Regulation (EC) No 593/2008 of the European Parliament and of the Council of 17 June 2008 on the law applicable to contractual obligations (Rome I), [2008] OJ L 177/6; → Rome Convention and Rome I Regulation), for example, the parties may only choose the law of a state, but not a non-state body of law, while according to § 187(2)(a) Restatement (Second) of Conflict of Laws (American Law Institute, Restatement of the Law, Second: Conflict of Laws 2d, St Paul 1971; → Restatement (First and Second) of Conflict of Laws) and § 1-301(e)(1) of the UCC (Uniform Commercial Code, American Law Institute, Uniform Commercial Code, Official Text with Comments, St Paul 2012), a choice-of-law clause will be respected only if the parties or the contract have a relationship to the chosen law. All these restrictions unnecessarily limit regulatory competition by reducing the number of available contract laws. It has therefore been suggested that they be removed (Giesela Rühl, 'The Choice of Law Framework for Efficient Regulatory Competition in Contract Law' in Horst Eidenmüller (ed), *Regulatory Competition in Contract Law and Dispute Resolution* (CH Beck 2013) 287).

b) The race to the bottom scenario
In the race to the bottom scenario, private international law may help to regulate regulatory competition by restricting freedom of choice. If it manages to ensure that a choice of law mirrors the preferences of all parties involved in and affected by the choice, it may prevent states from enacting laws that cater to the preferences of some people at the expense of others. In current private international law regimes, such provisions are already commonplace. For example, many national and international private international law regimes restrict the parties' choice if one of the parties is perceived as weaker than the other or if the choice affects the rights of third parties. According to art 6(2) Rome I Regulation, for example, a choice of law may not deprive consumers of the protection afforded to them by the mandatory provisions of the law of their habitual residence (→ Consumer contracts) and according to art 3(2), 3rd sentence Rome I Regulation, a choice of law entered into after the conclusion of the contract may not adversely affect the rights of third parties. Both provisions ensure that a choice of law accounts for the interests of weaker parties, ie consumers and third parties not directly involved in the choice. Thus, lawmakers may not ignore these interests when enacting rules of substantive contract law. As a result, private international law may guarantee the proper functioning of regulatory competition, just as competition law guarantees the proper functioning of competition in markets for goods and services. However, the effectiveness of private international law to avoid a race to the bottom varies depending on whether regulatory competition is horizontal or vertical and depending on whether the choice-of-law rules are of national or supranational origin.

Private international law is the most effective in avoiding a progressive deterioration if regulatory competition is horizontal. This is because horizontal regulatory competition takes place between national contract laws and is brought about by a choice of law on the level of private international law. In contrast, private international law's ability to avoid such a negative development is less obvious if regulatory competition is vertical. This is because vertical regulatory competition takes place between national contract laws and international or supranational contract laws, and is brought about by a choice of an optional instrument. However, the choice of an optional instrument may be subject to the rules of private international law, or alternatively the choice may be subject to the rules of the optional instrument itself. Take, for example, the original Draft for a Common European Sales Law (Proposal of 11 October 2011 for a Regulation of the European Parliament and of the European Council on a Common European Sales Law COM(2011) 635 final; → CESL). According to art 3, the Common European Sales Law may be chosen by the parties. However, according to art 8 CESL-D, this choice will be subject to the rules of the Common European Sales Law and not to the rules of private international law. Accordingly, the rules of private international law, notably the Rome I Regulation, will not be capable of regulating the resulting – vertical – regulatory competition between the Common European Sales Law and the contract laws of the Member States.

However, in addition, the effectiveness of private international law in avoiding a race to the bottom varies depending on who actually enacts the pertaining choice-of-law rules. Private international law is less influential in this regard if it is of national origin, ie if choice-of-law rules are enacted by national regulators. This is because states, just like individuals, pursue their own interests, and these interests are not necessarily directed towards efficient regulatory competition. Just like competitors on markets for goods and services, states might rather have an interest in preventing or at least impeding regulatory competition. Accordingly, private international law may be more effective in avoiding a race to the bottom if it is not enacted by states, ie the competitors themselves, but rather by international or supranational institutions seeking to balance the state interests involved. Against this background, it is to be welcomed that the European legislature has recently adopted a number of Regulations which provide for uniform choice-of-law rules for contractual and non-contractual obligations, divorce and → succession law. In addition, the → Hague Conference on Private International Law has added substantially to a growing body of globally accepted choice-of-law rules, of which many, albeit not all, embrace the freedom of choice principle. Certainly this does not mean that private international law cannot contribute to efficient regulatory competition if it is enacted by individual states. Provided that private international law is disciplined, for example, by constitutional principles, it may help to avoid a race to the bottom even if it is of national origin. However, the likelihood that it will actually do so is significantly lower.

2. *The role of substantive law*

The above discussion has focused on the ability of private international law to promote and regulate private international law. However, it should not be ignored that in addition to private international law, substantive law may also contribute to promoting regulatory competition and ensure that it actually leads to better laws. As regards the promotion of regulatory competition, international and supranational lawmakers may, for example, offer additional (optional) substantive legal regimes and thereby increase the number of laws available for party choice. Within the EU, this course of action has already proved to be successful in many areas of law, notably corporate and IP law. In addition, the United Nations Convention on the International Sale of Goods (United Nations Convention of 11 April 1980 on Contracts for the International Sale of Goods, 1489 UNTS 3; → CISG), the Principles of European Contract Law (Lando and Beale, Principles of European Contract Law (Parts I and II, Kluwer Law International 1999) and the UNIDROIT Principles for International Commercial Contracts (→ UNIDROIT) have influenced national and international legislation in the field of contract law and hence have stimulated regulatory competition. Should the Common European Sales Law (→ CESL) ever be enacted, it might promote regulatory competition in the field of contract law. This competition naturally differs from the competition between national laws, in that it is not horizontal, but rather vertical. It takes place not between national laws, but between national laws on the one hand and international or supranational laws on the other, and inevitably for vertical regulatory competition to have positive effects, certain conditions need to be met. Most importantly, the optional instrument in question must be efficiently designed to avoid network effects leading to inefficiently low market standards (Horst Eidenmüller, 'What Can Be Wrong with an Option? An Optional European Sales Law as a Regulatory Tool' (2013) 50 CMLR 69). However, provided these conditions are met, optional instruments may be driving forces on the market for laws (Stefan Leible, 'Kollisionsrecht und vertikaler Regulierungswettbewerb' (2012) 76 RabelsZ 374).

As regards the regulation of regulatory competition, the harmonization of substantive laws may play a part in avoiding a race to the bottom. Just like optional legal regimes, harmonizing measures are usually adopted by international or supranational lawmakers. They require states to adjust their substantive laws to comply with minimum standards set by the international community, or in Europe by the EU. Provided that these minimum standards reflect the preferences of society at large, harmonization may effectively prevent states from enacting one-sided laws apt to induce a race to the bottom. However, the problem with regulating regulatory competition at the level of substantive law is that its reach is frequently limited. With EU Directives, for example, the effects of harmonization are confined to the laws of the Member States. It follows that a race to the bottom cannot be avoided if the laws of a non-Member State apply, for example, by way of a choice of law which by its nature does not necessarily account for the interests of weaker and third parties. It follows that regulatory competition needs additional regulation on the level of private international law where the interests of weaker and third parties are at stake.

V. Conclusion

Regulatory competition is a powerful concept that improves our understanding of law and the lawmaking process. It explains how market forces may shape the existence and the content of legal rules and regulations. However, a number of questions still remain to be resolved and supported by empirical evidence. The most important challenge that yet remains is to define when and under what conditions regulatory competition will actually induce a race to the top or a race to the bottom. If we achieve clarity in this regard, private international law may be used to both promote and regulate regulatory competition – for the benefit of all parties involved and society at large.

GIESELA RÜHL

Literature

William Bratton and Joseph McCahery, 'The New Economics of Jurisdictional Competition: Devolutionary Federalism in a Second Best World' (1997) 86 Geo.L.J. 201; Horst Eidenmüller, 'The Transnational Law Market, Regulatory Competition, and Transnational Corporations' (2011) 18 Ind.J. Global L.Stud. 707; Horst Eidenmüller (ed), *Regulatory Competition in Contract Law and Dispute Resolution* (CH Beck 2013); Eva-Maria Kieninger, *Wettbewerb der Privatrechtsordnungen im Europäischen Binnenmarkt* (Mohr Siebeck 2002); Larry Ribstein and Erin O'Hara, *The Law Market* (OUP 2008); Wolf-Georg Ringe, 'Corporate Mobility in the European Union – A Flash in the Pan? An Empirical Study on the Success of Law Making and Regulatory Competition' [2013] ECFR 230; Roberta Romano, *The Genius of American Corporate Law* (Aei Press 1993); Giesela Rühl, *Statut und Effizienz* (Mohr Siebeck 2011); Giesela Rühl, 'Regulatory Competition in Contract Law: Empirical Evidence and Normative Implications' [2013] 9 ERCL 61; Charles Tiebout, 'A Pure Theory of Local Expenditure' (1956) 64 J.Pol.Econ. 416; Joel Trachtman, 'Regulatory Competition and Regulatory Jurisdiction' (2000) 3 J.Int'l Econ.L. 331; Stefan Vogenauer, 'Regulatory Competition through Choice of Contract Law and Choice of Forum in Europe: Theory and Evidence' (2013) 21 ERPL 13.

Reinsurance contracts

I. Introduction

An insurer's capacity to carry risk and to neutralize it through risk pooling is limited by the available (regulatory) capital held in reserve to cover potential losses. In light of this, reinsurance is essentially a tool for insurance companies to expand their risk-bearing capacity by passing on some of the volatility in loss claims arising from the policies they underwrite. Two basic types of reinsurance contracts must be distinguished as they present considerable differences under both substantive law and private international law. The first category, 'facultative reinsurance', describes tailor-made contracts covering a single risk stemming from a specific insurance policy. Therefore, the vast majority of these facultative reinsurance contracts are proportional, meaning that the risk covered by the reinsurer represents a certain percentage of the liability of the reinsured under each individual insurance policy. Insurance companies use these contracts to reinsure atypical risks or risks that are excluded or only partly covered by 'treaty reinsurance'. This second category, 'treaty reinsurance', covers multiple or even an entire portfolio of → insurance contracts under a single agreement. Treaty reinsurance involves a two-stage contractual process given that apart from the general treaty itself, the individual risks included are only being detailed successively in separate agreements or 'declarations' to the treaty. Treaty reinsurance takes two basic forms. Under proportional contracts, the reinsurer covers a certain quota of the liability incurred by the reinsured under each of its individual insurance policies. By contrast, non-proportional reinsurance treaties are detached from the individual insurance policies in that the reinsurer only promises to step in when the aggregated overall liability of the reinsured exceeds a predefined threshold (with regard to the aforementioned distinctions, see eg Colin Edelman and Andrew Burns, *The Law of Reinsurance* (OUP 2013) 11 *et seq*). These differences between treaty and facultative reinsurance as well as between proportional and non-proportional reinsurance must be borne in mind when characterizing these contracts under private international law. Given that the London market is the most important reinsurance market (cf Jeffrey E Thomas and others (eds), *New Appleman on Insurance Law, Vol 7: Reinsurance* (LexisNexis 2013) § 79), this entry focuses on the European private international law. Moreover, the rules on choice of law and jurisdiction in the relevant US and Bermuda reinsurance markets will be illustrated and compared to their European counterparts.

II. Party autonomy and reinsurance

1. Article 3 Rome I Regulation

Although the European legislator introduced a choice-of-law rule for insurance contracts in art 7, reinsurance contracts are explicitly excluded from the ambit of this provision by virtue of art 7(1) Rome I Regulation (Regulation (EC) No 593/2008 of the European Parliament and of the Council of 17 June 2008 on the law applicable to contractual obligations (Rome I), [2008] OJ L 177/6; → Rome Convention and Rome I Regulation (contractual obligations)). Hence, the law applicable to the different types of reinsurance agreements must be determined according to the general choice-of-law rules (see eg Jan D Lüttringhaus, 'Art 1' in Franco Ferrari (ed), *Rome I Regulation* (Sellier 2014) para 92). Against this backdrop, art 3 is the key provision for reinsurance contracts under the Rome I Regulation: according to art 3(1) Rome I Regulation, a contract shall be governed by the law chosen by the parties. In practice, most reinsurance contracts contain an explicit choice-of-law clause. Even where the parties failed to include such a clause, the choice may, pursuant to art 3(1) Rome I Regulation, also be 'clearly demonstrated by the terms of the contract or the circumstances of the case'. Although the wording of art 3(1) Rome I Regulation departs from its predecessor in art 3 Rome Convention insofar as the requirement of an implicit choice 'demonstrated with reasonable certainty' has now been replaced by 'clearly demonstrated', this implies no major change in substance.

The courts in the crucial London reinsurance market in particular will therefore be able to uphold their long-standing practice of deducing a → choice of law from, *inter alia*, jurisdiction or arbitration agreements (cf eg *Maritime Insurance v Assekuranz-Union von 1865* (1935) 53 Ll L Rep 16; *King v Brandywine Reinsurance* [2005] EWCA Civ 235; see also Rob Merkin, 'The Rome I Regulation and Reinsurance' (2009) 5 J Priv Int L 69, 72 *et seq*). With regard to jurisdiction clauses, Recital (12) Rome I Regulation states that those agreements 'should be one of the factors to be taken into account in determining whether a choice of law has been clearly demonstrated'. Arbitration agreements, by contrast, are excluded from the ambit of the Rome I Regulation by virtue of its art 1(2)(e). The law governing these agreements must therefore be determined separately and independently from the reinsurance contract according to the applicable national law. However, this does not prevent a court from taking into account the arbitration clause as one among other 'circumstances of the case' for the purposes of determining the law applicable to the reinsurance contract itself (Rob Merkin, 'The Rome I Regulation and Reinsurance' (2009) 5 J Priv Int L 69, 70 and 75 *et seq*; Raymond Cox, Louise Merrett and Marcus Smith, *Private international law of Reinsurance and Insurance* (Informa 2006) 228 *et seq*).

Other 'circumstances of the case' indicating a tacit choice of law under art 3(1) Rome I Regulation may include, for example, the use of standard form clauses commonly found in a particular jurisdiction, negotiations and other dealings between the parties, as well as the market where the reinsurance contract is being placed and administered. Hence, whenever reinsurance contracts were negotiated and placed in the important London market by the predominant English brokers using domestic standard form clauses, UK courts have usually held that English law should govern these contracts (see eg *Gan Insurance v Tai Ping Insurance* [1999] EWCA Civ 1524; *Stonebridge Underwriting v Ontario Municipal Insurance Exchange* [2010] EWHC 2279 (Comm); see also Peter Mankowski, 'Internationales Rückversicherungsvertragsrecht' [2002] VersR 1177 *et seq*; Rob Merkin, 'The Rome I Regulation and Reinsurance' (2009) 5 J Priv Int L 69, 70).

a) Party autonomy in facultative reinsurance and the 'full reinsurance clause'

Given that facultative reinsurance serves as a tool for insurers to pass on a specific (portion of) risk underwritten in an individual contract to a reinsurer, facultative reinsurance contracts usually contain a 'full reinsurance clause'. At the level of substantive law, such a clause basically amounts to incorporating all the terms of the direct insurance contract into the facultative reinsurance agreement (Özlem Gürses and Rob Merkin, 'Facultative Reinsurance and the Full Reinsurance Clause' [2008] LMCLQ 366; Rob Merkin, 'The Rome I Regulation and Reinsurance' (2009) 5 J

Priv Int L 69, 73 and 78 *et seq*). This 'back-to-back' construction of the facultative reinsurance contract serves the goal of achieving a truly proportional coverage by the reinsurer of all the risks underwritten by the reinsured under the initial insurance policy. The accessory nature of the facultative reinsurance agreement with regard to the direct insurance policy may also play a role in private international law: the 'full reinsurance clause' could namely be read as also implying the incorporation of choice-of-law clauses contained in the direct insurance contract into the facultative reinsurance agreement. While a choice-of-law provision in one contract may, at least in principle, also take effect for another agreement where the provision is expressly referred to (cf ECJ Case C-543/10 *Axa* [2013] ECR I-0000, paras 24 *et seq*; cf also *Burrows v Jamaica Private Power* [2001] EWHC 488 (Comm); *Sea Trade Maritime Corporation v Hellenic Mutual War Risks Association (Bermuda), The Athena (No 2)* [2006] EWHC 2530 (Comm)), it is unclear whether or not the mere existence of a 'full reinsurance clause' should be construed as including choice-of-law clauses in the direct insurance policy. The ECJ has recently held with regard to choice-of-jurisdiction clauses that such a clause agreed upon by the parties to one contract may only be imposed on another party in a chain of contracts if the latter, in turn, accepts the particular choice (ECJ Case C-543/10 *Axa* [2013] ECR I-0000, paras 24 *et seq*). The same reasoning should apply to the incorporation of choice-of-law clauses: the choice should only be regarded as binding at the reinsurance level where the parties to the facultative reinsurance contract, in addition to inserting the 'full reinsurance clause', have also made reference to the choice of law included in the direct insurance agreement (see Peter Mankowski, 'Internationales Rückversicherungsvertragsrecht' [2002] VersR 1177 *et seq*; Rob Merkin, 'The Rome I Regulation and Reinsurance' (2009) 5 J Priv Int L 69, 73 *et seq*; cf also *Lexington Insurance v AGF Insurance & WASA International Insurance* [2009] UKHL 40).

Moreover, a choice-of-law clause in a direct insurance contract on its own merits does not 'clearly demonstrate' a → choice of law in the reinsurance agreement under art 3(1) Rome I Regulation. However, this does not prevent courts from taking this clause into account as one of many 'circumstances of the case'. It is noteworthy that the courts in the English reinsurance market have developed a 'back-to-back' cover principle for proportional facultative reinsurance contracts that leads to a consistent interpretation of the reinsurance and direct insurance policies, regardless of the applicable laws (see eg *Forsakringsaktieselskapet Vesta v Butcher* [1989] UKHL 5; *Ace Insurance v Zurich Insurance* [2001] EWCA Civ 173; *Lexington Insurance v AGF Insurance & WASA International Insurance* [2009] UKHL 40). This principle amounts to a rule of construction on the level of substantive law and reduces potential friction that may arise from diverging national (re)insurance laws (as to the different implications of and exceptions to this rule, see Rob Merkin, 'The Rome I Regulation and Reinsurance' (2009) 5 J Priv Int L 69, 78 *et seq*).

b) Problematic issues with regard to treaty reinsurance

As already pointed out, a reinsurance treaty involves (at least) two steps: at the first stage, the parties enter into the treaty, the extent and risk coverage of which is detailed, but only at the second contractual stage involving so-called 'declarations' to the treaty. This dual nature of reinsurance treaties must also be taken into account at the level of private international law: the question is whether the two agreements may be regarded as a single transaction or if they should be treated separately for the purposes of determining the applicable law. The fact that different types of insurance treaties exist adds to the complexity: under so-called 'obligatory' reinsurance treaties, any risk accepted by the reinsured is automatically transferred to the treaty without requiring consent by the reinsurer. By contrast, reinsurance treaties may also be 'facultative' for both sides, meaning that the reinsured is free to declare any risk and the reinsurer, in turn, has the discretion to refuse coverage for that particular risk. Finally, a reinsurance treaty can also be 'facultative-obligatory' in that the reinsured is free to declare a specific risk, but the reinsurer, for his part, must accept all declarations made (as to this distinction, see Rob Merkin, 'The Rome I Regulation and Reinsurance' (2009) 5 J Priv Int L 69, 83 *et seq*).

Along the lines of their substantive nature, the aforementioned types of reinsurance treaties should be characterised differently: first, in substance, obligatory reinsurance treaties really are single agreements establishing an automatic inclusion of the risk accepted by the reinsured to the respective treaty. The law applicable to the obligatory reinsurance treaty by virtue of a choice-of-law clause therefore governs the entire transaction (Rob Merkin, 'The Rome I Regulation and Reinsurance' (2009) 5 J Priv Int L 69, 83). The same reasoning should apply to facultative-obligatory treaties: these contracts only confer discretion to the reinsured to unilaterally define the extent of the contractual performance owed by the reinsurer. The reinsured is simply exercising a right granted to him under the reinsurance treaty. Hence, the treaty and the declarations should be regarded as a single contract for the purposes of choice of law. The law applicable to the treaty should therefore also govern the unilateral declarations by the reinsured (*contra*, however, Rob Merkin, 'The Rome I Regulation and Reinsurance' (2009) 5 J Priv Int L 69, 84: 'each declaration takes effect as a separate contract of reinsurance').

However, the case is different with regard to facultative reinsurance treaties: the individual declarations amount to an offer of the reinsured which requires acceptance by the reinsurer. Each of these agreements therefore stands as a contract in its own right for which the applicable law must, at least in principle, be determined separately. Usually, the parties to a reinsurance treaty will incorporate a choice-of-law or at least a choice-of-jurisdiction/arbitration clause into their agreement that also expressly covers the individual declarations and is referred to in these agreements. As a consequence, the same law will apply to the treaty and the declarations despite the independent nature of these contracts (Rob Merkin, 'The Rome I Regulation and Reinsurance' (2009) 5 J Priv Int L 69, 83 *et seq*).

2. *Party autonomy under US and Bermuda choice-of-law rules*

In the USA, all courts will usually enforce an express choice-of-law clause in a reinsurance contract provided that the law selected by the parties has sufficient contacts with the reinsurance transaction (eg *American Special Risk Insurance v Delta American Re Insurance*, 836 F.Supp. 183 (SDNY 1993); *Acceptance Insurance v Granite Reinsurance*, 567 F.3d 369 (8th Cir 2009); *Onebeacon America Insurance v Commercial Union Assurance Co of Canada*, 684 F.3d 237, 241 (1st Cir 2012); see Jeffrey E Thomas and others (eds), *New Appleman on Insurance Law, Vol 7: Reinsurance* (LexisNexis 2013) § 72.02[7][a] and § 77.03[4][a]). In any event, a choice-of-law clause may be set aside where the enforcement of the agreement would violate a fundamental public policy of the forum (cf *Nevada v Hall*, 440 US 410, 421 *et seq* (1979); *American Special Risk Insurance v Delta American Re Insurance*, 836 F.Supp. 183 (SDNY 1993); see also Steven Plitt and others (eds), *Couch on Insurance* (3rd edn, Thomson 2013) § 9:14). Unlike their European counterparts, courts in the USA seem to be reluctant to infer a tacit choice-of-law from, for example, jurisdiction or arbitration agreements (cf *Reliance Insurance v Raybestos Products*, 1:97-cv-00027-RLY/TAB, US Dis. LEXIS 5487 (SD Ind. 24 January 2007); Jeffrey E Thomas and others (eds), *New Appleman on Insurance Law, Vol 7: Reinsurance* (LexisNexis 2013) § 72.02[7][a]). Moreover, US courts have not ruled on the question whether a 'full reinsurance clause' in facultative reinsurance should be read as implying the incorporation of choice-of-law clauses from the direct insurance policies. However, in a recent case, a US court seemed willing to interpret reinsurance agreements 'back-to-back' with the direct insurance contracts (cf *Pacific Employers Insurance v Global Reinsurance*, 693 F.3d 417 (3rd Cir 2012); see also Jeffrey E Thomas and others (eds), *New Appleman on Insurance Law, Vol 7: Reinsurance* (LexisNexis 2013) § 72.02[7][b]). If applied to a 'full reinsurance clause', this approach would differ from the view taken by English courts (see *Lexington Insurance v AGF Insurance & WASA International Insurance* [2009] UKHL 40; see also II.1.a) above).

As regards choice-of-law rules in the important Bermuda reinsurance market, the old rules of English common law continue to apply (see Ian RC Kawakey, *Offshore Commercial Law in Bermuda* (Wildy, Simmonds and Hill 2013) 460 *et seq*). Under this concept of 'proper law' (→ Proper law (doctrine)), the law expressly or tacitly chosen by the parties will govern the reinsurance agreement. A choice of law may also be inferred from the circumstances and, in particular, from arbitration or jurisdiction clauses (see eg Terry O'Neill and Jan W Woloniecki, *The Law of Reinsurance in England and Bermuda* (2nd edn, Sweet & Maxwell 2004) 647 *et seq*). In sum, this choice-of-law regime essentially mirrors the English case-law, which, at least as far as the courts in the predominant London market are concerned, still has considerable bearing under the Rome I Regulation (cf II.1. above).

III. The law applicable in the absence of choice

1. Article 4 Rome I Regulation and reinsurance

Where the parties to a reinsurance contract have not explicitly or tacitly chosen the applicable law or have only designated the law applicable to part of their contract pursuant to art 3(1), the courts have to draw upon art 4 Rome I Regulation. A reinsurance contract is 'a contract for the provision of services' under art 4(1)(b) Rome I Regulation and shall therefore be 'governed by the law of the country where the service provider has his habitual residence'. Pursuant to Recitals (7) and (17) Rome I Regulation, the term 'service contract' must be interpreted autonomously and consistently with the Brussels I Regulation (recast) (Regulation (EU) No 1215/2012 of the European Parliament and of the Council of 12 December 2012 on jurisdiction and the recognition and enforcement of judgments in civil and commercial matters (recast), [2012] OJ L 351/1; → Brussels I (Convention and Regulation)). Under the European rules on jurisdiction, the concept of 'service' implies, at the very least, that the party who provides the service carries out a particular activity in return for remuneration (cf ECJ Case C-533/07 *Falco Privatstiftung and Thomas Rabitsch v Gisela Weller-Lindhorst* [2009] ECR I-3327, para 29). A reinsurance contract satisfies these requirements since the reinsurer provides the service of covering specific risks in return for a reinsurance premium. Hence, art 4(1)(b) Rome I Regulation calls for the application of the law of the country where the reinsurer has his habitual residence (Rob Merkin, 'The Rome I Regulation and Reinsurance' (2009) 5 J Priv Int L 69, 74; Dirk Looschelders, 'Grundfragen des deutschen und internationalen Rückversicherungsvertragsrechts' [2012] VersR 1, 3; see also eg Klaus H Basedow, *Le Droit International Privé des Assurances* (LGDJ 1939) 157; Peter Mankowski, 'Internationales Rückversicherungsvertragsrecht' [2002] VersR 1177 *et seq*). Pursuant to art 19(1) and (3) Rome I Regulation, the habitual residence (→ Domicile, habitual residence and establishment) of → companies shall be the place of central administration at the time of the conclusion of the contract. Moreover, it is noteworthy that if the reinsurance agreement is concluded or performed in the course of the operations of a branch, agency or any other establishment of the reinsurer, the place where this specific establishment is located shall be treated as the place of habitual residence according to art 19(2) Rome I Regulation.

Since the law governing the reinsurance contract may already be determined under art 4(1)(b), there is no need to draw upon art 4(2) Rome I Regulation. The contrary view according to which art 4(2) should not only apply but also be construed as pointing to the law at the habitual residence of the reinsured appears to be based on the misconception that reinsurance coverage is always 'back-to-back', ie proportional, with regard to the direct insurance policies. Hence, this approach not only ignores art 4(1)(b) Rome I Regulation, but also fails to distinguish between the various types of reinsurance.

Article 4(3) Rome I Regulation may only be relied upon '[w]here it is clear from all the circumstances of the case that the contract is manifestly more closely connected with a country other than' the habitual residence of the reinsurer. This → escape clause is narrowly tailored and can become relevant only under exceptional circumstances, eg if there are a multiplicity of subscribing reinsurance companies (see III.1.b) below). The same holds for art 4(4) given that the applicable law can usually be determined under art 4(1)(b) Rome I Regulation. There are, however, scenarios that present certain difficulties and that must be addressed in light of the specificities of different reinsurance contracts.

a) Multiplicity of reinsurers and/or reinsured

Reinsurance policies may not only involve more than one reinsured party but are also often underwritten by several reinsurance companies (Rob Merkin, 'The Rome I Regulation and Reinsurance' (2009) 5 J Priv Int L 69, 72). Given that art 4(1)(b) Rome I Regulation points to the law of the country where the service provider, ie the reinsurer, has his habitual residence, a multiplicity of reinsurance policyholders usually does not affect the law governing the reinsurance agreement. The case is different, however, where the reinsurance policy is underwritten by more than one reinsurer and where the habitual residence, ie the place of central administration or the relevant branch (art 19(1), (2) Rome I Regulation), of these subscribing reinsurers is located in different countries. Even where there is a leading underwriter acting on behalf of the entire reinsurer side of the transaction, at least the courts in the relevant English reinsurance market have held that each subscription of a reinsurance policy with a different reinsurer must be treated as a contract in its own right (*Lincoln National Life Insurance v Employers Reinsurance Corporation* [2002] EWHC 28 (Comm); see also Rob Merkin, 'The Rome I Regulation and Reinsurance' (2009) 5 J Priv Int L 69, 72). It is therefore far from certain that the leading underwriter will be deemed the only relevant service provider acting on behalf of all of the following market. However, at least under art 4(1)(b) Rome I Regulation, this approach would be the only way to apply a single law to the whole transaction, namely the law of the country where the leading reinsurer has his place of central administration. If each subscription were to be characterized separately, art 4(1)(b) Rome I Regulation would lead to a multiplicity of different laws, depending on the location of the administration of the respective reinsurer. This is hardly desirable, especially from the point of view of the reinsured, who do not expect a single claim against the reinsurers to be governed by different laws. In order to avoid this outcome and to account for the reasonable expectation of the parties involved in the transaction, the courts should apply art 4(4) Rome I Regulation: factors that may constitute a manifestly closer connection are, apart from the habitual residence of the leading insurer, the country where the reinsurance contract is negotiated, placed and administered (cf *Lincoln National Life Insurance v Employers Reinsurance Corporation* [2002] EWHC 28 (Comm); see also Rob Merkin, 'The Rome I Regulation and Reinsurance' (2009) 5 J Priv Int L 69, 72). The courts may also take into account whether the agreement has 'a very close relationship with another contract or contracts' (cf Recital (21) Rome I Regulation; see also Lord Collins of Mapesbury and others (eds), *Dicey, Morris & Collins on the Conflict of Laws*, vol 2 (15th edn, Sweet & Maxwell 2012) 33–245).

b) Treaty reinsurance
As already pointed out (see III.3. above), 'obligatory' as well as 'facultative-obligatory' reinsurance treaties should be treated as single contracts for the purposes of private international law. Hence, the law applicable must be determined in accordance with the principles discussed with regard to art 4 Rome I Regulation (see IV.1. below). The case is more complicated where the parties to a 'facultative' reinsurance treaty have neither expressly nor tacitly chosen the law governing the treaty and/or the individual declarations assigning the risks to the treaty. For example, whereas the law applicable to the treaty itself may be the law of the country where the reinsurer has his habitual residence pursuant to art 4(1)(b) Rome I Regulation, the individual risks declared by the reinsured and accepted by the reinsurer may emanate from various jurisdictions. For the purposes of art 4 Rome I Regulation, it could therefore be argued that the individual declarations should be treated and characterized independently (with regard to 'facultative' reinsurance treaties, cf Rob Merkin, 'The Rome I Regulation and Reinsurance' (2009) 5 J Priv Int L 69, 83). However, there is no need to deviate from the general rule under art 4(1)(b) Rome I Regulation: although the declarations may be treated as independent contracts, they still fall within the context of the reinsurance treaty because the declarations aim at specifying the content as well as the extent of the performance owed by the reinsurer. Hence, the declarations, although potentially relating to risks from different jurisdictions and constituting separate contracts, are intrinsically linked to the reinsurance treaty. Each and every declaration aims at contouring this 'contract for the provision of services'. Since neither art 4(1)(b) nor art 4(2) leads to satisfactory results, the courts should draw upon art 4(3) Rome I Regulation to apply the law of the country which also governs the reinsurance treaty, given that the declarations are manifestly more closely connected to this country. This approach is in line with Recital (20) Rome I Regulation, pursuant to which account should be taken 'of whether the contract in question has a very close relationship with another contract or contracts'.

2. Choice of law in the absence of an agreement in the USA and Bermuda

Absent an express → choice of law, US courts take different approaches in determining the law applicable to a reinsurance contract. Many US jurisdictions follow the Restatement (Second) of Conflict of Laws (American Law Institute, Restatement of the Law, Second: Conflict of Laws 2d, St Paul 1971; → Restatement (First and Second) of Conflict of Laws), which leads to the application of the law presenting the 'most significant relationship' to the reinsurance transaction. The relevant points of contact include, *inter alia*, the place of negotiation, contracting and performance as well as the location of the subject matter of the contract and the domicile and place of business of the parties to the reinsurance agreement (cf § 188(2) Restatement (Second) of Conflict of Laws). Under this test, US courts tend to focus on the place where the reinsurance contract was issued and the state where performance is expected (cf eg *Progressive Casualty Insurance v Reaseguradora Nacional de Venezuela*, 991 F.2d 42, 46 (2nd Cir 1993); *Pacific Employers Insurance v Global Reinsurance*, 693 F.3d 417 (3rd Cir 2012); see also Jeffrey E Thomas and others (eds), *New Appleman on Insurance Law, Vol 7: Reinsurance* (LexisNexis 2013) § 77.03[4][c]). Other US jurisdictions rely on the 'lex loci contractus' test which usually points to the law where the agreement was executed. However, some courts have applied the law of the place where the reinsurance contract was issued instead (cf *Fortress Re v Central National Insurance*, 595 F.Supp. 334 (EDNC 1983)). Finally, other US courts apply the governmental interests test (cf *American Insurance v American Re-Insurance*, No C 05-01218 JSW, 2006 US Dist. LEXIS 95801 (ND Cal 27 November 2006) or combine different approaches (see Jeffrey E Thomas and others (eds), *New Appleman on Insurance Law, Vol 7: Reinsurance* (LexisNexis 2013) § 77.03[4][d]). In sum, there is no generally accepted rule as to the determination of the law applicable to a reinsurance contract in the absence of an explicit choice by the parties.

As already mentioned, the choice-of-law rules in the Bermuda reinsurance market are based on the English common law principles (see II.2. above). In the absence of an express or implicit choice of law by the parties to a reinsurance agreement, the courts in this jurisdiction will determine the 'proper law' by looking for the law that presents the closest and most real connection to the transaction (see Terry O'Neill and Jan W Woloniecki, *The Law of Reinsurance in England and Bermuda* (2nd edn, Sweet & Maxwell 2004) 647 *et seq*). Again, the outcome of this approach is likely to be in line with the English case-law regarding the law applicable to reinsurance contracts entered into in the London market (cf III.1. above).

IV. Arbitration and jurisdiction in reinsurance transactions

1. The paramount role of arbitration in reinsurance

Most reinsurance contracts contain an arbitration clause given that the parties usually want their disputes to be decided by arbitrators with in-depth knowledge of the reinsurance industry. From the European perspective, the private international law issues arising in this context are, for the most part, neither subject to the Rome I Regulation (cf art 1(2) (2) Rome I Regulation) nor to the Brussels I Regulation (recast) (cf art 1(2)(d) Brussels I Regulation (recast)). Instead, the rules contained in international treaties as well as the national provisions relating to arbitration apply (→ Arbitration, international commercial; with regard to reinsurance arbitration in England, see eg Rob Merkin, 'The Rome I Regulation and Reinsurance' (2009) 5 J Priv Int L 69, 75 *et seq*; Raymond Cox, Louise Merrett and Marcus Smith, *Private international law of Reinsurance and Insurance* (Informa 2006) 195 *et seq*). These rules also govern the recognition of arbitral awards (→ Arbitration, recognition of awards). Similarly, reinsurance arbitration is subject to the general rules on arbitration in the USA (see eg Jeffrey E Thomas and others (eds), *New Appleman on Insurance Law, Vol 7: Reinsurance* (LexisNexis 2013) § 77.04; Steven Plitt and others (eds), *Couch on Insurance* (3rd edn, Thomson 2013) §§ 9:34 *et seq*) and Bermuda (see eg Terry O'Neill and Jan W Woloniecki, *The Law of Reinsurance in England and Bermuda* (2nd edn, Sweet & Maxwell 2004) 767 *et seq*; Ian RC Kawakey, *Offshore Commercial Law in Bermuda* (Wildy, Simmonds and Hill 2013) 223 *et seq* and 305 *et seq*).

2. European rules on jurisdiction and enforcement: the Brussels I Regulation (recast)

Within the scope of application of the Brussels I Regulation (recast) (→ Brussels I (Convention and Regulation)), the special rules on jurisdiction in arts 10 *et seq* neither apply to disputes between a reinsured and his reinsurer nor to disputes between reinsurance companies (cf ECJ Case C-412/98 *Group Josi Reinsurance Company SA v Universal General Insurance Company (UGIC)* [2000] ECR I-5925). Thus, the parties to a reinsurance contract may enter into a jurisdiction agreement according to art 25 without the severe restrictions imposed by art 15 Brussels I Regulation (recast). Where a reinsurance contract does not contain a jurisdiction clause, in addition to the general rule in art 4, art 7(1)(b) Brussels I Regulation (recast) as the special provision for contracts on the 'provision of services' will usually apply. However, the case may be different in disputes relating to the portion of the risk assumed by individual members of a reinsurance pool (cf with regard to art 5(1)(a) Brussels I Regulation eg Higher Regional Court (OLG) of Cologne [2009] BeckRS 14010).

Under the Brussels I Regulation (recast), recognition and enforcement of foreign judgments is subject to the rules in arts 36 *et seq*. Particular problems arise in the context of reinsurance and English solvent schemes of arrangement given that these instruments are also used in the reinsurance run-off market. The German Federal Court of Justice has recently refused to recognize an English scheme under the Brussels I Regulation (see with regard to a direct insurance policy German Federal Court of Justice (BGH) [2012] NJW 2113; *contra*, however, Regional Court (LG) Rottweil [2010] BeckRS 13330).

3. *Rules on jurisdiction and enforcement in the USA and Bermuda*

US courts will usually enforce forum selection clauses incorporated into a reinsurance contract. Federal courts commonly exercise jurisdiction over reinsurance disputes under the diversity jurisdiction statute in 28 USC § 1332 (as to the requirements and specificities, see eg Jeffrey E Thomas and others (eds), *New Appleman on Insurance Law, Vol 7: Reinsurance* (LexisNexis 2013) §§ 77.03[1] *et seq*). However, US courts may dismiss actions on the grounds of → *forum non conveniens* where there is a more appropriate forum available to the parties of the reinsurance contract. The recognition of foreign judgments varies according to the states, although it usually follows the approach set out in the Uniform Foreign Money Judgments Recognition Act (→ Recognition and enforcement of judgments (common law)).

The Bermuda Supreme Court has jurisdiction for a reinsurance contract pursuant to Order 11(1)(d)(iv) RSC (Government Notice 470/1985) where the parties inserted a choice-of-forum clause into their agreement to that effect. The same applies, for example, where the contract was made in this jurisdiction (Order 11(1)(d)(i) RSC) or is 'by its terms, or by implication, governed by the law of Bermuda' (Order 11(1)(d)(iv) RSC). The Bermuda Supreme Court may also dismiss actions on grounds of *forum non conveniens*. The enforcement of judgments from the UK and certain Commonwealth countries is subject to the Judgments (Reciprocal Enforcement) Act 1958 (1958:103, available at <www.bermudalaws.bm>), whereas common law rules apply to foreign judgments from other countries (for more detail on this, see Terry O'Neill and Jan W Woloniecki, *The Law of Reinsurance in England and Bermuda* (2nd edn, Sweet & Maxwell 2004) 673 and 709 *et seq*).

V. Cross-border portfolio transfer and private international law

Reinsurers may transfer their portfolios of reinsurance contracts across borders to other EU/EEA reinsurers pursuant to art 39 Solvency II Directive (Directive 2009/138/EC of the European Parliament and of the Council of 25 November 2009 on the taking-up and pursuit of the business of Insurance and Reinsurance (Solvency II), [2009] OJ L 335/1). The transfer only requires the authorization of the supervisory authorities in the home Member State of the transferring company (cf, however, art 12 Solvency II Directive). Whereas international administrative law aspects are thus dealt with in EU Directives, the various private international law issues are first and foremost subject to the choice-of-law provisions of the Rome I Regulation. However, in the context of cross-border portfolio transfers, certain interdependencies may exist between international administrative law and the applicable choice-of-law rules (as to all of the above, see Jan D Lüttringhaus, 'Neue Wege zur internationalen Restrukturierung europäischer Erst- und Rückversicherungsunternehmen. Die Erweiterung des gemeinschaftsrechtlichen Rahmens für grenzüberschreitende Umwandlungen und Bestandsübertragungen' [2008] VersR 1036 *et seq*). Private international law issues may also arise with regard to the transfer of certain assets covering the portfolio.

VI. Continuing divergence and future challenges

There is important, although hardly surprising international convergence of the choice-of-law regimes for reinsurance contracts: party autonomy is most prominent across all jurisdictions. By contrast, already the conditions under which national courts are willing to deduce a choice of law from a reinsurance agreement vary, eg in the USA compared to the London or Bermuda reinsurance markets. Differences as well as uncertainties persist, especially when it comes to determining the law applicable in the absence of an express or implicit choice of law by the parties of a reinsurance contract.

In Europe, for example, just as reinsurance contracts remain excluded from the scope of projects to create a uniform substantive insurance law (see with regard to art 1:101(2) PEICL Jürgen Basedow and others (eds), *Principles of European Insurance Contract Law* (Sellier 2009) 31 referring to an 'internationally broadly established *lex mercatoria*' in this field), the legislator decided to bar reinsurance contracts from the ambit of the special choice-of-law rule in art 7 Rome I Regulation. Whereas it is sensible on the one hand to grant parties to a reinsurance contract the utmost → party autonomy under art 3 Rome I Regulation, the particular nature and design of reinsurance transactions may on the other hand lead to difficulties where the parties have not chosen the applicable law. This holds true, in particular, for reinsurance treaties, but also for facultative reinsurance involving a multiplicity of parties. Some commentators have even argued that the choice-of-law regime in art 4 Rome I Regulation 'is singularly inappropriate to this form of contract' (Rob Merkin, 'The Rome I Regulation and Reinsurance' (2009) 5 J Priv Int L 69, 84). On closer inspection, however, the general rule in art 4 Rome I Regulation offers sufficient flexibility to deal with special choice-of-law issues arising, for example, in the context of the subscription of a reinsurance policy by multiple reinsurers from different countries. Moreover, in practice, most reinsurance contracts contain an explicit or at least an implicit choice of the applicable law by the parties. Jurisdiction and arbitration clauses play an important role in this context since they may – in conjunction with other factors – indicate a tacit choice of law (cf Recital (12) Rome I Regulation).

Whereas reinsurance and retrocession contracts still dominate the risk transfer market, the importance of so-called Alternative Risk Transfer (ART) is growing steadily. These ART vehicles may serve as a substitute or a complement to traditional reinsurance contracts. In the future, the question will arise as to how the various instruments and reinsurance-linked transactions are to be characterized, eg under the Rome I Regulation. This concerns heterogeneous contracts relating to, for example, financial reinsurance, reinsurance sidecars, longevity and mortality swaps as well as life insurance securitizations.

JAN D LÜTTRINGHAUS

Literature

Klaus H Basedow, *Le Droit International Privé des Assurances* (LGDJ 1939); Lord Collins of Mapesbury and others (eds), *Dicey, Morris & Collins on the Conflict of Laws*, vol 2 (15th edn, Sweet & Maxwell 2012) 33; Raymond Cox, Louise Merrett and Marcus Smith, *Private international law of Reinsurance and Insurance* (Informa 2006); *Couch on Insurance* (3rd edn Thomson 2013) § 9; Colin Edelman and Andrew Burns, *The Law of Reinsurance* (OUP 2013); Özlem Gürses and Rob Merkin, 'Facultative Reinsurance and the Full Reinsurance Clause' [2008] LMCLQ 366; Ian RC Kawakey, *Offshore Commercial Law in Bermuda* (Wildy, Simmonds and Hill 2013); Dirk Looschelders, 'Grundfragen des deutschen und internationalen Rückversicherungsvertragsrechts' [2012] VersR 1; Jan D Lüttringhaus, 'Neue Wege zur internationalen Restrukturierung europäischer Erst- und Rückversicherungsunternehmen. Die Erweiterung des gemeinschaftsrechtlichen Rahmens für grenzüberschreitende Umwandlungen und Bestandsübertragungen' [2008] VersR 1036; Jan D Lüttringhaus, 'Art 1' in Franco Ferrari (ed), *Rome I Regulation* (Sellier 2014); Peter Mankowski, 'Internationales Rückversicherungsvertragsrecht' [2002] VersR 1177; Rob Merkin, 'The Rome I Regulation and Reinsurance' (2009) 5 J Priv Int L 69; Terry O'Neill and Jan W Woloniecki, *The Law of Reinsurance in England and Bermuda* (2nd edn, Sweet & Maxwell 2004); Jeffrey E Thomas and others (eds), *New Appleman on Insurance Law, Vol 7: Reinsurance* (LexisNexis 2013) §§ 72 et seq.

Remedies

I. Introduction

Obtaining an effective and enforceable remedy is the key objective of the claimant in any piece of civil litigation and, correspondingly, resisting the grant of such relief is the main goal of the defendant. Remedies as a discrete topic has been subject to little systematic analysis in private international law. Instead, it has been typically examined in the context of jurisdiction or procedure (in the case of interim or provisional relief such as anti-suit injunctions (→ Anti-suit injunctions) or freezing orders (→ Freezing injunctions and search orders)) or substantive causes of action such as tort or contract (in the case of final relief such as damages, declarations and specific performance). For the purposes of analysis in this chapter, the distinction between interim (or provisional) and final relief will be adopted.

II. The nature of the remedy

A general point to be noted concerning the awarding of remedies in transnational litigation is that a claimant can only obtain remedies that are available under forum law. The rationale of this view is that remedies are part of the court's machinery for resolving disputes and it is not practical for the forum to have to implement foreign remedies. The form of the remedy sought in litigation is therefore governed by forum law: *Phrantzes v Argenti* [1960] 2 QB 19; *Slater v Mexican National Railroad*, 194 US 120 (1904). EU law embodies this principle by providing in art 15(d) → Rome II Regulation (Regulation (EC) No 864/2007 of the European Parliament and of the Council of 11 July 2007 on the law applicable to non-contractual obligations (Rome II), [2007] OJ L 199/40) and art 12(1)(c) Rome I Regulation (Regulation (EC) No 593/2008 of the European Parliament and of the Council of 17 June 2008 on the law applicable to contractual obligations (Rome I), [2008] OJ L 177/6; → Rome Convention and Rome I Regulation (contractual obligations)) that any remedy sought must be within the limits conferred by the forum's procedural law. Modern commentary on private international law agrees that once a remedy is found to exist within the forum's armoury, its availability on the given facts of a case should, as far as possible, depend upon the applicable law of the obligation (Richard Garnett, *Substance and Procedure in Private international law* (OUP 2012) 296–297; George Panagopoulos, *Restitution in Private international law* (Hart 2000) 68). Such an approach helps to minimize forum shopping and to avoid unnecessary applicable law → *dépeçage* between substantive right and remedy.

III. Interim remedies

The most common forms of interim relief in transnational litigation are freezing orders and anti-suit injunctions, both of which are comprehensively discussed in the entries → Injunction, → Freezing injunctions and search orders and → Anti-suit injunctions. Two points should initially be noted about anti-suit injunctions. The first is that the award of anti-suit injunctions is generally confined to common law countries and the second is that a court of an EU Member State has no power to issue an anti-suit injunction to restrain proceedings in another Member State (*Turner v Grovit* [2005] 1 AC 101), but such injunctions may be granted to restrain actions in non-EU Member States (*Ust-Kamenogorsk Hydropower Plant JSC v AES Ust-Kamenogorsk Hydropower Plant LLP* [2013] UKSC 35).

1. Applicable law

In terms of applicable law, the availability of interim relief is almost universally considered a procedural matter and so is governed exclusively by forum law. Such a view is clearly justified where such remedies are integrally related to the conduct of proceedings in the forum, for example, where an anti-suit injunction is sought to restrain the pursuit of foreign litigation that may interfere with proceedings in the forum or where local or foreign assets are sought to be frozen to satisfy a future judgment given on the merits in the forum. However, such an unqualified application of forum law may be less justified where, for example, the basis of an anti-suit injunction is that the foreign proceedings are 'vexatious or oppressive' in terms of equity or where such proceedings are alleged to be in breach of contract (for example, an exclusive jurisdiction clause). In these two latter cases, a stronger argument in favour of the law of the obligation may be made, given the proximity of the relief to the rights and liabilities of the parties. Such a view is supported by art 15(d) Rome II Regulation, which provides that the law of the obligation applies to a 'measure designed to prevent or terminate injury or damage', which would likely include an anti-suit injunction issued to enforce equitable rights. However, interlocutory relief is not covered by the Rome I Regulation and so national law rules must apply to cases in which interim relief is sought in relation to contracts subject to the Regulation. Article 15(d) Rome II Regulation may also have the effect of reversing the traditional view that freezing orders are governed by forum law as matters of procedure, since they would also seem to be a 'measure to ensure the provision of compensation'. If that view is correct, then the law of the obligation will apply to determine whether such a measure is granted.

2. *Jurisdiction*

Under EU law, jurisdiction to award interim relief (most commonly freezing orders) is conferred on the court of a Member State that has jurisdiction over the substance of the case in accordance with arts 4 *et seq* Brussels I Regulation (recast) (Regulation (EU) No 1215/2012 of the European Parliament and of the Council of 12 December 2012 on jurisdiction and the recognition and enforcement of judgments in civil and commercial matters (recast), [2012] OJ L 351/1; → Brussels I (Convention and Regulation)) (Case C-391/95 *Van Uden Maritime BV v Firma Deco-Line* [1998] ECR I-7019, para 19). Second, art 35 Brussels I Regulation (recast) provides a further basis of jurisdiction to a court to order interim relief, even where it does not have jurisdiction as to the substance of the case, where such relief is sought in aid of proceedings before another Member State's court. However, such jurisdiction is only permissible where there is 'a real connecting link' between the subject matter of the relief sought and the territory of the Member State before which the measures are sought (Case C-391/95 *Van Uden Maritime BV v Firma Deco-Line* [1998] ECR I-7019, para 40).

In the case of interim relief sought outside the European jurisdictional regime, an English court will have jurisdiction to grant such relief where it is ancillary to substantive proceedings in the forum (*Masri v Consolidated Contractors International SAL* [2008] EWCA Civ 303) and also where it is sought in aid of foreign proceedings (see s 25 of the Civil Jurisdiction and Judgments Act 1982 (c 27)) provided that, again, a genuine connecting link with the forum exists. A genuine link will exist where the freezing order sought is confined to assets within the jurisdiction (*Mobil Cerro Negro Ltd v Petroleos de Venezuela SA* [2008] 1 Lloyd's Rep 684). In the case of assets outside the forum, English courts have generally required that the defendant whose conduct was sought to be restrained be present in the territory of the granting court (see *Banco Nacional de Comercio Exterior SNC v Empresa de Telecommunicaciones de Cuba SA* [2007] EWCA Civ 662; *Credit Suisse Fides Trust SA v Cuoghi* [1998] QB 818; for a fuller discussion of this issue, see → Injunction). In such cases, service may be made upon a defendant both within and (with the permission of the court) outside the jurisdiction.

In the case of anti-suit injunctions, English courts have also required that the forum court must also be shown to have a 'necessary interest in or connection with the matter in question' before exercising jurisdiction to grant such relief, out of respect for the foreign interests involved and the need for → comity (*Airbus Industries GIE v Patel* [1999] 1 AC 119, 138).

3. *Enforcement*

Enforcement of interim relief can be difficult unless the defendant is present in the forum in which the orders were granted or has assets there that may be seized in the event of non-compliance. If the defendant resides outside the forum in which the orders were issued and has no local assets there, enforcement is complicated by the fact that most countries' legal systems (especially common law jurisdictions) do not allow for the enforcement of foreign judgments for interim remedies. In order to be enforceable, a foreign judgment must normally be 'final and conclusive', which means not capable of variation or amendment in the granting court. However, a line of authority has developed in common law countries whereby interim relief granted in foreign common law countries' 'equitable' jurisdictions may be recognized by the granting of equivalent or parallel remedies in the country of enforcement. Such a principle has allowed Australian courts, for example, to recognize the appointment of a receiver by a US court to recover assets in Australia (*White v Verkouille* [1989] 2 Qd R 191) and to grant a freezing order in support of similar relief issued by a Bahamas court over the defendant's assets worldwide, including assets in Australia (*Davis v Turning Properties Pty Ltd* (2005) 222 ALR 676).

RICHARD GARNETT

Of course, such decisions may be seen alternatively as examples of interim relief being granted in aid of foreign proceedings, the permissibility of which, as noted above, is recognized by statute in England and in EU law (art 35 Brussels I Regulation (recast)).

However, EU law makes it clear in a separate provision in the Brussels I Regulation (recast) that interim relief granted by the court of one Member State may be directly enforceable in the court of another Member State under art 36 of the Regulation. This result is achieved by the Regulation defining the term 'judgment' in art 2(a) as including 'provisional, including protective measures ordered by a court or tribunal which, by virtue of this Regulation, has jurisdiction as to the substance of the matter'.

IV. Final relief

1. Applicable law

a) Non-monetary remedies

In common law countries, final non-monetary relief, such as orders for specific performance, rescission of contracts, declarations and permanent injunctions, has historically been governed by forum law because it originated in the medieval equitable jurisdiction based on conscience (see *Paramasivam v Flynn* (1998) 160 ALR 203; *National Commercial Bank v Wimborne* (1978) 5 BPR 11958). This approach had a serious consequence where equitable remedies such as specific performance and → injunction are sought in aid of 'non-equitable' rights, for example, to enforce a contract or restrain commission of a tort. In such cases, even where foreign law governs the obligation, the equitable remedy will only be granted if the conditions under forum law for its being ordered are satisfied: see *Baschet v London Illustrated Standard Co* [1900] 1 Ch 73. Consequently, the remedy may not be granted even if it would have been ordered under the law of the obligation: *Warner Brothers Pictures Inc v Nelson* [1937] 1 KB 209.

The 'conscience' principle underlying equity also meant that where purely equitable rights were involved, such as fiduciary duties or confidence, both substantive right and remedy have been traditionally governed by forum law. However, recent commentary and the majority of US decisions have cast doubt on this approach, arguing that equitable rights and obligations should no longer be governed by the law of the forum, but by the nearest analogous cause of action on the facts (Tiong Min Yeo, *Choice of Law for Equitable Doctrines* (OUP 2004)). Hence, for example, in the case of a breach of fiduciary duties, the applicable law rules for contract may be applied by analogy or, in the case of breach of confidence, the contract or tort rules may be the appropriate category depending upon the facts. Such a change in applicable law analysis to equitable rights has also led commentators to assert that, logically, the availability of final equitable remedies should also no longer be governed by forum law, but should instead, where possible, be subject to the law of the accompanying obligation (Adrian Briggs, 'Conflict of Laws and Commercial Remedies' in Andrew Burrows and Edwin Peel (eds), *Commercial Remedies: Current Issues and Problems* (OUP 2003) 271; George Panagopoulos, *Restitution in Private international law* (Hart 2000)).

Under EU law, the law of the obligation is applied to non-monetary relief: provided that the remedy exists 'under the forum's procedural law', the law of the obligation determines whether such relief should be granted. For example, art 12(1)(c) Rome I Regulation applies the law of the contractual obligation to the 'consequences of a total or partial breach of obligations' and art 15(d) Rome II Regulation applies the law of the non-contractual obligation to 'a measure designed to prevent or terminate injury or damage'. Hence, under EU law, a claimant's right to a final injunction to restrain commission of a civil wrong or an order for specific performance to enforce a contract will be determined by the law of the obligation. The traditional common law position is therefore almost entirely rejected and a view is taken similar to the recent commentary mentioned above. It will be interesting to see if the EU principles have a harmonizing or 'reflexive' effect on the common law so that an internationally consistent approach will be achieved.

A constructive trust is an equitable remedy imposed by a common law court in respect of property that has been acquired by a defendant in circumstances that are regarded as unconscionable in equity (for example, fraud) with such property declared to be held on trust for the claimant. While authority is not uniform, the availability of this remedy is now best regarded as being governed by the law of the obligation (for example, unjust enrichment) the breach of which gives rise to the duty to make relief (see *Chase Manhattan Bank NA v Israel-British Bank (London) Ltd* [1981] Ch 105). The position is also likely the same under EU law, where such a trust arises out of → unjust enrichment as this remedy would arguably be a 'measure which a court may take to prevent or terminate injury or damage, or to ensure the provision of compensation' under art 15(d) Rome II Regulation. However, the situation that has arisen before English courts is where the law of the obligation does not recognize the remedy of the constructive trust (as is the case in most civil law countries). The approach taken by English courts is to examine whether the foreign law of the obligation would impose a liability similar to that under English law, namely, that the defendant disgorge an unjustly acquired benefit. If such a liability exists under the law of the obligation, then a constructive trust may be imposed as it would be consistent with the objectives of the foreign law (see *First Laser Ltd v Fujian Enterprises (Holdings) Co Ltd* [2012] HKCFA 52 paras 65–69; *Kuwait Oil Tanker SAK v Al Bader* [2000] 2 All ER (Comm) 271). It is doubtful whether such an approach is permissible in EU law under the Rome II Regulation.

In common law countries the right to → set-off has historically been governed by forum law as a procedural matter, whereas in civil law countries a distinction has been drawn between cases where the effect of the defendant's claim to set-off is to discharge or extinguish its liability to the claimant on the original claim (substantive) and where a cross-claim is merely brought by the defendant in the same proceeding (procedural). EU law considers all questions of set-off as substantive issues and provides that where the right to set-off is not agreed by the parties, it shall be governed by the law applicable to the claim against which the right to set-off is asserted (see art 17 Rome I Regulation). Where the right to set-off is agreed between the parties, the general rules on choice of law in contract under arts 3 and 4 Rome I Regulation apply to determine the scope and validity of the right (see further the entry on → Set-off).

The issue of final non-monetary remedies would not be complete without reference to the → CISG (United Nations Convention of 11 April 1980 on Contracts for the International Sale of Goods, 1489 UNTS 3). The CISG operates as a set of transnational autonomous rules which override domestic law in contracts to which the Convention applies and includes a number of innovative remedies. The CISG gives the buyer the right to reduce the purchase price for the goods if the goods delivered do not conform with the contract (art 50) and the right to require delivery of substitute goods in the event of non-conformity and where such non-conformity amounts to a fundamental breach (art 46(2)). The CISG also provides both parties with a right to avoid the contract in the case of a fundamental breach (arts 49(1) and 64(1)) and the remedy of specific performance (arts 46(1) and 62). Each party may also grant the other (breaching) party an additional period of time for performance (arts 47 and 63).

b) Damages

In the area of → damages for breach of contractual and non-contractual obligations there has been a similar movement towards greater control by the law of the cause of action as opposed to the law of the forum. In common law and civil law jurisdictions it is well established that the issue of available heads of damages (for example, for economic loss or physical injury) are governed by the law of the obligation (see *Boys v Chaplin* [1971] AC 356; *Cox v Ergo Versicherung AG* [2014] 2 WLR 948; *Breavington v Godleman* (1988) 169 CLR 41). There is also a general consensus that the right to pre-judgment interest, that is, interest by way of damages dating from the accrual of the cause of action or on a contractual debt, is governed by the law of the obligation. The question of whether benefits may be deducted from an award of damages is also now likely, in most cases, to be determined by the law of the obligation (*Cox v Ergo Versicherung AG* [2014] 2 WLR 948). Where the right to damages has been abolished by statute and replaced by a no-fault administrative scheme, all jurisdictions accept that the scheme must be applied as part of the law of the obligation.

On the issue of quantification or assessment of damages, the traditional common law approach has been to refer all such questions to the law of the forum, both where the issue concerns the calculation of damages and where the legislature imposes a limitation or 'cap' on damages, unless such a cap is a provision in a contract. Such an approach is still followed in English and Canadian common law (*Harding v Wealands* [2007] 2 AC 1). By contrast, in Australia, it has been held that 'all questions about the ... amount of damages' are governed by the law of the obligation (*John Pfeiffer Pty Ltd v Rogerson* (2000) 203 CLR 503). Interestingly, the approach taken in Australia is also mirrored in EU law. Article 15(c) Rome II Regulation provides that the applicable law of the non-contractual obligation shall 'govern ... the existence, nature and assessment of damage or the remedy claimed' and art 12(1)(c) Rome I Regulation uses similar language in relation to contract. The effect of such language is that available heads of damages, caps on damages, deductibility of benefits and the right to an award of pre-judgment interest are all governed by the law of the obligation. Questions of assessment or calculation of damages are also resolved by this law (for a fuller discussion of this issue, see the entries on → Damages and → Substance and procedure).

Article 74 CISG imposes an autonomous rule for the award of damages in contracts to which the Convention applies.

2. Jurisdiction

For a court to have the ability to award final relief, it must first have personal jurisdiction in the action brought against the defendant. In the case of EU domiciled defendants, the principles of the Brussels I Regulation (recast) now apply with any defendant being able to be sued in the country of domicile or alternative forums in arts 4 *et seq* of the Regulation.

In the case of non-EU domiciled defendants, the personal jurisdiction principles of national law apply. In England the jurisdiction of courts is invoked by service of the claim form either on a defendant present within England or (with the permission of the court) on a defendant outside the EU where a relevant connection with England is established (see the Civil Procedure Rules). Examples of such grounds include where a claim is made for an injunction ordering the defendant to do or refrain from doing an act within the jurisdiction or where a claim is made in tort or contract and the obligation has a specified link to the forum.

In the case of an action against a non-EU domiciled defendant, the defendant may also seek a stay of English proceedings on the basis that a 'more appropriate forum' exists elsewhere, that is, a country 'in which the case may be tried more suitably for the interests of all the parties and ends of justice' (*Spiliada Maritime Corporation v Cansulex Ltd* [1987] 1 AC 460).

In applying this test of *forum non conveniens*, an English court will consider whether there is a 'legitimate personal or juridical advantage' to the claimant in having the proceeding heard in the local court. Generally speaking, the fact that a claimant could receive higher damages in English proceedings than before a foreign court is not normally a sufficient advantage, by itself, to avoid a stay (*Spiliada Maritime Corporation v Cansulex Ltd* [1987] 1 AC 460, 483; *Cooley v Ramsey* [2008] EWHC 129, para 57). Yet, in a number of cases, English courts have refused to stay their proceedings in favour of a foreign court where the difference between the damages that could be recovered in England and in the foreign jurisdiction has been shown to be great (*The Vishva Abha* [1990] 2 Lloyd's Rep 312; *Caltex Singapore Pte Ltd v BP Shipping Ltd* [1996] 1 Lloyd's Rep 286). Such decisions show that on occasion there can be an important link between available final remedies and a common law court's decision to exercise jurisdiction. Given the absence of any doctrine of *forum non conveniens* under EU law or in civil law countries, such an issue does not generally arise.

3. Enforcement

The question of enforcement of final remedies in foreign courts is partly well settled and partly in a state of reappraisal in common law countries. The traditional approach has been that a foreign judgment will only be recognized and enforced where it requires a defendant to pay a sum of money to the judgment creditor/claimant, such as an award of damages (*Sadler v Robins* [1808] 1 Camp. 853). However, such a rule has always been subject to the → public policy (*ordre public*) of the forum so that, for example, in some jurisdictions a foreign award of exemplary or punitive damages will not be enforced.

The requirement that an enforceable foreign judgment must be for a fixed sum of money (→ Money and currency) historically precluded enforcement in the forum of foreign orders for specific performance, declarations or final injunctions. Yet recently in Canada, it has been suggested that the 'fixed sum' rule is outdated in a time of increased technological change and modern communications, and when national courts need to cooperate with one another in the resolution of transnational disputes. Consequently, a foreign non-money judgment may now be enforced in Canada where: (i) the foreign order was clear and specific as to its territorial scope and the rights, duties and obligations that it imposes on the defendant; and (ii) it does not impose an undue burden on the Canadian justice system or the rights of third parties (*Pro Swing Inc v Elta Golf Inc* [2006] 2 SCR 612). Application of the above principles would allow injunctions, specific performance orders and declarations (for example, for constructive trust: *Bienstock v Adenyo Inc* [2014] ONSC 4997) to be recognized and enforced. Significantly, the Canadian approach has been adopted in Jersey (*Brunei Investment Agency and Bandone Sdn Bhd v Fidlis Nominees Ltd* [2008] JRC 1520) and in the Australia-New Zealand Agreement on Trans-Tasman Court Proceedings and Regulatory Enforcement (Agreement between the Government of Australia and the Government of New Zealand on Trans-Tasman Court Proceedings and Regulatory Enforcement [2013] ATS 32) where final and conclusive non-monetary judgments from each country may now be enforced in the other country's courts (see s 66 Trans-Tasman Proceedings Act 2010 (Cth)).

The principle that a court may enforce foreign non-money judgments is also consistent with the position under EU law. Under art 36(1) Brussels I Regulation (recast), a judgment given in a court of one Member State shall be recognized in other Member States, with 'judgment' pertinently defined as 'any judgment given by a court or tribunal of a Member State, whatever the judgment may be called, including a decree, order, decision or … writ of execution'. Such a provision again shows the potential for the harmonization of common law and EU law approaches.

RICHARD GARNETT

Literature

Bernard Audit, *Droit International Privé* (3rd edn, Economica 2005); Adrian Briggs, 'Conflict of Laws and Commercial Remedies' in Andrew Burrows and Edwin Peel (eds), *Commercial Remedies: Current Issues and Problems* (OUP 2003) 271; Lord Collins of Mapesbury and others (eds), *Dicey, Morris & Collins on the Conflict of Laws* (15th edn, Sweet & Maxwell 2012); Andrew Dickinson, *The Rome II Regulation* (OUP 2008); James Fawcett, Janeen Carruthers and Peter North, *Cheshire, North & Fawcett's Private international law* (14th edn, OUP 2008); Richard Fentiman, *International Commercial Litigation* (OUP 2010); Richard Fentiman, 'The Scope of Transnational Injunctions' [2013] NZJPIL 323; Richard Garnett, *Substance and Procedure in Private international law* (OUP 2012); Konstantinos Kerameus, 'Provisional Remedies in Transnational Litigation' in International Association of Procedural Law (ed), *Transnational Aspects of Procedural Law*, vol 3 (Giuffrè 1998) 1169; George Panagopoulos, *Restitution in Private international law* (Hart 2000); Richard Plender and Michael Wilderspin, *The European Private international law of Obligations* (3rd edn, Sweet & Maxwell 2009); Adam Rushworth, 'Remedies and the Rome II Regulation' in John Ahern and William Binchy (eds), *The Rome II Regulation on the Law Applicable to Non-contractual Obligations* (Martinus Nijhoff 2009) 199; Janet Walker, *Castel & Walker Canadian Conflict of Laws* (6th edn, LexisNexis Butterworths 2005); Tiong Min Yeo, *Choice of Law for Equitable Doctrines* (OUP 2004).

Renvoi

I. Concept and notion

1. References to the conflict-of-laws rules or references to the substantive law

The problem of *renvoi* concerns the question of whether a reference to a foreign legal system encompasses that system's substantive law or its conflict-of-laws rules. In the first case, the substantive law of the designated state is applicable. However, if the reference directs to the conflict-of-laws rules, there are three possibilities. First, this law may refer to itself, in that according to this law, for example, the nationality or habitual residence are also relevant for determining the applicable law. In such a case, the substantive rules of the law, designated by the law of the forum (→ *Lex fori*), are applicable. The so-designated law accepts the reference by the law of the forum. This also holds true in cases where the second law does not utilize the same → connecting factor such as nationality, but a different connecting factor such as habitual residence, that also directs to itself. Second, it is possible that the designated law itself refers back to the law of the forum, or as a third possibility refers further to a yet third law. In the latter case, the additional question arises of whether only remissions to the law of the forum (→ *Lex fori*) or also transmissions to the law of a third country have to be observed.

Both legal problems – that is, the above-mentioned question of whether a reference to a foreign legal system encompasses that system's substantive law or its conflict-of-laws rules, and the problem concerning remissions and transmissions – are collectively known as *renvoi*.

2. Remission to the law of the forum

In cases of remission to the law of the forum, the next question is whether the forum will accept and apply its own substantive law. This is the solution adopted by most legal systems that employ the doctrine of *renvoi*. German law, for example, accepts references to German law and applies German substantive law even if, according to German conflict-of-laws rules, the law of another country applies (see art 4(1), sentence 2 of the Introductory Act to the German Civil Code (Einführungsgesetz zum Bürgerlichen Gesetzbuche of 21 September 1994, BGBl. I 2494, as amended, henceforth EGBGB)) (→ Germany). This solution also holds true for example in → Austria, → France, → Italy, → Bulgaria, → Romania, → Slovenia, → Estonia, → Latvia, → Croatia, → Bosnia and Herzegovina, → Serbia and → Turkey.

By contrast, according to the so-called doctrine of double *renvoi*, the case will be decided in the manner of a judge in the state to which the law of the forum refers. This is because a legal system that applies the doctrine of double *renvoi* declines remission to its own conflict-of-laws rules and instead applies the substantive law of the state to which the conflict-of-laws rules of the *lex fori* refer. Japanese courts used to decide at least partially in this way until the reform of Japanese private international law in 2006.

The so-called foreign court theory involves yet another step. According to this theory, the judge has to decide the case in the same manner as a judge of the state whose law is applicable by virtue of the forum's conflict-of-laws rules. This theory goes a step beyond the doctrine of double *renvoi* because the judge even approaches the question of *renvoi* in the same way as a judge of the state to which the law of the *lex fori* refers. The foreign court theory was developed in England and is still applicable, for example, in England, → Australia and Louisiana.

3. Transmission to a third law

In cases of transmission to a third legal system, the substantive law of the third system will be applied when the reference to the third system covers only the substantive rules of that system. If the reference to the third system covers only the conflict-of-laws rules of that legal system, the possibilities are the same as where the law of the forum refers to the conflict-of-laws rules of another legal system: the third legal system can accept the *renvoi*, it can refer back (to the law of the forum or the second system) or it can refer to a fourth system. The question of whether also these references back to the first or the second system or the reference further to a fourth system have to be followed cannot be answered uniformly because there are myriad possibilities to reach a decision (see Michael Sonnentag, *Der Renvoi im Internationalen Privatrecht* (Mohr Siebeck 2001) 15 ff, 291 ff, 297 ff, 300 ff).

II. Historical development

The problem of *renvoi* was primarily seen in jurisprudence. Apart from a few earlier decisions in the 17th and 18th centuries, the courts of various countries began during the 19th century to examine the question of whether a remission by the foreign law to the → *lex fori* has to be followed. One of the most famous first decisions is the case *Forgo* (Cass. civ., 24 June 1878 (*arrêt Forgo*), Sirey 1878.1.429–431), decided by the French *Cour de cassation*. François-Xavier Forgo was born in Bavaria in 1801 and died in France in 1869. *Forgo* had not created a will, so legal succession was applied. According to Bavarian law, relatives of *Forgo*'s mother would have been appointed as heirs, whereas according to French law, the estate passed to the French treasury. Starting from French private international law as → *lex fori*, Bavarian law was designated because *Forgo* originated from Bavaria. *Forgo* had no French domicile permit and accordingly lacked legal domicile in France. However, according to Bavarian private international law, the actual domicile – and not the legal domicile– was decisive, so that Bavarian law referred back to French law. Accordingly, French substantive law was applied by the French *Cour de cassation* with the consequence that *Forgo's* estate passed to the French treasury. Subsequently, the decision of the *Cour de cassation* was vehemently criticized in legal literature, on the grounds that the *renvoi* was utilized to encourage a particular substantive result, ie inheritance by the French treasury instead of the relatives of *Forgo's* mother.

The first academic essays on *renvoi* were published shortly after the *Forgo* decision, with one of the first scholars to publish being *Pasquale Stanislao Mancini* (→ *Mancini, Pasquale Stanislao*) in 1879. From its very outset, the *renvoi* discussion was highly controversial.

Also in the second half of the 19th century, the first codifications of the doctrine of *renvoi* were created. The very first codification to contain the *renvoi* doctrine was the Legal Code in the Canton of Zurich in Switzerland. This regulation set the example for various Swiss cantonal codes, which were themselves replaced by Swiss federal law in 1891. In 1894 the *renvoi* doctrine was introduced in the Marriage Act of Hungary and in 1896 in the German EGBGB.

III. Reasons for and against the doctrine of *renvoi*

1. International uniformity of decisions

The doctrine of *renvoi* serves the purpose of achieving international uniformity of decisions by strengthening the likelihood that a case will be decided in a uniform manner irrespective of where an action is brought. International uniformity of decisions holds two important advantages. First, application of the same law irrespective of the competent court helps to avoid limping legal relationships, ie legal relationships which are recognized in one country but not in another. Second, it enhances the legal certainty and predictability of the applicable law. Parties to an international relationship accordingly know the law that governs their legal relationship. Naturally, *renvoi* does not always achieve international uniformity of decisions, but its application at least strengthens the likelihood of such uniformity (Michael Sonnentag, *Der Renvoi im Internationalen Privatrecht* (Mohr Siebeck 2001) 116 ff).

2. Homeward trend

In addition to international uniformity of decisions, a reference to conflict-of-laws rules serves the so-called homeward trend, in that it leads to the application of the *lex fori* in cases of remission rather than in cases of exclusive reference to substantive law. In the latter case, references to a foreign law always direct to the application of foreign substantive law. However, in most cases it is easier to apply foreign private international law and the substantive law of the forum than the substantive law of a foreign country. This is because judges are naturally more familiar with the application of their own (substantive) law, whereas the ascertainment and application of foreign (substantive) law poses difficulties (Michael Sonnentag, *Der Renvoi im Internationalen Privatrecht* (Mohr Siebeck 2001) 141 ff) (→ Foreign law, application and ascertainment).

3. Correction of substantive law which is contrary to the ordre public by the way of renvoi?

In contrast, disapplying the substantive law of a foreign country because it triggers results that are contrary to the *ordre public* of the forum is no purpose of *renvoi*. The appropriate means to correct a substantive result which is contrary to the *ordre public* is not *renvoi*, but the *ordre public* itself (→ Public policy (*ordre public*)). In contrast, application of the doctrine of *renvoi* would break with accepted principles of private international law (see Jan von Hein, 'Der Renvoi im europäischen Kollisionsrecht' in Stefan Leible and Hannes Unberath (eds), *Brauchen wir eine Rom 0-Verordnung?* (Jenaer Wissenschaftliche Verlagsgesellschaft 2013) 341, 347).

4. Undermining specific substantive ideas of justice

In contrast to the interests arguing for references to conflict-of-laws, the interest of not undermining substantive ideas of justice to be implemented by conflict-of-laws rules militates in favour of a reference to substantive law. However, conflict-of-laws rules are always intended to implement ideas of substantive justice in cases with a relationship to foreign countries. Accordingly, such an undermining only comes into question when conflict-of-laws rules implement special substantive ideas of justice. That is the case when the lawmaker creates a certain connection on special substantive grounds. This holds true, for example, in cases of alternative connecting factors, because the lawmaker chooses more than one → connecting factor in provisions intended to obtain a specific substantive result. The formal validity of legal acts, for example, is governed by the law of the place where the contract was made (*lex loci contractus*) or the law applicable to the main issue (*lex causae*). The lawmaker chooses this alternative connecting factor in order to support the formal validity of the legal act. This purpose would be frustrated if a legal act were formally valid only according to the *lex causae* and not the *lex loci contractus*, whereas the conflict-of-laws rules of the *lex causae* would direct the case to the *lex loci contractus*, with the ultimate effect that the legal act would not be formally valid in consequence of the *renvoi*. The question whether such special substantive ideas of justice exist is an issue of the specific subject matter of the particular conflict-of-laws rule (Michael Sonnentag, *Der Renvoi im Internationalen Privatrecht* (Mohr Siebeck 2001) 148 ff, 150 ff).

5. Decision between provisions referring to the conflict-of-laws rules and provisions referring to substantive law due to a balancing of interests

There is an inherent tension between the interests that speak in favour of the doctrine of *renvoi*, ie the achievement of international uniformity of decisions and the homeward trend, on the one hand, and those that militate against it, ie the implementation of specific substantive ideas of justice by conflict-of-laws rules, on the other hand. These interests cannot be realized simultaneously. A legislative choice to apply the doctrine of *renvoi* accords priority to the achievement of international uniformity of decisions and the homeward trend over the implementation of specific substantive ideas of justice by means of conflict-of-laws rules. By contrast, a legislative provision for references to substantive law accords precedence to the implementation of substantive ideas of justice by means of conflict-of-laws rules (Michael Sonnentag, *Der Renvoi im Internationalen Privatrecht* (Mohr Siebeck 2001) 164 ff).

IV. Legal sources and current regulation

1. National

a) Exclusion of renvoi

Some legal systems exclude *renvoi*, with the consequence that remissions and transmissions are impossible. Such regulations are found, for example, in → Denmark, → Greece and → Sweden, in some Arabic countries (eg in → Egypt, Jordan, Kuwait, → Tunisia, Syria and Iraq), in the Canadian province of Quebec (→ Canada) and also in some Latin American countries (eg → Brazil and → Peru).

b) Acceptance of renvoi

Most legal systems accept the doctrine of *renvoi*, but they differ regarding their regulatory systems. This is shown by the fact that in principle some of these countries enable references to conflict-of-laws rules, but – to different degrees – also arrange references to substantive law if it is expressly so ordered in the law or if it follows from the rationale of the conflict-of-laws rule without an express legislative provision. Such regulations are found in → Argentina (remissions and transmissions), → Austria (remissions and transmissions), → Bosnia and Herzegovina (remissions and transmissions), → Bulgaria (remissions and transmissions), → Cuba (remissions and transmissions), → Croatia (remissions and transmissions), → Estonia (only remissions), → Finland (remissions and transmissions), → France (remissions and transmissions), → Hungary (only remissions), → Iran (only remissions), → Italy (remissions and transmissions), → Latvia (remissions and transmissions), → Luxembourg (remissions and transmissions), → Macedonia (remissions and transmissions), → Poland (only remissions), → Romania (remissions and transmissions), → Slovenia (remissions and transmissions) and moreover in → Serbia (remissions and transmissions), South Korea (only remissions), → Thailand (only remissions) and → Venezuela (remissions, but transmissions only in the case of the acceptance by the law of the third state). English (remissions and transmissions), Irish (remissions and transmissions), Australian (remissions and transmissions) and Canadian courts also have decided for references to conflict-of-laws rules (→ Australia, → Canada, → Ireland, → United Kingdom).

c) Provisions to substantive law with a limited number of exceptions

In principle other countries implement references to substantive law, but accept a limited number of exceptions in cases of provisions in law or due to jurisdiction. This is the case, for example, in the → Netherlands → Portugal (remissions and transmissions), → Lithuania (only remissions), → Switzerland (remissions and transmissions) and → Turkey (remissions and transmissions in the rights of individuals and in family law, but a transmission is always regarded as a reference to the substantive law of the third country).

d) Decision between acceptance and exclusion of renvoi due to specific criteria
Some legal systems follow a separate path by distinguishing between references to substantive law and conflict-of-laws rules depending on special criteria. Such systems include the law of the federal district of Mexico and the Mexican federal state Nuevo León (remissions and transmissions as references to substantive law) as well as the law of the Slovak Republic (remissions and transmissions) (→ Mexico; → Slovakia). They also include German law (remissions and transmissions), which contains a regulation in art 4(1), sentence 1 EGBGB according to which in the case of a reference to a foreign country, that country's conflict-of-laws rules should be applied, provided such application is not contrary to the rationale of the reference (→ Germany). The consequence is that the German legislature – aside from the circumstances in which *renvoi* is expressly excluded – makes no express decision between references either to substantive law or conflict-of-laws rules. It has to be determined for each conflict-of-laws rule whether *renvoi* is in conformity with or contrary to the rationale of that conflict-of-laws rule. To arrive at this determination, the concerned interests have to be balanced for each particular conflict-of-laws rule. More specifically, it has to be determined whether the legislature gives priority to the interests that accompany the *renvoi* doctrine, ie uniformity of decisions and homeward trend, or those following from an exclusion of *renvoi*. The latter is the case when it is crucial for the legislature not to have specific substantive ideas of justice undermined by conflict-of-laws rules rather than achieving international uniformity of decisions. If the legislature instead wishes to achieve international uniformity of decisions, the provision refers to conflict-of-laws rules. The question of which interests are preferred by the legislature is a matter of interpretation. The more a conflict-of-laws rule is supported by substantive ideas of justice, the less plausible it is to relinquish these ideas in favour of the observance of a *renvoi*. The interest of achieving international uniformity of decisions is more important when status relationships are involved and less important regarding legal matters which are directed towards a unique liquidation (see Michael Sonnentag, *Der Renvoi im Internationalen Privatrecht* (Mohr Siebeck 2001) 95 ff, 164 ff).

2. *International*

In international treaties containing uniform conflict-of-laws rules, *renvoi* is usually excluded. As a result of the harmonization within the concerned Member States, the problem of *renvoi* no longer arises among these states.

Exceptions to this rule are rare but do exist: for example, *renvoi* is accepted in art 1 of the Hague Marriage Convention of 1902 (Convention of 12 June 1902 relating to the settlement of the conflict of the laws concerning marriage) that remains in force between → Germany and → Italy, as well as in art 2(1), sentence 2 of the Geneva Convention of 7 June 1930 for the Settlement of Certain Conflicts of Laws in connection with Bills of Exchange and Promissory Notes (143 LNTS 317), in art 2(1), sentence 2 of the Geneva Convention of 19 March 1931 for the Settlement of Certain Conflicts of Laws in connection with Cheques (143 LNTS 407), in art 3(1)(a) of the Hague Child Abduction Convention (Hague Convention of 25 October 1980 on the Civil Aspects of International Child Abduction, 1343 UNTS 89), as well as in art 21(2) of the Hague Child Protection Convention (Hague Convention of 19 October 1996 on Jurisdiction, Applicable Law, Recognition, Enforcement and Co-operation in Respect of Parental Responsibility and Measures for the Protection of Children, 35 ILM 1391).

However, international uniformity of decisions should not be neglected in relation to third countries. Therefore, conflict-of-laws rules in treaties, as far as they are enshrined as *lois uniformes*, *de lege ferenda*, should implement references to conflict-of-laws rules in status matters. Uniformity of decisions can be achieved with references to conflict-of-laws rules in treaties – concerning third countries – rather than with references to substantive law if conflict-of-laws rules in treaties are not to implement specific substantive ideas of justice.

3. *European*

The provisions in the Rome I Regulation (see art 20) (Regulation (EC) No 593/2008 of the European Parliament and of the Council of

17 June 2008 on the law applicable to contractual obligations (Rome I), [2008] OJ L 177/6; → Rome Convention and Rome I Regulation (contractual obligations)), → Rome II Regulation (see art 24) (Regulation (EC) No 864/2007 of the European Parliament and of the Council of 11 July 2007 on the law applicable to non-contractual obligations (Rome II), [2007] OJ L 199/40) and → Rome III Regulation (see art 11) (Council Regulation (EU) No 1259/2010 of 20 December 2010 implementing enhanced cooperation in the area of the law applicable to divorce and legal separation, [2010] OJ L 343/10) as well as in the Maintenance Regulation (Council Regulation (EC) No 4/2009 of 18 December 2008 on jurisdiction, applicable law, recognition and enforcement of decisions and cooperation in matters relating to maintenance obligations, [2009] OJ L 7/1) in association with the Hague Maintenance Protocol 2007 (see art 12 Hague Maintenance Protocol) (Hague Protocol of 23 November 2007 on the law applicable to maintenance obligations, [2009] OJ L 331/19) are references to substantive law and hence exclude *renvoi* (→ Maintenance obligations). Furthermore, the provisions in the Matrimonial Property Regulation (see art 32) (Council Regulation (EU) No 2016/1103 of 24 June 2016 implementing enhanced cooperation in the area of jurisdiction, applicable law and the recognition and enforcement of decisions in matters of matrimonial property regimes, [2016] OJ L 183/1) and in the Registered Partnerships Property Regulation (see art 32) (Council Regulation (EU) No 2016/1104 of 24 June 2016 implementing enhanced cooperation in the area of jurisdiction, applicable law and the recognition and enforcement of decisions in matters of the property consequences of registered partnerships, [2016] OJ L 183/30) only provide for references to substantive law (→ Matrimonial property, → Registered partnerships).

In contrast to these regulations, the provisions of the Succession Regulation (→ Rome IV Regulation) (Regulation (EU) No 650/2012 of the European Parliament and of the Council of 4 July 2012 on jurisdiction, applicable law, recognition and enforcement of decisions and acceptance and enforcement of authentic instruments in matters of succession and on the creation of a European Certificate of Succession, [2012] OJ L 201/107) refer to the substantive rules unless the rules of the designated third state make a *renvoi* to the law of a Member State of the Succession Regulation or if the rules of the designated law by the Succession Regulation make a *renvoi* to the law of another third state which would apply its own law (see art 34(1) Succession Regulation). But the provisions listed in art 34(2) Succession Regulation – for example, concerning the formal validity of dispositions of property upon death made in writing according to art 27 Succession Regulation – only refer to the substantive law.

Reasons for a different treatment of *renvoi* in the Succession Regulation and in the Matrimonial Property Regulation are neither evident nor indicated. As a result, a coherent legal regulation of *renvoi* in European private international law is still missing.

V. Basis for a coherent regulation in European private international law

1. Distinction between provisions which are favourable to renvoi *and which are hostile to* renvoi*?*

De lege ferenda, a fundamental distinction between provisions which are favourable to *renvoi* and those which are hostile is inadvisable (see Jan von Hein, 'Der Renvoi im europäischen Kollisionsrecht' in Stefan Leible and Hannes Unberath (eds), *Brauchen wir eine Rom 0-Verordnung?* (Jenaer Wissenschaftliche Verlagsgesellschaft 2013) 341, 358; Michael Sonnentag, *Der Renvoi im Internationalen Privatrecht* (Mohr Siebeck 2001) 108–112; dissenting Paul Heinrich Neuhaus, *Die Grundbegriffe des Internationalen Privatrechts* (2nd edn, Mohr 1976) § 36).

At first sight it would seem that the principle of party autonomy is hostile to *renvoi* because the parties, assuming they choose the applicable law, as a rule intend the substantive law of a specific state. This can differ in individual cases, eg in the case of an arbitral procedure (§ 1051(1), sentence 2 German Code of Civil Procedure (Zivilprozessordnung of 5 December 2005, BGBl. I 3202, as amended)). Concerning the choice of a specific legal system, it is necessary in contrast to ordinary civil proceedings to draw a distinction because arbitration courts do not have to emanate from a specific national law, whereas the judge in ordinary civil proceedings has to emanate from the *lex fori*.

The → connecting factor of → nationality is not in itself favourable to *renvoi*, just as the connection to the domicile or habitual residence

(→ Domicile, habitual residence and establishment) is not in itself hostile. This is because the domicile or habitual residence establishes a factual legal relation between a person and a legal system, while the connection to citizenship establishes a legal relation to a specific state. If the law of the forum designates the law of nationality but does not govern civil legal consequences to the citizenship, then a *renvoi* which is ordered by the law of nationality should rather (albeit not definitely) be observed. In contrast, this rationale for *renvoi* does not exist for the connection to the domicile or habitual residence. Nonetheless, *renvoi* may be appropriate concerning the connection to the domicile or habitual residence, eg with a view to achieving uniformity of decisions. Therefore, in view of provisions which are favourable and those which are hostile to *renvoi*, generalizations are not advisable in cases of connections to citizenship and to the domicile or habitual residence.

2. Distinction between areas of law

Rather than either accepting or excluding *renvoi*, the European legislature should adopt a more nuanced approach. The same holds true for international treaties containing uniform conflict-of-laws rules. So far as status matters are concerned, in particular in family law and the rights of individuals, but also in the law of companies, the risk of limping legal relationships arises. In these fields of law, recognition of *renvoi* makes sense with a view to achieving international uniformity of decisions. This also holds true for international property law and succession law. But if the implementation of specific substantive ideas of justice is more important than the international uniformity of decisions, *renvoi* should be excluded.

In the field of international contract law and the law of non-contractual obligations, *renvoi* is no longer important. Since conflict-of-laws rules under the law of obligations have become progressively more elaborate and implement specific ideas of justice in private international law, these ideas should not be undermined by *renvoi*. Thus, *renvoi* should be excluded in the law of obligations.

3. Multiple connecting factors

a) Alternative connecting factors

If conflict-of-laws rules apply alternative → connecting factors, the legislature should permit *renvoi*, because such rules are based on the favourability principle.

De lege lata, *renvoi* should not be applied in these cases to achieve a certain substantive result when it would be achieved only with the aid of *renvoi*. Otherwise the legislature's decision for several certain connecting factors – and the exclusion of *renvoi* in such cases – would be ignored. Currently, alternative connecting factors are provided, for example, in art 11(1) Rome I Regulation or art 27 Succession Regulation. If, for example, other alternative connecting factors were admitted in addition to the alternative connecting factor of form, the protective function of formal requirements (→ Formal requirements and validity) – at least for one party – would be ignored.

De lege ferenda, the European legislature could also consider introducing *renvoi in favorem*, ie in order to obtain an intended substantive result. The alternative connecting factors concerning the formal validity of wills, for example, intend to fulfil the intentions of the deceased whenever possible. If only the observance of the *renvoi* directs to a substantive law ensuring formal validity, could the legislature adopt a regulation which provides that a *renvoi in favorem* to the formal validity of a will has to be observed, whereas this solution is not possible *de lege lata*.

b) Subsidiary connecting factors

Regarding conflict-of-laws rules that utilize subsidiary → connecting factors, a distinction has to be drawn. If the subsidiary connecting factor is made for reasons of conflict of laws, the provision *de lege ferenda* should permit *renvoi*, provided the provision does not exclude *renvoi* for other reasons. Such a subsidiary connecting factor for reasons of the conflict of laws exists when the first step of the cascade is not able to determine the applicable law. That is, for example, the case when a divorce is primarily linked to the common habitual residence or common nationality of the spouses, but when the spouses have neither. In these cases at least one further – namely subsidiary – connecting factor is required in order to determine the applicable law.

Concerning a subsidiary connecting factor for reasons of substantive law, ie to achieve a certain substantive result, *de lege ferenda*, a reference to conflict-of-laws rules should exist at the first step of the cascade, the so-called primary connection, provided there is no reference to substantive law for special reasons irrespective of the subsidiary connection. Concerning the further provided subsidiary connecting factors, *de lege ferenda*, there should be a reference to substantive law because this reference is selected for substantive reasons, ie to achieve a certain substantive result. That is, for example, the case when the maintenance for a person is primarily linked to the law of the country in which the creditor has habitual residence, but this law does not grant the title of maintenance so that out of substantive reasons, namely to be preferably entitled to maintenance, one or even more connecting factors are provided subsidiarily in order to achieve the intended substantive result.

c) Cumulative connecting factors
Finally, if conflict-of-laws rules rely on cumulative → connecting factors, a distinction is necessary. If a cumulative connecting factor primarily serves to achieve international uniformity of decisions, the provision *de lege ferenda* should refer to conflict-of-laws rules. If, in contrast, the function of the cumulative connecting factor exists in impeding a certain substantive result or at least making it more difficult, the cumulative connecting factor *de lege ferenda* should be a reference to substantive law.

4. Accessory connecting factors

The question of whether accessory → connecting factors *de lege ferenda* should provide references to the substantive law of the controlling statute cannot be answered uniformly in all cases because accessory connecting factors can pursue varying purposes. It is possible that the accessory connecting factor strives for a uniform substantive assessment of legal issues that belong together – for example, the accessory connection of the formal validity to the *lex causae*. This suggests a reference to substantive law of the controlling statute because this unity would be destroyed by the doctrine of *renvoi*. However, it is also conceivable that the accessory provision is intended to extend the area of application of a conflict-of-laws rule without the uniform substantive assessment being absolutely necessary. Then a *renvoi* by virtue of a deviating → classification (characterization) would not be barred if the controlling statute expresses the *renvoi* for the dependent statute. Potentially the reference to another conflict-of-laws rule is merely intended to avoid repetitions of the wording of the law. In that case it is a pure legislative technique so that the *renvoi* is also not barred. It depends on the purpose of the accessory connecting factor in relation to the interest of achieving international uniformity of decisions if the accessory connecting factor is a reference to substantive law or to conflict-of-laws rules. It is necessary to draw a distinction between the question of whether the dependent statute concerning accessory connecting factors accessorily refers to the conflict-of-laws rules or to the substantive law of the controlling statute on the one hand, and the question whether the controlling statute has to be determined by a reference to substantive law or by a reference to conflict-of-laws rules on the other hand. The accessory connecting factor may be a reference to the substantive law of the controlling statute; however, a *renvoi* has to be borne in mind for the determination of the controlling statute. As far as a *renvoi* has to be observed for the ascertainment of the controlling statute, this *renvoi* indirectly affects the ascertainment of the dependent statute if the reference to the controlling statute is a reference to the substantive provisions of this law. By contrast, if the accessory connected statute refers to the conflict-of-laws rules of the controlling statute, a *renvoi* which has to be observed for the determination of the controlling statute can be considered. The answer to the question of whether it has to be observed depends on the reasons why the legislature has established an accessory connection. Therefore, this question cannot be answered uniformly in all cases (Michael Sonnentag, *Der Renvoi im Internationalen Privatrecht* (Mohr Siebeck 2001) 180 ff).

5. Connecting factor of the closest connection

Concerning the → connecting factor of the closest connection, the decision between acceptance and exclusion of *renvoi* depends on the answer to the question of which purpose the legislature pursued with the connecting factor to the closest connection. If the connecting factor to the law of the closest connection is an escape clause to a rigid connecting factor and the escape clause directs to a rigid connection again – in other words, a hardly flexible connecting factor – then this by itself is no reason for a reference to substantive law because in this case the concrete connection is again determined by typecasting criteria. If the meaning of the connecting factor to the closest connection exists in determining the applicable law individually, which means under consideration of all circumstances of the individual case, then the escape clause refers to the substantive law because otherwise the individual connection would again be questioned. A closer connection than the closest does not exist.

6. *Introduction of a clause according to which provisions to a foreign law refer to its conflict-of-laws rules, unless it is contrary to the rationale of the provision*

As far as possible, the European legislature should decide for each conflict-of-laws rule whether a provision refers to substantive law or to the conflict-of-laws rules.

Nevertheless, a clause should be introduced such as art 4(1), sentence 1 EGBGB, according to which provisions to a foreign law refer to its conflict-of-laws rules unless it is contrary to the rationale of the provision (Michael Sonnentag, *Der Renvoi im Internationalen Privatrecht* (Mohr Siebeck 2001) 271 f, 289 f). Since this rule has proved to be successful and enables flexible results, this regulation should persist and be considered at a European level. There are two reasons for this. First, there will always be gaps in the legislative framework which will have to be filled. Even if the European legislature has the intention of adopting a comprehensive system of private international law or even a Code on Private international law, new fields of law will be created. It is therefore preferable to have a general rule that decides whether a conflict-of-laws rule refers to the substantive law or the conflict-of-laws rules of the designated country. Second, also in the future, there will be cases that require a purposive interpretation of conflict-of-laws rules. This in turn can lead to the creation of a new conflict-of-laws rule. In these cases the question of *renvoi* will again have to be answered. Such a clause, according to which provisions to a foreign law refer to its conflict-of-laws rules unless it is contrary to the rationale of the provision, will also help to find appropriate results for these conflict-of-laws rules.

MICHAEL SONNENTAG

Literature

Eric Agostini, 'Le mécanisme du renvoi' (2013) 102 Rev.crit.DIP 545; Adrian Briggs, 'In Praise and Defence of Renvoi' (1998) 47 ICLQ 877; Angelo Davì, 'Le renvoi en droit international privé contemporain' (2010) 352 Rec. des Cours, 9; Dieter Henrich, 'Der Renvoi: Zeit für einen Abgesang?' in Herbert Kronke and Karsten Thorn (eds), *Grenzen überwinden – Prinzipien bewahren. Festschrift für Bernd von Hoffmann* (Gieseking 2011) 159; David Alexander Hughes, 'The Insolubility of Renvoi and its Consequences' (2010) 6 J Priv Int L 195; Larry Kramer, 'Return of the Renvoi' (1991) 66 N.Y.U.L.Rev. 979; J Georges Sauveplanne, 'Renvoi' in Kurt Lipstein (ed), *International Encyclopedia of Comparative Law, Vol. III: Private international law* (JCB Mohr 1990) ch 6; Haimo Schack, 'Was bleibt vom renvoi?' [2013] IPRax 315; Dennis Solomon, 'Die Renaissance des Renvoi im Europäischen Internationalen Privatrecht' in Ralf Michaels and Dennis Solomon (eds), *Liber Amicorum Klaus Schurig zum 70. Geburtstag* (Sellier 2012) 237; Michael Sonnentag, *Der Renvoi im Internationalen Privatrecht* (Mohr Siebeck 2001); Jan von Hein, 'Der Renvoi im europäischen Kollisionsrecht' in Stefan Leible and Hannes Unberath (eds), *Brauchen wir eine Rom 0-Verordnung?* (Jenaer Wissenschaftliche Verlagsgesellschaft 2013) 341.

Restatement (First and Second) of Conflict of Laws

I. Restatements of the Law

In the American legal lexicon, a *Restatement of the Law* is a document that resembles a code in the sense that it is a comprehensive and relatively systematic treatment of a legal subject, but also differs in many respects, not the least of which is that it is not a statute. It is promulgated not by a governmental authority, but rather by the American Law Institute (ALI), a non-governmental organization of up to 4,000 lawyers, judges and academics, which was founded in 1923 'to promote the clarification and simplification of the law and its better adaptation to social needs' (ALI Charter (1923, available at <www.ali.org>)). In addition to systematically restating and clarifying the common law, a restatement may also pre-state what the law ought to be, at least when judicial precedents are lacking, conflicting or ambiguous. Although the restatements are not binding authority in any state, they can be highly persuasive, depending on their intrinsic quality, and some of them enjoy wide judicial following.

Currently, there are three completed series of restatements, and a fourth under way, covering more than 30 legal subjects. This entry discusses the two Restatements of the law of conflict of laws, the first of which was promulgated in 1933 (American Law Institute, Restatement of the Law Conflict of Laws, St Paul 1934) and the second in 1969 (American Law Institute, Restatement of the Law, Second: Conflict of Laws 2d, St Paul 1971).

II. The Restatement (First)

1. Beale's *Restatement*

The drafting of the first conflicts Restatement began in 1923 and was completed in 1933. The Reporter and principal drafter was *Joseph H Beale* (1861–1943), a professor at the Harvard Law School. *Beale* was erudite and prolific, but also dogmatic, a scholar who dominated the American choice-of-law landscape for 50 years. He was the first professor to teach a conflict-of-laws course in the USA (1893) and to publish a casebook on the subject, which was adopted in most American law schools of that time (see Joseph H Beale, *Collection of Cases on the Conflict of Laws*, 3 vols (1900–1902)). His treatise (see Joseph Beale, *A Treatise on the Conflict of Laws* (Baker, Voorhis & Co 1935)), while still in manuscript form, was the model for the Restatement in both structure and content. Thus, the Restatement is inextricably tied to *Beale*. In many respects, it was a pre-statement of his views, rather than a restatement of the common law, conceived and executed through deduction from the principles he espoused instead of through induction from the cases (Symeon C Symeonides, 'The First Conflicts Restatement through the Eyes of Old: As Bad as its Reputation?' (2007) 32 S.Ill.U.L.J. 39).

2. *Overarching principles: territoriality and vested rights*

The Restatement consists of 625 black-letter sections accompanied by explanatory comments and illustrations, and arranged in 12 chapters covering all three parts of conflicts law – jurisdiction, → choice of law and recognition of judgments. However, the most consequential part of the Restatement, as well as the one that has attracted the most criticism, is the part on choice of law.

The two philosophical principles underlying the Restatement's choice-of-law part are the principles of → territoriality and vested rights (→ Vested rights theory). The very first section of the Restatement restates the territoriality principle as follows:

> No state can make a law which by its own force is operative in another state; the only law in force in the sovereign state is its own law, but by the law of each state rights or other interests in that state may, in certain cases, depend upon the law in force in some other state or states. (Restatement (First) of Conflict of Laws § 1)

Section 384 reflects the vested rights principle in the context of tort conflicts:

> if a cause of action in tort is created at the place of wrong, a cause of action will be recognized in other states. If no cause of action is created at the place of wrong, no recovery in tort can be had in any other state. (Restatement (First) of Conflict of Laws § 384)

Virtually all of the Restatement's choice-of-law rules are deduced from these two principles. For example, for → torts, the basic rule is the *lex loci delicti*, which is defined as the law of the place of injury and, more specifically, the place 'where the last event necessary to make an actor liable for an alleged tort' took place (Restatement (First) §§ 377–378). For virtually all issues of property (→ Property and proprietary rights), the basic rule is the *lex rei sitae* (Restatement (First) §§ 208–254), and for all contract issues the *lex loci contractus* (Restatement (First) § 332) or *solutionis* (Restatement (First) § 358), without any exceptions for issues such as capacity (Restatement (First) §333; → Capacity and emancipation) or any concessions to the parties' freedom to choose the applicable law (→ Party autonomy).

Ironically, the ALI membership did not question these overarching principles and did not discuss the *lex loci delicti* rule at all, which later became the target of the American choice-of-law revolution (Symeon C Symeonides, 'The First Conflicts Restatement through the Eyes of Old: As Bad as its Reputation?' (2007) 32 S.Ill.U.L.J. 39, 66–74; → (American) Conflict of laws revolution). Although at that time territoriality was the favourite principle in the Anglo-American world, neither the case-law nor the doctrinal writers had accepted it unexceptionally across the board. In contrast, the Restatement made this principle the exclusive foundation for its rules, allowing fewer if any 'personal' exceptions than most continental systems, which had adopted the personality principle for most matters of capacity (→ Capacity and emancipation), → personal status and → succession at death, and had recognized → party autonomy in contract conflicts.

Beale and his fellow drafters saw the world as a neatly laid-out, black-and-white chessboard in which the critical event would always occur entirely in either the black or the white squares. Of course, if the world were that simple or if law operated in such a simplistic manner, we would not need conflicts law. *Beale* never accepted the proposition that in some cases, for some issues, the law of a person's home state may have a legitimate claim of application (personality principle), even if the dispute is triggered by events occurring in another state. *Beale* thought that territoriality was the 'modern' principle and personality the medieval principle. Had he been a better student of history or a better comparatist, he would have realized that any system that completely banishes either one of these two grand principles will inevitably run into an impasse and that the key is to know when and how to compromise the two principles. Even in the 1930s, the Restatement's fixation with territoriality was odd for a country like the USA, which purported to be 'one nation, indivisible', notwithstanding its internal boundaries. With the subsequent advent of new means of transportation and communication, and the increased mobility of people, state boundaries became even less important and the Restatement's insistence on territoriality as the dominant principle made even less sense than before.

3. Criticisms

Perceptive academic authors have criticized the Restatement since its inception (see David F Cavers, 'Restatement of the Law of Conflict of Laws' (1935) 44 Yale L.J. 1478; Walter W Cook, 'The Jurisdiction of Sovereign States and the Conflict of Laws' (1931) 31 Colum.L.Rev. 368). As time went by, academic criticisms intensified and judicial discontent succeeded the initial favourable reception.

Indeed, the list of the Restatement's flaws is quite long. The Restatement was a system of mechanical and rigid rules that: (i) completely sacrificed flexibility on the altar of ostensible certainty and predictability, which eventually proved illusory; (ii) ignored the lessons of experience in favour of the pursuit of an ill-conceived theoretical purity; and (iii) completely eliminated judicial discretion, even as they purported to be a distillation of the courts' experience. The Restatement's choice-of-law rules – despite their name – were not designed to choose among conflicting laws. Instead, they *a priori* assigned 'legislative jurisdiction' to a particular state, based solely on a single, pre-designated, territorial contact. Subject only to limited post-choice exceptions, the law of the designated state applied almost automatically, regardless of its content, its underlying policy or the substantive quality of the solution it would bring to the case at hand. The only thing that mattered was whether that state had the specified contact, even if its presence there was entirely fortuitous, and even if that state had no real interest in the outcome. As *David Cavers* observed as early as 1933, the Restatement was not much different from a slot machine programmed to find the 'right' state in a 'blindfold' and random fashion. Indeed, the Restatement's goal was to find what it considered the spatially appropriate law ('conflicts justice') rather than to ensure a substantively appropriate result in a particular case ('material justice') (David F Cavers, 'A Critique of the Choice-of-Law Problem' (1933) 47 Harv.L.Rev. 173, 191–192). It did not occur to *Beale* that in order to intelligently resolve any conflict, one must first ascertain what the conflict is about, and what are the conflicting objectives and claims, if any. In turn, this requires looking into the content of the conflicting laws, identifying their purposes or policies and then proceeding from there.

4. Judicial acceptance

The initial judicial reaction to the Restatement ranged from favourable to conformist. However, this initial judicial acceptance was hardly a validation of the Restatement's quality. The courts accepted the Restatement because it was the only game in town. It was the first comprehensive and complete treatment of a previously obscure subject. Most courts encounter conflicts cases only infrequently and thus do not have the opportunity or the incentive to develop the necessary expertise. They do not have the time to read and evaluate the numerous conflicting academic commentaries. The availability of an authoritative-sounding document like the Restatement, which bears the prestigious imprimatur of the ALI, obviates the need to look elsewhere.

In any event, the courts' allegiance to the Restatement was not as deep as the numbers might suggest. Courts gradually began deviating from the Restatement's dictates by employing various 'escape devices', such as characterization,

→ *renvoi* and the → public policy exception (see eg *Grant v McAuliffe*, 264 P.2d 944 (Cal. 1953); *Haumschild v Continental Cas Co*, 95 N.W.2d 814 (Wis. 1959); *Kilberg v Northeast Airlines, Inc*, 172 N.E.2d 526 (N.Y. 1961)). The first overt departures from the Restatement occurred in 1954, when the New York Court of Appeals rejected the *lex loci contractus* rule, and 1963, when the same court rejected the *lex loci delicti* rule (see *Auten v Auten*, 124 N.E.2d 99 (N.Y. 1954); *Babcock v Jackson*, 191 N.E.2d 279 (N.Y. 1963)). This was the beginning of the widely hailed American choice-of-law revolution (see Symeon C Symeonides, *The American Choice-of-Law Revolution: Past, Present and Future* (Martinus Nijhoff 2006)).

However, the Restatement continued to command a majority of states as late as 1979 in tort conflicts and as late as 1984 in contract conflicts. Even today, it continues to be followed in ten states in tort conflicts (Alabama, Georgia, Kansas, Maryland, New Mexico, North Carolina, South Carolina, Virginia, West Virginia and Wyoming) and 12 states in contract conflicts (Alabama, Florida, Georgia, Kansas, Maryland, New Mexico, Oklahoma, Rhode Island, South Carolina, Tennessee, Virginia and Wyoming) (see Symeon C Symeonides, 'Choice of Law in the American Courts in 2014: Twenty-Eighth Annual Survey' (2015) 63 Am.J.Comp.L. 299, 351). Nevertheless, in some of these states, the courts follow the Restatement in name only, considering how often they evade its results through the various escape devices (see Symeon C Symeonides, *The American Choice-of-Law Revolution: Past, Present and Future* (Martinus Nijhoff 2006) 50–62).

5. *The first Restatement's contribution*

Despite its many flaws, the Restatement also made some positive contributions to the development of American conflicts law. They include the following:

(a) The Restatement unified American conflicts law, which until then had been scattered in the law reports, some of which were not widely available. Even if the judicial acceptance of the Restatement was less than enthusiastic, it did occur and was widespread. The Restatement dominated American conflicts law for more than a generation. At least in conflicts law, this consensus is a rare phenomenon and is unlikely to be repeated. For the first time, it was possible to speak of a single American conflicts law, despite small variations from state to state. Ironically, this unification and dominance, besides the Restatement's content, both caused and facilitated the choice-of-law revolution.

(b) The Restatement pulled American conflicts law out of its relative obscurity and raised the level of awareness about it among the members of the bar and the bench. Had it not been for *Beale's* stature in the 1920s, conflicts law would not have been one of the first four subjects chosen for a restatement. Because of *Beale* and the Restatement, conflicts law gained its rightful place in the curriculum of all American law schools and this, in turn, made possible the renaissance of American conflicts law during the next generation. One of the unintended by-products of the Restatement was to galvanize the opposition among the Restatement's critics, especially the legal realists. This led to the production of several outstanding scholarly articles giving conflicts law the attention that it might not have otherwise received. While these articles did not win the battle against the Restatement, they sowed the seeds of the revolution, eventually leading to, but not ending with, the Restatement (Second). Of course, without the first Restatement, there would be no need for revolution, but that is another matter.

(c) The first Restatement was a comprehensive and complete system. It provided a complete, organized and disciplined network of bilateral, fixed, neutral and detailed choice-of-law rules designed to provide solutions for all possible conflicts situations. This was the first time that such a comprehensive and complete work on conflicts law had been produced on American soil. According to one contemporary commentator, the Restatement was 'a system, something tangible out of the chaos of cases, a point of departure, a beginning, systematic, rational, and withal not inconsistent with what is implicit in most American precedents and explicit in many of the decisions of the last twenty years' (Frederick L de Sloovère, 'On Looking into Mr. Beale's Conflict of Laws' (1936) 13 N.Y.U. L.Q. Rev. 333, 345).

(d) The Restatement was non-parochial, even if it was not particularly internationalist.

Unlike most of the American approaches proposed since then (but not before), the Restatement did not give preference to the forum state *qua* forum. It purported to be, and in many respects was, impartial vis-à-vis forum and foreign law. Its explicit aspiration was not different from *Savigny's* and *Story's* goal of eliminating or curtailing forum shopping and fostering international or interstate uniformity of result by ensuring that a case would be resolved in the same way regardless of where it was litigated. That this aspiration never fully materialized cannot be blamed on the Restatement.

III. The Restatement (Second)

1. Introduction

Responding to the challenge of the choice-of-law revolution, the ALI began drafting the Restatement (Second) of Conflict of Laws, in 1952. The new Reporter was *Willis LM Reese*, a brilliant and open-minded professor at Columbia Law School, who was a member of the new school of conflicts thought, although not of its revolutionary branch. *Reese* agreed with many of the criticisms levelled against the first Restatement, but, more importantly, he was receptive to the criticisms of his own drafts of the Restatement (Second). A cursory look at the successive versions of what eventually became § 6 of the Restatement (Second) reveals this evolution in the reporter's own thinking, as well as the gradual gains of the new school over the old. The final version of the Restatement (Second) promulgated in 1969 did not join the revolution, but was a conscious compromise and synthesis between the old and the new schools, as well as among the various branches of the new schools.

2. The cornerstone: section 6

The Restatement (Second) consists of 423 black-letter sections accompanied by explanatory comments, illustrations and reporter's notes, and arranged in 14 chapters covering all parts of conflicts law – jurisdiction, choice of law and recognition of judgments. However, as with the first Restatement, the most consequential part of the Restatement (Second) is the one on choice of law. The cornerstone of the Restatement (Second) is § 6. It is a primary example of an 'approach' (as opposed to a dispositive rule) because, rather than designating the applicable law, it simply lists the factors that a court should consider in searching for that law. Section 6 provides that, unless a statutory or constitutional rule dictates otherwise:

> the factors relevant to the choice of the applicable rule of law include:
>
> (a) the needs of the interstate and international systems,
> (b) the relevant policies of the forum,
> (c) the relevant policies of other interested states and the relative interests of those states in the determination of the particular issue,
> (d) the protection of justified expectations,
> (e) the basic policies underlying the particular field of law,
> (f) certainty, predictability and uniformity of result, and
> (g) ease in the determination and application of the law to be applied. (American Law Institute, Restatement of the Law, Second: Conflict of Laws 2d (St Paul 1971) § 6(2))

From a philosophical viewpoint, § 6 is important in that it establishes the ideology of the Restatement (Second), which distinguishes it from other modern theories, particularly *Brainerd Currie's* (1912–1965) interest analysis (→ Currie, Brainerd; → Interest and policy analysis in private international law). The list of § 6 policies is broader than the policies relied upon by interest analysis, which focuses on the policies mentioned in the above-quoted clauses (b), (c) and (e), and de-emphasizes or expressly rejects the rest, including 'uniformity of result' and 'the needs of the interstate and international systems'. To *Currie's* ethnocentric attitude towards both these goals, the Restatement (Second) juxtaposes a universalistic perception of conflicts law reflected in the statement that 'the most important function of choice-of-law rules is to make the interstate and international systems work well ... to further harmonious relations between states and to facilitate commercial intercourse between them' (Restatement (Second) § 6 cmt (d)). The contrast is hardly surprising since, unlike interest analysis, which *Currie* conceived from the perspective of the forum judge confined to the role of the 'handmaiden' of the forum legislature, the Restatement (Second) was drafted from the perspective of a neutral forum, under the auspices of the ALI, a body that strives for national uniformity.

From a methodological viewpoint, § 6 is important in that it provides a guiding, as well as a validating, test for applying almost all other sections of the Restatement (Second), most of which incorporate § 6 by reference. For example, § 145 provides that a tort issue is governed by the law of the state that, with respect to that issue, has the most significant relationship to the occurrence and the parties 'under the principles stated in § 6'. Because the § 6 factors are not listed in a hierarchical order and may well point in different directions in a given case (Restatement (Second) § 6 cmt (c)), they fall short of providing the court with an actual choice of law. Nevertheless, these factors can help steer courts away from a state-selecting choice that is based solely on factual contacts. Although the specific sections of the Restatement (Second) call for the application of the law of the state with the 'most significant relationship' – a term that evokes jurisdiction-selecting notions – the choice of that state is to be made 'under the principles stated in § 6', and by taking into account the contacts listed in the specific sections (Restatement (Second) § 14). This constantly repeated cross-reference to § 6 also helps to supplement the multilateral approach of the specific Restatement sections with elements from a unilateral approach.

3. The 'most-significant-relationship' formula

The 'most-significant-relationship' formula is the other cornerstone of the Restatement (Second). While § 6 articulates the principles and policies that should guide the choice-of-law process, the ubiquitous most-significant-relationship formula describes the objective of that process – to apply the law of the state that, with regard to the particular issue, has the most significant relationship with the parties and the dispute.

4. Rules

In relatively few cases, the Restatement (Second) identifies *a priori* the state of the most significant relationship through black-letter rules. This is the case with most of the sections devoted to property and successions issues (see Restatement (Second) §§ 260–265 (succession to movables), §§ 245–255 (*inter vivos* transactions involving movables)). In cases involving land, the applicable law is almost invariably the 'law that would be applied by the courts of the situs' (see Restatement (Second) §§ 223, 225–232 (*inter vivos* transactions involving land), §§ 236, 239–242 (succession to land)). The quoted phrase is often accompanied by the prediction that the *situs* courts will 'usually' apply their own law. This is as close as the Restatement (Second) comes to prescribing black-letter rules.

5. Presumptive rules

In other cases, the Restatement (Second) identifies the state of the most significant relationship only tentatively, through presumptive rules that instruct the court to apply the law of a certain state, unless it appears that in the particular case, another state has a more significant relationship. For example, all ten of the sections that designate the law governing different types of torts conclude with the following escape clause: 'unless, with respect to the particular issue, some other state has a more significant relationship under the principles stated in § 6 to the occurrence and the parties, in which event the local law of the other state will be applied'. Thus, in an action for an invasion of privacy, the applicable law is the local law of the state where the invasion occurred, 'unless, with respect to the particular issue, some other state has a more significant relationship' (Restatement (Second) § 152). This clause is one of the most-repeated phrases in the entire Restatement (Second) (see eg Restatement (Second) §§ 146–151, 153–155, 175).

In contracts, the Restatement (Second) departs from the hostile position of the first Restatement on party autonomy and, in § 187, expressly authorizes the application of the law chosen by the parties, subject to limited exceptions. Courts in virtually all states, including those that do not otherwise follow the Restatement (Second), have adopted § 187. For most contracts not containing a choice-of-law clause, the Restatement (Second) designates the applicable law through presumptive rules (or pointers described below), subject always to the 'unless' clause described earlier (see eg Restatement (Second) §§ 189–193, 196).

6. Pointers

In some instances, the presumptive rules of the Restatement (Second) are even more equivocal and amount to no more than mere pointers in the direction of the likely applicable law. The pertinent sections provide that the state with the 'most significant relationship' will 'usually' be one particular state. For example, in the area of tort conflicts, 11 of the 19 sections devoted to specific tort issues conclude with the adage that: 'The applicable law will usually be the local law of the state where the injury occurred' (see Restatement (Second) § 156, tortious character of conduct; § 157, standard of care; § 158, interest entitled to legal protection; § 159, duty owed to plaintiff; § 160, legal cause; § 162, specific conditions of liability; § 164, contributory fault; § 165, assumption of risk; § 166, imputed negligence; and § 172, joint torts). One section, § 169, provides that for intra-family immunity, the applicable law 'will usually be the local law of the state of the parties' domicil'. Only the remaining seven sections (§§ 161, 163, 168, 170–171 and 173–174) are unaided by such a presumption.

In contract conflicts, § 188 provides that, subject to some exceptions: 'If the place of negotiating the contract and the place of performance are in the same state, the local law of this state will usually be applied.' Similarly, § 198 provides that '[t]he capacity of a party to contract will usually be upheld if he has such capacity under the local law of the state of his domicil', while § 199 provides that contractual '[f]ormalities which meet the requirements of the place where the parties execute the contract will usually be acceptable'. Similar language is found in many other sections of the Restatement (Second).

7. Ad hoc *analysis*

Finally, in the remaining and most difficult cases, the Restatement (Second) provides neither presumptive rules nor pointers. It simply provides a non-exclusive, non-hierarchical list of the factual contacts that should be 'taken into account' by the court in choosing the applicable law. On this point, the Restatement (Second) differs drastically from the first Restatement, which made the choice of the applicable law dependent on a single physical contact. The contacts to be taken into account in applying the Restatement (Second) vary from one subject matter to another. In torts, these contacts include the place of the injury, the place of the conduct causing the injury, the domicile, residence (→ Domicile, habitual residence and establishment), the nationality and place of business of the parties, and the place where the relationship, if any, between the parties is centred (see Restatement (Second) § 145(2)). In contracts, these contacts include the places of contracting, negotiation and performance of the contract, the location of the subject matter, and the domicile, residence (→ Domicile, habitual residence and establishment), nationality or place of business of the parties (see Restatement (Second) § 188(2)).

The determination of the state with the most significant relationship is to be made 'under the principles stated in § 6' by 'taking into account' the above factual contacts 'according to their relative importance with respect to the particular issue' (see eg Restatement (Second) §§ 145, 188). This language suggests that the policy part of this analysis should carry more weight than the evaluation of the factual contacts. Yet, courts tend to do it the other way around, by first focusing on the factual contacts listed in the pertinent section of the Restatement (Second) and then, if ever, on the policies of § 6. When the contacts of state A are clearly more numerous than are those of state B, some courts tend to assume that state A is the one that has the more significant relationship, without testing that assumption under the principles of § 6. In contrast, when the factual contacts are evenly divided between the two states, the courts look to the policies of § 6, but many courts pay lip service to most of the policies listed therein and confine themselves to examining 'the relative policies of the forum [and] of other interested states' (Restatement (Second) § 6).

8. *Judicial acceptance*

After a slow start, the Restatement (Second) managed to gain judicial acceptance in a plurality of states. In 2014, 24 states followed the Restatement (Second) in tort conflicts, and 23 states did likewise in contract conflicts (see Symeon C Symeonides, 'Choice of Law in the American Courts in 2014: Twenty-Eighth Annual Survey' (2015) 63 Am.J.Comp.L. 299, 351). In addition, the Restatement (Second) is followed in part by several other states that have adopted a 'mixed' approach, as well as by many federal courts in federal-question cases (see Symeon C Symeonides, *The American Choice-of-Law Revolution: Past, Present and Future* (Martinus Nijhoff 2006) §§ 80–87).

Thus, almost half a century after its official promulgation, the Restatement (Second) has prevailed over rival approaches proposed by individual scholars, such as *Brainerd Currie* or *Robert Leflar*. The fact that the Restatement (Second) carries the prestigious imprimatur of the ALI is only one of the reasons for this.

Another reason is that, unlike other approaches which provide no more than a single, good-for-all, 'methodology' for tort and contract cases, the Restatement (Second) is a comprehensive and complete document that covers the entire spectrum of conflicts cases. Moreover, in contrast to those approaches which are biased in favour of the *lex fori* or in favour of plaintiffs, the Restatement (Second) is ideologically neutral, even though it does not reduce the possibility of ideologically biased results and, indeed, it provides perfect camouflage for them. But perhaps the most important reason for the Restatement's popularity among judges is that it provides them with virtually unlimited discretion (see Symeon C Symeonides, 'The Judicial Acceptance of the Second Conflicts Restatement: A Mixed Blessing' (1997) 56 Md.L.Rev. 1248, 1269–1277).

IV. The need for a new restatement

Despite the Restatement (Second)'s apparent popularity among judges and regardless of the reasons for it, there is a legitimate question as to whether it is time to begin drafting a new restatement. The debate on this question began at the 1997 annual meeting of the Association of American Law Schools (AALS) Section on Conflict of Laws and continued at the 1999 and 2000 meetings (see Symposium, 'The Silver Anniversary of the Second Conflicts Restatement' (1997) 56 Md.L.Rev. 1193; Symposium, 'Preparing for the Next Century – A New Restatement of Conflicts' (2000) 75 Indiana L.J. 399–686; Symposium, 'American Conflicts Law at the Dawn of the 21st Century' (2001) 37 Willamette L.Rev. 1–298). The majority of speakers supported a new restatement, despite some disagreements about timing and some other respects.

Indeed, a new restatement is necessary, if not overdue. The Restatement (Second) was drafted during a period of transition from an inflexible territorialist approach to flexible policy-based approaches. As its drafter acknowledged, it was intended to be 'a transitional work' (Willis Reese, 'The Second Restatement of Conflict of Laws Revisited' (1983) 34 Mercer L.Rev. 501, 519). It was 'written during a time of turmoil and crisis ... when rival theories were being fiercely debated, and when serious doubt was expressed about the practicality, and indeed the desirability, of having any rules at all' (Willis Reese, 'The Second Restatement of Conflict of Laws Revisited' (1983) 34 Mercer L.Rev. 501, 518–19). The Restatement (Second) served its transitional purpose of helping liberate American courts from the straitjacket of the first Restatement and opening up new ways of thinking. However, as its critics predicted and its drafters acknowledged, the Restatement (Second) brought about an increased degree of unevenness and unpredictability. A new restatement will correct this imbalance and restore a much-needed modicum of predictability.

Moreover, in the intervening four decades, the American conflicts landscape has changed dramatically. For example, in 1969, when the Restatement (Second) was completed, American courts decided 520 conflicts cases. In 2014, the number of cases grew to 4,898 cases (see Symeon C Symeonides, 'Choice of Law in the American Courts in 2014: Twenty-Eighth Annual Survey' (2015) 63 Am.J.Comp.L. 299, 301).

This is more than a tenfold increase, but more important than the growth in volume is the change in the type of cases that now come before American courts. Among them are cyberspace conflicts, conflicts arising from same-sex relations, conflicts involving 'mega' or 'mass' → torts, → products liability, punitive damages, insurance coverage for environmental pollution and more international conflicts than ever before. The Restatement (Second) has little to say on these conflicts.

The process of drafting a new restatement will provide an opportunity for assessing the accumulated interstate and international experience in conflicts involving the above cases and issues, and extracting from it choice-of-law rules or guidelines that meet today's needs. It will also be an opportunity to revisit the Restatement (Second)'s anachronistic rules, such as the *situs* rule for all matters involving immovables, and to reduce the rule's vast scope by carving out appropriate exceptions from it.

More generally, the process of drafting a new restatement will provide an opportunity to: (i) extract, articulate and evaluate the lessons of the choice-of-law revolution, both positive and negative; and (ii) seek a new and proper equilibrium between the conflicting needs of certainty and flexibility.

SYMEON C SYMEONIDES

Literature

Joseph Beale, *A Treatise on the Conflict of Laws* (Baker, Voorhis & Co 1935); Lea Brilmayer, 'Hard

Cases, Single Factor Theories, and a Second Look at the Restatement 2d of Conflicts' (2015) 2015 U.Ill.L.Rev. 1969; David F Cavers, 'Restatement of the Law of Conflict of Laws' (1935) 44 Yale L.J. 1478; David Cavers, 'Re-restating the Conflict of Laws: The Chapter on Contracts' in Kurt Hans Nadelmann, Arthur Taylor Von Mehren and John Newbold Hazard (eds), *XXth Century Comparative and Conflicts Law, Legal Essays in Honor of Hessel E. Yntema* (AW Sythoff 1961) 349; Walter W Cook, *The Logical and Legal Bases of the Conflict of Laws* (HUP 1942); Albert Ehrenzweig, 'The Second Conflicts Restatement: A Last Appeal for its Withdrawal' (1965) 113 U.Pa.L.Rev. 123; Ernest G Lorenzen and Raymond J Heilman, 'The Restatement of the Conflict of Laws' (1935) 83 U.Pa.L.Rev. 555; John Morris, 'Law and Reason Triumphant or: How Not to Review a Restatement' (1973) 21 Am.J.Comp.L. 322; Willis Reese, 'Conflict of Laws and the Restatement, Second' (1963) 28 LCP 679; Willis Reese, 'The Second Restatement of Conflict of Laws Revisited' (1983) 34 Mercer L.Rev. 501; Symeon C Symeonides, 'The First Conflicts Restatement through the Eyes of Old: As Bad as its Reputation?' (2007) 32 S.Ill.U.L.J. 39; Symeon C Symeonides, 'A New Conflicts Restatement: Why Not?' (2009) 5 J Priv Int L 383; Symeon C Symeonides, 'The Choice-of-Law Revolution Fifty Years after Currie: An End and a Beginning' (2015) 2015 U.Ill.L.Rev. 1847; Symposium, 'The Silver Anniversary of the Second Conflicts Restatement' (1997) 56 Md.L.Rev. 1193; Symposium, 'Preparing for the Next Century – A New Restatement of Conflicts' (2000) 75 Indiana L.J. 399; Symposium, 'American Conflicts Law at the Dawn of the 21st Century' (2001) 37 Willamette L.Rev. 1; Michael Traynor, 'The First Restatements and the Vision of the American Law Institute, Then and Now' (2007) 32 S.Ill.U.L.J. 145; Louise Weinberg, 'A Radically Transformed Restatement for Conflicts' (2015) 2015 U.Ill.L.Rev. 1999; Hessel E Yntema, 'The Restatement of the Law of Conflict of Laws' (1936) 36 Colum.L.Rev. 183.

Afterword. After this manuscript was finalized, the American Law Institute authorized work for the Third Restatement of Conflict of Laws. As with the previous restatements, the drafting and approval process is expected to last several years.

Rome Convention and Rome I Regulation (contractual obligations)

I. Introduction

The Rome I Regulation (Regulation (EC) No 593/2008 of the European Parliament and of the Council of 17 June 2008 on the law applicable to contractual obligations (Rome I), [2008] OJ L 177/6) lays down a uniform framework of choice-of-law rules on → contractual obligations within the EU. This instrument has general application, and is fully binding and directly applicable in all Member States (art 288 TFEU (Treaty on the Functioning of the European Union (consolidated version), [2012] OJ C 326/47)). It therefore ensures that the same law will be applied to any contract irrespective of the court hearing the case. Its economic rationale is linked to the proper functioning of the EU market. A set of uniform choice-of-law rules ensures the cross-border protection of property rights (→ Property and proprietary rights) and the enforcement of contracts, which in turn facilitates the voluntary exchange of goods and services and therefore the proper functioning of the European market. In addition, it discourages *ex post* opportunistic behaviours, in particular forum shopping (see, with further references, Gralf-Peter Calliess, in Gralf-Peter Calliess (ed), *Rome Regulations: Commentary on the European Rules of the Conflict of Laws* (Kluwer Law International 2011) 3–6).

The Rome I Regulation has its predecessor in the Rome Convention, which was opened for signature in Rome on 19 June 1980 and entered into force on 1 April 1991 (Rome Convention on the law applicable to contractual obligations (consolidated version), [1998] OJ C 27/34). The Convention established a common system of choice-of-law rules on → contractual obligations, which was applied by EU Member States until 17 December 2009, when it was replaced by the Rome I Regulation. Beyond the change of legal nature, the Regulation introduced important amendments to the provisions of the Convention. As the legal basis is found in arts 61 and 65 TEC (Consolidated version of the Treaty establishing the European Community (2002) [2002] OJ C 325/33) (art 81 TFEU), the positions of the UK and Ireland, on the one hand, and Denmark on the other, are subject to special rules (see art 69 TEC, and currently Protocols nos 21 and 22 TFEU). The UK and Ireland have exercised their right to opt-in, and are therefore bound by the Regulation. Denmark has no opt-in right. The Regulation does not apply to this Member State, and therefore Danish courts continue to apply the Rome Convention. In the same way, the Convention remains in force in the Member State overseas territories referred to in art 349 TFEU.

Uniform rules must be uniformly interpreted. The ECJ provides an institutional guarantee for this objective, since it has jurisdiction to give preliminary rulings concerning the validity and interpretation of the Regulation pursuant to art 267 TFEU. Furthermore, the Rome I Regulation is subject to the general principles of interpretation applicable to secondary law. The Rome I Regulation is part of the EU private international law system, and this system provides the 'hermeneutic circle' within which the Regulation must be understood (see, for example, Recital (7)). The provisions of the Rome I Regulation must be interpreted and construed in a way consistent with the Brussels I Regulation (Regulation (EC) No 1215/2012 on 12 December 2012 of 22 December 2000 on jurisdiction and the recognition and enforcement of judgments in civil and commercial matters, [2012] OJ L 351); → Brussels I (Convention and Regulation)), and the → Rome II Regulation (Regulation (EC) No 864/2007 of the European Parliament and of the Council of 11 July 2007 on the law applicable to non-contractual obligations (Rome II), [2007] OJ L 199/40). These three instruments are complementary and together form a systematic unity. This means, for example, that when a legal concept is used by more than one instrument, it is in principle presumed to have the same meaning in all of them (this is, however, an 'in principle' argument, see Francisco Garcimartín, 'Hermeneutic Dialogue between Rome I and Rome II: General Principles and Argumentative Rules', in *A Commitment to Private international law. Essays in Honour of Hans Van Loon* (Intersentia 2013) 169 *et seq*, with further references). In addition, the Rome Convention provides the genetic criteria of interpretation, which means the Explanatory Report of the Convention (also known as Giuliano-Lagarde Report (Report on the Convention on the law applicable to contractual obligations by Mario Giuliano, Professor, University of Milan, and Paul Lagarde, Professor, University of Paris I, [1980] OJ C 282/1)), alongside the Commission's Proposal of 15 December 2005 (Proposal for a Regulation of the European Parliament and the Council on the law applicable to contractual obligations (Rome I), COM(2005) 650 final) and the Green Paper on the Conversion of the Rome Convention into a Community instrument (Green paper on the conversion of the Rome Convention of 1980 on the law applicable to contractual obligations into a Community instrument and its modernisation, COM(2002) 654 final) remain highly useful documents for interpreting the Regulation (on the interpretation of the Rome I Regulation, see in general Gralf-Peter Calliess (ed), *Rome Regulations: Commentary on the European Rules of the Conflict of Laws* (Kluwer Law International 2011) 11–14; Dieter Martiny, 'Vor Art 1 Rom I-VO' in J Säcker, R Rixecker and H Oetker (ed), *Münchener Kommentar zum Bürgerlichen Gesetzbuch* (5th edn, CH Beck 2010) paras 14–15; Richard Plender and Michael Wilderspin, *The European Private international law of Obligations* (3rd edn, Sweet & Maxwell 2009) 433–461).

II. Scope of application

The scope of application of the Rome I Regulation can be defined in the following terms. The Regulation determines the law applicable to contractual obligations in civil and commercial matters (see below 1.) with universal character (see below 2.). Furthermore, it applies only to situations involving a conflict of laws (see below 3.), but gives preference to existing international conventions and other EU instruments (see below 4.).

1. Sphere of substantive application

The Rome I Regulation determines the law applicable to contractual obligations in civil and commercial matters (art 1(1)). The concept of → civil and commercial matters is an autonomous concept, whose meaning must be uniform and independent of the national laws of Member States. In this regard, the ECJ has specified some of the aspects of that term in the context of the Brussels I Regulation, which must be taken into account when applying the Rome I Regulation. In particular, the Regulation does not apply when a public authority is acting in the exercise of its public powers and the case derives from that act (see eg Case C-49/12 *The Commissioners for Her Majesty's Revenue & Customs v Sunico ApS, M*

& B Holding ApS, Sunil Kumar Harwani [2013] OJ C 325/6). Hence, public contracts that meet this condition are excluded from the scope of the Rome I Regulation.

The term 'contractual obligations' is also an autonomous concept, and the ECJ's definition of this concept in the context of the Brussels I Regulation is equally relevant to the application of the Rome I Regulation. The ECJ has stated that contractual obligations, as opposed to non-contractual ones, are 'obligations freely consented to by one party towards another' (see eg Case C-147/12 *Östergötlands Fastigheter AB v Frank Koot, Evergreen Investments BV* [2013] OJ C 260/14). In other words, a contractual obligation arises where one party freely assumes towards another an obligation that otherwise would not exist (Ulrich Magnus, 'Anmerkungen zum sachlichen Anwendungsbereich der Rom I Verordnung' in Otto Sandrock and others (eds), *Festschrift für Gunther Kühne zum 70. Geburtstag* (Deutscher Fachverlag 2009) 779, 783). However, the Regulation contains a list of exclusions (art 1(2)). The Rome I Regulation does not apply, in particular: (i) to the status and legal capacity of natural persons (with the exception of art 13, which is aimed at protecting a party who believe in good faith believes himself to be making a contract with a person of full capacity in accordance to the local law; → Capacity and emancipation); (ii) to obligations arising from family relationships, → maintenance obligations, matrimonial property or wills and succession; (iii) to obligations arising from → bills of exchange, → cheques, promissory notes and other negotiable instruments to the extent that they arise out of their negotiable character (see also Recital (9)); (iv) to choice of law and arbitration agreements; (v) to questions governed by the law of → companies; (vi) to the external aspect of → agency contracts and representation; (vii) to the constitution of a → trust and the relationships between settlors, trustees and beneficiaries; and (viii) to certain collective → insurance contracts. → *Culpa in contrahendo* is also formally excluded. However, art 12 Rome II Regulation contains a cross-reference to the law governing the hypothetical contract, determined in accordance with the Rome I Regulation, as the relevant connecting factor for determining the law applicable to that issue.

2. Universal character

Like the Rome Convention, the Rome I Regulation has universal character (art 2). The law designated by its choice-of-law rules must be applied regardless of whether or not it is the law of a Member State. This means that the Regulation is applicable without any additional link to the EU if Member State courts are competent to hear a case. As a result, within its scope of application, the Regulation takes the place of the choice-of-law rules of the Member States.

3. International, European and domestic contracts

The Regulation applies to situations where there is a conflict of laws, ie contractual relationships that involve more than one legal system. While it does not define when a connection to a foreign legal system is sufficiently relevant to give rise to a conflict of laws, the Regulation nevertheless includes a rule specifically for those cases where the internationality of the relationship is purely based on the choice of the parties (art 3(3) and Recital (15)). The purpose of this provision is to prevent parties from internationalizing a domestic case merely by choosing a foreign law. Pursuant to that provision, where all other elements of the situation are located in one country other than the country whose law has been chosen, the choice is valid, but without prejudice to the application of the (internal) mandatory rules, ie the former country's rules that cannot be derogated from by agreement. Furthermore, the Regulation extends the same principle to harmonized sectors of EU law (art 3(4)). Where all the elements of the cases are located in two or more different Member States, choice by the parties of the law of a third state will not debar the application of the mandatory rules laid down by EU law. This prevents parties from 'evading' common EU standards by choosing the law of a third country (see Proposal for a Regulation of the European Parliament and the Council on the law applicable to contractual obligations (Rome I), COM(2005) 650 final, p 5). However, this provision has given rise to serious problems, since the application of EU mandatory rules does not usually require that all the elements be located within the EU (see Francisco Garcimartín, 'The Rome I Regulation: Much Ado about Nothing?' [2-2008] Eu.L.F. 1, 4). In addition, the Regulation expressly states that when the harmonized rules are contained in a Directive, which has no direct effect between private parties, the provisions of the forum Member State implementing the Directive will apply.

4. Relationship with other instruments

In its relationship with other instruments which contain choice-of-law rules, the Rome I Regulation distinguishes between international conventions and other provisions of EU law. On the one hand, the Rome I Regulation respects the pre-existing international conventions between Member States and third countries, such as the Hague Sales Convention (Hague Convention of 15 June 1955 on the law applicable to international sales of goods, 510 UNTS 147), but prevails over any conventions concluded exclusively between two or more Member States (art 25). In relation to other EU instruments, the Regulation is based on the *lex specialis* principle (art 23 and Recital (40)). The Rome I Regulation has no detrimental effects on the application of other EU instruments which for particular matters lay down conflict rules relating to contractual obligations. Legal literature has nevertheless pointed out the problems that may derive from the interplay between the Rome I Regulation and the Directives on consumer protection or a future optional instrument on contractual obligation (see eg Francisco Garcimartín, 'The Rome I Regulation: Much Ado about Nothing?' [2-2008] Eu.L.F. 1, 5–6; Eva-Maria Kieninger, 'Der grenzüberschreitende Verbrauchervertrag zwischen Richtlinienkollisionsrecht und Rome I-Verordnung' in Jan von Hein and others (eds), *Die richtige Ordnung. Festschrift für Jan Kropholler zum 70. Geburtstag* (Mohr Siebeck 2008) 499 *et seq*; Dieter Martiny, 'Neuanfang im Europäischen Internationalen Vertragsrecht mit der Rom I-Verordnung' [2010] ZEuP 747 *et seq*, 753 *et seq*; Sixto Sánchez-Lorenzo, 'Common European Sales Law and Private international law: Some Critical Remarks' [2013] J.P.I.L. 191 *et seq*).

III. Choice-of-law rules: structure

The Regulation maintains the same structure for the rules on choice of laws as the Rome Convention. This structure is based on three elements. First, it establishes a general framework which combines the principle of freedom of choice and a set of choice-of-law rules applicable by default, rooted in the principle of the proper law of the contract (arts 3–4). Second, it adds four special rules for situations where there is a need to protect one of the parties to the contract (arts 5–8). Third, it guarantees the protection of general or public interests by safeguarding the application of → overriding mandatory provisions (art 9).

IV. General rule: autonomy of the parties

The Regulation is based on the principle of freedom of choice, ie a contract will be governed by the law chosen by the parties (art 3). According to Recital (11), the parties' freedom to choose the applicable law is one of the cornerstones of the Regulation. It allows parties to select the legal system that is best tailored to their transactional needs (including a neutral law), promotes regulatory competition and also ensures certainty and predictability. The parties are absolutely free to choose any state law, so that no objective connection between the law chosen and their contractual relationship is required. The parties can also change the applicable law at any time (art 3(2)) and can choose different laws for different parts of the contract, ie *depeçage* is permitted (art 3(1) *in fine*). While they cannot choose a non-state law as *lex contractus*, the parties are allowed to incorporate by reference a non-state body of law or an international convention (see Recital (13)). This incorporation by reference is permissible within the limits of the domestic mandatory provisions of the state law applicable as *lex contractus*. It implies an exercise of substantive-law autonomy.

The regime applicable to the choice-of-law agreement is also flexible in a number of ways. No specific form is required. The choice of the parties can be either express or implied provided that the choice can be 'clearly demonstrated by the terms of the contract or the circumstances of the case' (art 3(1)). The court cannot decide on the basis of purely hypothetical or putative choices. Recital (12) specifies that an exclusive choice of court agreement is only one of the factors that the court must take into account when considering whether the parties have impliedly chosen the law governing their contract. Those aspects related to the validity of the consent of the parties to the choice-of-law agreement are to be determined by the national law designated by arts 10, 11 and 13 of the Regulation (art 3(5)).

V. Default rules

1. Introduction

In the absence of a choice-of-law agreement, the Regulation establishes a catalogue of types of contracts and sets out the applicable law for each one. This solution is intended to dispel the ambiguities that emerged from the parallel provision of the Rome Convention, and instead of fixing the principle of the closest connection as a starting point, the Regulation establishes a contractual typology (art 4(1); on the problems raised by the Rome Convention, see the Green Paper on the conversion of the Rome Convention of 1980 on the law applicable to contractual obligations into a Community instrument and its modernisation, COM(2002) 654 final, 25–26; Peter Mankowski, 'Die Ausweichklausel des Art. 4 V EVÜ und das System des EVÜ' [2003] IPRax 464 *et seq*; Richard Plender and Michael Wilderspin, *The European Private international law of Obligations* (3rd edn, Sweet & Maxwell 2009) 172–176). The Regulation then adds a solution for those contracts falling into none of the eight types of contract it identifies (art 4(2)). And finally the provision ends with an 'escape clause' based on the principle of closest connection (art 4(3)). This combination of rigid rules and escape clause seeks to achieve a balance between providing: (i) certainty and predictability to the parties; and (ii) the necessary discretion to adapt the solution to individual cases (see ECJ Case C-133/08 *Intercontainer Interfrigo SC (ICF) v Balkenende Oosthuizen BV and MIC Operations BV* [2009] ECR I-9687, para 59).

2. Contractual typology

The Regulation identifies the most common types of contract in practice and for each one designates the legal system in which it in principle has its 'centre of gravity' (though as regards franchise and distribution contracts, a particular policy of protection underlies the provision).

Specifically, the Regulation lays down a list of eight types of contract and the laws applicable to them, which can be summarized as follows: (i) contracts of sale of goods (→ Sale contracts and sale of goods) and contracts for provision of services are to be governed by the law of the country where the seller or the service provider has his habitual residence (art 4(1)(a)–(b)). Recital (17) clarifies that those terms should be interpreted in the same way as in art 5(1) Brussels I Regulation; (ii) contracts relating to a right *in rem* in immovable property (→ Property and proprietary rights) or to tenancy of immovable property (→ Lease contracts and tenancies) are to be governed by the law of the country where the property is located, unless these are tenancies concluded for temporary private use, which are governed by the national law of the landlord's habitual residence, provided that the tenant is a natural person and both parties have their habitual residence in the same country (art 4(1)(c)–(d); see art 22(1) Brussels I Regulation); (iii) franchise and distribution contracts are to be governed by the law of the country where the franchisee or the distributor have their habitual residence (art 4(1)(e)–(f)); and finally (iv) contracts of sale of goods by auction are to be governed by the law of the country where the action takes place and contracts concluded in organized financial markets, eg a stock exchange, by the law governing the market (art 4(1)(g)–(h); see also Recital (18)).

Contracts that fit into none of these categories, such as contracts relating to intellectual property rights, are to be governed by the law of the country where the party required to effect the characteristic performance of the contract has habitual residence. The same rule applies to contracts that are classifiable under more than one category (art 4(2)).

The Regulation includes a definition of the concept of habitual residence (→ Domicile, habitual residence and establishment). For legal persons, the habitual residence is the place of central administration, and for natural persons acting in the course of their business activities, the principal place of business (art 19(1)). Nevertheless, if the contract is concluded in the course of operations of a secondary establishment or if under the contract the performance is the responsibility of that establishment, then this establishment is to be considered to be the place of habitual residence (art 19(2)). The relevant date for determining the habitual residence location is the time of conclusion of the contract (art 19(3)). This implies that a movement of the habitual residence after the conclusion of the contract does not entail a change in the applicable law.

3. The principle of closest connection

The Regulation includes an 'escape clause' similar to that in the Rome II Regulation, under which, where it is clear from all the circumstances of the case that the contract is manifestly more closely connected to a country other than that indicated in any of the rules listed above, the law of that country will apply (art 4(3)). This escape clause provides the rule with some flexibility in order to avoid inappropriate results in particular cases from a conflict-of-laws perspective. However, the expressions 'it is clear' and 'manifestly' are intended to convey the idea that the application of this clause should be restricted to exceptional cases (see eg and with further references Martin Gebauer in Gralf-Peter Calliess (ed), *Rome Regulations: Commentary on the European Rules of the Conflict of Laws* (Kluwer Law International, 2011) 98–99; or Stefan Leible, 'Artikel 4 Rom I' in Rainer Hüßtege and Heinz-Peter Mansel, *Rom-Verordnungen* (Nomos 2014) paras 70–78). In practice, the provision should work as a rebuttable presumption in a strong sense, in that the law applicable to the contract is that designated by paragraphs 1 and 2 of art 4, unless the court is clearly convinced that the contract is manifestly more closely connected to a different country.

Furthermore, the Regulation also retains the closest connection principle to determine the law applicable to those contracts involving mutual performance by the parties in terms that qualify as characteristic on both sides, such as barter contracts (art 4(4)).

In both cases, the application of the closest connection principle calls for the court to: (i) take into account all the circumstances of the case; (ii) identify the connections of the contract with the different countries; and (iii) balance these connections under the general principles of contract law and, in particular, the parties' reasonable expectations (see Dieter Martiny, 'Art 4 Rom I-VO' in J Säcker, R Rixecker and H Oetker (eds), *Münchener Kommentar zum Bürgerlichen Gesetzbuch* (5th edn, CH Beck 2010) paras 14–15, 245 *et seq*; Stefan Leible, 'Artikel 4 Rom I' in Rainer Hüßtege and Heinz-Peter Mansel, *Rom-Verordnungen* (Nomos 2014) paras 79–80; see also ECJ Case C-133/08 *Intercontainer Interfrigo SC (ICF) v Balkenende Oosthuizen BV and MIC Operations BV* [2009] ECR I-9687, paras 60–63). Recital (21) *in fine* clarifies that when applying this clause, courts shall, among other circumstances, take into account whether the contract in question has a close relationship with another contract or contracts.

VI. Special rules: protection of the weaker party

The Rome I Regulation envisages special rules for certain categories of contracts: transport contracts (art 5), consumer contracts (art 6), insurance contracts (art 7) and employment contracts (art 8). Leaving aside contracts for the carriage of goods (art 5(1)), the rest of the provisions deal with situations characterized by an inequality of bargaining power between the parties. All the provisions have two features in common, in that, first, they limit albeit by different means the parties' freedom to choose the applicable law and, second, they designate as the law applicable by default a law close to the weaker party. The first feature reduces the risk of abuse by the more sophisticated party at the expense of their counterparty, either by applying the principle of more favourable law (arts 6 and 8) or by limiting the menu of eligible laws (arts 5 and 7). Absent a → choice of law, the application of a law close to the weaker party protects his legitimate expectations and reduces their cost of access to justice. The economic rationale behind these rules is the existence of a market failure, in that due to the asymmetric position of the parties in certain categories of contract, the freedom of choice may not produce an efficient outcome (see Giesela Rühl, 'Consumer Protection in Choice of Law' (2011) 44 Cornell Int'l L.J. 569 *et seq*). This policy is particularly relevant in the areas of consumer and employment contracts.

1. Consumer contracts

The special rule for → consumer contracts is contained in art 6 of the Regulation. This provision is based on the 'principle of most favourable law', ie a choice of law in a consumer contract is valid, but may not deprive the consumer of the protection afforded to him by the law applicable by default. As regards the Rome Convention, the Regulation extends the material scope of application of the rule and clarifies the definition of 'passive consumer'. These elements are taken from art 17 Brussels I Regulation.

The scope of application of this rule is defined by a material element in that it applies only to consumer contracts, and by a territorial element in that it protects only the so-called 'passive or sedentary consumers'. Those consumer contracts that fail to meet these conditions are governed by the general rules, ie arts 3 and 4.

Article 6 applies to any contract regardless of its object. The only relevant element is subjective, in that one of the parties must be a professional and the other a 'natural' person acting outside his trade or profession, ie a consumer. The provision therefore includes b2c and, arguably, c2b contracts, but not c2c contracts. The expression 'for the purpose that can be regarded as being outside his trade or profession' derives from the Rome Convention and is intended to protect the reasonable expectations of the professional. If a natural person, albeit acting for a private purpose, holds himself out as the professional, the good faith of the other party is protected and the case will not be governed by art 6 (see Report on the Convention on the law applicable to contractual obligations by Mario Giuliano, Professor, University of Milan, and Paul Lagarde, Professor, University of Paris I, [1980] OJ C 282/1, Commentary to art 5). However, the Regulation contains a list of exclusions (art 6(2)) related to contracts for the supply of services where a service is supplied exclusively in a country other than that in which the consumer has his habitual residence (typical examples, accommodation in a hotel or a language course), contracts of carriage, contracts for → immovable property, → financial instruments and financial markets.

Within that material scope, art 6 Rome I Regulation protects only the so-called 'passive consumer', ie those cases where rather than the consumer going to the professional's market, the professional goes or directs his activities to the consumer's market. The key element is the 'targeted activity criterion' (see elaborating this idea and with further references Peter Mankowski, 'Consumer Contracts under Article 6 of the Rome I Regulation' in Eleanor Cashin Ritaine and Andreas Bonomi (eds), *Le nouveau règlement européen Rome I relatif à la loi applicable aux obligations contractuelles* (Schulthess Verlag 2008) 121, 125–138). Following the formulation of art 17 Brussels I Regulation, the provision foresees two hypotheses. The first hypothesis is where the professional pursues his commercial or professional activities in the country of the consumer's habitual residence and the contract falls within the scope of such activities (art 6(1)(a)). The residence condition is highly relevant to understand the precise scope of this provision (see Recital (25)). A typical case would be when the professional has a branch or establishment in the consumer's country of habitual residence and the contract is concluded in or through this particular establishment. However, it does not hold where the contract is concluded in a different country, for instance, in the course of a journey by the consumer, even if the professional also has a branch in the country of the consumer's habitual residence. In such a case, it cannot be said that the contract was concluded in the framework of the particular activities that the professional is carrying out in the consumer's country. The second hypothesis is where the professional, by any means, directs such activities to the consumer's country of habitual residence, or to several countries including that country, and the contract falls within the scope of such activities (art 6(1)(b)). The typical fact pattern here is that the professional has no branch in the consumer's country, but directs his activities to that country and the contract is concluded at a distance or in person following a specific invitation addressed to the consumer or consumers of that country (ie under the framework of these activities). The concept of 'directs its activities' is defined in Recital (24) Rome I Regulation by a reference to the Brussels I Regulation. It states that 'the mere fact that an internet site is accessible is not sufficient ... although a fact will be that this internet site solicits the conclusion of distance contracts and that a contract has actually been concluded at a distance, by whatever means. In this respect, the language or currency which a website uses does not constitute a relevant factor' (for the application of this provision, ECJ case-law in the context of the Brussels I Regulation must be taken into account; see eg Joined Cases C-585/08 and C-144/09 *Peter Pammer v Reederei Karl Schlüter GmbH & Co KG* (C-585/08) and *Hotel Alpenhof GesmbH v Oliver Heller* (C-144/09) [2010] ECR I-12527; Case C-190/11 *Daniela Mühlleitner v Ahmad Yusufi and Wadat Yusufi* (6 September 2012); C-218/12 *Lokman Emrek v Vlado Sabranovic* [2013] OJ C 367/14).

Provided those circumstances are met, the law applicable absent a choice of law is the law of the country of the consumer's habitual residence. Conversely, if the parties have included a choice-of-law clause, then the law applicable is that chosen by the parties, although this may not result in depriving the consumer of the protection afforded by such legal provisions applicable by default that cannot be derogated from by contract (art 6(2)). Thus, the law of the country of the consumer's habitual residence sets the minimum protection standard.

Francisco Garcimartín Alférez

2. Employment contracts

For individual employment contracts, the Rome I Regulation follows the same approach as for consumer contracts, ie the most favourable law principle. The parties can choose the applicable law according to art 3. However, the application of the chosen law may not have the result of depriving the employee of the protection afforded by the mandatory rules of the law applicable by default, ie absent choice (art 8(1)). Party autonomy works only in favour of the weaker party. Naturally the comparison is made between the content of the law chosen by the parties and the mandatory rules, ie the rules that cannot be derogated from by contract, of the law applicable had the parties not made a choice.

The law applicable by default is the *lex loci laboris*, namely, the law of the country 'in which' or, failing that, 'from which' the employee habitually carries out their work in performance of the contract (art 8(2)). Following the ECJ case-law on art 21 Brussels I Regulation, the expression 'from which' has been introduced for employees who do not carry out their job in the territory of only one country, but where there is a country which constitutes a form of 'base of operations', such as in the case of employees who work on aircraft. Here, the law of the country which serves as a base for the worker is to be considered as *lex loci laboris* (see ECJ Case C-29/10 *Heiko Koelzsch v État du Grand-Duché de Luxembourg* [2011] ECR I-1595; Case C-384/10 *Jan Voogsgeerd v Navimer SA* [2012] OJ C 39/4). Furthermore, the provision clarifies that the country where the employee habitually works is not deemed to have changed merely because he (the employee) is temporarily posted to another country (art 8(2) *in fine*). This clarification also derives from ECJ case-law in the context of the Brussels I Regulation (Case C-437/00 *Giulia Pugliese v Finmeccanica SpA, Betriebsteil Alenia Aerospazio* [2003] ECR I-3573). Recital (36) points out that the concept of 'temporarily posted' has to be interpreted in a subjective *ex ante* manner (if the employee 'is expected' to resume working in the country of origin after carrying out his task abroad) and echoes the idea that the mere conclusion of a new contract with the original employer or with another employer belonging to the same group of companies should not mean that the employee is not temporarily posted to another country. The formula is sufficiently flexible to allow courts to adapt it to different work environments.

If according to these rules the employee cannot be considered as habitually carrying out his work in a country, then the contract is governed by the law of the country where the establishment through which the employee was engaged is situated (art 8(3)). Finally, the provision ends with an escape clause whereby if it appears from the circumstances as a whole that the contract is most closely connected to a country other than that indicated according to the above-mentioned rules, then the law of that country will apply. The wording of this clause is more flexible than for the escape clause contained in art 4(3) (above), as there is no repetition of the adverbs 'clear' and 'manifestly'. The intention was to give the courts greater leeway in areas of employment contracts, where the interests at stake may be different than in those contracts subject to the general rule of art 4 (see ECJ Case C-64/12 *Anton Schlecker v Melitta Josefa Boedeker* (12 September 2013)).

VII. Overriding mandatory provisions

The protection of general or public interests is guaranteed by art 9 Rome I Regulation. This provision deals with → overriding mandatory provisions. Unlike the Rome Convention, the Regulation incorporates a definition of this concept, the purpose of which is to reduce the scope of art 9 and therefore to minimize the risks that courts could invoke this clause to frustrate the general application of the conflict-of-law rules of the Regulation. Article 9 Rome I Regulation encompasses only 'ordo-political rules' or *Eingriffsrechte*, ie it can only be invoked when 'public policy interests' are at stake. Hence, 'overriding mandatory rules' are defined as those provisions the respect for which is regarded as crucial by a country for safeguarding its public interests, such as its political, social or economic organization, to such an extent that they are applicable to any situation falling within their scope, irrespective of the law otherwise applicable to the contract under this Regulation. This definition is inspired by the ECJ judgment in the *Arblade* case (see ECJ Joined Cases C-369/96 and C-376/96 *Criminal Proceedings against Jean-Claude Arblade and Arblade & Fils SARL* and *Bernard Leloup, Serge Leloup and Sofrage SARL* [1999] ECR I-8453; also Case C-184/12 *United Antwerp Maritime Agencies (UNAMAR)*

NV v Navigation Maritime Bulgare [2013] OJ C 367/12).

Following the scheme of the Convention, art 9 Rome I Regulation distinguishes between overriding mandatory rules of the forum and overriding mandatory rules of third countries. On the one hand, overriding mandatory rules of the forum state apply irrespective of the law governing the contract. According to art 9(1), 'nothing in this Regulation shall restrict the application of the overriding mandatory provisions of the law of the forum'. On the other hand, the Regulation also foresees the possibility of giving effect to the overriding mandatory provisions of a third country as a faculty of the court ('effects may be given'). Nevertheless, unlike the Convention, the new text limits the catalogue of mandatory rules that can be considered. First, not all rules can be considered, but only those of 'the country where the obligations arising out of the contract have to be or have been performed' and, second, only 'insofar as these overriding mandatory provisions render the performance of the contract unlawful'. These two specifications were considered necessary to reduce the uncertainty associated with the formula adopted in the Rome Convention. The material criteria that a court has to take into account to make a decision on this issue is the same in both texts, whereby 'regard shall be had to their nature and purpose and to the consequences of their application or non-application'.

VIII. Scope of the applicable law

The Regulation contains rules defining the scope of application of the *lex contractus* (art 12) and special connections for particular issues: the material validity of the contract or of any of its terms, including consent (art 10), formal validity (art 11), capacity (art 13) and → burden of proof (art 18). Furthermore, it clarifies the law applicable in tri-party situations: voluntary assignment and contractual subrogation (art 14), legal subrogation (art 15) and multiple debtors (art 16). It also contains a rule on the law applicable to → set-off rights (art 17).

IX. Final clauses

Finally, the Regulation includes three clauses on general problems for the application of conflict rules, namely the exception of public policy (art 21), the clarification of its application to multi-unit states (art 22) and the exclusion of → *renvoi* (art 20). In the provision on *renvoi*, a sentence has been added to ensure consistency with one of the choice-of-law rules on insurance contracts (art 7(3)).

X. Conclusion

The Rome I Regulation converted the Rome Convention on the law applicable to contractual obligations into an EU instrument. In addition to the change of legal nature, it introduced important amendments to the original text. Together with the Rome II Regulation and the Brussels I Regulation, this instrument constitutes the backbone of the EU private international law and therefore provides an effective legal framework to ensure the smooth functioning of the EU market.

FRANCISCO GARCIMARTÍN ALFÉREZ

Literature

Alexander J Belohlávek, *Rome Convention. Rome I Regulation* (Juris Publishing 2010); Gralf-Peter Calliess (ed), *Rome Regulations: Commentary on the European Rules of the Conflict of Laws* (Kluwer Law International, 2011); Franco Ferrari and others, *Internationales Vertragsrecht* (CH Beck 2012); Francisco Garcimartín, 'The Rome I Regulation: Much Ado about Nothing?' [2-2008] Eu.L.F. 1 *et seq*; Francisco Garcimartín, 'Hermeneutic Dialogue between Rome I and Rome II: General Principles and Argumentative Rules' in Hague Conference on Private International Law (ed), *A Commitment to Private international law: Essays in Honour of Hans Van Loon* (Intersentia 2013) 169 *et seq*; Rainer Hüßtege and Heinz-Peter Mansel, *Rom-Verordnungen* (Nomos 2014); Eva-Maria Kieninger, 'Der grenzüberschreitende Verbrauchervertrag zwischen Richtlinienkollisionsrecht und Rome I-Verordnung' in Jan von Hein and others (eds), *Die richtige Ordnung. Festschrift für Jan Kropholler zum 70. Geburtstag* (Mohr Siebeck 2008) 499 *et seq*; Ulrich Magnus, 'Anmerkungen zum *sachlichen* Anwendungsbereich der Rom I Verordnung' in Otto Sandrock and others (eds), *Festschrift für Gunther Kühne zum 70. Geburtstag* (Deutscher Fachverlag 2009) 779 *et seq*; Peter Mankowski, 'Die Ausweichklausel des Art. 4 V EVÜ und das System des EVÜ' [2003] IPRax 464 *et seq*; Peter Mankowski, 'Consumer Contracts under Article 6 of the Rome I Regulation' in Eleanor Cashin Ritaine and Andreas Bonomi (eds), *Le nouveau règlement européen Rome I relatif à la loi applicable aux obligations contractuelles* (Schulthess Verlag 2008) 121 *et seq*; Dieter Martiny, 'Neuanfang im Europäischen Internationalen Vertragsrecht mit der Rom I-Verordnung' [2010]

ZEuP 747 et seq; Richard Plender and Michael Wilderspin, *The European Private international law of Obligations* (3rd edn, Sweet & Maxwell 2009); Christoph Reithmann and Dieter Martiny, *Internationales Vertragsrecht* (7th edn, Verlag Dr Otto Schmidt 2010); Giesela Rühl, 'Consumer Protection in Choice of Law' (2011) 44 Cornell Int'l L.J. 569 et seq; J Säcker, R Rixecker and H Oetker (eds), *Münchener Kommentar zum Bürgerlichen Gesetzbuch* (5th edn, CH Beck 2010); Sixto Sánchez-Lorenzo, 'Common European Sales Law and Private international law: Some Critical Remarks' [2013] *J.P.I.L.* 191 et seq; *J von Staudingers Kommentar zum Bürgerlichen Gesetzbuch: Staudinger BGB. Einleitung zur Rom I-VO* (14th edn, Sellier/De Gruyter 2011).

Rome II Regulation (non-contractual obligations)

I. Background and context

The Rome II Regulation was adopted on 11 July 2007 and applies to events giving rise to damage occurring on or after 11 January 2009 (Regulation (EC) No 864/2007 of the European Parliament and of the Council of 11 July 2007 on the law applicable to non-contractual obligations (Rome II), [2007] OJ L 199/40). Upon its adoption, it was rightly considered as an important missing piece in the EU's private international law jigsaw, a necessary complement to the Brussels I Regulation (Regulation (EC) No 44/2001 of 22 December 2000 on jurisdiction and the recognition and enforcement of judgments in civil and commercial matters, [2001] OJ L 12/1; now recast as Regulation (EU) No 1215/2012 of the European Parliament and of the Council of 12 December 2012 on jurisdiction and the recognition and enforcement of judgments in civil and commercial matters (recast), [2012] OJ L 351/1; → Brussels I (Convention and Regulation)) and the Rome Convention (Rome Convention on the law applicable to contractual obligations (consolidated version), [1998] OJ C 27/34; since superseded in 2008 by the Rome I Regulation (Regulation (EC) No 593/2008 of the European Parliament and of the Council of 11 July 2007 on the law applicable to contractual obligations (Rome II), [2008] OJ L 177/6; → Rome Convention and Rome I Regulation (contractual obligations)). It is a quirk of EU legislative jargon that the first of the two Regulations containing rules of applicable law for obligations generally should carry the higher Roman numeral.

The history of the Rome II Regulation can be traced back to 1967, at which time the Commission (prompted by the Benelux states, which already cooperated to a significant degree in private international law matters) invited the then six Member States to consider common action to harmonize conflict-of-laws rules. This invitation came during the latter stages of the negotiations under art 220 EEC Treaty (Treaty of 25 March 1957 establishing the European Economic Community, 294–298 UNTS; now the TFEU (Treaty on the Functioning of the European Union (consolidated version) [2012] OJ C 326/47), art 293), which resulted in the conclusion of the Brussels Convention (Brussels Convention of 27 September 1968 on jurisdiction and the enforcement of judgments in civil and commercial matters, [1972] OJ L 299/32, consolidated version, [1998] OJ C 27/1).

Despite lofty ambitions, the harmonization project moved slowly. Some progress was made in the area of the law applicable to contractual and non-contractual obligations, with a preliminary draft Convention and report being produced in 1972 by a working group headed by Professors *Mario Giuliano* and *Paul Lagarde* and *Mr van Sasse van Ysselt* of the Netherlands Ministry of Justice (Commission of the European Communities, 'Draft Convention on the Law Applicable to Contractual and Non-contractual Obligations' (1973) 21 Am.J.Comp.L. 587 et seq). In 1978, however, and following the accession to the EEC of → Denmark, → Ireland and the → United Kingdom, the group of experts decided for reasons of time to focus their work in the area of → contractual obligations. The fruit of their efforts was the Rome Convention (→ Rome Convention and Rome I Regulation (contractual obligations)), which was concluded in 1980.

The non-contractual aspect of the project would not be revived for nearly two decades, almost matching the slumbers of *Rip van Winkle*. Its reawakening was triggered by the entry into force in 1993 of the Treaty of Maastricht (Treaty on the European Union, signed at Maastricht on 7 February 1992, [1992] OJ C 191/1) creating a framework for wider cooperation in matters of civil justice. In 1996, the Council identified as among its priorities in this area the possibility of a

Convention on the law applicable to non-contractual obligations. Early work on a draft Convention was overtaken by the conclusion and entry into force of the Treaty of Amsterdam (Treaty amending the Treaty on European Union, signed at Amsterdam on 2 October 1997, [1997] OJ C 340/1), giving legislative competence to the EC in civil justice matters, including measures to promote the compatibility of conflict-of-laws rules insofar as necessary for the proper functioning of the Internal Market (EC Treaty, as amended following the Treaty of Amsterdam, arts 61 and 65). Grasping the initiative, the Commission prepared a Green Paper (which was never published, apparently due to internal disagreements between DGs) and preliminary draft proposal (published as a consultation document in 2002, Commission preliminary draft proposal for the Rome II Regulation (2002), available at <http://ec.europa.eu/justice>). A formal proposal for a Regulation followed on 22 July 2003 (Commission of the European Communities, 'Proposal for a Regulation of the European Parliament and the Council on the law applicable to non-contractual obligations ("Rome II")', COM(2003) 427 final).

The legislative process was prolonged and bumpy, with both the Council and (notably) the European Parliament proposing significant changes to the Commission's proposal, prompting an amended proposal by the Commission in February 2006 (Commission of the European Communities, 'Amended Proposal for European Parliament and Council Regulation on the law applicable to non-contractual obligations ("Rome II")', COM(2006) 83 final) and a series of 'trilogues' between the Commission, the Council and the European Parliament in an effort to resolve differences, in particular between the positions of the Member States in the Council and the Parliament. Although most of these issues were resolved in favour of the Council's position, the compromises reached at this stage have left their mark on the Regulation and, in particular, on its review clause (art 30).

The question of Community competence to adopt the Regulation was controversial during negotiations. The → United Kingdom, in particular, argued that the adoption of universally applicable rules for determining the law applicable to non-contractual obligations was not necessary for the proper functioning of the Internal Market and that some territorial restriction on the situations to which the Regulation's rules would apply was appropriate. Although that position was apparently supported by a legal opinion given by the Council's legal service (Opinion of the Council Legal Service on the proposal for a Regulation on the law applicable to non-contractual obligations ("ROME II") of 2 March 2004, 7015/04), the Commission, with the support of the vast majority of Member States, fiercely resisted limits of this kind. Its wish ultimately prevailed, and a challenge to the vires of the Regulation now appears a remote prospect given the broadening of EU competence in the area of justice by the Lisbon Treaty (see now art 81 TFEU).

II. Scope and structure

Four elements of the Regulation's scope merit further comment: the geographical, temporal and subject matter/material scope of the Regulation, and its interrelationship with international conflict-of-laws conventions and other EU instruments.

First, the Regulation applies in 27 of the 28 Member States of the EU, with the sole exception of → Denmark (Recital (40) and art 1(4)). It is to be applied by the courts and tribunals of those Member States, irrespective of their nature (Recital (8)). Although the Rome II Regulation has no explicit arbitration exception (cf art 1(2)(d) Brussels I Regulation), its provisions do not in all likelihood bind arbitral tribunals even where the seat of the arbitration is in a Member State because they are not tribunals *of* a Member State.

Second, as noted above, the Regulation applies only in cases where the event giving rise to damage (or equivalent event: art 2(1)) occurs after 11 January 2009, irrespective of when the damage (or equivalent) occurred or when proceedings were issued or judgment was given. After some initial doubts arising from the unclear drafting of arts 31 and 32 of the Regulation, this interpretation was adopted by the Court of Justice in Case C-412/10 *Deo Antoine Homawoo v GMF Assurances SA* [2011] ECR I-11603. It remains to be seen what solution will be adopted in more complex cases where the relevant conduct occurred both before and after this start date.

Third, subject to a number of listed exceptions (see below), the Regulation applies: (a) in situations involving a conflict of laws; (b) to non-contractual obligations; and (c) in → civil and commercial matters (art 1(1)). Requirement (a) seems unlikely to present any difficulties: if the circumstances are such that a question as to whether there is a conflict of laws needs to be asked, a positive answer will invariably follow. Certainly, the Regulation does not require connections to two or more Member States in order to apply. Requirement (c) is a familiar one in the EU private international law instruments and will fall to be answered in line with the principles developed by the CJEU (→ Court of Justice of the European Union) in relation to the corresponding provisions in the Brussels Convention and the Brussels I Regulation (see Recital (7) Rome II Regulation), excluding from its scope only those cases where the claim is founded upon the exercise of public powers by a public authority or its representative (→ Brussels I (Convention and Regulation)). Article 1(1) specifically excludes from the Regulation's scope revenue, customs and administrative matters, and the liability of the state for acts and omissions in the exercise of state authority (*acta iure imperii*). These appear to be clarifications, for the avoidance of doubt, rather than additional restrictions on the category of → civil and commercial matters.

Much greater difficulty flows from requirement (b), the concept of a non-contractual obligation with which the Regulation concerns itself. The concept has positive and negative elements. On the one hand, it has a binary relationship with that of contractual obligation used in the Rome I Regulation. The two concepts are to be understood autonomously and consistently with one another (Recitals (7) and (11) Rome II Regulation; Recital (7) Rome I Regulation). If, therefore, an obligation is properly classified as contractual in nature, it will automatically fall outside the material scope of the Rome II Regulation.

However, that is not to say that the same factual situation cannot give rise to both contractual and non-contractual obligations – the parties to an arrangement which is obviously contractual and gives rise to contractual obligations will, at the same time, owe each other obligations which are properly classified as non-contractual. This, of course, begs the critical question where the line is to be drawn, and the two Regulations provide only limited guidance as to how that question is to be answered. In many cases, of course, the answer will be obvious, but more difficult cases arise at the borderline, when there is a contract or other voluntary relationship between the parties, but the obligation which forms the basis of proceedings is imposed on the person claimed to be liable by a legal rule which defines the content of the obligation otherwise than by reference to the parties' intentions. How, for example, are statutory duties imposed on an employer to ensure the safety of his employees, or not to discriminate against them, to be classified? What about the high standards of legal responsibility imposed on those who take on positions which may be described as fiduciary in character? Can careless, damage causing conduct in the performance of a contract generate liability for breach of concurrent contractual and non-contractual (tortious) obligations?

It is to be expected that the CJEU will be called upon in questions of this kind in the not too distant future. In answering those questions, while noting the difference in wording between the instruments, the Court will look to its case-law concerning the definition of 'matters relating to a contract' in art 5(1) Brussels Convention and the Brussels I Regulation (Joined Cases C-359/14 etc, *Ergo Insurance SE v If P&C Insurance AS* [2016] ECLI:EU:C:2016:40, para 43). In that case-law, the Court has frequently deployed the notion of obligations freely assumed, accepted or consented to (see eg Case C-419/11 *Česká spořitelna, as v Gerald Feichter* [2013] ECLI:EU:C:2013:165, paras 46–49). In a recent case, in which the existence of a contractual relationship between the parties was undisputed, the Court chose to focus, albeit rather too cryptically, on the question whether the legal basis of the claimant's claim could reasonably be regarded as asserting a breach of the rights and obligations of that contract, including within this category of 'matters relating to a contract' a case in which the interpretation of the contract was indispensable to establishing the lawful or unlawful nature of the defendant's conduct, irrespective of the classification of the claim under national law (Case C-548/12 *Marc Brogsitter v Fabrication de Montres Normandes EURL, Karsten Fräßdorf* [2014] ECLI:EU:C:2014:148, paras 24–26).

At least three possible general approaches to this problem of characterization may be suggested. Most narrowly, the Court could insist that the content of the obligation in question has been freely accepted, being derived from the parties' expression of their contractual intention (Joined Cases C-359/14 etc, *Ergo*

Insurance SE v If P&C Insurance AS [2016] ECLI:EU:C:2016:40, para 44), such that terms and other duties whose content is dictated by a legal rule (including eg terms implied as a matter of law) could be classified as involving a non-contractual obligation. At the other end, the Court could treat as contractual not only obligations 'freely assumed' in the narrow sense just described but also other legal obligations arising between the same parties and which have a direct link to their 'contractual' relationship. A more nuanced approach between these two positions would be to ask whether the obligation in question is one which arises as an incident of, or is closely dependent on, a 'contractual' relationship, or (viewed in the other direction) whether the existence of such a relationship is an *essential* prerequisite for the existence of an obligation of that type. This intermediate solution may be more readily supportable on teleological grounds, as it will not withdraw from the Rome II Regulation obligations which, although connected to a contract, raise issues of a kind that are better dealt with by rules targeted at non-contractual obligations, for example, those concerning the scope of the applicable law and → direct actions against insurers (arts 15 and 18 Rome II Regulation).

The positive aspect of the concept of non-contractual obligation in the Rome II Regulation must also be noted (Joined Cases C-359/14 etc, *Ergo Insurance SE v If P&C Insurance AS* [2016] ECLI:EU:C:2016:40, para 45). The Regulation's rules of applicable law, described in section III. below, cover only non-contractual obligations arising out of tort/delict (arts 5–9), unjust enrichment (art 10), unauthorized intervention in the affairs of another (→ *negotiorum gestio*) (art 11) and pre-contractual dealings (*culpa in contrahendo*) (art 12). There is no residual sweep-up rule for other non-contractual obligations, for example, customary or statutory payment obligations attached to the ownership of property (→ Property and proprietary rights).

Article 1(2) Rome II Regulation specifically excludes from its scope non-contractual obligations in the areas of: (a) family relationships and relationships deemed to have comparable effect; (b) matrimonial property (and comparable) regimes, wills and → succession; (c) → bills of exchange, → cheques and promissory notes and (to a more limited extent) other negotiable instruments; (d) the law of → companies and other bodies corporate; (e) voluntarily created trusts; (f) nuclear damage (→ Nuclear liability); and (g) violations of privacy and rights relating to personality, including defamation. The latter exclusion was particularly controversial during the passage of the Regulation and is specifically addressed in the review clause (art 31(2)). The European Parliament has since adopted a resolution advocating the introduction of a special rule for defamation and privacy cases (European Parliament Resolution of 10 May 2012 with recommendations to the Commission on the amendment of Regulation (EC) No 864/2007 on the law applicable to non-contractual obligations (Rome II) (2009/2170(INI)) [2013] OJ C 261 E/17). The separate carve-out of matters of evidence and procedure (art 1(3)) will be returned to below (see section III.11.).

Fourth, according to art 28(1), the Regulation is not to prejudice the application by Member States of pre-existing international Conventions which lay down conflict-of-law rules relating to non-contractual obligations. An indicative list of these Conventions is to be found in the Official Journal of the European Communities (Notifications under Article 29(1) of Regulation (EC) No 864/2007 on the law applicable to non-contractual obligations (Rome II) [2010] OJ C 343/7). Those having the most significant (and potentially prejudicial – see art 30(1)(ii)) effect upon the application of the Regulation would appear to be the Hague Traffic Accidents Convention (→ Traffic accidents), with 13 Member States parties, and the Hague Products Liability Convention (Hague Convention of 2 October 1973 on the law applicable to products liability 1056 UNTS 191) (→ Products liability), with seven Member States parties. The substantive provisions of international Conventions, which are not addressed in art 28, may take effect as → overriding mandatory provisions (see below, section III.13.).

According to art 27, the Regulation also takes effect subject to EU legislative instruments containing conflict-of-laws rules relating to non-contractual obligations. Recital (27) addresses, more generally, the relationship with Internal Market instruments such as the e-Commerce Directive (Directive 2000/31/EC of the European Parliament and of the Council of 8 June 2000 on certain legal aspects of information society services, in particular electronic commerce, in the Internal Market (Directive on electronic commerce) [2000] OJ L178/1; see Joined Cases C-509/09 and C-161/10 *eDate Advertising GmbH v X (C-509/09) and Oliver Martinez and Robert Martinez v MGN Ltd* [2011] ECR I-10629) (→ Electronic commerce).

ANDREW DICKINSON

The Regulation is to be interpreted in the same way as other EU legislative instruments, having regard to the legislative text in various different languages, the objectives appearing from its Recitals and general principles of EU law (→ Interpretation, autonomous). In Case C-412/10 *Deo Antoine Homawoo v GMF Assurances SA* [2011] ECR I-11603, the ECJ drew particular attention to Recitals (6), (13), (14) and (16). The latter Recital, drawing attention to the twin objectives of enhancing the foreseeability of court decisions and ensuring a reasonable balance between the interests of the person claimed to be liable and the person who has sustained damage, may prove to be especially influential (see Case C-350/14 *Lazar v Allianz SpA* [2015] ECLI:EU:C:2015:802, para 23). Recital (7), which refers to the need for consistency between the substantive scope and provisions of the Brussels I, Rome I and Rome II Regulations, will also likely prove significant (Joined Cases C-359/14 etc, *Ergo Insurance SE v If P&C Insurance AS* [2016] ECLI:EU:C:2016:40, para 43). Finally, attention must be paid to the specific definitions in art 2 (damage, event giving rise to damage) and art 23 (habitual residence of companies and other bodies corporate or unincorporated, and of natural persons acting in the course of a business) (see below, section III.1.).

The rules of applicable law in the Rome II Regulation are divided into three chapters: Chapter II concerns non-contractual obligations arising out of a tort/delict, Chapter III concerns non-contractual obligations arising out of unjust enrichment (→ Unjust enrichment (restitution)), → *negotiorum gestio* and → *culpa in contrahendo*, and Chapter IV allows the parties in certain cases to choose the law applicable to non-contractual obligations. Chapters V and VI of the Regulation contain rules common to all non-contractual obligations within its scope, including provisions concerning the scope of the law applicable (art 15), the forum's overriding mandatory provisions (art 16) and public policy (art 26), rules of safety and conduct (art 17), direct actions against insurers (art 18), subrogation (art 19), multiple liability (art 20), formal validity (art 21) and → burden of proof (art 22), the definition of habitual residence (art 23), the exclusion of *renvoi* (art 24), states with more than one legal system (art 25) and the Regulation's relationship with conflict-of-laws rules in other EU legislative instruments (art 27) and international conventions (art 28).

III. Content

The Regulation's rules of applicable law apply whether the law that they specify is the law of a Member State or the law of a non-Member State (art 3). They only permit the application of the law of a country (ie a territorial unit of a state having its own rules of law in respect of non-contractual obligations: art 25(1)) and not non-state rules of law. The doctrine of *renvoi* is excluded – reference to the law of a country means its rules of law rather than its rules of private international law (art 24).

The cornerstone of the Regulation is art 4 (see below, section III.1.), which contains a general rule for determining the law applicable to non-contractual obligations arising out of a tort/delict. It is suggested that this concept of a 'tort/delict' is to be understood as including obligations which are not contractual (see above, section II.) and which seek to establish the defendant's responsibility for the (adverse) consequences of a particular act (whether his own or another's) or other event (see arts 2(1), 4(1), 15(f) and 15(g)). It includes cases of strict liability (Recital (11)).

As its opening words make clear, art 4 does not apply if the non-contractual obligation in question falls within another, special rule in the Regulation. This requires account to be taken not only of the specific rules (Recital (19)) for particular kinds of tort/delict in arts 5–9 (product liability, competition matters, environmental damage, infringement of intellectual property rights and industrial action), but also the provision for non-contractual obligations arising out of dealings prior to the conclusion of a contract (→ *Culpa in contrahendo*) in art 12 (see below, sections III.2., III.6. and III.9.). The other two categories of non-contractual obligation dealt with in arts 10–11 (unjust enrichment and *negotiorum gestio*) (see below, sections III.7–8.) appear largely distinct and unlikely to affect the material scope of art 4.

1. *General rule for tort/delict*

Article 4 (see Recitals (16)–(18)) consists of a basic rule (art 4(1)), and two rules of displacement (art 4(2) and (3)). The rules must be applied in sequence.

First, under art 4(1), the law generally applicable is that of the country in which damage occurs, irrespective of the country in which the event giving rise to the damage occurred and irrespective of the country or countries in which the indirect consequences of that event occur. This formulation is inspired by the case-law of the ECJ in relation to art 5(3) Brussels Convention, originating in Case 21/76 *Handelskwekerij GJ Bier BV v Mines de potasse d'Alsace SA* [1976] ECR 1735. As that case-law and the qualifications in the text of art 4(1) make clear, the rule points to the law of the country in which the direct consequences of the relevant act or event for which the defendant is claimed to be responsible occurred, and not that of the place of acting or the place where the claimant is adversely affected in a way which merely reflects that suffered by the direct victim (Case C-220/88 *Dumez France SA and Tracoba SARL v Hessische Landesbank and Others* [1990] ECR I-49) or which is merely consequential upon the initial damage suffered by the claimant elsewhere (Case C-364/93 *Antonio Marinari v Lloyd's Bank plc and Zubaidi Trading Company* [1995] ECR I-2719). In cases of personal injury or damage to property, the country in which the damage occurs should be that where the personal injury was sustained by the immediate victim or the property damaged (Recital (17); Case C-350/14 *Lazar v Allianz SpA* [2015] ECLI:EU:C:2015:802). Needless to say, the direct damage will be more difficult to locate in cases of financial injury. Here it will be necessary for the court to isolate and locate one or more facts among the consequences of the event giving rise to the claim (see art 2(1)). The objectives of the Regulation, of enhancing the foreseeability of court decisions and ensuring a reasonable balance between the interests of the person claimed to be liable and the person who has sustained damage (Recital (16)), suggest that the fact (or facts) identified as constituting the relevant 'damage' must both be significant in the context of a tort/delict of that kind and have an outward (objective) manifestation, being reasonably ascertainable at the time of the events in question and subsequently. If relevant damage occurs in more than one country, it appears that the laws of those countries must, so far as possible, be applied cumulatively according to the principle known as *Mosaikbetrachtung*, although the courts may strive to avoid this conclusion (Case C-350/14 *Lazar v Allianz SpA* [2015] ECLI:EU:C:2015:802, para 29). The detailed application of this principle, particularly in cases where non-monetary relief is sought, is unclear.

Second, under art 4(2), where the person claimed to be liable and the person sustaining damage both have their habitual residence in the same country at the time when the damage occurs, the law of that country shall apply. The concept of habitual residence is to be understood, in the case of corporate and unincorporated bodies and of natural persons acting in the course of a business activity, in accordance with the definition in art 23. For a corporate etc body, the relevant place will be that of its central administration unless the event giving rise to damage occurs in the course of operation of a particular branch, agency or other establishment, in which case the relevant place will be that of the branch, etc (art 23(1)). For natural persons engaging in business activity, the relevant place will be that of the principal place of business (art 23(2)). The habitual residence of natural persons acting otherwise than in the course of business is not defined, and will need to be shaped by national courts and the ECJ, having regard to the meaning given to the concept elsewhere in EU law. A sensible starting point would be to look to the country in which the interests of a person are permanently or habitually centred. The rule of displacement in art 4(2) applies only if there is commonality in the habitual residence of the person claimed to be liable and the person sustaining damage at the time when the damage (understood as that referred to in art 4(1)) occurred.

A number of unanswered questions remain. First, is the person claimed to be liable: (a) the named defendant; (b) the person claimed to be legally responsible for the damage; or (c) another person (eg an employee) whose conduct gives rise to the claim? Option (b) seems the best fit with the terminology used (see also art 15(g)). Second, is the person sustaining damage: (a) the claimant; (b) the person sustaining the damage in respect of which the claim is brought; or (c) the person sustaining the direct damage, if different? Option (c) seems the more likely here (see arts 4(1) and 15(f)). Third, how does the rule apply where there are many persons claimed to be liable or sustaining damage? Here, the better view, which avoids tactical decisions on joinder affecting the law ultimately applicable, is that art 4(2) should be applied between each pair of parties by analogy with the approach taken to → *lis alibi pendens* in the Brussels Convention and Brussels I Regulation (Case C-406/92 *The Owners of the Cargo Lately Laden on Board the Ship 'Tatry' v The Owners of the Ship 'Maciej Rataj'* [1994] ECR I-5439).

ANDREW DICKINSON

Third, art 4(3) contains an 'escape clause' (Recital (18)) which applies where it is clear from all the circumstances of the case that the tort/delict is manifestly more closely connected with a country other than that to which art 4(1) or 4(2), as applicable, refers. In such a case, the law of that other country shall apply. A manifestly closer connection with another country might be based in particular on a pre-existing relationship between the parties, such as a contract, that is closely connected with the tort/delict in question, but art 4(3) is not limited to cases of this kind. The language used suggests that there must be a clear preponderance, in terms of their overall significance, of the factors linking the tort/delict to another country, when compared to the factors linking the tort/delict to the country whose law applies under art 4(1) or 4(2).

The Hague Traffic Accident Convention (Hague Convention of 4 May 1971 on the law applicable to traffic accidents 965 UNTS 415) and not the Rome II Regulation will apply in Member States party to that Convention (→ Traffic accidents).

2. Product liability

Article 5 (see Recital (20)) concerns non-contractual obligations arising out of damage caused by a product (→ Products liability). For these purposes, 'product' means, most obviously, a tangible movable (cf art 2 Products Liability Directive (Council Directive 85/374/EEC of 25 July 1985 on the approximation of the laws, regulations and administrative provisions of the Member States concerning liability for defective products [1985] OJ L 210/29)). This provision includes, but is apparently not limited to, defective product claims (cf the Spanish and Portuguese texts). In contrast with the Directive, it is not apparently limited to claims for personal injury or property damage or to claims by consumers. Nevertheless, to avoid an overly broad interpretation that would extend to all claims where a thing is the instrument of injury (covering eg all traffic accidents or misrepresentation claims), its material scope must probably be limited to claims against persons involved in the supply chain (including manufacturers, suppliers, retailers and repairers) and to claims which concern the physical characteristics of the product.

Article 5 contains a rather confusing cascade of applicable law rules, which apply as follows. First, if the person claimed to be liable and the person sustaining damage are habitually resident in the same country, the rule set out in art 4(2) (see above, section III.1.) applies, resulting in the application of the law of that country, apparently without the possibility of escape (art 5(1), opening words). Second, if the product (albeit not necessarily the item which caused the damage) was marketed in the country in which the person sustaining the damage had his habitual residence when the damage occurred, the law of that country will apply, unless the person claimed to be liable discharges the burden of proving that he could not reasonably foresee that the product, or a product of the same type (albeit not necessarily identical), would be marketed in that country (art 5(1)(a)). Third, failing that, if the product (again, not necessarily the item which caused the damage) was marketed in the law of the country in which the product (here, necessarily the item which caused the damage) was acquired, the law of that country will apply, unless the person claimed to be liable could not reasonably foresee that the product, or a product of the same type (albeit not necessarily identical), would be marketed in that country (art 5(1)(b)). Fourth, failing that, if the product (again, not necessarily the item which caused the damage) was marketed in the law of the country in which the damage occurred, the law of that country will apply, unless the person claimed to be liable could not reasonably foresee that the product, or a product of the same type (albeit not necessarily identical), would be marketed in that country (art 5(1)(c)). Fifth, if the person claimed to be liable could not reasonably foresee that the product (again, not necessarily the item which caused damage), or a product of the same type (albeit not necessarily identical), would be marketed in any of the country or countries specified in art 5(1)(a), (b) or (c), the law of that person's country of habitual residence will apply instead. Although not dealt with expressly, it is suggested that the same law should apply if (likely to be a rare case) the product was not, in fact, marketed in any of those countries at all. Sixth, by an escape clause which mirrors art 4(3) (see above, section III.1.), the law applicable under the preceding steps may be displaced in favour of the application of the law of a country with which the tort/delict is manifestly more closely connected.

The Hague Products Liability Convention, and not the Rome II Regulation, will apply in

3. Unfair competition and acts restricting free competition

Article 6 (see Recitals (21)–(23)) concerns non-contractual obligations arising out of acts of unfair competition (→ Competition, unfair) and acts restricting free competition. It is, very arguably, the least satisfactory rule in the entire Regulation.

Article 6(1) and (2) concerns acts of unfair competition, a concept which is to be understood autonomously (see eg art 10bis Paris Convention for the protection of industrial property, 828 UNTS 305 (1883, as amended) and art 1 of the World Intellectual Property Organization's Model Provisions on protection against unfair competition, WIPO Publication No 832(E)). If the act of unfair competition affects only the interests of a specific competitor (eg inducing a third party to break a contract or stealing trade secrets), the general rule in art 4 (see above, section III.1.) will apply (art 6(2)). In other cases (eg misleading advertising or passing off), a non-contractual obligation arising out of an act of unfair competition shall be the law of the country where competitive relations or the collective interests of consumers are, or are likely to be, affected (art 6(1)). Although art 6(1) does not say so, this may refer to the location of the market in which competition takes place or in which consumers collectively engage with suppliers, giving rise to the difficulties of application referred to below in the discussion on art 6(3) (but cf Case C-191/15, Verein für Konsumentinformation v Amazon EU Sàrl [2016] ECLI:EU:C:2016:612, para 43, adopting a more targeted approach).

Article 6(3) concerns acts restricting free competition, including infringements of both national and EU competition law (see Recitals (22) and (23)). In such cases, the law that is generally applicable shall be the law of the country in which the relevant market is or is likely to be situated (art 6(1)(a)). However, as Recital (22) acknowledges and as the EU's very existence demonstrates, markets in products and services are frequently not segregated along national borders, presenting an immediate problem. This is compounded by the fact that the task of locating a market geographically is an extremely difficult one, involving legal and economic criteria of some complexity (see Commission Notice on the definition of relevant market for the purposes of Commission competition law [1997] OJ C 372/5). Furthermore, if a market is identified as crossing national borders, art 6(3) provides no indication of the basis upon which the laws of the relevant countries are to be applied in a particular case, whether individually or cumulatively. Against this background, there will be an obvious temptation for Member State courts to define markets as operating in a single country, but it remains to be seen what approach the CJEU will take.

The difficulties raised by art 6(3)(a) (but not art 6(1)) are tempered to a degree by art 6(3)(b), which gives a person seeking compensation who sues in a court in the Member State of domicile of one of the defendants the option to elect the exclusive application to the claim of the law of the country in which the court sits, provided that the market in that country is amongst those directly and substantially affected by the restriction of competition. This provision, coupled with the possibility of claims for negative declaratory relief by those claimed to be liable (Case C-133/11 *Folien Fischer AG and Fofitec AG v Ritrama SpA* [2012] ECLI:EU:C:2012:664), may encourage → forum (and law) shopping of a kind which the Regulation set out to deter (see above, section I.). The mode of exercise of the option is a matter for the procedural law of the court seised (cf Recital (25)).

Article 6(4) excludes the possibility of the parties choosing, under art 14 (see below, section III.10.), the law applicable to non-contractual obligations to which art 6(1) or 6(3) applies, but this probably does not extend to cases falling within art 6(2) and for which the law applicable is determined by the provisions of art 4.

4. Environmental damage

Article 7 (see Recitals (24)–(26)) concerns non-contractual obligations arising out of environmental damage or damage sustained by persons or property as a result of such damage (→ Environmental liability). For these purposes, 'environmental damage' should be understood as meaning adverse change in a natural resource, such as water, land or air, impairment of a function performed by that resource for the benefit of another natural resource or the public, or impairment of the variability among living organisms (Recital (24)).

Article 7 seeks to ensure a high level of environmental protection consistently with the objectives set out in art 191 TFEU (see Recital

(23), referring to art 174 EEC Treaty). It does so through the application (via art 4(1)) of the law of the country in which the environmental damage occurred, while giving the person seeking compensation the option to have the law of the country in which the event giving rise to the damage occurred applied instead. The mode of exercise of the option is a matter for the procedural law of the court seised (Recital (25)).

5. Infringements of intellectual property rights

Article 8 (see Recital (28)) concerns non-contractual obligations arising from an infringement of an intellectual property right, including (for example) copyright, related rights, the *sui generis* right for the protection of databases and industrial property rights (→ Intellectual property, applicable law).

In general, the law applicable to a non-contractual obligation arising from an infringement of an intellectual property right shall be the law of the country for which protection is claimed (*lex loci protectionis*) (art 8(1)). This rule affords the claimant a certain flexibility in formulating his case in the most favourable way, although it would appear to be implicit in the formulation and the underlying conception of intellectual property rights as being territorial in nature that the alleged infringement (including its consequences) must have some connection to the territory of the country whose intellectual property law is relied on (see Case C-173/11 *Football Dataco Ltd, Scottish Premier League Ltd, Scottish Football League, PA Sport UK Ltd v Sportradar GmbH, Sportradar AG* [2012] ECLI:EU:C:2012:642, paras 27, 31–32).

A different rule applies to cases involving infringements of unitary Community intellectual property rights (Community trade marks, design rights, and plant variety rights). In such cases, the law applicable is governed primarily by the relevant EU legislative instrument (Community Trade Mark Regulation (Council Regulation (EC) No 2007/2009 of 26 February 2009 on the Community trade mark [2009] OJ L 78/1); Community Design Regulation (Council Regulation (EC) No 6/2002 of 12 December 2001 on Community designs [2002] OJ L 3/1); Community Plant Regulation (Council Regulation (EC) No 2100/94 of 27 July 1994 on Community plant variety rights [1994] OJ L 227/1); see also Unitary Patent Regulation (Regulation (EU) No 1257/2012 of the European Parliament and of the Council of 17 December 2012 implementing enhanced cooperation in the area of the creation of unitary patent protection [2012] OJ L 361/1)); and, for any question not governed by the relevant instrument, by the law of the country in which the act of infringement occurred (art 8(2); cf Case C-360/12 *Coty Germany GmbH v First Note Perfumes NB* [2014] ECLI:EU:C:2014:1318).

Article 8(3) excludes the possibility of the parties choosing, under art 14 (see below, section III.10.), the law applicable to non-contractual obligations to which art 8 applies.

6. Industrial action

Article 9 (see Recitals (27)–(28)) concerns non-contractual obligations in respect of the liability of a person in the capacity of a worker or an employer or the organizations representing their professional interests for → damages caused by an industrial action, pending or carried out (→ Employment, industrial disputes). The latter words make clear that art 9 applies not only to actions seeking compensation, but also actions for an → injunction to restrain industrial action or other non-monetary relief. For these purposes, the Regulation recognizes that the concept of industrial action may vary between Member States (strikes and lock-outs are given as examples) and the concept is therefore to be understood non-autonomously by reference to the law of the country where the action was or is to be taken (Recital (27)). That country's law also applies to non-contractual obligations falling within art 9, subject to a single exception: if the person claimed to be liable and the person sustaining damage have their habitual residence in the same country, the rule set out in art 4(2) (see above, section III.1.) applies, leading to the application of the law of that country, apparently without the possibility of escape.

The Rome II Regulation only concerns the law applicable to non-contractual obligations and is without prejudice to the conditions relating to the exercise of such action in accordance with national law and without prejudice to the legal status of trade unions or of the representative organizations of workers as provided for in the law of the Member States (Recital (28)).

7. Unjust enrichment

The material scope of art 10, concerning non-contractual obligations arising out of unjust enrichment (→ Unjust enrichment (restitution)), including by way of example payment of amounts wrongly received, is qualified in one and, possibly, two ways. First, under art 12(1)(e) Rome I Regulation, the consequences of nullity of a contract are a matter falling within the scope of that Regulation and not art 10 of the Rome II Regulation. Second, it appears strongly arguable that claims for gain-based remedies for tort/delict should be treated as falling within arts 4–9 or 12 Rome II Regulation, and not art 10, notwithstanding the reference in art 10(1) to a relationship arising out of a tort/delict (see below).

Article 10 contains a cascade of rules, which apply as follows. First, if the obligation in question concerns a relationship existing between the parties, such as one arising out of a contract or a tort/delict, that is closely connected with that unjust enrichment, it shall be governed by the law that governs that relationship (art 10(1)). Second, failing that, if the parties have their habitual residence in the same country where the event giving rise to unjust enrichment occurs, the law of that country shall apply (cf art 4(2); see above, section III.1.) (art 10(2)). Third, failing that, the law of the country in which the (allegedly) unjust enrichment took place shall apply (art 10(3)). Fourth, the law applicable under the preceding steps may be displaced in favour of the application of the law of a country with which the non-contractual obligation arising out of unjust enrichment is manifestly more closely connected (art 10(4)).

8. Negotiorum gestio

Article 11, a provision of very limited significance in the overall scheme of the Regulation, concerns non-contractual obligations arising out of an act performed without due authority in connection with the affairs of another (→ *Negotiorum gestio*). A cascade of rules (mirroring art 10) applies as follows. First, where the obligation in question concerns a relationship existing between the parties, such as one arising out of a contract or a tort/delict, that is closely connected with that unjust enrichment, it shall be governed by the law that governs that relationship (art 11(1)). Second, failing that, if the parties have their habitual residence in the same country when the event giving rise to the damage (ie the relevant act) occurs, the law of that country shall apply (art 11(2). cf art 4(2), above, section III.1.). Third, failing that, the law of the country in which the relevant act took place shall apply (art 11(3)). Fourth, the law applicable under the preceding steps may be displaced in favour of the application of the law of a country with which the non-contractual obligation is manifestly more closely connected (art 11(4)).

9. Culpa in contrahendo

Article 12 (see Recital (30)) is the most important of the rules of applicable law in Chapter III of the Regulation. It concerns non-contractual obligations arising out of dealings prior to the conclusion of a contract, whether the contract was actually concluded or not. Recital (30) makes clear that the scope of art 12 is to be determined autonomously, rather than in accordance with national law conceptions of → *culpa in contrahendo*. It is to include, for example, violations of the duty of disclosure and the breakdown of contractual obligations, as well as non-contractual obligations arising from other forms of pre-contractual misconduct, including, for example, misrepresentation and acts of duress. However, art 12 covers only non-contractual obligations presenting a direct link with the dealings prior to the conclusion of a contract, with the consequence that a different provision will apply (most likely art 4) if a person suffers personal injury while a contract is being negotiated. Moreover, art 12 does not extend to questions as to whether a valid contract has been formed or not, or as to the consequences of a finding of invalidity, even where the parties' pre-contractual behaviour is in issue. Such questions fall instead within arts 10 and 12(1)(e) of the Rome I Regulation. Finally, the connecting factor used in art 12 suggests that its scope is limited to obligations arising as between the parties to an actual or contemplated contract, rather than obligations owed by or to their representatives.

If a contract has been concluded between the parties, non-contractual obligations arising out of their pre-contractual dealings will be governed by the law applicable to that contract, most likely determined in accordance with the Rome I Regulation (art 12(1), art 12(2) having no possible application in this case).

If no contract has been concluded between the parties, non-contractual obligations arising out of their pre-contractual dealings will be governed by the law that would have applied to that contract had it been entered into, most likely determined in accordance with the Rome I Regulation, but only if the court is able to determine that law to a sufficient degree of certainty (art 12(1)). Failing that, art 12(2) refers to a set of rules for determining the law applicable to non-contractual obligations arising out of the parties' pre-contractual dealings which correspond closely to those in art 4 (see above, section III.1.), save that the relevant time for determining whether the parties shared a common habitual residence is the time of the event giving rise to the damage rather than the time of the damage (cf art 4(2)).

10. Freedom of choice

Article 14 is an important provision, which extends the principle of party autonomy, as recognized for contractual obligations in the Rome I Regulation, to non-contractual obligations other than those falling within arts 6(1), 6(3) and 8 (see above, sections III.3. and III.5.).

However, there exist a number of restrictions on the freedom of choice. First, the agreement must be entered into either: (a) by an agreement entered into after the event giving rise to the damage occurred; or (b) where all the parties are pursuing a commercial activity, by an agreement freely negotiated (ie otherwise on standard terms) before the event giving rise to the damage occurred. Second, following the test set out in art 3(1) Rome Convention (see now art 3(1) Rome I Regulation), the choice shall be expressed or demonstrated with reasonable certainty by the circumstances of the case. Since the Rome II Regulation was adopted, it has become increasingly common for commercial agreements to contain an express → choice of law for non-contractual obligations. Third, the choice shall not prejudice the rights of third parties (for example, insurers). Fourth, art 14(2) and (3) contains provisions, similar to those now to be found in art 3(3) and (4) Rome I Regulation, which preserve the effect of non-derogable rules of national (or EU) law in circumstances where, at the time of the event giving rise to damage, the relevant circumstances are located in a single country (or exclusively in the Member States) and the parties have chosen the law of another country (or a non-Member State).

11. Scope of the law applicable

The Rome II Regulation governs non-contractual obligations. It does not, for example, govern questions of property law or personal status. Article 15 provides a non-exhaustive list of the matters to which the law applicable under the rules described in the preceding paragraphs is to apply as follows: (a) the basis and extent of liability, including the determination of persons who may be held liable for acts performed by them; (b) the grounds for exemption from liability, any limitation of liability and any division of liability; (c) the existence, the nature and the assessment of damage or the remedy claimed (see also Recital (33), which does not contradict or undermine the requirement to apply the designated law to questions of assessment); (d) the measures which a court may take to prevent or terminate injury or damage or to ensure the provision of compensation, within the limits of powers conferred on the court by its procedural law; (e) the question whether a right to claim damages or a remedy may be transferred, including by inheritance (but arguably not by assignment, which is governed instead by art 14 Rome I Regulation); (f) persons entitled to compensation for damage sustained personally; (g) liability for the acts of another person; and (h) the manner in which an obligation may be extinguished and rules of → prescription and limitation, including rules relating to the commencement, interruption and suspension of a period of prescription or limitation.

To this list may be added: (1) provision for a direct action against an insurer, as an alternative to the law applicable to the insurance contract (art 18); (2) questions of formal validity of acts intended to have legal effect relating to a non-contractual obligation (such as a release of liability) as an alternative to the law of the country in which the relevant act was performed (art 21; see also art 22(2)); and (3) questions concerning legal presumptions of the burden of proof (art 22(1)).

The exclusion of matters of evidence and procedure from the scope of the Regulation must be understood in light of this list, even though art 1(3) expresses that exclusion to be subject only to arts 21 and 22. In particular, within the limits of the court's procedural powers, questions of remedy, the basis for the assessment of damages or the application of time bars can no longer be characterized for the purposes of the Regulation as procedural and matters for the law of the forum (→ *Lex fori*) rather than the law which applies under the rules described above. In this connection, due account must also be taken of the principle of effectiveness in EU law, which has the consequence here that the rules of evidence and procedure must not make it impossible or excessively difficult to identify and apply the law applicable under the Regulation to the matters listed above (cf Case C-365/88 *Kongress Agentur Hagen GmbH v Zeehaghe BV* [1990] ECR I-1845, para 20). This may be of particular significance in considering rules on the introduction and ascertainment of foreign law in court proceedings, as to which Member State practice varies greatly (see art 30(1)(i)).

12. Rules of safety and conduct

As noted above (section III.1.), the cornerstone provision in art 4 of the Regulation makes a policy choice to apply the law of the country (or countries) in which the damage occurred rather than the law of the country (or countries) in which the event giving rise to the damage occurred. The latter place will normally be where the person claimed to be liable acted. In striking the balance between the interests of that person and the person sustaining damage, art 17 of the Regulation requires that, in assessing the conduct of the person claimed to be liable, account shall be taken of the rules of safety and conduct which were in force at the place and time of the event giving rise to the liability, but only as a matter of fact and insofar as it is appropriate under the relevant rules of the applicable law. Rules of safety and conduct include, for example, traffic or factory safety regulations and environmental standards. Although not expressly addressed in art 17, there appears no reason why a similar approach may not be taken in assessing the conduct of the claimant, most obviously in matters of contributory negligence.

13. Overriding mandatory provisions and public policy of the forum

According to arts 16 and 26, the law applicable under the Regulation may be overridden or its application refused on the basis of: (a) provisions of the law of the forum which are → overriding mandatory provisions in the sense that they apply irrespective of the law applicable to the non-contractual obligation in question; or (b) a manifest incompatibility with the → public policy of the forum. Recital (32) emphasizes that these limitations are intended to be exceptional, but acknowledges that the public policy exception might be invoked by a Member State if that application of a provision of the law designated by this Regulation which would have the effect of causing non-compensatory exemplary or punitive damages of an excessive nature to be awarded is offensive to its legal order. It is expected that the CJEU will place limits upon the limited autonomy granted to the Member States under these provisions, in line with its case-law concerning similar qualifications in the Rome Convention, the Brussels Convention and the Brussels I Regulation (see Case C-184/12 *United Antwerp Maritime Agencies (UNAMAR) NV v Navigation Maritime Bulgare* [2013] ECLI:EU:C:2013:663; Case C-619/10 *Trade Agency Ltd v Seramico Investments Ltd* [2012] ECLI:EU:C:2012:531).

IV. Significance

It is too early to determine whether the Rome II Regulation will be as successful as other EU private international law instruments, in particular the Brussels I and Rome I Regulations and their predecessor conventions (→ Brussels I (Convention and Regulation); Rome Convention and Rome I Regulation). In particular, the CJEU has only just begun to provide guidance concerning the application of the Regulation's key provisions, including art 4 (Case C-350/14 *Lazar v Allianz SpA* [2015] ECLI:EU:C:2015:802), and its relationship with the Rome I Regulation. Moreover, the preceding commentary has highlighted a number of important issues which the text and Recitals of the Regulation do not satisfactorily resolve. Nevertheless, the Regulation can be justifiably described as an important and on the whole positive step for European private international law. It can also be seen as an important precedent internationally, being the first modern multilateral instrument to deal comprehensively with this subject matter.

Andrew Dickinson

Literature

John Ahern and William Binchy (eds), *The Rome II Regulation on the Law Applicable to Non-contractual Obligations: A New International Litigation Regime* (Martinus Nijhoff 2009); Fabrizio

Marongiu Buonaiuti, *Le obbligazioni non contrattuali nel diritto internazionale privato* (Giuffrè 2013); Gralf-Peter Calliess (ed), *Rome Regulations: Commentary on the European Rules of the Conflict of Laws* (2nd edn, Wolters-Kluwer 2015) pt II; Alfonso-Luis Calvo Caravaca and Javier Carrascosa González, *Las obligaciones extracontractuales en derecho internacional privado. El Reglamento Roma II* (Editorial Comares 2008); Lord Collins of Mapesbury and others (eds), *Dicey, Morris & Collins on the Conflict of Laws* (15th edn, Sweet & Maxwell 2012, supplement 2016) chs 34–36; Sabine Corneloup and Natalie Joubert (eds), *Le règlement communautaire 'Rome II' sur la loi applicable aux obligations non contractuelles* (LexisNexis 2008); Andrew Dickinson, *The Rome II Regulation* (OUP 2008, supplement 2010); Pietro Franzina, 'Il regolamento n. 864/2007/CE sulla legge applicabile alle obbligazioni extracontrattuali ("Roma II")' [2008] *Le nuove leggi civili commentate* 971; Peter Huber (ed), *Rome II Regulation: Pocket Commentary* (Sellier 2011); Richard Plender and Michael Wilderspin, *The European Private international law of Obligations* (4th edn, Sweet & Maxwell 2014) chs 2, 16–29; Thomas Rauscher (ed), *Europäisches Zivilprozess- und Kollisionsrecht, Rom I-VO, Rom II-VO* (Sellier 2011); Adam Rushworth and Andrew Scott, 'Rome II: Choice of Law for Non-contractual Obligations' [2008] LMCLQ 274; Jan von Hein (ed), *Münchener Kommentar zum Bürgerlichen Gesetzbuch, vol 10, IPR, Rom I-VO, Rom II-VO, Rom III* (6th edn, CH Beck 2014).

Rome III Regulation (divorce)

I. Background and objectives

Council Regulation (EU) 1259/2012 of 20 December 2010 implementing enhanced cooperation in the area of the law applicable to divorce and legal separation, [2010] OJ L 343/10 is also known as the Rome III Regulation.

The legal basis for the adoption of this Regulation is art 81 TFEU (Treaty on the Functioning of the European Union (consolidated version), [2012] OJ C 326/47), which develops the means to achieve the objective of maintaining and developing an area of freedom, security and justice in which the free movement of persons is assured. This provision allows the EU institutions to adopt measures specifically aimed at ensuring compatibility of the rules applicable in the Member States concerning → choice of law, among other measures relating to judicial cooperation in civil matters having cross-border implications, and particularly when necessary for the proper functioning of the Internal Market.

Thus, as with the other 'Rome' Regulations, the Rome III Regulation seeks unification of the conflict-of-laws rules (in a given matter) within the EU, as instrumental to the free movement of judgments (in that matter) between the Member States. Indeed, in order to promote free movement of judgments, it was first deemed necessary to establish common rules not only on recognition and enforcement, but also on jurisdiction to adjudicate. The so-called 'Brussels' Regulations have been enacted with this aim, as 'double' instruments: they settle rules governing the jurisdiction of courts and the recognition and enforcement of decisions. Following that, unification of the rules for determining the applicable law was also considered necessary in the matters covered by the 'Brussels' Regulations in order to avoid forum shopping (→ Forum (and law) shopping). In fact, as the 'Brussels' Regulations endorse (different forms of) → party autonomy on jurisdiction, they trigger the election of the courts of a given Member State may depend on the law that these courts apply to the merits. As the Rome III Regulation itself declares, this instrument 'should create a clear, comprehensive legal framework in the area of the law applicable to divorce and legal separation in the participating Member States, provide citizens with appropriate outcomes in terms of legal certainty, predictability and flexibility, and prevent a situation from arising where one of the spouses applies for divorce [→ Divorce and personal separation] before the other one does in order to ensure that the proceeding is governed by a given law which he or she considers more favourable to his or her own interests' (Recital (9)). In this sense, the Rome III Regulation is complementary to art 2 → Brussels IIa Regulation (Council Regulation (EC) No 2201/2003 of 27 November 2003 concerning jurisdiction and the recognition and enforcement of judgments in matrimonial matters and the matters of parental responsibility, repealing Regulation (EC) No 1347/2000, [2003] OJ L 338/1) (→ Brussels IIa Regulation). However, the result does not fully satisfy this objective, having regard to its limited substantial (see section II. below) and territorial scope.

Indeed, the Rome III Regulation is not binding on the entire EU, but rather is an enhanced cooperation Regulation; in fact, it is the first such enhanced cooperation Regulation in the history of the EU. The reason is that an agreement on the Regulation proposed by the Commission (Proposal of the Commission of 17 July 2006 (Commission, 'Proposal for a Council Regulation amending Regulation (EC) No 2201/2003 as regards jurisdiction and introducing new rules concerning applicable law in matrimonial matters' COM(2006) 399 final), elaborated after a public consultation on the Green Paper on applicable law and jurisdiction in divorce matters (COM(2005) 82 final) also adopted by the Commission on 14 March 2005) was not possible within the Council. The difficulties were considered insurmountable and accordingly, in the light of the lack of agreement and the conviction that unanimity would be impossible, certain Member States decided to address a request to the Commission, indicating their intention to establish enhanced cooperation among themselves. This cooperation was authorized by the Council on 20 July 2010 (Council Decision 2010/405/EU of 12 July 2010 authorising enhanced cooperation in the area of the law applicable to divorce and legal separation, [2010] OJ L 189/12), and the Rome III Regulation was adopted five months later. Since then, some Member States have decided to participate in the Regulation, while others have not. Participation is open to all at any time, but while some Member States apply other domestic or conventional instruments, the Rome III Regulation is binding in its entirety and directly applicable only in the participating Member States.

II. Scope of application

For the Rome III Regulation to be applicable, it is necessary that the situation involves any international element other than the mere fact that the parties have designated a foreign law as the law applicable to their divorce or legal separation, according to the choice that the Regulation allows (see section III.1. below). But the spatial application of the instrument does not depend on the countries that the situation is related to. The Rome III Regulation is an instrument of universal application. When art 4 states that 'the law designated by this Regulation shall apply whether or not it is the law of a participating Member State', it means that the Regulation applies without any condition of → reciprocity and independently of the links of the situation to any particular state. The Regulation is applicable in every participating Member State to determine the law applicable to the divorce or legal separation of any marriage, without regard to the → nationality, domicile or habitual residence (→ Domicile, habitual residence and establishment) of the spouses, the place of celebration of the marriage, or the law under which the marriage was celebrated, and, of course, regardless of the law applicable to the divorce or legal separation according to the Regulation, ie whether or not it is the law of a participating Member State. Thus, if the divorce or the legal separation is brought before the competent court of a participating Member State (according to the Brussels IIa Regulation), the law applicable to the merits has to be determined according to the Rome III Regulation in every situation; also, for instance, when the spouses, being US citizens (or Chilean or Chinese), celebrated the marriage in their country of origin, according to the law of a state of the → USA (or → Chile or → China). The fact that this Regulation has a universal character is as essential to achieve the conflictual unification pursued (at least between the participating Member States) as it is also fundamental for this aim to exclude → *renvoi* (art 11) and to limit the applicability of the → public policy clause to the situations where the application of the foreign law designated by the Regulation 'is *manifestly incompatible* with the public policy of the forum' (art 12, emphasis added). The inconveniences for an effective unification of the conflict-of-laws solutions converge with the limits on the above-mentioned territorial scope and also on the substantive scope.

Even if the Regulation should be consistent regarding its substantive scope with the Brussels IIa Regulation, there is a paramount difference between them. The Brussels IIa Regulation regulates the jurisdiction as well as the recognition and enforcement of decisions in matters of divorce, legal separation and marriage annulment. However, the Rome III Regulation only applies to divorce and legal separation of spouses (including → same-sex marriages, but not registered partnerships), whereas the annulment of a marriage is expressly excluded according to art 1(2)(c). This asymmetry in the treatment of the matter is not justified. Whereas this Regulation aims at preventing a 'race to the court' and eliminating the legal uncertainty caused by the lack of uniform solutions as to the law applicable (see reference above), these aims are equally pertinent to claims for legal separation, divorce and annulment of a marriage. Indeed, none of the justifications given for excluding the regulation of annulment of marriage is convincing. First, if the problem is that the Rome III Regulation allows for party autonomy, and if this solution is only convenient for legal separation and divorce, it would have sufficed to develop a different, specific conflict-of-laws rule for annulment. Second, it is also irrelevant that in some Member States the annulment of marriage is unknown, as legal separation is also unknown in others, and, as said, it is included within the scope of the Rome III Regulation. Nor is it satisfactory that the Rome III Regulation provides no rules on the celebration of marriage, because nothing would prevent each Member State from retaining its own rules on the celebration, even if these rules are different from the rules on annulment. In the light of the differences among the various Member States (and participating Member States) regarding the very concept of → marriage, unification of the rules on the law applicable to the annulment of marriage was arguably even more necessary than of the rules for divorce or legal separation. Indeed, only specific rules could prevent the courts of a Member State (for instance, → Italy) from declaring the nullity of a marriage validly celebrated in another Member State (for example, a Spanish same-sex marriage) by means of a judgment that has to be recognized (except for the application of the public policy clause) under the Brussels IIa Regulation in the Member State where the marriage was lawfully celebrated and is perfectly valid.

Other matters expressly excluded by art 1(2) Rome III Regulation are: (i) the legal capacity of natural persons (→ Capacity and emancipation); (ii) the existence, validity and recognition of a → marriage; (iii) the name of the spouse; (iv) the property consequences of the marriage; (v) parental responsibility; (vi) → maintenance obligations; and (vii) → trust or → successions.

As to the kind of conflicts of laws that the Rome III Regulation envisages, it is worth mentioning that, in the participating Member States in which different systems of law or sets of rules apply to divorce or legal separation, the Regulation is not compulsorily applicable to internal conflicts of law (art 16).

As to its temporal scope of application, the general rule states that the Rome III Regulation has been applicable to legal proceedings instituted before a court (according to art 1(3), a 'court' can be either a judicial or an administrative body) as from 21 June 2012. However, when the parties have concluded an agreement regarding the law applicable to the divorce or the legal separation before this date, the Regulation would also apply in order to give effect to the agreement, provided it complies with arts 6 and 7 (art 18(1)). If the court has been seised before the date mentioned, the validity and enforceability of the agreement are subject to the law of the forum (art 18(2)).

Finally, as to the relationship with international conventions which lay down conflict-of-laws rules relating to divorce or legal separation, should a convention obligate the participating Member State of the forum, it would apply instead of the Rome III Regulation only if the participating Member State was already party to the convention before the Regulation entered into force (art 19(1)), and whenever the convention's contracting states are not exclusively participating Member States (art 19(2)).

III. Conflict-of-laws rules

1. Party autonomy

A basic principle of the Rome III Regulation is the informed choice of the parties. Being aware of the legal and social implications of the application of a given law to the divorce or the legal separation, the spouses would attain a higher degree of certainty and better access to justice by means of their agreement to apply such law (Recitals (18) and (19)). Thus, the two spouses have the possibility of agreeing on the law applicable to their divorce or legal separation (art 5). The agreement is subject to limits as to the laws that can be chosen; it must comply with certain substantive and formal requirements, and there might also be constraints on the moment when the choice has to be made.

The choice of the law applicable to the divorce or the legal separation is limited to a law which has a particular connection with the spouses. Only four laws can alternatively be designated (art 5): either the law of the state where the spouses are habitually resident at the time that the agreement is concluded; or the law of the state where the spouses were last habitually resident, insofar as one of them still resides there at the time that the agreement is concluded; or the law of the state of nationality of either spouse at the time that the agreement is concluded; or the law of the forum.

Second, the validity of the agreement is subject to requirements as to the substance and to the form. The law which would govern the agreement under the Regulation if the agreement were valid is the law that would apply to its existence and substantial validity (art 6(1)). This means that the law designated in the agreement as the law applicable to the divorce or legal separation is the law applicable to the existence and validity of the agreement. But, as the conduct of one of the spouses may have a given effect according to the chosen law (such as their silence may be equivalent to acceptance, so that the agreement exists because they did not expressly reject the offer), it would not be reasonable to infer the same legal consequence according to the law of that spouse's country of residence (where, for instance, silence never amounts to acceptance), it is possible for that spouse to rely upon this law in order to reject the said effect (art 6(2)).

As to the formal validity, there are minimum requirements settled by the Regulation: the agreement must be expressed in writing (including electronic means, as long as they provide a durable record of the agreement), dated and signed by both spouses (art 7). These requirements are conceived as safeguards to ensure that spouses are aware of both the choice and its implications. But additional formal requirements (→ Formal requirements and validity), such as the agreement being formalized in a public deed, may also be applicable, depending on the spouses' place of residence. These additional requirements might be the additional requirements settled (if any) in the law of the participating Member States where the spouses have their common habitual residence at the time that the agreement is concluded (art 7(2)); or the law of (just) one of the participating Member States where the spouses have their habitual residence at the time that the agreement is concluded if they are habitually resident in a different participating Member State (art 7(3)); or the law of the participating Member State where one of the spouses has their habitual residence at the time that the agreement is concluded if the other is not resident in a participating Member State (art 7(4)). As a result, if both spouses have their habitual residence in a country other than a participating Member State, the only formal requirements applicable to their agreement are the said minimum requirements settled by the Rome III Regulation. However, in the event that the choice of the law is made during the course of the proceedings, it is sufficient that it is recorded in court in accordance with the law of the forum.

Finally, the Regulation allows that the spouses come to an agreement, and also modify the agreement already made, at any time before the completion of the application (art 5(2)). But the possibility of also concluding or modifying the agreement during the course of the proceedings depends on the law of the forum (art 5(3)). The possibility of making or modifying the agreement once the court has already been seised depends on the law of the participating Member States where the divorce or legal separation is sought. Thus, the uniform regulation of the agreement is also defective in this sense. As a result, there is not only legal uncertainty as to the immutable nature of any agreement, but also a possible ground for a particular type of forum shopping in that the couple could apply before the court of given participating Member States (or a Member State) solely because in that state, said possibility of amendment is granted (amendment is permissible in that state).

2. *The law applicable in the absence of choice*

a) *Conflict-of-laws rules*
Where there is no (valid) agreement between the spouses as to the law applicable, this law is determined according to the objective conflict-of-laws rules settled by the Rome III Regulation. There is a general rule (art 8) and a special rule for the conversion of legal separation into divorce (art 9).

The general rule establishes a scale of successive → connecting factors based on the existence of a close connection between the spouses and the law concerned. In the first place, the law applicable to the divorce or the legal separation is the law of the state where the spouses are habitually resident at the time that the court is seised. Failing that, the law of the state where the spouses were last habitually resident applies, provided that the period of residence did not end more than one year before the court was seised, and provided that one of the spouses still resides in that state at the time that the court is seised. Failing that, the law applies of the state of which both spouses are nationals at the time the court is seised. Failing that, the law of the forum applies.

The special rule is settled for conversion of legal separation into divorce, which is applicable only where there is no valid agreement between the spouses concerning the law applicable to the conversion. According to this rule, if the spouses are legally separated, the conversion of the legal separation into divorce is governed by the law which was applied to the legal separation, provided that the law provides for such conversion (art 9(1)). This continuity aims at promoting predictability for the parties and increasing legal certainty. Where the law applied to the legal separation does not provide for the conversion of legal separation into divorce, the law applicable will be determined according to the general rule (art 9(2)).

b) *Rules on the application of the conflict-of-laws rules*
The operation of the connecting factors employed by the Rome III Regulation may cause some difficulties. The connecting factor 'habitual residence', being of a factual nature, is intended to pose few problems as to its determination in given situations, although in reality it may at times be extremely difficult to determine the habitual residence of a couple in the context of an international family conflict. But the Regulation pays particular attention to the connecting factor 'nationality' of the spouses. Recital (22) envisages the situation where the spouses have multiple nationalities and it asserts that the solution (which nationality is to prevail) is left to national laws, but in full observance of the general principles of the EU. Thus, the national solutions have to be consistent with the ECJ doctrine on the application of the state conflict-of-law rules in cases of multiple nationalities. This application of the ECJ case-law would be reaffirmed having regard to the said necessity that the application of the terms of the Rome III Regulation are consistent with the Brussels IIa Regulation (Recital (10)). Thus, on the one hand, the ECJ has recognized the possibility for the individuals who have the nationality of two Member States to choose the application of the law of one of the Member States in rulings where the application of the national solutions to the cases of multiple nationalities was tested, as in Case C-148/02 *Carlos Garcia Avello v Belgian State* [2003] ECR I-11613 and Case C-353/06 *Stefan Grunkin and Dorothee Regina Paul* [2008] ECR I-7639. On the other hand, this impossibility of solving the issue by means of the application of the more effective nationality, contrary to the parties' will, has also been asserted in a case where the ECJ was asked to give a ruling on the interpretation of the Brussels IIa Regulation (Case C-168/08 *Hadadi v Hadadi* [2009] ECR I-6871). Thus, if the spouses choose the law of a given common nationality, this is the law that the participating Member State courts have to apply, as they are not allowed to solve the issue of the double nationality by means of the application of a divergent national solution, such as the principle of the more effective nationality.

The Rome III Regulation also establishes a rule for the cases where the state whose law is applicable according to the Regulation is a state which comprises several territorial units concerning legal separation or divorce (such as the UK, the USA or Mexico), and another rule for the situation where the state whose law is applicable has two or more systems of law, or sets of rules applicable to different categories of persons concerning legal separation or divorce (such as → Greece, → Israel or → India). If the state whose law is applicable comprises several territorial units, each of which has its own system of law, any reference made to the law of that state is to be construed as referring to the law in force in the relevant territorial unit (art 14). Thus, for instance, if the spouses have no common habitual residence in a given state, but one of them still resides in the state where the spouses were last habitually resident, and in this state there are several territorial units with different laws (such as in the UK), the law applicable absent a choice (art 8) is the law of the territorial unit where they were last habitually resident (England, Wales, Scotland or Northern Ireland). The same solution (ie direct reference to the territorial unit) is employed whenever the connecting factor is 'habitual residence'. For instance, in the example above, according to art 7, the spouses might have agreed that the law applicable to the legal separation or divorce is the law of the territory where the spouses were habitually resident (for instance, Scotland). But this 'direct' solution does not work where the connecting factor employed is 'nationality'. Returning to the example, if one of the spouses is a US citizen, art 7 confers on them the possibility of choosing the law of the USA, but a US law on legal separation or divorce does not exist, and the reference to nationality cannot be construed as referring to the law in force in a particular territory or state of the USA, as there is no 'nationality' of a sister state. Thus, a possible ('indirect') solution, which is the solution settled by the Rome III Regulation, consists in applying the rules established in this state (the

USA) for the resolution of internal conflicts of laws. But, as it is not unusual that there is not a single state set of rules of internal conflicts of laws (in the USA, each sister state has its own conflict-of-laws rules, applicable to both interstate and international situations), a closing solution is needed. This solution is established in art 7(c) Rome III Regulation, which declares that absent such rules, the law applicable is the law of the territorial unit chosen by the parties, or the law with the closest connection to the spouse or spouses. Thus, in the example, the spouses have the possibility of agreeing that the law applicable to their legal separation or divorce is the law of one of the sister states. This 'indirect' solution is also given to the situation where the applicable law, according to the Regulation, is the law of a state where there are two or more laws on legal separation or divorce, whose application depends on a given category of person (eg this person's creed or religion). Thus, if the state has specific rules to determine the personal law which is to be applied to the particular person, the solution will come from the application of these interpersonal conflict-of-laws rules (art 15). In their absence, the law applicable will be the law with which the spouse or spouses have the closest relationship.

There are two possible reasons not to apply the law determined according to the Rome III Regulation. The first is that the applicable law makes no provision for divorce or does not grant one of the spouses equal access to divorce or legal separation on the grounds of his or her sex. In this case, the court seised will apply its own law, without prejudice to the public policy clause (art 10). The other reason is, indeed, recognized in the public policy clause (art 12): the application of a provision of a foreign law will be disregarded where such application would be manifestly incompatible with the public policy of the forum. However, the clause cannot be applied where disregarding the applicable law would be contrary to the EU Charter of Fundamental Rights (Charter of Fundamental Rights of the European Union of 18 December 2000, [2000] OJ C 364/1 (consolidated version 2012/C 326/02, [2012] OJ C 326/391)) and in particular its art 21, which prohibits all forms of discrimination.

Finally, in order to achieve a higher degree of unification of the conflict-of-laws rules, → *renvoi* is excluded (art 11). This means that the reference to the law designated by the Regulation (either by means of an agreement on the law applicable to the divorce or the legal separation or by means of the rule applicable in the absence of a choice) is a reference to the substantive provisions of such law. Accordingly, it is not possible to apply the law of the forum or the law of another state to the divorce or the legal separation by means of the application of the conflict-of-laws rules of the state whose law is applicable.

3. The other relevant rule: obstacle to the principle of mutual recognition

'The existence, validity or recognition of a marriage' is one of the issues excluded from the scope of the Rome III Regulation. Accordingly, the reiteration may come as a surprise that regarding the recognition of marriage implies the provision of art 13, under which no court of a participating Member State is bound to recognize the validity of the marriage, in order to decide on the divorce or the legal separation (the text indicates nothing about the legal separation, but Recital (26) also refers to it in this context). Thus, the court of the participating Member State seised may apply the private international law rules of the forum, according to which the marriage may be non-existent or invalid. But this rule has its rationale. Through its enactment, the possibility of a future (jurisdictional) extension of the principle of mutual recognition to the issue of the validity of marriages celebrated in other Member States has been blocked. Indeed, the application of this principle would have amounted to giving prevalence to the most permissive laws; it would have obliged every Member State to recognize the validity of marriages celebrated under the law of any other Member State. On the contrary, the more restrictive standard has been adopted. The Rome III Regulation protects the participating Member States reluctant not only to legalize same-sex marriages, but also to acknowledge their validity when celebrated according to the law of another Member State.

Article 13 also states that if the law of the participating Member State whose courts have been seised does not have the institution of divorce, such courts should not be obliged to pronounce a divorce by virtue of the Regulation. This provision was called the 'Malta provision', because Malta was the only Member State where divorce was not legal at the time that the Regulation was approved. Thus, by establishing this rule, Malta would not be compelled to introduce divorce into its substantive law by virtue of an EU instrument. However, as Malta has already recognized the possibility of dissolution of marriages, the provision has no practical application now.

PATRICIA OREJUDO PRIETO DE LOS MOZOS

Literature

Nynke A Baarsma, 'European Choice of Law on Divorce (Rome III): Where Did it Go Wrong?' (2009) 27 NIPR 9; Katarina Boele-Woelki, 'For Better or for Worse: The Europanization of International Divorce Law' (2010) 2 YbPIL 11; Sabine Courneloup (ed), *Droit Européen du divorce. European Divorce Law, Université de Bourgogne, Travaux du CREDIMI*, vol 39 (LexisNexis Litec 2013); Aude Fiorini, 'Rome III – Un modèle a suivre?' in Mélina Douchy-Oudot and Emmanuel Guinchard (eds), *La Justicie civil européenne en marche* (Dalloz 2012) 79; Pietro Franzina, 'The Law Applicable to Divorce and Legal Separation under Regulation (EU) N° 1259/2010 of 10 December' (2011) 3 CTL 2; Cristina González Beilfuss, 'The Unification of Private international law in Europe: A Success History?' in Katharina Boele-Woelki, Jo Miles and Jens Scherpe (eds), *The Future of Family Property in Europe* (Intersentia 2011) 329; Patricia Orejudo Prieto de los Mozos, 'La nueva regulación de la ley aplicable a la separación judicial y al divorcio: aplicación del Reglamento Roma III en España' (2012) 7913 La Ley 1; Steve Peters, 'Divorce, European Style: The First Authorisation of Enhanced Cooperation' (2010) 6 European Constitutional Law Review 339.

Rome IV Regulation (succession)

I. Background and context

The establishment of the Succession Regulation (Regulation (EU) No 650/2012 of the European Parliament and of the Council of 4 July 2012 on jurisdiction, applicable law, recognition and enforcement of decisions and acceptance and enforcement of authentic instruments in matters of succession and on the creation of a European Certificate of Succession, [2012] OJ L 201/107) exemplifies the EU objective of developing and maintaining an area of freedom, security and justice in which the free movement of persons is secured. The Succession Regulation is one of the measures relating to judicial cooperation in civil matters with cross-border implications and it is deemed necessary for the proper functioning of the Internal Market.

According to the deliberations preparatory to the Succession Regulation (Recital (7)), the proper functioning of the Internal Market should be facilitated by removing obstacles to the free movement of persons who currently face difficulties asserting their rights in the context of succession with cross-border implications. In the European area of justice, it must be possible for citizens to organize their succession in advance. The rights of heirs and legatees, of other persons close to the deceased and of creditors of the succession must be effectively guaranteed. These objectives can only be met by way of common rules governing international successions, which must be uniform in order to guarantee legal certainty and predictability for the citizens of the EU Member States.

For this purpose, the Regulation contains rules on jurisdiction, applicable law, recognition or, as the case may be, acceptance, enforceability and enforcement of decisions, authentic instruments and court settlements and on the creation of a European Certificate of Succession (Recital (8)).

The preparatory work for the Regulation commenced with the excellent 'Study on international successions in the European Union' (available at <www.successions.org>) in 2002 by the German Notary Institute (Dr *Wolfgang Riering*) in cooperation with Professor *Heinrich Dörner* and Professor *Paul Lagarde*. This was followed by the Commission's Green Paper on successions and wills (COM(2005) 65 final) on 1 March 2005, which generated some 60 replies and culminated in a public hearing on 30 November 2006. A group of experts ([2006] OJ C 51/3) met on seven occasions between 2006 and 2008, and the Commission organized a meeting of national experts on 30 June 2008. All this led to the European Commission conclusion that there was a need for a Community instrument in this area (available at <http://ec.europa.eu/justice_home/news/consulting_public/successions/contributions/summary_contributions_successions_fr.pdf>). This opinion was supported by the European Parliament (Resolution of 16 November 2006, P6_TA(2006)0496) and the European Economic and Social Committee (Opinion of 26 October 2005, [2006] OJ C 28/1). On 14 October 2009, the Commission launched a proposal for a Succession Regulation, which was accompanied by an impact assessment. The final text of the proposal was established in the Succession Regulation.

II. Scope and structure

1. Substantive scope of application

The Regulation applies to succession relating to the estate of deceased persons (art 1(1)). The scope of the Regulation includes all civil law aspects of succession to the estate of a deceased person, ie all forms of transfer of assets, rights and obligations by reason of death, whether by way of a voluntary transfer under a disposition of property upon death or a transfer through intestate succession (Recital (9)). Excluded from the scope of the Regulation according to art 1(3) are: (i) the status of natural persons as well as family relationships; (ii) the legal capacity of natural persons (→ Capacity and emancipation); (iii) questions relating to the disappearance, absence or presumed death of a natural person (→ Absence (disappearance, presumed death)); (iv) questions relating to → matrimonial property regimes and property regimes of other relationships; (v) maintenance obligations; (vi) the formal validity of dispositions of property made orally upon death; (vii) property rights, interests and assets created or transferred otherwise than by succession; (viii) questions governed by the law of → companies and other bodies; (ix) the dissolution, extinction and merger of companies and other bodies; the creation, administration and dissolution of trusts; (x) the nature of rights *in rem*; as well as (xi) any recording in a register of rights in immovable or movable property, including the legal requirements for such recording, and the effects of recording or failing to record such rights in a register.

As stated above, the Regulation does not cover the matrimonial property regime, but nevertheless if the deceased was married, the authorities dealing with a given succession should first determine the law applicable to the matrimonial property regime. Although preparations are under way for regulations regarding matrimonial property regimes and property regimes of registered partners at the EU level, these rules will only apply to marriages and partnerships entered into once those regulations apply. Until then, each Member State will apply its national conflict rules. Since the settlement of the estate will in principle take place at the deceased's last habitual residence, the conflict rules of this country will in fact decide which law applies to the matrimonial property regime. Since the matrimonial property regimes within the EU vary enormously, this should be an important point for legal practitioners to deal with in advance. Authorities in other EU Member States accepting a European Succession Certificate should continue to apply their own conflict rules to this matter.

The Succession Regulation allows for the creation of, or the transfer by succession of, a right to immovable or movable property (→ Property and proprietary rights) as provided for in the law applicable to the succession. However, such a right cannot affect the limited number (*numerus clausus*) of rights *in rem* known in the national law of a Member State. A Member State should not be required to recognize a right *in rem* relating to property located in that Member State if the right *in rem* in question is not known in its law (Recital (15)). In this situation, Member States should provide for the adaptation of an unknown right *in rem* to the closest equivalent right *in rem* known under its law. For the purpose of determining the closest equivalent national right *in rem*, the authorities or competent persons of the state whose law applied to the succession may be contacted for further information on the nature and the effects of the right (Recital (16)).

The recording of a right to immovable or movable property in a register is excluded from the scope of this Regulation. This aspect and the effects of the recording of a right in a register are governed by the law of the country where the register is kept.

By way of secondary qualification, art 23 determines which aspects are governed by the succession law applicable according to conflict rules set out in arts 21 and 22. This law governs in particular: (i) the causes, time and place of the opening of the succession; (ii) the determination of the beneficiaries, their respective shares, the obligations which may be imposed on them by the deceased, and the determination of other succession rights, including the succession rights of the surviving spouse or partner; (iii) the capacity to inherit; (iv) disinheritance; (v) the transfer of the estate to the heirs, including the conditions and effects of the acceptance or waiver of the succession or of a legacy; (vi) the powers of the heirs, the executors of the wills and other administrators of the estate; (vii) liability for the debts under the succession; (viii) the disposable part of the estate, the reserved shares and other restrictions on the disposal of property upon death as well as claims which persons close to the deceased may have against the estate or the heirs; and (ix) any obligation to restore or account for gifts, advancements or legacies when determining the shares of the different beneficiaries; and the sharing-out of the estate. As such, the Succession Regulation has a much broader substantive scope than the Hague Succession Convention (Hague Convention of 1 August 1989 on the Law Applicable to Succession to the Estates of Deceased Persons, available at <www.hcch.net>), which concerns devolution only.

2. Territorial scope of application

As far as the applicable law is concerned, the Succession Regulation has a universal scope of application (art 20). Any law deemed applicable according to the conflict rules of the Regulation will be applied, irrespective of whether it is the law of a Member State.

The Regulation does not affect the application of international conventions to which one or more Member States are party. However, in any relationship between Member States, the Regulation takes precedence, except for the Hague Testamentary Dispositions Convention (Hague Convention of 5 October 1961 on the conflicts of laws relating to the form of testamentary dispositions, 510 UNTS 175) and the 1934 Nordic Convention on Succession and Wills (Nordic Convention on Succession and Wills (also Convention concerning Inheritance, Testamentary Dispositions and the Administration of Estates of Deceased Persons) of 19 November 1934, 164 LNTS 243, amended 1975 (amended by a new Convention 1 June 2012, which has not entered into force)). The bilateral agreements of some Member States with non-EU countries still have to be applied by these Member States. This concerns, for instance, the bilateral agreements of → Austria with respect to → Iran (1966) and the USSR (1958), → Germany with regard to Iran (1929), → Turkey (1929) and the USSR (1958) and → Italy in relation to Turkey (1929). These conventions may hinder the proper application of the Succession Regulation when property is scattered over several EU countries and nationals of these third countries are involved.

3. Application in time

Although the Succession Regulation entered into force on 16 August 2012, the rules of the Regulation will apply to the succession of persons who pass away on or after 17 August 2015, except for arts 77 and 78, which have applied since 16 January 2014, and arts 79, 80 and 81, which have applied since 5 July 2012 (art 84). The Succession Regulation is in force in all EU Member States, with the exception of → Denmark, the → United Kingdom and → Ireland.

4. Structure

The structure of the Regulation consists of a Preamble with considerations and 84 articles divided into seven chapters. Chapter I determines the scope of the Regulation and provides for several definitions. Chapter II deals with matters of jurisdiction. Chapter III is the heart of the Regulation and contains the conflict rules according to which the applicable law has to be determined. Chapter IV pertains to the recognition, enforceability and enforcement of decisions. Chapter V provides rules regarding authentic instruments and court settlements. In Chapter VI the Regulation creates a European Certificate of Succession and gives further rules with respect to such an instrument. The final Chapter VII contains general and final provisions, including transitional provisions.

III. Jurisdiction

According to art 4, the courts of the Member State of the deceased's habitual residence at the time of death will have jurisdiction to rule on the succession as a whole. Since the systems in Member States dealing with succession differ, the term 'court' has a broad meaning. As well as covering courts as such, exercising judicial functions, it includes also the notaries or registry offices in certain Member States with similar judicial functions in certain matters of succession, as well as the notaries and legal professionals of other Member States whose exercise of judicial functions in a given succession is based on a delegation of power by a court (Recital (20)). This does not imply that every civil law notary is deemed to be a court. This is only the case if the notary has the authority to exercise judicial functions, which means that, for example, a German or a Dutch notary would not qualify as a court. In consequence, notaries who do not exercise judicial functions are in this respect not bound by the jurisdiction rules (Recital (22)).

The European legislature brought about a concurrence (*Gleichlauf*) between competence and applicable law. Primarily competent is the court of the habitual residence of the deceased at the time of death (art 4), while the succession is governed by the same law (art 21). This ensures on the one hand the proper administration of justice within the EU, and on the other hand a genuine connection between the succession and the Member State in which jurisdiction is exercised.

In accordance with the *Gleichlauf* concept, art 5 states that if a testator has chosen the law of a particular Member State to be applicable, the parties may select a relevant court of that state in an ensuing procedure. It is obvious that the *Gleichlauf* principle cannot be applied if the deceased did not have his last habitual residence in a Member State. The courts of a Member State in which goods of the estate are situated are nevertheless (secondarily) competent to rule on the succession as a whole if the deceased was a national of that state (art 10(1)(a)). If a testator is not a national but resided habitually in that Member State (within a period of five years prior to the proceedings), then the relevant court of that Member State will have jurisdiction regarding the entire succession (art 10(1)(b)).

The application of this provision can be problematic as it is not always possible to establish the former place of habitual residence of a deceased. Indeed, it is possible that a person has in the past resided habitually in more than one Member State. It should be noted that if a court has jurisdiction under para 1(a), the courts of other Member States cannot be granted jurisdiction under para 1(b). If no court has jurisdiction in accordance with para 1, then the court of the Member State in which the property is located may accept jurisdiction with regard to that property (art 10(2)). Article 10 allocates jurisdiction in such a way that the courts of Member States cannot deal with the same property simultaneously.

The Regulation provides for a *forum necessitatis* in case it proves impossible to initiate proceedings in a third state, or when it is not feasible to require a beneficiary to initiate proceedings in that country. However, it is still required that the dispute be sufficiently connected with the Member State of the court called upon (art 11).

When an estate includes property located in a Member State as well as in a third country and it is expected that a ruling from the court of that Member State will not have effect in that third country, the court concerned may decide, at the request of one of the parties, to decline to render a ruling on the property located in the third country (art 12).

The Regulation provides detailed rules on the important matter of acceptation and waiver of the succession. Heirs and legatees can undertake all the necessary legal steps at the court dealing with the succession, but art 13 provides the opportunity to undertake these steps at the relevant court or authority of the Member State where the heir or legatee has habitual residence. The courts of the Member State where the succession is dealt with must, in accordance with Recital (32), be informed within the time period applicable there. This is a reasonable requirement since the terms of that country apply and not those of the courts where the heir or legatee has habitual residence.

Chapter II of the Succession Regulation further contains numerous typical jurisdictional provisions, such as the examination of a court on its own motion of jurisdiction, examination as to admissibility, *lis pendens* (→ *Lis alibi pendens*), connexity, and provisional and protective measures.

IV. Applicable law

1. General

The European legislature presumes a so-called unitary system in its Succession Regulation, whereby movable and immovable assets are inherited under the same law. This system promotes legal certainty and averts the fragmentation of the estate. It applies to assets worldwide, including those located in third countries. Objective directives must ensure that successions are governed by a legal system which is foreseeable and most closely connected to these successions. This has resulted in the designation of the deceased's last habitual place of residence. The nationality of the testator plays a role only with regard to the → choice of law.

A person has the authority to designate the law applicable (art 22) and absent such designation, the law of the last habitual residence will apply (art 21).

2. Professio juris

Article 22 Succession Regulation provides a person with the authority to manage their succession in advance through the option of choosing of the applicable law. This choice is limited to that of a state of which the deceased is a national. Contrary to the Hague Succession Convention, the choice of the law of the habitual residence is not possible. For the → Netherlands, this limited choice of law is to the detriment of estate planning possibilities. Other Member States do not acknowledge this authority, which also signifies a major change in estate planning. As a compromise, the Regulation provides the testator with the authority to choose the law of the state of his → nationality at the time of designation or at the time of death, as applicable to the entire inheritance. A person who holds more than one nationality may choose the law of one of the states of which he is a national at the time the choice is made.

Recital (38) states that:

> This Regulation should enable citizens to organise their succession in advance by choosing the law applicable to their succession. That choice should be limited to the law of a state of their nationality in order to ensure a connection between the deceased and the law chosen and to avoid a law being chosen with the intention of frustrating the legitimate expectations of persons entitled to a reserved share.

This consideration also applies to the habitual residence, but does not explain why such a choice-of-law option is not included. The fear of impeding the right to legitimate portions seems to have been influential. Whether this means the doctrine of *fraud à la loi* is introduced is questionable. Indeed, this doctrine does not comply with *Savigny*-based (→ *Savigny, Friedrich Carl von*) European private international law.

The choice of law must be made clearly in a declaration in the form of a disposition of property upon death or must be evident in the terms of such a disposition (art (2)). The latter is at times difficult to determine in practice. But references to certain rules of national law or the mentioning of them may, according to the preamble, be acknowledged as a choice for that law. The substantive validity of the act by which the choice is made is determined by the chosen law (art 22(3)). The amendment or repeal of the law chosen must meet the formal requirements for the modification or revocation of a will (art 22(4)).

3. Applicable law in the absence of a professio juris

Where a testator has made no choice of law, then according to art 21 Succession Regulation, the law of the last habitual residence will apply, unless another law would appear to be more closely connected.

The Regulation correctly gives no definition of *habitual residence*. In order to determine the habitual residence, all the circumstances of the life of the deceased during the years preceding death and at the time of death are to be taken into account, including all relevant factual elements, in particular the duration and regularity of the deceased's presence in the state concerned and the conditions and reasons for that presence. The determined habitual residence should, in accordance with the specific aims of the Regulation (Recital (23)), reveal a close and stable connection with the state concerned. Using the habitual residence as a connecting factor ensures a genuine connection between the succession and the Member State in which the deceased had his *centre of gravity*. The choice-of-law rule of art 21 is thus based on the principle of the closest connection.

The Preamble mentions two complex situations in which it may prove difficult to determine the deceased's habitual residence. First, it may be that the deceased had gone to live abroad to work for professional or economic reasons, sometimes for a long period, but had nevertheless maintained a close and stable connection with his state of origin. In such a case, the deceased could, depending on the circumstances of the case, still be considered to have habitual residence in the state of origin where the centre of interest of the family and social life was located. Second, complex cases may arise where the deceased lived in several states alternately or travelled from one state to another without settling permanently in any of them. If the deceased was a national of one of those states or had all his principal assets in one of those states, his nationality or the location of those assets could be a special factor in the overall assessment of all the factual circumstances (Recital (24)).

Determining the habitual residence according to such criteria will normally not be problematic. However, cases appear regularly in legal practice in which it can be extremely difficult to determine the centre of gravity of a person's life. An example would be if someone lives close to a border. One must also bear in mind that notarial and other legal practitioners often have to advise long in advance and have to provide legal certainty in doing so. The Regulation provides no sound solution for this type of case. A rebuttable presumption that a person has his habitual residence in a particular country when he has been resident there for a certain period of time could have helped to solve this problem.

In exceptional cases, when, from all the circumstances of the case, it is clear that, at the time of death, the deceased was manifestly more closely connected with a state other than the state whose law would be applicable under para 1, then the law applicable to the succession will be the law of that other state. This would, for instance, be the case if the deceased had moved to the state of his habitual residence recently before death and all the circumstances of the case indicate that the deceased was manifestly more closely connected with another state.

The Succession Regulation sets out a number of special conflicts-of-laws rules regarding disposition of property upon death. The admissibility and substantive validity of a final disposition that is not an agreement on succession is governed by the law which, under this Regulation, would have been applicable to the succession of the person who made the disposition if death had occurred on the day on which the disposition was made (art 24(1)). This is the law of the habitual residence. However, with regard to these aspects, the testator is free to designate the law chosen in accordance with art 22 (art 24(2)).

As an agreement as to succession is not a permissible form of disposition of property upon death in all Member States, art 25 deals with the law applicable in such circumstances, the legal consequences for the parties and the conditions for dissolution of such agreements.

Article 26 specifies the notion of substantive validity of disposition of property upon death. It relates to the capacity of the person making the disposition (→ Capacity and emancipation), the admissibility of representation for the purposes of making a disposition of property upon death, the interpretation of the disposition and fraud, duress, mistake and any other questions relating to the consent or intention of the person making the disposition.

As to the form of dispositions of property upon death, the Regulation is consistent with the Hague Testamentary Dispositions Convention, hereby introducing the *favor testamenti* principle for EU Member States that are not party to this Convention.

In addition, the Regulation contains a comprehensive set of rules on the appointment and powers of an administrator of the estate in certain situations (art 29). It introduces a specific rule for special succession regimes, in conformity with art 15 of the Hague Succession Convention. In addition to a rule regarding *commorientes* (art 32) and estates without a claimant (art 33), art 31 expressly stipulates that, when a person invokes a right *in rem* to which he is entitled under the law applicable to the succession, and when the law of the Member State in which the right is invoked does not know the right *in rem* in question, then, if necessary and to the extent possible, that right will be adapted to the closest equivalent right *in rem* under the law of that state, taking into account the aims and the interests pursued by the specific right *in rem* and the effects attached to it. This provision will evoke the same questions in legal practice as currently exist and, as such, the apparent benefit of uniform conflict-of-laws rules of the Succession Regulation is somewhat counterbalanced.

Article 34 regulates the issue of reversion and referral (→ *Renvoi*). According to Recital (57), *renvoi* should be accepted 'in order to ensure international consistency' if the conflict-of-laws rules laid down in the Regulation refer to the law of a non-Member State and the choice-of-law rules of that state refer to either the law of a Member State or to the law of a third state which would apply its own law to the succession. *Renvoi* should, however, be excluded in situations where the deceased had made a choice of law in favour of the law of a third state. Even so, no theoretical legal justification for this provision is given.

Chapter III of the Regulation closes with familiar rules on public policy and states with more than one legal system.

V. Recognition, enforceability and enforcement of decisions

Chapter IV governs the recognition, enforceability and enforcement of decisions. Given the primary objective of the Regulation, ie the mutual recognition of decisions on succession in Member States, arts 39–42 provide rules regarding recognition and arts 43–58 provide rules on enforceability. The starting point is that a decision given in a Member State will be recognized in the other Member States without any special procedure being required (art 39(1)). As is common in other regulations, art 40 Succession Regulation provides for specific grounds of non-recognition of decisions. A decision will not be recognized: (i) if such recognition is manifestly contrary to → public policy (*ordre public*) in the Member State in which recognition is sought; (ii) where the decision was given in default of appearance, if the defendant was not served with the document which instituted the proceedings or with an equivalent document in sufficient time and in such a way as to enable it to arrange for its defence, unless the defendant failed to commence proceedings to challenge the decision when it was possible for it to do so; (iii) if the decision is irreconcilable with a decision given in proceedings between the same parties in the Member State in which recognition is sought; (iv) if the decision is irreconcilable with an earlier decision given in another Member State or in a third state in proceedings involving the same cause of action and between the same parties, provided that the earlier decision fulfils the conditions necessary for its recognition in the Member State in which recognition is sought.

Decisions enforceable in a Member State shall, at the request of any interested party, be enforceable in another Member State when they have been declared enforceable there (art 43). If the decision on the application for a declaration of enforceability is appealed against, the court shall refuse or revoke a declaration of enforceability only on one of the grounds specified in art 40. It shall give its decision without delay (art 52).

VI. Authentic instruments and court settlements

The Succession Regulation is, moreover, aimed at safeguarding the acceptance and enforceability of authentic instruments in all Member States. Chapter V of the Regulation gives an elaborate scheme for this. The assumption is that authentic instruments should have the same evidentiary effects in another Member State as they have in the Member State of origin, or the most comparable effects (Recital (61)). The law of the country of origin therefore determines which evidentiary effect an authentic instrument should have in another Member State. An authentic instrument that is enforceable in the Member State of origin can be declared the same in another Member State at the request of a party concerned. This similarly applies to court settlements.

VII. European Certificate of Succession

The Succession Regulation, in art 62(1), provides for the creation of a uniform certificate, the European Certificate of Succession (henceforth 'the Certificate'). This is a certificate to be issued in a cross-border succession case in one Member State for use in another Member State. The Certificate should settle such succession speedily, smoothly and efficiently. The heirs, legatees, executors of the will or administrators of the estate should be able to easily demonstrate their status and/or rights and powers in another Member State, for instance, in a Member State in which succession property is located (Recital (67)). However, the Certificate does not replace the already existing national documents for similar purposes in the Member States.

The use of the Certificate is not mandatory. Other instruments provided by the Regulation are at a party's disposal, such as judgments, authentic instruments and court settlements. But when a Certificate is provided to an authority in another Member State, it cannot request one of the above instruments instead of the Certificate. As defined in art 69, a Certificate which has been issued for use in one Member State shall have similar effect in the Member State of issue.

The Certificate is for use by heirs, legatees having direct rights in the succession and executors of wills or administrators of the estate who, in another Member State, need to invoke their status or to exercise respectively their rights as heirs or legatees and/or their powers as executors of wills or administrators of the estate (art 63(1)). By means of the Certificate, those concerned can demonstrate their legal status and/or the rights as well as the attribution of a specific asset or specific assets, prove their respective shares of the estate and demonstrate their powers to execute the will or administer the estate (art 63(2)).

The Certificate is issued upon request by heirs, legatees having direct rights in the succession and executors of wills or administrators of the estate. The application can be submitted using a standard form provided by the European Commission and must contain at least the information specified in art 65(3). Upon receipt of the application, the issuing authority verifies this information and carries out any inquiries necessary for that verification of its own motion if this is required according to its own law (art 66(1)). The issuing authority may ask the competent authorities of other Member States to provide information held, for example, in the land registers, the civil status registers and registers recording documents, and facts of relevance for the succession or for the matrimonial property regime or an equivalent property regime of the deceased (art 66(5)).

In accordance with art 64, the Certificate can be issued in the Member State whose courts have jurisdiction under art 4, art 7, art 10 or art 11.

The issuing authority must issue the Certificate without delay as soon as the elements to be certified have been established under the law applicable to the succession or under any other law applicable to specific elements (art 67(1)). These Certificates are to be issued as outlined by the European Commission. Such Certificates will not have the form of a notarial deed, as is customary in several Member States for national certificates. In addition to details concerning the deceased and the applicant, the Certificate must contain, for instance, information on the law applicable to the matrimonial property and, if appropriate, the prenuptial agreement. It must also give particulars on the law applicable to the succession and the elements on the basis of which that law is determined, as well as information as to whether the succession is testate or intestate, including information concerning the elements giving rise to the rights and/or powers of the heirs, legatees, executors of wills or administrators of the estate. If relevant, the Certificate must give information about the nature of the acceptance or waiver of the succession by the beneficiaries. Additionally, it must identify the share for each heir and, if applicable, the list of rights and/or assets for any given heir, as well as the list of rights and/or assets for any given legatee and the restrictions on the rights of the heir(s) and, as appropriate, legatee(s) under the law applicable to the succession and/or under the disposition of property upon death. Furthermore, the Certificate must provide information about the powers of the executor of the will and/or the administrator of the estate and the restrictions on those powers under the law applicable to the succession and/or under the disposition of property upon death (art 68).

The original of the Certificate is held by the issuing authority, but this authority can provide one or more certified copies to the applicant or to any person demonstrating a legitimate interest (art 70). In principle, these certified copies are valid for a limited period of six months. However, any person in possession of a certified copy can request an extension of the period of validity or a new certified copy.

The Regulation also provides for the possibility of appeal against the decisions of the issuing authority about whether or not to issue a Certificate.

The Certificate produces its effects in all Member States without any special procedure being required (art 69). It does not constitute an enforcement order, but it is primarily aimed at providing proof of the information required. The probative value of the Certificate does not extend to items that are not covered by the Regulation. The Regulation also provides rules on the protection of parties who have made payments or delivered goods in good faith on the basis of a Certificate of Succession.

Ultimately, it is the objective of the *Conseil de l'Union des Notariats Europeénne* to create a European register for European Certificates of Succession.

VIII. General and final provisions, among which transitional provisions

It must be noted that, of the general and final provisions, the transitional provisions are extremely important for legal practitioners. According to art 83(1), the Regulation applies to the succession of persons who die on or after 17 August 2015. This gives rise to the question of how to deal with dispositions and choice of laws made before then. The premise is that the present regime should be favoured as much as possible with regard to the validity of dispositions and choices of law. The faith of citizens with respect to the preceding private international law regime should be protected. According to art 83(2) a choice of law is valid if: (i) it meets the conditions laid down in Chapter III; or (ii) it is admissible and valid in substantive terms and as regards form in the application of the rules of private international law which were in force, at the time the disposition was made, either in the state in which the deceased had habitual residence, or in any of the states whose nationality he possessed, or in the Member State of the authority dealing with the succession.

If, for example, a person (whether Dutch, German, Belgian or Austrian for that matter) with the → Netherlands as habitual residence exercises the extensive authority that the Hague Succession Convention affords to make a → choice of law and may have validly chosen Dutch law to be applicable. This choice of law must be honoured if the person were to move back to his homeland and die there after 17 August 2015. The same holds for a choice of law made by a Dutchman living in → Belgium.

IX. Significance

1. Significance for private international law theory

The Succession Regulation is styled as is customary for European regulations. A large part of the provisions are a representation of or based on those of the Hague Succession Convention. And although some basic principles of private international law can be identified in various provisions, an extensive theoretical private international law foundation is absent, as is the case with other regulations as well. The system laid down in this Regulation aims primarily at regulating the international aspects of succession in a practical way.

2. Significance for private international law practice

The Succession Regulation aims to make the life of EU citizens easier whenever they are in a cross-border situation and inheritance issues arise. This Regulation makes a major contribution to achieving this goal, but, nevertheless, the different approaches to property law in matters of succession will still in practice pose various challenges.

MATHIJS TEN WOLDE

Literature

Andrea Bonomi and Patrick Wautelet (in collaboration with Ilaria Pretelli and Azadi Öztürk), *Le droit européen des successions. Commentaire du Règlement No. 650/2012 du 4 juillet 2012* (Bruylant 2013); Anatol Dutta and Sebastian Herrler (eds), *Die Europäische Erbrechtsverordnung* (CH Beck 2014); Jonathan Fitchen, 'Recognition, Acceptance and Enforcement of Authentic Instruments in the Succession Regulation' (2012) 8 J Priv Int L 323; Marion Greeske, *Die Kollisionsnormen der neuen EU-Erbrechtsverordnung* (CH Beck 2014); Jens Kleinschmidt, 'Optionales Erbrecht: Das Europäische Nachlasszeugnis als Herausforderung an das Kollisionsrecht' (2013) 77 RabelsZ 723; Ulrich Simon and Markus Buschbaum, 'Die neue EU-Erbrechtsverordnung' [2012] NJW 2393.

Sale contracts and sale of goods

I. Contracts for the international sale of goods and the 1955 Hague Sales Convention

Scholars have always devoted a lot of attention to international sales contracts and, in particular, to contracts for the international sale of goods. In light of the importance of the latter type of sales contracts, considered to be the 'mercantile contract *par excellence*', the 'lifeblood of international commerce', and therefore 'the pillar of the entire system of commercial relations', this is unsurprising. And it is equally unsurprising that it is these sales contracts that have garnered the most attention from those attempting to promote certainty and predictability, 'the bedrock desiderata of [any] commercial law' (Robert Scott, 'The Uniformity Norm in Commercial Law: A Comparative Analysis of Common Law and Code Methodologies' in Jody Kraus and Steven Walt (eds), *The Jurisprudential Foundations of Corporate and Commercial Law* (CUP 2000) 149, 149, 176 note 3), let alone international commercial law, by attempting to create uniform rules. In this respect, reference has to be made to attempts to achieve certainty and predictability by creating a uniform set of substantive rules with the intention of overcoming the economic players' supposedly worst enemy, namely national borders and the differences between national legal systems, which constituted (and still constitute) 'an obstacle to economic relationships which constantly increase among citizens of different countries; an obstacle above all for the enterprises that are involved in international commerce and that acquire primary resources or distribute goods in different countries which all have different law' (Francesco Galgano, 'Il diritto uniforme: la vendita internazionale' in Francesco Galgano and others (eds), *Atlante di diritto privato comparato* (5th edn, Zanichelli 2011) 245).

However, this approach, focused on creating a set of uniform substantive law rules (→ Uniform substantive law and private international law), such as those contained in the → CISG (United Nations Convention of 11 April 1980 on Contracts for the International Sale of Goods, 1489 UNTS 3), is not the only approach that may result in predictability and certainty. The drafting of uniform rules of private international law also may lead to predictability and certainty. Unlike uniform substantive law, which aims at guaranteeing that all parties from countries where the uniform substantive law is in force have equal access to the substantive law solutions, uniform private international law, by making sure 'that courts will apply the same legal rules no matter where the parties litigate the dispute', 'assures a business entering into a contract with a foreign enterprise that no matter what forum a dispute is brought before, the uniform choice-of-law rules will apply the same country's substantive law' (Peter Winship, 'Private international law and the UN Sales Convention' [1988] Cornell Int'l L.J. 487).

In respect of the attempts to unify the private international law rules of contracts for the international sale of goods, one has to mention those made by the → Hague Conference on Private International Law. These efforts first resulted in the adoption, in 1955, of the Hague Sales Convention (Hague Convention of 15 June 1955 on the law applicable to international sales of goods, 510 UNTS 147) and, in 1986, in that of a successor convention. While the latter has never come into force, the former is in force today in → Denmark, → Finland, → France, → Italy, → Norway, → Sweden and → Switzerland.

The 1955 Hague Sales Convention being in force in the above-mentioned countries creates a conflict between the Convention on the one hand and some other instruments on the other. This is true in respect, for instance, of the Rome Convention (Rome Convention on the law applicable to contractual obligations (consolidated version), [1998] OJ C 27/34), which still applies in → Denmark, even to contracts concluded on or after 17 December 2009, the date that in the other EU Member States triggers the need to resort to the Rome I Regulation (Regulation (EC) No 593/2008 of the European Parliament and of the Council of 17 June 2008 on the law applicable to contractual obligations (Rome I), [2008] OJ L 177/6; → Rome Convention and Rome I Regulation (contractual obligations)) for the purpose of identifying the applicable law.

Given the foregoing conflict, when Danish courts are tasked with the identification of the law applicable to contracts for the international sale of goods, they will first have to determine which set of private international law rules to have recourse to. Article 21 Rome Convention is helpful in solving this dilemma, as it sets forth a 'generous' conflict-of-conventions rule. Pursuant to this rule, the Rome 'Convention will not prejudice the application of any other international agreement, present or future, to which a Contracting State is or becomes party' (Giuliano-Lagarde Report (Report on the Convention on the law applicable to contractual obligations by Mario Giuliano, Professor, University of Milan, and Paul Lagarde, Professor, University of Paris I, [1980] OJ C 282/1)), at least in those instances where the international agreement constitutes *lex specialis* vis-à-vis the Rome Convention. This has led both commentators and courts to state that recourse to the Hague Sales Convention prevails over resort to the Rome Convention, since the former Convention constitutes a *lex specialis* (see Trib Vigevano, 12 July 2000 (2001) 20 J.L.& Com. 209).

However, the 1955 Hague Sales Convention prevails not only over the Rome Convention, but also over the Rome I Regulation (see Ole Lando and Peter Arnt Nielsen, 'The Rome I Regulation' (2008) 45 CMLR 1687, 1705; Stefan Leible and Matthias Lehmann, 'Die Rom-I-Verordnung' [2008] RIW 528, 532). This can be derived from the Rome I Regulation's equivalent to art 21 Rome Convention, namely art 25(1), the provision that applies to solve the conflict at hand. Pursuant to art 25(1), the 'Regulation shall not prejudice the application of international conventions to which one or more Member States are parties at the time when this Regulation is adopted and which lay down conflict-of-laws rules relating to contractual obligations'. It is worth pointing out that art 25(2), which also sets forth a conflict-of-conventions rule and, more specifically, a conflict-of-conventions rule that lets the Regulation take precedence over bilateral or multilateral conventions concluded exclusively between Member States, cannot apply to solve the conflict at hand, given that the Hague Sales Convention is not one 'exclusively between Member States', as the foregoing list of contracting states unmistakably shows.

However, this does not mean that the Rome instruments are necessarily completely displaced in the courts of those countries where the Hague Sales Convention is also in force. This is due, on the one hand, to the limited sphere of application of the Hague Sales Convention and, on the other hand, to the Convention setting forth only a limited number of rules, thus leaving a lot of issues unsettled.

As regards the Convention's limited sphere of application, it can easily be derived from the Convention itself. Although the Convention applies to contracts for the international sale of goods generally (art 1), it does, among other things, 'not apply to sales of securities, to sales of ships and of registered boats or aircraft, or to sales upon judicial order or by way of execution', although it does 'apply to sales based on documents' (art 1). This means that where the Convention does not apply to a given contract for the 'sale of goods' – to be defined autonomously rather than on the basis of the domestic law of the forum – resort to the Rome instruments, where in force in the forum country, is to be had.

However, resort to the Rome instruments is also to be had when the Hague Sales Convention is applicable, but does not resolve a given issue. In this line of cases, resort is to be had once again to the Rome instruments, provided that they deal with a given issue. This occurs, for instance, in respect of the form issue. Pursuant to art 5(2), the Hague Sales Convention 'shall not apply to ... the form of the contract'. Thus, in order to determine the formal validity of contracts falling under the sphere of application of the Hague Sales Convention, resort is to be had to the Rome instruments. Similarly, resort is to be had to arts 18 and 20 of the Rome Convention and the Rome I Regulation respectively to decide whether the application of the law of the country specified by the Hague Sales Convention also requires the courts to apply the rules of private international law of that country. This is necessary since the Hague Sales Convention does not take a position on *renvoi*.

To the extent that the Hague Sales Convention applies and deals with a given issue, the results reached are, at least to a large degree, comparable to those reached under the Rome instruments. By way of example, it is worth pointing out that in its art 2, the Hague Sales Convention acknowledges the parties' freedom to choose the law applicable, thus codifying the principle of party autonomy and acknowledging, as do the Rome instruments, that the freedom to choose the law constitutes 'one of the cornerstones of the system of conflict-of-law rules in matters of contractual obligations' (Recital (11) Rome I Regulation). Still, art 2 Hague Sales Convention differs from its Rome instruments counterparts in that it makes unmistakably clear that the parties cannot choose non-state law to govern their contract, since art 2 states that a 'sale shall be governed by the domestic law of the country designated by the contracting parties' (in case-law, see Trib Padova, 11 January 2005 [2005] Riv.Dir.Int'le Priv. & Proc. 791).

Absent a (valid) choice of law, art 3(1) makes the law of the seller applicable. Although this appears to be in line with the solution to be derived from the Rome instruments (discussed below), the Hague Sales Convention rule differs from its Rome instruments counterparts in that it does not constitute a presumption. Thus, the law of the seller applies irrespective of a closer link to a different country. 'Nevertheless, a sale shall be governed by the domestic law of the country in which the purchaser has his habitual residence, or in which he has the establishment that has given the order, if the order has been received in such country, whether by the vendor or by his representative, agent or commercial traveler' (art 3(2)).

The Hague Sales Convention also sets forth a rule regarding sales of goods at exchanges or public auctions, making applicable the domestic law of the country in which the exchange is situated or the auction takes place.

II. Sale contracts and the Rome Convention

Unlike the Hague Sales Convention, the Rome Convention, which, as mentioned, is still applicable to contracts concluded prior to 17 December 2009, where, as in → Denmark, it is not applicable to contracts concluded even thereafter, covers not only contracts for the sale of goods, but all type of sales contracts.

The Rome Convention's starting point, where the sale does not constitute a consumer contract (→ Consumer contracts), a category not to be discussed in this chapter, is not different from that of the Hague Sales Convention: it allows the parties to freely choose the applicable law, irrespective of whether the sale is for movable goods, immovable goods or intangibles. Pursuant to art 3, the parties can choose to (expressly or implicitly) subject their contract to any law, even a neutral one, as long as it is, at least according to the majority view, a state law (Trib Padova, 11 January 2005 [2005] Riv.Dir.Int'le Priv. & Proc. 791), even after the conclusion of the contract (art 3(2) Rome Convention). Not only, the parties may also choose to apply different laws to one and the same contract (art 3(1) Rome Convention).

The differences between the regimes of the Hague Sales Convention and the Rome Convention become more evident where the parties have not – or not validly – chosen the law applicable. While, as already mentioned, the Hague Sales Convention makes the law of the seller applicable, provided that the seller (or his representative, agent or commercial traveller) has not received the order in the buyer's country, in which case the buyer's law will apply, the Rome Convention imposes recourse to a multi-step approach that is much more complicated and does not necessarily lead to the same solutions as the Hague Sales Convention.

Pursuant to art 4(1) Rome Convention, resort is to be had to the closest connection to identify the applicable law. The closest connection is, according to many commentators, that provision's principal → connecting factor. Although this is certainly true from a doctrinal point of view, statistically speaking recourse to that connecting factor occurs only in exceptional cases, since, in practice, recourse to the presumptions set forth in paras (2), (3) and (4) prevails. In effect, the general rule requiring resort to the closest connection applies 'directly' only where the law applicable cannot be determined by means of one of the aforementioned presumptions. By virtue of art 4(5), recourse to the closest connection is also to be had where it appears from the circumstances as a whole that the contract is more closely connected with a country other than that identified by virtue of one of the presumptions of paras (2)–(4). From a statistical point of view, this does not happen often either, and it is this principle's scarce application in practice that has led some commentators to propose that it be eliminated. However, in this author's opinion, the scarce practical importance of the principle of closest connection does not constitute a valid reason for denying its central role under the Rome Convention, because it allows courts to always be able to determine the law applicable to a contract, without exception. In other words, it is this connecting factor that makes any recourse to external connecting factors not contained in art 4 unnecessary.

The 'closest connection' is not defined in art 4 Rome Convention. From art 4(1), one can only derive that what counts is the 'closest connection' between the contract and a country, which in turn has two consequences: on the one hand, that art 4 cannot lead to the application of non-state law and, on the other hand, that elements that do not have any impact on the connection between the contract and a given country (such as the substantive law solution to be found in that country) cannot be relevant in determining the applicable law.

However, these consequences do not help to define the concept in question, which is so vague as to only have little meaning; therefore, the concept at hand needs to be 'give[n] greater precision' (Richard Plender and Michael Wilderspin, *The European Contracts Convention: The Rome Convention on the Law Applicable to Contractual Obligations* (2nd edn, Sweet & Maxwell 2001) 114). In this light, the concept is nothing but an 'empty formula', 'devoid of any innate, objectively ascertainable meaning'.

It is to give greater precision to the concept of 'closest connection' that the drafters of the Rome Convention have introduced the presumptions set forth in paras (2), (3) and (4) (see German Federal Court of Justice (BGH), 26 July 2004 [2005] IHR 79), to which one always has to resort – except in those cases that do fall into the primary sphere of application of the principle of closest connection – in order to determine the 'closest connection'. Still, these presumptions do not always lead to the law of the country that *de facto* presents the closest connection with the contract. This is due 'on the one hand, to the large number of types of contract that exist ... and, on the other hand, to the very diverse contexts in which they are embedded' (Dieter Martiny, in Christoph Reithmann and Dieter Martiny, *Internationales Vertragsrecht* (6th edn, Schmidt Verlag 2004) para 157). In order to always ensure the application of the law of the country most closely connected with the contract, as required by art 4(1), the drafters of the Rome Convention introduced a 'get-out clause', pursuant to which 'the presumptions in paragraphs 2, 3 and 4 shall be disregarded if it appears from the circumstances as a whole that the contract is more closely connected with another country' (art 4(5) Rome Convention; in the case-law, see German Federal Court of Justice (BGH), 26 July 2004 [2005] IHR 80). In this author's opinion, the fact that this means to 'leav[e] the judge a margin of discretion as to whether a set of circumstances exists in each specific case justifying the non-application of the presumptions in paragraphs 2, 3 and 4' (Giuliano-Lagarde Report) is consistent with the goal of this get-out clause. The uncertainty derived from it is to be accepted because of the scarce application of the get-out clause.

According to various commentators, the get-out clause in art 4(5) Rome Convention constitutes an exception to the presumptions established in art 4(2)–(4). In this author's opinion, this view can be endorsed only to the extent that it reflects a statistical evaluation of the instances in which the law is determined on the basis of the get-out clause. However, it does not follow that the get-out clause should be ranked any differently than the presumptions of art 4(2)–(4) in the hierarchy of the art 4 choice-of-law rules. Since both these presumptions and para (5) pursue the same goal – the application of the law of the country which is most closely connected to the contract – and since there can be no closer connection than the closest connection, the presumptions of art 4(2)–(4) and the get-out clause have the same standing with respect to the hierarchy of the choice-of-law rules laid down in art 4 Rome Convention. As a result, the law identified as the law applicable pursuant to one of the aforementioned presumptions does not necessarily apply. Rather, the courts must also – *ex officio* – decide whether the contract is, at the time of its conclusion and in light of the circumstances as a whole, *de facto* more closely connected to another country. Only where no such closer connection exists will the law identified pursuant to one of the presumptions apply. In other words, the absence of a closer connection with a country other than the one identified pursuant to one of the presumptions of art 4(2)–(4) constitutes a negative applicability requirement of the law of that (latter) country. Thus, where the contract (or, according to art 4(1), second sentence of the Rome Convention, a separable part of it) has a closer connection to a different country, the law of that country is to be applied (see Case C-64/12 *Anton Schlecker v Melitta Josefa Boedeker* (12 September 2013) para 54).

As regards sale contracts in particular, this means that courts have to first determine which law would apply pursuant to either art 4(2) (if the sale is one of movable goods or rights) or art 4(3) (if the sale relates to → immovable property) and then verify whether it appears from the circumstances as a whole that the contract is more closely connected with a country other than that the law of which would be applicable pursuant to the relevant presumption.

As regards contracts for the sale of goods and rights, what has just been said requires courts to first determine (on the basis of art 4(2)) what party has to effect the characteristic performance. In contracts for the sale of the type at hand, it is the seller who has to effect the characteristic performance, consisting of the transfer of ownership and, in the case of sale of goods, the delivery of the goods, since the buyer basically has to perform a monetary obligation, which is generally not characteristic of a given type of contract. However, the courts cannot stop there. They will have to determine whether it appears from the circumstances as a whole that the contract is more closely connected with a country other than that of the seller. If so, the law of that other country will apply. According to some commentators, this is the case in respect of contracts for the sale of ships. In this line of cases, the law of the country of the → flag or port of registry of the ship should apply, since this country appears to be more closely connected to the contract than that of the seller (Peter Mankowski, *Seerechtliche Vertragsverhältnisse im Internationalen Privatrecht* (Mohr Siebeck 1995) 434 ff).

Where the sale concerns immovable property, the presumption to be resorted to is that set forth in art 4(3) Rome Convention, pursuant to which the law of the country applies where the immovable property is situated. However, the *lex rei sitae* does not necessarily apply. Rather, the courts have to determine whether, in light of all the circumstances, it appears that the contract is more closely connected with a different country. Where this is the case, the law of that other country applies. By way of example, it may suffice to refer to a contract for the sale of immovable property situated in England that is concluded in → Germany in the presence of a German notary between two German citizens who have their habitual residences in Germany. Although the immovable property is located in England, the country that appears to be more closely connected to the contract is Germany, which is why German law should apply.

III. Sale contracts and the Rome I Regulation

Like the Rome Convention, the Rome I Regulation sets forth private international law rules applicable to contracts for the sale of goods, → immovable property and rights. And like its predecessor, it allows the parties to choose the law applicable to their contract, irrespective of the object of the sale. Therefore, under the Rome I Regulation as well, the parties are free to subject their sale contract to one or more (state) laws, expressly or implicitly, even after the conclusion of the contract. Thus, in the case of a → choice-of-law agreement, the solutions reached under the Rome I Regulation basically mirror those reached under the Rome Convention.

However, where the parties have not (or not validly) chosen the applicable law, the approach taken by the Rome I Regulation differs from that of its predecessor as outlined in the previous section.

Article 4(1) Rome I Regulation provides for eight special rules for as many types of contract, including rules relating to sale contracts. These special rules, not unlike the presumptions contained in art 4 Rome Convention, are not rigid. This results from art 4(3) Rome I Regulation, which contains a get-out clause similar to the one in art 4(5) Rome Convention. In effect, pursuant to art 4(3) Rome I Regulation: 'Where it is clear from all the circumstances of the case that the contract is manifestly more closely connected with a country other than [country], the law of that other country shall apply.' From this wording, it clearly follows that the special rules laid down in art 4(1) Rome I Regulation are as flexible as the presumptions of art 4 Rome Convention. The European legislator has merely raised the bar with regard to the standard that has to be met in order for the courts to apply the law of a country other than that indicated in one of the special rules (or the default rule set forth in art 4(2)). As a result, it appears that the new get-out clause is much more restrictive than that of art 4(5) Rome Convention; therefore, it creates less uncertainty and should be able to appease even the most fervent critics of art 4(5) Rome Convention. However, in this author's opinion, not much has changed, since the get-out clause of art 4(5) Rome Convention has been *de facto* applied almost exclusively in circumstances which will also trigger the application of the get-out clause contained in art 4(3) Rome I Regulation. Still, the wording is different and this cannot be disregarded. Yet, from a systemic point of view, not much has changed: even under art 4 Rome I Regulation, the courts have – *ex officio* – to look into whether the circumstances of the case connect the contract with the law of a country other than that first identified through resort to one of the special rules. As regards sale contracts, the relevant special rules are contained in arts 4(1)(a), 4(1)(c) and 4(1)(g) governing contracts for the sale of goods, the sale of immovable property and the sale of goods by auction respectively. As far as the sales of rights are concerned, they fall under the sphere of application of art 4(2).

Pursuant to art 4(1)(a) Rome I Regulation, contracts for the sale of goods shall be governed by the law of the country where the seller has his habitual residence (to be determined in accordance with art 19 Rome I Regulation). This corresponds to the result reached in the application of art 4(2) Rome Convention. But even though art 4(1)(a) Rome I Regulation and its counterpart in the Rome Convention lead to the same outcome, the provisions differ from each other to the extent that art 4(1)(a) Rome I Regulation sets forth a clear rule that expressly identifies the law of the seller's country as the law applicable to contracts for the sale of goods. However, the introduction of the rule, aimed at improving legal certainty, comes at a price: it requires an exact determination of its substantive sphere of application and thus of the concept of 'contract for the sale of goods', which is unnecessary when applying the characteristic performance rule under art 4(2) Rome Convention. The new rule requires an autonomous interpretation (→ Interpretation, autonomous) of the aforementioned concept; resort to domestic definitions is not to be had. When defining the contract for 'the sale of goods', Recital (17) has to be taken into account, according to which '"sale of goods" should be interpreted in the same way as when applying art 5 of Regulation (EC) No 44/2001 in so far as sale of goods [is] covered by that Regulation'. In this author's opinion, this allows one to resort to the definition elaborated in connection to the CISG, as that definition is relied upon both by commentators and courts in interpreting the Brussels I Regulation (see Trib Padova, 10 January 2006, CISG-online no 1157). Pursuant to this definition, a sales contract is a contract 'pursuant to which one party – the seller – is bound to deliver the goods and transfer the property in the goods sold and the other party – the buyer – is obliged to pay the price and accept the goods' (Trib Forlì, 16 February 2009, CISG-online no 1780).

As far as the concept of 'goods' is concerned, it covers all goods that, at the time of delivery, are movable and tangible, even those that do not typically form the subject of sales contracts. It must be noted that the sphere of application of art 4(1)(a) Rome I Regulation covers not only the sale of ready-made goods, but also that of goods to be manufactured or produced, as long as the buyer does not contribute himself a 'substantial part' of the material necessary for the manufacture or production of the goods. This can be derived from art 3(1) CISG, which should also be resorted to when autonomously defining what constitutes a 'contract of sale of goods' under the Rome I Regulation (see ECJ Case C-381/08 *Car Trim GmbH v KeySafety Systems Srl* [2010] ECR I-1255, paras 36 and 40). In addition, contracts requiring the supply of labour or other services on top of the transfer of title and delivery of goods are subject to the rule set forth in art 4(1)(a), provided that the obligation to supply labour or other services does not constitute the preponderant part of the obligations of the party who furnishes the goods (art 3(2) CISG). If this were the case, art 4(1)(b) Rome I Regulation would have to be resorted to rather than art 4(1)(a).

The sale of rights (including intellectual property rights) and → immovable property does not constitute a sale of goods; thus, to determine the applicable law, resort to rules other than that laid down in art 4(1)(a) is to be had.

Absent a (valid) choice of law, the European legislator, like the drafters of the Rome Convention, has decided to subject contracts for the sale of immovable property (as well as certain other types of contracts relating to immovable property) for various reasons (such as the immovability of the real estate, public interests and the applicability of mandatory provisions) to the law of the country where the property is situated (art 4(1)(c) Rome I Regulation). Consequently, not unlike under art 4(3) Rome Convention, the *lex rei sitae* applies to contracts for the sale of immovable property, provided, of course, that it is not clear from the circumstances of the case that the contract is manifestly more closely connected to a country other than that where the immovable property is located (art 4(3) Rome I Regulation).

The Rome I Regulation also provides for a specific rule regarding certain sale of goods by auction. Pursuant to that rule, this type of contract is governed by the law of the country where the auction takes place (art 4(1)(g)). Thus, the Rome I Regulation reaches the same result reached under the Rome Convention. However, while under the Rome I Regulation, this result is based upon the specific rule, under the Rome Convention, the aforementioned result is based upon the application of the get-out clause to be found in art 4(5) Rome Convention and, thus, amounts to a deviation from the presumptive result reached via art 4(2) Rome Convention, which requires the application of the law of the seller. Still, also when determining the applicable law pursuant to art 4(1)(g) Rome I Regulation, one has to take into account the get-out clause set forth in art 4(3) Rome I Regulation.

In respect of art 4(1)(g) Rome I Regulation, it is worth pointing out that it does not define 'auction'. This does not mean that resort can be had to domestic understandings of that concept. Rather, that expression, not unlike many other ones contained in the Rome I Regulation, has to be interpreted autonomously. Therefore, for the purposes of the Rome I Regulation, a sale by auction can be defined as the publicly made sale by tender to the highest bidder, ie a sale that offers an opportunity for outbidding other participants. Since online auctions, too, allow for outbidding, art 4(1)(g) Rome I Regulation also applies to this type of auction sales (subject to the qualifications to be made hereinafter). However, art 4(1) (g) Rome I Regulation does not apply to judicial sales as these are excluded from the sphere of application of the Rome I Regulation.

Article 4(1)(g) Rome I Regulation, which prevails over art 4(1)(a) Rome I Regulation due to the former being more specific, only applies where the auction sale concerns movable goods as defined earlier. Furthermore, the application of art 4(1)(g) Rome I Regulation requires that the place of the auction can be determined. If this is not the case, as may at times – although not necessarily always – be the case for Internet auctions, the law applicable has to be determined on the basis of art 4(1)(a) Rome I Regulation rather than art 4(2) Rome I Regulation. For the purpose of determining the law applicable to sales of goods by auction, art 4(2) Rome I Regulation can only be referred to where the applicability requirements of art 4(1)(g) are met, but the law of the country where the auction takes place cannot be applied due, for instance, to a negative choice of that law.

The Rome I Regulation's special rules referred to thus far do not apply to contracts for the sale of rights. To determine the law applicable to these sales, resort is to be had to art 4(2) Rome I Regulation, pursuant to 'which the contract shall be governed by the law of the country where the party required to effect the characteristic performance of the contract has his habitual residence'. This provision leads to the same results as art 4(2) Rome Convention. Thus, as regards reciprocal contracts, where the counterperformance by one of the parties takes the form of money, under the Rome I Regulation as well, the monetary performance does not constitute the one characterizing the contract. It is the performance for which the payment is due that constitutes the characteristic one, although, in exceptional cases, the monetary performance can be characteristic. This is true, for instance, in respect of loan agreements, where the lending is characteristic. Therefore, the law of the party granting the loan (and thus generally the law of the bank) will apply by virtue of art 4(2) Rome I Regulation. However, as regards the sale of rights, the payment obligation does not constitute the characteristic one, which is why the law of the seller applies to the sales at hand, provided that art 4(3) Rome I Regulation does not lead to a different law.

FRANCO FERRARI

Literature

Michael Bridge, *The International Sale of Goods* (3rd edn, OUP 2013); James Fawcett, *International Sale of Goods in the Conflict of Laws* (OUP 2005); Franco Ferrari, 'PIL and CISG: Friends or Foes?' [2012] IHR 89; Jean-Michel Jacquet, 'Le droit de la vente internationale de marchandises: le mélange des sources' in Charles Leben and others (eds), *Mélanges en honneur de Philippe Kahn* (CREDIMI 2000) 75; Dieter Martiny, 'Lex Rei Sitae as a Connecting Factor in EU Private international law' [2012] IPRax 119; Kurt Nadelman, 'Choice of Law Resolved by Rules or Presumptions with an Escape Clause' (1985) Am.J.Comp.L. 297; Michel Pelichet, 'La vente internationale de marchandises et le conflit de lois' [1987] Rec. des Cours 9.

Salvage

I. The concept and notion of salvage

Salvage may be defined as the activity undertaken by a person, the 'salvor', to assist properties and/or persons in danger. When the above-mentioned activity is successful, the salvor is entitled to remuneration, the amount of which may also have been determined in advance by the parties through a binding agreement.

The principle underlying this rule is that protection of property and lives is of paramount importance and salvage must therefore be encouraged (see, with specific reference to maritime salvage, Christopher Hill, *Maritime Law* (6th edn, Informa Law from Routledge 2003) 335).

Civil salvage is distinguished from military salvage, which involves the rescue of property from an enemy in times of war (nowadays of virtually no practical importance, see Francis Rose, *Kennedy and Rose Law of Salvage* (8th edn, Sweet & Maxwell 2013) 10).

The ancient law on salvage particularly concerned civil maritime salvage, ie the salvage of persons and maritime property at sea. Accordingly, the notion of salvage is traditionally linked to shipping and navigation of the seas.

Various notions of salvage have been adopted in national legal systems. Under common law, salvage comprises all activities necessary to save maritime property or lives of persons belonging to any vessel when in danger. Some civil law legal systems have drawn a distinction between 'assistance' (*assistance* in French or *assistenza* in Italian) and 'salvage' (*sauvetage* in French or *ricupero* and *ritrovamento* in Italian; see Francesco Berlingieri, *Le convenzioni internazionali di diritto marittimo e il codice della navigazione* (Guiffrè 2011) 459, 464–7). This distinction was formally acknowledged by the first international uniform convention on salvage (1910 Salvage Convention (International Convention of 23 September 1910 for the Unification of certain Rules of Law related to Assistance and Salvage at Sea, in K Zweigert and J Kropholler, *Sources of International Uniform Law*, vol 2 (AW Sijthoff 1972) 7; 206 LNTS 220)). This Convention expressly covers both salvage and assistance, providing for the same regime for both. However, this Convention has progressively become obsolete and at international level the common law interpretation of the notion of salvage has prevailed. In effect, the last international convention adopted on salvage (1989 Salvage Convention (International Convention of 28 April 1989 on Salvage, 1953 UNTS 165)) makes no express reference to assistance and defines a salvage operation as 'any act or activity undertaken to assist a vessel or any other property in danger in navigable waters or in any other water whatsoever' (art 1 1989 Salvage Convention).

II. The international law of salvage: the 1989 Salvage Convention and its wide sphere of application

Although salvage has ancient origins (see Tjard-Niklas Trümper, 'Salvage' in Jürgen Basedow and others (eds), *The Max Planck Encyclopedia of European Private Law*, vol 2 (OUP 2012) 1517, 1518), it became a particular concern of international law at the beginning of the 20th century.

As mentioned, the first international uniform law instrument adopted is the 1910 Salvage Convention, which originated with the Comité Maritime International. This Convention was extended to salvage of aircraft, by way of a second international instrument, the 1938 Brussels Convention on salvage of aircraft (Convention for Unification of Rules Relating to Assistance and Salvage of Aircraft or by Aircraft at Sea of 19 September 1938, available at <www.mlaus.org/download/1340.pdf>; see Arnold Knauth, 'The Aviation Salvage at Sea Convention of 1938' (1939) 10 *Air Law Review* 146) and to salvage by or to warships and state-owned ships by the Protocol of 27 May 1967 to amend the Convention for the Unification of Certain Rules of Law relating to Assistance and Salvage at Sea of 23 September 1910 (available at <www.admiraltylawguide.com>).

When the *Amoco Cadiz* disaster occurred in 1978, the international community was required to revise the 1910 Salvage Convention, so as to minimize the negative impact of maritime traffic on the environment. The principal defect of the 1910 Salvage Convention was that a salvor acting independently to prevent pollution as opposed to saving property had no entitlement to remuneration. Thus there was little incentive for the salvor to undertake such operations.

This problem was partially solved at contractual level through the insertion within the contractual standard form (LOF; acronym for Lloyd's Open Form) of a specific clause providing a remuneration to the salvor even in the absence of cure (ie the so-called 'safety net'). It was then addressed expressly in the course of revising the 1910 Salvage Convention.

The 1938 Brussels Convention on salvage of aircraft is the third attempt to codify the law of salvage at international level. This Convention expressly envisages the possibility of a 'safety net' for the salvor and it also introduces specific rules regarding state-owned ships as well as warships and state-owned cargos. However, this Convention makes no express reference to aircraft.

The 1989 Salvage Convention takes precedence over the previous 1910 Salvage Convention in regulating the relationship among states having ratified both Conventions (by virtue of the principle *lex posterior derogat legi anteriori*). Pursuant to its art 2, the 1989 Salvage Convention is to be applied *erga omnes*, in all (judicial and arbitral) proceedings on salvage taking place in a Member State of the Convention, regardless of the → nationality of the ships involved.

As for judicial proceedings, this means that the 1989 Salvage Convention applies as → *lex fori*, regardless of the existence of international subjective or objective elements, and that it takes precedence over national law and, more precisely, over national substantive as well as choice-of-law rules.

As for arbitral proceedings, art 2 states that the arbitrators of an arbitral proceeding seated in a Member State of the Convention are bound to apply the 1989 Salvage Convention. However, the 1989 Salvage Convention will certainly be applied in arbitral proceedings when the applicable law (chosen by the parties, or in the rare cases where party choice is absent, that determined by the relevant choice-of-law rules) is the law of a state which is party to the Convention itself. This is because the law of the state necessarily includes not only the *lex mercatoria*, but also the mandatory uniform rules of the 1989 Salvage Convention (Andrea La Mattina, *L'arbitrato marittimo e i principi del commercio internazionale* (Giuffrè 2012) 46, 213–14 and 214 fn 123).

Central to the definition of the sphere of application of the 1989 Salvage Convention is the definition of salvage, which, as mentioned, is based on a common law definition (art 1). No distinction is drawn between vessels, their apparel, cargo or wreck. Pursuant to art 1 'vessel' means any ship or craft, or any structure capable of navigation, while 'property' means any property not permanently and intentionally attached to the shoreline, including freight at risk (art 1). As pointed out by the German delegate during the drafting of the Convention, the 1989 Salvage Convention's purpose is to go beyond the sphere of application of the 1910 Salvage Convention and not to confine itself to vessels and their cargo. Thus, 'any property outside the vessel which is not intentionally and permanently attached to the shoreline' can be a separate object of salvage, so it can be a diamond, a car or a helicopter plunging into the water' (see *Travaux préparatoires of the 1989 London Salvage Convention*, p 56, available at <www.comitemaritime.org>; see also Francesco Berlingieri, *Le convenzioni internazionali di diritto marittimo e il codice della navigazione* (Guiffrè 2011) 459, 471).

In light of the foregoing, the 1989 Salvage Convention may be applied also to the salvage of an aircraft, despite the absence of express reference to aircraft (which, as mentioned, were by contrast expressly considered by the 1938 Brussels Convention on salvage of aircraft, extending to them the regime of the 1910 Salvage Convention).

At the same time under art 3 1989 Salvage Convention, properties permanently and voluntarily linked to the shoreline, fixed or floating platforms or mobile offshore drilling units, when engaged in exploration, exploitation or production of sea-bed mineral resources clearly fall outside the scope of application of the 1989 Salvage Convention.

By way of reservation, however, any state may decide not to apply the Convention to certain specific cases, such as (i) when the salvage operation takes place in inland waters and the vessels involved are of inland navigation or no vessels are involved, (ii) when the interested parties are nationals of that state, (iii) when the property involved is maritime cultural property of prehistoric, archaeological or historic interest and is located on the sea-bed (art 30).

Given its broad sphere of application and the small number of reservations made under art 30(d), the 1989 Salvage Convention needs to be coordinated with other existing international conventions on the law of the sea. More precisely, the 1989 Salvage Convention takes priority over the UNCLOS (United Nations Convention of 10 December 1982 on the Law of the Sea, 1833 UNTS 396). Thus art 303 of the UNCLOS expressly states that '[n]othing in this article affects the rights of identifiable owners, the law of salvage or other rules of admiralty, or laws and practices with respect to cultural exchanges'. The 1989 Convention also takes priority over the 1992 CLC (International Convention of 27 November 1992 on civil liability for oil pollution damage, 1956 UNTS 255) and over the 1971 Fund Convention (International Convention on the Establishment of an International Fund for Compensation for Oil Pollution Damage of 18 December 1971, ceased to be in force 24 May 2002, 1110 UNTS 57). While under the 1910 Salvage Convention the criterion used in order to understand which regime of compensation should be applied was that adopted by the Italian judges in the *Patmos* case (ie to identify the primary purpose of the measures taken, see Trib Messina, 30 July 1986, *Esso Italiana S.p.A. e altri c. Patmos Shipping Corp. e altri* [1986] Dir Marit 996 and Corte di Appello Messina, 24 December 1993 [1994] Dir Marit 1076), under the 1989 Salvage Convention it is now clear that, at least when contractual salvage arises, the Convention takes priority by virtue of the application of its art 8 and 14 (see Francesco Berlingieri, *Le convenzioni internazionali di diritto marittimo e il codice della navigazione* (Guiffrè 2011) 459, 496). Otherwise, when salvage is spontaneous, the regime to be applied should be identified having regard to the specific features of the salvage operations at stake. This reasoning may be applied for example when considering whether the 1989 Salvage Convention prevails over other relevant international conventions such as the Bunker Convention 2001 (International Convention of 23 March 2001 on civil liability for bunker oil pollution damage, IMO Doc LEG/CONF 12/19, 40 ILM 1406), the HNS Convention (International Convention of 3 May 1996 on liability and compensation for damage in connection with the carriage of hazardous and noxious substances by sea, 35 ILM 1406; as amended by the Protocol of 20 April 2010 to the International Convention on liability and compensation for damage in connection with the carriage of hazardous and noxious substances by sea, IMO Doc LEG/CONF.17/DC/1 (29 April 2010)) and the Removal of Wrecks Convention (Nairobi International Convention of 18 May 2007 on the Removal of Wrecks, IMO Doc LEG/CONF 16/17, 46 ILM 697). In other cases, specific rules should be provided – for example, when it is necessary to establish how the 1989 Salvage Convention is to be coordinated with (i) the 1969 Intervention

Convention (International Convention of 29 November 1969 Relating to Intervention on the High Seas in Cases of Oil Pollution Casualties, 970 UNTS 211) and its 1973 Intervention Protocol (Protocol relating to intervention on the high seas in cases of pollution by substances other than oil of 2 November 1973, 1313 UNTS 3), as well as with (ii) the UNESCO Convention of 2 November 2001 on the Protection of the Underwater Cultural Heritage (2562 UNTS 3; on this latter, see G Brice, 'Draft Protocol to the Salvage Convention 1989' [1999] CMI Yearbook 360 and RE Japikse, 'First Report on Unesco Draft Convention on the Protection of Underwater Cultural Heritage' [2001] CMI Yearbook 254).

III. The 1989 Salvage Convention: an overview of its substantive rules

Three categories of salvage operation were foreseen by the 1989 Salvage Convention: (i) mandatory salvage, arising when the master of the ship – so far as possible without serious danger to the vessel and persons thereon – is bound to render assistance when persons are in danger of being lost at sea (art 10); (ii) spontaneous or volunteer salvage, which happens when the salvor, facing a situation of danger for a ship and its cargo, offers salvage services without a contractual obligation to do so and even when unreasonably the master of the endangered ship expressly refuses any help; (iii) contractual salvage, when a contract for salvage operation has been concluded by the master (on behalf of the owner of the vessel) and the salvor. The transformation from volunteer to contract salvage is very frequent in practice, in that the salvor often starts the salvage operations on a volunteer basis and then concludes a contract with the master.

However, in all three categories of salvage operations considered by the 1989 Salvage Convention, the relationships between the person rendering the salvage services and the person receiving them are private in nature, save when regulated by the contract, rights and duties of the parties involved in salvage operation are governed by art 8 of the 1989 Salvage Convention.

Regarding contractual salvage, the use of standard contract forms is frequent (but not mandatory), formalizing parties' rights and duties as well as compensation rules. The latest version of the standard contract is the Lloyd's Open Form of Salvage Agreement (LOF 2011, see John Reeder, *Brice on Maritime Law of Salvage* (5th edn, Sweet & Maxwell 2011) 532 and Appendix 5), a document in two parts, the first of which has to be completed with the essential information related to the contract (such as the salvage contractors, the property to be salved, whether the SCOPIC clause – an acronym for special compensation protection and indemnity clause – is incorporated or not into the agreement), while the second part lays down the salvage contractual terms, many of them referring expressly to the rules of the 1989 Salvage Convention (see Emilio Piombino, 'Il Lloyd's open form 2000 e la Scopic clause' [2001] Dir Marit 1233–43 and 'Notiziario' [2012] Dir Marit 330).

As regards compensation, the 1989 Salvage Convention expressly confirms the 'no cure – no pay' principle, originally stated by the 1910 Salvage Convention, whereby a certain degree of success in the salvage operation is sufficient and at the same time necessary to claim compensation. The actual amount of compensation will be calculated taking into account several criteria, expressly listed in art 13 (such as the salved value of the vessel and other properties, the skill and efforts of the salvors in preventing or minimizing damage to the environment, the measure of success obtained by the salvor, the nature and degree of danger, the skill and effort of the salvors in salving the vessel, other properties). However, the list is not intended to be exhaustive and other elements may be considered. The only restriction expressly provided for is that compensation (aside from interest and legal expenses) may not exceed the value of the ship or properties saved.

As an exception to the general 'no cure – no pay' principle, art 14 envisages the special compensation rule, whereby the salvor preventing or avoiding → damages to the environment will be granted a special compensation (ie an increase up to 30 per cent of the expenses incurred by the salvor or even more, provided that the total increase is not over 100 per cent of the expenses incurred by the salvor).

The impact of this rule has been mitigated by the well-known decision of the then House of Lords in the ship salvage case *Nagasaki Spirit* (*Semco Salvage & Marine Pte Ltd v Lancer Navigation Co Ltd (The Nagasaki Spirit)* [1997] 1 Lloyd's Rep 323), where it was stated that the notion of 'fair rate for equipment, personnel actually and reasonably used in the salvage operation' under art 14.3 meant a fair rate of expenditure and did not include any element of profit. More precisely, as *Lord Mustill* stated (*Semco Salvage & Marine Pte Ltd v Lancer Navigation Co Ltd (The Nagasaki Spirit)* [1997] 1 Lloyd's Rep 323, 332),

> the promoters of the Convention did not choose, as they might have done, to create an entirely new and distinct category of environmental salvage, which would finance the owners of vessels and gear to keep them in readiness simply for preventing damage to the environment. Paragraphs 1, 2 and 3 of article 14 all make it clear that the right to special compensation depends on the performance of salvage operations which . . . are defined by article 1(a) as operations to assist a vessel in distress. Thus although article 14 is undoubtedly concerned to encourage professional salvors to keep vessels readily available, this is still for the purposes of a salvage, for which the primary incentive remains a traditional salvage award.

The *Nagasaki Spirit* decision therefore required a high standard of proof, ie that the environmental damage would have resulted but for the salvor's intervention and also regarding the extent of damage had the operation been unsuccessful. However, in order to overcome the difficulties encountered in the application of the special compensation regime provided by the 1989 Salvage Convention, a specific clause (called the SCOPIC clause), has been introduced in the latest version of LOF. The SCOPIC clause makes possible the application of pre-established criteria for the calculation of the special compensation which the owner of the saved properties has to pay in favour of the salvor. The SCOPIC clause will be applied only when it gives rise to a compensation higher than that deriving from the application of art 13 of the 1989 Salvage Convention.

It should finally be considered that the 1989 Salvage Convention does not introduce the concept of liability salvage. In other words, the Convention does not consider the ship's interest in avoiding third-party liabilities as in itself relevant, and accordingly does not extend the salvage concept to take account of salvage potentially preventing or minimizing damage to third-party interests.

IV. Jurisdiction

As mentioned, under its art 2, the 1989 Salvage Convention should apply whenever a judge of a State Party to the Convention (as well as – within the limits stated under section II. above – an arbitrator of an arbitral proceeding with seat in a State Party to the Convention) is called upon to decide a salvage dispute. However, with modern salvage operations largely governed by LOF 2011, which incorporates an arbitration clause, the number of cases coming before the courts has considerably decreased (Francis Rose, *Kennedy and Rose Law of Salvage* (8th edn, Sweet & Maxwell 2013) 4).

However, despite the reduced number of salvage cases being litigated, when an EU Member State court is seized with a salvage dispute and the defendant's domicile is within the EU judicial area, then the rules of the Brussels I Regulation (recast) (Regulation (EU) No 1215/2012 of the European Parliament and of the Council of 12 December 2012 on jurisdiction and the recognition and enforcement of judgments in civil and commercial matters (recast), [2012] OJ L 351/1; → Brussels I (Convention and Regulation)) will apply, as salvage falls within the notion of civil and commercial matters, and art 7(7) provides an express title of jurisdiction for the payment of salvage remuneration.

An EU Member State court may have jurisdiction in the first place by virtue of choice-of-court agreement. However, apart from standard contracts incorporating arbitration clauses, the parties may reach agreement on the salvage operations even when the operations have already started, and grant jurisdiction to a specific court within the EU (art 25 Brussels I Regulation (recast)).

Where no express or implied choice has been made by the parties, the general jurisdiction rule of the defendant's domicile applies (art 4 Brussels I Regulation (recast)).

As alternatives to the general forum of the defendant's domicile and depending on the object of the dispute (ie concerning contractual or non-contractual obligations arising from salvage operations), art 7(1) or art 7(3) of the Brussels I Regulation (recast) may apply. For example, the dispute on contractual salvage between salvor and shipowner may fall within art 7(1), while cargo interests may sue a would-be salvor under art 7(3) for negligence (see Peter Mankowski, 'Art 5' in Ulrich Magnus and Peter Mankowski (eds), *Brussels Ibis Regulation* (Ottoschmidt 2016), 367).

However, as mentioned, a specific forum for disputes concerning the payment of salvage remuneration is envisaged by art 7(7) of Brussels I Regulation (recast). The provision was originally included in the Brussels Convention (Brussels Convention of 27 September 1968 on jurisdiction and the enforcement of judgments in civil and commercial matters, [1972] OJ L 299/32, consolidated version, [1998] OJ C 27/1) on the occasion of the accession of the → United Kingdom, → Ireland and → Denmark (1978), on specific request of the maritime community in the City of London in order to acknowledge the established practice with maritime dispute, especially in salvage, centred in London (see Schlosser Report (Peter Schlosser, 'Report on the Convention on the Association of the Kingdom of Denmark, Ireland and the United Kingdom of Great Britain and Northern Ireland to the Convention on jurisdiction and the enforcement of judgments in civil and commercial matters and to the Protocol on its interpretation by the Court of Justice, signed at Luxembourg, 9 October 1978' [1979] OJ C 59/71) 108).

Art 7(7) Brussels I Regulation (recast) states that, with specific regard to disputes concerning the payment of remuneration claimed in respect of the salvage of a cargo or freight, the person with domicile in an EU Member State may be sued

> in the court under the authority of which the cargo or freight in question (a) has been arrested to secure such payment or (b) could have been so arrested, but bail or other security has been given; provided that this provision shall apply only if it is claimed that the defendant has an interest in the cargo or freight or has such an interest at the time of salvage.

The same rule is provided in the 1988 → Lugano Convention (Lugano Convention of 16 September 1988 on jurisdiction and the enforcement of judgments in civil and commercial matters, [1988] OJ L 319/9) and 2007 Lugano Convention (Lugano Convention of 30 October 2007 on jurisdiction and the recognition and enforcement of judgments in civil and commercial matters, [2007] OJ L 339/3) (see art 5(7) of both Conventions).

This rule envisages the so-called *forum arresti*, whereby the judge ordering the arrest of the cargo or freight, or alternatively the judge who would have arrested the cargo or freight but for the grant of a bail or other security, will have jurisdiction on the merits of the case in relation to which the → provisional measures of the arrest has been issued.

In this way, the *forum arresti* of the cargo or freight under art 7(7) may be considered as a further alternative forum to the *forum arresti* of the ship envisaged by the 1952 Arrest Convention (International Convention of 10 May 1952 relating to the Arrest of Seagoing Ships, 439 UNTS 193), for those EU Member States which ratified the latter (ie → Belgium, → Croatia, → Finland, → France, → Germany, → Greece, → Italy, → Netherlands, → Portugal and → United Kingdom).

Furthermore, the provision of art 7(7) of the Brussels I Regulation (recast) on the one hand clearly confirms the special character of maritime law, which derogating from general rules traditionally justifies the exercise of jurisdiction on the merits on the basis of the mere existence (or even potential existence) of jurisdiction on provisional measures. On the other hand it states that only those defendants with an interest in the cargo or freight saved may benefit from the *forum arresti* (see Sergio M Carbone, and Chiara Enrica Tuo, *Il nuovo spazio giudiziario europeo in materia civile e commerciale. Il Regolamento UE n. 1215/2012* (Giappichelli 2016) 151). Thus the *forum arresti* generally benefits the arresting salvor who on the one hand is not bound to follow the general rule under art 4, and on the other has the opportunity to heavily influence the location of the *forum arresti* itself (see Peter Mankowski, 'Article 5' in Ulrich Magnus and Peter Mankowski (eds), *Brussels Ibis Regulation* (Ottoschmidt 2016), 367).

In this respect, art 7(7) strictly depends on the determination of the jurisdiction on arresting proceedings, which ought to be determined according to national law (art 35 Brussels I Regulation (recast)). Relevant to this purpose is art 7(e) of the 1952 Arrest Convention (→ Arrest of vessels), which has been ratified by certain EU Member States (see above). However, for those states which have signed but not yet ratified the Convention (Ireland, Latvia, Luxembourg, Poland, Romania, Slovenia, Sweden) or have rejected it (Spain on 28 March 2011; see [2013] CMI Yearbook 620–22) or have not even signed it (Austria, Bulgaria, Cyprus, Czech Republic, Denmark, Estonia, Hungary, Lithuania, Malta, Slovakia), their national law will apply.

More precisely, art 7(7) may come into operation not only if an arrest takes place, but also if there is a possibility of arresting the cargo or freight, but the applicant decides not to start the arresting proceeding since some security has been provided. In doing so, art 7(7) goes beyond the ideas of the 1952 Arrest Convention (see Fausto Pocar, 'La giurisdizione sulle controversie marittime nello sviluppo della convenzione di Bruxelles del 1968' [1999] Dir Marit 188).

The *forum arresti* exists against the persons interested in freight or cargo (*actio in personam*), not against the ship (*action in rem*). The interest in freight or cargo may be ascertained when the suit commences or at the time of the salvage (ie the entire duration of the salvage operation). Therefore, a proper defendant under art 7(7) is any person with an interest in cargo or freight at any point of time between the beginning and the end of the salvage operation. The notion of defendant under art 7(7), focusing on the interests in the freight, includes every creditor of the freight claim, who may be the shipowner, as well as a charterer or a bank. It is disputed whether art 7(7) applies to proceedings where the shipowner is not the defendant but the plaintiff. Here for example reference is made to the case of a shipowner claiming the restitution of the compensation exceeding the costs of salvage operations from the salvor.

Finally, it is worth pointing out that the *forum arresti* is particularly relevant in those legal orders not envisaging any common liability on the shipowner's behalf for the salvage remuneration (Francesco Berlingieri, 'Entrata in vigore della Convenzione relativa all'adesione della Danimarca, dell'Irlanda, del Regno Unito alla convenzione del 1968 sulla competenza giurisdizionale e l'esecuzione delle decisioni in materia civile e commerciale' [1987] Dir Marit 166).

V. Choice-of-law rules

By virtue of art 2, the 1989 Salvage Convention applies to judicial or arbitral proceedings relating to salvage brought in a State Party, regardless of the existence of any international element or nature of the dispute at stake. Article 2 must be considered a mandatory provision (see Pierangelo Celle, 'Note sull'applicazione delle Convenzione di Londra del 1989 sul soccorso in mare' in Francesco Berlingieri (ed), *Scritti in onore di Francesco Berlingieri* (Il diritto marittimo 2010) 890), aimed at granting the necessary application of the 1989 Salvage Convention to salvage operations. In consequence, the 1989 Salvage Convention applies as → *lex fori*, taking precedence over national law (both substantive law and private international law) in the majority of EU countries, with the exception of nine Member States which have not ratified it (Austria, Cyprus, Czech Republic, Hungary, Luxembourg, Malta, Portugal, Slovakia as it results from the status of conventions as to 13 July 2016, see the official website of the International Maritime Organization). More precisely, this means that in the majority of EU countries, the 1980 Salvage Convention takes precedence over the EU private international law rules contained in the Rome I Regulation (Regulation (EC) No 593/2008 of the European Parliament and of the Council of 17 June 2008 on the law applicable to contractual obligations (Rome I), [2008] OJ L 177/6; → Rome Convention and Rome I Regulation) and the → Rome II Regulation (Regulation (EC) No 864/2007 of the European Parliament and of the Council of 11 July 2007 on the law applicable to non-contractual obligations (Rome II), [2007] OJ L 199/40). It must be also considered that, even if the list includes land-locked states, ships may nevertheless sail under their flag thereby triggering the choice-of-law issue on salvage.

Despite its uniform and *erga omnes* character, the 1989 Salvage Convention provides for a measure of flexibility.

First, under art 30 Member States are free to limit the sphere of application of the 1989 Salvage Convention, by way of reserving the right not to apply its provisions to specific cases. More precisely, Member States may decide not to apply the 1989 Salvage Convention to specific salvage operations, such as (i) those taking place in inland waters and vessels involved in inland navigation, (ii) those taking place in inland waters with no vessel involved, (iii) those interesting parties who are national of the same state and (iv) those involving maritime cultural property of prehistoric, archaeological or historic interest located on the sea bed.

Second, in certain cases instead of directly regulating some aspects of salvage, the 1989 Salvage Convention introduces choice-of-law rules identifying the applicable law. More precisely: under art 5(3), in salvage operations controlled by public authorities, the state where the authority is located determines the extent to which the authority itself is under a duty to perform salvage operations. Also, under art 15(2), the law of the flag determines the apportionment of reward between owner, master and other persons. Finally, under art 24, the law of the state in which the tribunal is seized determines the salvor's right to interest on any payment due under the 1989 Salvage Convention.

Third, Member States as well as parties involved in salvage operations have discretion to derogate certain rules of the 1989 Salvage Convention. For example art 13(2) states that, even if payment of a reward is to be made by all of the vessels and other property interests in proportion to their respective salved value, then a State Party may under its national law provide that the payment has to be made by one of these interests, subject to a right of recourse of this interest against other interests. An analogous principle has been stated by art 16(1), which with reference to salvage of persons states that no remuneration is due from persons whose lives are saved, but provisions on national laws are not affected on this subject. Finally under art 6(1), the parties involved in salvage operations may derogate the application of certain rules of the Convention by contract, expressly or impliedly. Reference may be made not only to certain substantive rules of the 1989 Salvage Convention, but also to its private international law rules (such as arts 5(2), 15(2) and 24 mentioned above). In consequence, the parties to a salvage contract may choose a different law from that provided by the uniform private international law of the 1989 Salvage Convention (see Pierangelo Celle, 'Note sull'applicazione delle Convenzione di Londra del 1989 sul soccorso in mare' in Franceco Berlingieri (ed), *Scritti in onore di Francesco Berlingieri* (Il diritto marittimo 2010) 894). On the one hand art 6(1) safeguards the use of standard form contracts such as Lloyd's Form where parties so agree, but on the other the general reference to 'a contract' makes it possible for the parties to regulate salvage operations also in a charter party or in a contract for the → carriage of goods by sea (Francis Rose, *Kennedy and Rose Law of Salvage* (8th edn, Sweet & Maxwell 2013)).

Apart from the flexibility mechanisms mentioned, the uniform regime of the 1989 Salvage Convention – as well as any other instrument of international uniform law – does not itself exclude the application of choice-of-law rules. On the one hand, despite its wide scope of application, there may be aspects not covered by the Convention. On the other hand, even though the majority of EU Member States has ratified the Convention, a significant number of countries have not and accordingly have to apply choice-of-law rules.

In disputes regarding contractual salvage operations, under art 3 of Rome I Regulation, EU Member State courts are to give priority to the *lex voluntatis*, ie to the law chosen by the parties. As for the contractual salvages regulated by the LOF 2011, the *lex voluntatis* is English law: under the clause headed 'Governing law', LOF 2011 expressly provides: '[t]his agreement and any arbitration hereunder shall be governed by English law' (see Francis Rose, *Kennedy and Rose Law of Salvage* (8th edn, Sweet & Maxwell 2013) 43). As for contracts for salvage operations not using the standard form and for other contracts also regulating salvage operations among others (such as charter parties or contracts for the carriage of goods), the choice of law must be expressed or clearly demonstrated by the terms of the contract or the circumstances of the case. Absent a choice or a valid choice, the applicable law is that of the salvor's habitual residence (art 4(1)(b) Rome I Regulation). Where the contract includes salvage operations among others, it will be governed by the law of the country of habitual residence of the party required to effect the characteristic performance (Recital (19) and art 4(2) Rome I Regulation).

Regarding non-contractual salvage, during the debate on the first Commission's proposal of the Rome II Regulation, the issue of a specific conflict of law provision was expressly considered and the Hamburg Group for Private international law (see Hamburg Group for Private international law, 'Comments on the European Commission's Draft Proposal for a Council Regulation on the Law Applicable to Non Contractual Obligations' (2003) 67 RabelsZ 1, 32) pointed out the following in this regard:

> The most commonly discussed case of *negotiorum gestio* in the choice of law was the case of a ship rendering help to another ship. Nevertheless it is not advisable to design a rule especially for this case. In modern times such cases mostly fall into the realm of contract and are not left to *negotiorum gestio*. The small remainder not ruled by contract will most likely be governed by the Convention on Salvage. It appears even more unnecessary to provide for a specific conflicts rule since there would be a kind of deadlock to choose between the flag of the helping ship and the flag of the ship to which help is rendered, as the appropriate connecting factor.

Ultimately, no specific provision is envisaged in the Rome II Regulation for disputes regarding non-contractual salvage operations, and in consequence art 11 Rome II Regulation on → *negotiorum gestio* will apply. More precisely, the obligations arising from the salvage will be governed by (i) the law of the common habitual residence of the parties involved in salvage operations (art 11(2)), (ii) absent a common habitual residence of the parties, the law of the country where the salvage operation takes place (place of performance) (art 11(3)), (iii) the law of the manifestly most closely connected country (art 11(4)).

The → place of performance criterion under art 11(3) raises questions with regard to successive acts of a cross-border intervention, such as the transportation of the ship salved. One solution may be to search for the place where the benevolent intervention of the salvor was substantially performed or had its centre of gravity; the other may be to apply the law of the country in which the performance started. The latter seems to be best suited to promote legal certainty. However, given the lack in the Rome II Regulation of a specific rule stating that a ship on the high seas which is registered in a state should be treated as being the territory of that state (see art 18 of European Commission, 'Proposal for a Regulation of the European Parliament and the Council on the Law Applicable to Non-Contractual Obligations ("Rome II")' COM(2003) 427 final), art 11(3) seems to be inoperable with regard to salvage measures in international waters, even if one assumes the saved ship as the place of salvage performance. In this case, the law of the most closely connected country under art 11(4) with regard to salvage operations is likely to be (i) the law of the place of registration of the ship, or (ii) the law of the flag state of the saved ship, or (iii) the law of its home port.

Despite the wide scope of application of the Rome II Regulation, obligations arising from the duty of the master to render assistance to any person in danger of being lost at sea under art 10 of the 1989 Salvage Convention (the above-mentioned mandatory salvage) may be considered to fall outside the relevant notion of non-contractual obligation. In such a case, national private international law rules apply. With specific reference to the Italian legal system (→ Italy), as far as salvage in the territorial sea is concerned, the law of the state where the damage occurred will apply (under art 61 of the Italian Law No 218/1995 in Gazzetta Ufficiale della Repubblica Italiana, 3 June 1995; Supplemento ordinario n 128; see Franco Mosconi and Cristina Campiglio, *Diritto internazionale privato e processuale, Volume I, Parte generale e obbligazioni* (Utet Giuridica 2015) 504; Antonio Lefebvre D'Ovidio, Leopoldo Tullio and Gabriele Pescatore, *Manuale di diritto della navigazione* (Giuffrè 2011) 678), while, in the case of salvage on the high sea, the law of the flag will apply (art 13 of the Italian Codice della Navigazione (Regio decreto-legge 30 marzo 1942, n 327)).

LAURA CARPANETO

Literature

Reuben Balzan, Keith A Borg and Carlos Bugeja, 'Collisions and Maritime Salvage' in Evangelos Vassilakakis, Nikolay Natov and Reuben Balzan (eds), *Regulations Rome I and Rome II and Maritime Law* (Giappichelli 2013) 123; Francesco Berlingieri, 'Entrata in vigore della Convenzione relativa all'adesione della Danimarca, dell'Irlanda, del Regno Unito alla convenzione del 1968 sulla competenza giurisdizionale e l'esecuzione delle decisioni in materia civile e commerciale' [1987] Dir Marit 166; Francesco Berlingieri, *Le convenzioni internazionali di diritto marittimo e il codice della navigazione* (Giuffrè 2011) 459; Gralf Peter Callies, *Rome Regulations, Commentary on the European Rules of the Conflict of Laws* (Kluwer Law International 2011) 513, 520, 521; Sergio Maria Carbone and Chiara Enrica Tuo, *Il nuovo spazio giudiziario europeo in materia civile e commerciale*. Il Regolamento n. 1215/2012, (Giappichelli 2016); Sergio Maria Carbone and Lorenzo Schiano di Pepe, *Conflitti di sovranità e di leggi nei traffici marittimi tra diritto internazionale e diritto dell'Unione europea* (Giappichelli 2010); Pierangelo Celle, 'Note sull'applicazione delle Convenzione di Londra del 1989 sul soccorso in mare' in Francesco Berlingieri (ed), *Scritti in onore di Francesco Berlingieri* (Il diritto marittimo 2010) 887; Andrew Dickinson, *The Rome II Regulation: The Law Applicable to Non-contractual Obligations* (OUP 2008); Andrew Dickinson, *The Rome II Regulation: The Law Applicable to Non-contractual Obligations, Updating Supplement* (OUP 2010) 89; Antonio Lefebvre D'Ovidio, Leopoldo Tullio and Gabriele Pescatore, *Manuale di diritto della navigazione* (Giuffrè 2011) 678; Peter Mankowski, 'Art 5' in Ulrich Magnus and Peter Mankowski (eds), *Brussels Ibis Regulation* (Ottoschmidt 2016) 367; Franco Mosconi and Cristina Campiglio, *Diritto internazionale privato e processuale, Volume I, Parte generale e obbligazioni* (Utet Giuridica 2015) 504; Fausto Pocar, 'La giurisdizione sulle controversie marittime nello sviluppo della convenzione di Bruxelles del 1968' [1999] Dir

Marit 183; John Reeder, *Brice on Maritime Law of Salvage* (5th edn, Sweet & Maxwell 2011); Francis Rose, *Kennedy and Rose Law of Salvage* (8th edn, Sweet & Maxwell 2013); Christopher Julius Starforth Hill, *Maritime Law* (6th edition, Informa Law from Routledge 2003); Mathijs ten Wolde, Jan Ger Knot and Francesca Ragno, 'Art 5.7' in Thomas Simons and Rainer Hausmann (eds), *Regolamento Bruxelles I. Commento al Regolamento (CE) 44/2001 e alla Convenzione di Lugano* (IPR Verlag 2012) 280; Tjard-Niklas Trümper, 'Salvage' in Jürgen Basedow and others (eds), *The Max Planck Encyclopedia of European Private Law*, vol 2 (OUP 2012) 1517.

Same-sex marriages

I. Concept and notion, historical development

Traditionally → marriage was conceived as a union between persons of different sex. Same-sex relationships were disregarded by the law or even criminalized. But in the 1970s the mentality in some countries changed. In → Sweden a commission investigated the legal status of same-sex couples. Despite finding that living in a same-sex relationship was a 'perfectly acceptable form of family life', same-sex marriage and registered partnership were rejected by the commission. But in 1987 the rules on cohabitation were extended to same-sex couples (see Jens M Scherpe, 'Same-Sex Relationships' in Jürgen Basedow and others (eds), *The Max Planck Encyclopedia of European Private Law*, vol 2 (OUP 2012) 1522; Peter Dopffel and Jens M Scherpe 'Gleichgeschlechtliche Lebensgemeinschaften im Recht der nordischen Länder' in Jürgen Basedow and others (eds), *Die Rechtsstellung gleichgeschlechtlicher Lebensgemeinschaften* (Mohr Siebeck 2000) 9). In 1989 → Denmark as the first country in the world introduced a registered partnership for same-sex couples (→ registered partnerships) as a functional equivalent of marriage. This example was followed by several European jurisdictions, but in scope and content the enacted statutes differed enormously. In some jurisdictions, as for example in the Nordic countries and → Germany, the new legal regimes for registered partnerships were only open to same-sex couples; by contrast, in other jurisdictions, such as → Belgium, the → Netherlands and France, they were also open to partners of different sex. As regards the content of the legal rules, some registered partnerships had legal effects comparable to those of marriage (for example as in the Nordic countries and the → United Kingdom and, to a lesser extent, in Germany), whereas others only had rather limited consequences in private law but more significant ones in social and tax law (eg Belgium and → France). But even in those jurisdictions where marriage and registered partnerships had almost the same effects, there was continued criticism that same-sex and opposite-sex couples were treated differently, particularly where registered partnership was open to couples of the opposite sex as well. Here opposite-sex couples could choose between marriage and registered partnership, whereas same-sex couples had no such choice. Compared to marriage, registered partnership was seen as having a lower social status (see eg the reasoning in the English case England and Wales High Court (Family Division), *Wilkinson v Kitzinger* [2006] EWHC 2022 (Fam)). These were some of the reasons which led the Netherlands, as the first country in the world, to open up marriage to same-sex couples in 2001. The Dutch example was followed in Europe by Belgium in 2003, → Spain in 2005, → Norway in 2008, Sweden in 2009, → Iceland and → Portugal in 2010, Denmark in 2012, France in 2013, England and Wales and Scotland in 2014, → Luxembourg in 2015 and → Finland in 2017. In → Ireland a referendum was held on 22 May 2015 and 62 per cent of voters voted in favour of changing the constitution to permit same-sex marriages. Outside Europe, same-sex marriage was introduced for example in → Argentina, → Brazil, → Canada, → Columbia, → New Zealand, → Uruguay, → South Africa. Also, several US states have introduced same-sex marriage, and in 2015 in the landmark decision of *Obergfell v Hodges* (576 U.S. ___(2015)) the US Supreme Court held that the Fourteenth Amendment to the United States Constitution requires the US states to license a marriage between two people of the same sex and to recognize a marriage between two people of the same sex when their marriage was lawfully licensed and performed out-of-state.

It is also worth noting that the ECtHR held in *Vallianatos and Others v Greece* (App Nos 29381/09 and 32684/09 (ECtHR, 7 November 2013)) that the exclusion of same-sex couples from the Greek civil union was a violation of art 8 ECHR (European Convention of 4 November 1950 for the Protection of Human Rights and Fundamental Freedoms, 213 UNTS

221). In *Oliari and Others v Italy* (App Nos 18766/11 and 36030/11 (ECtHR, 21 July 2015)) the ECtHR went even further and found that, at least in the Italian context, there was a positive obligation under the ECHR to provide a protective legal framework for same-sex couples and that the failure of Italy to do so was a violation of art 8 ECHR. As a result, legislative action now is required in many European jurisdictions, and this may lead to further jurisdictions opening up marriage or providing an alternative legal framework (on this see Jens M Scherpe and Andrew Hayward (eds), *The Future of Registered Partnerships* (Intersentia 2017)).

Private international law could simply refer to the rules concerning opposite-sex → marriage. But considering that the national laws of foreign spouses often do not admit same-sex marriage, legal systems using nationality as the traditional connecting factor had to find other solutions.

II. Purpose and function

Choice-of-law rules designate the applicable law to provide legal security, to guarantee a valid marriage in order to avoid a 'limping marriage'. Since the legal systems did not create a second category of marriage but simply opened marriage for same-sex persons, the conflict rules also do not make a distinction between marriages between persons of different or the same sex and thus the general conflict rules on marriage apply. But in legal systems where the nationality is the → connecting factor, this approach excludes a person having the nationality of a state whose law does not permit same-sex marriage. Therefore, the legal systems often use an alternative connecting factor – or consider that a law not permitting same-sex marriage violates public policy. Hence the right to marry prevails. Still, this solution leads to a distinction between different-sex marriage and same-sex marriage in the field of private international law (Patrick Wautelet, 'Private international law Aspects of Same-Sex Marriages and Partnerships in Europe: Divided We Stand?' in Katharina Boele-Woelki and Angelika Fuchs (eds), *Legal Recognition of Same-Sex Relationships in Europe: National, Cross-Border and European Perspectives* (2nd edn, Intersentia 2012) 147).

It is in the interest of same-sex couples that their marriage is recognized in states other than the state of celebration. This is accepted in legal systems having opened up marriage to such couples. But in other jurisdictions public policy often is an impediment, and some legal systems opt for other solutions such as the 'downgrading' of same-sex marriage to a registered partnership.

III. Legal sources

1. National

Most of the states having opened up → marriage to same-sex couples have not adopted specific rules and in principle apply the normal choice-of-law rule governing marriage (as for example Belgium, the Netherlands, Norway, Spain and Sweden). But some systems have provided for additional rules to facilitate same-sex marriages (for example Belgium (art 46 (2) Belgian Code of Private international law (Code de Droit International Privé, Loi du 16 juillet 2004 portant le Code de droit international privé, MB 27 July 2004, 57344, as amended, henceforth Belgian PILA)), England and Wales (Marriage (Same Sex Couples) Act 2013 (c 30)) and France (art 202-1 (2) Civil Code (Code Civil of 21 March 1804, as amended, henceforth French CC))).

States which do not permit same-sex marriages have not enacted private international law rules to deal with such cases but often public policy will be used to refuse the celebration or the recognition of a same-sex marriage. Some jurisdictions even have amended their constitutions, defining marriage as a union between and man and a woman, in order to ban same-sex marriages in their jurisdictions (eg art 46 Constitution of Bulgaria; art 28 Constitution of Lithuania; art 18 Constitution of Poland; art 110 Constitution of the Republic of Latvia; art 62 Constitution of Serbia; art L Constitution of Hungary; art 62(2) Constitution of Croatia; art 41 Constitution of Slovakia). In Europe only the Republic of Ireland went in the opposite direction and changed the constitution to permit same-sex marriages after a public referendum (see above).

2. International

The Hague Marriage Convention (Hague Convention of 14 March 1978 on Celebration and Recognition of the Validity of Marriages, 1901 UNTS 131) has, considering its date, not expressly taken same-sex marriages into account, but the connecting factor offers possibilities to deal with such marriages (*infra* IV.1.).

3. *European*

a) Brussels IIa Regulation

In deciding whether same-sex marriages fall within the scope of the → Brussels IIa Regulation (Council Regulation (EC) No 2201/2003 of 27 November 2003 concerning jurisdiction and the recognition and enforcement of judgments in matrimonial matters and the matters of parental responsibility, repealing Regulation (EC) No 1347/2000, [2003] OJ L 338/1) the concept of marriage has to be interpreted autonomously. This means that the content of the concept 'marriage' cannot be defined by means of the national law concerned, but that an interpretation has to be sought in a European context. The legislative process leading to the Brussels Convention and the Brussels II Regulation (Council Regulation (EC) No 1347/2000 of 29 May 2000 on jurisdiction and the recognition and enforcement of judgements in matrimonial matters and in matters of parental responsibility for children of both spouses, [2000] OJ L 160/19) took place at a time when same-sex marriages were unknown in the European Union. Therefore, a traditional marriage concept was the basis for those instruments (Haimo Schack, 'Das neue Internationale Eheverfahrensrecht in Europa' [2001] RabelsZ 615, 620 *et seq*). However, when implementing the Brussels IIa Regulation, the European legislator was aware of the developments in Belgium and in the Netherlands at the time but did not expressly consider them. Therefore, a historical interpretation would lead to the conclusion that same-sex marriages are excluded from the scope of the Regulation. While autonomous interpretation does not exclude a teleological interpretation, the well-established case-law of the Court of Justice states that a common core among the Member States or at least a strong tendency in a certain direction has to be detected (Case C-122/99 *D and the Kingdom of Sweden v Council of Ministers* [2002] ECR I-4319, I-4353). Consequently, at current an interpretation which includes same-sex marriages probably is not yet possible since only some 11 legal systems out of 29 have made marriage accessible to same-sex partners. The common core has to be followed (Walter Pintens, Art. 1, in Ulrich Magnus and Peter Mankowski (eds), *Brussels IIbis Regulation* (Sellier 2012) 58; Patrick Wautelet, 'Private international law Aspects of Same-Sex Marriages and Partnerships in Europe: Divided We Stand?' in Katharina Boele-Woelki and Angelika Fuchs (eds), *Legal Recognition of Same-Sex Relationships in Europe: National, Cross-Border and European Perspectives* (2nd edn, Intersentia 2012) 160). But this also implies that should more jurisdictions provide a broader meaning to marriage, a teleological interpretation which includes same-sex marriages in the scope of the Regulation would be possible, provided this then forms a common core or at least a strong tendency (cf Katharina Boele-Woelki, 'Die Verordnung über die Zuständigkeit und die Anerkennung von Entscheidungen in Ehesachen' [2001] ZfRV 121, 127; Hans Ulrich Jessurun d'Oliveira, 'Freedom of Movement of Spouses and Registered Partners in the European Union' in Jürgen Basedow and others (eds), *Liber Amicorum Kurt Siehr* (TMC Asser Press 2000) 527, 534; PMM Mostermans, 'De wederzijdse erkenning van echtscheidingen binnen de Europese Unie' [2002] NIPR 263, 266). From an equality point of view, it is not easy to find sociological, anthropological or ethical grounds to exclude same-sex marriages from the scope of the Regulation since they lead to the same consequences with the same rights and same obligations. In the long run this situation therefore needs to be reviewed (Walter Pintens, 'Marriage and Partnership in the Brussels IIa Regulation' in Vesna Tomljenovic, Johan A Erauw and Paul Volken (eds), *Liber Memorialis Petar Šarčević* (Sellier 2006) 338).

b) Rome III Regulation

A similar question arises under the → Rome III Regulation (Council Regulation (EU) No 1259/2010 of 20 December 2010 implementing enhanced cooperation in the area of the law applicable to divorce and legal separation, [2010] OJ L 343/10). The competent court deciding on the divorce petition (→ Divorce and personal separation) has first to recognize the marriage. But this preliminary question is excluded from the scope of the Regulation (art 1(2)(b)). The court will thus apply national choice-of-law rules, and if the result is the non-recognition of the marriage, the divorce will be refused. Although the preliminary question is excluded from the scope of the Regulation, art 13 confirms this solution by stipulating that nothing in the Regulation shall oblige the courts of a participating Member State whose law does not deem the marriage in question valid for the purposes of divorce proceedings to pronounce a divorce by virtue of the application of this Regulation. This superfluous stipulation was an initiative to satisfy the Member States refusing to recognize same-sex marriages but restricts the free movement of citizens (Katharina Boele-Woelki, 'For Better or for Worse: The Europeanization of International Divorce Law' (2010) 12 YbPIL 22).

c) Maintenance Regulation

Concerning the Maintenance Regulation (Council Regulation (EC) No 4/2009 of 18 December 2008 on jurisdiction, applicable law, recognition and enforcement of decisions and cooperation in matters relating to maintenance obligations, [2009] OJ L 7/1) it has been advocated that a same-sex marriage falls under its scope since this instrument is not restricted to → maintenance obligations arising from a marriage but also from other family relations (Ian Curry-Sumner, 'Same-Sex Relationships in Europe: Trends Towards Tolerance?' (2011) 3 *Amsterdam Law Forum* 55).

d) EU Regulation on matrimonial property regimes

The EU Regulation on matrimonial property regimes (Council Regulation (EU) 2016/1103 of 24 June 2016 implementing enhanced cooperation in the area of jurisdiction, applicable law and the recognition and enforcement of decisions in matters of matrimonial property regimes, OJ l183/1 of 8 July 2016; → Matrimonial property) is gender neutral and covers not only opposite-sex marriage but also same-sex marriages. But the proposal is only defining the scope of the regulation and does not define 'marriage', which is left to national law (Recital (17)). This means that 'marriage' will not be interpreted autonomously as in Regulation Brussels IIa but that each Member State has to decide whether it will apply the Regulation to same-sex marriages.

IV. Current regulation

1. International jurisdiction

In general the same rules on international jurisdiction apply for same-sex and opposite-sex marriages. For example, Belgian authorities have jurisdiction to celebrate the marriage in Belgium if one of the prospective spouses has Belgian nationality or has his domicile in Belgium or has had his habitual residence in Belgium for more than three months when the marriage is celebrated (art 44 Belgian PILA). Under Dutch law at least one of the spouses must have Dutch citizenship or domicile in the Netherlands (art 1:43 Dutch New Civil Code (Nieuw Burgerlijk Wetboek of 1 January 1992, henceforth Dutch CC). France has widened the jurisdiction of the civil-status registrar; originally the marriage had to be celebrated in the place of domicile or residence of one of the spouses or their parents (art 74 French CC). Now the marriage can also be celebrated in France if the marriage cannot be celebrated in the state of residence and the French diplomats and consuls have no authority to celebrate the marriage in that state (art 171-9 French CC).

2. Applicable law

The rules governing the formal requirements (→ Formal requirements and validity) of marriage are applied to same-sex marriages as well. Generally the *lex loci celebrationis* applies (eg art 47 Belgian PILA; art 10:30 Dutch CC, incorporating art 2 Hague Marriage Convention; art 202 French CC).

The same rule applies for the substantial validity of the marriage. In principle the choice-of-law rules for marriage apply. This means that in most legal systems a distributive application of the personal statute is made and that for the most part the conditions regarding the validity of the marriage are governed, for each spouse, by the law of the state of the spouse's → nationality when the marriage is celebrated (cf eg art 46 (1) Belgian CC). Each spouse must have the necessary capacity to marry (cf eg art 46(1) Belgian PILA; art 202-1 French CC). English law uses domicile instead of nationality as a connecting factor and makes a distributive application of the law of domicile. However, there is not always a strong link between nationality or domicile and the actual life of the future spouses. Therefore, some legal systems do not only use the *lex loci celebrationis* for the formal validity but also for the substantial validity. This is the solution adopted by the Hague Marriage Convention, which is in force in Luxembourg and the Netherlands. The future spouses have to meet the substantive requirements of the internal law of the state of celebration and one of them has to have the nationality of that state or habitually reside there. Alternatively, the future spouses can meet the substantive requirements of the internal law designated by the choice-of-law rules of the state of celebration (art 3). The → *lex fori* is also used in Sweden, when one of the future spouses has Swedish nationality or domicile in Sweden (§ 1 Act on Certain International Marriages (Lag (1904:26 s.1) om vissa internationella rättsförhållanden rörande äktenskap och förmynderskap, SFS 1904:26 s.1)). With the introduction of same-sex marriage this rule was widened to include all marriages. If none of the spouses has Swedish nationality or domicile in Sweden, the future spouses in addition have to fulfil the requirements of one of the laws of the state of nationality or habitual residence of one of the future spouses. But at the request of both parties only Swedish law may apply when specific reasons are invoked (§ 1 para 2 Act on Certain International Marriages).

The application of national law has the disadvantage that if one of the persons residing in a state that allows same-sex marriage has the nationality of a state that does not do so, they cannot enter in such marriage. Therefore, some states have broadened their conflict rules by a specific rule on same-sex marriages. Under Belgian law a provision of the law designated by the nationality of one of the future spouses which does not allow same-sex marriage is considered as contrary to international public policy. If one of the persons has the nationality of a state of which the law allows such marriage or has his habitual residence on the territory of such state, the marriage will be celebrated (art 46 (2) Belgian PILA). In France a comparable rule was introduced (art 202-1 (2) French CC). A *Circulaire* of the Minister of Justice refused to apply this rule in case of bilateral conventions with certain countries prescribing the application of the personal law of the spouses since these conventions take precedence over national law. However, in a 2013 decision the Court of Appeal of Chambéry while recognizing the primacy of international conventions in principle nevertheless ruled that the Franco-Moroccan Agreement of 10 August 1981 (JO 1 June 1983) could not apply to a Franco-Moroccan same-sex marriage because the Agreement violates French international public policy ([2013] Sem. J. 2056, commented by A Devers). This decision was confirmed by the Cour de Cassation on 28 January 105, No 13–50.059. Similarly, in Spain public policy is used by the *Direccion General de Registros y el Notariado* to ignore a law prohibiting same-sex marriage and to allow a same-sex marriage when one of the spouses has his or her habitual residence in Spain. Hence these jurisdictions accept that this practice will create 'limping marriages' but give priority to the right to marry.

All those legal systems have not adopted specific conflict rules for the effects of a same-sex marriage. Those effects are governed by the traditional conflict rules on the rights and duties of the spouse (→ matrimonial property, divorce (→ Divorce and personal separation), → maintenance obligations etc).

If the national laws of both future spouses permit same-sex marriage, it generally will not be possible to celebrate the marriage in a state using → nationality as → connecting factor if this state itself does not permit marriage of same-sex couples. This state will rely on the public policy exception to avoid the application of its choice-of-law rule and will thus refuse the celebration of the marriage. Some states even do not allow that same-sex marriages are celebrated in foreign embassies or consulates on their territory (see Patrick Wautelet, 'Private international law Aspects of Same-Sex Marriages and Partnerships in Europe: Divided We Stand?' in Katharina Boele-Woelki and Angelika Fuchs (eds), *Legal Recognition of Same-Sex Relationships in Europe: National, Cross-Border and European Perspectives* (2nd edn, Intersentia 2012) 151).

3. Recognition

States having introduced same-sex marriages will recognize foreign same-sex marriages under the same conditions as opposite-sex marriages. This will also be the case in Luxembourg and the Netherlands who are bound by the Hague Marriage Convention, which requires that a marriage validly entered into under the law of the state of celebration or which subsequently becomes valid under that law shall be considered as such in all contracting states (art 9). However, in most countries no specific rules for the recognition of same-sex marriages exist and a pragmatic approach is taken. For example, a marriage celebrated abroad is recognized in Belgium if the national law of each spouse has been applied or, when that law prohibits same-sex marriage, if one of the spouses has the nationality of or residence in a country permitting such a marriage.

Difficulties concerning the recognition of same-sex marriages of course arise in jurisdictions which have not themselves opened up marriage to same-sex couples. Some jurisdictions generally refuse to recognize same-sex marriage because they do not consider such a union as a marriage on the basis of constitutional tradition or public policy. Examples can be found in

Irish and Italian case-law (see Patrick Wautelet, 'Private international law Aspects of Same-Sex Marriages and Partnerships in Europe: Divided We Stand?' in Katharina Boele-Woelki and Angelika Fuchs (eds), *Legal Recognition of Same-Sex Relationships in Europe: National, Cross-Border and European Perspectives* (2nd edn, Intersentia 2012) 149). It is not even necessary to invoke public policy in legal systems where courts apply a *révision au fond* and conclude that the applied choice-of-law rules differ from domestic conflict rules. The *Verwaltungsgericht* Karlsruhe refused recognition of a Chinese-Dutch marriage celebrated in the Netherlands since art 13 Introductory Act to the German Civil Code (Einführungsgesetz zum Bürgerlichen Gesetzbuche of 21 September 1994, BGBl. I 2494, as amended, henceforth EGBGB) required a distributive application of the national law of the future spouses and Chinese law did not allow same-sex marriage (Administrative Court (Verwaltungsgericht) of Karlsruhe, 9 September 2004, [2006] IPrax 284). Other legal systems 'downgrade' same-sex marriages by merely recognizing them as registered partnerships. This solution is expressly regulated in Swiss law (art 45(3) Swiss PILA) and accepted by German case-law and doctrine which apply art 17 b (4) EGBGB analogously (Higher Regional Court (OLG) of Zweibrücken, 21 March 2011, [2011] StAZ 189). This effectively 'downgrades' the effects of a foreign marriage to the effects of a German/Swiss → registered partnership. Still, this means that at least to a certain extent a foreign marriage is recognized. Indeed, it would be illogical to recognize a foreign registered partnership but to deny any effect to foreign same-sex marriage (Dieter Martiny, 'Private international law Aspects of Same-Sex Couples under German Law' in Katharina Boele-Woelki and Angelika Fuchs (eds), *Legal Recognition of Same-Sex Relationships in Europe: National, Cross-Border and European Perspectives* (2nd edn, Intersentia 2012) 198).

WALTER PINTENS AND JENS M SCHERPE

Literature

Katharina Boele-Woelki and Angelika Fuchs (eds), *Legal Recognition of Same-Sex Relationships in Europe: National, Cross-Border and European Perspectives* (2nd edn, Intersentia 2012). Michael Bogdan, 'Private international law Aspects of the Introduction of Same-Sex Marriages in Sweden' [2009] *Nordic Journal of International Law* 253; Katharina Boele-Woelki and Angelika Fuchs (eds), *Same-Sex Relationships and Beyond* (Intersentia 2017); Stuart Davis, 'New Approaches to Same-Sex Marriage: The End of Nationality as a Connecting Factor' in Katharina Boele-Woelki, Nina Dethloff and Werner Gephart (eds), *Family Law and Culture in Europe* (Intersentia 2014) 263; Gerard-René de Groot 'Private international law Aspects Relating to Homosexual Couples' in Katharina Boele-Woelki and Sjef van Erp (eds), *General Reports of the XVIIth Congress of the International Academy of Comparative Law* (Eleven International Publishing 2007) 325; Christina Gonzáles Beilfuss, *Parejas de hecho y matrimonio del mismo sexo* (Marcial Pons 2004); Maarit Jänterä-Jareborg, 'Sweden: The Same-Sex Marriage Reform with Special Regard to Concerns of Religion' [2010] FamRZ 1505; Patricia Orejudo Prieto de Los Mozos, 'Private international law Problems Relating to the Celebration of Same-Sex Marriages' [2006] YbPIL 299; Walter Pintens and Jens Scherpe, 'Gleichgeschlechtliche Ehen im belgischen internationalen Privatrecht' [2004] IPRax 290.

Savigny, Friedrich Carl von

Friedrich Carl von Savigny was, alongside *Joseph Story* (→ Story, Joseph) and *Pasquale Stanislao Mancini* (→ Mancini, Pasquale Stanislao) one of the three most significant private international law scholars of the 19th century.

I. Life and work

Friedrich Carl von Savigny was born on 21 February 1779 in Frankfurt am Main. In 1795 he commenced his legal studies at the University of Marburg, graduating in 1799 and obtaining his doctorate on 31 October 1800. Subsequently he lectured as extraordinary professor on criminal law at the University of Marburg and subsequently turned to Roman law, legal history and methodology. In 1808 he accepted a chair at the University of Landshut. In 1810 he moved to the Friedrich-Wilhelm-University of Berlin, where he stayed until 1842. Moreover he became a member of the Prussian Privy Council in 1817. In 1842 he was appointed Minister of State and Minister of Justice as well as in 1847 President of the Privy Council and of the State Ministry. He resigned from the office during the revolution of 1848 (see Mathias Freiherr von Rosenberg, *Friedrich Carl von Savigny*

(1779–1861) im Urteil seiner Zeit (Peter Lang 2000) 2). During *Savigny's* membership and his eventual presidency of the Privy Council, he probably signed no treaties concerning foreign affairs, and also therefore none concerning private international law (see Fritz Sturm, 'Savigny und das internationale Privatrecht seiner Zeit' (1979) VIII Ius Commune 92, 96). *Savigny* died on 25 October 1861 in Berlin at the age of 82.

Savigny's seminal work, in which he developed the so-called seat theory (*Sitztheorie*), was the eighth and final volume of the '*System des heutigen römischen Rechts*' (System of Modern Roman Law; see William Guthrie, *Private international law. A Treatise on the Conflict of Laws and the Limits of Their Operation in Respect of Place and Time (by Friedrich Carl von Savigny), translation with notes* (T & T Clark, Law Publishers, Stevens & Sons 1869) IX, henceforth Guthrie). The eight volumes were published in stages from 1840 to 1849, with volume eight appearing in 1849. This is significant in view of the intense liberalization process taking place at the time, which also found expression in the system of private law, and consequently also in private international law. Taken as a whole, *Savigny* conceives of the '*System des heutigen römischen Rechts*' as a general part of private law. Private international law is discussed in the eighth volume under the title 'Authority of the Rules of Law over the Legal Relations' (see also Guthrie, 5; 'Herrschaft der Rechtsregeln über die Rechtsverhältnisse' (see Friedrich Carl von Savigny, *System des heutigen römischen Rechts*, vol 8 (Veit 1849) 1, henceforth von Savigny, vol 8)). In this volume *Savigny* deals – besides the 'Limits in Time of the Authority of Rules of Law over Legal Relations' (Guthrie, 277; von Savigny, vol 8, 368) – especially with 'Local Limits of the Authority of Rules of Law over the Legal Relations' (Guthrie, 11; von Savigny, vol 8, 27).

II. *Savigny's* contribution to private international law

1. Foundation of the seat theory

Savigny's doctrine is known as the 'Copernican revolution' of private international law (see Paul Heinrich Neuhaus, 'Savigny und die Rechtsfindung aus der Natur der Sache' (1949/50) 15 RabelsZ 364, 366). Since the Middle Ages the so-called statute theory (→ Unilateralism) had been applied, a theory based on the issue of whether a single legal norm can also be applied to cases involving foreign elements. In individual cases this question is problematic, because the legislature rarely considers cases with foreign elements when promulgating substantive legal norms. The statute theory was based on the → territoriality principle and preferred its own substantive law rules in contrast to foreign law (Marc-Philippe Weller, 'Anknüpfungsprinzipien im Europäischen Kollisionsrecht: Abschied von der "klassischen" IPR-Dogmatik?' [2011] IPRax 429, 430).

In contrast to the statute theory, *Savigny* did not enquire whether a legal norm was applicable to a case with relations to other states, but rather sought the seat of the legal relationship (*Sitz der Rechtsverhältnisse*; von Savigny, vol 8, 108). He posed the question of the applicability of domestic or foreign law and thereby approached the problem from the opposite direction and formulated the question of the applicable law from the converse standpoint. His approach proceeded not from a single norm, asking which legal relationship is included by that norm, but rather commenced from a legal relationship to examine which legal norm was accordingly applicable. Thus *Savigny* proceeded not from the law, but from the legal relationship.

This change represents a highly significant achievement on *Savigny's* part (see Paul Heinrich Neuhaus, 'Abschied von Savigny?' (1982) 46 RabelsZ 4, 8 f). Nevertheless, rather than seeking to revolutionize the private international law system, he intended to remain in conformity with the traditional system. According to *Savigny* only the starting point (law or legal relationship) should be changed (see Daniel Zimmer, 'Savigny und das internationale Privatrecht unserer Zeit' in Faculté de Droit de Lausanne under the direction of Jean-François Gerkens and others (eds), *Mélanges Fritz Sturm*, vol 2 (Editions Juridiques de l'Université de Liège 1999) 1709, 1710). Accordingly the results of his doctrine remained relatively unchanged in major respects when compared to the conventional method. But this is not crucial, in that *Savigny* was the first private international law scholar able to describe the system of conflict of laws in such a clear manner that he was designated as the 'founding father' of modern private international law (see Giesela Rühl, 'Methods and Approaches in Choice of Law: An Economic Perspective' (2006) 24 Berkeley J.Int'l L. 801, 821). The consequence of his theory is that, rather than the legislature deciding whether its legal norm is applicable, the actual situation is regarded as decisive for choosing the appropriate legislature (cf Ralf Michaels, 'Globalizing Savigny? The State in Savigny's Private international law and the Challenge of Europeanization and Globalization' Duke Law School Legal Studies, Research Paper Series, Research Paper No 74, September 2005, 15).

a) Starting point: an international common law of nations

Savigny developed his doctrine from the starting point 'of an international common law of nations having intercourse with one another' (*'eine völkerrechtliche Gemeinschaft mit einander verkehrenden Nationen'*, von Savigny, vol 8, 27; translation according to Guthrie, 27). This perspective on cooperation among states allowed him to neglect the public (political) interests of different states as he established his system of private international law. *Savigny* did not deny and reject private law as state law. Rather he rejected the idea of private law – and therefore also private international law – based on politics. For him, private law always has to be apolitical (see Ralf Michaels, 'Globalizing Savigny? The State in Savigny's Private international law and the Challenge of Europeanization and Globalization' Duke Law School Legal Studies, Research Paper Series, Research Paper No 74, September 2005, 11, 12). In consequence, *Savigny* based his system not on the superiority of the forum's legal system but rather on the equality of forum and foreign law. According to *Savigny*, domestic and foreign law have to be treated equally. Furthermore, *Savigny* not only considered the various states and legal systems as of equal import, but also the various persons involved, whether domestic or foreign.

b) Seat of the legal relationship

By attempting 'to discover for every legal relation (case) that legal territory to which, in its proper nature, it belongs or is subject in (in which it has its seat)', *Savigny* formulated as a methodological principle the question of the seat of the legal relationship (*'bei jedem Rechtsverhältniß dasjenige Rechtsgebiet aufgesucht werde, welchem dieses Rechtsverhältniß seiner eigenthümlichen Natur nach angehört oder unterworfen ist (worin dasselbe seinen Sitz hat)'*, von Savigny, vol 8, 108; see also 28; translation according to Guthrie, 89). *Savigny* utilizes the picture of the 'seat' of the legal relationship to connect a real situation (person, thing or action) with the applicable law. For this he applies four elements, ie the domicile of a person, the place of a thing, the place of an act and the place of a court (see von Savigny, vol 8, 120 f; Ralf Michaels, 'Globalizing Savigny? The State in Savigny's Private international law and the Challenge of Europeanization and Globalization' Duke Law School Legal Studies, Research Paper Series, Research Paper No. 74 September 2005, 17).

c) International uniformity of decisions

According to *Savigny* and in line with *Kant's* categorical imperative, conflict-of-laws rules should be suitable for standardization, since *Savigny* pursues an internationalization of private international law. He sees the international uniformity of decisions as essential. He postulates the ideal that 'in cases of conflict of laws, the same legal relations (cases) have to expect the same decision, whether the judgment be pronounced in this state or in that' (translation according to Guthrie, 27; von Savigny, vol 8, 27).

International uniformity of decisions is important and one of the principal objectives of private international law to this day. International uniformity of decisions brings two considerable advantages. First, there is a need to decide cases consistently irrespective of which country's courts have jurisdiction, because it is necessary to prevent limping legal relationships, ie legal relationships which are recognized in one country but not in another. Second, the parties must know which law governs their legal relationship in order to be aware of their rights and obligations.

d) Savigny's conflict-of-laws rules: an overview

From this basic methodological statement *Savigny* derives the following conflict-of-laws rules:

Legal capacity (→ Capacity and emancipation) and other matters of → personal status are governed by the law of their domicile (von Savigny, vol 8, 134 f; see also Fritz Sturm, 'Savigny und das internationale Privatrecht seiner Zeit' (1979) VIII Ius Commune 92, 99).

According to *Savigny* the legal relationships of the property law, regardless of whether it is personal or real property, are governed by the *lex rei sitae* (von Savigny, vol 8, 169 ff).

Corresponding to *Savigny*, the legal relationship of the law of obligations is ruled by the → place of performance. When no determination is possible, the debtor's domicile is decisive (von Savigny, vol 8, 247; see also Ulrike Seif, 'Savigny und das Internationale Privatrecht des 19. Jahrhunderts' (2001) 65 RabelsZ 492, 498). Long-term business relationships are connected to the management seat (von Savigny, vol 8, 247).

According to *Savigny* the form of a legal act is governed by the law of the place where the contract was made (*lex loci actus*; von Savigny, vol 8, 348 ff, 350 f). *Savigny* rejects the application of the *lex causae*, that is the applicable law of the principal issue, on the grounds that the formalities of that law can only be observed if at all with difficulty at the place where the contract is made (von Savigny, vol 8, 350).

Concerning torts/delicts, due to the proximity to criminal law *Savigny* regards not the place of tort, but rather the → *lex fori* as decisive (von Savigny, vol 8, 278 ff).

All cases of succession, regardless of whether personal or real property (→ Property and proprietary rights) is involved, are governed by the law of the testator's domicile at the time of death (von Savigny, vol 8, 295 ff, 302 ff).

Concerning family law, *Savigny* assigns all cases to the law of the husband's or father's domicile (von Savigny, vol 8, 324 ff).

2. Exceptions to the equality of domestic and foreign law

Savigny identified two exceptions, accepted to this day, to the principle of the equality of domestic and foreign law: on the one hand → overriding mandatory provisions and on the other hand → public policy (*ordre public*).

a) Overriding mandatory provisions

The first exception is → overriding mandatory provisions. *Savigny* labels them as 'Laws of a strictly positive, imperative nature which are consequently inconsistent with that freedom of application which pays no regard to the limits of particular states' (Guthrie, 34; see also von Savigny, vol 8, 33). *Savigny* describes such provisions in more detail as 'one class of absolute laws [that] has no other reason and end than to secure the administration of justice by fixed rules, so that they are enacted merely for the sake of persons (*Gründe 'des öffentlichen Wohls (publica utilitas)*'; von Savigny, vol 8, 35 f) who are the possessors of right' (translation by Guthrie, 35). According to our contemporary understanding, for example, a ban on exports and the provisions of the protection of cultural objects (→ Cultural objects, protection of) constitute overriding mandatory provisions.

Overriding mandatory provisions were and remain exceptions to *Savigny's* seat theory. In these cases, the question to be answered is not which legal norm is applicable to a legal relationship (in contrast to the application of the seat theory), but rather the question whether a single legal norm of the *lex fori* has to be applied to a case involving foreign elements and governed by foreign law – apart from the overriding mandatory provision. Referring to a domestic overriding mandatory provision, it has to be scrutinized whether it is also mandatory in cases with foreign elements, even though foreign law is applicable to this legal relation apart from the overriding mandatory provision. It is not sufficient that the provision is mandatory in the state of the forum in cases without relations to other countries, but rather it is necessary that it is mandatory internationally. Consequently it has to be an overriding mandatory provision which is, according to the intention of the legislative authority, intended to be applicable also in cases involving foreign elements and despite the application of foreign law (→ Foreign law, application and ascertainment).

Under currently valid European private international law, a regulation concerning overriding mandatory provisions is to be found for example in art 9(1) Rome I Regulation (Regulation (EC) No 593/2008 of the European Parliament and of the Council of 17 June 2008 on the law applicable to contractual obligations (Rome I), [2008] OJ L 177/6; → Rome Convention and Rome I Regulation (contractual obligations)). According to this rule, overriding mandatory provisions are provisions the respect for which is regarded as crucial by a country for safeguarding its public interests, such as its political, social or economic organization, to such an extent that they are applicable to any situation falling within their scope, irrespective of the law otherwise applicable to the contract under the Rome I Regulation. According to art 9(2) Rome I Regulation, nothing in the Rome I Regulation shall restrict the application of the overriding mandatory provisions of the law of the forum.

b) Ordre public

Moreover *Savigny* describes, without using the term, another, still accepted today, exception to the equality of domestic and foreign law: an infringement of the → public policy (*ordre public*). He explains that 'legal institutions of a foreign state, of which the existence is not at all recognised in ours, and which, therefore, have no claim to the protection of our courts' (translated by Guthrie, 34), are not legally valid in the domestic legal system (von Savigny, vol 8, 33). As a graphic and memorable example *Savigny* mentioned slavery (von Savigny, vol 8, 37). Another example is the civil death (von Savigny, vol 8, 37).

III. *Savigny's* influence on private international law

1. At the time

a) Relevance of the closest connection in continental Europe and in Latin America

Private international law in continental Europe – unharmonized or harmonized as a result of regulations of the European Union as much as treaties, especially by the Hague Academy of International Law – is fundamentally based, until today, on the doctrine of *Savigny* – by still seeking the law with the closest connection. In Austria, for example, § 1 Austrian Federal Code on Private international law (Bundesgesetz über das internationale Privatrecht of 15 June 1978, BGBl. No 304/1978, as amended) expressly provides that the law has to be applied of the country to which the strongest connection exists. Other countries, such as → France or → Germany do not regulate this basic principle expressly, but also assume this basic rule. In principle, this also holds true for the conflict-of-laws rules in the Rome I Regulation, → Rome II Regulation (Regulation (EC) No 864/2007 of the European Parliament and of the Council of 11 July 2007 on the law applicable to non-contractual obligations (Rome II), [2007] OJ L 199/40), → Rome III Regulation (Council Regulation (EU) No 1259/2010 of 20 December 2010 implementing enhanced cooperation in the area of the law applicable to divorce and legal separation, [2010] OJ L 343/10) and the Succession Regulation (Regulation (EU) No 650/2012 of the European Parliament and of the Council of 4 July 2012 on jurisdiction, applicable law, recognition and enforcement of decisions and acceptance and enforcement of authentic instruments in matters of succession and on the creation of a European Certificate of Succession, [2012] OJ L 201/107; → Rome IV Regulation). Also in Latin America, the system of private international law is based on *Savigny's* system of conflict of laws.

However, despite the still valid and applicable principle of the closest connection, there have been at times significant changes in the conflict-of-laws rules since *Savigny*. Thus the basic principle and methodological statement remain the same, while the interests and ideas of justice, essential for answering the question to which legal system the closest connection exists, have changed, in some instances fundamentally, since *Savigny's* day. For example, the equality of men and women directs to completely different conflict-of-laws rules in private international family law to those followed under *Savigny's* conflict-of-laws system, where the husband's or father's domicile were considered as decisive in all cases concerning family law. But the methodological basic statement is still the same.

b) Rejection of Savigny's *system of private international law in the USA*

By contrast to its reception in the legal systems in continental Europe and in Latin America, the *Savigny* doctrine met with criticism in the → USA in the second half of the 20th century (see Fritz Sturm, 'Savigny und das internationale Privatrecht seiner Zeit' (1979) VIII Ius Commune 92, 94 f; Daniel Zimmer, 'Savigny und das internationale Privatrecht unserer Zeit' in Faculté de Droit de Lausanne under the direction of Jean-François Gerkens and others (eds), *Mélanges Fritz Sturm*, vol 2 (Editions Juridiques de l'Université de Liège 1999) 1709, 1714; Albert A Ehrenzweig, *Private international law* (AW Sijthoff 1967) 50 f). The reason for this development in the USA was the localized understanding of the seat theory, on which the Restatement (First) of Conflict of Laws (American Law Institute, Restatement of the Law, First: Conflict of Laws, St. Paul 1934; → Restatement (First and Second) of Conflict of Laws), created by the American Law Institute (with the reporter *Joseph Beale*), was based. Instead of seeing *Savigny's* doctrine as a basic methodological statement, *Savigny's* doctrine was misunderstood. This excessively regional interpretation was the reason why the local reference points to different legal systems implied in the case were analysed and (over)estimated. Some of the obtained results seemed accidental and others arbitrary. The occasion for the denial of *Savigny's* doctrine was the landmark case *Babcock vs Jackson* (191 N.E. 2d 279 (N.Y. Court of Appeals, 9 May 1963)). Subsequently a somewhat confusing theoretical dispute arose in the USA, commonly referred to as the → (American) Conflict of laws revolution. This dispute generated a plurality of theories for the determination of the applicable law. According to one body of legal opinion, for example, private international law would be required to realize more legal policy objectives (the so-called 'governmental interest analysis' of *Brainerd Currie*; see Brainerd Currie, *Selected Essays on the Conflict of Laws* (Duke University Press 1963) 183, 621) (→ Currie, Brainerd; → Interest and policy analysis in private international law). According to another legal opinion, the substantive 'better law' was to be applied (the so-called → 'better law approach' of *Robert Leflar* (see Robert Leflar, 'Choice-Influencing Considerations in Conflicts Law' (1966) 41 N.Y.U.L.Rev. 267, 295 ff; Robert Leflar, 'Conflict Law: More on Choice-Influencing Considerations' (1966) 54 Cal.L.Rev. 1584, 1587)). Courts often used the confusing multiplicity of approaches to fall back on application of the → *lex fori*, an approach also supported by legal doctrinal opinion (the so-called 'lex fori approach' of Albert A Ehrenzweig, *Private international law* (AW Sijthoff 1967) 91 ff) (→ *Lex fori*).

c) *Further development of* Savigny's *private international law in Europe*
The criticism in the USA also provoked discussions in Europe. Unlike in the → USA, however, *Savigny's* doctrine was not rejected outright. In fact Europe remained faithful to the traditional method as outlined above, but set out to refine it, recognizing that not only spatial aspects are relevant for the determination of the applicable law, so the seat of the legal relation but, rather, the interests touched by the legal relationship. It was realized that private international law is responsible for the enforcement of the functions of substantive law in cases with foreign elements. In order to implement substantive ideas of justice in private international law, the specific conflict-of-laws rules were partially differentiated in yet more detail, as can be seen for example in art 3 ff Rome I Regulation and in art 4 ff Rome II Regulation. Furthermore, multiple connecting factors such as alternative connecting factors, subsidiary connecting factors and cumulative connecting factors were established in conflict-of-laws rules so as to prefer or avoid a specific substantive objective in several cases. For example, the alternative connecting factors concerning the formal validity of a will reflect the intention of the substantive law to whenever possible realize the intentions of the decedent. Or the formal validity of legal acts should be encouraged by the alternative connection to the *lex causae* or the *lex loci actus*. By contrast concerning cumulative connecting factors, the attainment of a specific substantive objective should depend on higher requirements by applying two legal systems to the legal relationship at the same time.

2. *In the long run*
European private international law, be it unharmonized or harmonized by regulations, still cherishes the search for the closest connection in the sense of seeking the seat of a legal relation. Nevertheless, modern European private international law as harmonized by Regulations threatens to depart from *Savigny's* theory in another way. Whereas *Savigny* postulated the equality of all legal systems, that is one's own legal system is basically no more important than a foreign legal system, the European legislature at times tends to prefer the application of the law of the EU Member States to application of the law of non-EU Member States. This is expressed for example by art 8(d) Rome III Regulation, which for divorce cases (→ Divorce and personal separation) provides that, absent a choice of law by the parties, absent a common habitual residence of the spouses at the time of seizing the court or within the last year before seizing the court, and absent a common citizenship of both spouses at the time the court is seized, then the divorce is governed by the law of the state of the seized court (→ *lex fori*). The *lex fori* is privileged in these cases, although the other spouse (the opposing party) has potentially no connection to this law. This solution is particularly unjust when the plaintiff, according to art 3(1)(a) fifth indent → Brussels IIa Regulation (Council Regulation (EC) No 2201/2003 of 27 November 2003 concerning jurisdiction and the recognition and enforcement of judgments in matrimonial matters and the matters of parental responsibility, repealing Regulation (EC) No 1347/2000, [2003] OJ L 338/1), can only sue in a EU Member State because he (the plaintiff) has abandoned the → marriage, has had habitual residence in a EU Member State for over one year, whereas the other spouse (the opposing party) has no connection to this EU Member State. In this way a place of jurisdiction is created for the plaintiff, but also the unilateral possibility to choose the applicable law. As a result the law of the

respective EU Member State is accorded undue preference over the law of the non-EU Member State. A similar preference of the law of the EU Member State arises in cases which deal with → consumer contracts, when the connection to the law of the EU Member State is low, but nevertheless this connection is rated higher than the connection to the law of a non-EU Member State. This danger of the preference for the law of the EU Member States exists because, when framing European private international law, the EU legislature particularly intends the effective functioning of the internal market pursuant to art 81(2) of the TFEU (The Treaty on the Functioning of the European Union (consolidated version), [2012] OJ C 326/47), and tends to rate this interest as overriding the realization of the interests of the parties.

De lege ferenda the European legislature should cherish the equality of the legal systems of EU Member States and non-EU Member States in the sense of *Savigny's* theory.

MICHAEL SONNENTAG

Literature

Helmut Coing, 'Rechtsverhältnis und Rechtsinstitution im Allgemeinen und Internationalen Privatrecht bei Savigny' in Law Faculty of the University of Athens (ed), *Eranion in honorem Georgii S. Maridakis*, vol 3 ([Universitas] Athenis 1964) 19; William Guthrie, *Private international law. A Treatise on the Conflict of Laws and the Limits of Their Operation in Respect of Place and Time (by Friedrich Carl von Savigny)*, translation with notes (T & T Clark, Law Publishers, Stevens & Sons 1869); Max Gutzwiller, *Der Einfluß Savignys auf die Entwicklung des Internationalprivatrechts* (Gschwend, Tschopp & Co 1923); Max Gutzwiller, 'Internationalprivatrecht: Die drei Grossen des 19. Jahrhunderts' in Peter Böckli and others (eds), *Festschrift für Frank Vischer zum 60. Geburtstag* (Schulthess 1983) 131; Ralf Michaels, 'Globalizing Savigny? The State in Savigny's Private international law and the Challenge of Europeanization and Globalization' Duke Law School Legal Studies, Research Paper Series, Research Paper No 74, September 2005; Paul Heinrich Neuhaus, 'Abschied von Savigny?' (1982) 46 RabelsZ 4; Mathias Freiherr von Rosenberg, *Friedrich Carl von Savigny (1779–1861) im Urteil seiner Zeit* (Peter Lang 2000); Friedrich Carl von Savigny, *System des heutigen römischen Rechts*, vol 8 (Veit 1849); Ulrike Seif, 'Savigny und das Internationale Privatrecht des 19. Jahrhunderts' (2001) 65 RabelsZ 492; Fritz Sturm, 'Savigny und das internationale Privatrecht seiner Zeit' (1979) VIII Ius Commune 92; Marc-Philippe Weller, 'Anknüpfungsprinzipien im Europäischen Kollisionsrecht: Abschied von der "klassischen" IPR-Dogmatik?' [2011] IPRax 429; Daniel Zimmer, 'Savigny und das internationale Privatrecht unserer Zeit' in Faculté de Droit de Lausanne under the direction of Jean-François Gerkens and others (eds), *Mélanges Fritz Sturm*, vol 2 (Editions Juridiques de l'Université de Liège 1999) 1709.

Sea waybills and other transport documents

I. Sea waybills and applicable law

Carriage of goods through the world is usually covered by a variety of documents which sometimes differ considerably.

In relation to → carriage of goods by sea the first document that came into use since 1700 (or even before, according to some theories) is the → bill of lading that is quite different from the most recent sea waybill which looks very similar to the waybills normally used in other modes of transport (ie carriage of goods by air, road and rail).

The use of different models has given rise to peculiar questions in respect of the law applicable to those transport documents and to the contracts evidenced by them.

Talking particularly about sea waybills, it must be first of all pointed out that, among the general categories of shipping documents, sea waybills must be distinguished from all the models of bills of lading used in the sea transportation field – which are normally issued in the forms of the 'order' bill of lading or in the form of the 'straight' bill of lading – for the following reasons.

The 'to order' bill of lading is the traditional document that contains, or is evidence, of the terms of the contract of carriage: according to this bill of lading the goods described in the document are to be delivered by the carrier to whomever presents an original bill of lading, duly and regularly endorsed. The 'to order' bill of lading is often used in commercial transactions between a seller and buyer as it is negotiable and transferrable: in fact, in a typical commercial transaction the 'to order' bill of lading is endorsed by the seller/consignor and then sent to an intermediary (mostly a commercial bank) who then delivers the endorsed → bill of lading to the buyer/consignee in exchange for payment → sales contracts and sale of goods. The buyer/consignee can then obtain delivery of the goods from the carrier by surrendering the endorsed bill of lading to the carrier.

The 'straight' bill of lading is similar to the 'to order' bill of lading in that it also contains the terms of the contract of carriage and must likewise be surrendered to the carrier to obtain delivery of the goods. It differs from the 'to order' bill of lading in that a straight bill of lading is made out to a named person/consignee; straight bills of lading are seldom used in commercial transactions.

Both 'to order' and 'straight' bills of lading – as well as the 'bearer' bill of lading, which, however, is not used in maritime traffics for it is considered too dangerous – are considered true bills of lading because they can be exchanged for the goods described within them and are therefore documents of title.

A sea waybill is similar to the abovementioned models of bills of lading in that it usually contains the terms of the contract of carriage and certifies receipt of the goods loaded on board. However, it is also quite different in that the carrier has to deliver the goods carried to the person named in the sea waybill upon proof of identity alone; in other words, the carrier shall have the burden of using due diligence to check the identity of the consignee and the original sea waybill shall not be, and need not be, surrendered to the carrier to obtain delivery of the goods (*JI MacWilliam Co Inc v Mediterranean Shipping Co SA (The Rafaela S)* (2005) 1 Lloyd's Rep 347): a sea waybill – which normally is identified by the writing 'not negotiable' printed on the first page – contains in fact a clause which attests that the goods shipped under this sea waybill will be delivered to the party named as consignee, or its authorized agent, on production of proof of identity without any documentary formalities.

Therefore, it appears that the sea waybill differs considerably from all the models of bills of lading for these latter have to be surrendered to the carrier for the purpose of obtaining delivery of the cargo, whereas the presentation of the document is not required when a sea waybill is issued.

It follows that the sea waybill – which is not negotiable and is not a document of title – has to be considered simply as a non-negotiable receipt for the goods loaded on board the carrying vessel at the port of loading, as well as evidence of the terms and conditions of the contract of carriage. (In this respect, see for example the UK's Carriage of Goods by Sea Act 1992 (c 50) which describes the sea waybill as 'any document which is not a bill of lading but (a) is such a receipt for goods as contains or evidences a contract for the → carriage of goods by sea; and (b) identifies the person to whom delivery of the goods is to be made by the carrier in accordance with that contract' (s 1(3) – see also § 526(2) of the German Commercial Code (Handelsgesetzbuch of 10 May 1897, RGBl. 219, as amended in 2013)).

Owing to the above-mentioned characteristics, it has to be noted that the sea waybill has met with success, particularly in the carriage of containers by sea whenever the goods stuffed into the container are not to be sold through a bank negotiation (in fact, because the sea waybill is a non-negotiable document, generally banks involved in documentary credit sales do not allow for the use of sea waybills in such transactions, especially where the cargo concerned has to be sold and resold one or more times while it is in transit).

When a sea waybill is adopted, some disadvantages or costs typical of the → bill of lading, are avoided; for instance, by adopting a sea waybill – which does not circulate – the risks of loss or theft of that document during the transit as well as the possible frauds connected with the documentary credits system are avoided; moreover, a sea waybill is much better suited to electronic data communications (→ Electronic commerce). On the other hand, it must be pointed out that a further burden is imposed on carriers who have the task of exercising due diligence in identifying the real consignee.

The differences between sea waybills and bills of lading have important consequences for the application of some international rules, such as the Hague-Visby Rules (International Convention for the Unification of Certain Rules relating to Bills of Lading signed at Brussels, 25 August 1924, as amended by the 1968 Visby Protocol and the 1979 Brussels Protocol).

II. The international rules on carriage of goods by sea and their application to sea waybills

Owing to their peculiar contents and functions, full attention must be given to the problems concerning the legal regime applicable to sea waybills. This relates in particular to the applicability of the relevant international Conventions governing the → carriage of goods by sea, ie International Convention of 25 August 1924 for the unification of certain rules relating to bills of lading, 25 August 1924 (120 LNTS 155, the so-called Hague Rules) as amended by the 1968 Visby Protocol (Protocol of 23 February 1968 to amend the International Convention for the unification of certain rules of law relating to bills of lading signed at Brussels on 25 August 1924 (Hague Rules), 1412 UNTS 128) and by the 1979 Brussels Protocol (Protocol of 21 December 1979 to amend the International Convention for the unification of certain rules to bills of lading (Hague Rules) as modified by the Amending Protocol of 23 February 1968 (Visby Protocol), 1412 UNTS 146), the United Nations Convention of 31 March 1978 on the carriage of goods by sea (1695 UNTS 3, the so-called Hamburg Rules) as well as the United Nations Convention of 11 December 2008 on contracts for the international carriage of goods wholly or partly by sea (not yet in force, UN Doc A/RES/63/122, 63 UNTS 122, the so-called Rotterdam Rules; → Carriage of goods by sea).

1. The Hague-Visby Rules

a) Direct application
The application of the Hague-Visby Rules to a contract for the international carriage of goods by sea depends upon art X which states that the provisions of the said Rules apply to every → bill of lading relating to the carriage of goods between ports in two different states if: (i) the bill of lading is issued in a contracting state, or (ii) the carriage sets out from a port in a contracting state, or (iii) the contract contained in, or evidenced by, the bill of lading provides that the Rules or a legislation of any state giving effect to them are to govern the contract, whatever may be the → nationality of the ship, the carrier, the shipper, the consignee or any other interested person.

It must also be recalled that art II of the Hague-Visby Rules states that, subject to the provisions of art VI, under every contract of carriage of goods by sea carriers are subject to the responsibilities and liabilities and are entitled to the rights and immunities set forth in the Rules themselves, in relation to the loading, handling, stowage, carriage, custody, care and discharge of such goods.

Therefore, pursuant to the above-mentioned articles, it appears that the Hague-Visby Rules apply where there is a 'contract of carriage' and the relevant bill of lading is issued in a contracting state or relates to a carriage from a contracting state, or where the contract contained in, or evidenced by, the bill of lading incorporates the said Rules: in fact, even if the term 'bill of lading' is not defined in the Rules, however, art I (b) clearly defines the term 'contract of carriage' stating:

> contract of carriage applies only to contracts of carriage covered by a bill of lading or any similar document of title, in so far as such document relates to the carriage of goods by water, including any bill of lading or any similar document as aforesaid issued under, or pursuant to, a charter-party from the moment at which such bill of lading or similar document of title regulates the relations between a carrier and a holder of the same.

As 'contract of carriage' refers only to 'contracts of carriage covered by a bill of lading or any similar document of title', it results that the Rules can govern only bills of lading or similar documents of title.

This would preclude the application of the Rules to contracts of carriage under sea waybills for they are not documents of title. Actually, sea waybills are not considered by most authors to be governed by the Hague or Hague-Visby Rules (Bernard Eder and others, *Scrutton on Charterparties and Bills of Lading* (22nd edn Sweet & Maxwell 2014) 201; see, however, the contrary opinion expressed by William Tetley, 'Waybills: The Modern Contract of Carriage of Goods by Sea' [1983] J.Mar.L.& Com. 456, 471). This position finds support in several decisions such as *Harland & Wolf v Burns & Laird Lines* [1931] 40 Ll.L.Rep 286; *Hugh Mack & Co v Burns & Laird Lines* [1944] 77 Ll.L.Rep. 377; *Browner International Ltd v Monarch Shipping Co Ltd (The European Enterprise)* [1989] 2 Lloyd's Rep 185, 188; *Starrag vs Maersk, Inc*, 486 F.3d 607 (9th Cir 2007); *The Maurice Desgagnés* [1977] 1 F.C. 215; *The Westwood Anette* [2009] F.C. 664.

b) Indirect application by means of contractual incorporation
Because the sea waybill is, in the opinion of most maritime authors, not a 'bill of lading' or a 'similar document of title', the general view is that the Hague and Hague-Visby regimes for carriage by sea do not govern sea waybills by their own force, but only if some contractual incorporation or a national law renders one of

those Rules applicable to the contract of carriage which the sea waybill evidences.

Where this is the case, also sea waybills can be governed by the Hague and/or Hague-Visby Rules regime concerning the sea carriers' liabilities, exonerations and limits of liability.

First, the Hague and Hague-Visby Rules regimes may be made applicable to contracts of carriage evidenced by a sea waybill by way of a contractual incorporation of those Rules into those documents: in this respect, it has to be pointed out that it is usual that standard forms of sea waybills contain a clause expressly incorporating the Hague or the Hague-Visby Rules.

The said regimes may be made applicable to contracts of carriage evidenced by a sea waybill also by way of an incorporation of some other international Rules referring to the Hague-Visby Rules which can be voluntarily inserted into the sea waybill: for instance, sea waybills may attract by reference the CMI Uniform Rules for Sea Waybills (issued by the Comité Maritime International (CMI) in 1990, see *CMI Yearbook 1990*), ie a set of provisions for carriage by sea evidenced by sea waybills, adopted by the Comité Maritime International (CMI), which carriers may voluntarily incorporate into their sea waybills.

On this subject it must be recalled that Rule 1(ii) provides that the mentioned CMI Rules apply when incorporated into a contract of carriage which is not covered by a → bill of lading or similar document of title, whether the contract is in writing or not.

In this case, according to art 4(i), the carriage of goods is subject to 'any International Convention or National Law which is, or if the contract of carriage had been covered by a bill of lading or similar document of title would have been, compulsorily applicable thereto. Such convention or law shall apply notwithstanding anything inconsistent therewith in the contract of carriage'; subject always to the above-mentioned provision, the said contracts of carriage are also governed, according to art 4(ii) and (iii): a) by the said CMI Rules; b) unless otherwise agreed, by the carrier's standard terms and conditions for the trade, if any, including any terms and conditions relating to the non-sea part of the carriage, provided they are incorporated in the sea waybill; c) by any other terms and conditions agreed by the parties.

Whereas the legal sources mentioned by art 4 of the CMI Rules govern specifically rights, obligations, liabilities and limits of liabilities, the said Rules govern particularly some typical aspects of sea carriage for which a sea waybill is issued; for instance, peculiar attention is drawn on the right of control on the goods as well as the delivery of the goods upon proper identification of the consignee and also the evidentiary value of sea waybills.

As far as these items are concerned, it must be briefly recalled that, according to art 6, the shipper is the party entitled to give the carrier instructions in relation to the contract of carriage and even to change the name of the consignee, unless he exercises the option, not later than on receipt of the goods by the carrier, of transferring the right of control to the consignee; the exercise of this option has to be noted on the sea waybill, or similar document. As regards delivery of the goods, art 7 states that the carrier has to deliver the cargo to the consignee upon production of proper identification and must exercise reasonable care to ascertain that the party claiming to be the consignee is really that party. Moreover art 5, dealing with the description of goods, states that in the absence of reservations by the carrier, any statement in sea waybills or similar documents as to the quantity or conditions of the goods shall be *prima facie* evidence of receipt of the goods as so stated as between the carrier and the shipper and shall be conclusive evidence of that as between the carrier and the consignee, provided that this latter has acted in good faith.

The CMI Uniform Rules for Sea Waybills have already been incorporated in several standard forms for sea waybills such as, for instance, the Bimco Non-Negotiable General Sea Waybill 1995 ('Genwaybill'), the Non-Negotiable Liner Sea Waybill ('Linewaybill') and the Combined Transport Sea Waybill 1995 ('Combiconwaybill').

Considering that modern waybills may cover not only carriage of goods by sea but even multimodal transport, it has to be added that those documents can also be governed by UNCTAD/ICC Rules for Multimodal Transports Documents (issued by the United Nations Commission on Trade and Development and International Chamber of Commerce in 1992. See UNCTAD Documentation – Trade/Wp.4/INF.117/corr.1) which apply when they are incorporated into a multimodal contract of carriage; in this case, and in the event that a MT waybill be issued, the liability regime provided for by the said Rules in art 5 (paras 1, 2, 3, 4), as well as the MTO's limits of liability contained in art 6, are applicable to the entire carriage of goods effected by at least two different modes of transport → Multimodal carriage contracts. As regards the maritime stage of a multimodal carriage, it must be noted that the regime of the UNCTAD/ICC Rules appears to be similar to that contained in the Hague-Visby Rules in that the same limits of liability are provided for.

c) Indirect application by means of national legislation

It must further be added that in a number of countries some national legislations render the Hague-Visby legal regime (or a national modification of it) applicable to the maritime carriage of goods under sea waybills for they extend the said regime to the contracts of carriage evidenced by sea waybills. For instance, in the United Kingdom, the Carriage of Goods by Sea Act, giving the force of law to the Hague-Visby Rules, already in the 1971 edition had provided at s 1(6)(b) that without prejudice to art X(c) of the Rules, the same have the force of law in relation to any receipt which is a non-negotiable document marked as such, if the contract contained in, or evidenced by it, is a contract for the → carriage of goods by sea which expressly provides that the Rules are to govern the contract as if the receipt were a → bill of lading. The more recent 1992 edition confirms the above trend at ss 1(1) and 5(1) clearly equalizing bills of lading and sea waybills for the purpose of applying the above-mentioned Rules.

In some other countries too, carriage of goods under sea waybills is regulated by national statutes which incorporate the Hague-Visby Rules and expressly extend them to sea waybills: examples may be found in → Australia, → New Zealand, → Singapore and → South Africa.

The very fact that many countries considered it necessary to enact specific legislation to bring sea waybills within the ambit of their compulsorily applicable national maritime carriage of goods regimes is further evidence of the general worldwide view that sea waybills are not automatically subject to the Hague or Hague-Visby Rules.

2. The Hamburg Rules

In contrast, more modern international Conventions on the → carriage of goods by sea appear to show a different approach in respect to sea waybills.

The Hamburg Rules, for example, by art 2(1), generally apply to 'all contracts of carriage between two different states', which evidently would include sea waybills, inasmuch as they show evidence of a contract of carriage of goods by sea (see also art 18 which clearly states that documents other than bills of lading can be issued).

It is therefore possible to conclude that in states which are party to the Hamburg Rules, sea waybills are subject to that international Convention (see the present status of ratifications at <www.uncitral.org>): in this case, they will be governed by the said Rules as far as carriers' obligations, liabilities and limits of liabilities are concerned.

It has to be added that these Rules also contain provisions on jurisdiction stating at art 21.1 that actions may be instituted before a competent court in the principal place of business (or the habitual residence) of the defendant or the place where the contract was made (provided that the defendant has there a place of business, branch or → agency through which the contract was made), or in the port of loading or in the port of discharge or in any additional place designated for that purpose in the contract of carriage. An action may also be instituted (art 21.2) before the court of any port or place in a contracting state at which the carrying vessel or any other vessel of the same ownership may have been arrested. According to art 22, the disputes arising from the contract of carriage may also be referred to arbitration.

3. The Rotterdam Rules

On the other hand, the new Rotterdam Rules define 'transport document' in such a way as to include any document issued under a contract of carriage which evidences or contains a contract of carriage (art 1(14)). Those Rules expressly apply to a 'non-negotiable transport document' and a 'non-negotiable electronic transport record' (arts 1(16) and art 1(20)) as well as to a 'negotiable transport document' and a 'negotiable electronic transport record' (art 1(15) and art 1(19)).

It is therefore self-evident that sea waybills (printed or electronic) will be covered, as well as bills of lading (printed or electronic) by the Rotterdam Rules as soon as they enter into force (see the present status of ratifications at <www. rotterdamrules2009.com>); consequently the basic obligations (see particularly chs 4 and 9), as well as the liability principles (see particularly ch 5) and the limits of liability (see ch 12) contained in the Rotterdam Rules will be applicable to sea waybills and to multimodal waybills (covering a carriage partly by sea).

As far as jurisdiction is concerned and unless the contract of carriage contains an exclusive choice of court agreement (complying with the Rules' provisions), ch 14 will be applicable. Parties will also be allowed to refer disputes arising from the contract of carriage to arbitration according to ch 15.

III. Some residual aspects concerning the application of national laws to sea waybills and jurisdiction

In practice, standard forms of sea waybills expressly incorporate the Hague or Hague-Visby Rules with the consequence that the regime provided for by the said Rules is applicable to the contracts of carriage in respect of which those documents are issued. However, as usual in bills of lading forms, many sea waybills contain on the reverse page also a clause making express reference to a national law for the purpose of governing those aspects of the contract of carriage which are not covered by the above-mentioned uniform Rules (when incorporated) or regulating the entire contract, in addition to the inserted clauses, in the event that the said Rules are not incorporated or not applicable.

The same clause (or, sometimes, an adjoining clause) also solve problems of jurisdiction. Thus, for instance, some waybill forms state that disputes arising under those documents are determined by the courts and in accordance with the law at the place where the carrier has its principal place of business (see, for instance, the Bimco standard form of Multimodal Transport Waybill 'Multiwaybill 1995'). The above provision appears to be self-explanatory in that it clearly not only indicates the law designated either to cover those aspects not dealt with by uniform Rules (where applicable) or to give a correct interpretation to the inserted clauses, but also indicates the forum to be chosen (or even the arbitration procedure) to solve possible disputes between the parties: it has to be added that such a provision may also fill the gap emerging from some international Rules – such as the Hague-Visby Rules – which do not contain any provision on jurisdiction or arbitration.

IV. Other transport documents and their regulation

Waybills which are normally used in modes of transport different from the carriage by sea (such as carriage of goods by road, air and rail) are usually governed by the uniform Rules that are in force in relation to each mode of transport.

Thus, in respect of international carriage of goods by road the Convention of 19 May 1956 on the contract for the international carriage of goods by road (CMR, 399 UNTS 189), as amended by the Protocol of 5 July 1978 (Protocol to the convention on the contract for the international carriage of goods by road (CMR) of 5 July 1978, 1208 UNTS 427) is applicable and in respect of carriage of goods by rail the COTIF (Convention of 9 May 1980 concerning international carriage by rail, 1396 UNTS 2, in the version of the Protocol of Modification of 3 June 1999, available at <www.otif.org>) and particularly its Appendix B (Uniform Rules concerning the contract of international carriage of goods by rail (CIM)) applies; as regards carriage by inland waterway, the CMNI (International Convention of 22 June 2001 on the contract of carriage of goods by inland waterway, UN Doc A/CN.9/645) has to be mentioned (→ Carriage of goods by road, rail and inland waterways). International carriage of goods by air is now governed by the Montreal Convention (Convention of 28 May 1999 for the unification of certain rules relating to international carriage by air, 2242 UNTS 309, see the status of ratifications at <www.icao.int/secretariat/legal>, → Air law (uniform law)).

Where the above uniform Rules are not applicable, reference must be made for the European Union to the Rome I Regulation (Regulation (EC) No 593/2008 of the European Parliament and of the Council of 17 June 2008 on the law applicable to contractual obligations (Rome I), [2008] OJ L 177/6; → Rome Convention and Rome I Regulation (contractual obligations)).

GIORGIA M BOI

Literature

Giorgia M Boi, *La lettera di trasporto marittimo: Studi per una disciplina uniforme* (Giuffrè 1995);

Leo D'Arcy, *Ridley's Law of Carriage of Goods by Land, Sea and Air* (7th edn, Shaw & Sons 1992); Charles De Battista, 'Waybills: Conclusive Evidence with Respect to Details of the Cargo' [1989] Dir Marit 127; Charles De Battista, 'Sea Waybills and the Carriage of Goods by Sea Act' [1989] LMCLQ 47; Bernard Eder and others, *Scrutton on Charterparties and Bills of Lading* (22nd edn, Sweet & Maxwell 2011); Nicholas Gaskell, Regina Asariotis and Yvonne Baatz, *Bills of Lading: Law and Contracts* (LLP 2000); Kurt Grönfors, *Towards a Transferable Sea Waybill* (Akademiförlaget 1991); Jan Ramberg, 'Documentation: Sea Waybills and Electronic Transmission' in Franceso Berlingieri and others (eds), *The Hamburg Rules: A Choice for the E.E.C.?* (Maklu 1994) 101; William Tetley, 'Waybills: The Modern Contract of Carriage of Goods by Sea' [1983] J.Mar.L.& Com. 456; William Tetley, *Marine Cargo Claims* (4th edn, Carswell 2008); Paul Todd, *Modern Bills of Lading* (3rd edn, Blackwell Scientific Publications 2002); John F Wilson, 'Legal Problems at Common Law Associated with the Use of the Seawaybill' [1994] Dir Marit 115; David Yates, *Contracts for the Carriage of Goods* (LLP 1993); Georgios Zekos and Jo Carby-Hall, 'Sea Waybills: A New Marketable Name for Straight Bills of Lading' [1994] Dir Marit 714.

Security interests in mobile equipment (uniform law)

I. Notion of 'mobile equipment'

'Mobile equipment' is a legal term that was introduced by the Cape Town Convention (Convention of 16 November 2001 on international interests in mobile equipment, 2307 UNTS 285). The text and current status of the Cape Town Convention and the adjacent Protocols can be found at <www.unidroit.org>. The Cape Town Convention gives no definition of 'mobile equipment', such a definition being unnecessary in that the Convention is applicable only to those categories of equipment for which a specific Protocol implementing the Convention exists. So far, there are protocols on Aircraft Equipment (Protocol of 16 November 2001 to the Convention on international interests in mobile equipment on matters specific to aircraft equipment, 2307 UNTS 615) covering airframes, aircraft engines and certain categories of helicopters, on Railway Rolling Stock (Luxembourg Protocol of 23 February 2007 to the Convention on international interests in mobile equipment on matters specific to railway rolling stock (23 February 2007), <www.unidroit.org>, last accessed on 8 February 2014) and on Space Assets (Protocol of 9 March 2012 to the Convention on international interests in mobile equipment on matters specific to space assets, <www.unidroit.org>, last accessed on 8 February 2014). The Governing Council of → UNIDROIT, under whose auspices the Cape Town Convention has been elaborated, is currently contemplating the possibilities for a further protocol on agricultural, mining and construction equipment. All these categories of movables have in common that they usually consist of high value, single items of property, which are capable of being individually identified and registered, for example through their serial number, and which frequently cross national borders or are temporarily or even regularly (as in the case of space assets) situated outside any national territory. These common features make the creation of an internationally registered, uniform security right at once feasible and highly desirable.

II. Private international law and the divergencies of national secured transactions laws

Principally, proprietary rights (→ Property and proprietary rights) in mobile equipment are subject to the same private international law rules as movables in general (*lex rei sitae* rule). However, many jurisdictions have specific rules for certain categories of mobile equipment, mostly transport vehicles such as aircraft and ships, sometimes also railways. Given the fact that there is still no European Regulation on international property law (as to the necessity see Ulrich Drobnig, 'A Plea for European Conflict Rules on Proprietary Security' in Michael J Bonell, Marie-Louise Holle and Peter A Nielsen (eds), *Liber Amicorum Ole Lando* (DJØF 2012) 85 *et seq*) it is for the autonomous private international law of the Member States to decide which kind of transport vehicle is subject to a special rule, and to which law it is in fact subject. Article 45(1) Introductory Act to the German Civil Code (Einführungsgesetz zum Bürgerlichen Gesetzbuche of 21 September 1994, BGBl. I 2494, as amended) provides that rights in airplanes, ships and trains are subject to the law of the country of origin, which is determined by nationality in the case of airplanes, by the place of registration in the case of ships and by the place of licensing in the case of railway rolling stock. There is a similar rule in Belgium (art 89 Belgian Private international law Act (Wet houdende het Wetboek von international privaatrecht/Code de droit international privé of 16 July 2004, BS 27 July 2004, pp 57344, 57366)) whereby proprietary rights (→ Property and proprietary rights) in ships, aircraft and other means of transportation which are publicly registered are to be governed by the law of the state of registration. Although one could argue that automobiles are usually also means of transportation which are publicly registered, they do not fall under the Belgian rule (see Caroline Clijmans, 'Article 89 – Recht toepasselijk op transportmiddelen' in Johan Erauw and others (eds), *Het Wetboek Internationaal Privaatrecht Becommentarieerd* (Intersentia 2006) 457, 458). Other jurisdictions follow the same line: the Dutch rule extends to ships and aircraft (see art 10:127 (2) and (3) Dutch New Civil Code (Nieuw Burgerlijk Wetboek of 1 January 1992)); the Austrian and Spanish provisions encompass ships, aircraft and railway rolling stock (see art 33 Austrian Federal Code on Private international law (Bundesgesetz über das internationale Privatrecht of 15 June 1978, BGBl. No 304/1978, as amended), art 10(2) Spanish Civil Code (Código Civil of 24 July 1889, Gaceta de Madrid No 206, 25 July 1889)). The same approach is followed in Romania (art 2.620 and 2.621 Romanian Civil Code (Law 287/2009, published in the Official Gazette No 511 of 24 July 2009, and subsequently amended and supplemented by Law 71/2011, published in the Official Gazette No 409 of 10 June 2011)) and Poland (art 42 Polish Private international law Act (Official Journal 2011 No 80, pos 432)). By contrast, the Italian Private international law Act (Riforma del Sistema italiano di diritto internazionale private, Act No 218 of 31 May 1995 in Gazz.Uff., Supplemento Ordinario No 128 of 3 June l995, as amended) does not contain a specific exemption from the general *lex situs* rule for means of transportation. Also English law lacks a special conflicts rule for ships and aircraft, so that the applicable law depends on the *situs* of the object. However, it has been held in England that, since no national law can be applied when a vehicle is not on or above national territory, a ship is deemed to be situated at her port of registry when the vessel is upon the high seas. Likewise, an aircraft is deemed to be at its country of registration when it is in fact over the high seas or over (or on) territory which is not under the sovereignty of any state (see Lord Collins of Mapesbury and others (eds), *Dicey, Morris and Collins on the Conflict of Laws* (15th edn, Sweet & Maxwell 2012) para 22-058 and 22E-061).

Thus, although the problem of a *conflit mobile* or *Statutenwechsel* (a right *in rem* created under the law of state A has to be enforced under the law of state B as the new *lex situs* after the property has been brought to state B) can partly be solved by selecting a more stable → connecting factor such as the place of registration, the flag, the home port etc. This solution can by no means satisfy the level of legal safety needed by the parties to a secured transaction where high-value property is involved. First, as the preceding paragraph has demonstrated, there is no uniformity with regard to special private international law rules relating to mobile equipment. Second, those rules for the most part only pertain to ships and aircraft, sometimes also to railways, whereas other means of transportation and other single high-value equipment are left out. Third, even if the state of registration, the home port or another stable connecting factor is selected, the substantive laws relating to secured transactions are so diverse, especially with respect to the kinds of transactions allowed (*numerus clausus*) and with respect to publicity (for an overview see Harry C Sigman and Eva-Maria Kieninger, *Cross-Border Security over Tangibles* (Sellier 2007); Eva-Maria Kieninger, *Security Rights in Movable Property in European Private Law* (CUP 2004)) that foreign substantive law will always run the risk of being disregarded on grounds of public policy of the forum state. Fourth, the main purpose of security rights is their possible enforcement against the debtor in case of default, whether in or outside insolvency. As long as the available remedies are solely determined by autonomous national law there can be no basis for a proper calculation and pricing of risks (see R Goode, 'Transcending the Boundaries of Earth and Space: The Preliminary Draft Unidroit Convention on International Interests in Mobile Equipment' [1998] Unif.L.Rev. 52 *et seq*).

III. Earlier international conventions relating to aircraft and ships

1. The Conventions on maritime liens and mortgages (1926 and 1993)

The first step in setting up a system of international recognition of security rights in vessels (mortgages, hypothecs, charges) was made by the 1926 Maritime Liens and Mortgages Convention (International Convention of 10 April 1926 for the unification of certain rules relating to maritime liens and mortgages, 120 LNTS 187) which is still in force in more than 20 states around the world, from Algeria to Zaire. It is basically a conflict of laws convention (Roy Goode and others, *Transnational Commercial Law: International Instruments and Commentary* (2nd edn, OUP 2012) 528 *et seq*) obligating the contracting states in its art 1 to regard as valid and to respect 'mortgages, hypothecations and other similar charges upon vessels, duly effected in accordance with the law of the Contracting State to which the vessel belongs, and registered in a public register . . .'. After a failed attempt in 1967 to modernize it, the 1926 Convention is to be replaced by the 1993 Maritime Liens and Mortgages Convention (International Convention of 6 May 1993 on maritime liens and mortgages, 2276 UNTS 39), which was elaborated under the auspices of the UN, came into force on 5 September 2004, and now has 17 members among them three EU Member States (→ Spain, → Estonia and → Lithuania). In contrast to the 1926 Convention, it is unnecessary for the application of the 1993 treaty that the ship is registered in a contracting state (art 13(1) 1993 Maritime Liens and Mortgages Convention). Instead, the treaty applies to all ships which are the subject of litigation in a contracting state. The Convention establishes rules for the recognition and ranking of foreign ship mortgages by contracting states (art 1(f)), establishes several basic rules for the forced sale of ships (art 11(f)) and determines the relationship between the rights of creditors and registered ship mortgages (art 4). Ship creditor rights are unregistered property rights which arise by virtue of the law to secure financial claims resulting from the operation of the ship.

2. The Geneva Aircraft Convention (1948)

Regarding aircraft, for most EU Member States (→ Belgium, → Croatia, → Czech Republic, → Denmark, Estonia, → France, → Germany, → Greece, → Hungary, → Italy, the → Netherlands with the exception of the Netherlands Antilles, → Portugal, Romania, → Slovenia and → Sweden), the relevant international source remains the Geneva Aircraft Convention (Convention on the International Recognition of Rights in Aircraft, 310 UNTS 151), signed at Geneva on 19 June 1948. This Convention is in force in 89 countries from Algeria to Zimbabwe (<www.icao.int>). For those states which are also contracting states of the Cape Town Convention and the 2001 Aircraft Protocol (→ Ireland and → Luxembourg), however, the Geneva Aircraft Convention is superseded by the more recent instruments except insofar as rights or interests covered by the Geneva Aircraft Convention are not covered or affected by the Cape Town Convention, see art XXIII Aircraft Protocol.

In contrast to the Cape Town instruments, the Geneva Aircraft Convention establishes no uniform international security interest nor sets up an international registry. It merely obliges the contracting states to recognize certain national security interests which are effective and registered in another contracting state, art I Geneva Aircraft Convention. Default remedies in and outside insolvency as well as priority conflicts with other holders of contractual or statutory security interests are only minimally harmonized (see arts IV and VII).

IV. The Cape Town Convention and its supplementing Protocols

1. Entry into force and membership

The Convention on international interests in mobile equipment was concluded on 16 November 2001 in Cape Town. It came into force on 1 March 2006 and to date (February 2017) already applies to 63 states, among them the → USA, → Canada, → China, → India and Russia (→ Russian Federation). In the EU, so far only Denmark, Ireland, Latvia, Luxembourg, Malta, Spain, Sweden and the United Kingdom have ratified the Convention. On 28 April 2009 the EU acceded to the Convention as an organization under art 48, and its membership came into force on 1 August 2009. However, the EU membership extends only to those provisions relating to jurisdiction, including interim relief, for which the EU has exclusive competence, so that accession by each individual Member State is still necessary. See on the somewhat complex EU relationship to the Convention: Karl Kreuzer, 'Internationale Mobiliarsicherungsrechte an Luftfahrzeugausrüstung' in Ingeborg Schwenzer and Günter Hager (eds), *Festschrift für Peter Schlechtriem* (Mohr Siebeck 2003) 869, 875 *et seq*; Roy Goode, *Official Commentary on the Convention on International Interests in Mobile Equipment and the Protocol thereto on Space*

Assets (UNIDROIT Books 2013) para 2.239 *et seq*). The Aircraft Protocol came into force simultaneously with the Convention and now (February 2017) has 65 contracting states (within the EU: Denmark, Ireland, Latvia, Luxembourg, Spain, Sweden and the United Kingdom). Neither the Rail nor the Space Protocols are yet in force.

2. Two-instruments structure

Early in the drafting process it became apparent that it would be difficult to create a single instrument that would equally meet the differing needs of the various financiers of aircraft, railways, space assets etc. Also, the aircraft industry which received considerable support from the International Air Transport Association (IATA) and the International Civil Aviation Organization (→ ICAO) wanted to move forward more quickly. The solution finally approved at the Diplomatic Conference in Cape Town, was to create a framework convention setting out the basic, equipment-neutral provisions with respect to the creation of an international interest, its rules on perfection and priority as well as its → remedies, while leaving all equipment-specific provisions to separate Protocols which could be elaborated step by step. Principally, the framework convention and the additional protocols are to be read and interpreted together as a single convention, according to art 6(1) Cape Town Convention. Nevertheless, as the more specific instruments, the Protocols may not merely supplement but also openly modify the Cape Town Convention. The Protocols prevail if there is any inconsistency between the two sets of rules, see art 6(2) Cape Town Convention (see on the history and the structure Roy Goode, 'Transcending the Boundaries of Earth and Space: The Preliminary draft UNIDROIT Convention on International Interests in Mobile Equipment' [1998] Unif.L.Rev. 52 *et seq*; Roy Goode, *Official Commentary on the Convention on International Interests in Mobile Equipment and the Protocol thereto on Matters Specific to Aircraft Equipment* (3rd edn, UNIDROIT Books 2013) para 2.12 *et seq*).

3. Scope of application

a) Territorial application

For the Cape Town Convention to be territorially applicable, only the debtor (usually the person seeking to finance the acquisition of mobile equipment) needs to be situated in a contracting state at the time of conclusion of the agreement creating the international security interest, see art 3 Cape Town Convention. The place where the debtor is situated is defined by art 4. It refers alternatively to the place of incorporation, the seat of the registered office or statutory seat, the centre of administration or the place of business. Both the place of business of the creditor and the location of the object are irrelevant. It is important to note that, as a consequence of these rules, the Cape Town Convention and the Aircraft and Railway Protocols can be used as a basis for the financing of aircraft and railways also by sellers, banks or other financial institutions which are situated in states that have not yet ratified the Convention and the relevant Protocols provided that the debtor is situated in a contracting state.

Thus, application of the Cape Town Convention by a state court still depends on the → *lex fori*: if the state in question is a contracting state, the Convention will apply if its substantive and territorial criteria are fulfilled, irrespective of the national private international law rules of the *lex fori*. Where the court is situated in a non-contracting state, applicability of the Convention depends on the forum private international law (see IV.1. above). If it leads to the application of the law of a contracting state and the Convention is applicable under its own rules, the court will apply the Convention (see Roy Goode, *Official Commentary on the Convention on International Interests in Mobile Equipment and the Protocol thereto on Matters Specific to Aircraft Equipment* (3rd edn, UNIDROIT Books 2013) para 2.26 *et seq*). Therefore, as long as the Convention is not in force worldwide, its practical effectiveness depends to a large extent on the question of jurisdiction. Arts 42–45 Cape Town Convention and arts XXI and XXII Aircraft Protocol contain special rules on jurisdiction, mostly relating to forum selection clauses.

b) Substantive application

From the substantive viewpoint, the interest in question must vest in an object which comes under one of the Protocols. Since, for the time being, only the Aircraft Protocol is in force, the interest must relate to an 'aircraft object' (art II(1) of the Aircraft Protocol) as defined in art I(2)(c), thus comprising airframes as defined in (e), aircraft engines as defined in (b) and helicopters as defined in (l). Note that under the Protocol, the aircraft is divided into the airframe and the aircraft engine, taking account of the fact that the engines are separable from the airframe and also are usually financed separately. When entering into force, the Luxembourg Railway Protocol will render the Convention applicable to railway rolling stock, meaning 'vehicles movable on a fixed railway track or directly on, above or below a guideway, together with traction systems, engines, brakes . . .', see art I(2)(e) Rail Protocol. The Rail Protocol includes simplified requirements for the identification of the collateral object in the security interest agreement, but it nevertheless requires that the entry in the register be unequivocal as to the object of the security interest. The concept is due to the fact that railway equipment, unlike airplane equipment, does not always have identification numbers.

Space Assets are defined by the Space Protocol, art I(2)(k), as meaning 'any man-made uniquely identifiable asset in space or designed to be launched into space, and comprising . . . a spacecraft, such as a satellite, space station, space module, space capsule, space vehicle or reusable launch vehicle . . .' with several separable units being capable of separate international interests.

4. The international interest and its creation

Essentially, the Convention creates a uniform international interest without, however, neglecting the fact that in different jurisdictions, different categories of security rights have been developed over time. It refrains from introducing the uniform, functionally defined security interest of art 9 Uniform Commercial Code (American Law Institute, Uniform Commercial Code, Official Text with Comments, St. Paul 2012). Instead, art 2(2)(a) to (c) of the Cape Town Convention unites a charge under a security agreement, a conditional sale under a title reservation agreement and the rights of a lessor under a leasing agreement under the umbrella of the 'international interest'. The creation and perfection mechanisms are equivalent for all three sub-categories of international interest, but there are differences with respect to the default remedies, see arts 8–10 Cape Town Convention. Thus, insofar as a distinction needs to be drawn between the three categories, it is for the court seized to (re-)characterize the agreement according to the *lex fori*. Article 2(2) at the end seeks to avoid a double characterization (Roy Goode, *Official Commentary on the Convention on International Interests in Mobile Equipment and the Protocol thereto on Space Assets* (UNIDROIT Books 2013) para 2.50 *et seq*).

The security interest is created by a written agreement between the parties, which must relate to an object as defined by one of the Protocols and of which the grantor has power to dispose, see art 7 Cape Town Convention. Principally, the international interest is effective from the moment of conclusion of the agreement (but see below IV.5.), the general effectiveness of the agreement being subject to the law designated by the forum private international law rules, such as the Rome I Regulation (Regulation (EC) No 593/2008 of the European Parliament and of the Council of 17 June 2008 on the law applicable to contractual obligations (Rome I), [2008] OJ L 177/6; → Rome Convention and Rome I Regulation (contractual obligations)) for EU Member States.

5. Perfection and priority

In order to become effective vis-à-vis third parties, particularly against the insolvency administrator, the international interest must be perfected (registered) under arts 16 *et seq* Cape Town Convention. Article 29(1) Cape Town Convention sets out the basic principles with respect to priority: a registered interest takes priority over an unregistered one and of two registered interests the time of registration determines priority; priority extends to proceeds, see art 29(6) Cape Town Convention. These rules apply even if the holder of the registered interest, upon acquisition and/or registration had actual knowledge of an earlier unregistered interest in the same asset, see art 29(2). Furthermore, according to art 29(3) a purchaser for value without notice is also subject to the registered interest. These rules apply irrespective of whether the interest was at all registrable. Therefore, interests according to national law which are not entered or incapable of being entered into the international registry set up by the Convention are subordinated to registered international interests (Roy Goode, *Official Commentary on the Convention on International Interests in Mobile Equipment and the Protocol thereto on Matters Specific to Aircraft Equipment* (3rd edn, UNIDROIT Books 2013) para 2.157 *et seq*; Michel Dechamps, 'The Perfection and Priority Rules of the Cape Town Convention and the Aircraft Protocol: A Comparative Law Analysis' (2013) 2 *Cape Town Convention Journal* 51 *et seq*).

These rules are of crucial importance for the publicity and the legal safety which the registry wishes to establish.

Registration is to take place in a special international register which is exclusively electronic and asset-based rather than debtor-based. The register is established separately for each type of mobile equipment. The framework Cape Town Convention includes general rules for organization of the register, whereas the additional protocols contain specific rules for different kinds of equipment. Access to the register is available both for new entries as well as for Internet searches. It follows that substantive information upon which the effectiveness of a security right in other respects depends is not checked by the registrar. It is not necessary to submit copies of the contractual documents, but rather the provision of certain information about the collateral and the parties to the security agreement suffices. Registration can be made under art 20(1) Cape Town Convention by either party to the agreement with written consent of the other party. Registration becomes effective on complete entry of the required data and their acceptance by the system. The entry remains effective until deleted or until a predetermined removal date set at the time of registration. According to art 22 Cape Town Convention, anyone may search the register. It must, however, be remembered that the register is asset-based, so that entries of security interests must be identified by serial numbers or other identification numbers pertaining to the collateral.

The aircraft register is available on the Internet at <http://internationalregistry.aero>. It is supervised by the International Civil Aviation Organization (→ ICAO), which participated in the creation of the Aircraft Protocol. The register has its seat in Dublin and is managed as a joint venture between a private firm and the Irish government. The establishment, running and supervision of the register for railway rolling stock will be under the auspices of an institution created by the contracting states, as the Intergovernmental Organisation for International Carriage by Rail (OTIF) does not operate worldwide. The seat of the new institution is to be Luxembourg.

6. *Default remedies*

a) *Outside insolvency*
Absent agreement by the parties, art 11(2) Cape Town Convention provides that a 'default' is an event 'which substantially deprives the creditor of what it is entitled to expect under the agreement'. With respect to the remedies upon default the Cape Town Convention distinguishes between charges, conditional sales and leasing agreements. Arts 8 and 9 Cape Town Convention set out in a detailed fashion the remedies for international interests by way of a charge. For leasing agreements and conditional sales, the comparatively brief art 10 states that the lessor or seller may terminate the agreement and take possession or control of the collateral. Article IX(1) Aircraft Protocol and art VII(1) Rail Protocol modify the Cape Town Convention rules and add to the list of remedies the export and physical transfer of the equipment from the territory in which it is located. Principally, the exercise of remedies must be in conformity with the procedure prescribed by the law of the place where the remedy is to be exercised, art 14 Cape Town Convention. However, in relation to the crucial question whether self-help by the creditor is allowed, the Cape Town Convention is more specific: the remedies of the Convention may be exercised against the defaulting debtor without court intervention even if the law of the state where the remedy is exercised generally requires leave of the court. However, upon accession to or ratification of the Cape Town Convention, a contracting state may reserve the right to require court intervention, see art 54(2) Cape Town Convention (see in detail Roy Goode, *Official Commentary on the Convention on International Interests in Mobile Equipment and the Protocol thereto on Matters Specific to Aircraft Equipment* (3rd edn, UNIDROIT Books 2013) para 2.81).

b) *In insolvency*
Article 30 Cape Town Convention deals with the effects of debtor insolvency on the international interest: according to art 30(1), a registered international interest is principally effective as against the insolvency administrator, whereas any procedural rules relating to the enforcement of proprietary rights are left to the autonomous *lex fori concursus* (art 13(3)(b) Cape Town Convention). Article XI Aircraft Protocol seeks to introduce a degree of uniformity also in relation to a creditor's remedies in insolvency, which is of course a key element in any secured transactions law. However, its applicability depends on an opt-in decision by the contracting state which is the primary insolvency jurisdiction (→ Insolvency,

jurisdiction and *vis attractiva*), see art XI(1) Aircraft Protocol. Moreover, art XI presents two different alternatives, A and B, between which the contracting state must decide upon ratification or accession (see in more detail Eva-Maria Kieninger, 'Effects in Insolvency of the International Interest in Mobile Equipment' [1999] Unif.L.Rev. 397). The Rail Protocol even introduces a choice between three alternative sets of rules (art IX, Alternatives A, B and C). Hopes to establish Alternative C as a basic rule binding for all contracting states have not materialized.

7. Assignments

As a starting point, the Cape Town Convention respects that, under most jurisdictions, security rights are secondary to the secured debt, so that an assignment of the international interest will take the form of an assignment of the secured debt with the international interest following automatically (partly critical Roy Goode, *Official Commentary on the Convention on International Interests in Mobile Equipment and the Protocol thereto on Matters Specific to Aircraft Equipment* (3rd edn, UNIDROIT Books 2013) para 2.189 *et seq*). On the other hand, it cannot be denied that it will largely be the international interest in the aircraft object or the railway rolling stock that is the commercially significant subject of the transaction. Under the Cape Town Convention, the secured debt is called the 'associated right', see art 1(a) Cape Town Convention, and an 'assignment' is defined as a contract which by way of security or otherwise, confers on the assignee associated rights (art 1(b) Cape Town Convention). Not being a convention on assignment as such (see on this subject the UNCITRAL Assignment of Receivables Convention (United Nations Convention on the Assignment of Receivables in International Trade, concluded 12 December 2001, adopted by resolution A/RES/56/8)), the Cape Town Convention does not deal with the requirements and effects of assignments in general, but rather confines itself to the effects which an assignment or subrogation may have on the international interest, see arts 31 *et seq*. The Convention itself only requires an assignment to be in writing and to render the associated rights identifiable (art 32(1) Cape Town Convention). In the case of an international interest created by a security agreement, the Cape Town Convention does not allow for an isolated transfer of the international interests without at least a partial assignment of the associated right, art 32(2) Convention. There are no such restrictions in the case of a conditional sale or leasing contract. Conversely, it is always open to the parties to assign a debt without at the same time transferring the international interest relating to it (Roy Goode, *Official Commentary on the Convention on International Interests in Mobile Equipment and the Protocol thereto on Space Assets* (UNIDROIT Books 2013) para 2.194). Article 35 solves priority conflicts in case of competing assignments of the same claim and, in contracting states, supersedes national priority rules (for details see Roy Goode, *Official Commentary on the Convention on International Interests in Mobile Equipment and the Protocol thereto on Matters Specific to Aircraft Equipment* (3rd edn, UNIDROIT Books 2013) para 2.200 *et seq*).

EVA-MARIA KIENINGER

Literature

Benjamin von Bodungen, *Mobiliarsicherungsrechte an Luftfahrzeugen und Eisenbahnrollmaterial im nationalen und internationalen Rechtsverkehr* (LIT 2009); Rob Cowan and Donald Gallagher, 'The International Registry for Aircraft Equipment: Breaking New Ground' [2012] Unif.L.Rev. 579; Michel Dechamps, 'The Perfection and Priority Rules of the Cape Town Convention and the Aircraft Protocol: A Comparative Law Analysis' (2013) 2 *Cape Town Convention Journal* 51; Roy Goode, *Official Commentary on the Convention on International Interests in Mobile Equipment and the Protocol thereto on Matters Specific to Aircraft Equipment* (3rd edn, UNIDROIT Books 2013); Roy Goode, *Official Commentary on the Convention on International Interests in Mobile Equipment and the Protocol thereto on Space Assets* (UNIDROIT Books 2013); Roy Goode, *Official Commentary on the Convention on International Interests in Mobile Equipment and Luxembourg Protocol thereto on Matters specific to Railway Rolling Stock* (2nd edn, UNIDROIT Books 2014); Roy Goode and others, *Transnational Commercial Law: International Instruments and Commentary* (2nd edn, OUP 2012); Eva-Maria Kieninger, *Security Rights in Movable Property in European Private Law* (CUP 2004); Karl Kreuzer, 'Internationale Mobiliarsicherungsrechte an Luftfahrzeugausrüstung' in Ingeborg Schwenzer and Günter Hager (eds), *Festschrift für Peter Schlechtriem* (Mohr Siebeck 2003) 869; Howard Rosen, Martin Fleetwood and Benjamin von Bodungen, 'The Luxembourg Rail Protocol: Extending Cape Town Benefits to the Rail Industry' [2012] Unif.L.Rev. 609; Harry C Sigman and Eva-Maria Kieninger, *Cross-Border Security over Tangibles* (Sellier 2007); see also the topical issue of [2007] Unif.L.Rev. 417 *et seq* on the Luxembourg Railway Protocol and the *Cape Town Convention Journal* (Hart Publishing; since 2012). See also the extensive list on <www.unidroit.org/biblio-2001capetown>.

Service of documents

I. Background and context

Every procedural system provides rules on how the written communication between the court and the parties is to be conducted ('service of documents') and, in particular, how to give notice of the initiation of proceedings to the defendant ('service of process'). However, since service of process is classified – at least by the traditional view in continental Europe – as an official act, such provisions designed for mere domestic cases cannot be applied offhand to international disputes in which the defendant resides outside the forum. Rather, service abroad requires the cooperation of the affected state or, at any rate, its acquiescence.

Hence, sovereignty interests are a characteristic feature of international law on service, but the same is true for the tension between the right to effective access to justice of the party interested in proper service on the one hand, and the right to be heard of the recipient on the other hand: the party interested in proper service, ordinarily the plaintiff, desires speedy transmission. The recipient, usually the defendant, is required to respond, frequently even within a certain time limit, to the served document; he thus puts emphasis on a reasonable opportunity to take note of the document as well as comprehensibility. These interests have to be reconciled with the principle of economic proceedings: this requires simple, cost-effective and expeditious service, but likewise that mistakes are avoided which could compromise the success of subsequent proceedings, namely the recognition and enforcement of the expected decision abroad.

A special function of the rules on service not discussed in this entry arises in relation to international jurisdiction (→ Jurisdiction, foundations): according to the traditional perception of the common law, personal service of process upon a defendant within the forum state may establish jurisdiction to adjudicate even if the defendant is only temporarily present within the forum (the so-called transient rule or tag jurisdiction).

II. Legal sources

The law on service has always been one of the big issues in international judicial cooperation in → civil and commercial matters. The Treaty concerning the Union of South American States in respect of Procedural Law of 11 January 1889, signed at Montevideo (United Nations Register of Texts of Conventions and other Instruments concerning International Trade Law, vol II, 1973, 5), as well as its successor, the Treaty on International Procedural Law of 19 March 1940 (United Nations Register of Texts of Conventions and other Instruments concerning International Trade Law, vol II, 1973, 21), already dealt with this topic. And, of course, the → Hague Conference on Private International Law concerned itself from the beginning with the development of rules on communication of judicial and extrajudicial documents: cross-border service was addressed in the very first Hague Convention, namely the Convention on Civil Procedure of 14 November 1896 (Convention de droit international privé du 14 novembre 1896, available at <www.hcch.net>), the Hague Convention on Civil Procedure of 17 July 1905 (Convention du 17 juillet 1905 relative à la procédure civile; RGBl. 1909, 409, available at <www.hcch.net>) and the Hague Civil Procedure Convention (Hague Convention of 1 March 1954 on civil procedure, 286 UNTS 265).

While these early conventions still dealt in general with different fundamental questions concerning mutual judicial assistance, the need for specialized rules soon became apparent. The result was the Hague Service Convention (Hague Convention of 15 November 1965 on the service abroad of judicial and extrajudicial documents in civil or commercial matters, 658 UNTS 163), which remains very important today and is in force in over 50 Member States of the Hague Conference as well as several non-Member States. It is an instrument of classic mutual judicial assistance, which prioritizes the interests of well-organized cross-border legal relations over national sovereignty considerations, but does not completely exclude them. This is illustrated by the fact that according to art 13(1) of the Hague Service Convention the state addressed may refuse to execute a request for service, even though it complies with the terms of the Convention, if it deems that compliance would infringe on its sovereignty or security. The applicability of this public policy clause has been much discussed in recent times in cases concerning service of process of US actions in Europe which aim at punitive damages or conducting a class action (cf from a German perspective: Federal Constitutional Court of Germany (BVerfG), 9 January 2013 [2013] NJW 990).

Multilateral conventions such as the Hague Service Convention have always been supplemented with both a network of additional bilateral agreements to simplify legal relations, and independent bilateral treaties on mutual judicial assistance. In order to facilitate closer cooperation and to clarify the legal situation, subsidiary multilateral agreements were negotiated at a regional level. This led to the Inter-American Convention of 30 January 1975 on Letters Rogatory (1438 UNTS 287), as supplemented by the Additional Protocol of 8 May 1979 (Additional Protocol to the Inter-American Convention on letters rogatory of 8 May 1979, 1438 UNTS 322), and in Europe to the Convention on the service in the Member States of the European Union of judicial and extrajudicial documents in civil or commercial matters of 26 May 1997 ([1997] OJ C 261/2). That Convention, however, never entered into force, but, shortly after the entry into force of the Treaty of Amsterdam (Treaty of Amsterdam amending the Treaty on the European Union, the Treaties establishing the European Communities and certain related acts (consolidated version), [1997] OJ C 340/01), it was in substance taken over by the similarly titled Regulation (EC) No 1348/2000 of 29 May 2000 on the service in the Member States of judicial and extrajudicial documents in civil or commercial matters ([2000] OJ L 160/37). This Regulation in turn was repealed by the current European Service Regulation (Regulation (EC) No 1393/2007 of the European Parliament and of the Council of 13 November 2007 on the service in the Member States of judicial and extrajudicial documents in civil or commercial matters (service of documents), and repealing Council Regulation (EC) No 1348/2000, [2007] OJ L 324/79).

The European Regulation applies in all EU Member States (regarding Denmark's special position, see the Agreement between the European Community and the Kingdom of Denmark on the service of judicial and extrajudicial documents in civil or commercial matters of 19 October 2005, [2005] OJ L 300/55, and the notice of the Commission, [2008] OJ L 331/21) and takes precedence over international treaties and national laws of the Member States. The Member States are, however, entitled to conclude or maintain bilateral agreements to achieve further acceleration and simplification of transmission (art 20 European Service Regulation). The Regulation basically distinguishes between service of documents by means of mutual judicial assistance (art 4 *et seq* European Service Regulation) and service of documents without involving foreign authorities (art 12 *et seq* European Service Regulation). Compared to the Hague Conventions, important progress has been achieved through the possibility of service by post (art 14 European Service Regulation) and the abolition of the public policy clause. With regard to the applicability to extrajudicial documents (*in casu*: a notarial deed) outside court proceedings, see ECJ Case C-14/08 *Roda Golf & Beach Resort SL* [2009] ECR I-5439.

In case the initial document has to be transmitted abroad, further legislative acts make reference to the mentioned provisions on international service of process in EU or Convention Law (cf art 26 Brussels I Regulation (Regulation (EC) No 44/2001 of 22 December 2000 on jurisdiction and the recognition and enforcement of judgments in civil and commercial matters, [2001] OJ L 12/1), respectively art 28 Brussels I Regulation (recast) (Regulation (EU) No 1215/2012 of the European Parliament and of the Council of 12 December 2012 on jurisdiction and the recognition and enforcement of judgments in civil and commercial matters (recast), [2012] OJ L 351/1) (→ Brussels I (Convention and Regulation)), art 18 → Brussels IIa Regulation (Council Regulation (EC) No 2201/2003 of 27 November 2003 concerning jurisdiction and the recognition and enforcement of judgments in matrimonial matters and the matters of parental responsibility, repealing Regulation (EC) No 1347/2000, [2003] OJ L 338/1) and art 11 Maintenance Regulation (Council Regulation (EC) No 4/2009 of 18 December 2008 on jurisdiction, applicable law, recognition and enforcement of decisions and cooperation in matters relating to maintenance obligations, [2009] OJ L 7/1); see below under IV.). Moreover, it must be kept in mind that the European Enforcement Order

Regulation (Regulation (EC) No 805/2004 of the European Parliament and of the Council of 21 April 2004 creating a European Enforcement Order for uncontested claims, [2004] OJ L 143/15, art 13 *et seq*) and the European Payment Order Regulation (Regulation (EC) No 1896/2006 of the European Parliament and of the Council of 12 December 2006 creating a European order for payment procedure, [2001] OJ L 399/1, art 13 *et seq*) contain minimum requirements for the service of process necessary in their respective scope (see ECJ Case C-119/13 *eco cosmetics v Virginie Laetitia Barbara Dupuy* and C-120/13 *Raiffeisenbank St. Georgen v Tetyana Bonchyk* [2014] OJ C 395/10).

Given the tight net of provisions in EU and Convention Law, national law on service is of only marginal importance today. Even in relation to states with which mutual judicial assistance has not been established, certain practices are commonly accepted. Many states tolerate, for example, that a foreign court serves documents informally on citizens of the forum state. This practice might even have become customary international law already.

III. Channels of transmission

Service of process via consular or diplomatic authorities has always occurred: the foreign office of the forum state contacts the authorities in the receiving state, which then administer service of process. The procedure was considerably simplified by the introduction of direct communication via Central Authorities (cf art 2 *et seq* Hague Service Convention). Direct transmission of judicial documents between the transmitting and receiving agency provided for in art 4 European Service Regulation provides further acceleration: ideally, this allows for direct communication between the court where the proceedings are pending and the authority responsible for service at the recipient's place of residence.

Service abroad by mutual judicial assistance via Central Authorities or other transmitting authorities requires a request, which is to be addressed to the foreign authority in charge of the administration of service. This authority is then obliged to carry out the request. Lest the requesting court exceptionally insists on observing certain formal requirements (→ Formal requirements and validity), the foreign authority may either serve the document informally, by simply delivering the document to the recipient willing to accept the document (cf eg art 5(2) Hague Service Convention), or formally according to the rules applicable in the receiving state (cf art 5(1) lit a Hague Service Convention). For example, service is possible by depositing the document in the postbox if the law of the receiving state provides for such a method. Since an initially informal service by simple delivery might fail due to the recipient's refusal of acceptance, it is advisable to request formal service of documents at the same time.

Much easier and faster than service via mutual judicial assistance is service by post. This method was already provided for in the Hague Convention on Civil Procedure signed on 17 July 1905 (Convention du 17 juillet 1905 relative à la procédure civile; RGBl. 1909, 409, available at <www.hcch.net>), but this Convention – like its successors – allowed for objections (cf art 10 lit a Hague Service Convention). Such an objection was, for example, declared by Germany, so that service of documents by post to Germany is prohibited. Within the EU, art 14 European Service Regulation now guarantees the possibility of service by registered letter with acknowledgement of receipt. This is not just a subsidiary means of service, since the European Service Regulation does not provide for a hierarchy between service of documents according to art 3 *et seq* and service according to art 14. If service is delivered in both ways, the moment of the earlier service is decisive (ECJ Case C-473/04 *Plumex v Young Sports NV* [2006] ECR I-1417). An even faster method of international service, namely service of documents by email has been approved by American courts in exceptional cases. Due to the primacy of the Hague Service Convention this is, however, only admissible when the Central Authorities are involved (for a different view see eg, *Gurung v Malhotra*, 279 F.R.D. 215 (SDNY 2011)).

Irrespective of the parties' → nationality, courts normally communicate in an official language of the forum state. In principle, this also applies for all orders and decisions of the court. In cases of service abroad, it can, however, be necessary that the document is accompanied by a translation (cf arts 5 and 8 European Service Regulation; art 5(3) Hague Service Convention). Art 8 European Service Regulation insists on the right of the recipient to refuse acceptance if the document is drafted in a language he does not comprehend and is not accompanied by a translation. In determining whether the recipient understands the language, in the sense of art 8(1) lit a European Service Regulation, no presumption is created by the recipient's acceptance of a language for the purposes of the contract, although this is a consideration which the court may take into account (cf ECJ Case C-14/07 *Ingenieurbüro Michael Weiss und Partner GbR v Industrie- und Handelskammer Berlin* [2008] ECR I-3367). If the recipient declines acceptance (if necessary by returning the document), service only becomes valid when the document has been served once again along with the required translation. In this case, art 8(3) European Service Regulation ensures that the consignor does not suffer any disadvantage with regard to deadlines to be observed. A standardized form instructs the recipient about his rights (cf art 8(1) and (5) with Annex II European Service Regulation).

IV. Safeguards for defendants

In order that completion of service can be formally certified, the relevant legislative acts provide for special certificates of service (eg art 6 Hague Service Convention, art 10 European Service Regulation). If no such certificate is received by the requesting court or if only the failure or infeasibility has been certified, a repetition of service abroad, if necessary by different means of transmission or a formal service of documents, is possible depending on the circumstances of the individual case.

Based on the model of art 15 Hague Service Convention, art 19 European Service Regulation requires that where a writ of summons or an equivalent document has to be transmitted to another Member State for the purpose of service and the defendant has not appeared, the court must stay the proceedings until it is established by a certificate of service or any other information that service was timely and proper. Provisions referring to art 19 European Service Regulation can be found in other secondary legislation (cf art 26 Brussels I Regulation, respectively art 28 Brussels I Regulation (recast), art 18 Brussels IIa Regulation, art 11 Maintenance Regulation) and Convention Law (cf art 16 Lugano Convention of 30 October 2007 on jurisdiction and the recognition and enforcement of judgments in civil and commercial matters, [2007] OJ L 339/3). The aim of the legislator is to hinder fictitious service abroad (see V.). The proceedings stayed may be continued even if proper service cannot be certified if: (i) the document was transmitted in accordance with the relevant provisions; (ii) a period of time of no less than six months, considered adequate by the judge in the particular case, has elapsed since the date of the transmission of the document; and (iii) no certificate of any kind has been received, even though every reasonable effort has been made to obtain it through the competent authorities or bodies of the Member State addressed (cf art 15(2) Hague Service Convention, art 19(2) European Service Regulation). The proceedings remain stayed, however, although service of documents can be certified, if service was not timely enough thereby compromising the defendant's opportunity to defend himself adequately. In such a case, the response period must be extended and/or a new date for trial must be set.

Many national procedural systems contain provisions according to which deficiencies in service abroad can be cured in accordance with the respective → *lex fori*. Accordingly, appearance of the defendant without objection to the procedure, or proof that the document actually reached the defendant can be sufficient. It is remarkable that convention law, namely the Hague Service Convention, does not address the question of curing defects in service. Against this backdrop it is not surprising that there is no consistent opinion on whether recourse to national provisions is appropriate (cf from a German perspective: German Federal Court of Justice (BGH), 14 September 2011 [2011] NJW 3581: curing of defects in service is possible according to German law if it is not the provisions of the Hague Service Convention that have been violated but only those of the receiving state applicable according to art 5(1) lit a Hague Service Convention). Even the European Service Regulation does not contain provisions on curing defects but allows – besides art 8(3) and art 19 European Service Regulation – space for respective national provisions. A special provision on curing defects is, however, contained in art 18 of the European Enforcement Order Regulation.

If service of process is defective and cannot be cured during subsequent proceedings, this can be an obstacle to the recognition and declaration of enforceability of a subsequent decision in another country. To illustrate this, art 34 Brussels I Regulation reads:

> A judgment shall not be recognised: . . . 2. where it was given in default of appearance, if the defendant was not served with the document which instituted the proceedings or with an equivalent

document in sufficient time and in such a way as to enable him to arrange for his defence, unless the defendant failed to commence proceedings to challenge the judgment when it was possible for him to do so; . . . .

Hence, according to this and similar provisions (art 45(1) lit b Brussels I Regulation (recast), art 22 lit b and 23 lit c Brussels IIa Regulation, art 24 lit b Maintenance Regulation), a violation of the right to be heard at the initiation of the procedure in the state of origin can bar recognition. This is a special manifestation of the procedural public policy clause: a decision is not recognized if the defendant could not sufficiently influence that decision for want of timely information on the initiation of the procedure. Therefore, it is not so much the appropriateness of service which matters, but rather whether a defect in service impairs the recipient's ability to defend (ECJ Case-420/07 *Meletis Apostolides v David Charles Orams and Linda Elizabeth Orams* [2009] ECR I-3571, paras 72 *et seq*). Even if the court in the forum state recorded the date of service in a certificate according to art 54 Brussels I Regulation (now: art 53 Brussels I Regulation (recast)), this does not discharge the court in the executing state of an examination according to art 34 No 2 Brussels I Regulation (ECJ Case C-619/10 *Trade Agency v Seramico Investments* [2012] OJ C 331/3).

Special requirements apply if European law renders a declaration of enforceability in the executing state unnecessary, because this involves enhanced demands on the examination of proper service in the forum state. So the court concerned with certifying a European Enforcement Order must examine according to art 6(1) lit c European Enforcement Order Regulation whether service of process met the requirements as set out in art 12 *et seq* European Enforcement Order Regulation. If the certificate has been rendered, the debtor can claim in the state of origin based on art 19 European Enforcement Order Regulation that his rights of defence have been curtailed and achieve a suspension or restriction of enforcement in the executing state (art 23 European Enforcement Order Regulation). Similar protective provisions are contained in the EU Maintenance Regulation (art 19 and art 21(3)), in the European → Payment Order Regulation (art 18(1) s 2, art 20(1) and art 23) and in the European Small Claims Procedure Regulation (Regulation (EC) No 861/2007 of the European Parliament and of the Council of 11 July 2007 establishing a European Small Claims Procedure, [2007] OJ L 199/1, art 28 and art 23).

V. Avoidance of serving process abroad

Since service of documents abroad is considered to be complicated and time-consuming, most courts welcome opportunities to avoid it. This can be achieved by requesting the party residing abroad that he names an authorized recipient within the forum state. If the party meets this demand, further communication can be made via the authorized recipient. If no authorized recipient is named, sanctions can be imposed. One example is § 184 of the German Code of Civil Procedure (Zivilprozessordnung of 5 December 2005, BGBl. I 3202, as amended, henceforth German CCP) which reads:

(1) For service pursuant to section 183, the court may order the party to name, within a reasonable period of time, an authorised recipient who is a resident of Germany or who has business premises in Germany, unless the party has appointed an attorney of record. Should no authorised recipient be named and until such recipient is named retroactively, documents may be served subsequently by being mailed to the address of the party.
(2) Two weeks after it has been mailed, the document shall be deemed served. The court may set a longer period. In the order issued pursuant to subsection (1), attention is to be drawn to these legal consequences. By way of recording proof of the documents having been served, it is to be noted in the files at which time and to which address the document was mailed.

According to this rule (and different from the cases of art 14 European Service Regulation), service is performed not by delivering the document to the recipient abroad by post, but rather by the court delivering the document to the postal agency in the forum state ('by being mailed') and then waiting two weeks. Hence, this is a case of a fictitious domestic service of documents. Consequently, this provision is in accordance with the Hague Service Convention, which only concerns service abroad (see also German Federal Court of Justice (BGH), 26 June 2012 [2012] NJW 2588, paras 13 *et seq*, dealing with the compatibility of § 184 with the fundamental rights of the Basic Law for the Federal Republic of Germany (Grundgesetz of 23 May 1949, BGBl. 1, as amended) and the ECHR (European Convention of 4 November

1950 for the Protection of Human Rights and Fundamental Freedoms, 213 UNTS 221) as well as other international law). There has been intensive discussion on the question whether fictitious domestic service is compatible with European Service Regulation and can therefore be admissible within Europe. With regard to fictitious service of the document initiating proceedings, this question must be answered in the negative, but it might be considered with regard to service of further documents during the proceedings. Even to this extent, however, the ECJ has made it clear in the meantime that the priority of European Service Regulation normally bars recourse to national provisions on fictitious domestic service (ECJ Case C-325/11 *Krystyna Alder and Ewald Alder v Sabina Orlowska and Czeslaw Orlowski* [2013] OJ C 46/7). This position finds support in the light of the prohibition of discrimination according to art 18 TFEU (The Treaty on the Functioning of the European Union (consolidated version), [2016] OJ C 202/47).

Only as an exception, service may be replaced by public notification if service abroad is infeasible or carries no guarantee of success. German law once again provides an example, namely § 185 German CCP, which reads:

> The documents may be served by publishing a notice (service by publication) wherever: 1. the abode of a person is unknown and it is not possible to serve the documents upon a representative or authorised recipient, . . . 3. it is not possible to serve documents abroad, or if such services do not hold out any prospect of success . . . .

This again might be regarded as a case of fictitious service. However, neither the European Service Regulation (cf art 1(2)) nor the Hague Service Convention (cf art 1(2)) are an obstacle to the application of such a national provision, and in consequence to the delivery of a judgment by default, if the defendant's place of abode is unknown although the court has made sure that all inquiries necessary to meet the principles of due care and good faith remained unsuccessful (ECJ Case C-292/10 *G v Cornelius de Visser* [2012] OJ C 133/5, also regarding the point that a judgment by default rendered against a defendant whose address is unknown may not be certified as a European Enforcement Order).

VI. Future developments

Special Commissions regularly deal with the practical operation of the Hague Service Convention (cf the recent Hague Conference on Private International Law (ed), Conclusions and Recommendations of the 2009 Special Commission on the practical operation of the Hague Apostille, Service, Taking of Evidence and Access to Justice Conventions, The Hague 2009). Currently a 2013 questionnaire addressed to Members and non-Member contracting states is being evaluated. The focus of future discussions will primarily lie on the impact of information technology.

In the view of the Commission as stated in the report published at the end of 2013 (Commission, 'Report from the Commission to the European Parliament, the Council and the European Economic and Social Committee on the Application of Regulation (EC) No 1393/2007 of the European Parliament and of the Council on the service in the Member States of judicial and extrajudicial documents in civil or commercial matters (service of documents)' COM(2013) 858 final), the European Service Regulation has proved itself in practice. It is considered, however, whether in the light of the entire framework of judicial cooperation in civil justice matters, particularly in the light of the abolition of *exequatur*, minimum standards on service (on which documents should be served on foreign parties, on whom such service may take place, and at which moment in time service should take place) should be prepared. This would mean that the legislation of the EU would no longer confine itself to rules on service abroad. A further acceleration of service, in particular by using electronic service as a new method, is also desired.

Furthermore, the topic 'service and due notice of proceedings' is among the pilot projects of the cooperation of ELI and → UNIDROIT aiming at adopting European Principles of Transnational Civil procedure.

WOLFGANG HAU

Literature

Christophe Bernasconi and Laurence Thébault, *Practical Handbook on the Operation of the Hague Service Convention* (Wilson & Lafleur 2006); Christophe Bernasconi, Mayela Celis and Alexander Kunzelmann, 'Of Luddites and Luminaries: The Use of Modern Technologies under the Hague Legal Co-operation Conventions' in The Permanent Bureau of the Hague Conference on Private International Law (ed), *A Commitment to Private international law: Essays in Honour of Hans van Loon* (Intersentia 2013) 31;

Fernando Gascón Inhausti, 'Electronic Service of Documents: National and International Aspects' in Miklós Kengyel and Zoltán Nemessányi (eds), *Electronic Technology and Civil Procedure: New Paths to Justice from around the World* (Springer 2012) 137; Burkhard Hess, 'Justizielle Kooperation/Judicial Cooperation' in Peter Gottwald and Burkhard Hess (eds), *Procedural Justice* (Gieseking 2014) 387; Klaus J Hopt, Rainer Kulms and Jan von Hein, *Rechtshilfe und Rechtsstaat – Die Zustellung einer US-amerikanischen class action in Deutschland* (Mohr Siebeck 2006); Wendy Kennett, 'Service of Documents in Europe' (1998) 17 CJQ 284; Hartmut Linke, 'Die Probleme der internationalen Zustellung' in Peter Gottwald (ed), *Grundfragen der Gerichtsverfassung – Internationale Zustellung* (Gieseking 1999) 95; Stephen C McCaffrey and Thomas O Main, *Transnational Litigation in Comparative Perspective: Theory and Application* (OUP 2010) 368; David McLean, *International Co-operation in Civil and Criminal Matters* (3rd edn, OUP 2012) 23; Hans-Eric Rasmussen-Bonne, 'The Pendulum Swings Back: The Cooperative Approach of German Courts to International Service of Process' in Peter Hay and others (eds), *Resolving International Conflicts: Liber Amicorum Tibor Várady* (CEU Press 2009) 231; Thomas Rauscher, 'Der Wandel von Zustellungsstandards zu Zustellungsvorschriften im Europäischen Zivilprozessrecht' in Dietmar Baetge and others (eds), *Die richtige Ordnung. Festschrift für Jan Kropholler zum 70. Geburtstag* (Mohr Siebeck 2008) 851; Bruno A Ristau, 'Service of Process Abroad' in Peter Gottwald (ed), *Grundfragen der Gerichtsverfassung – Internationale Zustellung* (Gieseking 1999) 71; Haimo Schack, 'Transnational Service of Process' (2001) 6 Unif.L.Rev. 827; Peter Schlosser, 'Jurisdiction and International Judicial and Administrative Co-operation' (2000) 284 Rec. des Cours 13; Gabriele Springer, *Die direkte Postzustellung gerichtlicher Schriftstücke nach der Europäischen Zustellungsverordnung (EG) Nr. 1348/2000* (Nomos 2008); David P Stewart and Anna Conley, 'E-Mail Service on Foreign Defendants: Time for an International Approach?' (2007) 38 Geo. J. Int'l L. 755; Michael Stürner, 'Fiktive Inlandszustellungen und europäisches Recht' (2013) 126 ZZP 137.

Set-off

I. Concept and function

Set-off is a defence that can be used by a defendant against a plaintiff's claim. If set-off is allowed the sum that plaintiff owes defendant should be deducted from the plaintiff's claim. The following simple example can serve to illustrate the functioning of set-off: a claims payment of EUR 10,000 from B for the rent of office premises. B claims an offset of EUR 1,000 for repairs that B had to make in order to be able to use the premises for the agreed purpose. If set-off is allowed B will only have to pay A the net sum of EUR 9,000. Although set-off in certain laws in theory operates automatically, in practice set-off has to be invoked. This use of set-off as a defence characterizes the terminology. Hence the party claiming set-off is referred to as the debtor and the other party is referred to as the creditor. The claim against which set-off is invoked is referred to as the principal claim (or sometimes the passive claim) and the claim that is used for offsetting is referred to as the counterclaim (or sometimes the active claim).

The claims that are to be set off against each other can be either contractual or non-contractual or both. For example, A's claim against B may be contractual and B's claim against A may be non-contractual. In fact, any combination of the two is possible. If we turn back to the example given above we may add to the factual circumstances that B remains in the premises after the rental contract has been terminated and still does not pay the rent. A's claim against B for remuneration for the use of office space after the termination of the rental contract will be non-contractual – depending on the applicable law the claim can be characterized as one under unjust enrichment or in tort.

The various claims that the parties have may be governed by different laws. A's claim for the payment of rent may be governed by a law other than B's claim for reimbursement for repairs. The question arises which law should be applied to the right to set-off itself and this entry of the Encyclopaedia will deal with the law applicable to set-off between contractual obligations, between non-contractual obligations, mixed obligations and the particular case of set-off in insolvency.

What is more, different courts could have jurisdiction to hear the claims. For instance, if the parties have different domiciles and the claims are based on contracts with different places of performance arts 4 and 7(1) of the Brussels I Regulation (recast) (Regulation (EU) No 1215/2012 of the European Parliament and of the Council of 12 December 2012 on jurisdiction and the recognition and enforcement of judgments in civil and commercial matters (recast), [2012] OJ L 351/1; → Brussels I (Convention and Regulation)) would not point in the direction of one court being competent to hear all claims. As we will see later in this entry, jurisdiction to entertain a request for set-off depends on whether it is formulated as a counterclaim in the procedural sense of the expression or merely as a defence which would result in a sum being deducted from the plaintiff's claim.

II. The law applicable to set-off between contractual obligations

1. The Rome I Regulation

In the European Union, the law applicable to → contractual obligations is determined according to the rules in the Rome I Regulation (Regulation (EC) No 593/2008 of the European Parliament and of the Council of 17 June 2008 on the law applicable to contractual obligations (Rome I), [2008] OJ L 177/6; → Rome Convention and Rome I Regulation (contractual obligations)). In this context it is worth mentioning that the → CISG (United Nations Convention of 11 April 1980 on Contracts for the International Sale of Goods, 1489 UNTS 3) does not contain any rules on set-off. This means that even if the laws of two contracting states are applicable – and the CISG according to its art 1(1)(b) applies – the matter will be left to national law. In other words, choice of law matters.

Article 17 of the Rome I Regulation contains a specific rule on the law applicable to set-off by operation of law. This is a novelty in comparison to the Rome Convention (Rome Convention on the law applicable to contractual obligations (consolidated version), [1998] OJ C 27/34), which did not contain an explicit rule concerning set-off. However, it was generally held that the question was covered by art 10(1)(d), according to which the various ways of extinguishing obligations were included in the scope of the applicable law. However, this solution carried with it an inherent uncertainty when the two or more obligations involved were governed by different laws with different rules concerning set-off. Which of the laws determined the conditions for and effects of set-off? In art 17 Rome I Regulation it has now been clarified that set-off shall be governed by the law applicable to the claim against which the right to set-off is asserted – the principal claim.

Set-off may take place either by operation of law or because the parties have agreed on set-off. The Rome I Regulation covers both these situations but it is only the first situation that is dealt with in art 17. The law applicable to contractual set-off is determined by the general rules of the Regulation. Having said this, both situations deserve our attention. Contractual set-off plays a great practical role in particular in connection with payment systems and financial markets.

2. Set-off by operation of law

a) General approaches to the law applicable to set-off

Prior to the inclusion of an explicit rule in the Rome I Regulation, various different approaches to the issue of the law applicable to contractual set-off were taken and advocated throughout Europe. The three main approaches were (i) application of the law of the forum; (ii) a cumulative application of the laws involved; and (iii) application of the law of the principal claim – the solution chosen in the Rome I Regulation.

Prior to the entry into force of the Rome I Regulation in English and Scots private international law (→ United Kingdom) a claim would be set off against the principal claim only if this were possible according to the law of the forum. The advantage of applying the law of the forum is obvious: it is simple and reduces the cost of proceedings. The problems inherent in the application of the law of the forum are also obvious. First, the law of the forum need not have any connection whatsoever to the contractual obligations involved in the set-off. Applying the → *lex fori* could therefore be quite inequitable. What is more, applying the law of the forum encourages forum shopping (→ Forum (and law) shopping) and the possibility of forum shopping in its turn leads to a race to the courts.

The cumulative solution was favoured in French (→ France) and Italian (→ Italy) private international law. Set-off would only be allowed if it were possible under both the law applicable to the principal claim and the law applicable to the counterclaim. The main argument for a cumulation of laws is one of equity – if the extinction of two debts is involved it is only fair that the conditions for their extinction must be satisfied for both. This rule allegedly applies in all legal systems in internal situations and should therefore also apply when two or more laws govern the different debts. The law governing the counterclaim is as worthy of consideration as the law governing the principal claim. Another argument in favour of the cumulative solution is that it is neutral in relation to which of the parties that first brings an action and thus renders his claim the status of 'principal'. If one applies the law of the principal claim to set-off, a party, A, that has reason to fear that his debtor, B, would bring a counterclaim for set-off could stand to gain from being the first to sue if the law applicable to A's claim against B does not allow it. This could lead to a race to the courts. Using the cumulative approach there would be nothing to gain from suing first; the result would always be the same irrespective of which claim is regarded as 'principal'.

The solution chosen in the Rome I Regulation is that the law applicable to the principal claim determines the right to set-off. This solution goes particularly well within systems in which set-off has to be declared by a party. It also appears to have been somewhat of a majority opinion in → Germany and the Scandinavian countries. It is also the solution chosen in art 148(2) of the Swiss Private international law Act (Bundesgesetz über das Internationale Privatrecht of 18 December 1987, 1988 BBl I 5, as amended). The rationale behind applying the law of the claim against which set-off is declared is that the (main) creditor cannot defend himself against the extinction of his claim and therefore should have the benefit of the protective rules of the law applicable to his own claim. The rule protects the party facing set-off.

b) Scope of the law applicable to set-off
The law applicable to the issue of set-off should in principle govern all matters connected therewith – irrespective of the fact that set-off might be characterized as procedural in the applicable law. Only procedural issues *sensu strictu*, such as the question of at what point in time in proceedings a declaration of set-off must be made and what form it should have, should be governed by the *lex fori*.

It is for the law of the principal claim to decide whether set-off is allowed or whether set-off is prohibited due to the character of the claim. In many legal orders there is a prohibition to set off against a claim for, by way of example, salary or maintenance. In this context it should be noted that such a prohibition could be internationally mandatory and find application through art 9 of the Regulation.

It is also for the law governing the principal claim to decide the prerequisites for set-off, in particular:

- whether there is a requirement of mutuality, ie the creditor for the principal claim is the same as the debtor for the counterclaim;
- whether there is a requirement of homogeneity, ie to which extent the two claims involved must concern matters of (more or less) the same kind, eg money;
- the effect of connexity, ie a strong link between the two claims for instance through the fact that they arise from the same contract or linked contracts;
- whether there is a requirement of liquidity, ie that the counterclaim is either exactly determined or can readily and without difficulty be computed;
- to which extent there is a requirement of maturity, ie whether one or both of the claims must be due; and
- the effect of limitation or → prescription; note that the question of whether a claim has expired or not is an incidental question to be determined by the law applicable to that claim.

It is also for the law governing the principal claim to determine questions of when and how set-off could be invoked (for strictly procedural issues concerning form etc, see above). Can set-off only be invoked through a counterclaim in court, or is an out of court declaration sufficient?

Finally it is for the law governing the principal claim to decide the effects of set-off, in particular from which point in time it takes effect. The alternatives here would be from the time when the two claims came into existence, from the time a declaration for set-off is made, from the time a counterclaim is made in court or from the time of a court decision.

It is for the law governing the counterclaim itself to determine to which extent this claim exists at all and whether it is mature, expired etc. These are all incidental questions pertaining to the quality of the counterclaim itself.

A disputed question is whether it is for the law governing the principal claim, ie the law governing set-off, or the law governing the counterclaim to determine whether the counterclaim is extinguished by the set-off or not. It could be said that art 17 only determines the right to set-off and its effects on the principal claim. Should the law governing the counterclaim not allow or even know set-off the counterclaim would still exist. The only way to escape the counterclaim would then be to invoke → unjust enrichment, → estoppel or the like. This author would strongly oppose such an interpretation, which runs counter to the very purpose of the rule, *viz* to bring about the greatest possible certainty as regards the law applicable to and the effects of set-off.

3. Contractual set-off

Even before the advent of the Rome I Regulation, there appears to have been full consensus in legal writing that the law applicable to agreements to allow set-off should be the law governing the agreement itself. Now this is also made clear in art 17 Rome I, which is only applicable when 'the right to set-off is not agreed by the parties'. This means that the applicable law will be determined according to the general rules in arts 3 and 4.

If the parties choose the law in accordance with art 3 then that law will apply. Article 3(1) *in fine* also allows the parties to make a separate → choice of law for the question of set-off. We are not aware that this should be common practice.

A complicating factor when discussing set-off agreements is their heterogeneity both in name and in nature. There is a multitude of types of contracts that contain agreements on set-off but very few go under the name of set-off agreements. Popular terms in business and banking circles are 'clearing' and 'netting', which regularly are understood to mean set-off. Other typical types of agreements involving contractual set-off are contracts for the opening of an account or credit with a bank, postal or bank giro accounts, revolving credit facilities etc. It is simply not possible to make sweeping statements on the law applicable to all kinds of contracts that include the question of set-off. Such contracts will have to be analysed on a case-to-case basis or at least according to their typology.

If we look at art 4 it is clear that to the extent that a contract containing provisions concerning set-off fits in with one of the various classes of contracts given in para 1 that rule will apply. If a contract for the sale of goods (→ Sale contracts and sale of goods) also contains provisions concerning set-off it follows from art 4(1)(a) that the law of the country where the seller has his habitual residence will apply, also to the matter of set-off. If the contract is one for the provision of services, according to art 4(1)(b) the law of the habitual residence of the service provider will apply etc.

If the contract does not fall under the typology in para 1 or under several of the categories therein, the contract, including its set-off provisions will be governed by the law of the country in which the party required to effect the characteristic performance of the contract has his habitual residence. If a characteristic performance cannot be determined for the contract we are left with trying to identify the country with which it is most closely connected and apply that law.

The contracts described above that include a financial institution keeping an account could be considered to be contracts for the provision of (financial) services and would hence fall under art 4(1)(b). We would apply the law of the habitual residence of the service provider, ie the financial institution. Even if the concept 'contract for the provision of services' were to be given a narrow interpretation, and we doubt it, the financial institution would be the party effecting the characteristic performance of the contract and the result would be the same.

A problem arises if both or none of the parties to such a contract are credit institutions, which is not uncommon. If one of them is the keeper of the account then we would argue that it is that party that effects the characteristic performance (or is even the service provider) and we should apply the law of its habitual residence.

If we turn to trade in financial instruments we find that there is a special rule in art 4(1)(h), which is concerned with the law applicable to trade in financial markets as defined in the MiFID (Markets in Financial Instruments Directive (Directive 2004/39/EC of the European Parliament and of the Council of 21 April 2004 on markets in financial instruments amending Council Directives 85/611/EEC and 93/6/EEC and Directive 2000/12/EC of the European Parliament and of the Council and repealing Council Directive 93/22/EEC, [2004] OJ L 145/1)). According to art 36(4) of the MiFID the public law applicable to a financial market should be the law of its home Member State. The Rome I Regulation takes this rule one step further and provides that that law should also govern any contracts concluded within such a system. However, set-off never takes place within such systems, only outside them. For the purposes of determining the law applicable to set-off this rule is irrelevant. Set-off becomes relevant in the context of trade in financial instruments either between the seller and the buyer or between a buyer and an authorized operator on a market, for instance a stockbroker.

It is important to point out that art 4(1)(h) has no bearing on the legal relationship between a buyer and a stockbroker as the provision only applies to contracts concluded within the financial market. The netting that occurs on accounts held by stockbrokers on behalf of their clients, which could for that matter cover trade on several financial markets, would instead fall under art 4(1)(b) since it is covered by a contract for the provision of financial services. Hence, to the extent that the parties have not agreed on the applicable law such a contract will be governed by the law of the service provider, ie the stockbroker.

As indicated above, set-off also occurs between parties that trade directly with securities. Independently of whether the trade has taken place on a regulated financial market or over-the-counter, trade is followed by settlement, which is the procedure whereby the securities are delivered and paid for. This procedure today almost invariably takes place electronically through a settlement system. Settlement can either take the form of so-called gross settlement, aka trade for trade settlement, or through various forms of netting, ie set-off. Settlement systems fall under the Settlement Finality Directive (Directive 2009/44/EC of the European Parliament and of the Council of 6 May 2009 amending Directive 98/26/EC on settlement finality in payment and securities settlement systems and Directive 2002/47/EC on financial collateral arrangements as regards linked systems and credit claims, [2009] OJ L 146/37) and, according to art 2(a), second indent of the Directive, the law of the Member State that the participants have chosen shall govern the settlement system – and they have to choose one. Since the parties will always have chosen the applicable law, it follows from art 3 Rome I Regulation that this choice will be respected. There is therefore no need for a rule similar to art 4(1)(h); but taking the belt and braces approach to ensure that this is understood by extremely risk-sensitive markets Recital (31) of Rome I makes it clear that the Regulation does not preclude the operation of a formal arrangement designated as a system under the Settlement Finality Directive.

At this moment it could be useful to call the reader's attention to the fact that the exemption from scope in art 1(2)(d) of the Rome I Regulation for obligations arising under → bills of exchange, → cheques and promissory notes and 'other negotiable instruments' is of no relevance in the context of settlement. Securities qualify as negotiable instruments but for this latter category the exemption from scope is limited to 'the extent that the obligations under such other negotiable instruments arise out of their negotiable character'. Factors relevant to us in the context of set-off such as whether there actually exists a contract for the purchase of certain securities and payment of the price remain within the scope of the Regulation. Obligations specific to the negotiable character that fall outside the scope of Rome I would include the bearer's right upon the issuer/drawer, irrespective of there ever being a contractual obligation between the two.

We finally turn to the question of 'naked' set-off agreements. Such an agreement is an agreement that is only concerned with set-off. A typical example would be when a party claims set-off of a counterclaim and the other party agrees or does not object. This would (or in the case of non-objection could, depending on the applicable law) constitute a set-off agreement pure. The question is what law governs such an agreement. The contract clearly does not fall under art 4(1) of the Rome I Regulation nor can it be said that either of the parties effects a characteristic performance. Hence art 4(2) is also not applicable. We are then left with art 4(4) and trying to find the country to which the contract is most closely connected.

If both claims are governed by one and the same law it would make sense to apply that law also to the set-off agreement. If in the context of the agreement one claim can be said to constitute the principal claim and one claim the counterclaim, we would argue that it makes sense to apply the law of the principal claim. Thus there would be no difference in the applicable law depending on whether there is an agreement or not and there would at least not be a private international law incentive to bring spurious claims that there is an agreement to set off. For all other cases we are left with simply trying to find the closest connection to the issue of set-off. Obviously this would have to be decided on a case-by-case basis.

MICHAEL HELLNER

III. The law applicable to set-off between non-contractual obligations

Although not as common as set-off between → contractual obligations, set-off between non-contractual obligations does occur. A practically important situation is between insurance companies netting their obligations towards each other for payments made to various policyholders.

It follows from art 1(1) Rome I Regulation that it is only applicable to contractual obligations. The answer to the question of the right to set-off between non-contractual obligations will therefore have to be sought elsewhere, *viz* in the → Rome II Regulation (Regulation (EC) No 864/2007 of the European Parliament and of the Council of 11 July 2007 on the law applicable to non-contractual obligations (Rome II), [2007] OJ L 199/40). The problem is that the Rome II Regulation, as opposed to the Rome I Regulation, does not contain an explicit rule concerning the law applicable to set-off. However, according to art 15(h) Rome II Regulation the question of the manner in which an obligation may be extinguished is included in the scope of the applicable law. This leaves us in the same situation as we were in when trying to interpret the Rome Convention, *viz* that we do not know which law if there are different laws applicable to claim and counterclaim.

The Rome I Regulation still contains a similar provision concerning the extinguishing of obligations in art 12(1)(d). It still has a role to play in spite of art 17 Rome I Regulation since after all set-off is not the only way to extinguish a contractual obligation. Article 17 should therefore be interpreted as a clarification of art 12(1)(d). Given that what is said in art 17 was already at the time of the Rome Convention the majority interpretation and that the Rome I Regulation was adopted after the Rome II Regulation we would strongly advise against any *a contrario* conclusions induced by the absence of an explicit rule on set-off in Rome II. On the contrary we would submit that the only reasonable interpretation is that art 15(h) of Rome II should by way of analogy with Rome I be read to mean that the law of the principal claim is applicable to the right to set-off. An argument in favour of this interpretation is that Recital (7) of Rome I stipulates that the provisions of the Regulation are intended to be consistent with those of Rome II. There is a similar Recital (7) in Rome II that for obvious reasons – Rome II was adopted before Rome I – only refers to Brussels I (Brussels I Regulation, Regulation (EC) No 44/2001 of 22 December 2000 on jurisdiction and the recognition and enforcement of judgments in civil and commercial matters, [2001] OJ L 12/1) and not to Rome I. However, the message is clear: similar issues should be solved in the same manner in the two Regulations.

If the parties agree on set-off they have concluded a contract. Even if this contract concerns the setting off of two non-contractual obligations this contract will be subject to the rules in the Rome I Regulation since the right to set-off has been made contractual (see II.3. above on 'Contractual Set-off').

IV. The law applicable to set-off between contractual and non-contractual obligations

A tricky situation arises if one of the two claims involved in set-off is contractual and the other is non-contractual. One example would be a claim under contract with a counterclaim under product liability. A, with habitual residence in country X, has delivered several machines to be installed in B's factory. The factory is located in country Y, which is the country in which B also has his habitual residence. One of the machines is defective and injures one of the workers. B incurs costs of EUR 200,000 for compensating the worker. After having repaired the machine, A demands a payment of EUR 4,000,000. B wishes to set off his counterclaim of EUR 200,000.

If we apply the Rome I Regulation to the contractual claim, art 4(1)(a) – or possibly 4(2) if the contract is for a combination of sale and installation – tells us that the law of B's habitual residence, ie country X, governs the contract. For the counterclaim under product liability art 5(1)(a) of the Rome II Regulation indicates that the law of Y, being the place of the habitual residence of the person sustaining damage, should apply. We thus have a situation where we have a claim in contract, a counterclaim in tort and two different laws apply to the two claims.

We have previously established that the solution is to apply the law of the principal claim to this issue, irrespective of whether Rome I or Rome II is applicable to the two claims involved in set-off. However, in a situation such as this one could argue that neither of the two instruments is applicable. The question of set-off between a contractual and a non-contractual claim falls outside the scope of both since they are limited to contractual and non-contractual

MICHAEL HELLNER

claims respectively. The logical consequence if such is the case would be to say that the matter is left to national law.

Having said this we would nonetheless submit that that is an unsatisfactory answer. As a matter of policy it is very difficult to defend that the question of the law applicable to set-off will be answered differently depending on the characterization of the claims involved. What is more, we find it highly unlikely that the Court of Justice would leave the issue to national law if ever confronted with the problem. An alternative, but in our view less logical, solution would therefore be to let the characterization of the principal claim decide whether Rome I or Rome II is applicable. In that way there will be no *lacunae*. This solution is also in line with the view in art 17 (applied directly in the case of Rome I, or by way of analogy in the case of Rome II) that the law of the principal claim determines all aspects of set-off – in this case the characterization of the entire set-off situation as either contractual or non-contractual.

V. The law applicable to set-off in insolvency proceedings

In insolvency proceedings both the insolvent debtor as well as creditors may wish to demand set-off of their claims. It follows from art 4(2)(d) of the Insolvency Regulation (Council Regulation (EC) No 1346/2000 of 29 May 2000 on insolvency proceedings, [2000] OJ L 160/1) that the *lex fori concursus* shall determine 'the conditions under which set-offs may be invoked'. This rule could, like any other rule involving the application of the *lex fori*, lead to forum shopping and to a certain extent does art 3 of the Insolvency Regulation make this possible. A creditor could chose to open insolvency proceedings either in the country where the debtor has its main interests or where the debtor has an establishment, but then limited to assets situated in the territory of that Member State. If the insolvency debtor has claims against the insolvency creditor it could be interesting to open insolvency proceedings in a country in which it would not be possible to offset those claims against those of the insolvency creditor. Such could be the case for the reason that under the *lex fori* a set-off is not allowed between the two claims in question or for the reason that this law excludes set-off in the case of insolvency proceedings.

The possibility for forum shopping (→ Forum (and law) shopping) is an undesired consequence of the rule and the argument that application of the *lex fori concursus* would keep the cost of the proceedings down remains unconvincing, in particular since art 6(1) could lead to the application of foreign law (→ Foreign law, application and ascertainment) to the question of the right to set-off anyway. In the 2012 proposal for a revision of the Insolvency Regulation (Proposal for a Regulation of the European Parliament and of the Council amending Council Regulation (EC) No 1346/2000 on insolvency proceedings, COM(2012) 744 final, at the time of writing still negotiated), no change is suggested but for a new art 6a on the law applicable to netting agreements, which stipulates that such agreements are exclusively subject to the law applicable to them (to be determined by the rules in the Rome I Regulation) – and not to the law applicable to the insolvency.

Article 6(1) of the Insolvency Regulation is a rule that protects insolvency creditors from the effects of insolvency in the case their right to set off should be adversely affected thereby. In the case of insolvency they will still have the right to demand the set-off of their claims if such a set-off is permitted under the law applicable to the insolvency debtor's claim, ie the principal claim. A limitation is that the rule is only applicable to claims that have arisen before the opening of insolvency proceedings. Should the parties have agreed on set-off the law applicable to that agreement, as determined by the Rome I Regulation, will continue to apply. In a sense the rule can be described as a rule protecting 'vested rights'. The insolvency should not deprive the insolvency creditor of a right to set-off that he would otherwise have had. As it is, the Regulation extends double protection to insolvency creditors. Either they can demand set-off of their claims according to the *lex fori concursus* or they could use their right under art 6(1) to do the same.

According to their wording arts 4(2)(d) and 6(1) only apply to the question of the right to set-off and not to the effects of set-off, most importantly the question of from which point in time it takes effect. How should the law applicable to that question be determined? As concerns art 4(2)(d) we are saved by the fact that the provision is not exhaustive. The *lex fori concursus* governs 'in particular' the question of the conditions for set-off but this does not exclude that it also governs the issue of the effects thereof. Applying the law of the insolvency proceedings to all matters concerning set-off also corresponds to the *telos* of the rule, *viz* that (practically) all issues should be governed by one law. We see no reason why the legislator should have wanted → *dépeçage*.

If we turn to art 6(1) the limitation of the rule to the right to demand set-off is not a problem since the rule is identical with that of the Rome I Regulation. Whether it is art 17 of the Rome I Regulation or art 6(1) of the Insolvency Regulation that is applied to determine the law applicable to the effects of set-off is therefore mainly of academic interest.

VI. Jurisdiction to try claims for set-off

One could imagine a case in which the court, according to art 7(1) of the Brussels I Regulation (recast), assumes jurisdiction to hear A's contractual claim against B on the basis that the contractual obligation in question is to be performed where the court is located. If in that procedure B invokes set-off against another contract according to which B has a claim against A, that is to be performed elsewhere, does the court have jurisdiction to hear also the claim for set-off? The problem is that while the court has jurisdiction to try the principal claim it would appear that it lacks jurisdiction to try the counterclaim.

There is a particular rule in the Brussels I Regulation that deals with counterclaims, *viz* art 8(3). According to this provision a court will have jurisdiction to hear a counterclaim if it arises 'from the same contract or facts on which the original claim was based'. Article 14(2) gives the same right under the same conditions for insurance disputes, art 18(3) does the same for consumer disputes and art 22(2) for employment disputes. The problem lies in the restriction to the same contract or facts, which would bar courts from trying a counterclaim for set-off even if such connexity is not required by the applicable law.

Article 8(3) is applicable to counterclaims. Here, the terminology becomes a bit confusing. The terms used when describing set-off are usually 'principal claim' and 'counterclaim'. However, not all (counter) claims for set-off qualify as counterclaims under the Brussels I Regulation (recast). The Court of Justice has distinguished between counterclaims and claims raised in defence during the proceedings (Case C-341/93 *Danværn Production A/S gegen Schuhfabriken Otterbeck GmbH & Co*

[1995] ECR I-2053). The purpose of a counterclaim in its procedural meaning is to obtain an enforceable judgment. Set-off, when used as a defence in proceedings, can only be used to deduct from the plaintiff's claim and the sum set off can therefore never exceed the principal claim. To which extent procedural set-off is allowed is determined by the law of the forum and if it allows it the rules on jurisdiction in the Brussels I Regulation (recast) constitute no obstacle.

MICHAEL HELLNER

Literature

Klaus Peter Berger, *Der Aufrechnungsvertrag* (Mohr 1996); Hans Dölle, 'Die Kompensation im internationalen Privatrecht' (1924) 13 *Rheinische Zeitschrift für Zivil- und Prozeßrecht* 32; Heiko Eujen, *Die Aufrechnung im internationalen Verkehr zwischen Deutschland, Frankreich und England* (Metzner 1975); Michael Hellner, 'Set-off' in Franco Ferrari and Stefan Leible (eds), *Rome I Regulation: The Law Applicable to Contractual Obligations in Europe* (European Law Publishers/NCTM 2009) 251; Mathias Kannengiesser, *Die Aufrechnung im Internationalen Privat- und Verfahrensrecht* (Mohr Siebeck 1998); Ole Lando, 'Chapter 24 Contracts' in Kurt Lipstein (ed), *International Encyclopedia of Comparative Law*, vol 3 (Mohr 1976); Ulrich Magnus, 'Internationale Aufrechnung' in Stefan Leible (ed), *Das Grünbuch zum Internationalen Vertragsrecht* (Sellier 2004) 210; Ulrich Magnus, 'Aufrechnung und Gesamtschuldnerausgleich' in Franco Ferrari and Stefan Leible (eds), *Ein neues Internationales Vertragsrecht für Europa – Der Vorschlag für eine Rom I-Verordnung* (JWV Jenaer Wissenschaftliche Verlagsgesellschaft 2007) 201; Rodolfo de Nova, *L'estinzione delle obbligazioni convenzionali nel diritto internazionale private* (Università di Pavia 1930).

Small Claims Regulation

I. Legislative history

In 2002, the European Commission launched the Green Paper on measures to simplify and speed up small claims litigation (Commission, 'Green Paper on a European order for payment procedure and on measures to simplify and speed up small claims litigation' COM(2002) 746 final) based on the 'programme of measures for implementation of the principle of mutual recognition of decisions in civil and commercial matters' of 15 January 2001. Due to arts 61(c), 65(c), 67 EEC Treaty (Treaty of 25 March 1957 establishing the European Economic Community, 294–8 UNTS) this programme focused primarily on facilitating the recognition and enforcement of judgments delivered in another Member State. However, with the Green Paper concerning the speeding up of small claims litigation, the European Commission prepared to follow a new approach, ie harmonization of procedural law. Consequently, the introduction of a specific procedure for the speedy and efficient recovery of uncontested claims as well as the simplification and acceleration of small claims litigation was the first initiative to directly address the procedural rules governing the obtaining of enforceable decisions.

After a public consultation, the European Commission on 15 March 2005 presented a Proposal for a Regulation of the European Parliament and of the Council establishing a European Small Claims Procedure (COM(2005) 87 final). The most contested point was the proposed application of the Regulation to purely internal cases. Discussion ended with the final opinion of the Council Legal Service of 30 June 2005 opting for a scope of application limited to cross-border cases. After the appropriate amendments, European Small Claims Procedure Regulation (Regulation (EC) No 861/2007 of the European Parliament and of the Council of 11 July 2007 establishing a European Small Claims Procedure, [2007] OJ L 199/1), was enacted on 11 July 2007, and it entered into force on 1 January 2009 (henceforth old version). The Regulation was adopted under art 61(c) EEC Treaty, providing that the Council is to adopt measures in the field of judicial cooperation in civil matters and art 67(1) EEC Treaty defining the legislative procedure to be followed (henceforth revised version).

According to its art 1(1) sentence 1, the European Small Claims Procedure Regulation intends 'to simplify and speed up litigation concerning small claims in cross-border cases, and to reduce costs'. The European Small Claims Procedure will be available to litigants as an alternative to the procedures existing under Member State laws (sentence 2). It has thus been dubbed 'European Civil Procedure en miniature' (Wolfgang Hau, 'Das neue europäische Verfahren zur Beitreibung geringfügiger Forderungen' [2008] *Juristische Schulung* 1056).

II. Revision of the European Small Claims Procedure

Five years after the entry into force of the European Small Claims Procedure Regulation in 2009, empirical statements on the application of the Regulation by Member State courts were rare. As the number of applications differed widely between the Member States, there was the presumption that the significance of the Regulation in national procedural law was to a large extent marginal. In a special Eurobarometer on the European Small Claims Procedure of 2012, 86 per cent of respondents (of all Member States) said that they had never heard of such a procedure. One reason might be the Regulation's limitation to cross-border cases, another the considerable lack of knowledge among legal practitioners and – more seriously – consumers. The finding was surprising because consumer interests were the Regulation's primary focus. However, several points remained unsatisfactory and required further reform efforts in order to improve the practical importance of the Regulation.

Accordingly, the European Commission, pursuant to art 28, on 19 November 2013 presented a 'Report on the application of Regulation (EC) No 861/2007 of the European Parliament and of the Council establishing a European Small Claims Procedure' (COM(2013) 795 final) which was accompanied by a proposal for revision of the European Small Claims Procedure Regulation (European Commission, 'Proposal for a Regulation of the European Parliament and of the Council of 19 November 2013 amending Regulation (EC) No 861/2007 of the European Parliament and the Council of 11 July 2007 establishing a European Small Claims Procedure and Regulation (EC) No 1896/2006 of the European Parliament and the Council of 12 December 2006 creating a European order for payment procedure' COM(2013) 794 final), in order to improve usefulness of the procedure. The amended version of the Small Claims Regulation (Regulation (EU) 2015/2421 of the European Parliament and of the Council of 16 December 2015 amending Regulation (EC) No 861/2007 establishing a European Small Claims Procedure) entered into force on 24 December 2015 ([2015] OJ L 341/1).

The revision of the European Small Claims Procedure Regulation introduces several practical changes to the way the procedure operates, such as raising the threshold for filing a 'small claim' from EUR 2,000.00 up to EUR 5,000.00. It seemed that the Commission believes in the benefits for SMEs as business claims under the procedure should be raised up from 20 per cent today to 50 per cent. Furthermore, the Commission aimed to cap court fees that under the existing procedure could have been disproportionate.

Another point that had to be improved was the limited scope of application. In its report the Commission noted that the Regulation applied only to disputes where at least one of the parties was domiciled or was habitually resident in a Member State other than the Member State of the court or tribunal seized. That means that where a claimant under the Brussels I Regulation (recast) exercised his right to choose the jurisdiction of the courts of the Member State of the parties' common domicile he was deprived of the possibility to use the European Small Claims Jurisdiction. Consequently, disputes involving parties domiciled in the same Member State which had an important cross-border element, such as the place of performance in another Member State, were left outside the scope of the European Small Claims Procedure Regulation.

Further, nationals of third countries could not so far benefit from the Regulation. The Commission therefore proposed to extend the scope of application by making the European Small Claims Procedure available in all cross-border cases, including those involving third countries. In doing so the Commission expected that both the costs and duration of litigation could be reduced in those cases where, for example, experts need to be heard in the Member State of the place of performance.

Moreover, claimants are to be enabled to launch the procedure online so that paperwork and travel costs can be minimized, seen as particularly important in long-distance cases.

Finally, the Commission in its report identified a considerable lack of awareness of the existence and operation of the European Small Claims Procedure among citizens, courts and other organizations. The Commission referred to the statistical data presented above according to which 86 per cent of European citizens have never heard about the procedure. The Commission was trying to address this problem by a range of measures such as publishing information together with interactive forms on several EU websites.

III. Scope of application

1. Cross-border cases

The first question in the Commission's 2002 Green Paper was whether the European instrument on small claims should be applicable only to cross-border cases or also to purely internal litigation. In its 2005 Proposal, the European Commission presented the opinion that the term 'matters' (instead of 'measures') in art 65 EEC Treaty indicates cross-border implications. This interpretation is said to be confirmed by art 65(c) EEC Treaty, providing that measures in the field of judicial cooperation in civil matters include eliminating obstacles to the good functioning of civil proceedings.

Furthermore, the European Commission explained that even measures applying to purely internal cases have 'necessarily cross-border implications since the putting in place of an efficient Small Claims Procedure in every Member State will facilitate access to justice under equal conditions' (COM(2005) 87 final, 6). It was therefore not only deemed 'inappropriate' but even 'counterproductive' to restrict the scope of application of the European Small Claims Procedure to cross-border cases (COM(2005) 87 final, 6). However, this was opposed by Member States, primarily based on the fact that the wording of art 65 EEC Treaty expressly focused on 'civil matters having cross-border implications' and that the cross-border requirement must be a real and present one. Accordingly, the European legislator decided to confine the Regulation to cross-border cases.

The question when the criterion 'cross-border cases' in art 1(1) European Small Claims Procedure Regulation is met is answered by art 3(1), according to which a cross-border case 'is one in which at least one of the parties is domiciled or habitually resident in a Member State other than the Member State of the court or tribunal seized'. The term 'domicile' should be interpreted in accordance with arts 62, 63 Brussels I Regulation (recast) (Regulation (EU) No 1215/2012 of 12 December 2012 on jurisdiction and the recognition and enforcement of judgments in civil and commercial matters, [2012] OJ L 351/1; → Brussels I (Convention and Regulation)). Under this definition the cross-border element is not only met where both parties are domiciled in different Member States, but also is deemed sufficient where the parties are domiciled in the same Member State while applying to a court in another Member

State. Furthermore, the requirements of art 3(1) European Small Claims Procedure Regulation are met if at least one of the parties is domiciled in a Member State (other than the Member State of the court seized) and the other party is resident in a third country.

2. Substantive scope

Regarding the substantive scope of the European Small Claims Procedure Regulation, the original version of art 2(1) defined a 'small claim' as one whose (net) value does not exceed EUR 2,000.00 at the time when the claim form is received by the court or tribunal with jurisdiction. The much debated threshold of EUR 2,000.00 could be seen as a compromise between the different values governed by the national procedural laws. In the revised version of art 2(1) the net value was raised up to EUR 5,000.00. Increasing the threshold up to EUR 5,000.00 is said to 'improve access to an effective and cost-efficient judicial remedy for cross-border disputes, in particular for SMEs' (Recital (4)).

Article 2(1) European Small Claims Procedure Regulation is expressly limited to 'civil and commercial matters, whatever the nature of the court or tribunal' (→ Civil and commercial matters). Thus, the Regulation expressly excludes customs or administrative matters. Furthermore, art 2(2) in a negative way determines all matters outside the Regulation's scope, such as the status or legal capacity of natural persons (art 2(2)(a); → Capacity and emancipation), the rights in property arising out of a matrimonial relationship, → maintenance obligations, wills and → succession (art 2(2)(d)), bankruptcy and proceedings relating to the winding-up of insolvent companies or other legal persons, judicial arrangements, compositions and analogous proceedings (art 2(2)(e)), social security (art 2(2)(f)), arbitration (art 2(2)(g)), employment law (art 2(2)(h)), tenancies (→ Lease contracts and tenancies) of → immovable property, with the exception of actions on monetary claims (art 2(2)(i)) or the violations of privacy and of rights relating to personality, including defamation (art 2(2)(j)).

IV. Procedure and jurisdiction

1. Commencement of the procedure

A small claims procedure cannot be initiated in an informal manner. On the contrary, the European legislator considered it efficient to base the whole communication between the parties on standard forms that are attached to the European Small Claims Procedure Regulation. At the very beginning there is the standard claim form A (as set out in Annex I) that should be filled in by the claimant and be lodged with the competent court directly, by post or by any other means of communication, such as fax or e-mail, provided it is acceptable to the Member State in which the procedure is commenced (art 4(1) European Small Claims Procedure Regulation). Pursuant to art 11 the Member States must ensure that the parties receive practical assistance in filling in the forms. According to art 4(2) the claim form must include a description of evidence supporting the claim and be accompanied, where appropriate, by any relevant supporting documents. However, the claimant is permitted, where appropriate, to submit further evidence during the procedure.

Interestingly, although the claimant needs to determine the court of jurisdiction to deal with the claim, the Regulation itself provides no rules on jurisdiction. Rather, the corresponding rules are to be found in the Brussels I Regulation (recast), or, where the claimant has no habitual residence in a Member State, in the national procedural law. If a claim falls outside the scope of the Regulation, the court or tribunal must inform the claimant to that effect and proceed in accordance with national law, unless the claimant withdraws the claim (art 4(3) European Small Claims Procedure Regulation). This rule must be seen in relation to a *lis pendens* as provided for in art 29(1) Brussels I Regulation (recast). That means that where proceedings involving the same cause of action and between the same parties are brought in the courts of other Member States, then any other court must stay its proceedings until jurisdiction of the court first seized is established.

According to art 4(4) sentence 1 European Small Claims Procedure Regulation, where the information provided by the claimant is to be considered inadequate or insufficiently clear or where the claim form is not properly completed, then, unless the claim appears to be clearly unfounded or the application inadmissible, the court must give the claimant the opportunity (i) to complete or rectify the claim form, or (ii) to supply supplementary information or documents, or (iii) to withdraw the claim. Furthermore, sentence 2 gives the court the right to dismiss the application if the claim appears to be clearly unfounded or the application inadmissible, or if the claimant fails to complete or rectify at this stage of proceedings neither knows the defendant's conclusion or answer nor has it gathered the required evidence to determine whether the claim is 'clearly unfounded'. The provision is even said to violate the individual's right of access to justice. However, in the revised version, art 4(2) was supplemented in such a way that the claimant is to be informed of the dismissal and whether an appeal is available against such dismissal.

2. Conduct and conclusion of the procedure

Provided the application has not been dismissed pursuant to art 4(3) and (4), then within 14 days of receipt of the properly filled-in claim form the court grants the defendant access to the proceedings by serving them a copy of the claim form and, where applicable, of the supporting documents and the answer form thus filled in (art 5(2)). Pursuant to art 5(1), the small claims procedure is a written procedure. However, art 5(3) allows the defendant to submit the response by using the standard answer form C. If the court receives no response from the defendant within the 30-day limit, it renders a judgment on the claim or counterclaim pursuant to art 7(3).

The written form requirement does not prevent the court from holding an oral hearing. Pursuant to art 5(1a) sentence 2, the court may hold an oral hearing as it considers necessary or where a party so requests. However, a party's request may be refused under sentence 3 if the court 'considers that with regard to the circumstances of the case, an oral hearing is not necessary for the fair conduct of the proceedings'. Under the former version of art 5(3) the refusal required the oral hearing being 'obviously' not necessary. However, the notion of the term 'obvious' could have been problematic in that courts would in many cases tend to deny the necessity for oral hearings on grounds of their workload. Thus it was doubted whether art 5(1) conforms to the right to a fair trial as it is guaranteed by art 6 European Convention on Human Rights (Convention of 4 November 1950 for the Protection of Human Rights and Fundamental Freedoms, 213 UNTS 221) and art 47 EU Charter of Fundamental Rights (Charter of Fundamental Rights of the European Union of 18 December 2000, [2000] OJ C 364/1). Nevertheless art 47(2) expressly states that 'everyone is entitled to a fair and public hearing within a reasonable time by an independent and impartial tribunal previously established by law'.

According to art 7(1) European Small Claims Procedure Regulation, the court or tribunal is to either (i) render judgment in a timely manner and within 30 days of receipt of defendant's or claimant's response, or (ii) to demand further details concerning the claim form from the parties within a time period not exceeding 30 days (art7(1)(a)), or (iii) take evidence in accordance with art 9 (art 7(1)(b)), or (iv) summon the parties to an oral hearing to be held within 30 days of the summons (art 7(1)(c)). Regarding the taking of evidence, Recital (7) prefers the use of modern communication technology. The court or tribunal should use the simplest and least costly method of taking evidence, and in this regard, art 9(1) sentence 1 provides for broad discretion on the part of the court, according to which it may 'determine the means of taking evidence and the extent of the evidence necessary for its judgment'. Subparagraph 2 expressly names only the taking of evidence through written statements of witnesses, experts or parties. Again, art 9(1) reflects the written procedure principle that underlies the Regulation. If the taking of evidence has cross-border relevance, then the Evidence Regulation (Regulation (EC) No 1206/2001 of 28 May 2001 on cooperation between the courts of the Member States in the taking of evidence in civil or commercial matters, [2001]OJ L 174/1) applies.

V. Judgment, appeal and enforcement

1. Judgment

According to art 7(1) European Small Claims Procedure Regulation, the court is to render judgment within 30 days of receipt of the defendant's or claimant's response. The court is to issue a certificate concerning the judgment using standard form D if so requested by one of the parties (art 20(2) European Small Claims Procedure Regulation). It is up to the party seeking enforcement of the judgment to produce such a certificate referred to in art 20(2).

Regarding potential appeal by the unsuccessful party, the Regulation is admittedly too specific because it omits to provide for an autonomous review proceeding. Rather, art 17 provides that Member States are to inform the Commission whether an appeal is available under their procedural law against a judgment given pursuant to the European Small Claims Procedure as well as the time limit for such an appeal. Review proceedings are therefore exclusively governed by the → *lex fori*. It is unclear why the European Commission did not opt for a uniform appeal mechanism. However, art 18 European Small Claims Procedure Regulation offers some minimum standards for 'review of the judgment in exceptional cases', and according to art 18(1), the defendant is entitled to apply for review of the judgment before the court or tribunal with jurisdiction of the Member State where (a) the claim form or summons to an oral hearing were served by a method without proof of defendant's personal receipt and service was, without any fault on his part effected too late to enable defendant to arrange a defence or (b) the defendant was prevented from objecting to the claim by reason of *force majeure*, or due to extraordinary circumstances without fault on his part. This rule is created to guarantee minimum standards for the review of a judgment in situations where the defendant was unable to contest a claim. However, such 'standards for review' have no suspensive or devolutive effect as familiar from appeal proceedings. According to art 16, which also applies to any appeal (art 17(2)) costs of the proceedings must be borne by the unsuccessful party. However, art 15a(2) ensures that the court fees are not disproportionate and are not higher than the court fees charged for national simplified court procedures in that Member State.

2. *Recognition and enforcement*

Articles 20 *et seq* European Small Claims Procedure Regulation take into account the aims of the Regulation, ie to simplify and expedite small claims litigation in cross-border cases as well as to reduce costs (art 1(1)). Consequently, art 20(1) is based on the direct recognition and enforcement of judgments given in a Member State under the European Small Claims Procedure. That means that judgments are to be recognized and enforced in another Member State without the need for a declaration of enforceability and without any possibility of opposing its recognition.

According to art 21(1) European Small Claims Procedure Regulation, the enforcement procedures are governed by the law of the Member State of enforcement and the judgment is to be enforced under the same conditions as a national judgment (using standard form D).

Article 21(1) can therefore be regarded as a contribution to the discussion on the abolition of *exequatur* proceedings and the implementation of the mutual trust principle. In consequence of the abolition of *exequatur* proceedings, it is for the parties to protect their interests in proceedings pending before the court of origin. Article 21(2) exhaustively determines which documents the party seeking enforcement must produce, that is authentic copies of the judgment and of certificate mentioned in art 20(2), where necessary translated into the official language of the Member State of enforcement or into another language the Member State has indicated. According to art 21a(1) each Member State may indicate the official language or languages of the institutions of the Union, other than its own, which it can accept for the certificate referred to in art 20(2). Article 21(3)–(4) contain specific manifestations of the prohibition on discrimination laid down in art 21 TFEU (The Treaty on the Functioning of the European Union (consolidated version), [2012] OJ C 326/47). The party seeking the enforcement of a judgment is not required to have an authorized representative, a postal address or a security, bond or deposit.

Article 22 European Small Claims Procedure Regulation lays down the grounds for refusal of enforcement, namely first the incompatibility of the judgment given in the small claims procedure with an earlier judgment given in any Member State or a third country, provided that the earlier judgment involved the same cause of action and was between the same parties (art 22(a)), second, if the judgment was rendered in the Member State of enforcement or fulfils the conditions necessary for its recognition in that state (art 22(b)) and, third, if the irreconcilability was not and could not have been raised as an objection in the Member State court or tribunal proceedings where the judgment under the European Small Claims Procedure was rendered (art 22(c)). In line with art 52 Brussels I Regulation (recast), art 22(2) European Small Claims Procedure Regulation constitutes a prohibition of *révision au fond*, providing that no judgment given under the European Small Claims Procedure may under any circumstances be reviewed substantively in the Member State of enforcement. However, unlike art 34(1) Brussels I Regulation (recast), the Regulation contains no public policy exception. Article 23(1) European Small Claims Procedure Regulation allows the court upon application of the party against whom enforcement is sought to limit enforcement proceedings to protective measures, to make them conditional on the provision of security or, under exceptional circumstances, to stay proceedings if a party has challenged a judgment, if such a challenge is still possible or a party has made an application for review within the meaning of art 18. Article 34a(1) makes statute the principle of mutual recognition providing that a court settlement approved by or concluded before a court or tribunal in the course of a Small Claims Procedure and that is enforceable in the Member State in which the procedure was conducted shall be recognized and enforced in another Member State under the same conditions as a judgment given under the Procedure.

KATHRIN KROLL-LUDWIGS

Literature

David-Christoph Bittmann, *Vom Exequatur zum qualifizierten Klauselerteilungsverfahren – Die Implementierung des Europäischen Vollstreckungstitels für unbestrittene Forderungen in den nationalen Zivilprozessordnungen* (Nomos 2008); Pablo Cortes, 'Does the Proposed European Procedure Enhance the Resolution of Small Claims?' (2008) 27 CJQ 83; Manfred Cuypers, 'Internationale Zuständigkeit, Brüssel I und small claims regulation' [2009] GPR 34; Aude Fiorini, 'Facilitating Cross-Border Debt Recovery: The European Payment Order and Small Claims Regulation' (2008) 57 ICLQ 449; Franco Frattini, 'European Area of Civil Justice: Has the Community Reached the Limits?' [2006] ZEuP 225; Robert Freitag and Stefan Leible, 'Erleichterungen der grenzüberschreitenden Forderungsbeitreibung in Europa: Das europäische Verfahren für geringfügige Forderungen' [2009] *Betriebs-Berater* 1; Georg Haibach, 'Zur Einführung des ersten europäischen Zivilprozessverfahrens: V erordnung (EG) Nr. 861/2007' [2008] EuZW 137; Wolfgang Hau, 'Das neue europäische Verfahren zur Beitreibung geringfügiger Forderungen' [2008] *Juristische Schulung* 1056; Wolfgang Hau, 'Experience of German and Austrian Courts and Legal Practice in Applying the European Small Claims Procedure' (2013) <www.eu2013.lt/uploads/documents/Prezentacijos/Hau%20Small%20Claims%20Germany%20text%20%282013-09-18%29.pdf>; Burkhard Hess and David-Christoph Bittmann, 'Die Verordnungen zur Einführung eines Europäischen Verfahrens für geringfügige Forderungen – ein substantieller Integrationsschritt im Europäischen Zivilprozessrecht' [2008] IPRax 305; Isabel Jahn 'Das Europäische Verfahren für geringfügige Forderungen' [2007] NJW 2890; Xandra Kramer, 'The Proposal for a European Small Claims Procedure' [2006] Int'l Lis 109; Xandra Kramer, 'The European Small Claims Procedure: Striking the Balance between Simplicity and Fairness in European Litigation' [2008] ZEuP 355; Xandra Kramer, 'Small Claims, Simple Recovery? The European Small Claims Procedure and its Implementation in the Member States' (2011) 1 Journal of European Law 119; István Varga, 'EG-BagatellVO' in Thomas Rauscher (ed), *EuZPR/EuIPR* (4th edn, Dr. Otto Schmidt 2015).

Social protection and private international law

Social protection is a major objective of modern legislation, which accordingly has a far-reaching impact, not only on substantive legislation, but also on private international law. This influence becomes evident in the context of various practical problems. However, the social protective strand of private international law has yet to assume a clearly elaborated and adequately identified position within theoretical discussion. The main discussion is found in German and French doctrine.

I. Contentious topics

1. Social policy and private law

Social protection is not only a basic, all-encompassing aim of today's public policy, but also arises in various practical contexts, including private international law. As all modern societies, to the extent they are part of the United Nations legal system, are legally established on the basis of universally guaranteed human rights (→ Human rights and private international law), national legislation of the entire world is expected to foster the personal freedom of each individual and at the same time to guarantee social welfare and social security to each individual. This is irrespective of divergent content and aspiration of national legislations.

Personal liberty is expressed in the various institutions of private law, such as contract, property, tort, family and succession. Social aims are to be promoted by the structures of social welfare and social security, which are to emphasize the elementary social human rights to which each individual is also entitled. These social human rights rank equally with civil human rights, so that both types of right have to be mutually compatible and at the same time internationally effective. This is to be achieved by means of private international law.

2. Three dimensions of interrelations between social protection and private law

Even though private law and social protection are embedded in different legal institutions and driven by different normative imperatives, neither institution is entirely isolated from the other. On the contrary, private law and social protection are deeply interrelated and these relations can be elucidated in different patterns. As social protection sets limits to private law and is based above all upon private law institutions, private international law rules also pursue an important role in the normative context of social protection.

First, private law and social protection can concur with regard to their legislative framework. For example, the protection of workers against the physical and economic risks deriving from work is governed by both labour and social security law. By the same token, the minimum level of subsistence for victims of → torts and family members is to be safeguarded by both private family or tort law and by social security and social welfare law.

Second, private law relations underlie a substantial series of entitlements to social security benefits. For instance, the social protection of widows depends on a pre-existing, valid marriage with the deceased insured person. If a social insurance system delivers services or payments to a tort victim, the question arises whether the victim's right to compensation by the tortfeasor is transferred on the basis of a → cessio legis to the social insurance body, as the burden of compensating the victim must and has been borne by the public institution. Accordingly, it is appropriate to grant the right to compensation against the tortfeasor to the institution, which not only must but also has effectively secured the victim's compensation.

Third, private international law provides a conceptual framework for choice-of-law rules, helping to explain international social security law. For EU Member States this law was created in 1959 by the EU's supranational legislation, or more precisely Regulations 3 and 4/58 (Verordnung Nr. 3 über die Soziale Sicherheit der Wanderarbeitnehmer, [1958] OJ 30/561, and Verordnung Nr. 4 zur Durchführung der Verordnung Nr. 3 über die Soziale Sicherheit der Wanderarbeitnehmer, [1958] OJ 30/597 (both only available in Dutch, French and German)), which were the first substantive legal provisions enacted within the Community.

These provisions were established by the European Council in order to fulfil the requirement, enshrined in art 51 EEC Treaty (Treaty of 25 March 1957 establishing the European Economic Community, 294–8 UNTS), under which the EEC was committed to establishing a multilateral framework of choice of law on a Community law basis and to coordinating social security provisions so as to safeguard acquired social security rights for those exercising the fundamental freedoms of the EU, in particular freedom of movement. These European laws harmonize the choice-of-law rules among the social protection legislation of all Member States and they establish harmonized rules on the coordination of welfare and social security benefit rights and commitments. EU social security coordination protects the vested rights (→ Vested rights theory) in social security as it facilitates intra-EU mobility and guards against any coincidental loss of accrued rights to social protection.

3. Prospect for further analysis

The following observations address the common features of private international law and social protection (II.), analyse the preliminary questions of private international law for social welfare or social security law (III.) and, finally, illustrate the conceptual impact of private international law on international social security law (IV.).

II. Common tasks and positions

1. Protective goals of private and social protection law

While social welfare and social security law have a protective strand, this objective can also be identified within private law, in that private law strives for deepening social justice. Private law legislation on employment seeks to afford substantive protection to each employee. Employment laws were specifically framed to establish fair labour standards, ie standards sufficient to protect the worker health and safety, participation in management of the enterprise and a fair remuneration for their work. This means in the context of employment law that the employee is perceived as the weak party, requiring substantive protection against the deemed stronger party, the employer.

The same tendency is apparent in family law, where the intention prevails in legislation on alimony or maintenance among actual or former family members to assist the needy party, that is generally speaking the dependent spouse (often the wife) or children and somewhat infrequently the parents. The same protective strand becomes apparent in the private law context, in that family law deals with economic inequalities and imbalances and seeks to strengthen the capabilities of the persons in need.

Tort law also deals with social protection of the victims of unlawful acts or verified risks. Thus those indulging in a risky investment may be held liable to compensate the losses caused to the victims. The principal intention of tort law is to find satisfying solutions from the victim's point of view: as the victims render a sacrifice and bear the consequences of the outcomes of unlawful or risky acts, it is for the law to protect and support them.

2. Similarities to determine the connecting factor

These similarities between private law and social protective law also find their expression in private international law. The choice-of-law rules of both branches of law are based on the same connecting factors. While not identical, the choice-of-law rules for both employment and social security law are largely based on the same principles, in that both are driven by the *lex loci laboris* rule that the workplace is the decisive → connecting factor.

The connecting factor in family law as well as in social welfare law is the domicile or habitual residence (→ Domicile, habitual residence and establishment) of the beneficiary, based on the *lex domicilii* rule. This connecting factor is justified by the argument that the beneficiary's need is to be satisfied in the social context in which these needs arise. In the context of international tort law, the victim's interest in adequate compensation finds its expression in the application of the law of the place where the victim actually suffered the loss or where the damage occurred (eg art 4(1) → Rome II Regulation (Regulation (EC) No 864/2007 of the European Parliament and of the Council of 11 July 2007 on the law applicable to non-contractual obligations (Rome II), [2007] OJ L 199/40)).

Thus speaking more generally, the protective strand of private international law is translated into connecting factors for choice-of-law rules. They have to ensure that the protective function of the applicable law can be achieved by taking into the fullest possible account all circumstances stemming from the sphere of the protective intention of the applicable law.

3. Preferential law approach

A further component of social protection by means of private international law is associated with the so-called 'preferential' law approach. Originally implemented in international tort law, this approach intends to give the victims of torts the most generous compensation ever to be acquired under the legislation of the competing states. Today, the preferential law approach is a key element in international contract law aimed at achieving an optimal protection for both workers and consumers under the rules of international employment and consumer law (arts 8 and 6 Rome I Regulation (Regulation (EC) No 593/2008 of the European Parliament and of the Council of 17 June 2008 on the law applicable to contractual obligations (Rome I), [2008] OJ L 177/6; → Rome Convention and Rome I Regulation (contractual obligations))). The overall purpose of these rules is to give to the weaker party the privilege of being treated on the basis of the most favourable legislation, regarded as potentially applicable law.

In the context of the coordination of European social security schemes, the preferential law approach is also broadly acknowledged on the basis of consistent case-law over decades (Case C-24/75 *Teresa and Silvana Petroni v Office national des pensions pour travailleurs salariés (ONPTS), Bruxelles* [1975] ECR 1149; Case C-352/06 *Brigitte Bosmann v Bundesagentur für Arbeit – Familienkasse Aachen* [2008] ECR I-3827; joined Cases C-611/10 and C-612/10 *Waldemar Hudzinski v Agentur für Arbeit Wesel – Familienkasse (C-611/10) and Jaroslaw Wawrzyniak v Agentur für Arbeit Mönchengladbach – Familienkasse (C-612/10)* [2012] ECR I-339). In the context of social security coordination, the preferential law approach is justified on the rationale that EU coordination has always and necessarily been a benevolent and never an adverse influence on beneficiary rights.

The preferential law approach aims at enforcing by means of choice-of-law rules the substantive social values that social law is committed to. The approach is a specific response under private international law to strengthen and elaborate the protective element that social security law is founded upon. It has to create choice-of-law rules which give the fullest possible protection of the weaker party, which is deserving of (merits) protection under the express assumptions of the legal programme the applicable legal matter is committed to pursue. Thus, the preferential law approach makes a true contribution to social purposes in private international law.

III. Preliminary issues

1. Preliminary issues regarding social welfare or security law

As social protection is based on private law institutions, private international law also has to contribute to the determination of social legal entitlements. A telling example relates to the issue of whether and to which extent the spouses of a polygamous → marriage are entitled to widow's benefits on the death of their insured husband, and to health care where married couples are jointly entitled to health insurance on the basis of the employment of one working spouse. Comparable issues arise in relation to marriages regarded as lawful under the law of one country and as unlawful under the law of another (Federal Constitutional Court of Germany (BVerfG), 23 November 1982, 62 BVerfGE 320, 322). The same problem is to be found in unemployment insurance, where it is common to disqualify unemployed persons if their unemployment stems from an industrial dispute. This exclusionary rule is an issue if a posted worker becomes unemployed as the result of an industrial dispute originating in a foreign country. Finally it must be asked whether a → *cessio legis* in favour of a social insurance administration could ever become effective as a right of the beneficiary under foreign tort law, where the *lex causae* does not permit transfer of the right to third parties. This issue is to be resolved on the basis that, due to the administration's responsibility to compensate for the consequences of tort resulting in damage, the transfer of the right must be determined by the law applicable to the administrations' actions. In all these cases, the social administration is confronted with preliminary private international law issues (→ incidental (preliminary) questions), but it remains unclear how these issues are to be resolved.

2. General rule: private international law also applies within social protection law

Section 34 German Social Code I (Erstes Buch Sozialgesetzbuch (SGB I) of 11 December 1975, BGBl. I 3015, as amended, henceforth SGB I) provides for a relatively general rule on how to deal with preliminary issues. Where in international cases a social security entitlement under German law depends on the existence of a family relationship, private international law determines the law applicable to the family relationship. If the relationship is governed by foreign law, it will be treated as if established under German law provided it is compatible with the corresponding family relationship under German law.

This provision articulates a profound insight into the interrelation of private international law and social protection law. It may be generalized in at least two directions. First, the underlying principle of the provision is restricted not only to international family law, but has to be extended to all preliminary private law relations. Second, as implicitly respected by many countries (Cour d'appel de Chambéry [1962] Rev. crit.DIP 496; *Din v National Assistance Board* [1967] 1 All ER 750 (QB); Cour de Cassation [1958] Rev.crit.DIP 110; Law Commission, *Family Law Report on Polygamous Marriages* (Law Com No 42, 1971)), the provision cannot be confined to German law, but rather should be accepted as a general and universal principle.

3. Substitution and adaptation

When in private international law a legal relationship under foreign law is conceived as equivalent to the corresponding relationship under domestic law, in private international law this operation is termed → substitution. This concept is not relevant within the framework of → choice of law, but has a role to play in the context of the application of substantive law. Substitution concerns the replacement of a legal institution of the forum by a comparable institution of a foreign state.

Each act of substitution is based upon on a comparative analysis of the laws of two states. If the comparison can elucidate the equivalence of the compared institutions in the light of the provision to be applied, then a substitution may and will be effected. If the comparison reveals a disparity, then rather than substitution an adjustment (→ Adjustment/Adaption (*Anpassung*)) takes place.

How those operations proceed may be illustrated by referring to the examples previously discussed. If an industrial dispute under foreign law was also regarded as lawful under domestic law, the dispute would lead to the same consequences in domestic unemployment insurance regarding waiver of the beneficiary's rights by virtue of a substitution. However, if a widow's pension after death of the insured husband is based upon the assumption that he could only have one surviving wife at any time, then a polygamous marriage allows for no substitution as it is not equivalent to a monogamous marriage. Thus, due to lack of equivalence, an adaptation is to be considered. Adaptation can be found in specific social security law provisions. Under § 34 II SGB I the same rule applies to bilateral social security treaties between Western countries as to countries where polygamous marriages are lawful. The solution treats all deceased married husbands alike, so that each widow is entitled to a pension, while the amount of the pension results from a division of the allotted sum in equal shares. To combat → *dépeçage*, divergent legal provisions on the effects of a → *cessio legis* are to be circumvented by the determination of an all-embracing statute. EU law rules integrate both social security and tort law (art 85 Coordination of Social Security Systems Regulation (Regulation (EC) No 883/2004 of the European Parliament and of the Council of 29 April 2004 on the coordination of social security systems, [2004] OJ L 166/1) = art 19 Rome II Regulation). This means the provision in the tort law statute on the invalidity of a *cessio legis* is irrelevant if the prevailing social security statute provides for a *cessio legis* on the right deriving from tort. This can be justified, as the social security administration must and does compensate the losses induced by tort.

IV. Conceptual similarities between private international and international social protection law

1. Choice-of-law rules versus principle of territoriality

The conceptual framework of private international law also helps to shed light on the principles and rules governing international social security law. Social security law is frequently understood as the result of the 'principle of territoriality'. Regarding this assumption, the international scope of national law stems from the territorial restrictions on the state power imposed by the international order. According to this idea, any fact and person is relevant for national social policy to the extent they are addressed by state action. As such facts and persons can only exist within a state's territorial limits, they only become relevant for national social policy when occurring within the borders of a given state.

However, this theory is profoundly misleading. The international scope of national social policy cannot be equated with the limits to national state power. Rather it is based on normative principles determined by the international community through international cooperation and coordination and established by international law. Seen from this perspective, international social security law can be understood as a system of choice-of-law rules, which is built upon similar structures as private international law, in that both branches of international law employ choice-of-law rules to determine the international scope of national law. These norms single out specific branches of law with a connecting factor to determine the applicable national law. To identify the content of the branch of law referred to in choice-of-law norms, the methods of → classification qualification are used. To understand the main structure of international social security law, the conceptual framework of private international law is thus helpful, as it makes key elements of this branch of international law understandable.

2. Differences between the choice-of-law rules

A profound difference may be noted between private international and international social security law with regard to the legal character of the choice-of-law rules. Whereas private international law is built upon multilateral choice-of-law rules, the respective rules in international social security law are unilateral in nature. From this difference it follows that only private international law judgments can be based upon foreign law, whereas, in the context of social administration, courts and authorities are bound to the application of their own law.

This difference can be explained by the divergent functions of the law applied in private and public law. Whereas a private law case can be assessed in the light of the universal plurality of existing private laws and the judge is expected to find a solution on the basis of the most appropriate national law, in public administration the applicable law is determined by the state, which creates the administration, and even by reference to various national welfare and social security regimes worldwide.

3. Rules of equivalence as alternatives to universal choice-of-law rules

Despite the unilateral character of international social security law, it is not ultimately isolated from the world. This is because international social security law has developed an alternative to unilateral choice-of-law rules, so-called rules of equivalence, which help to integrate foreigners and foreign facts and legal relations into the ambit of a state law. This instrument is termed in private international law → substitution or adaption → (Adjustment/Adaptation (*Anpassung*)), and it leads to the application of a given state law, whereas the conditions of this law are fulfilled not only by local but also by foreign data. Rules of equivalence open the national legislation for foreigners and foreign elements, facts, relations and vested rights. They provide for antidiscrimination rules (→ Antidiscrimination) regarding the → nationality of a covered person, which generally is entirely irrelevant for social protection (arts 4 Coordination of Social Security Systems Regulation). Further examples for a rule of equivalence are provisions on the export of benefits in cash (art 7 Coordination of Social Security Systems Regulation), the totalization of periods of coverage (art 6 Coordination of Social Security Systems Regulation) and provisions giving access to services in kind (arts 17–20 Coordination of Social Security Systems Regulation). The latter legal effect of getting access to services in kind results from regarding membership in a national system of social protection as equivalent to the protection in the system of the Member State where the protection is considered. For a number of years under art 5 Coordination of Social Security Systems Regulation, the principle of equivalence has been exposed as a general principle of international social security law. In the terminology of private international law this rule is dealt with in the concepts of substitution and adaptation.

V. Conclusion

Social protection and private international law have much more in common than the conventional wisdom recognizes. There are substantial similarities in choice-of-law rules, interdependencies based on preliminary relations as well as substantial conceptual analogies. Deeper examination of the interrelations helps to reveal social protection as an overall feature in modern law, as well as to elucidate the common targets and principles of the various branches of international law.

EBERHARD EICHENHOFER

Literature

Olaf Deinert, *Internationales Arbeitsrecht* (Tübingen 2013); Willy van Eeckhoutte, *International Encyclopaedia for Social Security Law* (Kluwer Law and Taxation Publishers 1994); Eberhard Eichenhofer, *Internationales Sozialrecht und Internationales Privatrecht* (Nomos Verlagsgesellschaft 1987); Eberhard Eichenhofer, *Sozialrecht der Europäischen Union* (5th edn, Erich Schmidt 2013); Charles Freyria, 'Sécurité sociale et droit international privé' [1956] Rev.crit.DIP 409; International Labour Office (ILO), *Social Security and the Rule of Law* (International Labour Office 2011); Kurt Lipstein, 'Conflicts of Laws in Matters of Social Security under the EEC Treaty' in Francis Geoffrey Jacobs (ed), *European Law and the Individual* (North-Holland 1976) 55; Dieter Martiny, *Unterhaltsrang und -rückgriff* (Mohr Siebeck 2000); Bernd von Maydell, *Sach- und Kollisionsnormen im internationalen Sozialversicherungsrecht* (Duncker & Humblot 1967); Guy Perrin, 'Les fondements du droit international de la sécurité sociale' [1974] Droit social 479; Alexandre Pilenko, 'Droit spatial et droit international privé' (1953) 5 *Jus Gentium – Diritto Internazionale* 34; Rolf Schuler, *Das internationale Sozialrecht der Bundesrepublik Deutschland* (Nomos 1988); Klaus Vogel, *Der räumliche Anwendungsbereich der Verwaltungsrechtsnorm* (Metzner 1965); Jean Wiebault, 'Le droit de la sécurité sociale et la notion du conflict de lois' [1965] Droit social 318.

States, failed and non-recognized

I. Failed states

The term 'failed state' does not have a technical meaning in international law. It has in recent years become popularized as a means of referring to states without functional governmental systems, particularly in the context of (controversial) arguments for intervention (military or otherwise) in such states. For the purposes of this note, a failed state is understood to mean a state without a functional private law legal system, which may have particular implications for issues of private international law both in the context of jurisdiction and choice of law. No special issues regarding recognition and enforcement of foreign judgments arise – to the extent that any such judgment has been rendered, the civil justice system has in fact functioned, and that judgment will be subject to the usual rules and defences concerning recognition or enforcement in other states. If there are doubts over the legitimacy of the body which has issued the judgment (whether it is indeed a valid governmental authority), such issues are dealt with in accordance with the rules examined below under the heading of 'Non-recognized states and governments'.

In the context of jurisdiction, the possibility that a foreign state may lack a functional civil justice system raises difficulties concerning the usual → comity which is shown between legal systems. The courts of a state will often not take jurisdiction where it is determined that a foreign court is a more appropriate forum for the dispute. This may be through a rigid rule, which specifies the circumstances in which a foreign court is considered more appropriate (for example, based on the foreign subject matter of the dispute), or through a discretionary doctrine such as → *forum non conveniens*, which requires the court to take a number of factors into consideration in making this determination. Rules on jurisdiction will also almost universally take into consideration the wishes of the parties expressed through a jurisdiction agreement, under the doctrine of party autonomy, including through declining to hear a case where the parties have agreed that a foreign forum should have exclusive jurisdiction. However, where these rules or such an agreement point to a foreign state without a functional civil legal order, adherence to comity or deference to the parties' own agreement could leave the claimant without any forum in which their claim might practically be adjudicated. To put this another way, there would be a risk of a 'denial of justice' for the claimant.

For this reason, jurisdictional rules commonly provide for exceptions directed to avoiding this risk. Such an exception is, for example, built into the English *forum non conveniens* discretion, under which the court will not stay proceedings in favour of a foreign more appropriate forum if to do so would deny the claimant justice, either substantively or practically. This approach does not enlarge a court's potential jurisdiction, but instead enlarges the category of cases in which the court will exercise its jurisdiction. An alternative formulation of such an exception is a forum of necessity rule, such as that in Switzerland or the Netherlands, under which the courts will take jurisdiction (subject to certain conditions) where the claimant would otherwise not have a forum in which to bring their claim. Under this approach, the claimant's need for a forum can enlarge the potential jurisdiction of the court, although this may remain subject to limitations. (Under Swiss law, for example, it is necessary that the case has 'a sufficient connection' with Switzerland for the court to exercise 'forum of necessity' jurisdiction – art 3 Swiss Private international law Act (Bundesgesetz über das Internationale Privatrecht of 18 December 1987, 1988 BBl I 5, as amended).) However formulated, one particular context in which such rules will come into play is where jurisdictional rules would otherwise suggest an inappropriate deference to the courts of a failed state, which are in practice unavailable.

The existence of a failed state may also have an impact on private international law in the context of choice-of-law rules – where those rules, applied in the courts of another state, point to the application of the law of the failed state. In many cases, such as where an existing legal and governmental order has collapsed, a failed state will still have law which is identifiable and theoretically applicable, but which is no longer practically enforceable. This situation is unlikely, however, to present significant difficulties to a foreign court, which will still be able to identify and apply the relevant applicable law. The more difficult case is where a foreign legal system has failed to the point where there is no identifiable applicable law. Such circumstances will traditionally not be taken into consideration in the choice-of-law process itself, except under those US approaches which take into consideration the content of the substantive applicable law in determining which law to apply. Under such approaches, a dysfunctional legal order would not be likely to be considered the 'better law' to resolve a dispute between the parties. Where a more traditional approach is taken to determining the applicable law, blind to its content, the issue is more likely to be dealt with through the rules on the proof of foreign law. If there is indeed no identifiable foreign law, because the legal order of the foreign state has collapsed, then this may be considered as a situation where the content of foreign law has not been (and cannot be) proven satisfactorily. In such cases, a traditional starting point in the common law has been that the law of the forum should apply as a default law. Although there are doubts as to whether this approach is always appropriate, those doubts principally arise from the possibility that a claimant may benefit from a strategic failure to establish a foreign law which would be disadvantageous to their claim. Such a concern does not arise where there has been a default to local law in place of the usual applicable law because choice-of-law rules point to a state whose system of private law simply cannot be established.

II. Non-recognized states and governments

The issue of non-recognized states and governments presents a distinct and broader problem. The concern often arises where the very existence of a foreign state is contested. Similar issues are also encountered where a foreign state is recognized as existing, but a dispute arises over who is the legitimate government of the territory of that state (either as a whole, or in relevant part), either because of an internal conflict between governmental authorities, or because of foreign occupation. Outside the realm of private international law, questions as to who is entitled to act on behalf of a foreign state may arise in a range of contexts, from the appointment of diplomats to the issue of entitlement to control state-owned property or → companies. Within private international law, the key problem is generally whether to apply the laws or recognize the judgments of an unrecognized foreign state, or more generally an unrecognized foreign governmental authority.

The term 'non-recognized' is, of course, somewhat question-begging, as courts themselves are considering whether to 'recognize' a foreign state or governmental authority through according effect to its private law acts or the judgments of its courts. The issue is generally that the courts are considering a foreign legal order which may not be recognized as valid by the executive branch of the legal system of which the courts form a constituent part. The danger for a contemplated 'judicial recognition' is that the courts, in giving effect to the acts of the foreign legal order in the context of private law, might find themselves acting inconsistently with the foreign policy position of the executive branch of government, under which that foreign legal order should not be recognized as valid or effective. The executive branch of government (perhaps in conjunction with parliament) will generally have domestic constitutional responsibility for the conduct of foreign policy, and the courts will be wary of interfering with that authority on grounds of the constitutional 'separation of powers'.

The traditional starting point in this area is therefore one of deference to the executive. In the common law tradition, this is known as the 'one voice' doctrine – the courts have generally deferred to the position of the executive on questions of whether a foreign legal system should be recognized. 'Our Sovereign has to decide whom he will recognize as a fellow sovereign in the family of States; and the relations of the foreign State with ours . . . must flow from that decision alone' (*Government of Republic of Spain v S.S. Arantzazu Mendi and Others*, '*The Arantzazu Mendi*', [1939] AC 256, 264). If necessary, the courts have prompted an executive determination of a disputed question of foreign statehood through requesting an executive certificate (generally from the relevant department of foreign affairs), which, if issued, is considered to be determinative of any questions it addresses. Recent practice in a number of states is that executive certificates are not generally issued in relation to the question of who is the government of a foreign state, only the question of statehood itself, although this practice is not universal. In the United Kingdom, for example, the courts have had to develop their own test for determining who is the government of a foreign state (*Republic of Somalia v Woodhouse Drake and Carey* [1993] QB 54), but they will continue to defer to executive certificates where they are exceptionally issued on such questions (*British Arab Commercial Bank v National Transitional Council of the State of Libya* [2011] EWHC 2274 (Comm)).

While this doctrine of deference to the executive may be sensible and relatively unproblematic in matters of interstate public or diplomatic relations, it has proven more unsatisfactory in the context of private law. This is because the lack of recognition accorded to a foreign legal order by the executive may appear to have unsatisfactory or unjust consequences for private parties who are nevertheless practically bound to adhere to that foreign legal order. For example, parties who live in a non-recognized but reasonably functional state and obtain a divorce (→ Divorce and personal separation) from a judge of that state might find that this divorce goes unrecognized in a foreign legal order, even though there was no alternative available forum through which they might have divorced (see, eg, *Adams v Adams* [1970] 3 All ER 572). Particularly in cases where the non-recognition of the foreign state is a consequence of an unlawful occupation which denies the self-determination rights of the people of the affected territory, there is a risk that the remedy – non-recognition – would actually doubly victimize the population. Not only would they lack self-governance as a matter of public law, but non-recognition of their private rights and status would further undermine the effectiveness of their private legal ordering.

Historically, one partial response to this issue was a distinction between the recognition of *de jure* and *de facto* governments, particularly in the practice of common law states – the former relating to the political question of who is the legitimate government of a territory, and the latter relating to the practical question of who has factual control over the territory. If a question arose concerning private rights within the foreign state, it would be the acts of the *de facto* rather than *de jure* government which would prevail. The nationalization of property within the Soviet Union was thus recognized by the English courts in 1921, on the basis of the *de facto* recognition of the Soviet government, even though *de jure* recognition was not granted until 1924 (*Luther v Sagor* [1921] 3 KB 532). If, however, a question arose concerning rights to property outside the foreign state, it would be the *de jure* rather than *de facto* government which would be considered the legitimate representative of the foreign state. Thus, the deposed Ethiopian emperor *Haile Selassie* was initially considered to have title to Ethiopian property in England, despite the *de facto* recognition of Italian occupation in 1936, although this was subsequently reversed by a recognition in 1938 that the Italian government had *de jure* status over Ethiopia, with retrospective effect (*Haile Selassie v Cable and Wireless* [1939] Ch 182).

The *de facto* / *de jure* distinction, adopted by certain states as part of their practice of recognition of foreign governments, thus provided a helpful way to acknowledge the practical effect of a foreign authority, even if the authority was considered to be illegitimate as a matter of international law or politics. However, the practice of distinguishing between *de jure* and *de facto* governments was not consistently adopted and has not generally been sustained. Indeed, as noted above, many states have adopted a practice of generally not recognizing foreign governments at all, passing the issue to the courts. The distinction between *de jure* and *de facto* governments was also of little assistance when dealing with the problem of an unrecognized state. The general issue thus remained that the non-recognition of a foreign state or government, because of its considered illegitimacy, could be in tension with the practical reality of the exercise of territorial control and legal power.

Faced with this problem, courts have strived to develop exceptions to their traditional deference to executive non-recognition. One particular (although somewhat narrowly applicable) example is where the non-recognized state or government may nevertheless be viewed as exercising authority on behalf of a legitimate and recognized state. For example, while East Germany was not recognized as a state by the United Kingdom, the House of Lords found that the East German government was in fact acting as an agent of the Soviet Union, the body recognized (in the post-Second World War settlement) as having legitimate authority over the territory (*Carl Zeiss Stiftung v Rayner and Keeler Ltd (No. 2)* [1967] 1 AC 853). Thus, 'the acts of the German Democratic Republic [are recognized] not because they are acts of a sovereign state, but because they are acts done by a subordinate body which the U.S.S.R. set up to act on its behalf' (pp 906 f). East German law could thus (conveniently) be recognized by the courts without recognizing East Germany. A similar approach was followed by the English courts in relation to Ciskei, an unrecognized 'Bantustan' territory created by apartheid South Africa as a means of segregating black South Africans and removing their citizenship, which was nevertheless recognized as having standing in the English courts (for the purposes of certain proceedings) as an effective agency of the South African government (*Gur Corporation v Trust Bank of Africa Ltd* [1987] QB 599).

This type of 'agency' argument is, however, both a stretch of legal logic and only available in a narrow set of factual circumstances, so cannot present an entirely satisfactory response to the potentially problematic consequences of non-recognition. The need for a more general exception, particularly in the context of private law rights, was noted by Lord Wilberforce in the Carl Zeiss case, who suggested that:

> if the consequences of non-recognition of the East German 'government' were to bring in question the validity of its legislative acts, I should wish seriously to consider whether the invalidity so brought about is total, or whether some mitigation of the severity of this result can be found. . . . [W]here private rights, or acts of everyday occurrence, or perfunctory acts of administration are concerned (the scope of these exceptions has never been precisely defined) the courts may, in the interests of justice and common sense, where no consideration of public policy to the contrary has to prevail, give recognition to the actual facts or realities found to exist in the territory in question. (*Carl Zeiss Stiftung v Rayner and Keeler Ltd (No. 2)* [1967] 1 AC 853, 954)

As *Lord Wilberforce* noted, such an exception had indeed received earlier recognition in US courts – perhaps starting with the practical recognition that many laws and decisions adopted by Confederate authorities during the Civil War should (subject to the Constitution) be given effect (*Texas v White*, 74 U.S. 700 (1868)). This approach had since been clarified as well as extended to international cases. It was discussed, for example, by the New York courts in the aftermath of the Soviet revolution – accepting that recognition might be given to the regulatory acts of the Soviet government, even though that government had not itself been recognized by the United States (*Sokoloff v National City Bank of New York* (1924) 239 N.Y. 158). A similar approach was developed around the same time by the Swiss courts, in *Banque internationale de Petrograd v Hausner* (1924), BGE 50 II 507, also accepting that possible effect might be given to domestic regulatory acts by the Soviet authorities even in the absence of Swiss recognition of those authorities as the government of Russia. The position was later summarized by the New York courts, in *Upright v Mercury Business Machines Co*, 213 N.Y.S.2d 417 (1961), as follows:

> A foreign government, although not recognized by the political arm of the United States Government, may nevertheless have *de facto* existence which is juridically cognizable. The acts of such a *de facto* government may affect private rights and obligations arising either as a result of activity in, or with persons or corporations within, the territory controlled by such *de facto* government. (p 419)

This approach received international support from the International Court of Justice in its Advisory Opinion on Legal Consequences for States of the Continued Presence of South Africa in Namibia Notwithstanding SC Res. 276 ((1971) ICJ Rep 16). Namibia had been a German colony prior to the First World War, following which it was established as a League of Nations mandate territory under the control of South Africa. While the mandate system was generally intended to establish a 'trustee' relationship, South Africa instead occupied the territory of Namibia, effectively (although not formally) integrating it within its own boundaries. The ICJ determined, consistently with widespread opinion, that this occupation was in violation of international law, and that states were under an obligation not to recognize South Africa's administration of the Namibian territory. However, the court also held as follows:

> In general, the non-recognition of South Africa's administration of the Territory should not result in depriving the people of Namibia of any advantages derived from international co-operation. In particular, while official acts performed by the Government of South Africa on behalf of or concerning Namibia after the termination of the Mandate are illegal and invalid, this invalidity cannot be extended to those acts, such as, for instance, the registration of births, deaths and marriages, the effects of which can be ignored only to the detriment of the inhabitants of the Territory. ([125])

The ICJ thus invited states to distinguish between the public and private dimensions of recognition, avoiding non-recognition of private rights where to do so would lead to injustice. National and regional courts have subsequently adopted this practice, which has sometimes been expressly referred to as the 'Namibia exception'. For example, in *Warenzeichenverband Regelungstechnik v Ministero dell'industria, del commercio e dell'artigianato* (1975) 77 ILR 571, the Italian Corte di Cassazione held (in relation to East Germany) that:

> [W]here the question arises of establishing the effects in Italy of an act of private law executed abroad, it is irrelevant whether or not a State maintains diplomatic relations with another State whose rule of private international law is to be

enforced, or whether or not the latter State is recognized by the former. (p 579)

The practice has developed perhaps most prominently in relation to the north of Cyprus, under Turkish occupation since 1974 (although formally self-administered as the Turkish Republic of Northern Cyprus (henceforth TRNC)). The generally accepted position (outside Turkey) is that states are under an obligation as a matter of international law not to recognize the TRNC or Turkish occupation, but the courts have developed exceptions for matters of private law. The English courts held, for example, that

> the courts of this country can recognise the laws or acts of a body which is in effective control of a territory even though it has not been recognised by Her Majesty's Government *de jure* or *de facto*: at any rate, in regard to the laws which regulate the day to day affairs of the people, such as their marriages, their divorces, their leases, their occupations, and so forth. (*Hesperides Hotels v Aegean Turkish Holidays* [1978] QB 205, 218, per Lord Denning)

In the case of *Emin v Yeldag* [2002] 1 FLR 956, the English courts thus recognized the validity of a divorce (→ Divorce and personal separation) granted by the courts of the TRNC.

The European Court of Human Rights has also endorsed the finding of the ICJ in the Namibia Opinion, supporting its conclusion that 'international law recognises the legitimacy of certain legal arrangements and transactions in such a situation [of foreign occupation], for instance as regards the registration of births, deaths and marriages' (*Loizidou v Turkey (Merits)* ECHR 1996-VI 2241, para 45). The position was put perhaps even more forcefully by the same Court in the case of *Cyprus v Turkey* [2001] ECHR 331, holding (para 96) that:

> [T]he obligation to disregard acts of *de facto* entities is far from absolute. Life goes on in the territory concerned for its inhabitants. That life must be made tolerable and be protected by the *de facto* authorities, including their courts; and, in the very interest of the inhabitants, the acts of these authorities related thereto cannot be simply ignored by third States or by international institutions, especially courts, including this one.

This approach has been extended by statute in Australia and the United Kingdom to include recognition of the legal personality of foreign corporations established under non-recognized legal systems, through the Foreign Corporations (Application of Laws) Act 1989 (Aust.) and the Foreign Corporations Act 1991 (UK).

US practice is reflected in § 205(3) Restatement (Third) of the Foreign Relations Law of the United States (American Law Institute, St. Paul 1987), which similarly provides:

> [C]ourts in the United States ordinarily give effect to acts of a regime representing an entity not recognized as a state, or of a regime not recognized as the government of a state, if those acts apply to territory under the control of that regime and relate to domestic matters only.

Another context in which these issues have commonly arisen is in relation to Taiwan, which is not formally recognized by the majority of states but is nevertheless in practice an important trading partner for many states. Unlike the TRNC, the existence of a separate administration in Taiwan is not the product of an unlawful use of force by a foreign state, and therefore no equivalent obligation to refuse recognition is generally considered to exist as a matter of international law (although it is perhaps arguable that any such recognition could constitute an unlawful interference in Chinese 'internal' affairs). The approach adopted by foreign states in relation to Taiwan has largely been consistent with the above distinction between public and private law questions, with private (particularly commercial) legal relations continuing to function, without such relations being considered to constitute recognition of Taiwan as a state or the Taiwanese administration as a legitimate government. In the USA, for example, the Taiwan Relations Act 1979 (93 Stat. 14) preserved the status of Taiwan's private law and the recognition of Taiwanese companies, despite withdrawal of recognition of the Taiwanese government. Such recognition of the status of Taiwanese companies gives them the capacity to sue and be sued in US courts (an equivalent effect to the Australian and UK statutes noted above). The courts of Hong Kong have also recognized the appointment by a Taiwanese court of a trustee to a bankrupt party, accepting that effect may be given in some circumstances to orders of unrecognized courts (*Chen Li Hung v Ting Lei Miao* [2000] 1 HKLRD 252). It has, however, proven more contentious whether this should also extend to accepting that a Taiwanese company exercising governmental authority possesses state → immunity

ALEX MILLS

(see, for example, *Civil Aeronautics Administration v Singapore Airlines Ltd* [2004] 1 SLR 570 (Singapore), but see also *Parent v Singapore Airlines Ltd and the Civil Aeronautics Administration* (2003) 133 ILR 264 (Quebec Superior Court, Canada)).

While the courts have thus embraced the possibility of recognizing the effect on private rights of an otherwise unrecognized foreign legal order, they remain cautious. A clear statement of the principle, and of the need for caution in regard to it, is provided in the UK case of *Caglar v Billingham (Inspector of Taxes)* [1996] S.T.C. (SCD) 150, in which it was held:

> [T]he courts may acknowledge the existence of an unrecognised foreign government in the context of the enforcement of laws relating to commercial obligations or matters of private law between individuals or matters of routine administration such as the registration of births, marriages or deaths. This principle is in line with that adopted in the Foreign Corporations Act 1991. However, the courts will not acknowledge the existence of an unrecognised state if to do so would involve them in acting inconsistently with the foreign policy or diplomatic stance of this country. ([121])

In this case, the court consequently refused to recognize a representative of the Turkish Republic of Northern Cyprus in London as a diplomat entitled to an exemption from income tax. In the case of *Regina v Minister for Agriculture, Fisheries and Food ex parte Anastasiou (Pissouri) Limited and others* (Case C-432/92, [1994] ECR I-3087), the European Court of Justice similarly found that certificates issued by the customs authorities of the TRNC could not be recognized, as this would constitute improper recognition of the status of that territory. In *Dag v Home Secretary* (2001) 122 ILR 529, it was confirmed (by a UK Immigration Appeal Tribunal) that this also excluded recognition for immigration purposes of a 'passport' issued by the TRNC, as no 'nationality' could arise in relation to an unrecognized state. In the decision of *R (on the application of Yollari) v Secretary of State for Transport* [2009] EWHC 1918 (Admin) the English courts again followed this practice, approving a decision of the Secretary of State for Transport to refuse to consider granting permission for a Turkish charter airline to fly from the United Kingdom to the north of Cyprus. The court held:

> the grant of permits would amount to implied recognition that the Government in control of the TRNC was sovereign over the territory which it effectively controls. The grant of permits would, in my judgment, completely undermine the express statements from the United Kingdom Government to the effect that it does not recognise the TRNC. ([79])

This would be particularly problematic because:

> there is a duty, as a matter of customary international law, not to recognise the TRNC as legal or lawful. The upshot is, of course, that the United Kingdom Government is under a legal duty not to recognise the TRNC. I have found that the grant of the permits sought by the Claimant would constitute acts of recognition. It follows that the grant of the permits sought would render the United Kingdom Government in breach of its duty not to recognise the TRNC. ([84])

The applicant appealed, including on the basis that the 'private rights' exception to non-recognition (the 'Namibia exception') should be invoked in this case, as individual passengers might be inconvenienced by their inability to fly directly from the north of Cyprus to the United Kingdom. The Court of Appeal, however, emphasized that the exception was inapplicable in a 'public' context such as this, holding:

> [T]he issue in the present case falls well outside the ambit of the Namibia exception, however precisely the principle may be formulated for the purposes of its application in domestic law. This case is not concerned with private rights, acts of everyday occurrence, routine acts of administration, day to day activities having legal consequences, or matters of that kind. The case involves public functions in the field of international civil aviation and the lawfulness of a public law decision. The issues in the case are issues of public law, concerning the question whether it is lawful to grant a permit for international flights to and from northern Cyprus contrary to the wishes (and, as I would hold, the treaty rights) of the recognised state of which that territory forms part. . . . This is not the kind of subject-matter at which the Namibia exception is directed. (*R (on the application of Yollari) v Secretary of State for Transport* [2010] EWCA Civ 1093 [79])

In summary, courts will generally not recognize the legal acts of unrecognized foreign states (or governments), as that would risk undermining the foreign policy position of the executive. This would be particularly problematic where the non-recognition is a matter of obligation under international law, such as in the context of an unlawful occupation of territory, as acts of recognition by the court could put the state in breach of international law. In the context of private international law, this rule was traditionally understood to mean that the law of an unrecognized foreign state could not be applied, nor could its judgments be recognized. However, an exception has developed, recognized by both the International Court of Justice and by national courts, under which the effect of the law of an unrecognized state on private rights and obligations may nevertheless be recognized, where this is necessary to do justice, provided the issues remain within the realm of private law. In the context of private international law, courts are thus likely to focus where possible not on questions of the 'legitimacy' of a foreign legal order, but rather on the facts on the ground – the reality of which legal order holds practical sway over the parties – in order to insulate the parties from the potentially harmful side-effects of the vagaries of global politics.

ALEX MILLS

Literature

Lawrence Collins, 'Foreign Relations and the Judiciary' (2002) 51 ICLQ 485; James Crawford, *Brownlie's Principles of Public International Law* (8th edn, OUP 2012) chapter 6; Fritz A Mann, *Foreign Affairs in English Courts* (Clarendon Press 1986); Fritz A Mann, 'The Judicial Recognition of an Unrecognised State' (1987) 36 ICLQ 348; Campbell McLachlan, *Foreign Relations Law* (CUP 2014) chapter 10; Zaim M Nedjati, 'Acts of Unrecognised Governments' (1981) 30 ICLQ 388; Elias A Olufemi, 'The International Status of Taiwan in the Courts of Canada and Singapore' (2004) 8 SYBIL 93; Stefan Talmon, *Recognition of Governments in International Law* (OUP 1998); Joe Verhoeven, 'Relations internationales de droit privé en l'absence de reconnaissance d'un Etat, d'un gouvernement ou d'une situation' (1985) 192 Recueil des cours 9; Colin Warbrick, 'The New British Policy on Recognition of Governments' (1981) 30 ICLQ 568; Colin Warbrick, 'British Policy and the National Transitional Council of Libya' (2012) 61 ICLQ 247.

Story, Joseph

Joseph Story (1779–1845) was one of the greatest and most influential American lawyers of all time. Both as a Supreme Court Justice and as a professor at Harvard Law School, his work and thought were, and still are, of great importance. Today's private international law would look different without him, both in the → USA and in the rest of the world. At the same time, his approach to the field cannot be properly understood unless placed within his broader work on law, and the specific American background against which it was developed.

I. Life and work

1. Life, positions

Joseph Story was born in 1779, the same year as *Carl Friedrich von Savigny* (1779–1861) (→ Savigny, Friedrich Carl von), in Marblehead, Massachusetts, then with about 5,000 inhabitants the eighth biggest city in the young USA. Both the importance of commerce and the international connections of New England influenced him throughout his life. He went to study at Harvard College where he graduated second in his class. At the time, law was taught at almost no US universities, so he read law with a practising attorney at Marblehead with great ambition, studying 14 hours a day. In 1801 he was admitted to the Bar in Salem and practised, successfully, as a lawyer in Essex County. As one of few Jeffersonian Republican lawyers in Massachusetts, he was an outsider, but his politics helped him gain the support of the influential *Crowninshield* family. Like many lawyers of his time he went into politics and was elected to the Massachusetts House of Representatives in 1805; in 1811 he became its speaker. His greatest pride from this position was to have originated a law that doubled the salary of judges at the Supreme Judicial Court. From December 1808 to March 1809 he served, briefly, as a representative in the US Congress to replace *Jacob Crowninshield* (1770–1808); in this brief time he managed to win President *Thomas Jefferson's* (1743–1826) enmity over the President's repeal of an embargo against the British.

Despite *Jefferson's* reservations, President *James Madison* (1751–1836), in need of a Republican from Massachusetts, appointed *Story*, in November 1811, to the US Supreme Court – at age 32 the youngest US Supreme Court Justice ever. He remained on the Court until his death in 1845. His first years on the Court were his happiest; he got along especially well with Chief Justice *John Marshall* (1755–1835). When *Marshall* died in 1832, President

Andrew Jackson (1767–1845) chose *Roger Brooke Taney* (1777–1864) as Chief Justice over *Story*, whom he considered 'the most dangerous man in America', perhaps because of *Story's* demonstrated independence from partisanship. Though *Story* worked well with *Taney*, he became less happy with his other colleagues and with the increasingly political role of the Court, and considered retiring. Indeed, work as a Supreme Court Justice was strenuous. Washington, DC, where the judges were active for six to twelve weeks each year without their families, was a most uninspiring place. In addition, Supreme Court Justices spent much time each year riding the circuits (for *Story* this meant Rhode Island, Massachusetts, Maine and New Hampshire) and serving as federal appeals court judges. *Story* was proud of his work as a Circuit Justice and went on to publish his own opinions.

While remaining on the bench, *Story* took up, in 1829, a position as Dane professor at the Harvard Law School. The school, founded in 1817 (making it the oldest continuing university law school in the country), was fledgling; when *Story* joined in 1824, it had a mere 12 students. *Story*, in addition to his ongoing judicial work, turned out to be a prolific writer, a successful and enthusiastic teacher of law and a harbinger of educational reform at Harvard. All of this paid off: during *Story's* time, the law school began to prosper; when he died, enrolment was up to 154 students. *Story's* aim, to turn Harvard into a national law school (and thereby enhance a national, as opposed to state-based, legal education) was a successful strategy, until our time.

The strains of this life took their toll on *Story*. In 1845, he announced his plans to retire, but died before he could put this plan into practice.

2. *Contributions in general*

Story's influence on American law is so great because he worked in two areas–scholarship and judicial works–and both activities for him were mutually influential. On the one hand, *Story* wanted to establish American law as a science in which judges discovered principles through reason (insofar not unlike European jurists, though he criticized the Europeans' overly abstract and theoretical style). On the other hand, *Story's* scholarly work aimed at providing comprehensive treatment of individual legal areas on the basis of existing American case-law.

a) Judicial opinions

As a Supreme Court Justice, *Story* wrote no less than 286 opinions, many of them influential (see H Jefferson Powell, 'Joseph Story' in Melvin I Urofsky (ed), *The Supreme Court Justices: A Biographical Dictionary* (Routledge 2006) 435). The decisions span a wide variety of fields, though a certain emphasis is on areas of commercial law, representing the expertise for which he had been appointed.

In general, *Story's* jurisprudence can be described by three elements. First, it was scholarly. *Story* took pride in working precisely and on the basis of existing case-law, even where the outcome went against his own personal preferences or those of the politics of the moment; in this, he considered himself 'the last of the old race of judges'. At the same time, this meant that his opinions were usually meticulously researched. *Story's* erudition in the law provided him with a particularly scholarly approach to lawyering that contrasted with the sometimes more aphoristic style of his colleagues.

Second, *Story* was a nationalist, meaning that as between the states and the federation he would often prioritize the latter. In one of his most influential decisions in this regard, *Martin v Hunter's Lessee* (1 Wheaton 304 (1816)), he emphasized that federal power came from the people and not from the states. As a consequence, the Supreme Court could review state court decisions concerning federal law. Elsewhere, he extended federal jurisdiction, for example in admiralty (*De Lovio v Boit*, 2 Gall. 398 (1815)).

Third, and relatedly, *Story* favoured the protection of private rights and the growth of private commerce unencumbered by politics. To this goal, he emphasized the constitutional protection of private corporations against interferences from the states (*Dartmouth College v Woodward*, 4 Wheaton 518 (1819)) and the protection of rights granted by the states against changing political preferences (*Charles River Bridge v Warren Bridge Co*, 11 Peters 420 (1837), Story J dissenting). In his view, the states with their sometimes peculiar and parochial approaches to legal questions could stand in the way of both private rights and general freedom of commerce; national (or, where possible, even global) solutions were better equipped for the trans-border character of commerce.

b) Scholarship

Story's other great influence came as a scholar, especially while at Harvard. *Nathan Dane*

(1752–1835), the founder of *Story's* chair, had stipulated that the donated money be used, in part, for the writing of comprehensive books on topics of American law. *Story* fulfilled this wish dutifully and with enthusiasm and wrote treatises in a wide variety of fields, all with several editions. These include treatises on bailments (Hilliard and Brown 1832; 9th edn, Little, Brown & Co 1888), the US Constitution (3 vols, Hilliard, Gray & Co 1833; 5th edn, Little, Brown & Co 1905), conflict of laws (Hilliard, Gray & Co 1834; 8th edn, Little, Brown & Co 1883), equity jurisprudence (2 vols, Hilliard, Gray & Co 1836; 14th edn, Little, Brown & Co 1918), equity pleadings (Little, Brown & Co 1838; 10th edn, Little, Brown & Co 1892), agency (Little, Brown & Co 1839; 9th edn, Little, Brown & Co 1882), partnership (Little, Brown & Co 1841; 7th edn, Little, Brown & Co 1881), bills of exchange (Little, Brown & Co 1843; 4th edn, Little, Brown & Co 1860) and promissory notes (Little, Brown & Co 1845; 7th edn, Little, Brown & Co 1878). He had planned additional books on shipping, insurance, equity practice, admiralty and public international law, when he died in 1845. The treatise on the Constitution has remained a standard work; it is still cited frequently. Remarkably, all other treatises (with the exception of conflict of laws) concerned areas of federal common law (which had a much broader scope then than today) and thus had no need to deal with different state laws. In content they were often based on the law of the New England states, which was, however, stripped of its local character and thereby nationalized.

Story was not the sole originator of the treatise as a type of literature on US law. *James Kent* (1743–1847) (whom *Story* admired and to whom he dedicated his treatise on the conflict of laws) had begun to write commentaries before. *Nathan Dane* himself had made the money that funded *Story's* chair at Harvard through the success of his 'General Abridgement and Digest of American Law', much like *Charles Viner* (1678–1756) had funded *Blackstone's* chair at Oxford with money made from the publication of a similar work. *Story's* work, however, was more comprehensive than *Kent's* four volumes, and more systematic than *Dane's* Abridgement. Although *Story* frequently criticized civilian writers for their abstract reasoning (and himself indeed relied mostly on existing case-law), he shared with the continental treatise literature the attention to system and the desire to demonstrate underlying principles. In this, *Story's* approach was more systematic than original: his treatises display knowledge and order more than new thoughts. At the same time, they served as something akin to civil codes, albeit (of course) non-legislative ones. Indeed, *Story* was an avid supporter of codification of the common law and presented, in 1837, a report on such a project for the governor of Massachusetts. The project did not come to fruition after he declared himself unable to serve as drafter. All in all, *Story's* treatises created a significant boost towards a more comprehensive understanding of US law and introduced what has later been called, in the → USA, classical legal thought.

II. Contributions to private international law

Story made important contributions to many areas, but at least globally, his influence rests primarily on his treatise on the conflict of laws. As in other areas, *Story's* work in private international law consisted also on judicial opinions, and both jurisprudence and scholarship mutually influenced each other.

1. Story's *commentaries on the conflict of laws*

a) Precursors

In his inaugural lecture at Harvard, *Story* announced that he planned a work on the conflict of laws in which he would 'venture far more than has been usual with publicists'. When he began work, he expected it to be his 'best Law work'. Indeed, at the time, the field as an intellectual discipline lay dormant, especially in the English language. As concerns England, this was understandable: although English courts had had to deal with issues of private international law repeatedly, the procedural nature of the common law at the time had prevented the development of a coherent doctrinal framework. In the United States, by contrast, relations between the states had led to a fast-growing case-law that called for treatment. Nonetheless, *Story* could draw on very little scholarly material. *James Kent* had dealt with the conflict of laws in his commentaries. *Story* himself had written a brief treatment for a Digest of American Law (Kurt Nadelmann (ed), 'Extract from Joseph Story's Manuscript "Digest of Law"' (1961) 5 Am. J. Legal Hist.

265–75); he had also treated the subject briefly in some of his other earlier treatises. Beyond this, the only relevant American treatment of the field was a treatise by *Samuel Livermore* (1732–1803), a Louisiana lawyer, written in response to a case in which *Livermore's* defence of the theory of statutes, drawing extensively on civilian literature, had not prevailed (see Rodolfo de Nova, 'The First American Book on Conflict of Laws' (1964) 8 Am. J. Legal Hist. 136–56).

Livermore had donated his library to Harvard Law School and thereby provided *Story* with ample scholarly material for his treatise. *Story* made good use of the material – he read Latin, French and Spanish though not German – and even introduced the most important works in the beginning of his treatise. But he found that the civilian writings 'abound with theoretical distinctions, which serve little other purpose than to provoke idle discussions, and with metaphysical subtleties, which perplex, if they do not confound, the inquirer' (Joseph Story, *Commentaries on the Conflict of Laws, Foreign and Domestic, in Regard to Contracts, Rights and Remedies, and Especially in Regard to Marriages, Wills, Successions, and Judgments* (1st edn, 1834) § 11, p 10, henceforth Story, *Commentaries on the Conflict of Laws* (1st edn, 1834)). Instead, he drew primarily, or at least in significant addition, on English and American case-law, of which, at the time of his writing, there was a lot. To some extent he also used judicial opinions from other jurisdictions. The book was, therefore, very comparative in nature, but at the same time remained explicitly Anglo-American in its focus: *Story* aimed at demonstrating the approach of the USA to the conflict of laws, not a general theory or an assumed universal law of conflicts.

b) The role of comity

Despite *Story's* opposition to abstract theorizing, the treatise does contain a theoretical part in its chapter 2 ('general maxims'). Here, *Story* adopted three maxims that he borrowed from *Ulricus Huber* (1636–94; → Huber, Ulrik):

(i) every nation possesses an exclusive sovereignty and jurisdiction within its own territory (Story, *Commentaries on the Conflict of Laws* (1st edn, 1834) § 18, p 19);
(ii) no state or nation can, by its laws, directly affect, or bind property out of its own territory, or persons not resident therein, whether they are natural born subjects or others (Story, *Commentaries on the Conflict of Laws* (1st edn, 1834) § 20, p 21);
(iii) whatever force and obligations the laws of one country have in another depends solely upon the laws, and municipal regulations of the latter, that is to say, upon its own proper jurisprudence and polity, and upon its own express or tacit consent (Story, *Commentaries on the Conflict of Laws* (1st edn, 1834) § 23, p 24).

This meant that questions of conflict of laws had to be resolved not by determining whether a statute was real or personal (as had been done under the theory of statutes), but instead, first and foremost, on the basis of a country's written or customary law. Only where these two were silent, the decision had to be made on the basis of general considerations of mutual interest and utility and a moral necessity to do justice (mainly by recognizing rights) (Story, *Commentaries on the Conflict of Laws* (1st edn, 1834) p 34).

States thus had no duty to apply foreign law; they did so out of → comity. This theoretical approach, though it is discussed frequently, was in reality neither new nor particularly relevant. It was not new because *Huber's* laying out of these principles had, as *Story* himself pointed out, been widely accepted in the USA; a reporter had even appended a translation of *Huber's* treatise to one of the US Supreme Court's early decisions. It has been suggested that *Story* misunderstood *Huber*, for whom comity was a binding obligation (Alan Watson, *Joseph Story and the Comity of Errors* (University of Georgia Press 1992)). Whether this was so matters little because an understanding of comity as nonbinding was widespread at *Story's* time. It was also in accordance with both the federalism of the USA and *Story's* interest, shared by others, in restraining the (extraterritorial) powers of the states (see G Blaine Baker, 'Interstate Choice of Law and Early American Constitutional Nationalism' (1993) 38 McGill L.J. 454).

The theoretical approach was not particularly relevant for three reasons. First, what *Story* had in mind was 'not the comity of courts, but the comity of the nation', meaning that judges had no discretion in determining whether or not to apply foreign law. The doctrine thus served as an explanation of what states do, but not as an empowerment for judges to rule as they pleased. Second, comity was very vague; *Story* pointed out that, 'from its generality, it leaves behind many grave questions as to its application'. The importance of the work lay not in this general basis but in the rules that *Story* developed. Third, comity functioned, in *Story's* treatise, less as a basis of developing doctrines and more as a check on general conflict-of-laws rules, akin to what would later become the → public policy exception. Comity was the small public law element in a treatise otherwise dedicated to private law in its international and interstate dimension. It is rarely taken up in the later parts of the treatise.

One could think that *Story's* idea of comity, giving states freedom to refuse to apply foreign law, should stand in the way of his preference for national rules over state rules and for uniformity. That would be a misunderstanding. Comity was indeed a way to weaken the power of individual states, because it prevented states from imposing their laws on other states. And it did not stand in the way of uniformity, because it enhanced the legitimacy of application of foreign law: although conflicts rules were quasi-universal, their adoption rested on the decision of each state.

c) Content of the treatise

Story's general maxims play no great role for the rest of his treatise. What sets the treatise apart from earlier literature is not its theory but *Story's* comprehensive treatment of all areas of the law. Apart from the first two chapters, dealing with, respectively, introductory remarks and general maxims, *Story* groups the remaining 15 chapters into eight areas (Story, *Commentaries on the Conflict of Laws* (1st edn, 1834) § 39, p 39): persons, including marriage and divorce (chs 3–7), contracts generally (ch 8), personal and real property (chs 9–10), wills and → succession (chs 11–12), persons acting for others ('*in autre droit*') (ch 13), remedies and judicial sentences (including jurisdiction and foreign judgments) (chs 14–15), penal laws and offences (ch 16) and evidence and proofs (ch 17). Notably absent is tort law Structuring analysis around areas of the law rather than types of statutes (real, personal, mixed) was a novelty. It was very much in accordance with viewing private international law as dealing not with conflicts between sovereigns nor with the characterization of statutes (real and personal) and more with the application of private laws across space – an approach later emulated by *Savigny* (→ Savigny, Friedrich Carl von). At the same time, it reflected the general shift in common law doctrine away from individual causes of action and towards subject matter substantive doctrine.

All in all, *Story's* treatise displays a number of characteristics. First, *Story* conceived of conflicts of laws as more than just conflicts of statutes; by including conflicts between different local common laws he significantly enhanced the scope and importance of the field, especially for the common law. Second, he endorsed a strong territorialism over the (partial) personalism that had characterized the theory of statutes (→ Unilateralism). → Connecting factors were almost always territorial – the place of the tort, the place of the contract, the place of the → marriage and so forth. Indeed, in his earlier digest and in his Harvard inaugural lecture, *Story* had described the scope of conflict of laws as the conflicts between → *lex fori* and *lex loci*, not mentioning personal statutes at all. Third, he emphasized the importance of private rights (especially contract and property): those take up the largest part of the treatise, and he was the first to call the discipline 'private international law'. Both the application of foreign law and the enforcement of foreign judgments served, first and foremost, private interests and the protection of private rights – they were not, as they had been for earlier theorists, matters of respective recognition of sovereign acts. Fourth, despite his emphasis on → comity and the discretion of states in applying foreign law, *Story* strove very much towards nationally uniform choice-of-law rules (as a second best to substantive law unification). Fifth, *Story* did not distinguish between interstate and international conflicts, thus placing his approach to conflict of laws in a global framework, in accordance with the foreign literature which he cited.

2. *Story's judicial decisions*

Story's importance for the conflict of laws is not confined to his scholarship. As a circuit judge he rendered 11 decisions on interstate conflicts, showing his interest in the subject area in an almost treatise-like decision on the law applicable to contracts in 1820 (*Le Roy v Crowninshield*, 2 Mason 151). On the Supreme Court, the very first decision assigned to him concerned a conflict of laws (*U.S. v Crosby*, 11. U.S. (7 Cranch) 115 (1812)). He went on to author six more and participated in 23 more decisions. His two most important Supreme Court decisions for the discipline, both rendered in 1842, were not technically private international law decisions. Despite this, and although both were later overruled, they maintain crucial relevance for the field and are therefore here discussed individually.

a) Federal common law: Swift v Tyson

Story's most important decision, *Swift v Tyson* (41 U.S. 1 (1842)), claimed the existence of a general common law that trumped state common laws. At stake was a → bill of exchange that was valid under accepted general principles of commercial law but invalid according to New York case-law. Under the Judiciary Act, federal courts had to apply 'the laws of the several states' in common law cases. *Story* limited the term 'laws' to state statutes and rights and titles of a permanent locality, leaving out the common law, in particular contracts. In cases presenting common law questions, federal courts therefore had to decide not on the basis of local case-law but instead on the basis of general legal reasoning. The consequence would be a 'general commercial law' that would not be merely national but actually global, 'not the law of a single country only, but of the commercial world' (*Swift v Tyson* (41 U.S. 1 (1842) at 19)).

Swift v Tyson thus demonstrated both *Story's* nationalism (as opposed to the individual states) and his protection of commercial freedom from state interference, discussed above. The opinion could be viewed as expressing a preference of uniform law (like → *lex mercatoria* or → *ius gentium*) as an alternative to conflict of laws, but that would be an exaggeration. In reality, *Story* was very aware that different states had different common laws. The decision resolved, first and foremost, a conflict between parochial state laws on the one hand and trans-border commercial law, in favour of the latter, at least for federal courts. At the same time, however, it did posit the existence of some universal background law against which local laws are made, in this sense not unlike the European *ius commune*. Although later overruled (*Erie Railroad v Tompkins*, 304 U.S. 64 (1938)), the decision thus remains important.

b) Slavery: Prigg v Pennsylvania

Story's other important private international law decision concerned slavery, one of the most important conflict-of-laws issues in the *antebellum* Republic. Slaves who crossed the border from Southern states (where slavery was legal) to Northern states (where it had been abolished) created complex status questions – could they gain, and then keep, their freedom? Did they lose their status as property? The Constitution provided that slaves who escaped into another state were not thereby free from service but had to be returned (U.S. Const art IV sec 2 cl 3). The federal Fugitive Slave Act of 1793 (An Act respecting fugitives from justice, and persons escaping from the service of their masters, Annals of Congress, 2nd Congress, 2nd Session (November 5, 1792 to March 2, 1793), pp 1414–15, available at <www.ushistory.org/presidentshouse/history/slaveact1793.htm>) provided for enforceability of the clause.

In *Prigg v Pennsylvania* (41 U.S. 539 (1842)), a slave catcher had caught fugitive slaves in Pennsylvania (which had abolished slavery and even had a law declaring most slaves free once on Pennsylvania territory). *Story* held in his favour. Under his → comity approach, *Story* could have declared Pennsylvania free to ignore, within its territory, the slavery laws of other states: '[under] the general law of nations, no nation is bound to recognize the state of slavery', so '[t]he state of slavery is deemed to be a mere municipal regulation, founded upon and limited to the range of the territorial laws' (41 U.S. 611). The fugitive slave clause in the Constitution, however, changed the matter as positive law:

> the clause contains a positive and unqualified recognition of the right of the owner in the slave, unaffected by any state law or regulation whatsoever, because there is no qualification or restriction of it to be found therein . . . the owner must, therefore, have the right to seize and repossess the slave, which the local laws of his own state confer upon him as property. (41 U.S. 612)

Because this was a consequence of federal law, it was up to the federal government to enforce rendition.

Story has been much criticized for his decision, both in his time and today. Abolitionists thought *Story*, who earlier had considered slavery 'repugnant to the general principles of justice and humanity' (*U.S. v La Jeune Eugenie*, 26 F.Cas. 832 (1822)) should have limited slavery. One explanation of the decision is that *Story's* nationalism and interest in maintaining the Union won over his opposition to slavery. Another is that he hoped, by vesting enforcement of the fugitive slave clause in the federal government, he could effectively enable its limitation. Both, however, are political analyses of what was first and foremost the application of the law: *Story* read the fugitive slave clause as an implicit federal conflict-of-laws rule that he, as a judge, had to apply. Decisions over slavery were left to the process of amending the Constitution – which is what happened with the abolition of slavery after the Civil War.

III. Story's influence

1. At the time

The immediate influence of *Story's* treatise influence was tremendous. In the → USA, it instantly became the standard reference for courts and scholars dealing with private international law, and remained so for a long time. The Supreme Court (in a decision not authored by *Story*) explicitly adopted his comity-based approach (*Bank of Augusta v Earle*, 28 U.S. 519 (1839)). Not surprisingly, therefore, *Story* soon had occasion for a second edition (1841) that was not only enlarged (it almost doubled in size) but also contained a number of significant changes. It enabled him to account not just for growing case-law but also for the emerging new European scholarship (much of which was inspired by his treatise) (Kurt Nadelmann, 'Bicentennial Observations on the Second Edition of Joseph Story's Commentaries on the Conflict of Laws' (1980) 28 Am.J.Comp.L. 67–77). In the foreword to the second edition, *Story* announced that he would not have much more to say on the topic; a third edition from 1846 was thus mostly a reprint of the second, containing *Story's* latest edits. Five more editions were published until the eighth edition in 1883. Indeed, the importance of the work can be viewed from the fact that no other similarly comprehensive treatise was published in the USA for more than a hundred years, and when one finally was published – *Joseph H Beale's* (1861–1943) treatise – it was dedicated to *Story*, in memory of the centenary of *Story's* first edition. Around the same time, *Ernest G Lorenzen* (1876–1952) could demonstrate how many of the rules set up by *Story* had survived (Ernest Lorenzen, 'Story's Commentaries on the Conflict of Laws: One Hundred Years After' (1934) 48 Harv.L.Rev. 15, 20–26).

Story's influence was not confined to the USA. His treatise became the first American scholarly treatise to be cited by English courts, and it was indeed cited frequently. In England, unlike in the USA, it spurred a number of treatises on the subject, which, however, were not able to surpass it in importance for a long time. The Commentaries also wielded considerable influence on the law in Canada.

This influence in common law countries may seem less remarkable than the fact that *Story's* treatise was immediately influential in Europe. The German immigrant *Francis Lieber* (1800–1872) sent a copy of *Story's* Commentaries to *Carl Joseph Anton Mittermaier* (1787–1867) in Germany, who promptly reviewed the book extensively in his journal. *Mittermaier* announced to *Story* that a young lawyer from Heidelberg was preparing a translation into German. That translation, though announced by the publisher, never materialized, presumably due to the translator's death. *Story's* treatise spurred the first treatises in Germany: both *Wilhelm Schaeffner* (1815–97) and *Savigny* (→ Savigny, Friedrich Carl von) admitted *Story's* great influence on their own treatises. (For *Wächter* (→ Wächter, Carl Georg von), by contrast, with his own positivist and noncomparative approach, *Story's* work was not relevant.) *Savigny* himself provided, however, a different concept of → comity from *Story's*, and indeed, the many treatises in the field that were published in 19th-century Germany took, doctrinally, a different direction.

In France, *Jean-Jacques Gaspard Foelix* (1791–1853) demonstrated the great impression that *Story's* treatise had left on him not just in a letter to *Story* and a review of his work in his journal ((1834) 1 *Revue étrangère* 758; cf 13 Am. Jurist & L. Mag. 237 (1835)), but also in his own treatise (Jean-Jacques Gaspard Foelix, *Traité du droit international privé*, vol 1 (Joubert 1843)). The influence shows already in the title, in the basis of private international in the idea of comity, and in several specific doctrines – even though *Foelix* remained in the structure of different kinds of statutes. Less influence seems to exist on Italy. A translation of the second edition of *Story's* treatise exists in manuscript but has never, it appears, been published (Kurt Nadelmann, 'Bicentennial Observations on the Second Edition of Joseph Story's Commentaries on the Conflict of Laws' (1980) 28 Am.J.Comp.L. 67, 74). *Pasquale Stanislao Mancini* (1817–88) (→ Mancini, Pasquale Stanislao), the foundational Italian scholar of private international law, was aware of *Story's* work but objected to his theory of comity.

RALF MICHAELS

Story's greatest influence outside the USA existed in Latin America, and it is only here that translations of his treatise were published (see Haroldo Valladão, 'The Influence of Joseph Story on Latin-American Rules of Conflict of Laws' (1954) 3 Am.J.Comp.L. 27). In 1880, *Hilario S Gabilondo* (ca 1849–93) published a Spanish translation in → Mexico (see Kurt Nadelmann, 'Una traducciòn Mexicana de los Comentarios sobre los Conflictos de Leyes de Joseph Story' (1983) 15 *Jurídica – Anuario del Departamento de Derecho de la Universidad Iberoamericana* 221 with republication of the translators' foreword and chapter 2). A more important translation of the eighth edition was made in 1891 in Argentina by *Clodomiro Quiroga* (1838–99). Even earlier, *Story's* treatise had left clear traces in the provisions on private international law of the Argentinian civil code of 1869 (see the synopsis in Haroldo Valladão, 'The Influence of Joseph Story on Latin-American Rules of Conflict of Laws' (1954) 3 Am.J.Comp.L. 27, 34–8) and thereby, indirectly, on private international law in Paraguay, which adopted the code in 1889. Several private international law conventions also demonstrate such influence.

2. *In the long run*

In the long run, *Story's* influence is great though, in many ways, indirect. In the → USA, the so-called → (American) Conflict of laws revolution destroyed not just the formalism of the → vested rights theory but also the classicism of *Joseph Story*. At the same time, contemporary conflict of laws in the USA still shows its roots in *Story's* theories, even though they have altered those considerably. Many specific doctrines in US law – at least outside of contract and tort law, the main *foci* of the American conflict of laws revolution – remain, largely, unchanged. More importantly, perhaps, four of *Story's* foundations remain dominant in US conflicts thinking. First, the idea that laws are, first and foremost, territorial, and that therefore the most important → connecting factors must be territorial as well, is still stronger in the USA than in many other jurisdictions (→ Territoriality). Second, → comity still plays a greater role in the USA than in other legal systems – a greater role in fact than it did for *Story*. Comity has emerged as a broad basis of conflicts decisions: that the application of foreign law is a matter not of obligation is a perspective that permeates US thinking in conflict of laws (→ Foreign law, application and ascertainment). Third (and relatedly), modern interest and policy analysis adopts an idea that *Story* already emphasized at various places, namely that the conflict of laws is about policies and interests and that no nation is obliged to yield its own policies and interests to those of other states. The difference is that *Story* aimed at limiting the reach of such policies, whereas modern → choice of law enforces them. Fourth, for contemporary conflict of laws in the USA, like for *Story*, interstate and international conflicts are treated similarly, and the model is the latter. All in all, despite all changes and evolutions and revolutions, there is still remarkable continuity between *Story* and modern conflict of laws.

This has been somewhat less so in the rest of the world, which is not surprising, given that *Story* wrote against the background of the US federal system. Although *Story* initiated the emergence of the field, the field moved on beyond him. Outside the USA, *Story's* most lasting contribution was, somewhat ironically, the name of the discipline – private international law. *Story* introduced the name almost in passing (Story, *Commentaries on the Conflict of Laws* (1st edn, 1834) § 9, p 9) whereupon it was adopted in Germany via *Schaeffner* and *Savigny* (→ Savigny, Friedrich Carl von) and in France via *Foelix*, while the common law stuck with the original name conflict of laws. Beyond the name, *Story* introduced the specifically private conception of private international law that has come to dominate the field outside the USA. Methodologically, his decision to structure the field alongside areas of the law rather than types of statutes was an early precursor of the modern idea of specialized conflict-of-laws rules.

RALF MICHAELS

Literature

G Blaine Baker, 'Interstate Choice of Law and Early-American Constitutional Nationalism. An Essay on Joseph Story and the Comity of Errors: A Case Study in Conflict of Laws' (1993) 38 McGill L.J. 454; Gerhard Kegel, 'Joseph Story' (1979) 43 RabelsZ 609; Gerhard Kegel, 'Wohnsitz und Belegenheit bei Story und Savigny' (1988) 52 RabelsZ 431; Gerhard Kegel, 'Story and Savigny' (1989) 37 Am.J.Comp.L. 39, translated as 'Story und Savigny' in *Festschrift der Rechtswissenschaftlichen Fakultät zur 600-Jahr-Feier der Universität zu Köln* (Heymanns 1988) 65; Édouard Lambert and JR Xirau, *L'ancêtre américain du droit comparé, la doctrine du juge Story* (Librairie du Recueil Sirey 1947); Ernest G Lorenzen, 'Story's Commentaries on the Conflict of Laws: One Hundred Years After' (1934) 48 Harv.L.Rev. 15 (French translation as 'A propos du centenaire des Commentaires de Story sur les conflits de lois' [1935] Rev. crit.DIP 295); Kurt Nadelmann (ed), 'Extract from Joseph Story's Manuscript "Digest of Law"' (1961) 5 Am. J. Legal Hist. 265; Kurt H Nadelmann, 'Joseph Story's Contribution to American Conflicts Law: A Comment' (1961) 5 Am. J. Legal Hist. 230; Kurt H Nadelmann, 'Bicentennial Observations on the Second Edition of Joseph Story's Commentaries on the Conflict of Laws' (1980) 28 Am.J.Comp.L. 66 (French translation as 'Observations sur la seconde edition des Commentaries on the Conflict of Laws de Joseph Story à l'occasion de son bicentennaire' [1981] Rev.crit.DIP 1; R Kent Newmyer, *Supreme Court Justice Joseph Story: Statesman of the New Republic* (University of North Carolina Press 1986); Joseph Story, *Commentaries on the Conflict of Laws, Foreign and Domestic, in Regard to Contracts, Rights and Remedies, and Especially in Regard to Marriages, Wills, Successions, and Judgments* (1st edn, 1834; 8th edn, Bigelow 1883); William W Story (ed), *Life and Letters of Joseph Story* (2 vols, John Chapman 1851); Haroldo Valladão, 'The Influence of Joseph Story on Latin-American Rules of Conflict of Laws' (1954) 3 Am.J.Comp.L. 27; Alan Watson, *Joseph Story and the Comity of Errors* (University of Georgia Press 1992); Konrad Zweigert, 'Die Gestalt Joseph Story's' (1949) 105 *Zeitschrift für die gesamte Staatswissenschaft* 590.

Substance and procedure

I. Introduction

The distinction between substance and procedure lies at the heart of all major systems of private international law. Matters of procedure are governed by the law of the forum and matters of substance are subjected to the law of the cause of action or obligation, selected by application of the appropriate choice-of-law rule of the forum. The distinction between substance and procedure must also be analysed against the wider context of private international law, whose objectives are the pursuit of uniformity of outcome in decisions of national courts and the discouragement of forum shopping. Such aims are compromised when national systems of choice of law allow too wide a scope for the operation of forum law at the expense of foreign rules. Accordingly, a narrow and limited definition of procedure focusing on the idea of the conduct or regulation of court proceedings is increasingly being adopted by most national and transnational legal systems in recognition of these concerns. In the case of forum law-specific choice-of-law rules, however, there is no need to employ the substance–procedure distinction, since forum law is also the law of the cause of action. It is also important to mention that conventions on uniform substantive law (→ Uniform substantive law and private international law), such as the CISG (United Nations Convention of 11 April 1980 on Contracts for the International Sale of Goods, 1489 UNTS 3), can render the substance–procedure dichotomy redundant by creating autonomous rules on certain matters.

II. Historical development

The rule that forum law governs procedural matters (*lex fori regit processum*) is of great antiquity, having been first pronounced by *Balduinus* of the glossator school in the 13th century. He drew the distinction between norms which the judge used to conduct the proceeding and those employed to resolve the merits of the dispute before the court. Later, European writers continued to follow the distinction which is now the universally admitted position in civil law countries (*Audit*). Common law countries, by contrast, did not adopt the rule that forum law governs procedure until the 18th century and even upon doing so, gave a much wider scope to the concept of procedure, holding that it embraced all aspects of relief and enforcement in a suit (the remedy) (*Huber v Steiner* [1835] 2 Bing 202, 210). Under the common law approach, it was only matters involving the abrogation of 'the right' as opposed to the remedy, which were considered substantive and so could be governed by foreign law. The consequence, therefore, was that a greater range of matters were referred to forum under the common law interpretation of procedure than under the more restrictive civil law view. It is unclear, however, whether the common law right-remedy analysis of substance and procedure has been entirely abandoned and it is arguable that this view still represents the law in Commonwealth countries apart from → Australia and → Canada. By contrast, EU instruments on choice of law such as the Rome I Regulation (Regulation (EC) No 593/2008 of the European Parliament and of the Council of 17 June 2008 on the law applicable to contractual obligations (Rome I), [2008] OJ L 177/6; → Rome Convention and Rome I Regulation) and the → Rome II Regulation (Regulation (EC) No 864/2007 of the European Parliament and of the Council of 11 July 2007 on the law applicable to non-contractual obligations (Rome II), [2007] OJ L 199/40), grant a wide field of operation to the law of the obligation and so implicitly construe procedure in line with the narrow civil law view, for example, see the scope of the applicable law in art 15 of Rome II Regulation and art 12 of Rome I Regulation.

III. The current position and general principles

As described in section II. above, there has traditionally been a divide between civil law countries who adopted a narrow 'mechanics of litigation' view of procedure and common law jurisdictions who favoured an approach based on enforcement and remedy. More recently, however, there are signs of this strict common law/civil law dichotomy breaking down with an approach developed in Australia and Canada that is very similar to that adopted in European civil law countries. Matters affecting the mode, conduct or regulation of court proceedings are classified as procedural but matters affecting the existence, extent or enforceability of the rights and duties of the parties to an action are substantive: *John Pfeiffer Pty Ltd v Rogerson* [2000] 203 CLR 503; *Tolofson v Jensen* [1994] 120 DLR (4th) 289. The effect of this reformulation of the distinction in Australian and Canadian law has been to reduce the number of issues which are regarded as procedural and subjected to forum law. In other Commonwealth jurisdictions, however, including England, → Hong Kong and → New Zealand, the traditional right-remedy approach has been generally maintained (*Harding v Wealands* [2007] 2 AC 1), although in England the impact of EU law has altered the position.

In the → USA perhaps the most widely accepted view is that taken in the 1971 Restatement (Second) of Conflict of Laws (American Law Institute, Restatement of the Law, Second: Conflict of Laws 2d, St. Paul 1971; → Restatement (First and Second) of Conflict of Laws). Under the Restatement (Second) of Conflict of Laws no attempt is made to classify issues according to whether they are substantive or procedural, but instead the focus is on defining the scope of operation of forum law in respect of individual issues. Significantly, however, in determining whether forum law should govern, the Restatement (Second) of Conflict of Laws adopts criteria similar to those seen in the recent Australian/Canadian approach; for example, a provision of forum law will not be applied where its purpose is found to 'affect the decision of the issue' or 'the ultimate result' (Restatement (Second) of Conflict of Laws § 122, comment a.). Where, by contrast, a provision merely concerns 'the conduct of the trial', then forum law should be applied.

The trend in US law to marginalize the substance–procedure distinction is also increasingly seen in recent EU codifications on → choice of law – in particular the Rome I and II Regulations referred to above. The provisions in both instruments dealing with choice of law in matters at the interface of substance and procedure are similar, with the drafters conspicuously excluding matters relating to evidence and procedure from the scope of the Regulations (art 1(3) Rome I Regulation and art 1(3) Rome II Regulation). Instead, certain issues are directly subjected to the applicable law of the obligation. The overall effect of the EU approach is to reduce the scope of forum law, especially when compared to the common law right-remedy approach. Such an outcome is consistent with the intention of the drafters of the EU texts, namely, to promote uniformity of result within the EU and to leave less to depend on national choice-of-law rules. Yet, it is important to note that the scope of Rome I and II Regulation is limited – confined to contractual and non-contractual obligations respectively – which means that choice-of-law issues will continue to arise requiring resolution according to national law principles.

In applying the substance–procedure distinction courts have also had to examine important questions of → classification. First, it is generally accepted among common law courts that when characterizing an issue as substantive or procedural the law of the forum applies, not the law of the cause of action. Hence, in the case of 'self-characterizing' provisions, where the legislature expressly states that a provision in a statute is substantive or procedural, the prevailing view is that where such a provision forms part of the law of the cause of action, it is to be ignored and forum law principles of classification are to be applied to determine its effect.

IV. The principles applied

With these general principles in mind, attention will now shift to examining the application of the substance–procedure distinction to specific issues. The test which will be predominantly employed is that based on the narrow conduct of court proceedings view of procedure, which applies in civil law countries and increasingly represents the preferred approach in common law jurisdictions, as outlined above. The impact of EU law, principally through the Rome I and II Regulations, will also be addressed.

1. Service of process and jurisdiction

It is well established that the manner of effecting service of originating process on a defendant is governed by the law of the forum court. Where, however, service out of the jurisdiction on a foreign defendant is involved the laws of most countries and international instruments (see, for example, the Hague Service Convention (Hague Convention of 15 November 1965 on the service abroad of judicial and extrajudicial documents in civil or commercial matters, 658 UNTS 163) and the European Service Regulation (Regulation (EC) No 1393/2007 of the European Parliament and of the Council of 13 November 2007 on the service in the Member States of judicial and extrajudicial documents in civil or commercial matters (service of documents), and repealing Council Regulation (EC) No 1348/2000, [2007] OJ L 324/79) now also require the forum court to have regard to the law of the country where service is to be effected (law of the country of service).

It is also well established that the rules governing the jurisdiction of a country's courts are procedural and governed by the law of the forum, although on occasion, may require the application of foreign substantive law, for example art 7(1) of the Brussels I Regulation (recast) (Regulation (EU) No 1215/2012 of the European Parliament and of the Council of 12 December 2012 on jurisdiction and the recognition and enforcement of judgments in civil and commercial matters (recast), [2012] OJ L 351/1; → Brussels I (Convention and Regulation)). Two exceptions, however, exist to this principle. The first arises in the case of a jurisdiction or choice-of-court clause whose interpretation and validity is governed by the law applicable to the clause (subject to overriding mandatory rules of the forum). The second exception concerns immunity from jurisdiction under foreign and forum law. Given the severity of the impact of immunity on the rights of the parties – in that no litigation can be brought against the defendant – a substantive classification is warranted. Consequently, immunity under foreign law only applies in the forum if it forms part of the law of the cause of action. In the case of rules of foreign state immunity under forum law, however, because such laws emanate from non-derogable rules of public international law, they must nevertheless be applied as overriding mandatory rules of the forum.

2. Parties to litigation

The question of whether a claimant or defendant has separate legal personality or capacity to sue is substantive, as it directly affects the parties' rights and is governed by the law of the entity's domicile or country of formation. By contrast, the question of whether the claimant or defendant is the type of entity that can be a party to litigation in the forum is procedural and governed by forum law, given its proximity to the conduct of court proceedings. The question of whether the claimant or defendant is the proper party to particular litigation is governed by the law of the cause of action. Consequently, the right of a claimant to sue directly the tortfeasor's liability insurer is substantive and governed by the law of the country creating such obligation. This position also applies under EU law; see art 18 Rome II Regulation. The right of a tortfeasor to recover contribution from another tortfeasor arising from a primary wrong is substantive, as it directly relates to the rights and liabilities of the parties. This position also applies under EU law, see art 15(b) Rome II Regulation. A claimant's right to subrogation is also substantive and governed by the law of the obligation under national law rules (and also under EU law, art 19 Rome II Regulation) as is the issue of vicarious liability (under EU law art 15(g) Rome II Regulation) and the question of whether a right to sue for → damages survives the death of the victim and passes to his or her estate (see again Rome II Regulation, art 15(e)).

An issue which has divided common law courts is the status of a statutory derivative action, that is, a claim brought by a minority shareholder against a company for a wrong done to the company. While some courts have held that the right to bring a derivative action is procedural, others have suggested (correctly) that it is substantive, being intrinsically related to the rights and obligations of the parties: *Konamaneni v Rolls Royce Industrial Power (India) Ltd* [2002] 1 WLR 1269.

3. Judicial administration

Issues concerning the constitution and competence of courts, the rules governing how an action is commenced, rules governing the form and requirements of pleadings, court powers to manage and conduct the proceedings, whether legal representation is required, and the rules governing dismissal for abuse of process are all procedural. Also procedural are the right to a jury trial or a public hearing, whether a party has a right to appeal, and any duty on a claimant to give notice to the defendant before commencing proceedings (at least where a failure to do so does not extinguish the cause of action). The right to recover costs and legal expenses is also best classified as procedural as a tool in the management and control of the litigation process, although some US courts have held the issue to be substantive. Under the → CISG also, some courts have held the right to recover costs and legal expenses to be an item of 'damages' falling under art 74 CISG.

Questions relating to the administration and distribution of a debtor's assets, including issues of priority between creditors, are procedural matters governed by the law of the forum. The rationale for this view is practicality and efficiency, especially where the administration involves large numbers of claims by creditors from different jurisdictions. Authority is, however, split on the nature and status of the right of the creditor who makes a claim to a fund (for example relying on a maritime lien). Some English and Australian decisions have regarded such a right as procedural and not applicable where it arises under the law of the cause of action. Canadian and US courts, by contrast, favour a substantive classification on the basis that the recognition of foreign security interests has little to do with the conduct of court proceedings but impacts significantly on the rights and liabilities of the parties: *The Strandhill* [1926] SCR 680. This view is to be preferred and would likely be adopted in European civil law countries. Under EU law, where a maritime lien arises in the context of a contract, it would likely be one of 'the consequences of a breach' (art 12(1)(c) Rome I Regulation) or if in the context of a non-contractual obligation, it would arguably be a 'measure . . . to ensure the provision of compensation' (art 15(d) Rome II Regulation).

The form and requirements of a judgment and methods of enforcing a court's orders are procedural, as they fall within the rubric of the forum's power of management and control of its proceedings.

4. Evidence

The law of evidence is partly procedural and partly substantive. The issue as to what are the material facts in a given case to prove, such as whether a contract exists, is substantive and governed by the law of the obligation. By contrast, the matter of how the facts in issue are to be proved, including the methods of proof which may be used (whether by oral or documentary evidence) is procedural. The question of admissibility of evidence has been traditionally regarded as procedural in common law countries. Yet in the US and some European civil law countries, there is a noticeable trend in favour of a substantive classification on the basis that a decision as to whether an item of evidence is admissible may have a direct impact on the outcome of the litigation and so should be determined by the law of the obligation. In the case of admissibility of documentary evidence, common law courts have also treated such an issue as procedural. Again in contrast, many European civil law countries appear to take the view that if a document is formally valid according to the law of the place of its execution (*lex loci actus*) then it should be admitted into evidence in the forum. The rationale for such a view is that the parties, at the time of executing the document, are more likely to have the place of execution in mind than the ultimate forum which will adjudicate the matter. EU instruments, such as the Rome I Regulation, take a slightly ambivalent view on the question with art 18(2) providing that a contract or an act intended to have legal effect may be proved by any mode of proof recognized by either the law of the forum, the law of the obligation or the law of the place of execution under which that contract or act is formally valid. Article 11 of the CISG provides an autonomous rule to the effect that a contract to which the Convention applies may be proved by any means, including witnesses.

Common law countries have also traditionally drawn a distinction between extrinsic evidence relied upon to interpret a document and such evidence which adds to or varies the document's terms. The first situation is classified as an issue of interpretation of the instrument and governed by the law of the cause of action but the second case is seen as an issue of admissibility of evidence and governed by forum law. The consequence of this view is that the common law parole evidence rule – by which oral evidence may not be admitted to contradict the terms of a subsequent written agreement – will apply to a contract governed by the law of a civil law country where no such rule exists. Once again, the CISG provides a solution that overrides domestic law: the parole evidence rule does not apply to contracts subject to the → CISG (see art 11 CISG again). By contrast, the position increasingly taken in common law and European civil law countries is to consider the issues of both interpretation and variation to be substantive given their equally clear impact on the rights and liabilities of the parties as they determine the meaning and existence of the terms of an agreement. Article 18(2) of the Rome I Regulation (referred to above) offers some support for a substantive view of the issue.

The issue of → burden of proof was originally considered by common law countries to be procedural, but more recently there has been a movement in favour of a substantive classification, driven by the fact that the question of which party bears the burden of proof can have a plainly outcome determinative effect in certain cases: *Fiona Trust and Holding Corporation v Privalov* [2010] EWHC 3199 (Comm) para. An example is where a claimant can provide no evidence of a right which he or she claims, yet under the law of the obligation which creates the right, the burden of proof would rest on the person denying the right to prevent the claimant succeeding. The substantive analysis is adopted by most courts and commentators in the US (see Restatement (Second) of Conflict of Laws § 133) and in European civil law countries. Under the EU Rome I and II Regulations, the applicable law of the obligation will apply to the extent that it contains, in the law of the obligation, rules which determine the burden of proof. Presumptions are treated in the same manner as the burden of proof at least where they are not linked to the conduct or regulation of the forum court's proceedings in which case a procedural view will be adopted.

A statutory provision which requires that, for a transaction to be enforceable, it must be evidenced in writing has long been regarded as procedural in common law countries. Yet, as this issue clearly affects the rights of the parties and the outcome of litigation, a substantive classification is appropriate – which is the approach taken in the USA and recent decisions in Canada and Australia: *Tipperary Developments Pty Ltd v the State of Western Australia* [2009] 38 WAR 488. The view of European civil law countries is likely to be the same on this issue. Article 11 of the CISG provides an autonomous rule that a contract of sale need not be concluded in or evidenced by writing and is not subject to any other requirement as to form.

The question of whether a witness is competent or compellable to testify is clearly procedural and governed by forum law. Also, issues such as the weight or value to be given to admitted evidence, rights to disclosure, summons against third parties, search and seizure orders, expert reports, the method by which witness evidence is to be received and whether examination of witnesses may occur are all procedural issues as they lie at the heart of the forum's conduct of its proceedings. The Rome I (art 18(2)) and II (art 22(2)) Regulations suggest that this view would also apply under EU law by providing that any mode of proof must be capable of being administered by the forum.

5. Estoppel

The status of the doctrine of → estoppel is more complex. Issue estoppel arises where a particular matter has been decided in earlier proceedings and a party is precluded from raising it in subsequent proceedings and cause of action estoppel (*res judicata*) prevents a subsequent suit being brought on the same cause of action. In respect of both such estoppels it is universally accepted that such matters are procedural and governed by the law of the forum of adjudication. In the context of issue and cause of action estoppel based on a foreign judgment, however, English, US and some Commonwealth courts have accepted that the law of the country in which the judgment was rendered should also be applied to determine whether the judgment was 'final and conclusive' and so eligible for recognition in the forum: *Carl-Zeiss Stiftung v Rayner and Keeler Ltd* (No 2) [1967] 1 AC 853. To that extent, therefore, both the law of the forum and the law of the country of rendition apply.

Other common law estoppels, such as estoppel by representation of existing fact, estoppel by convention, promissory and proprietary estoppel, are best regarded as substantive, given their close connection to the rights and liabilities of the parties.

6. Privilege

Another possible exception to the exclusivity of forum law in the area of taking evidence concerns privilege and other bars on disclosure of evidence. Article 11 of the Hague Evidence Convention (Hague Convention of 18 March 1970 on the taking of evidence abroad in civil or commercial matters, 847 UNTS 241) allows a party to resist disclosure in the context of a request for oral testimony or production of documents where a privilege exists under the law of the requesting or requested states or where there is a duty or obligation not to provide evidence under either or both laws. Article 14 of the Evidence Regulation (Council Regulation (EC) No 1206/2001 of 28 May 2001 on cooperation between the courts of the Member States in the taking of evidence in civil or commercial matters, [2001] OJ L 174/1) is to the same effect. Common law countries have also examined the more general question as to whether lawyer–client privilege should be classified as substantive or procedural and what law should be applied. Privilege has traditionally been seen as a question of admissibility of evidence and governed exclusively by forum law with the result that any privilege available under the law of the cause of action would not be relevant. Query, however, whether this view will continue to apply in countries such as Canada and Australia, where it may be argued that privilege should now be considered substantive, at least where it is likely to affect the outcome of a case.

7. Statutes of limitation

The traditional common law approach to limitation questions was based on the right-remedy view of substance and procedure. Where a limitation provision merely 'barred the remedy' such as where it was expressed in terms such as 'an action shall not be brought except within X period' it was considered procedural and not applicable in the forum where it was part of a foreign law of the cause of action. It was only where the limitation statute extinguished the claimant's action that it was classified as substantive and applied as part of the law of the cause of action. Such a view no longer applies in English law after the Foreign Limitation Periods Act 1984 (c 16) or in Australia and Canada who now treat all limitation provisions as substantive and applicable as part of the law of the cause of action: *John Pfeiffer Pty Ltd v Rogerson* [2000] 203 CLR 503. The law of the cause of action also determines whether a party has a right to an extension of time. The same approach has long applied in European civil law countries and also under EU law: see art 12(1)(d) Rome I Regulation and art 15(h) Rome II Regulation. Note, however, that forum law may still apply where the effect of applying a foreign limitation provision would be to cause the claimant or defendant great hardship or where it would be otherwise manifestly contrary to public policy. Something more than the fact that the forum's limitation period is more generous than the foreign provision is required to establish hardship, however, such as where the claimant was misled by the defendant as to the operation of the provision. Note that the UNCITRAL Limitation Convention (Convention of 14 June 1974 on the Limitation Period in the International Sale of Goods, 1151 UNTS 3; 13 ILM 952) imposes an autonomous rule for limitations in contracts to which the Convention applies.

Time provisions other than limitations by contrast, such as the period for filing a defence or an appeal, are universally regarded as procedural as they fall within the scope of the court's powers to manage litigation.

8. Remedies: non-monetary relief

The position in common law countries has long been that a claimant can only obtain → remedies which are available under forum law. The rationale for this view is that remedies are part of the court's machinery for resolving disputes and it is not practical for the forum to have to implement foreign remedies alien to the forum's traditions and processes. The form of the remedy sought in litigation is therefore a matter of procedure: *Phrantzes v Argenti* [1960] 2 QB 19. Once, however, it is established that the remedy sought exists under forum law and the law of the cause of action it is then for the latter law to determine whether such relief may be granted on the facts of the case. Such a result is consistent with the view that remedies have a direct impact on the rights and liabilities of the parties and so are at least partly substantive. EU law arguably draws a similar distinction with art 15(d) of the Rome II Regulation providing that the law of the obligation applies to 'a measure designed to prevent or terminate injury or damage' and art 12(1)(c) of Rome I Regulation providing that the same law applies to 'the consequences of a . . . breach of obligations' but that in both cases any remedy sought must be 'within the limits conferred by the forum's procedural law'.

a) Interim relief
The traditional position in common law countries is that the availability of all interim measures such as interlocutory injunctions (→ Injunction), freezing or search orders (→ Freezing injunctions and search orders) and → anti-suit injunctions are procedural and hence governed by forum law. Such a view is justifiable where such remedies are integrally related to the conduct of proceedings in the forum. The absoluteness of this procedural classification, however, must now be questioned. First in the case of anti-suit injunctions, where the injunction is sought only to protect the processes of the forum court, a procedural analysis is appropriate but where enforcement of contractual or equitable rights is involved, a substantive classification is more appropriate. The position under EU law is likely to be similar, with art 15(d) of the Rome II Regulation providing that the law of the obligation applies to 'a measure designed to prevent or terminate injury or damage', which would likely be the case with an anti-suit injunction designed to enforce equitable rights. Interlocutory relief is not, however, covered by the Rome I Regulation and so national law rules must apply to cases in which interim relief is sought in relation to contracts subject to the Regulation. In common law countries, where an interlocutory injunction is sought to restrain a breach of contract or a tort, the law of the obligation will be applied to determine whether a breach has occurred at least to the level of an arguable case. Once this is shown, principles of forum law are then applied to determine whether the injunction will be granted on the facts. In the case of freezing and search orders, however, art 15(d) of the Rome II Regulation arguably goes further in applying the law of the obligation, since such orders would seem to be 'measures . . . to ensure the provision of compensation'. The effect of this provision is that provided that such a remedy exists under both the laws of the forum and the obligation, it is for the law of the obligation to determine whether it will be granted in the specific case.

b) Final relief
In common law countries, final non-monetary relief such as orders for specific performance, rescission, declarations and → injunctions have historically been regarded as procedural because they originated in the medieval equitable jurisdiction based on conscience. More recent commentary and the majority of US courts, however, assert that final relief, where closely connected to the merits of the case, should be classified as substantive and governed by the law of the cause of action. Such a view also applies in EU law. Under art 12(1)(c) of the Rome I Regulation, the law of the obligation applies to 'the consequences of a total or partial breach of obligations' (which would include all final remedies in relation to contracts). Likewise, art 15(d) of the Rome II Regulation applies the law of the obligation to a measure designed to prevent or terminate injury or damage. Under both instruments again, however, the remedy sought must be 'within the limits conferred by the forum's procedural law', which requires the form of relief at least to exist within the forum's armoury.

In common law countries, → set-off was historically regarded as procedural while in European civil law countries, a distinction has been drawn between a case where the effect of the defendant's claim of set-off was to discharge or extinguish its liability to the claimant on the original claim (regarded as substantive), and where a cross claim is merely brought by the defendant in the same proceeding (procedural). There has been a recent movement in common law countries, in particular the USA (see Restatement (Second) of Conflict of Laws § 128) to follow the civil law approach. In EU law, it appears that set-off is to be generally classified as substantive without regard to whether it extinguishes the original liability. Article 17 of the Rome I Regulation provides that where the right to set-off is not agreed by the parties, set-off shall be governed by the law applicable to the claim against which the right to set-off is asserted.

RICHARD GARNETT

9. Damages

In the area of → damages for tort and contract, the distinction between substance and procedure has arisen frequently. In common law and civil law jurisdictions it is well established that the issue of available heads of damages (economic loss, physical injury) is classified as substantive and governed by the law of the cause of action. It is also universally accepted that the right to claim interest on a contractual debt is substantive and governed by the law applicable to the contract. A substantive classification also applies in the case of the right to pre-judgment interest, that is, interest by way of damages dating from the time of accrual of the cause of action, although some English courts maintain that the issue is procedural. The classification of the rate of pre-judgment interest has also divided common law courts with Canadian tribunals favouring a substantive view but English courts considering the issue to be procedural. The question of deductibility from an award of damages of benefits already received by the claimant now appears to be accepted as substantive by most common law countries; see *Cox v Ergo Versicherung AG* [2014] 2 WLR 948. European civil law countries, in line with their narrower 'process' idea of procedure, would likely take a substantive view of these questions. All jurisdictions also accept that where general tort law recovery has been abolished by statute and replaced by a no fault administrative scheme then such a scheme is substantive and applicable as part of the law of the cause of action.

Perhaps the most difficult question in relation to damages concerns quantification and assessment. English courts have long regarded the issue of assessment of damages as wholly procedural. Such an approach not only embraces the computational aspect of assessment of, but also the situation where the legislature imposes a cap on damages, unless such a cap is included in a contract. So, for example, if a foreign law of the cause of action restricted damages for non-economic loss an English court could ignore such a limitation on the ground that it is procedural: *Harding v Wealands* [2007] 2 AC 1. While Canadian courts have taken a similar approach, in Australia this view has been rejected with the High Court declaring that 'all questions about the ... amount of damages that may be recovered ... be treated as substantive issues': *John Pfeiffer Pty Ltd v Rogerson* [2000] 203 CLR 503. According to this approach, any issue regarding the assessment of damages is determined by the law of the cause of action. In applying this test, the forum court may receive evidence from foreign experts as to the likely ranges of recovery in the event that the matter went to trial in the foreign country. There is evidence of such an approach also being taken in European civil law countries which suggests a confluence with the Australian position. All jurisdictions would agree, however, that the forum cannot apply a rule under foreign law which requires a body such as a jury or special assessor to conduct an assessment as this would be beyond its procedural powers.

The position taken in European civil law countries and Australia also likely applies under EU law. Article 15(c) of the Rome II Regulation provides that the applicable law of the non-contractual obligation 'shall govern in particular ... the existence, nature and the assessment of damage or the remedy claimed' and art 12(1)(c) of the Rome I Regulation uses similar language in relation to contract. The effect of such provisions is that the available heads of damages and limitations or caps on damages are subjected to the law of the obligation. Further, all questions relating to the award of pre-judgment interest including the right to claim such interest and at what rate, are also so classified. The issue of deductibility of benefits would also likely fall within art 15(c) of the Rome II Regulation as a matter relating to the assessment of damages.

The more complex question again under EU law is whether all issues relating to the assessment of damages are referred to the applicable law. Since both art 15(d) of the Rome II Regulation and art 12(1)(c) of Rome I provide that the forum is only obliged to act within the limits of its procedural powers, a forum court would not apply a rule under foreign law which requires a body such as a jury to conduct an assessment. Yet, in assessing damages under the law of the obligation a court could again receive evidence from foreign experts as to likely ranges of recovery. The position under EU law is therefore close to that which applies in Australia and may be evidence of an emerging global trend. Finally, art 74 of the CISG imposes an autonomous rule for the award of damages in contracts to which the Convention applies.

RICHARD GARNETT

Literature

Edgar Ailes, 'Substance and Procedure in the Conflict of Laws' (1941) 39 Mich.L.Rev. 392; Bernard Audit, *Droit International Privé* (3rd edn, Economica 2005); Adrian Briggs, 'Conflict of Laws and Commercial Remedies' in Andrew Burrows and Edwin Peel (eds), *Commercial Remedies: Current Issues and Problems* (OUP 2003) 271; Alfonso-Luis Caravaca and Javier González, *Derecho Internacional Privado*, vol 1 (6th edn, Editorial Conares 2005); Lord Collins of Mapesbury and others (eds), *Dicey, Morris and Collins on the Conflict of Laws* (15th edn, Sweet & Maxwell 2012); Walter Cook, '"Substance" and "Procedure" in the Conflict of Laws' (1933) 42 Yale L.J. 333; Andrew Dickinson, *The Rome II Regulation* (OUP 2008); James Fawcett and Janeen Carruthers, *Cheshire, North and Fawcett Private international law* (14th edn, OUP 2008); Richard Garnett, *Substance and Procedure in Private international law* (OUP 2012); Reinhold Geimer, *International Zivilprozessrecht* (5th edn, Verlag Dr Otto Schmidt 2005); Martin Illmer, 'Neutrality Matters: Some Thoughts about the Rome Regulations and the So-called Dichotomy of Substance and Procedure in European Private international law' (2009) 28 CJQ 237; Mary Keyes, 'Substance and Procedure in Multistate Tort Litigation' (2010) 18 Torts L.J. 201; David McClean, *International Co-operation in Civil and Criminal Matters* (OUP 2002); Luther L McDougal, Robert L Felix and Ralph U Whitten, *American Conflicts Law* (5th edn, Transnational Publishers 2001); Marie-Laure Niboyet, 'Contre Le Dogme de La Lex Fori en Matière de Procédure' in Tristan Azzi (ed), *Vers de Nouveaux Equilibres Entre Ordres Juridiques Mélanges en L'Honneur d'Hélène Gaudemet-Tallon* (Dalloz 2008) 363; Richard Plender and Michael Wilderspin, *The European Private international law of Obligations* (3rd edn, Sweet and Maxwell 2009); Elsabe Schoeman, 'Rome II and the Substance-Procedure Dichotomy' [2010] LMCLQ 81; Istvan Szászy, *International Civil Procedure: A Comparative Study* (Sijthoff 1967); Janet Walker, *Castel & Walker Canadian Conflict of Laws* (6th edn, LexisNexis Butterworths 2005); Russell J Weintraub, *Commentary on the Conflict of Laws* (4th edn, Foundation Press 2001).

Substitution

I. General outline

1. Concept

Substitution describes a problem that occurs whenever the substantive law applicable by virtue of the choice-of-law rules requires a certain legal act or other legally relevant element (eg notarization) which, in the international scenario at hand, has been accomplished in a foreign legal system (for example, authentication by a foreign notary). Hence, the question is whether this foreign element meets the requirements set out by the applicable law and may therefore substitute for eg a corresponding legal act under the *lex causae* (see, for example, Hans Lewald, 'Règles generals des conflits de lois' (1939) 69 Rec. des Cours 5, 130 *et seq*; Jürgen Basedow, 'Qualifikation, Vorfrage und Anpassung im Internationalen Zivilverfahrensrecht' in Peter Schlosser (ed), *Materielles Recht und Prozeßrecht und die Auswirkungen der Unterscheidung im Recht der internationalen Zwangsvollstreckung* (Gieseking 1992) 131, 148; Erik Jayme, 'La substitution et le principe d'équivalence en droit international privé' (2007) 72 *Annuaire de l'Institut de droit international – Session de Santiago du Chili* 1). Substitution must be distinguished from neighbouring concepts in private international law: first, unlike in the case of adjustment/adaptation (→ Adjustment/Adaptation (*Anpassung*)), substitution only applies to situations where there is no doubt about the applicability of a specific substantive law by virtue of the choice-of-law rules. Second, the fact that substitution only relates to a question of substantive law and does not require a separate operation of choice-of-law rules distinguishes this concept from → incidental (preliminary) questions (see eg Paul Heinrich Neuhaus, *Die Grundbegriffe des internationalen Privatrechts* (2nd edn, Mohr Siebeck 1976) 351 *et seq*).

2. History, terminology and international acceptance

In the context of private international law, the term substitution was first used by *Hans Lewald* (Hans Lewald, 'Règles generals des conflits de lois' (1939) 69 Rec. des Cours 5, 130 *et seq*: 'Le problème consiste dans la question de savoir si l'on peut substituer à un rapport de droit interne, considéré par la loi interne comme condition préjudicielle d'un effet juridique determiné, un rapport analogue du droit étranger'. Cf also Wilhelm Wengler, 'Die Vorfrage im Kollisionsrecht' (1934) 8 RabelsZ 148, 159 *et seq*). Substitution has since that time not only become a well-established concept of private international law (see eg Bernard Audit and Louis d'Avout, *Droit international privé* (7th edn, Economica 2013) paras 379 *et seq*; Pierre Callé, L'acte public en droit international privé (Economica 2004) paras 163 *et seq*; Antoon Victor Marie Struycken, 'La substitution et le principe d'équivalence en droit international privé' (2007) 72 *Annuaire de l'Institut de droit international – Session de Santiago du Chili* 20) but the notion is also subject to a recent resolution of the Institut de Droit International (Resolution of the Institut de Droit International on Substitution and Equivalence in Private international law/La substitution et l'équivalence en droit international privé, Session de Santiago – 27 Octobre 2007 (1ère Commission), see *infra* V.). However, although the underlying problem is universal, not all jurisdictions use the term substitution to describe this phenomenon. Some scholars treat questions relating to substitution as a facet of adjustment/adaptation instead (cf eg Georges AL Droz, 'Regards sur le droit international privé comparé' (1991) 229 Rec. des Cours 370 *et seq*; → Adjustment/Adaptation (*Anpassung*)). Moreover, the concept of substitution is often deemed alien to common law jurisdictions (eg Peter North, in 'La substitution et le principe d'équivalence en droit international privé' (2007) 72 *Annuaire de l'Institut de droit international – Session de Santiago du Chili* 30, does 'not believe that "substitution" is a technique which is recognised in theory or decisions in the English system of private international law'). Still, many problems which are usually treated as questions relating to substitution in civil law systems may also occur in common law jurisdictions: it is, for instance, a general question whether the authentication of a legal act by a foreign notary is to be considered equivalent to the authentication required under national law. In particular, US state legislators and courts often have to substitute the notarization required under the law of a particular US state with an authentication by a notary public from another US state (see eg § 33–501 Arizona Revised Statutes (of 9 January 1956, as amended) and §§ 4(a), 6(a) Uniform Law on Notarial Acts (Uniform Law on Notarial Acts, drafted by the National Conference of Commissioners on Uniform State Laws and approved and recommended for enactment in all the States at its annual conference meeting in its 91st year in Monterey, California, July 30 – August 6, 1982). See as to the details *infra* IV.2.). Similarly, the question if, for example, a foreign polygamous marriage may substitute for the requirement of a 'marriage' laid down in the provision of the domestic law applicable by virtue of the choice-of-law rules is a problem also known to common law jurisdictions (cf with regard to questions relating to legitimacy of children and → succession by children or spouses under various English statutes, eg *Bamgbose v Daniel* [1955] AC 107; *Re Sehota* [1978] 1 WLR 1506. See also Lord Collins of Mapesbury and others (eds), *Dicey, Morris and Collins on the Conflict of Laws*, vol 2 (15th edn, Sweet & Maxwell 2012) paras 17–193 *et seq* and *infra* III.2.).

3. *Neighbouring concepts*

a) Substitution in international administrative law and criminal proceedings

Questions relating to substitution may also occur in the context of, for example, international administrative law and transnational criminal proceedings (see with regard to the influence of foreign proceedings on the limitation of time under national criminal law eg Federal Constitutional Court of Germany (BVerfG), 3 September 2009, [2009] EuGRZ 686; German Federal Court of Justice (BGH), 18 February 2010 [2010] NStZ-RR 177; Higher Regional Court (OLG) of Munich, 7 March 2013 [2013] NStZ-RR 179 and see as to procedural law in general *infra* III.4.). Substitution in the context of administrative law is sometimes also mandated by European Union law. For example, EU banking and insurance regulation is based on the 'single license' or 'single passport' principle. This system allows banks and insurance companies legally established in one EU Member State to provide their services in other Member States without further authorization requirements (cf with regard to (re)insurance companies eg Recital (11) and arts 14 *et seq* Solvency II Directive (Directive 2009/138/EC of the European Parliament and of the Council of 25 November 2009 on the taking-up and pursuit of the business of Insurance and Reinsurance (Solvency II), [2009] OJ L 335/1)). By consequence, foreign banking or insurance licences have to be treated as an equivalent of domestic authorizations and therefore serve as fully-fledged substitutes under national administrative law. Another case of substitution – taken in the widest sense of the term – is the recognition of professional qualifications and diplomas from other Member States: under certain preconditions, qualifications from other Member States have, at least in principle, to be treated as equivalents which may substitute for the national diplomas, qualifications etc required for regulated professions (cf Directive 2005/36/EC (Directive 2005/36/EC of the European Parliament and of the Council of 7 September 2005 on the recognition of professional qualifications, [2005] OJ L 255/22, as amended) and eg case C-19/92 *Kraus v Land Baden Wuerttemberg* [1993] ECR I-1663, paras 17 *et seq*; case C-285/01 *Isabel Burbaud v Ministère de l'Emploi et de la Solidarité* [2003] ECR I-8219, paras 57 *et seq*). The driving forces behind these facets of substitution are the freedoms of the European single market and, in particular, the freedom of establishment and the freedom to provide services. Although the aforementioned issues are a matter of international administrative law, they may also be linked to private international law. This is, for example, the case whenever a cross-border insurance portfolio transfer authorized by the regulatory authority of one Member State affects → insurance contracts to which the law of another Member State is applicable by virtue of the Rome I Regulation (Regulation (EC) No 593/2008 of the European Parliament and of the Council of 17 June 2008 on the law applicable to contractual obligations (Rome I), [2008] OJ L 177/6; → Rome Convention and Rome I Regulation (contractual obligations)) (see as to the details Jan D Lüttringhaus, 'Neue Wege zur internationalen Restrukturierung europäischer Erst- und Rückversicherungsunternehmen. Die Erweiterung des gemeinschaftsrechtlichen Rahmens für grenzüberschreitende Umwandlungen und Bestandsübertragungen' [2008] VersR 1036 *et seq*).

b) Apostille Convention regarding foreign public documents
One of the questions most frequently associated with substitution is whether an authentication by a foreign notary may be treated as equivalent to a domestic notarization. Although the Apostille Convention (Hague Convention of 5 October 1961 abolishing the requirement of legalization for foreign public documents, 527 UNTS 189) applies to 'notarial acts' pursuant to its art 1(c), this international convention does not touch upon the issue of substitution. In respect to its signatory states, the Apostille Convention abolished the legalization procedure and only requires that an apostille is affixed to the document in question by a competent authority of the state where the document originated. However, a foreign notarized document bearing the apostille merely obliges other signatory states to accept the notarization itself as being authentic and prevents them from setting further legalization requirements. By contrast, the Convention does not in any way stipulate an obligation such that notarizations required under the provisions of national private law may be replaced by a foreign authentication. For example, the Apostille Convention does not oblige Germany as one of the signatory states to accept an authentication by a notary from another signatory state as being equivalent to the notarization by a German notary required for the transfer of real estate pursuant to §§ 873, 925 German Civil Code (Bürgerliches Gesetzbuch of 2 January 2002, BGBl. I 42, as amended, henceforth German CC) (cf also *infra* III.1.a)).

II. Comparative law and equivalence as prerequisites of substitution

Hans Lewald already identified the hub of the problems associated with substitution: 'Le problème indiqué peut se poser dans les situations les plus diverses qui, toutefois, conduisent toutes à la question de savoir si les deux rapports en question – le rapport du droit interne et le rapport du droit étranger – peuvent être considérés comme équivalents, problème dont la solution relève, en fin de compte, du droit comparé' (Hans Lewald, 'Règles generals des conflits de lois' (1939) 69 Rec. des Cours 5, 130 *et seq*). Hence, in addition to the notion of equivalence, comparative law (→ Comparative law and private international law) is another instrument indispensable in the process of substitution. First, the substitutability of national legal requirements with foreign phenomena implies that the latter are – at least to a certain extent – functionally equivalent to the former (Heinz-Peter Mansel, 'Substitution im deutschen Zwangsvollstreckungsrecht' in Bernhard Pfister and Michael R Will (eds), *Festschrift für Werner Lorenz zum 70. Geburtstag* (Mohr Siebeck 1991) 689 *et seq*). By consequence, substitution can only operate where the legal act or other legally relevant phenomenon accomplished in a foreign legal system approximately corresponds to the element required under the applicable substantive law. Second, in the process of determining whether there is equivalence, comparative law comes into play as the other key prerequisite for substitution: by comparing the foreign phenomenon to its counterpart initially addressed by the relevant provision of the *lex causae*, it must be ascertained if the foreign element meets the requirements set out by the applicable substantive law (see Hans Lewald, 'Règles generals des conflits de lois' (1939) 69 Rec. des Cours 5, 130 *et seq*; Bernard Audit and Louis d'Avout, *Droit international privé* (7th edn, Economica 2013) para 380). It is only where this question is answered in the affirmative that substitution may take place. This process of assessing equivalence by comparing the phenomenon at hand in both legal systems therefore necessarily raises the question as to the minimum level of equivalence required by the respective rules of the *lex causae*. Hence, the process of substitution also involves the interpretation of the specific provision of the *lex causae* as to whether that provision's aim and purpose allow its requirements to be fulfilled under a foreign law (see eg Jürgen Basedow, 'Qualifikation, Vorfrage und Anpassung im Internationalen Zivilverfahrensrecht' in Peter Schlosser (ed), *Materielles Recht und Prozeßrecht und die Auswirkungen der Unterscheidung im Recht der internationalen Zwangsvollstreckung* (Gieseking 1992) 131, 148; Jan Kropholler, *Internationales Privatrecht* (6th edn, Mohr Siebeck 2006) 231).

III. Examples and common fields of application of substitution

1. Notarization

As already pointed out, the substitutability of a domestic with a foreign notarization is one of the questions most frequently associated with substitution. Some US states, for example, have codified rules regarding the equivalence of notarizations by notaries public from other US states (cf with regard to eg § 33–501 Arizona Revised Statutes *infra* IV.2.). By contrast, → Germany and → France rely on case-law when it comes to determining whether a notarization requirement under their respective substantive law may be substituted with an authentication by a foreign notary. The German BGH (German Federal Court of Justice (BGH), 16 February 1981, 80 BGHZ 76, 78), has developed an equivalence test: a notarization is deemed to be equivalent where the foreign notary has (i) an education as well as (ii) a professional position that is similar to that of a German notary and is, when notarizing a document, (iii) bound by procedural rules that mirror the fundamental principles governing German notarizations. In France, a similar approach is taken (see, for example, Hélène Gaudemet-Tallon, 'La substitution et le principe d'équivalence en droit international privé' (2007) 72 *Annuaire de l'Institut de droit international – Session de Santiago du Chili* 13 *et seq*, who stresses that it is common practice 'd'examiner si les conditions dans lesquelles cet acte a été dressé à l'étranger donnent des garanties équivalentes à celles qu'aurait procurées un acte authentique dressé en France'). As a rule of thumb, in France and Germany, notarizations from 'latin notaries' are usually treated as equivalent to domestic notarizations. The case is different, however, when it comes to, for example, an authentication by a notary public from a US state: French and German courts both refuse to substitute these notarizations for domestic ones by denying equivalence (cf eg Higher Regional Court (OLG) of Stuttgart, 17 May 2000 [2001] NZG 40, 43. See also Pierre Callé, *L'acte public en droit international privé* (Economica 2004) paras 574 *et seq*). However, the Hoge Raad in the Netherlands has, at least in a certain scenario, substituted a domestic notarization with an authentication by a notary public from a US state (cf Hoge Raad du 21 novembre, [1958] Rev.crit.DIP 512).

a) Transfer of immovable property

Where national law requires a notarization as a prerequisite for a valid transfer of title in real estate transactions, a substitution with a foreign notarization is usually denied. For example, §§ 873, 925 German CC, require that the declarations made by the parties regarding the transfer of real property must be notarized and German courts have repeatedly refused to substitute domestic with foreign notarizations (eg Kammergericht (KG) Berlin, 27 May 1986, 1 W 2627/85, [1986] NJW-RR 1462). The situation is similar, for example, in France when it comes to the notarization requirement with regard to mortgages on French soil under art 2417 French Civil Code (Code Civil of 21 March 1804; henceforth French CC) (see Hélène Gaudemet-Tallon and others, 'La substitution et le principe d'équivalence en droit international privé' (2007) 72 *Annuaire de l'Institut de droit international – Session de Santiago du Chili* 14. Cf also Cass civ 1ère [1999] 1 Bull. civ. no 21).

b) Company law issues

As regards the transfer of shares of a German limited liability company, the authentication of the agreement by a domestic notary required by § 15(3) German Companies Act (Gesetz betreffend die Gesellschaften mit beschränkter Haftung of 20. April 1892, RGBl. 477, as amended) may be replaced by, for example, a notarization by a Swiss or a Dutch notary (see eg German Federal Court of Justice (BGH), 22 May 1989 [1989] NJW-RR 1259, 1261; German Federal Court of Justice (BGH), 17 December 2013 [2014] NZG 219; Higher Regional Court (OLG) of Düsseldorf, 25 January 1989 [1989] NJW 2200). However, an authentication by a notary public from a US state is not considered to be equivalent given that the training varies substantially from the education required for 'latin notaries' (cf eg OLG Stuttgart, [2001] NZG 40, 43). Similar rules apply with respect to the notarization of a modification of the statutes of a German limited liability company in Switzerland by a Swiss notary (German Federal Court of Justice (BGH), 16 February 1981, 80 BGHZ 76).

2. Marriage

Where spouses live in a polygamous → marriage entered into under a foreign law, the question arises whether for the purpose of domestic provisions relating to matters such as alimony, → succession or filiation, the various spouses as well as the children born in these relationships should be entitled to alimony payments or may become heirs (cf eg in France Cass civ 1ère [1958] Rev.crit.DIP 110; Cass civ 1ère [1963] Rev.crit.DIP 559; Cass civ 1ère [1980] Rev.crit. DIP 331. See in the UK eg *Bamgbose v Daniel* [1955] AC 107; *Re Sehota* [1978] 1 WLR 1506. See also Lord Collins of Mapesbury and others (eds), *Dicey, Morris and Collins on the Conflict of Laws*, vol 2 (15th edn, Sweet & Maxwell 2012) paras 17–193 *et seq*; Paul Lagarde, 'La substitution et le principe d'équivalence en droit international privé' (2007) 72 *Annuaire de l'Institut de droit international – Session de Santiago du Chili* 27). The same problem occurs in respect to certain social security benefits for spouses in a polygamous marriage (cf with regard to a widow's pension eg *Bibi v Chief Adjudication Officer* [1998] 1 FLR 375; German Federal Social Court (BSG), 30 August 2000 [2003] IPRax 267). It is important to note, however, that most legal systems impose certain limits with regard to the substitutability of a marriage with a polygamous relationship (cf eg Hessisches Landessozialgericht (Hess. LSG), 29 June 2004 [2005] IPRax 43; Cass civ 1ère [1983] Rev.crit.DIP 275. See also Lord Collins of Mapesbury and others (eds), *Dicey, Morris and Collins on the Conflict of Laws*, vol 2 (15th edn, Sweet & Maxwell 2012) paras 17–199 *et seq*).

3. Succession

Substitution may also be mandated at the intersection of → succession and → adoption law. For example, a person adopted pursuant to the rules of a foreign law shall be entitled to inherit under the German substantive law as a 'child' of the deceased (cf § 1924 German CC) only if the foreign adoption is an equivalent to the type of adoption required under German succession law (cf Higher Regional Court (OLG) of Düsseldorf, 5 June 1998 [1999] IPRax 380. Cf also German Federal Court of Justice (BGH), 14 December 1988 [1989] NJW 2197). Another case of substitution in the context of succession may be found in French law: notably, the requirement set out in art 1008 French CC that an heir designated by a hand-written testament must be attributed possession of the estate by an order (*ordonnance*) of the president of a French court can be substituted provided that the will was drafted in the US or in the UK and has, moreover, been subject to a probate judgement. In this scenario, the foreign probate judgment is considered to be an equivalent to the *ordonnance* required under art 1008 French CC (see TGI Paris [1977] Rev.crit. DIP 324; Paul Lagarde, 'La substitution et le principe d'équivalence en droit international privé' (2007) 72 *Annuaire de l'Institut de droit international – Session de Santiago du Chili* 29).

4. Matters relating to civil procedure and the execution of judgments

a) Substitution of requirements under national provision on jurisdiction

The legal technique of substitution is not limited to substantive law but may be applied also in the context of civil procedure and jurisdiction: for example, where § 38(1) German Code of Civil Procedure (Zivilprozessordnung of 5 December 2005, BGBl. I 3202, as amended, henceforth German CCP) is applicable, the (international) jurisdiction of a court of first instance may, *inter alia*, be grounded on an explicit or tacit agreement provided that the parties are merchants. Where one of the parties is from a foreign state, the question may arise whether his status under foreign law meets the requirements set out in § 38(1) German CCP with regard to merchants (cf eg Higher Regional Court (OLG) of Saarbrücken, 13 October 1999 [2000] NJW 671; Higher Regional Court (OLG) of Munich, 23 March 2000 [2001] OLGR 27. Hans Joachim Herrmann, Jürgen Basedow and Jan Kropholler (eds), *Handbuch des Internationalen Zivilverfahrensrechts*, vol 1 (Mohr Siebeck 1982) paras 498 *et seq*).

b) Effects of foreign civil procedures on a statute of limitation
Certain phenomena at the juncture of civil procedure and substantive private law can raise the question of substitutability (eg Jürgen Basedow, 'Qualifikation, Vorfrage und Anpassung im Internationalen Zivilverfahrensrecht' in Peter Schlosser (ed), *Materielles Recht und Prozeßrecht und die Auswirkungen der Unterscheidung im Recht der internationalen Zwangsvollstreckung* (Gieseking 1992) 131, 148 *et seq*). Under German law, for example, the statute of limitation period is suspended by an order for payment (*Mahnbescheid*) issued by a court (cf § 204(1) no 3 German CC). Therefore, it is a question of substitution whether, for example, a foreign order for payment may also trigger the suspension of the statute of limitation period. German courts have at least treated the Swiss *Zahlungsbefehl* as an equivalent of the German order for payment which may therefore substitute for the latter for the purpose of § 204(1) no 3 German CC (see eg Higher Regional Court (OLG) of Cologne, 18 September 1980 [1980] RIW 877; German Federal Court of Justice (BGH), 17 April 2002 [2002] NJW-RR 937). Similar questions of substitution arise, for example, with regard to the effects of a third-party notice before a foreign court on the statute of limitation period in § 204(1) no 6 German CC (see in the context of a third-party notice involving a Dutch court, Imperial Court of Justice (*Reichsgericht*), 20 October 1905, 61 RGZ 390, 393) and, with respect to § 204(1) no 7 German CC, the consequences of foreign proceedings for the preservation of evidence (cf Regional Court (LG) of Hamburg, 15 September 1998, [2001] IPRax 45).

c) Forced execution and substitution
Finally, questions relating to substitution may also arise in the context of forced execution. For example, § 864(2) German CCP applies to forced execution with regard to co-owned → immovable property only in cases of joint tenancy (*Miteigentum*). Moreover, § 740 *et seq* German CCP relate to forced execution in cases where the matrimonial property regime of 'community of property' (*Gütergemeinschaft*) applies to spouses owning immovable property (see Heinz-Peter Mansel, 'Substitution im deutschen Zwangsvollstreckungsrecht' in Bernhard Pfister and Michael R Will (eds), *Festschrift für Werner Lorenz zum 70. Geburtstag* (Mohr Siebeck 1991) 689, 707 *et seq*). Where spouses have immovable property in Germany and their matrimonial property regime is governed by a foreign law, the question may arise whether this matrimonial property regime is an equivalent of the German categories and may therefore substitute for the requirements regarding ownership set out under the aforementioned German provisions on forced execution (see as to the details with respect to the Italian *communione legale* Heinz-Peter Mansel, 'Substitution im deutschen Zwangsvollstreckungsrecht' in Bernhard Pfister and Michael R Will (eds), *Festschrift für Werner Lorenz zum 70. Geburtstag* (Mohr Siebeck 1991) 689, 711 *et seq*). Similar questions arise under the Regulation on the cross-border freezing of bank accounts (Regulation (EU) No 655/2014 of the European Parliament and of the Council of 15 May 2014 establishing a European Account Preservation Order procedure to facilitate cross-border debt recovery in civil and commercial matters, [2014] OJ L 189/59. See Jan D Lüttringhaus, 'Die Europäisierung des Zwangsvollstreckungsrechts im Bereich der vorläufigen Kontenpfändung - Der Europäische Beschluss zur vorläufigen Kontenpfändung und seine Wechselwirkungen mit der deutschen Zivilprozessordnung' [2016] 129 ZZP, 187, 210 *et seq*.).

IV. Codified cases of substitution in national law

Examples of national provisions expressly laying down rules for the substitution of national with foreign legal phenomena are scarce. However, legislators in, for example, Germany as well as in some US states have codified certain cases of substitution.

1. German Pfandbrief *Act, social security law, payment order*

Pursuant to § 18(1) German *Pfandbrief* Act (Pfandbriefgesetz of 22 May 2005, BGBl.

I 1373, as amended), foreign mortgages and land charges are to be treated as an equivalent to the German *Hypothek* and *Grundschuld* under the condition that they provide a comparable security right and that the creditor may satisfy his claim by liquidating the collateral. Moreover, § 13(1) German *Pfandbrief* Act provides that a mortgage may also attach to foreign rights *in rem* under the condition that the foreign rights *in rem* are equivalent to those available under German law. Another example for a codified case of substitution can be found in German social security law: in cases where a provision of German social security law requires a family relation, § 34(1) German Social Code, first volume (Erstes Buch Sozialgesetzbuch (SGB I) of 11 December 1975, BGBl. I 3015, as amended) deems sufficient a family relation that has been legally established under a foreign law applicable pursuant to the choice-of-law rules and which is, moreover, equivalent to the family relations under German law. Finally, the German legislator expressly states that, at least with regard to the suspension of the statute of limitation period pursuant to § 204(1) no 3 German CC, a German payment order may be substituted with a European order for payment issued pursuant to the European → Payment Order Regulation (Regulation (EC) No 1896/2006 of the European Parliament and of the Council of 12 December 2006 creating a European order for payment procedure, [2006] OJ L 399/1) creating a European order for payment procedure.

2. US state law on notarizations in other states

US state legislators and courts often have to substitute the notarization required under the law of a particular US state with an authentication by a notary public from another US state. In light of this, the law of, for example, Arizona expressly provides in § 33–501 Arizona Revised Statutes that '[n]otarial acts may be performed outside this state for use in this state with the same effect as if performed by a notary public of this state' by a certain number of persons authorized pursuant to the laws and regulations of other governments. Similar provisions may be found in other US states as well since they are usually modelled on §§ 4(a), 6(a) Uniform Law on Notarial Acts (cf as to the issues associated with notarization in cross-border scenarios eg T David Hoyle, 'Seal of Disapproval: International Implications of South Carolina's Notary Statute' (2006) 3 SCJILB 1 *et seq*).

V. International conventions relating to substitution

There is presently no international convention dedicated exclusively to substitution. However, certain international instruments also deal with cases of substitution: for example, pursuant to art IX of the Protocol on Uniformity of Powers of Attorney (Protocol on Uniformity of Powers of Attorney Which Are to be Utilized Abroad. Opened for signature at the Pan American Union in Washington, on 17 February 1940, (1953) 161 UNTS 229), which has been adopted by certain Member States of the Organization of American States, 'notaries duly commissioned under the laws of their respective countries shall be deemed to have authority to exercise functions and powers equivalent to those accorded to native notaries by the laws and regulations' of other signatory states (see eg Stojan A Bayitch and José Luis Siqueiros, *Conflict of Laws: Mexico and the United States* (University of Miami Press 1968) 134 *et seq*).

Finally, it is noteworthy that, in the course of its 2007 session in Santiago, the *Institut de Droit International* adopted a resolution on 'Substitution and Equivalence in Private international law' (see as to the details and the initial proposal Erik Jayme, 'La substitution et le principe d'équivalence en droit international privé' (2007) 72 *Annuaire de l'Institut de droit international – Session de Santiago du Chili* 64 *et seq*). This resolution is centred around the definition of substitution and the concept of equivalence (arts 1 and 2 Resolution of the *Institut de Droit International*). Moreover, the resolution provides guidance regarding the process of substitution and the determination of equivalence (arts 3 *et seq* Resolution of the *Institut de Droit International*). However, it is important to stress that resolutions of the *Institut de Droit International* have no binding effect whatsoever but may merely serve as guidelines.

JAN D LÜTTRINGHAUS

Literature

Bernard Audit and Louis d'Avout, *Droit international privé* (7th edn, Economica 2013); Jürgen Basedow, 'Qualifikation, Vorfrage und Anpassung im Internationalen Zivilverfahrensrecht' in Peter

Schlosser (ed), *Materielles Recht und Prozeßrecht und die Auswirkungen der Unterscheidung im Recht der internationalen Zwangsvollstreckung* (Gieseking 1992) 131; Stojan A Bayitch and José Luis Siqueiros, *Conflict of Laws: Mexico and the United States* (University of Miami Press 1968) 134; Pierre Callé, *L'acte public en droit international privé* (Economica 2004); Lord Collins of Mapesbury and others (eds), *Dicey, Morris and Collins on the Conflict of Laws* (15th edn, Sweet & Maxwell 2012); Georges AL Droz, 'Regards sur le droit international privé comparé' (1991) 229 Rec. des Cours 9; Hans Joachim Herrmann, Jürgen Basedow and Jan Kropholler (eds), *Handbuch des Internationalen Zivilverfahrensrechts*, vol 1 (Mohr Siebeck 1982); T David Hoyle, 'Seal of Disapproval: International Implications of South Carolina's Notary Statute' (2006) 3 SCJILB 1; Erik Jayme and others, 'La substitution et le principe d'équivalence en droit international privé' in *Session de Santiago* (Institut de Droit International 2007) 1; Jan Kropholler, *Internationales Privatrecht* (6th edn, Mohr Siebeck 2006); Hans Lewald, 'Règles generals des conflits de lois' (1939) 69 Rec. des Cours 5; Jan D Lüttringhaus, 'Neue Wege zur internationalen Restrukturierung europäischer Erst- und Rückversicherungsunternehmen. Die Erweiterung des gemeinschaftsrechtlichen Rahmens für grenzüberschreitende Umwandlungen und Bestandsübertragungen' [2008] VersR 1036; Jan D Lüttringhaus, 'Die Europäisierung des Zwangsvollstreckungsrechts im Bereich der vorläufigen Kontenpfändung - Der Europäische Beschluss zur vorläufigen Kontenpfändung und seine Wechselwirkungen mit der deutschen Zivilprozessordnung' [2016] 129 ZZP, 187; Heinz-Peter Mansel, 'Substitution im deutschen Zwangsvollstreckungsrecht' in Bernhard Pfister and Michael R Will (eds), *Festschrift für Werner Lorenz zum 70. Geburtstag* (Mohr Siebeck 1991) 689; Paul Heinrich Neuhaus, *Die Grundbegriffe des internationalen Privatrechts* (2nd edn, Mohr Siebeck 1976); Wilhelm Wengler, 'Die Vorfrage im Kollisionsrecht' [1934] 8 RabelsZ 148.

Succession

I. Introduction

While limited in the past to rare instances involving few wealthy individuals, the phenomenon of international successions has become popularized over the last decades.

Several sociological and economic factors have contributed to this development. In the second half of the 20th century, economic growth together with the diffusion of the welfare state and of social security systems led to the accumulation of significant wealth, even in middle-class families. While the present crisis has slowed down this evolution, it did not bring it to a halt. At the same time, internationalization has increased dramatically under the combined effect of the free movement and migration of workers, the globalization (→ Globalization and private international law) of the economy as well as the steady growth of several emerging countries. The diffusion of mass tourism and of low-cost flights also played a significant role: the purchase of a holiday flat abroad – once the luxury of some upper-class families – has become in certain countries a new aspect of the consumer society.

In this framework, courts and legal professionals increasingly face the complexities of cross-border succession cases. International estate planning is also becoming more popular, at least in certain countries.

When it tackled the problem, the European Commission estimated that around 450,000 international successions of an estimated value of 123.3 billion Euros are dealt with in Europe each year.

Notwithstanding this evolution, substantive succession law has not changed significantly. Its sources are still mostly domestic. They reflect a rich variety of solutions, shaped by history and local traditions. Thus, important disparities exist among national laws regarding very central succession law issues, such as beneficiary rights in an intestate succession, the existence of forced heirship rights or other restrictions of the testator's freedom, the admissibility of mutual wills and agreements as to successions, as well as the administration of the estate and the heir's liability for debts.

Notwithstanding this diversity, harmonization efforts at the substantive law level have been scant until now. Only two texts deserve to be mentioned: the Council of Europe Convention of 16 May 1972 on the Establishment of a Scheme of Registration of Wills (CETS No 77), in force in 12 European states, and the UNIDROIT Convention of 26 October 1973 Providing a Uniform Law on the Form of an International Will (available at <www.unidroit.org/instruments/succession>), ratified by about 20 states.

That being so, the search for uniform and predictable solutions is entirely left to private international law. However, significant disparities also exist among the national systems regarding international jurisdiction and choice-of-law issues.

II. Uniform private international law instruments

Until recently, the efforts of unification of private international law rules in the area of successions were not very successful.

The → Hague Conference on Private International Law was very active in this field and elaborated three, increasingly ambitious international conventions. The Hague Testamentary Dispositions Convention (Hague Convention of 5 October 1961 on the conflicts of laws relating to the form of testamentary dispositions, 510 UNTS 175) was ratified by 41 European and non-European states. By contrast, the Hague Estates Administration Convention (Hague Convention of 2 October 1973 concerning the international administration of the estates of deceased persons, 1856 UNTS 5) is in force in only three states (→ Czech Republic, → Portugal and → Slovenia). The most recent Hague Convention of 1 August 1989 on the Law Applicable to Succession to the Estates of Deceased Persons (available at <www.hcch.net>, henceforth Hague Succession Convention), which includes uniform rules on the law applicable to all aspects of an international succession, was ratified by only one state, the → Netherlands, and never entered into force.

In this framework, the adoption of the European Succession Regulation (Regulation (EU) No 650/2012 of the European Parliament and of the Council of 4 July 2012 on jurisdiction, applicable law, recognition and enforcement of decisions and acceptance and enforcement of authentic instruments in matters of succession and on the creation of a European Certificate of Succession, [2012] OJ L 201/107; → Rome IV Regulation) is a very important step towards international uniformity. Even if three EU states (→ Denmark, → Ireland and the → United Kingdom) are not bound by this instrument, the Regulation unifies the rules on conflict of laws and conflict of jurisdictions in 25 Member States of the European Union. This very conspicuous instrument includes more than 80 articles and covers all main issues of private international law that could arise in an international succession case, such as jurisdiction, applicable law, recognition and enforcement of foreign decisions, as well as acceptance and enforcement of foreign authentic instruments. It also institutes and regulates in detail a European Succession Certificate. Many provisions of this Regulation, in particular those relating to jurisdiction and applicable law, enjoy a universal scope of application, ie they apply even to relationships with non-Member States of the EU (art 20 and Recital (30) Succession Regulation); therefore, these rules entirely replace the national private international law rules of the Member States with respect to the issues they cover. By contrast, the provisions of the Regulation on parallel proceedings (*lis pendens* and related actions (→ *Lis alibi pendens*)) as well as those on recognition and enforcement of decisions and authentic instruments are only applicable among the Member States. The Regulation is only applicable from 17 August 2015, to the successions of persons deceased on or after 17 August 2015 (arts 83 and 84).

III. Determining the law applicable to successions: a comparative law perspective

In a global comparative perspective, the national and international rules on the determination of the law applicable to a succession can be classified as part of the unitary system or the dualistic system.

1. The unitary approach

Under the unitary approach, one single law governs all assets belonging to an estate, wherever they are situated. Along the same lines, the applicable law also governs all different aspects of the succession, including the issues relating to the administration of the estate. The unitary approach thus avoids a scission of the succession and the complicated problems related to the simultaneous application of different laws to separate parts and distinct aspects of one single estate.

The systems based on the unitary approach are divided into different subgroups, depending on the connecting factor that is adopted for the determination of the applicable law.

Certain countries submit the succession to the law of the state of the deceased's → nationality at the time of death. This solution was still very common in several EU Member States before the application of the Succession Regulation. It is also adopted in some non-European countries, in particular in → Japan, → South Korea and most Arabic countries. The application of the deceased's national law normally ensures foreseeability and stability as to the rules governing the succession. As a matter of fact, the nationality of a person is generally quite easy to determine and does not change very frequently; in particular, under this system the law applicable to the succession is not affected by a change of the deceased's domicile or habitual residence (→ Domicile, habitual residence and establishment) during his lifetime. However, a difficult question arises when the deceased possessed two or more nationalities. In a world of increased mobility, nationality does not always reflect a serious and substantial link between a person and a state; therefore, this → connecting factor can lead to the application of a law with which there is no significant connection, thereby producing surprising results for the parties involved in the succession.

Other systems of private international law prefer the application of the law of the state of the deceased's last domicile or last habitual residence. This solution, which is followed in several Nordic states, has also been adopted by the Succession Regulation; under art 21(1) of the Regulation, the law applicable in the absence of a choice is that of the last habitual residence of the deceased. This approach is also widespread in Latin American countries, where the relevant criterion is generally the last domicile of the deceased. The most obvious advantage to this solution is that it leads to the application of the law of a country with a real and significant connection not only for the deceased but also for most other persons interested in the succession (members of the family, potential heirs, legatees, creditors etc). Moreover, since the administration of the estate normally takes place, at least in part, at the place of the last domicile or of the last habitual residence of the deceased, these connecting factors often lead to the application of the domestic law of the state of the competent authority, thus avoiding or reducing the instances in which a foreign law is applicable. However, this approach also has its downsides. The most evident drawback relates to the mutability of the applicable law in the case of a change of domicile or habitual residence by the deceased during his lifetime: to avoid this, these connecting factors are sometimes 'corrected' by special choice-of-law rules in order to grant the foreseeability needed for estate planning purposes (in particular with respect to the enforceability of dispositions upon death, see *infra* V.2.). Another shortcoming of this approach results from the practical difficulties linked to the determination of the last domicile or habitual residence where the deceased, during his lifetime, simultaneously lived in different countries.

2. The dualistic or scissionist approach

Dualistic (or scissionist) systems are based on the idea that the succession of → immovable property should be governed by the law of the country where the property is located (*lex rei sitae*, *lex situs*). This reflects the traditional and almost universally accepted application of the *lex situs* to property rights over immovables: in dualistic countries, the → connecting factor of the *situs rei* also covers the issues relating to succession over immovable property. As a consequence, immovable assets situated in different countries are not dealt with as part of one single, unitary estate, but as part of separate estates, each of them being governed by its own law.

Since the application of the *lex situs* to movable property would make the system even more complicated, it has been replaced in the course of history by a unitary connection of movables. Thus, in most scissionist countries the succession of movable property is governed by the law of the state of the deceased's last domicile or last habitual residence. This was the case in → Belgium, → France and → Luxembourg before the application of the Succession Regulation. The same solution is also adopted in most common law jurisdictions as well as in → China, Russia (→ Russian Federation) and several African countries. However, behind this apparent uniformity the concrete solutions may be very different, in particular because of the distinct understanding of the notion of domicile in civil and common law jurisdictions.

A few dualistic countries submit movable property to the law of the nationality of the deceased (eg Monaco and → Turkey) or to the *lex rei sitae* (eg the state of Massachusetts in the → USA and → Uruguay).

The scission of the deceased's estate which results from the application of the *lex situs* and from the dualistic approach raises difficult problems and is often perceived as the most serious drawback of the scissionist approach. The shortcomings of a scission of the succession are particularly evident when the substantive rules on succession under the governing laws are based on the consideration of the estate as a whole. This is for instance the case when one of the applicable laws provides for forced heirship rights, the calculation of which requires an assessment of the value of the entire estate and all financial provisions made by the deceased in favour of his/her close relatives. A unitary approach is also desirable when the issue at stake is the validity of a will or another *mortis causa* disposition by which the testator intended to dispose of the whole of the estate or assets situated in several countries. In such instances, the application of different laws to the individual assets belonging to the deceased's estate may lead to improper results and even cause injustice. To avoid this, some dualistic systems use correction mechanisms to overcome the undesirable effects of a scission.

IV. The corrections of the main connecting factor

In many jurisdictions, irrespective whether they are based on a unitary or dualistic approach, the → connecting factors adopted for the determination of the law applicable to the succession are subject to several exceptions. These have different goals; sometimes they are used to correct the improper results of a scission.

1. The doctrine of renvoi

Many private international law systems recognize, to some extent, the doctrine of → *renvoi*. It is worth mentioning that the *renvoi* doctrine was first developed both by French and English courts in succession cases.

Some jurisdictions accept *renvoi* very broadly and do so also in the area of successions: this is for instance the case in → France, → Germany, → Italy and in several common law jurisdictions. In other jurisdictions, which are more reticent to accept *renvoi*, this doctrine is sometimes specifically followed in the area of successions: an example is Swiss law (see art 91(2) Swiss Private international law Act (Bundesgesetz über das Internationale Privatrecht of 18 December 1987, RS 291, henceforth Swiss PILA)). This is due to the fact that *renvoi* is supposed to promote international uniformity of solutions, a goal which is often regarded as paramount in the area of international successions.

It is therefore not surprising that – contrary to all other existing European regulations in the field of conflict of laws – the Succession Regulation adopts the *renvoi* doctrine. Under art 34(1) of the Regulation, *renvoi* is first relevant when it leads to the application of the law of the forum or the law of another Member State (letter a); it must also be followed when it leads to the law of a third state, provided that this state considers its own law as applicable to the case at hand (letter b). As compared to some national systems, which limit the application of *renvoi* to cases where this leads to the application of the → *lex fori* ('reference back'; eg → Spain), the solution in the Regulation is very '*renvoi*-friendly'. According to Recital (57), the underlying purpose is 'to ensure international consistency'.

A difficult problem arises when all states concerned by the succession are prepared to apply *renvoi*. To put an end to the resulting vicious circle, the courts can either accept the 'reference back' resulting from the foreign *lex causae* and thus apply the substantive rules of their domestic law ('simple *renvoi*'), or they can follow the solution, which would be adopted by the courts of the other state concerned ('double *renvoi*' or 'foreign court theory'). The first solution is more frequently adopted in civil law jurisdictions, whereas the second one – more consistent with the goal of promoting international uniformity – is typical of common law jurisdictions. The Succession Regulation is silent in this respect.

The *renvoi* doctrine can also lead to a result, which alters the fundamental choices of a unitary or dualistic system. Thus, in a unitary system, *renvoi* can lead to a scission of the succession ('imported scission'), whereas in a dualistic system it can favour a unitary solution. In some national systems, the *renvoi* doctrine is followed in the field of successions only when it preserves (or re-creates) the unity of the succession. This ingenious solution was adopted by the Spanish and French courts (Tribunal supremo, 15 November 1996, *Lowenthal*; 21 May 1999, *Denney*; 23 September 2002, *François Marie James W*; Cass, 11 February 2009, *Riley* [2009] Rev.crit.DIP 512), as well as by the Belgian legislator (art 78(2) of the Belgian Private international law Act (Wet houdende het Wetboek von international privaatrecht/Code de droit international privé of 16 July 2004, BS 27 July 2004, pp 57344, 57366)). The Succession Regulation has not endorsed this particular use of *renvoi*; it seems, therefore, that the latter can lead to a scission of the succession, and this in contradiction with the unitary approach followed by the European legislator.

2. The escape clause

In most national private international law systems, the choice-of-law rules relating to successions are 'hard-and-fast rules', based on the application of the 'rigid' connecting factors mentioned above (domicile, habitual residence (→ Domicile, habitual residence and establishment), nationality, *situs rei*). Even in those common law jurisdictions in which the determination of the applicable law is normally based on rules involving a certain measure of court discretion (such as the USA), a 'flexible' approach is only rarely used in the area of successions. Similarly, in civil law jurisdictions, like → Switzerland, where all choice-of-law rules are subject to a general → 'escape clause' (see art 15 Swiss PILA), this mechanism has not been used so far to derogate from the normal connecting factors adopted for succession.

The main reason, which is often advanced in favour of such a rigid approach, is that predictability is particularly important in successions law. In particular, it is argued that efficient estate planning is only possible when the would-be deceased is capable of anticipating the law that will govern his/her estate.

This is certainly true. However, even the traditional connecting factors used in this area of law do not always grant predictability, the main reason being that they can change during the lifetime of the would-be deceased. Legal certainty is particularly threatened when the relevant connecting factor is the last domicile or the last habitual residence of the deceased, since these factors can easily be modified before death. That being so, a limited degree of judicial discretion in the determination of the applicable law is not necessarily incompatible with the specific needs of international successions.

It is therefore not surprising that escape clauses have been included in the most important uniform law instruments elaborated in this area, ie the Hague Succession Convention (see art 3) and the Succession Regulation. In particular, art 21(2) of the Regulation allows the competent authority to derogate from the application of the law of the state of the last habitual residence of the deceased when 'it is clear from all the circumstances of the case that, at the time of death, the deceased was manifestly most closely connected' with a different state. This provision should, however, be used only 'in exceptional cases', eg 'where . . . the deceased had moved to the State of his habitual residence fairly recently before his death and all the circumstances of the case indicate that he was manifestly more closely connected with another State' (see Recital (25)).

V. Party autonomy

→ Party autonomy is traditionally accepted in several fields of private international law, such as contracts and → matrimonial property regimes. Its application to the area of successions is the result of a much more recent development.

With some notable exceptions (eg Switzerland: see arts 87 and 90 Swiss PILA), most countries previously rejected the idea that the would-be deceased could choose the law applicable to the succession, considering that such a choice could be abused for the purpose of evading mandatory rules, in particular forced heirship rights. In recent times, however, awareness has grown regarding the benefits of a limited recognition of party autonomy. In particular, when the deceased had designated the law governing his succession, the chosen law remains applicable notwithstanding a subsequent change of domicile, habitual residence or nationality, thus granting the stability and predictability required for efficient estate planning.

That being so, the Hague Succession Convention of 1989 and certain national private international law legislations recognized in the course of the last decades a limited right to select the applicable law. Contrary to the extensive freedom of choice recognized for contracts or → trusts, the available options generally only include the laws of countries having a close connection to the deceased and/or the estate, such as the countries of the deceased's → nationality or his/her habitual residence or, less frequently, the country where the estate's assets are located. Moreover, certain private international law systems (such as those of Belgium, Italy and Quebec) limit the testator's freedom, providing that the choice of law cannot derogate from mandatory forced heirship rules of the otherwise applicable law.

The Succession Regulation also allows for the choice of the applicable law (art 22) in order to 'enable citizens to organize their succession in advance' (Recital (38)). The only available choice is that of the law of the would-be deceased's national state (or states, in the case of multiple nationalities). However, no specific limitation is provided with the purpose of protecting forced heirship rights: only public policy can be invoked to that effect, if and when the exclusion of the deceased's close relatives from the estate amounts to a violation of a fundamental principle of the forum.

In jurisdictions where → choice of law is allowed, it must be made in the form required for a valid disposition upon death. In general the choice is included in a will or in an agreement as to succession ('*pacte successoral*'). In some systems, a tacit choice is also possible provided that it is demonstrated by the terms of a *mortis causa* disposition (see art 22(3) of the Succession Regulation, and the decision of the Swiss Federal Court, ATF 125 III 35). If this is the case, the reference to specific rules, legal notions or institutions of a certain system of law can be construed as a tacit choice of that law (eg the constitution of a testamentary trust can in some circumstances be interpreted as an indication of the intention to submit the estate to the law of a common law jurisdiction).

In systems based on a unitary approach, the law designated by the deceased is normally applicable to the whole of the estate: this is in principle the case under art 22(1) of the Succession Regulation. However, certain national systems allow a voluntary scission, whereby the law applicable to only a part of the estate or different laws for separate parts of the estate are selected. Under Swiss law, for example, a Swiss citizen domiciled abroad can submit, to Swiss law, the whole of the estate or only the part that is situated in Switzerland (art 87(2) Swiss PILA). Such a *depeçage* brings about all the complexities of a scission. Following the model of the Hague Succession Convention (see art 11), arts 24(2) and 25(3) of the Succession Regulation allow for a partial choice of law, the effects of which are limited to issues of admissibility and substantive validity of a disposition upon death; in this case, all other issues remain subject to the law designated by the objective conflict rules.

The → choice of law may sometimes have an impact on jurisdiction. Under Swiss law, for instance, Swiss courts automatically have jurisdiction when a Swiss citizen domiciled abroad chooses Swiss law (art 87(2) Swiss PILA). The Succession Regulation provides for a much more complex mechanism, the purpose of which is 'to ensure that the authority dealing with the succession will . . . be applying its own law': under art 5, the 'parties concerned' (ie the heirs, legatees etc) can confer jurisdiction to the court(s) of the state whose law was designated by the would-be deceased as applicable to the succession. This means that the choice of law by the would-be deceased can be combined with a choice-of-court agreement entered into by the parties to the proceedings.

VI. The scope of the law applicable to the succession

1. Succession and administration of the estate

Significant differences exist with respect to the scope of the law applicable to the succession. In common law jurisdictions, a clear-cut difference is made between the succession and the administration of the estate. The law applicable to the succession (ie the *lex situs* for immovables and the *lex domicilii* for movables) only governs the issues relating to the determination of heirs, legatees and other beneficiaries of the estate: this includes *inter alia* the rules on intestate succession, all issues relating to the validity and effects of dispositions upon death, as well as the right of family members and dependents to request a proper financial provision. On the other hand, the administration of the estate is always governed by the *lex fori*: this includes all issues concerning the appointment and the powers of a personal representative of the estate, the collection and administration of the assets, the payment of the creditors and the distribution of the property to the heirs. The application of internal law to these issues is justified by the fact that they are dealt with in the framework of the probate procedure, which takes place under the close supervision of the courts.

By contrast, unitary systems tend to submit all issues relating both to the devolution and the administration of the estate to one single law. This approach is typical of civil law jurisdictions, which generally do not provide for an 'organized', court-driven procedure for the administration of the estate, but confer administration rights and liabilities to the heirs ('*saisine*' system). The Succession Regulation exemplifies this well. According to its art 23, the law designated by the choice-of-law rules of the Regulation (ie the law of the last habitual residence, the law which is most closely connected or the law chosen by the would-be deceased) governs the succession as a whole; it does not only determine the rights of heirs, legatees and other beneficiaries, but also governs all issues relating to the transfer and the administration of the properties, the liability for debts under the succession and the division of the estate. This solution successfully avoids *dépeçage*, but the court may still have to adapt the measures provided by a foreign succession law to the procedural framework of the *lex fori*, a task which can be quite challenging.

Other unitary systems are less draconian and provide that certain specific issues relating to the administration of the estate are subject to a law other than that which is applicable to the succession. In particular, it is quite common that specific procedural measures relating to the appointment of an administrator or liquidator of the estate, or relating to the inventory of the assets, are entirely governed by the law of the forum (this is for instance the case in Swiss law under art 92(2) Swiss PILA). In certain systems, questions relating to the transfer of property to the heirs (Germany) or the functioning of the community of heirs (France) may be subject to the law of the location of the property.

2. Dispositions upon death

In many legal systems, dispositions upon death are governed by the law applicable to the succession determined at the moment of death. This means that the validity and effects of a disposition, which was presumably established in conformity with the law that would have been applicable to the succession at the time of the disposition (eg the law of the would-be deceased's habitual residence at the time of the disposition), might be submitted after death to a different law (eg the law of the deceased's habitual residence at the time of death). Such a discrepancy can lead to unexpected results and represents a serious obstacle to efficient estate planning.

To avoid this, several private international law systems provide for special choice-of-law rules aimed at ensuring the validity of dispositions upon death. These special provisions typically provide for the submission of *mortis causa* dispositions to the law that would have governed the succession if the person who made the disposition had died on the day when the disposition was made (this is the so-called 'hypothetical' succession law; in German, '*Errichtungsstatut*').

Sometimes, such specific rules only apply to agreements as to succession, as is the case under the Hague Succession Convention (see art 9(1)) and under Swiss law (art 95(1) Swiss PILA). More frequently, they also cover wills and other dispositions upon death, as is the case under the Succession Regulation (art 24(1) and 25(1) and (2)).

This prevents a change of the applicable law after the establishment of a disposition upon death and thus preserves the latter's validity. Normally, it only applies to the admissibility and substantive validity of *mortis causa* dispositions and to some specific effects thereof, such as their binding character. By contrast, all other issues relating to the succession are still governed by the law determined at the time of death (in particular, this is the case of forced heirship rights): this *dépeçage*, which could raise complicated classification and adaptation issues, is the main downside of this solution.

Several systems also allow for a limited choice of the law governing dispositions upon death. This is a partial choice, which only concerns the admissibility or substantive validity of the *mortis causa* disposition without affecting the law applicable to the other issues under the succession (see art 11 of the Hague Succession Convention, arts 24(2) and 25(3) Succession Regulation and art 95(2) Swiss PILA). Therefore, it must be distinguished from a choice of the law applicable to the succession as a whole.

Specific rules sometimes regulate the admissibility of bilateral succession agreements and mutual wills. These particular dispositions upon death relate to the estate of two or more persons and these may be governed by different laws; in particular, this is the case when these persons have their domicile or habitual residence in different countries, or the nationality of different states. It is possible therefore that the disposition at hand is valid under one of these laws but void under the other. The most common solution is then to submit the admissibility of such dispositions to the cumulative application of the law governing the succession of all persons concerned, subject to a choice of law by the parties (see art 10 of the Hague Succession Convention; art 25(2) of the Succession Regulation; art 95(3) Swiss PILA).

With respect to the formal validity of dispositions upon death, the Hague Testamentary Dispositions Convention provides for alternative → connecting factors, with the consequence that a will is valid when it complies with the formal requirements (→ Formal requirements and validity) of at least one of several laws (the *lex loci actus*; the laws of the nationality, of the domicile and of the habitual residence of the testator at the time of the disposition or at the time of death; the law of the location of immovable property). Under some national systems, this solution aimed at favouring the formal validity of the disposition has been extended to succession agreements and other dispositions upon death (see art 26(4) of the Introductory Act to the German Civil Code (Einführungsgesetz zum Bürgerlichen Gesetzbuche of 21 September 1994, BGBl. I 2494, as amended) and art 93(2) Swiss PILA). The same solution has also been adopted by art 27 of the Succession Regulation.

3. Other specific rules

Specific rules are sometimes needed to tackle particular issues relating to a succession for which the applicable law cannot provide a satisfactory answer.

This is for instance the case of *commorientes*, ie 'where two or more persons whose successions are governed by different laws die in circumstances in which it is uncertain in what order their deaths occurred, and where those laws provide differently for that situation or make no provision for it at all' (art 32 Succession Regulation). Failing a solution based on the law(s) applicable to the succession, the Succession Regulation provides for a material rule pursuant to which 'none of the deceased persons shall have any rights to the succession of the other or others'.

A specific rule is provided in some private international law systems to determine the rights on *bona vacantia* when, under the law applicable to the succession, there is no heir and no other person is entitled to the estate properties. In certain legal systems, the state or another public law entity is entitled to the assets as a sort of 'necessary' heir in the absence of a will and of other relatives of the deceased. By contrast, in other jurisdictions the state has the right to appropriate the *bona vacantia* situated on its territory, even if the succession is governed by a foreign law. In case of conflict between competing claims of different states based on such rules, priority is most frequently given to the state where the properties are located (see art 33 Succession Regulation; on the relationship between the law applicable to the succession and the law governing real property rights → Immovable property).

4. Issues outside the scope of the law applicable to the succession

The law applicable to the succession only governs issues which can be characterized as pertaining to succession law. By contrast, it does not regulate questions pertaining to other areas of law, although these may also arise in the framework of a succession or be closely related to it.

Thus, the law applicable to the succession does not govern the status of a natural person nor the family relationships between the deceased and his/her relatives (see art 1(2)(a) Succession Regulation), although the existence and the validity of such status and relationships can become relevant as incidental questions for the purpose of determining the beneficiaries of inheritance rights (→ Incidental (preliminary) question).

The law applicable to the succession does not necessarily govern the matrimonial property regime (art 1(2)(d) Succession Regulation), even though the substantive rules in these two areas of law are often closely interrelated. Thus, the financial provisions included in a marriage contract in favour of the surviving spouse are generally regarded as pertaining to the law applicable to the matrimonial property regime; however, the possible claims of the beneficiary of forced heirship rights against the surviving spouse depend on the law governing the succession.

A simultaneous application of different laws to related issues is also provided for in many jurisdictions with respect to 'claw-back' claims, which can be directed toward the beneficiaries of gifts or other *inter vivos* property dispositions in case of violation of forced heirship rights. Such claims are governed by the law applicable to the succession, even though a different law governs the validity and effects of the *inter vivos* disposition (see art 1(2)(g) Succession Regulation and its Recital (14); see also art 15(c) of the Hague Trust Convention (Hague Convention of 1 July 1985 on the Law Applicable to Trusts and on their Recognition, 1664 UNTS 311)).

VII. Jurisdictional issues

In most private international law systems, the jurisdiction of courts and other authorities

ANDREA BONOMI

in succession matters is largely influenced by the solutions adopted for the → choice of law issues.

Thus, the choice for a unitary or dualist approach generally affects the extension of the court's jurisdiction: in a unitary system, the competent court's jurisdiction will normally cover the entire estate, including assets situated abroad, while in a dualistic system the extension of jurisdiction will vary depending on the nature and location of the assets. In particular, in most common law jurisdictions, the mandatory application of the *lex situs* to the succession over immovables is made effective through the allocation of exclusive jurisdiction to the courts of the *situs*. Conversely, the courts of these countries are often deprived of jurisdiction over foreign immovables because these are governed by a foreign law. The same approach is followed in some dualistic civil law systems (such as French law before the application of the Succession Regulation).

However, a comparative law overview (→ Comparative law and private international law) reveals that the jurisdictional grounds for succession matters do not always entirely coincide with, and are generally broader than, the connecting factors used for the determination of the applicable law. Therefore, in many systems, courts may have jurisdiction on an international succession case even though the choice-of-law rules lead to the application of a foreign law.

The German and Italian systems were illustrative: in these countries (before the application of the Succession Regulation), the deceased's national law was, in principle, applicable to the succession. However, the jurisdiction of local courts in an international succession case could be based not only on the deceased's → nationality but also – *inter alia* – on his/her last domicile and on the location of a part of the assets. When a German or Italian court had jurisdiction based on one of these grounds, it would have to apply a foreign law to the succession.

This is also true in some common law jurisdictions. In these systems, the succession over movable property is governed by the law of the deceased's last domicile. However, in England and other common law countries, a probate procedure is normally started when there is local property (including movable property) to be administered, even if the deceased's domicile was abroad. In such a case, the beneficiaries of inheritance rights will have to be determined in accordance with the foreign *lex domicilii*.

Under the Succession Regulation, jurisdiction is also quite broad. The jurisdiction of a Member State's courts can be based not only on the deceased's last habitual residence, but also, when the last habitual residence was not in a Member State, on the location of estate assets (both movables and immovables). In this case, the court's jurisdiction covers the entire succession (including assets situated abroad) when the deceased had the nationality of that Member State or, failing that, had in that State a previous habitual residence in the five years preceding the moment when the court is seized (art 10(1) Succession Regulation). Failing that, the court's jurisdiction is restricted to local assets (art 10(2) Succession Regulation).

In order to limit the jurisdictional reach of the courts, common law jurisdictions can make use of *forum non conveniens*. In civil law systems, specific rules may be used by the courts to decline jurisdiction over foreign immovables when these are subject to the exclusive jurisdiction of a foreign court (see art 86(2) Swiss PILA) or, more generally, over assets located abroad when it can be expected that the local decision will not be recognized in the foreign country (see art 12 Succession Regulation). Apart from these rules, the general mechanisms of international *lis pendens* and related actions are available in certain jurisdictions to avoid parallel proceedings (see arts 17 and 18 Succession Regulation, which are, however, only applicable among Member States).

Recognition and enforcement of foreign decisions relating to succession matters are normally subject to the general rules. The rules provided to this effect in the Succession Regulation (ch IV) are similar to those applicable under the Brussels I Regulation (Regulation (EC) No 44/2001 of 22 December 2000 on jurisdiction and the recognition and enforcement of judgments in civil and commercial matters, [2001] OJ L 12/1; → Brussels I (Convention and Regulation)).

From a practical point of view, authentic instruments (such as notarial acts) and succession certificates are very important in the area of successions. These documents are used in many jurisdictions for several purposes (dispositions upon death, acceptance or waiver of the inheritance, establishment of an inventory, non-contentious sharing of the estate, proof of an heir's status, proof of an executor's or administrator's powers). Their circulation is not always granted because of the existing disparities with respect to the modalities of their establishment. Only few national systems have specific rules relating to recognition of such documents (for an example, see art 96 Swiss PILA). The Succession Regulation grants among the Member States the 'acceptance' of the evidentiary effects of authentic acts (art 59 Succession Regulation) and regulates in detail the issuing and effects of the European Certificate of Succession (ch VI).

ANDREA BONOMI

Literature

Andrea Bonomi, 'Successions internationales: conflits de lois et conflits de juridictions' (2010) 350 Rec. des Cours 71; Andrea Bonomi and Patrick Wautelet, *Le droit européen des successions. Commentaire du Règlement No. 650/2012 du 4 juillet 2012* (Bruylant 2013); François Boulanger, *Droit international des successions: nouvelles approches comparatives et jurisprudentielles* (Economica 2004); Tim Brandi, *Das Haager Abkommen von 1989 über das auf die Erbfolge anzuwendende Recht* (Duncker und Humblot 1996); Angelo Daví, 'Riflessioni sul futuro diritto internazionale privato europeo delle successioni' [2005] Riv.Dir.Int. 297; Eva-Maria Derstadt, *Die Notwendigkeit der Anpassung bei Nachlassspaltung im internationalen Erbrecht* (Nomos 1998); Heinrich Dörner, 'Internationales Erbrecht, art 25, 26 EGBGB' in Karl-Dietrier Albrecht and others (eds), *J. von Staudingers Kommentar zum Bürgerlichen Gesetzbuch* (Sellier – de Gruyter 2007); Anatol Dutta, 'Succession and Wills in the Conflict of Laws on the Eve of Europeanisation' [2009] RabelsZ 547; Murad Ferid, 'Le rattachement autonome de la transmission successorale en droit international privé' (1974) 142 Rec. des Cours 71; Atle Grahl-Madsen, 'Conflict between the Principle of Unitary Succession and the System of Scission' [1979] ICLQ 598; Georges Khairallah and Mariel Revillard (eds), *Droit européen et international des successions: le règlement du 4 juillet 2012* (Defrénois 2013); Paul Lagarde, 'Les principes de base du nouveau règlement sur les successions' [2012] Rev.crit.DIP 691; Haopei Li, 'Some Recent Developments in the Conflict of Law of Succession' (1990) 224 Rec. des Cours 9; Mariel Revillard, *Droit international privé et communautaire: pratique notariale* (7th edn, Répertoire Defrénois 2010); Eugene Scoles, 'Choice of Law in Family Property Transactions' (1988) 209 Rec. des Cours 9.

Surrogacy

I. Concept and kinds

Surrogacy is a practice to which couples resort when the female partner is unable to carry a baby, or when gay couples and single men aim to be parents on their own. These commissioning couples or single parents (the intended parents) reach an arrangement with a woman (the surrogate mother) who will get pregnant and will hand over the baby to the intended parents once she gives birth, renouncing parental rights to the child.

Heterosexual couples may resort to surrogacy in order to have biologically linked (to both) children, when the female partner only suffers from uterine infertility. By means of assisted reproductive technology (henceforth ART), an embryo is created from the female eggs fertilized with the semen of the male partner, either naturally, through artificial insemination, or *in vitro*. The embryo is then transferred to the womb of the surrogate mother. The surrogate mother does not share biological links with the baby. She just agrees to a sort of 'womb renting'. This practice is known as gestational surrogacy. In the other cases, ie when the woman is wholly infertile or when there is no intended mother, the male partner of the heterosexual couple, or the single intended father, or any of the intended parents if they are both males, provides his gametes for the fertilization of a female donor's eggs. This donor can be a woman different to the carrier (again, gestational surrogacy), but the surrogate mother herself can also supply the genetic material (genetic surrogacy or surrogate motherhood). In all these situations, the employment of the genetic material of the intended father (or one of them, in case they are a couple) makes it possible to have biologically related (to the male or one of the males) offspring. The surrogate mother may act on a profit basis (commercial surrogacy), or just on grounds of sympathy or compassion for a friend or familiar (altruistic surrogacy).

Human ART techniques are sometimes also used by same-sex female marriages or partnerships, in which one of the women gets pregnant and gives birth to a baby who is genetically linked to the other woman and a male donor. But, as in these cases the carrier (surrogate mother) coincides with (one of) the intended mothers, there is no surrogacy practice properly speaking.

Surrogate parenting is not a recent phenomenon (a reference can be found in the Bible, Genesis 30:1–30:3), but it has extensively expanded since the late 1970s. Diverse factors have triggered the growth, such as the development of human ART, the ease of international travel and the worldwide dissemination and availability of information, essentially by means of the Internet. These elements, together with the diversity of the state legal approaches to the practice, have amounted to the emergence of an 'international surrogacy market'. Informed intended parents cross borders in order to have their offspring for economic or legal reasons: sometimes just because the surrogacy process is easier, quicker or cheaper abroad, others because the practice is unknown or illegal in their country of origin or residence or for the reason that the intended parents do not meet the legal requirements of the law of this country.

The employment of the term 'market' gives a hint of the ethical objections that surrogacy, especially commercial genetic surrogacy, raises. The fear of a commodification of children and the deterrence of women's exploitation are the main reasons for some countries to ban surrogate motherhood. On the other hand, some countries have approved specific legislation, in whose promulgation, in many cases, underlies the basic idea that it is preferable to regulate the practice than to adopt absolute prohibitions. The prevalent concern here is to avoid the rising of black markets where women could be even more exploited. But there are also jurisdictions where the debate has been clearly settled in favour of the ethical admissibility of the practice, and where, therefore, specific rules have already been enacted or announced.

Indeed, the international map of surrogacy shows no territorial, cultural or legal patterns: a (non-exhaustive) picture of the situation illustrates that, at this moment, surrogacy is regulated by means of either specific rules, a legislative framework setting standards or case-law, in countries of Europe (→ Greece and the → United Kingdom), Africa (→ South Africa), America (the states of Texas, Utah, Virginia, Florida, Illinois, Massachusetts, Nevada, Washington, New Hampshire, Ohio and California in the USA; the Mexican state of Tabasco), Oceania (→ Australia and → New Zealand) and Asia (→ Israel, → Ukraine and Russia (→ Russian Federation)). The practice takes place legally, although on an unregulated basis, in other countries, such as → India, → Thailand or Uganda. Among the countries where the practice is neither expressly banned nor expressly permitted are → Belgium, → Finland, the → Netherlands, → Spain, → Japan, Guatemala and → Argentina. Finally, other countries such as → Germany, → France, → China, and the states of New York and Michigan have an express ban against the practice in all its forms. Nevertheless, this picture is changing, especially because the number of jurisdictions with a surrogacy-friendly approach is growing.

Where surrogacy is either regulated or just practised on an unregulated basis, the surrogate mother is not regarded as the legal mother of the child(ren). The intended parents will be considered the legal parents, either *ex lege* or by means of the decision of a judicial or administrative authority. For this reason, where a surrogacy-friendly legislation has no requirements as to the nationality or residence of the intended parents (and it often happens in states where commercial surrogacy is allowed), foreign nationals or residents come from abroad. They come to an agreement on the practice and have their children, and they also achieve the legal recognition of their parent–child relationship pursued. Afterwards they seek recognition of the relationship also in their country of origin, even if the practice is banned in that country. This lack of a voluntary acceptance of the consequences of their acts is a clear sign of the fact that their behaviour cannot be qualified as civil disobedience. Surrogate motherhood is rather the object of a flourishing new sort of legal tourism: procreative tourism.

II. State regulations on surrogacy in jurisdictions favourable to the practice

1. Substantive regulation

There are many different and complex issues to tackle when elaborating specific rules on surrogacy. The existing statutes are far from being homogeneous, both as to the matters that are expressly regulated and the way in which they are envisaged. Nevertheless, in the majority of cases, a special attention is paid to the kinds of surrogacy permitted, the agents involved in the process, the surrogacy agreement, the rights of the child(ren) and the administrative and/or penal consequences of the violation of the legal conditions.

a) Kinds of surrogacy

First of all, it is necessary to define the types of surrogacy allowed. As said before, surrogacy can be performed by the surrogate mother with either altruistic or commercial purposes. Where state laws just allow altruistic surrogacy (it is the case in the vast majority of countries), no payment can be made to the surrogate mother, beyond the reimbursement of the reasonable expenses related to pregnancy and birth. Where commercial surrogacy is allowed, an additional compensation is given to the surrogate mother. Another relevant issue to regulate is whether surrogacy is subject to pre-approval or to an *a posteriori* assessment. In the first case, the relevant (administrative or judicial) authority has to declare before the birth of the child(ren) takes place that the intended parents will be considered the legal parents once the children are born, if the legal requirements are met. In the second case, the practice is subject to control *ex post facto*, ie, after the birth of the children, upon request to the relevant authority of the recognition of the legal parentage.

b) Agents involved

A high number and variety of agents may be involved in the practice, besides the surrogate mother and the intended parents, such as agencies or mediators, public (administrative and judicial) authorities, medical staff and legal advisors. The intervention in the process of these agents is often addressed by the state regulations.

Thus, administrative bodies might be established in order to monitor the process and assess the accomplishment of the legal requirements. These bodies, when settled, are sometimes also entrusted with the task of approving the surrogate agreement. However, the control of the whole process might be finally performed by judicial authorities, whose positive decision will be required for the establishment of legal links between the child(ren) and the intended parents. As said before, this decision is sometimes made prior to the birth; in other occasions, once the birth has taken place, within a given time.

If it is always advisable for the intended parents and surrogate mother to seek legal advice, the existence of a previous counsel might be settled as a legal requirement. Indeed, an attorney 'letter of compliance' with the provisions of the surrogacy law is one of the documents that is requested, according to some regulations, by the administrative body or the court entrusted with the approval of the process.

Clinics or hospitals also intervene in the vast majority of the processes, as the employment of human ART is not only commonly necessary, but sometimes also legally compulsory. They facilitate the pregnancy, and sometimes they carry out the psychological and medical evaluations of the surrogate mother and of the intended parents that the legal regulations require. Regulations often establish special requirements for the intervening clinics or hospitals, such as being public or certified; in some cases, the clinics need to have a special licence which specifies issues such as the activities covered by the licence, the premises in which the activities may be performed and the name of the responsible person.

Finally, in the countries where commercial surrogacy is allowed, it is habitual that commercial agencies are involved in the process. In these cases, specific administrative requirements may also be imposed by state regulations to the agencies through which the intended parents meet the surrogate mother. These agencies usually also help with the development of the whole process, by means of providing advice and facilitating the contacts with the rest of the agents (lawyers, clinics, courts etc). Where surrogacy is permitted and regulated, but only on a non-commercial basis, as the practice is to be kept 'within the family', restraints are usually imposed on commercial agencies and advertising surrogacy services.

c) The surrogacy agreement

A paramount element in the surrogacy process is the agreement between the intended parents and the surrogate mother. Regulations usually address the conditions for the agreement to be valid and enforceable.

First, the special object of the agreement makes it necessary to add requirements to the ordinary legal capacity of the parties (→ Capacity and emancipation). Further subjective conditions are established relating both parties to the agreement. As regards the intended parents, the requirements usually concern their maximum and minimum age, civil status (married or unmarried couples, singles), sex (open to same-sex couples or limited to opposite-sex couples) and psychological ability. There is an overwhelming trend relating to them: that a genetic link between at least one of the intended parents and the child(ren) is required. For the intended mother it is usually also required that she is unable to carry a pregnancy. As regards the surrogate mother, the conditions relate to her maximum and minimum age, her civil status (and the necessity of her husband's consent, in case she is married), the number of previous living children required (if any), the maximum number of previous surrogate practices (successfully or unsuccessfully) accomplished, and her psychological and medical condition. It is also usual that the rules on surrogacy clarify if biological links between the surrogate mother and the baby are either required or allowed (ie genetic surrogacy is permitted), or banned (just gestational surrogacy being tolerated). And other additional requirements regarding the surrogate mother and the intended mother are sometimes established, so that they have to be close relatives (ie the surrogate mother has to be the mother, sister or daughter of the intended mother), or they are required to practise the same religion.

As regards formal requirements, the agreement is usually deemed to be in writing, so as to gain certainty regarding a paramount element of the process: consent of the surrogate mother and the intended parents. As said before, another formal requirement of validity of the agreement might be its confirmation by the competent administrative body or court, usually before the surrogate mother is artificially inseminated.

The main obligation of the intended parents towards the surrogate mother is the reimbursement of the expenses which she may have directly incurred (medical insurance and fees, medicines, compensation for labour leave, maintenance during pregnancy, transport, special clothes and diet) and, in commercial surrogacy, if allowed, the extra amount agreed. Moreover, the intended parents also assume the rest of the expenses of the whole process: medical and psychological reports and intervention, legal counselling, the commissioning agency, insurance, travel, judicial or administrative fees etc. The surrogate mother's main obligation is to bring the pregnancy to its end, hand over the child(ren) to the intended parents and renounce her parental rights. Other usual provisions include the event of a divorce (→ Divorce and personal separation) or death of the intended parents; the contact, care, upbringing and general welfare of the child (including the future contacts between the child and the surrogate parents); termination of pregnancy (possible causes, and compensations due in case the pregnancy is disrupted, depending on the reasons and deciding party); and enforceability or unenforceability of the agreement, ie possibility of the surrogate mother changing her mind and refusing to surrender the child at birth, or possibility of the intended parents rejecting the newborn, because she or he is born with unexpected handicaps. Although being a private agreement, the parties are not entirely free to agree on all these terms: state surrogacy regulations contain many mandatory rules. Besides, the best interests of the child will always prevail over provisions that do not conform to this principle.

As regards the rights of the child, the most relevant issue that surrogacy regulations have to envisage relates to her or his right to information about her or his parentage, ie the possible anonymity of the surrogate mother and/or donor, and the access rights of the child to medical information concerning his or her genetic parents.

d) Administrative and/or penal sanctions

A complete regulation on surrogacy also envisages the administrative or penal sanctions for violation of the settled legal conditions. Such sanctions concern the possible infringement of the duties of any of the agents involved, but often also penalize advertising for surrogacy, which is an activity usually banned or subject to limitations. This activity is usually only allowed in the jurisdictions where commercial surrogacy is legally possible.

2. Private international law rules

Most of the existing statutes on surrogacy set a single provision dealing with transnational situations, which aims at preventing limping relationships. The rule addresses choice-of-law issues: there are neither specific rules on jurisdiction, nor on recognition and enforcement of judgments. According to the rule mentioned, in order to legally accomplish the practice, the intended parents and/or the surrogate mother must have a given connexion with the forum: → nationality, habitual residence or domicile (sometimes of a given length prior to filling the application). This requirement might nevertheless sometimes be legally relaxed if that is consistent with the child's best interest.

Another general feature is the lack of specific choice-of-law rules applicable to surrogacy. A factual unilateral approach as to the law applicable to the whole process is adopted, according to which the law of the forum is applied to all the above-mentioned issues.

III. State regulations on surrogacy in countries contrary to the practice: legal implications of reproductive tourism

As said before, there are countries where the practice is not allowed and in principle the legal consequences sought by the persons involved may not be achieved. Among them, some lack an express ban on the matter but, either expressly or under general law principles, consider the surrogate agreement void and unenforceable and with no effects on parentage. Thus, the parturient is always the mother of the child(ren), notwithstanding the fact that she could not be the genetic mother (in gestational surrogacy). Therefore, as regards the practice, these countries just reaffirm the principle *mater semper certa est*. Other jurisdictions have a clearer anti-surrogacy approach, as they expressly criminalize participation in and/or brokering of a surrogacy agreement.

Most of these countries, however, face requests for the recognition of the parent–child relationship established under foreign law or by foreign authorities, with regard to children born as a result of a surrogacy agreement. Such requests are usually addressed to the national consular authorities, to which the intended parents apply for a passport or travel document for the child(ren) to come back home. In other instances, they are addressed to the authorities competent for the recognition of the relationship (civil registers, courts), once the family has already returned to their place of residence.

So far, two different kinds of solutions have been given to these requests. On the one hand, there are countries where the relevant private international law rules of the forum are applied. This first solution usually leads to the denial of recognition of the legal parentage as established abroad – especially of the intended mother's legal link with the child(ren) – on grounds of the violation of the public policy of the forum. But, in order to attend the best interests of the child(ren), it is also habitual to establish some remedies, such as to accord the recognition of the biological links with the intended father who provided the genetic material, and allow the other intended father or mother to adopt the child(ren).

On the other hand, other countries apply the substantive → *lex fori*, even extraterritorially, to the issue of parentage. Thus, denial of the legal parentage as established in the foreign country is also habitual according to this second solution, except where the requested country allows for an *ex post facto* assessed surrogacy: in this case, the requested authorities could give effect to the surrogacy agreement if it meets the requirements laid down by the *lex fori*. But again here, where the surrogacy agreement has in principle no effects in the requested jurisdiction, domestic → adoption procedures are often available, so that at the end it is feasible to avoid that the limping relationship leads to the denial of any right to the child and the intended parents in the requested country. Nevertheless, as far as countries parties to the ECHR are concerned, the national solutions could soon evolve, in accordance with the most recent case-law of the ECtHR (see *infra*).

IV. International and EU instruments

So far, the only international conventions that deal with matters related to surrogacy are instruments on assisted reproduction and biomedicine, such as the Council of Europe's Convention on Human Rights and Biomedicine, adopted by the Committee of Ministers on 19 November 1996 and opened for signature on 4 April 1997 (Oviedo Convention, available at <http://conventions.coe.int/Treaty/en/Treaties/html/164.htm>). This Convention regulates issues such as equitable access to health, guarantee of the professional obligations and standards in health interventions, free and informed consent by any person prior to a medical intervention, prohibitions on sex selection and human genome modification (unless for therapeutic reasons), ban on embryo creation for research purposes and prohibition on the use of the human body and its parts for financial gain. But there is no specific regulation on the matter. Nevertheless, in light of the transnational problems arising as a result of international surrogacy agreements, the Permanent Bureau of the Hague Conference on Private International Law is currently studying the private international law issues being encountered in relation to international surrogacy arrangements.

As regards EU law, it is worth mentioning that surrogacy is still not contemplated in EU legislation of any kind. And it is an unknown phenomenon also with regard to the EU Directives that regulate labour rights derived from motherhood, such as the Council Directive 92/85/EEC of 19 October 1992 on the introduction of measures to encourage improvements in the safety and health at work of pregnant workers and workers who have recently given birth or are breastfeeding ([1992] OJ L 348/1), the Directive 2006/54/EC of the European Parliament and of the Council of 5 July 2006 on the implementation of the principle of equal opportunities and equal treatment of men and women in matters of employment and occupation ([2006] OJ L 204/23) and Council Directive 2000/78/EC of 27 November 2000 establishing a general framework for equal treatment in employment and occupation ([2000] OJ L 303/16). Indeed, the ECJ, in its judgments of 18 March 2014 (Case C-167/12 *CD v ST* [2012] OJ C 194/9; Case C-363/12 *Z v A Government department, The Board of management of a community school* [2014] OJ C 142/7) has denied the possibility of considering that any of these Directives oblige the Member States to equate an intended mother to the woman who has been pregnant and given birth for purposes of granting paid leave equivalent to maternity leave or adoptive leave.

Finally, it is also important to draw attention to the fact that the ECtHR condemned France, by means of its judgment of 26 June 2014, *Mennesson v France* (App No 65192/11), to compensate the moral prejudice caused to two twins, daughters of a French couple (the Mennesson), which resorted to gestational surrogacy in California, for violation of art 8 ECHR. The ECtHR has considered that the effects of non-recognition in French law of the parentage between the children born following surrogacy treatment abroad and the couples who had the treatment, not only raised a serious question of compatibility with the best interests of children, respect for which must guide all decisions affecting them, but also entailed serious consequences on the identity of the children. Therefore the ECtHR concluded that the children's right to respect for their private life had been infringed as a consequence of the non-recognition under French law of the legal parent–child relationship established in the USA. A similar result was also reached by the ECtHR in its judgment of 26 June 2014, *Labassee v France* (App no 65941/11).

Patricia Orejudo Prieto de los Mozos

Literature

Sonya Bychkov Green, 'Interstate Intercourse: How Modern Reproductive Technologies Challenge the Traditional Realm of Conflicts of Laws', Selected Works of Berkeley Electronic Press: <http://works.bepress.com/sonia_green/1/>; Cristina Campiglio, 'Lo stato di figlio nato da contratto internazionale di maternità' [2009] Riv.Dir.Int'le Priv. & Proc. 589; Rachel Cook and Shelly Day Sclater with Felicity Kaganas (eds), *Surrogate Motherhood: International Perspectives* (Hart Publishing 2003); J Flauss-Diem, 'Maternité de substitution et transfert de parenté en Angleterre' [1996] R.I.D.C. 855; Frédérique Granet, 'L'établissement de la filiation maternelle et les maternités de substitution dans les Etats de la CIEC' <www.ciec1.org/Documentation/NotePMA.pdf>; Guido Pennings, 'Reproductive Tourism as Moral Pluralism in Motion' [2002] 28 *Journal of Medical Ethics* 337; Katarina Trimmings and Paul Beaumont (eds), *International Surrogacy Arrangements: Legal Regulation at the International Level* (Hart Publishing 2013).

Taxation, international

I. General characterization

International taxation means the taxation of cross-border activities by the affected states according to their own national law which includes bilateral → double taxation treaties; this broad statement also applies to the European Union. Despite its international aspect, national sovereignty is still the core of fiscal regulation in this sphere. International cooperation merely constrains the financial interests of the sovereign. In contrast with international private law, in international tax law the participating states are biased as lawmakers. Because of globalization, international taxation has, however, experienced a worldwide increase of importance since the Second World War, supported by international organizations, namely by the International Chamber of Commerce and the League of Nations in the 1920s, the OECD from the 1960s and furthermore by the United Nations.

International tax law has two main functions: first the prevention of double and multiple taxation and second the prevention of tax evasion by well-advised taxpayers who sometimes pursue aggressive tax planning. Complementing the first function is the prevention of double non-taxation (resulting in so-called white income). However, international tax law primarily protects the taxpayer from uncoordinated exactions of more than one treasury: bans on discrimination and bans on restriction of tax benefits to the taxing authority's own nationals add to this protection in favour of foreign taxpayers. The latter function, ie the prevention of tax evasion, secures tax revenue and contributes to uniformity and equality of taxation. It has generated multiple provisions combating abuse, the amending process amounting to a permanent race between taxpayers and tax authorities. The overall aims of this process, however, are a fair division of the power to impose taxes between the states and the prevention of disadvantageous tax competition. These fiscal interests can be combined with other interests, such as European integration, development aid or the promotion of exports of the national economy and of investment in foreign countries.

In terms of the systematics of the tax regime, international tax law is closely linked to the law of company taxation. But income from employment or self-employment and to some extent more private activities such as inheritance or → donation are also covered. Specific rules exist for shipping companies and air carriers. Most → double taxation treaties deal with taxes on income or net worth of individuals, partnerships and corporations. Private consumption, on the other hand, lies outside of the thematic horizon (possibly, because the → USA does not have a federal turnover tax). Expenditure taxes, transfer taxes and excise taxes seem to be better grounded in national legislation without the need for treaties. Supranational harmonization of turnover taxation as an operating condition for the European single market as well as typically transnationally organized, criminal sales tax roundabouts shall, however, be explicitly pointed out. Customs law is a branch of international tax law that will not be further covered because of its singularity.

For all these types of taxes, tax law includes both substantive law and procedural law. Individual tax liability is paramount. Third-party liability, however, for example that of banks, and other obligors of the taxpayer is also covered. Among the procedural details of international taxation are rules governing mutual administrative assistance, communication between the involved tax authorities and extended duties of the taxpayer to cooperate and provide evidence. The functions and legal powers of specialist agencies, such as in Germany the Federal Central Tax Office (*Bundeszentralamt für Steuern*), in which necessarily high expertise and language skills are bundled, must also be addressed in tax law.

International tax law can be the reason for, but also the solution of conflict, and it is partially national, partially international law. Whether the term 'international taxation' covers all these aspects, or is to be limited to conflict-solving double taxation treaties, has been the subject matter of inconclusive academic dispute. On the other hand, the bundling of such different aspects makes the specifically demanded treatment more difficult, and, for instance, affects matters of interpreting applicable law.

II. Basic issues of international taxation

1. Criteria for cross-border cases

In tax law the distinction between national and cross-border cases depends on criteria with respect to which the community of states has reached general consensus, even if these criteria are nowhere defined as generally binding. A case is considered cross-border if the taxable entity and the taxable object are allocated in different states. The differentiation between the state of residence and the state of source as well as the differentiation between non-resident and resident taxpayers are fundamental.

2. Connecting factors for taxable fact situations

The state of residence is determined according to German law by the domicile (→ Domicile, habitual residence and establishment) or habitual place of residence, by the place of management or the corporate seat of the taxable entity. Nationality, and employment in the civil service of a state, are of little relevance in international tax law (exception: citizenship in the → USA). The state of source is the state to which a source of income, outside of the state of residence, is assigned. Additionally a specific stability of the relation is required for this assignment. For commercial income it therefore depends on the realization in a foreign permanent establishment, and for income from employment on the employment for 183 or more days of a year in this state. In interlaced structures of multinational corporate groups, in → electronic commerce and with regard to intellectual property this assignment is easily diminished.

A state imposes taxes on income of which it is the source, as determined under its law. Non-residents with income sourced in the taxing state may enjoy limited tax liability (principle of source state taxation, principle of origin, principle of territoriality). The state of source has the competence to impose taxes, because the income was obtained using its infrastructure. This justifies a general competence, but not the concrete specifics of taxation. If the state of residence limited its taxation to sources of income situated in its territory, the problem of double taxation would be minor (just as there would be minor problems if the country of source limited itself to the taxation of its residents, or if the power of taxation on sources would be restricted). Many states of residence are, however, not willing to do so. In order to increase their tax revenue and to fully exhaust the taxpayer's ability to pay, many states impose taxes on the worldwide income of their residents (an exception is eg the UK (→ United Kingdom) which does not tax the non-UK-source income of those residents who have no domicile (→ Domicile, habitual residence and establishment) in the UK). Residents are fully liable for taxes on their entire worldwide income (principle of universality and principle of totality). This is generally believed to be a permissible connection and within the limitation of international public law, namely the jurisdiction to prescribe.

3. The resulting problem: double taxation

In doing so, a combination of unlimited liability to pay taxes in the state of residence and limited tax liability in the state of source can easily be the result. Double taxation in legal terms exists, if comparable taxes are imposed on the same taxpayer for the same period of time in two or more countries. Since the main reason for double taxation is unlimited liability, it is up to the state of residence and not to the state of source to solve the problem (see Moris Lehner, 'Internationale Reichweite staatlicher Besteuerungshoheit' in Josef Isensee and Paul Kirchhof (eds), *Handbuch des Staatsrechts*, vol 11 (3rd edn, CF Müller 2013) § 251 para 41). A solution to this problem could be found unilaterally (by the state of residence) or bilaterally, by either exempting income in the state of source from taxation in the state of residence (exemption method) or by crediting the taxes paid to the state of source against the tax liability in the state of residence (credit method). These two methods are by far the most important.

4. Tax evasion

The residence of the taxpayer and the location of the tax base can change. Here, inbound and outbound cases are to be distinguished. An important example is the diversion of profits to a foreign subsidiary that as a corporate body is supposed to shelter from being subjected to domestic taxation (transfer pricing). Most states agree that the shifting of income and assets for reasonable financial motives should be distinguished from that which pursues the mere purpose of tax savings; some states may deny this but even those that accept this principle do not all agree on its proper application. Such application measures are considered a part of the law of international taxation (in German *Außensteuerrecht* as opposed to *Doppelbesteuerungsrecht*, in the US Controlled Foreign Corporation (CFC) rules (26 U.S.C. § 957)). Just how crediting and exemption are typical instruments of double taxation legislation, imputational taxation and non-consideration of losses incurred abroad are instruments of international taxation designed to combat tax evasion.

III. States as main actors of international taxation

The main actors in international taxation are states. International tax law is created by them, unilaterally or bilaterally, and it is enforced by them according to international public law, namely within the general boundary of the jurisdiction to enforce. Because of this boundary they render each other administrative, informative and enforcement assistance and impose cooperative duties on the taxpayer. Thus § 90(2) of the Fiscal Code of Germany (Abgabenordnung of 16 March 1976, BGBl. I 613, as amended) states:

> Where circumstances relating to transactions effected outside the territory of application of this Code are to be established and subjected to the provisions of tax law, the participants shall clarify these circumstances and procure the necessary evidence. In doing so, they shall exhaust all legal and practical means available to them. Where there are objectively recognizable indications to assume that the taxpayer has business relations with financial institutions in a State or territory with which there is no agreement to provide information in accordance with art 26 of the OECD Model Tax Convention on Income and on Capital (2010) . . ., or the state or the territory does not provide information to a comparable extent or is not willing to

engage in a corresponding provision of information, the taxpayer shall at the revenue authority's request make a sworn statement affirming the correctness and completeness of the details provided by him . . . . A participant may not plead inability to clarify circumstances or to submit evidence when he, depending on the case, could, in structuring his circumstances, have afforded himself or have himself given the opportunity to do so. (English translation available at <www.gesetze-im-internet.de>, last accessed on 14 April 2014).

According to § 146 of the Fiscal Code accounts and records otherwise required shall be kept and stored within the territory of application of this Code (para 2). Exceptions require the authorization by the revenue authority (para 2a). For persons related to the taxpayer, especially for corporations that own or are owned directly or indirectly by the taxpayer, the requirements of § 90(2) have been intensified in paragraph 3.

Federal states raise special problems. Tax jurisdiction of the central state and the member states can overlap, resulting in problematic situations similar to those in international taxation. A solution to double taxation problems is mainly achieved by a division of jurisdiction in the national constitution. For instance art 105(2a) of the Basic Law for the Federal Republic of Germany (Grundgesetz of 23 May 1949, BGBl. 1, as amended) states that the German *Länder* shall have power to legislate with regard to local taxes on consumption and expenditures so long and insofar as such taxes are not substantially similar to taxes regulated by federal law. The problem of a race to the top or a race to the bottom of tax rates can be countered by harmonizing measures of the federation. Another path to solve federal problems would be to conclude → double taxation treaties between federal states. The first German double taxation treaty, maybe the first double taxation treaty worldwide, was effected between Prussia and Saxony on 16 April 1869.

IV. European Union, OECD and UN

In a way the European Union carves out exceptions to many of the general features of international taxation. On behalf of the effective functioning of the Internal Market it deals with the harmonization of indirect taxes, mainly the value added tax (arts 110–113 TFEU (The Treaty on the Functioning of the European Union (consolidated version), [2012] OJ C 326/47), Directive on the VAT (Council Directive 2006/112/EC of 28 November 2006 on the common system of value added tax [2006] OJ L 347/1), Directive on the General Arrangements for Excise Duty (Council Directive 92/12/EEC of 25 February 1992 on the general arrangements for products subject to excise duty and on the holding, movement and monitoring of such products [1992] OJ L 76/1), Structural Directives (Council Directive 92/83/EEC of 19 October 1992 on the harmonization of the structures of excise duties on alcohol and alcoholic beverages [1992] OJ L 316/21; Council Directive 95/59/EC of 27 November 1995 on taxes other than turnover taxes which affect the consumption of manufactured tobacco [1995] OJ L 291/40; Council Directive 2003/96/EC of 27 October 2003 restructuring the Community framework for the taxation of energy products and electricity [2003] OJ L 283/51)), and is a customs union (arts 28–33 TFEU). However, it does not have a say in income and net worth taxation, which are the main matters of international tax law. The internal market competence of art 114 TFEU excludes taxes in paragraph 2. The former obligation of art 293 TEC to prevent double taxation was deleted without explanation in 2009 by the Lisbon Treaty (Treaty of Lisbon amending the Treaty on European Union and the Treaty establishing the European Community, signed at Lisbon, 13 December 2007, [2007] OJ C 306/1, consolidated version, [2012] OJ C 326/1). In order to contain the financial appetite of the EU for the multi-year financial framework (art 320 TFEU) from 2014 to 2020 the Member States made sure that the financial trees of the EU do not grow to heaven. The EU, like many other international organizations, has its own power to levy income tax only for its employees who are accordingly excluded from taxation by the Member States. Attempts to assign revenues from financial market taxes to the EU failed. The harmonization of the income taxation of the Member States is proceeding hesitantly. There are five legal acts concerning special matters of taxation of → companies and interests (Merger Directive (Council Directive 90/434/EEC of 23 July 1990 on the common system of taxation applicable to mergers, divisions, transfers of assets and exchanges of shares concerning companies of different Member States [1990] OJ L 225/1), Parent-Subsidiary

Directive (Council Directive 2011/96/EU of 30 November 2011 on the common system of taxation applicable in the case of parent companies and subsidiaries of different Member States [2011] OJ L 345/8), Arbitration Convention (Convention 90/436/EEC on the elimination of double taxation in connection with the adjustment of profits of associated enterprises [1990] OJ L 225/10), Savings Taxation Directive (Council Directive 2003/48/EC of 3 June 2003 on taxation of savings income in the form of interest payments [2003] OJ L 157/38), Interest and Royalties Directive (Council Directive 2003/49/EC of 3 June 2003 on a common system of taxation applicable to interest and royalty payments made between associated companies of different Member States [2003] OJ L 157/49)). A code of conduct against unfair tax competition from 1 December 1997 [1998] OJ C 2/1 is soft law. If the draft directive 'The Common Consolidated Corporate Tax Base' (Proposal for a Council Directive on a Common Consolidated Corporate Tax Base (CCCTB), (COM(2011) 121/4)) will ever become reality is questionable despite the 15-year long preparatory work. The influence of the European Union on accounting law is also to be mentioned.

In addition to legislative powers the EU also has judicial powers. The European Court of Justice developed the fundamental freedoms and furthermore, supported by the Commission, the prohibition of state aid into prohibitions of discrimination and restriction also relevant in tax matters that were temporarily viewed as bothersome restrictions of tax sovereignty by the Member States. In 20 years, since the early 1990s, case-law has been developed especially on the basis of the freedom of establishment (→ Freedom of establishment/persons (European Union) and private international law) and the free movement of capital. Keywords are: limited tax liability, losses incurred abroad, diversion of profits, allocation and accounting of hidden reserves. From an EU perspective the core problem is unequal treatment of resident and non-resident taxpayers. If there is an interference of national tax laws with fundamental freedoms, the European Court of Justice has repeatedly censured national tax laws providing for a gradual negative harmonization; but the Court has more recently also justified such restrictions thereby granting more importance to the Member States' power to impose taxes (cf Andreas Musil, 'Rechtsprechungswende des EuGH bei den Ertragsteuern? – Eine Analyse aktueller Leitentscheidungen des EuGH' (2009) DB 1037 ff).

Model agreements for double taxation treaties have been a trademark of the OECD since 1963. They are continuously updated, officially commented and completed with a range of reports and statements by its tax committee. The Andean Group, a union of Latin American countries, and the Economic and Social Council of the United Nations have also represented model agreements. The speciality of the Latin American proposal is its preference for taxation according to the principle of the state of source. The UN takes the concerns of developing countries more prominently into account reflecting the asymmetrical economic relations that are typical of countries with capital import and source taxation countries. Furthermore, other individual states, such as the → USA for the first time in 1976, propose model conventions that express choices favourable to their particular interests. A model agreement of the European Union does not exist.

V. Sources of international tax law

International tax law is partly specific international public law, partly autonomous, ie unilateral national law, partly case-law of national administrative and financial courts and of international arbitral courts. For further details relating to double taxation see → double taxation treaties. States lacking a clear hierarchy of legal sources that impose taxes by means of administrative regulations or administrative practices which are not necessarily published create remarkable problems of legal certainty for the affected taxpayers.

General international public law and the primary law of the European Union give little information and do not prohibit double taxation. The minimum contact requirements relating to the connecting factors used by states for taxing certain events correlate with the 'genuine link' requirement of general public international law (cf Moris Lehner and Christian Waldhoff, in Paul Kirchhof, Hartmut Söhn and Rudolf Mellinghoff (eds), *EStG Kommentar*, vol 1 (CF Müller 2013) § 1 para A 464–71). The European treaties do not specifically demand a continuous harmonization of the tax systems. International taxation only has few points of contact with the protection of human rights (→ Human rights and private international law). In the law of → immunity international taxation is, however, an independent item, dealing with diplomats, consuls or members of military deployment (for diplomats see Markus Heintzen, 'Die Befreiung ausländischer Diplomaten von deutscher Besteuerung' (2007) 45 AVR 455).

Therefore → double taxation treaties that are mainly bilateral and national legal norms on taxation are the main sources. Some of the national legal norms explicitly refer to cases with cross-border dimension and others affect such cases without explicitly referring to them. An example for the latter is the problem of transfer prices in corporate groups that is also an issue in domestic cases. The main reason for the small number of multilateral conventions and the numerical dominance of bilateral double taxation treaties are the unlike fiscal interests of the contracting parties that can be balanced better in the latter. Within the national legal tax system international tax law should not been regarded as a distinguishable subarea with its own separate laws. Relevant provisions are in fact inserted predominantly in particular tax laws, such as income or corporate income tax laws, and apply to all issues of the respective taxable event, thus taxable entity, taxable object, tax base and tax rate.

VI. Relation to international private law and comparative law

The dynamics of international taxation is based on the ability to shape contractually cross-border economic activity which connects to international private law. Contractual ordering indicates an economic capacity that for its part justifies taxation. It is acknowledged by tax law with the limitation that it shall not be abused. Problems can come up, if divergent legal choices of other states used for private transactions lead to results which are to be recognized. This does not mean that national financial authorities apply foreign law (especially foreign tax law), since such cases do not exist (for private international law problems in the procedure of tax assessment cf Rene Dauven, 'Ausländische Rechtsnormen im Besteuerungsverfahren' [2014] IStR 196 ff). There is no choice of law in international tax law.

The term conflict of laws has a different meaning in this case. The question is whether a foreign legal phenomenon can be treated as an equivalent to the domestic fact situation targeted by a national provision which, for this purpose, has been defined broadly such as to fit for international matters. The term 'trust' can serve as an example. It is not a coincidence that the Venezuela decision relating to the comparison of certain types of national and foreign corporations was not made by the *Reichsgericht* (German Imperial Court of Justice) but the *Reichsfinanzgericht* (Imperial Financial Court of Justice) (decision, 12 February 1930, VI A 899/27, [1930] RStBl. 444). The Venezuela decision clarifies that a foreign company can only be subject to German corporate taxation if it is isomorphous or comparable to a domestic entity. Another example is the question whether revenues are classified as interests or dividends. Unlike for some other areas of the law, eg social security law (in Germany see § 34 SGB I (German Social Code, first volume (Erstes Buch Sozialgesetzbuch (SGB I) of 11 December 1975, BGBl. I 3015, as amended))) there is no general rule permitting the substitution of foreign legal institutions for the domestic ones referred to in German tax law. The general problem of the dependency of taxation on the legal form, the differentiation between company and shareholder level, translates into the international context. If the states involved have diverging opinions about the qualification of a legal entity, double non-taxation can be the result. Germany responds by suspending the exemption of revenue covered by a double taxation treaty but not effectively taxed by the other contracting state (§ 50d(9) German Income Tax Law (Einkommensteuergesetz of 8 October 2009, BGBl. I 3366, as amended)).

Internationality of taxation is, similar to internationality of private legal relations, a motive for the comparison of laws, whereas in tax law the competition of fiscal interests of the states involved is an additional motive. International taxation increases the awareness for common problems and for a limited *repertoire* of solutions to such problems. A web of double taxation treaties based on model conventions provides for harmonization. That tax law is nonetheless a national matter may finally be illustrated by the fact that there is no complete translation of the German Income Tax Law into the English language. Its continuous changes would most likely not only frustrate interpreters but also lawyers. Even so, English is the working language of international taxation.

MARKUS HEINTZEN

Literature

Hugh Ault and Brian Arnold, *Comparative Income Taxation: A Structural Analysis* (3rd edn, Kluwer Law 2010); Rene Dauven, 'Ausländische Rechtsnormen im Besteuerungsverfahren' [2014] IStR 196; Gerrit Frotscher, *Internationales Steuerrecht* (3rd edn, CH Beck 2009); Florian Haase, *Internationales und Europäisches Steuerrecht* (4th edn, CF Müller 2014); Markus Heintzen, 'Die Befreiung ausländischer Diplomaten von deutscher Besteuerung' (2007) 45 AVR 455; Otto H Jacobs, *Internationale Unternehmensbesteuerung* (7th edn, CH Beck 2011); Moris Lehner, 'Internationale Reichweite staatlicher Besteuerungshoheit' in Josef Isensee and Paul Kirchhof (eds), *Handbuch des Staatsrechts*, vol 11 (3rd edn, CF Müller 2013); Moris Lehner and Christian Waldhoff, in Paul Kirchhof, Hartmut Söhn and Rudolf Mellinghoff (eds), *EStG Kommentar*, vol 1 (CF Müller 2013); Jörg Manfred Mössner and others, *Steuerrecht international tätiger Unternehmen* (4th edn, Dr. Otto Schmidt 2012); Andreas Musil, 'Rechtsprechungswende des EuGH bei den Ertragsteuern? – Eine Analyse aktueller Leitentscheidungen des EuGH' [2009] DB 1037; Ekkehart Reimer, 'Internationales Finanzrecht' in Josef Isensee and Paul Kirchhof, *Handbuch des Staatsrechts*, vol 11 (3rd edn, CF Müller 2013); Harald Schaumburg, *Internationales Steuerrecht* (3rd edn, Dr. Otto Schmidt 2011); Harald Schaumburg and Sebastian Peters, *Internationales Steuerstrafrecht* (Dr. Otto Schmidt 2014); Wolfgang Schön, 'International Tax Coordination for a Second-Best World' [2009] WTJ 67 and [2010] WTJ 65, 227; Klaus Tipke and others, *Steuerrecht* (21st edn, Dr. Otto Schmidt 2013); Matthias Valta, *Das Internationale Steuerrecht zwischen Effizienz, Gerechtigkeit und Entwicklungshilfe* (Mohr Siebeck 2014); Klaus Vogel and Moris Lehner, *Doppelbesteuerungsabkommen Kommentar* (5th edn, CH Beck 2008); Franz Wassermeyer, Stefan Richter and Helder Schnittker (eds), *Personengesellschaften im Internationalen Steuerrecht* (2nd edn, Dr. Otto Schmidt 2014).

Territoriality

I. Territoriality in private international law

Territoriality has, as a corollary of the sovereignty of a state, multiple connotations in private international law. First, territoriality is a jurisdictional concept. Judicial authority to resolve a case with a foreign element could be seen as emanating from state territorial sovereignty. Therefore, courts can assume jurisdiction over certain facts in the territory of the forum.

In the context of the application of law, territoriality has various connotations. First, territoriality could mean that all individuals and institutions in a particular state are subject to the regulations applicable in the territory of that state. Second, territoriality could define the spatial reach of domestic statutes. This issue would arise when states are willing to extend the territorial reach of their own regulations over acts which are committed abroad. Third, territoriality concerns the methodology of applying law. This function could be further distinguished between two types. First, states apply their own laws unilaterally, ie without recourse to choice-of-law rules. Public laws, for example, are effectuated once the criteria of applicability set out in that particular statute are met, or when designated procedural requirements are met (eg filing of a petition to the competent governmental agency). Second, a more refined methodology of choice between pertinent private law statutes of different states has evolved over time. Choice-of-law rules usually refer to a specific connecting factor which then points to a particular domestic or supranational law. Also in this context, there are nuanced differences. For example, a type of connecting factor leads to application of forum law (→ *lex fori*) to materialize the interests of the forum state, while in another type of connecting factor, such as the location of property (*locus rei sitae*), place of celebration (*locus celebrations*) or place of tort (*locus delicti*), territoriality is abstracted in different territorial concepts. The interpretation of such territorial connecting factors varies to a great extent in the jurisprudence of national courts.

II. Presumption against extraterritoriality

The activities of private individuals and multinational corporations often spill over the borders of several states. This can cause many difficulties for national regulatory authorities due to the limited territorial reach of the local statutes.

In common law countries, there is a long-standing practice of the so-called 'presumption against extraterritoriality doctrine'. It means that domestic statutes do not apply to the activities abroad, unless it is made explicitly clear in the statute itself. The original traces of this doctrine can be found in the medieval case-law of common law courts in admiralty cases. For instance, in early common law criminal cases such as Lacy's case ((1582)1 Leon. 270) courts were not able to adjudicate the case, if any matters constituting the elements of crime occurred outside England. If an element of the crime occurred abroad then the crime itself was deemed to be extraterritorial. Such crimes were not subject to the court's jurisdiction, unless there was an act of parliament clearly stating that domestic criminal statutes apply towards such extraterritorial crimes. In the 18th century, courts started to push common law jurisdiction forwards by asserting jurisdiction over claims in cases when a man received a fatal wound at sea but died in territorial waters. Yet, the presumption against extraterritoriality remained as a bedrock principle in regulating any cross-border wrongful conduct.

In the modern-day international law arena, the principle of territoriality has been triggered by the willingness of some states to apply their domestic statutes in cases concerning wrongful acts committed in the territory of another state. This is often based on the 'effects theory' which assumes that the foreign acts of the defendant which produces effects within the state confer jurisdiction upon the courts.

The effects theory has often been applied in antitrust cases decided by American courts. In a landmark case, *US v Aluminum Co of America* (148 F.2d 416 (2d Cir 1945)), it was held that 'any state may impose liabilities . . . for conduct outside its borders that has consequences within its borders which the state reprehends'. Over time, the effects doctrine was 'refined' by adding an intention requirement. US law has gradually become rather hostile towards foreign corporations who feared broad pre-trial discovery proceedings and treble → damages awards. As a reaction to that, US courts added additional criteria such as a balancing test and a jurisdictional rule of reason which aimed to ensure that US courts would exercise jurisdiction, only when foreign acts have significant effects in the US.

To be mentioned in this context is the US Supreme Court decision in *Hoffman-LaRoche Ltd v Empagran* (542 U.S. 155 (2004)). In this case, exceptions of non-applicability of the Sherman Act for conduct that significantly harms imports, domestic commerce or American exporters created by the Foreign Trade Antitrust Improvement Act of 1982 (FTAIA, § 402, 15 U.S.C. § 6a (1982)) were at stake. In this case, vitamin purchasers filed a class action against a number of domestic and foreign vitamin manufacturers and distributors for a massive and long-running conspiracy to fix the price of vitamin globally and sought compensation for damages under US antitrust laws. The defendants argued that the case should be dismissed because the defendants' conduct affecting the plaintiffs occurred entirely abroad and that none of the plaintiffs suffered injuries as a result of participation in US commerce. The Supreme Court unanimously held that foreign plaintiffs couldn't bring claims for treble damages based solely on a foreign effect. The price-fixing conduct significantly and adversely affects customers both outside and within the US, but the adverse foreign effect is independent of any adverse domestic effect.

The presumption against extraterritoriality is followed not only in antitrust disputes, but also in other situations where the territorial reach of American statutes governing various areas of economic activity is unclear. For example, § 271(f)(1) of the US Patent Act (35 U.S.C. §§ 1 *et seq* (consolidated Patent Laws as of September 2007)) was a source of controversy, which provided that infringement does occur when one 'suppl[ies] . . . from the United States', for a 'combination' abroad a patented invention's 'components'. This provision has often been invoked by US patent holders who sought compensation for alleged infringers liable under US law for acts that took place abroad (see eg *Microsoft v AT&T Corp*, 127 S.Ct. 1746 (2006)). The Supreme Court has several times restated its cautious approach and noted that the presumption against extraterritoriality in patent law should be understood in the potential differences of foreign states' approaches towards the relative rights of inventors, patentees and the public.

Another prominent example in the debate about extraterritoriality is the US Alien Tort Statute (henceforth ATS, 28 U.S.C. § 1350). It provides that '[T]he district courts shall have original jurisdiction of any action by an alien for a tort only, committed in violation of the law of nation or a treaty of the US'. The ATS, adopted in 1789 as a part of the Judiciary Act, became widely applied since the 1980 decision of the Court of Appeals for the Second Circuit in *Filartiga v Pena Irala* (630 F.2d 876 (2d Cir 1980)). In *Filartiga*, a claim was brought by two citizens of → Paraguay against a Paraguayan police chief for alleged torture and murder of family members. At the time of the proceedings, all parties were resident in the USA. The US Court of Appeals the Second Circuit held that federal courts had jurisdiction, because the law of nations 'has always been a part of the federal common law'. Furthermore, the court referred to the prohibition of torture under multilateral treaties as well as UN declarations.

Since *Filartiga*, more than a dozen cases were decided on the basis of the ATS, some of which reached the US Supreme Court. In *Sosa v Alvarez-Machain*, 542 U.S. 692 (2004), the Supreme Court confirmed that only violations of well-established rules of international law such as genocide, crimes against humanity, war crimes, slavery as well as other abuses by government officials could be invoked by private individuals.

Among many controversies surrounding the application of the ATS is the question whether corporations could be held liable for the violations of human rights, environmental harm and other injuries abroad. The 2013 decision of the US Supreme Court in *Kiobel v Royal Dutch Petroleum Co*, 133 S.Ct. 1659 (2013) concerns this issue. The plaintiffs as Nigerian citizens claimed that Dutch, British and Nigerian oil-exploration corporations aided and abetted the Nigerian government in committing violations under customary international law during the 1990s. In particular, it was argued that Royal Dutch Shell compelled its subsidiary in Nigeria to cooperate with the government to crush local community resistance to an oil development project. One of the main tenets of the *Kiobel* litigation was the presumption against extraterritorial application. The Supreme Court held that 'this presumption serves to protect against unintended clashes between the United States' laws and those of other nations which could result in international discord' and noted that nothing in the ATS rebutted the presumption against extraterritorial application. The issue of corporate liability for human rights violations was to be decided under the rules and principles of customary international law; and the Supreme Court refused to hold Shell liable for human rights violations.

III. Territoriality and international enforcement of intellectual property law

The principle of the territoriality of IP law has deep historical roots. Various privileges related to economic activities (eg printing or producing of certain goods such as alcohol) were granted by kings or princes to a particular merchant or tradesman. Such royal privileges had effects only within the territorial boundaries of the town-states or monarchies simply because granting kings had no sovereign powers in foreign territories. This idea of individual privileges granted by sovereign kings underwent a remarkable transformation during the time of the Industrial Revolution. The case-by-case granting of privileges gradually turned into a more formalized system where copyright protection was enshrined in domestic statutory provisions. By the mid-19th century almost all countries in Europe and some in the Americas had their own copyright legislation. Although domestic copyright statutes aimed to achieve similar objectives, the means for realizing them varied from state to state.

In the 19th century, it became clear that a closer cooperation among states was inevitable. However, the differences among national laws were so great that the idea of unification of substantive laws was not feasible. Accordingly, a decision was made to retain the idea of national treatment, conjoined with minimum rights. Issues related to the protection of industrial property rights were harmonized in the Paris Convention for the Protection of Industrial Property (20 March 1883, with later amendments, 828 UNTS 305) while the protection of literary and artistic works was subject to the regulations of the Berne Convention for the Protection of Literary and Artistic Works of 9 September 1886 (completed at Paris on 4 May 1896, revised at Berlin on 13 November 1908, completed at Berne on 20 March 1914, revised at Rome on 2 June 1928, revised at Brussels on 26 June 1948, revised at Stockholm on 14 July 1967 and revised at Paris on 24 July 1971, 1161 UNTS 3 and amended in 1979 Treaty Doc No 99-27, and 1985, 828 UNTS 221). Many more multilateral conventions were drafted in the second half of the 20th century both on an international level and as part of regional endeavours for economic integration.

Under the current IP regime, the minimum requirements for obtaining IP protection are harmonized internationally. Three main principles underpin the functioning of international IP treaties. First, the principle of national treatment aims to make sure that foreign nationals can trust that they will enjoy similarly favourable national treatment as domestic creators. The second principle common to multilateral IP conventions is territoriality. Just like medieval privileges, IP rights obtained in a Member State of a treaty have legal effects within that particular country. The rights conferred as well as the extent of the protection in those countries will be determined by the laws of the place for which protection is sought. The third principle is the so-called independence of IP rights. This principle is intended to retain a relatively level playing field for states and their economic, social and cultural interests.

Although the granting of IP rights has been harmonized to a significant extent, international treaties in the area of IP do not provide for a comprehensive mechanism to help proprietors efficiently protect their rights on an international level. The territoriality of IP rights dictates that the right holder has to take active steps before each and every state in which protection is sought. The most challenging issue in the current international IP regime concerns the cross-border exploitation of IP rights. Cross-border exploitation and enforcement of IP rights involves intricate private international law questions: which court decides? Which state law should be applied?

In common law countries, subject matter jurisdiction must be satisfied. One of the earliest cases, which became a landmark precedent on subject matter jurisdiction for international adjudication of multistate IP cases, was decided by the High Court of Australia in 1905, *Potter v Broken Hill Pty Co Ltd* (1906) 3 CLR 479. The High Court adopted a distinction between local and transitory actions which was first introduced by an English Court in the late 19th-century case, *British South Africa Co v Compania de Moçambique* ([1893] AC 602). Local actions were related to the facts occurring in a particular place (eg land, trespass). Such local actions were subject to the jurisdiction of the courts where those facts occurred. A similar logic was applied by the Australian court in the *Potter* case where patent rights were deemed to be tantamount to land rights. Consequently, the Court considered New South Wales and Victoria as different states and decided that an action for an infringement of a patent granted in New South Wales cannot be justiciable in a Victorian court. In subsequent judgments, common law countries all around the globe followed the *Potter* rationale and usually adhered to the non-justiciability of the foreign IP rights idea. For more than a century, common law courts consistently refused to adjudicate claims concerning foreign IP rights, indicating that they do not possess subject matter jurisdiction.

The same logic was applied to foreign copyright in the judgment of the High Court in *Lucasfilm Ltd v Ainsworth* ([2008] EWHC 1878 (Ch) (31 July 2008)) where at the centre of this dispute was the protection of some Imperial storm trooper helmets that were used in the 1977 film, *Star Wars*. The High Court stated that even if the defendant habitually resides in the UK, the UK court cannot adjudicate, since infringement of US copyright is the issue of the case. However, the UK Supreme Court in 2011 ([2011] UKSC 39 (27 July 2011)) found that there are no impediments for English courts to hear actions for the infringement of foreign copyrights. It held that the act of state doctrine was outdated and that traditional approaches should be reconciled in the light of changing market realities. If – and how – this judgment would affect other courts in the Commonwealth needs further observation.

Also in the USA, a territorial approach has been adopted. Hence, the US courts will exercise jurisdiction over infringements of IP rights only if the infringing acts occurred in the USA. For instance, in the case of *Subafilms Ltd v MGM-Pathe Communications Co* (24 F.3d 1088 (9th Cir 1994)), which concerned the exploitation of the Beatles' single Yellow Submarine in a cartoon, it was held that it could grant the plaintiff monetary relief only for infringements which occurred within the USA. To be noted however, was the fact that the Court did not pay attention to the foreign nature of the rights.

In civil law countries, exclusive jurisdiction performs a similar function. Article 22(4) of the Brussels I Regulation (Regulation (EC) No 44/2001 of 22 December 2000 on jurisdiction and the recognition and enforcement of judgments in civil and commercial matters, [2001] OJ L 12/1; → Brussels I (Convention and Regulation)) provided for exclusive jurisdiction of the country of registration over procedures on the registration and validity of IP rights. A question arose regarding the scope of this provision in the case C-4/03 *GAT v LuK* ([2006] ECR I-6509), concerning a dispute between two German companies. *LuK* considered that *GAT* infringed *LuK's* French patents. *GAT* sued *LuK* before the German courts and filed a declaratory action for non-infringement arguing that *LuK's* French patents were invalid. The European Court of Justice clarified that exclusive jurisdiction is applicable to any case, as long as the validity of the IP rights is at stake, irrespective of whether the issue is raised by way of an action or as a defence. The text of art 24(4) of the Brussels I Regulation (recast) (Regulation (EU) No 1215/2012 of the European Parliament and of the Council of 12 December 2012 on jurisdiction and the recognition and enforcement of judgments in civil and commercial matters (recast), [2012] OJ L 351/1; → Brussels I (Convention and Regulation)) includes now that clarification. The Japanese Code of Civil Procedure (Act No 109 of 26 June 26 1996, as amended, henceforth CCP) has a similar provision in arts 3–5 para 3 of the CCP, but the precise scope of this provision is not clear.

In the 21st century, multiple infringements of substantially identical IP rights could easily occur by making certain works available to the public on the Internet via Internet providers without the right holder's authorization or by coordinating a number of persons' actions in each of the states where the rights exist. In complex IP cases, where the IP rights are infringed by multiple parties, the possibility of suing multiple foreign defendants before one court is limited (→ Intellectual property, jurisdiction).

The approach taken by the US courts could be best illustrated by a decision in *Voda v Cordis*, 476 F.3d 887 (Fed. Cir 2007). In that case, the plaintiff, *Voda*, owned patents for identical inventions in the USA, Canada, the United Kingdom, Germany and France. The defendant, *Cordis*, was a US-based corporation established in Florida with foreign affiliates in France, Germany, Italy and the Netherlands. *Voda* instituted judicial proceedings against all related corporate infringers before a US court alleging infringements of its American, British, French, German and Canadian patents. The district court decided it had supplemental jurisdiction pursuant to 28 U.S.C. § 1367(c) to hear foreign patent infringement claims. Yet, regardless of *Voda's* arguments that a consolidated multinational patent adjudication would be more efficient, the Federal Circuit ruled that the district court abused its discretion by asserting jurisdiction and held that considerations of comity, judicial economy, convenience, fairness and other exceptional circumstances constituted compelling reasons to decline jurisdiction. In coming to this conclusion, the Federal Circuit relied on such notions as the independence of national patents, stating that 'only a British court, applying British law, can determine the validity and infringement of British patents'.

In the EU, the Brussels I Regulation (recast) does not provide for joinder of claims, but according to art 8(1), under certain conditions, a person domiciled in a Member State may also be sued, where he is one of a number of defendants, in the courts for the place where any one of them is domiciled. This provision would enable a plaintiff to sue several defendants in one court. However, in Case C-539/03 *Roche Nederland BV and Others v Frederick Primus and Milton Goldenberg* ([2006] ECR I-6535), where a US-firm tried to consolidate infringement claims against eight companies that belong to the same corporate group, the European Court of Justice stated that art 8(1) does not apply to such a case. Such a strictly territorial approach towards the adjudication of multistate IP disputes has been the object of some disagreement on the grounds that dissatisfaction with mosaic state-by-state litigation creates high costs.

Even if the court finds that it has jurisdiction over the case, several additional complications may arise with regard to the determination of the governing law. In the case of *Card Reader* (*Fujimoto v Neuron Co. Ltd* (Card Reader), Supreme Court of Japan, September 26, 2002, Minshu Vol 56, No 7, 1551) for instance, the plaintiff was a Japanese national residing in Japan who owned a patent in the USA. The defendant, another Japanese company with its principal place of business in Japan, produced an infringing product in Japan and exported it to the USA through a wholly owned subsidiary. Having found that the infringing product was sold in the USA, the proprietor of the patent sued in Japan seeking an injunction against production and export of the infringing products to the USA, destruction of the infringing products and compensation for damages. The Supreme Court of Japan stated in its 2002 judgment (*Card Reader*) that the law of the country where the patent is registered should be applied to the question of an injunction. According to sec 271 of the US Patent Law, both the infringer and the person who induced the infringement overseas are liable. However, the Japanese Supreme Court was of the opinion that the extraterritorial application of the US Patent Law would undermine the public policy of Japan and refused to grant the injunction. The claim for damages was also denied by applying a double-actionability clause.

The cases discussed above indicate some of the problems that arise when it comes to the enforcement of IP rights. The lack of harmonization with regard to the enforcement of IP rights leads to quite burdensome and costly situations. In this context it is easy to note the clear conflict between the global market and territorial jurisdiction. The open question remains how should the principle of territoriality be adjusted to meet the needs of a global market.

Due to difficulties in unifying the aspect of the enforcement of IP rights, a possible solution might be to adopt uniform rules on international jurisdiction and applicable law in areas related to IP.

Several scholarly projects have published draft principles or draft legislation advancing such a view. These include the ALI Intellectual Property Principles (American Law Institute, *Intellectual Property: Principles Governing Jurisdiction, Choice of Law and Judgments in Transnational Disputes*, St. Paul 2008) and the CLIP Principles (European Max Planck Group on Conflict of Laws in Intellectual Property, *Conflict of Laws in Intellectual Property: The CLIP Principles and Commentary*, Oxford 2013; → CLIP).

After these projects were completed, the Committee on IP and Private international law was established under the auspices of the International Law Association. Since 2011, this Committee has been drafting guidelines which would be valid worldwide, covering the outcome of the preceding projects as well as new issues with which the preceding projects did not deal.

IV. Territoriality and cross-border insolvencies

An insolvency proceeding has the nature of collective enforcement: once an insolvency proceeding is commenced following a debtor's non-payment, his creditors are, in principle, not allowed to individually exercise their rights to claim and enforce; the trustee appointed by a court should collectively exercise their rights on behalf of all creditors; the trustee is usually provided with such power that, under certain conditions, he could even cancel a debtor's prior transactions if it is in the collective interests of creditors. Since the insolvency proceeding as an enforcement represents the sovereign power, its scope and effects should be limited to the territory of the particular state. Territorialism is thus currently the international law of bankruptcy and the basic principle of cross-border insolvency. A good example of territorialism was art 3 of the Japanese Bankruptcy Act (Act No 75 of June 2, 2004, as last amended by Act No 109 of 15 December 2006) before it was amended in 2000.

However, as a result of globalization (→ Globalization and private international law), many corporations have expanded their activities throughout the world. These corporations have and will have their assets in multiple jurisdictions. Still, under strict territorialism, an insolvency proceeding must be commenced in each jurisdiction wherever the debtor has assets, ie there is a lack of cross-border cooperation. However it would cause problems, especially if a debtor company wants to collect its assets in one jurisdiction to restart its business.

The standard argument against territorialism is universalism, under which, ideally, there should be only one forum which deals with all of the assets of a debtor, irrespective of their location and their distribution, and only one country's laws govern the insolvency. The proponents of universalism claim that a universalist system would promote greater efficiency than a territorial system and that a universalist rule has the potential to bring greater returns to all creditors. In addition, a universalist system would produce more equality of distribution among creditors and would serve a global standard of fairness.

A pure universalism, under which one insolvency proceeding commences and other nations cooperate with that proceeding, does not work under the current legal systems in the world. Universalism therefore needs certain modifications, for example by reserving to local courts the discretion to evaluate the fairness of the home country's procedures and to protect the interests of local creditors.

→ UNCITRAL adopted the Model Law on Cross-Border Insolvency in 1997 (UNCITRAL (ed), *Model Law on Cross-Border Insolvency with Guide to Enactment* (1997): Model Law on Cross-Border Insolvency of the United Commission on International Trade Law, Resolution 52/158 adopted by the General Assembly, 30 January 1998, No E.99.V.3, General Assembly Resolution 52/158 of 15 December 1997). The Model Law has four features: access, recognition, relief and cooperation. The 'centrality of cooperation' in cross-border insolvency cases is emphasized in order to achieve the efficient conduct of proceedings and to ensure an optimal result. But the Model Law does not specify how that cooperation and communication might be achieved, but rather leaves that up to each jurisdiction and the application of its own domestic laws and practices. Still at least such countries as → Australia, → Canada, → Chile, → Colombia, Eritrea, Greece, Japan, Mauritius, Mexico, Montenegro, New Zealand, Poland, Republic of → Korea, → Romania, → Serbia, → Slovenia, → South Africa, Uganda, → United Kingdom, → USA, amended their insolvency laws under the influence of the Model Law. In this sense, the idea of universalism has been influential in recent law reforms in this area.

Among some basic concepts and ideals of the Model Law, the COMI (Center of Main Interest) is the decisive factor for a foreign proceeding to be a foreign 'main' proceeding (art 2(b)). Thus the representative appointed in that foreign proceeding could be recognized and reach the debtor's assets located in other jurisdictions. The Model Law presumes the debtor's registered office as the COMI (art 16(3)). But after the adoption of the Model Law, due to diverse judgments in some important jurisdictions, clarification became necessary. The Guide to Enactment and Interpretation of the UNCITRAL Model Law confirms that the 'concept of a debtor's centre of main interests is fundamental to the operation of the Model Law'. However, in a case where the debtor's COMI may not coincide with the place of registration, the COMI will be identified by other factors. In most cases, the location (i) where the central administration of the debtor takes place and (ii) which is readily ascertainable by creditors could be identified as COMI. If this does not work, a number of additional factors concerning the debtor's business may also be considered.

Large business could be operated by a group of enterprises, each of which is an independent juridical entity. A key question is how to conceptualize the COMI for this entire group. One view states that the COMI should be adapted as it applies to an individual debtor to the situation of an enterprise group, enabling all proceedings with respect to group members to be commenced in, and administered from, a single centre through one court and subject to a single governing law. Another suggestion is to identify a coordination centre for the group, which might be determined by reference to the location of the parent of the group or to permit group members to apply for insolvency in the state where proceedings have commenced with respect to the insolvent parent of the group.

On a regional level, a good example of universalism is the European Insolvency Regulation (Council Regulation (EC) No 1346/2000 of 29 May 2000 on insolvency proceedings, [2000] OJ L 160/1). According to this Regulation, activities of undertakings have more and more cross-border effects, so there is a greater need for a Community act requiring coordination of the measures to be taken regarding an insolvent debtor's assets. This Regulation adopts a mechanism combining insolvency jurisdiction (art 3) and the recognition of foreign insolvency proceedings (art 16), and provides for general and special rules on applicable laws (arts 4–15).

V. **Future of territoriality**

Territoriality remains the guiding benchmark of the international legal system and conflict of laws. Territorial → connecting factors are crucial in determining the governing law and asserting judicial competence over cases with foreign elements. While many disputes can be resolved by domestic courts applying national statutes, the expansion of global business models and cross-border activities will bring about challenging territoriality-based notions in the future. As the examples of cross-border insolvencies or intellectual property disputes show, territoriality may come at a huge cost. Mere splitting of cases depending on territorial connections often leads to a mosaic of adjudication schemes, a high risk of abuse and discordant solutions. Yet, in the absence of a unitary lawmaker at an international level, territoriality will remain the bedrock for the conflict of law. Territorial limitations could be overcome, at least to some degree, if more emphasis is given to the enhancement of institutional cooperation between courts and governmental agencies. The development of mutual trust-based regimes could be a great task for developments in the near future.

TOSHIYUKI KONO

Literature

Christian Von Bar and Peter Mankowski, *Internationales Privatrecht* (Beck 2001) ch 4; Jürgen Basedow, 'Foundations of Private international law in Intellectual Property' in Jürgen Basedow, Toshiyuki Kono and Axel Metzger (eds), *Intellectual Property in the .Global Arena* (Mohr Siebeck 2010) 3; Graeme Dinwoodie, 'Developing a

Private International Intellectual Property Law: The Demise of Territoriality?' [2009] Wm. & Mary L.Rev. 711; William S Dodge, 'Extraterritoriality and Conflict of Laws Theory: An Argument for Judicial Unilateralism' [1998] Harv.Int'l L.J. 102; Paul Goldstein and Bernt Hugenholtz, *International Copyright* (OUP 2013) ch 4; Lynn M LoPucki, 'The Case for Cooperative Territoriality in International Bankruptcy' [2000] Mich.L.Rev. 2216; Ralf Michaels, 'Two Paradigms of Jurisdiction' [2005–2006] Mich.J.Int'l L. 1003; Alex Mills, *Confluence of Public and Private international law* (CUP 2009) 234; Robert K Rasmussen, 'Resolving Transnational Insolvencies through Private Ordering' [2000] Mich.L.Rev. 2252; Dan Jerker B Svantesson, *Extraterritoriality in Data Privacy Law* (Ex Tuto 2013).

Torts

I. Introduction

On the substantive law level, rules on extra-contractual liability, tort or delict vary considerably between countries (for detailed information on the substantive tort law regimes, see the publications of the European Group on Tort Law, available at <www.egtl.org> and of the European Centre of Tort and Insurance Law (ECTIL), and in particular the Digests and Yearbooks on European Tort Law, available at <www.ectil.org>; see also Christian von Bar, Eric Clive and Hans Schulte-Nölke (eds), *Principles, Definitions and Model Rules of European Private Law: Draft Common Frame of Reference*, vol 4 (Sellier 2009); Walter van Gerven, Pierre Larouche and Jeremy Lever, *Cases, Materials and Text on National, Supranational and International Tort Law* (Hart Publishing 2000); Cees van Dam, *European Tort Law* (2nd edn, OUP 2013)). Thus it is often crucial in cross-border tort cases to know which national liability system applies. In private international law, the law of torts was for a long time overshadowed by criminal liability and for centuries remained a neglected topic. However, this changed drastically in the second half of the 20th century as the number of cross-border situations involving non-contractual liability multiplied. Road traffic accidents abroad (→ Traffic accidents), sports accidents in foreign countries, damage caused by defective products (→ Products liability), cross-border environmental damage (→ Environmental liability), acts restricting free competition in an international context, cross-border infringements of intellectual property rights (→ Intellectual property, applicable law), as well as infringements of privacy rights by media (printed or online) have multiplied and have come into the focus of private international law. Following the multiplication of situations raising issues of applicable law, the private international law rules on torts became more differentiated and more specific rules were introduced in numerous countries, either by means of legislation or through case-law. These rules differed from one jurisdiction to another in many respects (see Thomas Kadner Graziano, *Gemeineuropäisches Internationales Privatrecht (am Beispiel der ausservertraglichen Haftung für Schäden)* (Mohr Siebeck 2002); Thomas Kadner Graziano, *Europäisches Internationales Deliktsrecht* (Mohr Siebeck 2003); Thomas Kadner Graziano, *La responsabilité délictuelle en droit international privé européen* (Helbing Lichtenhahn 2004)). On a European scale, the existence of rules designating different applicable laws meant that the outcome of a particular case could vary according to the forum in which the case was brought. This in turn led to considerable uncertainty and a lack of predictability of the applicable law. In such circumstances, claimants and their lawyers had the opportunity to assess their options and choose the most favourable forum, engaging in what is termed 'forum shopping' (→ Forum (and law) shopping).

This state of the law was considered unsatisfactory and initiatives were taken to unify private international law rules in the field of torts, initially by the → Hague Conference on Private International Law, then by the EC and later the EU.

Two Hague Conventions were adopted, one on the law applicable to traffic accidents (Hague Convention of 4 May 1971 on the law applicable to traffic accidents, 965 UNTS 415, Hague Traffic Accident Convention), the other designating the law applicable to products liability (Hague Convention of 2 October 1973 on the law applicable to products liability, 1056 UNTS 191, Hague Products Liability Convention; text and status charts available at <www.hcch.net>). While the Hague Traffic Accident Convention has been highly successful with 21 contracting states (→ Traffic accidents), the Hague Products Liability Convention has been less so, with 11 contracting states (→ Products liability).

In 2009, the → Rome II Regulation (Regulation (EC) No 864/2007 of the European Parliament and of the Council of 11 July 2007 on the law applicable to non-contractual obligations (Rome II), [2007] OJ L 199/40) entered into force in the EU Member States. It has universal application and so applies even when the designated law is not that of an EU Member State. The Rome II Regulation introduced, for the first time in modern history, common rules setting out the applicable law in non-contractual matters in all EU Member States except Denmark. It designates the same national law, irrespective of the country where the case is brought. For the issues covered, Rome II establishes foreseeability of the outcome, creates legal certainty as to the applicable law, and eliminates forum shopping within Europe.

However, according to art 28(1) of the Rome II Regulation, the two Hague Conventions on traffic accidents (→ Traffic accidents) and product liability (→ Products liability) prevail over the Regulation in their respective contracting states. With respect to traffic accidents and to products liability, two different sets of private international law rules thus coexist within Europe. For these two areas of considerable practical importance, the unification of private international law rules by the Rome II Regulation so far remains only partial.

II. General principles of private international law of torts

Specific chapters in this Encyclopedia are dedicated to the Rome II Regulation, to traffic accidents and to product liability. This chapter will instead focus on general principles of private international law of torts, as they have evolved over the centuries (see II.1. below) or during the second half of the 20th century (see II.2. to II.4. below).

1. The lex loci delicti commissi *rule*

The first principle of almost global importance to be identified in the private international law of tort is the application of the law of the place where the tort was committed, the so-called *lex loci delicti commissi* rule. From the beginning of private international law in the 12th and 13th centuries until well into the 20th century, the *lex loci delicti rule* was seen on the European continent as the (only) reasonable rule to follow in torts. It thus ranks among the oldest rules of private international law. However, until the mid-19th century, the legal analysis often focused on the question of which law to apply to criminal sanctions, while compensation was regarded as a secondary issue, governed by the law applicable in criminal law. In the 19th and the 20th centuries, when accident and compensation law was emancipated from criminal law, new statutes and case-law endorsed the *lex loci delicti* rule for compensatory tort claims in continental Europe and eg South America. Before the entry into force of the → Rome II Regulation, and despite modern tendencies towards more specific or more flexible rules, the *lex loci* rule was in force in almost all European countries from → Poland to → Portugal, from the → Netherlands to → Greece, and from England (→ United Kingdom) to the Baltic States (→ Estonia, → Latvia, → Lithuania) and Russia (→ Russian Federation). The same is true for the private international law of torts in many jurisdictions around the world. The Hague Traffic Accident Convention (→ Traffic accidents) and the → Rome II Regulation also retain the place of the accident as a central criterion for determining the law applicable in torts.

The place where the tort was committed is currently used as the general rule, for example, in art 4(1) Rome II Regulation, art 3 Hague Traffic Accident Convention, art 1219(1) Russian Civil Code (The Civil Code of the Russian Federation of 26 November 2001, No 146-FZ – Part 3, as amended by Federal Law No 260-FZ of 30 September 2013, henceforth Russian CC), art 1129(1) Civil Code of Belarus (Law No 218-Z of 7 December 1998, henceforth Belarus CC), art 17(1) Japanese Act on General Rules for Application of Laws (Hōno Tekiyō ni Kansuru Tsūsokuhō, Law No 10 of 1898, as newly titled and amended by Act No 78 of 21 June 2006, henceforth Japanese PILA), art 44 Law of the People's Republic of China on the Laws Applicable to Foreign-Related Civil Relations (Statute of Application of Law to Foreign Civil Relations adopted at the 17th session of the Standing Committee of the 11th National People's Congress on 28 October 2010, effective 1 April 2011, henceforth Chinese PILA). Other examples are art 3126(1) Civil Code of Québec (L.Q. 1991, ch 64, henceforth Québec CC); art 21 first sentence Civil Code of Egypt (Law No 131/1948 of 16 July 1948, al qānūn al madanī); arts 70 and 73(1) Tunisian Code of Private international law (Law No 98-97 of 27 November 1998, Official Journal of the Republic of Tunisia, 1 December, p 2332, henceforth Tunisian PILA); art 20(1) Civil Code of Algeria (Ordonnance No 75-58 du 20 Ramadhan correspondant au 26 septembre 1975 portant code civil, modifiée et complétée) and § 13 Civil Foreign Relations Act of South Korea (Law No 966 of 15 January 1962 and Law No 6465 of 7 April 2001, Amending the Conflict of Laws Act of the Republic of Korea). In other jurisdictions, the *lex loci delicti* is applied as a default rule, used where no other, more specific → connecting factors apply. This is the case in art 133(2) Swiss Private international law Act (Bundesgesetz über das Internationale Privatrecht of 18 December 1987, 1988 BBl I 5, as amended, henceforth Swiss PILA). In the USA, the *lex loci* rule was followed unanimously until the mid-1960s.

There is a strong rationale for the *lex loci delicti* rule. First, in situations where the parties had no contact with each other before the damaging event occurred, which is the case eg in many road traffic accidents or sports accidents, the place of the accident is the only link between them. Second, the law of the place of the tort or accident is simple to apply, efficient and favours legal certainty. Parties know even before a tort is committed which law will apply to potential liability, and they might adapt their insurance cover accordingly. Third, application of the *lex loci delicti* is a neutral solution favouring neither party. Fourth, it is in conformity with the interests of the state in which the damage occurred to have certain victims of accidents compensated, particularly those resident there. Lastly, this solution generally corresponds to the parties' expectations and interests, and is usually fair and recognized as such by the parties.

2. *Exceptions to the* lex loci delicti *rule*

A second general principle common to almost all modern systems on private international law of torts is that, under certain circumstances, exceptions are made to the *lex loci delicti* rule. In a series of influential publications from the 1950s onwards, proposals were made to deviate from the *lex loci delicti* in cases where the victim on the one hand and the person claimed to be liable on the other originated from the same jurisdiction or lived in the same legal environment, distinct from the one in force at the place of the tort (see JHC Morris, 'The Proper Law of Tort' [1951] Harv.L.Rev. 881–95; Heinz Binder, 'Zur Auflockerung des Deliktsstatuts (1955) 20 RabelsZ 401–99; Pierre Bourel, *Les conflits de lois en matière d'obligations extracontractuelles* (Bruylant 1961), 45 *et seq*; Jan Kropholler, 'Ein Anknüpfungssystem für das Deliktsstatut' (1969) 33 RabelsZ 601–53).

The single most famous case illustrating this development is certainly the New York Court of Appeals case *Babcock v Jackson*, 191 N.E.2d 279 (NY 1963). The *Jacksons*, a couple from New York, went with a friend, *Babcock*, on a trip by car from New York to Ontario, Canada, where they had a traffic accident. *Babcock* sued *Jackson*, the driver of the car, before the courts in New York, claiming that *Jackson* had negligently caused the accident. The law of Ontario, ie the law of the place of the accident, prohibited a passenger from suing the driver, so that under the *lex loci delicti* rule, then applicable in New York, the claim would have failed. The law of New York, on the contrary, provided no such → immunity. The court found that the parties lacked a substantial connection with Ontario and that application of the *lex loci delicti* under the circumstances would be fortuitous and unfair. Accordingly the court held that the jurisdiction most closely connected to the case was New York and applied New York law.

In later years, exceptions were made in the large majority of European jurisdictions, either through legislation or case-law. Only a few countries (such as → France, → Spain, → Greece, → Sweden and → Denmark) continued to apply the *lex loci delicti* rule without exception. In other countries, deviations from the *lex loci* rule were made particularly in cases where the parties had their habitual residence in the same jurisdiction when the damage occurred, or where the parties were linked in a close relationship, such as by contract, which the tort violated; in this case, the law governing this relationship was also applied to tortious liability (the so-called *rattachement accessoire* or accessory connection mechanism).

The → Rome II Regulation follows these examples and provides for exceptions to the *lex loci delicti* rule pursuant to art 4(2) where the parties have their habitual residence in the same country, or pursuant to art 4(3) where there is a manifestly closer connection with another country, in particular a pre-existing relationship between the parties, such as a contractual relationship.

An exception where the parties have their habitual residence in the same state was already made in art 133(1) Swiss PILA, and is today also to be found for example in art 1219(2) Russian CC, art 20 Japanese PILA, art 44 2 Chinese PILA, art 3126(2) Québec CC and in art 70(3) Tunisian PILA. Thus, the common habitual residence exception is today a standard feature of modern codifications, whereas the *rattachement accessoire* is less widespread, and exists for example in art 133(3) of the Swiss PILA, art 20 Japanese PILA, and in art 3127 Québec CC.

There are good reasons for making exceptions to the *lex loci delicti* principle. A rule designating the law of the parties' common habitual residence has the advantage that the applicable tort rules are familiar to parties by virtue of their both living in this jurisdiction. Additionally, this is the jurisdiction in which the parties will bear the consequences of the tort. Under the exception rule, the accident is thus treated as though it had occurred in the state in which the parties are habitually resident. The more superficial the link between the parties and the place of accident, the more justified this exception to the *lex loci delicti* rule appears.

There is also a strong rationale for applying the law governing contractual relations to a potential claim in torts, ie to practise *rattachement accessoire*. Many national tort law regimes, such as English, German, Swiss or Italian law, allow concurrent actions in contract and tort. In domestic law, the systems of contractual and extra-contractual liability are usually well-coordinated. Given that the private international law rules for tortious and contractual matters differ (for example, the habitual residence of the seller or service provider in contractual matters, and the *lex loci delicti* in tort), the application of different private international law rules in contract and tort may lead to contract and tort claims between the parties being governed by different laws, even though they are based on the same facts and events. This risks undermining the balance that exists in each national system between claims in contracts and torts. On the other hand, the accessory connection mechanism leads to the application of one single law for all claims between the parties and avoids friction between the two liability systems. Lastly, this exception is generally in line with the parties' expectation that their relationships will be governed by the law of a single jurisdiction.

In Europe, the conditions for making exceptions to the *lex loci* rule are thus clearly defined. The development took another direction in the USA. Following scenarios such as that in *Babcock v Jackson*, the *lex loci* rule was replaced in many states by a flexible, policy-oriented case-by-case analysis taking into consideration a wide range of interests and policies. Accordingly, § 6(2) Restatement (Second) of Conflict of Laws (American Law Institute, Restatement of the Law, Second: Conflict of Laws 2d, St. Paul 1971; → Restatement (First and Second) of Conflict of Laws) provides that

> [t]he factors relevant to the choice of the applicable law include (a) the needs of the interstate and international systems, (b) the relevant policies of the forum, (c) the relevant policies of other interested states and the relevant interests of those states in the determination of the particular issue, (d) the protection of justified expectations, (e) the basic policies underlying the particular field of law, (f) certainty, predictability and uniformity of result, and (g) ease in the determination and application of the law to be applied.

The price of such an open-ended approach in US private international law is a considerable lack of foreseeability regarding the law applicable in torts.

3. Party autonomy

Since the late 1970s, → party autonomy has occupied an ever-increasing place in statutory provisions in the European private international law of tort. Practically all modern European statutes that expressly addressed this issue from the 1980s onwards allowed to a certain extent the parties to choose the applicable law in tort. Some national systems provided the choice only after the tort had occurred (→ Germany, → Belgium, → Lithuania, Russia, and outside Europe the Tunisian PILA). The Swiss PILA and the Japanese PILA allow an *ex post* choice of the *lex fori*.

In other countries, the parties were free to choose the applicable law both *ex ante* and *ex post*, ie before or after the injury occurred, provided they were already in contact at that time (→ Austria, → Liechtenstein and the → Netherlands). Article 14 Rome II Regulation follows this development. Under the Rome II Regulation, the parties are free to choose *ex post* and under certain circumstances also *ex ante*. They may choose the law of the forum or any law they consider appropriate to govern their relationships (→ Rome II Regulation). Consequently, when applying Rome II, the first question to be asked is whether the parties have agreed on the applicable law.

Some scholars have predicted that rules on party autonomy will turn out to remain dead letter in the field of torts given that the chosen law would necessarily favour one party so that the other would never agree to the choice. However, European case-law proves the contrary. In what is probably the most famous case in the European private international law of torts (Rechtbank Rotterdam, 23 September 1988, *Bier v Mines de Potasse d'Alsace* [1989] NJ 743, [1989] RabelsZ 699; Case C-21/76 SCJEC *Handelskwekerij GJ Bier BV v Mines de Potasse d'Alsace SA* [1976] ECR 1735), the *Mines de potasse d'Alsace*, situated in France, had released saline residue into the Rhine. A Dutch horticultural company which used water from the river for irrigation purposes was consequently forced to install a water purification system. The Dutch claimants brought a claim for → damages and an injunction against the *Mines de Potasse d'Alsace* before the Dutch courts. At the first stage of proceedings, each party wanted the law of its own country to apply. However, the parties eventually agreed on the application of Dutch law. This was because application of a foreign law could not be appealed against before the Dutch courts, so that by choosing Dutch law the parties left open the possibility of a review of the application of the substantive law by the higher courts.

This case illustrates that choosing the applicable law, particularly the law of the forum, may constitute an attractive option for parties, largely for reasons of procedure and practical convenience. Even parties for whom the chosen substantive law initially appears somewhat unfavourable may have good reason to agree upon the choice. This is the case, for example, if the chosen law can be more quickly, easily and reliably established than the law which would apply in the absence of choice, thus reducing the costs of litigation, or it may provide specific presumptions that ease a party's → burden of proof. Choosing the law of the forum is also an attractive option when, as in *Bier*, application of a foreign law cannot be appealed against. Consequently, for practical purposes, reaching agreement on the applicable law may be an attractive option in almost all cases where the private international law of the forum would lead to application of a foreign law.

There are good reasons to extend the party freedom of choice to a choice *ex ante*, as provided under certain circumstances in art 14(1)(b) Rome II Regulation. Where there is a pre-tortious relationship between the parties, in particular where they are bound by a contract (such as a complex construction contract or where they are in an ongoing business relationship), they may have an interest in determining in advance the law applicable to all their relationships, including future extra-contractual liability. An *ex ante* choice of the applicable law means that the parties are clear on the applicable liability law from the outset. The parties will consequently have the possibility to submit all their legal relations, contractual and non-contractual, to a single law.

It is true that the *rattachement accessoire*, or accessory connection mechanism (see II.2. above), often also indirectly leads to the result that the law governing the contractual relationship between the parties will eventually apply to their liability in tort. It therefore has been questioned whether there is a need to also permit *ex ante* choice of law in tort and delict.

However, a rule that extends → party autonomy in tort to the choice of the applicable law *ex ante* and that clearly defines the limits of this freedom is preferable to introducing party autonomy only 'through the backdoor'. Such a rule provides the parties with precise information necessary for them to organize their relationships efficiently and also reinforces legal certainty. Finally, rules on the *ex ante* choice of law in tort are needed where the parties' contractual relations are governed by international uniform contract law, in particular by the United Nations Convention on Contracts for the International Sale of Goods (United Nations Convention of 11 April 1980 on Contracts for the International Sale of Goods, 1489 UNTS 3; → CISG), or where the parties have agreed to submit their contractual relations to non-state rules such as the European Principles of Contract Law or the UNIDROIT Principles of International Commercial Contracts (International Institute for the Unification of Private Law/Institut international pour l'unification du droit privé (ed), UNIDROIT Principles of International Commercial Contracts 2010 (3rd edn, UNIDROIT 2010)). In the future, the same need could arise where parties choose to apply a future EU instrument on contract law. Given that neither the → CISG nor these non-state rules contain provisions on tort or delict, an accessory connection is ruled out when these contractual regimes apply. Finally, given that the injured party always has the possibility to decide whether to bring a claim at all and that parties can compromise and settle out of court, the injured party should also be able to determine the applicable law in agreement with the person claimed to be liable. Ultimately, the parties are best placed to know which applicable law would most effectively protect their interests and lead to the desired outcome. Hence, there are indeed good reasons for party autonomy in the private international law of torts.

Before entry into force of the Rome II Regulation, when parties argued in the course of the proceedings on the basis of the *lex fori*, courts in some jurisdictions inferred from this an implied tacit choice in favour of the law of the forum. Article 14(1) second sentence Rome II Regulation requires that the choice of law 'shall be expressed or demonstrated with reasonable certainty by the circumstances of the case', ruling out such a practice, and rightly so. In reality, courts and lawyers still often overlook the impact of private international law and, in particular, the potential application of a foreign law. Inferring a choice of law from mere silence would therefore constitute a sheer fiction with no relation to actual party intentions in many cases.

Finally, modern statutes accepting party autonomy in torts expressly state that the choice of the applicable law may not prejudice third-party rights. These provisions relate in particular to the insurer of the tortfeasor, see for example art 14(1) *in fine* Rome II Regulation or art 21 second sentence Japanese PILA.

4. Complex torts

A fourth significant development in the private international law of torts took place in the last decades of the 20th century regarding so-called 'complex torts'.

In the absence of a choice of the applicable law by the parties (see II.3. above), tortious liability is generally governed by the law of the place where the tort was committed, the *lex loci delicti* (see II.1. above). In the most common cases of extra-contractual liability, the place where the person committing a tort or delict either acts, or refrains from acting, is also the place where the damage occurs. This is true of road traffic accidents (→ Traffic accidents) and of sports accidents. In other situations, there is a distance in time and space between one person's behaviour and the resulting damage to another. When the event giving rise to damage takes place entirely or partly in one jurisdiction but the damage occurs in one or several other jurisdictions, we speak of a 'double or multiple locality case', 'multilocal tort' or 'complex tort' (*Distanzdelikt, délit à distance, illeciti complessi* or *a distanza, afstandsdelicten, ilícitos a distancia*). Determining the law that is to govern complex torts has proven to be one of the most difficult issues in the private international law of torts in the 20th century.

a) Complex torts in general

When the event giving rise to damage takes place in one jurisdiction and the damage occurs in another, the question is whether (i) the law of the place where the person claimed to be liable acted should apply, or rather (ii) the law of the place where the injury to the protected interest occurred, or alternatively (iii) whether both criteria should be combined and the tort localized at both places (so-called rule of ubiquity), and the law most favourable to the victim be applied. The second fundamental question is whether the criteria for torts in general should apply to all categories of complex torts, or whether, for different categories of complex torts, separate and more specific rules are needed (below, II.4.b)).

In the late 19th and early 20th centuries, applying the law of the place of acting was so widespread on the European continent that it was considered 'the civil law rule' for complex torts (Ernst Rabel, *The Conflict of Laws: A Comparative Study*, vol 2 (2nd edn, University of Michigan Press 1960) 303–304). On the other hand, from the 1880s onwards, German courts applied a rule of ubiquity, leading to the application of the law most favourable to the victim. In the 20th century, jurisdictions in central and eastern European countries applied similar ubiquity rules. In 1976, the ubiquity rule was adopted by the ECJ in the seminal *Bier* case (Case C-21/76, [1976] ECR 1735) for the purpose of jurisdiction under what is now art 7(2) of the Brussels I Regulation (recast) (Regulation (EU) No 1215/2012 of the European Parliament and of the Council of 12 December 2012 on jurisdiction and the recognition and enforcement of judgments in civil and commercial matters (recast), [2012] OJ L 351/ 1; → Brussels I (Convention and Regulation)). With respect to the applicable law, however, in the second half of the 20th century, applying the law of the place of injury became increasingly widespread in Europe, and this solution was eventually adopted in the Rome II Regulation: according to art 4(1) Rome II Regulation, complex torts are ordinarily to be governed by the law 'of the country in which the damage occurs irrespective of the country in which the event giving rise to the damage occurred and irrespective of the country or countries in which the indirect consequences of the event occur'. If the damage occurs in several countries, the laws of these countries will be applied to the damage that occurred in each country respectively (the so-called *application distributive* or mosaic principle).

There are numerous reasons for applying the law of the place of injury as opposed to that of the place of acting or a rule of ubiquity: a person causing damage in a foreign country must conform to the rules of the country in which his actions produce their effects. In fact, every actor must take into consideration the potential victims' legitimate expectations to be protected according to the level of protection provided by the law of the state where his goods and interests are located and the injury occurs. Moreover, from a prevention and deterrence perspective, the law of the place where the damage occurred is the most appropriate, in that national tort laws are in principle directed at behaviour that has its effects within the territory of the state in question. This means that actions with consequences in another country ought to be governed by the tort law rules in force in the place where the damage occurs. The preventive function of the substantive tort law of this country would be lost if persons acting from abroad had to comply only with the rules of the country in which they are acting. Accordingly, both the compensatory and the preventive functions of tort law favour application of the law of the place where the damage occurs.

For these reasons, the place of injury rule (as opposed to the place of acting rule or ubiquity rules) is also gaining wider acceptance in other jurisdictions worldwide, for example it was recently adopted in art 17 Japanese PILA and in art 44 of the Chinese PILA.

For cross-border torts caused by omission, this signifies that the determining factor is to be not the place where the alleged tortfeasor ought to have acted, but rather the place where the damage he ought to have prevented occurs.

In Europe, there has always been a widespread consensus that neither the place where purely preparatory acts took place nor the place where consequential damage occurred are to be taken into consideration when determining jurisdiction and the applicable law in tort. If, for example, an Italian citizen undergoes surgery in Hungary, and complications occur after his return to Italy entailing further medical treatment, then the place of injury relevant for determining jurisdiction and the law applicable for a claim in tort is Hungary, and not Italy where the consequential damage occurred (see for the purpose of jurisdiction also: Case C-364/93 *Antonio Marinari v Lloyd's Bank plc and Zubaidi Trading Co* [1995] ECR I-2719; Case C-220/88 *Dumez France SA and Tracoba SARL v Hessische Landesbank* [1990] ECR I-49; art 4(1) *in fine* of the Rome II Regulation). If, in Spain, a motor boat driven by a Belgian collides with a Frenchman who is harpoon fishing, leading to amputation of the victim's arm or leg, and if the victim is subsequently hospitalized in Nice where he later dies as a result of the accident, then Spanish courts (as opposed to French) would have jurisdiction under art 7 no 2 of the Brussels I Regulation (recast), and a claim brought by the widow in tort for damages to herself and any children would be governed by Spanish (as opposed to French) law, ie by the law of the place of the accident and of the initial injury (compare the scenario of the French case – Cour de Cassation, 21 October 1981, Bull. civ., I., no 303).

b) Specific rules for specific torts
Complex torts occur frequently in cases of products liability, environmental damage, violations of privacy and other → personality rights (in particular by mass media and/ or via the Internet), unfair competition and infringements of intellectual property rights. In these categories of cases, the criteria of the 'place where the damage occurred' is, as a → connecting factor, frequently vague. It is, for example, far from clear where the damage is to be localized for violations of personality rights through mass media, infringements of intellectual property rights or in situations of cross-border unfair competition. For several specific categories of complex torts, the place of the tort (the *locus delicti*) either needs

further specification or is simply inadequate, as in the case of products liability (→ Products liability).

In the second half of the 20th century, the conviction that certain categories of complex torts need to be governed by specific rules has gained ground in many jurisdictions. Introducing such specific rules became one of the most important developments in the private international law of torts. The development started with the Swiss PILA, which provides specific rules for products liability, unfair competition, restrictions of trade, damage to the environment, violations of personality rights and infringements of intellectual property rights. Before the entry into force of the Rome II Regulation, specific rules for complex torts were also introduced in varying numbers in → Austria, → Belgium, → Italy, → Liechtenstein, the → Netherlands, → Spain, and in many central and eastern European countries, such as → Lithuania, → Estonia, → Romania, Russia (→ Russian Federation) and → Belarus (for references, see Marc Fallon, 'The Law Applicable to Specific Torts' in Jürgen Basedow, Harald Baum and Yuko Nishitani (eds), *Japanese and European Private international law in Comparative Perspective* (Mohr Siebeck 2008) 261–77; Thomas Kadner Graziano, *Europäisches Internationales Deliktsrecht* (Mohr Siebeck 2003) 55–109; Thomas Kadner Graziano, *La responsabilité délictuelle en droit international privé européen* (Helbing Lichtenhahn 2004) 54–103; Thomas Kadner Graziano, 'General Principles of Private international law of Tort in Europe' in Jürgen Basedow, Harald Baum and Yuko Nishitani (eds), *Japanese and European Private international law in Comparative Perspective* (Mohr Siebeck 2008) 254–6).

In countries that did not adopt specific rules for the various categories of complex torts, eg → France, considerable uncertainty persisted before entry into force of the Rome II Regulation with respect to the law applicable to complex torts.

With a view to improving predictability and legal certainty regarding the applicable law, and in accordance with the above-mentioned trend towards specific rules for different categories of complex torts, arts 5 to 9 Rome II Regulation provide rules for products liability (→ Products liability), unfair competition and acts restricting free competition, environmental damage, infringement of intellectual property rights and industrial action (→ Rome II Regulation). The Regulation thereby contributes significantly to predictability of the applicable law and to legal certainty.

On the other hand, no agreement could be reached on the intricate question of which law to apply to infringements of personality rights, including infringements via the Internet. The Rome II Regulation currently expressly excludes this issue from its scope of application, pursuant to art 1(1)(g). Consequently, the traditional private international law rules on torts continue to apply in each country (for these rules, varying considerably between countries, see with references, Thomas Kadner Graziano, *Europäisches Internationales Deliktsrecht* (Mohr Siebeck 2003) 79–90; Thomas Kadner Graziano, *La responsabilité délictuelle en droit international privé européen* (Helbing Lichtenhahn 2004) 75–86).

In other parts of the world, legislatures also took the position that at least some specific torts need to be governed by specific rules. Both the new Japanese PILA and the new Chinese PILA provide specific rules for the two most difficult issues of complex torts, ie product liability (art 19 Japanese PILA; art 45 Chinese PILA) and defamation (art 20 Japanese PILA; art 46 Chinese PILA). The Chinese Act further contains specific rules on infringements of intellectual property rights (arts 48–50). Special rules on products liability are further found in art 1221 Russian CC, art 1130 Belarus CC, art 3128 Québec CC and in art 72 of the Tunisian PILA. Article 1222 of the Russian CC further contains a rule on unfair competition.

III. Conclusions

For many centuries, the *lex loci delicti* rule was considered the only reasonable rule to follow in the private international law of torts. From the 1950s onwards, in certain situations the *lex loci* rule was considered too rigid. In many countries, deviations from the *lex loci* rule were made, particularly in cases where the parties both had their habitual residence in the same country when the damage occurred, or where the parties were in a close relationship, such as a contractual relationship, which the tort violated. In these situations, the law governing this relationship was also applied to tortious liability.

From the 1980s onwards, → party autonomy gained ground in the European private international law of torts. Initially an *ex post* choice of the applicable law was recognized. Later, in situations where the parties were in contact before the damaging event occurred, the option to choose the applicable law in tort *ex ante* was, under certain circumstances, accepted.

Other important developments took place with regard to complex torts. In the early 20th century, many courts in Europe applied the law of the place of acting to potential liability in tort. In other countries the tort was located both at the place where the alleged tortfeasor had acted and the place where the protected interest suffered injury. This so-called ubiquity rule continues to apply with respect to jurisdiction under the Brussels I Regulation (recast) (→ Brussels I (Convention and Regulation)) and the → Lugano Convention (Lugano Convention of 30 October 2007 on jurisdiction and the recognition and enforcement of judgments in civil and commercial matters, [2007] OJ L 339/3). With regard to the applicable law, in a growing number of jurisdictions and under the Rome II Regulation, complex torts are for many good reasons governed by the law of the place where the injury occurred (as opposed to the place where the alleged tortfeasor has acted). In the second half of the 20th century, introducing special rules for separate categories of complex torts became a further and possibly the most important development in the private international law of torts.

All these developments have led to numerous clarifications and principled refinement of the rules in torts, thereby contributing to legal certainty. The Rome II Regulation adopted all of these modern developments. Since its entry into force, the discussions and deliberations in this field take place on a higher, more sophisticated level, allowing the achievement of more justice and fairness in transnational tort cases.

THOMAS KADNER GRAZIANO

Literature

Jürgen Basedow, Harald Baum and Yuko Nishitani (eds), *Japanese and European Private international law in Comparative Perspective* (Mohr Siebeck 2008); William Binchy and John Ahern (eds), *The Rome II Regulation on the Law Applicable to Non-Contractual Obligations: A New Tort Litigation Regime* (Martinus Nijhoff 2009); Andrew Dickinson, *The Rome II Regulation on the Law Applicable to Non-Contractual Obligations* (OUP 2008); Marc Fallon, 'The Law Applicable to Specific Torts' in Jürgen Basedow, Harald Baum and Yuko Nishitani (eds), *Japanese and European Private international law in Comparative Perspective* (Mohr Siebeck 2008) 261; Jan von Hein, 'Protecting Victims of Cross-Border Torts under Article 7 No. 2 Brussels I *bis*: Towards a More Differentiated and Balanced Approach' [2014/2015] YbPIL 241; Jin Huang and others, 'The Chinese Private international law Act: Some Selected Issues' [2012/2013] YbPIL 269; Thomas Kadner Graziano, *Gemeineuropäisches Internationales Privatrecht (am Beispiel der ausservertraglichen Haftung für Schäden)* (Mohr Siebeck 2002); Thomas Kadner Graziano, *Europäisches Internationales Deliktsrecht* (Mohr Siebeck 2003); Thomas Kadner Graziano, *La responsabilité délictuelle en droit international privé européen* (Helbing Lichtenhahn 2004); Thomas Kadner Graziano, 'General Principles of Private international law of Tort in Europe' in Jürgen Basedow, Harald Baum and Yuko Nishitani (eds), *Japanese and European Private international law in Comparative Perspective* (Mohr Siebeck 2008) 243; Thomas Kadner Graziano, 'Freedom to Choose the Applicable Law in Tort: Articles 14 and 4(3) of the Rome II Regulation' in William Binchy and John Ahern (eds), *The Rome II Regulation on the Law Applicable to Non-Contractual Obligations* (Martinus Nijhoff 2009) 113; Jan Kropholler and others, *Aussereuropäische IPR-Gesetze, Textausgabe* (Deutsches Notarinstitut und Max-Planck-Institut für ausländisches und Internationales Privatrecht 1999); JHC Morris, 'The Proper Law of Tort' [1951] Harv.L.Rev. 881; Yasuhiro Okuda, 'New Provisions on International Jurisdiction of Japanese Courts' [2011] YbPIL 367; Michel Reymond, *La Compétence internationale en cas d'atteinte à la personalité par Internet* (Schwethness 2015); Symeon Symeonides, 'Rome II and Tort Conflicts: A Missed Opportunity' [2008] Am.J.Comp.L. 173; Symeon Symeonides, 'Party Autonomy in Rome I and II from a Comparative Perspective' in Katharina Boele-Woelki and others (eds), *Convergence and Divergence in Private international law: Liber Amicorum Kurt Siehr* (Schulthess 2010) 513; also published in [2010] *Nederlands Internationaal Privaatrecht* 191; Russell J Weintraub, *Commentary on the Conflict of Laws* (6th edn, Foundation Press/Thomson Reuters 2010) ch 6.

Traffic accidents

I. Introduction

Road traffic accidents are the most common cause of personal injury and of extracontractual liability claims brought before European courts. Regarding liability for traffic accidents, domestic laws vary considerably between countries. For example, in most European countries the liability for personal injury suffered in a motor accident is strict, whereas in England and Ireland liability is still fault-based. In Belgium, liability is also fault-based, but certain victims benefit from insurance coverage which is independent of the traditional tort liability system. In jurisdictions using strict liability regimes, the circle of those entitled to compensation varies from one country to another. Other differences concern the damage covered and the amounts due, in particular with respect to loss of earnings or compensation of immaterial harm (in most jurisdictions, compensation is due for the entire actual loss suffered by the victim, whereas in Spain and Portugal the amounts, eg for loss of earnings, are fixed in *Baremos* providing flat-rates and caps). Finally, limitation periods vary considerably, ranging from one year to ten years (or more) depending on the country (for a comparative overview with numerous references, see Thomas Kadner Graziano and Christoph Oertel, 'Ein europäisches Haftungsrecht für Schäden im Straßenverkehr? – Eckpunkte de lege lata und Überlegungen de lege ferenda' [2008] ZVglRWiss 113–63). Consequently, the question of the applicable law might well be crucial for the outcome of a case, both with respect to the conditions for liability as well as the amount of compensation that is due.

II. The applicable law in road traffic accidents

In Europe, the law applicable to road traffic accidents is determined either by the → Rome II Regulation (Regulation (EC) No 864/2007 of the European Parliament and of the Council of 11 July 2007 on the law applicable to non-contractual obligations (Rome II), [2007] OJ L 199/40), or the Hague Traffic Accident Convention (Hague Convention of 4 May 1971 on the law applicable to traffic accidents, 965 UNTS 415).

1. The relationship between the Rome II Regulation and the Hague Traffic Accident Convention

The rules laid down in the Rome II Regulation on the law applicable to non-contractual obligations also apply in principle to road traffic accidents. However, in this area of great practical importance, unification of the private international law rules by the Rome II Regulation has remained partial at best. In fact, according to art 28(1), the Rome II Regulation 'shall not prejudice the application of international conventions to which one or more Member States are parties at the time when this Regulation is adopted and which lay down choice-of-law rules relating to non-contractual obligations', such as the Hague Traffic Accident Convention. With a view to respecting the international commitments of Member States (see Recital (36) Rome II Regulation), art 28 thus leads to the coexistence of two different sets of private international law rules within Europe.

The 13 EU Member States that are also contracting states of the Hague Traffic Accident Convention will thus continue to apply the Convention (text and list of contracting states in <www.hcch.net>). The 15 other EU Member States will designate the applicable law in accordance with the → Rome II Regulation. Consequently, the French (→ France), Spanish (→ Spain), Belgian (→ Belgium), Luxembourgish (→ Luxembourg), Dutch (the → Netherlands), Austrian (→ Austria), Polish (→ Poland), Lithuanian (→ Lithuania), Latvian (→ Latvia), Czech (→ Czech Republic), Slovak (→ Slovakia), Slovenian (→ Slovenia) and Croatian (→ Croatia) courts (as well as, outside the EU, the courts in Switzerland and the countries succeeding the former Yugoslavia) will determine the law applicable to road accidents through the application of the Hague Traffic Accident Convention (see eg French Cour de Cassation, 30 April 2014, no 13-11932). In contracting states of the Hague Traffic Accident Convention, the rules of the Rome II Regulation will only have to be taken into consideration where the matter is not, or is not yet, before a court, but the courts both in contracting states and in non-contracting states would have jurisdiction, ie particularly where an out-of-court settlement is negotiated. On the other hand, courts in the → United Kingdom, → Ireland, → Germany, → Finland, → Denmark, → Sweden, → Estonia, → Portugal, → Italy, → Greece, → Hungary, → Romania, → Bulgaria, → Malta and Cyprus will determine the law applicable to road traffic accidents according to the Rome II Regulation. Given that the rules on the applicable law used in the Rome II Regulation and in the Hague Traffic Accident Convention differ, the applicable law and the compensation that is due in an actual case might depend on the applicable private international law regime. As a result, the possibility of forum shopping in such cases will persist (→ Forum (and law) shopping).

2. Differences between the Rome II Regulation and the Hague Traffic Accident Convention

As a starting point, according to both the Rome II Regulation and the Hague Traffic Accident Convention, liability following a road traffic accident is in principle governed by the law of the jurisdiction where the accident occurred, under both art 4(1) of the Rome II Regulation and art 3 of the Hague Traffic Accident Convention.

A first difference between the two instruments exists with respect to the role of → party autonomy (→ Choice of law). In the case of traffic accidents, the parties might have a considerable interest in choosing the applicable law (usually *ex post*), in particular if the forum's private international law rules designate a foreign law.

The Rome II Regulation allows choice of the applicable law under art 14, whereas party autonomy in torts was not yet on the agenda in 1971 so that the Hague Traffic Accident Convention makes no mention of such a possibility. According to some scholars, the parties cannot exclude the law applicable under the Convention and choose another law instead (Adrian Rufener 'Article 134' in Heinrich Honsell and others (eds), *Basler Kommentar, Internationales Privatrecht* (2nd edn, 2007) no 29). The opposing opinion is that a choice of applicable law is permitted (Austrian Supreme Court of Justice (OGH), 26 January 1995 [1995] ZfRV 36, 212; French Cour de cassation, *Roho v Caron*, 19 April 1988 [1989] Rev.crit.DIP 68, note *Batiffol*). It is indeed difficult to see why the parties' agreement on the applicable law should not be respected under the Hague Traffic Accident Convention, especially in view of the marked current trend towards party autonomy in both contract and tort law, as expressed in art 14 Rome II Regulation (→ Torts).

A second major difference between the Rome II Regulation and the Hague Traffic Accident Convention concerns the conditions under which both instruments make exceptions to the application of the law of the place in which the accident occurred. For example when both the alleged tortfeasor and the injured party have their habitual residence in the same country at the time the damage occurred, art 4(2) of the Rome II Regulation provides for the application of the law of that country instead of the *lex loci delicti*. On the other hand, a rather complex exception clause in art 4 Hague Traffic Accident Convention focuses on the state of registration of the vehicle(s) involved in the accident. According to art 4(b) eg, where several vehicles are involved, the law of the state of registration is only applicable if all the vehicles are registered in the same state which is also a state other than that where the accident occurred. Under art 4(c), where persons that were outside a vehicle are involved in an accident, the exception to the *lex loci delicti* rule only applies if all these persons have their habitual residence in the state of registration. The exception to the application of the *lex loci delicti* rule therefore depends on the state of registration of the vehicles involved, even if the alleged tortfeasor and the injured person are habitually resident in the same country. Conversely, in such a case, the law of the country of the parties' common habitual residence would be applicable to their extra-contractual obligations under the Rome II Regulation.

A third difference is relevant in cases where the parties involved in the road traffic accident are in a contractual relationship with each other (eg a contract of transport or carriage). Under art 4(3) Rome II Regulation, the law applicable to the contract is also applicable to extra-contractual liability, so-called *rattachement accessoire* (→ Torts), whereas the Hague Traffic Accident Convention does not provide for a similar synchronous treatment of claims in contracts and torts.

3. The major differences between the two instruments in practice – four case studies

Four case studies inspired by case-law of the European courts illustrate the practical consequences of having different rules on the applicable law for traffic accidents in Europe in the Rome II Regulation on the one hand and the Hague Traffic Accident Convention on the other.

a) Road traffic accident: one single car involved

In a first scenario, inspired by the case-law of European courts, an accident happened in France involving a single hire car registered in Belgium. The car was carrying several people, all of whom were habitually resident in Spain. A claim for → damages was brought by passengers against the driver of the car.

The case was brought before the courts in France, a contracting state to the Hague Traffic Accident Convention (Cour de cassation crim, *R Casielles-Iglesias et J Feyaerts*, 6 May 1981 [1981] Rev.crit.DIP 679, note *Bourel*). Given that only one vehicle was involved and that this vehicle was registered in a state other than that where the accident occurred, the law of the state of registration, Belgian law, was applicable to the driver's liability to the passengers, pursuant to art 4(a) of the Hague Traffic Accident Convention. (For a critical evaluation of this solution, and an opinion in favour of the application of Spanish law to the facts, see Bourel, [1981] Rev.crit.DIP 681, 685; Werner Lorenz, 'Das außervertragliche Haftungsrecht der Haager Konventionen' (1993) 57 RabelsZ 175, 180 ff.) Should such a case be brought before the courts in Belgium or Spain (both contracting states to the Hague Convention), they would also apply the Convention (leading to Belgian law).

Conversely, in such a situation, art 4(2) Rome II Regulation would lead to the application of the law of the country of habitual residence of the person(s) to be liable and the person(s) having suffered damage, ie Spanish law.

b) Road traffic accident: two cars involved, claim brought by passengers against driver or keeper of the other car
In a second example, a car driver with habitual residence in France attempted, contrary to the rules of the road, to overtake an articulated lorry on a German road. Another car, going in the other direction and carrying two brothers also with habitual residence in France, was forced to make an emergency stop. The brothers' car skidded and crashed into the lorry, causing the death of one brother and serious injury to the other. Both cars were registered in France whereas the lorry was registered in another state. The surviving brother and his father brought a claim against the driver of the other car and its keeper for pecuniary damages and for damages for loss of a loved one (bereavement damages). The latter would be awarded under French but not under German law (see the scenario of French Cour de cassation, *Kieger v Amigues*, 30 May 1967 [1967] Rev.crit. DIP 728).

In such a case, the German courts (with jurisdiction according to art 7(2) Brussels I Regulation (recast) (Regulation (EU) No 1215/2012 of the European Parliament and of the Council of 12 December 2012 on jurisdiction and the recognition and enforcement of judgments in civil and commercial matters (recast), [2012] OJ L 351/1; → Brussels I (Convention and Regulation)) since the accident happened in Germany) would apply the Rome II Regulation. This would lead to application of French law, pursuant to art 4(2) of the Rome II Regulation, as the alleged tortfeasor and the injured passenger both had their habitual residence in France.

On the other hand, the French courts, also with jurisdiction according to art 4(1) Brussels I Regulation (recast) since the defendant was domiciled in France, designated (and continue to designate) the law according to the Hague Traffic Accident Convention, as opposed to the Rome II Regulation (see art 28 of the Rome II Regulation and above, II.1.). The Hague Convention stipulates that if all vehicles involved in an accident are registered in the same state, then under art 4(b) read in accordance with art 4(a) of the Convention, the law applicable to driver and passenger claims is the law of the state of registration. However, in this case, only the two cars were registered in France, unlike the lorry which was registered in another state. In this instance, given that the lorry was not registered in France, not all the vehicles were registered in the same state, so the requirements of art 4 Hague Traffic Accident Convention, allowing an exception to the *lex loci delicti* rule, were not met. Therefore the French courts, applying the Hague Traffic Accident Convention, designated German law (ie the *lex loci delicti*) as the applicable law.

To conclude, in such cases, courts in EU Member States that are not Contracting States to the Hague Traffic Accident Convention and those that are would apply different laws to the same traffic accident case. In this case study, according to the Rome II Regulation German courts would apply French law since both the alleged tortfeasor and the injured person had their habitual residence in France, whereas in accordance with the Hague Traffic Accident Convention French courts would designate German law since the accident happened in Germany and the vehicles involved were not all registered in the same state. Given the divergences between the laws of the two countries in the compensation awarded in such a case, particularly for non-pecuniary loss following the loss or severe injury of a one (*tort moral*/bereavement damages), victims of such accidents and their relatives would be well advised to opt for proceedings before the German courts in order for French law to be applied.

c) Road traffic accident: more than one car involved, claim of passenger against driver or keeper of the car he was in

Often accidents involve several vehicles but passengers bring an action against the driver, keeper or owner of the vehicle in which they were travelling. This situation can be illustrated by a third scenario. A car registered in Austria carrying passengers, all with habitual residence in Austria, crashes in Italy into a stationary vehicle registered in Italy. The passengers claim compensation for their injuries from the driver's insurance company. According to established case-law, even a parked car playing a purely passive role in the accident is deemed to be 'involved in the accident' in the sense of art 4 Hague Traffic Accident Convention, since it might transpire during proceedings that the car was wrongly parked, giving rise to liability of its keeper. However, it would be very inconvenient if the issue of whether the car was wrongly parked had an impact on the applicable law, thus possibly leading to a change of the applicable law once the finding of facts advances during proceedings. In order to avoid this effect, the stationary vehicle is thus also regarded as being 'involved' in the accident. Given that in the above scenario not all the involved vehicles were registered in one single state other than that where the accident occurred, the requirements of art 4(a) are not met and, pursuant to art 3, the Hague Traffic Accident Convention leads to application of the law of the place where the accident occurred. Before Austrian courts, the case would thus be governed by the law of the place of the accident in Italy (see eg the cases Austrian Supreme Court of Justice (OGH), 21 May 1985, IPRE 2/90; 20 June 1989, IPRE 3/72: an accident in Hungary involving vehicles registered in Hungary and Austria respectively; claim for damages by the passenger against the driver of the vehicle and his liability insurance: application of the *lex loci delicti*; similarly, Belgian Hof van Cassatie, 15 March 1993 [1992/1993] RW 1446 and French Cour de cassation, *GAN Incendie-Accidents, Daniel Dubois c/ Delle Pascale Marchot et Caisse primaire d'assurance maladie de l'Essonne*, 4 April 1991 [1991] Clunet 981: collision between a motorbike registered in France and a car registered in Germany occurred in Yugoslavia; the passenger on the motorbike claimed damages from the driver of the motorbike and his insurer; application of Yugoslav law, ie the *lex loci delicti*; similarly, French Cour de cassation, *Mutuelle Parisienne de garantie et autres v Delfino et autres*, 24 March 1987 [1987] Rev. crit.DIP 577; Cour de cassation France, 6 December 1988 [1990] Rev.crit.DIP 786; Cour de cassation France, *L'Union et le Phénix espagnol et autres./. Mlle Beau*, 6 June 1990 [1991] Rev.crit.DIP 354).

Alternatively, if the case were brought before the Italian courts, the Rome II Regulation would apply and under art 4(2) the law of the country of the common habitual residence of the injured person and the person claimed to be liable would be applicable, ie Austrian law.

d) Road traffic accident: one car involved, victims outside the car

The fourth example is inspired by the first case in which the English High Court considered the application of the Rome II Regulation. A person with habitual residence in England was on holiday in Spain, where in a supermarket car park he was hit by a car and was severely injured. The car was registered in England and kept, owned and driven by a person living in Spain. Spain is a contracting state to the Hague Traffic Accident Convention, whereas the UK is not.

Spanish courts would determine the applicable law under the Hague Traffic Accident Convention. Under art 3, liability for traffic accidents is in principle determined according to the law of the place of the accident. Given that only one car was involved in the accident and the claim was brought by a victim who was outside the vehicle, the possibility arises under art 4(a) of an exception to the *lex loci delicti*. Article 4(a) provides that

> [w]here only one vehicle is involved in the accident and it is registered in a State [England] other than that where the accident occurred [Spain], the internal law of the State of registration [English law] is applicable ... towards a victim who is outside the vehicle at the place of the accident and whose habitual residence is in the State of registration.

In the example, the victim was on in car park and outside the car that caused the accident, and also had his habitual residence in England, the state in which the car that caused his injury was registered. Thus, the conditions for an exception under art 4(a) Hague Traffic Accident Convention are met, so the Spanish courts would apply English law to the victim's claim.

On the other hand, the English courts would apply the Rome II Regulation in order to determine the applicable law. According to art 4(1) the law of the place of the accident applies, except when 'the person claimed to be liable and the person sustaining damage both have their habitual residence in the same country at the time when the damage occurs', in which case 'the law of that country shall apply', art 4(2). In the example, the victim had his habitual residence in England whereas the driver of the car that caused the accident lived in Spain. Thus, the conditions for an exception under art 4(2) Rome II Regulation are not met and English courts would decide the case according to Spanish law.

Here again, the applicable law issue is particularly interesting in view of the specific features of the respective liability laws. English law applies the principle of full compensation with respect to all → damages, including eg loss of earnings. On the other hand, under Spanish law, compensation for certain personal injury and for loss of income and immaterial harm is calculated on the basis of a table using fixed lump sums (*Baremo*). The amounts are calculated on the basis of data collected annually in Spain, and might be considerably lower than the damage that a foreign victim actually suffered.

4. *Applicable law:* résumé

These examples demonstrate that for traffic accidents, frequent as they are in practice, the dual system of regimes compromises the objective of unifying the rules on the law applicable to traffic accidents in Europe as well as compromising the foreseeability of solutions on a European scale.

5. *A way out of the dilemma?*

The question arises how the Rome II Regulation and Hague Traffic Accident Convention could be better coordinated so as to achieve legal certainty and foreseeability of the applicable law on a European scale.

For example, one alternative would be that cases involving persons all with habitual residence in the EU would be governed by the Rome II Regulation, whereas the Hague Traffic Accident Convention would continue to govern cases where at least one of the parties is resident in an EU non-Member State, such as Switzerland. Under this solution, in the first scenario concerning an accident in France with a car rented in Belgium, before all courts in the EU, the claims of the Spanish victims against the Spanish driver of the car would be governed by Spanish law given that the parties had their habitual residence in EU Member States. In the second scenario of an accident in Germany involving persons all habitually resident in France, the case would also be resolved differently: the law applicable to the case between the surviving brother and his father on the one hand and the driver of the other car on the other, would, whether brought in France or Germany, be decided according to the Rome II Regulation and French law would apply given that the parties had their habitual residence in an EU Member State. Conversely, the applicable law in an action between parties with their habitual residence in, for example, France and Switzerland, would be determined by the Hague Traffic Accident Convention before the courts in either country. The applicable law in the third and fourth scenarios would also be the same whether the case be brought before the courts in Austria or Italy (third scenario) or in Spain or England (fourth scenario), all these states being EU Member States.

To achieve this outcome, art 28 of the Rome II Regulation would need to be complemented eg by the following paragraph: 'Where the person claimed to be liable and the injured person have their habitual residence in EU Member States at the time the damage occurred, this Regulation will take precedence over other conventions to which the Member States are or become party' (compare the proposal in Thomas Kadner Graziano, 'The Rome II Regulation and the Hague Conventions on Tort Law: Interaction, Conflicts and Future Perspectives' [2008] NIPR 425–9). However, such a modification would necessarily imply the renegotiation of the scope of application of the Hague Traffic Accident Convention between the EU and the Hague Conference.

III. Jurisdiction

1. Introduction

If a traffic accident victim brings a claim against the driver, keeper or owner of the vehicle involved in causing the damage, jurisdiction in the courts in Europe is determined either according to the Brussels I Regulation (recast) (→ Brussels I (Convention and Regulation)) or the → Lugano Convention (Lugano Convention of 30 October 2007 on jurisdiction and the recognition and enforcement of judgments in civil and commercial matters, [2007] OJ L 339/3). A claim can in principle be brought either under art 4(1) Brussels I Regulation (recast)/ art 2(1) Lugano Convention, before the courts of the state of the defendant's domicile, or under art 7(2) Brussels I Regulation (recast)/ art 5 No 3 Lugano Convention before the courts of the place where the accident occurred.

With traffic accident cases in Europe, the victim has the further option to bring a direct claim against the liability insurer of the car involved in causing the damage (see art 18 Directive 2009/103/EC of the European Parliament and of the Council of 16 September 2009 relating to insurance against civil liability in respect of the use of motor vehicles, and the enforcement of the obligation to insure against such liability [2009] OJ L 263/11). In practice, the claim is indeed usually brought directly against the insurer (→ Direct action).

2. Heads of jurisdiction for direct claims against liability insurers

According to the Brussels I Regulation (recast) and the Lugano Convention, a claim against an insurer domiciled in an EU Member State or in a contracting state of the Lugano Convention, may be brought in the courts of the state of the insurer's domicile, under art 11(1)(a) Brussels I Regulation (recast)/ art 9(1)(a) Lugano Convention. 'In respect of liability insurance . . ., the insurer may in addition be sued in the courts for the place where the harmful event occurred', under art 12 Brussels I Regulation (recast)/ art 10 Lugano Convention. These two heads of jurisdiction correspond to the general rules for jurisdiction (see III.1. above) and take their place for claims against insurers.

A road traffic accident victim has the further option of bringing a claim against the liability insurer before the courts of the place 'where the claimant is domiciled', under art 13(2) in conjunction with art 11(1)(b) Brussels I Regulation (recast)/ art 11(2) with art 9(1)(b) Lugano Convention. The ECJ has confirmed that this forum at the claimant's domicile is available to persons benefitting from a direct claim against an insurer following a road traffic accident (Case C-463/06 *FBTO Schadenverzekeringen NV v Jack Odenbreit* [2007] ECR I-11321). In practice, in the case of an accident in a foreign country, parties almost always prefer a forum in the country of their domicile to a forum at the foreign place of accident, thus benefitting substantially from the forum at their own domicile confirmed in *Odenbreit*.

If the accident happened in a country that is not the one of the victim's domicile and the plaintiff brings the claim in his country of domicile, the courts there will often have to apply foreign law. If for example, as was the case in *Odenbreit*, an accident occurs in the Netherlands, between a car registered and insured in the Netherlands and driven by a person domiciled there, and a car registered in Germany driven by a person domiciled there, and if a claim is brought by the German victim against the Dutch insurer of the other party before the German courts (ie the courts of the victim's domicile), then according to art 4(1) Rome II Regulation, this claim is governed by Dutch law.

If a road accident victim has (as in the *Odenbreit* case) the choice between bringing the claim before the courts of a contracting state of the Hague Convention (such as the Netherlands) and those of a non-contracting state (such as Germany), the above-mentioned differences between the connecting factors of the Hague Convention and of the Rome II Regulation might have an impact on the applicable law and the outcome of the case so that there is again a potential for → forum (and law) shopping.

On the other hand, the forum of the claimant's domicile is not available for a social security insurer that has paid compensation to a victim of a traffic accident and that brings an action for recourse against the car's civil liability insurer. The ECJ held that, whereas the victim is generally in a weak position justifying a forum for the plaintiff, a social security insurer is not (C-347/08 *Vorarlberger Gebietskrankenkasse v WGV-Schwäbische Allgemeine Versicherungs AG* [2009] ECR I-8661).

The *Odenbreit* decision confirming the forum at the victim's domicile has important consequences for the insured driver, keeper or owner of a vehicle himself. The Brussels I Regulation (recast) and the Lugano Convention both state that '[i]f the law governing such direct actions provides that the policyholder or the insured may be joined as a party to the action, the same court shall have jurisdiction over them', art 13(3) Brussels I Regulation (recast)/ art 11(3) Lugano Convention. The purpose of this provision is to prevent conflicting decisions. Consequently, if the victim brings a claim before the courts of the country of his domicile, and if the insured is joined in this action, then according to art 13(3) Brussels I Regulation (recast)/ art 11(3) Lugano Convention in conjunction with the applicable national law, the insured party will have to defend their interests before the (foreign) court of the claimant's domicile. The forum at the place 'where the claimant is domiciled' is available for a claim against the liability insurer even if, under the applicable law, the insured party is required to join proceedings that are brought against his insurer (which is the case eg in Italian law, see eg the German case of the Higher Regional Court (OLG) of Nuremberg, 10 April 2012 [2012] NJW-RR 1178).

IV. The law applicable to direct claims against civil liability insurers

The further question is which law governs the issue of whether the victim can bring a direct claim against the liability insurer of the person claimed to be responsible (→ Direct action).

Before entry into force of the Rome II Regulation, the law applicable to the insurance contract in some countries determined whether there was a direct claim against the insurer. A formerly widespread solution was to determine this issue under the law governing liability for the accident (the applicable tort law). The most recent solution (adopted eg under art 141 Swiss Private international law Act (Bundesgesetz über das Internationale Privatrecht of 18 December 1987, 1988 BBl I 5, as amended)) is to allow a direct action against the insurer if either the law applicable to liability or the law applicable to the insurance contract provides for a direct claim.

1. Law applicable under the Rome II Regulation

With a view to protecting the injured party, art 18 Rome II Regulation adopts the third of the above solutions, providing for an alternative private international law rule in favour of the person who suffered damage. This solution is considered entirely compatible with the interests of the insurer. The direct action has no influence on the existence or scope of his obligation given that the insurer's duty to provide coverage is always determined by the law applicable to the insurance contract, whereas any obligation to compensate the victim is always governed by the law applicable to the victim's claims against the tortfeasor, ie the car's driver, keeper or, in some jurisdictions, its owner.

2. Law applicable under the Hague Traffic Accident Convention

The Hague Traffic Accident Convention provides a multi-layer or cascade test: According to art 9, first sentence Hague Traffic Accident Convention, '[p]ersons who have suffered injury or damage shall have a right of direct action against the insurer of the person liable if they have such a right under the law applicable according to arts 3, 4 or 5' of the Convention, ie according to the case under examination, the law of the state where the accident occurred or the law of the registration state of the involved car(s). Alternatively, '[i]f the law of the State of registration is applicable under arts 4 or 5 and that law provides no right of direct action, such a right shall nevertheless exist if it is provided by the internal law of the State where the accident occurred', under art 9, second sentence, and ultimately, '[i]f neither of these laws provides any such right it shall exist if it is provided by the law governing the contract of insurance', according to art 9, third sentence.

To conclude, in Europe this question has lost much of its practical importance since in all EU Member States, as well as for example in Switzerland, the road traffic accident victim today has a direct claim against the insurer of the vehicle that caused the accident.

V. Secondary victims

1. The place of injury in cases where damage is suffered by secondary victims

In the event of a serious accident, the primary victim, ie the person who is involved at the scene of the accident, is often not the only person to suffer damage. The primary victim's relatives may also suffer damage in the form of loss of financial support and non-pecuniary loss (bereavement damages, *tort moral*). The issue then arises as whether, for the purpose of jurisdiction and the applicable law, the place of injury suffered by secondary victims should be the same as that applied to primary victims, or whether the secondary victims' place of injury should be determined autonomously and in particular may be located at the place of their domicile (→ Domicile, habitual residence and establishment).

Before entry into force of the Rome II Regulation, the French *Cour de cassation* had to determine the conflict of law rule to be used for bereavement damages of secondary victims: a French travel agency organized a tour of Cambodia. During an excursion on the Mekong, a canoe carrying French tourists capsized and four tourists were killed. The victims' relatives, domiciled in France, brought an action against the travel agency and their insurance company for compensation of their non-pecuniary loss.

The *Cour de cassation* clearly opted for submitting all damage (ie initial damage and damage suffered by secondary victims) to the law of the place where the event of their common cause of action had taken place (in the example Cambodia), thereby declining to treat primary and secondary victims differently (Cour de cassation, *Pays-Fourvel v Société Axa Courtage* [2004] Rev.crit.DIP 82, note *Bureau*, [2004] Clunet 499, note *Légier*, [2004] JCP II 10006, note *Lardeux*, [2003] Petites affiches no 255 p 11, note *Ancel*, [2006] IPRax 307, note *Kadner Graziano*).

According to art 15(f) Rome II Regulation '[t]he law applicable to non-contractual obligations under this Regulation shall govern in particular ... (f) persons entitled to compensation for damage sustained personally'. It may be inferred from this provision that the law applicable to claims by primary victims also governs claims by secondary victims. Article 4(1) of the Rome II Regulation, which states that the applicable law is generally the law of the country in which the damage occurs 'irrespective of the country or countries in which the indirect consequences of that event occur', might be understood as reinforcing this argument further.

In a judgment of 10 December 2015 (ECJ Case C-350/14 *Florin Lazar v Allianz SpA* [20] ECLI:EU:C:2015:802), the ECJ followed this same line of reasoning. The ECJ held that damage suffered by secondary victims following the death of a close relative in a road traffic accident is to be regarded as an 'indirect consequence' of the accident. The place where secondary victims suffer their own loss is thus irrelevant in determining the applicable law under art 4(1) of the Rome II Regulation. On the contrary, the law that governs, or would govern, claims of primary victims is also to apply to claims brought by secondary victims.

This solution is persuasive in view of the interests at stake. If the place of injury suffered by secondary victims were to be determined autonomously at their own domicile, every car accident occurring in the EU could have worldwide implications regarding the applicable law, depending on the secondary victims' domicile. Arguments relating to the foreseeability of the applicable law, simplicity and consistency all favour application of the same law for primary and secondary victims.

2. Compulsory insurance against civil liability in respect of the use of motor vehicles (First Motor Insurance Directive and Third Motor Insurance Directive): coverage with respect to secondary victims

In a 2013 ruling, the ECJ held that, if the applicable law provides compensation for the immaterial harm suffered by secondary victims following a road traffic accident, then the mandatory insurance against civil liability for damage caused by the use of motor vehicles must also cover the damage suffered by the secondary victims (Case C-22/12 *Katarína Haasová v Rastislav Petrík, Blanka Holingová* [2013] OJ C 367/5).

VI. Conclusions

Following an international road traffic accident, the injured party often has a choice between the courts of the state of the defendant's domicile and those of the place where the accident occurred. For claims against the defendant's liability insurer, the injured party has the further option of the courts of his or her own domicile.

In Europe, the law applicable to road traffic accident liability is determined either by the Rome II Regulation or by the 1971 Hague Traffic Accident Convention. There are significant differences between the connecting factors under the Rome II Regulation and the Hague Convention, though either instrument may be used to determine the applicable law, depending on the state where the claim is brought.

Scenarios drawn from the practice of courts in Europe demonstrate that the choice of the forum might have a significant impact on the applicable law, and, given the differences in domestic substantive laws on road traffic accident liability, on the outcome of a given case. Consequently, as long as the Rome II Regulation and the Hague Traffic Convention coexist, careful analysis of the plaintiff's options might considerably enhance their chances of success in litigation, in turn prolonging the opportunity for forum shopping.

THOMAS KADNER GRAZIANO

Literature

Vincent Brulhart, 'Le projet de Règlement "Rome II" sur la loi applicable aux obligations non contractuelles: son incidence en matière de circulation routière, notamment à la lumière du droit suisse' [2007] (Schweizerische) Haftung und Versicherung (HAVE/REAS) 3; European Commission, 'Rome II Study on compensation of cross-border victims in the EU. Compensation of victims of cross-border road traffic accidents in the EU: comparison of national practices, analysis of problems and evaluation of options for improving the position of cross-border victims. Final report prepared for the European Commission DG Internal Market and Services. Final version of the final report – Part II – Analysis' (2008) 20, available at <http://ec.europa.eu/civiljustice/news/docs/study_compensation_road_victims_en.pdf>; European Commission, 'Consultation Paper on the Compensation of Victims of Cross-Border Road Traffic Accidents in the European Union' (2009), available at <http://ec.europa.eu/internal_market/consultations/docs/2009/cross-border-accidents/rome2study_en.pdf>; Robert Fucik, 'Checkliste zum Haager Strassenverkehrsübereinkommen' [2011] (Österreichische) Zeitschrift für Verkehrsrecht (ZVR) 47; Hague Conference on Private International Law, 'Convention on the Law Applicable to Traffic Accidents, Explanatory Report' (by Eric W Essén), available at <www.hcch.net/upload/expl19e.pdf>; Jan von Hein, 'Article 4 and Traffic Accidents' in William Binchy and John Ahern (eds), *The Rome II Regulation on the Law Applicable to Non-Contractual Obligations: A New Tort Litigation Regime* (Martinus Nijhoff 2009) 153; Thomas Kadner Graziano, 'Le nouveau droit international privé communautaire en matière de responsabilité extracontractuelle' [2008] Rev.crit. DIP 445; Thomas Kadner Graziano, 'The Rome II Regulation and the Hague Conventions on Tort Law: Interaction, Conflicts and Future Perspectives' [2008] NIPR 425; Thomas Kadner Graziano, 'Das auf außervertragliche Schuldverhältnisse anwendbare Recht nach Inkrafttreten der Rom II-Verordnung' [2009] RabelsZ 1; Thomas Kadner Graziano, 'Internationale Straßenverkehrsunfälle im Lichte von Brüssel I, Rom II und des Haager Straßenverkehrsübereinkommens' [2011] ZVR 40; Thomas Kadner Graziano and Christoph Oertel, 'Ein europäisches Haftungsrecht für Schäden im Strassenverkehr? – Eckpunkte de lege lata und Überlegungen de lege ferenda' [2008] ZVglRWiss 113; Beate Lemke-Geis and Martin Müller, 'Internationale Unfallregulierung in der Europäischen Union' [2009] SVR 241; Werner Lorenz, 'Das außervertragliche Haftungsrecht der Haager Konventionen' [1993] RabelsZ 175; Csondor Istvan Nagy, 'The Rome II Regulation and Traffic Accidents: Uniform Conflict Rules with Some Room for Forum Shopping – How So?' [2010] J Priv Int L 93; Jenny Papettas, 'Direct Actions against Insurers of Intra-Community Cross-Border Traffic Accidents: Rome II and the Motor Insurance Directives' [2012] J Priv Int L 297; Nora Reisinger, *Internationale Verkehrsunfälle: Gerichtszuständigkeit und anwendbares Recht* (LexisNexis 2011); Thomas Thiede, 'Strassenverkehrsunfall mit Auslandsberührung – Internationale Zuständigkeit und anwendbares Recht' [2013] ZAK 407; Thomas Thiede and Markus Kellner, 'Forum shopping zwischen dem Haager Übereinkommen über das auf Verkehrsunfälle anzuwendende Recht und der Rom II-Verordnung' [2007] VersR 1624; Thomas Thiede and Katarzyna Ludwichowska, 'Kfz-Haftpflichtversicherung' [2008] VersR 631.

Transport law (uniform law)

I. Concept and function

Uniform transport law refers to the body of law which covers all aspects of carriage of goods and passengers through a uniform set of substantive legal rules such as that on the rights and obligations of the parties to a carriage contract, liability in case of an accident, safety and security issues and environmental protection.

1. Public international law

In the area of public international law, uniform sets of rules on the protection of the environment and safety and security measures for specific types of transport have been agreed upon. These rules are generally adopted in multilateral conventions; for maritime transport eg SOLAS (International Convention of 1 November 1974 for the safety of life at sea, 1184 UNTS 278 and the SOLAS Protocol 1978 (Protocol of 17 February 1978 relating to the International Convention for the safety of life at sea, 1226 UNTS 237)), COLREG (Convention on the

International Regulations for preventing collisions at sea of 20 October 1972, 1050 UNTS 16), MARPOL (International Convention of 2 November 1973 on the prevention of pollution from ships, 1340 UNTS 184, as modified by the Protocol of 17 February 1978 relating thereto, 1340 UNTS 61), SAR Convention (International Convention of 27 April 1979 on maritime search and rescue, 1405 UNTS 97), UNCLOS (United Nations Convention of 10 December 1982 on the law of the sea, 1833 UNTS 396); and for air transport eg the Chicago Convention (Convention of 7 December 1944 on international civil aviation, 15 UNTS 295), Convention of 1 March 1991 on the marking of plastic explosives for the purpose of detection (2122 UNTS 359), Convention of 10 September 2010 on the suppression of unlawful acts relating to international civil aviation (ICAO Doc No 9960). The unification of transport law is almost invariably the result of the work of international organizations established by international treaties. Leading organizations are the → IMO for sea transport, → ICAO for air transport and OTIF for rail transport, as well as, on occasion UNECE and UNCITRAL. However, NGOs such as the CMI and the IATA also play an important part in the unification efforts.

Unification of transport law in the area of public international law also takes place at the regional level. Several conventions have been adopted eg for the protection of the marine environment in certain regions, such as the OSPAR Convention (Convention of 22 September 1992 for the protection of the marine environment of the North-East Atlantic, 2354 UNTS 67), the Helsinki Convention (Convention of 9 April 1992 on the protection of the marine environment of the Baltic Sea area, 2009 UNTS 197) and the Bucharest Convention (Bucharest Convention of 21 April 1992 for the protection of the Black Sea against pollution, 1764 UNTS 3). Last but not least, the EU has been increasingly active in the unification of transport law. It has laid down rules for the regulation of the Internal Market (eg Council Regulation (EEC) No 2407/92 of 23 July 1992 on licensing of air carriers ([1992] OJ L 240/1) and Commission Regulation (EC) No 2096/2005 of 20 December 2005 laying down common requirements for the provision of air navigation services ([2005] OJ L 335/13) for the air transport sector, Regulation (EC) No 1073/2009 of the European Parliament and of the Council of 21 October 2009 on common rules for access to the international market for coach and bus services, and amending Regulation (EC) No 561/2006 ([2009] OJ L 300/88) for the road transport sector, Council Regulation (EEC) No 3577/92 of 7 December 1992 applying the principle of freedom to provide services to maritime transport within Member States (maritime cabotage) ([1992] OJ L 364/7) for the maritime transport sector), regarding safety issues and for environmental protection (eg Regulation (EC) No 216/2008 of the European Parliament and of the Council of 20 February 2008 on common rules in the field of civil aviation and establishing a European Aviation Safety Agency, and repealing Council Directive 91/670/EEC, Regulation (EC) No 1592/2002 and Directive 2004/36/EC ([2008] OJ L 79/1) for air transport, Regulation (EC) No 391/2009 of the European Parliament and of the Council of 23 April 2009 on common rules and standards for ship inspection and survey organisations ([2009] OJ L 131/11), Regulation (EC) No 530/2012 of the European Parliament and of the Council of 13 June 2012 on the accelerated phasing-in of double-hull or equivalent design requirements for single-hull oil tankers (recast) ([2012] OJ L 172/3) and Regulation (EC) No 336/2006 of the European Parliament and of the Council of 15 February 2006 on the implementation of the International Safety Management Code within the Community and repealing Council Regulation (EC) No 3051/95 ([2006] OJ L 64/1) for maritime transport) and for security issues (eg Regulation (EC) No 300/2008 of the European Parliament and of the Council of 11 March 2008 on common rules in the field of civil aviation security and repealing Regulation (EC) No 2320/2002 ([2008] OJ L 97/72) in the area of air transport, Regulation (EC) No 725/2004 of the European Parliament and of the Council of 31 March 2004 on enhancing ship and port facility security ([2004] OJ L 129/6) in the area of maritime transport).

2. Private international law

For the purposes of private international law, uniform transport law indicates the set of rules intended for the regulation of liability in tort, contractual relations pertaining to carriage of goods and passengers and rights *in rem* in transport vehicles. The need for unification emerges from the international character of transportation. Application of isolated national regulations causes severe problems such as forum selection and unpredictability in international commercial relations. Hence, unification of transport law plays a vital role as a means of avoiding unfair outcomes, promoting certainty of law for the international transportation sector and for the regulation of risk allocation.

The need for unification in transport law is predominantly met by unified substantive law rules in international conventions. These international conventions generally have a limited territorial and personal scope of application, they are only applicable to cases involving more than one country. Article 1 para 1 Montreal Convention (Convention of 28 May 1999 for the unification of certain rules relating to international carriage by air, 2242 UNTS 309) states for instance that the convention is applicable to international carriages by air. Similarly, art 2 Athens Convention 2002 (Athens Convention of 1 November 2002 relating to the carriage of passengers and their luggage by sea, IMO Doc LEG/CONF.13/20 (19 November 2002)) provides that the convention is applicable to international carriage of passengers by sea. However, some transport law conventions are configured as unlimited substantive law unification, ie applicable also to national issues such as the 1976 LLMC (Convention of 19 November 1976 on limitation of liability for maritime claims, 1456 UNTS 221, as amended by the 1996 Protocol, 35 ILM 1433, and in 2012 by the amendment adopted by the Legal Committee of IMO at its ninety-ninth session (April 2012) by resolution LEG.5(99); art 15) and the 1999 Arrest Convention (International Convention of 12 March 1999 on arrest of ships, 2797 UNTS I-44196; art 8). Under some of these conventions, however, it is still possible to reserve the right to regulate purely domestic issues in a different way (eg art 15 para 3 1976 LLMC).

In addition to unified substantive law rules, some international conventions on transport law also adopt private international law rules, such as for jurisdiction (eg art 46 CIM (Uniform Rules concerning the contract of international carriage of goods by rail (Appendix B to the Convention of 9 May 1980 concerning international carriage by rail (COTIF), 1396 UNTS 2, in the version of the Protocol of Modification of 3 June 1999, available at <www.otif.org>)) and *lis alibi pendens* (art 21 para 4 Hamburg Rules (United Nations Convention of 31 March 1978 on the carriage of goods by sea, 1695 UNTS 3)). Nevertheless, the private international law rules of the forum must still be applied as international conventions on transport law do not cover every single issue. Therefore, national laws as identified pursuant to the conflict of laws rules of the → *lex fori* remain subsidiarily applicable.

II. Historical development

Although the earliest mode of transport is carriage by sea, the first work in the sense of modern unification took place in the area of transport by rail. After the first railways began operating in the early 19th century, the lack of a unified regulation caused economic losses due to the need for the re-consignment of the goods at each border (Joseph Haenni, 'Carriage by Rail' in René Rodière and Rolf Herber (eds), *International Encyclopedia of Comparative Law, vol XII: Law of Transport* (Mohr 1973) 12). This led to the very first piece of uniform transport law in order to solve the problem: the Berne Convention concerning carriage of goods which was signed in 1890 and entered into force in 1893 (Berne Convention of 14 October 1890 concerning carriage of goods by rail, [1893] ZIEV 1). The carriage of passengers by rail was not internationally regulated until 1924. After several amendments, both conventions were ultimately merged, as annexes, into a single convention, the COTIF (Convention of 9 May 1980 concerning international carriage by rail, 1396 UNTS 2), adopted in 1980 (→ Carriage of goods by road, rail and inland waterways).

The unification of law relating to air carriage was not promoted until after regular passenger carriage started in the 1920s. Even though airlines were mostly subsidized by the states during the infancy of the aviation industry, national legislation of this new mode of transport was either lacking or insufficient. Thus, the CITEJA, a committee to delineate unified rules, was established. Consequently, the Warsaw Convention which lays down the liability regime for the international carriage of passengers and goods was adopted in 1929 (Convention of 12 October 1929 for the unification of certain rules relating to international carriage by air, 137 LNTS 11). However, soon after its entry into force in 1933, the Convention proved to be inadequate especially due to the liability limits being rendered unrealistically low because of the rapid development of aviation technology and the strength gained by the aviation industry. Therefore, the Convention was amended by the Hague Protocol (Protocol of 28 September 1955 to amend the Convention for the unification of certain rules relating to international carriage by air, 478 UNTS 371). Further attempts to raise liability limits for passenger transport followed, until in 1999 a completely new air transport convention was agreed, the Montreal Convention, which is intended to replace the Warsaw Convention. Another matter involving air transport was the damage caused by aircraft to third parties on the surface. This issue was first regulated in the Rome Convention 1933 (Convention of 29 May 1933 for the unification of certain rules relating to damage caused by aircraft to third parties on the surface, (1937) 8 JAL 312). However, due to the lack of wide international support, a new convention, the Convention of 7 October 1952 on damage caused by foreign aircraft to third parties on the surface was adopted (310 UNTS 181). Consideration of the issue of aircraft being used for unlawful purposes (triggered by the 9/11 attacks) led to the adoption of two separate conventions for damage caused by aircrafts and damage resulting from the unlawful interference involving aircraft in 2009 (→ Air law (uniform law)).

In maritime transport, the first unification work began in the late 19th century. It started with the work of the ILA but was soon transferred to the CMI. Under the auspices of the CMI, the first results of unification efforts were the Collision Convention and the Salvage Convention, both dated 1910. The Collision Convention (International Convention of 23 September 1910 for the unification of certain rules of law related to collision between vessels, in K Zweigert and J Kropholler, *Sources of International Uniform Law*, vol 2 (AW Sijthoff 1972) 3) abolished differing national liability schemes for collisions at sea by the proportionate fault principle. From the varying principles of common and civil law for → salvage matters, the common law understanding of salvage was adopted as international regime under the Salvage Convention (International Convention of 23 September 1910 for the unification of certain rules of law related to assistance and salvage at sea, in K Zweigert and J Kropholler, *Sources of International Uniform Law*, vol 2 (AW Sijthoff 1972) 7) (William Tetley, 'Maritime Transportation' in Rolf Herber (ed), *International Encyclopedia of Comparative Law, vol XII: Law of Transport* (Mohr Siebeck 2002) 66–9, 95–7). Unification of the liability regime for the → carriage of goods by sea was not achieved until 1924. The Hague Rules of 1924 (International Convention of 25 August 1924 for the unification of certain rules relating to bills of lading, 120 LNTS 155) were a result of the pressure created by national legislations, which had been adopted to change the late 19th-century practice of maritime carriers exonerating themselves from absolute liability by contractual clauses. The Hague Rules were amended, in response to the so-called container revolution, by the 1968 Visby Protocol (Protocol of 23 February 1968 to amend the International Convention for the unification of certain rules of law relating to bills of lading signed at Brussels on 25 August 1924 (Hague Rules), 1412 UNTS 128). An attempt to create a completely new regime in the Hamburg Rules of 1978 led to a further distortion of international uniformity which the Rotterdam Rules of 2009 (United Nations Convention of 11 December 2008 on contracts for the international carriage of goods wholly or partly by sea, UN Doc A/RES/63/122, 63 UNTS 122) are meant to restore (→ Carriage of goods by sea). The rules on another important matter were unified in 1924 as well: the 1924 Limitation Convention (International Convention of 25 August 1924 for the unification of certain rules relating to the limitation of liability of owners of seagoing vessels, 120 LNTS 123). The regime set by this Convention has subsequently been modified by the 1957 Limitation Convention (International Convention of 10 October 1957 relating to the limitation of the liability of owners of seagoing ships, 1412 UNTS 73) and the 1976 LLMC (→ Liability, limitation of maritime). In the field of carriage of passengers and their luggage by sea, the unified rules were not adopted until the second half of the 20th century. After unsuccessful attempts to unify the carrier's liability in separate conventions for passengers (International Convention of 29 April 1961 for the unification of certain rules relating to carriage of passengers by sea, 1411 UNTS 81) and for their luggage (International Convention of 27 May 1967 for the unification of certain rules relating to carriage of passengers' luggage by sea, RMC.I.5.160, II.5.160; [1968] I CMI Documents 12) the international community finally adopted the Athens Convention 1974 (Athens Convention of 13 December 1974 relating to the carriage of passengers and their luggage by sea, 1463 UNTS 20) which was substantially amended by a Protocol in 2002 (Protocol of 1 November 2002 to the Athens Convention relating to the carriage of passengers and their luggage by sea, IMO Doc LEG/CONF.13/20 (19 November 2002)) (→ Carriage of passengers).

Despite the fact that road transport was in pressing need of standardization, the uniform law rules were not adopted until after the Second World War due to strongly conflicting interests. Preparatory work undertaken by the UNECE resulted in the CMR in 1956 (Convention of 19 May 1956 on the contract for the international carriage of goods by road, 399 UNTS 189). Over the years, it became one of the most successful conventions which is in force for almost all European as well as for some central Asian and northern African states. The CMR, like in maritime carriage, only unifies the rules for the carriage of goods (→ Carriage of goods by road, rail and inland waterways). The rules for passenger carriage by road were unified in 1973 by the CVR (Convention of 1 March 1973 on the contract for the international carriage of passengers and luggage by road, 1774 UNTS 109) which was again the result of the UNECE efforts.

As a final point, the unification in the field of inland navigation is also based on UNECE efforts. The CANI (Convention of 15 March 1960 relating to the unification of certain rules concerning collisions in inland navigation, 572 UNTS 133), signed in 1960 was the first result of this work. Although efforts to unify the law on the carriage of goods by inland waterways first started in the 1950s (→ Carriage of goods by road, rail and inland waterways), it was not until 2001 that the CMNI (International Convention of 22 June 2001 on the contract of carriage of goods by inland waterway, UN Doc A/CN.9/645) was adopted to this end.

III. Carriage of passengers

1. Air

With respect to carriage of passengers by air, there are two basic international conventions, namely the Warsaw Convention (1929) and the Montreal Convention (1999). The Warsaw Convention, which entered into force on 13 February 1933, set a fault-based liability system with a reversal of the → burden of proof for injury or death of passengers and for delay (arts 17–21) as well as maximum amounts limiting the air carrier's liability (art 22). However, not only some aspects of the liability regime, but also the liability limits soon became obsolete. Therefore, the Warsaw Convention was amended several times by the following instruments (which are currently in force): the Hague Protocol, the Guadalajara Supplementary Convention (Convention of 18 September 1961, supplementary to the Warsaw Convention, for the unification of certain rules relating to international carriage by air performed by a person other than the contracting carrier, 500 UNTS 31), the Montreal Additional Protocol No 1 (Additional Protocol No 1 of 25 September 1975 to amend the Convention for the unification of certain rules relating to international carriage by air signed at Warsaw on 12 October 1929, 2097 UNTS 23), the Montreal Additional Protocol No 2 (Additional Protocol No 2 of 25 September 1975 to amend the Convention for the unification of certain rules relating to international carriage by air signed at Warsaw on 12 October 1929 as amended by the Protocol done at The Hague on 28 September 1955, 2097 UNTS 64) and the Montreal Protocol No 4 (Montreal Protocol No 4 of 25 September 1975 to amend the Convention for the unification of certain rules relating to international carriage by air signed at Warsaw on 12 October 1929 as amended by the Protocol done at The Hague on 28 September 1955, 2145 UNTS 31). Some of these instruments (Hague Protocol, Guadalajara Supplementary Convention, Montreal Additional Protocol No 1) amend only the Warsaw Convention while others (Montreal Additional Protocol No 2, Montreal Additional Protocol No 4) amend the Warsaw Convention as already amended by the Hague Protocol. Inflation in the contracting states of the concurrently existing versions of the Warsaw system and the desire to improve the existing regime as well as to establish a single unified regime of liability led to the adoption of the Montreal Convention in 1999 which entered into force on 4 November 2003. The Convention effected a strict liability system up to a specified amount for the injury or death of passengers. For → damages exceeding the specified amount and for delay the – unlimited – liability of the carrier is based on presumed fault (arts 17 to 22).

Currently 152 states are party to the Warsaw Convention, 137 states to the Hague Protocol, 86 states to the Guadalajara Supplementary Convention, 51 states to the Montreal Additional Protocol No 1, 52 states to the Montreal Additional Protocol No 2 and 60 states to the Montreal Protocol No 4. To date,

123 parties have acceded to the Montreal Convention including the EU (by virtue of the Council Decision of 5 April 2001 (Council, 'Council Decision of 5 April 2001 on the conclusion by the European Community of the Convention for the Unification of Certain Rules for International Carriage by Air (the Montreal Convention)' [2001] OJ L 194/38)). Determining which liability system is applicable – whether the Warsaw regime or the Montreal regime of 1999 – and which version of the Warsaw system to apply is not always an easy task (JD McClean and others (eds), *Shawcross and Beaumont: Air Law*, vol 1 (looseleaf, LexisNexis Butterworths 1991) para VII 328–9 [issue 103]).

The EU has put the Montreal Convention's liability regime with respect to passengers and their luggage into effect by means of Regulation (EC) No 889/2002 of the European Parliament and of the Council of 13 May 2002 amending Council Regulation (EC) No 2027/97 on air carrier liability in the event of accidents ([2002] OJ L 140/2), thereby extending the scope of the regime to domestic air transport. Furthermore, compulsory insurance must be maintained by air carriers in respect of contractual and tort liability (Regulation (EC) No 785/2004 of the European Parliament and of the Council of 21 April 2004 on insurance requirements for air carriers and aircraft operators, [2004] OJ L 138/1). Last but not least, the Passenger Rights Regulation (Regulation (EC) No 261/2004 of the European Parliament and of the Council of 11 February 2004 establishing common rules on compensation and assistance to passengers in the event of denied boarding and of cancellation or long delay of flights, and repealing Regulation (EEC) No 295/91, [2004] OJ L 46/1) set uniform rules to ensure that passengers are adequately compensated in cases of denied boarding, cancellation or long delay of a flight. This Regulation will undergo important modifications in the near future (Proposal for a Regulation of the European Parliament and of the Council amending Regulation (EC) No 261/2004 establishing common rules on compensation and assistance to passengers in the event of denied boarding and of cancellation or long delay of flights and Regulation (EC) No 2027/97 on air carrier liability in respect of the carriage of passengers and their baggage by air, COM/2013/0130 final).

2. Sea

The unified rules for the carriage of passengers by sea are currently to be found in the Athens Convention 1974 and 2002. The Athens Convention 1974 combined the 1961 and 1967 conventions, and doubled the limitation amounts. It set principally a fault-based liability system for passengers and their luggage, however with no reversal of the → burden of proof (art 3 paras 1–2). Fault on the part of the carrier is only presumed for shipping accidents (art 3 para 3). The general dissatisfaction with the fault-based liability system and the limitation amounts which gradually became quite outdated resulted in the adoption of the Athens Convention of 2002. The Convention fundamentally changes the liability regime: the carrier is strictly liable for shipping incidents (art 3 para 5) up to a certain amount (art 3 para 1). For losses exceeding the strict liability amount, the carrier's liability is based on fault with a reversal of the burden of proof (art 3 para 1). With regard to loss arising from events other than shipping incidents, the carrier's liability is again based on fault, however with no reversal of the burden of proof (art 3 para 2).

The Athens Convention 1974 entered into force on 28 April 1987; currently 25 states representing 32 per cent of the world's tonnage are contracting parties. The Athens Convention of 2002 entered into force on 23 April 2014. The 12-year delay in taking effect is due to a problem encountered with the issue of compulsory insurance. Once the issue was solved, the EU became party to the Convention (by virtue of the Council Decision of 12 December 2011 concerning the accession of the European Union to the Protocol of 2002 to the Athens Convention relating to the carriage of passengers and their luggage by sea, 1974, with the exception of Articles 10 and 11 thereof, [2012] OJ L 8/1). Currently 27 states representing 44.54 per cent of the world's tonnage are party to the Convention, with further ratifications expected. Finally, the EU has made the liability regime set by the Athens Convention of 2002 a part of European legislation (Athens Regulation (Regulation (EC) No 392/2009 of the European Parliament and of the Council of 23 April 2009 on the liability of carriers of passengers by sea in the event of accidents, [2009] OJ L 131/24) which is also applicable to almost all domestic passenger carriage by sea in Member States.

3. Rail

As to carriage by rail, transport law is unified through the COTIF (1980) which entered into force on 1 May 1985. The Vilnius Protocol (Protocol of 3 June 1999 for the modification of the Convention concerning international carriage by rail, UNTS registration No A-23353), which essentially amends the Convention, was adopted in 1999 and entered into force on 1 July 2006. To date, 48 states and the EU (see Council Decision of 16 June 2011 on the signing and conclusion of the Agreement between the European Union and the Intergovernmental Organisation for International Carriage by Rail on the Accession of the European Union to the Convention concerning International Carriage by Rail (COTIF) of 9 May 1980, as amended by the Vilnius Protocol of 3 June 1999, [2013] OJ L 51/1) are party to the COTIF. By virtue of the States Parties, the legal regime for the carriage by rail is unified in Europe, Asia and North Africa. COTIF has several appendixes including the CIV (Appendix A) which sets uniform rules with respect to carriage of passengers and their luggage. Both the 1980 and the 1999 versions of the CIV stipulate liability based on presumed fault with the duty of utmost care for cases involving physical injury or death of passengers (art 26) and for luggage (art 35 CIV 1980, art 36 CIV 1999). As in every international instrument regarding transport law, the carrier is entitled to limit its liability (arts 30 para 2, 38–41 CIV 1980, arts 30 para 2, 41–6 CIV 1999). The liability regime of the CIV 1999 is also applicable to → carriage of passengers by rail in the EU including domestic carriage within the Member States (arts 1–2, 11 Regulation (EC) No 1371/2007 of the European Parliament and of the Council of 23 October 2007 on rail passengers' rights and obligations ([2007] OJ L 315/14)).

4. Road

Unlike other transport modes, carriage of passengers by road has not been subject to extensive unification work. The only international instrument to this end is the CVR adopted in 1973 that entered into force on 12 April 1994. Of the nine States Parties to this Convention, most are southeastern and eastern European countries. Recently, Moldova (2012) and Ukraine (2005) have acceded to the Convention. The CVR employs a liability regime based on presumed fault with a duty of high degree of care in cases of physical injury or death of passengers (arts 11, 17) and for luggage (art 14). The carrier is entitled to limitation of liability (arts 13, 16). The EU decided to take another route and adopted Regulation (EU) No 181/2011 of the European Parliament and of the Council of 16 February 2011 concerning the rights of passengers in bus and coach transport and amending Regulation (EC) No 2006/2004 ([2011] OJ L 55/1). This Regulation does not enact a comprehensive liability regime, but sets some minimum requirements. Regarding death or personal injury to passengers and loss of or damage to luggage, the Regulation refers to the applicable national law for liability issues (art 7 para 1), but provides for minimum limitation amounts for compensation (art 7 para 2). It further grants rights in cases of cancellation and delay (arts 19–21) additional to those provided by national laws (art 22).

IV. Carriage of goods

1. Air

As outlined above (III.1.), the liability regime for the carriage of goods and passengers by air is set by the Warsaw Convention (1929) and its Protocols as well as by the Montreal Convention (1999). The Warsaw Convention adopts a fault-based liability regime with a reversal of the → burden of proof for damage to or loss of goods as well as for delay (arts 18–19), combined with the right to limit liability (art 22). Differing from the carriage of passengers, a carrier was able to relieve itself from liability by proving negligent pilotage (art 20 para 2). By the Hague Protocol of 1955 this defence was removed and the limitation amounts were raised. However, the liability regime has been significantly altered by the Montreal Protocol No 4. Under the amended regime, the carrier is principally liable for damage to or loss of goods (art 18 para 2) and for damage caused by delay (art 19). The carrier can be relieved of liability only if the damage or loss is caused by specific reasons listed in art 18 para 3, such as an inherent defect of the goods, or in case of damage caused by delay, if all necessary measures had been taken (art 20). Furthermore, the carrier can be wholly or partly exonerated from liability if the damage was caused by the contributory negligence of the claimant (art 21 para 2). Another important modification by the Montreal Protocol No 4 was that liability limits were made unbreakable for cargo damage (art

25). This liability regime remained unchanged in the Montreal Convention.

2. Sea

The law on the carriage of goods by sea was first unified by the Hague Rules. Adopted as a Brussels Convention in 1924, the Hague Rules entered into force on 2 June 1931 and are currently in force for 76 states. They are applicable to international contracts of carriage covered by a → bill of lading or similar document of title (art I para b) and set the obligations and the duties of the parties to such a contract. The carrier is liable for damage to or loss of goods except for certain reasons regulated in art IV such as force majeure or nautical fault. The burden of proof that the damage was caused without its actual fault or privity rests with the carrier (art IV). However, the carrier is entitled to limit its liability to certain sums calculated per package or weight unit (art IV para 5). The liability regime is mandatory for the tackle-to-tackle period (art VII).

The container revolution starting in the 1950s and the low liability limits made the amendment of the Hague Rules inevitable, leading to the adoption of the 1968 Visby Protocol. The Protocol entered into force on 23 June 1977 and currently 30 states are party to it. The 1968 Visby Protocol does not change the basics of the liability regime set by the Hague Rules: it merely increases the liability limits and includes a provision specifying the calculation of the limitation amount per package for carriage with containers (art IV para 5c).

Though major maritime nations were satisfied with the unification achieved by the Hague-Visby Rules (International Convention for the unification of certain rules relating to bills of lading signed at Brussels, 25 August 1924, as amended by the 1968 Visby Protocol and the 1979 Brussels Protocol), the disadvantageous position of developing countries as shippers under the Hague-Visby regime and developments in shipping, construction, navigation, loading and documentation techniques triggered a revision of the existing system. The work of → UNCITRAL to this end resulted in the Hamburg Rules (1978). As these are more advantageous for shippers and drafted in a more civil law fashion, many major maritime countries have not ratified the Hamburg Rules. They entered into force on 1 November 1992 and currently 34 states are contracting parties. Unlike the Hague-Visby Rules, which require the contract of carriage being covered by a bill of lading or similar document of title, the Hamburg Rules are applicable to contracts of carriage by sea at large (art 1 no 6). Compared to the Hague-Visby regime, the period and basis of liability have also undergone important changes. Basically, the carrier's liability is based on presumed fault combined with a duty of high degree of care (art 5). The liability period was stretched to the port-to-port period (art 4). Finally, liability limits are set in art 6 of the Rules.

3. Rail

As explained earlier (III.3.) COTIF and its appendixes unify carriage by rail. The obligations of the parties and the liability regime are set by CIM in the 1980 and 1999 versions. The liability system established by both versions of the CIM adopts the same principle: the liability of the carrier is based on presumed fault coupled with the duty of utmost care (arts 36–7 CIM 1980, arts 23, 25 CIM 1999) and the carrier has the right to limit liability (arts 40–4 CIM 1980, arts 30–6 CIM 1999). Nevertheless, there are some important changes in the overall picture. Maybe the most important modification is the abolishment of the obligation to carry (art 3 CIM 1980) in the CIM 1999 due to the liberalization of the railway market in Europe.

4. Road

Under the CMR regime, the carrier is liable for the loss of or damage to goods occurring during carriage and for delay in delivery. However, if the carrier can prove that the loss, damage or delay was unpreventable despite showing the utmost care, or from the fault or neglect of the claimant, it will be relieved of liability (arts 17–18). Therefore, the liability of the carrier under the CMR is based on the presumed fault of the carrier, coupled with the duty of utmost care. Limitation of liability amounts are set in arts 23 to 25 of the Convention. The CMR entered into force on 2 July 1961, and to date, 55 states are party to the Convention, effectively achieving unification between almost all European states and some additional Asian and African states.

DUYGU DAMAR

5. Inland waterways

After UNECE efforts had endured for almost half a decade, the unification of the liability regime for the carriage of goods by inland waterways was achieved by the CMNI in 2001 (→ Carriage of goods by road, rail and inland waterways). The Convention entered into force on 1 April 2005 and currently 15 states are party to the Convention. As in other conventions on the carriage of goods, the carrier's liability for damage to or loss of goods or for delay is based on presumed fault (art 16). Nevertheless, if there are any of the special circumstances or risks listed in art 18 (eg carriage on deck), the carrier will be exonerated from liability unless it can prove that the loss suffered did not result from one of the circumstances or risks listed. If the carrier is found liable, the compensation amount payable may not exceed the limitation amounts specified in art 20 of the Convention.

V. Non-contractual liability and salvage

1. Maritime torts

The law on the collision of ships and civil liability for pollution damage has been unified on an international level mainly for water-born transport. Unification by the very first convention in the area of maritime transport, namely by the Collision Convention (1910) has been so successful that it has never been amended. The Convention took effect on 1 March 1913 and is currently in force for 83 states. Under its liability regime, every vessel involved in the collision is liable according to its degree of fault (art 4). The shipowner remains liable, even if the collision was caused by the fault of a compulsory pilot (art 5). The CANI (1960) which entered into force on 13 September 1966 adopts the same principles with respect to collisions between inland navigation vessels, and 13 states are party to it.

The unification of rules governing compensation for marine pollution damage was achieved for (i) oil pollution damage, (ii) bunker oil pollution damage and (iii) pollution damage caused by hazardous and noxious substances. Big tanker disasters such as the Torrey Canyon in 1967 triggered unification work for the compensation of damage caused by oil pollution. To this end, unification was achieved in 1969 (1969 CLC (International Convention on civil liability for oil pollution damage of 29 November 1969, 973 UNTS 3)), but the relevant instrument underwent several amendments. Currently, with 136 states parties representing 97.43 per cent of the world's tonnage, the 1992 CLC (International Convention of 27 November 1992 on civil liability for oil pollution damage, 1956 UNTS 255, entry into force 30 May 1996) is the essential legal instrument in setting the liability regime. However, the 1992 CLC does not cover pollution damage caused by oil used as fuel for a vessel, ie bunker pollution damage. Therefore, a specific convention, namely the Bunker Convention, was adopted in 2001 in order to unify the rules on the liability regime for bunker pollution damage (International Convention of 23 March 2001 on civil liability for bunker oil pollution damage, IMO Doc LEG/CONF 12/19, 40 ILM 1406). Currently 83 states representing 92.58 per cent of the world's tonnage are party to this Convention which entered into force on 21 November 2008. Finally, the HNS Convention was adopted in 1996 (International Convention of 3 May 1996 on liability and compensation for damage in connection with the carriage of hazardous and noxious substances by sea, 35 ILM 1406). Although it was amended by a Protocol of 2010 (Protocol of 20 April 2010 to the International Convention on liability and compensation for damage in connection with the carriage of hazardous and noxious substances by sea, IMO Doc LEG/CONF.17/DC/1 (29 April 2010)), the HNS Convention did not gain the necessary support and has not yet become effective.

All three documents make the shipowner subject to strict liability for any pollution damage (art III 1992 CLC, art 7 HNS Convention, art 3 Bunker Convention 2001). Under the regime of these conventions, the shipowner is entitled to limitation of liability (art V 1992 CLC, art 9 HNS Convention, art 6 Bunker Convention 2001). For damage caused by oil pollution, damage above the shipowner's liability limit is compensated by the IOPC Funds. The main rationale for this system is that the damage is compensated by the various industries which benefit from the carriage of oil by sea. The damage up to the liability limits by the shipowner, ie the shipping industry, and the remaining damage is to be compensated by the IOPC Funds, ie by the oil industry.

2. Salvage

The Salvage Convention of 1910 adopts the principle of 'no cure, no pay', ie if the → salvage service had no beneficial result, no remuneration is to be paid (art 2). The Convention, further, sets the principles upon which the amount of remuneration should be fixed (art 8). Currently, 78 states are party to the Convention which entered into force on 1 March 1913. The 1989 Salvage Convention (International Convention of 28 April 1989 on salvage, 1953 UNTS 165) adheres to the same principles (arts 12–13). Additionally the Convention of 1989 employs the concept of special compensation in art 14 according to which a salvor is entitled to adequate reward if it provided salvage services to a ship which by itself or its cargo threatened damage to the environment even when the salvage operation was unsuccessful. Currently 69 states representing 52 per cent of the world's tonnage are party to the Convention which entered into force on 14 July 1996.

3. Damage caused by aircraft

The Convention on damage caused by foreign aircraft to third parties on the surface was adopted in 1952. It entered into force on 4 February 1958 and has currently 49 contracting states. According to the Convention, the operator of the aircraft (art 2) is strictly liable for damage on the surface caused by the aircraft (art 1). However, the liability of the operator is limited to an amount to be calculated according to the weight of the aircraft (art 11). The limitation amounts were raised by a Protocol of 1978 (Protocol of 23 September 1978 to amend the Convention on damage caused by foreign aircraft to third parties on the surface, ICAO Doc No 9257) which became effective as late as 25 July 2002 and has 12 contracting states. Recently, two new conventions on the issue were adopted in Montreal: the Convention of 2 May 2009 on compensation for damage caused by aircraft to third parties (ICAO Doc No 9919) and the Convention of 2 May 2009 on compensation for damage to third parties, resulting from acts of unlawful interference involving aircraft (ICAO Doc No 9920). The Convention for damage caused by aircraft also adheres to the strict liability principle; it adopts, however, higher liability limits. The Convention for damage caused by unlawful interference, on the other hand, provides for a liability and compensation scheme similar to the IOPC Fund regime for oil pollution damage (see above V.1.). To date, eight states ratified the Convention for damage caused by aircraft, and seven states the Convention for damage caused by unlawful interference.

VI. Limitation of liability

This category covers the unification of transport law regarding global limitation of liability. Limitation of liability for the carriage of passengers and goods is addressed earlier (under II.1. and IV.). It must be noted that the global limitation of liability only effects water-borne transport.

There are three international conventions on the limitation of liability relating to seagoing ships: the 1924 Limitation Convention (see above II.), the 1957 Limitation Convention and the 1976 LLMC (1976) together with its Protocol of 1996. Currently only eight contracting states to the 1924 Convention are left; therefore unification in this area is effected basically by the 1957 Limitation Convention and the 1976 LLMC. The 1957 Limitation Convention which entered into force on 31 May 1968 has 35 contracting states. The Convention entitles shipowners (and other persons, see art 6 of the Convention), to limit their liability for personal and property claims (art 1 para 2) to a limitation fund, the amount of which is calculated according to the tonnage of the ship (art 3), unless the claim resulted from the actual fault or privity of the owner (art 1 para 1). However, the course of time has necessitated a revision of this regime due, *inter alia*, to the limitation amounts having become unrealistically low because of depreciation of monetary values, to the increase in the size of ships and to the general dissatisfaction with the 'actual fault or privity' standard. Thus the 1976 LLMC was adopted in 1976; it entered into force on 1 December 1986 and has currently 54 contracting states representing 55.63 per cent of the world's tonnage. The 1976 LLMC grants a category of persons (mainly shipowners) and salvors the right to limit their liability (art 1) by creating a limitation fund the amount of which is calculated according to the tonnage of the ship (arts 6 *et seq*). The limitation amounts are higher than those of the 1957 Limitation Convention. The 1976 LLMC also covers a wider range of personal and property claims (art 2) and makes limitation amounts almost unbreakable by adopting a higher degree of culpability, ie wilful misconduct (art 4). The 1996 Protocol further increased the limitation amounts.

DUYGU DAMAR

The rules and principles of the 1976 LLMC were adopted for inland navigation with the CLNI (Strasbourg Convention of 4 November 1988 on the limitation of liability of owners of inland navigation vessels, in *International Transport Treaties* (Kluwer Law International) II-87 (supplement 13 – March 1989)) which has been in force since 1 September 1997. Currently, four states are party to the Convention as it is geographically limited to the Rhine and the Moselle (art 15 para 1a). A new international convention (under the same name: CLNI) concluded on 27 September 2012 (Strasbourg Convention of 27 September 2012 on the limitation of liability of owners of inland navigation vessels, UNECE Doc SC.3 No 4 (10 October 2012)), abolished the geographical restriction (art 15) and the limitation amounts have been increased (arts 6–8). The Convention is not yet in force.

VII. Rights *in rem*

One of the most problematic areas in international commercial law is that of rights *in rem*, more specifically securities *in rem* over transport vehicles which are by nature not located in a specific place. The first unification work to overcome the difficulties with regard to seagoing ships was the 1926 Maritime Liens and Mortgages Convention (International Convention of 10 April 1926 for the unification of certain rules relating to maritime liens and mortgages, 120 LNTS 187) which entered into force on 2 June 1931 and currently has 24 contracting states. This Convention sets the conditions under which mortgages and hypothecs on vessels registered in contracting states should be recognized and enforced in others. It further determines claims secured by a maritime lien on the vessel and the security provided by maritime liens. The 1993 Maritime Liens and Mortgages Convention (International Convention of 6 May 1993 on maritime liens and mortgages, 2276 UNTS 39) to which currently 18 states are party, entered into force on 5 September 2004. With this Convention some ambiguities under the 1926 Maritime Liens and Mortgages Convention have been clarified, eg the effects of forced sale on mortgages and hypothecs (art 12) and the category of persons against whom a claim relating to a vessel is secured by a maritime lien (art 4 para 1). New provisions have been adopted on some previously unregulated issues, eg the ranking of mortgages and hypothecs *inter se* (art 2).

The recognition of rights *in rem* in aircrafts was first facilitated by the Geneva Aircraft Convention (Convention of 19 June 1948 on the international recognition of rights in aircraft, 310 UNTS 151) which entered into force on 17 September 1953 and currently has 89 contracting states. According to the Convention, registered rights *in rem* and recorded rights to possession under leases (→ Lease contracts and tenancies) should be recognized in other contracting states (arts I–II). Charges based on claims for → salvage reward and for extraordinary expenses for the preservation of the aircraft should in principle also be recognized (art IV). The Convention prohibits the transfer of an aircraft to another registry without the consent of the holder of registered rights (art IX) and further adopts provisions on the procedure and effects of the judicial sale of aircrafts (arts VI–X).

The latest unification work in the area of rights and securities *in rem* is the Cape Town Convention (Convention of 16 November 2001 on international interests in mobile equipment, 2307 UNTS 285, → Security interests in mobile equipment (uniform law)). By means of this Convention (and its protocols: Aircraft Protocol (Protocol of 16 November 2001 to the Convention on international interests in mobile equipment on matters specific to aircraft equipment, 2307 UNTS 615); Luxembourg Protocol of 23 February 2007 to the Convention on international interests in mobile equipment on matters specific to railway rolling stock (23 February 2007), available at <www.unidroit.org> (last accessed on 19 January 2017); Protocol of 9 March 2012 to the Convention on international interests in mobile equipment on matters specific to space assets, available at <www.unidroit.org> (last accessed on 19 January 2017)) a system for internationally recognized securities (arts 2–15) over aircraft equipment, railway rolling stock and space assets is created, along with an international registry to support it (arts 16–17). The Convention to which 73 states are party and its Protocol specific to aircraft equipment to which 65 states are party entered into force on 1 March 2006. The Luxembourg Protocol on railway rolling stock (2007) and the Berlin Protocol on space assets (2012) are not yet in force.

VIII. Modern trends

Especially in the → carriage of passengers, the development in the 20th century clearly shows the growing importance attached to human life. Fault-based liability regimes laid down in international instruments have generally been changed into either strict liability (as under the Montreal Convention and the Athens Convention 2002) or into fault-based liability coupled with the duty of utmost care (as under the CIV system). This development is also characteristic of the consumer rights and consumer protection era. However, it is doubtful how much the patchwork of conventions and protocols in air carriage contributes to a protective purpose. The high number of protocols to the Warsaw Convention makes the prospect of a real unification quite distant. Hopefully the number of contracting states to the Montreal Convention will continue increasing.

Another basic concern in the development of unified transport law has been the protection of the marine environment which is evident in the unification work regarding civil liability for marine pollution. The growing importance of protecting the marine environment is likewise an underlying principle in special compensation (art 14 1989 Salvage Convention).

With respect to carriage of goods, there are international conventions on every mode of transport. However, the reality in the carriage of goods has drastically changed since the container revolution. Due to the common usage of containers wherever possible, it has become rather unusual for carriage to be undertaken by way of a single mode of transport. Unimodal transport conventions generally address the issue to a certain extent (eg art 2 CMR, art 18 para 4 Montreal Convention, art 1 para 3 CIM 1999), but the need for an international unification is obvious. The Geneva Multimodal Transport Convention (United Nations Convention of 24 May 1980 on international multimodal transport of goods, UN Doc TD/MT/CONF/16) unfortunately failed to achieve the long-desired unification, as it did not receive the required number of ratifications. Therefore, the work undertaken by UNCITRAL to prepare an international instrument proposing legal solutions to the modern needs of the carriage of goods by sea followed the trend of expanding the carrier's period of responsibility. The tackle-to-tackle period in art I para (e) Hague-Visby Rules had already been extended to port-to-port by art 4 Hamburg Rules. The Rotterdam Rules which were adopted in 2009 took another step forward and stretched responsibility to the door-to-door period (arts 12 and 79) for carriages with a sea leg (art 26). However, the Rotterdam Rules are not yet in force, as to date, only three states have ratified them. If they enter into force in the future, the fault-based liability regime of previous conventions will not undergo any changes.

DUYGU DAMAR

Literature

Jürgen Basedow, *Der Transportvertrag* (Mohr 1987); Francesco Berlingieri, 'The Convention on Maritime Liens and Mortgages, 1993' [1996] CMI Yearbook 225; Malcolm A Clarke, *International Carriage of Goods by Road: CMR* (6th edn, Informa 2014); Malcolm A Clarke and David Yates, *Contracts of Carriage by Land and Air* (2nd edn, Informa 2008); G Beate Czerwenka, 'Das Budapester Übereinkommen über den Vertrag über die Güterbeförderungen in der Binnenschiffahrt (CMNI)' [2001] TranspR 277; Duygu Damar, *Wilful Misconduct in International Transport Law* (Springer 2011); Franco Ferrari, 'Uniform Law' in J Basedow and others (eds), *The Max Planck Encyclopedia of European Private Law*, vol 2 (OUP 2012) 1732; Roy Goode, 'The Cape Town Convention on International Interests in Mobile Equipment: A Driving Force for International Asset-Based Financing' [2002] Unif.L.Rev. 3; P Griggs and others, *Limitation of Liability for Maritime Claims* (4th edn, LLP 2005); Joseph Haenni, 'Carriage by Rail' in René Rodière and Rolf Herber (eds) *International Encyclopedia of Comparative Law, vol XII: Law of Transport* (Mohr 1973); A Lilar and C van den Bosch, *International Maritime Committee: 1897–1972* (CMI 1972); JD McClean and others (eds), *Shawcross and Beaumont: Air Law*, vol 1 (looseleaf, LexisNexis Butterworths 1991); Walter Müller, 'Inland Navigation' in Rolf Herber (ed), *International Encyclopedia of Comparative Law, vol XII: Law of Transport* (Mohr Siebeck 2002); Susan Schubert, *Die Haftung für Reisende und ihr Gepäck auf Schiffen* (Lang 1981); Barış Soyer, 'Sundry Considerations on the Draft Protocol to the Athens Convention Relating to the Carriage of Passengers and Their Luggage by Sea 1974' (2002) 33 J.Mar.L.&Com. 519; Michael F Sturley, 'The History of COGSA and the Hague Rules' (1991) 22 J.Mar.L.&Com. 1; MF Sturley and others, *The Rotterdam Rules* (Sweet & Maxwell 2010); William Tetley, 'Maritime Transportation' in Rolf Herber (ed), *International Encyclopedia of Comparative Law, vol XII: Law of Transport* (Mohr Siebeck 2002); Cécile Tournaye, 'Adoption of the CLNI 2012:

What Has Changed Compared with CLNI 1988?' [2013] TranspR 213. Information on the States Parties to conventions is available at the UNTS (<https://treaties.un.org>), IMO (<www.imo.org/About/Conventions/StatusOfConventions/Pages/Default.aspx>), ICAO (<www.icao.int/secretariat/legal/Lists/Current%20lists%20of%20parties/AllItems.aspx>), OTIF (<www.otif.org>), CCNR (<www.ccr-zkr.org/12050400-en.html>), UNECE (<www.unece.org/trans/conventn/legalinst.html>) and the UNIDROIT (<www.unidroit.org/>) websites (all accessed in January 2017) and in the latest issue of the CMI Yearbook.

Transsexual and transgender persons

I. Concept and notion

Following Stephen Whittle's terminological approach (Whittle, *Respect and Equality: Transsexual and Transgender Rights* (Routledge-Cavendish 2002) xxii f), the term 'transgender person' in this entry is meant to indicate all persons who live, or desire to live in the role of a gender which is not the one designated to that person at birth; 'transsexual person' is meant to refer to those transgender persons who desire or have undergone gender reassignment treatment/surgery.

That said, this entry deals with the legal gender of persons, and more specifically with the possibilities of changing a person's legal gender once it has been allocated. The legal situation of persons who were not allocated a legal gender at birth (a possibility recently introduced in Germany by the Gesetz zur Änderung personenstandsrechtlicher Vorschriften, [2013] BGBl. I 122) if it was not possible to unequivocally classify that person as either male or female because of the physical sexual characteristics of that person, or who desire a gender allocation that is neither 'male' nor 'female', both often referred to as 'intersex', are beyond the scope of this entry.

As this entry mainly is concerned with legal aspects, the terms 'changing legal gender' or 'recognition of preferred gender' will be used to describe the acts that in the eyes of the law 'change' the gender of a person, while of course being fully aware that in actuality the persons concerned did not, as is often referred to in the public discourse, 'change their gender' as they continue to be the very same person they were before the legal act.

II. Purpose and function

Until very recently, in all European jurisdictions (as mentioned Germany so far being an exception in Europe) the legal gender of a person was determined and classified shortly after birth as either male or female. The legal gender of a person is one of the constituents of the legal status of a person. Many legal provisions are gendered in the sense that they will only apply if a person has a specified gender, for example in family law (eg provisions using terms like mother and father, or marriage in many jurisdictions still being considered the union of a man and a woman → same-sex marriage), social security law (eg maternity leave), criminal law (eg the crime of rape), pensions etc. Hence, the legal gender of a person continues to matter (even though admittedly it matters less than it did some 50 years ago), but one might very well question whether this should be the case.

III. Historical development

Traditionally, it was the case that once a person's legal gender was fixed it was immutable (except in cases where there had been a mistake in the registration). However, with considerable delay the law began to follow the findings in other disciplines (especially medicine and psychology) and jurisdictions gradually started to provide for the possibility of a change of legal gender under certain conditions.

The earliest statute enacted in this regard was the Swedish Act on determination of gender in certain cases (Lag (1972:119) om fastställande av könstillhörighet i vissa fall). This Act allowed the change of legal gender under restrictive conditions, such as the requirement for gender reassignment surgery, including sterilization. Since 1972, the Swedish law has been amended on a number of occasions, with the strict surgery requirements being only recently removed. In 1980, Germany followed Sweden by enacting the Act on the change of given names and determination of gender in specific cases (Gesetz über die Änderung der Vornamen und die Feststellung der Geschlechtszugehörigkeit in besonderen Fällen (Transsexuellengesetz), [1980] BGBl. I 1654). The 1980 Act initially introduced similarly restrictive rules but many of these have now been challenged successfully in the German Constitutional Court, including the surgery requirement (Federal Constitutional Court of Germany (BVerfG), 11 January 2011, 128 BVerfGE 109), minimum age (Federal Constitutional Court of Germany (BVerfG), 16 March 1982, 60 BVerfGE 123, 26 January 1993, 88 BVerfGE 87), nationality requirements (Federal Constitutional Court of Germany (BVerfG), 18 July 2006, 116 BVerfGE 243) and the requirement to dissolve an existing marriage before the preferred gender can be recognized (Federal Constitutional Court of Germany (BVerfG), 27 May 2008, 121 BVerfGE 175). In the following years, several European jurisdictions enacted statutes in this area: eg Italy in 1982: Norme in materia di rettificazione di attribuzione di sesso, legge 14 April 1982, n 164; the Netherlands in 1985: (then) art 1:29a–d Nieuw Burgerlijk Wetboek of 1 January 1992, henceforth NBW (now art 1:28–28c), Turkey in 1988: (then) art 19 of the Turkish Civil Code (Law No 4721 of 7 December 2002 as amended by Law No 4963 of 6 August 2003 published in official Gazette No 25192 of 7 August 2003; now art 40); Finland in 2002: Laki transseksuaalin sukupuolen vahvistamiseta/Lag om fastställande av transsexuella personers könstillhörighet, 28 June 2002/563; the United Kingdom in 2004: Gender Recognition Act 2004 (2004 ch 7); Belgium and Spain in 2007: Arts 57, 62bis, 62ter, 99, 100 Burgerlijk Wetboek (Law of 10 May 2007, Belgisch Staatsblad 11 July 2007) and Ley 3/2007, de 15 de marzo, reguladora de la rectificación registral de la mención al sexo de las personas; Ireland in 2015: Gender Recognition Act 2015 (No 25 of 2015); Malta in 2015: Gender Identity, Gender Expression and Sex Characteristics Act 2015 (Act No XI of 2015). Other European jurisdictions have not enacted extensive statutory provisions but, rather, have dealt with these issues either by administrative procedure (eg for Austria, see Erlaß Zahl 36.250/66-IV/4/596 and Verwaltungsgerichtshof, 30 September 1997, [1999] ZfRV 185), by amending the provisions for civil registration (as is the case with Denmark's recent Lov Nr 752 af 25.6.2014 om ændring af Lov om Det Centrale Personregister) or by action *d'état* (eg for France, Cour de Cassation, Assemblée plénière, 11 December 1992, Bull.civ. No 13; Gazette du Palais 1993, 180 concl).

In 1989, the European Parliament passed Resolution of 12 September 1989 on discrimination against transsexuals ([1989] OJ C 256/33) which declared 'that human dignity and personal rights must include the right to live according to one's sexual identity'. A few years later, the European Court of Justice in *P v S and Cornwall City Council* (Case C-13/94 *P v S and Cornwall City Council* [1996] ECR I-2143) held that the provisions in Directive 76/207 concerning discrimination on the grounds of gender in the workplace (Council Directive 76/207/EEC of 9 February 1976 on the implementation of the principle of equal treatment for men and women as regards access to employment, vocational training and promotion, and working conditions, [1976] OJ L 39/40) applied to persons who had changed or intended to change their legal gender. The scope of the Directive could not 'be confined simply to discrimination based on the fact that a person is of one or other sex. It must extend to discrimination arising from gender reassignment, which is based, essentially if not exclusively, on the sex of the person concerned'. To dismiss a person on the ground that 'he or she intends to undergo, or has undergone, gender reassignment' was found to be treating 'him or her unfavourably by comparison with persons of the sex to which he or she was deemed to belong to before that operation'. In Case C-117/01 *KB v National Health Service Pensions Agency* ([2004] ECR I-541) the ECJ later continued this line of reasoning.

During the same period, a significant number of cases were brought before the European Court of Human Rights. The Court at first took a rather cautious approach, affording contracting states a wide margin of appreciation (see van *Oosterwijck v Belgium* (1981) 3 EHRR 557; *Rees v United Kingdom* (1986) 9 EHRR 56; *B v France* (1993) 16 EHRR 1; *X, Y and Z v the United Kingdom* (1997) 24 EHRR 143; *Cossey v United Kingdom* (1991) 13 EHRR 622; *Sheffield and Horsham v United Kingdom* (1999) 27 EHRR 163). However, in the light of the developments in European jurisdictions outlined above, this margin consistently decreased until, finally, in *Christine Goodwin v United Kingdom* (2002) 35 EHRR 447 and *I v United Kingdom* (2003) 36 EHRR 967, both decided on 11 July 2002, the ECtHR unanimously found that not allowing a change of legal gender under any circumstances (and prohibiting the person concerned from marrying once the change of legal gender was finalized) was a violation of art 8 ECHR (and art 12 ECHR). This of course means that all contracting states of the ECHR must now provide for the possibility of change of the legal gender. However, since the decisions did not stipulate particular requirements for allowing a change of legal gender, the contracting states retain a margin of appreciation in this respect, as recently confirmed in *Hämäläinen v Finland* (2014) ECHR 877. Here, the Court had a first opportunity to decide on the modalities of gender recognition and, somewhat disappointingly, held that the requirement, under Finnish law, to convert an existing marriage (which in Finland until 1 March 2017 is only open to opposite sex couples) into a registered partnership (for same-sex couples) was within the margin of appreciation of the contracting state. Interestingly, the German Federal Constitutional Court ((BVerfG), 27 May 2008, 121 BVerfGE 175) and Italian Constitutional Court (No 170/2014, 11 June 2014) previously had decided that forcing a person to choose between a constitutionally protected marriage and the recognition of preferred gender identity amounted to a violation of the respective constitutions.

IV. Legal sources and current legislation

1. National

As already outlined above, following the European Court of Human Rights decision in *Goodwin*, all contracting states of the ECHR are now obliged to provide mechanisms for the change of legal gender. As the decision did not mandate specific requirements or procedures, the approaches in the European jurisdictions unsurprisingly vary greatly – both in substance and in procedure. Space precludes a detailed discussion, or even a list of the relevant provisions (but see Jens M Scherpe (ed), *The Legal Status of Transsexual and Transgender Persons* (Intersentia 2015), and Jürgen Basedow and Jens M Scherpe (eds), *Transsexualität, Staatsangehörigkeit und internationales Privatrecht* (Mohr Siebeck 2004)). Given the topic of this volume, the focus in the following sections will be on private international law aspects.

The underlying political, as well as practical, problem lies in the fact that it is of course the home state of every person that is responsible for issuing personal identity documents etc; as regards birth certificates, it is the state in which the birth was registered. But the place in which the person concerned lives and desires to be recognized in his or her preferred gender might be a different jurisdiction. The question for the jurisdiction concerned, therefore, is how to deal with this situation, particularly if the law of the home state does not allow for a change of legal gender, or at least not under circumstances which the particular applicant can meet.

The early statutes (such as the 1972 Swedish or the 1980 German Acts) had a very straightforward answer, which was deemed necessary at the time for reasons of → comity: only nationals of the state in which the change of legal gender was sought could apply for and be granted such a change of status. Therefore, the policy was that each state should be responsible for the recognition of the (preferred) gender of its citizens. However, this position came under increasing political and legal pressure, and the German Constitutional Court's decision (Federal Constitutional Court of Germany (BVerfG), 18 July 2006, 116 BVerfGE 243) can be seen as a paradigm example of this movement. The German Court unanimously held that restricting recognition of preferred gender to German nationals constituted a violation of basic human rights (→ Human rights and private international law), as enshrined in the German Constitution. There was no sufficient justification for treating German and foreign citizens differently. Germany could obviously not issue personal identification documents or birth certificates for foreign citizens, nor could it require foreign states to do so. The German state could, however, recognize the preferred gender of foreign nationals for all intents and purposes on the German territory and for German law. The fact that the home state might not recognize the preferred gender and that, therefore, this might cause certain difficulties was recognized by the Court. However, the judges concluded that it undoubtedly would be more important for the person concerned to be able to live according to their preferred gender in Germany. Hence any person now in Germany can apply for the recognition of their preferred gender. After *Goodwin* this must be the case in all European contracting states of the ECHR.

The question therefore merely is how this is to be dealt with from a private international law point of view.

One possibility (which is fairly common, not least because of legislative inertia in this field) is to have no specific regulation. That means that the starting point for civil status matters continues to be that the law of the applicant's → nationality applies. However, should that law not allow for a change of legal gender, this would be deemed to violate the *ordre public* and, thus, the law of the state in which the application is made becomes applicable so that gender recognition can be affected (see for examples on this approach in France Cour d'appel Paris, 14 June 1994, [1995] 84 Rev.crit.DIP 308; in Italy Tribunale di Milano, 4 July 2000, [2000] Famiglia e Diritto 608 ff; Tribunale di Milano, 14 July 1997, [1998] Riv.Dir. Int'le Priv. & Proc. 508 and in Austria VwGH, 30 September 1997, [1999] ZfRV 185).

Another possibility is to enact specific legislation. This legislation then might still refer to nationality as the connecting factor, which results in the *ordre public* exception being applied in some cases as just described (cf for example Belgium art 35ter Belgian Private international law Act (Wet houdende het Wetboek van internationaal privaatrecht/Code de droit international privé of 16 July 2004, BS 27 July 2004, pp 57344, 57366)). The more modern approach, however, is to apply the law of the country in which the applicant is habitually resident, as for example is the case in the Netherlands (art 1: 28 para 3 NBW, requiring a minimum residency period of one year before the application) and Finland (on which see Pimenoff and Will, 'Zum neuen finnischen Transsexuellengesetz' [2003] StAZ 71). The United Kingdom's Gender Recognition Act 2004 goes even further and does not expressly stipulate any specific nationality or residency requirements.

The recognition of foreign acts or decisions concerning the change of legal gender (and of subsequent → marriages etc in that gender) in most jurisdictions are not the subject of specific private international law rules and thus are governed by the general law provisions on recognition of civil status acts (for example in the Netherlands art 431 para 2 Dutch Code of Civil Procedure (Wetboek van Burgerlijke Rechtsvordering, available at <http://wetten. overheid.nl>) which applies to all such acts and decisions, except those from Spain for which the CIEC Convention No 29 applies (available at <www.ciec1.org/Conventions/Conv29.pdf> (French) and <http://ciec1.org/Conventions/ Conv29Angl.pdf> (English), see below).

2. International

a) CIEC Convention No 29

There are currently almost no international conventions or agreements regarding the change of legal gender. The only exception is the Convention No 29 of the CIEC on the recognition of decisions recording a gender reassignment (Convention No 29 relative à la reconnaissance des décisions constatant un changement de sexe) by the International Commission on Civil Status (Commission Internationale de l'État Civil, → CIEC/ICCS (International Commission on Civil Status)), adopted on 16 September 1999 in Lisbon and signed on 12 September 2000 in Vienna – and thus almost two years before the seminal decision of the ECtHR in *Goodwin v UK* (*Christine Goodwin v United Kingdom* (2002) 35 EHRR 447) was handed down. This also explains why the substance of the CIEC Convention in many respects today appears unduly narrow. It certainly does not reflect current legal or medical developments and essentially is out of date.

So far, only five states have signed the CIEC Convention (→ Austria, → Greece, the → Netherlands, → Spain and → Germany), and only Spain and the Netherlands have ratified it. Therefore, the Convention has been in force since 1 March 2011 only in those two jurisdictions. Given that legal and medical understanding of gender identity has developed significantly since the Convention was drafted, it is unlikely that there will be any future signatures, ratifications or accessions.

The purpose of the CIEC Convention is to facilitate the → recognition of administrative acts or court decisions made by competent authorities in a contracting state 'regarding a person's sex reassignment', provided that the person concerned was a national of, or habitually resident in, the state where the decision was taken (art 1). Under the CIEC Convention, therefore, the nationality of an applicant for recognition is not the exclusive connecting factor and habitual residence may suffice.

The commentary to the CIEC Convention makes clear that 'sex reassignment means a physical adaptation such that the person concerned must be considered from a legal point of view as no longer belonging to his or her original sex', and, indeed, art 2(a) expressly refers to 'the physical adaptation' and states that recognition may be refused if such adaptation 'has not been carried out and recorded in the decision in question'. While this is not defined any further, it seems to suggest that some form of gender reassignment/confirmation surgery might be required, or at the very least hormonal treatment which alters the physical appearance. While it may be doubted whether such a requirement was appropriate at the time of drafting, it certainly is not appropriate at the time this chapter is written. This is despite the fact that some national laws continue to require such medical treatment. The decision by the German Constitutional Court on this matter (Federal Constitutional Court of Germany (BVerfG), 11 January 2011, 128 BVerfGE 109) is most instructive and represents the emerging legal view. The German Court held that requiring surgery and/or sterility for legal recognition of the preferred gender violates a person's fundamental human rights, as the person concerned otherwise must make a 'choice' between accepting a violation of his or her physical integrity, through surgery that is not desired, or refusing such surgical intervention and losing the right to legal gender recognition. This essentially forces the person concerned to 'sacrifice' one of the protected human rights to gain the other, which is unacceptable. Similarly, the Italian Supreme Court in 2015 (Decision No 15138 of 20 July 2015) held that medical intervention and sterilization are not necessary prerequisites for legally changing one's gender and that 'medical treatment' in the 1982 Act must be interpreted accordingly. Modern statutory provisions (such as the recent Danish, Dutch Maltese, Argentinian and Irish statutes, the United Kingdom's Gender Recognition Act, as well as amendments in Sweden) no longer contain requirements for surgery etc.

According to art 2(b) and (c) of the Convention recognition may also be refused if 'such recognition is contrary to public policy in the Contracting State in which the decision is relied on' or 'when the decision has been obtained by fraudulent means'.

If none of the grounds for refusal apply, art 3 obliges the respective state to 'update' the birth certificate of the person concerned if it has been drawn up in that state or transcribed into the civil status registers.

b) Yogyakarta Principles
The Yogyakarta Principles on the application of international human rights law in relation to sexual orientation and gender identity (available at <www.yogyakartaprinciples.org/>) were drafted in 2006 by an international panel of 29 experts in the areas of international human rights law and sexual orientation and gender identity. The panel members came from 25 jurisdictions and included the former Irish President and United Nations High Commissioner of Human Rights Mary Robinson. The Yogyakarta Principles, named for the city of Yogyakarta in which they were drawn up, are not a convention or treaty, and cannot claim any legal authority. However, they certainly carry considerable moral and persuasive authority and have been considered and referred to by the highest courts (see eg the dissenting opinions of Judges Sajó, Keller and Lemmens in the ECtHR case of *Hämäläinen v Finland* (2014) ECHR 877) and government reform commissions in a number of jurisdictions (eg in Sweden, cf Departementsserien (Ds) 2012:46, pp 44–5 and 52). These Principles contain, amongst other things, the right to equality and non-discrimination and the right to recognition. They do not, however, include a specific provision relating to private international law.

Yogyakarta Principle No 3 states:

. . . Each person's self-defined sexual orientation and gender identity is integral to their personality and is one of the most basic aspects of self-determination, dignity and freedom. No one shall be forced to undergo medical procedures, including sex reassignment surgery, sterilisation or hormonal therapy, as a requirement for legal recognition of their gender identity. No status, such as marriage or parenthood, may be invoked as such to prevent the legal recognition of a person's gender identity. . . .

Principle No. 3 continues that states shall:

. . . B. Take all necessary legislative, administrative and other measures to fully respect and legally recognise each person's self-defined gender identity;

C. Take all necessary legislative, administrative and other measures to ensure that procedures exist whereby all State-issued identity papers which indicate a person's gender/sex – including birth certificates, passports, electoral records and other documents – reflect the person's profound self-defined gender identity;

D. Ensure that such procedures are efficient, fair and non-discriminatory, and respect the dignity and privacy of the person concerned;

E. Ensure that changes to identity documents will be recognised in all contexts where the identification or disaggregation of persons by gender is required by law or policy; . . .

The Yogyakarta Principles therefore mandate not only the recognition of an individual's preferred gender but also the recognition of foreign decisions, acts or documents to that effect.

3. European

There are no legislative acts on the European level directly applicable to the recognition of the preferred gender/change of legal gender. However, the European Court of Justice has extended the application of Directives and Regulations concerning gender discrimination to the situation of transsexual and transgender persons (see above).

What is clear is that following the decision of the European Court of Human Rights in *Goodwin*, contracting states are obliged to provide the possibility to change the legal gender of a person. However, as explained above, the particular modalities of that recognition have not been prescribed by the Strasbourg Court. Furthermore, it is also clear that once an EU Member State does recognize and document the preferred legal gender of an individual, other Member States must recognize and respect this civil status act – any other response would impede the free movement of workers and therefore violate the European Union Treaties. Similarly, the refusal to respect the preferred gender (and thus the gender identity) of a person recognized by a competent authority elsewhere surely must be a violation of the respect to private life protected by art 8 ECHR.

V. Modern trends

The legal recognition of preferred gender (ie allowing the change of the legal gender of a person) is mandatory for all contracting states of the ECHR following the *Goodwin* decision. However, there still appears to be a significant margin of appreciation for the states concerning the modalities, including in relation to private international law rules. While in most states there are no existing legal provisions on this issue, and thus the 'traditional' connecting factor of nationality determines the applicable law for status-defining elements such as gender (including an *ordre public* exception where the law so designated does not allow for such a change), more recently enacted statutory provisions prefer habitual residence as the connecting factor.

JENS M SCHERPE

Literature

Jürgen Basedow and Jens M Scherpe (eds), *Transsexualität, Staatsangehörigkeit und internationales Privatrecht* (Mohr Siebeck 2004); Commission Internationale de l'État Civil, 'Le transsexualisme en Europe' [2002] available at <www.ciec1.org/Etudes/Transsexualisme/Transsexualisme EnEuropeNoteSynthese 2avecMAJau20-9-02.pdf>; Salvatore Patti and Michael R Will (eds), *Mutamento di sesso e tutela della persona – Saggi di diritto civile e comparato* (CEDAM 1986); Jens M Scherpe (ed), *The Legal Status of Transsexual and Transgender Persons* (Intersentia 2015); Jens M. Scherpe, The Legal Status of Intersex Persons (Intersentia 2017); Stephen Whittle, *Respect and Equality: Transsexual and Transgender Rights* (Routledge-Cavendish 2002).

Treaties in private international law

I. Introduction

It is fair to say that, until the 1950s, treaties in private international law were quite exceptional. Private international law was traditionally regulated by domestic, autonomous conflict rules, either developed by courts or codified in normative instruments (see, for instance, Erik Jayme, 'Internationalprivatrechtliche, staatsrechtliche, völkerrechtliche Aspekte – 14. Tagung der Deutschen Gesellschaft für Völkerrecht in Göttingen am 10. und 11. April 1975' in Erik Jayme and Karl M Meessen, *Staatsverträge zum Internationalen Privatrecht* (CF Müller 1975) 7, 9). In the past decades, however, there has been a notable tendency for states to replace their unilateral sources in this area with a network of treaties in the different sectors of private international law.

According to the Vienna Convention on the Law of Treaties (Vienna Convention on the Law of Treaties of 23 May 1969, 1155 UNTS 331), a treaty is 'an international agreement concluded between states in written form and governed by international law, whether embodied in a single instrument or in two or more related instruments and whatever its particular designation'. The key elements that characterize a particular instrument as a treaty are its international character, a wide variety of forms that reflect the flexible nature of international law (the instrument's title is not a determinative factor – treaty, convention, protocol, covenant, charter, statute, act, declaration, concordat, exchange of notes, agreed minute, memorandum of agreement, *modus vivendi* or any other appellation) and its adherence to international law. While the Vienna Convention on the Law of Treaties explicitly refers to states as the subjects of treaties, other subjects of international law, such as a Regional Economic Integration Organization, contract with each other or with states by means of treaties (United Nations, *Yearbook of the International Law Commission 1962*, vol 2 (United Nations Publication 1964, Sales No 62. V 5) 161; see also Ian Brownlie, *Principles of Public International Law* (6th edn, OUP 2003) 580; Anthony Aust, *Modern Treaty Law and Practice* (2nd edn, CUP 2007) 16).

According to art 38(1)(a) of the ICJ Statute (Statute of the International Court of Justice of 26 June 1945, 15 UNTS 355), conventions (or treaties as described above) are one of the main sources of public international law, besides international custom and general principles of law recognized by civilized nations. The reference to 'public international law' in art 38(1) of the ICJ Statute is not to be understood as separate from or excluding private international law as, in this context, private international law is a sub-category of public international law.

II. Why treaties to regulate private international law?

The particular objective of private international law, ie the regulation of the interests of citizens in situations connected with more than one state, is adequately served by treaties as these arrangements are meant to be uniformly applied in more than one state (Hans van Loon, 'Unification and Co-operation in Family Law' in Alegría Borrás and others (eds), *E Pluribus Unum. Liber Amicorum Georges A L Droz. On the Progressive Unification of Private international law. Sur L'Unification Progressive du Droit International Privé* (Martinus Nijhoff 1996) 175). For instance, in the particular area of civil procedure, a state may provide for recognition of foreign judgments or foreign official documents, but it cannot ensure the recognition by other states of its own judgments and official documents. To reach such a goal, international cooperation is needed, either by entering into an arrangement with one given party, leading to a bilateral treaty, or between three or more parties (a multilateral treaty). More generally, addressing the issues arising from different legal rules applicable to cross-border situations (with regard to either international civil procedure and/or the conflict of laws) at the international plane is beneficial in terms of increased predictability and legal certainty for citizens involved in international situations. A treaty which contains provisions relating to the different areas of private international law – ie provisions on the governing law, provisions regarding the determination of international jurisdiction, provisions regarding the recognition and enforcement of judgments as well as provisions on cross-border cooperation between relevant authorities to ensure a proper application of the treaty itself – ensure a very high level of legal certainty for citizens facing legal diversity (Mattijs Herbert Van Hoogstraten, 'La codification par traités en droit international privé dans le cadre de la Conférence de la Haye' (1967) 122 Rec. des Cours 337). The Hague Child Protection Convention (Hague Convention of 19 October 1996 on jurisdiction, applicable law, recognition, enforcement and co-operation in respect of parental responsibility and measures for the protection of children, 35 ILM 1391) is one such example of a comprehensive treaty which improves the cross-border protection of children by addressing a variety of private international law issues.

At the same time, treaties are only one category of public international law sources which may regulate private international legal issues. States or other subjects of international law may also revert to alternative mechanisms in order to develop uniform private international law.

The past decades have indeed been characterized by a proliferation of non-binding instruments in the area of private international law, such as model laws, legislative guides, principles etc. Such instruments do not involve the creation of *per se* legally binding norms, yet they still contribute to the unification of private international law. In other words, they share the same objective as treaties in private international law but they are different as to their formation or binding nature. Their greater degree of adaptability to the domestic systems of private international law are essential advantages when states or other subjects of international law pursue the development of unified international standards. Conversely, states or other subjects of international law cannot become party to an instrument which is developed as a non-binding standard. They can instead consider such an instrument as a model for the development or reform of their domestic legislation. The prevailing view appears to indicate that a non-binding instrument cannot be given the status of a treaty in the sense of the Vienna Convention on the

Law of Treaties because the reference to a treaty as a norm which is 'governed by international law' (art 2(1)(a) Vienna Convention on the Law of Treaties) presupposes that such norm is capable of creating obligations under international law (Anthony Aust, *Modern Treaty Law and Practice* (2nd edn, CUP 2007) 20). Accordingly, instruments developed in the framework of international professional and/ or academic groupings such as the International Law Association or the International Law Institute cannot be considered to be treaties in private international law, even though they serve the same goal of approximation or unification of the rules in this area. Examples of such instruments are *inter alia* the CLIP Principles (European Max Planck Group on Conflict of Laws in Intellectual Property, *Conflict of Laws in Intellectual Property: The CLIP Principles and Commentary*, OUP 2013) and several influential ILA or ILI Resolutions relating to key aspects of private international law (to refer to some recent ones, Resolution No 1/2000 of the ILA on Declining and Referring Jurisdiction in Civil or Commercial Matters, available at www.ila-hq.org; or the ILI 1995 Resolution on Cooperation between State Authorities Combating the Unlawful Displacement of Children, available at <www.justitiaetpace. org>). Similarly, the development of such instruments within intergovernmental organizations such as the → Hague Conference on Private International Law or the International Institute for the Unification of Private Law (→ UNIDROIT) and their adoption pursuant to the rules of procedure of the corresponding intergovernmental organization does not influence their characterization: they are still not to be considered 'treaties' (United Nations, *Yearbook of the International Law Commission 1962*, vol 2 (United Nations Publication 1964, Sales No 62. V 5) 31; Georges Droz, 'La Conférence de La Haye de droit international privé et les méthodes d'unification du droit: traités internationaux ou lois modèles' [1961] R.D.I.D.C. 511). The Hague Principles on Choice of Law in International Commercial Contracts (approved on 19 March 2015, available at <www.hcch.net>) may constitute the most recent example of a non-binding instrument – and hence not a treaty – in private international law (see, for further details, Permanent Bureau of the Hague Conference on Private International Law, 'Choice of Law in International Commercial Contracts: Hague Principles?' [2010] Unif.L.Rev. 883–903, in particular at 886 and the bibliography on this instrument available at <www.hcch.net>).

Furthermore, in the specific context of the EU, the relevance of treaties in private international law has notably decreased since the EU gained legislative competences to develop regulations, directives and other instruments of EU law. The Treaty of Amsterdam (Treaty of Amsterdam amending the Treaty on the European Union, the Treaties establishing the European Communities and certain related acts (consolidated version), [1997] OJ C 340/01) is generally considered to be the turning point for this evolution: several fundamental treaties in private international law, which came into existence before 1997, have since been superseded by regulations. For example, the Brussels Convention (Brussels Convention of 27 September 1968 on jurisdiction and the enforcement of judgments in civil and commercial matters, [1972] OJ L 299/32, consolidated version, [1998] OJ C 27/1), being the cornerstone of EU private international law, gave way first to the Brussels I Regulation (Regulation (EC) No 44/2001 of 22 December 2000 on jurisdiction and the recognition and enforcement of judgments in civil and commercial matters, [2001] OJ L 12/1) and subsequently to the Brussels I Regulation (recast) (Regulation (EU) No 1215/2012 of the European Parliament and of the Council of 12 December 2012 on jurisdiction and the recognition and enforcement of judgments in civil and commercial matters (recast), [2012] OJ L 351/1).

At present, EU instruments cover extensive areas of private international law. Furthermore, such instruments operate differently than treaties as the latter may have direct legal effect without being subject to ratification or any other process at the domestic level. The prevalence of EU instruments in the private international law arena has furthermore given rise to interesting legal issues of articulation between treaties and EU instruments (see *inter alia* Alegría Borrás, 'Les clauses de déconnexion et le droit international privé communautaire' in Heinz-Peter Mansel and others (eds), *Festschrift für Erik Jayme* (Sellier 2004) 51–72; Jan-Jaap Kuipers, 'The European Union and the Hague Conference on Private International Law: Forced Marriage or Fortunate Partnership?' in Henri de Waele and Jan-Jaap Kuipers (eds), *The European Union's Emerging International Identity: Views from the Global Arena* (Brill Nijhoff 2013) 181–3). In certain cases, treaties contain so-called 'disconnection clauses' to ensure that EU instruments prevail. Examples of this coordination technique can be found in art 51(4) of the Hague Maintenance Convention 2007 (Hague Convention of 23 November 2007 on the international recovery of child support and other forms of family maintenance, [2011] OJ L 192/51), which 'gives way' to the application of the Maintenance Regulation (Council Regulation (EC) No 4/2009 of 18 December 2008 on jurisdiction, applicable law, recognition and enforcement of decisions and cooperation in matters relating to maintenance obligations, [2009] OJ L 7/1), or art 64 of the → Lugano Convention (Lugano Convention of 30 October 2007 on jurisdiction and the recognition and enforcement of judgments in civil and commercial matters, [2007] OJ L 339/3), which gives primacy to the Brussels I Regulation. In other cases, a treaty and an EU instrument apply in a coordinated fashion, for example, by an explicit referral to a treaty in an EU Regulation (for instance, art 15 of the Maintenance Regulation 'gives way' to the Hague Maintenance Protocol 2007 (Hague Protocol of 23 November 2007 on the law applicable to maintenance obligations, [2009] OJ L 331/19) in the Member States bound by that instrument). The interaction of a treaty and an EU instrument may also be a matter of careful delimitation of the relevant instruments, such as the interaction between the Hague Child Protection Convention (Hague Convention of 19 October 1996 on jurisdiction, applicable law, recognition, enforcement and co-operation in respect of parental responsibility and measures for the protection of children, 35 ILM 1391), the Hague Child Abduction Convention (Hague Convention of 25 October 1980 on the civil aspects of international child abduction, 1343 UNTS 89) and the Brussels IIa Regulation (Council Regulation (EC) No 2201/2003 of 27 November 2003 concerning jurisdiction and the recognition and enforcement of judgments in matrimonial matters and the matters of parental responsibility, repealing Regulation (EC) No 1347/2000, [2003] OJ L 338/1). The interwoven application of such instruments is further determined pursuant to Opinion 1/13 rendered by the CJEU (→ Court of Justice of the European Union) on 14 October 2014 on the competence to accept the accessions to a treaty (*in casu* the Hague Child Abduction Convention) by states outside the EU (available at <http://curia.europa.eu>). The CJEU, which was requested to decide whether it is for the EU or for the Member States to accept such accessions, ruled in favour of the exclusive competence of the EU. The CJEU's Opinion reaffirmed its prior case-law on external competence of the EU and, in line with art 3(2) TFEU (The Treaty on the Functioning of the European Union (consolidated version), [2012] OJ C 326/47), confirmed that the EU enjoys exclusive competence where an international treaty affects EU rules or alters their scope. With regard to international → child abduction rules, they are indeed both contained in the Hague Child Abduction Convention and in the Brussels IIa Regulation. Furthermore, according to the CJEU, 'the scope and effectiveness of the common rules laid down by the regulation are likely to be affected when the Member States individually make separate declarations accepting third-State accessions to the 1980 Hague Convention'. While the legal reasoning followed by the CJEU is open to criticisms (see *inter alia* Alegría Borrás, 'La aceptación de las adhesiones al Convenio de La Haya sobre sustracción de menores: el Dictamen del TJUE de 14 de octubre de 2014' (2014) 21 La Ley Unión Europea 42), the Opinion has to be welcomed as representing the end of an institutional deadlock to the application of a relevant treaty to specific child abduction cases, and thus to children in need. It is now for the EU institutions to speedily take up their responsibilities as regards any newly acceded state and contribute to the best possible operation of this treaty.

While treaties and EU instruments are normally set to coexist, a treaty can be denounced further to the adoption of an EU instrument on the same subject matter. For example, the → Netherlands had ratified the Hague Succession Convention (Hague Convention of 1 August 1989 on the Law Applicable to Succession to the Estates of Deceased Persons, available at <www.hcch.net>) (for the Kingdom in Europe only). However, as an indirect consequence to the entry into force of the Succession Regulation (Regulation (EU) No 650/2012 of the European Parliament and of the Council of 4 July 2012 on jurisdiction, applicable law, recognition and enforcement of decisions and acceptance and enforcement of authentic instruments in matters of succession and on the creation of a European Certificate of Succession, [2012] OJ L 201/107; → Rome IV Regulation), the Netherlands denounced the Convention on 17 December 2014, with effect as per 1 April 2015.

Marta Pertegás

III. Treaty techniques in the area of private international law

The process of negotiating, adopting, consenting to and bringing a treaty into effect falls outside the scope of this contribution as these processes are regulated by public international law. It suffices to say that treaties in private international law, like treaties in other branches of international law, are governed by the 1969 Vienna Convention on the law of the treaties more generally.

However, it is interesting to review which treaty techniques are more often used by negotiators in the area of private international law. An overview of some of the most important instruments shows that multilateral treaties concluded in the framework of an intergovernmental organization are generally open to the signature of at least all states that negotiated and concluded the treaty. These multilateral treaties can be 'open' to other states so that states which did not conclude the treaty can accede to it without further conditions. An example of such an 'open' treaty is the Hague Choice of Court Convention (Hague Convention of 30 June 2005 on choice of court agreements, 44 ILM 1294), which stipulates in art 27 that the Convention is 'open for signature by all States [and] subject to ratification, acceptance or approval by the signatory States', as well as 'open for accession by all States'.

Alternatively, accession to the treaty for non-negotiating states can be subject to conditions, either in the form of an acceptance of accession or in the form of an objection to accession.

In the first case (acceptance of accession or 'opt-in' approach), the treaty enters into force between an acceding state and a contracting state if the latter declares acceptance of the former's accession. An example of such an 'opt-in' system can be found in art 39 of the Hague Evidence Convention (Hague Convention of 18 March 1970 on the taking of evidence abroad in civil or commercial matters, 847 UNTS 241), which stipulates that the Hague Evidence Convention will have effect 'only as regards the relations between the acceding State and such Contracting States as will have declared their acceptance of the accession'.

In the second case (objection to accession or 'opt-out' approach), the treaty will only enter into force between the acceding state and those contracting states that have not raised an objection to the accession of that state. The treaty should contain further indications as to how the objection should be raised. For example, art 58 of the Hague Maintenance Convention 2007 allows for a period of 12 months after the date of the accession's notification by the Convention's depositary or at the time when states 'ratify, accept or approve the Convention after an accession'.

Finally, it is rather unusual for a treaty in private international law to follow the 'veto approach', ie a system which requires that no contracting state objects to a given state's accession. Article 29 of the Hague Recognition and Enforcement Convention (Hague Convention of 1 February 1971 on the recognition and enforcement of foreign judgments in civil and commercial matters, 1144 UNTS 258) provides an illustration of this approach as 'the Convention shall enter into force for such a State in the absence of any objection from a State which has ratified the Convention before such deposit . . .'. The same Hague Recognition and Enforcement Convention provides an example of another restricting technique for the instrument to enter into force, ie a requirement of a supplementary agreement being concluded between two States Parties to the Convention (the 'bilateralization approach'). Consequently, the Hague Recognition and Enforcement Convention never entered into force, as some anticipated a long time ago (Karl M Meessen, 'Völkerrechtliche und verfassungsrechtliche Aspekte – 14. Tagung der Deutschen Gesellschaft für Völkerrecht in Göttingen am 10. und 11. April 1975' in Erik Jayme and Karl M Meessen, *Staatsverträge zum Internationalen Privatrecht* (CF Müller 1975) 49, 53).

Besides the above-mentioned approaches, most treaties in private international law use reservations and/or declarations to 'customize' the legal effect of certain provisions of the treaty in their application in the state that makes the reservation. Reservations are defined in art 2(1)(d) of the Vienna Convention on the Law of Treaties while declarations are not. It is therefore often difficult to make a distinction between a declaration and a reservation, especially when the legal effects of such principally unilateral acts extend, by operation of the reciprocity principle, to other contracting states (Alfred E Von Overbeck, 'L'application par le juge interne des conventions de droit international privé' [1971] Rec. des Cours 1, 34). Certain Conventions do not permit the operation of reservations at all (see, for instance, art 21 of the Hague

Securities Convention (Hague Convention of 5 July 2006 on the law applicable to certain rights in respect of securities held with an intermediary, 46 ILM 649)).

MARTA PERTEGÁS

Literature

Anthony Aust, *Modern Treaty Law and Practice* (2nd edn, CUP 2007); Alegría Borrás, 'La aceptación de las adhesiones al Convenio de La Haya sobre sustracción de menores: el Dictamen del TJUE de 14 de octubre de 2014' (2014) 21 La Ley Unión Europea 42; Alegría Borrás and others (eds), *E Pluribus Unum. Liber Amicorum Georges A L Droz. On the Progressive Unification of Private international law. Sur L'Unification Progressive du Droit International Privé* (Martinus Nijhoff 1996); Ian Brownlie, *Principles of Public International Law* (6th edn, OUP 2003); Erik Jayme, 'Internationalprivatrechtliche, staatsrechtliche, völkerrechtliche Aspekte – 14. Tagung der Deutschen Gesellschaft für Völkerrecht in Göttingen am 10. und 11. April 1975' in Erik Jayme and Karl M Meessen, *Staatsverträge zum Internationalen Privatrecht* (CF Müller 1975) 7; Karl M Meessen, 'Völkerrechtliche und verfassungsrechtliche Aspekte – 14. Tagung der Deutschen Gesellschaft für Völkerrecht in Göttingen am 10. und 11. April 1975' in Erik Jayme and Karl M Meessen, *Staatsverträge zum Internationalen Privatrecht* (CF Müller 1975) 49; Antoon VM Struycken, 'Coordination and Co-operation in Respectful Disagreement: General Course on Private international law' (2004) 311 Rec. des Cours 5; United Nations, 'Report of the Commission to the General Assembly' UNGAOR 17th Session, Supp No 9 UN Doc A/5209 (1962), reprinted in [1962] 2 *Yearbook of the International Law Commission* 157, UN Sales No 62. V 5; Mattijs Herbert Van Hoogstraten, 'La codification par traités en droit international privé dans le cadre de la Conférence de la Haye' (1967) 122 Rec. des Cours 337; Alfred Verdross and Bruno Simma, *Universelles Völkerrecht: Theorie und Praxis* (3rd edn, Duncker & Humblot 1984); Alfred E Von Overbeck, 'L'application par le juge interne des conventions de droit international privé' [1971] Rec. des Cours 1;.

TRIPS

I. Background

The Agreement of 15 April 1994 on Trade Related Aspects of Intellectual Property Rights (TRIPS, 1869 UNTS 299) is part of the WTO's Final Act of the 1986–94 Uruguay Round of trade negotiations. TRIPS contains a framework of fundamental principles on substantive issues of intellectual property and on enforcement measures to be respected by all WTO members (→ WTO and private international law). TRIPS negotiations introduced intellectual property issues to the realm of international trade policy. The agreement incorporates the most significant older international conventions on intellectual property, particularly the Berne Convention for the Protection of Literary and Artistic Works of 1886, last revised 1971 (Berne Convention for the Protection of Literary and Artistic Works of 9 September 1886, completed at Paris on 4 May 1896, revised at Berlin on 13 November 1908, completed at Berne on 20 March 1914, revised at Rome on 2 June 1928, revised at Brussels on 26 June 1948, revised at Stockholm on 14 July 1967 and revised at Paris on 24 July 1971, 1161 UNTS 3 and amended in 1979 Treaty Doc No 99-27, and 1985, 828 UNTS 221), and the Paris Convention for the Protection of Industrial Property of 1883, last revised 1967 (Paris Convention for the Protection of Industrial Property, 20 March 1883, with later amendments, 828 UNTS 305), but goes beyond the standard of protection under these older conventions (so-called Berne-plus and Paris-plus approaches). Many developing countries and emerging markets were not member to these older intellectual property conventions before TRIPS. As part of a larger negotiation package comprising free trade of goods, free trade of services and intellectual property, developing countries finally accepted the high level of intellectual property protection established by TRIPS. However, developing countries and emerging markets insist in the current Doha Round of trade negotiations at WTO that intellectual property should not restrict access to technology and knowledge, particularly with regard to pharmaceuticals. TRIPS is binding on all 164 WTO members (as of 26 July 2016) comprising all major economies, including China and Russia. The EU also has member status at WTO (→ WTO and private international law).

II. Overview of the substantive rules

1. Structure and general provisions

TRIPS comprises six parts. Part I of the Agreement provides general provisions and basic principles. Article 1 clarifies the minimum standard approach of agreement, under which

TRIPS members are at liberty to implement more extensive protection than provided for in the Agreement. Article 2 obliges Member States to comply with the substantive provisions of the Paris Convention. Article 3 codifies the principle of national treatment as previously laid down in the older intellectual property conventions, whereby nationals of other party states must be given treatment with regard to intellectual property protection no less favourable than that accorded to a state's own nationals. Article 4 contains a 'most-favoured-nation' clause, a novelty in an international intellectual property agreement, under which any advantage a party gives to the nationals of another country must be extended immediately and unconditionally to the nationals of all other parties, even if such treatment is more favourable than that given to its own nationals. Unfortunately Member States could not agree on the introduction of an internationally binding exhaustion rule. Although art 6 has the sub-title 'exhaustion', the provision merely excludes the exhaustion issue from application of WTO dispute settlement rules without laying down a substantive standard. The result is that Member States are free to establish their own regime for exhaustion. Arts 7 and 8 contain the general objectives which may be used for interpretation of the Agreement.

2. Material standards of intellectual property law

Part II addresses substantive issues relating to the most significant intellectual property rights. With respect to copyright, parties are required to comply with the substantive provisions of the Berne Convention, except for the provisions on moral rights in art 6bis Berne Convention. The USA opposed any reference to moral rights. Article 10 ensures that computer programs and data bases are protected as literary works under the Berne Convention. Article 12 provides that, whenever the term of protection of a work is calculated on a basis other than the life of a natural person, then that term may be no less than 50 years from the end of the calendar year of authorized publication, or failing such authorized publication within 50 years of creation of the work, 50 years from the end of the calendar year of creation. The provision supplements art 7 Berne Convention, which determines that the term of protection is in principle the life of the author and 50 years after their death. Article 14 obliges Member States to grant protection for performing artists against unauthorized recording and broadcasting of live performances. Producers of phonograms enjoy the right to authorize or prohibit the direct or indirect reproduction of their products. The protection of neighbouring rights under art 14 fills an important gap of protection for performing artists and electronic recording producers from states such as the → USA which was not signatory to the International Convention for the Protection of Performers, Producers of Phonograms and Broadcasting Organisations of 26 October 1961 (496 UNTS 43).

Arts 15 to 21 address trade marks and service marks. Article 15 defines what types of signs are eligible for protection as a trade mark, whereby, as under EU law, the list of eligible signs is open. Article 16 specifies the rights conferred on the owner of a trade mark, whereby well-known trade marks enjoy additional protection. Article 19 sets a legal framework for national provisions which require the use of the trade mark to maintain registration. Under such provisions, a registration may in principle be cancelled only after an uninterrupted period of at least three years of non-use of the trade mark. An interesting provision is found in art 2 with regard to licences and assignments, under which Member States may in principle determine the conditions for the licensing and assignment of trade marks. However, the owner of a registered trade mark has the right to assign the trade mark with or without transfer of the business to which the trade mark belongs. This solution deviates substantially from the traditional approach followed in many jurisdictions according to which trade marks and businesses could not be transferred separately.

Article 22 obliges Member States to protect geographical indications where a given quality, reputation or other characteristic of the good is essentially attributable to its geographical origin. Article 23 provides a higher level of protection for geographical indications for wines and spirits. These provisions establish the first binding recognition of such rights on an international level. Arts 25 and 26 lay down fundamental principles of protection for industrial designs, including a protection period under the Agreement of ten years.

Under art 27, patents must be available for any inventions, whether products or processes, in all fields of technology, provided that they are new, involve an inventive step and are capable of industrial application. The provision has obliged some Member States to introduce product patents in the pharmaceutical sector, most significantly → India with its strong drug industry. The provision has been relied upon in other jurisdictions, particularly Europe, to argue for more extensive patent protection in the IT sector. Inventions may be excluded from patentability if their commercial exploitation is prohibited for reasons of public order or morality. Further permissible grounds for exclusion cover diagnostic, therapeutic and surgical methods, as well as plants and animals and essentially biological processes for the production of plants or animals. Plant varieties must be protectable either by patents or by a *sui generis* system as under the Community Plant Regulation (Council Regulation (EC) No 2100/94 of 27 July 1994 on Community plant variety rights [1994] OJ L 227/1). Article 28 defines the minimum rights conferred on patent holders. A point of political controversy has been the compulsory licence provision in art 31, which allows use of a protected technology under a compulsory licence regime only for supply of the domestic market of the Member State authorizing such use. Thus, third countries would not be permitted to produce goods, particularly pharmaceuticals, in response to an emergency in another state. This controversial issue was addressed by the WTO Declaration on the TRIPS agreement and public health of 2001, as well as further instruments on public health issues under TRIPS. The protection of layout designs of integrated circuits according to art 35 has not proven to be of major importance for the IT sector. Article 39 provides for protection of undisclosed information of commercial value. Finally, art 40 addresses anti-competitive practices in contractual licences.

3. Procedures and remedies

Part III of the Agreement sets out Member State obligations with regard to procedures and → remedies under their domestic law to ensure the effective enforcement of intellectual property rights. The remedies and procedural rules of this part of the Agreement are applicable to all forms of intellectual property right. As the first comprehensive international instrument on remedies and procedures in intellectual property disputes, arts 41 to 61 have proven highly influential, particularly in Europe where the legislature implemented their provisions through Directive 2004/48/EC of 29 April 2004 on the enforcement of intellectual property rights ([2004] OJ L 157/45).

According to art 41, procedures must permit effective action against intellectual property rights infringement but at the same time be fair and equitable, be neither unnecessarily complicated nor costly, and should entail no unreasonable time-limits or unwarranted delays. The provisions are to be applied in such a manner as to avoid creating barriers to legitimate trade and to provide for safeguards against their abuse. The civil procedures and remedies in art 43 include provisions on evidence which allow courts to order evidence which lies in the opposing party's control by that party. According to art 44, the provision on injunctions, judicial authorities have the authority to order a party to desist from an infringement. However, Member States have no obligation to grant injunctions against a person dealing in a certain subject matter prior to that person knowing or having reasonable grounds to know that this would constitute infringement of an intellectual property right. Article 45, the provision on damages, sets out several alternatives for assessing the damage caused by an infringer who knowingly, or with reasonable grounds to know (with actual or constructive knowledge), engaged in infringing activity. Other remedies under art 46 TRIPS include the right of judicial authorities to order the disposal or destruction of infringing goods. Under art 50, judicial authorities must also have the authority to order prompt and effective → provisional measures. Where appropriate such provisional measures may even be taken without prior hearing of the other party, in particular where any delay is likely to cause irreparable harm to the rights holder, or there is a demonstrable risk of evidence being destroyed. Arts 51 to 60 oblige Member States to introduce specific border measures for counterfeit trade mark or pirated copyright goods. Finally, according to art 61 Member States must provide for criminal procedures and penalties to be applied at least in cases of wilful trade mark counterfeiting or copyright piracy on a commercial scale. Remedies are to include imprisonment and fines sufficient to act as a deterrent. The EU has yet to implement such criminal sanctions.

4. Final parts

Part IV TRIPS provides rules on procedures and formalities regarding the acquisition and maintenance of intellectual property rights and related inter-party procedures. Part V concerns dispute prevention and settlement. It obliges Member States to publish final judicial decisions and administrative rulings. Moreover, the dispute settlement procedures as developed for the GATT system and elaborated in the Dispute Settlement Understanding (Understanding on rules and procedures governing the settlement of Disputes, available at <www.wto.org>) are applicable for dispute resolution under TRIPS. Parts V and VI regulate transitional and institutional arrangements.

III. TRIPS and private international law

TRIPS as such entails no provisions on jurisdiction or private international law. Its principal focus is to promote effective protection of intellectual property rights by harmonizing the substantive provisions of the Member States and the EU, and to provide measures and procedures to enforce intellectual property rights. However, since TRIPS incorporates the main older conventions on intellectual property, namely the Berne and Paris Convention, conflict rules embedded in these older conventions would also be applicable within the WTO framework.

It is widely held, though not undisputed, that the concept of territorially restricted intellectual property rights is enshrined in the main international conventions for intellectual property protection. It is true that the Paris and Berne Convention aimed not at unification of conflict rules, but rather the national treatment of authors and right holders coming from other Member States as well as minimum standards of protection. However, the conventions make repeated reference to the 'law of the country where protection is claimed', which can be interpreted as a reference to the law of the country for which protection is sought. The most prominent reference is to be found in art 5(2) Berne Convention, according to which the 'extent of protection, as well as the means of redress afforded to the author to protect his rights, shall be governed exclusively by the laws of the country where protection is claimed'. Similar references may be found in art 6bis(2) with regard to moral rights, eg 'The rights granted to the author in accordance with the preceding paragraph . . . shall be exercisable by the persons or institutions authorized by the legislation of the country where protection is claimed', art 6bis(3): 'The means of redress for safeguarding the rights granted by this Article shall be governed by the legislation of the country where protection is claimed', or with regard to the term of protection in art 7(8): 'In any case, the term shall be governed by the legislation of the country where protection is claimed; however, unless the legislation of that country otherwise provides, the term shall not exceed the term fixed in the country of origin of the work', in art 10bis(1) with regard to the exception for press reproductions: 'The legal consequences of a breach of this obligation shall be determined by the legislation of the country where protection is claimed', in art 14bis(2)(a) with regard to the ownership of cinematographic works: 'Ownership of copyright in a cinematographic work shall be a matter for legislation in the country where protection is claimed' and in art 18(2) regarding works existing on the Convention's entry into force: 'If, however, through the expiry of the term of protection which was previously granted, a work has fallen into the public domain of the country where protection is claimed, that work shall not be protected anew.' Thus, reference is made to the law of the country where protection is claimed for a broad range of copyright law topics.

However, the ambiguous drafting of the provisions has left scope for divergent interpretations. According to some authors, the reference to the law of the country 'where' protection is claimed is to be understood as a reference to the *lex fori*, including the private international law rules of the forum. But such an interpretation is not supported by a close reading of the cited provisions, which refer expressly or by implication to the substantive legislation of the country where protection is claimed. In this regard, it is of particular interest that the → Court of Justice of the European Union applied the *lex loci protectionis* principle in a cross-border broadcasting case and based its judgment on the 'principle of the territoriality of those rights, which is recognised in international law and also in the EC Treaty' (Case C-192/04 *Lagardère Active Broadcast v Société pour la perception de la rémunération équitable (SPRE) and Gesellschaft zur Verwertung von Leistungsschutzrechten mbH (GVL)* [2005]

ECR I-7199, para 46). Unfortunately the Court omitted to clarify whether the → territoriality principle has to be seen as an integral part of the WTO system. The Court also failed to elaborate on the question of which aspects of intellectual property disputes should be covered by the *lex loci protectionis*. However, the Court gave a clear indication that it considers the territoriality principle as being codified on the international level and as such binding on EU institutions.

IV. TRIPS reform and free trade agreements

Since the conclusion of the TRIPS Agreement in 1994, industries have constantly lobbied for a higher level of protection of intellectual property on an international scale. These attempts have been unsuccessful within the WTO framework because of the opposing interests of the less developed countries and user groups represented by NGOs. Countries with only minor creative and engineering industries have no interest in a higher level of intellectual property protection. Such countries primarily seek enhanced access to protected contents, technologies and other subject matters through fair use exceptions, compulsory licence schemes etc. These countervailing interests have blocked negotiations of the WTO Doha round since the late 1990s. The reaction of industrial states has been to negotiate bilateral free trade agreements aimed at a higher level of protection, such as the 2007 free trade agreement between the USA and South Korea ('KORUS', available at <www.ustr.gov/trade-agreements/free-trade-agreements/korus-fta/final-text>), which includes a detailed chapter on the protection of intellectual property. On a multilateral level, the Anti-Counterfeiting Trade Agreement (Anti-Counterfeiting Trade Agreement (ACTA) of 15 November 2010 (see text in Proposal for a Council Decision on the conclusion of the Agreement of 24 June 2011, COM(2011) 380 final)) would have committed the participating parties to intellectual property protection which goes beyond TRIPS. The European Parliament rejected ACTA in summer 2012 with a clear vote of 478 MEPs against ACTA, 39 in favour, and 165 abstaining. The EU has negotiated in the last years a free trade agreement with the USA and Canada (CETA and TTIP), which include. Thus, the current tendency in international intellectual property policy is to bypass the competent international fora, especially WTO (→ WTO and private international law) and WIPO (→ WIPO and private international law), and to proceed on a bilateral or multilateral basis.

AXEL METZGER

Literature

Lorand Bartels and Federico Ortino (eds), *Regional Trade Agreements and the WTO Legal System* (OUP 2006); Jan Busche, Peter-Tobias Stoll and Andreas Wiebe (eds), *TRIPS – internationales und europäisches Recht des geistigen Eigentums* (2nd edn, Heymann 2013); Carlos Maria Correa, *Trade Related Aspects of Intellectual Property Rights* (OUP 2008); Daniel Gervais, *The TRIPS Agreement: Drafting History and Analysis* (3rd edn, Sweet & Maxwell 2008); Jane C Ginsburg and Sam Ricketson, *International Copyright and Neighbouring Rights* (2nd edn, OUP 2006); Henning Grosse Ruse-Khan, 'The Role of TRIPS in a Fragmented IP World' (2012) 43 IIC 881; Silke von Lewinski, *International Copyright Law and Policy* (OUP 2008); Justin Malbon, Charles Lawson and Mark Davison, *The WTO Agreement on Trade-related Aspects of Intellectual Property: A Commentary* (Edward Elgar 2014); Axel Metzger, 'A Primer on ACTA: What Europeans Should Fear about the Anti-Counterfeiting Trade Agreement' (2010) 1 JIPITEC 109; Antony Taubman, Hannu Wager and Jayashree Watal (eds), *A Handbook on the WTO TRIPS Agreement* (CUP 2012); Peter-Tobias Stoll (ed), *WTO: Trade-related Aspects of Intellectual Property Rights* (Nijhoff 2009).

Trust

I. Introduction

Trusts pose a particular challenge for private international law. They are an institution traditionally known only to common law jurisdictions, although some civil law jurisdictions (eg the → Czech Republic, → Liechtenstein, → Luxembourg, Québec) have incorporated the trust into their legal systems. A trust describes a situation in which property is legally held by a trustee forming a separate fund in favour of a beneficiary, which has a beneficial interest in the property (→ Property and proprietary rights). The trust can be established by the original owner of the property to be held in trust as the settlor of the trust. Such an express trust requires a unilateral declaration by the settlor and – if the settlor is not to act as trustee himself – a transfer of the property to the trustee as a third party. Trusts can, however, also be created by operation of law (see V. below). However, it is not merely the 'common law versus civil law' dichotomy which poses problems in private international law in the area of trusts. Rather challenging for private international lawyers is also the variety of trust forms, which touch upon different areas of law – areas of law, which – in civilian jurisdictions – based on a *lex fori* characterization are potentially subject to different conflict rules, for example, the conflict rules for family law, succession law, property law and contract law. Trusts are multifunctional instruments: they are a flexible tool to organize the rights and duties of several persons in certain property, be it in a private, commercial, family or charitable context.

II. The Hague Trust Convention

The only international instrument directly addressing the private international law of trusts is the 1985 Hague Trust Convention (Hague Convention of 1 July 1985 on the Law Applicable to Trusts and on their Recognition, 1664 UNTS 311). The Hague Trust Convention particularly aims to integrate trusts into jurisdictions without a trust tradition. It not only determines the law applicable to trusts (see II.2. below) but also regulates their 'recognition' (see II.3. below), see art 1 of the Hague Trust Convention. The Convention has attracted only a few ratifications although the number of contracting states has been growing during the past years. In the meantime, the Convention is applicable in → Australia, → Canada, Hong Kong (→ Hong Kong, S.A.R. of China), → Italy, → Liechtenstein, → Luxembourg, → Malta, Monaco, the → Netherlands, San Marino, → Switzerland and the → United Kingdom, hence not only classic common law jurisdictions but also some civil law systems. The reluctance to adopt the Hague Trust Convention can probably be explained by a number of technical deficiencies, ambiguities and redundancies.

1. The scope: 'trusts'

The Hague Trust Convention applies to trusts as defined autonomously in its art 2. The notion of trusts within the Convention is clearly inspired by the common law trust but not necessarily restricted to that concept. It may even cover institutions which are functional equivalents to trusts in civil law jurisdictions as the French *fiducie* or the German *Treuhand*, although the preamble of the Convention describes the trust as 'a unique legal institution' of the common law systems which has been 'developed in courts of equity in common law jurisdictions and adopted with some modifications in other jurisdictions', referring at first sight to the common law original only.

Article 2(1) Hague Trust Convention clarifies that a trust in the sense of the Hague Trust Convention concerns 'the legal relationships created – *inter vivos* or on death – by a person, the settlor, when assets have been placed under the control of a trustee for the benefit of a beneficiary or for a specified purpose'. Hence, only express trusts (see I. above) are covered, as art 3 Hague Trust Convention also clarifies by restricting the scope of the Convention to 'trusts created voluntarily and evidenced in writing'. Constructive trusts or other statutory trusts which are established by the operation of law are clearly excluded. This exclusion applies, for example in the area of successions to the position of the personal representative administrating the estate of the deceased, see also art 15(c) Hague Trust Convention. Moreover trusts created by a court decision, for example as part of an order regulating the financial consequences of divorce or the family provision of the deceased's dependents, lie outside the scope of the Hague Trust Convention. However, a contracting state can extend the scope of the Convention to such 'trusts declared by judicial decisions' unilaterally, see art 20 Hague Trust Convention. By contrast, it can be derived from the *travaux préparatoires* that resulting trusts which are based on the presumed intention of the settlor might fall within the scope of the Convention (see Alfred van Overbeck, 'Explanatory Report' (1984) 2 *Proceedings of the Fifteenth Session* 370, 380, para 51).

Furthermore, art 2(2) of the Convention describes some of the characteristics of a trust required to be subject to the Hague Trust Convention. Thus the trust funds have to be separated from the trustee's other assets (art 2(2)(a) Hague Trust Convention), the trustee must be the legal owner of the property held in trust (art 2(2)(b) Hague Trust Convention) and the trustee must have the power and obligation to administrate the fund (art 2(2)(c)

Hague Trust Convention). The fact that the settlor retains certain rights or powers towards the trust property and the fact that the trustee is also one of the beneficiaries does not exclude application of the Convention, see art 2(3). Those characteristics can also be met by civil law equivalents. For example, the *fideicommissarische Substitution* in Austria, the *libéralité graduelle* or *résiduelle* in France, or the *Vor- und Nacherbschaft* in Germany and Switzerland – all cases of subsequent succession – could be regarded as a testamentary trust in the sense of the Convention with the first heir acting as a trustee and the final heir as a beneficiary.

However, the Hague Trust Convention contains two important restrictions of its scope. On the one hand the Convention does not apply to any transfer of property to the trustee, be it *inter vivos* or upon death, as art 4 Hague Trust Convention clarifies. Those preliminary issues are governed by the conflict rules of the *lex fori*, often the *lex rei sitae* or the *lex successionis*. On the other hand, according to its art 5, the Convention only determines the applicable law and establishes a duty to recognize a trust if the conflict rules of the Convention (see next section) refer to a law which provides for trusts (as defined in the Convention). Hence, if the *lex causae* does not know such trusts the private international law of the forum decides on the validity and effects of the attempt to create a trust. The governing law must not be the law of a contracting state, see art 21 Hague Trust Convention *e contrario* which reserves the right of the contracting state to recognize only those trusts the validity of which is governed by the law of a contracting state (see for details II.3. below).

2. The applicable law

The second chapter of the Hague Trust Convention is dedicated to determination of the law applicable to the trust – excluding a → *renvoi* and referring only to the substantive provisions of the governing law, see art 17 Hague Trust Convention.

The Hague Trust Convention stresses the → party autonomy of the settlor. The settlor can expressly or impliedly choose the law applicable to the trust, art 6(1) Hague Trust Convention. However, here again the Convention seeks to ensure that a law applies which contains provisions on trusts (again in the autonomous sense of the Convention, see II.1. above). In addition art 6(2) Hague Trust Convention invalidates the settlor's choice of law if the law chosen makes no provision for trusts (see already II.1.).

If the settlor does not (validly) choose the applicable law, art 7 Hague Trust Convention determines the law governing the trust by referring in subpara 1 to the law to which the trust is most closely connected. Article 7(2) of the Convention seeks to provide guidance when applying this rather vague conflict rule by highlighting certain aspects to be considered when deciding on the close connection, namely the place of administration of the trust designated by the settlor (art 7(2)(a) Hague Trust Convention), the *situs* of the assets of the trust (art 7(2)(b) Hague Trust Convention), the place of residence or business of the trustee (art 7(2)(c) Hague Trust Convention) and the objects of the trust and the places where they are to be fulfilled (art 7(2)(d) Hague Trust Convention). Where the objectively applicable law does not know trusts, the Convention is not applicable and the internal conflict rules of the contracting state apply (see already II.1.).

The scope of the applicable law is determined in art 8 Hague Trust Convention. This provision emphasizes in subpara 1 that the law determined under the Hague Convention applies only to the 'validity of the trust, its construction, its effects, and the administration of the trust'. As already stressed, the transfer of the trust property to the trustee is regarded as an incidental question not governed by the Convention (see II.1. above). Certain issues falling under the applicable law are listed in art 8(2) Hague Trust Convention. Article 9 of the Convention provides for a → *dépeçage* by allowing 'a severable aspect of the trust, particularly matters of administration', to be governed by a different law, be it on the basis of a → choice of law by the settlor (art 6 Hague Trust Convention) or a most close connection (art 7 Hague Trust Convention). A rather surprising conflict rule is contained in art 10 of the Hague Convention: the law governing the validity of the trust decides 'whether that law or the law governing a severable aspect of the trust may be replaced by another law'. It may be asked whether this provision refers to the private international law of the *lex causae* (which would be contrary to the general exclusion of *renvoi* in art 17 Hague Trust Convention). The substantive law will not address the question whether a change of the applicable law is admissible. Apparently, the drafters of the Convention sought to address the question whether the trustee has the power, presumably according to substantive law, to change the applicable law (Alfred van Overbeck, 'Explanatory Report' (1984) 2 *Proceedings of the Fifteenth Session* 370, 392, para 98).

3. The 'recognition' of trusts

The third chapter of the Hague Trust Convention provides for a 'recognition' of trusts. A trust validly established in accordance with the law applicable under the conflict rules of the Convention (see II.2.) will be recognized as a trust, art 11(1) of the Convention. However, the use of the term 'recognition' is rather misleading in this context. Recognition under the Convention is not understood technically in the sense of a recognition of a foreign judgment or other judicial or administrative act. Rather the term recognition within the Convention refers to certain minimum effects which have to be granted by the contracting states to the trust to be recognized under the Convention. However, as already mentioned, the contracting state can reserve the right to recognize only trusts which are governed – under the conflict rules of the Convention – by the law of a contracting state (art 21 Hague Trust Convention). Hence, the universal application of the conflict rules is indirectly limited introducing a kind of → reciprocity requirement reminiscent of the old Hague Conventions but already abandoned by subsequent conventions. If the conflict rules contained in chapter II refer to the law of a non-contracting state, the duty of recognition under chapter III is suspended.

The duty to recognize the trust relates for example to the separation of the trust fund from the remaining property of the trustee and to the capacity of the trustee to act as a trustee (art 11(2) Hague Trust Convention; see also art 12 Hague Trust Convention). Furthermore, art 11(3) of the Convention specifies (i) that the trust funds are protected against the creditors of the trustee, whether or not subject to insolvency, (ii) that the trust funds are not part of the trustee's property for purposes of → matrimonial property or succession law, (iii) that, subject to the protection of third parties under the law applicable according to the forum's conflict rules, the trust funds can be recovered if the trustee mingles trust property with own assets or alienates objects of the trust property in violation of the duties as a trustee. However, at least the effects mentioned in art 11(3) Hague Trust Convention are subject to the governing law determined under chapter II of the Convention ('In so far as the law applicable to the trust requires or provides, such recognition shall imply . . .'). Hence, those effects do not exceed the effects under the law applicable to the trust as specified in the second chapter of the Convention. An important restriction of the duty to recognize can be found in art 13 of the Convention: a contracting state is not bound to recognize the trust under chapter III if the trust is more closely connected to a state whose law does not provide for trusts, whereby in determining the closer connection the settlor's choice of the applicable law, the place of administration and the trustee's habitual residence have to be disregarded. It does not surprise that, for example, Switzerland has explicitly stipulated in its Private international law Act (Bundesgesetz über das Internationale Privatrecht of 18 December 1987, 1988 BBl I 5, as amended; art 149c) that this exception – which due to its vagueness causes considerable insecurity – shall not be applied. Finally, the duty to recognize does not prevent a court from applying a law 'more favourable to the recognition of trusts', art 14 Hague Trust Convention. This can only be a clarification that beyond the minimum effects to be recognized under chapter III the law governing the trust under chapter II can be applied.

The precise purpose of the duty to 'recognize' trusts under chapter III is not entirely clear: already the conflict rules contained in the second chapter of the Convention would oblige the contracting states to apply a certain law to the trust, including the effects of a trust under the applicable law. There is no particular need to recognize the trust, in particular, as far as, the effects of the trust to be recognized may not exceed the effects under the applicable law. It appears that the duty to recognize has been adopted for instructional reasons (*'aus pädagogischen Gründen'*, Hein Kötz, 'Die 15. Haager Konferenz und das Kollisionsrecht des trust' (1986) 50 RabelsZ 562, 577). In particular, arts 11 *et seq* Hague Trust Convention should alert lawyers and courts in civilian systems to the fact that trusts established under foreign law have certain effects which should be recognized.

4. General limitations to foreign trusts

The Hague Trust Convention does not oblige the contracting states to apply foreign trust law (see II.2.) or to recognize foreign trusts (see II.3.) unlimitedly. On the one hand the Convention contains the customary public policy exception in art 18 Hague Trust Convention. On the other hand internationally mandatory provisions of the forum and possibly third states (art 16 Hague Trust Convention) as well as tax law (art 19 Hague Trust Convention) may not be affected by the operation of the Convention.

An important restriction on the duty to apply foreign trust law or to recognize foreign trusts is contained in art 15 Hague Trust Convention, which ensures that (internally) mandatory provisions applicable according to the conflict rules of the forum are enforced even in situations involving trusts. Those provisions have to be applied to the extent they cannot be derogated from by unilateral acts. This applies in particular to mandatory provisions regarding the protection of minors and persons lacking capacity (art 1(a) Hague Trust Convention), family and succession law (art 1(b) and (c) Hague Trust Convention), property law (art 1(d) and (f) Hague Trust Convention) and insolvency law (art 1(e) Hague Trust Convention) – a list which is not exhaustive. Hence, art 15 Hague Trust Convention converts internally mandatory provisions for purposes of a trust into internationally mandatory provisions. However, where recognition of a foreign trust is restricted by such mandatory provisions, the Convention obliges the court 'to give effect to the objects of the trust by other means', art 15(2) Hague Trust Convention. The aims of the settlor have to be implemented as far as possible, for example by adapting or transforming the trusts to other equivalent instruments ('by other means').

III. Common law jurisdictions

The conflict rules of the Hague Trust Convention (see II.2. above) widely reflect the traditional solutions in the common law jurisdictions – solutions which are still relevant to the extent those jurisdictions are not bound by the Convention. The common law traditionally follows a proper law approach (→ Proper law (doctrine)), at least for express trusts regarding movables. Thus absent an express or implied choice by the settlor a trust is governed by the law with which it has the closest and most real connection (see eg *Chellaram v Chelleram* [2002] EWHC 632). Also in the US the Restatement (Second) of Conflict of Laws (American Law Institute, Restatement of the Law, Second: Conflict of Laws 2d, St. Paul 1971; → Restatement (First and Second) of Conflict of Laws) highlights party autonomy of the settlor (see § 269(b)(i), § 270(a), see also § 271(a), § 272(a)). Absent a valid choice by the settlor, the Restatement (Second) of Conflict of Laws differentiates between trusts created by will and trusts established *inter vivos*, whereby the latter are governed by the law with which the trust has 'its most significant relationship' (see § 270(b), see also § 272(b)), and testamentary trusts are subject to the law of the last domicile of the testator (see § 269(b)(ii), see also § 271(b)). For trusts regarding immovable property the Restatement (Second) of Conflict of Law refers to the *lex situs* (see § 278, see also § 279).

IV. Civil law jurisdictions

Whereas in the common law and the Hague Trust Convention trusts can be addressed by a comprehensive system of conflict rules, civil law jurisdictions largely have to follow a functional approach, especially if their substantive laws do not know the concept of trusts or their private international law makes no provision for a special (statutory) conflict rule for trusts. Trusts are characterized as their functional equivalents in the relevant jurisdiction, and subjected to the conflict rules pertinent for those functional equivalents. Hence for example, testamentary trusts are often regarded as testamentary dispositions governed by the law applicable to the succession upon death (see eg German Federal Court of Justice (BGH), 2 June 1976 [1976] WM 811; Cass Civ, 3 November 1983, 73 [1984] Rev.crit.DIP 336). If the law applicable is unfamiliar with testamentary trusts, they are often transformed into the closest equivalent under *lex causae*, for example in a testamentary execution or subsequent succession (see Higher Regional Court (OLG) of Frankfurt am Main, 22 September 1965 [1966/67] IPRspr. No 168a; Bayerisches Oberstes Landesgericht, 18 March 2003 [2003] IPRspr. No 99). *Inter vivos* trusts are often characterized as → contractual obligations subject party autonomy of the settlor and trustee (see German Federal Court of Justice (BGH), 15 April 1959 [1959] NJW 1317; German Federal Court of Justice (BGH), 10 June 1968 [1968] WM 1170). However, as the trust property forms a separate fund in the hands of the trustee, one could also apply the conflict rules for → companies or other juridical persons to trusts. The property law consequences of a trust on the other hand are governed by the *lex rei sitae* of the property held in trust.

Some civilian jurisdictions, notably in the modern private international law codifications, contain special conflict rules for trusts. This for example applies to Belgian law, where art 124 § 1(1) of the Belgian Private international law Act (Wetboek von international privaatrecht/Code de droit international privé of 16 July 2004, BS 27 July 2004, pp 57344, 57366, henceforth Belgian PILA) accepts for trusts (as defined in art 122 Belgian PILA) a choice of law by the settlor, whereby absent such choice, the law of the settlor's habitual residence applies, art 124 § 2 Belgian PILA. However, also Belgian law is not prepared to integrate foreign trusts fully in a civilian system. On the one hand the Belgian PILA clarifies that a foreign trust cannot be used to circumvent forced heirship rights under the law applicable to the succession upon death, art 124 § 3 Belgian PILA. On the other hand Belgian law stresses that the property consequence of the trust are still governed by the *lex rei sitae*, see art 125 § 2, art 87 § 1(1) Belgian PILA.

V. Private international law of the European Union

European private international law does not as yet expressly address trusts, at least not on the conflict of laws level. Rather it is only the Brussels I Regulation (recast) (Regulation (EU) No 1215/2012 of the European Parliament and of the Council of 12 December 2012 on jurisdiction and the recognition and enforcement of judgments in civil and commercial matters (recast), [2012] OJ L 351/1; → Brussels I (Convention and Regulation)), dealing with jurisdiction and the recognition and enforcement of foreign judgements, which contains special jurisdiction rules for trusts. On the one hand art 7(6) of the Brussels I Regulation (recast) vests special jurisdiction in the court where the trust is domiciled (see art 63(3)), and on the other hand art 25(3) Brussels I Regulation (recast) allows the settlor of the trust to select the forum for 'proceedings brought against a settlor, trustee or beneficiary, if relations between those persons or their rights or obligations under the trust are involved'. Apart from those special rules, the general provisions of the Brussels I Regulation (recast) on jurisdiction apply. The ECJ has ruled that the beneficial interest of the beneficiary in the trust funds may not be characterized as a right *in rem* (Case C-294/92 *George Lawrence Webb v Lawrence Desmond Webb* [1994] ECR I-1733), so that trusts involving → immovable property are not subject to an exclusive jurisdiction of the courts where the property is situated under art 24(1) of the Brussels I Regulation (recast).

Most private international law instruments dealing with questions of the applicable law exclude trusts from their scope, see art 1(2)(h) of the Rome I Regulation (Regulation (EC) No 593/2008 of the European Parliament and of the Council of 17 June 2008 on the law applicable to contractual obligations (Rome I), [2008] OJ L 177/6; → Rome Convention and Rome I Regulation), art 1(2)(e) of the → Rome II Regulation (Regulation (EC) No 864/2007 of the European Parliament and of the Council of 11 July 2007 on the law applicable to non-contractual obligations (Rome II), [2007] OJ L 199/40), art 1(2)(h) of the → Rome III Regulation (Council Regulation (EU) No 1259/2010 of 20 December 2010 implementing enhanced cooperation in the area of the law applicable to divorce and legal separation, [2010] OJ L 343/10), art 1(2)(j) of the Succession Regulation (Regulation (EU) No 650/2012 of the European Parliament and of the Council of 4 July 2012 on jurisdiction, applicable law, recognition and enforcement of decisions and acceptance and enforcement of authentic instruments in matters of succession and on the creation of a European Certificate of Succession, [2012] OJ L 201/107; → Rome IV Regulation). However, those exclusions should not conceal the fact that trusts also play a role within some of those instruments. Two examples may be given. First although trusts are expressly excluded from the scope of the Succession Regulation, Recital (13) of that Regulation clarifies that art 1(2) (j) Succession Regulation 'should not be understood as a general exclusion of trusts. Where a trust is created under a will or under statute in connection with intestate succession the law applicable to the succession under this Regulation should apply with respect to the devolution of the assets and the determination of the beneficiaries.' Hence, succession-related trusts are at least partly governed by the *lex successionis* from a European perspective. Second, trusts can also be covered by the Rome II Regulation. This applies, for example, for constructive trusts which are established by the operation of law in order to grant an equitable interest in certain property to a person. Such trusts can be characterized as a non-contractual obligation. They are not excluded by art 1(2)(e) of the Rome II Regulation which only covers a 'trust created voluntarily', hence, in particular express trusts.

Until now it is an open question whether the fundamental freedoms within the EU oblige Member States to recognize trusts validly established under the law of a Member State. The answer to that question in particular depends on whether the ECJ case-law regarding the freedom of establishment guaranteed according to arts 49, 54 of the TFEU (The Treaty on the Functioning of the European Union (consolidated version), [2012] OJ C 326/47) in *Centros* (Case 212/97 *Centros Ltd v Erhvervs- og Selskabsstyrelsen* [1999] ECR I-1459), *Überseering* (Case C-208/00 *Überseering BV v Nordic Construction Company Baumanagement GmbH* [2002] ECR I-9943) and *Inspire Art* (Case C-167/01 *Kamer van Koophandel en Fabrieken voor Amsterdam v Inspire Art Ltd* [2003] ECR I-10195) can also be applied to trusts. The EFTA Court held in a recent decision that the freedom of establishment granted under the parallel provision of the EEA Agreement (Agreement on the European Economic Area, [1994] OJ L 1/3) also covers trusts if 'the trust pursues a real and genuine economic activity' (see EFTA Court of 9 July 2014, Joined Cases E-3/13 and E-20/13 *Fred. Olsen and Others and Petter Olsen and Others v The Norwegian State, represented by the Central Tax Office for Large Enterprises and the Directorate of Taxes* [2015] OJ C 68/5). If the fundamental freedoms also apply to trusts, it appears inevitable that the Member States would be bound to recognize trusts from other Member States – a duty of recognition which would go far beyond the duty to 'recognize' under the Hague Trust Convention (see II.3. above). The validity and effects of the trust would be governed by the law under which the trust was established. If such a duty to recognize trusts under primary EU law exists, in the interests of legal security the European legislature should consider creating common conflict rules for trusts within the EU under art 81 TFEU, be it by adopting the Hague Trust Convention (II. above) or better by drafting an own instrument.

ANATOL DUTTA

Literature

Le Trust en droit international privé – Perspectives suisses et étrangères, Actes de la 17ème Journée de droit international privé du 18 mars 2005 à Lausanne (Schulthess 2005); Aldo Berlinguer, 'The Italian Road to Trusts' (2007) 15 ERPL 533; Adeline Chong, 'The Common Law Choice of Law Rules for Resulting and Constructive Trusts' [2005] *I* 855; Lord Collins of Mapesbury and others (eds), *Dicey, Morris and Collins on the Conflict of Laws* (15th edn, Sweet & Maxwell 2012) ch 29; Adair Dyer, 'International Recognition and Adaptation of Trusts: The Influence of the Hague Convention' [1999] Vand.J. Transnat'l L. 989; Emmanuel Gaillard and Donald T Trautman, 'Trusts in Non-Trust Countries: Conflict of Laws and the Hague Convention on Trusts' (1987) 35 Am.J.Comp.L. 307; Jonathan Harris, *The Hague Trust Convention: Scope, Application and Preliminary Issues* (Hart Publishing 2002); Jonathan Harris, 'The Trust in Private international law' in James Fawcett (ed), *Reform and Development of Private international law: Essays in Honour of Sir Peter North* (OUP 2002) 187; Jonathan Harris, 'Constructive Trusts and Private international law: Determining the Applicable Law' (2012) 18 *Trusts & Trustees* 965; David Hayton, 'The Hague Convention on the Law Applicable to Trusts and on their Recognition' (1987) 36 ICLQ 260; David Hayton, '"Trusts" in Private international law' (2014) 366 Rec. des Cours 9; Hein Kötz, 'Die 15. Haager Konferenz und das Kollisionsrecht des trust' (1986) 50 RabelsZ 562; Hans van Loon, 'L'actualité de la convention de La Haye relative à la loi applicable au trust et à sa reconnaissance' in Jean-Paul Béraudo and others (eds), *Mélanges en l'honneur de Mariel Revillard* (Défrenois 2007) 323; Maurizio Lupoi, 'The Hague Convention, the Civil Law and the Italian Experience' (2007) 21 *Trust Law International* 80; Alfred van Overbeck, 'Explanatory Report' (1984) 2 *Proceedings of the Fifteenth Session* 370; David B Parker and Anthony R Mellows, *The Modern Law of Trusts* (9th edn, Sweet & Maxwell 2008) ch 23; Anne Wallace, 'Choice of Law for Trusts in Australia and the United Kingdom' [1987] ICLQ 454.

UNCITRAL

I. Background and structure

On 17 December 1966, the United Nations Commission on International Trade Law, UNCITRAL, was set up at Hungary's request by the United Nations General Assembly by its Resolution 2205 (XXI) of 17 December 1966. Originally headquartered in New York and relocated to Vienna in 1979, UNCITRAL consists of a limited, but steadily increasing number of member states of the United Nations. When it was created, UNCITRAL was composed of 29 Member States of the United Nations; subsequently, membership was expanded to 36 (1973) and thereafter to 60 (2002) states. The increase in the number of Member States (elected for terms of six years) makes it easier to guarantee that the various geographic regions and the principal economic and legal systems of the world are represented. This becomes apparent if one considers that the 60 states include 14 African states, 14 Asian states, 8 Eastern European states, 10 Latin American states and Caribbean states and 14 Western European and other states.

UNCITRAL's secretariat is provided by the International Trade Law Division of the United Nations Office of Legal Affairs (OLA), whose director also serves as the Secretary to UNCITRAL. The secretariat has different tasks, including the preparation of studies, reports and draft texts on issues that are being considered for potential inclusion in UNCITRAL's work programme. It is also responsible for elaborating and revising working papers and legislative texts on issues already included in the work programme. The secretariat is also tasked with reporting on the annual meetings of UNCITRAL (the venues of which alternate between Vienna and New York) as well as on the meetings of the various Working Groups which carry out the substantive preparatory work on the issues included in UNCITRAL's work programme.

At present, there are five Working Groups, specifically dealing with 'micro, small and medium-sized enterprises', 'dispute settlement', 'electronic commerce', 'insolvency law' and 'security interests'. These Working Groups, which are responsible for the actual work on the issues included in UNCITRAL's work programme, meet once or twice a year, with the venue again alternating between Vienna and New York. Generally, the Working Groups go about their work without intervention from the Commission. This does not mean that the Working Groups cannot ask the Commission for guidance or request the Commission to take certain decisions with respect to their work, such as clarifying the mandate of a Working Group on a particular topic or approving the policy settings of a particular text.

As regards the membership of the Working Groups, it obviously includes all of UNCITRAL's Member States. Non-Member States and accredited international and regional organizations are allowed to participate in the sessions of the Working Groups, and even though all decision-making power solely rests with the Member States, the contribution of non-Member States and accredited organizations may well have an impact on the output of the Working Groups due to their persuasiveness.

As for the decisions of the Working Group, they have traditionally been taken by consensus and not by vote. In 2010, the Commission formalized this long-standing practice, 'resolving that decisions should be reached by consensus as far as possible; in the absence of consensus, decisions are to be taken by voting in accordance with the relevant rules of procedure of the General Assembly' (Official Records of the General Assembly, Sixty-fifth session, Supplement No 17 (A/65/17) (2010), Annex III: UNCITRAL Rules of procedure and methods of work, Summary of conclusions, para 2).

It is worth pointing out that on several occasions, substantive work has not been carried out by a Working Group, but rather by the secretariat itself. This is true, for instance, as regards the Legislative Guide on Privately Financed Infrastructure Projects draft chapters which were prepared directly by the secretariat and reviewed and adopted by the Commission.

II. UNCITRAL's mandate

As per the United Nations General Assembly Resolution 2205 (XXI), UNCITRAL's mandate is to achieve the aforementioned goal of promoting international trade via efforts made 'towards the progressive harmonization and unification of the law of international trade'. The Resolution also describes how that progressive harmonization and unification of the law of international trade shall be achieved. In this respect, reference is made, for example, to the need to coordinate the work of organizations active in the field of harmonization and unification of the law of international trade. One must wonder, however, precisely how such coordination is to be accomplished, especially the coordination with the work of those organizations that are not integrated into the United Nations system and, therefore, cannot be obliged by either the United Nations or UNCITRAL to be subject to UNCITRAL's coordination efforts. It appears that these coordination efforts may only take the form of equal-footed cooperation which may be achieved, for instance, by allowing UNCITRAL to participate – as an observer – in the work of these organizations and vice versa. These organizations include the → Hague Conference on Private International Law, → UNIDROIT, the International Maritime Committee (CMI), the Organization of American States (OAS), the Organisation for Economic Cooperation and Development

(OECD), the United Nations regional commissions, UNCTAD, the World Bank, the World Customs Organization (WCO), the World Intellectual Property Organization (WIPO) and the World Trade Organization (WTO).

While there are examples of useful coordination with organizations that are not integrated into the United Nations system, there are instances that show that the coordination aimed at is not always successful. As an example of the former, it suffices to recall the coordinated activities of UNCITRAL, UNIDROIT and the Hague Conference on Private International Law in the area of security interests, which have been documented in a joint publication of 2012 entitled 'UNCITRAL, Hague Conference and UNIDROIT Texts on Security Interests. Comparison and analysis of major features of international instruments relating to secured transactions'.

In this author's opinion, the fact that UNCITRAL has produced instruments that do overlap with instruments drafted by other organizations is evidence of unsuccessful coordination. By way of example, it may suffice to recall the potential conflicts between the UNCITRAL Assignment of Receivables Convention (United Nations Convention on the Assignment of Receivables in International Trade, concluded 12 December 2001, adopted by resolution A/RES/56/8) and the UNIDROIT Convention on International Factoring of 28 May 1988 (2323 UNTS 373; 27 ILM 943; → Factoring (uniform law)), which UNCITRAL sought to solve through a rather aggressive conflict-of-conventions rule stating in part that the Assignment of Receivables 'Convention prevails over the UNIDROIT Convention on International Factoring' (art 38(2)).

The coordination of UNCITRAL's activities with other bodies and special organizations of the United Nations is much easier. For example, recall the close cooperation between UNCITRAL and the United Nations Conference on Trade and Development (UNCTAD), upon the suggestion of which the working group on international legislation on shipping was established, which then elaborated the 1978 United Nations Convention on the Carriage of Goods by Sea – the 'Hamburg Rules' (United Nations Convention of 31 March 1978 on the carriage of goods by sea, 1695 UNTS 3), in force since 1992.

Pursuant to United Nations General Assembly Resolution 2205 (XXI), UNCITRAL is also supposed to promote 'the progressive harmonization and unification of the law of international trade' by 'encouraging cooperation' among the various organizations. This cooperation occurs not only through participation on the part of other organizations – albeit only with observer status – in UNCITRAL Working Group sessions, but also in a more direct way. By way of an example of such active cooperation, it is worth recalling that the Permanent Bureau of the → Hague Conference on Private International Law submitted an expert report upon which the private international law rule on the law applicable to competing rights contained in art 22 of the United Nations Convention on the Assignment of Receivables in International Trade is based (see Group of Experts Report Prepared by the Permanent Bureau of the Hague Conference on Private International Law, UNCITRAL A/CN.9/WG.II/WP90 (10 July 1998) para 4.4).

Occasionally, UNCITRAL efforts 'towards the progressive harmonization and unification of the law of international trade' have taken other forms. It is common knowledge that in the elaboration of the United Nations Convention on Contracts for the International Sale of Goods, the → CISG (United Nations Convention of 11 April 1980 on Contracts for the International Sale of Goods, 1489 UNTS 3), the drafters heavily relied on two conventions drafted by UNIDROIT, annexed to which were the ULIS (Convention of 1 July 1964 relating to a Uniform Law for the International Sale of Goods, 834 UNTS 107) and the ULF (Convention of 1 July 1964 relating to a Uniform Law on the Formation of Contracts for the International Sale of Goods, 834 UNTS 169) (→ Sale contracts and sale of goods). Similarly, during the drafting process of what ultimately became the United Nations Convention on International Bills of Exchange and International Promissory Notes (United Nations Convention on International Bills of Exchange and International Promissory Notes of 9 December 1988, Doc A/RES/43/165), UNCITRAL relied on preparatory work done by → UNIDROIT in the early 1950s. A similar method was resorted to in respect of the Rotterdam Rules (United Nations Convention on Contracts for the International Carriage of Goods Wholly or Partly by Sea, UN Doc A/RES/63/122, 63 UNTS 122), for which UNCITRAL relied on initial work done by the CMI. Also, as regards the rules of private international law contained in Chapter V of the United Nations Convention on Assignment of

Receivables in International Trade, the drafters borrowed from the Rome Convention (Rome Convention on the law applicable to contractual obligations (consolidated version), [1998] OJ C 27/34). In effect, '[w]ith some important refinements . . ., Chapter V follows article 12 of the Rome Convention on the appropriate law to govern assignor/assignee and assignee/debtor relations, with the former governed by the proper law of the contract of assignment, and the latter by the law governing the original contract which generated the receivable' (Catherine Walsh, 'Receivables Financing and the Conflict of Laws: The UNCITRAL Draft Convention on the Assignment of Receivables in International Trade' (2001) 106 Dick.L.Rev. 159, 164). The UNCITRAL Convention deals, however, also with some private international law issues not expressly dealt with in the Rome Convention – or the Rome I Regulation (Regulation (EC) No 593/2008 of the European Parliament and of the Council of 17 June 2008 on the law applicable to contractual obligations (Rome I), [2008] OJ L 177/6; → Rome Convention and Rome I Regulation (contractual obligations)), for that matter (see Dorothea Heine, *Das Kollisionsrecht der Forderungsabtretung: UNCITRAL-Abtretungskonvention und Rom I-Verordnung* (Peter Lang 2012)).

Furthermore, UNCITRAL fosters co-operation through endorsements of text of other organizations. By way of recent examples, it may suffice to recall that in 2012 UNCITRAL endorsed both the 2012 version of the UNIDROIT Principles of International Commercial Contracts and the 2010 version of the ICC Incoterms.

III. UNCITRAL's legislative activities

As stated in the United Nations General Assembly Resolution 2205 (XXI), UNCITRAL is not only meant to further the progressive harmonization and unification of the law of international trade by coordinating the work of organizations engaged in the field, but also by promoting wider participation in existing international conventions and wider acceptance of existing model laws and uniform law instruments as well as by carrying out legislative activities of its own. This last type of activities appears to have been one of UNCITRAL's preferred means of trying to reach its overall goal. And this became clear as early as on the occasion of the first session in 1968, on the occasion of which UNCITRAL adopted nine subject areas as the basis of its future work programme, namely international sale of goods (→ Sale contracts and sale of goods), international commercial arbitration (→ Arbitration, international commercial), transportation, insurance, international payments, intellectual property, elimination of discrimination in laws affecting international trade, → agency, and legalization of documents (→ Legalization of public documents). While some of these subject areas have not been taken up at all by UNCITRAL (elimination of discrimination in laws affecting international trade, agency and legalization of documents), others have been focused on extensively over the years (international sale of goods, transportation, international commercial arbitration and international payments), and other subject areas in which UNCITRAL has done extensive work have been added at a later stage (government contracts, insolvency, electronic commerce, → online dispute resolution, microfinance).

As regards UNCITRAL's legislative activity, it has produced various types of texts: conventions, model laws, legislative guides and model provisions, which all have different advantages and disadvantages. It may suffice to point out that conventions, for instance, are capable of achieving a very high degree of unification. This is due to the fact that the states which adopt such conventions may only adopt them as a whole. In other words, a convention can only be adopted *tel quel*, without any modifications. In some instances, the rigidity of international conventions, an advantage in those cases where a specific area of law is best governed by rules that are fully identical in at least two jurisdictions, may constitute a disadvantage. This rigidity may push a legislature to reject the international convention as a whole, simply because of the presence of a single provision, since the all-or-nothing principle applied to international conventions also mandates application of that single provision. Model laws, on the other hand, are sources of international uniform law that are much more flexible than international conventions; they are legislative texts that are recommended to states for adoption as part of their national law (with no obligation whatsoever for enactment). The flexibility that characterizes model laws (and that international conventions are missing) allows states to conform their domestic legislation to specific domestic needs and, thus, avoid the concerns that may be triggered by a unification of law based on the aforementioned all-or-nothing principle. This adaptability, which also allows states to unilaterally modify the rules enacted, promotes the willingness of states to participate in the unification efforts. It bears a risk, however: legal rules intended to create uniformity may develop differently in the various states due to their being adapted to fit different needs and situations.

In the area of international sale of goods, UNCITRAL's efforts first led to the UNCITRAL Limitation Convention (Convention of 14 June 1974 on the Limitation Period in the International Sale of Goods, 1151 UNTS 3; 13 ILM 952); thereafter, they led to UNCITRAL's most successful uniform law instrument, the → CISG, which is in force today in 80 countries and governs more than two-thirds of the overall trade of goods. It is worth mentioning that the adoption of the CISG made a revision of the UNCITRAL Limitation Convention necessary, which is why the Limitation Convention was amended by a Protocol adopted in 1980 by the Diplomatic Conference that adopted the CISG. Both the original Limitation Convention and the Convention as amended by the Protocol entered into force on 1 August 1988 (1511 UNTS 77). In the area of transportation, both the Hamburg Rules and the recent 2008 Convention on Contracts for the International Carriage of Goods Wholly or Partly by Sea ought to be mentioned. UNCITRAL has also been particularly active in the area of international commercial arbitration since its founding. In 1976, it adopted the Arbitration Rules (Official Records of the General Assembly, Thirty-first Session, Supplement No 17 (A/31/17)), widely used both in ad hoc arbitrations and administered arbitrations, which provide a comprehensive set of procedural rules upon which parties may agree for the conduct of arbitral proceedings arising out of their commercial relationship. UNCITRAL's major achievement in this area is, however, the 1985 UNCITRAL Model Law on International Commercial Arbitration, amended in 2006 (with a view towards the modernization of the form requirement of an arbitration agreement to better conform with international contract practices) (UNCITRAL Arbitration Model Law, United Nations Commission on International Trade Law, UNCITRAL Model Law on International Commercial Arbitration as adopted on 21 June 1985, and as amended on 7 July 2006, UN Doc A/40/17 and A/61/17; → Arbitration,

(UNCITRAL) Model Law). The Model Law, which covers all stages of the arbitral process, has been developed with the objective of providing national legislators with an ideology free and globally suitable model for the drafting of national rules on international commercial arbitration. Considering that the arbitration legislation of more than 60 states is based upon the Model Law, it appears that UNCITRAL has achieved its goal. UNCITRAL's work in this area has also led to the 1996 UNCITRAL Notes on Organizing Arbitral Proceedings (UNCITRAL Yearbook, vol. XXVII: 1996, part three, annex I), designed to assist arbitration practitioners by providing an annotated list of issues in relation to which decisions of the arbitral tribunal are desirable, including the determination of the set of arbitration rules, the language and place of arbitration and questions relating to confidentiality, as well as other matters. It is well known that the subject of commercial conciliation is closely related to that of commercial arbitration. It is therefore unsurprising that UNCITRAL has also worked, and continues to work, in the area of commercial conciliation, and has one working group, Working Group II, specifically dedicated to 'international arbitration and conciliation'. As a result of UNCITRAL's efforts in this specific area, the UNCITRAL Conciliation Rules (United Nations General Assembly Resolution 35/52 of 4 December 1980) and the UNCITRAL Model Law on International Commercial Conciliation (United Nations General Assembly Resolution 57/18 of 19 November 2002) were adopted in 1980 and 2002 respectively.

As for UNCITRAL's work in the area of international payments, the adoption of the following uniform law instruments should be mentioned: the 1988 United Nations Convention on International Bills of Exchange and International Promissory Notes (of 9 December 1988, Doc A/RES/43/165), the 1992 Model Law on International Credit Transfers (United Nations General Assembly Resolution 47/34 of 25 November 1992) and the United Nations Convention of 11 December 1995 on Independent Guarantees and Stand-by Letters of Credit (2169 UNTS 163). The fact that UNCITRAL focused its attention mainly on the aforementioned areas does not mean that UNCITRAL has ignored other areas. For instance, consider the work done on security interests, an area in which efforts have been underway since the very first session of the

Commission. In 2001, this work resulted in the adoption of the United Nations Convention on the Assignment of Receivables in International Trade. As mentioned previously, over the years, UNCITRAL has also become active in areas not listed in the 1968 work programme. This is true, for instance, for the area of electronic commerce, to which, for obvious reasons, no thought had been given in 1968. The efforts undertaken in this area have resulted in various instruments, namely the 1996 Model Law on Electronic Commerce (UNCITRAL Model Law on Electronic Commerce, UNCITRAL (ed): Model Law on Electronic Commerce with Guide to Enactment 1996, New York 1997, amended in 1998), the 2001 Model Law on Electronic Signatures (UNCITRAL Model Law on Electronic Signatures, UNCITRAL Model Law on Electronic Signatures of 2001, available at <www.uncitral.org/pdf/english/texts/electcom/ml-elecsig-e.pdf>) and the 2005 Convention on the Use of Electronic Communications in International Contracts (UNCITRAL Electronic Communications Convention, United Nations Convention of 23 November 2005 on the Use of Electronic Communications in International Contracts, adopted on 23 November 2005 during the 53rd plenary meeting of the General Assembly by resolution A/60/21, text available in UN doc A/60/515). Likewise, insolvency law is an area UNCITRAL has been concerned with for some time now, although it did not start looking into the subject until 1993. The efforts in this field allowed, however, for the adoption in 1997 of the UNCITRAL Model Law on Cross-Border Insolvency (United Nations General Assembly Resolution 52/158 of 15 December 1997), an instrument designed to assist states to equip their insolvency laws with a modern, harmonized and fair framework to address instances of cross-border insolvency more effectively.

At times, it is not possible to draft specific provisions in a given area. In these situations, it may be more beneficial not to try to elaborate conventions or model laws, but to draft legislative guides and recommendations. These texts offer a number of possible legislative solutions to specific issues without promoting any one specific solution in particular. Where it seems appropriate, the texts include variants to mirror the varying policy choices that can be made vis-à-vis a given issue. 'By discussing the advantages and disadvantages of different policy choices, the text [can] assist the reader to evaluate different approaches and to choose the one most suitable in a particular national context' (A Guide to UNCITRAL (United Nations 2013) 16). As regards this type of instruments, it may suffice to recall just a few, such as the UNCITRAL Legislative Guide on Secured Transactions (United Nations General Assembly Resolution 63/121 of 11 December 2008), the UNCITRAL Legislative Guide on Insolvency Law (United Nations General Assembly Resolution 59/40 of 2 December 2004; United Nations General Assembly Resolution 65/24 of 6 December 2010; United Nations General Assembly Resolution 68/107 of 16 December 2013) and the UNCITRAL Legislative Guide on Privately Financed Infrastructure Projects (United Nations General Assembly Resolution 56/79 of 12 December 2001).

IV. UNCITRAL's legislative activity and private international law

As can be easily gathered from the text of the United Nations General Assembly Resolution 2205 (XXI), the UNCITRAL's legislative activity has to focus on international trade law. According to many, this requires UNCITRAL to merely focus on substantive rules rather than on rules of private international law. This limitation may be due to the realization that other organizations exist that appear institutionally better suited to tackle private international issues, such as the Hague Conference on Private International Law. This may, however, also be due to the assumption, apparently behind the drafting of all early uniform substantive law conventions (→ Uniform substantive law and private international law), that the drafting of substantive rules makes international trade easier, namely by avoiding the need to resort to private international law – considered to be rather complicated. It is generally held that this type of uniform law promotes certainty of law, makes business decisions easier and facilitates risk assessment. According to the prevailing view, this leads to a reduction of costs, benefiting not only the parties involved but the economy as a whole.

In light of the foregoing, it cannot surprise that many of UNCITRAL's early conventions are uniform substantive law conventions that do not include any private international law rules. Where the texts of these conventions refer to 'private international law' at all (as do, for instance, art 3(1)(b) Convention on the Limitation Period in the International Sale of Goods, art 1(1)(b) CISG, etc), they refer to the rules of private international law of the forum.

However, the assumption that uniform substantive law avoids the need to resort to private international law cannot be embraced. This is due in part to the fact that international uniform substantive law is not exhaustive; it does not constitute a substantive law capable of dealing with all legal issues arising from the relationships a given uniform substantive law instrument addresses, thus making resort to the applicable domestic law necessary. This means that private international law is indispensable, as the applicable domestic law needed to fill gaps must be determined by means of the private international law (of the forum).

It seems that UNCITRAL has started to realize this, which is why some UNCITRAL conventions do contain some private international law rules. In this respect it may be worth referring to Chapter VI (arts 21 and 22) of the Convention on Independent Guarantees and Stand-by Letters of Credit, which sets forth the rules of private international law governing the independent guarantee and the stand-by letter of credit.

The most elaborate set of rules of private international law can, however, be found in the United Nations Convention on the Assignment of Receivables in International Trade. This Convention contains not only a private international law rule for priority (art 22), but also what has been labelled a 'mini-convention' of private international law. While the rule for priority applies whenever the Convention itself applies due to all of its applicability requirements being met, Chapter V, containing, as mentioned earlier, an elaborate set of rules (dealing with the law applicable to the formal requirements (→ Formal requirements and validity) of the assignment, the law applicable to the mutual rights and obligations of the assignor and the assignee, as well as the law applicable to the rights and obligations of the assignee and the debtor) mostly modelled after art 12 Rome Convention, to the extent that the Rome Convention addresses the issues, has a much broader sphere of application. Although Chapter V applies to determine which substantive law to resort to where gaps in the Convention have to be filled, in the courts of contracting states, Chapter V also applies as long as one of the alternatively listed internationality requirements set forth in the Convention (art 1(4)) is met, and this is even if the other applicability requirements (such as those *ratione materiae*) are not met. In effect,

> it may happen that litigation involving an assignment which satisfies the criteria of internationality is heard in a Contracting State but the application of the Convention is not triggered . . . In such cases, Chapter V is meant to add an additional layer of international harmony by providing an independently applicable uniform conflicts regime (albeit one subject to an opt-out by Contracting States) to determine the applicable law. (Catherine Walsh, 'Receivables Financing and the Conflict of Laws: The UNCITRAL Draft Convention on the Assignment of Receivables in International Trade' (2001) 106 Dick.L.Rev. 159, 167)

It is worth pointing out that in the arbitration area UNCITRAL has produced rules of private international law for some time, long before it started to insert private international law rules into its uniform substantive law conventions. In this regard, UNCITRAL's most famous private international law provision is probably art 28 of the Model Law on International Commercial Arbitration, identifying the rules applicable to the substance of a dispute brought before an arbitral tribunal

V. UNCITRAL's additional activities

UNCITRAL's mandate is, however, not limited to the aforementioned coordination and codification activities. Pursuant to United Nations General Assembly Resolution 2205 (XXI), UNCITRAL shall also promote 'ways and means of ensuring a uniform interpretation and application of international conventions and uniform laws in the field of the law of international trade'.

The need to look into how to promote a uniform interpretation and application arises from the realization that the mere drafting of uniform texts does not by itself create uniform law. Rather, it is necessary that uniform texts also be interpreted and applied in the same manner throughout the states where it is in force. To make sure that its instruments are interpreted with that goal in mind, many UNCITRAL instruments contain a provision mandating exactly that, ie that in their interpretation 'regard is to be had to [their] international character and to the need to promote uniformity in [their] application' (art 7(1) CISG; art 7(1) United Nations Convention on the Assignment of Receivables in International Trade; art 5(1) United Nations Convention on the Use of Electronic Communications in International Contracts).

This requires that interpreters generally not read the international instruments through the lenses of domestic law but rather 'autonomously'. But an autonomous interpretation cannot, by itself, guarantee uniformity (→ Interpretation, autonomous). To 'promote uniformity in [their] application', it is insufficient to consider the international instruments' autonomous bodies of rules. To achieve uniformity, it is also necessary to consider the practice of other jurisdictions, ie what others have already done. This is why it cannot surprise that it has been advocated that courts resort to decisions rendered by foreign judicial bodies. However, requiring interpreters to consider foreign decisions creates practical difficulties, for two main reasons: foreign case-law is not readily available, and even where it can be retrieved, it is often written in a language unknown to the interpreter. To overcome these practical obstacles, UNCITRAL created in 1988 a system for the gathering and distribution (in all official languages of the United Nations) of information concerning the case-law on UNCITRAL texts rendered in various countries. This system is known as 'CLOUT', the acronym for 'Case-Law on UNCITRAL Texts', and comprises abstracts of court decisions rendered in application of texts drafted by UNCITRAL, in particular the → CISG and the Model Law on International Commercial Arbitration (→ Arbitration, international commercial). These abstracts are drafted in one of the official United Nations languages by national reporters appointed by the different governments and are then sent to the secretariat, which edits and translates them into the other official United Nations languages.

The CLOUT system is, however, not the only UNCITRAL project intended to further the uniform interpretation and application of UNCITRAL texts. On the basis of a decision taken during the 2001 Commission session, UNCITRAL prepared, with the help of a number of experts, an 'UNCITRAL Digest of Case Law on the United Nations Convention on the International Sale of Goods', first published in June 2004 and revised in 2008, 2012 and, most recently, in 2016. The Digest is meant to reflect the evolution of case-law by offering a synopsis of the relevant case-law, highlighting common views and reporting any divergent approach, thus enabling the interpreters to become aware of how a particular Convention is interpreted and applied around the world. This is certainly useful, which is why a Digest has also been produced in an area other than sales law, namely the 'UNCITRAL Digest of Case Law on the Model Law on International Commercial Arbitration'. One has to wonder, however, whether this kind of publication can really promote the uniform interpretation and application of the uniform texts that they relate to, since it does nothing but promote knowledge of foreign case-law which is insufficient to create uniformity. A critical evaluation of the court decisions, which is absent due to a conscious decision taken by UNCITRAL to avoid any criticism – or any praise for that matter – would certainly have been helpful in guiding the interpreters through the vast case-law that is, at times, contradictory. Thus, the Digests do not allow the interpreters to distinguish between case-law that should and case-law that should not be followed. Regrettably, UNCITRAL missed the chance to truly promote uniform interpretation and application of its text to which the Digests relate.

FRANCO FERRARI

Literature

Spiros V Bazinas, 'Harmonisation of International and Regional Trade Law: The UNCITRAL Experience' [2003] Unif.L.Rev. 53; Spiros V Bazinas, 'Towards Global Harmonization of Conflict-of-Laws Rules in the Area of Secured Financing: The Conflict-of-Laws Recommendations of the UNCITRAL Legislative Guide on Secured Transactions' in The Permanent Bureau of the Hague Conference on Private International Law (ed), *A Commitment to Private international law: Essays in Honour of Hans van Loon* (Intersentia 2013) 1; Jacques Bischoff, 'Allgemeine Erfahrung bei der Rechtsvereinheitlichung in der UNCITRAL' [1993] SZIER 623; Allan E Farnsworth, 'UNCITRAL' (1972) 20 Am.J.Comp.L. 314; Geoff Fischer, 'UNCITRAL Gives International Trade Law CLOUT' [1993] Austr.Bus.L.Rev. 362; Dorothea Heine, *Das Kollisionsrecht der Forderungsabtretung: UNCITRAL-Abtretungskonvention und Rom I-Verordnung* (Peter Lang 2012); Gerold Herrmann, 'The Contribution of UNCITRAL to the Development of International Trade' in Norbert Horn and Clive M Schmitthoff (eds), *The Transnational Law of International Commercial Transactions* (Kluwer 1982) 35; Gerold Herrmann, 'The Role of UNCITRAL' in Ian Fletcher, Loukas Mistelis and Marise Cremona (eds), *Foundations and Perspectives of International Trade Law* (Sweet &

Maxwell 2001) 28; Gerold Herrmann, 'A Vision for UNCITRAL: Global Commerce Needs a Global Uniform Law' [2001] B.L.I. 249; Bernardine WM Trompenaars, 'UNCITRAL en har mandaat' [1989] *Molengrafica* 3; Bernardine WM Trompenaars, *Pluriforme unificatie en uniforme interpretatie: In het bijzonder de bijdrage van UNCITRAL aan de internationale unificatie van het privaatrecht* (Kluwer 1989).

UNIDROIT[1]

I. History, purposes, Member States

The International Institute for the Unification of Private Law, better known as UNIDROIT, the abbreviation of the organization's French name, Institut International pour l'Unification du Droit Privé, was founded in 1926 as one of six specialized agencies (*bureaux*) of the League of Nations. The initiative had been taken by *Vittorio Scialoja*, professor of Roman law and senator. The first Statute of 1926 (as the one of 1993 presently in force) describes the objectives of the organization as follows: 'The purposes ... are to examine ways of harmonising and coordinating the private law of States and groups of States, and to prepare gradually for the adoption by the various States of uniform rules of private law ....'

The Council of the League of Nations appointed the Institute's Governing Council, while Italy provided the historic Villa Aldobrandini, enlarged by an important library building, as its seat as well as the budgetary means for the carrying out of its activities. On 30 May 1928, the Institute commenced its work with the official inauguration, attended by King *Victor Emmanuel III* and his Prime Minister *Benito Mussolini*, and the Governing Council's first session. *Ernst Rabel* (→ Rabel, Ernst), under whose direction the former Kaiser Wilhelm Institute for Comparative Law and Private international law was founded also in 1926 in Berlin (today Max Planck Institute, Hamburg), was a member of the first Governing Council. He emphasized the need to focus available resources on work aiming at the unification of the law of the sale of goods (→ Sale contracts and sale of goods). Apart from this, priority items on the agenda were the law of → bills of exchange and → cheques, culminating in the Geneva Conventions of 1930 and 1931 (Convention providing a Uniform Law for Bills of Exchange and Promissory Notes of 7 June 1930, 143 LNTS 259; Convention of 7 June 1930 for the Settlement of certain Conflicts of Laws in connection with Bills of Exchange and Promissory Notes, 143 LNTS 317; Convention of 19 March 1931 providing a Uniform Law for Cheques, 143 LNTS 355; Geneva Cheques Convention (Convention of 19 March 1931 for the Settlement of certain Conflicts of Laws in connection with Cheques, 143 LNTS 407)), arbitration and the enforcement of → maintenance obligations. When work on sale of goods was about to come to fruition, → Italy and → Germany left the League of Nations. *Ernst Rabel's* forced emigration set a temporary end to the work.

UNIDROIT's new constitutional arrangement as an intergovernmental organization is a multilateral treaty, the Statute of 1940, which entered into force in the same year for 23 Member States. However, there is no evidence for it to be more than a mere shell and that any substantial activity was carried out prior to the end of the Second World War.

While the European Member States were predominant both in numbers and with respect to pro-active involvement in the Institute's work until the 1960s (only → Japan and a number of Latin American states represented non-European regions from the beginning), today, with 63 Member States from all four corners of the world, the organization is truly a global one. The two states that acceded most recently (2008) – → Saudi Arabia and → Indonesia – are particularly significant examples of the growing attraction to being involved in coordinated efforts for law reform.

A peculiarity worth mentioning is that only as late as 1988 instruments developed by UNIDROIT were actually named after the organization (UNIDROIT Convention on International Factoring of 28 May 1988, 2323 UNTS 373, 27 ILM 943, and UNIDROIT Convention of 28 May 1988 on International Financial Leasing, 2312 UNTS 195, 27 ILM 931). Prior to that, the organization rather considered itself an academic forum where conventions were conceived and elaborated by experts only to be handed over to other organizations (eg the UN and its specialized agencies, the Council of Europe, the → Hague Conference on Private International Law etc) for the purpose of being adopted. Prominent examples of its

---

[1] This entry is an amended version of 'Unidroit' by Herbert Kronke, published in Jürgen Basedow and others (eds), *The Max Planck Encyclopedia of European Private Law*, vol 2 (OUP 2012) 1723 et seq. The entry is current as of 2014.

role as an academic back office are the CMR (Convention of 19 May 1956 on the contract for the international carriage of goods by road, 399 UNTS 189) and the 1964 Hague Conventions on International Sale of Goods (ULIS (Convention of 1 July 1964 relating to a Uniform Law for the International Sale of Goods, 834 UNTS 107); ULF (Convention of 1 July 1964 relating to a Uniform Law on the Formation of Contracts for the International Sale of Goods, 834 UNTS 169)).

II. Legal status, languages

UNIDROIT is an independent intergovernmental organization governed by its Statute, currently in its 1993 version (Statute of UNIDROIT as amended on 26 March 1993, available at <www.unidroit.org>, henceforth the Statute). According to its provisions

> [t]he Institute shall enjoy, in the territory of each participating Government, the necessary legal capacity to enable it to exercise its functions and to realise its purposes. The privileges and immunities which the Institute and its agents and officers shall enjoy shall be defined in agreements to be concluded with the participating Governments.

Of crucial importance is the Headquarters Agreement with the Italian Republic of 1967 (Legge 12 dicembre 1969 No 1074, Approvazione ed esecuzione dell'Accordo tra il Governo italiano e l'Istituto internazionale per l'unificazione del diritto privato sui privilegi e le immunità dell'Istituto concluso a Roma il 20 luglio 1967, Gazzetta Ufficiale della Republica Italiana No 21 of 26 January 1970) as amended, most recently in 1995. Jurisdiction in internal matters, notably in matters concerning the staff's status and labour relations vests in the UNDROIT Administrative Tribunal whose judges are elected by the General Assembly.

Cooperation agreements govern relationships with the United Nations and a number of other international and regional organizations.

According to the Statute the official languages are English, French, German, Italian and Spanish, a reflection of the importance of German-, Italian- and Spanish-speaking scholars during the early decades of the Institute's history. Today, the working languages are English and French. A number of instruments are, however, available in the other official as well as numerous other languages.

III. Organizational structure

The Statute provides for three organs: the General Assembly, the Governing Council elected by the Assembly, and the Secretariat.

The General Assembly, the supreme organ of the Institute, consists of the representatives of all Member States (currently 63). They are the ambassadors of the Member States in Italy or diplomats delegated by them. The ambassador of one of them, chosen according to a system of rotation from among the states of one world region, exercises the office of President of the General Assembly. Its competence is general. However, the most important acts are the approval of the annual budget, the triennial work programme, the Strategic Plan and its amendments and, every five years and particularly important, the election of the members of the Governing Council. The General Assembly moreover deliberates and adopts internal regulations regarding administrative, financial and staff matters. Committees, such as the Finance Committee, which oversees the development of the budget, and *ad hoc* committees tasked, eg with the preparation of amendments to the regulations assist the Assembly in carrying out its functions. The General Assembly is convened once a year for its ordinary session. It may also be convened for an extraordinary session, as for example when it adopted, in November 2008, in a joint session with a Committee of governmental experts (see VI. below) the UNIDROIT Model Law on Leasing (UNIDROIT (ed), Model Law on Leasing (13 November 2008), available under <www.unidroit.org>).

The Governing Council is a unique body that distinguishes UNIDROIT from other organizations. It is its composition, its competences and its working methods to which the organization owes its historic nickname 'Republic of scholars'. Twenty-five members elected for a term of office of five years and an honorary President appointed by the Italian government also for five years formulate strategic objectives, discuss and submit proposals for the working programme to the General Assembly, monitor the development of each project and make key decisions with respect to Secretariat officials. The Council moreover forwards the draft budget, as proposed by the Secretariat, to the General Assembly with its comments and recommendations. The Council's members are typically eminent scholars, high-ranking members of the judiciary or senior government officials or diplomats. Each government follows its own traditions in selecting and proposing its candidate, and recently there would appear to be a tendency to ensure a stronger presence of governments as such. Traditionally, members of the Council, while having been elected upon nomination from their respective government, once elected saw themselves not so much as its representative but rather as experts in matters of private law who served in that personal capacity and independently from any instructions. As long as a member was a civil servant – as has traditionally been the case in the continental European countries, → China, → Japan and → Australia – the difference was but nominal. Where, however, members of the Council were academics or judges who insisted on their independence, this potentially impaired the effectiveness of communication between the Member State and the organization. The aforementioned more recent tendency in selecting candidates is in all likelihood a reaction. The price for enhanced effectiveness may be diminished originality and scholarliness of programmatic and substantive discussions at the Council's sessions.

The Secretariat is the executive organ. The Secretary-General is appointed by the Governing Council on the nomination of the President for a term of office of five years. The President's proposal is based on the decision of an *ad hoc* committee which concludes an open international selection procedure. The Secretariat consists furthermore of one or two Deputy Secretaries-General of different nationalities, a staff of qualified lawyers from various jurisdictions and legal families, as well as qualified librarians and clerical staff. In 2008, nationals from 12 countries served on the Secretariat. The Secretary-General is *ex officio* Secretary of the General Assembly, the Governing Council and all Diplomatic Conferences convened by UNIDROIT. The Secretariat's tasks and responsibilities include (i) the organization and preparation of all legislative activities, such as receiving and analysing proposals for the work programme submitted by Member States' governments, industry and academics, enquiries with relevant circles as to the need for an instrument, feasibility studies, opinions assisting the Governing Council and the General Assembly with their decisions, etc, (ii) the composition of working groups, in particular the identification of potential members with the requisite expertise, preparation and follow-up work of the groups' working sessions, assisting the chairpersons, (iii) the organization of sessions of committees of governmental experts, including the production of drafts, reports and commentaries, keeping of minutes and reports on the sessions, (iv) preparation and organization of diplomatic conferences for the adoption of conventions, (v) once an instrument has been finalized, its promotion and assistance in its implementation. The Secretariat furthermore carries out all non-legislative activities (see VIII. below). Apart from work on individual projects, the most resource-consuming activity is the care for the relationship with Member States' governments, governments of states contemplating accession to the UNIDROIT Statute as well as with other intergovernmental and non-governmental organizations. Close cooperation and coordination of work with the other two 'sister' organizations – → Hague Conference on Private International Law and → UNCITRAL – and related work carried out within their framework enjoys highest priority. The Secretariat represents UNIDROIT as observer with the two mentioned organizations as well as with other international and regional organizations engaged in activities relevant for its own projects.

IV. Organization of work on the part of Member States

Locally, Member States' embassies or trade missions in Italy are in charge of ensuring communication with their governments as well as all routine consultations, such as attending to the Finance Committee's and the General Assembly's business. Conversely, a wide range of organizational models for substantive involvement can be found in capitals. In some cases (eg in the majority of Latin American Member States, a few European countries, such as → Greece and → Italy, in → India, Pakistan, → South Africa and the → USA) the ministry of foreign affairs has primary competence for all matters concerning UNIDROIT. In others it is the ministry of justice or the Attorney General (examples are → Australia, → Canada, the majority of states in continental Europe, → Japan and → Nigeria) or the ministry of trade, industry, the economy or some specific branch of economic regulation (eg as in → China, → Poland, the → Russian Federation or the → United Kingdom). The key criterion seems to be whether the ministry of justice has comprehensive competence for all areas of legislation – as eg in Germany – or whether its focus is – as eg in

Italy – on the organization of the judiciary and penitentiaries.

Typically, it is the ministry with primary competence that takes care of internal coordination for the government as a whole, consultation with that country's industry and other interested circles etc. In this respect, fundamentally different approaches and priorities have a significant impact. Governments of countries whose policies and objectives regarding all activities relevant for private and economic law in all organizations – from UNIDROIT and its 'sisters' to the World Bank and regional development banks, the International Monetary Fund, the OECD and regional economic integration organizations, such as the European Union – are formulated or coordinated by one department or office and where continual presence of governmental and private-sector interests in internal preparation and on negotiating delegations is ensured typically contribute most effectively to negotiations and secure the strongest impact on the outcome.

V. Working methods

Thanks to the exceedingly low degree of regulation typical of an independent organization, the organization and administration of any work process is extremely flexible. There is, obviously, a fundamental difference in approach flowing from the decision as to whether an international convention, ie a treaty (hard law), or one of the various types of soft law, such as model laws, general principles, a guide etc, will ultimately be the nature of the instrument.

Proposals from member governments, international organizations, central banks, industry, academia or members of the Governing Council that have been included in the work programme are submitted to a Study Group consisting of independent experts (scholars and practitioners) after having been the subject of further analysis on the basis of comparative law reports (→ Comparative law and private international law), feasibility studies, economic impact assessment studies, etc carried out or commissioned by the Secretariat. Apart from excellence the only criterion for being invited to serve on a Study Group is the desire to have expertise from the major legal families and from jurisdictions likely to be most strongly affected by or to profit the most from the particular project. Traditionally, Study Groups were very small (four to seven experts). More recently and where considered useful for the particular project (eg secured transactions, financial markets law), up to 14 experts have been invited to participate. The result of a Study Group's work – eg a position paper, a first draft of a future convention – is submitted to the Governing Council for examination and, if approved, transmitted to a Committee of governmental experts. Only now, during this second phase, do Member States' governments become directly involved. International organizations, international trade and other professional associations as well as non-Member States may be invited to attend the Committee's sessions as observers. Again, the result of this phase, usually a reasonably mature draft convention, will be examined by the Governing Council and, if approved, transmitted to a Diplomatic Conference, for final deliberation and adoption. Diplomatic Conferences are hosted by a Member State (during the period 1988–2012 the hosts were → Canada, → Italy, → South Africa, → Luxembourg, → Switzerland and → Germany) and all UN Member States and relevant international organizations are invited to attend. For the text adopted by such a conference to become law it requires ratification or accession according to the constitutionally provided for procedures.

Beginning in the 1980s there is a tendency to use – provided the subject matter area permits or requires to do so – more frequently one of the many types of non-binding instrument. The flagship of this movement are the UNIDROIT Principles (International Institute for the Unification of Private Law/Institut international pour l'unification du droit privé (ed), *UNIDROIT Principles of International Commercial Contracts 2010* (3rd edn, UNIDROIT 2010)) (first version 1994; second, enlarged edition 2004; third, again enlarged edition 2010). This 'international Restatement' is elaborated without any governmental involvement by a group of 17 (2004) or 21 (third version) experts (scholars, eminent practitioners and judges with the participation of the most important arbitration institutions). In this case, a finalized draft of black letter rules and detailed explanatory text ('comments') is laid before the Governing Council and adopted by that body.

The two model laws elaborated so far by UNIDROIT, the Model Franchise Disclosure Law (adopted in Rome on 25 September 2002, [2002] Unif.L.Rev. 1060–139 (with Explanatory Report)) and the UNIDROIT Model Law on

Leasing of 2008, were, after the first stage, finalized and adopted by a Committee of governmental experts. As regards the latter, the Committee had been convened in a joint session with the General Assembly with a view to emphasizing the political importance, in particular for the intended users in developing countries and transition economies.

The development of the Guide to Master Franchise Arrangements (UNIDROIT Guide to International Master Franchise Arrangements, 1998, second edition 2007, available at <www.unidroit.org>) permitted an even more informal process: a restricted group of experts formulated the individual chapters, and the Council just authorized the publication.

Coordination of the work with that in other intergovernmental organizations is of utmost importance in order to avoid duplication and achieve efficient use of scarce resources. With respect to the Hague Conference on Private International Law and UNCITRAL coordination occurs on the one hand by way of reciprocal participation in the sister organizations' meetings and, on the other hand, by means of an annual meeting of the three Secretaries-General geared at exchange of information and fine tuning of planned progress of the various projects. In 2012, a common guide to the instruments on secured credit transactions developed by the three organizations was published.

UNIDROIT attaches importance to efficient and rational coordination with work on private law carried out by regional organizations (eg Organization of American States – OAS; Organisation pour l'Harmonisation du Droit des Affaires en Afrique – OHADA; Common Market of the South – MERCOSUR/MERCOSUL; possibly other organizations in Africa and Asia). Such coordination is more difficult and complex where – as in the case of the European Union/European Communities – Member States of a regional supranational organization have transferred legislative competences to that organization. Here, unanimity regarding the exact scope of the (transferred) competence and a clear mandate for the negotiating organ (*in casu* the European Commission) are needed. Moreover, the Europeans must understand that they cannot impose timelines and content on the rest of the world because a given subject matter for which a globally applicable instrument is under preparation requires deeper and more detailed harmonization in the framework of the Internal Market.

VI. Important instruments

It is impossible to list even only those of the more than 75 studies carried out since the 1920s that actually entered into force. Worth mentioning are the CMR (1956 – in cooperation with UN/UNECE and the International Chamber of Commerce), the two Hague Uniform Laws on Sale (1964) (ULIS (Convention of 1 July 1964 relating to a Uniform Law for the International Sale of Goods, 834 UNTS 107) and ULF (Convention of 1 July 1964 relating to a Uniform Law on the Formation of Contracts for the International Sale of Goods, 834 UNTS 169)), predecessors of the → CISG (United Nations Convention of 11 April 1980 on Contracts for the International Sale of Goods, 1489 UNTS 3), the UNIDROIT Conventions on International Factoring and International Leasing (1988), the UNIDROIT Principles of International Commercial Contracts (1994, 2004, 2010), the UNIDROIT Convention on Restitution of Stolen or Illegally Exported Cultural Objects (UNIDROIT Convention on stolen or illegally exported cultural objects of 24 June 1995, 2421 UNTS 457), UNIDROIT Guide to International Master Franchise Arrangements (1998, second edition 2007), Cape Town Convention (2001 – in cooperation with ICAO) (Convention of 16 November 2001 on international interests in mobile equipment, 2307 UNTS 285 and Aircraft Protocol (Protocol of 16 November 2001 to the Convention on international interests in mobile equipment on matters specific to aircraft equipment, 2307 UNTS 615)), Luxembourg Protocol on Matters Specific to Railway Rolling Stock (2007 – in cooperation with OTIF) (Luxembourg Protocol of 23 February 2007 to the Convention on international interests in mobile equipment on matters specific to railway rolling stock (23 February 2007) available at <www.unidroit.org>), Protocol of 9 March 2012 to the Convention on international interests in mobile equipment on matters specific to space assets (2012) (available at <www.unidroit.org>), ALI/UNIDROIT Principles of Transnational Civil Procedure (2004) (ALI/UNIDROIT Rules of Transnational Civil Procedure (text of the Principles and the accompanying commentary were adopted by the American Law Institute (ALI) in May 2004 and by the International Institute for the Unification of Private Law (UNIDROIT) in April 2004 (2004) 4 Unif.L.Rev. 758)), Draft Uniform Act on Contract Law for the Member States of OHADA (2004/

2007) (OHADA Uniform Act on Contract Law Preliminary Draft of September 2004, available at <www.unidroit.org>, Colloquium on the Harmonisation of OHADA Contract Law of 15–17 November 2007, available at <www.unidroit.org>), UNIDROIT Convention on Substantive Rules for Intermediated Securities (2009) (available at <www.unidroit.org>), UNIDROIT Model Law on Leasing (2008); the UNIDROIT Principles on the Operation of Close-out Netting Provisions (2013) (available at <www.unidroit.org>).

VII. UNIDROIT instruments and conflict of laws

While in the early decades of the movement for internationally coordinated law reform in the areas of private law and, in particular, commercial law there were no clearly defined remits of the various international organizations involved, more recently limits of their respective expertise are acknowledged. This is reflected in the various organizations' work. UNIDROIT's expertise being focused on substantive law, it is the organization's practice to seek close cooperation with the Hague Conference on Private International Law and to refrain from formulating conflicts provisions. Examples are art 5(3) of the Cape Town Convention, which refers for the determination of the applicable law to the rules of private international law of the forum state. In a similar vein, art 2(2) of the UNIDROIT Convention on Substantive Rules for Intermediated Securities provides that the Convention (ie domestic law implementing the Convention) applies whenever the applicable conflict-of-laws rules designate the law in force in a contracting state as the applicable law. Other instruments provide themselves for conflict-of-laws rules, albeit in a rather limited manner. By way of example, it may suffice to refer to arts 4(2) and 7(3) of the UNIDROIT Financial Leasing Convention (→ Financial leasing (uniform law)).

VIII. Non-legislative activities

The Statute provides for the Institute to maintain a library which currently holds about 300,000 volumes and which, notwithstanding permanent lack of funding, continues to be world standard specifically in the area of harmonization of private law. Among other publications the Uniform Law Review/Revue de droit uniforme (New Series since 1996) stands out. The data base UNILEX, devoted to the UNIDROIT Contract Principles and the → CISG, is maintained in association with the Institute. Another data base, UNILAW, devoted primarily to the law of carriage of goods is being developed. UNIDROIT's programme of legal assistance rests on two pillars: first, scholarships for young scholars, government officials or practitioners, in particular from developing countries and transition economies, permitting them to work in Rome on projects of their own choice and, second, assistance with the development and the implementation of instruments of uniform private and commercial law in such states.

HERBERT KRONKE

Literature

René David, 'The International Unification of Private Law' in René David (ed), *International Encyclopedia of Comparative Law*, vol 2 (Mohr Siebeck 1971) ch 5; Roy Goode, Herbert Kronke and Ewan McKendrick, *Transnational Commercial Law: Text, Cases, and Materials* (OUP 2007) ch 5, 191; Herbert Kronke, 'Ziele – Methoden, Kosten – Nutzen: Perspektiven der Privatrechtsharmonisierung nach 75 Jahren UNIDROIT' [2001] JZ 1149; Herbert Kronke, 'Methodical Freedom and Organizational Constraints in the Development of Transnational Commercial Law' (2005) 51 Loy.L.A.L.Rev. 287; Riccardo Monaco, 'L'unification du droit dans le cadre d'Unidroit (1926–1986)' [1986] Rev.Dr.Unif. I 46; Gonzalo Parra-Arranguren, 'La importancia del Instituto para la Unificación del Derecho Privado (UNIDROIT) en la futura uniformidad juridica del hemisferio americano' (1992) 86 *Revista de la Facultad de Ciencias Jurídicas y Políticas* 34; Lena Peters, 'International Institute for the Unification of Private Law (UNIDROIT)' in Roger Blanpain and Jan Wouters (eds), *International Encyclopedia of Laws: Intergovernmental Organizations*, vol 2, supp 23 (Wolters Kluwer 2005); Ernst Rabel, 'On Institutes for Comparative Law' in Hans G Leser (ed), *Ernst Rabel, Gesammelte Aufsätze*, vol 3 (Mohr Siebeck 1967) 235; Walter Rodinò, 'Malcolm Evans and UNIDROIT: A Chronology' [1998] Unif.L.Rev. 249; Walter Rodinò, 'UNIDROIT' in Sacco Rodolfo, *Digesto Discipline Privatistiche Sezione Civile* (4th edn, UTET 2000) 742; Pierre Widmer, 'The International Institute for the Unification of Private Law: Shipyard for World-wide Unification of Private Law' [1999] Eur.J.L.Ref. 181; Peter Winship, 'International Harmonization of Private Law' in Marylin J Raisch and Roberta I Shaffer (eds), *Introduction to Transnational Legal Transactions* (Oceana Publications 1995) 159.

HERBERT KRONKE

Uniform substantive law and private international law

I. Definition of uniform law – and types of uniform law

The expression 'uniform law' indicates a set of identically worded legal rules that are binding on a general level in more than one jurisdiction where they are also supposed to be interpreted and applied in the same manner. Actually, for such sets of rules to be considered uniform law, they must have been created with the intention to be interpreted and applied in one and the same manner throughout the jurisdictions where they are in force. Where this so-called *animus unificandi* is lacking, it may well be possible for the laws of different jurisdictions to be identical to each other, but they will nevertheless not constitute uniform law. This is why, for instance, the spontaneous, unintentional creation of identically worded legal rules in different jurisdictions as an answer to similar problems arising in practice do not constitute uniform law. The same is true as regards the unilateral reception of foreign legal rules – even though this may lead to legal rules of various jurisdictions being identical.

Law that is simply 'harmonized', that is, law that has not been created with the intention of getting rid of the existing differences, but rather with the goal of merely reducing those differences (as is the case for the law originating from most EU directives), does not constitute uniform law. This does not mean that only those legal rules that fully correspond to each other can be considered uniform law. If this were the case, it would be impossible to ever speak of uniform law, as fully corresponding legal rules are very rare, even where the wording of the legal rules is identical. The reasons for divergence are manifold, such as the fact that the uniform texts are often drafted in different languages and are interpreted and applied differently in practice (see Tribunale di Rimini, 26 November 2002 [2003] Giur. it. 896). Therefore, the starting point for determining whether there is uniform law is the degree of intended similarity of the legal rules in question. Where the maximum degree is intended, ie where the law is supposed to be one and the same, uniform law may exist despite any factors that may have a negative impact on the uniformity aimed at. Where, however, from the outset, the efforts are merely aimed at the creation of a similar, harmonized law, one cannot speak of uniform law.

While, as just mentioned, the intended identity of the legal rules defines uniform law, for the purpose of that definition the area of law to be unified is utterly irrelevant. This is due to the fact that the expression 'uniform law' indicates not so much an area of the law as a status, but how the law is (supposed to be). Consequently, efforts towards the creation of uniform law can relate to the most disparate areas of law. For the purpose of this entry, it is relevant to point out by way of example that they can relate to the areas of private international law as well as substantive law.

As regards the latter, a distinction has to be made between unlimited and limited uniform substantive law. Unlimited uniform substantive law is constituted by those legal rules that also govern purely domestic situations, which is why this kind of uniform substantive law is rather rare (although there are a few examples of such uniform law, such as the rules laid down by the Convention of 7 June 1930 for the Settlement of certain Conflicts of Laws in connection with Bills of Exchange and Promissory Notes (143 LNTS 317) and the Geneva Cheques Convention (Convention of 19 March 1931 for the Settlement of certain Conflicts of Laws in connection with Cheques, 143 LNTS 407)). Limited uniform substantive law, on the other hand, solely governs trans-border situations, that is, situations that have a relationship to more than one country. Unlike unlimited uniform substantive law, limited uniform substantive law does not *per se* have an impact on domestic law. This is an advantage insofar as it allows a given state to enter a limited uniform substantive law instrument into force even where it contrasts with that state's domestic law. This means that the adoption of limited uniform substantive law does not require a high degree of compatibility vis-à-vis the domestic substantive law. The same is true with uniform private international law because it has an impact solely at the conflict-of-laws level rather than the substantive one. Such uniform private international law may, however, override domestic private international law rules, which, at times, may cause problems, as this entry will show.

A high degree of compatibility is, however, a prerequisite for the success of any effort towards the creation of unlimited uniform substantive law, which is why there are areas of law in relation to which unlimited uniform substantive law will be nearly impossible. In this respect, it may

Franco Ferrari

suffice to mention areas such as family law and the law of → succession – areas characterized by national particularities originating from nation-specific social, ideological, religious and cultural values and backgrounds which national legislatures will hardly give up. Even though limited uniform substantive law would not impact on the existing national particularities in these areas, insofar as the domestic law would still apply to (purely) domestic situations, limited uniform substantive law in these areas is very rare as well since these areas are far too influenced by the aforementioned values to allow for even the creation of a limited uniform substantive law.

In the aforementioned areas, one can find, however, uniform private international law. This is due to the fact that private international law is – as much as its → connecting factors – influenced to a much lesser extent than its substantive counterpart by such particularities and values. In other words, it is much easier to forego domestic private international law rules than substantive rules, since the former are rarely the expression of deeply rooted cultural, sociological, ideological or religious beliefs. This is why, to give just a few examples, there is a Hague Convention of 24 October 1956 on the law applicable to maintenance obligations towards children (510 UNTS 161), but no substantive law convention addressing those obligations. The same can be said in respect of substantive law conventions (and the lack thereof) governing the topics addressed in other private international law conventions, such as the Hague Testamentary Dispositions Convention (Hague Convention of 5 October 1961 on the conflicts of laws relating to the form of testamentary dispositions, 510 UNTS 175), the Hague Matrimonial Property Convention (Hague Convention of 14 March 1978 on the law applicable to matrimonial property regimes, 16 ILM 14), and the Hague Marriage Convention (Hague Convention of 14 March 1978 on Celebration and Recognition of the Validity of Marriages, 1901 UNTS 131) etc.

II. Aims and goals of uniform substantive law versus those of uniform private international law

At this point one must wonder what goals the unification of law pursues and whether the distinction between uniform substantive law and uniform private international law influences not only the possibility of unifying certain areas of law, but also has an impact on the goals behind the unification process. The starting point is the realization that unification of law does not in itself constitute a goal that is to be pursued at all costs, independently from any valid justification. Instead, unification of law has to aim at more than 'just' obtaining unified law. The issue of which other goals may justify the unification of law depends, in part, on the area of law (such as private international or substantive law) to be unified, as the goals of unification of one area may differ from those of a different area.

Of course, efforts towards the unification of different areas of law may also pursue the same goals. For example, one of the goals behind the unification of both substantive law and private international law is to avoid the unequal treatment to which the application of different legal rules may lead to in a specific instance. This does not mean, however, that in light of that common goal, the distinction between private international law and substantive law becomes irrelevant. This is due to the fact that private international law and substantive law have an impact on different levels. With respect to avoiding unequal treatment, uniform private international law guarantees that the courts of the states in which it is in force apply the same substantive law. This leads to uniformity on a conflict-of-laws level. Consequently, parties have (apart from the cases of → *dépeçage*) merely to provide for the application of one substantive law. There is a downside to this: courts may well have to apply an unfamiliar law, which leads to uncertainty and costs arising from the determination of the contents of that unfamiliar (foreign) law. In any case, it should be mentioned that uniform private international law cannot prevent all unequal treatment. For example, the party whose law will ultimately be applicable will have an advantage, insofar as that party will have no difficulties nor will that party incur any costs in determining the contents of the applicable law. Uniform substantive law, on the other hand, guarantees that all parties from countries where it is in force will have equal access to the substantive law solutions, thus 'levelling the playing field' – at least among the parties of states in which that uniform law is in force. The fact that uniform substantive law always deals with the situations falling within its sphere of application in the same manner (at least as a starting point), while uniform private international law merely guarantees resort to the same substantive law, also avoids unequal treatment.

The goal of uniform substantive law for international situations most often referred to is a different one. It involves making the application of law easier by creating a (substantive) law that, according to the prevailing view, avoids the need to resort both to private international law – considered to be rather complicated – and to the applicable law determined by means of that very same private international law. This promotes certainty of law, makes business decisions easier and facilitates risk assessment. According to the prevailing view, this leads to a reduction of costs, benefiting not only the parties involved but the economy as a whole. Therefore, where no resort to private international law is had, an important source of uncertainty is avoided which, in turn, certainly saves costs.

The foregoing assumption leads some commentators to suggest that the unification of substantive law rules is, where at all possible, to be preferred over the unification of private international law rules, on the grounds that uniform substantive law rules are 'of a higher level' or 'superior' vis-à-vis uniform private international law rules. Whether this is true or not is not relevant here. What is relevant, however, is that whenever the court of a contracting state to a given uniform substantive law convention has to determine the substantive rules to apply to an international situation *prima facie* governed by that convention, the court must first look into whether that convention applies rather than resort to its own private international law rules. This result has been justified both by commentators and courts on two grounds: first, that the rules of a uniform substantive law convention are more specific insofar as their sphere of application is more limited; and further, that they lead directly to a substantive solution, while resort to private international law requires a two-step approach, that is, the identification of the applicable law and the application thereof (see Tribunale di Vigevano, 12 July 2000 (2001) 20 J.L.& Com. 209).

It must be pointed out, however, that this prevalence of uniform substantive law vis-à-vis private international law (irrespective of whether it is uniform or not) does not necessarily lead to the conclusion, incorrectly drawn by some commentators, that resort to private international law is irreconcilable with the uniform substantive law approach. This statement, not unlike similar ones suggesting that uniform substantive law can do away with recourse to private international law, is incorrect. It is time to recognize that there are many reasons why a private international law analysis cannot be excluded despite the existence of uniform substantive law conventions. And this is true even in respect of uniform substantive law instruments, such as the ULIS (Convention of 1 July 1964 relating to a Uniform Law for the International Sale of Goods, 834 UNTS 107) and the ULF (Convention of 1 July 1964 relating to a Uniform Law on the Formation of Contracts for the International Sale of Goods, 834 UNTS 169), which contain provisions explicitly stating that for the purposes of their application private international law rules are to be excluded. In effect, even under these instruments it was incorrect to state that resort to private international law rules was precluded. As one commentator correctly pointed out in respect of the ULIS and ULF, '[e]ven the adoption of the Uniform Law[s] everywhere in the world would not exclude the need for conflicts rules . . . . In the end, the blackballed rules of private international law will have to be rediscovered and resorted to' (Kurt Nadelman, 'The Conflicts Problems of the Uniform Law on the International Sale of Goods' [1965] Am.J.Comp.L. 236, 239–40). But it cannot be doubted that provisions such as the aforementioned ones make it more difficult to depart from the more traditional way of seeing the relationship between uniform substantive law and private international law as an antagonistic one and, thus, to see that there is room for resort to private international law even where a uniform substantive law instrument is in force in the forum state.

III. Express and implicit references to private international law in uniform substantive law conventions

One reason why it is incorrect to state that resort to private international law can be completely forgone where uniform substantive law conventions exist is due to the fact that many uniform substantive law conventions, albeit neither the ULIS nor the ULF, refer themselves to private international law, where they do not put forth private international law rules themselves.

By way of example of the latter, it may be worth referring to the UNIDROIT Financial Leasing Convention (UNIDROIT Convention of 28 May 1988 on International Financial Leasing, 2312 UNTS 195; → Financial leasing (uniform law)), which itself sets forth a rule of private international law, namely art 7(3). That provision identifies the law applicable to decide which, if any, public notice requirements must be met in order for the lessor's real rights in the equipment leased to be valid against execution creditors or the lessee's trustee in bankruptcy. Similarly, chapter VI of the Convention on Independent Guarantees and Stand-by Letters of Credit (2196 UNTS 163) sets forth the rules of private international law. The most elaborate set of rules of private international law can, however, be found in the UNCITRAL Assignment of Receivables Convention (United Nations Convention on the Assignment of Receivables in International Trade, concluded 12 December 2001, adopted by resolution A/RES/56/8). This Convention contains not only a private international law rule for priority (art 22), but also what has been labelled a 'mini-convention' of private international law. While the rule for priority applies whenever the Convention itself applies due to all of its applicability requirements being met, Chapter V, which contains an elaborate set of rules (dealing with the law applicable to the formal requirements of the assignment, the law applicable to the mutual rights and obligations of the assignor and the assignee, as well as the law applicable to the rights and obligations of the assignee and the debtor) has a much broader sphere of application, as it also applies as long as one of the alternatively listed internationality requirements set forth in the Convention (art 1(4)) is met, and this is even if the other applicability requirements (such as those *ratione materiae*) are not met.

As regards the references to private international law in uniform substantive law conventions, there are many, including many express ones. The UNIDROIT Convention on International Financial Leasing, for instance, expressly refers to 'private international law' on several occasions, namely in arts 6(2), 7(5) (b) and 8(4) (→ Financial leasing (uniform law)). Express references to 'private international law' can also be found in other uniform substantive conventions, such as the → CISG (United Nations Convention of 11 April 1980 on Contracts for the International Sale of Goods, 1489 UNTS 3), the Ottawa Factoring Convention (UNIDROIT Convention on International Factoring of 28 May 1988, 2323 UNTS 373, 27 ILM 943) (→ Factoring (uniform law)) etc. Where these instruments refer to 'private international law', the reference is to be understood as to the 'private international law' of the forum, unless, of course, a given instrument provides for private international law rules itself.

If one looks at the context in which such express references are made as well as at the context in which some of these instruments rely on a private international law analysis, as do, for instance, the UNIDROIT Convention on International Financial Leasing in art 3(1) (b), and the Ottawa Factoring Convention in art 2(1)(b), one can see how important resort to private international law is. In effect, the provisions just mentioned are particularly important, as they show that the applicability of the foregoing conventions themselves depends (where these conventions are not applicable due to all parties to the contract having their relevant place of business in contracting states) on a private international law analysis. The same is true, for instance, in respect of art 1(1)(b) CISG, which states that the CISG applies 'when the rules of private international law lead to the law of a contracting State'. These provisions unambiguously show that resort to private international law may be necessary even for the purpose of applying a uniform substantive law convention.

IV. Limitations to the sphere of application as a reason for the need to resort to private international law

As mentioned earlier, all recent uniform substantive law conventions merely set forth limited uniform law, ie uniform law that only governs situations linked to more than one jurisdiction. Furthermore, all conventions that are limited in the aforementioned way define internationality in a given way. This means, *inter alia*, that where a relationship is not international as per the definition contained in the relevant convention, the convention cannot *per se* be applicable, even though the relationship may still be international. This, in turn, requires resort to a private international law analysis to determine which law applies to that relationship.

By way of example, it may suffice to recall the definition of internationality found in art 2(1) of the UNIDROIT Convention on International Factoring. Unlike, for instance, the → CISG, the Ottawa Factoring Convention (→ Factoring (uniform law)) does not define internationality on the basis of the location of the place of business of the parties to the contract it governs. Therefore, even factoring contracts concluded between parties having their places of business in the same state can be subject to the Convention *de quo*, provided that the 'internationality' requirement, as well as all the other requirements, are met. According to the Convention, the internationality of a factoring contract depends on an objective rather than a subjective element. By virtue of art 2(1), a factoring contract is international when the receivables assigned arise either from an 'international' contract for the sale of goods (between suppliers and debtors with places of business in different states) (→ Sale contracts and sale of goods) or an 'international' contract for the supply of services (the parties to which have their places of business in different states). Consequently, the Convention's applicability depends not as much upon the 'internationality' of the factoring contract as upon the 'internationality' of the receivables. This means, however, that the assignment of domestic receivables between suppliers and factors who have their relevant place of business in different states cannot fall under the Convention's international sphere of application, even though the factoring contract is certainly 'international'. For these types of situations, resort to private international law is necessary to identify the applicable law.

The CMR (Convention of 19 May 1956 on the contract for the international carriage of goods by road, 399 UNTS 189) also does not define the internationality of the contracts it governs on the basis of the location of the place of business of the parties. In effect, pursuant to that Convention, the contracts for carriage of goods are international, 'when the place of taking over of the goods and the place designated for delivery, as specified in the contract, are situated in two different countries' (art 1(1) CMR). This, of course, excludes very many types of international contracts for the carriage of goods by road from that Convention's international sphere of application, thus making it necessary to often determine the applicable law on the basis of the rules of private international law (of the forum) (→ Carriage of goods by road, rail and inland waterways).

At this point, it is worth pointing out that not only is the international sphere of application of all recent uniform substantive law conventions limited, but so too is their substantive sphere of application, thus making it again necessary to identify the law applicable to the international contracts falling outside a particular convention's substantive sphere of application (at least where no other uniform substantive law convention governs).

By way of example, it suffices to recall the limitations to the substantive sphere of application found in art 2 CISG. Pursuant to this provision, the → CISG does not extend to the sale of ships, airplanes, stocks, shares, investment securities, negotiable instruments, money, electricity as well as the sale by auction, sales on execution or otherwise by authority of law. It further does not apply to the sale of goods bought for personal, family or household use, unless the seller, at any time before or at the conclusion of the contract, neither knew nor ought to have known that the goods were bought for any such use. Other conventions have similar carve-outs. The CMR, for instance, expressly states that it does not apply 'to carriage performed under the terms of any international postal convention, funeral consignments and furniture removal' (art 1(4) CMR). The UNIDROIT Financial Leasing Convention excludes, for instance, leasing contracts that take the form of operating leasing from its sphere of application. Although this is not expressly stated in the Convention, it can be derived from the fact that the Convention only applies to leasing contracts where the rentals payable under the leasing agreement are calculated so as to take into account in particular the amortization of the whole or a substantial part of the cost of the equipment, since operating leasing is from the outset not aimed at full or substantial amortization of the assets. By way of final example, it is worth recalling that the Ottawa Factoring Convention only governs factoring contracts requiring, among others, that notice of assignment be given to the debtor (art 1(2)(c)), thus excluding the Convention's application to non-notification factoring contracts. Furthermore, as per its art 1(2)(a), the Convention does not apply where the receivables assigned arise from contracts for the sale of goods bought primarily for their personal, family or household use, thus limiting the substantive sphere of application to notification factoring.

FRANCO FERRARI

V. The impact of reservations on the need to have recourse to private international law

Most recent uniform substantive law conventions allow contracting states to declare a limited number of reservations, so as to provide some flexibility to a type of instrument the rigidity of which would otherwise lead some states to outright reject it. The possibility to declare such reservations impacts, however, on the uniformity aimed at. Furthermore, where states declare such reservations, they also trigger the need to resort to a private international law analysis.

The reservation contained in a uniform substantive law convention that has probably drawn the most attention is the reservation declared by various contracting states to the → CISG in relation to art 95. Pursuant to this provision, contracting states may declare that they will not be bound by art 1(1)(b) CISG, pursuant to which the CISG also applies 'when the rules of private international law lead to the law of a Contracting State'. Although there is disagreement as to the exact effects of declaring this type of reservation, there is agreement on the fact that it has private international law implications.

Although other uniform substantive law conventions contain provisions comparable to art 1(1)(b) CISG (such as art 2(1)(b) Ottawa Factoring Convention and art 3(1)(b) UNIDROIT Convention on International Financial Leasing), these conventions do not provide for the possibility to declare a reservation relating to the operation of those provisions. There are, however, some reservations that all recent uniform substantive law conventions allow contracting states to declare. In this respect, it may be sufficient to refer to the so-called 'federal state clause', contained, for instance in art 93 CISG, art 18 ILC, art 17 IFC as well as in art 18 of the UNCITRAL Electronic Communications Convention (United Nations Convention of 23 November 2005 on the Use of Electronic Communications in International Contracts, adopted on 23 November 2005 during the 53rd plenary meeting of the General Assembly by resolution A/60/21, text available in UN doc A/60/515) and art 35 of the UNCITRAL Assignment of Receivables Convention. These provisions all allow a state that is divided into several territorial units in which, according to that state's constitution, different systems of law are applicable in relation to the matters dealt with in the relevant convention, to make a declaration pursuant to which the convention does not extend to all territorial units. Where a state made such a declaration and a party to a contract has its place in a territorial unit to which the convention does not extend, that party is considered to have its place of business in a non-contracting state, thus triggering, once again, a private international law analysis which may either lead to the application of the convention or to a domestic law.

Many recent uniform substantive law conventions also allow states to declare another reservation that has private international law consequences. For instance, pursuant to art 94 CISG, art 17 IFC and art 19 ILC, contracting states which have the same or closely related legal rules on matters governed by the relevant convention may declare that the convention is not to apply where the parties to the contract the convention governs and, in the case of the IFC and the ILC, the parties to the underlying contract, have their place of business in those states. The rationale behind this provision is to render the conventions inapplicable to contractual relationships between parties that have their places of business in states that have a law that is largely uniform, thus allowing regional unification efforts not to be overridden by the existence of the conventions drafted on a more global level. Consequently, where the potentially applicable convention does not apply, resort is once again to be made to the private international law rules of the forum to determine the applicable law.

Some conventions also allow states to declare reservations that, unlike the aforementioned ones, do not have an impact on the status of a contracting state, but rather on the substance. Despite the different impact, what these reservations have in common is that they all trigger the need for a private international law analysis. By way of example, it may suffice to recall the art 96 reservation, which has an impact on the formal validity of contracts for the international sale of goods generally governed by art 11 of the CISG, which sets forth the principle of freedom from form requirements. This principle does not necessarily apply where at least one of the parties to the contract governed by the → CISG has its place of business in a state that has declared a reservation under art 96 CISG. In this line of cases, any provision 'that allows a contract of sale or its modification or termination by agreement or any offer, acceptance or other indication of intention to be made in any form other than in writing does not apply'. What consequences this has on the applicable writing requirements is subject to dispute. What is undisputed, however, is the fact that a private international law analysis is required to determine whether any form requirements have to be met.

It may be worth pointing out that the IFC also allows for a reservation with substantive effects. Pursuant to art 18, states may at any time make a declaration that an assignment made in breach of a non-assignment clause shall not be effective against the debtor when, at the time of conclusion of the contract of sale of goods, the debtor has its place of business in that state. This provision does not, however, require resort to private international law, at least not in the courts of states declaring the reservation at hand, as the provision itself sets forth the substantive consequences of declaring the art 18 reservation.

VI. Limitations to the scope of application and party autonomy as reasons for resort to private international law

All uniform substantive law conventions, without exception, fail to constitute exhaustive bodies of rules. In other words, no uniform substantive law convention provides solutions to all matters that may arise in relation to the specific relationships it governs. This, however, means that resort to private international law may be necessary to determine the law applicable to the issues falling outside a given convention's scope of application.

In effect, it is generally through resort to private international law that the law applicable to matters excluded from the limited scope of application of these conventions, the so-called 'external gaps', are to be settled. This is provided, of course, that no other uniform substantive convention takes precedence, as does, under certain conditions, the 1974 Convention on the Limitation Period in the International Sale of Goods (Convention of 14 June 1974 on the Limitation Period in the International Sale of Goods, 1151 UNTS 3; 13 ILM 952) in relation to the statute of limitations issue not governed by the → CISG.

The private international law approach is completely different from the one to be adopted in respect of the so-called 'internal gaps', ie matters governed by a convention which, however, are not expressly settled in it, which requires resort to private international law only as *ultima ratio*, when it is not possible to solve the matter from within the relevant convention, that is through recourse to the general principles upon which the convention is based. From the foregoing, it becomes apparent how important the distinction between the various types of gaps and their identification really is. Unfortunately, however, the various uniform substantive law conventions do not set forth specific criteria on the basis of which to make the distinction. Some conventions do, however, expressly list some issues that they do not settle. Article 4 CISG, for instance, provides a (non-exhaustive) list of matters with which the CISG is not concerned. This includes the validity (other than the formal validity) of the contract or of any of its provisions or of any usage as well as the effect which the contract may have on the property in the goods sold. Article 5 CISG also lists a matter with which the CISG is not concerned, namely the liability for death or personal injury caused by the goods to any person. The ILC, too, expressly identifies some issues with which it is not concerned, such as the liability of the lessor in respect of the equipment in his capacity as owner (art 8(1)(c)) and accounting and taxation issues (Preamble).

Although some conventions do not contain a list of matters not governed by them, their scope of application is still limited. In this respect, it may suffice to point out that the IFC, for instance, does not deal with matters of general contract law, such as formation of contract, validity, damages, statute of limitations etc. Nor does the IFC deal with all matters more specifically relating to factoring, such as the third-party effectiveness of assignments of receivables and the priority among conflicting claimants as to the accounts receivable. These matters have to be settled through the law applicable pursuant to the rules of private international law.

Of course, the fact that some of the conventions contain a list of matters excluded from their scope does not limit the matters excluded to the ones listed. Among the matters identified by courts and commentators as not being at all governed for instance by the → CISG are, among others, the validity of a choice of forum clause (→ Choice of forum and submission to jurisdiction), the validity of a penalty clause, the validity of a settlement agreement, the assignment of receivables, the assignment of contract, the issue of whether a court has jurisdiction and, generally, any other issue of procedural law, the assumption of debts, the acknowledgement of debts, third-party rights, the effects of the contract on third parties, as well as the issue of whether one is jointly liable.

It should be noted that even where all of the positive applicability requirements of a given uniform substantive law convention are met and the matters to be dealt with fall into that convention's scope of application, resort to private international law may still not be superfluous. This is due to the fact that many uniform substantive law conventions are not mandatory. In other words, many conventions allow the parties involved to opt out of it, but making it necessary to identify the applicable law by means of private international law. As regards the → CISG, the possibility to opt out of it is set forth in art 6, which allows the parties to 'exclude the application of this Convention or, subject to art 12, derogate from or vary the effect of any of its provisions'. By providing for this possibility, the drafters of the CISG reaffirmed the CISG's dispositive nature and the central role which → party autonomy plays in international sales. Of course, where the parties exercise their power to exclude the CISG, the applicable substantive rules have to be determined by means of the applicable private international law rules. Similarly, art 5 ILC allows for the exclusion of the ILC, but only if each of the parties to the supply agreement and each of the parties to the leasing agreement agree to it. The IFC, too, allows for its exclusion – but only as a whole (art 3(2)) – by the parties to the international factoring contract or by the parties to the contract for the sale of goods, as regards receivables arising at or after the time when the factor has been given notice in writing of such exclusion. Where the parties take advantage of the autonomy granted to them to exclude the IFC, the applicable substantive rules have to be determined by means of the applicable private international law rules.

From all of the foregoing it clearly follows that it is an oversimplification to state that where uniform substantive law exists resort to private international law is superfluous. Only when there is awareness as to the many limitations of uniform substantive law conventions and, consequently, their non-autarkic character, can one really understand the relationship between these conventions on private international law – which is not an antagonistic one. These uniform substantive law conventions and the rules of private international law necessarily co-exist.

FRANCO FERRARI

Literature

Didier Opertti Badan, 'Conflit de lois et droit uniforme dans le droit international privé contemporain: dilemme ou convergence?' (2013) 359 Rec. des Cours 9; Ted M de Boer, 'The Relation between Uniform Substantive Law and Private international law' in Arthur S Hartkamp and others (eds), *Towards a European Civil Code* (Kluwer 1994) 51; Franco Ferrari, 'Forum Shopping Despite International Uniform Contract Law Conventions' (2002) 51 ICLQ 689; Franco Ferrari, 'La Convention de Vienne sur la vente internationale et le droit international privé' (2006) 27 J.Dr.Int'l 27; Franco Ferrari, 'PIL and CISG: Friends of Foes?' [2012] IHR 89; Herbert Kronke, 'Zur Komplementarität von IPR und Einheitsrecht bei der Modernisierung des Wirtschaftsrechts: eine Fallstudie' in Jürgen Basedow and others, *Aufbruch nach Europa: 75 Jahre Max-Planck-Institut für Privatrecht* (Mohr Siebeck 2001) 757; Holger Lerche, *Konkurrenz von Einheitsrecht und nationalem Privatrecht* (Kovac 2007); Sylvain Marchand, *Les limites de l'uniformisation matérielle du droit de la vente internationale: mise en oeuvre de la Convention des Nations Unies du 11 avril 1980 sur la vente internationale de marchandises dans le contexte juridique suisse* (Helbing & Lichtenhahn 1994); Karl August von Sachsen-Gessaphe, *Internationales Privatrecht und UN-Kaufrecht* (2nd edn, BWV 2007).

Unilateralism

I. Definition and historical development

Unilateralism is a theory of private international law, which is often opposed to multilateralism. In order to identify the applicable law, multilateralism tends to localize the 'seat' of each legal relationship or situation, or in more contemporary terms, the legal system with which the situation presents the closest connection. Multilateralism thus allocates each legal relationship to a legal order via a multilateral conflict rule. Unilateralism, in contrast, proposes to resolve conflict of laws via the spatial scope of the substantive rules in conflict. From a unilateralist perspective, the question is whether the law commands its application to a specific situation. Unilateralism thus rests on the premise that the spatial scope of rules can be determined from their content or nature and that conflict of laws should be solved on this basis.

Throughout history, unilateralism has taken various forms. It is commonly accepted that unilateralism was the method used to solve conflict of laws from the 12th century until the second part of the 19th century. The 19th century was marked by *Savigny* (→ Savigny, Friedrich Carl von) 'Copernican revolution', but unilateralism never disappeared in Europe, or in the USA.

1. Statutist period – 12th to 19th centuries

The question of choice-of-law rules has arguably been identified since Italian cities gained relative independence within the Empire and started developing their own legal provisions (or *statuta*) in some areas. Early forms of globalization (→ Globalization and private international law), materialized in international/inter-city commerce, as well as individuals travelling and migrating, forcing scholars and courts to consider the application of their own statutes or of those of other municipalities in situations that were not purely domestic. The first solutions were derived from Roman law and in particular from the *Corpus Juris* of *Justinian* and a passage thereof, well known under its first terms: *Cunctos populos* (*Cunctos populos quos clementiae nostrae regit imperium, in tali sanctissima volumus religion versari, quam divinum Patrum apostolum tradidisse Romanis*, stating in short that subjects of the Roman empire should embrace the Christian faith). A scholar called *Karolus de Tocco*, interpreting the *lex cunctos populos*, concluded that statutes are obligatory for those who are submitted to them or to the authority enacting them ('*Statutum non ligat nisi subditos*'; Eduard Maurits Meijers, 'L'histoire des principes fondamentaux du droit international privé à partir du Moyen Age spécialement dans l'Europe occidentale' (1934) 49 Rec. des Cours 534, 594). From there, the 'conflict' of statute was envisioned as a process of identification of those who were submitted to a specific statute and thus of determination of the statute's scope. The identification of the statute's scope operated with reference to its nature or content and statutes were progressively classified in, more or less precise, categories according to their content and their corresponding reach. With the passing of time, the accumulation of case-law, the categories of statutes progressively gave rise to a 'fairly coherent system of principles and rules' restated by → *Bartolus* in the 14th century (Rodolfo de Nova, 'Historical and Comparative Introduction to Conflict of Laws' (1966) 118 Rec. des Cours 435, 446). A corresponding 'French' statutist school, in the meanwhile, had developed according to rather similar terms (Eduard Maurits Meijers, 'L'histoire des principes fondamentaux du droit international privé à partir du Moyen Age spécialement dans l'Europe occidentale' (1934) 49 Rec. des Cours 596–7), but it is the later version thereof that is usually referred to in literature, citing especially the work of *d'Argentré* (16th century). *D'Argentré* classified all the statutes in only two categories, according to their effect: *statuta realia*, the dominant category applying territorially, and *statuta personalia*, potentially applying extra-territorially. *D'Argentré's* extensive conception of → territoriality was later received in Holland and inspired the three famous maxims of *Ulrik Huber* (→ Huber, Ulrik). In 1689, *Huber* was the first to concentrate on conflicts between the laws of different states (Ulrich Huber, 'De conflictu legum diversarum in diversis imperiis' in *Paelectiones juris romani et hodierni* (1689, reproduced by Ernest G Lorenzen: Ernest G Lorenzen, 'Huber's De Conflictu Legum' (1919) 13 *Illinois Law Review* 375)) and to formulate the idea of *comitas* and of vested rights (→ Vested rights theory).

Irrespective of the very general nature of the statute categories (especially as described by *d'Argentré*), statutists can be considered as incarnating the first unilateralist period because of the process of reasoning adopted at the time. As *Gutzwiller* phrased it: 'for them the problem lies in the rule of decision. Rules (or statutes) are the sole object of consideration. No specific provision regulates conflict of laws, because the solutions are inherent to the text of the statutes' (Max Gutzwiller, 'Le développement historique du droit international privé' (1929) 29 Rec. des Cours 291, 312, the translation is ours).

2. Rise of multilateralism – Europe from the middle of the 19th century

Two important developments took place in the middle of the 19th century, under the influence of which private international law progressively abandoned the statutist school and its unilateral roots. On the one hand, in Italy, *Pasquale Stanislao Mancini* (→ Mancini,

Pasquale Stanislao) proposed new grounds for private international law, ie the model of the nation state and the corresponding generalization of nationality as a factor for designating the applicable law. On the other hand, *Savigny* completed his *opus* on private law with a book dedicated to conflict of laws. *Savigny* is commonly considered the father of multilateralism, even if he probably restated ideas that were circulating at the time. For *Savigny*, each legal relationship has a natural seat (*Sitz*), ie a place where it belongs in regard to its characteristics. *Savigny* anchors relationships within legal systems, with the help of connecting factors designed for each type of legal relationship. In contrast, the statutists were identifying the spatial scope of statutes by reference to their content and object. *Savigny* held the two ways of conceptualizing the conflict-of-law issue ('who is submitted to a specific statute?' or 'which law applies to a specific person?') for equivalent and as leading to identical results (Friedrich Carl von Savigny, *System des heutigen römischen Rechts*, vol 8 (Veit und Comp 1849) 48, 55). The equivalence between the two methods can be explained by *Savigny's* conception of law and legal systems, and the reason why he favoured the second method (now called multilateral) a result of the spirit of the time. *Savigny's* system is rooted in the belief that different statutes are merely various expressions of common legal concepts (in *Savigny's* vocabulary, '*Institutionen*') shared by all Christian nations influenced by Roman law. Legal relationships are themselves the visible form of these common concepts and the expression of a legal community rooted in a society shaped by Roman and Catholic heritage (the '*Volksgeist*'). For this reason, statutes are interchangeable and the spatial scope of the one naturally corresponds to the spatial scope of the other. It is therefore possible to identify the 'seat' of a legal relationship, because all the relevant statutes will apprehend this relationship in similar terms and identify their own scope in similar ways. Within the limits of this legal community, the (now called) unilateral and multilateral methods are thus equivalent and *Savigny* favoured the method consisting of identifying the seat of a legal relationship, as a mirror image of the domicile (*Sitz* in German) of individuals. Indeed his whole conception was also inspired by the liberal spirit of the time and therefore focused on the individual and the expressions of its free will. Since legal relationships are considered a mere extension of individuals, *Savigny* localizes legal relationships, as he localizes individuals, on the basis of their connection to a legal community, ie their seat (for more details see Pierre Gothot, 'Simples réflexions à propos de la saga du conflit de lois' in Marie-Noelle Jobard-Bachellier and Pierre Mayer, *Le droit international privé: esprit et méthodes – Mélanges en l'honneur de Paul Lagarde* (Dalloz 2005) 343, 349–54).

What remains of *Savigny's* legacy is the multilateral method, detached from the reasons why *Savigny* conceived it in the first place. The idea of a legal community has been long abandoned and intensive migrations have shown that even for individuals, the identification of a seat can be a thorny issue. Nevertheless the multilateral method has proven very useful and received tremendous success in court rooms, as well as in codification. Multilateralism dominates the conflict-of-laws practice and debates in Europe. Interestingly, despite this clear dominance of multilateralism, unilateralism remained part of the debate, be it in order to advocate a unilateralist system or to highlight incoherencies of multilateralism (an almost comprehensive overview until the middle of the 20th century can be found in Rudolf Wiethölter, *Einseitige Kollisionsnormen als Grundlage des Internationales Privatrechts* (Walter de Gruyter & Co 1956); *Wiethölter* was unaware of the writings of *Quadri*). Repeatedly, scholars proposed (sometimes for different reasons) unilateralist systems.

Like the statutists, *Pillet* attempted to identify the proper scope of statutes by reference to their social function and to organize statutes in two categories: laws that apply to everyone present in the forum, even foreigners, and laws that follow the nationals even when they are abroad. Potential conflicts between laws were to be solved, in his view, via public international law (→ Public international law and private international law) imposing a mutual respect for equal sovereigns and favouring the application of the law of the state, having the highest interest in the application of its law. Based on totally different premises, his follower, *Niboyet*, proposed to implement unilateralism in a controversial project of codification of French private international law that was never adopted (cf *Les travaux de la réforme du Code Civil*, année 1948–49 (Sirey 1950) 716). Before him, in Germany, authors like *Schnell* and *Niedner* believed that private international law had the sole function of setting the limits of the substantive law of the forum and not to decide when foreign law should apply (Alexander Niedner, *Einführungsgesetz vom 18.8.1896 (Kommentar)* (2nd edn, Heyman 1901); Julius Schnell, 'Über die Zuständigkeit zum Erlaß von gesetzlichen Vorschriften über die räumliche Herrschaft der Rechtsnormen' [1895] *Niemeyers Zeitschrift für internationales Recht* 337). In the same period, the German *Bundesrat* adopted a first codification of private international law, mainly composed of unilateral rules.

Pilenko and *Quadri* are two interesting examples of modern forms of unilateralism in Europe. For *Pilenko* (a Russian professor), laws are necessarily composed of three aspects: a substantive aspect, a temporal aspect and a spatial aspect (Aleksandr A Pilenko, 'Droit spatial et droit international privé' (1954) 5 *Jus Gentium* 35–59; 'Le Droit spatial et le Droit international privé dans le projet du nouveau Code Civil français' (1953) 6 R.H.D.I. 319–55). Those three elements are interdependent and cannot exist without one another. The question of spatial reach of laws is therefore a matter of domestic law, not of private international law, and is necessarily solved in unilateral terms (by 'monovalent rules' forming the '*droit spatial*', ie the branch of law considering the spatial reach of domestic rules). *Pilenko* shows with examples that acknowledging the spatial scope of rules actually prevents conflicts (in terms that anticipate those later used by *Brainerd Currie* (→ Currie, Brainerd) about false conflicts. It is only when the internal spatial delineation of two laws of different origin collide that private international law and its 'polyvalent' rules come into play, thus late in the reasoning. *Pilenko*'s system, even though it leaves room for multilateral rules obtained through a process of generalization of the unilateral/monovalent rules, is unilateralist in its premises because it starts with the observation of the spatial reach of internal rules. In contrast, *Rolando Quadri*'s system is entirely unilateralist (Rolando Quadri, *Lezione di diritto internazionale privato* (5th edn, Liguori 1969); and the famous article of Pierre Gothot, 'Le renouveau de la tendance unilatéraliste en droit international privé' (1971) 60 Rev.crit.DIP. 1, 209, 415, who introduced *Quadri*'s system in the French literature). It rests on an elaborated conception of laws: as the result of accumulated social experiences, laws regulate specific situations and intend to command individual actions. As such, laws, by nature, determine their own scope of application, including in their spatial aspects. Laws are seen as the direct product of social experience. Therefore applying laws without consideration for the way they describe their own scope of application denatures them and leads to absurd situations where foreign laws are applied to situations they were not intended to cover. Also, as for *Pilenko*, conflicts occur only when the laws of different countries intend to cover the same situation. Forum law is recognized as having priority when the situation falls within its scope. For the rest, each system recognizes foreign legal systems and coexists with them in an autonomous way, but also searches for coordination and respect for the imperativity of foreign norms which apply according to their own terms through a process of '*auto-collegamento*', a sort of 'self-designation'. *Quadri*'s system, together with *Currie*'s system, will be explained in more detail *infra* since it probably incarnates best the contemporary unilateralist thinking (II.).

3. A contrasted picture – the USA as from the 19th century

Almost a contemporary of *Quadri*, Brainerd Currie launched a vast unilateralist movement in the USA in the 1950s and early 1960s. *Currie* fought against the formalism of the first Restatement (Restatement (First) of Conflict of Laws, American Law Institute, Restatement of the Law, First: Conflict of Laws, St. Paul 1934). *Story* had in the 19th century imported the three maxims of *Huber* (→ Huber, Ulrik) and explained on their basis the complicated case-law of common law countries on conflict of laws (Joseph Story, *Commentaries on the Conflict of Laws, Foreign and Domestic* (Little & Brown 1834)). On the basis of *Story*'s writing and influenced by *Dicey*'s (→ Dicey, Albert Venn) idea of vested rights, *Beale* elaborated the first Conflict Restatement. The first Restatement identified through rigid rules (usually resting on territorial connecting factors) the competent state for creating the rights and obligations. In contrast, *Currie* saw the conflict problem not as a matter of vested rights but as a conflict between laws of different states whose interests might be at stake, or not, depending on the factual situation. The application of a law should only be considered if an 'interest analysis' (→ Interest and policy analysis in private international law) reveals that this law commands its application to the case at hand in regard of its purpose and of the facts pattern

(Brainerd Currie, *Selected Essays on the Conflict of Laws* (Duke University Press 1963)). *Currie's* system, inspired by legal realism (and prompted among others by *Cook's* seminal article: Walter Wheeler Cook, 'The Logical and Legal Basis of the Conflict of Laws' [1924] Yale L.J. 457), is thus based on the premise that states express political, social and economic interest in their statutes and that any conflict-of-laws solution should start with identifying these interests. It also empowers the judge with the role of interpreting the statutes in order to distinguish false conflict (when only one state is interested) from true conflicts (when more than one state is interested).

Currie's conception of laws echoes *Quadri's* even though he was not aware of the Italian scholar's writings and despite the fact that his methodology was not formulated in view of the unilateralism v multilateralism debate. His idea of state interests and of a need for consideration for the substantive and political content of the rules at stake has been shared by many of his US colleagues, even though each of them proposed alternative solutions, mainly in regard of true conflicts, in order to depart from *Currie's* tendency to favour forum law. *Baxter's* 'comparative impairment' approach, *Leflar's* → 'better law approach', *Caver's* 'principle of preference', *Von Mehren* and *Trautman's* 'functional analysis', *Weintraub's* 'consequences based approach' share the conception of laws bearing a political content having an impact on their spatial scope. Later American scholars thus followed *Currie's* intuition in various ways (see Symeon C Symeonides, 'The American Choice-of-Law Revolution in the Courts: Today or Tomorrow' (2003) 298 Rec. des Cours 1, 48–58). The Second Conflicts Restatement (Restatement (Second) of Conflict of Laws, American Law Institute, Restatement of the Law, Second: Conflict of Laws 2d, St. Paul 1972) tries to find a balance between the premises highlighted by *Currie* and the need for rules, in identifying the law with which the situation presents the 'most significant relationship' in regard to a series of factors enumerated in its § 6 referring, among others, to the state's interest.

II. Theoretical background and concepts

As a general theory, unilateralism proposes a system of ideas explaining the problem of private international law and the appropriate solutions thereof. The theory rests on two paradigms deeply rooted in legal theory and leads to consequences regarding the way of solving conflict of laws (II.1., II.2.). Depending on the historical period of time and on the scholars, unilateralism has been considered capable of grounding a system of private international law (II.3.) or simply as the basis for specific tools of private international law, ie for a method illustrated in specific conflict rules (II.2., III.).

1. Unilateralist paradigms

Despite the diversity of its protagonists and of their slightly differing conceptions, unilateralist theory (or rather all unilateralist theories) rests on the idea that laws prescribe their own scope of application for domestic as well as international situations. This idea constitutes the first paradigm of unilateralism. The delineation of the scope of application derives from the substantive content of the rule, from its goal and purposes, and as such can only be addressed by the law itself, either in a specific and express rule or as an inherent and implicit part of the normative (substantial) content.

The second paradigm of unilateralism derives from the first one. It is for each legal order to prescribe for itself when and to what extent its rules should apply to international (as well as domestic) situations. Therefore no legal order can decide that a foreign law applies to a specific relationship if this law does not command its application. Correlatively, it is for each legal system to decide when and how it considers the application of a foreign rule that covers the situation. Obviously, the range of foreign laws to be taken into consideration is limited to those in the scope of which the situation falls. However nothing compels a given legal system to apply those rules, but for an autonomous decision to consider their application.

Unilateralist theory is therefore first and foremost enshrined in a specific conception of the law. Be they of public or private nature, laws are seen as bearing a substantive content aiming to achieve specific goals and therefore covering specific situations. As such, they are not 'neutral' (as they can be considered in the multilateralist theory, *infra*, III.). For instance, in France, *Pillet* expressed this in his concept of the 'social function of laws', and in the USA, *Currie*, in his 'interest analysis'.

Beyond a specific conception of rules, unilateralism has been, time and again, depending on doctrinal readings, considered as deriving from sovereignty. More recently, unilateralism has been considered the private international law version of pluralism, understood as a general theory of relationships between legal orders (the idea is present though not formulated as such in the famous article of Pierre Gothot, 'Le renouveau de la tendance unilatéraliste' (1971) 60 Rev.crit.DIP 1–36, 209–43, 415–50, resting on the conceptions of *Quadri* and *Santi Romano*; see later Didier Boden, 'Le pluralisme juridique en droit international privé' (2005) 49 A.P.D. 275–316, for a more detailed explanation of the link between pluralism and unilateralism).

2. *Unilateralist method*

In describing the paradigms of unilateralism and their theoretical roots, much has already been said about the unilateralist method. The essence of the method is to take stock of the 'will of application' of the laws in presence. As a result, conflicts of laws exist only if two (or more) laws from different legal systems intend to regulate the situation. In the unilateralist vision based on sovereignty, and nourished by a universalist conception of private international law (ie the belief that common conflict solutions could be found outside of each legal system), the conflict is merely potential: it is avoided through allocation rules deriving from rationality or public international law. For later unilateralists, the concept of conflict of laws is not a potentiality but rather a reality that occurs, in practical terms, in specific situations. For *Currie*, 'true conflicts' arise when more than one state is 'interested' in applying its law, as the result of a match between the substantive policies of the state on the one hand and the factual specificities of the case on the other hand. For *Quadri*, conflicts of laws arise when two substantive laws from different origins cover the same situation.

Leaving aside the statutist period, scholars who proposed a unilateral system commonly agreed on two steps of reasoning. The first step considers the application of forum law. If the situation falls within the spatial reach of forum law, it should be applied. If forum law does not regulate the situation, the second step consists in analysing the application of foreign laws (→ Foreign law, application and ascertainment). The task is thus to identify relevant foreign law or laws that intend to regulate the specific situation at hand. Divergences can be traced regarding the way in which the scope of application of forum law is determined and regarding the way in which to deal with conflicts of foreign laws.

On this basis, several characteristics of unilateralism can be identified.

First, the applicability of a law is determined by its own spatial reach, or its 'own intent of application'. This scope of application is inherent to every law, either expressly or implicitly, and must be derived from the law itself. The same method is therefore used to select the applicable law, be it the *lex fori* or foreign law: by reference to the predetermined scope of application of this law. The difference between forum and foreign law lies in the natural priority reserved to forum law.

Second, unilateralism aims at applying foreign law without distorting it. The ground for applying foreign law lies indeed in what foreign law states/says about itself, ie whether it requires its own application or not. A common feature of unilateralist tenets is to consider that forum law (including forum conflict rules) cannot determine the hypothesis of application of foreign law. This idea, which is fundamental in contemporary unilateralism, was not so clear in earlier versions of unilateralism based on sovereignty because → *ius* gentium or higher principles were believed to limit sovereignty (and thus the spatial scope of rules) for every sovereign equally.

Third, unilateralism in its different versions considers that the coordination with foreign legal systems is an integral part of the reasoning process, even when ascertaining the application of forum law. In coordinating with foreign legal systems, the stability of individual situations should be protected. This concern was formulated in various ways over time. *Pillet* was looking for a principle of 'common conciliation' in order to ensure the highest level of respect of sovereignty. *Currie* developed the 'moderate and restrained approach', according to which a state, in ascertaining its interest in applying its own law, should take into account the legitimate interest of other states to have their law applied to the case at hand. For *Quadri*, a principle of coordination with foreign legal systems guides each national system of private international law with the view of ensuring the stability of individual situations or, in other words, the uniformity of decisions. This principle, however, is not derived from higher norms of conduct (such as → *ius gentium* or → comity), but constitutes an inherent part of national systems of private international law.

STÉPHANIE FRANCQ

Fourth, unilateralism obviously needs to develop alternative solutions for true conflicts, ie the hypothesis where two (or more) foreign laws require their application to the case at hand. This is certainly the trickiest issue for unilateralism. *Currie* finally proposed that the judge seized with what he called a problem of 'disinterested third State' should decline jurisdiction on → *forum non conveniens* grounds or apply forum law (Brainerd Currie, 'The Disinterested Third State' (1963) 28 LCP 754). His followers developed more convincing models, like the comparative impairment approach of *Baxter*. *Pilenko* renounced unilateralism at this stage and considered that this is the only question resorting to private international law and to be solved with multilateral rules (which could be obtained through generalizing the unilateral forum rule). The problem is equally insurmountable for unilateralism based on sovereignty: any solution amounts to bowing to one sovereign's affirmation of power over another sovereign's affirmation of power. But tenets of this school partially denied the possibility of such conflicts, since the allocation of sovereignty (coming from *jus gentium* or some other superior rationale) was deemed to prevent them. When unilateralism is rooted in the conception of the law, as for *Quadri*, concurring claims of different states for applying their own laws are less problematic. For *Quadri*, if the system rests on the respect of what each state decides for itself, it is also based on a pragmatic evaluation of the facts in order to ensure the stability of the individual situation. Therefore, a search for effectiveness favours the application of the law that in practice has the best chance of applying and that corresponds (as a consequence) to the expectation of the parties (Rolando Quadri, *Lezione di diritto internazionale privato* (5th edn, Liguori 1969) 221).

Fifth, unilateralism encounters another difficulty, called *lacuna* or, in *Currie's* vocabulary, the 'unprovided for' case, ie situations where no law claims its application. Applying the *lex fori* solves this problem. *Niboyet* grounded this solution in the territoriality principle. *Currie* justified this solution as a matter of convenience for the judge and of common sense, because no other option can really be considered as a more favourable alternative. In order to promote the stability of individual situations, *Quadri* added (to the option of applying forum law) the option of applying the law which the parties thought applicable and according to which they had behaved.

3. Unilateralist system

A unilateralist system is a system of private international law entirely derived from the unilateralist paradigm and resting exclusively on the unilateralist method. Such a system has been proposed repeatedly throughout history but has barely materialized, with the notable exception of the statutist period. The true point of divergence between a unilateralist and a multilateralist system concerns the designation of foreign law: for unilateralism, forum law cannot determine the hypothesis of application of foreign law (→ Foreign law, application and ascertainment), this can only be done by foreign law. The reluctance of private international law systems to select foreign applicable law on the sole ground of its 'intention' to apply is the reason why a comprehensive unilateralist system is lacking.

In Europe, attempts to create a unilateral system have taken the form of unilateral rules on the application of forum law. But concerning the application of foreign law, national judges have developed an analogy reasoning, called 'multilateralization', using the applicability criteria of forum law as a factor for designating the foreign law applicable irrespective of what the latter indicates about its own applicability. For instance, the early codification of private international law in → Germany was at first conceived on a unilateralist mode, but when confronted with the need for solving cases where German law was not applicable, German judges had recourse to the analogy reasoning. The same phenomenon occurred in → France and → Belgium where the few provisions of the Civil Code (the '*Code Napoléon*') dedicated to international situations were formulated in a unilateral way, but were later submitted to an analogy reasoning allowing for the application of foreign law (for France and Germany: Gérard Vivier, 'Le caractère bilatéral des règles de conflit' [1953] Rev.crit.DIP 655, 656–8 [1954] 73, 86–7). The natural tendency towards 'multilateralization' of unilateral rules has been explained by the need for judges to find a legal basis for applying foreign rules in positivist systems (Marc Fallon, 'L'application de l'article 3, alinéa 3, du Code civil par la jurisprudence belge du 19e siècle' in Colloque

François Laurent, Gand, 4–8 September 1987 (Story 1989) 765).

In the USA, only two states still practise the approach advocated by *Currie* (California and District of Columbia, where interest analysis is used for torts: Symeon C Symeonides, 'Choice of Law in the American Courts in 2013: Twenty-seventh Annual Survey' (2014) 62 Am.J.Comp.L. 2). However, as *Symeonides* has shown, most of the current approaches in the USA are, at least partially, based on unilateralism in the sense that 'the purposes, policies, or interests underlying the laws from which the selection is to be made' are taken into consideration (Symeon C Symeonides, 'The American Choice-of-Law Revolution in the Courts: Today or Tomorrow' (2003) 298 Rec. des Cours 1, 365, 375). In particular, § 6 of the Restatement (Second) of Conflict of Laws places the relevant policies of the forum and other interested states among the factors guiding the selection of the applicable law. In practice, courts tend to emphasize the factors of § 6 dealing with states' interests, so that *Currie's* influence on the current practice of conflict of laws in the USA remains remarkable.

Interestingly, despite the absence of a comprehensive unilateralist system, unilateralism has remained vivid in various ways. First, unilateralism remains, even recently, a strong source of inspiration for doctrinal writings, be it for proposing a new system, for explaining new techniques or new phenomena. Second, legislators (both in the EU and in the USA) have enacted statutes that are obvious examples of the unilateralist method. As *Gothot* and *Wiethölter* underlined, unilateralism also offers an opportunity for challenging and re-conceptualizing the dominant multilateral theory (Pierre Gothot, 'Le renouveau de la tendance unilatéraliste' (1971) 60 Rev.crit.DIP 1, 6; Rudolf Wiethölter, *Einseitige Kollisionsnormen als Grundlage des Internationalen Privatrechts* (Walter de Gruyter & Co 1956) 122), which will now be compared.

4. Unilateralism v multilateralism

Points of divergence between unilateralism and multilateralism have been mentioned above but need to be summarized as a conclusion on the theoretical background.

The fundamental difference between multilateralism and unilateralism is the conception of the rule of law. After the idea of a legal community, which grounded *Savigny's* conception (*supra*), had been abandoned, multilateralism has received alternative foundations. The most convincing ground for multilateralism lies in a concept of rules of law as being the incarnation of rationality, thus a neutral, non-political object and virtually universal. Laws are thus unable to determine their own spatial scope of application for the reason that as purely rational objects, they can encompass any situation corresponding to their hypothesis, irrespective of the geographical and personal features of the situation. The unlimited character of laws explains why it is possible to apply foreign laws and why forum law can apply to facts localized outside the forum (Pierre Mayer, 'Le phénomène de la coordination des ordres juridiques étatiques en droit privé' (2007) 327 Rec. des Cours 1, 140–51). To put it in short, law is more a model for action of individuals, than a practical command of their action (Pierre Mayer, 'Le phénomène de la coordination des ordres juridiques étatiques en droit privé' (2007) 327 Rec. des Cours 1, 149). As shown above, the unilateralist concept of laws differs profoundly from this vision, also because unilateralists probably have a more pragmatic rather than abstract approach to law.

As a result of the diverging concept of laws, unilateralism and multilateralism have opposing views on conflict of laws: in a multilateral system, national laws, because they do not limit their scope, are considered as virtually always in a state of conflict, whereas in a unilateralist system, conflicts occur only when two laws are proved to effectively cover the same factual situation. The first role of the judge in a unilateralist system is thus to identify the conflict.

Finally, the methods for solving conflicts differ in nature. The preceding section (*supra* II.2.) shows that the unilateralist method is closer to an 'approach' than a set of rules: the system rests upon an observation of laws in conflict with adaptation mechanisms for true conflict and *lacuna*. In contrast, multilateralism must give rise to a set of rules because the judge needs to refer to a rule delimiting the scope of application of the laws virtually in conflict. Such conflict rules are thus necessary in every field of law.

III. Practical contemporary implications

Even if unilateralism is a marginal theory in contemporary private international law, most systems of private international law use some unilateral tools. As many of these tools or methods are discussed in other entries of the Encyclopedia, we will only mention here how and why they echo unilateralism. These various examples illustrate how lawmakers regularly feel the need to identify the international scope of their norms.

1. Unilateral conflict rules

Unilateral conflict rules are conflict rules having the sole function of designating the *lex fori* (or more generally the law of the state having enacted them). Truly unilateral conflict rules are formulated in terms that render their multilateralization impossible and are therefore rather rare. Indeed most conflict rules initially formulated in unilateral terms (such as the provisions of the first Introductory Act to the German Civil Code (Einführungsgesetz zum Bürgerlichen Gesetzbuche of 21 September 1994, BGBl. I 2494, as amended) or art 3 of the French Civil Code (Code Civil of 21 March 1804; henceforth French CC) were easily submitted to a multilateralization process. In contrast, rules like the former art 330 of the French CC cannot lead to the designation of foreign law through analogy reasoning. Now replaced by the → Rome III Regulation (Regulation (EC) No 864/2007 of the European Parliament and of the Council of 11 July 2007 on the law applicable to non-contractual obligations (Rome II), [2007] OJ L 199/40), art 330 of the French CC states that divorce and legal separation are submitted to French law:

when both spouses are French nationals
when both spouses have their domicile on the French territory
when no other law finds itself competent and French courts have jurisdiction over the divorce or legal separation.

To a certain extent, these unilateral conflict rules are comparable to the overriding mandatory rules mechanism. Indeed a unilateral conflict rule delineates the scope of forum law and ensures its application to the situations covered. Unilateral conflict rules however determine the hypothesis of application not only of a specific statute (like overriding mandatory rules), but of an unlimited amount of provisions (like the rules on divorce or legal separation (→ Divorce and personal separation)). Also, in contrast to international mandatory rules, the provisions designated by the unilateral conflict rules are not necessarily imperative.

Unilateral conflict rules are thus an expression of unilateralism in the sense that they determine the scope of application of forum law, without deciding on the hypothesis of application of foreign law (→ Foreign law, application and ascertainment).

2. Rules of applicability, self-limited rules, substantive rules of private international law

Rules of applicability are rules which determine the scope of a specific set of provisions, like a domestic statute, an international agreement or a piece of European secondary law (on this notion: Marc Fallon, 'Les règles d'applicabilité en droit international privé' in *Mélanges offerts à Raymond Vander Elst*, vol 1 (Nemesis 1986) 285). The various aspects of the scope of application (time, space, substance) are usually spread in various provisions. The most relevant of them, for private international law purposes, is the rule concerning the spatial scope, ie identifying the situations covered by the set of provisions with regard to their connections with one or more contracting states (for international conventions) or the state or legal system to which the rule belongs (for domestic statute and EU rules). Rules of applicability are necessarily unilateral: they state when a specific statute of state A applies to an international situation. This role is very close to the one of unilateral conflict rules with the only difference that rules of applicability refer to a specific (and not unlimited) set of provisions. They may determine the scope of mandatory provisions (as in overriding mandatory rules, *infra* III.3.), as well as non-mandatory provisions.

Examples of applicability of rules are as diverse as art 2 of the Athens Regulation (Regulation (EC) No 392/2009 of the European Parliament and of the Council of 23 April 2009 on the liability of carriers of passengers by sea in the event of accidents, [2009] OJ L 131/24) (stating that the regulation applies to international carriage 'where the ship is flying the → flag of or is registered in a Member State or, the contract of carriage has been made in a Member State or the place of departure or destination... is in a Member State'), art 1 (1) a) of the → CISG (United Nations Convention of 11 April 1980 on Contracts for the International Sale of Goods, 1489 UNTS 3) (stating that the Convention applies to international sales contracts when the two parties are established in contracting states) or art L-3122-1 of the French public health code (Ordonnance 2000-548 of 15 June 2000 on the legislative part of the Code of Public Health, JORF No 143, 22 June 2000, p 9340) (limiting the scope of the fund established for victims having been infected by HIV after a blood transfusion to cases were the transfusion occurred on the territory of the French Republic; see Cass Civ II France, 3 February 2005 (2005 II) 24 Bulletin 22).

The doctrine (with some diversity in the vocabulary) usually distinguishes between rules of applicability influencing the conflict-of-laws solutions and rules of applicability that are relevant only after the law of the state they belong to has been selected as the applicable law. Self-limited rule and substantive rules of private international law belong to the second category. A self-limited rule restricts the reach of a specific statute to some determined domestic situations (for instance, a specific statute that would apply only in part of the territory of a state). It thus operates a distinction between a special statute and other more general statutes or, in some countries, the common law. Substantive rules of private international law are those domestic rules whose content makes sense only for international situations, without identifying precisely those situations and thus without impacting the conflict-of-law reasoning. For instance, in → Belgium, a provision on employee protection states that when the employee works abroad, he may choose to be paid in the currency valid in Belgium or in the state where he works (art 4 of the Law of 12 April 1965 on the protection of remuneration (Loi du 12 avril 1965 sur la protection de la rémunération des travailleurs, MB, 30 April 1965, 4710)).

Of course, despite the nuances, these various provisions express the need felt by the legislature to identify the scope of its provisions, in regard of international or domestic situations. When they relate to identified international situations, rules of applicability obviously have an influence on the conflict-of-law process. As special rules, they derogate to the general multilateral choice-of-law rules.

3. Overriding mandatory rules

Overriding mandatory rules are the most widespread example of using unilateralism as a tool in private international law and probably the best accepted in contemporary legislation on private international law (*lois de police/ Eingriffsnormen*). Indeed, specific provisions on international mandatory rules can be found in EU Regulations (art 9 Rome I Regulation (Regulation (EC) No 593/2008 of the European Parliament and of the Council of 17 June 2008 on the law applicable to contractual obligations (Rome I), [2008] OJ L 177/6; → Rome Convention and Rome I Regulation), art 16 → Rome II Regulation (Regulation (EC) No 864/2007 of the European Parliament and of the Council of 11 July 2007 on the law applicable to non-contractual obligations (Rome II), [2007] OJ L 199/40)), in national codifications (for instance, art 10:7 of the Dutch New Civil Code (Boek 10 Burgerlijk Wetboek, Wet van 19 mei 2011 tot vaststelling en invoering van Boek 10 (Internationaal privaatrecht) van het Burgerlijk Wetboek (Vaststellings- en Invoeringswet Boek 10 Burgerlijk Wetboek), Staatsblad 2011, 272), art 19 Swiss Private international law Act (Bundesgesetz über das Internationale Privatrecht of 18 December 1987, 1988 BBl I 5), art 20 of the Belgian Private international law Act (Wet houdende het Wetboek von international privaatrecht/Code de droit international privé of 16 July 2004, BS 27 July 2004, pp 57344, 57366), art 4 Statute of Application of Law to Foreign Civil Relations (adopted at the 17th session of the Standing Committee of the 11th National People's Congress on 28 October 2010, effective 1 April 2011)), as well as in international conventions (for instance, art 11 of the Inter-American Contracts Convention (Inter-American Convention of 17 March 1994 on the Law Applicable to International Contracts, 33 ILM 732); art 16 of the Hague Agency Convention (Hague Convention of 14 March 1978 on the law applicable to agency, Hague Conference of Private international law (ed), *Collection of Conventions (1951–2009)* (Intersentia 2009) 268); art 17 of the Hague Convention of 22 December 1986 on the law applicable to contracts for the international sale of goods ((1985) 24 ILM 1575); art 11 of the Hague Securities Convention (Hague Convention of 5 July 2006 on the law applicable to certain rights in respect of securities held with an intermediary, 46 ILM 649)) and model laws (for instance, art 11 of the Hague Principles on Choice of Law in International Commercial Contracts (approved on 19 March 2015, available at <www.hcch.net>); art 1.4. of the UNIDROIT Principles (International Institute for the Unification of Private Law/

Institut international pour l'unification du droit privé, *UNIDROIT Principles of International Commercial Contracts 2010* (3rd edn, UNIDROIT 2010))). These provisions systematically allow the application of international mandatory rules of the forum, but not always those of other interested states.

Overriding mandatory rules are a topical example of unilateralism. As identified in the definition proposed by *Francescakis* (Phocion Francescakis, 'Conflits de lois (principes généraux)' in Dalloz, *Encyclopédie juridique, Repertoire de droit international*, vol 1 (Dalloz 1968) no 137) and later by the ECJ (Joined Cases C-369/96 and C-376/96 *Criminal proceedings against Jean-Claude Arblade and Arblade & Fils SARL* and *Bernard Leloup, Serge Leloup and Sofrage SARL* [1999] ECR I-8453) and by the European lawmakers in art 9(1) of the Rome I Regulation, they are characterized by three components. First, they fix their own scope of application through an implicit or explicit applicability rule. Second, their scope of application reflects their specific purpose, aiming at the protection of essential interests of the state. Third, this purpose justifies their need to derogate from the general conflict rules.

Overriding mandatory rules are thus the most direct expression of the link between the aim of a statute and its scope regarding international matters. The mandatory aspect of those rules (displacing party autonomy and the designation operated by objective conflict rules) might have led to some confusion, in the sense that doctrine tends to assimilate any statute stating its scope of application with an overriding mandatory rule. However, the expression of the scope of applicability of a statute and its degree of imperativity are different matters (Stéphanie Francq, *L'applicabilité du droit communautaire dérivé au regard des méthodes du droit international privé* (Bruylant/LGDJ 2005) 421–41, 575–6, 643).

The most perfect example of unilateralism (and the most controversial) occurs when a system of law is ready to apply international mandatory rules belonging to a system of law that has not been designated by the multilateral conflict rule. In this case, there are only two identifiable bases for applying a foreign mandatory rule. First, the latter requests its application to the case at hand. In other words, foreign law applies according to its own terms. Second, the forum wishes to harmonize with the foreign legal system, thus furthering the other system's policies.

4. Renvoi

Though it is not a direct product of unilateralism, the technique of *renvoi* expresses the concern of unilateralism towards the opinion of foreign systems on the application of their own rules. In other words, *renvoi* is based not only on the idea of uniformity of result, but also on an attempt to prevent the 'forced' application of foreign substantive norms when the system they belong to does not consider them applicable to a specific situation.

5. EU regulations and directives

Within the European Union, EU regulations and directives (ie secondary Union law) offer another illustration of unilateralism in the sense that they determine their own scope of application, through implicit or explicit rules of applicability. Examples of recent explicit rules of applicability are found in regulations as well as directives (for a regulation, see among others: art 1 of Regulation (EU) No 236/2012 of the European Parliament and of the Council of 14 March 2012 on short selling and certain aspects of credit default swaps ([2012] OJ L 86/1); art 1, 3 of Directive 2014/17 on credit agreement for consumers relating to residential immovable property (Directive 2014/17 of the European Parliament and of the Council of 4 February 2014 on credit agreements for consumers relating to residential immovable property and amending Directives 2008/48/EC and 2013/36/EU and Regulation 1093/2010, [2014] OJ L 60/34)). Even in the absence of an explicit rule, the scope of application of EU secondary legislation derives from its purpose and can be identified through a literal or teleological interpretation process (Stéphanie Francq, *L'applicabilité du droit communautaire dérivé au regard des méthodes du droit international privé* (Bruylant/LGDJ 2005)). The reasons for this extensive use of the unilateral method in European law are debatable. On the one hand, regarding the wide margin of appreciation of the EU lawmaker, the principle of limited power cannot offer a final explanation. On the other hand, since party autonomy is not systematically excluded, EU legislation determining its own scope of application cannot be entirely assimilated to overriding mandatory norms. In the end, EU regulations and directives illustrate the spontaneous use of the unilateral method by a lawmaker thinking in functional terms.

STÉPHANIE FRANCQ

Preoccupied with achieving a specific social or economic goal, the EU lawmaker tends to provide indications on the international scope of its statute. The ECJ has shown how the scope of the agency directive, for instance, directly resulted from its purpose in the famous and controversial *Ingmar* case (Case C-381/98 *Ingmar GB Ltd v Eaton Leonard Technologies Inc* [2000] ECR I-9325, Opinion of G Léger I-9307) and established the link between the purpose and substantive content of a directive on the one hand and the interpretation of the provisions of its scope of application in the *Google* case on the other (Case C-131/12 *Google Spain SL and Google Inc v Agencia Española de Protección de Datos (AEPD) and Mario Costeja González* (13 May 2014) § 52, 53, 57). Since the reasons why the EU lawmaker uses unilateralism are valid for any law, the author considers that unilateralism should receive wider acceptance.

IV. Theoretical contemporary significance

As mentioned earlier, unilateralism continually questions the dominant multilateral system. The concerns carried out by unilateralism regarding the link between the scope and the aims of a statute, respect for foreign legislature's conceptions about the scope of their own laws, and consistency of private situations are echoed in contemporary discussions on the theory and methods of private international law (→ Private international law, methods of). Again, the following lines simply highlight how traces of unilateralism can be found in modern theoretical debates, rather than providing for a full account of those debates.

1. International economic law / Wirtschaftskollisionsrecht

In the field of international economic law, unilateralism is dominant (Jürgen Basedow, 'Wirtschaftskollisionsrecht – Theoretischer Versuch über die ordnungspolitischen Normen des Forumstaates' (1988) 52 RabelsZ 8). As the states became increasingly concerned with the potential negative impact of pure liberalism on individuals and on their own economic market, they developed regulatory intervention motivated by a political (often protective) purpose. Doing so, they naturally used the unilateralist method to assert the application of these regulations concerning for instance, competition, transport or employment.

The theory of international economic law is close to the French theory of the '*lois de police*' (overriding mandatory rules), since all the statutes which are considered as belonging to international economic law could be qualified as '*lois de police*'. But the theory of international economic law tends to allocate a field of law to unilateralism, in contrast to the theory of '*lois de police*' where the overriding mandatory norms are identified on a case-by-case basis.

2. Conflict-of-systems theory

At the intersection of multilateralism and unilateralism, the conflict-of-systems theory tends to identify a system of law under the auspices of which the situation should be treated. Therefore the designation covers not only the substantive law, but also the rules of conflict of jurisdiction (or authorities) and conflict of laws (Paolo Picone, 'La méthode de coordination entre ordres juridiques en droit international privé' (1999) 276 Rec. des Cours 229). Even if the designation operates on a multilateral basis, its object is the foreign system as a whole in consideration of the foreign approach to the appropriate treatment of the situation in private international law terms. Foreign law should not apply unless it is required to do so. Presenting similarities with *renvoi*, but with an extension to conflict of jurisdiction, the theory integrates part of the unilateral concern with respecting foreign systems, but also the stability of individual situations. In this respect, the theory tends to favour the recognition of situations formed by a competent authority (in regard to its own system).

3. The method of recognition

Under the influence of several important decisions of the ECJ and the ECHR (for instance: Case C-148/02 *Carlos Garcia Avello v État belge* [2003] ECR I-11613; Case C-353/06 *Stefan Grunkin and Dorothee Regina Paul* [2008] ECR I-7639; *Wagner and JMWL v Luxembourg* App No 76240/01 (ECHR, 28 June 2007); *Negrepontis-Giannisis v Greece* App No 56759/08 (ECHR, 3 May 2011)), it has been proposed to treat private situations that have been 'crystallized' (after the term of Pierre Mayer: Pierre Mayer, 'Les méthodes de la reconnaissance en droit international privé' in Marie-Noelle Jobard-Bachellier and

Pierre Mayer, *Le droit international privé: esprit et méthodes – Mélanges en l'honneur de Paul Lagarde* (Dalloz 2005) 547, 562) in a foreign legal system in the same way as judgments rather than testing their validity under the law designated by the conflict-of-law rules of the forum. Such 'foreign' situations would, accordingly, be automatically recognized in the forum unless they contravene specific non-recognition grounds (that would need to be identified). The so-called method of recognition (Paul Lagarde, *La reconnaissance des situations en droit international privé: actes du colloque international de la Haye du 18 janvier 2013* (Pédone 2013)) presents similarities with the doctrine of vested rights even though the respect of vested rights was thought of as the object of a multilateral conflict rule. Like the conflict-of-systems theory, it echoes unilateralism in its search for the respect of stability of individual situations and in the trust placed in the foreign system. It is for the foreign system to solve the question of the applicable law and once it has done so, the forum in its recognition process will not revise this choice, nor project its own identification of the applicable law on a situation already existing and established in the foreign system.

4. The natural role of unilateralism

In contemporary doctrine, several authors argue for a more coherent integration of the unilateralist doctrine. These approaches consider it necessary to leave some room (the extent of which depends on the author) to unilateralism, in the theoretical conception of private international law and/or at the more practical level of conceiving conflict rules (in addition to Francq, see: Didier Boden, 'Le pluralisme juridique en droit international privé' (2005) 49 A.P.D. 275–316; Andreas Bucher, 'La dimension sociale du droit international privé' (2009) 341 Rec. des Cours 9–526; Andreas Bucher 'Vers l'adoption de la méthode des intérêts ? Réflexions à la lumière des codifications récentes', *Travaux du Comité français de droit international privé 1994–1995* (Pedone 1996) 209–37; Louis d'Avout, *Sur les solutions du conflit de lois en droit des biens* (Economica 2006); Gian Paolo Romano, *L'unilateralismo nel diritto internazionale privato moderno* (Schulthess 2014); Symeon C Symeonides, 'Accommodative Unilateralism as a Starting Premise in Choice of Law' in Hans-Eric Rasmussen-Bonne, Richard Freer, Wolfgang Lüke and Wolfgang Weitnauer (eds), *Balancing of Interests: Liber Amicorum Peter Hay zum 70. Geburtstag* (Verlag Recht und Wirtschaft 2005) 417).

STÉPHANIE FRANCQ

Literature

Brainerd Currie, *Selected Essays on the Conflict of Laws* (Duke University Press 1963); Phocion Francescakis, 'Quelques précisions sur les lois d'application immédiate et leur rapports avec les règles de conflit de lois' [1966] Rev.crit.DIP 1; Stéphanie Francq, *L'applicabilité du droit communautaire dérivé au regard des méthodes du droit international privé* (Bruylant/LGDJ 2005); Pierre Gothot, 'Le renouveau de la tendance unilatéraliste' (1971) 60 Rev.crit.DIP 1, 209, 415; Pierre Mayer, 'Les lois de police étrangères' [1981] J.Dr. Int'l 278; Jean Paulin Niboyet, *Travaux de la commission de réforme du Code civil, 1948–1949* (Sirey 1950); Alexander Niedner, *Einführungsgesetz vom 18.8.1896 (Kommentar)* (2nd edn, Heyman 1901); Alexandre Pilenko, 'Droit spatial et droit international privé' [1954] *Jus Gentium* 1; Antoine Pillet, *Principes de droit international privé* (Pedone 1903); Rolando Quadri, *Lezione di diritto internazionale privato* (5th edn, Liguori 1969); Santi Romano, *Il Ordinamente giuridico* (2nd edn, GC Sansoni 1946; French translation, 2nd edn, Dalloz 2002); Julius Schnell, 'Über die Zuständigkeit zum Erlaß von gesetzlichen Vorschriften über die raümliche Herrschaft der Rechtsnormen' [1895] Zeitschr Int Priv & StrafR 337; Symeon C Symeonides, 'The American Choice-of-Law Revolution in the Courts: Today or Tomorrow' (2003) 298 Rec. des Cours 1; Gérard Vivier, 'Le caractère bilatéral des règles de conflit' [1953] Rev.crit.DIP 655, [1954] 73; Rudolf Wiethölter, *Einseitige Kollisionsnormen als Grundlage des Internationalen Privatrechts* (Walter de Gruyter & Co 1956).

Unitary intellectual property rights and jurisdiction

I. Concept

For the concepts and characteristics of unitary rights as well as the respective choice-of-law provisions, see → Unitary intellectual property rights and private international law. The following entry presents the jurisdictional rules for EU unitary intellectual property rights.

II. Unitary rights and jurisdiction

1. Community trade mark, Community design, Community plant variety right

The Community Trade Mark Regulation (Council Regulation (EC) No 207/2009 of 26 February on the Community trade mark, [2009] OJ L 78/1) and the Community Design Regulation (Council Regulation (EC) No 6/2002 of 12 December 2001 on Community designs, [2002] OJ L 3/1) concentrate jurisdiction in respect of infringement and validity of the respective unitary rights (art 96 Community Trade Mark Regulation; art 82 Community Design Regulation) in a limited number of national courts which the Member States have designated as 'Community trade mark (design) courts' (art 95 Community Trade Mark Regulation; art 81 Community Design Regulation). For the jurisdiction of these courts, the Community Trade Mark Regulation and the Community Design Regulation establish rules which as *leges speciales* (ECJ Case C-360/12 *Coty Germany GmbH v First Note Perfumes NV*, ECLI:EU:2014:1318, para 27) largely pre-empt application of the general regime of the Brussels I Regulation (recast) (Regulation (EU) No 1215/2012 of the European Parliament and of the Council of 12 December 2012 on jurisdiction and the recognition and enforcement of judgments in civil and commercial matters, [2012] OJ L 351/1; → Brussels I (Convention and Regulation)) (art 94(2) Community Trade Mark Regulation; art 79(2) Community Design Regulation). Moreover, the jurisdictional rules of the Community rights regulations, unlike the Brussels rules, also apply to third-state domiciled defendants, as the reference to national law in art 6 Brussels I Regulation (recast) is excluded (art 94(2)(a) Community Trade Mark Regulation; art 79(2)(a) Community Design Regulation). For issues other than infringement and validity of the Community unitary rights, the Brussels I Regulation (recast) remains largely unaffected (see arts 106–7, 94(1) Community Trade Mark Regulation; arts 93–4, 79(1) Community Design Regulation and art 80 Brussels I Regulation (recast); for enforcement and insolvency see also arts 20(2), 21 Community Trade Mark Regulation and arts 30(2); 31 Community Design Regulation).

In their structure, the jurisdictional rules of the Community unitary rights regulations resemble the Brussels I regime, but with certain significant differences. General jurisdiction, for example, is not only vested in the courts of the defendant's domicile (defined as in the Brussels I Regulation; art 94(1) Community Trade Mark Regulation; art 79(1) Community Design Regulation; art 102(3) Community Plant Regulation (Council Regulation (EC) No 2100/94 of 27 July 1994 on Community plant variety rights [1994] OJ L 227/1)), but also in the courts of the defendant's establishment in the EU (art 97(1) Community Trade Mark Regulation; art 82(1) Community Design Regulation; art 101(2)(a) Community Plant Regulation) and, for defendants not domiciled or established in the EU, in the courts of the plaintiff's domicile or establishment in the EU (art 97(2) Community Trade Mark Regulation; art 82(2) Community Design Regulation; art 101(2)(b) Community Plant Regulation), or failing that, in the courts of the Member State where the respective Harmonization Office has its seat (art 97(3) Community Trade Mark Regulation; art 82(3) Community Design Regulation: Alicante, Spain; art 101(2)(c) Community Plant Regulation: Angers, France). Such broad general jurisdiction may be explained by the desire to preserve jurisdiction for Community unitary rights disputes in EU courts, even if the alleged infringer and even if both parties are not domiciled or established in the EU.

Another important ground of jurisdiction is jurisdiction based on agreement or appearance in an EU court for which the Community unitary rights regulations refer to the respective Brussels I rules (art 25, 26 Brussels I Regulation (recast)) or, in case of the Community Plant Regulation, Lugano provisions (art 102(2) Community Plant Regulation). In order to preserve the purpose of concentration of Community Trade Mark (and Design) actions to specialized courts, the Community Trade Mark Regulation and the Community Design Regulation restrict prorogation to courts defined by the Member States as Community Trade Mark (or Design) courts (art 97(4) Community Trade Mark Regulation; art 82(4) Community Design Regulation; see Austrian Federal Court of Justice, 11 December 2007 [2009] GRUR Int. 74, 75, under para 2.2, *Personal Shop*).

A further venue is jurisdiction 'in the courts of the Member State in which the act of infringement has been committed or threatened' (art 97(5) Community Trade Mark Regulation; art 82(5) Community Design Regulation) or, in the Community Plant Regulation, 'in the courts for the place where the harmful event occurred' (art 101(3) Community Plant Regulation). In contrast to the term 'place where the harmful event occurred' in art 7(2) Brussels I Regulation (recast) and art 101(3) Community Plant Regulation, the term 'act of infringement' in art 97(5) Community Trade Mark Regulation; art 82(5) Community Design Regulation does not refer both to the place of the event giving rise to the damage and the place where the damage occurred. Rather, the Court has held that the concept of 'act of infringement' 'relates to active conduct on the part of the person causing that infringement. Therefore, the linking factor provided for by that provision refers to the Member State where the act giving rise to the alleged infringement occurred or may occur, not the Member State where that infringement produces its effects' (ECJ Case C-360/12 *Coty Germany GmbH v First Note Perfumes NV*, ECLI:EU:2014:1318 at [34], [37]). Consequently, if an allegedly infringing product is sold and delivered in Member State A, followed by a resale by the purchaser in another Member State B, art 97(5) Community Trade Mark Regulation / art 82(5) Community Design Regulation do not grant jurisdiction for an infringement action against an original seller who did not itself act in the Member State B where the court seized is situated (ECJ Case C-360/12 *Coty Germany GmbH v First Note Perfumes NV*, ECLI:EU:2014:1318, para 38).

As concerns the scope, jurisdiction based on domicile or establishment and agreement or appearance encompasses all acts of infringement committed in the territory of any Member State (art 98(1) Community Trade Mark Regulation; art 84(1) Community Design Regulation; art 101(2) final sentence Community Plant Regulation), whereas jurisdiction at the 'act of infringement' (or place where the harmful event occurred') excludes actions for a declaration of non-infringement and applies only 'in respect of acts committed or threatened within the territory of the Member State in which that court is situated' (art 98(2) Community Trade Mark Regulation; art 84(2) Community Design Regulation; art 101(3) 2nd sentence Community Plant Regulation).

Finally, the Community Trade Mark Regulation and Community Design Regulation allow application of certain special grounds of jurisdiction found in the Brussels I Regulation recast (in particular art 8(1) Brussels I Regulation (recast) on joint defendants, for a list see art 94(1) Community Trade Mark Regulation; art 79(1) Community Design Regulation), and permit → provisional measures to be granted also by courts other than Community Trade Mark (Design) courts (art 103(1) Community Trade Mark Regulation; art 90(1) Community Design Regulation). However, only provisional measures granted by courts competent under art 97(1)–(4) Community Trade Mark Regulation / art 82(1)–(4) Community Design Regulation are eligible for cross-border recognition and enforcement in all EU Member States (art 103(2) Community Trade Mark Regulation; art 90(3) Community Design Regulation), whereas provisional measures based on other grounds of jurisdiction are limited to the territory of the state to which the rendering court belongs.

For coordination of proceedings, the unitary rights regulations include provisions which are limited to a conflict between infringement and validity proceedings (art 104 Community Trade Mark Regulation; art 91 Community Design Regulation; art 106 Community Plant Regulation; on the interpretation of 'special grounds' to continue infringement proceedings in art 104 Community Trade Mark Regulation see *Starbucks (UK) Ltd v British Sky Broadcasting Group plc; EMI (IP) Ltd v British Sky Broadcasting Group plc* [2012] EWCA Civ 1201, [102]–[112]), or infringement actions involving the same cause of action between the same parties, where one court is seized on the basis of a Community unitary right and the other is seized on the basis of a parallel national trade mark or design (art 109, Recital (17) Community Trade Mark Regulation; art 95 Community Design Regulation; on the limitation to 'infringement proceedings' see *Prudential Assurance v Prudential Insurance* [2003] EWCA Civ 327, [44–5], *contra* James Fawcett and Paul Torremans, *Intellectual Property and Private international law* (2nd edn, OUP 2011) para 8.71). For other scenarios which the *lis pendens* provisions (→ *Lis alibi pendens*) of the unitary rights regulations do not cover, it would seem appropriate to apply the corresponding provisions of the Brussels I Regulation (recast) (art 29, 30 Brussels I Regulation (recast); Austrian Federal Court of Justice, 28 September 2006 [2007] GRURInt. 433, 434 under para 4.1, *Cilgin Boga* = [2008] IIC 245).

2. European patents and European patents with unitary effect

Whereas the jurisdictional rules of the Community Trade Mark Regulation, the Community Design Regulation and the Community Plant Regulation deviate in some respects from the general rules of the Brussels regime, the general rules of European civil procedure continue to apply to European patents, subject only to a minor exception for claims for grant of a European patent, for which the Protocol on Jurisdiction and the Recognition of Decisions in respect of the Right to the Grant of a European Patent ((Protocol on Jurisdiction and Recognition) of 5 October 1973, available at <www.epo.org>) applies.

This situation will change significantly once the 'European Patent Package' consisting of the UPC Agreement (Agreement of 19 February 2013 on a Unified Patent Court, [2013] OJ C 175/1), the Unitary Patent Regulation (Regulation (EU) No 1257/2012 of the European Parliament and of the Council of 17 December 2012 implementing enhanced cooperation in the area of the creation of unitary patent protection, [2012] OJ L 361/1) and the Translation Regulation (Council Regulation (EU) No 1260/2012 of 17 December 2012 implementing enhanced cooperation in the area of the creation of unitary patent protection with regard to the applicable translation arrangements, [2012] OJ L 361/89) enters into force (see also → Unitary intellectual property rights and private international law). The Patent Package is intended to complement the existing unified granting procedure under the European Patent Convention (Convention on the Grant of European Patents of 5 October 1973 as revised by the Act revising Article 63 EPC of 17 December 1991 and the Act revising the EPC of 29 November 2000) by establishing a new Unified Patent Court (UPC) with multinational panels (art 8 UPC Agreement) as a court common to all contracting Member States (art 1, 2nd sentence UPC Agreement). Subject to a possible opt-out in the seven-year transitional period (art 83(1), (3) UPC Agreement), the Patent Package will bring about two core changes, namely the creation of a European patent with unitary effect (by the Unitary Patent Regulation) and the concentration of infringement litigation over simple European (European Patent Convention-granted) patents and over European patents with unitary effect in a single Unified Patent Court with its own substantive and procedural provisions (UPC Agreement; Statute of the Unified Patent Court, [2013] OJ C 175/29; Rules of Procedure of the Unified Patent Court).

This new common court will consist of a Court of First Instance, a Court of Appeal in Luxembourg and a Registry at the seat of the Court of Appeal (art 6 UPC Agreement). The Court of First Instance will be decentralized and consist of a central division in Paris with branches in London and Munich, as well as local and regional divisions. Local divisions may be established upon request by each contracting state, with, depending on the number of patent cases, up to four local divisions per contracting state. Regional divisions may be set up by two or more contracting states (for details see art 7 UPC Agreement). The division of competence between the central division and the local or regional divisions is spelled out in art 33 UPC Agreement.

For issues of international jurisdiction, the relationship between the new instruments of the Patent Package and the general corpus of EU civil procedure is simplified by the fact that the Unitary Patent Regulation does not include jurisdictional provisions. Rather, art 31 UPC Agreement makes clear that '[t]he international jurisdiction of the [Unified Patent] Court shall be established in accordance with Regulation (EU) No. 1215/2012 or, where applicable, on the basis of the Convention on jurisdiction and the recognition and enforcement of judgments in civil and commercial matters (Lugano Convention)', while the 'internal allocation of proceedings' among the divisions of the Unified Patent Court is governed by art 33 UPC Agreement (Recital (5) Regulation 542/2014 (Regulation (EU) No 542/2014 of the European Parliament and of the Council of 15 May 2014 amending Regulation (EU) No 1215/2012 as regards the rules to be applied with respect to the Unified Patent Court and the Benelux Court of Justice, [2014] OJ L 163/1)).

Even if the Brussels I Regulation (recast) thus governs international jurisdiction for European patents and European patents with a unitary character, the adoption of the Patent Package made certain changes in the Brussels framework inevitable (see art 89(1) UPC Agreement). These changes were implemented by Regulation 542/2014, which has inserted four new arts as arts 71a–71d into the Brussels I Regulation (recast). Article 71a(1) Brussels I Regulation (recast) makes clear that a 'court common to several Member States', such as the Unified Patent Court, 'shall be deemed to be a court of a Member State when, pursuant to the instrument establishing it, such a common court exercises jurisdiction in matters falling within the scope of this Regulation'. This change was considered necessary as the internal allocation of jurisdiction within the different divisions of the Unified Patent Court may lead to jurisdiction in a UPC Agreement contracting state different from the state which would have jurisdiction under the Brussels I Regulation (recast) (European Commission, 'Proposal of 26 July 2013 for a Regulation of the European Parliament and of the Council amending Regulation (EU) No 1215/2012 on jurisdiction and the recognition and enforcement of judgments in civil and commercial matters' COM(2013) 554 final, pp 4–5; for doubts as to the compatibility with the as yet unamended → Lugano Convention see Pedro de Miguel Asensio, 'Regulation (EU) No. 542/2014 and the International Jurisdiction of the Unified Patent Court' [2014] IIC 868, 873–4).

The jurisdiction of the Unified Patent Court as a common court is then determined by art 71b Brussels I Regulation (recast). For defendants domiciled in an EU Member State, the Unified Patent Court has jurisdiction where, under the Brussels I Regulation (recast) (eg arts 4, 24(4), 25, 26 Brussels I Regulation (recast)), 'the courts of a Member State party to the instrument establishing the common court would have jurisdiction in a matter governed by that instrument' (art 71b(1) Brussels I Regulation (recast)). For defendants not domiciled in an EU Member State, for which the Brussels I Regulation (recast) in general does not apply and only exceptionally confers jurisdiction (eg under arts 24(4), 25 Brussels I Regulation (recast)), art 71b(2) Brussels I Regulation (recast) adds that ch II of the Brussels I Regulation (recast) 'shall apply as appropriate regardless of the defendant's domicile'. Moreover, '[a]pplication may be made to a common court for provisional, including protective, measures even if the courts of a third State have jurisdiction as to the substance of the matter'. Article 71b(2) thus provides for a universal application of the Brussels regime also in relation to defendants from third states, a proposal which failed in the reform of the general rules. Finally, for defendants not domiciled in an EU Member State, art 71b(3) Brussels I Regulation (recast) establishes a supplementary forum which is different from the *forum actoris* found in the Community Trade Mark, Design and Plant Variety Regulations: art 71b(3) Brussels I Regulation (recast) provides that 'where a common court has jurisdiction over a defendant under point 2 [ie under ch II of the Brussels I Regulation (recast)] in a dispute relating to an infringement of a European Patent giving rise to damage within the Union, that court may also exercise jurisdiction in relation to damage arising outside the Union from such an infringement'. However, '[s]uch jurisdiction may only be established if property belonging to the defendant is located in any Member State party to the instrument establishing the common court, and the dispute has a sufficient connection with any such Member State'. Recital (7) Brussels I Regulation (recast) explains when such a 'sufficient connection' may be established, 'for example because the claimant is domiciled there or the evidence relating to the dispute is available there'. Moreover, 'in establishing its jurisdiction, the common court should have regard to the value of the property in question, which should not be insignificant and which should be such as to make it possible to enforce the judgment, at least in part, in the Member States parties to the instrument establishing the common court'. This new supplementary forum, which was probably included to extend jurisdiction of the Unified Patent Court to infringements outside the EU and to make the Court a more patentee-friendly venue (Pedro de Miguel Asensio, 'Regulation (EU) No. 542/2014 and the International Jurisdiction of the Unified Patent Court' [2014] IIC 868, 879), goes beyond tort jurisdiction under art 7(2) Brussels I Regulation (recast) (which already establishes jurisdiction for infringements in all Member States if the event giving rise to the damage occurred in the forum state, see ECJ Case C-523/10 *Wintersteiger AG v Products 4U Sondermaschinenbau GmbH*, ECLI:EU:C:2012:220 para 30). Rather, similar to an objective joinder provision, on condition that the defendant has sufficient assets (unrelated to the infringement) in the forum state, art 71b(3) Brussels I Regulation (recast) extends the jurisdiction of the Unified Patent Court 'to damage arising outside the Union from such an infringement'. The wording of this provision could be interpreted in two ways. On the one hand, one might argue that the provision aims at extending jurisdiction to subsequent (economic) damage arising outside the EU resulting from an infringement happening inside the EU. However, such an understanding would be contrary to the interpretation of damage in art 7(2) Brussels

I Regulation (recast), for which the ECJ has held that the 'place where the damage occurred' is (only) the country of registration (for registered rights, ECJ Case C-523/10 *Wintersteiger AG v Products 4U Sondermaschinenbau GmbH*, ECLI:EU:C:2012:220, paras 27–9), and in particular does not 'encompass any place where the adverse consequences can be felt of an event which has already caused damage actually arising elsewhere' (ECJ Case C-364/93 *Antonio Marinari v Lloyds Bank plc and Zubaidi Trading Company* [1995] ECR I-2719, para 14). Accordingly, it is more likely that art 71b(3) Brussels I Regulation (recast) aims at extending jurisdiction of the Unified Patent Court to infringements of European patents occurring outside the EU. In other words, provided that the Unified Patent Court has jurisdiction because an EPC patent granted for a UPC contracting state has been infringed, art 71b(3) Brussels I Regulation seems to extend this jurisdiction also to infringements of parallel EPC patents granted for EPC contracting states outside the EU (for a criticism as exorbitant see Pedro de Miguel Asensio, 'Regulation (EU) No. 542/2014 and the International Jurisdiction of the Unified Patent Court' [2014] IIC 868, 879–83; for a more positive view Paul Torremans, 'An International Perspective II: A View from Private international law' in Justine Pila and Christopher Wadlow (eds), *The Unitary EU Patent System* (Hart Publishing 2015) 161, 173–4).

Moreover, art 71c Brussels I Regulation (recast) extends the application of the *lis pendens* provisions of the Brussels I Regulation (recast) (arts 29–32) to proceedings brought in the Unified Patent Court and in another Member State court. Finally, art 71d Brussels I Regulation (recast) renders the Brussels I recognition and enforcement provisions applicable to the recognition and enforcement of 'judgments given by a common court which are to be recognized and enforced in a Member State not party to the instrument establishing the common court' (for Member States party to the instrument, art 82 UPC Agreement applies; see art 71d, 2nd sentence Brussels I Regulation (recast)), and *vice versa* to 'judgments given by the courts of a Member State not party to the instrument establishing the common court which are to be recognised and enforced in a Member State party to that instrument'.

CHRISTIAN HEINZE

Literature

See entry → Unitary intellectual property rights and private international law.

Unitary intellectual property rights and private international law

I. Concept

1. EU unitary intellectual property rights

The late 20th century saw the rise of regional organizations of economic and political integration, most prominently the European Union, driven, not exclusively but strongly, by the desire to integrate national markets into a larger economic area. In this process of integration towards a single market, certain national rights, in particular intellectual property rights, were perceived as a 'barrier of territoriality', which could neither be overcome under the guarantee of the free movement of goods and services of the EU Treaties (see art 36 TFEU (The Treaty on the Functioning of the European Union (consolidated version), [2012] OJ C 326/47)) nor 'be removed by approximation of laws' (Recital (4) Community Trade Mark Regulation (Council Regulation (EC) No 207/2009 of 26 February on the Community trade mark, [2009] OJ L 78/1); Jürgen Basedow 'The Law of Open Societies: Private Ordering and Public Regulation of International Relations' (2012) 360 Rec. des Cours 11, 225 para 283: 'territorial confinement of intellectual property rights as such is considered as flowing from the territorial limitation of sovereignty'). Even under fully harmonized national intellectual property laws, it is possible that a certain invention or sign is protected only in some Member States of the integrated market (eg due to registration only in certain states). The EU sought to solve this problem by creation of rights with a unitary character 'to which uniform protection is given and which produce their effect throughout the entire area of the Community' (Recital (3) Community Trade Mark Regulation). These rights can be obtained 'by means of one procedural system' and 'shall have equal effect throughout the Community', ie they 'shall not be registered, transferred or surrendered or be the subject of a decision revoking the rights of the proprietor or declaring it invalid, nor shall its use be prohibited, save in respect of the whole Community' (art 1(2), Recital (3) Community Trade Mark Regulation; see also art 2 Community Plant Regulation (Council Regulation (EC) No 2100/94 of 27 July 1994 on Community plant variety rights [1994] OJ L 227/1); art 1(3), Recitals (4) and (5) Community Design Regulation (Council Regulation (EC) No 6/2002 of 12 December 2001 on Community designs, [2002] OJ L 3/1) and art 3(2), Recital (7) Unitary Patent Regulation (Regulation (EU) No 1257/2012 of the European Parliament and of the Council of 17 December 2012 implementing enhanced cooperation in the area of the creation of unitary patent protection, [2012] OJ L 361/1)). The first of these unitary rights were the Community Trade Mark (created under Council Regulation (EC) No 40/94 of 20 December 1993 on the Community trade mark, [1994] OJ L 11/1, now Community Trade Mark Regulation) and the Community Plant Variety Right (created under Community Plant Regulation). More recent unitary rights are the Community Design (created under Community Design Regulation), and most recently the Unitary Patent (created under the Unitary Patent Regulation, see also Regulation 1260/2012 (Council Regulation (EU) No 1260/2012 of 17 December 2012 implementing enhanced cooperation in the area of the creation of unitary patent protection with regard to the applicable translation arrangements, [2012] OJ L 361/89)). Depending on the understanding of geographical indications, one may also include in this list designations of origin and geographical indications registered on the EU level (see Recital (24) and art 13 Regulation 1151/2012 (Regulation (EU) No 1151/2012 of the European Parliament and of the Council of 21 November 2012 on quality schemes for agricultural products and foodstuffs, [2012] OJ L 343/1)). Early predecessors to the EU unitary rights regimes were the Convention Benelux en matière de marques de produits du 19 mars 1962 and the Convention Benelux en matière de dessins ou modèles du 25 octobre 1966, which have been superseded by the Convention Benelux en matière de propriété intellectuelle (Marques et dessins ou modèles) or Benelux-Verdrag inzake de intellectuele eigendom (merken en tekeningen of modellen) of 2006 (available at <www.wipo.int>). These Conventions create a single and indivisible trade mark for the entire territory of → Belgium, the → Netherlands and → Luxembourg (see art 2.25(3) and (4), art 2.31(2)(b), art 2.9(1), art 3.21(4) and art 3.25(2)(b) Convention Benelux en matière de propriété intellectuelle (Marques et dessins ou modèles)).

2. Characteristics of unitary rights

On the basis of the existing unitary rights regimes in the EU, it is possible to identify essentially two common traits which seem to be characteristic of a unitary right (for a definition see also Colin Birss, 'Unitary Rights and Judicial Respect in the EU: "Bringing Cool Back"' (2013) 3 *Queen Mary Journal of Intellectual Property Law* 195, 196: 'one piece of property has supranational effect across part or all of the territory of Europe'). First, for registered rights it is essential that the right be obtained through a single granting procedure administered by a single agency (see arts 25 *et seq* Community Trade Mark Regulation; arts 35 *et seq* Community Design Regulation: Office for Harmonisation in the Internal Market; arts 49 *et seq* Community Plant Regulation: Community Plant Variety Office; art 9 and Recitals (5), (7) Unitary Patent Regulation: European Patent Office (EPO); for gaps in the administrative procedure law see the reference to 'principles of procedural law generally recognised in the Member States' in art 83 Community Trade Mark Regulation; art 68 Community Design Regulation; art 81(1) Community Plant Regulation). However, as the example of the simple European patent granted by the European Patent Office shows, this alone will not be sufficient to justify talk of a unitary right.

As a second element, it is necessary that the right has 'equal effect' throughout the entire territory of the supranational organization in question. Equal effect, in turn, has two facets. One element of equal effect concerns the existence of the right and its use as a piece of property, so that a unitary right can only be registered, transferred, surrendered, revoked, declared invalid or its use be prohibited for the entire territory of the supranational organization (art 1(2) Community Trade Mark Regulation; ECJ Case C-235/09 *DHL Express France v Chronopost* [2009] ECR I-2801, paras 39–41; art 1(3) Community Design Regulation; art 2 Community Plant Regulation; art 3(2) Unitary Patent Regulation). It is thus not possible to split the right by transferring merely the right for a specific sub-division (eg one country) of the supranational organization. The unitary character extends also to proprietary aspects of such rights. A unitary intellectual property right is subject in its entirety and for the whole EU area to the same law, be it the proprietary provisions of the Regulations or a national law as determined by a conflict rule (art 16(1) Community Trade Mark Regulation: '[u]nless Articles 17 to 24 provide otherwise, a Community trade mark as an object of property shall be dealt with in its entirety and for the whole area of the Community, as a national trade mark . . .'; see also art 27(1) Community Design Regulation and art 22(1) Community Plant Regulation; art 7(1) Unitary Patent Regulation). As a consequence of the unitary character of the right, decisions regarding validity and infringement must in principle have effect in the entire area of the supranational organization in question (for certain exceptions as concerns the uniform scope of protection see next paragraph), and contradictory judgments in actions should be avoided which involve the same acts and the same parties and which are brought on the basis of a Community trade mark and parallel national trade marks (Recitals (15) and (16) Community Trade Mark Regulation). However, equal effect as concerns the existence of the right does not extend to licences which – as for national rights – may still be granted for only part of the territory of protection (art 22(1) Community Trade Mark Regulation; art 32(1) Community Design Regulation; art 27(1) Community Plant Regulation; art 3(2) Unitary Patent Regulation).

The second facet of unitary effect concerns its scope of protection. In general, the unitary right must grant uniform protection, ie the scope of protection, the prohibited acts and the limitations and exceptions must, in principle, be the same in the entire territory where the unitary right is in force (arts 9–13, 14(1) Community Trade Mark Regulation: 'effects of Community trade marks shall be governed solely by the provisions of this Regulation'; arts 19–23 Community Design Regulation; arts 13–18 Community Plant Regulation). For political reasons, namely due to concerns about an involvement of the → Court of Justice of the European Union (CJEU) in the interpretation of substantive patent law, a different regime was adopted for the European patent with unitary effect. The extent of protection of such a right, in particular the interpretation of patent claims, will, as it is a patent granted under the European Patent Convention (Convention on the Grant of European Patents (European Patent Convention) of 5 October 1973 as revised by the Act revising Article 63 EPC of 17 December 1991 and the Act revising the EPC of 29 November 2000) be determined by art 69 European Patent Convention. For the acts against which the patent provides protection and its limitations, art 5(2) Unitary Patent Regulation states that these 'shall be uniform in all participating Member States in which the patent has unitary effect'. However, the provisions on scope and limitations of the European patent with unitary effect, except for exhaustion (art 6 Unitary Patent Regulation), are not included in the Unitary Patent Regulation itself. Rather, according to art 5(3) Unitary Patent Regulation,

> [t]he acts against which the patent provides protection . . . and the applicable limitations shall be those defined by the law applied to European patents with unitary effect in the participating Member State whose national law is applicable to the European patent with unitary effect as an object of property in accordance with Article 7.

Thus, art 5(3) and art 7 Unitary Patent Regulation refer to the national law of the participating Member States, which is harmonized by an international convention, the UPC Agreement (Agreement of 19 February 2013 on a Unified Patent Court, [2013] OJ C 175/1), in particular its arts 25–9 on the rights conferred by a patent and its limitations. All in all, it may thus be summarized that the unitary effect in case of the EU patent is achieved by reference not to EU law, but to national law as harmonized by two international conventions (European Patent Convention, UPC Agreement) and interpreted by a court common to all participating Member States (the Unified Patent Court established under the UPC Agreement).

3. Limits of unitary effect

The principle of uniform protection, however, is subject to certain limits. An important institutional limitation stems from the fact that, except for the new European patent with unitary effect, for which a new Unified Patent Court has been created, all EU unitary rights have to be litigated and enforced in national courts. Even if the CJEU may guide on the uniform interpretation of the respective EU texts under art 267 TFEU, the risk of divergent interpretation and application is necessarily higher than in an integrated court system of a single state. Moreover, on the level of substantive law, uniform protection covers only actions based on the intellectual property right itself, whereas parallel actions based on national law of civil liability and unfair competition (→ Competition, unfair) are still governed by national law and thus outside the uniform effect (see art 14(2) Community Trade Mark Regulation; art 96(1) Community Design Regulation). Also, particularly in trade mark law, uniform protection of the unitary right 'may not extend beyond what that right allows its proprietor to do in order to protect his trade mark, that is, to prohibit only uses which are liable to affect the functions of the trade mark' (ECJ Case C-235/09 *DHL Express France v Chronopost* [2009] ECR I-2801, para 47). As a consequence, if a court hearing an infringement action finds that the acts of infringement are limited to a single Member State, for example because a likelihood of confusion arises for linguistic reasons only in one Member State or because the plaintiff has restricted the territorial scope of its action, then the court 'must limit the territorial scope of the prohibition which it issues' (ECJ Case C-235/09 *DHL Express France v Chronopost* [2009] ECR I-2801, para 48). Finally, unitary effect of a Community right does not imply that the requirements for protection and preservation of the right are fulfilled in all parts of the entire Community. For example, it is sufficient to establish a trade mark with a 'reputation in the Community' in the sense of art 9(1)(c) Community Trade Mark Regulation (protection of well-known trade marks) if the trade mark 'has a reputation in a substantial part of the territory of the Community' which has been held to be fulfilled if a trade mark has reputation throughout the territory of one Member State (→ Austria) (ECJ C-301/07 *Pago International GmbH v Tirolmilch registrierte Genossenschaft mbH* [2009] ECR I-9429, paras 27-9; see also first question in Case C-125/14 *Iron & Smith Kft v Unilever NV*, ECLI:EU:C:2015:195 on the question whether the reputation has to be enjoyed in the state in which the protection of the mark is relied upon). Similarly, if a trade mark is descriptive and lacks distinctive character in one linguistic area, the trade mark may acquire distinctive character through use if in that linguistic area 'the relevant class of persons, or at least a significant proportion thereof, identifies the product or service in question as originating from a particular undertaking because of the trade mark' (ECJ C-108/05 *Bovemij Verzekeringen NV v Benelux-Merkenbureau* [2006] ECR I-7605, para 27; see also ECJ C-98/11 P *Chocoladefabriken Lindt & Sprüngli AG v Office for Harmonisation in the Internal Market (Trade Marks and Designs) (OHIM)*, ECLI:EU:C:2012:307, para 62). On the other hand, the Court has held 'that the territorial borders of the Member States should be disregarded in the assessment of whether a trade mark has been put to' genuine use in the Community 'within the meaning of' art 15(1) Community Trade Mark Regulation (ECJ C-149/11 *Leno Merken BV v Hagelkruis Beheer BV*, ECLI:EU:C:2012:816, para 57). This means that genuine use in only one Member State is not necessarily sufficient for genuine use of the Community Trade Mark, but rather the Community mark must be 'used in accordance with its essential function and for the purpose of maintaining or creating market share within the Community for the goods or services covered by it', which is for the national court to assess, 'taking account of all the relevant facts and circumstances, including the characteristics of the market concerned, the nature of the goods or services protected by the trade mark and the territorial extent and the scale of the use as well as its frequency and regularity' (ECJ C-149/11 *Leno Merken BV v Hagelkruis Beheer BV*, ECLI:EU:C:2012:816, para 58).

Lastly, uniform protection does not imply full uniformity of → remedies and procedure in infringement proceedings. Rather, the unitary rights regulations refer for most aspects of remedies (arts 101(2), 102(2) Community Trade Mark Regulation; arts 89(1)(d), 88(2) Community Design Regulation; art 97(1), (2) Community Plant Regulation) and procedure (art 101(3) Community Trade Mark Regulation; art 88(3) Community Design Regulation; art 103 Community Plant Regulation) to the law of the Member States including their rules of private international law. A different stance is taken for the unitary patent where remedies and procedure of the Unified Patent Court are largely governed by the provisions of the UPC Agreement (see arts 59-72 UPC Agreement). As a final point, it may be mentioned that all aspects which go beyond the intellectual property right as such are outside the scope of unification, in particular → contractual obligations between parties of licensing or transfer contracts.

CHRISTIAN HEINZE

4. Unitary rights outside the EU

Outside Europe, regional integration has progressed at a slower pace. Nevertheless, for some regional organizations it is debatable whether they have created rights which go beyond mere harmonization of national laws and may already be considered as unitary rights. The African Organization for Intellectual Property (OAPI), for example, is sometimes said to have established a 'unitary system for the protection of intellectual property rights effective in all 17 OAPI member states' which is based on the Treaty of Bangui (Treaty of Bangui of 2 March 1977 Establishing the African Intellectual Property Organization (OAPI), available at <www.wipo.int>), in particular on the annexes to this Treaty (Marius Schneider and Vanessa Ferguson, 'Cross-border Enforcement of Intellectual Property Rights: Africa' in Paul Torremans (ed), *Research Handbook on Cross-border Enforcement of Intellectual Property* (Edward Elgar 2014) 329, 347). In particular, the OAPI serves as a national industrial property service for all participating states (art 2(2) Treaty of Bangui), intellectual property rights such as patents, utility models etc 'shall produce the [uniform] effects provided for in this Agreement and its Annexes' (art 8(4) Treaty of Bangui) and '[f]inal legal decisions relating to the validity of titles and rendered in one Member State under the provisions of Annexes I to X of this Agreement shall be binding on all other member States' (art 18 Treaty of Bangui).

The finding of a truly unitary right, however, stands in a certain tension with art 3(1) of the Treaty of Bangui, which suggests that the Treaty adheres to the traditional concept of harmonized but independent national rights ('Rights relating to the fields of intellectual property, as provided for in the Annexes to this Agreement, shall be independent national rights subject to the legislation of each of the member States in which they have effect', see also [1982] IIC 685, 686: 'A patent grant by the Organization creates a bundle of national rights'; Philippe Baechtold, Tomoko Miyamoto and Thomas Henninger, 'International Patent Law: Principles, Major Instruments and Institutional Aspects' in Daniel Gervais (ed), *International Intellectual Property: A Handbook of Contemporary Research* (Edward Elgar 2015) 37, 62: 'infringement of intellectual property rights is a matter dealt with by the courts of each member state'). Therefore, this instrument would not seem to create a unitary right comparable to the rights created by EU regulations, but rather a mere bundle of harmonized uniform but parallel national rights (see also Preamble (1) Treaty of Bangui: '[c]onsidering the advantages of establishing a uniform system for the protection of literary and artistic property').

Another example sometimes mentioned as a non-EU unitary right is a patent granted under the Eurasian Patent Convention of 9 September 1994 (available at <www.wipo.int>). In the light of art 13(2) Eurasian Patent Convention ('Each Contracting State shall, in the case of infringement of a Eurasian patent, provide for the same civil or other liability as in the case of a national patent'), however, it seems that the Eurasian patent falls short of the characteristics of a truly unitary right (see also art 13(1) Eurasian Patent Convention: '[a]ny dispute arising from the validity, in a given Contracting State, or the infringement, in a given Contracting State, of a Eurasian patent shall be resolved by the national courts or other competent authorities of that State on the basis of this Convention and the Patent Regulations. The decision shall have effect only in the territory of the Contracting State').

5. Neighbouring concepts: harmonization of intellectual property law, federal intellectual property law, unitary rights outside intellectual property

While, subject to certain exceptions, unitary intellectual property rights create a single right for the entire supranational community, the mere harmonization of intellectual property rights by international conventions or EU directives still leaves the bundle of national rights of the right holder intact (Graeme Dinwoodie 'art 2:605' in European Max Planck Group on Conflict of Laws in Intellectual Property (ed), *Conflict of Laws in Intellectual Property: The CLIP Principles and Commentary* (OUP 2013) para 2:605.C13). Even if the consequence of harmonization may be a far-reaching parallelism of the national intellectual property laws, the rights still derive from several different national laws and not from a single unitary right. Unitary rights are therefore more akin to intellectual property rights created by federal legislation in a state which comprises several territorial units, each of which at least partly has its own rules of law in respect of intellectual property or neighbouring areas (eg general tort or contract law, procedure, unfair competition etc).

Finally, the concept of a unitary right is not only conceivable in the field of intellectual property. For instance, a federal or supranational legislature may also identify a need for a statute of organization for → companies on the federal or supranational level. In comparing unitary intellectual property rights and other forms of 'unitary' supranational entities such as companies, one may identify certain common conceptual questions such as the competence of the federal or supranational legislator to create a 'unitary right', the need for such a supranational entity, the definition of its scope of application including whether a cross-border element is required, the interplay of supranational and national law, the relationship to private international law, the filling of gaps in the unitary rights instrument or the general → regulatory competition in the vertical relationship (for these questions, from the perspective of EU optional instruments, see Jürgen Basedow 'The Law of Open Societies: Private Ordering and Public Regulation of International Relations' (2012) 360 Rec. des Cours 11, 220 para 227; Holger Fleischer, 'Optionales europäisches Privatrecht ("28. Modell")' (2012) 76 RabelsZ 235, 242–51). As the private international law aspects depend on the drafting of the instrument in question, the following entry will focus only on unitary intellectual property rights.

II. Unitary rights and private international law

Even if all EU unitary intellectual property rights claim to be of unitary character, none of the instruments provides a comprehensive set of rules for all questions of substantive and procedural law which may arise in dealing with such a right. Therefore, the instruments cannot dispense with provisions on → choice of law and on jurisdiction (for the latter, see → Unitary intellectual property rights and jurisdiction).

1. Community trade mark, Community design, Community plant right

For the choice-of-law rules of the Community Trade Mark Regulation, the Community Design Regulation and the Community Plant Regulation, the law applicable for filling gaps in the respective Community unitary rights regulations (see a) below) must be distinguished from the applicability of the unitary rights regulation itself (see b) below).

a) The law applicable for filling gaps in the Community unitary rights regulations

The choice-of-law rules of the EU unitary rights regulations – which take precedence over the general provisions of the → Rome II Regulation (Regulation (EC) No 864/2007 of the European Parliament and of the Council of 11 July 2007 on the law applicable to non-contractual obligations (Rome II), [2007] OJ L 199/40) (art 27 Rome II Regulation; German Federal Court of Justice (BGH), 22 April 2010 [2010] GRURInt. 1072, paras 51–61, *Verlängerte Limousinen*; 28 September 2011 [2012] GRUR 512, paras 55–8, *Kinderwagen*) – presuppose that the respective Community regulation is applicable and answer only questions of applicable law which concern issues which are not covered by the regulation. In such a situation of a gap within the applicable regulation, the conflict rules of the Community Trade Mark Regulation and the Community Design Regulation refer (i) for rules of procedure (and enforcement) to the → *lex fori* of the respective (Community Trade Mark/Design) court (arts 101(3), 102(1), 2nd sentence Community Trade Mark Regulation; arts 88(3), 89(2) Community Design Regulation), (ii) for sanctions for infringement which are not harmonized by the regulations (for harmonized sanctions see art 102(1) Community Trade Mark Regulation; art 89(1)(a)–(c) Community Design Regulation) 'to the law of the Member State in which the acts of infringement or threatened infringement were committed, including the private international law' (art 102(2) Community Trade Mark Regulation; art 89(1)(d) Community Design Regulation) and (iii) for all other matters not covered by the regulation (eg defences such as → prescription, ECJ C-479/12 *H Gautzsch Großhandel GmbH & Co KG v Münchener Boulevard Möbel Joseph Duna GmbH*, ECLI:EU:C:2014:75, para 49) to the national law of the Community Trade Mark (Design) court, including its private international law (art 101(2) Community Trade Mark Regulation; art 88(2) and Recital (22) Community Design Regulation). Surprisingly, the Court of Justice (ECJ Case C-479/12 *H Gautzsch Großhandel GmbH & Co KG v Münchener Boulevard Möbel Joseph Duna GmbH*, ECLI:EU:C:2014:75, para 54) seems to regard a claim for damages not as a sanction in the sense of art 89(1)(d) Community

Design Regulation, but rather as part of 'all other matters' in art 88(2) Community Design Regulation. Ultimately this seems to make no difference as the conflict rules of the Member States for all non-contractual obligations are now harmonized by art 8(2) Rome II Regulation, thus making it less relevant whether the unitary rights regulation refers to the conflict rules of the Member State in which the acts of infringement were committed (as art 102(2) Community Trade Mark Regulation; art 89(1)(d) Community Design Regulation) or to the conflict rules of the Member State in which the Community Trade Mark (Design) court is situated (as art 101(3) Community Trade Mark Regulation; art 88(2) Community Design Regulation). Less differentiated are the conflict rules of the Community Plant Variety Regulation, which refer to the *lex fori* for procedure (art 103 Community Plant Regulation) and, for certain remedies to the 'national law, including their private international law' of the competent courts (art 97(2), (3) Community Plant Regulation), a solution which should be applied for all gaps in the Community Plant Regulation.

All references to the applicable national law are subject to the overriding principles of equivalence and effectiveness, as the application of national rules may not render the enforcement of a Community right ineffective (ECJ Case C-479/12 *H Gautzsch Großhandel GmbH & Co KG v Münchener Boulevard Möbel Joseph Duna GmbH*, ECLI:EU:C:2014:75, para 49). Following adoption of the Rome II Regulation, the reference to the Member States' private international law (in particular for sanctions in art 102(2) Community Trade Mark Regulation and art 88(3) Community Design Regulation, but also for other matters in the sense of art 101(3) Community Trade Mark Regulation, art 88(2) Community Design Regulation such as prescription, see art 15(h) Rome II Regulation) has been replaced by the uniform rule of art 8(2) Rome II Regulation, stating that '[i]n the case of a non-contractual obligation arising from an infringement of a unitary Community intellectual property right, the law applicable shall, for any question that is not governed by the relevant Community instrument, be the law of the country in which the act of infringement was committed'.

The reference to the law of the country in which the act of infringement was committed raises essentially two questions. First, it has to be decided whether 'act of infringement' in art 102(2) Community Trade Mark Regulation is to be understood in a natural or legal sense. A 'natural' understanding of the 'act' would point to the place where the alleged infringer has in fact acted (Jürgen Basedow, 'Foundations of Private international law in Intellectual Property' in Jürgen Basedow, Toshiyuki Kono and Axel Metzger (eds), *Intellectual Property in the Global Arena* (Mohr Siebeck 2010) 3, 26; Josef Drexl, 'Internationales Immaterialgüterrecht' in Franz Jürgen Säcker, Roland Rixecker and Hartmut Oetker (eds), *Münchener Kommentar zum Bürgerlichen Gesetzbuch*, vol 11 (6th edn, CH Beck 2015) para 140), which may also be in a third state outside the EU. A 'legal' understanding, on the other hand, would understand 'act of infringement' in art 8(2) Rome II in the same sense as the infringing acts are defined in the substantive provisions of art 9 Community Trade Mark Regulation, art 19 Community Design Regulation and art 13 Community Plant Regulation, ie in the same sense in which the acts which may be prohibited by the owner of a trade mark (or design, or plant variety right) are defined. If for example a sign registered as a Community Trade Mark is used by a company resident in → Switzerland for Internet advertisement in → Germany directed to German customers, the natural understanding would localize the 'act of infringement' in Switzerland (from where the advertisement was in fact initiated), while the legal understanding would find an 'act of infringement' in the sense of art 102(2) Community Trade Mark Regulation only inside the EU territory, ie in the country to which the advertisement was targeted, that is Germany in the example (for this understanding, albeit in substantive trade mark law, ECJ Case C-324/09 *L'Oréal v eBay* [2011] ECR I-6011, paras 63–7). In order to avoid finding an 'act of infringement' in a non-EU Member State (and thus application of a third state's sanctions to infringement of a Community trade mark, at least if art 8(2) Rome II Regulation is applied literally, for a teleological limitation of art 8(2) Rome II Regulation Josef Drexl 'Internationales Immaterialgüterrecht' in Franz Jürgen Säcker, Roland Rixecker and Hartmut Oetker (eds), *Münchener Kommentar zum Bürgerlichen Gesetzbuch*, vol 11 (6th edn, CH Beck 2015) para 140; see also the alternative proposal of the Hamburg Group for Private international law, 'Comments on the European Commission's Draft Proposal for a Council

Regulation on the Law Applicable to Non-Contractual Obligations' (2003) 67 RabelsZ 1, 21, referring to the 'law of the Member State where the infringement affects the right' instead of the place of the 'act of infringement') and also for reasons of systematic coherence, namely using the same criteria to localize the act of infringement in substantive trade mark law and in art 8(2) Rome II Regulation, it seems preferable to adopt the 'legal' understanding of 'act of infringement' in art 8(2) Rome II Regulation. On the other hand, the recent ECJ decision on the interpretation of 'act of infringement' in the parallel jurisdictional provision of art 97(5) Community Trade Mark Regulation (ECJ Case C-360/12 *Coty Germany GmbH v First Note Perfumes NV*, ECLI:EU:2014:1318, para 34) refers to 'active conduct on the part of the person causing that infringement', which tends more towards a natural understanding of the term. However, it should be borne in mind that if the term 'act of infringement' in art 8(2) Rome II Regulation is to be interpreted in the same way as 'place of the event giving rise to the damage' in art 7(2) Brussels I Regulation (recast) (Regulation (EU) No 1215/2012 of the European Parliament and of the Council of 12 December 2012 on jurisdiction and the recognition and enforcement of judgments in civil and commercial matters (recast), [2012] OJ L 351/1; → Brussels I (Convention and Regulation)), this will in most cases lead to the place of establishment of the alleged infringer where the decision about the activity leading to the infringement is made (see ECJ Case C-523/10 *Wintersteiger v Products 4U*, ECLI:EU:C:2012:220, paras 36–7). In other words, it will be the law of the alleged infringer's place of establishment which will govern those sanctions not covered by the Community rights regulations.

Finally, if the 'act of infringement' is not to be concentrated at the infringer's residence, the question arises which law applies if a Community unitary right has been infringed by several acts in different EU Member States (eg production, advertisement, sale), which from an economic point of view cause a single damage. In order to avoid a mosaic of several national laws being applicable due to the different acts of infringement in different countries, it has been proposed to apply the law of the defendant's domicile (Axel Metzger, 'Community IP Rights and Conflict of Laws: Community Trade Mark, Community Design, Community Patent – Applicable Law for Claims for Damages' in

Josef Drexl and Annette Kur (eds), *Intellectual Property and Private international law: Heading for the Future* (Hart 2005) 215, 223), the law of closest connection (eg of the place from which the infringer's actions were directed or where the decisions about distribution were made, see Higher Regional Court (OLG) of Hamburg, 27 January 2005 [2005] GRUR-RR 251, 255, *The Home Depot*, *contra* German Federal Court of Justice (BGH), 13 September 2007 [2008] GRUR 254, para 42, *The Home Depot*; Josef Drexl, 'Internationales Immaterialgüterrecht' in Franz Jürgen Säcker, Roland Rixecker and Hartmut Oetker (eds), *Münchener Kommentar zum Bürgerlichen Gesetzbuch*, vol 11 (6th edn, CH Beck 2015) para 143) or the law of the forum (*de lege ferenda* Marta Pertegás Sender, 'Intellectual Property and Choice of Law Rules' in Alberto Malatesta (ed), *The Unification of Choice of Law Rules on Torts and other Non-Contractual Obligations in Europe* (CEDAM 2006) 221, 246). While all these proposals are commendable, they are difficult to square with the words 'act of infringement' of art 8(2) Rome II (critical for the substitution of the wording of legislation by 'judicial gloss' Guy Tritton, *Intellectual Property in Europe* (4th edn, Butterworths 2014) Preface p xi). Therefore, a potential concentration on a single law should be achieved by focusing only on the last act of infringement directly causing the damage for which compensation is claimed, which will normally be the act of distribution (for injunctions, the problem is less relevant as art 102(1) Community Trade Mark Regulation and art 89(1) Community Design Regulation already provide EU unitary remedies).

b) Applicability of the unitary rights regulations themselves

Whereas the conflict rules of the unitary rights regulations cover the gap filling process in the absence of EU rules, they do not address the question under which circumstances the unitary rights regulations themselves are applicable. Article 101(1) Community Trade Mark Regulation and art 88(1) Community Design Regulation merely state that the 'Community trade mark courts shall apply the provisions of this Regulation', but do not define the geographic scope of application of these Regulations. As the ECJ has accepted that the territorial scope of prohibitions based on unitary Community rights must be limited to part of the territory of the EU if acts of infringement of a

Community Trade Mark are limited to this territory (ECJ Case C-235/09 *DHL Express France v Chronopost* [2011] ECR I-2801, para 48), and as an infringement of a European intellectual property right requires that the corresponding territory of protection is targeted or at least affected by the alleged infringing act (for trade marks ECJ Case C-324/09 *L'Oréal v eBay* [2011] ECR I-6011, para 65; for copyright ECJ Case C-5/11 *Strafverfahren gegen Titus Alexander Donner* ECLI:EU:C:2012:370, para 28; for database rights ECJ Case C-173/11 *Football Dataco Ltd and Others v Sportradar GmbH and Sportradar AG* ECLI:EU:C:2012:642, para 39; for the general acceptance of the principle of territoriality in EU law ECJ Case C-9/93 *IHT Internationale Heiztechnik GmbH and Uwe Danzinger v Ideal-Standard GmbH and Wabco Standard GmbH* [1994] ECR I-2789, para 22 (trade marks); ECJ Case C-192/04 *Lagardère Active Broadcast v Société pour la perception de la rémunération équitable (SPRE) and Gesellschaft zur Verwertung von Leistungsschutzrechten mbH (GVL)* [2005] ECR I-7199, para 46 (copyright)), consequently the silence of the unitary rights regulations as concerns their geographic scope of application vis-à-vis third states allows to resort to the general *lex loci protectionis* principle of art 8(1) Rome II Regulation (see also Recital (26) Rome II Regulation: 'universally acknowledged principle of the *lex loci protectionis*'). Thus, the unitary rights regulations are applicable only if the claimant claims protection under an EU unitary right. If he does so, the court will have to apply the EU unitary rights regulations, and for gaps in these regulations have to resort to the conflict provisions of these regulations (for procedure art 101(3) Community Trade Mark Regulation, art 88(3) Community Design Regulation, art 103 Community Plant Regulation; for sanctions for infringement art 102(2) Community Trade Mark Regulation, art 89(1)(d) Community Design Regulation; for other matters art 101(2) Community Trade Mark Regulation, art 88(2) Community Design Regulation), which are, for sanctions for infringement, complemented by the reference to the law of the country in which the act of infringement was committed in art 8(2) Rome II Regulation (see a) above).

2. *European patents*

While patents granted on the basis of the European Patent Convention (Convention on the Grant of European Patents of 5 October 1973 as revised by the Act revising Article 63 EPC of 17 December 1991 and the Act revising the EPC of 29 November 2000) are at present largely equivalent to national patents (arts 2(2), 64(1), (3) European Patent Convention) and thus governed by art 8(1) Rome II Regulation, with only few specific provisions (see art 60(1), (2) European Patent Convention for ownership of employee inventions and art 74 European Patent Convention for patent applications as an object of property), the new 'European Patent Package' consisting of the UPC Agreement (Agreement of 19 February 2013 on a Unified Patent Court, [2013] OJ C 175/1), the Unitary Patent Regulation (Regulation (EU) No 1257/2012 of the European Parliament and of the Council of 17 December 2012 implementing enhanced cooperation in the area of the creation of unitary patent protection, [2012] OJ L 361/1) and the Translation Regulation (Council Regulation (EU) No 1260/2012 of 17 December 2012 implementing enhanced cooperation in the area of the creation of unitary patent protection with regard to the applicable translation arrangements, [2012] OJ L 361/89) will significantly change this situation. The UPC Agreement will apply to all European patents (ie patents granted under the provisions of the European Patent Convention, art 2(e) UPC Agreement, subject however to an opt-out in the transitional period of seven years, art 83(1), (3) UPC Agreement) and all European patents with unitary effect (ie patents granted under the provisions of the European Patent Convention which benefit from unitary effect by virtue of Unitary Patent Regulation, art 2(f) UPC Agreement) as well as corresponding supplementary protection certificates or patent applications (art 3 UPC Agreement). For European patents with unitary effect two additional EU regulations come into play, namely the Unitary Patent Regulation and the Translation Regulation, which define how a European patent with unitary effect may be obtained and which law is applicable to such a unitary right. The Patent Package is intended to complement the existing unified granting procedure under the European Patent Convention (Convention on the Grant of European Patents of 5 October 1973 as revised by the Act revising Article 63 EPC of 17 December 1991 and the Act revising the EPC of 29 November 2000) by establishing a new Unified Patent Court (UPC) with multinational panels (art 8 UPC Agreement) as a court common to all contracting Member

States (art 1, 2nd sentence UPC Agreement). The Patent Package will bring about two core changes, namely the creation of a European patent with unitary effect (by the Unitary Patent Regulation) and the concentration of infringement litigation over simple European (European Patent Convention-granted) patents and over European patents with unitary effect in a single Unified Patent Court with its own substantive and procedural provisions (UPC Agreement, Statute of the Unified Patent Court, [2013] OJ C 175/29, Rules of Procedure of the Unified Patent Court).

From a private international law perspective, before turning to potential specific private international law provisions in Unitary Patent Regulation and the UPC Agreement, the question arises of how the new instruments relate to the general corpus of European private international law, in particular the Rome I Regulation (Regulation (EC) No 593/2008 of the European Parliament and of the Council of 17 June 2008 on the law applicable to contractual obligations (Rome I), [2008] OJ L 177/6; → Rome Convention and Rome I Regulation (contractual obligations)) and the Rome II Regulation.

a) European patents with unitary effect (Unitary Patent Regulation)

Concerning European patents with unitary effect, it may be noted that the Unitary Patent Regulation and the Translation Regulation create a right with unitary effect which, unlike the Community trade mark, design and plant variety rights, does not cover the entire EU, but is limited to 'those participating Member States in which the Unified Patent Court has exclusive jurisdiction with regard to European patents with unitary effect at the date of registration' (art 18(2) 2nd sentence Unitary Patent Regulation). Moreover, for political reasons, in particular a reluctance to entrust the interpretation of substantive patent law to the ECJ, art 5(1) and (2) Unitary Patent Regulation merely state that the European patent with unitary effect confers on its proprietor an exclusive right and that the 'scope of that right and its limitations shall be uniform'. The exact definitions of the 'acts against which the patent provides protection . . . and the applicable limitations' are, with few exceptions such as exhaustion (art 6 Unitary Patent Regulation), not spelled out in Unitary Patent Regulation. Rather, art 5(3) Unitary Patent Regulation refers for these issues to 'the law applied to European Patents with unitary effect in the participating Member State whose national law is applicable to the European Patent with unitary effect as an object of property in accordance with Article 7'. Article 7(1) Unitary Patent Regulation, in turn, refers to the substantive, ie law excluding its conflict-of-law provisions, of the place in a participating Member State where the patent applicant had its residence or principal place of business or place of business on the date of filing of the patent application. Where no applicant has its residence, principal place of business or place of business in a participating Member State in which the patent has unitary effect, the European patent with unitary effect 'shall be treated . . . as a national patent of the State where the European Patent Organization has its headquarters' (art 7(3) Unitary Patent Regulation), ie as a German patent. The desired unification of the prohibited acts and limitations is thus achieved by reference to the national law of a participating Member State which is harmonized by the UPC Agreement (arts 25 et seq UPC Agreement) as an international convention to be ratified by all participating Member States for which unitary effect is granted (art 18(2) 2nd sentence Unitary Patent Regulation).

From a private international law perspective, the conflict rules in arts 5(3) and 7 Unitary Patent Regulation seem to overlap with the general rules of the Rome Regulations only in so far as the 'acts against which the [unitary] patent provides protection and the applicable limitations' are considered to fall under the Rome II Regulation (because they define the 'basis and extent of liability' in the sense of art 15(1)(a) Rome II Regulation). For these issues, arts 5(3) and 7 Unitary Patent Regulation will arguably have to be given precedence for the participating Member States over the general conflict rules of the Rome I and II Regulations, in particular over art 8(2) Rome II Regulation either on the basis of art 27 Rome II Regulation or as a *lex specialis* for reasons of effectiveness of the Unitary Patent Regulation (for the parallel debate for provisions in transport law regulations Johannes Schilling, 'Materielles Einheitsrecht und Europäisches Schuldvertrags-IPR. Das Verhältnis der Rom I-Verordnung zu internationalen Sachrechtsakten' [2011] EuZW 776, 778) or, concerning art 8(2) Rome II

Regulation, for reason of the caveat in that provision ('for any question that is not governed by the relevant Community instrument').

For all matters other than prohibited acts, limitations and proprietary aspects which are not covered by the Unitary Patent Regulation and the Translation Regulation (such as sanctions, eg calculation of damages), Recital (9) 2nd sentence Unitary Patent Regulation states that 'the provisions of the EPC, the Agreement on a Unified Patent Court, including its provisions defining the scope of that right and its limitations, and national law, including rules of private international law, should apply'. While Recital (9) seems to suggest that the European Patent Convention und UPC Agreement are applied directly and not as part of the applicable national law (as defined by private international law rules), Recital (13) Unitary Patent Regulation adds that '[t]he regime applicable to damages should be governed by the laws of the participating Member States, in particular the provisions implementing article 13 of Directive 2004/48/EC', which suggests, on the contrary, an application of the damages provisions in the UPC Agreement as part of the national law of the participating Member States. Recitals, however, are not the operative part of a Regulation, so that the Unitary Patent Regulation does not include a conflict rule except for the matters covered by art 5(3) and art 7 Unitary Patent Regulation (Josef Drexl, 'Internationales Immaterialgüterrecht' in Franz Jürgen Säcker, Roland Rixecker and Hartmut Oetker (eds), *Münchener Kommentar zum Bürgerlichen Gesetzbuch*, vol 11 (6th edn, CH Beck 2015) para 147, who proposes to apply art 8(2) Rome II Regulation for matters not covered by art 5(3) Unitary Patent Regulation such as sanctions).

b) 'Simple' European patents
(UPC Agreement)
The limited scope of the conflict rules in Unitary Patent Regulation shifts the focus to the provisions which define the law to be applied under the Agreement on a Unified Patent Court, namely arts 3 and 24 Agreement on a Unified Patent Court which are relevant both for European patents with unitary effect and 'simple' European patents (art 2(e), (f), art 3 UPC Agreement).

(1) Relationship with general EU choice-of-law provisions (Rome I Regulation and Rome II Regulation) Before turning to arts 3 and 24 UPC Agreement, it has to be decided whether these provisions can be applied immediately or whether they apply only subject to the general EU choice-of-law provisions as incorporated in particular in the Rome I Regulation and the Rome II Regulation. In this respect, it has to be noted that technically the UPC Agreement constitutes an international convention which did not yet exist when the Rome I Regulation and the Rome II Regulation were adopted. Therefore, it cannot claim precedence over these Regulations under art 28(1) Rome II Regulation (art 25(1) Rome I Regulation). Moreover, the precedence of the Rome Regulations over arts 3 and 24 UPC Agreement arguably finds further support in their nature as part of EU law which is specifically preserved by art 20 and art 24(1) first half-sentence as well as art 24(1)(a) UPC Agreement. The primacy of EU law, if it is extended to choice-of-law provisions, would indeed suggest that the applicable law is determined by the Rome Regulations, with the UPC Agreement only being applied if it is part of the substantive law referred to by the Rome Regulations. This view was apparently the position held in the legislative procedure. In the Commission's non-paper on 'Compatibility of the draft agreement on the Unified Patent Court with the Union *acquis*' (Council Document 14191/11 of 20 September 2011), it is stated that '[t]he Agreement on a Unified Patent Court does not contain conflict rules in matters governed by the Rome I and Rome II Regulations', while '[t]he Agreement on a Unified Patent Court does contain harmonized rules of substantive law'. The Commission further wrote that '[i]t needs to be ascertained that, in case the Rome Regulations lead to the applicability of the national law of a non-participating State, this law is applied, even if its rules differ from the rules provided for in the UPC Agreement'. The consequences of this interpretation, which is probably founded on the desire to preserve full primacy of EU law as a requirement for compatibility of the UPC Agreement with EU law, were later implemented in the UPC Agreement: the title of ch V – formerly IIIB – was changed from 'Applicable Law' to 'Sources of Law', and the applicability of the law of a non-participating state made possible (Council Document 13751/11 COR 2 of 23 September 2011, 20–21; see also Council Document 15487/11 of 13 October 2011, 20–21).

Against this view, however, it may be pointed out that the UPC Agreement does not only lay down choice-of-law rules, but rather aims at substantive and procedural harmonization. Therefore, it may benefit from the argument that international conventions aiming at substantive law harmonization (as concluded by the Member States in the realm of their competences) may not be barred by the Rome I Regulation and the Rome II Regulation and thus be able to define their own scope of application (for an analogous argument concerning uniform transport law conventions (→ Transport law (uniform law)) in relation to Rome II Regulation see Jürgen Basedow, 'Rome II at Sea: General Aspects of Maritime Torts' (2010) 74 RabelsZ 118, 127–8, stating that uniform substantive law conventions (→ Uniform substantive law and private international law) exclude 'situations involving a conflict of laws' in the sense of art 1(1) Rome II Regulation and make the EU conflict rules not applicable). For the UPC Agreement, it could be added that arts 5(3), 18 and Recital (9) Unitary Patent Regulation expressly refer to the UPC Agreement and thus include it into the EU accepted corpus of international conventions. Finally, one may point to the order of art 24(1) and (2) Agreement on a Unified Patent Court, where the second para of art 24 Agreement on a Unified Patent Court mentions general EU private international law rules (such as Rome I and Rome II) only after EU law, including Unitary Patent Regulation and Regulation 1260/2012, the UPC Agreement, the European Patent Convention and other international conventions. This suggests an *e contrario* argument that the Unified Patent Court should apply the instruments mentioned in art 24(1)(a)–(d) UPC Agreement (substantive EU law, UPC Agreement, European Patent Convention, other international conventions) without a detour via private international law, with the general rules of EU and national choice-of-law provisions coming into play only where the Unified Patent Court has to resort to national law (art 24(1)(e) UPC Agreement). Moreover, if the Rome II Regulation was applied before resorting to arts 3, 24 UPC Agreement, the references in art 24(1), (2) UPC Agreement could be regarded as conflicting with the exclusion of *renvoi* in art 24 Rome II Regulation. Following this line of argument, arts 3, 24 UPC Agreement could be considered as a uniform law *lex specialis* to the Rome Regulations, the latter coming into play only where the UPC Agreement refers to national law (art 24(1)(e), (2) UPC Agreement).

For practical purposes, the difficult question of primacy of either arts 3, 24 UPC Agreement or the Rome Regulations can probably be left open in most cases: according to art 3 UPC Agreement, the Agreement applies only to European patents with unitary effect, European patents and related supplementary protection certificates or patent applications. Moreover, the jurisdiction of the Unified Patent Court (art 32(1) UPC Agreement) – subject to objective joinder under art 71b(3) Brussels I Regulation (recast) (Regulation (EU) No 1215/2012 of the European Parliament and of the Council of 12 December 2012 on jurisdiction and the recognition and enforcement of judgments in civil and commercial matters (recast), [2012] OJ L 351/1 (→ Brussels I (Convention and Regulation)) as amended by Regulation (EU) No 542/2014 of the European Parliament and of the Council of 15 May 2014 amending Regulation (EU) No 1215/2012 as regards the rules to be applied with respect to the Unified Patent Court and the Benelux Court of Justice, [2014] OJ L 163/1) – covers only actions concerning infringement and/or revocation of 'patents' and certain related actions in the sense of the Unified Patent Court, ie European patents or European patents with unitary effect (art 2(g) UPC Agreement). Accordingly, to fall within the scope of the UPC Agreement and to establish jurisdiction of the Unified Patent Court, the claimant will have to sue under and thus claim protection (or the defendant non-infringement) of a 'patent' in the sense of the UPC Agreement. This, however, would also be sufficient under art 8(1) Rome II Regulation to make the law of the country for which protection is claimed applicable. Further, if the plaintiff sues and thus claims protection under a 'patent' in the sense of the UPC Agreement, this will be a participating state, as otherwise the action would fail for lack of infringement in the territory of protection. In the state of protection, the UPC Agreement will thus have been implemented so that the UPC Agreement and the European Patent Convention will either apply directly under art 24(1)(b) and (c) UPC Agreement, or under art 8(1) Rome II Regulation apply as part of the *lex protectionis*, so that in either case the question of primacy can be left open.

The same probably holds true for art 8(2) Rome II Regulation, to the extent the European patent with unitary effect is concerned, provided the 'act of infringement' is claimed to have occurred in those Member States where the unitary effect has come into existence, as these Member States, according to art 18(2) 2nd sentence Unitary Patent Regulation, will also have to be contracting states where the Unified Patent Court has jurisdiction and thus the UPC Agreement has been implemented into national law, so that it applies both under art 24(1)(b) UPC Agreement and art 8(2) Rome II Regulation (see also Josef Drexl 'Internationales Immaterialgüterrecht' in Franz Jürgen Säcker, Roland Rixecker and Hartmut Oetker (eds), *Münchener Kommentar zum Bürgerlichen Gesetzbuch*, vol 11 (6th edn, CH Beck 2015) para 147, who argues that the country of protection and the country where the act of infringement happened are identical if that country is a participating Member State). Differences may remain only if the 'act of infringement' occurred in a non-participating state. Moreover, a minor technical difference stems from the fact that under art 8(2) Rome II Regulation, the various national implementing laws of the UPC Agreement at the different 'acts of infringement' are applicable, whereas under a direct application via art 24(1) UPC Agreement, one could argue that the UPC Agreement as such applies.

(2) Source of law under art 24 UPC Agreement The substantive and procedural law of the Unified Patent Court under the UPC Agreement is described by art 24(1) UPC Agreement. According to this provision, the Unified Patent Court must,

> in full compliance with article 20 [primacy of EU law], when hearing a case brought before it under this Agreement . . ., base its decisions on (a) Union law, including Regulation (EU) No 1257/2012 and Regulation (EU) No 1260/2012; (b) this Agreement; (c) the EPC [eg art 69 European Patent Convention on the scope of patents]; (d) other international agreements applicable to patents and binding on all the Contracting Member States [eg Paris Industrial Property Convention (Paris Convention for the Protection of Industrial Property, 20 March 1883, with later amendments, 828 UNTS 305)]; and (e) national law.

For the determination of the applicable national law, which may be relevant for all aspects not covered by the UPC Agreement, eg transfer of a European patent without unitary effect, art 24(2) UPC Agreement adds that

> [t]o the extent that the Court shall base its decisions on national law, including where relevant the law of non-contracting States, the applicable law shall be determined: (a) by directly applicable provisions of Union law containing private international law rules [eg Rome I and Rome II Regulations], or (b) in the absence of directly applicable provisions of Union law or where the latter do not apply, by international instruments containing private international law rules [the order in art 24(2) Agreement on a Unified Patent Court is probably not meant to change the precedence of existing choice-of-law conventions over the Rome I and II Regulations under art 28 Rome II, art 25 Rome I]; or (c) in the absence of provisions referred to in points (a) and (b), by national provisions on private international law as determined by the Court.

The latter reference to court-determined national private international law provisions raises the question how the Unified Patent Court is to determine the applicable national conflict rules. As the determination of a conflict rule accepted in most or even all Member States will probably in most cases be impossible, and as application of the conflict rules at the seat of the respective division will lead to different rules being applicable to the same patent depending on the seat of the division, it seems most convincing to draw an analogy to art 7 Unitary Patent Regulation and apply the conflict rules of the country where the patent applicant was resident at the time of application. Finally, art 24(3) UPC Agreement clarifies that

> [t]he law of non-contracting States shall apply when designated by application of the rules referred to in paragraph 2, in particular in relation to articles 25 to 28 [right to prevent direct and indirect use of invention and limitations], 54 [burden of proof], 55 [reversal of burden of proof], 64 [corrective measures in infringement proceedings], 68 [award of damages] and 72 [period of limitation].

As the substantive law of non-contracting states is unlikely to include the mentioned provisions of the UPC Agreement, art 24(3) UPC Agreement is probably intended as a form of qualification provision, stating that the matters in the mentioned UPC Agreement provisions are to be considered as substantive (as opposed to procedural) law in nature. Finally, it may be noted that art 82(3) UPC Agreement refers for enforcement procedures to the law of the contracting Member State where the enforcement takes place.

CHRISTIAN HEINZE

Literature

Philippe Baechtold, Tomoko Miyamoto and Thomas Henninger, 'International Patent Law: Principles, Major Instruments and Institutional Aspects' in Daniel Gervais (ed), *International Intellectual Property: A Handbook of Contemporary Research* (Edward Elgar 2015) 37; Jürgen Basedow, 'Foundations of Private international law in Intellectual Property' in Jürgen Basedow, Toshiyuki Kono and Axel Metzger (eds), *Intellectual Property in the Global Arena* (Mohr Siebeck 2010) 3; Jürgen Basedow, 'The Law of Open Societies: Private Ordering and Public Regulation of International Relations' (2012) 360 Rec. des Cours 11; Colin Birss, 'Unitary Rights and Judicial Respect in the EU: "Bringing Cool Back"' (2013) 3 *Queen Mary Journal of Intellectual Property Law* 195; Josef Drexl, 'Internationales Immaterialgüterrecht' in Franz Jürgen Säcker, Roland Rixecker and Hartmut Oetker (eds), *Münchener Kommentar zum Bürgerlichen Gesetzbuch*, vol 11 (6th edn, CH Beck 2015); European Max Planck Group on Conflict of Laws in Intellectual Property, *Conflict of Laws in Intellectual Property: The CLIP Principles and Commentary* (OUP 2013) art 2:605: Unitary regional rights, p 186; James Fawcett and Paul Torremans, *Intellectual Property and Private international law* (2nd edn, OUP 2011); Holger Fleischer 'Optionales europäisches Privatrecht ("28. Modell")' (2012) 76 RabelsZ 235; Hamburg Group for Private international law, 'Comments on the European Commission's Draft Proposal for a Council Regulation on the Law Applicable to Non-Contractual Obligations' (2003) 67 RabelsZ 1; Axel Metzger, 'Community IP Rights and Conflict of Laws: Community Trade Mark, Community Design, Community Patent – Applicable Law for Claims for Damages' in Josef Drexl and Annette Kur (eds), *Intellectual Property and Private international law: Heading for the Future* (Hart 2005) 215; Pedro de Miguel Asensio, 'Regulation (EU) No. 542/2014 and the International Jurisdiction of the Unified Patent Court' [2014] IIC 868; Marta Pertegás Sender, 'Intellectual Property and Choice of Law Rules' in Alberto Malatesta (ed), *The Unification of Choice of Law Rules on Torts and other Non-Contractual Obligations in Europe* (CEDAM 2006) 221; Marius Schneider and Vanessa Ferguson, 'Cross-border Enforcement of Intellectual Property Rights: Africa' in Paul Torremans (ed), *Research Handbook on Cross-border Enforcement of Intellectual Property* (Edward Elgar 2014) 329; Paul Torremans, 'An International Perspective II: A View from Private international law' in Justine Pila and Christopher Wadlow (eds), *The Unitary EU Patent System* (Hart Publishing 2015) 161; Guy Tritton, *Intellectual Property in Europe* (4th edn, Butterworths 2014).

Unjust enrichment (restitution)

I. Generalities

Unjust enrichment, or restitution to use the traditional English expression, is a specific kind of extra-contractual obligation. Accordingly, it is governed by the → Rome II Regulation (Regulation (EC) No 864/2007 of the European Parliament and of the Council of 11 July 2007 on the law applicable to non-contractual obligations (Rome II), [2007] OJ L 199/40), which devotes its art 10 to this topic. Article 10 Rome II Regulation deliberately avoids the more technical term of 'restitution', which might be regarded as a synonym for 'unjust enrichment' but could also be reduced to a more specific understanding under English common law. 'Unjust enrichment' might be slightly broader and is definitely more in line with the terminology used in the legal orders of continental Europe. Unjust enrichment as a topic addressed and regulated also appears for example in art 128 Swiss Private international law Act (Bundesgesetz über das Internationale Privatrecht of 18 December 1987, 1988 BBl I 5, as amended, henceforth Swiss PILA), art 1223 Civil Code of the Russian Federation (as amended by Federal Law No 260-FZ on 30 September 2013, henceforth Russian CC), art 39 Turkish Private international law Code (Code on Private International and International Civil Procedure Law of 27 November 2007 (Act No 5718) (Milletlerarası Özel Hukuk ve Usul Hukuku Hakkında Kanun), Resmî Gazete No 26728 of 12 December 2007, henceforth Turkish PILA), art 14 Japanese Act on General Rules for Application of Laws (Hōno Tekiyō ni Kansuru Tsūsokuhō, Law No 10 of 1898, as newly titled and amended by Act No 78 of 21 June 2006, henceforth Japanese PILA), art 31 Korean Private international law Act (Law 6465 of 7 April 2001, Amending the Conflict of Laws Act of the Republic of Korea, henceforth Korean PILA) and art 47 Chinese Private international law Act (Statute of Application of Law to Foreign Civil Relations (adopted at the 17th session of the Standing Committee of the 11th National People's Congress on 28 October 2010, effective 1 April 2011, henceforth Chinese PILA).

II. Characterization issues

1. In general

Article 10 Rome II Regulation contains neither an express definition of unjust enrichment nor even an attempt in this regard. Comparative law (→ Comparative law and private international law) evinces that the substantive laws of the states of the world employ and pursue different approaches, always assuming that any concept of unjust enrichment is even recognized. Basically, in distinguishing between unjust enrichment and other kinds of claim, particularly those in tort, two basic approaches can be identified. The first looks at the cause of action whereas the second takes the consequences as its starting point. Recital (11) Rome II Regulation calls for an autonomous concept for the term 'non-contractual obligation', but Recital (29) Rome II Regulation only mentions unjust enrichment in passing without further exploration and explanation.

2. *Specific issues*

Specific issues of characterization are discussed with less intensity than that enjoyed by → torts. Article 15 Rome II Regulation demonstrates this in that it is formulated in terms associated with torts such as liability, damage or compensation for damage, whereas unjust enrichment would require the use of a different terminology. It would have been appropriate to insert a separate characterization rule specifically designed for unjust enrichment, just as a separate, complete and comprehensive Chapter would have been useful with the same degree of systematic treatment as that given to tort. A particular difficulty might arise in drawing an acceptable borderline between unjust enrichment and the law of property (see before the advent of the Rome II Regulation *Macmillan Inc v Bishopsgate Investment Trust Plc* (No 3) [1995] EWCA 55, (1996) 1 WLR 387, (1996) 1 All ER 585).

III. Connecting factors

Article 11 Rome II Regulation might be as good as any rule that regulates the private international law of unjust enrichment. It indicates the most elaborate approach currently visible in the market of conflict laws. Article 11 Rome II Regulation employs a five-step approach to ascertaining the law applicable to a certain unjust enrichment.

1. Condictio indebiti *after performing an invalid contract*

A significant exclusion has to be stressed as a preliminary, in that the *condictio indebiti* ensuing from performing an invalid contract is governed by the Rome I Regulation (Regulation (EC) No 593/2008 of the European Parliament and of the Council of 17 June 2008 on the law applicable to contractual obligations (Rome I), [2008] OJ L 177/6; → Rome Convention and Rome I Regulation (contractual obligations)) by virtue of art 12(1)(e), under which it is to be classified as a consequence of the nullity of the contract. Accordingly art 12(1)(e) Rome I Regulation serves as *lex specialis* taking precedence over art 10 Rome II Regulation. This has also consequences for the extent to which the parties may choose a law: assigning the *condictio indebiti* to the realm of contract liberates → party autonomy from the restrictions found in art 14 Rome II Regulation, and allows application of art 3 Rome I Regulation (with various restrictions in arts 5(2), 6(2), 7(3), 8(1) Rome I Regulation). Article 31 sentence 1 Korean PILA, unconcerned with any interrelation with another act dealing with the private international law of contracts, submits the *condictio indebiti* also to the *lex causae* of the obligation performed but wrongly assumed. Even absent a codification, following a breakdown of the contract the proper law (→ Proper law (doctrine)) of restitutionary obligations is assumed to be the same as the proper law of the contract (*Dervan v Concept Fiduciaries Ltd* [2013–14] Guernsey L.R. 1).

2. *Party choice of law*

The first step in the process of ascertaining the applicable law under the Rome II Regulation must have regard to a possible → choice of law by the parties within the confines of art 14 Rome II Regulation. This rule is equally applicable in unjust enrichment as in tort. Party autonomy has not been expressly granted in art 10 Rome II Regulation, since that would have been an unnecessary reduplication, given the overall structure of the Regulation with its art 14 covering all kinds of non-contractual obligations including unjust enrichment. Applying art 14 Rome II Regulation includes all restrictions which this rule places on party autonomy, particularly its severe limitations on B2C relationships. On its wording, art 47 sentence 1 Chinese PILA grants the parties unrestricted autonomy to choose the law applicable to an unjust enrichment. Article 128(2) *in fine* Swiss PILA and art 1223(1) sentence 2 Russian CC permit the parties to choose the *lex fori*, without providing more liberally for party autonomy.

3. Accessory connection to a leading relationship

By virtue of art 10(1) Rome I Regulation, if a non-contractual obligation arising out of unjust enrichment, including payment of accounts wrongly received, concerns a relationship existing between the parties such as one arising out of a contract or a tort/delict that is closely connected with that unjust enrichment, then the obligation will be governed by the law that governs that relationship. The underlying rationale is expediency, in that it is deemed preferable for the entire legal situation to be governed by the same law (European Commission, 'Proposal for a Regulation of the European Parliament and the Council on the Law Applicable to Non-Contractual Obligations ("Rome II")' COM(2003) 427 final, p 21). Furthermore, an accessory connection enhances consistency between the legal treatment of concurring claims with different causes of action. Article 1223(2) Russian CC operates along the same lines, and art 128(1) Swiss PILA adopts the same approach establishing a connection accessory to an existing or presumed leading relationship. For the sake of formulating a general rule, art 10(1) Rome II Regulation does not expressly exclude unjust enrichment in the field of contracts from its scope of application. However, this does not alter the relation to art 12(1)(e) Rome I Regulation, in which the latter takes precedence as *lex specialis*, and does not draw *condictiones indebiti* into the realm of art 10 Rome II Regulation.

Contracts and torts are merely examples of potential candidates for constituting a leading relationship. Relationships stemming from family law are equally feasible if one disregards relationships arising out of family relations, → matrimonial property regimes or → successions as excluded from the scope of the Rome II Regulation pursuant to its art 1(2)(a) and (b).

Whether the leading relationship must be a pre-existing one is a difficult and open question subject to discussion. It is of particular relevance with regard to torts committed *uno actu* with the act giving rise to the unjust enrichment.

Eingriffskondiktion and tort are close neighbours and will frequently occur in the same cases. The basic rationales of pursuing expediency and consistency militate in favour of recognizing the tort as the leading relationship, even if it originates *uno actu* with the unjust enrichment.

Where there is more than one relationship, the relationship with the closest connection to the unjust enrichment should take precedence. It is immaterial whether the law applicable to the leading relationship is determined following the parties' choice of the law as recognized by the relevant private international law rules, or is ascertained by an objective determination. This means in particular that the greater extent of party autonomy granted in the realm of contracts by arts 3–9 Rome I Regulation also gains importance in the field of unjust enrichment.

4. Parties' common habitual residence

The third step is to be found in art 10(2) Rome II Regulation: '[w]here the law applicable cannot be determined on the basis of paragraph 1, and the parties have their habitual residence in the same country when the event giving rise to unjust enrichment occurs, the law of that country, [not the same place,] will apply'. However, if they live in different countries the required → connecting factor under art 10(2) Rome II Regulation becomes a specified expression of a particularly strong connection. This reflects the same idea as under art 4(2) in tort. However, the relevant point in time is when the event giving rise to the unjust enrichment occurs. Article 47 sentence 2 Chinese PILA seizes on the parties' common habitual residence on the second tier.

5. Default rule: country where the unjust enrichment took place

Article 10(3) Rome II Regulation serves as a default rule. It declares applicable the law of the country where the unjust enrichment took place. Provisions to the same effect are art 128(2) Swiss PILA, art 39(1) sentence 2 Turkish PILA, art 1223(1) sentence 1 Russian CC, art 31 sentence 1 Korean PILA and art 47 sentence 3 Chinese PILA. On the other hand art 14 Japanese PILA establishes the place where the events causing the non-contractual claims occurred as a connecting factor. The notion of the country where the unjust enrichment took place is not clear beyond any reasonable doubt, but allows of two possible explanations, either the place of enrichment itself relating to the result, or the place of the event causing the enrichment itself relating to the activity. The tension might be dismissed as simply a matter of wording, however the underlying implications differ in that the result will be felt in the enriched person's sphere whereas the event causing the enrichment might possibly take place in the sphere of the person from which the transferred assets derive. Either approach might favour either debtor or creditor.

If the place of enrichment is preferred, the task arises in consequence of identifying the *situs* of enrichment. Basically, one should focus on the particular asset rather than seeking a notional centre of the enriched person's wealth. As with tort, indirect or remote consequences are not relevant, but only the direct and immediate enrichment matters. For example, interest generated in one country on a sum received in another country is not relevant, but only the said sum received.

Multiple enrichments in different states call for either identifying a form of centre or establishing a mosaic approach.

6. Escape clause

The final step consists of an → escape clause as laid down in art 10(4) Rome II Regulation: '[w]here it is clear from the circumstances of the case that the non-contractual obligation arising out of unjust enrichment is manifestly more closely connected with a country other than that indicated in paragraphs 1, 2 and 3, the law of that other country shall apply'. As with all escape clauses, this rule has to be employed with extreme caution and may not be misused as granting liberty to deviate at will from the preceding rules. The main case for the escape clause might be that the intervener paid another person's debt to a third party, leading to the application of the law governing the debt paid where appropriate.

IV. Multi-party scenarios

Triangular situations and multi-party scenarios can pose almost insoluble problems on the substantive level in the law of unjust enrichment. The potential scenarios are so diverse and multi-faceted that any attempt to draft comprehensive rules is thwarted from the outset. Accordingly, Article 10 Rome I Regulation makes no such attempt, but rather one has to cope with its provisions basically designed to address bilateral situations and to adapt them to the multi-party cases as well as possible. The goal is a relative but not absolute optimum. The legislative decision not to include a provision specifically addressing multi-party cases is a wise one. Such cases are rare in cross-border settings and would not merit a specific regulation with the attendant danger of verbosity. The fundamental distinction to be drawn is between either a main approach of separating the legal treatment of individual bilateral relationships or of assessing the ensemble and entirety of all relationships concerned, this by means of some form of proper law approach (→ Proper law (doctrine)). The technical means for such an approach could be provided by art 10(4) Rome II Regulation, although this to an extent contradicts the general concept of an escape clause. The approach of separating individual relationships would seek to employ art 10(1)–(3) Rome II Regulation wherever possible and feasible.

PETER MANKOWSKI

Literature

Tim Behrens, *Bereicherungsrechtliche Mehrpersonenverhältnisse im Internationalen Privatrecht* (Sellier European Law Publisher 2011); Rolf Birk and others, 'Arts 1–24 EGBGB' in Hans-Jürgen Sonnenberger (ed) *Münchener Kommentar zum BGB*, vol 10 (5th edn, CH Beck 2010); Gralff-Peter Calliess (ed), *Rome Regulations* (Alphen aan den Rijn 2011); Adeline Chong, Choice of Law for Unjust Enrichment/Restitution and the Rome II Regulation (2008) 57 ICLQ 863; Andrew Dickinson, *The Rome II Regulation* (OUP 2008); Gerfried Fischer, 'Ungerechtfertigte Bereicherung und Geschäftsführung ohne Auftrag im europäischen Internationalen Privatrecht' in Jörn Bernreuther, Robert Freitag and Stefan Leible, *Festschrift für Ulrich Spellenberg* (Sellier European Law Publishers 2010) 151; Peter Huber, *Rome II Regulation* (Sellier European Law Publishers 2011); George Panagopoulos, *Restitution in Private international law* (Hart Publishing 2000); Stephen Pitel, 'Choice of Law for Unjust Enrichment: Rome II and the Common Law' (2008) 26 NIPR 456; Stephen Pitel, 'Rome II and Choice of Law for Unjust Enrichment' in John Ahern and William Binchy (eds), *The Rome II Regulation on the Law Applicable to Non-Contractual Obligations* (Martinus Nijhoff Publishers 2009) 231; Pattarapas Tudsri, 'Characterization of Proprietary Restitution in the Conflict of Laws' (2012–13) 44 Ottawa L.Rev. 263.

Vested rights theory

I. Concept

According to the theory of vested rights, private international law does not determine the application of any specific law, potentially a foreign law, to a given dispute; rather, it ensures the recognition of individual rights acquired and 'vested' abroad. While this approach has enjoyed a particular notoriety in private international law (see I.2. below), it is in other fields of law where the concept of vested rights (*iura quaesita*, *droits acquis*, *wohlerworbene Rechte*) emerged and still has a certain significance (see I.1. below).

1. Historical background

The rise of absolutism in 17th- and 18th-century Europe aroused the demand for a counter-balance, for a limitation of the ruler's absolutist powers and for the protection of some basic rights of subjects and citizens. The intellectual construction which could provide that counter-balance and which became popular and even dominant in those centuries was the theory of natural law. *Inter alia* it postulated the existence of certain innate rights of the individual (*iura cognata*) which are protected from curtailment by the ruler's will; some authors would grant the same protection to rights which the individual had acquired in a particular way, ie vested rights (*iura quaesita*). Authors of the latter group paved the way for the recognition of human and fundamental rights in the French Revolution and in the US Bill of Rights as well as in later constitutions. According to this tradition, vested rights operate within a given jurisdiction; they are of a public law and constitutional nature and protect the individual from the sovereign, in particular against the retroactive effect of laws which deprive him or her of those rights or somehow restrict their recognition (Burkhard Hess, *Intertemporales Privatrecht* (Mohr Siebeck 1998) 70 ff). Or, as the US Supreme Court put it in 1898: 'It is not within the power of a legislature to take away rights which have been once vested by a judgment' (*McCullough v Virginia*, 172 U.S. 102, 123 ff (1898)).

As the discipline of public international law (→ Public international law and private international law) was evolving, the protection afforded to the individual at the domestic level was extended to his or her relation to other sovereigns, especially those which appropriate the rule over a given territory from another state (Georges Kaeckenbeck, 'La protection internationale des droits acquis' (1937) 59 Rec. des cours 317; Jacques Barde, *La notion des droits acquis en droit international public* (Presses Universitaires de France 1981) ff). In the context of state succession it was soon generally agreed that the succeeding state has to recognize the private rights of individuals and private corporate bodies acquired under the rule of a previous sovereign. Thus, the Permanent Court of International Justice, in its 1926 judgment on German interests in Polish Upper Silesia, highlighted the 'principle of respect for vested rights, a principle which, as the Court has already had occasion to observe, forms part of generally accepted international law . . .' (Permanent Court of International Justice, Certain German interests in Polish Upper Silesia, 25 May 1926, PCIJ Series A, No 7, 42). Consequently this principle serves as a guideline for the interpretation of international treaties.

2. Vested rights in private international law

In cases of state succession the conflict of legal rules is one of a temporal nature; it is engendered by the sequence of different sovereigns in the same territory. This is a matter of public international law. Where the conflict arises from the existence of diverse rules of law in different jurisdictions, we are in the domain of private international law. From an historical perspective, the systematic difference was not generally acknowledged before the 20th century and then only at different times in the various countries.

In private international law, the vested rights theory was particularly well-received, elaborated and influential in Anglo-Saxon jurisdictions. Adopting a sovereignty-based publicist approach to → choice of law, they had great difficulty in accommodating the undisputed need to give effect to foreign private law in appropriate cases. While *Huber's* (→ Huber, Ulrik) recourse to → comity was readily accepted as an escape permitting exceptions from the otherwise inevitable application of the *lex fori*, it was often considered unsatisfactory because of its vagueness and the resulting lack of legal certainty. The vested rights theory appeared to reconcile the conflicting objectives and to offer

JÜRGEN BASEDOW

a solution that would allow granting legal certainty without openly applying foreign law.

In England *Albert Venn Dicey* (→ Dicey, Albert Venn) clearly enunciated this concern in 1896: 'The Courts, eg, of England, never in strictness enforce foreign law; when they are said to do so, they enforce not foreign laws, but rights acquired under foreign laws' (Albert Venn Dicey, *A Digest of the Law of England with Reference to the Conflict of Laws* (Stevens 1896) 10). This approach was applauded in a book review by *Joseph Beale* in the USA (Joseph Beale, 'Dicey's "Conflict of Laws"' (1896/97) 10 Harv.L.Rev. 168). *Beale*, who taught a whole generation of American conflicts lawyers and later served as Reporter to the Restatement (First) on the Conflict of Laws (→ Restatement (First and Second) of Conflict of Laws), summarized his views on private international law repeatedly and in an even more pointed way:

> The topic called 'Conflict of Laws' deals with the recognition and enforcement of foreign created rights. In the legal sense, all rights must be created by some law... When a right has been created by law, this right itself becomes a fact; and its existence may be a factor in an event which the same or some other law makes the condition of a new right. In other words, a right may be changed by the law that created it, or by any other law having power over it. If no law having power to do so has changed a right, the existing right should everywhere be recognized; since to do so is merely to recognize the existence of a fact. (Joseph Beale, *A Selection of Cases on the Conflict of Laws*, vol 3 (Harvard University Press 1902) 501; Joseph Beale, *A Treatise on the Conflict of Laws or Private international law* (Harvard University Press 1916) 106 ff)

The crucial question arising from this line of argument is: which law creates the right in question? It is answered by *Beale* in a strictly territorial sense:

> For the creation of rights, as has been seen, there must exist some law with power to create them... Not only must every political society have some law, but it must have only one law... Since there can be but one law in a place..., it follows that every question there arising must be determined by the law of that place. (Joseph Beale, *A Selection of Cases on the Conflict of Laws*, vol 3 (Harvard University Press 1902) 501–504).

He further elaborated the territorial approach in his voluminous treatise of 1935 (Joseph Beale, *A Treatise on the Conflict of Laws*, vol 1 (Baker, Voorhis & Co 1935) 308 ff). Thus, the vested rights theory which was influential in England and the USA up to the middle of the 20th century combined the idea of pre-created, 'vested' rights originating in the period of natural law, with a claim to strict → territoriality of the application of law and a duty of other states to recognize such rights.

On the European continent, approaches that at first blush appear similar to the vested rights theory have been predicated by various authors ever since around 1700 (Carl Georg von Wächter, 'Ueber die Collision der Privatrechtsgesetze verschiedener Staaten' (1842) 25 AcP 1–2; Ralf Michaels, 'EU Law as Private international law? Reconceptualising the Country-of-Origin Principle as Vested-Rights Theory' (2006) 2 J Priv Int L 195, 214–220). Here as well, the heyday of such approaches was shortly after 1900. In France, *Antoine Pillet* advocated this doctrine in his 1925 Hague course on the general theory of acquired rights. He postulated that

> whenever a right has regularly been acquired in some country, this right shall be respected and the effects it produces shall be ensured in another country which, like the first one, forms part of the international community. This is an absolutely inevitable necessity, a principle without which no international commerce would be possible. (Antoine Pillet, 'La théorie générale des droits acquis' (1925) 8 Rec. des cours 485, 492; author's translation)

The key issue in this line of reasoning concerns the 'regular' acquisition of a right; which law determines the regularity? *Pillet* clearly identifies the hidden choice-of-law question and asks whether the relevant law is the one designated by the choice-of-law rules of the country of origin regarding the right in question or the one which would be applicable in accordance with the choice-of-law rules of the country where the right is asserted. His answer is unambiguous:

> There is no doubt that on a question like this which touches upon the scope of application of the law and, consequently, of sovereignty, the only binding formula is the one given by the *lex fori*; there is no reason to be concerned with the law considered to govern in the country of the creation [of the right]... (Antoine Pillet, 'La théorie générale des droits acquis' (1925) 8 Rec. des cours 485, 497; author's translation.)

Where the creation of the right is thus determined by the law designated by the forum's choice-of-law rules, the alleged second step consisting of the recognition of the right is, however, reduced to naught; in fact this recognition is the immediate consequence of the application of the foreign law to the creation of the right in question. *Pillet's* approach therefore differs profoundly from the one advocated by *Dicey* and *Beale*.

II. Critique and further development

While the vested rights theory had several followers also in Germany, *von Wächter* (→ Wächter, Carl Georg von) and *von Savigny* (→ Savigny, Friedrich Carl von) raised fundamental criticisms as early as the 1840s, and the theory did not recover from that critique. As *von Wächter* pointed out, the alleged principle of the protection of vested rights depends upon the prior assertion of what is a vested right, an assertion that cannot entirely be left to a foreign state and its law, but has to be decided by the forum state and its choice-of-law rules. For that reason, *von Wächter* declared the purported principle of the protection of vested rights a *petitio principii*; 'it presupposes what still has to be proved, in particular that the legal relation is governed by foreign and not by domestic law' (Carl Georg von Wächter, 'Ueber die Collision der Privatrechtsgesetze verschiedener Staaten' (1842) 25 AcP 1, 4–5, author's translation). Some years later, *von Savigny* reiterated and deepened this criticism: 'This principle leads into a complete circle; for we can only know what are vested rights, if we know beforehand by what local law we are to decide as to their complete acquisition' (Friedrich Carl von Savigny, *A Treatise on the Conflict of Laws and the Limits of their Operation in Respect of Place and Time* (William Guthrie tr, 2nd edn, Clark 1880) § 361, 147).

This critique is based on logic, but it contains elements of valuation. *Von Wächter* asks whether the forum state, in accordance with the vested rights theory, should recognize rights to slavery, to interest at usurious rates, or to debts arising from gambling for the sole reason that they have been acquired and 'vested' in a foreign country (Carl Georg von Wächter, 'Ueber die Collision der Privatrechtsgesetze verschiedener Staaten' (1842) 25 AcP 1, 6). The rhetorical question is meant to provide support to his assertion that it is up to the forum state (and not to the law of origin) to decide which rights can be recognized as 'vested'. More than 80 years later *Pillet* (see I.2. above) highlighted the dominant role of the forum state on a similar note, although rather stressing the sovereignty of the forum state.

In modern times the vested rights theory has also been criticized for its rejection of a potential → *renvoi* element in the ascertainment of a right possibly vested in a foreign jurisdiction. Where the courts in the jurisdiction of origin (A) would not apply their own law but, in accordance with their choice-of-law rules, the law of a different country (B), the disregard by the court of the forum state (C) of the choice-of-law rules of state A leads to the recognition of a right which may not even exist in state A (Kurt Siehr, 'Renvoi und wohlerworbene Rechte' in Isaak Meier and Kurt Siehr (eds), *Rechtskollisionen – Festschrift für Anton Heini zum 65. Geburtstag* (Schulthess 1995) 407, 419). On a similar note, the inflexibility and the lack of consistency of the vested rights theory have been highlighted. Where, for example, an occurrence giving rise to a right takes place partly in state A and partly in state B, a correct appreciation of the resulting right is not possible without giving one of the territorial laws an extraterritorial effect (Elliott E Cheatham, 'American Theories of Conflict of Laws: Their Role and Utility' (1945) 58 Harv.L.Rev. 361, here cited after the reprint in Maurice S Culp (ed), *Selected Readings in Conflict of Laws* (West Publishing 1956) 48, 60–61; Pierre Arminjon, 'La notion des droits acquis en droit international privé' (1933) 44 Rec. des cours 1, 22–23).

In the final result it turned out that the vested rights theory could not subsist without the elaboration of choice-of-law rules referring to the law that determined the creation of the right. Since those choice-of-law rules imply the recognition of the right emerging from the designated law, the recognition as the second, allegedly independent and principal element of the vested rights theory becomes redundant: the court always ends up in a 'conflict of laws the solution of which is justified without any need to have recourse to the notion of vested rights. In all cases, the only point to resolve is that of the applicable law' (Pierre Arminjon, 'La notion des droits acquis en droit international privé' (1933) 44 Rec. des cours 1, 60, author's translation). At present the vested rights theory therefore appears to be an approach of the past that is no longer defended as the general basis of private international law (Ralf Michaels, 'EU Law as Private international law? Reconceptualising the Country-of-Origin Principle as Vested-Rights Theory' (2006) 2 J Priv Int L 195, 227 regarding English law).

JÜRGEN BASEDOW

From a present perspective the former adherence to the vested rights theory may be explained by a number of what now appear as amalgamations and inaccuracies. First, several writers amalgamated policy objectives and legal principles. The vested rights theory was accepted because it was beneficial to international exchange and commerce, a generally accepted goal. The recognition of rights acquired abroad can still be regarded as a policy objective that, alongside and in possible conflict with other objectives, inspires many choice-of-law rules; but it should not be taken for a legal rule itself. It is rather pursued through the operation of rules on jurisdiction, the selection of the applicable law, and recognition (→ Private international law, methods of). A second amalgamation originates in the natural law origin of the vested rights theory (see I. above): the idea of *ius quaesitum* was intended to protect individual rights from interference by 'the state'. In a liberal fashion, this included both the successor of a domestic sovereign and the foreign state where the recognition of a right acquired at home might become an issue; public international law and private international law (→ Public international law and private international law) were not yet clearly separated. A third amalgamation concerns the 'right' that was allegedly vested; there is no clear distinction in the early sources between a foreign judgment acknowledging such rights and rights which arise from legal transactions and contacts without being identified in any formalized way. Thus, the demise of the vested rights theory may be interpreted as resulting from a growing precision and awareness among conflicts lawyers of appropriate distinctions. That demise did not, however, exclude a certain revitalization of the theory in federal entities in more recent times.

III. Contemporary significance

1. The resuscitation of the vested rights theory in federal entities

As pointed out above, a major criticism of the vested rights theory highlights the excessive exposure to foreign law and values: it requires the court to recognize rights created abroad, perhaps subject solely to the → public policy exception, which it would not have acknowledged in the framework of its own legal system. This critique may be perceived as less urgent where the countries involved form part of a federal entity governed by basic common values. Here, the divergence between the values enshrined in the foreign law giving rise to the rights in question and the values of the forum where they are asserted is moderated or is overcome by the merits of competing values, in particular by the aspiration towards the unity or further development of the federal entity. Hence, the recognition of such rights may appear more acceptable.

Michaels has alluded to a certain resuscitation of the vested rights theory, albeit differently named, in federal entities (Ralf Michaels, 'EU Law as Private international law? Reconceptualising the Country-of-Origin Principle as Vested-Rights Theory' (2006) 2 J Priv Int L 195, 213–239). As to the USA he refers to the Due Process clause and the → Full Faith and Credit clause of the US Constitution, which are said to have served in the early 20th century as the legal basis for the Supreme Court when establishing a duty of the individual US courts to recognize foreign-created rights or to apply foreign law (Ralf Michaels, 'EU Law as Private international law? Reconceptualising the Country-of-Origin Principle as Vested-Rights Theory' (2006) 2 J Priv Int L 195, 220–221). Whatever may be said about this interpretation, it lost its significance when the Supreme Court decided in 1981 that the choice-of-law decision by a court cannot be challenged as long as there is a significant contact creating state interests, such that the choice of the law applied is neither arbitrary nor fundamentally unfair (*Allstate Insurance Co v Hague*, 449 U.S. 302, 313 (1981)). As *Michaels* concludes, this decision has deprived the vested rights theory in the USA of its constitutional underpinnings.

2. European Union: the country-of-origin principle

a) Country-of-origin principle and vested rights theory

With regards to the European Union a similarity of the vested rights theory with the so-called country-of-origin principle has been suggested (Ralf Michaels, 'EU Law as Private international law? Reconceptualising the Country-of-Origin Principle as Vested-Rights Theory' (2006) 2 J Priv Int L 195, 198, 221 ff). This principle has emerged from the case law of the European Court of Justice on the basic freedoms enshrined in the EU Treaties (→ Country of origin rule). In respect of the free movement of goods (now: art 34 TFEU (The Treaty on the Functioning of the European Union (consolidated version), [2012] OJ C 326/47)) the Court was asked in 1979 whether German provisions on the minimum alcohol content of a liqueur could possibly serve as a legal basis for the prohibition of the import of Cassis de Dijon from France. It answered in the negative:

> There is ... no valid reason why, provided that they have been lawfully produced and marketed in one of the Member States, alcoholic beverages should not be introduced into any other Member State; the sale of such products may not be subject to a legal prohibition on the marketing of beverages with an alcohol content lower than the limit set by the national rules. (Case 120/78 *REWE v Bundesmonopolverwaltung für Branntwein* [1979] ECR 649, para 14)

On a similar note the Court held with regard to services (now: art 56 TFEU) that 'the Treaty requires ... the abolition of any restriction ... when it is liable to ... impede the activities of a provider of services established in another Member State where he lawfully provides similar services' (Case C-76/90 *Säger v Dennemeyer* [1991] ECR I-4221, para 12). Subject to certain limitations, the Court's practice has the effect of requiring the Member States to recognize the right of any supplier established in another Member State to trade in goods or services produced or marketed in accordance with the law of its country of origin in their national markets. Other directly applicable rules of primary EU law have been held to produce similar effects (see III.3. below).

The duty to respect such rights acquired abroad may indeed be considered as similar to the court's obligation, postulated by the vested rights theory, to recognize rights created in a foreign jurisdiction. There is, however, a fundamental difference: the exponents of the vested rights theory in private international law refer to private rights asserted by private persons against other private persons, eg ownership, → marriage, maintenance, a right to → damages etc. No one ever invoked the vested rights theory to protect rights acquired abroad from sovereign intervention in the forum state. By contrast, the country-of-origin principle has been enunciated by the Court of Justice in cases opposing private persons and states, ie in a public law context. Although the *Säger* opinion arose from a civil litigation, the legal rule at issue was one of public market regulation which allegedly prohibited the defendant *Dennemeyer* from providing the services of patent renewal in → Germany. The crucial objection raised against the vested rights theory, ie that the law giving rise to the right in question still has to be determined under choice-of-law rules and that the theory therefore leads into a vicious circle (see II. above), does not hold true in public law. In public law matters there is no doubt about the territorial application of the law; the country of origin and its law which created the right in question are always clear.

b) Application to private law issues

So far the Court of Justice has expanded the scope of the country-of-origin principle only to a few issues of private law. This has occurred in the field of unfair competition (→ Competition, unfair). Here, the Court has declared that a law of the target or host state prohibiting advertising practices which are lawful in the country of origin of the advertising firm may be incompatible with basic freedoms (Case C-362/88 *GB-Inno-BM v Confédération du commerce luxembourgeois* [1990] ECR I-667; Case C-126/91 *Schutzverband gegen Unwesen in der Wirtschaft v Yves Rocher* [1993] ECR I-2384). The law of advertising is generally subject to the territorial regime of the market concerned, either under the choice-of-law rules of private international law (see art 6 → Rome II Regulation (Regulation (EC) No 864/2007 of the European Parliament and of the Council of 11 July 2007 on the law applicable to non-contractual obligations (Rome II), [2007] OJ L 199/40)) or as a consequence of the territorial application of public market regulations. The recognition, by the Court of Justice, of an undertaking's right to employ the advertising practices of its home market also in the target or host market, irrespective of the divergent laws of the latter, may therefore be interpreted as the recognition, by the host state, of a right 'vested' in the country of origin. But again, this has happened in an area where the 'country of origin' and thereby the law giving rise to the right of advertising are unambiguously identified.

It is still unclear whether the country-of-origin principle, as applied to private law issues, is a choice-of-law rule or rather a rule of EU law impacting choice of law. The progressive codification of private international law at EU level renders this question largely immaterial. The role of the country-of-origin principle may perhaps be extrapolated from the interpretation of the E-Commerce Directive (Directive 2000/31/EC of the European Parliament and of the Council of 8 June 2000 on certain legal aspects of information society services, in particular electronic commerce, in the Internal Market (Directive on electronic commerce) [2000] OJ L178/1) by the Court of Justice. Against the background of a very complex setting, Recital (22) of that Directive points out that 'information society services should in principle be subject to the law of the Member State in which the service provider is established', while art 1(4) explicitly states that this 'Directive does not establish additional rules on private international law . . .'. Under art 3(2) Member States may not, 'for reasons falling within the coordinated field, restrict the freedom to provide information society services from another Member State', and the definition of art 2(h)(i), second indent includes issues concerning the service provider's liability in the coordinated field that should be subject to the law of the country of origin (Recital (22), see above). In a case involving such liability the Court of Justice was called upon to reconcile those divergent indications of the Directive. It pointed out that art 3 need not be interpreted as requiring transposition in the form of a choice-of-law rule referring to the law of the country of origin, but that Member States must ensure that a service provider, except for particular reasons specified in the Directive, is not 'subject to stricter requirements than those provided for by the substantive law applicable in the Member State in which that service provider is established' (Joined cases C-509/09 and C-161/10 *eDate advertising v X* [2011] ECR I-10269, paras 60–68). Arguably this substantive law limitation also applies where the country-of-origin principle follows from primary EU law.

3. *European Union: the principle of mutual recognition*

The Anglo-Saxon variant of the vested rights theory consists of two elements: the territorial approach to the ascertainment of the acquisition of a right – which is an equivalent to the country-of-origin principle – and the court's duty to recognize such foreign-created rights. The principle of (mutual) recognition becomes increasingly significant in EU law, both in case law and in legislation.

a) Case law of the ECJ
The impact of the principle of recognition is particularly visible in company law. According to the choice-of-law rules of some Member States the law applicable to a company is determined not by the statutory seat, but by the location of the actual administration, the 'real seat'. A transfer of the headquarters to another country will therefore lead to a change of the applicable law. Since the company was not founded in accordance with the new applicable law, the relocation may engender the loss of the company's legal personality, ie a loss of its capacity to hold rights and to appear in court (→ Capacity and emancipation) unless it is reincorporated under the new law. According to the Court of Justice such

> requirement of reincorporation . . . is tantamount to outright negation of freedom of establishment [under art 49 and 54 TFEU]. In those circumstances, the refusal by a host Member State . . . to recognise the legal capacity of a company formed in accordance with the law of another Member State . . . constitutes a restriction of the freedom of establishment. (Case C-208/00 *Überseering BV v NCC* [2002] ECR I-9919, paras 81–82)

Put in other words, Member States are under a duty to recognize the legal capacity of a company established in another Member State, ie a right vested abroad. The bearing of this jurisprudence on the other various aspects of company law is still unclear. The criticism voiced against the vested rights theory (II. above) does not hold water in the present context because the country of origin of a company and the law bestowing legal personality on it unambiguously emerge from the entry into the foreign company register.

A further area of private law that is affected by what may appear as a revival of the vested rights theory concerns the → names of individuals. German parents living in → Denmark had registered their new-born child, who was a German national as well, under the family name *Grunkin-Paul*. In accordance with Danish law this name was composed of the family names of the father and the mother. When they later moved to → Germany, the German registry office refused to register the child with this family name, insisting, because of the child's → nationality, on the application of German law which did not allow a child's surname to be composed of each of the parents' family names, but required the parents to choose between their surnames. The dispute went to court and up to the Court of Justice. It pointed out that the need to use a surname in the country of which the child is a national differing from the surname conferred and registered in the country of birth hampered the exercise of the right of free movement of an EU citizen (now: art 21 TFEU). The Court concluded that the right to free movement flowing from EU citizenship 'precludes the authorities of a Member State . . . from refusing to recognise a child's surname, as determined and registered in a second Member State in which the child . . . was born and has been resident since birth' (Case C-353/06 *Grunkin and Paul* [2008] ECR I-7639, para 39). Again, the Court uses a term of recognition familiar from the vested rights theory. And again this occurs in respect of a right registered in a foreign country.

b) Legislation
It might appear that the following general principle can be inferred from the cases reported above: a legal situation that has crystallized through registration or other proceedings in one Member State shall be recognized in other Member States irrespective of choice-of-law rules, perhaps subject to a public policy reservation. In fact, such principle might be regarded to be in line with the Union's mission expressed in art 81 TFEU to 'develop judicial cooperation in civil matters . . ., based on the principle of mutual recognition of judgments and of decisions in extrajudicial cases'. The reference to 'decisions in extrajudicial cases' makes clear that the principle of mutual recognition does not relate to legal situations which arise from the application of a substantive law without the stabilization and solidification resulting from administrative or judicial proceedings. Put in other words, a contract concluded or a holographic will executed in a foreign country is not capable of being 'recognized'; it is valid or invalid in accordance with the law applicable under the relevant choice-of-law rules.

It is, however, doubtful whether the principle enunciated above is already sufficiently underpinned by specific experience in the various fields of law. Apart from the legal capacity of → companies and the → names of individuals, EU law has not yet established many duties of recognition bearing substantive effects. A duty of enforcement is enshrined in art 58 Brussels I Regulation (recast) (Regulation (EU) No 1215/2012 of the European Parliament and of the Council of 12 December 2012 on jurisdiction and the recognition and enforcement of judgments in civil and commercial matters (recast), [2012] OJ L 351/1; → Brussels I (Convention and Regulation)) and art 46 → Brussels IIa Regulation (Council Regulation (EC) No 2201/2003 of 27 November 2003 concerning jurisdiction and the recognition and enforcement of judgments in matrimonial matters and the matters of parental responsibility, repealing Regulation (EC) No 1347/2000, [2003] OJ L 338/1) with regard to authentic acts, court settlements and certain agreements enforceable in the country of origin. And arts 59 and 60 of the Succession Regulation (Regulation (EU) No 650/2012 of the European Parliament and of the Council of 4 July 2012 on jurisdiction, applicable law, recognition and enforcement of decisions and acceptance and enforcement of authentic instruments in matters of succession and on the creation of a European Certificate of Succession, [2012] OJ L 201/107; → Rome IV Regulation) extend the evidentiary and enforcement effect of authentic instruments executed in a Member State and relating to matters of succession to all other participating Member States. But would all legally relevant facts and occurrences evidenced in some kind of public document be susceptible of being recognized and of producing their substantive effects in all other Member States for the sole reason of the principle of mutual recognition mentioned above (→ Recognition of legal situations evidenced by documents)? In a Green Paper of 2010 the EU Commission contemplated such an extension of the principle with regard to matters of civil status such as kinship relations (→ Kinship and legitimation), → marriage, → adoption and acknowledgement of paternity (European Commission, 'Green Paper: Less bureaucracy for citizens: promoting free movement of public documents and recognition for the effects of civil status records of 14 December 2010' COM(2010) 747 final, part 4). However, the proposal resulting from the public consultation abandoned the idea and exclusively aims at ensuring the free movement of public documents by reducing formalities (European Commission, 'Proposal for a Regulation of the European Parliament and of the Council on promoting the free movement of citizens and businesses by simplifying the acceptance of certain public documents in the European Union and amending Regulation (EU) No 1024/2012 of 24 April 2013' COM(2013) 228 final, see in particular Recital (6)).

It is characteristic of the recognition of legal situations that a state where the consequences of such situation are asserted does not apply its own choice-of-law rules (Paul Lagarde,

'Introduction au thème de la reconnaissance des situations: Rappel des points les plus discutés' in Paul Lagarde (ed), *La reconnaissance des situations en droit international privé* (Pedone 2013) 19). In Dutch private international law this is indeed what the law provides for:

> In the Netherlands, the same legal consequences may be attributed to a fact to which legal consequences are attributed pursuant to the law which is applicable under the private international law of a foreign state involved, in contravention to the law applicable to Dutch private international law, as far as not attaching those consequences would constitute an unacceptable violation of the legitimate expectations of the parties or of legal certainty. (art 10:9 Dutch New Civil Code (Nieuw Burgerlijk Wetboek of 1 January 1992))

Thus the principle of recognition of vested rights is an equitable solution that applies under uncertain conditions. But it encounters the criticism voiced against the vested rights theory reported above (see II. above). When is a foreign state involved? This cannot be ascertained without legal provisions of the forum state that determine which involvement is relevant and which is not. The EU appears well-advised to further study the interplay of private international law and basic freedoms before adopting a similar rule.

JÜRGEN BASEDOW

Literature

Pierre Arminjon, 'La notion des droits acquis en droit international privé' (1933) 44 Rec. des cours 1; Jacques Barde, *La notion des droits acquis en droit international public* (Presses Universitaires de France 1981); Joseph Beale, 'Dicey's Conflict of Laws' (1896/97) 10 Harv.L.Rev. 168; Joseph Beale, *A Selection of Cases on the Conflict of Laws*, vols 1–3 (Harvard University Press 1902–1907); Joseph Beale, *A Treatise on the Conflict of Laws or Private international law* (Harvard University Press 1916); Joseph Beale, *A Treatise on the Conflict of Laws*, vols 1–3 (Baker, Voorhis & Co 1935); Elliott E Cheatham, 'American Theories of Conflict of Laws: Their Role and Utility' (1945) 58 Harv.L.Rev. 361, here cited after the reprint in Maurice S Culp (ed), *Selected Readings in Conflict of Laws* (West Publishing 1956) 48; Albert Venn Dicey, *A Digest of the Law of England with Reference to the Conflict of Laws* (Stevens 1896); Burkhard Hess, *Intertemporales Privatrecht* (Mohr Siebeck 1998); Georges Kaeckenbeeck, 'La protection internationale des droits acquis' (1937) 59 Rec. des cours 317; Paul Lagarde (ed), *La reconnaissance des situations en droit international privé* (Pedone 2013); Ralf Michaels, 'EU Law as Private international law? Reconceptualising the Country-of-Origin Principle as Vested-Rights Theory' (2006) 2 J Priv Int L 195; Antoine Pillet, 'La théorie générale des droits acquis' (1925) 8 Rec. des cours 485; Friedrich Carl von Savigny, *A Treatise on the Conflict of Laws and the Limits of their Operation in Place and Time* (William Guthrie tr, 2nd edn, Clark 1880); Kurt Siehr, 'Renvoi und wohlerworbene Rechte' in Isaak Meier and Kurt Siehr (eds), *Rechtskollisionen – Festschrift für Anton Heini zum 65. Geburtstag* (Schulthess 1995) 407; Carl Georg von Wächter, 'Ueber die Collision der Privatrechtsgesetze verschiedener Staaten' (1841) 24 AcP 230 and (1842) 25 AcP 1.

Voet, Paulus and Johannes

Paulus and *Johannes Voet*, father and son, were two of the main proponents of the statutist theory as it was developed and theoretically underpinned in the Netherlands in the course of the 17th century.

I. Paulus Voet

1. Life and work

Paulus Voet lived from 1619 to 1667. He was born on 7 June 1619 in Heusden as the son of *Deliana Jans* and *Gijsbert Voet*, a clergyman who became a professor of theology at the University of Utrecht in 1634. *Paul* studied philosophy and law at the University of Utrecht and received his *Magister Artium* from the Law Faculty there in 1640. He was appointed professor extraordinarius in metaphysics in Utrecht on 24 May 1641 and with the addition of logic and Greek to his teaching commitments, attained full professor status there in 1644. He had, in the meantime, furthered his knowledge in the study of law and was awarded the title of *Juris Doctor Utriusque* in 1645. He was commissioned to teach at the Faculty of Law and was appointed full professor of law on 21 April 1654. His studies focused specifically on the Institutes. In addition to his academic career, *Paulus Voet* was also a judge at the Court in Vianen.

2. Contribution to private international law

Paulus Voet first expressed his thoughts on the cross-border effects of law in '*De Statutis eorumque Concursu, liber singularis*' (Ex officina Johannis à Waesberge 1661; reprinted in 1700 and 1715). *Voet* describes the classification of the articles and their operation in this work. Besides using the, until then, accepted format based on objective and ratio in real (*statuta realia*) and personal statutes (*statuta personalia*), *Voet* differentiates a third group of articles (*statuta mixta*) based on their functioning. *Voet* was criticized by *Abraham van Wesel* (*Commentarius ad Novellas Constitutiones Ultraiectinas*, 1666) because of his divergent views, but took the opportunity to defend and further elucidate his ideas in his *Rebus Mobilibus et Immobilibus* (1666).

In line with the then general view, *Voet* argues that a classification into real and personal statutes is most logical when the objective is the starting point. According to *Voet* only two categories remain viable based on this criterion because ultimately each law relates to either a right or a person, even if a law concerns formalities. However, according to *Voet*, a third category, the *statuta mixta*, should be distinguished if the effect of a statute is taken as the starting point.

Because it is difficult to determine whether a statutory provision qualifies as real, personal or mixed, *Voet* provides a number of auxiliary norms through which the main topic of each relevant statutory provision can first and foremost be determined. Moreover, it is not so much the wording of the provision, but the intention of the legislature which is decisive. This means that a statute can be real, even if the wording relates to people, or can be personal, even if it refers to goods. A similar view was already expressed by *d'Argentré*, *Burgundus* and *Rodenburg* (Johannes Philippus Suijling, *De Statutentheorie in Nederland gedurende de XVIIde eeuw* (Robijns 1893) 42). According to *Paulus Voet*, one should come to the following classification based on the objective and effect of statutes: *Statuta realia* are the laws that apply to everyone, but only within the limits of their own territory. *Voet* expresses it as the laws which are invalid beyond the boundaries of the area of those making the law. These laws are not binding for persons in relation to real estate outside the territory.

Statuta personalia are laws that apply only in respect of a state's subjects (the people residing within its territory). These laws have extraterritorial effect; the state and the authority granted to a person by his *lex domicilii* follows such person everywhere. *Voet* makes an exception if this concerns → immovable property situated in a foreign country. In this connection the real statute pertains because the sovereignty of the state of the *situs* disallows the domination of a foreign law.

Statuta Mixta are laws that have effect both within and beyond a state's territory. Within the territory, they are binding on both its own subjects and on foreigners operating there, as well as having legal effect with regard to goods located anywhere outside the state's territory. The consequences (effects) of these laws are similar for both real and personal laws.

Voet gives precedence to the principle of sovereignty in this. The absolute sovereignty of states stands in the way of any extraterritorial effect of foreign statutes: 'Laws are statements of independent supreme powers that have no obligation to each other at all. Thus, the laws of one State can never be legally binding within the territory of the other' (Johannes Philippus Suijling, *De Statutentheorie in Nederland gedurende de XVIIde eeuw* (Robijns 1893) 50).

However, the established practice in Utrecht and the other provinces of the Republic of the Seven United Netherlands was different. So, on what basis did their judges apply the law of other Provinces? *Rodenburg*, one of the predecessors of *Voet*, was of the opinion that '*ex rei natura*' a legal obligation for sovereign states existed to apply foreign law. *Voet*, in contrast, endeavours to explain and justify the practice of law while still maintaining the principle of sovereignty (Roeland D Kollewijn, *Geschiedenis van de Nederlandse wetenschap van het internationaal privaatrecht tot 1880* (Noord-Hollandse Uitg Mij 1937) 82). It is '*ex comitate*' rather than any legal obligation that states tolerate the validity and application of foreign law (→ Foreign law, application and ascertainment) within their territory. *Voet* was the first to utilize *comitas* in this context whereby application of foreign law does not take place because of an obligation between one state and another. It is rather an expression of goodwill which goes beyond the scope of international law. A legal (international law) basis for such application does not exist.

On the one hand, *Voet* emphasizes the freedom of one state to tolerate the law of another, but on the other hand he insists on rules by which to determine when judges are obliged to apply foreign law. These rules may be made or approved by the legislature of the state concerned, but can also result from the requirements of fairness (*aequitas*), civility (*humanitas*)

MATHIJS TEN WOLDE

or a need for rights relating to international social and legal traffic (interaction).

The *comitas* is nothing more than the extraterritorial side of these rules, indicating that the application of foreign law is a matter of benevolence rather than of submission. In the courtroom, however, these rules are binding for both the parties and the court (with reference to the excellent analysis of Roeland D Kollewijn, *Geschiedenis van de Nederlandse wetenschap van het internationaal privaatrecht tot 1880* (Noord-Hollandse Uitg Mij 1937) 83 ff).

3. Influence on private international law

Through the theory of *Paulus Voet*, private international law slowly but surely starts to liberate itself from the Roman legal idea that private international law should be universal. It is a first step towards the development of national private international law (Roeland D Kollewijn, *Geschiedenis van de Nederlandse wetenschap van het internationaal privaatrecht tot 1880* (Noord-Hollandse Uitg Mij 1937) 88).

Voet's great significance for private international law lies in the discovery of the *comitas* as a basis for the application of foreign law within a state's territory. His ideas propelled his contemporaries to respond and counter them but also inspired further development. His ideology was expanded and elaborated by his son *Johannes*.

Paulus Voet's theory has little significance to modern Dutch private international law which is primarily based on the conflict theory of *Savigny* (→ Savigny, Friedrich Carl von). The doctrine of *comitas* has, however, influenced the Anglo-American private international law through case law. More specifically that of Scotland, England and the USA, as well as legal doctrine in the USA. The work of *Paulus Voet* contributed mightily to building the foundations of South African private international law (A Basil Edwards, *The Selective Paulus Voet* (University of South Africa 2007) 3).

II. Johannes Voet

1. Life and work

Johannes Voet lived from 1647 to 1714. He was born in Utrecht on 3 October 1647 to *Elisabeth van Winssen* and *Paulus Voet* who was a professor of law in Utrecht. *Johannes* was educated at the College of Utrecht, where he studied law. He worked briefly as a professor at the College (*Gymnasium*) of Herborn before being appointed professor at the College of Utrecht (*Hogeschool Utrecht*) on 11 May 1673 on the condition that he would receive no salary for the first two years. However, it was only on 25 August 1674 that *Johannes Voet* formally accepted the professorship and held his inaugural speech titled '*De Advocatis*'. Five years later he became dean (*Rector Magnificus*) of the College, shortly following which, in 1680, he was appointed professor at Leiden University.

The College of Utrecht attempted unsuccessfully to entice *Voet* to return to Utrecht in December 1687 by offering him a salary of 2,000 guilders a year. However, his salary in Leiden was significantly increased because of the offer. *Johannes Voet* was *Rector Magnificus* of the College of Leiden (*Hogeschool Leiden*) in 1681, 1686 and 1709. *Voet* was the first to combine Roman law teaching with contemporary law, for which purpose he used *Hugo Grotius' Inleydinge tot de Hollantsche rechtsgeleertheit* (Den Haag 1631) (Introduction to the laws of Holland) as the starting point. This was directly influenced by the extension of his teaching commitments in 1688 to include 'the practice of law'. His writings demonstrate his knowledge of classical literature and feudal law (*leenrecht*) (Abraham Jacob van der Aa, *Biographisch Woordenboek der Nederlanden* (Brederode 1852–78), part 19, p 303; Jef J van Kuyk, *Nieuw Nederlandsch Biografisch Woordenboek* (Sijthoff 1911–37), part 3, p 1328).

Voet published many works from 1670 onwards, of which '*Commentarius ad Pandectas*' (Leiden 1698), dealing, among other things, with private international law, is most important. As a result of this book he became a scholar of renown in Europe.

2. Contribution to private international law

Johannes Voet follows his father *Paulus'* line of thinking, but *Johannes'* works are better organized and easier to read. This helped him garner more fame in the field of private international law than his father had. It is, nevertheless, important to recognize that *Paulus Voet* was the original thinker, whose son *Johannes* perfected his father's theories, turning them into a comprehensive system.

Johannes Voet first discusses private international law in his extensive '*Commentarius ad Pandectas*'. It was a subject he had deliberately ignored in earlier works. He follows the threefold division of the statutes based on the criteria distinguished by his father (*De Statutis eorumque Concursu, liber singularis*) in the first book, Title IV, Part 2, of his *Commentarius*. The intention of the legislature plays an important role in determining the nature of the relevant statute and he considers a state's sovereignty to be paramount.

The *statuta personalia* are the laws intended by the legislator to govern the state and the authority of a person, regardless of whether they refer to a person and/or goods. Such laws determine, for example, if a person is the subject of a particular state, is competent to make a will, or whether a married woman or minor can enter into a contract without the consent of spouse or guardian.

Statuta realia relate primarily to goods and are designed to regulate the status thereof. Once again, the intention of the legislator is decisive. In this category, among other elements in this set, *Voet* includes rules governing entitlement under intestate succession and whether or not gifts between spouses are allowed.

Statuta mixta determine the form, the manner and the order of official proceedings (solemnities) regarding goods conducted by persons, both in and outside of court proceedings, rather than the persons or goods themselves. *Johannes Voet* refers explicitly to his father with regard to the term *statuta mixta*.

As with his father, *Johannes Voet* presumes the absolute sovereignty of a state regarding the force and effect of laws outside a legislator's territory. The consequence of this strict principle, says *Voet*, is that laws, whether personal, real or mixed, have no inherent cross-border effect. Laws may indeed have no more power than the legislature has attributed to them, and because the power of the legislature is limited to its own territory, it is clear that the power of these laws is limited to that territory.

Regarding the *statuta realia*, authors were in agreement that territorial restriction is self-explanatory and that it is unnecessary to expound further on the subject. Various authors endorsed the view that personal laws extend beyond the boundaries of a legislature's territory, but *Voet* argues that those views lack reasoning and are not in accordance with Roman law. *Personal statuta* are territorial by nature as well, simply because the legislator's powers do not extend beyond its borders. According to *Voet*, the same reasoning should be followed with regard to the *statuta mixta*.

The above implies that no court is compelled to apply foreign law in respect of property (→ Property and proprietary rights) situated within its own state's territory. This does not, however, hinder a court to apply foreign law under the *comitas*.

In the same way as his father, *Johannes Voet* considers the *comitas* to be a reciprocal concession by states, based on the goodwill of one sovereign state towards another. The *comitas* stems from the own interests of a state in the pursuit of mutual benefit between states. *Voet* makes the comparison of a private person granting favours to others and receiving favours in return. If such a person did not do this, pursuing only his own interests instead, he would only be making his own life difficult.

The *comitas* tempers the strict territorial application of statutes. In order to determine the extent of the *comitas* one must identify the situations in which the *jus strictum* is relinquished. The rule that real estate is governed by the local law is the first example of such a circumstance. While *Paulus Voet* still considers this rule to be a *lex suprema* binding on all states, it is *Johannes Voet* who correlates it to a *comitas* situation (Roeland D Kollewijn, *Geschiedenis van de Nederlandse wetenschap van het internationaal privaatrecht tot 1880* (Noord-Hollandse Uitg Mij 1937) 113). The rule by which movables follow their owner (*mobilia sequuntur personam*) has, according to *Voet*, become a conflict law common in the different countries and should therefore be treated as such. Despite the lack of a common legislator for this rule, it is, nonetheless, based on *comitas gentium*. The same can be said, according to *Voet*, for the permission to allow the judgments from Utrecht to be executed in Holland and vice versa for example. Following the same line of thought, it is agreed upon that an executor, appointed in the place of residence of a deceased or a bankrupt person, can exercise his authority in another country as well.

The *locus regit actum* rule, based as it is on the *comitas*, forms a generally accepted exception to the strict territorial application of the law as well. The different states have accepted this rule particularly on grounds of efficacy. However, it is not valid if someone acts in *fraudem statuti* of his place of residence. *Voet* names other exceptions to the *locus regit actum* rule in cases where, instead of following the prescribed procedures of the place where legal action took place, those of the place of the domicile or of the place where the real estate is actually situated have been followed in their place.

Mathijs ten Wolde

A testament made in another country, not in accordance with local formalities but in accordance with the solemnities of the place of residence, must be recognized *ex aequo et bono* by the judge of the place of residence. Again, *Johannes Voet* follows the view of his father in this matter (Roeland D Kollewijn, *Geschiedenis van de Nederlandse wetenschap van het internationaal privaatrecht tot 1880* (Noord-Hollandse Uitg Mij 1937) 117). However, where *Paulus Voet* was of the opinion that a testament regarding real estate, made in one country, not being that of the *situs*, but in accordance with the laws of the situs, is invalid, *Johannes Voet* defended the view that such a testament would be valid. He did not make use of strict law in this but argued that deviation from the *comitas* did not cause any disruption to something which had been effected legally elsewhere and would therefore not be detrimental to another state.

As his father before him, *Johannes Voet* held the view that, although it is possible, with here and there an exception, to identify general directives, valid in all *states* regarding the working of the *comitas* in real and mixed laws, this is not sufficiently possible in the case of personal laws. The rules involved in this cannot be deduced from universally accepted, mutually understood principles and, as such, their existence must be determined for each legal institution separately.

Voet concludes his treatise over private international law with a discourse on the question whether and the extent to which it is permissible for private persons to deviate, even though in mutual agreement, from the law. He differentiates in this between regulations covering public law matters and those with a private law character. Regulations covering public law matters have a mandatory character and therefore cannot be deviated from, without any exceptions. As far as the regulations covering private law matters are concerned, *Voet* is of the opinion that they can, even so, be partly disregarded where they comprise supplementary law.

3. *Influence on private international law*

a) At the time
Johannes Voet was, during his life, a scholar of renown in Europe. He perfected the theories of his father and in doing so enabled the *comitas* theory to reach its climax. Dutch lawyers of the 17th and 18th centuries generally accepted his doctrine almost without question. In fact there was practically no discussion on its underlying principles following *Johannes Voet's* clarification. Any debate to be found in legal literature of this period is usually only related to the effect of the chosen principles in actual cases.

b) In the long run
Like that of his father *Paulus*, *Johannes Voet's* theory has little significance to modern Dutch private international law which is primarily based on the theory of *Savigny*. The doctrine of *comitas* has, however, influenced the Anglo-American private international law through case law. More specifically that of → Scotland, → England and the United States, as well as legal doctrine in the → USA. The work of both *Johannes Voet* and of his father *Paulus Voet* contributed mightily to building the foundations of South African private international law (A Basil Edwards, *The Selective Paulus Voet* (University of South Africa 2007) 3).

MATHIJS TEN WOLDE

Literature

Abraham Jacob van der Aa, *Biographisch Woordenboek der Nederlanden* (Brederode 1852–78), part 19, p 303 (Johannes Voet) and p 304 (Paulus Voet); ThM de Boer, 'Living Apart Together: The Relationship between Public and Private international law' (2010) 57 NILR 183; A Basil Edwards, *The Selective Paulus Voet* (University of South Africa 2007); Roeland D Kollewijn, *Geschiedenis van de Nederlandse wetenschap van het internationaal privaatrecht tot 1880* (Noord-Hollandse Uitg Mij 1937); Jef J van Kuyk, *Nieuw Nederlandsch Biografisch Woordenboek (NNBW)* (Sijthoff 1911–37), part 3, p 1328 (Johannes Voet) and pp 1329–30 (Paulus Voet); Kurt H Nadelmann, 'Joseph Story's Contribution to American Conflicts Law: A Comment' (1962) 5 Am.J.Legal Hist. 230; Johannes MB Scholten, *Het begrip comitas in het internationaal privaatrecht van de Hollandse juristenschool der zeventiende eeuw* (Dekker & van de Vegt 1949); Johannes Philippus Suijling, *De Statutentheorie in Nederland gedurende de XVIIde eeuw* (Robijns 1893).

Wächter, Carl Georg von

Carl Georg von Wächter (1797–1880) was once considered 'one of the greatest German jurists of all times' (Ernst Landsberg, *Geschichte der*

Deutschen Rechtswissenschaft, vol 3/2 (Verl Oldenbourg 1910) 386), but was all but forgotten in the 20th century, despite an excellent dissertation on his work in private international law (Nikolaus Sandmann, *Grundlagen und Einfluss der internationalprivatrechtlichen Lehre Carl Georg von Wächters (1797–1880)* (Diss Münster 1979)). In private international law, he is known mainly for his refutation of earlier theories, in particular the theory of statutes. Positively, *Wächter* is mainly (and not accurately) known as a proponent of a strong preference for the → *lex fori* and as such mainly presented in opposition to *Friedrich Carl von Savigny's* theory (→ Savigny, Friedrich Carl von). Only recently has there been renewed interest in him. And in rereading, *Wächter* proves to be prescient for today's state of the discipline.

I. *Wächter's* life and work

1. Life

Wächter was born in 1797 in Württemberg, where his father worked in the state administration. He would have liked to study medicine or theology, but the king ordered him to study law. *Wächter* mostly studied in Tübingen, then the only university available to citizens of Württemberg, but was able to spend one semester abroad in Heidelberg, which had a far better university. Here, he was influenced especially by *Carl Theodor Welcker* (1790–1869), a proponent of the historical school, and *Anton Friedrich Justus Thibaut* (1772–1840), an early proponent of legislative codification. In September 1818 *Wächter* passed his university exam in Tübingen; in March 1819 he became a judge; in the same year he was, at age 21, appointed a professor at Tübingen. These developments were consequences not just of his brilliance but also of the political turmoil in Württemberg and the dire needs of the struggling university. As soon as 1825, he became rector of the university but left after five years because his loyalty to the government and opposition against greater autonomy of the university did not find enough support. *Wächter* accepted a chair at Leipzig for three years (1833–36) before returning to Tübingen, where he became chancellor, extraordinary government representative and 'First Professor of Law'. As such, he was also a member, and from 1839 the President, of Württemberg's chamber of representatives. After the 1848 revolution led to a more liberal government, *Wächter* refused both his post in the newly constituted chamber of representatives and, in 1851, his office as university chancellor. To escape the new political environment he adopted a post as president of the Supreme Appellate Court of the Free Cities in Lübeck. However, he stayed for less than a year before taking up a chair again at the University of Leipzig in 1852, where he remained until his death. During this time, he was instrumental in the establishment of the German Lawyers Association in 1860, and presided over its inaugural session in Berlin as well as four other sessions. After a breakdown in 1872, *Wächter* reduced his academic obligations but kept working until his death in 1880. Numerous obituaries, including three of book length (by his Leipzig successor *Bernhard Windscheid* (1817–92), his son *Oskar von Wächter* (1825–1902) and *Heinrich Dernburg* (1829–1907)) demonstrate the high esteem in which he had been held.

2. Work

Wächter's work is broad, and private international law only concerns a small element in it; in fact, most biographies devote very little space to it. *Wächter* was in many ways a conservative: his work is characterized by legal positivism, informed by his loyalty to the state with its monarchy and its laws and distrust in popular democracy. At the same time, he supported constitutional principles of separation and power, positions that had more affinity with liberal principles. Moreover, he cannot be neatly placed in the virulent dispute between Germanists and Romanists. What is clear is that he was a nationalist and had little interest in comparative law beyond German borders. Similarly, although, as a positivist, he was clearly influenced by *Thibaut*, he nonetheless shared with *Savigny* an interest in law as it had developed historically. All in all, his interest was more in actual law than in its theories. His use of legal sources was more thorough than that of many others, while he largely ignored philosophical and theoretical literature as well as theories of natural law. Despite his interest in legal history he insisted on separating both the history of law and the law as it should be from the law currently in force.

All of this may explain both the high esteem for him during his lifetime and the relative lack of interest in him after his death. Almost all of Wächter's publications were written also with practical interests in mind: to help practitioners in their daily work, but also with a view to potential or actual legislation. In this sense, Wächter's significant involvement in legislation and his academic work were closely interrelated, more so than for other scholars of his time. Windscheid's assessment is instructive: 'There have been more erudite jurists than Wächter. There have been more profound jurists than Wächter. But there has not been, among the great German jurists, a more juristic jurist – a jurist in whom everything is combined that is necessary for the practice of law' (Bernhard Windscheid, Carl Georg von Wächter (Duncker & Humblot 1880) 79).

Although Wächter always read widely, he began his scholarly career with a specific emphasis on criminal law. In 1825 and 1826 he published a treatise on Roman–German criminal law, later a number of articles in this area. A second edition of the treatise, entitled 'Common Law of Germany' (1842), included also private law and signalled a shift to that field; between 1838 and 1842 he published his important Handbook of Private Law in Württemberg (Carl Georg von Wächter, Handbuch des im Königreiche Württemberg geltenden Privatrechts, vols 1 and 2 (Metzler 1839–42)). His declared goal was to describe the actual law valid in Württemberg as a whole, without distinction between local and imported (Roman) law; it was meant as a preparation for a possible codification. Wächter continued his interests in both criminal and private law after his move to Leipzig. During that time, he wrote a critique of the Saxon draft civil code (Carl Georg von Wächter, Der Entwurf eines bürgerlichen Gesetzbuches für das Königreich Sachsen: ein Beitrag zur Beurtheilung desselben (Tauchnitz 1853)). He also published parts towards a Handbook on the Criminal Law of Saxony and Thuringia (Carl Georg von Wächter, Das Königlich Sächsische und das Thüringische Strafrecht: Ein Handbuch – Einleitung und Allgemeiner Teil (Metzler 1857)), which has been considered the founding text for an emerging scientific approach to criminal law (see Lars Jungemann, Carl Georg von Wächter (1797–1880) und das Strafrecht des 19. Jahrhunderts. Strafrechtliche Lehre und Wirkungsgeschichte (Duncker & Humblot 1999)). He continued to publish widely, often in close relation to his teaching; important among his later publications is a treatise on the Pandects (Carl Georg von Wächter, Pandekten Vol 1: Allgemeine Lehren (Breitkopf und Härtel 1880)).

Wächter's scholarly interests went further than the doctrine of criminal law and private law, however: he published several texts in favour of a codification and of German legal unification. In 1847 he received a royal mandate to negotiate with several German governments the possibility of unified codifications in criminal law, private law and procedure – a project brought to its end by the 1848 revolutions. In addition, Wächter's oeuvre includes several articles dedicated to issues of legislation.

Wächter's most important contribution to private international law lies in a treatise-like article of 238 pages published in several instalments in the Archiv für die civilistische Praxis in 1841 and 1842 (Carl Georg von Wächter, 'Ueber die Collision der Privatrechtsgesetze verschiedener Staaten' (1841) 24 AcP 230, (1842) 25 AcP 1, 161, 361). The article emerged from his research towards his handbook of Wurttembergian private law (but was published separately, perhaps because Wächter rightly felt it could be of broader interest). A summary of the findings is found in the handbook (Carl Georg von Wächter, Handbuch des im Königreiche Württemberg geltenden Privatrechts, vol 2 (Metzler 1842) 79–119). Shortly before his death, in his treatise on the Pandects, Wächter addressed responses to his article, especially by Savigny and von Bar; he saw no reason to alter his views from 40 years earlier (Carl Georg von Wächter, Pandekten Vol 1: Allgemeine Lehren (Breitkopf und Härtel 1880) 146–7). Wächter also applied his findings on the territorial scope of criminal law (Carl Georg von Wächter, Das Königlich Sächsische und das Thüringische Strafrecht: Ein Handbuch – Einleitung und Allgemeiner Teil (Metzler 1857) 125–75).

II. Contribution to private international law

1. Background

Wächter's fame in private international law rests entirely on that aforementioned article from 1841 and 1842. The article was the first comprehensive modern German treatise-size elaboration in over 100 years and thus can well be viewed as the founding text of a modern academic approach to German private international law. This is so although (or maybe because) Wächter mostly did not set out to establish a theoretical approach – much of the quality of his article lies in the extent to which it established existing private international law on the basis of existing materials.

Wächter's contribution is often presented as largely negative – he helped overcome the theory of statutes and the → vested rights theory. His positive contribution is often limited to a → *lex fori* principle, which is viewed as unattractive. This presentation overestimates *Wächter's* role in overcoming old theories (which had already lost influence). On the other hand, and perhaps more importantly, it underestimates his constructive contribution.

The novelty of *Wächter's* approach is best understood in comparison with other approaches of his time. A first approach, the strict *lex fori* approach, held that the only valid law in a state was the law of that state, so a judge would never apply foreign law. A second theory was the Italian theory of statutes, which suggested that each statute designates its own scope of application (which could be found through statutory interpretation) (→ Unilateralism). Closely related was the → vested rights theory, which suggested that a right acquired under one legal system is binding everywhere else. A third approach, building on the first, was the theory of → comity, developed in the → Netherlands and adopted in the → USA, whereby each state would have exclusive sovereignty over its territory, and foreign law would be applied only on the basis of extralegal considerations of courtesy and comity. A fourth approach, made famous by *Savigny* but to be found already in earlier authors, suggested that the applicable law could be determined on the basis of the nature of things (*Natur der Sache*). (A fifth approach, the suggestion of public international law as a source for private international law, emerged after *Wächter's* article with *Mancini* (→ Mancini, Pasquale Stanislao).)

Wächter combined elements from all of these approaches. He agreed with the strict *lex fori* theory that a judge was bound only by his home law – but disagreed that this would mean the exclusive application of the *lex fori*. Instead, he suggested, domestic law might be interpreted so as to designate foreign law to apply. He rejected the idea behind the theory of statutes that a foreign legislator could, by defining the scope of a legislation, bind another state – but he agreed with the method of statutory interpretation to answer questions of private international law. He disagreed with comity as a basis for applying foreign law, but he agreed that it was up to each state's sovereign designation whether and when to apply foreign law. Similarly, he agreed that 'the nature of things' was an important criterion to determine the applicable law, but he thought that this nature had to be determined not in the abstract but from the perspective of the *lex fori*.

Wächter's own approach, then, was novel. He treated questions of private international law as questions of law. However, that law was neither the statute whose application was in question, nor was it public international law (→ Public international law and private international law). Instead, it was the *lex fori*. Where the *lex fori* had an explicit private international law rule, that rule was to be applied. Where the *lex fori* had no such explicit private international law rule, such a rule had to be developed by analogy to existing substantive law. Only where neither path led to a result would the substantive law of the *lex fori* be applied as a residual solution. This approach, though deficient in some ways, was instrumental for the development of our modern understanding or private international law as a national law different from substantive law.

2. Refutations: theory of statutes and theory of vested rights

Often, *Wächter's* main contribution is seen in his refutation of the theory of statutes ((1841) 24 AcP 270 ff, § 11). That theory held, essentially, that statutes themselves designate the scope of their application and can therefore be distinguished in three types – real statutes that have a territorial application, personal statutes that go with a person, and mixed statutes that are treated in diverse ways. Indeed, after *Wächter's* article was published, the theory of statutes was virtually dead in Germany, but *Wächter* himself acknowledged that such a theory had already lost most support when he wrote ((1841) 24 AcP 298 note 138). What makes *Wächter's* refutation relevant is that he based it not just on the numerous exceptions that the theory required, but on a foundational argument that one country cannot bind others with regard to the scope of application of its laws ((1841) 24 AcP 288–9).

In the context of these arguments, *Wächter* also rejected the → vested rights theory (*Theorie der wohlerworbenen Rechte*). That theory suggests, in essence, that rights acquired anywhere under local law are enforceable elsewhere. *Wächter* pointed out that such a theory is circular: we cannot say whether a right has been acquired under a certain law until we know whether that law is applicable in the first place ((1842) 25 AcP 1–9, § 14; the relevant passage is translated in Kurt H Nadelmann, 'Some Historical Notes on the Doctrinal Sources of American Conflict' in Kurt H Nadelmann (ed), *Conflict of Laws: International and Interstate. Selected Essays* (Nijhoff 1972) 1, 16). Again, the refusal is linked to *Wächter's* general suggestion that it is up to the forum to determine whether foreign law is applicable. It is therefore consequential (though often overlooked) that *Wächter* in fact defended a vested rights theory as between states within a federal state, because a state is required to make sure that rights established within one of its sub-units are recognized everywhere within the state (Carl Georg von Wächter, *Pandekten Vol 1: Allgemeine Lehren* (Breitkopf und Härtel 1880) 152–3; see already (1842) 25 AcP 3 note 170, § 14).

3. *Foundation: positivism*

For his own approach, *Wächter* suggested that the question as to what law applies requires a prior question: 'From what sources shall the judge take the answer to this question?' *Wächter's* response was unreserved: 'Without any doubt from the laws to which he is subject, that is, from the laws in force in his state' ((1841) 24 AcP 237, § 2). Because of this, *Wächter* is often viewed as a proponent of a *lex fori* approach to private international law, but his approach is better called a positivist one. In reality, *Wächter* agreed with many other authors' suggestions on principles guiding private international law: international → comity, the protection of vested rights, etc. However, unlike other authors, he viewed these as guidelines only for the legislator, and he asked to balance them against interests in ensuring the enforcement of the forum's policies. The judge, by contrast, had to rest his decisions on the basis of the *lex fori* ((1841) 24 AcP 240, § 2; (1842) 25 AcP 12–15, § 16).

Wächter's theory for judges has three elements. First and foremost, a judge must apply explicit choice-of-law rules of the forum ((1841) 24 AcP 239–40, § 2; 261, § 9). *Wächter* postulated that a legislator, in drafting such rules, would have two considerations: on the one hand protection of its own substantive law, on the other international relations and deference. Such a priority for existing choice-of-law rules was the common view of the time. However, explicit rules were rare at the time. To fill the gap, many authors sought to develop an extensive system of common law rules of private international law. *Wächter* expressed doubts that such rules could be found. Roman law itself had very little to say about private international law. Germanic law was not uniform after the decline of personal (tribal) laws. And *Wächter* was sceptical about attempts to claim existence of a contemporary German customary law.

Given that a common law of conflicts did not exist, what did a judge have to do outside the forum's existing positive choice-of-law rules? *Wächter's* second principle, his most ingenious contribution, remained a positivist one: the judge 'must seek the solution in the meaning and the spirit of those special laws in force in his state which as such cover the relationship put before him' ((1841) 24 AcP 261, § 9).

> This means in particular that the judge must first determine for every statute of his state dealing with the legal relationship brought before him whether it accords with the meaning of the statute that it be applied absolutely even if the relation was created abroad or a foreigner is involved, or that the statute need not. ((1841) 24 AcP 263, § 9.)

This is, however, not an explicit priority for the substantive *lex fori*. *Wächter's* own examples make it clear that what he was thinking of were mainly mandatory laws of the *lex fori*. And he criticized those who regularly postulated application of the *lex fori* ((1841) 24 AcP 265, § 9). In fact, the really interesting aspect of the second principle was *Wächter's* suggestion to derive actual choice-of-law rules that designate foreign law from the forum's own substantive law: 'our judge . . . has to apply foreign law where . . . the contents, spirit, and direction of the specific [substantive] law covering the legal issue in question . . . lead to application and recognition of foreign law' ((1841) 24 AcP 230, 268, § 10). Later, *Wächter* reformulated slightly: the judge must find the applicable law from the spirit of our law and its general principles and the nature of the legal relation (Carl Georg von Wächter, *Pandekten Vol 1: Allgemeine Lehren* (Breitkopf und Härtel 1880), 147).

Wächter's preference for the substantive *lex fori* can be found only in his third principle: 'If, however, no definite decision can be reached for the question derived from the aim, the sense, and the spirit of the specific statute involved, the judge must in case of doubt apply the law of his state.' The importance of this third principle was not great. Although *Wächter* did suggest that application of foreign law (→ Foreign law, application and ascertainment) would remain an exception ((1842) 25 AcP 267, § 10), his examples demonstrate that he gave, in practice, rather wide scope for foreign law. He formulated this principle mainly for mandatory law ('*leges cogentes*') and, as his explanation makes clear, rules of *ordre public* (→ Public policy (*ordre public*)) and as a description of the (very real) tendency of judges to get to the application of their own law (see the discussion in Nikolaus Sandmann, *Grundlagen und Einfluss der internationalprivatrechtlichen Lehre Carl Georg von Wächters (1797–1880)* (Diss Münster 1979) 110–14).

All in all, viewing *Wächter* as a proponent of the *lex fori* is in many ways a misunderstanding. For *Wächter*, the *lex fori* was not the primarily applicable substantive law. Instead, the *lex fori* was the basis for the applicable choice-of-law rules. Where those choice-of-law rules were not explicit, they had to be developed from the policies underlying existing substantive rules of the *lex fori*.

4. Specific doctrines

The greater part of *Wächter's* text was dedicated not to questions of theory but to doctrines on the applicable law in specific areas, which he covered comprehensively. Here, his specific solutions often did not differ dramatically from those of other authors – another sign that his *lex fori* theory did not lead to significantly greater application of the forum's substantive law. What made his solutions novel was that he frequently justified them as emerging from interpretation of the forum's substantive laws. With this approach, he also made distinctions between truly international conflicts on the one hand and interregional conflicts on the other. And what made his contribution path breaking was that he was the first, in Germany, to treat almost all areas of conflict of laws comprehensively.

Although *Wächter's* solutions for specific questions were often in accordance with existing views, he sometimes proposed novelties, some of which were influential. Thus, he proposed to distinguish the existence of a → personal status (eg minor age) and its consequences. Similarly, he proposed a more flexible approach to questions of statutes of limitations than exclusive application of either *lex fori* or *lex obligationis*. In property law (→ Property and proprietary rights), his solution was application of the *lex rei sitae* for both land and chattel. *Wächter's* solutions in family law were dominated by domicile (frequently that of the husband) and → party autonomy (for matters of marital property). In the law of → succession, *Wächter* focused on the deceased's domicile, but allowed for exceptions for special assets. Finally, *Wächter* treated (briefly) the recognition of foreign judgments. He viewed (consistently with his general approach) no duty to enforce such decisions, and emphasized, in addition to the requirements of → reciprocity and indirect jurisdiction of the rendering court (→ jurisdiction, foundations), a basic compatibility with the enforcing court's own laws ((1842) 25 AcP 417–19, § 32).

One of *Wächter's* most important contributions was his detailed treatment of → choice of law for delicts, which had before usually been treated together with criminal law. This analytical distinction was an important novelty, although *Wächter's* solution, in practice, was largely not novel: he suggested that the applicable law should usually be the *lex fori*, but proposed a double actionability rule for certain situations. His extensive treatment of international criminal law, which remained a standard reference for decades to come, also emphasized the *lex fori* (Carl Georg von Wächter, *Das Königlich Sächsische und das Thüringische Strafrecht: Ein Handbuch – Einleitung und Allgemeiner Teil* (Metzler 1857) 125–75).

Another important (and underappreciated) contribution was *Wächter's* defence of the parties' power to designate the applicable law in contracts and beyond (for marital property). That designation was, for him, limited to non-mandatory laws and in this sense a mere extension of contractual freedom. Nonetheless, *Wächter* laid the foundations for the rise of → party autonomy in private international law of contracts and beyond.

III. *Wächter's* influence

1. Influence at the time

Wächter's article proved to be a turning point in German private international law. His most important influence at the time was that he, together with *Schaeffner* (whose treatise was published concurrently), (re-)established private international law as an academic field, after it had lain dormant in Germany for more than a century. Further, *Wächter's* comprehensive (though sometimes questionable) refutation of older theories proved fatal to these, and they were no longer defended in Germany. Moreover, this creation of a blank slate helped pave the way for new theoretical approaches, including approaches that differed from his (like those of more famous authors like *Savigny* and *Ludwig von Bar*).

Today, *Wächter* is often juxtaposed with *Savigny*. A common judgment is that *Wächter's* contribution was merely that of critique, and that *Savigny's* formulation of a positive theory carried the day. This judgment appears inexact in more than one way. First, it underestimates the great influence that *Wächter's* article had on *Savigny's* treatment of the topic, which closely follows *Wächter's* structure and many of his findings. Both were, in fact, friends. Second, it underestimates the degree to which *Wächter* and *Savigny* come to identical results on concrete questions (as *Wächter* himself later pointed out: Carl Georg von Wächter, *Pandekten Vol 1: Allgemeine Lehren* (Breitkopf und Härtel 1880) 146). Third, it ignores that *Wächter* and *Savigny* agreed, actually, on the role of the seat of the legal relation and the importance of comity and decisional harmony for private international law. Where they differed, most importantly, was in their assessment whether the judge is entitled to make such considerations or whether they are the exclusive domain of the legislator. *Savigny*, in the spirit of 19th-century liberalism, took the former position and posited a (weak) internationalist super-law of private international law (while conceding that explicit state rules on private international law would trump). *Wächter*, as a sovereigntist, held the latter view.

Fourth, it is not actually clear that *Savigny* was, in the long run, more influential than *Wächter*, the 'source of the second mainstream in modern conflict of laws theories' (Frank Vischer, 'General Course on Private international law' (1992) 232 Rec. des Cours 9, 34). Although *Savigny's* formulation of the 'seat' of a legal relation received, over time, near universal scholarly acceptance, his transnationalized and depoliticized view of private international law fell out of favour, effectively, already towards the end of the 19th century. Instead, what emerged were (i) a tendency towards legislation in private international law and (ii) the emergence of the idea that private international law rules actually incorporate domestic policies, to be established by the legislator. Not surprisingly, therefore, *Wächter* found favour in the nationalist school of private international law, which emerged in Germany towards the end of the 19th century; he has also been influential on the legislation of the German codification of private international law (see Nikolaus Sandmann, *Grundlagen und Einfluss der internationalprivatrechtlichen Lehre Carl Georg von Wächters (1797–1880)* (Diss Münster 1979) 296–306).

2. *Influence abroad*

Wächter's influence on foreign legal discussions was less pronounced – although he was read and discussed in several countries, in the long run he remained less influential than *Savigny* and *von Bar*. (Curiously, in the common law he was long viewed as a proponent of the → vested rights theory, due to a misattribution in Thomas Erskine Holland, *The Elements of Jurisprudence* (Clarendon Press 1880) 188 no 1; see Kurt H Nadelmann, 'Some Historical Notes on the Doctrinal Sources of American Conflict' in Kurt H Nadelmann (ed), *Conflict of Laws: International and Interstate. Selected Essays* (Nijhoff 1972) 1, 15–18). There may be two reasons for the relative lack of attention: first, publication in a journal made his work less accessible abroad. Second, *Wächter's* insistence on a positivist approach, and his refusal to use foreign sources, may have made his work seem less relevant abroad. Nonetheless, he is often discussed at least in historical treatments of private international law.

What has enabled reception are translations. The greater part of the original essay (up until § 25) was translated, by *Quintín Alfonsín*, into Spanish ((1951) 2 Revista de la Facultad de Derecho y Ciencias Sociales Montevideo 949–1020, and (1954) 5 Revista de la Facultad de Derecho y Ciencias Sociales Montevideo 39–104, 907–50). This led to a significant interest in *Wächter* in Latin American discussions. The sections of Wächter's article on theory and on obligation (§§ 2 (in part), 9, 10, 28), as well as the passage from the Pandects treatise, were translated into English by *Kurt Nadelmann* (Kurt H Nadelmann, 'Wächter's Essay on the Collision of Private Laws of Different States' (1964) 13 Am.J.Comp.L. 414, 417–28), together with an excellent brief foreword by the same author (Kurt H Nadelmann, 'Wächter's Essay on the Collision of Private Laws of Different States' (1964) 13 Am.J.Comp.L. 414–17).

3. Importance in the long run

In the long run, *Wächter's* importance has been overshadowed by *Savigny's* fame. *Savigny's* conception of private international law, in promoting a priority of the legal relation over its regulation by the state, was a good fit for the emerging liberal order of the 19th century with its strict separation of a private and a public sphere, and with its emphasis to limit the state's ability to regulate, actively, private relations. It is not, however, in many ways such a good fit for contemporary understanding of private international law as emerging from sovereignty (nationalization) and as instrumental in the promotion of certain values (politicization). For our time, *Wächter's* formulations provide us with a model of current private international law that is in many ways more adequate – even where a direct influence is doubtful.

Wächter's most important legacy is the priority of the *lex fori* as the starting point of private international law thinking. This implies not only the priority of explicit choice-of-law rules, which was never seriously in doubt. It implies especially the suggestion that choice-of-law decisions are allocated with the legislator and thus deserve legislative treatment. The emergence of national private international law codifications worldwide is evidence of this.

Related to this is *Wächter's* insight into the absence of truly universal rules of private international law, be they derived from the nature of things or public international law. Although scholars have long deplored the absence of uniformity, most of the doctrine today agrees with *Wächter* that such uniformity is only one of several policies (see, eg American Law Institute, Restatement of the Law, Second: Conflict of Laws 2d, St. Paul 1971, section 6).

Positing private international law within a state's own law made possible another development of contemporary private international law, namely its politicization. Here, *Wächter's* approach has some affinity with US legal thought. It is related in particular to *Brainerd Currie's* governmental interest theory (→ Currie, Brainerd; → Interest and policy analysis in private international law), which likewise derives application from underlying policies (Hans Baade, 'Foreword' (1963) 28 LCP 673, 675 note 9). Later, *Albert Ehrenzweig* explicitly invoked *Wächter* as an ancestor for his own *lex fori* theory (→ Ehrenzweig, Albert A), according to which a judge should, ordinarily, apply his own law (Albert A Ehrenzweig, 'Lex Fori: Basic Rule in the Conflict of Laws' (1959–60) 58 Mich.L.Rev. 637, 659–60; see Kurt Lipstein, 'The General Principles of Private international law' (1972) 135 Rec. des Cours 97, 144–7; Kurt Siehr, 'Die lex-fori-Theorie heute' in Rolf Serick and others (eds), *Albert A Ehrenzweig und das internationale Privatrecht* (Winter 1986) 35, 57–8).

Wächter's suggestion to derive choice-of-law policies from substantive law policies still finds much application in legislation and occasionally in case law. The protection of weaker parties in substantive law, for example, is naturally extended into private international law. Otherwise, however, modern → interest and policy analysis in private international law has developed new and specific choice-of-law-related policies.

Wächter's defence of the substantive *lex fori* as the residual law has met with a lot of opposition, especially in continental Europe. It did and does, however, describe an actual judicial tendency to apply one's own law where possible (the so-called homeward trend). And it exists occasionally in doctrine, for example when the content of foreign law cannot be ascertained, and as generally residually applicable law (eg art 10 of the → Rome III Regulation (Council Regulation (EU) No 1259/2010 of 20 December 2010 implementing enhanced cooperation in the area of the law applicable to divorce and legal separation, [2010] OJ L 343/10)).

Wächter's most important contribution was, arguably, one he made in passing, namely his distinction between interlocal and international conflicts. His suggestion that a vested rights theory could be justified for conflicts within one sovereignty proved prescient for the country-of-origin principle in the European Union (→ Country of origin rule), which is best understood as such a reborn vested rights theory (Ralf Michaels, 'EU Law as Private international law? Reconceptualising the Country-of-Origin Principle as Vested Rights Theory' (2006) 2 J Priv Int L 195–242).

RALF MICHAELS

Literature

Bernd Rüdiger Kern (ed), *Zwischen Romanistik und Germanistik. Carl Georg von Wächter (1797–1880)* (Duncker & Humblot 2000); Christoph Mauntel, *Carl Georg von Wächter (1797–1880). Rechtswissenschaft im Frühkonstitutionalismus* (Schöningh 2004); Enrico Cattellani, 'L'opera di Giorgio v. Wächter nel diritto internazionale privato' in *Atti del Reale Istituto Veneto di scienze, lettere ed arti, Anno accademico 1899-1900 vol. IX part 2*, 527–586; Kurt H Nadelmann, 'Wächter's Essay on the Collision of Private Laws of Different States' (1964) 13 *Am.J.Comp.L.* 414; Kurt H Nadelmann, 'Some Historical Notes on the Doctrinal Sources of American Conflict' in Kurt H Nadelmann (ed), *Conflict of Laws: International and Interstate. Selected Essays* (Nijhoff 1972) 1; Nikolaus Sandmann, *Grundlagen und Einfluss der internationalprivatrechtlichen Lehre Carl Georg von Wächters (1797–1880)* (Diss Münster 1979); Paul Volken, 'Wenn Wächter mit Story' in Jürgen Basedow and others (eds), *Private Law in the International Arena: Liber amicorum Kurt Siehr* (TMC Asser Press 2000) 815; Carl Georg von Wächter, 'Ueber die Collision der Privatrechtsgesetze verschiedener Staaten' (1841) 24 AcP 230, (1842) 25 AcP 1, 161, 361 (also as reprint Vico Verlag 2008); Carl Georg von Wächter, *Handbuch des im Königreiche Württemberg geltenden Privatrechts*, vols 1 and 2 (Metzler 1839–42); Carl Georg von Wächter, *Das Königlich Sächsische und das Thüringische Strafrecht: Ein Handbuch – Einleitung und Allgemeiner Teil* (Metzler 1857); Carl Georg von Wächter, *Pandekten Vol 1: Allgemeine Lehren* (Breitkopf und Härtel 1880); Oskar von Wächter, *Carl Georg von Wächter. Leben eines deutschen Juristen* (Breitkopf und Härtel 1881); Bernhard Windscheid, *Carl Georg von Wächter* (Duncker & Humblot 1880).

West Balkan Convention

I. Introduction

At a Regional Conference of Ministers of the Interior and of Justice, held in Belgrade on 12 April 2013, the representatives of → Albania, → Bosnia and Herzegovina, → Macedonia, → Montenegro and → Serbia signed a letter of intent for the signature and ratification of a Regional Convention on jurisdiction and the mutual recognition and enforcement of judgments (→ Recognition and enforcement of judgments (civil law)) in → civil and commercial matters. After a stand-still period, negotiations for finalizing the process were resumed at the turn of the year 2014/2015 and Albania, Bosnia and Herzegovina, Macedonia and Montenegro confirmed their intention of signing the Convention. On the other hand, Serbia has in the meantime withdrawn its consent, referring to the beginning of accession negotiations with the EU and the related burden of harmonizing its national law with the *acquis* as well as shortage of resources. The project has been substantially supported throughout by the Open Regional Fund for South East Europe – Legal Reform of the *Deutsche Gesellschaft für Internationale Zusammenarbeit (GIZ) GmbH*.

II. Background

The plans for a Regional Convention go back to a Slovenian initiative, put forward in Brdo pri Kranju on 15 April 2011, for strengthening judicial cooperation in → civil and commercial matters in West Balkan countries. As a consequence, on 19–20 July 2011, a regional conference was convened in Hotel Europa in Sarajevo to discuss possible options. Various strategies were considered at the time. Participants initially focused on the possibility of accession of the West Balkan countries to the → Lugano Convention (Lugano Convention of 30 October 2007 on jurisdiction and the recognition and enforcement of judgments in civil and commercial matters, [2007] OJ L 339/3). By accession to the Lugano Convention, the West Balkan countries would become fully integrated into the European regime for jurisdiction and the recognition and enforcement of judgments in civil and commercial matters. Application of the standards laid down in the Lugano Convention would substantially facilitate cross-border enforcement within the West Balkan region. Even more important, it would dramatically facilitate cross-border enforcement in relations between the West Balkan countries and the EU Member States as well as the Member States to the European Free Trade Association (EFTA). So far, in some EU Member States judgments in → civil and commercial matters originating from certain West Balkan countries cannot in principle be enforced (eg for the recognition of foreign judgments, the Austrian law in Section 79 of the Act on the Enforcement of Judgments (Exekutionsordnung of 27 May 1896, Reichsgesetzblatt No 79/1896, last amended by Bundesgesetzblatt No I 69/2014) requires formal reciprocity, which is not guaranteed among others in relation to Serbia. Exceptions to this rule are provided only in matters relating to civil status or to maintenance. Lastly, by accession to the Lugano Convention the West Balkan countries would emphasize their wish of approximation to the EU.

However, accession to the Lugano Convention on principle requires that each candidate state the unanimous agreement of all existing Member States (see art 72(3) and (4) of

Lugano Convention). The procedure could be extremely time consuming while the outcome could prove unpredictable. Therefore the conclusion was reached that it would be preferable to conclude a regional convention that would be framed on the Lugano Convention model. Such a 'parallel' convention could be useful in several aspects. First, it would considerably improve legal relations between the countries of the West Balkans. Second, by practising the mechanism of the Lugano Convention among themselves, the participating states could demonstrate that such a convention works on a regional level and thereby enhance confidence in the judiciary of the countries concerned, paving the way for their joint accession to the Lugano Convention at some future date. An additional advantage would be to familiarize the states concerned with a system that corresponds to the Brussels I Regulation (Regulation (EC) No 44/2001 of 22 December 2000 on jurisdiction and the recognition and enforcement of judgments in civil and commercial matters, [2001] OJ L 12/1; → Brussels I (Convention and Regulation)). This might in turn facilitate EU accession of the West Balkan states.

III. Contracting states

The Draft Convention was elaborated by an international team of experts in cooperation with the Ministries of Justice of the target countries in a series of working meetings in Sarajevo, Bucharest, Pržno/Montenegro, The Hague and Belgrade. Representatives of the EU as well as of the → Hague Conference on Private International Law participated and provided valuable comments. The Draft provides that the Regional Convention will be open for signature by Member States of the Central European Free Trade Agreement (CEFTA, available at <www.cefta.int>) and is to enter into force within six months following the date on which a minimum of three states deposit their instruments of ratification. After entering into force the Convention will be open to (i) Members of CEFTA, (ii) any contracting party to the Lugano Convention and (iii) other states. Invitation of states to accede will require the unanimous agreement of all states which are already contracting parties to the Regional Convention. CEFTA Members and Members to the Lugano Convention could then accede under a simplified procedure. Other states could also join but would be subject to prior examination regarding their judicial system and their civil procedure law, including private international law relating to civil procedure.

CEFTA is a trade agreement between countries of southeast Europe which have not yet joined the EU. At present, this includes the following: → Albania, → Bosnia and Herzegovina, → Macedonia, Moldova, → Montenegro, → Serbia and Kosovo. So far, from these only Albania, Macedonia and Montenegro have recognized the Republic of Kosovo as an independent state, which fact would complicate simultaneous accession of certain actual CEFTA states to the Regional Convention. For this reason the Convention emphasized a step-by-step approach. Not only will it be possible to admit additional members in future. The Convention also expressly acknowledges the right of any contracting party to the Convention to expand the application of the Convention bilaterally, by way of a bilateral treaty with any other state.

Considering the intensive economic and other relations between the Yugoslav successor states, it would be desirable for the region to have → Croatia and → Slovenia ratify the new Convention, even though these two states no longer belong to CEFTA. However, since Croatia and Slovenia have already become EU Member States, they will under the EU law no longer be entitled to join a regional convention on a matter which falls under the exclusive jurisdiction of the EU.

IV. Outline

The contents of the Draft Regional Convention may be summarized as follows. While the scope is the same as for the → Lugano Convention, it is not the same as for the Brussels I Regulation, in so far as the Regional Convention applies also to maintenance issues, which on the level of the EU fall under the scope of the Maintenance Regulation (Council Regulation (EC) No 4/2009 of 18 December 2008 on jurisdiction, applicable law, recognition and enforcement of decisions and cooperation in matters relating to maintenance obligations, [2009] OJ L 7/1) (→ Maintenance obligations). The Draft Regional Convention applies in → civil and commercial matters, with the exception of (i) status or legal capacity of natural persons (→ Capacity and emancipation), rights in property (→ Property and proprietary rights), arising out of a matrimonial relationship, wills and succession, (ii) bankruptcy and analogous proceedings, (iii) social security and (iv) arbitration.

The general rule on → jurisdiction is determined on the basis of the defendant's domicile (→ Domicile, habitual residence and establishment). For certain case-groups the plaintiff may on their own choice bring the action in a contracting state other than at the defendant's domicile. Such special jurisdiction is in particular provided for in matters relating to a contract, to maintenance, to tort, delict or quasi-delict, actions arising out of a crime, actions arising out of the operation of company branch offices and some others. A separate set of rules applies for matters relating to insurance, to → consumer contracts as well as to individual contracts of employment. Exclusive jurisdiction, regardless of domicile, is provided for disputes on rights *in rem* in immovable property, on certain matters relating to companies, on entries in public registers and on intellectual property rights. The Draft also contains detailed rules on prorogation of jurisdiction as well as on → *lis alibi pendens*.

The provisions of the Draft Regional Convention on mutual → recognition and enforcement of judgments are equally modelled on the Lugano Convention and the Brussels I Regulation. For the West Balkan states, they contain far-reaching novelties. Thus, the Draft Regional Convention introduces the concept of automatic recognition. Review is on principle provided for only after grant of the declaration of enforceability, on appeal of the party against whom enforcement is sought. Under no circumstances may the foreign judgment be reviewed as to its substance.

West Balkan states have concluded among themselves a number of bilateral agreements on legal assistance which contain rules on recognition and enforcement of judgments. The scope of these agreements is typically broader than that of the Draft Regional Convention and extends also to matters of family law and → succession. On the other hand, their scope is also narrower in that they do not cover international jurisdiction. The Draft Regional Convention as between the contracting states is to supersede bilateral agreements covering the same matter. Conventions superseded are to be enumerated in an Annex. In relation to matters which are outside the scope of the Draft Regional Convention the bilateral agreements enumerated in the Annex will continue to have effect, as for example for the recognition and enforcement of judgments in matters of divorce (→ Divorce and personal separation) and of → succession.

As far as the relationship to other conventions is concerned, which in relation to particular matters govern jurisdiction or the recognition or enforcement of judgments, these are superseded by the provisions of the Regional Convention on recognition and enforcement. An exception is made in case the provisions on recognition and enforcement provided in such other convention are 'more favorable for the free circulation of judgments'. Therefore, the Regional Convention does not prevent the application of another convention which provides for a broader basis for recognition or for simplified procedures. This clause was inserted on the occasion of the entry into force of the Hague Maintenance Convention 2007 (Hague Convention of 23 November 2007 on the international recovery of child support and other forms of family maintenance, [2011] OJ L 192/51; 47 ILM 257) in Albania on 1 January 2013 and in Bosnia and Herzegovina on 1 February 2013.

Similar to the Lugano Convention, three Protocols are annexed to the Draft Regional Convention. In accordance with Protocol 2 'On the uniform interpretation of the Convention and on the Standing Committee', the Convention is to be applied and interpreted by the courts of the contracting states in due consideration of any relevant decisions rendered by the ECJ on the Brussels I Regulation, the Lugano Convention as well as the Brussels Convention (Brussels Convention of 27 September 1968 on jurisdiction and the enforcement of judgments in civil and commercial matters, [1972] OJ L 299/32, consolidated version, [1998] OJ C 27/1). A Standing Committee is to be set up to coordinate the efforts towards uniform interpretation; it will request information from the contracting states at regular intervals on the practice of the courts in those states with regard to the provisions of the Convention and promulgate such information among the contracting states.

The drafters of the convention were aware of the fact that from 10 January 2015 the Brussels I Regulation (recast) (Regulation (EU) No 1215/2012 of the European Parliament and of the Council of 12 December 2012 on jurisdiction and the recognition and enforcement of judgments in civil and commercial matters (recast), [2012] OJ L 351/1; → Brussels I (Convention and Regulation)) would apply. For application between CEFTA states it was considered appropriate to adhere for the time being to the regime of the Brussels I Regulation (which corresponds to that of the Lugano Convention). However, in Protocol 3 'On observing changes in the Brussels I Regulation', the contracting parties express their intent to harmonize the provisions of the Convention to the extent reasonable and possible with the Brussels I Regulation (recast).

In recognition of the fact that the Convention originates from an initial meeting held in the city of Sarajevo, the instruments of ratification are to be deposited with the Bosnia and Herzegovina's Ministry of Foreign Affairs, which will act as Depositary of the Convention.

CHRISTA JESSEL-HOLST

Literature

Christa Jessel-Holst, 'Recognition and Enforcement of Foreign Judgments: Some Comments on Recent Developments in Serbia and other West Balkan Countries from the Perspective of European and Comparative Private international law' (2012) 49/7–9 Pravo i privreda 13; Zlatan Meškić and Dženana Radončić, 'Brussels I Recast and the South-East Europe' (2013) 15/1 Revija za evropsko pravo 1; Dženana Radončić and Zlatan Meškić, 'Uredba (EU) br. 1215/2012 Evropskog parlamenta i Savjeta od 12. decembra 2012. godine o nadležnosti i priznanju i izvršenju sudskih odluka u građanskim i trgovačkim predmetima' (2013) 4/1 Nova pravna revija 46.

WIPO and private international law[1]

I. The World Intellectual Property Organization

The World Intellectual Property Organization (WIPO) is an international intergovernmental organization that was established 'to promote the protection of intellectual property throughout the world through cooperation among states and, where appropriate, in collaboration with any other international organization' (art 3(i) of the WIPO Convention (Convention of 14 July 1967 establishing the World Intellectual Property Organization (828 UNTS 4))).

The WIPO Convention defines intellectual property broadly as including

- literary, artistic and scientific works,
- performances of performing artists, phonograms, and broadcasts,
- inventions in all fields of human endeavour,
- scientific discoveries,
- industrial designs,
- trade marks, service marks, and commercial names and designations,
- protection against unfair competition,
- and all other rights resulting from intellectual activity in the industrial, scientific, literary or artistic fields (art 2(viii) WIPO Convention).

WIPO became a specialized agency of the United Nations in 1974. According to art 1 of the Agreement between the United Nations and the World Intellectual Property Organization (Agreement concerning the relations between the two organizations. Approved by the General Assembly of the World Intellectual Property Organization on 27 September 1974, and by the General Assembly of the United Nations on 17 December 1974, 956 UNTS 405), WIPO is responsible 'inter alia, for promoting creative intellectual activity and for facilitating the transfer of technology related to industrial property to the developing countries in order to accelerate economic, social and cultural development'.

Today, WIPO has become the global forum for intellectual property services, policy, information and cooperation with 189 Member States.

II. Origins of WIPO

Intellectual property rights are territorial so that rights established under a national law do not extend beyond the territory in which this law applies. Intellectual property rights are protected in individual countries, sometimes on a regional basis, but never on a global scale. Recognizing 'foreign' intellectual property rights would require a state to accept a foreign country's policy choices, as to which intangible assets can (or cannot) be protected by way of an exclusive right. So far, however, countries have been reluctant to give such acceptance, and innovative or creative products need to satisfy each country's requirements for protection. This territorial link is reinforced by registration requirements for some industrial property rights such as patents. → Territoriality also means that there can be different owners for the same or similar rights in different territories, which also means that if a trade mark has been registered in one country, third parties are not

---

[1] The views expressed in this contribution are entirely those of the author.

prevented from applying for protection for the exact same trade mark in another country.

The territoriality of intellectual property rights constitutes a stumbling block for international trade and motivated international normsetting in intellectual property. The origins of WIPO go back to the first wave of globalization that followed the Industrial Revolution and the expansion of international trade in the late 19th century. The first treaties concluded in this area were the Paris Industrial Property Convention (Paris Convention for the Protection of Industrial Property, 20 March 1883, with later amendments, 828 UNTS 305) (176 contracting parties in 2014) and the Berne Convention (Berne Convention for the Protection of Literary and Artistic Works of 9 September 1886, completed at Paris on 4 May 1896, revised at Berlin on 13 November 1908, completed at Berne on 20 March 1914, revised at Rome on 2 June 1928, revised at Brussels on 26 June 1948, revised at Stockholm on 14 July 1967 and revised at Paris on 24 July 1971, 1161 UNTS 3 and amended in 1979 Treaty Doc No 99-27, and 1985, 828 UNTS 221) (168 contracting parties in 2014). In 1893, an international organization called the United International Bureaux for the Protection of Intellectual Property (commonly known by its French acronym BIRPI) was established, the predecessor of WIPO. Since then, these two basic intellectual property conventions have been amended several times and a number of further treaties concluded. Today, WIPO administers 26 international intellectual property treaties. Another important international intellectual property agreement, the TRIPS (Agreement of 15 April 1994 on Trade-Related Aspects of Intellectual Property Rights, 1869 UNTS 299) is not administered by WIPO (→ TRIPS), but forms part of the World Trade Organization (→ WTO and private international law). In the Agreement between the World Intellectual Property Organization and the World Trade Organization of 1 January 1996 (available at <www.wipo.int/treaties/en/text.jsp?file_id=305457>), both organizations have regulated their cooperation in the area of intellectual property.

III. Basic approaches in international intellectual property normsetting

Since its origins, international normsetting in intellectual property has aimed at facilitating the protection of intellectual property rights across borders and at mitigating the trade-restricting effects of territoriality. The Paris Industrial Property Convention and the Berne Convention addressed these concerns by introducing a number of general principles of uniform application, most notably the principle of national treatment (see III.1. below), and by harmonizing national laws on the basis of certain minimum standards. All contracting parties form a 'Union' (art 1 Paris Industrial Property Convention, art 1 Berne Convention) thereby excluding, within their scope of application, the principle of reciprocity.

While intellectual property law has become one of the most internationalized areas of the law, private international law, which might require the application of foreign intellectual property law, hardly played a minimal role in this process. None of the international intellectual property treaties contains a clear, let alone comprehensive, treatment of private international law issues in the modern sense (James Fawcett and Paul Torremans, *Intellectual Property and Private international law* (2nd edn, OUP 2011) para 12.05). However, these treaties have developed specific ways of determining issues of applicable law that are largely based on the basic principles of national treatment and territoriality. In the following paragraphs, this approach will be demonstrated for the basic international intellectual property treaties, the Paris Industrial Property Convention and the Berne Convention (see the comprehensive treatment in James Fawcett and Paul Torremans, *Intellectual Property and Private international law* (2nd edn, OUP 2011) ch 12).

1. Industrial property: the Paris Industrial Property Convention of 1883

The Paris Industrial Property Convention applies to all industrial property rights listed in art 1(2), ie 'patents, utility models, industrial designs, trademarks, service marks, trade names, indications of source or appellations of origin, and the repression of unfair competition'. The connecting factor that triggers the Convention's application is the applicant's or owner's → nationality or domicile (art 3 Paris Industrial Property Convention) 'of a country of the Union'. Article 2(1) Paris Industrial Property Convention stipulates that

[n]ationals of any country of the Union shall, as regards the protection of industrial property,

enjoy in all the other countries of the Union the advantages that their respective laws now grant, or may hereafter grant, to nationals; all without prejudice to the rights specially provided for by this Convention. Consequently, they shall have the same protection as the latter, and the same legal remedy against any infringement of their rights, provided that the conditions and formalities imposed upon nationals are complied with.

This norm contains first the national treatment principle for issues of substantive law regarding 'protection' and 'legal remedy', but it does not apply regarding administrative or judicial procedures or jurisdiction as art 2(3) Paris Industrial Property Convention specifies. This means that the Paris Industrial Property Convention does not require the application of a foreign intellectual property law, but rather the uniform application of domestic intellectual property law – even in cases that contain a foreign element. Furthermore, art 2(1) Paris Industrial Property Convention also contains a somewhat indirect or imperfect choice-of-law rule (Jürgen Basedow, 'Foundations of Private international law in Intellectual Property' in Jürgen Basedow, Toshiyuki Kono and Axel Metzger (eds), *Intellectual Property in the Global Arena* (Mohr Siebeck 2010) 3; James Fawcett and Paul Torremans, *Intellectual Property and Private international law* (2nd edn, OUP 2011) para 12.54; Eugen Ulmer, *Die Immaterialgüterrechte im internationalen Privatrecht* (Carl Heymanns 1975) 10) calling for the (uniform) application of the *lex loci protectionis*, since for matters of protection, each country is required to apply its substantive domestic industrial property law without differentiation as to nationality, and without → renvoi. This rule is reinforced by art 4bis Paris Industrial Property Convention (for patents) and art 6(3) Paris Industrial Property Convention (for marks), according to which the various national rights protected under the domestic laws of individual countries of the Paris Union are independent of each other. This means that the territorial scope of this protection is limited to the territory of the respective countries, and that the domestic law, shielded from external influences, determines protection. This expression of the → territoriality principle seems rather obvious here, since many of the industrial property rights covered by the Paris Industrial Property Convention are registered rights. On an international level, it leads to a 'patchwork' (James Fawcett and Paul Torremans, *Intellectual Property and Private international law* (2nd edn, OUP 2011) para 12.55), or rather a mosaic of national rights protected under the individual laws of the countries of the Paris Union. The national treatment principle guarantees that, wherever protection is needed, there is always an applicable law, regardless of the nationality (or country of origin) of the right holder, 'provided that the conditions and formalities imposed upon nationals are complied with' (art 2(1) Paris Industrial Property Convention).

In order to mitigate the difficulties of obtaining protection in more than one country, the Paris Industrial Property Convention also provides, in art 4, a right of priority for patents (and utility models), trade marks and industrial designs. Once an application for any of these rights has been filed in one contracting party, applicants are granted a certain period (12 months for patents (and utility models), six months for the other industrial property rights) during which they can file applications in the other countries of the Paris Union. All Union countries are required to consider such subsequent applications under their domestic laws as having been filed on the date of filing of the original application. In other words, the original application, a foreign element, must be treated as a domestic application. During the priority period, an application therefore preserves its original filing date throughout the Union and applicants are protected against intervening applications by other persons for the same invention, mark or design. Rather than having to file in all countries at the same time, they have six or 12 months at their disposal during which they can decide in which countries they require protection.

This interplay of the national treatment rule, the principle of independence of rights as an expression of territoriality, and the application of the *lex loci protectionis* does not (directly) lead to international harmonization, since it does not itself reduce the differences between national intellectual property laws. However, the international level of protection is further reinforced by a number of substantive rules ('rights specifically provided for by this Convention' in the terms of art 2(1) Paris Industrial Property Convention) that have a harmonizing effect by requiring that certain minimum standards of substantive protection be granted under the domestic laws of countries of the Paris Union.

JOHANNES CHRISTIAN WICHARD

Later treaties in the area of industrial property, such as the Madrid Agreement of 14 April 1891 concerning the international registration of marks (available at <www.wipo.int/treaties/en/text.jsp?file_id=283530>) and the Protocol of 27 June 1989 relating to the Madrid Agreement of 14 April 1891 concerning the international registration of marks (828 UNTS 389, available at <www.wipo.int/treaties/en/text.jsp?file_id=283484>), the Hague Agreement Concerning the International Registration of Industrial Designs of 6 November 1925 (WIPO Publication No 269), or the Patent Cooperation Treaty (PCT) of 19 June 1970 (WIPO Publication No 274, 1160 UNTS 231), all build on the Paris Industrial Property Convention and establish international mechanisms that centralize the application for the registration of certain types of industrial property rights in a multitude of Member States thus facilitating international protection.

2. *Copyright: the Berne Convention for the Protection of Literary and Artistic Works of 1886*

The approach chosen in the Berne Convention is similar but slightly more complex, partly due to the fact that copyright is more 'fluid' than industrial property in that it requires no registration. Like the Paris Industrial Property Convention, the Berne Convention determines its applicability by way of certain factors that connect the 'work' (definition in arts 2 and 2bis Berne Convention) to be protected to a Member State of the Berne Union. These factors most notably include the → nationality of the author, their place of habitual residence, or the place of first publication of the work in question (arts 3, 4 Berne Convention). The country so identified is considered the work's country of origin (art 5(4) Berne Convention). The work enjoys protection under the country of origin's domestic copyright law, independent of the author's nationality (art 5(3) Berne Convention). This is an expression of the national treatment principle. Article 5(1) Berne Convention extends the national treatment rule to all other countries of the Berne Union:

[a]uthors shall enjoy, in respect of works for which they are protected under this Convention, in countries of the Union other than the country of origin, the rights which their respective laws do now or may hereafter grant to their nationals, as well as the rights specially granted by this Convention.

Hence, copyright protection must be determined in accordance with each Member State's domestic law, not in accordance with the law of country of origin. This is confirmed by art 5(2) second sentence Berne Convention, which states that '[c]onsequently, apart from the provisions of this Convention, the extent of protection, as well as the means of redress afforded to the author to protect his rights, shall be governed exclusively by the laws of the country where protection is claimed'.

Article 5(2) Berne Convention clearly excludes application of the law of the country of origin, because referring issues of protection back to the country of origin might lead to a differential treatment between nationals and foreigners, a result that the Berne Convention seeks to prevent (Jürgen Basedow, 'Foundations of Private international law in Intellectual Property' in Jürgen Basedow, Toshiyuki Kono and Axel Metzger (eds), *Intellectual Property in the Global Arena* (Mohr Siebeck 2010) 3, 14). Cases where the country of origin – exceptionally – retains significance, are specifically provided for in the Berne Convention. They refer to industrial designs (art 2(7) Berne Convention), to the term of protection (art 7(8) Berne Convention) and the resale right or *droit de suite* (art 14 Berne Convention).

There has been some controversy whether the country of origin retains significance, at least for determining authorship or initial ownership of the work, as suggested by a 'universalist' approach which has advantages especially in the digital environment (proponents eg Haimo Schack, *Zur Anknüpfung des Urheberrechts im internationalen Privatrecht* (Duncker & Humblot 1979); Haimo Schack, *Urheber- und Urhebervertragsrecht* (6th edn, Mohr Siebeck 2013) para 1026 ff; Mireille van Eechoud, 'Alternatives to the lex protectionis for Initial Ownership of Copyright' in Josef Drexl and Anette Kur (eds), *Intellectual Property and Private international law* (Hart 2005) 289–306; Paul Goldstein and Bernt Hugenholtz, *International Copyright: Principles, Law, and Practice* (3rd edn, OUP 2013) 136–8; against this approach James Fawcett and Paul Torremans, *Intellectual Property and Private international law* (2nd edn, OUP 2011) paras 12.39–12.47; André Lucas, *Private international law Aspects of the Protection of Works and of the Subject*

Matter of Related Rights Transmitted over Digital Networks, WIPO document WIPO/PIL/01/1 PROV, 18 December 2000 (<www.wipo.int>) 10–12). Unlike with industrial property rights, copyright protection follows from the mere act of creation (in the case of nationals of a Union country) or the first act of publication in a country of the Union (this is also the reason why the Berne Convention, unlike the Paris Industrial Property Convention, has no need to address matters of priority). This protection would then, in principle, be valid in all countries of the Berne Union. At the same time, art 5(2) Berne Convention introduces a territorial element by stating that 'the extent of protection, as well as the means of redress afforded to the author to protect his rights' may vary between countries.

As for industrial property, the interplay between national treatment and → territoriality under the Berne Convention results, on the international level, in a bundle (or mosaic) of 'copyrights' protected under each Member State's domestic law (James Fawcett and Paul Torremans, *Intellectual Property and Private international law* (2nd edn, OUP 2011) para 12.31). This protection is independent of whether and how the work is protected in its country of origin. Thus art 5(2) first sentence Berne Convention states that '[t]he enjoyment and the exercise of these rights shall not be subject to any formality; such enjoyment and such exercise shall be independent of the existence of protection in the country of origin of the work'.

As a result, the Berne Convention refers to the *lex loci protectionis*. This is the law of the country where the extent of protection for the work needs to be determined because the work is about to be used or exploited there. It is not necessarily the law of the country, where the copyright is being infringed or enforced, for example through litigation (Jürgen Basedow, 'Foundations of Private international law in Intellectual Property' in Jürgen Basedow, Toshiyuki Kono and Axel Metzger (eds), *Intellectual Property in the Global Arena* (Mohr Siebeck 2010) 3, 12–13; James Fawcett and Paul Torremans, *Intellectual Property and Private international law* (2nd edn, OUP 2011) para 12.25–12.26; Eugen Ulmer, *Die Immaterialgüterrechte im internationalen Privatrecht* (Carl Heymanns 1975) 11). If, for example, a book is first published in France, it receives copyright protection under the French country of origin of the work, independent of the author's → nationality, domicile or residence (art 5(3) Berne Convention). If copies of the books are exported to England, English law determines the 'extent of protection' (art 5(2) Berne Convention), for example against unauthorized copying. If unauthorized copying in England was committed by a Belgian national, English law applies even if the infringer is sued in his home country. As with the Paris Industrial Property Convention, this choice-of-law rule in the Berne Convention is somewhat implicit, in that it leaves → territoriality intact and deals with the question whether the law where protection is requested should apply even though there is a foreign element. The Berne Convention does so 'from the inside' by requiring the uniform application of the *lex loci protectionis*, and excluding the law of the country of origin. What matters under both Conventions is that there is always a law that regulates protection, independent of questions of nationality or origin.

As under the Paris Industrial Property Convention, the level of protection granted by the Berne Convention is reinforced internationally by a number of substantive rules ('rights specifically provided for by this Convention' in the terms of art 2(1) Berne Convention) that have a harmonizing effect by requiring that certain minimum standards of substantive protection be granted under the domestic laws of countries of the Berne Union (art 19 Berne Convention).

3. *Common approach: the 'inside view'*

What is common in the treatment by both Conventions of international issues is that, perhaps contrary to expectations in private international law, they do not approach the question from an international perspective by determining which from among many national laws is applicable to a given fact pattern, in this case intellectual property protection. Rather the Conventions approach the issue 'from the inside', by regulating how a domestic law must treat intellectual property protection within its territory, namely without regard for the country of origin and for issues of nationality. Together with the territoriality principle, as also expressed in the principle of independence of (national) rights, this leads to a situation where there is an international patchwork – as large as the respective Unions – where national laws provide protection, based on certain common minimum standards. Thus wherever the issue of protection arises, there is an applicable law.

IV. Later developments: adapting territoriality to digitization and the Internet

While the basic Conventions provide a degree of guidance on private international law issues by pointing in essence to *lex loci protectionis*, it might still be said that, in consequence of the → territoriality principle and the subsequent efforts to mitigate its effects, intellectual property and private international law have a history of avoiding each other. International progress has been achieved by the establishment of common principles, by international harmonization, or by the establishment of international procedures. This approach has hardly changed. However, what has changed is the urgency with which international aspects have invaded intellectual property law in the context of the most recent wave of globalization (→ Globalization and private international law), which itself has largely been fuelled by digitization and the Internet. So far, the intellectual property rights most affected have been copyright and trade marks, and in both areas intellectual property-specific responses have been developed on the basis of the traditional structures.

1. Copyright: WIPO Copyright Treaty 1996 (WCT) and WIPO Performances and Phonograms Treaty 1996 (WPPT)

The WCT (WIPO Copyright Treaty (WCT) of 20 December 1996, WIPO Publication No 226) and the WPPT (WIPO Performances and Phonograms Treaty (WPPT) of 20 December 1996, WIPO Publication No 227) were the first reactions in international intellectual property normsetting to the challenges brought about by the Internet. The purpose of both Treaties is to extend the level of copyright protection (WCT) and of the protection for performances and phonograms (WPPT) to the Internet. Both Treaties do so on the basis of the traditional means of requiring the harmonization of national laws according to certain international standards. The WCT requires protection for computer programs as literary works (art 4 WCT) and databases provided they qualify as 'intellectual creations' (art 5 WCT). Both Treaties specify certain rights (distribution, rental), and introduce a new right of communication to the public (art 8 WCT, art 14 WPPT), in particular, on-demand, interactive communication through the Internet. Also new in both Treaties is the obligation on contracting parties to provide legal → remedies against the circumvention of technological protection measures (art 11 WCT, art 18 WPPT), and against the removal of electronic rights management information (art 12 WCT, art 19 WPPT). Neither Treaty addresses issues of private international law.

2. Trade marks

In the area of trade marks, WIPO has followed a dual approach. On the one hand, a Joint Recommendation (World Intellectual Property Organization, Joint Recommendation Concerning Provisions on the Protection of Marks, and Other Industrial Rights in Signs on the Internet, adopted by the Assembly of the Paris Union and the General Assembly of WIPO from 24 September to 3 October 2001 (WIPO Publication No 845, available at <www.wipo.int>)), a 'soft law instrument', was developed that seeks to translate trade mark protection to the Internet, by making its territorial basis Internet-compatible. On the other hand, a more radical departure from traditional intellectual property normsetting approaches introduces a new international alternative dispute resolution mechanism to remedy certain extreme cases of bad-faith trade mark infringements. Both will be explored in the following paragraphs.

a) The Joint Recommendation Concerning Protection of Marks, and Other Industrial Property Rights in Signs on the Internet 2001

The WIPO Joint Recommendation Concerning the Protection of Marks, and Other Industrial Property Rights in Signs on the Internet was adopted in September 2001 by the Assembly of the Paris Union for the Protection of Industrial Property and the General Assembly of WIPO (analysis in Graeme B Dinwoodie, *Private International Aspects of the Protection of Trademarks*, WIPO document WIPO/PIL/01/4, 19 January 2001 (available at <www.wipo.int/edocs/mdocs/mdocs/en/wipo_pil_01/wipo_pil_01_4.pdf>) paras 101–10; Johannes Christian Wichard, 'The Joint Recommendation Concerning Protection of Marks, and Other Industrial Property Rights in Signs, on the Internet' in Josef Drexl and Anette Kur (eds), *Intellectual Property and Private international law* (Hart 2005) 257–64). While the Joint Recommendation lacks the legal force of an international treaty, it has strong persuasive authority as an expression of international consensus in this particular area of the law.

The Joint Recommendation seeks to address problems that arise when trade marks and other distinctive signs, such as trade names or geographical indications, are used on the Internet. Three issues are addressed: (i) when the use of a sign on the Internet can be deemed to have taken place in the territory of a specific country; (ii) how conflicts between rights in signs that belong to different owners in different countries can be resolved, so that both owners can use their signs on the Internet without infringing each other's rights; (iii) how remedies for infringing use of a sign on the Internet can be limited to the territorial scope of protection of the infringed right.

In line with the tradition of international norm-setting in trade mark law, the Joint Recommendation addresses international dimensions of trade mark use within the framework of national trade mark laws. It accepts both the territorial character of existing trade mark laws as well as the global nature of the Internet as given factors, and resolves the issue 'from within' a given domestic law by providing guidance on how to apply it in a way that does justice to both factors in an 'Internet-compatible' way. The Joint Recommendation specifically states that it does not address choice-of-law issues (note 0.04 Joint Recommendation: 'The question of determining the applicable law is not addressed by the present provisions, but left to the private international laws of individual Member States').

(1) Legal relevance of Internet use Trade mark use is fundamentally territorial in that it must be linked to a particular territory in order to gain legal relevance. Use of a sign can only establish, maintain or infringe a trade mark in a particular country if the sign has been used in that country. This link may be difficult to establish where a sign has been used on the Internet. For the Joint Recommendation, this link consists in the 'commercial effect' of Internet use. Only use that has a 'commercial effect' in a particular territory will be treated as having occurred in that territory (art 2 Joint Recommendation). Mere visibility on a computer screen alone is insufficient. Article 3 Joint Recommendation provides a detailed, but non-exhaustive, list of factors that can be relevant for determining commercial effect, such as the interactivity of the website in question, registration under a country code Top-Level Domain (such as '.de' for Germany), etc. With a commercial effect, use on the Internet is relevant for establishing or maintaining trade mark rights under a national or regional trade mark law (art 5 Joint Recommendation). Similarly, such use can be regarded as infringing a right protected in the territory concerned (art 6 Joint Recommendation), while use without a commercial effect is legally irrelevant.

(2) Avoiding and resolving conflicts Because the scope of trade mark rights is territorially limited, different owners can hold rights in identical or similar signs in different countries. Such rights that coexist offline in different territories may enter into conflict on the Internet. Requiring a comprehensive worldwide search for conflicting registered and unregistered rights would in many instances be impossible or at least not commercially viable. To provide a practicable way for addressing such conflicts, the Joint Recommendation suggests a 'notice and avoidance of conflict' procedure (Part V, arts 9 to 15 Joint Recommendation). Under certain conditions, use of a sign on the Internet is exempt from liability up to the point when the user is notified of a conflicting right (art 9 Joint Recommendation), provided that the user owns a right in that sign, or that the use is legitimate under the law of a country to which the user has a close connection, for example because it is the user's personal name or because the term is considered generic or descriptive, and provided that such use has not been made in bad faith. Once a user has been notified of a conflicting right, they have to take certain measures in order to avoid liability. The Joint Recommendation suggests a qualified disclaimer (art 12 Joint Recommendation) as a sufficient measure and therefore provides a way to avoid the mutual blocking effect of conflicting rights.

(3) Proportionality of remedies The effect of an → injunction prohibiting every use of a sign on the Internet is as global as the Internet and far exceeds the territorial scope of the infringed right. → Remedies should, however, be limited as far as possible to the territory in which the right is recognized. These issues are addressed in Part VI (arts 13 to 15) of the Joint Recommendation, which introduces a general principle of proportionality. Injunctions should generally be limited to what is necessary to prevent or remove the commercial effect in the Member State (or Member States) in which the infringed right is protected, and damages should cover only use that has a commercial effect in the country concerned. The Joint

Recommendation mentions 'qualified disclaimers' (as set out in art 12), gateway webpages and the like. It recognizes that 'global injunctions' may be unavoidable in certain cases, for example if the user has targeted a well-known mark in bad faith (as in the case of 'cybersquatting'). Pursuant to art 15 Joint Recommendation, however, such global injunctions may not be granted against good-faith users who hold a right in the sign or who are otherwise permitted to use the sign.

(4) The 'inside view' In substance, the Joint Recommendation is an example of the traditional approach in international intellectual property law described above. Like the Paris Industrial Property Convention and the Berne Convention, the Joint Recommendation is concerned with the way a national intellectual property law is applied to certain international facts. Thus it takes an 'inside view', rather than determining which from among many national laws may be applicable to govern the case at hand. At the same time this approach bears some similarity to private international law methods, since it also seeks to link a certain fact pattern, in the case of the Joint Recommendation the use of a sign on the Internet, to a certain territory. However, its purpose is not to use this link as a means to determine the applicable law, but rather to locate the facts within the framework of a given substantive law. Thus 'use', a substantive legal requirement, is only relevant in a particular country if it has a 'commercial effect' in that country. At the same time, the factors listed in art 3 Joint Recommendation to assist in this determination may also be helpful wherever a certain activity on the Internet needs to be linked to a certain territory, for example, in the context of determining jurisdiction for Internet-related disputes.

b) Domain names: Uniform Domain Name Dispute Resolution Policy
The Uniform Domain Name Dispute Resolution Policy (UDRP; Uniform Domain Name Dispute Resolution Policy, as approved by ICANN on 24 October 1999 (<www.icann.org/en/help/dndr/udrp/policy>)) is an example of an approach that transcends territoriality and departs from traditional means of normsetting in intellectual property. The UDRP establishes an international dispute resolution system with a built-in enforcement mechanism that is only loosely connected to any national law. The UDRP is the product of WIPO recommendations (<www.wipo.int/amc/en/processes/process1/report/index.html>) that were made as a result of the WIPO Internet Domain Name Process, an international consultative process in which everyone, not only states, could participate. These recommendations were approved by WIPO's decision-making bodies and transmitted to the then newly established Internet Corporation for Assigned Names and Numbers (ICANN). The recommendations were largely adopted and implemented as the UDRP (<www.icann.org/en/help/dndr/udrp/policy>), which entered into effect in December 1999. The WIPO Arbitration and Mediation Centre was appointed as one among several dispute resolution providers under the UDRP. It has administered the highest caseload from among all providers, reaching a total of 35,000 disputes at the end of 2016.

The UDRP is an → alternative dispute resolution procedure that is based on a contractual agreement. Everyone who registers a domain name in one of the generic Top Level domains (such as '.com', '.org', '.biz'), submits, as part of the agreement, to the UDRP. The scope of the UDRP is clearly limited to cases of bad faith abusive registration of trade marks as domain names, so-called 'cybersquatting' – this was the international lowest common denominator at the time of the WIPO Internet Domain Name Process. The complainant must prove that he/she owns a (registered or unregistered) trade mark right in the alphanumerical string that was registered as a domain name, that the registrant has no right or even a 'legitimate interest' that would be recognized under any national law, and that the registration and use of the domain name took place in bad faith. In the words of s 2(a)(i)–(iii) UDRP (taking the perspective of a domain name registrant): '(i) your domain name is identical or confusingly similar to a trade mark or service mark in which the complainant has rights; and (ii) you have no rights or legitimate interests in respect of the domain name; and (iii) your domain name has been registered and is being used in bad faith'.

Whether the domain name registrant files a substantive response or not, a neutral and independent panellist (list of all WIPO panellists at <www.wipo.int/amc/en/domains/panel/panelists.html>) is appointed to decide the case on the basis of the arguments and documentary evidence submitted. The only remedies that can be granted under the UDRP are cancellation of the domain name or transfer to the complainant (see s 3(c) UDRP). These remedies can be implemented within the domain name system on the basis of the domain name registration contract, and no recourse to a national law enforcement agency is required. Unlike in arbitration, either party can bring the dispute before a competent national court of justice instead of a UDRP procedure, or to appeal its outcome. This happens only very rarely. The procedure is very effective; the overall duration of a typical UDRP procedure is around two months.

The UDRP establishes an international procedure that transcends → territoriality. It is almost 'supranational' in the sense that it is hardly connected to any national legal system. The UDRP relies on national laws only to determine whether the complainant holds a sufficient trade mark right, and whether the respondent has no right or legal interest under any national law. Its enforcement system, cancellation or transfer of the disputed domain name, does not rely on national law either. Over the years, an elaborate international case law has been established that is accessible through WIPO tools like the WIPO Overview of WIPO Panel Views on Selected UDRP Questions (<www.wipo.int/amc/en/domains/search/overview2.0/>), or the Index of WIPO UDRP Panel Decisions (<www.wipo.int/amc/en/domains/search/legalindex.jsp>), which provide guidance to parties and panellists and have contributed to ensuring a reasonable level of predictability and legal certainty. The UDRP has *de facto* become an (almost) self-contained international legal system – albeit with a very narrow substantive scope.

V. WIPO and private international law?

WIPO has addressed private international law issues directly only on two occasions by providing a forum for discussion among experts in both areas. In December 1998, WIPO convened a Group of Consultants on the Private international law Aspects of the Protection of Works and Objects of Related Rights Transmitted through Global Digital Networks (papers available at <www.wipo.int/edocs/mdocs/mdocs/en/gcpic/gcpic_2.pdf>). On 30 to 31 January 2001, WIPO organized a Forum on Private international law and Intellectual Property (all papers available at <www.wipo.int/meetings/en/details.jsp?meeting_id=4243>). This Forum was followed by a one-day consultation session organized by the → Hague Conference on Private International Law, on the proposed Hague Recognition and Enforcement Convention (Hague Convention of 1 February 1971 on the recognition and enforcement of foreign judgments in civil and commercial matters, 1144 UNTS 258). Negotiations on this draft instrument had stalled since no agreement could be reached on how to address intellectual property disputes (report at <www.hcch.net/upload/wop/jdgmpd13.pdf>).

The above remarks have demonstrated that WIPO has largely avoided addressing issues of private international law directly. In its normative activities, it has instead followed an approach that leaves the territorial basis of intellectual property rights unchallenged; the potentially negative impact of territoriality on international trade is addressed through the establishment of basic general principles (eg national treatment) and the harmonization of national laws. International issues are addressed from 'inside' national laws, and this approach has been followed even in response to new challenges brought about by the Internet and digitization. The UDRP is an exception; it is a 'policy' that relies on the basis of contracts established under private law, and provides a unique example for an international system that has been established almost completely outside any national legal system.

JOHANNES CHRISTIAN WICHARD

Literature

Graeme Austin, *Private international law and Intellectual Property Rights: A Common Law Overview*, WIPO document WIPO/PIL/01/5, 15 January 2001 (<www.wipo.int/edocs/mdocs/mdocs/en/wipo_pil_01/wipo_pil_01_5.pdf>); Jürgen Basedow, 'Foundations of Private international law in Intellectual Property' in Jürgen Basedow, Toshiyuki Kono and Axel Metzger (eds), *Intellectual Property in the Global Arena* (Mohr Siebeck 2010) 3; Adler Bernard, 'The Proposed New WIPO Treaty for Increased Protection for Audiovisual Performers: Its Provisions and Its Domestic and International Implications, Fordham Intellectual Property' [2002] Media and Entertainment Law Journal 1089; Torsten Bettinger, *Handbuch des Domainrechts: Nationale Schutzsysteme und internationale Streitbeilegung* (Carl Heymanns 2008); Torsten Bettinger, Tony Willougby and Sally Abel (eds), *Domain Name Law and Practice: An*

International Handbook (OUP 2005); Fritz Blumer, *Patent Law and International Private Law on Both Sides of the Atlantic*, WIPO document WIPO/PIL/01/3, 17 January 2001 (<www.wipo.int/edocs/mdocs/mdocs/en/wipo_pil_01/wipo_pil_01_3.pdf>); Georg Hendrik Christiaan Bodenhausen, *Guide to the Application of the Paris Convention for the Protection of Industrial Property* (BIRPI 1968); Graeme B Dinwoodie, *Private International Aspects of the Protection of Trademarks*, WIPO document WIPO/PIL/01/4, 19 January 2001 (<www.wipo.int/edocs/mdocs/mdocs/en/wipo_pil_01/wipo_pil_01_4.pdf>); Masato Dogauchi, *Private international law on Intellectual Property: A Civil Law Overview*, WIPO document WIPO/PIL/01/8, 24 January 2001 (<www.wipo.int/edocs/mdocs/mdocs/en/wipo_pil_01/wipo_pil_01_8.pdf>); Mireille van Eechoud, 'Alternatives to the lex protectionis for Initial Ownership of Copyright' in Josef Drexl and Anette Kur (eds), *Intellectual Property and Private international law* (Hart 2005) 289; James Fawcett and Paul Torremans, *Intellectual Property and Private international law* (2nd edn, OUP 2011); Jane Ginsburg, *Private international law Aspects of the Protection of Works and Objects of Related Rights Transmitted through Digital Networks* (2000 Update), WIPO document WIPO/PIL/01/2, 17 December 2000 (<www.wipo.int/edocs/mdocs/mdocs/en/wipo_pil_01/wipo_pil_01_2.pdf>); Paul Goldstein and Bernt Hugenholtz, *International Copyright: Principles, Law, and Practice* (3rd edn, OUP 2013); André Lucas, *Private international law Aspects of the Protection of Works and of the Subject Matter of Related Rights Transmitted over Digital Networks*, WIPO document WIPO/PIL/01/1 PROV, 18 December 2000 (<www.wipo.int/meetings/en/doc_details.jsp?doc_id=12385>); Haimo Schack, *Zur Anknüpfung des Urheberrechts im internationalen Privatrecht* (Duncker & Humblot 1979); Haimo Schack, *Urheber- und Urhebervertragsrecht* (6th edn, Mohr Siebeck 2013); Eugen Ulmer, *Die Immaterialgüterrechte im internationalen Privatrecht* (Carl Heymanns 1975); Johannes Christian Wichard, 'The Joint Recommendation Concerning Protection of Marks, and Other Industrial Property Rights in Signs, on the Internet' in Josef Drexl and Anette Kur (eds), *Intellectual Property and Private international law* (Hart 2005) 257; WIPO, *The Management of Internet Names and Addresses: Intellectual Property Issues. Final Report of the WIPO Internet Domain Name Process* (WIPO 30 April 1999); WIPO, 'The Management of Internet Names and Addresses: Intellectual Property Issues, Final Report of the WIPO Internet Domain Name Process', 1999 (<www.wipo.int/export/sites/www/amc/en/docs/report-final1.pdf>); WIPO, *Intellectual Property on the Internet: A Survey of Issues* (WIPO 2002); WIPO, *Guide to the Copyright and Related Rights Treaties Administered by WIPO and Glossary of Copyright and Related Rights Terms* (WIPO 2003); WIPO, Index of WIPO UDRP Panel Decisions (constantly updated) (<www.wipo.int/amc/en/domains/search/legalindex.jsp>); WIPO, Overview of WIPO Panel Views on Selected UDRP Questions, 2011 (<www.wipo.int/amc/en/domains/search/overview2.0/>).

WTO and private international law

I. Introduction: background and context

Traditionally, private international law and World Trade Organization (WTO) law have been viewed as separate areas. The scarcity of scholarly debate on the two fields' interplay is telling. Private international law (particularly → choice of law) is viewed as part of a country's national law. It is designed to determine the applicable law in cases involving foreign contacts. Under the traditional understanding, private international law is limited largely to private-party disputes and, hence, individual interests. WTO law, by contrast, is seen as a segment of public international law, an area to be kept strictly separate from national law. It concerns the rights and obligations of nation-states vis-à-vis one another. Private parties are neither directly protected nor endowed with individual rights.

But this impression of isolation is incorrect, primarily because private international law is no longer limited (if it ever was) to the resolution of private-party conflicts. By determining the applicable law, the choice-of-law norm also decides on the horizontal allocation of regulatory powers. In other words, determination of the *lex causae* includes a choice of which national policy to enforce. It is this 'regulatory function' of private international law that may conflict with a state's obligations under public international law (→ Public international law and private international law). This becomes a concern with respect to WTO law. The organization's central aim is to guarantee unhindered international trade. This is achieved through, *inter alia*, a strict prohibition on discrimination. While the mere choice of an applicable law as such does not restrict trade, it does decide which substantive law will govern. And depending on how this combined application of conflicts and substantive law plays out, imported goods, imported services or importing parties may be discriminated against. Barriers to trade will ensue.

Thus, at least regarding WTO law, the oft-enunciated separation between public and private international law is no longer as clear-cut as has been traditionally explained. On the contrary, a vertical osmosis between the different levels of international law seems logical, if not inevitable. It may therefore appear surprising that WTO law contains no express provisions on private international law. Indeed, it is far from clear whether implied rules exist (eg under the TRIPS Agreement (Agreement of 15 April 1994 on Trade-Related Aspects of Intellectual Property Rights, 1869 UNTS 299)) or what other influence WTO law may exert on Member States' laws.

II. WTO law: basic principles

The WTO was established in 1994 with the final act of the Uruguay Round of trade negotiations. It provides a common institutional framework for trade relations between its members. The organization has different responsibilities, including the supervision of several multilateral trade agreements and their practical workings. The General Agreement on Tariffs and Trade (GATT, General Agreement on Tariffs and Trade of 15 April 1994, 1867 UNTS 187) sits at the core of these agreements. Closely related are the General Agreement on Trade in Services (GATS, General Agreement on Trade in Services of 15 April 1994, 1869 UNTS 183) and the Agreement on Trade-Related Aspects of Intellectual Property Rights (→ TRIPS). In addition, the WTO provides for dispute resolution between Member States. The WTO's principles, which are summarized in the preamble to the 1994 agreement establishing the organization, include trade liberalization, non-discrimination in international trade, promotion of fair trade, transparency and special treatment for developing countries.

The WTO's most fundamental aim is to establish a system of transnational and international commerce that is unhindered by national protectionism. Accordingly, the reduction of barriers to trade is critically important. In this respect, WTO law distinguishes between admissible and inadmissible barriers. In the field of trade in goods, the traditional barriers are tariffs and quotas. While tariffs are generally allowed, members are supposed to reduce them through negotiations. Yet tariff reduction alone will not, in the long run, guarantee free trade.

Member States often resort to 'non-tariff barriers' to protect national interests. One example is the imposition of quotas for imports. Another important, albeit less obvious, restriction is the discriminatory conception or application of domestic laws. In order to avoid such protectionism, the WTO system adopts the so-called antidiscrimination model. This model requires Member States not to discriminate against foreign products in terms of the products' market access or internal regulation. It is reflected in two basic rules: the most-favoured-nation (MFN) rule and the national-treatment rule. The MFN rule is a basic principle contained in the 1994 GATT, the GATS and the TRIPS Agreement (*infra* IV.3.). It requires that any advantage or favour given to the products of one country must be given to those of all other WTO members. In essence, it obligates Member States not to discriminate against the products of other members. The second basis of non-discrimination – the principle of national treatment – can also be found in the 1994 GATT, the GATS and the TRIPS (*infra* IV.3.). Under the 1994 GATT, the principle requires that imported goods be treated the same as domestic goods once they have cleared customs and border procedures (John H Jackson, *The World Trading System: Law and Policy of International Relations* (2nd edn, MIT Press 1997) 213). Article III:1 provides:

> The contracting parties recognize that internal taxes and other internal charges, and laws, regulations and requirements affecting the internal sale, offering for sale, purchase, transportation, distribution or use of products, and internal quantitative regulations requiring the mixture, processing or use of products in specified amounts or proportions, should not be applied to imported or domestic products so as to afford protection to domestic production.

Further, art III:2 of the 1994 GATT prohibits the imposition of internal taxes on imports that exceed taxes on 'like domestic products'. Under art III:4, Member States must eventually accord imports 'treatment no less favourable than that accorded to like products of national origin in respect of all laws, regulations and requirements affecting their internal sale, offering for sale, purchase, transportation, distribution or use'. In essence, non-discrimination is the Magna Carta of the *par conditio concurrentium* in international trade. Notably, the national-treatment principle 'protects expectations not of any particular trade volume but rather of the equal competitive relationship between imported and domestic products' (Appellate Body, Report, Japan – *Alcoholic Beverages II*, WT/DS8/AB/R (4 October 1996), 16).

III. Foundations: the interplay between public and private international law

The WTO aims to uphold unrestricted international trade within a decentralized system of Member States' widely sovereign policy making and decision making. Such a stratification of regulatory capacities with respect to international and national transacting is not unique to the WTO. The European Union (EU), as well, aims at market liberalization, and its Member States are largely prohibited from implementing contrary policies. Given the structural similarities between the WTO and the EU, a comparative look is indicated (see Christian Joerges, 'Constitutionalism in Postnational Constellations: Contrasting Social Regulation in the EU and in the WTO' in Christian Joerges and Ernst-Ulrich Petersmann (eds), *Constitutionalism, Multilevel Trade Governance and Social Regulation* (Oxford Hart 2006) 491, 510). Such a comparison reveals, however, that WTO law is not as deeply implemented as EU law, and that vertical integration is not sufficiently advanced to cause a direct impact on Member States' private international law.

1. *EU law: a self-referential system of integration*

The issue of interplay between EU law and national private international law is intensely debated. For some time, it was contended that EU freedoms were neutral – even disinterested – with respect to choice of law (eg Harry Duintjer Tebbens, 'Les conflits de lois en matière de publicité déloyale à l'épreuve du droit communautaire' (1994) 83 Rev.crit.DIP 451, 476 *et seq*). Upon first look, this argument seems hard to contest. After all, choice of law is incomplete by definition. Without a substantive-law regime found to apply, there is no 'regulation' – and hence there cannot be a violation of EU law. Yet, as is acknowledged today, choice of law and the *lex causae* in tandem can effectuate outcomes that may violate EU law (see generally Hans-Jürgen Sonnenberger, 'Einleitung IPR' in Franz Jürgen Säcker and Poland Rixecker (eds), *Münchener Kommentar zum Bürgerlichen Gesetzbuch* (5th edn, CH Beck 2011) paras 135 *et seq*). While the details of this debate are irrelevant for this inquiry, one facet is important: supranational legal principles closely and directly interact with members' laws. EU law requires more than mere non-discrimination – it requires the elimination of nearly all obstacles to trade, whether discriminatory or not.

The Court of Justice explained this in 1974 in *Dassonville*: 'All trading rules enacted by Member States which are capable of hindering, directly or indirectly, actually or potentially, intra-Community trade are to be considered as measures having an effect equivalent to quantitative restrictions' (Case C-8/74, *Procureur du Roi v Benoît and Gustave Dassonville* [1974] ECR 837, para 5).

A regulation applicable to national and imported products alike may be subject to the prohibition 'if in practice it produces protective effects by favouring typical national products and, by the same token, operating to the detriment of certain types of products from other Member States' (C-16/83, *Criminal proceedings against Karl Prantl* [1984] ECR 1229, para 21). Any import limitation may qualify as undue protectionism (Joined Cases C-177 and C-178/82, *Criminal proceedings against Jan van de Haar and Keveka de Meern BV* [1984] ECR 1797, para 13). But *Dassonville* was partly restricted in 1993 following the *Keck* decision. As the new ruling established, national provisions restricting or prohibiting only certain selling arrangements should be subject to a lower standard of scrutiny. Beyond directly product-related regulation, therefore, the standard is one of non-discrimination, not a general non-hindrance of transacting. In other words, provisions of this kind are not deemed illegitimate restrictions as long as they 'apply to all relevant traders operating within the national territory and so long as they affect in the same manner, in law and in fact, the marketing of domestic products and of those from other Member States' (Joined Cases C-267/91 and C-268/91, *Criminal proceedings against Bernard Keck and Daniel Mithouard* [1994] ECR I-6097, para 16).

Although the *Keck* holding may have limited the scope of *Dassonville*, it has not changed the general paradigm. In essence, the EU has established a principle of mutual recognition among Member States, particularly with respect to the freedom of trade (Commission of the European Communities, 'Completing the Internal Market: White Paper from the Commission to the European Council (Milan, 28–29 June 1985)' COM(85) 310 final, paras 63, 65; Case C-184/96, *Commission of the European Communities v French Republic* [1998] ECR I-6197, para 28). All national legal and technical rules of one Member State must therefore be assumed equivalent to domestic regulation by other members. With respect to inter-EU trade, only exceptions under the TFEU (TFEU, The Treaty on the Functioning of the European Union (consolidated version), [2012] OJ C 326/47; eg art 36) or measures recognized as 'being necessary in order to satisfy mandatory requirements' (eg public health or consumer protection) under the *Cassis de Dijon* formula allow for the application of national regulatory standards (Case C-120/78, *Rewe-Zentral AG v Bundesmonopolverwaltung für Branntwein* [1979] ECR 649, para 8). This paradigm of integration concerns both the public and private law of Member States.

It also finds expression in the relationship between supranational and national levels. Even though EU law is understood as separate from Member States' national laws, both levels closely interact. Early on, the Court of Justice began developing a doctrine of the supremacy of EU law (see, eg, Case C-6/64, *Flaminio Costa v E.N.E.L.* [1964] ECR 585). Under this doctrine, if a Member State's law does not comply with EU law, it cannot be applied by the country's national authorities or its judiciary (see, eg, Joined Cases C-10/97 to C-22/97, *Ministero delle Finanze v IN.CO.GE. '90 Srl et al* [1998] ECR I-6307, para 21). Notably, EU freedoms have direct effect, even if there has been no formal internal transformation within the state (see, eg, Joined Cases C-46/93 and C-48/93, *Brasserie du Pêcheur SA* [1996] ECR I-1029, paras 52 *et seq*).

Member States' private international law is also supposed to incorporate EU law. Nineteenth- and 20th-century private international law sought to achieve conflicts justice by choosing the law most spatially and topically related to the parties' dispute. Content neutrality was a side effect. The impact of EU freedoms, however, has brought out a choice-of-law doctrine no longer framed in such formal-technical norms. Modern European conflicts law is loaded with substantive policies (Kurt Siehr, 'Vom universellen zum globalen IPR – Zur jüngsten Geschichte und Entwicklung des Internationalen Privatrechts' in Heinz-Peter Mansel and others (eds), *Festschrift für Erik Jayme*, vol 1 (Sellier 2004) 873, 879 *et seq*). Thus, choice of law – through its interplay with substantive policies – might take part in a violation of EU freedoms or of the non-hindrance principle. This might be the case, for instance, if the *lex causae* is determined on the basis of → nationality. Illegitimate discrimination could then result from different substantive laws to be applied. Also, the undue extension of national policies beyond a member's territory may be found a violation even if these policies as such are legitimate. The facts of the *Alpine Investments* case provide an illustration. There, a Dutch consumer-protection policy – *per se* limited to national territory – was nonetheless extended to consumers and transactions in another Member State (Case C-384/93, *Alpine Investments BV* [1995] ECR I-1141, para 43).

Internally, of course, Member States are free to choose the corrective measure in cases of discriminatory or unduly restricting conflicts resolution. They may allow for → party autonomy, refer to the country-of-origin regime as *lex causae*, or simply provide for non-application of the substantive norm at issue (see, eg, Jürgen Basedow, 'Der kollisionsrechtliche Gehalt der Produktfreiheiten im europäischen Binnenmarkt: favor offerentis' (1995) 59 RabelsZ 1, 27–8; Hans-Jürgen Sonnenberger, 'Einleitung IPR' in Franz Jürgen Säcker and Poland Rixecker (eds), *Münchener Kommentar zum Bürgerlichen Gesetzbuch* (5th edn, CH Beck 2011) paras 154 *et seq*, 172). Modification of members' choice of law is thus only one among several options for guaranteeing compliance with EU law. Nevertheless, the once-described isolation of national private international law has been 'pierced' by materialization. Private international law is predetermined by a strictly defined framework of integrative policies. And with respect to its practical implementation, this framework is procedurally consolidated in the EU judiciary's direct and final decision-making authority.

2. WTO law: liberalization through non-integrating coordination

The WTO has not established a comparable mechanism for integration. Indeed, neither the GATT nor the WTO has even managed to establish an unrestrained free-trade charter. The WTO system still plays out as a balancing between free trade and the antagonistic policies of independent sovereign policy makers. It focuses on trade and has, at least so far, no agenda of socio-economic harmonization (John O McGinnis and Mark L Movsesian, 'The World Trade Constitution' (2001) 114 Harv.L.Rev. 511, 549 *et seq*). Indeed, as the 2004 report *The Future of the WTO* makes clear, 'It is not that the WTO disallows market protection, only that it sets some strict disciplines under which governments may choose to respond to special interests' (Peter Sutherland and others, *The Future of the WTO (Report by the Consultative Board to the Director-General Supachai Panitchpakdi)* (WTO 2004), para 39). Accordingly, WTO law does not prohibit restrictions on trade altogether. Each member is largely free to regulate its internal affairs, even though this may ultimately bring out a barrier to international trade. While the EU aims to establish a single Internal Market under a uniform regulatory regime, the WTO still provides for a system of multiple markets determined by separate national policies (Joseph HH Weiler, *The EU, the WTO, and the NAFTA: Towards a Common Law of International Trade?* (OUP 2000) 201).

This difference also plays out with respect to the vertical implementation of Member States' WTO obligations. Interaction between national laws and WTO law is indirect at best. Article XVI:4 of the Treaty of Marrakesh (Marrakesh Agreement of 15 April 1994 establishing the World Trade Organization, 1867 UNTS 3) provides that '[e]ach Member shall ensure the conformity of its laws, regulations and administrative procedures with its obligations as provided in the annexed Agreements'. But there is no direct application of WTO law in Member States. The 1999 WTO panel report on the US Trade Act illustrates this:

> The most relevant [objects and purposes of the WTO] are those which relate to the creation of market conditions conducive to individual economic activity in national and global markets and to the provision of a secure and predictable multilateral trading system. Under the doctrine of direct effect, which has been found to exist most notably in the legal order of the [EU] . . ., obligations addressed to States are construed as creating legally enforceable rights and obligations for individuals. Neither the GATT nor the WTO has so far been interpreted . . . as a legal order producing direct effect. Following this approach, the GATT/WTO did not create a new legal order the subjects of which comprise both contracting parties or Members and their nationals. (Panel Report, WT/DS 152/R, 22 December 1999, US – Sections

301–10 of the Trade Act of 1974 para 7.71–2)

Member States, too, are hesitant to grant WTO law a direct effect and application within their national domains. This is the case particularly in Europe and the US (see, eg, Joined Case C-21 to C-24/72, *International Fruit Company NV and others v Produktschap voor Groenten en Fruit* [1972] ECR 1219, paras 19 *et seq*; Case C-69/89, *Nakajima All Precision Co. Ltd v Council of the European Communities* [1991] ECR I-2069, paras 27 *et seq*; Case C-149/96, *Portuguese Republic v Council of the European Union* [1999] ECR I-8395, paras 47 *et seq*; Case C-377/02, *Léon Van Parys NV v Belgisch Interventie- en Restitutiebureau (BIRB)* [2005] ECR I-1465, paras 53–4; for the US, see, eg, *Suramerica de Aleaciones Laminadas, CA v US*, 966 F.2d 660, 667–8 (Fed Cir 1992)). Consequently, WTO law must always be formally implemented into the national regime first.

For the interplay between WTO law and private international law, this is crucial in two respects. First, with regard to the standard of scrutiny, WTO law requires only non-discrimination; unlike the EU, the WTO does not prohibit all trade restrictions. Each member country is free to apply the *lex fori* with respect to foreign imports. Even if this may ultimately hurt importing parties, Member States are not obligated to avoid any and all obstacles to trade. Nor is there a duty to refer to the law of the country of production or origin (Wulf-Henning Roth, 'Welthandelsordnung und IPR' in Wolff Heintschel von Heinegg and others (eds), *Entschädigung nach bewaffneten Konflikten, Berichte der Deutschen Gesellschaft für Völkerrecht* (CF Müller 2003) 331, 343). Second, the procedural effectuation of WTO obligations is indirect at best. A Member State, when formulating its private international law, is obligated to consider its international obligation under the WTO (see art XVI:4 of the Treaty of Marrakesh), which requires giving regard to the interplay between → choice of law and *lex causae*. In addition, courts are obligated to construct choice-of-law norms – as all other law – in accordance with public international law (eg Case C-92/71, *Interfood GmbH v Hauptzollamt Hamburg-Ericus* [1972] ECR 231, para 6; Case C-83/94, *Criminal proceedings against Peter Leifer, Reinhold Otto Krauskopf and Otto Holzer* [1995] ECR I-3231, para 24). Yet choice of law will not be automatically invalidated for lack of compliance alone. The actual effects of public international legal obligations are a matter of the Member State's internal judicial review. If the state provides for a review of norms that contravene external obligations, a certain 'directness' is guaranteed. If no such corrective procedure is in place, a violation of WTO obligations will remain unheeded internally. It is during this last stage – ie when statutory choice of law and judicial practice fail to comply with obligations under public international law – that WTO dispute resolution comes into play.

IV. Application

At a practical level, the interplay between WTO law and private international law raises a number of questions. First, the combined application of choice of law and *lex causae* can lead to a violation of non-discrimination principles. Second, there are a number of exceptions under WTO law that allow Member States to treat foreign and domestic products unequally. The issue then is whether the national policies implemented to justify such restrictions may have extraterritorial reach. Finally, there are specific areas where a direct impact of WTO law on members' choice of law seems possible. This particularly concerns international corporate and intellectual property law.

1. The principle of non-discrimination

The interplay between a member's → choice of law and the *lex causae* may result in discrimination against foreign products or parties (*supra* III.2.). An obvious example of such a scenario is a choice-of-law norm that expressly provides for different treatment of nationals and foreigners. But it is not only formal (*de jure*) discrimination that may violate WTO law. Mere factual (*de facto*) discrimination may also qualify if it exerts the same competition-stifling effects (eg Appellate Body Report, Korea – *Various Measures on Beef* (2000), para 137; Panel Report, *Italian Agricultural Machinery* (1958), para 12).

One example of *de facto* discrimination in choice of law can be found in international product liability. A choice-of-law rule that provides for application of the law of the defendant's place of business may end up discriminating against imports. This would be the case if the foreign law is stricter than the law of the marketplace, for foreign producers would then bear higher costs. Therefore, as some have suggested, the principle of national treatment should be interpreted as allowing for application of the law of the importer's place of business only if it is more beneficial than the law of the importing state. Alternatively, it may require avoiding discrimination more categorically by applying the law of the marketplace without regard to product origin (Wulf-Henning Roth, 'Welthandelsordnung und IPR' in Wolff Heintschel von Heinegg and others (eds), *Entschädigung nach bewaffneten Konflikten, Berichte der Deutschen Gesellschaft für Völkerrecht* (CF Müller 2003) 331, 349 *et seq*; but cf Ralf Michaels, 'Public and Private international law: German Views on Global Issues' (2008) 4 J Priv Int L 121, 130–31 ('such extreme developments seem unlikely at this stage')).

But it is also the practical consequences of MFN treatment that point in this direction. If several producers competing in a market, each from a different state, are liable under the laws of their respective production countries, discrimination will result whenever the eligible laws differ on the liability standard. In the EU, this kind of unequal treatment is rarely problematic. Indeed, a consequent implementation of EU freedoms and of the policy of non-hindrance may even be understood to contain an inherent element of discrimination (Jürgen Basedow, 'Der kollisionsrechtliche Gehalt der Produktfreiheiten im europäischen Binnenmarkt: favor offerentis' (1995) 59 RabelsZ 1, 38–9; see also Joined Cases C-80 and C-159/85, *Nederlandse Bakkerij Stichting and others v Edah BV* [1986] ECR 3359). The convergence of socio-economic conditions, particularly the harmonization of substantive laws, keeps the actual effects of such discrimination small. In effect, this kind of inequality can spur further integration at the level of substantive law (Stefan Leible and Thomas Streinz, 'art 34 AEUV' in Eberhard Grabitz, Meinhard Hilf and Martin Nettesheim, *Das Recht der Europäischen Union* (54th edn, CH Beck 2014) para 34).

This is not the case at the international level, where socio-economic conditions vary significantly. The WTO is not designed to harmonize Member States' substantive laws. On the contrary – the divergence in national policies, *inter alia*, leads to differences in costs and hence to the comparative advantage described long ago by *Adam Smith* and *David Ricardo*. Against this backdrop, the obligation to grant MFN treatment can have drastic effects. Whenever a certain national law is applicable under a member's

→ choice of law, any other member can request application of this specific *lex causae* if it promises a more beneficial outcome than the law otherwise applied. In terms of product liability, this means that all importers may demand application of the most lenient liability regime among all eligible laws. By this means, MFN treatment will ultimately circumvent private international law. In other words, if choice of law provides for a multilateral rule that potentially determines different laws (depending on the origin of a product or party), it will always be the single most beneficial regime among all members' laws that governs. There will be no more actual 'choice'.

In effect, while national treatment avoids discrimination against imports, MFN treatment may discriminate against domestic products or parties. Unlike the EU, the WTO system has no integrative policy to be spurred by a 'race to the bottom'. Consequently, each WTO member is not only advised to avoid any factor of conflicts attachment that directly or indirectly refers to the origin of certain products or parties. In addition, in order to avoid 'inland discrimination', members should implement the marketplace principle as the choice-of-law rule.

2. *The territoriality of national policies*

The liberalization of international trade often conflicts with WTO members' national values and interests. Countries tend to legislate and adopt measures that protect their domestic constituencies. This is especially the case regarding issues of public health, consumer protection, environmental protection and national security. In order to reconcile conflicts between national law and WTO rules, WTO law includes a number of exceptions allowing for trade-restricting regulation (see, eg, arts XX, XXI 1994 GATT; arts XIV, XIVbis GATS).

A frequent question regarding the application of the general exceptions in art XX of the 1994 GATT (and art XIV of the GATS) is whether the national policies at issue should be viewed as having a strictly territorial scope or whether they might be extraterritorially extended. While some cases clearly have an extraterritorial element – such as trade in products of prison labour, as outlined in art XX(e) – others are more limited. The motivation for banning certain trade in products of prison labour is evidently concerned with the conditions in other members' penitentiary institutions – hence, the 'extraterritorial' scope of regulations banning such products. On the other hand, the exceptions outlined in art XX(d) and (f) have been interpreted as clearly territorially limited (Wulf-Henning Roth, 'Welthandelsordnung und IPR' in Wolff Heintschel von Heinegg and others (eds), *Entschädigung nach bewaffneten Konflikten, Berichte der Deutschen Gesellschaft für Völkerrecht* (CF Müller 2003) 331, 355–6).

However, other exceptions under art XX – particularly those in letters (a), (b), and (g) – are not as clear cut. Measures restricting international trade, for instance, may be allowed as measures 'relating to the conservation of exhaustible natural resources if such measures are made effective in conjunction with restrictions on domestic production or consumption' (lit g). In the 1998 *US-Shrimp* case, the WTO Appellate Body acknowledged that an extraterritorial dimension existed. The US had imposed an import ban on shrimp harvested with commercial fishing technology that had the potential to adversely affect sea turtles. As the Appellate Body explained:

> The sea turtle species here at stake ... are all known to occur in waters over which the United States exercises jurisdiction. Of course, it is not claimed that all populations of these species migrate to, or traverse, at one time or another, waters subject to United States jurisdiction. . . We do not pass upon the question of whether there is an implied jurisdictional limitation in Article XX(g), and if so, the nature or extent of that limitation. We note only that in the specific circumstances of the case before us, there is a sufficient nexus between the migratory and endangered marine populations involved and the United States for purposes of Article XX(g). (WTO, Report of the Appellate Body, WT/DS58/AB/R, 12 October 1998, United States – *Import Prohibition of Certain Shrimp and Shrimp Products*, para 133)

Similar issues are debated with respect to trade restrictions intended to protect human life or health. Extraterritoriality may result from restrictions that are justified by reference to the protection not of a member's own polity but of parties in another country (William J Davey, 'Non-Discrimination in the World Trade Organization: The Rules and Exceptions' (2012) 354 Rec. des Cours 183, 365; Lorand Bartels, 'Article XX of GATT and the Problem of Extraterritorial Jurisdiction: The Case of Trade Measures for the Protection of Human Rights' (2002) 36 J.W.T. 353 *et seq*).

Decentralized policy making is the engine of international trade insofar as it upholds members' sovereignty with respect to a determination of their domestic production standards and, accordingly, their exports' price competitiveness. Invasion into this strictly national domain must thus be avoided. This means that parochial protectionist policies must be kept limited, suggesting a general presumption against extraterritoriality (see John O McGinnis and Mark L Movsesian, 'The World Trade Constitution' (2001) 114 Harv.L.Rev. 511, 583 *et seq*; Wulf-Henning Roth, 'Welthandelsordnung und IPR' in Wolff Heintschel von Heinegg and others (eds), *Entschädigung nach bewaffneten Konflikten, Berichte der Deutschen Gesellschaft für Völkerrecht* (CF Müller 2003) 331, 356 *et seq*). And strict → territoriality means that an importing member's private international law must not require compliance with its own regulation of production conditions and circumstances; rather, it should acknowledge divergent standards in other Member States (Wulf-Henning Roth, 'Welthandelsordnung und IPR' in Wolff Heintschel von Heinegg and others (eds), *Entschädigung nach bewaffneten Konflikten, Berichte der Deutschen Gesellschaft für Völkerrecht* (CF Müller 2003) 331, 362).

3. Specific cases: corporations and intellectual property

Finally, there is extensive debate around two particular aspects. First, with respect to the → connecting factors used to determine the law applicable to corporations exists the question whether the GATS provides for an 'incorporation' or a 'seat rule' of choice of law. Second, the TRIPS Agreement is quite often understood to require application of the *lex loci protectionis* to intellectual property infringements.

a) Corporations and the GATS

The GATS may be interpreted as containing an implicit conflicts rule regarding the freedom of market access that it provides for services and service suppliers. While English and US law traditionally refer to the 'law of incorporation', civil-law jurisdictions (notably Germany) tend to apply the law of the place where the corporation has its seat. This is the place where the corporation's principal administration or management are located. Within the EU, this 'seat theory' has come under pressure, though, in recent Court of Justice decisions. In essence, the Court requires a corporation that has been validly established in the state of incorporation to be recognized in other Member States on the basis of the freedom of establishment (arts 49, 54 TFEU). While details are contested, it is acknowledged that, in general, Member States should not restrict a corporation's right of establishment by instituting requirements under their domestic law that are stricter than those under the law of the place of incorporation (see, eg, Case C-167/01, *Kamer van Koophandel en Fabrieken voor Amsterdam v Inspire Art Ltd* [2003] ECR I-10155; Case C-210/06, *Cartesio Oktató és Szolgáltató bt* [2008] ECR I-9641; Case C-378/10 *VALE Építési* [2012] OJ C 287/3).

A similar limitation of the seat theory may result from WTO law. Freedom of access under the GATS comprises, *inter alia*, the supplying of services by a supplier from one Member State through a commercial presence in the territory of another member (art I:2c GATS). Under this mode of supply, each Member State is obligated to accord services and service suppliers of any other member treatment no less favourable than that provided for under the terms, limitations and conditions agreed and specified in its schedule (art XVI:1 GATS).

Article XVI:2e further specifies:

> In sectors where market-access commitments are undertaken, the measures which a Member shall not maintain or adopt either on the basis of a regional subdivision or on the basis of its entire territory, unless otherwise specified in its Schedule, are defined as: . . . measures which restrict or require specific types of legal entity or joint venture through which a service supplier may supply a service.

On this basis, some scholars have concluded that the limitation on admissible measures requires that a corporate entity that is a 'juridical person of another Member' (art XXVIII (m) (i) GATS) may not be prohibited from establishing a branch in the Member State where it supplies its services, nor be prohibited from acting validly in the legal form that it has under the law of its state of incorporation (Jochen Hoffmann, 'Anhang zu art 12 EGBGB' in Thomas Heidel and others (eds), *NomosKommentar-BGB* (2nd edn, Nomos 2012), paras 154 *et seq*; Markus Kraus, *Die Auswirkungen des Welthandelsrechts auf das Internationale Kollisionsrecht* (Nomos 2008) 159 *et seq*). The majority opinion in theory and practice, however, rejects such an interpretation (German Federal Court of Justice (BGH), 27 October 2008 [2009] NJW 289 *et seq*; Peter Kindler, 'Internationales Handels- und Gesellschaftsrecht' in Franz Jürgen Säcker and Roland Rixecker (eds), *Münchener Kommentar zum Bürgerlichen Gesetzbuch*, vol 11 (6th edn, CH Beck 2015) paras 503–4). As the German *Bundesgerichtshof* argues, the GATS does not provide for individual rights of Member States' nationals or juridical persons. The GATS's policy is limited to fostering free trade; there is no international consensus on any additional purpose, particularly regarding impacts on members' private international law. The interpretation of national choice of law in accordance with public international law should, hence, not effectuate an alteration of the seat rule (German Federal Court of Justice (BGH), 27 October 2008 [2009] NJW 289, 290; Peter Kindler, 'Internationales Handels- und Gesellschaftsrecht' in Franz Jürgen Säcker and Roland Rixecker (eds), *Münchener Kommentar zum Bürgerlichen Gesetzbuch*, vol 11 (6th edn, CH Beck 2015) para 504). Ultimately – although this is not very likely to occur – interpretation of the GATS in this respect will be an issue for WTO dispute settlement (see *infra* III.2.).

b) TRIPS and intellectual property
There is debate over whether → TRIPS contains rules of private international law. This debate is situated in the context of other international intellectual property conventions (eg the Berne Convention (Berne Convention for the Protection of Literary and Artistic Works of 9 September 1886, completed at Paris on 4 May 1896, with later revisions and amendments, 1161 UNTS 3 and amended in 1979 Treaty Doc No 99-27, and 1985, 828 UNTS 221) and the Paris Industrial Property Convention (Paris Convention for the Protection of Industrial Property, 20 March 1883, with later amendments, 828 UNTS 305)) and their alleged impact on national choice of law. Most scholars agree that, on their face, these conventions lack an express obligation to adopt specific rules of private international law (see, eg, James Fawcett and Paul Torremans, *Intellectual Property and Private international law* (2nd edn, OUP 2011) para 12.05). Yet the effects of national and MFN treatment are still unclear.

As dominant commentary and practice contend, the principle of national treatment (eg art 2 of the Paris Industrial Property Convention; art 5(2) of the Berne Convention; art 3(1) of TRIPS) invariably demands application of the law of the country for which protection is claimed (Nerina Boschiero, 'Infringement of Intellectual Property Rights: A Commentary on Article 8 of the Rome II Regulation' (2007) 9 YbPIL 87, 95–6; Sierd Jurriaan Schaafsma, *Intellectuele eigendom in het conflictenrecht* (Kluwer 2009) 413 *et seq*; Josef Drexl, 'Internationales Immaterialgüterrecht' in Roland Rixecker and Franz Jürgen Säcker (eds), *Münchener Kommentar zum BGB*, vol 11 (6th edn, CH Beck 2015) paras 68, 79). With respect to copyrights, this dominant opinion also refers to the text of art 5(2) of the Berne Convention, as well as the accompanying note to art 3 of TRIPS, which provides that '[f]or the purposes of Articles 3 and 4, "protection" shall include matters affecting the availability, acquisition, scope, maintenance and enforcement of IP rights as well as those matters affecting the use of IP rights specifically addressed in this Agreement' (see James Fawcett and Paul Torremans, *Intellectual Property and Private international law* (2nd edn, OUP 2011) paras 12.17 *et seq*, 12.66 *et seq*; also, eg, German Federal Court of Justice (BGH), 17 June 1992, 118 BGHZ 394, 397; Cour de cassation France, 30 January 2007, *Tideworks v Waterworld*, chambre civil 1, No de pourvoi: 03-12354; Paul Goldstein, *International Copyright: Principles, Law, and Practice* (OUP 2001), 3.2, 3.3.2.1). In addition, as dominant opinion further contends, application of the *lex loci protectionis* is also required on the basis of MFN treatment (art 4 TRIPS; see, eg, Josef Drexl, 'Internationales Immaterialgüterrecht' in Roland Rixecker and Franz Jürgen Säcker (eds), *Münchener Kommentar zum BGB*, vol 11 (6th edn, CH Beck 2015) paras 68, 77 *et seq*). As it seems, the TRIPS principles of non-discrimination have established a directly applicable rule of choice of law.

The contrary opinion rejects such a role of the *lex loci protectionis*. Some within this camp have suggested that the national-treatment principle still requires equal treatment of nationals and foreigners at the level of → choice of law. Thus, nationality should not be used as a → connecting factor (Marta Pertegás, 'Intellectual Property and Choice of Law Rules' in Alberto Malatesta (ed), *The Unification of Choice of Law Rules on Torts and other Non-contractual Obligations in Europe: The "Rome II" Proposal* (CEDAM 2006) 221, 227–8). Others reject the effects of international conventions more radically. They define national treatment as relating to substantive law only (see, eg, Paul

Heinrich Neuhaus, 'Freiheit und Gleichheit im internationalen Immaterialgüterrecht' (1976) 40 RabelsZ 191, 193; Mireille MM van Eechoud, *Choice of Law in Copyright and Related Rights: Alternatives to the lex protectionis* (Kluwer Law International 2003), 106 et seq, 125–6; Richard Fentiman, 'Choice of Law and Intellectual Property' in Josef Drexl and Annette Kur (eds), *Intellectual Property and Private international law: Heading for the Future* (Hart 2005) 129, 134). This approach is illustrated in *Itar-Tass Russian News Agency v Russian Kurier Inc*, 153 F.3d 82 (2nd Cir 1998):

[T]he principle of national treatment is really not a conflicts rule at all; it does not direct application of the law of any country. It simply requires that the country in which protection is claimed must treat foreign and domestic authors alike. Whether US copyright law directs US courts to look to foreign or domestic law as to certain issues is irrelevant to national treatment, so long as the scope of protection would be extended equally to foreign and domestic authors. (*Itar-Tass Russian News Agency v Russian Kurier Inc*, 153 F3d 82, 90 para 8 (2nd Cir 1998))

The Court of Justice has also explained:

As is apparent from Article 5(1) of the Berne Convention, the purpose of that convention is not to determine the applicable law on the protection of literary and artistic works, but to establish, as a general rule, a system of national treatment of the rights appertaining to such works. (Case C-28/04, *Tod's SpA and Tod's France SARL v Heyraud SA* [2005] ECR I-57581, para 32)

In the same vein, European lawmakers seem to have chosen an express conflicts rule for intellectual property in art 8 of the → Rome II Regulation (Regulation (EC) No 864/2007 of the European Parliament and of the Council of 11 July 2007 on the law applicable to non-contractual obligations (Rome II), [2007] OJ L 199/40), implying that they did not expect a binding rule to be inferable from public international law (cf European Commission, 'Proposal for a Regulation of the European Parliament and the Council on the Law Applicable to Non-Contractual Obligations ("Rome II")' COM(2003) 427 final, 21).

Here, as well, extending the view on both national and MFN treatment explains not only the legal obligation but also a practical need to apply the *lex loci protectionis*. Still, however, none of these principles leads to a direct choice-of-law norm.

As our general analysis of national and MFN treatment in WTO law has revealed, underlying obligations do not constitute a direct choice-of-law rule (*supra*). This also holds true for TRIPS. None of the international conventions on intellectual property protection, including TRIPS, was adopted with the aim of establishing rules of private international law; none contains anything that comes even close to a coherent conflicts system (Mireille MM van Eechoud, *Choice of Law in Copyright and Related Rights: Alternatives to the lex protectionis* (Kluwer Law International 2003) 125; Nerina Boschiero, 'Infringement of Intellectual Property Rights: A Commentary on Article 8 of the Rome II Regulation' (2007) 9 YbPIL 87, 98). Moreover, TRIPS – like WTO law in general – is not generally seen as directly applicable in Member States (see, eg, Case C-300/98 and C-392/98, *Parfums Christian Dior SA v TUK Consultancy BV and Assco Gerüste GmbH et al* [2000] ECR I-11307, paras 46 *et seq*; Case C-89/99, *Schieving-Nijstad vof and Others v Robert Groeneveld* [2001] ECR I-5851, paras 51 *et seq*). Accordingly, choice-of-law rules hardly ensue directly from TRIPS.

Notwithstanding the lack of immediacy, national and MFN treatment jointly indicate application of the *lex loci protectionis*. Discrimination against foreign right owners must be avoided by granting national treatment under art 3. *De facto* discrimination may result from a choice-of-law norm allowing for different laws to apply depending on a right owner's nationality. One example of such a rule is the adoption of the *lex originis* for copyright protection. If the level of protection under the *lex originis* falls below the protection granted under the *lex fori*, foreign right owners are factually disadvantaged (Josef Drexl, 'Internationales Immaterialgüterrecht' in Roland Rixecker and Franz Jürgen Säcker (eds), *Münchener Kommentar zum BGB*, vol 11 (6th edn, CH Beck 2015) paras 68, 70). Hence, an obligation to interpret national law in accordance with public international law (for the EU see, eg, Case C-53/96, *Hermès International* [1998] ECR I-3603, para 28) requires application of the *lex loci protectionis*.

Further, the obligation of MFN treatment in art 4 implies application of the law of the place of infringement as well. Only the *lex loci protectionis* can secure the non-discrimination of national right owners. While the MFN principle can trigger a race to the bottom with respect to international trade (*supra*), under TRIPS, it can lead to a similarly unwelcome 'race to the top'. Foreign right owners can demand optimal treatment of their rights, in comparison with both national holders and those of other Member States. On this basis, any choice-of-law issue will ultimately be decided 'in favour' of the right owner by applying the most protective among the members' laws. Choice of law would yield to a rule of optimum protection. Not only would this effect contradict the concept of minimum protection so central to TRIPS (see art 1(1)) – it would be particularly paradoxical in light of the fierce debates that have been (and continue to be) fought between developed and developing countries with respect to protection levels. Seen in this light, the *lex loci protectionis* is the only rule that avoids the pitfalls of a multilateral choice of law. A multilateral conflicts rule only guarantees equal treatment *de jure*. The *lex loci protectionis*, however, is the only rule to also secure *de facto* non-discrimination. In addition, it is the approach that most closely replicates the marketplace rule avoiding the MFN-induced detriment of discrimination against national right owners.

TIM W DORNIS

Literature

Lorand Bartels, 'Article XX of GATT and the Problem of Extraterritorial Jurisdiction: The Case of Trade Measures for the Protection of Human Rights' (2002) 36 J.W.T. 353; Suzanne Basdevant, *La clause de la nation la plus favorisée: effets en droit international privé* (Librairie du recueil sirey 1929); Jürgen Basedow, 'Der kollisionsrechtliche Gehalt der Produktfreiheiten im europäischen Binnenmarkt: favor offerentis' (1995) 59 RabelsZ 1; Nerina Boschiero, 'Infringement of Intellectual Property Rights: A Commentary on Article 8 of the Rome II Regulation' (2007) 9 YbPIL 87; William J Davey, 'Non-Discrimination in the World Trade Organization: The Rules and Exceptions' (2012) 354 Rec. des Cours 183; Mireille MM van Eechoud, *Choice of Law in Copyright and Related Rights: Alternatives to the lex protectionis* (Kluwer Law International 2003); James J Fawcett and Paul Torremans, *Intellectual Property and Private international law* (2nd edn, OUP 2011); Richard Fentiman, 'Choice of Law and Intellectual Property' in Josef Drexl and Annette Kur (eds), *Intellectual Property and Private international law: Heading for the Future* (Hart 2005) 129; Paul Goldstein, *International Copyright: Principles, Law, and Practice* (OUP 2001); Eberhard Grabitz, Meinhard Hilf and Martin Nettesheim, *Das Recht der Europäischen Union* (54th edn, CH Beck 2014); Thomas Heidel and others (eds), *NomosKommentar-BGB* (2nd edn, Nomos 2012); John H Jackson, *The World Trading System: Law and Policy of International Relations* (2nd edn, MIT Press 1997); Christian Joerges, 'Constitutionalism in Postnational Constellations: Contrasting Social Regulation in the EU and in the WTO' in Christian Joerges and Ernst-Ulrich Petersmann (eds), *Constitutionalism, Multilevel Trade Governance and Social Regulation* (Oxford Hart 2006); Markus Kraus, *Die Auswirkungen des Welthandelsrechts auf das Internationale Kollisionsrecht* (Nomos 2008); Matthias Lehmann, 'Fällt die Sitztheorie jetzt auch international? – Zur Vereinbarkeit der kollisionsrechtlichen Anknüpfung an den Gesellschaftssitz mit dem GATS' [2004] RIW 816; Peter Mankowski, 'Binnenmarkt IPR – Eine Problemskizze' in Jürgen Basedow (ed), *Aufbruch nach Europa: 75 Jahre Max-Planck-Institut für Privatrecht* (Mohr Siebeck 2001) 595; John O McGinnis and Mark L Movsesian, 'The World Trade Constitution' (2001) 114 Harv.L.Rev. 511; Johan Meeusen, 'Le droit international privé et le principe de non-discrimination' (2012) 353 Rec. des Cours 10; Ralf Michaels, 'Public and Private international law: German Views on Global Issues' (2008) 4 J Priv Int L 121; Paul Heinrich Neuhaus, 'Freiheit und Gleichheit im internationalen Immaterialgüterrecht' (1976) 40 RabelsZ 191; Marta Pertegás, 'Intellectual Property and Choice of Law Rules' in Alberto Malatesta (ed), *The Unification of Choice of Law Rules on Torts and other Non-contractual Obligations in Europe: The "Rome II" Proposal* (CEDAM 2006) 221; Wulf-Henning Roth, 'Welthandelsordnung und IPR' in Wolff Heintschel von Heinegg and others (eds), *Entschädigung nach bewaffneten Konflikten, Berichte der Deutschen Gesellschaft für Völkerrecht* (CF Müller 2003) 331; Franz Jürgen Säcker and Roland Rixecker (eds), *Münchener Kommentar zum Bürgerlichen Gesetzbuch* (5th and 6th edn, CH Beck 2011 and 2015); Sierd Jurriaan Schaafsma, *Intellectuele eigendom in het conflictenrecht* (Kluwer 2009); Kurt Siehr, 'Vom universellen zum globalen IPR – Zur jüngsten Geschichte und Entwicklung des Internationalen Privatrechts' in Heinz-Peter Mansel and others (eds), *Festschrift für Erik Jayme*, vol 1 (Sellier 2004) 873; Peter Sutherland and others, *The Future of the WTO (Report by the Consultative Board to the Director-General Supachai Panitchpakdi)* (WTO 2004); Harry Duintjer Tebbens, 'Les conflits de lois en matière de publicité déloyale à l'épreuve du droit communautaire' (1994) 83 Rev.crit.DIP 451; Joseph HH Weiler, *The EU, the WTO, and the NAFTA: Towards a Common Law of International Trade?* (OUP 2000).